Annual Abstract
of Statistics

No 150
2014 Edition
Compiled by: Dandy Booksellers

Contacts

For information about the content of this publication, contact
Dandy Booksellers: Tel 020 7624 2993
Email: dandybooksellers@btconnect.com

Publications orders
To obtain the print version of this publication, please contact Dandy
Booksellers
Tel: 0207 624 2993
Email: dandybooksellers@btconnect.com
Fax: 0207 624 5049
Post: Unit 3&4, 31-33 Priory Park Road
      London, NW6 7UP
Web: www.dandybooksellers.com

Contents

5: Social Protection

6: External trade and investment

7: Research and development

8: Personal income, expenditure & wealth

9: Lifestyles

10: Environment

11: Housing

12: Banking and Finance

12: Banking and Finance

13: Service industry

14: Defence

15: Population and vital statistics

16: Health

17: Prices

18: Production

19: National Accounts

20: Education

20: Education

21: Crime and Justice

22: Transport

22: Transport

23:Government Finance

24:Agriculture

Units of measurement

Length

1 millimetre (mm)	= 0.03937 inch	
1 centimetre (cm)	= 10 millimetres	= 0.3937 inch
1 metre (m)	= 1,000 millimetres	= 1.094 yards
1 kilometre (km)	= 1,000 metres	= 0.6214 mile
1 inch (in.)		= 25.40 millimetres or 2.540 centimetres
1 foot (ft.)	= 12 inches	= 0.3048 metre
1 yard (yd.)	= 3 feet	= 0.9144 metre
1 mile	= 1,760 yards	= 1.609 kilometres

Area

1 square millimetre (mm2)		= 0.001550 square inch
1 square metre (m2)	= one million square millimetres	= 1.196 square yards
1 hectare (ha)	= 10,000 square metres	= 2.471 acres
1 square kilometre (km2)	= one million square metres	= 247.1 acres
1 square inch (sq. in.)		= 645.2 square millimetres or 6.452 square centimetres
1 square foot (sq. ft.)	= 144 square inches	= 0.09290 square metre or 929.0 square centimetres
1 square yard (sq. yd.)	= 9 square feet	= 0.8361 square metre
1 acre	= 4,840 square yards	= 4,046 square metres or 0.4047 hectare
1 square mile (sq. mile)	= 640 acres	= 2.590 square kilometres or 259.0 hectares

Volume

1 cubic centimetre (cm3)		= 0.06102 cubic inch
1 cubic decimetre (dm3)	= 1,000 cubic centimetres	= 0.03531 cubic foot
1 cubic metre (m3)	= one million cubic centimetres	= 1.308 cubic yards
1 cubic inch (cu.in.)		=16.39 cubic centimetres
1 cubic foot (cu. ft.)	= 1,728 cubic inches	= 0.02832 cubic metre or 28.32 cubic decimetres
1 cubic yard (cu. yd.)	= 27 cubic feet	= 0.7646 cubic metre

Capacity

1 litre (l)	= 1 cubic decimetre	= 0.2200 gallon
1 hectolitre (hl)	= 100 litres	= 22.00 gallons
1 pint		= 0.5682 litre
1 quart	= 2 pints	= 1.137 litres
1 gallon	= 8 pints	= 4.546 litres
1 bulk barrel	= 36 gallons (gal.)	= 1.637 hectolitres

Weight

1 gram (g)		= 0.03527 ounce avoirdupois
1 hectogram (hg)	= 100 grams	= 3.527 ounces or 0.2205 pound
1 kilogram (kg)	= 1,000 grams or 10 hectograms	= 2.205 pounds
1 tonne (t)	= 1,000 kilograms	= 1.102 short tons or 0.9842 long ton
1 ounce avoirdupois (oz.)	= 437.5 grains	= 28.35 grams
1 pound avoirdupois (lb.)	= 16 ounces	= 0.4536 kilogram
1 hundredweight (cwt.)	= 112 pounds	= 50.80 kilograms
1 short ton	= 2,000 pounds	= 907.2 kilograms or 0.9072 tonne
1 long ton (referred to as ton)	= 2,240 pounds	= 1,016 kilograms or 1.016 tonnes
1 ounce troy	= 480 grains	= 31.10 grams

Energy

British thermal unit (Btu)	= 0.2520 kilocalorie (kcal) = 1.055 kilojoule (kj)
Therm	= 105 British thermal units = 25,200 kcal = 105,506 kj
Megawatt hour (MWh)	= 106 watt hours (Wh)
Gigawatt hour (GWh)	= 106 kilowatt hours = 34,121 therms

Food and drink

Butter	23,310 litres milk	= 1 tonne butter (average)
Cheese	10,070 litres milk	= 1 tonne cheese
Condensed milk	2,550 litres milk	= 1 tonne full cream condensed milk
	2,953 litres skimmed milk	= 1 tonne skimmed condensed milk
Milk	1 million litres	= 1,030 tonnes
Milk powder	8,054 litres milk	= 1 tonne full cream milk powder
	10,740 litres skimmed milk	= 1 tonne skimmed milk powder
Eggs	17,126 eggs	= 1 tonne (approximate)
Sugar	100 tonnes sugar beet	= 92 tonnes refined sugar
	100 tonnes cane sugar	= 96 tonnes refined sugar

Shipping

Gross tonnage	= The total volume of all the enclosed spaces of a vessel, the unit of measurement being a 'ton' of 100 cubic feet.
Deadweight tonnage	= Deadweight tonnage is the total weight in tons of 2,240 lb. that a ship can legally carry, that is the total weight of cargo, bunkers, stores and crew.

Introduction

Welcome to the 2014 edition of the Annual Abstract of Statistics. This compendium draws together statistics from a wide range of official and other authoritative sources.

Dandy Booksellers have sourced and formatted these tables under instruction from various government departments/organisations

Current data for many of the series appearing in this Annual Abstract are contained in other ONS publications, such as Economic & Labour Market Review, Population Trends, Health Statistics Quarterly and Financial Statistics. These titles can be purchased through Dandy Booksellers.

Other ONS publications which contain related data are the Monthly Digest of Statistics and Social Trends.

These publications can be found at:
http://www.ons.gov.uk

The name (and telephone number, where this is available) of the organisation providing the statistics are shown under each table. In addition, a list of Sources is given at the back of the book, which sets out the official publications or other sources to which further reference can be made.

Identification codes

The four-letter identification code at the top of each data column, or at the side of each row is the ONS reference for this series of data on their database. Please quote the relevant code if you contact them requiring any further information about the data. On some tables it is not possible to include these codes, so please quote the table number in these cases.

Definitions and classification

Time series
So far as possible annual totals are given throughout, but quarterly or monthly figures are given where these are more suitable to the type of series.

Standard Industrial Classification

A Standard Industrial Classification (SIC) was first introduced into the UK in 1948 for use in classifying business establishments and other statistical units by the type of economic activity in which they are engaged. The classification provides a framework for the collection, tabulation, presentation and analysis of data about economic activities. Its use promotes uniformity of data collected by various government departments and agencies.

Since 1948 the classification has been revised in 1958, 1968, 1980, 1992, 2003 and 2007. One of the principal objectives of the 1980 revision was to eliminate differences from the activity classification issued by the Statistical Office of the European Communities (Eurostat) and entitled 'Nomenclature générale des activités économiques dans les Communautés Européennes', usually abbreviated to NACE.

In 1990 the European Communities introduced a new statistical classification of economic activities (NACE Rev 1) by regulation. The regulation made it obligatory for the UK to introduce a new Standard Industrial Classification SIC(92), based on NACE Rev 1. UK SIC(92) was based exactly on NACE Rev 1 but, where it was thought necessary or helpful, a fifth digit was added to form subclasses of the NACE 1 four digit system. Classification systems need to be revised periodically because, over time, new products, processes and industries emerge. In January 2003 a minor revision of NACE Rev 1, known as NACE Rev 1.1, was published in the Official Journal of the European Communities.

Consequently, the UK was obliged to introduce a new Standard Industrial Classification, SIC(2003) consistent with NACE Rev 1.1. The UK took the opportunity of the 2003 revision also to update the national Subclasses. Full details are available in UK Standard Industrial Classification of Economic Activities 2003 and the Indexes to the UK Standard Industrial Classification of Economic Activities 2003. These are the most recent that are currently used. The most up to date version is the UK Standard Industrial Classification of Economic activities 2007 (SIC2007). It will be implemented in five stages and came into effect on 1 January 2008.

- For reference year 2008, the Annual Business Inquiry (parts 1 & 2) will be based on SIC 2007

- PRODCOM will also be based on SIC 2007 from reference year 2008

- Other annual outputs will be based on SIC 2007 from reference year 2009, unless otherwise determined by regulation

- Quarterly and monthly surveys will be based on SIC 2007 from the first reference period in 2010, unless otherwise determined by regulation

- National Accounts will move to SIC 2007 in September 2011

Symbols and conventions used

Change of basis
Where consecutive figures have been compiled on different bases and are not strictly comparable, a footnote is added indicating the nature of the difference.

Geographic coverage
Statistics relate mainly to the UK. Where figures relate to other areas, this is indicated on the table.

Units of measurement
The various units of measurement used are listed after the Contents.

Rounding of figures
In tables where figures have been rounded to the nearest final digit, the constituent items may not add up exactly to the total.

Symbols
The following symbols have been used throughout:

  .. = not available or not applicable (also information supressed to avoid disclosure)

  - = nil or less than half the final digit shown

Office for National Statistics online:
www.ons.gov.uk
Web-based access to time series, cross-sectional data and metadata from across the Government Statistical Service (GSS), is available using the site search function from the homepage. Download many datasets, in whole or in part, or consult directory information for all GSS statistical resources, including censuses, surveys, periodicals and enquiry services. Information is posted as PDF electronic documents or in XLS and CSV formats, compatible with most spreadsheet packages.

Contact point
Dandy Booksellers welcomes any feedback on the content of the Annual Abstract, including comments on the format of the data and the selection of topics. Comments and requests for general information should be addressed to:

Dandy Booksellers
Unit 3&4
31-33 Priory Park Road
London
NW6 7UP
or
enquiries@dandybooksellers.com

02 September 2015

Area

Chapter 1

Area

The United Kingdom (UK) comprises Great Britain and Northern Ireland. Great Britain comprises England, Wales and Scotland.

Physical Features

The United Kingdom (UK) constitutes the greater part of the British Isles. The largest of the islands is Great Britain. The next largest comprises Northern Ireland and the Irish Republic. Western Scotland is fringed by the large island chain known as the Hebrides, and to the north east of the Scottish mainland are the Orkney and Shetland Islands. All these, along with the Isle of Wight, Anglesey and the Isles of Scilly, form part of the UK, but the Isle of Man, in the Irish Sea and the Channel Islands, between Great Britain and France are largely self-governing and are not part of the UK. The UK is one of the 28 member states of the European Union. With an area of about 243 000 sq km (about 94 000 sq miles), the UK is just under 1 000 km (about 600 miles) from the south coast to the extreme north of Scotland and just under 500 km (around 300 miles) across at the widest point.

- Highest mountain: Ben Nevis, in the highlands of Scotland, at 1 343 m (4 406 ft)
- Longest river: the Severn, 354 km (220 miles) long, which rises in central Wales and flows through Shrewsbury, Worcester and Gloucester in England to the Bristol Channel
- Largest lake: Lough Neagh, Northern Ireland, at 396 sq km (153 sq miles)
- Deepest lake: Loch Morar in the Highlands of Scotland, 310 m (1 017 ft) deep
- Highest waterfall: Eas a'Chual Aluinn, from Glas Bheinn, in the highlands of Scotland, with a drop of 200 m (660 ft)
- Deepest cave: Ogof Ffynnon Ddu, Wales, at 308 m (1 010 ft) deep
- Most northerly point on the British mainland: Dunnet Head, north-east Scotland
- Most southerly point on the British mainland: Lizard Point, Cornwall
- Closest point to mainland continental Europe: Dover, Kent. The Channel Tunnel, which links England and France, is a little over 50 km (31 miles) long, of which nearly 38 km (24 miles) are actually under the Channel

Area Measurements

I'd like to get area figures for all the local authorities in the UK. Where do I look?

UK Standard Area Measurements (SAM) are now available to download free of charge from the Open Geography portal in both MS Excel and CSV formats for a variety of administrative areas (countries, counties, local authority districts, electoral wards/divisions, regions, output areas, super output areas and workplace zones). The two questions below show some statistics taken from SAM 2013 (Extent of the Realm figures).

Which is the largest local authority in the UK?

- The largest anywhere in the UK is Highland (Scotland), at 2,648,436.34 hectares (ha).
- The largest in England is Northumberland, at 507,835.00 ha.
- The largest in Wales is Powys, at 519,543.65 ha.
- The largest in Northern Ireland is Fermanagh, at 187,125.95 ha.

Which is the smallest local authority in the UK?

- The smallest anywhere in the UK is the City of London, at 314.94 ha
- The smallest in Scotland is Dundee City, at 6,222.59 ha.
- The smallest in Wales is Blaenau Gwent, at 10,872.81 ha
- The smallest in Northern Ireland is North Down, at 8,150.19 ha.

UK Standard Area Measurements (SAM)

About UK Standard Area Measurements (SAM)

The SAM product provides a definitive list of measurements for administrative, health, Census, electoral and other geographic areas in the UK. SAM will change annually for some geographies, but for others it will be 'frozen' for several years.

The land measurement figures provided are defined by topographic boundaries (coastline and inland water), where available.

Measurements are reviewed annually and include information up to the end of December.

The measurements have been produced in conjunction with the following UK government statistical organisations and independent mapping agencies: National Records of Scotland (NRS), Northern Ireland Statistics and Research Agency (NISRA), Ordnance Survey®(OS) and Land & Property Services (LPS).

The SAM User Guide explains differences in methodology and base mapping between these agencies.

Product details

If you have any queries about this dataset, please contact:

ONS Geography Customer Services
Office for National Statistics
Segensworth Road
Titchfield
Fareham
Hampshire
PO15 5RR

Tel: 01329 444 971
Email: ons.geography@ons.gov.uk

1.1 Standard Area Measurement for UK Local Authority Districts as at 31/12/2013

	Code as at December 2013[1]	Extent of the realm (Km^2)	Area to mean high water (Km^2)	Inland water (Km^2)	Land only (Km^2)
United Kingdom	K02000001	248541	244178	1664	242514
Great Britain	K03000001	234411	230048	1097	228952
England	E92000001	132947	130458	152	130306
Hartlepool	E06000001	98	94	0	94
Middlesbrough	E06000002	55	54	0	54
Redcar and Cleveland	E06000003	254	245	0	245
Stockton-on-Tees	E06000004	210	204	0	204
Darlington	E06000005	197	197	0	197
Halton	E06000006	90	79	0	79
Warrington	E06000007	182	181	0	181
Blackburn with Darwen	E06000008	137	137	0	137
Blackpool	E06000009	43	35	0	35
Kingston upon Hull, City of	E06000010	81	71	0	71
East Riding of Yorkshire	E06000011	2495	2406	1	2405
North East Lincolnshire	E06000012	204	192	0	192
North Lincolnshire	E06000013	876	846	0	846
York	E06000014	272	272	0	272
Derby	E06000015	78	78	0	78
Leicester	E06000016	73	73	0	73
Rutland	E06000017	394	394	12	382
Nottingham	E06000018	75	75	0	75
Herefordshire, County of	E06000019	2180	2180	0	2180
Telford and Wrekin	E06000020	290	290	0	290
Stoke-on-Trent	E06000021	93	93	0	93
Bath and North East Somerset	E06000022	351	351	5	346
Bristol, City of	E06000023	235	110	0	110
North Somerset	E06000024	391	375	1	374
South Gloucestershire	E06000025	537	497	0	497
Plymouth	E06000026	84	80	0	80
Torbay	E06000027	119	63	0	63
Bournemouth	E06000028	47	46	0	46
Poole	E06000029	75	65	0	65
Swindon	E06000030	230	230	0	230
Peterborough	E06000031	343	343	0	343
Luton	E06000032	43	43	0	43
Southend-on-Sea	E06000033	68	42	0	42
Thurrock	E06000034	184	163	0	163
Medway	E06000035	269	194	0	194
Bracknell Forest	E06000036	109	109	0	109
West Berkshire	E06000037	704	704	0	704
Reading	E06000038	40	40	0	40
Slough	E06000039	33	33	0	33
Windsor and Maidenhead	E06000040	198	198	2	197
Wokingham	E06000041	179	179	0	179
Milton Keynes	E06000042	309	309	0	309
Brighton and Hove	E06000043	85	83	0	83
Portsmouth	E06000044	60	40	0	40
Southampton	E06000045	56	50	0	50
Isle of Wight	E06000046	395	380	0	380
County Durham	E06000047	2233	2232	6	2226
Cheshire East	E06000049	1166	1166	0	1166
Cheshire West and Chester	E06000050	941	917	0	917
Shropshire	E06000051	3197	3197	0	3197
Cornwall	E06000052	3613	3550	4	3546
Isles of Scilly	E06000053	23	16	0	16
Wiltshire	E06000054	3255	3255	0	3255
Bedford	E06000055	476	476	0	476
Central Bedfordshire	E06000056	716	716	0	716
Northumberland	E06000057	5078	5026	12	5014

1.1 Standard Area Measurement for UK Local Authority Districts as at 31/12/2013

	Code as at December 2013[1]	Extent of the realm (Km^2)	Area to mean high water (Km^2)	Inland water (Km^2)	Land only (Km^2)
Aylesbury Vale	E07000004	903	903	0	903
Chiltern	E07000005	196	196	0	196
South Bucks	E07000006	141	141	0	141
Wycombe	E07000007	325	325	0	325
Cambridge	E07000008	41	41	0	41
East Cambridgeshire	E07000009	652	651	0	651
Fenland	E07000010	547	546	0	546
Huntingdonshire	E07000011	913	912	6	906
South Cambridgeshire	E07000012	902	902	0	902
Allerdale	E07000026	1321	1258	16	1242
Barrow-in-Furness	E07000027	132	78	0	78
Carlisle	E07000028	1054	1039	0	1039
Copeland	E07000029	776	738	6	732
Eden	E07000030	2156	2156	14	2142
South Lakeland	E07000031	1743	1553	19	1534
Amber Valley	E07000032	265	265	0	265
Bolsover	E07000033	160	160	0	160
Chesterfield	E07000034	66	66	0	66
Derbyshire Dales	E07000035	795	795	3	792
Erewash	E07000036	110	110	0	110
High Peak	E07000037	540	540	1	539
North East Derbyshire	E07000038	276	276	0	276
South Derbyshire	E07000039	338	338	0	338
East Devon	E07000040	824	814	0	814
Exeter	E07000041	48	47	0	47
Mid Devon	E07000042	913	913	0	913
North Devon	E07000043	1105	1086	0	1086
South Hams	E07000044	905	886	0	886
Teignbridge	E07000045	681	674	0	674
Torridge	E07000046	996	985	1	984
West Devon	E07000047	1165	1161	1	1160
Christchurch	E07000048	52	50	0	50
East Dorset	E07000049	354	354	0	354
North Dorset	E07000050	609	609	0	609
Purbeck	E07000051	428	404	0	404
West Dorset	E07000052	1087	1081	0	1081
Weymouth and Portland	E07000053	43	42	0	42
Eastbourne	E07000061	46	44	0	44
Hastings	E07000062	31	30	0	30
Lewes	E07000063	294	292	0	292
Rother	E07000064	518	512	2	509
Wealden	E07000065	836	835	2	833
Basildon	E07000066	110	110	0	110
Braintree	E07000067	612	612	0	612
Brentwood	E07000068	153	153	0	153
Castle Point	E07000069	64	45	0	45
Chelmsford	E07000070	343	342	3	339
Colchester	E07000071	347	333	4	329
Epping Forest	E07000072	339	339	0	339
Harlow	E07000073	31	31	0	31
Maldon	E07000074	427	359	0	359
Rochford	E07000075	263	169	0	169
Tendring	E07000076	366	338	0	338
Uttlesford	E07000077	641	641	0	641
Cheltenham	E07000078	47	47	0	47
Cotswold	E07000079	1165	1165	0	1165
Forest of Dean	E07000080	561	526	0	526
Gloucester	E07000081	41	41	0	41
Stroud	E07000082	476	461	0	461
Tewkesbury	E07000083	415	414	0	414
Basingstoke and Deane	E07000084	634	634	0	634
East Hampshire	E07000085	514	514	0	514
Eastleigh	E07000086	85	80	0	80

1.1 Standard Area Measurement for UK Local Authority Districts as at 31/12/2013

	Code as at December 2013[1]	Extent of the realm (Km^2)	Area to mean high water (Km^2)	Inland water (Km^2)	Land only (Km^2)
Fareham	E07000087	78	74	0	74
Gosport	E07000088	28	25	0	25
Hart	E07000089	215	215	0	215
Havant	E07000090	79	55	0	55
New Forest	E07000091	777	753	0	753
Rushmoor	E07000092	39	39	0	39
Test Valley	E07000093	628	628	0	628
Winchester	E07000094	661	661	0	661
Broxbourne	E07000095	51	51	0	51
Dacorum	E07000096	212	212	0	212
Hertsmere	E07000098	101	101	0	101
North Hertfordshire	E07000099	375	375	0	375
Three Rivers	E07000102	89	89	0	89
Watford	E07000103	21	21	0	21
Ashford	E07000105	581	581	0	581
Canterbury	E07000106	321	309	0	309
Dartford	E07000107	76	73	0	73
Dover	E07000108	321	315	0	315
Gravesham	E07000109	105	99	0	99
Maidstone	E07000110	393	393	0	393
Sevenoaks	E07000111	370	370	1	369
Shepway	E07000112	365	357	0	357
Swale	E07000113	422	374	0	374
Thanet	E07000114	112	103	0	103
Tonbridge and Malling	E07000115	241	240	0	240
Tunbridge Wells	E07000116	331	331	0	331
Burnley	E07000117	111	111	0	111
Chorley	E07000118	203	203	0	203
Fylde	E07000119	183	166	0	166
Hyndburn	E07000120	73	73	0	73
Lancaster	E07000121	654	576	0	576
Pendle	E07000122	169	169	0	169
Preston	E07000123	143	142	0	142
Ribble Valley	E07000124	584	584	1	583
Rossendale	E07000125	138	138	0	138
South Ribble	E07000126	115	113	0	113
West Lancashire	E07000127	381	347	0	347
Wyre	E07000128	329	283	0	283
Blaby	E07000129	130	130	0	130
Charnwood	E07000130	279	279	0	279
Harborough	E07000131	593	593	1	592
Hinckley and Bosworth	E07000132	297	297	0	297
Melton	E07000133	481	481	0	481
North West Leicestershire	E07000134	279	279	0	279
Oadby and Wigston	E07000135	24	24	0	24
Boston	E07000136	398	365	0	365
East Lindsey	E07000137	1831	1765	0	1765
Lincoln	E07000138	36	36	0	36
North Kesteven	E07000139	922	922	0	922
South Holland	E07000140	816	751	0	751
South Kesteven	E07000141	943	943	0	943
West Lindsey	E07000142	1158	1156	0	1156
Breckland	E07000143	1305	1305	0	1305
Broadland	E07000144	553	552	0	552
Great Yarmouth	E07000145	182	174	0	174
King's Lynn and West Norfolk	E07000146	1528	1438	0	1438
North Norfolk	E07000147	991	965	2	963
Norwich	E07000148	41	39	0	39
South Norfolk	E07000149	909	908	0	908
Corby	E07000150	80	80	0	80
Daventry	E07000151	666	666	3	663
East Northamptonshire	E07000152	510	510	0	510
Kettering	E07000153	233	233	0	233

1.1 Standard Area Measurement for UK Local Authority Districts as at 31/12/2013

	Code as at December 2013[1]	Extent of the realm (Km^2)	Area to mean high water (Km^2)	Inland water (Km^2)	Land only (Km^2)
Northampton	E07000154	81	81	0	81
South Northamptonshire	E07000155	634	634	0	634
Wellingborough	E07000156	163	163	0	163
Craven	E07000163	1179	1179	1	1177
Hambleton	E07000164	1311	1311	0	1311
Harrogate	E07000165	1309	1309	1	1308
Richmondshire	E07000166	1319	1319	0	1319
Ryedale	E07000167	1507	1507	0	1507
Scarborough	E07000168	827	817	0	817
Selby	E07000169	602	599	0	599
Ashfield	E07000170	110	110	0	110
Bassetlaw	E07000171	639	638	0	638
Broxtowe	E07000172	80	80	0	80
Gedling	E07000173	120	120	0	120
Mansfield	E07000174	77	77	0	77
Newark and Sherwood	E07000175	652	651	0	651
Rushcliffe	E07000176	409	409	0	409
Cherwell	E07000177	589	589	0	589
Oxford	E07000178	46	46	0	46
South Oxfordshire	E07000179	679	679	0	679
Vale of White Horse	E07000180	579	579	1	578
West Oxfordshire	E07000181	714	714	0	714
Mendip	E07000187	739	739	0	739
Sedgemoor	E07000188	606	564	0	564
South Somerset	E07000189	959	959	0	959
Taunton Deane	E07000190	463	462	0	462
West Somerset	E07000191	747	727	1	725
Cannock Chase	E07000192	79	79	0	79
East Staffordshire	E07000193	390	390	3	387
Lichfield	E07000194	331	331	0	331
Newcastle-under-Lyme	E07000195	211	211	0	211
South Staffordshire	E07000196	407	407	0	407
Stafford	E07000197	598	598	0	598
Staffordshire Moorlands	E07000198	576	576	0	576
Tamworth	E07000199	31	31	0	31
Babergh	E07000200	612	595	1	594
Forest Heath	E07000201	378	378	0	378
Ipswich	E07000202	40	39	0	39
Mid Suffolk	E07000203	871	871	0	871
St Edmundsbury	E07000204	657	657	0	657
Suffolk Coastal	E07000205	921	891	0	891
Waveney	E07000206	375	370	0	370
Elmbridge	E07000207	96	96	1	95
Epsom and Ewell	E07000208	34	34	0	34
Guildford	E07000209	271	271	0	271
Mole Valley	E07000210	258	258	0	258
Reigate and Banstead	E07000211	129	129	0	129
Runnymede	E07000212	78	78	0	78
Spelthorne	E07000213	51	51	6	45
Surrey Heath	E07000214	95	95	0	95
Tandridge	E07000215	248	248	0	248
Waverley	E07000216	345	345	0	345
Woking	E07000217	64	64	0	64
North Warwickshire	E07000218	284	284	0	284
Nuneaton and Bedworth	E07000219	79	79	0	79
Rugby	E07000220	354	354	2	351
Stratford-on-Avon	E07000221	978	978	0	978
Warwick	E07000222	283	283	0	283
Adur	E07000223	44	42	0	42
Arun	E07000224	224	221	0	221
Chichester	E07000225	812	786	0	786
Crawley	E07000226	45	45	0	45
Horsham	E07000227	531	530	0	530

1.1 Standard Area Measurement for UK Local Authority Districts as at 31/12/2013

	Code as at December 2013[1]	Extent of the realm (Km^2)	Area to mean high water (Km^2)	Inland water (Km^2)	Land only (Km^2)
Mid Sussex	E07000228	334	334	0	334
Worthing	E07000229	34	32	0	32
Bromsgrove	E07000234	217	217	0	217
Malvern Hills	E07000235	577	577	0	577
Redditch	E07000236	54	54	0	54
Worcester	E07000237	33	33	0	33
Wychavon	E07000238	664	664	0	664
Wyre Forest	E07000239	195	195	0	195
St Albans	E07000240	161	161	0	161
Welwyn Hatfield	E07000241	130	130	0	130
East Hertfordshire	E07000242	476	476	0	476
Stevenage	E07000243	26	26	0	26
Bolton	E08000001	140	140	0	140
Bury	E08000002	99	99	0	99
Manchester	E08000003	116	116	0	116
Oldham	E08000004	142	142	0	142
Rochdale	E08000005	158	158	0	158
Salford	E08000006	97	97	0	97
Stockport	E08000007	126	126	0	126
Tameside	E08000008	103	103	0	103
Trafford	E08000009	106	106	0	106
Wigan	E08000010	188	188	0	188
Knowsley	E08000011	86	86	0	86
Liverpool	E08000012	134	112	0	112
St. Helens	E08000013	136	136	0	136
Sefton	E08000014	205	153	0	153
Wirral	E08000015	256	157	0	157
Barnsley	E08000016	329	329	0	329
Doncaster	E08000017	569	568	0	568
Rotherham	E08000018	287	287	0	287
Sheffield	E08000019	368	368	0	368
Newcastle upon Tyne	E08000021	115	113	0	113
North Tyneside	E08000022	85	82	0	82
South Tyneside	E08000023	67	64	0	64
Sunderland	E08000024	140	137	0	137
Birmingham	E08000025	268	268	0	268
Coventry	E08000026	99	99	0	99
Dudley	E08000027	98	98	0	98
Sandwell	E08000028	86	86	0	86
Solihull	E08000029	178	178	0	178
Walsall	E08000030	104	104	0	104
Wolverhampton	E08000031	69	69	0	69
Bradford	E08000032	366	366	0	366
Calderdale	E08000033	364	364	0	364
Kirklees	E08000034	409	409	0	409
Leeds	E08000035	552	552	0	552
Wakefield	E08000036	339	339	0	339
Gateshead	E08000037	144	142	0	142
City of London	E09000001	3	3	0	3
Barking and Dagenham	E09000002	38	36	0	36
Barnet	E09000003	87	87	0	87
Bexley	E09000004	64	61	0	61
Brent	E09000005	43	43	0	43
Bromley	E09000006	150	150	0	150
Camden	E09000007	22	22	0	22
Croydon	E09000008	86	86	0	86
Ealing	E09000009	56	56	0	56
Enfield	E09000010	82	82	1	81
Greenwich	E09000011	50	47	0	47
Hackney	E09000012	19	19	0	19
Hammersmith and Fulham	E09000013	17	16	0	16
Haringey	E09000014	30	30	0	30
Harrow	E09000015	50	50	0	50

1.1 Standard Area Measurement for UK Local Authority Districts as at 31/12/2013

	Code as at December 2013[1]	Extent of the realm (Km²)	Area to mean high water (Km²)	Inland water (Km²)	Land only (Km²)
Havering	E09000016	114	112	0	112
Hillingdon	E09000017	116	116	0	116
Hounslow	E09000018	57	56	0	56
Islington	E09000019	15	15	0	15
Kensington and Chelsea	E09000020	12	12	0	12
Kingston upon Thames	E09000021	37	37	0	37
Lambeth	E09000022	27	27	0	27
Lewisham	E09000023	35	35	0	35
Merton	E09000024	38	38	0	38
Newham	E09000025	39	36	0	36
Redbridge	E09000026	56	56	0	56
Richmond upon Thames	E09000027	59	57	0	57
Southwark	E09000028	30	29	0	29
Sutton	E09000029	44	44	0	44
Tower Hamlets	E09000030	22	20	0	20
Waltham Forest	E09000031	39	39	0	39
Wandsworth	E09000032	35	34	0	34
Westminster	E09000033	22	21	0	21
Scotland	S92000003	80240	78810	900	77910
Clackmannanshire	S12000005	164	159	0	159
Dumfries and Galloway	S12000006	6676	6438	11	6427
East Ayrshire	S12000008	1270	1270	8	1262
East Lothian	S12000010	701	679	0	679
East Renfrewshire	S12000011	174	174	0	174
Eilean Siar	S12000013	3269	3101	41	3060
Falkirk	S12000014	315	297	0	297
Fife	S12000015	1374	1325	0	1325
Highland	S12000017	26484	26162	506	25657
Inverclyde	S12000018	174	162	2	160
Midlothian	S12000019	355	355	2	354
Moray	S12000020	2257	2238	0	2238
North Ayrshire	S12000021	904	885	0	885
Orkney Islands	S12000023	1086	1013	25	989
Perth and Kinross	S12000024	5419	5384	98	5286
Scottish Borders	S12000026	4743	4739	7	4732
Shetland Islands	S12000027	1657	1468	1	1467
South Ayrshire	S12000028	1235	1224	2	1222
South Lanarkshire	S12000029	1774	1774	2	1772
Stirling	S12000030	2255	2253	66	2187
Aberdeen City	S12000033	206	186	0	186
Aberdeenshire	S12000034	6339	6318	5	6313
Argyll and Bute	S12000035	7164	7008	99	6909
City of Edinburgh	S12000036	273	263	0	263
Renfrewshire	S12000038	269	261	0	261
West Dunbartonshire	S12000039	183	177	19	159
West Lothian	S12000040	432	429	1	428
Angus	S12000041	2204	2185	4	2182
Dundee City	S12000042	62	60	0	60
North Lanarkshire	S12000044	472	472	2	470
East Dunbartonshire	S12000045	174	174	0	174
Glasgow City	S12000046	176	175	0	175

1.1 Standard Area Measurement for UK Local Authority Districts as at 31/12/2013

	Code as at December 2013[1]	Extent of the realm (Km²)	Area to mean high water (Km²)	Inland water (Km²)	Land only (Km²)
Wales	W92000004	21224	20780	45	20736
Isle of Anglesey	W06000001	749	714	3	711
Gwynedd	W06000002	2622	2548	13	2535
Conwy	W06000003	1153	1130	4	1126
Denbighshire	W06000004	846	839	2	837
Flintshire	W06000005	489	437	0	437
Wrexham	W06000006	504	504	0	504
Ceredigion	W06000008	1806	1789	3	1786
Pembrokeshire	W06000009	1650	1619	0	1619
Carmarthenshire	W06000010	2439	2371	1	2370
Swansea	W06000011	421	380	0	380
Neath Port Talbot	W06000012	452	442	1	441
Bridgend	W06000013	255	251	0	251
Vale of Glamorgan	W06000014	340	331	0	331
Cardiff	W06000015	150	140	0	140
Rhondda Cynon Taf	W06000016	424	424	0	424
Caerphilly	W06000018	277	277	0	277
Blaenau Gwent	W06000019	109	109	0	109
Torfaen	W06000020	126	126	1	126
Monmouthshire	W06000021	886	850	1	849
Newport	W06000022	218	191	0	191
Powys	W06000023	5195	5195	15	5181
Merthyr Tydfil	W06000024	112	112	1	111
Northern Ireland	N92000002	14130	14130	568	13562
Derry	95A	380	380	0	379
Limavady	95B	586	586	0	585
Coleraine	95C	484	484	1	483
Ballymoney	95D	418	418	0	418
Moyle	95E	494	494	0	494
Larne	95F	336	336	1	335
Ballymena	95G	632	632	2	630
Magherafelt	95H	573	573	9	563
Cookstown	95I	622	622	109	513
Strabane	95J	859	859	1	858
Omagh	95K	1130	1130	1	1129
Fermanagh	95L	1871	1871	154	1718
Dungannon	95M	784	784	12	771
Craigavon	95N	378	378	100	279
Armagh	95O	671	671	2	668
Newry and Mourne	95P	901	901	4	897
Banbridge	95Q	453	453	1	452
Down	95R	648	648	4	644
Lisburn	95S	447	447	5	442
Antrim	95T	577	577	156	421
Newtownabbey	95U	151	151	0	150
Carrickfergus	95V	82	82	1	81
North Down	95W	82	82	1	81
Ards	95X	378	378	1	377
Castlereagh	95Y	85	85	0	85
Belfast	95Z	110	110	1	109

Source: ONS Geography codes
Standard Area Measurement for Local Authority Districts as at 31/12/2013

1. Area codes implemented from 1 January 2011; in line with the GSS Coding and Naming Policy

Figures have been rounded to the nearest whole number

Parliamentary elections

Chapter 2

Parliamentary elections

This chapter covers parliamentary elections, by-elections and devolved assembly elections in the UK, Wales, Scotland and Northern Ireland.

Parliamentary elections (Table 2.1)

Information is supplied on the total electorate, average electorate and valid votes as a percentage of electorate. The number of seats by party is also listed.

Parliamentary by-elections (Table 2.2)

Information can be found on the votes recorded for each party and General Elections and subsequent by-elections between General Elections.

Devolved assembly elections (Tables 2.3 and 2.4)

Table 2.2 provides information on the devolved assembly elections in Wales and Scotland, listing information on the total electorate, average electorate and valid votes as a percentage of electorate. The number of seats by party is also listed. Table 2.4 provides information on the devolved assembly elections in Northern Ireland, listing information on the total electorate, average electorate and valid votes as a percentage of electorate. The number of seats by party is also listed.

2.1 Parliamentary elections[1]

United Kingdom
Thousands and percentages

		31-Mar 1966	18-Jun 1970[1]	28-Feb 1974		10-Oct 1974	03-May 1979	09-Jun 1983	11-Jun 1987	09-Apr 1992	01-May 1997	07-Jun 2001	05-May 2005	06-May 2010	07-May 2015
United Kingdom															
Electorate	DZ5P	35957	39615	40256	DZ6V	40256	41573	42704	43666	43719	43846	44403	44246	45597	46354
Average-electors per seat	DZ5T	57.1	62.9	63.4	DZ6R	63.4	65.5	66.7	67.2	67.2	66.5	67.4	68.5	70.1	71.3
Valid votes counted	DZ5X	27265	28345	31340	DZ6N	29189	31221	30671	32530	33614	31286	26367	27149	29688	30697.5
As percentage of electorate	DZ63	75.8	71.5	77.9	DZ6J	72.5	75.1	71.8	74.5	76.7	71.4	59.4	61.4	65.1	66.2
England and Wales															
Electorate	DZ5Q	31695	34931	35509	DZ6W	35509	36695	37708	38568	38648	38719	39228	39266	40565	40968
Average-electors per seat	DZ5U	57.9	63.9	64.3	DZ6S	64.3	66.5	67.2	68.8	68.8	68	68.9	69	70.8	71.6
Valid votes counted	DZ5Y	24116	24877	27735	DZ6O	25729	27609	27082	28832	29897	27679	23243	24097	26548	27034
As percentage of electorate	DZ64	76.1	71.2	78.1	DZ6K	72.5	75.2	71.8	74.8	77.5	71.5	59.3	61.4	65.4	66.0
Scotland															
Electorate	DZ5R	3360	3659	3705	DZ6X	3705	3837	3934	3995	3929	3949	3984	3840	3863	4100
Average-electors per seat	DZ5V	47.3	51.5	52.2	DZ6T	52.2	54	54.6	55.5	54.6	54.8	55.3	65.1	65.5	69.4963
Valid votes counted	DZ5Z	2553	2688	2887	DZ6P	2758	2917	2825	2968	2931	2817	2313	2334	2466	2910
As percentage of electorate	DZ65	76	73.5	77.9	DZ6L	74.5	76	71.8	74.3	74.2	71.3	58.1	60.8	63.8	71.0
Northern Ireland															
Electorate	DZ5S	902	1025	1027	DZ6Y	1037	1028	1050	1090	1141	1178	1191	1140	1169	1237
Average-electors per seat	DZ5W	75.2	85.4	85.6	DZ6U	86.4	85.6	61.8	64.1	67.1	65.4	66.2	63.3	65.0	68.7
Valid votes counted	DZ62	596	779	718	DZ6Q	702	696	765	730	785	791	810	718	674	718
As percentage of electorate	DZ66	66.1	76	69.9	DZ6M	67.7	67.7	72.9	67	68.8	67.1	68	62.9	57.6	58.1
Members of Parliament elected: (numbers)	DZV7	630	630	635	DZV8	635	635	650	650	651	659	659	646	650	650
Conservative	DZ67	253	330	296	DZ6D	276	339	396	375	336	165	166	198	306	331
Labour	DZ68	363	287	301	DZ6E	319	268	209	229	271	418	412	355	258	232
Liberal Democrat[2]	DZ69	12	6	14	DZ6F	13	11	23	22	20	46	52	62	57	8
Scottish National Party	DZ6A	–	1	7	DZ6G	11	2	2	3	3	6	5	6	6	56
Plaid Cymru	DZ6B	–	–	2	DZ6H	3	2	2	3	4	4	4	3	3	3
Other[3]	DZ6C	2	6	15	DZ6I	13	13	18	18	17	20	20	22	20	20

1 The Representation of the People Act 1969 lowered the minimum voting age from 21 to 18 years with effect from 16 February 1970.
2 Liberal before 1992. The figures for 1983 and 1987 include six and five MPs respectively who were elected for the Social Democratic Party.
3 Including the Speaker.

Source: British Electoral Facts 1832-2012
Plymouth University for the Electoral Commission: 01752 233207

2.2 Parliamentary by-elections

United Kingdom

	May 1997 - June 2001	General[1,2] Election May 1997	June 2001 - November 2004	General[1] Election June 2001	May 2005 - November 2009	General[1] Election May 2005	May 2010- November 2014	General[1] Election May 2010
Numbers of by-elections	17		6		14		21	
Votes recorded								
By party (percentages)								
Conservative	27.0	25.1	17.7	21.2	27.7	25.7	17.3	27.8
Labour	29.7	40.1	40.8	58.3	29.3	35.7	36.0	36.4
Liberal Democrat	22.1	14.4	31.3	13.7	20.0	20.6	8.3	18.8
Scottish National Party	6.0	4.1	-	-	9.5	6.2	1.5	0.7
Plaid Cymru	2.5	2.3	2.7	2.1	0.4	0.1	0.3	0.2
UKIP[3]							17.3	2.1
Other	12.7	14.1	7.4	4.7	13.0	11.7	19.3	13.9
Total votes recorded (percentages)	100	100	100	100	100	100	100	100
(thousands)	435	723	140	205	436	586	605	909

Source: Plymouth University for the Electoral Commission: 01752 233207

1 Votes recorded in the same seats in the previous General Election.
2 Proportions of 'other' votes inflated by the fact that votes were cast for the retiring Speaker as 'The Speaker seeking re-election' and not as a party
3 Figures for UKIP only recorded for by-elections since 2010

The Bradford West by-election of 29th March 2012 was won by the Respect candidate whose votes are included under "Other".
Similarly all votes cast in Northern Ireland by-elections have been included under "Other".

2.3 Devolved assembly elections
Wales and Scotland

Thousands and percentages

		06-May 1999	01-May 2003	03-May 2007	05-May 2011
Welsh Assembly					
Electorate	E28K	2205	2230	2248	2290
Average-electors per seat[1]	E28N	55.1	55.7	56.2	57.2
Valid votes counted	E28Q	1023	850	978	949
As percentage of electorate	E28T	46.4	38.1	43.5	41.5
Members elected:[2] (numbers)	E2XI	60	60	60	60
Conservative	E2WG	9	11	12	14
Labour	E2WU	28	30	26	30
Liberal Democrat	E2WW	6	6	6	5
Plaid Cymru	E2X3	17	12	15	11
Other	E2WY	–	1	1	-
Scottish Parliament					
Electorate	E28L	4024	3879	3899	3951
Average-electors per seat[1]	E28O	55.1	53.1	53.4	54.1
Valid votes counted	E28R	2342	1916	2017	1989
As percentage of electorate	E28U	58.2	49.4	51.7	50.3
Members elected:[3] (numbers)	E2XJ	129	129	129	129
Conservative	E2WH	18	18	17	15
Labour	E2WV	56	50	46	37
Liberal Democrat	E2WX	17	17	16	5
Scottish National Party	E2X4	35	27	47	69
Other	E2WZ	3	17	3	3

1 This is the average in each first-past-the-post constituency. Additional members are then elected on the basis of a regional 'list' vote.
2 Comprising 40 from constituencies and 20 from the regional 'list'.
3 Comprising 73 from constituencies and 56 from the regional 'list'.

Sources: British Electoral Facts 1832-2012;
Plymouth University for the Electoral Commission: 01752 233207

2.4 Devolved assembly elections
Northern Ireland

Thousands and percentages

		25-Jun 1998	26-Nov 2003	08-Mar 2007	05-May 2011
Electorate	E28M	1179	1098	1108	1210
Average-electors per seat[1]	E28P	65.5	61	61.6	67.2
Valid votes counted	E28S	810	692	692	662
As percentage of electorate	E28V	68.7	63	63	55.7
Members elected: (numbers)	E2XK	108	108	108	108
Alliance Party	E2X5	6	6		
SDLP	E2X6	24	18	16	14
Sinn Fein	E2X7	18	24	28	29
Democratic Unionist Party	E2X8	20	30	36	38
UK Unionist Party	E2X9	5	1	–	-
Ulster Unionist Party	E2XA	28	27	18	16
Other	E2X2	7	2		

1 This is the average in each Westminster constituency. Six members are
elected by single transferable vote (STV) in each constituency.

Sources: British Electoral Facts 1832-2012;
Plymouth University for the Electoral Commission: 01752233207

International development

Chapter 3

International development

Overseas development assistance

The Department for International Development (DFID) is the UK Government Department with lead responsibility for overseas development. DFID's aim is to eliminate poverty in poorer countries through achievement of the Millennium Development Goals (MDG's) by 2015. Statistics relating to international development are published on a financial year basis and on a calendar year basis. Statistics on a calendar year basis allow comparisons of aid expenditure with other donor countries. Aid flows can be measured before (gross) or after (net) deductions of repayments of principal on past loans. These tables show only the gross figures.

Aid is provided in two main ways: Bilateral funding is provided directly to partner countries while multilateral funding is provided through international organisations.

Funds can only be classified as multilateral if they are channelled through an organisation on a list in the OECD –

Development Assistance Committee (DAC) Statistical Reporting Directives – which identifies all multilateral organisations. This list also highlights some bodies that might appear to be multilateral but are actually bilateral (in particular this latter category includes some international non-governmental organisations such as the International Committee of the Red Cross and some Public-Private Partnerships). The DAC list of multilaterals is updated annually based on members nominations; organisations must be engaged in development work to be classified as multilateral aid channels although money may be classified as bilateral while a case is being made for a new multilateral organisation to be recognised.

While core funding to multilateral organisations is always classified as multilateral expenditure, additional funding channelled through multilaterals is often classified as bilateral expenditure. This would be the case in circumstances where a DFID country office transfers some money to a multilateral organisation (for example UN agency) for a particular programme in that country (or region). That is where DFID has control over what the money is being spent on and/or where it is being spent. Likewise, if DFID responds to an emergency appeal from an agency for a particular country or area, the funds will be allocated as bilateral spend to that country or region. As a result, some organisations, such as UN agencies have some of their DFID funding classified as bilateral and some as multilateral.

Bilateral assistance takes various forms:

Financial Aid – Poverty Reduction Budget Support (PRBS) – Funds provided to developing countries for them to spend in support of their expenditure programmes whose long-term objective is to reduce poverty; funds are spent using the overseas governments' own financial management, procurement and accountability systems to increase ownership and long term sustainability. PRBS can take the form of a general contribution to the overall budget – general budget support – or support with a more restricted focus which is earmarked for a specific sector – sector budget support.

Other Financial Aid – Funding of projects and programmes such as Sector Wide Programmes not classified as PRBS. Financial aid in its broader sense covers all bilateral aid expenditure other than technical cooperation and administrative costs but in SID we separately categorise this further.

Technical Co-operation – Activities designed to enhance the knowledge, intellectual skills, technical expertise or the productive capability of people in recipient countries. It also covers funding of services which contribute to the design or implementation of development projects and programmes.

This assistance is mainly delivered through research and development, the use of consultants, training (generally overseas partners visiting the UK or elsewhere for a training programme) and employment of 'other Personnel' (non-DFID experts on fixed term contracts). This latter category is growing less significant over time as existing contracted staff reach the end of their assignments.

Bilateral Aid Delivered Through a Multilateral Organisation – This category covers funding that is channelled through a multilateral organisation and DFID has control over the country, sector or theme that the funds will be spent on. For example, where a DFID country office transfers money to a multilateral organisation for a particular piece of work in that country. This also includes aid delivered through multi donor funds such as the United Nations Central Emergency Response Fund (CERF).

Bilateral Aid Delivered Through a Non-Governmental Organisation (NGO) – This category covers support to the international development work of UK and international not for profit organisations such as NGOs or Civil Society Organisations. This covers Partnership Programme Arrangements (PPAs), the Civil Society Challenge Fund and other grants.

Other Bilateral Aid – This category includes any aid not elsewhere classified such as funding to other donors for shared development purposes. More information on all of the above aid types is provided in the Glossary.

Humanitarian Assistance – Provides food, aid and other humanitarian assistance including shelter, medical care and advice in emergency situations and their aftermath. Work of the conflict pools is also included.

DFID Debt Relief – This includes sums for debt relief on DFID aid loans and cancellation of debt under the Commonwealth Debt Initiative (CDI). The non-CDI DFID debt relief is reported on the basis of the 'benefit to the recipient country'. This means that figures shown represent the money available to the country in the year in question that would otherwise have been spent on debt servicing. The CDI debt cancellation is reported on a 'lump sum' basis where all outstanding amounts on a loan are shown at the time the agreement to cancel is made.

CDC Gross Investments – **CDC Group PLC** is wholly government owned. Its investments must have a clear development objective. The net amount (that is equity purchase less equity sales) of

CDC investments in official development assistance (ODA)-eligible countries is reported as ODA and the gross amount (that is equity purchase only) is reported in GPEX.

Non-DFID Debt Relief – Comprises CDC Debt and ECGD Debt. CDC has a portfolio of loans to governments which can become eligible for debt relief under the Heavily Indebted Poor Countries (HIPC) or other debt relief deals. In 2005/06 £90 million of debts owed to CDC were reorganised. Export Credit Guarantee Department (ECGD) is the UK's official export credit agency providing insurance for exporters against the main risks in selling overseas and guarantees to banks providing export finance. It also negotiates debt relief arrangements on commercial debt.

The Foreign and Commonwealth Office (FCO) contributes to UK GPEX in a number of ways:

The FCO Strategic Programme Fund supports a range of the UK government's international goals. Where the programme funds projects which meet the required OECD definition these projects are included in UK GPEX statistics.

The FCO supports the British Council through grant-in-aid funding. This funding goes to support a range of initiatives including building the capacity and quality of English language teaching; supporting education systems; and using cultural exchange to improve economic welfare. UK GPEX statistics include the proportion of this work which is clearly focussed on delivering economic welfare and development in ODA eligible countries.

The British Council also manages, on behalf of the FCO, the Chevening Scholarships programme, which provides funding for postgraduate students or researchers from developing countries to study in UK universities. Funding from this scheme to students from ODA eligible countries are included in UK ODA and GPEX statistics.

The FCO makes annual contributions to UN and Commonwealth organisations. A proportion of these contributions are allowed to score as ODA in line with Annex 2 of the DAC Statistical Reporting Directives.

In addition to contributing directly to the Conflict Pool (see below) the FCO is also responsible for the UK contribution to the UN Department for Peacekeeping Operations (UNDPKO). In line with DAC rules 6 per cent of donor funding to UNDPKO is allowed to score as ODA. FCO also funds other bilateral peacekeeping missions including the Organisation for Security and Cooperation in Europe (OSCE) and the European Security and Defence Policy (ESDP) civilian missions; a proportion of which is reported as bilateral GPEX.

The Conflict Pool (CP) –is governed and jointly managed by DFID, the FCO and the Ministry of Defence (MoD) to bring together the UK government's development, diplomatic and defence interest and expertise to ensure a coherent response to conflict prevention. Some of the CP's expenditure is ODA eligible. All CP funds disbursed through DFID are included in GPEX and appear in these statistics as part of DFID expenditure. The remaining figures comprise the aggregate of FCO and MOD spending. Data on the ODA eligible CP funds disbursed by the FCO and MOD are collected by DFID in liaison with programme officers in the relevant departments.

Other –includes contributions from other government departments including: Department of Energy and Climate Change; Department of Health; Department for Environment, Food & Rural

Affairs; Department for Culture, Media and Sport; Scottish Government; and the Welsh Assembly Government. It also includes estimates of the UK Border Agency's costs of supporting refugees in the UK; as well as estimates of gift aid to NGOs and other official funding to NGOs.

Comparisons are available in the OECD Development Assistance Committee's annual report.

3.1a Total Gross Public Expenditure on Development 2008/09 - 2012/13

£ thousand

	2008/09	2009/10	2010/11 [1]	2011/12	2012/13 [1]
Total GPEX					
Total Bilateral GPEX	4 333 951	4 765 735	5 311 859	5 178 611	5 231 347
Total Multilateral GPEX	2 600 365	2 748 766	3 461 939	3 461 684	3 498 040
Of which: European Commission	1 407 901	1 424 089	1 431 849	1 355 553	1 194 602
World Bank	573 652	559 785	926 713	1 038 568	1 025 431
UN Agencies	308 154	278 619	417 317	434 462	424 145
Other Organisations	310 659	486 273	686 060	633 102	853 862
Total Admin	249 000	252 101	233 208	309 292	293 590
TOTAL GPEX ON DEVELOPMENT	**7 183 316**	**7 766 602**	**9 007 006**	8 949 587	9 022 977
of which: DFID Programme					
DFID Bilateral Programme	3 283 996	3 958 263	4 248 018	4 204 114	4 169 389
DFID Multilateral Programme	2 277 358	2 436 338	3 221 673	3 257 724	3 281 308
DFID Admin	237 899	234 398	219 457	220 352	220 220
TOTAL DFID PROGRAMME	**5 799 253**	**6 628 999**	**7 689 149**	7 682 191	7 670 916

Source: Department for International Development (DFID)

1. Section 1 of Statistics on International Development publication shows a reconciliation of 2012/13 GPEX and 2012/13 ODA

3.1b DFID Expenditure on Development 2008/09-2012/13

£thousands

	2008/09	2009/10	2010/11	2011/12	2012/13
DFID Bilateral Programme[1]					
Poverty Reduction Budget Support	648 668	634 101	643 671	536 662	410 133
of which					
General Budget Support	*392 748*	*383 150*	*360 467*	*242 290*	*167 343*
Sector Budget Support	*255 920*	*250 951*	*283 204*	*294 372*	*242 790*
Other Financial Aid	516 431	518 817	550 728	544 778	685 571
Technical Co-operation	514 235	419 911	467 939	527 907	638 258
Bilateral Aid Delivered though a Multilateral Organisation [2]	656 448	1 264 716	1 465 789	1 404 592	1 074 957
Bilateral Aid Delivered through a NGO	462 597	599 434	626 752	739 558	747 302
of which:					
Partnership Programme Agreements	*108 928*	*128 823*	*115 347*	*119 625*	*110 347*
Other CSO's	*353 669*	*470 612*	*511 405*	*619 933*	*636 955*
Other Bilateral Aid [3]	17 030	34 668	76 009	81 372	119 120
Humanitarian Assistance	449 163	434 556	350 669	354 293	476 878
DFID Debt Relief	19 425	52 061	66 460	14 954	17 169
Total DFID Bilateral Programme	**3 283 996**	**3 958 263**	**4 248 018**	**4 204 114**	**4 169 389**
DFID Multilateral Programme					
European Comission	1 153 892	1 186 303	1 268 563	1 220 076	1 085 769
World Bank	573 652	559 785	926 713	1 038 568	1 025 431
United Nations	251 903	216 315	355 337	376 708	360 304
Other Multilateral	297 911	473 934	671 061	622 373	809 804
Total DFID Multilateral Programme	**2 277 358**	**2 436 338**	**3 221 673**	**3 257 724**	**3 281 308**
Total DFID Programme (excl. Admin)	**5 561 355**	**6 394 601**	**7 475 391**	**7 461 839**	**7 450 696**
DFID Administration	237 899	234 398	219 457	220 352	220 220
Total DFID Programme	**5 799 253**	**6 628 999**	**7 689 149**	**7 682 191**	**7 670 916**

Source: Department for International Development (DFID)

1. Descriptions of aid types given in Technical Note 1.
2. This covers aid provided through multialteral organisations where the recipient country, region, sector, theme or specific project are known.
3. Other Bilateral Aid covers bilateral aid that does not fit into any other category.

3.2a Total DFID Expenditure and GPEX by Recipient Country (Africa) 2008/09 - 2012/13[1]

£ thousand

| | | Financial Aid | | | | | | | | | | | | |
		General Poverty Reduction Budget Support	Sector Poverty Reduction Budget Support	Other Financial Aid [5]	Technical Cooperation	Bilateral aid delivered through a Multilateral	Bilateral aid Delivered through an NGO	Other Bilateral Aid [2]	Humanitarian Assistance	DFID Debt Relief	Total DFID Bilateral Programme	Aid from other UK Official Sources [5]	Total Bilateral Gross Public Expenditure	UK Imputed Multilateral Shares [3]
Africa: North of Sahara														
Algeria	2008/09	-	-	-	-	-	-	-	-	-	-	1 169	1 169	1 560
	2009/10	-	-	-	-	-	-	-	230	-	230	2 314	2 545	6 479
	2010/11	-	-	-	-	-	-	-	-	-	-	1 481	1 481	10 173
	2011/12	-	-	-	-	-	-	-	-	-	-	1 533	1 533	-
	2012/13	-	-	-	-	-	-	-	-	-	-	1 894	1 894	
Egypt	2008/09	-	-	-	-	-	-	-	-	-	-	6 529	6 529	15 065
	2009/10	-	-	-	-	-	-	-	-	-	-	23 666	23 666	18 728
	2010/11	-	-	-	-	-	-	-	-	-	-	10 843	10 843	29 033
	2011/12	-	-	-	-	100	-	-	-	-	100	12 951	13 051	19 624
	2012/13	-	-	-	-	300	98	-	-	-	398	7 305	7 702	
Libyan Arab Republic	2008/09	-	-	-	-	-	-	-	-	-	-	630	630	691
	2009/10	-	-	-	-	-	-	-	-	-	-	1 187	1 187	75
	2010/11	-	-	-	-	-	-	-	28	-	28	1 020	1 048	1 833
	2011/12	-	-	-	2 107	156	-	-	5 305	-	7 568	6 245	13 813	4 770
	2012/13	-	-	-	578	500	139	-	304	-	1 521	5 411	6 932	
Morocco	2008/09	-	-	-	-	-	-	-	-	-	-	3 693	3 693	23 343
	2009/10	-	-	-	-	-	-	-	-	-	-	3 040	3 040	18 444
	2010/11	-	-	-	-	-	-	-	-	-	-	2 137	2 137	23 527
	2011/12	-	-	-	-	-	-	-	-	-	-	-	-	24 054
	2012/13	-	-	-	-	-	-	-	-	-	-	5 424	5 424	
Tunisia	2008/09	-	-	-	-	-	-	-	-	-	-	807	807	10 899
	2009/10	-	-	-	-	-	-	-	-	-	-	2 446	2 446	10 225
	2010/11	-	-	-	-	48	-	-	-	-	-	1 633	1 633	13 083
	2011/12	-	-	-	-	48	-	-	-	-	48	6 102	6 150	-
	2012/13	-	-	-	-	327	175	-	-	-	502	6 684	7 186	
North of Sahara Regional	2008/09	-	-	-	124	510	-	-	-	-	634	7 114	7 748	4 635
	2009/10	-	-	-	31	397	-	-	-	-	429	-	429	26 086
	2010/11	-	-	-	-	-	-	-	10 249	-	10 249	-	10 249	21 469
	2011/12	-	-	-	-	-	-	-	-	-	-	126	126	18 047
	2012/13	-	-	-	292	500		-	19	-	811	4 113	4 924	
Total North of Sahara	2008/09	-	-	-	124	510	-	-	-	-	634	19 942	20 576	56 192
	2009/10	-	-	-	31	397	-	-	230	-	659	32 653	33 312	80 037
	2010/11	-	-	-	-	-	-	-	10 277	-	10 277	17 113	27 391	99 117
	2011/12	-	-	-	2 107	304	-	-	5 305	-	7 716	30 615	38 331	66 495
	2012/13	-	-	-	870	1 627	412	-	323	-	3 232	30 830	34 062	
Angola	2008/09	-	-	-	114	465	1 638	-	1 048	-	3 265	164	3 428	12 619
	2009/10	-	-	-	176	2 350	866	-	348	-	3 741	78	3 818	2 450
	2010/11	-	-	-	-	-29	502	-	-	-	473	8 999	9 472	10 845
	2011/12	-	-	-	-	-	-	-	-	-	-	336	336	15 933
	2012/13	-	-	-	-	-	-	-	-	-	-	-	-	
Benin [4]	2008/09	-	-	-	-	-	-	-	-	-	-	-	-	15 666
	2009/10	-	-	-	-	-	-	-	-	-	-	17	17	14 537
	2010/11	-	-	-	-	3 257	-	-	66	-	3 323	-	3 323	25 873
	2011/12	-	-	-	-	-	-	-	26	-	26	-	26	24 533
	2012/13	-	-	-	-	-	-	-	-	-	-	381	381	
Botswana	2008/09	-	-	-	-	-	-	-	-	-	-	484	484	873
	2009/10	-	-	-	-	-	-	-	-	-	-	594	594	8 128
	2010/11	-	-	-	-	-	-	-	-	-	-	684	684	1 865
	2011/12	-	-	-	-	-	-	-	-	-	-	1 146	1 146	1 681
	2012/13	-	-	-	-	-	-	-	-	-	-	399	399	
Burkina Faso	2008/09	-	-	-	-	-	127	-	-	-	127	-	127	46 482
	2009/10	-	-	-	-	-	131	-	1 269	-	1 400	-	1 400	19 637
	2010/11	-	-	-	-	-	-	-	-	-	-	142	142	36 099
	2011/12	-	-	-	-	-	-	-	-	-	-	510	510	52 219
	2012/13	-	-	-	-	-	-	-	-	-	-	1 077	1 077	
Burundi [4]	2008/09	-	-	-	2 611	484	1 891	410	5 024	-	10 421	-	10 421	12 767
	2009/10	-	-	3 004	1 086	2 530	1 963	410	3 995	-	12 988	15	13 003	15 052
	2010/11	-	-	2 790	741	1 539	4 161	406	1 299	-	10 936	24	10 960	16 800
	2011/12	-	-	2 206	890	1 051	4 915	-	-	-	9 062	36	9 098	25 626
	2012/13	-	-	-	140	-2	104	-	-	-	242	33	275	
Cameroon	2008/09	-	-	-	28	5 618	1 204	-	-	-	6 850	1 057	7 907	16 148
	2009/10	-	-	-	-	-	240	-	-	-	240	709	949	21 193
	2010/11	-	-	-	-	319	-62	-	-	-	257	576	833	25 182
	2011/12	-	-	-	-	508	8	-	-	-	516	414	930	19 257
	2012/13	-	-	-	-	-	-	-	-	-	-	216	216	
Cape Verde	2008/09	-	-	-	-	-	-	-	-	449	449	-	449	7 338
	2009/10	-	-	-	-	-	-	-	71	456	527	-	527	2 368
	2010/11	-	-	-	-	-	-	-	-	581	581	-	581	3 966
	2011/12	-	-	-	-	-	-	-	-	620	620	31	651	2 432
	2012/13	-	-	-	-	-	-	-	-	-	-	-	-	
Central African Republic	2008/09	-	-	-	-	-	-	-	3 615	-	3 615	-	3 615	5 745
	2009/10	-	-	-	-	-	-	-	2 706	-	2 706	-	2 706	13 136
	2010/11	-	-	-	-	1 268	-	-	-	24	1 291	456	1 747	10 125
	2011/12	-	-	-	-	-	-	-	-	-	-	-	-	10 617
	2012/13	-	-	-	-	-	-	-	-	-	-	54	54	

3.2a Total DFID Expenditure and GPEX by Recipient Country (Africa) 2008/09 - 2012/13[1]

£ thousand

| | | Financial Aid | | | | | | | | | | | | |
		General Poverty Reduction Budget Support	Sector Poverty Reduction Budget Support	Other Financial Aid [5]	Technical Cooperation	Bilateral aid delivered through a Multilateral	Bilateral aid Delivered through an NGO	Other Bilateral Aid [2]	Humanitarian Assistance	DFID Debt Relief	Total DFID Bilateral Programme	Aid from other UK Official Sources [5]	Total Bilateral Gross Public Expenditure	UK Imputed Multilateral Shares [3]
Chad [4]	2008/09	-	-	-	-	-	-	-	6 331	-	6 331	-	6 331	6 978
	2009/10	-	-	-	-	900	-	-	4 893	-	5 793	-	5 793	12 526
	2010/11	-	-	-	-	-	-	-	149	-	149	10	159	22 484
	2011/12	-	-	-	-	-	-	-	66	-	66	-	66	29 374
	2012/13	-	-	-	-	-	-	-	-	-	-	68	68	
Comoros	2008/09	-	-	-	-	-	-	-	-	-	-	-	-	734
	2009/10	-	-	-	-	-	-	-	-	-	-	-	-	3 831
	2010/11	-	-	-	-	-	-	-	-	-	-	79	79	2 472
	2011/12	-	-	-	-	-	-	-	-	-	-	75	75	790
	2012/13	-	-	-	-	-	-	-	-	-	-	-	-	
Congo	2008/09	-	-	-	-	-	9	-	-	-	9	-	9	7 709
	2009/10	-	-	-	-	-	-	-	1 181	-	1 181	-	1 181	3 508
	2010/11	-	-	-	-	-	-	-	750	40 750	41 500	50 238	50 238	6 429
	2011/12	-	-	-	-	-	-	-	-	-	-	-	-	6 984
	2012/13	-	-	-	-	-	-	-	-	-	-	-	-	
Congo (Dem Rep) [4]	2008/09	-	-	-	3 551	21 899	28 737	6 751	32 778	176	93 892	5 753	99 645	38 602
	2009/10	-	-	2	3 994	34 848	25 117	4 116	40 979	-	109 055	7 728	116 783	68 987
	2010/11	-	-	-	8 992	38 487	32 980	5 425	47 089	-	132 973	910	133 883	88 195
	2011/12	-	-	-	20 296	46 127	49 458	2 976	27 002	-	145 859	93 453	239 312	108 767
	2012/13	-	-	-	25 667	21 723	36 206	74	49 259	-	132 930	242	133 171	
Cote d'Ivoire	2008/09	-	-	-	-	-	-	-	-	-	-	180	180	28 421
	2009/10	-	-	-	-	-	-	-	360	-	360	256	616	23 714
	2010/11	-	-	-	-	-	-	-	-	-	-	16 880	16 880	21 432
	2011/12	-	-	-	-	-	-	-	7 950	-	7 950	495	8 445	-
	2012/13	-	-	-	-	-	-	-	-	-	-	18 158	18 158	
Djibouti	2008/09	-	-	-	-	-	-	-	-	-	-	-	-	2 408
	2009/10	-	-	-	-	-	-	-	443	-	443	1 504	1 947	771
	2010/11	-	-	-	-	-	-	-	-	-	-	3	3	2 331
	2011/12	-	-	-	-	-	-	-	-	-	-	20	20	2 945
	2012/13	-	-	-	-	-	-	-	-	-	-	62	62	
Equatorial Guinea	2008/09	-	-	-	-	-	-	-	-	-	-	-	-	278
	2009/10	-	-	-	-	-	-	-	-	-	-	-	-	531
	2010/11	-	-	-	-	-	-	-	-	-	-	-	-	134
	2011/12	-	-	-	-	-	-	-	-	-	-	-	-	158
	2012/13	-	-	-	-	-	-	-	-	-	-	-	-	
Eritrea [4]	2008/09	-	-	-	-	-	-	-	3 692	-	3 692	357	4 049	2 857
	2009/10	-	-	-	-	-	-	-	3 176	-	3 176	47	3 222	9 734
	2010/11	-	-	-	-	-	-	-	4 187	-	4 187	270	4 457	5 380
	2011/12	-	-	-	-	-	-	-	3 686	-	3 686	29	3 715	4 838
	2012/13	-	-	-	-	-	-	-	4 630	-	4 630	34	4 663	
Ethiopia [4]	2008/09	-	105 184	16 248	1 930	4 860	3 600	-	33 699	-	165 521	3 086	168 607	61 574
	2009/10	-	93 030	39 895	1 920	13 738	1 094	1 000	63 609	-	214 286	1 401	215 688	76 226
	2010/11	-	94 700	95 501	5 374	42 004	1 085	5 989	5 900	-	250 553	1 342	251 895	105 665
	2011/12	-	132 800	65 000	4 222	57 612	1 447	6 500	56 850	-	324 430	1 359	325 789	73 362
	2012/13	-	128 500	72 086	13 031	9 105	2 050	4 110	31 860	-	260 743	2 913	263 656	
Gabon	2008/09	-	-	-	-	-	-	-	-	-	-	-	-	479
	2009/10	-	-	-	-	-	-	-	-	-	-	-	-	1 390
	2010/11	-	-	-	-	-	-	-	-	-	-	106	106	2 585
	2011/12	-	-	-	-	-	-	-	-	-	-	126	126	1 997
	2012/13	-	-	-	-	-	-	-	-	-	-	-	-	
Gambia [4]	2008/09	-	-	-	1 617	1	800	-	-	49	2 467	106	2 573	923
	2009/10	-	-	-	1 458	-1	643	-	59	-	2 159	83	2 243	2 237
	2010/11	-	-	-	852	-	192	-	-	-	1 044	10	1 054	7 945
	2011/12	-	-	-	487	-	94	-	-	-	581	4 805	5 386	7 216
	2012/13	-	-	-	-	-	-	-	-	-	-	8 902	8 902	
Ghana	2008/09	59 548	18 000	12 830	1 905	2 746	2 638	-	1 781	-	99 448	4 279	103 728	54 288
	2009/10	48 000	24 210	11 203	1 748	1 387	2 965	-	404	-	89 917	6 832	96 749	38 282
	2010/11	36 000	25 000	7 275	3 255	11 233	4 430	-	-	-	87 192	8 280	95 471	52 059
	2011/12	12 290	46 000	3 988	11 310	2 568	4 023	-	-	-	80 178	3 748	83 927	-
	2012/13	14 108	10 000	8 381	4 298	5 687	7 204	817	-	-	50 495	6 035	56 530	
Guinea	2008/09	-	-	-	-	-	434	-	246	-	680	271	951	1 789
	2009/10	-	-	-	-	-	120	-	629	-	749	139	888	1 778
	2010/11	-	-	-	-	2 658	-	-	-	7	2 666	-	2 666	2 684
	2011/12	-	-	-	-	-	-	-	-	-	-	192	192	25 105
	2012/13	-	-	-	-	-	-	-	-	-	-	998	998	
Guinea-Bissau	2008/09	-	-	-	-	-	-	-	42	-	42	25	67	3 657
	2009/10	-	-	-	-	-	-	-	-	-	-	85	85	4 381
	2010/11	-	-	-	-	-	-	-	-	-	-	47	47	4 761
	2011/12	-	-	-	-	-	-	-	-	-	-	75	75	2 902
	2012/13	-	-	-	-	-	-	-	-	-	-	28	28	
Kenya [4]	2008/09	-	-	12 152	8 194	35 572	30 618	-	15 795	-	102 331	7 498	109 829	4 921
	2009/10	-	-	7 651	7 006	10 375	23 872	1 600	13 716	-	64 219	11 466	75 685	50 032
	2010/11	-	-	451	11 671	25 401	24 041	2 000	5 536	-	69 099	4 750	73 849	67 636
	2011/12	-	-	1 425	10 027	24 776	38 750	396	22 740	-	98 115	9 216	107 331	79 295
	2012/13	-	-	1 428	4 209	21 865	45 692	4 000	14 970	-	92 164	18 874	111 038	

3.2a Total DFID Expenditure and GPEX by Recipient Country (Africa) 2008/09 - 2012/13[1]

£ thousand

| | | Financial Aid | | | | | | | | | | | | |
		General Poverty Reduction Budget Support	Sector Poverty Reduction Budget Support	Other Financial Aid [5]	Technical Cooperation	Bilateral aid delivered through a Multilateral	Bilateral aid Delivered through an NGO	Other Bilateral Aid [2]	Humanitarian Assistance	DFID Debt Relief	Total DFID Bilateral Programme	Aid from other UK Official Sources [5]	Total Bilateral Gross Public Expenditure	UK Imputed Multilateral Shares [3]
Lesotho [4]	2008/09	-	-	698	2 750	1 550	333	-	-	878	6 209	82	6 292	3 607
	2009/10	-	-	818	1 759	250	1 242	-	83	923	5 075	45	5 120	4 579
	2010/11	-	-	30	335	436	1 215	-	-	920	2 935	10	2 946	14 246
	2011/12	-	-	-	-	-	1 790	-	-	1 093	2 883	80	2 963	12 821
	2012/13	-	-	-	-	-	-	-	2 000	1 124	3 124	98	3 222	
Liberia	2008/09	-	-	2 166	1 557	1 250	3 421	-	4 757	3 548	16 698	329	17 027	7 859
	2009/10	-	-	165	2 151	4 910	4 000	-	739	-	11 965	611	12 576	17 865
	2010/11	-	-	4 000	214	6 220	80	-	1 000	-	11 514	3 530	15 044	17 005
	2011/12	-	-	3 000	-	5 000	-	-	10 959	-	18 959	100	19 059	21 061
	2012/13	-	-	7 000	54	1 750	-	-	1 004	-	9 809	207	10 016	
Madagascar	2008/09	-	-	-	-	9 029	-	-	311	-	9 341	904	10 245	51 072
	2009/10	-	-	-	-	-	-	-	2 521	-	2 521	-	2 521	2 636
	2010/11	-	-	-	-	6 869	-	-	-29	-	6 840	375	7 215	11 328
	2011/12	-	-	-	-	-	-	-	-	-	-	505	505	7 099
	2012/13	-	-	-	-	-	-	-	-	-	-	1 969	1 969	
Malawi [4]	2008/09	22 000	20 420	20 360	2 863	5 973	5 032	-	451	-	77 100	4 921	82 021	14 390
	2009/10	24 000	17 514	22 524	1 939	2 088	4 835	11	943	-	73 853	3 517	77 370	29 400
	2010/11	19 000	26 659	13 727	2 366	920	6 767	284	901	-	70 624	5 810	76 434	40 549
	2011/12	-	14 000	22 614	2 965	6 636	7 133	43	8 491	-	61 882	4 470	66 351	29 835
	2012/13	20 000	19 000	43 838	4 119	6 086	13 623	-	14 634	-	121 300	6 897	128 198	
Mali	2008/09	-	-	-	-	1 104	-	-	-	-	1 104	-	1 104	38 671
	2009/10	-	-	-	-	-	-	-	-	-	-	37	37	27 881
	2010/11	-	-	-	3	1 042	-	-	-	-	1 045	30	1 076	14 640
	2011/12	-	-	-	-	-	-	-	-	-	-	15	15	32 556
	2012/13	-	-	-	-	-	-	-	-	-	-	70	70	
Mauritania	2008/09	-	-	-	-	-	-	-	-	-	-	-	-	2 254
	2009/10	-	-	-	-	-	-	-	325	-	325	497	822	643
	2010/11	-	-	-	-	363	-	-	-	-	363	-	-	4 721
	2011/12	-	-	-	-	-	-	-	-	-	-	904	904	11 937
	2012/13	-	-	-	-	-	-	-	-	-	-	358	358	
Mauritius	2008/09	-	-	-	-	-	-	-	-	-	-	332	332	4 932
	2009/10	-	-	-	-	-	-	-	-	-	-	13 513	13 513	13 068
	2010/11	-	-	-	-	-	-	-	-	-	-	4 625	4 625	2 128
	2011/12	-	-	-	-	-	-	-	-	-	-	8 734	8 734	9 754
	2012/13	-	-	-	-	-	-	-	-	-	-	348	348	
Mayotte	2008/09	-	-	-	-	-	-	-	-	-	-	-	-	-
	2009/10	-	-	-	-	-	-	-	-	-	-	-	-	-
	2010/11	-	-	-	-	-	-	-	-	-	-	-	-	-
	2011/12	-	-	-	-	-	-	-	-	-	-	-	-	-
	2012/13	-	-	-	-	-	-	-	-	-	-	-	-	-
Mozambique [4]	2008/09	42 000	14 481	1 307	3 688	401	1 647	-	1 971	-	65 495	869	66 365	50 397
	2009/10	44 000	16 860	66	4 184	619	1 925	-	237	-	67 891	410	68 301	13 788
	2010/11	48 205	28 556	2 658	3 571	9 617	1 141	-	500	-	94 248	568	94 815	41 569
	2011/12	48 000	21 367	8 000	4 479	1 930	1 151	-	750	-	85 677	678	86 354	46 779
	2012/13	45 000	2 000	5 001	6 700	6 204	1 668	-	-	-	66 574	718	67 292	
Namibia	2008/09	-	-	280	12	70	173	-	-	-	535	221	755	2 924
	2009/10	-	-	-	-	-	-	-	195	-	195	178	373	609
	2010/11	-	-	-	-	-	-	-	-	-	-	362	362	14 384
	2011/12	-	-	-	-	-	-	-	-	-	-	153	153	
	2012/13	-	-	-	-	-	-	-	-	-	-	405	405	
Niger [4]	2008/09	-	986	-	-	2 007	-	-	4 553	-	7 546	-	7 546	29 577
	2009/10	-	868	-	-	-	-	-	4 275	-	5 143	-	5 143	6 052
	2010/11	-	-	-	-	1 737	958	-	5	-	2 700	-	2 700	16 213
	2011/12	-	33	-	-	-	9	-	-	-	42	-	42	40 746
	2012/13	-	-	-	-	-	-	-	-	-	-	6	6	
Nigeria	2008/09	-	-	2 106	97 155	5 406	4 806	-	551	-	110 025	21 612	131 637	54 211
	2009/10	-	-	160	94 327	15 379	3 499	-	860	-	114 226	16 369	130 594	88 405
	2010/11	-	-	57	104 200	16 903	4 091	16 700	-	-	141 952	39 063	181 015	52 330
	2011/12	-	-	40	127 159	24 343	5 879	4 368	-	-	161 789	44 405	206 194	
	2012/13	-	-	-	169 504	24 528	7 534	-	-	-	201 565	16 145	217 710	
Rwanda [4]	2008/09	33 000	2 180	9 270	2 697	21 126	1 800	-	8	-	70 081	489	70 570	25 417
	2009/10	33 000	5 680	4 001	4 306	5 068	711	-	-	-	52 766	936	53 702	23 407
	2010/11	35 750	10 540	9 716	16 330	16 877	121	567	-	-	89 901	998	90 898	46 524
	2011/12	37 000	23 172	9 981	3 340	100	1 838	567	-	-	75 997	942	76 939	37 835
	2012/13	8 000	16 990	26 778	2 850	647	615	567	1 918	-	58 365	1 572	59 937	
Sao Tome & Principe	2008/09	-	-	-	-	-	-	-	-	-	-	-	-	687
	2009/10	-	-	-	-	-	-	-	-	-	-	-	-	2 079
	2010/11	-	-	-	-	487	-	-	-	-	487	-	-	342
	2011/12	-	-	-	-	-	-	-	-	-	-	-	-	3 024
	2012/13	-	-	-	-	-	-	-	-	-	-	-	-	
Senegal	2008/09	-	-	-	-	-	163	-	-	-	163	415	578	22 862
	2009/10	-	-	-	-	-	137	-	-	-1,140	-1,002	3 981	2 978	20 152
	2010/11	-	-	-	-	-	-	-	-	-	-	1 005	1 492	19 179
	2011/12	-	-	-	-	-	-	-	-	-	-	1 614	1 614	26 255
	2012/13	-	-	-	-	-	-	-	-	-	-	2 908	2 908	
Seychelles	2007/08	-	-	-	-	-	-	-	-	-	-	17	17	17
	2009/10	-	-	-	-	-	-	-	-	-	-	38	38	2 317
	2010/11	-	-	-	-	-	-	-	-	-	-	28	28	231
	2011/12	-	-	-	-	-	-	-	-	-	-	72	72	66
	2012/13	-	-	-	-	-	-	-	-	-	-	1 211	1 211	

3.2a Total DFID Expenditure and GPEX by Recipient Country (Africa) 2008/09 - 2012/13[1]

£ thousand

| | | Financial Aid | | | | | | | | | | | |
		General Poverty Reduction Budget Support	Sector Poverty Reduction Budget Support	Other Financial Aid [5]	Technical Cooperation	Bilateral aid delivered through a Multilateral	Bilateral aid Delivered through an NGO	Other Bilateral Aid[2]	Humanitarian Assistance	DFID Debt Relief	Total DFID Bilateral Programme	Aid from other UK Official Sources [5]	Total Bilateral Gross Public Expenditure	UK Imputed Multilateral Shares[3]
Sierra Leone [4]	2008/09	20 000	-	114	15 394	5 405	5 063	-	1 794	-	47 770	582	48 352	9 499
	2009/10	12 150	-	7 559	12 338	8 154	4 243	-	213	-	44 655	2 030	46 686	5 528
	2010/11	8 000	-	12 647	12 447	14 192	3 998	-	7	-	51 291	2 270	53 561	21 642
	2011/12	12 500	-	3 240	9 896	23 147	3 795	-	-	-	52 578	704	53 282	17 981
	2012/13	2 000	-	2 330	9 851	35 825	3 581	-	2 067	-	55 653	3 054	58 707	
Somalia [4]	2008/09	-	-	-	227	9 376	5 579	-	18 288	-	33 471	129	33 600	12 192
	2009/10	-	-	-	361	8 110	4 061	-	31 900	-	44 431	744	45 176	10 380
	2010/11	-	-	-	454	10 595	5 156	-	29 855	-	46 060	1 529	47 588	8 746
	2011/12	-	-	-	202	12 467	9 721	-	79 093	-	101 483	2 359	103 842	30 264
	2012/13	-	-	-	486	29 818	12 972	-	36 419	-	79 694	5 107	84 801	
South Africa	2008/09	-	-	-	23 600	1 677	14 626	-	776	-	40 679	37 877	78 556	13 822
	2009/10	-	-	3 000	9 957	400	7 914	-	-7	-	21 265	18 139	39 404	16 009
	2010/11	-	-	4 000	6 880	1 061	5 274	-	196	-	17 411	33 965	51 376	29 147
	2011/12	-	-	4 000	8 015	-	7 324	-	-	-	19 339	3 902	23 241	26 464
	2012/13	-	-	500	12 261	1 500	3 831	-	-	-	18 093	18 099	36 192	
South Sudan [4,5]	2011/12	-	-	-	16 415	38 899	5 278	956	17 955	-	79 503	503	80 005	-
	2012/13	-	-	-	31 003	7 915	5 963	10 437	48 754	-	104 073	1 982	106 056	-
St Helena and Dependencies	2008/09	-	-	29 150	6 092	460	35	-	-	-	35 738	-	35 738	-
	2009/10	-	-	20 377	2 228	-	97	-	-	-	22 701	40	22 741	-
	2010/11	-	-	24 885	6 033	-	132	-	-	-	31 050	627	31 677	-
	2011/12	-	-	64 435	3 697	-	90	-	-	-	68 223	191	68 414	-
	2012/13	-	-	92 958	1 516	0	-	-	-	-	94 473	321	94 794	
Sudan [4]	2008/09	-	-	-	14 644	32 358	6 212	-	52 574	-	105 787	4 157	109 945	23 435
	2009/10	-	-	-	10 350	67 991	7 280	895	59 062	-	145 578	3 711	149 289	15 694
	2010/11	-	-	-	16 478	22 535	4 752	912	83 529	-	128 206	4 907	133 113	27 805
	2011/12	-	-	-	6 480	11 058	7 972	196	6 901	-	32 607	2 909	35 515	49 804
	2012/13	-	-	-	4 380	7 935	2 924	182	39 019	-	54 440	2 645	57 085	
Swaziland	2008/09	-	-	-	-	-	-	-	997	-	997	32	1 029	3 554
	2009/10	-	-	-	-	-	-	-	195	-	195	50	244	3 533
	2010/11	-	-	-	-	-	-	-	-	-	-	11	11	5 015
	2011/12	-	-	-	-	-	-	-	-	-	-	23	23	13 398
	2012/13	-	-	-	-	-	-	-	-	-	-	4 831	4 831	
Tanzania [4]	2008/09	103 500	-	11 651	501	11 275	4 864	-	550	-	132 341	9 958	142 299	52 243
	2009/10	103 500	-	12 785	2 869	9 715	5 719	815	8 245	-	143 648	2 381	146 029	93 424
	2010/11	103 512	-	8 449	8 514	17 811	5 358	445	1 956	-	146 045	3 726	149 771	87 596
	2011/12	80 000	-	17 850	9 000	8 150	16 334	7 630	-	-	138 964	9 804	148 768	75 679
	2012/13	50 000	30 000	28 609	13 920	3 043	15 540	3 641	4 785	-	149 537	6 588	156 125	
Togo	2008/09	-	-	-	-	-	67	-	-	-	67	4 859	4 926	11 212
	2009/10	-	-	-	-	-	-	-	-	-	-	6 668	6 668	8 090
	2010/11	-	-	-	-	-	-	-	-	13 076	13 076	20	13 096	15 136
	2011/12	-	-	-	-	-	-	-	-	-	-	1 202	1 202	15 847
	2012/13	-	-	-	-	-	-	-	-	-	-	28	28	
Uganda [4]	2008/09	35 000	-	7 815	2 903	5 574	3 747	125	15 508	-	70 672	1 458	72 131	44 763
	2009/10	32 500	-	5 313	2 801	15 722	1 915	1 313	8 477	-	68 041	10 090	78 131	45 817
	2010/11	27 200	-	11 455	4 563	44 839	1 896	4 450	-	-	94 402	1 618	96 020	35 868
	2011/12	20 000	5 000	8 916	7 505	21 496	4 687	6 000	2 966	-	76 571	4 805	81 376	36 754
	2012/13	7 635	6 600	2 725	13 781	14 303	3 101	27 782	4 125	-	80 053	8 005	88 057	
Zambia [4]	2008/09	27 700	-	7 487	2 847	758	4 128	-	3 671	-	46 590	2 876	49 466	43 326
	2009/10	36 000	-	7 192	2 163	726	1 692	769	18	615	49 176	1 177	50 353	11 417
	2010/11	32 800	-	4 767	1 947	3 769	3 354	5 270	6	-	51 912	1 070	52 982	18 779
	2011/12	12 500	-	4 462	5 736	8 586	5 596	5 788	-	-	42 668	2 684	45 352	33 952
	2012/13	20 600	-	5 416	3 782	7 587	6 401	9 926	-	-	53 712	1 741	55 453	
Zimbabwe [4]	2008/09	-	-	-	6 310	15 571	12 099	-	21 004	1 063	56 048	1 285	57 332	2 647
	2009/10	-	-	-	18 100	20 442	8 218	-	18 646	1 167	66 572	3 751	70 323	8 127
	2010/11	-	-	-	20 498	38 674	5 272	2 000	2 081	-	68 526	4 770	73 296	10 185
	2011/12	-	-	-	27 910	53 836	4 029	2 629	-	-	88 403	3 154	91 557	7 899
	2012/13	-	-	-	15 647	41 300	8 027	3 213	10 957	-	79 144	3 584	82 728	
East African Community	2008/09	-	-	-	180	209	-	-	-	-	389	475	864	-
	2009/10	-	-	-	64	1 491	-	-	-	-	1 555	559	2 115	-
	2010/11	-	-	-	-	840	-	-	-	-	840	419	419	-
	2011/12	-	-	-	-	60	-	-	-	-	60	65	125	-
	2012/13	-	-	-	-	-	-	-	-	-	-	-	-	
Southern Africa Dev Comm (SADC)	2008/09	-	-	-	149	1 100	8 658	-	150	-	10 057	-	10 057	-
	2009/10	-	-	-	-	2 000	5 275	-	-	-	7 275	-	7 275	-
	2010/11	-	-	-	-	1 200	10 643	2 800	-	-	14 643	-	14 643	-
	2011/12	-	-	-	-	-	4 800	-	-	-	4 800	168	4 968	-
	2012/13	-	-	-	-	-	-	-	-	-	-	-	-	

3.2a Total DFID Expenditure and GPEX by Recipient Country (Africa) 2008/09 - 2012/13[1]

£ thousand

| | | Financial Aid | | | | | | | | | | | | |
		General Poverty Reduction Budget Support	Sector Poverty Reduction Budget Support	Other Financial Aid [5]	Technical Cooperation	Bilateral aid delivered through a Multilateral	Bilateral aid Delivered through an NGO	Other Bilateral Aid [2]	Humanitarian Assistance	DFID Debt Relief	Total DFID Bilateral Programme	Aid from other UK Official Sources [5]	Total Bilateral Gross Public Expenditure	UK Imputed Multilateral Shares [3]
South of Sahara regional	2008/09	-	-	32	5 844	3 783	4 082	500	4 892	-	19 134	67	19 200	39 742
	2009/10	-	-	650	5 364	47 155	5 842	2 285	17 075	-	78 370	686	79 057	68 949
	2010/11	-	-	3 053	6 497	49 988	8 213	199	-	-	67 950	252	68 202	42 212
	2011/12	-	-	3 000	5 296	8 037	4 587	-	2 724	-	23 644	28 132	51 776	41 529
	2012/13	-	-	-	3 042	18 411	3 223	6 214	-	-	30 890	607	31 497	
Total South of Sahara	2008/09	342 748	161 252	133 665	209 364	207 108	158 231	7 786	236 858	6 163	1 463 174	117 227	1 580 402	898 575
	2009/10	333 150	158 163	146 365	192 648	276 347	125 616	13 213	291 836	2 022	1 539 360	121 113	1 660 472	934 277
	2010/11	310 467	185 454	205 460	242 213	393 112	135 751	47 445	184 984	55 358	1 760 245	205 393	1 965 639	1 120 466
	2011/12	222 290	242 372	222 158	285 327	356 386	190 709	38 047	248 159	1 713	1 807 161	239 342	2 046 503	1 125 369
	2012/13	167 343	213 090	297 050	340 240	265 232	180 258	70 965	266 401	1 124	1 801 704	147 975	1 949 679	
Africa regional	2008/09	-	-	2	6 013	36 976	17 480	142	3 671	4 759	69 043	91 322	160 365	1 130
	2009/10	-	-	5 500	6 594	55 997	23 587	7 475	1 527	6 785	107 463	112 986	220 449	144 407
	2010/11	-	-	6 500	6 374	44 383	22 487	424	16 471	-	96 640	24 382	121 022	38 581
	2011/12	-	-	-	10 625	30 037	22 292	6 998	6 865	-	76 817	17 412	94 229	54 240
	2012/13	-	-	-	27 652	49 363	26 990	5 635	51 140	-	160 780	48 962	209 742	
Total Africa	2008/09	342 748	161 252	133 667	215 501	244 594	175 711	7 928	240 530	10 922	1 532 852	228 491	1 761 343	955 897
	2009/10	333 150	158 163	151 865	199 273	332 740	149 203	20 688	293 593	8 807	1 647 482	266 751	1 914 233	1 158 720
	2010/11	310 467	185 454	211 960	248 588	437 496	158 238	47 869	211 732	55 358	1 867 162	246 889	2 114 051	1 258 164
	2011/12	222 290	242 372	222 158	298 059	386 727	213 000	45 046	260 329	1 713	1 891 694	287 369	2 179 063	1 246 104
	2012/13	167 343	213 090	297 050	368 762	316 221	207 659	76 600	317 864	1 124	1 965 716	227 767	2 193 483	

1. Descriptions of aid types given in Technical Note 1.
2. Other Bilateral Aid covers bilateral aid not elsewhere classified.
3. Details on DFID Imputed Multilateral Shares are in Section 2; 2012/13 data are not yet available.
4. Low Income Country. Income groups are classified using 2012 GNI per capita thresholds.
5. Pension payments have been reclassified from "Other Financial Aid" to "Aid from other UK Official Sources". This is consistent with the classification of spending under Department Expenditure Limits (DEL) agreed with Treasury.
6. South Sudan expenditure information reported in 2011/12 for the first time, following independence in 2011.

Source: Department for International Development (DFID)

3.2b Total DFID Expenditure and GPEX by Recipient Country (Americas) 2008/09 - 2012/2013

£ thousand

| | | Financial Aid | | | | | | | | | | | | |
		General Poverty Reduction Budget Support	Sector Poverty Reduction Budget Support	Other Financial Aid[5]	Technical Cooperation	Bilateral aid delivered through a Multilateral	Bilateral aid Delivered through an NGO	Other Bilateral Aid[2]	Humanitarian Assistance	DFID Debt Relief	Total DFID Bilateral Programme	Aid from other UK Official Sources[5]	Total Bilateral Gross Public Expenditure	UK Imputed Multilateral Shares[3]
North and Central America														
Costa Rica	2008/09	-	-	-	-	-	-	-	-	-	-	356	356	883
	2009/10	-	-	-	-	-	-	-	-	-	-	1 640	1 640	958
	2010/11	-	-	-	-	-	-	-	-	-	-	497	497	1 613
	2011/12	-	-	-	-	-	-	-	-	-	-	234	234	3 207
	2012/13	-	-	-	-	-	-	-	-	-	-	562	562	
Cuba	2008/09	-	-	-	-	-	-	-	-	-	-	132	132	471
	2009/10	-	-	-	-	-	-	-	250	-	250	362	612	4 685
	2010/11	-	-	-	-	-	-	-	-	-	-	250	250	2 030
	2011/12	-	-	-	-	-	-	-	-	-	-	272	272	1 719
	2012/13	-	-	-	-	-	-	-	850	-	850	-	850	
El Salvador	2008/09	-	-	-	-	-	-	-	-	-	-	39	39	626
	2009/10	-	-	-	-	-	-	-	372	-	372	21	393	6 419
	2010/11	-	-	-	-	-	-	-	-	-	-	-	-	4 866
	2011/12	-	-	-	-	-	-	-	-	-	-	10	10	7 913
	2012/13	-	-	-	-	-	-	-	-	-	-	62	62	
Guatemala	2008/09	-	-	-	-	-	256	-	-	-	256	36	292	2 221
	2009/10	-	-	-	-	-	194	-	744	-	938	228	1 167	5 413
	2010/11	-	-	-	-	-	-	-	100	-	100	-	100	4 888
	2011/12	-	-	-	-	-	-	-	-	-	-	95	95	5 871
	2012/13	-	-	-	-	-	-	-	-	-	-	9 276	9 276	
Haiti	2008/09	-	-	-	-	-	-	-	824	-	824	-	824	8 691
	2009/10	-	-	-	71	-	-	-	15 044	-	15 114	703	15 817	38 477
	2010/11	-	-	-	1	7 089	341	-	6 934	1 706	16 071	23	16 094	43 543
	2011/12	-	-	-	-	1 255	533	-	2 459	-	4 246	24	4 270	35 465
	2012/13	-	-	-	-	-	-	-	5 503	-	5 503	-	5 503	
Honduras	2008/09	-	-	-	-	-	-	-	-	-	-	18	18	12 146
	2009/10	-	-	-	-	-	111	-	189	-	300	4	304	3 153
	2010/11	-	-	-	-	-	-	-	-	-	-	16 286	16 286	11 633
	2011/12	-	-	-	-	-	-	-	-	-	-	20	20	18 244
	2012/13	-	-	-	-	-	-	-	-	-	-	6 879	6 879	
Mexico	2008/09	-	-	-	-	-	-	-	80	-	80	3 633	3 713	2 107
	2009/10	-	-	-	-	-	-	-	-	-	-	7 593	7 593	1 986
	2010/11	-	-	-	-	-	-	-	-	-	-	6 093	6 093	5 967
	2011/12	-	-	-	-	-	-	-	-	-	-	5 050	5 050	539
	2012/13	-	-	-	-	-	-	-	-	-	-	5 653	5 653	
Nicaragua	2008/09	-	-	-	-	-	-	-	-	-	3 854	18	3 872	7 123
	2009/10	-	-	-	-	-	-	-	-	-	3 802	26	3 829	5 604
	2010/11	-	-	-	-	-	-	-	-	-	4 695	-	4 695	8 077
	2011/12	-	-	-	-	-	-	-	-	-	-	29	29	8 814
	2012/13	-	-	-	-	-	-	-	-	-	-	11 389	11 389	
Panama	2008/09	-	-	-	-	-	-	-	-	-	-	20	20	271
	2009/10	-	-	-	-	-	-	-	-	-	-	48	48	1 592
	2010/11	-	-	-	-	-	-	-	-	-	-	26	26	241
	2011/12	-	-	-	-	-	-	-	-	-	-	202	202	451
	2012/13	-	-	-	-	-	-	-	-	-	-	268	268	
North & Central America, regional	2008/09	-	-	-	-	110	-	-	-	-	110	-	110	1 831
	2009/10	-	-	-	-	-53	-	-	-	-	-53	-	-53	6 748
	2010/11	-	-	-	-	-	-	-	-	-	-	84	84	1 499
	2011/12	-	-	-	-	-	-	-	-	-	-	3 427	3 427	1 977
	2012/13	-	-	-	-	-	-	-	-	-	-	2 083	2 083	
Total North and Central America	2008/09	-	-	-	712	953	300	995	3 158	-	5 123	4 252	9 375	36 370
	2009/10	-	-	-	265	2 222	336	995	16 905	-	20 723	10 626	31 349	75 033
	2010/11	-	-	-	1	9 089	341	2 695	7 034	1 706	20 866	23 259	44 125	84 356
	2011/12	1 450	-	-	-	1 255	533	-	2 459	-	4 246	9 362	13 609	84 202
	2012/13	-	-	-	-	-	-	-	6 353	-	6 353	36 172	42 525	
Caribbean														
Anguilla	2008/09	-	-	-	-	-	-	-	-	-	-	28	28	-
	2009/10	-	-	-	-	-	-	-	-	-	-	136	136	-
	2010/11	-	-	-	-	-	-	-	-	-	-	58	58	-
	2011/12	-	-	-	-	-	-	-	-	-	-	400	400	-
	2012/13	-	-	-	-	-	-	-	-	-	-	-	-	
Antigua and Barbuda	2008/09	-	-	-	-	-	-	-	-	-	-	11	11	-
	2009/10	-	-	-	-	-	-	-	-	-	-	4	4	514
	2010/11	-	-	-	-	-	-	-	-	-	-	3	3	1 313
	2011/12	-	-	-	-	-	-	-	-	-	-	2	2	-
	2012/13	-	-	-	-	-	-	-	-	-	-	9	9	
Barbados	2008/09	-	-	-	-	-	-	-	-	-	-	97	97	845
	2009/10	-	-	-	-	-	-	-	-	-	-	290	290	277
	2010/11	-	-	-	-	-	-	-	-	-	-	52	52	2 196
	2011/12	-	-	-	-	-	-	-	-	-	-	-	-	-
	2012/13	-	-	-	-	-	-	-	-	-	-	-	-	
Belize	2008/09	-	-	-	-	-	8	-	-	-	8	45	53	878
	2009/10	-	-	-	-	-	-	-	-	-	-	33	33	3 060
	2010/11	-	-	-	-	-	-	-	-	-	-	51	51	3 514
	2011/12	-	-	-	-	-	-	-	-	-	-	378	378	-
	2012/13	-	-	-	-	-	-	-	-	-	-	233	233	

3.2b Total DFID Expenditure and GPEX by Recipient Country (Americas) 2008/09 - 2012/013

£ thousand

| | | Financial Aid | | | | | | | | | | | | |
		General Poverty Reduction Budget Support	Sector Poverty Reduction Budget Support	Other Financial Aid[5]	Technical Cooperation	Bilateral aid delivered through a Multilateral	Bilateral aid Delivered through an NGO	Other Bilateral Aid[2]	Humanitarian Assistance	DFID Debt Relief	Total DFID Bilateral Programme	Aid from other UK Official Sources[5]	Total Bilateral Gross Public Expenditure	UK Imputed Multilateral Shares[3]
Dominica	2008/09	-	-	-	-	-	-	-	-	-	-	134	134	439
	2009/10	-	-	-	-	-	-	-	-	-	-	1	1	7
	2010/11	-	-	-	-	-	-	-	-	-	-	195	195	778
	2011/12	-	-	-	-	-	-	-	-	-	-	34	34	6
	2012/13	-	-	-	-	-	-	-	-	-	-	21	21	
Dominican Republic	2008/09	-	-	-	-	-	-	-	-	-	-	818	818	1 532
	2009/10	-	-	-	-	-	-	-	-	-	-	64	64	4 917
	2010/11	-	-	-	-	-	-	-	-	-	-	36	36	14 744
	2011/12	-	-	-	-	-	-	-	-	-	-	157	157	-
	2012/13	-	-	-	-	-	-	-	-	-	-	105	105	
Grenada	2008/09	-	-	-	-	-	-	-	-	-	-	12	12	411
	2009/10	-	-	-	-	-	-	-	-	-	-	16	16	862
	2010/11	-	-	-	-	-	-	-	-	-	-	1	1	745
	2011/12	-	-	-	-	-	-	-	-	-	-	1	1	1 821
	2012/13	-	-	-	-	-	-	-	-	-	-	11	11	
Guyana	2008/09	-	-	922	1 139	341	70	-	-	-	2 472	168	2 640	2 432
	2009/10	-	-	462	432	600	88	-	-	47	1 629	97	1 726	3 037
	2010/11	-	-	-	9	11 591	0	-	-	-	11 600	45	11 645	4 865
	2011/12	-	-	-	-	-	-	-	-	-	-	107	107	7 749
	2012/13	-	-	-	2	-	-	-	-	-	2	178	180	
Jamaica	2008/09	-	-	2 430	756	-	167	-	-	-	3 352	875	4 227	8 351
	2009/10	-	-	748	720	64	251	-	-	-	1 783	1 929	3 711	2 825
	2010/11	-	-	986	769	1 067	-	-	-	-	2 822	613	3 435	7 314
	2011/12	-	-	2 400	-	3 167	750	-	-	-	6 317	1 413	7 730	8 124
	2012/13	-	-	2 587	-	2 887	901	-	-	-	6 375	1 343	7 718	
Montserrat	2008/09	-	-	15 043	1 132	-	101	-	0	-	16 276	107	16 383	-
	2009/10	-	-	19 798	968	-	-	-	-	-	20 766	61	20 827	2
	2010/11	-	-	18 763	317	-	-	-	-	-	19 080	119	19 199	6
	2011/12	-	-	23 834	534	-	-	-	-	-	24 368	205	24 573	-
	2012/13	-	-	27 423	189	-	-	-	-	-	27 613	165	27 778	
St. Kitts-Nevis	2008/09	-	-	-	-	-	-	-	-	-	-	1	1	742
	2009/10	-	-	-	-	-	-	-	-	-	-	1	1	1 424
	2010/11	-	-	-	-	-	-	-	-	-	-	1	1	2 811
	2011/12	-	-	-	-	-	-	-	-	-	-	0	0	-
	2012/13	-	-	-	-	-	-	-	-	-	-	71	71	
St. Lucia	2008/09	-	-	-	-	-	-	-	-	-	-	38	38	768
	2009/10	-	-	-	-	-	-	-	-	-	-	8	8	134
	2010/11	-	-	-	-	213	-	-	-	-	213	11	224	513
	2011/12	-	-	-	-	-4	-	-	-	-	-4	33	29	2 896
	2012/13	-	-	-	-	-	-	-	-	-	-	22	22	
St.Vincent & Grenadines	2008/09	-	-	-	-	-	-	-	-	-	-	9	9	347
	2009/10	-	-	-	-	-	-	-	-	-	-	0	0	219
	2010/11	-	-	-	-	-	-	-	-	-	-	10	10	990
	2011/12	-	-	-	-	-	-	-	-	-	-	44	44	1 420
	2012/13	-	-	-	-	-	-	-	-	-	-	11	11	
Suriname	2008/09	-	-	-	-	-	-	-	-	-	-	-	-	329
	2009/10	-	-	-	-	-	-	-	-	-	-	-	-	2 176
	2010/11	-	-	-	-	-	-	-	-	-	-	-	-	389
	2011/12	-	-	-	-	-	-	-	-	-	-	-	-	524
	2012/13	-	-	-	-	-	-	-	-	-	-	-	-	
Trinidad and Tobago	2008/09	-	-	-	-	-	-	-	-	-	-	464	464	972
	2009/10	-	-	-	-	-	-	-	-	-	-	282	282	1 320
	2010/11	-	-	-	-	-	-	-	-	-	-	157	157	4 826
	2011/12	-	-	-	-	-	-	-	-	-	-	-	-	
	2012/13	-	-	-	-	-	-	-	-	-	-	-	-	
Turks and Caicos Islands	2008/09	-	-	1 000	-	-	-	-	-	-	1 000	-	1 000	-
	2009/10	-	-	4 000	520	-	-	-	170	-	4 690	-	4 690	-
	2010/11	-	-	-	581	-	110	-	-	-	691	-	691	-
	2011/12	-	-	160	1 694	-	208	-	-	-	2 061	-	2 061	-
	2012/13	-	-	112	1 865	-	201	-	-	-	2 178	-	2 178	
Windward Islands	2008/09	-	-	-	71	108	-	-	-	-	179	-	179	-
	2009/10	-	-	-	21	-	-	-	-	-	21	-	21	-
	2010/11	-	-	-	-	-	-	-	-	-	-	-	-	-
	2011/12	-	-	-	-	-	-	-	-	-	-	95	95	-
	2012/13	-	-	-	-	-	-	-	-	-	-	-	-	
Caribbean regional	2008/09	-	-	217	1 749	355	19	-	7 979	-	10 319	1 557	11 876	-
	2009/10	-	-	411	1 828	13 096	375	-	-4,750	-	10 960	34	10 994	153
	2010/11	-	-	-	603	7 449	609	475	340	-	9 476	281	9 757	4 210
	2011/12	-	-	-	591	9 107	243	526	78	-	10 545	162	10 707	-
	2012/13	-	-	218	295	8 882	648	364	30	-	10 436	165	10 601	
Overseas Territories (cross territory programmes)	2008/09	-	-	54	197	163	368	-	21	-	804	-	804	-
	2009/10	-	-	53	625	336	217	-	-	-	1 231	-	1 231	-
	2010/11	-	-	220	866	210	565	-	-	-	1 861	-	1 861	-
	2011/12	-	-	182	1 113	479	482	-	-	-	2 256	28	2 284	-
	2012/13	-	-	100	102	210	197	-	-	-	609	9	618	

3.2b Total DFID Expenditure and GPEX by Recipient Country (Americas) 2008/09 - 2012/2013

£ thousand

| | | Financial Aid | | | | | | | | | | | | |
		General Poverty Reduction Budget Support	Sector Poverty Reduction Budget Support	Other Financial Aid[5]	Technical Cooperation	Bilateral aid delivered through a Multilateral	Bilateral aid Delivered through an NGO	Other Bilateral Aid[2]	Humanitarian Assistance	DFID Debt Relief	Total DFID Bilateral Programme	Aid from other UK Official Sources[5]	Total Bilateral Gross Public Expenditure	UK Imputed Multilateral Shares[3]
Total Caribbean	2008/09	-	-	19 666	5 044	966	733	-	8 001	-	34 411	4 362	38 773	18 044
	2009/10	-	-	25 472	5 114	14 096	932	-	-4,580	47	41 081	2 955	44 036	20 927
	2010/11	-	-	19 969	3 145	20 530	1 284	475	340	-	45 742	1 632	47 374	49 214
	2011/12	-	-	26 576	3 932	12 749	1 683	526	78	-	45 543	3 061	48 604	22 539
	2012/13	-	-	30 440	2 453	11 979	1 947	364	30	-	47 213	2 343	49 556	
South America														
Argentina	2008/09	-	-	-	-	-	-	-	-	-	-	574	574	1 145
	2009/10	-	-	-	-	-	-	-	-	-	-	916	916	1 835
	2010/11	-	-	-	-	-	-	-	-	-	-	350	350	3 662
	2011/12	-	-	-	-	-	-	-	-	-	-	1 217	1 217	2 125
	2012/13	-	-	-	-	-	-	-	-	-	-	1 479	1 479	
Bolivia	2008/09	-	-	-	42	897	344	-	-	-	1 283	93	1 376	3 951
	2009/10	-	-	-	-	-	-	-	-	-	-	262	262	7 630
	2010/11	-	-	-	-	-	-	-	-	-	-	54	54	7 950
	2011/12	-	-	-	-	-	-	-	-	-	-	148	148	26 323
	2012/13	-	-	-	-	-	-	-	-	-	-	-	-	
Brazil	2008/09	-	-	-	291	-	569	-	-	-	860	6 737	7 597	2 622
	2009/10	-	-	216	424	-	286	-	-	-	927	9 895	10 823	4 262
	2010/11	-	-	134	24	-	-	-	-	-	158	29 533	29 691	3 492
	2011/12	-	-	-	-	-	-	-	-	-	-	36 595	36 595	2 462
	2012/13	-	-	-	-	-	-	-	-	-	-	44 465	44 465	
Chile	2008/09	-	-	-	-	-	-	-	-	-	-	264	264	720
	2009/10	-	-	-	-	-	-	-	250	-	250	383	633	238
	2010/11	-	-	-	-	-	-	-	67	-	67	110	178	1 473
	2011/12	-	-	-	-	-	-	-	-	-	-	564	564	274
	2012/13	-	-	-	-	-	-	-	-	-	-	885	885	
Colombia	2008/09	-	-	-	-	-	219	-	-	-	219	1 617	1 836	4 154
	2009/10	-	-	-	-	-	-	-	1 269	-	1 269	4 915	6 184	3 626
	2010/11	-	-	-	-	-	-	-	-	-	-	1 709	1 709	11 575
	2011/12	-	-	-	-	-	-	-	-	-	-	3 976	3 976	-
	2012/13	-	-	-	-	-	-	-	-	-	-	18 938	18 938	
Ecuador	2008/09	-	-	-348	-	-	102	-	-	-	-246	105	-141	5 061
	2009/10	-	-	-245	-	-	97	-	-	-	-147	20	-127	4 530
	2010/11	-	-	-	-	-	-	-	-	-	-	124	124	2 148
	2011/12	-	-	-	-	-	-	-	-	-	-	173	173	-
	2012/13	-	-	-	-	-	-	-	-	-	-	182	182	
Paraguay	2008/09	-	-	-	-	-	-	-	-	-	-	36	36	5 588
	2009/10	-	-	-	-	-	-	-	-	-	-	27	27	651
	2010/11	-	-	-	-	-	-	-	-	-	-	7	7	1 823
	2011/12	-	-	-	-	-	-	-	-	-	-	47	47	4 862
	2012/13	-	-	-	-	-	-	-	-	-	-	-	-	
Peru	2008/09	-	-	-	-40	-	510	-	21	-	492	1 424	1 915	1 163
	2009/10	-	-	-	-	-	311	-	-	-	311	412	723	9 839
	2010/11	-	-	-	-	-	-	-	-	-	-	718	718	2 694
	2011/12	-	-	-	-	-	-	-	-	-	-	557	557	-
	2012/13	-	-	-	-	-	-	-	-	-	-	2 080	2 080	
Uruguay	2008/09	-	-	-	-	-	-	-	-	-	-	80	80	383
	2009/10	-	-	-	-	-	-	-	-	-	-	26	26	202
	2010/11	-	-	-	-	-	-	-	-	-	-	43	43	233
	2011/12	-	-	-	-	-	-	-	-	-	-	97	97	1 140
	2012/13	-	-	-	-	-	-	-	-	-	-	103	103	
Venezuela	2008/09	-	-	-	-	-	-	-	-	-	-	285	285	1 259
	2009/10	-	-	-	-	-	-	-	-	-	-	1 384	1 384	1 782
	2010/11	-	-	-	-	-	-	-	-	-	-	705	705	467
	2011/12	-	-	-	-	-	-	-	-	-	-	798	798	230
	2012/13	-	-	-	-	-	-	-	-	-	-	1 227	1 227	
Latin America Regional	2008/09	-	-	-	2 759	2 401	654	-	82	-	5 895	16	5 911	6 714
	2009/10	-	-	-	99	-71	248	-	-	-	276	2 350	2 626	3 763
	2010/11	-	-	-	-	-	-	-	-	-	-	219	219	11 405
	2011/12	-	-	-	-	-	-	-	-	-	-	112	112	-
	2012/13	-	-	-	98	-	-	-	-	-	98	209	307	
Total South America	2008/09	-	-	-348	3 051	3 298	2 399	-	103	-	8 503	11 230	19 733	32 760
	2009/10	-	-	-28	524	-71	942	-	1 519	-	2 886	20 590	23 476	38 359
	2010/11	-	-	134	24	-	-	-	67	-	225	33 573	33 797	46 921
	2011/12	-	-	-	-	-	-	-	-	-	-	44 284	44 284	37 415
	2012/13	-	-	-	98	-	-	-	-	-	98	69 568	69 666	
America, regional	2008/09	-	-	-	-	-	-	-	-	-	-	7 495	7 495	6 166
	2009/10	-	-	-	-	-	-	-	-	-	-	-	-	18 736
	2010/11	-	-	-	-	-	-	-	-	-	-	6 738	6 738	30 535
	2011/12	-	-	-	-	-	-	-	-	-	-	146	146	20 376
	2012/13	-	-	-	-	-	-	-	-	-	-	217	217	
Total Americas	2008/09	-	-	19 319	8 807	5 217	3 432	-	11 262	47	48 036	27 339	75 376	93 340
	2009/10	-	-	25 444	5 903	16 248	2 209	995	13 844	47	64 690	34 171	98 861	153 055
	2010/11	-	-	25 803	3 170	29 618	1 624	3 170	7 442	1 706	66 833	65 202	132 035	211 026
	2011/12	-	-	26 576	3 932	14 004	2 215	526	2 537	-	49 789	56 853	106 642	164 532
	2012/13	-	-	30 440	2 552	11 979	1 947	364	6 383	-	53 665	108 300	161 965	

1. Descriptions of aid types are given in Technical Note 1.
2. Other Bilateral Aid covers bilateral aid not elsewhere classified.
3. Details on DFID Imputed Multilateral Shares are in Section 2; 2012/13 data are not yet available.
4. Low Income Country. Income groups are classified using 2012 GNI per capita thresholds.
5. Pension payments have been reclassified from "Other Financial Aid" to "Aid from other UK Official Sources". This is consistent with the classification of spending under Department Expenditure Limits (DEL) agreed with Treasury.

Source: Department for International Development (DFID)

3.2c Total DFID Expenditure and GPEX by Recipient Country (Asia) 2008/09 - 2012/2013

£ thousand

| | | Financial Aid | | | | | | | | | | | | |
		General Poverty Reduction Budget Support	Sector Poverty Reduction Budget Support	Other Financial Aid[5]	Technical Cooperation	Bilateral aid delivered through a Multilateral	Bilateral aid Delivered through an NGO	Other Bilateral Aid[2]	Humanitarian Assistance	DFID Debt Relief	Total DFID Bilateral Programme	Aid from other UK Official Sources[5]	Total Bilateral Gross Public Expenditure	UK Imputed Multilateral Shares[3]
Asia: Middle East														
Iran	2008/09	-	-	-	-	-	-	-	-	-	-	919	919	2 051
	2009/10	-	-	-	-	-	-	-	-	-	-	466	466	1 200
	2010/11	-	-	-	-	-	-	-	-	-	-	-	-	2 057
	2011/12	-	-	-	-	-	-	-	-	-	-	435	435	-
	2012/13	-	-	-	-	-	-	-	-	-	-	338	338	
Iraq	2008/09	-	-	81	15 509	-	1 223	-	16 000	-	32 812	304 665	337 477	14 012
	2009/10	-	-	-	10 009	600	1 981	-	7 648	-	20 238	9 767	30 005	7 865
	2010/11	-	-	-	4 859	2 650	-10	-	2 800	-	10 299	5 277	15 576	6 202
	2011/12	-	-	-	1 887	1 200	-	-	-	-	3 087	4 505	7 592	4 659
	2012/13	-	-	-	234	-	-	-	-	-	234	4 112	4 346	
Jordan	2008/09	-	-	-	-	-	-	-	-	-	-	2 454	2 454	8 603
	2009/10	-	-	-	-	-	-	-	-	-	-	974	974	8 571
	2010/11	-	-	178	-	-	-	-	-	-	178	1 619	1 797	10 911
	2011/12	-	-	-	-	-	-	-	-	-	-	2 523	2 523	-
	2012/13	-	-	-	-	-	332	-	1 477	-	1 809	3 014	4 823	
Lebanon	2008/09	-	-	-	-	-	39	-	-	-	39	1 364	1 403	9 177
	2009/10	-	-	-	-	-	-	-	-	-	-	3 450	3 450	5 880
	2010/11	-	-	-	-	-	-	-	-	-	-	2 565	2 565	7 859
	2011/12	-	-	-	-	-	-	-	-	-	-	2 064	2 064	9 063
	2012/13	-	-	-	-	-	-	-	359	-	359	3 475	3 834	
Oman	2008/09	-	-	-	-	-	-	-	-	-	-	308	308	33
	2009/10	-	-	-	-	-	-	-	-	-	-	410	410	25
	2010/11	-	-	-	-	-	-	-	-	-	-	602	602	20
	2011/12	-	-	-	-	-	-	-	-	-	-	-	-	
	2012/13	-	-	-	-	-	-	-	-	-	-	-	-	
Saudi Arabia	2008/09	-	-	-	-	-	-	-	-	-	-	-	-	-
	2009/10	-	-	-	-	-	-	-	-	-	-	-	-	-
	2010/11	-	-	-	-	-	-	-	-	-	-	-	-	-
	2011/12	-	-	-	-	-	-	-	-	-	-	-	-	-
	2012/13	-	-	-	-	-	-	-	-	-	-	-	-	
Syria	2008/09	-	-	-	-	-	-	-	-	-	-	1 263	1 263	2 979
	2009/10	-	-	-	-	-	-	-	490	-	490	672	1 162	6 313
	2010/11	-	-	-	-	-	-	-	-	-	-	1 260	1 260	9 810
	2011/12	-	-	-	-	-	-	-	2 011	-	2 011	2 018	4 029	1 942
	2012/13	-	-	-	-	-	190	-	55 207	-	55 397	1 977	57 374	
West Bank & Gaza	2008/09	-	-	896	3 621	23 950	-	-	12 847	-	41 314	1 243	42 557	50 933
	2009/10	-	-	340	3 952	38 500	-	-	14 838	-	57 630	4 973	62 603	72 818
	2010/11	-	-	1 000	5 018	36 751	216	-	3 587	-	46 572	5 214	51 786	77 309
	2011/12	-	-	48	2 384	49 163	1 135	-	236	-	52 966	3 455	56 421	55 135
	2012/13	-	-	598	1 478	41 885	1 893	158	1 707	-	47 719	4 747	52 466	
Yemen	2008/09	-	-	1 050	3 402	13 053	-	-	1 710	-	19 215	1 098	20 313	9 216
	2009/10	-	-	17 038	863	3 613	40	982	7 241	-	29 778	882	30 660	12 986
	2010/11	-	-	30 193	1 972	10 225	123	1 172	7 429	-	51 113	2 598	53 711	21 851
	2011/12	-	-	9 000	327	4 055	210	750	19 957	-	34 299	1 721	36 020	12 075
	2012/13	-	-	-	37	11 368	15 310	19	29 218	-	55 951	1 843	57 794	
Middle East, Regional	2008/09	-	-	-	-	976	75	-	-	-	1 051	14 594	15 645	979
	2009/10	-	-	-	55	2 653	1 135	-	-	-	3 843	69	3 912	2 202
	2010/11	-	-	-	-	2 852	968	-	-	-	3 820	2 883	6 703	7 234
	2011/12	-	-	-	8	6 897	210	-	-	-	7 114	32	7 147	5 064
	2012/13	-	-	-	1	17 981	210	-	17 193	-	35 384	63	35 447	
Total Middle East	2008/09	-	-	2 027	22 532	37 979	1 336	-	30 557	-	94 431	327 909	422 340	97 982
	2009/10	-	-	17 378	14 880	45 367	3 156	982	30 217	-	111 979	21 663	133 642	117 860
	2010/11	-	-	31 371	11 849	52 477	1 298	1 172	13 816	-	111 983	22 018	134 001	143 252
	2011/12	-	-	9 048	4 606	61 316	1 555	750	22 204	-	99 478	16 753	116 231	32 802
	2012/13	-	-	598	1 750	71 234	17 934	178	105 161	-	196 854	19 569	216 423	
Asia: South														
Afghanistan	2008/09	-	-	71 881	21 618	28 877	4 538	933	19 607	-	147 455	50 231	197 687	25 181
	2009/10	-	-	74 698	28 146	8 486	14 036	840	7 160	-	133 367	72 334	205 701	45 755
	2010/11	-	-	19 458	29 079	37 120	11 026	-	503	-	97 185	75 126	172 311	55 968
	2011/12	-	-	5 672	27 625	95 488	13 127	-	4 219	-	146 131	79 178	225 309	73 655
	2012/13	-	-	101 786	37 328	29 590	10 834	88	1 907	-	181 532	83 584	265 116	
Bangladesh	2008/09	-	-	20 568	38 111	15 107	50 916	916	7 324	-	132 941	2 745	135 686	86 475
	2009/10	-	-	31 914	33 881	15 009	63 524	3 258	1 222	-	148 808	2 368	151 176	25 863
	2010/11	-	-	27 325	28 733	44 409	64 976	5 476	3 472	-	174 391	4 174	178 565	79 981
	2011/12	-	-	30 000	28 272	72 138	82 843	5 482	539	-	219 273	4 379	223 652	251 060
	2012/13	-	-	25 028	25 071	48 973	80 280	5 633	1 232	-	186 217	5 956	192 173	
Bhutan	2008/09	-	-	-	-	-	-	-	-	-	-	-	-	629
	2009/10	-	-	-	-	-	-	-	71	-	71	-	71	1 102
	2010/11	-	-	-	-	-	-	-	-	-	-	-	-	4 437
	2011/12	-	-	-	-	-	-	-	-	-	-	-	-	1 394
	2012/13	-	-	-	-	-	-	-	-	-	-	-	-	
Burma	2008/09	-	-	-	1 894	7 115	1 987	-	45 666	-	56 661	940	57 601	5 583
	2009/10	-	-	-	1 409	13 726	9 978	-	3 061	-	28 175	844	29 019	5 403
	2010/11	-	-	-	1 092	20 689	5 088	-	4 616	-	31 485	1 053	32 538	13 113
	2011/12	-	-	-	1 015	25 099	7 507	-	2 528	-	36 150	1 179	37 329	-
	2012/13	-	-	-	1 375	14 164	11 851	1 249	4 321	-	32 959	1 405	34 364	

3.2c Total DFID Expenditure and GPEX by Recipient Country (Asia) 2008/09 - 2012/2013

£ thousand

| | | Financial Aid | | | | | | | | | | | | |
		General Poverty Reduction Budget Support	Sector Poverty Reduction Budget Support	Other Financial Aid[5]	Technical Cooperation	Bilateral aid delivered through a Multilateral	Bilateral aid Delivered through an NGO	Other Bilateral Aid[2]	Humanitarian Assistance	DFID Debt Relief	Total DFID Bilateral Programme	Aid from other UK Official Sources[5]	Total Bilateral Gross Public Expenditure	UK Imputed Multilateral Shares[3]
India	2008/09	-	54 000	194 292	17 871	27 673	2 807	-	386	-	297 028	105 211	402 239	73 974
	2009/10	-	52 000	177 152	19 360	42 023	4 584	-	-	-	295 119	61 371	356 490	35 761
	2010/11	-	46 000	185 226	26 016	15 802	5 892	-	-	-	278 936	149 148	428 084	273 161
	2011/12	-	-	220 451	29 469	30 269	4 170	-	-	-	284 359	87 030	371 389	211 882
	2012/13	-	-	142 148	28 589	18 375	7 294	-	-	-	196 405	87 092	283 497	
Maldives	2008/09	-	-	-	-	-	-	-	-	-	-	58	58	1 285
	2009/10	-	-	150	-	-	-	-	-	-	150	94	244	784
	2010/11	-	-	-	-	-	-	-	-	-	-	170	170	1 478
	2011/12	-	-	-	-	-	-	-	-	-	-	177	177	-
	2012/13	-	-	-	-	-	-	-	-	-	-	222	222	
Nepal	2008/09	-	9 018	6 858	14 965	5 123	13 859	-	5 596	2 579	57 999	519	58 518	11 048
	2009/10	-	5 239	12 247	16 496	15 415	7 350	1 020	6 013	3 082	66 862	1 625	68 487	15 231
	2010/11	-	7 000	5 603	20 295	14 985	9 653	873	25	3 391	61 825	1 168	62 993	27 723
	2011/12	-	14 000	6 897	24 262	11 143	10 896	6	-	3 477	70 682	708	71 389	34 163
	2012/13	-	-	9 245	24 454	10 513	9 790	1 955	-	3 567	59 523	953	60 476	
Pakistan	2008/09	30 000	25 700	26 977	8 082	13 994	4 416	-	10 775	-	119 942	9 771	129 713	20 570
	2009/10	30 000	22 500	7 029	6 617	21 645	23 164	-	29 444	-	140 398	10 846	151 244	102 099
	2010/11	30 000	32 500	28 075	11 129	11 459	7 059	-	82 715	-	202 937	8 923	211 860	69 800
	2011/12	-	38 000	15 500	15 330	77 920	5 596	-	59 337	-	211 682	13 167	224 849	-
	2012/13	-	29 700	62 774	25 854	7 282	10 737	-	34 591	-	170 938	17 355	188 293	
Sri Lanka	2008/09	-	-	-	-	-	-60	-	3 038	-	2 978	574	3 552	17 595
	2009/10	-	-	-	49	-	139	-	12 872	-	13 061	3 293	16 354	14 153
	2010/11	-	-	-	-	-	-	-	1 375	-	1 375	2 993	4 367	17 795
	2011/12	-	-	-	860	-	-	-	2	-	863	2 695	3 557	30 972
	2012/13	-	-	-	1 127	-	-	-	-	-	1 127	2 924	4 051	
South & Central Asia	2008/09	-	-	-	2 442	86	-	-	927	-	3 455	10 146	13 601	179
	2009/10	-	-	-	1 706	-	-	-	-	-	1 706	1 050	2 757	1 101
	2010/11	-	-	-	78	-	-	-	-	-	78	728	806	2 714
	2011/12	-	-	-	34	-	-	-	-	-	34	1 598	1 632	4 353
	2012/13	-	-	-	377	-	-	-	-	-	377	788	1 165	
Total South Asia	2008/09	30 000	88 718	320 576	104 983	97 974	78 462	1 849	93 319	2 579	818 460	180 195	998 655	242 518
	2009/10	30 000	79 739	303 190	107 665	116 303	122 776	5 118	59 844	3 082	827 717	153 826	981 543	247 251
	2010/11	30 000	85 500	265 687	116 421	144 463	103 694	6 349	92 707	3 391	843 211	243 484	1 091 695	546 170
	2011/12	-	52 000	278 521	126 867	312 056	124 140	5 488	66 625	3 477	969 174	190 111	1 159 285	603 126
	2012/13	-	29 700	340 981	144 174	128 896	130 785	8 924	42 051	3 567	829 078	200 279	1 029 357	
Asia: Far East														
Brunei	2008/09	-	-	-	-	-	-	-	-	-	-	3	3	-
	2009/10	-	-	-	-	-	-	-	-	-	-	3	3	-
	2010/11	-	-	-	-	-	-	-	-	-	-	-	-	-
	2011/12	-	-	-	-	-	-	-	-	-	-	-	-	-
	2012/13	-	-	-	-	-	-	-	-	-	-	-	-	-
Cambodia	2008/09	-	-	2 857	2 019	9 215	680	2 904	49	-	17 725	1 279	19 003	9 086
	2009/10	-	-	1 200	2 391	6 280	795	5 205	-	-	15 871	402	16 273	4 521
	2010/11	-	-	-	1 390	13 217	51	4 798	-	-	19 456	538	19 993	21 200
	2011/12	-	-	-	2 586	8 000	-	1 059	-	-	11 645	994	12 638	7 677
	2012/13	-	-	-	2 063	6 700	-	352	-	-	9 115	345	9 460	
China	2008/09	-	-	19 255	6 776	10 442	1 705	-	2 118	-	40 296	78 091	118 387	12 678
	2009/10	-	-	14 014	3 494	14 420	1 281	198	1 104	-	34 512	56 283	90 796	23 529
	2010/11	-	-	11 388	2 505	7 020	1 286	231	440	-	22 871	56 634	79 505	24 503
	2011/12	-	-	-747	128	-	110	-	-	-	-508	55 797	55 289	-
	2012/13	-	-	-	-	-	-	-	-	-	-	29 039	29 039	
East Timor	2008/09	-	-	-	-	2 057	72	-	-	-	2 129	21	2 150	1 713
	2009/10	-	-	-	-	-	-	-	-	-	-	20	20	1 404
	2010/11	-	-	-	-	1 145	-	-	-	-	1 145	-	1 145	7 537
	2011/12	-	-	-	-	-	-	-	-	-	-	75	75	-
	2012/13	-	-	-	-	-	-	-	-	-	-	37	37	
Indonesia	2008/09	-	-	4 562	462	15 130	1 404	-	15 106	-	36 665	20 733	57 397	24 482
	2009/10	-	-	756	430	15 613	2 630	-	5 628	-	25 058	8 110	33 167	25 929
	2010/11	-	-	3 318	779	3 000	2 470	-	592	-	10 159	22 762	32 921	17 359
	2011/12	-	-	2 716	1 422	-	3 251	4 965	-	-	12 355	10 782	23 137	8 876
	2012/13	-	-	2 082	1 842	118	3 729	2 800	-	-	10 570	8 716	19 286	
Japan	2008/09	-	-	-	-	-	-	-	-	-	-	-	-	-
	2009/10	-	-	-	-	-	-	-	-	-	-	-	-	-
	2010/11	-	-	-	-	-	-	-	1 380	-	1 380	-	1 380	-
	2011/12	-	-	-	-	-	-	-	-	-	-	-	-	-
	2012/13	-	-	-	-	-	-	-	-	-	-	-	-	-
Korea (North)	2008/09	-	-	-	-	-	-	-	-	-	-	185	185	935
	2009/10	-	-	-	-	-	-	-	2 822	-	2 822	32	2 853	1 309
	2010/11	-	-	-	-	-	-	-	-	-	-	264	264	4 832
	2011/12	-	-	-	-	-	-	-	-	-	-	620	620	1 952
	2012/13	-	-	-	-	-	-	-	-	-	-	583	583	
Laos	2008/09	-	-	-	-	-	145	-	100	-	245	-	245	5 733
	2009/10	-	-	-	-	-	153	-	567	-	720	-	720	2 878
	2010/11	-	-	-	58	-	-	-	-	-	58	-	58	11 248
	2011/12	-	-	-	1 206	-	-	-	-	-	1 206	-	1 206	7 293
	2012/13	-	-	-	903	-	-	-	-	-	903	11	914	

3.2c Total DFID Expenditure and GPEX by Recipient Country (Asia) 2008/09 - 2012/2013

£ thousand

| | | Financial Aid | | | | | | | | | | | | |
		General Poverty Reduction Budget Support	Sector Poverty Reduction Budget Support	Other Financial Aid[5]	Technical Cooperation	Bilateral aid delivered through a Multilateral	Bilateral aid Delivered through an NGO	Other Bilateral Aid[2]	Humanitarian Assistance	DFID Debt Relief	Total DFID Bilateral Programme	Aid from other UK Official Sources[5]	Total Bilateral Gross Public Expenditure	UK Imputed Multilateral Shares[3]
Malaysia	2008/09	-	-	-	-	-	-	-	-	-	-	11 922	11 922	995
	2009/10	-	-	-	-	-	-	-	-	-	-	2 929	2 929	393
	2010/11	-	-	-	-	-	-	-	-	-	-	2 742	2 742	1 556
	2011/12	-	-	-	-	-	-	-	-	-	-	5 177	5 177	369
	2012/13	-	-	-	-	-	-	-	-	-	-	6 216	6 216	
Mongolia	2008/09	-	-	-	-	2 508	-	-	-	307	2 815	354	3 170	1 509
	2009/10	-	-	-	-	-	-	-	-	331	331	306	637	2 402
	2010/11	-	-	-	-	1 969	-	-	-	375	2 344	163	2 507	6 488
	2011/12	-	-	-	-	-	-	-	-	477	477	181	658	5 401
	2012/13	-	-	-	-	-	-	-	-	-	-	2 381	2 381	
Philippines	2008/09	-	-	-5	12	-	13	-	-	-	20	823	844	4 837
	2009/10	-	-	-2	9	-	-	-	2 271	-	2 278	2 402	4 680	9 434
	2010/11	-	-	-	-	-	-	-	-	-	-	564	564	13 079
	2011/12	-	-	-	-	-	-	-	-	-	-	1 561	1 561	4 638
	2012/13	-	-	-	-	-	-	-	308	-	308	1 303	1 611	
Singapore	2008/09	-	-	-	-	-	-	-	-	-	-	26	26	-
	2009/10	-	-	-	-	-	-	-	-	-	-	31	31	-
	2010/11	-	-	-	-	-	-	-	-	-	-	-	-	-
	2011/12	-	-	-	-	-	-	-	-	-	-	-	-	-
	2012/13	-	-	-	-	-	-	-	-	-	-	-	-	-
Thailand	2008/09	-	-	-	-	-	52	-	-	-	-	1 207	1 207	2 261
	2009/10	-	-	-	-	-	52	-	-	-	52	6 326	6 378	4 496
	2010/11	-	-	-	-	-	52	-	-	-	-	4 667	4 667	3 741
	2011/12	-	-	-	-	-	-	-	-	-	-	2 864	2 864	
	2012/13	-	-	-	-	-	-	-	-	-	-	2 238	2 238	
Vietnam	2008/09	20 000	5 950	2 762	233	20 858	2 047	-	-	3 205	55 055	1 616	56 671	65 532
	2009/10	20 000	9 550	710	359	19 325	233	-	-	4 140	54 317	1 343	55 660	60 281
	2010/11	20 000	9 750	1 007	566	19 220	94	-	-	4 742	55 378	3 107	58 485	87 161
	2011/12	20 000	-	1 602	1 387	8 810	350	-	-	5 264	37 413	4 009	41 422	-
	2012/13	-	-	5 486	1 758	10 465	335	-51	-	6 215	24 208	4 249	28 457	
Far East Asia, regional	2008/09	-	-	-	-	803	-	-	-	-	803	-	803	-
	2009/10	-	-	-	-	-	-	-	-	-	-	-	-	
	2010/11	-	-	-	-	-	-	-	-	-	-	-	-	2 787
	2011/12	-	-	-	-	-	-	-	-	-	-	-	-	5 439
	2012/13	-	-	-	-	-	-	-	-	-	-	-	-	
Total Far East Asia	2008/09	20 000	5 950	29 430	9 503	61 014	6 067	2 904	17 374	3 513	155 754	116 259	272 012	129 762
	2009/10	20 000	9 550	16 678	6 684	55 638	5 144	5 404	12 392	4 471	135 961	78 187	214 148	136 574
	2010/11	20 000	9 750	15 713	5 298	45 571	3 901	5 029	2 412	5 117	112 790	91 441	204 231	201 490
	2011/12	20 000	-	3 571	6 730	16 810	3 712	6 024	-	5 741	62 588	82 060	144 648	39 694
	2012/13	-	-	7 568	6 566	17 283	4 063	3 101	308	6 215	45 104	55 118	100 222	
Asia: Central Asian Republics														
Kazakhstan	2008/09	-	-	-	-	-	-	-	-	-	-	2 996	2 996	1 634
	2009/10	-	-	-	-	-	-	-	-	-	-	4 446	4 446	1 813
	2010/11	-	-	-	-	-	-	-	-	-	-	1 113	1 113	5 190
	2011/12	-	-	-	-	-	-	-	-	-	-	2 199	2 199	1 591
	2012/13	-	-	-	-	-	-	-	-	-	-	2 140	2 140	
Kyrgyz Republic	2008/09	-	-	1 000	862	6 772	22	-	703	-	9 359	1 324	10 683	5 736
	2009/10	-	-	1 000	198	3 010	-	186	-	-	4 395	229	4 624	5 265
	2010/11	-	-	980	290	1 053	998	-	-	-	3 321	231	3 552	11 716
	2011/12	-	-	2 000	378	2 548	42	-	-	-	4 968	857	5 824	13 283
	2012/13	-	-	-	36	2 936	101	1 500	-	-	4 573	474	5 047	
Tajikistan	2008/09	-	-	3	1 372	2 627	-	-	1 092	-	5 093	278	5 372	3 031
	2009/10	-	-	-	570	3 547	221	-	511	-	4 849	205	5 054	4 958
	2010/11	-	-	-	489	8 150	168	800	94	-	9 701	718	10 419	11 247
	2011/12	-	-	-	70	4 224	-	3 000	12	-	7 306	96	7 402	4 922
	2012/13	-	-	-	98	4 253	272	3 800	362	-	8 785	102	8 887	
Turkmenistan	2008/09	-	-	-	-	-	-	-	-	-	-	218	218	752
	2009/10	-	-	-	-	-	-	-	-	-	-	218	218	137
	2010/11	-	-	-	-	-	-	-	-	-	-	39	39	2 718
	2011/12	-	-	-	-	-	-	-	-	-	-	150	150	950
	2012/13	-	-	-	-	-	-	-	-	-	-	179	179	
Uzbekistan	2008/09	-	-	-	-	-	-	-	-	-	-	551	551	4 746
	2009/10	-	-	-	-	-	-	-	-	-	-	1 183	1 183	8 639
	2010/11	-	-	-	-	-	-	-	-	-	-	797	797	9 252
	2011/12	-	-	-	-	-	-	-	-	-	-	859	859	-
	2012/13	-	-	-	-	-	-	-	-	-	-	729	729	
Central Asia, regional	2008/09	-	-	-	-	18	-	-	-	-	18	-	18	2 656
	2009/10	-	-	-	-	-	-	-	-	-	-	-	-	3 901
	2010/11	-	-	-	-	-	-	-	-	-	-	-	-	3 866
	2011/12	-	-	-	-	-	-	-	-	-	-	-	-	3 349
	2012/13	-	-	-	-	-	-	-	-	-	-	-	-	
Total Central Asian Republics	2008/09	-	-	1 003	2 234	9 416	22	-	1 795	-	14 470	5 367	19 837	18 556
	2009/10	-	-	1 000	768	6 557	221	186	511	-	9 244	6 281	15 525	24 713
	2010/11	-	-	980	780	9 203	1 166	800	94	-	13 022	2 897	15 920	43 989
	2011/12	-	-	2 000	448	6 772	42	3 000	12	-	12 274	4 161	16 434	24 095
	2012/13	-	-	-	134	7 190	372	5 300	362	-	13 358	3 624	16 982	

3.2c Total DFID Expenditure and GPEX by Recipient Country (Asia) 2008/09 - 2012/2013

£ thousand

| | | Financial Aid | | | | | | | | | | | | |
		General Poverty Reduction Budget Support	Sector Poverty Reduction Budget Support	Other Financial Aid[5]	Technical Cooperation	Bilateral aid delivered through a Multilateral	Bilateral aid Delivered through an NGO	Other Bilateral Aid[2]	Humanitarian Assistance	DFID Debt Relief	Total DFID Bilateral Programme	Aid from other UK Official Sources[5]	Total Bilateral Gross Public Expenditure	UK Imputed Multilateral Shares[3]
Asia, regional	2008/09	-	-	584	0	1 099	2 962	-	0	-	4 644	16 206	20 851	7 161
	2009/10	-	-	-	320	1 832	1 869	-	222	-	4 243	4 452	8 695	36 112
	2010/11	-	-	-	1 205	5 812	420	-	-	-	7 437	16 693	24 130	26 266
	2011/12	-	-	-	3 452	16 433	1 130	80	-	-	21 095	5 876	26 971	50 519
	2012/13	-	-	-	5 942	5 956	1 135	-	-	-	13 034	6 333	19 367	
Total Asia	2008/09	50 000	94 668	353 620	139 252	207 482	88 848	4 753	143 045	6 092	1 087 760	645 936	1 733 696	495 978
	2009/10	50 000	89 289	338 246	130 317	225 697	133 166	11 691	103 187	7 553	1 089 144	264 409	1 353 553	562 511
	2010/11	50 000	95 250	313 750	135 553	257 527	110 479	13 349	109 028	8 508	1 093 443	376 534	1 469 977	961 167
	2011/12	20 000	52 000	293 140	142 103	413 386	130 578	15 342	88 841	9 218	1 164 608	298 961	1 463 569	750 236
	2012/13	-	29 700	349 146	158 565	230 558	154 290	17 502	147 881	9 781	1 097 428	284 923	1 382 351	

1. Descriptions of aid types are given in Technical Note 1.
2. Other Bilateral Aid covers bilateral aid not elsewhere classified.
3. Details on DFID Imputed Multilateral Shares are in Section 2; 2012/13 data are not yet available.
4. Low Income Country. Income groups are classified using 2012 GNI per capita thresholds.
5. Pension payments have been reclassified from "Other Financial Aid" to "Aid from other UK Official Sources". This is consistent with the classification of spending under Department Expenditure Limits (DEL) agreed with Treasury.

Source: Department for International Development (DFID)

3.2d Total DFID Expenditure and GPEX by Recipient Country (Europe) 2008/09 - 2012/2013

£ thousand

| | | Financial Aid | | | | | | | | | | | | |
		General Poverty Reduction Budget Support	Sector Poverty Reduction Budget Support	Other Financial Aid [5]	Technical Cooperation	Bilateral aid delivered through a Multilateral	Bilateral aid Delivered through an NGO	Other Bilateral Aid [2]	Humanitarian Assistance	DFID Debt Relief	Total DFID Bilateral Programme	Aid from other UK Official Sources [5]	Total Bilateral Gross Public Expenditure	UK Imputed Multilateral Shares [3]
Europe														
Albania	2008/09	-	-	-	356	180	149	-	-	-	686	831	1 516	10 774
	2009/10	-	-	-	-	-	143	-	-	-	143	720	863	9 096
	2010/11	-	-	-	-	-	-	-	-	-	-	537	537	12 912
	2011/12	-	-	-	-	-	-	-	-	-	-	696	696	-
	2012/13	-	-	-	-	-	-	-	-	-	-	524	524	
Armenia	2008/09	-	-	200	1 492	-	246	-	-	860	2 798	407	3 204	4 030
	2009/10	-	-	-	-	-	-	-	24	-	24	380	404	14 359
	2010/11	-	-	-	-	-	-	-	-	-	-	405	405	4 898
	2011/12	-	-	-	-	-	-	-	-	-	-	358	358	9 688
	2012/13	-	-	-	-	-	-	-	-	-	-	345	345	
Azerbaijan	2008/09	-	-	-	-	-	-	-	-	-	-	1 033	1 033	8 296
	2009/10	-	-	-	-	-	-	-	-	-	-	918	918	5 378
	2010/11	-	-	-	-	-	-	-	-	-	-	559	559	7 269
	2011/12	-	-	-	-	-	-	-	-	-	-	978	978	-
	2012/13	-	-	-	-	-	-	-	-	-	-	1 066	1 066	-
Belarus	2008/09	-	-	-	-	-	-	-	-	-	-	601	601	1 394
	2009/10	-	-	-	-	-	-	-	-	-	-	392	392	2 058
	2010/11	-	-	-	-	-	-	-	-	-	-	238	238	3 768
	2011/12	-	-	-	-	-	-	-	-	-	-	127	127	3 502
	2012/13	-	-	-	-	-	-	-	-	-	-	94	94	
Bosnia-Herzegovina	2008/09	-	-	750	3 025	321	16	-	-	-	4 112	988	5 100	8 490
	2009/10	-	-	750	1 405	43	182	-	-	-	2 379	2 737	5 116	12 862
	2010/11	-	-	947	2 750	149	20	-	-	-	3 866	2 207	6 073	23 015
	2011/12	-	-	-	-	-	-	-	-	-	-	2 285	2 285	-
	2012/13	-	-	-	-	-	-	-	-	-	-	1 702	1 702	
Croatia	2008/09	-	-	-	-	-	-	-	-	-	-	779	779	14 018
	2009/10	-	-	-	-	-	-	-	-	-	-	1 200	1 200	17 029
	2010/11	-	-	-	-	-	-	-	-	-	-	679	679	21 283
	2011/12	-	-	-	-	-	-	-	-	-	-	-	-	
	2012/13	-	-	-	-	-	-	-	-	-	-	-	-	
Cyprus	2008/09	-	-	-	-	-	-	-	-	-	-	2	2	-
	2009/10	-	-	-	-	-	-	-	-	-	-	2	2	-
	2010/11	-	-	-	-	-	-	-	-	-	-	-	-	
	2011/12	-	-	-	-	-	-	-	-	-	-	-	-	
	2012/13	-	-	-	-	-	-	-	-	-	-	-	-	
Georgia	2008/09	-	-	1 500	2 342	-	-	-	3 199	784	7 825	408	8 234	20 314
	2009/10	-	-	-	165	-	-	-	948	-	1 113	2 037	3 149	21 665
	2010/11	-	-	-	-	-	-	-	-	-	-	2 223	2 223	18 583
	2011/12	-	-	-	-	-	-	-	-	-	-	2 221	2 221	14 547
	2012/13	-	-	-	-	-	-	-	-	-	-	2 507	2 507	
Gibraltar	2008/09	-	-	-	-	-	-	-	-	-	-	-	-	-
	2009/10	-	-	-	-	-	-	-	-	-	-	-	-	-
	2010/11	-	-	-	-	-	-	-	-	-	-	-	-	-
	2011/12	-	-	-	-	-	-	-	-	-	-	-	-	-
	2012/13	-	-	6 746	-	-	-	-	-	-	6 746	-	6 746	
Macedonia, FYR	2008/09	-	-	-	-	-	-	-	-	-	-	1 181	1 181	6 035
	2009/10	-	-	-	-	-	-	-	-	-	-	1 250	1 250	9 616
	2010/11	-	-	-	-	-	-	-	-	-	-	743	743	13 538
	2011/12	-	-	-	-	-	-	-	-	-	-	1 017	1 017	-
	2012/13	-	-	-	-	-	-	-	-	-	-	1 130	1 130	
Moldova	2007/08	-	-	-	1 824	2 706	114	-	-	176	1 790	153	1 942	10 701
	2009/10	-	3 500	-	1 216	157	122	-	140	297	5 432	415	5 847	10 090
	2010/11	-	2 500	-	2 396	480	57	-	26	365	5 825	169	5 994	38 444
	2011/12	-	-	-	-	-	-	-	-	378	378	196	574	18 206
	2012/13	-	-	-	-	-	-	-	-	-	-	252	252	
Russian Federation	2008/09	-	-	-	-	-	190	-	-	-	190	-	190	-
	2009/10	-	-	-	7	1 259	242	-	-	-	1 507	535	2 042	-
	2010/11	-	-	-	-	1 134	135	-	-	-	1 269	-	1 269	-
	2011/12	-	-	-	-	-	-	-	-	-	-	-	-	-
	2012/13	-	-	-	-	-	-	-	-	-	-	-	-	
Serbia	2008/09	-	-	144	1 638	896	192	-	-	-	2 869	1 018	3 888	41 081
	2009/10	-	-	326	545	648	202	-	-	-	1 721	3 685	5 406	22 438
	2010/11	-	-	291	8	377	277	55	-	-	1 008	1 830	2 837	28 945
	2011/12	-	-	-	-	-	-	-28	-	-	-28	2 370	2 342	24 381
	2012/13	-	-	-	-	-	-	-	-	-	-	2 194	2 194	
Kosovo	2008/09	-	-	154	2 891	250	8	-	-	-	3 304	364	3 668	-
	2009/10	-	-	-	2 729	50	243	-	-	-	3 022	4 294	7 316	27 348
	2010/11	-	-	1 000	1 857	6	438	-	-	-	3 301	3 547	6 848	24 135
	2011/12	-	-	-	3 230	244	326	-	-	-	3 799	4 022	7 821	31 342
	2012/13	-	-	-	2 305	782	193	-	-	-	3 280	4 750	8 030	
Montenegro	2008/09	-	-	-	-	-	-	-	-	-	-	407	407	2 665
	2009/10	-	-	-	-	-	-	-	-	-	-	292	292	3 887
	2010/11	-	-	-	-	-	-	-	-	-	-	135	135	4 817
	2011/12	-	-	-	-	-	-	-	-	-	-	333	333	4 111
	2012/13	-	-	-	-	-	-	-	-	-	-	454	454	

3.2d Total DFID Expenditure and GPEX by Recipient Country (Europe) 2008/09 - 2012/2013

£ thousand

| | | Financial Aid | | Other Financial Aid [5] | Technical Cooperation | Bilateral aid delivered through a Multilateral | Bilateral aid Delivered through an NGO | Other Bilateral Aid [2] | Humanitarian Assistance | DFID Debt Relief | Total DFID Bilateral Programme | Aid from other UK Official Sources [5] | Total Bilateral Gross Public Expenditure | UK Imputed Multilateral Shares [3] |
		General Poverty Reduction Budget Support	Sector Poverty Reduction Budget Support											
States Ex-Yugoslavia	2008/09	-	-	-	-	-	-	-	-	-	-	-	-	23
	2009/10	-	-	-	-	-	-	-	-	-	-	-	-	-
	2010/11	-	-	-	-	-	-	-	-	-	-	-	-	233
	2011/12	-	-	-	-	-	-	-	-	-	-	-	-	-
	2012/13	-	-	-	-	-	-	-	-	-	-	-	-	
Turkey	2008/09	-	-	105	-	-	-	-	-	-	105	2 859	2 964	155 971
	2009/10	-	-	-	-	-	-	-	-	-	-	1 743	1 743	63 260
	2010/11	-	-	-	-	-	-	-	-	-	-	2 429	2 429	95 661
	2011/12	-	-	-	-	-	-	-	425	-	425	5 302	5 727	99 681
	2012/13	-	-	-	-	-	-	-	7	-	7	7 455	7 462	
Ukraine	2008/09	-	-	-	153	-	126	-	-	-	279	608	887	14 088
	2009/10	-	-	-	-	-	34	-	-	-	34	1 633	1 667	20 939
	2010/11	-	-	-	-	-	9	-	-	-	9	543	552	22 349
	2011/12	-	-	-	-	-	18	-	-	-	18	1 359	1 377	27 117
	2012/13	-	-	-	-	-	-	-	-	-	-	2 154	2 154	
Balkan Regional	2008/09	-	-	-	371	2 847	178	-	-	-	3 397	7 483	10 880	-
	2009/10	-	-	-	300	1 650	-	-	-	-	1 950	122	2 071	-
	2010/11	-	-	-	20	2 497	-	-	-	-	2 517	91	2 608	-
	2011/12	-	-	-	-	-	-	-	-	-	-	-	-	-
	2012/13	-	-	-	-	-	-	-	-	-	-	112	112	
Europe, regional	2008/09	-	-	-	1 520	773	2 236	-	82	-	4 612	724	5 336	27 573
	2009/10	-	-	-	1 156	2 142	179	2	49	-	3 527	1 970	5 497	46 480
	2010/11	-	-	1	-	60	-	13	-	-	74	-	74	56 887
	2011/12	-	-	-	-	-	-	14	-	-	14	121	135	61 782
	2012/13	-	-	-	-	-	-	12	-	-	12	107	119	
Total Europe	2008/09	-	-	2 853	15 855	8 662	1 490	-	3 199	1 821	33 880	19 404	53 284	323 966
	2009/10	-	3 500	1 076	7 522	5 949	1 346	2	1 161	297	20 853	24 321	45 174	286 505
	2010/11	-	2 500	2 239	7 030	4 703	937	68	26	365	17 868	16 335	34 203	376 737
	2011/12	-	-	-	3 230	244	344	-14	425	378	4 607	21 385	25 992	327 728
	2012/13	-	-	6 746	2 305	782	193	12	7	-	10 046	24 846	34 892	

1. Descriptions of aid types are given in Tehnical Note 1.
2. Other Bilateral Aid covers bilateral aid not elsewhere classified.
3. Details on DFID Imputed Multilateral Shares are in Section 2; 2012/13 data are not yet available.
5. Pension payments have been reclassified from "Other Financial Aid" to "Aid from other UK Official Sources". This is consistent with the classification of spending under Department Expenditure Limits (DEL) agreed with Treasury.

Source: Department for International Development (DFID)

3.2e Total DFID Expenditure and GPEX by Recipient Country (Pacific) 2008/09 - 2012/2013

£ thousand

| | | Financial Aid | | Other Financial Aid [5] | Technical Cooperation | Bilateral aid delivered through a Multilateral | Bilateral aid Delivered through an NGO | Other Bilateral Aid [2] | Humanitarian Assistance | DFID Debt Relief | Total DFID Bilateral Programme | Aid from other UK Official Sources [5] | Total Bilateral Gross Public Expenditure | UK Imputed Multilateral Shares [3] |
		General Poverty Reduction Budget Support	Sector Poverty Reduction Budget Support											
Cook Islands	2008/09	-	-	-	-	-	-	-	-	-	-	-	-	35
	2009/10	-	-	-	-	-	-	-	-	-	-	-	-	113
	2010/11	-	-	-	-	-	-	-	-	-	-	-	-	53
	2011/12	-	-	-	-	-	-	-	-	-	-	-	-	97
	2012/13	-	-	-	-	-	-	-	-	-	-	-	-	
Fiji	2008/09	-	-	-	-	-	-	-	-	-	-	409	409	2 165
	2009/10	-	-	-	-	-	-	-	-	-	-	373	373	609
	2010/11	-	-	-	-	-	-	-	-	-	-	243	243	1 992
	2011/12	-	-	-	-	-	-	-	-	-	-	231	231	-
	2012/13	-	-	-	-	-	-	-	-	-	-	9 006	9 006	
Kiribati	2008/09	-	-	-	-	-	-	-	-	-	-	18	18	72
	2009/10	-	-	-	-	-	-	-	-	-	-	22	22	629
	2010/11	-	-	-	-	-	-	-	-	-	-	36	36	708
	2011/12	-	-	-	-	-	-	-	-	-	-	16	16	3 537
	2012/13	-	-	-	-	-	-	-	-	-	-	17	17	
Marshall Islands	2008/09	-	-	-	-	-	-	-	-	-	-	-	-	39
	2009/10	-	-	-	-	-	-	-	-	-	-	-	-	536
	2010/11	-	-	-	-	-	-	-	-	-	-	-	-	128
	2011/12	-	-	-	-	-	-	-	-	-	-	11	11	4
	2012/13	-	-	-	-	-	-	-	-	-	-	1	1	
Micronesia, Fed. States	2008/09	-	-	-	-	-	-	-	-	-	-	-	-	58
	2009/10	-	-	-	-	-	-	-	-	-	-	-	-	887
	2010/11	-	-	-	-	-	-	-	-	-	-	-	-	..
	2011/12	-	-	-	-	-	-	-	-	-	-	-	-	10
	2012/13	-	-	-	-	-	-	-	-	-	-	-	-	
Nauru	2008/09	-	-	-	-	-	-	-	-	-	-	-	-	16
	2009/10	-	-	-	-	-	-	-	-	-	-	-	-	300
	2010/11	-	-	-	-	-	-	-	-	-	-	8	8	..
	2011/12	-	-	-	-	-	-	-	-	-	-	-	-	76
	2012/13	-	-	-	-	-	-	-	-	-	-	-	-	
Niue	2008/09	-	-	-	-	-	-	-	-	-	-	-	-	-
	2009/10	-	-	-	-	-	-	-	-	-	-	-	-	402
	2010/11	-	-	-	-	-	-	-	-	-	-	-	-	3
	2011/12	-	-	-	-	-	-	-	-	-	-	-	-	-
	2012/13	-	-	-	-	-	-	-	-	-	-	-	-	
Palau	2008/09	-	-	-	-	-	-	-	-	-	-	55	55	20
	2009/10	-	-	-	-	-	-	-	-	-	-	-	-	296
	2010/11	-	-	-	-	-	-	-	-	-	-	12	12	-
	2011/12	-	-	-	-	-	-	-	-	-	-	-	-	1
	2012/13	-	-	-	-	-	-	-	-	-	-	-	-	
Papua New Guinea	2008/09	-	-	-	-	-	279	-	-	-	-	279	302	582	2 550
	2009/10	-	-	-	-	-	97	-	-	-	-	97	431	528	3 346
	2010/11	-	-	-	-	-	-	-	-	-	-	-	814	814	9 731
	2011/12	-	-	-	-	-	-	-	-	-	-	-	301	301	-
	2012/13	-	-	-	-	-	-	-	-	-	-	-	762	762	
Pitcairn Islands	2008/09	-	-	1 821	219	-	75	-	-	-	-	2 115	1	2 116	-
	2009/10	-	-	1 745	3	-	42	-	-	-	-	1 790	-	1 790	-
	2010/11	-	-	2 235	212	-	-	-	-	-	-	2 447	39	2 486	-
	2011/12	-	-	2 738	36	-	-	-	-	-	-	2 774	-	2 774	-
	2012/13	-	-	2 883	11	-	-	-	-	-	-	2 894	-	2 894	
Samoa	2008/09	-	-	-	-	-	-	-	-	-	111	111	-	111	573
	2009/10	-	-	-	-	-	-	-	-	100	115	215	-	215	2 065
	2010/11	-	-	-	-	-	-	-	-	-	150	150	-	150	3 806
	2011/12	-	-	-	-	-	-	-	-	-	170	170	85	254	1 524
	2012/13	-	-	-	-	-	-	-	-	-	166	166	8	174	
Solomon Islands	2008/09	-	-	-	-	-	-	-	-	-	-	-	137	137	253
	2009/10	-	-	-	-	-	-	-	-	-	-	-	146	146	1 316
	2010/11	-	-	-	-	-	-	-	-	-	-	-	144	144	3 793
	2011/12	-	-	-	-	-	-	-	-	-	-	-	139	139	606
	2012/13	-	-	-	-	-	-	-	-	150	-	150	186	336	
Tokelau	2008/09	-	-	-	-	-	-	-	-	-	-	-	-	-	-
	2009/10	-	-	-	-	-	-	-	-	-	-	-	-	-	14
	2010/11	-	-	-	-	-	-	-	-	-	-	-	-	-	9
	2011/12	-	-	-	-	-	-	-	-	-	-	-	-	-	2
	2012/13	-	-	-	-	-	-	-	-	-	-	-	-	-	
Tonga	2008/09	-	-	-	-	-	-	-	-	-	-	-	277	277	251
	2009/10	-	-	-	-	-	-	-	-	-	-	-	6	6	214
	2010/11	-	-	-	-	-	-	-	-	-	-	-	99	99	1 462
	2011/12	-	-	-	-	-	-	-	-	-	-	-	34	34	4 393
	2012/13	-	-	-	-	-	-	-	-	-	-	-	17	17	
Tuvalu	2008/09	-	-	-	-	-	-	-	-	-	-	-	-	-	47
	2009/10	-	-	-	-	-	-	-	-	-	-	-	-	-	548
	2010/11	-	-	-	-	-	-	-	-	-	-	-	28	28	219
	2011/12	-	-	-	-	-	-	-	-	-	-	-	51	51	1 399
	2012/13	-	-	-	-	-	-	-	-	-	-	-	-	-	

3.2e Total DFID Expenditure and GPEX by Recipient Country (Pacific) 2008/09 - 2012/2013

£ thousand

| | | Financial Aid | | | | | | | | | | | | |
		General Poverty Reduction Budget Support	Sector Poverty Reduction Budget Support	Other Financial Aid [5]	Technical Cooperation	Bilateral aid delivered through a Multilateral	Bilateral aid Delivered through an NGO	Other Bilateral Aid [2]	Humanitarian Assistance	DFID Debt Relief	Total DFID Bilateral Programme	Aid from other UK Official Sources [5]	Total Bilateral Gross Public Expenditure	UK Imputed Multilateral Shares [3]
Vanuatu	2008/09	-	-	-	-	-	-	-	-	33	33	18	51	112
	2009/10	-	-	-	-	-	-	-	-	40	40	22	62	1 070
	2010/11	-	-	-	-	-	-	-	-	42	42	17	58	60
	2011/12	-	-	-	-	-	-	-	-	42	42	31	73	291
	2012/13	-	-	-	-	-	-	-	-	-	-	14	14	
Wallis & Fortuna	2008/09	-	-	-	-	-	-	-	-	-	-	-	-	-
	2009/10	-	-	-	-	-	-	-	-	-	-	-	-	-
	2010/11	-	-	-	-	-	-	-	-	-	-	-	-	-
	2011/12	-	-	-	-	-	-	-	-	-	-	-	-	-
	2012/13	-	-	-	-	-	-	-	-	-	-	-	-	
South Pacific Regional	2008/09	-	-	-	156	-	95	-	-	-	251	-	251	-
	2009/10	-	-	-	-	-	-	-	-	-	-	-	-	-
	2010/11	-	-	-	-	-	-	-	-	-	-	-	-	-
	2011/12	-	-	-	-	-	-	-	-	-	-	60	60	12 794
	2012/13	-	-	-	-	-	-	-	-	-	-	-	-	
Oceania, regional	2008/09	-	-	-	-	-	-	-	-	-	-	-	-	475
	2009/10	-	-	-	-	-	-	-	-	-	-	-	-	3 535
	2010/11	-	-	-	-	-	-	-	-	-	-	103	103	7 391
	2011/12	-	-	-	-	-	-	-	-	-	-	101	101	275
	2012/13	-	-	-	-	-	-	-	-	-	-	69	69	
Total Pacific	2008/09	-	-	1 821	375	-	449	-	-	144	2 790	1 217	4 007	6 666
	2009/10	-	-	1 745	3	-	139	-	100	155	2 142	1 001	3 142	15 882
	2010/11	-	-	2 235	212	-	-	-	-	191	2 638	1 542	4 180	29 355
	2011/12	-	-	2 738	36	-	-	-	-	212	2 986	1 060	4 046	12 213
	2012/13	-	-	2 883	11	-	-	-	150	166	3 210	10 080	13 290	

1. Descriptions of aid types are given in Technical Note 1.
2. Other Bilateral Aid covers bilateral aid not elsewhere classified
3. Details on DFID Imputed Multilateral Shares are in Section 2; 2012/13 data are not yet available.
4. Low Income Country. Income groups are classified using 2012 GNI per capita thresholds.
5. Pension payments have been reclassified from "Other Financial Aid" to "Aid from other UK Official Sources". This is consistent with the classification of spending under Department Expenditure Limits (DEL) agreed with Treasury.

Source: Department for International Development (DFID)

3.3 DFID Bilateral Expenditure by Input Sector Code 2008/09 to 2012/13

£ thousand

Input Sector Code	2008/09	2009/10	2010/11	2011/12	2012/13
Education:					
11010 Education Poverty Reduction Budget Support	105 319	155 629	152 581	90,301	135,395
11020 Education Unallocable/Unspecified	281	1 489	8 718	51,403	6,399
11110 Education Policy and Administrative Management	63 585	53 549	68 527	122,537	63,369
11120 Facilities and Training Education	43 243	34 929	31 044	44,756	25,531
11130 Teacher Training	9 891	14 135	17 775	15,879	24,181
11220 Primary Education	179 650	111 045	210 797	231,124	143,204
11230 Basic Life Skills for Youth and Adults Education	11 248	3 749	10 933	11,426	25,215
11240 Pre-School	1 164	4 717	4 337	3,717	2,123
11320 Secondary Education	11 784	8 040	27 059	28,089	58,090
11330 Vocational Training	4 411	4 820	8 588	6,609	7,028
11420 Higher Education	20 075	2 677	20 237	19,267	21,146
11430 Advanced Technical and Managerial Training	323	269	312	281	562
Education Total	**450 973**	**395 049**	**560 907**	**625 389**	**512 243**
Health:					
12010 Health Poverty Reduction Budget Support	105 679	111 811	100 327	57,306	48,440
12020 Health Unallocable/Unspecified	1 827	2 585	3 712	13,504	8,346
12110 Health Policy and Administrative Management	48 784	46 829	58 667	43,590	56,090
12220 Basic Health Care	99 652	91 566	74 650	105,712	144,027
12240 Basic Nutrition	12 927	19 365	23 715	37,505	49,433
12250 Infectious Disease Control	69 169	61 487	73 853	146,612	105,375
12261 Health Education	19 842	19 919	26 392	31,717	34,434
12262 Malaria Control	35 060	42 295	101 393	86,181	111,521
12263 Tuberculosis Control	12 802	13 577	44 187	10,051	12,735
12281 Health Personnel Development	10 918	10 368	7 773	12,295	12,611
13010 Population Policy and Administrative Management	2 619	2 949	7 092	6,063	5,463
13021 Reproductive Health Care	36 466	43 196	47 962	108,852	36,746
13022 Maternal and Neonatal Health	61 645	49 376	49 987	121,362	125,862
13030 Family Planning	8 075	15 252	31 082	43,767	109,727
13041 HIV/AIDS including STD Prevention	147 863	122 036	119 094	69,002	50,271
13042 HIV/AIDS including STD Treatment and Care	10 113	24 002	52 717	27,331	40,160
13081 Personnel Development for Population and Reproductive Health	1 490	6 676	7 506	8,332	7,543
Health Total	**684 931**	**683 289**	**830 109**	**929 182**	**958 782**
Social Infrastructure and Services:					
16011 Social Protection	68 656	156 911	186 531	103,647	104,931
16012 Social Other	22 893	27 923	48 714	83,879	53,237
16020 Employment Policy & Admin Management	150	623	2 956	2,924	4,271
16030 Housing Policy and Admin Management	2 764	623	73	594	566
16040 Low-cost Housing	564	2 226	1 706	5,693	7,867
16070 Poverty Reduction Budget Support-Social infrastructure and services	18 647	23 319	18 273	12,940	7,078
52010 Food Aid and Food Security Programmes	51 148	26 468	52 145	50,622	47,148
Social Infrastructure and Services Total	**164 822**	**238 093**	**310 396**	**260 300**	**225 098**
Water Supply and Sanitation:					
14010 Water Resources Policy and Administrative Management	7 484	20 611	14 317	20,655	14,926
14015 Water Resources Protection	384	1 323	2 335	5,216	5,192
14020 Water Supply and Sanitation Large Systems	4 415	3 081	4 869	9,175	10,934
14021 Water Supply – Large Systems	-	54	4 039	5,100	-
14030 Basic Drinking Water	59 799	55 820	63 219	73,031	55,664
14031 Basic drinking water supply	-	72	964	891	2,581
14032 Basic sanitation	-	88	1 466	7,605	17,237
14040 River Development	1 359	5 439	3 688	1,360	29
14050 Waste Management and Disposal	110	2 900	2 669	2,519	3,737
14060 Water Poverty Reduction Budget Support	13 325	15 556	13 271	8,255	9,134
14070 Water Unallocable/Unspecified	484	718	868	6,976	9,623
14081 Education and Training	1 108	250	354	1,408	962
Water Supply and Sanitation Total	**88 467**	**105 912**	**112 061**	**142 191**	**130 020**
Government and Civil Society:					
15010 Government Poverty Reduction Budget Support	111 246	137 078	115 004	58,494	37,665
15020 Government Unallocated/ Unspecified	11 017	26 082	52 166	37,876	42,945
15110 Economic and Development Policy/Planning	135 931	114 791	121 076	90,314	86,146
15121 Public Sector Financial Management	118 112	113 514	105 996	132,449	126,422
15122 Corruption - Public Sector Financial Management	7 908	13 182	17 719	18,010	16,677
15130 Legal and Judicial Development	19 147	18 469	17 351	18,158	15,623

3.3 DFID Bilateral Expenditure by Input Sector Code 2008/09 to 2012/13

£ thousand

Input Sector Code	2008/09	2009/10	2010/11	2011/12	2012/13
15141 National Government Administration	21 657	16 791	30 876	33,736	49,375
15142 Local Government Administration	36 803	42 417	36 266	57,607	53,882
15150 Strengthening Civil Society	172 757	89 251	116 792	121,683	102,697
15161 Elections	30 456	18 539	33 880	28,920	1,877
15162 Human Rights	11 591	9 084	10 688	10,284	27,490
15163 Free Flow of Information	2 956	7 419	9 997	10,144	9,369
15164 Women's Equality Organisations and Institutions	3 748	6 138	12 306	11,742	13,170
15171 Culture and Recreation	-	143	82		-
15172 Statistical Capacity Building	12 262	27 935	40 395	31,102	15,752
15173 Narcotics Control	-	46	53	24	21,880
15210 Security System Management and Reform	13 050	13 338	19 285	27,065	34,429
15220 Civilian Peace-Building, Conflict Prevention and Resolution	61 327	39 409	20 497	21,597	38,480
15230 Post-Conflict Peace-Building (UN)	2 627	5 689	6 520	5,719	9,257
15240 Reintegration and SALW Control	1 343	6 377	4 683	754	269
15250 Land Mine Clearance	16 444	9 907	9 902	11,720	10,586
15261 Child Soldiers (Prevention and Demobilisation)	375	261	141	159	14
Government and Civil Society Total	**790 756**	**715 860**	**781 674**	**727 557**	**714 004**
Economic:					
Economic Infrastructure					
21010 Transport Policy and Administrative Management	37 973	39 007	65 697	42,208	53,921
21021 Road Transport: Excluding Rural Feeder Roads	623	36 408	37 096	26,548	24,630
21022 Road Transport: Rural Feeder Roads	9 868	8 745	15 224	17,222	9,427
21031 Other Transport	12 295	12 832	5 755	22,965	45,652
22010 Communications Policy and Administrative Management	8 190	8 150	6 065	1,680	1,649
22020 Telecommunications	73	9 439	8 596	8,892	1,444
22030 Radio/Television/Print Media: Communications	788	1 872	64	38	1
22040 Information and Communication Technology (ICT)	28	519	2 055	655	135
23010 Energy Policy and Administrative Management	22 815	23 993	35 208	12,887	14,973
23020 Power Generation/Non-Renewable Sources: Energy	23	7 439	11 809	9,760	3,628
23030 Power Generation/Renewable Sources: Energy	5 023	23 513	30 633	3,956	13,090
24010 Financial Policy and Administrative Management	30 268	24 223	26 098	27,913	26,940
24020 Monetary Institutions	1 593	205 870	1 319	3,111	1,409
24030 Formal Sector Financial Intermediaries	4 528	6 239	10 968	12,825	14,092
24040 Informal/Semi-Formal Financial Intermediaries	4 105	6 250	7 449	6,764	10,277
24081 Education/Training in Banking and Financial Services	1 297	2 382	2 471	4,877	3,518
25010 Business Support Services and Institutions	2 912	16 947	29 087	25,071	29,458
25020 Privatisation	17 009	5 765	7 896	5,479	4,626
Production Sectors					
31110 Agriculture Policy and Administrative Management	27 519	43 937	38 879	34,080	19,891
31120 Agricultural Development	18 122	26 089	18 023	37,625	18,877
31130 Agricultural Land Resources	11 972	7 555	11 033	4,115	3,639
31163 Livestock: Agriculture	4 914	3 231	2 281	2,895	5,133
31191 Agricultural Services	82	1 287	865	2,766	4,617
31210 Forestry Policy and Administrative Management	10 901	16 583	30 650	4,910	15,936
31220 Forestry Development	10 962	15 320	28 989	4,351	865
31310 Fishing Policy and Administrative Management	1 025	2 368	3 046	1,838	1,496
31320 Fishery Development	330	201	265	0	9
32110 Industrial Policy and Administrative Management	45	548	1 068	1,632	2,054
32120 Industrial Development	126	934	2 034	2,816	1,901
32130 Small and Medium-Sized Enterprises (SME): Development	31 730	24 765	30 011	25,575	20,686
32210 Mineral/Mining Policy and Administrative Management	1 101	679	369	8,663	5,287
32310 Construction Policy and Administrative Management	101	105	939	2,503	1,430
32350 Production Poverty Reduction Budget Support	34 501	34 237	30 984	18,803	15,905
33110 Trade Policy and Administrative Management	35 267	34 430	30 713	19,204	18,423
33120 Trade Facilitation	4 015	29 745	40 024	11,613	16,343
33130 Regional Trade Agreements (RTAs)	160	3 865	6 792	4,191	6,031
33140 Multilateral Trade Negotiations	1 982	741	120	273	1,742
33181 Trade Education/Training	31	360	613	838	400
33210 Tourism Policy and Administrative Management	13	829	1 272	2,215	1,345
43050 Non-Agricultural Alternative Development	211	550	818	1,692	2,132
Development Planning					
43020 Poverty Reduction Budget Support for Econ. Infrastructure & Dev. Planning	83 370	108 985	67 825	42,162	26,009
43030 Urban Development and Management	28 476	16 626	30 362	19,907	28,356
43040 Rural Development	55 536	51 502	68 083	55,302	53,854
Economic Total	**526 925**	**865 063**	**749 546**	**542 821**	**531 231**

3.3 DFID Bilateral Expenditure by Input Sector Code 2008/09 to 2012/13

£ thousand

Input Sector Code	2008/09	2009/10	2010/11	2011/12	2012/13
Environment Protection:					
41010 Environmental Policy and Administrative Management	11 587	15 071	16 512	9,506	7,029
41031 Bio-Diversity	1 533	1 869	198	3,264	963
41032 Climate Change	30 043	54 926	2 191	30,997	59,724
41033 Desertification	108	624	101 790		1,711
41040 Site Preservation	10	15	242		
41050 Flood Prevention/Control	472	188	22	898	
41060 Environment: Poverty Reduction Budget Support	2 990	3 359	377	1,418	627
41070 Environment Unallocable/Unspecified	217	38	1 846	3,104	6,011
41081 Environmental Education/ Training	4 737	1 804	1 905	2,591	2,302
41090 Climate Change - Low Carbon Emissions				55,772	12,688
41092 Climate Change - Cross Cutting				2,811	4,319
41093 Climate Change - Adaptation				99,048	141,088
74010 Disaster Prevention and Preparedness	8 838	21 450	10 142	7,896	1,784
Environment Protection Total	**60 536**	**99 344**	**135 226**	**217 304**	**238 246**
Research:					
80010 Economic Research	12 182	9 784	12 651	16,350	20,533
80011 Education Research	3 549	3 076	1 775	2,884	5,121
80012 Health Research	48 900	66 816	46 997	49,312	49,412
80013 Water Supply and Sanitation Research	1 622	908	2 064	1,502	1,748
80014 Governance Research	17 247	9 923	6 825	11,836	9,781
80015 Social Research	10 774	11 529	12 257	8,327	11,248
80016 Humanitarian Research	772	939	1 185	1,163	1,486
80017 Renewable Natural Resources Research	29 978	20 000	7 603	6,139	1,596
80018 Environment Research	4 538	5 044	6 883	8,968	11,375
80019 Energy Research	26	17	817	1,037	2,553
80020 Agricultural Research	3 141	11 397	19 624	22,073	33,287
80021 Forestry Research	17	403	269	54	
80022 Fishery Research		70	169		
80023 Technological Research and Development	3 284	2 436	1 541	1,210	1,670
80024 Unspecified/Unallocated Research	3 191	3 983	7 442	9,253	17,182
Research Total	**139 222**	**146 325**	**128 103**	**140 109**	**166 994**
Humanitarian Assistance:					
72010 Material Relief Assistance and Services	174 831	232 635	198 368	157,678	243,333
72040 Emergency Food Aid	80 354	96 986	68 862	106,548	145,762
72050 Relief Coordination, Protection and Support Services	46 535	56 769	61 763	38,336	69,742
73010 Reconstruction Relief and Rehabilitation	15 674	50 861	27 996	47,043	14,345
Humanitarian Assistance Total	**317 395**	**437 250**	**356 989**	**349 604**	**473 182**
Non Sector Allocable:					
11110 Education policy and administrative management					162
15220 Civilian peace-building, conflict preventiona and resolution					847
74010 Disaster prevention and preparedness					2000
10000 DFID Administrative Costs	-	-	220		
88889 Multilateral Capacity Building and Administration	1 893	27 836	17 850	42,463	2675
88890 Multilateral Institutions: Secondees to & Staffing of	485	1 163	1,838	4,673	5264
60010 Action Relating to Debt	19 619	50 992	66 483	15,110	17440
90010 Programme Partnership Agreements		129 557	116 100	91,508	124808
91010 Administrative Costs of Donors	902	559	1 236		
92000 Support to Non-Governmental Organisations (NGOs)	1 784	36 422	50 815	101,785	62436
93020 Aid to Refugees in Recipient Countries	19 479	2 348	9 164	2,344	2882
88888 Multilateral Core Contribution					-14249
99820 Promotion of Development Awareness	15 279	28 372	19 300	11,775	16008
Others					-684
Non Sector Allocable Total	**59 440**	**277 249**	**283 006**	**269 658**	**219 589**

Source: Department for International Development (DFID)

1. '-' means nil
   '0' means less than half the final digit shown
   '..' means not available
   'n/a' means not applicable
2. Figures are rounded to the nearest unit, therefore they may not add exactly to the rounded totals.
3. Negative amounts reflect accounting adjustments.

Labour market

Chapter 4

Labour Market

Labour Force Survey

Background

The Labour Force Survey (LFS) is the largest regular household survey in the UK. LFS interviews are conducted continuously throughout the year. In any three-month period, nationally representative samples of approximately 110,000 people aged 16 and over in around 50,000 households are interviewed. Each household is interviewed five times, at three-monthly intervals. The initial interview is done face-to-face by an interviewer visiting the address, except for residents north of the Caledonian Canal in Scotland. The other interviews are done by telephone wherever possible. The survey asks a series of questions about respondents' personal circumstances and their labour market activity. Most questions refer to activity in the week before the interview.

The LFS collects information on a sample of the population. To convert this information to give estimates for the population, the data must be grossed. This is achieved by calculating weighting factors (often referred to simply as weights) which can be applied to each sampled individual in such a way that the weighted-up results match estimates or projections of the total population in terms of age distribution, sex, and region of residence. There is a considerable amount of ongoing research to improve methodologies. Whenever methodologies are implemented the estimates may be revised.

The concepts and definitions used in the LFS are agreed by the International Labour Organisation (ILO) – an agency of the United Nations. The definitions are used by European Union member countries and members of the Organisation for Economic Co-operation and Development (OECD). The LFS was carried out every two years from 1973 to 1983. The ILO definition was first used in 1984. This was also the first year in which the survey was conducted on an annual basis with results available for every spring quarter (representing an average of the period from March to May). The survey moved to a continuous basis in spring 1992 in Great Britain and in winter 1994/95 in Northern Ireland, with average quarterly results published four times a year for seasonal quarters: spring (March to May), summer (June to August), autumn (September to November) and winter (December to February). From April 1998, results are published 12 times a year for the average of three consecutive months.

Strengths and limitations of the LFS

The LFS produces coherent labour market information on the basis of internationally standard concepts and definitions. It is a rich source of data on a wide variety of labour market and personal characteristics. It is the most suitable source for making comparisons between countries. The LFS is designed so that households interviewed in each three month period constitute a representative sample of UK households. The survey covers those living in private households and nurses in

National Health Service accommodation. Students living in halls of residence have been included since 1992, as information about them is collected at their parents' address.

However the LFS has its limitations. It is a sample survey and is therefore subject to sampling variability. The survey does not include people living in institutions such as hostels, hotels, boarding houses, mobile home sites or residential homes. 'Proxy' reporting (when members of the household are not present at the interview, another member of the household answers the questions on their behalf) can affect the quality of information on topics such as earnings, hours worked, benefit receipt and qualifications. Around a third of interviews are conducted 'by proxy', usually by a spouse or partner but sometimes by a parent or other near relation. LFS estimates are also potentially affected by non-response.

Sampling Variability

Survey estimates are prone to sampling variability. The easiest way to explain this concept is by example. In the September to November 1997 period, ILO unemployment in Great Britain (seasonally adjusted) stood at 1,847,000. If we drew another sample for the same period we could get a different result, perhaps 1,900,000 or 1,820,000.

In theory, we could draw many samples, and each would give a different result. This is because each sample would be made up of different people who would give different answers to the questions. The spread of these results is the sampling variability. Sampling variability is determined by a number of factors including the sample size, the variability of the population from which the sample is drawn and the sample design. Once we know the sampling variability we can calculate a range of values about the sample estimate that represents the expected variation with a given level of assurance. This is called a confidence interval. For a 95 per cent confidence interval we expect that in 95 per cent of the samples (19 times out of 20) the confidence interval will contain the true value that would be obtained by surveying the entire population. For the example given above, we can be 95 per cent confident that the true value was in the range 1,791,000 to 1,903,000.

Unreliable estimates

Estimates of small numbers have relatively wide confidence intervals making them unreliable. For this reason, the Office for National Statistics (ONS) does not currently publish LFS estimates below 10,000.

Non-response

All surveys are subject to non-response – that is respondents in the sample who either refuse to take part in the survey or who cannot be contacted. Non-response can introduce bias to a survey, particularly if the people not responding have characteristics that are different from those who do respond.

The LFS has a response rate of around 65 per cent to the first interview, and over 90 per cent of those who are interviewed once go on to complete all five interviews. These are relatively high levels for a household survey.

Any bias from non-response is minimised by weighting the results. Weighting (or grossing) converts sample data to represent the full population. In the LFS, the data are weighted separately by age, sex and area of residence to population estimates based on the census. Weighting also adjusts for people not in the survey and thus minimises non-response bias.

LFS concepts and definitions

Discouraged worker - A sub-group of the economically inactive population who said although they would like a job their main reason for not seeking work was because they believed there were no jobs available.

Economically active – People aged 16 and over who are either in employment or unemployed.

Economic activity rate – The number of people who are in employment or unemployed expressed as a percentage of the relevant population.

Economically inactive – People who are neither in employment nor unemployed. These include those who want a job but have not been seeking work in the last four weeks, those who want a job and are seeking work but not available to start, and those who do not want a job.

Employment – People aged 16 and over who did at least one hour of paid work in the reference week (as an employee or self-employed), those who had a job that they were temporarily away from, those on government-supported training and employment programmes, and those doing unpaid family work.

Employees – The division between employees and self employed is based on survey respondents' own assessment of their employment status.

Full Time – The classification of employees, self-employed and unpaid family workers in their main job as full-time or part-time is on the basis of self-assessment. However, people on government supported employment and training programmes that are at college in the reference week are classified, by convention, as part-time.

Government -supported training and employment programmes – Comprise all people aged 16 and over participating in one of the government's employment and training programmes (Youth Training, Training for Work and Community Action), together with those on similar programmes administered by Training and Enterprise Councils in England and Wales, or Local Enterprise Companies in Scotland.

Hours worked – Respondents to the LFS are asked a series of questions enabling the identification of both their usual hours and their actual hours. Total hours include overtime (paid and unpaid) and exclude lunch breaks.

Actual Hours Worked – Actual hours worked statistics measure how many hours were actually worked. These statistics are directly affected by changes in the number of people in employment and in the number of hours that individual works.

Usual Hours Worked – Usual hours worked statistics measure how many hours people usually work per week. Compared with actual hours worked, they are not affected by absences and so can provide a better measure of normal working patterns.

Unemployment – The number of unemployed people in the UK is measured through the LFS following the internationally agreed definition recommended by the International Labour Organisation (ILO), an agency of the United Nations.

Unemployed people are:

Without a job, have actively sought work in the last four weeks and are available to start work in the next two weeks, or

Out of work, have found a job and are waiting to start in the next two weeks

Unemployment (rate) – The number of unemployed people expressed as a percentage of the relevant economically active population.

Unemployment (duration) – The duration of respondents unemployment is defined as the shorter of the following two periods:

Duration of active search for work

Length of time since employment

Part-time – see full-time.

Second jobs – Jobs which LFS respondents hold in addition to a main full-time or part-time job.

Self-employment – See Employees.

Temporary employees – In the LFS these are defined as those employees who say that their main job is non permanent in one of the following ways: fixed period contract, agency temping, casual work, seasonal work or other temporary work.

Unpaid family workers – Persons doing unpaid work for a business they own or for a business that a relative owns.

International Employment Comparisons

All employment rates for European Union (EU) countries published by Eurostat (including the rate for the UK) are based on the population aged 15–64. The rates for Canada and Japan are also based on the population aged 15–64, but the rate for the US is for those aged 16–64. The employment rate for the UK published by ONS is based on the working age population aged 16–64 (men) and 16–59 (women) and therefore takes into account both the current school leaving age and state pension ages.

The unemployment rate published by Eurostat for most EU countries (but not for the UK), are calculated by extrapolating from the most recent LFS data using monthly registered unemployment data. A standard population basis (15–74) is used by Eurostat except for Spain and the UK (16–74). The unemployment rate for the US is based on those aged 16 and over, but the rates for Canada and Japan are for those aged 15 and over. All unemployment rates are seasonally adjusted.

The unemployment rate for the UK published by Eurostat is based on the population aged 16–74 while the unemployment rate for the UK published by ONS is based on those aged 16 and over. There are other minor definitional differences.

Jobseekers allowance claimant count

This is a count of all those people who are claiming Jobseeker's Allowance (JSA) at Jobcentre Plus local offices. People claiming JSA must declare that they are:

- out of work
- capable of work
- available for work
- actively seeking work

during the week in which the claim is made.

All people claiming JSA on the day of the monthly count are included in the claimant count, irrespective of whether they are actually receiving benefits. Also see table 5.6 in Social protection chapter.

Annual Survey of Hours and Earnings

The Annual Survey of Hours and Earnings (ASHE) is based on a one per cent sample of employee jobs taken from HM Revenue & Customs (HMRC) PAYE records. Information on earnings and paid hours worked is obtained from employers and treated confidentially. ASHE does not cover the self-employed nor does it cover employees not paid during the reference period.

The headline statistics for ASHE are based on the median rather than the mean. The median is the value below which 50 per cent of employees fall. It is ONS's preferred measure of average earnings as it is less affected by a relatively small number of very high earners and the skewed distribution of earnings. It therefore gives a better indication of typical pay than the mean.

The earnings information presented relates to gross pay before tax, National Insurance or other deductions, and excludes payments in kind. With the exception of annual earnings, the results are restricted to earnings relating to the survey pay period and so exclude payments of arrears from another period made during the survey period; any payments due as a result of a pay settlement but not yet paid at the time of the survey will also be excluded.

More detailed information is available on the National Statistics web site at:

www.statistics.gov.uk/StatBase/Product.asp?vlnk=13101

Average Weekly Earnings

The Average Weekly Earnings (AWE) indicator measures changes in the level of earnings in Great Britain. Average earnings are calculated as the total wages and salaries paid by firms, divided by the number of employees paid. It is given as a level, in pounds per employee per week. Annual growth rates are derived from the level of average weekly earnings.

The AWE data are now published on a SIC 2007 basis, and the historic time series have been re-estimated as a result. For more information, see the article available at:

www.statistics.gov.uk/downloads/theme_labour/average-week-earnings-sic2007.pdf

AWE is based on the Monthly wages and Salaries Survey (MWSS). As such, it is a timely indicator of changes in the level of earnings. The survey does not cover businesses with fewer than 20 employees; an adjustment is made to AWE to reflect these businesses. Note that the survey does not include Northern Ireland.

Unlike the previous measure of average earnings (the Average Earnings Index), changes in the composition of the workforce have an impact on AWE. If a high-paying sector of the economy employs more people, other things staying the same, average earnings will increase.

Average Weekly Earnings, like AEI before it, is a measure based on earnings per employee. If the number of paid hours worked per employee change, average earnings will also change.

Trade unions

The statistics relate to all organisations of workers known to the Certification Officer with head offices in Great Britain that fall within the appropriate definition of a trade union in the Trade Union and Labour Relations (Consolidation) Act 1992. Included in the data are home and overseas membership figures of contributory and non-contributory members. Employment status of members is not provided and the figures may therefore include some people who are self-employed, unemployed or retired.

4.1 Labour Force Summary by Sex: United Kingdom

		LFS household population[1]		Headline indicators					
				Employment		Unemployment		Inactivity	
				Level	Rate[2]	Level	Rate[3]	Level	Rate[4]
		All aged 16 & over	All aged 16 to 64	All aged 16 & over	All aged 16 to 64	All aged 16 & over	All aged 16 & over	All aged 16 to 64	All aged 16 to 64
People		MGSL	LF2O	MGRZ	LF24	MGSC	MGSX	LF2M	LF2S
	Aug-Oct 2011	50,258	40,171	29,102	70.3	2,637	8.3	9,321	23.2
	Aug-Oct 2012	50,625	40,204	29,601	71.2	2,510	7.8	9,072	22.6
	Nov-Jan 2013	50,717	40,220	29,732	71.5	2,516	7.8	8,954	22.3
	Feb-Apr 2013	50,809	40,237	29,756	71.5	2,511	7.8	8,994	22.4
	May-Jul 2013	50,901	40,253	29,836	71.6	2,487	7.7	8,961	22.3
	Aug-Oct 2013	**51,011**	**40,299**	**30,086**	**72.0**	**2,388**	**7.4**	**8,916**	**22.1**
	Change on quarter	*110*	*45*	*250*	*0.4*	*-99*	*-0.3*	*-45*	*-0.1*
	Change %	*0.2*	*0.1*	*0.8*		*-4.0*		*-0.5*	
	Change on year	*386*	*95*	*485*	*0.8*	*-121*	*-0.5*	*-156*	*-0.4*
	Change %	*0.8*	*0.2*	*1.6*		*-4.8*		*-1.7*	
Men		MGSM	YBTG	MGSA	MGSV	MGSD	MGSY	YBSO	YBTM
	Aug-Oct 2011	24,555	20,003	15,569	75.2	1,533	9.0	3,445	17.2
	Aug-Oct 2012	24,757	20,029	15,901	76.5	1,430	8.3	3,299	16.5
	Nov-Jan 2013	24,807	20,039	15,921	76.5	1,431	8.2	3,291	16.4
	Feb-Apr 2013	24,857	20,050	15,907	76.3	1,419	8.2	3,354	16.7
	May-Jul 2013	24,908	20,060	15,948	76.4	1,434	8.3	3,313	16.5
	Aug-Oct 2013	**24,974**	**20,092**	**16,103**	**77.0**	**1,350**	**7.7**	**3,291**	**16.4**
	Change on quarter	*66*	*32*	*155*	*0.6*	*-84*	*-0.5*	*-22*	*-0.1*
	Change %	*0.3*	*0.2*	*1.0*		*-5.9*		*-0.7*	
	Change on year	*217*	*63*	*202*	*0.5*	*-80*	*-0.5*	*-9*	*-0.1*
	Change %	*0.9*	*0.3*	*1.3*		*-5.6*		*-0.3*	
Women		MGSN	LF2P	MGSB	LF25	MGSE	MGSZ	LF2N	LF2T
	Aug-Oct 2011	25,703	20,168	13,533	65.5	1,104	7.5	5,876	29.1
	Aug-Oct 2012	25,868	20,175	13,700	66.1	1,080	7.3	5,773	28.6
	Nov-Jan 2013	25,910	20,181	13,810	66.6	1,085	7.3	5,663	28.1
	Feb-Apr 2013	25,952	20,187	13,848	66.7	1,092	7.3	5,640	27.9
	May-Jul 2013	25,993	20,193	13,887	66.9	1,053	7.0	5,648	28.0
	Aug-Oct 2013	**26,037**	**20,206**	**13,982**	**67.1**	**1,038**	**6.9**	**5,625**	**27.8**
	Change on quarter	*44*	*13*	*95*	*0.2*	*-15*	*-0.1*	*-23*	*-0.1*
	Change %	*0.2*	*0.1*	*0.7*		*-1.4*		*-0.4*	
	Change on year	*169*	*31*	*283*	*1.0*	*-41*	*-0.4*	*-148*	*-0.8*
	Change %	*0.7*	*0.2*	*2.1*		*-3.8*		*-2.6*	

Source: Labour Force Survey
Labour market statistics enquiries: labour.market@ons.gsi.gov.uk

1. The Labour Force Survey (LFS) is a survey of the population of private households, student halls of residence and NHS accommodation.
2. The headline employment rate is the number of people aged 16 to 64 in employment divided by the population aged 16 to 64.
3. The headline unemployment rate is the number of unemployed people (aged 16+) divided by the economically active population (aged 16+). The economically active population is defined as those in employment plus those who are unemployed.
4. The headline inactivity rate is the number of economically inactive people aged 16 to 64 divided by the population aged 16 to 64.

Note on headline employment, unemployment and inactivity rates
The headline employment and inactivity rates are based on the population aged 16 to 64 but the headline unemployment rate is based on the economically active population aged 16 and over. The employment and inactivity rates for those aged 16 and over are affected by the inclusion of the retired population in the denominators and are therefore less meaningful than the rates for those aged from 16 to 64. However, for the unemployment rate for those aged 16 and over, no such effect occurs as the denominator for the unemployment rate is the economically active population which only includes people in work or actively seeking and able to work.

Note on headline employment, unemployment and inactivity levels
The headline employment and unemployment levels are for those aged 16 and over; they measure all people in work or actively seeking and able to work. However, the headline inactivity level is for those aged 16 to 64. The inactivity level for those aged 16 and over is less meaningful as it includes elderly people who have retired from the labour force.

4.2 Full-time, part-time and temporary workers

United Kingdom (thousands) seasonally adjusted

	All in employment					Full-time and part-time workers[1]						Total workers with second jobs
	Total	Employees	Self employed	Unpaid family workers	Government supported training & employment programmes[2]	Total people working full-time	Total people working part-time	Employees working full-time	Employees working part-time	Self-employed people working full-time	Self-employed people working part-time	
	1	2	3	4	5	6	7	8	9	10	11	12
People	MGRZ	MGRN	MGRQ	MGRT	MGRW	YCBE	YCBH	YCBK	YCBN	YCBQ	YCBT	YCBW
Nov-Jan 2004	28,356	24,513	3,630	101	111	20,994	7,362	18,125	6,388	2,795	836	1,096
Dec-Feb 2004	28,394	24,559	3,622	107	107	21,004	7,391	18,147	6,412	2,787	835	1,105
Jan-Mar 2004	28,415	24,585	3,608	104	118	21,001	7,415	18,158	6,426	2,768	839	1,108
Feb-Apr 2004	28,404	24,553	3,622	108	122	21,011	7,393	18,144	6,409	2,791	831	1,103
Mar-May 2004	28,420	24,573	3,620	101	127	21,033	7,388	18,181	6,392	2,772	847	1,074
Apr-Jun 2004	28,425	24,539	3,665	97	123	21,061	7,364	18,159	6,380	2,821	844	1,070
May-Jul 2004	28,419	24,565	3,635	89	130	21,058	7,361	18,193	6,372	2,788	847	1,074
Jun-Aug 2004	28,433	24,587	3,627	87	132	21,073	7,360	18,205	6,383	2,788	839	1,075
Jul-Sep 2004	28,467	24,667	3,582	90	129	21,121	7,346	18,275	6,392	2,768	814	1,059
Aug-Oct 2004	28,491	24,651	3,616	94	130	21,175	7,316	18,294	6,358	2,801	814	1,045
Sep-Nov 2004	28,568	24,717	3,624	94	133	21,267	7,301	18,385	6,332	2,801	823	1,069
Oct-Dec 2004	28,615	24,777	3,615	97	125	21,314	7,301	18,446	6,331	2,790	825	1,054
Nov-Jan 2005	28,663	24,845	3,596	98	123	21,365	7,298	18,511	6,335	2,777	819	1,065
Dec-Feb 2005	28,727	24,883	3,612	105	127	21,441	7,286	18,569	6,314	2,792	820	1,063
Jan-Mar 2005	28,719	24,889	3,597	104	128	21,439	7,280	18,569	6,320	2,788	809	1,060
Feb-Apr 2005	28,687	24,860	3,602	103	122	21,400	7,287	18,528	6,332	2,791	812	1,064
Mar-May 2005	28,706	24,859	3,630	102	115	21,378	7,328	18,483	6,376	2,813	817	1,080
Apr-Jun 2005	28,726	24,904	3,609	99	114	21,392	7,334	18,510	6,394	2,800	809	1,075
May-Jul 2005	28,776	24,951	3,618	95	112	21,442	7,335	18,553	6,398	2,810	808	1,068
Jun-Aug 2005	28,826	25,003	3,629	85	108	21,515	7,310	18,641	6,361	2,803	826	1,063
Jul-Sep 2005	28,845	24,990	3,658	90	107	21,543	7,301	18,647	6,344	2,823	834	1,068
Aug-Oct 2005	28,827	24,995	3,637	92	103	21,541	7,285	18,665	6,329	2,805	832	1,059
Sep-Nov 2005	28,786	24,921	3,669	92	103	21,513	7,273	18,619	6,303	2,822	848	1,034
Oct-Dec 2005	28,788	24,915	3,674	90	110	21,533	7,255	18,635	6,279	2,824	849	1,028
Nov-Jan 2006	28,837	24,957	3,682	92	106	21,566	7,270	18,660	6,297	2,832	850	1,036
Dec-Feb 2006	28,889	25,002	3,704	88	96	21,582	7,307	18,673	6,329	2,841	863	1,044
Jan-Mar 2006	28,946	25,052	3,711	88	95	21,607	7,339	18,686	6,366	2,854	857	1,028
Feb-Apr 2006	28,982	25,077	3,727	84	93	21,658	7,324	18,728	6,349	2,863	863	1,031
Mar-May 2006	28,959	25,087	3,690	86	96	21,644	7,315	18,742	6,344	2,842	849	1,021
Apr-Jun 2006	28,999	25,115	3,699	91	94	21,641	7,358	18,736	6,379	2,843	856	1,044
May- Jul 2006	29,030	25,128	3,714	98	90	21,666	7,364	18,754	6,374	2,847	867	1,048
Jun-Aug 2006	29,110	25,182	3,736	105	87	21,717	7,394	18,781	6,401	2,869	867	1,056
Jul-Sep 2006	29,066	25,107	3,756	105	98	21,655	7,411	18,721	6,386	2,864	892	1,064
Aug-Oct 2006	29,072	25,090	3,783	98	102	21,601	7,472	18,656	6,434	2,877	905	1,063
Sep-Nov 2006	29,078	25,089	3,773	101	116	21,631	7,447	18,677	6,412	2,883	890	1,054
Oct-Dec 2006	29,089	25,107	3,774	102	106	21,634	7,455	18,684	6,423	2,884	891	1,075
Nov-Jan 2007	29,072	25,070	3,794	100	108	21,637	7,435	18,658	6,412	2,912	883	1,069
Dec-Feb 2007	29,045	25,039	3,801	99	106	21,632	7,413	18,656	6,383	2,909	892	1,073
Jan-Mar 2007	29,064	25,054	3,807	102	102	21,639	7,425	18,678	6,376	2,895	911	1,072
Feb-Apr 2007	29,098	25,092	3,806	100	100	21,679	7,419	18,723	6,369	2,892	913	1,091
Mar-May 2007	29,178	25,191	3,785	98	104	21,775	7,403	18,820	6,371	2,893	892	1,096
Apr-Jun 2007	29,178	25,184	3,785	97	111	21,774	7,403	18,823	6,361	2,891	894	1,103
May-Jul 2007	29,205	25,191	3,794	103	118	21,795	7,410	18,853	6,337	2,882	912	1,110
Jun-Aug 2007	29,222	25,194	3,813	102	113	21,817	7,405	18,866	6,327	2,889	924	1,111
Jul-Sep 2007	29,262	25,239	3,813	98	111	21,855	7,406	18,907	6,332	2,887	926	1,098
Aug-Oct 2007	29,313	25,275	3,829	97	111	21,902	7,410	18,941	6,335	2,901	928	1,110
Sep-Nov 2007	29,362	25,325	3,824	104	110	21,916	7,446	18,962	6,363	2,887	937	1,111
Oct-Dec 2007	29,408	25,372	3,816	106	114	21,935	7,474	18,977	6,395	2,884	931	1,118
Nov-Jan 2008	29,437	25,390	3,826	109	112	21,935	7,502	18,977	6,414	2,884	942	1,107
Dec-Feb 2008	29,499	25,402	3,870	109	118	21,983	7,516	18,971	6,431	2,937	933	1,121
Jan-Mar 2008	29,510	25,428	3,858	108	117	21,988	7,522	18,991	6,437	2,930	928	1,102
Feb-Apr 2008	29,528	25,466	3,830	114	118	22,010	7,518	19,016	6,450	2,923	907	1,117
Mar-May 2008	29,572	25,503	3,836	114	119	22,077	7,494	19,084	6,419	2,924	912	1,112
Apr-Jun 2008	29,536	25,481	3,835	109	110	22,032	7,504	19,039	6,442	2,927	908	1,127
May-Jul 2008	29,508	25,467	3,830	99	111	22,019	7,489	19,034	6,433	2,922	908	1,123
Jun-Aug 2008	29,418	25,418	3,805	90	105	21,924	7,494	18,977	6,441	2,895	909	1,115
Jul-Sep 2008	29,386	25,391	3,796	92	106	21,904	7,482	18,958	6,434	2,897	899	1,121
Aug-Oct 2008	29,346	25,365	3,782	92	106	21,854	7,492	18,928	6,437	2,877	906	1,123
Sep-Nov 2008	29,361	25,355	3,811	92	103	21,802	7,558	18,875	6,480	2,884	927	1,140
Oct-Dec 2008	29,329	25,332	3,803	94	99	21,793	7,535	18,870	6,462	2,878	925	1,131
Nov-Jan 2009	29,328	25,325	3,816	88	99	21,784	7,544	18,849	6,476	2,894	922	1,147
Dec-Feb 2009	29,228	25,244	3,797	85	103	21,686	7,542	18,734	6,510	2,894	903	1,150
Jan-Mar 2009	29,172	25,164	3,821	86	102	21,610	7,562	18,656	6,508	2,898	922	1,161
Feb-Apr 2009	29,078	25,053	3,834	87	104	21,559	7,520	18,612	6,441	2,890	945	1,151
Mar-May 2009	28,970	24,940	3,831	98	101	21,432	7,539	18,512	6,429	2,871	960	1,137
Apr-Jun 2009	28,900	24,886	3,817	94	103	21,326	7,575	18,423	6,462	2,847	971	1,121
May-Jul 2009	28,831	24,809	3,830	88	104	21,266	7,566	18,342	6,467	2,871	959	1,111
Jun-Aug 2009	28,875	24,815	3,865	85	111	21,286	7,589	18,331	6,484	2,899	966	1,133
Jul-Sep 2009	28,867	24,828	3,851	78	110	21,226	7,641	18,295	6,532	2,878	973	1,136
Aug-Oct 2009	28,885	24,842	3,856	84	104	21,190	7,695	18,251	6,591	2,890	966	1,141
Sep-Nov 2009	28,895	24,842	3,868	76	108	21,193	7,702	18,271	6,571	2,876	992	1,125
Oct-Dec 2009	28,901	24,819	3,882	87	114	21,199	7,703	18,256	6,563	2,892	989	1,125
Nov-Jan 2010	28,843	24,769	3,871	85	118	21,131	7,712	18,203	6,566	2,878	993	1,090
Dec-Feb 2010	28,823	24,732	3,881	91	119	21,137	7,686	18,196	6,537	2,892	989	1,076
Jan-Mar 2010	28,807	24,669	3,927	90	121	21,086	7,722	18,117	6,552	2,920	1,007	1,062
Feb-Apr 2010	28,842	24,679	3,948	90	124	21,075	7,767	18,095	6,584	2,931	1,017	1,092
Mar-May 2010	28,930	24,776	3,933	92	128	21,109	7,821	18,143	6,634	2,912	1,021	1,128

4.2 Full-time, part-time and temporary workers

United Kingdom (thousands) seasonally adjusted

	All in employment						Full-time and part-time workers[1]					
	Total	Employees	Self employed	Unpaid family workers	Government supported training & employment programmes[2]	Total people working full-time	Total people working part-time	Employees working full-time	Employees working part-time	Self-employed people working full-time	Self-employed people working part-time	Total workers with second jobs
	1	2	3	4	5	6	7	8	9	10	11	12
Apr-Jun 2010	28,975	24,831	3,924	89	131	21,143	7,832	18,178	6,653	2,908	1,015	1,134
May-Jul 2010	29,118	24,919	3,962	100	137	21,189	7,929	18,199	6,721	2,927	1,034	1,125
Jun-Aug 2010	29,128	24,921	3,963	110	134	21,162	7,966	18,163	6,757	2,937	1,026	1,117
Jul-Sep 2010	29,173	24,920	4,016	106	132	21,186	7,987	18,163	6,757	2,965	1,051	1,113
Aug-Oct 2010	29,109	24,920	3,958	101	131	21,149	7,961	18,180	6,740	2,915	1,043	1,110
Sep-Nov 2010	29,086	24,884	3,976	94	132	21,154	7,933	18,174	6,709	2,924	1,052	1,110
Oct-Dec 2010	29,120	24,929	3,976	92	123	21,197	7,923	18,233	6,696	2,913	1,062	1,119
Nov-Jan 2011	29,167	24,952	3,990	97	128	21,243	7,925	18,287	6,665	2,903	1,087	1,149
Dec-Feb 2011	29,242	25,019	4,003	96	124	21,310	7,932	18,362	6,657	2,902	1,101	1,166
Jan-Mar 2011	29,229	25,050	3,960	97	122	21,301	7,928	18,385	6,665	2,870	1,090	1,156
Feb-Apr 2011	29,228	25,036	3,986	91	114	21,287	7,941	18,363	6,673	2,879	1,107	1,142
Mar-May 2011	29,248	25,060	3,997	89	101	21,303	7,945	18,390	6,670	2,874	1,123	1,139
Apr-Jun 2011	29,224	25,054	3,984	93	94	21,328	7,896	18,397	6,656	2,891	1,093	1,131
May-Jul 2011	29,130	24,986	3,970	89	86	21,325	7,805	18,393	6,593	2,897	1,073	1,129
Jun-Aug 2011	29,080	24,882	4,013	101	83	21,305	7,776	18,340	6,542	2,926	1,087	1,119
Jul-Sep 2011	29,063	24,788	4,079	107	89	21,259	7,803	18,265	6,523	2,948	1,130	1,133
Aug-Oct 2011	29,102	24,773	4,126	111	92	21,271	7,831	18,212	6,561	3,005	1,121	1,138
Sep-Nov 2011	29,128	24,802	4,115	112	99	21,261	7,867	18,214	6,588	2,985	1,130	1,141
Oct-Dec 2011	29,146	24,868	4,075	108	94	21,260	7,886	18,244	6,624	2,962	1,113	1,125
Nov-Jan 2012	29,141	24,847	4,084	107	104	21,250	7,892	18,234	6,613	2,964	1,120	1,116
Dec-Feb 2012	29,210	24,865	4,132	97	116	21,255	7,955	18,221	6,645	2,977	1,155	1,140
Jan-Mar 2012	29,274	24,892	4,163	97	123	21,275	7,999	18,235	6,657	2,981	1,182	1,141
Feb-Apr 2012	29,324	24,927	4,171	98	128	21,335	7,989	18,277	6,650	2,998	1,173	1,138
Mar-May 2012	29,378	24,962	4,161	110	145	21,374	8,004	18,296	6,666	3,006	1,156	1,130
Apr-Jun 2012	29,476	25,020	4,202	109	144	21,405	8,070	18,308	6,712	3,020	1,182	1,124
May-Jul 2012	29,560	25,071	4,223	113	152	21,438	8,123	18,328	6,743	3,017	1,206	1,118
Jun-Aug 2012	29,590	25,124	4,196	112	158	21,462	8,129	18,386	6,738	2,988	1,209	1,119
Jul-Sep 2012	29,576	25,107	4,191	112	166	21,456	8,120	18,373	6,735	2,987	1,204	1,107
Aug-Oct 2012	29,601	25,118	4,200	111	171	21,482	8,119	18,376	6,743	3,010	1,191	1,122
Sep-Nov 2012	29,700	25,218	4,205	111	165	21,589	8,111	18,481	6,737	3,017	1,189	1,120
Oct-Dec 2012	29,751	25,258	4,218	111	163	21,669	8,081	18,553	6,705	3,023	1,195	1,149
Nov-Jan 2013	29,732	25,288	4,179	103	162	21,677	8,055	18,585	6,704	2,993	1,186	1,144
Dec-Feb 2013	29,698	25,240	4,204	102	151	21,649	8,049	18,545	6,695	3,006	1,198	1,114
Jan-Mar 2013	29,708	25,280	4,176	105	147	21,680	8,028	18,565	6,715	3,022	1,155	1,098
Feb-Apr 2013	29,756	25,294	4,200	105	156	21,692	8,064	18,581	6,713	3,025	1,175	1,084
Mar-May 2013	29,714	25,275	4,176	104	160	21,677	8,038	18,583	6,692	3,017	1,159	1,107
Apr-Jun 2013	29,777	25,320	4,182	111	164	21,711	8,066	18,616	6,704	3,011	1,171	1,120
May-Jul 2013	29,836	25,392	4,173	106	164	21,787	8,049	18,685	6,708	3,013	1,160	1,122
Jun-Aug 2013	29,869	25,376	4,209	116	168	21,824	8,045	18,684	6,693	3,047	1,162	1,159
Jul-Sep 2013	29,953	25,468	4,197	114	175	21,868	8,085	18,740	6,728	3,033	1,164	1,155
Aug-Oct 2013	30,086	25,547	4,253	116	170	21,942	8,144	18,789	6,758	3,065	1,188	1,161
Sep-Nov 2013	30,150	25,537	4,356	110	148	22,046	8,104	18,830	6,707	3,139	1,217	1,176
Oct-Dec 2013	**30,146**	**25,531**	**4,368**	**105**	**141**	**22,077**	**8,069**	**18,843**	**6,689**	**3,154**	**1,215**	**1,171**
Change on qtr	*193*	*63*	*172*	*-8*	*-33*	*209*	*-16*	*102*	*-39*	*121*	*51*	*17*
Change %	*0.6*	*0.2*	*4.1*	*-7.3*	*-19.1*	*1.0*	*-0.2*	*0.5*	*-0.6*	*4.0*	*4.4*	*1.5*
Change on year	*396*	*273*	*150*	*-6*	*-22*	*408*	*-12*	*289*	*-17*	*130*	*20*	*22*
Change %	*1.3*	*1.1*	*3.6*	*-5.0*	*-13.3*	*1.9*	*-0.1*	*1.6*	*-0.2*	*4.3*	*1.7*	*1.9*
Men	MGSA	MGRO	MGRR	MGRU	MGRX	YCBF	YCBI	YCBL	YCBO	YCBR	YCBU	YCBX
Nov-Jan 2004	15,309	12,548	2,658	40	64	13,735	1,574	11,369	1,179	2,318	340	462
Dec-Feb 2004	15,342	12,568	2,669	43	63	13,759	1,584	11,384	1,184	2,327	341	469
Jan-Mar 2004	15,362	12,611	2,639	44	68	13,750	1,612	11,400	1,211	2,297	342	472
Feb-Apr 2004	15,357	12,583	2,658	44	71	13,742	1,615	11,375	1,208	2,313	345	469
Mar-May 2004	15,379	12,607	2,656	41	75	13,743	1,636	11,390	1,217	2,302	354	454
Apr-Jun 2004	15,369	12,567	2,689	41	72	13,739	1,629	11,351	1,216	2,337	352	449
May-Jul 2004	15,380	12,597	2,673	36	74	13,749	1,631	11,389	1,208	2,312	361	451
Jun-Aug 2004	15,390	12,613	2,672	33	71	13,753	1,637	11,391	1,222	2,310	362	454
Jul-Sep 2004	15,406	12,656	2,641	34	76	13,765	1,641	11,421	1,235	2,295	346	452
Aug-Oct 2004	15,408	12,634	2,663	34	77	13,776	1,632	11,407	1,226	2,319	344	447
Sep-Nov 2004	15,444	12,657	2,668	38	81	13,827	1,617	11,444	1,213	2,329	339	461
Oct-Dec 2004	15,465	12,689	2,663	38	76	13,830	1,635	11,460	1,229	2,321	343	451
Nov-Jan 2005	15,489	12,730	2,646	40	73	13,839	1,651	11,479	1,251	2,311	336	454
Dec-Feb 2005	15,499	12,740	2,645	42	72	13,849	1,650	11,495	1,246	2,307	338	448
Jan-Mar 2005	15,514	12,761	2,640	42	70	13,859	1,655	11,509	1,252	2,301	339	453
Feb-Apr 2005	15,501	12,736	2,652	42	70	13,841	1,660	11,477	1,259	2,313	339	456
Mar-May 2005	15,492	12,714	2,669	40	69	13,838	1,654	11,453	1,261	2,332	336	466
Apr-Jun 2005	15,509	12,749	2,652	37	71	13,863	1,646	11,483	1,266	2,326	326	462
May-Jul 2005	15,521	12,763	2,652	35	70	13,878	1,643	11,502	1,261	2,325	327	463
Jun-Aug 2005	15,535	12,783	2,652	33	66	13,897	1,637	11,544	1,239	2,307	345	464
Jul-Sep 2005	15,551	12,785	2,672	32	63	13,912	1,639	11,543	1,241	2,323	348	458
Aug-Oct 2005	15,550	12,792	2,666	32	59	13,909	1,640	11,555	1,238	2,314	352	451
Sep-Nov 2005	15,543	12,768	2,686	30	59	13,893	1,650	11,520	1,247	2,331	356	435
Oct-Dec 2005	15,546	12,756	2,699	29	62	13,888	1,658	11,509	1,247	2,336	363	445
Nov-Jan 2006	15,577	12,776	2,709	32	60	13,923	1,654	11,532	1,244	2,346	363	455
Dec-Feb 2006	15,588	12,789	2,709	30	60	13,920	1,667	11,533	1,257	2,343	366	457
Jan-Mar 2006	15,582	12,802	2,689	31	59	13,927	1,655	11,548	1,254	2,335	354	440
Feb-Apr 2006	15,629	12,839	2,701	30	58	13,973	1,656	11,578	1,261	2,353	348	442

51

4.2 Full-time, part-time and temporary workers

United Kingdom (thousands) seasonally adjusted

| | All in employment | | | | | Full-time and part-time workers[1] | | | | | | |
	Total	Employees	Self employed	Unpaid family workers	Government supported training & employment programmes[2]	Total people working full-time	Total people working part-time	Employees working full-time	Employees working part-time	Self-employed people working full-time	Self-employed people working part-time	Total workers with second jobs
	1	2	3	4	5	6	7	8	9	10	11	12
Mar-May 2006	15,612	12,834	2,687	33	58	13,948	1,664	11,563	1,271	2,347	340	433
Apr-Jun 2006	15,625	12,845	2,689	36	55	13,949	1,676	11,565	1,280	2,346	342	448
May-Jul 2006	15,655	12,875	2,689	38	54	13,970	1,685	11,591	1,284	2,338	351	452
Jun-Aug 2006	15,693	12,900	2,701	42	49	14,014	1,678	11,622	1,279	2,351	351	448
Jul-Sep 2006	15,709	12,887	2,721	43	59	13,996	1,713	11,594	1,293	2,356	364	454
Aug-Oct 2006	15,708	12,871	2,735	43	60	13,965	1,743	11,556	1,316	2,364	371	455
Sep-Nov 2006	15,709	12,855	2,744	40	69	13,987	1,722	11,564	1,292	2,378	366	448
Oct-Dec 2006	15,715	12,877	2,736	41	60	13,999	1,715	11,583	1,294	2,375	361	461
Nov-Jan 2007	15,724	12,861	2,762	39	63	14,017	1,707	11,569	1,292	2,406	355	445
Dec-Feb 2007	15,719	12,863	2,757	40	59	14,006	1,713	11,573	1,290	2,392	365	459
Jan-Mar 2007	15,727	12,864	2,763	42	57	13,991	1,735	11,564	1,301	2,388	375	461
Feb-Apr 2007	15,749	12,891	2,761	39	57	14,018	1,730	11,600	1,291	2,381	380	459
Mar-May 2007	15,813	12,957	2,759	38	60	14,087	1,726	11,668	1,289	2,382	377	455
Apr-Jun 2007	15,803	12,941	2,763	36	63	14,074	1,729	11,657	1,285	2,380	383	456
May-Jul 2007	15,809	12,943	2,760	37	69	14,071	1,737	11,667	1,276	2,367	393	459
Jun-Aug 2007	15,820	12,960	2,759	39	62	14,086	1,734	11,673	1,287	2,377	383	455
Jul-Sep 2007	15,841	12,994	2,748	39	60	14,090	1,751	11,693	1,301	2,362	386	449
Aug-Oct 2007	15,862	13,000	2,769	37	56	14,127	1,734	11,710	1,289	2,385	384	458
Sep-Nov 2007	15,894	13,024	2,771	38	61	14,126	1,768	11,711	1,314	2,374	397	454
Oct-Dec 2007	15,898	13,020	2,775	39	64	14,126	1,772	11,695	1,325	2,384	391	448
Nov-Jan 2008	15,912	13,032	2,774	38	67	14,119	1,793	11,685	1,348	2,385	389	451
Dec-Feb 2008	15,942	13,018	2,809	39	75	14,138	1,804	11,669	1,350	2,421	389	460
Jan-Mar 2008	15,959	13,037	2,808	38	75	14,156	1,803	11,696	1,341	2,416	393	450
Feb-Apr 2008	15,977	13,073	2,792	41	71	14,171	1,806	11,723	1,350	2,403	389	457
Mar-May 2008	15,976	13,071	2,796	40	69	14,199	1,777	11,750	1,322	2,406	390	458
Apr-Jun 2008	15,964	13,066	2,794	39	64	14,157	1,808	11,709	1,357	2,408	387	463
May-Jul 2008	15,938	13,056	2,782	36	64	14,119	1,819	11,682	1,374	2,400	382	452
Jun-Aug 2008	15,876	13,020	2,761	31	64	14,045	1,831	11,638	1,382	2,375	386	451
Jul-Sep 2008	15,859	13,009	2,755	31	64	14,025	1,834	11,621	1,389	2,374	381	457
Aug-Oct 2008	15,818	12,987	2,730	33	67	13,973	1,844	11,592	1,395	2,350	381	453
Sep-Nov 2008	15,830	12,974	2,753	37	65	13,985	1,845	11,586	1,388	2,369	384	471
Oct-Dec 2008	15,814	12,954	2,756	41	64	13,954	1,860	11,557	1,398	2,370	386	469
Nov-Jan 2009	15,793	12,932	2,762	37	61	13,925	1,867	11,523	1,409	2,379	383	477
Dec-Feb 2009	15,732	12,889	2,749	32	62	13,876	1,857	11,465	1,425	2,379	371	481
Jan-Mar 2009	15,694	12,848	2,757	30	59	13,849	1,845	11,438	1,410	2,379	378	491
Feb-Apr 2009	15,636	12,784	2,760	32	60	13,786	1,850	11,380	1,405	2,374	386	499
Mar-May 2009	15,543	12,694	2,757	36	57	13,669	1,874	11,286	1,408	2,353	404	488
Apr-Jun 2009	15,475	12,639	2,738	39	59	13,587	1,887	11,228	1,411	2,324	414	482
May-Jul 2009	15,427	12,591	2,741	36	60	13,569	1,858	11,199	1,391	2,337	404	480
Jun-Aug 2009	15,423	12,579	2,749	34	61	13,562	1,861	11,171	1,408	2,355	394	492
Jul-Sep 2009	15,401	12,581	2,728	30	62	13,551	1,850	11,181	1,401	2,338	389	489
Aug-Oct 2009	15,402	12,556	2,753	33	59	13,540	1,862	11,151	1,405	2,359	395	494
Sep-Nov 2009	15,400	12,571	2,738	33	57	13,524	1,876	11,161	1,410	2,337	401	482
Oct-Dec 2009	15,398	12,550	2,750	37	61	13,514	1,884	11,142	1,408	2,344	406	485
Nov-Jan 2010	15,356	12,510	2,749	36	61	13,459	1,897	11,094	1,416	2,338	411	466
Dec-Feb 2010	15,360	12,512	2,746	40	63	13,467	1,893	11,100	1,412	2,339	407	456
Jan-Mar 2010	15,354	12,488	2,760	40	66	13,441	1,913	11,063	1,425	2,350	410	432
Feb-Apr 2010	15,378	12,502	2,766	41	69	13,457	1,921	11,071	1,431	2,356	410	452
Mar-May 2010	15,458	12,569	2,771	42	76	13,504	1,953	11,121	1,448	2,351	420	476
Apr-Jun 2010	15,497	12,607	2,774	41	76	13,519	1,978	11,131	1,476	2,355	419	474
May-Jul 2010	15,595	12,664	2,804	43	85	13,585	2,010	11,183	1,481	2,365	438	465
Jun-Aug 2010	15,610	12,664	2,820	44	83	13,575	2,035	11,157	1,506	2,379	441	460
Jul-Sep 2010	15,655	12,682	2,844	44	85	13,591	2,064	11,156	1,526	2,396	448	465
Aug-Oct 2010	15,620	12,698	2,795	44	84	13,555	2,065	11,176	1,522	2,347	448	460
Sep-Nov 2010	15,619	12,692	2,810	34	84	13,566	2,053	11,180	1,512	2,355	456	462
Oct-Dec 2010	15,644	12,722	2,812	34	76	13,594	2,050	11,206	1,516	2,357	455	470
Nov-Jan 2011	15,653	12,740	2,798	34	81	13,624	2,029	11,253	1,487	2,342	456	489
Dec-Feb 2011	15,670	12,754	2,807	32	77	13,661	2,009	11,296	1,458	2,341	467	506
Jan-Mar 2011	15,643	12,753	2,784	31	75	13,630	2,013	11,292	1,461	2,315	469	492
Feb-Apr 2011	15,695	12,782	2,816	27	70	13,647	2,048	11,291	1,491	2,337	479	485
Mar-May 2011	15,688	12,781	2,818	32	58	13,643	2,045	11,301	1,479	2,325	493	487
Apr-Jun 2011	15,675	12,758	2,825	37	55	13,638	2,036	11,280	1,478	2,340	485	487
May-Jul 2011	15,604	12,704	2,817	37	46	13,599	2,005	11,242	1,462	2,340	477	493
Jun-Aug 2011	15,564	12,652	2,825	41	46	13,607	1,957	11,234	1,418	2,353	472	478
Jul-Sep 2011	15,543	12,585	2,869	43	45	13,577	1,966	11,178	1,407	2,376	493	486
Aug-Oct 2011	15,569	12,577	2,904	41	46	13,588	1,981	11,137	1,440	2,423	482	492
Sep-Nov 2011	15,598	12,602	2,900	43	53	13,580	2,018	11,139	1,463	2,409	491	490
Oct-Dec 2011	15,603	12,647	2,862	41	53	13,582	2,022	11,169	1,478	2,382	480	479
Nov-Jan 2012	15,591	12,627	2,864	41	59	13,570	2,021	11,156	1,471	2,384	480	463
Dec-Feb 2012	15,660	12,665	2,894	36	65	13,579	2,081	11,143	1,522	2,399	495	487
Jan-Mar 2012	15,695	12,673	2,907	43	72	13,585	2,110	11,146	1,527	2,399	507	485
Feb-Apr 2012	15,739	12,697	2,920	45	77	13,615	2,124	11,156	1,541	2,418	502	489
Mar-May 2012	15,781	12,705	2,935	47	94	13,653	2,128	11,164	1,541	2,441	493	487
Apr-Jun 2012	15,838	12,743	2,963	41	91	13,687	2,151	11,178	1,565	2,460	503	490
May-Jul 2012	15,847	12,745	2,964	42	97	13,721	2,127	11,196	1,548	2,461	503	478
Jun-Aug 2012	15,875	12,777	2,950	46	102	13,733	2,142	11,236	1,541	2,436	514	479
Jul-Sep 2012	15,877	12,772	2,946	49	111	13,740	2,137	11,237	1,534	2,431	514	468
Aug-Oct 2012	15,901	12,777	2,960	47	117	13,780	2,121	11,259	1,519	2,448	512	466
Sep-Nov 2012	15,943	12,853	2,932	46	112	13,827	2,116	11,327	1,526	2,436	496	455
Oct-Dec 2012	15,947	12,864	2,929	45	110	13,844	2,103	11,348	1,516	2,431	497	458
Nov-Jan 2013	15,921	12,858	2,908	43	113	13,818	2,104	11,341	1,517	2,409	499	446

4.2 Full-time, part-time and temporary workers

	All in employment					Full-time and part-time workers[1]						Total workers with second jobs
	Total	Employees	Self employed	Unpaid family workers	Government supported training & employment programmes[2]	Total people working full-time	Total people working part-time	Employees working full-time	Employees working part-time	Self-employed people working full-time	Self-employed people working part-time	
	1	2	3	4	5	6	7	8	9	10	11	12
Dec-Feb 2013	15,887	12,810	2,931	39	107	13,804	2,082	11,321	1,489	2,414	517	437
Jan-Mar 2013	15,889	12,820	2,924	39	106	13,818	2,072	11,325	1,495	2,425	499	432
Feb-Apr 2013	15,907	12,829	2,931	39	109	13,787	2,120	11,314	1,514	2,416	515	445
Mar-May 2013	15,889	12,830	2,922	34	104	13,793	2,096	11,334	1,495	2,414	507	451
Apr-Jun 2013	15,914	12,845	2,919	41	108	13,806	2,108	11,356	1,489	2,401	518	454
May-Jul 2013	15,948	12,897	2,910	38	103	13,848	2,101	11,406	1,491	2,399	511	464
Jun-Aug 2013	15,979	12,903	2,928	45	104	13,862	2,117	11,402	1,500	2,418	510	492
Jul-Sep 2013	16,044	12,986	2,913	39	106	13,895	2,149	11,446	1,539	2,403	510	488
Aug-Oct 2013	16,103	13,008	2,947	41	107	13,935	2,168	11,463	1,544	2,427	520	489
Sep-Nov 2013	16,155	13,009	3,008	43	96	13,990	2,166	11,475	1,534	2,471	537	497
Oct-Dec 2013	**16,144**	**12,999**	**3,011**	**43**	**90**	**13,982**	**2,162**	**11,458**	**1,541**	**2,476**	**535**	**504**
Change on qtr	*100*	*13*	*98*	*4*	*-16*	*87*	*13*	*11*	*2*	*73*	*25*	*16*
Change %	*0.6*	*0.1*	*3.4*	*10.1*	*-14.8*	*0.6*	*0.6*	*0.1*	*0.1*	*3.0*	*5.0*	*3.3*
Change on year	*197*	*135*	*83*	*-1*	*-20*	*138*	*59*	*110*	*26*	*45*	*37*	*47*
Change %	*1.2*	*1.1*	*2.8*	*-3.3*	*-17.9*	*1.0*	*2.8*	*1.0*	*1.7*	*1.9*	*7.5*	*10.2*
Women	MGSB	MGRP	MGRS	MGRV	MGRY	YCBG	YCBJ	YCBM	YCBP	YCBS	YCBV	YCBY
Nov-Jan 2004	13,047	11,965	973	61	48	7,259	5,787	6,756	5,209	477	496	634
Dec-Feb 2004	13,052	11,991	953	63	45	7,245	5,807	6,763	5,228	459	494	636
Jan-Mar 2004	13,053	11,974	968	61	50	7,251	5,802	6,759	5,216	471	497	636
Feb-Apr 2004	13,047	11,969	963	64	51	7,269	5,778	6,768	5,201	477	486	634
Mar-May 2004	13,041	11,966	964	60	52	7,290	5,752	6,791	5,175	471	493	620
Apr-Jun 2004	13,056	11,973	977	57	51	7,322	5,735	6,808	5,165	484	492	621
May-Jul 2004	13,039	11,968	962	53	57	7,309	5,730	6,804	5,164	476	486	623
Jun-Aug 2004	13,043	11,974	955	54	61	7,320	5,723	6,814	5,160	477	477	621
Jul-Sep 2004	13,061	12,011	941	55	53	7,356	5,705	6,854	5,157	473	469	607
Aug-Oct 2004	13,083	12,018	953	60	53	7,399	5,684	6,886	5,131	483	470	598
Sep-Nov 2004	13,124	12,060	956	56	51	7,440	5,684	6,941	5,119	472	485	609
Oct-Dec 2004	13,150	12,088	952	60	50	7,484	5,666	6,986	5,103	470	482	603
Nov-Jan 2005	13,174	12,116	949	58	51	7,526	5,647	7,032	5,084	466	483	611
Dec-Feb 2005	13,228	12,143	967	63	55	7,592	5,636	7,075	5,069	485	482	615
Jan-Mar 2005	13,205	12,128	957	62	58	7,580	5,625	7,060	5,068	487	470	607
Feb-Apr 2005	13,186	12,123	950	61	52	7,559	5,628	7,051	5,073	477	473	609
Mar-May 2005	13,214	12,145	961	63	46	7,540	5,674	7,030	5,115	480	480	615
Apr-Jun 2005	13,217	12,155	957	62	43	7,529	5,688	7,028	5,128	473	483	613
May-Jul 2005	13,256	12,188	966	60	42	7,564	5,691	7,051	5,137	485	481	604
Jun-Aug 2005	13,291	12,220	977	52	42	7,618	5,673	7,098	5,122	496	481	599
Jul-Sep 2005	13,294	12,205	986	58	44	7,631	5,662	7,103	5,102	500	486	610
Aug-Oct 2005	13,277	12,202	971	60	43	7,632	5,645	7,110	5,092	492	480	608
Sep-Nov 2005	13,243	12,154	983	62	44	7,620	5,624	7,098	5,055	491	492	599
Oct-Dec 2005	13,242	12,159	975	61	48	7,645	5,597	7,126	5,032	488	486	583
Nov-Jan 2006	13,260	12,181	973	60	46	7,644	5,616	7,128	5,053	486	487	581
Dec-Feb 2006	13,301	12,213	995	58	35	7,662	5,639	7,141	5,072	498	497	587
Jan-Mar 2006	13,364	12,250	1,021	58	36	7,680	5,685	7,139	5,111	518	503	588
Feb-Apr 2006	13,353	12,238	1,025	54	35	7,684	5,669	7,150	5,088	510	516	589
Mar-May 2006	13,347	12,252	1,003	53	39	7,695	5,651	7,179	5,073	494	509	587
Apr-Jun 2006	13,374	12,270	1,010	54	39	7,692	5,682	7,172	5,098	496	514	596
May-Jul 2006	13,375	12,253	1,025	60	36	7,696	5,679	7,163	5,090	509	516	596
Jun-Aug 2006	13,418	12,282	1,035	63	38	7,702	5,715	7,160	5,122	518	516	608
Jul-Sep 2006	13,357	12,220	1,036	62	39	7,659	5,698	7,127	5,093	508	528	610
Aug-Oct 2006	13,364	12,219	1,048	55	42	7,636	5,728	7,101	5,118	513	535	608
Sep-Nov 2006	13,369	12,233	1,029	60	47	7,644	5,725	7,113	5,120	505	524	606
Oct-Dec 2006	13,375	12,230	1,038	60	46	7,635	5,740	7,102	5,128	509	530	614
Nov-Jan 2007	13,348	12,209	1,033	62	45	7,620	5,728	7,089	5,121	505	527	623
Dec-Feb 2007	13,326	12,176	1,044	59	47	7,626	5,701	7,083	5,093	518	527	614
Jan-Mar 2007	13,337	12,189	1,043	60	45	7,648	5,689	7,114	5,075	507	536	611
Feb-Apr 2007	13,350	12,201	1,045	61	42	7,661	5,689	7,123	5,079	511	533	631
Mar-May 2007	13,365	12,233	1,026	60	45	7,687	5,677	7,151	5,082	511	515	640
Apr-Jun 2007	13,375	12,243	1,023	61	49	7,701	5,674	7,166	5,077	511	512	647
May-Jul 2007	13,397	12,248	1,034	65	49	7,724	5,673	7,186	5,062	515	519	651
Jun-Aug 2007	13,402	12,233	1,054	63	51	7,731	5,671	7,193	5,040	512	541	656
Jul-Sep 2007	13,421	12,245	1,066	59	51	7,765	5,656	7,214	5,031	525	541	648
Aug-Oct 2007	13,451	12,276	1,060	60	55	7,775	5,676	7,230	5,045	517	544	652
Sep-Nov 2007	13,468	12,300	1,053	66	49	7,790	5,678	7,251	5,049	513	540	657
Oct-Dec 2007	13,510	12,352	1,041	67	50	7,809	5,701	7,282	5,070	500	541	670
Nov-Jan 2008	13,525	12,358	1,052	70	45	7,817	5,709	7,292	5,066	499	553	656
Dec-Feb 2008	13,557	12,384	1,061	70	42	7,845	5,712	7,303	5,082	516	545	662
Jan-Mar 2008	13,552	12,391	1,049	69	42	7,833	5,719	7,295	5,095	515	535	652
Feb-Apr 2008	13,551	12,393	1,039	73	46	7,839	5,712	7,293	5,100	520	518	660
Mar-May 2008	13,596	12,432	1,040	74	50	7,878	5,718	7,335	5,097	519	522	654
Apr-Jun 2008	13,571	12,415	1,041	70	46	7,875	5,696	7,330	5,085	520	521	664
May-Jul 2008	13,570	12,411	1,048	63	47	7,900	5,670	7,352	5,059	523	526	671
Jun-Aug 2008	13,542	12,398	1,044	59	41	7,879	5,663	7,340	5,059	520	524	664
Jul-Sep 2008	13,527	12,382	1,042	61	42	7,879	5,648	7,337	5,045	523	518	664
Aug-Oct 2008	13,528	12,378	1,052	59	39	7,881	5,647	7,335	5,043	527	525	670
Sep-Nov 2008	13,531	12,381	1,058	55	37	7,818	5,714	7,288	5,092	515	543	669
Oct-Dec 2008	13,514	12,378	1,047	54	36	7,839	5,675	7,313	5,065	507	539	662

4.2 Full-time, part-time and temporary workers

United Kingdom (thousands) seasonally adjusted

	All in employment					Full-time and part-time workers[1]						Total workers with second jobs
	Total	Employees	Self employed	Unpaid family workers	Government supported training & employment programmes[2]	Total people working full-time	Total people working part-time	Employees working full-time	Employees working part-time	Self-employed people working full-time	Self-employed people working part-time	
	1	2	3	4	5	6	7	8	9	10	11	12
Nov-Jan 2009	13,536	12,393	1,054	51	38	7,859	5,677	7,327	5,066	515	539	670
Dec-Feb 2009	13,496	12,354	1,048	52	41	7,810	5,686	7,269	5,085	516	532	669
Jan-Mar 2009	13,478	12,316	1,064	55	43	7,762	5,716	7,219	5,098	519	545	669
Feb-Apr 2009	13,442	12,269	1,074	55	44	7,772	5,670	7,233	5,036	516	558	653
Mar-May 2009	13,427	12,247	1,074	62	45	7,763	5,664	7,226	5,021	518	556	650
Apr-Jun 2009	13,426	12,247	1,079	56	44	7,738	5,687	7,195	5,052	523	556	638
May-Jul 2009	13,404	12,219	1,089	53	44	7,696	5,708	7,142	5,076	533	555	630
Jun-Aug 2009	13,452	12,235	1,115	51	50	7,725	5,728	7,159	5,076	543	572	641
Jul-Sep 2009	13,466	12,246	1,123	48	48	7,675	5,791	7,115	5,132	539	584	648
Aug-Oct 2009	13,483	12,286	1,102	50	44	7,651	5,832	7,101	5,186	531	571	647
Sep-Nov 2009	13,495	12,271	1,130	44	51	7,669	5,826	7,111	5,160	539	591	643
Oct-Dec 2009	13,504	12,269	1,132	50	53	7,685	5,819	7,114	5,155	549	583	641
Nov-Jan 2010	13,488	12,260	1,122	49	57	7,672	5,816	7,109	5,151	540	582	624
Dec-Feb 2010	13,463	12,220	1,135	51	56	7,670	5,793	7,096	5,125	553	582	620
Jan-Mar 2010	13,453	12,181	1,167	50	55	7,644	5,809	7,054	5,126	570	598	630
Feb-Apr 2010	13,464	12,177	1,182	49	55	7,618	5,846	7,024	5,153	575	608	640
Mar-May 2010	13,473	12,208	1,162	51	52	7,605	5,868	7,022	5,186	561	601	652
Apr-Jun 2010	13,477	12,224	1,150	48	55	7,623	5,854	7,047	5,177	553	597	659
May-Jul 2010	13,522	12,256	1,158	57	52	7,604	5,918	7,016	5,240	562	596	660
Jun-Aug 2010	13,518	12,257	1,143	67	50	7,587	5,931	7,006	5,251	558	585	657
Jul-Sep 2010	13,518	12,237	1,172	62	47	7,595	5,923	7,006	5,231	569	603	648
Aug-Oct 2010	13,489	12,222	1,163	57	47	7,593	5,896	7,004	5,218	569	595	650
Sep-Nov 2010	13,467	12,192	1,166	61	49	7,587	5,880	6,994	5,198	570	596	648
Oct-Dec 2010	13,477	12,207	1,164	58	48	7,604	5,873	7,027	5,180	556	608	649
Nov-Jan 2011	13,515	12,212	1,192	63	48	7,619	5,896	7,035	5,177	561	631	660
Dec-Feb 2011	13,572	12,264	1,196	65	47	7,649	5,923	7,066	5,199	562	634	660
Jan-Mar 2011	13,586	12,296	1,176	67	47	7,672	5,915	7,093	5,203	555	622	663
Feb-Apr 2011	13,533	12,254	1,171	64	44	7,640	5,893	7,073	5,182	542	628	657
Mar-May 2011	13,560	12,279	1,180	58	43	7,660	5,900	7,089	5,191	549	630	652
Apr-Jun 2011	13,549	12,296	1,159	56	39	7,690	5,860	7,117	5,178	551	608	644
May-Jul 2011	13,526	12,282	1,152	52	40	7,726	5,799	7,151	5,131	557	595	636
Jun-Aug 2011	13,516	12,231	1,188	60	37	7,698	5,818	7,106	5,125	573	615	641
Jul-Sep 2011	13,520	12,203	1,209	64	44	7,682	5,838	7,087	5,117	572	637	647
Aug-Oct 2011	13,533	12,196	1,222	70	46	7,683	5,850	7,075	5,121	582	640	646
Sep-Nov 2011	13,530	12, 200	1,216	69	46	7,682	5,849	7,075	5,125	576	640	652
Oct-Dec 2011	13,543	12,220	1,213	68	41	7,678	5,865	7,075	5,146	580	634	646
Nov-Jan 2012	13,550	12,220	1,220	66	45	7,680	5,871	7,078	5,142	580	640	654
Dec-Feb 2012	13,551	12,201	1,238	61	51	7,676	5,874	7,078	5,123	578	661	654
Jan-Mar 2012	13,579	12,219	1,256	54	51	7,691	5,889	7,089	5,130	582	675	656
Feb-Apr 2012	13,585	12,230	1,251	53	51	7,720	5,865	7,120	5,110	580	671	650
Mar-May 2012	13,597	12,257	1,227	63	51	7,721	5,876	7,132	5,124	564	663	644
Apr-Jun 2012	13,637	12,278	1,239	68	53	7,719	5,919	7,131	5,147	559	679	634
May-Jul 2012	13,713	12,327	1,259	72	55	7,717	5,996	7,132	5,195	556	703	640
Jun-Aug 2012	13,715	12,347	1,246	66	56	7,729	5,986	7,150	5,197	552	695	640
Jul-Sep 2012	13,699	12,336	1,245	63	56	7,717	5,982	7,135	5,200	556	689	640
Aug-Oct 2012	13,700	12,341	1,241	64	54	7,702	5,998	7,117	5,224	562	679	656
Sep-Nov 2012	13,757	12,365	1,274	65	54	7,762	5,995	7,154	5,211	581	693	666
Oct-Dec 2012	13,804	12,395	1,290	66	53	7,825	5,979	7,205	5,189	592	697	692
Nov-Jan 2013	13,810	12,430	1,271	60	49	7,859	5,952	7,244	5,186	584	687	698
Dec-Feb 2013	13,811	12,430	1,273	64	45	7,845	5,967	7,225	5,206	591	681	677
Jan-Mar 2013	13,819	12,460	1,252	66	41	7,862	5,957	7,240	5,220	597	655	666
Feb-Apr 2013	13,848	12,465	1,269	66	48	7,905	5,944	7,267	5,199	609	660	638
Mar-May 2013	13,825	12,445	1,254	70	56	7,884	5,942	7,249	5,196	603	651	656
Apr-Jun 2013	13,863	12,475	1,263	70	56	7,905	5,958	7,260	5,214	610	653	666
May-Jul 2013	13,887	12,496	1,263	68	61	7,939	5,949	7,279	5,217	614	649	658
Jun-Aug 2013	13,891	12,474	1,281	71	64	7,962	5,928	7,281	5,192	629	652	666
Jul-Sep 2013	13,909	12,482	1,284	74	69	7,973	5,936	7,294	5,189	629	654	667
Aug-Oct 2013	13,982	12,539	1,306	74	63	8,006	5,976	7,325	5,214	637	669	671
Sep-Nov 2013	13,995	12,528	1,348	67	52	8,056	5,938	7,355	5,173	668	679	679
Oct-Dec 2013	**14,003**	**12,532**	**1,357**	**62**	**51**	**8,095**	**5,908**	**7,385**	**5,147**	**678**	**680**	**667**
Change on qtr	*93*	*50*	*74*	*-12*	*-18*	*122*	*-28*	*91*	*-41*	*48*	*26*	*1*
Change %	*0.7*	*0.4*	*5.7*	*-16.5*	*-25.7*	*1.5*	*-0.5*	*1.2*	*-0.8*	*7.6*	*3.9*	*0.1*
Change on year	*199*	*137*	*68*	*-4*	*-2*	*270*	*-71*	*179*	*-42*	*85*	*-17*	*-25*
Change %	*1.4*	*1.1*	*5.3*	*-6.2*	*-3.9*	*3.4*	*-1.2*	*2.5*	*-0.8*	*14.4*	*-2.5*	*-3.6*

4.2 Full-time, part-time and temporary workers

United Kingdom (thousands) seasonally adjusted

	Temporary employees (reasons for temporary working)							Part-time workers (reasons for working part-time)[3]					
	Total	Total as % of all employees	Could not find permanent job	% that could not find permanent job	Did not want permanent job	Had a contract with period of training	Some other reason	Total[4]	Could not find full-time job	% that could not find full-time job	Did not want full-time job	Ill or disabled	Student or at school
	13	14	15	16	17	18	19	20	21	22	23	24	25
People	YCBZ	YCCC	YCCF	YCCI	YCCL	YCCO	YCCR	YCCU	YCCX	YCDA	YCDD	YCDG	YCDJ
Nov-Jan 2004	1,519	6.2	405	26.7	435	82	598	7,223	563	7.8	5,299	180	1,151
Dec-Feb 2004	1,516	6.2	404	26.7	436	87	588	7,247	560	7.7	5,318	186	1,154
Jan-Mar 2004	1,507	6.1	405	26.9	431	86	585	7,265	570	7.8	5,313	188	1,165
Feb-Apr 2004	1,503	6.1	394	26.2	434	86	588	7,240	568	7.8	5,289	185	1,168
Mar-May 2004	1,490	6.1	386	25.9	439	82	582	7,240	545	7.5	5,317	183	1,163
Apr-Jun 2004	1,510	6.2	390	25.8	440	89	591	7,224	533	7.4	5,327	182	1,150
May-Jul 2004	1,499	6.1	393	26.2	428	88	591	7,219	543	7.5	5,312	178	1,155
Jun-Aug 2004	1,535	6.2	385	25.1	431	92	627	7,221	547	7.6	5,306	176	1,163
Jul-Sep 2004	1,515	6.1	377	24.9	422	100	617	7,208	555	7.7	5,282	170	1,168
Aug-Oct 2004	1,519	6.2	371	24.4	421	103	624	7,173	555	7.7	5,246	171	1,169
Sep-Nov 2004	1,488	6.0	362	24.4	414	111	600	7,155	537	7.5	5,242	171	1,174
Oct-Dec 2004	1,507	6.1	364	24.2	430	116	596	7,154	537	7.5	5,246	166	1,175
Nov-Jan 2005	1,500	6.0	357	23.8	427	113	603	7,154	538	7.5	5,239	166	1,182
Dec-Feb 2005	1,502	6.0	357	23.7	419	113	614	7,134	549	7.7	5,228	166	1,161
Jan-Mar 2005	1,466	5.9	357	24.3	404	102	603	7,129	568	8.0	5,209	166	1,153
Feb-Apr 2005	1,444	5.8	357	24.7	385	104	599	7,143	563	7.9	5,225	176	1,146
Mar-May 2005	1,445	5.8	357	24.7	382	105	602	7,193	585	8.1	5,258	168	1,151
Apr-Jun 2005	1,450	5.8	356	24.5	387	98	609	7,202	588	8.2	5,243	165	1,173
May-Jul 2005	1,474	5.9	355	24.1	402	107	610	7,206	592	8.2	5,234	160	1,186
Jun-Aug 2005	1,471	5.9	378	25.7	397	100	596	7,188	589	8.2	5,234	165	1,164
Jul-Sep 2005	1,480	5.9	392	26.5	395	104	589	7,179	597	8.3	5,234	168	1,152
Aug-Oct 2005	1,433	5.7	386	26.9	388	100	559	7,162	593	8.3	5,226	170	1,143
Sep-Nov 2005	1,419	5.7	370	26.1	378	102	569	7,151	612	8.6	5,212	167	1,127
Oct-Dec 2005	1,387	5.6	347	25.0	375	94	572	7,126	604	8.5	5,206	168	1,113
Nov-Jan 2006	1,430	5.7	363	25.4	388	104	574	7,147	610	8.5	5,210	168	1,122
Dec-Feb 2006	1,450	5.8	363	25.0	402	102	583	7,191	618	8.6	5,217	177	1,141
Jan-Mar 2006	1,485	5.9	373	25.1	411	115	586	7,222	618	8.6	5,239	174	1,148
Feb-Apr 2006	1,484	5.9	369	24.8	418	115	583	7,213	617	8.6	5,229	171	1,157
Mar-May 2006	1,478	5.9	368	24.9	414	114	581	7,193	610	8.5	5,211	170	1,162
Apr-Jun 2006	1,463	5.8	369	25.2	419	110	565	7,234	623	8.6	5,225	170	1,178
May-Jul 2006	1,441	5.7	359	24.9	417	99	567	7,241	632	8.7	5,213	175	1,186
Jun-Aug 2006	1,468	5.8	362	24.7	434	96	576	7,268	644	8.9	5,215	184	1,198
Jul-Sep 2006	1,462	5.8	365	25.0	434	93	570	7,280	645	8.9	5,206	186	1,211
Aug-Oct 2006	1,476	5.9	383	26.0	429	88	576	7,340	659	9.0	5,238	187	1,217
Sep-Nov 2006	1,495	6.0	390	26.1	438	94	573	7,302	662	9.1	5,217	189	1,190
Oct-Dec 2006	1,510	6.0	391	25.9	448	92	579	7,311	663	9.1	5,221	193	1,192
Nov-Jan 2007	1,527	6.1	398	26.1	443	105	581	7,295	666	9.1	5,213	197	1,178
Dec-Feb 2007	1,520	6.1	396	26.1	441	106	578	7,275	645	8.9	5,232	191	1,171
Jan-Mar 2007	1,533	6.1	402	26.2	436	113	582	7,287	659	9.0	5,235	188	1,173
Feb-Apr 2007	1,513	6.0	401	26.5	427	104	581	7,283	669	9.2	5,242	177	1,162
Mar-May 2007	1,514	6.0	406	26.8	423	100	584	7,264	685	9.4	5,222	176	1,151
Apr-Jun 2007	1,506	6.0	415	27.5	411	97	584	7,255	683	9.4	5,224	174	1,141
May-Jul 2007	1,500	6.0	409	27.3	414	91	586	7,250	696	9.6	5,199	179	1,141
Jun-Aug 2007	1,488	5.9	403	27.1	417	86	581	7,251	696	9.6	5,217	164	1,139
Jul-Sep 2007	1,478	5.9	390	26.4	421	83	583	7,260	692	9.5	5,227	169	1,137
Aug-Oct 2007	1,458	5.8	383	26.2	421	84	570	7,262	698	9.6	5,226	167	1,134
Sep-Nov 2007	1,475	5.8	379	25.7	432	82	581	7,299	694	9.5	5,255	172	1,146
Oct-Dec 2007	1,491	5.9	380	25.5	447	80	583	7,324	725	9.9	5,229	170	1,160
Nov-Jan 2008	1,470	5.8	366	24.9	440	78	586	7,357	733	10.0	5,244	173	1,168
Dec-Feb 2008	1,443	5.7	362	25.1	429	83	569	7,365	724	9.8	5,245	177	1,178
Jan-Mar 2008	1,428	5.6	359	25.1	429	84	556	7,365	701	9.5	5,262	183	1,175
Feb-Apr 2008	1,438	5.6	357	24.8	433	85	563	7,358	690	9.4	5,246	185	1,192
Mar-May 2008	1,420	5.6	356	25.1	407	83	575	7,331	670	9.1	5,249	193	1,171
Apr-Jun 2008	1,397	5.5	345	24.7	407	84	560	7,350	683	9.3	5,247	203	1,175
May-Jul 2008	1,384	5.4	351	25.3	392	87	554	7,341	689	9.4	5,229	213	1,168
Jun-Aug 2008	1,376	5.4	351	25.5	401	82	542	7,350	701	9.5	5,254	213	1,145
Jul-Sep 2008	1,376	5.4	358	26.0	397	88	534	7,333	712	9.7	5,241	205	1,134
Aug-Oct 2008	1,361	5.4	348	25.5	403	83	528	7,342	727	9.9	5,244	195	1,133
Sep-Nov 2008	1,396	5.5	362	25.9	398	84	552	7,405	748	10.1	5,273	198	1,143
Oct-Dec 2008	1,404	5.5	380	27.1	389	86	549	7,386	768	10.4	5,241	197	1,135
Nov-Jan 2009	1,417	5.6	396	27.9	388	91	542	7,399	808	10.9	5,220	191	1,136
Dec-Feb 2009	1,420	5.6	419	29.5	385	84	533	7,414	844	11.4	5,220	183	1,125
Jan-Mar 2009	1,425	5.7	420	29.5	388	82	534	7,431	869	11.7	5,226	184	1,114
Feb-Apr 2009	1,416	5.7	419	29.6	381	86	530	7,386	893	12.1	5,167	190	1,095
Mar-May 2009	1,407	5.6	417	29.6	388	90	513	7,389	935	12.7	5,132	193	1,088
Apr-Jun 2009	1,435	5.8	429	29.9	392	88	527	7,433	966	13.0	5,130	189	1,096
May-Jul 2009	1,430	5.8	442	30.9	372	84	532	7,427	972	13.1	5,138	178	1,087
Jun-Aug 2009	1,430	5.8	445	31.2	374	89	521	7,450	975	13.1	5,141	183	1,102
Jul-Sep 2009	1,440	5.8	462	32.1	372	84	521	7,506	996	13.3	5,160	187	1,118
Aug-Oct 2009	1,434	5.8	467	32.5	367	86	515	7,557	1,011	13.4	5,165	189	1,149
Sep-Nov 2009	1,438	5.8	489	34.0	366	76	507	7,562	1,029	13.6	5,160	183	1,146
Oct-Dec 2009	1,445	5.8	498	34.5	362	77	508	7,552	1,027	13.6	5,159	187	1,138
Nov-Jan 2010	1,449	5.9	499	34.4	370	76	505	7,561	1,038	13.7	5,158	184	1,138
Dec-Feb 2010	1,474	6.0	511	34.7	364	82	516	7,526	1,043	13.9	5,121	179	1,142
Jan-Mar 2010	1,474	6.0	510	34.6	366	79	520	7,559	1,066	14.1	5,146	167	1,136
Feb-Apr 2010	1,490	6.0	536	36.0	362	81	512	7,601	1,083	14.2	5,171	172	1,132
Mar-May 2010	1,528	6.2	549	35.9	376	79	524	7,653	1,072	14.0	5,227	167	1,146
Apr-Jun 2010	1,559	6.3	565	36.2	378	81	535	7,667	1,072	14.0	5,254	172	1,130
May-Jul 2010	1,565	6.3	568	36.3	380	81	536	7,755	1,110	14.3	5,265	170	1,169

4.2 Full-time, part-time and temporary workers

United Kingdom (thousands) seasonally adjusted

	Temporary employees (reasons for temporary working)							Part-time workers (reasons for working part-time)[3]					
	Total	Total as % of all employees	Could not find permanent job	% that could not find permanent job	Did not want permanent job	Had a contract with period of training	Some other reason	Total[4]	Could not find full-time job	% that could not find full-time job	Did not want full-time job	Ill or disabled	Student or at school
	13	14	15	16	17	18	19	20	21	22	23	24	25
Jun-Aug 2010	1,569	6.3	591	37.7	367	87	524	7,784	1,130	14.5	5,258	169	1,181
Jul-Sep 2010	1,571	6.3	597	38.0	363	87	524	7,808	1,148	14.7	5,268	162	1,181
Aug-Oct 2010	1,584	6.4	588	37.1	370	92	534	7,783	1,167	15.0	5,270	164	1,129
Sep-Nov 2010	1,571	6.3	587	37.4	354	94	537	7,761	1,165	15.0	5,295	172	1,077
Oct-Dec 2010	1,544	6.2	579	37.5	339	95	531	7,759	1,181	15.2	5,271	164	1,091
Nov-Jan 2011	1,559	6.2	579	37.2	339	93	548	7,754	1,170	15.1	5,299	164	1,067
Dec-Feb 2011	1,565	6.3	570	36.4	349	94	551	7,758	1,172	15.1	5,307	172	1,050
Jan-Mar 2011	1,586	6.3	576	36.3	358	100	552	7,755	1,182	15.2	5,288	181	1,051
Feb-Apr 2011	1,589	6.3	580	36.5	357	93	559	7,779	1,220	15.7	5,262	184	1,060
Mar-May 2011	1,590	6.3	577	36.3	365	90	558	7,791	1,259	16.2	5,251	181	1,048
Apr-Jun 2011	1,591	6.3	600	37.7	358	86	547	7,747	1,263	16.3	5,212	180	1,034
May-Jul 2011	1,551	6.2	577	37.2	348	85	541	7,665	1,281	16.7	5,131	179	1,013
Jun-Aug 2011	1,520	6.1	585	38.5	312	81	541	7,629	1,268	16.6	5,125	178	1,007
Jul-Sep 2011	1,508	6.1	583	38.7	318	85	522	7,654	1,269	16.6	5,132	186	1,016
Aug-Oct 2011	1,523	6.1	602	39.5	324	85	512	7,683	1,280	16.7	5,154	183	1,019
Sep-Nov 2011	1,551	6.3	593	38.2	351	90	517	7,719	1,315	17.0	5,144	183	1,032
Oct-Dec 2011	1,549	6.2	606	39.1	346	91	506	7,739	1,349	17.4	5,136	188	1,023
Nov-Jan 2012	1,556	6.3	613	39.4	339	96	508	7,736	1,386	17.9	5,114	189	1,004
Dec-Feb 2012	1,575	6.3	631	40.0	344	95	506	7,800	1,398	17.9	5,148	182	1,026
Jan-Mar 2012	1,564	6.3	619	39.6	336	89	520	7,839	1,406	17.9	5,167	189	1,030
Feb-Apr 2012	1,550	6.2	608	39.2	331	94	517	7,822	1,400	17.9	5,149	190	1,034
Mar-May 2012	1,562	6.3	632	40.4	320	93	518	7,819	1,397	17.9	5,152	190	1,032
Apr-Jun 2012	1,580	6.3	631	39.9	323	101	526	7,891	1,422	18.0	5,186	183	1,051
May-Jul 2012	1,628	6.5	658	40.4	335	100	535	7,947	1,424	17.9	5,250	177	1,047
Jun-Aug 2012	1,621	6.5	649	40.0	334	100	538	7,946	1,411	17.8	5,256	178	1,054
Jul-Sep 2012	1,615	6.4	655	40.5	323	93	543	7,939	1,411	17.8	5,263	177	1,037
Aug-Oct 2012	1,620	6.4	650	40.1	325	93	552	7,935	1,405	17.7	5,273	184	1,018
Sep-Nov 2012	1,651	6.5	655	39.7	341	91	564	7,925	1,389	17.5	5,281	181	1,015
Oct-Dec 2012	1,660	6.6	662	39.9	338	97	563	7,900	1,382	17.5	5,274	183	998
Nov-Jan 2013	1,638	6.5	657	40.1	330	95	555	7,890	1,398	17.7	5,266	187	980
Dec-Feb 2013	1,595	6.3	641	40.2	331	98	526	7,892	1,411	17.9	5,260	184	982
Jan-Mar 2013	1,617	6.4	651	40.3	332	103	530	7,869	1,408	17.9	5,234	176	999
Feb-Apr 2013	1,594	6.3	634	39.7	339	98	523	7,889	1,422	18.0	5,214	180	1,019
Mar-May 2013	1,581	6.3	622	39.4	327	102	529	7,851	1,446	18.4	5,167	179	998
Apr-Jun 2013	1,547	6.1	596	38.6	321	106	523	7,875	1,433	18.2	5,209	187	986
May-Jul 2013	1,557	6.1	607	39.0	307	111	532	7,871	1,447	18.4	5,190	185	988
Jun-Aug 2013	1,572	6.2	611	38.9	299	121	541	7,855	1,450	18.5	5,205	188	950
Jul-Sep 2013	1,601	6.3	606	37.9	315	125	555	7,892	1,457	18.5	5,205	191	974
Aug-Oct 2013	1,584	6.2	593	37.4	323	121	547	7,945	1,472	18.5	5,272	194	984
Sep-Nov 2013	1,591	6.2	586	36.8	322	128	556	7,921	1,438	18.2	5,236	190	1,004
Oct-Dec 2013	**1,615**	**6.3**	**605**	**37.5**	**331**	**115**	**564**	**7,900**	**1,428**	**18.1**	**5,219**	**190**	**1,013**
Change on qtr	14	0.0	-1	-0.4	16	-10	8	9	-29	-0.4	14	-1	39
Change %	0.8		-0.2		5.0	-7.7	1.5	0.1	-2.0		0.3	-0.6	4.0
Change on year	-45	-0.2	-57	-2.4	-7	18	0	0	46	0.6	-55	7	15
Change %	-2.7		-8.6		-2.2	18.9	0.0	0.0	3.3		-1.0	3.8	1.5
Men	YCCA	YCCD	YCCG	YCCJ	YCCM	YCCP	YCCS	YCCV	YCCY	YCDB	YCDE	YCDH	YCDK
Nov-Jan 2004	707	5.6	236	33.3	172	33	266	1,519	249	16.4	704	76	482
Dec-Feb 2004	709	5.6	234	33.0	174	37	264	1,525	251	16.5	706	76	484
Jan-Mar 2004	698	5.5	233	33.3	168	37	260	1,553	265	17.1	718	73	488
Feb-Apr 2004	700	5.6	221	31.6	176	41	261	1,553	259	16.7	726	71	488
Mar-May 2004	695	5.5	221	31.8	178	41	256	1,571	253	16.1	742	72	496
Apr-Jun 2004	702	5.6	224	31.9	174	44	260	1,568	244	15.6	745	73	497
May-Jul 2004	701	5.6	227	32.4	172	43	258	1,569	243	15.5	751	69	498
Jun-Aug 2004	743	5.9	224	30.2	184	49	285	1,584	245	15.5	761	67	501
Jul-Sep 2004	723	5.7	218	30.2	175	55	274	1,581	246	15.5	762	64	501
Aug-Oct 2004	718	5.7	218	30.3	171	52	277	1,570	244	15.5	753	66	499
Sep-Nov 2004	691	5.5	209	30.2	169	51	262	1,551	232	14.9	742	69	500
Oct-Dec 2004	715	5.6	212	29.7	187	52	264	1,571	230	14.7	756	66	509
Nov-Jan 2005	709	5.6	203	28.6	187	54	265	1,587	228	14.4	754	65	529
Dec-Feb 2005	706	5.5	202	28.6	177	52	276	1,583	225	14.2	768	66	512
Jan-Mar 2005	697	5.5	202	28.9	175	52	268	1,591	232	14.6	768	69	510
Feb-Apr 2005	692	5.4	206	29.7	170	53	265	1,598	229	14.4	772	76	506
Mar-May 2005	691	5.4	211	30.5	161	57	263	1,597	236	14.8	766	72	510
Apr-Jun 2005	695	5.5	210	30.2	169	56	261	1,592	236	14.8	754	73	512
May-Jul 2005	696	5.5	208	29.8	174	60	254	1,589	242	15.2	747	73	512
Jun-Aug 2005	682	5.3	212	31.1	175	58	237	1,585	228	14.4	756	75	512
Jul-Sep 2005	684	5.3	213	31.1	169	59	243	1,590	228	14.4	770	76	506
Aug-Oct 2005	671	5.2	206	30.7	170	56	239	1,590	234	14.7	772	77	496
Sep-Nov 2005	663	5.2	202	30.5	166	51	243	1,603	248	15.5	778	76	490
Oct-Dec 2005	652	5.1	195	29.8	165	43	249	1,610	247	15.3	785	77	489
Nov-Jan 2006	655	5.1	196	29.9	164	50	245	1,607	245	15.2	784	75	489
Dec-Feb 2006	663	5.2	191	28.8	169	55	248	1,622	251	15.5	786	76	497
Jan-Mar 2006	669	5.2	192	28.8	169	61	247	1,608	247	15.4	777	76	495
Feb-Apr 2006	673	5.2	195	29.0	177	56	246	1,609	248	15.4	775	72	503
Mar-May 2006	670	5.2	188	28.1	175	55	252	1,611	249	15.5	774	73	503
Apr-Jun 2006	659	5.1	188	28.6	175	53	242	1,623	256	15.8	770	70	518

4.2 Full-time, part-time and temporary workers

United Kingdom (thousands) seasonally adjusted

	Temporary employees (reasons for temporary working)							Part-time workers (reasons for working part-time)[3]					
	Total	Total as % of all employees	Could not find permanent job	% that could not find permanent job	Did not want permanent job	Had a contract with period of training	Some other reason	Total[4]	Could not find full-time job	% that could not find full-time job	Did not want full-time job	Ill or disabled	Student or at school
	13	14	15	16	17	18	19	20	21	22	23	24	25
May-Jul 2006	650	5.0	181	27.8	170	48	250	1,635	258	15.8	771	74	523
Jun-Aug 2006	667	5.2	187	28.0	174	47	259	1,629	265	16.2	758	76	520
Jul-Sep 2006	671	5.2	194	28.9	175	47	255	1,658	272	16.4	767	74	533
Aug-Oct 2006	690	5.4	206	29.8	178	46	261	1,686	281	16.7	786	74	531
Sep-Nov 2006	705	5.5	211	30.0	184	50	260	1,658	281	17.0	779	75	510
Oct-Dec 2006	710	5.5	214	30.1	187	49	261	1,655	279	16.9	784	78	504
Nov-Jan 2007	716	5.6	210	29.3	188	57	262	1,647	281	17.1	769	83	503
Dec-Feb 2007	708	5.5	213	30.1	187	52	256	1,655	268	16.2	786	81	508
Jan-Mar 2007	718	5.6	215	29.9	185	55	263	1,676	276	16.4	797	81	512
Feb-Apr 2007	701	5.4	212	30.2	178	49	262	1,670	274	16.4	798	80	508
Mar-May 2007	702	5.4	220	31.4	176	43	263	1,666	279	16.8	802	76	498
Apr-Jun 2007	698	5.4	223	31.9	174	40	260	1,668	280	16.8	821	75	480
May-Jul 2007	696	5.4	220	31.6	179	39	258	1,669	284	17.0	831	79	463
Jun-Aug 2007	698	5.4	218	31.2	187	38	255	1,670	292	17.5	826	69	470
Jul-Sep 2007	686	5.3	207	30.2	191	37	251	1,687	293	17.4	828	72	480
Aug-Oct 2007	671	5.2	202	30.1	188	38	243	1,673	292	17.4	814	71	484
Sep-Nov 2007	687	5.3	203	29.6	193	42	248	1,710	288	16.8	831	71	508
Oct-Dec 2007	699	5.4	201	28.8	195	45	258	1,716	290	16.9	834	70	508
Nov-Jan 2008	689	5.3	189	27.4	192	44	265	1,737	290	16.7	855	68	511
Dec-Feb 2008	667	5.1	183	27.4	183	44	258	1,739	292	16.8	855	68	510
Jan-Mar 2008	660	5.1	183	27.7	185	41	251	1,734	288	16.6	858	68	506
Feb-Apr 2008	661	5.1	181	27.4	185	42	253	1,738	286	16.4	859	72	505
Mar-May 2008	654	5.0	180	27.6	168	44	261	1,711	270	15.8	858	77	490
Apr-Jun 2008	633	4.8	176	27.8	162	46	249	1,744	276	15.8	865	77	510
May-Jul 2008	619	4.7	184	29.6	147	48	241	1,756	292	16.6	857	81	512
Jun-Aug 2008	618	4.8	180	29.0	155	44	240	1,768	305	17.2	856	82	513
Jul-Sep 2008	635	4.9	185	29.1	157	47	246	1,769	316	17.8	857	80	503
Aug-Oct 2008	628	4.8	176	28.1	169	42	241	1,775	321	18.1	854	79	507
Sep-Nov 2008	636	4.9	186	29.2	156	42	252	1,772	332	18.7	844	79	501
Oct-Dec 2008	641	4.9	195	30.5	153	42	250	1,784	353	19.8	837	80	497
Nov-Jan 2009	660	5.1	215	32.6	155	48	242	1,793	376	21.0	829	77	494
Dec-Feb 2009	663	5.1	227	34.2	160	38	239	1,796	385	21.5	828	79	490
Jan-Mar 2009	666	5.2	231	34.6	158	38	239	1,788	393	22.0	820	78	484
Feb-Apr 2009	668	5.2	231	34.6	157	40	240	1,791	405	22.6	812	79	476
Mar-May 2009	658	5.2	223	33.8	156	47	233	1,812	427	23.6	806	83	477
Apr-Jun 2009	683	5.4	230	33.7	161	46	246	1,825	445	24.4	796	80	481
May-Jul 2009	689	5.5	233	33.8	155	45	256	1,795	442	24.6	790	72	474
Jun-Aug 2009	681	5.4	236	34.7	151	47	246	1,802	431	23.9	800	70	480
Jul-Sep 2009	674	5.4	243	36.0	146	44	241	1,790	433	24.2	784	78	477
Aug-Oct 2009	675	5.4	247	36.6	140	50	238	1,800	434	24.1	778	78	492
Sep-Nov 2009	690	5.5	264	38.3	146	43	237	1,812	448	24.7	785	76	486
Oct-Dec 2009	698	5.6	272	39.0	147	42	237	1,815	447	24.6	797	77	478
Nov-Jan 2010	689	5.5	262	38.1	149	41	237	1,827	451	24.7	809	74	476
Dec-Feb 2010	713	5.7	276	38.7	151	46	241	1,819	457	25.1	798	71	479
Jan-Mar 2010	709	5.7	270	38.0	152	43	245	1,835	466	25.4	805	68	484
Feb-Apr 2010	715	5.7	284	39.7	152	42	238	1,840	467	25.4	802	68	493
Mar-May 2010	733	5.8	291	39.7	159	41	243	1,868	464	24.8	828	63	503
Apr-Jun 2010	755	6.0	302	39.9	163	40	251	1,894	471	24.9	845	71	497
May-Jul 2010	756	6.0	302	39.9	160	41	253	1,919	481	25.1	842	70	513
Jun-Aug 2010	761	6.0	317	41.6	157	45	242	1,947	490	25.1	847	77	519
Jul-Sep 2010	757	6.0	321	42.5	148	46	241	1,974	502	25.4	857	71	527
Aug-Oct 2010	761	6.0	315	41.4	154	50	242	1,970	520	26.4	866	72	498
Sep-Nov 2010	749	5.9	306	40.8	150	53	240	1,968	519	26.4	873	77	483
Oct-Dec 2010	728	5.7	296	40.7	148	54	230	1,971	520	26.4	875	73	488
Nov-Jan 2011	744	5.8	303	40.7	146	51	244	1,944	511	26.3	874	72	470
Dec-Feb 2011	745	5.8	297	39.9	147	51	248	1,925	511	26.6	866	75	453
Jan-Mar 2011	752	5.9	301	40.0	148	56	248	1,930	525	27.2	863	80	440
Feb-Apr 2011	766	6.0	312	40.8	147	50	256	1,970	543	27.6	872	83	453
Mar-May 2011	766	6.0	311	40.6	150	47	258	1,971	558	28.3	880	75	439
Apr-Jun 2011	780	6.1	324	41.6	150	45	260	1,962	565	28.8	871	72	435
May-Jul 2011	756	6.0	306	40.4	152	46	253	1,939	579	29.9	854	70	417
Jun-Aug 2011	740	5.9	310	41.9	133	42	255	1,889	565	29.9	832	67	410
Jul-Sep 2011	733	5.8	306	41.8	137	43	246	1,900	556	29.3	845	66	415
Aug-Oct 2011	731	5.8	311	42.6	134	42	244	1,922	562	29.2	850	67	424
Sep-Nov 2011	735	5.8	303	41.3	149	42	241	1,954	577	29.5	853	67	437
Oct-Dec 2011	737	5.8	315	42.8	143	42	238	1,959	594	30.3	846	69	433
Nov-Jan 2012	739	5.9	319	43.1	140	44	236	1,951	606	31.1	836	72	424
Dec-Feb 2012	743	5.9	331	44.6	137	44	231	2,017	625	31.0	856	72	450
Jan-Mar 2012	744	5.9	324	43.5	138	43	239	2,034	637	31.3	861	72	453
Feb-Apr 2012	741	5.8	311	42.0	138	45	246	2,043	643	31.5	858	74	452
Mar-May 2012	734	5.8	322	43.9	133	44	235	2,033	638	31.4	853	76	449
Apr-Jun 2012	735	5.8	319	43.4	132	48	237	2,067	654	31.7	864	75	454
May-Jul 2012	753	5.9	336	44.6	131	50	236	2,050	645	31.4	869	70	449
Jun-Aug 2012	750	5.9	327	43.6	132	51	240	2,055	632	30.7	879	73	451
Jul-Sep 2012	758	5.9	335	44.2	126	47	250	2,049	637	31.1	880	69	442
Aug-Oct 2012	764	6.0	337	44.1	125	47	255	2,031	634	31.2	889	68	418
Sep-Nov 2012	783	6.1	347	44.3	131	42	263	2,023	633	31.3	886	62	415
Oct-Dec 2012	798	6.2	362	45.4	135	44	257	2,014	640	31.8	877	66	401
Nov-Jan 2013	783	6.1	354	45.2	137	41	251	2,016	643	31.9	887	63	396
Dec-Feb 2013	774	6.0	345	44.5	142	43	244	2,006	639	31.8	888	62	395
Jan-Mar 2013	761	5.9	343	45.1	138	41	239	1,994	639	32.0	872	59	400

4.2 Full-time, part-time and temporary workers

United Kingdom (thousands) seasonally adjusted

	Temporary employees (reasons for temporary working)							Part-time workers (reasons for working part-time)[3]					
	Total	Total as % of all employees	Could not find permanent job	% that could not find permanent job	Did not want permanent job	Had a contract with period of training	Some other reason	Total[4]	Could not find full-time job	% that could not find full-time job	Did not want full-time job	Ill or disabled	Student or at school
	13	14	15	16	17	18	19	20	21	22	23	24	25
Feb-Apr 2013	750	5.8	332	44.3	144	34	239	2,029	658	32.4	869	62	414
Mar-May 2013	749	5.8	324	43.3	137	42	246	2,003	659	32.9	855	64	398
Apr-Jun 2013	727	5.7	312	42.9	136	39	240	2,007	648	32.3	868	68	398
May-Jul 2013	738	5.7	318	43.1	129	48	243	2,003	653	32.6	868	64	396
Jun-Aug 2013	741	5.7	315	42.5	130	59	237	2,010	660	32.8	877	65	387
Jul-Sep 2013	756	5.8	311	41.1	134	67	244	2,049	668	32.6	892	70	395
Aug-Oct 2013	740	5.7	301	40.7	137	60	242	2,064	668	32.4	897	72	404
Sep-Nov 2013	755	5.8	300	39.7	133	63	259	2,071	662	32.0	894	75	423
Oct-Dec 2013	**774**	**6.0**	**305**	**39.4**	**142**	**61**	**265**	**2,075**	**645**	**31.1**	**902**	**76**	**433**
Change on qtr	*18*	*0.1*	*-6*	*-1.7*	*8*	*-5*	*21*	*26*	*-23*	*-1.5*	*11*	*6*	*38*
Change %	*2.4*		*-1.8*		*5.9*	*-8.0*	*8.7*	*1.3*	*-3.5*		*1.2*	*8.5*	*9.7*
Change on year	*-24*	*-0.2*	*-57*	*-6.0*	*7*	*17*	*9*	*62*	*4*	*-0.7*	*25*	*10*	*32*
Change %	*-3.0*		*-15.7*		*5.1*	*39.9*	*3.4*	*3.1*	*0.7*		*2.9*	*15.5*	*8.0*
Women	YCCB	YCCE	YCCH	YCCK	YCCN	YCCQ	YCCT	YCCW	YCCZ	YCDC	YCDF	YCDI	YCDL
Nov-Jan 2004	812	6.8	169	20.9	263	49	331	5,705	314	5.5	4,596	104	670
Dec-Feb 2004	808	6.7	170	21.1	262	50	325	5,722	310	5.4	4,612	110	670
Jan-Mar 2004	809	6.8	172	21.3	263	49	325	5,712	304	5.3	4,596	114	677
Feb-Apr 2004	803	6.7	173	21.5	258	45	327	5,687	309	5.4	4,563	114	680
Mar-May 2004	795	6.6	166	20.9	261	41	326	5,669	292	5.2	4,576	111	668
Apr-Jun 2004	809	6.8	167	20.6	266	45	330	5,656	289	5.1	4,583	109	653
May-Jul 2004	798	6.7	166	20.7	256	44	333	5,650	300	5.3	4,561	110	657
Jun-Aug 2004	792	6.6	160	20.2	247	43	342	5,637	302	5.4	4,545	109	661
Jul-Sep 2004	793	6.6	158	20.0	247	44	343	5,627	309	5.5	4,520	106	667
Aug-Oct 2004	801	6.7	153	19.1	250	51	347	5,602	311	5.6	4,493	105	669
Sep-Nov 2004	796	6.6	153	19.3	245	60	338	5,604	305	5.4	4,500	102	674
Oct-Dec 2004	792	6.5	152	19.2	243	64	333	5,582	307	5.5	4,490	100	666
Nov-Jan 2005	790	6.5	154	19.5	240	58	338	5,567	310	5.6	4,485	101	653
Dec-Feb 2005	796	6.6	155	19.4	242	62	338	5,551	323	5.8	4,460	100	649
Jan-Mar 2005	769	6.3	155	20.1	229	51	334	5,538	336	6.1	4,441	97	643
Feb-Apr 2005	752	6.2	151	20.1	215	51	335	5,545	333	6.0	4,453	99	640
Mar-May 2005	755	6.2	146	19.3	221	48	340	5,595	349	6.2	4,493	96	642
Apr-Jun 2005	755	6.2	146	19.3	218	42	349	5,611	351	6.3	4,489	92	661
May-Jul 2005	778	6.4	147	18.9	228	47	356	5,618	350	6.2	4,487	87	674
Jun-Aug 2005	789	6.5	165	21.0	222	42	359	5,603	361	6.4	4,478	91	651
Jul-Sep 2005	796	6.5	180	22.6	226	45	346	5,590	369	6.6	4,463	92	646
Aug-Oct 2005	762	6.2	179	23.5	218	44	320	5,572	359	6.4	4,454	93	647
Sep-Nov 2005	756	6.2	168	22.2	212	51	325	5,548	364	6.6	4,434	92	637
Oct-Dec 2005	735	6.0	152	20.7	209	51	323	5,516	357	6.5	4,421	92	624
Nov-Jan 2006	775	6.4	168	21.6	224	54	329	5,540	365	6.6	4,425	93	633
Dec-Feb 2006	787	6.4	172	21.8	233	47	335	5,569	368	6.6	4,431	101	644
Jan-Mar 2006	815	6.7	180	22.1	242	54	339	5,614	371	6.6	4,462	98	652
Feb-Apr 2006	811	6.6	174	21.4	241	59	337	5,604	369	6.6	4,454	99	654
Mar-May 2006	808	6.6	180	22.3	239	59	330	5,582	360	6.5	4,437	97	659
Apr-Jun 2006	804	6.6	181	22.5	244	56	322	5,612	368	6.6	4,455	101	661
May-Jul 2006	791	6.5	178	22.5	246	51	316	5,607	374	6.7	4,442	101	663
Jun-Aug 2006	800	6.5	175	21.9	260	48	317	5,639	379	6.7	4,456	108	677
Jul-Sep 2006	791	6.5	171	21.7	258	46	315	5,622	373	6.6	4,439	112	678
Aug-Oct 2006	786	6.4	178	22.6	252	42	315	5,653	378	6.7	4,451	113	686
Sep-Nov 2006	790	6.5	179	22.7	254	44	313	5,644	380	6.7	4,438	114	680
Oct-Dec 2006	799	6.5	178	22.2	261	43	318	5,655	384	6.8	4,436	115	688
Nov-Jan 2007	811	6.6	188	23.2	255	48	320	5,649	386	6.8	4,444	115	675
Dec-Feb 2007	812	6.7	183	22.5	254	54	322	5,620	377	6.7	4,445	110	663
Jan-Mar 2007	815	6.7	187	23.0	251	58	319	5,611	384	6.8	4,438	107	661
Feb-Apr 2007	812	6.7	190	23.4	249	55	318	5,612	395	7.0	4,444	97	654
Mar-May 2007	812	6.6	186	22.9	248	57	321	5,598	406	7.2	4,419	100	652
Apr-Jun 2007	809	6.6	192	23.7	237	56	324	5,588	403	7.2	4,403	99	661
May-Jul 2007	805	6.6	189	23.5	235	53	329	5,581	413	7.4	4,369	101	678
Jun-Aug 2007	790	6.5	185	23.4	230	48	327	5,581	404	7.2	4,391	95	669
Jul-Sep 2007	792	6.5	183	23.2	230	46	332	5,573	399	7.2	4,399	97	656
Aug-Oct 2007	786	6.4	180	22.9	233	45	327	5,589	406	7.3	4,412	97	649
Sep-Nov 2007	787	6.4	176	22.3	239	40	333	5,589	406	7.3	4,424	102	638
Oct-Dec 2007	791	6.4	179	22.6	252	35	325	5,608	435	7.8	4,395	100	652
Nov-Jan 2008	781	6.3	177	22.7	248	34	321	5,620	443	7.9	4,389	105	657
Dec-Feb 2008	776	6.3	179	23.1	246	39	311	5,627	432	7.7	4,390	109	668
Jan-Mar 2008	768	6.2	176	22.9	244	43	305	5,630	413	7.3	4,404	115	670
Feb-Apr 2008	777	6.3	176	22.7	248	43	310	5,619	404	7.2	4,387	113	687
Mar-May 2008	767	6.2	176	22.9	239	39	314	5,619	401	7.1	4,392	117	681
Apr-Jun 2008	763	6.1	169	22.2	245	38	312	5,606	406	7.2	4,382	125	665
May-Jul 2008	765	6.2	167	21.9	245	40	312	5,585	397	7.1	4,373	132	655
Jun-Aug 2008	757	6.1	171	22.6	246	38	302	5,582	396	7.1	4,398	131	631
Jul-Sep 2008	741	6.0	173	23.3	239	41	288	5,564	397	7.1	4,384	125	631
Aug-Oct 2008	733	5.9	171	23.4	234	41	287	5,567	406	7.3	4,390	116	626
Sep-Nov 2008	760	6.1	176	23.1	242	42	300	5,634	416	7.4	4,429	119	643
Oct-Dec 2008	763	6.2	185	24.3	236	43	299	5,602	415	7.4	4,403	117	638
Nov-Jan 2009	757	6.1	180	23.8	234	44	299	5,606	432	7.7	4,391	113	642
Dec-Feb 2009	757	6.1	192	25.4	225	46	294	5,618	459	8.2	4,392	105	635

4.2 Full-time, part-time and temporary workers

United Kingdom (thousands) seasonally adjusted

	Temporary employees (reasons for temporary working)							Part-time workers (reasons for working part-time)[3]					
	Total	Total as % of all employees	Could not find permanent job	% that could not find permanent job	Did not want permanent job	Had a contract with period of training	Some other reason	Total[4]	Could not find full-time job	% that could not find full-time job	Did not want full-time job	Ill or disabled	Student or at school
	13	14	15	16	17	18	19	20	21	22	23	24	25
Jan-Mar 2009	758	6.2	189	25.0	230	44	295	5,643	476	8.4	4,406	106	630
Feb-Apr 2009	747	6.1	188	25.1	224	46	289	5,595	488	8.7	4,355	110	619
Mar-May 2009	749	6.1	194	25.9	232	43	280	5,577	508	9.1	4,326	110	612
Apr-Jun 2009	752	6.1	198	26.4	231	42	281	5,608	521	9.3	4,334	109	615
May-Jul 2009	740	6.1	209	28.2	218	38	276	5,632	530	9.4	4,348	106	614
Jun-Aug 2009	749	6.1	209	27.9	223	41	275	5,648	544	9.6	4,341	113	622
Jul-Sep 2009	766	6.3	220	28.7	226	40	280	5,716	563	9.9	4,376	108	641
Aug-Oct 2009	759	6.2	219	28.9	227	36	277	5,757	578	10.0	4,387	111	657
Sep-Nov 2009	748	6.1	225	30.1	220	33	270	5,750	581	10.1	4,376	107	660
Oct-Dec 2009	747	6.1	226	30.2	215	35	272	5,737	580	10.1	4,362	110	659
Nov-Jan 2010	760	6.2	236	31.1	221	35	268	5,734	587	10.2	4,349	110	661
Dec-Feb 2010	761	6.2	236	31.0	213	37	275	5,707	586	10.3	4,323	108	664
Jan-Mar 2010	765	6.3	240	31.3	214	36	275	5,724	600	10.5	4,341	99	652
Feb-Apr 2010	775	6.4	252	32.5	210	39	274	5,761	616	10.7	4,370	104	639
Mar-May 2010	795	6.5	258	32.4	217	38	282	5,786	609	10.5	4,399	104	643
Apr-Jun 2010	804	6.6	263	32.7	216	41	284	5,773	601	10.4	4,409	101	633
May-Jul 2010	809	6.6	266	32.9	220	40	283	5,835	628	10.8	4,423	99	656
Jun-Aug 2010	808	6.6	274	33.9	210	42	282	5,836	641	11.0	4,411	92	662
Jul-Sep 2010	814	6.7	276	33.9	214	41	283	5,834	646	11.1	4,411	91	653
Aug-Oct 2010	823	6.7	273	33.1	216	43	292	5,813	647	11.1	4,404	92	631
Sep-Nov 2010	822	6.7	282	34.2	204	41	296	5,793	646	11.1	4,421	94	594
Oct-Dec 2010	816	6.7	283	34.6	191	42	301	5,788	661	11.4	4,395	91	603
Nov-Jan 2011	816	6.7	277	33.9	193	42	304	5,810	660	11.4	4,425	92	596
Dec-Feb 2011	820	6.7	273	33.3	202	43	303	5,833	661	11.3	4,441	97	598
Jan-Mar 2011	834	6.8	275	33.0	211	44	304	5,825	658	11.3	4,425	100	611
Feb-Apr 2011	823	6.7	268	32.5	210	43	303	5,809	677	11.7	4,390	101	608
Mar-May 2011	824	6.7	267	32.4	215	43	299	5,820	701	12.0	4,371	106	608
Apr-Jun 2011	811	6.6	276	34.0	208	41	287	5,785	698	12.1	4,342	108	599
May-Jul 2011	795	6.5	272	34.2	196	39	288	5,726	702	12.3	4,277	109	597
Jun-Aug 2011	780	6.4	275	35.3	180	39	287	5,740	703	12.3	4,293	112	597
Jul-Sep 2011	775	6.4	277	35.7	181	41	276	5,754	713	12.4	4,286	120	601
Aug-Oct 2011	793	6.5	291	36.7	190	43	268	5,762	718	12.5	4,304	116	594
Sep-Nov 2011	816	6.7	290	35.5	203	48	276	5,764	738	12.8	4,291	116	595
Oct-Dec 2011	812	6.6	291	35.8	203	49	269	5,780	755	13.1	4,290	119	590
Nov-Jan 2012	817	6.7	295	36.1	198	52	272	5,784	780	13.5	4,277	118	580
Dec-Feb 2012	832	6.8	299	36.0	207	50	275	5,784	773	13.4	4,292	110	576
Jan-Mar 2012	820	6.7	296	36.1	197	46	281	5,804	769	13.3	4,306	117	577
Feb-Apr 2012	810	6.6	296	36.6	194	48	271	5,780	757	13.1	4,291	115	582
Mar-May 2012	828	6.8	310	37.4	187	49	283	5,785	758	13.1	4,299	114	583
Apr-Jun 2012	845	6.9	312	36.9	191	53	290	5,824	768	13.2	4,322	109	597
May-Jul 2012	875	7.1	322	36.8	204	50	299	5,897	779	13.2	4,382	107	599
Jun-Aug 2012	871	7.1	322	36.9	202	49	298	5,891	780	13.2	4,377	104	603
Jul-Sep 2012	857	6.9	319	37.3	198	46	293	5,890	774	13.1	4,383	108	596
Aug-Oct 2012	856	6.9	313	36.6	200	45	297	5,904	771	13.1	4,384	116	600
Sep-Nov 2012	868	7.0	308	35.4	210	49	302	5,902	756	12.8	4,395	119	600
Oct-Dec 2012	862	7.0	300	34.8	203	53	307	5,886	741	12.6	4,397	117	597
Nov-Jan 2013	855	6.9	304	35.5	193	54	304	5,874	755	12.9	4,379	124	584
Dec-Feb 2013	822	6.6	296	36.0	189	54	282	5,886	772	13.1	4,372	122	587
Jan-Mar 2013	855	6.9	308	36.0	194	62	291	5,875	769	13.1	4,361	117	599
Feb-Apr 2013	845	6.8	301	35.7	195	64	284	5,860	764	13.0	4,345	118	604
Mar-May 2013	831	6.7	298	35.8	190	60	283	5,848	788	13.5	4,312	115	601
Apr-Jun 2013	819	6.6	284	34.7	186	66	283	5,868	784	13.4	4,340	119	588
May-Jul 2013	819	6.6	289	35.3	178	63	289	5,868	794	13.5	4,322	120	592
Jun-Aug 2013	831	6.7	296	35.6	169	62	304	5,845	790	13.5	4,327	123	563
Jul-Sep 2013	845	6.8	295	34.9	180	58	311	5,843	789	13.5	4,313	121	579
Aug-Oct 2013	843	6.7	292	34.6	186	61	305	5,881	803	13.7	4,376	122	580
Sep-Nov 2013	837	6.7	286	34.2	189	65	297	5,850	776	13.3	4,342	116	581
Oct-Dec 2013	**840**	**6.7**	**300**	**35.7**	**188**	**54**	**298**	**5,825**	**783**	**13.4**	**4,316**	**114**	**580**
Change on qtr	*-5*	*-0.1*	*5*	*0.7*	*8*	*-4*	*-13*	*-17*	*-6*	*-0.1*	*3*	*-7*	*1*
Change %	*-0.6*		*1.5*		*4.4*	*-7.4*	*-4.2*	*-0.3*	*-0.8*		*0.1*	*-5.8*	*0.2*
Change on year	*-22*	*-0.2*	*0*	*0.9*	*-14*	*1*	*-9*	*-61*	*42*	*0.8*	*-80*	*-3*	*-17*
Change %	*-2.5*		*0.1*		*-7.0*	*1.6*	*-2.8*	*-1.0*	*5.6*		*-1.8*	*-2.9*	*-2.8*

Relationship between columns: 1= 2+3+4+5; 1=6+7; 2=8+9; 3=10+11; 13=15+17+18+19; 20=21+23+24+25 ; 20=9+11 ;14=13/2; 16=15/13; 22=21/19

1. The split between full-time and part-time employment is based on respondents' self-classification.

2. This series does not include all people on these programmes; it only includes those engaging in any form of work, work experience or work-related training.

3. These series cover Employees and Self-employed only. These series include some temporary employees recorded in columns 13 to 19.

4. The total includes those who did not give a reason for working part-time and it therefore does not equal the sum of columns 21, 23, 24 and 25.

Further information

The Labour Force Survey is a survey of the population of private households, student halls of residence and NHS accommodation

Source: Labour Force Survey
Labour market statistics enquiries: labour.market@ons.gsi.gov.uk

4.3 Employment: by sex and age: United Kingdom

United Kingdom (thousands) seasonally adjusted

| | | Aged 16 and over | | | | | | Aged 16-64 | | | | | |
| | | Employment | | Unemployment | | Inactivity | | Employment | | Unemployment | | Inactivity | |
		Level	Rate	Level	Rate	Level	Rate	Level	Rate	Level	Rate	Level	Rate
People		MGRZ	MGSR	MGSC	MGSX	MGSI	YBTC	LF2G	LF24	LF2I	LF2Q	LF2M	LF2S
	Oct-Dec 2011	29,146	57.9	2,657	8.4	18,517	36.8	28,272	70.4	2,630	8.5	9,273	23.1
	Oct-Dec 2012	29,751	58.7	2,503	7.8	18,432	36.4	28,778	71.6	2,481	7.9	8,955	22.3
	Jan-Mar 2013	29,708	58.5	2,518	7.8	18,552	36.5	28,728	71.4	2,500	8.0	9,003	22.4
	Apr-Jun 2013	29,777	58.5	2,514	7.8	18,580	36.5	28,767	71.5	2,488	8.0	8,993	22.3
	Jul-Sep 2013	29,953	58.8	2,466	7.6	18,555	36.4	28,914	71.8	2,446	7.8	8,924	22.2
	Oct-Dec 2013	**30,146**	**59.0**	**2,342**	**7.2**	**18,597**	**36.4**	**29,084**	**72.1**	**2,312**	**7.4**	**8,932**	**22.1**
	Change on quarter	*193*	*0.3*	*-125*	*-0.4*	*42*	*0.0*	*171*	*0.3*	*-134*	*-0.4*	*8*	*0.0*
	Change %	*0.6*		*-5.1*		*0.2*		*0.6*		*-5.5*		*0.1*	
	Change on year	*396*	*0.3*	*-161*	*-0.6*	*165*	*0.0*	*307*	*0.6*	*-169*	*-0.6*	*-23*	*-0.1*
	Change %	*1.3*		*-6.5*		*0.9*		*1.1*		*-6.8*		*-0.3*	
Men		MGSA	MGSS	MGSD	MGSY	MGSJ	YBTD	YBSF	MGSV	YBSI	YBTJ	YBSO	YBTM
	Oct-Dec 2011	15,603	63.5	1,537	9.0	7,449	30.3	15,077	75.4	1,520	9.2	3,410	17.0
	Oct-Dec 2012	15,947	64.3	1,412	8.1	7,431	30.0	15,354	76.6	1,394	8.3	3,288	16.4
	Jan-Mar 2013	15,889	64.0	1,430	8.3	7,522	30.3	15,284	76.2	1,416	8.5	3,346	16.7
	Apr-Jun 2013	15,914	63.9	1,445	8.3	7,533	30.3	15,292	76.2	1,423	8.5	3,342	16.7
	Jul-Sep 2013	16,044	64.3	1,391	8.0	7,517	30.1	15,425	76.8	1,375	8.2	3,281	16.3
	Oct-Dec 2013	**16,144**	**64.5**	**1,326**	**7.6**	**7,549**	**30.2**	**15,507**	**77.1**	**1,309**	**7.8**	**3,298**	**16.4**
	Change on quarter	*100*	*0.2*	*-65*	*-0.4*	*31*	*0.0*	*82*	*0.3*	*-67*	*-0.4*	*17*	*0.1*
	Change %	*0.6*		*-4.7*		*0.4*		*0.5*		*-4.8*		*0.5*	
	Change on year	*197*	*0.2*	*-86*	*-0.5*	*118*	*0.2*	*153*	*0.5*	*-85*	*-0.5*	*10*	*0.0*
	Change %	*1.2*		*-6.1*		*1.6*		*1.0*		*-6.1*		*0.3*	
Women		MGSB	MGST	MGSE	MGSZ	MGSK	YBTE	LF2H	LF25	LF2J	LF2R	LF2N	LF2T
	Oct-Dec 2011	13,543	52.6	1,120	7.6	11,068	43.0	13,194	65.4	1,110	7.8	5,863	29.1
	Oct-Dec 2012	13,804	53.3	1,091	7.3	11,000	42.5	13,424	66.5	1,088	7.5	5,667	28.1
	Jan-Mar 2013	13,819	53.3	1,088	7.3	11,030	42.5	13,444	66.6	1,084	7.5	5,657	28.0
	Apr-Jun 2013	13,863	53.4	1,070	7.2	11,047	42.5	13,475	66.7	1,065	7.3	5,651	28.0
	Jul-Sep 2013	13,909	53.5	1,076	7.2	11,037	42.4	13,489	66.8	1,070	7.4	5,643	27.9
	Oct-Dec 2013	**14,003**	**53.7**	**1,016**	**6.8**	**11,048**	**42.4**	**13,577**	**67.2**	**1,003**	**6.9**	**5,634**	**27.9**
	Change on quarter	*93*	*0.3*	*-60*	*-0.4*	*11*	*0.0*	*89*	*0.4*	*-67*	*-0.5*	*-9*	*-0.1*
	Change %	*0.7*		*-5.6*		*0.1*		*0.7*		*-6.3*		*-0.2*	
	Change on year	*199*	*0.4*	*-76*	*-0.6*	*48*	*-0.1*	*154*	*0.6*	*-85*	*-0.6*	*-33*	*-0.2*
	Change %	*1.4*		*-6.9*		*0.4*		*1.1*		*-7.8*		*-0.6*	

| | | Aged 16-17 | | | | | | Aged 18-24 | | | | | |
| | | Employment | | Unemployment | | Inactivity | | Employment | | Unemployment | | Inactivity | |
		Level	Rate	Level	Rate	Level	Rate	Level	Rate	Level	Rate	Level	Rate
People		YBTO	YBUA	YBVH	YBVK	YCAS	LWEX	YBTR	YBUD	YBVN	YBVQ	YCAV	LWFA
	Oct-Dec 2011	345	23.4	211	37.9	921	62.4	3,295	56.6	822	20.0	1,703	29.3
	Oct-Dec 2012	327	22.3	197	37.6	941	64.2	3,393	58.7	778	18.6	1,613	27.9
	Jan-Mar 2013	317	21.7	190	37.5	958	65.4	3,357	58.2	768	18.6	1,644	28.5
	Apr-Jun 2013	317	21.7	196	38.1	952	65.0	3,265	56.7	778	19.2	1,713	29.8
	Jul-Sep 2013	321	22.0	182	36.2	960	65.6	3,311	57.6	782	19.1	1,654	28.8
	Oct-Dec 2013	**319**	**21.8**	**183**	**36.4**	**960**	**65.7**	**3,363**	**58.6**	**734**	**17.9**	**1,646**	**28.7**
	Change on quarter	*-2*	*-0.1*	*0*	*0.2*	*0*	*0.1*	*52*	*0.9*	*-48*	*-1.2*	*-9*	*-0.1*
	Change %	*-0.8*		*0.1*		*0.0*		*1.6*		*-6.1*		*-0.5*	
	Change on year	*-8*	*-0.5*	*-15*	*-1.2*	*19*	*1.5*	*-30*	*-0.1*	*-43*	*-0.7*	*32*	*0.8*
	Change %	*-2.5*		*-7.5*		*2.0*		*-0.9*		*-5.6*		*2.0*	
Men		YBTP	YBUB	YBVI	YBVL	YCAT	LWEY	YBTS	YBUE	YBVO	YBVR	YCAW	LWFB
	Oct-Dec 2011	159	21.0	109	40.7	488	64.5	1,691	57.2	514	23.3	751	25.4
	Oct-Dec 2012	140	18.7	108	43.6	502	66.9	1,747	59.5	462	20.9	726	24.7
	Jan-Mar 2013	141	18.9	100	41.5	508	67.7	1,734	59.2	445	20.4	750	25.6
	Apr-Jun 2013	142	18.9	103	42.2	505	67.3	1,676	57.4	463	21.7	781	26.8
	Jul-Sep 2013	142	19.0	95	40.1	510	68.2	1,705	58.4	466	21.5	747	25.6
	Oct-Dec 2013	**143**	**19.1**	**96**	**40.1**	**508**	**68.1**	**1,729**	**59.3**	**440**	**20.3**	**748**	**25.6**
	Change on quarter	*0*	*0.1*	*0*	*0.0*	*-3*	*-0.2*	*25*	*0.9*	*-26*	*-1.2*	*1*	*0.0*
	Change %	*0.2*		*0.3*		*-0.5*		*1.4*		*-5.6*		*0.1*	
	Change on year	*3*	*0.5*	*-13*	*-3.5*	*6*	*1.2*	*-18*	*-0.2*	*-23*	*-0.7*	*22*	*0.9*
	Change %	*2.1*		*-11.7*		*1.3*		*-1.0*		*-4.9*		*3.0*	
Women		YBTQ	YBUC	YBVJ	YBVM	YCAU	LWEZ	YBTT	YBUF	YBVP	YBVS	YCAX	LWFC
	Oct-Dec 2011	186	25.8	102	35.4	433	60.1	1,604	56.0	308	16.1	952	33.2
	Oct-Dec 2012	187	26.2	89	32.2	439	61.4	1,646	57.8	315	16.1	887	31.1
	Jan-Mar 2013	176	24.6	90	33.8	450	62.9	1,623	57.1	323	16.6	895	31.5
	Apr-Jun 2013	176	24.5	92	34.4	448	62.6	1,589	56.0	314	16.5	932	32.9
	Jul-Sep 2013	179	25.0	87	32.7	449	62.8	1,606	56.8	316	16.5	907	32.1
	Oct-Dec 2013	**176**	**24.6**	**87**	**33.1**	**452**	**63.2**	**1,634**	**57.8**	**295**	**15.3**	**897**	**31.8**
	Change on quarter	*-3*	*-0.4*	*0*	*0.3*	*2*	*0.4*	*27*	*1.0*	*-22*	*-1.2*	*-10*	*-0.3*
	Change %	*-1.5*		*-0.2*		*0.5*		*1.7*		*-6.8*		*-1.1*	
	Change on year	*-11*	*-1.5*	*-2*	*0.8*	*13*	*1.8*	*-12*	*0.0*	*-21*	*-0.8*	*10*	*0.6*
	Change %	*-5.9*		*-2.4*		*2.9*		*-0.8*		*-6.5*		*1.2*	

Source: Labour Force Survey

Labour market statistics enquiries: labour.market@ons.gsi.gov.uk

4.3 Employment: by sex and age: United Kingdom

United Kingdom (thousands) seasonally adjusted

| | | Aged 25-34 | | | | | | Aged 35-49 | | | | |
| | | Employment | | Unemployment | | Inactivity | | Employment | | Unemployment | | Inactivity | |
		Level	Rate	Level	Rate	Level	Rate	Level	Rate	Level	Rate	Level	Rate
People		YBTU	YBUG	YCGM	YCGP	YCAY	LWFD	YBTX	YBUJ	YCGS	YCGV	YCBB	LWFG
	Oct-Dec 2011	6,529	77.9	575	8.1	1,281	15.3	10,695	81.4	624	5.5	1,819	13.8
	Oct-Dec 2012	6,787	78.9	539	7.4	1,278	14.9	10,642	82.0	600	5.3	1,735	13.4
	Jan-Mar 2013	6,831	78.9	547	7.4	1,281	14.8	10,588	81.8	607	5.4	1,743	13.5
	Apr-Jun 2013	6,918	79.4	528	7.1	1,268	14.6	10,578	82.0	588	5.3	1,730	13.4
	Jul-Sep 2013	6,981	79.8	527	7.0	1,245	14.2	10,543	82.0	566	5.1	1,755	13.6
	Oct-Dec 2013	**7,010**	**79.8**	**506**	**6.7**	**1,267**	**14.4**	**10,530**	**82.0**	**528**	**4.8**	**1,779**	**13.9**
	Change on quarter	*30*	*0.1*	*-21*	*-0.3*	*21*	*0.2*	*-13*	*0.1*	*-38*	*-0.3*	*24*	*0.2*
	Change %	*0.4*		*-3.9*		*1.7*		*-0.1*		*-6.7*		*1.3*	
	Change on year	*223*	*0.9*	*-33*	*-0.6*	*-11*	*-0.4*	*-113*	*0.0*	*-72*	*-0.6*	*44*	*0.5*
	Change %	*3.3*		*-6.1*		*-0.9*		*-1.1*		*-12.0*		*2.5*	
Men		YBTV	YBUH	YCGN	YCGQ	YCAZ	LWFE	YBTY	YBUK	YCGT	YCGW	YCBC	LWFH
	Oct-Dec 2011	3,594	84.7	317	8.1	330	7.8	5,673	87.4	327	5.4	492	7.6
	Oct-Dec 2012	3,766	86.4	291	7.2	302	6.9	5,649	88.0	291	4.9	478	7.5
	Jan-Mar 2013	3,769	85.9	316	7.7	304	6.9	5,589	87.3	317	5.4	493	7.7
	Apr-Jun 2013	3,807	86.1	311	7.6	301	6.8	5,595	87.7	299	5.1	487	7.6
	Jul-Sep 2013	3,854	86.7	306	7.4	285	6.4	5,588	87.8	280	4.8	499	7.8
	Oct-Dec 2013	**3,875**	**86.8**	**298**	**7.1**	**294**	**6.6**	**5,582**	**87.9**	**263**	**4.5**	**508**	**8.0**
	Change on quarter	*21*	*0.0*	*-8*	*-0.2*	*9*	*0.2*	*-5*	*0.1*	*-16*	*-0.3*	*10*	*0.2*
	Change %	*0.6*		*-2.6*		*3.2*		*-0.1*		*-5.9*		*1.9*	
	Change on year	*109*	*0.4*	*7*	*0.0*	*-8*	*-0.4*	*-67*	*-0.2*	*-28*	*-0.4*	*30*	*0.5*
	Change %	*2.9*		*2.3*		*-2.8*		*-1.2*		*-9.5*		*6.2*	
Women		YBTW	YBUI	YCGO	YCGR	YCBA	LWFF	YBTZ	YBUL	YCGU	YCGX	YCBD	LWFI
	Oct-Dec 2011	2,935	70.8	258	8.1	952	23.0	5,022	75.6	298	5.6	1,327	20.0
	Oct-Dec 2012	3,021	71.2	248	7.6	976	23.0	4,994	76.1	309	5.8	1,257	19.2
	Jan-Mar 2013	3,062	71.7	231	7.0	977	22.9	4,998	76.5	290	5.5	1,250	19.1
	Apr-Jun 2013	3,111	72.4	217	6.5	967	22.5	4,983	76.5	290	5.5	1,243	19.1
	Jul-Sep 2013	3,127	72.6	221	6.6	961	22.3	4,955	76.3	286	5.5	1,257	19.3
	Oct-Dec 2013	**3,135**	**72.6**	**208**	**6.2**	**973**	**22.5**	**4,948**	**76.3**	**264**	**5.1**	**1,271**	**19.6**
	Change on quarter	*8*	*0.1*	*-13*	*-0.4*	*12*	*0.2*	*-8*	*0.1*	*-21*	*-0.4*	*14*	*0.3*
	Change %	*0.3*		*-5.7*		*1.3*		*-0.2*		*-7.5*		*1.1*	
	Change on year	*114*	*1.5*	*-40*	*-1.4*	*-3*	*-0.4*	*-46*	*0.2*	*-45*	*-0.8*	*14*	*0.4*
	Change %	*3.8*		*-16.1*		*-0.3*		*-0.9*		*-14.4*		*1.1*	

| | | Aged 50-64 | | | | | | Age 65+ | | | | |
| | | Employment | | Unemployment | | Inactivity | | Employment | | Unemployment | | Inactivity | |
		Level	Rate	Level	Rate	Level	Rate	Level	Rate	Level	Rate	Level	Rate
People		LF26	LF2U	LF28	LF2E	LF2A	LF2W	LFK4	LFK6	K5HU	K5HW	LFL4	LFL6
	Oct-Dec 2011	7,408	65.2	398	5.1	3,549	31.3	874	8.6	26	2.9	9,244	91.1
	Oct-Dec 2012	7,628	67.0	367	4.6	3,388	29.8	973	9.3	22	2.2	9,476	90.5
	Jan-Mar 2013	7,634	67.0	388	4.8	3,377	29.6	980	9.3	18	1.8	9,549	90.5
	Apr-Jun 2013	7,689	67.3	398	4.9	3,330	29.2	1,010	9.5	26	2.5	9,587	90.2
	Jul-Sep 2013	7,758	67.7	389	4.8	3,309	28.9	1,040	9.7	21	2.0	9,631	90.1
	Oct-Dec 2013	**7,862**	**68.3**	**361**	**4.4**	**3,281**	**28.5**	**1,062**	**9.9**	**30**	**2.7**	**9,665**	**89.9**
	Change on quarter	*105*	*0.6*	*-27*	*-0.4*	*-28*	*-0.4*	*22*	*0.1*	*9*	*0.7*	*34*	*-0.2*
	Change %	*1.3*		*-7.1*		*-0.8*		*2.1*		*42.1*		*0.4*	
	Change on year	*234*	*1.3*	*-6*	*-0.2*	*-107*	*-1.2*	*89*	*0.6*	*8*	*0.5*	*188*	*-0.6*
	Change %	*3.1*		*-1.6*		*-3.2*		*9.1*		*36.7*		*2.0*	
Men		MGUX	YBUN	MGVM	MGXF	MGWB	LWFK	MGVA	YBUQ	MGVP	MGXI	MGWE	LWFN
	Oct-Dec 2011	3,961	71.2	253	6.0	1,349	24.3	526	11.5	17	3.1	4,039	88.2
	Oct-Dec 2012	4,052	72.7	241	5.6	1,279	23.0	593	12.5	18	2.9	4,143	87.1
	Jan-Mar 2013	4,049	72.6	238	5.6	1,291	23.1	605	12.6	13	2.1	4,176	87.1
	Apr-Jun 2013	4,072	72.9	246	5.7	1,268	22.7	622	12.9	22	3.4	4,191	86.7
	Jul-Sep 2013	4,137	73.8	228	5.2	1,240	22.1	619	12.7	15	2.4	4,236	87.0
	Oct-Dec 2013	**4,177**	**74.2**	**212**	**4.8**	**1,240**	**22.0**	**637**	**13.0**	**17**	**2.6**	**4,251**	**86.7**
	Change on quarter	*41*	*0.4*	*-16*	*-0.4*	*0*	*-0.1*	*18*	*0.3*	*2*	*0.2*	*14*	*-0.3*
	Change %	*1.0*		*-7.0*		*0.0*		*2.9*		*11.2*		*0.3*	
	Change on year	*126*	*1.5*	*-29*	*-0.8*	*-39*	*-0.9*	*44*	*0.5*	*-1*	*-0.3*	*107*	*-0.5*
	Change %	*3.1*		*-11.8*		*-3.1*		*7.3*		*-5.1*		*2.6*	
Women		LF27	LF2V	LF29	LF2F	LF2B	LF2X	LFK5	LFK7	K5HV	K5HX	LFL5	LFL7
	Oct-Dec 2011	3,447	59.5	145	4.0	2,199	38.0	348	6.3	*	*	5,205	93.6
	Oct-Dec 2012	3,576	61.5	126	3.4	2,109	36.3	380	6.6	*	*	5,333	93.3
	Jan-Mar 2013	3,585	61.6	150	4.0	2,086	35.8	375	6.5	*	*	5,373	93.4
	Apr-Jun 2013	3,617	62.0	152	4.0	2,061	35.4	388	6.7	*	*	5,396	93.2
	Jul-Sep 2013	3,621	61.9	160	4.2	2,069	35.4	421	7.2	*	*	5,394	92.7
	Oct-Dec 2013	**3,685**	**62.7**	**149**	**3.9**	**2,041**	**34.7**	**425**	**7.3**	**12**	**2.8**	**5,414**	**92.5**
	Change on quarter	*64*	*0.8*	*-11*	*-0.4*	*-28*	*-0.6*	*4*	*0.0*	*	*	*20*	*-0.2*
	Change %	*1.8*		*-7.1*		*-1.4*		*1.1*		*		*0.4*	
	Change on year	*109*	*1.2*	*23*	*0.5*	*-68*	*-1.5*	*45*	*0.6*	*	*	*81*	*-0.8*
	Change %	*3.0*		*17.9*		*-3.2*		*11.9*		*		*1.5*	

Source: Labour Force Survey

Labour market statistics enquiries: labour.market@ons.gsi.gov.uk

4.4: All in employment by industry sector

Standard Industrial Classification (SIC) 2007 [1]

People

	All in employment[2]	Public sector[3]	Private sector	Agriculture, forestry & fishing	Mining, energy and water supply	Manufacturing	Construction	Wholesale, retail & repair of motor vehicles	Transport & storage	Accommodation and food services	Information & communication	Financial & insurance activities	Real estate activities	Professional, scientific & technical activities	Administrative & support services	Public admin & defence; social security	Education	Human health & social work activities	Other services
				A	B, D, E	C	F	G	H	I	J	K	L	M	N	O	P	Q	R, S, T
Jan-Mar 2004	28,327	6,768	21,423	260	368	3,379	2,295	4,240	1,517	1,331	1,044	1,215	228	1,753	1,253	1,882	2,695	3,327	1,460
Apr-Jun 2004	28,361	6,819	21,421	263	376	3,312	2,310	4,243	1,514	1,319	1,045	1,205	244	1,719	1,265	1,888	2,717	3,392	1,465
Jul-Sep 2004	28,577	6,853	21,605	273	409	3,384	2,370	4,250	1,521	1,335	1,048	1,200	234	1,692	1,297	1,945	2,668	3,408	1,455
Oct-Dec 2004	28,668	6,859	21,660	271	400	3,364	2,399	4,324	1,531	1,304	1,027	1,190	242	1,719	1,319	1,917	2,711	3,409	1,452
Jan-Mar 2005	28,635	6,932	21,554	288	399	3,294	2,392	4,249	1,530	1,303	1,025	1,217	224	1,732	1,346	1,945	2,725	3,456	1,411
Apr-Jun 2005	28,658	6,894	21,644	283	397	3,322	2,378	4,207	1,553	1,320	1,011	1,208	239	1,751	1,332	1,930	2,759	3,465	1,429
Jul-Sep 2005	28,953	6,992	21,846	282	404	3,302	2,453	4,235	1,570	1,283	1,021	1,286	248	1,778	1,320	1,973	2,709	3,556	1,446
Oct-Dec 2005	28,844	7,007	21,720	287	413	3,244	2,405	4,196	1,586	1,270	1,019	1,278	256	1,813	1,294	1,957	2,744	3,543	1,442
Jan-Mar 2006	28,863	7,095	21,667	272	402	3,225	2,425	4,156	1,556	1,290	1,011	1,268	252	1,828	1,270	2,009	2,823	3,558	1,421
Apr-Jun 2006	28,923	7,060	21,751	267	412	3,267	2,455	4,111	1,546	1,343	1,021	1,255	262	1,800	1,274	1,978	2,836	3,560	1,442
Jul-Sep 2006	29,174	6,980	22,087	291	422	3,260	2,505	4,146	1,565	1,384	1,042	1,249	247	1,818	1,316	1,959	2,745	3,608	1,525
Oct-Dec 2006	29,151	6,901	22,130	301	433	3,214	2,536	4,189	1,576	1,330	1,054	1,266	246	1,817	1,322	1,951	2,797	3,499	1,504
Jan-Mar 2007	28,976	6,914	21,949	287	447	3,195	2,519	4,109	1,558	1,323	1,052	1,259	255	1,867	1,297	1,968	2,782	3,478	1,469
Apr-Jun 2007	29,096	6,942	22,031	293	461	3,260	2,535	4,022	1,549	1,371	1,046	1,267	244	1,874	1,338	1,970	2,805	3,435	1,510
Jul-Sep 2007	29,370	6,868	22,363	295	465	3,247	2,549	4,076	1,547	1,407	1,058	1,300	265	1,902	1,420	1,974	2,763	3,478	1,508
Oct-Dec 2007	29,475	6,964	22,368	305	457	3,193	2,528	4,172	1,565	1,396	1,015	1,306	278	1,944	1,388	1,979	2,819	3,503	1,512
Jan-Mar 2008	29,417	6,992	22,280	332	448	3,124	2,523	4,164	1,592	1,381	1,019	1,282	262	1,930	1,385	1,993	2,828	3,538	1,505
Apr-Jun 2008	29,448	7,046	22,250	319	443	3,065	2,501	4,176	1,577	1,352	1,028	1,280	253	1,957	1,403	2,017	2,841	3,610	1,511
Jul-Sep 2008	29,497	6,980	22,380	311	460	3,046	2,573	4,230	1,593	1,351	1,059	1,266	258	1,909	1,393	2,012	2,785	3,615	1,524
Oct-Dec 2008	29,399	7,108	22,155	305	505	2,958	2,553	4,204	1,610	1,329	1,030	1,241	250	1,841	1,336	2,016	2,828	3,716	1,572
Jan-Mar 2009	29,074	7,165	21,771	320	486	2,831	2,470	4,088	1,556	1,317	1,027	1,224	272	1,833	1,300	1,990	2,897	3,739	1,566
Apr-Jun 2009	28,809	7,179	21,489	309	480	2,752	2,375	3,972	1,496	1,352	1,007	1,233	266	1,872	1,293	1,950	2,904	3,706	1,572
Jul-Sep 2009	28,972	7,216	21,609	327	488	2,790	2,302	4,015	1,450	1,420	1,011	1,243	263	1,880	1,290	1,960	2,937	3,744	1,586
Oct-Dec 2009	28,964	7,260	21,554	321	478	2,777	2,303	3,998	1,444	1,399	1,005	1,218	252	1,875	1,315	1,928	3,019	3,812	1,567
Jan-Mar 2010	28,712	7,192	21,341	334	467	2,791	2,201	3,920	1,448	1,381	1,002	1,207	261	1,872	1,305	1,915	3,036	3,787	1,537
Apr-Jun 2010	28,901	7,264	21,440	339	458	2,854	2,203	3,979	1,432	1,452	969	1,172	260	1,883	1,312	1,910	3,104	3,810	1,521
Jul-Sep 2010	29,279	7,240	21,828	367	470	2,868	2,228	4,083	1,474	1,492	1,036	1,165	299	1,840	1,327	1,909	3,095	3,787	1,583
Oct-Dec 2010	29,182	7,219	21,781	365	485	2,882	2,230	4,052	1,427	1,418	1,023	1,168	297	1,872	1,367	1,853	3,093	3,849	1,541
Jan-Mar 2011	29,134	7,254	21,688	355	494	2,840	2,201	4,004	1,442	1,407	1,052	1,176	296	1,847	1,287	1,860	3,095	3,932	1,527
Apr-Jun 2011	29,157	7,125	21,870	341	518	2,849	2,188	4,021	1,435	1,446	1,068	1,171	304	1,840	1,309	1,830	3,103	3,897	1,574
Jul-Sep 2011	29,171	6,953	22,068	367	516	2,824	2,227	3,990	1,417	1,488	1,054	1,190	298	1,876	1,327	1,839	2,959	3,947	1,628
Oct-Dec 2011	29,205	6,916	22,132	354	525	2,868	2,165	4,054	1,420	1,487	1,079	1,214	290	1,885	1,340	1,852	2,991	3,895	1,569
Jan-Mar 2012	29,178	6,898	22,077	372	533	2,835	2,141	3,993	1,421	1,426	1,118	1,198	331	1,893	1,357	1,835	3,061	3,832	1,542
Apr-Jun 2012	29,414	6,798	22,394	352	531	2,907	2,165	4,081	1,406	1,483	1,093	1,228	326	1,933	1,348	1,794	3,055	3,838	1,562
Jul-Sep 2012	29,692	6,839	22,608	355	547	2,922	2,170	4,108	1,448	1,514	1,106	1,218	328	1,974	1,363	1,818	2,997	3,918	1,596
Oct-Dec 2012	29,816	6,937	22,642	316	518	2,898	2,147	4,083	1,473	1,511	1,140	1,169	344	1,960	1,366	1,815	3,119	3,963	1,579
Jan-Mar 2013	29,600	6,943	22,401	303	535	2,912	2,100	4,012	1,479	1,492	1,153	1,150	342	1,993	1,346	1,842	3,091	3,959	1,575
Apr-Jun 2013	29,721	6,922	22,543	307	524	2,859	2,154	4,008	1,447	1,497	1,156	1,145	342	2,012	1,415	1,856	3,078	4,004	1,579
Jul-Sep 2013	30,068	6,968	22,851	323	509	2,949	2,185	3,985	1,512	1,562	1,172	1,179	325	2,061	1,445	1,871	3,057	4,010	1,631
Oct-Dec 2013	**30,241**	**6,863**	**23,147**	**321**	**510**	**2,951**	**2,203**	**4,083**	**1,535**	**1,548**	**1,195**	**1,171**	**340**	**2,085**	**1,431**	**1,810**	**3,074**	**4,039**	**1,629**
Change on year	425	-75	505	5	-8	52	56	0	63	37	55	3	-4	125	64	-4	-45	76	49
Change %	1.4	-1.1	2.2	1.7	-1.5	1.8	2.6	0.0	4.2	2.5	4.8	0.2	-1.3	6.4	4.7	-0.2	-1.4	1.9	3.1

4.4: All in employment by industry sector

United Kingdom (thousands) not seasonally adjusted

Standard Industrial Classification (SIC) 2007 [1]

Men

	All in employment[2]	Public sector[3]	Private sector	Agriculture, forestry & fishing	Mining, energy and water supply	Manufacturing	Construction	Wholesale, retail & repair of motor vehicles	Transport & storage	Accommodation and food services	Information & communication	Financial & insurance activities	Real estate activities	Professional, scientific & technical activities	Administrative & support services	Public admin & defence; social security	Education	Human health & social work activities	Other services
				A	B, D, E	C	F	G	H	I	J	K	L	M	N	O	P	Q	R, S, T
Jan-Mar 2004	15,289	2,431	12,787	198	289	2,589	2,009	2,120	1,247	578	723	605	114	993	700	981	787	657	650
Apr-Jun 2004	15,323	2,449	12,803	200	293	2,528	2,016	2,145	1,241	593	729	593	127	984	704	976	768	705	667
Jul-Sep 2004	15,492	2,460	12,964	199	320	2,595	2,072	2,154	1,241	598	733	587	124	954	720	999	756	718	667
Oct-Dec 2004	15,504	2,412	13,011	196	315	2,581	2,085	2,199	1,251	581	714	584	129	973	730	972	748	737	655
Jan-Mar 2005	15,443	2,478	12,882	209	316	2,521	2,076	2,128	1,237	593	715	610	117	986	735	994	753	755	639
Apr-Jun 2005	15,461	2,464	12,927	200	318	2,538	2,062	2,131	1,250	600	713	611	127	997	741	973	764	753	638
Jul-Sep 2005	15,635	2,528	13,036	201	323	2,528	2,133	2,141	1,274	568	721	638	127	993	754	1,009	768	748	650
Oct-Dec 2005	15,585	2,521	12,992	213	337	2,485	2,098	2,113	1,292	585	717	638	132	1,024	735	993	781	738	643
Jan-Mar 2006	15,513	2,552	12,894	198	320	2,479	2,101	2,080	1,255	589	722	640	134	1,022	712	1,010	806	752	629
Apr-Jun 2006	15,575	2,522	12,988	199	321	2,495	2,123	2,086	1,257	608	727	640	144	998	705	989	814	748	664
Jul-Sep 2006	15,791	2,504	13,223	217	326	2,479	2,179	2,144	1,260	634	741	631	124	1,027	710	991	782	775	713
Oct-Dec 2006	15,757	2,440	13,253	220	335	2,450	2,207	2,160	1,256	584	750	647	130	1,023	732	985	792	728	689
Jan-Mar 2007	15,657	2,426	13,172	203	344	2,438	2,205	2,137	1,237	591	756	664	125	1,023	733	996	767	713	662
Apr-Jun 2007	15,750	2,447	13,231	207	357	2,492	2,209	2,086	1,238	623	748	660	116	1,023	768	986	784	705	685
Jul-Sep 2007	15,923	2,410	13,437	213	361	2,449	2,237	2,105	1,239	653	754	683	127	1,050	823	997	780	699	688
Oct-Dec 2007	15,943	2,431	13,435	208	355	2,414	2,219	2,131	1,260	653	712	704	134	1,064	819	1,013	795	716	680
Jan-Mar 2008	15,885	2,470	13,335	221	349	2,364	2,196	2,131	1,284	635	721	693	130	1,059	800	1,032	783	752	667
Apr-Jun 2008	15,909	2,496	13,332	220	347	2,340	2,173	2,143	1,265	637	730	675	131	1,080	819	1,046	778	796	660
Jul-Sep 2008	15,944	2,475	13,388	217	368	2,302	2,241	2,178	1,266	624	752	650	142	1,065	800	1,030	738	801	705
Oct-Dec 2008	15,861	2,526	13,257	218	407	2,239	2,225	2,164	1,282	617	743	633	137	1,022	771	1,021	775	826	716
Jan-Mar 2009	15,618	2,561	12,979	246	389	2,128	2,204	2,104	1,246	605	719	627	132	1,069	713	997	801	824	719
Apr-Jun 2009	15,417	2,547	12,791	239	382	2,085	2,120	2,057	1,199	621	713	639	123	1,104	709	980	787	809	711
Jul-Sep 2009	15,482	2,561	12,834	251	387	2,113	2,059	2,091	1,163	648	722	646	122	1,093	693	991	827	802	725
Oct-Dec 2009	15,434	2,569	12,782	245	380	2,108	2,065	2,070	1,165	636	719	639	114	1,065	703	989	864	816	719
Jan-Mar 2010	15,282	2,523	12,660	251	376	2,139	1,967	2,038	1,171	647	706	631	118	1,091	703	979	853	788	693
Apr-Jun 2010	15,455	2,569	12,775	262	370	2,194	1,959	2,093	1,153	683	688	626	113	1,093	720	999	862	806	698
Jul-Sep 2010	15,736	2,593	13,016	282	378	2,200	1,989	2,157	1,167	687	746	628	131	1,069	755	990	871	801	736
Oct-Dec 2010	15,678	2,573	13,002	281	392	2,203	1,985	2,144	1,127	669	747	644	129	1,096	784	946	840	848	701
Jan-Mar 2011	15,569	2,571	12,890	269	410	2,168	1,947	2,111	1,160	643	755	650	131	1,091	721	959	845	849	693
Apr-Jun 2011	15,637	2,537	13,012	261	426	2,160	1,932	2,107	1,164	652	766	649	142	1,101	748	909	885	857	723
Jul-Sep 2011	15,624	2,443	13,104	270	420	2,159	1,997	2,079	1,141	680	752	654	153	1,105	738	902	837	845	759
Oct-Dec 2011	15,636	2,428	13,130	260	422	2,189	1,934	2,123	1,145	711	788	659	149	1,104	730	920	832	840	711
Jan-Mar 2012	15,619	2,421	13,089	269	433	2,145	1,905	2,091	1,152	678	810	640	176	1,117	740	911	865	819	694
Apr-Jun 2012	15,804	2,359	13,311	256	435	2,198	1,924	2,155	1,135	672	801	665	162	1,144	746	890	868	833	733
Jul-Sep 2012	15,961	2,387	13,415	256	440	2,215	1,939	2,162	1,168	680	803	677	156	1,152	753	922	851	837	744
Oct-Dec 2012	15,978	2,406	13,421	236	405	2,193	1,916	2,161	1,184	675	814	647	164	1,140	764	952	899	852	723
Jan-Mar 2013	15,799	2,379	13,259	219	417	2,224	1,859	2,084	1,196	693	826	641	169	1,180	745	956	865	829	705
Apr-Jun 2013	15,890	2,360	13,373	234	418	2,196	1,894	2,097	1,170	700	847	640	163	1,182	783	955	835	849	714
Jul-Sep 2013	16,135	2,404	13,585	236	400	2,242	1,910	2,115	1,223	752	850	657	148	1,209	807	957	857	861	738
Oct-Dec 2013	**16,196**	**2,324**	**13,744**	**234**	**409**	**2,227**	**1,940**	**2,131**	**1,247**	**734**	**844**	**659**	**144**	**1,242**	**805**	**920**	**848**	**860**	**763**
Change on year	218	-81	323	-2	5	34	24	-30	63	59	29	13	-19	102	42	-32	-51	7	40
Change %	1.4	-3.4	2.4	-1.0	1.1	1.5	1.3	-1.4	5.3	8.7	3.6	1.9	-11.8	9.0	5.5	-3.4	-5.7	0.9	5.5

4.4: All in employment by industry sector

United Kingdom (thousands) not seasonally adjusted

Standard Industrial Classification (SIC) 2007 [1]

Women	All in employment [2]	Public sector [3]	Private sector	Agriculture, forestry & fishing A	Mining, energy and water supply B, D, E	Manufacturing C	Construction F	Wholesale, retail & repair of motor vehicles G	Transport & storage H	Accommodation and food services I	Information & communication J	Financial & insurance activities K	Real estate activities L	Professional, scientific & technical activities M	Administrative & support services N	Public admin & defence; social security O	Education P	Human health & social work activities Q	Other services R, S, T
Jan-Mar 2004	13,038	4,336	8,636	62	79	790	286	2,120	270	753	321	610	114	760	552	901	1,908	2,669	809
Apr-Jun 2004	13,038	4,370	8,618	63	83	785	294	2,098	273	726	317	612	117	735	560	912	1,948	2,687	798
Jul-Sep 2004	13,085	4,393	8,640	74	88	789	297	2,095	280	737	316	612	111	738	577	946	1,912	2,690	788
Oct-Dec 2004	13,165	4,447	8,649	75	85	782	314	2,124	281	722	313	606	113	746	589	945	1,963	2,671	797
Jan-Mar 2005	13,191	4,454	8,672	79	83	773	316	2,121	293	711	309	607	107	746	611	951	1,971	2,701	772
Apr-Jun 2005	13,196	4,430	8,717	83	78	784	316	2,076	303	719	298	597	113	755	592	957	1,995	2,711	791
Jul-Sep 2005	13,319	4,465	8,811	82	81	774	320	2,094	296	715	299	648	121	785	566	964	1,941	2,808	796
Oct-Dec 2005	13,259	4,486	8,727	74	76	759	307	2,083	294	685	302	640	124	790	559	964	1,963	2,805	798
Jan-Mar 2006	13,350	4,542	8,773	67	82	746	324	2,076	301	701	289	628	118	806	558	1,000	2,017	2,807	792
Apr-Jun 2006	13,348	4,538	8,764	75	91	772	332	2,025	289	734	294	615	118	802	569	989	2,022	2,812	778
Jul-Sep 2006	13,383	4,477	8,865	75	95	781	325	2,001	305	750	301	619	122	790	605	968	1,962	2,834	812
Oct-Dec 2006	13,394	4,461	8,877	81	98	764	329	2,028	320	745	303	619	116	795	591	966	2,005	2,771	816
Jan-Mar 2007	13,319	4,487	8,776	84	103	757	314	1,972	320	732	296	595	130	844	564	971	2,016	2,765	807
Apr-Jun 2007	13,346	4,494	8,800	86	104	768	325	1,937	311	748	299	607	127	851	570	985	2,021	2,730	825
Jul-Sep 2007	13,447	4,458	8,926	83	105	797	311	1,971	308	754	305	617	138	852	598	977	1,982	2,779	820
Oct-Dec 2007	13,532	4,534	8,932	97	102	779	309	2,040	305	742	303	602	144	880	568	966	2,025	2,787	832
Jan-Mar 2008	13,531	4,522	8,945	111	99	761	328	2,034	308	745	298	589	132	871	585	962	2,045	2,785	838
Apr-Jun 2008	13,539	4,550	8,918	98	96	725	328	2,033	312	715	299	605	121	877	584	972	2,064	2,814	851
Jul-Sep 2008	13,554	4,505	8,992	94	92	744	332	2,052	327	727	307	617	116	844	593	983	2,047	2,814	819
Oct-Dec 2008	13,538	4,582	8,898	87	97	719	327	2,040	329	712	288	608	114	818	565	996	2,053	2,891	856
Jan-Mar 2009	13,456	4,604	8,792	75	97	704	266	1,984	311	712	307	597	140	764	587	994	2,096	2,914	847
Apr-Jun 2009	13,391	4,632	8,698	71	98	667	255	1,915	298	731	293	594	143	768	584	971	2,117	2,897	861
Jul-Sep 2009	13,490	4,656	8,775	76	101	678	243	1,924	287	772	289	597	142	786	597	970	2,110	2,942	861
Oct-Dec 2009	13,531	4,692	8,771	76	97	669	238	1,928	279	762	286	579	138	810	613	939	2,155	2,996	848
Jan-Mar 2010	13,431	4,669	8,682	83	91	653	235	1,882	277	734	295	575	143	782	602	935	2,183	2,999	845
Apr-Jun 2010	13,446	4,695	8,665	77	88	660	244	1,885	279	769	281	546	147	790	591	911	2,242	3,004	823
Jul-Sep 2010	13,544	4,646	8,812	85	92	667	240	1,927	307	805	290	537	168	772	572	919	2,224	2,986	847
Oct-Dec 2010	13,504	4,646	8,779	83	94	679	245	1,908	300	749	275	525	168	775	583	907	2,253	3,001	840
Jan-Mar 2011	13,565	4,683	8,797	86	84	673	254	1,893	281	764	298	526	165	755	566	902	2,250	3,083	835
Apr-Jun 2011	13,520	4,588	8,858	80	92	688	256	1,914	271	795	301	523	162	739	561	920	2,218	3,040	850
Jul-Sep 2011	13,546	4,510	8,964	98	96	665	230	1,911	276	807	302	536	145	771	588	937	2,122	3,102	869
Oct-Dec 2011	13,569	4,488	9,002	94	103	680	231	1,931	275	776	291	555	141	781	610	932	2,158	3,056	858
Jan-Mar 2012	13,559	4,477	8,988	100	100	690	235	1,902	270	748	308	558	155	776	617	924	2,196	3,013	847
Apr-Jun 2012	13,610	4,439	9,083	95	96	709	241	1,926	271	810	292	562	165	789	602	904	2,187	3,005	829
Jul-Sep 2012	13,730	4,452	9,193	99	107	707	230	1,947	280	834	304	540	172	822	610	896	2,146	3,080	852
Oct-Dec 2012	13,839	4,532	9,221	99	113	705	232	1,922	288	836	326	522	181	820	603	862	2,219	3,111	857
Jan-Mar 2013	13,801	4,564	9,142	80	118	688	242	1,928	282	800	327	508	173	813	601	886	2,226	3,130	870
Apr-Jun 2013	13,831	4,562	9,170	84	106	664	260	1,912	277	797	308	505	179	830	632	901	2,243	3,155	866
Jul-Sep 2013	13,932	4,564	9,266	73	110	707	275	1,870	289	809	322	522	176	852	638	915	2,200	3,149	893
Oct-Dec 2013	**14,045**	**4,538**	**9,403**	**87**	**100**	**724**	**263**	**1,952**	**288**	**814**	**351**	**512**	**195**	**843**	**625**	**890**	**2,226**	**3,179**	**866**
Change on year	207	6	182	8	-12	18	31	30	-1	-21	25	-10	15	22	22	28	6	68	9
Change %	1.5	0.1	2.0	9.4	-11.0	2.6	13.5	1.6	-0.2	-2.5	7.8	-1.9	8.2	2.7	3.7	3.2	0.3	2.2	1.1

Source: Labour Force Survey

[1] The breakdown by industry sector for Q1 2009 onwards is not entirely consistent with those of previous quarters. This is because:
(a) LFS data on industrial activity were coded directly to SIC 1992 for all quarters up to and including Q4 2008 and then mapped to the new industrial classification, SIC 2007, according to the assumed relationship between the two classifications;
(b) data for Q1 2009 onwards have been coded directly to SIC 2007; and
(c) a new, automatic coding tool was introduced in January 2009.

The effect of these changes on the time series was significant for some of the industry sectors shown. **Consequently some adjustments have been made to the pre-2009 estimates to account for the estimated combined effects of the new classification and the new coding tool.** This also means that the pre-2009 estimates in this table are not the same as those obtained from LFS microdata.

More information and analysis of these effects are available in the Labour Force Survey User Guide (Volume 1) and from Labour Force Assessment Branch (tel 01633 455839 or email labour.market.assessment@ons.gov.uk).

[2] Includes people with workplace outside UK and those who did not state their industry.

[3] In the LFS the distinction between public and private sector is based on respondents' views about the organisation for which they work. The public sector estimates provided here do not correspond to the official Public Sector Employment estimates which are based on National Accounts definitions.

4.5a International comparisons

		Latest period	Employment rate (%)[1][2]	Change on year %			Latest Period	Unemployment rate (%)[3]	Change on period %[6]	Change on year %
Employment rates as published by EUROSTAT: (not seasonally adjusted)					**Unemployment rates as published by EUROSTAT on 31 January 2014 (seasonally adjusted)**					
European Union (EU)					**European Union (EU)**					
Austria	YXSN	Jul-Sep 13	73.3	-0.3	Austria	ZXDS	Dec 13	4.9	0.1	0.2
Belgium	YXSO	Jul-Sep 13	62.3	0.2	Belgium	ZXDI	Dec 13	8.4	0.0	0.3
Bulgaria	A495	Jul-Sep 13	61.1	0.5	Bulgaria	A492	Dec 13	13.1	0.1	0.5
Croatia	GUMI	Jul-Sep 13	50.2	-2.3	Croatia	GUMJ	Dec 13	18.6	0.0	0.9
Cyprus	A4AC	Jul-Sep 13	61.8	-2.8	Cyprus	A4AN	Dec 13	17.5	0.2	3.6
Czech Republic	A4AD	Jul-Sep 13	68.0	0.9	Czech Republic	A4AO	Dec 13	6.7	-0.1	-0.5
Denmark	YXSP	Jul-Sep 13	73.0	0.2	Denmark	ZXDJ	Dec 13	6.9	0.1	-0.4
Estonia	A4AE	Jul-Sep 13	68.5	0.4	Estonia	A4AP	Nov 13	9.3	0.2	-0.4
Finland	YXSQ	Jul-Sep 13	69.9	-0.8	Finland	ZXDU	Dec 13	8.4	0.0	0.5
France	YXSR	Jul-Sep 13	64.5	0.1	France	ZXDN	Dec 13	10.8	0.0	0.1
Germany	YXSS	Jul-Sep 13	73.6	0.4	Germany	ZXDK	Dec 13	5.1	0.0	-0.3
Greece	YXST	Jul-Sep 13	49.6	-1.4	Greece	ZXDL	Oct 13	27.8	0.1	1.7
Hungary	A4AF	Jul-Sep 13	59.2	1.0	Hungary	A4AQ	Nov 13	9.3	-0.2	-1.7
Ireland	YXSU	Jul-Sep 13	61.1	2.1	Ireland	ZXDO	Dec 13	12.1	-0.2	-1.9
Italy	YXSV	Jul-Sep 13	55.6	-1.3	Italy	ZXDP	Dec 13	12.7	-0.1	1.2
Latvia	A4AG	Jul-Sep 13	66.0	1.6	Latvia	A4AR	Q3 2013	12.1	0.5	-1.9
Lithuania	A4AH	Jul-Sep 13	64.5	1.4	Lithuania	A4AS	Dec 13	11.4	0.3	-1.6
Luxembourg	YXSW	Jul-Sep 13	66.0	-0.6	Luxembourg	ZXDQ	Dec 13	6.2	0.1	0.8
Malta	A4AI	Jul-Sep 13	61.3	1.7	Malta	A4AT	Dec 13	6.7	0.2	0.3
Netherlands	YXSX	Jul-Sep 13	74.4	-0.9	Netherlands	ZXDR	Dec 13	7.0	0.1	1.2
Poland	A4AJ	Jul-Sep 13	60.7	0.5	Poland	A4AU	Dec 13	10.1	-0.1	-0.3
Portugal	YXSY	Jul-Sep 13	61.6	-0.4	Portugal	ZXDT	Dec 13	15.4	-0.1	-1.9
Romania	A494	Jul-Sep 13	61.0	0.2	Romania	A48Z	Dec 13	7.1	-0.2	0.4
Slovak Republic	A4AK	Jul-Sep 13	60.0	-0.1	Slovak Republic	A4AV	Dec 13	13.8	-0.2	-0.6
Slovenia	A4AL	Jul-Sep 13	64.5	0.2	Slovenia	A4AW	Dec 13	10.1	0.2	0.4
Spain	YXSZ	Jul-Sep 13	54.7	-0.9	Spain	ZXDM	Dec 13	25.8	-0.3	-0.5
Sweden	YXTA	Jul-Sep 13	75.8	0.8	Sweden	ZXDV	Dec 13	8.0	0.0	0.0
United Kingdom	ANZ6	Jul-Sep 13	71.1	0.6	United Kingdom[4]	ZXDW	Oct 13	7.2	-0.1	-0.5
Total EU[5]	**A496**	**Jul-Sep 13**	**64.5**	**0.0**	**Total EU[5]**	**A493**	**Dec 13**	**10.7**	**-0.1**	**-0.1**
Eurozone[5]	YXTC	Jul-Sep 13	63.8	-0.3	Eurozone[5]	ZXDH	Dec 13	12.0	0.0	0.1
Employment rates as published by national statistical offices					**Unemployment rates as published by national statistical offices (seasonally adjusted)**					
Canada (NSA)	IUUK	Oct-Dec 13	72.3	-0.1	Canada	ZXDZ	Jan 14	7.0	-0.2	0.0
Japan (NSA)	YXTF	Oct-Dec 13	72.3	1.4	Japan	ZXDY	Dec 13	3.7	-0.3	-0.6
United Kingdom (SA)	LF24	Oct-Dec 13	72.1	0.6	United Kingdom[4]	MGSX	Oct-Dec 13	7.2	-0.4	-0.6
United States (NSA)	YXTE	Oct-Dec 13	67.5	0.0	United States	ZXDX	Jan 14	6.6	-0.1	-1.3

Sources: Eurostat, national statistical offices. Labour market statistics enquiries: labour.market@ons.gsi.gov.uk

1. The UK employment rate shown in the lower part of the table - as published by the Office for National Statistics - is seasonally adjusted; all other employment rates are unadjusted.

2. All employment rates for EU countries published by EUROSTAT (including the rate for the UK) are based on the population aged 15-64. The rates for Canada and Japan are also based on the population aged 15-64, but the rate for the US is for those aged 16-64. The employment rate for the UK published by the Office for National Statistics is based on the population aged 16-64.

3. Unemployment rates published by EUROSTAT for most EU countries (but not for the UK), are calculated by extrapolating from the most recent LFS data using monthly registered unemployment data. A standard population basis (15-74) is used by EUROSTAT except for Spain, Italy and the UK (16-74). The unemployment rate for the US is based on those aged 16 and over, but the rates for Canada and Japan are for those aged 15 and over. All unemployment rates are seasonally adjusted.

4. The unemployment rate for the UK published by EUROSTAT is based on the population aged 16-74 but the unemployment rate for the UK published by the Office for National Statistics is based on those aged 16 and over. There are other minor definitional differences.

5. The "Total EU" series consist of all 28 EU countries. The Eurozone figures consist of the following EU countries: Austria, Belgium, Cyprus, Estonia, Finland, France, Germany, Greece, Ireland, Italy, Luxembourg, Malta, Netherlands, Portugal, Slovak Republic, Slovenia and Spain. Latvia joined the Eurozone on 1 January 2014 and it will be included in the Eurozone figures published in this table from the March 2014 edition of this Statistical Bulletin (when figures for January 2014 will be shown in this table).

6. Change on previous month except "Latvia" and "United Kingdom as published by national statistical office" (change on previous quarter).

4.5b Labour disputes

United Kingdom, not seasonally adjusted

		Working days lost (thousands)[1][2]	Working days lost in the Public Sector (thousands)[1][2]	Working days lost in the Private Sector (thousands)[1][2]	Number of stoppages[3][4]	Number of stoppages in the Public Sector[4]	Number of stoppages in the Private Sector[4]	Workers involved (thousands)[1][3]
		1	2	3	4	5	6	7
		BBFW	F8XZ	F8Y2	BLUU	F8Y3	F8Y4	BLUT
2011 Dec		7	2	5	15	7	8	7
2012 Dec		4	1	3	16	7	9	3
2013 Jan		5	1	4	8	4	4	1
Feb		3	2	0	9	6	3	2
Mar		87	87	0	12	7	5	100
Apr		30	27	3	15	7	8	61
May		12	11	1	16	10	6	13
Jun		79	76	2	21	10	11	96
Jul		7	3	3	16	5	11	4
Aug		5	4	2	13	6	7	5
Sep		9	4	5	19	8	11	9
Oct		156	130	26	10	6	4	186
Nov		14	11	3	12	6	6	23
Dec	(p)	38	6	32	8	4	4	55
Cumulative totals 12 months to:								
Dec 12		249	198	51	131	63	68	237
Dec 13	**(p)**	**445**	**363**	**82**	**114**	**50**	**64**	**397**

Relationship between columns 1=2+3; 4=5+6

Source: ONS Labour Disputes Inquiry Labour disputes enquiries 01633 456724

1. Estimates of working days lost and workers involved are shown to the nearest thousand. Unrounded estimates of less than 500 therefore round to zero.
2. Due to rounding the working days lost for the public and private sectors may not add up to the total working days lost.
3. The latest 12 month cumulative totals for the figures in these columns will not necessarily equal the sum of the 12 months as some disputes continue for over one month. These disputes appear in each month's data, but only once in the total.
4. These series exclude disputes which do not result in a stoppage of work, those involving fewer than ten workers or lasting less than one day unless the total number of working days lost in the dispute is 100 or more.

4.6 Civil Service employment; regional distribution by government department[1,2]

All employees

Headcount

	North West	North East	Yorkshire and the Humber	West Midlands	East Midlands	East of England	London	South East	South West	Scotland	Wales	Northern Ireland	Overseas	Not reported
31 March 2013														
Attorney General's Departments														
Attorney General's Office	0	0	0	0	0	0	40	0	0	0	0	0	0	0
Crown Prosecution Service	1,070	390	920	670	480	550	1,630	800	390	0	400	0	20	30
Crown Prosecution Service Inspectorate	0	0	10	0	0	0	30	0	0	0	0	0	0	0
Serious Fraud Office	0	0	0	0	0	0	300	0	0	0	0	0	0	0
Treasury Solicitor	0	0	0	0	0	0	990	0	0	0	0	0	0	0
Business, Innovation and Skills														
Business, Innovation and Skills (excl. agencies)	60	30	270	50	30	30	2,560	10	20	40	50	0	0	0
Advisory Conciliation and Arbitration Service	110	70	60	60	60	50	230	50	50	70	50	0	0	0
Companies House	0	0	0	0	0	0	10	0	0	30	910	20	0	0
Insolvency Service	230	70	150	460	90	190	410	140	150	40	70	0	0	0
Land Registry	630	420	240	430	600	250	290	10	1,210	0	440	0	0	0
Met Office	10	..	20	20	50	40	70	80	1,500	110	20	10	30	0
National Measurement Office	0	0	0	0	0	0	70	0	0	0	0	0	0	0
Office of Fair Trading	0	0	0	0	0	0	540	0	0	..	0	0	0	0
Office of Gas and Electricity Market	0	0	0	0	0	0	640	0	0	70	..	0	0	0
Ordnance Survey	30	10	20	20	20	20	20	910	20	30	20	0	0	0
Skills Funding Agency	130	80	110	540	50	50	180	120	70	0	0	0	0	0
UK Intellectual Property Office	0	0	0	0	0	0	50	0	0	0	920	0	0	0
UK Space Agency	0	0	0	0	0	0	10	0	40	0	0	0	0	0
Cabinet Office														
Cabinet Office (excl. agencies)	0	..	10	0	0	70	1,740	20	..	0	0	0	0	0
Other Cabinet Office agencies														
Office of the Parliamentary Counsel	0	0	0	0	0	0	110	0	0	0	0	0	0	0
Government Procurement Service	220	0	..	0	..	100	..	..	..	..	40	0	0	0
Chancellor's other departments														
Debt Management Office	0	0	0	0	0	0	110	0	0	0	0	0	0	0
Government Actuary's Department	0	0	0	0	0	0	120	0	0	0	0	0	0	0
National Savings and Investments	10	10	..	..	..	10	100	40	0	10	0	0	0	0
Charity Commission														
Charity Commission	150	0	0	0	0	0	70	0	100	0	10	0	0	0
Communities and Local Government														
Department for Communities and Local Government (excl. agencies)	70	40	50	70	20	90	1,280	20	90	0	0	0	0	0
Planning Inspectorate	0	0	0	0	0	0	0	0	700	0	40	0	0	0
Queen Elizabeth II Conference Centre	0	0	0	0	0	0	40	0	0	0	0	0	0	0
Culture, Media and Sport														
Department for Culture Media and Sport [4]	0	0	0	0	0	0	390	0	0	0	0	0	0	0
Royal Parks	0	0	0	0	0	0	120	0	0	0	0	0	0	0
Defence														
Ministry of Defence	1,900	320	2,900	2,790	1,730	4,110	3,830	9,260	13,940	4,040	930	1,520	1,820	..
Defence Support Group	0	0	110	960	..	90	10	90	660	80	360	10	130	0
Defence Science and Technology Laboratory	0	0	0	0	..	10	..	2,070	1,760	0	0	0	0	0
Royal Fleet Auxiliary	0	0	0	0	0	0	0	0	0	0	0	0	0	1,900
UK Hydrographic Office	0	0	0	0	0	0	0	0	1,100	0	0	0	0	0
Education														
Department for Education	290	380	450	100	30	0	1,400	0	..	0	0	0	0	0
Education Funding Agency	50	90	70	160	30	20	210	40	30	0	0	0	0	0
Standards and Testing Agency	0	0	0	60	..	0	30	0	0	0	0	0	0	0
The National College	10	0	..	..	190	0	10	0	0	0	0	0	0	0
The Teaching Agency	120	10	10	90	..	0	20	0	0	0	0	0	0	0
Energy and Climate Change														
Department of Energy and Climate Change	0	0	..	0	0	0	1,370	0	0	100	0	0	0	0
Environment, Food and Rural Affairs														
Department for Environment Food and Rural Affairs (excl. agencies)	30	60	370	20	10	20	1,510	20	130	0	0	0	0	0
Animal Health and Veterinary Laboratories Agency	170	50	70	380	110	100	50	780	290	140	200	0	0	0
Centre for Environment Fisheries and Aquaculture Science	..	0	10	0	0	420	..	0	140	0	0	0	0	0
Food and Environment Research Agency	10	..	760	40	..	40	20	20	50	0	..	0	0	0
Office of Water Services	0	0	0	170	0	0	20	0	0	0	0	0	0	0
Rural Payments Agency	760	270	350	40	20	40	10	440	330	0	..	..	0	0

4.6 Civil Service employment; regional distribution by government department[1,2]

All employees

Headcount

	North West	North East	Yorkshire and the Humber	West Midlands	East Midlands	East of England	London	South East	South West	Scotland	Wales	Northern Ireland	Overseas	Not reported
Veterinary Medicines Directorate	0	0	0	0	0	0	0	150	0	0	0	0	0	0
ESTYN														
ESTYN	0	0	0	0	0	0	0	0	0	0	110	0	0	0
Food Standards Agency														
Food Standards Agency	90	20	200	100	80	130	230	80	90	150	100	40	..	10
Foreign and Commonwealth Office														
Foreign and Commonwealth Office (excl. agencies)	0	0	0	0	0	0	2,610	320	0	0	0	0	1,910	0
FCO Services [5]	0	0	0	0	0	0	180	590	0	0	0	0	110	0
Wilton Park Executive Agency	0	0	0	0	0	0	0	70	0	0	0	0	0	0
Health														
Department of Health (excl. agencies)	60	10	740	10	10	10	1,370	20	10	0	0	0	0	40
Medicines and Healthcare Products Regulatory Agency	0	0	20	0	0	20	870	0	0	0	0	0	0	0
HM Revenue and Customs														
HM Revenue and Customs	13,160	12,650	4,820	4,060	3,630	3,930	7,760	4,680	2,770	9,440	3,920	1,900	0	20
Valuation Office	430	230	440	320	240	280	720	450	320	50	270	0	0	70
HM Treasury														
HM Treasury	0	0	0	0	0	30	1,210	0	0	..	0	0	..	0
Office for Budget Responsibility	0	0	0	0	0	0	20	0	0	0	0	0	0	0
Home Office														
Home Office (excl. agencies)	600	140	340	330	60	970	5,650	2,790	200	260	90	80	160	10
Identity and Passport Service	1,110	760	20	10	10	500	570	30	20	170	180	200	0	..
National Fraud Authority	0	0	0	0	0	0	50	0	0	0	0	0	0	0
UK Border Agency	1,960	150	1,840	410	120	200	5,550	320	110	260	200	50	..	0
International Development														
Department for International Development	0	0	0	0	0	0	730	0	0	550	0	0	530	0
Justice														
Ministry of Justice (excl. agencies)	240	40	120	200	90	30	2,510	60	60	380	760	0	0	..
Her Majesty's Courts and Tribunals Service	2,760	990	1,800	1,940	1,670	1,300	4,490	1,820	1,250	280	990	0	0	110
National Archives	0	0	0	0	0	..	620	0	0	0	0	0	0	0
National Offender Management Service	5,320	3,240	5,080	3,790	4,210	4,390	4,970	7,290	3,380	0	1,000	0	0	10
Office of the Public Guardian	0	0	0	330	120	0	30	0	0	0	0	0	0	0
UK Supreme Court	0	0	0	0	0	0	0	0	0	0	0	0	0	50
Northern Ireland Office														
Northern Ireland Office	0	0	0	0	0	0	50	0	0	0	0	50	0	0
Office for Standards in Education														
Office for Standards in Education	390	0	40	40	250	30	230	40	230	0	0	0	0	0
Office of Qualifications and Examinations Regulation														
Ofqual	0	0	0	150	0	0	0	0	0	0	0	..	0	0
Scottish Government														
Scottish Government (excl. agencies)	0	0	0	0	0	0	0	0	0	5,120	0	0	10	0
Crown Office and Procurator Fiscal Service	0	0	0	0	0	0	0	0	0	1,700	0	0	0	0
Disclosure Scotland	0	0	0	0	0	0	0	0	0	180	0	0	0	0
National Records of Scotland	0	0	0	0	0	0	0	0	0	400	0	0	0	0
Education Scotland	0	0	0	0	0	0	0	0	0	250	0	0	0	0
Historic Scotland	0	0	0	0	0	0	0	0	0	1,110	0	0	0	0
Office of Accountant in Bankruptcy	0	0	0	0	0	0	0	0	0	150	0	0	0	0
Office of the Scottish Charity Regulator	0	0	0	0	0	0	0	0	0	50	0	0	0	0
Registers of Scotland	0	0	0	0	0	0	0	0	0	1,010	0	0	0	0
Scottish Court Service	0	0	0	0	0	0	0	0	0	1,460	0	0	0	0
Scottish Housing Regulator	0	0	0	0	0	0	0	0	0	50	0	0	0	0
Scottish Prison Service	0	0	0	0	0	0	0	0	0	4,340	0	0	0	0
Scottish Public Pensions Agency	0	0	0	0	0	0	0	0	0	260	0	0	0	0
Student Awards Agency	0	0	0	0	0	0	0	0	0	200	0	0	0	0
Transport Scotland	0	0	0	0	0	0	0	0	0	380	0	0	0	0
Scotland Office														
Scotland Office	0	0	0	0	0	0	30	0	0	70	0	0	0	0
Security and Intelligence Services														
Security and Intelligence Services	0	0	0	0	0	0	0	0	5,450	0	0	0	0	0
Transport														
Department for Transport (excl. agencies)	0	10	10	..	20	0	1,520	180	10	0	0	0	..	20

4.6 Civil Service employment; regional distribution by government department[1,2]

All employees

Headcount

	North West	North East	Yorkshire and the Humber	West Midlands	East Midlands	East of England	London	South East	South West	Scotland	Wales	Northern Ireland	Overseas	Not reported
Driver and Vehicle Licensing Agency	150	60	100	90	110	130	120	100	120	120	5,360	0	0	0
Driving Standards Agency	220	320	160	180	410	210	280	240	150	160	120	0	0	0
Government Car and Despatch Agency	0	0	0	0	0	..	70	20	0	0	0	0	0	0
Highways Agency	480	20	420	850	110	420	80	580	360	0	0	0	0	0
Maritime and Coastguard Agency	40	20	50	0	..	50	20	440	140	160	130	40	0	0
Office of Rail Regulation	20	..	20	10	..	..	210	10	10	10	..	0	0	0
Vehicle and Operator Services Agency	230	70	270	190	130	200	130	220	370	170	290	0	0	0
Vehicle Certification Agency	0	0	0	0	50	0	0	..	100	0	0	0	10	0
United Kingdom Statistics Authority														
United Kingdom Statistics Authority	0	0	0	0	0	0	40	1,840	..	0	1,660	0	0	0
UK Export Finance														
UK Export Finance	0	0	0	0	0	0	200	0	0	0	..	0	0	0
Wales Office														
Wales Office	0	0	0	0	0	0	30	0	0	0	10	0	0	0
Welsh Government														
Welsh Government	0	0	0	0	0	0	10	0	0	0	5,540	0	10	0
Work and Pensions														
Department for Work and Pensions [3]	20,330	10,730	10,920	9,580	6,020	5,270	10,270	7,150	6,330	11,590	6,410	0	0	290
The Health and Safety Executive	1,370	80	350	140	480	150	210	130	130	260	110	0	0	0
Total employment	55,010	31,840	34,720	29,830	21,360	24,570	74,240	44,530	44,350	45,460	31,710	3,920	4,760	2,550

Source: Annual Civil Service Employment Survey

1 Numbers are rounded to the nearest ten, and cells containing between one and five employees are represented by "..".

2 Workplace postcode data are used to derive geographical information.

3 On 1 August 2012, Child Maintenance and Enforcement Commission become part of the Department for Work and Pensions.

4 Department for Culture Media and Sport now includes 102 Government Equalities Office employees, they were previously reported by the Home Office.

5 FCO Services were previously reported as part of the Foreign and Commonwealth Office, they are now reported separately.

4.7: Unemployment by sex, age and duration

United Kingdom (thousands) seasonally adjusted

	All aged 16 & over							All aged 16 - 64						
	All	Rate (%)[1]	Up to 6 months	Over 6 and up to 12 months	All over 12 months	% over 12 months	All over 24 months	All	Rate (%)[1]	Up to 6 months	Over 6 and up to 12 months	All over 12 months	% over 12 months	All over 24 months
	1	2	3	4	5	6	7	8	9	10	11	12	13	14
People	MGSC	MGSX	YBWF	YBWG	YBWH	YBWI	YBWL	LF2I	LF2Q	LF2Y	LF32	LF34	LF36	LF38
Nov-Jan 2005	1,428	4.7	926	221	281	19.7	133	1,413	4.8	917	219	277	19.6	129
Dec-Feb 2005	1,449	4.8	927	224	299	20.6	140	1,435	4.8	919	223	294	20.5	137
Jan-Mar 2005	1,419	4.7	908	215	296	20.9	137	1,406	4.8	901	215	291	20.7	135
Feb-Apr 2005	1,422	4.7	909	214	299	21.0	133	1,409	4.8	903	214	292	20.7	131
Mar-May 2005	1,437	4.8	918	214	304	21.2	139	1,426	4.8	915	213	297	20.8	136
Apr-Jun 2005	1,439	4.8	912	215	313	21.7	143	1,428	4.8	904	213	310	21.7	139
May-Jul 2005	1,426	4.7	902	217	306	21.5	141	1,413	4.8	896	216	301	21.3	137
Jun-Aug 2005	1,423	4.7	894	232	298	20.9	138	1,411	4.8	888	230	293	20.8	135
Jul-Sep 2005	1,439	4.8	908	242	290	20.1	134	1,424	4.8	901	241	282	19.8	130
Aug-Oct 2005	1,503	5.0	951	255	297	19.8	147	1,489	5.0	942	254	294	19.7	144
Sep-Nov 2005	1,542	5.1	971	252	319	20.7	159	1,524	5.1	963	250	311	20.4	154
Oct-Dec 2005	1,572	5.2	987	254	331	21.1	163	1,556	5.2	979	251	326	21.0	157
Nov-Jan 2006	1,555	5.1	970	259	326	21.0	163	1,539	5.2	960	255	324	21.1	159
Dec-Feb 2006	1,587	5.2	984	272	332	20.9	161	1,573	5.3	977	269	327	20.8	157
Jan-Mar 2006	1,607	5.3	988	281	339	21.1	164	1,592	5.3	981	278	334	20.9	159
Feb-Apr 2006	1,635	5.3	1,010	279	347	21.2	161	1,621	5.4	1,007	276	339	20.9	157
Mar-May 2006	1,665	5.4	1,015	296	354	21.3	171	1,651	5.5	1,010	293	347	21.0	167
Apr-Jun 2006	1,686	5.5	1,025	300	361	21.4	169	1,672	5.6	1,016	297	359	21.5	166
May-Jul 2006	1,700	5.5	1,023	304	373	21.9	174	1,683	5.6	1,012	301	369	21.9	171
Jun-Aug 2006	1,692	5.5	1,024	301	366	21.7	165	1,677	5.6	1,016	297	364	21.7	163
Jul-Sep 2006	1,696	5.5	1,017	289	389	23.0	181	1,680	5.6	1,011	286	383	22.8	178
Aug-Oct 2006	1,694	5.5	1,014	293	387	22.8	181	1,682	5.6	1,009	291	382	22.7	178
Sep-Nov 2006	1,677	5.5	1,004	283	390	23.2	184	1,665	5.5	1,000	282	383	23.0	180
Oct-Dec 2006	1,705	5.5	1,023	286	396	23.3	187	1,694	5.6	1,016	285	394	23.2	185
Nov-Jan 2007	1,704	5.5	1,030	275	399	23.4	184	1,693	5.6	1,021	274	397	23.5	181
Dec-Feb 2007	1,707	5.6	1,041	269	397	23.2	178	1,696	5.6	1,034	267	395	23.3	176
Jan-Mar 2007	1,701	5.5	1,033	277	391	23.0	178	1,687	5.6	1,026	275	386	22.9	174
Feb-Apr 2007	1,688	5.5	1,011	277	400	23.7	176	1,673	5.5	1,006	276	391	23.4	172
Mar-May 2007	1,663	5.4	996	269	397	23.9	180	1,648	5.5	990	269	389	23.6	176
Apr-Jun 2007	1,655	5.4	999	262	394	23.8	175	1,638	5.4	989	260	389	23.8	171
May-Jul 2007	1,643	5.3	988	261	393	23.9	178	1,628	5.4	981	260	387	23.8	175
Jun-Aug 2007	1,645	5.3	987	266	392	23.8	175	1,631	5.4	981	264	385	23.6	171
Jul-Sep 2007	1,650	5.3	991	268	391	23.7	176	1,638	5.4	984	268	385	23.5	173
Aug-Oct 2007	1,631	5.3	988	260	383	23.5	176	1,619	5.3	980	260	380	23.4	173
Sep-Nov 2007	1,636	5.3	987	258	392	23.9	176	1,624	5.4	982	257	385	23.7	173
Oct-Dec 2007	1,610	5.2	970	256	383	23.8	169	1,601	5.3	965	254	381	23.8	167
Nov-Jan 2008	1,619	5.2	977	261	381	23.5	179	1,608	5.3	969	258	381	23.7	177
Dec-Feb 2008	1,620	5.2	957	274	388	24.0	189	1,607	5.3	950	271	386	24.0	187
Jan-Mar 2008	1,618	5.2	954	267	396	24.5	198	1,605	5.3	949	264	392	24.4	195
Feb-Apr 2008	1,660	5.3	985	265	409	24.6	197	1,643	5.4	979	262	402	24.5	195
Mar-May 2008	1,614	5.2	949	262	403	25.0	190	1,599	5.2	943	258	398	24.9	189
Apr-Jun 2008	1,674	5.4	989	271	413	24.7	191	1,659	5.4	981	268	411	24.8	189
May-Jul 2008	1,719	5.5	1,011	275	433	25.2	204	1,706	5.6	1,006	271	428	25.1	202
Jun-Aug 2008	1,788	5.7	1,073	275	440	24.6	205	1,771	5.8	1,066	270	436	24.6	203
Jul-Sep 2008	1,836	5.9	1,110	285	440	24.0	202	1,817	6.0	1,101	282	434	23.9	201
Aug-Oct 2008	1,873	6.0	1,148	288	437	23.3	200	1,853	6.1	1,135	285	433	23.4	198
Sep-Nov 2008	1,943	6.2	1,192	313	438	22.5	198	1,924	6.3	1,181	311	432	22.4	195
Oct-Dec 2008	2,003	6.4	1,226	324	453	22.6	210	1,986	6.5	1,215	319	452	22.7	208
Nov-Jan 2009	2,059	6.6	1,255	345	459	22.3	207	2,044	6.7	1,244	341	459	22.4	205
Dec-Feb 2009	2,123	6.8	1,287	355	481	22.7	222	2,105	6.9	1,276	351	478	22.7	218
Jan-Mar 2009	2,225	7.1	1,336	382	507	22.8	231	2,206	7.2	1,327	379	501	22.7	228
Feb-Apr 2009	2,283	7.3	1,358	404	521	22.8	235	2,265	7.4	1,350	401	514	22.7	232
Mar-May 2009	2,377	7.6	1,408	437	532	22.4	236	2,359	7.7	1,400	433	526	22.3	234
Apr-Jun 2009	2,435	7.8	1,411	476	549	22.5	239	2,415	7.9	1,399	472	543	22.5	234
May-Jul 2009	2,469	7.9	1,398	492	579	23.4	245	2,446	8.0	1,387	488	571	23.3	240
Jun-Aug 2009	2,473	7.9	1,348	515	610	24.7	252	2,454	8.0	1,340	513	601	24.5	246
Jul-Sep 2009	2,462	7.9	1,296	536	629	25.6	236	2,437	8.0	1,287	532	618	25.4	229
Aug-Oct 2009	2,469	7.9	1,285	562	622	25.2	236	2,444	8.0	1,273	557	614	25.1	230
Sep-Nov 2009	2,442	7.8	1,248	559	634	26.0	235	2,415	7.9	1,237	551	627	26.0	230
Oct-Dec 2009	2,438	7.8	1,245	533	659	27.0	246	2,416	7.9	1,234	527	655	27.1	242
Nov-Jan 2010	2,428	7.8	1,197	548	682	28.1	246	2,403	7.9	1,184	541	678	28.2	241
Dec-Feb 2010	2,486	7.9	1,206	552	727	29.3	271	2,462	8.1	1,196	547	719	29.2	265
Jan-Mar 2010	2,512	8.0	1,206	542	764	30.4	283	2,487	8.2	1,198	537	752	30.2	276
Feb-Apr 2010	2,494	8.0	1,186	525	783	31.4	294	2,471	8.1	1,179	521	771	31.2	287
Mar-May 2010	2,491	7.9	1,176	518	797	32.0	302	2,469	8.1	1,169	514	785	31.8	295
Apr-Jun 2010	2,471	7.9	1,166	508	797	32.3	314	2,452	8.0	1,158	504	790	32.2	307
May-Jul 2010	2,475	7.8	1,187	489	799	32.3	321	2,456	8.0	1,179	486	791	32.2	314
Jun-Aug 2010	2,455	7.8	1,168	468	819	33.4	333	2,435	7.9	1,160	465	810	33.3	327
Jul-Sep 2010	2,442	7.7	1,181	445	816	33.4	328	2,424	7.9	1,176	443	805	33.2	323
Aug-Oct 2010	2,484	7.9	1,189	461	835	33.6	333	2,467	8.0	1,185	457	826	33.5	328
Sep-Nov 2010	2,476	7.8	1,204	441	831	33.6	335	2,455	8.0	1,197	436	822	33.5	328
Oct-Dec 2010	2,477	7.8	1,197	451	829	33.5	339	2,457	8.0	1,187	448	822	33.5	332

4.7: Unemployment by sex, age and duration

United Kingdom (thousands) seasonally adjusted

Nov-Jan 2011	2,507	7.9	1,213	451	843	33.6	346	2,487	8.1	1,204	449	834	33.5	339
Dec-Feb 2011	2,471	7.8	1,190	439	842	34.1	369	2,454	8.0	1,183	437	834	34.0	363
Jan-Mar 2011	2,460	7.8	1,173	437	850	34.5	386	2,443	7.9	1,169	435	838	34.3	381
Feb-Apr 2011	2,436	7.7	1,177	429	829	34.0	385	2,418	7.9	1,170	428	821	33.9	380
Mar-May 2011	2,470	7.8	1,218	442	809	32.8	383	2,452	8.0	1,213	443	796	32.5	378
Apr-Jun 2011	2,513	7.9	1,246	432	835	33.2	405	2,495	8.1	1,238	430	827	33.1	402
May-Jul 2011	2,531	8.0	1,236	444	851	33.6	415	2,509	8.2	1,227	442	840	33.5	411
Jun-Aug 2011	2,577	8.1	1,241	469	868	33.7	423	2,555	8.3	1,233	464	858	33.6	418
Jul-Sep 2011	2,624	8.3	1,260	497	868	33.1	421	2,598	8.4	1,248	492	857	33.0	416
Aug-Oct 2011	2,637	8.3	1,276	495	867	32.9	429	2,608	8.5	1,261	490	857	32.9	424
Sep-Nov 2011	2,675	8.4	1,306	512	858	32.1	424	2,647	8.6	1,289	506	852	32.2	419
Oct-Dec 2011	2,657	8.4	1,289	510	858	32.3	423	2,630	8.5	1,273	504	853	32.4	418
Nov-Jan 2012	2,652	8.3	1,289	510	853	32.1	405	2,628	8.5	1,274	506	848	32.3	400
Dec-Feb 2012	2,634	8.3	1,251	504	879	33.4	421	2,610	8.4	1,238	502	871	33.4	414
Jan-Mar 2012	2,610	8.2	1,215	515	881	33.8	426	2,582	8.3	1,204	510	867	33.6	419
Feb-Apr 2012	2,599	8.1	1,195	523	882	33.9	434	2,572	8.3	1,182	518	872	33.9	429
Mar-May 2012	2,577	8.1	1,183	511	883	34.3	443	2,554	8.2	1,173	506	875	34.3	440
Apr-Jun 2012	2,564	8.0	1,180	502	882	34.4	422	2,544	8.2	1,172	496	875	34.4	417
May-Jul 2012	2,592	8.1	1,184	504	904	34.9	443	2,569	8.2	1,179	499	891	34.7	435
Jun-Aug 2012	2,528	7.9	1,167	464	897	35.5	444	2,507	8.0	1,163	461	883	35.2	437
Jul-Sep 2012	2,514	7.8	1,168	452	894	35.5	443	2,494	8.0	1,164	450	880	35.3	436
Aug-Oct 2012	2,510	7.8	1,165	442	904	36.0	449	2,490	8.0	1,159	439	892	35.8	444
Sep-Nov 2012	2,493	7.7	1,177	424	892	35.8	435	2,469	7.9	1,168	420	882	35.7	429
Oct-Dec 2012	2,503	7.8	1,186	437	880	35.1	442	2,481	7.9	1,175	434	872	35.1	436
Nov-Jan 2013	2,516	7.8	1,183	447	887	35.3	451	2,499	8.0	1,173	445	882	35.3	446
Dec-Feb 2013	2,563	7.9	1,208	454	900	35.1	463	2,546	8.1	1,202	452	892	35.0	457
Jan-Mar 2013	2,518	7.8	1,189	427	902	35.8	464	2,500	8.0	1,185	424	891	35.6	458
Feb-Apr 2013	2,511	7.8	1,201	412	898	35.8	458	2,490	8.0	1,191	411	889	35.7	452
Mar-May 2013	2,505	7.8	1,174	417	915	36.5	474	2,484	8.0	1,161	415	908	36.5	468
Apr-Jun 2013	2,514	7.8	1,177	428	909	36.2	474	2,488	8.0	1,160	426	902	36.3	465
May-Jul 2013	2,487	7.7	1,140	448	899	36.1	469	2,463	7.9	1,125	447	891	36.2	462
Jun-Aug 2013	2,487	7.7	1,142	446	900	36.2	467	2,462	7.9	1,128	445	889	36.1	461
Jul-Sep 2013	2,466	7.6	1,148	428	890	36.1	458	2,446	7.8	1,139	427	880	36.0	456
Aug-Oct 2013	2,388	7.4	1,118	405	866	36.3	444	2,365	7.5	1,108	402	855	36.2	442
Sep-Nov 2013	2,320	7.1	1,087	395	839	36.2	449	2,298	7.3	1,073	391	833	36.3	446
Oct-Dec 2013	**2,342**	**7.2**	**1,098**	**398**	**845**	**36.1**	**451**	**2,312**	**7.4**	**1,078**	**394**	**840**	**36.3**	**448**
Change on qtr	*-125*	*-0.4*	*-50*	*-30*	*-45*	*0.0*	*-7*	*-134*	*-0.4*	*-60*	*-33*	*-40*	*0.3*	*-9*
Change %	*-5.1*		*-4.3*	*-7.1*	*-5.0*		*-1.5*	*-5.5*		*-5.3*	*-7.7*	*-4.6*		*-1.9*
Change on year	*-161*	*-0.6*	*-88*	*-40*	*-34*	*1.0*	*9*	*-169*	*-0.6*	*-97*	*-41*	*-31*	*1.2*	*12*
Change %	*-6.5*		*-7.4*	*-9.1*	*-3.9*		*2.0*	*-6.8*		*-8.3*	*-9.4*	*-3.6*		*2.7*

Men	MGSD	MGSY	MGYK	MGYM	MGYO	YBWJ	YBWM	YBSI	YBTJ	YBWP	YBWS	YBWV	YBWY	YBXB
Nov-Jan 2005	844	5.2	505	143	195	23.2	101	832	5.2	500	142	190	22.9	98
Dec-Feb 2005	847	5.2	498	144	205	24.3	101	837	5.2	492	142	202	24.2	99
Jan-Mar 2005	838	5.1	492	140	206	24.6	99	828	5.2	487	139	202	24.4	97
Feb-Apr 2005	836	5.1	486	143	206	24.7	98	826	5.2	481	142	202	24.5	96
Mar-May 2005	842	5.2	492	139	210	24.9	103	834	5.2	489	138	206	24.7	101
Apr-Jun 2005	837	5.1	483	137	217	25.9	105	830	5.2	479	136	214	25.8	102
May-Jul 2005	840	5.1	488	136	216	25.8	104	831	5.2	484	134	213	25.6	101
Jun-Aug 2005	847	5.2	493	140	215	25.3	103	838	5.2	488	139	211	25.2	101
Jul-Sep 2005	848	5.2	499	145	203	24.0	99	839	5.2	494	145	200	23.8	96
Aug-Oct 2005	890	5.4	533	145	212	23.8	109	881	5.5	528	145	209	23.7	106
Sep-Nov 2005	910	5.5	538	145	227	25.0	120	898	5.6	533	143	221	24.6	115
Oct-Dec 2005	932	5.7	545	146	241	25.8	124	920	5.7	541	144	234	25.5	119
Nov-Jan 2006	897	5.4	510	157	230	25.6	118	885	5.5	506	155	224	25.4	114
Dec-Feb 2006	918	5.6	525	163	230	25.1	115	908	5.6	522	161	225	24.8	111
Jan-Mar 2006	937	5.7	533	168	237	25.2	119	927	5.7	529	166	232	25.0	115
Feb-Apr 2006	952	5.7	548	159	245	25.8	119	942	5.8	546	157	240	25.4	115
Mar-May 2006	973	5.9	543	172	258	26.5	129	963	5.9	538	170	255	26.5	126
Apr-Jun 2006	976	5.9	541	175	259	26.5	125	965	6.0	536	173	256	26.5	122
May-Jul 2006	980	5.9	538	180	262	26.7	127	968	6.0	531	178	259	26.8	125
Jun-Aug 2006	971	5.8	544	179	248	25.5	116	961	5.9	539	176	246	25.6	114
Jul-Sep 2006	983	5.9	543	173	267	27.2	131	970	6.0	538	170	262	27.1	128
Aug-Oct 2006	983	5.9	540	177	266	27.1	132	973	6.0	536	175	262	26.9	129
Sep-Nov 2006	960	5.8	532	169	259	27.0	129	949	5.8	527	167	254	26.8	126
Oct-Dec 2006	978	5.9	541	169	268	27.4	132	971	6.0	537	169	265	27.3	129
Nov-Jan 2007	974	5.8	537	163	275	28.2	129	966	5.9	533	162	271	28.1	127
Dec-Feb 2007	980	5.9	545	156	278	28.4	127	971	6.0	541	154	276	28.4	125
Jan-Mar 2007	975	5.8	539	165	272	27.9	126	965	5.9	535	162	268	27.7	123
Feb-Apr 2007	972	5.8	531	164	277	28.5	126	960	5.9	527	162	271	28.3	122
Mar-May 2007	956	5.7	521	162	273	28.6	130	945	5.8	516	161	268	28.4	127
Apr-Jun 2007	945	5.6	522	152	270	28.6	124	932	5.7	517	152	264	28.3	120
May-Jul 2007	940	5.6	521	153	267	28.4	126	930	5.7	516	152	261	28.1	123
Jun-Aug 2007	940	5.6	520	153	267	28.4	124	930	5.7	515	153	262	28.2	121
Jul-Sep 2007	941	5.6	521	156	264	28.0	126	933	5.7	516	156	261	28.0	124
Aug-Oct 2007	925	5.5	511	155	260	28.1	130	916	5.6	505	154	256	28.0	127
Sep-Nov 2007	933	5.5	513	152	267	28.6	130	924	5.6	509	152	263	28.5	127
Oct-Dec 2007	917	5.5	505	152	259	28.3	122	911	5.6	503	150	257	28.2	120
Nov-Jan 2008	934	5.5	520	152	262	28.0	130	926	5.6	517	150	259	27.9	128

4.7: Unemployment by sex, age and duration

United Kingdom (thousands) seasonally adjusted

Dec-Feb 2008	938	5.6	509	163	266	28.3	140	929	5.6	506	161	263	28.3	138
Jan-Mar 2008	939	5.6	509	157	272	29.0	146	929	5.6	505	156	269	28.9	144
Feb-Apr 2008	948	5.6	515	155	277	29.3	142	936	5.7	509	153	274	29.3	141
Mar-May 2008	938	5.5	511	151	276	29.4	138	927	5.6	505	149	273	29.4	137
Apr-Jun 2008	981	5.8	534	158	289	29.5	142	971	5.9	530	155	286	29.4	139
May-Jul 2008	1,012	6.0	546	163	303	30.0	150	1,002	6.1	543	160	300	29.9	148
Jun-Aug 2008	1,054	6.2	581	163	310	29.4	149	1,042	6.3	575	159	308	29.6	148
Jul-Sep 2008	1,083	6.4	612	164	306	28.3	147	1,068	6.5	603	162	303	28.4	146
Aug-Oct 2008	1,110	6.6	647	163	300	27.0	143	1,095	6.6	637	160	297	27.2	142
Sep-Nov 2008	1,158	6.8	678	183	297	25.7	139	1,144	6.9	669	181	294	25.7	138
Oct-Dec 2008	1,201	7.1	700	191	310	25.8	151	1,190	7.2	693	189	308	25.9	150
Nov-Jan 2009	1,237	7.3	719	204	314	25.4	148	1,226	7.4	714	202	311	25.3	147
Dec-Feb 2009	1,276	7.5	742	209	325	25.5	157	1,264	7.6	736	207	321	25.4	156
Jan-Mar 2009	1,342	7.9	776	227	338	25.2	160	1,328	8.0	769	224	335	25.2	159
Feb-Apr 2009	1,383	8.1	795	248	341	24.7	164	1,370	8.3	788	244	338	24.7	162
Mar-May 2009	1,454	8.6	837	272	345	23.7	166	1,442	8.7	831	268	343	23.8	165
Apr-Jun 2009	1,494	8.8	837	303	354	23.7	164	1,480	9.0	830	300	350	23.7	161
May-Jul 2009	1,527	9.0	825	318	383	25.1	172	1,510	9.2	817	315	378	25.0	169
Jun-Aug 2009	1,538	9.1	787	343	408	26.6	180	1,522	9.2	779	341	402	26.4	176
Jul-Sep 2009	1,526	9.0	743	362	421	27.6	167	1,508	9.2	735	359	414	27.5	162
Aug-Oct 2009	1,529	9.0	731	382	416	27.2	166	1,509	9.2	723	377	409	27.1	161
Sep-Nov 2009	1,499	8.9	713	369	416	27.8	162	1,479	9.0	705	363	410	27.8	158
Oct-Dec 2009	1,487	8.8	706	343	438	29.5	170	1,472	9.0	699	339	433	29.5	167
Nov-Jan 2010	1,498	8.9	685	353	460	30.7	173	1,481	9.0	678	349	454	30.7	170
Dec-Feb 2010	1,522	9.0	672	352	497	32.6	192	1,504	9.2	666	348	490	32.6	188
Jan-Mar 2010	1,544	9.1	672	350	522	33.8	203	1,525	9.3	665	345	515	33.8	199
Feb-Apr 2010	1,523	9.0	651	335	536	35.2	211	1,506	9.2	646	332	529	35.1	207
Mar-May 2010	1,500	8.8	636	321	543	36.2	216	1,483	9.0	630	317	536	36.1	211
Apr-Jun 2010	1,478	8.7	623	308	547	37.0	223	1,464	8.9	618	305	541	36.9	218
May-Jul 2010	1,462	8.6	627	287	548	37.5	226	1,448	8.8	622	284	543	37.5	222
Jun-Aug 2010	1,440	8.4	615	267	558	38.8	235	1,426	8.6	609	265	553	38.8	231
Jul-Sep 2010	1,426	8.3	626	249	551	38.7	236	1,411	8.5	621	246	545	38.6	233
Aug-Oct 2010	1,450	8.5	635	257	559	38.5	239	1,436	8.7	631	253	552	38.5	236
Sep-Nov 2010	1,462	8.6	646	253	563	38.5	235	1,446	8.7	641	249	555	38.4	230
Oct-Dec 2010	1,451	8.5	636	256	559	38.5	237	1,436	8.7	632	253	551	38.4	232
Nov-Jan 2011	1,471	8.6	642	263	565	38.4	241	1,457	8.8	640	262	555	38.1	235
Dec-Feb 2011	1,444	8.4	628	252	564	39.1	262	1,432	8.6	625	249	557	38.9	258
Jan-Mar 2011	1,433	8.4	614	250	569	39.7	272	1,421	8.6	611	248	562	39.5	269
Feb-Apr 2011	1,420	8.3	621	245	554	39.0	278	1,407	8.5	616	243	548	38.9	274
Mar-May 2011	1,436	8.4	636	259	540	37.6	279	1,423	8.6	632	259	531	37.3	275
Apr-Jun 2011	1,458	8.5	659	245	554	38.0	288	1,447	8.7	655	244	547	37.8	286
May-Jul 2011	1,465	8.6	654	256	555	37.9	296	1,451	8.8	649	254	548	37.8	293
Jun-Aug 2011	1,502	8.8	672	266	565	37.6	302	1,489	9.0	668	262	559	37.5	299
Jul-Sep 2011	1,531	9.0	688	281	562	36.7	303	1,516	9.2	683	277	556	36.7	300
Aug-Oct 2011	1,533	9.0	694	280	559	36.5	306	1,517	9.2	687	277	553	36.4	301
Sep-Nov 2011	1,547	9.0	700	290	556	36.0	295	1,530	9.2	693	287	550	36.0	292
Oct-Dec 2011	1,537	9.0	694	289	554	36.0	291	1,520	9.2	687	285	548	36.0	286
Nov-Jan 2012	1,530	8.9	699	287	544	35.5	270	1,515	9.1	694	284	537	35.4	265
Dec-Feb 2012	1,506	8.8	667	286	553	36.7	285	1,490	9.0	661	284	545	36.6	279
Jan-Mar 2012	1,494	8.7	648	294	552	37.0	291	1,475	8.9	641	290	544	36.9	286
Feb-Apr 2012	1,482	8.6	629	297	556	37.5	299	1,464	8.8	620	294	550	37.5	295
Mar-May 2012	1,475	8.5	636	283	556	37.7	299	1,461	8.8	630	279	551	37.8	297
Apr-Jun 2012	1,464	8.5	627	280	558	38.1	286	1,453	8.7	625	276	552	38.0	281
May-Jul 2012	1,491	8.6	631	289	570	38.3	301	1,476	8.8	629	285	563	38.1	295
Jun-Aug 2012	1,444	8.3	623	263	558	38.7	303	1,430	8.5	619	260	551	38.5	297
Jul-Sep 2012	1,426	8.2	611	265	549	38.5	301	1,412	8.4	607	262	543	38.4	297
Aug-Oct 2012	1,430	8.3	609	262	559	39.1	311	1,413	8.4	603	258	553	39.1	307
Sep-Nov 2012	1,408	8.1	606	243	559	39.7	303	1,389	8.3	599	240	550	39.6	298
Oct-Dec 2012	1,412	8.1	614	241	557	39.4	306	1,394	8.3	608	239	547	39.2	300
Nov-Jan 2013	1,431	8.2	617	250	565	39.5	308	1,418	8.5	612	249	558	39.3	304
Dec-Feb 2013	1,445	8.3	632	251	562	38.9	306	1,433	8.6	628	249	556	38.8	303
Jan-Mar 2013	1,430	8.3	632	230	568	39.7	306	1,416	8.5	628	227	561	39.6	303
Feb-Apr 2013	1,419	8.2	639	218	562	39.6	302	1,403	8.4	633	217	554	39.5	298
Mar-May 2013	1,429	8.3	623	230	575	40.3	313	1,412	8.5	614	229	569	40.3	308
Apr-Jun 2013	1,445	8.3	634	240	571	39.5	313	1,423	8.5	620	240	563	39.5	307
May-Jul 2013	1,434	8.3	617	250	567	39.5	312	1,417	8.5	607	249	561	39.6	307
Jun-Aug 2013	1,420	8.2	612	250	559	39.4	311	1,401	8.4	600	248	552	39.4	306
Jul-Sep 2013	1,391	8.0	603	231	557	40.0	307	1,375	8.2	595	229	552	40.1	305
Aug-Oct 2013	1,350	7.7	597	221	533	39.4	293	1,333	7.9	587	219	527	39.5	291
Sep-Nov 2013	1,314	7.5	575	218	521	39.6	302	1,299	7.7	566	217	516	39.7	300
Oct-Dec 2013	**1,326**	**7.6**	**574**	**228**	**524**	**39.5**	**308**	**1,309**	**7.8**	**563**	**227**	**519**	**39.7**	**306**
Change on qtr	*-65*	*-0.4*	*-29*	*-3*	*-33*	*-0.5*	*1*	*-67*	*-0.4*	*-32*	*-2*	*-33*	*-0.5*	*1*
Change %	*-4.7*		*-4.8*	*-1.2*	*-5.9*		*0.2*	*-4.8*		*-5.3*	*-0.9*	*-6.0*		*0.2*
Change on year	*-86*	*-0.5*	*-39*	*-13*	*-33*	*0.1*	*2*	*-85*	*-0.5*	*-45*	*-12*	*-28*	*0.4*	*6*
Change %	*-6.1*		*-6.4*	*-5.6*	*-5.9*		*0.8*	*-6.1*		*-7.4*	*-5.2*	*-5.1*		*2.0*
Women	MGSE	MGSZ	MGYL	MGYN	MGYP	YBWK	YBWN	LF2J	LF2R	LF2Z	LF33	LF35	LF37	LF39
Nov-Jan 2005	584	4.2	421	78	85	14.6	32	581	4.3	417	77	86	14.8	31

4.7: Unemployment by sex, age and duration

United Kingdom (thousands) seasonally adjusted

Dec-Feb 2005	602	4.4	428	80	93	15.5	40	599	4.4	427	80	92	15.3	39
Jan-Mar 2005	581	4.2	416	76	90	15.5	38	578	4.3	414	75	89	15.3	37
Feb-Apr 2005	586	4.3	422	71	92	15.8	35	583	4.3	422	71	89	15.4	35
Mar-May 2005	595	4.3	426	75	94	15.9	36	592	4.4	426	75	91	15.3	35
Apr-Jun 2005	602	4.4	429	77	96	15.9	37	599	4.4	425	77	96	16.1	37
May-Jul 2005	586	4.2	414	81	90	15.4	37	582	4.3	412	81	89	15.2	36
Jun-Aug 2005	576	4.2	401	92	83	14.4	35	572	4.2	400	91	81	14.2	34
Jul-Sep 2005	591	4.3	409	96	86	14.6	35	585	4.3	407	96	83	14.1	35
Aug-Oct 2005	613	4.4	418	110	85	13.9	38	609	4.5	415	109	85	13.9	38
Sep-Nov 2005	632	4.6	433	107	92	14.6	39	626	4.6	429	107	90	14.4	39
Oct-Dec 2005	641	4.6	442	108	90	14.1	39	637	4.7	438	107	92	14.4	38
Nov-Jan 2006	658	4.7	460	101	97	14.7	45	653	4.8	454	100	99	15.2	45
Dec-Feb 2006	669	4.8	458	109	102	15.2	46	665	4.8	455	108	102	15.4	46
Jan-Mar 2006	670	4.8	455	113	102	15.2	44	666	4.8	452	112	102	15.3	44
Feb-Apr 2006	683	4.9	462	120	101	14.8	42	679	4.9	461	119	99	14.5	42
Mar-May 2006	692	4.9	472	124	96	13.9	42	688	5.0	472	124	93	13.5	41
Apr-Jun 2006	710	5.0	484	125	102	14.3	44	706	5.1	480	124	102	14.5	44
May-Jul 2006	720	5.1	485	124	111	15.4	47	715	5.2	481	124	109	15.3	46
Jun-Aug 2006	721	5.1	480	122	118	16.4	49	716	5.2	477	121	118	16.5	49
Jul-Sep 2006	713	5.1	474	116	122	17.2	50	710	5.1	473	116	120	16.9	50
Aug-Oct 2006	711	5.0	474	116	121	17.0	49	709	5.1	473	116	121	17.0	49
Sep-Nov 2006	718	5.1	473	114	130	18.2	55	716	5.2	473	114	128	17.9	55
Oct-Dec 2006	726	5.1	481	116	129	17.7	56	723	5.2	478	116	129	17.9	55
Nov-Jan 2007	730	5.2	493	113	125	17.1	55	727	5.3	489	112	127	17.4	54
Dec-Feb 2007	727	5.2	496	113	118	16.3	51	725	5.2	493	113	119	16.5	51
Jan-Mar 2007	726	5.2	494	112	119	16.4	51	722	5.2	491	113	118	16.4	51
Feb-Apr 2007	717	5.1	480	113	123	17.2	50	713	5.2	479	114	120	16.8	50
Mar-May 2007	708	5.0	476	108	124	17.5	50	703	5.1	474	108	121	17.2	49
Apr-Jun 2007	710	5.0	477	110	124	17.4	51	706	5.1	472	108	126	17.8	51
May-Jul 2007	703	5.0	468	109	127	18.0	53	698	5.0	465	108	126	18.0	52
Jun-Aug 2007	705	5.0	467	113	125	17.7	52	701	5.1	466	112	123	17.6	51
Jul-Sep 2007	709	5.0	470	112	127	18.0	50	705	5.1	469	112	125	17.7	49
Aug-Oct 2007	707	5.0	477	106	124	17.5	47	703	5.1	474	105	124	17.6	46
Sep-Nov 2007	704	5.0	474	105	125	17.7	47	701	5.0	473	105	122	17.4	46
Oct-Dec 2007	693	4.9	465	104	124	17.9	47	690	4.9	462	104	124	18.0	47
Nov-Jan 2008	684	4.8	456	109	119	17.4	49	682	4.9	451	108	122	17.9	48
Dec-Feb 2008	682	4.8	449	111	122	18.0	50	678	4.8	445	110	124	18.2	49
Jan-Mar 2008	680	4.8	445	110	124	18.3	52	676	4.8	444	109	124	18.3	52
Feb-Apr 2008	712	5.0	470	110	132	18.5	54	707	5.0	470	109	128	18.2	54
Mar-May 2008	676	4.7	438	111	127	18.9	52	672	4.8	437	110	125	18.6	52
Apr-Jun 2008	692	4.9	455	113	124	17.9	49	688	4.9	451	112	125	18.2	49
May-Jul 2008	707	5.0	465	113	129	18.3	54	703	5.0	464	112	128	18.2	54
Jun-Aug 2008	734	5.1	492	112	129	17.6	56	729	5.2	491	111	128	17.5	55
Jul-Sep 2008	753	5.3	498	121	134	17.8	56	749	5.3	498	120	131	17.5	55
Aug-Oct 2008	764	5.3	501	125	137	18.0	57	759	5.4	498	125	136	17.9	56
Sep-Nov 2008	785	5.5	514	130	141	17.9	59	780	5.5	512	130	138	17.7	58
Oct-Dec 2008	801	5.6	526	132	143	17.9	59	796	5.7	522	131	143	18.0	58
Nov-Jan 2009	822	5.7	536	141	145	17.6	59	817	5.8	530	139	148	18.1	58
Dec-Feb 2009	847	5.9	545	146	156	18.4	65	841	6.0	540	145	156	18.6	62
Jan-Mar 2009	884	6.2	560	155	169	19.1	71	879	6.2	558	155	166	18.9	69
Feb-Apr 2009	899	6.3	563	156	180	20.0	71	894	6.4	562	157	176	19.6	70
Mar-May 2009	923	6.4	571	165	187	20.3	70	917	6.5	569	165	183	19.9	69
Apr-Jun 2009	941	6.6	574	173	194	20.6	75	935	6.6	570	172	193	20.7	74
May-Jul 2009	941	6.6	572	173	195	20.8	73	936	6.7	570	173	193	20.6	71
Jun-Aug 2009	936	6.5	562	172	202	21.6	72	931	6.6	561	172	199	21.4	70
Jul-Sep 2009	936	6.5	554	174	208	22.2	68	930	6.6	552	174	204	21.9	67
Aug-Oct 2009	941	6.5	553	181	207	22.0	70	935	6.6	550	180	205	21.9	69
Sep-Nov 2009	942	6.5	535	190	218	23.1	73	936	6.6	531	188	217	23.2	72
Oct-Dec 2009	951	6.6	540	190	221	23.2	76	944	6.7	535	188	221	23.4	74
Nov-Jan 2010	930	6.4	513	195	222	23.9	73	922	6.5	506	192	224	24.3	71
Dec-Feb 2010	964	6.7	534	200	231	23.9	79	958	6.8	530	199	229	23.9	77
Jan-Mar 2010	969	6.7	534	193	242	25.0	80	962	6.8	533	193	237	24.6	77
Feb-Apr 2010	971	6.7	534	190	247	25.5	83	965	6.8	533	190	242	25.1	80
Mar-May 2010	991	6.9	540	197	254	25.6	86	986	7.0	539	197	249	25.3	84
Apr-Jun 2010	994	6.9	543	200	250	25.2	90	988	7.0	540	199	249	25.2	89
May-Jul 2010	1,013	7.0	560	202	251	24.8	94	1,008	7.1	557	202	248	24.6	93
Jun-Aug 2010	1,014	7.0	553	201	261	25.7	98	1,009	7.1	551	201	257	25.5	97
Jul-Sep 2010	1,017	7.0	555	197	264	26.0	92	1,013	7.1	555	197	260	25.7	91
Aug-Oct 2010	1,034	7.1	554	204	276	26.7	94	1,031	7.3	554	204	274	26.5	93
Sep-Nov 2010	1,014	7.0	559	188	268	26.4	99	1,010	7.1	556	187	267	26.4	98
Oct-Dec 2010	1,026	7.1	561	195	270	26.3	102	1,021	7.2	555	194	271	26.5	101
Nov-Jan 2011	1,037	7.1	571	188	278	26.8	105	1,030	7.3	564	187	279	27.1	103
Dec-Feb 2011	1,028	7.0	562	187	278	27.1	107	1,022	7.2	558	188	277	27.0	106
Jan-Mar 2011	1,027	7.0	559	187	281	27.4	113	1,022	7.2	558	187	277	27.1	112
Feb-Apr 2011	1,016	7.0	556	184	275	27.1	107	1,011	7.1	554	185	273	27.0	106
Mar-May 2011	1,034	7.1	582	183	269	26.0	104	1,029	7.2	580	184	265	25.8	103
Apr-Jun 2011	1,055	7.2	587	187	281	26.6	117	1,048	7.4	583	186	279	26.6	116
May-Jul 2011	1,065	7.3	582	188	296	27.8	119	1,058	7.4	578	188	292	27.6	117
Jun-Aug 2011	1,075	7.4	569	203	303	28.2	121	1,066	7.5	565	202	299	28.1	119
Jul-Sep 2011	1,093	7.5	572	216	306	28.0	119	1,081	7.6	565	215	301	27.8	117
Aug-Oct 2011	1,104	7.5	582	215	307	27.8	123	1,091	7.6	574	213	304	27.9	122

4.7: Unemployment by sex, age and duration

United Kingdom (thousands) seasonally adjusted

Period	All	Rate (%)	Up to 6	Over 6 & up to 12	All over 12	% over 12	All over 24	All	Rate (%)	Up to 6	Over 6 & up to 12	All over 12	% over 12	All over 24
Sep-Nov 2011	1,129	7.7	605	221	302	26.7	128	1,117	7.8	597	219	301	27.0	128
Oct-Dec 2011	1,120	7.6	595	221	304	27.2	132	1,110	7.8	586	218	306	27.5	131
Nov-Jan 2012	1,122	7.6	590	224	309	27.5	135	1,113	7.8	581	222	311	28.0	135
Dec-Feb 2012	1,128	7.7	584	218	327	29.0	136	1,120	7.8	577	218	326	29.1	135
Jan-Mar 2012	1,116	7.6	566	221	329	29.4	135	1,106	7.7	563	220	323	29.2	133
Feb-Apr 2012	1,117	7.6	566	225	326	29.2	135	1,108	7.7	562	224	322	29.1	134
Mar-May 2012	1,103	7.5	547	228	328	29.7	144	1,094	7.6	543	226	324	29.6	143
Apr-Jun 2012	1,099	7.5	553	222	324	29.5	136	1,091	7.6	547	220	323	29.6	136
May-Jul 2012	1,101	7.4	553	215	333	30.3	142	1,093	7.6	551	214	328	30.0	140
Jun-Aug 2012	1,084	7.3	544	201	338	31.2	141	1,077	7.5	544	201	332	30.8	140
Jul-Sep 2012	1,089	7.4	557	187	345	31.7	142	1,082	7.5	557	188	337	31.2	140
Aug-Oct 2012	1,080	7.3	555	180	344	31.9	138	1,076	7.5	556	181	339	31.5	137
Sep-Nov 2012	1,085	7.3	571	180	333	30.7	132	1,080	7.5	568	180	332	30.7	130
Oct-Dec 2012	1,091	7.3	572	196	323	29.6	137	1,088	7.5	568	195	325	29.9	136
Nov-Jan 2013	1,085	7.3	566	197	322	29.7	142	1,081	7.4	561	196	324	30.0	141
Dec-Feb 2013	1,118	7.5	577	203	338	30.3	156	1,113	7.6	574	203	336	30.2	155
Jan-Mar 2013	1,088	7.3	557	196	335	30.8	158	1,084	7.5	557	196	330	30.5	156
Feb-Apr 2013	1,092	7.3	562	194	337	30.8	156	1,087	7.5	558	194	335	30.8	154
Mar-May 2013	1,077	7.2	550	187	340	31.6	161	1,072	7.4	547	186	339	31.6	160
Apr-Jun 2013	1,070	7.2	544	187	339	31.7	160	1,065	7.3	540	186	339	31.9	159
May-Jul 2013	1,053	7.0	523	198	332	31.5	157	1,046	7.2	518	198	330	31.6	155
Jun-Aug 2013	1,067	7.1	530	196	341	31.9	156	1,061	7.3	528	196	337	31.7	155
Jul-Sep 2013	1,076	7.2	545	198	333	31.0	151	1,070	7.4	544	198	328	30.7	151
Aug-Oct 2013	1,038	6.9	521	184	333	32.1	151	1,032	7.1	521	183	328	31.8	151
Sep-Nov 2013	1,006	6.7	512	176	318	31.6	147	998	6.9	507	174	317	31.8	146
Oct-Dec 2013	**1,016**	**6.8**	**524**	**170**	**321**	**31.7**	**143**	**1,003**	**6.9**	**515**	**167**	**321**	**32.0**	**142**
Change on qtr	*-60*	*-0.4*	*-21*	*-28*	*-12*	*0.7*	*-8*	*-67*	*-0.5*	*-29*	*-31*	*-7*	*1.3*	*-9*
Change %	*-5.6*		*-3.8*	*-13.9*	*-3.6*		*-5.2*	*-6.3*		*-5.3*	*-15.6*	*-2.2*		*-6.1*
Change on year	*-76*	*-0.6*	*-48*	*-26*	*-1*	*2.1*	*6*	*-85*	*-0.6*	*-52*	*-28*	*-4*	*2.1*	*6*
Change %	*-6.9*		*-8.4*	*-13.4*	*-0.4*		*4.7*	*-7.8*		*-9.2*	*-14.5*	*-1.1*		*4.2*

	16-17							18-24						
	All	Rate (%)[1]	Up to 6 months	Over 6 and up to 12 months	All over 12 months	% over 12 months	All over 24 months	All	Rate (%)[1]	Up to 6 months	Over 6 and up to 12 months	All over 12 months	% over 12 months	All over 24 months
	15	16	17	18	19	20	21	22	23	24	25	26	27	28
People	YBVH	YBVK	YBXD	YBXG	YBXJ	YBXM	YBXP	YBVN	YBVQ	YBXS	YBXV	YBXY	YBYB	YBYE
Nov-Jan 2005	175	21.3	142	24	9	5.0	*	426	10.7	306	64	56	13.0	18
Dec-Feb 2005	176	21.5	142	25	9	5.2	*	435	10.9	315	63	58	13.2	19
Jan-Mar 2005	180	22.1	146	23	12	6.7	*	409	10.4	297	55	57	13.9	19
Feb-Apr 2005	175	21.8	143	22	11	6.1	*	415	10.5	298	58	59	14.2	21
Mar-May 2005	176	21.8	140	25	12	6.5	*	429	10.9	310	58	61	14.2	24
Apr-Jun 2005	176	21.9	139	24	13	7.4	*	437	11.0	312	58	66	15.2	28
May-Jul 2005	175	21.7	139	25	12	6.7	*	425	10.7	303	59	63	14.7	26
Jun-Aug 2005	175	22.3	137	27	11	6.2	*	428	10.8	294	68	66	15.5	28
Jul-Sep 2005	174	22.3	134	28	12	6.7	*	436	10.9	297	75	63	14.6	27
Aug-Oct 2005	182	23.8	139	31	11	6.2	*	472	11.8	323	79	70	14.7	30
Sep-Nov 2005	178	23.8	138	27	13	7.5	*	473	11.8	318	80	74	15.7	34
Oct-Dec 2005	185	25.1	145	29	11	6.0	*	480	12.0	322	83	75	15.7	35
Nov-Jan 2006	190	25.5	146	30	13	6.7	*	462	11.5	306	86	70	15.1	36
Dec-Feb 2006	190	25.3	146	33	11	5.9	*	469	11.6	318	82	69	14.7	31
Jan-Mar 2006	182	24.7	136	33	13	7.2	*	478	11.7	325	81	71	15.0	33
Feb-Apr 2006	183	24.3	134	35	14	7.6	*	488	11.9	344	73	72	14.7	29
Mar-May 2006	182	24.5	131	39	12	6.4	*	503	12.3	343	81	80	15.9	34
Apr-Jun 2006	178	24.0	129	35	14	7.8	*	518	12.6	353	85	80	15.4	33
May-Jul 2006	173	23.6	126	31	16	9.1	*	533	12.9	355	89	89	16.7	35
Jun-Aug 2006	171	23.4	127	25	19	10.9	*	522	12.5	349	93	81	15.5	30
Jul-Sep 2006	183	24.9	141	25	16	9.0	*	520	12.5	340	94	87	16.7	32
Aug-Oct 2006	184	25.1	144	24	16	8.6	*	510	12.3	329	100	81	15.8	32
Sep-Nov 2006	187	25.1	143	27	17	9.1	*	490	11.9	333	84	72	14.8	29
Oct-Dec 2006	187	24.9	144	27	16	8.5	*	511	12.3	357	80	74	14.5	28
Nov-Jan 2007	188	25.4	146	27	14	7.7	*	513	12.4	362	73	78	15.2	29
Dec-Feb 2007	192	26.2	149	29	15	7.6	*	519	12.5	360	70	88	16.9	31
Jan-Mar 2007	191	26.3	149	28	14	7.4	*	520	12.5	352	78	89	17.2	32
Feb-Apr 2007	188	25.9	146	27	15	8.0	*	523	12.6	345	86	92	17.5	28
Mar-May 2007	190	26.5	149	26	15	8.0	*	527	12.7	350	88	90	17.0	30
Apr-Jun 2007	195	27.4	152	29	14	7.4	*	520	12.5	342	85	93	17.8	30
May-Jul 2007	208	28.3	158	30	20	9.7	*	503	12.1	334	79	89	17.7	32
Jun-Aug 2007	206	28.0	152	35	19	9.2	*	507	12.2	338	74	95	18.7	36
Jul-Sep 2007	215	29.1	156	37	22	10.0	*	496	11.9	333	72	91	18.3	34
Aug-Oct 2007	204	27.6	148	41	14	7.1	*	493	11.8	331	69	94	19.1	35
Sep-Nov 2007	195	26.2	143	37	15	7.7	*	500	12.0	332	71	96	19.3	33
Oct-Dec 2007	188	25.0	138	34	16	8.6	*	497	11.9	328	71	97	19.6	37
Nov-Jan 2008	178	24.2	132	31	14	7.9	*	506	12.1	338	71	97	19.2	41
Dec-Feb 2008	176	24.2	130	33	13	7.3	*	503	12.0	336	75	92	18.4	40

73

4.7: Unemployment by sex, age and duration

United Kingdom (thousands) seasonally adjusted

Jan-Mar 2008	174	24.2	129	33	12	7.1	*	513	12.2	342	73	97	19.0	43
Feb-Apr 2008	182	24.8	135	34	13	7.3	*	515	12.3	343	66	107	20.7	41
Mar-May 2008	183	25.2	135	36	13	6.9	*	503	12.0	328	68	107	21.2	40
Apr-Jun 2008	187	26.0	145	32	11	5.7	*	526	12.6	346	75	105	20.0	36
May-Jul 2008	186	25.8	143	31	12	6.5	*	541	12.9	357	80	105	19.3	39
Jun-Aug 2008	190	26.4	152	27	11	5.9	*	556	13.3	363	82	111	20.0	40
Jul-Sep 2008	187	26.3	146	29	12	6.5	*	578	13.7	386	83	109	18.9	39
Aug-Oct 2008	189	27.0	152	25	12	6.6	*	591	14.0	399	93	98	16.6	35
Sep-Nov 2008	194	27.7	148	30	16	8.4	*	610	14.5	408	101	102	16.6	36
Oct-Dec 2008	193	28.2	145	32	16	8.2	*	619	14.7	410	104	105	16.9	37
Nov-Jan 2009	199	28.7	144	38	17	8.3	*	626	14.9	411	112	104	16.6	39
Dec-Feb 2009	188	27.7	136	35	17	8.9	*	633	15.2	414	112	107	16.9	40
Jan-Mar 2009	197	29.3	144	32	22	11.0	*	677	16.2	434	125	118	17.4	46
Feb-Apr 2009	188	29.0	134	33	22	11.5	*	698	16.8	435	131	132	18.9	51
Mar-May 2009	200	30.8	145	35	20	10.2	*	731	17.5	456	139	136	18.6	51
Apr-Jun 2009	206	32.0	145	39	21	10.4	*	719	17.3	431	146	143	19.8	51
May-Jul 2009	219	34.7	156	42	21	9.4	*	725	17.5	419	151	156	21.5	56
Jun-Aug 2009	210	33.9	142	45	23	11.1	*	729	17.6	411	157	160	22.0	57
Jul-Sep 2009	203	33.2	135	42	26	12.8	*	738	17.9	410	156	172	23.3	55
Aug-Oct 2009	197	32.3	128	40	29	14.5	*	741	18.1	426	153	163	21.9	51
Sep-Nov 2009	198	32.6	128	41	29	14.7	*	712	17.5	409	147	156	21.9	52
Oct-Dec 2009	196	33.0	130	37	29	14.6	*	712	17.4	411	142	159	22.3	53
Nov-Jan 2010	198	33.7	133	38	26	13.3	*	711	17.5	395	147	168	23.7	50
Dec-Feb 2010	198	34.1	133	35	30	15.1	*	725	17.8	393	158	174	24.1	59
Jan-Mar 2010	204	34.7	135	43	26	12.7	*	740	18.1	388	162	190	25.7	66
Feb-Apr 2010	215	36.2	141	48	25	11.8	*	729	17.7	380	154	195	26.8	72
Mar-May 2010	219	36.2	142	53	24	10.8	*	723	17.6	379	148	196	27.0	72
Apr-Jun 2010	197	33.5	131	44	22	11.3	*	732	17.8	404	141	187	25.5	74
May-Jul 2010	190	32.8	129	39	22	11.4	*	733	17.7	410	130	193	26.3	72
Jun-Aug 2010	181	31.6	123	33	24	13.2	*	740	17.8	407	126	208	28.1	72
Jul-Sep 2010	190	33.4	126	36	28	14.6	*	711	17.1	402	118	191	26.8	66
Aug-Oct 2010	208	35.7	138	40	30	14.4	*	732	17.6	402	131	198	27.1	69
Sep-Nov 2010	204	36.5	144	36	25	12.2	*	736	17.9	400	134	202	27.5	71
Oct-Dec 2010	211	37.4	151	35	25	12.0	*	745	18.0	395	141	208	27.9	76
Nov-Jan 2011	213	37.2	148	37	28	13.0	*	756	18.2	414	143	199	26.3	70
Dec-Feb 2011	214	37.3	149	39	26	12.2	*	743	17.9	410	135	198	26.6	76
Jan-Mar 2011	209	37.1	146	37	26	12.4	*	726	17.7	393	135	198	27.3	82
Feb-Apr 2011	204	36.2	140	39	26	12.6	*	700	17.1	393	122	186	26.5	82
Mar-May 2011	205	36.7	136	42	26	12.7	*	720	17.5	409	131	180	25.0	78
Apr-Jun 2011	208	37.1	143	39	25	12.2	*	749	18.2	418	129	201	26.9	93
May-Jul 2011	205	37.3	138	39	27	13.4	*	775	18.9	422	136	217	28.0	92
Jun-Aug 2011	208	37.6	136	41	31	14.7	*	790	19.2	416	146	228	28.8	98
Jul-Sep 2011	216	39.2	135	45	35	16.4	*	800	19.6	421	156	223	27.9	88
Aug-Oct 2011	211	39.0	134	45	32	15.2	*	815	19.8	430	158	226	27.8	98
Sep-Nov 2011	213	38.3	132	45	36	16.8	*	826	20.0	453	163	210	25.5	92
Oct-Dec 2011	211	37.9	132	46	33	15.5	*	822	20.0	443	166	213	25.9	94
Nov-Jan 2012	217	39.2	135	46	36	16.7	*	821	20.0	440	165	216	26.4	89
Dec-Feb 2012	212	38.1	135	45	32	15.2	*	812	19.8	416	169	227	28.0	96
Jan-Mar 2012	206	37.3	130	43	32	15.7	*	810	19.7	412	168	231	28.5	99
Feb-Apr 2012	202	36.6	133	40	30	14.7	*	808	19.7	405	180	223	27.6	97
Mar-May 2012	202	36.6	134	38	30	14.8	*	816	19.8	398	179	239	29.2	111
Apr-Jun 2012	203	36.5	135	38	29	14.3	*	809	19.5	396	176	236	29.2	98
May-Jul 2012	201	36.8	134	39	27	13.7	*	816	19.6	398	170	249	30.4	103
Jun-Aug 2012	193	35.5	126	37	30	15.4	*	764	18.5	383	140	241	31.5	105
Jul-Sep 2012	189	34.5	122	34	34	17.9	*	774	18.9	397	144	232	30.0	103
Aug-Oct 2012	198	36.3	128	35	35	17.6	*	747	18.2	381	135	231	30.9	101
Sep-Nov 2012	196	36.7	129	35	32	16.5	*	763	18.4	398	131	233	30.6	90
Oct-Dec 2012	197	37.6	131	38	29	14.5	*	778	18.6	399	131	248	31.8	102
Nov-Jan 2013	193	37.3	128	39	26	13.2	*	800	19.2	415	128	257	32.2	107
Dec-Feb 2013	192	37.9	130	36	26	13.5	*	787	19.0	405	130	252	32.1	108
Jan-Mar 2013	190	37.5	128	33	29	15.1	*	768	18.6	401	122	245	31.9	99
Feb-Apr 2013	185	36.4	125	30	30	16.2	*	766	18.6	409	121	235	30.7	95
Mar-May 2013	196	38.1	132	33	31	15.6	*	763	18.7	397	117	249	32.7	103
Apr-Jun 2013	196	38.1	136	35	24	12.4	*	778	19.2	400	127	250	32.2	109
May-Jul 2013	195	38.0	137	36	22	11.2	*	765	18.9	378	132	255	33.3	115
Jun-Aug 2013	185	36.3	129	32	25	13.5	*	773	19.1	381	145	247	32.0	115
Jul-Sep 2013	182	36.2	128	29	25	14.0	*	782	19.1	389	137	256	32.8	114
Aug-Oct 2013	183	35.5	123	33	27	14.7	*	758	18.6	380	138	240	31.7	106
Sep-Nov 2013	186	35.9	128	36	23	12.3	*	733	18.0	368	134	232	31.6	107
Oct-Dec 2013	**183**	**36.4**	**122**	**38**	**23**	**12.4**	*	**734**	**17.9**	**371**	**129**	**234**	**31.8**	**114**
Change on qtr	*0*	*0.2*	*-7*	*10*	*-3*	*-1.6*	*	*-48*	*-1.2*	*-17*	*-8*	*-22*	*-0.9*	*0*
Change %	*0.1*		*-5.1*	*33.2*	*-11.2*		*	*-6.1*		*-4.5*	*-5.9*	*-8.7*		*0.1*
Change on year	*-15*	*-1.2*	*-9*	*0*	*-6*	*-2.1*	*	*-43*	*-0.7*	*-27*	*-2*	*-14*	*0.0*	*13*
Change %	*-7.5*		*-7.0*	*0.8*	*-20.8*		*	*-5.6*		*-6.9*	*-1.7*	*-5.5*		*12.4*
Men	YBVI	YBVL	YBXE	YBXH	YBXK	YBXN	YBXQ	YBVO	YBVR	YBXT	YBXW	YBXZ	YBYC	YBYF
Nov-Jan 2005	93	22.6	73	14	6	6.2	*	263	12.4	182	39	42	16.0	15
Dec-Feb 2005	95	23.0	74	15	6	6.4	*	265	12.4	184	36	45	16.9	16
Jan-Mar 2005	97	23.5	75	12	9	9.5	*	254	11.9	176	34	44	17.5	16

4.7: Unemployment by sex, age and duration

United Kingdom (thousands) seasonally adjusted

Feb-Apr 2005	96	23.8	75	13	7	7.7	*	253	11.9	172	37	44	17.6	18
Mar-May 2005	94	23.3	72	14	8	8.4	*	265	12.5	180	39	47	17.7	20
Apr-Jun 2005	100	24.7	74	18	8	8.3	*	263	12.3	175	38	51	19.4	24
May-Jul 2005	100	24.6	75	17	8	8.0	*	261	12.2	174	38	49	18.8	21
Jun-Aug 2005	102	26.2	78	16	8	7.9	*	262	12.2	168	41	52	19.9	23
Jul-Sep 2005	103	26.4	79	15	9	8.4	*	268	12.5	173	47	48	18.0	21
Aug-Oct 2005	109	29.0	84	17	9	8.0	*	292	13.4	191	49	52	17.7	25
Sep-Nov 2005	101	27.4	75	16	10	9.5	*	293	13.5	188	49	56	19.2	28
Oct-Dec 2005	102	28.1	76	17	9	8.6	*	300	13.8	192	53	56	18.6	29
Nov-Jan 2006	104	28.5	75	20	9	8.2	*	274	12.7	171	53	50	18.3	28
Dec-Feb 2006	110	29.9	83	20	8	7.2	*	284	13.0	181	53	49	17.3	25
Jan-Mar 2006	111	30.5	81	21	9	8.2	*	288	13.2	183	51	55	18.9	28
Feb-Apr 2006	111	29.6	78	22	11	9.5	*	302	13.8	204	43	55	18.3	25
Mar-May 2006	111	29.9	77	25	9	7.8	*	303	13.8	194	47	61	20.3	30
Apr-Jun 2006	104	28.1	73	21	10	9.3	*	311	14.2	198	52	62	19.9	28
May-Jul 2006	100	27.2	70	19	10	10.5	*	315	14.2	190	57	69	21.9	32
Jun-Aug 2006	95	26.3	67	16	12	12.4	*	308	13.8	190	58	61	19.8	27
Jul-Sep 2006	104	28.6	75	18	11	10.4	*	312	13.9	187	60	65	20.8	30
Aug-Oct 2006	104	28.6	76	17	11	10.4	*	308	13.8	186	64	59	19.0	28
Sep-Nov 2006	108	29.2	79	19	10	9.6	*	295	13.3	189	54	51	17.4	24
Oct-Dec 2006	107	29.0	79	18	10	9.1	*	306	13.7	202	50	54	17.6	23
Nov-Jan 2007	108	29.7	80	18	10	9.0	*	307	13.6	201	47	59	19.2	22
Dec-Feb 2007	107	29.6	79	18	10	9.7	*	310	13.8	201	44	65	20.9	23
Jan-Mar 2007	106	29.2	79	17	10	9.0	*	309	13.7	195	51	63	20.4	23
Feb-Apr 2007	101	28.0	77	15	10	9.8	*	316	14.0	192	58	66	21.0	22
Mar-May 2007	106	29.6	81	15	11	10.0	*	315	13.9	193	58	65	20.5	23
Apr-Jun 2007	108	30.9	82	15	10	9.6	*	314	13.9	191	55	68	21.8	23
May-Jul 2007	116	32.1	86	18	12	10.5	*	298	13.4	185	50	63	21.2	25
Jun-Aug 2007	114	31.2	83	21	11	9.6	*	305	13.7	188	48	69	22.6	28
Jul-Sep 2007	116	31.4	80	23	13	11.5	*	302	13.5	191	45	65	21.7	27
Aug-Oct 2007	115	30.7	80	27	8	7.1	*	297	13.3	188	42	67	22.7	29
Sep-Nov 2007	110	28.8	78	22	10	9.4	*	300	13.4	188	44	68	22.6	28
Oct-Dec 2007	110	28.8	79	20	11	10.3	*	298	13.3	183	45	69	23.2	32
Nov-Jan 2008	103	27.2	71	19	12	11.3	*	306	13.6	190	46	71	23.1	35
Dec-Feb 2008	101	27.3	71	22	9	8.7	*	312	13.8	194	47	70	22.5	36
Jan-Mar 2008	98	26.7	69	22	8	8.4	*	320	14.1	200	46	74	23.1	39
Feb-Apr 2008	102	27.9	73	19	9	8.8	*	315	14.0	197	41	76	24.1	35
Mar-May 2008	101	28.2	75	18	9	8.6	*	307	13.6	188	44	75	24.3	32
Apr-Jun 2008	100	28.0	76	15	8	8.0	*	329	14.6	203	50	76	23.1	29
May-Jul 2008	101	27.8	77	16	7	7.4	*	344	15.2	215	53	76	22.0	30
Jun-Aug 2008	101	27.7	80	14	6	6.2	*	354	15.6	222	52	80	22.6	30
Jul-Sep 2008	102	27.9	84	12	6	5.9	*	363	16.0	230	54	79	21.9	29
Aug-Oct 2008	102	28.3	85	11	6	5.7	*	369	16.3	234	62	73	19.9	25
Sep-Nov 2008	106	29.7	82	16	8	8.0	*	380	16.7	238	66	76	19.9	26
Oct-Dec 2008	104	29.7	76	19	8	7.9	*	388	17.0	241	69	78	20.1	27
Nov-Jan 2009	107	30.6	76	21	10	9.3	*	395	17.3	244	74	78	19.8	29
Dec-Feb 2009	103	30.1	74	18	11	11.0	*	398	17.8	246	77	75	18.9	29
Jan-Mar 2009	108	31.8	79	14	14	13.4	*	418	18.7	253	83	82	19.5	34
Feb-Apr 2009	101	31.0	69	19	13	12.7	*	429	19.2	257	86	87	20.2	39
Mar-May 2009	110	33.7	76	20	13	11.9	*	451	20.1	271	92	89	19.6	39
Apr-Jun 2009	117	36.5	78	24	15	12.5	*	450	20.0	259	97	94	20.9	39
May-Jul 2009	121	38.7	80	26	15	12.5	*	464	20.7	251	103	110	23.7	44
Jun-Aug 2009	118	38.6	77	27	15	12.6	*	464	20.8	236	111	117	25.2	45
Jul-Sep 2009	108	37.2	68	26	14	12.7	*	465	21.0	231	110	123	26.4	42
Aug-Oct 2009	106	36.8	67	24	16	14.7	*	464	21.1	240	111	113	24.4	36
Sep-Nov 2009	109	39.1	69	26	14	12.9	*	439	20.1	229	99	111	25.4	40
Oct-Dec 2009	108	39.1	70	23	15	13.6	*	437	20.1	226	93	118	27.1	40
Nov-Jan 2010	109	39.9	72	23	13	11.9	*	436	20.1	215	92	129	29.6	41
Dec-Feb 2010	109	40.0	72	21	16	14.5	*	441	20.3	211	101	129	29.2	45
Jan-Mar 2010	115	41.5	74	28	14	11.9	*	455	20.8	212	104	140	30.7	52
Feb-Apr 2010	121	42.5	76	32	13	10.6	*	448	20.3	206	99	143	32.0	56
Mar-May 2010	123	41.5	75	34	14	11.1	*	439	19.9	202	92	145	33.0	57
Apr-Jun 2010	106	37.0	67	26	14	12.8	*	439	19.9	213	89	137	31.3	57
May-Jul 2010	103	36.5	68	22	13	12.7	*	433	19.4	213	81	139	32.1	55
Jun-Aug 2010	96	34.5	64	17	14	15.0	*	438	19.6	219	72	147	33.6	55
Jul-Sep 2010	101	36.6	65	21	16	15.8	*	414	18.4	219	65	130	31.5	49
Aug-Oct 2010	105	38.1	67	22	16	15.2	*	429	19.1	223	73	133	31.0	49
Sep-Nov 2010	108	39.6	74	19	15	13.5	*	436	19.5	219	80	137	31.4	47
Oct-Dec 2010	112	40.9	78	19	14	12.6	*	439	19.6	217	82	141	32.1	47
Nov-Jan 2011	116	40.7	77	21	18	15.3	*	438	19.6	220	87	131	29.9	43
Dec-Feb 2011	112	41.4	78	21	14	12.4	*	435	19.5	222	84	130	29.8	48
Jan-Mar 2011	107	40.4	75	18	15	13.5	*	434	19.7	214	86	134	30.7	54
Feb-Apr 2011	107	40.4	72	20	16	14.8	*	431	19.4	223	79	129	30.0	59
Mar-May 2011	107	40.3	66	25	17	15.5	*	438	19.7	230	85	122	27.9	56
Apr-Jun 2011	111	41.4	70	23	18	15.8	*	448	20.2	236	79	133	29.7	64
May-Jul 2011	107	41.9	67	22	18	17.0	*	458	20.8	230	86	142	31.0	65
Jun-Aug 2011	112	42.1	68	23	21	18.4	*	477	21.7	235	88	154	32.3	72
Jul-Sep 2011	119	44.5	72	25	22	18.3	*	488	22.3	245	95	148	30.4	67
Aug-Oct 2011	114	43.3	69	25	20	17.4	*	502	22.9	253	97	152	30.3	74
Sep-Nov 2011	111	41.7	64	23	24	21.1	*	509	23.2	268	101	140	27.5	67
Oct-Dec 2011	109	40.7	65	23	20	18.6	*	514	23.3	260	106	147	28.7	71

4.7: Unemployment by sex, age and duration

United Kingdom (thousands) seasonally adjusted

Nov-Jan 2012	117	43.7	71	23	22	19.0	*	516	23.5	263	104	149	28.9	64
Dec-Feb 2012	111	40.7	70	22	19	17.1	*	511	23.1	246	110	155	30.4	72
Jan-Mar 2012	106	39.1	67	21	18	17.0	*	504	22.9	239	107	158	31.3	73
Feb-Apr 2012	102	38.0	67	19	16	15.8	*	503	22.9	233	114	156	30.9	74
Mar-May 2012	105	38.8	73	16	16	15.0	*	509	23.0	228	114	167	32.9	80
Apr-Jun 2012	103	38.6	73	15	15	14.5	*	505	22.7	229	112	163	32.3	71
May-Jul 2012	98	37.7	70	17	10	10.3	*	506	22.6	227	112	168	33.1	74
Jun-Aug 2012	95	37.5	63	19	13	14.0	*	469	21.3	218	89	162	34.5	73
Jul-Sep 2012	93	37.0	59	20	14	15.2	*	473	21.5	224	91	158	33.4	71
Aug-Oct 2012	101	39.4	65	19	17	16.9	*	458	20.7	214	86	158	34.4	70
Sep-Nov 2012	104	41.8	69	19	16	15.3	*	461	20.8	213	84	165	35.7	66
Oct-Dec 2012	108	43.6	70	21	17	15.7	*	462	20.9	211	80	171	37.1	71
Nov-Jan 2013	102	41.2	66	22	14	13.7	*	476	21.6	223	81	172	36.2	72
Dec-Feb 2013	98	41.0	65	18	14	14.4	*	457	20.9	218	74	165	36.0	72
Jan-Mar 2013	100	41.5	67	19	15	15.3	*	445	20.4	217	63	165	37.1	68
Feb-Apr 2013	98	41.1	62	18	17	17.9	*	442	20.4	219	61	163	36.8	67
Mar-May 2013	102	42.6	65	21	16	15.7	*	448	20.8	218	62	167	37.3	70
Apr-Jun 2013	103	42.2	70	22	11	10.5	*	463	21.7	227	70	166	35.9	73
May-Jul 2013	108	43.4	75	23	10	9.6	*	456	21.2	217	74	166	36.3	80
Jun-Aug 2013	98	39.8	69	19	10	9.9	*	462	21.5	211	87	163	35.4	82
Jul-Sep 2013	95	40.1	68	17	11	11.2	*	466	21.5	216	83	167	35.9	81
Aug-Oct 2013	96	39.3	65	19	12	12.2	*	459	21.2	217	85	156	34.0	73
Sep-Nov 2013	102	41.0	70	21	11	10.7	*	435	20.1	202	81	152	34.8	77
Oct-Dec 2013	**96**	**40.1**	**64**	**21**	**10**	**10.7**	*	**440**	**20.3**	**201**	**80**	**158**	**35.9**	**84**
Change on qtr	*0*	*0.0*	*-3*	*4*	*0*	*-0.5*	*	*-26*	*-1.2*	*-15*	*-2*	*-10*	*-0.1*	*4*
Change %	*0.3*		*-5.0*	*23.9*	*-4.3*		*	*-5.6*		*-6.7*	*-2.5*	*-5.8*		*4.4*
Change on year	*-13*	*-3.5*	*-6*	*0*	*-7*	*-5.0*	*	*-23*	*-0.7*	*-9*	*0*	*-14*	*-1.2*	*13*
Change %	*-11.7*		*-8.4*	*-0.1*	*-39.8*		*	*-4.9*		*-4.5*	*0.4*	*-8.0*		*18.2*
Women	YBVJ	YBVM	YBXF	YBXI	YBXL	YBXO	YBXR	YBVP	YBVS	YBXU	YBXX	YBYA	YBYD	YBYG
Nov-Jan 2005	82	20.1	69	10	3	3.7	*	163	8.9	125	25	13	8.2	3
Dec-Feb 2005	81	19.9	69	10	3	3.8	*	170	9.2	131	27	13	7.5	2
Jan-Mar 2005	84	20.7	70	10	3	3.4	*	155	8.5	121	22	13	8.1	3
Feb-Apr 2005	80	19.9	68	9	3	4.3	*	162	8.9	126	21	14	8.9	2
Mar-May 2005	82	20.3	68	10	4	4.4	*	164	9.0	131	19	14	8.6	4
Apr-Jun 2005	76	19.1	65	6	5	6.1	*	173	9.5	137	21	15	8.8	4
May-Jul 2005	75	18.9	64	8	4	4.9	*	164	9.0	129	21	14	8.3	5
Jun-Aug 2005	73	18.4	59	11	3	3.9	*	167	9.1	125	27	14	8.6	5
Jul-Sep 2005	72	18.3	56	13	3	4.2	*	168	9.2	124	28	15	9.1	5
Aug-Oct 2005	73	18.8	56	15	2	3.4	*	180	9.8	132	30	18	9.9	6
Sep-Nov 2005	76	20.3	62	10	4	4.8	*	180	9.8	130	31	18	10.1	5
Oct-Dec 2005	83	22.2	70	11	2	2.9	*	180	9.8	130	30	19	10.8	6
Nov-Jan 2006	86	22.6	71	11	4	4.9	*	188	10.1	135	33	20	10.5	8
Dec-Feb 2006	79	20.9	63	13	3	4.1	*	185	9.9	137	28	19	10.5	6
Jan-Mar 2006	71	18.9	55	12	4	5.5	*	189	10.0	142	30	17	8.9	5
Feb-Apr 2006	72	19.1	55	13	3	4.5	*	187	9.9	140	30	17	8.9	3
Mar-May 2006	71	19.1	54	14	3	4.1	*	200	10.5	148	34	18	9.1	5
Apr-Jun 2006	74	19.9	56	13	4	5.6	*	206	10.8	156	33	18	8.6	4
May-Jul 2006	73	20.0	56	12	5	7.3	*	218	11.4	166	32	20	9.1	4
Jun-Aug 2006	76	20.6	61	8	7	9.0	*	214	11.1	159	35	20	9.4	3
Jul-Sep 2006	79	21.3	66	7	6	7.1	*	208	10.9	153	33	22	10.5	3
Aug-Oct 2006	80	21.7	68	7	5	6.3	*	201	10.5	143	36	22	10.9	4
Sep-Nov 2006	79	21.1	64	8	7	8.3	*	195	10.3	144	30	21	10.8	5
Oct-Dec 2006	80	20.9	64	9	6	7.8	*	205	10.7	155	30	20	9.8	6
Nov-Jan 2007	80	21.2	66	10	5	5.9	*	206	10.8	161	26	19	9.2	7
Dec-Feb 2007	85	22.8	70	11	4	4.9	*	209	11.0	159	26	23	11.1	8
Jan-Mar 2007	85	23.4	70	10	4	5.3	*	211	11.1	157	28	26	12.4	8
Feb-Apr 2007	86	23.8	69	13	5	5.8	*	208	10.9	154	29	25	12.3	7
Mar-May 2007	84	23.4	68	11	5	5.5	*	212	11.1	157	30	25	11.9	7
Apr-Jun 2007	87	24.0	70	13	4	4.7	*	207	10.8	152	31	24	11.7	7
May-Jul 2007	93	24.7	72	13	8	8.8	*	205	10.7	149	30	26	12.6	7
Jun-Aug 2007	92	24.9	69	15	8	8.6	*	202	10.5	150	26	26	12.9	8
Jul-Sep 2007	99	26.9	76	14	8	8.3	*	194	10.1	142	26	25	13.1	7
Aug-Oct 2007	89	24.4	68	15	6	7.0	*	197	10.2	143	27	27	13.6	7
Sep-Nov 2007	85	23.4	65	15	5	5.6	*	199	10.3	144	27	28	14.2	5
Oct-Dec 2007	77	21.1	59	14	5	6.2	*	198	10.3	145	26	28	14.3	5
Nov-Jan 2008	74	21.1	60	12	2	3.2	*	199	10.3	149	25	26	13.1	6
Dec-Feb 2008	75	21.1	59	11	4	5.3	*	191	9.9	141	28	22	11.6	4
Jan-Mar 2008	75	21.6	60	11	4	5.3	*	193	10.0	142	27	23	12.2	5
Feb-Apr 2008	81	21.8	61	15	4	5.3	*	201	10.4	145	25	31	15.3	6
Mar-May 2008	82	22.3	60	18	4	4.7	*	196	10.1	140	23	32	16.4	8
Apr-Jun 2008	87	24.0	68	16	3	3.1	*	197	10.2	143	25	29	14.6	7
May-Jul 2008	85	23.9	66	15	5	5.4	*	198	10.2	142	27	29	14.6	9
Jun-Aug 2008	89	25.1	71	13	5	5.6	*	202	10.5	142	30	31	15.3	10
Jul-Sep 2008	85	24.6	62	17	6	7.1	*	215	11.1	156	29	30	13.8	10
Aug-Oct 2008	88	25.6	66	15	7	7.6	*	222	11.5	165	32	25	11.1	10
Sep-Nov 2008	88	25.6	66	13	8	9.0	*	231	11.8	170	34	26	11.3	11
Oct-Dec 2008	89	26.7	69	13	8	8.5	*	232	11.9	169	36	27	11.6	11
Nov-Jan 2009	93	26.8	69	17	7	7.2	*	231	11.9	167	38	26	11.1	10

4.7: Unemployment by sex, age and duration

United Kingdom (thousands) seasonally adjusted

Dec-Feb 2009	85	25.3	62	17	5	6.3	*	235	12.2	167	35	32	13.6	11
Jan-Mar 2009	89	26.7	65	18	7	8.2	*	259	13.4	180	42	36	14.1	12
Feb-Apr 2009	87	27.1	65	14	9	10.1	*	269	13.9	178	45	45	16.9	13
Mar-May 2009	90	27.9	69	14	7	8.0	*	279	14.5	185	47	47	16.9	12
Apr-Jun 2009	89	27.5	67	15	7	7.6	*	270	14.1	172	49	49	18.0	13
May-Jul 2009	98	30.7	76	17	5	5.6	*	261	13.8	168	48	46	17.5	12
Jun-Aug 2009	92	29.2	65	18	8	9.2	*	265	13.9	175	46	44	16.5	12
Jul-Sep 2009	95	29.6	67	15	12	12.9	*	273	14.3	178	46	49	18.0	14
Aug-Oct 2009	90	28.3	62	16	13	14.2	*	277	14.7	186	42	49	17.8	15
Sep-Nov 2009	90	27.2	59	16	15	16.8	*	273	14.4	180	48	45	16.4	12
Oct-Dec 2009	88	27.7	60	14	14	15.9	*	275	14.4	186	49	40	14.7	13
Nov-Jan 2010	89	28.4	61	15	13	15.0	*	275	14.5	181	55	39	14.3	10
Dec-Feb 2010	89	28.8	61	14	14	15.9	*	284	14.9	182	57	46	16.0	13
Jan-Mar 2010	89	28.7	61	15	12	13.8	*	285	14.9	176	58	50	17.7	14
Feb-Apr 2010	94	30.4	65	16	13	13.4	*	281	14.7	174	55	52	18.5	16
Mar-May 2010	96	31.1	67	19	10	10.5	*	284	14.9	177	56	50	17.8	15
Apr-Jun 2010	91	30.2	64	19	9	9.4	*	293	15.3	191	52	49	16.8	16
May-Jul 2010	87	29.3	61	17	9	9.9	*	300	15.6	198	49	54	17.8	17
Jun-Aug 2010	85	29.0	59	16	9	11.2	*	302	15.6	188	54	60	19.9	17
Jul-Sep 2010	88	30.3	61	16	12	13.2	*	297	15.5	183	53	60	20.3	17
Aug-Oct 2010	103	33.5	71	18	14	13.7	*	302	15.9	179	58	65	21.5	20
Sep-Nov 2010	97	33.6	70	16	10	10.9	*	300	16.1	181	54	65	21.7	25
Oct-Dec 2010	99	34.2	73	16	11	11.2	*	305	16.1	179	59	67	21.9	29
Nov-Jan 2011	97	33.6	71	16	10	10.3	*	318	16.6	194	56	68	21.4	27
Dec-Feb 2011	102	33.7	72	18	12	11.9	*	307	16.1	187	52	68	22.2	28
Jan-Mar 2011	102	34.2	72	19	11	11.1	*	292	15.4	179	48	65	22.2	27
Feb-Apr 2011	97	32.5	68	19	10	10.0	*	270	14.4	170	43	57	21.1	23
Mar-May 2011	97	33.4	70	18	9	9.7	*	282	14.9	179	46	58	20.5	22
Apr-Jun 2011	96	33.1	73	16	8	8.1	*	301	15.8	182	50	68	22.7	29
May-Jul 2011	97	33.3	71	17	9	9.5	*	317	16.6	192	50	75	23.7	26
Jun-Aug 2011	96	33.5	67	19	10	10.4	*	312	16.4	182	57	73	23.5	26
Jul-Sep 2011	97	34.3	63	20	14	14.1	*	312	16.4	176	61	75	24.0	22
Aug-Oct 2011	97	34.8	64	20	12	12.6	*	312	16.2	177	61	74	23.7	24
Sep-Nov 2011	102	35.1	68	22	12	12.0	*	317	16.4	185	62	71	22.2	25
Oct-Dec 2011	102	35.4	66	23	12	12.2	*	308	16.1	182	60	65	21.2	23
Nov-Jan 2012	100	35.0	64	23	14	14.0	*	305	16.0	177	61	67	22.0	25
Dec-Feb 2012	101	35.6	64	24	13	13.0	*	302	15.8	170	60	72	24.0	24
Jan-Mar 2012	99	35.4	63	22	14	14.3	*	306	16.0	173	60	73	23.9	25
Feb-Apr 2012	100	35.3	66	21	14	13.5	*	305	16.0	172	66	67	22.1	23
Mar-May 2012	97	34.4	61	22	14	14.7	*	308	16.1	171	66	71	23.2	31
Apr-Jun 2012	100	34.7	62	23	14	14.0	*	304	15.9	167	64	73	24.0	27
May-Jul 2012	103	35.9	64	22	17	16.9	*	310	16.1	171	58	81	26.1	29
Jun-Aug 2012	98	33.8	63	18	16	16.7	*	295	15.4	165	50	79	26.8	33
Jul-Sep 2012	96	32.5	62	14	20	20.5	*	301	15.8	174	53	74	24.7	33
Aug-Oct 2012	97	33.6	63	16	18	18.3	*	289	15.2	167	49	73	25.2	32
Sep-Nov 2012	92	32.2	60	16	16	17.8	*	302	15.6	186	47	68	22.7	24
Oct-Dec 2012	89	32.2	61	17	12	13.0	*	315	16.1	188	51	76	24.1	30
Nov-Jan 2013	91	33.7	62	17	12	12.7	*	324	16.6	192	47	85	26.2	35
Dec-Feb 2013	94	35.2	65	17	12	12.6	*	330	16.9	187	56	88	26.6	36
Jan-Mar 2013	90	33.8	62	14	13	14.8	*	323	16.6	185	59	80	24.7	31
Feb-Apr 2013	87	32.1	63	11	12	14.3	*	323	16.6	190	60	73	22.5	28
Mar-May 2013	93	34.2	67	12	14	15.5	*	316	16.4	179	55	82	26.0	33
Apr-Jun 2013	92	34.4	66	13	13	14.4	*	314	16.5	173	57	84	26.7	36
May-Jul 2013	87	32.9	62	13	11	13.2	*	309	16.3	162	58	89	28.8	35
Jun-Aug 2013	87	33.1	60	12	15	17.4	*	311	16.4	170	57	84	27.1	32
Jul-Sep 2013	87	32.7	61	12	15	17.0	*	316	16.5	173	55	89	28.1	33
Aug-Oct 2013	87	32.2	58	14	15	17.5	*	300	15.6	163	53	84	28.1	33
Sep-Nov 2013	85	31.3	58	15	12	14.1	*	298	15.6	165	52	80	27.0	30
Oct-Dec 2013	**87**	**33.1**	**58**	**17**	**12**	**14.2**	*	**295**	**15.3**	**170**	**49**	**76**	**25.8**	**30**
Change on qtr	*0*	*0.3*	*-3*	*5*	*-2*	*-2.7*	*	*-22*	*-1.2*	*-3*	*-6*	*-13*	*-2.2*	*-3*
Change %	*-0.2*		*-5.3*	*46.9*	*-16.1*		*	*-6.8*		*-1.7*	*-11.0*	*-14.2*		*-10.2*
Change on year	*-2*	*0.8*	*-3*	*0*	*1*	*1.3*	*	*-21*	*-0.8*	*-18*	*-3*	*0*	*1.7*	*0*
Change %	*-2.4*		*-5.3*	*1.8*	*7.1*		*	*-6.5*		*-9.6*	*-5.1*	*0.0*		*-1.3*

4.7: Unemployment by sex, age and duration

United Kingdom (thousands) seasonally adjusted

	25-49							50 and over						
	All	Rate (%)[1]	Up to 6 months	Over 6 and up to 12 months	All over 12 months	% over 12 months	All over 24 months	All	Rate (%)[1]	Up to 6 months	Over 6 and up to 12 months	All over 12 months	% over 12 months	All over 24 months
	29	30	31	32	33	34	35	36	37	38	39	40	41	42
People	MGVI	MGXB	YBYH	YBYK	YBYN	YBYQ	YBYT	YBVT	YBVW	YBYW	YBYZ	YBZC	YBZF	YBZI
Nov-Jan 2005	617	3.5	372	100	145	23.4	71	210	2.8	105	33	72	34.2	45
Dec-Feb 2005	624	3.5	366	106	152	24.4	75	214	2.8	103	31	80	37.3	46
Jan-Mar 2005	617	3.5	365	106	146	23.7	71	212	2.8	100	31	81	38.0	47
Feb-Apr 2005	623	3.5	372	103	149	23.9	67	209	2.7	97	32	80	38.4	44
Mar-May 2005	630	3.5	377	100	153	24.2	72	201	2.6	92	30	79	39.2	43
Apr-Jun 2005	620	3.5	366	101	153	24.7	67	207	2.7	95	31	80	38.7	48
May-Jul 2005	616	3.5	362	101	152	24.8	67	210	2.8	98	32	80	37.9	47
Jun-Aug 2005	605	3.4	364	103	138	22.9	60	215	2.8	99	33	82	38.2	48
Jul-Sep 2005	613	3.4	373	104	136	22.2	60	216	2.8	103	35	79	36.4	46
Aug-Oct 2005	629	3.5	383	108	138	21.9	64	221	2.9	105	36	79	35.8	51
Sep-Nov 2005	664	3.7	409	107	148	22.2	68	228	3.0	106	38	84	36.8	56
Oct-Dec 2005	679	3.8	414	106	159	23.4	71	227	2.9	105	37	86	37.7	57
Nov-Jan 2006	679	3.8	413	105	160	23.6	72	225	2.9	105	37	84	37.2	55
Dec-Feb 2006	708	4.0	417	121	170	24.0	77	221	2.8	102	36	82	37.3	53
Jan-Mar 2006	722	4.0	425	129	167	23.2	75	226	2.9	102	37	87	38.5	56
Feb-Apr 2006	732	4.1	421	136	174	23.8	79	232	3.0	111	34	87	37.3	53
Mar-May 2006	743	4.1	420	139	184	24.7	88	237	3.0	121	37	79	33.4	48
Apr-Jun 2006	755	4.2	422	140	193	25.6	91	236	3.0	120	41	74	31.4	44
May-Jul 2006	755	4.2	424	141	190	25.2	90	238	3.0	117	44	78	32.7	48
Jun-Aug 2006	754	4.2	427	142	185	24.5	84	245	3.1	122	42	82	33.3	50
Jul-Sep 2006	744	4.1	418	129	198	26.6	92	248	3.1	119	41	88	35.7	55
Aug-Oct 2006	758	4.2	424	132	202	26.7	91	242	3.1	117	37	88	36.4	57
Sep-Nov 2006	767	4.3	426	135	206	26.9	93	233	3.0	102	37	94	40.3	61
Oct-Dec 2006	773	4.3	412	144	217	28.1	102	233	3.0	110	34	89	38.3	57
Nov-Jan 2007	765	4.3	406	141	219	28.6	101	238	3.0	116	35	88	37.0	54
Dec-Feb 2007	756	4.2	409	131	216	28.6	100	241	3.0	123	39	78	32.4	46
Jan-Mar 2007	745	4.1	410	128	208	27.9	100	245	3.1	121	44	80	32.7	46
Feb-Apr 2007	724	4.0	393	122	209	28.8	99	253	3.2	128	41	84	33.3	47
Mar-May 2007	699	3.9	383	115	200	28.6	101	247	3.1	114	40	92	37.4	48
Apr-Jun 2007	690	3.8	388	106	196	28.4	95	249	3.1	117	42	91	36.4	48
May-Jul 2007	685	3.8	383	108	193	28.2	96	247	3.1	113	43	91	36.8	48
Jun-Aug 2007	690	3.8	382	118	190	27.6	89	242	3.0	115	39	88	36.2	48
Jul-Sep 2007	696	3.9	387	123	186	26.7	89	244	3.0	115	36	92	37.9	51
Aug-Oct 2007	695	3.9	394	115	186	26.7	91	239	3.0	115	35	89	37.3	49
Sep-Nov 2007	702	3.9	396	115	191	27.2	91	240	3.0	116	35	90	37.4	52
Oct-Dec 2007	692	3.8	392	113	187	27.1	90	233	2.9	113	38	82	35.3	43
Nov-Jan 2008	705	3.9	394	123	188	26.6	96	230	2.9	112	37	82	35.6	43
Dec-Feb 2008	706	3.9	384	126	196	27.8	102	235	2.9	108	40	87	37.0	48
Jan-Mar 2008	702	3.9	378	125	199	28.3	101	231	2.8	106	37	88	38.2	52
Feb-Apr 2008	720	4.0	396	124	200	27.8	101	242	3.0	112	41	89	36.8	52
Mar-May 2008	701	3.9	381	121	200	28.5	99	227	2.8	105	37	84	37.0	50
Apr-Jun 2008	723	4.0	388	127	208	28.8	102	238	2.9	110	38	90	37.7	52
May-Jul 2008	747	4.1	402	126	219	29.4	108	245	3.0	109	39	97	39.5	57
Jun-Aug 2008	782	4.3	439	121	222	28.4	109	260	3.2	118	46	95	36.7	56
Jul-Sep 2008	801	4.4	450	124	227	28.3	111	270	3.3	129	49	92	34.2	53
Aug-Oct 2008	813	4.5	454	125	234	28.8	111	280	3.4	143	44	93	33.2	54
Sep-Nov 2008	843	4.7	480	139	224	26.6	109	295	3.6	155	44	96	32.5	53
Oct-Dec 2008	880	4.8	510	140	230	26.2	113	310	3.8	161	47	102	32.9	60
Nov-Jan 2009	919	5.0	536	144	239	26.0	114	314	3.8	164	51	99	31.5	56
Dec-Feb 2009	967	5.3	567	149	252	26.0	118	335	4.1	170	59	105	31.5	64
Jan-Mar 2009	1,005	5.5	581	164	260	25.8	122	346	4.2	177	61	108	31.1	62
Feb-Apr 2009	1,034	5.7	604	179	251	24.3	117	362	4.3	186	61	116	31.9	64
Mar-May 2009	1,089	6.0	625	197	267	24.5	126	357	4.3	182	66	109	30.5	58
Apr-Jun 2009	1,140	6.3	647	220	273	24.0	127	371	4.4	188	71	112	30.1	58
May-Jul 2009	1,151	6.3	634	226	291	25.3	133	373	4.5	189	73	111	29.8	55
Jun-Aug 2009	1,157	6.4	613	233	310	26.8	137	378	4.5	182	79	117	30.9	57
Jul-Sep 2009	1,147	6.3	586	249	312	27.2	124	374	4.5	166	89	119	31.9	56
Aug-Oct 2009	1,149	6.3	570	267	312	27.1	126	383	4.6	161	103	119	31.2	59
Sep-Nov 2009	1,143	6.3	548	270	325	28.4	121	388	4.6	163	101	124	32.0	61
Oct-Dec 2009	1,140	6.2	536	262	342	30.0	129	391	4.6	168	92	130	33.3	65
Nov-Jan 2010	1,129	6.2	511	267	351	31.1	130	390	4.6	158	96	136	35.0	66
Dec-Feb 2010	1,175	6.5	522	269	384	32.7	150	388	4.6	158	91	139	35.9	63
Jan-Mar 2010	1,183	6.5	532	248	403	34.0	153	386	4.6	150	90	145	37.7	64
Feb-Apr 2010	1,176	6.5	524	244	408	34.7	154	374	4.4	141	78	155	41.4	66
Mar-May 2010	1,160	6.4	510	241	409	35.3	155	388	4.6	144	75	169	43.4	74
Apr-Jun 2010	1,149	6.3	483	247	419	36.4	167	393	4.6	147	76	170	43.2	71
May-Jul 2010	1,154	6.3	495	245	414	35.9	170	398	4.6	152	75	171	42.9	76
Jun-Aug 2010	1,142	6.2	484	236	422	37.0	177	392	4.6	154	73	165	42.2	82
Jul-Sep 2010	1,149	6.3	501	223	426	37.1	183	393	4.6	153	69	171	43.6	78
Aug-Oct 2010	1,151	6.3	496	220	435	37.8	187	393	4.6	152	69	172	43.7	76
Sep-Nov 2010	1,151	6.3	509	204	438	38.1	185	385	4.5	151	68	166	43.1	75
Oct-Dec 2010	1,139	6.2	503	201	435	38.2	184	382	4.5	148	74	161	42.0	77
Nov-Jan 2011	1,151	6.3	505	199	448	38.9	196	387	4.5	146	73	168	43.5	78

4.7: Unemployment by sex, age and duration

United Kingdom (thousands) seasonally adjusted

Dec-Feb 2011	1,130	6.2	491	195	445	39.3	210	385	4.4	141	70	174	45.3	82
Jan-Mar 2011	1,130	6.2	484	201	446	39.4	210	394	4.6	150	65	180	45.6	91
Feb-Apr 2011	1,137	6.2	491	203	443	39.0	204	394	4.6	154	65	174	44.3	95
Mar-May 2011	1,152	6.3	514	203	435	37.7	205	393	4.5	159	66	168	42.8	97
Apr-Jun 2011	1,168	6.3	522	200	447	38.2	209	388	4.5	163	64	161	41.5	98
May-Jul 2011	1,165	6.3	518	202	446	38.3	218	386	4.5	158	67	160	41.6	101
Jun-Aug 2011	1,193	6.5	532	209	452	37.9	222	386	4.5	156	72	158	40.8	99
Jul-Sep 2011	1,197	6.5	539	218	440	36.8	227	412	4.8	165	77	170	41.2	105
Aug-Oct 2011	1,200	6.5	544	219	437	36.4	230	412	4.8	168	72	172	41.7	99
Sep-Nov 2011	1,204	6.5	548	227	429	35.7	222	433	5.0	173	77	183	42.3	105
Oct-Dec 2011	1,200	6.5	551	224	425	35.4	215	424	4.9	164	73	188	44.3	111
Nov-Jan 2012	1,188	6.4	545	227	416	35.0	204	426	4.9	169	73	184	43.2	111
Dec-Feb 2012	1,181	6.4	525	226	430	36.4	208	429	4.9	176	63	189	44.2	118
Jan-Mar 2012	1,175	6.4	511	234	430	36.6	209	419	4.8	162	69	188	44.9	117
Feb-Apr 2012	1,167	6.3	497	231	440	37.7	214	421	4.8	160	73	189	44.9	121
Mar-May 2012	1,152	6.2	489	222	441	38.3	222	407	4.6	162	71	174	42.6	108
Apr-Jun 2012	1,149	6.2	490	221	438	38.2	218	403	4.6	159	66	178	44.2	103
May-Jul 2012	1,162	6.3	506	220	436	37.5	222	413	4.7	147	75	192	46.4	113
Jun-Aug 2012	1,162	6.3	514	217	430	37.0	222	410	4.6	143	70	196	47.9	115
Jul-Sep 2012	1,155	6.2	515	204	436	37.7	222	397	4.5	134	70	192	48.4	115
Aug-Oct 2012	1,165	6.3	514	207	444	38.1	234	400	4.5	140	65	194	48.7	112
Sep-Nov 2012	1,138	6.1	507	191	439	38.6	232	396	4.4	142	66	188	47.5	108
Oct-Dec 2012	1,139	6.1	510	203	426	37.4	234	389	4.3	147	65	177	45.6	104
Nov-Jan 2013	1,134	6.1	491	215	428	37.7	237	390	4.3	149	64	176	45.2	104
Dec-Feb 2013	1,182	6.4	524	217	442	37.3	240	401	4.5	150	71	180	44.9	113
Jan-Mar 2013	1,154	6.2	502	205	446	38.7	250	406	4.5	157	67	182	44.9	112
Feb-Apr 2013	1,143	6.1	506	195	442	38.7	246	418	4.6	161	66	191	45.7	115
Mar-May 2013	1,129	6.1	485	199	444	39.4	251	418	4.6	159	68	191	45.7	115
Apr-Jun 2013	1,116	6.0	478	198	441	39.5	243	425	4.7	163	67	194	45.7	117
May-Jul 2013	1,113	6.0	471	213	429	38.5	236	415	4.5	154	67	194	46.7	115
Jun-Aug 2013	1,116	6.0	476	207	433	38.8	238	414	4.5	156	63	195	47.1	110
Jul-Sep 2013	1,092	5.9	472	203	418	38.3	235	409	4.4	159	59	191	46.5	107
Aug-Oct 2013	1,044	5.6	457	176	411	39.4	231	404	4.3	158	58	187	46.4	105
Sep-Nov 2013	1,018	5.5	441	167	409	40.2	235	383	4.1	150	58	175	45.7	104
Oct-Dec 2013	**1,034**	**5.6**	**451**	**170**	**413**	**39.9**	**233**	**391**	**4.2**	**155**	**60**	**176**	**45.0**	**103**
Change on qtr	*-59*	*-0.3*	*-21*	*-33*	*-5*	*1.7*	*-2*	*-19*	*-0.3*	*-5*	*1*	*-15*	*-1.5*	*-4*
Change %	*-5.4*		*-4.4*	*-16.1*	*-1.2*		*-0.8*	*-4.6*		*-3.0*	*1.5*	*-7.7*		*-3.7*
Change on year	*-105*	*-0.6*	*-59*	*-33*	*-13*	*2.5*	*-1*	*2*	*-0.1*	*8*	*-5*	*-1*	*-0.5*	*0*
Change %	*-9.2*		*-11.6*	*-16.3*	*-3.1*		*-0.2*	*0.5*		*5.4*	*-7.2*	*-0.7*		*-0.5*
Men	MGVJ	MGXC	YBYI	YBYL	YBYO	YBYR	YBYU	YBVU	YBVX	YBYX	YBZA	YBZD	YBZG	YBZJ
Nov-Jan 2005	349	3.7	184	69	96	27.5	52	138	3.3	66	21	51	37.2	33
Dec-Feb 2005	344	3.6	174	70	100	29.0	51	143	3.4	66	22	55	38.3	33
Jan-Mar 2005	343	3.6	175	69	98	28.6	49	144	3.4	66	24	54	37.7	33
Feb-Apr 2005	347	3.6	181	67	100	28.7	47	140	3.3	59	26	55	39.2	32
Mar-May 2005	348	3.7	186	61	101	28.9	50	134	3.1	55	24	54	40.5	32
Apr-Jun 2005	341	3.6	181	58	102	29.8	46	132	3.1	53	24	56	42.3	35
May-Jul 2005	342	3.6	182	57	103	30.1	48	137	3.2	57	23	57	41.2	35
Jun-Aug 2005	341	3.6	188	58	95	27.9	43	143	3.3	59	24	59	41.6	36
Jul-Sep 2005	337	3.5	189	59	89	26.5	41	140	3.3	58	25	57	40.9	35
Aug-Oct 2005	347	3.6	199	57	92	26.4	44	142	3.3	60	22	60	42.2	40
Sep-Nov 2005	367	3.8	214	56	97	26.4	46	148	3.4	60	24	64	43.3	46
Oct-Dec 2005	380	4.0	217	54	109	28.8	50	150	3.4	61	22	67	44.6	45
Nov-Jan 2006	372	3.9	206	58	108	28.9	49	147	3.4	58	26	63	43.0	41
Dec-Feb 2006	382	4.0	205	67	111	29.0	51	142	3.3	57	23	62	43.8	38
Jan-Mar 2006	397	4.1	217	72	108	27.1	49	141	3.3	52	23	65	46.3	43
Feb-Apr 2006	401	4.1	213	73	114	28.5	51	139	3.2	53	21	65	47.1	43
Mar-May 2006	414	4.3	209	75	129	31.1	60	145	3.3	62	24	59	40.7	39
Apr-Jun 2006	415	4.3	207	76	132	31.8	62	145	3.3	64	26	55	38.1	35
May-Jul 2006	417	4.3	211	77	128	30.8	61	148	3.4	67	27	54	36.5	34
Jun-Aug 2006	414	4.3	217	79	118	28.5	54	155	3.5	71	26	57	37.2	35
Jul-Sep 2006	406	4.2	210	67	128	31.5	61	160	3.7	70	27	63	39.4	40
Aug-Oct 2006	412	4.2	210	71	131	31.7	62	159	3.6	68	25	66	41.6	43
Sep-Nov 2006	411	4.2	210	72	129	31.5	59	147	3.3	54	24	68	46.6	46
Oct-Dec 2006	419	4.3	201	79	139	33.2	67	147	3.3	59	22	65	44.6	42
Nov-Jan 2007	411	4.2	194	76	140	34.1	66	149	3.4	61	22	66	44.2	40
Dec-Feb 2007	412	4.3	196	70	146	35.4	70	151	3.4	69	24	58	38.1	35
Jan-Mar 2007	403	4.2	193	69	140	34.9	67	158	3.6	71	28	59	37.4	36
Feb-Apr 2007	391	4.0	186	65	140	35.8	67	164	3.7	77	26	61	37.2	36
Mar-May 2007	376	3.9	179	66	131	34.8	70	158	3.6	68	23	67	42.5	36
Apr-Jun 2007	362	3.7	179	58	125	34.6	64	161	3.6	71	24	67	41.2	36
May-Jul 2007	368	3.8	183	58	127	34.4	64	159	3.6	67	27	65	41.0	36
Jun-Aug 2007	366	3.8	180	60	126	34.3	60	154	3.5	68	25	61	39.7	34
Jul-Sep 2007	367	3.8	184	63	120	32.8	61	157	3.5	66	26	65	41.2	36
Aug-Oct 2007	361	3.7	181	61	120	33.1	65	152	3.4	62	25	64	42.5	36
Sep-Nov 2007	366	3.8	183	61	122	33.3	62	156	3.5	63	26	67	42.9	39
Oct-Dec 2007	360	3.7	183	59	118	32.9	58	149	3.3	60	28	61	40.8	32
Nov-Jan 2008	372	3.8	194	61	118	31.6	63	152	3.4	64	27	62	40.5	32
Dec-Feb 2008	372	3.8	182	66	124	33.3	67	153	3.4	61	29	63	41.1	37

4.7: Unemployment by sex, age and duration

United Kingdom (thousands) seasonally adjusted

	MGVK	MGXD	YBYJ	YBYM	YBYP	YBYS	YBYV	YBVV	YBVY	YBYY	YBZB	YBZE	YBZH	YBZK
Jan-Mar 2008	372	3.8	180	65	127	34.1	66	148	3.3	61	24	63	42.4	40
Feb-Apr 2008	380	3.9	184	67	129	33.8	66	151	3.3	60	27	64	42.3	41
Mar-May 2008	379	3.9	187	64	128	33.8	67	151	3.3	61	26	64	42.6	39
Apr-Jun 2008	395	4.1	194	67	134	33.8	71	157	3.4	61	25	71	45.4	42
May-Jul 2008	404	4.1	193	70	141	34.9	73	164	3.6	61	24	79	48.1	48
Jun-Aug 2008	430	4.4	214	67	149	34.7	75	170	3.7	65	30	75	44.1	45
Jul-Sep 2008	441	4.5	224	67	150	34.1	76	175	3.8	74	31	70	40.1	41
Aug-Oct 2008	454	4.7	241	64	150	33.0	76	185	4.0	87	27	71	38.4	41
Sep-Nov 2008	475	4.9	257	75	143	30.1	76	197	4.3	102	25	71	35.7	38
Oct-Dec 2008	498	5.1	276	73	149	30.0	80	212	4.6	107	30	74	35.1	44
Nov-Jan 2009	524	5.3	294	75	156	29.7	79	211	4.6	106	35	70	33.3	40
Dec-Feb 2009	548	5.6	312	74	162	29.6	80	227	4.9	110	41	76	33.6	47
Jan-Mar 2009	576	5.9	327	87	162	28.2	81	240	5.2	116	44	80	33.3	45
Feb-Apr 2009	601	6.1	345	99	157	26.1	77	252	5.4	124	44	85	33.6	48
Mar-May 2009	638	6.5	366	111	162	25.4	83	255	5.5	124	49	82	32.0	44
Apr-Jun 2009	665	6.8	373	130	162	24.3	80	263	5.7	127	51	84	32.0	45
May-Jul 2009	678	6.9	369	135	175	25.8	85	264	5.7	125	55	83	31.6	43
Jun-Aug 2009	684	7.0	349	149	186	27.2	89	272	5.8	125	56	91	33.5	46
Jul-Sep 2009	686	7.0	332	159	195	28.4	82	268	5.8	111	66	90	33.7	43
Aug-Oct 2009	682	7.0	315	171	196	28.7	84	276	5.9	110	75	91	32.9	45
Sep-Nov 2009	677	6.9	307	170	200	29.6	77	275	5.9	108	75	91	33.1	45
Oct-Dec 2009	670	6.9	298	161	211	31.5	84	272	5.9	112	66	94	34.7	46
Nov-Jan 2010	678	6.9	291	169	218	32.2	85	276	5.9	106	69	100	36.3	47
Dec-Feb 2010	699	7.2	284	165	250	35.7	100	272	5.8	104	65	103	37.7	47
Jan-Mar 2010	702	7.2	286	156	261	37.2	102	271	5.8	101	63	107	39.6	49
Feb-Apr 2010	691	7.1	275	149	266	38.5	105	263	5.6	94	56	114	43.2	51
Mar-May 2010	670	6.9	262	142	267	39.8	106	268	5.7	97	53	118	44.0	53
Apr-Jun 2010	663	6.8	248	139	276	41.6	114	269	5.7	95	54	120	44.6	51
May-Jul 2010	655	6.7	247	132	275	42.0	116	271	5.7	99	52	121	44.5	55
Jun-Aug 2010	646	6.6	237	132	277	42.9	119	261	5.5	95	46	120	45.9	60
Jul-Sep 2010	644	6.6	246	120	277	43.1	128	267	5.6	96	43	127	47.8	58
Aug-Oct 2010	650	6.6	250	116	284	43.6	134	266	5.7	94	46	126	47.3	55
Sep-Nov 2010	653	6.6	258	108	287	43.9	130	265	5.6	95	46	125	47.1	57
Oct-Dec 2010	641	6.5	250	106	285	44.5	130	259	5.5	91	49	118	45.6	58
Nov-Jan 2011	653	6.6	252	108	293	44.9	138	264	5.6	92	48	124	46.8	58
Dec-Feb 2011	634	6.4	240	101	294	46.4	153	262	5.5	88	47	127	48.4	60
Jan-Mar 2011	625	6.3	231	103	291	46.5	151	266	5.6	93	43	130	48.9	66
Feb-Apr 2011	619	6.3	233	102	283	45.8	147	263	5.5	93	44	126	47.7	70
Mar-May 2011	627	6.3	246	106	276	44.0	147	264	5.5	94	44	126	47.7	74
Apr-Jun 2011	640	6.5	253	101	285	44.6	149	259	5.4	99	42	118	45.5	73
May-Jul 2011	644	6.5	260	104	280	43.5	152	256	5.4	97	44	115	44.8	75
Jun-Aug 2011	658	6.6	272	107	279	42.5	155	255	5.4	97	48	110	43.3	71
Jul-Sep 2011	652	6.6	273	109	270	41.5	157	272	5.8	98	52	122	44.7	75
Aug-Oct 2011	647	6.5	271	111	265	40.9	159	269	5.7	100	47	122	45.4	71
Sep-Nov 2011	647	6.5	268	116	263	40.6	150	280	5.9	100	49	131	46.7	75
Oct-Dec 2011	644	6.5	275	115	253	39.4	139	270	5.7	93	44	133	49.2	78
Nov-Jan 2012	627	6.3	266	116	245	39.1	129	270	5.7	100	43	127	47.0	76
Dec-Feb 2012	617	6.2	254	116	247	40.1	128	267	5.6	97	38	131	49.2	85
Jan-Mar 2012	616	6.2	249	121	247	40.0	132	267	5.6	94	44	130	48.6	85
Feb-Apr 2012	613	6.2	240	117	255	41.6	136	264	5.5	88	47	129	48.8	89
Mar-May 2012	607	6.1	241	107	259	42.6	144	253	5.3	94	45	114	44.9	75
Apr-Jun 2012	604	6.1	236	111	258	42.6	141	252	5.2	89	42	122	48.3	73
May-Jul 2012	625	6.2	252	110	263	42.0	146	263	5.4	83	50	130	49.6	81
Jun-Aug 2012	611	6.1	255	106	249	40.8	145	269	5.6	87	48	134	49.9	85
Jul-Sep 2012	599	6.0	250	104	245	41.0	143	261	5.4	79	51	131	50.3	87
Aug-Oct 2012	604	6.0	246	109	249	41.2	154	266	5.5	84	46	136	50.9	86
Sep-Nov 2012	579	5.8	240	95	244	42.2	154	264	5.4	84	46	134	50.9	81
Oct-Dec 2012	582	5.8	244	94	244	41.9	159	259	5.3	89	46	124	48.0	73
Nov-Jan 2013	592	5.9	238	101	252	42.6	159	262	5.3	90	45	126	48.3	75
Dec-Feb 2013	638	6.4	261	110	267	41.8	160	252	5.1	88	48	116	46.2	74
Jan-Mar 2013	633	6.3	257	104	272	43.0	165	251	5.1	92	44	115	45.9	72
Feb-Apr 2013	621	6.2	263	96	262	42.2	158	258	5.2	96	43	119	46.3	75
Mar-May 2013	617	6.2	242	104	271	43.9	163	261	5.3	97	43	121	46.3	76
Apr-Jun 2013	610	6.1	238	104	267	43.9	157	268	5.4	99	43	126	47.1	81
May-Jul 2013	614	6.1	239	111	264	43.0	150	256	5.2	86	43	127	49.6	81
Jun-Aug 2013	604	6.0	243	104	258	42.7	148	257	5.1	89	39	128	50.0	79
Jul-Sep 2013	586	5.8	234	96	255	43.6	151	244	4.9	86	35	124	50.7	73
Aug-Oct 2013	558	5.6	225	84	248	44.5	149	238	4.7	89	32	116	48.9	69
Sep-Nov 2013	552	5.5	219	83	251	45.4	155	225	4.5	84	33	108	47.9	68
Oct-Dec 2013	**561**	**5.6**	**218**	**95**	**248**	**44.3**	**155**	**230**	**4.6**	**91**	**31**	**107**	**46.8**	**67**
Change on qtr	*-25*	*-0.2*	*-16*	*-2*	*-7*	*0.7*	*3*	*-14*	*-0.3*	*5*	*-3*	*-16*	*-3.8*	*-6*
Change %	*-4.2*		*-6.9*	*-1.9*	*-2.6*		*2.2*	*-5.9*		*5.6*	*-8.9*	*-13.0*		*-7.8*
Change on year	*-21*	*-0.2*	*-26*	*0*	*4*	*2.3*	*-4*	*-29*	*-0.7*	*1*	*-14*	*-17*	*-1.2*	*-6*
Change %	*-3.6*		*-10.5*	*0.4*	*1.8*		*-2.6*	*-11.4*		*1.7*	*-30.9*	*-13.6*		*-8.3*
Women	MGVK	MGXD	YBYJ	YBYM	YBYP	YBYS	YBYV	YBVV	YBVY	YBYY	YBZB	YBZE	YBZH	YBZK
Nov-Jan 2005	268	3.3	188	31	48	18.1	18	72	2.2	40	12	20	28.6	12
Dec-Feb 2005	280	3.4	192	35	52	18.7	24	71	2.1	37	9	25	35.2	13
Jan-Mar 2005	274	3.3	190	36	48	17.7	22	68	2.0	34	8	26	38.6	14

4.7: Unemployment by sex, age and duration

United Kingdom (thousands) seasonally adjusted

Feb-Apr 2005	276	3.4	191	36	49	17.9	21	69	2.1	37	6	25	36.6	12
Mar-May 2005	282	3.4	191	39	52	18.4	21	67	2.0	37	6	25	36.6	11
Apr-Jun 2005	279	3.4	184	43	52	18.6	21	74	2.2	42	8	24	32.4	12
May-Jul 2005	274	3.3	180	44	50	18.1	20	73	2.2	41	9	23	31.6	12
Jun-Aug 2005	264	3.2	176	45	43	16.4	16	72	2.1	40	9	23	31.6	12
Jul-Sep 2005	276	3.3	184	45	47	16.9	18	76	2.2	44	10	21	28.2	10
Aug-Oct 2005	281	3.4	184	51	46	16.4	21	79	2.3	46	14	19	24.2	11
Sep-Nov 2005	297	3.6	195	51	51	17.0	23	80	2.4	46	14	20	24.6	11
Oct-Dec 2005	299	3.6	198	52	50	16.6	21	78	2.3	44	14	19	24.4	11
Nov-Jan 2006	306	3.7	207	47	53	17.2	23	78	2.3	47	11	20	26.2	15
Dec-Feb 2006	326	3.9	213	54	59	18.0	26	79	2.3	45	13	20	25.6	14
Jan-Mar 2006	325	3.9	208	57	60	18.4	27	85	2.5	50	13	22	25.5	13
Feb-Apr 2006	331	4.0	208	63	60	18.2	28	93	2.7	59	13	21	22.7	10
Mar-May 2006	329	4.0	211	64	55	16.7	27	91	2.6	59	13	20	21.7	9
Apr-Jun 2006	340	4.1	215	64	61	18.0	29	90	2.6	56	15	19	20.8	10
May-Jul 2006	338	4.1	213	63	62	18.3	29	91	2.6	49	17	24	26.5	14
Jun-Aug 2006	340	4.1	210	63	67	19.7	30	90	2.6	51	15	24	26.7	15
Jul-Sep 2006	339	4.1	207	62	70	20.6	31	88	2.5	49	14	25	28.8	15
Aug-Oct 2006	346	4.2	214	61	71	20.6	29	84	2.4	50	12	22	26.5	14
Sep-Nov 2006	356	4.3	216	63	77	21.6	34	87	2.5	48	13	26	29.8	15
Oct-Dec 2006	354	4.3	211	65	78	22.0	34	87	2.5	51	12	24	27.8	15
Nov-Jan 2007	355	4.3	212	64	79	22.2	36	89	2.5	54	13	22	24.8	13
Dec-Feb 2007	344	4.2	213	61	70	20.5	31	90	2.6	54	15	20	22.8	12
Jan-Mar 2007	342	4.1	216	59	67	19.7	32	87	2.5	50	16	21	24.2	11
Feb-Apr 2007	333	4.0	207	57	69	20.8	31	90	2.6	51	15	23	26.0	11
Mar-May 2007	323	3.9	204	49	69	21.4	30	89	2.5	46	17	25	28.3	12
Apr-Jun 2007	329	4.0	209	48	71	21.7	31	88	2.5	46	18	24	27.6	12
May-Jul 2007	317	3.8	200	50	67	21.1	32	88	2.5	46	16	26	29.3	13
Jun-Aug 2007	324	3.9	201	58	65	19.9	29	87	2.5	47	14	26	30.2	14
Jul-Sep 2007	329	4.0	203	60	66	20.0	28	87	2.5	49	10	28	31.9	15
Aug-Oct 2007	333	4.0	213	54	66	19.9	26	87	2.5	53	10	25	28.2	14
Sep-Nov 2007	336	4.0	213	54	69	20.5	29	84	2.4	52	9	23	27.0	13
Oct-Dec 2007	332	4.0	209	54	69	20.8	31	84	2.4	52	10	22	25.8	11
Nov-Jan 2008	332	4.0	200	62	70	21.1	33	78	2.2	48	10	20	26.1	11
Dec-Feb 2008	334	4.0	201	61	72	21.6	36	82	2.3	47	11	24	29.3	11
Jan-Mar 2008	329	3.9	198	59	72	21.7	35	82	2.3	45	12	25	30.8	12
Feb-Apr 2008	340	4.1	212	57	71	21.0	35	91	2.5	52	14	25	27.7	12
Mar-May 2008	323	3.9	194	57	72	22.2	33	76	2.1	44	12	20	25.9	11
Apr-Jun 2008	327	3.9	194	60	74	22.6	31	80	2.2	50	13	18	22.7	10
May-Jul 2008	343	4.1	209	56	78	22.8	35	81	2.2	48	15	18	21.7	10
Jun-Aug 2008	352	4.2	225	54	73	20.8	35	90	2.5	53	16	20	22.8	11
Jul-Sep 2008	359	4.3	226	57	76	21.3	35	94	2.6	55	18	22	23.4	11
Aug-Oct 2008	359	4.3	213	61	84	23.4	35	95	2.6	56	17	22	23.2	13
Sep-Nov 2008	369	4.4	223	64	81	22.1	33	98	2.7	54	19	25	26.0	15
Oct-Dec 2008	382	4.6	235	67	81	21.2	33	98	2.7	54	17	28	28.2	16
Nov-Jan 2009	395	4.7	242	70	84	21.2	35	103	2.8	58	16	29	27.8	16
Dec-Feb 2009	419	5.0	255	75	89	21.4	38	108	3.0	61	18	29	27.1	17
Jan-Mar 2009	429	5.1	254	78	97	22.6	42	106	2.9	61	18	28	26.1	16
Feb-Apr 2009	433	5.2	259	80	94	21.8	40	110	3.0	62	17	31	28.2	16
Mar-May 2009	451	5.4	259	87	106	23.4	42	102	2.8	58	17	27	26.5	14
Apr-Jun 2009	475	5.6	274	90	111	23.4	47	108	2.9	61	19	27	25.4	13
May-Jul 2009	473	5.6	265	91	116	24.6	48	109	2.9	64	18	28	25.4	12
Jun-Aug 2009	473	5.6	265	84	124	26.2	48	106	2.8	57	23	26	24.2	11
Jul-Sep 2009	462	5.5	254	90	118	25.5	42	106	2.9	55	23	29	27.3	13
Aug-Oct 2009	467	5.5	255	96	116	24.9	41	107	2.9	50	28	29	26.8	14
Sep-Nov 2009	466	5.5	241	100	125	26.7	44	114	3.0	54	26	33	29.4	17
Oct-Dec 2009	469	5.5	238	101	131	27.9	46	118	3.1	56	26	36	30.2	19
Nov-Jan 2010	451	5.3	220	98	133	29.5	46	114	3.0	51	27	36	31.8	19
Dec-Feb 2010	476	5.6	238	104	134	28.2	51	116	3.1	54	25	37	31.8	16
Jan-Mar 2010	481	5.7	247	92	141	29.4	51	115	3.0	50	27	38	33.2	15
Feb-Apr 2010	485	5.8	249	95	141	29.1	49	111	2.9	47	23	41	37.3	16
Mar-May 2010	490	5.8	248	99	143	29.1	49	120	3.2	47	22	51	42.2	21
Apr-Jun 2010	486	5.8	236	107	143	29.4	53	124	3.3	52	22	50	40.0	20
May-Jul 2010	499	5.9	248	112	139	27.9	55	127	3.3	53	24	50	39.5	21
Jun-Aug 2010	496	5.9	247	104	145	29.2	58	131	3.4	59	26	46	34.9	22
Jul-Sep 2010	505	6.0	254	102	148	29.4	56	126	3.3	57	25	44	34.9	20
Aug-Oct 2010	501	5.9	246	104	151	30.1	53	127	3.3	58	23	46	36.3	21
Sep-Nov 2010	498	5.9	251	96	151	30.4	55	120	3.1	57	22	41	34.2	18
Oct-Dec 2010	498	5.9	253	95	150	30.0	54	123	3.2	56	24	43	34.5	19
Nov-Jan 2011	499	5.9	253	91	155	31.1	58	123	3.2	54	25	45	36.5	19
Dec-Feb 2011	496	5.8	251	94	150	30.3	57	123	3.2	52	23	48	38.7	22
Jan-Mar 2011	505	5.9	253	98	155	30.7	59	128	3.3	56	22	50	38.8	25
Feb-Apr 2011	519	6.1	257	101	160	30.8	57	131	3.4	61	21	49	37.3	25
Mar-May 2011	525	6.2	268	98	159	30.3	58	129	3.3	64	22	43	33.0	23
Apr-Jun 2011	529	6.2	269	99	161	30.5	61	129	3.3	64	22	43	33.4	25
May-Jul 2011	522	6.1	258	98	166	31.8	65	129	3.3	61	23	46	35.3	26
Jun-Aug 2011	535	6.3	260	102	172	32.2	67	131	3.4	59	25	47	36.0	28
Jul-Sep 2011	545	6.4	266	109	169	31.1	69	139	3.5	66	25	48	34.3	29
Aug-Oct 2011	553	6.5	273	108	172	31.1	72	143	3.6	68	25	49	34.6	28
Sep-Nov 2011	557	6.6	280	110	167	29.9	72	153	3.9	73	28	52	34.3	30
Oct-Dec 2011	556	6.5	276	109	171	30.8	76	154	3.9	70	28	55	35.9	33

4.7: Unemployment by sex, age and duration

United Kingdom (thousands) seasonally adjusted

Nov-Jan 2012	561	6.6	279	111	171	30.4	75	156	3.9	69	29	57	36.7	35
Dec-Feb 2012	564	6.6	271	109	183	32.5	79	162	4.1	79	25	58	35.9	33
Jan-Mar 2012	559	6.6	263	113	183	32.8	77	152	3.8	68	26	58	38.2	32
Feb-Apr 2012	555	6.5	257	113	185	33.3	78	158	3.9	71	26	60	38.3	32
Mar-May 2012	544	6.4	247	115	182	33.5	79	154	3.9	68	26	60	38.8	33
Apr-Jun 2012	544	6.4	253	110	181	33.2	77	151	3.8	70	24	56	37.4	29
May-Jul 2012	537	6.3	254	110	173	32.3	77	151	3.7	64	25	62	40.9	32
Jun-Aug 2012	551	6.4	259	111	181	32.9	76	140	3.5	57	22	62	44.1	30
Jul-Sep 2012	556	6.5	265	100	190	34.2	79	136	3.4	55	20	61	44.7	29
Aug-Oct 2012	561	6.5	268	98	195	34.7	80	133	3.3	56	18	59	44.1	26
Sep-Nov 2012	558	6.5	267	97	195	34.8	78	132	3.3	58	20	54	40.8	27
Oct-Dec 2012	557	6.5	266	109	182	32.7	75	130	3.2	58	19	53	40.7	30
Nov-Jan 2013	542	6.3	253	113	176	32.4	77	128	3.1	59	19	50	39.0	29
Dec-Feb 2013	545	6.3	263	107	175	32.1	80	149	3.6	63	23	64	42.8	39
Jan-Mar 2013	521	6.1	246	101	175	33.5	84	154	3.8	65	23	67	43.4	40
Feb-Apr 2013	522	6.1	243	99	180	34.5	88	160	3.9	65	24	71	44.6	40
Mar-May 2013	512	6.0	243	96	173	33.8	88	156	3.8	62	25	70	44.8	38
Apr-Jun 2013	506	5.9	239	94	173	34.2	86	157	3.8	65	24	68	43.4	36
May-Jul 2013	499	5.8	232	102	165	33.0	85	159	3.8	68	24	67	42.0	34
Jun-Aug 2013	512	5.9	233	103	175	34.2	91	157	3.8	67	24	66	42.3	32
Jul-Sep 2013	507	5.9	238	106	163	32.1	84	166	3.9	74	25	67	40.5	34
Aug-Oct 2013	486	5.7	232	92	163	33.5	81	166	3.9	69	26	71	42.8	37
Sep-Nov 2013	466	5.4	222	85	159	34.0	81	158	3.7	66	25	67	42.6	37
Oct-Dec 2013	**473**	**5.5**	**233**	**75**	**165**	**34.8**	**79**	**161**	**3.8**	**64**	**29**	**68**	**42.4**	**36**
Change on qtr	*-34*	*-0.4*	*-5*	*-31*	*2*	*2.7*	*-5*	*-4*	*-0.2*	*-10*	*4*	*1*	*2.0*	*2*
Change %	*-6.7*		*-2.0*	*-29.0*	*1.1*		*-6.3*	*-2.6*		*-13.1*	*15.8*	*2.1*		*4.8*
Change on year	*-85*	*-1.0*	*-33*	*-33*	*-18*	*2.1*	*4*	*31*	*0.6*	*6*	*9*	*16*	*1.8*	*6*
Change %	*-15.2*		*-12.5*	*-30.7*	*-9.7*		*4.8*	*24.2*		*11.1*	*48.3*	*29.6*		*18.5*

Relationship between columns: 1=3+4+5; 8=10+11+12.

Source: Labour Force Survey
Labour market statistics enquiries: labour.market@ons.gsi.gov.uk

[1] Denominator = economically active for that age group.

* Sample size too small for reliable estimate.

Further information

The Labour Force Survey is a survey of the population of private households, student halls of residence and NHS accommodation

4.8 Regional labour market summary (employment, unemployment, economic activity, inactivity)

Thousands, seasonally adjusted

Headline estimates for October to December 2013

	Economically active		Employment		Unemployment		Economically inactive	
	Aged 16+	Aged 16-64	Aged 16+	Aged 16-64	Aged 16+	Aged 16+	Aged 16-64	Aged 16-64
	Level	Rate (%)[2]	Level	Rate (%)[2]	Level	Rate (%)[3]	Level	Rate (%)[2]
	1	2	3	4	5	6	7	8
North East	1,304	75.1	1,174	67.4	130	10.0	423	24.9
North West	3,423	74.9	3,146	68.6	277	8.1	1,117	25.1
Yorkshire and The Humber	2,781	78.0	2,541	71.2	240	8.6	763	22.0
East Midlands	2,328	78.1	2,166	72.6	162	6.9	631	21.9
West Midlands	2,712	75.7	2,486	69.2	226	8.3	835	24.3
East of England	3,141	80.4	2,961	75.7	180	5.7	734	19.6
London	4,352	77.6	4,001	71.3	351	8.1	1,224	22.4
South East	4,596	80.8	4,362	76.6	233	5.1	1,049	19.2
South West	2,736	79.8	2,559	74.6	177	6.5	664	20.2
England	27,373	78.0	25,396	72.3	1,977	7.2	7,440	22.0
Wales	1,492	76.3	1,387	70.8	105	7.1	447	23.7
Scotland	2,751	78.5	2,556	72.8	195	7.1	732	21.5
Great Britain	31,617	78.0	29,339	72.3	2,277	7.2	8,619	22.0
Northern Ireland	871	73.1	807	67.6	64	7.4	313	26.9
United Kingdom	32,488	77.9	30,146	72.1	2,342	7.2	8,932	22.1

Change on quarter (change since July to September 2013)[4]

	Economically active		Employment		Unemployment		Economically inactive	
	Aged 16+	Aged 16-64	Aged 16+	Aged 16-64	Aged 16+	Aged 16+	Aged 16-64	Aged 16-64
	Level	Rate (%)[2]	Level	Rate (%)[2]	Level	Rate (%)[3]	Level	Rate (%)[2]
North East	4	0.0	7	0.2	-3	-0.2	0	0.0
North West	0	0.0	6	0.2	-6	-0.2	0	0.0
Yorkshire and The Humber	7	0.1	15	0.3	-8	-0.3	-1	-0.1
East Midlands	3	0.0	7	0.1	-4	-0.2	0	0.0
West Midlands	6	-0.2	36	0.8	-31	-1.2	7	0.2
East of England	8	-0.1	8	0.0	-1	0.0	4	0.1
London	31	0.3	56	0.8	-25	-0.6	-14	-0.3
South East	3	-0.3	41	0.4	-37	-0.8	20	0.3
South West	6	0.3	3	0.2	3	0.1	-9	-0.3
England	67	0.0	178	0.4	-111	-0.4	8	0.0
Wales	-4	0.0	7	0.5	-12	-0.8	0	0.0
Scotland	6	-0.1	9	0.0	-3	-0.1	6	0.1
Great Britain	68	0.0	194	0.3	-126	-0.4	14	0.0
Northern Ireland	0	0.5	-1	0.4	1	0.1	-5	-0.5
United Kingdom	68	0.0	193	0.3	-125	-0.4	8	0.0

Change on year (change since October to December 2012)

	Economically active		Employment		Unemployment		Economically inactive	
	Aged 16+	Aged 16-64	Aged 16+	Aged 16-64	Aged 16+	Aged 16+	Aged 16-64	Aged 16-64
	Level	Rate (%)[2]	Level	Rate (%)[2]	Level	Rate (%)[3]	Level	Rate (%)[2]
North East	7	0.0	2	-0.3	5	0.3	1	0.0
North West	-56	-1.5	-37	-1.2	-18	-0.4	68	1.5
Yorkshire and The Humber	39	0.7	45	0.9	-5	-0.3	-22	-0.7
East Midlands	24	0.5	40	1.1	-16	-0.8	-13	-0.5
West Midlands	-48	-2.1	-36	-1.7	-11	-0.3	73	2.1
East of England	18	-0.1	50	0.8	-32	-1.1	6	0.1
London	51	0.6	63	0.8	-12	-0.4	-24	-0.6
South East	59	0.4	122	1.6	-62	-1.4	-16	-0.4
South West	32	0.5	5	-0.1	27	0.9	-15	-0.5
England	127	-0.1	252	0.3	-125	-0.5	58	0.1
Wales	21	1.1	42	2.1	-22	-1.6	-22	-1.1
Scotland	82	1.7	92	2.0	-10	-0.6	-57	-1.7
Great Britain	230	0.1	387	0.6	-158	-0.6	-20	-0.1
Northern Ireland	5	0.3	8	0.6	-4	-0.5	-3	-0.3
United Kingdom	234	0.1	396	0.6	-161	-0.6	-23	-0.1

Relationship between columns: 1=3+5

1. Labour Force Survey is tabulated by region of residence.

2. Denominator = all persons aged 16 to 64.

3. Denominator = Total economically active.

4. Quarter on quarter changes at regional level are particularly subject to sampling variability and should be interpreted in the context of changes over several quarters rather than in isolation.

Source: Labour Force Survey
Labour market statistics enquiries: labour.market@ons.gsi.gov.uk

4.9 claimant count rates: by region

ONS Crown Copyright Reserved [from Nomis on 8 June 2015]

Sex: Total
Rate: Workplace-based estimates

Area		January 2002 - December 2002 (inclusive)		January 2003 - December 2003 (inclusive)		January 2004 - December 2004 (inclusive)		January 2005 - December 2005 (inclusive)	
		number	rate	number	rate	number	rate	number	rate
England	E92000001	761,175	2.9	754,375	2.8	690,317	2.6	706,092	2.6
United Kingdom	K02000001	946,650	3.0	933,050	3.0	853,342	2.7	861,775	2.7
North East	E12000001	57,942	5.0	52,808	4.5	46,275	3.9	45,942	3.8
North West	E12000002	118,117	3.5	111,650	3.3	99,200	2.8	101,242	2.9
Yorkshire and The Humber	E12000003	88,808	3.6	83,708	3.3	73,400	2.8	76,017	2.9
East Midlands	E12000004	58,683	2.8	58,875	2.8	52,483	2.5	54,083	2.5
West Midlands	E12000005	93,708	3.5	94,675	3.5	88,258	3.2	93,958	3.4
East	E12000006	56,558	2.0	58,067	2.1	55,408	2.0	58,100	2.1
London	E12000007	166,017	3.5	170,692	3.6	162,750	3.4	162,950	3.4
South East	E12000008	71,242	1.6	75,558	1.7	70,675	1.6	71,625	1.6
South West	E12000009	50,100	1.9	48,342	1.8	41,867	1.6	42,175	1.6
Wales	W92000004	47,067	3.5	44,600	3.3	40,208	3.0	41,200	2.9
Scotland	S92000003	101,975	3.8	99,500	3.7	92,000	3.4	85,892	3.1
Northern Ireland	N92000002	36,433	4.4	34,575	4.1	30,817	3.6	28,592	3.3

Area		January 2006 - December 2006 (inclusive)		January 2007 - December 2007 (inclusive)		January 2008 - December 2008 (inclusive)		January 2009 - December 2009 (inclusive)	
		number	rate	number	rate	number	rate	number	rate
England	E92000001	785,550	2.9	723,100	2.6	754,108	2.7	1,275,583	4.6
United Kingdom	K02000001	944,967	2.9	864,467	2.6	906,083	2.7	1,527,683	4.6
North East	E12000001	50,233	4.0	49,275	4.0	53,717	4.3	83,775	6.7
North West	E12000002	115,550	3.3	110,092	3.1	119,708	3.4	191,708	5.3
Yorkshire and The Humber	E12000003	87,358	3.3	81,158	3.1	88,033	3.3	149,817	5.6
East Midlands	E12000004	61,975	2.8	58,483	2.6	61,408	2.7	108,300	4.8
West Midlands	E12000005	108,325	3.8	102,525	3.7	106,167	3.8	173,775	6.2
East	E12000006	65,583	2.2	61,225	2.1	63,625	2.2	115,992	3.9
London	E12000007	166,833	3.4	145,450	3.0	137,658	2.7	211,150	4.2
South East	E12000008	81,675	1.8	71,950	1.6	76,942	1.7	149,225	3.3
South West	E12000009	48,017	1.8	42,942	1.6	46,850	1.7	91,842	3.3
Wales	W92000004	44,217	3.1	40,692	2.8	45,517	3.2	77,133	5.3
Scotland	S92000003	87,258	3.1	76,300	2.7	78,633	2.8	125,958	4.5
Northern Ireland	N92000002	27,875	3.2	24,375	2.8	27,825	3.1	49,008	5.5

Area		January 2010 - December 2010 (inclusive)		January 2011 - December 2011 (inclusive)		January 2012 - December 2012 (inclusive)		January 2013 - December 2013 (inclusive)	
		number	rate	number	rate	number	rate	number	rate
England	E92000001	1,230,708	4.4	1,258,225	4.5	1,301,508	4.6	1,157,708	4.1
United Kingdom	K02000001	1,496,358	4.6	1,534,408	4.7	1,585,492	4.7	1,421,283	4.2
North East	E12000001	81,417	6.5	85,367	7.0	93,400	7.7	84,508	7.0
North West	E12000002	184,017	5.2	190,200	5.4	200,292	5.6	178,458	5.0
Yorkshire and The Humber	E12000003	148,008	5.6	153,267	5.8	164,067	6.2	149,925	5.6
East Midlands	E12000004	101,492	4.5	103,142	4.5	108,842	4.7	95,567	4.2
West Midlands	E12000005	163,667	5.9	164,025	6.0	164,992	5.9	149,217	5.4
East	E12000006	111,067	3.8	111,800	3.8	115,075	3.8	101,758	3.4
London	E12000007	217,283	4.3	228,000	4.5	226,683	4.3	202,108	3.7
South East	E12000008	139,858	3.1	137,242	3.0	139,308	3.0	119,550	2.6
South West	E12000009	83,900	3.0	85,183	3.1	88,850	3.2	76,617	2.7
Wales	W92000004	73,192	5.1	74,850	5.2	79,592	5.6	72,942	5.2
Scotland	S92000003	135,733	5.0	141,508	5.1	141,442	5.1	128,075	4.7
Northern Ireland	N92000002	56,725	6.2	59,825	6.6	62,950	7.1	62,558	7.1

Seasonally adjusted

Source: Office for National Statistics

Claimants of Universal Credit are not yet included in the Claimant Count. An article provides further information: http://www.ons.gov.uk/ons/guide-method/method-quality/specific/labour-market/claimant-count/list-of-jobcentre-plus-offices-under-universal-credit.pdf.
Rate figures for dates from 2013 onwards are calculated using mid-2013 workforce estimates.

4.10 Claimant count[1] by Unitary and Local Authority

	CLAIMANT COUNT ON 12th DECEMBER 2013						Change on year					
	Levels			Percentage of Pop[2]			Levels			Percentage[2]		
	Men	Women	People	Men	Women	People	Men	Women	People	Men	Women	People
	1	2	3	4	5	6	7	8	9	10	11	12
UNITED KINGDOM†	779,122	422,390	1,201,512	3.8	2.1	2.9	-223,118	-98,592	-321,710	-1.1	-0.5	-0.8
GREAT BRITAIN†	738,287	405,126	1,143,413	3.7	2.0	2.9	-218,421	-97,813	-316,234	-1.1	-0.5	-0.8
ENGLAND†	621,488	350,108	971,596	3.6	2.0	2.8	-191,033	-86,038	-277,071	-1.1	-0.5	-0.8
NORTH EAST	48,230	24,254	72,484	5.8	2.9	4.3	-15,169	-5,611	-20,780	-1.8	-0.7	-1.2
County Durham	7,907	3,977	11,884	4.8	2.4	3.6	-2,883	-1,220	-4,103	-1.8	-0.7	-1.2
Darlington	1,881	953	2,834	5.8	2.9	4.3	-585	-239	-824	-1.8	-0.7	-1.3
Hartlepool	2,630	1,307	3,937	9.2	4.4	6.8	-560	-218	-778	-2.0	-0.7	-1.3
Middlesbrough	4,238	1,911	6,149	9.5	4.2	6.9	-1,016	-454	-1,470	-2.3	-1.0	-1.6
Northumberland	4,297	2,266	6,563	4.5	2.3	3.3	-1,488	-631	-2,119	-1.5	-0.6	-1.1
Redcar and Cleveland	3,034	1,422	4,456	7.4	3.3	5.3	-919	-403	-1,322	-2.3	-0.9	-1.6
Stockton-on-Tees	3,980	1,882	5,862	6.5	3.0	4.7	-939	-323	-1,262	-1.5	-0.5	-1.0
Tyne and Wear	20,263	10,536	30,799	5.6	2.9	4.2	-6,779	-2,123	-8,902	-1.9	-0.6	-1.2
Gateshead	3,300	1,691	4,991	5.2	2.6	3.9	-1,200	-377	-1,577	-1.9	-0.6	-1.2
Newcastle upon Tyne	5,346	2,614	7,960	5.4	2.8	4.1	-1,279	-393	-1,672	-1.3	-0.4	-0.9
North Tyneside	3,105	1,526	4,631	4.9	2.3	3.6	-1,157	-448	-1,605	-1.8	-0.7	-1.2
South Tyneside	3,658	1,972	5,630	7.8	4.1	5.9	-1,219	-399	-1,618	-2.6	-0.8	-1.7
Sunderland	4,854	2,733	7,587	5.5	3.0	4.2	-1,924	-506	-2,430	-2.2	-0.6	-1.4
NORTH WEST†	98,930	50,916	149,846	4.4	2.2	3.3	-30,141	-11,487	-41,628	-1.3	-0.5	-0.9
Blackburn with Darwen	2,231	1,133	3,364	4.7	2.4	3.6	-767	-139	-906	-1.6	-0.3	-1.0
Blackpool	3,341	1,578	4,919	7.5	3.6	5.6	-874	-303	-1,177	-2.0	-0.7	-1.3
Cheshire East	2,840	1,475	4,315	2.5	1.3	1.9	-816	-296	-1,112	-0.7	-0.3	-0.5
Cheshire West and Chester	3,032	1,578	4,610	3.0	1.5	2.2	-1,249	-528	-1,777	-1.2	-0.5	-0.9
Halton	2,120	1,129	3,249	5.3	2.7	4.0	-557	-279	-836	-1.4	-0.7	-1.0
Warrington†	2,104	1,064	3,168	3.2	1.6	2.4	-859	-358	-1,217	-1.3	-0.6	-0.9
Cumbria	4,286	2,077	6,363	2.8	1.3	2.1	-1,518	-557	-2,075	-1.0	-0.4	-0.7
Allerdale	1,004	507	1,511	3.4	1.7	2.6	-299	-91	-390	-1.0	-0.3	-0.7
Barrow-in-Furness	1,006	429	1,435	4.7	2.0	3.3	-208	-118	-326	-1.0	-0.6	-0.8
Carlisle	889	493	1,382	2.6	1.4	2.0	-509	-177	-686	-1.5	-0.5	-1.0
Copeland	797	358	1,155	3.5	1.6	2.6	-272	-73	-345	-1.2	-0.3	-0.8
Eden	212	101	313	1.3	0.6	1.0	-41	-24	-65	-0.3	-0.1	-0.2
South Lakeland	378	189	567	1.2	0.6	0.9	-189	-74	-263	-0.6	-0.2	-0.4
Greater Manchester†	41,491	21,775	63,266	4.7	2.5	3.6	-13,657	-5,136	-18,793	-1.6	-0.6	-1.1
Bolton	4,713	2,536	7,249	5.4	2.9	4.1	-862	-198	-1,060	-1.0	-0.2	-0.6
Bury	2,458	1,295	3,753	4.2	2.2	3.2	-771	-194	-965	-1.3	-0.3	-0.8
Manchester	10,446	5,434	15,880	5.6	3.1	4.4	-2,842	-1,057	-3,899	-1.5	-0.6	-1.1
Oldham†	3,059	1,869	4,928	4.4	2.6	3.5	-1,839	-809	-2,648	-2.6	-1.1	-1.9
Rochdale	3,217	1,847	5,064	4.8	2.7	3.8	-1,431	-583	-2,014	-2.1	-0.9	-1.5
Salford	4,309	2,055	6,364	5.4	2.7	4.1	-1,177	-586	-1,763	-1.5	-0.8	-1.1
Stockport	3,275	1,551	4,826	3.7	1.7	2.7	-744	-157	-901	-0.8	-0.2	-0.5
Tameside†	3,135	1,753	4,888	4.5	2.5	3.5	-1,463	-565	-2,028	-2.1	-0.8	-1.4
Trafford	2,295	1,106	3,401	3.2	1.5	2.4	-756	-285	-1,041	-1.1	-0.4	-0.7
Wigan†	4,584	2,329	6,913	4.5	2.3	3.4	-1,772	-702	-2,474	-1.7	-0.7	-1.2
Lancashire	11,819	5,991	17,810	3.2	1.6	2.4	-3,464	-1,364	-4,828	-0.9	-0.4	-0.7
Burnley	1,304	748	2,052	4.8	2.7	3.7	-430	-174	-604	-1.6	-0.6	-1.1
Chorley	856	459	1,315	2.4	1.3	1.9	-295	-90	-385	-0.8	-0.3	-0.6
Fylde	657	303	960	2.9	1.3	2.1	-46	-26	-72	-0.2	-0.1	-0.2
Hyndburn	934	478	1,412	3.7	1.9	2.8	-400	-122	-522	-1.6	-0.5	-1.0
Lancaster	1,619	729	2,348	3.7	1.6	2.6	-246	-140	-386	-0.6	-0.3	-0.4
Pendle	980	532	1,512	3.5	1.9	2.7	-382	-138	-520	-1.4	-0.5	-0.9
Preston	1,766	862	2,628	3.7	1.9	2.8	-384	-132	-516	-0.8	-0.3	-0.5
Ribble Valley	230	127	357	1.3	0.7	1.0	-99	-41	-140	-0.6	-0.2	-0.4
Rossendale	717	351	1,068	3.3	1.6	2.4	-318	-138	-456	-1.5	-0.6	-1.0
South Ribble	694	416	1,110	2.0	1.2	1.6	-256	-95	-351	-0.8	-0.3	-0.5
West Lancashire	1,176	554	1,730	3.5	1.6	2.5	-367	-175	-542	-1.1	-0.5	-0.8
Wyre	886	432	1,318	2.8	1.3	2.1	-241	-93	-334	-0.8	-0.3	-0.5
Merseyside	25,666	13,116	38,782	5.8	2.9	4.3	-6,380	-2,527	-8,907	-1.4	-0.6	-1.0
Knowsley	2,893	1,693	4,586	6.5	3.4	4.9	-919	-424	-1,343	-2.1	-0.9	-1.4
Liverpool	11,196	5,796	16,992	6.9	3.6	5.2	-2,239	-899	-3,138	-1.4	-0.6	-1.0
Sefton	4,301	2,118	6,419	5.2	2.5	3.8	-1,376	-552	-1,928	-1.7	-0.6	-1.2
St. Helens	2,879	1,524	4,403	5.2	2.7	4.0	-792	-229	-1,021	-1.4	-0.4	-0.9
Wirral	4,397	1,985	6,382	4.6	2.0	3.2	-1,054	-423	-1,477	-1.1	-0.4	-0.7

4.10 Claimant count[1] by Unitary and Local Authority

not seasonally adjusted

	CLAIMANT COUNT ON 12th DECEMBER 2013						Change on year					
	Levels			Percentage of Pop[2]			Levels			Percentage[2]		
	Men	Women	People	Men	Women	People	Men	Women	People	Men	Women	People
	1	2	3	4	5	6	7	8	9	10	11	12
YORKSHIRE AND THE HUMBER	**84,342**	**43,649**	**127,991**	**5.0**	**2.6**	**3.8**	**-22,645**	**-8,872**	**-31,517**	**-1.3**	**-0.5**	**-0.9**
East Riding of Yorkshire	3,521	1,767	5,288	3.5	1.7	2.6	-1,093	-449	-1,542	-1.1	-0.4	-0.8
Kingston upon Hull, City of	7,997	3,827	11,824	9.1	4.6	6.9	-2,264	-860	-3,124	-2.6	-1.0	-1.8
North East Lincolnshire	3,448	1,745	5,193	6.9	3.5	5.2	-772	-333	-1,105	-1.6	-0.7	-1.1
North Lincolnshire	2,377	1,292	3,669	4.5	2.4	3.5	-662	-277	-939	-1.3	-0.5	-0.9
York	1,416	711	2,127	2.1	1.1	1.6	-505	-218	-723	-0.8	-0.3	-0.5
North Yorkshire	4,203	2,297	6,500	2.3	1.3	1.8	-1,532	-753	-2,285	-0.8	-0.4	-0.6
Craven	323	161	484	2.0	1.0	1.5	-116	-62	-178	-0.7	-0.4	-0.5
Hambleton	398	268	666	1.4	1.0	1.2	-174	-79	-253	-0.6	-0.3	-0.5
Harrogate	662	331	993	1.4	0.7	1.0	-317	-214	-531	-0.7	-0.4	-0.5
Richmondshire	241	175	416	1.2	1.2	1.2	-115	-47	-162	-0.6	-0.3	-0.5
Ryedale	325	188	513	2.1	1.2	1.7	-104	-78	-182	-0.7	-0.5	-0.6
Scarborough	1,622	746	2,368	5.1	2.3	3.6	-550	-221	-771	-1.7	-0.7	-1.2
Selby	632	428	1,060	2.4	1.6	2.0	-156	-52	-208	-0.6	-0.2	-0.4
South Yorkshire	22,928	11,790	34,718	5.3	2.7	4.0	-6,101	-2,255	-8,356	-1.4	-0.5	-1.0
Barnsley	3,685	2,016	5,701	5.0	2.7	3.8	-1,246	-532	-1,778	-1.7	-0.7	-1.2
Doncaster	5,149	2,908	8,057	5.3	3.0	4.2	-1,434	-565	-1,999	-1.5	-0.6	-1.0
Rotherham	4,647	2,378	7,025	5.8	2.9	4.3	-1,131	-425	-1,556	-1.4	-0.5	-1.0
Sheffield	9,447	4,488	13,935	5.1	2.5	3.8	-2,290	-733	-3,023	-1.2	-0.4	-0.8
West Yorkshire	38,452	20,220	58,672	5.3	2.8	4.1	-9,716	-3,727	-13,443	-1.3	-0.5	-0.9
Bradford	10,760	6,177	16,937	6.5	3.7	5.1	-1,981	-514	-2,495	-1.2	-0.3	-0.8
Calderdale	3,371	1,766	5,137	5.2	2.7	3.9	-955	-427	-1,382	-1.5	-0.6	-1.1
Kirklees	6,538	3,373	9,911	4.8	2.5	3.7	-2,012	-803	-2,815	-1.5	-0.6	-1.0
Leeds	13,264	6,505	19,769	5.3	2.6	3.9	-3,232	-1,286	-4,518	-1.3	-0.5	-0.9
Wakefield	4,519	2,399	6,918	4.3	2.3	3.3	-1,536	-697	-2,233	-1.5	-0.7	-1.1
EAST MIDLANDS	**50,292**	**28,044**	**78,336**	**3.5**	**1.9**	**2.7**	**-16,493**	**-7,597**	**-24,090**	**-1.1**	**-0.5**	**-0.8**
Derby	3,326	1,890	5,216	4.1	2.4	3.3	-1,688	-773	-2,461	-2.1	-1.0	-1.5
Leicester	5,925	3,710	9,635	5.3	3.3	4.3	-1,917	-603	-2,520	-1.7	-0.5	-1.1
Nottingham	7,441	3,820	11,261	6.7	3.6	5.2	-1,586	-621	-2,207	-1.4	-0.6	-1.0
Rutland	120	70	190	1.0	0.7	0.9	-68	-33	-101	-0.6	-0.3	-0.5
Derbyshire	6,629	3,656	10,285	2.7	1.5	2.1	-2,809	-1,306	-4,115	-1.2	-0.5	-0.8
Amber Valley	872	515	1,387	2.3	1.3	1.8	-568	-281	-849	-1.5	-0.7	-1.1
Bolsover	781	454	1,235	3.2	1.9	2.6	-117	-107	-224	-0.5	-0.4	-0.5
Chesterfield	1,291	616	1,907	3.9	1.9	2.9	-462	-195	-657	-1.4	-0.6	-1.0
Derbyshire Dales	261	172	433	1.2	0.8	1.0	-161	-61	-222	-0.7	-0.3	-0.5
Erewash	1,244	658	1,902	3.5	1.8	2.7	-540	-258	-798	-1.5	-0.7	-1.1
High Peak	812	426	1,238	2.8	1.5	2.1	-352	-144	-496	-1.2	-0.5	-0.9
North East Derbyshire	871	462	1,333	2.9	1.5	2.2	-334	-113	-447	-1.1	-0.4	-0.7
South Derbyshire	497	353	850	1.6	1.1	1.4	-275	-147	-422	-0.9	-0.5	-0.7
Leicestershire	4,066	2,358	6,424	1.9	1.1	1.5	-1,721	-910	-2,631	-0.8	-0.4	-0.6
Blaby	499	317	816	1.7	1.1	1.4	-253	-127	-380	-0.9	-0.4	-0.6
Charnwood	1,007	588	1,595	1.8	1.1	1.4	-514	-247	-761	-0.9	-0.5	-0.7
Harborough	273	167	440	1.0	0.6	0.8	-187	-85	-272	-0.7	-0.3	-0.5
Hinckley and Bosworth	750	441	1,191	2.3	1.3	1.8	-226	-143	-369	-0.7	-0.4	-0.6
Melton	286	168	454	1.8	1.0	1.4	-136	-90	-226	-0.9	-0.6	-0.7
North West Leicestershire	772	405	1,177	2.6	1.4	2.0	-285	-182	-467	-1.0	-0.6	-0.8
Oadby and Wigston	479	272	751	2.8	1.5	2.1	-120	-36	-156	-0.7	-0.2	-0.4
Lincolnshire	8,007	4,162	12,169	3.7	1.8	2.8	-1,517	-794	-2,311	-0.7	-0.4	-0.5
Boston	629	325	954	3.2	1.6	2.4	-129	-133	-262	-0.7	-0.7	-0.7
East Lindsey	1,910	993	2,903	5.0	2.5	3.7	-281	-145	-426	-0.7	-0.4	-0.5
Lincoln	1,807	848	2,655	5.6	2.6	4.1	-382	-143	-525	-1.2	-0.4	-0.8
North Kesteven	686	363	1,049	2.1	1.1	1.6	-147	-95	-242	-0.4	-0.3	-0.4
South Holland	676	440	1,116	2.6	1.6	2.1	-198	-84	-282	-0.8	-0.3	-0.5
South Kesteven	1,089	576	1,665	2.7	1.3	2.0	-247	-120	-367	-0.6	-0.3	-0.4
West Lindsey	1,210	617	1,827	4.5	2.2	3.3	-133	-74	-207	-0.5	-0.3	-0.4
Northamptonshire	6,727	3,990	10,717	3.0	1.8	2.4	-2,778	-1,391	-4,169	-1.2	-0.6	-0.9
Corby	779	476	1,255	3.8	2.3	3.1	-444	-280	-724	-2.2	-1.4	-1.8
Daventry	511	282	793	2.1	1.1	1.6	-207	-134	-341	-0.8	-0.5	-0.7
East Northamptonshire	623	372	995	2.3	1.4	1.8	-267	-166	-433	-1.0	-0.6	-0.8
Kettering	1,045	589	1,634	3.5	2.0	2.7	-391	-193	-584	-1.3	-0.6	-1.0
Northampton	2,611	1,489	4,100	3.7	2.1	2.9	-893	-436	-1,329	-1.3	-0.6	-0.9
South Northamptonshire	301	182	483	1.1	0.7	0.9	-104	-72	-176	-0.4	-0.3	-0.3

4.10 Claimant count[1] by Unitary and Local Authority

not seasonally adjusted

	CLAIMANT COUNT ON 12th DECEMBER 2013						Change on year					
	Levels			Percentage of Pop[2]			Levels			Percentage[2]		
	Men	Women	People	Men	Women	People	Men	Women	People	Men	Women	People
	1	2	3	4	5	6	7	8	9	10	11	12
Wellingborough	857	600	1,457	3.6	2.5	3.1	-472	-110	-582	-2.0	-0.5	-1.2
Nottinghamshire	8,051	4,388	12,439	3.2	1.8	2.5	-2,409	-1,166	-3,575	-1.0	-0.5	-0.7
Ashfield	1,484	859	2,343	3.9	2.2	3.1	-506	-228	-734	-1.3	-0.6	-1.0
Bassetlaw	1,237	707	1,944	3.5	2.0	2.7	-227	-80	-307	-0.6	-0.2	-0.4
Broxtowe	975	564	1,539	2.8	1.6	2.2	-435	-188	-623	-1.2	-0.5	-0.9
Gedling	1,175	572	1,747	3.3	1.6	2.4	-459	-210	-669	-1.3	-0.6	-0.9
Mansfield	1,538	799	2,337	4.6	2.4	3.5	-298	-178	-476	-0.9	-0.5	-0.7
Newark and Sherwood	961	557	1,518	2.7	1.5	2.1	-282	-152	-434	-0.8	-0.4	-0.6
Rushcliffe	681	330	1,011	2.0	1.0	1.5	-202	-130	-332	-0.6	-0.4	-0.5
WEST MIDLANDS†	81,626	45,649	127,275	4.6	2.6	3.6	-21,030	-8,743	-29,773	-1.2	-0.5	-0.8
Herefordshire, County of	1,147	685	1,832	2.0	1.2	1.6	-494	-206	-700	-0.9	-0.4	-0.6
Shropshire	2,392	1,280	3,672	2.5	1.4	1.9	-658	-312	-970	-0.7	-0.3	-0.5
Stoke-on-Trent	4,014	2,256	6,270	4.9	2.8	3.9	-1,247	-296	-1,543	-1.5	-0.4	-1.0
Telford and Wrekin	2,085	1,214	3,299	3.8	2.3	3.1	-687	-426	-1,113	-1.3	-0.8	-1.0
Staffordshire	5,816	3,530	9,346	2.2	1.3	1.7	-2,775	-1,191	-3,966	-1.0	-0.4	-0.7
Cannock Chase	915	513	1,428	2.9	1.6	2.3	-476	-231	-707	-1.5	-0.7	-1.1
East Staffordshire	679	464	1,143	1.8	1.3	1.6	-405	-147	-552	-1.1	-0.4	-0.8
Lichfield	497	324	821	1.6	1.0	1.3	-275	-169	-444	-0.9	-0.5	-0.7
Newcastle-under-Lyme	1,146	650	1,796	2.9	1.6	2.3	-217	-98	-315	-0.5	-0.2	-0.4
South Staffordshire	739	476	1,215	2.2	1.4	1.8	-344	-87	-431	-1.0	-0.3	-0.6
Stafford	791	411	1,202	1.9	1.0	1.4	-370	-188	-558	-0.9	-0.5	-0.7
Staffordshire Moorlands	567	321	888	1.9	1.1	1.5	-266	-86	-352	-0.9	-0.3	-0.6
Tamworth	482	371	853	2.0	1.5	1.7	-422	-185	-607	-1.7	-0.7	-1.2
Warwickshire†	3,729	2,149	5,878	2.2	1.2	1.7	-1,086	-530	-1,616	-0.6	-0.3	-0.5
North Warwickshire	389	231	620	2.0	1.2	1.6	-134	-131	-265	-0.7	-0.7	-0.7
Nuneaton and Bedworth	1,587	889	2,476	4.0	2.2	3.1	-206	-96	-302	-0.5	-0.2	-0.4
Rugby†	616	409	1,025	1.9	1.3	1.6	-178	-85	-263	-0.6	-0.3	-0.4
Stratford-on-Avon	372	208	580	1.1	0.6	0.8	-201	-93	-294	-0.6	-0.3	-0.4
Warwick	765	412	1,177	1.7	0.9	1.3	-367	-125	-492	-0.8	-0.3	-0.5
West Midlands (Metropolitan County)	57,465	31,905	89,370	6.6	3.6	5.1	-12,506	-5,113	-17,619	-1.4	-0.6	-1.0
Birmingham	26,856	14,417	41,273	7.8	4.1	5.9	-4,830	-1,976	-6,806	-1.4	-0.6	-1.0
Coventry	5,060	2,755	7,815	4.7	2.6	3.7	-1,127	-458	-1,585	-1.0	-0.4	-0.7
Dudley	5,309	2,692	8,001	5.5	2.8	4.1	-1,399	-664	-2,063	-1.4	-0.7	-1.1
Sandwell	6,829	3,988	10,817	7.0	4.0	5.5	-1,795	-734	-2,529	-1.8	-0.7	-1.3
Solihull	2,039	1,167	3,206	3.3	1.8	2.5	-618	-306	-924	-1.0	-0.5	-0.7
Walsall	4,943	3,073	8,016	5.9	3.7	4.8	-1,473	-496	-1,969	-1.8	-0.6	-1.2
Wolverhampton	6,429	3,813	10,242	8.0	4.8	6.4	-1,264	-479	-1,743	-1.6	-0.6	-1.1
Worcestershire	4,978	2,630	7,608	2.8	1.5	2.2	-1,577	-669	-2,246	-0.9	-0.4	-0.6
Bromsgrove	630	326	956	2.2	1.1	1.7	-198	-67	-265	-0.7	-0.2	-0.5
Malvern Hills	480	242	722	2.2	1.1	1.6	-119	-80	-199	-0.6	-0.4	-0.5
Redditch	842	539	1,381	3.1	1.9	2.5	-280	-114	-394	-1.0	-0.4	-0.7
Worcester	1,170	563	1,733	3.6	1.7	2.6	-233	-109	-342	-0.7	-0.3	-0.5
Wychavon	679	397	1,076	1.9	1.1	1.5	-423	-175	-598	-1.2	-0.5	-0.8
Wyre Forest	1,177	563	1,740	4.0	1.9	2.9	-324	-124	-448	-1.1	-0.4	-0.8
EAST OF ENGLAND	52,024	30,838	82,862	2.8	1.7	2.2	-18,003	-8,408	-26,411	-1.0	-0.5	-0.7
Bedford	1,927	1,143	3,070	3.9	2.2	3.0	-573	-341	-914	-1.1	-0.7	-0.9
Central Bedfordshire	1,593	1,070	2,663	1.9	1.3	1.6	-805	-318	-1,123	-1.0	-0.4	-0.7
Luton	2,446	1,740	4,186	3.6	2.6	3.1	-817	-288	-1,105	-1.2	-0.4	-0.8
Peterborough	2,420	1,678	4,098	4.0	2.8	3.4	-1,100	-523	-1,623	-1.8	-0.9	-1.4
Southend-on-Sea	2,541	1,368	3,909	4.6	2.5	3.6	-819	-277	-1,096	-1.5	-0.5	-1.0
Thurrock	1,880	1,360	3,240	3.6	2.6	3.1	-500	-221	-721	-1.0	-0.4	-0.7
Cambridgeshire	3,599	2,124	5,723	1.7	1.1	1.4	-1,718	-883	-2,601	-0.8	-0.4	-0.6
Cambridge	792	411	1,203	1.6	0.9	1.3	-311	-131	-442	-0.6	-0.3	-0.5
East Cambridgeshire	463	312	775	1.8	1.2	1.5	-199	-102	-301	-0.8	-0.4	-0.6
Fenland	848	560	1,408	2.9	1.9	2.4	-421	-226	-647	-1.4	-0.8	-1.1
Huntingdonshire	973	523	1,496	1.8	1.0	1.4	-511	-277	-788	-0.9	-0.5	-0.7
South Cambridgeshire	523	318	841	1.1	0.7	0.9	-276	-147	-423	-0.6	-0.3	-0.4
Essex	12,395	7,639	20,034	2.9	1.7	2.3	-3,953	-1,873	-5,826	-0.9	-0.4	-0.7
Basildon	2,147	1,411	3,558	3.9	2.5	3.2	-614	-301	-915	-1.1	-0.5	-0.8
Braintree	1,102	714	1,816	2.4	1.5	1.9	-457	-284	-741	-1.0	-0.6	-0.8
Brentwood	385	251	636	1.7	1.1	1.4	-147	-80	-227	-0.7	-0.3	-0.5

4.10 Claimant count[1] by Unitary and Local Authority

not seasonally adjusted

	CLAIMANT COUNT ON 12th DECEMBER 2013						Change on year					
	Levels			Percentage of Pop[2]			Levels			Percentage[2]		
	Men	Women	People	Men	Women	People	Men	Women	People	Men	Women	People
	1	2	3	4	5	6	7	8	9	10	11	12
Castle Point	681	451	1,132	2.6	1.7	2.1	-342	-95	-437	-1.3	-0.4	-0.8
Chelmsford	1,213	760	1,973	2.3	1.4	1.8	-483	-188	-671	-0.9	-0.3	-0.6
Colchester	1,537	829	2,366	2.7	1.4	2.1	-486	-233	-719	-0.9	-0.4	-0.6
Epping Forest	995	699	1,694	2.6	1.7	2.1	-292	-182	-474	-0.8	-0.4	-0.6
Harlow	1,220	754	1,974	4.7	2.8	3.7	-238	-134	-372	-0.9	-0.5	-0.7
Maldon	430	234	664	2.3	1.2	1.8	-131	-70	-201	-0.7	-0.4	-0.5
Rochford	484	325	809	1.9	1.3	1.6	-206	-99	-305	-0.8	-0.4	-0.6
Tendring	1,884	1,017	2,901	5.0	2.6	3.8	-411	-122	-533	-1.1	-0.3	-0.7
Uttlesford	317	194	511	1.3	0.8	1.0	-146	-85	-231	-0.6	-0.3	-0.5
Hertfordshire	7,897	4,878	12,775	2.2	1.3	1.8	-2,700	-1,400	-4,100	-0.8	-0.4	-0.6
Broxbourne	760	631	1,391	2.6	2.1	2.3	-381	-140	-521	-1.3	-0.5	-0.9
Dacorum	961	606	1,567	2.1	1.3	1.7	-230	-179	-409	-0.5	-0.4	-0.4
East Hertfordshire	761	436	1,197	1.7	1.0	1.3	-246	-156	-402	-0.6	-0.3	-0.5
Hertsmere	669	443	1,112	2.2	1.4	1.8	-206	-158	-364	-0.7	-0.5	-0.6
North Hertfordshire	932	542	1,474	2.3	1.3	1.8	-305	-157	-462	-0.8	-0.4	-0.6
St Albans	657	381	1,038	1.5	0.8	1.2	-267	-127	-394	-0.6	-0.3	-0.4
Stevenage	1,057	615	1,672	3.8	2.2	3.0	-344	-154	-498	-1.3	-0.6	-0.9
Three Rivers	466	265	731	1.7	0.9	1.3	-182	-97	-279	-0.7	-0.3	-0.5
Watford	795	465	1,260	2.6	1.5	2.1	-319	-149	-468	-1.0	-0.5	-0.8
Welwyn Hatfield	839	494	1,333	2.3	1.3	1.8	-220	-83	-303	-0.6	-0.2	-0.4
Norfolk	9,109	4,547	13,656	3.5	1.7	2.6	-2,758	-1,155	-3,913	-1.1	-0.4	-0.7
Breckland	1,078	592	1,670	2.7	1.5	2.1	-329	-172	-501	-0.8	-0.4	-0.6
Broadland	668	357	1,025	1.8	0.9	1.4	-264	-74	-338	-0.7	-0.2	-0.5
Great Yarmouth	2,160	978	3,138	7.4	3.3	5.3	-485	-291	-776	-1.7	-1.0	-1.3
King's Lynn and West Norfolk	1,530	814	2,344	3.5	1.8	2.7	-314	-147	-461	-0.7	-0.3	-0.5
North Norfolk	720	410	1,130	2.6	1.4	2.0	-273	-76	-349	-1.0	-0.3	-0.6
Norwich	2,203	1,000	3,203	4.8	2.2	3.5	-836	-285	-1,121	-1.8	-0.6	-1.2
South Norfolk	750	396	1,146	2.1	1.0	1.5	-257	-110	-367	-0.7	-0.3	-0.5
Suffolk	6,217	3,291	9,508	2.8	1.5	2.1	-2,260	-1,129	-3,389	-1.0	-0.5	-0.8
Babergh	524	343	867	2.0	1.3	1.7	-262	-117	-379	-1.0	-0.4	-0.7
Forest Heath	397	206	603	2.0	1.1	1.6	-185	-104	-289	-0.9	-0.5	-0.7
Ipswich	2,054	1,016	3,070	4.7	2.3	3.5	-561	-216	-777	-1.3	-0.5	-0.9
Mid Suffolk	489	318	807	1.7	1.1	1.4	-198	-98	-296	-0.7	-0.3	-0.5
St Edmundsbury	709	401	1,110	2.0	1.2	1.6	-266	-184	-450	-0.8	-0.5	-0.7
Suffolk Coastal	543	270	813	1.5	0.7	1.1	-299	-166	-465	-0.8	-0.5	-0.6
Waveney	1,501	737	2,238	4.5	2.2	3.3	-489	-244	-733	-1.5	-0.7	-1.1
LONDON†	100,239	69,394	169,633	3.5	2.4	3.0	-30,885	-18,773	-49,658	-1.1	-0.7	-0.9
Inner London†	48,301	32,811	81,112	4.0	2.8	3.4	-14,197	-8,492	-22,689	-1.2	-0.7	-1.0
Camden	2,331	1,525	3,856	2.9	1.9	2.4	-744	-474	-1,218	-0.9	-0.6	-0.7
City of London	58	32	90	1.8	1.3	1.6	-14	-11	-25	-0.4	-0.4	-0.4
Hackney	4,625	3,173	7,798	5.1	3.5	4.3	-1,321	-770	-2,091	-1.5	-0.8	-1.1
Hammersmith and Fulham†	2,360	1,654	4,014	3.6	2.4	3.0	-423	-333	-756	-0.7	-0.5	-0.6
Haringey	4,667	3,039	7,706	5.1	3.3	4.2	-1,120	-794	-1,914	-1.2	-0.9	-1.0
Islington	3,203	2,148	5,351	4.1	2.7	3.4	-918	-482	-1,400	-1.2	-0.6	-0.9
Kensington and Chelsea†	1,370	957	2,327	2.5	1.7	2.1	-367	-228	-595	-0.7	-0.4	-0.5
Lambeth	5,537	3,759	9,296	4.8	3.3	4.0	-1,341	-932	-2,273	-1.2	-0.8	-1.0
Lewisham	4,569	3,126	7,695	4.7	3.1	3.9	-1,473	-884	-2,357	-1.5	-0.9	-1.2
Newham	4,800	3,416	8,216	4.1	3.3	3.7	-1,853	-951	-2,804	-1.6	-0.9	-1.3
Southwark	4,931	3,406	8,337	4.6	3.1	3.9	-1,314	-791	-2,105	-1.2	-0.7	-1.0
Tower Hamlets	4,726	3,073	7,799	4.7	3.3	4.0	-1,911	-922	-2,833	-1.9	-1.0	-1.5
Wandsworth	2,961	2,022	4,983	2.7	1.7	2.2	-768	-474	-1,242	-0.7	-0.4	-0.5
Westminster	2,163	1,481	3,644	2.6	1.9	2.2	-630	-446	-1,076	-0.7	-0.6	-0.7
Outer London	51,938	36,583	88,521	3.2	2.2	2.7	-16,688	-10,281	-26,969	-1.0	-0.6	-0.8
Barking and Dagenham	2,960	2,193	5,153	5.0	3.5	4.3	-1,218	-760	-1,978	-2.1	-1.2	-1.6
Barnet	3,090	2,116	5,206	2.7	1.7	2.2	-729	-636	-1,365	-0.6	-0.5	-0.6
Bexley	1,787	1,434	3,221	2.5	1.9	2.2	-800	-364	-1,164	-1.1	-0.5	-0.8
Brent	4,734	2,997	7,731	4.3	2.8	3.6	-1,205	-733	-1,938	-1.1	-0.7	-0.9
Bromley	2,419	1,615	4,034	2.5	1.6	2.0	-973	-522	-1,495	-1.0	-0.5	-0.8
Croydon	4,232	2,986	7,218	3.6	2.4	3.0	-1,669	-1,033	-2,702	-1.4	-0.8	-1.1
Ealing	4,256	2,885	7,141	3.6	2.5	3.1	-897	-453	-1,350	-0.8	-0.4	-0.6
Enfield	4,260	3,431	7,691	4.3	3.2	3.7	-1,449	-1,009	-2,458	-1.5	-0.9	-1.2
Greenwich	3,538	2,428	5,966	4.0	2.8	3.4	-1,213	-715	-1,928	-1.4	-0.8	-1.1
Harrow	1,733	1,188	2,921	2.2	1.5	1.8	-404	-378	-782	-0.5	-0.5	-0.5
Havering	2,201	1,515	3,716	3.0	2.0	2.5	-907	-683	-1,590	-1.2	-0.9	-1.1
Hillingdon	2,252	1,669	3,921	2.4	1.8	2.1	-639	-251	-890	-0.7	-0.3	-0.5
Hounslow	2,344	1,579	3,923	2.6	1.8	2.2	-587	-399	-986	-0.6	-0.5	-0.6

4.10 Claimant count[1] by Unitary and Local Authority

not seasonally adjusted

	CLAIMANT COUNT ON 12th DECEMBER 2013						Change on year					
	Levels			Percentage of Pop[2]			Levels			Percentage[2]		
	Men	Women	People	Men	Women	People	Men	Women	People	Men	Women	People
	1	2	3	4	5	6	7	8	9	10	11	12
Kingston upon Thames	857	690	1,547	1.6	1.2	1.4	-327	-114	-441	-0.6	-0.2	-0.4
Merton	1,779	1,214	2,993	2.6	1.7	2.2	-447	-300	-747	-0.7	-0.4	-0.5
Redbridge	2,737	1,993	4,730	3.0	2.1	2.5	-1,128	-724	-1,852	-1.2	-0.8	-1.0
Richmond upon Thames	989	682	1,671	1.6	1.1	1.3	-173	-91	-264	-0.3	-0.1	-0.2
Sutton	1,436	1,037	2,473	2.3	1.6	2.0	-569	-307	-876	-0.9	-0.5	-0.7
Waltham Forest	4,334	2,931	7,265	4.8	3.3	4.0	-1,354	-809	-2,163	-1.5	-0.9	-1.2
SOUTH EAST	**63,156**	**35,297**	**98,453**	**2.3**	**1.3**	**1.8**	**-23,248**	**-10,176**	**-33,424**	**-0.8**	**-0.4**	**-0.6**
Bracknell Forest	668	428	1,096	1.7	1.1	1.4	-303	-157	-460	-0.8	-0.4	-0.6
Brighton and Hove	3,099	1,623	4,722	3.1	1.7	2.4	-875	-460	-1,335	-0.9	-0.5	-0.7
Isle of Wight	2,053	1,027	3,080	5.1	2.5	3.8	-422	-199	-621	-1.0	-0.5	-0.8
Medway	3,294	1,910	5,204	3.8	2.2	3.0	-1,056	-395	-1,451	-1.2	-0.5	-0.8
Milton Keynes	2,183	1,447	3,630	2.6	1.7	2.2	-1,019	-460	-1,479	-1.2	-0.6	-0.9
Portsmouth	2,516	1,329	3,845	3.5	2.0	2.7	-845	-336	-1,181	-1.2	-0.5	-0.8
Reading	1,490	845	2,335	2.7	1.6	2.2	-855	-396	-1,251	-1.6	-0.7	-1.2
Slough	1,609	1,078	2,687	3.4	2.3	2.9	-471	-198	-669	-1.0	-0.4	-0.7
Southampton	2,603	1,390	3,993	3.0	1.7	2.4	-986	-297	-1,283	-1.2	-0.4	-0.8
West Berkshire	665	352	1,017	1.4	0.7	1.0	-381	-222	-603	-0.8	-0.5	-0.6
Windsor and Maidenhead	770	438	1,208	1.7	1.0	1.3	-338	-157	-495	-0.7	-0.3	-0.5
Wokingham	548	309	857	1.1	0.6	0.9	-291	-158	-449	-0.6	-0.3	-0.5
Buckinghamshire	2,731	1,587	4,318	1.7	1.0	1.4	-1,118	-572	-1,690	-0.7	-0.4	-0.5
Aylesbury Vale	888	511	1,399	1.6	0.9	1.2	-365	-183	-548	-0.6	-0.3	-0.5
Chiltern	439	227	666	1.6	0.8	1.2	-127	-112	-239	-0.5	-0.4	-0.4
South Bucks	248	192	440	1.2	0.9	1.1	-131	-50	-181	-0.6	-0.2	-0.4
Wycombe	1,156	657	1,813	2.1	1.2	1.7	-495	-227	-722	-0.9	-0.4	-0.7
East Sussex	4,847	2,530	7,377	3.2	1.6	2.4	-1,486	-595	-2,081	-1.0	-0.4	-0.7
Eastbourne	1,195	594	1,789	4.1	2.0	3.0	-257	-72	-329	-0.9	-0.2	-0.6
Hastings	1,700	793	2,493	6.0	2.7	4.3	-558	-210	-768	-2.0	-0.7	-1.3
Lewes	691	384	1,075	2.4	1.3	1.8	-174	-95	-269	-0.6	-0.3	-0.5
Rother	676	411	1,087	2.8	1.6	2.2	-254	-119	-373	-1.0	-0.5	-0.7
Wealden	585	348	933	1.4	0.8	1.1	-243	-99	-342	-0.6	-0.2	-0.4
Hampshire	7,103	4,024	11,127	1.7	1.0	1.3	-3,190	-1,292	-4,482	-0.8	-0.3	-0.5
Basingstoke and Deane	890	551	1,441	1.6	1.0	1.3	-462	-191	-653	-0.8	-0.3	-0.6
East Hampshire	457	295	752	1.3	0.8	1.1	-214	-77	-291	-0.6	-0.2	-0.4
Eastleigh	635	326	961	1.6	0.8	1.2	-269	-163	-432	-0.7	-0.4	-0.5
Fareham	481	272	753	1.4	0.8	1.1	-262	-105	-367	-0.8	-0.3	-0.5
Gosport	725	349	1,074	2.8	1.3	2.1	-308	-160	-468	-1.2	-0.6	-0.9
Hart	281	166	447	1.0	0.6	0.8	-127	-72	-199	-0.4	-0.3	-0.3
Havant	1,207	648	1,855	3.4	1.8	2.5	-434	-117	-551	-1.2	-0.3	-0.8
New Forest	883	485	1,368	1.8	0.9	1.3	-360	-137	-497	-0.7	-0.3	-0.5
Rushmoor	616	384	1,000	1.9	1.2	1.6	-359	-144	-503	-1.1	-0.5	-0.8
Test Valley	479	336	815	1.3	0.9	1.1	-244	-32	-276	-0.7	-0.1	-0.4
Winchester	449	212	661	1.3	0.6	0.9	-151	-94	-245	-0.4	-0.3	-0.3
Kent	14,202	7,737	21,939	3.1	1.7	2.4	-4,127	-1,681	-5,808	-0.9	-0.4	-0.6
Ashford	952	542	1,494	2.6	1.4	2.0	-291	-116	-407	-0.8	-0.3	-0.6
Canterbury	1,197	579	1,776	2.5	1.2	1.8	-380	-115	-495	-0.8	-0.2	-0.5
Dartford	793	517	1,310	2.5	1.6	2.0	-271	-125	-396	-0.8	-0.4	-0.6
Dover	1,417	683	2,100	4.2	2.0	3.1	-316	-209	-525	-0.9	-0.6	-0.8
Gravesham	1,138	764	1,902	3.5	2.4	2.9	-431	-96	-527	-1.3	-0.3	-0.8
Maidstone	1,106	662	1,768	2.2	1.3	1.8	-425	-154	-579	-0.9	-0.3	-0.6
Sevenoaks	553	293	846	1.6	0.8	1.2	-190	-144	-334	-0.5	-0.4	-0.5
Shepway	1,406	721	2,127	4.3	2.2	3.2	-408	-195	-603	-1.2	-0.6	-0.9
Swale	1,757	969	2,726	4.1	2.3	3.2	-491	-138	-629	-1.1	-0.3	-0.7
Thanet	2,793	1,384	4,177	7.2	3.4	5.2	-452	-186	-638	-1.2	-0.5	-0.8
Tonbridge and Malling	653	384	1,037	1.8	1.0	1.4	-287	-110	-397	-0.8	-0.3	-0.5
Tunbridge Wells	437	239	676	1.2	0.7	0.9	-185	-93	-278	-0.5	-0.3	-0.4
Oxfordshire	3,009	1,692	4,701	1.4	0.8	1.1	-1,314	-547	-1,861	-0.6	-0.3	-0.4
Cherwell	529	336	865	1.2	0.7	0.9	-320	-129	-449	-0.7	-0.3	-0.5
Oxford	1,186	560	1,746	2.2	1.0	1.6	-438	-197	-635	-0.8	-0.4	-0.6
South Oxfordshire	416	290	706	1.0	0.7	0.8	-219	-97	-316	-0.5	-0.2	-0.4
Vale of White Horse	481	262	743	1.2	0.7	1.0	-155	-68	-223	-0.4	-0.2	-0.3
West Oxfordshire	397	244	641	1.2	0.7	1.0	-182	-56	-238	-0.5	-0.2	-0.4
Surrey	4,900	2,937	7,837	1.4	0.8	1.1	-2,236	-1,069	-3,305	-0.6	-0.3	-0.5
Elmbridge	455	295	750	1.2	0.7	0.9	-249	-76	-325	-0.6	-0.2	-0.4
Epsom and Ewell	340	202	542	1.5	0.8	1.1	-140	-89	-229	-0.6	-0.4	-0.5

4.10 Claimant count[1] by Unitary and Local Authority

not seasonally adjusted

	CLAIMANT COUNT ON 12th DECEMBER 2013						Change on year					
	Levels			Percentage of Pop[2]			Levels			Percentage[2]		
	Men	Women	People	Men	Women	People	Men	Women	People	Men	Women	People
	1	2	3	4	5	6	7	8	9	10	11	12
Guildford	586	317	903	1.3	0.7	1.0	-332	-199	-531	-0.7	-0.4	-0.6
Mole Valley	314	175	489	1.2	0.7	0.9	-128	-63	-191	-0.5	-0.2	-0.4
Reigate and Banstead	697	461	1,158	1.6	1.0	1.3	-275	-108	-383	-0.6	-0.2	-0.4
Runnymede	351	216	567	1.3	0.8	1.1	-143	-67	-210	-0.5	-0.2	-0.4
Spelthorne	504	311	815	1.6	1.0	1.3	-226	-119	-345	-0.7	-0.4	-0.6
Surrey Heath	392	239	631	1.4	0.9	1.2	-170	-63	-233	-0.6	-0.2	-0.4
Tandridge	377	236	613	1.5	0.9	1.2	-154	-104	-258	-0.6	-0.4	-0.5
Waverley	398	218	616	1.1	0.6	0.8	-226	-122	-348	-0.6	-0.3	-0.5
Woking	486	267	753	1.5	0.8	1.2	-193	-59	-252	-0.6	-0.2	-0.4
West Sussex	4,866	2,614	7,480	2.0	1.0	1.5	-1,935	-985	-2,920	-0.8	-0.4	-0.6
Adur	437	235	672	2.4	1.2	1.8	-170	-111	-281	-0.9	-0.6	-0.8
Arun	1,064	529	1,593	2.5	1.2	1.8	-421	-206	-627	-1.0	-0.5	-0.7
Chichester	619	386	1,005	1.9	1.1	1.5	-291	-122	-413	-0.9	-0.4	-0.6
Crawley	888	558	1,446	2.5	1.6	2.0	-258	-173	-431	-0.7	-0.5	-0.6
Horsham	602	260	862	1.5	0.6	1.1	-215	-119	-334	-0.5	-0.3	-0.4
Mid Sussex	459	243	702	1.1	0.6	0.8	-150	-91	-241	-0.3	-0.2	-0.3
Worthing	797	403	1,200	2.5	1.2	1.9	-430	-163	-593	-1.4	-0.5	-0.9
SOUTH WEST	42,649	22,067	64,716	2.6	1.3	2.0	-13,419	-6,371	-19,790	-0.8	-0.4	-0.6
Bath and North East Somerset	1,146	628	1,774	2.0	1.1	1.5	-374	-73	-447	-0.7	-0.1	-0.4
Bournemouth	2,045	981	3,026	3.2	1.6	2.4	-462	-154	-616	-0.7	-0.3	-0.5
Bristol, City of	5,932	3,019	8,951	4.0	2.1	3.0	-1,913	-955	-2,868	-1.3	-0.7	-1.0
Cornwall	4,668	2,465	7,133	2.9	1.5	2.2	-1,917	-905	-2,822	-1.2	-0.5	-0.9
Isles of Scilly	5	5	10	0.7	0.7	0.7	-2	-1	-3	-0.3	-0.1	-0.2
North Somerset	1,506	820	2,326	2.5	1.3	1.9	-677	-280	-957	-1.1	-0.4	-0.8
Plymouth	2,984	1,339	4,323	3.5	1.6	2.6	-981	-483	-1,464	-1.1	-0.6	-0.9
Poole	959	533	1,492	2.1	1.2	1.6	-143	-56	-199	-0.3	-0.1	-0.2
South Gloucestershire	1,537	909	2,446	1.8	1.1	1.4	-636	-350	-986	-0.7	-0.4	-0.6
Swindon	2,061	1,282	3,343	2.9	1.9	2.4	-328	-190	-518	-0.5	-0.3	-0.4
Torbay	1,791	844	2,635	4.7	2.1	3.4	-488	-249	-737	-1.3	-0.6	-1.0
Wiltshire	2,812	1,458	4,270	1.9	1.0	1.4	-818	-506	-1,324	-0.6	-0.3	-0.4
Devon	4,405	2,262	6,667	2.0	1.0	1.5	-1,806	-800	-2,606	-0.8	-0.3	-0.6
East Devon	585	305	890	1.6	0.8	1.2	-200	-97	-297	-0.5	-0.3	-0.4
Exeter	918	471	1,389	2.3	1.2	1.7	-352	-130	-482	-0.9	-0.3	-0.6
Mid Devon	406	222	628	1.8	0.9	1.3	-203	-56	-259	-0.9	-0.2	-0.5
North Devon	622	257	879	2.2	0.9	1.6	-298	-164	-462	-1.1	-0.6	-0.8
South Hams	324	215	539	1.3	0.8	1.1	-151	-59	-210	-0.6	-0.2	-0.4
Teignbridge	716	386	1,102	2.0	1.0	1.5	-270	-134	-404	-0.7	-0.4	-0.5
Torridge	607	264	871	3.2	1.3	2.3	-181	-96	-277	-1.0	-0.5	-0.7
West Devon	227	142	369	1.4	0.9	1.2	-151	-64	-215	-1.0	-0.4	-0.7
Dorset	2,072	1,111	3,183	1.7	0.9	1.3	-546	-263	-809	-0.5	-0.2	-0.3
Christchurch	282	135	417	2.2	1.0	1.6	-29	-12	-41	-0.2	-0.1	-0.2
East Dorset	307	183	490	1.3	0.7	1.0	-114	-35	-149	-0.5	-0.1	-0.3
North Dorset	235	152	387	1.1	0.7	0.9	-76	-36	-112	-0.4	-0.2	-0.3
Purbeck	202	120	322	1.5	0.9	1.2	-62	-39	-101	-0.5	-0.3	-0.4
West Dorset	338	198	536	1.2	0.7	0.9	-131	-70	-201	-0.5	-0.2	-0.4
Weymouth and Portland	708	323	1,031	3.5	1.7	2.6	-134	-71	-205	-0.7	-0.4	-0.5
Gloucestershire	5,061	2,571	7,632	2.7	1.4	2.0	-1,469	-730	-2,199	-0.8	-0.4	-0.6
Cheltenham	1,132	542	1,674	3.0	1.4	2.2	-454	-192	-646	-1.2	-0.5	-0.8
Cotswold	378	193	571	1.5	0.8	1.1	-93	-28	-121	-0.4	-0.1	-0.2
Forest of Dean	699	338	1,037	2.8	1.3	2.0	-151	-105	-256	-0.6	-0.4	-0.5
Gloucester	1,577	851	2,428	3.9	2.1	3.0	-432	-195	-627	-1.1	-0.5	-0.8
Stroud	698	342	1,040	2.0	1.0	1.5	-273	-135	-408	-0.8	-0.4	-0.6
Tewkesbury	577	305	882	2.3	1.2	1.7	-66	-75	-141	-0.3	-0.3	-0.3
Somerset	3,665	1,840	5,505	2.3	1.1	1.7	-859	-376	-1,235	-0.5	-0.2	-0.4
Mendip	631	295	926	1.9	0.9	1.4	-145	-110	-255	-0.4	-0.3	-0.4
Sedgemoor	1,161	647	1,808	3.3	1.8	2.6	-103	-39	-142	-0.3	-0.1	-0.2
South Somerset	817	402	1,219	1.7	0.8	1.3	-298	-105	-403	-0.6	-0.2	-0.4
Taunton Deane	834	365	1,199	2.5	1.1	1.8	-213	-116	-329	-0.6	-0.3	-0.5
West Somerset	222	131	353	2.4	1.3	1.8	-100	-6	-106	-1.1	-0.1	-0.5
WALES	42,276	21,257	63,533	4.4	2.2	3.3	-10,007	-3,937	-13,944	-1.0	-0.4	-0.7
Isle of Anglesey	1,154	549	1,703	5.5	2.6	4.1	-137	-78	-215	-0.7	-0.4	-0.5
Gwynedd	1,520	703	2,223	4.0	1.9	3.0	-210	-118	-328	-0.6	-0.3	-0.4
Conwy	1,596	747	2,343	4.8	2.2	3.5	-239	-56	-295	-0.7	-0.2	-0.4
Denbighshire	1,353	664	2,017	4.8	2.3	3.6	-265	-121	-386	-0.9	-0.4	-0.7

4.10 Claimant count[1] by Unitary and Local Authority

not seasonally adjusted

	CLAIMANT COUNT ON 12th DECEMBER 2013						Change on year					
	Levels			Percentage of Pop[2]			Levels			Percentage[2]		
	Men	Women	People	Men	Women	People	Men	Women	People	Men	Women	People
	1	2	3	4	5	6	7	8	9	10	11	12
Flintshire	1,594	926	2,520	3.3	1.9	2.6	-320	-160	-480	-0.7	-0.3	-0.5
Wrexham	1,959	1,017	2,976	4.5	2.4	3.5	-326	-72	-398	-0.8	-0.2	-0.5
Powys	878	453	1,331	2.2	1.2	1.7	-428	-184	-612	-1.1	-0.5	-0.8
Ceredigion	558	243	801	2.3	1.0	1.6	-117	-36	-153	-0.5	-0.2	-0.3
Pembrokeshire	1,489	710	2,199	4.1	1.9	3.0	-322	-55	-377	-0.9	-0.1	-0.5
Carmarthenshire	1,916	917	2,833	3.5	1.6	2.5	-409	-225	-634	-0.7	-0.4	-0.6
Swansea	2,878	1,316	4,194	3.7	1.7	2.7	-394	-212	-606	-0.5	-0.3	-0.4
Neath Port Talbot	1,786	882	2,668	4.1	2.0	3.0	-191	-126	-317	-0.4	-0.3	-0.4
Bridgend	1,701	864	2,565	3.8	2.0	2.9	-557	-242	-799	-1.3	-0.5	-0.9
The Vale of Glamorgan	1,430	652	2,082	3.7	1.6	2.6	-412	-144	-556	-1.1	-0.4	-0.7
Cardiff	5,761	2,789	8,550	4.9	2.3	3.6	-1,347	-392	-1,739	-1.1	-0.3	-0.7
Rhondda Cynon Taf	3,620	1,899	5,519	4.9	2.5	3.7	-1,164	-452	-1,616	-1.6	-0.6	-1.1
Merthyr Tydfil	1,162	631	1,793	6.3	3.3	4.7	-376	-136	-512	-2.0	-0.7	-1.4
Caerphilly	3,158	1,706	4,864	5.6	3.0	4.3	-820	-411	-1,231	-1.5	-0.7	-1.1
Blaenau Gwent	1,712	949	2,661	7.7	4.2	6.0	-541	-202	-743	-2.4	-0.9	-1.7
Torfaen	1,542	747	2,289	5.5	2.6	4.0	-494	-234	-728	-1.8	-0.8	-1.3
Monmouthshire	669	351	1,020	2.4	1.3	1.8	-261	-119	-380	-0.9	-0.4	-0.7
Newport	2,840	1,542	4,382	6.2	3.3	4.8	-677	-162	-839	-1.5	-0.3	-0.9
SCOTLAND†	74,523	33,761	108,284	4.4	1.9	3.1	-17,381	-7,838	-25,219	-1.0	-0.4	-0.7
Aberdeen City	1,548	724	2,272	1.9	0.9	1.4	-496	-223	-719	-0.6	-0.3	-0.5
Aberdeenshire	895	445	1,340	1.1	0.5	0.8	-350	-184	-534	-0.4	-0.2	-0.3
Angus	1,058	489	1,547	3.0	1.3	2.1	-377	-149	-526	-1.1	-0.4	-0.7
Argyll & Bute	1,049	432	1,481	4.0	1.6	2.8	-198	-149	-347	-0.8	-0.6	-0.7
Clackmannanshire	1,008	459	1,467	6.1	2.7	4.4	-114	-120	-234	-0.7	-0.7	-0.7
Dumfries & Galloway	1,714	853	2,567	3.8	1.8	2.8	-524	-263	-787	-1.2	-0.6	-0.9
Dundee City	3,147	1,238	4,385	6.5	2.4	4.4	-713	-196	-909	-1.5	-0.4	-0.9
East Ayrshire	2,678	1,176	3,854	6.9	2.9	4.9	-465	-227	-692	-1.2	-0.6	-0.9
East Dunbartonshire	738	328	1,066	2.3	1.0	1.6	-346	-143	-489	-1.1	-0.4	-0.7
East Lothian	1,116	531	1,647	3.6	1.6	2.6	-157	-128	-285	-0.5	-0.4	-0.4
East Renfrewshire	632	277	909	2.3	1.0	1.6	-206	-120	-326	-0.8	-0.4	-0.6
Edinburgh, City of	6,065	2,756	8,821	3.6	1.6	2.6	-1,202	-540	-1,742	-0.7	-0.3	-0.5
Na h-Eileanan an Iar	342	131	473	4.0	1.6	2.8	8	4	12	0.1	0.0	0.1
Falkirk	2,587	1,151	3,738	5.1	2.2	3.7	-363	-233	-596	-0.7	-0.5	-0.6
Fife	5,316	2,626	7,942	4.6	2.2	3.4	-1,152	-443	-1,595	-1.0	-0.4	-0.7
Glasgow City	12,860	5,451	18,311	6.3	2.6	4.4	-3,133	-1,476	-4,609	-1.5	-0.7	-1.1
Highland†	2,051	983	3,034	2.8	1.3	2.1	-710	-369	-1,079	-1.0	-0.5	-0.7
Inverclyde	1,222	477	1,699	4.8	1.8	3.3	-314	-257	-571	-1.2	-1.0	-1.1
Midlothian	1,095	505	1,600	4.2	1.8	3.0	-309	-145	-454	-1.2	-0.5	-0.8
Moray	644	332	976	2.2	1.1	1.7	-202	-96	-298	-0.7	-0.3	-0.5
North Ayrshire	3,084	1,497	4,581	7.5	3.3	5.3	-729	-303	-1,032	-1.8	-0.7	-1.2
North Lanarkshire	6,068	2,988	9,056	5.6	2.6	4.1	-1,657	-503	-2,160	-1.5	-0.4	-1.0
Orkney Islands	95	39	134	1.4	0.6	1.0	-17	-25	-42	-0.3	-0.4	-0.3
Perth & Kinross	1,144	520	1,664	2.5	1.1	1.8	-250	-78	-328	-0.5	-0.2	-0.4
Renfrewshire	3,098	1,293	4,391	5.6	2.2	3.9	-496	-205	-701	-0.9	-0.4	-0.6
Scottish Borders	1,167	540	1,707	3.4	1.5	2.5	-199	-78	-277	-0.6	-0.2	-0.4
Shetland Islands	101	38	139	1.3	0.5	0.9	-50	-26	-76	-0.7	-0.4	-0.5
South Ayrshire	1,806	821	2,627	5.4	2.3	3.8	-304	-140	-444	-0.9	-0.4	-0.6
South Lanarkshire	4,827	2,222	7,049	4.9	2.1	3.5	-1,199	-519	-1,718	-1.2	-0.5	-0.8
Stirling	1,012	501	1,513	3.6	1.6	2.6	-269	-84	-353	-0.9	-0.3	-0.6
West Dunbartonshire	2,188	924	3,112	7.7	3.0	5.3	-360	-119	-479	-1.3	-0.4	-0.8
West Lothian	2,168	1,014	3,182	3.8	1.7	2.8	-528	-301	-829	-0.9	-0.5	-0.7

Relationship between columns = 3=1+2; 9=7+8

Source: Jobcentre Plus administrative system

Labour market statistics enquiries: labour.market@ons.gov.uk

1. The Claimant Count is a measure of the number of people claiming Jobseeker's Allowance. Claimants of Universal Credit (which, for the December 2013 Claimant Count date, had been introduced in seven Jobcentre Plus offices) are not yet included in the Claimant Count. See Background Note 3 of the Statistical Bulletin for details. The level measures the number of claimants on the second Thursday of each month (the "count date").

† Area affected by the start of the introduction of Universal Credit.

2. Percentages of population aged from 16 to 64 based on mid-year 2012 population estimates.

NB. These are different from the national and regional claimant count rates shown in Tables 7 of HI01 to HI11 and of other headline indicators. See Concepts and Definitions.

More detailed estimates and time series are available from Nomis at: http://www.nomisweb.co.uk

Table 4.11a Weekly pay - Gross (£) - For all employee jobs[a] by Industry: United Kingdom, 2013

Description	Code	Number of jobs[b] (thousand)	Median	Annual % change	Mean	Annual % change	Percentiles 10	20	25	30	40	60	70	75	80	90
ALL EMPLOYEES		24,575	415.3	2.3	501.3	2.0	124.2	211.8	251.0	286.0	348.4	491.6	584.5	642.3	704.4	909.8
All Industries and Services		24,567	415.4	2.3	501.4	2.1	124.2	211.9	251.1	286.1	348.5	491.7	584.5	642.4	704.4	909.8
All Index of Production Industries		2,748	521.9	3.2	600.8	3.3	275.4	340.2	369.8	398.7	459.3	595.8	681.6	730.1	792.2	994.6
All Manufacturing		2,403	510.6	2.9	584.2	2.7	270.9	333.6	361.7	388.9	448.7	581.0	667.8	711.0	766.8	958.2
All Service Industries		20,875	394.3	2.2	485.1	1.8	113.2	191.7	230.6	265.9	328.7	471.5	566.2	622.4	689.9	893.5
AGRICULTURE, FORESTRY AND FISHING	A	121	356.2	7.9	392.1	8.2	122.9	200.2	240.2	264.3	307.5	401.7	468.9	501.5	536.6	678.1
Crop and animal production, hunting and related service activities	1	109	345.0	5.4	382.8	7.8	119.8	193.9	231.0	260.8	302.9	392.6	458.4	491.4	525.7	654.3
Forestry and logging	2	7	480.3	7.6	512.5	9.8	x	317.4	364.2	391.0	435.6	521.9	600.9	x	x	x
Fishing and aquaculture	3	x	x		435.9	14.3	x	x	x	x	x	x	x	x	x	x
MINING AND QUARRYING	B	46	722.0	0.5	904.3	8.0	382.8	460.9	490.2	550.7	622.9	849.1	969.3	1,108.9	1,217.2	x
Mining of coal and lignite	5	x	870.7	5.3	914.0	9.1	x	x	706.0	771.9	802.0	902.3	x	x	x	x
Extraction of crude petroleum and natural gas	6	8	1,222.2	10.5	1,298.6	2.1	x	636.4	711.3	813.7	980.3	#####	1,513.7	x	x	x
Mining of metal ores	7	:														
Other mining and quarrying	8	17	566.2	16.1	744.5	36.0	346.4	398.0	426.6	458.0	488.3	624.8	755.1	825.5	x	x
Mining support service activities	9	17	726.1	0.9	883.3	6.8	383.4	464.1	484.4	565.5	639.0	840.4	948.4	1,128.3	x	x
MANUFACTURING	C	2,403	510.6	2.9	584.2	2.7	270.9	333.6	361.7	388.9	448.7	581.0	667.8	711.0	766.8	958.2
Manufacture of food products	10	353	392.8	2.6	482.3	3.5	230.5	273.2	291.5	311.0	351.0	453.6	526.8	576.7	642.5	808.5
Manufacture of beverages	11	41	596.5	6.4	681.0	7.7	311.1	413.6	448.3	466.6	525.1	660.7	757.1	811.2	886.0	x
Manufacture of tobacco products	12	6	889.1	11.0	1,007.6	22.7	x	702.0	714.9	755.7	834.0	933.6	1,120.9	x	x	x
Manufacture of textiles	13	41	369.2	4.7	445.9	6.1	217.6	263.4	280.0	293.9	330.2	395.4	466.7	545.7	612.4	x
Manufacture of wearing apparel	14	17	283.9	4.8	347.0	1.8	112.3	147.6	155.8	177.6	242.0	336.3	385.1	422.3	x	x
Manufacture of leather and related products	15	8	345.5	3.8	429.2	6.2	x	254.9	279.9	285.5	317.4	395.3	x	x	x	x
Manufacture of wood and of products of wood and cork, except furniture; manufacture of articles of straw and plaiting materials	16	50	419.2	4.1	467.4	5.2	253.4	309.3	322.5	345.6	377.0	462.1	510.5	536.8	596.2	x
Manufacture of paper and paper products	17	58	487.3	-0.8	550.0	-1.1	274.2	332.2	365.5	390.8	443.1	538.3	599.6	650.5	708.1	x
Printing and reproduction of recorded media	18	98	451.3	0.7	506.5	0.8	241.4	313.6	337.3	360.1	407.3	504.8	574.9	611.5	655.1	804.9
Manufacture of coke and refined petroleum products	19	11	896.8	2.0	1,009.8	2.2	420.2	625.0	662.3	704.6	812.9	989.4	1,094.0	x	x	x
Manufacture of chemicals and chemical products	20	100	557.7	0.4	632.2	1.4	297.6	375.9	405.1	437.3	494.0	618.0	696.4	754.7	815.9	1,054.0
Manufacture of basic pharmaceutical products and pharmaceutical preparations	21	65	673.3	3.1	763.7	-0.7	390.5	464.8	498.5	536.8	602.6	765.5	874.0	938.1	1,020.3	x
Manufacture of rubber and plastic products	22	148	431.6	4.9	514.8	5.2	254.9	306.0	327.1	345.0	383.7	494.6	558.1	587.7	647.6	808.4
Manufacture of other non-metallic mineral products	23	86	521.7	7.2	558.8	0.0	286.2	340.4	374.6	405.3	453.4	584.7	656.5	687.5	731.5	862.7
Manufacture of basic metals	24	85	612.2	0.8	642.4	0.1	331.0	428.7	465.2	500.1	555.4	665.1	737.3	780.2	815.5	942.3
Manufacture of fabricated metal products, except machinery and equipment	25	267	487.1	4.0	531.6	1.8	269.2	331.9	360.0	383.3	430.0	536.5	604.5	650.1	697.5	835.7
Manufacture of computer, electronic and optical products	26	140	585.1	1.8	664.9	2.1	298.1	368.5	397.2	422.8	501.9	671.2	760.2	813.6	888.6	1,111.2
Manufacture of electrical equipment	27	94	476.4	5.8	563.6	7.7	276.8	325.8	351.7	378.2	421.8	535.0	612.6	651.9	704.5	x
Manufacture of machinery and equipment n.e.c.	28	207	560.6	2.2	627.4	1.6	324.3	383.9	413.7	443.4	495.9	625.9	695.4	736.9	791.9	958.4
Manufacture of motor vehicles, trailers and semi-trailers	29	160	601.4	6.0	682.6	6.9	331.3	408.5	441.5	481.4	537.9	679.0	759.2	818.0	874.4	1,077.3
Manufacture of other transport equipment	30	173	689.2	3.9	732.9	-1.5	425.2	504.5	538.3	570.0	641.6	735.7	794.1	839.6	885.5	1,066.7
Manufacture of furniture	31	53	395.2	-0.2	461.0	1.3	249.8	280.0	300.3	317.0	353.5	441.1	504.1	548.4	605.2	x
Other manufacturing	32	63	426.4	-0.8	484.6	-2.8	230.0	287.5	306.7	325.1	372.4	483.0	526.4	559.4	622.1	x
Repair and installation of machinery and equipment	33	81	622.3	5.5	700.7	2.8	315.8	400.0	430.7	463.9	536.4	704.3	811.4	890.8	964.2	x
ELECTRICITY, GAS, STEAM AND AIR CONDITIONING SUPPLY	D	168	685.8	12.3	761.1	9.9	343.2	418.5	464.5	493.2	593.4	792.0	903.3	961.6	1,044.4	1,243.2
Electricity, gas, steam and air conditioning supply	35	168	685.8	12.3	761.1	9.9	343.2	418.5	464.5	493.2	593.4	792.0	903.3	961.6	1,044.4	1,243.2
WATER SUPPLY; SEWERAGE, WASTE MANAGEMENT AND REMEDIATION ACTIVITIES	E	131	526.6	3.3	595.4	3.8	294.2	364.2	401.8	429.4	477.1	591.2	659.5	698.8	740.4	925.5
Water collection, treatment and supply	36	40	587.7	6.4	624.3	4.7	345.7	432.8	458.0	479.6	533.3	625.6	683.0	708.8	748.6	x
Sewerage	37	14	512.4	1.0	594.8	12.4	345.7	387.5	411.2	440.8	480.1	578.9	653.7	705.2	x	x
Waste collection, treatment and disposal activities; materials recovery	38	75	490.0	1.0	581.8	2.7	268.2	330.9	360.6	395.9	449.7	556.1	643.2	688.2	738.6	x
Remediation activities and other waste management services	39	x	x		539.9	-17.9	x	x	x	x	x	x	x	x	x	x
CONSTRUCTION	F	824	519.4	2.7	597.1	2.5	231.0	345.0	382.3	410.4	466.9	586.9	675.0	732.1	796.1	1,006.1
Construction of buildings	41	252	528.2	-3.2	641.5	-1.0	240.9	350.0	390.7	418.0	473.6	612.7	721.6	792.0	862.4	1,135.1

Table 4.11a   Weekly pay - Gross (£) - For all employee jobs[a] by Industry: United Kingdom, 2013

Description	Code	Number of jobs[b] (thousand)	Median	Annual % change	Mean	Annual % change	Percentiles 10	20	25	30	40	60	70	75	80	90
Civil engineering	42	181	566.5	8.0	655.8	5.8	287.7	382.5	419.1	446.5	498.3	647.5	764.1	813.0	872.7	1,079.8
Specialised construction activities	43	392	499.9	2.9	541.5	2.6	201.3	325.0	360.0	393.8	450.0	554.3	625.0	666.2	717.3	871.2
WHOLESALE AND RETAIL TRADE; REPAIR OF MOTOR VEHICLES AND MOTORCYCLES	G	3,569	307.6	3.5	387.3	4.4	98.8	143.4	168.8	200.7	260.1	360.7	431.9	479.0	536.5	726.9
Wholesale and retail trade and repair of motor vehicles and motorcycles	45	405	398.1	3.4	456.8	3.4	180.9	271.9	290.5	308.6	351.4	445.8	500.1	534.4	574.9	725.0
Wholesale trade, except of motor vehicles and motorcycles	46	966	443.2	2.7	556.5	3.3	235.3	300.0	323.7	345.0	386.6	507.1	594.1	651.6	725.0	977.4
Retail trade, except of motor vehicles and motorcycles	47	2,198	233.7	2.9	300.2	4.2	78.5	112.3	127.9	145.0	184.9	277.9	329.5	362.7	408.2	574.9
TRANSPORTATION AND STORAGE	H	1,063	493.6	1.4	565.4	3.0	267.0	349.2	380.8	399.6	445.3	551.6	623.3	667.3	728.0	910.8
Land transport and transport via pipelines	49	454	503.0	1.4	539.1	2.0	256.1	352.3	383.7	407.6	452.0	552.9	618.3	657.4	712.9	877.0
Water transport	50	11	506.5	0.2	600.5	2.1	x	350.7	385.7	421.1	466.0	588.1	651.2	x	x	x
Air transport	51	69	628.9	12.8	820.7	15.5	308.1	373.9	421.3	457.9	536.9	753.1	880.8	974.0	1,057.4	x
Warehousing and support activities for transportation	52	315	518.3	0.4	609.4	1.7	284.1	348.2	378.6	404.7	461.5	594.1	670.8	721.9	793.5	1,040.4
Postal and courier activities	53	214	438.3	2.2	472.2	2.1	253.4	333.2	368.7	393.7	399.7	474.3	526.4	556.8	588.2	695.9
ACCOMMODATION AND FOOD SERVICE ACTIVITIES	I	1,228	203.9	0.9	244.9	2.0	54.4	91.5	105.9	123.8	160.0	247.7	290.2	317.2	349.6	458.2
Accommodation	55	284	258.7	2.1	296.4	3.4	71.0	124.2	154.8	180.9	227.7	291.9	336.1	360.3	393.0	518.5
Food and beverage service activities	56	944	185.5	1.7	229.4	1.5	51.9	84.5	99.0	113.9	148.0	229.3	274.5	301.6	335.4	440.5
INFORMATION AND COMMUNICATION	J	959	623.2	-1.5	725.5	-0.8	269.2	375.7	421.6	460.0	536.6	713.1	832.6	908.4	993.6	1,288.4
Publishing activities	58	153	498.3	0.9	604.9	2.7	x	306.6	345.0	375.4	440.0	579.6	670.8	736.5	815.1	1,045.3
Motion picture, video and television programme production, sound recording and music publishing activities	59	49	432.1	-10.0	581.0	-8.3	95.1	145.3	183.0	244.5	356.7	520.1	632.4	699.1	796.0	x
Programming and broadcasting activities	60	45	701.7	4.7	794.2	0.4	398.6	471.5	519.8	557.0	643.4	773.6	854.8	885.7	952.0	x
Telecommunications	61	210	608.2	-7.5	707.3	-4.1	309.1	410.2	453.9	491.7	557.6	687.6	778.8	849.9	942.5	1,199.1
Computer programming, consultancy and related activities	62	438	676.8	0.3	775.3	0.0	287.5	394.9	449.7	482.0	574.9	785.1	910.3	990.5	1,070.2	1,372.2
Information service activities	63	65	709.3	2.1	794.5	-0.2	332.4	422.3	476.7	530.1	604.2	825.5	931.7	1,011.0	1,075.3	x
FINANCIAL AND INSURANCE ACTIVITIES	K	1,019	602.2	4.7	858.6	6.9	277.9	347.6	379.1	416.0	498.3	743.5	923.2	1,053.5	1,201.9	1,704.4
Financial service activities, except insurance and pension funding	64	561	602.2	5.4	873.8	8.3	273.3	340.5	372.3	407.9	493.6	765.4	955.2	1,078.5	1,245.7	1,730.9
Insurance, reinsurance and pension funding, except compulsory social security	65	132	574.9	5.5	769.4	2.6	290.7	358.4	396.2	428.2	499.5	691.0	821.4	919.9	1,066.6	1,451.2
Activities auxiliary to financial services and insurance activities	66	327	612.2	3.9	868.6	6.2	277.8	354.7	383.3	421.6	512.9	741.7	919.9	1,054.1	1,186.4	1,724.9
REAL ESTATE ACTIVITIES	L	316	432.4	2.4	496.9	0.9	167.1	269.2	306.6	331.2	383.3	486.4	545.6	587.7	636.9	826.9
Real estate activities	68	316	432.4	2.4	496.9	0.9	167.1	269.2	306.6	331.2	383.3	486.4	545.6	587.7	636.9	826.9
PROFESSIONAL, SCIENTIFIC AND TECHNICAL ACTIVITIES	M	1,479	546.2	-0.3	674.4	0.5	190.6	306.6	349.2	389.5	468.2	641.5	756.3	824.1	910.4	1,245.7
Legal and accounting activities	69	482	517.5	0.0	655.0	-0.2	204.5	295.9	327.9	364.1	431.1	613.3	730.2	804.9	902.4	1,245.7
Activities of head offices; management consultancy activities	70	279	543.9	-1.9	733.2	1.9	149.5	277.4	333.2	366.0	457.6	650.6	804.9	881.7	1,011.0	1,485.3
Architectural and engineering activities; technical testing and analysis	71	360	600.5	2.7	697.3	2.8	263.9	383.3	428.0	460.0	532.5	684.3	777.4	843.3	915.1	1,165.8
Scientific research and development	72	114	687.1	1.9	802.6	-3.1	391.2	475.4	509.3	538.3	621.0	769.3	866.4	942.3	1,027.4	x
Advertising and market research	73	113	493.5	2.2	643.8	1.8	101.4	264.9	336.0	367.8	426.1	567.6	673.2	747.4	840.9	x
Other professional, scientific and technical activities	74	88	423.0	-5.9	495.5	-3.9	115.7	182.3	230.0	276.7	355.1	488.7	574.9	639.6	709.7	x
Veterinary activities	75	43	356.2	-3.4	427.0	-1.9	135.2	199.5	231.7	260.4	306.2	415.8	520.9	578.8	658.0	x
ADMINISTRATIVE AND SUPPORT SERVICE ACTIVITIES	N	1,471	319.8	2.8	386.5	3.2	83.6	146.2	182.6	219.9	271.8	373.9	447.8	488.0	543.7	723.7
Rental and leasing activities	77	114	445.9	7.4	514.2	9.6	233.5	316.2	333.4	350.1	394.8	499.1	569.2	615.9	671.3	872.0
Employment activities	78	543	299.0	2.7	363.9	1.7	109.5	180.9	208.1	230.3	260.7	346.8	407.1	453.7	498.3	660.3
Travel agency, tour operator and other reservation service and related activities	79	49	427.1	17.2	562.3	18.1	224.3	287.8	313.8	342.6	380.0	510.4	582.3	630.2	707.6	x
Security and investigation activities	80	93	390.5	1.9	393.6	-3.2	139.9	234.4	270.4	302.1	349.8	440.0	475.2	492.7	516.9	600.4
Services to buildings and landscape activities	81	415	200.0	3.1	279.4	3.0	60.0	77.4	91.1	103.7	143.6	279.0	344.7	380.1	429.1	596.3
Office administrative, office support and other business support activities	82	258	401.8	4.8	514.3	5.0	143.4	242.9	268.3	286.2	338.6	475.1	574.9	637.8	718.7	966.1
PUBLIC ADMINISTRATION AND DEFENCE; COMPULSORY SOCIAL SECURITY	O	1,258	545.8	3.1	573.5	2.1	260.4	351.8	380.9	414.4	476.8	609.6	681.8	721.3	769.2	900.4
Public administration and defence; compulsory social security	84	1,258	545.8	3.1	573.5	2.1	260.4	351.8	380.9	414.4	476.8	609.6	681.8	721.3	769.2	900.4
EDUCATION	P	3,881	412.4	1.0	456.5	1.3	99.8	184.7	222.2	260.4	335.4	493.4	592.6	646.0	699.4	844.1

93

Table 4.11a   Weekly pay - Gross (£) - For all employee jobs[a] by Industry: United Kingdom, 2013

Description	Code	Number of jobs[b] (thousand)	Median	Annual % change	Mean	Annual % change	Percentiles 10	20	25	30	40	60	70	75	80	90
Education	85	3,881	412.4	1.0	456.5	1.3	99.8	184.7	222.2	260.4	335.4	493.4	592.6	646.0	699.4	844.1
HUMAN HEALTH AND SOCIAL WORK ACTIVITIES	Q	3,696	374.8	1.3	461.4	0.4	139.7	206.7	235.9	265.2	316.9	445.7	534.7	585.4	646.1	806.1
Human health activities	86	2,379	450.4	2.2	541.0	0.6	178.1	261.8	295.4	326.9	384.6	530.9	617.0	661.8	723.6	906.2
Residential care activities	87	676	270.1	1.5	310.7	0.4	115.7	162.1	184.7	204.3	235.8	302.9	348.8	381.6	425.4	560.3
Social work activities without accommodation	88	641	282.2	2.5	324.8	1.7	83.7	140.5	164.4	191.4	239.5	328.4	395.7	434.9	476.7	603.7
ARTS, ENTERTAINMENT AND RECREATION	R	472	282.7	1.1	362.9	-0.2	39.8	97.1	124.9	157.0	225.1	333.8	397.1	440.8	498.3	669.8
Creative, arts and entertainment activities	90	44	410.0	-6.8	492.7	1.9	113.1	191.1	250.2	287.5	351.8	483.2	551.1	594.1	673.6	x
Libraries, archives, museums and other cultural activities	91	56	392.6	-2.7	416.6	-3.1	86.7	174.1	213.4	266.4	328.2	443.3	511.1	557.0	592.4	x
Gambling and betting activities	92	107	296.9	3.0	363.7	3.9	116.4	188.2	208.7	225.8	262.0	331.3	379.9	410.9	458.0	x
Sports activities and amusement and recreation activities	93	265	224.5	0.4	329.7	-1.9	26.8	54.6	76.1	99.1	155.7	287.5	348.5	387.0	437.4	616.7
OTHER SERVICE ACTIVITIES	S	413	345.8	6.3	406.9	3.2	93.7	147.2	179.3	213.7	280.5	408.2	476.4	522.3	580.6	772.6
Activities of membership organisations	94	199	390.7	-2.7	447.7	1.4	74.2	155.3	204.8	246.8	326.2	446.5	536.4	581.9	655.1	826.3
Repair of computers and personal and household goods	95	38	494.6	15.0	580.7	9.2	240.2	336.5	364.2	384.3	439.9	561.3	626.0	709.4	804.9	x
Other personal service activities	96	176	263.8	5.8	323.4	0.2	96.2	126.1	146.0	166.3	216.7	316.4	383.3	416.8	456.9	595.6
ACTIVITIES OF HOUSEHOLDS AS EMPLOYERS; UNDIFFERENTIATED GOODS-AND SERVICES-PRODUCING ACTIVITIES OF HOUSEHOLDS FOR OWN USE	T	49	152.3	12.8	208.0	9.2	29.0	54.5	67.0	75.8	110.5	191.4	263.6	289.8	329.5	x
Activities of households as employers of domestic personnel	97	49	152.3	12.8	208.0	9.2	29.0	54.5	67.0	75.8	110.5	191.4	263.6	289.8	329.5	x
Undifferentiated goods- and services-producing activities of private households for own use	98	:														
ACTIVITIES OF EXTRATERRITORIAL ORGANISATIONS AND BODIES	U	x	x		522.0	-7.2	x	x	x	x	x	x	x	x	x	x
Activities of extraterritorial organisations and bodies	99	x	x		522.0	-7.2	x	x	x	x	x	x	x	x	x	x
NOT CLASSIFIED		8	201.8		254.6		x	106.1	120.4	139.9	167.0	x	x	x	x	x

a Employees on adult rates whose pay for the survey pay-period was not affected by absence.
b Figures for Number of Jobs are for indicative purposes only and should not be considered an accurate estimate of employee job counts.
KEY - The colour coding indicates the quality of each estimate; jobs, median, mean and percentiles but not the annual percentage change.
The quality of an estimate is measured by its coefficient of variation (CV), which is the ratio of the standard error of an estimate to the estimate.

Source: Annual Survey of Hours and Earnings, Office for National Statistics.

Key
CV <= 5%
CV > 5% and <= 10%
CV > 10% and <= 20%
x = unreliable
CV > 20% or unavailable
.. = disclosive
: = not applicable
- = nil or negligible

Table 4.11b   Hourly pay - Gross (£) - For all employee jobs[a] by Industry: United Kingdom, 2013

Description	Code	Number of jobs[b] (thousand)	Median	Annual % change	Mean	Annual % change	Percentiles 10	20	25	30	40	60	70	75	80	90
ALL EMPLOYEES		24,575	11.59	2.7	15.13	2.0	6.57	7.55	8.12	8.72	10.00	13.61	16.14	17.68	19.55	25.38
All Industries and Services		24,567	11.59	2.8	15.14	2.0	6.57	7.55	8.12	8.72	10.00	13.61	16.14	17.68	19.55	25.38
All Index of Production Industries		2,748	12.91	3.7	15.31	3.3	7.42	8.77	9.41	10.05	11.40	14.79	17.04	18.37	20.00	25.44
All Manufacturing		2,403	12.58	3.3	14.86	2.5	7.28	8.56	9.20	9.84	11.15	14.37	16.58	17.83	19.37	24.59
All Service Industries		20,875	11.32	2.0	15.14	1.8	6.50	7.42	7.94	8.50	9.79	13.42	16.02	17.65	19.55	25.45
AGRICULTURE, FORESTRY AND FISHING	A	121	8.83	5.3	10.40	6.3	6.31	7.00	7.18	7.50	8.09	9.88	10.72	11.31	12.32	15.68
Crop and animal production, hunting and related service activities	1	109	8.60	4.8	10.12	6.3	6.28	6.96	7.08	7.45	7.99	9.57	10.41	11.00	11.98	15.07
Forestry and logging	2	7	12.38	0.5	13.80	0.5	x	10.04	x	10.70	11.31	13.07	14.74	x	x	x
Fishing and aquaculture	3	x	9.07	5.8	12.13	18.4	x	x	x	8.52	8.80	x	x	x	x	x
MINING AND QUARRYING	B	46	17.84	3.2	22.01	9.6	9.58	11.00	12.00	13.04	15.58	20.40	23.81	25.23	29.68	x
Mining of coal and lignite	5	x	17.60	20.1	19.61	16.1	x	x	13.94	14.49	16.05	19.38	x	x	x	x
Extraction of crude petroleum and natural gas	6	8	33.20	14.0	35.76	2.3	x	18.91	21.27	22.42	25.02	x	41.94	x	x	x
Mining of metal ores	7	:														
Other mining and quarrying	8	17	12.27	14.9	17.07	35.9	8.20	9.30	9.63	10.01	10.79	13.85	16.82	18.78	x	x
Mining support service activities	9	17	19.35	1.3	22.41	7.3	10.96	12.88	14.58	15.27	16.80	20.41	23.28	x	x	x
MANUFACTURING	C	2,403	12.58	3.3	14.86	2.5	7.28	8.56	9.20	9.84	11.15	14.37	16.58	17.83	19.37	24.59
Manufacture of food products	10	353	9.46	2.7	12.15	3.3	6.49	7.08	7.43	7.75	8.46	10.65	12.41	13.73	15.51	20.10
Manufacture of beverages	11	41	15.62	10.3	17.78	8.1	9.02	11.03	11.61	11.99	13.18	17.09	18.86	20.08	22.47	x
Manufacture of tobacco products	12	6	23.49	14.0	27.25	25.7	x	19.26	20.07	20.94	22.23	24.25	x	x	x	x
Manufacture of textiles	13	41	9.24	2.3	11.78	5.4	6.40	7.05	7.42	7.79	8.58	10.19	12.08	12.89	14.40	x
Manufacture of wearing apparel	14	17	7.89	-2.5	10.69	1.0	6.19	6.39	6.57	6.84	7.30	8.76	10.14	10.80	x	x
Manufacture of leather and related products	15	8	8.65	-0.3	11.53	3.4	x	6.91	7.32	7.55	8.21	10.02	x	x	x	x
Manufacture of wood and of products of wood and cork, except furniture; manufacture of articles of straw and plaiting materials	16	50	9.97	5.6	11.47	4.9	7.00	7.76	8.20	8.46	9.16	10.71	11.84	12.16	13.47	x
Manufacture of paper and paper products	17	58	12.16	-0.9	14.17	-0.7	7.29	8.81	9.48	10.15	11.08	13.51	15.09	16.58	17.87	x
Printing and reproduction of recorded media	18	98	11.63	2.6	13.34	-0.5	7.38	8.62	8.97	9.34	10.50	12.81	14.31	15.32	16.28	20.15
Manufacture of coke and refined petroleum products	19	11	22.93	-0.6	25.50	0.9	10.27	15.44	17.61	18.71	20.46	25.05	x	x	x	x
Manufacture of chemicals and chemical products	20	100	14.30	-0.1	16.51	-0.2	8.09	9.83	10.37	11.22	12.73	16.21	18.22	19.67	21.10	27.30
Manufacture of basic pharmaceutical products and pharmaceutical preparations	21	65	17.63	3.8	20.12	-1.1	10.15	12.34	12.92	13.73	15.86	19.80	22.90	24.81	27.30	x
Manufacture of rubber and plastic products	22	148	10.62	3.6	12.99	4.8	6.95	7.80	8.27	8.68	9.66	12.05	13.77	14.85	15.74	20.18
Manufacture of other non-metallic mineral products	23	86	11.91	4.9	13.75	-2.2	7.59	8.67	9.12	9.75	10.89	13.46	16.10	16.77	17.84	x
Manufacture of basic metals	24	85	15.20	-0.4	16.15	0.2	8.68	10.69	11.45	12.33	13.71	16.65	17.92	19.58	21.04	24.52
Manufacture of fabricated metal products, except machinery and equipment	25	267	11.70	4.0	13.19	2.2	7.36	8.60	9.17	9.69	10.67	12.89	14.28	15.30	16.56	20.42
Manufacture of computer, electronic and optical products	26	140	15.32	2.8	17.55	2.3	8.11	9.74	10.47	11.20	13.17	17.31	19.40	21.27	22.98	29.73
Manufacture of electrical equipment	27	94	12.01	3.5	14.62	8.5	7.50	8.68	9.20	9.83	10.93	13.41	15.36	16.53	17.86	x
Manufacture of machinery and equipment n.e.c.	28	207	13.69	2.1	15.74	1.6	8.50	9.89	10.59	11.28	12.32	15.10	17.10	18.24	19.69	24.81
Manufacture of motor vehicles, trailers and semi-trailers	29	160	15.22	5.9	17.00	7.0	8.51	10.24	11.08	11.79	13.45	17.24	19.17	20.18	21.65	25.90
Manufacture of other transport equipment	30	173	17.60	4.1	18.79	-1.0	11.23	12.96	13.69	14.39	15.93	18.96	20.56	21.53	23.27	28.33
Manufacture of furniture	31	53	9.57	-1.6	11.57	0.0	6.68	7.18	7.62	8.01	8.87	10.59	11.72	12.78	14.19	x
Other manufacturing	32	63	10.97	-0.3	13.06	-1.6	7.00	7.77	8.26	8.62	9.97	12.13	13.36	14.70	16.45	x
Repair and installation of machinery and equipment	33	81	14.96	4.3	17.34	4.2	8.49	10.06	10.81	11.54	13.31	17.11	19.59	21.18	22.66	x
ELECTRICITY, GAS, STEAM AND AIR CONDITIONING SUPPLY	D	168	17.97	9.7	20.45	9.7	9.96	11.77	12.68	13.42	15.93	20.30	23.25	24.87	26.90	32.52
Electricity, gas, steam and air conditioning supply	35	168	17.97	9.7	20.45	9.7	9.96	11.77	12.68	13.42	15.93	20.30	23.25	24.87	26.90	32.52
WATER SUPPLY; SEWERAGE, WASTE MANAGEMENT AND REMEDIATION ACTIVITIES	E	131	12.65	5.5	14.74	4.7	7.83	8.97	9.68	10.25	11.37	14.21	16.05	17.38	18.78	23.75
Water collection, treatment and supply	36	40	14.58	0.4	16.45	4.4	9.98	11.42	12.04	12.52	13.67	15.89	17.46	18.41	19.46	x
Sewerage	37	14	13.18	12.5	14.75	10.5	8.14	9.41	10.14	10.61	11.49	14.14	15.43	x	x	x
Waste collection, treatment and disposal activities; materials recovery	38	75	11.25	2.6	13.93	4.0	7.31	8.33	8.73	9.13	10.18	12.60	14.61	16.20	18.26	x
Remediation activities and other waste management services	39	x	x		14.23	-15.9	x	x	x	x	x	x	x	x	x	x
CONSTRUCTION	F	824	12.68	1.7	15.12	1.9	7.82	9.25	9.97	10.41	11.54	14.05	15.91	17.32	18.89	24.16
Construction of buildings	41	252	13.28	-1.0	16.88	0.7	8.04	9.55	10.02	10.70	11.96	15.29	18.00	19.72	22.04	29.46
Civil engineering	42	181	13.08	6.9	15.80	5.2	8.00	9.73	10.10	10.74	11.77	14.78	17.34	18.75	20.18	25.44
Specialised construction activities	43	392	12.25	1.9	13.69	1.0	7.50	9.00	9.59	10.02	11.23	13.33	14.80	15.54	16.71	20.36

Table 4.11b Hourly pay - Gross (£) - For all employee jobs[a] by Industry: United Kingdom, 2013

Description	Code	Number of jobs[b] (thousand)	Annual % Median change		Annual % Mean change		Percentiles 10	20	25	30	40	60	70	75	80	90
WHOLESALE AND RETAIL TRADE; REPAIR OF MOTOR VEHICLES AND MOTORCYCLES	G	3,569	8.49	3.5	11.99	3.8	6.25	6.65	6.85	7.05	7.66	9.47	11.01	12.13	13.63	18.98
Wholesale and retail trade and repair of motor vehicles and motorcycles	45	405	9.74	2.4	11.74	3.2	6.31	7.17	7.50	7.91	8.76	10.71	12.05	12.82	13.76	17.78
Wholesale trade, except of motor vehicles and motorcycles	46	966	11.23	3.9	14.70	3.1	6.99	7.90	8.34	8.86	9.83	12.84	15.26	16.69	18.69	26.12
Retail trade, except of motor vehicles and motorcycles	47	2,198	7.50	2.0	10.49	3.7	6.19	6.42	6.61	6.75	7.03	8.21	9.13	9.82	10.83	15.17
TRANSPORTATION AND STORAGE	H	1,063	11.71	4.1	14.19	3.8	7.82	8.97	9.51	10.00	10.56	12.97	14.88	16.00	17.74	24.28
Land transport and transport via pipelines	49	454	11.14	2.5	13.00	2.9	7.55	8.67	9.00	9.43	10.20	12.40	14.09	15.33	16.67	22.84
Water transport	50	11	13.48	0.6	15.75	-3.2	7.87	8.58	9.26	9.76	11.35	14.98	17.16	x	x	x
Air transport	51	69	19.77	13.7	24.54	14.5	9.92	11.85	12.73	13.94	16.64	23.00	26.26	28.97	31.67	x
Warehousing and support activities for transportation	52	315	12.52	1.7	15.37	1.7	7.79	8.91	9.44	10.02	11.16	14.30	16.17	17.36	19.81	27.49
Postal and courier activities	53	214	10.75	3.9	12.17	5.2	8.24	9.77	10.09	10.09	10.22	11.70	12.52	13.04	13.80	16.07
ACCOMMODATION AND FOOD SERVICE ACTIVITIES	I	1,228	6.62	1.9	8.57	2.0	5.45	x	x	6.19	6.33	7.05	7.71	8.15	8.76	11.22
Accommodation	55	284	7.10	2.8	9.33	3.6	x	6.19	6.21	6.32	6.63	7.69	8.54	9.15	9.95	12.93
Food and beverage service activities	56	944	6.50	0.1	8.31	1.4	5.19	x	x	6.19	6.27	6.97	7.50	7.93	8.47	10.72
INFORMATION AND COMMUNICATION	J	959	16.82	-1.9	20.34	-0.8	8.59	10.75	11.93	12.90	14.76	19.24	22.43	24.10	26.58	34.68
Publishing activities	58	153	14.49	1.8	18.99	2.1	7.61	9.53	10.50	11.17	12.75	16.86	19.42	21.24	22.95	29.80
Motion picture, video and television programme production, sound recording and music publishing activities	59	49	12.05	-3.7	17.97	-3.2	6.19	6.65	7.32	8.02	9.80	13.94	16.81	19.13	21.17	x
Programming and broadcasting activities	60	45	19.44	1.4	22.11	-2.3	11.11	13.24	14.24	15.67	17.85	20.94	23.26	24.58	26.97	x
Telecommunications	61	210	15.81	-8.2	18.72	-4.4	8.97	11.14	12.20	13.15	14.48	17.40	19.54	21.46	23.70	30.76
Computer programming, consultancy and related activities	62	438	18.34	0.1	21.39	-0.2	9.09	11.45	12.65	13.59	15.81	20.98	24.27	26.42	28.49	36.79
Information service activities	63	65	19.06	5.2	21.94	1.2	9.56	11.97	13.15	14.41	16.35	22.30	25.23	27.58	29.81	x
FINANCIAL AND INSURANCE ACTIVITIES	K	1,019	17.25	5.4	25.13	7.3	8.99	10.50	11.28	12.23	14.49	21.22	26.35	29.76	34.01	47.94
Financial service activities, except insurance and pension funding	64	561	17.39	7.2	25.91	8.6	9.12	10.53	11.27	12.18	14.43	21.72	27.16	30.56	35.23	49.25
Insurance, reinsurance and pension funding, except compulsory social security	65	132	16.47	4.7	22.21	2.3	8.94	10.60	11.52	12.23	14.27	19.80	23.54	26.34	30.17	41.23
Activities auxiliary to financial services and insurance activities	66	327	17.38	4.1	25.00	6.7	8.71	10.40	11.23	12.26	14.69	21.02	26.13	29.55	33.67	48.17
REAL ESTATE ACTIVITIES	L	316	11.98	1.5	14.59	-0.5	7.34	8.61	9.20	9.68	10.75	13.44	15.13	16.36	17.68	23.27
Real estate activities	68	316	11.98	1.5	14.59	-0.5	7.34	8.61	9.20	9.68	10.75	13.44	15.13	16.36	17.68	23.27
PROFESSIONAL, SCIENTIFIC AND TECHNICAL ACTIVITIES	M	1,479	15.33	0.1	19.79	1.5	8.01	9.83	10.54	11.49	13.29	17.83	20.77	22.74	25.02	34.02
Legal and accounting activities	69	482	15.36	0.5	20.06	0.1	8.18	9.71	10.42	11.17	13.14	18.06	21.03	23.23	26.01	35.97
Activities of head offices; management consultancy activities	70	279	15.33	2.8	21.39	3.6	7.45	9.20	10.00	10.83	12.90	17.89	21.56	23.68	27.19	40.25
Architectural and engineering activities; technical testing and analysis	71	360	15.97	1.0	19.08	3.1	8.84	10.71	11.68	12.50	14.16	18.14	20.90	22.67	24.54	30.98
Scientific research and development	72	114	18.66	2.6	22.17	-1.8	11.02	13.11	14.07	14.95	16.73	20.68	23.57	25.29	27.81	36.59
Advertising and market research	73	113	14.20	5.8	20.03	4.8	7.70	9.21	10.00	10.54	12.29	15.63	19.04	20.69	23.57	x
Other professional, scientific and technical activities	74	88	12.50	-4.9	15.66	-3.2	7.13	8.34	9.01	10.00	10.98	14.24	16.77	18.27	20.21	x
Veterinary activities	75	43	10.35	-2.5	13.09	-1.1	7.00	7.62	7.99	8.41	9.32	12.44	14.90	16.34	18.43	x
ADMINISTRATIVE AND SUPPORT SERVICE ACTIVITIES	N	1,471	8.83	2.9	11.85	2.9	6.19	6.50	6.84	7.16	7.94	10.02	11.85	12.99	14.51	19.46
Rental and leasing activities	77	114	10.48	4.8	12.57	5.2	6.76	7.80	8.18	8.73	9.50	11.63	13.27	14.38	15.40	20.26
Employment activities	78	543	8.92	2.7	11.16	1.2	6.19	6.50	6.88	7.19	8.00	10.08	11.94	12.95	14.38	18.57
Travel agency, tour operator and other reservation service and related activities	79	49	12.00	17.1	15.61	11.9	7.32	8.19	8.62	9.26	10.26	13.64	15.32	16.45	18.38	x
Security and investigation activities	80	93	8.42	-0.7	9.52	-3.4	6.48	6.99	7.15	7.43	7.90	9.03	10.04	10.91	11.34	14.21
Services to buildings and landscape activities	81	415	7.36	5.0	10.32	3.3	6.19	6.20	6.30	6.48	6.78	8.03	9.23	9.97	10.94	15.20
Office administrative, office support and other business support activities	82	258	11.07	5.4	15.06	5.3	6.64	7.50	7.94	8.43	9.53	12.94	15.53	17.52	19.88	27.24
PUBLIC ADMINISTRATION AND DEFENCE; COMPULSORY SOCIAL SECURITY	O	1,258	14.53	1.3	16.00	1.5	9.24	10.38	11.16	11.94	13.22	15.95	17.66	18.64	19.75	23.19
Public administration and defence; compulsory social security	84	1,258	14.53	1.3	16.00	1.5	9.24	10.38	11.16	11.94	13.22	15.95	17.66	18.64	19.75	23.19
EDUCATION	P	3,881	13.60	1.5	16.16	0.9	7.24	8.33	8.90	9.64	11.29	16.18	18.93	20.68	22.20	27.02
Education	85	3,881	13.60	1.5	16.16	0.9	7.24	8.33	8.90	9.64	11.29	16.18	18.93	20.68	22.20	27.02
HUMAN HEALTH AND SOCIAL WORK ACTIVITIES	Q	3,696	11.80	1.5	14.67	0.2	6.84	7.86	8.38	8.91	10.21	13.91	16.06	17.47	18.54	22.72
Human health activities	86	2,379	14.27	1.0	17.00	0.6	8.31	9.58	10.11	10.94	12.58	16.23	17.99	19.22	20.72	25.20

Table 4.11b   Hourly pay - Gross (£) - For all employee jobs[a] by Industry: United Kingdom, 2013

Description	Code	Number of jobs[b] (thousand)	Median	Annual % change	Mean	Annual % change	Percentiles 10	20	25	30	40	60	70	75	80	90
Residential care activities	87	676	7.80	0.5	9.61	-0.5	6.24	6.48	6.63	6.82	7.21	8.60	9.84	10.80	11.85	14.51
Social work activities without accommodation	88	641	9.02	1.8	11.17	1.9	6.44	6.93	7.19	7.47	8.09	10.24	11.96	12.87	14.08	17.78
ARTS, ENTERTAINMENT AND RECREATION	R	472	8.80	0.9	12.85	0.7	6.19	6.56	6.93	7.25	7.98	9.91	11.63	12.95	14.52	19.51
Creative, arts and entertainment activities	90	44	12.04	-3.7	15.47	2.9	6.68	7.91	8.28	8.97	10.36	13.57	15.48	16.92	19.07	x
Libraries, archives, museums and other cultural activities	91	56	11.33	-1.4	13.63	1.7	6.70	8.00	8.41	8.95	10.11	12.80	14.79	15.97	17.04	x
Gambling and betting activities	92	107	7.94	1.5	10.66	1.2	6.28	6.50	6.72	7.00	7.62	8.61	9.50	10.12	11.02	x
Sports activities and amusement and recreation activities	93	265	8.56	0.7	13.32	0.2	6.19	6.35	6.65	7.00	7.67	9.55	11.24	12.56	14.22	19.55
OTHER SERVICE ACTIVITIES	S	413	10.22	2.2	13.43	3.1	6.20	6.97	7.45	7.92	8.95	11.60	13.74	15.13	16.83	22.20
Activities of membership organisations	94	199	11.79	0.3	15.52	2.3	6.80	7.99	8.56	9.14	10.42	13.78	16.17	17.68	19.73	23.85
Repair of computers and personal and household goods	95	38	12.80	15.1	15.49	11.2	7.66	9.15	9.81	10.23	11.18	14.69	16.43	18.88	21.13	x
Other personal service activities	96	176	8.24	3.5	10.65	0.1	6.19	6.25	6.50	6.76	7.50	9.21	10.50	11.27	12.17	16.24
ACTIVITIES OF HOUSEHOLDS AS EMPLOYERS; UNDIFFERENTIATED GOODS-AND SERVICES-PRODUCING ACTIVITIES OF HOUSEHOLDS FOR OWN USE	T	49	8.74	2.8	9.68	2.0	6.93	7.50	7.71	7.95	8.20	9.26	10.00	10.13	10.69	x
Activities of households as employers of domestic personnel	97	49	8.74	2.8	9.68	2.0	6.93	7.50	7.71	7.95	8.20	9.26	10.00	10.13	10.69	x
Undifferentiated goods- and services-producing activities of private households for own use	98	:														
ACTIVITIES OF EXTRATERRITORIAL ORGANISATIONS AND BODIES	U	x	14.25	-9.7	15.84	0.1	x	x	x	x	x	17.89	x	x	x	x
Activities of extraterritorial organisations and bodies	99	x	14.25	-9.7	15.84	0.1	x	x	x	x	x	17.89	x	x	x	x
NOT CLASSIFIED		8	8.04	-3.7	9.26	-16.3	x	6.21	6.44	6.60	7.00	9.16	x	x	x	x

a Employees on adult rates whose pay for the survey pay-period was not affected by absence.

b Figures for Number of Jobs are for indicative purposes only and should not be considered an accurate estimate of employee job counts.

KEY - The colour coding indicates the quality of each estimate; jobs, median, mean and percentiles but not the annual percentage change.

The quality of an estimate is measured by its coefficient of variation (CV), which is the ratio of the standard error of an estimate to the estimate.

Source: Annual Survey of Hours and Earnings, Office for National Statistics.

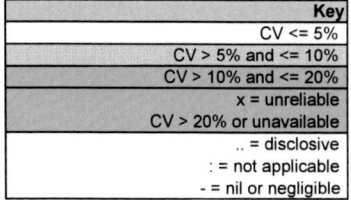

Key	
CV <= 5%	
CV > 5% and <= 10%	
CV > 10% and <= 20%	
x = unreliable	
CV > 20% or unavailable	
.. = disclosive	
: = not applicable	
- = nil or negligible	

Source: Annual Survey of Hours and Earnings, Office for National Statistics.

4.12a   Weekly pay - Gross (£) - For all employee jobs[a]: United Kingdom, 2013

Description	Number of jobs[b] (thousand)	Median	Annual % change	Mean	Annual % change	Percentiles									
						10	20	25	30	40	60	70	75	80	90
All Employees	24,575	415.3	2.3	501.3	2.0	124.2	211.8	251.0	286.0	348.4	491.6	584.5	642.3	704.4	909.8
Male	12,353	507.8	1.9	611.6	2.5	202.3	303.6	339.0	372.0	439.1	588.2	686.7	747.3	818.9	1,071.0
Female	12,222	327.2	2.4	389.8	1.9	97.0	153.6	184.2	214.3	271.2	389.4	469.5	519.4	577.3	741.9
Full-Time	17,592	517.4	2.2	620.2	2.0	287.5	342.5	368.1	395.5	453.0	589.3	676.2	729.1	794.7	1,020.0
Part-Time	6,983	159.8	3.0	201.7	2.0	49.9	83.5	99.0	111.3	137.0	186.8	222.5	245.5	276.2	392.2
Male Full-Time	10,653	556.2	1.9	677.0	2.5	306.5	368.1	398.9	427.5	488.4	633.5	729.0	789.7	862.4	1,126.9
Male Part-Time	1,700	149.4	2.5	201.7	-0.6	44.2	74.7	89.8	101.1	127.0	175.0	207.6	230.0	260.2	392.0
Female Full-Time	6,939	458.9	2.2	533.0	1.5	268.3	313.5	334.8	356.5	403.0	523.2	602.1	649.6	697.9	853.9
Female Part-Time	5,283	164.0	3.3	201.7	2.9	51.6	86.9	100.8	114.1	139.9	191.2	226.8	250.2	281.6	392.3

a Employees on adult rates whose pay for the survey pay-period was not affected by absence.

b Figures for Number of Jobs are for indicative purposes only and should not be considered an accurate estimate of employee job counts.

KEY - The colour coding indicates the quality of each estimate; jobs, median, mean and percentiles but not the annual percentage change.

The quality of an estimate is measured by its coefficient of variation (CV), which is the ratio of the standard error of an estimate to the estimate.

Source: Annual Survey of Hours and Earnings, Office for National Statistics.

Table 4.12b Hourly pay - Excluding overtime (£) - For all employee jobs[a]: United Kingdom, 2013

Description	Code	Number of jobs[b] (thousand)	Median	Annual % change	Mean	Annual % change	Percentiles 10	20	25	30	40	60	70	75	80	90
ALL EMPLOYEES		24,575	11.53	2.7	15.17	1.9	6.55	7.52	8.08	8.69	9.97	13.54	16.08	17.66	19.48	25.35
All Industries and Services		24,567	11.53	2.7	15.18	2.0	6.55	7.52	8.08	8.69	9.97	13.54	16.08	17.66	19.48	25.35
All Index of Production Industries		2,748	12.73	4.4	15.25	3.2	7.28	8.63	9.25	9.91	11.23	14.56	16.87	18.22	19.87	25.32
All Manufacturing		2,403	12.38	3.4	14.81	2.5	7.18	8.43	9.05	9.67	10.98	14.13	16.42	17.70	19.20	24.55
All Service Industries		20,875	11.28	2.0	15.20	1.7	6.50	7.40	7.92	8.49	9.76	13.39	16.00	17.64	19.51	25.42
AGRICULTURE, FORESTRY AND FISHING	A	121	8.57	5.7	10.31	6.6	6.26	6.89	7.04	7.40	8.00	9.39	10.45	11.15	12.22	15.68
Crop and animal production, hunting and related service activities	1	109	8.34	4.2	10.03	6.6	6.21	6.78	7.00	7.25	7.84	9.05	10.04	10.86	11.85	15.07
Forestry and logging	2	7	12.32	0.1	13.81	0.6	x	9.84	x	10.67	11.31	12.78	14.74	x	x	x
Fishing and aquaculture	3	x	9.02	9.4	12.01	18.4	x	x	7.94	8.61	x	x	x	x	x	x
MINING AND QUARRYING	B	46	17.39	0.1	22.37	9.1	9.14	11.00	11.70	12.66	14.92	20.40	23.57	24.84	29.68	x
Mining of coal and lignite	5	x	17.51	32.5	19.64	14.9	x	x	12.51	12.65	13.38	19.25	x	x	x	x
Extraction of crude petroleum and natural gas	6	8	33.20	14.0	35.78	2.4	x	18.91	21.27	22.42	24.30	x	41.94	x	x	x
Mining of metal ores	7	:														
Other mining and quarrying	8	17	12.17	14.7	17.36	38.5	7.98	8.74	9.20	9.71	10.69	13.68	16.82	18.80	x	x
Mining support service activities	9	17	18.97	0.9	22.43	6.7	10.96	12.78	14.22	14.94	16.53	20.41	22.89	x	x	x
MANUFACTURING	C	2,403	12.38	3.4	14.81	2.5	7.18	8.43	9.05	9.67	10.98	14.13	16.42	17.70	19.20	24.55
Manufacture of food products	10	353	9.29	3.1	12.13	3.3	6.43	7.00	7.27	7.59	8.31	10.57	12.31	13.66	15.33	20.07
Manufacture of beverages	11	41	15.67	11.0	17.82	8.4	8.85	11.06	11.59	11.97	13.07	17.04	18.77	20.00	22.47	x
Manufacture of tobacco products	12	6	23.19	15.4	26.99	26.8	x	19.20	x	20.12	21.31	23.79	x	x	x	x
Manufacture of textiles	13	41	9.20	2.0	11.71	5.1	6.32	7.00	7.27	7.66	8.48	10.03	11.71	12.65	14.18	x
Manufacture of wearing apparel	14	17	7.84	-1.3	10.67	1.0	6.19	6.39	6.57	6.81	7.30	8.85	10.14	10.80	x	x
Manufacture of leather and related products	15	8	8.65	-0.1	11.56	3.9	x	6.91	7.25	7.35	8.17	10.02	x	x	x	x
Manufacture of wood and of products of wood and cork, except furniture; manufacture of articles of straw and plaiting materials	16	50	9.69	5.7	11.43	5.4	6.91	7.61	8.00	8.19	9.00	10.50	11.65	12.07	13.34	x
Manufacture of paper and paper products	17	58	12.08	0.1	14.11	-0.7	7.19	8.64	9.14	9.72	11.01	13.39	14.98	16.25	17.52	x
Printing and reproduction of recorded media	18	98	11.56	3.4	13.30	-0.3	7.31	8.42	8.90	9.24	10.32	12.70	14.24	15.12	16.26	20.13
Manufacture of coke and refined petroleum products	19	11	22.93	-0.6	25.39	0.7	10.23	15.41	17.61	18.53	20.18	24.50	x	x	x	x
Manufacture of chemicals and chemical products	20	100	14.16	0.1	16.51	-0.3	7.98	9.63	10.23	11.13	12.55	16.09	18.19	19.42	21.08	27.30
Manufacture of basic pharmaceutical products and pharmaceutical preparations	21	65	17.48	3.8	20.11	-1.1	10.07	12.24	12.65	13.55	15.71	19.69	22.82	24.81	27.30	x
Manufacture of rubber and plastic products	22	148	10.46	3.7	12.95	4.6	6.79	7.72	8.12	8.58	9.47	11.97	13.56	14.68	15.62	20.31
Manufacture of other non-metallic mineral products	23	86	11.66	3.9	13.68	-2.8	7.47	8.40	8.99	9.45	10.58	13.26	15.93	16.57	17.52	x
Manufacture of basic metals	24	85	15.00	-0.7	16.17	0.2	8.67	10.51	11.19	12.10	13.58	16.35	17.83	19.58	21.04	24.52
Manufacture of fabricated metal products, except machinery and equipment	25	267	11.41	3.9	13.04	2.7	7.25	8.46	9.00	9.49	10.46	12.60	14.08	15.01	16.29	20.27
Manufacture of computer, electronic and optical products	26	140	15.13	2.5	17.54	2.2	7.98	9.59	10.35	11.05	13.12	17.18	19.34	20.95	22.91	29.57
Manufacture of electrical equipment	27	94	11.91	5.2	14.62	8.4	7.44	8.53	9.09	9.70	10.76	13.33	15.10	16.52	17.77	x
Manufacture of machinery and equipment n.e.c.	28	207	13.31	1.9	15.64	1.8	8.33	9.77	10.37	10.98	12.08	14.88	16.86	18.18	19.63	24.78
Manufacture of motor vehicles, trailers and semi-trailers	29	160	14.95	4.9	16.85	6.9	8.46	10.00	10.90	11.55	13.24	16.99	19.05	20.03	21.34	25.70
Manufacture of other transport equipment	30	173	17.34	3.2	18.78	-1.4	10.98	12.55	13.27	14.03	15.57	18.82	20.54	21.49	23.24	28.34
Manufacture of furniture	31	53	9.51	-0.1	11.51	0.1	6.58	7.13	7.50	7.93	8.73	10.52	11.56	12.74	13.88	x
Other manufacturing	32	63	10.93	-0.1	13.05	-1.7	7.00	7.77	8.24	8.62	9.92	12.07	13.35	14.63	16.42	x
Repair and installation of machinery and equipment	33	81	14.62	3.4	17.17	3.8	8.48	10.00	10.75	11.37	13.04	17.13	19.16	21.10	22.51	x
ELECTRICITY, GAS, STEAM AND AIR CONDITIONING SUPPLY	D	168	17.45	7.1	20.23	9.7	9.90	11.57	12.64	13.38	15.65	19.96	23.04	24.73	26.78	32.30
Electricity, gas, steam and air conditioning supply	35	168	17.45	7.1	20.23	9.7	9.90	11.57	12.64	13.38	15.65	19.96	23.04	24.73	26.78	32.30
WATER SUPPLY; SEWERAGE, WASTE MANAGEMENT AND REMEDIATION ACTIVITIES	E	131	12.60	6.6	14.71	4.9	7.63	8.83	9.44	10.00	11.24	13.90	15.94	17.26	18.50	23.75
Water collection, treatment and supply	36	40	14.35	0.6	16.40	4.3	9.67	11.34	11.97	12.48	13.37	15.86	17.44	18.44	19.42	x
Sewerage	37	14	13.18	12.3	14.89	10.0	8.00	9.09	9.96	10.25	11.38	13.97	15.29	x	x	x
Waste collection, treatment and disposal activities; materials recovery	38	75	11.06	4.3	13.84	4.5	7.22	8.11	8.54	9.00	9.96	12.31	14.55	16.11	18.16	x
Remediation activities and other waste management services	39	x	x		14.30		x	x	x	x	x	x	x	x	x	x
CONSTRUCTION	F	824	12.50	1.8	15.06	1.9	7.75	9.22	9.86	10.30	11.47	13.86	15.74	17.15	18.77	24.26
Construction of buildings	41	252	13.22	-0.2	16.91	0.8	8.00	9.49	10.00	10.59	11.86	15.02	17.98	19.58	22.03	29.10
Civil engineering	42	181	13.02	8.2	15.78	5.2	8.00	9.50	10.00	10.59	11.65	14.51	17.19	18.60	20.13	25.45
Specialised construction activities	43	392	12.07	0.8	13.53	0.8	7.50	8.97	9.50	10.00	11.06	13.03	14.50	15.27	16.45	20.17

Table 4.12b   Hourly pay - Excluding overtime (£) - For all employee jobs[a]: United Kingdom, 2013

Description	Code	Number of jobs[b] (thousand)	Median	Annual % change	Mean	Annual % change	Percentiles 10	20	25	30	40	60	70	75	80	90
WHOLESALE AND RETAIL TRADE; REPAIR OF MOTOR VEHICLES AND MOTORCYCLES	G	3,569	8.47	3.7	12.08	3.8	6.24	6.63	6.83	7.03	7.63	9.45	11.00	12.08	13.54	18.99
Wholesale and retail trade and repair of motor vehicles and motorcycles	45	405	9.64	1.8	11.71	3.1	6.29	7.08	7.50	7.86	8.70	10.54	11.98	12.75	13.59	17.70
Wholesale trade, except of motor vehicles and motorcycles	46	966	11.09	3.4	14.74	3.2	6.95	7.84	8.29	8.75	9.75	12.78	15.13	16.63	18.69	26.12
Retail trade, except of motor vehicles and motorcycles	47	2,198	7.50	1.9	10.59	3.7	6.19	6.41	6.59	6.73	7.02	8.21	9.14	9.85	10.89	15.19
TRANSPORTATION AND STORAGE	H	1,063	11.68	4.1	14.29	3.6	7.74	8.86	9.36	9.99	10.50	12.95	14.86	16.02	17.80	24.27
Land transport and transport via pipelines	49	454	11.11	3.3	12.99	2.9	7.50	8.50	8.91	9.27	10.10	12.33	14.00	15.22	16.67	22.84
Water transport	50	11	13.47	0.5	15.89	-2.1	7.59	8.60	9.26	9.76	11.35	14.84	17.09	x	x	x
Air transport	51	69	19.73	13.3	24.71	14.8	9.87	11.85	12.71	13.94	16.58	22.95	26.26	28.97	31.77	x
Warehousing and support activities for transportation	52	315	12.50	2.4	15.47	2.0	7.74	8.77	9.27	9.96	11.04	14.27	16.25	17.45	19.88	27.46
Postal and courier activities	53	214	10.74	3.7	12.26	3.9	8.22	9.76	10.09	10.09	10.22	11.82	12.57	13.24	13.96	16.20
ACCOMMODATION AND FOOD SERVICE ACTIVITIES	I	1,228	6.62	1.8	8.58	2.1	5.46	x	x	6.19	6.32	7.05	7.71	8.14	8.76	11.22
Accommodation	55	284	7.11	3.1	9.35	3.7	x	6.19	6.21	6.32	6.64	7.69	8.54	9.12	9.93	12.95
Food and beverage service activities	56	944	6.50	0.3	8.31	1.5	5.18	x	x	6.19	6.27	6.96	7.50	7.92	8.47	10.72
INFORMATION AND COMMUNICATION	J	959	16.78	-1.9	20.33	-0.8	8.58	10.73	11.86	12.84	14.56	19.17	22.36	24.02	26.54	34.68
Publishing activities	58	153	14.50	2.0	18.99	2.1	7.61	9.53	10.46	11.16	12.70	16.82	19.37	21.24	22.95	29.80
Motion picture, video and television programme production, sound recording and music publishing activities	59	49	11.99	-4.1	17.93	-3.1	6.19	6.65	7.32	8.02	9.80	13.93	16.81	19.13	21.17	x
Programming and broadcasting activities	60	45	19.41	2.0	22.11	-2.1	11.22	13.26	14.16	15.67	17.78	20.90	23.26	24.58	26.97	x
Telecommunications	61	210	15.68	-8.2	18.67	-4.5	8.94	11.02	12.03	13.02	13.80	17.34	19.44	21.36	23.62	30.76
Computer programming, consultancy and related activities	62	438	18.30	0.3	21.38	-0.3	9.07	11.44	12.55	13.53	15.71	20.95	24.09	26.25	28.49	36.79
Information service activities	63	65	19.06	5.2	21.95	1.2	9.56	11.92	13.15	14.41	16.34	22.30	25.23	27.18	29.60	x
FINANCIAL AND INSURANCE ACTIVITIES	K	1,019	17.21	5.9	25.21	7.4	8.94	10.40	11.21	12.16	14.39	21.18	26.26	29.60	33.96	47.97
Financial service activities, except insurance and pension funding	64	561	17.37	7.4	25.99	8.6	9.08	10.45	11.19	12.13	14.37	21.67	27.00	30.54	35.16	49.46
Insurance, reinsurance and pension funding, except compulsory social security	65	132	16.43	5.1	22.28	2.6	8.85	10.57	11.49	12.22	14.15	19.80	23.51	26.26	30.17	41.23
Activities auxiliary to financial services and insurance activities	66	327	17.37	4.1	25.09	6.8	8.69	10.32	11.11	12.23	14.63	20.99	26.11	29.43	33.70	48.17
REAL ESTATE ACTIVITIES	L	316	11.98	1.6	14.61	-0.6	7.33	8.60	9.18	9.63	10.73	13.38	15.04	16.31	17.66	23.27
Real estate activities	68	316	11.98	1.6	14.61	-0.6	7.33	8.60	9.18	9.63	10.73	13.38	15.04	16.31	17.66	23.27
PROFESSIONAL, SCIENTIFIC AND TECHNICAL ACTIVITIES	M	1,479	15.33	0.7	19.83	1.4	8.00	9.82	10.53	11.44	13.25	17.81	20.72	22.74	25.03	34.01
Legal and accounting activities	69	482	15.33	0.8	20.09	0.2	8.18	9.70	10.41	11.15	13.13	18.06	20.98	23.12	26.02	35.97
Activities of head offices; management consultancy activities	70	279	15.21	2.4	21.48	3.2	7.44	9.19	10.00	10.73	12.81	17.89	21.54	23.68	27.29	40.25
Architectural and engineering activities; technical testing and analysis	71	360	15.88	1.6	19.09	3.1	8.74	10.68	11.58	12.46	14.00	18.11	20.85	22.69	24.54	30.97
Scientific research and development	72	114	18.64	2.4	22.27	-2.0	10.97	13.13	13.88	14.95	16.70	20.62	23.59	25.49	27.81	36.59
Advertising and market research	73	113	14.17	5.6	20.05	4.7	7.71	9.21	10.00	10.54	12.29	15.63	19.09	20.69	23.57	x
Other professional, scientific and technical activities	74	88	12.50	-4.9	15.68	-3.2	7.01	8.34	9.03	9.98	10.96	14.19	16.79	18.40	20.21	x
Veterinary activities	75	43	10.32	-1.0	13.13	-1.0	7.00	7.61	7.95	8.37	9.36	12.39	14.81	16.34	18.41	x
ADMINISTRATIVE AND SUPPORT SERVICE ACTIVITIES	N	1,471	8.77	3.0	11.84	3.0	6.19	6.50	6.82	7.14	7.91	10.00	11.76	12.93	14.43	19.37
Rental and leasing activities	77	114	10.36	4.7	12.57	5.5	6.76	7.67	8.11	8.63	9.39	11.50	13.02	14.14	15.31	20.26
Employment activities	78	543	8.85	3.2	11.14	1.0	6.19	6.50	6.85	7.16	8.00	10.02	11.88	12.91	14.33	18.57
Travel agency, tour operator and other reservation service and related activities	79	49	11.94	16.7	15.67	12.6	7.32	8.19	8.63	9.26	10.26	13.58	15.37	16.45	18.38	x
Security and investigation activities	80	93	8.42	-0.8	9.48	-3.6	6.47	6.99	7.14	7.43	7.86	9.00	10.02	10.81	11.32	13.88
Services to buildings and landscape activities	81	415	7.34	4.9	10.26	3.5	6.19	6.20	6.29	6.47	6.76	8.02	9.18	9.88	10.86	15.18
Office administrative, office support and other business support activities	82	258	11.00	5.0	15.10	5.4	6.59	7.48	7.90	8.36	9.46	12.93	15.42	17.46	19.89	27.24
PUBLIC ADMINISTRATION AND DEFENCE; COMPULSORY SOCIAL SECURITY	O	1,258	14.52	1.5	15.99	1.9	9.23	10.35	11.16	11.94	13.22	15.95	17.59	18.55	19.68	23.19
Public administration and defence; compulsory social security	84	1,258	14.52	1.5	15.99	1.9	9.23	10.35	11.16	11.94	13.22	15.95	17.59	18.55	19.68	23.19
EDUCATION	P	3,881	13.56	1.3	16.21	0.8	7.23	8.32	8.89	9.62	11.27	16.18	18.93	20.67	22.17	27.02
Education	85	3,881	13.56	1.3	16.21	0.8	7.23	8.32	8.89	9.62	11.27	16.18	18.93	20.67	22.17	27.02
HUMAN HEALTH AND SOCIAL WORK ACTIVITIES	Q	3,696	11.81	1.4	14.68	0.1	6.83	7.85	8.38	8.91	10.21	13.93	16.06	17.46	18.51	22.66
Human health activities	86	2,379	14.27	1.0	16.96	0.5	8.31	9.58	10.11	10.94	12.58	16.23	17.97	19.18	20.72	25.14

Table 4.12b   Hourly pay - Excluding overtime (£) - For all employee jobs[a]: United Kingdom, 2013

Description	Code	Number of jobs[b] (thousand)	Annual Median	% change	Annual Mean	% change	Percentiles 10	20	25	30	40	60	70	75	80	90
Residential care activities	87	676	7.79	0.6	9.64	-0.6	6.24	6.48	6.62	6.80	7.20	8.60	9.85	10.80	11.85	14.50
Social work activities without accommodation	88	641	9.03	1.6	11.23	2.0	6.44	6.92	7.18	7.47	8.09	10.25	11.99	12.95	14.09	17.78
ARTS, ENTERTAINMENT AND RECREATION	R	472	8.75	0.7	12.96	0.7	6.20	6.50	6.88	7.22	7.92	9.86	11.56	12.91	14.55	19.51
Creative, arts and entertainment activities	90	44	11.91	-4.4	15.44	2.7	6.67	7.88	8.19	8.87	10.30	13.42	15.48	16.92	19.07	x
Libraries, archives, museums and other cultural activities	91	56	11.09	-3.0	13.63	1.6	6.70	8.00	8.42	8.95	9.96	12.80	14.84	15.97	17.04	x
Gambling and betting activities	92	107	7.90	2.5	10.84	1.6	6.28	6.45	6.60	6.90	7.51	8.60	9.44	10.06	11.05	x
Sports activities and amusement and recreation activities	93	265	8.55	0.7	13.37	0.0	6.19	6.35	6.65	7.00	7.66	9.52	11.16	12.53	14.24	19.54
OTHER SERVICE ACTIVITIES	S	413	10.19	1.9	13.45	3.1	6.20	6.97	7.44	7.90	8.95	11.59	13.70	15.06	16.82	22.18
Activities of membership organisations	94	199	11.79	0.3	15.54	2.4	6.80	7.96	8.56	9.14	10.42	13.78	16.14	17.68	19.73	23.85
Repair of computers and personal and household goods	95	38	12.50	13.9	15.45	11.1	7.51	9.05	9.62	10.20	11.18	14.52	16.48	18.47	21.51	x
Other personal service activities	96	176	8.24	4.3	10.65	0.2	6.19	6.25	6.50	6.75	7.50	9.20	10.48	11.27	12.17	16.24
ACTIVITIES OF HOUSEHOLDS AS EMPLOYERS; UNDIFFERENTIATED GOODS-AND SERVICES-PRODUCING ACTIVITIES OF HOUSEHOLDS FOR OWN USE	T	49	8.70	2.4	9.67	2.0	6.95	7.50	7.70	7.95	8.17	9.25	10.00	10.00	10.65	x
Activities of households as employers of domestic personnel	97	49	8.70	2.4	9.67	2.0	6.95	7.50	7.70	7.95	8.17	9.25	10.00	10.00	10.65	x
Undifferentiated goods- and services-producing activities of private households for own use	98	:														
ACTIVITIES OF EXTRATERRITORIAL ORGANISATIONS AND BODIES	U	x	14.25	-9.7	15.84	0.3	x	x	x	x	x	17.89	x	x	x	x
Activities of extraterritorial organisations and bodies	99	x	14.25	-9.7	15.84	0.3	x	x	x	x	x	17.89	x	x	x	x
NOT CLASSIFIED		8	8.04	-3.7	9.21	-16.5	x	6.20	6.32	6.49	7.00	9.18	x	x	x	x

a Employees on adult rates whose pay for the survey pay-period was not affected by absence.

b Figures for Number of Jobs are for indicative purposes only and should not be considered an accurate estimate of employee job counts.

KEY - The colour coding indicates the quality of each estimate; jobs, median, mean and percentiles but not the annual percentage change. The quality of an estimate is measured by its coefficient of variation (CV), which is the ratio of the standard error of an estimate to the estimate.

Key	
CV <= 5%	
CV > 5% and <= 10%	
CV > 10% and <= 20%	
x = unreliable	
CV > 20% or unavailable	
.. = disclosive	
: = not applicable	
- = nil or negligible	

Source: Annual Survey of Hours and Earnings, Office for National Statistics.

4.13 Average weekly earnings: main industrial sectors Great Britain
Great Britain
Standard Industrial Classification 2007

	Whole economy		Manufacturing		Construction		Services		Distribution Hotels and Restuarants	
	Actual	Seasonally adjusted	Actual	Seasonally adjusted	Actual	Seasonally adjusted	Actual	Seasonally adjusted	Actual	Seasonally adjusted
	KA46	KAB9	K55I	K5CA	K55L	K5CD	K55O	K5BZ	K55R	K5CG
2000	318	317	369	369	378	377	303	303	215	215
2001	335	334	383	383	407	407	320	320	223	223
2002	345	345	397	397	418	417	331	330	232	232
2003	356	356	412	411	436	436	342	341	237	237
2004	372	371	431	431	448	448	358	357	245	245
2005	389	388	447	447	461	461	375	375	254	254
2006	407	407	464	464	490	490	393	393	263	263
2007	427	427	483	483	522	522	413	412	279	279
2008	443	442	498	497	531	531	429	428	286	286
2009	442	441	503	503	536	536	427	427	290	290
2010	452	451	525	524	535	535	437	437	297	296
2011	463	463	532	531	542	541	450	449	300	300
2012	470	469	542	541	545	544	456	455	307	307
2013	475	475	554	553	546	546	461	460	315	315

	Finance and Business Industries		Private Sector		Public Sector		Private Sector Excl Financial Services	
	Actual	Seasonally adjusted	Actual	Seasonally adjusted	Actual	Seasonally adjusted	Actual	Seasonally adjusted
	K55U	K5C4	KA4O	KAC4	KA4R	KAC7	KA4U	KAD8
2000	389	390	319	318	314	313	314	314
2001	417	418	335	335	331	330	331	329
2002	423	424	345	345	344	342	344	342
2003	434	434	355	355	360	358	360	358
2004	458	458	371	370	376	374	375	374
2005	485	486	387	387	396	394	395	394
2006	519	519	406	406	410	408	410	408
2007	546	545	428	428	424	422	424	421
2008	573	570	443	443	439	437	438	436
2009	552	553	439	439	452	451	450	448
2010	579	579	448	447	467	467	459	459
2011	610	609	458	458	479	479	468	467
2012	612	611	465	464	487	487	476	476
	613	613	472	471	490	489	480	480

Source: Office for National Statistics: 01633 456780

4.14a Average Weekly Earnings by Industry (Not Seasonally Adjusted)

CDID	Agriculture, Forestry and Fishing (A)			Mining and Quarrying (B)			Manufacturing - Food Products, Beverages and Tobacco (C1)			Manufacturing - Textiles, Leather and Clothing (C2)		
	Average Weekly Earnings	of which Bonuses	Arrears	Average Weekly Earnings	Of which Bonuses	Arrears	Average Weekly Earnings	Of which Bonuses	Arrears	Average Weekly Earnings	Of which Bonuses	Arrears
	K57A	K57B	K57C	K57D	K57E	K57F	K57G	K57H	K57I	K57J	K57K	K57L
2009 Jan	339	8	0	1044	128	1	456	10	0	339	14	0
2009 Feb	332	12	0	1022	88	4	457	17	0	344	15	0
2009 Mar	341	7	2	1311	379	6	518	71	1	349	22	0
2009 Apr	330	3	0	1044	98	0	462	16	0	346	15	0
2009 May	342	2	0	989	52	0	456	9	0	340	11	1
2009 Jun	337	2	0	996	59	1	459	14	0	361	36	0
2009 Jul	330	11	0	992	46	0	459	16	2	336	9	0
2009 Aug	330	3	0	995	62	0	441	6	0	335	6	0
2009 Sep	346	9	0	988	40	2	463	21	1	335	9	0
2009 Oct	335	5	1	1002	56	0	448	9	0	344	8	0
2009 Nov	347	4	0	993	47	6	449	11	0	357	15	0
2009 Dec	376	31	0	1045	95	1	514	36	0	375	33	0
2010 Jan	343	4	0	1021	112	0	487	9	0	367	20	0
2010 Feb	358	26	0	1092	152	1	471	14	0	357	18	1
2010 Mar	360	17	0	1583	639	0	581	106	0	400	39	15
2010 Apr	340	7	0	1001	72	0	487	24	0	362	12	0
2010 May	322	2	0	966	51	0	462	8	0	360	12	0
2010 Jun	328	2	0	968	48	1	473	12	1	359	8	0
2010 Jul	336	4	0	971	36	3	465	12	0	369	14	0
2010 Aug	331	12	0	979	45	1	461	6	1	366	10	0
2010 Sep	328	4	0	976	59	0	482	32	0	361	6	0
2010 Oct	373	28	0	966	43	0	463	8	0	366	12	0
2010 Nov	365	8	0	975	53	2	461	7	1	363	9	0
2010 Dec	407	54	0	1029	115	0	510	47	1	370	20	0
2011 Jan	333	5	0	1052	110	0	466	6	3	364	14	0
2011 Feb	326	4	0	1093	173	1	464	11	0	361	15	0
2011 Mar	364	16	0	1584	657	1	550	86	0	386	39	1
2011 Apr	339	2	0	1066	133	0	502	30	0	361	13	0
2011 May	322	2	0	1026	66	1	464	6	0	363	8	0
2011 Jun	312	1	0	1013	56	0	472	14	0	366	10	0
2011 Jul	340	25	0	1057	97	1	458	5	0	363	8	0
2011 Aug	333	11	0	993	36	0	463	5	0	360	6	0
2011 Sep	317	2	0	1006	48	0	499	34	1	366	9	0
2011 Oct	337	11	0	1002	34	0	462	5	0	368	8	0
2011 Nov	330	6	0	1017	40	1	471	4	0	372	10	0
2011 Dec	378	39	0	1063	98	1	510	32	0	381	23	0
2012 Jan	329	3	0	1241	259	7	463	8	0	358	8	0
2012 Feb	333	7	0	1132	159	0	466	10	0	372	18	0
2012 Mar	345	18	0	1525	546	2	514	47	0	371	20	0
2012 Apr	319	3	0	1123	134	0	476	15	1	363	10	0
2012 May	319	5	0	1060	60	0	473	12	1	370	10	0
2012 Jun	328	3	0	1025	54	0	480	12	0	373	16	0
2012 Jul	349	14	0	1028	57	0	469	8	0	384	14	0
2012 Aug	342	8	0	1013	36	0	468	4	0	378	9	0
2012 Sep	340	6	0	1017	35	1	493	23	0	384	11	0
2012 Oct	333	4	1	1030	42	3	475	11	0	382	10	0
2012 Nov	339	5	0	1061	59	5	468	4	0	391	17	0
2012 Dec	364	28	2	1065	82	4	505	27	0	398	29	0
2013 Jan	345	7	0	1200	226	0	474	7	8	378	10	0
2013 Feb	350	5	0	1190	198	3	490	16	0	382	13	0
2013 Mar	347	3	0	1522	534	3	541	47	2	398	26	0
2013 Apr	357	4	0	1256	269	1	498	14	0	387	15	0
2013 May	352	3	0	1175	165	0	491	6	1	384	10	0
2013 Jun	339	3	0	1081	57	2	497	9	1	387	10	0
2013 Jul	341	2	0	1076	39	0	486	7	1	386	8	0
2013 Aug	339	3	0	1091	45	6	482	5	0	386	13	0
2013 Sep	346	3	0	1120	51	1	501	18	0	398	15	0
2013 Oct	351	2	0	1128	52	3	492	10	0	389	10	1
2013 Nov	339	3	0	1107	48	1	493	4	0	395	10	0
2013 Dec	395	54	0	1139	84	0	536	44	0	402	35	0
2014 Jan	344	3	0	1177	114	2	499	6	0	380	8	0
2014 Feb	355	5	0	1199	142	8	511	20	1	379	9	0
2014 Mar	357	2	1	1610	572	3	525	53	0	384	15	0
2014 Apr	349	3	0	1296	234	0	491	9	0	377	11	0
2014 May	338	3	0	1265	177	1	486	5	1	370	6	0
2014 Jun	340	5	0	1137	78	0	494	16	0	375	7	0
2014 Jul	351	13	0	1119	59	1	485	8	0	373	8	0
2014 Aug	335	2	0	1109	45	2	482	4	0	369	6	0
2014 Sep	341	5	0	1123	54	0	499	19	0	375	9	0
2014 Oct	349	3	0	1131	63	0	481	6	0	378	10	0
2014 Nov	347	3	0	1101	46	0	499	23	0	385	8	0
2014 Dec	400	43	1	1143	93	1	522	43	0	400	23	0
2015 Jan	357	13	0	1129	104	0	486	10	0	386	12	0
2015 Feb (r)	357	4	0	1166	126	0	496	18	0	385	11	0
2015 Mar (p)	374	7	0	1470	449	0	527	50	0	391	15	0

p = Provisional
r = Revised
All figures are in pounds (£)

Source: Monthly Wages & Salaries Survey

4.14a Average Weekly Earnings by Industry (Not Seasonally Adjusted)

	Manufacturing - Chemicals and Man-made Fibres (C3)			Manufacturing - Basic Metals and Metal Products (C4)			Manufacturing - Engineering and Allied Industries (C5)			Other Manufacturing (C6)		
	Average Weekly Earnings	Of which		Average Weekly Earnings	Of which		Average Weekly Earnings	Of which		Average Weekly Earnings	Of which	
		Bonuses	Arrears		Bonuses	Arrears		Bonuses	Arrears		Bonuses	Arrears
CDID	K57M	K57N	K57O	K57P	K57Q	K57R	K57S	K57T	K57U	K57V	K57W	K57X
2009 Jan	578	15	1	491	18	0	546	17	1	452	11	1
2009 Feb	595	36	1	491	23	0	563	34	1	449	10	0
2009 Mar	730	157	0	510	41	0	591	59	1	470	29	1
2009 Apr	690	110	0	495	21	1	562	28	1	453	12	0
2009 May	610	12	0	485	13	0	545	16	1	456	12	0
2009 Jun	639	23	1	500	17	0	544	13	1	461	11	0
2009 Jul	623	14	0	490	20	0	540	12	1	456	11	0
2009 Aug	609	7	0	481	8	0	544	10	3	455	10	0
2009 Sep	611	8	0	486	6	0	544	10	0	459	10	0
2009 Oct	614	12	0	492	10	0	552	9	0	463	12	0
2009 Nov	615	11	2	510	23	0	554	10	0	463	10	0
2009 Dec	663	48	0	513	23	0	576	28	0	476	22	0
2010 Jan	639	26	0	502	19	0	557	12	0	469	10	0
2010 Feb	673	62	1	529	24	2	577	31	1	477	20	0
2010 Mar	823	207	0	591	89	1	627	70	1	505	45	0
2010 Apr	670	61	1	528	25	0	582	24	1	470	11	0
2010 May	634	21	0	524	19	0	572	15	1	467	9	0
2010 Jun	635	15	1	523	21	1	569	11	1	472	11	0
2010 Jul	637	14	1	531	22	1	568	13	1	476	16	0
2010 Aug	622	11	0	513	10	0	569	10	0	468	9	0
2010 Sep	623	11	1	520	8	4	568	7	0	471	10	0
2010 Oct	650	18	1	524	20	0	572	11	0	475	13	1
2010 Nov	657	15	1	517	9	0	576	11	1	475	13	0
2010 Dec	682	35	0	512	14	0	594	29	1	485	26	0
2011 Jan	661	28	0	524	21	2	595	28	0	467	11	0
2011 Feb	661	27	0	515	15	1	591	31	1	478	21	0
2011 Mar	959	324	1	563	54	0	640	70	3	502	42	1
2011 Apr	698	68	1	525	22	0	596	30	1	471	15	0
2011 May	665	16	1	533	22	0	582	17	2	468	9	1
2011 Jun	664	18	1	530	14	0	592	24	1	471	14	0
2011 Jul	679	29	1	543	24	1	582	15	1	476	15	1
2011 Aug	661	11	1	519	7	1	573	9	1	470	9	0
2011 Sep	666	22	2	521	7	0	578	10	1	471	8	0
2011 Oct	656	14	1	533	16	1	584	9	5	473	12	0
2011 Nov	662	12	3	525	13	1	595	13	4	479	15	0
2011 Dec	688	36	4	528	29	1	597	24	2	490	26	0
2012 Jan	677	26	10	531	20	0	595	20	1	473	14	0
2012 Feb	668	25	2	526	16	0	614	42	1	478	17	0
2012 Mar	907	265	0	555	39	0	645	66	1	515	46	1
2012 Apr	736	85	1	556	37	1	610	27	2	488	20	0
2012 May	675	19	1	543	24	1	602	18	1	482	13	0
2012 Jun	683	24	1	532	21	0	615	28	1	482	13	1
2012 Jul	683	22	4	539	21	0	603	17	0	478	12	0
2012 Aug	678	19	1	516	8	0	597	13	1	479	10	0
2012 Sep	668	13	1	518	9	0	593	7	4	481	10	0
2012 Oct	674	17	0	522	12	0	598	8	1	482	13	0
2012 Nov	689	17	2	529	14	2	601	15	1	488	15	0
2012 Dec	722	36	1	536	24	4	611	27	0	494	23	0
2013 Jan	704	21	6	530	13	6	606	20	0	481	12	0
2013 Feb	708	31	0	525	17	4	617	28	0	488	16	0
2013 Mar	955	271	0	555	41	1	669	78	1	521	45	0
2013 Apr	823	152	1	541	25	0	635	36	1	501	26	1
2013 May	698	22	2	533	20	0	616	16	1	487	13	0
2013 Jun	701	15	0	532	21	0	646	43	1	485	11	0
2013 Jul	697	12	0	526	17	0	628	23	2	486	13	0
2013 Aug	704	17	0	510	6	0	614	15	1	484	9	1
2013 Sep	693	21	1	524	11	0	603	6	0	487	11	1
2013 Oct	692	17	1	534	12	0	612	11	1	489	10	1
2013 Nov	694	16	0	541	17	0	622	14	1	495	16	2
2013 Dec	712	28	1	559	33	9	628	23	1	508	26	0
2014 Jan	678	21	0	536	15	0	643	30	3	494	13	1
2014 Feb	690	23	0	542	20	0	644	25	2	497	18	1
2014 Mar	1027	352	1	558	34	0	695	76	1	534	52	1
2014 Apr	789	116	1	541	18	0	654	32	1	513	28	1
2014 May	700	14	1	544	17	1	638	20	1	503	15	1
2014 Jun	697	15	1	550	22	0	670	46	3	503	13	0
2014 Jul	712	35	1	548	18	0	640	23	0	496	13	1
2014 Aug	707	29	0	527	6	2	622	8	1	497	12	0
2014 Sep	703	24	1	545	12	4	623	9	0	500	13	1
2014 Oct	694	16	1	551	14	0	628	9	0	498	11	0
2014 Nov	676	13	0	553	15	0	632	10	1	500	13	0
2014 Dec	693	31	0	571	39	1	664	41	2	514	31	0
2015 Jan	686	25	0	549	17	0	643	16	2	498	19	0
2015 Feb (r)	719	38	1	542	12	7	646	18	1	499	16	0
2015 Mar (p)	1019	337	1	576	39	6	711	79	2	533	51	0

p = Provisional

r = Revised

All figures are in pounds (£)

Source: Monthly Wages & Salaries Survey

4.14a Average Weekly Earnings by Industry (Not Seasonally Adjusted)

	Electricity, Gas and Water Supply			Construction			Wholesale Trade			Retail Trade and Repairs		
	(D , E)			(F)			(G46)			(G45 & G47)		
	Average Weekly Earnings	Of which		Average Weekly Earnings	Of which		Average Weekly Earnings	Of which		Average Weekly Earnings	Of which	
		Bonuses	Arrears		Bonuses	Arrears		Bonuses	Arrears		Bonuses	Arrears
CDID	K57Y	K57Z	K582	K583	K584	K585	K586	K587	K588	K589	K58A	K58B
2009 Jan	577	16	0	530	13	0	518	51	0	252	11	0
2009 Feb	581	21	0	528	14	0	528	61	0	258	18	0
2009 Mar	639	72	0	559	41	0	537	69	2	265	24	0
2009 Apr	599	40	0	535	19	0	497	35	0	258	17	0
2009 May	589	24	0	525	12	0	494	30	0	257	15	0
2009 Jun	636	66	1	526	17	0	498	33	0	260	18	0
2009 Jul	618	47	3	530	17	0	494	31	0	258	16	0
2009 Aug	588	19	0	524	12	0	491	28	0	256	13	0
2009 Sep	590	19	0	531	16	0	493	27	0	254	10	0
2009 Oct	592	20	0	537	15	0	497	28	0	256	14	0
2009 Nov	606	25	1	543	22	0	507	37	0	250	12	0
2009 Dec	594	18	1	559	38	1	523	50	0	250	11	0
2010 Jan	595	20	1	540	15	0	512	42	1	258	13	0
2010 Feb	601	22	1	537	14	0	523	58	0	266	22	0
2010 Mar	670	83	2	592	67	0	610	136	2	294	46	0
2010 Apr	608	31	1	535	12	1	503	34	0	270	23	0
2010 May	595	21	0	527	12	0	496	29	0	261	14	0
2010 Jun	661	81	3	531	14	0	497	32	0	267	16	0
2010 Jul	621	29	4	525	14	0	501	34	0	265	15	0
2010 Aug	599	22	2	515	9	0	489	27	0	261	11	0
2010 Sep	600	21	3	531	19	0	489	25	0	260	8	0
2010 Oct	606	21	1	526	8	0	490	29	0	257	12	0
2010 Nov	613	26	1	531	15	0	490	29	0	258	12	0
2010 Dec	622	36	1	532	25	0	516	58	0	256	12	0
2011 Jan	608	27	1	539	14	0	510	43	0	263	12	0
2011 Feb	606	24	3	546	21	1	504	45	0	265	19	0
2011 Mar	646	81	1	583	55	0	565	99	0	286	38	0
2011 Apr	617	43	1	530	14	0	503	37	0	272	18	0
2011 May	584	17	5	530	11	0	501	30	1	270	16	0
2011 Jun	656	90	3	543	18	0	522	53	1	272	20	0
2011 Jul	640	69	0	535	12	0	519	48	1	267	16	0
2011 Aug	596	31	2	528	9	0	507	38	0	262	10	0
2011 Sep	596	20	2	542	19	0	501	30	0	260	9	0
2011 Oct	601	18	1	535	12	0	511	34	0	264	13	0
2011 Nov	611	21	6	546	21	0	505	27	1	261	11	0
2011 Dec	616	25	3	545	27	0	540	61	0	258	10	0
2012 Jan	608	24	0	539	13	0	538	56	0	265	12	0
2012 Feb	608	32	1	540	14	0	533	54	0	270	18	0
2012 Mar	665	87	1	589	50	3	585	103	1	288	34	0
2012 Apr	625	36	0	544	16	0	527	42	0	274	18	1
2012 May	602	17	2	548	13	0	527	39	1	274	16	0
2012 Jun	667	80	1	554	22	0	543	54	0	276	16	0
2012 Jul	647	60	2	545	16	0	534	43	1	272	15	0
2012 Aug	600	15	1	526	8	0	532	43	0	271	15	0
2012 Sep	605	17	2	538	18	0	524	34	0	267	10	0
2012 Oct	619	19	5	536	15	0	535	38	1	271	15	0
2012 Nov	626	24	2	542	17	0	528	31	1	267	14	0
2012 Dec	621	22	1	540	25	0	542	49	1	266	14	0
2013 Jan	610	20	0	527	12	1	558	58	0	269	13	0
2013 Feb	622	26	4	539	13	1	559	63	0	270	19	0
2013 Mar	665	74	0	559	28	1	585	82	2	291	35	0
2013 Apr	651	48	1	566	28	1	593	83	0	279	21	1
2013 May	621	24	0	546	14	1	551	42	1	282	23	0
2013 Jun	678	71	1	551	20	1	564	53	0	279	16	0
2013 Jul	653	55	0	543	16	1	571	60	1	283	18	0
2013 Aug	626	24	1	538	11	1	559	50	0	284	21	0
2013 Sep	612	11	2	553	24	1	547	39	0	275	11	0
2013 Oct	624	18	2	537	13	1	554	38	0	281	18	0
2013 Nov	629	14	7	545	17	1	544	43	0	275	13	0
2013 Dec	631	20	3	552	25	1	574	65	0	274	13	0
2014 Jan	637	20	1	558	16	1	592	60	1	281	14	0
2014 Feb	638	19	1	546	15	0	551	49	0	278	14	0
2014 Mar	710	83	5	568	40	0	613	110	1	304	38	0
2014 Apr	681	49	12	544	19	0	564	62	1	295	24	0
2014 May	643	23	2	539	13	0	534	31	0	297	24	0
2014 Jun	690	73	1	555	22	0	555	54	0	287	14	0
2014 Jul	678	58	3	565	28	0	547	49	1	287	16	0
2014 Aug	653	27	2	545	14	1	534	42	1	287	14	0
2014 Sep	636	18	2	565	29	1	540	38	0	288	11	0
2014 Oct	637	14	2	551	14	0	541	39	0	293	18	0
2014 Nov	652	18	8	561	22	0	537	39	0	289	16	0
2014 Dec	639	14	1	570	34	1	565	66	1	287	13	0
2015 Jan	643	21	1	548	16	0	564	60	0	303	18	0
2015 Feb (r)	663	38	6	553	13	0	563	65	0	299	15	0
2015 Mar (p)	695	75	2	602	46	0	655	152	0	335	49	0

p = Provisional

r = Revised

All figures are in pounds (£)

Source: Monthly Wages & Salaries Survey

4.14a Average Weekly Earnings by Industry (Not Seasonally Adjusted)

	Transport and Storage			Accommodation and Food Service Activities			Information and Communication			Financial & Insurance Activities		
	(H)			(I)			(J)			(K)		
	Average Weekly Earnings	Of which		Average Weekly Earnings	Of which		Average Weekly Earnings	Of which		Average Weekly Earnings	Of which	
		Bonuses	Arrears		Bonuses	Arrears		Bonuses	Arrears		Bonuses	Arrears
CDID	K58F	K58G	K58H	K58C	K58D	K58E	K5E9	K5EA	K5EB	K58I	K58J	K58K
2009 Jan	480	7	0	206	2	0	710	60	2	1033	365	1
2009 Feb	477	6	4	215	7	0	752	94	1	1229	554	1
2009 Mar	490	19	3	213	5	0	803	145	1	1170	496	2
2009 Apr	494	19	0	212	3	0	747	80	1	803	115	12
2009 May	542	63	0	217	6	0	729	66	0	760	78	1
2009 Jun	500	20	0	211	3	0	749	91	0	846	166	3
2009 Jul	484	6	1	214	3	0	713	63	0	755	71	1
2009 Aug	486	4	0	211	2	0	725	72	0	749	61	2
2009 Sep	492	7	0	210	2	0	719	62	0	785	96	1
2009 Oct	487	5	1	212	3	0	696	48	1	754	61	2
2009 Nov	485	5	1	213	6	0	693	50	0	780	68	14
2009 Dec	503	15	1	219	5	0	704	66	0	922	227	1
2010 Jan	488	5	0	213	4	0	713	59	1	984	283	1
2010 Feb	491	8	2	222	8	0	746	95	1	1694	975	10
2010 Mar	517	29	1	221	7	0	827	169	1	1438	714	2
2010 Apr	497	9	2	217	4	0	704	46	2	789	71	1
2010 May	496	8	1	221	8	0	725	59	1	887	162	2
2010 Jun	521	32	1	215	3	0	782	114	1	975	239	5
2010 Jul	500	6	1	215	4	0	728	55	0	804	60	2
2010 Aug	499	4	0	223	3	0	736	58	6	780	47	1
2010 Sep	501	3	0	221	3	0	728	54	2	839	112	1
2010 Oct	503	6	0	226	4	0	722	45	1	793	57	1
2010 Nov	507	6	1	220	7	0	729	48	1	787	54	1
2010 Dec	515	10	1	222	7	0	745	66	0	878	138	0
2011 Jan	507	7	0	219	5	0	759	72	2	1235	473	0
2011 Feb	506	7	0	226	9	0	771	83	1	1662	901	1
2011 Mar	527	31	1	225	8	0	867	180	1	1541	783	2
2011 Apr	516	14	1	223	5	0	743	56	1	850	86	0
2011 May	515	10	1	227	8	0	755	61	1	892	121	1
2011 Jun	518	14	3	224	3	1	816	129	1	1064	296	1
2011 Jul	523	18	2	225	6	1	752	62	1	878	114	1
2011 Aug	512	6	1	223	3	0	791	97	1	815	50	2
2011 Sep	512	5	2	222	4	0	746	52	1	871	105	1
2011 Oct	511	5	1	223	5	1	754	65	1	830	51	1
2011 Nov	522	6	7	227	9	1	754	58	0	825	47	0
2011 Dec	526	10	2	229	8	0	756	65	1	903	121	0
2012 Jan	517	8	0	231	6	0	771	83	1	1093	325	0
2012 Feb	529	17	0	236	11	0	792	98	1	1488	713	2
2012 Mar	539	26	0	228	7	0	870	171	2	1505	728	3
2012 Apr	538	17	1	228	5	1	766	71	1	897	117	0
2012 May	533	9	1	232	8	0	777	80	2	875	95	1
2012 Jun	553	27	2	230	4	0	826	137	2	1000	225	3
2012 Jul	534	6	1	232	5	0	778	81	1	861	88	0
2012 Aug	548	18	1	233	4	0	788	82	1	842	67	1
2012 Sep	538	12	0	230	3	0	777	71	3	856	85	1
2012 Oct	538	13	1	227	5	0	755	51	1	819	47	1
2012 Nov	533	7	2	231	6	0	775	66	1	819	41	1
2012 Dec	555	23	2	235	8	1	765	56	1	899	115	0
2013 Jan	530	7	0	223	5	1	787	79	2	1134	354	1
2013 Feb	534	15	0	227	8	0	817	105	2	1534	748	1
2013 Mar	550	26	1	228	7	0	846	139	1	1551	762	0
2013 Apr	554	21	5	231	8	0	819	101	2	1062	265	1
2013 May	546	9	1	235	9	0	784	63	2	969	171	0
2013 Jun	570	34	1	229	4	0	838	112	6	1050	259	0
2013 Jul	543	10	1	232	5	0	785	64	2	865	75	1
2013 Aug	543	13	1	232	4	0	797	71	2	852	65	0
2013 Sep	538	5	1	231	4	0	787	67	1	875	88	0
2013 Oct	542	7	2	230	3	0	777	54	2	839	51	1
2013 Nov	547	7	5	233	6	0	769	49	1	841	53	1
2013 Dec	577	35	1	238	8	1	781	54	1	939	142	1
2014 Jan	539	7	1	233	7	1	801	77	3	1139	353	0
2014 Feb	639	39	68	235	8	0	825	99	2	1656	855	3
2014 Mar	562	29	1	233	7	0	861	143	2	1640	824	3
2014 Apr	561	20	1	233	7	0	833	108	2	940	130	1
2014 May	556	13	1	239	11	0	791	70	1	960	156	1
2014 Jun	573	33	2	233	8	0	847	115	2	990	187	1
2014 Jul	564	24	0	233	6	0	781	49	3	863	60	2
2014 Aug	545	5	0	232	4	0	807	75	2	901	66	2
2014 Sep	544	5	1	229	5	1	769	39	2	931	91	1
2014 Oct	553	13	1	232	4	1	794	59	1	895	53	3
2014 Nov	554	7	1	235	8	1	794	59	2	896	54	0
2014 Dec	584	31	0	243	12	1	823	65	2	1054	201	2
2015 Jan	552	9	3	238	5	1	834	86	4	1188	340	1
2015 Feb (r)	559	18	0	243	10	1	865	108	3	1588	730	5
2015 Mar (p)	559	19	1	242	9	1	910	149	1	1747	888	1

p = Provisional

r = Revised

All figures are in pounds (£)

Source: Monthly Wages & Salaries Survey

4.14a Average Weekly Earnings by Industry (Not Seasonally Adjusted)

CDID	Real Estate Activities (L) Average Weekly Earnings	Of which Bonuses	Of which Arrears	Professional, Scientific & Technical Activities (M) Average Weekly Earnings	Of which Bonuses	Of which Arrears	Administrative and Support Service Activities (N) Average Weekly Earnings	Of which Bonuses	Of which Arrears	Public Administration (O) Average Weekly Earnings	Of which Bonuses	Of which Arrears
	K58L	K58M	K58N	K5EC	K5ED	K5EE	K5EF	K5EG	K5EH	K58O	K58P	K58Q
2009 Jan	449	22	1	632	30	2	341	14	0	502	1	2
2009 Feb	430	16	0	638	30	1	337	12	0	524	3	16
2009 Mar	483	62	1	670	65	0	345	17	0	505	1	4
2009 Apr	450	22	3	632	27	0	344	10	0	508	1	1
2009 May	439	17	0	629	21	0	345	12	0	512	1	3
2009 Jun	439	22	1	633	25	1	344	7	0	507	1	2
2009 Jul	459	43	0	637	30	0	346	11	0	508	3	7
2009 Aug	433	24	0	620	15	0	346	9	0	513	3	2
2009 Sep	449	29	1	619	14	0	333	7	0	505	1	1
2009 Oct	453	30	1	628	21	0	336	9	0	508	1	7
2009 Nov	460	35	1	626	17	1	334	8	0	514	3	3
2009 Dec	471	42	0	653	42	1	335	11	0	520	10	2
2010 Jan	456	28	0	637	23	1	343	11	0	521	1	1
2010 Feb	456	15	1	652	37	1	333	13	0	521	1	1
2010 Mar	521	83	0	719	96	3	353	23	0	521	2	1
2010 Apr	451	15	0	648	28	0	342	12	0	522	1	0
2010 May	454	14	0	635	18	0	341	9	0	522	2	0
2010 Jun	463	24	0	641	22	1	334	8	0	524	3	1
2010 Jul	481	34	3	634	31	1	339	15	0	532	3	1
2010 Aug	466	27	0	635	20	1	332	10	0	535	11	0
2010 Sep	468	27	1	636	18	1	330	9	0	528	1	1
2010 Oct	473	30	0	645	28	1	334	11	0	529	1	0
2010 Nov	474	30	0	655	31	1	329	9	0	533	3	1
2010 Dec	484	34	0	685	56	1	331	14	0	537	8	0
2011 Jan	493	34	1	658	29	0	338	13	0	536	1	0
2011 Feb	484	26	1	671	35	1	329	12	0	534	2	0
2011 Mar	534	70	1	777	143	1	352	33	0	537	4	0
2011 Apr	500	34	0	667	28	0	326	13	0	537	2	0
2011 May	490	27	0	671	31	0	330	8	0	537	2	0
2011 Jun	512	48	0	669	33	0	340	14	0	542	6	0
2011 Jul	506	42	1	696	56	0	344	16	0	539	5	0
2011 Aug	491	35	0	658	21	1	340	13	0	545	11	0
2011 Sep	484	28	0	661	18	0	332	9	0	545	1	0
2011 Oct	494	36	0	676	29	0	339	11	0	538	1	0
2011 Nov	507	43	3	682	35	1	335	10	0	537	2	0
2011 Dec	517	49	1	709	58	0	355	24	0	540	6	0
2012 Jan	493	30	0	682	38	1	351	12	0	535	1	0
2012 Feb	504	39	0	695	49	1	353	13	0	538	1	0
2012 Mar	612	142	0	785	134	1	381	39	0	541	2	0
2012 Apr	505	34	0	692	41	0	351	13	0	545	0	0
2012 May	494	32	0	680	30	0	350	10	0	543	1	0
2012 Jun	518	52	0	685	29	0	348	10	0	550	5	0
2012 Jul	521	56	0	708	61	1	352	12	0	551	5	0
2012 Aug	488	29	0	674	26	1	353	9	0	547	3	0
2012 Sep	502	38	1	666	23	1	347	9	0	554	7	1
2012 Oct	504	41	0	661	24	1	350	10	0	547	2	1
2012 Nov	501	38	0	667	28	1	348	8	0	544	2	0
2012 Dec	515	54	0	706	71	1	360	21	0	543	2	2
2013 Jan	506	50	2	655	23	0	350	11	0	546	1	1
2013 Feb	486	34	1	677	36	1	352	13	0	535	0	0
2013 Mar	543	87	1	735	88	2	374	37	0	536	3	0
2013 Apr	543	84	0	701	55	2	360	21	0	537	1	0
2013 May	510	48	0	667	32	1	360	15	0	537	0	0
2013 Jun	514	49	0	671	38	1	348	9	0	540	3	0
2013 Jul	532	69	0	686	47	2	357	15	0	543	6	0
2013 Aug	510	47	1	656	23	0	354	9	0	540	1	4
2013 Sep	502	47	0	664	29	1	346	9	0	547	7	0
2013 Oct	510	52	0	664	24	1	347	10	0	537	1	0
2013 Nov	494	44	0	662	22	1	346	8	0	537	1	0
2013 Dec	521	53	0	708	66	0	368	26	0	540	2	1
2014 Jan	498	42	0	661	21	1	362	19	1	545	1	1
2014 Feb	490	34	0	669	34	0	352	16	0	541	1	1
2014 Mar	573	108	1	743	102	1	373	34	0	548	2	4
2014 Apr	536	70	2	687	45	1	355	18	0	553	7	3
2014 May	519	54	0	678	42	1	358	12	0	547	1	1
2014 Jun	526	53	2	692	56	1	359	13	0	549	3	0
2014 Jul	549	81	1	683	46	1	364	13	0	549	4	3
2014 Aug	506	40	0	664	27	1	368	10	0	547	3	1
2014 Sep	506	32	1	664	26	1	370	10	0	555	7	0
2014 Oct	518	43	1	674	26	1	378	13	0	552	1	1
2014 Nov	509	36	0	669	25	1	367	10	0	549	1	1
2014 Dec	551	72	1	729	84	1	382	28	0	554	1	1
2015 Jan	515	37	0	665	21	1	372	14	0	551	0	1
2015 Feb (r)	512	41	1	702	53	0	384	24	1	551	2	1
2015 Mar (p)	626	157	1	763	115	1	395	34	0	548	2	0

p = Provisional
r = Revised
All figures are in pounds (£)

Source: Monthly Wages & Salaries Survey

4.14a Average Weekly Earnings by Industry (Not Seasonally Adjusted)

CDID	Education (P) Average Weekly Earnings	Of which Bonuses	Of which Arrears	Health and Social Work (Q) Average Weekly Earnings	Of which Bonuses	Of which Arrears	Arts, Entertainment and Recreation (R) Average Weekly Earnings	Of which Bonuses	Of which Arrears	Other Service Activities (S) Average Weekly Earnings	Of which Bonuses	Of which Arrears
	K58R	K58S	K58T	K58U	K58V	K58W	K5EI	K5EJ	K5EK	K58X	K58Y	K58Z
2009 Jan	391	1	3	387	1	1	293	10	1	380	23	2
2009 Feb	390	1	1	384	1	0	291	9	0	376	16	0
2009 Mar	388	1	1	385	1	1	301	18	0	387	28	0
2009 Apr	393	1	1	392	0	0	303	10	6	382	13	0
2009 May	392	1	0	394	1	1	295	7	0	367	13	0
2009 Jun	394	1	0	396	0	0	308	12	0	361	10	0
2009 Jul	398	1	1	391	0	0	305	14	0	368	11	0
2009 Aug	399	1	0	386	0	0	297	7	0	366	10	0
2009 Sep	402	1	0	390	0	0	295	5	1	362	6	0
2009 Oct	401	1	4	391	1	1	300	9	3	365	7	1
2009 Nov	396	1	1	390	1	0	312	19	0	370	11	1
2009 Dec	398	1	2	393	1	0	317	22	1	378	12	0
2010 Jan	393	1	1	388	1	0	322	17	0	401	16	0
2010 Feb	392	1	0	392	1	0	307	9	0	368	14	0
2010 Mar	393	2	0	390	1	0	333	35	0	411	63	1
2010 Apr	395	1	0	397	0	0	302	8	0	365	15	0
2010 May	394	1	0	398	0	0	304	8	0	353	11	0
2010 Jun	394	1	0	399	0	0	309	11	1	360	8	1
2010 Jul	397	2	0	396	0	0	319	10	1	356	7	0
2010 Aug	398	1	0	395	0	0	325	10	0	359	11	0
2010 Sep	404	1	1	397	0	0	323	6	0	352	8	0
2010 Oct	401	1	1	396	0	0	315	5	0	345	8	0
2010 Nov	400	1	1	398	0	0	317	8	0	354	13	0
2010 Dec	401	1	0	398	1	0	328	15	0	353	10	0
2011 Jan	397	0	0	398	0	0	329	13	0	351	14	1
2011 Feb	398	0	1	399	1	1	319	15	1	362	17	1
2011 Mar	401	2	0	398	1	0	331	23	0	401	50	1
2011 Apr	404	1	0	400	1	0	314	9	0	364	12	0
2011 May	401	1	0	401	0	0	311	10	2	356	10	1
2011 Jun	401	1	0	402	0	0	312	9	0	359	8	1
2011 Jul	402	1	0	400	1	0	320	13	0	364	11	1
2011 Aug	407	1	0	398	0	0	326	17	0	359	8	1
2011 Sep	409	1	0	400	1	0	322	12	0	358	8	0
2011 Oct	404	1	0	399	1	0	312	5	0	360	7	0
2011 Nov	402	1	0	401	0	0	322	9	0	367	14	1
2011 Dec	402	2	0	402	1	0	337	13	0	369	14	0
2012 Jan	396	0	0	402	0	0	340	16	0	356	15	1
2012 Feb	396	1	0	403	1	0	330	7	0	354	19	0
2012 Mar	398	1	0	403	2	0	338	26	0	354	22	0
2012 Apr	400	1	0	404	0	0	329	10	1	348	12	0
2012 May	399	1	0	407	0	0	332	10	0	347	12	0
2012 Jun	402	1	0	404	0	0	360	24	0	352	15	0
2012 Jul	402	1	0	405	1	0	344	11	1	348	13	0
2012 Aug	409	1	0	404	1	0	356	10	0	351	13	0
2012 Sep	411	1	0	403	1	0	360	13	0	339	7	0
2012 Oct	407	0	0	404	1	0	348	6	0	337	9	0
2012 Nov	406	0	0	406	0	0	354	13	0	346	13	0
2012 Dec	407	1	1	407	1	0	370	14	0	350	14	0
2013 Jan	402	1	1	409	0	0	363	16	0	352	12	0
2013 Feb	399	0	0	401	1	0	353	5	0	348	11	0
2013 Mar	400	2	0	403	2	0	356	19	0	354	21	0
2013 Apr	403	0	0	410	1	0	361	18	0	357	14	0
2013 May	404	1	0	407	1	0	364	19	0	357	10	0
2013 Jun	404	1	0	406	1	0	372	18	0	360	7	0
2013 Jul	406	1	0	405	1	0	361	10	0	358	10	0
2013 Aug	411	1	1	400	0	0	365	12	0	359	9	0
2013 Sep	414	0	0	403	1	0	363	19	0	352	6	0
2013 Oct	413	1	1	403	1	0	348	4	0	364	6	6
2013 Nov	411	1	1	403	1	0	350	13	0	367	10	1
2013 Dec	415	1	1	405	1	0	346	14	0	371	10	0
2014 Jan	408	0	0	408	1	0	363	12	1	374	13	1
2014 Feb	409	0	0	404	1	0	334	6	0	453	83	0
2014 Mar	410	3	0	402	1	0	330	13	0	401	30	2
2014 Apr	412	1	1	407	1	0	352	14	0	381	15	0
2014 May	413	1	2	408	1	0	346	13	0	379	12	1
2014 Jun	412	1	0	407	1	0	356	15	0	376	8	0
2014 Jul	413	1	0	405	0	0	352	7	0	381	13	0
2014 Aug	421	1	0	402	1	0	341	6	1	385	12	0
2014 Sep	424	1	0	407	1	0	347	16	0	385	8	1
2014 Oct	420	1	0	406	0	0	337	9	1	384	9	0
2014 Nov	418	1	0	407	1	0	341	8	1	368	10	0
2014 Dec	425	2	2	408	1	0	346	19	1	375	15	0
2015 Jan	419	1	0	409	1	0	357	15	1	371	17	0
2015 Feb (r)	416	0	0	407	0	0	336	11	0	373	18	0
2015 Mar (p)	420	3	0	408	1	0	345	20	0	387	32	0

p = Provisional

r = Revised

All figures are in pounds (£)

Source: Monthly Wages & Salaries Survey

4.14b Average Weekly Earnings - regular pay[1]

Seasonally adjusted

Standard Industrial Classification (2007)

Great Britain

	Whole Economy			Private sector [3][4][5]			Public sector [3][4][5]		
	Weekly Earnings (£)	% changes year on year		Weekly Earnings (£)	% changes year on year		Weekly Earnings (£)	% changes year on year	
		Single month	3 month average [2]		Single month	3 month average [2]		Single month	3 month average [2]
	KAI7	KAI8	KAI9	KAJ2	KAJ3	KAJ4	KAJ5	KAJ6	KAJ7
Jan 02	323	4.5	4.6	320	4.4	4.4	335	4.9	5.2
Feb 02	325	5.2	4.7	323	5.4	4.6	336	4.5	5.0
Mar 02	326	4.8	4.8	323	4.9	4.9	337	4.3	4.6
Apr 02	327	4.2	4.7	324	4.3	4.8	337	3.6	4.1
May 02	327	4.1	4.4	324	4.2	4.5	339	3.5	3.8
Jun 02	329	4.5	4.3	326	4.7	4.4	340	3.7	3.6
Jul 02	329	4.0	4.2	326	4.0	4.3	342	3.9	3.7
Aug 02	328	3.1	3.9	326	3.2	4.0	341	2.5	3.4
Sep 02	329	3.4	3.5	326	3.4	3.5	342	3.1	3.2
Oct 02	330	3.2	3.2	326	3.0	3.2	344	3.6	3.1
Nov 02	331	3.0	3.2	327	2.7	3.0	346	4.2	3.6
Dec 02	331	2.9	3.0	326	2.4	2.7	347	4.3	4.0
Jan 03	334	3.4	3.1	330	3.2	2.8	348	4.1	4.2
Feb 03	335	2.9	3.1	331	2.5	2.7	350	4.4	4.3
Mar 03	335	2.9	3.1	331	2.4	2.7	351	4.3	4.3
Apr 03	336	3.0	3.0	332	2.6	2.5	352	4.5	4.4
May 03	337	3.3	3.1	333	3.0	2.7	353	4.3	4.4
Jun 03	338	2.9	3.1	334	2.3	2.6	355	4.4	4.4
Jul 03	339	2.9	3.0	334	2.4	2.6	359	4.8	4.5
Aug 03	340	3.6	3.1	334	2.7	2.5	362	6.3	5.2
Sep 03	341	3.6	3.4	336	3.0	2.7	361	5.6	5.6
Oct 03	342	3.7	3.6	337	3.2	3.0	361	4.9	5.6
Nov 03	344	3.8	3.7	338	3.4	3.2	363	4.9	5.2
Dec 03	345	4.3	3.9	340	4.1	3.6	363	4.6	4.8
Jan 04	345	3.4	3.8	340	3.1	3.5	364	4.5	4.7
Feb 04	346	3.3	3.7	340	2.8	3.3	365	4.1	4.4
Mar 04	347	3.4	3.4	341	3.1	3.0	366	4.3	4.3
Apr 04	348	3.5	3.4	343	3.2	3.0	369	4.7	4.4
May 04	350	3.6	3.5	344	3.2	3.2	370	4.9	4.6
Jun 04	351	3.7	3.6	345	3.4	3.3	371	4.5	4.7
Jul 04	352	3.8	3.7	346	3.7	3.4	373	4.0	4.5
Aug 04	353	3.9	3.8	348	4.0	3.7	375	3.5	4.0
Sep 04	354	3.7	3.8	348	3.5	3.7	376	4.2	3.9
Oct 04	356	3.9	3.8	350	3.7	3.8	378	4.7	4.1
Nov 04	356	3.7	3.8	350	3.5	3.6	379	4.3	4.4
Dec 04	359	4.1	3.9	354	4.1	3.8	378	4.1	4.4
Jan 05	360	4.2	4.0	353	3.9	3.8	382	4.9	4.4
Feb 05	360	4.2	4.1	354	4.2	4.0	383	4.9	4.7
Mar 05	362	4.4	4.3	356	4.2	4.1	386	5.4	5.1
Apr 05	363	4.3	4.3	357	4.0	4.1	389	5.4	5.3
May 05	364	4.2	4.3	357	3.7	4.0	391	5.5	5.4
Jun 05	365	4.2	4.2	358	3.9	3.9	391	5.3	5.4
Jul 05	367	4.4	4.3	361	4.2	3.9	392	5.1	5.3
Aug 05	369	4.4	4.3	362	4.1	4.1	394	5.0	5.1
Sep 05	370	4.6	4.5	363	4.4	4.2	396	5.2	5.1
Oct 05	371	4.2	4.4	364	4.0	4.2	397	5.1	5.1
Nov 05	371	4.2	4.3	364	4.0	4.1	398	5.2	5.2
Dec 05	372	3.7	4.0	365	3.3	3.8	400	5.7	5.3
Jan 06	374	4.1	4.0	367	4.0	3.8	400	4.8	5.2
Feb 06	375	4.2	4.0	368	4.0	3.7	403	5.2	5.2
Mar 06	376	3.8	4.1	370	4.0	4.0	400	3.6	4.5
Apr 06	377	3.7	3.9	371	4.0	4.0	401	3.0	3.9
May 06	379	4.0	3.8	373	4.5	4.1	401	2.6	3.1
Jun 06	381	4.2	4.0	374	4.5	4.3	404	3.4	3.0
Jul 06	381	3.6	3.9	374	3.7	4.2	405	3.3	3.1
Aug 06	381	3.4	3.7	375	3.6	3.9	405	3.0	3.3
Sep 06	383	3.5	3.5	377	3.9	3.7	406	2.7	3.0
Oct 06	386	4.0	3.7	380	4.4	4.0	409	2.9	2.9
Nov 06	386	4.0	3.8	380	4.4	4.2	409	2.7	2.8
Dec 06	388	4.1	4.0	382	4.5	4.4	412	2.9	2.9
Jan 07	388	3.7	3.9	381	3.8	4.2	414	3.5	3.0
Feb 07	390	3.8	3.9	384	4.2	4.1	413	2.7	3.0
Mar 07	392	4.2	3.9	386	4.3	4.1	415	3.7	3.3
Apr 07	392	4.0	4.0	386	4.2	4.2	414	3.3	3.2
May 07	395	4.2	4.1	389	4.4	4.3	416	3.7	3.6
Jun 07	397	4.2	4.1	391	4.5	4.4	417	3.1	3.4
Jul 07	398	4.6	4.3	393	5.1	4.7	417	3.1	3.3
Aug 07	400	4.9	4.6	395	5.2	4.9	419	3.4	3.2
Sep 07	400	4.5	4.7	395	4.8	5.1	420	3.3	3.3
Oct 07	401	3.9	4.4	395	4.1	4.7	421	3.0	3.2
Nov 07	403	4.2	4.2	397	4.5	4.5	423	3.3	3.2
Dec 07	403	4.0	4.0	397	4.1	4.3	425	3.2	3.2
Jan 08	404	4.1	4.1	398	4.5	4.4	426	2.9	3.2
Feb 08	406	4.2	4.1	401	4.4	4.3	429	3.8	3.3
Mar 08	408	4.1	4.1	402	4.1	4.3	430	3.8	3.5
Apr 08	411	4.8	4.4	405	4.8	4.4	432	4.5	4.0
May 08	409	3.8	4.2	404	3.7	4.2	431	3.6	4.0
Jun 08	411	3.5	4.0	405	3.7	4.1	429	2.9	3.7

109

4.14b Average Weekly Earnings - regular pay[1]

Seasonally adjusted
Standard Industrial Classification (2007)

Great Britain

	Whole Economy			Private sector [3][4][5]			Public sector [3][4][5]		
	Weekly Earnings (£)	% changes year on year		Weekly Earnings (£)	% changes year on year		Weekly Earnings (£)	% changes year on year	
		Single month	3 month average [2]		Single month	3 month average [2]		Single month	3 month average [2]
	KAI7	KAI8	KAI9	KAJ2	KAJ3	KAJ4	KAJ5	KAJ6	KAJ7
Jul 08	412	3.4	3.6	406	3.2	3.5	434	3.9	3.5
Aug 08	413	3.3	3.4	407	3.1	3.3	435	3.7	3.5
Sep 08	414	3.3	3.3	408	3.1	3.2	436	3.8	3.8
Oct 08	415	3.6	3.4	409	3.6	3.3	436	3.6	3.7
Nov 08	416	3.2	3.4	410	3.1	3.3	437	3.5	3.6
Dec 08	416	3.1	3.3	410	3.1	3.2	438	3.1	3.4
Jan 09	416	2.8	3.1	409	2.8	3.0	439	3.0	3.2
Feb 09	417	2.6	2.9	410	2.4	2.8	442	3.0	3.0
Mar 09	417	2.2	2.5	410	2.2	2.5	440	2.3	2.7
Apr 09	418	1.8	2.2	411	1.5	2.0	444	2.6	2.6
May 09	419	2.3	2.1	411	1.9	1.9	446	3.5	2.8
Jun 09	419	2.0	2.0	411	1.4	1.6	448	4.4	3.5
Jul 09	418	1.4	1.9	408	0.6	1.3	450	3.7	3.9
Aug 09	418	1.3	1.6	409	0.4	0.8	451	3.8	4.0
Sep 09	419	1.4	1.4	410	0.5	0.5	452	3.7	3.7
Oct 09	419	1.0	1.2	410	0.1	0.3	452	3.8	3.8
Nov 09	420	1.0	1.1	409	0.0	0.2	454	3.9	3.8
Dec 09	421	1.3	1.1	411	0.4	0.2	455	3.9	3.9
Jan 10	423	1.8	1.4	413	1.0	0.5	457	4.2	4.0
Feb 10	423	1.5	1.6	413	0.6	0.7	459	3.8	4.0
Mar 10	425	2.1	1.8	416	1.3	1.0	457	3.9	4.0
Apr 10	424	1.4	1.7	414	0.7	0.9	460	3.6	3.7
May 10	424	1.2	1.6	413	0.4	0.8	460	3.3	3.6
Jun 10	425	1.4	1.3	414	0.8	0.6	460	2.6	3.1
Jul 10	427	2.2	1.6	416	1.9	1.0	462	2.6	2.8
Aug 10	428	2.3	2.0	418	2.2	1.6	463	2.5	2.6
Sep 10	429	2.2	2.2	418	1.9	2.0	464	2.7	2.6
Oct 10	429	2.3	2.3	418	2.0	2.0	466	3.0	2.7
Nov 10	430	2.4	2.3	419	2.2	2.0	467	2.8	2.8
Dec 10	430	2.0	2.2	418	1.6	1.9	468	2.9	2.9
Jan 11	433	2.3	2.2	422	2.0	2.0	470	2.8	2.8
Feb 11	432	2.2	2.2	421	2.0	1.9	471	2.6	2.7
Mar 11	433	1.8	2.1	421	1.3	1.8	472	3.2	2.9
Apr 11	433	2.2	2.1	422	2.0	1.8	472	2.6	2.8
May 11	434	2.4	2.1	423	2.5	1.9	472	2.5	2.8
Jun 11	434	2.1	2.3	423	2.1	2.2	471	2.5	2.5
Jul 11	434	1.7	2.1	424	1.8	2.1	471	2.0	2.3
Aug 11	435	1.6	1.8	424	1.5	1.8	472	2.1	2.2
Sep 11	436	1.8	1.7	426	1.9	1.7	474	2.1	2.1
Oct 11	437	2.0	1.8	426	2.0	1.8	475	1.9	2.0
Nov 11	438	1.9	1.9	427	2.1	2.0	475	1.8	1.9
Dec 11	438	2.0	1.9	428	2.3	2.1	475	1.3	1.7
Jan 12	438	1.0	1.6	427	1.3	1.9	475	1.0	1.4
Feb 12	440	1.8	1.6	429	2.0	1.9	476	1.2	1.2
Mar 12	441	2.0	1.6	431	2.3	1.9	477	1.2	1.1
Apr 12	441	1.7	1.8	430	2.0	2.1	478	1.4	1.3
May 12	442	1.7	1.8	431	2.0	2.1	479	1.4	1.3
Jun 12	442	2.0	1.8	432	2.2	2.1	482	2.3	1.7
Jul 12	443	1.9	1.9	432	1.9	2.0	484	2.7	2.2
Aug 12	444	2.1	2.0	433	2.1	2.1	486	3.1	2.7
Sep 12	443	1.6	1.9	432	1.6	1.9	484	2.2	2.6
Oct 12	443	1.3	1.7	432	1.4	1.7	484	1.9	2.4
Nov 12	444	1.4	1.4	434	1.5	1.5	484	1.8	1.9
Dec 12	444	1.3	1.3	433	1.3	1.4	483	1.8	1.8
Jan 13	442	1.1	1.2	431	1.0	1.2	483	1.9	1.8
Feb 13	443	0.8	1.0	433	0.8	1.0	482	1.2	1.6
Mar 13	444	0.6	0.8	433	0.6	0.8	483	1.3	1.4
Apr 13	447	1.4	0.9	437	1.5	1.0	485	1.4	1.3
May 13	446	1.1	1.0	436	1.1	1.1	486	1.4	1.4
Jun 13	447	0.9	1.1	437	1.1	1.2	485	0.5	1.1
Jul 13	447	1.1	1.0	438	1.3	1.2	485	0.2	0.7
Aug 13	447	0.7	0.9	437	1.0	1.1	483	-0.7	0.0
Sep 13	447	0.8	0.8	437	1.0	1.1	485	0.1	-0.2
Oct 13	448	1.0	0.8	438	1.4	1.1	487	0.6	0.0
Nov 13	447	0.8	0.8	438	1.0	1.1	486	0.3	0.4
Dec 13	449	1.2	1.0	440	1.6	1.3	488	0.9	0.6
Jan 14 (r)	450	1.8	1.3	441	2.2	1.6	488	0.9	0.7

1. Estimates of regular pay exclude bonuses and arrears of pay.

2. The three month average figures are the changes in the average seasonally adjusted values for the three months ending with the relevant month compared with the same period a year earlier.

3. From July 2009 Royal Bank of Scotland Group plc is classified to the public sector; for earlier time periods it is classified to the private sector. Between July 2009 and March 2014 Lloyds Banking Group plc is classified to the public sector; it is classified to the private sector for earlier and later time periods.

4. Between June 2010 and May 2012 English Further Education Corporations and Sixth Form College Corporations are classified to the public sector. Before June 2010 and after May 2012 they are classified to the private sector.

5. From October 2013 Royal Mail plc is classified to the private sector; previously it is in the public sector.

Source: Monthly Wages & Salaries Survey
Earnings enquiries: 01633 456773
Email: ster@ons.gsi.gov.uk

4.14b Average Weekly Earnings - regular pay[1]

Seasonally adjusted

Great Britain

Standard Industrial Classification (2007)

	Services, SIC 2007 sections G-S			Finance and business services, SIC 2007 sections K-N			Public sector excluding financial services [4][5]		
	Weekly Earnings (£)	% changes year on year		Weekly Earnings (£)	% changes year on year		Weekly Earnings (£)	% changes year on year	
		Single month	3 month average [2]		Single month	3 month average [2]		Single month	3 month average [2]
	K5DL	K5DM	K5DN	K5DO	K5DP	K5DQ	KAK6	KAK7	KAK8
Jan 02	308	5.0	5.0	377	4.6	4.8	334	4.7	5.1
Feb 02	310	5.7	5.2	381	6.4	5.1	335	4.4	4.9
Mar 02	312	5.4	5.3	381	5.2	5.4	336	4.3	4.5
Apr 02	312	4.7	5.2	382	4.8	5.5	337	3.7	4.1
May 02	312	4.5	4.8	380	3.8	4.6	338	3.6	3.8
Jun 02	314	4.9	4.7	383	4.1	4.3	340	3.6	3.6
Jul 02	314	4.4	4.6	383	3.5	3.8	342	4.0	3.7
Aug 02	313	3.3	4.2	382	2.5	3.4	340	2.3	3.3
Sep 02	314	3.6	3.8	384	3.5	3.2	342	3.3	3.2
Oct 02	315	3.5	3.5	385	3.6	3.2	344	3.4	3.0
Nov 02	316	3.2	3.4	387	2.5	3.2	346	4.1	3.6
Dec 02	316	3.0	3.2	382	1.3	2.4	347	4.5	4.0
Jan 03	319	3.7	3.3	390	3.4	2.4	348	4.2	4.3
Feb 03	320	3.1	3.3	392	2.9	2.5	350	4.3	4.3
Mar 03	321	2.9	3.3	392	2.9	3.1	351	4.3	4.3
Apr 03	322	3.3	3.1	393	3.0	2.9	352	4.6	4.4
May 03	323	3.5	3.3	395	3.9	3.3	352	4.1	4.3
Jun 03	324	2.9	3.3	393	2.7	3.2	355	4.6	4.4
Jul 03	324	3.2	3.2	393	2.7	3.1	359	4.7	4.4
Aug 03	326	4.0	3.4	393	2.8	2.7	362	6.4	5.2
Sep 03	327	3.9	3.7	395	2.8	2.8	361	5.6	5.6
Oct 03	328	4.0	4.0	398	3.3	3.0	361	5.0	5.7
Nov 03	329	4.0	4.0	398	3.0	3.0	362	4.8	5.2
Dec 03	330	4.6	4.2	399	4.4	3.6	364	4.7	4.9
Jan 04	331	3.5	4.0	399	2.5	3.3	363	4.3	4.6
Feb 04	331	3.3	3.8	398	1.7	2.8	366	4.7	4.6
Mar 04	331	3.3	3.4	400	2.1	2.1	367	4.5	4.5
Apr 04	333	3.6	3.4	402	2.1	2.0	369	4.6	4.6
May 04	334	3.7	3.5	405	2.6	2.3	370	5.0	4.7
Jun 04	336	3.8	3.7	404	2.6	2.5	371	4.5	4.7
Jul 04	337	3.9	3.8	405	3.0	2.8	372	3.9	4.4
Aug 04	338	3.9	3.8	407	3.6	3.1	375	3.6	4.0
Sep 04	339	3.8	3.9	409	3.4	3.3	376	4.1	3.9
Oct 04	341	4.2	4.0	410	3.1	3.4	378	4.6	4.1
Nov 04	341	3.9	4.0	411	3.2	3.2	379	4.5	4.4
Dec 04	345	4.5	4.2	415	4.1	3.5	379	4.0	4.4
Jan 05	345	4.4	4.2	416	4.2	3.8	382	5.0	4.5
Feb 05	346	4.7	4.5	420	5.5	4.6	382	4.3	4.5
Mar 05	348	5.1	4.7	422	5.4	5.0	386	5.3	4.9
Apr 05	349	4.8	4.8	423	5.2	5.4	388	5.4	5.0
May 05	350	4.7	4.8	423	4.5	5.0	391	5.7	5.4
Jun 05	351	4.7	4.7	423	4.7	4.8	390	5.2	5.4
Jul 05	354	5.0	4.8	429	5.9	5.0	392	5.2	5.4
Aug 05	355	4.8	4.8	429	5.3	5.3	394	5.1	5.1
Sep 05	356	5.0	4.9	430	5.3	5.5	396	5.2	5.1
Oct 05	356	4.4	4.7	430	4.9	5.1	397	5.1	5.1
Nov 05	357	4.5	4.6	431	4.7	5.0	398	5.2	5.2
Dec 05	358	3.8	4.2	430	3.5	4.4	399	5.5	5.3
Jan 06	360	4.4	4.2	435	4.5	4.3	400	4.7	5.1
Feb 06	360	4.1	4.1	433	3.1	3.7	402	5.4	5.2
Mar 06	361	3.9	4.1	439	4.0	3.8	400	3.6	4.5
Apr 06	362	3.6	3.9	439	3.9	3.7	400	3.1	4.0
May 06	363	3.7	3.7	440	4.0	4.0	401	2.6	3.1
Jun 06	366	4.1	3.8	443	4.9	4.3	404	3.4	3.0
Jul 06	366	3.4	3.7	443	3.3	4.0	405	3.5	3.2
Aug 06	366	3.3	3.6	445	3.8	4.0	405	2.9	3.3
Sep 06	368	3.4	3.3	446	3.6	3.6	406	2.7	3.0
Oct 06	370	4.0	3.5	447	4.0	3.8	408	2.8	2.8
Nov 06	371	4.0	3.8	448	3.9	3.8	409	2.8	2.8
Dec 06	373	4.2	4.1	451	5.0	4.3	411	3.0	2.9
Jan 07	372	3.5	3.9	444	2.2	3.7	414	3.7	3.1
Feb 07	375	4.1	3.9	450	4.0	3.7	413	2.7	3.1
Mar 07	376	4.1	3.9	452	3.1	3.1	414	3.7	3.4
Apr 07	377	4.2	4.1	455	3.7	3.6	413	3.3	3.2
May 07	380	4.6	4.3	459	4.2	3.6	415	3.6	3.5
Jun 07	381	4.3	4.4	461	4.0	3.9	416	3.1	3.3
Jul 07	382	4.5	4.5	463	4.5	4.2	417	2.8	3.2
Aug 07	384	4.8	4.6	464	4.1	4.2	419	3.5	3.1
Sep 07	385	4.6	4.6	467	4.8	4.5	420	3.3	3.2
Oct 07	385	3.9	4.4	468	4.6	4.5	421	3.1	3.3
Nov 07	387	4.3	4.3	471	5.3	4.9	422	3.1	3.2
Dec 07	388	4.0	4.1	473	4.7	4.8	425	3.4	3.2
Jan 08	389	4.3	4.2	470	5.8	5.2	426	2.8	3.1
Feb 08	390	4.1	4.1	475	5.5	5.3	428	3.6	3.3
Mar 08	393	4.3	4.2	476	5.2	5.5	430	3.8	3.4
Apr 08	395	4.9	4.4	479	5.2	5.3	431	4.4	3.9
May 08	394	3.7	4.3	477	4.0	4.8	431	3.7	4.0
Jun 08	395	3.5	4.0	483	4.7	4.6	428	2.9	3.7

4.14b Average Weekly Earnings - regular pay[1]

Seasonally adjusted

Great Britain

Standard Industrial Classification (2007)

	Services, SIC 2007 sections G-S			Finance and business services, SIC 2007 sections K-N			Public sector excluding financial services [4][5]		
	Weekly Earnings (£)	% changes year on year		Weekly Earnings (£)	% changes year on year		Weekly Earnings (£)	% changes year on year	
		Single month	3 month average [2]		Single month	3 month average [2]		Single month	3 month average [2]
	K5DL	K5DM	K5DN	K5DO	K5DP	K5DQ	KAK6	KAK7	KAK8
Jul 08	396	3.7	3.6	486	5.1	4.6	434	4.0	3.6
Aug 08	398	3.6	3.6	489	5.4	5.1	434	3.6	3.5
Sep 08	399	3.6	3.7	489	4.7	5.1	435	3.8	3.8
Oct 08	400	3.9	3.7	490	4.7	4.9	436	3.5	3.6
Nov 08	400	3.3	3.6	490	4.0	4.5	437	3.6	3.6
Dec 08	400	3.3	3.5	488	3.3	4.0	438	3.0	3.4
Jan 09	400	3.0	3.2	490	4.4	3.9	439	3.0	3.2
Feb 09	402	3.1	3.1	491	3.4	3.7	441	3.1	3.1
Mar 09	402	2.3	2.8	493	3.6	3.8	439	2.0	2.7
Apr 09	403	2.0	2.5	494	3.1	3.4	443	2.8	2.6
May 09	404	2.6	2.3	494	3.6	3.4	445	3.3	2.7
Jun 09	404	2.4	2.3	494	2.5	3.1	447	4.3	3.5
Jul 09	404	1.8	2.3	494	1.6	2.5	446	2.9	3.5
Aug 09	403	1.4	1.9	494	1.2	1.7	447	3.1	3.4
Sep 09	404	1.5	1.6	495	1.2	1.3	448	2.8	2.9
Oct 09	404	1.1	1.3	495	1.0	1.1	448	2.9	2.9
Nov 09	404	1.1	1.2	498	1.6	1.3	450	2.8	2.8
Dec 09	405	1.2	1.1	498	2.0	1.5	451	2.8	2.8
Jan 10	408	1.8	1.4	502	2.3	1.9	452	2.9	2.9
Feb 10	407	1.2	1.4	498	1.3	1.8	453	2.7	2.8
Mar 10	409	1.8	1.6	506	2.7	2.1	452	3.1	2.9
Apr 10	408	1.2	1.4	503	1.9	2.0	454	2.5	2.8
May 10	408	1.1	1.4	504	2.0	2.2	456	2.4	2.6
Jun 10	409	1.2	1.2	504	1.9	1.9	454	1.5	2.1
Jul 10	412	2.1	1.5	511	3.5	2.4	457	2.4	2.1
Aug 10	413	2.3	1.9	513	3.7	3.0	457	2.0	2.0
Sep 10	414	2.3	2.3	515	4.2	3.8	459	2.7	2.4
Oct 10	414	2.4	2.4	518	4.6	4.2	460	2.6	2.4
Nov 10	415	2.6	2.5	519	4.3	4.4	462	2.7	2.7
Dec 10	415	2.5	2.5	523	4.9	4.6	463	2.8	2.7
Jan 11	419	2.7	2.6	529	5.6	4.9	464	2.8	2.8
Feb 11	418	2.6	2.6	525	5.5	5.3	465	2.5	2.7
Mar 11	418	2.2	2.5	525	3.7	4.9	466	3.1	2.8
Apr 11	419	2.7	2.5	527	4.8	4.7	465	2.4	2.6
May 11	420	2.8	2.6	531	5.4	4.6	465	2.0	2.5
Jun 11	419	2.5	2.7	530	5.3	5.1	465	2.5	2.3
Jul 11	420	1.9	2.4	531	3.8	4.8	464	1.6	2.0
Aug 11	420	1.7	2.0	529	3.1	4.1	466	2.1	2.1
Sep 11	422	1.9	1.8	533	3.4	3.4	467	1.6	1.8
Oct 11	423	2.2	1.9	537	3.8	3.4	467	1.5	1.8
Nov 11	423	2.0	2.0	537	3.5	3.6	467	1.1	1.4
Dec 11	424	2.1	2.1	541	3.5	3.6	467	0.8	1.1
Jan 12	423	1.1	1.8	537	1.5	2.8	466	0.4	0.8
Feb 12	426	1.8	1.7	541	2.9	2.6	469	0.9	0.7
Mar 12	426	2.0	1.6	543	3.4	2.6	470	0.8	0.7
Apr 12	426	1.6	1.8	541	2.7	3.0	470	1.0	0.9
May 12	427	1.6	1.7	541	1.8	2.7	470	1.2	1.0
Jun 12	428	1.9	1.7	542	2.3	2.3	474	2.1	1.4
Jul 12	428	1.9	1.8	540	1.8	2.0	476	2.6	2.0
Aug 12	429	2.3	2.0	542	2.6	2.2	479	2.7	2.5
Sep 12	429	1.6	1.9	541	1.6	2.0	477	2.1	2.5
Oct 12	428	1.3	1.7	539	0.2	1.4	477	2.0	2.3
Nov 12	430	1.5	1.5	540	0.6	0.8	477	2.0	2.1
Dec 12	430	1.3	1.4	538	-0.5	0.1	476	1.9	2.0
Jan 13	428	1.2	1.3	538	0.0	0.0	476	2.1	2.0
Feb 13	428	0.6	1.0	539	-0.2	-0.2	474	1.0	1.7
Mar 13	428	0.5	0.7	539	-0.8	-0.3	475	1.2	1.4
Apr 13	431	1.2	0.7	541	-0.1	-0.4	477	1.5	1.2
May 13	431	1.0	0.9	539	-0.3	-0.4	478	1.5	1.4
Jun 13	431	0.8	1.0	537	-1.0	-0.5	477	0.6	1.2
Jul 13	432	1.0	1.0	538	-0.3	-0.5	478	0.4	0.8
Aug 13	431	0.5	0.8	537	-1.0	-0.8	477	-0.3	0.2
Sep 13	431	0.6	0.7	535	-1.2	-0.9	478	0.3	0.1
Oct 13	432	0.9	0.7	534	-0.8	-1.0	481	0.9	0.3
Nov 13	432	0.5	0.7	534	-1.0	-1.0	480	0.8	0.7
Dec 13	434	1.1	0.8	539	0.2	-0.6	481	1.2	0.9
Jan 14	434	1.3	0.9	536	-0.3	-0.4	482	1.4	1.1

1. Estimates of regular pay exclude bonuses and arrears of pay.

2. The three month average figures are the changes in the average seasonally adjusted values for the three months ending with the relevant month compared with the same period a year earlier.

3. From July 2009 Royal Bank of Scotland Group plc is classified to the public sector; for earlier time periods it is classified to the private sector. Between July 2009 and March 2014 Lloyds Banking Group plc is classified to the public sector; it is classified to the private sector for earlier and later time periods.

4. Between June 2010 and May 2012 English Further Education Corporations and Sixth Form College Corporations are classified to the public sector. Before June 2010 and after May 2012 they are classified to the private sector.

5. From October 2013 Royal Mail plc is classified to the private sector; previously it is in the public sector.

Source: Monthly Wages & Salaries Survey

Earnings enquiries: 01633 456773

Email: ster@ons.gsi.gov.uk

4.14b Average Weekly Earnings - regular pay[1]

Seasonally adjusted

	Manufacturing, SIC 2007 section C			Construction, SIC 2007 section F			Wholesaling, retailing, hotels & restaurants, SIC 2007 sections G & I		
	Weekly Earnings (£)	% changes year on year		Weekly Earnings (£)	% changes year on year		Weekly Earnings (£)	% changes year on year	
		Single month	3 month average [2]		Single month	3 month average [2]		Single month	3 month average [2]
	K5DU	K5DV	K5DW	K5DX	K5DY	K5DZ	K5E2	K5E3	K5E4
Jan 02	377	3.7	4.0	391	3.7	5.4	211	3.1	2.8
Feb 02	379	3.9	3.9	399	7.0	5.5	213	3.4	3.0
Mar 02	378	3.4	3.6	396	4.1	4.9	214	3.9	3.5
Apr 02	381	3.4	3.6	397	4.1	5.0	215	3.9	3.7
May 02	383	4.2	3.7	398	3.8	4.0	216	4.7	4.2
Jun 02	384	4.2	3.9	400	3.0	3.6	219	5.6	4.7
Jul 02	385	4.5	4.3	401	1.7	2.8	219	4.6	5.0
Aug 02	386	4.1	4.3	393	0.8	1.8	219	4.3	4.8
Sep 02	385	3.6	4.1	400	1.9	1.5	219	4.2	4.4
Oct 02	387	3.5	3.7	398	0.9	1.2	219	4.1	4.2
Nov 02	386	2.9	3.3	407	2.5	1.8	220	4.1	4.1
Dec 02	389	3.7	3.4	404	1.8	1.7	219	4.1	4.1
Jan 03	389	3.1	3.2	408	4.5	2.9	223	5.4	4.5
Feb 03	390	2.9	3.2	411	3.0	3.1	221	4.1	4.5
Mar 03	389	2.9	3.0	414	4.5	4.0	221	3.2	4.2
Apr 03	392	2.9	2.9	413	4.1	3.9	222	3.4	3.6
May 03	394	2.8	2.9	411	3.5	4.0	223	3.5	3.4
Jun 03	396	3.0	2.9	419	4.9	4.2	223	1.6	2.8
Jul 03	397	2.9	2.9	416	3.6	4.0	222	1.5	2.2
Aug 03	398	3.2	3.1	409	4.0	4.2	223	1.6	1.6
Sep 03	401	4.0	3.4	420	5.0	4.2	224	2.1	1.8
Oct 03	401	3.6	3.6	420	5.3	4.8	223	1.8	1.9
Nov 03	402	4.3	4.0	423	4.0	4.8	224	2.1	2.0
Dec 03	405	4.1	4.0	427	5.8	5.0	226	3.2	2.4
Jan 04	406	4.4	4.2	427	4.6	4.8	226	1.7	2.3
Feb 04	407	4.5	4.3	427	3.8	4.7	227	2.6	2.5
Mar 04	410	5.2	4.7	434	4.8	4.4	227	2.8	2.4
Apr 04	409	4.4	4.7	431	4.3	4.3	229	3.3	2.9
May 04	412	4.6	4.8	431	4.7	4.6	230	3.1	3.1
Jun 04	414	4.6	4.5	427	1.9	3.6	231	3.7	3.4
Jul 04	416	4.9	4.7	429	3.1	3.2	232	4.2	3.7
Aug 04	417	4.7	4.7	427	4.4	3.1	232	4.1	4.0
Sep 04	418	4.4	4.7	427	1.7	3.1	232	3.8	4.0
Oct 04	421	5.0	4.7	423	0.7	2.3	234	4.7	4.2
Nov 04	422	4.8	4.7	428	1.2	1.2	234	4.2	4.2
Dec 04	421	4.0	4.6	429	0.3	0.7	236	4.5	4.5
Jan 05	422	4.0	4.2	439	2.9	1.5	237	4.5	4.4
Feb 05	423	3.9	3.9	425	-0.4	0.9	237	4.5	4.5
Mar 05	426	3.9	3.9	428	-1.4	0.4	238	4.6	4.5
Apr 05	427	4.5	4.1	431	0.0	-0.6	239	4.1	4.4
May 05	427	3.7	4.0	432	0.3	-0.4	237	2.9	3.9
Jun 05	428	3.6	3.9	434	1.7	0.7	239	3.3	3.5
Jul 05	430	3.4	3.5	436	1.7	1.2	240	3.6	3.3
Aug 05	432	3.7	3.6	437	2.4	1.9	242	4.6	3.8
Sep 05	434	3.7	3.6	444	4.1	2.7	241	4.0	4.1
Oct 05	434	3.2	3.5	446	5.5	4.0	244	4.3	4.3
Nov 05	435	3.1	3.3	451	5.5	5.0	244	4.6	4.3
Dec 05	437	3.7	3.3	446	4.0	5.0	244	3.4	4.1
Jan 06	436	3.3	3.4	453	3.0	4.2	245	3.7	3.9
Feb 06	442	4.5	3.8	455	7.2	4.7	246	3.5	3.5
Mar 06	441	3.5	3.8	456	6.4	5.5	245	3.1	3.4
Apr 06	443	3.7	3.9	459	6.5	6.7	245	2.6	3.1
May 06	446	4.3	3.8	466	7.8	6.9	248	4.5	3.4
Jun 06	444	3.6	3.9	470	8.1	7.5	248	3.8	3.7
Jul 06	442	2.7	3.5	473	8.6	8.2	248	3.5	3.9
Aug 06	446	3.2	3.2	463	5.8	7.5	248	2.3	3.2
Sep 06	448	3.4	3.1	473	6.5	6.9	250	3.7	3.2
Oct 06	450	3.7	3.4	474	6.3	6.2	253	3.6	3.2
Nov 06	451	3.7	3.6	475	5.3	6.0	255	4.3	3.9
Dec 06	450	3.0	3.5	476	6.6	6.1	256	4.8	4.2
Jan 07	456	4.6	3.8	476	5.3	5.8	254	3.5	4.2
Feb 07	457	3.4	3.7	471	3.4	5.1	257	4.7	4.3
Mar 07	460	4.5	4.2	481	5.5	4.7	258	5.2	4.5
Apr 07	457	3.3	3.7	478	4.2	4.4	260	5.9	5.3
May 07	459	2.9	3.6	480	3.1	4.2	260	4.8	5.3
Jun 07	461	3.7	3.3	488	3.9	3.7	261	5.3	5.3
Jul 07	462	4.7	3.8	506	7.0	4.7	262	5.6	5.2
Aug 07	462	3.6	4.0	502	8.5	6.5	263	6.2	5.7
Sep 07	463	3.2	3.8	509	7.7	7.7	263	5.0	5.6
Oct 07	464	3.2	3.3	502	5.8	7.3	264	4.4	5.2
Nov 07	464	3.0	3.1	506	6.4	6.6	264	3.6	4.3
Dec 07	465	3.3	3.2	503	5.7	6.0	263	2.8	3.6
Jan 08	469	2.8	3.0	494	3.8	5.3	265	4.4	3.6
Feb 08	472	3.2	3.1	502	6.6	5.3	265	3.0	3.4
Mar 08	472	2.5	2.8	498	3.5	4.6	268	3.7	3.7
Apr 08	474	3.6	3.1	507	6.1	5.4	271	4.2	3.6
May 08	474	3.3	3.2	505	5.3	5.0	269	3.5	3.8
Jun 08	475	3.1	3.3	512	5.0	5.5	268	2.9	3.6

4.14b Average Weekly Earnings - regular pay[1]

Seasonally adjusted

Great Britain

	Manufacturing, SIC 2007 section C			Construction, SIC 2007 section F			Wholesaling, retailing, hotels & restaurants, SIC 2007 sections G & I		
	Weekly Earnings (£)	% changes year on year		Weekly Earnings (£)	% changes year on year		Weekly Earnings (£)	% changes year on year	
		Single month	3 month average[2]		Single month	3 month average[2]		Single month	3 month average[2]
	K5DU	K5DV	K5DW	K5DX	K5DY	K5DZ	K5E2	K5E3	K5E4
Jul 08	476	3.0	3.2	510	0.7	3.6	267	2.0	2.8
Aug 08	476	2.9	3.0	498	-0.8	1.6	269	2.1	2.3
Sep 08	476	2.9	2.9	510	0.2	0.0	270	2.9	2.3
Oct 08	477	2.8	2.9	515	2.7	0.7	269	2.2	2.4
Nov 08	481	3.5	3.1	514	1.7	1.6	268	1.5	2.2
Dec 08	480	3.2	3.2	511	1.8	2.1	271	2.9	2.2
Jan 09	479	2.1	2.9	517	4.6	2.7	271	2.2	2.2
Feb 09	478	1.2	2.2	514	2.4	2.9	274	3.5	2.8
Mar 09	478	1.2	1.5	517	4.0	3.7	272	1.7	2.5
Apr 09	480	1.3	1.2	516	1.7	2.7	271	0.1	1.7
May 09	481	1.6	1.4	513	1.6	2.4	272	1.1	1.0
Jun 09	484	2.0	1.6	509	-0.6	0.9	272	1.3	0.8
Jul 09	480	0.8	1.4	513	0.7	0.5	273	2.0	1.4
Aug 09	484	1.7	1.5	512	2.9	0.9	272	1.3	1.5
Sep 09	486	2.1	1.5	515	0.9	1.5	274	1.2	1.5
Oct 09	488	2.2	2.0	522	1.2	1.7	274	1.8	1.4
Nov 09	488	1.7	2.0	521	1.3	1.1	274	2.2	1.8
Dec 09	499	4.0	2.6	521	1.8	1.4	276	1.9	2.0
Jan 10	499	4.2	3.3	525	1.4	1.5	275	1.7	1.9
Feb 10	500	4.8	4.3	523	1.8	1.7	277	1.2	1.6
Mar 10	504	5.4	4.8	524	1.4	1.5	279	2.4	1.8
Apr 10	501	4.5	4.9	522	1.2	1.5	277	2.1	1.9
May 10	501	4.1	4.7	515	0.4	1.0	276	1.4	2.0
Jun 10	502	3.7	4.1	517	1.6	1.1	278	2.2	1.9
Jul 10	501	4.4	4.1	511	-0.3	0.6	278	2.0	1.9
Aug 10	504	4.3	4.1	506	-1.1	0.0	279	2.6	2.3
Sep 10	504	3.7	4.1	512	-0.5	-0.7	279	2.1	2.2
Oct 10	504	3.3	3.8	517	-0.8	-0.8	278	1.3	2.0
Nov 10	504	3.2	3.4	516	-1.0	-0.8	278	1.5	1.6
Dec 10	505	1.2	2.6	507	-2.7	-1.5	277	0.5	1.1
Jan 11	507	1.6	2.0	524	0.0	-1.2	279	1.4	1.1
Feb 11	505	1.0	1.2	524	0.3	-0.8	279	0.5	0.8
Mar 11	507	0.6	1.0	527	0.5	0.3	279	0.0	0.6
Apr 11	506	0.9	0.8	516	-1.2	-0.1	281	1.6	0.7
May 11	507	1.2	0.9	519	0.6	0.0	282	2.3	1.3
Jun 11	508	1.2	1.1	525	1.4	0.3	280	1.0	1.6
Jul 11	510	1.7	1.4	522	2.1	1.4	280	0.8	1.4
Aug 11	511	1.3	1.4	519	2.6	2.0	281	0.6	0.8
Sep 11	513	1.8	1.6	522	2.0	2.2	281	0.5	0.6
Oct 11	512	1.6	1.6	522	0.9	1.8	283	1.7	0.9
Nov 11	514	2.0	1.8	524	1.7	1.5	284	2.2	1.4
Dec 11	513	1.7	1.7	518	2.2	1.6	284	2.4	2.1
Jan 12	513	1.2	1.6	526	0.3	1.4	285	2.1	2.2
Feb 12	514	1.7	1.5	525	0.2	0.9	287	2.9	2.5
Mar 12	516	1.9	1.6	536	1.7	0.7	286	2.7	2.6
Apr 12	517	2.2	1.9	528	2.3	1.4	286	1.7	2.4
May 12	519	2.4	2.2	535	3.1	2.4	287	1.9	2.1
Jun 12	519	2.2	2.3	532	1.3	2.2	289	3.1	2.2
Jul 12	521	2.2	2.3	529	1.3	1.9	289	2.9	2.6
Aug 12	522	2.2	2.2	518	-0.3	0.8	288	2.5	2.8
Sep 12	522	1.8	2.1	520	-0.4	0.2	288	2.6	2.7
Oct 12	523	2.1	2.0	521	-0.2	-0.3	289	2.2	2.4
Nov 12	521	1.4	1.7	524	0.0	-0.2	291	2.3	2.3
Dec 12	524	2.1	1.8	515	-0.5	-0.2	289	1.9	2.1
Jan 13	523	1.9	1.8	514	-2.2	-0.9	287	0.6	1.6
Feb 13	527	2.5	2.2	525	-0.2	-1.0	287	0.3	0.9
Mar 13	529	2.4	2.3	530	-1.2	-1.2	290	1.3	0.7
Apr 13	530	2.4	2.4	537	1.8	0.1	291	1.8	1.1
May 13	530	2.1	2.3	532	-0.5	0.0	292	1.5	1.5
Jun 13	531	2.2	2.2	529	-0.5	0.3	294	1.7	1.7
Jul 13	532	2.1	2.1	527	-0.4	-0.4	296	2.7	2.0
Aug 13	531	1.7	2.0	526	1.6	0.3	296	2.8	2.4
Sep 13	531	1.7	1.8	529	1.7	1.0	296	2.7	2.7
Oct 13	534	2.1	1.8	523	0.4	1.2	297	3.0	2.8
Nov 13	536	2.9	2.2	528	0.7	0.9	297	2.1	2.6
Dec 13	537	2.4	2.5	526	2.2	1.1	298	2.9	2.7
Jan 14	539	3.2 (r)	2.8	542	5.5	2.8	300	4.6	3.2

1. Estimates of regular pay exclude bonuses and arrears of pay.

2. The three month average figures are the changes in the average seasonally adjusted values for the three months ending with the relevant month compared with the same period a year earlier.

3. From July 2009 Royal Bank of Scotland Group plc is classified to the public sector; for earlier time periods it is classified to the private sector.

Between July 2009 and March 2014 Lloyds Banking Group plc is classified to the public sector; it is classified to the private sector for earlier and later time periods.

4. Between June 2010 and May 2012 English Further Education Corporations and Sixth Form College Corporations are classified to the public sector.

Before June 2010 and after May 2012 they are classified to the private sector.

5. From October 2013 Royal Mail plc is classified to the private sector; previously it is in the public sector.

Source: Monthly Wages & Salaries Survey

Earnings enquiries: 01633 456773

Email: ster@ons.gsi.gov.uk

4.14c Average Weekly Earnings - bonus pay

Seasonally adjusted

Standard Industrial Classification (2007)

Great Britain

	Whole Economy			Private sector [234]			Public sector [234]		
	Weekly Earnings (£)	% changes year on year		Weekly Earnings (£)	% changes year on year		Weekly Earnings (£)	% changes year on year	
		Single month	3 month average [1]		Single month	3 month average [1]		Single month	3 month average [1]
	KAF4	KAF5	KAF6	KAF7	KAF8	KAF9	KAG2	KAG3	KAG4
Jan 02	19	-7.3	-8.4	20	-11.5	-8.7	3	0.1	-17.3
Feb 02	18	-14.2	-11.1	20	-14.7	-12.2	4	7.0	-0.3
Mar 02	17	-15.7	-12.4	19	-15.6	-13.9	3	-2.8	1.5
Apr 02	18	-10.2	-13.4	21	-8.0	-12.8	4	31.0	10.6
May 02	18	-5.9	-10.7	21	-7.1	-10.3	4	18.0	14.4
Jun 02	18	-11.4	-9.2	20	-10.8	-8.7	3	6.3	18.3
Jul 02	18	1.1	-5.6	21	1.9	-5.5	3	30.2	17.7
Aug 02	18	1.0	-3.4	22	3.0	-2.2	3	-2.9	10.5
Sep 02	18	-1.7	0.1	21	-1.1	1.3	3	17.0	14.1
Oct 02	18	-6.3	-2.4	20	-5.8	-1.4	3	21.6	11.6
Nov 02	18	-3.0	-3.7	21	-0.9	-2.6	3	36.4	24.5
Dec 02	18	-3.9	-4.4	21	-2.5	-3.1	3	152.2	51.6
Jan 03	16	-13.5	-6.8	16	-18.2	-7.0	3	-14.7	32.4
Feb 03	17	-3.2	-6.9	19	-3.2	-7.9	3	-21.8	6.6
Mar 03	20	18.8	0.2	24	20.8	-0.4	3	-3.5	-13.7
Apr 03	16	-11.3	1.2	20	-5.6	3.7	3	-23.2	-16.7
May 03	17	-8.9	-0.8	19	-6.2	2.6	3	-23.3	-17.3
Jun 03	17	-4.0	-8.0	20	-4.3	-5.4	4	34.9	-6.1
Jul 03	18	-2.3	-5.1	22	2.0	-2.8	3	-8.9	-0.9
Aug 03	17	-7.1	-4.5	20	-6.0	-2.8	3	12.1	12.0
Sep 03	18	0.8	-2.9	22	3.6	-0.2	3	-7.2	-2.1
Oct 03	20	14.2	2.5	24	18.1	5.0	3	-10.8	-2.7
Nov 03	18	0.8	5.3	22	6.5	9.3	2	-28.1	-15.4
Dec 03	17	-0.7	4.8	21	4.7	9.7	3	6.2	-11.5
Jan 04	21	27.2	8.6	30	83.2	27.5	3	24.2	-0.9
Feb 04	17	-1.9	7.8	21	7.4	28.4	3	-6.3	7.8
Mar 04	21	3.2	8.8	25	5.4	27.5	3	10.0	9.1
Apr 04	21	34.0	10.7	24	21.7	11.1	3	9.4	4.5
May 04	20	20.8	18.0	26	31.9	18.7	3	9.4	9.6
Jun 04	20	13.5	22.4	24	20.8	24.7	3	-21.6	-3.7
Jul 04	20	10.8	14.9	23	5.7	18.9	3	-0.3	-6.4
Aug 04	20	21.0	15.0	23	15.1	13.6	3	4.5	-7.4
Sep 04	22	21.4	17.7	26	17.9	12.8	3	1.6	1.9
Oct 04	24	18.5	20.2	27	11.6	14.7	3	-0.9	1.8
Nov 04	22	25.1	21.5	26	15.1	14.7	3	38.7	11.2
Dec 04	22	24.1	22.4	24	12.7	13.1	3	8.3	13.6
Jan 05	23	11.0	19.6	31	3.7	9.8	3	-2.6	12.2
Feb 05	21	23.0	18.8	25	20.2	11.1	3	18.3	7.2
Mar 05	21	2.5	11.4	25	2.3	7.8	3	-7.8	1.5
Apr 05	22	5.2	9.4	26	8.2	9.7	4	21.5	9.7
May 05	22	11.0	6.2	26	1.0	3.8	3	12.2	8.1
Jun 05	21	8.8	8.3	26	8.3	5.7	4	19.4	17.7
Jul 05	22	13.2	11.0	26	14.0	7.5	4	27.3	19.6
Aug 05	26	26.1	16.2	30	26.8	16.3	4	35.8	27.6
Sep 05	24	8.9	15.9	28	9.2	16.4	5	50.1	37.7
Oct 05	24	-0.4	10.9	28	2.6	12.3	5	65.2	49.8
Nov 05	25	13.0	7.0	30	16.0	9.2	4	21.2	44.6
Dec 05	25	14.8	8.9	29	18.7	12.2	5	41.9	42.0
Jan 06	23	1.0	9.5	29	-4.9	8.8	5	57.1	40.1
Feb 06	25	21.9	12.2	30	18.7	9.6	5	54.8	51.1
Mar 06	27	25.2	15.6	32	24.6	11.5	5	49.1	53.7
Apr 06	26	17.7	21.5	31	18.4	20.6	5	36.7	46.3
May 06	26	17.5	20.1	30	17.0	20.0	5	43.8	42.8
Jun 06	29	33.9	22.9	34	32.4	22.6	5	22.6	34.0
Jul 06	29	28.3	26.5	34	29.2	26.2	5	29.9	31.7
Aug 06	28	8.6	22.7	32	9.7	23.1	5	8.2	19.7
Sep 06	25	6.0	13.8	29	5.3	14.3	4	-16.7	5.9
Oct 06	27	12.0	8.9	32	15.2	10.0	5	8.0	-0.1
Nov 06	28	9.1	9.1	33	11.6	10.7	3	-14.1	-7.0
Dec 06	32	27.3	16.2	38	32.2	19.6	5	-2.6	-2.2
Jan 07	31	33.9	23.1	39	32.5	25.3	4	-18.5	-11.7
Feb 07	33	31.2	30.7	38	29.0	31.2	4	-28.9	-16.7
Mar 07	29	9.4	24.3	34	8.0	22.8	6	17.1	-10.7
Apr 07	29	11.3	17.1	34	12.2	16.1	5	3.7	-2.9
May 07	29	11.0	10.6	35	14.6	11.5	5	9.5	9.9
Jun 07	30	5.0	9.0	35	4.7	10.2	6	26.1	12.8
Jul 07	31	7.0	7.6	36	8.0	8.9	5	-5.0	9.9
Aug 07	31	10.7	7.5	37	12.9	8.5	5	1.6	7.2
Sep 07	34	35.3	17.0	40	35.2	18.1	5	24.1	5.4
Oct 07	30	14.4	19.7	37	16.1	21.0	3	-46.8	-10.5
Nov 07	32	17.1	21.9	39	18.2	22.8	5	47.1	0.6
Dec 07	29	-8.1	7.0	36	-6.3	8.5	5	1.4	-5.8
Jan 08	30	-1.2	2.0	40	2.3	4.1	4	-6.7	11.2
Feb 08	35	7.2	-0.6	40	4.9	0.3	5	30.3	6.7
Mar 08	32	8.7	4.9	36	6.2	4.4	4	-31.4	-7.2
Apr 08	32	9.2	8.3	38	10.6	7.1	4	-24.2	-13.6
May 08	33	13.0	10.3	41	18.1	11.7	5	-4.8	-20.1
Jun 08	30	0.9	7.6	37	3.4	10.6	5	-13.6	-14.1

4.14c Average Weekly Earnings - bonus pay

Seasonally adjusted

Great Britain

Standard Industrial Classification (2007)

	Whole Economy			Private sector [234]			Public sector [234]		
	Weekly Earnings (£)	% changes year on year		Weekly Earnings (£)	% changes year on year		Weekly Earnings (£)	% changes year on year	
		Single month	3 month average [1]		Single month	3 month average [1]		Single month	3 month average [1]
	KAF4	KAF5	KAF6	KAF7	KAF8	KAF9	KAG2	KAG3	KAG4
Jul 08	31	-0.1	4.5	37	0.4	7.1	6	26.6	1.3
Aug 08	30	-4.0	-1.1	36	-1.9	0.6	6	15.9	8.0
Sep 08	30	-12.8	-5.9	34	-13.5	-5.3	5	10.5	17.7
Oct 08	30	0.0	-5.9	37	-0.6	-5.5	5	79.7	28.2
Nov 08	27	-17.9	-10.5	32	-18.2	-11.0	6	22.8	30.8
Dec 08	27	-6.4	-8.3	34	-4.6	-8.1	6	16.6	33.0
Jan 09	27	-12.5	-12.5	25	-37.2	-20.6	6	41.2	25.9
Feb 09	18	-48.9	-24.2	21	-47.3	-30.7	5	10.0	21.6
Mar 09	18	-42.4	-35.4	26	-27.3	-37.6	6	54.2	33.6
Apr 09	30	-3.6	-32.3	38	-1.6	-25.8	6	51.9	37.1
May 09	26	-21.1	-22.4	30	-25.8	-18.3	4	-18.7	24.2
Jun 09	21	-29.5	-18.0	32	-11.6	-13.3	4	-21.0	0.1
Jul 09	25	-17.8	-22.8	30	-17.8	-18.6	4	-39.0	-26.9
Aug 09	26	-14.1	-20.5	31	-14.2	-14.5	4	-32.4	-31.3
Sep 09	24	-17.5	-16.5	31	-11.1	-14.4	5	1.1	-24.4
Oct 09	25	-18.1	-16.6	31	-15.7	-13.7	5	3.1	-10.2
Nov 09	27	0.4	-12.2	33	2.6	-8.5	5	-23.6	-7.6
Dec 09	28	2.6	-5.5	34	-0.3	-4.9	4	-29.8	-17.7
Jan 10	22	-16.5	-4.4	23	-7.7	-1.3	5	-3.0	-19.0
Feb 10	27	51.7	7.9	33	56.8	12.4	5	6.6	-9.3
Mar 10	26	43.3	20.4	36	35.0	26.5	4	-25.9	-8.1
Apr 10	24	-20.4	16.5	30	-20.0	16.1	5	-10.9	-10.8
May 10	26	-0.6	2.1	34	13.6	6.2	6	32.0	-5.0
Jun 10	24	12.8	-4.7	28	-13.1	-7.6	5	19.0	10.2
Jul 10	23	-8.4	0.6	28	-6.4	-2.2	5	35.7	28.7
Aug 10	23	-8.3	-2.1	28	-8.4	-9.4	5	25.1	26.3
Sep 10	25	3.8	-4.4	32	3.7	-3.7	5	-13.5	12.2
Oct 10	25	1.3	-1.1	31	1.1	-1.2	6	13.3	6.5
Nov 10	25	-4.7	0.0	32	-4.9	-0.2	6	24.0	7.3
Dec 10	26	-8.9	-4.3	32	-6.3	-3.5	5	29.7	21.6
Jan 11	30	36.5	5.7	35	49.1	8.5	5	-10.2	12.4
Feb 11	27	-1.7	6.6	33	0.5	10.5	6	12.2	8.6
Mar 11	28	7.2	12.6	36	1.2	13.0	6	45.7	13.7
Apr 11	26	7.3	4.1	32	6.1	2.4	5	-0.5	17.2
May 11	26	1.6	5.4	34	-1.8	1.6	5	-12.3	8.2
Jun 11	29	22.4	10.2	36	26.2	9.3	6	26.4	3.6
Jul 11	32	37.7	19.9	36	26.8	15.8	20	292.6	98.9
Aug 11	27	17.0	25.6	34	18.5	23.8	5	13.4	113.3
Sep 11	26	2.4	18.5	32	0.2	14.5	5	14.7	111.2
Oct 11	27	7.0	8.6	33	6.6	8.1	4	-24.0	-0.6
Nov 11	27	6.0	5.2	33	5.2	4.0	5	-8.0	-7.4
Dec 11	26	1.7	4.9	32	1.2	4.4	6	10.8	-7.9
Jan 12	27	-12.9	-2.4	31	-9.3	-1.2	6	27.0	8.8
Feb 12	26	-5.6	-6.0	32	-5.1	-4.5	4	-30.7	0.1
Mar 12	27	-3.8	-7.6	34	-5.8	-6.7	5	-18.2	-9.8
Apr 12	29	11.0	0.3	34	7.0	-1.5	4	-17.3	-22.2
May 12	27	1.1	2.6	33	-3.6	-1.0	6	12.6	-8.8
Jun 12	27	-7.3	1.2	33	-7.5	-1.6	5	-11.7	-6.3
Jul 12	29	-7.7	-4.9	36	-0.5	-3.8	6	-72.1	-46.6
Aug 12	29	5.2	-3.6	34	0.3	-2.6	10	74.0	-34.8
Sep 12	28	6.1	0.7	33	4.2	1.2	6	20.4	-29.9
Oct 12	27	0.0	3.8	32	-3.8	0.2	10	122.5	69.7
Nov 12	27	1.0	2.3	33	-0.7	-0.2	6	17.7	49.6
Dec 12	26	1.1	0.7	32	-1.6	-2.0	10	76.9	69.4
Jan 13	27	1.0	1.0	32	3.3	0.3	5	-17.5	24.5
Feb 13	26	1.6	1.2	32	1.9	1.2	3	-24.5	14.0
Mar 13	25	-6.9	-1.5	31	-7.7	-1.0	4	-12.9	-17.9
Apr 13	46	59.1	19.2	52	51.8	15.7	4	-3.5	-13.3
May 13	32	20.0	24.9	38	16.8	20.4	5	-7.9	-8.3
Jun 13	28	2.8	28.0	34	1.9	23.9	5	-4.9	-5.6
Jul 13	28	-4.2	5.8	34	-3.1	5.0	4	-23.0	-12.0
Aug 13	29	0.6	-0.3	35	4.4	1.0	5	-48.8	-30.2
Sep 13	29	5.3	0.5	35	5.1	2.1	5	-16.9	-32.6
Oct 13	28	3.6	3.1	33	3.4	4.3	4	-62.3	-46.2
Nov 13	27	-0.2	2.9	33	-1.3	2.4	4	-35.3	-42.0
Dec 13	28	6.8	3.3	33	6.0	2.7	2	-77.8	-61.7
Jan 14 (r)	27	2.0	2.8	34	5.3	3.3	5	-7.9	-48.6

1. The three month average figures are the changes in the average seasonally adjusted values for the three months ending with the relevant month compared with the same period a year earlier.

2. From July 2009 Royal Bank of Scotland Group plc is classified to the public sector; for earlier time periods it is classified to the private sector.

Between July 2009 and March 2014 Lloyds Banking Group plc is classified to the public sector; it is classified to the private sector for earlier and later time periods.

3. Between June 2010 and May 2012 English Further Education Corporations and Sixth Form College Corporations are classified to the public sector.

Before June 2010 and after May 2012 they are classified to the private sector.

4. From October 2013 Royal Mail plc is classified to the private sector; previously it is in the public sector.

Source: Monthly Wages & Salaries Survey

Earnings enquiries: 01633 456773

Email: ster@ons.gsi.gov.uk

4.14c Average Weekly Earnings - bonus pay

Seasonally adjusted

Great Britain

	Services, SIC 2007 sections G-S			Finance and business services, SIC 2007 sections K-N			Public sector excluding financial services [3][4]		
	Weekly Earnings (£)	% changes year on year		Weekly Earnings (£)	% changes year on year		Weekly Earnings (£)	% changes year on year	
		Single month	3 month average [1]		Single month	3 month average [1]		Single month	3 month average [1]
	K5CS	K5CT	K5CU	K5CV	K5CW	K5CX	KAH3	KAH4	KAH5
Jan 02	19	-8.9	-9.6	42	-15.9	-15.7	2	-3.1	-18.6
Feb 02	19	-13.3	-11.6	42	-15.0	-16.0	2	-10.4	-10.3
Mar 02	16	-22.2	-14.7	36	-26.7	-19.2	2	1.7	-4.1
Apr 02	19	-13.1	-16.1	39	-20.8	-20.8	3	14.6	1.4
May 02	19	-6.0	-13.8	40	-9.8	-19.4	3	20.5	12.1
Jun 02	18	-12.9	-10.7	41	-41.2	-26.4	2	5.1	13.6
Jul 02	19	1.2	-6.2	44	4.5	-19.8	2	24.0	16.5
Aug 02	19	1.4	-3.8	41	-2.6	-18.0	2	-11.4	6.0
Sep 02	19	-0.9	0.5	44	-1.4	0.2	2	21.8	11.6
Oct 02	18	-4.5	-1.4	41	-6.5	-3.5	2	21.2	10.6
Nov 02	19	-2.2	-2.5	41	-2.1	-3.3	2	32.2	24.8
Dec 02	18	-5.6	-4.1	38	-9.6	-6.1	2	174.8	52.5
Jan 03	16	-19.5	-9.1	31	-24.8	-12.2	2	-14.5	33.3
Feb 03	18	-5.1	-10.1	41	-2.4	-12.2	2	-9.1	15.6
Mar 03	18	14.1	-4.5	42	14.5	-5.1	2	-13.9	-12.5
Apr 03	17	-10.5	-1.2	38	-3.7	2.4	2	-24.4	-16.1
May 03	17	-9.5	-2.8	39	-3.1	2.2	2	-29.4	-22.9
Jun 03	18	-4.4	-8.2	37	-9.0	-5.3	3	36.6	-8.3
Jul 03	18	-4.3	-6.1	40	-10.1	-7.5	2	-12.5	-4.0
Aug 03	17	-9.9	-6.2	38	-7.7	-9.0	2	24.3	14.4
Sep 03	18	-4.4	-6.2	38	-12.5	-10.1	2	-10.3	-2.1
Oct 03	20	12.1	-0.9	47	14.3	-2.2	2	-9.8	-0.9
Nov 03	18	-3.0	1.4	42	2.6	1.1	2	-30.8	-16.9
Dec 03	18	-2.3	2.2	31	-18.9	-0.3	2	1.2	-13.5
Jan 04	20	27.9	6.5	49	56.9	10.5	2	14.6	-6.3
Feb 04	18	-0.5	7.5	38	-7.0	6.9	2	-0.5	4.9
Mar 04	20	10.9	12.1	50	20.9	20.7	2	11.1	8.3
Apr 04	23	37.0	15.3	54	44.1	18.6	2	6.5	5.7
May 04	20	16.1	21.0	54	39.6	34.5	2	9.5	9.1
Jun 04	20	13.9	22.2	47	27.6	37.2	2	-21.7	-5.0
Jul 04	20	10.0	13.3	50	26.0	31.1	2	-5.4	-8.3
Aug 04	20	19.1	14.2	38	0.4	18.1	2	7.6	-8.3
Sep 04	22	22.2	17.0	47	21.9	16.3	2	-4.8	-0.9
Oct 04	24	20.2	20.5	65	38.9	21.8	2	-0.2	0.9
Nov 04	22	25.0	22.4	51	22.8	28.5	2	34.5	7.7
Dec 04	22	26.5	23.7	53	70.4	41.5	2	8.4	12.4
Jan 05	22	9.7	20.0	55	11.0	30.2	2	-3.6	10.9
Feb 05	22	24.9	19.9	51	32.9	33.7	2	4.3	3.0
Mar 05	21	3.1	12.0	52	4.4	14.7	2	-5.1	-1.6
Apr 05	23	-0.5	8.1	54	0.1	10.4	2	12.0	3.5
May 05	23	13.2	5.0	51	-6.6	-0.9	2	14.8	6.9
Jun 05	22	8.8	6.8	60	27.4	6.0	2	4.4	10.1
Jul 05	22	12.3	11.5	54	7.7	8.7	3	32.8	16.6
Aug 05	26	27.1	16.1	67	76.8	33.9	3	27.3	20.9
Sep 05	23	7.7	15.5	64	37.3	37.4	3	50.9	36.6
Oct 05	23	-2.9	9.8	60	-8.2	27.6	3	53.0	43.2
Nov 05	25	13.2	5.8	67	31.7	17.4	3	19.6	40.9
Dec 05	26	14.7	8.1	62	16.6	11.7	3	30.8	34.2
Jan 06	22	-0.8	9.1	57	4.5	17.3	4	72.6	40.7
Feb 06	28	27.1	13.7	65	28.0	16.1	4	75.1	58.6
Mar 06	27	28.5	18.2	71	35.8	22.5	3	49.4	65.7
Apr 06	26	14.5	23.2	70	28.7	30.8	3	36.5	53.2
May 06	27	18.7	20.3	71	39.0	34.4	3	35.4	40.1
Jun 06	29	34.7	22.4	96	60.4	43.4	3	25.6	32.4
Jul 06	30	31.6	28.2	82	51.5	50.9	3	17.3	25.8
Aug 06	28	7.9	23.8	77	15.5	41.2	3	6.6	15.9
Sep 06	24	2.3	13.5	61	-4.5	19.1	2	-21.5	-0.1
Oct 06	26	9.4	6.6	73	23.0	11.1	4	17.7	1.1
Nov 06	28	9.4	7.1	81	20.3	12.8	2	-21.6	-7.3
Dec 06	35	37.5	19.0	107	72.6	38.3	3	4.6	1.7
Jan 07	30	36.8	27.5	81	42.7	44.5	3	-22.4	-13.3
Feb 07	38	36.4	36.9	84	28.2	47.6	3	-24.7	-15.3
Mar 07	29	7.0	26.2	75	4.7	23.8	3	-2.0	-17.1
Apr 07	29	10.3	18.2	78	10.6	14.1	3	-3.4	-10.9
May 07	29	8.9	8.7	75	5.5	6.9	3	5.7	0.1
Jun 07	30	1.0	6.5	75	-22.0	-4.1	4	19.6	7.2
Jul 07	31	3.7	4.4	77	-5.3	-8.7	3	0.7	8.6
Aug 07	31	10.2	4.9	80	3.9	-8.8	3	1.5	7.2
Sep 07	33	39.3	16.4	91	49.2	13.1	3	23.8	7.4
Oct 07	30	18.1	21.8	74	1.1	16.0	2	-50.9	-14.2
Nov 07	32	14.1	23.2	80	-1.1	13.9	3	53.4	-3.4
Dec 07	29	-16.6	3.0	75	-29.9	-12.3	3	-10.2	-13.0
Jan 08	30	-0.3	-2.2	80	-1.5	-12.7	3	-0.8	9.0
Feb 08	42	9.1	-2.4	88	4.6	-10.8	2	-14.7	-8.6
Mar 08	32	9.2	6.3	83	11.5	4.7	2	-41.7	-19.7
Apr 08	31	7.9	8.8	79	2.0	6.0	3	2.3	-18.3
May 08	32	10.6	9.2	92	22.7	11.9	3	-9.7	-16.3
Jun 08	30	2.3	6.9	92	22.8	15.7	3	-14.7	-7.9

4.14c Average Weekly Earnings - bonus pay

Seasonally adjusted

Great Britain

	Services, SIC 2007 sections G-S			Finance and business services, SIC 2007 sections K-N			Public sector excluding financial services [3] [4]		
	Weekly Earnings (£)	% changes year on year		Weekly Earnings (£)	% changes year on year		Weekly Earnings (£)	% changes year on year	
		Single month	3 month average [1]		Single month	3 month average [1]		Single month	3 month average [1]
	K5CS	K5CT	K5CU	K5CV	K5CW	K5CX	KAH3	KAH4	KAH5
Jul 08	30	-1.2	3.8	79	1.9	15.6	4	20.1	-2.3
Aug 08	30	-2.6	-0.5	73	-8.7	5.0	4	19.0	7.0
Sep 08	29	-12.6	-5.7	82	-10.0	-5.9	3	15.3	18.2
Oct 08	31	2.6	-4.5	88	18.6	-0.9	3	79.1	31.7
Nov 08	27	-15.5	-8.8	65	-19.5	-4.5	4	26.9	34.8
Dec 08	29	-2.6	-5.3	80	7.0	1.5	3	14.4	34.7
Jan 09	27	-8.0	-8.9	77	-3.7	-5.7	3	0.8	14.4
Feb 09	20	-51.6	-24.6	44	-49.3	-16.8	4	56.6	22.1
Mar 09	18	-43.1	-36.5	47	-43.1	-32.6	3	92.3	43.2
Apr 09	30	-3.6	-34.7	86	8.9	-28.8	5	50.8	63.0
May 09	26	-19.5	-22.1	53	-42.4	-26.6	3	-14.6	35.3
Jun 09	21	-30.7	-17.8	55	-40.8	-26.4	2	-25.2	3.8
Jul 09	25	-17.2	-22.4	62	-21.0	-35.4	2	-47.1	-30.2
Aug 09	26	-14.2	-20.7	67	-7.8	-24.5	2	-53.6	-43.0
Sep 09	25	-14.2	-15.3	60	-27.1	-19.0	3	-13.0	-38.6
Oct 09	25	-19.4	-16.0	64	-27.5	-21.4	2	-40.6	-36.2
Nov 09	27	-0.6	-11.9	69	6.8	-17.9	2	-54.0	-36.7
Dec 10	29	1.0	-6.8	84	4.2	-7.0	2	-44.5	-46.8
Jan 10	23	-17.3	-5.5	62	-19.3	-3.2	3	-3.5	-36.6
Feb 10	30	48.3	7.1	76	69.9	9.7	2	-55.3	-36.7
Mar 10	26	44.1	19.9	66	38.7	20.4	4	15.4	-16.2
Apr 10	24	-20.5	16.9	63	-26.8	14.8	1	-70.8	-40.7
May 10	26	0.2	2.4	78	47.5	10.9	2	-28.3	-32.6
Jun 10	25	16.7	-3.4	68	23.9	7.7	2	-14.4	-45.7
Jul 10	23	-7.3	2.4	58	-7.7	19.6	2	-21.7	-21.7
Aug 10	23	-8.1	-0.6	66	-2.8	3.4	2	-1.1	-13.0
Sep 10	26	3.0	-4.2	73	22.3	3.5	2	-47.8	-28.0
Oct 10	25	1.5	-1.3	72	12.8	10.2	2	1.7	-21.1
Nov 10	26	-2.0	0.8	73	5.3	13.0	2	-0.6	-20.7
Dec 10	26	-10.8	-4.1	69	-17.9	-1.4	2	-5.1	-1.3
Jan 11	32	39.8	6.8	98	57.8	11.5	1	-48.6	-22.7
Feb 11	29	-5.2	5.2	75	-0.2	9.5	2	24.6	-16.4
Mar 11	29	10.3	12.8	78	18.1	23.5	2	-52.7	-36.1
Apr 11	26	6.5	3.3	68	8.3	8.3	2	60.6	-12.5
May 11	27	3.1	6.6	73	-6.3	5.9	2	-13.4	-21.3
Jun 11	30	23.7	10.9	87	29.0	9.6	1	-44.3	-5.8
Jul 11	33	40.9	21.8	87	51.3	21.8	4	128.5	16.2
Aug 11	28	20.1	28.1	71	7.6	28.4	2	10.1	24.7
Sep 11	26	2.4	20.5	72	-2.3	16.7	2	4.2	46.6
Oct 11	28	11.0	10.9	73	1.3	2.0	1	-26.6	-5.6
Nov 11	28	5.3	6.2	76	4.9	1.3	2	4.9	-7.1
Dec 11	27	3.2	6.4	71	3.0	3.1	2	-4.9	-9.6
Jan 12	27	-14.1	-2.7	72	-26.4	-8.5	2	51.9	14.9
Feb 12	26	-7.9	-6.8	66	-12.1	-13.6	2	-23.8	2.9
Mar 12	28	-2.4	-8.3	74	-4.6	-15.4	2	-13.7	-0.4
Apr 12	30	15.4	1.2	76	11.5	-2.2	1	-31.5	-23.4
May 12	27	0.0	4.0	61	-16.8	-3.7	2	7.8	-14.4
Jun 12	28	-8.5	1.7	68	-22.4	-10.5	2	56.1	1.1
Jul 12	30	-7.7	-5.6	79	-9.5	-16.2	2	-51.1	-17.1
Aug 12	30	6.2	-3.7	77	9.6	-8.6	2	23.9	-11.6
Sep 12	29	9.7	2.0	69	-4.0	-1.9	2	32.0	-12.2
Oct 12	28	-1.1	4.8	68	-6.8	-0.5	4	189.1	75.5
Nov 12	28	1.3	3.2	67	-12.0	-7.7	2	19.0	73.6
Dec 12	27	2.5	0.9	71	0.6	-6.2	3	82.7	90.1
Jan 13	28	1.9	1.9	72	0.0	-4.0	2	-17.7	23.6
Feb 13	27	0.8	1.7	67	1.5	0.7	1	-30.7	9.2
Mar 13	26	-6.9	-1.5	68	-7.5	-2.1	2	13.1	-12.1
Apr 13	49	66.7	21.4	134	76.4	24.8	2	33.1	4.8
May 13	33	22.6	28.3	87	43.1	37.4	2	14.4	19.7
Jun 13	29	3.8	31.9	76	12.8	45.5	2	22.2	22.8
Jul 13	29	-3.3	7.2	71	-9.7	13.1	2	-7.4	9.7
Aug 13	30	-0.4	-0.1	74	-4.1	-1.0	2	-33.2	-8.9
Sep 13	30	4.9	0.3	75	9.7	-1.9	2	-23.9	-22.8
Oct 13	29	3.7	2.7	73	7.1	3.9	1	-73.9	-50.8
Nov 13	28	1.0	3.2	70	4.0	7.0	1	-55.6	-56.8
Dec 13	29	7.3	4.0	74	3.7	4.9	1	-71.9	-69.0
Jan 14 (r)	28	2.7	3.6	71	-1.5	2.0	1	-27.0	-55.4

1. The three month average figures are the changes in the average seasonally adjusted values for the three months ending with the relevant month compared with the same period a year earlier.

2. From July 2009 Royal Bank of Scotland Group plc is classified to the public sector; for earlier time periods it is classified to the private sector.

Between July 2009 and March 2014 Lloyds Banking Group plc is classified to the public sector; it is classified to the private sector for earlier and later time periods.

3. Between June 2010 and May 2012 English Further Education Corporations and Sixth Form College Corporations are classified to the public sector.

Before June 2010 and after May 2012 they are classified to the private sector.

4. From October 2013 Royal Mail plc is classified to the private sector; previously it is in the public sector.

Source: Monthly Wages & Salaries Survey

Earnings enquiries: 01633 456773

Email: ster@ons.gsi.gov.uk

4.14c Average Weekly Earnings - bonus pay

Seasonally adjusted

	Manufacturing, SIC 2007 section C			Construction, SIC 2007 section F			Wholesaling, retailing, hotels & restaurants, SIC 2007 sections G & I		
	Weekly Earnings (£)	% changes year on year		Weekly Earnings (£)	% changes year on year		Weekly Earnings (£)	% changes year on year	
		Single month	3 month average [1]		Single month	3 month average [1]		Single month	3 month average [1]
	K5D3	K5D4	K5D5	K5D6	K5D7	K5D8	K5D9	K5DA	K5DB
Jan 02	13	-10.6	-8.4	16	-24.6	-11.4	16	12.1	8.5
Feb 02	14	-11.5	-9.1	20	6.7	-12.8	15	-2.1	4.9
Mar 02	15	6.4	-5.5	20	35.3	2.3	15	-9.0	-0.2
Apr 02	15	6.7	0.1	27	39.8	27.0	15	-4.0	-5.1
May 02	14	-6.5	2.1	19	-10.3	19.7	16	-4.8	-6.0
Jun 02	16	7.7	2.5	21	-25.5	-2.2	17	11.4	0.5
Jul 02	14	0.3	0.5	21	2.6	-12.6	14	-5.9	0.0
Aug 02	14	-5.9	0.7	23	-2.9	-10.1	16	-8.9	-1.5
Sep 02	14	-5.2	-3.6	20	-5.6	-2.1	16	-2.7	-5.9
Oct 02	14	-4.3	-5.1	17	-25.1	-11.2	16	13.1	-0.2
Nov 02	15	3.2	-2.1	17	-26.8	-19.4	16	-1.3	2.6
Dec 02	15	4.8	1.2	19	-1.1	-18.5	15	-2.4	2.7
Jan 03	16	16.9	8.0	22	36.2	-1.0	16	-0.5	-1.4
Feb 03	17	25.9	15.6	20	2.4	10.9	15	2.8	-0.1
Mar 03	16	5.6	15.8	24	18.5	17.8	14	-5.1	-0.9
Apr 03	13	-11.3	6.4	20	-27.3	-5.0	12	-20.2	-7.7
May 03	16	14.8	2.9	17	-11.0	-8.9	13	-19.7	-15.1
Jun 03	13	-16.8	-5.1	18	-11.0	-17.7	14	-16.6	-18.8
Jul 03	17	16.5	4.0	19	-9.2	-10.4	15	2.9	-11.7
Aug 03	17	24.9	7.1	20	-13.4	-11.3	13	-15.2	-10.1
Sep 03	16	11.0	17.4	22	9.5	-4.8	14	-9.2	-7.5
Oct 03	16	11.3	15.7	24	40.1	9.4	15	-5.8	-10.0
Nov 03	19	31.0	18.0	22	29.8	25.4	13	-16.7	-10.6
Dec 03	15	-3.7	12.7	21	8.8	25.6	18	20.8	-1.0
Jan 04	17	8.5	11.7	21	-3.5	10.3	14	-12.3	-3.2
Feb 04	14	-18.1	-5.0	20	1.8	2.1	15	0.4	2.7
Mar 04	16	-0.3	-3.8	23	-2.6	-1.5	14	-4.4	-5.6
Apr 04	16	23.8	-0.3	21	4.8	1.1	15	24.4	5.8
May 04	19	19.8	13.7	25	52.0	15.0	14	9.2	9.0
Jun 04	16	24.6	22.5	20	6.9	19.8	15	6.3	13.0
Jul 04	17	3.1	15.1	22	12.7	22.8	15	1.2	5.4
Aug 04	18	6.8	10.5	18	-10.6	2.7	15	14.3	7.1
Sep 04	20	27.7	12.2	15	-33.1	-11.6	17	17.6	10.9
Oct 04	19	16.3	16.6	18	-23.4	-22.9	15	-1.5	9.8
Nov 04	17	-12.0	9.0	26	21.5	-12.4	15	11.2	8.9
Dec 04	22	45.1	13.8	20	-1.6	-2.0	16	-13.9	-2.7
Jan 05	18	7.7	11.0	24	14.7	11.6	16	13.3	1.8
Feb 05	17	19.8	23.6	23	14.2	9.0	16	4.5	0.0
Mar 05	17	5.7	10.7	25	10.5	13.0	13	-4.7	4.4
Apr 05	18	16.1	13.6	24	14.1	12.8	15	-1.0	-0.3
May 05	17	-11.7	2.5	26	4.4	9.4	15	8.1	0.8
Jun 05	16	-0.5	0.5	23	16.5	11.1	14	-2.3	1.5
Jul 05	18	6.8	-2.2	24	9.6	9.7	14	-4.0	0.5
Aug 05	19	1.5	2.6	20	11.1	12.4	14	-5.4	-3.9
Sep 05	17	-16.7	-3.4	21	41.8	19.0	15	-9.4	-6.4
Oct 05	18	-4.5	-6.8	25	34.7	28.5	15	2.0	-4.5
Nov 05	19	13.5	-3.3	26	-0.7	20.9	15	0.0	-2.7
Dec 05	19	-11.3	-1.7	25	21.6	16.3	16	4.9	2.4
Jan 06	19	6.9	2.0	26	7.7	8.6	15	-5.8	-0.3
Feb 06	21	22.5	4.7	27	17.1	15.2	13	-15.5	-5.5
Mar 06	19	13.1	14.0	23	-8.2	5.2	15	13.8	-3.5
Apr 06	20	10.8	15.4	24	0.6	2.8	15	-3.9	-2.8
May 06	19	14.4	12.7	25	-6.0	-4.7	14	-7.2	0.2
Jun 06	20	20.1	14.9	27	16.0	3.0	15	5.2	-2.1
Jul 06	19	2.7	12.0	27	15.6	7.9	17	18.9	5.3
Aug 06	18	-1.9	6.4	27	38.4	22.6	15	4.0	9.3
Sep 06	21	24.9	8.0	21	-1.0	17.2	15	-1.4	7.0
Oct 06	24	36.6	19.4	25	2.8	12.3	15	0.1	0.8
Nov 06	20	0.9	20.1	23	-11.7	-3.5	15	1.4	0.0
Dec 06	20	2.8	12.8	25	1.5	-2.6	16	-4.2	-1.0
Jan 07	21	9.7	4.5	25	-1.9	-4.1	16	9.2	1.9
Feb 07	22	4.4	5.6	46	67.6	23.5	17	27.0	9.6
Mar 07	21	8.0	7.3	26	9.8	26.6	19	28.4	21.3
Apr 07	21	1.4	4.5	29	20.0	34.2	18	24.7	26.7
May 07	22	17.5	8.8	31	25.1	18.4	19	36.5	29.8
Jun 07	24	21.3	13.2	35	32.6	26.1	21	37.3	32.9
Jul 07	23	24.6	21.1	29	4.8	20.6	20	20.4	30.9
Aug 07	23	23.2	23.0	28	0.8	12.5	18	20.4	25.9
Sep 07	23	10.9	19.3	33	56.5	17.7	21	40.6	26.9
Oct 07	23	-5.4	8.2	29	15.1	21.6	21	41.7	34.3
Nov 07	24	23.9	8.8	33	45.4	37.7	20	30.2	37.5
Dec 07	24	23.2	12.5	35	37.9	32.4	19	23.1	31.5
Jan 08	22	2.9	16.3	32	28.6	37.1	17	7.4	20.0
Feb 08	23	3.6	9.5	31	-31.8	2.3	18	9.1	13.1
Mar 08	20	-6.1	0.2	28	8.5	-5.4	20	6.5	7.6
Apr 08	24	13.9	3.8	25	-11.2	-15.6	20	8.0	7.8
May 08	34	54.1	21.5	27	-11.4	-5.4	20	3.5	6.0
Jun 08	24	2.0	23.1	23	-35.3	-20.2	19	-10.3	0.0

4.14c Average Weekly Earnings - bonus pay

Seasonally adjusted

Great Britain

	Manufacturing, SIC 2007 section C			Construction, SIC 2007 section F			Wholesaling, retailing, hotels & restaurants, SIC 2007 sections G & I		
	Weekly Earnings (£)	% changes year on year		Weekly Earnings (£)	% changes year on year		Weekly Earnings (£)	% changes year on year	
		Single month	3 month average [1]		Single month	3 month average [1]		Single month	3 month average [1]
	K5D3	K5D4	K5D5	K5D6	K5D7	K5D8	K5D9	K5DA	K5DB
Jul 08	27	16.3	23.6	23	-18.4	-22.4	19	-8.7	-5.3
Aug 08	22	-3.5	5.0	26	-6.1	-21.2	17	-3.4	-7.7
Sep 08	22	-5.4	2.6	28	-14.2	-13.0	16	-21.5	-11.6
Oct 08	24	5.5	-1.1	23	-23.0	-14.6	16	-26.5	-17.9
Nov 08	19	-20.4	-7.0	22	-33.4	-23.6	18	-6.6	-18.5
Dec 08	21	-11.9	-9.2	21	-39.9	-32.6	17	-12.1	-15.4
Jan 09	21	-3.9	-12.3	18	-42.8	-38.7	18	5.5	-4.8
Feb 09	19	-18.6	-11.6	21	-34.0	-39.0	18	-2.5	-3.3
Mar 09	22	10.5	-4.7	24	-14.3	-31.1	17	-18.4	-5.8
Apr 09	25	5.0	-1.5	24	-5.2	-18.8	17	-14.2	-12.0
May 09	20	-41.0	-14.0	18	-34.0	-18.1	17	-14.6	-15.8
Jun 09	19	-22.1	-22.2	19	-16.0	-18.9	17	-9.4	-12.8
Jul 09	18	-33.8	-33.4	19	-18.0	-23.3	16	-12.1	-12.1
Aug 09	19	-13.5	-23.9	20	-23.8	-19.4	18	2.5	-6.5
Sep 09	20	-9.9	-20.2	18	-35.8	-26.4	17	4.7	-2.0
Oct 09	18	-25.6	-16.6	20	-9.4	-24.0	17	9.4	5.4
Nov 09	21	7.2	-10.6	22	0.2	-16.7	17	-5.4	2.5
Dec 09	21	-3.7	-8.6	21	-0.9	-3.4	17	1.2	1.3
Jan 10	20	-4.0	-0.4	22	18.7	5.4	18	-1.0	-1.8
Feb 10	22	18.2	2.9	20	-0.6	5.3	19	7.2	2.4
Mar 10	22	4.3	5.6	24	-1.0	4.9	23	38.3	14.1
Apr 10	19	-22.9	-2.2	16	-35.5	-13.1	18	8.9	17.7
May 10	20	-0.6	-7.3	18	1.9	-12.8	17	-1.0	15.2
Jun 10	15	-19.1	-14.7	14	-25.0	-21.2	16	-2.0	1.9
Jul 10	22	23.1	0.8	18	-5.2	-9.6	17	2.9	-0.1
Aug 10	22	18.5	7.3	18	-9.6	-13.2	15	-13.2	-4.3
Sep 10	22	11.3	17.5	17	-4.0	-6.3	17	-2.5	-4.5
Oct 10	26	43.1	23.8	14	-30.5	-15.2	17	-2.3	-6.1
Nov 10	20	-2.3	16.2	16	-29.1	-22.1	19	6.5	0.6
Dec 10	23	9.9	15.7	18	-12.8	-24.3	19	10.5	4.9
Jan 11	23	15.6	7.7	19	-12.8	-18.4	17	-4.6	4.0
Feb 11	21	-2.9	7.3	24	16.7	-3.2	19	-4.0	0.4
Mar 11	23	0.3	4.0	20	-14.6	-4.3	19	-18.4	-9.7
Apr 11	22	15.0	3.6	17	9.7	2.5	16	-11.4	-11.7
May 11	21	2.3	5.5	17	-5.4	-5.1	18	6.2	-9.1
Jun 11	20	32.6	15.2	19	32.0	10.6	23	39.2	10.5
Jul 11	22	0.7	9.7	16	-11.8	2.9	21	22.6	22.5
Aug 11	19	-12.9	3.8	18	-1.9	4.2	17	10.0	24.2
Sep 11	24	11.2	-0.4	18	4.0	-3.4	19	10.4	14.5
Oct 11	21	-19.6	-7.8	21	46.5	14.0	19	11.8	10.8
Nov 11	22	6.6	-1.8	22	38.7	28.3	18	-4.0	5.7
Dec 11	21	-5.2	-7.1	19	7.1	29.1	19	-0.9	1.9
Jan 12	21	-10.2	-3.3	18	-6.6	11.6	20	13.8	2.7
Feb 12	24	13.1	-1.1	17	-28.8	-11.2	20	6.4	6.2
Mar 12	19	-14.7	-4.3	19	-7.4	-15.3	18	-2.2	5.8
Apr 12	23	2.6	0.1	19	12.0	-10.4	16	0.7	1.7
May 12	25	20.6	2.4	20	16.8	6.4	19	7.4	1.9
Jun 12	22	11.2	11.3	22	17.4	15.5	20	-11.8	-2.2
Jul 12	21	-4.1	8.9	20	23.6	19.1	18	-11.2	-6.0
Aug 12	25	27.6	10.8	17	-3.2	12.4	21	23.4	-1.8
Sep 12	21	-15.2	1.2	16	-8.9	3.1	21	11.4	6.7
Oct 12	22	4.7	4.1	24	16.4	2.2	21	10.6	14.9
Nov 12	23	7.7	-1.6	18	-20.0	-4.3	20	11.8	11.3
Dec 12	20	-4.7	2.5	18	-8.3	-4.2	19	1.5	7.9
Jan 13	18	-12.4	-3.0	17	-7.4	-12.4	20	2.0	4.9
Feb 13	21	-12.8	-10.1	16	-6.5	-7.4	21	6.9	3.5
Mar 13	21	7.8	-6.5	11	-41.9	-19.1	17	-5.7	1.3
Apr 13	28	22.1	5.2	33	73.7	9.5	25	51.9	16.2
May 13	22	-11.2	5.6	21	4.5	12.5	23	21.4	21.4
Jun 13	25	11.0	6.7	21	-7.7	21.5	20	-1.8	21.9
Jul 13	22	1.3	-0.1	19	-2.6	-2.1	23	28.0	15.4
Aug 13	25	1.8	4.7	21	25.3	3.5	27	31.0	18.9
Sep 13	21	1.0	1.4	21	27.1	15.5	22	7.8	22.1
Oct 13	22	2.3	1.7	21	-14.5	9.1	22	5.6	14.8
Nov 13	23	-2.6	0.1	17	-1.9	1.1	22	8.8	7.4
Dec 13	23	11.5	3.4	18	-1.2	-6.8	21	11.2	8.5
Jan 14 (r)	24	32.0	12.3	21	29.4	8.4	21	5.9	8.6

1. The three month average figures are the changes in the average seasonally adjusted values for the three months ending with the relevant month compared with the same period a year earlier.

2. From July 2009 Royal Bank of Scotland Group plc is classified to the public sector; for earlier time periods it is classified to the private sector.

Between July 2009 and March 2014 Lloyds Banking Group plc is classified to the public sector; it is classified to the private sector for earlier and later time periods.

3. Between June 2010 and May 2012 English Further Education Corporations and Sixth Form College Corporations are classified to the public sector.

Before June 2010 and after May 2012 they are classified to the private sector.

4. From October 2013 Royal Mail plc is classified to the private sector; previously it is in the public sector.

Source: Monthly Wages & Salaries Survey

Earnings enquiries: 01633 456773

Email: ster@ons.gsi.gov.uk

4.14d Average Weekly Earnings in the public sector for selected activities (Not Seasonally Adjusted)

	Public Administration (Public Sector) (O)			Education (Public Sector) (P)			Health and Social Work (Public Sector) (Q)			Arts, Entertainment and Recreation (Public Sector) (R)		
	Average Weekly Earnings	Of which		Average Weekly Earnings	Of which		Average Weekly Earnings	Of which		Average Weekly Earnings	Of which	
		Bonuses	Arrears		Bonuses	Arrears		Bonuses	Arrears		Bonuses	Arrears
CDID	K5BE	K5BF	K5BG	K5BH	K5BI	K5BJ	K5BK	K5BL	K5BM	K5BN	K5BO	K5BP
2009 Jan	503	1	2	364	0	4	491	0	1	392	0	0
2009 Feb	526	3	16	361	0	1	494	0	0	400	0	5
2009 Mar	506	1	4	358	1	1	496	0	1	400	0	3
2009 Apr	510	1	1	367	1	1	508	0	0	403	1	0
2009 May	511	1	3	365	0	0	510	0	1	406	0	1
2009 Jun	505	1	2	366	1	0	513	0	1	415	10	1
2009 Jul	506	3	8	368	1	1	507	0	0	400	1	0
2009 Aug	511	3	2	370	1	0	500	0	0	416	10	0
2009 Sep	503	1	1	373	1	0	504	0	0	415	4	4
2009 Oct	508	1	7	376	1	5	505	0	1	403	1	1
2009 Nov	514	3	3	371	1	1	509	0	0	415	1	2
2009 Dec	521	11	2	374	1	2	507	0	0	414	4	2
2010 Jan	520	1	1	369	0	0	505	0	0	415	0	4
2010 Feb	520	1	1	371	0	0	509	0	0	412	0	0
2010 Mar	521	2	1	371	1	0	502	0	0	409	1	0
2010 Apr	522	1	0	374	1	0	516	0	0	413	1	0
2010 May	521	2	0	372	0	0	522	0	0	418	9	0
2010 Jun	524	3	1	371	0	0	524	0	0	420	11	0
2010 Jul	530	3	1	373	1	0	521	0	0	412	6	2
2010 Aug	535	11	0	374	1	0	514	0	0	414	1	0
2010 Sep	528	1	1	380	1	1	520	0	0	416	0	0
2010 Oct	529	1	0	378	0	1	520	0	0	418	0	0
2010 Nov	534	3	1	379	0	1	522	0	0	420	0	2
2010 Dec	538	8	0	381	1	0	525	0	0	424	2	0
2011 Jan	537	1	0	377	0	0	527	0	0	427	2	0
2011 Feb	535	2	0	378	0	0	527	0	0	423	0	0
2011 Mar	534	1	0	381	0	0	527	0	0	430	0	0
2011 Apr	537	1	0	384	0	1	530	0	1	433	5	0
2011 May	538	1	0	378	0	0	532	0	0	458	29	1
2011 Jun	542	6	0	379	0	0	534	0	0	428	3	0
2011 Jul	539	5	0	380	1	0	528	0	0	421	0	0
2011 Aug	545	11	0	383	0	0	524	0	0	424	4	0
2011 Sep	545	1	0	384	0	0	528	0	0	418	0	0
2011 Oct	538	1	0	381	1	0	529	0	0	419	0	0
2011 Nov	537	2	0	380	0	1	533	0	0	423	1	1
2011 Dec	540	6	0	379	0	0	533	0	0	427	0	0
2012 Jan	535	1	0	375	0	0	534	0	0	435	1	0
2012 Feb	538	1	0	377	0	0	537	0	0	463	0	0
2012 Mar	541	2	0	377	0	0	536	0	0	462	0	0
2012 Apr	545	0	0	381	0	0	540	0	0	463	1	1
2012 May	543	1	0	379	0	0	543	0	0	501	44	0
2012 Jun	550	5	0	381	0	0	541	0	0	463	5	0
2012 Jul	551	5	0	382	1	0	542	0	0	461	0	2
2012 Aug	547	3	0	387	0	0	536	0	0	455	0	0
2012 Sep	554	7	1	388	0	0	537	0	0	437	3	1
2012 Oct	547	2	1	385	0	0	536	0	0	462	41	0
2012 Nov	544	2	0	385	0	0	538	0	0	442	1	2
2012 Dec	543	2	2	385	0	0	537	0	0	444	5	0
2013 Jan	546	1	1	381	0	0	540	0	0	442	0	2
2013 Feb	535	0	0	380	0	0	538	0	0	441	0	0
2013 Mar	536	3	0	379	0	0	538	0	0	451	0	0
2013 Apr	537	1	0	384	0	0	547	0	0	450	3	0
2013 May	537	0	0	383	0	0	546	0	0	447	5	0
2013 Jun	540	3	0	382	0	0	545	0	0	449	4	1
2013 Jul	543	6	0	384	1	0	546	0	0	449	4	3
2013 Aug	540	1	4	386	0	1	536	0	0	442	1	1
2013 Sep	547	7	0	390	0	1	541	0	0	439	1	0
2013 Oct	537	1	0	390	0	1	543	0	0	441	1	1
2013 Nov	537	1	0	387	0	1	543	0	0	450	1	0
2013 Dec	540	2	1	391	0	1	543	0	0	444	0	0

p = Provisional

r = Revised

All figures are in pounds (£)

Source: Monthly Wages & Salaries Survey

Earnings enquiries: 01633 456773

Email: ster@ons.gsi.gov.uk

Table 4.15a   Weekly pay - Gross (£) - For all employee jobs[a] by age group and occupation: United Kingdom, 2013

Description	Code	Number of jobs[b] (thousand)	Median	Annual % change	Mean	Annual % change	10	20	25	30	40	60	70	75	80	90
All employees		24,575	415.3	2.3	501.3	2.0	124.2	211.8	251.0	286.0	348.4	491.6	584.5	642.3	704.4	909.8
18-21		1,245	171.2	-1.7	193.9	0.9	42.9	69.7	84.1	98.7	130.0	219.1	257.0	274.5	295.8	358.4
22-29		4,145	366.4	1.4	401.4	1.8	140.0	229.2	257.7	282.3	323.8	419.3	479.1	511.0	548.5	663.9
30-39		5,572	483.0	0.8	552.1	1.5	167.5	271.8	311.0	345.5	413.0	563.8	651.6	699.1	757.8	955.9
40-49		6,485	476.9	1.8	576.3	1.9	151.3	247.3	288.2	327.9	399.5	564.9	670.8	728.3	800.0	1,044.7
50-59		5,116	444.6	3.2	551.0	2.3	148.9	237.2	275.1	308.6	375.1	529.6	635.3	694.2	766.6	993.6
60+		1,829	329.0	3.2	419.7	3.5	80.7	136.4	163.8	198.1	264.0	399.7	483.0	536.8	605.1	809.3
18-21 ALL OCCUPATIONS		1,245	171.2	-1.7	193.9	0.9	42.9	69.7	84.1	98.7	130.0	219.1	257.0	274.5	295.8	358.4
18-21 Managers, directors and senior officials	1	17	312.0	2.7	404.9	32.8	x	x	x	251.9	273.6	366.7	417.1	x	x	x
18-21 Corporate managers and directors	11	12	282.8	-11.1	346.0	5.1	x	x	x	246.2	262.7	332.4	x	x	x	x
18-21 Other managers and proprietors	12	x	x		x		x	x	x	x	x	x	x	x	x	x
18-21 Professional occupations	2	28	361.3	3.8	373.0	9.6	209.0	268.3	290.6	307.6	325.4	384.3	422.5	455.5	481.9	540.3
18-21 Science, research, engineering and technology professionals	21	15	362.7	18.3	392.5	20.6	x	300.9	307.6	313.8	339.0	383.3	429.4	470.3	484.2	x
18-21 Health professionals	22	x	x		303.7	-13.8	x	x	x	x	x	x	x	x	x	x
18-21 Teaching and educational professionals	23	x	x		343.1		x	x	x	x	x	x	x	x	x	x
18-21 Business, media and public service professionals	24	x	359.9		400.2	-3.9	x	x	x	x	x	x	x	x	x	x
18-21 Associate professional and technical occupations	3	66	274.3	-2.9	270.2	-14.8	27.6	x	x	144.3	230.4	314.5	355.0	383.3	410.0	489.1
18-21 Science, engineering and technology associate professionals	31	14	314.0	3.5	322.7	6.0	x	242.0	254.7	266.4	290.5	345.0	374.5	387.1	x	x
18-21 Health and social care associate professionals	32	7	x		x		x	x	x	x	x	x	x	x	x	x
18-21 Protective service occupations	33	x	429.1	-5.4	472.2	-1.3	x	x	x	x	x	x	x	x	x	x
18-21 Culture, media and sports occupations	34	14	x		130.0		x	x	x	x	x	x	x	x	x	x
18-21 Business and public service associate professionals	35	29	319.2	3.8	332.5	8.1	x	188.8	230.7	252.5	287.5	352.7	394.1	412.0	436.5	x
18-21 Administrative and secretarial occupations	4	128	257.8	3.1	239.3	2.0	61.1	121.2	146.6	181.1	230.0	277.9	300.0	312.0	331.6	372.8
18-21 Administrative occupations	41	106	259.9	1.0	242.3	1.3	69.7	130.8	151.0	191.2	232.2	282.1	302.6	316.6	335.0	373.1
18-21 Secretarial and related occupations	42	22	248.3	13.6	225.1	5.7	48.1	x	x	151.4	210.8	268.3	286.0	296.1	315.2	x
18-21 Skilled trades occupations	5	77	300.0	2.0	321.9	2.4	159.0	213.5	230.2	243.7	266.8	319.6	353.9	371.3	399.6	492.8
18-21 Skilled agricultural and related trades	51	x	263.7	-1.0	240.9	-9.6	x	x	x	x	278.5	x	x	x	x	
18-21 Skilled metal, electrical and electronic trades	52	34	330.9	-1.9	377.7	2.9	193.4	239.7	256.6	268.8	304.1	360.7	401.9	429.1	457.9	x
18-21 Skilled construction and building trades	53	12	303.6	7.8	336.2	8.0	200.1	229.1	251.5	261.3	289.4	327.4	360.0	397.8	x	x
18-21 Textiles, printing and other skilled trades	54	26	253.7	-0.3	254.0	-0.6	x	166.4	185.8	202.4	240.4	278.9	308.3	316.2	327.7	x
18-21 Caring, leisure and other service occupations	6	150	205.4	-1.4	198.6	-0.2	41.3	90.9	112.6	131.5	174.0	234.1	256.8	271.1	285.6	328.0
18-21 Caring personal service occupations	61	111	211.9	-2.1	203.7	-0.4	46.0	97.5	122.7	143.0	186.6	239.9	262.2	273.9	287.6	330.3
18-21 Leisure, travel and related personal service occupations	62	39	186.9	3.4	184.3	0.3	x	75.2	96.0	111.1	141.2	209.3	241.2	249.8	274.6	x
18-21 Sales and customer service occupations	7	328	118.0	-0.8	143.5	0.6	46.0	61.9	71.5	80.3	99.0	140.2	180.0	203.8	230.3	278.9
18-21 Sales occupations	71	284	111.1	0.0	135.1	1.3	44.4	59.6	67.3	76.7	93.3	132.6	166.2	187.6	212.6	264.4
18-21 Customer service occupations	72	43	191.8	-5.0	198.5	-2.0	62.9	90.8	103.0	113.3	137.9	243.0	268.3	287.3	296.8	329.7
18-21 Process, plant and machine operatives	8	34	284.6	8.4	294.2	9.2	114.7	186.9	212.9	230.8	261.7	316.7	346.4	360.9	384.0	474.3
18-21 Process, plant and machine operatives	81	29	292.5	8.6	307.4	10.5	151.2	215.2	231.3	247.2	273.1	327.9	349.8	361.6	387.1	475.6
18-21 Transport and mobile machine drivers and operatives	82	6	204.4		231.1	-2.4	x	x	x	x	x	x	x	x	x	x
18-21 Elementary occupations	9	417	127.0	-2.3	153.5	-0.8	32.4	55.9	65.7	76.5	98.7	160.2	203.9	224.3	247.6	298.2
18-21 Elementary trades and related occupations	91	31	269.3	-1.9	267.4	-5.0	103.3	151.2	191.9	218.3	247.3	286.8	317.7	327.8	346.8	x
18-21 Elementary administration and service occupations	92	386	120.6	-0.8	144.4	0.5	31.3	53.0	62.1	73.5	93.4	149.6	187.8	210.1	232.1	283.0
22-29 ALL OCCUPATIONS		4,145	366.4	1.4	401.4	1.8	140.0	229.2	257.7	282.3	323.8	419.3	479.1	511.0	548.5	663.9
22-29 Managers, directors and senior officials	1	208	462.0	3.5	552.2	5.2	288.4	335.4	354.4	371.5	412.0	517.5	577.2	617.5	681.8	919.9
22-29 Corporate managers and directors	11	156	488.7	4.1	592.2	6.0	297.1	345.0	365.1	384.7	440.3	548.4	612.9	670.8	754.4	1,008.2
22-29 Other managers and proprietors	12	52	394.6	1.1	432.8	3.5	262.8	316.7	330.2	345.0	364.4	430.4	488.8	517.4	534.3	x
22-29 Professional occupations	2	811	537.4	0.9	563.0	1.0	337.5	413.7	441.5	460.0	501.7	574.9	625.1	658.3	702.1	820.7
22-29 Science, research, engineering and technology professionals	21	190	557.5	0.3	591.9	1.1	369.0	429.6	450.8	474.7	513.4	596.1	653.1	690.5	737.9	844.1
22-29 Health professionals	22	191	553.7	2.3	572.2	1.2	329.6	430.4	458.4	483.3	520.9	596.5	642.0	670.8	717.8	845.0
22-29 Teaching and educational professionals	23	207	482.3	-1.1	481.5	-0.4	241.6	403.8	413.7	427.2	449.7	519.4	560.4	578.7	604.7	670.7
22-29 Business, media and public service professionals	24	223	565.4	1.7	606.1	2.0	345.2	425.8	460.0	479.1	521.3	613.3	676.0	718.7	766.6	904.3
22-29 Associate professional and technical occupations	3	640	463.7	1.4	507.3	2.0	284.6	345.0	364.1	383.3	422.2	503.6	558.9	586.3	618.0	729.5
22-29 Science, engineering and technology associate professionals	31	122	432.1	1.8	457.9	2.6	286.9	333.9	353.7	365.8	401.8	468.1	503.6	536.6	579.8	672.1
22-29 Health and social care associate professionals	32	49	396.5	1.4	380.7	4.3	x	228.6	283.1	315.9	347.2	425.9	460.5	486.6	506.3	x
22-29 Protective service occupations	33	52	584.4	1.4	575.4	-1.3	410.8	484.7	509.3	529.0	567.3	611.8	637.1	653.2	677.6	x
22-29 Culture, media and sports occupations	34	60	391.5	3.3	540.8	6.2	98.0	213.9	272.5	295.9	351.7	440.8	479.1	493.1	527.0	x
22-29 Business and public service associate professionals	35	358	479.1	1.0	526.0	1.7	310.1	359.9	383.3	402.0	440.8	520.6	574.9	609.4	649.3	788.4
22-29 Administrative and secretarial occupations	4	516	343.9	2.3	351.8	1.4	170.9	250.9	273.9	289.4	316.2	367.8	402.5	421.6	449.0	524.2
22-29 Administrative occupations	41	433	347.5	1.7	360.2	1.4	185.6	263.9	286.8	299.0	324.1	373.7	408.6	427.1	454.5	527.8
22-29 Secretarial and related occupations	42	83	298.9	2.2	307.9	2.2	123.6	184.1	219.8	244.6	268.3	325.8	361.0	383.3	414.5	493.4
22-29 Skilled trades occupations	5	356	407.3	2.8	437.8	3.2	255.3	301.1	317.4	333.1	370.5	447.0	496.8	519.4	554.2	663.7
22-29 Skilled agricultural and related trades	51	15	317.0	-3.1	326.4	-4.2	242.9	270.6	281.6	287.9	298.5	334.0	365.7	373.6	391.6	x
22-29 Skilled metal, electrical and electronic trades	52	170	473.8	4.4	505.1	4.3	305.6	357.9	381.2	400.0	435.5	516.2	563.9	592.1	628.6	743.5
22-29 Skilled construction and building trades	53	67	446.1	3.1	469.9	3.8	288.6	339.6	360.0	376.0	410.7	479.1	513.2	527.7	574.7	x
22-29 Textiles, printing and other skilled trades	54	105	319.1	-0.3	323.9	-0.2	182.8	243.3	262.0	275.3	300.4	340.3	365.7	384.8	403.4	460.0
22-29 Caring, leisure and other service occupations	6	428	256.6	1.3	256.7	0.6	99.9	148.7	173.4	191.6	227.9	285.6	311.6	328.3	346.9	405.7
22-29 Caring personal service occupations	61	346	255.5	1.2	254.8	0.8	101.1	152.3	175.5	192.9	226.8	282.7	307.8	323.4	341.2	400.0
22-29 Leisure, travel and related personal service occupations	62	82	262.3	1.2	264.7	0.1	99.0	132.6	158.9	186.6	232.9	297.1	329.0	345.3	358.6	425.5
22-29 Sales and customer service occupations	7	481	248.9	-0.2	250.0	0.5	96.8	126.3	145.0	164.0	211.4	278.8	309.8	327.5	348.0	409.5

Table 4.15a Weekly pay - Gross (£) - For all employee jobs[a] by age group and occupation: United Kingdom, 2013

Description	Code	Number of jobs[b] (thousand)	Median	Annual % change	Mean	Annual % change	Percentiles 10	20	25	30	40	60	70	75	80	90
22-29 Sales occupations	71	358	222.2	0.1	226.3	-0.6	84.9	112.7	128.3	144.4	179.4	253.5	284.5	301.2	318.0	371.4
22-29 Customer service occupations	72	123	316.2	4.0	319.1	3.4	147.9	219.3	248.9	262.7	287.5	342.0	368.5	387.5	407.4	474.8
22-29 Process, plant and machine operatives	8	192	356.5	1.9	388.6	4.0	232.1	268.6	281.9	299.3	325.8	395.1	440.0	476.0	502.4	588.3
22-29 Process, plant and machine operatives	81	136	348.0	3.8	381.3	4.2	235.6	267.7	280.1	295.7	316.2	383.6	429.9	461.0	491.7	576.9
22-29 Transport and mobile machine drivers and operatives	82	56	383.4	1.8	406.5	4.4	224.9	272.5	292.7	314.8	345.0	418.6	471.4	496.7	522.2	620.7
22-29 Elementary occupations	9	514	245.9	-1.3	244.8	-1.8	72.4	115.7	136.7	163.7	208.7	272.5	306.6	324.7	347.7	415.5
22-29 Elementary trades and related occupations	91	69	320.5	0.2	325.9	-1.5	168.0	244.8	252.8	263.0	290.9	342.9	374.5	393.7	421.5	485.3
22-29 Elementary administration and service occupations	92	445	232.1	-0.8	232.3	-1.2	66.9	106.3	126.2	148.6	191.9	259.8	293.0	310.5	330.6	398.3
30-39 ALL OCCUPATIONS		5,572	483.0	0.8	552.1	1.5	167.5	271.8	311.0	345.5	413.0	563.8	651.6	699.1	757.8	955.9
30-39 Managers, directors and senior officials	1	577	714.1	2.6	876.6	3.1	342.5	435.0	479.1	529.0	613.3	824.8	980.7	1,091.5	1,196.2	1,619.6
30-39 Corporate managers and directors	11	479	773.5	3.0	936.3	3.4	354.3	474.3	528.0	574.9	670.8	897.1	1,064.4	1,153.5	1,274.1	1,690.8
30-39 Other managers and proprietors	12	98	499.8	0.3	582.8	0.8	287.6	363.5	377.1	401.7	455.1	574.9	643.2	693.0	737.9	x
30-39 Professional occupations	2	1,451	664.2	0.2	708.2	0.3	342.1	464.5	506.8	545.3	609.7	727.0	795.3	843.3	900.8	1,092.4
30-39 Science, research, engineering and technology professionals	21	355	729.1	2.5	782.6	1.6	467.9	549.8	579.2	617.3	671.9	797.3	868.1	927.5	978.9	1,149.9
30-39 Health professionals	22	346	602.1	0.1	659.3	-2.1	278.0	387.5	432.7	475.3	541.5	658.4	731.1	777.3	856.2	1,128.4
30-39 Teaching and educational professionals	23	372	655.1	0.0	620.8	1.3	271.7	406.7	446.8	498.2	598.2	703.7	747.2	773.8	806.0	904.5
30-39 Business, media and public service professionals	24	378	676.0	-1.1	769.1	0.4	402.5	498.1	538.5	572.9	624.3	747.4	842.4	900.5	966.8	1,227.6
30-39 Associate professional and technical occupations	3	998	579.4	0.5	638.7	1.5	316.5	408.6	440.8	471.5	527.0	637.9	708.2	749.1	802.8	968.3
30-39 Science, engineering and technology associate professionals	31	167	536.6	0.4	578.7	3.1	338.7	409.1	434.5	455.0	491.6	583.3	640.5	670.8	709.5	840.4
30-39 Health and social care associate professionals	32	83	449.6	1.2	435.3	-1.4	151.3	244.9	295.3	335.9	411.7	490.8	526.9	549.0	577.9	675.2
30-39 Protective service occupations	33	135	665.8	-0.4	672.0	-1.3	479.1	558.6	576.7	600.0	630.6	705.1	738.3	763.3	796.4	884.1
30-39 Culture, media and sports occupations	34	59	488.1	1.9	481.4	-2.5	111.2	284.4	336.0	377.8	430.7	536.6	597.0	620.1	655.2	x
30-39 Business and public service associate professionals	35	554	600.1	0.7	695.8	2.1	334.0	417.8	450.3	479.6	539.0	670.8	760.9	809.3	882.4	1,130.9
30-39 Administrative and secretarial occupations	4	600	361.0	0.9	383.3	0.7	148.3	210.5	243.8	272.5	322.8	402.5	448.2	479.1	514.3	628.9
30-39 Administrative occupations	41	495	367.8	1.0	394.8	1.1	160.0	230.0	262.1	289.7	333.9	412.0	456.6	484.4	522.5	632.8
30-39 Secretarial and related occupations	42	105	303.8	-3.5	329.2	-0.5	115.0	150.8	173.2	189.0	251.4	356.2	409.9	434.3	476.0	594.6
30-39 Skilled trades occupations	5	403	455.3	0.2	490.1	0.4	260.8	330.8	356.8	375.6	418.6	502.1	560.3	597.5	640.0	758.3
30-39 Skilled agricultural and related trades	51	21	356.4	3.7	362.7	1.8	264.3	299.6	309.5	322.6	337.1	373.9	386.3	399.3	421.3	x
30-39 Skilled metal, electrical and electronic trades	52	205	549.0	4.6	579.8	3.4	359.8	418.7	435.3	455.3	498.3	596.0	651.4	681.9	727.4	833.4
30-39 Skilled construction and building trades	53	62	466.9	0.2	498.1	-1.5	326.6	373.9	390.6	403.0	439.4	499.3	536.5	550.0	572.2	x
30-39 Textiles, printing and other skilled trades	54	115	344.8	0.0	348.8	-4.8	148.6	214.2	250.2	271.1	312.8	374.0	408.4	429.3	450.0	536.8
30-39 Caring, leisure and other service occupations	6	439	252.3	1.4	272.4	1.2	99.0	143.0	162.8	183.1	218.9	291.3	332.4	357.1	383.3	463.7
30-39 Caring personal service occupations	61	371	246.8	2.6	261.8	1.3	93.8	142.0	162.4	180.7	212.8	281.8	319.2	342.5	369.4	443.5
30-39 Leisure, travel and related personal service occupations	62	68	311.2	3.3	330.5	2.4	109.3	148.8	165.0	193.6	246.0	355.2	408.1	448.3	479.1	590.1
30-39 Sales and customer service occupations	7	332	272.2	1.5	294.1	-0.9	103.1	136.2	152.5	177.7	225.2	313.1	360.2	385.0	418.4	513.3
30-39 Sales occupations	71	225	230.3	-1.0	257.3	-1.0	98.0	120.0	133.1	147.2	183.7	273.4	315.4	340.9	368.5	454.8
30-39 Customer service occupations	72	107	352.5	1.2	371.6	-1.2	153.9	215.8	248.5	274.4	314.5	397.1	441.7	471.0	500.0	581.7
30-39 Process, plant and machine operatives	8	291	418.9	3.2	448.9	2.8	251.7	300.3	321.2	340.1	378.6	463.9	517.6	547.8	586.3	687.8
30-39 Process, plant and machine operatives	81	162	401.3	4.8	439.6	3.1	252.1	294.7	311.4	326.4	358.2	442.6	500.3	532.6	573.1	673.8
30-39 Transport and mobile machine drivers and operatives	82	129	440.8	1.2	460.5	2.4	248.2	310.8	343.1	362.0	401.3	488.5	532.4	562.9	601.1	691.4
30-39 Elementary occupations	9	482	264.3	-0.1	271.1	0.4	64.6	105.5	127.8	151.8	214.8	304.0	350.9	377.6	401.7	484.3
30-39 Elementary trades and related occupations	91	62	338.5	0.2	346.2	-0.7	168.7	242.9	255.6	272.4	300.3	368.9	402.0	424.6	452.8	523.1
30-39 Elementary administration and service occupations	92	420	249.0	0.6	260.0	0.9	61.9	99.0	117.6	137.7	191.7	293.6	338.9	366.4	393.7	475.9
40-49 ALL OCCUPATIONS		6,485	476.9	1.8	576.3	1.9	151.3	247.3	288.2	327.9	399.5	564.9	670.8	728.3	800.0	1,044.7
40-49 Managers, directors and senior officials	1	805	804.9	5.0	1,003.6	3.6	345.0	478.4	537.4	584.6	690.1	945.8	1,111.6	1,219.9	1,379.9	1,839.0
40-49 Corporate managers and directors	11	687	859.9	6.4	1,058.1	3.9	353.4	510.8	574.9	633.3	741.1	1005.4	1,172.9	1,293.6	1,455.3	1,913.2
40-49 Other managers and proprietors	12	118	575.5	0.1	687.8	0.5	290.7	374.2	420.2	454.2	510.4	665.9	755.5	819.4	876.4	1,159.9
40-49 Professional occupations	2	1,438	693.2	0.6	755.0	0.1	326.2	456.8	506.2	548.8	624.3	766.6	847.2	892.7	958.2	1,202.1
40-49 Science, research, engineering and technology professionals	21	323	801.2	1.7	858.5	0.8	491.6	591.3	630.2	670.8	741.1	862.4	945.8	1,006.8	1,069.3	1,267.2
40-49 Health professionals	22	415	610.8	0.5	715.8	-0.6	271.0	391.9	439.8	476.5	541.6	671.9	752.0	788.8	848.5	1,281.0
40-49 Teaching and educational professionals	23	370	686.1	1.0	664.8	1.4	246.1	399.2	446.4	511.5	609.0	747.6	815.1	854.9	886.9	1,021.9
40-49 Business, media and public service professionals	24	329	695.6	-0.3	804.3	-1.1	378.9	486.2	528.3	568.5	627.9	782.6	878.0	953.6	1,035.9	1,325.4
40-49 Associate professional and technical occupations	3	989	601.3	0.1	678.5	0.4	298.9	405.7	440.9	472.9	536.6	680.1	758.0	803.8	861.7	1,081.6
40-49 Science, engineering and technology associate professionals	31	168	536.7	-3.0	573.4	-1.6	294.1	366.9	406.5	436.5	488.3	595.1	652.3	691.8	726.8	867.9
40-49 Health and social care associate professionals	32	103	444.3	1.2	460.7	4.4	184.6	288.8	328.0	366.5	399.7	488.1	533.7	563.6	608.4	729.0
40-49 Protective service occupations	33	140	734.2	0.9	736.6	-1.2	515.4	582.4	613.0	647.0	699.9	780.4	819.5	846.4	863.3	948.1
40-49 Culture, media and sports occupations	34	49	421.6	-11.2	462.8	-6.4	34.0	x	154.1	211.9	356.2	515.4	601.2	646.7	708.3	x
40-49 Business and public service associate professionals	35	529	632.4	1.1	758.8	1.6	344.1	433.0	464.9	497.8	561.2	715.9	814.6	882.3	970.5	1,301.8
40-49 Administrative and secretarial occupations	4	769	342.2	-0.2	373.0	-0.5	143.7	196.5	226.1	254.1	300.5	383.3	435.6	465.6	500.2	624.1
40-49 Administrative occupations	41	598	353.7	0.4	384.8	-1.0	147.2	209.0	239.5	269.8	315.1	392.0	445.9	475.4	508.7	634.6
40-49 Secretarial and related occupations	42	171	296.0	1.0	331.9	2.5	134.5	173.5	192.5	214.1	256.1	339.1	395.9	426.2	464.2	586.6
40-49 Skilled trades occupations	5	477	488.4	0.1	524.6	0.8	250.1	340.0	371.3	396.3	441.4	537.7	597.8	637.8	688.2	825.6
40-49 Skilled agricultural and related trades	51	27	375.4	2.9	410.3	5.7	268.4	300.2	314.0	328.6	352.1	401.4	444.2	485.2	509.6	x
40-49 Skilled metal, electrical and electronic trades	52	253	560.9	0.2	609.0	1.9	366.5	423.2	445.1	466.1	510.5	614.4	685.3	716.2	764.1	912.9
40-49 Skilled construction and building trades	53	79	501.6	0.9	541.1	-0.1	347.4	401.4	418.8	434.5	470.1	537.8	588.8	613.0	653.2	x
40-49 Textiles, printing and other skilled trades	54	118	334.1	2.0	358.3	-1.2	144.0	192.4	220.1	243.0	289.1	378.7	421.6	450.2	485.2	577.7
40-49 Caring, leisure and other service occupations	6	639	256.2	2.0	278.7	1.4	105.7	148.8	169.7	188.3	221.5	292.0	334.2	362.1	387.3	468.2

123

Table 4.15a Weekly pay - Gross (£) - For all employee jobs[a] by age group and occupation: United Kingdom, 2013

Description	Code	Number of jobs[b] (thousand)	Median	Annual % change	Mean	Annual % change	Percentiles									
							10	20	25	30	40	60	70	75	80	90
40-49 Caring personal service occupations	61	545	248.4	0.7	265.7	0.5	105.8	148.1	167.9	186.7	216.6	282.7	323.3	348.7	373.5	442.7
40-49 Leisure, travel and related personal service occupations	62	94	311.9	6.4	354.5	5.6	101.4	154.6	184.4	212.4	264.5	356.6	431.3	468.5	516.5	675.7
40-49 Sales and customer service occupations	7	343	242.8	0.8	281.8	0.0	101.2	131.5	148.1	164.2	202.4	285.7	333.3	358.4	395.1	509.9
40-49 Sales occupations	71	250	212.3	4.0	246.9	1.4	96.5	123.5	134.5	147.8	176.4	246.9	287.0	313.0	340.9	441.9
40-49 Customer service occupations	72	93	348.0	0.9	375.9	-1.3	139.0	197.9	234.8	266.9	310.4	383.2	436.6	463.8	507.8	618.5
40-49 Process, plant and machine operatives	8	414	454.9	2.6	485.4	2.4	264.5	321.8	345.0	363.1	411.3	501.2	557.1	594.4	630.6	758.2
40-49 Process, plant and machine operatives	81	190	430.2	0.9	469.6	2.5	249.1	303.1	320.0	342.0	387.9	485.2	539.4	576.2	617.0	735.0
40-49 Transport and mobile machine drivers and operatives	82	224	471.5	2.9	498.7	2.3	278.8	345.0	363.4	384.9	426.1	518.2	570.0	600.3	639.0	779.6
40-49 Elementary occupations	9	612	242.0	-2.3	261.7	-0.9	56.1	96.0	113.9	133.4	184.6	292.4	348.1	376.3	400.3	491.9
40-49 Elementary trades and related occupations	91	72	363.7	1.5	385.1	0.5	216.8	262.7	280.8	295.2	330.8	394.5	445.4	474.9	505.2	588.3
40-49 Elementary administration and service occupations	92	540	216.2	-2.0	245.3	-0.6	51.5	86.5	103.0	122.7	162.0	267.3	328.0	358.7	390.7	471.5
50-59 ALL OCCUPATIONS		5,116	444.6	3.2	551.0	2.3	148.9	237.2	275.1	308.6	375.1	529.6	635.3	694.2	766.6	993.6
50-59 Managers, directors and senior officials	1	603	769.4	-0.8	985.1	-2.0	293.6	438.8	499.1	557.1	663.0	896.0	1,062.2	1,166.7	1,336.8	1,773.2
50-59 Corporate managers and directors	11	500	820.2	-1.2	1,047.8	-1.7	299.0	460.0	527.1	585.8	703.0	958.2	1,146.9	1,271.0	1,437.4	1,859.0
50-59 Other managers and proprietors	12	103	586.0	0.0	680.0	-3.0	282.7	382.6	425.7	460.1	528.0	666.8	764.0	829.9	889.0	x
50-59 Professional occupations	2	1,114	691.8	0.5	752.0	1.1	287.2	422.7	480.7	536.5	624.0	769.6	848.6	900.8	968.2	1,203.3
50-59 Science, research, engineering and technology professionals	21	220	794.4	3.1	862.4	1.6	467.2	579.9	617.9	657.3	721.9	879.1	968.4	1,029.7	1,098.4	1,323.5
50-59 Health professionals	22	324	602.0	2.9	720.5	1.5	257.1	365.7	403.4	446.2	529.4	665.9	763.8	792.0	861.5	1,196.0
50-59 Teaching and educational professionals	23	328	704.4	0.0	697.4	-0.3	203.3	398.2	456.2	539.4	655.4	775.9	844.0	877.2	921.9	1,082.0
50-59 Business, media and public service professionals	24	243	685.1	2.6	768.1	1.4	316.3	438.6	497.7	548.5	622.6	766.6	866.8	943.7	1,019.4	1,279.2
50-59 Associate professional and technical occupations	3	635	562.1	1.4	630.7	2.8	285.0	374.2	412.1	440.8	499.7	625.4	708.1	759.6	815.8	1,010.1
50-59 Science, engineering and technology associate professionals	31	124	558.7	3.4	580.7	2.3	303.7	376.2	416.2	447.2	503.2	603.4	668.3	695.6	743.1	880.5
50-59 Health and social care associate professionals	32	90	430.5	5.2	442.0	4.9	187.7	274.0	305.6	334.3	392.7	474.6	520.8	548.8	585.5	687.3
50-59 Protective service occupations	33	55	706.1	1.4	700.7	1.1	383.4	491.9	541.7	565.5	620.3	750.5	793.5	840.9	884.4	x
50-59 Culture, media and sports occupations	34	25	422.9	6.0	540.2	16.0	x	x	x	x	306.3	495.9	608.5	688.3	x	x
50-59 Business and public service associate professionals	35	342	594.6	0.7	693.5	1.8	320.7	406.3	440.8	469.2	527.6	670.8	764.1	820.0	890.2	1,149.9
50-59 Administrative and secretarial occupations	4	731	340.8	1.8	366.3	-0.1	146.7	199.8	229.0	255.2	302.2	379.7	424.8	453.9	490.3	597.6
50-59 Administrative occupations	41	553	355.6	1.5	381.2	-0.3	149.5	215.7	244.7	276.0	316.6	393.1	440.8	470.1	502.6	613.1
50-59 Secretarial and related occupations	42	178	292.7	0.9	320.0	0.7	135.1	170.2	187.1	209.3	255.2	332.2	372.3	406.9	428.1	536.8
50-59 Skilled trades occupations	5	380	500.0	3.7	523.1	2.6	246.9	338.9	371.3	400.9	450.0	554.4	617.5	651.5	687.0	807.9
50-59 Skilled agricultural and related trades	51	21	356.4	8.4	368.4	5.6	176.6	257.9	287.9	301.8	324.9	382.1	402.6	417.2	436.4	x
50-59 Skilled metal, electrical and electronic trades	52	220	573.4	2.6	600.1	2.3	369.8	432.6	459.3	481.7	523.4	624.2	670.7	701.0	741.5	864.2
50-59 Skilled construction and building trades	53	54	516.0	7.3	557.3	6.4	348.8	414.8	434.1	448.2	479.4	559.0	611.4	645.0	674.9	x
50-59 Textiles, printing and other skilled trades	54	85	317.7	-0.5	339.7	-1.9	140.3	181.8	213.0	237.3	280.0	352.6	394.1	414.4	451.5	569.4
50-59 Caring, leisure and other service occupations	6	511	269.2	0.1	287.0	0.5	106.0	158.5	179.7	198.5	234.0	307.9	347.9	369.1	396.0	474.2
50-59 Caring personal service occupations	61	431	265.9	0.2	279.3	0.1	107.2	159.4	180.1	198.4	232.1	302.0	340.9	362.6	387.6	456.0
50-59 Leisure, travel and related personal service occupations	62	80	300.0	2.3	328.3	3.4	99.7	149.0	177.7	198.9	250.8	347.3	387.3	421.4	456.1	587.8
50-59 Sales and customer service occupations	7	299	231.5	6.8	266.7	4.4	100.1	130.4	145.0	159.4	192.5	268.3	309.1	334.9	366.5	477.5
50-59 Sales occupations	71	223	201.0	6.1	234.1	4.8	95.9	121.0	132.6	144.2	169.1	240.1	273.1	291.1	317.3	399.7
50-59 Customer service occupations	72	76	333.6	5.4	361.9	2.4	145.8	195.1	218.9	243.7	287.5	368.5	416.6	445.1	488.7	622.6
50-59 Process, plant and machine operatives	8	343	432.8	2.0	458.2	1.1	234.7	294.1	315.2	339.7	385.0	480.3	530.3	561.6	601.4	719.1
50-59 Process, plant and machine operatives	81	159	412.5	1.3	449.0	0.1	235.2	281.4	300.7	316.1	362.7	464.1	518.9	550.9	595.0	730.8
50-59 Transport and mobile machine drivers and operatives	82	184	448.8	3.0	466.0	1.9	230.1	309.5	335.3	359.6	403.4	493.2	538.6	572.9	610.9	713.1
50-59 Elementary occupations	9	499	258.7	6.6	272.1	5.6	62.6	100.6	123.8	144.6	202.7	307.4	360.4	388.8	412.4	495.8
50-59 Elementary trades and related occupations	91	62	362.8	4.6	385.4	4.7	224.3	262.9	276.9	293.8	329.4	397.9	439.7	468.8	499.9	582.4
50-59 Elementary administration and service occupations	92	437	237.7	9.5	256.1	5.7	59.9	93.0	110.5	130.0	176.4	287.7	342.7	373.3	400.4	478.7
60+ ALL OCCUPATIONS		1,829	329.0	3.2	419.7	3.5	80.7	136.4	163.8	198.1	264.0	399.7	483.0	536.8	605.1	809.3
60+ Managers, directors and senior officials	1	203	593.4	2.0	790.1	1.4	183.9	280.9	335.3	383.3	485.5	705.0	847.9	927.1	1,092.1	1,490.8
60+ Corporate managers and directors	11	162	629.5	2.2	840.4	1.9	171.0	276.0	340.2	395.8	506.5	758.9	908.1	1,012.9	1,168.1	1,620.1
60+ Other managers and proprietors	12	41	498.0	0.5	590.5	-1.8	210.0	287.5	320.7	362.6	444.8	579.4	652.2	697.5	743.1	x
60+ Professional occupations	2	310	537.1	-0.7	618.5	-1.1	124.7	243.0	296.1	346.4	440.4	639.4	737.5	798.8	875.4	1,176.6
60+ Science, research, engineering and technology professionals	21	53	728.6	1.4	738.9	-2.1	301.5	455.2	502.7	556.4	637.4	796.5	887.1	945.3	991.8	x
60+ Health professionals	22	73	450.4	3.2	620.6	3.1	176.9	249.3	282.2	320.9	389.3	529.4	650.0	690.6	772.0	x
60+ Teaching and educational professionals	23	110	442.9	-12.6	539.5	-5.3	74.3	134.7	178.3	226.9	321.3	587.8	704.4	759.9	851.2	1,066.5
60+ Business, media and public service professionals	24	75	584.4	1.6	647.7	1.2	197.6	335.1	375.3	416.7	503.3	640.5	713.1	766.6	862.5	x
60+ Associate professional and technical occupations	3	175	461.4	1.1	499.2	-1.3	146.8	244.6	288.5	328.1	396.8	522.0	599.5	643.6	692.5	859.6
60+ Science, engineering and technology associate professionals	31	37	490.0	3.7	517.5	3.6	220.6	321.5	350.9	376.3	449.0	536.4	609.0	644.2	691.2	x
60+ Health and social care associate professionals	32	22	306.5	-1.4	324.7	1.8	x	136.8	161.8	190.9	248.0	379.6	421.4	476.0	499.3	x
60+ Protective service occupations	33	10	444.5	-6.7	475.4	-1.9	x	305.9	359.4	366.6	387.3	514.5	549.0	x	x	x
60+ Culture, media and sports occupations	34	10	x		310.5	2.6	x	x	x	x	x	x	x	x	x	x
60+ Business and public service associate professionals	35	97	490.1	-7.0	553.4	-3.9	167.9	288.0	322.3	354.2	429.0	574.9	652.6	700.1	767.9	943.0
60+ Administrative and secretarial occupations	4	287	255.4	1.4	287.0	0.6	62.0	119.9	143.5	161.0	206.6	310.9	359.2	387.6	421.9	534.7
60+ Administrative occupations	41	205	269.1	2.4	293.8	1.1	54.8	120.5	147.2	168.4	218.4	325.8	370.8	402.4	430.1	535.9
60+ Secretarial and related occupations	42	82	230.7	3.2	269.9	-0.4	85.2	118.2	133.4	149.9	191.4	279.8	322.0	356.7	393.4	528.5
60+ Skilled trades occupations	5	148	447.2	2.8	464.4	2.2	176.5	282.7	316.5	345.6	401.2	492.0	555.8	600.0	635.2	746.4
60+ Skilled agricultural and related trades	51	13	287.5	3.2	289.4	3.5	x	150.2	164.9	179.6	254.7	307.5	345.0	361.8	x	x
60+ Skilled metal, electrical and electronic trades	52	80	521.1	5.0	543.8	2.6	312.2	388.6	416.6	439.3	479.4	572.6	630.0	660.6	695.8	788.8
60+ Skilled construction and building trades	53	25	464.0	2.5	506.2	3.4	288.2	369.6	391.3	407.9	427.5	491.5	550.0	585.5	620.2	x

Table 4.15a Weekly pay - Gross (£) - For all employee jobs[a] by age group and occupation: United Kingdom, 2013

Description	Code	Number of jobs[b] (thousand)	Annual Median	% change	Annual Mean	% change	Percentiles 10	20	25	30	40	60	70	75	80	90
60+ Textiles, printing and other skilled trades	54	30	286.1	0.1	295.0	0.3	86.1	135.2	155.5	175.8	223.2	317.7	362.0	383.8	418.5	x
60+ Caring, leisure and other service occupations	6	180	217.0	3.8	235.6	1.5	57.9	102.3	122.9	140.3	178.7	256.5	303.9	330.4	360.1	432.9
60+ Caring personal service occupations	61	134	218.1	4.8	232.1	1.2	58.1	108.9	129.3	145.9	183.3	254.2	293.0	321.3	346.6	417.8
60+ Leisure, travel and related personal service occupations	62	46	210.7	-2.3	245.8	2.4	55.5	89.9	100.7	121.4	165.5	276.8	329.2	367.8	385.9	x
60+ Sales and customer service occupations	7	131	156.4	1.0	199.8	2.0	69.9	95.6	104.0	113.0	134.5	188.9	231.7	256.7	284.0	378.7
60+ Sales occupations	71	107	151.9	4.4	184.1	-0.3	68.1	94.8	102.4	111.5	128.0	175.0	213.1	235.3	258.6	337.1
60+ Customer service occupations	72	24	225.6	7.1	268.4	11.0	76.9	98.5	113.0	128.1	175.6	290.1	344.6	365.3	387.1	x
60+ Process, plant and machine operatives	8	160	351.9	5.7	365.0	3.4	118.0	192.8	229.2	254.0	300.3	400.0	450.5	479.8	512.1	620.4
60+ Process, plant and machine operatives	81	56	352.0	6.1	375.4	3.9	153.1	235.1	251.1	268.0	309.5	392.2	452.3	471.5	508.6	631.6
60+ Transport and mobile machine drivers and operatives	82	105	351.4	5.4	359.5	2.9	103.8	165.1	204.6	245.0	298.2	403.8	449.8	481.4	514.3	610.2
60+ Elementary occupations	9	235	168.8	13.2	213.0	6.9	46.5	69.7	80.9	94.4	123.8	231.6	287.7	318.2	346.4	429.0
60+ Elementary trades and related occupations	91	24	321.9	2.6	333.1	2.9	115.0	196.3	251.0	275.0	299.1	357.5	399.0	416.0	454.2	x
60+ Elementary administration and service occupations	92	212	151.0	11.8	199.5	7.7	44.2	65.8	76.9	86.4	112.7	202.0	264.9	295.1	329.1	410.1
Not Classified		:														

a Employees on adult rates whose pay for the survey pay-period was not affected by absence.

b Figures for Number of Jobs are for indicative purposes only and should not be considered an accurate estimate of employee job counts.

KEY - The colour coding indicates the quality of each estimate; jobs, median, mean and percentiles but not the annual percentage change.

The quality of an estimate is measured by its coefficient of variation (CV), which is the ratio of the standard error of an estimate to the estimate.

Source: Annual Survey of Hours and Earnings, Office for National Statistics.

Key
CV <= 5%
CV > 5% and <= 10%
CV > 10% and <= 20%
x = unreliable
CV > 20% or unavailable
.. = disclosive
: = not applicable
- = nil or negligible

Table 4.15b Hourly pay - Gross (£) - For all employee jobs^a by age group and occupation: United Kingdom, 2013

Description	Code	Number of jobs^b (thousand)	Median	Annual % change	Mean	Annual % change	10	20	25	30	40	60	70	75	80	90
All employees		24,575	11.59	2.7	15.13	2.0	6.57	7.55	8.12	8.72	10.00	13.61	16.14	17.68	19.55	25.38
18-21		1,245	6.72	2.2	7.62	1.9	5.20	6.14	6.19	6.20	6.41	7.07	7.59	8.00	8.44	10.00
22-29		4,145	9.82	2.3	11.59	1.8	6.41	7.10	7.50	7.90	8.76	11.14	12.78	13.74	14.81	17.99
30-39		5,572	13.33	1.3	16.02	1.5	7.07	8.49	9.19	9.91	11.46	15.40	17.83	19.25	20.90	26.59
40-49		6,485	13.18	2.3	16.98	2.0	7.03	8.35	9.00	9.75	11.25	15.51	18.29	20.00	21.87	28.74
50-59		5,116	12.49	3.5	16.43	1.8	7.00	8.19	8.81	9.41	10.81	14.65	17.58	19.22	21.28	27.87
60+		1,829	10.67	4.5	14.59	3.0	6.63	7.42	7.88	8.34	9.45	12.29	14.81	16.44	18.41	24.99
18-21 ALL OCCUPATIONS		1,245	6.72	2.2	7.62	1.9	5.20	6.14	6.19	6.20	6.41	7.07	7.59	8.00	8.44	10.00
18-21 Managers, directors and senior officials	1	17	7.69	-2.9	11.07	30.1	x	x	6.75	6.79	6.96	8.82	10.39	x	x	x
18-21 Corporate managers and directors	11	12	7.54	-7.5	9.12	6.5	x	x	x	6.74	6.96	7.79	x	x	x	x
18-21 Other managers and proprietors	12	x	x		x		x	x	x	x	x	x	x	x	x	x
18-21 Professional occupations	2	28	11.00	9.4	11.24	4.0	7.18	7.73	8.11	8.50	9.45	12.52	12.87	13.20	14.33	17.07
18-21 Science, research, engineering and technology professionals	21	15	9.94	17.9	10.95	15.3	x	7.70	7.80	8.19	8.65	12.18	12.87	13.14	x	x
18-21 Health professionals	22	x	8.29	-19.5	10.16	-7.5	x	x	x	x	x	x	x	x	x	x
18-21 Teaching and educational professionals	23	x	13.49	-1.4	14.61	13.2	x	x	x	x	x	14.01	x	x	x	x
18-21 Business, media and public service professionals	24	x	9.65	-15.3	11.09	-10.4	x	x	x	x	x	x	x	x	x	x
18-21 Associate professional and technical occupations	3	66	8.69	3.9	9.67	-8.1	6.19	6.94	7.16	7.44	8.00	9.33	10.21	10.62	11.51	13.24
18-21 Science, engineering and technology associate professionals	31	14	8.50	3.0	9.08	3.6	6.35	6.96	7.11	7.49	8.24	9.25	10.27	10.85	x	x
18-21 Health and social care associate professionals	32	7	8.29	-3.0	9.58	0.8	x	x	7.45	7.53	8.15	8.84	9.24	x	x	x
18-21 Protective service occupations	33	x	10.34	-13.9	11.09	-4.6	x	x	x	x	x	x	x	x	x	x
18-21 Culture, media and sports occupations	34	14	8.06	5.3	9.06		5.83	6.25	6.32	6.63	7.24	9.94	10.17	10.36	x	x
18-21 Business and public service associate professionals	35	29	8.72	4.7	10.03	5.7	6.19	6.93	7.14	7.45	7.99	9.33	10.24	10.62	11.32	x
18-21 Administrative and secretarial occupations	4	128	7.78	2.4	8.11	3.4	6.17	6.40	6.64	6.91	7.31	8.22	8.73	9.12	9.39	10.77
18-21 Administrative occupations	41	106	7.93	3.1	8.18	2.9	6.19	6.49	6.75	7.00	7.45	8.33	8.82	9.20	9.49	10.69
18-21 Secretarial and related occupations	42	22	7.19	5.7	7.75	6.0	5.57	6.19	6.31	6.43	6.91	7.73	8.21	8.55	9.05	x
18-21 Skilled trades occupations	5	77	7.20	-2.3	8.26	1.2	5.32	6.19	6.20	6.36	6.69	7.71	8.50	8.94	9.82	12.10
18-21 Skilled agricultural and related trades	51	x	6.75	0.4	7.13	3.1	x	x	x	x	6.54	7.11	x	x	x	x
18-21 Skilled metal, electrical and electronic trades	52	34	8.00	-4.8	9.18	1.8	5.03	6.24	6.50	6.66	7.42	8.87	10.12	10.52	11.50	x
18-21 Skilled construction and building trades	53	12	7.51	-2.0	8.30	3.4	x	5.90	6.08	6.30	6.99	8.50	9.20	9.49	x	x
18-21 Textiles, printing and other skilled trades	54	26	6.61	-1.8	7.02	-2.0	5.51	x	x	6.19	6.32	6.94	7.19	7.45	7.69	x
18-21 Caring, leisure and other service occupations	6	150	6.97	5.1	7.31	2.6	5.72	6.19	6.24	6.35	6.58	7.28	7.74	8.02	8.33	9.81
18-21 Caring personal service occupations	61	111	6.99	4.3	7.31	2.5	5.95	6.21	6.31	6.43	6.65	7.30	7.79	8.09	8.50	10.00
18-21 Leisure, travel and related personal service occupations	62	39	6.76	4.7	7.28	3.0	5.09	6.18	6.19	6.20	6.37	7.17	7.62	7.93	8.23	x
18-21 Sales and customer service occupations	7	328	6.65	2.1	7.01	1.6	5.32	6.17	6.19	6.25	6.42	6.87	7.12	7.31	7.57	8.58
18-21 Sales occupations	71	284	6.61	1.7	6.90	1.7	5.23	6.09	6.19	6.22	6.39	6.82	7.01	7.20	7.43	8.46
18-21 Customer service occupations	72	43	7.14	5.9	7.57	1.4	6.10	6.31	6.41	6.49	6.84	7.41	7.73	7.95	8.35	x
18-21 Process, plant and machine operatives	8	34	7.46	7.6	8.22	8.2	6.02	6.21	6.35	6.52	6.85	8.00	8.72	9.29	9.71	11.37
18-21 Process, plant and machine operatives	81	29	7.46	6.6	8.23	7.7	6.00	6.22	6.36	6.57	6.82	8.00	8.73	9.30	9.72	11.59
18-21 Transport and mobile machine drivers and operatives	82	6	7.17	10.3	8.17	10.0	x	6.19	6.22	6.49	6.85	7.74	8.65	9.00	x	x
18-21 Elementary occupations	9	417	6.23	1.8	6.73	1.2	5.00	5.37	5.82	6.13	6.19	6.44	6.75	7.00	7.25	8.43
18-21 Elementary trades and related occupations	91	31	6.90	-2.7	7.54	-0.3	6.18	6.19	6.21	6.32	6.56	7.17	7.52	7.92	8.53	x
18-21 Elementary administration and service occupations	92	386	6.20	1.6	6.63	1.6	5.00	5.31	5.68	6.05	6.19	6.38	6.67	6.92	7.19	8.23
22-29 ALL OCCUPATIONS		4,145	9.82	2.3	11.59	1.8	6.41	7.10	7.50	7.90	8.76	11.14	12.78	13.74	14.81	17.99
22-29 Managers, directors and senior officials	1	208	11.73	2.4	14.23	4.0	7.55	8.46	8.88	9.24	10.32	13.08	15.04	16.35	17.96	24.37
22-29 Corporate managers and directors	11	156	12.51	2.7	15.40	4.6	7.78	8.79	9.19	9.74	11.03	14.17	16.42	17.91	19.92	27.56
22-29 Other managers and proprietors	12	52	9.69	0.1	10.85	3.2	7.12	7.91	8.10	8.40	9.07	10.80	12.08	12.72	13.48	x
22-29 Professional occupations	2	811	15.27	0.5	16.10	0.9	10.42	12.18	12.77	13.29	14.35	16.54	17.93	18.85	19.98	22.92
22-29 Science, research, engineering and technology professionals	21	190	14.50	-0.1	15.49	0.6	9.81	11.25	11.96	12.45	13.44	15.54	17.30	18.22	19.30	22.09
22-29 Health professionals	22	191	14.95	1.9	15.62	0.6	10.96	12.40	13.00	13.32	14.18	15.66	16.99	17.86	18.81	21.35
22-29 Teaching and educational professionals	23	207	16.60	0.3	16.67	0.8	11.99	13.34	13.77	14.41	15.61	17.57	18.68	19.76	20.76	23.76
22-29 Business, media and public service professionals	24	223	15.33	1.3	16.63	1.7	9.79	11.64	12.29	12.93	14.24	16.65	18.40	19.60	20.79	25.04
22-29 Associate professional and technical occupations	3	640	12.47	2.1	13.89	2.1	8.26	9.47	9.92	10.46	11.50	13.51	14.75	15.37	16.38	19.34
22-29 Science, engineering and technology associate professionals	31	122	11.30	2.6	12.08	2.9	7.85	8.83	9.33	9.72	10.51	12.22	13.24	13.75	14.71	17.12
22-29 Health and social care associate professionals	32	49	11.15	1.3	11.85	2.2	7.86	8.80	9.21	9.48	10.47	11.91	12.77	13.27	13.76	x
22-29 Protective service occupations	33	52	14.65	2.0	14.64	-0.1	11.51	12.97	13.32	13.67	14.23	15.09	15.63	16.21	16.95	x
22-29 Culture, media and sports occupations	34	60	11.80	5.8	16.88	6.8	7.39	8.69	9.22	9.62	10.95	12.70	13.45	14.10	15.00	x
22-29 Business and public service associate professionals	35	358	12.78	0.7	14.22	1.6	8.50	9.68	10.18	10.65	11.77	14.00	15.38	16.39	17.45	21.47
22-29 Administrative and secretarial occupations	4	516	9.40	2.0	10.24	1.0	6.96	7.68	8.01	8.31	8.85	10.01	10.88	11.34	12.04	14.18
22-29 Administrative occupations	41	433	9.58	2.5	10.39	1.1	7.17	7.91	8.20	8.50	9.00	10.16	11.01	11.50	12.19	14.29
22-29 Secretarial and related occupations	42	83	8.49	1.3	9.43	0.2	6.39	6.94	7.16	7.43	7.92	9.06	10.00	10.54	11.04	13.28
22-29 Skilled trades occupations	5	356	9.86	3.8	10.69	2.8	6.78	7.50	7.78	8.11	8.87	10.69	11.88	12.46	13.24	15.20
22-29 Skilled agricultural and related trades	51	15	7.90	-0.7	8.40	-0.9	6.71	7.01	7.10	7.25	7.57	8.38	8.86	9.10	9.37	x
22-29 Skilled metal, electrical and electronic trades	52	170	11.58	6.3	12.04	4.0	7.59	8.62	9.13	9.58	10.50	12.50	13.68	14.22	14.77	17.01
22-29 Skilled construction and building trades	53	67	10.60	1.3	11.22	2.5	7.45	8.50	9.00	9.48	10.02	11.46	12.00	12.36	13.01	x
22-29 Textiles, printing and other skilled trades	54	105	7.75	1.1	8.28	-0.4	6.30	6.69	6.92	7.06	7.45	8.09	8.58	8.99	9.31	10.55
22-29 Caring, leisure and other service occupations	6	428	7.78	-0.2	8.39	0.6	6.25	6.57	6.75	6.94	7.31	8.25	8.94	9.36	9.91	11.53
22-29 Caring personal service occupations	61	346	7.78	-0.3	8.35	0.2	6.28	6.60	6.78	6.96	7.32	8.26	8.99	9.40	9.94	11.46
22-29 Leisure, travel and related personal service occupations	62	82	7.77	1.2	8.55	2.1	6.20	6.39	6.61	6.85	7.19	8.23	8.80	9.18	9.75	11.72
22-29 Sales and customer service occupations	7	481	7.41	1.1	8.31	0.9	6.20	6.41	6.57	6.72	7.00	7.88	8.54	8.90	9.40	10.82

Table 4.15b Hourly pay - Gross (£) - For all employee jobs[a] by age group and occupation: United Kingdom, 2013

Description	Code	Number of jobs[b] (thousand)	Annual % Median change		Annual % Mean change		Percentiles 10	20	25	30	40	60	70	75	80	90
22-29 Sales occupations	71	358	7.06	0.2	7.88	0.1	6.19	6.35	6.44	6.58	6.83	7.48	7.95	8.33	8.69	9.97
22-29 Customer service occupations	72	123	8.74	3.3	9.35	2.8	6.49	7.09	7.35	7.56	8.14	9.33	10.00	10.38	10.82	12.30
22-29 Process, plant and machine operatives	8	192	8.58	3.3	9.51	3.7	6.33	6.88	7.08	7.37	8.00	9.29	10.19	10.85	11.47	13.58
22-29 Process, plant and machine operatives	81	136	8.46	3.2	9.44	3.7	6.32	6.81	7.05	7.32	7.91	9.26	10.17	10.83	11.46	13.59
22-29 Transport and mobile machine drivers and operatives	82	56	8.76	2.6	9.67	4.0	6.39	6.92	7.18	7.50	8.15	9.43	10.30	10.94	11.59	x
22-29 Elementary occupations	9	514	7.00	0.0	7.82	-0.1	6.19	6.20	6.25	6.34	6.58	7.46	8.00	8.36	8.81	10.09
22-29 Elementary trades and related occupations	91	69	7.71	1.1	8.21	0.2	6.19	6.37	6.56	6.87	7.24	8.12	8.60	8.92	9.33	10.63
22-29 Elementary administration and service occupations	92	445	6.90	1.0	7.74	0.0	6.19	6.19	6.22	6.30	6.51	7.30	7.88	8.25	8.72	10.08
30-39 ALL OCCUPATIONS		5,572	13.33	1.3	16.02	1.5	7.07	8.49	9.19	9.91	11.46	15.40	17.83	19.25	20.90	26.59
30-39 Managers, directors and senior officials	1	577	18.87	2.6	23.27	2.7	8.93	11.23	12.38	13.62	16.06	21.87	26.32	29.10	32.73	43.99
30-39 Corporate managers and directors	11	479	20.51	3.1	24.97	3.0	9.44	12.29	13.70	14.98	17.69	23.91	28.46	31.37	34.89	46.51
30-39 Other managers and proprietors	12	98	12.74	1.9	15.14	0.7	8.01	9.16	9.70	10.28	11.23	14.51	16.63	17.82	19.17	x
30-39 Professional occupations	2	1,451	19.55	1.6	21.13	1.0	12.82	14.89	15.82	16.60	17.97	21.15	23.16	24.53	26.19	31.28
30-39 Science, research, engineering and technology professionals	21	355	19.44	1.9	20.94	2.0	12.99	14.95	15.84	16.65	17.98	20.95	23.01	24.49	25.75	30.42
30-39 Health professionals	22	346	17.84	1.3	20.12	-0.7	12.75	14.27	14.87	15.51	16.78	19.13	20.97	22.44	24.06	30.92
30-39 Teaching and educational professionals	23	372	21.65	0.7	21.85	1.2	14.06	17.13	18.19	18.73	20.22	22.97	24.66	25.87	27.18	30.56
30-39 Business, media and public service professionals	24	378	18.91	-0.2	21.59	1.0	12.05	14.29	15.22	16.06	17.28	20.72	23.03	24.67	26.61	33.67
30-39 Associate professional and technical occupations	3	998	15.51	0.6	17.57	1.2	9.94	11.59	12.28	12.98	14.27	16.90	18.54	19.68	20.85	25.96
30-39 Science, engineering and technology associate professionals	31	167	14.08	0.3	15.34	1.9	9.38	10.81	11.41	12.11	12.98	15.35	16.58	17.39	18.41	21.84
30-39 Health and social care associate professionals	32	83	12.86	2.1	13.72	1.2	9.00	10.30	10.75	11.15	12.01	13.79	14.81	15.22	16.28	18.24
30-39 Protective service occupations	33	135	16.40	-1.4	16.65	-1.4	13.04	14.13	14.53	15.03	15.70	17.42	18.04	18.61	19.28	20.67
30-39 Culture, media and sports occupations	34	59	13.65	-2.9	14.78	-4.8	8.90	10.41	10.85	11.51	12.58	15.00	16.46	17.56	18.86	x
30-39 Business and public service associate professionals	35	554	16.37	1.0	19.30	1.9	10.06	11.86	12.59	13.32	14.84	18.18	20.51	21.86	23.76	31.15
30-39 Administrative and secretarial occupations	4	600	10.54	0.8	12.00	0.1	7.47	8.39	8.80	9.15	9.80	11.44	12.58	13.31	14.33	17.38
30-39 Administrative occupations	41	495	10.64	0.3	12.13	0.0	7.62	8.61	8.95	9.29	9.91	11.58	12.77	13.51	14.45	17.49
30-39 Secretarial and related occupations	42	105	9.85	-0.6	11.31	1.0	7.00	7.74	8.03	8.41	9.09	10.77	11.85	12.40	13.28	16.41
30-39 Skilled trades occupations	5	403	11.09	0.0	12.11	0.6	7.21	8.38	8.82	9.29	10.21	12.10	13.22	14.00	14.83	17.58
30-39 Skilled agricultural and related trades	51	21	9.09	2.6	9.46	-0.6	7.01	7.59	7.77	8.28	8.68	9.56	9.86	10.19	10.58	x
30-39 Skilled metal, electrical and electronic trades	52	205	12.91	3.2	13.74	2.5	9.00	10.22	10.69	11.05	12.00	13.94	15.00	15.71	16.90	19.57
30-39 Skilled construction and building trades	53	62	11.21	-0.8	11.92	-2.5	8.28	9.17	9.68	10.00	10.64	11.93	12.87	13.12	13.79	x
30-39 Textiles, printing and other skilled trades	54	115	8.47	0.5	9.42	-1.9	6.40	6.79	7.05	7.40	7.93	9.06	9.99	10.37	11.11	12.81
30-39 Caring, leisure and other service occupations	6	439	8.59	1.2	9.47	0.4	6.46	6.96	7.21	7.46	8.01	9.27	10.06	10.63	11.26	13.05
30-39 Caring personal service occupations	61	371	8.49	1.5	9.21	0.4	6.47	6.92	7.17	7.40	7.96	9.13	9.94	10.42	11.01	12.69
30-39 Leisure, travel and related personal service occupations	62	68	9.23	0.3	10.80	1.5	6.35	7.23	7.59	7.95	8.56	9.95	11.30	12.10	12.97	15.87
30-39 Sales and customer service occupations	7	332	8.16	1.6	9.68	-0.3	6.26	6.63	6.82	7.00	7.52	8.94	9.97	10.57	11.31	13.71
30-39 Sales occupations	71	225	7.50	1.2	8.88	0.0	6.20	6.43	6.63	6.76	7.05	8.02	8.79	9.25	9.82	11.94
30-39 Customer service occupations	72	107	10.17	1.6	11.16	-1.2	6.73	7.68	8.08	8.52	9.39	11.00	11.99	12.73	13.42	15.65
30-39 Process, plant and machine operatives	8	291	9.69	1.4	10.68	2.3	6.69	7.49	7.87	8.24	8.96	10.53	11.63	12.25	12.99	15.29
30-39 Process, plant and machine operatives	81	162	9.54	2.2	10.73	2.2	6.59	7.27	7.69	8.02	8.71	10.48	11.84	12.59	13.54	15.84
30-39 Transport and mobile machine drivers and operatives	82	129	9.83	1.4	10.62	2.3	6.85	7.66	8.05	8.45	9.11	10.57	11.47	12.02	12.52	14.75
30-39 Elementary occupations	9	482	7.59	1.2	8.73	1.2	6.19	6.30	6.47	6.64	7.05	8.23	9.06	9.54	10.09	11.73
30-39 Elementary trades and related occupations	91	62	8.09	0.2	8.85	0.4	6.21	6.52	6.80	7.00	7.53	8.80	9.56	10.00	10.53	11.72
30-39 Elementary administration and service occupations	92	420	7.50	1.3	8.71	1.4	6.19	6.28	6.44	6.60	7.00	8.11	9.00	9.42	10.06	11.73
40-49 ALL OCCUPATIONS		6,485	13.18	2.3	16.98	2.0	7.03	8.35	9.00	9.75	11.25	15.51	18.29	20.00	21.87	28.74
40-49 Managers, directors and senior officials	1	805	21.23	3.9	26.89	3.3	9.79	12.81	14.27	15.56	18.23	25.03	29.54	32.61	36.92	50.01
40-49 Corporate managers and directors	11	687	22.54	3.7	28.39	3.6	10.24	13.73	15.25	16.63	19.54	26.43	31.09	34.58	39.32	52.02
40-49 Other managers and proprietors	12	118	15.14	1.7	18.26	-0.4	8.39	10.10	11.01	11.88	13.48	16.99	19.55	21.27	23.25	30.93
40-49 Professional occupations	2	1,438	20.63	0.6	22.91	0.0	13.10	15.42	16.37	17.25	18.75	22.29	24.53	26.08	28.08	34.70
40-49 Science, research, engineering and technology professionals	21	323	21.46	0.8	23.19	1.1	13.87	16.12	17.01	17.96	19.88	23.31	25.38	27.04	28.70	33.77
40-49 Health professionals	22	415	18.42	2.2	22.28	-0.4	12.79	14.54	15.22	16.06	17.49	20.04	21.43	22.80	24.19	36.84
40-49 Teaching and educational professionals	23	370	22.83	1.5	23.43	0.6	14.36	17.64	18.66	19.50	21.51	24.31	26.49	27.75	29.06	33.69
40-49 Business, media and public service professionals	24	329	19.64	-0.6	22.89	-0.8	12.18	14.58	15.58	16.35	17.71	21.69	24.36	26.18	28.33	36.22
40-49 Associate professional and technical occupations	3	989	16.18	0.3	18.83	0.6	9.97	11.83	12.55	13.25	14.68	17.89	19.71	20.81	22.44	28.95
40-49 Science, engineering and technology associate professionals	31	168	14.17	-2.5	15.41	-1.3	8.85	10.13	10.99	11.67	12.79	15.69	16.78	17.65	18.93	22.13
40-49 Health and social care associate professionals	32	103	12.98	1.1	14.10	1.2	8.98	10.17	10.73	11.12	12.02	14.00	15.18	16.08	17.32	19.22
40-49 Protective service occupations	33	140	18.16	0.2	18.03	-1.2	13.32	14.55	15.21	15.92	17.50	19.05	19.86	20.40	21.12	23.08
40-49 Culture, media and sports occupations	34	49	15.01	0.7	17.03	-1.2	9.13	10.92	11.88	12.44	13.74	17.16	19.14	20.00	20.74	x
40-49 Business and public service associate professionals	35	529	17.12	0.4	21.17	1.7	10.53	12.27	13.01	13.89	15.43	19.27	22.15	23.94	26.37	35.18
40-49 Administrative and secretarial occupations	4	769	10.48	1.4	12.10	0.1	7.49	8.35	8.74	9.04	9.76	11.35	12.57	13.30	14.24	17.56
40-49 Administrative occupations	41	598	10.69	1.8	12.31	0.0	7.63	8.60	8.91	9.25	9.86	11.58	12.77	13.50	14.37	17.65
40-49 Secretarial and related occupations	42	171	9.82	1.2	11.32	0.9	7.06	7.79	8.08	8.42	9.01	10.75	11.51	12.50	13.60	17.12
40-49 Skilled trades occupations	5	477	11.97	1.1	13.01	0.7	7.47	8.71	9.24	9.83	10.87	12.98	14.13	14.86	15.92	18.86
40-49 Skilled agricultural and related trades	51	27	9.49	1.0	10.38	3.5	7.10	7.61	8.15	8.48	8.95	10.03	10.84	11.72	12.63	x
40-49 Skilled metal, electrical and electronic trades	52	253	13.31	0.3	14.37	1.2	9.10	10.45	10.98	11.48	12.46	14.29	15.69	16.51	17.50	20.40
40-49 Skilled construction and building trades	53	79	12.50	3.4	13.17	1.0	8.99	10.00	10.38	10.73	11.74	13.05	13.99	14.62	15.33	x
40-49 Textiles, printing and other skilled trades	54	118	8.54	-2.1	10.08	-1.2	6.32	6.98	7.26	7.50	8.00	9.26	10.35	11.03	11.87	13.94
40-49 Caring, leisure and other service occupations	6	639	8.65	-0.1	9.70	0.6	6.55	7.04	7.30	7.54	8.07	9.33	10.19	10.75	11.36	13.34

Table 4.15b Hourly pay - Gross (£) - For all employee jobs[a] by age group and occupation: United Kingdom, 2013

Description	Code	Number of jobs[b] (thousand)	Median	Annual % change	Mean	Annual % change	Percentiles 10	20	25	30	40	60	70	75	80	90
40-49 Caring personal service occupations	61	545	8.59	-0.2	9.33	0.0	6.57	7.05	7.29	7.51	8.02	9.25	10.09	10.52	11.10	12.72
40-49 Leisure, travel and related personal service occupations	62	94	9.00	1.2	11.73	2.9	6.45	7.03	7.46	7.74	8.34	10.00	12.03	13.47	14.95	x
40-49 Sales and customer service occupations	7	343	7.80	2.6	9.62	0.9	6.25	6.57	6.71	6.87	7.24	8.60	9.59	10.15	10.99	13.66
40-49 Sales occupations	71	250	7.28	3.3	8.78	2.3	6.20	6.47	6.61	6.70	6.96	7.80	8.55	8.95	9.54	11.68
40-49 Customer service occupations	72	93	10.06	1.7	11.57	-0.9	6.57	7.59	8.00	8.48	9.32	11.11	12.00	12.87	13.64	16.57
40-49 Process, plant and machine operatives	8	414	10.14	1.4	11.29	1.7	7.00	7.92	8.31	8.66	9.43	11.00	12.17	12.92	13.88	16.56
40-49 Process, plant and machine operatives	81	190	10.23	-0.5	11.45	1.2	6.69	7.63	8.14	8.46	9.30	11.30	12.67	13.64	14.61	17.05
40-49 Transport and mobile machine drivers and operatives	82	224	10.08	1.9	11.17	2.2	7.30	8.10	8.50	8.82	9.50	10.83	11.78	12.41	13.30	16.19
40-49 Elementary occupations	9	612	7.59	1.1	8.94	1.6	6.19	6.36	6.50	6.67	7.08	8.25	9.18	9.80	10.12	11.87
40-49 Elementary trades and related occupations	91	72	9.00	4.4	9.64	1.4	6.31	6.88	7.17	7.46	8.16	9.56	10.30	10.76	11.55	13.11
40-49 Elementary administration and service occupations	92	540	7.50	1.4	8.81	1.8	6.19	6.32	6.47	6.61	7.00	8.09	8.95	9.52	10.09	11.57
50-59 ALL OCCUPATIONS		5,116	12.49	3.5	16.43	1.8	7.00	8.19	8.81	9.41	10.81	14.65	17.58	19.22	21.28	27.87
50-59 Managers, directors and senior officials	1	603	20.73	-0.9	26.84	-1.7	9.14	12.37	13.80	15.02	17.73	23.91	28.51	31.39	35.95	48.17
50-59 Corporate managers and directors	11	500	22.04	-0.9	28.53	-1.5	9.32	13.02	14.42	15.99	18.85	25.64	30.62	34.08	38.47	50.62
50-59 Other managers and proprietors	12	103	15.88	2.5	18.59	-2.6	8.49	10.45	11.48	12.49	14.17	17.91	20.56	22.06	23.90	29.41
50-59 Professional occupations	2	1,114	20.74	1.1	23.18	1.0	12.76	15.38	16.45	17.38	18.84	22.49	24.98	26.55	28.60	35.40
50-59 Science, research, engineering and technology professionals	21	220	21.28	3.2	23.20	2.4	13.42	15.97	16.91	17.81	19.36	23.33	25.67	27.35	29.13	34.70
50-59 Health professionals	22	324	18.44	1.5	22.76	0.4	12.47	14.35	15.06	15.97	17.49	20.19	21.42	22.65	24.39	37.02
50-59 Teaching and educational professionals	23	328	23.62	1.3	24.73	0.5	14.98	18.53	19.19	20.42	21.75	25.18	27.50	28.94	30.48	35.77
50-59 Business, media and public service professionals	24	243	19.03	1.3	22.00	1.7	10.95	13.74	15.04	16.00	17.41	21.10	23.84	25.43	27.49	34.66
50-59 Associate professional and technical occupations	3	635	15.20	0.3	17.75	1.8	9.51	11.20	11.98	12.63	13.83	16.90	18.97	20.10	21.60	26.98
50-59 Science, engineering and technology associate professionals	31	124	14.51	0.6	15.45	1.3	8.89	10.44	11.14	11.77	13.20	15.69	17.31	18.26	19.32	22.16
50-59 Health and social care associate professionals	32	90	12.63	2.1	13.72	2.1	8.96	9.96	10.55	11.08	11.89	13.61	14.59	15.36	16.34	18.84
50-59 Protective service occupations	33	55	17.82	0.8	17.88	1.2	11.22	13.55	14.25	14.52	15.95	19.00	20.05	21.13	21.97	x
50-59 Culture, media and sports occupations	34	25	15.00	0.0	20.49	10.6	8.92	11.06	11.66	12.33	13.72	16.88	19.84	20.85	22.73	x
50-59 Business and public service associate professionals	35	342	16.14	0.5	19.41	1.4	9.91	11.96	12.62	13.03	14.62	18.06	20.54	22.07	24.08	31.44
50-59 Administrative and secretarial occupations	4	731	10.26	0.8	11.82	-0.3	7.54	8.37	8.73	8.99	9.67	11.16	12.23	12.89	13.71	16.87
50-59 Administrative occupations	41	553	10.56	1.9	12.09	-0.4	7.73	8.60	8.91	9.17	9.85	11.43	12.55	13.25	14.05	17.16
50-59 Secretarial and related occupations	42	178	9.61	1.2	10.93	-0.3	7.19	7.87	8.15	8.45	8.99	10.23	11.25	11.60	12.50	15.30
50-59 Skilled trades occupations	5	380	12.29	2.7	13.22	2.4	7.52	8.88	9.53	10.09	11.21	13.33	14.66	15.44	16.43	19.15
50-59 Skilled agricultural and related trades	51	21	9.44	6.4	10.16	4.1	6.93	7.58	8.00	8.25	8.86	9.86	10.47	10.94	11.67	x
50-59 Skilled metal, electrical and electronic trades	52	220	13.67	2.5	14.44	2.1	9.36	10.86	11.25	11.89	12.79	14.74	16.01	16.70	17.59	20.40
50-59 Skilled construction and building trades	53	54	12.61	4.0	13.37	3.5	8.97	10.25	10.69	11.16	11.73	13.35	14.45	14.90	15.70	x
50-59 Textiles, printing and other skilled trades	54	85	8.73	0.1	10.02	0.0	6.49	7.10	7.31	7.54	8.04	9.28	10.16	10.83	11.52	13.85
50-59 Caring, leisure and other service occupations	6	511	8.89	1.0	9.77	0.5	6.62	7.24	7.53	7.76	8.31	9.57	10.46	11.01	11.55	13.23
50-59 Caring personal service occupations	61	431	8.89	1.0	9.57	0.2	6.63	7.23	7.53	7.78	8.32	9.57	10.44	10.95	11.44	12.92
50-59 Leisure, travel and related personal service occupations	62	80	8.83	1.1	10.78	2.2	6.61	7.25	7.50	7.67	8.20	9.58	10.64	11.38	12.24	15.93
50-59 Sales and customer service occupations	7	299	7.50	3.0	9.22	3.4	6.25	6.47	6.63	6.77	7.04	8.18	9.00	9.57	10.33	12.73
50-59 Sales occupations	71	223	7.14	2.5	8.40	3.7	6.20	6.40	6.50	6.63	6.84	7.53	8.15	8.58	8.99	10.85
50-59 Customer service occupations	72	76	9.82	3.4	11.29	2.1	6.41	7.22	7.68	8.18	9.00	10.67	11.68	12.49	13.37	16.58
50-59 Process, plant and machine operatives	8	343	9.95	1.5	11.00	1.1	6.77	7.55	8.00	8.30	9.05	10.84	11.88	12.55	13.44	16.23
50-59 Process, plant and machine operatives	81	159	10.03	-0.4	11.31	0.3	6.65	7.33	7.74	8.10	9.01	11.17	12.52	13.43	14.53	17.08
50-59 Transport and mobile machine drivers and operatives	82	184	9.91	2.4	10.75	1.9	6.97	7.76	8.20	8.51	9.06	10.58	11.42	12.08	12.75	15.04
50-59 Elementary occupations	9	499	7.72	2.9	9.03	3.4	6.19	6.44	6.57	6.80	7.22	8.33	9.25	9.96	10.33	12.11
50-59 Elementary trades and related occupations	91	62	8.63	3.4	9.55	2.5	6.26	6.86	7.11	7.50	8.00	9.52	10.41	10.84	11.47	13.37
50-59 Elementary administration and service occupations	92	437	7.62	2.9	8.92	3.5	6.19	6.40	6.52	6.74	7.15	8.22	9.04	9.74	10.18	11.87
60+ ALL OCCUPATIONS		1,829	10.67	4.5	14.59	3.0	6.63	7.42	7.88	8.34	9.45	12.29	14.81	16.44	18.41	24.99
60+ Managers, directors and senior officials	1	203	17.27	-0.2	23.38	2.0	7.99	10.00	10.94	11.85	14.45	20.00	24.27	27.76	31.50	43.43
60+ Corporate managers and directors	11	162	18.28	-2.8	25.01	2.9	8.01	10.41	11.31	12.50	15.21	21.78	26.20	29.86	33.23	45.59
60+ Other managers and proprietors	12	41	14.12	0.2	17.10	-2.7	7.84	8.96	9.90	10.53	11.99	16.22	18.22	19.34	21.71	x
60+ Professional occupations	2	310	20.45	0.3	23.12	1.3	12.01	14.81	16.01	16.98	18.45	22.49	25.31	27.05	29.06	37.80
60+ Science, research, engineering and technology professionals	21	53	20.25	-2.0	21.38	-3.1	12.16	14.95	15.79	16.83	18.41	22.26	24.47	25.59	27.05	x
60+ Health professionals	22	73	17.79	1.0	23.90	2.8	11.63	13.58	14.27	14.85	16.94	19.72	21.59	23.42	26.26	x
60+ Teaching and educational professionals	23	110	23.71	0.9	25.85	0.5	14.83	18.04	18.73	20.16	21.69	26.03	28.22	29.65	31.96	38.76
60+ Business, media and public service professionals	24	75	18.09	1.1	21.12	5.2	10.51	12.80	14.19	15.56	16.90	19.77	22.74	24.48	26.65	x
60+ Associate professional and technical occupations	3	175	14.08	0.8	16.07	-2.1	8.70	10.16	10.86	11.47	12.71	15.45	17.27	18.73	20.25	24.84
60+ Science, engineering and technology associate professionals	31	37	13.64	2.0	14.53	0.0	8.67	9.98	10.61	11.25	12.24	14.56	15.96	16.84	17.43	x
60+ Health and social care associate professionals	32	22	12.29	6.9	12.85	2.7	8.02	9.25	9.72	10.16	11.15	13.18	14.04	14.43	15.75	x
60+ Protective service occupations	33	10	14.14	1.5	14.13	2.1	9.22	9.48	10.78	11.38	12.83	14.43	16.23	x	x	x
60+ Culture, media and sports occupations	34	10	13.67	14.2	16.56	15.2	x	9.90	10.00	10.86	11.59	16.53	19.82	x	x	x
60+ Business and public service associate professionals	35	97	14.88	-2.4	17.48	-4.4	8.91	10.73	11.39	12.23	13.49	16.70	19.10	20.48	21.98	27.77
60+ Administrative and secretarial occupations	4	287	9.97	2.1	11.46	0.9	7.25	8.03	8.36	8.71	9.34	10.70	11.76	12.48	13.31	16.26
60+ Administrative occupations	41	205	10.00	1.2	11.52	1.3	7.23	8.06	8.45	8.78	9.50	10.79	11.89	12.50	13.40	16.30
60+ Secretarial and related occupations	42	82	9.83	2.4	11.29	-0.4	7.31	8.00	8.24	8.51	9.00	10.47	11.30	12.14	13.02	16.14
60+ Skilled trades occupations	5	148	11.38	2.9	12.42	2.0	7.16	8.42	8.96	9.50	10.50	12.32	13.49	14.26	15.17	17.64
60+ Skilled agricultural and related trades	51	13	8.29	2.9	9.17	3.7	6.43	6.72	6.90	7.34	7.82	8.80	9.55	9.94	x	x
60+ Skilled metal, electrical and electronic trades	52	80	12.85	4.7	13.50	1.7	8.77	10.27	10.72	11.16	12.00	13.75	15.06	15.52	16.26	18.51
60+ Skilled construction and building trades	53	25	11.82	2.7	12.94	4.3	9.11	10.12	10.43	10.78	11.04	12.48	13.19	14.09	14.69	x

128

Table 4.15b Hourly pay - Gross (£) - For all employee jobs[a] by age group and occupation: United Kingdom, 2013

Description	Code	Number of jobs[b] (thousand)	Annual % Median change		Annual % Mean change		Percentiles 10	20	25	30	40	60	70	75	80	90
60+ Textiles, printing and other skilled trades	54	30	8.34	2.1	9.58	0.1	6.50	6.95	7.15	7.25	7.84	8.98	9.60	10.01	10.35	x
60+ Caring, leisure and other service occupations	6	180	8.58	-0.7	9.37	-0.4	6.57	7.09	7.32	7.52	8.03	9.10	9.91	10.37	10.93	12.63
60+ Caring personal service occupations	61	134	8.74	0.8	9.27	-1.0	6.59	7.11	7.33	7.56	8.12	9.17	9.92	10.39	10.90	12.49
60+ Leisure, travel and related personal service occupations	62	46	8.30	-1.6	9.66	1.4	6.50	7.00	7.27	7.49	7.98	8.82	9.76	10.22	11.01	x
60+ Sales and customer service occupations	7	131	7.17	2.7	8.55	2.1	6.20	6.41	6.55	6.64	6.87	7.54	8.25	8.67	9.16	11.13
60+ Sales occupations	71	107	7.03	2.8	8.09	0.6	6.19	6.40	6.50	6.63	6.80	7.35	7.82	8.21	8.65	10.36
60+ Customer service occupations	72	24	8.50	2.3	10.30	7.0	6.41	6.71	6.90	7.06	7.87	9.24	10.23	10.80	11.57	x
60+ Process, plant and machine operatives	8	160	8.97	3.1	10.02	3.1	6.44	7.00	7.25	7.55	8.20	9.79	10.55	11.10	11.70	13.49
60+ Process, plant and machine operatives	81	56	9.29	4.2	10.41	2.8	6.50	7.02	7.27	7.57	8.48	10.42	11.46	11.97	12.59	15.15
60+ Transport and mobile machine drivers and operatives	82	105	8.80	2.6	9.82	3.0	6.32	6.97	7.25	7.52	8.15	9.58	10.23	10.54	11.11	12.79
60+ Elementary occupations	9	235	7.30	2.8	8.50	2.7	6.19	6.34	6.48	6.58	6.93	7.78	8.47	8.91	9.50	10.98
60+ Elementary trades and related occupations	91	24	8.41	3.2	9.24	0.6	6.50	6.98	7.10	7.36	7.84	8.93	9.83	10.35	10.96	x
60+ Elementary administration and service occupations	92	212	7.19	2.3	8.38	3.2	6.19	6.30	6.43	6.52	6.85	7.67	8.27	8.76	9.25	10.73
Not Classified		:														

a Employees on adult rates whose pay for the survey pay-period was not affected by absence.

b Figures for Number of Jobs are for indicative purposes only and should not be considered an accurate estimate of employee job counts.

KEY - The colour coding indicates the quality of each estimate; jobs, median, mean and percentiles but not the annual percentage change.

The quality of an estimate is measured by its coefficient of variation (CV), which is the ratio of the standard error of an estimate to the estimate.

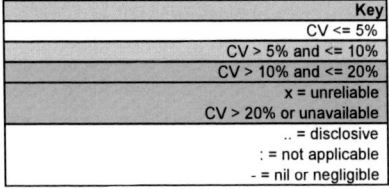

Key
CV <= 5%
CV > 5% and <= 10%
CV > 10% and <= 20%
x = unreliable
CV > 20% or unavailable
.. = disclosive
: = not applicable
- = nil or negligible

Source: Annual Survey of Hours and Earnings, Office for National Statistics.

4.16 Median[1] weekly and hourly earnings of full-time employees[2] by age group: United Kingdom April 2006 to 2013

	18-21	22-29	30-39	40-49	50-59	60+
Median gross weekly earnings						
All	**JRG9**	**JRH2**	**JRH3**	**JRH4**	**JEH5**	**JRH6**
2006	250.6	376.5	496.1	502.5	465.4	400.0
2007	265.5	387.8	509.0	517.3	479.1	418.7
2008	271.6	400.0	532.7	539.9	504.1	437.5
2009	277.5	407.1	541.8	550.5	514.0	446.3
2010	277.4	411.2	547.8	559.6	528.2	457.3
2011	277.8	406.6	553.7	564.7	531.8	466.1
2012	279.7	412.0	557.7	573.1	535.9	476.1
2013	287.5	420.6	562.9	579.9	551.0	490.4
Men	**JRH8**	**JRH9**	**JRI2**	**JRI3**	**JRI4**	**JRI5**
2006	261.5	390.6	525.0	558.7	516.0	421.6
2007	275.9	402.5	539.0	574.9	534.4	440.9
2008	280.0	416.7	566.3	599.1	563.6	462.6
2009	285.7	421.6	571.1	605.2	569.7	469.0
2010	285.9	421.2	573.7	613.7	582.7	483.0
2011	288.2	413.7	574.9	618.9	586.7	496.3
2012	295.4	420.6	574.9	622.9	598.2	508.3
2013	299.0	430.6	579.6	637.8	613.3	527.5
Women	**JRI7**	**JRI8**	**JRI9**	**JRJ2**	**JRJ3**	**JRJ4**
2006	240.4	362.7	444.0	410.2	385.0	343.7
2007	254.3	374.1	460.6	420.3	395.6	356.1
2008	258.8	384.7	480.9	437.3	419.7	376.4
2009	268.3	392.9	497.9	457.7	432.8	382.1
2010	268.3	401.3	507.9	472.2	440.9	389.0
2011	264.7	398.5	519.4	477.1	449.1	399.6
2012	266.3	402.5	527.0	484.4	446.0	407.4
2013	276.2	405.7	533.8	494.1	463.5	416.1

4.16 Median[1] weekly and hourly earnings of full-time employees[2] by age group: United Kingdom April 2006 to 2013

	18-21	22-29	30-39	40-49	50-59	60+
Median hourly earnings (excluding overtime)						
All	JRJ6	JRJ7	JRJ8	JRJ9	JRK2	JRK3
2006	6.31	9.50	12.43	12.49	11.50	9.72
2007	6.60	9.80	12.77	12.77	11.87	10.09
2008	6.75	10.12	13.34	13.31	12.53	10.57
2009	7.00	10.43	13.82	13.83	12.95	10.97
2010	7.00	10.34	13.91	14.01	13.19	11.18
2011	6.97	10.23	14.07	14.16	13.34	11.46
2012	7.00	10.34	14.23	14.37	13.55	11.83
2013	7.20	10.60	14.37	14.63	13.89	12.13
Men	JRK5	JRK6	JRK7	JRK8	JRK9	JRL2
2006	6.37	9.51	12.78	13.46	12.28	9.96
2007	6.65	9.80	13.10	13.77	12.79	10.31
2008	6.85	10.13	13.70	14.37	13.52	10.89
2009	7.09	10.45	14.15	14.95	13.91	11.25
2010	7.05	10.26	14.07	14.95	14.25	11.50
2011	7.07	10.08	14.14	15.14	14.31	11.84
2012	7.24	10.22	14.28	15.27	14.68	12.15
2013	7.27	10.57	14.43	15.62	15.00	12.61
Women	JRL4	JRL5	JRL6	JRL7	JRL8	JRL9
2006	6.24	9.48	11.87	10.95	10.24	9.17
2007	6.55	9.79	12.28	11.14	10.54	9.48
2008	6.64	10.12	12.78	11.57	11.10	9.82
2009	6.93	10.40	13.29	12.21	11.52	10.23
2010	6.90	10.48	13.66	12.54	11.84	10.40
2011	6.76	10.45	13.99	12.77	12.02	10.64
2012	6.82	10.53	14.18	12.93	11.99	10.99
2013	7.15	10.64	14.28	13.18	12.38	11.10

1. Median values are less affected by extremes of earnings at either ends of the scale with half the employees earning above the stated amount and half below.
2. Data relate to full-time employees on adult rates whose pay for the survey pay-period was not affected by absence.

Source: Annual Survey of Hours and Earnings: 01633 456 120

4.17 Trade Unions

Trade unions: distribution by size

Number of Members	Number of Unions	Membership	Number of Unions		Membership of all Unions	
			Per cent	Cumulative Per cent	Per cent	Cumulative Per cent
Under 100	30	1,202	18.1	18.1	0.0	0.0
100-499	30	8,287	18.1	36.1	0.1	0.1
500-999	15	11,083	9.0	45.2	0.2	0.3
1,000-2,499	23	37,912	13.9	59.0	0.5	0.8
2,500-4,999	15	54,875	9.0	68.1	0.8	1.6
5,000-9,999	11	85,025	6.6	74.7	1.2	2.8
10,000-14,999	2	23,848	1.2	75.9	0.3	3.2
15,000-24,999	11	225,061	6.6	82.5	3.2	6.3
25,000-49,999	12	404,427	7.2	89.8	5.7	12.0
50,000-99,999	4	268,726	2.4	92.2	3.8	15.8
100,000-249,999	5	797,381	3.0	95.2	11.3	27.1
250,000 and over	8	5,168,289	4.8	100.0	72.9	100.0
Total	166	7,086,116	100	100	100	100

The recorded trade union membership of 7,086,116 in 2013-14, compares to 7,197,415 reported in the previous period. This indicates a decrease of 111,299 members or 1.55%. The total recorded membership of around 7.1 million compares with a peak of 13.2 million in 1979, a fall of about 46%.

The following table shows unions whose membership has increased or decreased by 10,000 or more since the previous reporting period.

Trade Union: Changes in Membership

	Total Membership (000's)		
	2012-2013	2011-2012	% changes
Increases			
Union of Shop Distributive and Allied Workers	425,652	412,441	+ 3.2
Decreases			
UNISON:	1,301,500	1,317,500	- 1.2
Unite the Union	1,424,303	1,510,026	- 5.7
Public and Commercial Service Union	262,819	280,547	- 6.3

The annual returns submitted by unions to the Certification Officer require each union to provide figures for both total membership and members who pay contributions. There can be significant differences between these figures. This is usually the result of total membership figures including retired and unemployed members, members on long term sick and maternity/child care leave and those on career breaks. The returns submitted by unions during this reporting period show that the total number of contributing members was around 90.9% of the total number of members. This compared to 90.5% in the preceding year.

Source: Certification Officer Annual Report

Social protection

Chapter 5

Social Protection

(Tables 5.2 to 5.11, 5.13 and 5.15 to 5.19)

Tables 5.2 to 5.6, 5.9 to 5.11 and 5.13 to 5.19 give details of contributors and beneficiaries under the National Insurance and Industrial Injury Acts, supplementary benefits and war pensions.

There are four classes of National Insurance Contributions (NICs):

Class 1 Earnings-related contributions paid on earnings from employment. Employees pay primary Class 1 contributions and employers pay secondary Class 1 contributions. Payment of Class 1 contributions builds up entitlement to contributory benefits which include Basic State Pension; Additional State Pension (State Earnings Related Pension Scheme SERPS and from April 2002, State Second Pension, S2P); Contribution Based Jobseeker's Allowance; Bereavement Benefits; Incapacity Benefit; and the new Employment and Support Allowance.

Primary class 1 contributions stop at State Pension age, but not Class 1 secondary contributions paid by employers. There are reduced contribution rates where the employee contracts out of S2P (previously SERPS). They still receive a Basic State Pension but an Occupational or Personal Pension instead of the Additional State Second Pension.

Class 2 Flat rate contributions paid by the self-employed whose profits are above the small earnings exception. Payment of Class 2 contributions builds up entitlement to the contributory benefits which include Basic State Pension; Bereavement Benefits; Maternity Allowance; Incapacity Benefit; and the Employment and Support Allowance, but not Additional State Second Pension or Contribution Based Jobseeker's Allowance (JSA).

Class 2 contributions stop at State Pension age.

Class 3 Flat rate voluntary contributions, which can be paid by someone whose contribution record is insufficient. Payment of Class 3 contributions builds up entitlement to contributory benefits which include Basic State Pension and Bereavement Benefits. (Tables 5.2 to 5.11, 5.13 and 5.15 to 5.19) Tables 5.2 to 5.6, 5.9 to 5.11 and 5.13 to 5.19 give details of contributors and beneficiaries under the National Insurance and Industrial Injury Acts, supplementary benefits and war pensions.

Class 4 Profit-related contributions paid by the self employed in addition to Class 2 contributions. Class 4 contributions stop at State Pension age. Under some circumstances people who are not in employment do not have to make voluntary contributions to accrue a qualifying year for Basic State Pension.

Home Responsibilities Protection

Home Responsibilities Protection (HRP) was introduced to help to protect the basic State Pension of those precluded from regular employment because they are caring for children or a sick or disabled person at home. To be entitled to HRP, a person must have been precluded from regular employment for a full tax year. HRP reduces the amount of qualifying years a person would otherwise need for a Basic State Pension. The scheme ceased on the 6th April 2010 and has been replaced by new weekly credits which can be claimed if qualifying criteria are met.

National Insurance Credits

In addition to paying, or being treated as having paid contributions, a person can be credited with National Insurance contributions (NIC) credits. Contribution credits help to protect people's rights to State Retirement Pension and other Social Security Benefits.

A person is likely to be entitled to contributions credits if they are: a student in full time education or training, in receipt of Jobseeker's Allowance, unable to work due to sickness or disability, entitled to Statutory Maternity Pay or Statutory Adoption Pay, or they have received Carer's Allowance.

Credits are automatically awarded for men aged 60 to 65 provided they are not liable to pay Class 1 or 2 NICs, and to young people for the tax years containing their 16th, 17th and 18th birthdays.

Jobseeker's Allowance (Table 5.6)

Jobseeker's Allowance (JSA) replaced Unemployment Benefit and Income Support for unemployed claimants on 7 October 1996. It is a unified benefit with two routes of entry: contribution-based, which depends mainly upon National Insurance contributions, and income-based, which depends mainly upon a means test. Some claimants can qualify by either route. In practice they receive income-based JSA but have an underlying entitlement to the contribution based element.

Employment and Support Allowance, Invalidity Benefit and Incapacity Benefit (Table 5.7)

Incapacity Benefit replaced Sickness Benefit and Invalidity Benefit from 13 April 1995. The first condition for entitlement to these contributory benefits is that the claimants are incapable of work because of illness or disablement. The second is that they satisfy the contribution conditions, which depend on contributions paid as an employed (Class 1) or self-employed person (Class 2). Under Sickness and Invalidity Benefits the contribution conditions were automatically treated as satisfied if a person was incapable of work because of an industrial accident or prescribed disease. Under Incapacity Benefit those who do not satisfy the contribution conditions do not have them treated as satisfied. Class 1A contributions paid by employers are in respect of the benefit of cars provided for the private use of employees, and the free fuel provided for private use. These contributions do not provide any type of benefit cover.

Since 6 April 1983, most people working for an employer and paying National Insurance contributions as employed persons receive Statutory Sick Pay (SSP) from their employer when they are off work sick. Until 5 April 1986 SSP was payable for a maximum of eight weeks, since this date SSP has been payable for 28 weeks. People who do not work for an employer, and employees who are excluded from the SSP scheme, or those who have run out of SSP before reaching the maximum of 28 weeks and are still sick, can claim benefit. Any period of SSP is excluded from the tables.

Spells of incapacity of three days or less do not count as periods of interruption of employment and are excluded from the tables. Exceptions are where people are receiving regular weekly treatment by dialysis or treatment by radiotherapy, chemotherapy or plasmapheresis where two days in any six consecutive days make up a period of interruption of employment, and those whose incapacity for work ends within three days of the end of SSP entitlement.

At the beginning of a period of incapacity, benefit is subject to three waiting days, except where there was an earlier spell of incapacity of more than three days in the previous eight weeks. Employees entitled to SSP for less than 28 weeks and who are still sick can get Sickness Benefit or Incapacity Benefit Short Term (Low) until they reach a total of 28 weeks provided they satisfy the conditions.

After 28 weeks of SSP and/or Sickness Benefit (SB), Invalidity Benefit (IVB) was payable up to pension age for as long as the incapacity lasted. From pension age, IVB was paid at the person's State Pension rate, until entitlement ceased when SP was paid, or until deemed pension age (70 for a man, 65 for a woman). People who were on Sickness or Invalidity Benefit on 12 April 1995 were automatically transferred to Incapacity Benefit, payable on the same basis as before.

For people on Incapacity Benefit under State Pension age there are two short-term rates: the lower rate is paid for the first 28 weeks of sickness and the higher rate for weeks 29 to 52. From week 53 the Long Term rate Incapacity Benefit is payable. The Short Term rate Incapacity Benefit is based on State Pension entitlement for people over State Pension age and is paid for up to a year if incapacity began before pension age.

The long-term rate of Incapacity Benefit applies to people under State Pension age who have been sick for more than a year. People with a terminal illness, or who are receiving the higher rate care component of Disability Living Allowance, will get the Long Term rate. The Long Term rate is not paid for people over pension age.

Under Incapacity Benefit, for the first 28 weeks of incapacity, people previously in work will be assessed on the 'own occupation' test – the claimant's ability to do their own job. Otherwise, incapacity will be based on a personal capability assessment, which will assess ability to carry out a range of work-related activities. The test will apply after 28 weeks of incapacity or from the start of the claim for people who did not previously have a job. Certain people will be exempted from this test.

The tables exclude all men aged over 65 and women aged over 60 who are in receipt of State Pension, and all people over deemed pension age (70 for a man and 65 for a woman), members of the armed forces, mariners while at sea, and married women and certain widows who have chosen not to be insured for sickness benefit. The tables include a number of individuals who were unemployed prior to incapacity.

The Short Term (Higher) and Long Term rates of Incapacity Benefit are treated as taxable income. There were transitional provisions for people who were on Sickness or Invalidity Benefit on 12 April 1995. They were automatically transferred to Incapacity Benefit, payable on the same basis as before. Former IVB recipients continue to get Additional Pension entitlement, but frozen at 1994 levels. Also their IVB is not subject to tax. If they were over State Pension age on 12 April 1995 they may get Incapacity Benefit for up to five years beyond pension age.

Employment and Support Allowance (ESA) replaced Incapacity Benefit and Income Support paid on the grounds of incapacity for new claims from 27 October 2008. ESA consists of two phases. The first, the assessment phase rate, is paid for the first 13 weeks of the claim whilst a decision is made on the claimants capability through the 'Work Capability Asessment'. The second, or main phase begins after 14 weeks, but only if the 'Work Capability Assesment' has deemed the claimants illness or disability as a limitation on their ability to work.

Within the main phase there are two groups, 'The Work Related Activity Group' and 'The Support Group'. If a claimant is placed in the first, they are expected to take part in work focused interviews with a personal advisor. They will be given support to help them prepare for work and on gaining work will receive a work related activity component in addition to their basic rate. If the claimant is placed in the second group due to their illness or disability having a severe effect upon their ability to work, the claimant will not be expected to work at all, but can do so on a voluntary basis. These claimants will receive a support component in addition to their basic rate.

Child Benefits (Table 5.9a and 5.9b)

You get child benefit if you are responsible for a child under 16 (or under 20 if they stay in approved education or training.
Approved education
Education must be full-time (more than an average of 12 hours a week supervised study or course-related work experience) and can include:
A levels or similar - eg Pre-U, International Baccalaureate
Scottish Highers
NVQs and other vocational qualifications up to level 3
home education - if started before your child turned 16
traineeships in England
Courses are not approved if paid for by an employer or 'advanced', eg a university degree or BTEC Higher National Certificate.

Approved training
Approved training should be unpaid and can include:
Access to Apprenticeships in England
Foundation Apprenticeships or Traineeships in Wales
Employability Fund programmes or Get Ready for Work (if started before 1 April 2013) in Scotland
Training for Success, Pathways to Success or Collaboration and Innovation Programme in Northern Ireland
Courses that are part of a job contract are not approved.

Guardian's Allowance is an additional allowance for people bringing up a child because one or both of their parents has died. They must be getting Child Benefit (CB) for the child. The table shows the number of families in the UK in receipt of CB. The numbers shown in the table are estimates based on a random 5 per cent sample of awards current at 31 August, and are therefore subject to sampling error. The figures take no account of new claims, or revisions to claims that were received or processed after 31 August, even if they are backdated to start before 31 August.

Child and Working Tax Credits (New Tax Credits) (Table 5.10 and 5.11)

Child and Working Tax Credits (CTC and WTC) replaced Working Families' Tax Credit (WFTC) from 6th April 2003. CTC and WTC are claimed by individuals, or jointly by couples, whether or not they have children.

CTC provides support to families for the children (up to the 31 August after their 16th birthday) and the 'qualifying' young people (in full-time non-advanced education until their 20th birthday) for which they are responsible. It is paid in addition to CB.

WTC tops up the earnings of families on low or moderate incomes. People working for at least 16 hours a week can claim it if they: (a) are responsible for at least one child or qualifying young person, (b) have a disability which puts them at a disadvantage in getting a job or, (c) in the first year of work, having returned to work aged at least 50 after a period of at least six months receiving out-of-work benefits. Other adults also qualify if they are aged at least 25 and work for at least 30 hours a week.

Widow's Allowance and Bereavement Benefit (Table 5.12 and 5.13)

Widow's Allowance is payable to women widowed on or after 11 April 1988 and up to and including 8 April 2001. There are three types of Widow's Benefits: Widow's Payment, Widowed Mother's Allowance and Widow's Pension. Women widowed before 11 April 1988 continue to receive Widow's Benefit based on the rules that existed before that date. Bereavement Benefit was introduced on 9 April 2001 as a replacement for Widow's Benefit, payable to both men and women widowed on or after 9 April 2001. There are three types of Bereavement Benefits available: Bereavement Payment, Widowed Parent's Allowance and Bereavement Allowance.

5.1 National Insurance Fund (Great Britain and Northern Ireland)

Years ended 31 March

£ million

		2002 /03	2003 /04	2004 /05	2005 /06	2006 /07	2007 /08	2008 /09	2009 /10	2010 /11	2011 /12	2012 /13
Receipts												
Opening balance	KJFB	24177	27267	27816	29804	34940	39243	50288	53046	48457	43164[3]	38594
Contributions	JXVM	59658	59827	62863	67786	69599	77224	74453	73817	74182	78424	79120
State Scheme Premiums[1]	C59W	194	147	115	117	76	79	67	52	47	37	31
Grant from Consolidated Fund	KOTF	..	..	..	..	..	..	..	..	..	..	..
Compensation for SSP/SMP	KJQM	775	1346	1470	1392	1197	1919	1626	1684	2052	3009	2560
Transfers from Great Britian	KOTG	350	260	270	185	630	452	505	395	125	145	334
Income from investments	KJFE	1457	1292	1288	1399	1867	2453	1957	237	204	189	162
Other receipts	KJFF	80	82	72	66	54	57	50	49	47	46	36
Redundancy receipts	KIBQ	24	28	32	38	43	37	39	40	49	49	38
Total	JYJO	86716	90249	93926	100787	108406	121464	128985	129320	125163	125063	120876
Expenditure												
Total benefits	JYJP	54201	56255	58572	61304	63695	67443	70487	75410	77800	82358	87465
Jobseeker's Allowance (Contributory)	LUQW	519	512	455	497	493	435	703	1106	812	758	669
Incapacity	JYXL	7104	7116	6910	7028	7009	6945	6600	6177	5599	4981	3355
Maternity	KETY	70	128	153	128	180	250	320	343	343	367	396
Bereavement Benefits	KEWU	1142	1033	946	903	826	759	683	647	615	605	598
Guardian's allowances and Child's special allowance[2]	KJFK	2	2	1	2	2	2	2	2	2	2	2
State pensions	JYJV	45240	47339	49979	52578	55053	58921	61301	66442	69347	74111	80009
Other payments	KAAZ	27	34	30	33	40	61	97	126	149	150	164
Administration	KABE	1280	1794	1521	1464	1473	1430	1326	1401	1420	1125	917
Transfers to Northern Ireland	KABF	350	260	270	185	630	452	505	395	125	145	334
Redundancy payments	KIBR	255	243	222	295	248	215	428	531	446	407	454
Personal Pensions	C59X	3336	3847	3508	2566	3076	2557	2629	2623	2314	2139	2125
Total	JYJU	59449	62433	64123	65847	69161	72027	74594	79793	81172	84790	89023
Accumulated funds	KABH	27267	27816	29804	34940	39245	50288	53046	48457	42834[3]	38594	29083

1 State Scheme Premiums are payable in respect of employed persons who cease to be covered, in certain circumstances, by a contracted out pension scheme.
2 Includes Child's special allowance for Northern Ireland
3 opening balance has been restated based on analysis of prior year data as better management information has become available

Sources: HM Revenue and Customs
https://www.gov.uk/government/uploads/system/uploads/attachment_data/file/229082/1107.pdf
Department for Work and Pensions:01253 856123 Ext 62436

5.2 Persons[1] who paid National Insurance contributions[2,3] in a tax year:[4] by sex

Millions

United Kingdom

		Total					Men					Women			
		2005 /06	2006 /07	2007 /08	2008 /09		2005 /06	2006 /07	2007 /08	2008 /09		2005 /06	2006 /07	2007 /08	2008 /09
Total	KABI	29.02	28.91	28.98	29.39	KEYF	15.89	15.8	15.82	15.97	KEYP	13.13	13.08	13.17	13.42
Class 1	KABJ	24.5	24.5	24.77	25.21	KEYG	13.03	13.49	13.16	13.39	KEYQ	11.47	11.47	11.61	11.82
Not contracted out[5]	KABK	17.47	17.88	18.54	18.73	KEYH	9.69	9.64	10.35	10.43	KEYR	7.79	7.93	8.19	8.30
Contracted out	KABL	7.03	6.62	6.23	6.48	KEYI	3.35	3.34	2.81	2.96	KEYS	3.68	3.54	3.42	3.52
Mixed contracted in/out[6]	KABM	1.18	1.1	1.06	1.10	KEYJ	0.5	0.52	0.43	0.43	KEYT	0.68	0.63	0.63	0.67
Class 1 Reduced rate (including standard rate)	KABO	0.04	0.03	0.02	0.02	KEYL	–	–	–	–	KEYV	0.04	0.03	0.02	0.02
Class 2 exclusively[7]	KABP	2.38	2.4	2.36	2.32	KEYM	1.8	1.77	1.75	1.69	KEYW	0.59	0.6	0.62	0.63
Mixed Class 1 and Class 2	KABQ	0.71	0.7	0.7	0.69	KEYN	0.47	0.46	0.45	0.44	KEYX	0.24	0.25	0.25	0.26
Class 3 exclusively[8]	KABR	0.16	0.13	0.07	0.05	KEYO	0.07	0.06	0.03	0.02	KEYY	0.09	0.07	0.04	0.03
Mixed Class 1, 2 and 3[9]	I6CH	0.06	0.05	0.01	0.01	I6CK	0.02	0.02	–	–	I6CN	0.03	0.03	0.01	–

1 Based on all persons making contributions and not only if they have a qualifying year.
2 Estimates obtained from DWP Infor mation Directorate: Lifetime Labour Market Data Tabulation Tool which uses a 1% sample of the National Insurance Recording System (NIRS2) summer 2010 extract.
3 Components may not sum to totals as a result of rounding.
4 The tax year commences on 6 April and ends on 5 April the following year.

5 Includes those persons with an Appropriate Personal Pension (such persons pay contributions at the not contracted out rate but then receive a rebate paid directly to their scheme).
6 Not included in the above rows.
7 Persons who paid a mixture of Class 2 contributions and others are not included in this category.
8 Persons who paid a mixture of Class 3 contributions and others are not included in this category.
9 Persons with a mixture of class 1,2 or 3 contributions.
Source: HM:Revenue and Customs:020 7147 3045
Department for Work and Pensions;

Contributions and Qualifying Years People contributing (Thousands) : Contribution type by Gender

Time Series=APR2011

	Total	Gender	
		Female	Male
	People contributing (Thousands)	People contributing (Thousands)	People contributing (Thousands)
Total	**28,557**	**13,157**	**15,399**
Contribution type			
Class 1 only - Contracted In	**18,894**	8,331	10,562
Class 1 only - Contracted Out	**5,853**	3,336	2,517
Class 1 only - Contracted Out and In	**909**	560	349
Reduced Rate	**3**	3	
Class 1 and Class 2	**617**	243	375
Class 2 only	**2,264**	676	1,588
Class 3 only	**16**	8	-
Combinations of class 1 2 or 3	* 1	-	-
No contributions	-	-	-

DEFINITIONS AND CONVENTIONS: "*" Figures are subject to a high degree of sampling error and should only be used as a guide"-" Nil or Negligible; "." Not applicable.
Caseload figures are rounded to the nearest thousand and displayed in thousands. Totals may not sum due to rounding.
Figures for the two most up-to-date releases should be regarded as provisional and may be subject to changes in future releases.
As these statistics are taken from a 1% sample, they are subject to sampling variation. The Quality document at http://statistics.dwp.gov.uk/asd/index.php?page=stpp_cq contains details of indicative confidence intervals. SOURCE: DWP Information Governance and Security Directorate: Lifetime Labour Market Database (L2) 1% sample of the National Insurance Recording System (NIRS2)

2011 is the latest data available. Data issues with the Second Tier Pension Provision and Contributions and Qualifying Years tabulation tools for the financial year 2012 to 2013 resulted in DWP statisticians deciding to postpone the release of the statistics while investigations take place.

5.3 Main Features of National Insurance Contributions (NCIS) 1999-2000 to 2014-15

	Rate in 1999-2000	Rate in 2000-2001	Rate in 2001-2002	Rate in 2002-2003	Rate in 2003-2004	Rate in 2004-2005	Rate in 2005-2006	Rate in 2006-2007	Rate in 2007-2008	Rate in 2008-2009
Class 1										
Lower earnings limit (LEL) – a week	£66	£67	£72	£75	£77	£79	£82	£84	£87	£90
Primary threshold (PT) – a week	-	£76	£87	£89	£89	£91	£94	£97	£100	£105
Secondary threshold (ST) – a week	£83	£84	£87	£89	£89	£91	£94	£97	£100	£105
Upper accruals Point (UAP) – a week (1)	-	-	-	-	-	-	-	-	-	-
Upper earnings limit (UEL) – a week (2)	£500	£535	£575	£585	£595	£610	£630	£645	£670	£770
Primary contributions (employee)										
Main contribution rate (PT to UEL) (3)	10.0%	10.0%	10.0%	10.0%	11.0%	11.0%	11.0%	11.0%	11.0%	11.0%
Additional contribution rate (above UEL)	-	-	-	-	1.0%	1.0%	1.0%	1.0%	1.0%	1.0%
Contracted out rebate (LEL to UAP/UEL) (4) (5)	1.6%	1.6%	1.6%	1.6%	1.6%	1.6%	1.6%	1.6%	1.6%	1.6%
Reduced rate for married women and widow optants (6)	3.85%	3.85%	3.85%	3.85%	4.85%	4.85%	4.85%	4.85%	4.85%	4.85%
Secondary contributions (employer)										
Contribution rate (above ST)	12.2%	12.2%	11.9%	11.8%	12.8%	12.8%	12.8%	12.8%	12.8%	12.8%
Contracted out rebate (LEL to UAP/UEL) (5)										
- COSRS	3.0%	3.0%	3.0%	3.5%	3.5%	3.5%	3.5%	3.5%	3.7%	3.7%
- COMPS (7)	0.6%	0.6%	0.6%	1.0%	1.0%	1.0%	1.0%	1.0%	1.4%	1.4%
Class 1A and 1B										
Contribution rate (8)	12.2%	12.2%	11.9%	11.8%	12.8%	12.8%	12.8%	12.8%	12.8%	12.8%
Class 2										
Flat-rate contribution – a week	£6.55	£2.00	£2.00	£2.00	£2.00	£2.05	£2.10	£2.10	£2.20	£2.30
Small earnings exception – a year	£3,770	£3,825	£3,955	£4,025	£4,095	£4,215	£4,345	£4,465	£4,635	£4,825
Class 3										
Flat-rate contribution – a week (9)	£6.45	£6.55	£6.75	£6.85	£6.95	£7.15	£7.35	£7.55	£7.80	£8.10
Class 4										
Lower profits limit (LPL) – a year	£7,530	£4,385	£4,535	£4,615	£4,615	£4,745	£4,895	£5,035	£5,225	£5,435
Upper profits limit (UPL) – a year (2)	£26,000	£27,820	£29,900	£30,420	£30,940	£31,720	£32,760	£33,540	£34,840	£40,040
Main contribution rate (LPL to UPL)	6%	7%	7%	7%	8%	8%	8%	8%	8%	8%
Additional contribution rate (above UPL)	-	-	-	-	1%	1%	1%	1%	1%	1%

Source: HM Revenue and Customs.

5.3 Main Features of National Insurance Contributions (NCIS) 1999-2000 to 2014-15

	Rate in 2009-2010	Rate in 2010-11	Rate in 2011-12	Rate in 2012-13 (10)	Rate in 2013-14 (10)	Rate in 2014-15 (10)
Class 1						
Lower earnings limit (LEL) – a week	£95	£97	£102	£107	£109	£111
Primary threshold (PT) – a week	£110	£110	£139	£146	£149	£153
Secondary threshold (ST) – a week	£110	£110	£136	£144	£148	£153
Upper accruals Point (UAP) – a week (1)	£770	£770	£770	£770	£770	£770
Upper earnings limit (UEL) – a week (2)	£844	£844	£817	£817	£797	£805
Primary contributions (employee)						
Main contribution rate (PT to UEL) (3)	11.0%	11.0%	12.0%	12.0%	12.0%	12.0%
Additional contribution rate (above UEL)	1.0%	1.0%	2.0%	2.0%	2.0%	2.0%
Contracted out rebate (LEL to UAP/UEL) (4) (5)	1.6%	1.6%	1.6%	1.4%	1.4%	1.4%
Reduced rate for married women and widow optants (6)	4.85%	4.85%	5.85%	5.85%	5.85%	5.85%
Secondary contributions (employer)						
Contribution rate (above ST)	12.8%	12.8%	13.8%	13.8%	13.8%	13.8%
Contracted out rebate (LEL to UAP/UEL) (5)						
- COSRS	3.7%	3.7%	3.7%	3.4%	3.4%	3.4%
- COMPS (7)	1.4%	1.4%	1.4%	-	-	-
Class 1A and 1B						
Contribution rate (8)	12.8%	12.8%	13.8%	13.8%	13.8%	13.8%
Class 2						
Flat-rate contribution – a week	£2.40	£2.40	£2.50	£2.65	£2.70	£2.75
Small earnings exception – a year	£5,075	£5,075	£5,315	£5,595	£5,725	£5,885
Class 3						
Flat-rate contribution – a week (9)	£12.05	£12.05	£12.60	£13.25	£13.55	£13.90
Class 4						
Lower profits limit (LPL) – a year	£5,715	£5,715	£7,225	£7,605	£7,755	£7,956
Upper profits limit (UPL) – a year (2)	£43,875	£43,875	£42,475	£42,475	£41,450	£41,865
Main contribution rate (LPL to UPL)	8%	8%	9%	9%	9%	9%
Additional contribution rate (above UPL)	1%	1%	2%	2%	2%	2%

Source: HM Revenue and Customs

5.3 Main Features of National Insurance Contributions (NCIS) 1999-2000 to 2014-15

(1) The upper accruals point was introduced in April 2009.

(2) From April 2009 the upper earnings limit and upper profits limit were aligned to the income tax higher rate threshold.

(3) Between LEL and UEL for 1999-2000.

(4) For Appropriate Personal Pension Schemes (APPS) both employer and employee pay NICs at the full contracted-out rate and in the following tax year on submission of the end-of-year returns HMRC pay an age related rebate direct to the schemes. The employee's share of this rebate is 1.6%.

(5) Up to and including 2008-09, the rebate applies between the LEL and the UEL. From 2009-10 onwards the rebate applies between the LEL and UAP.

(6) Married women opting to pay contributions at the reduced rate earn no entitlement to contributory National Insurance benefits as a result of these contributions. No women have been allowed to exercise this option since 1977.

(7) For employers operating a COMPS, in addition to the reduction shown in secondary Class 1 contributions, in the following tax year on submission of end-of-year returns, HMRC pay an additional "top-up" rebate direct to the scheme. As with APPS, this rebate is age related. COMPs are abolished from 2012-13 onwards.

(8) From April 2000 the Class 1A liability for employers was extended from company cars and fuel to include other taxable benefits not already attracting a Class 1 liability. Class 1A and Class 1B contributions are paid in the year following accrual.

(9) Class 3 contribution rules changed in 2009-10 to allow those reaching state pension age before April 2015 with 20 qualifying years to purchase up to 6 additional years.

(10) From 2012-13 the default indexation assumption for NICs is CPI (excluding the secondary threshold).

Notes:

Class 1 National Insurance Contributions (NICs)

Class 1 NICs are earnings related contributions paid by employed earners who are below State Pension age and their employers. The contributions are paid at either the contracted-out rate or the not contracted-out rate. The contracted-out rate is payable only where the employee is a member of a contracted-out occupational scheme in place of State Second Pension (formerly SERPS). Class 1 NICs are collected by HMRC along with income tax under the Pay As You Earn (PAYE) scheme.

Class 1A National Insurance Contributions (NICs)

Class 1A NICs are paid only by employers on the value of most taxable benefits-in-kind provided to employees, such as private use of company cars and fuel, private medical insurance, accommodation and loan benefits. They do not give any benefit rights.

Class 1B National Insurance Contributions (NICs)

Class 1B NICs were introduced on 6 April 1999. Like Class 1A they are also paid only by employers and cover PAYE Settlement Agreements (PSA) under which employers agree to meet the income tax liability arising on a restricted range of benefits. Class 1B is payable on the value of the items included in the PSA that would otherwise attract a Class 1 or Class 1A liability and the value of the income tax met by the employer. They do not give any benefit rights.

Class 2 National Insurance Contributions (NICs)

Class 2 contributions are a flat rate weekly liability payable by all self-employed people over 16 (up to State Pension age) unless they have applied for and been granted a "small earnings exception" (SEE) because their earnings from self-employment are expected to be low, although they may still pay if they choose to. Class 2 NICs can be paid up to six years after the tax year in which they are due. Class 4 NICS may also have to be paid if their profits for the year are over the lower profits limit (see below).

Class 3 National Insurance Contributions (NICs)

Class 3 NICs may be paid voluntarily by people aged 16 and over (but below State Pension age) to help them qualify for State Pension and Bereavement Benefits if their contribution record would not otherwise be sufficient. Contributions are flat rate and can be paid up to six years after the year in which they are due.

Class 4 National Insurance Contributions (NICs)

Class 4 NICS are paid by the self-employed whose profits are above the lower profits limit. They are profit related and do not count for any benefits themselves.

5.4 The Department for Work and Pensions - Social Security Benefit Up-rating

Schedule of proposed benefit rates from April 2013

(Weekly rates unless otherwise shown)	RATES 2012	RATES 2013
ATTENDANCE ALLOWANCE		
higher rate	77.45	79.15
lower rate	51.85	53.00
BEREAVEMENT BENEFIT		
Bereavement payment (lump sum)	2000.00	2000.00
Widowed parent's allowance	105.95	108.30
Bereavement Allowance		
standard rate	105.95	108.30
age-related		
age 54	98.53	100.72
53	91.12	93.14
52	83.70	85.56
51	76.28	77.98
50	68.87	70.40
49	61.45	62.81
48	54.03	55.23
47	46.62	47.65
46	39.20	40.07
45	31.79	32.49

CAPITAL LIMITS - rules common to Income Support, income based Jobseeker's Allowance, income-related Employment and Support Allowance, Pension Credit, and Housing Benefit unless stated otherwise

upper limit	16000.00	16000.00
upper limit - Pension Credit guarantee credit and those getting HB/CTB and Pension Credit guarantee credit	No limit	No limit
Amount disregarded - all benefits except Pension Credit and Housing Benefit for those above the qualifying age for Guarantee Credit	6000.00	6000.00
Amount disregarded - Pension Credit and Housing Benefit for those above the qualifying age for Pension Credit	10000.00	10000.00
child disregard (not Pension Credit or Employment and Support Allowance)	3000.00	3000.00
amt disregarded (living in RC/NH)	10000.00	10000.00

Tariff income
    £1 for every £250, or part thereof, between the amount of
    capital disregarded and the capital upper limit

Tariff income - Pension Credit and HB/CTB where clmt/ptner is over Guarantee Credit qualifying age
    £1 for every £500, or part thereof, between the amount of
    capital disregarded and capital upper limit

5.4 The Department for Work and Pensions - Social Security Benefit Up-rating

Schedule of proposed benefit rates from April 2013

(Weekly rates unless otherwise shown)	RATES 2012	RATES 2013
CARER'S ALLOWANCE	58.45	59.75

DEDUCTIONS - rules common to Income Support, Jobseeker's Allowance, Employment and Support Allowance, Pension Credit and Housing Benefit unless stated otherwise

	RATES 2012	RATES 2013
Non-dependant deductions from housing benefit and from IS, JSA(IB), ESA(IR) and Pension Credit		
aged 25 and over in receipt of IS and JSA(IB), in receipt of main phase ESA(IR), aged 18 or over, not in remunerative work	11.45	13.60
aged 18 or over and in remunerative work		
- gross income: less than £124.00	11.45	13.60
- gross income: £124 to £182.99	26.25	31.25
- gross income: £183 to £237.99	36.10	42.90
- gross income: £238 to £315.99	59.05	70.20
- gross income: £316 to £393.99	67.25	79.95
- gross income: £394 and above	73.85	87.75
Deductions from housing benefit		
Service charges for fuel		
heating	25.50	25.60
hot water	2.95	2.95
lighting	2.05	2.05
cooking	2.95	2.95
Amount ineligible for meals		
three or more meals a day		
single claimant	25.30	25.85
each person in family aged 16 or over	25.30	25.85
each child under 16	12.80	13.10
less than three meals a day		
single claimant	16.85	17.20
each person in family aged 16 or over	16.85	17.20
each child under 16	8.45	8.65
breakfast only - claimant and each member of the family	3.10	3.15
Amount for personal expenses (not HB/CTB)	23.25	23.50
Third party deductions from IS, JSA(IB), ESA(IR) and Pension Credit for;		
arrears of housing, fuel and water costs council tax etc. and deductions for ELDS and ILS.	3.55	3.60
child support, contribution towards maintenance (CTM)		
standard deduction	7.10	7.20
lower deduction	3.55	3.60
arrears of Community Charge		
court order against claimant	3.55	3.60
court order against couple	5.60	5.65
fine or compensation order		

5.4 The Department for Work and Pensions - Social Security Benefit Up-rating

Schedule of proposed benefit rates from April 2013

(Weekly rates unless otherwise shown)	RATES 2012	RATES 2013
standard rate	5.00	5.00
lower rate	3.55	3.60
Maximum deduction rates for recovery of overpayments (not CTB/JSA(C)/ESA(C))		
ordinary overpayments	10.65	10.80
where claimant convicted of fraud	17.75	18.00
Deductions from JSA(C) and ESA (C)		
Arrears of Comm. Charge, Council Tax, fines & overpayment recovery		
Age 16 - 24	18.75	18.93
Age 25 +	23.66	23.90
Max. dedn for arrears of Child Maintenance (CTM)		
Age 16 - 24	18.75	18.93
Age 25 +	23.66	23.90

DEPENDENCY INCREASES

Adult dependency increases for spouse or person looking after after children - payable with;

	RATES 2012	RATES 2013
State Pension on own insurance (Cat A or B)	61.85	63.20
long term Incapacity Benefit	57.60	58.85
Severe Disablement Allowance	34.60	35.35
Carers Allowance	34.40	35.15
short-term Incapacity Benefit (over state pension age)	55.45	56.65
short-term Incapacity Benefit (under State Pension age)	44.85	45.85

	RATES 2012	RATES 2013
Child Dependency Increases - payable with; State Pension; Widowed Mothers/Parents Allowance; short-term Incapacity benefit - higher rate or over state pension age; long-term Incapacity Benefit; Carer's Allowance; Severe Disablement Allowance; Industrial Death Benefit (higher rate);	11.35	11.35
NB - The rate of child dependency increase is adjusted where it is payable for the eldest child for whom child benefit is also paid. The weekly rate in such cases is reduced by the difference (less £3.65) between the ChB rates for the eldest and subsequent children.	8.10	8.10

DISABILITY LIVING ALLOWANCE

	RATES 2012	RATES 2013
Care Component		
Highest	77.45	79.15
Middle	51.85	53.00
Lowest	20.55	21.00
Mobility Component		
Higher	54.05	55.25
Lower	20.55	21.00

5.4 The Department for Work and Pensions - Social Security Benefit Up-rating

Schedule of proposed benefit rates from April 2013

(Weekly rates unless otherwise shown)	RATES 2012	RATES 2013
DISREGARDS		
Housing Benefit		
Earnings disregards		
standard (single claimant)	5.00	5.00
couple	10.00	10.00
higher (special occupations/circumstances)	20.00	20.00
lone parent	25.00	25.00
childcare charges	175.00	175.00
childcare charges (2 or more children)	300.00	300.00
permitted work higher	97.50	99.50
permitted work lower	20.00	20.00
Other Income disregards		
adult maintenance disregard	15.00	15.00
war disablement pension and war widows pension	10.00	10.00
widowed mothers/parents allowance	15.00	15.00
Armed Forces Compensation Scheme	10.00	10.00
student loan	10.00	10.00
student's covenanted income	5.00	5.00
income from boarders (plus 50% of the balance)	20.00	20.00
additional earnings disregard	17.10	17.10
income from subtenants (£20 fixed from April 08)	20.00	20.00
Income Support, income-based Jobseeker's Allowance, income-related Employment and Support Allowance and Pension Credit		
Earnings disregards		
standard (single claimant)	5.00	5.00
couple	10.00	10.00
higher (special occupations/circumstances)	20.00	20.00
Other Income disregards		
war disablement pension and war widows pension	10.00	10.00
widowed mothers/parents allowance	10.00	10.00
Armed Forces Compensation Scheme	10.00	10.00
student loan (not Pension Credit)	10.00	10.00
student's covenanted income (not Pension Credit)	5.00	5.00
income from boarders (plus 50% of the balance)	20.00	20.00
income from subtenants (£20 fixed from April 08)	20.00	20.00
EARNINGS RULES		
Carers Allowance	100.00	100.00
Limit of earnings from councillor's allowance	97.50	99.50
Permitted work earnings limit - higher	97.50	99.50
- lower	20.00	20.00
Industrial injuries unemployability supplement permitted earnings level (annual amount)	5070.00	5174.00
Earnings level at which adult dependency (ADI) increases are affected with:		
short-term incap.benefit where claimant is (a) under state pension age	44.85	45.85

5.4 The Department for Work and Pensions - Social Security Benefit Up-rating

Schedule of proposed benefit rates from April 2013

(Weekly rates unless otherwise shown)	RATES 2012	RATES 2013
(b) over state pension age	55.45	56.65
state pension, long term incapacity benefit, severe disablement allowance, unemployability supplement - payable when dependant		
(a) is living with claimant	71.00	71.70
(b) still qualifies for the tapered earnings rule	45.09	45.09
Earnings level at which ADI is affected when dependent is not living with claimant;		
state pension,	61.85	63.20
long-term incapacity benefit,	57.60	58.85
unemployability supplement,	58.45	59.75
severe disablement allowance	34.60	35.35
Carers allowance	34.40	35.15
Earnings level at which child dependency increases are affected		
for first child	215.00	220.00
additional amount for each subsequent child	28.00	29.00
Pension income threshold for incapacity benefit	85.00	85.00
Pension income threshold for contributory Employment Support Allowance	85.00	85.00

EMPLOYMENT AND SUPPORT ALLOWANCE

	RATES 2012	RATES 2013
Personal Allowances		
Single		
under 25	56.25	56.80
25 or over	71.00	71.70
lone parent		
under 18	56.25	56.80
18 or over	71.00	71.70
couple		
both under 18	56.25	56.80
both under 18 with child	84.95	85.80
both under 18 (main phase)	71.00	71.70
both under 18 with child (main phase)	111.45	112.55
one 18 or over, one under 18 (certain conditions apply)	111.45	112.55
both over 18	111.45	112.55
claimant under 25, partner under 18	56.25	56.80
claimant 25 or over, partner under 18	71.00	71.70
claimant (main phase), partner under 18	71.00	71.70
Premiums		
enhanced disability		
single	14.80	15.15
couple	21.30	21.75
severe disability		

5.4 The Department for Work and Pensions - Social Security Benefit Up-rating

Schedule of proposed benefit rates from April 2013

(Weekly rates unless otherwise shown)	RATES 2012	RATES 2013
single	58.20	59.50
couple (lower rate)	58.20	59.50
couple (higher rate)	116.40	119.00
carer	32.60	33.30
pensioner		
single with WRAC	43.55	45.25
single with support component	37.65	38.90
single with no component	71.70	73.70
couple with WRAC	78.30	81.05
couple with support component	72.40	74.70
couple with no component	106.45	109.50
Components		
Work-related Activity	28.15	28.45
Support	34.05	34.80

HOUSING BENEFIT

Personal allowances		
single		
under 25	56.25	56.80
25 or over	71.00	71.70
entitled to main phase ESA	71.00	71.70
lone parent		
under 18	56.25	56.80
18 or over	71.00	71.70
entitled to main phase ESA	71.00	71.70
couple		
both under 18	84.95	85.80
one or both 18 or over	111.45	112.55
claimant entitled to main phase ESA	111.45	112.55
dependent children	64.99	65.62
pensioner		
single/lone parent has attained the qualifying age for Pension Credit but under 65.	142.70	145.40
couple – one or both has attained the qualifying age for Pension Credit but both under 65	217.90	222.05
single / lone parent - 65 and over	161.25	163.50
couple - one or both 65 and over	241.65	244.95
Premiums		
family	17.40	17.40
family (lone parent rate)	22.20	22.20
disability		
single	30.35	31.00

5.4 The Department for Work and Pensions - Social Security Benefit Up-rating

Schedule of proposed benefit rates from April 2013

(Weekly rates unless otherwise shown)	RATES 2012	RATES 2013
couple	43.25	44.20
enhanced disability		
single	14.80	15.15
disabled child	22.89	23.45
couple	21.30	21.75
severe disability		
single	58.20	59.50
couple (lower rate)	58.20	59.50
couple (higher rate)	116.40	119.00
disabled child	56.63	57.89
carer	32.60	33.30
ESA components		
work-related activity	28.15	28.45
support	34.05	34.80
INCAPACITY BENEFIT		
Long-term Incapacity Benefit	99.15	101.35
Short-term Incapacity Benefit (under state pension age)		
lower rate	74.80	76.45
higher rate	88.55	90.50
Short-term Incapacity Benefit (over state pension age)		
lower rate	95.15	97.25
higher rate	99.15	101.35
Increase of Long-term Incapacity Benefit for age		
higher rate	11.70	10.70
lower rate	5.90	6.00
Invalidity Allowance (Transitional)		
higher rate	11.70	10.70
middle rate	5.90	6.00
lower rate	5.90	6.00
INCOME SUPPORT		
Personal Allowances		
single		
under 25	56.25	56.80
25 or over	71.00	71.70
lone parent		
under 18	56.25	56.80
18 or over	71.00	71.70
couple		
both under 18	56.25	56.80
both under 18 - higher rate	84.95	85.80

5.4 The Department for Work and Pensions - Social Security Benefit Up-rating

Schedule of proposed benefit rates from April 2013

(Weekly rates unless otherwise shown)	RATES 2012	RATES 2013
one under 18, one under 25	56.25	56.80
one under 18, one 25 and over	71.00	71.70
both 18 or over	111.45	112.55
dependent children	64.99	65.62
Premiums		
family / lone parent	17.40	17.40
pensioner (applies to couples only)	106.45	109.50
disability		
single	30.35	31.00
couple	43.25	44.20
enhanced disability		
single	14.80	15.15
disabled child	22.89	23.45
couple	21.30	21.75
severe disability		
single	58.20	59.50
couple (lower rate)	58.20	59.50
couple (higher rate)	116.40	119.00
disabled child	56.63	57.89
carer	32.60	33.30
Relevant sum for strikers	38.00	39.00

INDUSTRIAL DEATH BENEFIT

Widow's pension		
higher rate	107.45	110.15
lower rate	32.24	33.05
Widower's pension	107.45	110.15

INDUSTRIAL INJURIES DISABLEMENT BENEFIT

Standard rate		
100%	158.10	161.60
90%	142.29	145.44
80%	126.48	129.28
70%	110.67	113.12
60%	94.86	96.96
50%	79.05	80.80
40%	63.24	64.64
30%	47.43	48.48
20%	31.62	32.32
Maximum life gratuity (lump sum)	10500.00	10730.00
Unemployability Supplement	97.75	99.90

5.4 The Department for Work and Pensions - Social Security Benefit Up-rating

Schedule of proposed benefit rates from April 2013

(Weekly rates unless otherwise shown)	RATES 2012	RATES 2013
increase for early incapacity		
higher rate	20.25	20.70
middle rate	13.00	13.30
lower rate	6.50	6.65
Maximum reduced earnings allowance	63.24	64.64
Maximum retirement allowance	15.81	16.16
Constant attendance allowance		
exceptional rate	126.60	129.40
intermediate rate	94.95	97.05
normal maximum rate	63.30	64.70
part-time rate	31.65	32.35
Exceptionally severe disablement allowance	63.30	64.70
JOBSEEKER'S ALLOWANCE		
Contribution based JSA - Personal rates		
under 25	56.25	56.80
25 or over	71.00	71.70
Income-based JSA - personal allowances		
under 25	56.25	56.80
25 or over	71.00	71.70
lone parent		
under 18	56.25	56.80
18 or over	71.00	71.70
couple		
both under 18	56.25	56.80
both under 18 - higher rate	84.95	85.80
one under 18, one under 25	56.25	56.80
one under 18, one 25 and over	71.00	71.70
both 18 or over	111.45	112.55
dependent children	64.99	65.62
Premiums		
family / lone parent	17.40	17.40
pensioner		
single	71.70	73.70
couple	106.45	109.50
disability		
single	30.35	31.00
couple	43.25	44.20
enhanced disability		
single	14.80	15.15
disabled child	22.89	23.45

5.4 The Department for Work and Pensions - Social Security Benefit Up-rating

Schedule of proposed benefit rates from April 2013

(Weekly rates unless otherwise shown)	RATES 2012	RATES 2013
couple	21.30	21.75
severe disability		
single	58.20	59.50
couple (lower rate)	58.20	59.50
couple (higher rate)	116.40	119.00
disabled child	56.63	57.89
carer	32.60	33.30
Prescribed sum for strikers	38.00	39.00
MATERNITY ALLOWANCE		
Standard rate	135.45	136.78
MA threshold	30.00	30.00
PENSION CREDIT		
Standard minimum guarantee		
single	142.70	145.40
couple	217.90	222.05
Additional amount for severe disability		
single	58.20	59.50
couple (one qualifies)	58.20	59.50
couple (both qualify)	116.40	119.00
Additional amount for carers	32.60	33.30
Savings credit		
threshold - single	111.80	115.30
threshold - couple	178.35	183.90
maximum - single	18.54	18.06
maximum - couple	23.73	22.89
Amount for claimant and first spouse in polygamous marriage	217.90	222.05
Additional amount for additional spouse	75.20	76.65
Non-State Pensions (for Pension Credit purposes)		
Statutory minimum increase to non-state pensions	Increase by	2.20%
SEVERE DISABLEMENT ALLOWANCE		
Basic rate	69.00	71.80
Age-related addition (from Dec 90)		
Higher rate	11.70	10.70
Middle rate	5.90	6.00
Lower rate	5.90	6.00

5.4 The Department for Work and Pensions - Social Security Benefit Up-rating

Schedule of proposed benefit rates from April 2013

(Weekly rates unless otherwise shown)	RATES 2012	RATES 2013
STATE PENSION		
Category A or B	107.45	110.15
Category B(lower) - spouse or civil partner's insurance	64.40	66.00
Category C or D - non-contributory	64.40	66.00
Additional pension	Increase by	2.20%
Increments to:-		
Basic pension	Increase by	2.20%
Additional pension	Increase by	2.20%
Graduated Retirement Benefit (GRB)	Increase by	2.20%
Inheritable lump sum	Increase by	2.20%
Contracted-out Deduction from AP in respect of pre-April 1988 contracted-out earnings	Nil	Nil
Contracted-out Deduction from AP in respect of contracted-out earnings from April 1988 to 1997	Increase by	2.20%
Graduated Retirement Benefit (unit)	0.1251	0.1279
Increase of long term incapacity for age	Increase by	2.20%
Addition at age 80	0.25	0.25
Increase of Long-term incapacity for age		
higher rate	20.25	20.70
lower rate	10.15	10.35
Invalidity Allowance (Transitional) for State Pension recipients		
higher rate	20.25	20.70
middle rate	13.00	13.30
lower rate	6.50	6.65
STATUTORY ADOPTION PAY		
Earnings threshold	107.00	109.00
Standard Rate	135.45	136.78
STATUTORY MATERNITY PAY		
Earnings threshold	107.00	109.00
Standard rate	135.45	136.78
STATUTORY PATERNITY PAY		
Earnings threshold	107.00	109.00
Standard Rate	135.45	136.78
Additional statutory paternity pay	135.45	136.78
STATUTORY SICK PAY		
Earnings threshold	107.00	109.00
Standard rate	85.85	86.70

5.4 The Department for Work and Pensions - Social Security Benefit Up-rating

Schedule of proposed benefit rates from April 2013

(Weekly rates unless otherwise shown)	RATES 2012	RATES 2013
WIDOW'S BENEFIT		
Widowed mother's allowance	105.95	108.30
Widow's pension		
standard rate	105.95	108.30
age-related		
age 54 (49)	98.53	100.72
53 (48)	91.12	93.14
52 (47)	83.70	85.56
51 (46)	76.28	77.98
50 (45)	68.87	70.40
49 (44)	61.45	62.81
48 (43)	54.03	55.23
47 (42)	46.62	47.65
46 (41)	39.20	40.07
45 (40)	31.79	32.49

Note: For deaths occurring before 11 April 1988
refer to age-points shown in brackets.

Source: Department for Work and Pensions

5.5 Number of persons claiming benefits: Caseloads by age group, thousands

	2002/03 Outturn	2003/04 Outturn	2004/05 Outturn	2005/06 Outturn	2006/07 Outturn	2007/08 Outturn	2008/09 Outturn	2009/10 Outturn	2010/11 Outturn	2011/12 Outturn	2012/13 Outturn
Benefits directed at Children											
Attendance Allowance (in payment)	-	-	-	-	-	-	-	-	-	-	-
Child Benefit & One Parent Benefit	7,042	-	-	-	-	-	-	-	-	-	-
number of children covered	12,622	-	-	-	-	-	-	-	-	-	-
Disability Living Allowance	258	270	279	286	292	300	310	322	331	339	350
of which in payment	258	270	279	286	292	300	310	322	331	339	350
of which entitlement without payment	-	-	-	-	-	-	-	-	-	-	-
Mobility Allowance	-	-	-	-	-	-	-	-	-	-	-
Benefits Directed at People of Working Age											
Armed Forces Independence Payment											
Attendance Allowance (in payment)	-	-	-	-	-	-	-	-	-	-	-
Bereavement Benefits	227	203	180	163	147	129	117	108	101	95	91
Carer's Allowance	433	455	467	475	485	496	519	550	584	615	650
of which in payment	-	386	407	422	432	442	462	491	523	558	595
of which entitlement without payment	-	69	60	53	52	54	57	59	61	57	55
Christmas Bonus - non-contributory	1,719	1,854	1,921	1,912	1,920	2,003	3,164	3,246	3,227	3,212	3,240
Council Tax Benefit	2,268	2,358	2,473	2,603	2,570	2,533	2,566	2,940	3,172	3,254	3,368
Disability Living Allowance	1,491	1,553	1,596	1,627	1,657	1,692	1,733	1,780	1,819	1,847	1,877
of which in payment	1,477	1,539	1,582	1,612	1,641	1,676	1,715	1,761	1,800	1,828	1,858
of which entitlement without payment	14	14	14	15	16	16	17	19	19	20	20
Disability Working Allowance	-	-	-	-	-	-	-	-	-	-	-
Employment and Support Allowance	-	-	-	-	-	-	136	391	579	811	1,365
of which contributory	-	-	-	-	-	-	59	145	199	262	364
of which contributory and income-based	-	-	-	-	-	-	6	22	38	59	103
of which income-based	-	-	-	-	-	-	56	168	275	424	784
of which credits only	-	-	-	-	-	-	16	56	67	65	114
Family Credit	-	-	-	-	-	-	-	-	-	-	-
Housing Benefit	2,194	2,267	2,387	2,495	2,518	2,527	2,625	2,981	3,224	3,356	3,502
Incapacity Benefit, Invalidity Benefit & Sickness Benefit	2,483	2,504	2,510	2,475	2,443	2,415	2,332	2,031	1,827	1,577	965
of which in payment	1,586	1,570	1,543	1,500	1,456	1,413	1,346	1,177	1,054	909	566
of which credits only	898	934	967	975	987	1,002	986	854	773	668	399
Income Support	2,213	2,218	2,187	2,142	2,135	2,117	2,087	1,935	1,803	1,619	1,254
Industrial Injuries Disablement Benefit	-	192	187	182	176	170	163	156	152	145	137
Jobseeker's Allowance	920	898	819	870	927	818	1,025	1,538	1,415	1,515	1,507
of which contributory	190	185	158	165	157	142	244	321	234	212	178
of which contributory and income-based	19	18	14	15	15	13	21	30	22	19	18
of which income-based	646	631	588	632	691	609	695	1,072	1,069	1,208	1,242
of which credits only	65	64	59	58	64	54	66	114	91	77	69
Maternity Allowance	15	22	26	29	27	44	54	56	54	57	60
Mobility Allowance	-	-	-	-	-	-	-	-	-	-	-
Personal Independence Payment											
of which in payment	-	-	-	-	-	-	-	-	-	-	-
of which entitlement without payment	-	-	-	-	-	-	-	-	-	-	-
Severe Disablement Allowance	289	274	260	246	234	221	210	200	191	184	177
Statutory Maternity Pay	86	104	137	154	154	197	248	253	274	273	276
Unemployment Benefit	-	-	-	-	-	-	-	-	-	-	-
Benefits Directed at Pensioners											
Attendance Allowance	1,510	1,547	1,589	1,629	1,666	1,700	1,737	1,776	1,782	1,756	1,710
of which in payment	1,304	1,343	1,400	1,445	1,489	1,528	1,568	1,607	1,619	1,597	1,553
of which entitlement without payment	206	204	189	184	177	172	169	169	163	160	158
Bereavement Benefits	29	27	26	23	21	19	14	11	11	11	11
Carer's Allowance	-	178	235	279	319	356	388	411	420	417	405
of which in payment	-	20	22	24	26	28	30	31	30	26	22
of which entitlement without payment	-	158	213	255	292	327	357	381	390	391	383
Christmas Bonus - contributory	12,002	12,232	12,302	12,387	12,586	12,728	11,754	12,123	12,239	12,335	12,346
Council Tax Benefit	2,357	2,335	2,442	2,426	2,510	2,535	2,592	2,631	2,633	2,620	2,544
Disability Living Allowance	741	784	826	864	903	949	991	1,031	1,055	1,066	1,079
of which in payment	736	779	821	859	897	942	984	1,023	1,046	1,057	1,070
of which entitlement without payment	5	5	5	5	6	6	7	8	9	9	9
Housing Benefit	1,612	1,546	1,554	1,491	1,503	1,509	1,541	1,566	1,574	1,576	1,551
Incapacity Benefit, Invalidity Benefit & Sickness Benefit	-	-	-	-	-	-	-	-	-	-	-
of which in payment	-	-	-	-	-	-	-	-	-	-	-
of which credits only	-	-	-	-	-	-	-	-	-	-	-
Industrial Injuries Disablement Benefit	-	150	153	156	159	171	172	176	182	185	187

5.5 Number of persons claiming benefits: Caseloads by age group, thousands

	2002/03 Outturn	2003/04 Outturn	2004/05 Outturn	2005/06 Outturn	2006/07 Outturn	2007/08 Outturn	2008/09 Outturn	2009/10 Outturn	2010/11 Outturn	2011/12 Outturn	2012/13 Outturn
Income Support	1,776	-	-	-	-	-	-	-	-	-	-
Mobility Allowance	-	-	-	-	-	-	-	-	-	-	-
Over-75 TV Licence	3,790	3,839	3,892	3,965	3,982	3,993	4,079	4,206	4,236	4,277	4,316
Pension Credit	-	1,979	2,594	2,700	2,729	2,732	2,724	2,736	2,718	2,649	2,505
Personal Independence Payment	-	-	-	-	-	-	-	-	-	-	-
of which in payment	-	-	-	-	-	-	-	-	-	-	-
of which entitlement without payment	-	-	-	-	-	-	-	-	-	-	-
State Pension	11,195	11,320	11,477	11,585	11,715	11,938	12,160	12,410	12,566	12,667	12,810
of which contributory	11,195	11,320	11,477	11,585	11,715	11,938	12,160	12,410	12,566	12,667	12,810
of which basic element	11,102	11,231	11,384	11,492	11,617	11,837	12,053	12,285	12,460	12,556	12,737
of which earnings-related element ("Additional Pension", "SERPS" or "S2P")	6,851	7,122	7,425	7,700	7,963	8,324	8,673	9,052	9,320	9,549	9,848
of which Graduated Retirement Benefit	8,961	9,117	9,296	9,439	9,594	9,842	10,087	10,358	10,563	10,702	10,874
of which lump sums (covering all contributory elements)	-	-	-	-	8	24	46	58	66	59	56
of which new State Pension Pension (excluding protected payments)											
of which new State Pension Protected Payments (including inherited elements)											
of which non-contributory ("Category D")	24	23	23	23	23	25	26	28	29	33	35
Severe Disablement Allowance	41	41	42	42	42	42	41	40	39	36	34
Winter Fuel Payments	11,358	11,486	11,430	11,555	11,750	12,123	12,421	12,681	12,783	12,686	12,683

Source: Department for Work and Pensions (DWP)

5.6 Jobseeker's Allowance[1,2,3] claimants: by benefit entitlement Great Britain

As at May

Thousands

All Persons		2002	2003	2004	2005	2006	2007	2008	2009	2010	2011	2012	2013 *
All with benefit - total	KXDX	790.4	797.9	699.6	728.3	812	730.8	718	1316.4	1237.3	1298.3	1377	1433
Contribution-based JSA only	KXDY	155.3	160.4	131	139.5	134.6	113.6	127.8	341.8	205.3	182.7	159.5	142.4
Contribution based JSA & income-based JSA	KXDZ	18.5	18.1	13.5	13.5	13	11.9	12.8	34.6	21.1	19.9	16.8	14.9
Income-based JSA only payment	KXEA	616.6	619.4	555.1	575.3	664.5	605.3	577.4	940	1010.9	1096	1201	1156
No benefit in payment	KXEB	87.0	87.9	77.8	72.4	83.9	76.4	69.9	126.6	117.3	105.8	107.2	119.4
Males													
All with benefit - total	KXED	606.2	605.6	527.2	545.3	606.8	537.8	529.9	978.9	890.9	879.8	930	938.4
Contribution-based JSA only	KXEE	110.8	114.1	93.8	99.5	95.8	79.6	90.6	248.7	143.4	118.9	103.5	94.1
Contribution based JSA & income-based JSA	KXEF	16.7	15.9	12.3	12.6	12	10.7	11.7	31.2	18.1	16.9	13.7	12.6
Income-based JSA only payment	KXEG	478.7	475.6	421.1	433.2	498.9	447.5	427.6	698.9	729.5	744	812.8	753
No benefit in payment	KXEH	59.5	60.3	52.7	49.8	56.6	51.7	46.7	88.8	82.2	69.3	71.6	78.7
Females													
All with benefit - total	KXEJ	184.2	192.3	172.4	182.9	205.3	193	188.1	337.6	346.4	418.4	447	494.3
Contribution-based JSA only	KXEK	44.5	46.3	37.2	40	38.7	34	37.2	93.1	61.9	63.7	56	48.3
Contribution based JSA & income-based JSA	KXEL	1.8	2.2	1.2	0.8	1	1.2	1.2	3.4	3.0	3	3.1	2.3
Income-based JSA only payment	KXEM	137.9	143.8	134	142.1	165.5	157.8	149.8	241.1	281.4	351.7	387.9	403
No benefit in payment	KXEN	27.5	27.6	25	22.6	27.2	24.8	23.2	37.7	35.1	36.5	35.5	40.7

Source: Department for Work and Pensions

1. Jobseeker's Allowance (JSA) has two routes of entry: contrbution-based which depends mainly upon national insurance contributions and income-based which depends mainly on a means test. Some claimants can qualify by either route. In practice they receive income-based JSA but have an under lying entitlement to the contribution-based element.

2 Figures are given at May each year and have been derived by applying 5% proportions to 100% totals taken from the DWP 100% Work and Pensions Longitudinal Study (WPLS).

3 Figures are rounded to the nearest hundred and quoted in thousands. They may not sum due to rounding.

* 5% sample data - DWP recommends that, where the detail is only available on the 5% sample data, the proportions derived should be applied to the overall 100% total for the benefit.

5.7 Employment and Support Allowance and Incapacity Benefit[1,2,3] claimants: by sex, age and duration of spell
Great Britain and Overseas (excluding Northern Ireland).

At end of May   Thousands

		2001	2002	2003	2004	2005	2006	2007	2008[4]	2009	2010	2011	2012	2013
Males														
All durations: All ages	KJJA	1512.24	1526.17	1525.02	1517.62	1492.38	1455.52	1428.65	1399.58	1419.43	1409.10	1358.24	1,312.25	1,252.36
Under 20	KJJB	11.33	21.79	21.81	22.04	21.45	19.95	18.66	17.25	18.09	17.33	15.6	15.66	15.90
20-29	KJJC	129.02	133.83	138.54	142.68	143.24	141.8	146.07	149.47	159.1	160.91	156.22	156.71	159.44
30-39	KJJD	245.71	250.79	254.3	253.32	245.61	233.7	224.29	215.51	215.95	213.57	201.58	195.39	189.43
40-49	KJJE	298.04	304.47	311.85	318.04	320.77	319.77	320.24	319.22	330.96	335.93	328.57	319.31	304.49
50-59	KJJF	482.18	478.01	472.03	463.37	451.93	439.54	418.26	404.76	405.59	403.61	391.96	384.28	369.52
60-64	KJJG	345.87	337.22	326.45	318.12	309.36	300.73	301.1	293.33	289.57	277.30	263.8	240.26	212.72
65 and over	KJJH	0.09	0.05	0.05	0.05	0.04	0.02	0.03	0.04	0.17	0.46	0.48	0.60	0.82
Unknown												0.04	0.03	0.03
Over six months: All ages	KJJI	1338.11	1346.8	1359.53	1359.08	1347.43	1323.2	1291.32	1266.8	1253.91	1251.24	1213.77	1,050.73	950.15
Under 20	KJJJ	3.52	6.91	13.4	13.78	13.51	12.85	11.7	10.9	10.42	10.50	9.29	9.46	9.50
20-29	KJJK	94.86	96.61	105.72	110.85	114.57	115.21	117.83	121.9	124.5	128.76	125.36	115.47	114.37
30-39	KJJL	207.75	213.19	217.05	217.81	213.91	205.36	195.22	188.25	182.41	180.52	170.92	145.09	139.67
40-49	KJJM	264.41	271.25	278.53	285.9	290.72	291.36	289.94	289.72	293.13	298.29	294.15	249.83	230.62
50-59	KJJN	439.78	438.55	434.04	427.06	418.6	409.46	387.76	374.75	368.48	367.26	360.03	311.58	278.75
60-64	KJJO	327.73	320.26	310.75	303.64	296.1	288.93	288.85	281.25	274.93	265.52	253.54	218.74	176.44
65 and over	KJJP	0.06	0.03	0.03	0.04	0.02	0.02	0.03	0.03	0.05	0.39	0.43	0.53	0.76
Unknown												0.04	0.03	0.03
Females														
All durations: All ages	KJJQ	908.03	944.44	969.44	990.84	998.2	994.33	988.93	982.33	998.74	1007.13	1026.38	1,037.34	1,033.19
Under 20	KJJR	13.68	21.51	21.49	21.48	20.51	18.92	17.86	16.79	15.68	14.54	13.05	13.01	13.26
20-29	KJJS	92.79	96.66	100.78	105.02	108.61	109.73	114.42	117.91	121.5	122.82	121.54	121.56	123.93
30-39	KJJT	172.04	175.37	177.7	177.91	173.45	167.36	162.39	156.95	156.85	157.74	157.34	155.59	156.43
40-49	KJJU	243.27	252.82	262.2	270.9	276.62	279.32	283.45	285.84	296.87	305.06	305.31	299.72	287.89
50-59	KJJV	386.21	398.06	407.24	415.52	418.99	418.99	410.8	404.82	407.82	406.97	401.12	397.31	381.70
60 and over	KJJW	0.04	0.03	0.03	0.02	0.02	0.02	0.02	0.02	0.02	0.01	27.98	50.13	69.96
Unknown												0.03	0.02	0.02
Over six months: All ages	KJJX	795.67	825.25	858.03	880.52	894.57	896.33	885.69	881.41	882.94	888.73	905.11	817.68	787.01
Under 20	KJJY	4.74	7.41	12.35	12.4	12.1	11.13	10.2	9.55	8.75	8.15	7.16	7.31	7.46
20-29	KJJZ	70.88	72.32	79.63	84.02	88.98	90.99	93.6	97.24	99.15	100.81	99.22	90.34	89.68
30-39	KJKA	148.19	151.59	154.19	154.95	152.48	148	142.28	137.59	134.9	134.29	131.11	116.57	116.53
40-49	KJKB	216.19	225.65	234.71	243.52	250.11	253.5	255.99	258.74	263.7	269.48	269.38	234.09	222.46
50-59	KJKC	355.64	368.25	377.12	385.61	390.88	392.69	383.6	378.27	376.43	375.99	371.76	322.89	293.82
60 and over	KJKD	0.04	0.03	0.03	0.02	0.02	0.02	0.02	0.02	0.02	0.02	26.45	46.46	57.03
Unknown												0.03	0.02	0.02
Unknown Gender														
All durations	EW44	0.62	0.54	0.44	0.31	0.26	0.15	0.13	0.11	0.23	3.86	-	-	-
Over 6 months	EW45	0.28	0.29	0.21	0.16	0.13	0.1	0.09	0.09	0.1	3.67	-	-	-

Source: Department for Work and Pensions Work and Pensions Longitudinal Study 100% data

Definitions and conventions. Caseload figures are rounded to the nearest ten and displayed in thousands. Totals may not sum due to rounding.
1 Figures are given at May each year.
2 Table includes Employment and Support Allowance and Incapacity Benefit ONLY claimants and not those claiming Severe Disablement Allowance (SDA).
3 From 27th October 2008, new claims to Incapacity Benefit can also be allocated, on incapacity grounds, to the newly introduced Employment and Support Allowance (ESA).
4 Due to rounding errors several figures have been revised for May 2008.
5 2011 figures provided by IGS in relation to FOI 2013-2248 therefore 'Unknown' categories are different to previous years but match IGS published information on IB and ESA

5.8 Attendance allowance - cases in payment[1]: Age and gender of claimant Great Britain

At May each year

Thousands

		2004	2005	2006	2007	2008	2009	2010	2011	2012	2013
Males: All ages	JT9Z	418.5	436.9	459.5	478.4	497.2	516.5	531.5	530.00	526.1	504.92
Unknown age	JTA2	–	–	–	–	–	–	–	0.02	0.02	0.02
65 - 69	JTA3	21.4	22	22.3	22.8	23.5	24.4	24.8	23.8	23.3	21.2
70 - 74	JTA4	59.8	61.6	64.2	66.8	70.2	73.7	74.9	71.9	68.8	63.6
75 - 79	JTA5	103.8	104.2	104.8	106.3	109.1	112.4	114.9	113.7	112.3	107.3
80 - 84	JTA6	121.7	125.3	130.4	133.1	135.4	137.8	139.9	137.6	135.3	130.0
85 - 89	JTA7	70.1	78.7	89.4	98.5	107.7	116	118.1	118.00	117.0	112.7
90 and over	JTA8	41.7	45.1	48.4	50.8	51.2	52.2	58.9	65.00	69.4	70.1
Females: All ages	JTA9	958.9	982.6	1006.2	1029.1	1049.5	1069.3	1082.8	1069.1	1047.5	997.9
Unknown age	JTB2	–	–	–	–	–	–	–	0.03	0.03	0.03
65 - 69	JTB3	27.3	27.7	28.3	28.4	29.1	30	30.3	28.7	27.2	23.8
70 - 74	JTB4	91.5	92	93.6	96.4	99.6	103.5	104.5	99.7	93.9	85.3
75 - 79	JTB5	190.9	189.1	186.8	185.8	186.7	188.4	188.4	182.2	176.5	166.3
80 - 84	JTB6	282.5	282	279.4	278.3	277.7	277.7	277.0	269.2	259.8	244.9
85 - 89	JTB7	204.7	221.4	241.6	259.3	276.7	290.9	286.6	279.8	271.7	258.8
90 and over	JTB8	162	170.4	176.4	180.9	179.6	178.8	196.0	209.6	218.5	218.7

1 Totals show the number of people in receipt of allowance, and exclude people
with entitlement where the payment has been suspended, for example if they are in hospital.

Sources: DWP Information, Governance and Security,
Work and Pensions Longitudinal Study

Caseload figures are rounded to the nearest ten

Thousands

5.9a: Families and children receiving Child Benefit, in each country and English Region, 2003 to 2013

Time Series	United Kingdom [1]	Great Britain	England and Wales	England	North East	North West	Yorkshire and the Humber	East Midlands	West Midlands	East	London	South East	South West	Wales	Scotland	Northern Ireland	Foreign and not known
				England													
Area Codes [2]	K02000001	K03000001	K04000001	E92000001	E12000001	E12000002	E12000003	E12000004	E12000005	E12000006	E12000007	E12000008	E12000009	W92000004	S92000003	N92000002	n/a
Number of families																	
August 2003	7,246,335	7,000,770	6,394,870	6,037,500	318,470	861,775	619,630	517,590	663,400	653,695	876,120	956,080	570,735	357,370	605,900	225,885	19,675
August 2004	7,296,495	7,055,160	6,448,355	6,087,500	317,515	863,070	622,065	520,870	667,175	660,390	894,090	965,480	576,845	360,855	606,805	226,850	14,485
August 2005	7,315,165	7,074,665	6,470,575	6,110,190	315,855	860,660	622,475	522,195	667,565	664,155	909,045	970,225	578,015	360,385	604,085	226,800	13,705
August 2006	7,413,475	7,129,720	6,528,205	6,168,010	316,665	864,650	626,740	527,105	672,220	671,850	926,055	981,015	581,705	360,195	601,515	230,140	53,615
August 2007	7,475,035	7,212,565	6,605,270	6,241,895	318,020	869,475	631,995	535,775	678,300	683,780	937,480	995,990	591,085	363,375	607,290	230,825	31,650
August 2008	7,582,990	7,320,990	6,708,080	6,341,345	319,815	876,795	640,670	543,350	686,910	696,485	964,180	1,013,595	599,550	366,735	612,910	233,830	28,165
August 2009	7,769,880	7,485,730	6,864,935	6,492,290	324,525	892,240	653,645	554,925	701,070	713,455	1,002,815	1,038,010	611,600	372,650	620,795	238,605	45,545
August 2010	7,841,675	7,557,305	6,935,695	6,562,705	324,265	894,940	657,700	559,645	705,640	723,030	1,028,265	1,051,885	617,340	372,985	621,615	240,985	43,385
August 2011	7,884,760	7,600,115	6,979,465	6,606,285	323,155	895,670	659,240	561,885	708,325	730,180	1,044,355	1,061,870	621,605	373,180	620,650	242,310	42,335
August 2012	7,920,495	7,641,575	7,022,780	6,650,070	321,310	895,845	661,370	564,385	711,110	737,485	1,061,620	1,071,795	625,145	372,705	618,795	243,185	35,735
August 2013	7,550,265	7,279,100	6,691,985	6,328,460	311,725	868,775	643,560	545,720	692,110	690,410	996,490	979,075	600,590	363,525	587,115	239,125	32,040
Number of children																	
August 2003	13,138,075	12,670,975	11,625,050	10,983,290	552,970	1,549,900	1,116,630	934,450	1,219,985	1,200,175	1,613,235	1,754,585	1,041,360	641,755	1,045,925	439,870	27,230
August 2004	13,096,760	12,635,505	11,600,380	10,960,280	544,840	1,534,595	1,109,155	930,920	1,214,695	1,200,175	1,632,425	1,752,995	1,040,475	640,100	1,035,125	435,690	25,565
August 2005	13,111,665	12,654,135	11,626,490	10,988,765	540,940	1,528,255	1,109,150	932,310	1,215,315	1,204,750	1,658,755	1,758,520	1,040,780	637,725	1,027,640	431,995	25,535
August 2006	13,233,320	12,706,365	11,685,995	11,050,975	540,980	1,529,585	1,113,190	936,980	1,219,915	1,212,530	1,686,375	1,768,965	1,042,445	635,020	1,020,370	435,485	91,475
August 2007	13,267,355	12,778,460	11,754,415	11,117,770	540,610	1,529,060	1,117,760	946,090	1,225,025	1,225,485	1,699,215	1,782,530	1,052,000	636,645	1,024,045	433,370	55,525
August 2008	13,340,565	12,857,555	11,831,255	11,194,420	539,840	1,528,890	1,124,420	951,000	1,231,190	1,235,400	1,732,120	1,795,225	1,056,340	636,835	1,026,300	434,390	48,625
August 2009	13,604,375	13,088,240	12,054,140	11,409,950	546,125	1,549,625	1,143,245	967,010	1,251,900	1,258,520	1,794,220	1,827,530	1,071,775	644,190	1,034,095	440,570	75,565
August 2010	13,685,250	13,170,155	12,138,365	11,495,395	544,775	1,551,080	1,147,440	971,690	1,257,180	1,269,870	1,831,965	1,843,465	1,077,930	642,965	1,031,795	443,110	71,985
August 2011	13,721,160	13,207,465	12,179,715	11,537,505	542,680	1,549,475	1,148,450	973,310	1,259,770	1,276,525	1,853,670	1,852,950	1,080,680	642,210	1,027,750	444,285	69,410
August 2012	13,771,635	13,267,355	12,243,960	11,602,370	540,060	1,550,880	1,153,480	976,870	1,265,765	1,284,980	1,880,560	1,865,335	1,084,435	641,590	1,023,390	445,220	59,055
August 2013	13,107,460	12,618,675	11,651,810	11,026,465	525,215	1,505,780	1,124,295	943,980	1,233,780	1,198,215	1,763,895	1,693,670	1,037,630	625,345	966,865	437,440	51,345

Source: HM Revenue and Customs

Footnotes

[1] Includes Foreign and not known

[2] Area codes implemented from 1 January 2011; in line with the new GSS Coding and Naming policy.

5.9b Families receiving Child Benefit nationally, in each country and English Region, August 2013

Area names	Area Codes [1]	Number of families, by size						Number of children in these families, by age				
		Total	One child	Two children	Three children	Four children	Five or more children	Total	Under 5	5-10	11-15	16 and over
United Kingdom [2]	K02000001	7,550,265	3,615,465	2,760,290	853,760	234,045	86,700	13,107,460	3,686,230	4,197,945	3,334,055	1,889,230
Great Britain	K03000001	7,279,100	3,492,780	2,662,850	816,295	223,625	83,550	12,618,675	3,550,910	4,045,795	3,210,990	1,810,975
England and Wales	K04000001	6,691,985	3,189,745	2,452,780	758,885	210,680	79,895	11,651,810	3,283,025	3,731,520	2,951,485	1,685,780
England	E92000001	6,328,460	3,014,125	2,319,485	718,390	200,205	76,250	11,026,465	3,113,370	3,534,560	2,789,195	1,589,340
North East	E12000001	311,725	157,415	110,905	32,065	8,325	3,010	525,215	145,400	166,955	133,965	78,890
North West	E12000002	868,775	423,585	308,715	97,500	27,870	11,105	1,505,780	420,280	480,735	381,870	222,890
Yorkshire and the Humber	E12000003	643,560	307,545	233,080	72,835	21,805	8,295	1,124,295	318,760	360,110	283,525	161,895
East Midlands	E12000004	545,720	260,290	203,395	59,915	16,095	6,030	943,980	263,840	300,520	242,400	137,225
West Midlands	E12000005	692,110	324,405	247,560	82,870	26,115	11,160	1,233,780	345,955	395,235	313,005	179,585
East	E12000006	690,410	321,380	265,035	78,025	19,740	6,230	1,198,215	335,610	382,305	306,650	173,650
London	E12000007	996,490	482,290	340,525	120,655	36,425	16,595	1,763,895	521,110	579,850	426,220	236,715
South East	E12000008	979,075	456,495	378,070	108,730	27,325	8,455	1,693,670	474,625	542,295	433,190	243,565
South West	E12000009	600,590	280,725	232,195	65,795	16,505	5,370	1,037,630	287,790	326,550	268,370	154,920
Wales	W92000004	363,525	175,615	133,300	40,490	10,475	3,645	625,345	169,655	196,960	162,290	96,440
Scotland	S92000003	587,115	303,035	210,065	57,410	12,945	3,655	966,865	267,880	314,275	259,510	125,195
Northern Ireland	N92000002	239,125	104,975	86,725	34,670	9,785	2,970	437,440	120,260	135,770	110,790	70,620
Foreign and not known	n/a	32,040	17,710	10,715	2,795	640	180	51,345	15,060	16,375	12,270	7,635

Source: HM Revenue and Customs

Footnotes

[1] Area codes implemented from 1 January 2011; in line with the new GSS Coding and Naming policy.

[2] Includes Foreign and not known.

5.10 Child Tax Credit or Working Tax Credit elements and thresholds

Annual rate (£), except where specified

	2003-04	2004-05	2005-06	2006-07	2007-08	2008-09	2009-10	2010-11	2011-12	2012-13	2013-14
Child Tax Credit											
Family element	545	545	545	545	545	545	545	545	545	545	545
Family element, baby addition[1]	545	545	545	545	545	545	545	545	-	-	-
Child element[2]	1,445	1,625	1,690	1,765	1,845	2,085	2,235	2,300	2,555	2,690	2,720
Disabled child additional element[3]	2,155	2,215	2,285	2,350	2,440	2,540	2,670	2,715	2,800	2,950	3,015
Severely disabled child additional element[4]	865	890	920	945	980	1,020	1,075	1,095	1,130	1,190	1,220
Working Tax Credit											
Basic element	1,525	1,570	1,620	1,665	1,730	1,800	1,890	1,920	1,920	1,920	1,920
Couples and lone parent element	1,500	1,545	1,595	1,640	1,700	1,770	1,860	1,890	1,950	1,950	1,970
30 hour element[5]	620	640	660	680	705	735	775	790	790	790	790
Disabled worker element	2,040	2,100	2,165	2,225	2,310	2,405	2,530	2,570	2,650	2,790	2,855
Severely disabled adult element	865	890	920	945	980	1,020	1,075	1,095	1,130	1,190	1,220
50+ return to work payment[6]											
16 but less than 30 hours per week	1,045	1,075	1,110	1,140	1,185	1,235	1,300	1,320	1,365	-	-
at least 30 hours per week	1,565	1,610	1,660	1,705	1,770	1,840	1,935	1,965	2,030	-	-
Childcare element											
Maximum eligible costs allowed (£ per week)											
Eligible costs incurred for 1 child	135	135	175	175	175	175	175	175	175	175	175
Eligible costs incurred for 2+ children	200	200	300	300	300	300	300	300	300	300	300
Percentage of eligible costs covered	*70%*	*70%*	*70%*	*80%*	*80%*	*80%*	*80%*	*80%*	*70%*	*70%*	*70%*
Common features											
First income threshold[7]	5,060	5,060	5,220	5,220	5,220	6,420	6,420	6,420	6,420	6,420	6,420
First withdrawal rate	*37%*	*37%*	*37%*	*37%*	*37%*	*39%*	*39%*	*39%*	*41%*	*41%*	*41%*
Second income threshold[8]	50,000	50,000	50,000	50,000	50,000	50,000	50,000	50,000	40,000	-	-
Second withdrawal rate	*1 in 15*	*1 in 15*	*1 in 15*	*1 in 15*	*1 in 15*	*1 in 15*	*1 in 15*	*1 in 15*	*41%*	-	-
First income threshold for those entitled to Child Tax Credit only[9]	13,230	13,480	13,910	14,155	14,495	15,575	16,040	16,190	15,860	15,860	15,910
Income increase disregard	2,500	2,500	2,500	25,000	25,000	25,000	25,000	25,000	10,000	10,000	5,000
Income fall disregard[10]										2,500	2,500
Minimum award payable	26	26	26	26	26	26	26	26	26	26	26

Source: HM Revenue and Customs

[1] Payable to families for any period during which they have one or more children aged under 1. Abolished 6 April 2011.

[2] Payable for each child up to 31 August after their 16th birthday, and for each young person for any period in which they are aged under 20 (under 19 to 2005-06) and in full-time non-advanced education, or under 19 and in their first 20 weeks of registration with the Careers service or Connexions.

[3] Payable in addition to the child element for each disabled child.

[4] Payable in addition to the disabled child element for each severely disabled child.

[5] Payable for any period during which normal hours worked (for a couple, summed over the two partners) is at least 30 per week.

[6] Payable for each qualifying adult for the first 12 months following a return to work. Abolished 6 April 2012.

[7] Income is net of pension contributions, and excludes Child Benefit, Housing benefit, Council tax benefit, maintenance and the first £300 of family income other than from work or benefits. The award is reduced by the excess of income over the first threshold, multiplied by the first withdrawal rate.

[8] For those entitled to the Child Tax Credit, the award is reduced only down to the family element, plus the baby addition where relevant, less the excess of income over the second threshold multiplied by the second withdrawal rate. Abolished 6 April 2012.

[9] Those also receiving Income Support, income-based Jobseeker's Allowance or Pension Credit are passported to maximum CTC with no tapering.

[10] Introduced from 6 April 2012, this drop in income is disregarded in the calculation of Tax Credit awards.

5.11: Number of families and children with Child Tax Credit or Working Tax Credit, by level of award[3]

Thousands

	Area Codes[1]	Total out-of-work families	In-work families With children Receiving WTC and CTC	In-work families With children Receiving CTC only	Of which, lone parents	With no children Receiving WTC only	Total in receipt (out-of-work and in-work families)	Number of children in recipient families Total out-of-work families	In-work families Receiving WTC and CTC	In-work families Receiving CTC only
United Kingdom[2]	K02000001	1397	1780	838	1134	512	4,528	2,663	3218	1706
Great Britain	K03000001	1335	1718	806	1093	491	4,350	2,546	3107	1636
England and Wales	K04000001	1229	1586	743	993	441	3,999	2,359	2892	1512
England	E92000001	1155	1497	698	935	410	3,761	2,220	2736	1422
North East	E12000001	67	78	34	52	30	209	125	133	67
North West	E12000002	173	230	95	146	75	573	329	416	190
Yorkshire and the Humber	E12000003	124	171	77	99	53	425	241	315	154
East Midlands	E12000004	92	131	70	81	40	333	178	234	141
West Midlands	E12000005	139	175	82	100	47	443	277	331	168
East	E12000006	108	142	79	91	34	363	206	255	163
London	E12000007	225	246	80	152	47	597	432	475	163
South East	E12000008	140	189	102	127	43	474	267	338	212
South West	E12000009	88	135	79	85	42	344	165	238	164
Wales	W92000004	74	89	44	58	30	238	139	156	89
Scotland	S92000003	107	131	63	100	50	352	187	214	125
Northern Ireland	N92000002	52	59	30	39	19	160	98	105	64
Foreign and not known	n/a	9	1	2	1	1	12	17	2	4

Footnotes

[1] Area codes implemented from 1 January 2011 in line with the new GSS Coding and Naming policy.

[2] Includes Foreign and not known

[3] All figures are rounded to the nearest integer therefore not all totals may exactly equal the sums of their respective components.

Source: HM Revenue and Customs

5.12 Widows' Allowance (excluding bereavement payment[1,2,3]): by type of benefit Great Britain

Number in receipt of widows benefit as at May each year

Thousands

		2005	2006	2007	2008	2009	2010	2011	2012	2013
All Widows' Benefit (excluding bereavement allowance)										
All ages	KJGA	139	117.7	96.89	77.9	62.14	50.75	44	38	33
Unknown Age	EW4O	–	–	0.02	–	–	–	–	–	–
18 - 24	EW4P	–	–	–	–	–	–	–	–	–
25 - 29	EW4Q	0.1	0.1	0.04	0.02	0.01	–	–	–	–
30 - 34	EW4R	0.8	0.5	0.32	0.2	0.13	0.08	0.05	0.02	0.01
35 - 39	EW4S	2.9	2.1	1.53	1.08	0.74	0.50	0.34	0.22	0.14
40 - 44	EW4T	6.1	4.9	3.93	3.04	2.31	1.72	1.22	0.84	0.59
45 - 49	EW4U	11	9.1	7.58	6.26	5.14	4.20	3.38	2.71	2.07
50 - 54	EW4V	26.9	21.8	17.69	14.42	11.72	9.76	8.09	6.77	5.60
55 - 59	EW4W	66.9	57.3	45.78	36.86	30.37	24.62	20.00	16.31	13.26
60 - 64	EW4X	24.3	21.8	20.01	16.01	11.71	9.86	10.93	11.13	11.24
Widowed parents' allowance - with dependant children										
All ages	KJGG	23.2	19	15.6	12.6	9.98	7.91	6.11	4.61	3.35
Unknown Age	EW4Y	–	–	–	–	–	–	–	–	–
18 - 24	EW4Z	–	–	–	–	–	–	–	–	–
25 - 29	EW52	0.1	0.1	0.03	0.02	0.01	–	–	–	–
30 - 34	EW53	0.8	0.5	0.31	0.19	0.12	0.07	0.04	0.02	0.01
35 - 39	EW54	2.8	2.1	1.49	1.05	0.72	0.49	0.32	0.21	0.13
40 - 44	EW55	5.7	4.6	3.75	2.92	2.23	1.65	1.18	0.80	0.57
45 - 49	EW56	6.7	5.6	4.71	3.87	3.13	2.61	2.04	1.56	1.12
50 - 54	EW57	4.8	4.1	3.58	3.1	2.53	2.08	1.68	1.32	1.00
55 - 59	EW58	2	1.8	1.57	1.33	1.13	0.92	0.75	0.62	0.45
60 - 64	EW59	0.3	0.2	0.17	0.13	0.1	0.09	0.09	0.08	0.07
Widowed parents' allowance - without dependant children										
All ages	KJGM	1.1	0.8	0.69	0.54	0.46	0.39	0.28	0.22	0.17
Unknown Age	EW5A	–	–	–	–	–	–	–	–	–
18 - 24	EW5B	–	–	–	–	–	–	–	–	–
25 - 29	EW5C	–	–	–	–	–	–	–	–	–
30 - 34	EW5D	–	–	0.01	0.01	0.01	0.01	–	–	–
35 - 39	EW5E	0.1	0.1	0.04	0.03	0.02	0.02	0.01	0.01	0.01
40 - 44	EW5F	0.2	0.2	0.13	0.09	0.07	0.06	0.04	0.03	0.02
45 - 49	EW5G	0.3	0.2	0.21	0.17	0.15	0.12	0.09	0.07	0.05
50 - 54	EW5H	0.3	0.2	0.17	0.13	0.13	0.12	0.08	0.06	0.05
55 - 59	EW5I	0.2	0.1	0.11	0.1	0.07	0.06	0.04	0.04	0.02
60 - 64	EW5J	–	–	0.02	0.01	0.01	0.01	0.01	0.01	0.01
Age-related bereavement allowance										
All ages	KJGS	96.6	84	70.13	57.37	46.58	38.55	34.2	30.16	26.7
Unknown Age	EW5K	–	–	0.01	–	–	–	–	–	–
18 - 24	EW5L	–	–	–	–	–	–	–	–	–
25 - 29	EW5M	–	–	–	–	–	–	–	–	–
30 - 34	EW5N	–	–	–	–	–	–	–	–	–
35 - 39	EW5O	–	–	–	–	–	–	–	–	–
40 - 44	EW5P	0.2	0.1	0.06	0.03	0.01	–	–	–	–
45 - 49	EW5Q	4	3.3	2.66	2.23	1.86	1.47	1.24	1.08	0.90
50 - 54	EW5R	21.4	17.2	13.75	11.08	9.01	7.55	6.32	5.39	4.55
55 - 59	EW5S	59	50.9	40.57	32.61	26.83	21.74	17.71	14.44	11.80
60 - 64	EW5T	12	12.5	13.08	11.42	8.87	7.78	6.92	9.25	9.47
Bereavement allowance (Not age related)										
All ages	KJGW	18.1	13.9	10.47	7.39	5.12	3.90	3.41	3.02	2.67
Unknown Age	EW5U	–	–	–	–	–	–	–	–	–
18 - 24	EW5V	–	–	–	–	–	–	–	–	–
25 - 29	EW5W	–	–	–	–	–	–	–	–	–
30 - 34	EW5X	–	–	–	–	–	–	–	–	–
35 - 39	EW5Y	–	–	–	–	–	–	–	–	–
40 - 44	EW5Z	–	–	–	–	–	–	–	–	–
45 - 49	EW62	–	–	–	–	–	–	–	–	–
50 - 54	EW63	0.5	0.3	0.2	0.11	0.05	0.01	0.01	–	–
55 - 59	EW64	5.6	4.4	3.53	2.82	2.33	1.90	1.5	1.22	0.99
60 - 64	EW65	12	9.1	6.74	4.45	2.74	1.98	1.91	1.79	1.69

Sources: DWP Information, Governance and Security, Work and Pensions Longitudinal Study.

1 "-" Nil or Negligible; "." Not applicable; Caseload figures are rounded to the nearest ten; Some additional disclosure control has also been applied. Average amounts are shown as pounds per week and rounded to the nearest penny. Totals may not sum due to rounding.
2 Caseload (Thousands) All Claimants of Widows Benefit are female. No new claims for WA have been accepted since April 2001 when it was replaced by Bereavement Allowance
3 Figures include overseas cases.

STATE PENSION AGE: The age at which women reach State Pension age is gradually increasing from 60 to 65 between April 2010 and April 2016 to November 2018. Under current legislation, State Pension age for men and women is planned to increase to: 66 between November 2018 and October 2020; 67 between 2034 and 2036; 68 between 2044 and 2046. This will introduce a small increase to the number of working age benefit recipients and a small reduction to the number of pension age recipients. Figures from May 2010 onwards reflect this change. For more information see http://statistics.dwp.gov.uk/asd/espa.pdf.

5.13 Bereavement Allowance[1,2] (excluding bereavement payment): by sex, type of benefit and age of widow/er Great Britain.

Thousands

		Males						Females				
		2009	2010	2011	2012	2013		2009	2010	2011	2012	2013
All Bereavement Benefit (excluding bereavement allowance)												
All ages	WLSX	18.6	18.67	18.59	18.78	18.76	WLTC	43.32	44.64	46.18	47.40	48.79
18 - 24	EVW9	-	-	-	.	.	EVY2	0.06	0.04	0.05	0.05	0.04
25 - 29	EVX2	0.06	0.05	0.06	0.05	0.04	EVY3	0.53	0.52	0.48	0.47	0.48
30 - 34	EVX3	0.25	0.26	0.24	0.25	0.26	EVY4	1.68	1.71	1.67	1.69	1.78
35 - 39	EVX4	1.06	0.99	0.88	0.84	0.79	EVY5	4.3	4.27	4.01	3.86	3.82
40 - 44	EVX5	2.47	2.32	2.13	2.15	2.10	EVY6	7.61	7.74	7.77	7.76	7.67
45 - 49	EVX6	3.92	3.98	4.00	3.92	3.81	EVY7	10.22	10.78	11.09	11.30	11.17
50 - 54	EVX7	3.68	3.77	3.82	3.97	4.10	EVY8	9.64	10.3	10.58	10.76	10.94
55 - 59	EVX8	3.38	3.42	3.41	3.53	3.57	EVY9	9.28	9.18	9.38	9.51	9.79
60 - 64	EVX9	3.77	3.87	4.05	4.08	4.08	EVZ2	-	0.11	1.15	1.99	3.11
Widowed parents' allowance - with dependant children												
All ages	WLUD	11.81	11.78	11.58	11.68	11.64	WLUH	31.08	32.47	33.27	33.90	34.30
18 - 24	EVZ3	-	-	-	.	.	EW24	0.06	0.04	0.05	0.05	0.04
25 - 29	EVZ4	0.06	0.05	0.06	0.05	0.04	EW25	0.53	0.52	0.48	0.46	0.47
30 - 34	EVZ5	0.25	0.26	0.24	0.25	0.26	EW26	1.66	1.7	1.66	1.68	1.76
35 - 39	EVZ6	1.06	0.99	0.88	0.84	0.79	EW27	4.26	4.24	3.98	3.85	3.81
40 - 44	EVZ7	2.46	2.31	2.12	2.15	2.09	EW28	7.54	7.69	0.73	7.73	7.64
45 - 49	EVZ8	3.39	3.47	3.51	3.41	3.33	EW29	8.7	9.22	9.56	9.81	9.81
50 - 54	EVZ9	2.62	2.67	2.7	2.86	2.97	EW2A	5.97	6.58	6.97	7.12	7.31
55 - 59	EW22	1.38	1.42	1.45	1.46	1.49	EW2B	2.36	2.47	2.69	2.93	3.09
60 - 64	EW23	0.59	0.61	0.63	0.66	0.65	EW2C	-	0.01	0.14	0.25	0.37
Widowed parents' allowance - without dependant children												
All ages	WLVK	0.04	0.04	0.03	0.03	0.02	WMMR	0.28	0.25	0.21	0.18	0.16
18 - 24	EW2D	-	-	-	.	.	EW2M	-	-	-	.	.
25 - 29	EW2E	-	-	-	.	.	EW2N	0.01	-	-	.	.
30 - 34	EW2F	-	-	-	.	.	EW2O	0.02	0.01	0.01	0.01	0.01
35 - 39	EW2G	-	-	-	.	.	EW2P	0.04	0.03	0.02	0.01	0.01
40 - 44	EW2H	0.01	0.01	0.01	0.01	0.01	EW2Q	0.06	0.05	0.04	0.04	0.03
45 - 49	EW2I	0.01	0.01	0.01	0.01	0.01	EW2R	0.08	0.07	0.06	0.06	0.05
50 - 54	EW2J	0.01	0.01	0.01	.	.	EW2S	0.05	0.04	0.05	0.04	0.04
55 - 59	EW2K	0.01	0.01	0.01	.	.	EW2T	0.03	0.03	0.02	0.01	0.01
60 - 64	EW2L	-	-	-	.	.	EW2U	-	-	-	.	.
Age-related bereavement allowance												
All ages	WMOB	1.74	1.76	1.75	1.75	1.75	WMOC	5.59	5.63	5.51	5.53	5.38
18 - 24	EW2V	-	-	-	.	.	EW36	-	-	-	.	.
25 - 29	EW2W	-	-	-	.	.	EW37	-	-	-	.	.
30 - 34	EW2X	-	-	-	.	.	EW38	-	-	-	.	.
35 - 39	EW2Y	-	-	-	.	.	EW39	-	-	-	.	.
40 - 44	EW2Z	-	-	-	.	.	EW3A	-	-	-	.	.
45 - 49	EW32	0.52	0.5	0.49	0.49	0.47	EW3B	1.45	1.48	1.46	1.43	1.32
50 - 54	EW33	1.06	1.1	1.11	0.11	0.12	EW3C	3.62	3.67	3.56	3.60	3.59
55 - 59	EW34	0.16	0.16	0.15	0.15	0.15	EW3D	0.52	0.47	0.49	0.51	0.48
60 - 64	EW35	-	-	-	.	.	EW3E	-	-	-	.	.
Bereavement allowance (not age related)												
All ages	WMOX	5.01	5.09	5.22	5.33	5.35	WMOY	6.36	6.3	7.19	7.80	8.94
18 - 24	EW3F	-	-	-	.	.	EW3O	-	-	-	.	.
25 - 29	EW3G	-	-	-	.	.	EW3P	-	-	-	.	.
30 - 34	EW3H	-	-	-	.	.	EW3Q	-	-	-	.	.
35 - 39	EW3I	-	-	-	.	.	EW3R	-	-	-	.	.
40 - 44	EW3J	-	-	-	.	.	EW3S	-	-	-	.	.
45 - 49	EW3K	-	-	-	.	.	EW3T	-	-	-	.	.
50 - 54	EW3L	-	-	-	.	.	EW3U	-	-	-	.	.
55 - 59	EW3M	1.83	1.83	1.8	1.91	1.91	EW3V	6.36	6.2	6.18	6.06	6.21
60 - 64	EW3N	3.18	3.26	3.42	3.42	3.43	EW3W	-	0.1	1.00	1.73	2.74

Sources: DWP Information, Governance and Security, Work and Pensions Longitudinal Study

1 Figures include overseas cases.

2 Figures are given at May each year and are taken from the DWP 100% Work and Pensions Longitudinal Study (WPLS).

"-" Nil or Negligible; "." Not applicable; Caseload figures are rounded to the nearest ten; Some additional disclosure control has also been applied. Average amounts are shown as pounds per week and rounded to the nearest penny. Totals may not sum due to rounding.

Notes:

Type of BA *The category 'WPA with dependants' will include clients getting paid at the personal rate only due to the introduction of of Child Tax Credits in April 2003. To obtain figures for those who still receive Child Dependancy Increases, under the transitional protection arrangements, use the 'type of dependant' option.*

STATE PENSION AGE: The age at which women reach State Pension age is gradually increasing from 60 to 65 between April 2010 and April 2016 to November 2018. Under current legislation, State Pension age for men and women is planned to increase to: 66 between November 2018 and October 2020; 67 between 2034 and 2036; 68 between 2044 and 2046. This will introduce a small increase to the number of working age benefit recipients and a small reduction to the number of pension age recipients. Figures from May 2010 onwards reflect this change. For more information see http://statistics.dwp.gov.uk/asd/espa.pdf.

5.14 Contributory and non-contributory retirement pensions:[1,2] by sex and age of claimant Great Britain and Overseas.

At May each year.   Thousands and percentages

		2004	2005	2006	2007	2008	2009	2010	2011	2012	2013
Men:											
Age-groups:											
65-69	KJSB	1354.3	1364.1	1341.5	1332.77	1350.61	1389.85	1,441.17	1,498.78	1,629.37	1705.34
Percentage	KJSC	31.6	31.4	30.6	30.03	29.84	29.99	30.28	30.77	32.14	32.59
70-74	KJSD	1140.3	1150	1160.1	1177.96	1205.7	1232.97	1,252.63	1249.42	1,256.65	1286.51
Percentage	KJSE	26.6	26.5	26.5	26.54	26.63	26.61	26.32	25.65	24.79	24.58
75-79	KJSF	875	887.1	903	918.47	932.17	942.03	958.54	975.17	996.90	1025.20
Percentage	KJSG	20.4	20.4	20.6	20.7	20.59	20.33	20.14	20.02	19.67	19.59
80-84	KJSH	593.7	593.3	596.9	604.74	614.77	627.28	644.94	663.35	680.67	695.95
Percentage	KJSI	13.9	13.7	13.6	13.63	13.58	13.54	13.55	13.62	13.43	13.30
85-89	KJSJ	221.4	246.4	273.1	296.36	317.9	335.49	340.87	348.51	357.78	365.24
Percentage	KJSK	5.2	5.7	6.2	6.68	7.02	7.24	7.16	7.16	7.06	6.98
90 and over	KJSL	95.5	100.2	103.6	106.13	105.33	105.62	120.82	135.62	147.15	154.43
Percentage	KJSM	2.2	2.3	2.4	2.39	2.33	2.28	2.54	2.79	2.90	2.95
Unknown age	EW3Y	0.8	1.1	1.2	1.45	0.19	0.24	0.23	0.27	0.27	0.29
Percentage	EW3Z	–	–	–	–	–	–	–	.	.	–
Total all ages	KJSA	4281.1	4342.2	4379.5	4437.99	4526.79	4633.62	4,759.36	4871.26	5068.96	5233.15
Women:											
Age-groups:											
60-64	KJSO	1451.3	1498.7	1524	1628.19	1695.88	1734.92	1,747.21	1621.44	1391.16	1178.35
Percentage	KJSP	20.3	20.8	21	21.98	22.47	22.62	22.45	20.94	18.07	15.45
65-69	KJSQ	1452.7	1464.2	1453.1	1456.08	1484.8	1527.47	1,576.10	1632.12	1768.96	1847.19
Percentage	KJSR	20.4	20.3	20	19.65	19.67	19.91	20.25	21.1	22.98	24.22
70-74	KJSS	1319.2	1314.5	1312.7	1322.14	1343.22	1366.91	1,382.42	1377.54	1385.36	1415.89
Percentage	KJST	18.5	18.2	18.1	17.85	17.8	17.82	17.77	17.79	18.00	18.56
75-79	KJSU	1156.7	1158.6	1165.5	1168.86	1170.01	1166.2	1,168.83	1172.33	1185.64	1207.02
Percentage	KJSV	16.2	16.1	16	15.78	15.5	15.2	15.02	15.14	15.40	15.82
80-84	KJSW	973.9	951.6	933.3	923.7	919.11	921.01	931.08	942.31	950.53	955.31
Percentage	KJSX	13.6	13.2	12.9	12.47	12.18	12.01	11.97	12.17	12.35	12.52
85-89	KJSY	473.1	511	552.7	587.91	621.15	643.5	634.29	628.71	626.68	625.48
Percentage	KJSZ	6.6	7.1	7.6	7.94	8.23	8.39	8.15	8.12	8.14	8.20
90 and over	KJTA	307.2	314.9	319.4	319.9	313.66	310.07	341.10	370.18	389.38	398.29
Percentage	KJTB	4.3	4.4	4.4	4.32	4.16	4.04	4.38	4.78	5.06	5.22
Unknown age	EW42	1.1	1.3	1.5	1.67	0.37	0.38	0.35	0.35	0.35	0.43
Percentage	EW43	–	–	–	–	–	–	–	.	.	–
Total all ages	KJSN	7135.1	7214.7	7262.3	7408.44	7548.2	7670.44	7,781.39	7744.98	7698.12	7627.94

Source: DWP Information, Governance and Security, Work and Pensions Longitudinal Study.

1 See chapter text.

2 Caseloads include both contributory and non-contributory state pensioners.

"-" Nil or Negligible; "." Not applicable; Caseload figures are rounded to the nearest ten; Some additional disclosure control has also been applied. Average amounts are shown as pounds per week and rounded to the nearest penny. Totals may not sum due to rounding.

STATE PENSION AGE: *The age at which women reach State Pension age is gradually increasing from 60 to 65 between April 2010 and April 2016 to November 2018. Under current legislation, State Pension age for men and women is planned to increase to: 66 between November 2018 and October 2020; 67 between 2034 and 2036; 68 between 2044 and 2046. This will introduce a small increase to the number of working age benefit recipients and a small reduction to the number of pension age recipients. Figures from May 2010 onwards reflect this change. For more information see http://statistics.dwp.gov.uk/asd/espa.pdf.*

5.15a War pensions: estimated number of pensioners[1] Great Britain

At 31 March each year   Thousands

		2002	2003	2004	2005	'2006[2]	2007	2008	2009	2010	2011	2012	2013
Disablement	KADH	221.8	212.18	201.55	191.75	182.8	173.85	165.17	157.13	148.95	141.72	134.43	127.60
Widows and dependants	KADI	50.98	48.61	46.04	43.55	41.05	38.69	36.1	33.62	31.45	29.20	27.11	25.10
Total	KADG	272.78	260.79	247.59	235.3	223.85	212.54	201.27	190.75	180.40	170.92	161.54	152.70

Source: Ministry of Defence/DASA

1 See chapter text. From 1914 war, 1939 war and later service.

2 The discontinuity between 2005 and 2006 is due to improvements in data processing.

5.15b: War Pensions in payment by type of pension, gender and financial year end, 31 March 2009 to 31 March 2013, numbers

	Awards in payment at:				
	31-Mar-09	31-Mar-10	31-Mar-11	31-Mar-12	31-Mar-13
ALL IN PAYMENT	**190,745**	**180,400**	**170,910**	**161,535**	**152,695**
Men	**150,655**	**142,770**	**135,740**	**128,720**	**122,105**
Women	**40,090**	**37,630**	**35,175**	**32,820**	**30,590**
Disablement Pensioners	**157,125**	**148,945**	**141,715**	**134,430**	**127,590**
Men	150,005	142,135	135,120	128,130	121,530
Women	7,120	6,810	6,595	6,305	6,060
War Widow(er)s	**32,790**	**30,655**	**28,425**	**26,375**	**24,415**
Men	70	75	75	80	85
Women	32,715	30,580	28,350	26,295	24,330
Other Pensioners	**830**	**795**	**770**	**730**	**690**
Men	580	555	540	510	490
Women	255	240	230	220	200

Source: Ministry of Defence/DASA

5.16 Income support[1],[2] by statistical group[3]: number of claimants receiving weekly payment

Great Britain

Thousands[4]

		2005	2006	2007	2008	2009	2010	2011	2012	2013
All income support claimants (including MIG from 2003)[5]	F8YY	2150.8	2125.1	2128.4	2102.3	1990.0	1852.3	1703.2	1417.1	1021.9
Incapacity Benefits	F8YZ	1202.8	1191.7	1193.5	1191.4	1097.0	996.6	924.9	654.13	328.09
Lone Parent	F8Z2	789.3	774.9	765.6	738.6	720.5	679.2	595.4	577.08	499.73
Carer	F8Z3	80.5	81.7	84.3	87.3	93.8	103.9	115.7	129.75	145.84
Others on Income Related Benefits	F8Z4	78.1	76.8	84.9	85.0	78.9	72.7	67.2	56.1	48.2

Sources: DWP Information, Governance and Security, Work and Pensions Longitudinal Study

1 Figures are given at May each year and are taken from the DWP 100% Work and Pensions Longitudinal Study (WPLS).

2 From 27th October 2008, new claims to Income Support can also be allocated, on incapacity grounds, to the newly introduced Employment and Support Allowance (ESA).

3 Statistical Group is a hierarchical variable. A person who fits into more than one category will only appear in the top-most one for which they are eligible. These statistical groups differ from the groups shown in the 5% sample tables. Lone Parents are defined as claimants on Income Support with child under 16 and no partner. Lone Parent Obligations were introduced from 24th November 2008 affecting the eligibility criteria based on the age of the youngest child. For more information see http://83.244.183.180/100pc/is/tabtool_is.html.

4 Figures are rounded to the nearest hundred and quoted in thousands.

5 Totals may not sum due to rounding.

"-" Nil or Negligible; "." Not applicable; Caseload figures are rounded to the nearest ten; Some additional disclosure control has also been applied.

STATE PENSION AGE: The age at which women reach State Pension age is gradually increasing from 60 to 65 between April 2010 and April 2016 to November 2018. Under current legislation, State Pension age for men and women is planned to increase to: 66 between November 2018 and October 2020; 67 between 2034 and 2036; 68 between 2044 and 2046. This will introduce a small increase to the number of working age benefit recipients and a small reduction to the number of pension age recipients. Figures from May 2010 onwards reflect this change. For more information see http://statistics.dwp.gov.uk/asd/espa.pdf.

5.17 Pension Credit[1]: number of claimants

Great Britain
End of May

		2005	2006	2007	2008	2009	2010	2011	2012	Thousands[2] 2013
All Pension Credit	F8Z5	2682.7	2717.4	2733.5	2719.1	2730.6	2734.2	2674.7	2541.5	2413.9
Guarantee Credit Only	F8Z6	767.3	775.6	805.7	882.1	925.7	954.4	937	1015.9	968.4
Guarantee Credit and Savings Credit	F8Z7	1321.7	1343.2	1330.1	1246.2	1205.2	1202.4	1148.1	964.3	906.6
Savings Credit	F8Z8	593.7	598.6	597.7	590.8	599.6	577.4	589.6	561.4	538.8

1 Source: DWP 100% Work and Pensions Longitudinal study (WPLS).

2 Figures are rounded to the nearest hundred and expressed in thousands.

Source: DWP Information, Governance and Security, Work and Pensions Longitudinal Study.

Caseload - number of claimants (Thousands) - Pension Credit was introduced on 6 October 2003 and replaced Minimum Income Guarantee (Income Support for people aged 60 or over). The vast majority of people who were previously in receipt of the Minimum Income Guarantee transferred to Pension Credit in October 2003. These Pension Credit statistics are produced on a different basis to the Early Estimates. The latter are more timely but operational processing times mean that a number of claim commencements and terminations are not reflected in them.

Type of Pension Credit - Certain aspects of the April 2012 uprating for Pension Credit were applied to the administrative computer system in advance, before the February 2012 statistics were extracted. Hence, the statistics in February 2012 show the Pension Credit type based on 2012/13 rates. However, the amounts in payment had not been adjusted and claimants were still being paid the correct rate of benefit, based on 2011/12 rates.

STATE PENSION AGE: The age at which women reach State Pension age is gradually increasing from 60 to 65 between April 2010 and April 2016 to November 2018. Under current legislation, State Pension age for men and women is planned to increase to: 66 between November 2018 and October 2020; 67 between 2034 and 2036; 68 between 2044 and 2046. This will introduce a small increase to the number of working age benefit recipients and a small reduction to the number of pension age recipients. Figures from May 2010 onwards reflect this change. For more information see http://statistics.dwp.gov.uk/asd/espa.pdf.

5.18 Income support: average weekly amounts of benefit[1,2,3]

Great Britain
As at May

		2004	2005	2006	2007	2008	2009	2010	2011	2012	£ per week 2013
All income support claimants	F8ZF	91.14	85.89	83.54	82.45	82.55	85.17	85.01	84.88	83.93	76.42
Incapacity benefits[4]	F8ZG	77.84	77.12	78.35	80.04	81.85	89.22	91.81	93.66	93.69	82.12
Lone Parent[4]	F8ZH	114.96	102.85	94.88	89.70	87.37	82.79	79.02	75.94	76.54	74.09
Carer[4]	F8ZI	77.22	73.03	71.13	70.82	70.21	71.85	70.90	69.94	72.23	72.32
Others on income related benefits[4]	F8ZJ	64.24	62.81	62.78	62.47	63.02	66.35	67.87	68.82	73.19	74.11

1 Figures are given at May each year and are taken from the DWP 100% Work and Pensions Longitudinal Study (WPLS).

Source: DWP Information, Governance and Security, Work and Pensions Longitudinal Study.

2 The amount of Income Support is affected by the introduction in April 2003 of Child Tax Credit. From that date there were no new child dependency increases awarded to IS claimants, although existing CDIs were transitionally protected.

3 Average amounts are shown as pounds per week and rounded to the nearest penny.

4 Statistical Group is a hierarchical variable. A person who fits into more than one category will only appear in the top-most one for which they are eligible. These statistical groups differ from the groups shown in the 5% sample tables. Lone Parents are defined as claimants on Income Support with child under 16 and no partner. Lone Parent Obligations were introduced from 24th November 2008 affecting the eligibility criteria based on the age of the youngest child. For more information see http://83.244.183.180/100pc/is/tabtool_is.html.

5.19 Pension Credit: average weekly amounts of benefit[1]

Great Britain
As at May

		2005	2006	2007	2008	2009	2010	2011	2012	£ per week[2] 2013
All Pension Credit	F8ZA	43.62	46.75	50.04	52.69	55.56	57.39	57.74	57.60	57.12
Guarantee Credit Only	F8ZB	75.43	79.56	83.74	85.07	88.86	90.73	92.51	90.12	90.06
Guarantee Credit and Savings Credit	F8ZC	39.87	43.11	46.11	48.29	50.81	51.75	52.04	52.26	49.41
Savings Credit only	F8ZD	10.83	12.39	13.36	13.62	13.71	14.01	13.57	11.36	10.87

1 Figures are given in each May and are taken from the DWP 100% Work and Pensions Longitudinal Study (WPLS).

2 Average amounts are shown as pounds per week and rounded to the nearest penny.

Source: DWP Information, Governance and Security, Work and Pensions Longitudinal Study.

Certain aspects of the April 2012 uprating for Pension Credit were applied to the administrative computer system in advance, before the February 2012 statistics were extracted. Hence, the statistics in February 2012 show the Pension Credit type based on 2012/13 rates. However, the amounts in payment had not been adjusted and claimants were still being paid the correct rate of benefit, based on 2011/12 rates.

STATE PENSION AGE: The age at which women reach State Pension age is gradually increasing from 60 to 65 between April 2010 and April 2016 to November 2018. Under current legislation, State Pension age for men and women is planned to increase to: 66 between November 2018 and October 2020; 67 between 2034 and 2036; 68 between 2044 and 2046. This will introduce a small increase to the number of working age benefit recipients and a small reduction to the number of pension age recipients. Figures from May 2010 onwards reflect this change. For more information see http://statistics.dwp.gov.uk/asd/espa.pdf.

External trade and investment

External trade and investment

External trade (Table 6.1 and 6.3 to 6.6)

The statistics in this section are on the basis of Balance of Payments (BoP). They are compiled from information provided to HM Revenue and Customs (HMRC) by importers and exporters on the basis of Overseas Trade Statistics (OTS) which values exports 'f.o.b.' (free on board) and imports 'c.i.f.' (including insurance and freight). In addition to deducting these freight costs and insurance premiums from the OTS figures, coverage adjustments are made to convert the OTS data to a BoP basis. Adjustments are also made to the level of all exports and European Union (EU) imports to take account of estimated under-recording. The adjustments are set out and described in the annual United Kingdom *Balance of Payments Pink Book* (Office for National Statistics (ONS)). These adjustments are made to conform to the definitions in the 5th edition of the IMF Balance of Payments Manual.

Aggregate estimates of trade in goods, seasonally adjusted and on a BoP basis, are published monthly in the ONS statistical bulletin UK Trade. More detailed figures are available from time series data on the ONS website (www.ons.gov.uk) and are also published in the *Monthly Review of External Trade Statistics*. Detailed figures for EU and non-EU trade on an OTS basis are published in *Overseas trade statistics: United Kingdom trade with the European Community and the world* (HMRC).

A fuller description of how trade statistics are compiled can be found in Statistics on Trade in Goods (Government Statistical Service Methodological Series) available at: www.statistics.gov.uk/STATBASE/Product.asp?vlnk=14943

Overseas Trade Statistics

HMRC provide accurate and up to date information via the website: www.uktradeinfo.com
They also produce publications entitled 'Overseas Trade Statistics'.

Import penetration and export sales ratios (Table 6.2)

The ratios were first introduced in the August 1977 edition of *Economic Trends* in an article entitled 'The Home and Export Performance of United Kingdom Industries'. The article described the conceptual and methodological problems involved in measuring such variables as import penetration.

The industries are grouped according to the 2007 Standard Industrial Classification at 2-digit level.

Table 6.3 to 6.6

The series are now available as datasets in the UK Trade release, which is updated monthly

International trade in services (Tables 6.7 and 6.8)

These data relate to overseas trade in services and cover both production and non-production industries (excluding the public sector). In terms of the types of services traded these include royalties, various forms of consultancy, computing and telecommunications services, advertising and market research and other business services. A separate inquiry covers the film and television industries. The surveys cover receipts from the provision of services to residents of other countries (exports) and payments to residents of other countries for services rendered (imports).

Sources of data

The International Trade in Services (ITIS) surveys (which consist of a quarterly component addressed to the largest businesses and an annual component for the remainder) are based on a sample of companies derived from the Inter-departmental Business Register in addition to a reference list and from 2007 onwards a sample of approximately 5000 contributors from the Annual Business Inquiry (ABI). The companies are asked to show the amounts for their imports and exports against the geographical area to which they were paid or from which they were received, irrespective of where they were first earned.

The purpose of the ITIS survey is to record international transactions which impact on the UK's BoP. Exports and imports of goods are generally excluded, as they will have been counted in the estimate for trade in goods. However earnings from third country trade – that is, from arranging the sale of goods between two countries other than the UK and where the goods never physically enter the UK (known as merchanting) – are included. Earnings from commodity trading are also included. Together, these two comprise trade related services.

Royalties are a large part of the total trade in services collected in the ITIS survey. These cover transactions for items such as printed matter, sound recordings, performing rights, patents, licences, trademarks, designs, copyrights, manufacturing rights, the use of technical know-how and technical assistance.

Balance of Payments (Tables 6.9 to 6.12)

Tables 6.9 to 6.12 are derived from *United Kingdom Balance of Payments: The Pink Book* 2013 edition. The following general notes to the tables provide brief definitions and explanations of the figures and terms used. Further notes are included in the Pink Book.

Summary of Balance of Payments

The BoP consists of the current account, the capital account, the financial account and the International Investment Position (IIP). The current account consists of trade in goods and services, income, and current transfers. Income consists of investment income and compensation of employees. The capital account mainly consists of capital transfers and the financial account covers financial transactions. The IIP covers balance sheet levels of UK external assets and liabilities. Every credit entry in the balance of payments accounts should, in theory, be matched by a corresponding debit entry so that total current, capital and financial account credits should be equal to, and therefore offset by, total debits. In practice there is a discrepancy termed net errors and omissions.

Current account

Trade in goods
The goods account covers exports and imports of goods. Imports of motor cars from Japan, for example, are recorded as debits in the trade in goods account, whereas exports of vehicles manufactured in the UK are recorded as credits. Trade in goods forms a component of the expenditure measure of gross domestic product (GDP).

Trade in services
The services account covers exports and imports of services, for example civil aviation. Passenger tickets for travel on UK aircraft sold abroad, for example, are recorded as credits in the services account, whereas the purchases of airline tickets from foreign airlines by UK passengers are recorded as debits. Trade in services, along with trade in goods, forms a component of the expenditure measure of GDP.

Income
The income account consists of compensation of employees and investment income and is dominated by the latter. Compensation of employees covers employment income from cross-border and seasonal workers which is less significant in the UK than in other countries. Investment income covers earnings (for example, profits, dividends and interest payments and receipts) arising from cross-border investment in financial assets and liabilities. For example, earnings on foreign bonds and shares held by financial institutions based in the UK are recorded as credits in the investment income account, whereas earnings on UK company securities held abroad are recorded as investment income debits. Investment income forms a component of gross national income (GNI) but not GDP.

Current transfers

Current transfers are composed of central government transfers (for example, taxes and payments to and receipts from, the EU) and other transfers (for example gifts in cash or kind received by private individuals from abroad or receipts from the EU where the UK government acts as an agent for the ultimate beneficiary of the transfer). Current transfers do not form a component either of GDP or of GNI. For example, payments to the UK farming industry under the EU Agricultural Guarantee Fund are recorded as credits in the current transfers account, while payments of EU agricultural levies by the UK farming industry are recorded as debits in the current transfers account.

Capital account

Capital account transactions involve transfers of ownership of fixed assets, transfers of funds associated with acquisition or disposal of fixed assets and cancellation of liabilities by creditors without any counterparts being received in return. The main components are migrants transfers, EU transfers relating to fixed capital formation (regional development fund and agricultural guidance fund) and debt forgiveness. Funds brought into the UK by new immigrants would, for example, be recorded as credits in the capital account, while funds sent abroad by UK residents emigrating to other countries would be recorded as debits in the capital account. The size of capital account transactions are quite minor compared with the current and financial accounts.

Financial account

While investment income covers earnings arising from cross-border investments in financial assets and liabilities, the financial account of the balance of payments covers the flows of such investments. Earnings on foreign bonds and shares held by financial institutions based in the UK are, for example, recorded as credits in the investment income account, but the acquisition of such foreign securities by UK-based financial institutions are recorded as net debits in the financial account or portfolio investment abroad. Similarly, the acquisitions of UK company securities held by foreign residents are recorded in the financial account as net credits or portfolio investment in the UK.

International Investment Position

While the financial account covers the flows of foreign investments and financial assets and liabilities, the IIP records the levels of external assets and liabilities. While the acquisition of foreign securities by UK-based financial institutions are recorded in the financial account as net debits, the total holdings of foreign securities by UK-based financial institutions are recorded as levels of UK external assets. Similarly, the holdings of UK company securities held by foreign residents are recorded as levels of UK liabilities.

Foreign direct investment (Tables 6.13 to 6.18)

Direct investment refers to investment that adds to, deducts from, or acquires a lasting interest in an enterprise operating in an economy other than that of the investor – the investor's purpose being to have an effective voice in the management of the enterprise. (For the purposes of the statistical inquiry, an effective voice is taken as equivalent to a holding of 10 per cent or more in the foreign enterprise.) Other investments in which the investor does not have an effective voice in the management of the enterprise are mainly portfolio investments and these are not covered here.

Direct investment is a financial concept and is not the same as capital expenditure on fixed assets. It covers only the money invested in a related concern by the parent company and the concern will then decide how to use the money. A related concern may also raise money locally without reference to the parent company.

The investment figures are published on a net basis; that is they consist of investments net of disinvestments by a company into its foreign subsidiaries, associate companies and branches.

Definitional changes from 1997

The new European System of Accounts (ESA(95)) definitions were introduced from the 1997 estimates. The changes were as follows:

i.   Previously, for the measurement of direct investment, an effective voice in the management of an enterprise was taken as the equivalent of a 20 per cent shareholding. This is now 10 per cent

ii.   The Channel Islands and the Isle of Man have been excluded from the definition of the economic territory of the UK. Prior to 1987 these islands were considered to be part of the UK

iii.   Interest received or paid was replaced by interest accrued in the figures on earnings from direct investment. There is deemed to be little or no impact arising from this definitional change on the estimates

A further change caused by the move to ESA(95) is that withholding taxes payable on direct investment earnings are now measured. Earnings were shown gross of these taxes in the Balance of Payments 2005 Pink Book. However, for the purposes of this business monitor earnings are calculated net of tax, as before.

New register sources available from 1998 have led to revisions of the figures from that year onwards. These sources gave an improved estimate of the population satisfying the criteria for foreign direct investment.

From the 2005 surveys new data sources have allowed the inclusion of data for the previously excluded Private Property (outward & inward surveys) and Public Corporations (outward surveys) sectors. From the 2006 surveys the tax data previously excluded from the FDI surveys are now also included in the final earnings figures for both the outward & inward surveys. This now means that there are no coherence issues between the FDI annual surveys and the quarterly Balance of Payments figures as published in the latest Balance of Payments Pink Book.

Definitional changes have been introduced from 1997 and the register changes from 1998. Data prior to these years have not been reworked in Tables 6.13 to 6.18. For clarity, the Offshore Islands are identified separately on the tables. Breaks in the series for the other definitional changes are not quantified but are relatively small. More detailed information on the effect of these changes appears in the business monitor MA4 – Foreign Direct Investment 2002, which was published in February 2003 and is available from the ONS website.

Sources of data

The figures in Tables 6.13 to 6.18 are based on annual inquiries into foreign direct investment for 2009. These were sample surveys which involved sending approximately 1530 forms to UK businesses investing abroad, and 2370 forms to UK businesses in which foreign parents and associates had invested. The tables also contain some revisions to 2008 as a result of new information coming to light in the course of the latest surveys. Further details from the latest annual surveys, including analyses by industry and by components of direct investment, are available in business monitor MA4. Initial figures were published on the ONS website in a statistical bulletin Foreign Direct Investment 2009 in December 2010 Data for 2010 will be published in a statistical bulletin in December 2011, followed by the full business monitor MA4 in February 2012.

Country allocation

The analysis of inward investment is based on the country of ownership of the immediate parent company. Thus, inward investment in a UK company may be attributed to the country of the intervening overseas subsidiary, rather than the country of the ultimate parent. Similarly, the country analysis of outward investment is based on the country of ownership of the immediate subsidiary; for example, to the extent that overseas investment in the UK is channelled through holding companies in the Netherlands, the underlying flow of investment from this country is overstated and the inflow from originating countries is understated.

Further information

More detailed statistics on foreign direct investment are available on request from Richard Tonkin, Office for National Statistics, International Transactions Branch, Room 2.364, Government

Buildings, Cardiff Road, Newport, South Wales, United Kingdom, NP10 8XG. Telephone: +44 (0)1633 456082, fax: +44 (0)1633 812855, email Richard.tonkin@ons.gov.uk

6.1 Trade in goods[1]
United Kingdom
Balance of payments basis

£million and Indices 2011=100

		2001	2002	2003	2004	2005	2006	2007	2008	2009	2010	2011	2012	2013
Value (£ million)														
Exports of goods	BOKG	189746	187792	189489	191410	212741	244848	222462	254965	230746	270816	309184	305142	306765
Imports of goods	BOKH	231284	234830	238327	254360	282375	322269	315758	351380	314337	368226	405699	414114	419364
Balance on trade in goods	BOKI	-41538	-47038	-48838	-62950	-69634	-77421	-93296	-96415	-83591	-97410	-96515	-108972	-112599
Price index numbers														
Exports of goods	BQKR	71.6	70.6	71.9	72.2	74.8	76	75.6	86	86.9	92.7	100	99.8	100.9
Imports of goods	BQKS	73.9	72	71.6	71	74	76.3	76.2	86.9	87.8	92	100	99.8	100.4
Terms of trade[2]	BQKT	96.9	98.1	100.4	101.7	101.1	99.6	99.2	99	99	100.8	100	100	100.5
Volume index numbers														
Exports of goods	BQKU	81.4	82	81.3	82	89	101	92.3	94	84.5	93.6	100	99.2	98.7
Imports of goods	BQKV	74.8	78.3	80	85.9	91.9	102.2	99.9	98.2	87.6	98.3	100	102.6	103.3

Source: Office for National Statistics: 01633 456294

1 See chapter text. Statistics of trade in goods on a balance of payments basis are obtained by making certain adjustments in respect of valuation and coverage to the statistics recorded in the Overseas Trade Statistics. These adjustments are described in detail in The Pink Book.
2 Export price index as a percentage of the import price index.

Table 6.1 may show revisions to data going back over time. This is mainly to reflect revised data from HMRC and other data suppliers, later survey data and a re-assessment of seasonal factors.

6.2 Sales of products manufactured in the United Kingdom by Industry Division

		S - Suppressed as disclosive		
				£ Thousands
Industry	SIC(07) Division[1]	2010	2011	2012
Other mining and quarrying	8	2,409,112	2,348,023	2,186,507
Manufacture of food products	10	58,468,601	60,663,124	62,670,273
Manufacture of beverages	11	12,397,869	12,875,926	12,704,895
Manufacture of tobacco products	12	1,625,505	1,672,839	1,793,420
Manufacture of textiles	13	3,887,733	4,047,168	4,130,189
Manufacture of wearing apparel	14	1,568,459	1,490,960	1,601,349
Manufacture of leather and related products	15	S	618,239	637,880
Manufacture of wood and of products of wood and cork, except furniture; manufacture of articles of straw and plaiting materials	16	S	5,577,606	S
Manufacture of paper and paper products	17	9,689,632	S	10,443,693
Printing and reproduction of recorded media	18	8,715,583	8,927,210	8,786,224
Manufacture of chemicals and chemical products	20	23,074,946	S	24,040,531
Manufacture of basic pharmaceutical products and pharmaceutical preparations	21	14,723,163	13,901,544	12,460,883
Manufacture of rubber and plastic products	22	S	S	S
Manufacture of other non-metallic mineral products	23	9,733,216	10,249,359	10,163,904
Manufacture of fabricated metal products, except machinery and equipment	25	S	S	S
Manufacture of computer, electronic and optical products	26	13,458,189	12,857,258	S
Manufacture of electrical equipment	27	10,963,840	11,864,709	11,831,864
Manufacture of machinery and equipment n.e.c.	28	22,769,955	S	26,775,816
Manufacture of motor vehicles, trailers and semi-trailers	29	S	38,446,099	39,430,045
Manufacture of other transport equipment	30	20,531,722	21,392,793	23,116,357
Manufacture of furniture	31	5,643,486	S	6,094,702
Other manufacturing	32	4,541,098	S	S
Repair and installation of machinery and equipment	33	11,809,272	12,589,466	S
Publishing activities	58	16,122,672	N/A*	10,156,325
Total		333,850,505	337,144,227	339,213,626

Source: Office for National Statistics

Note:

[1] Division 07 (Mining of metal ores), Division 19 (manufacture of coke and refined petroleum products) and Division 24 (Manufacture of basic metals) do not form part of this analysis.

* Product sales within this division were not collected in 2011

*** data for division 30 excludes SIC(07) 30400 Manufacture of military fighting machines

2010 and 2011 data are final estimates
2012 data are intermediate estimates

Tables 6.2b, c, d and e are no longer included in this publication. The import penetration and export sales ratios are no longer published by the ONS as a result of potential data differences with trade data which feed into the ratios.

6.3 United Kingdom exports: by commodity[1,2]

Seasonally adjusted

£ million

		2003	2004	2005	2006	2007	2008	2009	2010	2011	2012	2013
0. Food and live animals	BOGG	6708	6711	6932	6872	7774	9082	9482	11623	14142	12103	12983
01. Meat and meat preparations	BOGS	599	662	717	724	789	1086	1166	1311	1569	1455	1691
02. Dairy products and eggs	BQMS	769	790	723	718	808	887	836	1037	1248	1167	1378
04 & 08. Cereals and animal feeding stuffs	BQMT	1697	1568	1554	1575	1781	2291	2371	2586	2746	2776	2830
05. Vegetables and fruit	BQMU	472	506	514	588	608	695	761	814	882	855	783
1. Beverages and tobacco	BQMZ	4439	4145	4111	4182	4386	5030	5353	5950	6962	6935	7265
11. Beverages	BQNB	3515	3386	3497	3717	4085	4582	4951	5626	6819	6861	6999
12. Tobacco	BQOW	924	759	614	465	301	448	402	324	143	74	266
2. Crude materials	BQOX	2896	3438	3610	4615	5167	6247	4795	6915	8551	7984	7154
of which:												
24. Wood, lumber and cork	BQOY	102	116	131	145	143	125	83	111	113	107	154
25. Pulp and waste paper	BQOZ	178	243	282	338	415	478	354	542	623	544	503
26. Textile fibres	BQPA	476	508	497	545	497	540	573	674	782	821	764
28. Metal ores	BQPB	1115	1558	1642	2415	2877	3659	2512	4114	5074	4517	4059
3. Fuels	BOPN	16478	17808	21464	24757	24369	35428	26970	35115	42713	43714	42878
33. Petroleum and petroleum products	ELBL	14491	16092	19741	22594	22397	31857	24568	31288	37966	39516	39292
32, 34 & 35. Coal, gas and electricity	BOQI	1987	1716	1723	2163	1972	3571	2402	3827	4747	4198	3586
4. Animal and vegetable oils and fats	BQPI	265	198	235	273	326	360	375	421	440	480	492
5. Chemicals	ENDG	31179	31831	33115	37128	38814	43792	46927	50821	53065	52953	48992
of which:												
51. Organic chemicals	BQPJ	6042	6001	6676	7987	7567	8376	9071	8838	9163	9013	7688
52. Inorganic chemicals	BQPK	1474	1555	1564	2145	2819	2978	2834	3481	3018	2885	2564
53. Colouring materials	CSCE	1607	1606	1605	1600	1669	1844	1693	1951	2165	1995	2033
54. Medicinal products	BQPL	11802	12265	12203	13773	14555	17301	20457	22319	22823	23467	20532
55. Toilet preparations	CSCF	3122	3108	3208	3444	3677	3940	4128	4292	4843	4843	5313
57 & 58. Plastics	BQQA	3659	3791	4220	4438	4593	4847	4389	5310	5854	5627	5546
6. Manufactures classified chiefly by material	BQQB	23151	24511	26492	27632	29246	32293	24452	29140	34767	32273	31817
of which:												
63. Wood and cork manufactures	BQQC	319	289	249	276	273	243	220	224	253	265	247
64. Paper and paperboard manufactures	BQQD	2108	2010	2053	2015	2112	2338	2281	2338	2376	2289	2281
65. Textile manufactures	BQQE	2942	2833	2632	2687	2582	2593	2371	2596	2791	2735	2805
67. Iron and steel	BQQF	3307	4230	5148	5121	5995	6841	4572	5032	6027	5754	6096
68. Non-ferrous metals	BQQG	2579	3249	3882	4828	5762	6843	3965	5832	8574	6824	7160
69. Metal manufactures	BQQH	3759	3848	4037	4489	4616	4983	4190	4437	4761	4823	4782
7. Machinery and transport equipment[3]	BQQI	79333	77969	88923	110094	82200	88724	79169	92411	103106	104227	109703
71-716, 72, 73 & 74. Mechanical machinery	BQQK	24168	23716	25609	28104	28850	32178	29265	32786	38493	39355	41662
716, 75, 76 & 77. Electrical machinery	BQQL	30494	28519	37093	55168	23917	24966	23919	25587	25962	24009	24034
78. Road vehicles	BQQM	17374	18220	19158	19335	21035	22433	17006	23322	27366	28948	31511
79. Other transport equipment	BQQN	7297	7514	7063	7487	8398	9147	8979	10716	11285	11915	12496
8. Miscellaneous manufactures[3]	BQQO	22472	22850	25049	25928	26630	28431	27686	31249	33534	35696	36964
of which:												
84. Clothing	CSCN	2677	2702	2694	2860	3085	3300	3423	3659	4208	4448	5158
85. Footwear	CSCP	420	417	469	523	543	622	723	852	932	1035	1245
87 & 88. Scientific and photographic	BQQQ	7241	7016	7228	7347	7035	8038	8281	9275	10177	10373	11132
9. Other commodities and transactions	BOQL	2568	1949	2810	3367	3550	5578	5537	7171	11904	8777	8517
Total United Kingdom exports	BOKG	189489	191410	212741	244848	222462	254965	230746	270816	309184	305142	306765

Source: Office for National Statistics: 01633 456294

1 See chapter text. The numbers on the left hand side of the table refer to the code numbers of the Standard International Trade Classification, Revision 3, which was introduced in January 1988.
2 Balance of payments consistent basis.
3 Sections 7 and 8 are shown by broad economic category in table G2 of the Monthly Review of External Trade Statistics.

Table 6.3 may show revisions to data going back over time. This is mainly to reflect revised data from HMRC and other data suppliers, later survey data and a re-assessment of seasonal factors.

6.4 United Kingdom imports: by commodity [1,2]

Seasonally adjusted

		2003	2004	2005	2006	2007	2008	2009	2010	2011	2012	2013
0. Food and live animals	BQQR	16435	17215	18623	19761	21298	25285	26327	27147	29438	30130	31160
of which:												
01. Meat and meat preparations	BQQS	3297	3469	3658	3788	3980	4607	4910	5006	5617	5621	5511
02. Dairy products and eggs	BQQT	1513	1631	1724	1802	1836	2289	2321	2429	2546	2621	2914
04 & 08. Cereals and animal feeding stuffs	BQQU	2229	2323	2383	2482	2909	3809	3922	3973	4142	4624	5565
05. Vegetables and fruit	BQQV	4683	4827	5360	5768	6207	7050	7039	7431	7897	8002	7339
1. Beverages and tobacco	BQQW	4702	4929	5088	5147	5367	5815	5954	6296	6482	6459	7733
11. Beverages	EGAT	3214	3464	3608	3646	3882	4300	4360	4613	4875	5033	5155
12. Tobacco	EMAI	1488	1465	1480	1501	1485	1515	1594	1683	1607	1426	2578
2. Crude materials	ENVB	5541	5720	6150	7088	8630	9583	6542	9119	10407	9259	11089
of which:												
24. Wood, lumber and cork	ENVC	1378	1350	1375	1452	1801	1408	1169	1465	1430	1460	2329
25. Pulp and waste paper	EQAH	487	479	474	533	516	612	452	596	629	518	519
26. Textile fibres	EQAP	322	323	303	299	322	338	290	355	455	379	402
28. Metalores	EHAA	1446	1652	2008	2649	3760	4646	2257	3887	4748	3944	4783
3. Fuels	BQAT	12624	18049	26415	31366	32294	48990	35466	44882	61837	65287	61701
33. Petroleum and petroleum products	ENXO	11575	15717	22403	26447	27120	38390	28020	36010	49461	53896	49300
32, 34 & 35. Coal, gas and electricity	BPBI	1049	2332	4012	4919	5174	10600	7446	8872	12376	11391	12401
4. Animal and vegetable oils and fats	EHAB	613	625	646	778	897	1397	1052	1128	1493	1415	1388
5. Chemicals	ENGA	27987	29995	31198	33215	36737	40406	41662	47161	52295	53296	51029
of which:												
51. Organic chemicals	EHAC	6196	6872	7323	7697	8643	8449	8277	9378	10091	10110	8163
52. Inorganic chemicals	EHAE	1102	1387	1533	2130	2692	2762	2745	2952	3612	3197	2543
53. Colouring materials	CSCR	1006	1063	1078	1084	1157	1227	1144	1253	1325	1362	1380
54. Medicinal products	EHAF	9874	10271	10233	10728	12045	13531	15886	17670	19794	21564	20954
55. Toilet preparations	CSCS	2762	2912	3071	3325	3438	3921	4157	4416	4654	4749	5065
57 & 58. Plastics	EHAG	4424	4773	5073	5354	5687	6221	5556	6847	7741	7527	7977
6. Manufactures classified chiefly by material	EHAH	29692	32044	33282	37630	39713	41887	35885	43540	49123	49878	46647
of which:												
63. Wood and cork manufactures	EHAI	1468	1614	1533	1581	1738	1729	1477	1664	1690	1662	1799
64. Paper and paperboard manufactures	EHAJ	4767	4872	4842	5022	5235	5482	5501	5885	6020	5701	5871
65. Textile manufactures	EHAK	3899	3940	3664	3996	4074	4081	3823	4289	4605	4525	4751
67. Iron and steel	EHAL	3163	4120	4348	5070	5924	6555	3850	5162	6487	6182	5364
68. Non-ferrous metals	EHAM	3338	3625	3938	6177	6231	6430	6354	8668	10139	12581	9608
69. Metal manufactures	EHAN	4767	4961	5354	5843	6543	6968	5957	6865	7532	7607	8055
7.Machinery and transport equipment[3]	EHAO	101662	103952	117170	139447	117403	120747	107210	129086	128752	131270	142470
71 - 716, 72, 73 & 74. Mechanical machinery	EHAQ	18754	19599	21891	22308	25495	29054	24407	28732	32773	34348	35976
716, 75, 76 & 77. Electrical machinery	EHAR	43937	45582	55438	75106	46004	47191	44515	50943	51164	50682	52380
78. Road vehicles	EHAS	29957	30731	31475	32557	36522	33883	26158	33649	36715	36638	43070
79. Other transport equipment	EHAT	9014	8040	8366	9476	9382	10619	12130	15762	8100	9602	11044
8. Miscellaneous manufactures[3]	EHAU	37072	38701	41096	44801	47929	51027	50058	54701	58630	59635	61246
of which:												
84. Clothing	CSDR	9345	9581	10208	11956	12361	13191	13840	14821	16143	15837	16741
85. Footwear	CSDS	2398	2473	2605	2713	2681	2843	3100	3605	3700	3858	4074
87 & 88. Scientific and photographic	EHAW	7060	7290	7482	7614	7526	8445	8493	9112	9571	10083	10768
9. Other commodities and transactions	BQAW	1999	3130	2707	3036	5490	6243	4181	5166	7242	7485	4901
Total United Kingdom imports	BOKH	238327	254360	282375	322269	315758	351380	314337	368226	405699	414114	419364

Source: Office for National Statistics: 01633 456294

1 See chapter text. The numbers on the left hand side of the table refer to the code numbers of the Standard International Trade Classification, Revision 3,which was introduced in January 1988.

2 Balance of payments consistent basis

3 Sections 7 and 8 are shown by broad economic category in table G2 of the Monthly Review of External Trade Statistics.

Table 6.4 may show revisions to data going back over time. This is mainly to reflect revised data from HMRC and other data suppliers, later survey data and a re-assessment of seasonal factors.

6.5 United Kingdom exports: by area[1,2]

Seasonally adjusted

£ million

		2003	2004	2005	2006	2007	2008	2009	2010	2011	2012	2013
European Union:[3]	LGCK	112166	112668	122892	151558	128245	142396	125347	144841	164880	152939	154474
EMU members:	QAKW	101819	101852	111166	135767	115212	127506	112443	128440	146603	136298	136404
Austria	CHMY	1267	1097	1336	1670	1362	1467	1282	1465	1693	1563	1659
Belgium & Luxembourg	CHNQ	11425	10575	11443	14627	12042	13553	11056	13566	16197	14521	14199
Cyprus	BQGN	315	321	355	1038	414	535	618	565	693	444	459
Finland	CHMZ	1495	1365	1522	1805	1944	1903	1321	1557	1587	1530	1572
France	ENYL	18910	18614	19983	28832	17992	18013	17165	19154	21958	21028	21090
Germany	ENYO	21225	22059	23624	27171	25177	28392	24930	28806	35764	33423	30712
Greece	CHNT	1300	1460	1446	1481	1429	1742	1698	2304	2430	1418	1368
Irish Republic	CHNS	12247	14179	16342	17086	17663	19036	15883	16841	17819	17346	18870
Italy	CHNO	8761	8562	9039	9482	9392	9587	8369	8841	10043	8103	8631
Malta	BQGY	256	256	239	316	362	448	400	394	449	396	454
Netherlands	CHNP	13718	12156	12888	16554	15172	20068	18290	22389	25345	25547	26187
Portugal	CHNU	1453	1589	1704	2317	1467	1634	1536	1832	1751	1382	1376
Slovakia	BQHB	235	222	259	275	380	453	377	468	554	531	479
Slovenia	BQHE	158	160	167	194	204	222	176	221	242	220	209
Spain	CHNV	8961	9131	10704	12451	9984	10233	9203	9904	9729	8530	8806
Non-EMU members:[3]	BQIA	10440	10922	11841	16259	13261	15110	13052	16605	18749	17028	18403
of which:												
Bulgaria	WYUF	152	155	220	226	202	252	198	250	326	313	405
Czech Rep	FKML	1004	982	1086	1560	1385	1544	1439	1820	1918	1839	1960
Denmark	CHNR	2187	2047	2322	3826	2163	2584	2473	2684	3077	2730	3100
Estonia	AUEV	93	106	115	468	228	220	145	194	280	291	333
Hungary	QALC	857	941	844	829	857	1002	840	1085	1187	1099	1256
Latvia	BQGQ	160	139	174	607	229	280	109	172	237	258	383
Lithuania	BQGU	187	142	166	236	311	282	171	226	269	380	331
Poland	ERDR	1462	1422	1661	2767	2354	2999	2788	3784	4311	3439	3891
Romania	WMDB	512	615	651	602	662	752	684	781	953	948	947
Sweden	CHNA	3826	4373	4602	5138	4870	5195	4205	5548	6260	5756	5797
Other Western Europe:	HCJD	6764	7119	9701	9455	9282	10836	9717	12532	14205	15199	14437
of which:												
Iceland	EPLW	142	170	176	190	201	186	128	132	149	191	171
Norway	EPLX	1892	1943	2177	2154	2675	2800	2719	3099	3373	3572	3484
Switzerland	EPLV	2894	2909	5016	4331	3852	4775	4083	5534	6138	7095	6080
Turkey	EOBA	1654	1915	2136	2474	2308	2579	2363	3251	3929	3702	4101
North America:	HBZQ	32644	32336	34829	36968	36863	40014	38012	43351	46325	46780	45181
of which:												
Canada	EOBC	3147	3233	3157	3859	3220	3213	3325	4128	4748	4174	4017
Mexico	EPJX	666	609	616	735	749	897	752	952	1006	1134	1178
USA inc Puerto Rica	J9C5	28831	28493	31056	32373	32893	35883	33935	38230	40495	41472	39983
Other OECD countries:	HCII	7645	8020	8324	8706	8514	9864	9041	10464	12337	15264	15094
of which:												
Australia	EPMA	2236	2393	2505	2482	2539	3072	2959	3361	4389	4753	4337
Japan	EOBD	3613	3765	3782	4107	3796	3877	3563	4343	4721	4943	4833
New Zealand	EPMB	342	407	406	375	347	381	350	414	542	618	654
South Korea	ERDM	1445	1446	1626	1742	1828	2534	2169	2346	2685	4950	5218
Oil exporting countries:	HDII	7527	7823	10736	9272	9592	11658	11594	12634	13815	15476	16887
of which:												
Brunei	QALF	123	67	43	80	849	62	61	159	55	52	81
UAE inc Dubai	J8YH	2006	2622	5365	3621	2703	3786	3661	4064	4864	5392	6227
Indonesia	FKMR	451	390	365	317	283	388	366	460	672	657	703
Kuwait	QATB	374	347	419	444	447	541	472	556	527	616	562
Nigeria	QATE	726	741	782	831	993	1506	1315	1424	1609	1518	1508
Saudi Arabia	ERDI	1835	1603	1586	1736	1880	2291	2442	2564	2808	3187	3468

6.5 United Kingdom exports: by area[1,2]

Seasonally adjusted

		2003	2004	2005	2006	2007	2008	2009	2010	2011	2012	£ million 2013
Rest of the World	**HCHW**	22598	23315	26134	28745	29795	39972	36814	46811	57282	59242	60587
of which:												
Brazil	FKMO	799	773	808	909	1051	1674	1789	2220	2465	2674	2730
China	ERDN	2431	2644	3190	3952	4319	6001	6236	8387	10592	11602	13292
Egypt	QALL	447	654	531	578	678	936	1006	1200	1102	963	978
Hong Kong	ERDG	2414	2560	2983	2856	2605	3624	3735	4461	5377	5404	5665
India	ERDJ	2892	2566	3271	3530	3634	5271	3952	4975	7150	5801	6129
Israel	ERDL	1328	1354	1303	1310	1219	1324	1146	1389	1651	1554	1429
Malaysia	ERDK	999	972	1049	881	934	1124	1051	1273	1484	1542	1656
Pakistan	FKMU	278	334	451	490	416	469	478	462	533	564	493
Philippines	FKMX	373	308	267	240	243	242	267	284	293	329	381
Russia	ERDQ	1449	1494	1914	2093	2883	4390	2537	3670	5156	5675	5380
Singapore	ERDH	1535	1667	2011	2312	2397	2784	2926	3411	3739	4408	4248
South Africa	EPME	1715	1826	2002	2178	2117	2622	2253	2889	3459	3231	2583
Taiwan	ERDP	869	929	910	909	920	879	796	1115	1385	1158	1243
Thailand	ERDO	556	625	614	564	587	750	914	1137	1414	2003	1978

1 See chapter text.

Source: Office for National Statistics: 01633 456294

2 Balance of payments consistent basis.

3 Includes Austria, Belgium, Bulgaria, Cyprus, Czech Republic, Denmark, Estonia, Finland, France, Germany, Greece, Hungary, Irish Republic, Italy, Latvia, Lithuania, Luxemburg, Malta, Netherlands, Poland, Portugal, Romania, Slovakia, Slovenia, Spain and Sweden.

Table 6.5 may show revisions to data going back over time. This is mainly to reflect revised data from HMRC and other data suppliers, later survey data and a re-assessment of seasonal factors.

6.6 United Kingdom imports: by area[1,2]
Seasonally adjusted

£ million

		2003	2004	2005	2006	2007	2008	2009	2010	2011	2012	2013
European Union:[3]	LGDC	140156	145851	161557	184567	172018	184200	165139	188411	205535	209566	223585
EMU members	QAKX	126208	130405	143271	160709	151866	160824	143047	161347	174203	176777	191189
Austria	CHNB	2835	2404	2518	2790	2523	2383	2314	2668	2998	2639	3123
Belgium & Luxembourg	CHNY	13353	14049	15336	18072	15880	17496	15847	18225	20364	19223	20994
Cyprus	BQGO	254	212	281	1718	196	156	123	106	143	168	134
Finland	CHNC	2719	2388	2479	3081	2653	2826	2142	2180	2482	2192	2512
France	ENYP	20809	20602	22473	26790	22182	23574	20740	21824	23401	22899	24498
Germany	ENYS	34373	36257	40013	42110	45211	45568	40642	47094	51403	53648	58525
Greece	CHOB	661	685	739	811	658	672	563	713	680	696	762
Irish Republic	CHOA	10128	10377	10626	10760	11461	12444	12610	13019	13263	13068	12435
Italy	CHNW	11723	12482	12953	12929	13486	14401	12509	14132	14322	14544	15438
Malta	BQGZ	186	186	181	166	181	135	106	170	170	128	107
Netherlands	CHNX	17029	18629	20893	22533	23447	26314	22283	26771	29020	31847	35435
Portugal	CHOC	2002	1969	2065	3182	1528	1770	1445	1771	1835	1776	1998
Slovakia	BQHC	261	267	382	847	1286	1655	1627	1642	1537	1610	1863
Slovenia	BQHN	171	171	206	752	319	326	255	360	367	347	332
Spain	CHOD	9435	9337	11754	12049	10615	10953	9713	10506	11993	11754	12841
Non-EMU members:[3]	BQIB	14217	15836	18658	25977	20392	23527	22220	27230	31557	33027	32588
of which:												
Bulgaria	WYUT	126	150	174	198	239	215	183	232	290	286	417
Czech Rep	FKMM	1447	1326	1921	2959	3018	3646	3385	4037	4311	4557	4710
Denmark	CHNZ	3465	3438	4505	6535	3485	3986	3893	4166	6182	5941	5878
Estonia	BQGL	269	390	372	2119	240	151	128	166	225	238	192
Hungary	QALD	1148	1621	1898	2369	2406	2573	2577	3291	3139	2685	2666
Latvia	BQGR	528	708	736	801	636	421	340	441	451	412	599
Lithuania	BQGV	288	279	284	284	312	360	373	559	614	843	907
Poland	ERED	1580	1876	2369	3679	3738	4381	4736	6186	7199	7540	8063
Romania	WMDC	697	806	822	829	953	821	796	1259	1308	1295	1507
Sweden	CHND	4669	5242	5577	6204	5365	6973	5809	6893	7838	9230	7649
Other Western Europe:	HBTS	13375	15903	20087	23714	24953	33089	26954	34537	39182	37994	32236
of which:												
Iceland	EPMW	303	357	347	408	419	471	489	433	418	391	378
Norway	EPMX	6541	8648	12234	14757	14683	22016	16235	21081	25241	22368	17506
Switzerland	EPMV	3760	3504	3830	4399	4971	5477	5366	7517	7757	9210	7933
Turkey	EOBU	2613	3261	3493	3977	4703	4961	4659	5347	5560	5774	6200
North America:	HCRB	26586	26248	26155	30812	32066	32062	29439	33785	36016	36269	34172
of which:												
Canada	EOBW	3585	4103	4069	4924	5811	5725	4463	5767	6145	5552	5755
Mexico	EPJY	472	395	425	431	559	780	757	1034	1086	722	761
USA inc Puerto Rica	J9C6	22529	21750	21661	25457	25695	25557	24219	26982	28763	29969	27656
Other OECD countries:	HDJQ	12654	13316	14040	13593	13790	15201	12575	13820	14801	15135	14161
of which:												
Australia	EPNA	1701	1799	2026	2082	2198	2383	2224	2311	2440	2426	2232
Japan	EOBX	7916	7931	8459	7843	7929	8554	6671	8105	8872	8558	7630
New Zealand	EPNB	536	567	573	603	661	752	819	843	872	896	891
South Korea	ERDY	2501	3019	2982	3065	3002	3512	2861	2561	2617	3255	3408

6.6 United Kingdom imports: by area[1,2]

Seasonally adjusted

£ million

		2003	2004	2005	2006	2007	2008	2009	2010	2011	2012	2013
Oil exporting countries:	HCPC	4021	4955	6202	7310	6794	8318	7893	11669	16717	19132	20133
of which:												
Brunei	QALG	54	65	28	72	50	28	48	20	32	58	56
UAE inc Dubai	J8YI	1005	1041	1266	1015	1014	957	1126	1632	1891	2193	2602
Indonesia	FKMS	952	964	904	1033	1011	1220	1238	1392	1351	1283	1257
Kuwait	QATC	332	407	383	789	764	1125	762	1033	1522	1519	1742
Nigeria	QATF	61	87	132	193	317	926	645	885	2311	4002	3380
Saudi Arabia	ERDU	728	1229	1840	1314	1016	803	644	833	1192	1830	2645
Rest of the World	HCIF	41489	48036	54284	62206	66063	78422	72259	85906	93342	95940	94950
of which:												
Brazil	FKMP	1461	1551	1737	1935	2071	2656	2567	3110	2725	2458	2560
China	ERDZ	8898	10765	13464	16245	19533	24418	24993	31326	32879	32896	33925
Egypt	QALM	418	484	332	664	539	648	687	658	827	652	809
Hong Kong	ERDS	5463	5757	6571	7462	7015	8172	7759	8173	7631	7421	7389
India	ERDV	2221	2903	3136	3570	5261	5996	5068	6674	7785	7862	7107
Israel	ERDX	822	898	979	959	1047	1171	1098	1564	2268	2422	1913
Malaysia	ERDW	1856	2021	1798	1921	1711	1897	1667	1838	1779	1725	1688
Pakistan	FKMV	512	543	473	511	500	636	702	810	887	848	959
Philippines	FKMY	710	655	708	747	724	638	396	526	479	455	404
Russia	EREC	2408	3478	4966	5793	5465	6995	4643	5250	7458	8478	7138
Singapore	ERDT	2641	3371	3800	3803	4099	4051	3589	4140	3884	3746	2711
South Africa	EPNE	2925	3267	3926	3952	3156	4800	3854	4425	2956	3319	2144
Taiwan	EREB	2194	2344	2223	2387	2426	2633	2267	3114	3487	3977	3635
Thailand	EREA	1640	1767	1715	1960	2026	2457	2323	2683	2595	2631	2734

1 See chapter text.

2 Balance of payments consistent basis.

3 Includes Austria, Belguim, Bulgaria, Cyprus, Czech Republic, Denmark, Estonia, Finland, France, Germany, Greece, Hungary, Irish Republic, Italy, Latvia, Lithuania, Luxemburg, Malta, Netherlands, Poland, Portugal, Romania, Slovakia, Slovenia, Spain and Sweden.

Source: Office for National Statistics: 01633 456294

Table 6.6 may show revisions to data going back over time. This is mainly to reflect revised data from HMRC and other data suppliers, later survey data and a re-assessment of seasonal factors.

6.7 Total International Trade in Services all industries (excluding travel, transport and banking) analysed by product 2010 - 2012

£ million

	Exports			Imports			Balances		
	2010	2011	2012	2010	2011	2012	2010	2011	2012
Agricultural, Mining and On-site Processing Services									
Agricultural	69	28	37	14	78	22	55	-50	15
Mining	243	151	181	46	28	28	197	122	153
Waste treatment and depollution	7	14	9	4	15	18	3	-	-9
Other on-site processing services	647	727	874	155	206	228	493	521	646
Total Agricultural, Mining and On-site Processing Services	**966**	**920**	**1,102**	**219**	**327**	**296**	**747**	**593**	**806**
Business and Professional Services									
Accountancy, auditing, bookkeeping and tax consulting services	1,111	1,118	1,170	409	475	666	702	642	503
Advertising	2,392	2,749	2,838	1,821	1,598	1,664	572	1,151	1,173
Management consulting	1,563	1,641	1,893	853	653	693	710	989	1,200
Public relations services	438	437	393	178	183	121	260	254	272
Recruitment	787	722	931	406	236	299	382	486	632
Other business management	1,622	1,781	2,214	1,288	1,361	1,637	334	420	577
Legal services	3,267	3,510	3,835	654	601	877	2,613	2,910	2,958
Market research and public opinion polling	526	552	641	368	413	385	158	138	257
Operational leasing services	362	367	327	462	354	477	-100	12	-150
Procurement	157	152	188	276	239	262	-119	-87	-75
Property management	157	155	218	34	44	42	123	111	175
Research and development	5,683	5,736	5,559	4,217	4,025	3,523	1,465	1,711	2,037
Services between related enterprises	12,482	13,758	17,308	6,892	7,996	9,027	5,590	5,762	8,282
Other business and professional services	2,931	3,592	4,573	1,520	1,847	2,179	1,410	1,745	2,394
Total Business and Professional Services	**33,478**	**36,270**	**42,088**	**19,378**	**20,026**	**21,853**	**14,100**	**16,245**	**20,235**
Communications Services									
Postal and courier	809	812	916	413	372	486	396	440	430
Telecommunications	4,818	4,656	5,397	4,148	3,467	3,606	670	1,189	1,792
Total Communications Services	**5,627**	**5,468**	**6,313**	**4,561**	**3,840**	**4,092**	**1,066**	**1,628**	**2,222**
Computer and Information Services									
Computers	6,654	7,279	7,674	3,784	3,688	4,200	2,869	3,591	3,474
News agency services	435	416	397	65	38	38	370	378	359
Publishing services	513	615	638	80	107	91	433	508	547
Other information provision services	638	887	868	230	434	444	408	453	424
Total Computer and Information Services	**8,240**	**9,196**	**9,578**	**4,160**	**4,267**	**4,774**	**4,080**	**4,930**	**4,804**
Construction Goods and Services									
Construction in the UK	103	133	170	521	378	783	-418	-245	-613
Construction outside the UK	1,053	1,471	1,452	475	502	491	578	969	961
Total Construction Goods and Services	**1,156**	**1,604**	**1,622**	**996**	**880**	**1,274**	**160**	**724**	**348**
Financial Services									
Financial	9,318	9,847	11,629	1,477	1,903	1,826	7,841	7,944	9,803
Insurance Services									
Insurance Claims	2,253	2,494	3,009				2,253	2,494	3,009
Insurance Premiums				894	502	671	-894	-502	-671
Merchanting and Other Trade related Services									
Merchanting	3,712	7,635	3,025	133	329	306	3,579	7,305	2,719
Other trade - related services	1,059	964	975	517	634	569	543	329	405
Total Merchanting and Other Trade related Services	**4,771**	**8,598**	**4,000**	**649**	**964**	**875**	**4,122**	**7,634**	**3,124**
Personal, Cultural and Recreational Services									
Audio- Visual and related services	1,784	1,863	1,678	362	346	410	1,422	1,518	1,268
Health Services	59	65	38	58	32	20	1	32	18
Training and educational services	454	279	321	41	43	58	414	237	263
Other personal, cultural and recreational services	578	453	418	175	162	119	403	291	299
Total Personal, Cultural and Recreational Services	**2,875**	**2,660**	**2,456**	**635**	**582**	**607**	**2,240**	**2,078**	**1,849**
Royalties and Licenses									
Use of franchise and similar rights fees	2,408	2,129	2,527	1,784	1,590	1,625	624	539	902
Other royalties and license fees	7,160	6,660	5,495	3,811	4,980	3,882	3,349	1,680	1,613
Purchases and sales of franchises and similar rights	490	191	212	229	212	91	262	-21	121
Purchases and sales of other royalties and licenses	800	1,086	1,500	1,008	870	1,275	-209	216	225
Total Royalties and Licenses	**10,858**	**10,066**	**9,733**	**6,832**	**7,652**	**6,872**	**4,026**	**2,414**	**2,861**
Technical services									
Architectural	378	369	351	25	30	37	354	339	314
Engineering	4,850	5,409	5,627	1,123	1,113	1,503	3,727	4,296	4,124
Surveying	183	250	203	69	125	96	115	125	107
Other technical services	1,724	1,345	1,652	522	512	642	1,203	833	1,010
Total Technical Services	**7,136**	**7,373**	**7,834**	**1,738**	**1,779**	**2,279**	**5,398**	**5,594**	**5,555**
Other Trade in Services									
Other trade in services	2,844	2,815	4,465	535	844	979	2,309	1,971	3,487
World Total		**97,311**	**103,828**	**42,074**	**43,564**	**46,399**	**47,449**	**53,746**	**57,430**

Note: World Total Exports 2010 = 89,523

Source: Office for National Statistics

-   Denotes nil or less than £500,000

..   Denotes disclosive data

6.7 Total International Trade in Services all industries (excluding travel, transport and banking) analysed by product 2013

£ million

	Exports	Imports	Balance
	2013	2013	2013
Agricultural and Mining Services			
Agricultural, forestry and fishing	15	25	-10
Mining and oil and gas extraction services	1,180	145	1,035
Total Agricultural and Mining services	1,196	170	1,025
Manufacturing, Maintenance and On-site Processing Services			
Waste treatment and depolution services	34	44	-10
Manufacturing services on goods owned by others	2,555	760	1,795
Maintenance and repair services	1,366	463	903
Total Manufacturing, Maintenance and On-site Processing services	3,956	1,267	2,688
Business and Professional Services			
Accountancy, auditing, bookkeeping and tax consulting services	1,680	806	874
Advertising, market research and public opinion polling services	4,337	2,911	1,426
Business management and management consulting services	6,302	3,129	3,173
Public relations services	428	132	296
Recruitment services	1,412	763	649
Legal services	4,074	845	3,229
Operating leasing services	483	942	-459
Procurement services	100	267	-167
Property management services	371	134	238
Other business and professional services	4,480	2,539	1,942
Services between related enterprises	11,662	8,424	3,239
Total Business and Professional Services	35,330	20,891	14,439
Research and Development Services			
Provision of R&D services	5,141	3,828	1,313
Provision of product development and testing activities	784	256	528
Total Research and Development Services	5,925	4,084	1,841
Intellectual Property			
Trade marks, franchises, brands or design rights			
Outright sales and purchases	668	660	8
Charges or payments for the use of	4,388	2,894	1,494
Copyrighted literary works, sound recordings, films, television prgrammes and databases			
Outright sales and purchases	720	510	210
Charges or payments for the use of	4,390	2,663	1,727
Patents and other intellectual property that are the end result of research and development			
Outright sales and purchases	119	70	49
Charges or payments for the use of	1,446	669	776
Total intellectual property	11,730	7,466	4,265
Telecommunication, Computer and Information Services			
Postal and courier	1,056	629	427
Telecommunications	5,978	3,616	2,362
Computer Services	6,696	4,689	2,008
Publishing Services	740	90	651
News agency Services	459	97	361
Information Services	1,422	501	921
Total Telecommunication, Computer and Information Services	16,352	9,622	6,730
Construction Services			
Construction in the UK	147	889	-742
Construction outside the UK	2,101	567	1,534
Total Construction Services	2,248	1,456	792

6.7 Total International Trade in Services all industries (excluding travel, transport and banking) analysed by product 2013

£ million

	Exports	Imports	Balance
	2013	2013	2013
Financial Services			
Financial	14,909	2,935	11,974
Insurance and Pension Services			
Insurance and Pension Services Claims	3,435		3,435
Insurance and Pension Services Premiums		742	-742
Merchanting and Other Trade related Services			
Merchanting	3,585	437	3,147
Other trade - related services	1,516	629	887
Total Merchanting and Other Trade related Services	5,101	1,067	4,034
Personal, Cultural and Recreational Services			
Audio- Visual and related services	1,307	580	726
Medical Services	57	18	39
Training and educational services	265	119	146
Heritage and recreational services	349	31	319
Social, domestic and other personal services	36	17	18
Total Personal, Cultural and Recreational Services	2,014	765	1,248
Technical and Scientific Services			
Architectural services	483	111	372
Engineering Services	7,068	1,241	5,827
Scientific and other techinical services inc surveying	1,845	487	1,358
Total Technical Services	9,395	1,839	7,556
Other Trade in Services			
Other trade in services	5,603	1,083	4,520
Total International Trade in Services	**117,193**	**53,387**	**63,806**

Source: Office for National Statistics

- Denotes nil or less than £500,000

.. Denotes disclosive data

The sum of constituent items may not always agree exactly with the totals shown due to rounding

Data from 2013 has been collected in accordance with BPM6 regulations

6.8 Total International Trade in Services (excluding travel, transport and banking) analysed by continents and countries 2011 - 2013

£ million

	Exports			Imports			Balances		
	2011	2012	2013	2011	2012	2013	2011	2012	2013
Europe									
European Union (EU)									
Austria	641	340	365	198	158	245	444	183	120
Belgium	1,399	1,596	2,064	943	1,007	1,199	456	589	865
Bulgaria	73	77	93	86	37	87	-13	40	6
Croatia			45			25			20
Cyprus	272	301	456	129	110	285	143	191	171
Czech Republic	322	313	351	160	144	243	162	168	108
Denmark	1,158	1,237	1,539	444	441	563	714	796	976
Estonia	29	38	30	15	15	29	14	22	1
Finland	755	719	624	195	211	229	560	508	395
France	4,061	4,547	4,798	3,395	3,518	3,274	667	1,029	1,524
Germany	5,471	6,018	7,490	3,760	4,102	4,736	1,710	1,915	2,754
Greece	564	434	438	102	122	152	462	312	286
Hungary	341	342	248	225	238	196	116	104	52
Irish Republic	6,094	6,346	6,697	1,873	2,597	4,084	4,221	3,748	2,613
Italy	1,904	1,928	2,411	1,191	1,415	1,324	713	513	1,087
Latvia	36	32	46	11	9	25	25	24	21
Lithuania	45	29	61	50	20	24	-5	9	37
Luxembourg	1,704	1,683	2,090	1,191	1,182	1,404	514	501	686
Malta	227	183	265	62	37	65	165	146	200
Netherlands	4,838	5,373	5,584	1,494	1,657	2,727	3,344	3,717	2,857
Poland	739	636	679	394	407	521	344	229	158
Portugal	323	289	474	154	156	195	168	133	279
Romania	170	211	242	70	94	125	100	117	117
Slovakia	378	199	205	34	48	83	344	151	122
Slovenia	..	..	..	..	..	..	..	..	30
Spain	1,589	1,791	1,863	911	1,056	1,305	678	735	558
Sweden	1,816	1,686	1,930	1,403	1,381	1,183	413	305	747
EU Institutions	..	..	..	..	..	..	..	..	16
Total European Union (EU)	**35,071**	**36,497**	**41,148**	**18,592**	**20,281**	**24,342**	**16,479**	**16,217**	**16,806**
European Free Trade Association (EFTA)									
Iceland	69	84	74	73	14	9	-4	69	65
Liechtenstein	40	55	32	6	3	3	34	52	29
Norway	1,463	1,723	2,194	470	441	459	993	1,282	1,735
Switzerland	6,001	6,248	7,712	1,301	1,307	2,179	4,700	4,941	5,533
Total EFTA	**7,572**	**8,109**	**10,012**	**1,850**	**1,765**	**2,650**	**5,722**	**6,344**	**7,362**
Other Europe									
Russia	753	754	944	342	210	390	411	544	554
Channel Islands	1,339	2,073	1,843	244	255	232	1,095	1,818	1,611
Isle of Man	65	68	93	22	12	13	43	56	80
Turkey	647	549	564	107	121	188	541	429	376
Rest of Europe	1,030	900	622	163	223	241	868	677	381
Europe Unallocated	2,431	3,013	1,924	1,006	1,326	1,303	1,425	1,687	621
Total Europe	**48,909**	**51,963**	**57,150**	**22,325**	**24,192**	**29,359**	**26,583**	**27,771**	**27,791**
America									
Brazil	556	743	819	183	183	140	373	560	679
Canada	1,362	1,368	1,815	975	583	760	387	785	1,055
Mexico	175	171	224	54	59	43	121	112	181
USA	20,670	22,759	26,504	9,471	10,654	11,642	11,200	12,104	14,862
Rest of America	3,299	3,184	3,182	425	599	697	2,874	2,585	2,485
America Unallocated	666	580	371	109	114	54	557	466	317
Total America	**26,729**	**28,805**	**32,915**	**11,217**	**12,193**	**13,336**	**15,512**	**16,612**	**19,579**
Asia									
China	1,007	1,183	1,180	325	427	591	682	757	589
Hong Kong	578	757	895	610	637	638	-31	120	257
India	1,087	717	863	1,355	1,241	1,355	-268	-524	-492
Indonesia	108	141	167	30	25	43	77	116	124
Israel	549	433	329	348	333	363	201	100	-34
Japan	2,056	1,995	2,140	2,793	1,579	1,238	-737	417	902
Malaysia	391	413	498	111	88	60	280	325	438

6.8 Total International Trade in Services (excluding travel, transport and banking) analysed by continents and countries 2011 - 2013

£ million

	Exports			Imports			Balances		
	2011	2012	2013	2011	2012	2013	2011	2012	2013
Pakistan	103	103	104	23	40	106	79	63	-2
Philippines	70	84	92	81	124	121	-11	-40	-29
Saudi Arabia	1,525	3,483	5,315	156	322	113	1,369	3,162	5,202
Singapore	2,547	1,346	1,411	900	1,070	1,192	1,647	275	219
South Korea	480	626	700	158	201	203	322	425	497
Taiwan	388	387	366	47	72	87	341	316	279
Thailand	185	213	294	51	56	57	134	157	237
Rest of Asia	3,382	3,616	4,580	924	1,005	1,452	2,458	2,611	3,128
Asia Unallocated	989	786	726	337	588	418	652	198	308
Total Asia	**15,445**	**16,284**	**19,660**	**8,250**	**7,807**	**8,037**	**7,195**	**8,477**	**11,623**
Australasia and Oceania									
Australia	1,642	1,785	..	744	855	..	898	931	1,101
New Zealand	89	154	219	42	46	75	47	109	144
Rest of Australia and Oceania	162	224	..	27	13	..	135	211	152
Oceania Unallocated	14	21	-	4	5	-	10	16	-
Total Australasia and Oceania	**1,907**	**2,185**	**2,365**	**816**	**918**	**968**	**1,090**	**1,266**	**1,397**
Africa									
Nigeria	543	507	562	50	140	297	492	367	265
South Africa	868	1,127	968	253	307	332	615	820	636
Rest of Africa	2,539	2,453	2,793	410	371	637	2,129	2,082	2,156
Africa Unallocated	244	326	233	183	279	239	61	47	-6
Total Africa	**4,194**	**4,412**	**4,556**	**897**	**1,097**	**1,505**	**3,297**	**3,316**	**3,051**
Total Unallocated	..	180	547	..	192	182	..	-12	365
International Organisations	..	-	-	..	-	-	..	-	-
TOTAL INTERNATIONAL TRADE IN SERVICES	**97,311**	**103,828**	**117,193**	**43,564**	**46,399**	**53,387**	**53,746**	**57,430**	**63,806**

Source: Office for National Statistics

- Denotes nil or less than £500,000

.. Denotes disclosive data

The sum of constituent items may not always agree exactly with the totals shown due to rounding

Data from 2013 has been collected in accordance with BPM6 regulation

See background notes for geographical groupings

Excludes the activities of banking and travel industries

Estimates for Croatia have been published for the first time in 2013. Previously this was included in the Rest of Europe.

6.9 Summary of balance of payments in 2012

£ million

	Credits	Debits
1. Current account		
A. Goods and services	492 810	526 711
1. Goods	299 457	407 350
2. Services	193 353	119 361
2.1. Transportation	22 072	21 047
2.2. Travel	23 178	32 585
2.3. Communications	6 008	4 482
2.4. Construction	1 509	1 459
2.5. Insurance	15 078	3 503
2.6. Financial	45 960	11 217
2.7. Computer and information	9 449	4 319
2.8. Royalties and licence fees	7 993	5 323
2.9. Other business	56 490	31 043
2.10. Personal, cultural and recreational	3 405	451
2.11. Government	2 211	3 932
B. Income	161 980	164 234
1. Compensation of employees	1 124	1 272
2. Investment income	160 856	162 962
2.1 Direct investment	80 962	43 489
2.2 Portfolio investment	47 979	73 050
2.3 Other investment	31 221	46 423
2.4 Reserve assets	694	
C. Current transfers	17 519	40 574
1. General government	3 715	20 086
2. Other sectors	13 804	20 488
Total current account	**672 309**	**731 519**
2. Capital and financial accounts		
A. Capital account	6 140	2 352
1. Capital transfers	4 450	1 023
2. Acquisition/disposal of non-produced, non-financial assets	1 690	1 329
B. Financial account	−26 970	−75 183
1. Direct investment	39 365	48 250
Abroad		48 250
1.1. Equity capital		9 339
1.2. Reinvested earnings		29 232
1.3. Other capital[1]		9 679
In United Kingdom	39 365	
1.1. Equity capital	28 411	
1.2. Reinvested earnings	11 334	
1.3. Other capital[2]	−380	
2. Portfolio investment	−92 489	118 756
Assets		118 756
2.1. Equity securities		32 487
2.2. Debt securities		86 269
Liabilities	−92 489	
2.1. Equity securities	−26 325	
2.2. Debt securities	−66 164	
3. Financial derivatives (net)		−26 757
4. Other investment	26 154	−223 074
Assets		−223 074
4.1 Trade credits		−94
4.2 Loans		−32 234
4.3 Currency and deposits		−191 702
4.4 Other assets		956
Liabilities	26 154	
4.1. Trade credits	–	
4.2. Loans	145 119	
4.3. Currency and deposits	−119 158	
4.4. Other liabilities	193	
5. Reserve assets		7 642
5.1. Monetary gold		–
5.2. Special drawing rights		111
5.3. Reserve position in the IMF		556
5.4. Foreign exchange		6 980
5.5. Other claims		−5
Total capital and financial accounts	**−20 830**	**−72 831**
Total current, capital and financial accounts	**651 479**	**658 688**
Net errors and omissions	7 209	

Source: Office for National Statistics - United Kingdom Balance of payments 2013

1 Other capital transaction on direct investment abroad represents claims on affiliated enterprises less liabilities to affiliated enterprises.

2 Other capital transactions on direct investment in the United Kingdom represents liabilities to direct investors less claims on direct investors.

6.10   Summary of Balance of payments: balances (credits less debits)[1]

£ million

| | | | Total goods | Compensati- | | | | | Current | | | |
| | Trade in | Trade in | and | on of | Investment | Total | Current | Current | balance as | Capital | Financial | Net errors |
	goods	services	services	employees	income	income	transfers	balance	% of GDP[1]	account	account	& omissions
	LQCT	KTMS	KTMY	KTMP	HMBM	HMBP	KTNF	HBOG	AA6H	FKMJ	HBNT	HHDH
1946	−101	−274	−375	−20	76	56	166	−153	..	−21	181	−7
1947	−358	−197	−555	−19	140	121	123	−311	..	−21	552	−220
1948	−152	−64	−216	−20	223	203	96	83	0.7	−17	−58	−8
1949	−137	−43	−180	−20	206	186	29	35	0.3	−12	−103	80
1950	−54	−4	−58	−21	378	357	39	338	2.6	−10	−447	119
1951	−692	32	−660	−21	322	301	29	−330	−2.3	−15	426	−81
1952	−272	123	−149	−22	231	209	169	229	1.4	−15	−229	15
1953	−244	123	−121	−25	207	182	143	204	1.2	−13	−177	−14
1954	−210	115	−95	−27	227	200	55	160	0.9	−13	−174	27
1955	−315	42	−273	−27	149	122	43	−108	−0.6	−15	34	89
1956	50	26	76	−30	203	173	2	251	1.2	−13	−250	12
1957	−29	121	92	−32	223	191	−5	278	1.3	−13	−313	48
1958	34	119	153	−34	261	227	4	384	1.7	−10	−411	37
1959	−116	118	2	−37	233	196	−	198	0.8	−5	−68	−125
1960	−404	39	−365	−35	201	166	−6	−205	−0.8	−6	−7	218
1961	−144	51	−93	−35	223	188	−9	86	0.3	−12	23	−97
1962	−104	50	−54	−37	301	264	−14	196	0.7	−12	−195	11
1963	−123	4	−119	−38	364	326	−37	170	0.6	−16	−30	−124
1964	−551	−34	−585	−33	365	332	−74	−327	−1.0	−17	392	−48
1965	−263	−66	−329	−34	405	371	−75	−33	−0.1	−18	49	2
1966	−111	44	−67	−39	358	319	−91	161	0.4	−19	22	−164
1967	−601	157	−444	−39	354	315	−118	−247	−0.6	−25	179	93
1968	−708	341	−367	−48	303	255	−119	−231	−0.5	−26	688	−431
1969	−214	392	178	−47	468	421	−109	490	1.0	−23	−794	327
1970	−18	455	437	−56	527	471	−89	819	1.6	−22	−818	21
1971	205	617	822	−63	454	391	−90	1 123	2.0	−23	−1 330	230
1972	−736	722	−14	−52	350	298	−142	142	0.2	−35	477	−584
1973	−2 573	907	−1 666	−68	970	902	−336	−1 100	−1.5	−39	1 031	108
1974	−5 241	1 292	−3 949	−92	1 010	918	−302	−3 333	−4.0	−34	3 185	182
1975	−3 245	1 708	−1 537	−102	257	155	−313	−1 695	−1.6	−36	1 569	162
1976	−3 930	2 872	−1 058	−140	760	620	−534	−972	−0.8	−12	507	477
1977	−2 271	3 704	1 433	−152	−678	−830	−889	−286	−0.2	11	−3 286	3 561
1978	−1 534	4 215	2 681	−140	−300	−440	−1 420	821	0.5	−79	−2 655	1 913
1979	−3 326	4 573	1 247	−130	−342	−472	−1 777	−1 002	−0.5	−103	864	241
1980	1 329	4 414	5 743	−82	−2 268	−2 350	−1 653	1 740	0.8	−4	−2 157	421
1981	3 238	4 776	8 014	−66	−1 883	−1 949	−1 219	4 846	1.9	−79	−5 312	545
1982	1 879	4 261	6 140	−95	−2 336	−2 431	−1 476	2 233	0.8	6	−1 233	−1 006
1983	−1 618	5 406	3 788	−89	−1 050	−1 139	−1 391	1 258	0.4	75	−3 287	1 954
1984	−5 409	6 101	692	−94	−326	−420	−1 566	−1 294	−0.4	107	−7 130	8 317
1985	−3 416	8 499	5 083	−120	−2 609	−2 729	−2 924	−570	−0.2	185	−1 657	2 042
1986	−9 617	8 182	−1 435	−156	71	−85	−2 094	−3 614	−0.9	135	−122	3 601
1987	−11 698	9 163	−2 535	−174	−855	−1 029	−3 437	−7 001	−1.6	333	10 606	−3 938
1988	−21 553	7 506	−14 047	−64	−1 438	−1 502	−3 293	−18 842	−3.9	235	16 989	1 618
1989	−24 724	7 543	−17 181	−138	−2 683	−2 821	−4 228	−24 230	−4.6	270	13 614	10 346
1990	−18 707	8 879	−9 828	−110	−5 085	−5 195	−4 802	−19 825	−3.5	497	22 272	−2 944
1991	−10 223	9 106	−1 117	−63	−6 266	−6 329	−999	−8 445	−1.4	290	7 855	300
1992	−13 050	9 706	−3 344	−49	−1 786	−1 835	−5 228	−10 407	−1.7	421	16 311	−6 325
1993	−13 066	12 086	−980	35	−3 420	−3 385	−5 056	−9 421	−1.4	309	22 278	−13 166
1994	−11 126	12 632	1 506	−170	523	353	−5 187	−3 328	−0.5	33	−3 240	6 535
1995	−12 023	16 195	4 172	−296	−1 669	−1 965	−7 363	−5 156	−0.7	533	−1 717	6 340
1996	−13 722	17 249	3 527	93	−3 494	−3 401	−4 539	−4 413	−0.6	1 260	−940	4 093
1997	−12 347	18 071	5 724	83	−1 244	−1 161	−5 525	−962	−0.1	958	−7 204	7 208
1998	−21 761	16 098	−5 663	−10	10 306	10 296	−8 111	−3 538	−0.4	489	4 535	−1 486
1999	−29 126	15 448	−13 678	201	−4 247	−4 046	−7 322	−25 046	−2.7	767	29 478	−5 199
2000	−33 264	15 000	−18 264	150	−435	−285	−9 775	−28 324	−2.9	1 703	17 135	9 486
2001	−41 277	17 930	−23 347	66	5 765	5 831	−6 392	−23 908	−2.3	1 318	26 715	−4 125
2002	−47 619	18 339	−29 280	67	15 499	15 566	−8 459	−22 173	−2.1	971	15 489	5 713
2003	−48 605	22 649	−25 956	59	16 475	16 534	−9 569	−18 991	−1.7	1 466	29 773	−12 248
2004	−61 078	28 115	−32 963	−494	18 907	18 413	−9 817	−24 367	−2.0	2 064	33 765	−11 462
2005	−69 149	33 569	−35 580	−610	24 376	23 766	−11 746	−23 560	−1.8	1 503	37 181	−15 124
2006	−76 842	41 643	−35 199	−958	9 603	8 645	−11 788	−38 342	−2.8	975	36 966	401
2007	−90 535	53 802	−36 733	−734	19 719	18 985	−13 456	−31 204	−2.2	2 566	43 303	−14 665
2008	−94 261	61 689	−32 572	−715	33 203	32 488	−13 697	−13 781	−0.9	3 241	10 143	397
2009	−82 933	59 560	−23 373	−259	18 641	18 382	−15 060	−20 051	−1.4	3 637	11 298	5 116
2010	−98 585	65 733	−32 852	−389	13 799	13 410	−20 570	−40 012	−2.7	3 861	32 024	4 127
2011	−100 092	76 832	−23 260	−172	22 666	22 494	−21 709	−22 475	−1.5	4 020	11 477	6 978
2012	−107 893	73 992	−33 901	−148	−2 106	−2 254	−23 055	−59 210	−3.8	3 788	48 213	7 209

1 Using series YBHA: GDP at current market prices.

Source: Office for National Statistics - United Kingdom Balance of Payments 2013

6.11 Balance of payments: current account
United Kingdom

£ million

		1991	1992	1993	1994	1995	1996	1997	1998	1999	2000	2001
Credits												
Exports of goods and services												
Exports of goods	LQAD	103 939	107 863	122 229	135 143	153 577	167 196	171 924	163 482	165 451	187 133	188 391
Exports of services	KTMQ	37 768	41 271	47 868	52 944	59 051	64 934	67 653	70 753	76 909	82 435	89 341
Total exports of goods and services	KTMW	141 707	149 134	170 097	188 087	212 628	232 130	239 577	234 235	242 360	269 568	277 732
Income												
Compensation of employees	KTMN	551	551	595	681	887	911	1 007	840	960	1 032	1 087
Investment income	HMBN	73 652	65 168	70 944	72 585	85 490	89 794	93 360	102 548	100 733	131 902	137 447
Total income	HMBQ	74 203	65 719	71 539	73 266	86 377	90 705	94 367	103 388	101 693	132 934	138 534
Current transfers												
General government	FJUM	4 892	2 180	2 826	2 138	1 730	2 828	2 393	1 767	3 542	2 465	4 991
Other sectors	FJUN	7 234	9 945	9 085	8 918	10 213	11 372	11 646	11 446	9 056	8 882	8 733
Total current transfers	KTND	12 126	12 125	11 911	11 056	11 943	14 200	14 039	13 213	12 598	11 347	13 724
Total	HBOE	**228 036**	**226 978**	**253 547**	**272 409**	**310 948**	**337 035**	**347 983**	**350 836**	**356 651**	**413 849**	**429 990**
Debits												
Imports of goods and services												
Imports of goods	LQBL	114 162	120 913	135 295	146 269	165 600	180 918	184 271	185 243	194 577	220 397	229 668
Imports of services	KTMR	28 662	31 565	35 782	40 312	42 856	47 685	49 582	54 655	61 461	67 435	71 411
Total imports of goods and services	KTMX	142 824	152 478	171 077	186 581	208 456	228 603	233 853	239 898	256 038	287 832	301 079
Income												
Compensation of employees	KTMO	614	600	560	851	1 183	818	924	850	759	882	1 021
Investment income	HMBO	79 918	66 954	74 364	72 062	87 159	93 288	94 604	92 242	104 980	132 337	131 682
Total income	HMBR	80 532	67 554	74 924	72 913	88 342	94 106	95 528	93 092	105 739	133 219	132 703
Current transfers												
General government	FJUO	3 218	3 506	4 156	4 795	4 811	5 081	5 087	6 585	7 271	7 778	7 559
Other sectors	FJUP	9 907	13 847	12 811	11 448	14 495	13 658	14 477	14 799	12 649	13 344	12 557
Total current transfers	KTNE	13 125	17 353	16 967	16 243	19 306	18 739	19 564	21 384	19 920	21 122	20 116
Total	HBOF	**236 481**	**237 385**	**262 968**	**275 737**	**316 104**	**341 448**	**348 945**	**354 374**	**381 697**	**442 173**	**453 898**
Balances												
Trade in goods and services												
Trade in goods	LQCT	−10 223	−13 050	−13 066	−11 126	−12 023	−13 722	−12 347	−21 761	−29 126	−33 264	−41 277
Trade in services	KTMS	9 106	9 706	12 086	12 632	16 195	17 249	18 071	16 098	15 448	15 000	17 930
Total trade in goods and services	KTMY	−1 117	−3 344	−980	1 506	4 172	3 527	5 724	−5 663	−13 678	−18 264	−23 347
Income												
Compensation of employees	KTMP	−63	−49	35	−170	−296	93	83	−10	201	150	66
Investment income	HMBM	−6 266	−1 786	−3 420	523	−1 669	−3 494	−1 244	10 306	−4 247	−435	5 765
Total income	HMBP	−6 329	−1 835	−3 385	353	−1 965	−3 401	−1 161	10 296	−4 046	−285	5 831
Current transfers												
General government	FJUQ	1 674	−1 326	−1 330	−2 657	−3 081	−2 253	−2 694	−4 818	−3 729	−5 313	−2 568
Other sectors	FJUR	−2 673	−3 902	−3 726	−2 530	−4 282	−2 286	−2 831	−3 353	−3 593	−4 462	−3 824
Total current transfers	KTNF	−999	−5 228	−5 056	−5 187	−7 363	−4 539	−5 525	−8 171	−7 322	−9 775	−6 392
Total (Current balance)	HBOG	**−8 445**	**−10 407**	**−9 421**	**−3 328**	**−5 156**	**−4 413**	**−962**	**−3 538**	**−25 046**	**−28 324**	**−23 908**

6.11 Balance of payments: current account
United Kingdom

£ million

		2002	2003	2004	2005	2006	2007	2008	2009	2010	2011	2012
Credits												
Exports of goods and services												
Exports of goods	LQAD	185 857	187 554	190 099	210 704	242 899	219 981	251 565	227 727	265 243	298 421	299 457
Exports of services	KTMQ	94 138	105 527	115 722	129 139	144 686	160 535	178 193	174 444	182 026	194 463	193 353
Total exports of goods and services	KTMW	279 995	293 081	305 821	339 843	387 585	380 516	429 758	402 171	447 269	492 884	492 810
Income												
Compensation of employees	KTMN	1 121	1 116	931	974	938	984	1 046	1 176	1 097	1 121	1 124
Investment income	HMBN	120 543	121 974	137 548	186 115	237 522	289 986	260 855	167 220	160 134	191 250	160 856
Total income	HMBQ	121 664	123 090	138 479	187 089	238 460	290 970	261 901	168 396	161 231	192 371	161 980
Current transfers												
General government	FJUM	3 663	3 968	4 299	4 385	4 471	4 408	5 720	6 271	3 842	3 525	3 715
Other sectors	FJUN	10 660	11 396	12 026	14 065	19 055	12 363	17 647	15 020	13 258	13 154	13 804
Total current transfers	KTND	14 323	15 364	16 325	18 450	23 526	16 771	23 367	21 291	17 100	16 679	17 519
Total	HBOE	**415 982**	**431 535**	**460 625**	**545 382**	**649 571**	**688 257**	**715 026**	**591 858**	**625 600**	**701 934**	**672 309**
Debits												
Imports of goods and services												
Imports of goods	LQBL	233 476	236 159	251 177	279 853	319 741	310 516	345 826	310 660	363 828	398 513	407 350
Imports of services	KTMR	75 799	82 878	87 607	95 570	103 043	106 733	116 504	114 884	116 293	117 631	119 361
Total imports of goods and services	KTMX	309 275	319 037	338 784	375 423	422 784	417 249	462 330	425 544	480 121	516 144	526 711
Income												
Compensation of employees	KTMO	1 054	1 057	1 425	1 584	1 896	1 718	1 761	1 435	1 486	1 293	1 272
Investment income	HMBO	105 044	105 499	118 641	161 739	227 919	270 267	227 652	148 579	146 335	168 584	162 962
Total income	HMBR	106 098	106 556	120 066	163 323	229 815	271 985	229 413	150 014	147 821	169 877	164 234
Current transfers												
General government	FJUO	9 205	10 927	12 020	13 625	13 874	14 082	14 714	17 665	18 680	19 783	20 086
Other sectors	FJUP	13 577	14 006	14 122	16 571	21 440	16 145	22 350	18 686	18 990	18 605	20 488
Total current transfers	KTNE	22 782	24 933	26 142	30 196	35 314	30 227	37 064	36 351	37 670	38 388	40 574
Total	HBOF	**438 155**	**450 526**	**484 992**	**568 942**	**687 913**	**719 461**	**728 807**	**611 909**	**665 612**	**724 409**	**731 519**
Balances												
Trade in goods and services												
Trade in goods	LQCT	−47 619	−48 605	−61 078	−69 149	−76 842	−90 535	−94 261	−82 933	−98 585	−100 092	−107 893
Trade in services	KTMS	18 339	22 649	28 115	33 569	41 643	53 802	61 689	59 560	65 733	76 832	73 992
Total trade in goods and services	KTMY	−29 280	−25 956	−32 963	−35 580	−35 199	−36 733	−32 572	−23 373	−32 852	−23 260	−33 901
Income												
Compensation of employees	KTMP	67	59	−494	−610	−958	−734	−715	−259	−389	−172	−148
Investment income	HMBM	15 499	16 475	18 907	24 376	9 603	19 719	33 203	18 641	13 799	22 666	−2 106
Total income	HMBP	15 566	16 534	18 413	23 766	8 645	18 985	32 488	18 382	13 410	22 494	−2 254
Current transfers												
General government	FJUQ	−5 542	−6 959	−7 721	−9 240	−9 403	−9 674	−8 994	−11 394	−14 838	−16 258	−16 371
Other sectors	FJUR	−2 917	−2 610	−2 096	−2 506	−2 385	−3 782	−4 703	−3 666	−5 732	−5 451	−6 684
Total current transfers	KTNF	−8 459	−9 569	−9 817	−11 746	−11 788	−13 456	−13 697	−15 060	−20 570	−21 709	−23 055
Total (Current balance)	HBOG	**−22 173**	**−18 991**	**−24 367**	**−23 560**	**−38 342**	**−31 204**	**−13 781**	**−20 051**	**−40 012**	**−22 475**	**−59 210**

Source: Office for National Statistics - United Kingdom Balance of Payments 2013

6.12 Balance of payments: financial account and investment income.
Summary of international investment position, financial account and investment income

£ billion

		2002	2003	2004	2005	2006	2007	2008	2009	2010	2011	2012
Investment abroad												
International investment position												
Direct investment	HBWD	637.2	691.1	678.1	705.9	733.1	899.8	1 068.7	975.3	1 044.8	1 097.1	1 137.0
Portfolio investment	HHZZ	844.0	935.8	1 092.1	1 360.9	1 531.0	1 689.7	1 664.3	1 875.3	2 070.3	2 075.9	2 251.3
Financial derivatives	JX96	–	–	709.4	820.1	853.7	1 378.1	4 040.2	2 176.4	2 962.8	3 617.8	3 060.4
Other investment	HLXV	1 545.2	1 813.7	2 118.0	2 714.8	2 917.3	3 683.5	4 147.9	3 461.2	3 747.0	4 034.7	3 712.5
Reserve assets	LTEB	25.5	23.8	23.2	24.7	22.9	26.7	36.3	40.1	49.7	56.8	61.7
Total	HBQA	**3 051.9**	**3 464.5**	**4 620.8**	**5 626.4**	**6 058.1**	**7 677.8**	**10 957.4**	**8 528.3**	**9 874.6**	**10 882.3**	**10 222.9**
Financial account transactions												
Direct investment	-HJYP	35.0	40.9	51.5	44.0	45.0	162.6	99.6	25.2	25.5	66.6	48.2
Portfolio investment	-HHZC	1.0	36.3	141.0	151.0	138.8	91.5	–123.2	164.7	76.8	7.3	118.8
Financial derivatives (net)	-ZPNN	–1.0	5.4	6.8	–5.8	–20.6	27.0	121.7	–29.1	–32.8	2.9	–26.8
Other investment	-XBMM	71.1	260.9	325.4	501.3	396.6	664.7	–645.8	–358.7	240.0	105.1	–223.1
Reserve assets	-LTCV	–0.5	–1.6	0.2	0.7	–0.4	1.2	–1.3	5.8	6.1	4.9	7.6
Total	-HBNR	**105.7**	**341.9**	**524.8**	**691.1**	**559.4**	**947.0**	**–549.0**	**–192.1**	**315.6**	**186.8**	**–75.2**
Investment income												
Direct investment	HJYW	51.5	55.1	63.3	79.2	83.6	91.4	69.5	67.9	80.3	100.9	81.0
Portfolio investment	HLYX	32.5	32.5	36.7	45.4	55.1	66.1	67.5	54.6	47.1	51.0	48.0
Other investment	AIOP	35.8	33.5	36.8	60.9	98.2	131.9	123.1	43.9	32.0	38.6	31.2
Reserve assets	HHCB	0.8	0.8	0.7	0.7	0.6	0.6	0.8	0.8	0.7	0.8	0.7
Total	HMBN	**120.5**	**122.0**	**137.5**	**186.1**	**237.5**	**290.0**	**260.9**	**167.2**	**160.1**	**191.2**	**160.9**
Investment in the UK												
International investment position												
Direct investment	HBWI	340.6	355.5	383.3	494.2	577.3	613.8	660.4	681.8	725.6	766.2	839.5
Portfolio investment	HLXW	925.3	1 091.2	1 249.5	1 489.2	1 722.4	2 006.5	2 022.7	2 417.8	2 554.3	2 469.3	2 503.2
Financial derivatives	JX97	–	–	715.0	831.1	890.5	1 392.2	3 915.3	2 096.8	2 895.0	3 554.9	3 032.6
Other investment	HLYD	1 892.1	2 102.7	2 437.6	2 946.2	3 085.6	3 883.7	4 283.4	3 516.7	3 772.1	4 081.9	3 989.3
Total	HBQB	**3 158.0**	**3 549.5**	**4 785.5**	**5 760.7**	**6 275.8**	**7 896.3**	**10 881.7**	**8 713.1**	**9 946.9**	**10 872.3**	**10 364.5**
Financial account transactions												
Direct investment	HJYU	16.8	16.8	31.2	97.8	84.9	100.0	48.4	49.0	32.1	31.9	39.4
Portfolio investment	HHZF	49.8	131.3	143.8	205.0	195.7	203.1	128.9	211.0	94.9	–19.9	–92.5
Other investment	XBMN	54.6	223.6	383.6	425.5	315.8	687.3	–716.2	–440.8	220.6	186.2	26.2
Total	HBNS	**121.2**	**371.7**	**558.6**	**728.3**	**596.4**	**990.3**	**–538.8**	**–180.8**	**347.6**	**198.3**	**–27.0**
Investment income												
Direct investment	HJYX	16.0	21.9	27.6	36.2	51.6	45.1	3.1	26.6	37.6	43.4	43.5
Portfolio investment	HLZC	33.3	32.8	38.7	47.6	60.2	69.1	75.5	59.9	62.4	72.1	73.1
Other investment	HLZN	55.7	50.7	52.3	78.0	116.1	156.1	149.0	62.2	46.3	53.2	46.4
Total	HMBO	**105.0**	**105.5**	**118.6**	**161.7**	**227.9**	**270.3**	**227.7**	**148.6**	**146.3**	**168.6**	**163.0**
Net investment												
International investment position												
Direct investment	HBWQ	296.6	335.6	294.7	211.7	155.8	285.9	408.4	293.5	319.2	331.0	297.5
Portfolio investment	CGNH	–81.3	–155.4	–157.4	–128.2	–191.4	–316.8	–358.3	–542.5	–483.9	–393.4	–251.9
Financial derivatives	JX98	–	–	–5.6	–11.0	–36.8	–14.1	124.9	79.6	67.8	62.9	27.8
Other investment	CGNG	–346.9	–289.0	–319.7	–231.4	–168.2	–200.1	–135.5	–55.5	–25.1	–47.2	–276.7
Reserve assets	LTEB	25.5	23.8	23.2	24.7	22.9	26.7	36.3	40.1	49.7	56.8	61.7
Net investment position	HBQC	**–106.1**	**–85.0**	**–164.7**	**–134.3**	**–217.7**	**–218.4**	**75.7**	**–184.8**	**–72.3**	**10.0**	**–141.6**
Financial account transactions												
Direct investment	HJYV	–18.3	–24.1	–20.3	53.8	39.9	–62.7	–51.2	23.8	6.6	–34.7	–8.9
Portfolio investment	HHZD	48.8	95.0	2.8	54.0	56.9	111.5	252.1	46.3	18.1	–27.2	–211.2
Financial derivatives	ZPNN	1.0	–5.4	–6.8	5.8	20.6	–27.0	–121.7	29.1	32.8	–2.9	26.8
Other investment	HHYR	–16.5	–37.3	58.3	–75.8	–80.8	22.6	–70.4	–82.1	–19.4	81.2	249.2
Reserve assets	LTCV	0.5	1.6	–0.2	–0.7	0.4	–1.2	1.3	–5.8	–6.1	–4.9	–7.6
Net transactions	HBNT	**15.5**	**29.8**	**33.8**	**37.2**	**37.0**	**43.3**	**10.1**	**11.3**	**32.0**	**11.5**	**48.2**
Investment income												
Direct investment	HJYE	35.5	33.2	35.7	43.0	32.0	46.3	66.4	41.4	42.7	57.5	37.5
Portfolio investment	HLZX	–0.8	–0.3	–2.0	–2.2	–5.1	–3.0	–8.0	–5.3	–15.3	–21.1	–25.1
Other investment	CGNA	–20.0	–17.2	–15.4	–17.1	–17.9	–24.2	–25.9	–18.2	–14.3	–14.5	–15.2
Reserve assets	HHCB	0.8	0.8	0.7	0.7	0.6	0.6	0.8	0.8	0.7	0.8	0.7
Net earnings	HMBM	**15.5**	**16.5**	**18.9**	**24.4**	**9.6**	**19.7**	**33.2**	**18.6**	**13.8**	**22.7**	**–2.1**

Source: Office for National Statistics - United Kingdom Balance of Payments 2013

6.13 Net foreign direct investment flows abroad analysed by area and main country, 2004 to 2013[1,2] (Directional)

£ million

	2004	2005	2006	2007	2008	2009	2010	2011	2012	2013
EUROPE	**10,814**	**12,105**	**16,899**	**90,683**	**50,863**	**15,690**	**11,374**	**27,312**	**2,008**	**-17,582**
EU	11,917	13,337	4,038	69,836	47,298	-7,047	9,761	15,856	-2,262	-12,430
AUSTRIA	1,322	-301	-94	110	-159	-154	2,389	-16	-576	-120
BELGIUM	-544	970	-4,356	1,037	1,656	-1,307	7,594	5,575	1,359	-4,250
BULGARIA	0	11	-5	..	43	11	-80	-1	-6	-3
CROATIA	..	..	..	..	..	..	..	..	12	1
CYPRUS	18	69	98	365	294	63	-290	-184	-19	24
CZECH REPUBLIC	23	24	-160	59	371	-105	-182	-80	829	221
DENMARK	569	391	1,529	539	2,774	-2,170	511	-240	96	-158
ESTONIA	21	2	3	-3	-20	38	9	0	6	10
FINLAND	-37	707	106	268	63	-95	-41	-393	3	46
FRANCE	793	3,138	1,175	4,536	5,979	-1,248	3,382	1,823	8,100	-8,865
GERMANY	-366	-479	3,186	2,260	2,268	3,186	-1,644	444	-1,209	1,393
GREECE	-253	63	15	286	362	-366	33	-230	-105	26
HUNGARY	336	1,821	39	88	164	76	85	50	59	-213
IRISH REPUBLIC	3,325	-1,181	5,161	3,995	-2,098	3,530	-7,731	3,260	5,431	-1,709
ITALY	667	191	-397	2,904	463	-3,801	362	-92	-718	-498
LATVIA	1	-1	4	65	142	-51	-19	-24	37	26
LITHUANIA	1	-4	1	..	..	..	3	6	3	1
LUXEMBOURG	-1,022	-1,213	-14,131	25,453	6,094	4,874	5,820	7,947	-4,350	-8,520
MALTA	178	142	891	-1,952	..	..	..	..	-230	290
NETHERLANDS	4,805	4,821	1,350	22,176	11,056	-14,072	-638	-1,194	-10,609	8,500
POLAND	182	150	397	-500	-128	1,261	73	134	208	776
PORTUGAL	444	603	314	278	341	277	576	104	115	163
ROMANIA	11	101	40	117	211	27	22	61	-3	78
SLOVAKIA	18	21	18	90	104	-29	-17	23	34	301
SLOVENIA	-5	-5	14	9	12	9	..	..	-56	7
SPAIN	1,131	564	2,177	4,155	12,974	1,628	2,148	-566	122	-883
SWEDEN	299	2,732	6,669	3,501	3,155	1,314	-2,025	-454	-781	925
EFTA	-6,667	547	6,926	3,620	2,476	4,550	1,468	1,834	4,600	611
of which										
NORWAY	367	-831	3	1,060	1,556	1,693	-759	1,045	322	-720
SWITZERLAND	-7,007	1,330	6,948	2,653	1,054	2,956	2,221	791	4,291	1,322
OTHER EUROPEAN COUNTRIES	5,564	-1,779	5,935	17,227	1,088	18,188	145	9,621	-331	-5,763
of which										
RUSSIA	1,831	349	-13	1,334	3,919	-353	-1,859	467	-2,662	-9,627
UK OFFSHORE ISLANDS[3]	3,528	-2,341	5,023	14,752	-4,278	17,848	1,036	8,468	1,720	3,522
THE AMERICAS	**24,321**	**20,689**	**19,100**	**53,837**	**33,574**	**-2,218**	**-13,814**	**14,675**	**15,791**	**27,997**
of which										
BERMUDA	6,242	653	908	2,082	3,913	-2,160	-479	-1,238	494	1,726
BRAZIL	386	48	354	791	832	525	1,605	1,723	521	-293
CANADA	1,143	3,372	8,130	15,468	-1,075	-2,732	-8,528	1,372	5,408	-4,169
CHILE	675	790	25	110	-315	59	204	469	14	81
COLOMBIA	225	-687	315	126	157	311	402	-769	..	66
MEXICO	1,386	168	334	128	409	57	503	1,015	541	727
PANAMA	12	27	7	-18	-4	60	40	36	25	58
USA	9,732	15,041	-1,803	30,820	27,568	7,851	-9,025	12,055	9,321	28,271
ASIA	**7,689**	**5,399**	**7,992**	**7,734**	**6,364**	**8,575**	**8,401**	**20,526**	**-3,099**	**-4,165**
NEAR & MIDDLE EAST COUNTRIES	486	398	1,219	2,044	2,884	1,330	-1,136	4,754	-7,356	-5,354
of which										
GULF ARABIAN COUNTRIES	293	577	329	482	544	1,424	830	167	-294	4,733
OTHER ASIAN COUNTRIES	7,203	5,001	6,773	5,689	3,480	7,245	9,538	15,772	4,257	1,188
of which										
CHINA	539	598	374	1,138	290	343	797	1,311	506	347
HONG KONG	5,303	1,547	1,674	1,503	305	1,798	2,180	3,475	3,760	3,613
INDIA	274	616	104	650	437	695	1,856	7,090	-228	488
INDONESIA	-289	-116	196	-140	-68	594	1,021	3,308	1,190	269
JAPAN	37	247	440	1,141	-140	923	-568	1,996	499	-1,721
MALAYSIA	428	244	241	216	321	337	603	585	84	267
SINGAPORE	-161	-508	2,621	-1,265	183	-582	392	-4,733	-1,698	-1,054

6.13 Net foreign direct investment flows abroad analysed by area and main country, 2004 to 2013[1,2] (Directional)

£ million

	2004	2005	2006	2007	2008	2009	2010	2011	2012	2013
SOUTH KOREA	278	2,247	679	488	810	566	833	411	528	354
THAILAND	181	228	536	3	192	331	154	178	158	169
AUSTRALASIA & OCEANIA	**1,026**	**423**	**3,132**	**2,149**	**7,662**	**-3,543**	**11,704**	**803**	**1,139**	**8,064**
of which										
AUSTRALIA	408	444	2,743	2,012	6,590	-4,625	11,487	338	983	7,885
NEW ZEALAND	258	-56	405	125	126	1,078	156	373	140	118
AFRICA	**5,863**	**5,843**	**-235**	**4,726**	**881**	**6,590**	**7,822**	**-3,186**	**11,554**	**2,923**
of which										
KENYA	47	73	62	97	67	115	195	63	-35	89
NIGERIA	-44	-108	44	56	273	763	228	354	76	-874
SOUTH AFRICA	3,840	4,368	1,466	1,734	1,317	994	2,459	1,814	5,163	1,333
ZIMBABWE	91	18	8	4	-6	1	12	25	18	8
WORLD TOTAL	**49,713**	**44,458**	**46,887**	**159,129**	**99,322**	**25,094**	**25,486**	**60,130**	**27,392**	**17,237**
OECD	18,355	35,305	21,276	125,975	83,393	1,164	7,674	36,119	20,257	19,459
CENTRAL & EASTERN EUROPE[4]	36	158	76	0	53	40	-26	-3	10	55

1 Net foreign direct investment includes unremitted profits.

2 A negative sign before values indicates a net disinvestment abroad (i.e. a decrease in the amount due to the UK).

3 The UK Offshore Islands consist of the Channel Islands & the Isle of Man, excluded from the definition of the economic territory of the UK from 1997.

4 Central & Eastern Europe prior to 2007 includes data for Bulgaria and Romania.

5 Data between 2004-2011 are on a Balance of Payments Manual 5 basis; data for 2012 and 2013 are on a Balance of Payments Manual 6 basis. The largest change between methods is a shift from a directional to asset/liability. However, there are a number of additional methodological changes that have been undertaken between BPM5 and BPM6, outlined here: http://www.ons.gov.uk/ons/rel/naa1-rd/national-accounts-articles/impact-of-new-international-measurement-guidelines--balance-of-payments-manual-6--on-the-uk-s-balance-of-payments/index.html

.. Indicates data are disclosive.

.- Indicates nil returns.

Source: Office for National Statistics

6.14 FDI international investment position abroad analysed by area and main country, 2004 to 2013 [1]

£ million

	2004	2005	2006	2007	2008	2009	2010	2011	2012	2013
EUROPE	382,104	387,324	402,593	527,997	600,375	552,235	612,848	614,775	572,301	528,941
EU	348,576	339,691	314,481	412,024	513,506	477,747	539,683	533,266	495,633	447,425
AUSTRIA	4,102	4,005	2,402	2,579	2,707	3,746	1,054	999	347	786
BELGIUM	7,828	13,492	4,380	6,887	11,207	14,615	41,128	38,027	16,702	9,309
BULGARIA	22	53	46	46	143	117	104	88	55	120
CROATIA	..	..	..	..	..	..	..	..	185	251
CYPRUS	64	59	561	683	363	498	560	643	1,260	528
CZECH REPUBLIC	793	823	523	632	1,011	510	533	438	1,347	1,694
DENMARK	5,256	5,090	7,782	6,220	10,809	6,995	7,940	7,152	24,496	7,482
ESTONIA	78	7	-1	7	25	33	62	86	63	97
FINLAND	695	2,465	1,287	2,329	609	396	1,190	1,533	193	486
FRANCE	35,313	47,348	36,327	39,598	42,111	39,944	54,841	53,459	66,165	54,105
GERMANY	12,164	20,753	17,602	19,766	30,550	26,896	22,476	20,482	15,586	20,859
GREECE	456	625	562	864	1,047	910	2,028	1,417	1,308	1,571
HUNGARY	1,506	2,491	1,795	1,870	2,136	697	635	1,007	1,039	594
IRISH REPUBLIC	29,059	26,824	26,432	25,362	30,529	34,859	40,927	44,844	44,380	43,453
ITALY	11,322	10,872	7,924	12,786	10,734	11,689	11,971	11,708	10,585	11,790
LATVIA	25	22	27	..	95	1	-26	48	71	141
LITHUANIA	22	16	6	11	..	25	..	41	45	54
LUXEMBOURG	81,709	97,260	62,355	95,915	137,065	124,582	140,457	137,410	122,127	96,703
MALTA	1,528	-459	2,399	3,263	..	1,467	824	333	1,766	253
NETHERLANDS	131,143	64,511	92,783	138,769	160,172	146,027	145,279	144,966	129,036	122,237
POLAND	2,316	1,974	2,519	2,078	2,914	3,723	3,647	3,796	4,056	4,797
PORTUGAL	1,664	2,702	3,167	3,366	3,528	3,311	3,665	3,014	2,853	2,590
ROMANIA	260	356	247	402	675	558	549	530	591	707
SLOVAKIA	103	93	136	184	392	253	262	275	203	..
SLOVENIA	54	3	53	..	52	52	..	320	262	115
SPAIN	11,318	25,604	25,233	30,879	37,105	32,552	35,836	37,343	31,528	35,012
SWEDEN	9,776	12,702	17,935	17,388	26,069	23,289	23,305	23,309	19,570	20,688
EFTA	14,468	12,933	12,637	17,745	20,119	25,927	26,373	23,761	25,206	16,030
of which										
NORWAY	4,934	4,498	2,116	2,370	3,927	5,310	5,532	4,664	4,782	3,932
SWITZERLAND	9,104	7,979	10,239	15,124	15,790	20,202	20,813	19,071	20,404	12,060
OTHER EUROPEAN COUNTRIES	19,060	34,700	75,475	98,228	66,750	48,561	46,792	57,747	51,462	65,486
of which										
RUSSIA	1,627	1,814	6,054	7,182	10,380	10,042	10,019	7,863	5,688	13,819
UK OFFSHORE ISLANDS [2]	15,678	29,954	65,814	86,482	49,921	31,225	29,483	41,723	35,263	43,213
THE AMERICAS	182,091	216,343	256,423	292,687	354,745	300,175	265,351	286,481	283,762	318,642
of which										
BERMUDA	7,561	10,604	13,889	13,839	24,027	15,707	16,123	15,625	15,349	12,372
BRAZIL	3,922	3,220	2,824	3,717	6,502	4,602	6,442	14,113	14,079	11,315
CANADA	8,922	12,812	19,188	28,980	29,216	28,879	32,546	27,602	30,936	27,892
CHILE	2,133	2,814	563	439	320	226	506	744	721	865
COLOMBIA	1,874	1,132	985	1,109	1,520	1,975	2,553	439	-117	633
MEXICO	2,461	2,860	2,337	3,791	3,548	2,489	3,088	5,007	4,076	5,121
PANAMA	132	166	..	..	168	182	183	297	..	424
USA	140,321	164,405	180,629	202,117	246,063	224,957	184,788	205,481	190,418	241,220
ASIA	47,311	54,919	54,377	60,887	77,412	80,647	105,706	121,635	101,521	108,422
NEAR & MIDDLE EAST COUNTRIES	3,008	3,733	6,874	9,984	14,690	18,514	24,084	28,544	13,064	11,743
of which										
GULF ARABIAN COUNTRIES	2,062	3,013	4,756	6,320	8,926	12,800	16,153	20,598	10,194	7,045
OTHER ASIAN COUNTRIES	44,303	51,187	47,503	50,903	62,723	62,133	81,622	93,091	88,456	96,679
of which										
CHINA	1,882	2,685	2,228	2,719	4,571	4,446	5,760	6,337	6,509	5,991
HONG KONG	19,165	20,432	22,256	25,517	28,666	24,342	27,675	31,015	36,701	46,175
INDIA	1,682	2,126	1,977	2,942	3,475	9,287	10,890	13,618	5,090	3,606
INDONESIA	1,178	1,168	982	825	1,035	1,848	2,651	5,457	4,091	2,829
JAPAN	5,829	6,076	2,485	592	1,901	2,943	2,588	5,833	6,306	3,573
MALAYSIA	1,592	1,455	1,174	1,233	891	884	1,364	1,736	1,912	4,024
SINGAPORE	6,610	7,144	6,684	6,220	10,479	6,284	7,969	9,538	9,046	11,748
SOUTH KOREA	1,218	4,586	3,763	4,457	3,048	3,243	4,160	4,403	4,470	4,332
THAILAND	947	1,281	1,407	1,456	1,708	1,201	1,288	1,363	1,492	2,050
AUSTRALASIA & OCEANIA	16,888	16,694	12,665	16,173	19,930	18,893	32,051	37,161	43,532	45,769
of which										
AUSTRALIA	14,586	14,627	11,571	15,391	18,024	16,091	31,490	36,201	42,430	44,599
NEW ZEALAND	1,459	1,176	923	682	580	1,509	457	641	665	658

6.14 FDI international investment position abroad analysed by area and main country, 2004 to 2013 [1]

£ million

	2004	2005	2006	2007	2008	2009	2010	2011	2012	2013
AFRICA	**17,350**	**20,834**	**15,105**	**18,516**	**21,104**	**29,548**	**30,143**	**30,848**	**42,292**	**33,252**
of which										
KENYA	238	281	313	331	372	396	474	579	479	881
NIGERIA	950	924	1,011	744	1,349	2,071	1,858	2,175	1,743	1,173
SOUTH AFRICA	10,964	13,733	8,255	9,533	10,994	14,404	10,245	10,609	13,015	8,114
ZIMBABWE	103	50	58	32	35	29	15	14	32	..
WORLD TOTAL	**645,744**	**696,113**	**741,163**	**916,261**	**1,073,613**	**981,481**	**1,046,098**	**1,090,900**	**1,043,408**	**1,035,026**
OECD	537,109	561,694	547,303	684,619	837,804	785,854	827,827	845,859	803,561	796,106
CENTRAL & EASTERN EUROPE [3]	534	640	515	65	275	312	239	245	-7	130

1. A negative sign before values indicates a net disinvestment abroad (ie a decrease in the amount due to the UK).

2. The UK Offshore Islands consist of the Channel Islands & the Isle of Man, excluded from the definition of the economic territory of the UK from 1997.

3. Central & Eastern Europe prior to 2007 includes data for Bulgaria and Romania.

4. Data between 2004-2011 are on a Balance of Payments Manual 5 basis; data for 2012 and 2013 are on a Balance of Payments Manual 6 basis.

The largest change between methods is a shift from a directional to asset/liability. However, there are a number of additional methodological changes that have been undertaken between BPM5 and BPM6, outlined here: http://www.ons.gov.uk/ons/rel/naa1-rd/national-accounts-articles/impact-of-new-international-measurement-guidelines--balance-of-payments-manual-6--on-the-uk-s-balance-of-payments/index.html

.. Indicates data are disclosive.
.- Indicates nil returns.

Source: Office for National Statistics

6.15 Earnings from foreign direct investment abroad analysed by area and main country, 2004 to 2013 [1]

£ million

	2004	2005	2006	2007	2008	2009	2010	2011	2012	2013
EUROPE	**25,782**	**32,186**	**38,957**	**44,062**	**43,598**	**34,944**	**30,867**	**45,661**	**27,436**	**26,706**
EU	20,708	23,904	28,337	34,284	37,521	28,673	20,889	35,899	22,165	22,471
AUSTRIA	296	301	186	247	169	259	139	0	-149	-149
BELGIUM	653	818	875	1,312	1,568	1,443	1,171	1,853	1,357	352
BULGARIA	0	9	3	-9	-3	5	0	8	0	21
CROATIA	..	..	..	..	..	..	..	..	-3	12
CYPRUS	22	37	171	366	92	57	-8	-58	138	19
CZECH REPUBLIC	110	108	-64	72	-134	-127	-70	42	212	167
DENMARK	272	387	411	580	530	216	628	586	474	394
ESTONIA	3	..	11	5	6	26	17	23	14	5
FINLAND	112	103	69	281	131	120	184	218	56	37
FRANCE	2,107	2,957	3,344	3,007	1,769	1,437	3,419	3,531	2,661	1,993
GERMANY	2,328	2,685	2,189	2,890	3,116	2,732	1,492	1,649	52	1,286
GREECE	102	160	151	223	102	208	-51	19	-39	52
HUNGARY	202	295	83	96	77	32	22	94	114	52
IRISH REPUBLIC	2,461	2,835	2,525	3,049	1,879	-2,747	-10,064	-756	1,207	2,337
ITALY	708	732	696	837	311	32	630	251	349	307
LATVIA	0	..	5	4	-18	-26	..	..	33	29
LITHUANIA	0	-	-	2	-	0	2	4	4	3
LUXEMBOURG	2,191	4,006	7,626	8,030	13,185	11,547	10,357	12,002	7,329	4,085
MALTA	60	31	-185	-56	50	334	27	-21	69	..
NETHERLANDS	6,651	5,344	7,251	9,725	9,460	8,210	9,743	12,658	4,593	8,182
POLAND	218	293	373	256	414	693	363	486	543	583
PORTUGAL	191	297	234	264	271	155	292	38	278	13
ROMANIA	19	26	43	76	111	92	12	66	76	47
SLOVAKIA	..	34	24	103	20	22	37	42	29	39
SLOVENIA	..	17	5	11	14	5	..	..	-38	..
SPAIN	694	1,023	918	1,021	1,083	764	-53	463	-531	726
SWEDEN	1,271	1,395	1,395	1,896	3,325	3,187	2,475	2,715	3,333	2,314
EFTA	2,382	3,334	3,759	4,987	4,765	3,311	5,577	5,183	3,361	1,615
of which										
NORWAY	297	937	345	296	578	577	537	515	-420	328
SWITZERLAND	2,084	2,396	3,411	4,377	3,872	2,460	4,849	4,667	3,788	1,285
OTHER EUROPEAN COUNTRIES	2,692	4,948	6,861	4,791	1,312	2,959	4,401	4,578	1,911	2,620
of which										
RUSSIA	841	1,681	1,715	1,180	1,811	1,492	1,584	2,996	311	1,658
UK OFFSHORE ISLANDS[2]	1,602	3,017	4,580	3,138	-993	707	2,401	1,058	1,090	625
THE AMERICAS	**21,113**	**26,585**	**26,461**	**28,527**	**9,871**	**13,450**	**21,476**	**26,635**	**24,058**	**19,272**
of which										
BERMUDA	1,629	1,561	..	1,557	1,558	1,178	2,338	1,450	2,159	2,612
BRAZIL	652	866	577	712	725	1,225	1,063	1,303	1,059	243
CANADA	1,340	1,895	1,769	1,653	-2,501	-477	468	-42	417	-3,991
CHILE	820	1,164	771	777	678	531	125	322	89	88
COLOMBIA	379	414	274	190	320	137	280	..	-441	26
MEXICO	485	536	531	563	293	260	545	1,364	756	731
PANAMA	44	50	23	42	..	65	53	83	61	76
USA	14,332	18,244	17,112	19,110	6,034	8,865	14,634	20,127	17,758	17,238
ASIA	**8,001**	**10,975**	**11,621**	**11,389**	**9,129**	**11,917**	**15,901**	**18,952**	**17,030**	**13,969**
NEAR & MIDDLE EAST COUNTRIES	692	1,053	1,430	2,563	2,341	1,744	2,049	2,704	862	2,945
of which										
GULF ARABIAN COUNTRIES	549	688	717	983	405	868	773	975	722	1,714
OTHER ASIAN COUNTRIES	7,309	9,922	10,191	8,826	6,788	10,173	13,852	16,248	16,168	11,024
of which										
CHINA	370	580	445	504	265	579	815	821	1,291	530
HONG KONG	2,541	3,553	3,786	4,163	1,448	1,316	3,119	4,362	4,846	5,109
INDIA	427	626	715	798	690	1,046	1,647	1,794	1,459	1,481
INDONESIA	155	226	336	153	105	420	562	1,091	1,094	555
JAPAN	440	482	388	145	304	344	284	366	213	297
MALAYSIA	525	508	494	595	526	731	810	592	571	600

6.15 Earnings from foreign direct investment abroad analysed by area and main country, 2004 to 2013 [1]

£ million

	2004	2005	2006	2007	2008	2009	2010	2011	2012	2013
SINGAPORE	1,651	2,510	2,285	478	1,663	2,553	2,469	3,267	2,963	-288
SOUTH KOREA	340	683	532	519	536	568	907	609	763	653
THAILAND	159	171	-121	23	-132	199	221	222	246	285
AUSTRALASIA & OCEANIA	**3,623**	**3,157**	**3,065**	**3,716**	**3,134**	**4,323**	**6,007**	**2,359**	**3,809**	**3,646**
of which										
AUSTRALIA	3,108	2,681	2,665	3,294	2,734	3,843	5,545	2,044	3,512	3,366
NEW ZEALAND	279	359	388	379	329	402	371	209	236	205
AFRICA	3,958	5,764	3,488	4,548	3,765	3,298	6,084	6,355	7,535	5,072
of which										
KENYA	64	70	88	89	100	141	174	144	8	110
NIGERIA	153	197	133	78	212	108	660	1,045	1,263	375
SOUTH AFRICA	2,706	3,768	1,620	2,236	1,143	1,199	2,588	2,596	3,192	2,217
ZIMBABWE	87	16	10	6	-5	-4	5	23	23	12
WORLD TOTAL	**62,476**	**78,667**	**83,591**	**92,242**	**69,500**	**67,942**	**80,334**	**99,962**	**79,869**	**68,665**
OECD	43,453	52,138	55,675	64,794	50,006	45,802	49,160	66,062	49,223	43,168
CENTRAL & EASTERN EUROPE[3]	74	76	62	-11	25	28	-3	0	-3	1

1. Net earnings equal profits of foreign branches plus United Kingdom companies' receipts of interest and their share of profits of foreign subsidiaries and associates. Earnings are after deduction of provisions for depreciation and foreign taxes on profits, dividends and interest.

2. The UK Offshore Islands consist of the Channel Islands & the Isle of Man, excluded from the definition of the economic territory of the UK from 1997.

3. Central & Eastern Europe prior to 2007 includes data for Bulgaria and Romania.

A negative sign before values indicates a net disinvestment abroad (ie a decrease in the amount due to the UK).

4. Data between 2004-2011 are on a Balance of Payments Manual 5 basis; data for 2012 and 2013 are on a Balance of Payments Manual 6 basis.

The largest change between methods is a shift from a directional to asset/liability. However, there are a number of additional methodological changes that have been undertaken between BPM5 and BPM6, outlined here: http://www.ons.gov.uk/ons/rel/naa1-rd/national-accounts-articles/impact-of-new-international-measurement-guidelines--balance-of-payments-manual-6--on-the-uk-s-balance-of-payments/index.html

.. Indicates data are disclosive.

.- Indicates nil returns.

Source: Office for National Statistics

6.16 Foreign direct investment flows into the United Kingdom analysed by area and main country, 2004 to 2013 [5]

£ million

	2004	2005	2006	2007	2008	2009	2010	2011	2012	2013
EUROPE	**29,901**	**80,087**	**53,837**	**49,752**	**25,258**	**32,075**	**355**	**12,736**	**23,032**	**12,498**
EU	26,384	71,034	47,698	39,348	24,122	25,739	-6,574	17,688	15,052	4,673
AUSTRIA	..	..	..	..	..	..	84	..	-126	79
BELGIUM	1,542	23	670	317	-547	367	146	9,057	2,018	2,810
BULGARIA	..	..	..	1	..	..	..	..	-2	0
CROATIA	..	..	..	..	..	..	..	..	..	..
CYPRUS	0	7	18	75	30	19	47	97	-206	218
CZECH REPUBLIC	..	..	..	..	..	..	0	..	9	..
DENMARK	-11	-1,246	13	-18	1,577	-414	-209	79	408	-1,249
ESTONIA	-	-	-	-	..	-	..	..	..	..
FINLAND	32	238	44	21	-25	131	64	63	-10	125
FRANCE	..	..	..	..	..	..	-4,523	..	6,933	-2,789
GERMANY	11,131	7,279	5,566	16,616	4,454	5,473	2,711	-4,171	2,886	2,943
GREECE	13	14	17	17	11	74	197	99	59	-45
HUNGARY	..	1	3	1	-	0	0	1	..	-81
IRISH REPUBLIC	..	..	..	..	..	..	1,238	..	717	-10
ITALY	1,327	-42	282	288	-282	-655	146	399	750	503
LATVIA	-	..	..	0	..	-	-	-	..	..
LITHUANIA	..	0	0	-	-	-	-	-	..	..
LUXEMBOURG	..	..	..	..	..	..	-3,490	..	4,648	-908
MALTA	0	1	2	6	1	-14	4	27	-58	-10
NETHERLANDS	1,226	50,366	13,715	2,471	17,668	-9,977	-4,216	12,068	-2,602	2,400
POLAND	0	1	50	-29	7	0	2	4	-7	22
PORTUGAL	..	..	..	..	..	..	44	..	-1	-2
ROMANIA	-34	..	..	4	-	..	..	1	-9	0
SLOVAKIA	..	..	..	1	..	..	..	..	0	..
SLOVENIA	..	..	..	3	-	..	..	0	0	1
SPAIN	..	..	..	..	..	..	889	..	-378	117
SWEDEN	-14	393	508	-117	575	56	294	803	172	569
EFTA	3,016	9,050	5,321	8,793	-4,082	1,973	2,567	-2,396	6,432	8,438
of which										
NORWAY	..	..	..	..	..	..	216	..	-495	548
SWITZERLAND	3,488	7,405	4,786	8,159	-3,094	1,839	1,876	-2,000	6,904	8,023
OTHER EUROPEAN COUNTRIES	501	3	817	1,611	5,219	4,363	4,362	-2,555	1,548	-614
of which										
RUSSIA	..	..	..	..	..	..	..	..	-87	105
UK OFFSHORE ISLANDS[3]	476	-60	733	1,248	4,208	4,255	3,984	-2,717	-772	-721
THE AMERICAS	**-4,792**	**17,422**	**17,242**	**32,460**	**18,614**	**16,774**	**28,636**	**11,621**	**8,129**	**14,283**
of which										
BRAZIL	..	6	..	2	1	..	..	1	-7	-22
CANADA	683	1,632	3,509	799	343	-1,265	3,680	-231	1,700	631
USA	-5,727	15,589	12,313	27,975	18,135	15,175	22,829	12,268	6,013	13,451
ASIA	**4,081**	**-4,168**	**11,806**	**9,938**	**4,026**	**-2,330**	**5,324**	**2,842**	**3,735**	**2,756**
NEAR & MIDDLE EAST COUNTRIES	384	736	5,034	-979	-635	274	335	-895	464	589
OTHER ASIAN COUNTRIES	3,697	-4,904	6,772	10,919	4,662	-2,604	4,988	3,738	3,271	2,167
of which										
CHINA	-26	13	12	16	-20	123	9	..	809	14
HONG KONG	..	315	92	-1,919	737	-152	2,995	2,004	596	1,006
INDIA	-15	138	265	151	2,638	20	48	563	-15	-264
JAPAN	..	..	..	..	..	..	-90	..	859	1,979
SINGAPORE	14	46	..	6,749	268	136	1	-467	20	-292
SOUTH KOREA	193	175	-85	5	247	11	..	38	106	-1

6.16 Foreign direct investment flows into the United Kingdom analysed by area and main country, 2004 to 2013 [5]

£ million

	2004	2005	2006	2007	2008	2009	2010	2011	2012	2013
AUSTRALASIA & OCEANIA	..	..	..	..	..	..	**-2,388**	..	**10,020**	**14,027**
of which										
AUSTRALIA	1,412	3,396	1,479	588	-66	2,471	-2,392	1,597	10,020	..
NEW ZEALAND	8	-	54	-48	-20	-20	4	9	-11	..
AFRICA	**-43**	**66**	**131**	**459**	**1,083**	**18**	**181**	**75**	**-319**	**159**
of which										
SOUTH AFRICA	-35	25	101	438	..	31	35	81	-359	160
WORLD TOTAL	**30,566**	**96,803**	**84,885**	**93,148**	**48,875**	**48,986**	**32,106**	**28,883**	**44,596**	**43,723**
OECD	26,762	95,187	73,961	83,165	39,384	41,296	21,921	30,096	40,447	43,359
CENTRAL & EASTERN EUROPE[4]	..	..	..	..	..	..	..	..	..	..

1   Net foreign direct investment includes unremitted profits.

2   A negative sign before values indicates a net disinvestment abroad (i.e. a decrease in the amount due to the UK).

3   The UK Offshore Islands consist of the Channel Islands & the Isle of Man, excluded from the definition of the economic territory of the UK from 1997

4   Central & Eastern Europe prior to 2007 includes data for Bulgaria and Romania.

5 Data between 2004-2011 are on a Balance of Payments Manual 5 basis, data for 2012 and 2013 are on a Balance of Payments Manual 6 basis. The largest change between methods is a shift from a directional to asset/liability principle. However, there are a number of additional methodological changes that have been undertaken between BPM5 and BPM6, outlined here: http://www.ons.gov.uk/ons/rel/naa1-rd/national-accounts-articles/impact-of-new-international-measurement-guidelines--balance-of-payments-manual-6--on-the-uk-s-balance-of-payments/index.html

.. Indicates data are disclosive.
 - Indicates nil returns.

Source: Office for National Statistics

6.17 FDI International positions in the United Kingdom analysed by area and main country, 2004 to 2013 [4]

£ million

	2004	2005	2006	2007	2008	2009	2010	2011	2012	2013
EUROPE	**181,198**	**277,027**	**332,077**	**354,382**	**389,925**	**416,484**	**417,201**	**447,608**	**553,813**	**547,701**
EU	161,395	244,392	299,906	308,996	335,526	362,673	353,741	371,932	464,790	452,525
AUSTRIA	366	561	848	1,030	840	935	1,076	2,435	5,296	2,267
BELGIUM	4,338	4,481	5,609	4,545	4,121	4,341	7,846	16,177	10,787	16,466
BULGARIA	..	..	..	..	..	..	..	..	..	10
CROATIA	..	..	..	..	..	..	..	..	..	..
CYPRUS	78	100	162	437	494	316	2,307	2,536	4,090	3,539
CZECH REPUBLIC	6	3	..	8	18	1	7	26	103	25
DENMARK	2,359	1,404	4,344	5,530	8,706	5,357	3,140	3,710	6,020	4,021
ESTONIA	-	-	-	..	..	-	..	..	..	..
FINLAND	886	756	817	708	736	753	780	875	2,178	1,395
FRANCE	41,100	56,309	59,998	54,303	51,838	73,534	67,241	61,236	78,547	77,798
GERMANY	39,300	51,469	54,382	64,558	71,755	67,784	51,677	50,046	66,966	58,129
GREECE	100	103	121	174	221	456	668	805	325	414
HUNGARY	12	9	12	12	20	5	10	14	86	334
IRISH REPUBLIC	5,021	7,146	8,186	8,839	10,204	10,886	9,524	11,013	9,314	11,120
ITALY	6,708	6,122	4,482	4,901	6,258	4,854	753	2,106	9,147	8,438
LATVIA	-	..	..	..	..	-	-	-	..	..
LITHUANIA	..	-	..	-	-	..	-	-	..	..
LUXEMBOURG	5,963	7,880	16,021	20,399	26,833	48,756	58,233	47,941	57,046	54,650
MALTA	5	12	12	62	69	48	172	292	974	760
NETHERLANDS	47,579	95,579	119,843	110,903	137,248	110,878	112,291	126,715	148,987	150,598
POLAND	7	21	96	75	76	16	26	98	198	216
PORTUGAL	113	111	122	222	308	600	892	302	571	452
ROMANIA	..	..	..	..	..	..	..	11	76	7
SLOVAKIA	..	-	-	..	..	..	..	..	..	5
SLOVENIA	..	..	..	9	13	..	7	0	..	7
SPAIN	4,536	8,782	20,658	27,876	11,178	26,781	33,344	40,447	56,300	53,663
SWEDEN	2,849	3,467	4,113	4,312	4,453	6,265	3,680	5,141	7,716	8,177
EFTA	15,752	25,033	22,358	32,570	29,931	29,654	35,771	41,470	35,521	42,295
of which										
NORWAY	242	1,085	969	1,522	1,789	1,776	1,723	2,400	4,913	3,563
SWITZERLAND	14,685	21,624	19,033	28,936	26,783	26,885	33,043	36,140	29,722	35,925
OTHER EUROPEAN COUNTRIES	4,051	7,602	9,813	12,816	24,468	24,158	27,689	34,205	53,502	52,880
of which										
RUSSIA	..	..	..	179	1,581	743	1,200	1,343	912	..
UK OFFSHORE ISLANDS [2]	3,500	7,059	9,111	11,963	22,026	23,025	26,120	32,183	45,100	49,203
THE AMERICAS	**140,090**	**174,037**	**200,709**	**202,062**	**209,792**	**208,475**	**242,270**	**263,464**	**305,076**	**319,293**
of which										
BRAZIL	..	77	134	21	9	..	..	17	-10	88
CANADA	12,108	15,587	19,369	20,835	21,333	19,535	19,259	18,028	14,637	16,162
USA	122,069	149,759	170,880	167,008	168,689	170,206	198,163	219,181	260,518	262,464
ASIA	**24,800**	**24,101**	**39,436**	**53,166**	**50,419**	**42,521**	**54,791**	**66,426**	**67,698**	**67,305**
NEAR & MIDDLE EAST COUNTRIES	2,765	2,970	10,160	6,449	5,389	3,780	4,498	5,137	3,772	4,538
OTHER ASIAN COUNTRIES	22,035	21,131	29,275	46,717	45,030	38,741	50,293	61,289	63,926	62,767
of which										
CHINA	119	111	99	202	427	618	378	780	1,151	950
HONG KONG	..	..	..	..	..	6,641	9,579	20,504	10,322	11,628
INDIA	164	518	798	1,376	3,591	1,900	2,846	2,921	2,072	1,890
JAPAN	12,300	10,513	14,766	25,479	30,643	24,646	27,638	31,512	40,667	40,729
SINGAPORE	925	1,034	4,046	12,197	1,555	3,526	6,115	3,829	4,125	3,311
SOUTH KOREA	635	638	798	779	914	703	2,867	953	2,516	2,404

6.17 FDI International positions in the United Kingdom analysed by area and main country, 2004 to 2013 [4]

£ million

	2004	2005	2006	2007	2008	2009	2010	2011	2012	2013
AUSTRALASIA & OCEANIA	**16,804**	**12,537**	**7,623**	**9,412**	**8,122**	**12,705**	**9,721**	**12,941**	**32,074**	**39,261**
of which										
AUSTRALIA	16,631	12,313	7,093	8,974	7,842	12,466	9,478	11,926	31,478	..
NEW ZEALAND	153	224	428	430	279	239	239	289	579	..
AFRICA	**530**	**510**	**469**	**1,397**	**2,115**	**1,088**	**1,574**	**2,220**	**1,430**	**1,872**
of which										
SOUTH AFRICA	296	186	130	900	1,600	501	570	1,124	353	873
WORLD TOTAL	**363,422**	**488,212**	**580,313**	**620,419**	**660,373**	**681,273**	**725,557**	**792,660**	**960,091**	**975,431**
OECD	340,870	458,185	535,218	564,201	594,466	619,512	644,444	690,293	845,903	849,622
CENTRAL & EASTERN EUROPE [3]	..	..	..	6	..	..	..	..	..	..

1. A negative sign before values indicates a net disinvestment abroad (ie a decrease in the amount due to the UK).

2. The UK Offshore Islands consist of the Channel Islands & the Isle of Man, excluded from the definition of the economic territory of the UK from 1997.

3. Central & Eastern Europe prior to 2007 includes data for Bulgaria and Romania.

4 Data between 2004-2011 are on a Balance of Payments Manual 5 basis, data for 2012 and 2013 are on a Balance of Payments Manual 6 basis. The largest change between methods is a shift from a directional to asset/liability principle. However, there are a number of additional methodological changes that have been undertaken between BPM5 and BPM6, outlined here: http://www.ons.gov.uk/ons/rel/naa1-rd/national-accounts-articles/impact-of-new-international-measurement-guidelines--balance-of-payments-manual-6--on-the-uk-s-balance-of-payments/index.html

.. Indicates data are disclosive

- Indicates nil returns.

Source: Office for National Statistics

6.18 Earnings from foreign direct investment in the United Kingdom analysed by area and main country, 2004 to 2013 [5]

£ million

	2004	2005	2006	2007	2008	2009	2010	2011	2012	2013
EUROPE	**12,676**	**17,592**	**27,447**	**26,174**	**-17,381**	**9,438**	**20,481**	**21,139**	**24,000**	**31,543**
EU	11,330	15,278	22,919	24,144	-3,729	9,817	15,301	17,607	22,510	27,982
AUSTRIA	61	60	207	211	-45	85	112	171	207	181
BELGIUM	269	367	646	577	286	-218	488	1,020	950	868
BULGARIA	..	-	-	..	..	..	..	..	0	1
CROATIA	..	..	..	..	..	..	..	..	..	..
CYPRUS	20	24	44	66	57	33	147	124	198	250
CZECH REPUBLIC	0	0	..	1	1	..	0	18	..	7
DENMARK	311	326	204	-70	-175	-257	91	-91	175	514
ESTONIA	-	-	-	..	..	-	..	..	..	..
FINLAND	62	61	93	181	50	96	98	76	198	144
FRANCE	3,842	5,121	5,329	3,489	1,351	9,249	4,670	5,119	2,850	3,252
GERMANY	2,900	4,037	4,541	5,789	-823	-1,902	4,945	3,778	6,275	7,220
GREECE	-4	49	70	104	212	193	338	67	124	120
HUNGARY	0	1	3	1	..	..	1	1	1	20
IRISH REPUBLIC	471	724	1,012	1,202	-132	-1,785	-2,598	333	521	693
ITALY	408	483	477	577	466	430	269	174	1,147	1,012
LATVIA	-	..	..	..	..	-	-	-	..	0
LITHUANIA	..	1	1	-	-	-	-	-	..	..
LUXEMBOURG	289	214	79	463	619	937	1,500	699	2,084	1,803
MALTA	0	0	3	7	28	22	46	47	92	45
NETHERLANDS	2,585	2,800	7,283	8,393	-7,297	-464	2,962	4,180	4,343	7,921
POLAND	0	1	8	6	3	1	2	4	5	10
PORTUGAL	47	30	48	54	50	42	52	-66	68	53
ROMANIA	..	..	..	..	..	..	..	1	0	1
SLOVAKIA	..	5	5	3	..	..	..	..	0	..
SLOVENIA	..	..	..	..	..	..	0	1	-1	1
SPAIN	37	773	2,536	2,696	1,255	3,023	1,636	1,359	2,697	3,138
SWEDEN	21	182	316	386	368	337	541	592	575	729
EFTA	849	1,495	3,366	264	-16,382	-2,352	1,029	1,419	-559	951
of which										
NORWAY	-20	82	169	194	262	15	29	215	399	731
SWITZERLAND	819	1,320	2,933	-286	-15,112	-2,411	528	821	-941	36
OTHER EUROPEAN COUNTRIES	497	819	1,162	1,767	2,731	1,975	4,152	2,113	2,050	2,609
of which										
RUSSIA	..	..	..	7	-77	-14	40	101	-47	41
UK OFFSHORE ISLANDS[2]	468	757	1,107	1,752	2,891	1,939	4,090	2,001	1,878	2,445
THE AMERICAS	**12,278**	**16,460**	**20,154**	**17,158**	**21,033**	**18,584**	**17,333**	**20,121**	**21,109**	**18,375**
of which										
BRAZIL	1	-4	-4	6	-6	..	32	9	12	16
CANADA	1,021	1,348	1,458	-250	-2,856	350	912	453	790	1,159
USA	10,981	14,156	16,828	15,060	22,518	16,931	14,993	17,920	19,165	15,721
ASIA	**168**	**937**	**2,710**	**447**	**-1,316**	**-3,631**	**-202**	**2,835**	**3,871**	**3,216**
NEAR & MIDDLE EAST COUNTRIES	188	354	564	237	216	101	135	483	468	650
OTHER ASIAN COUNTRIES	-19	583	2,145	210	-1,533	-3,731	-337	2,352	3,403	2,566
of which										
CHINA	8	-63	-35	17	-38	34	25	31	121	176
HONG KONG	..	..	-597	..	-337	-89	549	55	591	1,229
INDIA	-2	65	132	140	261	89	161	700	118	108
JAPAN	608	1,089	1,956	-216	-2,000	-3,979	-1,646	394	2,062	1,341
SINGAPORE	32	85	259	609	166	-213	-64	821	231	-231
SOUTH KOREA	23	72	104	125	134	59	116	49	100	153

6.18 Earnings from foreign direct investment in the United Kingdom analysed by area and main country, 2004 to 2013 [5]

£ million

	2004	2005	2006	2007	2008	2009	2010	2011	2012	2013
AUSTRALASIA & OCEANIA	**695**	**535**	**1,259**	**1,222**	**613**	**2,143**	**-30**	**140**	**224**	**1,111**
of which										
AUSTRALIA	690	521	876	1,196	629	2,152	-47	154	195	1,061
NEW ZEALAND	5	13	46	25	-13	-4	18	6	20	189
AFRICA	**59**	**65**	**80**	**137**	**166**	**47**	**51**	**152**	**-322**	**80**
of which										
SOUTH AFRICA	26	25	31	82	126	67	23	82	-364	9
WORLD TOTAL	**25,876**	**35,588**	**51,650**	**45,138**	**3,113**	**26,581**	**37,631**	**44,388**	**48,882**	**54,325**
OECD	25,471	33,927	47,476	40,242	-1,792	22,914	30,470	37,463	44,024	48,206
CENTRAL & EASTERN EUROPE[3]	1	..	..	1	..	..	0	..	..	..

1 Net earnings equal profits of foreign branches plus United Kingdom companies' receipts of interest and their share of profits of foreign subsidiaries and associates. Earnings are after deduction of provisions for depreciation and foreign taxes on profits, dividends and interest.

2 The UK Offshore Islands consist of the Channel Islands & the Isle of Man, excluded from the definition of the economic territory of the UK from 1997

3 Central & Eastern Europe prior to 2007 includes data for Bulgaria and Romania.

4 A negative sign before values indicates a net disinvestment abroad (i.e. a decrease in the amount due to the UK).

5 Data between 2004-2011 are on a Balance of Payments Manual 5 basis, data for 2012 and 2013 are on a Balance of Payments Manual 6 basis. The largest change between methods is a shift from a directional to asset/liability principle. However, there are a number of additional methodological changes that have been undertaken between BPM5 and BPM6, outlined here: http://www.ons.gov.uk/ons/rel/naa1-rd/national-accounts-articles/impact-of-new-international-measurement-guidelines--balance-of-payments-manual-6--on-the-uk-s-balance-of-payments/index.html

.. Indicates data are disclosive.

- Indicates nil returns.

Source: Office for National Statistics

Research and development

Chapter 7

Research and development

(Tables 7.1 to 7.5)

Research and experimental development (R&D) is defined for statistical purposes as 'creative work undertaken on a systematic basis in order to increase the stock of knowledge, including knowledge of man, culture and society, and the use of this stock of knowledge to devise new applications'.

R&D is financed and carried out mainly by businesses, the Government, and institutions of higher education. A small amount is performed by non-profit-making bodies. Gross Expenditure on R&D (GERD) is an indicator of the total amount of R&D performed within the UK: it has been approximately 2 per cent of GDP in recent years. Detailed figures are reported each year in a statistical bulletin published in March. Table 7.1 shows the main components of GERD.

ONS conducts an annual survey of expenditure and employment on R&D performed by government, and of government funding of R&D. The survey collects data for the reference period along with future estimates. Until 1993 the detailed results were reported in the *Annual Review of Government Funded R&D*. From 1997 the results have appeared in the Science, Engineering and Technology (SET) Statistics published by the Department for Business, Innovation and Skills (BIS). Table 7.2 gives some broad totals for gross expenditure by government (expenditure before deducting funds received by government for R&D). Table 7.3 gives a breakdown of net expenditure (receipts are deducted).

The ONS conducts an annual survey of R&D in business. Tables 7.4 and 7.5 give a summary of the main trends up to 2013.

Statistics on expenditure and employment on R&D in higher education institutions (HEIs) are based on information collected by Higher Education Funding Councils and the Higher Education Statistics Agency (HESA). In 1994 a new methodology was introduced to estimate expenditure on R&D in HEIs. This is based on the allocation of various Funding Council Grants. Full details of the new methodology are contained in science, engineering and technology (SET) Statistics available on the BIS website at: https://www.gov.uk/government/collections/science-engineering-and-technology-statistics

The most comprehensive international comparisons of resources devoted to R&D appear in Main Science and Technology Indicators published by the Organisation for Economic Co-operation and Development (OECD). The Statistical Office of the European Union and the United Nations also compile R&D statistics based on figures supplied by member states.

To make international comparisons more reliable the OECD have published a series of manuals giving guidance on how to measure various components of R&D inputs and outputs. The most important of these is the Frascati Manual, which defines R&D and recommends how resources for R&D should be measured. The UK follows the Frascati Manual as far as possible.

For information on available aggregated data on Research and Development please call Office for National Statistics on 01633 456728.

7.1a R&D Performed in the UK in each sector according to source of funding, 2012

Current prices		Sector performing the R&D						£ million
	Government	Research Councils	Higher Education	Business Enterprise	Private Non-Profit	Total	Overseas
Sector providing the funds							
Government	948	103	406	1,346	67	**2,871**	481
Research Councils	68	578	1,955	2	85	**2,688**	206
Higher Education Funding Councils	-	-	2,185	-	-	**2,185**	-
Higher Education	2	10	284	-	14	**310**	-
Business Enterprise	243	28	292	11,666	88	**12,317**	2,243
Private Non-Profit	4	44	1,022	37	170	**1,277**	-
Overseas	96	49	1,068	4,055	91	**5,358**	-
TOTAL	**1,360**	**813**	**7,211**	**17,107**	**515**	**27,006**	-
of which:							
Civil	1,210	813	7,178	15,518	513	**25,232**	-
Defence	150	-	34	1,588	2	**1,774**	-

Source: Office for National Statistics

- denotes nil, figures unavailable or too small to display.

7.1b Expenditure on research and development in the UK by sector of performance: 2004 to 2012

										£ million
		2004	2005	2006	2007	2008	2009	2010	2011	2012
Sector performing the R&D										
Current prices										
TOTAL	**GLBA**	**20,242**	**22,106**	**22,993**	**24,696**	**25,345**	**25,632**	**26,173** [†]	**27,459**	**27,006**
Government	**GLBK**	1,240	1,238	1,252	1,320	1,348	1,406	1,372 [†]	1,321	1,360
Research Councils	**DMRS**	930	1,051	1,061	1,034	1,041	1,097	1,141	1,040	813
Business Enterprise	**GLBL**	12,662	13,734	14,144	15,676	15,814	15,532	16,045 [†]	17,468	17,107
Higher Education	**GLBM**	5,004	5,580	6,022	6,119	6,545	6,931	6,963 [†]	7,133	7,211
Private Non-Profit	**GLBN**	406	502	513	546	595	666	652	496	515
As % of GDP		1.65	1.71	1.68	1.71	1.76	1.79	1.74	1.77	1.72
		2004	2005	2006	2007	2008	2009	2010	2011	2012
Sector performing the R&D										
Constant prices (2012)										
TOTAL		**24,538**	**26,317**	**26,609**	**27,878**	**27,825**	**27,389**	**27,255**	**27,944**	**27,006**
Government		1,503	1,474	1,449	1,490	1,480	1,502	1,429	1,344	1,360
Research Councils		1,127	1,251	1,228	1,167	1,143	1,172	1,188	1,058	813
Business Enterprise		15,349	16,350	16,368	17,696	17,361	16,596	16,708	17,776	17,107
Higher Education		6,066	6,643	6,969	6,907	7,185	7,406	7,251	7,259	7,211
Private Non-Profit		492	598	594	616	653	712	679	505	515

Source: Office for National Statistics

[†] crosses denote earliest data revision.

7.2 Gross central government expenditure on research and development

United Kingdom

£ million

	2007/08		2008/09		2009/10		2010/11		2011/12r		2012/13r	
	Intra-mural[2]	Extra-mural	Intra-mural	Extra-mural	Intra-mural	Extra-mural	Intra-mural	Extra-mural	Intra-mural	Extra-mural	Intra-mural	Extra-mural
Defence	279	1941	262	1812	288	1551	226	1556	158	1190	150	1353
Research councils	1034	2005	1041	2297	1097	2434	1141	2414	1035	2440	804	2487
Higher education institutes	-	2234	-	2227	-	2395	-	2303	-	2257	-	2185
Other programmes	410	1019	419	1064	421	1276	400	1236	418	1411	444	1443
Total (excluding NHS)	1723	7199	1722	7400	1806	7656	1767	7509	1611	7298	1398	7468

Source: Office for National Statistics 01633 456763

1. Extramural Includes work performed overseas
2. From 2007/08 expenditure data no longer includes VAT

r - revised data

7.3 UK Government Net expenditure on R&D by Socio-Economic Objective, Percentage Share: 2007 to 2013

Current prices

£ million

	2007	2008	2009	2010	2011		2012	2013
TOTAL	8,825	9,107	9,371	9,260	8,995	†	8,943	9,832

	2007	2008	2009	2010	2011		2012	2013
Per cent								
TOTAL	**100**	**100**	**100**	**100**	**100**		**100**	**100**
Agriculture	3	3	4	3	4		4	4
Industrial production and technology	-	1	2	1	2	†	1	2
Energy	1	1	1	1	2	†	2	2
Transport, telecommunication, other infrastructure	1	1	1	1	3	†	3	3
Environment	2	3	3	3	3		3	3
Health	17	18	19	21	22	†	22	22
Education	1	1	1	1	-		-	-
Exploration and exploitation of the earth	3	3	3	3	3		3	3
General advancement of knowledge: R&D financed from General University Funds	25	24	26	25	25		24	23
Exploration and exploitation of space	2	2	2	2	3		4 †	4
Defence	24	22	19	18	15		16	16
Culture, recreation, religion and mass media	2	2	2	2	2		2	2
Political and social systems, structures and processes	1	2	2	2	1		1 †	1
General advancement of knowledge: R&D financed from other sources	18	18	17	18	13	†	13	13

Source: Office for National Statistics

denotes nil, figures unavailable or too small to display.
denotes earliest data revision.

7.4 Expenditure on Civil and Defence R&D performed in UK businesses: Broad product groups, 2010 - 2012

£ million

		Civil					Defence			
		2010	2011	2012	2013		2010	2011	2012	2013
CURRENT PRICES										
TOTAL	DLBV	14,392	15,667 †	15,539	16,734	DLBW	1,653	1,785 †	1,604	1,713
Manufacturing	DLEP	10,036	10,815 †	10,807	11,318	DLEX	1,549	1,647 †	1,511	1,502
Chemicals	DLEQ	..	..	..	..	DLEY	..	..	..	..
Mechanical engineering	DLER	456	520	600 †	628	DLEZ	446	572	526 †	527
Electrical machinery	DLES	751	847	1,069 †	1,197	DLFA	393	353	270 †	194
Transport equipment	DLET	..	..	..	..	DLFB	..	..	..	..
Aerospace	DLEU	1,018	1,036	1,167	1,240	DLFC	419	402	351 †	416
Other manufacturing	DLEV	1,168	1,398 †	1,383	1,453	DLFD	127	98 †	124	114
Services	DLEW	..	4,425 †	..	4,857	DLFE	..	138	..	212
Other: Total	LDIL	..	426	..	559	LDJJ	..	-	..	-
Agriculture, hunting & forestry; Fishing	LDIN	102	133	132	124	LDJL	-	-	-	-
Extractive industries	LDIS	152	195	206	225	LDKF	-	-	-	-
Electricity, gas & water supply; Waste management	LDJB	..	68	..	139	LDKG	..	-	..	-
Construction	LDJG	..	31	..	72	LDKS	..	-	..	-

£ million

	2010	2011	2012	2013		2010	2011	2012	2013
CONSTANT PRICES (2013)									
TOTAL	15,168	16,222	15,825	16,734		1,742	1,848	1,634	1,713
Manufacturing	10,577	11,198	11,006	11,318		1,633	1,705	1,539	1,502
Chemicals	..	..	..	..		..	..	..	..
Mechanical engineering	481	538	611	628		470	592	536	527
Electrical machinery	792	877	1,089	1,197		414	366	275	194
Transport equipment	..	..	..	..		..	..	..	..
Aerospace	1,073	1,073	1,189	1,240		442	416	357	416
Other manufacturing	1,231	1,448	1,408	1,453		134	101	126	114
Services	..	4,582	..	4,857		..	143	..	212
Other: Total	..	441	..	559		..	-	..	-
Agriculture, hunting & forestry; Fishing	108	138	134	124		-	-	-	-
Extractive industries	160	202	210	225		-	-	-	-
Electricity, gas & water supply; Waste management	..	70	..	139		..	-	..	-
Construction	..	32	..	72		..	-	..	-

	2010	2011	2012	2013		2010	2011	2012	2013
GDP deflator used to convert current prices to constant prices	94.882	96.580	98.190	100.000		94.882	96.580	98.190	100.000

1. - denotes nil, figures unavailable or too small to display.
2. .. denotes disclosive figures.
3. † crosses denote earliest data revision.

Source: Office for National Statistics

209

7.5a Sources of funds for R&D performed in UK businesses 2010 to 2013

CURRENT PRICES

		2010	2011	2012	2013
£ Million					
TOTAL	**DLBX**	**16,045**	**17,452** †	**17,144**	**18,448**
UK Government	DLDO	1,407	1,513 †	1,380	1,649
Overseas total of which:	DLHK	3,789	3,939	3,957 †	3,965
EC Programmes	DLDQ	62	55 †	47	44
All other funding from abroad	DLDS	3,727	3,884	3,910 †	3,920
Other UK Business	DLDU	718	595 †	358	381
Own funds	DLDW	10,129	11,283 †	11,381	12,368
Other	DLDY	3	122	67 †	84

	2010	2011	2012	2013
Per cent				
TOTAL	**100**	**100**	**100**	**100**
UK Government	9	9	8	9
Overseas total of which:	24	23	23 †	21
EC Programmes	-	-	-	-
All other funding from abroad	23	22	23	21
Other UK Business	4	3	2	2
Own funds	63	65	65 †	67
Other	-	1	-	-

Source: Office for National Statistics

1. - denotes nil, figures unavailable or too small to display.
2. † crosses denote earliest data revision.
3. The sum of percentages may be more or less than 100 due to rounding.
4. 'Other' includes funds from UK Private Non-Profit organisations and
   Higher Education establishments, and from 2011, international organisations.

7.5b Sources of funds for R&D performed in UK businesses: Civil and Defence, 2010 to 2013

CURRENT PRICES   £ million

		Civil					Defence			
		2010	2011	2012	2013		2010	2011	2012	2013
UK Government	DLFG	410	394	315 †	518	DLFN	996	1,119 †	1,065	1,131
Overseas total of which:	DLHS	3,584	3,788 †	3,800	3,805	DLIF	205	151 †	157	160
EC Programmes	DLFH	60	53	45 †	42	DLFO	2	3	2	3
All other funding from abroad	DLFI	3,524	3,735 †	3,755	3,763	DLFP	203	149 †	155	157
Other UK Business	DLFJ	607	485	286 †	..	DLFQ	111	109	72	..
Own	DLFK	9,787	10,922 †	11,076	12,052	DLFR	341	361 †	304	317
Other	DLFL	3	78	62	..	DLFS	1	44	6 †	..
TOTAL	**DLBV**	**14,392**	**15,667** †	**15,539**	**16,734**	**DLBW**	**1,653**	**1,785** †	**1,604**	**1,713**

Source: Office for National Statistics

1. - denotes nil, figures unavailable or too small to display.
2. .. denotes disclosive figures.
3. † crosses denote earliest data revision.
4. 'Other' includes funds from UK Private Non-Profit organisations and
 Higher Education establishments, and from 2011, international organisations.

this page is intentionally blank

Income and wealth

Chapter 8

Personal income, expenditure and wealth

Distribution of total incomes (Table 8.1)

The information shown in Table 8.1 comes from the Survey of Personal Income 2011/12. This is an annual survey covering approximately 600,000 individuals across the whole of the UK. It is based on administrative data held by HM Revenue & Customs (HMRC) on individuals who could be liable for tax. The table relates only to those individuals who are taxpayers. The distributions only cover incomes as computed for tax purposes, and above a level which for each year corresponds approximately to the single person's allowance. Incomes below these levels are not shown because the information about them is incomplete.

Some components of investment income (for example interest and dividends), from which tax has been deducted at source, are not always held on HMRC business systems. Estimates of missing bank and building society interest and dividends from UK companies are included in these tables. The missing investment income is distributed to cases, so that the population as a whole has amounts consistent with evidence from other sources. For example, amounts of tax accounted for by deposit takers and the tendency to hold interest-bearing accounts as indicated by household surveys.

Superannuation contributions are estimated and included in total income. They have been distributed among earners in the Survey of Personal Incomes sample, by a method consistent with information about the number of employees who are contracted in or out of the State Earnings Related Pension Scheme (SERPS) and the proportion of their earnings contributed.

When comparing results of these surveys across years, it should be noted that the Survey of Personal Incomes is not a longitudinal survey. However, sample sizes have increased in recent years to increase precision.

Average incomes of households (Table 8.2)

Original income is the total income in cash of all the members of the household before receipt of state benefits or the deduction of taxes. It includes income from employment, self-employment, investment income and occupational pensions. Gross income is original income plus cash benefits received from government (retirement pensions, child benefit, and so on). Disposal income is the income available for consumption; it is equal to gross income less direct taxes (which include income tax, national insurance contributions, and council tax). By further allowing for taxes paid on goods and services purchased, such as VAT, an estimate of post-tax income is derived. These income figures are derived from estimates made by the Office for National Statistics (ONS) based largely on information from the Living Costs and Food Survey (LFC) and published each year on the ONS website.

In Table 8.2, a retired household is defined as one where the combined income of retired members amounts to at least half the total gross income of the household; where a retired person is defined as anyone who describes themselves as retired, or anyone over the minimum National Insurance (NI) pension age describing themselves as 'unoccupied' or 'sick or injured but not intending to seek work.

Children are defined as persons aged under 16 or between 16 and 18, unmarried and receiving full-time non-advanced further education.

Living Costs and Food Survey (Tables 8.3–8.5)

The Living Costs and Food Survey (LCF) is a sample survey of private households in the UK.The LCF sample is representative of all regions of the UK and of different types of households. The survey is continuous, with interviews spread evenly over the year to ensure that estimates are not biased by seasonal variation. The survey results show how households spend their money; how much goes on food, clothing and so on, how spending patterns vary depending upon income, household composition, and regional location of households. From January 2006 the survey has been conducted on a calendar-year basis, therefore the latest results refer to the January to December 2013 period.

One of the main purposes of the LCF is to define the 'basket of goods' for the Retail Prices Index (RPI) and the Consumer Prices Index (CPI). The RPI has a vital role in the up rating of state pensions and welfare benefits, while the CPI is a key instrument of the Government's monetary policy. Information from the survey is also a major source for estimates of household expenditure in the UK National Accounts. In addition, many other government departments use LCF data as a basis for policy making, for example in the areas of housing and transport. The Department for Environment, Food and Rural Affairs (Defra) uses LCF data to report on trends in food consumption and nutrient intake within the UK. Users of the LCF outside government include independent research institutes, academic researchers and business and market researchers. Like all surveys based on a sample of the population, its results are subject to sampling variability and potentially to some bias due to non-response. The results of the survey are published in an annual report the latest being The Family Spending 2014 edition. The report includes a list of definitions used in the survey, items on which information is collected, and a brief account of the fieldwork procedure.

8.1 Distribution of total income before and after tax by gender, 2011-12

Taxpayers only
Numbers: thousands; Amounts: £ million

Total

Range of total income (lower limit) £	Before tax, by range of total income before tax				After tax, by range of total income after tax			
	No. of taxpayers	Total income before tax	Total tax	Total income after tax	No. of taxpayers	Total income before tax	Total tax	Total income after tax
7,475	609	4,710	27	4,680	736	5,730	40	5,690
8,000	2,120	19,000	570	18,400	2,570	24,000	868	23,100
10,000	2,870	31,500	1,450	30,100	3,520	40,900	2,240	38,700
12,000	3,940	53,100	3,950	49,200	4,640	68,200	5,810	62,400
15,000	5,530	96,300	9,890	86,400	6,100	119,000	13,400	106,000
20,000	7,000	171,000	22,200	149,000	6,720	190,000	26,200	164,000
30,000	5,850	222,000	33,400	189,000	4,810	216,000	36,100	180,000
50,000	1,460	84,600	17,100	67,400	919	70,300	17,000	53,300
70,000	708	58,400	14,700	43,800	430	49,700	14,800	34,800
100,000	372	44,600	13,500	31,100	186	33,400	11,400	22,000
150,000	130	22,300	7,410	14,800	52	14,300	5,350	8,970
200,000	84	20,200	7,440	12,800	36	14,400	5,630	8,720
300,000	46	17,500	6,910	10,600	20	13,000	5,330	7,690
500,000	24	16,200	6,720	9,430	10	12,200	5,140	7,050
1,000,000	11	24,300	10,400	13,900	4	14,800	6,180	8,650
All ranges	30,800	886,000	156,000	731,000	30,800	886,000	156,000	731,000

Male

Range of total income (lower limit) £	Before tax, by range of total income before tax				After tax, by range of total income after tax			
	No. of taxpayers	Total income before tax	Total tax	Total income after tax	No. of taxpayers	Total income before tax	Total tax	Total income after tax
7,475	270	2,090	12	2,080	326	2,540	18	2,520
8,000	863	7,750	238	7,510	1,050	9,770	361	9,410
10,000	1,230	13,600	604	13,000	1,550	18,000	968	17,000
12,000	1,870	25,200	1,830	23,400	2,290	33,800	2,840	30,900
15,000	2,930	51,100	5,190	45,900	3,410	66,800	7,490	59,300
20,000	4,210	103,000	13,400	89,800	4,170	118,000	16,400	102,000
30,000	3,820	146,000	22,000	124,000	3,250	147,000	25,000	122,000
50,000	1,060	61,300	12,600	48,800	684	52,600	12,800	39,700
70,000	534	44,100	11,100	33,000	337	39,100	11,800	27,300
100,000	295	35,400	10,800	24,700	152	27,500	9,430	18,100
150,000	107	18,300	6,100	12,200	45	12,400	4,640	7,760
200,000	72	17,300	6,360	10,900	31	12,500	4,910	7,580
300,000	41	15,300	6,040	9,280	18	11,700	4,790	6,910
500,000	21	14,500	6,030	8,470	10	11,300	4,760	6,510
1,000,000	10	22,300	9,580	12,700	3	13,500	5,640	7,880
All ranges	17,300	577,000	112,000	465,000	17,300	577,000	112,000	465,000

8.1 Distribution of total income before and after tax by gender, 2011-12

Taxpayers only

Numbers: thousands; Amounts: £ million

Range of total income (lower limit) £	Female							
	Before tax, by range of total income before tax				After tax, by range of total income after tax			
	No. of taxpayers	Total income before tax	Total tax	Total income after tax	No. of taxpayers	Total income before tax	Total tax	Total income after tax
7,475	339	2,620	14	2,610	410	3,190	22	3,170
8,000	1,250	11,300	333	10,900	1,530	14,200	507	13,700
10,000	1,640	18,000	843	17,100	1,970	22,900	1,270	21,600
12,000	2,070	27,900	2,110	25,800	2,350	34,500	2,970	31,500
15,000	2,600	45,200	4,700	40,500	2,700	52,500	5,950	46,500
20,000	2,790	67,900	8,750	59,200	2,550	71,600	9,790	61,800
30,000	2,040	76,800	11,400	65,400	1,560	68,700	11,100	57,600
50,000	403	23,200	4,560	18,700	235	17,700	4,160	13,600
70,000	174	14,400	3,520	10,800	93	10,600	3,070	7,520
100,000	77	9,120	2,710	6,410	33	5,870	1,970	3,900
150,000	23	3,950	1,320	2,630	7	1,920	713	1,210
200,000	12	2,970	1,090	1,880	5	1,860	726	1,130
300,000	6	2,200	872	1,330	2	1,330	545	780
500,000	2	1,660	695	961	1	920	375	545
1,000,000	1	2,000	836	1,160	-	1,310	540	771
All ranges	13,400	309,000	43,800	265,000	13,400	309,000	43,800	265,000

Source: Survey of Personal Incomes 2011-12, HMRC

Table updated January 2014

Notes on the Table
Distribution of total income before and after tax by gender, 2011-12

1. This table only covers individuals with some liability to tax.

2. It should be noted that individuals may not necessarily fall into the same total income range for before and after tax breakdowns. Total income before tax is used to assign people to an income range for columns 2 to 5, whereas total income after the deduction of tax is used to assign individuals to an income band for columns 6 to 9.

3. For more information about the SPI and symbols used in this table, please refer to
Personal Income Statistics release

8.2: Summary of the effects of taxes and benefits, by household type,[1] 2012/13

	Retired households					Non-Retired households		
	1 adult Men	1 adult Women	All 1 adult	2 or more adults		1 adult Men[2]	1 adult Women[2]	All 1 adult[2]
Average per household (£ per year)								
Original income	10 241	5 741	7 212	15 125		21 390	18 150	20 045
plus Cash benefits	8 992	9 455	9 303	12 662		2 704	3 049	2 847
Gross income	19 233	15 195	16 515	27 786		24 094	21 199	22 891
less Direct taxes and employees' NIC	2 640	1 493	1 868	3 401		5 132	4 253	4 767
Disposable income	16 593	13 702	14 648	24 386		18 961	16 946	18 124
Equivalised[3] disposable income	*24 876*	*20 526*	*21 948*	*23 362*		*28 442*	*25 419*	*27 187*
less Indirect taxes	3 010	2 334	2 555	5 463		3 806	3 216	3 561
Post-tax income	13 583	11 368	12 092	18 923		15 155	13 730	14 563
plus Benefits in kind	4 472	4 863	4 735	7 287		1 446	1 623	1 519
Final income	18 055	16 231	16 827	26 209		16 601	15 354	16 083

	Non-Retired households							
	2 adults[2]	3 or more adults[2]	1 adult with children	2 adults with 1 child	2 adults with 2 children	2 adults with 3 or more children	3 or more adults with children	All house-holds
Average per household (£ per year)								
Original income	46 603	54 619	11 834	44 760	51 741	44 591	49 496	32 108
plus Cash benefits	2 613	3 430	10 602	3 954	4 371	8 470	6 540	5 990
Gross income	49 216	58 049	22 436	48 713	56 112	53 061	56 036	38 098
less Direct taxes and employees' NIC	11 026	11 348	1 967	10 651	13 102	9 397	10 178	7 418
Disposable income	38 189	46 700	20 469	38 063	43 010	43 664	45 858	30 680
Equivalised[3] disposable income	*38 189*	*32 325*	*19 898*	*31 019*	*29 654*	*25 089*	*25 304*	*28 676*
less Indirect taxes	6 839	8 878	3 659	6 275	7 293	7 317	8 564	5 623
Post-tax income	31 351	37 823	16 809	31 787	35 717	36 348	37 294	25 057
plus Benefits in kind	3 399	6 938	11 090	7 933	13 633	20 189	16 357	6 777
Final income	34 749	44 761	27 899	39 721	49 350	56 537	53 652	31 834

Source: Office for National Statistics

Notes:
1 See Further Analysis and Methodology section for definitions of retired households, adults and children.
2 Without children.
3 Using the modified-OECD scale.

8.3 Income and source of income, 1970 to 2013

United Kingdom

	Weighted number of house-holds	Number of house-holds in the sample	Weekly household income[1]				Source of income					
			Current prices		Constant prices[2]		Wages and salaries	Self employ-ment	Invest-ments	Annuities and pensions[3]	Social security benefits[4]	Other sources
			Dispo-sable	Gross	Dispo-sable	Gross						
	(000s)	Number	£	£	£	£	Percentage of gross weekly household income					
1970		6,390	28	34	290	349	77	7	4	3	9	1
1980		6,940	115	140	345	423	75	6	3	3	13	1
1990		7,050	258	317	455	559	67	10	6	5	11	1
1995-96		6,800	307	381	447	555	64	9	5	7	14	2
1996-97		6,420	325	397	463	565	65	9	4	7	14	1
1997-98		6,410	343	421	480	590	67	8	4	7	13	1
1998-99[5]	24,660	6,630	371	457	512	630	68	8	4	7	12	1
1999-2000	25,340	7,100	391	480	533	654	66	10	5	7	12	1
2000-01	25,030	6,640	409	503	553	680	67	9	4	7	12	1
2001-02[6]	24,450	7,470	447	547	596	729	68	8	4	7	12	1
2002-03	24,350	6,930	453	552	597	728	68	8	3	7	12	1
2003-04	24,670	7,050	464	570	603	742	67	9	3	7	13	1
2004-05	24,430	6,800	489	601	627	770	68	8	3	7	13	1
2005-06	24,800	6,790	500	616	628	773	67	8	3	7	13	1
2006[7]	24,790	6,650	521	642	642	791	67	9	3	7	12	1
2006[8]	25,440	6,650	515	635	635	782	67	9	3	7	13	1
2007	25,350	6,140	534	659	643	794	67	8	4	7	13	1
2008	25,690	5,850	582	713	676	829	67	9	4	7	12	1
2009	25,980	5,830	558	683	635	776	66	8	3	8	14	1
2010	26,320	5,260	578	700	637	772	65	10	2	8	14	1
2011	26,110	5,690	587	713	618	752	66	7	2	9	14	1
2012	26,410	5,600	597	720	612	738	65	8	3	9	14	1
2013	26,840	5,140	614	739	614	739	65	7	3	9	14	1

1 Does not include imputed income from owner-occupied and rent-free households.

2 Constant prices have been deflated using the CPI All Items Index for years from 1998. Before 1988, the index is based on modelled or indicative data.

3 Other than social security benefits.

4 Excluding housing benefit and council tax benefit (rates rebate in Northern Ireland) and their predecessors in earlier years

5 Based on weighted data from 1998-99 onwards.

6 From 2001-02 onwards, weighting is based on the population estimates from the 2001 Census.

7 From 1998-99 to this version of 2006, figures shown are based on weighted data using non-response weights based on the 1991 Census and population figures from the 1991 and 2001 Censuses.

8 From this version of 2006, figures shown are based on weighted data using updated weights, with non-response weights and population figures based on the 2001 Census.

Source: ONS, Family Spending 2013, © Crown copyright 2014

8.4 Household expenditure based on COICOP classification, 2001-02 to 2013 at 2013 prices[1]

United Kingdom

	2001-02	2002-03	2003-04	2004-05	2005-06	2006[2]	2006[3]	2007	2008	2009	2010	2011	2012	2013
Weighted number of households (thousands)	24,450	24,350	24,670	24,430	24,800	24,790	25,440	25,350	25,690	25,980	26,320	26,110	26,410	26,840
Total number of households in sample	7,470	6,930	7,050	6,800	6,790	6,650	6,650	6,140	5,850	5,830	5,260	5,690	5,600	5,140
Total number of persons in sample	18,120	16,590	16,970	16,260	16,090	15,850	15,850	14,650	13,830	13,740	12,180	13,430	13,180	12,120
Total number of adults in sample	13,450	12,450	12,620	12,260	12,170	12,000	12,000	11,220	10,640	10,650	9,430	10,330	10,200	9,350
Weighted average number of persons per household	2.4	2.4	2.4	2.4	2.4	2.4	2.3	2.4	2.4	2.3	2.3	2.4	2.3	2.4

Commodity or service	Average weekly household expenditure (£)													
1 Food & non-alcoholic drinks	62.10	63.70	63.60	65.20	65.10	65.80	65.00	64.60	62.40	60.90	60.10	58.70	58.90	58.80
2 Alcoholic drinks, tobacco & narcotics	18.20	17.90	18.10	17.20	16.00	16.10	16.10	15.70	14.60	14.40	14.50	13.50	13.30	12.00
3 Clothing & footwear	15.40	16.10	17.00	18.80	18.90	19.90	19.60	19.50	20.50	21.60	24.30	22.10	23.60	22.60
4 Housing (net)[4], fuel & power	61.70	61.90	64.20	63.70	65.30	65.40	65.40	67.90	64.00	66.30	69.60	69.20	70.70	74.40
5 Household goods & services	36.00	35.80	37.10	37.60	35.80	36.30	35.90	36.20	34.80	31.20	34.10	28.20	28.70	33.10
6 Health	6.30	6.50	6.60	6.40	6.90	7.20	7.20	6.80	5.90	5.90	5.50	7.00	6.50	6.20
7 Transport	88.00	88.60	88.20	83.60	83.10	82.10	80.50	79.20	77.10	70.50	72.20	67.90	64.80	70.40
8 Communication	11.30	11.50	12.10	12.80	13.20	13.10	12.90	13.70	14.10	13.60	14.50	14.20	14.20	14.50
9 Recreation & culture	53.80	55.30	57.10	59.40	58.70	60.20	59.20	59.60	62.80	59.70	58.90	64.70	62.20	63.90
10 Education	14.20	12.50	11.80	14.00	13.40	13.90	13.50	11.50	9.40	9.80	13.40	9.00	7.90	8.80
11 Restaurants & hotels	48.50	49.80	47.60	47.90	47.00	47.40	47.00	45.00	43.90	43.70	43.40	42.00	41.60	40.40
12 Miscellaneous goods & services	41.50	43.70	43.20	43.40	41.30	41.70	41.30	40.00	39.50	38.00	38.00	39.90	38.80	39.10
1-12 All expenditure groups	457.00	463.30	466.80	470.00	464.80	469.10	463.60	459.80	449.00	435.80	448.50	436.30	431.30	444.30
13 Other expenditure items[5]	78.30	75.90	76.80	77.10	80.10	78.30	76.20	71.90	75.30	78.40	72.00	72.60	69.70	73.00
Total expenditure	535.30	539.20	543.60	547.10	544.90	547.40	539.80	531.70	524.40	514.10	520.50	508.90	501.00	517.30

Average weekly expenditure per person (£)														
Total expenditure	225.30	226.40	230.60	229.20	231.10	231.50	230.90	225.60	222.40	219.70	223.30	216.20	213.90	219.40

Average weekly household income (£)														
Gross income (£)	729	728	742	770	773	791	782	794	829	776	772	752	738	739
Disposable income (£)	596	597	603	627	628	642	635	643	676	635	637	618	612	614

Note: The commodity and service categories are not comparable to those in publications before 2001-02.

1 Figures have been deflated to 2013 prices using deflators specific to the COICOP category.

2 From 2001-02 to this version of 2006, figures shown are based on weighted data using non-response weights based on the 1991 Census and population figures from the 1991 and 2001 Censuses.

3 From this version of 2006, figures shown are based on weighted data using updated weights, with non-response weights and population figures based on the 2001 Census.

4 Excluding mortgage interest payments, council tax and Northern Ireland rates.

5 An improvement to the imputation of mortgage interest payments has been implemented for 2006 data onwards. This means there is a slight discontinuity between 2006 and earlier years.

Source: ONS, Family Spending 2013, © Crown copyright 2014

8.5 Percentage of households with durable goods 1998/99 to 2013
United Kingdom

	Car/ van	Central heating[1]	Washing machine	Tumble dryer	Dish-washer	Micro-wave	Tele-phone	Mobile phone	DVD Player	Home computer	Internet connection
1998-99[2]	72	89	92	51	23	79	95	27	--	33	10
1999-2000	71	90	91	52	23	80	95	44	--	38	19
2000-01	72	91	93	53	25	84	93	47	--	44	32
2001-02[3]	74	92	93	54	27	86	94	64	--	49	39
2002-03	74	93	94	56	29	87	94	70	31	55	45
2003-04	75	94	94	57	31	89	92	76	50	58	49
2004-05	75	95	95	58	33	90	93	78	67	62	53
2005-06	74	94	95	58	35	91	92	79	79	65	55
2006[4]	76	95	96	59	38	91	91	80	83	67	59
2006[5]	74	95	96	59	37	91	91	79	83	67	58
2007	75	95	96	57	37	91	89	78	86	70	61
2008	74	95	96	59	37	92	90	79	88	72	66
2009	76	95	96	58	39	93	88	81	90	75	71
2010	75	96	96	57	40	92	87	80	88	77	73
2011	75	96	97	56	41	92	88	87	88	79	77
2012	75	96	97	56	42	93	88	87	87	81	79
2013	76	96	97	56	42	92	89	92	85	83	82

-- Data not available.

1 Full or partial.

2 From this version of 1998-99, figures shown are based on weighted data and including children's expenditure.

3 From 2001-02 onwards, weighting is based on the population figures from the 2001 census.

4 From 1998-99 to this version of 2006, figures shown are based on weighted data using non-response weights based on the 1991 Census and population figures from the 1991 and 2001 Census.

5 From this version of 2006, figures shown are based on weighted data using updated weights, with non-response weights and population figures based on the 2001 Census.

Source: ONS, Family Spending 2013, © Crown copyright 2014

this page is intentionally blank

Chapter 9

Lifestyles

Lifestyles

Expenditure by the Department for Culture, Media and Sport (Table 9.1)
The figures in this table are taken from the department's Annual Report and are outturn figures for each of the headings shown (later figures are the estimated outturn). The department's planned expenditure for future years is also shown.

International tourism and holidays abroad (Tables 9.8 and 9.9)
The figures in these tables are compiled using data from the International Passenger Survey (IPS). A holiday abroad is a visit made for holiday purposes. Business trips and visits to friends and relatives are excluded.

Domestic tourism (Table 9.10)
The figures in this table are compiled using data from the UK Tourism Survey (UKTS) and represent trips of one or more nights away from home. The UKTS changed survey methodology in 2000 and 2005. Data from 1995 to 1999 were reworked to allow comparisons to be made with 2000 to 2004 data. Data for 2004 should be used and interpreted with caution. Data for 2005 is not comparable with previous years.

Gambling (Table 9.12)
The National Lottery figures in this table are the latest figures released by The National Lottery Commission at the time of going to press. They represent ticket sales (money staked1) for each of the games which comprise the lottery. The figures have been adjusted to real terms using the Retail Prices Index (RPI).
The National Lottery started on the 19 November 1994 with the first instant ticket being sold in March 1995. The sum of the individual games may not agree exactly with the figures for total sales which also include the Easy Play games which started in 1998 but were dropped in 1999. The other gambling figures in this table are obtained from the Gambling Commission (formerly the Gaming Board) and HM Revenue & Customs (HMRC). The figures have been adjusted to real terms using the Retail Prices Index (RPI).

9.1 Expenditure by the Department for Culture, Media and Sport

Resource DEL (£'000s)	2007-08 Outturn	2008-09 Outturn	2009-10 Outturn	2010-11 Outturn	2011-12 Outturn	2012-13 Outturn	2013-14 Outturn	2014-15 Plans	2015-16 Plans
Support for the Museums and Galleries sector	12,619	4,230	4,170	3,831	13,336	12,664	16,267	17,478	17,367
Museums and Galleries sponsored ALBs (net)	334,044	278,988	357,425	361,853	306,816	359,754	354,959	412,336	388,803
Libraries sponsored ALBs (net)	99,452	104,277	103,587	106,243	113,172	110,753	101,374	112,196	109,378
Museums, libraries and archives council (net)	59,804	61,838	58,376	64,474	43,741	8,632	-	-	-
Support for the Arts sector	3,088	(1,273)	(3,821)	(1,737)	2,373	(53,218)	(67,219)	(61,175)	421
Arts and culture ALBs (net)	402,293	413,791	420,612	420,204	380,835	446,545	442,838	434,221	358,336
Support for the Sports sector	8,525	2,203	8,801	1,098	5,394	6,847	21,147	16,874	14,374
Sport sponsored ALBs (net)	141,744	161,154	151,945	148,362	136,077	144,942	114,967	120,269	108,121
Ceremonial and support for the Heritage sector	19,064	20,633	18,555	22,200	13,946	22,161	16,690	30,607	29,281
Heritage sponsored ALBs (net)	141,608	151,149	151,825	144,270	130,737	97,567	92,975	97,311	84,024
The Royal Parks	18,999	20,092	18,487	15,759	17,162	16,955	13,637	14,767	13,730
Support for the Tourism sector	1,985	2,230	127	2,362	16	70	10	-	-
Tourism sponsored ALBs (net)	53,848	52,985	50,450	39,479	45,494	47,824	48,200	27,591	28,006
Support for the Broadcasting and Media sector	4,417	2,722	2,624	1,561	3,218	15,161	12,063	10,190	13,946
Broadcasting and Media sponsored ALBs (net)	118,109	129,542	136,260	138,139	170,893	183,597	93,543	91,042	95,979
Administration and Research	53,309	56,476	56,448	53,406	58,429	51,679	34,863	37,630	39,949
Support for Horseracing and the Gambling sector	(11,518)	(5,121)	(3,732)	(4,020)	2,700	(1,560)	(1,603)	(2,817)	-
Gambling Commission(net)	16,610	7,927	5,801	4,107	4,722	1,959	3,097	3,765	1,234
Olympics - legacy programmes	459	(67)	524	13,022	65,868	501,628	(18,083)	178	-
London 2012(net)	24,130	(2,703)	(35,363)	(18,700)	45,399	1,575,240	(29,477)	100	-
Government Equalities Office	5,969	10,333	13,998	11,611	7,080	15,283	7,298	18,900	11,000
Equalitiy and Human Rights Commission (net)	74,129	59,395	55,700	52,800	42,982	26,683	19,230	24,785	23,317
Spectrum Management Receipts	-	-	-	-	-	(60,142)	(54,535)	(62,600)	(61,800)
Total resource DEL	**1,582,687**	**1,530,801**	**1,572,799**	**1,580,324**	**1,610,390**	**3,531,024**	**1,222,241**	**1,343,648**	**1,275,466**

Resource DEL (£'000s)	2007-08 Outturn	2008-09 Outturn	2009-10 Outturn	2010-11 Outturn	2011-12 Outturn	2012-13 Outturn	2013-14 Outturn	2014-15 Plans	2015-16 Plans
Total resource DEL (brought forward)	**1,582,687**	**1,530,801**	**1,572,799**	**1,580,324**	**1,610,390**	**3,531,024**	**1,222,241**	**1,343,648**	**1,275,466**
Of which:									
Staff costs	632,674	585,335	604,087	606,177	648,611	593,804	560,591	213,687	219,842
Purchase of goods and services	817,214	852,475	795,638	745,002	931,655	849,574	979,159	571,777	479,095
Income from sales of goods and services	(400,225)	(435,149)	(371,751)	(364,397)	(402,992)	(273,532)	(474,637)	(23,000)	-
Current grants to local government (net)	48,672	91,378	38,415	57,507	(26,931)	10,603	(7,008)	-	-
Current grants to persons and non-profit bodies (net)	575,071	580,437	649,477	606,302	585,540	786,028	502,356	508,414	427,911
Current grants abroad (net)	(12,410)	906	493	823	136	-	(1,528)	-	-
Subsidies to private sector companies	-	-	-	-	-	-	157	-	-
Subsidies to public corporations	-	-	-	82,590	74,880	522,976	10,026	2,689	(10)
Rentals	-	-	-	800	6,346	3,545	33,199	-	-
Depreciation [1]	107,081	28,571	115,617	109,300	114,120	1,443,884	133,696	176,200	179,328
Change in pension scheme liabilities [2]	-	-	-	100	471	12	(44)	-	-
Other resource	(185,390)	(173,152)	(259,177)	(263,880)	(321,446)	(405,870)	(513,726)	(106,119)	(30,700)

Resource AME (£'000s)	2007-08 Outturn	2008-09 Outturn	2009-10 Outturn	2010-11 Outturn	2011-12 Outturn	2012-13 Outturn	2013-14 Outturn	2014-15 Plans	2015-16 Plans
British Broadcasting Corporation(net)	2,962,800	2,868,987	3,020,000	3,121,360	2,608,460	3,224,802	2,794,569	3,471,499	3,305,146
Provisions, Impairments and other AME spend	6,786	(276)	13,027	96,255	35,957	19,449	16,854	62,071	-
Lottery Grants	882,351	1,010,728	1,000,814	994,845	1,334,509	1,450,239	1,399,564	1,401,425	994,222
London 2012(net)	(507)	13,667	26,057	156,592	(155,839)	(30,996)	102,138	-	-
Gambling levy bodies	-	-	-	-	(30,535)	(10,268)	(2,721)	-	-
Total resource AME	**3,851,430**	**3,893,106**	**4,059,898**	**4,369,052**	**3,792,552**	**4,653,226**	**4,310,404**	**4,934,995**	**4,299,368**

9.1 Expenditure by the Department for Culture, Media and Sport

Resource AME (£'000s)	2007-08 Outturn	2008-09 Outturn	2009-10 Outturn	2010-11 Outturn	2011-12 Outturn	2012-13 Outturn	2013-14 Outturn	2014-15 Plans	2015-16 Plans
Total resource AME	3,851,430	3,893,106	4,059,898	4,369,052	3,792,552	4,653,226	4,310,404	4,934,995	4,299,368
Of which:									
Staff costs	1,097,800	974,130	1,248,000	1,053,000	1,199,758	921,649	884,993	1,323,577	1,051,440
Purchase of goods and services	2,375,000	2,410,870	2,279,000	2,630,510	1,973,067	2,812,655	2,498,563	3,041,000	2,780,175
Income from sales of goods and services	-	-	-	-	-	(328,808)	-	(392,474)	-
Current grants to local government (net)	43,953	102,440	79,898	73,666	57,497	20,812	34,896	62,530	95,050
Current grants to persons and non-profit bodies (net)	729,672	784,288	784,245	761,179	961,726	557,133	452,521	1,338,895	899,172
Subsidies to public corporations	-	-	-	-	-	-	24	-	-
Rentals	-	-	-	-	-	80,775	104,496	-	-
Depreciation [1]	35,000	84,787	93,000	69,585	124,644	237,372	273,208	221,881	159,146
Take up of provisions	12,911	17,283	41,771	292,898	(96,968)	592,197	870,437	2,850	-
Release of provision	(6,632)	(3,892)	(2,687)	(6,041)	(16,345)	(40,604)	(11,576)	-	-
Change in pension scheme liabilities[2]	-	-	-	-	-	162,422	178,831	-	-
Unwinding of the discount rate on pension scheme liabilities[2]	-	-	-	-	560,222	730,035	82,412	-	-
Release of provisions covering payments of pension benefits	-	-	-	-	-	(234)	(14,336)	-	-
Other resource	(436,274)	(476,800)	(463,329)	(505,745)	(971,049)	(1,092,178)	(1,044,065)	(663,264)	(685,615)
Total resource budget	5,434,117	5,423,907	5,632,697	5,949,376	5,402,942	8,184,250	5,532,645	6,278,643	5,574,834
Of which: Depreciation[1]	142,081	113,358	208,617	178,885	238,764	1,681,256	406,904	398,081	338,474

Source: Department for Culture, Media and Sport

1 Depreciation includes impairment

2 Pension schemes report under IAS19 Employee Benefits accounting requirements. These figures, therefore, include cash payments made and contributions received, as well as certain non-cash items.

9.2 Estimates of Average Issue Readership of National Daily Newspapers

rolling 12 months' periods ending

000's

		2010 Mar	2010 Jun	2010 Sep	2010 Dec	2011 Mar	2011 Jun	2011 Sept	2011 Dec	2012 Mar	2012 Jun	2012 Sep	2012 Dec	2013 Mar	2013 Jun	2013 Sep	2013 Dec	2014 Mar
The Sun	WSDV	7,751	7,694	7,700	7,722	7,722	7,683	7,652	7,480	7,331	7,244	7,084	7,007	6,707	6,435	6,123	5,841	5,685
Daily Mail	WSEI	4,881	4,896	4,739	4,741	4,775	4,622	4,561	4,455	4,426	4,385	4,320	4,258	4,245	4,298	4,269	4,215	4,074
Daily Mirror/Daily Record	WSEH	4,288	4,170	4,004	3,947	4,026	3,997	4,114	4,053	4,046	3,995	3,849	3,773	3,614	3,512	3,357	3,167	2,975
Daily Mirror	WSEM	3,381	3,244	3,117	3,087	3,163	3,163	3,251	3,200	3,196	3,178	3,062	2,995	2,856	2,775	2,639	2,456	2,309
The Daily Telegraph	WSEN	1,840	1,796	1,751	1,680	1,693	1,688	1,584	1,562	1,468	1,387	1,394	1,346	1,352	1,348	1,312	1,318	1,313
The Times	WSES	1,768	1,673	1,613	1,571	1,552	1,486	1,435	1,385	1,359	1,302	1,310	1,311	1,300	1,261	1,240	1,147	1,155
Daily Express	WSEP	1,617	1,586	1,551	1,565	1,504	1,457	1,439	1,417	1,329	1,304	1,265	1,192	1,157	1,123	1,114	1,095	1,114
Daily Star	WSEQ	1,529	1,463	1,423	1,427	1,488	1,498	1,506	1,452	1,409	1,439	1,421	1,358	1,279	1,211	1,158	1,113	1,090
The Guardian	WSET	1,124	1,132	1,130	1,103	1,154	1,143	1,119	1,120	1,058	1,081	1,062	1,050	1,027	935	890	843	793
i		-	-	-	-	-	-	-	-	-	564	561	612	579	545	568	559	563
The Independent	WSEU	635	607	556	532	562	535	541	530	533	537	506	490	443	397	393	348	309
Financial Times[1]	WSEY	418	404	391	364	367	344	325	317	301	300	285	319	312	305	296	235	-
Any national morning	WSEZ	20,404	20,207	19,841	19,690	19,751	19,481	19,391	19,124	18,679	18,466	18,069	17,825	17,403	20,852	20,181	19,347	19,092

Source: National Readership Surveys Ltd.

1. NRS ceased to publish estimates for Financial Times as of 2014 data, so data cannot be provided for March 2014 onwards.

9.3 Employment in the Creative Economy in 2012

By Group

Group	Employment in Creative Industries	95% Confidence Interval (+/-)	Creative Jobs outside of the Creative Industries	95% Confidence Interval (+/-)	Employment in the Creative Economy	95% Confidence Interval (+/-)
1. Advertising and marketing	143,000	12,000	322,000	18,000	465,000	22,000
2. Architecture	89,000	10,000	30,000	6,000	120,000	11,000
3. Crafts	7,000	3,000	95,000	10,000	102,000	10,000
4. Design: product, graphic and fashion design	116,000	11,000	50,000	7,000	166,000	13,000
5. Film, TV, video, radio and photography	238,000	16,000	28,000	6,000	266,000	16,000
6. IT, software and computer services	558,000	23,000	233,000	15,000	791,000	28,000
7. Publishing	223,000	15,000	32,000	6,000	255,000	16,000
8. Museums, galleries and libraries	85,000	10,000	22,000	5,000	108,000	11,000
9. Music, performing and visual arts	224,000	15,000	53,000	8,000	277,000	17,000
Total	1,684,000	40,000	866,000	29,000	2,550,000	48,000
Wider UK Economy Total	-		-		30,150,000	

Notes

1: Source – Annual Population Survey 2012

2: Figures have been rounded to the nearest thousand, and therefore estimates may not sum across rows or columns to equal totals

9.4 Selected activities performed in free time, by age, 2013/14 England

	Age					
	16-24	25-44	45-64	65-74	75+	All aged 16+
	%	%	%	%	%	%
Free time activities						
Watching TV	86.8	88.3	91.9	93.8	94.6	90.4
Spending time with friends/family	89.9	90.7	88.1	88.2	86.5	89.1
Listening to music	89.1	80.7	78.0	72.5	67.9	78.9
Shopping	74.9	77.2	76.3	81.8	75.8	77.0
Eating out at restaurants	74.5	75.3	74.3	76.6	69.1	74.4
Internet/emailing	85.7	81.4	69.8	53.9	25.2	69.9
Reading	57.8	66.4	71.7	78.3	75.1	69.0
Days out or visits to places	63.3	73.0	68.5	72.6	57.7	68.7
Sport/exercise	65.6	63.8	56.0	52.2	33.9	57.4
Going to the cinema	73.3	61.3	49.2	38.4	22.1	52.9
Going to pubs/bars/clubs	61.0	55.6	49.6	42.4	28.9	50.4
Gardening	13.7	42.1	63.5	69.9	60.6	49.5
Theatre/music concerts	39.7	42.2	49.5	51.0	33.0	44.2
DIY	17.9	44.0	53.4	44.6	24.5	41.3
Visiting historic sites	21.7	39.5	47.2	54.0	32.1	40.2
Visiting museums/galleries	22.7	39.6	43.7	46.9	28.8	38.2
Playing computer games	49.6	34.0	24.0	17.8	7.9	28.8
Arts and crafts	20.8	22.7	23.4	28.2	22.3	23.2
Playing a musical instrument	17.2	10.8	9.3	8.0	5.1	10.4

Source: Taking Part 2013/14. Department for Culture, Media and Sport

9.5 Films

United Kingdom

Numbers and £ million

	Production of UK films[1,4]		Expenditure on feature films (Expressed in 2012 Pounds)			
	Films produced in the UK (numbers)	Production costs (current prices)	UK box office	Video[2] rental	Video[2] retail[3]	Video on Demand
	KWGD	KWGE	KWHU	KWHV	KWHW	
1998	83	389	547	437	453	33
1999	92	507	563	408	451	40
2000	80	578	583	444	601	50
2001	74	379	645	494	821	65
2002	119	551	755	494	1,175	63
2003	198	1,119	742	462	1,392	68
2004	173	875	770	476	1,557	73
2005	174	582	770	389	1,399	74
2006	139	826	762	327	1,302	67
2007	136	836	821	280	1,440	75
2008	143	721.6 [4]	850	265	1,454	101
2009	163	1123.0 [4]	944	263	1,311	120 r
2010	141	1292.8 [4]	988	253	1,267	130 r
2011	166	1274.0 [4]	1,040	246	1,165	150 r
2012	173	994 [4]	1,099	229	968	236

Source:BFI RSU analysis, BVA, Official Charts Company, Attentional, IHS

1 Includes films with a production budget of £500,000 or more.

2 Video includes only rental and retail of physical discs, and does not include downloads.

3 In 2005 the British Video Association changed its methodology for producing market value which has necessitated a change to historical figures quoted.

4. Prior to 2010, the Research and Statistics Unit tracked all features shooting in the UK with a minimum budget of £500,000. However, evidence from a variety of sources (data on British film certification and the 2008 UK Film Council report Low and Micro-Budget Film Production in the UK) revealed a substantial number of films produced below this budget level. In order to broaden the evidence base, production tracking was extended to include feature films with budgets under £500,000 and data was collected from 2008 onwards.

r: Revised data since the last edition

9.6 Box office top 20 films released in the UK and Republic of Ireland, 2012

	Title	Country of origin	Box office gross (£ million)	Distributor
1	Skyfall*	UK/USA	102.8	Sony Pictures
2	The Dark Knight Rises	UK/USA	56.3	Warner Bros
3	The Hobbit: An Unexpected Journey*	USA/NZ	52.2	Warner Bros
4	Marvel Avengers Assemble	USA	51.9	Walt Disney
5	The Twilight Saga: Breaking Dawn – Part 2	USA	35.8	eOne Films
6	Ted	USA	30.4	Universal
7	Ice Age 4: Continental Drift	USA	30.3	20th Century Fox
8	Life of Pi*	USA/Can	28.7	20th Century Fox
9	The Amazing Spider-Man	USA	26.0	Sony Pictures
10	Prometheus	UK/USA	24.8	20th Century Fox
11	The Hunger Games	USA	24.0	Lionsgate
12	Taken 2	Fra	23.5	20th Century Fox
13	Madagascar 3: Europe's Most Wanted	USA	22.7	Paramount
14	Men in Black 3	USA	22.3	Sony Pictures
15	Brave	USA	22.2	Walt Disney
16	The Woman in Black	UK/USA/Swe	21.3	Momentum
17	The Best Exotic Marigold Hotel	UK/USA/Ind	20.4	20th Century Fox
18	War Horse	UK/USA	18.6	Walt Disney
19	American Pie: Reunion	USA	17.0	Universal
20	The Muppets	USA	16.8	Walt Disney

Notes:
Box office gross = cumulative total up to 17 February 2013.
Films with an asterisk (*) were still on release on 17 February 2013.

Source: Rentrak, BFI RSU analysis.

9.7 Full year accommodation usage figures by visitors from overseas for 2004 - 2012

Data	Accommodation	Year								
		2004	2005	2006	2007	2008	2009	2010	2011	2012
Total Visits (000s)	All staying visits	25,677	28,038	30,654	30,871	30,142	28,208	28,300	29,197	29,282
	Bed & Breakfast	1,177	1,221	1,242	1,174	1,118	1,065	1,083	996	1,003
	Camping/mobile home	295	381	425	394	298	333	312	302	284
	Free guest with relatives or friends	10,174	11,144	12,081	11,944	12,056	11,165	10,570	10,646	10,811
	Holiday village/Centre	37	60	44	67	59	77	41	49	59
	Hostel/university/school	949	1,096	1,167	1,203	1,138	1,218	1,102	1,180	1,174
	Hotel/guest house	11,451	12,465	13,939	14,156	13,472	13,001	13,841	14,446	14,406
	Other	1,815	1,855	2,143	2,073	1,930	1,470	1,518	1,360	1,439
	Own home	413	412	466	446	418	385	358	392	364
	Paying guest family or friends house	610	616	595	567	650	461	465	577	537
	Rented house	740	806	832	836	868	934	882	958	1,002
Total Nights (000s)	All staying visits	227,406	249,181	273,417	251,522	245,775	229,391	227,960	234,363	230,149
	Bed & Breakfast	8,576	7,840	7,411	7,078	6,500	5,804	6,341	5,639	5,307
	Camping/mobile home	3,015	4,705	4,350	4,182	2,988	3,296	2,904	3,229	2,757
	Free guest with relatives or friends	113,736	121,487	133,209	121,272	122,898	111,947	107,642	108,703	107,575
	Holiday village/Centre	222	346	336	576	329	448	321	321	393
	Hostel/university/school	16,757	17,863	21,103	15,680	15,443	16,775	16,305	18,670	18,236
	Hotel/guest house	45,291	51,069	57,540	57,174	55,133	54,246	58,741	60,365	60,081
	Other	5,546	7,078	6,930	6,452	6,597	4,397	4,982	4,990	4,635
	Own home	4,638	5,507	7,895	5,169	5,110	4,524	5,068	5,625	4,895
	Paying guest family or friends house	8,807	8,716	9,692	8,240	7,961	5,423	5,148	6,574	7,433
	Rented house	20,818	24,570	24,950	25,695	22,817	22,362	20,482	20,237	18,838
Total Spend (£m)	All staying visits	12,798	14,011	15,759	15,699	16,058	16,354	16,649	17,666	18,245
	Bed & Breakfast	481	511	512	488	470	459	522	470	457
	Camping/mobile home	97	112	142	146	111	144	129	128	111
	Free guest with relatives or friends	3,822	3,972	4,498	4,207	4,501	4,425	4,254	4,371	4,515
	Holiday village/Centre	9	12	17	27	22	27	23	23	27
	Hostel/university/school	739	848	937	829	813	1,055	1,004	1,122	1,083
	Hotel/guest house	5,826	6,547	7,580	7,916	7,914	7,773	8,577	9,138	9,626
	Other	263	308	245	328	337	328	272	307	265
	Own home	354	357	412	402	429	531	354	377	505
	Paying guest family or friends house	345	393	439	385	379	364	340	426	475
	Rented house	861	951	977	971	1,084	1,245	1,172	1,305	1,181
Sample	All staying visits	37,321	39,977	40,410	36,432	31,854	41,952	41,948	38,144	37,666
	Bed & Breakfast	1,570	1,617	1,471	1,266	1,137	1,469	1,518	1,252	1,224
	Camping/mobile home	250	322	339	320	298	363	378	379	325
	Free guest with relatives or friends	15,167	16,363	16,256	14,386	12,831	16,976	16,003	14,233	14,207
	Holiday village/Centre	45	64	53	59	46	99	49	55	82
	Hostel/university/school	1,232	1,372	1,348	1,261	1,153	1,616	1,510	1,382	1,381
	Hotel/guest house	18,716	19,971	20,585	18,560	15,641	20,885	21,998	19,765	19,458
	Other	965	893	910	864	873	1,008	1,033	1,136	1,174
	Own home	730	744	740	645	522	656	637	545	594
	Paying guest family or friends house	562	599	527	487	507	529	538	637	548
	Rented house	1,101	1,161	1,164	1,034	973	1,457	1,397	1,291	1,334

International Passenger Survey, Office for National Statistics

NB: For 2013 the accommodation categories were reduced therefore this data is shown separately. The ONS will revert to the full accommodation options for 2014 data.

9.7 Full year accommodation usage figures by visitors from overseas for 2013

Full year accommodation usage figures for 2013 - staying visits (000s)

	ALL STAYING VISITS	Own Home	Hotels or similar	Camp/caravan sites	Other Short Term Rented	Friends or Relatives	Other (Non Rented or Long Term Rented)
ALL STAYING VISITS	31,169	359	16,880	496	2,115	10,584	2,348
TOTAL ENGLAND	28,602	318	15,568	395	1,910	9,706	1,925
*LONDON	16,784	159	10,839	121	948	4,424	412
*REST OF ENGLAND	13,629	161	5,619	294	1,007	5,626	1,581
- ENGLAND'S NORTH COUNTRY	3,791	30	1,830	46	162	1,425	412
- CENTRAL ENGLAND	4,766	55	1,690	84	249	2,051	727
- SOUTHERN ENGLAND	6,350	76	2,560	210	616	2,476	643
NORTH EAST	431	6	190	8	22	167	41
NORTH WEST	2,415	13	1,264	30	91	832	237
YORKSHIRE	1,220	11	523	14	53	478	158
WEST MIDLANDS	1,869	20	723	29	81	651	382
EAST MIDLANDS	1,077	11	340	22	64	469	174
EAST OF ENGLAND	2,006	24	681	38	106	986	203
SOUTH WEST	2,230	21	961	114	229	842	153
SOUTH EAST	4,587	55	1,846	124	405	1,726	504
SCOTLAND	2,443	25	1,517	92	181	687	110
WALES	884	14	345	59	61	303	111
NORTHERN IRELAND	366	3	85	1	11	67	204

Full year accommodation usage figures for 2013 - nights (000s)

	ALL STAYING VISITS	Own Home	Hotels or similar	Camp/caravan sites	Other Short Term Rented	Friends or Relatives	Other (Non Rented or Long Term Rented)
ALL STAYING VISITS	245,230	5,350	77,447	4,120	34,569	105,701	18,042
TOTAL ENGLAND	216,975	4,601	67,154	3,029	31,719	95,049	15,423
*LONDON	97,439	1,830	43,291	568	12,270	35,576	3,904
*REST OF ENGLAND	119,536	2,771	23,864	2,460	19,449	59,472	11,519
- ENGLAND'S NORTH COUNTRY	30,890	480	6,715	473	3,907	15,922	3,393
- CENTRAL ENGLAND	38,245	811	6,404	567	5,849	20,936	3,679
- SOUTHERN ENGLAND	50,397	1,481	10,744	1,419	9,693	22,615	4,446
NORTH EAST	3,398	55	643	26	401	1,639	635
NORTH WEST	17,100	180	4,358	382	1,864	8,463	1,853
YORKSHIRE	10,391	245	1,714	65	1,642	5,820	905
WEST MIDLANDS	14,796	332	2,932	179	2,206	7,168	1,979
EAST MIDLANDS	9,160	267	1,174	172	1,442	5,230	875
EAST OF ENGLAND	14,289	212	2,298	215	2,201	8,538	826
SOUTH WEST	18,577	411	4,205	807	3,540	7,630	1,984
SOUTH EAST	31,820	1,070	6,540	611	6,153	14,984	2,462
SCOTLAND	19,361	479	8,386	754	1,902	7,029	811
WALES	5,932	256	1,322	315	845	2,704	490
NORTHERN IRELAND	2,133	14	424	11	100	728	857

Full year accommodation usage figures for 2013 - spend (£m)

	ALL STAYING VISITS	Own Home	Hotels or similar	Camp/caravan sites	Other Short Term Rented	Friends or Relatives	Other (Non Rented or Long Term Rented)
ALL STAYING VISITS	£20,691	£505	£11,821	£230	£2,472	£4,607	£1,054
TOTAL ENGLAND	£18,397	£465	£10,490	£171	£2,293	£4,128	£850
*LONDON	£11,256	£342	£7,642	£55	£1,141	£1,830	£247
*REST OF ENGLAND	£7,141	£122	£2,849	£116	£1,152	£2,298	£603
- ENGLAND'S NORTH COUNTRY	£1,868	£28	£832	£21	£194	£593	£200
- CENTRAL ENGLAND	£2,175	£34	£774	£31	£356	£780	£200
- SOUTHERN ENGLAND	£3,097	£60	£1,243	£65	£601	£925	£203
NORTH EAST	£208	£7	£88	£1	£16	£70	£27
NORTH WEST	£1,076	£16	£537	£16	£85	£329	£94
YORKSHIRE	£584	£5	£207	£4	£93	£195	£79
WEST MIDLANDS	£844	£15	£330	£10	£149	£237	£104
EAST MIDLANDS	£459	£6	£157	£10	£69	£178	£39
EAST OF ENGLAND	£873	£14	£287	£12	£138	£366	£57
SOUTH WEST	£1,097	£19	£431	£39	£228	£292	£88
SOUTH EAST	£2,000	£41	£812	£26	£374	£634	£115
SCOTLAND	£1,680	£26	£1,118	£45	£123	£336	£32
WALES	£353	£15	£156	£14	£48	£103	£18
NORTHERN IRELAND	£208	£0	£41	£0	£6	£32	£129

Full year accommodation usage figures for 2013 - sample size

	ALL STAYING VISITS	Own Home	Hotels or similar	Camp / Caravan sites	Other Short Term Rented	Friends or Relatives	Other (Non Rented or Long Term Rented)
ALL STAYING VISITS	39,416	566	22,514	602	2,561	13,609	1,910
TOTAL ENGLAND	36,565	503	20,872	452	2,303	12,512	1,692
*LONDON	21,835	257	14,488	148	1,162	5,519	428
*REST OF ENGLAND	17,488	249	7,788	321	1,196	7,548	1,313
- ENGLAND'S NORTH COUNTRY	5,340	53	2,784	86	241	2,036	333
- CENTRAL ENGLAND	5,790	73	2,250	86	294	2,627	582
- SOUTHERN ENGLAND	8,060	123	3,424	190	692	3,390	542
NORTH EAST	557	8	273	20	30	202	34
NORTH WEST	3,556	27	1,977	50	130	1,263	190
YORKSHIRE	1,682	19	780	36	87	664	130
WEST MIDLANDS	2,251	27	978	32	98	853	290
EAST MIDLANDS	1,266	14	454	26	67	570	140
EAST OF ENGLAND	2,516	32	893	35	135	1,284	176
SOUTH WEST	3,017	39	1,307	105	287	1,256	142
SOUTH EAST	5,605	84	2,390	108	425	2,272	413
SCOTLAND	3,148	37	1,991	154	234	855	101
WALES	1,226	24	539	60	76	461	80
NORTHERN IRELAND	250	3	123	1	13	88	27

Source: International Passenger Survey, Office for National Statistics

Sample Size

Figures for a number of areas / accommodation types are based on small sample sizes (i.e. low numbers of this type of visitor were interviewed).

Danger!
If sample size is less than 30 it will appear **red** - it

Caution
If sample size is between 30 and 100 it will appear **amber** - it is recommended to only use

OK
If sample size is over 100 it will appear **green** - this is the recommended level of data to use

NB: For 2013 the accommodation categories were reduced therefore this data is shown separately. The ONS will revert to the full accommodation options for 2014 data.

What to do if sample size is low
You may find it helpful to consider looking at three year averages, or widening results by selecting fewer categories

9.8 International tourism[1]

Thousands and £ million

		Spending in the UK by overseas residents			Spending overseas by UK residents	
	Visits to the UK by overseas residents (thousands)	Current prices	Constant 1995 prices	Visits overseas by UK residents (thousands)	Current prices	Constant 1995 prices
	GMAA	GMAK	CQPR	GMAF	GMAM	CQPS
2000	25,207	12,806	11,102	56,837	24,250	27,281
2001	22,832	11,305	9,528	58,281	25,332	27,710
2002	24,392	11,737	9,641	59,498	26,962	29,311
2003	24,874	11,856	9,451	61,334	28,550	28,677
2004	27,755	13,047	10,146	64,194	30,285	30,444
2005	29,970	14,248	10,714	66,441	32,154	30,954
2006	32,713	16,002	11,641	69,536	34,411	30,904
2007	32,778	15,960	11,389	69,450	35,013	32,477
2008	31,888	16,323	11,276	69,011	36,838	28,657
2009	29,889	16,592	11,032	58,614	31,694	22,673
2010	29,803	16,899	10,644	55,562	31,820	22,116
2011	30,798	17,998	10,870	56,836	31,701	20,569
2012	31,084	18,640	10,842	56,538	32,450	22,024
2013	32,812	21,011	11,780	58,509	34,900	24,063

1 See chapter text

Sources: International Passenger Survey
Office for National Statistics;
01633 456032

9.9 Holidays abroad:[1] by destination

Percentages

		2001	2002	2003	2004	2005	2006	2007	2008	2009	2010	2011	2012	2013
Spain	JTKC	27.9	28.5	29.8	28.4	27.2	27.8	26.5	26.6	26.5	25.9	25.8	27.0	27.5
France	JTKD	18.3	19	18.1	17.3	16.6	15.9	16.7	16.7	18.6	18.3	17.4	17.2	16.4
Greece	JTKF	7.8	7	6.6	5.7	5.1	5.0	5.0	4.2	4.4	4.8	4.8	4.5	4.4
USA	JTKE	6.3	5.4	5.5	6.1	6.0	5.1	5.2	5.4	5.4	4.9	5.2	5.2	5.0
Italy	JTKG	4.3	4.6	5	5	5.4	5.4	5.6	5.2	4.7	4.6	4.5	5.0	5.3
Irish Republic	JTKI	4.1	4.1	3.7	3.8	3.8	4.0	3.3	3.2	3.2	2.5	2.9	2.3	2.2
Portugal	JTKH	3.6	4	4	3.5	3.6	3.7	4.1	4.8	4.1	4.4	4.5	4.5	4.8
Cyprus	JTKL	3.5	3	2.7	2.6	2.8	2.4	2.4	2.4	2.1	2.1	2.2	2.0	1.5
Netherlands	JTKK	2.6	2.8	2.6	2.6	2.5	2.7	2.4	2.1	2.2	2.2	2.6	2.6	2.7
Turkey	JTKJ	2	2.2	2.3	2.3	2.7	2.7	2.8	3.7	3.5	4.7	3.7	3.3	2.8
Belgium	JTKM	2.1	2	2.2	1.8	1.9	2.0	2.2	2.0	1.9	1.7	2	2.5	2.3
Germany	JTKN	1.4	1.5	1.2	1.6	1.7	1.7	2.0	1.9	1.7	1.7	2.2	2.0	2.3
Austria	JTKP	1.1	1.4	1.1	1.4	1.3	1.2	1.2	1.4	1.4	1.5	1	1.1	1.2
Malta	JTKO	1	1			1.1	1.0	0.9	0.9	0.8	1.0	1	1.0	1.2
Other countries	JTKQ	13.8	13.6	14.2	16.8	18.4	20	19.6	19.5	19.5	19.6	20.2	13.3	13.4

Sources: International Passenger Survey, Office for National Statistics;

1 See chapter text.

01633 456032

9.10 All Tourism

	2008	2009	2010	2011	2012	2013	2014
TRIPS (millions)	114.442	122.537	115.711	126.635	126.019	122.905	114.242
BEDNIGHTS (millions)	367.635	387.448	361.398	387.329	388.24	373.607	349.546
EXPENDITURE (£ millions)	£20,168	£20,971	£19,797	£22,666	£23,976	£23,294	£22,692
Av. Trip Length	3.21	3.16	3.12	3.06	3.08	3.04	3.06
Av. £ / Night	£55	£54	£55	£59	£62	£62	£65
Av. £ / Trip	£176	£171	£171	£179	£190	£190	£199

Source: Visit England

latest results are provisional and subject to minor changed in subsequent months due to trip-takers returning from late trips. Pre-2014 results are based on full year data so will not change

All expenditure figures are in historic prices

9.11 All Tourism in Great Britain

	TRIPS				NIGHTS				SPEND			
	GB	England	Scotland	Wales	GB	England	Scotland	Wales	GB	England	Scotland	Wales
		Millions				Millions				Millions		
All Tourism - 2012	126.02	104.46	12.75	9.60	388.2	310.2	43.3	34.7	£23,976	£19,497	£2,891	£1,588
All Tourism - 2013	122.91	101.76	12.12	9.93	373.6	297.2	42.7	33.7	£23,294	£18,710	£2,889	£1,696
PURPOSE												
Leisure	101.20	83.12	9.95	8.84	323.0	255.7	36.1	31.2	£18,319	£14,540	£2,310	£1,469
Holiday (total)	82.62	66.87	8.80	7.65	277.7	216.3	32.9	28.5	£16,457	£12,925	£2,172	£1,361
Holiday / pleasure / leisure	56.97	44.93	6.48	6.09	198.2	149.7	24.4	24.1	£13,472	£10,463	£1,814	£1,195
Visiting friends & relatives – mainly holiday	25.65	21.94	2.32	1.56	79.5	66.6	8.5	4.4	£2,985	£2,462	£357	£166
Visiting friends & relatives – mainly other	18.55	16.25	1.15	1.19	45.3	39.4	3.2	2.7	£1,862	£1,616	£138	£108
Visiting friends or relatives (total)	44.20	38.19	3.47	2.75	124.8	105.9	11.7	7.1	£4,847	£4,078	£496	£274
Business (total)	18.29	15.59	1.97	0.88	41.5	33.5	6.0	2.0	£4,514	£3,770	£542	£203
Business travel	17.77	15.12	1.93	0.87	40.1	32.3	5.9	2.0	£4,388	£3,655	£531	£702

The GB Tourist 2013

British residents made an estimated 123 million trips in Great Britain in 2013, representing 374 million bed nights and £23 billion in spending.

Holidays (including visiting friends and relatives) are the main purpose of trips taken, accounting for two thirds (67%) of trips taken and are even more important in terms of nights (74%) and spending (71%).

Visits to friends and relatives (VFR) for mainly holiday purposes account for one in five trips and nights away (21%) but are less important in terms of spending (13%).

Business and work is the main purpose for around one in seven trips (15%) accounting for one in nine nights (11%). These are higher spending trips, accounting for a fifth (19%) of all tourism spending.

Friends' and relatives' homes (including owned second homes) are a widely used type of accommodation accounting for almost four in ten of all trips (36%). This reflects not only visits to friends and relatives as such, but also holidays spent staying with friends and relatives. With no real accommodation costs, trips staying at friends' and relatives' homes account for only a fifth (18%) of spending on all tourism trips.

Commercial accommodation is used on almost three-fifths of trips (59%), but these trips represent a much higher share of spending (78%). Commercial accommodation is mainly serviced (41% of trips) where trips tend to be shorter in duration (30% of nights) but higher spending (55%). Hotels and motels account for 35% of trips and 45% of spend; Guest houses and B&Bs account for 4% of trips and 5% of spend.

Self catering rented accommodation is used on a lower volume of trips (18%), but these trips are longer (27% of nights) and slightly above average in terms of spending (22%).

The car is the dominant form of transport with 73% of trips using a private car for the longest part of the journey from home to the destination.

Firm bookings are made before more than half of all trips (56%), but this figure would be higher were it not for the high level of staying at friends and relatives' homes and using personal transport, where advance booking is less relevant.

Large cities/large towns (41%) are the major destinations of tourism trips, followed by small towns (23%), the seaside (19%) and countryside/villages (19%).

9.12 Gambling[1]
United Kingdom

£ million[2] and numbers

		2000 /01	2001 /02	2002 /03	2003 /04	2004 /05	2005 /06	2006 /07	2007 /08	2008 /09	2009 /10	2010 /11	2011 /12	2012 /13
Money staked on gambling														
National Lottery -Total[3]	C229	5,315	5,029	4,670	4,614	4,757	5,000	4,911	4,966	5,149	5,477	5,825	6,503	6,977
Lotto including on-line	C3PU	4,416	4,038	3,479	3,225	3,225	3,021	2,858	2,752	2,698	2,661	2,667	2,475	2,345
Lotto Plus 5[8]		-	-	-	-	-	-	-	-	-	-	-	101.7	78.7
Instants[4] (Scratchcards)	C3PV	590	606	592	641	729	804	943	1,109	1,221	1,340	1,436	1,726	2,062
Thunderball	C3PW	257	254	287	351	343	355	329	309	297	286	356	331	314
Lottery Extra[5]	C3PX	51	131	90	78	77	57	12	0	-	-	-	-	-
HotPicks	C3PY	..	..	222	244	219	228	222	210	211	210	206	200	193
Euromillions	C3Q2	..	..	..	15	104	427	464	476	618	881	1,056	1,666	1,984
Daily Play	C3Q3	..	..	..	45	59	54	49	50	50	49	46	4.3	-
Dream number[6]		..	..	..	..	..	..	59	59	54	50	39	-	-
Number operating in GB:														
Casinos	JE55	117	122	126	131	138	140	138	144	145	141	149	146	144
betting shops[7]	JE5B	..	..	..	..	..	..	..	8,800	8,862	8,822	9,067	9128	9,076

1 See chapter text.

2 Adjusted to real terms using the Retail Prices Index.

3 Includes Easy Play tickets which are not shown separately.

4 From 2003/04 includes Inter-active Instant Win Games

5 Discontinued games

6 Started July 2006

7 The Gambling Commission started regulating the betting industry from 1 September 2007, the number of betting shops is an ABB estimate.

8 launched in February 2011

Sources: National Lottery Commission;
Gambling Commission: 0121 230 6666;
Department for Culture, Media and Sport: 020 7211 6451

		General Remote Data (£m) - turnover and gross gambling yield					
		2008/09	**2009/10**	**2010/11**	**2011/12**	**2012/13**	**2013/14**
Betting	Turnover	10,263.69	10,825.64	12,999.82	14,098.91	19,550.73	25,411.26
	GGY	640.77	460.85	492.25	563.96	751.70	980.40
Betting Exchange	Turnover	n/a	n/a	n/a	n/a	n/a	n/a
	GGY	142.54	146.91	145.93	46.04	32.51	31.13
Bingo	Turnover	3.94	20.44	26.24	28.17	33.78	44.40
	GGY	0.47	1.51	2.19	2.03	2.46	4.32
Casino	Turnover	950.07	685.49	340.57	512.25	861.39	697.72
	GGY	33.08	22.95	12.69	20.23	42.49	30.31
Pool Betting	Turnover	n/a	n/a	n/a	154.11	184.73	207.63
	GGY	n/a	n/a	n/a	77.92	103.45	93.22

		Betting Data (£m) - turnover and gross gambling yield					
		2008/09	**2009/10**	**2010/11**	**2011/12**	**2012/13**	**2013/14**
Cricket	Turnover	n/a	n/a	n/a	320.77	333.44	490.62
	GGY	n/a	n/a	n/a	6.16	9.23	6.34
Dogs	Turnover	n/a	83.79	71.50	59.33	90.93	127.70
	GGY	n/a	11.06	9.44	5.83	8.05	9.91
Financials	Turnover	n/a	n/a	n/a	205.41	314.47	342.66
	GGY	n/a	n/a	n/a	2.73	8.96	8.65
Football	Turnover	n/a	4,130.06	5,402.97	5,396.85	7,770.87	10,189.41
	GGY	n/a	172.19	271.19	281.23	377.22	489.08
Golf	Turnover	n/a	n/a	n/a	52.25	60.18	103.49
	GGY	n/a	n/a	n/a	2.50	1.17	2.93
Horses	Turnover	n/a	2,402.45	2,441.95	1,956.56	1,881.32	1,988.82
	GGY	n/a	201.29	105.97	92.21	111.99	114.99
Tennis	Turnover	n/a	n/a	n/a	2,071.02	3,948.78	5,156.05
	GGY	n/a	n/a	n/a	68.81	121.61	166.16
Other	Turnover	n/a	4,209.34	5,083.39	4,190.83	5,314.06	7,220.16
	GGY	n/a	223.22	251.59	228.44	249.42	306.70

9.12 Gambling[1]

United Kingdom

Casino Data (£m) - turnover and gross gambling yield							
		2008/09	2009/10	2010/11	2011/12	2012/13	2013/14
Card Game	Turnover	n/a	48.90	43.71	27.84	56.26	45.08
	GGY	n/a	1.47	1.59	1.10	2.55	1.69
Peer to Peer	Turnover	n/a	0.78	0.01	0.02	0.00	0.00
	GGY	n/a	0.78	0.01	0.01	0.00	0.00
Slots	Turnover	n/a	86.08	102.18	200.50	405.95	366.13
	GGY	n/a	5.11	6.24	12.44	25.52	22.08
Table Game	Turnover	n/a	508.21	144.16	238.00	404.72	283.29
	GGY	n/a	13.41	3.24	4.95	10.32	6.43
Other	Turnover	n/a	41.52	50.50	45.89	15.87	3.23
	GGY	n/a	2.18	1.61	1.73	4.10	0.11

Gambling Software Income (£m)							
		2008/09	2009/10	2010/11	2011/12	2012/13	2013/14
Game	Sales	n/a	n/a	n/a	3.85	3.68	7.32
	Shared Income	n/a	n/a	n/a	14.87	15.21	16.21
	Total Revenue	n/a	n/a	n/a	18.73	18.89	23.53
Platform	Sales	n/a	n/a	n/a	65.18	62.91	73.82
	Shared Income	n/a	n/a	n/a	20.84	19.59	20.89
	Total Revenue	n/a	n/a	n/a	86.03	82.50	94.71
Other	Sales	n/a	n/a	n/a	1.72	0.65	9.80
	Shared Income	n/a	n/a	n/a	0.73	2.32	4.24
	Total Revenue	n/a	n/a	n/a	2.45	2.97	14.04

Number of employees						
	at 31 Mar 2009	at 31 Mar 2010	at 31 Mar 2011	at 31 Mar 2012	at 31 Mar 2013	at 31 Mar 2014
Number of employees	n/a	7,496	6,438	5,832	4,725	4,973

Accounts						
	2008/09	2009/10	2010/11	2011/12	2012/13	2013/14
Customer accounts	16.14	16.57	14.92	15.18	16.53	16.99
Active customer accounts	4.92	4.19	3.50	3.99	4.66	4.88
New player registrations	4.22	3.95	3.31	3.83	4.62	5.68
Funds held in customer accounts (£m)	281.02	256.76	265.95	147.13	185.09	205.08

Social responsibility data						
	2008/09	2009/10	2010/11	2011/12	2012/13	2013/14
Self-exclusions	46,359	40,358	33,953	34,321	37,746	69,413
Known breaches of self-exclusion	7,198	7,480	2,533	2,317	2,031	2,126
Number of individuals who cancelled their self-exclusion after minimum period	1,540	1,525	1,581	1,508	1,984	3,800
Challenged when attempting to gamble but unable to prove age	159	109	74			
Challenged having gambled but unable to prove age				188	432	493

Notes on the data in this section:

1. All years above refer to the period April-March unless otherwise stated.
2. The betting exchange sector saw a large decrease from April 2009-March 2010 to April 2011-March 2012. This is a result of Betfair moving its' previously Commission regulated business offshore during quarter 1 of 2011/12.
3. In 2008/09, betting data was not collected on individual sports. It wasn't until 2011/12 when the Commission collected data onthe full list of sports in the table above. Between 2009/10 and 2010/11 data on cricket, financials, golf and tenniswere captured under under 'Other'. Similarly, casino data was not collected on individual games in 2008/09.
4. The decrease in employee numbers is in part due to the clarification of operators on the classification of staff directly associated with remote gambling activities.
5. Customers will often have accounts with more than one operator and therefore the datain the accounts table above relates to accounts rather than the individuals holding those accounts.
6. The number of people who have self excluded and the number of people who have cancelled their self exclusion may be lower than these figures as individuals may have self excluded from more than one site or operator and therefore been counted more than once. The number of breaches represents the number of separate incidents, rather than the number of individuals. The majority of the figures in the 'known breaches / attempted breaches of self exclusion' field are incidents where a customer has attempted to breach their self exclusion but has been successfully detected and prevented from gambling by the operator.
7. As of October 2011, the question 'challenged when attempting to gamble but unable to prove age' and the guidance issued in association with this question changed to 'challenged having gambled and unable to prove age'.
8. The Commission began collecting data on gambling software licence holders in 2011.
9. Shared Income includes income generated from gambling software provided to organisations for which royalties are received.
10. The above data only relates to operators licensed by the Commission.
11. In previous publications, headcount figures were averaged dependent upon the number of returns submitted within the reporting period. This publication however uses the figures detailed on the last regulatory return submitted before the reporting date.

9.13 Most Popular Boy and Girl Baby Names in England and Wales, 2012

Rank	Boys Name	Rank	Boys Name	Rank	Girls Name	Rank	Girls Name
1	HARRY	51	CALLUM	1	AMELIA	51	AMELIE *
2	OLIVER	52	ARTHUR *	2	OLIVIA	52	GRACIE *
3	JACK	53	MICHAEL	3	JESSICA	53	MAYA *
4	CHARLIE	54	JENSON *	4	EMILY	54	HOLLIE
5	JACOB	55	TOMMY *	5	LILY	55	GEORGIA
6	THOMAS	56	NATHAN	6	AVA *	56	EMILIA *
7	ALFIE	57	BOBBY *	7	MIA	57	EVELYN *
8	RILEY	58	CONNOR	8	ISLA *	58	BELLA *
9	WILLIAM	59	DAVID	9	SOPHIE	59	BROOKE *
10	JAMES	60	MOHAMMAD	10	ISABELLA	59	AMBER
11	JOSHUA	61	LUCA *	11	EVIE	61	ELIZA *
12	GEORGE	62	CHARLES	12	RUBY	62	AMY
13	ETHAN	63	KAI	13	POPPY	63	ELEANOR
14	NOAH *	64	JAMIE	14	GRACE	63	LEAH
15	SAMUEL	65	ALEX	15	SOPHIA	65	ESME *
16	DANIEL	66	BLAKE *	16	CHLOE	66	KATIE
17	OSCAR	67	FRANKIE *	17	ISABELLE	67	HARRIET
18	MAX	68	REUBEN *	18	ELLA	68	ANNA
19	MUHAMMAD	69	AARON	19	FREYA	69	WILLOW *
19	LEO	70	DEXTER *	20	CHARLOTTE	70	ELSIE *
21	TYLER	71	JUDE *	21	SCARLETT *	71	ZARA
22	JOSEPH	72	LEON	22	DAISY	72	ANNABELLE *
23	ARCHIE	73	OLLIE *	23	LOLA *	73	BETHANY
24	HENRY	74	STANLEY *	24	EVA *	74	FAITH *
25	LUCAS	74	ELLIOT	25	HOLLY	75	MADISON
26	MOHAMMED	76	GABRIEL	26	MILLIE	76	ISABEL
27	ALEXANDER	77	CAMERON	27	LUCY	77	MARTHA *
28	DYLAN	78	OWEN	28	PHOEBE	78	ROSE *
29	LOGAN *	79	LOUIE *	29	LAYLA *	79	JULIA *
30	ISAAC	80	AIDEN *	30	MAISIE	80	PAIGE
31	MASON	81	LOUIS	31	SIENNA *	81	MARYAM *
32	BENJAMIN	82	ELIJAH *	32	ALICE	82	MADDISON *
33	JAKE	83	FINLAY	33	LILLY *	83	HEIDI *
34	FINLEY	84	RHYS	34	FLORENCE *	84	MOLLIE
35	HARRISON	85	CALEB *	35	ELLIE	85	NIAMH
36	EDWARD	86	EVAN *	36	ERIN	86	SKYE *
37	JAYDEN *	87	FREDERICK *	37	IMOGEN	87	AISHA *
38	FREDDIE *	88	HUGO *	38	ELIZABETH	88	IVY *
39	ADAM	89	KIAN	39	MOLLY	89	DARCEY *
40	ZACHARY	90	SONNY *	40	SUMMER *	90	FRANCESCA
41	SEBASTIAN	91	SETH *	41	MEGAN	91	ZOE
42	RYAN	92	KAYDEN *	42	HANNAH	92	KEIRA *
43	LEWIS	93	TAYLOR	43	SOFIA *	93	TILLY *
44	THEO *	94	KYLE	44	ABIGAIL	93	MARIA *
45	LUKE	95	ELLIOTT *	45	JASMINE	95	SARAH
46	HARLEY *	96	ROBERT	46	LEXI *	96	LYDIA
47	MATTHEW	97	THEODORE *	47	MATILDA *	97	CAITLIN
48	HARVEY	98	BAILEY	48	ROSIE	98	ISOBEL
49	TOBY	99	RORY *	49	LACEY *	99	SARA *
50	LIAM	100	ELLIS	50	EMMA	100	VIOLET *

Source: Office for National Statistics (ONS)

Notes:

These rankings have been produced using the exact spelling of the name given at birth registration. Similar names with different spellings have been counted separately.

Births where the name was not stated have been excluded from these figures. Of the 374,346 baby boys and 355,328 baby girls in the 2012 dataset, 9 girls and 16 boys were excluded for this reason

* denotes new entry to top 100

9.14a Libraries overview
Great Britain

Percentages

	2005/06	2006/07	2007/08	2008/09	2009/10	2010/11	2011/12	2012/13
						%	%	%
	%	%	%	%	%	(1)	(1)	(1)
Has visited a public library in the last year (2)	48.2	46.1	45.0	41.1	39.4	**39.7**	**38.8**	**37.0**
Frequency of attendance [2]								
1-2 times a year	10.4	10.3	10.5	8.9	7.9	**8.9**	**8.4**	**8.7**
3-4 times a year	13.4	12.9	13.0	11.4	10.9	**11.6**	**12.2**	**10.8**
At least once a month	16.4	15.7	14.9	13.3	12.8	**13.4**	**12.4**	**12.4**
At least once a week	7.9	7.2	6.7	5.9	5.4	**5.8**	**5.7**	**5.0**
Has not visited	51.8	53.9	55.0	60.5	63.0	**60.3**	**61.2**	**63.0**

Notes
(1) Figures in bold indicate a significant change from 2005/06.
(2) Figures exclude people who have visited a library for the purposes of paid work or academic study

Source: DCMS Taking Part Survey 2013/14 Q1
https://www.gov.uk/government/statistics/taking-part-201314-quarter-1-statistical-release

9.14b Proportion who have visited a public library in the last year - area-level breakdown

percentages

	2005/06	2006/07	2007/08	2008/09	2009/10	2010/11	2011/12	2012/13
						%	%	%
	%	%			%	(1)	(1)	(1)
Index of deprivation								
1- Most deprived	N/A	N/A	N/A	N/A	37.6	39.8	37.3	40.1
2	N/A	N/A	N/A	N/A	32.8	38.2	37.0	35.7
3	N/A	N/A	N/A	N/A	38.3	39.2	39.2	33.5
4	N/A	N/A	N/A	N/A	36.1	41.2	39.1	35.0
5	N/A	N/A	N/A	N/A	42.1	38.4	40.6	35.3
6	N/A	N/A	N/A	N/A	38.7	36.4	38.3	37.5
7	N/A	N/A	N/A	N/A	39.9	40.7	40.4	34.8
8	N/A	N/A	N/A	N/A	34.6	40.1	33.8	37.1
9	N/A	N/A	N/A	N/A	45.4	**38.7**	42.2	41.8
10- Least deprived	N/A	N/A	N/A	N/A	46.3	43.5	39.8	**38.4**
Region								
North East	44.9	43.9	40.1	37.1	42.9	**38.8**	**36.3**	**38.2**
North West	46.9	46.2	45.0	42.1	41.4	**43.0**	**37.5**	**37.8**
Yorkshire and Humberside	42.1	40.5	36.6	33.7	30.0	**33.6**	**33.4**	**34.9**
East Midlands	44.7	42.9	44.3	38.8	42.7	**35.8**	**37.7**	**34.9**
West Midlands	47.6	47.1	43.5	39.3	38.0	**36.6**	**40.1**	**35.5**
East of England	50.5	47.5	45.5	42.9	39.5	**42.4**	**41.2**	**37.5**
London	52.6	49.2	49.5	43.6	38.1	**43.1**	**43.1**	**41.9**
South East	51.0	48.3	48.5	44.5	43.5	**40.5**	**37.4**	**34.6**
South West	47.9	45.1	45.5	41.8	38.8	**38.8**	**40.0**	**36.3**
Urban	48.5	46.5	45.6	41.6	40.1	**40.0**	**39.2**	**37.8**
Rural	47.1	44.7	42.8	38.9	36.5	**38.2**	**36.9**	**33.7**
ACORN								
Wealthy Achievers	50.9	48.9	47.4	42.1	39.9	**40.7**	**40.6**	**38.4**
Urban Prosperity	57.3	51.0	52.0	41.8	42.6	**43.9**	**41.9**	**39.2**
Comfortably Off	48.5	46.4	44.2	41.9	41.9	**38.2**	**37.9**	**35.4**
Moderate Means	45.3	45.0	42.4	41.5	37.7	**41.3**	**38.9**	**36.9**
Hard-pressed	40.9	39.8	41.0	37.5	33.9	**36.9**	**35.8**	**36.4**
Unclassified	61.7	50.0	62.7	46.9	*	*	*	*
All	48.2	46.1	45.0	41.1	39.4	**39.7**	**38.8**	**37.0**

Notes
(1) Figures in bold indicate a significant change from 2005/06.
(2) Index of deprivation data not available pre-2009/10. For Index of Deprivation data, figures in bold indicate a significant change from 2009/10.
(3) *= N too small to report

Source: DCMS Taking Part Survey 2013/14 Q1
https://www.gov.uk/government/statistics/taking-part-201314-quarter-1-statistical-release

9.14c Proportion who have visited a public library in the last year - demographic breakdown

Percentages

	2005/06	2006/07	2007/08	2008/09	2009/10	2010/11	2011/12	2012/13
						%	%	%
	%	%	%	%	%	(1)	(1)	(1)
Age								
16-24	51.0	47.1	45.4	42.8	40.0	**34.4**	**34.5**	**32.3**
25-44	51.2	50.2	49.5	43.7	40.9	**44.6**	**44.0**	**42.2**
45-64	45.7	44.3	42.1	38.8	39.5	**36.0**	**36.1**	**33.1**
65-74	46.7	44.4	44.7	42.0	39.3	44.3	**35.8**	**38.6**
75+	42.3	37.1	37.6	35.0	32.9	**37.1**	38.9	**36.5**
Sex								
Male	43.8	42.1	40.2	35.3	35.5	**34.3**	**33.6**	**31.4**
Female	52.3	49.9	49.6	46.5	43.2	**44.8**	**43.8**	**42.3**
NS-SEC								
Upper socio-economic group	52.1	50.2	48.0	43.3	43.1	**43.9**	**42.3**	**39.7**
Lower socio-economic group	40.1	38.1	38.7	35.1	32.3	**33.6**	**33.5**	**33.0**
Employment status								
Not working	49.7	46.7	46.6	44.0	42.4	**42.9**	**41.7**	**41.0**
Working	47.2	45.7	44.0	39.0	37.4	**37.5**	**36.8**	**34.3**
Tenure								
Owners	48.7	46.4	44.8	41.1	39.8	**40.1**	**39.2**	**37.0**
Social rented sector	41.9	40.5	42.2	39.0	36.8	**37.0**	**37.2**	38.6
Private rented sector	53.3	51.0	49.2	43.0	39.8	**40.2**	**38.7**	**35.8**
Ethnicity								
White	47.2	44.9	43.6	40.1	37.9	**38.3**	**37.8**	**35.9**
Black or ethnic minority	57.5	56.7	57.9	50.2	50.6	**50.0**	**46.5**	**45.1**
Religion								
No religion	46.8	45.5	45.3	40.1	35.2	**37.8**	**36.8**	**33.2**
Christian	47.3	44.8	43.7	40.3	39.7	**39.2**	**38.8**	**37.7**
Other religion	58.2	58.9	57.1	52.7	53.0	**48.2**	**44.4**	**46.9**
Long-standing illness or disability								
No	50.0	48.0	46.0	42.1	40.4	**40.1**	**39.2**	**36.9**
Yes	43.8	41.5	42.4	38.4	36.8	**38.5**	**37.9**	**37.3**
All	48.2	46.1	45.0	41.1	39.4	**39.7**	**38.8**	**37.0**

Notes

(1) Figures in bold indicate a significant change from 2005/06.

Source: DCMS Taking part Survey 2013/14 Q1
https://www.gov.uk/government/statistics/taking-part-201314-quarter-1-statistical-release

9.15 Museums and Galleries Overview (adults)

Percentages

	2006/07	2007/08	2008/09	2009/10	2010/11	2011/12	2012/13
					%	%	%
	%	%	%	%	(1)	(1)	(1)
Has visited a museum or gallery in the last year [2]	41.5	**43.5**	43.4	**46.0**	**46.3**	48.9	52.8
Frequency of attendance [2]							
1-2 times a year	25.3	26.3	26.1	**27.9**	**27.4**	29.6	31.3
3-4 times a year	12.9	13.8	13.9	14.1	**14.7**	15.3	17.2
At least once a month	2.8	3.2	2.9	3.6	**3.6**	3.4	3.5
At least once a week	**0.4**	0.3	0.4	0.4	**0.5**	**0.5**	**0.6**
Has not visited	58.5	**56.5**	56.7	**54.0**	**53.7**	51.1	47.2

Notes

(1) Figures in bold indicate a significant change from 2005/06. For purpose of visit data, figures in bold indicate a significant change from 2008/09.

(2) Figures exclude people who have visited a library for the purposes of paid work or academic study

Source: DCMS Taking Part Survey 2013/14 Q1
https://www.gov.uk/government/statistics/taking-part-201314-quarter-1-statistical-release

9.16 Participation in voluntary activities, 2003 to 2013/14
England

Percentages

	At least once a month							
	2003	2005	2007/08	2008/09	2009/10	2010/11	2012/13	2013/14
Informal volunteering[1]	37	37	35	35	29	29	36	35
Formal volunteering[2]	28	29	27	26	25	25	29	27
Any volunteering[3]	**50**	**50**	**48**	**47**	**42**	**41**	**49**	**48**
	At least once in last year							
Informal volunteering	63	68	64	62	54	55	62	64
Formal volunteering	42	44	43	41	40	39	44	41
Any volunteering	**73**	**76**	**73**	**71**	**66**	**65**	**72**	**74**

Source: Community Life Survey 2013/14, Cabinet Office

1 Informal volunteering: Giving unpaid help as an individual to people who are not relatives.

2 Formal volunteering: Giving unpaid help through groups, clubs or organisations to benefit other people or the environment.

3 Participated in either formal or informal volunteering.

9.17 UK residents' visits to friends and relatives[1] abroad: by destination
United Kingdom

Percentages[2]

	2003	2006	2009	2011	2012	2013
Irish Republic	16	15	14	13	10	10
France	13	11	11	10	10	10
Poland	1	6	9	9	9	9
Spain	9	9	8	7	8	8
Germany	6	6	5	5	5	5
USA	7	6	5	5	4	4
India	3	3	4	4	4	4
Italy	4	4	4	3	4	4
Netherlands	4	3	3	3	3	3
Pakistan	3	3	3	3	3	3
Other countries	34	35	36	39	39	39
All destinations (=100%) (millions)	8.5	12.0	11.6	11.6	11.8	12.3

Source: International Passenger Survey, Office for National Statistics

1 As a proportion of all visits to friends and relatives taken abroad by residents of the UK.
Excludes business trips and other miscellaneous visits.

2 Percentages may not add up to 100 per cent due to rounding.

9.18 The Internet

Internet activities by age group and sex, 2013 %

	16-24	25-34	35-44	45-54	55-64	65+	Men	Women	All
Sending/receiving emails	87	89	86	81	72	44	78	72	**75**
Finding information about goods and services	65	77	77	74	69	41	69	64	**66**
Reading or downloading online news, newspapers or magazines	69	72	66	57	49	23	60	49	**55**
Social networking, eg Facebook or Twitter	93	84	66	50	29	11	52	55	**53**
Using services related to travel or travel related accommodation	46	65	58	56	51	29	50	50	**50**
Internet banking	55	76	62	50	43	23	54	47	**50**
Seeking health related information	46	59	56	41	41	21	39	46	**43**
Consulting wikis	60	55	52	44	40	18	48	39	**43**
Looking for information about education, training or course offers	62	40	38	31	17	8	30	32	**31**
Downloading software (other than games software)	55	47	35	27	18	10	40	22	**31**
Selling goods or services over the Internet	33	45	34	31	19	10	32	24	**28**
Telephoning or making video calls over the Internet via a webcam	40	39	28	22	18	9	26	24	**25**
Looking for a job or sending a job application	45	39	30	23	12	1	25	22	**24**
Participating in professional networks	16	23	23	17	13	3	19	12	**15**
Posting opinions on civic or political issues	13	15	12	8	8	5	12	8	**10**
Doing an online course	18	9	14	8	6	1	11	7	**9**
Taking part in online consultations or voting on civic or political issues	6	8	10	7	8	6	8	7	**7**

Base: Adults (aged 16+) in Great Britain | Source: Office for National Statistics

Purchases made over the Internet, by age group and sex, 2013 %

	16-24	25-34	35-44	45-54	55-64	65+	Men	Women	All
Clothes, sports goods	62	68	59	52	40	14	45	50	**47**
Household goods	32	65	63	46	38	18	44	43	**43**
Films and music	46	52	52	38	29	9	40	33	**36**
Books, magazines, newspapers	28	42	47	37	35	18	33	35	**34**
Holiday accommodation	19	45	46	39	34	15	35	31	**33**
Other travel arrangements	24	41	41	38	34	15	33	31	**32**
Tickets for events	30	44	43	36	27	11	31	31	**31**
Food or groceries	15	35	34	23	14	6	20	22	**21**
Electronic equipment	20	31	28	22	16	7	26	14	**20**
Video games software and upgrades	30	33	29	18	8	2	26	13	**19**
Share purchases, insurance policies etc	8	26	26	22	18	7	22	13	**18**
Other computer software and upgrades	19	22	23	22	14	8	25	11	**18**
Telecommunication services	10	21	21	19	13	6	19	10	**15**
Computer hardware	10	12	17	12	9	4	16	5	**10**
Medicine	5	10	9	11	8	4	8	7	**8**
E-learning material	10	7	9				6	5	**5**

Adults (aged 16+) in Great Britain | Source: Office for National Statistics

Households with Internet Access, 2005 to 2013 %

Year	
2005	55
2006	57
2007	61
2008	65
2009	70
2010	73
2011	77
2012	80
2013	83

All GB households | Source: Office for National Statistics

9.19 Radio Listening

	Adult (15+) Population '000	Weekly Reach '000's	Weekly Reach %	Average Hours Per Head	Average Hours Per Listener	Total Hours ('000's)	Share of Listening %
Quarterly Summary of Radio Listening - Survey period ending June 2014							
ALL RADIO	53,502	48,052	90	19.2	21.4	1,025,971	100
ALL BBC	53,502	35,227	66	10.2	15.5	546,723	53.3
BBC Local/Regional	53,502	8,985	17	1.5	8.8	79,478	7.7
ALL COMMERCIAL	53,502	34,408	64	8.3	12.9	443,326	43.2
All National Commercial	53,502	17,106	32	2.5	7.7	132,325	12.9
All Local Commercial (National TSA)	53,502	27,494	51	5.8	11.3	311,001	30.3
All BBC Network Radio	53,502	32,255	60	8.7	14.5	467,245	45.5
BBC Radio 1	53,502	10,795	20	1.3	6.4	69,481	6.8
BBC Radio 2	53,502	15,496	29	3.4	11.7	181,168	17.7
BBC Radio 3	53,502	1,884	4	0.2	5.6	10,598	1
BBC Radio 4	53,502	10,528	20	2.2	11.3	119,223	11.6
BBC Radio 4 (including 4 Extra)	53,502	10,786	20	2.4	11.9	128,047	12.5
BBC Radio 4 Extra	53,502	1,570	3	0.2	5.6	8,824	0.9
BBC Radio FIVE LIVE	53,502	6,276	12	0.8	6.8	42,408	4.1
BBC Radio FIVE LIVE (inc SPORTS EXTRA)	53,502	6,442	12	0.9	7.1	45,554	4.4
FIVE LIVE SPORTS EXTRA	53,502	919	2	0.1	3.4	3,145	0.3
BBC 6 Music	53,502	1,891	4	0.3	8.6	16,252	1.6
1Xtra from the BBC	53,502	937	2	0.1	5.3	4,997	0.5
BBC Asian Network UK	53,502	552	1	0.1	6.2	3,410	0.3
BBC World Service	53,502	1,372	3	0.1	5.2	7,157	0.7

STATION SUMMARY ANALYSIS - RAJAR REPORTING PERIOD 2014 Q1
(Report 1690) All Radio, Total Sample
Quarterly Weighted Data

		Age Group of Respondent						
	Total	**10-14**	**15-24**	**25-34**	**35-44**	**45-54**	**55-64**	**65+**
Unw. Sample	26557	908	2857	3000	3820	4708	4543	6721
Est. Pop'n	56726	3521	8313	8864	8495	9049	7296	11187
ALL RADIO								
Weekly Reach 000s	51307	3244	7285	7754	7893	8502	6819	9810
Weekly Reach %	90.4	92.1	87.6	87.5	92.9	94	93.5	87.7
Total Hours	1065631	30299	113282	138838	167691	198569	163339	253615
Average Hours Per Head	18.79	8.6	13.63	15.66	19.74	21.94	22.39	22.67
Average Hours Per Listener	20.77	9.34	15.55	17.91	21.24	23.36	23.95	25.85

Source: RAJAR

Environment

Chapter 10

Environment

Air emissions (Table 10.2 to 10.8)

Emissions of air pollutants arise from a wide variety of sources. The National Atmospheric Emissions Inventory (NAEI) is prepared annually for the Government and the devolved administrations by AEA Energy and Environment, with the work being co-ordinated by the Department of Energy and Climate Change (DECC). Information is available for a range of point sources including the most significant polluters. However, a different approach has to be taken for diffuse sources such as transport and domestic emissions, where this type of information is not available. Estimates for these are derived from statistical information and from research on emission factors for stationary and mobile sources. Although for any given year considerable uncertainties surround the emission estimates for each pollutant, trends over time are likely to be more reliable.

UK national emission estimates are updated annually and any developments in methodology are applied retrospectively to earlier years. Adjustments in the methodology are made to accommodate new technical information and to improve international comparability.

Three different classification systems are used in the tables presented here; a National Accounts basis (Table 10.2), the format required by the Inter-governmental Panel on Climate Change (IPCC) (Table 10.3) and the National Communications (NC) categories (Tables 10.5-10.7).

The NC source categories are detailed below together with details of the main sources of these emissions:

Energy supply total: Power stations, refineries, manufacture of solid fuels and other energy industries, solid fuel transformation, exploration, production and transport of oils, offshore oil and gas – venting and flaring, power stations - FGD, coal mining and handling, and exploration, production and transport of gas.

Business total: Iron and steel – combustion, other industrial combustion, miscellaneous industrial and commercial combustion, energy recovery from waste fuels, refrigeration and air conditioning, foams, fire fighting, solvents, one components foams, and electronics, electrical insulation and sporting goods.

Transport total: Civil aviation (domestic, landing and take off, and cruise), passenger cars, light duty vehicles, buses, HGVs, mopeds & motorcycles, LPG emissions (all vehicles), other road vehicle engines, railways, railways – stationary combustion, national navigation, fishing vessels, military aircraft and shipping, and aircraft – support vehicles.

Residential total: Residential combustion, use of non aerosol consumer products, accidental vehicle fires, and aerosols and metered dose inhalers.

Agriculture total: Stationary and mobile combustion, breakdown of pesticides, enteric fermentation (cattle, sheep, goats, horses, pigs, and deer), wastes (cattle, sheep, goats, horses, pigs, poultry, and deer), manure liquid systems, manure solid storage and dry lot, other manure management, direct soil emission, and field burning of agricultural wastes.

Industrial process total: Sinter production, cement production, lime production, limestone and dolomite use, soda ash production and use, fletton bricks, ammonia production, iron and steel, nitric acid production, adipic acid production, other – chemical industry, halocarbon production, and magnesiun cover gas.

Land-use change: Forest land remaining forest land, forest land biomass burning, land converted to forest land, direct N2O emissions from N fertilisation of forest land, cropland liming, cropland remaining cropland, cropland biomass burning, land converted to cropland, N2O emissions from disturbance associated with land-use conversion to cropland, grassland biomass burning, grassland liming, grassland remaining grassland, land converted to grassland, wetlands remaining wetland, Non-CO2 emissions from drainage of soils and wetlands, settlements biomass burning, land converted to settlements, and harvested wood.

Waste management total: Landfill, waste-water handling, and waste incineration.

Atmospheric emissions on a National Accounts basis (Table 10.2)
The air and energy accounts are produced for ONS by AEA Technology plc based on data compiled for the National Atmospheric Emissions Inventory (NAEI)7 and UK Greenhouse Gas Inventory (GHGI)8. Every year a programme of development work is undertaken to optimise the methodologies employed in compiling the accounts. Assessments in previous years have indicated that a number of splits used to apportion road transport source data to more than one industry should be reviewed. The results of this review have been implemented in the 2011 UK Environmental Accounts for reference period 2009 and years back to 1990.

The industry breakdown used in the accounts has moved to using the Standard Industrial Classification 2007 (SIC 2007). Historically, the accounts were based on Environmental Accounts codes (EAcodes) based on SIC 2003. This change will allow the accounts which are broken down by industry to be more readily compared with other economic statistics. A methodology article that outlines this change in more detail was published on the ONS website in May 2011: http//www.statistics.gov.uk/cci/article.asp?id=2694. As a result while names given to the breakdown maybe similar they are not necessarily the same.

The National Accounts figures in Table 10.2 differ from those on an IPCC basis, in that they include estimated emissions from fuels purchased by UK resident households and companies either at home or abroad (including emissions from UK international shipping and aircraft operators), and exclude emissions in the UK resulting from the activities of non-residents. This allows for a more consistent comparison with key National Accounts indicators such as Gross Domestic Product (GDP).

Greenhouse gases include carbon dioxide, methane, nitrous oxide, hydro-fluorocarbons, perfluorocarbons and sulphur hexafluoride which are expressed in thousand tonnes of carbon dioxide equivalent.

Acid rain precursors include sulphur dioxide, nitrogen oxides and ammonia which are expressed as thousand tonnes of sulphur dioxide equivalent.

Estimated total emissions of greenhouse gases on an IPCC basis (Table 10.3)
The IPCC classification is used to report greenhouse gas emissions under the UN Framework Convention on Climate Change (UNFCCC) and includes Land Use Change and all emissions from Domestic aviation and shipping, but excludes International aviation and shipping bunkers. Estimates of the relative contribution to global warming of the main greenhouse gases, or classes of gases, are presented weighted by their global warming potential.

Greenhouse gas emissions bridging table (Table 10.4)
National Accounts measure to UNFCCC measure
The air and energy accounts are produced for ONS by AEA Technology plc based on data compiled for the National Atmospheric Emissions Inventory (NAEI)7 and UK Greenhouse Gas Inventory (GHGI)8. Every year a programme of development work is undertaken to optimise the methodologies employed in compiling the accounts. Assessments in previous years have indicated that a number of splits used to apportion road transport source data to more than one industry should be reviewed. The results of this review have been implemented in the 2011 UK Environmental Accounts for reference period 2009 and years back to 1990.

There are a number of formats for the reporting and recording of atmospheric emissions data, including those used by the Department of Energy and Climate Change (DECC) for reporting greenhouse gases under UNFCCC and the Kyoto Protocol, and for reporting air pollutant emissions to the UN Economic Commission for Europe (UNECE), which differ from the National Accounts consistent measure published by the Office for National Statistics (ONS).
Differences between the National Accounts measure and those for reporting under UNFCCC and the Kyoto Protocol, following the guidance of the IPCC, are shown in Table 10.4.

Emissions of carbon dioxide (Table 10.5)
Carbon dioxide is the main man-made contributor to global warming. The UK contributes about 2 per cent to global man-made emissions which, according to the IPCC, was estimated to be 38 billion tonnes of carbon dioxide in 2004. Carbon dioxide emissions accounted for about 84 per cent of the UK's man-made greenhouse gas emissions in 2009.

Emissions of methane (Table 10.6)
Weighted by global warming potential, methane accounted for about 8 per cent of the UK's greenhouse gas emissions in 2009. Methane emissions, excluding those from natural sources, were 61 per cent below 1990 levels. In 2009, the main sources of methane emissions were agriculture (41 per cent of the total) and landfill sites (37 per cent). Emissions from landfill have reduced by 72 per cent and emissions from agriculture by 19 per cent since 1990.

Emissions of nitrous oxide (Table 10.7)
Weighted by global warming potential, nitrous oxide emissions accounted for about 6 per cent of the UK's man-made greenhouse gas emissions in 2009. Nitrous oxide emissions fell by 49 per cent between 1990 and 2009. The largest reductions were in emissions from adipic acid production between 1998 and 1999 (down 95 per cent). This leaves agriculture as the main source in 2009, accounting for 79 per cent of emissions, mainly from agricultural soils.

Annual rainfall (Table 10.9)
Regional rainfall is derived by the Met Office's National Climate Information Centre for the National Hydrological Monitoring Programme at the Centre for Ecology and Hydrology. These monthly area rainfalls are based initially on a subset of rain gauges (circa 350) but are updated after four to five months with figures using the majority of the UK's rain gauge network.
The regions of England shown in this table correspond to the original nine English regions of the National Rivers Authority (NRA). The NRA became part of the Environment Agency on its creation in April 1996. The figures in this table relate to the country of Wales, not the Environment Agency Welsh Region.

UK weather summary (Table 10.10)
For 2010, initial averages use data available from about 200 observing sites available on 1 January 2011. They represent an initial assessment of the weather that was experienced across the UK during 2010 and how it compares with the 1961 to 1990 average.
For all other years, final averages use quality controlled data from the UK climate network of observing stations. They show the Met Office's best assessment of the weather that was experienced across the UK during the years and how it compares with the 1961 to 1990 average. The columns headed 'Anom' (anomaly) show the difference from, or percentage of, the 1961 to 1990 long-term average.

Biological and chemical quality of rivers and canals (Table 10.11)

Table 10.11 shows a Summary of River Basin District Ecological and Chemical Status from 2009-2013. It looks at each river basin district in terms of Percent of surface water bodies that are at good chemical status or better and also Percent of surface water bodies are at good ecological status/potential or better. Improvements are measured in terms of the number of water bodies meeting good status

Status of Rivers anf Canals in Scotland (Table 10.12)

Looks at the overall status of rivers & canals in Scotland, including water quality.

Reservoir stocks in England and Wales (Table 10.13)

Data are collected for a network of major reservoirs (or reservoir groups) in England and Wales for the National Hydrological Monitoring Programme at the Centre for Ecology and Hydrology. Figures of usable capacity are supplied by the Water PLCs and the Environment Agency at the start of each month and are aggregated to provide an index of the total reservoir stocks for England and Wales.

Water industry expenditure (Table 10.14)

The data is taken from the annual regulatory accounts (and the June return submission to Ofwat) of water and sewerage companies and water companies of England and Wales.

Operating expenditure includes: employment costs, power, Environment Agency charges, bulk supply imports, general overheads, customer services, scientific services, local authority rates, local authority sewerage agencies, materials and consumables, charge for bad and doubtful debts, current cost depreciation and the infrastructure renewals charge.

Capital expenditure figures represent all capital additions (both maintenance and enhancement) but exclude infrastructure renewals expenditure. Figures quoted are before deducting grants and contributions, typically received from developers. Adopted assets at nil cost are not included.

Water pollution incidents (Table 10.15)

The Environment Agency responds to complaints and reported incidents of pollution in England and Wales. Each incident is then logged and categorised according to its severity. The category describes the impact of each incident on water, land and air. The impact of an incident on each medium is considered and reported separately. If no impact has occurred for a particular medium, the incident is reported as a category 4. Before 1999, the reporting system was used only for water pollution incidents; thus the total number of substantiated incidents was lower, as it did not include   incidents not relating to the water environment.

Bathing waters (Table 10.16)

Under the EC Bathing Water Directive 76/160/EEC, 11 physical, chemical and microbiological parameters are measured including total and faecal coliforms which are generally considered to be the most important indicators of the extent to which water is contaminated by sewage. The mandatory value for total coliforms is 10,000 per 100 ml, and for faecal coliforms 2,000 per 100 ml. For a bathing water to comply with the coliform standards, the Directive requires that at least 95 per cent of samples taken for each of these parameters over the bathing season are less than or equal to the mandatory values. In the UK a minimum of 20 samples are normally taken at each site. In practice this means that where 20 samples are taken, a maximum of only one sample may exceed the mandatory value for the bathing water to comply, and where less than 20 samples are taken none may exceed the mandatory value for the bathing water to comply.

The bathing water season is from mid-May to end-September in England and Wales, but shorter in Scotland and Northern Ireland. Bathing waters which are closed for the season are excluded for that year.

The table shows Environment Agency regions for England and Wales, the boundaries of which are based on river catchment areas and not county borders. In particular, the figures shown for Wales are the Environment Agency Welsh Region, the boundary of which does not coincide with the boundary of Wales.

Surface and groundwater abstractions (Table 10.17)

Significant changes in the way data is collected and/or reported were made in 1991 (due to the Water Resources Act 1991) and 1999 (commission of National Abstraction Licensing Database). Figures are therefore not strictly comparable with those in previous/intervening years. From 1999, data have been stored and retrieved from one system nationally and are therefore more accurate and reliable. Some regions report licensed and actual abstracts for financial rather than calendar years. As figures represent an average for the whole year expressed as daily amounts, differences between amounts reported for financial and calendar years are small.

Under the Water Act 2003, abstraction of less than 20 m3/day became exempt from the requirement to hold a licence as of 1 April 2005. As a result over 22,000 licences were deregulated, mainly for agricultural or private water supply purposes. However, due to the small volumes involved, this has had a minimal affect on the estimated licensed and actual abstraction totals.

The following changes have occurred in the classification of individual sources:
• Spray irrigation: this category includes small amounts of non-agricultural spray irrigation
• Mineral washing: from 1999 this was not reported as a separate category; licences for 'Mineral washing' are now contained in 'Other industry'
• Private water supply: this was shown as separate category from 1992 and includes private abstractions for domestic use and individual households
• Fish farming, cress growing, amenity ponds: includes amenity ponds, but excludes miscellaneous from 1991

Estimates of remaining recoverable oil and gas reserves (Table 10.18)

Only a small proportion of the estimated remaining recoverable reserves of oil and gas are known with any degree of certainty. The latest oil and gas data for 2012 shows that the upper range of total UK oil reserves was estimated to be around 2.4 billion tonnes, while UK gas reserves were around 1709 billion cubic metres. Of these, proven reserves of oil were 0.4 billion tonnes and proven reserves of gas were 244 billion cubic metres.

Local authority collected (Table 10.19)

Local authority collected includes household and non-household waste that is collected and disposed of by local authorities. It includes regular household collections, specific recycling collections, and special collections of bulky items, waste received at civic amenity sites, and waste collected from non-household sources that come under the control of local authorities.

Amounts of different materials from household sources collected for recycling (Table 10.20)

Household recycling includes those materials collected for recycling, composting or reuse by local authorities and those collected from household sources by 'private/voluntary' organisations where this material comes under the possession or control of local authorities. It includes residual waste from the household stream which was diverted for recycling by sorting or further treatment.

'Bring sites' are facilities where members of the public can bring recyclable materials (such as paper, glass, cans, textiles, shoes, etc). These are often located at supermarkets or similar locations, but exclude civic amenity sites.

'Civic Amenity sites' refers to household waste collected at sites provided by local authorities for the disposal of excess household and garden waste free of charge, as required by the Refuse Disposal (Amenity) Act 1978. These are also known as Household Waste Recycling Centres.

Material flows (Table 10.22)

Economy-wide material flow accounts record the total mass of natural resources and products that are used by the UK economy, either directly in the production and distribution of products and services, or indirectly through the movement of materials which are displaced in order for production to take place.

The direct movement of materials into the economy derives primarily from domestic extraction. This covers: biomass (agricultural harvest, timber, fish and animal grazing); fossil fuel extraction (such as coal, crude oil and natural gas); mineral extraction (metal ores, industrial minerals such as pottery clay; and construction material such as crushed rock, sand and gravel). This domestic extraction is supplemented by the imports of products, which may be raw materials such as unprocessed agricultural products, but can also be semi-manufactured or finished products. In a similar way the UK produces exports of raw materials, semi-manufactured and finished goods which can be viewed as inputs to the production and consumption of overseas economies. Indirect flows of natural resources consist of the unused material resulting from domestic extraction, such as mining and quarrying overburden and the soil removed during construction and dredging activities. They also include the movement of used and unused material overseas which is associated with the production and delivery of imports. Water, except for that included directly in products, is excluded.

There are three main indicators used to measure inputs. The Direct Material Input measures the input of used materials into the economy that is all materials which are of economic value and are used in production and consumption activities (including the production of exports). Domestic Material Consumption measures the total amount of material directly used in the economy that is it includes imports but excludes exports. The Total Material Requirement (TMR) measures the total material basis of the economy that is the total primary resource requirements of all the production and consumption activities. It includes not only the direct use of resources for producing exports, but also indirect flows from the production of imports and the indirect flows associated with domestic extraction. Although TMR is widely favoured as a resource use indicator, the estimates of indirect flows are less reliable than those for materials directly used by the economy, and the indicator therefore needs to be considered alongside other indicators. Between 2007 and 2008 the quantity of natural resources used by the UK economy, known as domestic material consumption, fell by 67 million tonnes (9.9 per cent) to 613 million tonnes. This is the largest recorded fall since records began in 1970. It follows 10 years where resource use has remained broadly unchanged. This means that, with rising levels of economic activity, UK material productivity has been increasing.

The fall in domestic material consumption mainly reflects decreases in the domestic extraction of minerals, with a decrease of 57 million tonnes (19.3 per cent) driven by a sharp fall in the extraction of primary aggregates – crushed stone, sand and gravel – as demand was impacted by the economic downturn. Imports of minerals also fell in 2008, by 10.9 per cent.

Much of the period 1990 to 2007 had seen strong economic growth in the UK and material productivity increased, with material use falling in relation to the level of economic activity. This in part reflects the increasing importance of the service industries in the UK economy. Gross Domestic Product overall continued to increase in 2008 (by 0.5 per cent) and material use fell. The fall in demand for primary aggregates coincides with the contraction in output of the construction   industry in 2008.

10.1 Atmospheric emissions[1] 2012

	Total greenhouse gas emissions	Carbon Dioxide (CO2)	Methane (CH4)	Nitrous Oxide (N2O)	Hydrofluoro-carbons (HFCs)	Perfluoro-carbons (PFCs)	Sulphur hexafluoride (SF6)
Thousand tonnes CO2 equivalent							
Agriculture, forestry and fishing	58,621	6,225	22,118	30,241	36	..	..
Mining and quarrying	20,412	16,751	3,307	345	10	..	..
Manufacturing	91,071	88,694	229	689	1,020	199	240
Electricity, gas, steam & air conditioning supply; water supply, sewerage, waste management activities & remediation services	203,084	176,181	23,977	2,468	180	9	268
Construction	10,401	9,715	16	330	341	..	..
Wholesale & retail trade; repair of motor vehicles & motorcycles	17,679	12,952	9	139	4,579	..	..
Transport & storage; information & communication	84,306	82,540	169	820	777	..	..
Accommodation and food services	3,204	2,597	5	20	583	..	..
Financial and insurance activities	222	117	..	13	91	..	..
Real estate activities; professional scientific & technical activities; administration & support service activities	5,606	4,745	5	36	785	..	34
Public administration & defence; compulsory social security	6,612	6,337	8	53	214	..	..
Education	4,493	4,228	7	19	238	..	..
Human health and social work activities	6,082	5,691	11	9	370	..	..
Arts, entertainment and recreation; other service activities	2,548	2,311	3	16	218	..	..
Activities of households as employers; undifferentiated goods & services-producing activities of households for own use	232	230	1	1	..	..	..
Consumer expenditure	141,697	136,124	571	566	4,436	..	..
Total	656,269	555,439	50,437	35,766	13,877	208	542
of which, emissions from road transport[2]	112,734	111,761	55	918	..	..	..

	Total acid rain precursors	Sulphur Dioxide (SO2)	Nitrogen Oxides (NOx)	Ammonia (NH3)
Thousand tonnes SO2 equivalent				
Agriculture, forestry and fishing	461	..	22	439
Mining and quarrying	54	8	46	..
Manufacturing	258	134	114	11
Electricity, gas, steam & air conditioning supply; water supply, sewerage, waste management activities & remediation services	462	228	209	26
Construction	32	..	31	..
Wholesale & retail trade; repair of motor vehicles & motorcycles	30	..	30	..
Transport & storage; information & communication	457	127	330	1
Accommodation and food services	3	..	3	..
Financial and insurance activities	1	..	1	..
Real estate activities; professional scientific & technical activities; administrative & support service activities	10	..	9	1
Public administration and defence; compulsory social security	31	6	20	6
Education	8	4		..
Human health and social work activities	6	..	5	..
Arts, entertainment and recreation; other service activities	12	1	4	8
Activities of households as employers; undifferentiated goods & services-producing activities of households for own use	..	..	..	..
Consumer expenditure	207	40	127	41
Total (excluding Natural World)	2032	547	954	531
of which, emissions from road transport[2]	251	1	235	15

	Thousand tonnes						Tonnes		
	PM10[3]	PM2.5[3]	CO	NMVOC[4]	Benzene	Butadiene	Lead	Cadmium	Mercury
Agriculture, forestry and fishing	20.06	9.54	74.54	157.21	0.12	0.05	0.43	0.04	0.02
Mining and quarrying	7.54	1.89	27.04	92.08	0.37	..	0.36	0.04	0.02
Manufacturing	22.85	15.19	518.68	262.83	1.92	0.31	45.74	1.15	2.35
Electricity, gas, steam & air conditioning supply; water supply, sewerage, waste management activities & remediation services	9.62	5.71	97.78	75.58	1.62	0.07	6.17	0.18	2.21
Construction	4.38	3.23	170.52	47.36	0.48	0.14	0.3	0.04	0.02
Wholesale & retail trade; repair of motor vehicles & motorcycles	2.88	2.09	20.34	38.48	0.11	0.05	1.52	0.04	0.02
Transport & storage; information & communication	30.8	28.12	92.43	27.49	1.98	0.24	2.77	1.13	0.12
Accommodation and food services	0.24	0.21	2.32	0.64	0.02	..	0.02	..	..
Financial and insurance activities	0.09	0.08	0.55	0.2	..	..	0.01	..	..
Real estate activities; professional scientific & technical activities; administration & support service activities	0.84	0.66	20.45	1.65	0.07	0.02	0.05	0.01	0.01
Public administration & defence: compulsory social security	0.97	0.89	21	2.42	0.16	0.03	0.15	0.02	0.01
Education	0.57	0.53	3.04	0.32	0.02	..	0.69	0.01	0.07
Human health and social work activities	0.22	0.2	2.83	1.1	0.02	..	0.02	0.01	..
Arts, entertainment and recreation; other service activities	0.35	0.29	5.3	1.98	0.02	0.01	0.09	0.01	0.67
Activities of households as employers; undifferentiated goods & services-producing activities of households for own use	..	..	48.95	2.32	0.16	0.03	..	..	..
Consumer expenditure	35.2	30.85	923.26	200.59	2.73	0.5	5.15	0.41	0.34
Total (excluding Natural World)	136.6	99.48	2029.04	912.23	9.79	1.46	63.45	3.07	5.84
of which, emissions from road transport[2]	22.77	16.18	649.58	40.09	1.7	0.63	1.65	0.35	0.23

1. Components may not sum to totals due to rounding.
2. Includes emissions from fuel sources which are used by road vehicles (eg HGVs, LGVs, cars and motorcycles) across all industries.
3. PM10 is particulate matter arising from various sources including fuel combustion, quarrying and construction, and formation of 'secondary' particles in the atmosphere from reactions involving other pollutants - sulphur dioxide, nitrogen oxides, ammonia and NMVOCs.
4. Non-methane Volatile Compounds, including benzene and 1,3-butadien

Source: AEA Energy & Environment, ONS

251

10.2 Road Transport[1] Emissions: by Pollutant, 1999 to 2012

All weights in thousand tonnes, unless specified
Greenhouse gases are made up of carbon dioxide, methane and nitrous oxide. Weight in carbon dioxide equivalent
Acid rain precursors are made of sulphur dioxide, nitrogen oxides and ammonia. Weight in sulphur dioxide equivalent

Pollutant	1999	2000	2001	2002	2003	2004	2005	2006	2007	2008	2009	2010	2011	2012
Greenhouse gases	**119,354.0**	**118,493.3**	**118,178.0**	**120,504.8**	**120,100.8**	**120,816.2**	**121,565.6**	**121,901.4**	**125,207.1**	**119,465.2**	**115,698.7**	**114,897.0**	**113,271.5**	**112,733.6**
of which														
Carbon dioxide	117,550.5	116,765.6	116,584.8	118,983.0	118,686.9	119,473.8	120,286.7	120,687.1	124,017.6	118,472.5	114,792.1	113,987.2	112,335.6	111,761.2
Methane	345.6	300.6	259.1	233.9	206.3	184.9	169.3	151.9	139.4	118.2	84.5	72.0	62.9	54.8
Nitrous oxide	1,457.9	1,427.2	1,334.1	1,287.9	1,207.6	1,157.5	1,109.6	1,062.4	1,050.1	874.5	822.1	837.8	873.0	917.6
Acid rain precursors	**602.6**	**561.1**	**531.3**	**500.9**	**471.3**	**448.7**	**425.7**	**408.9**	**389.6**	**362.5**	**299.8**	**282.8**	**264.9**	**250.6**
of which														
Sulphur dioxide	13.6	5.9	3.4	3.0	3.0	2.7	2.4	2.1	1.7	1.0	0.5	0.5	0.5	0.5
Nitrogen Oxides as NO2	558.6	511.0	486.8	459.3	433.2	413.2	393.2	378.7	362.2	338.6	277.5	263.0	247.3	234.9
Ammonia	30.3	44.2	41.1	38.5	35.1	32.8	30.2	28.1	25.7	22.8	21.8	19.3	17.2	15.2
PM_{10}	39.0	35.0	34.4	33.2	32.5	31.8	30.9	30.0	29.1	27.8	26.4	25.6	23.9	22.8
$PM_{2.5}$	31.6	27.8	27.2	26.0	25.2	24.5	23.7	22.8	21.9	20.7	19.5	18.8	17.2	16.2
Carbon monoxide	4,437.7	3,852.7	3,465.0	3,089.9	2,757.1	2,457.8	2,141.1	1,883.6	1,602.3	1,432.1	1,071.9	904.4	739.5	649.6
Non Methane VOC	483.7	405.5	362.6	306.3	255.5	213.0	177.6	151.0	126.2	108.4	71.5	58.8	47.6	40.1
Benzene	19.8	12.2	12.2	11.5	10.7	9.7	8.5	7.4	6.0	5.2	3.7	2.8	2.2	1.7
1,3-Butadiene	7.0	5.9	5.0	4.3	3.6	3.1	2.7	2.4	2.0	1.8	1.1	0.9	0.8	0.6
Cadmium (*tonnes*)	0.4	0.4	0.4	0.4	0.4	0.4	0.4	0.4	0.4	0.4	0.4	0.4	0.4	0.4
Lead (*tonnes*)	323.3	2.3	2.1	2.1	2.1	2.1	2.2	2.2	1.8	1.7	1.7	1.7	1.6	1.7
Mercury (*tonnes*)	0.3	0.3	0.3	0.3	0.3	0.3	0.3	0.3	0.3	0.2	0.2	0.2	0.2	0.2

Source: Ricardo-AEA, Office for National Statistics

[1] Emissions from fuel sources which are used by road vehicles across industry groups.

10.3 UK Greenhouse Gas Emissions 1998-2012, headline results

Greenhouse gas emissions: actual emissions in tonnes

	Units (tonnes)	1998	1999	2000	2001	2002	2003	2004	2005	2006	2007	2008	2009	2010	2011	2012
Net CO_2 emissions (emissions minus removals)	Million	552.5	544.6	552.2	562.3	545.1	555.6	556.2	552.8	552.3	544.9	527.3	477.9	495.2	454.0	474.1
Methane (CH_4)	Million	4.3	4.0	3.7	3.6	3.5	3.3	3.1	3.0	2.9	2.8	2.8	2.7	2.5	2.5	2.4
Nitrous Oxide (N_2O)	Million	0.2	0.2	0.2	0.1	0.1	0.1	0.1	0.1	0.1	0.1	0.1	0.1	0.1	0.1	0.1
Hydrofluorocarbons (HFC)	Thousand	4.33	3.92	4.48	5.09	5.54	6.22	6.47	6.96	7.37	7.55	7.91	8.10	8.24	8.36	8.43
Perfluorocarbons (PFC)	Thousand	0.05	0.05	0.06	0.05	0.04	0.04	0.05	0.04	0.04	0.03	0.03	0.02	0.03	0.05	0.03
Sulphur hexafluoride (SF_6)	Thousand	0.05	0.06	0.07	0.06	0.06	0.05	0.04	0.04	0.03	0.03	0.02	0.02	0.03	0.02	0.02

Greenhouse gas emissions: weighted by global warming potential (million tonnes carbon dioxide equivalent)

	Baseline	1998	1999	2000	2001	2002	2003	2004	2005	2006	2007	2008	2009	2010	2011	2012
Net CO_2 emissions (emissions minus removals)		552.5	544.6	552.2	562.3	545.1	555.6	556.2	552.8	552.3	544.9	527.3	477.9	495.2	454.0	474.1
Methane (CH_4)		90.0	83.8	78.2	74.8	74.0	69.3	65.1	62.3	61.2	59.2	58.0	55.7	52.5	51.7	50.6
Nitrous Oxide (N_2O)		59.8	49.2	48.3	45.6	43.8	43.3	43.8	42.9	40.8	40.0	39.0	36.8	37.7	36.3	36.0
Hydrofluorocarbons (HFC)		16.7	9.9	8.8	9.7	10.1	11.2	10.4	11.2	11.9	12.2	12.7	13.1	13.5	13.8	13.9
Perfluorocarbons (PFC)		0.4	0.4	0.5	0.4	0.3	0.3	0.3	0.3	0.3	0.2	0.2	0.1	0.2	0.3	0.2
Sulphur hexafluoride (SF_6)		1.3	1.4	1.8	1.4	1.4	1.3	1.0	1.0	0.7	0.7	0.6	0.6	0.6	0.6	0.5
Kyoto greenhouse gas basket	779.9	721.1 '	690.2 '	692.2 '	697.6 '	678.9 '	685.3 '	682.3 '	676.3 '	673.2 '	663.7 '	644.2 '	590.7 '	606.2 '	563.2 '	581.1 '

Source: Department for Energy and Climate Change

Notes:

1. Figures for each individual gas include the Land Use, Land-Use Change and Forestry sector (LULUCF). These emissions cover the UK and Crown Dependencies, but exclude emissions from UK Overseas Territories.

2. Kyoto basket total differs slightly from sum of individual pollutants above as the basket uses a narrower definition for the Land Use, Land-Use Change and Forestry sector (LULUCF) and has a slightly different geographical coverage. This includes emissions from the UK, Crown Dependencies and UK Overseas Territories, as well as emissions from flights between the UK, Crown Dependencies, and Overseas Territories.

3. Kyoto base year consists of emissions of CO_2, CH_4 and N_2O in 1990, and of HFCs, PFCs and SF_6 in 1995. Includes an allowance for net emissions from LULUCF in 1990.

4. The entire time series is revised each year to take account of methodological improvements in the UK emissions inventory.

5. Emissions in the bottom table are presented as carbon dioxide equivalent in line with international reporting and carbon trading. To convert Carbon dioxide into carbon equivalents, divide figures by 44/12.

6. Figures shown do not include any adjustment for the effect of the EU Emissions Trading Scheme (EUETS), which was introduced in 2005.

r The Kyoto greenhouse gas basket figures were revised on the 27th March 2014 to correct a minor error. The largest revision is 0.1Mt for 2012.

10.4 Greenhouse Gas Emissions Bridging Table

UK [5 6 9]   Thousand tonnes CO_2 equivalent

	1990	1995	2000	2005	2010	2012
Greenhouse gases[2] - CO_2, CH_4, N_2O, HFCs, PFCs SF_6 and NF_3						
Environmental Account	841,966	799,824	777,951	774,946	687,085	656,541
less						
Bunker emissions[3]	24,195	28,251	36,917	42,814	40,874	40,988
CO2 biomass[4]	2,545	4,327	5,087	8,749	16,062	17,081
Cross-boundary[5]	11,663	11,949	16,026	25,628	14,350	13,119
plus						
Crown Dependencies[6]	1,861	2,015	2,041	1,754	1,815	1,813
Land-Use, Land-Use Change and Forestry (LULUCF)[7]	3,989	3,298	865	-2,909	-4,279	-4,956
DECC reported (Excluding Overseas Territories)[8 9]	809,413	760,609	722,827	696,599	613,334	582,209
plus						
Overseas Territories (including net emissions from land use change/forestry)	1,793	1,764	1,853	2,119	2,170	2,056
UNFCCC reported in the UK Greenhouse Gas Inventory[8]	811,206	762,373	724,680	698,719	615,504	584,265
Kyoto greenhouse gas basket (baseline taken from the Assigned Amount Report)[8 9]	*782,211*	*731,138*	*702,892*	*686,279*	*610,300*	*583,126*

Source: Ricardo-AEA, DECC, ONS

1 United Nations Framework Convention on Climate Change http://unfccc.int/2860.php

2 Carbon dioxide, methane, nitrous oxide, hydrofluorocarbons, perfluorocarbons, sulphur hexafluoride and nitrogen trifluoride expressed as thousand tonnes of carbon dioxide equivalent

3 Bunker emissions include IPCC memo items International Aviation and International Shipping

4 Emissions arising from wood, straw, biogases and poultry litter combustion for energy production

5 Emissions generated by UK households and business transport and travel abroad, net of emissions generated by non-residents travel and transport in the UK

6 Emissions of Crown dependancies; Guernsey, Jersey, Isle of Man.

7 Emissions from deforestation, soils and changes in forest and other woody biomass.

8 https://www.gov.uk/government/statistics/final-uk-emissions-estimates

9 This is the UK total for the sum of the 7 pollutants and differs slightly from the Kyoto greenhouse gas basket totals which uses a narrower definition of Land Use, Land Use Change and Forestry and includes emissions from UK Overseas Territories (Gibraltar, the Falkland Islands, the Cayman Islands, Montserrat, Bermuda)

10.5 Estimated emissions of carbon dioxide (CO_2), 1997-2012

UK and Crown Dependencies

Units: Million Tonnes

NC Category	1997	1998	1999	2000	2001	2002	2003	2004	2005	2006	2007	2008	2009	2010	2011	2012
Energy Supply	198.3	203.4	193.1	203.6	214.0	212.0	219.4	217.4	218.7	224.4	219.3	213.0	190.0	196.4	182.3	193.3
Business	109.1	108.0	110.3	109.7	107.5	96.5	99.1	98.3	97.1	94.1	92.3	89.5	76.3	79.3	73.4	72.9
Transport	125.8	124.9	126.0	124.9	125.1	127.6	127.2	128.5	129.3	129.9	131.3	125.7	120.9	119.3	117.5	116.9
Public	13.9	12.9	12.8	12.0	12.2	10.3	10.2	11.2	11.1	10.1	9.4	10.7	9.2	9.7	9.3	9.3
Residential	84.1	86.0	85.8	86.1	88.4	85.0	85.8	87.2	83.0	80.3	76.8	78.6	75.3	84.9	64.9	74.4
Agriculture	6.9	6.3	6.2	5.8	5.8	5.8	5.9	5.7	5.6	5.4	5.4	4.9	5.2	5.2	5.4	5.1
Industrial Process	17.5	17.5	17.6	17.1	15.7	14.8	15.6	16.0	16.4	15.5	16.8	15.1	10.0	10.6	10.1	9.9
Land Use Change	1.4	0.9	0.8	-0.2	-1.1	-2.1	-2.5	-3.3	-3.8	-4.4	-4.8	-4.9	-4.9	-5.1	-5.6	-5.8
Waste Management	0.5	0.5	0.5	0.5	0.5	0.5	0.5	0.4	0.4	0.3	0.3	0.3	0.3	0.3	0.3	0.2
Grand Total	557.6	560.6	553.0	559.5	568.0	550.4	561.3	561.5	557.8	555.6	546.7	532.9	482.2	500.8	457.5	476.3

Source: Department for Energy and Climate Change

Notes:

1. The entire time series is revised each year to take account of methodological improvements.

10.6: Estimated emissions of methane (CH$_4$), 2000-2012

UK and Crown Dependencies, thousand tonnes

Thousand tonnes

NC Category	2000	2001	2002	2003	2004	2005	2006	2007	2008	2009	2010	2011	2012
Energy Supply	656.2	606.7	584.2	522.3	510.9	443.9	411.3	392.9	375.4	372.2	361.0	352.3	349.3
Business	4.9	5.0	4.9	5.4	4.8	4.7	4.5	4.5	4.7	4.0	4.3	4.3	4.2
Transport	14.7	12.7	11.5	10.2	9.2	8.5	7.7	7.0	6.1	4.5	3.9	3.4	3.0
Public	1.1	1.1	0.9	0.9	1.0	1.0	0.9	0.8	0.9	0.8	0.8	0.8	0.8
Residential	32.0	28.6	23.6	21.9	20.8	18.7	19.4	21.1	22.4	21.6	24.6	21.8	23.3
Agriculture	1240.3	1172.6	1149.8	1157.9	1166.4	1151.2	1143.8	1130.4	1104.9	1088.6	1094.3	1089.2	1085.2
Industrial Process	6.1	5.9	6.0	6.7	5.9	5.1	5.1	5.6	4.3	4.7	4.8	4.3	4.7
Land Use Change	1.8	1.8	1.8	3.0	1.9	2.2	1.8	2.3	1.8	2.0	1.9	1.6	2.7
Waste Management	2598.7	2536.2	2502.5	2354.0	2173.1	2048.2	1932.1	1804.9	1613.1	1376.8	1184.4	1080.3	974.9
Grand Total	**4,555.7**	**4,370.7**	**4,285.1**	**4,082.3**	**3,893.9**	**3,683.4**	**3,526.6**	**3,369.4**	**3,133.6**	**2,875.2**	**2,680.1**	**2,558.0**	**2,448.2**

Notes:

1. The entire time series is revised each year to take account of methodological improvements.

Source: Department for Energy and Climate Change

10.7 Estimated emissions of nitrous oxide (N$_2$O), 1998-2012

UK and Crown Dependencies 1998-2012, Mt CO$_2$e

Mt CO$_2$e

NC Category	1998	1999	2000	2001	2002	2003	2004	2005	2006	2007	2008	2009	2010	2011	2012
Energy Supply	1.5	1.3	1.4	1.5	1.5	1.6	1.5	1.5	1.6	1.5	1.4	1.2	1.2	1.3	1.5
Business	1.1	1.1	1.1	1.1	1.1	1.1	1.2	1.2	1.2	1.2	1.1	0.9	0.9	0.8	0.9
Transport	1.5	1.5	1.5	1.4	1.3	1.3	1.2	1.2	1.1	1.1	1.0	0.9	0.9	0.9	1.0
Public	0.0	0.0	0.0	0.0	0.0	0.0	0.0	0.0	0.0	0.0	0.0	0.0	0.0	0.0	0.0
Residential	0.2	0.2	0.2	0.2	0.1	0.1	0.1	0.1	0.1	0.1	0.1	0.1	0.1	0.1	0.1
Agriculture	25.7	25.4	24.6	23.5	23.7	23.5	23.3	22.9	22.5	22.0	21.8	21.7	22.0	21.9	21.7
Industrial Process	14.7	5.2	5.4	4.7	2.7	2.9	3.7	2.9	2.3	2.7	2.5	1.2	1.3	0.2	0.1
Land Use Change	1.1	1.0	1.0	1.0	0.9	0.9	0.9	0.9	0.8	0.8	0.8	0.8	0.7	0.7	0.7
Waste Management	1.3	1.3	1.3	1.3	1.3	1.3	1.4	1.4	1.4	1.5	1.5	1.6	1.6	1.6	1.7
Grand Total	**47.1**	**37.1**	**36.6**	**34.7**	**32.9**	**32.7**	**33.3**	**32.2**	**31.2**	**30.9**	**30.2**	**28.5**	**28.9**	**27.7**	**27.7**

Notes:

1. The entire time series is revised each year to take account of methodolog

Source: Department for Energy and Climate Change

10.8 Material flow account for the United Kingdom 2000 to 2012

1,000 Metric tonnes

Domestic extraction[1]	2000	2001	2002	2003	2004	2005	2006	2007	2008	2009	2010	2011	2012
Biomass	**168,692**	**161,166**	**169,644**	**164,928**	**165,838**	**160,262**	**162,569**	**161,489**	**168,704**	**169,414**	**167,286**	**173,854**	**164,517**
Crops	44,495	39,352	44,746	42,338	42,747	41,629	39,700	37,146	43,700	42,334	39,746	42,796	37,390
Crop residues (used), fodder crops and grazed biomass	118,667	116,201	119,372	116,991	117,314	112,751	117,110	118,238	119,271	121,218	120,997	124,353	120,330
Wood	4,623	4,672	4,617	4,775	4,915	5,039	4,963	5,311	4,958	5,092	5,730	5,907	5,963
Wild fish catch and aquatic plants/animals	907	940	908	826	862	843	796	794	775	770	814	799	835
Metal ores (gross ores)	**9**	**7**	**6**	**6**	**5**	**3**	**3**	**3**	**3**	**3**	**3**	**4**	**1**
Iron	1	1	0	1	1	0	0	0	0	:	:	:	:
Non-ferrous metal	8	7	6	6	4	3	3	3	3	3	3	4	1
Non-metallic minerals	**305,147**	**310,881**	**293,164**	**287,885**	**300,018**	**290,601**	**291,300**	**295,217**	**261,611**	**210,789**	**208,484**	**209,330**	**195,574**
Limestone and gypsum	85,848	89,938	82,388	80,635	83,334	79,296	81,928	85,191	75,843	61,810	61,907	59,630	56,538
Clays and kaolin	14,944	14,140	13,925	14,224	14,504	14,221	13,437	13,135	11,014	7,226	8,084	8,536	7,493
Sand and gravel	174,729	176,727	167,856	164,899	174,227	170,603	169,275	173,861	155,993	126,935	122,203	125,050	115,539
Other	29,626	30,076	28,995	28,127	27,953	26,481	26,660	23,030	18,762	14,818	16,290	16,114	16,004
Fossil energy materials/carriers	**264,956**	**253,916**	**248,665**	**236,833**	**216,186**	**192,960**	**174,777**	**165,159**	**158,828**	**145,426**	**138,268**	**115,383**	**100,216**
Coal and other solid energy materials/carriers	31,936	32,755	30,431	29,183	25,664	21,175	19,234	17,405	18,396	18,273	18,868	18,713	17,219
Crude oil, condensate and natural gas liquids	126,043	116,678	115,944	106,073	95,374	84,721	76,579	76,575	71,665	68,198	62,962	51,972	44,573
Natural gas	106,977	104,483	102,289	101,578	95,148	87,063	78,964	71,179	68,767	58,954	56,438	44,698	38,424
Total domestic extraction	**738,804**	**725,969**	**711,478**	**689,653**	**682,046**	**643,826**	**628,649**	**621,869**	**589,147**	**525,631**	**514,041**	**498,570**	**460,307**

Sources: Department for Environment, Food and Rural Affairs; Food and Agriculture Organization of the United Nations; Eurostat; European Forest Institute; Kentish Cobnuts Association; British Geological Survey

1,000 Metric tonnes

Imports[1]	2000	2001	2002	2003	2004	2005	2006	2007	2008	2009	2010	2011	2012
Biomass and biomass products	46,097	49,668	50,184	52,631	53,671	53,935	53,710	53,867	52,312	49,423	51,425	50,468	52,387
Metal ores and concentrates, raw and processed	40,943	42,167	41,035	42,348	45,964	43,623	45,291	47,862	42,607	26,955	32,936	33,523	33,855
Non-metallic minerals, raw and processed	13,607	14,845	17,013	16,240	16,989	16,752	16,454	17,160	16,337	12,684	15,078	15,904	13,904
Fossil energy materials/carriers, raw and processed	93,100	109,127	105,309	113,301	138,367	148,165	159,123	159,103	152,461	148,598	148,028	161,053	171,578
Other products	16,418	16,832	15,170	15,793	18,258	16,915	17,167	17,038	16,469	14,858	16,543	15,611	15,102
Waste imported for final treatment and disposal	3	1	4	2	1	1	15	10	13	19	22	5	5
Total imports	210,167	232,640	228,715	240,314	273,252	279,392	291,760	295,039	280,199	252,537	264,032	276,563	286,830

1,000 Metric tonnes

Exports[1]	2000	2001	2002	2003	2004	2005	2006	2007	2008	2009	2010	2011	2012
Biomass and biomass products	18,130	13,850	15,688	20,289	19,118	20,005	20,704	21,374	21,543	20,159	22,413	21,950	22,103
Metal ores and concentrates, raw and processed	23,997	21,870	22,155	24,952	26,677	26,355	27,216	27,335	27,176	20,709	23,502	24,502	23,991
Non-metallic minerals, raw and processed	20,715	21,867	20,445	20,312	21,928	22,634	23,591	22,840	21,170	17,094	16,681	17,034	14,444
Fossil energy materials/carriers, raw and processed	123,229	127,540	129,791	114,128	108,739	98,716	93,760	90,402	89,444	87,836	95,693	92,063	88,728
Other products	8,428	8,832	8,596	8,934	8,685	9,423	8,072	9,539	8,754	7,721	7,716	7,739	7,705
Waste exported for final treatment and disposal	0	0	5	2	4	2	3	0	1	3	3	4	5
Total exports	194,500	193,959	196,680	188,616	185,150	177,134	173,346	171,491	168,087	153,523	166,007	163,291	156,976

1.Totals may not sum due to rounding.

Sources: HM Revenue & Customs

10.8 Material flow account for the United Kingdom 2000 to 2012

1,000 Metric tonnes

Indicators[1,2]	2000	2001	2002	2003	2004	2005	2006	2007	2008	2009	2010	2011	2012
Domestic Material Consumption (Domestic extraction + Imports - Exports)	754,472	764,650	743,513	741,350	770,148	746,084	747,063	745,418	701,258	624,645	612,066	611,842	590,162
of which													
Biomass	196,659	196,984	204,140	197,271	200,391	194,192	195,575	193,982	199,473	198,678	196,299	202,371	194,801
Metal ores	16,956	20,304	18,886	17,403	19,293	17,271	18,079	20,530	15,435	6,248	9,437	9,024	9,865
Non-metallic minerals	298,039	303,860	289,732	283,813	295,080	284,720	284,162	289,537	256,778	206,378	206,880	208,201	195,033
Fossil fuels	234,827	235,503	224,182	236,006	245,814	242,409	240,140	233,860	221,846	206,188	190,603	184,373	183,066
Physical Trade Balance (Imports-Exports)	15,668	38,681	32,035	51,698	88,101	102,258	118,414	123,549	112,111	99,014	98,025	113,273	129,854
Direct Material Input (Domestic extraction + Imports)	948,971	958,609	940,193	929,967	955,298	923,218	920,409	916,908	869,346	778,168	778,073	775,133	747,138
Raw Material Consumption[3]	856,457	887,004	871,562	839,627	805,422	739,684	737,199	740,993	682,544	531,156	553,092	543,787	531,743
of which													
Biomass	212,603	216,159	218,291	213,679	212,743	204,068	202,306	203,191	206,423	211,958	207,168	213,021	207,923
Metal ores	50,619	76,555	75,039	58,856	50,897	39,007	55,411	67,220	51,630	42,323	52,533	40,936	54,636
Non-metallic minerals	318,900	324,223	307,880	309,259	310,230	292,311	292,397	294,647	257,477	209,531	225,194	234,768	222,409
Fossil fuels	274,336	270,066	270,352	257,834	231,553	204,298	187,086	175,934	167,014	67,344	68,196	55,062	46,777
Raw Material Consumption (excluding fossil fuels)	582,122	616,937	601,210	581,794	573,869	535,386	550,113	565,059	515,530	463,812	484,896	488,725	484,967

1. Indicators were calculated using unrounded data.
2. Estimates for indirect flows are currently under development and are likely to be included in Environmental Accounts, 2015. It has not therefore been possible to include the Total Material Requirement (TMR) (Direct Material Input + Indirect flows) indicator in this table.
3. Raw Material Consumption estimates are calculated by the Department for Environment, Food and Rural Affairs. They are experimental statistics and the methodology used to produce them is currently under development.

Sources: Office for National Statistics; Department for Environment, Food and Rural Affairs

Metric tonnes

Per capita (person)	2000	2001	2002	2003	2004	2005	2006	2007	2008	2009	2010	2011	2012
Mid-year population estimates (persons)[1]	58,886,065	59,113,016	59,365,677	59,636,662	59,950,364	60,413,276	60,827,067	61,319,075	61,823,772	62,260,486	62,759,456	63,285,145	63,705,030
Domestic extraction	12.5	12.3	12	11.6	11.4	10.7	10.3	10.1	9.5	8.4	8.2	7.9	7.2
Total imports	3.6	3.9	3.9	4	4.6	4.6	4.8	4.8	4.5	4.1	4.2	4.4	4.5
Total exports	3.3	3.3	3.3	3.2	3.1	2.9	2.8	2.8	2.7	2.5	2.6	2.6	2.5
Domestic Material Consumption (DMC)	12.8	12.9	12.5	12.4	12.8	12.3	12.3	12.2	11.3	10	9.8	9.7	9.3
Direct Material Input (DMI)	16.1	16.2	15.8	15.6	15.9	15.3	15.1	15	14.1	12.5	12.4	12.2	11.7

1. Available here: http://www.ons.gov.uk/ons/about-ons/business-transparency/freedom-of-information/what-can-i-request/published-ad-hoc-data/pop/march-2014/uk-population-estimates-1851-2012.xls

The symbol '..' denotes that the data are not available

The symbol ': ' denotes that the data are not applicable (or zero)

10.9 Annual rainfall: by region

United Kingdom

Millimetres and percentages

Region		1971 - 2000[2] rainfall average (= 100%) millimetres	1999	2000	2001	2002	2003	2004	2005	2006	2007	2008	2009	2010	2011	2012	2013
United Kingdom	JSJB	1084	114	123	97	118	83	112	100	109	111	120	112	88	108	123	101
North West	JSJC	1177	111	132	94	121	85	116	96	114	110	126	113	84	116	136	97
Northumbria	JSJD	831	106	132	106	124	80	120	111	101	105	135	116	105	104	144	106
Severn Trent[1]	JSJE	759	120	132	104	119	81	110	92	103	123	121	103	84	74	139	100
Yorkshire	JSJF	814	110	136	100	126	82	114	96	110	115	130	105	91	89	143	91
Anglian	JSJG	603	113	129	124	118	86	115	89	102	118	116	99	97	73	138	93
Thames	JSLK	700	111	137	116	128	81	103	79	106	118	115	104	87	79	134	101
Southern	JSLL	782	105	148	114	129	85	97	79	101	106	108	109	94	81	130	107
Wessex	JSLM	866	118	136	100	132	83	98	89	100	113	116	107	80	84	140	101
South West	JSLN	1208	113	128	92	121	78	99	90	92	110	112	110	83	86	133	103
England	JSLO	819	113	133	105	123	83	109	91	103	114	120	107	89	87	137	99
Wales	JSLP	1373	116	133	98	119	83	108	95	107	108	121	109	82	94	124	98
Scotland	JSLQ	1440	116	113	91	112	84	117	110	114	109	120	117	87	131	112	102
Northern Ireland	JSLR	1111	111	110	81	127	84	98	96	104	99	114	114	94	115	107	103

Sources: Met Office; National Hydrological Monitoring Programme, Centre for Ecology and Hydrology

[1] The regions of England shown in this table correspond to the original nine English regions of the National Rivers Authority (NRA); the NRA became part of the Environment Agency upon its creation in April 1996. The exception to this is the Severn Trent region, part of which (the upper Severn) lies in Wales.

[2] 1971-2000 averages have been derived using arithmetic averages of Met Office areal rainfall.

10.10 UK Annual Weather Summary

	Max Temp		Min Temp		Mean Temp		Sunshine		Rainfall	
	Actual (degrees celsius)	Anomaly (degrees celsius)	Actual (degrees celsius)	Anomaly (degrees celsius)	Actual (degrees celsius)	Anomaly (degrees celsius)	Actual (hours/ day)	Anomaly (%)	Actual (mm)	Anomaly (%)
	WLRL	WLRM	WLRO	WLRP	WLRR	WLRS	WLRX	WLRY	WLSH	WLSI
1990	13.1	1.2	5.8	0.9	9.4	1.1	1490.7	111.4	1172.8	106.7
1991	12.1	0.3	5.1	0.2	8.6	0.3	1302.0	97.3	998.2	90.8
1992	12.3	0.4	5.2	0.4	8.7	0.4	1290.8	96.5	1186.8	107.9
1993	11.8	-0.1	5.0	0.1	8.4	0.0	1218.6	91.1	1121.1	102.0
1994	12.4	0.5	5.5	0.6	8.9	0.6	1366.9	102.2	1184.7	107.7
1995	13.0	1.1	5.4	0.6	9.2	0.9	1588.5	118.7	1023.7	93.1
1996	11.7	-0.1	4.7	-0.1	8.2	-0.2	1403.5	104.9	916.6	83.4
1997	13.1	1.3	5.8	1.0	9.4	1.1	1430.3	106.9	1024.0	93.1
1998	12.6	0.8	5.8	1.0	9.1	0.8	1268.4	94.8	1265.1	115.1
1999	13.0	1.1	5.9	1.0	9.4	1.1	1419.4	106.1	1239.1	112.5
2000	12.7	0.8	5.6	0.8	9.1	0.8	1367.5	102.2	1337.3	121.5
2001	12.4	0.6	5.3	0.5	8.8	0.5	1411.9	105.5	1052.8	95.5
2002	13.0	1.1	6.0	1.2	9.5	1.2	1304.0	97.5	1283.7	116.5
2003	13.5	1.6	5.6	0.7	9.5	1.2	1587.4	118.7	904.2	82.0
2004	13.0	1.2	6.0	1.2	9.5	1.2	1361.4	101.8	1210.1	110.1
2005	13.1	1.2	5.9	1.1	9.5	1.1	1399.2	104.6	1083.0	98.4
2006	13.4	1.5	6.1	1.3	9.7	1.4	1495.9	111.8	1175.9	106.8
2007	13.3	1.4	6.0	1.1	9.6	1.3	1450.7	108.4	1197.1	108.8
2008	12.7	0.8	5.5	0.6	9.1	0.7	1388.8	103.8	1295.0	117.7
2009	12.8	1.0	5.6	0.7	9.2	0.9	1467.4	109.7	1213.3	110.2
2010	11.7	-0.1	4.2	-0.6	8.0	-0.4	1456.0	108.8	950.5	86.4
2011	13.5	1.5	6.0	1.2	9.6	1.3	1406.2	105.0	1172.5	107
2012	12.4	0.5	5.2	0.4	8.8	0.4	1340.5	100	1334.8	121
2013	12.4	0.5	5.2	0.4	8.8	0.5	1421.1	106	1091	99

Source: Met Office

10.11 Summary of River Basin District Ecological and Chemical Status 2009-2013

River Basin District	Percent of surface water bodies are at good chemical status or better				
	2009	2010	2011	2012	2013
Solway Tweed	50	89	89	88	91
Northumbria	50	68	72	68	70
Humber	77	79	83	77	76
Anglian	85	89	92	87	84
Thames	75	76	79	74	72
South East	88	91	93	88	88
South West	77	80	83	84	79
Severn	78	83	88	82	82
Dee	75	92	92	87	82
North West	70	75	72	71	74

River Basin District	Percent of surface water bodies are at good ecological status/potential or better				
	2009	2010	2011	2012	2013
Solway Tweed	44	43	45	48	41
Northumbria	43	41	43	40	42
Humber	18	16	17	18	17
Anglian	18	19	18	18	17
Thames	23	22	22	18	19
South East	19	15	16	15	15
South West	33	31	34	32	31
Severn	29	30	30	30	29
Dee	28	26	30	30	25
North West	30	31	30	29	30

Source: Environment Agency

Improvements measured in terms of the number of water bodies meeting good status

10.12 Overall status of rivers & canals in Scotland, 2012

	High	Max EP	Good	Good EP	Moderate	Moderate EP	Poor	Poor EP	Bad	Bad EP
No. of river water bodies	203	1	1011	140	447	54	298	55	123	74
Length of river water bodies (km)	1559.9	6.4	10341	1312.8	5668	470.7	3038.1	575.3	1333.3	806.9
% of length of river water bodies	6.2%	0.0%	41.2%	5.2%	22.6%	1.9%	12.1%	2.3%	5.3%	3.2%

Water Quality 2012

	High	Good	Moderate	Poor	Bad
No. of river water bodies	837	725	395	70	3
Length of river water bodies (km)	8622	7760.5	4598	784.1	31.7
% of length of river water bodies	39.6%	35.6%	21.1%	3.6%	0.1%

Source: Scottish Environment Protection Agency

10.13 Monthly reservoir stocks for England & Wales[1]

Percentages

		2001	2002	2003	2004	2005	2006	2007	2008	2009	2010	2011	2012	2013
January	JTAS	94.4	93.7	95.0	93.8	92.3	88.7	93.7	95.7	95.3	92.4	89.8	90.4	96.7
February	JTAT	95.0	95.5	92.1	92.1	92.1	91.2	96.7	95.6	93.4	91.8	93.7	92.0	93.8
March	JTAU	95.5	94.5	92.3	94.4	93.6	96.2	95.2	97.3	94.5	94.1	92.2	89.2	92.0
April	JTAV	96.7	91.9	88.6	94.7	95.0	93.4	91.9	95.1	92.0	91.9	88.9	94.0	94.5
May	JTAW	91.9	97.0	93.1	90.5	93.0	94.4	91.1	92.6	93.3	86.2	87.4	93.6	94.5
June	JTAX	85.1	94.9	87.0	84.8	85.6	88.4	94.4	90.6	88.6	79.0	86.7	97.8	90.8
July	JTAY	80.7	91.1	81.1	78.5	77.9	77.2	93.5	92.0	91.1	77.3	84.7	96.8	83.7
August	JTAZ	77.9	85.9	69.9	82.4	71.5	70.7	88.3	92.5	89.7	75.5	79.9	96.0	82.2
September	JTBA	77.0	77.3	60.4	84.2	67.4	67.8	86.1	90.9	84.0	81.1	81.0	95.3	77.7
October	JTBB	85.5	82.9	53.0	87.5	77.2	80.0	81.2	93.8	82.3	82.0	80.0	94.3	87.6
November	JTBC	87.9	91.8	60.9	86.2	83.8	89.8	82.4	93.1	93.0	86.9	79.7	95.8	88.3
December	JTBD	86.5	95.1	79.9	91.2	85.9	92.2	89.8	92.4	90.6	84.3	88.6	97.6	95.4

1 Reservoir stocks are the percentage of useable capacity based on a representative
selection of reservoirs; the percentages relate to the end of each month.

Sources: Water PLCs;
Environment Agency;
National Hydrological Monitoring Programme, Centre for Ecology and Hydrology: 01491 838800

10.14a Water Industry Current cost profit and loss account for the 12 months ended 31 March 2014 (appointed business only)

Description	Anglian	Welsh	Northumbrian	Severn Trent	Southern	South West	Thames	United Utilities	Wessex	Yorkshire	Bournemouth	Bristol	Cambridge	Dee Valley	Portsmouth	South East	South Staffs	Sutton and East Surrey	Affinity	Northern Ireland	Scottish
				WaSC										WoC							
Water																					
Turnover																					
Unmeasured - household	121.112	163.300	220.400	351.100	45.500	59.400	497.600	378.500	70.400	208.500	11.501	58.500	6.126		20.984	79.832	52.914	30.811	129.145		381.700
Unmeasured - non-household	0.662	2.500	2.900	3.600	1.200	4.300	7.400	4.400	2.500	1.400	0.530	1.500	0.526		0.346	1.804	0.893	0.259	2.698		100.300
Measured - household	239.909	59.100	112.100	200.900	105.600	109.900	208.600	174.500	63.400	125.000	17.544	34.400	9.495		5.700	82.903	22.293	17.990	102.870		
Measured - non-household	77.476	69.100	67.100	133.700	31.700	49.400	174.500	137.200	42.100	80.900	9.510	21.000	6.308		8.594	39.718	17.827	9.096	55.341		
Trade effluent	0.000									0.000	0.000		0.000		0.000	0.000	0.000	0.000	0.000		
Bulk supplies/inter company payments	7.685	9.300	0.600	5.300	3.000	7.400	3.600	0.700	0.400	0.200	0.023	0.700	0.040		0.631	0.000	0.416	0.034	2.040		
Other third party services (incl non-potable water)	12.170	15.000	10.500	36.600	5.800	4.500	3.100	6.000	0.100	0.300	0.193	0.400	0.099		0.735	0.000	0.618	1.334	0.884		
Other sources	36.157	6.800	28.800	1.100	7.400	0.000	40.400	57.300	13.300	34.800	5.236	5.300	0.000		0.066	5.206	0.434	1.201	0.000		3.000
Total turnover	495.171	325.100	442.400	732.300	200.200	234.900	935.200	758.600	192.200	451.100	44.537	121.800	22.594		37.056	209.463	95.395	60.725	292.978		485.000
Current cost operating costs - wholesale	-313.742	-223.000	-269.700	-462.700	-142.700	-124.800	-99.500	-444.700	-112.300	-294.000	-27.689	-93.100	-13.376		-27.493	-124.143	-62.613	-39.480	-197.791		
Current cost operating costs - retail	-36.532	-28.000	-41.700	-60.400	-31.600	-17.600	-607.000	-76.200	-15.000	-28.700	-4.496	-10.800	-2.720		-4.888	-20.075	-14.641	-6.580	-32.419		
Operating income	0.318	0.300	0.900	2.500	-0.200	1.200	11.900	-12.900	-0.200	2.800	-0.083	-0.500	-0.202		-0.017	-0.127	-0.018	14.665	-1.674		
Working capital adjustment	-0.154	0.100	-0.600	-2.600	0.100	-0.200	4.000	0.500	-0.200	0.800		0.400	0.171		0.152	0.217	0.248	-1.025	0.841		
Current cost operating profit	145.061	74.500	131.300	209.100	25.800	93.500	244.600	225.300	64.500	132.000	12.269	17.800	6.467		4.810	65.335	18.371	13.640	61.935		
Other income	0.000			0.000		0.000	1.100					0.300	0.032		-0.750	0.591	0.000	-0.023	0.000		
Net Interest	0.000	-79.800		0.000		0.000					-5.231	-12.700	-0.906		-3.936	-46.753	-10.366	-10.522	-40.187		
Financing adjustment	0.000	16.500		0.000		0.000					1.930	4.500	1.278		0.030	17.317	-0.452	0.614	20.592		
Current cost profit before taxation	145.061	11.200		0.000		93.500					8.968	9.900	6.871		0.154	36.490	7.553	3.709	42.340		
Net revenue movement out of tariff basket	0.048	0.200	0.000	-1.000	-0.200	0.000	0.500	0.800	0.000	0.900	0.050	0.200	0.000		0.149	-0.030	-0.093	0.000	0.010		
Back-billing amount identified	0.000		0.000	0.600	0.000	0.000		4.000	0.000	0.000	0.000		0.016		0.000	0.269	0.423	0.000	2.703		
Sewerage																					
Turnover																					
Unmeasured - household	191.647	229.500	165.000	371.500	208.200	72.900	508.100	404.300	138.500	251.000											412.300
Unmeasured - non-household	1.470	3.200	4.600	9.600	5.300	5.500	7.500	5.800	3.400	2.700											177.700
Measured - household	390.162	93.200	53.900	186.300	275.700	144.500	271.900	202.200	113.600	152.800											
Measured - non-household	76.986	57.100	61.900	170.500	80.800	42.300	137.200	245.300	50.600	73.600											
Trade effluent	7.333	9.700	2.600	10.900	7.100	4.500	8.400	21.800	4.200	9.100											
Bulk supplies/inter company payments	1.720	8.700		0.000	0.000	9.000		0.100	0.100	0.000											
Other third party services (incl non-potable water)	0.000		0.300	39.600	3.600	3.000	1.300	0.000	0.800	0.800											
Other sources	33.435		19.600	3.900	18.800	0.000	42.900	51.700	13.500	32.400											3.000
Total turnover	702.753	401.400	307.900	792.300	599.500	281.700	977.300	931.200	324.700	522.400											593.000
Current cost operating costs - wholesale	-463.230	-225.100	-178.500	-456.700	-374.000	-168.500	-76.000	-534.100	-175.700	-386.200											
Current cost operating costs - retail	-45.877	-34.600	-16.500	-66.800	-56.300	-17.900	-622.400	-84.800	-15.200	-33.300											
Operating income	0.158	0.400	-0.700	2.800	-0.300	0.600	11.700	-6.900	-1.900	1.300											
Working capital adjustment	-0.154	0.200	-0.400	-2.900	0.600	-0.300	3.900	0.600	-0.400	1.000											
Current cost operating profit	193.650	142.300	111.800	268.700	169.500	95.600	294.500	306.000	131.500	105.200											
Other income	0.000			0.000		0.000	1.200														
Net Interest	0.000	-82.600		0.000		0.000															
Financing adjustment	0.000	17.000		0.000		0.000															
Current cost profit before taxation	193.650	76.700		0.000		95.600															
Net revenue movement out of tariff basket	0.655		-0.200	1.000	-0.100	0.000	0.200	-2.200	-0.300	-0.200											
Back-billing amount identified	0.000		0.000	1.000	0.000	0.000		4.200	0.000	0.100											
Total																					
Turnover																					
Unmeasured - household	312.759	392.800	385.400	722.600	253.700	132.300	1,005.700	782.800	208.900	459.500	11.501	58.500	6.126		20.984	79.832	52.914	30.811	129.145		794.000
Unmeasured - non-household	2.132	5.700	7.500	13.200	6.500	9.800	14.900	10.200	5.900	4.100	0.530	1.500	0.526		0.346	1.804	0.893	0.259	2.698		278.000
Measured - household	630.071	152.300	166.000	387.200	381.300	254.400	480.500	376.700	177.000	277.800	17.544	34.400	9.495		5.700	82.903	22.293	17.990	102.870		
Measured - non-household	154.462	126.200	129.000	304.200	112.500	91.700	311.700	382.500	92.700	154.500	9.510	21.000	6.308		8.594	39.718	17.827	9.096	55.341		
Trade effluent	7.333	9.700	2.600	10.900	7.100	4.500	8.400	21.800	4.200	9.100	0.000		0.000		0.000	0.000	0.000	0.000	0.000		
Bulk supplies/inter company payments	9.405	18.000	0.600	5.300	3.000	16.400	3.600	0.800	0.500	0.200	0.023	0.700	0.040		0.631	0.000	0.416	0.034	2.040		

10.14a Water Industry Current cost profit and loss account for the 12 months ended 31 March 2014 (appointed business only)

Description	WaSC										WoC									Northern Ireland	Scottish
	Anglian	Welsh	Northumbrian	Severn Trent	Southern	South West	Thames	United Utilities	Wessex	Yorkshire	Bournemouth	Bristol	Cambridge	Dee Valley	Portsmouth	South East	South Staffs	Sutton and East Surrey	Affinity		
Other third party services (incl non-potable water)	12.170	15.000	10.800	76.200	9.400	7.500	4.400	6.000	0.900	1.100	0.193	0.400	0.099		0.735	0.000	0.618	1.334	0.884		
Other sources	69.592	6.800	48.400	5.000	26.200	0.000	83.300	109.000	26.800	67.200	5.236	5.300	0.000		0.066	5.206	0.434	1.201	0.000		6.000
Total turnover	1,197.924	726.500		1,524.600	799.700	516.600	1,912.500	1,689.800	516.900	973.500	44.537	121.800	22.594		37.056	209.463	95.395	60.725	292.978	361.313	1,078.000
Current cost operating costs - wholesale	-776.972	-448.100	-448.200	-919.400	-516.700	-293.300	-175.500	-978.800	-288.000	-680.200	-27.689	-93.100	-13.376		-27.493	-124.143	-62.613	-39.480	-197.791	-343.723	
Current cost operating costs - retail	-82.410	-62.600	-58.200	-127.200	-87.900	-35.500	-1,229.400	-161.000	-30.200	-62.000	-4.496	-10.800	-2.720		-4.888	-20.075	-14.641	-6.580	-32.419		
Operating income	0.476	0.700	0.200	5.300	-0.500	1.800	23.600	-19.800	-2.100	4.100		-0.500	-0.202		-0.017	-0.127	-0.018	14.665	-1.674		
Current cost profit on disposal of fixed assets																				208.000	
Working capital adjustment	-0.307	0.300	-1.000	-5.500	0.700	-0.500	7.900	1.100	-0.600	1.800	-0.083	0.400	0.171		0.152	0.217	0.248	-1.025	0.841	2.001	
Current cost operating profit	338.711	216.800		477.800	195.300	189.100	539.100	531.300	196.000	237.200	12.269	17.800	6.467		4.810	65.335	18.371	13.640	61.935	19.799	
Other income	0.000	0.200	0.200	1.800	0.200	0.300	2.300	0.300	0.400	2.200	0.032	0.300	0.032		-0.750	0.591	0.000	-0.023	0.000		
Net Interest	-139.127	-162.400	-130.000	-238.000	-167.300	-57.700	-417.700	-139.900	-77.800	-188.000	-5.231	-12.700	-0.906		-3.936	-46.753	-10.366	-10.522	-40.187	-48.580	
Financing adjustment	10.209	33.500	46.700	80.500	80.000	43.500	60.200	78.700	26.100	16.200	1.930	4.500	1.278		0.030	17.317	-0.452	0.614	20.592	23.962	
Current cost profit before taxation	209.793	87.900		322.100	108.200	175.200	183.900	470.400	144.700	67.600	8.968	9.900	6.871		0.154	36.490	7.553	3.709	42.340	-4.819	
Net revenue movement out of tariff basket	0.702	0.200	-0.200	0.000	-0.300	0.000	0.700	-1.400	-0.300	0.700	0.050	0.200	0.000		0.149	-0.030	-0.093	0.000	0.010		
Back-billing amount identified	0.000	0.000	0.000	1.600	0.000	0.000	3.500	8.200	0.000	0.100	0.000	0.000	0.016		0.000	0.269	0.423	0.000	2.703		

10.14b Water Industry Regulatory Capital Values at 2013-14 prices

£m	2013-14	2014-15
RCV at 31 March 2013 as published on website for 2012-13 update	61,223	
Indexation	1,502	
Opening RCV	62,725	63,894
Capital expenditure (excluding IRE)	4,288	3,495
Infrastructure renewals expenditure	1,132	1,061
Infrastructure renewals charge	-1,001	-1,002
Grants & contributions	-234	-245
Depreciation	-2,767	-2,779
Outperformance of regulatory assumptions	-248	-248
Other adjustments (CC referral)	0.1	-7.4
Closing RCV	63,894	64,168
Average Year RCV	62,547	63,260

Source: OFWAT

Numbers may not add due to rounding

10.15 Overall summary of pollution incident results by region, medium and incident category 2013

Water	Anglian	Midlands	North East	North West	South East	South West	Total
Cat 1	4	6	10	6	13	6	45
Cat 2	46	43	57	45	76	65	332
Cat 3	1074	1584	1068	792	2327	1235	8080
Cat 4	1465	2018	1678	1103	3424	1284	10972
Total	2589	3651	2813	1946	5840	2590	19429
						Cat 1 & 2 Total	**377**

Land	Anglian	Midlands	North East	North West	South East	South West	Total
Cat 1	0	2	1	0	0	0	3
Cat 2	14	21	15	39	23	19	131
Cat 3	529	802	705	454	1393	721	4604
Cat 4	2046	2826	2092	1453	4424	1850	14691
Total	2589	3651	2813	1946	5840	2590	19429
						Cat 1 & 2 Total	**134**

Air	Anglian	Midlands	North East	North West	South East	South West	Total
Cat 1	0	3	1	1	1	0	6
Cat 2	18	65	30	24	38	46	221
Cat 3	625	806	632	360	912	521	3856
Cat 4	1946	2777	2150	1561	4889	2023	15346
Total	2589	3651	2813	1946	5840	2590	19429
						Cat 1 & 2 Total	**227**

Source: Environment Agency

10.16a 2013 mandatory compliance[1] results for bathing waters in the UK

Coastal Bathing Waters (results for 2012 are in brackets)

Region *	Mandatory Pass	Fail	Total	Compliance%
North East	54 (47)	0 (7)	54 (54)	100 (87.0)
Anglian	40 (40)	0 (0)	40 (40)	100 (100)
South East	90 (90)	0 (0)	90 (90)	100 (100)
South West	191 (177)	1 (16)	192 (193)	99.5 (91.7)
North West	25 (24)	4 (6)	29 (30)	86.2 (80.0)
England	**400 (378)**	**5 (29)**	**405 (407)**	**98.8 (92.9)**
Wales	**99 (97)**	**1 (3)**	**100 (100)**	**99.0 (97.0)**
Scotland	**80 (74)**	**0 (2)**	**80 (80)**	**100 (97.5)**
Northern Ireland	**23 (22)**	**0 (1)**	**23 (23)**	**100 (95.7)**
UK COASTAL WATERS	**602 (575)**	**6 (35)**	**608 (610)**	**99.0 (94.3)**

Inland Bathing Waters (results for 2012 are in brackets)

Region*	Mandatory Pass	Fail	Total	Compliance %
Midland	1 (-)	0 (-)	1 (0)	100 (-)
South East	6 (6)	0 (0)	6 (6)	100 (100)
North West	3 (3)	0 (0)	3 (3)	100 (100)
England	**10 (9)**	**0 (0)**	**10 (9)**	**100 (100)**
Scotland	**3 (3)**	**0 (0)**	**3 (3)**	**100 (100)**
UK INLAND WATERS	**13 (12)**	**0 (0)**	**13 (12)**	**100 (100)**

[1] Figures shown are for compliance with the mandatory microbiological standards set by the EC Bathing Water Directive (76/160/EEC)

* Environment Agency operational regions. The bathing water in Midlands region has been designated in 2013.

Source: Department for Environment, Food and Rural Affairs

10.16b 2013 guideline[2] compliance results for bathing waters in the UK

Coastal Bathing Waters (results for 2012 are in brackets)

Region *	Guideline Pass	Fail	Total	Compliance %
North East	46 (25)	8 (29)	54 (54)	85.2 (46.3)
Anglian	34 (33)	6 (7)	40 (40)	85.0 (82.5)
South East	78 (62)	12 (28)	90 (90)	86.7 (68.9)
South West	174 (117)	18 (76)	192 (193)	90.6 (60.6)
North West	6 (3)	23 (27)	29 (30)	20.7 (10.0)
England	**338 (240)**	**67(167)**	**405 (407)**	**83.5 (59.0)**
Wales	**89 (75)**	**11 (25)**	**100 (100)**	**89.0 (75.0)**
Scotland	**47 (32)**	**33 (41)**	**80 (80)**	**58.8 (40.0)**
Northern Ireland	**20 (16)**	**3 (4)**	**23 (23)**	**87.0 (69.6)**
UK COASTAL WATERS	**494 (363)**	**114 (247)**	**608 (610)**	**81.3 (59.5)**

Inland Bathing Waters (Results for 2012 are in brackets)

Region *	Guideline Pass	Fail	Total	Compliance %
Midlands	1 (-)	0 (-)	1 (0)	100 (-)
South East	1 (2)	5 (4)	6 (6)	16.7 (33.3)
North West	2 (1)	1 (2)	3 (3)	66.7 (33.3)
England	**4 (3)**	**6 (6)**	**10 (9)**	**40.0 (33.3)**
Scotland	**0 (0)**	**3 (3)**	**3 (3)**	**0 (0)**
UK INLAND WATERS	**4 (3)**	**9 (9)**	**13 (12)**	**30.8 (25.0)**

[2] These figures show compliance with the equivalent single standard that is being used during the transitional period from 2012 - 2014 as the revised Directive (2006/7/EC) is implemented.

* Environment Agency operational regions. The bathing water in Midlands region has been designated in 2013

Source: Department for Environment, Food and Rural Affairs

10.17 Estimated abstractions from all surface and groundwater sources: by purpose[1]

England and Wales

million cubic metres

		2001	2002	2003	2004	2005	2006	2007	2008	2009	2010	2011	2012	2013
Public water supply	JZLA	5,923	6,183	6,036	6,298	6,342	6,207	5,979	5,944	5,768	5,977	5,829	5,844	5,879
Spray irrigation [a]	JZLB	94	91	116	83	81	101	58	58	86	106	117	49	100
Agriculture (excl spray irrigation)	JZLC	40	44	49	44	22	18	26	14	17	24	26	25	26
Electricity supply industry[2] [b]	JZLD	11,777	12,938	11,555	11,189	10,956	11,737	11,856	12,128	10,977	10,868	10,716	13,309	13,343
Other industry[3]	JZLE	1,743	1,784	2,160	2,409	2,314	2,379	1,886	1,814	2,065	1,815	1,737	2,011	1,728
Fish farming, cress growing, amenity ponds	JYXG	1,700	1,173	1,241	1,490	1,334	1,322	1,245	1,043	953	1,059	848	974	947
Private water supply	JZLG	32	20	15	10	9	14	11	9	9	8	9	10	9
Other	JZLH	40	28	27	28	22	32	41	27	28	22	22	27	33
Total	JZLI	21,348	22,259	21,199	21,552	21,080	21,809	21,105	21,036	19,899	19,875	19,304	22,251	22,065

1 See chapter text.

Source: Environment Agency

2 Increased electricity supply abstraction from 2002 due to issue of 2 new abstraction licences

3 Three abstraction licences in 2003 re-assigned to "other industry" from "electricty supply"

(a) Includes small amounts of non-agricultural spray irrigation

(b) The Electricity Supply Industry category includes hydropower licences.

10.18 Estimates of remaining recoverable oil & gas reserves and resources, 2002-2012

United Kingdom

		2002	2003	2004	2005	2006	2007	2008	2009	2010	2011	2012
OIL (million tonnes)												
Discovered reserves												
Proven	JKOV	595	571	533	516	479	452	408	378	374	413	405
Probable	JKOW	325	286	283	300	298	328	361	390	377	374	405
Proven plus Probable	JKOX	920	857	816	816	776	780	770	769	751	788	811
Possible	JKOY	425	410	512	451	478	399	360	343	342	319	253
Maximum	JKOZ	1,345	1,267	1,328	1,267	1,254	1,179	1,130	1,112	1,093	1,106	1,064
Range of undiscovered resources												
Lower	JKNY	272	323	396	346	438	379	454	397	475	422	455
Upper	JKNZ	1,770	1,826	1,830	1,581	1,637	1,577	1,561	1,477	1,374	1,321	1,342
Range of total reserves and resources												
Lower[1]	JKOA	867	894	929	862	917	831	862	775	849	835	860
Upper[2]	JKOB	3,115	3,093	3,158	2,848	2,891	2,756	2,691	2,589	2,467	2,427	2,406
Expected level of reserves[3]												
Opening stocks	JKOC	955	920	857	816	816	776	780	770	769	751	788
Extraction[4]	JKOD	-116	-106	-95	-85	-77	-77	-72	-68	-63	-52	-45
Other volume changes	JKOE	81	43	54	85	37	81	62	67	45	89	68
Closing stocks	JKOF	920	857	816	816	776	780	770	769	751	788	811
GAS (billion cubic metres)												
Discovered reserves												
Proven	JKOH	630	590	531	481	412	343	292	256	253	246	244
Probable	JKOI	370	315	296	247	272	304	309	308	267	246	217
Proven plus Probable	JKOJ	1,000	905	826	728	684	647	601	564	520	493	461
Possible	JKOK	330	336	343	278	283	293	306	276	261	216	238
Maximum	JKOL	1,330	1,241	1,169	1,006	967	940	907	840	781	709	699
Range of undiscovered resources												
Lower	JKOM	238	279	293	226	301	280	319	300	363	353	369
Upper	JKON	1,386	1,259	1,245	1,035	1,049	1,039	1,043	949	1,021	977	1,010
Range of total reserves and resources												
Lower[1]	JKOO	868	869	824	707	713	623	611	556	616	599	613
Upper[2]	JKOP	2,716	2,500	2,414	2,041	2,016	1,979	1,950	1,789	1,802	1,686	1,709
Expected Level of Reserves[3]												
Opening stocks	JKOQ	1,100	1,000	905	826	728	684	647	601	564	520	493
Extraction[4]	JKOR	-102	-102	-95	-86	-78	-70	-68	-57	-55	-43	-37
Other volume changes	JKOS	2	7	16	-12	34	33	22	20	10	16	5
Closing stocks	JKOT	1,000	905	826	728	684	647	601	564	520	493	461

Sources: Office for National Statistics, Department of Energy and Climate Change

All data refer to end of year.

Components may not sum to totals due to rounding.

1. The lower end of the range of total reserves and resources has been calculated as the sum of proven reserves and the lower end of the range of undiscovered resources.

2. The upper end of the range of total reserves and resources is the sum of proven, probable and possible reserves and the upper end of the range of undiscovered resources.

3. Expected reserves are the sum of proven and probable reserves.

4. The negative of extraction is shown here for the purposes of the calculation only. Of itself, extraction should be considered as a positive value.

10.19a Local Authority Collected Waste England from 2000/01 to 2012/13

England   *Thousand tonnes*

Household waste from:	2000/01	2001/02	2002/03	2003/04	2004/05	2005/06	2006/07r	2007/08	2008/09r	2009/10	2010/11	2011/12	2012/13
Regular household collection	16,655	16,683	16,528	16,066	15,470	14,616	14,050	13,046	12,076	11,432	11,048	10,586	10,317
Other household sources	1,381	1,277	1,351	1,244	1,205	1,314	1,173	1,073	1,026	1,070	1,047	997	1,027
Civic amenity sites	4,234	4,367	4,213	3,616	3,198	2,726	2,576	2,434	2,086	1,765	1,635	1,470	1,477
Household recycling	2,809	3,197	3,740	4,521	5,785	6,796	7,976	8,735	9,146	9,398	9,724	9,846	9,759
Total household	**25,079**	**25,524**	**25,832**	**25,448**	**25,658**	**25,454**	**25,775**	**25,287**	**24,334**	**23,666**	**23,454**	**22,899**	**22,580**
Non household sources (excl. recycling)	2,342	2,656	2,730	2,650	2,795	2,289	2,408	2,250	2,063	1,999	1,882	1,654	1,558
Non household recycling	636	724	832	1,016	1,167	1,003	961	969	936	877	864	866	817
Total LA collected waste	**28,057**	**28,905**	**29,394**	**29,114**	**29,619**	**28,745**	**29,144**	**28,506**	**27,334**	**26,541**	**26,200**	**25,419**	**24,955**

Source: Department for Environment, Food & Rural Affairs

There has been a revision to 2008/09 to include asbestos in "Other household sources" instead of "Non household sources".

2010/11 data has been revised slightly due to data issues.

10.19b Waste managed by type and year (Wales) (a)

Thousand tonnes

	2008-09	2009-10	2010-11	2011-12	2012-13
Composted	214	233	264	291	285
Recycled	433	443	471	493	531
Incineration	32	35	38	51	72
Landfill	1,035	931	826	710	641
Other (b)	12	16	14	15	36
Total	**1,724**	**1,659**	**1,613**	**1,560**	**1,565**

Source: WasteDataFlow

(a) Includes household and non-household waste. Excluding abandoned vehicles.

(b) Includes refuse derived fuel, and mechanical biological treatment (MBT)

Waste managed (tonnes) by management method and year 2012-13 onwards

		2012-13	2013-14
Total Municipal Waste Collected/Generated		1553511.534	1557229
Total Waste Reused/Recycled/Composted (Statutory Target) (1)		811865.985	846091
Total Waste Reused/Recycled/Composted (Statutory Target) (1)			
	Household Waste Reused/Recycled (2)	499946.4776	429863
	Household Waste Composted (3)	265133.1467	274265
	Non-Household Waste Reused/Recycled (4)	28622.11644	128310
	Non-Household Waste Composted (5)	18164.2443	13653
Waste sent for other recovery (6)		1801.856	4532
Waste Incinerated with Energy Recovery		71887.638	89907
Waste Incinerated without Energy Recovery		363.827	341
Waste Landfilled		640904.458	587390
Percentage of Waste Reused/Recycled/Composted (Statutory Target) (7)		52.26005519	54.33310793
Percentage of Waste Reused/Recycled/Composted (Statutory Target) (7)			
	Percentage of Household Waste Reused/Recycled (8)	32.18170362	27.60425396
	Percentage of Household Waste Composted (9)	17.0666996	17.61241588
	Percentage of Non-Household Waste Reused/Recycled (10)	1.842414157	8.239625335
	Percentage of Non-Household Waste Composted (11)	1.169237814	0.876876969

Source: WasteDataFlow, Natural Resources Wales

1. Total waste reused/recycled/composted as defined by the Statutory Local Authority Recovery Target (LART)

2. Household waste sent to be reused/recycled as defined by the Statutory Local Authority Recovery Target (LART)

3. Household waste sent to be composted as defined by the Statutory Local Authority Recovery Target (LART)

4. Non-Household waste sent to be reused/recycled as defined by the Statutory Local Authority Recovery Target (LART)

5. Non-Household waste sent to be composted as defined by the Statutory Local Authority Recovery Target (LART)

6. Other waste sent for recycling and/or composting that is not included in the statutory target definition

7. Total waste reused/recycled/composted (as defined by the Statutory Local Authority Recovery Target, LART), as a percentage of total municipal waste collected/generated

8. Household waste sent to be reused/recycled (as defined by the Statutory Local Authority Recovery Target, LART), as a percentage of total municipal waste collected/generated

9. Household waste sent to be composted (as defined by the Statutory Local Authority Recovery Target, LART), as a percentage of total municipal waste collected/generated

10. Non-Household waste sent to be reused/recycled (as defined by the Statutory Local Authority Recovery Target, LART), as a percentage of total municipal waste collected/generated

11. Non-Household waste sent to be composted (as defined by the Statutory Local Authority Recovery Target, LART), as a percentage of total municipal waste collected/generated

From 1 April 2012, there have been changes in definitions relating to local authority municipal waste. These changes affect the total amount of local authority municipal waste generated and the percentage reused, recycled or composted in Wales. A detailed description of these definition changes and their impacts can be found in the Statistical article Local Authority Municipal Waste Management

10.19c Household waste WasteDataFlow data 2013 CALENDAR YEAR[1]

2012

Local Authority	HOUSEHOLD WASTE[2] Generated (tonnes)	HOUSEHOLD WASTE Recycled / Composted[1] (tonnes)	Percentage HOUSEHOLD WASTE Recycled / Composted (%)	HOUSEHOLD WASTE Other Waste Diverted from Landfill (tonnes)[3]	Percentage HOUSEHOLD WASTE Other Waste Diverted from Landfill (%)	HOUSEHOLD WASTE Landfilled (tonnes)[4]	Percentage HOUSEHOLD WASTE Landfilled (%)	Percentage HOUSEHOLD WASTE Recycled / Composted (%)
Aberdeen City	94,117	34,956	37.1	109	0.1	59,051	62.7	37.3
Aberdeenshire	131,811	47,220	35.8	170	0.1	84,421	64.0	35.6
Angus	54,258	23,416	43.2	5,578	10.3	25,265	46.6	40.1
Argyll & Bute	49,244	17,773	36.1	6,283	12.8	25,188	51.1	31.5
Clackmannanshire	26,797	16,044	59.9	1,755	6.5	9,018	33.7	58.9
Dumfries & Galloway	75,501	18,082	23.9	25,418	33.7	30,923	41.0	22.2
Dundee City	61,485	19,111	31.1	15,579	25.3	26,795	43.6	29.7
East Ayrshire	58,282	28,456	48.8	1,263	2.2	28,567	49.0	44.4
East Dunbartonshire	51,997	23,363	44.9	3,295	6.3	25,340	48.7	38.7
East Lothian	49,335	20,879	42.3	0	0.0	28,456	57.7	44.8
East Renfrewshire	44,057	24,817	56.3	0	0.0	19,239	43.7	54.2
Edinburgh, City of	184,360	70,189	38.1	0	0.0	114,172	61.9	36.7
Eilean Siar	12,738	4,281	33.6	0	0.0	8,457	66.4	29.7
Falkirk	71,950	38,162	53.0	1,954	2.7	31,834	44.2	55.2
Fife	190,784	106,602	55.9	965	0.5	83,217	43.6	52.8
Glasgow City	227,940	61,310	26.9	0	0.0	166,631	73.1	29.5
Highland	125,651	56,584	45.0	2,936	2.3	66,169	52.7	44.3
Inverclyde	29,183	16,184	55.5	32	0.1	12,968	44.4	50.7
Midlothian	40,177	17,012	42.3	0	0.0	23,165	57.7	45.3
Moray	47,533	24,424	51.4	0	0.0	23,110	48.6	51.9
North Ayrshire	61,908	34,704	56.1	640	1.0	26,566	42.9	51.8
North Lanarkshire	152,729	64,571	42.3	11,663	7.6	76,494	50.1	39.8
Orkney Islands	9,923	3,053	30.8	4,459	44.9	2,700	27.2	22.5
Perth & Kinross	74,267	40,088	54.0	2,555	3.4	31,622	42.6	55.0
Renfrewshire	78,417	34,742	44.3	3,176	4.0	40,500	51.6	38.9
Scottish Borders	51,242	21,178	41.3	1,250	2.4	28,821	56.2	42.8
Shetland Islands	10,141	1,235	12.2	6,636	65.4	2,269	22.4	13.5
South Ayrshire	55,423	24,574	44.3	3,801	6.9	27,048	48.8	47.5
South Lanarkshire	144,734	56,529	39.1	0	0.0	88,205	60.9	37.4
Stirling	39,923	21,448	53.7	3,958	9.9	16,052	40.2	55.7
West Dunbartonshire	36,206	15,933	44.0	251	0.7	20,027	55.3	44.1
West Lothian	70,592	31,290	44.3	640	0.9	38,539	54.6	43.0
TOTAL SCOTLAND	**2,412,706**	**1,018,208**	**42.2**	**104,366**	**4.3**	**1,290,829**	**53.5**	**41.2**

Source: Scottish Environment Protection Agency

[1] All the figures are calculated according to the   Zero Waste Plan - guidance for local authorities

[2] Household waste is waste generated by households (see full definition in par 1.2 of the Zero Waste Plan - guidance for local authorities).

[3] Other waste diverted from landfill is the fate of waste material not reused, recycled or landfilled. It includes household waste treated by incineration, mechanical biological and heat treatment. It also includes any Incinerator Bottom Ash and Metals recycled as a result of treatment, and excludes the residue from incineration which is landfilled. It also includes any weight loss during the treatment process. It does not include temporary storage of treated waste pending a recycling or disposal market.

[4] Includes household waste disposed of instead of being recycled and residues from incineration that are landfilled.

* Treated waste sent to interim storage pending a recycling or disposal market. More waste will be recorded as generated than managed.

** Treated waste sent from interim storage to final recycling or disposal. More waste will be recorded as managed than generated.

Please note local authorities report the management of waste in the same period when that waste is collected to avoid discrepancies with the total waste generated and managed. The figures are accurate at the time of publication. However the data may be updated if further revisions are necessary.

10.19d Municipal waste sent for recycling & composting, KPI(e), and landfilled, KPI(f), for Northern Ireland, 2012/13

	KPI(j)						KPI(e)		KPI(f)				
Area	LAC municipal waste arisings (tonnes)	LAC municipal dry recycling (tonnes)	LAC municipal composting (tonnes)	Total LAC municipal dry recycling & composting (tonnes)	LAC municipal dry recycling rate	LAC municipal composting rate	LAC municipal waste sent for recycling (inc composting) as a % of LAC municipal waste arisings	LAC municipal waste landfilled (tonnes)	LAC municipal waste landfilled as a % of total LAC municipal waste arisings	LAC municipal waste energy recovery (mixed residual LACMW) (tonnes)	LAC municipal waste energy recovery (specific streams e.g. wood) (tonnes)	LAC municipal waste preparing for reuse (tonnes)	LAC municipal waste unclassified (tonnes)
arc21													
Antrim	33,091	9,657	8,096	17,753	29.2%	24.5%	53.6%	14,596	44.1%	175	369	92	106
Ards	41,712	6,702	8,140	14,842	16.1%	19.5%	35.6%	25,883	62.1%	196	783	7	1
Ballymena	30,315	6,171	7,291	13,462	20.4%	24.1%	44.4%	16,704	55.1%	0	147	2	0
Belfast	144,497	27,770	15,220	42,990	19.2%	10.5%	29.8%	82,998	57.4%	13,820	19	77	4,593
Carrickfergus	21,470	5,307	3,446	8,753	24.7%	16.1%	40.8%	12,557	58.5%	0	159	0	0
Castlereagh	29,463	5,827	6,215	12,042	19.8%	21.1%	40.9%	16,946	57.5%	84	213	16	161
Down	33,607	6,559	4,201	10,760	19.5%	12.5%	32.0%	22,066	65.7%	162	618	0	0
Larne	19,935	6,699	3,828	10,528	33.6%	19.2%	52.8%	8,157	40.9%	709	469	23	48
Lisburn	55,806	10,149	10,963	21,112	18.2%	19.6%	37.8%	32,770	58.7%	605	1,064	48	207
Newtownabbey	44,323	9,748	9,197	18,945	22.0%	20.7%	42.7%	23,133	52.2%	1,168	858	0	219
North Down	48,503	12,113	9,242	21,355	25.0%	19.1%	44.0%	25,947	53.5%	214	821	166	1
All arc21	**502,722**	**106,703**	**85,840**	**192,543**	**21.2%**	**17.1%**	**38.3%**	**281,758**	**56.0%**	**17,133**	**5,520**	**432**	**5,337**
NWRWMG													
Ballymoney	14,655	2,810	1,997	4,808	19.2%	13.6%	32.8%	9,336	63.7%	306	206	0	0
Coleraine	33,434	8,196	4,036	12,232	24.5%	12.1%	36.6%	17,702	52.9%	2,918	583	0	0
Derry	54,211	13,812	1,423	15,235	25.5%	2.6%	28.1%	26,087	48.1%	10,301	2,520	0	68
Limavady	16,296	5,207	1,665	6,872	32.0%	10.2%	42.2%	7,272	44.6%	1,880	137	134	1
Magherafelt	23,638	7,255	5,853	13,107	30.7%	24.8%	55.4%	6,098	25.8%	3,951	481	0	1
Moyle	9,272	2,276	1,141	3,418	24.5%	12.3%	36.9%	5,489	59.2%	176	190	0	0
Strabane	17,590	4,105	877	4,982	23.3%	5.0%	28.3%	10,720	60.9%	1,144	643	0	101
All NWRWMG	**169,097**	**43,661**	**16,992**	**60,653**	**25.8%**	**10.0%**	**35.9%**	**82,705**	**48.9%**	**20,675**	**4,760**	**134**	**170**
SWaMP2008													
Armagh	27,001	6,453	4,610	11,063	23.9%	17.1%	41.0%	14,693	54.4%	1,083	4	78	81
Banbridge	25,545	5,967	8,094	14,061	23.4%	31.7%	55.0%	10,511	41.1%	738	183	0	52
Cookstown	19,301	4,519	3,521	8,040	23.4%	18.2%	41.7%	10,832	56.1%	352	55	0	21
Craigavon	45,284	13,685	7,370	21,055	30.2%	16.3%	46.5%	14,376	31.7%	9,332	70	11	441
Dungannon	28,351	6,559	4,830	11,389	23.1%	17.0%	40.2%	15,392	54.3%	1,462	73	2	33
Fermanagh	27,335	7,804	2,317	10,121	28.5%	8.5%	37.0%	16,748	61.3%	204	126	77	59
Newry & Mourne	45,285	9,447	5,536	14,983	20.9%	12.2%	33.1%	29,540	65.2%	631	0	0	131
Omagh	23,626	6,365	3,690	10,054	26.9%	15.6%	42.6%	12,883	54.5%	282	360	0	46
All SWaMP2008	**241,728**	**60,799**	**39,966**	**100,765**	**25.2%**	**16.5%**	**41.7%**	**124,975**	**51.7%**	**14,084**	**871**	**168**	**865**
Northern Ireland	**913,546**	**211,163**	**142,798**	**353,961**	**23.1%**	**15.6%**	**38.7%**	**489,437**	**53.6%**	**51,892**	**11,151**	**734**	**6,372**

Source: NIEA

Note: Rates calculated by dividing total tonnage of LAC municipal waste sent for recycling, composting and landfill by total LAC municipal waste arisings.

Note: Unclassified waste is calculated as a residual amount of municipal waste after municipal waste sent to landfill, sent for recycling (including composting), sent for energy recovery and preparing for reuse have been accounted for, instead of being extracted directly from the WasteDataFlow system. The majority of the total unclassified tonnage can be attributed to moisture and/or gaseous losses.

Note: The sum of the tonnages for recycling and composting, landfill, energy recovery, preparing for reuse and unclassified may not equal waste arisings due to rounding.

10.19d Household waste sent for recycling and composting, KPI(a), for Northern Ireland, 2012/13

Area	Household waste arisings (tonnes)	Household dry recycling (tonnes)	Household composting (tonnes)	Total household dry recyling & composting (tonnes)	Household dry recycling rate	Household composting rate	KPI (a) Household waste sent for recycling (inc composting) as a % of household waste arisings
arc21							
Antrim	27,679	5,533	8,096	13,628	20.0%	29.2%	49.2%
Ards	38,637	6,454	8,140	14,594	16.7%	21.1%	37.8%
Ballymena	27,379	4,861	7,291	12,152	17.8%	26.6%	44.4%
Belfast	117,750	25,452	14,633	40,085	21.6%	12.4%	34.0%
Carrickfergus	17,819	3,420	3,446	6,866	19.2%	19.3%	38.5%
Castlereagh	27,626	5,032	6,214	11,246	18.2%	22.5%	40.7%
Down	31,511	6,408	4,135	10,543	20.3%	13.1%	33.5%
Larne	17,018	4,685	3,828	8,514	27.5%	22.5%	50.0%
Lisburn	50,408	8,182	10,963	19,144	16.2%	21.7%	38.0%
Newtownabbey	39,210	8,412	9,074	17,486	21.5%	23.1%	44.6%
North Down	39,506	8,202	9,039	17,241	20.8%	22.9%	43.6%
All arc21	**434,544**	**86,640**	**84,860**	**171,500**	**19.9%**	**19.5%**	**39.5%**
NWRWMG							
Ballymoney	13,241	2,418	1,997	4,415	18.3%	15.1%	33.3%
Coleraine	29,477	7,665	4,036	11,701	26.0%	13.7%	39.7%
Derry	47,284	11,245	1,418	12,663	23.8%	3.0%	26.8%
Limavady	14,856	4,051	1,665	5,716	27.3%	11.2%	38.5%
Magherafelt	20,759	5,788	5,853	11,640	27.9%	28.2%	56.1%
Moyle	8,392	2,132	1,141	3,273	25.4%	13.6%	39.0%
Strabane	15,599	3,906	877	4,782	25.0%	5.6%	30.7%
All NWRWMG	**149,607**	**37,204**	**16,987**	**54,190**	**24.9%**	**11.4%**	**36.2%**
SWaMP2008							
Armagh	24,309	5,338	4,526	9,864	22.0%	18.6%	40.6%
Banbridge	23,888	4,769	7,880	12,649	20.0%	33.0%	53.0%
Cookstown	16,915	3,491	3,521	7,011	20.6%	20.8%	41.4%
Craigavon	41,558	12,380	7,282	19,662	29.8%	17.5%	47.3%
Dungannon	26,726	6,411	4,830	11,241	24.0%	18.1%	42.1%
Fermanagh	24,254	6,113	2,317	8,430	25.2%	9.6%	34.8%
Newry & Mourne	40,026	9,347	5,536	14,883	23.4%	13.8%	37.2%
Omagh	21,797	5,725	3,690	9,415	26.3%	16.9%	43.2%
All SWaMP2008	**219,472**	**53,574**	**39,582**	**93,156**	**24.4%**	**18.0%**	**42.4%**
Northern Ireland	**803,624**	**177,418**	**141,428**	**318,846**	**22.1%**	**17.6%**	**39.7%**

Source: NIEA

Note: Rates calculated by dividing total tonnage of household waste sent for recycling and composting by total household waste arisings.

Note: The tonnages of recycled (including composted) and landfilled waste may not always equal the waste arisings because the recycling measures were defined to capture outputs from recovery processes which excludes reuse.

Note: The percentage of recycled (including composted) and landfilled waste may not always equal 100% because the recycling measures were defined to capture outputs from recovery processes which excludes reuse.

10.19d: Household waste landfilled, KPI(b), and generated per household, KPI(h), and per capita, KPI(p), in Northern Ireland, 2012/13

Area	KPI (b)		KPI(h)		KPI(p)	
	Household waste landfilled (tonnes)	Household waste landfilled as a % of household waste arisings	Estimated households (March 2013)	Annual household waste collected per household (tonnes)	Population (2012)	Annual household waste collected per capita (kilogrammes)
arc21						
Antrim	13,332	48.2%	20,427	1.355	53,835	514
Ards	23,105	59.8%	31,901	1.211	78,550	492
Ballymena	15,088	55.1%	25,218	1.086	64,551	424
Belfast	63,555	54.0%	121,504	0.969	280,537	420
Carrickfergus	10,793	60.6%	16,285	1.094	39,096	456
Castlereagh	15,921	57.6%	28,070	0.984	67,716	408
Down	20,202	64.1%	26,543	1.187	70,440	447
Larne	7,379	43.4%	13,473	1.263	32,191	529
Lisburn	29,424	58.4%	46,734	1.079	121,687	414
Newtownabbey	19,706	50.3%	34,491	1.137	85,322	460
North Down	21,140	53.5%	33,681	1.173	79,420	497
All arc21	**239,645**	**55.1%**	**398,327**	**1.091**	**973,345**	**446**
NWRWMG						
Ballymoney	8,346	63.0%	11,616	1.140	31,551	420
Coleraine	14,758	50.1%	23,867	1.235	58,993	500
Derry	23,109	48.9%	41,446	1.141	108,586	435
Limavady	7,048	47.4%	12,279	1.210	33,761	440
Magherafelt	5,286	25.5%	15,474	1.342	45,450	457
Moyle	4,768	56.8%	6,775	1.239	17,129	490
Strabane	9,157	58.7%	14,967	1.042	40,033	390
All NWRWMG	**72,471**	**48.4%**	**126,424**	**1.183**	**335,503**	**446**
SWaMP2008						
Armagh	13,308	54.7%	22,127	1.099	60,147	404
Banbridge	10,290	43.1%	18,686	1.278	48,730	490
Cookstown	9,522	56.3%	13,224	1.279	37,411	452
Craigavon	13,004	31.3%	36,478	1.139	94,597	439
Dungannon	14,047	52.6%	20,963	1.275	58,813	454
Fermanagh	15,407	63.5%	23,813	1.019	62,400	389
Newry & Mourne	24,513	61.2%	35,991	1.112	100,858	397
Omagh	11,723	53.8%	18,738	1.163	51,830	421
All SWaMP2008	**111,814**	**50.9%**	**190,020**	**1.155**	**514,786**	**426**
Northern Ireland	**423,931**	**52.8%**	**714,771**	**1.124**	**1,823,634**	**441**

Source: NIEA, NISRA, DSD

Note: Rates calculated by dividing total tonnage of household waste sent to landfill by total household waste arisings.

10.20a Amounts of different materials from household sources collected for recycling (including reuse) by collection method 2012/13, England

(Thousand tonnes)

2012/13	Paper & Card	Glass	Compost	Scrap & White Goods	Textiles	Cans	Plastic	Co-mingled	Other	Total
Kerbside	789.6	334.9	2924.9	12.6	13.8	45.9	57.7	2,581.1	17.9	6,778.3
Bring site collection	91.1	185.2	5.2	1.7	47.5	4.3	8.5	18.7	6.9	369.0
Civic amenity site collection	191.5	38.5	957.0	437.8	48.6	8.1	31.9	4.3	676.0	2,393.6
Private/voluntary collection schemes*	0.1	0.1	33.5	0.0	-	0.0	0.1	0.8	97.6	132.2
Total	**1,072.2**	**558.7**	**3,920.6**	**452.0**	**109.8**	**58.3**	**98.1**	**2,604.9**	**798.4**	**9,673.0**

Sources: WasteDataFlow, Department for Environment Food and Rural affairs

1.* Based on Includes street sweepings, street recycling bins, gully waste, community skips and household green waste collected by private/voluntary schemes

2 Total amount of household waste collected for recycling is greater than the amount collected and sent for recycling as some material is subsequently rejected during sorting or by the reprocessor.

10.20b Total Houshold recycling by material and source, Wales

Materials	Kerbside collection (tonnes)						
	2006-07	2007-08	2008-09	2009-10	2010-11	2011-12	2012-13
All paper and Card	69,581.5	84,592.8	61,161.1	60,908.1	58,790.1	59670.6	57119.0
Ferrous food & beverage cans (1)	5,857.0	7,808.7	7,083.2	6,193.9	5,846.2	5927.8	5670.9
Food (5)	0.0	0.0	0.0	15,957.1	35,486.5	62216.1	76347.4
Garden waste (2)	63,409.7	85,402.8	107,069.8	118,959.4	138,226.2	137393.0	131374.4
Glass	28,052.1	36,709.5	33,393.1	32,321.5	29,956.7	30280.5	35466.6
Miscellaneous	24,201.4	28,276.3	78,314.4	102,333.6	119,930.2	132460.5	146728.9
Non-ferrous metal	321.3	888.4	486.4	393.7	564.2	752.8	926.4
Other ferrous metal (3)	750.7	559.8	50.1	78.6	67.0	82.2	144.9
Plastics	9,569.5	12,740.8	9,105.2	8,094.2	11,267.0	13663.1	14012.5
Textiles and shoes	807.2	725.7	726.1	622.7	631.1	690.5	776.7
WEEE (4)	1,723.9	1,690.1	1,532.6	1,340.5	1,466.6	356.4	252.3
Wood	423.6	574.1	69.2	9.1	124.8	318.6	110.1
TOTAL	204,697.7	259,969.0	298,991.2	347,212.4	402,356.7	443812.1	468930.0

Materials	Bring and Civic Amenity sites (tonnes)						
	2006-07	2007-08	2008-09	2009-10	2010-11	2011-12	2012-13
All paper and Card	33,116.0	32,994.4	31,282.1	28,596.9	24,816.0	22154.5	20782.4
Ferrous food & beverage cans (1)	1,323.2	884.5	753.6	843.5	748.2	559.3	422.9
Food (5)	0.0	0.0	0.0	0.0	275.9	0.0	148.5
Garden waste (2)	61,864.9	62,988.0	63,381.3	61,667.5	58,991.5	56222.8	55275.4
Glass	18,815.5	20,613.1	20,283.4	19,256.6	17,213.5	16366.0	13495.8
Miscellaneous	6,235.5	18,033.3	10,227.8	15,675.3	15,694.2	92309.3	92984.1
Non-ferrous metal	52.2	70.8	61.3	141.2	26.3	56.5	24.3
Other ferrous metal (3)	23,078.6	21,460.4	17,076.9	16,895.6	16,110.8	14411.0	13495.6
Plastics	3,855.9	3,844.6	4,390.6	4,499.5	5,240.5	5678.1	5486.6
Textiles and shoes	3,876.9	4,292.6	4,771.4	5,323.1	5,484.8	5615.8	4024.4
WEEE (4)	13,484.0	17,016.0	19,627.8	21,539.1	21,558.4	18451.1	17309.3
Wood	39,696.3	46,557.9	53,673.2	52,615.6	53,621.0	54471.0	54074.4
TOTAL	205,398.9	228,755.6	225,529.4	227,054.0	219,780.9	286295.5	277523.7

Materials	Total Kerbside, Bring and Civic Amenity sites (tonnes)						
	2006-07	2007-08	2008-09	2009-10	2010-11	2011-12	2012-13
All paper and Card	102,697.5	117,587.2	92,443.2	89,505.0	83,606.1	81825.2	77901.4
Ferrous food & beverage cans (1)	7,180.2	8,693.2	7,836.8	7,037.4	6,594.4	6487.1	6093.8
Food (5)	0.0	0.0	0.0	15,957.1	35,762.5	62216.1	76495.9
Garden waste (2)	125,274.6	148,390.9	170,451.2	180,626.9	197,217.7	193615.8	186649.8
Glass	46,867.6	57,322.6	53,676.5	51,578.1	47,170.1	46646.6	48962.5
Miscellaneous	30,436.9	46,309.5	88,542.2	118,008.9	135,624.4	224769.8	239713.0
Non-ferrous metal	373.4	959.3	547.7	535.0	590.5	809.3	950.6
Other ferrous metal (3)	23,829.3	22,020.2	17,127.0	16,974.2	16,177.8	14493.1	13640.5
Plastics	13,425.3	16,585.4	13,495.8	12,593.8	16,507.5	19341.2	19499.1
Textiles and shoes	4,684.1	5,018.3	5,497.5	5,945.8	6,115.8	6306.3	4801.1
WEEE (4)	15,207.9	18,706.1	21,160.4	22,879.6	23,025.0	18807.5	17561.6
Wood	40,119.9	47,132.0	53,742.3	52,624.7	53,745.8	54789.7	54184.4
TOTAL	410,096.6	488,724.6	524,520.6	574,266.4	622,137.6	730107.6	746453.7

10.20b Total Houshold recycling by material and source, Wales

Materials	Voluntary/Private collection/Other (tonnes)						
	2006-07	2007-08	2008-09	2009-10	2010-11	2011-12	2012-13
All paper and Card	1,652.6	914.2	297.5	87.1	73.0	44.6	45.8
Ferrous food & beverage cans (1)	242.7	95.2	30.3	0.0	0.0	2.2	2.7
Food (5)	0.0	0.0	0.0	0.0	0.0	0.0	0
Garden waste (2)	3,165.8	6,238.1	5,165.5	7,582.7	863.9	0.0	0
Glass	977.4	328.2	109.1	0.3	0.4	140.3	154.1
Miscellaneous	1,710.8	2,024.7	2,628.3	3,700.9	2,981.3	4565.4	4412.2
Non-ferrous metal	14.2	1.4	0.0	0.0	0.0	0.0	0.0
Other ferrous metal (3)	65.6	9.5	22.1	38.6	2.0	138.4	1.5
Plastics	268.4	123.5	47.0	0.0	0.0	2.3	1.5
Textiles and shoes	385.6	434.2	354.6	519.7	543.0	120.9	158.4
WEEE (4)	198.1	125.3	333.3	206.0	284.7	108.6	177.5
Wood	57.4	21.4	227.2	69.4	398.7	412.2	418.7
TOTAL	8,738.7	10,315.8	9,214.8	12,204.8	5,147.1	5534.9	5372.5

Materials	Total household recycled / composted (tonnes)						
	2006-07	2007-08	2008-09	2009-10	2010-11	2011-12	2012-13
All paper and Card	104,350.1	118,501.5	92,740.6	89,592.0	83,679.1	81869.8	77947.2
Ferrous food & beverage cans (1)	7,422.8	8,788.4	7,867.0	7,037.4	6,594.4	6489.2	6096.4
Food (5)	0.0	0.0	0.0	15,957.1	35,762.5	62216.1	76495.9
Garden waste (2)	128,440.4	154,629.0	175,616.7	188,209.6	198,081.7	193615.8	186649.8
Glass	47,845.0	57,650.8	53,785.6	51,578.4	47,170.5	46786.8	49116.6
Miscellaneous	32,147.7	48,334.2	91,170.5	121,709.8	138,605.8	229335.2	244125.2
Non-ferrous metal	387.7	960.7	547.7	535.0	590.5	809.3	950.6
Other ferrous metal (3)	23,894.9	22,029.7	17,149.0	17,012.8	16,179.8	14631.5	13642.0
Plastics	13,693.7	16,708.9	13,542.8	12,593.8	16,507.5	19343.6	19500.6
Textiles and shoes	5,069.8	5,452.5	5,852.0	6,465.6	6,658.9	6427.2	4959.5
WEEE (4)	15,406.0	18,831.3	21,493.8	23,085.6	23,309.7	18916.1	17739.2
Wood	40,177.3	47,153.5	53,969.6	52,694.2	54,144.5	55201.9	54603.1
TOTAL	418,835.3	499,040.4	533,735.3	586,471.2	627,284.7	735642.5	751826.2

Source: WasteDataFlow, Natural Resources Wales

1. Includes mixed cans

2. Includes mixed food and garden waste

3. Includes scrap metal

4. Waste Electronic and Electrical Equipment

5. food waste that is separately collected only

10.20c Waste Collections in Scotland - Kerbside Collections 2013

Tonnage collected

Kerbside Collection	Collected for Recycling	Collected for Reuse
Green glass	7109.01	0
Brown glass	2256.66	0
Mixed glass	21972.423	0
Paper	18270.14	0
Card	5324.67	0
Books	0	0
Mixed paper & card	34331.18	0
Steel cans	737.37	0
Aluminium cans	181.11	0
Mixed cans	811.12	0
Plastics	796.78	0
Mixed Plastic Bottles	1178.97	0
PET [1]	0	0
HDPE [2]	0	0
PVC [3]	0	0
LDPE [4]	0	0
PP [5]	0	0
PS [6]	0	0
OTHER PLASTICS [7]	471.31	0
Waste food only	24319.11	0
Mixed garden and food waste	86842.03	0
Wood for Composting	0	0
Other compostable waste	0	0
Wood	433.97	0
Chipboard and mdf	0	0
Composite wood materials	1118.89	0
WEEE - Large Domestic App	33.65	0
WEEE - Small Domestic App	240.24	0
WEEE - Cathode Ray Tubes	0	0
WEEE - Flourescent tubes and other light bulbs	0	0
WEEE - Fridges & Freezers	577.52	2.77
Other Scrap metal	417.89	0
Automotive batteries	0	0
Post consumer, non automotive batteries	6.557	0
Car tyres	0	0
Van tyres	0	0
Large vehicle tyres	0	0
Mixed tyres	0	0
Furniture	400.13	1036.91
Rubble	0	0
Soil	17.66	0
Plasterboard	0	0
Vegetable Oil	0	0
Mineral Oil	0	0
Aluminium foil	0	0
Aerosols	0	0
Bric-a-brac	53.77	0
Composite food and beverage cartons	0	0
Fire extinguishers	0	0
Gas bottles	0	0
Ink & toner cartridges	0	0
Mattresses	0	752.11
Paint	0	0
Textiles & footwear	147.74	84.37
Video tapes, DVDs and CDs	0	0
Yellow Pages	0	0
Other materials	0	0
Bicycles	0	0
Co mingled materials	202399.464	0
Absorbent Hygiene Products (AHP)	20.84	0
Carpets	0	0

Source: WasteDataFlow, Scottish Environment Protection Agency
Data is subject to change. Only included for the selected authorities and periods if returns have been completed.

10.20c Waste Collections in Scotland - Civic Amenity Site Collections 2013

Civic Amenity Site Collection	Tonnage collected	
	Collected for Recycling	Collected for Reuse
Green glass	432.617	0
Brown glass	223.61	0
Clear glass	467.26	0
Mixed glass	393.91	0
Plasterboard	430.24	0
Wood for composting	0	0
Paper	735.66	0
Card	3892.91	0
Books	32.74	4.89
Mixed paper & card	593.71	0
Steel cans	0	0
Aluminium cans	14.30	0
Mixed cans	218.99	0
Plastics	311.31	0
Mixed Plastic Bottles	201.16	0
PET [1]	0	0
HDPE [2]	0	0
PVC [3]	0	0
LDPE [4]	0	0
PP [5]	0	0
PS [6]	0	0
OTHER PLASTICS [7]	52.78	0
Green garden waste only	29823.73	0
Waste food only	0	0
Mixed garden and food waste	0	0
Other compostable waste	466.26	0
Wood	23234.85	0
Chipboard and mdf	5191.98	0
Composite wood materials	0	0
WEEE - Large Domestic App	3006.60	0
WEEE - Small Domestic App	4316.84	0
WEEE - Cathode Ray Tubes	2957.245	0
WEEE - Flourescent tubes and other light bulbs	16.39	0
WEEE - Fridges & Freezers	2539.37	32.02
Other Scrap metal	10526.442	0
Automotive batteries	146.23	0
Post consumer, non automotive batteries	23.24	0
Car tyres	86.46	0
Van tyres	0	0
Large vehicle tyres	0	0
Mixed tyres	481.81	0
Furniture	141.03	30.737
Rubble	32170.7	0.00
Soil	4804.81	0
Vegetable Oil	49.21	0
Mineral Oil	306.11	0
Aluminium foil	0	0
Aerosols	0	0
Bric-a-brac	22.29	0
Composite food and beverage cartons	24.05	0
Fire extinguishers	0	0
Gas bottles	41.45	18.93
Ink & toner cartridges	0	0
Mattresses	270.38	0
Paint	40.99	0
Textiles & footwear	1027.606	144.29
Video tapes, DVDs and CDs	2.54	0
Yellow Pages	0	0
Other materials	0	0
Bicycles	30.03	18.50
Co mingled materials	3949.34	0
Absorbent Hygiene Products (AHP)	0	0
Carpets	465.09	0

Source: WasteDataFlow, Scottish Environment Protection Agency

Data is subject to change. Only included for the selected authorities and periods if returns have been completed.

10.20c Waste Collections in Scotland- Bring Site Collections 2013

Bring Site Collection	Collected for Recycling	Tonnage collected Collected for Reuse
Green glass	4212.422	0
Brown glass	1753.625	0
Clear glass	4446.02	0
Mixed glass	3050.75	0
Paper	3181.717	0
Card	867.97	0
Books	106.70	9.56
Mixed paper & card	2579.26	0
Steel cans	199.88	0
Aluminium cans	119.74	0
Mixed cans	99.28	0
Plastics	0.00	0
Mixed Plastic Bottles	344.28	0
PET [1]	0	0
HDPE [2]	0	0
PVC [3]	0	0
LDPE [4]	0	0
PP [5]	0	0
PS [6]	0	0
OTHER PLASTICS [7]	1.74	0
Green garden waste only	1030.30	0
Waste food only	90.34	0
Mixed garden and food waste	0	0
Wood for composting	316.32	0
Other compostable waste	0.00	0
Wood	329.42	0
Chipboard and mdf	0	0
Composite wood materials	0	0
WEEE - Large Domestic App	181.25	0
WEEE - Small Domestic App	170.45	0
WEEE - Cathode Ray Tubes	126.29	0
WEEE - Flourescent tubes and other light bulbs	1.197	0
WEEE - Fridges & Freezers	95.01	0
Other Scrap metal	268.62	0
Automotive batteries	5.76	0
Post consumer, non automotive batteries	4.739	0
Car tyres	0	0
Van tyres	0	0
Large vehicle tyres	0	0
Mixed tyres	0	0
Furniture	0	0
Rubble	475.03	0
Soil	317.76	0
Plasterboard	0	0
Vegetable Oil	3.65	0
Mineral Oil	7.83	0
Aluminium foil	0	0
Aerosols	0	0
Bric-a-brac	0	0
Composite food and beverage cartons	18.476	0
Fire extinguishers	0	0
Gas bottles	0.00	0
Ink & toner cartridges	0	0
Mattresses	0	0
Paint	0	0
Textiles & footwear	3423.121	117.69
Video tapes, DVDs and CDs	0	0
Yellow Pages	0	0
Other materials	0	0
Bicycles	0	0
Co mingled materials	998.63	0
Absorbent Hygiene Products (AHP)	0	0
Carpets	0	0

Source: WasteDataFlow, Scottish Environment Protection Agency

Data is subject to change. Only included for the selected authorities and periods if returns have been completed.

10.20d Material types collected for recycling (inc composting) at kerbside in Northern Ireland, 2012/13

Unit: Tonnes

Area	Glass	Metal	Paper and card	Plastic	Compostable (excluding all wood)	Electrical Goods	Construction, Demolition and Excavation	Textiles	Wood	Unclassified	All recycled materials
arc21											
Antrim	0	107	1,771	182	3,794	0	0	0	0	0	5,855
Ards	0	187	3,085	318	5,667	0	0	0	0	0	9,257
Ballymena	896	270	1,953	415	5,931	1	0	15	0	1	9,483
Belfast	1,263	567	8,438	1,051	11,425	0	0	16	26	3	22,790
Carrickfergus	714	119	1,009	210	2,988	1	0	10	0	0	5,051
Castlereagh	814	218	2,088	336	5,239	58	0	11	0	0	8,764
Down	0	149	2,476	255	2,799	0	0	0	0	0	5,679
Larne	464	77	1,331	131	2,524	0	0	0	0	0	4,527
Lisburn	0	256	4,252	437	9,358	0	0	0	0	0	14,304
Newtownabbey	1,483	252	2,449	661	6,775	2	0	23	0	0	11,646
North Down	0	202	3,413	346	5,930	0	0	0	0	0	9,891
All arc21	5,635	2,404	32,266	4,343	62,430	63	0	75	26	5	107,245
NWRWMG											
Ballymoney	258	64	1,099	218	1,094	0	0	4	0	253	2,990
Coleraine	824	157	2,151	482	0	1	0	8	0	512	4,136
Derry	1,032	461	4,427	750	0	8	0	22	0	610	7,311
Limavady	380	114	1,247	184	755	0	0	5	0	256	2,941
Magherafelt	506	118	1,753	323	3,753	0	0	0	0	114	6,567
Moyle	241	38	585	143	568	0	0	2	0	163	1,740
Strabane	238	117	1,727	341	0	1	0	2	0	198	2,625
All NWRWMG	3,478	1,069	12,989	2,441	6,170	11	0	43	0	2,107	28,309
SWaMP2008											
Armagh	911	158	1,308	304	3,233	2	0	0	0	0	5,916
Banbridge	924	91	1,559	396	5,944	0	0	0	0	52	8,965
Cookstown	57	139	1,492	330	1,253	2	0	60	0	0	3,333
Craigavon	244	200	3,424	615	4,492	0	0	0	0	432	9,407
Dungannon	180	231	2,441	518	2,400	2	0	3	0	0	5,775
Fermanagh	714	173	3,013	1,041	0	0	0	0	0	66	5,006
Newry & Mourne	1,427	149	3,562	498	3,249	3	0	7	3	432	9,329
Omagh	240	214	2,211	513	2,045	2	0	10	0	0	5,235
All SWaMP2008	4,697	1,354	19,010	4,215	22,617	11	0	80	3	982	52,968
Northern Ireland	13,809	4,827	64,265	10,998	91,216	85	0	198	29	3,094	188,521

Source: NIEA

10.20d Material types collected for recycling (inc composting) at bring sites in Northern Ireland, 2012/13

Unit: Tonnes

Area	Glass	Metal	Paper and card	Plastic	Compostable (excluding all wood)	Electrical Goods	Construction, Demolition and Excavation	Textiles	Wood	Unclassified	All recycled materials collected
arc21											
Antrim	87	3	1	0	0	0	0	6	0	0	97
Ards	632	1	0	0	0	0	0	20	0	0	653
Ballymena	103	4	39	0	0	0	0	25	0	0	171
Belfast	774	2	130	0	0	0	0	1,335	0	0	2,241
Carrickfergus	81	2	121	0	0	0	0	0	0	0	204
Castlereagh	174	2	9	1	0	0	0	17	0	0	202
Down	728	2	1	0	0	0	0	15	0	0	746
Larne	127	1	0	0	0	0	0	15	0	0	144
Lisburn	527	0	9	0	0	0	0	17	0	0	554
Newtownabbey	53	1	7	0	0	0	0	21	0	0	82
North Down	710	1	14	0	0	0	0	15	0	0	740
All arc21	3,996	19	332	1	0	0	0	1,485	0	0	5,832
NWRWMG											
Ballymoney	81	0	5	0	0	0	0	12	0	0	99
Coleraine	94	2	19	0	0	0	0	25	0	0	139
Derry	123	2	0	0	0	0	0	11	0	0	136
Limavady	158	0	0	0	0	0	0	14	0	0	172
Magherafelt	19	0	0	0	0	0	0	18	0	0	38
Moyle	64	0	0	0	0	0	0	32	0	0	97
Strabane	292	7	52	0	0	0	0	24	0	0	375
All NWRWMG	831	12	76	0	0	0	0	137	0	0	1,055
SWaMP2008											
Armagh	34	1	0	1	0	0	0	0	0	0	36
Banbridge	0	0	0	0	0	0	0	58	0	0	59
Cookstown	200	2	5	0	0	0	0	28	0	0	236
Craigavon	414	1	0	0	0	0	0	50	0	0	465
Dungannon	228	0	0	0	0	0	0	33	0	0	261
Fermanagh	356	1	0	0	0	0	0	0	0	0	357
Newry & Mourne	397	7	33	0	0	0	0	73	0	0	510
Omagh	212	1	1	0	0	0	0	28	0	0	242
All SWaMP2008	1,841	13	40	1	0	0	0	271	0	0	2,165
Northern Ireland	6,668	43	447	2	0	0	0	1,893	0	0	9,052

Source: NIEA

10.20d Material types collected for recycling (inc composting) at civic amenity sites in Northern Ireland, 2012/13

Unit: Tonnes

Area	Glass	Metal	Paper and card	Plastic	Compostable (excluding all wood)	Electrical Goods	Construction, Demolition and Excavation	Textiles	Wood	Unclassified	All recycled materials collected
arc21											
Antrim	280	324	204	44	4,301	510	4,058	70	1,505	99	11,396
Ards	432	388	215	0	2,473	773	0	52	1,080	128	5,540
Ballymena	0	169	195	0	1,361	346	948	0	580	17	3,615
Belfast	1,150	852	910	94	3,288	1,449	36	204	3,838	215	12,034
Carrickfergus	11	132	58	0	458	251	1,887	0	800	60	3,658
Castlereagh	181	185	263	8	976	313	788	33	418	59	3,225
Down	229	233	95	0	1,336	499	0	25	671	61	3,149
Larne	81	246	214	4	1,305	371	1,385	32	766	77	4,480
Lisburn	271	399	181	42	1,604	844	1,916	69	1,330	161	6,818
Newtownabbey	86	390	360	50	2,299	639	878	51	1,071	87	5,912
North Down	403	502	269	94	3,174	724	3,495	75	2,016	104	10,856
All arc21	**3,124**	**3,822**	**2,964**	**336**	**22,576**	**6,719**	**15,390**	**610**	**14,075**	**1,066**	**70,683**
NWRWMG											
Ballymoney	27	88	62	0	904	162	366	12	273	37	1,932
Coleraine	105	222	165	0	4,036	431	0	41	834	85	5,918
Derry	189	337	449	0	1,575	797	2,009	42	942	351	6,692
Limavady	38	51	349	124	910	190	1,050	16	279	48	3,055
Magherafelt	122	135	207	18	2,099	283	1,101	24	535	92	4,615
Moyle	5	50	0	0	573	84	9	3	125	24	874
Strabane	70	75	34	0	877	176	21	11	430	57	1,751
All NWRWMG	**556**	**958**	**1,266**	**142**	**10,974**	**2,123**	**4,556**	**149**	**3,417**	**695**	**24,837**
SWaMP2008											
Armagh	156	231	579	63	1,293	306	1,032	0	728	64	4,453
Banbridge	278	211	490	88	2,069	362	1,028	46	299	45	4,916
Cookstown	81	130	196	70	1,845	217	925	33	423	324	4,243
Craigavon	212	433	258	243	2,790	742	584	66	1,128	125	6,581
Dungannon	143	191	185	74	2,429	316	45	33	780	62	4,258
Fermanagh	7	249	2	281	2,317	421	14	49	803	531	4,672
Newry & Mourne	248	334	469	96	2,287	553	6	51	897	117	5,058
Omagh	162	252	458	130	1,644	375	614	57	625	347	4,663
All SWaMP2008	**1,287**	**2,029**	**2,637**	**1,045**	**16,675**	**3,293**	**4,248**	**334**	**5,682**	**1,613**	**38,844**
Northern Ireland	**4,967**	**6,810**	**6,867**	**1,524**	**50,226**	**12,135**	**24,195**	**1,092**	**23,175**	**3,374**	**134,364**

Source: NIEA

10.21 CIEH Survey of Local Authority Noise Enforcement Activity 2012-13

England and Wales Data represents 159 (46%) of 348 local authorities

	INDUSTRY		COMMERCE / LEISURE			RESIDENTIAL			CONSTRUCTION ETC	VME's	TOTAL'S	
	Agricultural Premises	Industrial / Warehousing / Distribution Premises	"On"-licensed Premises e.g. Pubs, Clubs, Restaurants	Commercial Premises e.g. Offices, Shops, Public transport	Leisure Premises e.g. Sports Facilities, Funfairs	Single Family House / Bungalow	Flats / Maisonettes	Other Residential e.g. Hostels, HMOs, Boarding Schools	Construction / Demolition Sites	Vehicles, Machinery and Equipment in Streets	SUM OF COLUMNS [4]	TOTAL OF ALL COMPLAINTS [5]
COMPLAINTS												
Number of Noise Complaints Received in Year	1,054	2,307	10,579	8,503	3,151	85,977	32,203	4,152	6,799	8,111	162,836	194,501
Number of Noise Complaints Resolved in Year	890	1,890	8,305	7,405	2,502	73,640	22,436	3,568	5,865	6,864	133,365	158,095
Number of Noise Incidents Complained-of	839	1,705	7,823	6,640	2,519	70,915	23,657	3,280	4,904	5,882	128,164	142,993
Number of Noise Incidents Per Million Population	57	82	358	313	123	3,252	1,180	185	229	270	6,049	6,291
Incidents Confirmed as Potentially Actionable [1,2]	245	627	2,752	2,441	746	25,674	7,642	927	1,601	1,120	43,775	
STATUTORY NUISANCES REMEDIED WITHOUT A NOTICE [3,6]												
Nuisance Ceased and Not Likely to Recur	28	95	329	320	128	3,420	580	61	171	141	5,273	
Referred to Other Services	13	15	74	73	34	388	179	11	24	33	844	
Resolved Informally	52	136	534	630	160	3,894	1,228	120	371	127	7,252	
No Action Possible	27	77	378	282	120	3,164	1,121	54	146	164	5,533	
NOTICES SERVED [6]												
S.80 EPA 1990 Abatement Notice	2	22	253	140	27	1,613	687	223	31	150	3,148	8,931
S.60 & S.61 CoPA 1974 Control of Construction Noise									990	2	992	1,026
Noise Act 1996 Warning Notice			3			134	20	98			255	258
Noise Act 1996 Fixed Penalty							2	9			11	11
S.80(4A) EPA 1990 Fixed Penalty (Lond)		1		1		2			1		5	27
APPEALS AGAINST NOTICES [6]												
Number of Appeals Allowed in Whole or in Part			3		1	1					5	
PROSECUTIONS BEGUN [6]												
Breach of Abatement Notice			37	14	2	197	112		4	6	372	1,108
Breach of Restriction on, or Prior Consent for, Construction Noise									12		12	35
Noise Act 1996											0	
Convictions Gained			12	2	7	82	42		6		151	
OTHER REMEDIES [6]												
Nuisance Remedied by the LA in Default			1	8	2	85	25	13		44	178	317
Number of Seizures			4	1	1	77	55				138	

[1] Incidents Confirmed as Potentially Actionable includes all those 'triggers' giving rise to formal enforcement power (described previously as "incidents confirmed as statutory nuisances etc")

[2] The sum of actions taken to resolve nuisances may exceed the Incidents Confirmed as Potentially Actionable figure because not all local authorities could provide data on incidents and more than one formal action may be taken to resolve a nuisance

[3] "Nuisances" here means statutory nuisances

[4] The sum of columns value is calculated, information provided by local authorities providing sub-total data only is not included here

[5] The Total of all Complaints column includes noise activity unaccounted for in previous columns

[6] Figures reported from 2005-06 may seem lower than previous years as they have not been subject to a 'grossing' calculation. Before 2005-06, where responding authorities were not able to provide data on the questions concerning outcome of noise incidents, estimates were made by pro-rating on number of noise incidents complained of

Source: Chartered Institute of Environmental Health.
Website: http://www.cieh.org

10.22 Government revenue from environmental taxes in the UK, 2002 to 2013

£ million

Environmental tax	2002	2003	2004	2005	2006	2007	2008	2009	2010	2011	2012	2013
Energy taxes	**23,179**	**23,730**	**24,685**	**24,666**	**24,859**	**26,035**	**26,503**	**27,743**	**29,166**	**29,362**	**30,012**	**31,113**
Tax on Hydrocarbon oils	22,070	22,476	23,412	23,346	23,448	24,512	24,790	25,894	27,013	26,923	26,703	26,697
including												
Unleaded petrol [1,3]	:	:	:	:	:	:	:	:	:	:	:	:
Leaded petrol/LRP [2]	103	69	67	20	15	13	10	9	10	11	9	9
Ultra low sulphur petrol	12,624	12,183	12,160	11,688	11,299	11,314	11,114	11,175	11,001	10,580	10,530	9,926
Diesel [3]	:	:	:	:	:	:	:	:	:	:	:	:
Ultra low sulphur diesel	9,029	9,523	10,168	10,796	11,236	12,131	12,216	12,718	13,923	14,240	15,073	15,422
Climate Change Levy [4]	825	828	756	747	711	690	717	693	666	675	624	1,071
Fossil Fuel Levy	32	:	:	:	:	:	:	:	:	:	:	:
Gas Levy	:	:	:	:	:	:	:	:	:	:	:	:
Hydro-Benefit	44	44	40	10	:	:	:	:	:	:	:	:
Renewable Energy Obligations	208	382	477	563	700	833	996	1,099	1,243	1,423	1,842	2,388
Emmisions Trading Scheme (EU-ETS)	:	:	:	:	:	:	:	57	244	341	257	356
Carbon Reduction Commitment	:	:	:	:	:	:	:	:	:	:	586	601
Transport taxes	**5,261**	**5,662**	**5,824**	**5,756**	**6,096**	**7,526**	**7,704**	**7,944**	**8,742**	**9,434**	**9,930**	**10,348**
Air Passenger Duty	814	781	856	896	961	1,883	1,876	1,800	2,094	2,605	2,766	2,960
Rail Franchise Premia	153	161	205	98	125	244	285	496	792	993	1,275	1,271
Northern Ireland Driver Vehicle Agency	:	:	:	:	:	15	19	18	16	16	16	16
Motor vehicle duties paid by businesses	724	797	808	809	865	878	885	908	937	931	940	977
Motor vehicle duty paid by households	3,570	3,923	3,955	3,953	4,145	4,506	4,639	4,722	4,903	4,889	4,933	5,124
Boat Licenses	:	:	:	:	:	:	:	:	:	:	:	:
Pollution/Resources taxes	**770**	**964**	**1,019**	**1,080**	**1,145**	**1,236**	**1,308**	**1,137**	**1,375**	**1,403**	**1,379**	**1,521**
Landfill Tax	541	607	672	733	804	877	954	842	1,065	1,090	1,094	1,221
Fishing Licenses	16	17	19	20	20	20	20	20	20	23	21	21
Aggregates levy	213	340	328	327	321	339	334	275	290	290	264	279
Total environmental taxes	**29,210**	**30,356**	**31,528**	**31,502**	**32,100**	**34,797**	**35,515**	**36,824**	**39,283**	**40,199**	**41,321**	**42,982**
As a percentage of total taxes and social contributions	7.8	7.7	7.5	7.0	6.6	6.8	6.8	7.6	7.5	7.3	7.4	7.5
As a percentage of Gross Domestic Product (GDP)												
Energy	2.1	2.1	2.0	1.9	1.8	1.8	1.8	2.0	2.0	1.9	1.9	1.9
Transport	0.5	0.5	0.5	0.5	0.5	0.5	0.5	0.6	0.6	0.6	0.6	0.6
Pollution/Resources	0.1	0.1	0.1	0.1	0.1	0.1	0.1	0.1	0.1	0.1	0.1	0.1
Total environmental taxes	2.7	2.6	2.6	2.5	2.4	2.4	2.4	2.6	2.6	2.6	2.7	2.7

Source: ONS; Department for Energy and Climate Change

1 Unleaded petrol includes super unleaded petrol.

2 Lead Replacement Petrol (the alternative to 4-Star petrol introduced in 2000) is lead-free.

3 Duty incentives have concentrated production on ultra low sulphur varieties.

4 Includes Carbon Price Floor from 2013.

The symbol ':' denotes 'not applicable'.

this page is intentionally blank

Housing

Chapter 11

Housing

Permanent dwellings (Table 11.1, 11.3)
Local housing authorities include: the Commission for the New Towns and New Towns Development Corporations; Communities Scotland; and the Northern Ireland Housing Executive. The figures shown for housing associations include dwellings provided by housing associations other than the Communities Scotland and the Northern Ireland Housing Executive and include those provided or authorised by government departments for the families of police, prison staff, the Armed Forces and certain other services.

Mortgage possession actions by region (Table 11.6)
The table shows mortgage possession actions in the county courts of England and Wales and excludes a small number of mortgage actions in the High Court.

A claimant begins an action for an order for possession of a property by issuing a claim in the county court, either by using the Possession Claim Online system or locally through a county court. In mortgage possession cases, the usual procedure is for the claim being issued to be given a hearing date before a district judge. The court, following a judicial hearing, may grant an order for possession immediately. This entitles the claimants to apply for a warrant to have the defendant evicted. However, even where a warrant for possession is issued, the parties can still negotiate a compromise to prevent eviction.

Frequently the court grants the claimant possession but suspends the operation of the order. Provided the defendant complies with the terms of suspension, which usually require the defendant to pay the current mortgage instalments plus some of the accrued arrears, the possession order cannot be enforced.

The mortgage possession figures do not indicate how many houses have actually been repossessed through the courts. Repossessions can occur without a court order being made while not all court orders result in repossession.

A new mortgage pre-action protocol (MPAP), approved by the Master of the Rolls, was introduced for possession claims in the County Courts with effect from 19 November 2008. The MPAP gives clear guidance on what the courts expect lenders and borrowers to have done prior to a claim being issued.

Evidence from administrative records from Qtr4 2008 suggests that this date coincided with a fall of around 50% in the daily and weekly numbers of new mortgage repossession claims being issued in the courts.

It therefore seems highly likely that the launch of the MPAP has led to a fall in the number of new claims being issued since introduction of MPAP (19th November to 31st December 2008). Mortgage possession orders are typically made (where necessary) around 8 weeks after the corresponding claims are issued.

Households in Temporary Accommodation under homelessness provisions (Tables 11.7, 11.8, 11.9)
Comprises households in accommodation arranged by local authorities pending enquiries or after being accepted as owed a main homeless duty under the 1996 Act (includes residual cases awaiting re-housing under the 1985 Act). Excludes "homeless at home" cases. The data shown for Wales includes "homeless at home" cases.

11.1a Dwelling stock: by tenure[1], England

Thousands of dwellings

	Owner Occupied	Rented Privately or with a job or business	Rented from Private Registered Providers	Rented from Local Authorities	Other public sector dwellings	All Dwellings
31 March [3]						
1999	14,408	2,086	1,146	3,178	110	**20,927**
2000	14,600	2,089	1,273	3,012	101	**21,075**
2001	14,735	2,133	1,424	2,812	103	**21,207**
2002	14,846	2,197	1,492	2,706	112	**21,354**
2003 [4]	14,752	2,549	1,651	2,457	104	**21,513**
2004 [4]	14,986	2,578	1,702	2,335	83	**21,684**
2005 [4]	15,100	2,720	1,802	2,166	82	**21,870**
2006 [4]	15,052	2,987	1,865	2,087	82	**22,073**
2007 [4]	15,093	3,182	1,951	1,987	75	**22,288**
2008 [4]	15,067	3,443	2,056	1,870	74	**22,511**
2009 [4]	14,968	3,705	2,128	1,820	74	**22,694**
2010 [4]	14,895	3,912	2,180	1,786	66	**22,839**
2011 [4]	14,827	4,105	2,255	1,726	63	**22,976**
2012 [4] [R]	14,754	4,286	2,304	1,693	75	**23,111**
2013 [4] [R]	14,685	4,465	2,331	1,682	73	**23,236**

Source: Department for Communities and Local Government

Contact: 0303 44 41864

1. For detailed definitions of all tenures, see Definitions of housing terms in Housing Statistics home page.　　E-Mail: housing.statistics@communities.gsi.gov.uk

2. Figures for census years are based on census output.

3. Series from 1992 to 2001 for England has been adjusted so that the 2001 total dwelling estimate matches the 2001 Census.

　Series from 2002 to 2011 for England has been adjusted so that the 2011 total dwelling estimate matches the 2011 Census.

　Estimates from 2002 are based on local authority and Private Registered Provider (housing association) dwelling counts,

　the Labour Force Survey and, from 2003, the English Housing Survey. Estimates may not be strictly comparable between periods.

4. From 2003 the figures for owner-occupied and the private rental sector for England have been produced using a new

　improved methodology as detailed in the dwelling stock release. Previous to this vacancy was not accounted for.

R- Revised from previous publication

P - Provisional

Data for earlier years are less reliable and definitions may not be consistent throughout the series

Stock estimates are expressed to the nearest thousand but should not be regarded as accurate to the last digit Components may not sum to totals due to rounding

11.1b Dwelling stock: by tenure[1,2], Wales

Thousands of dwellings

	Owner Occupied	Rented Privately or with a job or business	Rented from Housing Associations	Rented from Local Authorities	All Dwellings
31 March					
1999 [5]	926	84	52	197	1,259
2000 [5]	914	106	54	193	1,267
2001 [5]	941	90	55	188	1,275
2002 [5]	957	89	57	183	1,285
2003 [5]	966	97	57	176	1,296
2004 [5]	980	103	64	160	1,307
2005 [5]	990	108	65	156	1,319
2006 [5]	998	113	66	154	1,331
2007 [5]	1,002	122	67	153	1,343
2008 [5]	1,001	135	89	130	1,355
2009 [5]	989	157	107	113	1,366
2010 [5]	983	171	110	111	1,375
2011 [5]	980	181	134	89	1,384
2012 [5]	975	191	135	88	1,389
2013 [5]	982	190	135	88	1,394

Source: Welsh Assembly Government

Contact: 0303 44 41864

E-Mail: housing.statistics@communities.gsi.gov.uk

1. For detailed definitions of all tenures, see Definitions of housing terms in Housing Statistics home page.

2. Owner-occupied tenure includes owner-occupied, intermediate and other.

3. April data for census years are based on census output.

4. Data for years 1969 to 1990 sourced from Department of Environment publications:
   Housing and Construction Statistics, 1967-1979, 1977-1987,1980-1990 and 1990-1997.

5. The tenure split between owner-occupied and privately rented dwellings has been calculated from 1997 onwards using information from the Labour Force Survey. These figures were revised in January 2011 following a re-weighting of the Labour Force Survey data.

R - Revised

P - Provisional

These data are produced and published separately by the Welsh Assembly Government, and although the figures in this table are correct at the time of its latest update they may be superseded before the next update.

Data for earlier years are less reliable and definitions may not be consistent throughout the series.

Stock estimates are expressed to the nearest thousand but should not be regarded as accurate to the last digit.

Components may not sum to totals due to rounding.

11.1c Dwelling stock: by tenure[1,2,3,4,5], Scotland

Thousands of dwellings

	Owner Occupied	Rented Privately or with a job or business	Rented from Housing Associations	Rented from Local Authorities	All Dwellings
31 December[4]					
1999	1,435	155	131	583	**2,303**
2000	1,472	155	137	557	**2,322**
31 March[4]					
2001 [R]	1,439	181	139	553	**2,312**
2002 [R]	1,477	179	143	531	**2,329**
2003 [R]	1,505	188	238	416	**2,347**
2004 [R]	1,513	213	251	389	**2,367**
2005 [R]	1,536	225	251	374	**2,387**
2006 [R]	1,559	234	251	362	**2,406**
2007 [R]	1,562	259	261	346	**2,428**
2008 [R]	1,592	259	269	330	**2,451**
2009 [R]	1,590	285	268	326	**2,469**
2010 [R]	1,584	303	272	323	**2,482**
2011 [R]	1,580	320	275	320	**2,495**
2012 [R]	1,545	366	277	319	**2,508**
2013 [R]	1,537	389	277	318	**2,521**

Source: Scottish Government

Contact: 0303 44 41864

E-Mail: housing.statistics@communities.gsi.gov.uk

1. For detailed definitions of all tenures, see Definitions of housing terms in Housing Statistics home page

2. April data for census years are based on census output

3. Data for years 1969 to 1989 sourced from Department of Environment publications:
   Housing and Construction Statistics, 1967-1979, 1977-1987,1980-1990 and 1990-1997.

4. Estimates from 1990 onwards are based on the Census (1991, 2001, 2011), council tax records and exemptions,
   social sector stock counts, and private tenure splits from the Scottish Household Survey and are not strictly comparable
   with earlier figures. These are not all collected for the same timescales and may not be exact counts, even rounded to the nearest thousand.

5. In order to include vacant private sector dwellings in table 107, estimates for vacant private sector stock in the Scottish
   statistics have been apportioned according to the % of occupied dwellings for the private sector tenures.

R- Revised from previous publication

P- Provisional

These data are produced and published separately by the Scottish Government, and although the figures in this table are correct at the time of its latest update they may be superseded before the next update.

Data for earlier years are less reliable and definitions may not be consistent throughout the series. Stock estimates are expressed to the nearest thousand but should not be regarded as accurate to the last digit.Components may not sum to totals due to rounding.

11.1d Dwelling stock: by tenure[1], Northern Ireland

Thousands of dwellings

	Owner Occupied	Rented Privately or with a job or business	Rented from Housing Associations	Rented from Local Authorities	All Dwellings
31 December[3]					
1999	455	32	17	131	**636**
2000	488	37	19	129	**674**
31 March					
2002 [4]	481	47	20	120	**668**
2003 [4]	491	54	21	113	**679**
2004 [4]	501	61	22	100	**684**
2005 [4]	505	68	22	102	**698**
2006 [4]	508	76	23	99	**706**
2007 [4]	523	69	24	97	**713**
2008 [4]	524	83	26	97	**730**
2009 [4]	517	97	28	96	**737**
2010 [4]	521	106	29	96	**752**
2011 [4]	512	121	30	95	**759**
2012 [4]	514	121	31	93	**759**
2013 [4]	510	130	32	92	**763**
2014 [4]	513	130	33	91	**767**

Source: Department for Social Development (NI)
Contact: 0303 44 41864
E-Mail: housing.statistics@communities.gsi.gov.uk

1. For detailed definitions of all tenures, see Definitions of housing terms in Housing Statistics home page

2. April data for census years are based on census output.

3. Data for years 1980 to 1997 sourced from Department of Environment publications: Housing and Construction Statistics, 1980-1990 and 1990-1997.

4. To include estimates for vacant dwellings, stock figures from Northern Ireland Housing Statistics 2013/14 table 1.2 have been apportioned according to the % of occupied dwellings for each of the tenures given in table 1.2

R- Revised from previous publication
P- Provisional

These data are produced and published separately by the Northern Ireland Department for Social Development, and although the figures in this table are correct at the time of its latest update they may be superseded before the next update.

Data for earlier years are less reliable and definitions may not be consistent throughout the series. Stock estimates are expressed to the nearest thousand but should not be regarded as accurate to the last digit.

11.2 Dwelling stock: by tenure1, Great Britain

Thousands of dwellings

	Owner Occupied	Rented Privately or with a job or business	Rented from Housing Associations	Rented from Local Authorities	Other public sector dwellings	All Dwellings
31 December [3]						
1981	11,936	2,288	468	6,388	..	21,077
1982	12,357	2,201	480	6,196	..	21,233
1983	12,740	2,121	497	6,060	..	21,419
1984	13,099	2,040	516	5,959	..	21,615
1985	13,440	1,963	537	5,863	..	21,803
1986	13,790	1,885	551	5,776	..	22,002
1987	13,968	2,139	586	5,599	..	22,293
1988	14,424	2,077	614	5,412	..	22,527
1989	14,832	2,069	652	5,190	..	22,743
1990	15,099	2,123	702	5,015	..	22,940
31 March [3,4]						
1991	15,155	1,990	701	4,966	167	22,979
1992	15,367	2,058	733	4,879	151	23,190
1993	15,523	2,120	811	4,759	153	23,366
1994	15,695	2,184	884	4,634	150	23,546
1995	15,869	2,255	976	4,496	145	23,739
1996	16,013	2,332	1,078	4,369	141	23,931
1997	16,215	2,361	1,132	4,273	132	24,113
1998	16,461	2,367	1,205	4,140	121	24,296
1999	16,734	2,324	1,319	3,983	110	24,469
2000	16,949	2,350	1,458	3,788	101	24,645
2001 R	17,115	2,404	1,618	3,553	103	24,794
2002 R	17,280	2,465	1,692	3,420	112	24,968
2003[5] R	17,223	2,834	1,946	3,049	104	25,156
2004[5] R	17,479	2,894	2,017	2,884	83	25,358
2005[5] R	17,626	3,053	2,118	2,696	82	25,576
2006[5] R	17,609	3,334	2,182	2,603	82	25,810
2007[5] R	17,657	3,563	2,279	2,486	75	26,059
2008[5] R	17,660	3,837	2,414	2,330	74	26,317
2009[5] R	17,547	4,147	2,503	2,259	74	26,529
2010[5] R	17,462	4,386	2,562	2,220	66	26,696
2011[5] R	17,387	4,606	2,664	2,135	63	26,855
2012 R	17,274	4,843	2,716	2,100	75	27,008

1. For detailed definitions of all tenures, see Definitions of housing terms in Housing Statistics home page. 'Other public sector dwellings' figures are currently only available for England.

2. Figures for census years are based on census output

3. Data for years 1969 to 1990 sourced from Department of Environment publications:
   Housing and Construction Statistics, 1967-1979, 1977-1987,1980-1990 and 1990-1997.
   Great Britain totals from 2002 are derived by summing country totals at 31st March.
   For 1991 to 2001 Scotland stock levels from the year before is added into the UK total.

4. Series from 1992 to 2011 for England has been adjusted so that the 2001 and 2011 total dwelling estimate matches the 2001 and 2011 Census.
   Estimates from 2002 are based on local authority and housing association dwelling counts,
   the Labour Force Survey and, from 2003, the English Housing Survey. Estimates may not be strictly comparable between periods.

5. From 2003 the figures for owner-occupied and the private rental sector for England have been produced using a new improved
   methodology as detailed in the dwelling stock release. Previous to this vacancy was not accounted for.

R- Revised from previous publication
P- Provisional

Contact: 0303 44 41864
E-Mail: housing.statistics@Communities.gsi.gov.uk

Source:

Department for Communities and Local Government
Welsh Assembly Government
Scottish Government
Department for Social Development (Northern Ireland)

Data for earlier years are less reliable and definitions
may not be consistent throughout the series
Stock estimates are expressed to the nearest thousand
but should not be regarded as accurate to the last digit
Components may not sum to totals due to rounding

11.3 House building: permanent dwellings completed, by tenure[1] and country[2]

Number of dwellings

	Financial Year	United Kingdom	England	Wales	Scotland	Northern Ireland
All Dwellings	1992-93	178,420	142,460	9,400	18,990	7,560
	1993-94	186,850	147,710	9,870	22,110	7,160
	1994-95	195,580	157,970	9,070	21,810	6,730
	1995-96	197,710	154,600	9,170	24,690	9,250
	1996-97	185,940	146,250	10,090	20,700	8,910
	1997-98	190,760	149,560	8,430	22,590	10,180
	1998-99	178,290	140,260	7,740	20,660	9,640
	1999-00	184,010	141,800	8,710	23,110	10,400
	2000-01	175,370	133,260	8,330	22,110	11,670
	2001-02	174,200	129,870	8,270	22,570	13,490
	2002-03	183,210	137,740	8,310	22,750	14,420
	2003-04	190,590	143,960	8,300	23,820	14,510
	2004-05	206,620	155,890	8,490	26,470	15,770
	2005-06 [3]	214,000	163,400	8,250	24,950	17,410
	2006-07 [3]	219,070	167,680	9,330	24,260	17,800
	2007-08	218,530	170,610	8,660	25,790	13,480
	2008-09	178,790	140,990	7,120	20,950	9,720
	2009-10 R	152,950	119,910	6,170	17,120	9,750
	2010-11 R	137,440	107,870	5,510	16,420	7,640
	2011-12	146,850	118,510	5,580	15,970	6,800
	2012-13	135,510	107,980	5,450	14,060	8,030
Private Enterprise	1992-93	143,980	115,910	6,690	15,620	5,760
	1993-94	146,750	116,050	6,650	18,310	5,730
	1994-95	155,290	125,740	6,300	17,890	5,350
	1995-96	156,540	123,620	6,880	19,200	6,850
	1996-97	153,450	121,170	7,520	17,490	7,270
	1997-98	160,680	127,840	6,490	17,980	8,370
	1998-99	154,560	121,190	6,440	18,780	8,140
	1999-00	160,520	124,470	7,860	19,070	9,120
	2000-01	152,740	116,640	7,390	18,200	10,510
	2001-02	153,580	115,700	7,490	18,310	12,070
	2002-03	164,300	124,460	7,520	18,940	13,390
	2003-04	172,360	130,100	7,860	20,450	13,950
	2004-05	184,500	139,130	7,990	22,440	14,940
	2005-06 [3]	189,700	144,940	7,880	20,250	16,630
	2006-07 [3]	192,170	145,680	8,990	21,030	16,470
	2007-08	189,660	147,170	8,320	21,660	12,510
	2008-09	144,920	113,800	6,430	16,040	8,650
	2009-10 R	117,980	93,030	5,290	11,130	8,530
	2010-11 R	104,770	83,180	4,510	10,690	6,380
	2011-12	109,620	89,120	4,750	10,080	5,680
	2012-13	106,030	84,550	4,710	9,850	6,920
Housing Associations	1992-93	30,010	23,970	2,590	2,600	850
	1993-94	36,580	30,210	3,010	2,820	550
	1994-95	37,240	31,380	2,570	2,790	500
	1995-96	38,170	30,230	2,130	4,780	1,040
	1996-97	30,950	24,630	2,550	2,960	810
	1997-98	28,550	21,400	1,940	4,490	730
	1998-99	22,870	18,890	1,270	1,750	960
	1999-00	23,170	17,270	850	3,960	1,090
	2000-01	22,250	16,430	900	3,800	1,110
	2001-02	20,400	14,100	710	4,200	1,390
	2002-03	18,610	13,080	780	3,720	1,030
	2003-04	18,020	13,670	420	3,370	560
	2004-05	21,990	16,660	480	4,020	830

11.3 House building: permanent dwellings completed, by tenure[1] and country[2]

Number of dwellings

	Financial Year	United Kingdom	England	Wales	Scotland	Northern Ireland
	2005-06 [3]	23,990	18,160	350	4,700	780
	2006-07 [3]	26,650	21,750	350	3,230	1,330
	2007-08	28,630	23,220	340	4,100	970
	2008-09	33,040	26,690	690	4,580	1,070
	2009-10	34,190	26,520	880	5,580	1,210
	2010-11	30,920	23,550	990	5,110	1,270
	2011-12	34,190	27,460	830	4,780	1,120
	2012-13	27,160	22,060	740	3,240	1,110
Local Authorities	1992-93	4,420	2,580	120	770	950
	1993-94	3,530	1,450	210	980	890
	1994-95	3,060	850	200	1,130	880
	1995-96	3,010	760	160	720	1,360
	1996-97	1,540	450	20	240	820
	1997-98	1,520	320	-	110	1,080
	1998-99	870	180	30	120	540
	1999-00	320	60	-	70	190
	2000-01	380	180	50	110	50
	2001-02	230	60	70	70	30
	2002-03	300	200	10	90	-
	2003-04	210	190	20	-	-
	2004-05	130	100	30	-	-
	2005-06 [3]	320	300	20	-	-
	2006-07 [3]	260	250	-	10	-
	2007-08	250	220	10	30	-
	2008-09	830	490	-	340	-
	2009-10	780	370	-	410	-
	2010-11	1,760	1,140	-	610	-
	2011-12	3,080	1,960	-	1,110	-
	2012-13	2,330	1,360	-	960	-

1. For detailed definitions of all tenures see definitions of housing terms on Housing Statistics home page

2. Northern Ireland Housing Executive are in the process of a methodological review for housebuilding data. Results of this review will be available in May 2015 and no data will be published until this review has concluded. The results for the UK will only be revised and not extended during this time.

3. Figures from October 2005 to March 2007 in England are missing a small number of starts and completions that were inspected by independent approved inspectors. These data are included from 'June 2007

Totals may not equal the sum of component parts due to rounding to the nearest 10

- Less than 5 dwellings

P Figure provisional and subject to revision

R Revised from previous release

.. Not available

Contact:
Telephone: 0303 444 1864
Email: housing.statistics@communities.gsi.gov.uk

Source:
P2 returns from local authorities
National House-Building Council (NHBC)
Approved inspector data returns
Welsh Assembly Government
Scottish Government
Department for Social Development (NI), Northern Ireland Housing
Executive, Local Authority Building Control (NI)

11.4a Housebuilding: permanent dwellings completed, by house and flat, number of bedroom and tenure[1], ENGLAND

Percentage of all dwellings

Financial Year		2000/01	2001/02[2]	2002/03[2]	2003/04[2]	2004/05[2]	2005/06[2]	2006/07[2]	2007/08[2]	2008/09[2]	2009/10[2]	2010/11[2]	2011/12[2]	2012/13[2]
Private Enterprise														
Houses	1 bedroom	1	0	0	0	0	0	-00	0	0	1	1	1	1
	2 bedrooms	13	9	9	8	7	6	6	7	8	8	9	10	10
	3 bedrooms	33	30	29	28	28	26	27	26	25	28	33	32	33
	4 or more bedrooms	36	39	36	31	25	22	22	21	21	24	27	26	28
	All	83	78	74	67	60	55	56	55	54	60	70	69	71
Flats	1 bedroom	4	6	5	7	9	9	9	9	12	11	6	8	7
	2 bedrooms	12	15	19	24	30	35	34	35	33	28	23	22	20
	3 bedrooms	1	1	1	1	1	1	1	1	1	1	1	1	1
	4 or more bedrooms	0	0	0	0	0	0	0	0	0	0	0	0	0
	All	17	22	26	33	40	45	44	45	46	40	30	31	29
Houses and flats	1 bedroom	5	6	6	8	9	9	9	10	12	11	7	8	8
	2 bedrooms	24	24	28	32	37	41	40	41	41	35	33	32	30
	3 bedrooms	35	31	30	29	29	28	28	27	26	29	34	33	34
	4 or more bedrooms	36	39	36	32	25	22	22	22	21	25	27	27	28
	All	100	100	100	100	100	100	100	100	100	100	100	100	100
Housing Associations														
Houses	1 bedroom	3	2	2	1	1	1	0	0	0	1	1	0	1
	2 bedrooms	29	29	24	23	19	18	15	15	17	16	19	21	22
	3 bedrooms	27	28	27	24	22	19	16	15	17	19	23	24	25
	4 or more bedrooms	4	5	8	6	5	4	3	3	3	5	6	5	5
	All	63	64	62	54	47	42	34	34	37	40	50	51	53
Flats	1 bedroom	17	15	14	13	17	18	23	18	17	17	13	11	12
	2 bedrooms	17	20	22	31	34	38	41	45	44	38	34	33	31
	3 bedrooms	3	1	2	1	2	2	1	2	2	3	3	4	4
	4 or more bedrooms	0	0	1	1	0	0	0	1	0	1	1	1	1
	All	37	36	39	46	53	58	66	66	63	60	50	49	47
Houses and flats	1 bedroom	19	17	17	14	18	19	24	18	17	18	14	12	13
	2 bedrooms	46	49	45	54	52	56	56	60	61	54	54	54	53
	3 bedrooms	30	28	29	25	24	21	17	18	18	22	26	28	29
	4 or more bedrooms	5	5	9	7	5	4	3	4	4	6	7	6	6
	All	100	100	100	100	100	100	100	100	100	100	100	100	100
All tenures														
Houses	1 bedroom	1	0	1	0	0	0	0	0	0	1	1	1	1
	2 bedrooms	15	11	10	9	8	8	8	8	10	10	12	13	12
	3 bedrooms	32	28	29	28	27	26	25	25	23	25	30	30	31
	4 or more bedrooms	32	37	34	30	23	20	20	19	16	19	22	21	23
	All	80	77	73	66	59	54	53	52	50	55	65	64	67
Flats	1 bedroom	6	6	6	8	10	10	11	11	13	12	8	9	8
	2 bedrooms	12	15	19	24	30	35	35	36	36	31	26	25	22
	3 bedrooms	2	1	1	1	1	1	1	1	1	1	1	2	2
	4 or more bedrooms	0	0	0	0	0	0	0	0	0	0	0	0	0
	All	20	23	27	34	41	46	47	48	50	45	35	36	33
Houses and flats	1 bedroom	7	7	6	8	10	10	11	11	13	13	8	9	9
	2 bedrooms	27	25	29	33	38	42	42	44	46	40	38	38	35
	3 bedrooms	34	31	30	29	28	27	27	26	24	27	32	32	33
	4 or more bedrooms	32	37	34	30	23	21	20	19	17	20	22	21	23
	All	100	100	100	100	100	100	100	100	100	100	100	100	100

Source: Department for Communities & Local Government

1. For detailed definitions of all tenures, see Definitions of housing terms in Housing Statistics home page
2. Figures for 2001/02 onwards are based on NHBC data only, so there is some degree of variability owing to partial coverage.
3. The England worksheet and charts have been corrected following initial publication.

Contact:

Telephone: 0303 444 1864
E-Mail: housing.statistics@communities.gsi.gov.uk

11.4b Housebuilding completions: by number of bedrooms , Wales

Percentages

Wales[1]		1999 /00	2000 /01	2001 /02	2002 /03	2003 /04	2004 /05	2005 /06	2006 /07	2007 /08	2008 /09	2009 /10	2010 /11	2011 /12	2012 /13
1 bedroom	JUWO	5	5	4	6	6	7	9	11	10	16	11	10	11	7
2 bedrooms	JUWP	19	18	19	18	20	21	27	28	30	33	33	29	28	24
3 bedrooms	JUWQ	43	42	39	35	37	35	35	33	33	30	36	39	36	39
4 or more bedrooms	JUWR	34	34	38	41	37	37	30	28	27	22	20	22	25	29
All houses and flats	JUWS	100	100	100	100	100	100	100	100	100	100	100	100	100	100

Sources: Welsh Government

1 Figures for all years for Wales are based on the reports of local authority building inspectors and the National House Building Council (NHBC). It does not include information from other private approved inspector.

11.5 Mortgage possession workload in the county courts of England and Wales, 2002 - 2013

Year	Quarter	Claims Issued	Orders			Warrants	Repossessions by county court bailiffs	Properties taken into possession[2]
			Outright	Suspended	Total			
2002		62,862	16,656	25,127	41,783	34,360	8,800	12,000
2003		65,373	16,495	24,547	41,042	31,481	6,692	8,500
2004		76,993	20,048	26,639	46,687	33,042	7,074	8,200
2005		114,733	32,757	38,211	70,968	48,513	12,794	14,500
2006		131,248	46,288	44,895	91,183	66,060	20,960	21,000
2007		137,725	58,250	49,259	107,509	73,890	23,831	25,900
2008		142,741	70,804	61,994	132,798	89,748	35,792	40,000
2009		93,533	44,856	38,039	82,895	77,461	32,457	48,300
2010		75,431	32,940	29,235	62,175	63,532	23,612	38,100
2011		73,181	30,190	29,697	59,887	65,371	25,463	37,100
2012		59,877	24,129	23,935	48,064	59,040	19,728	34,000
2013		53,659	20,717	19,585	40,302	52,292	15,689	
2009	Q1	23,968	10,610	9,210	19,820	21,350	9,284	13,000
	Q2	26,419	11,757	10,026	21,783	20,087	8,040	12,000
	Q3	24,938	13,186	10,664	23,850	20,057	8,157	12,400
	Q4	18,208	9,303	8,139	17,442	15,967	6,976	10,900
2010	Q1	18,805	8,322	7,225	15,547	16,397	6,889	10,800
	Q2	18,395	7,959	6,804	14,763	16,071	5,927	9,800
	Q3	20,384	8,849	7,799	16,648	16,690	5,898	9,300
	Q4	17,847	7,810	7,407	15,217	14,374	4,898	8,200
2011	Q1	19,608	8,122	7,732	15,854	17,330	6,538	9,600
	Q2	18,339	7,388	7,336	14,724	16,403	6,170	9,300
	Q3	18,763	7,790	7,762	15,552	16,409	7,274	9,500
	Q4	16,471	6,890	6,867	13,757	15,229	5,481	8,700
2012	Q1	16,963	6,763	7,116	13,879	16,136	6,072	9,600
	Q2	14,615	6,032	6,152	12,184	14,373	4,825	8,500
	Q3	14,168	5,556	5,437	10,993	14,557	4,676	8,200
	Q4	14,131	5,778	5,230	11,008	13,974	4,155	7,700
2013	Q1	14,375	5,674	5,260	10,934	13,580	4,474	8,000
	Q2	12,881	5,187	5,059	10,246	13,529	4,087	7,600
	Q3	14,256	4,974	4,723	9,697	13,039	3,733	7,200
	Q4	12,147	4,882	4,543	9,425	12,144	3,395	

Source:

HM Courts and Tribunals Service CaseMan, Possession Claim OnLine (PCOL) and Council of Mortgage Lenders (CML)

Notes:

[1] Data relating to 1999 onwards are sourced from county court administrative systems and exclude duplicate observations.

[2] Council of Mortgage Lenders (CML) statistics for the latest quarter are unavailable prior to this bulletin being published as the MoJ does not have pre-release access to them. Please also note this figure relates to repossessions made in the United Kingdom whereas all other statistics in this bulletin relate to England and Wales. It should also be noted that these figures are rounded by the CML to the nearest hundred. Please see the CML website http://www.cml.org.uk/cml/statistics for more information about these statistics.

11.6 Mortgage arrears and repossessions

Year	2002	2003	2004	2005	2006	2007	2008	2009	2010	2011	2012	2013
Number of mortgages at year end (000s)	11,368	11,452	11,515	11,608	11,746	11,852	11,667	11,504	11,478	11,384	11,284	11,186
Repossessions during year	12,000	8,500	8,200	14,500	21,000	25,900	40,000	48,900	38,500	37,300	33,900	28,900
Cases in mortgage arrears												
12+ months arrears	16,500	12,600	11,000	15,000	15,700	15,300	29,500	69,500	63,700	54,400	48,500	41,100
6 - 12 months arrears	34,100	31,000	29,900	38,600	34,900	40,500	72,000	93,900	80,500	72,200	69,900	60,700
3 - 6 months arrears	66,600	55,800	60,500	69,400	64,900	71,700	117,400	112,400	103,300	99,000	97,200	86,600
3 - 5 months arrears	–	–	–	–	–	–	–	–	–	–	–	–

Sources: Compendium of Housing Finance Statistics & Housing Finance, Council of Mortgage Lenders, Janet Ford, Roof (3-5 months arrears).

Notes: Properties taken into possession include those voluntarily surrendered. The CML 3-6, 6-12 & 12+ months arrears figures are for the end of the year. Changes in the mortgage rate have the effect of changing monthly mortgage repayments and hence the number of months in arrears which a given amount represents.

The Janet Ford figures for 3-5 months arrears are for the March of the year; her survey of mortgage arrears was discontinued from following the introduction of the CML 3-6 months arrears series.

11.7 Households in temporary accommodation[1] by type of accommodation, at the end of each quarter, England

		Total in TA[1] (Temporary Accommodation)					Bed and breakfast hotels[2]							Hostels (including women's refuges)		
		(seasonally adjusted)	(not seasonally adjusted)	on same quarter in previous year	of which: with children[4]	Total number of children[5]	Total	% of Total TA	of which: with children[4]	with children and resident more than 6 weeks	of which: pending review/appeal	of which: headed by a 16/17 year old	of which: resident more than 6 weeks	Total	% of Total TA	of which: with children[4]
Number and percentage of total households in TA (%)																
2000	Q1	65,130	**65,170**	15%	..	..	8,680	13%	..	..	..	..	..	10,300	16%	..
	Q2	67,750	**67,520**	16%	..	..	8,910	13%	..	..	..	..	..	10,320	15%	..
	Q3	71,070	**71,860**	17%	..	..	9,420	13%	..	..	..	..	..	10,460	15%	..
	Q4	73,690	**73,080**	18%	..	..	9,870	14%	..	..	..	..	..	10,800	15%	..
2001	Q1	75,160	**75,200**	15%	..	..	10,860	14%	..	..	..	..	..	10,610	14%	..
	Q2	76,120	**75,920**	12%	..	..	11,390	15%	..	..	..	..	..	10,320	14%	..
	Q3	77,020	**77,800**	8%	..	..	12,220	16%	..	..	..	..	..	11,270	14%	..
	Q4	78,120	**77,510**	6%	..	..	11,860	15%	..	..	..	..	..	10,680	14%	..
2002	Q1	80,200	**80,200**	7%	54,660	..	12,710	16%	6,960		..	..	..	9,570	12%	5,540
	Q2	81,810	**81,660**	8%	58,870	..	12,720	16%	6,830	..	..	..	..	9,770	12%	6,030
	Q3	84,260	**85,010**	9%	61,740	..	13,950	16%	6,970	..	..	..	..	9,720	11%	6,280
	Q4	85,720	**85,140**	10%	60,310	..	13,240	16%	5,870	3,050	..	..	..	9,650	11%	5,770
2003	Q1	89,100	**89,040**	11%	61,510	..	12,440	14%	5,230	2,910	..	..	..	10,050	11%	6,040
	Q2	91,970	**91,870**	13%	65,040	..	11,380	12%	3,940	2,120	..	..	..	10,420	11%	6,360
	Q3	93,730	**94,440**	11%	67,260	..	10,310	11%	3,200	1,590	..	..	..	10,800	11%	6,450
	Q4	95,120	**94,610**	11%	67,540	..	8,420	9%	1,730	940	..	..	..	10,370	11%	6,060
2004	Q1	97,820	**97,680**	10%	70,580	..	7,090	7%	820	30	..	..	..	10,790	11%	6,280
	Q2	99,570	**99,530**	8%	71,640	121,590	7,240	7%	1,100	60	..	..	..	10,570	11%	6,090
	Q3	100,650	**101,300**	7%	72,510	122,530	7,450	7%	1,420	180	..	..	..	10,380	10%	5,960
	Q4	101,470	**101,030**	7%	72,800	124,630	6,450	6%	820	100	..	..	..	10,070	10%	5,650
2005	Q1	101,260	**101,070**	3%	72,670	125,860	6,780	7%	1,180	110	..	..	..	10,280	10%	5,830
	Q2	100,990	**100,970**	1%	72,810	124,900	6,290	6%	1,300	130	50	..	..	9,870	10%	5,440
	Q3	100,420	**101,020**	0%	74,180	127,990	6,100	6%	1,470	150	40	..	..	10,020	10%	5,410
	Q4	99,110	**98,730**	-2%	72,920	127,620	4,950	5%	820	140	30	..	..	9,230	9%	4,990
2006	Q1	96,580	**96,370**	-5%	71,560	127,650	5,150	5%	1,020	110	30	..	..	9,010	9%	4,960
	Q2	93,910	**93,910**	-7%	69,790	130,470	4,890	5%	1,050	100	50	..	..	8,940	10%	4,820
	Q3	92,530	**93,090**	-8%	69,500	129,340	4,900	5%	1,100	120	40	..	..	8,460	9%	4,460
	Q4	89,870	**89,510**	-9%	65,770	122,080	4,210	5%	650	110	40	..	..	7,850	9%	3,950
2007	Q1	87,310	**87,120**	-10%	65,210	125,430	4,310	5%	980	80	30	..	..	7,640	9%	4,030
	Q2	84,890	**84,900**	-10%	64,020	117,340	4,070	5%	940	100	30	670	300	7,230	9%	3,890
	Q3	82,220	**82,750**	-11%	62,830	117,090	4,090	5%	900	130	30	690	300	7,180	9%	3,850
	Q4	79,890	**79,500**	-11%	59,990	112,260	3,530	4%	700	120	20	550	270	6,620	8%	3,490
2008	Q1	77,660	**77,510**	-11%	59,230	110,360	3,840	5%	1,030	160	30	560	250	6,450	8%	3,580
	Q2	74,650	**74,690**	-12%	57,210	107,050	3,440	5%	1,030	180	30	420	160	6,020	8%	3,350
	Q3	71,640	**72,130**	-13%	55,850	104,640	3,230	4%	940	160	30	400	150	5,800	8%	3,190
	Q4	67,920	**67,480**	-15%	52,290	98,880	2,560	4%	520	100	20	330	150	5,250	8%	2,830
2009	Q1	64,090	**64,000**	-17%	49,030	92,590	2,450	4%	470	70	10	340	120	5,170	8%	2,740
	Q2	60,150	**60,230**	-19%	45,940	87,030	2,150	4%	510	80	20	310	130	4,710	8%	2,430
	Q3	56,460	**56,920**	-21%	43,400	82,780	2,050	4%	510	130	20	230	100	4,480	8%	2,330
	Q4	53,870	**53,370**	-21%	40,560	77,990	1,880	4%	400	120	10	170	70	4,150	8%	2,150
2010	Q1	51,350	**51,310**	-20%	39,200	74,610	2,050	4%	630	100	10	180	60	4,240	8%	2,270
	Q2	50,290	**50,400**	-16%	37,940	72,590	2,410	5%	740	160	10	190	70	4,320	9%	2,380
	Q3	49,240	**49,680**	-13%	37,620	71,460	2,660	5%	930	140	10	210	80	4,360	9%	2,440
	Q4	48,550	**48,010**	-10%	36,230	69,050	2,310	5%	660	150	10	140	50	4,160	9%	2,270
2011	Q1	48,250	**48,240**	-6%	36,640	69,660	2,750	6%	1,030	200	10	160	50	4,250	9%	2,330
	Q2	48,190	**48,330**	-4%	35,950	68,770	3,120	6%	1,210	240	20	150	40	4,370	9%	2,340
	Q3	48,680	**49,100**	-1%	36,680	69,850	3,370	7%	1,340	310	40	140	50	4,380	9%	2,370
	Q4	49,510	**48,920**	2%	36,600	69,460	3,170	6%	1,310	450	60	100	30	4,310	9%	2,380
2012	Q1	50,420	**50,430**	5%	37,190	70,090	3,960	8%	1,660	480	60	150	50	4,360	9%	2,350
	Q2	51,460	**51,630**	7%	39,470	73,890	4,230	8%	1,900	680	70	140	50	4,350	8%	2,610
	Q3	52,550	**52,960**	8%	40,090	75,460	4,120	8%	1,920	870	100	120	50	4,390	8%	2,690
	Q4	53,740	**53,140**	9%	40,830	76,740	3,820	7%	1,600	770	100	80	50	4,280	8%	2,610
2013	Q1	55,290	**55,320**	10%	40,450	76,040	4,510	8%	1,970	760	50	100	40	4,480	8%	2,710
	Q2	56,100	**56,290**	9%	43,140	79,710	4,330	8%	2,080	740	70	80	20	4,590	8%	2,890
	Q3	57,030	**57,420**	8%	42,190	78,760	4,610	8%	2,110	800	80	80	20	4,710	8%	2,960
	Q4	57,560	**56,940**	7%	43,750	80,970	3,920	7%	1,560	500	60	90	20	4,710	8%	2,950

11.7 Households in temporary accommodation[1] by type of accommodation, at the end of each quarter, England

		Local Authority or Housing Association (LA/HA) stock[6]			Leased from the Private Sector by an LA or HA[6]			Other Private Sector accommodation[2] (incl. private landlord)			Of which: in TA in another local authority district	Duty owed, no accommodation secured[3]					
		Total	% of Total TA	of which: with children[4]	Total	% of Total TA	of which: with children[4]	Total	% of Total TA	of which: with children[4]		a main duty accepted	% change from previous quarter	of which: with children[4]	All incl. decision pending	% change from previous quarter	Total with children[4], incl. decision
Number and percentage of total households in TA (%)																	
2000	Q1	21,370	33%	..	17,070	26%	..	7,750	12%	..	5,870	6,580	2.2%	..	11,150	7%	..
	Q2	22,490	33%	..	19,720	29%	..	6,080	9%	..	5,660	6,600	0.3%	..	11,270	1%	..
	Q3	23,700	33%	..	18,580	26%	..	9,710	14%	..	6,120	7,160	8.5%	..	12,570	11.6%	..
	Q4	24,320	33%	..	21,620	30%	..	6,490	9%	..	5,470	7,610	6.2%	..	12,220	-2.8%	..
2001	Q1	25,480	34%	..	21,900	29%	..	6,350	8%	..	6,150	8,420	10.6%	..	12,730	4.1%	..
	Q2	25,450	34%	..	21,970	29%	..	6,790	9%	..	7,440	8,870	5.4%	..	13,240	4.0%	..
	Q3	25,930	33%	..	20,050	26%	..	8,320	11%	..	8,240	8,090	-8.8%	..	11,820	-10.7%	..
	Q4	26,580	34%	..	20,600	27%	..	7,800	10%	..	8,460	8,600	6.4%	..	12,000	1.5%	..
2002	Q1	27,760	35%	19,160	20,660	26%	17,070	9,500	12%	5,930	9,670	8,620	0.2%	..	11,990	-0.1%	3,320
	Q2	28,470	35%	21,360	22,610	28%	18,570	8,090	10%	6,090	8,190	8,890	3.1%	..	12,440	3.8%	4,450
	Q3	28,870	34%	21,130	23,850	28%	20,600	8,620	10%	6,760	11,550	10,390	16.9%	..	14,440	16.1%	6,760
	Q4	27,580	32%	20,380	25,940	30%	21,630	8,740	10%	6,660	12,310	9,760	-6.1%	..	14,800	2.5%	5,830
2003	Q1	28,250	32%	19,690	28,370	32%	23,240	9,920	11%	7,310	11,470	10,580	8.4%	..	16,280	10.0%	7,550
	Q2	27,590	30%	19,900	31,460	34%	26,630	11,020	12%	8,220	10,880	13,310	25.9%	..	19,380	19.0%	9,410
	Q3	27,560	29%	19,650	35,140	37%	29,950	10,640	11%	8,020	9,880	15,370	15.4%	..	23,060	19.0%	10,140
	Q4	27,480	29%	19,450	38,730	41%	33,340	9,620	10%	6,960	10,440	17,500	13.9%	..	23,070	0.0%	10,990
2004	Q1	27,890	29%	20,120	42,390	43%	36,390	9,530	10%	6,970	9,850	15,870	-9.3%	..	21,940	-4.9%	11,610
	Q2	27,960	28%	20,070	42,630	43%	35,900	11,130	11%	8,480	9,480	17,030	7.3%	..	23,000	4.9%	13,230
	Q3	28,220	28%	20,070	43,720	43%	36,650	11,530	11%	8,420	10,030	17,100	0.4%	..	23,200	0.9%	13,400
	Q4	27,730	27%	19,730	46,140	46%	38,750	10,640	11%	7,840	8,610	16,100	-5.9%	..	20,930	-9.8%	11,880
2005	Q1	26,630	26%	18,610	46,530	46%	39,170	10,860	11%	7,880	11,660	15,290	-5.0%	..	20,910	-0.1%	12,850
	Q2	27,430	27%	19,070	46,990	47%	39,600	10,390	10%	7,390	11,790	16,020	4.8%	10,470	..	..	..
	Q3	25,030	25%	17,620	48,860	48%	41,500	11,020	11%	8,190	13,430	15,140	-5.5%	10,270	..	..	..
	Q4	24,220	25%	17,110	49,910	51%	42,310	10,420	11%	7,700	10,700	11,570	-23.5%	7,840	..	..	..
2006	Q1	22,350	23%	16,080	49,660	52%	41,960	10,200	11%	7,550	11,080	11,010	-4.8%	7,210	..	..	..
	Q2	20,790	22%	14,880	49,320	53%	41,740	9,970	11%	7,290	11,590	10,210	-7.3%	6,920	..	..	..
	Q3	20,180	22%	14,830	49,700	53%	41,980	9,850	11%	7,140	11,620	9,720	-4.8%	6,550	..	..	..
	Q4	18,840	21%	13,930	48,850	55%	40,130	9,770	11%	7,120	9,950	8,470	-12.9%	5,740	..	..	..
2007	Q1	18,040	21%	13,510	45,600	52%	38,600	11,540	13%	8,090	10,130	8,780	3.7%	5,910	..	..	..
	Q2	17,240	20%	12,970	44,610	53%	37,920	11,750	14%	8,290	10,490	9,150	4.1%	6,280	..	..	..
	Q3	16,490	20%	12,410	43,430	52%	37,100	11,570	14%	8,580	11,130	9,540	4.3%	6,300	..	..	..
	Q4	15,910	20%	11,780	41,730	52%	35,380	11,710	15%	8,640	10,820	8,080	-15.4%	5,510	..	..	..
2008	Q1	14,740	19%	11,080	40,480	52%	34,610	12,000	15%	8,930	10,200	7,470	-7.5%	5,180	..	..	..
	Q2	14,030	19%	10,660	41,130	55%	34,900	10,070	13%	7,270	8,720	7,890	5.7%	5,630	..	..	..
	Q3	13,420	19%	10,240	39,990	55%	34,390	9,710	13%	7,090	7,620	6,740	-14.6%	4,520	..	..	..
	Q4	11,930	18%	8,990	38,790	57%	33,560	8,950	13%	6,400	7,360	6,070	-9.9%	4,030	..	..	..
2009	Q1	10,480	16%	7,800	37,450	59%	32,050	8,460	13%	5,970	7,960	5,560	-8.5%	3,740	..	..	..
	Q2	9,520	16%	6,970	35,920	60%	30,620	7,930	13%	5,410	7,880	4,560	-17.9%	2,940	..	..	..
	Q3	8,780	15%	6,390	34,130	60%	29,090	7,490	13%	5,080	6,550	4,350	-4.5%	2,770	..	..	..
	Q4	8,180	15%	5,950	32,430	61%	27,540	6,730	13%	4,520	5,780	4,150	-4.6%	2,540	..	..	..
2010	Q1	7,790	15%	5,790	30,920	60%	26,310	6,320	12%	4,210	5,430	3,710	-10.6%	2,320	..	..	..
	Q2	7,650	15%	5,570	29,820	59%	25,210	6,200	12%	4,040	5,630	3,780	1.9%	2,510	..	..	..
	Q3	7,610	15%	5,480	28,740	58%	24,570	6,320	13%	4,200	5,880	4,100	8.4%	2,700	..	..	..
	Q4	7,430	15%	5,440	27,730	58%	23,620	6,380	13%	4,250	5,810	4,410	7.6%	2,970	..	..	..
2011	Q1	7,490	16%	5,500	26,960	56%	23,170	6,790	14%	4,620	6,300	4,770	8.1%	3,270	..	..	..
	Q2	7,570	16%	5,460	26,240	54%	22,170	7,050	15%	4,780	6,290	4,770	0.1%	3,420	..	..	..
	Q3	7,890	16%	5,810	26,380	54%	22,250	7,090	14%	4,910	6,850	5,110	7.0%	3,590	..	..	..
	Q4	7,990	16%	5,840	26,080	53%	21,800	7,370	15%	5,280	7,350	5,490	7.5%	3,550	..	..	..
2012	Q1	8,270	16%	6,000	26,040	52%	21,490	7,810	15%	5,690	7,870	5,400	-1.7%	3,860	..	..	..
	Q2	8,600	17%	6,470	25,960	50%	22,240	8,500	16%	6,250	8,170	5,500	1.9%	3,830	..	..	..
	Q3	8,930	17%	6,730	26,290	50%	21,880	9,230	17%	6,860	8,520	5,560	1.1%	4,080	..	..	..
	Q4	9,090	17%	6,830	26,310	50%	22,490	9,630	18%	7,300	9,270	5,690	2.3%	3,950	..	..	..
2013	Q1	9,270	17%	7,020	26,260	47%	21,020	10,810	20%	7,730	9,130	5,930	4.2%	4,270	..	..	..
	Q2	9,790	17%	7,650	25,520	45%	21,760	12,070	21%	8,750	11,310	5,530	-6.8%	3,890	..	..	..
	Q3	9,810	17%	7,290	25,660	45%	21,450	12,630	22%	8,390	11,860	5,170	-6.4%	3,610	..	..	..
	Q4	9,560	17%	7,280	25,460	45%	21,450	13,290	23%	10,520	12,190	4,930	-4.8%	3,460	..	..	..

Notes:

1. Households in accommodation arranged by local authorities pending enquiries or after being accepted as homeless under the 1996 Act (includes residual cases awaiting re-housing under the 1985 Act).

2. Other private sector accommodation includes accommodation that has been leased directly by the household from a private landlord where this arrangement is temporary, supported lodgings, and mobile homes such as caravans. From 2002 Q1, some self-contained accommodation in Annex-style units previously recorded under B&B is now more appropriately attributed to Private Sector Accommodation. The Homelessness (Suitability of Accommodation) (England) Order 2003 came into force on 1 April 2004. This prohibits the use of B&B accommodation for families except in an emergency and even then for no longer than six weeks.

3. "Duty owed, but no accommodation has been secured" are households accepted as owed a main duty but able to remain in their existing accommodation for the immediate future. Cases in the final two columns include those households awaiting a decision on their application. Since Q2 2005, this can only apply once an appeal has been accepted as owed a main duty.

4. Includes expectant mothers with no other dependent children.
5. Includes expected children.
6. Housing Association (HA) - this was previously known as "Registered Social Landlord".
P. Provisional data
R. Revised data
.. Data not collected
- Not calculated

Source: Department for Communities and Local Government
Totals may not equal the sum of components because of rounding.
DCLG P1E Homelessness returns (quarterly)
Contact: 0303 444 2259

11.8 Homeless Households in temporary accommodation at the end of the period - as at 31 March each year
(a) (b): Wales

Number of households

		2001-02 Annual	2002-03 Annual	2003-04 Annual	2004-05 Annual	2005-06 Annual	2006-07 Annual	2007-08 Annual	2008-09 Annual	2009-10 Annual	2010-11 Annual	2011-12 Annual	2012-13 Annual
Total accommodated at the end of quarter	Private sector accommodation (c)	130	175	255	415	505	710	900	1070	1050	1080	1065	1010
	Public sector accommodation (d)	395	455	355	460	615	575	445	415	390	435	380	380
	Hostels and women's refuges	195	230	310	310	450	405	475	510	400	415	485	505
	Bed and breakfast	125	300	690	760	595	380	280	255	235	240	310	300
	Other (e)	30	110	145	170	300	230	190	105	*	*	5	10
	Homeless at home	430	220	1130	1230	980	855	585	465	415	470	525	320
	Accommodation type unknown	.	.	.	.	.	.	.	.	.	.	.	.
Total accommodated at the end of quarter		1310	1490	2890	3350	3440	3150	2880	2815	2490	2640	2770	2525

Source: Welsh Government - Statutory Homelessness data collection from local authorities

(a) All the figures are rounded independently to the nearest 5 to protect the identity of individuals. As a result, there may be a difference between the sum of the constituent items and the total.

(b) Under Part VII of the Housing Act 1996

(c) Includes households placed directly with a private sector landlord, private sector accommodation leased by local authorities and private sector accommodation leased by registered social landlords.

(d) Includes local authority stock and registered social landlord stock on assured shorthold tenancies

(e) Prior to the April to June quarter 2009 the 'Other' category was used by some local authorities who were unable to were unable to distinguish the exact accommodation type for all households in temporary accommodation. Following a validation exercise all authorities are now able to provide this information.

* The data item is disclosive or not sufficiently robust for publication

11.9 Households in temporary accommodation type: Scotland

All households		Social sector accommodation[1]		Hostel		Bed & Breakfast		Other[2]		Total	
		Number	%	Number	%	Number	%	Number	%	Number	%
2003	as at 31 March	2,984	55	1,380	26	898	17	141	3	5,403	100
	as at 30 June	3,224	58	1,218	22	986	18	112	2	5,540	100
	as at 30 September	3,329	56	1,519	25	1,061	18	85	1	5,994	100
	as at 31 December	3,475	56	1,601	26	983	16	116	2	6,175	100
2004	as at 31 March	3,537	55	1,586	25	1,190	18	132	2	6,445	100
	as at 30 June	3,754	56	1,514	23	1,273	19	105	2	6,646	100
	as at 30 September	3,894	56	1,590	23	1,331	19	110	2	6,925	100
	as at 31 December	4,071	59	1,521	22	1,243	18	117	2	6,952	100
2005	as at 31 March	4,136	57	1,490	20	1,516	21	159	2	7,301	100
	as at 30 June	4,324	59	1,340	18	1,413	19	264	4	7,341	100
	as at 30 September	4,606	60	1,320	17	1,424	19	333	4	7,683	100
	as at 31 December	4,525	60	1,295	17	1,323	18	356	5	7,499	100
2006	as at 31 March	4,747	59	1,328	17	1,494	19	416	5	7,985	100
	as at 30 June	4,732	60	1,342	17	1,362	17	452	6	7,888	100
	as at 30 September	4,880	60	1,301	16	1,491	18	439	5	8,111	100
	as at 31 December	4,981	62	1,235	15	1,391	17	482	6	8,089	100
2007	as at 31 March	5,164	60	1,242	14	1,528	18	643	7	8,577	100
	as at 30 June	5,075	60	1,170	14	1,588	19	690	8	8,523	100
	as at 30 September	5,104	61	1,134	13	1,492	18	671	8	8,401	100
	as at 31 December	5,460	63	1,104	13	1,348	16	721	8	8,633	100
2008	as at 31 March[3]	6,134	64	1,079	11	1,609	17	713	7	9,535	100
	as at 30 June	6,079	62	1,064	11	1,791	18	815	8	9,749	100
	as at 30 September	6,131	62	1,058	11	1,780	18	848	9	9,817	100
	as at 31 December	5,931	62	1,019	11	1,662	17	924	10	9,536	100
2009	as at 31 March	6,355	63	994	10	1,748	17	956	10	10,053	100
	as at 30 June	6,294	62	1,186	12	1,654	16	1,072	11	10,206	100
	as at 30 September	6,438	62	1,221	12	1,584	15	1,100	11	10,343	100
	as at 31 December	6,378	62	1,234	12	1,515	15	1,151	11	10,278	100
2010	as at 31 March	6,775	63	1,217	11	1,765	16	972	9	10,729	100
	as at 30 June	6,938	62	1,267	11	1,940	17	958	9	11,103	100
	as at 30 September	7,124	63	1,369	12	1,673	15	1,098	10	11,264	100
	as at 31 December	7,272	66	1,339	12	1,418	13	1,066	10	11,095	100
2011	as at 31 March	7,215	64	1,371	12	1,544	14	1,124	10	11,254	100
	as at 30 June	7,443	67	1,349	12	1,414	13	953	9	11,159	100
	as at 30 September	7,382	67	1,329	12	1,433	13	916	8	11,060	100
	as at 31 December	7,102	66	1,310	12	1,232	12	1,041	10	10,685	100
2012	as at 31 March	7,093	66	1,333	12	1,281	12	1,043	10	10,750	100
	as at 30 June	7,106	68	1,190	11	1,205	12	965	9	10,466	100
	as at 30 September	7,146	68	1,333	13	1,090	10	977	9	10,546	100
	as at 31 December	6,920	67	1,292	13	1,063	10	977	10	10,252	100
2013	as at 31 March	7,061	67	1,290	12	1,170	11	950	9	10,471	100
	as at 30 June	6,965	66	1,451	14	1,104	11	972	9	10,492	100
	as at 30 September	6,877	67	1,503	15	1,001	10	887	9	10,268	100
	as at 31 December	6,687	67	1,496	15	932	9	848	9	9,963	100

Source: Scottish Government

1. Includes Glasgow Housing Association stock from 2003, and all other housing associations from June 2005 onward.

2. The category 'other' includes mainly private landlords. Prior to June 1999 the figures may also include an unknown number of local authority-owned chalets or mobile homes.

3. From 31 March 2008 there is a break in comparability in numbers in temporary accommodation in Glasgow-see notes page.

Banking, insurance

Chapter 12

Banking, insurance

Bank lending to, and bank deposits from, UK residents
(Tables 12.4 and 12.5)

These are series statistics based on the Standard Industrial Classification (SIC) 1992 (which was revised slightly in 2003).

Table 12.4. Until the third quarter of 2007, the analysis of lending covered loans, advances (including under reverse repos), finance leasing, acceptances and facilities (all in Sterling and other currencies) provided by reporting banks to their UK resident non-bank non-building society customers, as well as bank holdings of sterling and euro commercial paper issued by these resident customers. Following a review of statistical data collected, acceptances and holdings of sterling and euro commercial paper are no longer collected at the industry level detail with effect from fourth quarter 2007 data. Total lending therefore reflects loans and advances (including under reverse repos) only, from fourth quarter 2007 data.

Table 12.5 includes borrowing under sale and repo. Adjustments for transit items are not included. Figures for both tables are supplied by monthly reporting banks and grossed to cover quarterly reporters. Following the transition of building societies' statistical reporting from the Financial Services Authority to the Bank of England on 1st January 2008, both tables will include data reported by building societies from the first quarter of 2008 onwards. They exclude lending to building societies and to residents of the Channel Islands and Isle of Man.

Consumer credit (Excluding Student Loans)
(Table 12.12)

Following an ONS review in August 1997, data for 'other specialist lenders' were improved and revised back to January 1995. Total outstanding consumer credit was revised upwards by £2.6bn. Flows were break adjusted. Monthly data are available for lending by retailers from January 1997 but are not available for lending by insurance companies. The missing monthly data have been interpolated from quarterly data.

Within total consumer credit (excluding student loans) outstanding, credit card lending had been underestimated and 'other' consumer credit overestimated prior to January 1999 as a result of a longstanding inconsistency. The credit card element had previously covered sterling credit card lending to the UK household sector by only UK banks and building societies. Credit card lending by other specialist lenders and retailers (where they finance lending themselves) could not be separately identified and so was included within the 'other' consumer credit component.

From January 1999 onwards this inconsistency has been corrected, as credit card lending by other specialist lenders can be separately identified. As a result, data from January 1999 onwards for credit card lending and for 'other' consumer credit are not directly comparable with those for earlier periods. The change affects all three measures of credit card lending (gross, net and amounts outstanding), with an equal offsetting change to 'other' consumer credit. In non-seasonally adjusted terms, gross credit card lending was on average around £800 million per month higher since January 1999, whilst the amount outstanding of credit card debt was boosted by £4.8 billion in January 1999. The changes to net credit card lending are much smaller in absolute terms, with no discernible change to trend.

From November 2006, the Bank of England ceased to update the separate data on consumer credit provided by other specialist lenders, retailers, and insurance companies, previously contained in Table A5.6 of Monetary and Financial Statistics. The final month for which separate data are available on the Bank's Statistical Interactive Database is November 2006. The three categories have been merged into "other consumer credit lenders".

Prior to January 2008, building societies' lending was unsecured lending to individuals including sterling bridging loans (prior to October 1998 this was class 3 lending to individuals). Building societies gross lending through overdrafts is no longer included from January 2008.

http://www.bankofengland.co.uk/boeapps/iadb/newintermed.asp

12.1a Central bank's balance sheet - Bank of England 'Bank return'

£ millions   Not seasonally adjusted

Amounts outstanding of consolidated Issue and Banking department liabilities

	Sterling notes in circulation total	Sterling reserve balance liabilities	Sterling short-term open market operations with Bank of England counterparties	one week sterling	fine-tuning sterling	other maturity within maintenance period sterling	Foreign currency public securities issued total	Sterling cash ratio deposits from monetary financial institutions	Other liabilities total	Total liabilities
					of which:					
	RPWB55A [d] [e]	RPWB56A [d]	RPWB9R6	RPWB9R8	RPWB58A [d]	RPWBV79	RPWB59A [d]	RPWB62A [a] [b]	RPWB63A [a] [b]	RPWB75A [a] [b]
03-Jul-13	59,522	290,697	-	-	-	-	3,941	4,013	45,679	403,852
10-Jul-13	59,521	294,490	-	-	-	-	4,024	4,013	41,916	403,965
17-Jul-13	59,710	294,217	-	-	-	-	3,966	4,013	41,882	403,789
24-Jul-13	59,747	293,962	-	-	-	-	3,917	4,013	42,416	404,055
31-Jul-13	59,945	294,511	-	-	-	-	3,967	4,013	42,453	404,889
07-Aug-13	59,900	295,309	-	-	-	-	3,878	4,013	41,895	404,995
14-Aug-13	59,824	295,269	-	-	-	-	3,870	4,013	41,590	404,566
21-Aug-13	59,976	298,658	-	-	-	-	3,831	4,013	37,899	404,377
28-Aug-13	60,475	296,693	-	-	-	-	3,866	4,013	39,545	404,591
04-Sep-13	60,050	297,861	-	-	-	-	3,842	4,013	38,221	403,987
11-Sep-13	59,821	294,157	-	-	-	-	3,796	4,013	41,163	402,949
18-Sep-13	59,684	294,143	-	-	-	-	3,763	4,013	41,659	403,261
25-Sep-13	59,817	294,255	-	-	-	-	3,745	4,013	41,159	402,990
02-Oct-13	59,853	298,608	-	-	-	-	3,710	4,013	36,092	402,275
09-Oct-13	59,759	299,406	-	-	-	-	3,777	4,013	36,291	403,246
16-Oct-13	59,737	299,272	-	-	-	-	3,778	4,013	36,416	403,215
23-Oct-13	59,809	298,058	-	-	-	-	3,726	4,013	37,344	402,950
30-Oct-13	60,226	302,460	-	-	-	-	3,747	4,013	32,845	403,291
06-Nov-13	60,224	302,399	-	-	-	-	3,744	4,013	33,960	404,340
13-Nov-13	60,092	303,169	-	-	-	-	3,763	4,013	33,830	404,868
20-Nov-13	60,273	302,828	-	-	-	-	3,723	4,013	33,435	404,272
27-Nov-13	60,617	300,503	-	-	-	-	3,698	4,013	34,599	403,430
04-Dec-13	61,171	301,488	-	-	-	-	3,683	4,078	31,552	401,973
11-Dec-13	61,489	298,923	-	-	-	-	3,676	4,078	33,223	401,388
18-Dec-13	62,117	297,716	-	-	-	-	3,669	4,078	33,899	401,479
25-Dec-13	63,425	297,183	-	-	-	-	3,670	4,078	33,372	401,729
01-Jan-14	62,470	297,036	-	-	-	-	3,634	4,078	34,043	401,261
08-Jan-14	60,517	299,413	-	-	-	-	3,647	4,078	33,817	401,472
15-Jan-14	59,688	300,820	-	-	-	-	3,674	4,078	33,361	401,622
22-Jan-14	59,438	300,583	-	-	-	-	3,624	4,078	34,145	401,867
29-Jan-14	59,478	302,310	-	-	-	-	3,632	4,078	32,782	402,280
05-Feb-14	59,528	302,188	-	-	-	-	3,687	4,078	33,332	402,814
12-Feb-14	59,444	303,994	-	-	-	-	3,624	4,078	31,022	402,162
19-Feb-14	59,391	305,951	-	-	-	-	3,597	4,078	30,072	403,089
26-Feb-14	59,610	305,743	-	-	-	-	3,612	4,078	30,573	403,617
05-Mar-14	59,721	306,104	-	-	-	-	3,592	4,078	30,213	403,709
12-Mar-14	59,758	295,540	-	-	-	-	3,620	4,073	42,321	405,312
19-Mar-14	59,820	299,620	-	-	-	-	3,616	4,073	37,175	404,304
26-Mar-14	60,104	300,100	-	-	-	-	3,624	4,073	35,885	403,786
02-Apr-14	60,447	299,696	-	-	-	-	3,608	4,073	36,202	404,026
09-Apr-14	60,479	300,649	-	-	-	-	3,587	4,073	35,100	403,888
16-Apr-14	61,421	299,695	-	-	-	-	3,580	4,078	34,948	403,722
23-Apr-14	61,661	303,399	-	-	-	-	3,581	4,078	30,615	403,335
30-Apr-14	61,255	303,808	-	-	-	-	3,560	4,078	30,913	403,613
07-May-14	61,436	304,262	-	-	-	-	3,544	4,078	30,089	403,409
14-May-14	60,778	304,876	-	-	-	-	3,589	4,078	29,464	402,786
21-May-14	60,993	304,879	-	-	-	-	3,567	4,078	29,657	403,174
28-May-14	61,436	305,548	-	-	-	-	3,605	4,078	28,758	403,425
04-Jun-14	61,175	305,980	-	-	-	-	3,590	4,128	28,306	403,179
11-Jun-14	61,157	303,405	-	-	-	-	3,581	4,128	31,101	403,371
18-Jun-14	61,164	303,435	-	-	-	-	3,547	4,128	32,006	404,280
25-Jun-14	61,410	303,599	-	-	-	-	3,540	4,128	32,120	404,797

Notes to table

[a] Following Bank of England money market reform on 18 May 2006 the Bank of England 'Bank Return' was changed. This series forms part of the new Bank Return, with data starting on 24 May 2006. More information on changes made to the Bank's monetary policy operations and their impact on published data can be found in `The implications of money market reform for data published in Monetary and Financial Statistics' in the June 2006 issue of Bank of England: Monetary and Financial Statistics.

[b] This series was discontinued in September 2014. For more information, please see www.bankofengland.co.uk/publications/Pages/news/2014/095.aspx.

[c] This series increased by around £1.5bn on 25 November 2009 as a result of the additional backing by Bank of England notes for commercial banknote issue in Scotland and Nothern Ireland. For details, see the October 2009 article in Monetary & Financial Statistics at; http://www.bankofengland.co.uk/statistics/pages/ms/articles.aspx (25 Nov 2009)

[d] This series formed part of the Bank Return, which was published between 24 May 2006 and 29 September 2014, and now forms part of the Weekly Report. More information on changes made to the Bank's monetary policy operations and their impact on published data can be found in `The implications of money market reform for data published in Monetary and Financial Statistics' in the June 2006 issue of Bank of England: Monetary and Financial Statistics.
see the October 2009 article in Monetary and Financial Statistics at; http://www.bankofengland.co.uk/statistics/pages/ms/articles.aspx (25 Nov 2009)

[f] As part of the Bank of England's reformed framework for implementing monetary policy, the Bank announced in May 2006 its intention to conduct open market operations to make outright purchases of gilts and high-quality foreign currency government bonds. The first of these gilt-purchase open market operations took place in January 2008.

© Bank of England.

12.1b Central bank's balance sheet - Bank of England 'Bank return'

£ millions   Not seasonally adjusted

Amounts outstanding of consolidated Issue and Banking Department assets

		of which:		Sterling long-term operations with Bank of England counterparties	Sterling Ways and Means advances to HM government	Bonds and other securities acquired via market transactions	Other assets	Total assets
Short-term open market operations with Bank of England counterparties	One week sterling reverse repos with Bank of England counterparties	Sterling fine-tuning reverse repos with Bank of England counterparties	Sterling other maturity within maintenance period reverse repos with Bank of England counterparties					
RPWB66A	RPWB67A	RPWB68A	RPWBL59	RPWB69A	RPWB72A	RPWB73A	RPWB74A	RPWB75A
[d]	[d]	[d]		[d]	[e] [a] [b]	[f] [a] [b]	[a] [b]	[a] [b]
03-Jul-13	-	-	-	-	325	370	14,523	388,634	403,852
10-Jul-13	-	-	-	-	325	370	14,588	388,681	403,965
17-Jul-13	-	-	-	-	380	370	14,630	388,409	403,789
24-Jul-13	-	-	-	-	380	370	14,648	388,656	404,055
31-Jul-13	-	-	-	-	380	370	15,070	389,070	404,889
07-Aug-13	-	-	-	-	380	370	15,654	388,591	404,995
14-Aug-13	-	-	-	-	380	370	15,947	387,870	404,566
21-Aug-13	-	-	-	-	180	370	16,344	387,483	404,377
28-Aug-13	-	-	-	-	180	370	17,099	386,943	404,591
04-Sep-13	-	-	-	-	180	370	16,825	386,612	403,987
11-Sep-13	-	-	-	-	180	370	16,749	385,650	402,949
18-Sep-13	-	-	-	-	215	370	17,091	385,585	403,261
25-Sep-13	-	-	-	-	215	370	17,460	384,945	402,990
02-Oct-13	-	-	-	-	215	370	16,709	384,982	402,275
09-Oct-13	-	-	-	-	215	370	16,996	385,665	403,246
16-Oct-13	-	-	-	-	155	370	17,063	385,627	403,215
23-Oct-13	-	-	-	-	155	370	17,272	385,153	402,950
30-Oct-13	-	-	-	-	155	370	17,462	385,304	403,291
06-Nov-13	-	-	-	-	155	370	17,198	386,617	404,340
13-Nov-13	-	-	-	-	155	370	17,294	387,049	404,868
20-Nov-13	-	-	-	-	105	370	17,114	386,683	404,272
27-Nov-13	-	-	-	-	105	370	16,967	385,989	403,430
04-Dec-13	-	-	-	-	105	370	16,410	385,088	401,973
11-Dec-13	-	-	-	-	105	370	16,388	384,525	401,388
18-Dec-13	-	-	-	-	125	370	16,492	384,492	401,479
25-Dec-13	-	-	-	-	125	370	16,438	384,796	401,729
01-Jan-14	-	-	-	-	125	370	16,400	384,366	401,261
08-Jan-14	-	-	-	-	125	370	16,141	384,836	401,472
15-Jan-14	-	-	-	-	325	370	16,240	384,687	401,622
22-Jan-14	-	-	-	-	325	370	16,157	385,015	401,867
29-Jan-14	-	-	-	-	325	370	16,165	385,420	402,280
05-Feb-14	-	-	-	-	325	370	16,413	385,706	402,814
12-Feb-14	-	-	-	-	325	370	16,162	385,305	402,162
19-Feb-14	-	-	-	-	1,165	370	16,312	385,242	403,089
26-Feb-14	-	-	-	-	1,165	370	16,589	385,493	403,617
05-Mar-14	-	-	-	-	1,165	370	15,871	386,303	403,709
12-Mar-14	-	-	-	-	1,165	370	17,187	386,590	405,312
19-Mar-14	-	-	-	-	1,313	370	17,242	385,379	404,304
26-Mar-14	-	-	-	-	1,313	370	17,237	384,866	403,786
02-Apr-14	-	-	-	-	1,313	370	17,161	385,182	404,026
09-Apr-14	-	-	-	-	1,313	370	17,169	385,036	403,888
16-Apr-14	-	-	-	-	1,313	370	17,190	384,850	403,722
23-Apr-14	-	-	-	-	1,313	370	17,189	384,463	403,335
30-Apr-14	-	-	-	-	1,313	370	16,904	385,026	403,613
07-May-14	-	-	-	-	1,313	370	16,895	384,832	403,409
14-May-14	-	-	-	-	1,313	370	16,927	384,176	402,786
21-May-14	-	-	-	-	1,473	370	16,858	384,473	403,174
28-May-14	-	-	-	-	1,473	370	16,933	384,649	403,425
04-Jun-14	-	-	-	-	1,473	370	16,560	384,776	403,179
11-Jun-14	-	-	-	-	1,473	370	16,769	384,760	403,371
18-Jun-14	-	-	-	-	1,908	370	16,615	385,387	404,280
25-Jun-14	-	-	-	-	1,908	370	16,674	385,845	404,797

Notes to table

[a] Following Bank of England money market reform on 18 May 2006 the Bank of England 'Bank Return' was changed. This series forms part of the new Bank Return, with data starting on 24 May 2006. More information on changes made to the Bank's monetary policy operations and their impact on published data can be found in `The implications of money market reform for data published in Monetary and Financial Statistics' in the June 2006 issue of Bank of England: Monetary and Financial Statistics.

[b] This series was discontinued in September 2014. For more information, please see www.bankofengland.co.uk/publications/Pages/news/2014/095.aspx.

[c] This series increased by around £1.5bn on 25 November 2009 as a result of the additional backing by Bank of England notes for commercial banknote issue in Scotland and Nothern Ireland. For details, see the October 2009 article in Monetary & Financial Statistics at; http://www.bankofengland.co.uk/statistics/pages/ms/articles.aspx (25 Nov 2009)

[d] This series formed part of the Bank Return, which was published between 24 May 2006 and 29 September 2014, and now forms part of the Weekly Report. More information on changes made to the Bank's monetary policy operations and their impact on published data can be found in `The implications of money market reform for data published in Monetary and Financial Statistics' in the June 2006 issue of Bank of England: Monetary and Financial Statistics.

[e] The Debt Management Office announced on 24 January 2008 that HM Treasury had instructed an initial part repayment of the Ways and Means balance, with a payment to the Bank of England of £4.0bn, which is first shown in this table on 30 January 2008. The Ways and Means facility is the central government's overdraft facility at the Bank of England.

[f] As part of the Bank of England's reformed framework for implementing monetary policy, the Bank announced in May 2006 its intention to conduct open market operations to make outright purchases of gilts and high-quality foreign currency government bonds. The first of these gilt-purchase open market operations took place in January 2008.

Source: Bank of England

12.1c Central bank's balance sheet - Bank of England 'Bank return'

£ millions   Not seasonally adjusted

Amounts outstanding of Issue Department liabilities

	Weekly amounts outstanding of Bank of England Issue Department		
	Sterling notes in circulation total **RPWAEFA** [a] [b] [c]	Sterling notes in Bank of England Banking Department **RPWAEFB** [d] [a] [b]	Total liabilities RPWBL37 [a] [b]
03-Jul-13	59522	-	59522
10-Jul-13	59521	-	59521
17-Jul-13	59710	-	59710
24-Jul-13	59747	-	59747
31-Jul-13	59945	-	59945
07-Aug-13	59900	-	59900
14-Aug-13	59824	-	59824
21-Aug-13	59976	-	59976
28-Aug-13	60475	-	60475
04-Sep-13	60050	-	60050
11-Sep-13	59821	-	59821
18-Sep-13	59684	-	59684
25-Sep-13	59817	-	59817
02-Oct-13	59853	-	59853
09-Oct-13	59759	-	59759
16-Oct-13	59737	-	59737
23-Oct-13	59809	-	59809
30-Oct-13	60226	-	60226
06-Nov-13	60224	-	60224
13-Nov-13	60092	-	60092
20-Nov-13	60273	-	60273
27-Nov-13	60617	-	60617
04-Dec-13	61171	-	61171
11-Dec-13	61489	-	61489
18-Dec-13	62117	-	62117
25-Dec-13	63425	-	63425
01-Jan-14	62470	-	62470
08-Jan-14	60517	-	60517
15-Jan-14	59688	-	59688
22-Jan-14	59438	-	59438
29-Jan-14	59478	-	59478
05-Feb-14	59528	-	59528
12-Feb-14	59444	-	59444
19-Feb-14	59391	-	59391
26-Feb-14	59610	-	59610
05-Mar-14	59721	-	59721
12-Mar-14	59758	-	59758
19-Mar-14	59820	-	59820
26-Mar-14	60104	-	60104
02-Apr-14	60447	-	60447
09-Apr-14	60479	-	60479
16-Apr-14	61421	-	61421
23-Apr-14	61661	-	61661
30-Apr-14	61255	-	61255
07-May-14	61436	-	61436
14-May-14	60778	-	60778
21-May-14	60993	-	60993
28-May-14	61436	-	61436
04-Jun-14	61175	-	61175
11-Jun-14	61157	-	61157
18-Jun-14	61164	-	61164
25-Jun-14	61410	-	61410

Notes to table   Source: Bank of England

[a] Following Bank of England money market reform on 18 May 2006 the Bank of England 'Bank Return' was changed. This series forms part of the new Bank Return, with data starting on 24 May 2006. More information on changes made to the Bank's monetary policy operations and their impact on published data can be found in 'The implications of money market reform for data published in Monetary and Financial Statistics' in the June 2006 issue of Bank of England: Monetary and Financial Statistics.

[b] This series was discontinued in September 2014. For more information, please see www.bankofengland.co.uk/publications/Pages/news/2014/095.aspx.

[c] This series increased by around £1.5bn on 25 November 2009 as a result of the additional backing by Bank of England notes for commercial banknote issue in Scotland and Nothern Ireland. For details, see the October 2009 article in Monetary & Financial Statistics at; http://www.bankofengland.co.uk/statistics/pages/ms/articles.aspx (25 Nov 2009)

[d] On 1 August 2006, the Bank ceased using 'Notes in Banking Department' in the Issue Department balance sheet as a balancing item to ensure that the total liabilities of Issue Department were rounded-up to the nearest £10 million. Consequently, the total liabilities of Issue Department are now equal to 'Notes in circulation', which are notes that have been issued and paid for. The entry for 'Notes in Banking Department' does not reflect the value of physical notes held on Bank premises.

© Bank of England.

Banking and finance

12.1d Central bank's balance sheet - Bank of England 'Bank return'

£ millions   Not seasonally adjusted

Amounts outstanding of Issue Department assets

	Weekly amounts outstanding of Bank of England Issue Department							
	Sterling short-term open market operations with Bank of England counterparties	of which:		Sterling longer-term reverse repos with Bank of England counterparties	Sterling Ways and Means advances to HM government	Bonds and other securities acquired via market transactions	Other assets total	Total assets
		one week sterling reverse repos with Bank of England counterparties	Sterling fine-tuning reverse repos with Bank of England counterparties					
	RPWBL29	RPWBL32	RPWBL33	RPWBL34	RPWB54A	RPWBL35	RPWBL36	RPWBL37
	[b] [c]	[b] [c]	[b] [c]	[b] [c]	[a] [b] [c]	[d] [b] [c]	[b] [b] [c]	[b] [c]
03-Jul-13	-	-	-	0	370	4,847	54,305	59,522
10-Jul-13	-	-	-	0	370	4,847	54,304	59,521
17-Jul-13	-	-	-	40	370	4,847	54,453	59,710
24-Jul-13	-	-	-	40	370	4,847	54,490	59,747
31-Jul-13	-	-	-	40	370	4,847	54,688	59,945
07-Aug-13	-	-	-	40	370	4,847	54,643	59,900
14-Aug-13	-	-	-	40	370	4,847	54,567	59,824
21-Aug-13	-	-	-	40	370	4,847	54,719	59,976
28-Aug-13	-	-	-	40	370	4,847	55,217	60,475
04-Sep-13	-	-	-	40	370	4,668	54,972	60,050
11-Sep-13	-	-	-	40	370	4,668	54,743	59,821
18-Sep-13	-	-	-	45	370	4,668	54,601	59,684
25-Sep-13	-	-	-	45	370	4,668	54,735	59,817
02-Oct-13	-	-	-	45	370	4,279	55,159	59,853
09-Oct-13	-	-	-	45	370	4,279	55,065	59,759
16-Oct-13	-	-	-	5	370	4,279	55,083	59,737
23-Oct-13	-	-	-	5	370	4,279	55,156	59,809
30-Oct-13	-	-	-	5	370	4,279	55,572	60,226
06-Nov-13	-	-	-	5	370	4,279	55,570	60,224
13-Nov-13	-	-	-	5	370	4,279	55,438	60,092
20-Nov-13	-	-	-	5	370	4,279	55,619	60,273
27-Nov-13	-	-	-	5	370	4,279	55,963	60,617
04-Dec-13	-	-	-	5	370	4,247	56,549	61,171
11-Dec-13	-	-	-	5	370	4,247	56,866	61,489
18-Dec-13	-	-	-	55	370	4,247	57,444	62,117
25-Dec-13	-	-	-	55	370	4,247	58,752	63,425
01-Jan-14	-	-	-	55	370	4,247	57,797	62,470
08-Jan-14	-	-	-	55	370	4,247	55,845	60,517
15-Jan-14	-	-	-	255	370	4,247	54,815	59,688
22-Jan-14	-	-	-	255	370	4,247	54,565	59,438
29-Jan-14	-	-	-	255	370	4,247	54,606	59,478
05-Feb-14	-	-	-	255	370	4,247	54,656	59,528
12-Feb-14	-	-	-	255	370	4,247	54,572	59,444
19-Feb-14	-	-	-	495	370	4,247	54,279	59,391
26-Feb-14	-	-	-	495	370	4,247	54,498	59,610
05-Mar-14	-	-	-	495	370	4,224	54,633	59,721
12-Mar-14	-	-	-	495	370	4,224	54,669	59,758
19-Mar-14	-	-	-	588	370	4,224	54,639	59,820
26-Mar-14	-	-	-	588	370	4,224	54,922	60,104
02-Apr-14	-	-	-	588	370	4,224	55,265	60,447
09-Apr-14	-	-	-	588	370	4,224	55,297	60,479
16-Apr-14	-	-	-	513	370	4,224	56,314	61,421
23-Apr-14	-	-	-	513	370	4,224	56,555	61,661
30-Apr-14	-	-	-	513	370	4,224	56,148	61,255
07-May-14	-	-	-	513	370	4,224	56,330	61,436
14-May-14	-	-	-	513	370	4,224	55,672	60,778
21-May-14	-	-	-	623	370	4,224	55,776	60,993
28-May-14	-	-	-	623	370	4,224	56,219	61,436
04-Jun-14	-	-	-	623	370	4,217	55,965	61,175
11-Jun-14	-	-	-	623	370	4,217	55,947	61,157
18-Jun-14	-	-	-	763	370	4,217	55,815	61,164
25-Jun-14	-	-	-	763	370	4,217	56,060	61,410

Notes to table

Source: Bank of England

[a] The Debt Management Office announced on 24 January 2008 that HM Treasury had instructed an initial part repayment of the Ways and Means balance, with a payment to the Bank of England of £4.0bn, which is first shown in this table on 30 January 2008. The Ways and Means facility is the central government's overdraft facility at the Bank of England.

[b] Following Bank of England money market reform on 18 May 2006 the Bank of England 'Bank Return' was changed. This series forms part of the new Bank Return, with data starting on 24 May 2006. More information on changes made to the Bank's monetary policy operations and their impact on published data can be found in `The implications of money market reform for data published in Monetary and Financial Statistics' in the June 2006 issue of Bank of England: Monetary and Financial Statistics.

[c] This series was discontinued in September 2014. For more information, please see www.bankofengland.co.uk/publications/Pages/news/2014/095.aspx.

[d] As part of the Bank of England's reformed framework for implementing monetary policy, the Bank announced in May 2006 its intention to conduct open market operations to make outright purchases of gilts and high-quality foreign currency government bonds. The first of these gilt-purchase open market operations took place in January 2008.

© Bank of England.

12.1e Central bank's balance sheet - Bank of England 'Bank return'

£ millions   Not seasonally adjusted

Amounts outstanding of Banking Department liabilities

	Weekly amounts outstanding of Bank of England Banking Department								
	Sterling reserve balance liabilities	Short-term open market operations	of which:			Foreign currency public securities issued	Cash ratio deposits from monetary financial institutions	Other liabilities	Total liabilities
			one week sterling	fine-tuning sterling	other maturity within maintenance period sterling				
	RPWBL38	RPWB9R5	RPWB9R7	RPWBL42	RPWBV78	RPWBL43	RPWBL44	RPWBL45	RPWBL56
	[b] [a]	[a]	[a]	[b] [a]	[a]	[b] [a]	[b] [a]	[b] [a]	[b] [a]
03-Jul-13	290,697	-	-	-	-	3,941	4,013	99,984	398,635
10-Jul-13	294,490	-	-	-	-	4,024	4,013	96,220	398,748
17-Jul-13	294,217	-	-	-	-	3,966	4,013	96,336	398,532
24-Jul-13	293,962	-	-	-	-	3,917	4,013	96,906	398,797
31-Jul-13	294,511	-	-	-	-	3,967	4,013	97,141	399,632
07-Aug-13	295,309	-	-	-	-	3,878	4,013	96,539	399,738
14-Aug-13	295,269	-	-	-	-	3,870	4,013	96,158	399,309
21-Aug-13	298,658	-	-	-	-	3,831	4,013	92,618	399,119
28-Aug-13	296,693	-	-	-	-	3,866	4,013	94,763	399,334
04-Sep-13	297,861	-	-	-	-	3,842	4,013	93,193	398,910
11-Sep-13	294,157	-	-	-	-	3,796	4,013	95,906	397,872
18-Sep-13	294,143	-	-	-	-	3,763	4,013	96,259	398,179
25-Sep-13	294,255	-	-	-	-	3,745	4,013	95,894	397,907
02-Oct-13	298,608	-	-	-	-	3,710	4,013	91,251	397,582
09-Oct-13	299,406	-	-	-	-	3,777	4,013	91,357	398,552
16-Oct-13	299,272	-	-	-	-	3,778	4,013	91,499	398,562
23-Oct-13	298,058	-	-	-	-	3,726	4,013	92,500	398,296
30-Oct-13	302,460	-	-	-	-	3,747	4,013	88,418	398,637
06-Nov-13	302,399	-	-	-	-	3,744	4,013	89,530	399,687
13-Nov-13	303,169	-	-	-	-	3,763	4,013	89,268	400,214
20-Nov-13	302,828	-	-	-	-	3,723	4,013	89,054	399,618
27-Nov-13	300,503	-	-	-	-	3,698	4,013	90,562	398,777
04-Dec-13	301,488	-	-	-	-	3,683	4,078	88,101	397,351
11-Dec-13	298,923	-	-	-	-	3,676	4,078	90,089	396,766
18-Dec-13	297,716	-	-	-	-	3,669	4,078	91,344	396,807
25-Dec-13	297,183	-	-	-	-	3,670	4,078	92,125	397,056
01-Jan-14	297,036	-	-	-	-	3,634	4,078	91,840	396,588
08-Jan-14	299,413	-	-	-	-	3,647	4,078	89,662	396,800
15-Jan-14	300,820	-	-	-	-	3,674	4,078	88,177	396,750
22-Jan-14	300,583	-	-	-	-	3,624	4,078	88,710	396,995
29-Jan-14	302,310	-	-	-	-	3,632	4,078	87,387	397,407
05-Feb-14	302,188	-	-	-	-	3,687	4,078	87,988	397,942
12-Feb-14	303,994	-	-	-	-	3,624	4,078	85,593	397,290
19-Feb-14	305,951	-	-	-	-	3,597	4,078	84,351	397,977
26-Feb-14	305,743	-	-	-	-	3,612	4,078	85,071	398,505
05-Mar-14	306,104	-	-	-	-	3,592	4,078	84,846	398,620
12-Mar-14	295,540	-	-	-	-	3,620	4,073	96,991	400,223
19-Mar-14	299,620	-	-	-	-	3,616	4,073	91,814	399,122
26-Mar-14	300,100	-	-	-	-	3,624	4,073	90,807	398,604
02-Apr-14	299,696	-	-	-	-	3,608	4,073	91,467	398,844
09-Apr-14	300,649	-	-	-	-	3,587	4,073	90,397	398,706
16-Apr-14	299,695	-	-	-	-	3,580	4,078	91,262	398,616
23-Apr-14	303,399	-	-	-	-	3,581	4,078	87,170	398,228
30-Apr-14	303,808	-	-	-	-	3,560	4,078	87,061	398,506
07-May-14	304,262	-	-	-	-	3,544	4,078	86,419	398,303
14-May-14	304,876	-	-	-	-	3,589	4,078	85,136	397,680
21-May-14	304,879	-	-	-	-	3,567	4,078	85,433	397,958
28-May-14	305,548	-	-	-	-	3,605	4,078	84,977	398,208
04-Jun-14	305,980	-	-	-	-	3,590	4,128	84,271	397,969
11-Jun-14	303,405	-	-	-	-	3,581	4,128	87,048	398,162
18-Jun-14	303,435	-	-	-	-	3,547	4,128	87,820	398,930
25-Jun-14	303,599	-	-	-	-	3,540	4,128	88,180	399,447

Notes to table   Source: Bank of England

[a] This series was discontinued in September 2014. For more information, please see www.bankofengland.co.uk/publications/Pages/news/2014/095.aspx.

[b] Following Bank of England money market reform on 18 May 2006 the Bank of England 'Bank Return' was changed. This series forms part of the new Bank Return, with data starting on 24 May 2006. More information on changes made to the Bank's monetary policy operations and their impact on published data can be found in `The implications of money market reform for data published in Monetary and Financial Statistics' in the June 2006 issue of Bank of England: Monetary and Financial Statistics.

12.1f Central bank's balance sheet - Bank of England 'Bank return'

£ millions   Not seasonally adjusted

Amounts outstanding of Banking Department assets

	Weekly amounts outstanding of Bank of England Banking Department								
			of which:						
	Sterling Short-term open market operations with Bank of England counterparties	one week sterling reverse repos with Bank of England counterparties	Sterling fine-tuning reverse repos with Bank of England counterparties	Other maturity reverse repos with Bank of England counterparties	Longer-term reverse repos with Bank of England counterparties	Bonds and other securities acquired via market transactions	Sterling notes issued by Bank of England Issue Department	Other assets total	Total assets
	RPWBL48	RPWBL49	RPWBL52	RPWBL98	RPWB3J2	RPWBL53	RPWBL54	RPWBL55	RPWBL56
	[b] [a]	[b] [a]	[b] [a]	[a]	[a]	[b] [a]	[c] [b] [a]	[b] [a]	[b] [a]
03-Jul-13	-	-	-	-	325	9,676	-	388,634	398,635
10-Jul-13	-	-	-	-	325	9,741	-	388,681	398,748
17-Jul-13	-	-	-	-	340	9,783	-	388,409	398,532
24-Jul-13	-	-	-	-	340	9,801	-	388,656	398,797
31-Jul-13	-	-	-	-	340	10,222	-	389,070	399,632
07-Aug-13	-	-	-	-	340	10,807	-	388,591	399,738
14-Aug-13	-	-	-	-	340	11,100	-	387,870	399,309
21-Aug-13	-	-	-	-	140	11,497	-	387,483	399,119
28-Aug-13	-	-	-	-	140	12,252	-	386,943	399,334
04-Sep-13	-	-	-	-	140	12,158	-	386,612	398,910
11-Sep-13	-	-	-	-	140	12,082	-	385,650	397,872
18-Sep-13	-	-	-	-	170	12,424	-	385,585	398,179
25-Sep-13	-	-	-	-	170	12,792	-	384,945	397,907
02-Oct-13	-	-	-	-	170	12,430	-	384,982	397,582
09-Oct-13	-	-	-	-	170	12,717	-	385,665	398,552
16-Oct-13	-	-	-	-	150	12,785	-	385,627	398,562
23-Oct-13	-	-	-	-	150	12,993	-	385,153	398,296
30-Oct-13	-	-	-	-	150	13,183	-	385,304	398,637
06-Nov-13	-	-	-	-	150	12,919	-	386,617	399,687
13-Nov-13	-	-	-	-	150	13,015	-	387,049	400,214
20-Nov-13	-	-	-	-	100	12,835	-	386,683	399,618
27-Nov-13	-	-	-	-	100	12,688	-	385,989	398,777
04-Dec-13	-	-	-	-	100	12,163	-	385,088	397,351
11-Dec-13	-	-	-	-	100	12,141	-	384,525	396,766
18-Dec-13	-	-	-	-	70	12,245	-	384,492	396,807
25-Dec-13	-	-	-	-	70	12,191	-	384,796	397,056
01-Jan-14	-	-	-	-	70	12,153	-	384,366	396,588
08-Jan-14	-	-	-	-	70	11,894	-	384,836	396,800
15-Jan-14	-	-	-	-	70	11,992	-	384,687	396,750
22-Jan-14	-	-	-	-	70	11,909	-	385,015	396,995
29-Jan-14	-	-	-	-	70	11,918	-	385,420	397,407
05-Feb-14	-	-	-	-	70	12,165	-	385,706	397,942
12-Feb-14	-	-	-	-	70	11,915	-	385,305	397,290
19-Feb-14	-	-	-	-	670	12,065	-	385,242	397,977
26-Feb-14	-	-	-	-	670	12,342	-	385,493	398,505
05-Mar-14	-	-	-	-	670	11,647	-	386,303	398,620
12-Mar-14	-	-	-	-	670	12,963	-	386,590	400,223
19-Mar-14	-	-	-	-	725	13,018	-	385,379	399,122
26-Mar-14	-	-	-	-	725	13,013	-	384,866	398,604
02-Apr-14	-	-	-	-	725	12,937	-	385,182	398,844
09-Apr-14	-	-	-	-	725	12,945	-	385,036	398,706
16-Apr-14	-	-	-	-	800	12,966	-	384,850	398,616
23-Apr-14	-	-	-	-	800	12,965	-	384,463	398,228
30-Apr-14	-	-	-	-	800	12,680	-	385,026	398,506
07-May-14	-	-	-	-	800	12,671	-	384,832	398,303
14-May-14	-	-	-	-	800	12,703	-	384,176	397,680
21-May-14	-	-	-	-	850	12,634	-	384,473	397,958
28-May-14	-	-	-	-	850	12,710	-	384,649	398,208
04-Jun-14	-	-	-	-	850	12,343	-	384,776	397,969
11-Jun-14	-	-	-	-	850	12,552	-	384,760	398,162
18-Jun-14	-	-	-	-	1,145	12,398	-	385,387	398,930
25-Jun-14	-	-	-	-	1,145	12,457	-	385,845	399,447

Notes to table   Source: Bank of England

[a] This series was discontinued in September 2014. For more information, please see www.bankofengland.co.uk/publications/Pages/news/2014/095.aspx.

[b] Following Bank of England money market reform on 18 May 2006 the Bank of England 'Bank Return' was changed. This series forms part of the new Bank Return, with data starting on 24 May 2006. More information on changes made to the Bank's monetary policy operations and their impact on published data can be found in 'The implications of money market reform for data published in Monetary and Financial Statistics' in the June 2006 issue of Bank of England: Monetary and Financial Statistics.

[c] On 1 August 2006, the Bank ceased using 'Notes in Banking Department' in the Issue Department balance sheet as a balancing item to ensure that the total liabilities of Issue Department were rounded-up to the nearest £10 million. Consequently, the total liabilities of Issue Department are now equal to 'Notes in circulation', which are notes that have been issued and paid for. The entry for 'Notes in Banking Department' does not reflect the value of physical notes held on Bank premises.

12.2a Annual clearing volumes and values

Clearing volumes thousands

	Annual volumes		
	2013	2014	Change 2014 on 2013 %
Bacs			
Standing orders	18,405	18,678	1%
Direct Credits	2,151,718	2,150,557	-
Direct Debits	3,524,905	3,671,995	4%
Total BACS	**5,695,028**	**5,841,230**	**3%**
CHAPS Clearing Company			
Retail and Commercial (MT 103)	27,557	28,689	4%
Wholesale Financial (MT202)	7,419	7,833	6%
Total CHAPS	**34,976**	**36,521**	**4%**
Faster Payments			
Standing Order Payments	312,995	329,858	5%
Single Immediate Payments	502,025	609,879	21%
Forward Dated Payments	150,381	159,153	6%
Return Payments	2,228	2,040	-8%
Total Faster Payments	**967,629**	**1,100,930**	**14%**
Cheque and Credit Clearing Company			
Cheques	525,295	464,191	-12%
Credits	40,569	34,962	-14%
Euro debits	131	108	17%
Total Cheque & Credit	**565,995**	**499,262**	**-12%**
Currency Clearing: US Dollar	26.9	21.6	20%
Total all Clearing Companies	**7,263,655**	**7,477,965**	**3%**

Clearing values £ millions

	Annual values		
	2013	2014	Change 2014 on 2013 %
Bacs			
Standing orders and Bacs Direct Credits	3,103,579	3,253,279	5%
Direct Debits	1,115,065	1,167,266	5%
Total BACS	**4,218,644**	4,420,546	**5%**
CHAPS Clearing Company			
Retail and Commercial (MT 103)	15,509,721	14,886,852	-4%
Wholesale Financial (MT202)	54,629,206	53,072,638	-3%
Total CHAPS	**70,138,927**	**67,959,491**	**-3%**
Faster Payments			
Standing Order Payments	88,885	97,121	9%
Single Immediate Payments	423,571	517,641	22%
Forward Dated Payments	257,794	288,034	12%
Return Payments	1,111	999	-10%
Total Faster Payments	**771,361**	903,794	**17%**
Cheque and Credit Clearing Company			
Cheques	535,513	498,729	-7%
Credits	21,109	19,659	-7%
Euro debits	1,166	1,289	11%
Total	557,787	519,677	-7%
Currency Clearing: US Dollar	**328**	249	**-24%**
Total all Clearing Companies	**75,687,047**	73,803,757	**-2%**

Source: UK Payments Administration Ltd

(a) Totals, averages and percentages are calculated using unrounded data. The values of all euro and US Dollar clearings are shown as £ sterling equivalent.

(b) 253 clearing days were used to calculate the average daily statistics for both 2013 and 2014. In terms of Faster Payments, 253 clearing days were used for Standing Orders and 365 days for other payment types.

(c) A description of the United Kingdom payment clearings together with more comprehensive statistics over a longer period is available from the Information Management team. These data are published annually in UK Payment Statistics

12.2b Average daily volumes and values

Average volumes thousands

	Peak daily volumes		Average daily volumes	
	2013	2014	2013	2014
Bacs Payment Schemes Limited				
Standing orders	34,794}	22,688}	73	74
Bacs Direct Credits			8,505	8,500
Direct Debits	78,542	83,236	13,932	14,514
Total Bacs Payment Schemes Limited			**22,510**	**23,088**
CHAPS Clearing Company Limited				
Retail and commercial (MT103)	210	187	108.9	113.4
Wholesale financial (MT202)	45	47	29.3	31.0
Total CHAPS Clearing Company Limited			**138.2**	**144.4**
Faster Payments Scheme Limited				
Standing Order Payments	9,210	8,492	1,237.1	1,303.8
Single Immediate Payments	5,599	6,018	1,375.4	1,670.9
Forward Dated Payments	1,770	1,967	412.0	436.0
Return Payments	137	45	6.1	5.6
Cheque and Credit Clearing Company Limited				
Cheques exchanged in Great Britain	3,430	2,806	2,076	1,835
Euro debits exchanged in Great Britain	1.0	1.0	0.5	0.4
Credits (paper bank giro credits) exchanged in Great Britain	341	263	160	138
Total			**2,237**	**1,973**

Average clearing values

	Average values			
	Daily £ millions		Per item £	
	2013	2014	2013	2014
Bacs Payment Schemes Limited				
Standing orders and Bacs Direct Credits	12,267	12,859	1,430	1,500
Direct Debits	4,407	4,614	316	318
Total Bacs Payment Schemes Limited	**16,674**	**17,473**	**741**	**757**
CHAPS Clearing Company Limited				
Retail and commercial (MT103)	61,303	58,841	562,828	518,913
Wholesale financial (MT202)	215,926	209,773	7,363,128	6,775,822
Total CHAPS Clearing Company Limited	**277,229**	**268,615**	**2,005,341**	**1,860,824**
Faster Payments Scheme Limited				
Standing Order Payments	351.3	383.9	284	294
Single Immediate Payments	1160.5	1418.2	844	849
Forward Dated Payments	706.3	789.1	1,714	1,810
Return Payments	3.0	2.7	499	490
Total			797	821
Cheque and Credit Clearing Company Limited				
Cheques exchanged in Great Britain	2,117	1,971	1,019	1,074
Euro debits exchanged in Great Britain	4.6	5.1	8,923	11,881
Credits (paper bank giro credits) exchanged in Great Britain	83	78	520	562
Total	**2,205**	**2,054**	**985**	**1,041**
Total all Clearing Companies			**10,420**	**9,869**

Source: UK Payments Administration Ltd

253 days were used to calculate the average daily statistics for both 2013 and 2014. In terms of Faster Payments, 253 days were used for Standing Orders and 365 days were used for the other payment types.

A description and full list of members of referenced payment systems is available in the Annual Summary of Payment Statistics 2014 at: http://www.paymentscouncil.org.uk/resources_and_publications/publications/reports/

12.2c Bacs volumes and values

Annual volumes thousands

	Standing orders		Bacs Direct Credits		Bacs Euro Credits		Direct Debits		Total volumes	
	Number	% Change	Number	% Change	Number	% Change	Number	% Change	Number	% Change
2003	288,443	5.6	1,341,945	14.4	54	45.0	2,429,915	6.2	4,060,357	8.7
2004	301,879	4.7	1,710,673	27.5	84	55.5	2,589,934	6.6	4,602,570	13.4
2005	318,022	5.3	2,093,859	22.4	12	48.6	2,722,245	5.1	5,134,250	11.6
2006	332,245	4.5	2,171,586	3.7	157	25.9	2,857,761	5.0	5,361,749	4.4
2007	347,347	4.5	2,233,106	2.8	181	15.8	2,296,474	3.7	5,544,109	3.4
2008	323,843	-6.8	2,254,875	1.0	176	-3.2	3,076,857	3.8	5,655,751	2.0
2009	199,759	-38.3	2,289,813	1.5	193	10.0	3,149,153	2.3	5,638,919	-0.3
2010	150,307	-24.8	2,292,942	0.1	143	26.0	3,229,338	2.5	5,672,730	0.6
2011	123,652	-17.7	2,270,987	-1.0			3,322,360	2.9	5,716,999	0.8
2012	17,074	-86.2	2,182,667	-3.9			3,416,651	2.8	5,616,392	-1.8
2013	18,405	8%	2,151,718	-1.0			3,524,905	3.0	5,695,028	1.0
2014	18,678	1%	2,150,557	-			3,671,995	4.0	5,841,230	3.0

Average values £ millions

	Bacs Direct Credits [a]		Bacs Euro Credits		Direct Debits		Total volumes	
	Number	% Change	Number	% Change	Number	% Change	Number	% Change
2003	1,910,251	8.3	1,924	53.9	662,192	7.3	2,574,367	8.1
2004	2,131,031	11.6	2,040	6.0	750,381	13.3	2,883,452	12.0
2005	2,350,644	10.3	2,524	23.7	797,039	6.2	3,150,207	9.3
2006	2,581,682	9.8	2,819	11.7	844,832	6.0	3,429,333	8.9
2007	2,808,349	8.8	3,965	40.6	883,592	4.6	3,695,906	7.8
2008	3,006,159	7.0	4,806	21.2	935,356	5.9	3,946,321	6.8
2009	2,969,711	-1.2	5,255	9.3	885,708	-5.3	3,860,674	-2.2
2010	3,111,218	4.8	3,033	-42.3	948,137	7.0	4,062,388	5.2
2011	3,318,536	6.7			1,044,677	10.2	4,363,214	7.4
2012	3,036,714	-8.5			1,075,507	3.0	4,112,222	-5.8
2013	3,103,579	2.0			1,115,065	4.0	4,218,644	3.0
2014	3,253,279	5.0			1,167,266	5.0	4,420,546	5.0

Source: UK Payments Administration Ltd

(a) Values represent standing orders and Bacs Direct Credits combined

Bacs has 16 members and is responsible for the processing of bulk payments through its two principle payment schemes; Direct Debit and Bacs Direct Credit.

The Euro Debit Credit Service ceased operation on 29 October 2010

12.2d CHAPS volumes and values

Annual volumes thousands

	CHAPS Sterling [a]		CHAPS Euro						Total volumes [a]	
			Domestic (a)		Target					
					Transmitted to		Received from			
Year	Number	% Change	Number	% Change	Number	% Change	Number	% Change	Number	% Change
2003	27,215	6.5	1,399	13.1	2,904	19.2	1,685	4.7	33,202	7.6
2004	28,322	4.1	1,378	-1.5	3,314	14.1	1,849	9.7	34,862	5.0
2005	29,686	4.8	1,484	7.7	3,597	8.6	1,988	7.5	36,756	5.4
2006	33,030	11.3	1,461	-1.6	4,115	14.4	2,080	4.6	40,686	10.7
2007	35,588	7.7	1,455	-0.3	4,263	3.6	2,229	7.1	43,535	7.0
2008	34,606	-2.8	220	-84.9	379	-91.1	593	-73.4	35,797	-17.8
2009	31,926	-7.7							31,926	-10.8
2010	32,169	0.8							32,169	0.8
2011	34,024	5.8							34,024	5.8
2012	33,936	-0.3							33,936	-0.3
2013	34,976	3.0							34,976	3.0
2014	36,521	4.0							36,521	4.0

Annual Values £ millions

	CHAPS Sterling [a]		CHAPS Euro (sterling equivalent)						Total values [a]	
			Domestic (a)		Target					
					Transmitted to		Received from			
Year	Number	% Change	Number	% Change	Number	% Change	Number	% Change	Number	% Change
2003	51,613,456	-0.5	5,114,198	22.7	15,924,879	21.5	15,923,974	21.5	88,576,506	7.7
2004	52,347,525	1.4	4,509,924	-11.8	17,238,602	8.2	17,238,737	8.3	91,334,788	3.1
2005	52,671,592	0.6	6,069,146	34.6	19,180,194	11.3	19,179,273	11.3	97,100,206	6.3
2006	59,437,370	12.8	7,365,558	21.4	21,415,027	11.7	21,419,195	11.7	109,637,149	12.9
2007	69,352,322	16.7	6,781,942	-7.9	25,266,729	18.0	25,268,856	18.0	126,669,848	15.5
2008	73,625,908	6.2	574,610	-91.5	4,413,570	-82.5	4,403,022	-82.6	83,017,110	-34.5
2009	64,616,956	-12.2							64,616,956	-22.2
2010	61,587,609	-4.7							61,587,609	-4.7
2011	63,876,772	3.7							63,876,772	3.7
2012	71,716,857	12.3							71,716,857	12.3
2013	70,138,927	-2.0							70,138,927	-2.0
2014	67,959,491	-3.0							67,959,491	-3.0

Source: UK Payments Administration Ltd

(a) NewCHAPS was launched on 27 August 2001 and since his date CHAPS Sterling and CHAPS Euro Domestic figures include all CHAPS traffic

The CHAPS Scheme enables same-day bank-to-bank payments in sterling and has 21 direct participants

12.2e CHAPS value band analysis: 2014

Annual volume thousands

Upper Value (£/€)	Number	% of total
100,000	28,168	77.1
300,000	3,964	10.9
1,000,000	2,092	5.7
3,000,000	928	2.5
10,000,000	656	1.8
30,000,000	356	1.0
100,000,000	224	0.6
300,000,000	97	0.3
1,000,000,000	31	0.1
100,000,000,000	5	..
Total	36,521	

Annual value £ millions

Upper Value (£/€)	Value	% of total
100,000	379,015	0.6
300,000	696,681	1.0
1,000,000	1,187,609	1.7
3,000,000	1,668,795	2.5
10,000,000	3,733,710	5.5
30,000,000	6,318,608	9.3
100,000,000	12,547,658	18.5
300,000,000	16,709,940	24.6
1,000,000,000	15,161,009	22.3
100,000,000,000	9,556,466	14.1
Total	67,959,491	

Source: UK Payments Administration Ltd

The Bank of England and SWIFT provide services to CHAPS Co in operation of the CHAPS system. The Bank of England provides the real-time gross settlement process and SWIFT provides the secure communication network.

12.2f Faster Payments volumes and values

Annual volumes thousands

	Standing Order Payments		Single Immediate Payments		Forward Dated Payments		Return Payments		Total volumes(a)	
	Number	% Change	Number	% Change	Number	% Change	Number	% Change	Number	% Change
2003										
2004										
2005										
2006										
2007										
2008	37,574	*	36,325	*	8,708	*	182	*	82,789	*
2009	156,865	*	109,337	*	27,912	*	673	*	294,787	*
2010	203,055	29.4	181,195	65.7	40,632	45.6	880	30.6	425,761	44.4
2011	235,654	16.1	237,718	31.2	50,861	25.2	1,092	24.2	525,325	23.4
2012	299,630	27.1	379,844	59.8	129,829	155.3	1,788	63.6	811,090	54.4
2013	312,995	4.0	502,025	32.0	150,381	16.0	2,228	25.0	967,629	19.0
2014	329,858	5.0	609,879	21.0	159,153	6.0	2,040	- 8.0	1,100,930	14.0

Annual values £ millions

	Standing Order Payments		Single Immediate Payments		Forward Dated Payments		Return Payments		Total values(a)	
	Value	% Change	Value	% Change	Value	% Change	Value	% Change	Value	% Change
2003										
2004										
2005										
2006										
2007										
2008	3,341	*	22,015	*	7,473	*	42	*	32,871	*
2009	26,527	*	59,015	*	20,544	*	136	*	106,223	*
2010	38,963	46.9	92,847	57.3	32,193	56.7	208	52.9	164,211	54.6
2011	50,206	28.9	135,101	45.5	49,429	53.5	308	47.9	235,044	43.1
2012	80,009	59.4	328,685	143.3	208,252	321.3	965	213.0	617,911	162.9
2013	88,885	11.0	423,571	29.0	257,794	24.0	1,111	15.0	771,361	25.0
2014	97,121	9.0	517,641	22.0	288,034	12.0	999	-10.0	903,794	17.0

Source: UK Payments Administration Ltd

(a) The UK Faster Payments Service was launched on 27 May 2008.

The Faster Payments Service enables internet, mobile and telephone banking payments, as well as standing orders, to be processed almost instantaneously, 24 hours a day, 7 days a week. 10 banks and building societies operated in the service in 2014.

12.2g Inter-bank cheque volumes and values

Annual volumes thousands

	Exchanged in Great Britain				Total volumes	
	Cheques		Euro debits			
	Number	% Change	Number	% Change	Number	% Change
2003	1,519,117	-6.3	759	3.6	1,519,876	-6.3
2004	1,423,742	-6.3	724	-4.6	1,424,465	-6.3
2005	1,325,762	-6.9	637	-12.0	1,326,399	-6.9
2006	1,237,401	-6.7	586	-7.9	1,237,987	-6.7
2007	1,124,869	-9.1	531	-9.5	1,125,400	-9.1
2008	1,007,379	-10.4	445	-16.1	1,007,824	-10.4
2009	875,533	-13.1	351	-21.2	875,884	-13.1
2010	775,643	-11.4	279	-20.5	775,922	-11.4
2011	682,082	-12.1	223	-20.1	682,305	-12.1
2012	597,076	-12.5	165	-25.7	597,241	-12.5
2013	525,295	-12.0	131	-21.0	525,426	-12.0
2014	464,191	-12.0	108	-17.0	464,299	-12.0

Annual values £ millions

	Exchanged in Great Britain				Total values	
	Cheques		Euro debits			
	Value	% Change	Value	% Change	Value	% Change
2003	1,240,685	-3.2	3,898	13.8	1,244,583	-3.1
2004	1,210,057	-2.5	3,456	-11.4	1,213,513	-2.5
2005	1,152,256	-4.8	3,206	-7.2	1,155,462	-4.8
2006	1,171,062	1.6	3,111	-3.0	1,174,174	1.6
2007	1,156,684	-1.2	2,970	-4.6	1,159,653	-1.2
2008	1,075,694	-7.0	2,980	0.4	1,078,674	-7.0
2009	870,591	-19.1	2,993	0.4	873,584	-19.0
2010	761,081	-12.6	1,767	-41.0	762,848	-12.7
2011	675,706	-11.2	1,559	-11.8	677,266	-11.2
2012	601,256	-11.0	1,188	-23.9	602,444	-11.0
2013	535,513	-11.0	1,166	-2.0	536,679	-11.0
2014	498,729	- 7.0	1,289	11.0	500,018	- 7.0

Source: UK Payments Administration Ltd

The Cheque & Credit Clearing Company was established in 1985 and took over responsibility for managing the operation of the two bulk paper clearings for England and Wales.

From December 1996 the Cheque and Credit Clearing Company also took over responsibility for managing the operation of the inter-bank clearings in Scotland. The clearing of cheque and credit payments in Northern Ireland is managed by the Belfast Bankers' Clearing Company Limited (BBCCL)

12.2h Inter-bank credit volumes and values

Annual volumes thousands

	Exchanged in Great Britain		Total volumes	
	Number	% Change	Number	% Change
2003	140,792	-6.4	140,792	-6.4
2004	132,899	-5.6	132,899	-5.6
2005	123,280	-7.2	123,280	-7.2
2006	108,309	-12.1	108,309	-12.1
2007	96,290	-11.1	96,290	-11.1
2008	86,442	-10.2	86,442	-10.2
2009	73,686	-14.8	73,686	-14.8
2010	61,662	-16.3	61,662	-16.3
2011	53,934	-12.5	53,934	-12.5
2012	46,927	-12.9	46,927	-12.9
2013	40,569	-14.0	40,569	-14.0
2014	34,962	-14.0	40,569	-14.0

Annual values £ millions

	Exchanged in Great Britain		Total values	
	Value	% Change	Value	% Change
2003	74,366	-7.6	74,366	-7.6
2004	68,261	-8.2	68,261	-8.2
2005	61,844	-9.4	61,844	-9.4
2006	59,309	-4.1	59,309	-4.1
2007	57,347	-3.3	57,347	-3.3
2008	51,641	-9.9	51,641	-9.9
2009	41,624	-19.4	41,624	-19.4
2010	32,312	-22.4	32,312	-22.4
2011	27,990	-13.4	27,990	-13.4
2012	23,802	-15.0	23,802	-15.0
2013	21,109	-11.0	21,109	-11.0
2014	19,659	-7.0	19,659	- 7.0

Source: UK Payments Administration Ltd

The Cheque & Credit Clearing Company was established in 1985 and took over responsibility for managing the operation of the two bulk paper clearings for England and Wales.

From December 1996 the Cheque and Credit Clearing Company also took over responsibility for managing the operation of the inter-bank clearings in Scotland. The clearing of cheque and credit payments in Northern Ireland is managed by the Belfast Bankers' Clearing Company Limited (BBCCL)

12.2i Inter-bank values: UK summary £ billions

	Total bulk paper clearings•• inter-bank cheque and credit				Bulk electronic values	
	Great Britain	Northern•• Ireland[a]••	Total		Bacs	
	Value	Value	Value	% Change	Value	% Change
2004	1,282	28	1,310	-2.8	2,883	12.0
2005	1,217	27	1,244	-5.0	3,150	9.3
2006	1,234	27	1,261	1.3	3,429	8.9
2007	1,217	27	1,244	-1.3	3,696	7.8
2008	1,130	45	1,175	-5.5	3,946	6.8
2009	915	36	952	-19.1	3,861	-2.2
2010	795	31	826	-13.2	4,062	5.2
2011	705	27	733	-11.3	4,363	7.4
2012	626	25	652	-11.0	4,112	-5.8
2013	558	23	581	-10.9	4,219	2.6
2014	520	22	542	-6.7	4,421	4.8

	Total bulk values		Same-day values				Grand total all UK inter-bank values	
			CHAPS[b]		Faster Payments[c]			
	Value	% Change	Value	% Change	Value	% Change	Value	% Change
2004	4,193	6.9	91,335	3.1			95,528	3.3
2005	4,394	4.8	97,100	6.3			101,495	6.2
2006	4,690	6.7	109,637	12.9			114,327	12.6
2007	4,940	5.3	126,670	15.5			131,609	15.1
2008	5,122	3.7	83,017	-34.5	33	*	88,172	-33.0
2009	4,812	-6.0	64,617	-22.2	106	*	69,535	-21.1
2010	4,888	1.6	61,588	-4.7	164	54.6	66,640	-4.2
2011	5,096	4.3	63,877	3.7	235	43.1	69,208	3.9
2012	4,764	-6.5	71,717	12.3	618	162.9	77,099	11.4
2013	4,799	0.7	70,139	-2.2	771	24.8	75,710	-1.8
2014	4,962	3.4	67,959	-3.1	904	17.2	73,825	-2.5

Source: UK Payments Administration Ltd

[a] The clearing of cheque and credit payments in Northern Ireland is managed by the Belfast Bankers' Clearing Company (BBCCL). Figures from 2004 – 2007 are estimated, but those for 2008 onwards were provided by BBCCL.

[b] CHAPS Euro ceased operation on 16 May 2008.

[c] The Faster Payments Service was launched on 27 May 2008.

12.2j Inter-bank volumes: UK summary millions

	Total bulk paper clearings•• inter-bank cheque and credit				Bulk electronic volumes	
	Great Britain	Northern•• Ireland(a)••	Total		Bacs	
	Number	Number	Number	% Change	Number	% Change
2004	1,557.4	41.3	1,598.7	-6.2	4,602.6	13.4
2005	1,449.7	38.4	1,488.1	-6.9	5,134.3	11.6
2006	1,346.3	35.7	1,382.0	-7.1	5,361.7	4.4
2007	1,221.7	32.4	1,254.1	-9.3	5,544.1	3.4
2008	1,094.3	25.1	1,119.4	-10.7	5,655.8	2.0
2009	949.6	22.4	972.0	-13.2	5,638.9	-0.3
2010	837.6	20.2	857.8	-11.8	5,672.7	0.6
2011	736.2	18.7	754.9	-12.0	5,717.0	0.8
2012	644.2	16.8	661.0	-12.4	5,616.4	-1.8
2013	566.0	15.2	581.2	-12.1	5,695.0	1.4
2014	499.3	13.9	513.2	-11.7	5,841.2	2.6

	Total bulk volumes		Same-day volumes				Grand total all UK inter-bank volumes	
			CHAPS(b)		Faster Payments(c)			
	Number	% Change	Number	% Change	Number	% Change	Number	% Change
2004	6,201.2	7.6	34.9	5.0			6,236.1	7.6
2005	6,622.4	6.8	36.8	5.4			6,659.1	6.8
2006	6,743.8	1.8	40.7	10.7			6,784.4	1.9
2007	6,798.2	0.8	43.5	7.0			6,841.8	0.8
2008	6,775.2	-0.3	35.8	-17.8	82.8	*	6,893.7	0.8
2009	6,610.9	-2.4	31.9	-10.8	294.8	*	6,937.6	0.6
2010	6,530.5	-1.2	32.2	0.8	425.8	44.4	6,988.4	0.7
2011	6,471.9	-0.9	34.0	5.8	525.3	23.4	7,031.3	0.6
2012	6,277.4	-3.0	33.9	-0.3	811.1	54.4	7,122.4	1.3
2013	6,276.2	..	35.0	3.1	967.6	19.3	7,278.8	2.2
2014	6,354.4	1.2	36.5	4.4	1,100.9	13.8	7,491.9	2.9

Source: UK Payments Administration Ltd

(a) The clearing of cheque and credit payments in Northern Ireland is managed by the Belfast Bankers' Clearing Company (BBCCL). Figures from 2004 - 2007 are estimated, but those for 2008 onwards were provided by BBCCL.

(b) CHAPS Euro ceased operation on 16 May 2008.

(c) The Faster Payments Service was launched on 27 May 2008.

12.3a Monetary financial institutions' (excluding central bank) balance sheet

£ millions

Amounts outstanding of sterling liabilities

| | Notes outstanding and cash loaded cards | Sight deposits | | | | | Time deposits | | | | | | |
| | | UK MFIs | of which intragroup banks | UK public sector | Other UK residents | Non-residents | UK MFIs | of which intragroup banks | UK public sector | Other UK residents | of which SAYE | of which cash ISAs | Non-residents |
RPM	B3LM	B3GL	B8ZC	B3MM	B3NM	B3OM	B3HL	B8ZE	B3PM	B3QM	B3RM	B3SM	B3TM
2013 May	6,538	208,690	190,089	14,111	983,445	133,836	284,486	272,159	19,556	879,500	1,174	224,054	230,125
Jun	6,764	212,376	194,879	13,663	999,197	142,652	288,101	275,987	20,012	872,963	1,182	224,809	221,273
Jul	6,518	206,604	187,937	14,172	1,001,659	136,036	291,824	280,412	20,928	872,433 (e)	1,182	225,042	221,612
Aug	6,520	211,825	193,324	14,417	1,013,348	134,012	284,256	273,064	20,495	874,454	1,114	225,557	212,371
Sep	6,621	225,781	206,927	14,424	1,029,192	140,523	307,027 (b)	296,833 (b)	20,219	871,381	1,104	225,537	209,340
Oct	6,600	231,924	213,336	14,609	1,034,283	138,835	311,672	301,047	19,552	864,113	1,172	225,103	206,311
Nov	6,731	223,826	207,376	13,901	1,052,684	140,565	322,299	311,654	18,793	856,271	1,053	224,672	202,109
Dec	7,022	216,160	200,806	14,122	1,062,647	145,396	314,861	304,318	17,360	827,075	1,009	224,086	217,722
2014 Jan	6,645	135,994 (a)	119,869 (a)	15,586	1,058,759	137,481	153,610 (c)(d)	144,081 (c)(d)	16,950	814,211	978	223,427	214,684
Feb	6,622	126,599	110,727	14,508	1,067,657	140,432	151,400	142,239	17,452	812,966	971	223,012	206,514
Mar	6,649	120,924	105,533	13,601	1,092,620	143,337	142,310	134,996	16,249	787,852	1,078	224,697	192,593
Apr	6,645	98,730	83,422	16,726	1,087,024	131,123	143,122	134,711	18,919	774,390	1,188	229,896	196,148
May	6,713	106,531	90,274	15,336	1,099,700	141,090	138,836	131,530	19,914	761,630	1,096	230,987	194,642
Jun	6,720	105,876	89,695	14,575	1,117,183	144,330	139,657	132,963	20,289	755,540	1,211	230,752	190,299
Jul	6,732	94,126	79,727	15,164	1,105,619	145,022	136,755	129,078	21,055	759,777	1,225	238,593	186,191
Aug	6,801	95,817	81,188	14,227	1,112,259	140,505	135,735	128,223	20,807	759,558	1,236	241,719	189,966
Sep	6,764	98,245	83,644	13,938	1,126,047	146,254	137,628	130,140	20,154	755,280	1,108	243,485	185,874
Oct	6,803	96,691	82,111	14,560	1,123,571	144,177	138,696	131,345	20,113	741,933	1,154	244,899	183,831
Nov	6,836	100,007	85,192	13,940	1,135,456	145,187	146,538	140,001	19,386	735,317	1,202	245,850	182,894
Dec	7,095	107,959	93,751	14,227	1,147,349	150,731	141,205	135,640	17,791	737,138	1,289	246,432	191,528
2015 Jan	6,824	119,954	102,936	15,486	1,145,137	146,519	140,938	135,129	17,783	710,220	1,209	246,469	187,336
Feb	6,769	116,303	100,489	14,678	1,144,242	142,548	133,454	127,645	17,958	705,161	1,100	246,515	182,625
Mar	6,820	125,471	108,555	13,851	1,174,283	158,621	137,078	131,363	17,009	704,124	1,112	249,476	183,664
Apr	6,812	126,438	110,184	15,305	1,163,182	143,995	131,872	126,545	18,338	708,726	1,091	256,422	195,170

Source: Bank of England

12.3a Monetary financial institutions' (excluding central bank) balance sheet

£ millions

Amounts outstanding of sterling liabilities

	UK MFIs	of which intragroup banks	Sale and repurchase agreements UK public sector	Other UK residents	Non-residents	Acceptances granted	CDs and other paper issued CDs and Commercial paper	Bonds with maturity of up to and incl. 5 years	Bonds with maturity of greater than 5 years	Total	Total sterling deposits	Sterling items in suspense and transmission	Net derivatives	Accrued amounts payable	Sterling capital and other internal funds	Total sterling liabilities
RPM	B3IL	B8ZA	B3UM	B3VM	B3WM	B3XM	B2TL	B6OI	B2TM	B3VM	B3ZM	B3GN	B3HN	B3N	B3JN	B3KN
2013 May	68,594	41,259	5,361	115,194	67,606	305	79,704	26,203	44,373	150,280	3,161,089	47,032	3,877	21,806	429,946	3,670,289
Jun	63,066	41,283	5,301	107,570	58,630	258	79,684	25,039	45,110	149,833	3,154,896	49,844	16,135	22,808	412,951	3,663,398
Jul	66,316	42,748	9,896	115,827	64,952	252	75,672	25,684	44,995	146,351	3,168,862	38,715	18,687	20,158	412,937	3,665,877
Aug	64,177	40,852	5,653	124,419	56,214	118	72,645	25,253	44,469	142,367	3,158,126	44,196	11	21,078	416,011	3,645,941
Sep	68,514	46,261	2,255	124,418	61,852	130	72,386	25,497	44,704	142,587	3,217,643	45,750	-13,478	19,244	392,842 (g)	3,668,623
Oct	66,674	42,900	6,425	125,305	58,969	131	68,801	25,433	44,552	138,787	3,217,590	46,769	664	19,259	397,159	3,688,042
Nov	73,714	47,828	5,611	121,666	62,714	151	70,175	25,062	44,468	139,705	3,234,008	44,895	-8,417	20,680	390,475	3,688,371
Dec	73,318	48,111	3,442	96,875	61,028	153	75,378	24,904	43,042	143,323	3,193,484	23,939	-6,900	19,623	389,906	3,627,073
2014 Jan	84,148	49,239	13,308	130,564 (f)	65,436	158	79,837	25,376	43,428	148,641	2,989,530 (a)(c)(d)(f)	55,917	-11,259	25,682	430,004 (h)(i)	3,496,519 (a)(c)(d)(f)(h)(i)
Feb	92,709	52,531	13,444	144,813	58,003	150	79,240	24,838	42,818	146,897	2,993,546	56,786	-14,556	26,222	451,236	3,519,855
Mar	86,755	55,087	8,946	112,803	66,588	166	77,122	23,837	42,794	143,754	2,928,498	51,822	-8,986	24,466	442,276	3,444,724
Apr	75,791	45,968	2,241	121,696	73,832	159	81,388	23,423	42,475	147,286	2,887,186	51,613	-23,639	23,934	447,226	3,392,965
May	83,097	53,532	1,557	122,157	72,957	154	82,240	22,975	42,091	147,306	2,904,905	40,498	-14,765	24,954	455,739	3,418,043
Jun	84,149	55,113	1,279	117,067	75,286	124	80,517	21,533	41,585	143,634	2,909,286	40,747	-21,088	22,849	445,697	3,404,212
Jul	74,417	44,245	4,282	119,798	76,224	150	82,355	22,319	42,705	147,380	2,885,961	47,185	-22,785	23,681	422,472 (j)(k)	3,363,246 (j)(k)
Aug	74,076	47,099	7,518	125,388	70,518	152	81,730	22,030	41,626	145,386	2,891,911	42,174	-9,817	23,937	426,393 (l)	3,381,400 (l)
Sep	56,811	36,268	796	103,057	68,517	162	81,884	23,103	41,203	146,190	2,858,953	49,388	-14,052	26,884	405,101	3,333,038
Oct	59,600	37,737	4,440	116,195	66,614	173	81,953	22,994	41,674	146,621	2,857,214	38,432	-12,151	23,829	431,089	3,345,216
Nov	60,997	38,054	5,372	115,389	63,626	169	80,333	23,459	39,942	143,734	2,868,012	39,932	-1,693	24,095	430,706	3,367,887
Dec	64,292	36,212	2,870	95,762	69,829	167	85,318	23,143	39,128	147,589	2,888,435	19,975	7	25,080	435,739	3,376,331
2015 Jan	75,875	46,874	2,822	103,421	70,008	159	86,166	23,279	39,572	149,016	2,884,674	44,328	-4,499	25,759	454,083	3,411,169
Feb	74,528	45,580	3,224	105,481	66,160	162	87,650	23,833	38,815	150,297	2,856,821	46,097	-26,705	27,881	453,300	3,364,163
Mar	72,399	46,430	2,872	94,351	67,154	171	94,278	23,959	37,596	155,834	2,906,882	42,791	-1,434	24,463	423,012	3,402,534
Apr	72,534	42,171	6,081	99,656	72,625	180	97,381	24,909	38,897	161,187	2,915,286	42,951	-26,380	22,109	413,996	3,374,774

Source: Bank of England

Notes to table

Movements in amounts outstanding can reflect breaks in data series as well as underlying flows. For changes data, users are recommended to refer directly to the appropriate series or data tables. Further explanation can be found at: www.bankofengland.co.uk/statistics/Pages/iadb/notesiadb/Changes_flows_growth_rates.aspx.

(a) Due to improvements in reporting at one institution, the amounts outstanding decreased by £85bn. This effect has been adjusted out of the flows for January 2014.

(b) Due to improvements in reporting at one institution, the amounts outstanding increased by £12bn. The effect has been adjusted out of the flows for September 2013.

(c) Due to improvements in reporting at one institution, the amounts outstanding decreased by £26bn. This effect has been adjusted out of the flows for January 2014.

(d) Due to improvements in reporting at one institution, the amounts outstanding decreased by £129bn. This effect has been adjusted out of the flows for January 2014.

(e) Due to improvements in reporting at one institution, the amounts outstanding increased by £8bn. This effect has been adjusted out of the flows for July 2013.

(f) Due to a change in treatment at one institution, the amounts outstanding increased by £19bn. This effect has been adjusted out of the flows for January 2014.

(g) Due to a change in treatment at one institution, the amounts outstanding increased by £19bn. This effect has been adjusted out of the flows for January 2014.

(h) Due to improvements in reporting at one institution, the amounts outstanding decreased by £8bn. The effect has been adjusted out of the flows for September 2013.

(i) Due to improvements in reporting at one institution, the amounts outstanding increased by £18bn. This effect has been adjusted out of the flows for January 2014.

(j) Due to improvements in reporting at one institution, the amounts outstanding decreased by £18bn. This effect has been adjusted out of the flows for January 2014.

(k) Due to improvements in reporting at one institution, the amounts outstanding decreased by £36bn. This effect has been adjusted out of the flows for July 2014.

(l) Due to improvements in reporting at one institution, the amounts outstanding decreased by £16bn. This effect has been adjusted out of the flows for July 2014. This effect has been adjusted out of the flows for August 2014.

12.3b Monetary financial institutions' (excluding central bank) balance sheet: group detail - UK

£ millions   Not seasonally adjusted

Amounts outstanding of foreign currency liabilities (including euro)

RPM	Sight and time deposits					Acceptances granted	Sale and repurchase agreements				
	MFIs	of which intragroup banks	UK public sector	Other UK residents	Non-residents		MFIs	of which intragroup banks	UK public sector	Other UK residents	Non-residents
	B3JLUKIN	B8ZMUKIN	B2UPUKIN	B2UVUKIN	B3NNUKIN	B3KQUKIN	B3KLUKIN	B8ZKUKIN	B3PNUKIN	B3QNUKIN	B3RNUKIN
2013 May	46,229	28,710	647	151,334	577,354	1,126	26,768	2,785	169	58,469	323,948
Jun	46,471	29,269	604	145,563	564,497	1,409	23,778	2,877	-	62,102	340,726
Jul	43,303	29,920	604	146,347	522,734	1,313	25,476	3,581	-	64,686	308,690
Aug	42,023	28,761	627	143,001	500,064	1,219	24,237	3,781	-	65,309	304,032
Sep	42,244	29,941	509	139,322	477,123	1,238	25,003	4,643	679	61,205	281,339
Oct	43,337	29,857	496	137,485	484,214	1,407	25,209	4,139	666	53,842	276,859
Nov	40,957	28,521	615	134,339	464,272	1,634	25,284	5,822	-	59,627	264,741
Dec	41,233	30,168	446	126,170	453,229	1,834	25,126	6,266	-	54,628	249,001
2014 Jan	45,222	31,347	473	135,832	454,312	1,709	23,716	5,892	-	45,985	268,776
Feb	44,892	31,552	457	138,752	457,527	1,638	24,748	7,735	-	52,579	261,186
Mar	44,581	31,665	376	125,864	437,751	2,005	24,202	6,662	-	45,096	261,273
Apr	42,654	30,908	462	123,709	436,250	1,673	21,956	3,472	-	51,762	248,860
May	42,675	31,292	422	123,038	444,618	1,708	17,586	1,535	-	49,893	253,389
Jun	43,271	31,482	428	111,530	435,482	1,764	16,663	997	-	46,190	231,308
Jul	42,994	30,523	436	111,031	428,962	1,885	19,745	918	-	43,370	241,915
Aug	43,241	29,353	695	110,262	442,190	2,121	19,170	798	-	52,475	245,624
Sep	43,567	29,715	713	110,669	446,128	2,278	19,056	855	-	50,762	244,625
Oct	44,263	30,698	1,376	110,591	444,364	1,779	21,511	936	-	48,048	243,076
Nov	45,529	32,169	1,344	118,202	461,132	1,595	17,382	506	-	47,220	234,339
Dec	46,343	33,871	1,132	114,480	438,439	1,415	14,797	481	962	35,772	212,213
2015 Jan	48,551	33,833	1,112	116,642	468,972	1,311	15,857	463	-	44,179	222,620
Feb	46,007	33,465	1,013	117,140	449,197	1,274	14,573	446	-	45,375	229,075
Mar	49,015	34,186	1,016	122,653	448,477	1,387	16,295	455	-	41,130	214,586
Apr	50,815	35,352	1,037	120,009	455,770	1,312	15,867	458	-	41,643	219,232

Source: Bank of England

12.3b Monetary financial institutions' (excluding central bank) balance sheet: group detail - UK

£ millions

Amounts outstanding of foreign currency liabilities (including euro)

RPM	CDs and Commercial paper	CDs and other paper Issued: Bonds with maturity of up to and incl. 5 years	Bonds with maturity of greater than 5 years	Total	Total foreign currency deposits	Items in suspense and transmission	Net derivatives	Accrued amounts payable	Capital and other internal funds	Total foreign currency liabilities	Total liabilities
	B2TPUKIN	B6OKUKIN	B2TQUKIN	B3SNUKIN	B3TNUKIN	B3UNUKIN	B3VNUKIN	B3WNUKIN	B3XNUKIN	B3YNUKIN	B3ZNUKIN
2013 May	36,773	109,618	119,324	265,716	1,451,761	81,286	-10,654	5,830	147,091	1,675,313	4,421,725
Jun	27,078	108,102	117,119	252,299	1,437,449	64,739	-14,103	5,629	152,023	1,645,737	4,370,390
Jul	36,410	110,364	118,858	265,632	1,378,784	65,827	-12,950	5,216	143,174	1,580,052	4,319,548
Aug	38,524	103,766	116,190	258,479	1,338,992	62,969	-3,240	5,525	138,471	1,542,717	4,277,622
Sep	28,766	100,145	112,838	241,748	1,269,732	68,073	-2,623	5,681	161,166 (l)	1,502,030	4,261,665
Oct	28,364	103,347	111,017	242,727	1,266,255	69,502	-6,452	5,633	158,615	1,493,553	4,268,148
Nov	26,799	98,525	110,983	236,307	1,228,443	60,791	-2,293	5,085	162,472	1,454,497	4,237,756
Dec	25,059	97,419	104,731	227,208	1,178,876	40,598	-1,479	5,288	175,003	1,398,286	4,140,366
2014 Jan	29,183	94,604	101,507	225,294	1,201,320	61,750	7,832	4,674	129,008	1,404,584 (n)(o)(p)(q)(r)(s)	3,989,747
Feb	28,197	95,622	102,070	225,889	1,207,667	61,676	6,687	4,763	110,765	1,391,559	3,998,818
Mar	21,709	96,124	102,263	220,097	1,161,244	58,218	-757	4,864	111,950	1,335,520	3,882,006
Apr	28,122	93,648	102,209	223,979	1,151,304	59,917	11,589	4,477	97,301	1,324,588	3,821,433
May	29,398	89,792	104,289	223,479	1,156,807	64,835	5,723	5,011	91,904	1,324,281	3,841,635
Jun	21,024	88,690	103,797	213,511	1,100,148	58,327	3,288	5,280	107,736	1,274,779	3,795,237
Jul	27,242	85,597	102,419	215,257	1,100,595	58,584	8,694	5,420	79,143	1,257,436 (m)	3,742,677 (m)(t)(u)
Aug	30,547	85,555	102,990	219,093	1,134,871	51,470	9,500	5,461	66,185	1,267,488	3,754,663 (v)
Sep	22,586	81,029	99,929	203,545	1,121,343	48,457	11,139	3,633	96,260	1,280,834	3,723,821
Oct	29,887	77,485	100,054	207,425	1,122,433	47,883	11,893	5,743	77,654	1,265,606	3,711,304
Nov	30,823	77,386	102,384	210,593	1,137,337	45,108	6,570	6,781	87,357	1,283,154	3,729,662
Dec	23,437	75,198	100,594	199,229	1,064,783	17,483	2,923	5,875	76,081	1,167,145	3,630,907
2015 Jan	30,566	71,428	100,398	202,392	1,121,637	52,307	15,682	4,828	64,549	1,259,003	3,728,685
Feb	35,249	68,273	98,356	201,877	1,105,531	48,815	15,002	2,759	70,858	1,242,965	3,699,523
Mar	27,165	67,827	108,875	203,868	1,098,427	38,709	9,834	4,412	90,362	1,241,745	3,696,890
Apr	34,570	64,905	106,975	206,450	1,112,136	50,580	22,642	4,496	98,962	1,288,816	3,718,410

Source: Bank of England

Notes to table

Movements in amounts outstanding can reflect breaks in data series as well as underlying flows. Further explanation can be found at: www.bankofengland.co.uk/statistics/Pages/iadb/notesiadb/Changes_flows_growth_rates.aspx.

(l) Due to improvements in reporting at one institution, the amounts outstanding increased by £8bn in September 2013.

(m) Due to improvements in reporting at one institution, the amounts outstanding decreased by £11bn in July 2014.

(n) Due to improvements in reporting at one institution, the amounts outstanding increased by £18bn in January 2014.

(o) Due to improvements in reporting at one institution, the amounts outstanding decreased by £18bn in January 2014.

(p) Due to improvements in reporting at one institution, the amounts outstanding decreased by £85bn in January 2014.

(q) Due to improvements in reporting at one institution, the amounts outstanding decreased by £26bn in January 2014.

(r) Due to improvements in reporting at one institution, the amounts outstanding decreased by £129bn in January 2014.

(s) Due to a change in treatment at one institution, the amounts outstanding increased by £19bn in January 2014.

(t) Due to improvements in reporting at one institution, the amounts outstanding decreased by £36bn in July 2014.

(u) Due to improvements in reporting at one institution, the amounts outstanding decreased by £16bn in July 2014.

(v) Due to improvements in reporting at one institution, the amounts outstanding increased by £9bn in August 2014.

12.3c Monetary financial institutions' (excluding central bank) balance sheet: group detail - UK

£ millions   Not seasonally adjusted

Amounts outstanding of sterling assets

RPM	Notes coin	With UK central bank: Cash ratio deposits	With UK central bank: Other	Loans: UK MFIs	Loans: of which intragroup banks	Loans: UK MFIs CDs	Loans: UK MFIs commercial paper	Loans: Non-residents	Acceptances granted: UK MFIs	Acceptances granted: UK public sector	Acceptances granted: Other UK residents	Acceptances granted: Non-residents
	B3UOUKIN	B3VOUKIN	B3WOUKIN	B3NLUKIN	B8ZIUKIN	B3OLUKIN	B3PLUKIN	B3XOUKIN	B3QLUKIN	B3YOUKIN	B3ZOUKIN	B3GPUKIN
2013 May	6,969	2,019	184,415	412,244	396,305	4,831	14	18,701	27	-	133	10
Jun	6,579	3,104	172,536	414,876	400,679	4,979	17	21,005	20	-	87	11
Jul	6,494	3,104	195,681	412,272	398,959	4,832	22	19,072	20	-	87	12
Aug	6,688	3,104	195,499	414,035	400,723	4,795	22	18,022	20	-	92	13
Sep	6,196	3,104	193,453	446,551 (y)	432,773 (y)	4,332	22	18,358	29	-	108	10
Oct	6,612	3,104	196,213	458,026	444,155	4,003	22	18,729	29	-	103	15
Nov	6,399	3,115	182,954	460,533	448,435	3,929	30	18,879	28	-	122	13
Dec	7,123	3,176	176,199	465,951	454,406	3,648	35	16,619	28	-	124	12
2014 Jan	6,229	3,176	181,452	227,827 (z)(aa)	217,000 (z)(aa)	3,905	70	17,864	28	-	128	12
Feb	6,132	3,176	187,060	219,091	207,701	3,948	30	18,242	28	-	127	7
Mar	5,914	3,176	177,222	206,734	197,175	4,001	34	17,042	43	-	143	8
Apr	6,405	3,176	183,803	186,064	176,498	4,071	42	18,777	43	-	136	9
May	6,306	3,176	184,277	190,910	180,487	4,114	50	19,460	43	-	135	6
Jun	5,870	3,186	177,604	194,119	184,192	4,361	59	18,938	23	-	105	5
Jul	6,320	3,186	184,632	184,092	174,953	4,483	122	19,265	23	-	125	6
Aug	6,312	3,187	189,839	186,893	176,738	4,525	75	23,753	24	-	123	6
Sep	6,234	3,187	179,937	186,058	175,928	3,682	128	20,326	24	-	129	5
Oct	6,328	3,187	195,213	186,063	175,410	3,546	146	18,754	23	-	136	8
Nov	6,012	3,196	188,549	195,526	183,976	3,222	176	18,843	23	-	132	8
Dec	7,019	3,135	175,133	199,607	187,293	2,955	186	17,074	24	-	134	7
2015 Jan	6,086	3,135	188,048	200,936	185,529	2,884	183	17,068	15	-	122	6
Feb	5,943	3,135	195,388	202,444	190,206	2,948	175	17,511	15	-	127	5
Mar	6,284	3,135	183,931	208,471	195,134	2,949	133	17,815	15	-	134	5
Apr	6,432	3,134	192,148	207,071	193,925	3,099	128	16,247	14	-	142	6

Source: Bank of England

12.3c Monetary financial institutions' (excluding central bank) balance sheet: group detail - UK

£ millions

Amounts outstanding of sterling assets

	Bills				Sales and repurchase agreements					Advances		
	Treasury bills	UK MFIs bills	Other UK residents	Non-residents	UK MFIs	of which intragroup banks	UK public sector	Other UK residents	Non-residents	UK public sector	Other UK residents	Non-residents
RPM	B3HPUKIN	B3RLUKIN	B3IPUKIN	B3JPUKIN	B3SLUKIN	B8ZGUKIN	B3KPUKIN	B3LPUKIN	B3MPUKIN	B2UKUKIN	B3OPUKIN	B3PPUKIN
2013 May	1,947	6	327	3,939	32,451	20,475	208	71,056	19,018	6,142	1,486,488	36,206
Jun	1,601	6	415	3,875	26,617	19,588	744	72,526	22,548	6,141	1,486,274	36,182
Jul	2,174	5	220	3,786	29,933	21,586	92	65,337	26,226	6,089	1,497,329	36,536
Aug	1,406	5	215	3,772	29,611	20,764	-	68,770	27,309	6,138	1,506,422	33,720
Sep	1,933	5	227	3,749	37,298	27,690	998	78,168	19,698	6,165	1,509,356	33,021
Oct	1,395	2	240	4,034	35,791	25,872	1,093	69,956	20,881	6,136	1,513,609	33,859
Nov	-372	2	323	4,055	43,330	30,711	566	71,404	25,275	6,115	1,512,468	34,423
Dec	-1,777	8	272	3,774	45,235	31,884	77	63,070	26,828	6,276	1,496,208	40,706
2014 Jan	-631	10	269	3,790	47,695	31,466	652	78,369 (ab)	30,316	6,254	1,489,017	40,897
Feb	857	17	256	3,756	55,227	33,658	3	82,618	30,044	6,320	1,490,497	41,296
Mar	692	16	232	3,706	52,250	35,626	21	79,105	25,222	6,267	1,454,509	40,886
Apr	1,188	25	279	3,434	38,740	24,029	-	77,011	25,517	6,424	1,441,564	37,174
May	2,009	32	263	3,647	49,166	33,720	-	82,413	25,425	6,427	1,433,927	40,867
Jun	1,164	40	258	3,668	57,067	38,651	-	86,570	27,663	6,409	1,432,954	41,444
Jul	880	33	325	3,734	45,773	29,155	97	85,765	27,609	6,321	1,434,783	35,674
Aug	2,503	43	217	4,231	44,969	31,566	1,175	79,697	30,135	6,341	1,435,296	40,764
Sep	2,078	34	204	3,708	29,714	20,531	26	85,049	28,669	6,426	1,429,654	42,061
Oct	3,152	42	209	1,340	34,000	24,663	-	81,775	28,789	6,632	1,424,538	40,388
Nov	3,785	53	218	1,353	36,260	24,990	-	82,789	28,071	6,596	1,415,976	40,599
Dec	3,007	54	229	1,412	41,287	24,135	24	74,768	29,338	6,635	1,411,428	38,601
2015 Jan	2,779	50	132	1,242	51,761	33,917	-	76,342	29,617	6,619	1,410,743	38,779
Feb	3,226	63	116	1,140	49,019	32,813	8	77,793	31,185	6,671	1,408,490	39,547
Mar	1,949	51	99	1,042	46,409	33,972	5	82,529	28,036	6,570	1,419,898	36,025
Apr	2,284	48	85	1,318	44,488	30,826	7	82,229	32,747	6,642	1,418,393	33,027

Source: Bank of England

12.3c Monetary financial institutions' (excluding central bank) balance sheet: group detail - UK

£ millions

Amounts outstanding of sterling assets

RPM	UK government bonds	Other UK public sector	Investments UK MFIs	Other UK residents	Non-residents	Items in suspense and collection	Accrued amounts receivable	Other assets	Total sterling assets
	B3QPUKIN	B3RPUKIN	B3TLUKIN	B3SPUKIN	B3TPUKIN	B3UPUKIN	B3VPUKIN	B3WPUKIN	B3XPUKIN
2013 May	91,902	10	77,371	206,244	31,206	24,045	10,292	19,484	2,747,676
Jun	93,228	43	77,589	206,242	25,242	24,751	10,922	19,559	2,737,699
Jul	95,810	8	77,329	208,001	23,961	17,606	12,569	18,178	2,762,763
Aug	94,924	1	76,362	208,058	21,077	20,431	12,184	17,658	2,770,333
Sep	97,410	-1	76,496	206,502	20,767	21,417	11,359	18,032	2,814,732
Oct	103,187	39	76,715	197,721	22,674	21,788	11,998	17,945	2,825,890
Nov	107,589	23	76,577	201,354	23,042	19,158	12,113	18,708	2,832,127
Dec	108,558	15	77,279	194,973	21,348	11,361	10,490	19,375	2,796,962 (z)(aa)(ab)
2014 Jan	109,860	8	74,460	194,318	27,076	23,434	11,264	18,932	2,596,651
Feb	108,788	8	75,355	190,122	26,970	22,258	11,645	18,881	2,602,731
Mar	104,979	2	76,644	188,215	26,789	23,530	9,681	18,807	2,525,827
Apr	106,582	13	76,732	182,154	25,736	20,438	8,507	19,438	2,473,438
May	107,038	24	76,358	184,649	27,397	19,048	8,855	20,773	2,496,750
Jun	107,428	11	77,797	186,110	26,717	20,022	8,834	20,740	2,509,143
Jul	108,453	26	29,304 (ac)(ad)	187,851	26,708	22,919	8,143	20,671	2,447,300 (ac)(ad)
Aug	108,563	24	34,584 (ae)	186,893	26,212	21,035	9,125	20,825	2,467,343 (ae)
Sep	105,489	20	34,834	185,201	27,751	31,132	8,051	20,674	2,440,459
Oct	112,167	32	35,068	180,382	27,983	18,236	8,170	20,744	2,437,028
Nov	117,669	30	35,430	180,352	26,868	22,329	9,286	20,845	2,444,175
Dec	116,968	30	36,557	194,846	30,151	13,183	7,871	20,941	2,432,583
2015 Jan	117,052	24	38,442	176,818	30,848	21,609	7,530	21,066	2,449,922
Feb	108,855	6	39,370	173,652	30,992	20,233	7,302	20,922	2,446,265
Mar	105,858	16	40,168	166,920	31,414	22,097	6,746	21,279	2,439,971
Apr	104,689	20	39,883	167,555	30,863	19,818	6,850	21,589	2,440,940

Source: Bank of England

Notes to table

Movements in amounts outstanding can reflect breaks in data series as well as underlying flows. Further explanation can be found at:
www.bankofengland.co.uk/statistics/Pages/iadb/notesiadb/Changes_flows_growth_rates.aspx.

(y) Due to improvements in reporting at one institution, the amounts outstanding increased by £12bn in September 2013.
(z) Due to improvements in reporting at one institution, the amounts outstanding decreased by £129bn in January 2014.
(aa) Due to improvements in reporting at one institution, the amounts outstanding decreased by £111bn in January 2014.
(ab) Due to a change in treatment at one institution, the amounts outstanding increased by £19bn in January 2014.
(ac) Due to improvements in reporting at one institution, the amounts outstanding decreased by £36bn in July 2014.
(ad) Due to improvements in reporting at one institution, the amounts outstanding decreased by £13bn in July 2014.
(ae) Due to improvements in reporting at one institution, the amounts outstanding increased by £9bn in August 2014.

12.3d Monetary financial institutions' (excluding central bank) balance sheet: group detail - UK

£ millions   Not seasonally adjusted

Amounts outstanding of foreign currency assets (including euro)

RPM	Loans and advances						Sale and repurchase agreements					Acceptances granted	Bills
	UK MFIs	of which intragroup banks	UK MFIs' CDs etc.	UK public sector	Other UK residents	Non-residents	UK MFIs	of which intragroup banks	UK public sector	Other UK residents	Non-residents		
	B3ULUKIN	B8ZQUKIN	B3VLUKIN	B2UNUKIN	B3ZPUKIN	B2UHUKIN	B3WLUKIN	B8ZOUKIN	B3HQUKIN	B3IQUKIN	B3JQUKIN	B3KQUKIN	B3LQUKIN
2013 May	47,623	29,016	339	8	154,764	670,336	21,377	2,785	-	67,720	346,747	1,126	25,977
Jun	45,917	29,599	341	9	136,420	651,645	20,161	2,877	-	69,912	345,208	1,409	22,410
Jul	48,687	30,045	332	6	124,685	612,256	20,879	3,581	-	68,552	326,378	1,313	21,859
Aug	46,286	28,502	467	6	122,045	579,438	19,266	3,781	-	61,284	324,364	1,219	22,007
Sep	46,419	29,635	419	7	121,160	545,666	18,586	4,643	-	57,237	306,465	1,238	19,228
Oct	47,128	29,623	861	7	126,955	530,292	18,968	4,139	-	62,329	298,751	1,407	18,980
Nov	44,704	28,275	1,148	7	122,437	526,018	17,295	5,822	-	57,298	286,685	1,634	19,083
Dec	42,661	29,852	1,251	7	122,068	507,322	17,728	6,266	-	55,259	272,012	1,834	19,981
2014 Jan	45,888	30,577	752	7	126,079	527,337	21,149	5,892	-	56,952	279,002	1,709	18,156
Feb	44,629	30,793	837	7	127,265	545,147	21,516	7,735	-	54,055	267,275	1,638	21,418
Mar	44,220	30,753	460	-	111,692	513,589	20,212	6,638	-	49,774	274,241	2,005	21,940
Apr	42,265	29,812	489	-	113,301	516,678	16,165	3,472	-	56,216	260,556	1,673	21,475
May	41,970	30,381	364	2	110,768	519,204	13,960	1,543	-	50,142	262,094	1,708	19,961
Jun	42,501	30,289	376	2	97,007	493,411	18,784	997	-	50,999	248,650	1,764	18,586
Jul	42,703	30,111	431	-	98,442	504,068	16,754	918	-	49,141	264,057	1,885	16,250
Aug	41,752	28,844	257	-	99,620	510,901	15,192	798	-	57,085	261,436	2,121	16,674
Sep	42,545	29,405	231	-	103,042	495,828	15,836	855	-	55,788	257,934	2,278	20,128
Oct	42,038	29,912	56	778	102,134	497,778	16,092	953	-	54,680	243,621	1,779	18,422
Nov	45,196	31,086	58	795	102,186	516,440	14,129	506	-	51,842	232,014	1,595	21,039
Dec	46,764	33,409	55	709	101,760	488,935	11,720	481	-	41,982	230,165	1,415	21,702
2015 Jan	48,972	33,348	68	623	106,419	513,575	12,391	463	-	45,817	225,471	1,311	21,712
Feb	47,034	33,099	64	579	105,825	496,347	12,424	446	-	45,550	225,536	1,274	21,462
Mar	49,350	33,895	80	516	103,895	504,213	13,978	455	-	43,324	221,719	1,387	23,031
Apr	51,631	35,056	129	470	106,433	520,702	12,499	458	-	49,096	213,423	1,312	24,547

Source: Bank of England

12.3d Monetary financial institutions' (excluding central bank) balance sheet: group detail - UK

£ millions

Amounts outstanding of foreign currency assets (including euro)

RPM	UK government bonds	Other UK public	Investments UK MFIs	Other UK residents	Non-residents	Items in suspense and collection	Accrued amounts receivable	Other assets	Total foreign currency	Total assets	Holdings of own sterling	Holdings of own foreign currency
	B3MQUKIN	B3NQUKIN	B3XLUKIN	B3OQUKIN	B3PQUKIN	B3QQUKIN	B3RQUKIN	B3SQUKIN	B3TQUKIN	B3UQUKIN	B3IMUKIN	B3JMUKIN
2013 May	-	-	6,235	24,835	217,271	70,909	3,998	14,782	1,674,048	4,421,725	78	1,055
Jun	-	-	6,658	25,341	228,299	57,585	4,023	17,353	1,632,691	4,370,390	60	1,023
Jul	-	-	6,546	26,053	224,775	53,640	2,977	17,846	1,556,784	4,319,548	71	1,087
Aug	-	-	6,368	25,601	222,644	54,393	3,115	18,785	1,507,289	4,277,622	77	935
Sep	1	-	5,856	25,548	222,338	56,055	2,906	17,804	1,446,933	4,261,665	84	865
Oct	63	-	6,814	26,079	224,673	58,099	3,106	17,744	1,442,258	4,268,148	93	1,039
Nov	62	-	7,233	25,156	225,093	52,353	3,000	16,424	1,405,629	4,237,756	106	881
Dec	61	-	6,830	26,370	221,953	28,068	3,150	16,850	1,343,404	4,140,366	104	831
2014 Jan	67	-	9,128	21,841	197,584	68,466	2,762	16,218	1,393,097	3,989,748 (ag)(ah)(ai)	114	883
Feb	66	-	9,307	21,723	194,570	69,467	2,834	14,334	1,396,087	3,998,819	114	847
Mar	85	-	9,301	22,133	204,019	63,527	2,899	16,081	1,356,179	3,882,006	113	969
Apr	78	1	9,199	21,871	202,864	66,695	3,061	15,408	1,347,996	3,821,433	120	1,050
May	78	-	9,290	21,796	208,717	69,313	3,169	12,347	1,344,885	3,841,635	121	1,137
Jun	66	-	8,961	22,177	203,748	63,537	3,051	12,474	1,286,094	3,795,237	111	1,045
Jul	47	-	16,680	18,440	187,082	65,118	2,911	11,369	1,295,376 (af)	3,742,677 (af)(aj)(ak)	106	977
Aug	35	-	8,917	18,494	186,694	52,994	3,126	12,021	1,287,320	3,754,663 (al)	114	883
Sep	19	-	8,361	18,821	201,152	48,236	2,911	10,253	1,283,362	3,723,821	136	947
Oct	131	-	7,971	18,708	207,882	50,405	2,989	8,812	1,274,275	3,711,304	132	978
Nov	189	-	8,069	19,142	211,152	49,310	3,382	8,949	1,285,488	3,729,662	149	924
Dec	189	-	6,285	8,111	209,277	19,899	3,085	6,271	1,198,324	3,630,907	147	1,041
2015 Jan	157	-	5,909	7,955	219,832	58,091	2,798	7,664	1,278,763	3,728,685	113	1,101
Feb	102	-	5,638	7,739	221,459	52,457	2,981	6,786	1,253,258	3,699,523	112	1,051
Mar	159	-	5,535	8,202	229,860	41,938	3,243	6,492	1,256,920	3,696,890	120	1,252
Apr	155	-	5,598	7,963	219,424	55,012	2,884	6,191	1,277,470	3,718,410	121	1,009

Notes to table

Movements in amounts outstanding can reflect breaks in data series as well as underlying flows. Further explanation can be found at: www.bankofengland.co.uk/statistics/Pages/iadb/notesiadb/Changes_flows_growth_rates.aspx.

(af) Due to improvements in reporting at one institution, the amounts outstanding decreased by £11bn in July 2014.

(ag) Due to improvements in reporting at one institution, the amounts outstanding decreased by £129bn in January 2014.

(ah) Due to improvements in reporting at one institution, the amounts outstanding decreased by £111bn in January 2014.

(ai) Due to a change in treatment at one institution, the amounts outstanding increased by £19bn in January 2014.

(aj) Due to improvements in reporting at one institution, the amounts outstanding decreased by £36bn in July 2014.

(ak) Due to improvements in reporting at one institution, the amounts outstanding decreased by £13bn in July 2014.

(al) Due to improvements in reporting at one institution, the amounts outstanding increased by £9bn in August 2014.

Source: Bank of England

Source: Bank of England

12.3e Monetary financial institutions' (excluding central bank) balance sheet

£ millions   Not seasonally adjusted

Changes in sterling liabilities

	Notes outstanding & cash loaded cards	Sight deposits					Time deposits						
		UK MFIs	of which intragroup banks	UK public sector	Other UK residents	Non-residents	UK MFIs	of which intragroup banks	UK public sector	Other UK residents	of which SAYE	of which cash ISAs	Non-residents
RPM	B4IJ	B4GA	B8ZD	B4CF	B4BH	B4DD	B4HA	B8ZF	B4DF	B4CH	B4FH	B4DH	B4ED
2013 May	95	10,263	12,683	-829	5,300	6,864	-1,808	-1,708	1,065	-4,049	32	2,155	-4,443
Jun	226	3,686	4,790	-448	14,803	8,816	3,615	3,828	455	-5,675	8	755	-8,642
Jul	-246	-5,773	-6,942	508	3,278	-6,616	3,723	4,425	917	-9,887	-	233	339
Aug	2	5,222	5,387	246	10,289	-943	-7,568	-7,348	-434	1,814	-68	433	-5,425
Sep	101	13,956	13,604	7	15,841	6,525	11,271	12,269	-276	-3,173	-9	-19	-2,668
Oct	-21	6,143	6,409	185	2,621	-1,688	4,645	4,214	-667	-4,797	68	-434	-3,028
Nov	130	-8,098	-5,961	-1,060	20,359	1,815	10,627	10,607	-759	-7,218	-119	-431	-4,142
Dec	291	-8,324	-7,228	97	6,680	4,762	-7,438	-7,335	-1,409	-23,421	-44	-612	15,109
2014 Jan	-377	4,771	3,999	1,463	-3,852	-7,915	-6,644	-5,630	-410	-12,864	-31	-659	-3,039
Feb	-23	-9,340	-9,142	-1,051	6,830	2,808	-2,210	-1,842	502	847	-7	-415	-7,395
Mar	27	-5,675	-5,194	-907	24,962	2,905	-8,496	-6,649	-1,203	-25,069	108	1,685	-13,968
Apr	-4	-22,194	-22,111	3,125	-5,595	-12,213	812	-285	2,670	-13,546	109	5,199	3,843
May	68	7,801	6,852	-1,390	12,677	9,967	-4,286	-3,181	1,055	-12,280	-92	1,091	-1,505
Jun	7	-655	-579	-732	17,453	1,340	821	1,433	375	-6,118	115	-235	-4,360
Jul	12	-11,750	-9,967	639	-12,470	77	-2,901	-3,885	778	2,725	14	7,841	-4,108
Aug	69	1,691	1,461	-937	5,796	-4,536	-1,021	-854	-248	-219	11	3,125	3,775
Sep	-37	2,427	2,456	-289	13,547	5,730	1,893	1,917	-699	-4,231	-128	1,766	-4,092
Oct	38	-1,519	-1,532	-300	-1,589	-2,078	1,068	1,205	-41	-13,978	46	1,414	-2,043
Nov	33	3,422	3,080	-620	12,838	1,230	7,842	8,656	-676	-6,384	48	926	-936
Dec	259	7,952	8,559	287	11,892	5,543	-4,931	-4,361	-1,595	1,419	87	582	8,634
2015 Jan	-270	11,995	9,185	1,259	-3,467	-4,211	-266	-511	-7	-24,348	-80	37	-3,392
Feb	-56	-3,651	-2,448	-808	-843	-3,972	-7,484	-7,484	174	-6,163	-109	46	-4,710
Mar	51	9,168	8,067	-809	27,221	15,294	3,624	3,718	-949	188	12	2,961	804
Apr	-7	966	1,629	1,454	-7,145	-14,626	-5,207	-4,819	1,329	4,602	-21	6,946	11,506

Source: Bank of England

Full explanatory notes to this table can be found on the Bank of England website: http://www.bankofengland.co.uk/statistics/Pages/iadb/notesiadb/MFIs_exICB.aspx

12.3e Monetary financial institutions' (excluding central bank) balance sheet

£ millions

Changes in sterling liabilities

| RPM | UK MFIs | Liabilities under sale and repurchase agreements | | | | Acceptances granted | CDs and other paper issued | | | | Total sterling deposits | Sterling items in suspense and transmission | Net derivatives | Accrued amounts payable | Sterling capital and other internal funds | Total sterling liabilities |
		of which intragroup banks	UK public sector	Other UK residents	Non-residents		CDs and Commercial paper	Bonds with maturity of up to and incl. 5 years	Bonds with maturity of greater than 5 years	Total						
	B4IA	B8ZB	B4EF	B4EH	B4FD	B4BK	B2SU	B6OH	B2TK	B4EJ	B4FJ	B4AK	B4GJ	B4CJ	B4DJ	B4J
2013 May	2,712	-1,780	548	185	-1,129	-14	1,576	1,715	-1,723	1,567	16,232	3,102	4,819	-918	-7,180	16,150
Jun	-5,527	24	-60	-7,624	-8,976	-47	-20	-1,164	737	-447	-6,070	2,811	12,257	1,002	-10,913	-686
Jul	3,249	1,465	4,595	8,257	6,321	-5	-4,012	645	-114	-3,482	5,425	-11,129	2,980	-2,650	2,315	-3,305
Aug	-2,139	-2,004	-4,243	8,592	-8,738	4	-3,027	-430	-526	-3,984	-7,308	5,481	-18,677	270	10,618	-9,613
Sep	5,035	5,409	-3,397	-1	5,639	12	-259	244	235	219	48,990	434	-13,488	-1,005	-14,832	20,199
Oct	-1,608	-3,361	4,170	887	-3,116	1	-3,585	-64	-152	-3,800	-53	1,019	14,142	15	1,720	16,822
Nov	7,040	4,929	-814	-3,640	3,746	20	1,374	-404	-52	919	18,795	-1,904	-8,981	1,550	-2,088	7,502
Dec	-396	282	-2,169	-24,791	-1,686	2	3,074	-158	-1,426	1,489	-41,495	-20,955	1,267	-197	6,395	-54,695
2014 Jan	7,382	1,128	9,866	14,858	4,408	5	4,459	473	386	5,318	13,347	36,069	-5,967	2,360	40,430	85,861
Feb	8,561	3,293	137	14,248	-7,433	-8	-597	-486	-610	-1,693	4,803	446	-3,296	526	23,504	25,959
Mar	-5,954	2,556	-4,498	-32,010	8,585	15	-2,118	-1,001	-24	-3,143	-64,456	-4,964	5,570	-1,756	-6,614	-72,193
Apr	-10,965	-9,119	-6,705	8,893	7,243	-7	4,266	-414	-320	3,532	-41,107	-209	-14,653	-532	3,700	-52,804
May	7,306	7,564	-685	461	-874	-5	872	-445	-384	43	18,285	-11,115	8,874	1,023	8,765	25,899
Jun	1,052	1,581	-278	-5,090	2,329	-30	-1,723	-1,443	-603	-3,769	2,339	249	-6,193	-2,107	-7,388	-13,093
Jul	-9,732	-10,868	3,003	2,731	939	25	1,838	787	1,120	3,745	-26,296	6,438	-1,697	837	29,896	9,190
Aug	-341	2,854	3,235	5,589	-5,706	2	-625	-289	-1,080	-1,994	5,087	-5,011	12,968	256	-9,508	3,861
Sep	-17,264	-10,831	-6,722	-23,782	-550	10	153	1,073	-422	804	-33,217	7,215	-4,236	2,947	-18,869	-46,197
Oct	2,789	1,469	3,645	13,138	-1,903	11	69	-109	471	431	-2,369	-10,956	1,901	-2,426	22,547	8,735
Nov	1,396	317	932	-806	-2,988	-4	-1,620	465	-1,732	-2,887	12,359	1,500	10,458	266	-6,610	18,005
Dec	3,296	-1,842	-2,502	-19,628	6,204	-2	4,985	-316	-814	3,855	20,425	-19,957	1,730	1,028	6,290	9,774
2015 Jan	11,582	10,663	-48	7,659	179	-7	848	-664	444	628	-2,447	24,353	-4,506	679	9,161	26,969
Feb	-1,347	-1,295	401	2,061	-3,848	2	1,484	1	-204	1,281	-28,906	1,769	-22,206	2,123	9,547	-37,729
Mar	-2,128	851	-352	-11,130	994	10	3,724	127	-1,355	2,495	44,429	-3,306	20,886	-3,282	-22,399	36,379
Apr	134	-4,259	3,209	5,305	5,472	9	3,103	949	1,301	5,353	12,360	161	-24,946	-2,354	6,795	-7,993

Source: Bank of England

Full explanatory notes to this table can be found on the Bank of England website: http://www.bankofengland.co.uk/statistics/Pages/iadb/notesiadb/MFIs_exlCB.aspx

12.3f Monetary financial institutions' (excluding central bank) balance sheet

£ millions   Not seasonally adjusted

Changes in foreign currency liabilities (including euro)

RPM	Sight and time deposits					Acceptances granted	Sale and repurchase agreements				
	UK MFIs	of which intragroup banks	UK public sector	Other UK residents	Non-residents		UK MFIs	of which intragroup banks	UK public sector	Other UK residents	Non-residents
	B4GB	B8ZN	B2VP	B2VV	B2VJ	B4HM	B4HB	B8ZL	B4GG	B4GI	B4HE
2013 May	-7,632	-8,102	-235	-4,466	-48,166	-126	-147	-1,003	274	15,800	-1,543
Jun	2,068	2,363	-135	716	-58,853	405	-3,775	-1,681	-221	-4,332	-12,443
Jul	-1,157	-1,991	14	-1,709	-68,451	47	-475	-1,103	-198	-8,982	-31,346
Aug	-8,034	-7,530	17	-4,391	-36,069	18	-6,951	-2,836	-223	3,555	7,693
Sep	6,132	8,510	61	-16,577	21,031	-12	-7,925	-4,660	-318	-8,544	-22,461
Oct	7,885	7,130	52	-831	13,774	196	11,101	10,842	794	-6,152	-5,710
Nov	-3,168	-3,608	98	1,855	-19,536	28	3,612	5,017	368	12,178	-2,041
Dec	13,601	13,300	-264	-4,468	-1,756	164	-15,400	-9,452	582	-7,669	-27,878
2014 Jan	499	-1,360	19	4,905	-6,414	-118	3,878	3,606	-107	-1,664	38,567
Feb	7,075	9,696	420	9,890	-20,111	56	-3,936	-2,654	333	3,427	-6,721
Mar	-3,909	-3,129	-74	-12,463	1,305	298	-7,159	-4,884	755	-6,356	-11,132
Apr	6,757	11,280	48	93	7,448	-274	4,375	2,227	-1,576	3,989	-2,655
May	-13,676	-10,656	-74	708	23,675	-58	-10,293	-8,371	-26	1,428	9,133
Jun	13,848	12,626	-68	-9,704	-4,122	208	3,330	3,668	-200	-4,217	-22,975
Jul	-6,572	-7,513	-19	-3,017	6,684	103	709	-4,949	-133	-6,386	19,110
Aug	7,257	4,836	281	-10,326	3,694	216	6,676	8,560	222	13,763	1,617
Sep	-941	-317	-57	-1,674	7,890	-35	-8,507	-2,871	584	218	-17,754
Oct	-7,719	-7,069	159	-3,086	-11,387	-442	-2,731	-4,802	984	-7,747	-8,763
Nov	512	-2,304	-36	9,904	50,968	-257	-8,925	-6,088	-1,187	3,676	1,377
Dec	9,753	6,747	-450	894	-39,875	-202	628	5,184	464	-16,536	-21,765
2015 Jan	9,222	674	57	-1,387	66,347	-80	7,082	4,395	-1,262	7,416	10,048
Feb	10,644	15,079	309	3,980	-25,550	-47	1,062	866	-653	8,107	40,296
Mar	1,293	-3,191	-546	334	-21,076	117	-255	1,097	1,761	-4,217	-35,380
Apr	6,527	5,677	5	3,944	9,694	-81	4,474	894	-1,695	-3,116	21,843

Source: Bank of England

Full explanatory notes to this table can be found on the Bank of England website: http://www.bankofengland.co.uk/statistics/Pages/iadb/notesiadb/MFIs_exICB.aspx

12.3f Monetary financial institutions' (excluding central bank) balance sheet

£ millions

Changes in foreign currency liabilities (including euro)

RPM	CDs and Commercial paper	CDs and other paper Issued Bonds with maturity of up to and incl. 5 years	Bonds with maturity of greater than 5 years	Total	Total foreign currency deposits	Items in suspense and transmission	Net derivatives	Accrued amounts payable	Capital and other internal funds	Total foreign currency liabilities	Total liabilities
	B2TN	B6OJ	B2TO	B3CM	B4DM	B4GM	B4EM	B4AM	B4BM	B4FM	B4JM
2013 May	3,405	-5,143	-3,299	-5,037	-51,280	-16,021	-6,285	869	5,221	-67,496	-51,346
Jun	-10,990	-9,785	-6,121	-26,896	-103,467	-22,575	-13,067	172	15,390	-123,546	-124,232
Jul	6,479	-419	1,419	7,479	-104,776	-21,529	3,727	-1,261	13,838	-110,002	-113,306
Aug	-1,718	-2,920	-2,396	-7,034	-51,419	-955	15,065	1,569	-4,742	-40,481	-50,094
Sep	-4,821	-1,989	1,690	-5,121	-33,734	24,614	12,885	-1,194	7,191	9,761	29,960
Oct	-1,336	4,038	-1,893	809	21,918	12,965	-16,403	-443	-12,477	5,559	22,381
Nov	2,161	-1,490	3,059	3,730	-2,876	-42,420	8,821	-893	26,873	-10,494	-2,992
Dec	-5,377	-3,177	-7,015	-15,569	-58,658	-79,634	-1,351	-1,182	-1,225	-142,051	-196,745
2014 Jan	9,548	-177	-5,072	4,299	43,864	138,158	9,133	-1,184	-43,764	146,207	232,068
Feb	38	5,049	2,314	7,401	-2,166	-1,352	6,523	-917	-36,625	-34,536	-8,577
Mar	-9,380	521	-3,041	-11,900	-50,635	-10,615	-12,003	788	8,883	-63,581	-135,774
Apr	11,061	1,863	5,324	18,247	36,452	24,421	8,000	-393	-2,198	66,282	13,478
May	4,760	-2,108	4,317	6,970	17,787	-32,772	6,619	791	-19,379	-26,954	-1,055
Jun	-3,722	-4,915	1,656	-6,980	-30,880	-24,741	3,086	860	15,145	-36,529	-49,622
Jul	9,926	-3,974	-384	5,568	16,048	9,119	984	-170	-22,049	3,932	13,122
Aug	4,249	1,072	1,283	6,604	30,004	-5,915	-9,306	424	-12,632	2,575	6,436
Sep	-6,848	-646	1,075	-6,419	-26,695	-2,333	3,022	-2,164	34,295	6,125	-40,072
Oct	1,330	-3,318	27	-1,961	-42,694	-11,441	3,440	2,067	-34,577	-83,204	-74,469
Nov	1,411	13	3,660	5,083	61,113	-10,111	-13,845	98	2,007	39,263	57,268
Dec	-9,822	-2,329	-2,017	-14,168	-81,256	-83,243	2,642	-1,077	-8,572	-171,506	-161,732
2015 Jan	6,962	-6,361	1,863	2,464	99,907	124,833	11,562	-193	-36,219	199,890	226,859
Feb	3,941	-985	4,091	7,047	45,194	-8,686	22,309	-2,092	6,693	63,417	25,688
Mar	-11,660	-1,130	6,647	-6,143	-64,111	-16,661	-18,463	1,988	16,241	-81,005	-44,626
Apr	7,185	-5,226	3,379	5,337	46,931	23,208	22,541	-500	15,855	108,037	100,044

Source: Bank of England

Full explanatory notes to this table can be found on the Bank of England website: http://www.bankofengland.co.uk/statistics/Pages/iadb/notesiadb/MFIs_exlCB.aspx

12.3g Monetary financial institutions' (excluding central bank) balance sheet

£ millions   Not seasonally adjusted

Changes in sterling assets

	Notes and coin	With UK central bank		Loans					Acceptances granted			
		Cash ratio deposits	Other	UK MFIs	of which intragroup banks	UK MFIs' CDs etc	UK MFIs commercial paper	Non-residents	UK MFIs	UK public sector	Other UK residents	Non-residents
RPM	B4II	B3YR	B3ZR	B4DC	B8ZJ	B4JB	B4BC	B4BD	B4EC	B4FF	B3TR	B4GD
2013 May	-3	134	2,132	8,959	10,688	-27	4	5,024	-	-	-13	-2
Jun	-440	1,416	-3,331	8,787	10,479	-38	3	4,249	-8	-	-41	1
Jul	48	-	8,650	-3,121	-2,338	-269	5	-4,367	-	-	-4	-1
Aug	461	-	-3,057	-2,295	-2,518	-115	-	4,036	-	-	3	1
Sep	-742	-	270	26,805	27,151	-531	-	-1,929	9	-	5	-2
Oct	509	-	11,330	12,460	11,237	-582	-	-2,167	-	-	-4	6
Nov	-31	11	-4,939	3,075	5,735	-118	8	-2,166	-	-	20	-
Dec	1,220	50	5,668	-15,191	-14,856	-438	6	-5,493	-	-	3	-1
2014 Jan	-1,401	-1	-4,707	-1,299	39	274	34	3,256	-	-	4	-
Feb	-236	-	550	-13,076	-12,625	194	-40	4,856	-	-	-3	-5
Mar	-124	1	-9,264	-11,954	-8,999	272	4	-3,898	14	-	1	-
Apr	617	-	13,993	-21,976	-22,105	-336	8	-4,213	-	-	-8	1
May	-294	3	-3,724	3,440	3,463	-97	9	6,512	-	-	-1	-3
Jun	-591	49	1,231	1,718	1,432	278	8	-7,596	-20	-	-10	-
Jul	491	-	-1,432	-16,234	-13,725	24	62	-2,520	-	-	20	6
Aug	-163	-2	2,746	1,208	225	-241	-46	7,891	-	-	-3	5
Sep	13	2	-10,455	3,799	4,107	-738	53	-716	-	-	7	4
Oct	185	1	14,241	-542	-773	-323	21	-543	1	-	7	4
Nov	-356	10	201	13,374	12,117	-415	27	-866	-1	-	-4	1
Dec	2,329	-41	-3,043	4,460	4,548	-355	60	-1,227	-	-	-	-2
2015 Jan	-1,684	-	4,014	10,631	7,446	551	4	1,140	-8	-	-1	2
Feb	-346	-	3,780	-11,900	-9,393	90	-16	-2,673	-	-	3	-1
Mar	429	-	-3,537	12,516	12,054	213	-42	9,993	-	-	8	2
Apr	128	-1	5,654	-2,948	-3,341	268	-63	-1,087	-	-	8	1

Source: Bank of England

Full explanatory notes to this table can be found on the Bank of England website: http://www.bankofengland.co.uk/statistics/Pages/iadb/notesiadb/MFIs_exICB.aspx

12.3g Monetary financial institutions' (excluding central bank) balance sheet

£ millions

Changes in sterling assets

	Bills				Claims under sale and repurchase agreements					Advances		
	Treasury bills	UK MFIs bills	Other UK	Non-residents	UK MFIs	of which intragroup banks	UK public sector	Other UK residents	Non-residents	UK public sector	Other UK residents	Non-residents
RPM	B4BA	B4IB	B4HG	B4IC	B4FA	B8ZH	B4BF	B4AH	B4CD	B2VK	B2VQ	B4HC
2013 May	1,556	-	-12	-172	1,639	-1,535	247	3,270	-2,722	-91	-6,030	1,718
Jun	-265	-	107	-49	-4,235	-182	466	-3,034	2,320	-32	-3,728	-1,150
Jul	-1,019	-1	-212	-86	1,662	1,442	-334	-4,571	-2,138	-108	5,159	134
Aug	-612	-	25	50	-1,950	-1,953	-317	5,009	58	-136	9,368	-2,534
Sep	642	19	-16	-103	6,094	5,371	915	8,137	-4,927	208	2,139	1,121
Oct	-972	-22	17	400	-2,316	-3,360	83	-11,427	2,765	204	5,888	996
Nov	-275	-	94	-40	6,849	4,947	-534	2,741	4,559	-447	2,104	85
Dec	-1,102	6	-44	-333	-1,144	273	-491	-9,859	2,327	72	-16,121	5,991
2014 Jan	1,538	2	-3	23	7,789	1,096	575	-4,825	3,781	-35	-3,665	683
Feb	1,846	7	-26	2	6,991	3,306	-489	-530	1,808	89	4,711	2,368
Mar	575	-1	-34	-93	-4,824	2,570	-58	-4,310	-2,590	172	-41,833	2,178
Apr	-1,143	9	49	-218	-8,689	-9,152	-94	264	-2,357	192	-13,615	-4,431
May	-1,245	7	-15	261	7,881	7,642	82	4,612	-965	-197	-4,853	6,491
Jun	-1,836	8	-2	70	29	1,547	-91	4,487	4,129	186	1,212	1,277
Jul	-1,424	-7	78	46	-10,461	-10,894	101	-1,076	-480	-86	4,439	-9,201
Aug	2,658	10	-110	488	-73	2,872	1,101	-3,659	4,110	18	4,593	7,073
Sep	-831	-9	-12	-564	-17,656	-10,843	-1,114	2,894	-4,513	1	-4,185	1,481
Oct	1,530	8	41	-2,294	2,772	1,422	-90	-123	1,662	-158	-4,317	-1,089
Nov	958	11	44	-50	1,143	426	190	1,473	-433	262	-5,776	109
Dec	-972	1	-29	6	3,256	-1,941	-165	-8,578	3,160	-181	-5,207	-1,018
2015 Jan	-962	-4	-61	-164	12,273	10,998	-5	4,960	-1,600	105	5,212	4,461
Feb	818	13	-76	-105	-3,397	-1,254	-12	-407	850	-22	3,549	2,212
Mar	-1,380	-12	-20	-105	-4,491	942	-3	5,135	-2,903	145	7,823	-3,198
Apr	-277	-3	46	291	-3,079	-4,264	3	-951	4,961	-30	1,889	-2,127

Full explanatory notes to this table can be found on the Bank of England website: http://www.bankofengland.co.uk/statistics/Pages/iadb/notesiadb/MFIs_exICB.aspx

Source: Bank of England

12.3g Monetary financial institutions' (excluding central bank) balance sheet

£ millions

Changes in sterling assets

RPM	UK government bonds	Other UK public sector	Investments UK MFIs	Other UK residents	Non-residents	Items in suspense and collection	Accrued amounts receivable	Other assets	Total sterling assets
	B4CA	B4IE	B4CC	B4IG	B4JC	B4BJ	B4HI	B4JI	B4AJ
2013 May	4,348	-43	-236	-3,645	-1,649	5,425	178	-335	19,654
Jun	4,947	34	95	12	-5,672	2,078	2,381	194	5,068
Jul	7,139	-39	-529	1,251	-364	-15,014	69	-628	-8,689
Aug	1,023	-16	-276	2,913	-1,516	5,724	-146	-504	15,198
Sep	2,431	-	372	-3,588	803	3,159	-405	391	41,277
Oct	6,927	53	-622	-9,761	1,608	125	-631	-11	14,856
Nov	5,918	-20	787	2,517	1,477	-4,687	625	778	18,391
Dec	575	-16	682	-6,118	-1,287	-18,652	-2,336	627	-61,401
2014 Jan	2,797	-8	1,031	-198	1,653	34,112	735	-445	41,699
Feb	2,269	-15	1,366	-8,733	-384	2,482	779	-24	6,758
Mar	-6,753	26	970	-3,142	-262	-4,688	-2,093	38	-91,669
Apr	634	-7	1,011	-2,174	-2,339	-3,217	-1,810	566	-49,283
May	451	16	-99	5,361	1,931	-9,032	1,110	-757	16,887
Jun	1,767	-2	900	-4,264	443	-1,099	-57	11	2,235
Jul	2,245	7	1,448	5,245	581	5,622	-906	-105	-23,517
Aug	-979	12	-4,057	-4,676	-2,460	-2,080	1,780	146	15,290
Sep	-4,138	2	288	-3,989	1,878	9,329	-1,532	-323	-31,026
Oct	6,588	13	797	-7,483	227	-12,409	-293	582	-987
Nov	4,431	24	539	2,043	-2,858	895	1,567	163	16,707
Dec	-3,025	23	971	12,110	1,566	-20,069	-1,732	115	-17,586
2015 Jan	-6,643	-39	1,666	-23,026	-1,992	22,783	-72	145	31,685
Feb	-4,657	-29	1,076	-2,082	2,370	-1,416	664	-182	-11,894
Mar	-2,683	8	390	-3,126	-466	-1,208	-820	391	13,060
Apr	3,094	-	697	2,297	1,117	-1,016	-351	401	8,920

Source: Bank of England

Full explanatory notes to this table can be found on the Bank of England website: http://www.bankofengland.co.uk/statistics/Pages/iadb/notesiadb/MFIs_exICB.aspx

12.3h Monetary financial institutions' (excluding central bank) balance sheet

£ millions   Not seasonally adjusted

Changes in foreign currency assets (including euro)

RPM	Loans and advances						Claims under sale and repurchase agreements					Acceptances granted	Total Bills
	UK MFIs	of which intragroup banks	UK MFIs' CDs etc.	UK public sector	Other UK residents	Non-residents	UK MFIs	of which intragroup banks	UK public sector	Other UK residents	Non-residents		
	B4EB	B8ZR	B4AF	B2VN	B2VT	B2VH	B4FB	B8ZP	B4EG	B4EI	B4FE	B4HM	B4GL
2013 May	-9,420	-7,878	212	-42	10,352	-60,937	-1,787	-1,323	142	4,780	2,918	-126	374
Jun	-4,751	2,397	91	-16	-25,376	-19,089	-834	-1,949	151	-12,209	-26,383	405	-5,007
Jul	2,381	-2,441	118	5	-2,841	-60,856	181	-1,021	124	-10,352	-11,317	47	1,152
Aug	-7,574	-7,057	224	-9	-3,935	-44,743	-7,132	-2,745	-140	4,826	-4,237	18	-1,496
Sep	6,238	8,203	32	20	-4,644	3,754	-9,792	-4,570	-223	321	-11,872	-12	-4,056
Oct	8,345	7,231	-48	32	1,761	-34,967	12,230	10,679	-38	-3,085	-5,707	196	-833
Nov	-5,939	-3,520	-103	-47	766	6,738	1,910	5,004	128	5,011	-6,218	28	-662
Dec	7,246	12,662	-38	46	-130	-6,641	-11,803	-9,459	740	-8,427	-12,931	164	2,208
2014 Jan	1,395	-2,051	-389	-41	3,187	24,081	5,748	3,495	1,377	3,395	12,514	-118	-3,251
Feb	6,176	8,986	-14	19	2,819	11,045	-9,463	-2,605	-590	-6,714	-9,846	56	3,151
Mar	-2,563	-3,767	-531	-33	-7,947	-11,798	-6,396	-4,820	-551	-11,678	13,980	298	1,231
Apr	7,584	11,204	250	4	4,551	11,869	1,871	2,203	-232	12,730	-7,744	-274	-1,931
May	-13,642	-10,478	-296	-	-160	27,812	-8,176	-8,320	1,038	-2,240	100	-58	-179
Jun	13,212	12,184	-543	12	-12,465	-17,305	4,295	3,645	-646	-6,242	-9,277	208	-25
Jul	-4,806	-7,072	-589	-24	-3,048	30,962	229	-4,928	29	-1,517	14,431	103	-2,375
Aug	7,505	5,516	-696	7	-5,345	2,092	5,003	8,541	-515	1,932	-345	216	-502
Sep	-1,187	-510	108	-6	4,774	-309	-7,764	-2,864	165	1,974	-11,290	-35	3,411
Oct	-8,864	-7,734	-525	-20	-8,329	-20,492	-3,450	-4,746	600	-1,231	-20,824	-442	-2,280
Nov	1,602	-2,765	233	21	4,620	34,826	-7,870	-6,396	499	126	-7,926	-257	1,267
Dec	6,247	7,120	-30	-119	3,023	-12,363	-2,859	5,421	-866	-17,598	-3,609	-202	644
2015 Jan	9,455	924	436	-111	6,340	28,096	7,929	4,043	206	5,081	1,474	-80	-558
Feb	13,810	14,543	301	-70	1,495	-20,813	2,934	1,041	-423	8,896	28,398	-47	782
Mar	2,215	-1,685	-165	-13	917	-156	763	1,327	1,594	-4,005	-29,483	117	689
Apr	8,371	5,586	301	-104	5,808	39,186	3,324	808	-1,420	5,801	3,197	-81	2,100

Source: Bank of England

Full explanatory notes to this table can be found on the Bank of England website: http://www.bankofengland.co.uk/statistics/Pages/iadb/notesiadb/MFIs_exlCB.aspx

12.3h Monetary financial institutions' (excluding central bank) balance sheet

£ millions

Changes in foreign currency assets (including euro)

RPM	UK government bonds	Other UK public sector	Investments UK MFIs	Other UK residents	Non-residents	Items in suspense and collection	Accrued amounts receivable	Other assets	Total foreign currency assets	Total assets	Holdings of own sterling acceptances	Holdings of own foreign currency acceptances
	B4EA	B4CG	B4AG	B4CI	B4DE	B4JL	B4FL	B4HL	B4IL	B4IM	B3VR	B3XR
2013 May	-21	-2	-600	2,001	3,621	-19,571	1,274	-4,152	-70,983	-51,329	-	40
Jun	-	10	222	-209	-14,557	-16,582	-834	-4,282	-129,249	-124,182	-19	-86
Jul	-	-2	-880	-165	612	-30,574	-1,229	8,970	-104,627	-113,315	12	83
Aug	-	-13	-345	2,156	-2,791	2,286	1,082	-3,441	-65,263	-50,065	6	-29
Sep	1	-2	-651	620	-12,977	24,758	-1,178	-1,670	-11,335	29,942	7	-50
Oct	62	-	1,006	-517	16,154	12,841	27	45	7,503	22,359	9	163
Nov	22	-	503	-300	17,852	-39,477	-320	-1,258	-21,365	-2,974	14	-102
Dec	-22	-	562	428	-24,378	-84,158	265	1,530	-135,338	-196,739	-2	-26
2014 Jan	6	6	-403	-3,092	-2,532	150,149	-1,740	61	190,353	232,052	10	82
Feb	-	4	-51	-121	-8,530	-4,646	-90	1,325	-15,469	-8,711	-	-58
Mar	18	-8	-212	597	-6,373	-11,569	804	-1,389	-44,119	-135,788	-1	169
Apr	-6	11	-401	-553	4,600	29,823	661	-58	62,756	13,474	7	106
May	-	-21	1,355	380	15,612	-38,260	162	-1,387	-17,961	-1,074	-	28
Jun	-11	-21	-479	-151	2,401	-25,684	425	439	-51,856	-49,621	-10	-94
Jul	-14	67	-474	-250	-5,787	12,488	-381	-2,405	36,640	13,123	-5	-47
Aug	-18	-8	1,673	-344	-3,527	-16,720	258	453	-8,881	6,409	8	-135
Sep	-17	4	-1,385	-66	8,267	-2,639	-200	-2,829	-9,029	-40,055	22	51
Oct	56	-13	-961	-977	6,933	-11,037	-522	-1,118	-73,496	-74,482	-4	-50
Nov	78	-21	826	385	19,271	-5,970	-848	678	40,540	57,247	17	-4
Dec	13	-	-2,324	-12,504	-13,225	-86,076	-1,547	-755	-144,147	-161,733	-2	11
2015 Jan	-41	-	-676	-986	10,760	127,535	-1,283	1,561	195,137	226,822	-34	57
Feb	-39	-	-211	-548	10,417	-6,792	1,073	-1,568	37,594	25,700	-1	-40
Mar	88	-	-720	-759	-10,833	-18,219	222	42	-57,705	-44,644	8	149
Apr	-5	-	195	-481	-1,715	26,781	695	-807	91,147	100,067	-	-221

Source: Bank of England

Full explanatory notes to this table can be found on the Bank of England website: http://www.bankofengland.co.uk/statistics/Pages/iadb/notesiadb/MFIs_exICB.aspx

12.4a Industrial analysis of monetary financial institutions' lending to UK residents

£ millions   Not seasonally adjusted

Amounts outstanding of lending in sterling

RPM	Agriculture, hunting and forestry	Fishing	Mining and quarrying	Manufacturing									Electricity, gas and water supply			Total
				Food, beverages and tobacco	Textiles, wearing apparel and leather	Pulp, paper, and printing	Chemicals, pharmaceuticals, rubber and plastics	Non-metallic mineral products and metals	Machinery, equipment and transport equipment	Electrical, medical and optical equipment	Other manufacturing	Total	Electricity, gas steam and air conditioning	Water collection and sewerage	Waste management related services and remediation activities	
	TBUC	TBUD	TBUE	TBUG	TBUH	TBUI	TBUJ	TBUK	TBUL	TBUM	TBUN	TBUF	TBUO	TBUP	B3F9	B3FN
2013 May	13,846	241	1,427	4,496	584	1,850	2,232	3,242	5,090	1,587	2,773	21,854	5,007	2,310	1,886	9,203
Jun	14,036	241	2,308	4,429	596	1,826	2,166	3,512	4,712 (a)	1,611	2,724	21,573 (a)	4,961	2,259	1,856	9,076
Jul	14,296	240	2,317	4,387	564	1,802	2,236	3,554	4,295	1,629	2,710	21,179	5,653	2,259	1,867	9,779
Aug	14,416	237	2,276	4,322	562	1,818	2,281	3,551	4,230	1,734	2,669	21,167	5,548	2,227	1,859	9,634
Sep	14,563	236	2,581	4,318	551	1,988	2,156	3,345	4,447	1,659	2,681	21,145	6,217	2,511	1,789	10,518
Oct	14,709	234	2,647	4,407	564	1,954	2,316	3,430	4,474	1,601	2,680	21,426	6,415	2,551	1,887	10,853
Nov	14,880	232	2,792	5,274	551	1,911	2,304	3,407	4,375	1,628	2,502	21,951	6,500	2,552	1,861	10,913
Dec	14,243	227	2,773	5,703	538	1,980	2,322	3,176	4,289	1,456	2,477	21,940	7,888	2,609	1,937	12,434
2014 Jan	14,424	224	2,775	5,248	553	1,910	2,475	3,277	4,412	1,545	2,467	21,888	7,553	2,657	2,003	12,213
Feb	14,526	227	2,854	5,692	565	1,944	2,371	3,366	4,710	1,671	2,462	22,780	7,357	2,613	2,048	12,019
Mar	14,663	227	2,889	4,351	559	1,917	2,290	3,455	4,912	1,466 (b)	2,432	21,382 (b)	7,857	2,690	1,939	12,486
Apr	14,900	261	2,564	4,107	545	1,833	2,395	3,395	4,881	1,475	2,433	21,064	7,837	2,662	1,927	12,426
May	15,124	244	2,594	3,853	537	1,993	2,473	3,470	5,218	1,839	2,432	21,815	7,846	2,660	2,011	12,517
Jun	15,376	252	2,553	3,897	567	2,012	2,719	3,420	4,861	1,836	2,398	21,711	8,018	2,603	1,991	12,612
Jul	15,571	258	2,594	3,967	584	1,841	2,728	3,475	5,185	1,965	2,433	22,178	8,057	2,625	1,936	12,618
Aug	15,692	255	2,607	4,323	576	1,937	2,721	3,492	5,328	1,833	2,443	22,651	7,823	2,672	1,972	12,467
Sep	15,812	254	2,682	4,420	562	1,995	2,768	3,771	5,649	1,875	2,411	23,451	7,857	2,685	1,944	12,486
Oct	16,055	255	2,763	4,461	553	1,982	2,845	3,722	5,887	1,907	2,409	23,767	8,075	2,700	1,973	12,748
Nov	16,212	253	2,704	5,250	540	1,993	2,841	3,532	5,621	1,926	2,478	24,182	7,848	2,606	1,967	12,421
Dec	15,684	244	2,553	4,962	591	2,031	2,811	3,405	5,001	1,774	2,463	23,038	8,767	2,581	1,844	13,192
2015 Jan	15,761	238	2,646	4,533	600	2,070	2,822	3,419	5,116	1,878	2,449	22,888	8,775	2,715	1,908	13,399
Feb	15,894	238	2,609	4,927	616	2,039	2,806	3,514	5,119	1,845	2,522	23,388	8,442	2,886	1,921	13,249
Mar	16,121	240	2,474	4,521	663	1,999	2,848	3,573	5,293	1,869	2,606	23,372	8,576	3,232	2,022	13,830
Apr	16,235	230	2,538	4,702	681	2,038	2,948	3,458	5,134	1,909	2,560	23,430	8,534	2,731	2,040	13,305

Source: Bank of England

12.4a Industrial analysis of monetary financial institutions' lending to UK residents

£ millions

Amounts outstanding of lending in sterling

| | Development of buildings | Construction | | | | | Wholesale and retail trade | | | | Accommodation and food service activities | Transport, storage and communication | | |
		Construction of commercial buildings	Construction of domestic buildings	Civil Engineering	Other construction activities	Total	Wholesale and retail trade and repair of motor vehicles and motorcycles	Wholesale trade, excluding motor vehicles and motor cycles	Retail trade excluding motor vehicles and motor cycles	Total		Transportation and storage	Information and communication	Total
RPM	B7EB	B3I6	B3LX	B4PK	B4PX	TBUQ	TBUS	TBUT	TBUU	TBUR	TBUV	B5PK	B5PR	TBUW
2013 May	30,505	4,148	4,556	3,090	7,499	49,797	9,926	10,209	15,533	35,668	24,313	12,906	9,671	22,577
Jun	30,437	3,849	4,100	2,770	7,313	48,469	10,375 (g)	10,027	15,558	35,960 (g)	24,367	12,770	9,066	21,836
Jul	30,206	4,035	4,105	2,998	7,278	48,622	10,591	10,000	15,563	36,154	24,304	12,716	9,233	21,950
Aug	29,912	4,138	4,193	3,056	7,275	48,575	10,153	10,359	15,516	36,029	24,189	12,690	9,242	21,931
Sep	29,769	4,228	4,229	3,089	7,264	48,578	8,944 (h)	10,772	15,753	35,469 (h)	23,854	12,557	9,336	21,893
Oct	29,696	4,592	4,208	3,145	6,926	48,567	8,718	10,637	15,661	35,016	23,548	12,820	10,267	23,087
Nov	35,194 (c)	5,585 (e)	4,349	3,171	6,120 (f)	54,419 (c)	8,764	10,840	16,067	35,672	25,188 (k)	12,810	10,301	23,111
Dec	34,040	5,170	4,006	2,416	5,834	51,466	8,832	10,956	15,951	35,739	24,740	12,678	10,930	23,608
2014 Jan	33,934	5,339	4,147	2,768	5,804	51,992	9,306	10,633	16,533	36,471	25,045	12,628	10,510	23,137
Feb	33,697	5,330	4,384	2,822	5,914	52,147	10,654	10,782	17,037	38,473	24,884	12,146	9,320	21,466
Mar	33,031	5,278	4,311	2,908	5,865	51,394	9,327	10,577	17,050	36,954	24,041	12,141	9,254	21,395
Apr	32,455	5,310	4,310	3,002	5,928	51,005	9,437	10,541	16,952	36,930	23,593	12,262	8,866	21,128
May	32,036	5,217	4,385	3,074	5,938	50,650	9,556	10,402	16,566	36,523	23,473	12,353	9,356	21,709
Jun	31,861	4,948	3,988	2,548	5,943	49,287	9,749	10,333	16,932	37,015	23,436	12,364	8,713	21,077
Jul	31,490	5,073	4,015	2,835	5,991	49,405	10,087	10,444	16,658	37,189	23,664	12,062	8,438	20,500
Aug	31,392	5,019	4,048	2,997	6,042	49,499	10,576	10,406	17,000 (i)	37,982 (i)	23,377	11,719	8,355	20,074
Sep	31,012	5,067	4,100	2,999	6,011	49,188	9,655	10,094	17,112	36,861	22,871	11,944	8,432	20,377
Oct	30,538	5,072	4,241	3,100	5,896	48,846	9,009	10,436	17,348	36,792	22,903	11,923	8,452	20,374
Nov	30,126	5,106	4,185	2,603	5,579	47,598	9,465	10,568	17,047	37,081	22,189	11,551	8,548	20,099
Dec	28,946	4,614	3,689	2,161	5,443	44,852	9,841	10,005	17,510	37,356	22,196	11,988	8,745	20,733
2015 Jan	19,780 (d)	4,713	4,031	2,376	5,477	36,377 (d)	10,128	10,043	17,869	38,039	22,414	12,063	8,364	20,427
Feb	19,270	4,763	4,158	2,294	5,550	36,035	11,424	10,258	17,128	38,809	22,262	12,263	8,513	20,776
Mar	18,801	4,849	4,320	2,571	5,503	36,044	10,605	10,200	18,336	39,141	21,992	12,503	9,187	21,690
Apr	18,705	4,883	4,438	2,563	5,689	36,278	10,303	10,083	14,626 (j)	35,012 (j)	22,653	12,300	8,919	21,219

Source: Bank of England

12.4a Industrial analysis of monetary financial institutions' lending to UK residents

£ millions

Amounts outstanding of lending in sterling

| | Real estate, professional services and support activities | | | | Public administration and defence | Education | Human health and social work | Recreational, personal and community service activities | | | Financial intermediation (excluding insurance and pension funds) | | | | |
| | Buying, selling and renting of real estate | Professional, scientific and technical activities | Administrative and support services | Total | | | | Recreational, cultural and sporting activities | Personal and community service activities | Total | Financial leasing corporations | Non-bank credit grantors excluding credit unions and SPVs | Credit unions | Factoring corporations | Mortgage and housing credit corporations excluding SPVs |
RPM	TBUY	B6PD	B6PO	TBUX	TBVD	TBVE	TBVF	TBVH	TBVG	B6PT	TBVJ	TBVK	TBVL	TBVM	TBVN
2013 May	162,102	15,052	14,758	191,912	7,974	11,431	21,010	6,353	3,549	9,902	23,958	12,311	-	7,633	55,385
Jun	161,347	15,077	14,801	191,226	8,418	11,494	21,008	5,868	3,506	9,374	23,909	12,193	5	8,183	55,586
Jul	159,293	15,469	15,050	189,812	8,022	11,292	20,951	5,884	3,497	9,381	23,412	12,063	-	7,905	55,974
Aug	156,471 (l)	15,714	15,152	187,337 (l)	7,733	11,331	20,773	5,831	3,478	9,308	22,421	12,106	1	8,015	55,745
Sep	155,518	15,860	15,309	186,687	8,733	11,247	20,908	5,913	3,481	9,394	22,555	12,283	1	7,680	55,937
Oct	154,169	16,080	15,049	185,298	8,916	11,274	20,835	6,022	3,482	9,504	21,989	12,362	1	8,004	55,029
Nov	144,172 (m)	14,360 (f)	19,077 (r)	177,609 (r)(s)	8,075	11,191	20,804	5,992	3,273	9,265	22,214	12,317	1	4,753 (u)	51,656 (v)
Dec	143,408	13,869	20,017	177,295	7,819	10,911	20,585	5,990	3,245	9,235	22,552	12,551	1	4,828	50,446 (w)
2014 Jan	142,120	14,185	19,393	175,698	8,345	10,781	20,567	5,927	3,280	9,208	22,294	12,153	-	4,005	50,573
Feb	141,331	14,436	19,274	175,041	7,937	10,764	20,573	5,939	3,323	9,262	22,328	12,393	1	4,313	50,600
Mar	139,528	14,224	19,135	172,887	7,834	10,824	20,461	5,818	3,255	9,073	23,245	12,552	1	4,353	50,867
Apr	139,012	14,317	19,081	172,410	7,991	10,879	20,243	5,801	3,330	9,131	24,241	12,053	1	4,507	48,441
May	138,201	14,276	19,538	172,015	7,919	10,845	20,133	5,819	3,343	9,162	24,034	12,110	-	4,573	48,960
Jun	137,261	15,502 (q)	19,633	172,397 (q)	7,861	10,865	20,341	5,481	3,355	8,835	24,300	12,260	-	4,733	49,165
Jul	136,158	16,542	19,805	172,505	7,874	10,998	20,289	5,459	3,316	8,775	24,359	12,506	-	4,720	49,997
Aug	135,893	16,902	20,027	172,821	8,979	11,014	20,199	5,436	3,338	8,774	24,207	17,337 (t)	1	4,814	49,136
Sep	134,157	16,437	19,908	170,503	8,031	10,861	19,788	5,423	3,270	8,694	24,281	17,409	1	4,998	48,658
Oct	131,737	16,125	20,118	167,980	8,440	10,918	19,685	5,410	3,223	8,632	24,284	15,655	1	4,820	48,391
Nov	130,514	16,446	20,784	167,744	8,689	10,849	19,736	5,461	3,329	8,790	24,323	15,744	-	5,058	47,938
Dec	128,986 (n)	15,911	19,990	164,887 (n)	8,487	10,966	19,676	5,426	3,245	8,671	24,915	15,479	1	4,864	48,052
2015 Jan	137,300 (o)	16,819	19,953	174,071 (o)	8,588	10,777	19,681	5,298	3,237	8,535	24,877	15,381	1	4,459	48,351
Feb	137,055	17,270	20,019	174,343	8,525	10,857	19,672	5,237	3,271	8,507	25,095	17,021	1	4,710	48,646
Mar	136,161	17,475	19,610	173,247	8,594	10,943	19,818	5,183	3,243	8,426	24,643	17,066	1	4,459	49,340
Apr	136,624 (p)	17,186	19,180	172,990 (p)	8,595	11,023	19,850	5,261	3,245	8,506	24,354	17,192	1	4,464	49,775

Source: Bank of England

12.4a Industrial analysis of monetary financial institutions' lending to UK residents

£ millions

Amounts outstanding of lending in sterling

	Financial intermediation (excluding insurance and pension funds)								Insurance companies & pension funds			Fund management activities	Activities auxiliary to financial intermediation			Total
	Investment and unit trusts excluding money market mutual funds	Money market mutual funds	Bank holding companies	Securities dealers	SPVs related to securitisation	Other financial intermediaries	of which intragroup activity	Total	Insurance companies	Pension funds	Total		Central clearing counterparties	Other auxiliary activities	Total	
RPM	TBVO	TBVP	TBVQ	TBVR	B6PY	TBVS	B3U8	TBVI	B3V6	B3W4	TBVT	TBVU	B7FX	B8FD	TBVV	B8FJ
2013 May	6,547	62	24,385	20,467	18,692	147,028	139,508	316,468	9,166	13,340	22,506	38,702	74,400	3,290	77,690	116,392
Jun	7,284	64	24,499	19,931	18,516	144,791	137,565	314,961	9,257	13,544	22,801	38,994	67,903	3,148	71,051	110,045
Jul	7,707	65	29,796	21,441	19,694	146,075 (y)	138,813 (y)	324,133	8,340	12,738	21,078	40,238	61,693	3,208	64,901	105,139
Aug	8,262	60	33,102	20,527	19,903	146,810	139,710	326,952	7,456	12,557	20,012	42,355	69,439	3,416	72,855	115,210
Sep	8,503	62	35,483	18,571	19,459	146,607	140,187	327,140	7,076 (ac)	13,504	20,580 (ac)	43,248	73,219	5,314	78,533	121,782
Oct	7,659	62	35,415	20,893	19,637	148,334	141,502	329,386	7,635	13,022	20,657	44,746	63,098 (af)	3,249 (ah)	66,347	111,093
Nov	7,648	62	35,427	21,851	20,044	147,682 (u)	140,861 (u)	323,655 (v)(ab)	7,785	12,939	20,704	45,741	63,093	3,098	66,191	111,931
Dec	8,651	63	35,779	21,586	20,073	126,349	119,400	302,880 (w)	11,850	11,673	23,522	48,241	50,823	3,075	53,898	102,139
2014 Jan	8,498	64	35,753	25,138	14,528 (x)	126,918 (z)	120,985 (z)	299,925 (xl)(z)	11,615	7,741	19,356	46,936	66,131 (ag)	2,967	69,098 (ag)	116,034 (ag)
Feb	8,467	68	35,657	27,171	14,461	127,411	121,257	302,869	11,371	7,823	19,194	48,699	62,902	2,970	65,873	114,572
Mar	5,097	67	35,329	23,944	14,876	92,516	86,284	262,847	10,553	7,956	18,509	46,983	61,273	2,936	64,208	111,191
Apr	4,761	72	36,219	26,906	14,770	79,211 (aa)	71,563	251,181 (aa)	8,970	7,640	16,610	48,708	59,347	2,908	62,255	110,963
May	4,513	76	34,033	25,930	14,606	72,669	64,987	241,501	8,767	7,251	16,018	52,051	62,578	2,878	65,456	117,507
Jun	4,243	73	32,931	29,491	14,581	68,951	61,265	240,730	7,894	8,499	16,392	56,788	62,981	2,973	65,954	122,742
Jul	4,182	31	32,949	27,450	13,965	69,735	62,493	239,894	7,806	7,981	15,787	58,266	61,572	2,823	64,395	122,661
Aug	4,359	18	32,759	28,141	15,142	68,756	61,153	244,668 (t)	8,862	7,686	16,548	57,475	57,214	2,964	60,178	117,653
Sep	4,561	17	29,461	25,372	15,234	66,238	58,478	236,231	9,932	9,221	19,153	54,436 (ad)	64,111	2,935	67,046	121,482 (ad)
Oct	4,766	18	30,443	23,684	14,345	62,550	54,966	228,957	9,298	9,849	19,147	55,572	64,097	2,922	67,019	122,591
Nov	4,729	18	19,442	23,179	14,458	63,759	56,133	218,649	9,576	8,735	18,310	59,069	65,451	2,930	68,381	127,450
Dec	4,741	18	18,069	22,498	16,457	59,905	52,339	215,000	9,396	9,473	18,870	61,003	52,526	2,977	55,503	116,506
2015 Jan	3,711	19	18,099	22,508	14,843	60,187	51,496	212,434	11,569	9,693	21,262	64,034	56,724	3,196	59,920	123,954
Feb	3,845	27	18,035	25,378	14,643	59,098	50,735	216,499	10,236	8,894	19,130	61,968	56,939	3,128	60,067	122,035
Mar	4,240	27	18,830	22,876	14,315	66,274	57,814	222,072	11,285	10,477	21,762	68,163 (ae)	55,549	3,138	58,687	126,850 (ae)
Apr	4,268	38	19,746	22,906	14,418	64,011	55,669	221,172	11,817	9,610	21,427	67,895	55,537	3,296	58,833	126,728

Source: Bank of England

12.4a Industrial analysis of monetary financial institutions' lending to UK residents

£ millions

Amounts outstanding of lending in sterling

RPM	Total financial and non-financial businesses	Individuals and individual trusts — Lending secured on dwellings inc. bridging finance	Other loans and advances	Total	Total UK residents
	Z949	TBVX	TBVY	TBVW	TBUA
2013 May	876,521	1,029,108	105,114	1,134,222	2,010,743
Jun	867,191	1,030,938	105,554	1,136,492	2,003,683
Jul	868,650 (ai)	1,032,668	107,664 (an)	1,140,332 (ar)	2,008,982 (ai)(ar)
Aug	877,111	1,034,121	107,881	1,142,003	2,019,113
Sep	885,308	1,035,329	109,162	1,144,491	2,029,799
Oct	877,050	1,038,101	108,583	1,146,684	2,023,734
Nov	872,393 (u)(v)	1,042,057 (aj)(ak)	108,915	1,150,972 (aj)(ak)	2,023,366 (u)(v)(ak)
Dec	841,557 (w)	1,043,121	108,865	1,151,986	1,993,543 (w)
2014 Jan	848,083 (x)(z)(ag)	1,045,411	107,765	1,153,176	2,001,259 (x)(z)(ag)
Feb	849,587	1,046,414	107,550	1,153,965	2,003,552
Mar	799,057 (b)	1,048,651	108,129	1,156,780	1,955,837 (b)
Apr	783,275 (aa)	1,050,612	108,609	1,159,220	1,942,496 (aa)
May	779,751	1,052,455	108,749	1,161,203	1,940,954
Jun	783,480 (q)	1,054,852	109,519	1,164,371	1,947,851 (q)
Jul	782,761	1,058,195	109,985	1,168,180	1,950,941
Aug	785,260 (i)(t)	1,060,446	110,293	1,170,739	1,955,999 (i)(t)
Sep	778,725 (ad)	1,062,676	112,685 (ao)	1,175,360 (as)	1,954,085 (ad)(as)
Oct	770,853	1,065,274	114,788 (ap)	1,180,061 (ap)	1,950,915 (ap)
Nov	762,957	1,067,277	115,586	1,182,863	1,945,820
Dec	742,911 (n)	1,068,894	116,615	1,185,509	1,928,420 (n)
2015 Jan	751,491	1,068,314 (al)	115,939	1,184,253 (al)	1,935,745 (al)
Feb	752,828	1,070,289 (am)	115,256 (aq)	1,185,545	1,938,373
Mar	766,615 (ae)	1,071,350	116,757	1,188,107	1,954,722 (ae)
Apr	761,190 (j)	1,072,722	116,988	1,189,710	1,950,900 (j)

Source: Bank of England

Movements in amounts outstanding can reflect breaks in data series as well as underlying flows. For changes data, users are recommended to refer directly to the appropriate series or data tables. www.bankofengland.co.uk/statistics/Pages/iadb/notesiadb/Changes_flows_growth_rates.aspx.

Notes to table

(a) Due to improvements in reporting at one institution, the amounts outstanding decreased by £0.7bn. This effect has been adjusted out of the flows for June 2013.
(b) Due to a change in accounting treatment at one reporting institution, the amounts outstanding decreased by £2bn. This effect has been adjusted out of the flows for March 2014.
(c) Due to improvements in reporting at one institution, the amounts outstanding increased by £6bn. This effect has been adjusted out of the flows for November 2013.
(d) Due to improvements in reporting at one institution, the amounts outstanding decreased by £9bn. This effect has been adjusted out of the flows for January 2015.
(e) Due to improvements in reporting at one institution, the amounts outstanding increased by £9bn. This effect has been adjusted out of the flows for November 2013.
(f) Due to improvements in reporting at one institution, the amounts outstanding decreased by £1bn. This effect has been adjusted out of the flows for November 2013.
(g) Due to improvements in reporting at one institution, the amounts outstanding increased by £1bn. This effect has been adjusted out of the flows for June 2013.
(h) Due to a reclassification by one reporting institution, the amounts outstanding increased by £0.4bn. This effect has been adjusted out of the flows for September 2013.
(i) Due to a change in treatment at one institution, the amounts outstanding decreased by £1bn. This effect has been adjusted out of the flows for August 2014.
(j) Due to a change in treatment at one institution, the amounts outstanding decreased by £4bn. This effect has been adjusted out of the flows for April 2015.
(k) Due to improvements in reporting at one institution, the amounts outstanding increased by £2bn. This effect has been adjusted out of the flows for November 2013.
(l) Due to loan transfers out of the UK MFI population, the amounts outstanding decreased by £2bn. This effect has been adjusted out of the flows for August 2013.
(m) Due to improvements in reporting at one institution, the amounts outstanding decreased by £7bn. This effect has been adjusted out of the flows for November 2013.
(n) Due to a loan transfer by one reporting institution, the amounts outstanding decreased by £1bn. This effect has been adjusted out of the flows for December 2014.
(o) Due to improvements in reporting at one institution the amounts outstanding increased by £9bn. This effect has been adjusted out of the flows for January 2015.
(p) Due to a change in the reporting population, the amounts outstanding increased by £1bn. This effect has been adjusted out of the flows for April 2015.
(q) Due to a change in accounting treatment at one reporting institution, the amounts outstanding increased by £2bn. This effect has been adjusted out of the flows for June 2014.
(r) Due to a restructuring at one reporting institution, the amounts outstanding increased by £3bn. This effect has been adjusted out of the flows for November 2013.
(s) Due to improvements in reporting at one institution, the amounts outstanding decreased by £8bn. This effect has been adjusted out of the flows for November 2013.
(t) Due to improvements in reporting at one institution, the amounts outstanding increased by £4bn. This effect has been adjusted out of the flows for August 2014.
(u) Due to a restructuring at one reporting institution, the amounts outstanding decreased by £3bn. This effect has been adjusted out of the flows for November 2013.
(v) Due to improvements in reporting at one institution, the amounts outstanding decreased by £1bn. This effect has been adjusted out of the flows for November 2013.
(w) Due to improvements in reporting at one institution, the amounts outstanding decreased by £2bn. This effect has been adjusted out of the flows for December 2013.
(x) Due to improvements in reporting at one institution, the amounts outstanding decreased by £4bn. This effect has been adjusted out of the flows for November 2013.
(y) Due to improvements in reporting at one institution, the amounts outstanding increased by £2bn. This effect has been adjusted out of the flows for July 2013.
(z) Due to improvements in reporting at one institution, the amounts outstanding increased by £2bn. This effect has been adjusted out of the flows for January 2014.
(aa) Due to improvements in reporting at one institution, the amounts outstanding increased by £1bn. This effect has been adjusted out of the flows for April 2014.
(ab) Due to a restructuring at one reporting institution, the amounts outstanding decreased by £6bn. This effect has been adjusted out of the flows for November 2013.
(ac) Due to a reclassification by one reporting institution, the amounts outstanding increased by £1bn. This effect has been adjusted out of the flows for November 2013.
(ad) Due to improvements in reporting at one institution, the amounts outstanding increased by £1bn. This effect has been adjusted out of the flows for September 2014.
(ae) Due to improvements in reporting at one institution, the amounts outstanding increased by £2bn. This effect has been adjusted out of the flows for March 2015.
(af) Due to improvements in reporting at one institution, the amounts outstanding increased by £2bn. This effect has been adjusted out of the flows for October 2013.
(ag) Due to a change in treatment at one institution, the amounts outstanding increased by £17bn. This effect has been adjusted out of the flows for January 2014.
(ah) Due to improvements in reporting at one institution, the amounts outstanding decreased by £2bn. This effect has been adjusted out of the flows for October 2013.
(ai) Due to improvements in reporting at one institution, the amounts outstanding increased by £5bn. This effect has been adjusted out of the flows for July 2013.
(aj) Due to improvements in reporting at one institution, the amounts outstanding increased by £2bn. This effect has been adjusted out of the flows for November 2013.
(ak) Following a purchase of loans by one reporting institution, the amounts outstanding increased by £2bn. This effect has been adjusted out of the flows for November 2013.
(al) Due to a loan transfer by one reporting institution, the amounts outstanding decreased by £2bn. This effect has been adjusted out of the flows for January 2015.
(am) Due to improvements in reporting at one institution, the amounts outstanding increased by £1bn. This effect has been adjusted out of the flows for February 2015.
(an) Following a purchase of loans by one reporting institution, the amounts outstanding increased by £2bn. This effect has been adjusted out of the flows for September 2014.
(ao) Due to a change in the reporting population, the amounts outstanding increased by £2bn. This effect has been adjusted out of the flows for September 2014.
(ap) Due to a loan transfer by one reporting institution, the amounts outstanding increased by £2bn. This effect has been adjusted out of the flows for October 2014.
(aq) Due to improvements in reporting at one institution, the amounts outstanding decreased by £1bn. This effect has been adjusted out of the flows for February 2015.
(ar) Following a purchase of loans by one reporting institution, the amounts outstanding increased by £2bn. This effect has been adjusted out of the flows for July 2013.
(as) Due to a change in the reporting population, the amounts outstanding increased by £2bn. This effect has been adjusted out of the flows for September 2014.

12.4b Industrial analysis of monetary financial institutions' lending to UK residents

£ millions   Not seasonally adjusted

Amounts outstanding of lending in all currencies

	Agriculture, hunting and forestry	Fishing	Mining and quarrying	Food, beverages and tobacco	Textiles, wearing apparel and leather	Pulp, paper, and printing	Chemicals, pharmaceuticals, rubber and plastics	Manufacturing Non-metallic mineral products and metals	Machinery, equipment and transport equipment	Electrical, medical and optical equipment	Other manufacturing	Total	Electricity, gas steam and air conditioning	Water collection and sewerage	Electricity, gas and water supply Waste management related services and remediation activities	Total
RPM	TBSC	TBSD	TBSE	TBSG	TBSH	TBSI	TBSJ	TBSK	TBSL	TBSM	TBSN	TBSF	TBSO	TBSP	B3FA	B3FO
2013 May	14,087	246	5,121	5,425	1,020	2,542	4,697	4,737	7,872	3,752	3,667	33,712	5,930	2,314	1,949	10,193
Jun	14,252	246	5,937	5,366	1,039	2,515	4,594	4,959	7,073 (be)	3,770	3,615	32,932 (be)	5,803	2,280	1,941	10,025
Jul	14,514	245	6,239	5,650	1,015	2,415	5,238	5,066	7,024	3,920	3,583	33,911	6,660	2,281	2,023	10,964
Aug	14,642	241	5,757	5,336	986	2,401	5,142	5,028	6,657	3,861	3,516	32,928	6,547	2,248	1,968	10,763
Sep	14,767	240	5,516	5,598	954	2,682	4,884	4,721	6,953	3,649	3,468	32,908	6,818	2,532	1,884	11,234
Oct	14,948	238	5,993	5,480	969	2,451	5,038	4,823	7,038	3,774	3,565	33,137	6,967	2,572	1,975	11,514
Nov	15,156	236	5,866	6,189	927	2,429	4,936	4,582	6,582	3,614	3,228	32,487	7,108	2,572	1,914	11,595
Dec	14,469	232	5,674	6,863	866	2,538	4,643	4,457	6,647	3,359	3,224	32,597	8,540	2,628	1,985	13,154
2014 Jan	14,668	228	6,021	6,172	887	2,406	5,307	4,537	6,760	3,422	3,214	32,705	8,277	2,675	2,088	13,040
Feb	14,745	231	6,276	6,502	892	2,439	5,019	4,771	6,883	3,595	3,287	33,388	8,099	2,632	2,139	12,869
Mar	14,918	231	6,358	5,348	914	2,398	5,307	4,923	7,188	2,237 (bf)	3,223	31,538 (bf)	8,694	2,710	2,015	13,418
Apr	15,163	264	5,858	5,079	898	2,229	5,276	4,823	7,287	2,265	3,360	31,217	8,568	2,682	2,077	13,327
May	15,386	248	5,366	4,758	881	2,599	5,281	4,878	7,633	2,837	3,685	32,552	8,620	2,679	2,084	13,383
Jun	15,625	256	5,512	4,783	909	2,626	5,445	4,812	7,401	2,944	3,512	32,432	8,693	2,622	2,012	13,327
Jul	15,779	262	5,403	4,978	985	2,681	5,432	4,841	7,620	2,976	3,560	33,073	8,818	2,643	1,971	13,432
Aug	15,901	258	5,286	5,216	981	2,771	5,475	4,911	7,587	2,850	3,576	33,367	8,556	2,690	2,034	13,280
Sep	16,028	257	5,832	5,505	997	2,704	5,720	5,245	8,564	2,876	3,428	35,038	8,496	2,702	1,984	13,183
Oct	16,289	258	5,980	5,593	994	2,502	5,691	5,325	8,599	2,884	3,435	35,024	8,617	2,718	2,000	13,334
Nov	16,467	257	6,008	6,446	976	2,697	5,730	5,369	8,254	2,879	3,419	35,767	8,434	2,623	2,026	13,084
Dec	15,909	247	5,877	6,439	995	2,776	5,641	5,266	7,768	2,760	3,404	35,049	9,304	2,595	1,855	13,754
2015 Jan	15,997	242	6,338	5,813	1,039	2,813	5,593	5,191	8,026	2,879	3,541	34,894	9,289	2,717	2,036	14,042
Feb	16,117	242	6,314	6,290	1,044	2,763	5,767	5,291	7,935	2,787	3,553	35,430	8,935	2,887	1,974	13,796
Mar	16,408	244	6,910	5,795	1,124	2,672	5,822	5,368	8,261	2,840	3,668	35,550	9,143	3,234	2,063	14,439
Apr	16,541	234	6,710	5,700	1,068	2,565	5,836	5,155	7,927	2,833	3,586	34,670	9,078	2,733	2,123	13,934

Source: Bank of England

12.4b Industrial analysis of monetary financial institutions' lending to UK residents

£ millions

Amounts outstanding of lending in all currencies

RPM	Development of buildings	Construction					Wholesale and retail trade				Accommodation and food service activities	Transport, storage and communication		
		Construction of commercial buildings	Construction of domestic buildings	Civil Engineering	Other construction activities	Total	Wholesale and retail trade and repair of motor vehicles and motorcycles	Wholesale trade, excluding motor vehicles and motor cycles	Retail trade excluding motor vehicles and motor cycles	Total		Transportation and storage	Information and communication	Total
	B7EC	B3I7	B3LY	B4PL	B4PY	TBSQ	TBSS	TBST	TBSU	TBSR	TBSV	B5PL	B5PS	TBSW
2013 May	30,836	4,211	4,556	3,183	7,626	50,412	10,129	13,694	16,978	40,801	24,585	17,655	12,322	29,977
Jun	30,776	3,912	4,101	2,877	7,450	49,116	11,090 (bk)	13,741	16,905	41,736 (bk)	24,653	16,735	11,868	28,603
Jul	30,550	4,099	4,105	3,129	7,516	49,400	11,128	14,132	17,095	42,355	24,655	16,398	12,005	28,403
Aug	30,234	4,234	4,194	3,172	7,440	49,274	10,655	13,896	17,188	41,739	24,536	16,424	11,705	28,129
Sep	30,082	4,318	4,229	3,197	7,461	49,287	9,358 (bl)	14,613	17,269	41,239 (bl)	24,188	16,295	11,810	28,105
Oct	30,001	4,665	4,208	3,274	7,123	49,271	9,132	14,386	17,167	40,685	23,864	16,565	12,782	29,347
Nov	35,877 (bg)	5,644 (bi)	4,350	3,260	6,280 (bj)	55,410 (bg)	9,169	14,574	17,668	41,411	25,467 (bo)	16,013	12,921	28,934
Dec	34,508	5,246	4,006	2,505	5,995	52,261	9,345	14,423	17,729	41,497	25,064	16,018	14,031	30,049
2014 Jan	34,368	5,415	4,147	2,899	5,930	52,759	9,757	14,342	17,944	42,043	25,397	15,798	13,139	28,937
Feb	34,037	5,407	4,385	2,970	6,046	52,846	11,182	14,580	18,445	44,207	25,267	15,219	11,854	27,074
Mar	33,350	5,342	4,312	3,032	6,029	52,065	9,824	14,476	18,511	42,811	24,413	15,216	11,946	27,161
Apr	32,771	5,373	4,310	3,131	6,072	51,658	9,889	13,954	18,327	42,169	23,949	15,185	11,875	27,060
May	32,335	5,281	4,385	3,239	6,082	51,322	10,162	13,682	17,960	41,803	23,796	15,733	12,219	27,951
Jun	32,139	5,011	3,988	2,715	6,086	49,940	10,256	13,637	18,351	42,244	23,850	15,412	11,017	26,429
Jul	31,763	5,136	4,015	3,137	6,116	50,167	10,531	13,784	18,182	42,497	24,156	15,159	11,249	26,408
Aug	31,688	5,083	4,049	3,286	6,175	50,280	10,991	14,164	18,431 (bm)	43,586 (bm)	23,951	14,946	11,220	26,166
Sep	31,309	5,126	4,100	3,267	6,136	49,940	10,056	14,327	18,554	42,936	23,459	15,040	11,595	26,635
Oct	30,852	5,133	4,241	3,271	6,020	49,517	9,431	14,759	18,948	43,138	23,413	15,175	12,101	27,276
Nov	30,427	5,169	4,185	2,929	5,701	48,411	9,914	15,177	18,580	43,671	22,728	14,814	12,374	27,187
Dec	29,130	4,669	3,689	2,456	5,599	45,543	10,426	14,398	19,119	43,942	22,751	15,223	12,587	27,810
2015 Jan	19,957 (bh)	4,779	4,032	2,667	5,642	37,076 (bh)	10,663	14,006	19,160	43,829	23,007	15,486	12,527	28,013
Feb	19,440	4,827	4,159	2,588	5,665	36,678	11,909	13,982	18,431	44,322	22,835	15,439	12,635	28,074
Mar	18,965	4,906	4,320	2,876	5,615	36,682	11,121	14,456	19,862	45,438	22,546	15,308	13,365	28,673
Apr	18,866	4,952	4,438	2,862	5,818	36,935	10,919	14,378	15,900 (bn)	41,197 (bn)	23,236	15,147	13,685	28,832

Source: Bank of England

12.4b Industrial analysis of monetary financial institutions' lending to UK residents

£ millions

Amounts outstanding of lending in all currencies

	Real estate, professional services and support activities				Public administration and defence	Education	Human health and social work	Recreational, personal and community service activities			Financial intermediation (excluding insurance and pension funds)				
	Buying, selling and renting of real estate	Professional, scientific and technical activities	Administrative and support services	Total				Recreational, cultural and sporting activities	Personal and community service activities	Total	Financial leasing corporations	Non-bank credit grantors excluding credit unions and SPVs	Credit unions	Factoring corporations	Mortgage and housing credit corporations excluding SPVs
RPM	TBSY	B6PE	B6PP	TBSX	TBTD	TBTE	TBTF	TBTH	TBTG	B6H5	TBTJ	TBTK	TBTL	TBTM	TBTN
2013 May	165,109	17,724	18,808	201,640	9,398	11,548	21,223	6,808	3,682	10,491	29,016	12,539	1	8,039	55,790
Jun	164,435	18,224	18,983	201,642	9,979	11,605	21,186	6,528	3,624	10,152	28,699	12,349	6	8,750	55,964
Jul	162,362	18,202	19,488	200,052	9,748	11,380	21,135	6,659	3,612	10,271	28,230	12,372	1	8,321	56,370
Aug	159,319 (bp)	18,497	19,299	197,116 (bp)	9,276	11,605	20,958	6,561	3,589	10,149	26,975	12,293	1	8,385	56,119
Sep	158,304	18,514	19,225	196,043	10,043	11,354	21,058	6,578	3,592	10,170	26,807	12,423	1	8,052	56,285
Oct	156,596	18,675	18,792	194,062	10,232	11,352	20,977	6,643	3,593	10,236	26,184	12,503	1	8,398	55,376
Nov	146,058 (bq)	16,447 (bi)	22,904 (bv)	185,409 (bv)(bw)	9,449	11,246	20,945	6,412	3,381	9,793	26,315	12,492	1	5,147 (by)	52,017 (bz)
Dec	145,148	15,816	23,661	184,625	9,976	10,969	20,740	6,377	3,349	9,726	26,160	12,787	1	5,302	50,786 (ca)
2014 Jan	143,764	16,163	22,834	182,761	11,807	10,829	20,740	6,311	3,384	9,695	25,827	12,370	1	4,426	50,739
Feb	142,946	16,356	22,406	181,708	10,827	10,818	20,715	6,348	3,426	9,774	25,687	12,576	1	4,717	50,764
Mar	140,762	16,398	22,343	179,502	10,173	10,886	20,589	6,230	3,412	9,642	26,681	12,729	1	4,743	51,033
Apr	140,138	16,441	22,446	179,025	10,083	10,922	20,374	6,205	3,415	9,620	28,223	12,215	2	4,819	48,789
May	139,304	16,764	23,218	179,287	11,035	10,890	20,273	6,205	3,435	9,640	28,077	12,261	1	4,934	49,340
Jun	138,325	18,452 (bu)	23,302	180,078 (bu)	10,288	10,917	20,486	5,818	3,442	9,261	27,880	12,450	1	5,208	49,542
Jul	137,224	19,991	23,651	180,865	10,322	11,045	20,438	5,793	3,417	9,210	28,043	12,687	1	5,100	50,364
Aug	137,112	20,320	23,862	181,294	10,930	11,058	20,366	5,567	3,439	9,006	28,461	17,528 (bx)	1	5,210	49,493
Sep	135,341	19,432	23,803	178,577	10,143	10,904	19,998	5,547	3,371	8,918	28,607	17,636	1	5,454	49,073
Oct	132,950	19,146	23,495	175,590	12,406	10,962	19,894	5,541	3,343	8,883	28,591	15,889	1	5,234	48,824
Nov	131,562	20,158	24,187	175,907	12,271	10,892	19,942	5,595	3,482	9,076	28,716	15,979	1	5,557	48,287
Dec	129,844 (br)	19,991	23,316	173,150 (br)	11,033	11,017	19,873	5,551	3,369	8,919	28,830	15,768	1	5,299	48,251
2015 Jan	138,200 (bs)	20,794	23,278	182,272 (bs)	11,184	10,816	19,886	5,439	3,363	8,802	28,773	15,675	1	4,881	48,549
Feb	138,004	21,226	23,199	182,429	10,553	10,892	19,853	5,376	3,389	8,765	28,960	17,350	1	5,112	48,845
Mar	137,171	21,818	22,625	181,614	12,191	10,988	20,017	5,563	3,328	8,891	28,431	17,375	1	4,879	50,134
Apr	137,715 (bt)	21,482	22,002	181,199 (bt)	10,687	11,071	20,055	5,625	3,332	8,957	27,928	17,598	1	4,840	50,560

Source: Bank of England

12.4b Industrial analysis of monetary financial institutions' lending to UK residents

£ millions

Amounts outstanding of lending in all currencies

RPM	Investment and unit trusts excluding money market mutual funds	Money market mutual funds	Bank holding companies	Securities dealers	SPVs related to securitisation	Other financial intermediaries	of which intragroup activity	Total	Insurance companies	Pension funds	Total
	TBTO	TBTP	TBTQ	TBTR	B6PZ	TBTS	B3U9	TBTI	B3V7	B3W5	TBTT
2013 May	17,845	136	31,694	170,801	19,823	259,290	230,697	604,974	12,597	14,050	26,648
Jun	19,962	106	31,591	155,505	19,585	245,915	217,564	578,433	12,558	14,218	26,776
Jul	20,952	133	36,468	152,882	20,600	239,693 (cf)	221,647 (cj)	576,022	11,503	13,407	24,909
Aug	19,238	154	39,283	149,153	20,837	235,271	218,266	567,708	10,500	13,292	23,793
Sep	21,051	143	42,726	133,127	20,889	226,313	210,721	547,817	10,187 (cl)	14,329	24,516 (cl)
Oct	21,263	140	44,701	138,469	21,081	228,405	213,284	556,521	10,412	13,671	24,083
Nov	14,885 (cb)	116	42,204	143,684	21,420	226,951 (by)	210,945 (by)	545,233 (bz)(cb)(ck)	10,943	13,586	24,529
Dec	16,186	107	44,362	138,630	21,351	201,458	185,634	517,130 (ca)	14,291	12,174	26,465
2014 Jan	15,584	127	44,478	142,248 (cd)	15,729 (ce)	201,278 (cg)	186,700 (cg)	512,806 (cd)(ce)(cg)	14,108	8,243	22,350
Feb	13,887	139	44,473	144,745	15,857	198,863	184,605	511,710	13,607	8,481	22,088
Mar	10,001	134	44,144	141,332	16,087	149,761	135,813	456,646	12,704	8,412	21,116
Apr	9,147	124	45,444	150,518	16,003	129,210 (ch)(ci)	113,507 (ch)	444,494 (ch)(ci)	11,363	8,087	19,450
May	9,679	118	44,296	142,793	16,036	121,703	106,404	429,239	11,121	7,679	18,800
Jun	7,939	111	42,616	147,038	15,992	106,993	91,051	415,770	10,301	8,997	19,297
Jul	8,116	37	41,687	142,748	14,894	107,756	92,213	411,434	10,363	8,675	19,038
Aug	7,771	22	41,749	133,473	16,088	107,181	91,251	406,977 (bx)	11,986	8,468	20,454
Sep	8,735	17	38,283	134,047	17,308	104,498	88,807	403,658	12,900	10,540	23,439
Oct	9,071	18	39,448	132,475	15,735	101,792	86,211	397,077	12,495	10,723	23,218
Nov	9,375	18	28,023	134,762	15,860	102,115	87,474	388,694	13,339	9,728	23,067
Dec	9,735	18	27,156	128,568	17,793	98,143	83,678	379,561	13,154	10,484	23,638
2015 Jan	7,379 (cc)	58	27,285	136,980	16,106	97,343	81,328	383,030 (cc)	15,961	11,085	27,046
Feb	8,057	77	26,675	140,078	15,846	96,202	80,766	387,203	15,140	10,431	25,571
Mar	8,445	98	26,914	142,655	15,562	100,021	84,832	394,515	16,459	11,681	28,141
Apr	9,072	186	30,903	142,518	15,625	97,859	82,707	397,089	18,309	10,933	29,242

Source: Bank of England

12.4b Industrial analysis of monetary financial institutions' lending to UK residents

£ millions

Amounts outstanding of lending in all currencies

	Fund management activities	Activities auxiliary to financial intermediation				Total financial and non-financial businesses	Individuals and individual trusts			Total UK residents
		Other			Total		Lending secured on dwellings inc. bridging finance	Other loans and advances	Total	
		Central clearing counterparties	Other auxiliary activities	Total						
RPM	TBTU	B3X2	B8FE	TBTV	B5H8	Z92T	TBTX	TBTY	TBTW	TBSA
2013 May	94,195	154,236	5,121	159,357	253,552	1,348,607	1,029,707	105,920	1,135,627	2,484,234
Jun	86,030	144,030	5,017	149,047	235,077	1,302,352	1,031,523	106,383	1,137,906	2,440,258
Jul	86,119	130,543	4,932	135,474	221,593	1,285,796 (cv)	1,033,249	108,473 (da)	1,141,723 (de)	2,427,519
Aug	91,222	140,963	5,126	146,088	237,311	1,285,924	1,034,692	108,662	1,143,354	2,429,278
Sep	91,504	149,348	7,720	157,068	248,572	1,277,057	1,035,877	109,931	1,145,808	2,422,866
Oct	89,425	140,124 (cq)	5,166 (ct)	145,290	234,715	1,271,175	1,038,641	109,319	1,147,960	2,419,135
Nov	92,638 (cm)	145,113	4,650	149,763	242,401 (cm)	1,265,568 (by)(bz)	1,042,602 (cw)(cx)	109,642	1,152,244 (cw)(cx)	2,417,812 (by)(bz)(cx)
Dec	96,914	128,421	4,970	133,391	230,305	1,224,934 (ca)	1,043,652	109,619	1,153,271	2,378,205 (ca)
2014 Jan	95,536	151,261 (cr)(cs)	4,696	155,957 (cr)(cs)	251,494 (cr)(cs)	1,238,281 (cd)(ce)(cg)(cr)(cs)	1,045,938	109,136	1,155,074	2,393,355 (cd)(ce)(cg)(cr)(cs)
Feb	98,438	143,300	4,703	148,002	246,441	1,230,984	1,046,938	108,891	1,155,829	2,386,813
Mar	99,490	135,056	4,529	139,586	239,076	1,160,542 (bf)	1,049,186	109,472	1,158,658	2,319,200 (bf)
Apr	103,114	141,936	9,286 (cu)	151,222 (cu)	254,336 (cu)	1,158,969 (ci)	1,051,150	109,940	1,161,090	2,320,060 (ci)
May	107,870	145,466	9,393	154,859	262,729	1,153,700	1,052,982	110,074	1,163,057	2,316,757
Jun	110,012	137,408	9,575	146,983	256,995	1,132,706 (bu)	1,055,361	110,868	1,166,230	2,298,935 (bu)
Jul	108,181	136,692	10,170	146,862	255,042	1,128,572	1,058,682	111,329	1,170,010	2,298,583
Aug	113,319	133,848	10,567	144,415	257,734	1,129,894 (bm)(bx)	1,060,928	111,646	1,172,574	2,302,468 (bm)(bx)
Sep	111,979 (cn)	138,614	10,801	149,415	261,394 (cn)	1,130,339 (cn)	1,063,163	114,061 (db)	1,177,224 (df)	2,307,563 (cn)(df)
Oct	102,795	140,126	10,982	151,107	253,902	1,116,160	1,065,770	116,199 (dc)	1,181,969 (dc)	2,298,129 (dc)
Nov	111,306	140,795	11,912	152,707	264,013	1,117,443	1,067,783	117,026	1,184,809	2,302,252
Dec	110,496	118,290	12,202	130,493	240,989	1,079,062 (br)	1,069,391	118,020	1,187,412	2,266,473 (br)
2015 Jan	115,774 (co)	126,346	12,758	139,104	254,878 (co)	1,101,351	1,068,790 (cy)	117,340	1,186,130 (cy)	2,287,481 (cy)
Feb	113,350	127,000	12,455	139,456	252,805	1,101,880	1,070,509 (cz)	116,590 (dd)	1,187,098	2,288,979
Mar	125,233 (cp)	120,069	12,600	132,669	257,902 (cp)	1,121,149 (cp)	1,071,564	118,147	1,189,710	2,310,859 (cp)
Apr	124,756	123,470	12,438	135,908	260,664	1,121,252 (bn)	1,072,915	118,364	1,191,279	2,312,531 (bn)

Source: Bank of England

12.4b Industrial analysis of monetary financial institutions' lending to UK residents

(be) Due to improvements in reporting at one institution, the amounts outstanding decreased by £1bn. This effect has been adjusted out of the flows for June 2013.

(bf) Due to a change in accounting treatment at one reporting institution, the amounts outstanding decreased by £1bn. This effect has been adjusted out of the flows for March 2014.

(bg) Due to improvements in reporting at one institution, the amounts outstanding decreased by £6bn. This effect has been adjusted out of the flows for November 2013.

(bh) Due to improvements in reporting at one institution, the amounts outstanding decreased by £9bn. This effect has been adjusted out of the flows for January 2015.

(bi) Due to improvements in reporting at one institution, the amounts outstanding increased by £1bn. This effect has been adjusted out of the flows for November 2013.

(bj) Due to improvements in reporting at one institution, the amounts outstanding decreased by £1bn. This effect has been adjusted out of the flows for November 2013.

(bk) Due to improvements in reporting at one institution, the amounts outstanding increased by £0.7bn. This effect has been adjusted out of the flows for June 2013.

(bl) Due to a reclassification by one reporting institution, the amounts outstanding decreased by £1bn. This effect has been adjusted out of the flows for September 2013.

(bm) Due to a change in treatment at one institution, the amounts outstanding increased by £4bn. This effect has been adjusted out of the flows for August 2014.

(bn) Due to a change in treatment at one institution, the amounts outstanding increased by £2bn. This effect has been adjusted out of the flows for April 2015.

(bo) Due to improvements in reporting at one institution, the amounts outstanding increased by £2bn. This effect has been adjusted out of the flows for November 2013.

(bp) Due to loan transfers out of the UK MFI population, the amounts outstanding decreased by £2bn. This effect has been adjusted out of the flows for August 2013.

(bq) Due to improvements in reporting at one institution, the amounts outstanding decreased by £7bn. This effect has been adjusted out of the flows for November 2013.

(br) Due to a loan transfer by one reporting institution, the amounts outstanding decreased by £1bn. This effect has been adjusted out of the flows for December 2014.

(bs) Due to improvements in reporting at one institution the amounts outstanding increased by £9bn. This effect has been adjusted out of the flows for January 2015.

(bt) Due to a change in the reporting population, the amounts outstanding increased by £1bn. This effect has been adjusted out of the flows for April 2015.

(bu) Due to a change in accounting treatment at one reporting institution, the amounts outstanding increased by £2bn. This effect has been adjusted out of the flows for June 2014.

(bv) Due to a restructuring at one reporting institution, the amounts outstanding increased by £3bn. This effect has been adjusted out of the flows for November 2013.

(bw) Due to improvements in reporting at one institution, the amounts outstanding decreased by £8bn. This effect has been adjusted out of the flows for November 2013.

(bx) Due to improvements in reporting at one institution, the amounts outstanding increased by £4bn. This effect has been adjusted out of the flows for August 2014.

(by) Due to a restructuring at one reporting institution, the amounts outstanding decreased by £3bn. This effect has been adjusted out of the flows for November 2013.

(bz) Due to improvements in reporting at one institution, the amounts outstanding decreased by £1bn. This effect has been adjusted out of the flows for November 2013.

(ca) Due to improvements in reporting at one institution, the amounts outstanding decreased by £2bn. This effect has been adjusted out of the flows for December 2013.

(cb) Due to improvements in reporting at one institution, the amounts outstanding decreased by £4bn. This effect has been adjusted out of the flows for November 2013.

(cc) Due to improvements in reporting at one reporting institution, the amounts outstanding decreased by £2bn. This effect has been adjusted out of the flows for January 2015.

(cd) Due to a restructuring at one reporting institution, the amounts outstanding decreased by £3bn. This effect has been adjusted out of the flows for January 2014.

(ce) Due to improvements in reporting at one institution, the amounts outstanding decreased by £4bn. This effect has been adjusted out of the flows for January 2014.

(cf) Due to improvements in reporting at one institution, the amounts outstanding decreased by £7bn. This effect has been adjusted out of the flows for July 2013.

(cg) Due to improvements in reporting at one institution, the amounts outstanding increased by £2bn. This effect has been adjusted out of the flows for January 2014.

(ch) Due to improvements in reporting at one institution, the amounts outstanding decreased by £4bn. This effect has been adjusted out of the flows for April 2014.

(ci) Due to improvements in reporting at one institution, the amounts outstanding increased by £1bn. This effect has been adjusted out of the flows for April 2014.

(cj) Due to improvements in reporting at one institution, the amounts outstanding increased by £2bn. This effect has been adjusted out of the flows for July 2013.

(ck) Due to a restructuring at one reporting institution, the amounts outstanding decreased by £6bn. This effect has been adjusted out of the flows for November 2013.

(cl) Due to a reclassification by one reporting institution, the amounts outstanding increased by £1bn. This effect has been adjusted out of the flows for September 2013.

(cm) Due to improvements in reporting at one institution, the amounts outstanding decreased by £4bn. This effect has been adjusted out of the flows for November 2013.

(cn) Due to improvements in reporting at one institution, the amounts outstanding increased by £1bn. This effect has been adjusted out of the flows for September 2014.

(co) Due to improvements in reporting at one reporting institution, the amounts outstanding increased by £2bn. This effect has been adjusted out of the flows for January 2015.

(cp) Due to improvements in reporting at one institution, the amounts outstanding increased by £2bn. This effect has been adjusted out of the flows for March 2015.

(cq) Due to improvements in reporting at one institution, the amounts outstanding increased by £2bn. This effect has been adjusted out of the flows for October 2013.

(cr) Due to a change in treatment at one institution, the amounts outstanding increased by £17bn. This effect has been adjusted out of the flows for January 2014.

(cs) Due to a change in treatment at one institution, the amounts outstanding increased by £2bn. This effect has been adjusted out of the flows for January 2014.

(ct) Due to improvements in reporting at one institution, the amounts outstanding decreased by £2bn. This effect has been adjusted out of the flows for October 2013.

(cu) Due to improvements in reporting at one institution, the amounts outstanding increased by £4bn. This effect has been adjusted out of the flows for April 2014.

(cv) Due to improvements in reporting at one institution, the amounts outstanding decreased by £4bn. This effect has been adjusted out of the flows for July 2013.

(cw) Due to improvements in reporting at one institution, the amounts outstanding decreased by £1bn. This effect has been adjusted out of the flows for November 2013.

(cx) Following a purchase of loans by one reporting institution, the amounts outstanding increased by £2bn. This effect has been adjusted out of the flows for November 2013.

(cy) Due to a loan transfer by one reporting institution, the amounts outstanding decreased by £2bn. This effect has been adjusted out of the flows for January 2015.

(cz) Due to improvements in reporting at one institution, the amounts outstanding increased by £1bn. This effect has been adjusted out of the flows for February 2015.

(da) Following a purchase of loans by one reporting institution, the amounts outstanding increased by £2bn. This effect has been adjusted out of the flows for July 2013.

(db) Due to a change in the reporting population, the amounts outstanding increased by £2bn. This effect has been adjusted out of the flows for September 2014.

(dc) Due to a loan transfer by one reporting institution, the amounts outstanding increased by £2bn. This effect has been adjusted out of the flows for October 2014.

(dd) Due to improvements in reporting at one institution, the amounts outstanding decreased by £1bn. This effect has been adjusted out of the flows for February 2015.

(de) Following a purchase of loans by one reporting institution, the amounts outstanding increased by £2bn. This effect has been adjusted out of the flows for July 2013.

(df) Due to a change in the reporting population, the amounts outstanding increased by £2bn. This effect has been adjusted out of the flows for September 2014.

12.4c Industrial analysis of monetary financial institutions' lending to UK residents

£ millions   Not seasonally adjusted

Amounts outstanding of facilities granted in sterling

	Agriculture, hunting and forestry	Fishing	Mining and quarrying	Manufacturing									Electricity, gas and water supply			Total
				Food, beverages and tobacco	Textiles, wearing apparel and leather	Pulp, paper, and printing	Chemicals, pharmaceuticals, rubber and plastics	Non-metallic mineral products and metals	Machinery, equipment and transport equipment	Electrical, medical and optical equipment	Other manufacturing	Total	Electricity, gas steam and air conditioning	Water collection and sewerage	Waste management related services and remediation activities	
RPM	TCCC	TCCD	TCCE	TCCG	TCCH	TCCI	TCCJ	TCCK	TCCL	TCCM	TCCN	TCCF	TCCO	TCCP	B3FE	B3FS
2013 May	16,572	276	2,454	7,771	842	2,503	7,304	4,822	8,762	2,756	3,833	38,593	10,022	5,175	2,675	17,872
Jun	16,723	272	3,410	7,547	852	2,456	7,181	4,749	8,523 (dh)	2,754	3,983	38,044 (dh)	10,109	5,153	2,698	17,960
Jul	16,872	269	3,384	7,572	810	2,403	7,432	4,738	8,383	2,763	4,046	38,148	10,953	5,214	2,723	18,890
Aug	16,993	266	3,383	7,398	822	2,418	7,928	4,868	8,396	2,781	4,003	38,614	10,996	5,185	2,617	18,798
Sep	17,171	268	3,529	7,480	783	2,626	7,329	4,753	8,697	2,618	3,996	38,283	11,181	5,330	2,482	18,994
Oct	17,301	268	3,542	7,526	850	2,695	7,536	4,808	8,723	2,619	4,002	38,760	11,372	5,386	2,583	19,341
Nov	17,414	267	3,716	8,369	866	2,555	7,570	4,841	8,600	2,637	3,859	39,297	11,479	5,411	2,593	19,483
Dec	17,401	274	3,752	8,684	816	2,512	6,834	4,696	8,277	2,557	3,948	38,323	12,662	5,455	2,939	21,056
2014 Jan	17,443	267	3,751	8,380	843	2,493	6,901	4,724	8,397	2,747	3,691	38,174	12,231	5,522	3,070	20,823
Feb	17,531	269	3,757	8,528	874	2,479	6,825	4,801	8,664	2,888	3,658	38,718	12,252	5,567	3,029	20,849
Mar	17,625	288	3,841	7,585	840	2,467	6,895	4,885	8,986	2,615 (di)	3,572	37,845 (di)	12,840	5,628	2,874	21,341
Apr	17,819	295	3,775	7,144	837	2,513	6,785	4,997	8,933	2,588	3,524	37,320	12,365	5,579	2,840	20,784
May	18,031	287	3,822	6,957	793	2,656	6,650	5,131	9,334	3,026	3,542	38,088	12,362	5,615	2,872	20,850
Jun	18,356	280	3,813	7,485	842	2,677	6,947	5,190	8,990	3,096	3,583	38,811	13,326	5,865	2,838	22,029
Jul	18,287	293	3,690	7,752	857	2,396	7,077	5,195	9,270	3,192	3,695	39,434	13,304	5,927	2,676	21,907
Aug	18,541	291	3,687	7,824	854	2,466	7,025	5,339	9,436	3,063	3,744	39,752	13,136	5,940	2,666	21,742
Sep	18,537	289	3,706	7,850	875	2,670	7,132	5,625	9,865	3,059	3,747	40,824	13,339	5,841	2,665	21,845
Oct	18,736	291	3,847	7,902	828	2,832	7,207	5,742	10,131	3,027	3,634	41,303	13,436	5,968	2,692	22,096
Nov	18,890	288	3,783	8,640	824	2,731	7,254	5,530	9,853	3,040	3,759	41,630	13,099	5,778	2,716	21,594
Dec	18,900	284	3,722	8,336	882	2,737	7,242	5,347	9,568	3,001	3,839	40,951	13,755	6,078	2,681	22,515
2015 Jan	18,880	279	3,766	8,021	896	2,757	7,243	5,255	9,561	2,998	3,810	40,542	13,610	5,996	2,630	22,236
Feb	18,921	277	3,786	8,233	905	2,724	7,036	5,407	9,650	2,954	3,888	40,797	13,646	6,234	2,662	22,542
Mar	18,988	280	3,606	8,064	990	2,800	7,197	5,497	9,709	3,040	3,930	41,227	13,735	6,502	2,775	23,013
Apr	22,653 (dg)	285	3,704	8,819	1,047	3,093	7,441	5,637	10,192	3,112	3,923	43,264	13,908	6,481	2,910	23,299

Source: Bank of England

12.4c Industrial analysis of monetary financial institutions' lending to UK residents

£ millions

Amounts outstanding of facilities granted in sterling

RPM	Development of buildings B7EG	Construction of commercial buildings B3ID	Construction of domestic buildings B4PC	Civil Engineering B4PP	Other construction activities B5QH	Total TCCQ	Wholesale and retail trade and repair of motor vehicles and motorcycles TCCS	Wholesale trade, excluding motor vehicles and motor cycles TCCT	Retail trade excluding motor vehicles and motor cycles TCCU	Total TCCR	Accommodation and food service activities TCCV	Transportation and storage B5PP	Information and communication B5PW	Total TCCW
2013 May	34,909	5,134	7,355	4,826	9,688	61,912	11,685	15,564	23,591	50,840	27,305	18,725	13,394	32,119
Jun	34,866	4,972	7,274	4,763	9,511	61,386	12,126 (dn)	15,527	23,324	50,978 (dn)	27,220	18,890	13,062	31,952
Jul	34,593	5,061	7,051	4,734	9,451	60,890	12,433	15,047	23,118	50,597	27,225	18,938	13,612	32,551
Aug	34,298	5,195	7,173	4,717	9,516	60,900	12,069	15,677	22,634	50,379	27,176	18,812	13,424	32,235
Sep	34,065	5,276	7,279	4,657	9,477	60,754	10,894 (do)	15,811	22,895	49,600 (do)	27,010	19,125	13,753	32,879
Oct	34,472	5,598	7,193	4,941	9,052	61,256	10,747	15,624	22,706	49,076	26,675	19,228	13,864	33,092
Nov	41,106 (dj)	7,071 (dl)	7,287	4,953	7,950 (dm)	68,367 (dj)	10,776	15,855	23,057	49,688	28,313 (dt)	19,203	14,086	33,289
Dec	39,867	6,577	7,301	4,543	7,688	65,976	10,677	16,009	23,156	49,842	27,856	19,952	14,899	34,851
2014 Jan	39,696	6,750	7,375	4,700	7,516	66,038	11,216	15,660	23,792	50,668	27,845	19,672	14,362	34,034
Feb	39,153	6,690	7,646	4,747	7,528	65,764	12,665	15,846	24,314	52,825	27,721	19,283	13,262	32,545
Mar	38,993	6,639	7,695	5,293	7,607	66,228	11,291	15,521	24,181	50,993	26,847	19,626	13,123	32,748
Apr	38,249	6,719	7,604	4,949	7,742	65,263	11,775	15,444	24,148	51,366	26,961	19,884	12,908	32,792
May	37,885	6,626	7,673	4,800	7,677	64,660	11,561	15,492	24,254	51,306	26,794	20,361	13,495	33,856
Jun	38,028	6,728	7,664	4,517	7,664	64,601	11,885	15,650	24,468	52,003	26,441	21,184 (dv)	13,125	34,309 (dv)
Jul	37,439	6,751	7,674	4,763	7,646	64,274	12,049	15,724	24,367	52,141	26,847	20,842	13,056	33,898
Aug	37,127	6,660	7,698	4,855	7,722	64,062	12,704	15,734	24,896	53,334 (ds)	26,589	20,820	12,790	33,609
Sep	36,865	6,674	7,732	4,608	7,752	63,630	11,722	15,922	26,092	53,736	26,394	21,142	13,340	34,482
Oct	36,598	6,579	7,683	4,671	7,677	63,208	11,143	16,084	26,684	53,912	26,146	21,149	13,631	34,780
Nov	36,235	6,569	7,463	4,571	7,313	62,150	11,442	15,938	26,632	54,012	25,616	20,297	13,281	33,578
Dec	34,700	6,217	7,422	4,534	7,221	60,094	11,816	15,603	27,224	54,644	25,566	20,416	13,662	34,078
2015 Jan	23,294 (dk)	6,141	7,153	4,563	7,162	48,314 (dk)	12,197	15,285	27,295	54,778	25,556	20,523	13,580	34,104
Feb	23,017	6,123	7,100	4,366	7,176	47,782	13,569	15,517	26,821	55,908	25,382	20,506	13,720	34,226
Mar	22,627	6,133	7,150	4,575	7,105	47,590	12,761	15,557	27,665	55,983	25,361	20,789	15,791	36,581
Apr	23,076	6,219	7,405	4,557	7,622	48,879	12,972	17,165 (dp)	25,534 (dq)(dr)	55,671 (dp)(dq)(dr)	27,284 (du)	20,575	15,786	36,361

Source: Bank of England

12.4c Industrial analysis of monetary financial institutions' lending to UK residents

£ millions

Amounts outstanding of facilities granted in sterling

	Real estate, professional services and support activities				Public administration and defence	Education	Human health and social work	Recreational, personal and community service activities			Financial intermediation (excluding insurance and pension funds)				
	Buying, selling and renting of real estate	Professional, scientific and technical activities	Administrative and support services	Total				Recreational, cultural and sporting activities	Personal and community service activities	Total	Financial leasing corporations	Non-bank credit grantors excluding credit unions and SPVs	Credit unions	Factoring corporations	Mortgage and housing credit corporations excluding SPVs
RPM	TCCY	B6PH	B3S2	TCCX	TCDD	TCDE	TCDF	TCDH	TCDG	B3SR	TCDJ	TCDK	TCDL	TCDM	TCDN
2013 May	182,289	20,568	21,002	223,859	10,099	13,757	24,716	7,833	4,246	12,079	26,023	13,282	2	7,923	56,505
Jun	181,694	20,814	21,069	223,576	10,629	13,734	24,690	7,311	4,206	11,517	25,943	13,103	6	8,415	56,711
Jul	179,755	20,623	21,373	221,751	10,112	13,378	24,523	7,250	4,251	11,501	25,408	13,075	2	8,137	57,061
Aug	176,692 (dw)	20,548	21,604	218,843 (dw)	9,706	13,457	24,467	7,387	4,297	11,685	24,362	13,280	2	8,242	56,850
Sep	175,783	20,905	21,766	218,453	10,756	13,349	24,466	7,417	4,318	11,735	24,453	13,409	2	7,917	57,048
Oct	174,722	21,285	21,918	217,925	10,773	13,263	24,300	7,497	4,277	11,774	23,902	13,431	2	8,275	56,076
Nov	164,024 (dx)	19,612 (dm)	25,824 (ee)	209,460 (ee)(eg)	9,914	13,123	23,924	7,394	4,045	11,439	24,155	14,146	2	5,004 (el)	52,655 (em)
Dec	163,340	20,022	26,262	209,623	9,349	12,660	23,399	7,449	3,921	11,369	24,406	14,233	2	5,104	51,450 (en)
2014 Jan	162,302	20,259	25,690	208,251	9,957	12,765	23,362	7,459	3,929	11,389	24,327	13,788	2	4,260	51,578
Feb	161,562	20,432	25,573	207,567	9,447	12,744	23,383	7,435	3,938	11,374	24,388	13,893	2	4,551	51,602
Mar	159,749	20,116	25,546	205,411	9,801	12,796	23,005	7,324	3,860	11,183	25,299	14,022	2	4,606	51,819
Apr	158,880	20,328	25,378	204,586	9,481	13,075	22,653	7,292	3,936	11,228	26,387	13,523	2	4,762	49,373
May	158,236	20,877	25,692	204,805	9,226	12,953	22,393	7,457	3,889	11,346	26,077	13,680	1	4,818	49,893
Jun	157,178	22,255 (ec)	26,010	205,443 (ec)	9,457	12,939	22,505	6,927	3,895	10,822	26,250	13,813	1	4,960	50,088
Jul	156,235	22,819	26,082	205,136	9,564	13,117	22,582	6,892	3,891	10,784	26,345	14,009	1	4,955	51,265
Aug	156,298	23,111	26,592	206,002	10,513	13,135	22,655	7,002	3,885	10,887	26,679	18,647 (ej)	2	5,059	50,202
Sep	153,985	22,558	26,388	202,931	9,526	13,117	22,018	6,896	3,802	10,698	26,182	18,620	2	5,254	49,669
Oct	152,721	22,450	27,039	202,209	9,944	13,058	21,855	6,853	3,821	10,674	26,341	17,429	2	5,094	49,357
Nov	151,198	22,795	27,257	201,250	10,393	13,008	21,786	6,786	3,883	10,669	26,358	17,437	2	5,320	48,990
Dec	149,533 (dy)	22,166	26,725	198,423 (dy)	10,223	13,126	21,750	6,868	3,894	10,762	26,934	17,040	2	5,126	49,081
2015 Jan	159,766 (dz)	22,795	26,861	209,421 (dz)	10,427	12,909	21,864	6,667	3,803	10,470	26,880	17,019	2	4,789	49,365
Feb	159,239	23,018	26,359	208,616	10,427	13,023	21,866	6,655	3,824	10,479	27,201	18,693	2	4,961	49,453
Mar	159,075	23,362	25,929	208,366	10,808	13,189	22,045	6,689	3,788	10,477	26,746	18,366	2	4,745	50,252
Apr	163,769 (ea)(eb)	24,166 (ed)	26,887 (ef)	214,821 (ea)(eb)(ed)(ef)	11,057	13,841	23,199 (eh)	7,017	4,161	11,178	28,864 (ei)	23,279 (ek)	2	4,966	50,670

Source: Bank of England

347

12.4c Industrial analysis of monetary financial institutions' lending to UK residents

£ millions

Amounts outstanding of facilities granted in sterling

RPM	Investment and unit trusts excluding money market mutual funds	Money market mutual funds	Financial intermediation (excluding insurance and pension funds)						Insurance companies & pension funds		
			Bank holding companies	Securities dealers	SPVs related to securitisation	Other financial intermediaries	of which intragroup activity	Total	Insurance companies	Pension funds	Total
	TCDO	TCDP	TCDQ	TCDR	B8EX	TCDS	B7FF	TCDI	B7FK	B3W9	TCDT
2013 May	8,638	65	24,424	21,043	20,299	151,754	139,754	329,958	13,209	13,899	27,108
Jun	9,472	66	24,535	20,552	20,164	149,571	137,757	328,539	13,014	14,148	27,162
Jul	9,940	67	29,830	22,066	21,365	151,087 (ep)	139,004 (ep)	338,036	11,949	13,339	25,288
Aug	10,287	63	33,134	21,087	21,407	151,991	139,923	340,706	10,998	13,183	24,181
Sep	10,463	64	35,512	19,211	21,092	151,757	140,384	340,927	10,534 (es)	14,124	24,658 (es)
Oct	9,707	64	35,443	21,503	21,225	153,594	141,693	343,222	11,071	13,634	24,705
Nov	9,833	65	35,454	22,469	21,601	152,590 (el)	141,054 (el)	337,975 (em)(er)	11,490	13,564	25,054
Dec	11,099	66	35,802	22,223	21,386	131,265	119,639	317,036 (en)	15,560	12,311	27,871
2014 Jan	10,915	68	35,773	25,759	15,474 (eo)	131,769 (eq)	121,129 (eq)	313,714 (eo)(eq)	15,293	8,372	23,665
Feb	10,780	73	35,666	27,705	15,436	132,325	121,463	316,421	15,071	8,504	23,575
Mar	7,249	120	35,346	24,571	15,759	97,262	86,481	276,055	14,673	8,601	23,274
Apr	6,738	125	36,228	27,637	15,649	82,792	71,576	263,218	12,964	8,364	21,328
May	6,468	130	34,041	26,532	15,520	76,252	65,263	253,413	12,910	7,807	20,717
Jun	6,321	128	32,978	31,112 (dv)	15,460	72,777	61,778	253,888 (dv)	12,708	9,056	21,764
Jul	6,278	85	32,959	28,931	14,846	73,300	63,006	252,974	12,590	8,527	21,117
Aug	6,397	72	32,867	29,646	16,021	72,275	61,751	257,868 (ej)	13,531	8,141	21,672
Sep	5,707	71	29,571	25,860	17,163	70,165	58,996	248,263	14,589	9,633	24,222
Oct	5,983	21	30,594	24,224	16,070	67,046	55,555	242,162	14,050	10,263	24,313
Nov	6,067	21	19,643	23,661	16,156	67,683	56,719	231,339	14,364	9,156	23,521
Dec	6,019	21	18,125	22,986	18,251	64,165	52,974	227,749	14,414	9,895	24,310
2015 Jan	4,961	28	18,142	23,144	17,094	64,279	52,132	225,704	16,618	10,108	26,726
Feb	5,275	36	18,039	25,987	16,510	63,024	51,367	229,181	15,564	9,306	24,870
Mar	5,511	36	18,833	23,528	16,247	70,268	58,440	234,534	16,567	10,944	27,511
Apr	5,717	45	19,777	23,572	16,225	68,046	56,287	241,161 (ei)(ek)	17,020	10,246	27,266

Source: Bank of England

12.4c Industrial analysis of monetary financial institutions' lending to UK residents

£ millions

Amounts outstanding of facilities granted in sterling

RPM	Fund management activities	Activities auxiliary to financial intermediation			Total	Total financial and non-financial businesses	Individuals and individual trusts			Total UK residents
		Central clearing counterparties	Other auxiliary activities	Total			Lending secured on dwellings inc. bridging finance	Other loans and advances	Total	
	TCDU	B3X6	B3Y4	TCDV	B8FO	Z94D	TCDX	TCDY	TCDW	TCCA
2013 May	39,397	74,400	4,096	78,496	117,894	1,007,414	1,084,719	160,088	1,244,808	2,252,222
Jun	39,673	67,905	4,022	71,928	111,601	999,394	1,087,611	160,609	1,248,221	2,247,614
Jul	40,957	61,694	3,942	65,636	106,593	1,000,009 (ey)	1,089,650	162,714 (ff)	1,252,364 (ff)	2,252,373
Aug	43,066	69,439	4,217	73,656	116,722	1,008,509	1,091,354	163,302	1,254,656	2,263,165
Sep	43,978	73,219	6,050	79,269	123,247	1,016,079	1,093,039	164,224	1,257,263	2,273,342
Oct	45,387	63,098 (ev)	3,982 (ex)	67,080	112,467	1,007,741	1,096,774	163,863	1,260,636	2,268,377
Nov	46,415	63,093	3,841	66,935	113,349	1,004,072 (el)(em)	1,102,019 (fa)(fb)	164,258	1,266,277 (fa)(fb)	2,270,350 (el)(em)(fb)
Dec	48,975	50,823	3,886	54,709	103,684	974,324 (en)	1,102,718	163,624	1,266,342	2,240,666 (en)
2014 Jan	47,795	66,131 (ew)	3,771	69,902 (ew)	117,697 (ew)	979,843 (eo)(eq)(ew)	1,103,036	163,738	1,266,773	2,246,616 (eo)(eq)(ew)
Feb	49,527	62,902	3,892	66,794	116,322	980,813	1,104,296	164,877	1,269,173	2,249,986
Mar	47,832	61,273	3,874	65,146	112,978	932,261 (di)	1,108,103	164,464	1,272,568	2,204,829 (di)
Apr	49,632	59,347	4,051	63,398	113,030	914,973	1,110,773	165,478	1,276,251	2,191,225
May	53,213	62,579	4,061	66,639	119,852	912,401	1,112,799	165,978	1,278,777	2,191,177
Jun	57,654	63,097	4,220	67,317	124,971	922,435 (ec)(ez)	1,115,321	166,843	1,282,164	2,204,599 (ec)(ez)
Jul	59,178	61,647	4,160	65,807	124,985	921,031	1,120,432	167,052	1,287,484	2,208,515
Aug	58,284	57,282	4,259	61,540	119,825	924,164 (ds)(ej)	1,121,704	167,309	1,289,012	2,213,177 (ds)(ej)
Sep	55,130 (et)	64,229	4,352	68,581	123,711 (et)	917,930 (et)	1,122,302	170,098 (fg)	1,292,400 (fg)	2,210,329 (et)(fg)
Oct	56,474	64,215	4,388	68,603	125,077	913,610	1,124,991	181,071 (fh)	1,306,063 (fh)	2,219,673 (fh)
Nov	59,908	65,573	4,424	69,997	129,906	903,412	1,126,436	182,214	1,308,650	2,212,062
Dec	62,179	52,542	4,244	56,786	118,965	886,063 (dy)	1,126,593	183,173	1,309,765	2,195,828 (dy)
2015 Jan	65,442	56,735	4,242	60,978	126,420	892,395	1,123,698 (fc)	182,864	1,306,561 (fc)	2,198,956 (fc)
Feb	63,294	56,947	4,277	61,224	124,519	892,602	1,125,080 (fd)	181,847 (fi)	1,306,928	2,199,529
Mar	69,449 (eu)	55,563	4,164	59,727	129,175 (eu)	908,735 (eu)	1,128,080	183,213	1,311,292	2,220,027 (eu)
Apr	69,247	55,592	4,395	59,988	129,235	933,159 (dg)(dp)(dq)(ei)(ek)	1,127,213 (fe)	190,863 (fi)	1,318,077 (fe)(fi)	2,251,236 (dg)(dp)(dq)(ei)(ek)(fe)(fi)

Source: Bank of England

Notes to table

Movements in amounts outstanding can reflect breaks in data series as well as underlying flows. For changes data, users are recommended to refer directly to the appropriate series or data tables.

Further explanation can be found at: www.bankofengland.co.uk/statistics/Pages/iadb/notesiadb/Changes_flows_growth_rates.aspx.

12.4c Industrial analysis of monetary financial institutions' lending to UK residents

(dg) Due to improvements in reporting at one institution, the amounts outstanding increased by £3bn. This effect has been adjusted out of the flows for April 2015.

(dh) Due to improvements in reporting at one institution, the amounts outstanding decreased by £0.7bn. This effect has been adjusted out of the flows for June 2013.

(di) Due to a change in accounting treatment at one reporting institution, the amounts outstanding decreased by £1bn. This effect has been adjusted out of the flows for March 2014.

(dj) Due to improvements in reporting at one institution, the amounts outstanding increased by £6bn. This effect has been adjusted out of the flows for November 2013.

(dk) Due to improvements in reporting at one institution the amounts outstanding decreased by £11bn. This effect has been adjusted out of the flows for January 2015.

(dl) Due to improvements in reporting at one institution, the amounts outstanding decreased by £1bn. This effect has been adjusted out of the flows for November 2013.

(dm) Due to improvements in reporting at one institution, the amounts outstanding decreased by £1bn. This effect has been adjusted out of the flows for November 2013.

(dn) Due to improvements in reporting at one institution, the amounts outstanding increased by £0.4bn. This effect has been adjusted out of the flows for June 2013.

(do) Due to a reclassification by one reporting institution, the amounts outstanding decreased by £1bn. This effect has been adjusted out of the flows for September 2013.

(dp) Due to improvements in reporting at one institution, the amounts outstanding increased by £2bn. This effect has been adjusted out of the flows for April 2015.

(dq) Due to a change in treatment at one institution, the amounts outstanding decreased by £4bn. This has been adjusted out of the flows for April 2015,

(dr) Due to improvements in reporting at one institution, the amounts outstanding increased by £1bn. This effect has been adjusted out of the flows for April 2015.

(ds) Due to a change in treatment at one institution, the amounts outstanding increased by £1bn. This effect has been adjusted out of the flows for August 2014.

(dt) Due to improvements in reporting at one institution, the amounts outstanding increased by £2bn. This effect has been adjusted out of the flows for November 2013.

(du) Due to improvements in reporting at one institution, the amounts outstanding increased by £1bn. This effect has been adjusted out of the flows for April 2015.

(dv) Due to improvements in reporting at one institution, the amounts outstanding increased by £1bn. This effect has been adjusted out of the flows for June 2014.

(dw) Due to loan transfers out of the UK MFI population, the amounts outstanding decreased by £2bn. This effect has been adjusted out of the flows for August 2013.

(dx) Due to improvements in reporting at one institution, the amounts outstanding decreased by £7bn. This effect has been adjusted out of the flows for November 2013.

(dy) Due to a loan transfer by one reporting institution, the amounts outstanding decreased by £1bn. This effect has been adjusted out of the flows for December 2014.

(dz) Due to improvements in reporting at one institution, the amounts outstanding increased by £11bn. This effect has been adjusted out of the flows for January 2015.

(ea) Due to improvements in reporting at one institution, the amounts outstanding increased by £3bn. This effect has been adjusted out of the flows for April 2015.

(eb) Due to a change in the reporting population, the amounts outstanding increased by £1bn. This effect has been adjusted out of the flows for April 2015.

(ec) Due to a change in accounting treatment at one reporting institution, the amounts outstanding increased by £2bn. This effect has been adjusted out of the flows for June 2014.

(ed) Due to improvements in reporting at one institution, the amounts outstanding increased by £1bn. This effect has been adjusted out of the flows for April 2015.

(ee) Due to a restructuring at one reporting institution, the amounts outstanding increased by £3bn. This effect has been adjusted out of the flows for November 2013.

(ef) Due to improvements in reporting at one institution, the amounts outstanding increased by £1bn. This effect has been adjusted out of the flows for April 2015.

(eg) Due to improvements in reporting at one institution, the amounts outstanding decreased by £8bn. This effect has been adjusted out of the flows for November 2013.

(eh) Due to improvements in reporting at one institution, the amounts outstanding increased by £1bn. This effect has been adjusted out of the flows for April 2015.

(ei) Due to improvements in reporting at one institution, the amounts outstanding increased by £2bn. This effect has been adjusted out of the flows for April 2015.

(ej) Due to improvements in reporting at one institution, the amounts outstanding increased by £4bn. This effect has been adjusted out of the flows for August 2014.

(ek) Due to improvements in reporting at one institution, the amounts outstanding increased by £5bn. This effect has been adjusted out of the flows for April 2015.

(el) Due to a restructuring at one reporting institution, the amounts outstanding decreased by £3bn. This effect has been adjusted out of the flows for November 2013.

(em) Due to improvements in reporting at one institution, the amounts outstanding increased by £1bn. This effect has been adjusted out of the flows for November 2013.

(en) Due to improvements in reporting at one institution, the amounts outstanding decreased by £2bn. This effect has been adjusted out of the flows for December 2013.

(eo) Due to improvements in reporting at one institution, the amounts outstanding decreased by £4bn. This effect has been adjusted out of the flows for January 2014.

(ep) Due to improvements in reporting at one institution, the amounts outstanding increased by £2bn. This effect has been adjusted out of the flows for July 2013.

(eq) Due to improvements in reporting at one institution, the amounts outstanding increased by £2bn. This effect has been adjusted out of the flows for January 2014.

(er) Due to a restructuring at one reporting institution, the amounts outstanding decreased by £6bn. This effect has been adjusted out of the flows for November 2013.

(es) Due to a reclassification by one reporting institution, the amounts outstanding increased by £1bn. This effect has been adjusted out of the flows for September 2013.

(et) Due to improvements in reporting at one institution, the amounts outstanding increased by £1bn. This effect has been adjusted out of the flows for September 2014.

(eu) Due to improvements in reporting at one institution, the amounts outstanding increased by £2bn. This effect has been adjusted out of the flows for March 2015.

(ev) Due to improvements in reporting at one institution, the amounts outstanding increased by £2bn. This effect has been adjusted out of the flows for October 2013.

(ew) Due to a change in treatment at one institution, the amounts outstanding increased by £17bn. This effect has been adjusted out of the flows for January 2014.

(ex) Due to improvements in reporting at one institution, the amounts outstanding decreased by £2bn. This effect has been adjusted out of the flows for October 2013.

(ey) Due to improvements in reporting at one institution, the amounts outstanding increased by £5bn. This effect has been adjusted out of the flows for July 2013.

(ez) Due to improvements in reporting at one institution, the amounts outstanding increased by £2bn. This effect has been adjusted out of the flows for June 2014.

(fa) Following a purchase of loans by one reporting institution, the amounts outstanding increased by £2bn. This effect has been adjusted out of the flows for November 2013.

(fb) Following a purchase of loans by one reporting institution, the amounts outstanding increased by £2bn. This effect has been adjusted out of the flows for November 2013.

(fc) Due to a loan transfer by one reporting institution, the amounts outstanding decreased by £2bn. This effect has been adjusted out of the flows for January 2015.

(fd) Due to improvements in reporting at one institution, the amounts outstanding increased by £1bn. This effect has been adjusted out of the flows for February 2015.

(fe) Due to improvements in reporting at one institution, the amounts outstanding decreased by £4bn. This effect has been adjusted out of the flows for April 2015.

(ff) Following a purchase of loans by one reporting institution, the amounts outstanding increased by £2bn. This effect has been adjusted out of the flows for July 2013.

(fg) Due to a change in the reporting population, the amounts outstanding increased by £2bn. This effect has been adjusted out of the flows for September 2014.

(fh) Due to a loan transfer by one reporting institution, the amounts outstanding increased by £10bn. This effect has been adjusted out of the flows for October 2014.

(fi) Due to improvements in reporting at one institution, the amounts outstanding decreased by £1bn. This effect has been adjusted out of the flows for February 2015.

(fj) Due to improvements in reporting at one institution, the amounts outstanding increased by £7bn. This effect has been adjusted out of the flows for April 2015.

12.4d Industrial analysis of monetary financial institutions' lending to UK residents

£ millions Not seasonally adjusted

Amounts outstanding of facilities granted in all currencies

RPM	Agriculture, hunting and forestry	Fishing	Mining and quarrying	Manufacturing									Electricity, gas and water supply			
				Food, beverages and tobacco	Textiles, wearing apparel and leather	Pulp, paper, and printing	Chemicals, pharmaceuticals, rubber and plastics	Non-metallic mineral products and metals	Machinery, equipment and transport equipment	Electrical, medical and optical equipment	Other manufacturing	Total	Electricity, gas steam and air conditioning	Water collection and sewerage	Waste management related services and remediation activities	Total
	TCAC	TCAD	TCAE	TCAG	TCAH	TCAI	TCAJ	TCAK	TCAL	TCAM	TCAN	TCAF	TCAO	TCAP	B3FF	B3FT
2013 May	16,920	288	25,810	15,920	1,485	3,949	15,585	8,704	14,782	5,789	5,285	71,500	16,021	5,559	2,915	24,495
Jun	17,065	284	26,533	15,824	1,511	3,889	15,794	8,458	13,875 (fl)	5,824	5,444	70,620 (fl)	16,110	5,582	2,951	24,643
Jul	17,219	281	26,943	16,183	1,483	3,714	16,207	8,520	13,978	5,922	5,487	71,494	17,828	5,647	3,051	26,526
Aug	17,365	277	25,472	16,032	1,502	3,602	16,412	8,466	13,704	5,728	5,409	70,854	19,160	5,611	2,906	27,677
Sep	17,511	279	24,395	15,993	1,423	3,898	15,465	8,206	14,007	5,382	5,306	69,679	19,091	5,735	2,816	27,642
Oct	17,654	278	25,260	15,939	1,522	3,860	15,975	8,279	14,126	5,561	5,379	70,640	18,883	5,813	2,925	27,620
Nov	17,771	276	24,656	16,308	1,549	3,779	15,907	8,318	13,863	5,467	5,079	70,269	18,568	5,816	2,898	27,282
Dec	17,746	284	25,394	16,046	1,440	3,756	14,862	8,088	13,780	5,383	5,219	68,574	19,639	5,800	3,232	28,671
2014 Jan	17,787	277	25,537	15,937	1,477	3,665	15,434	8,018	14,004	5,670	5,025	69,228	19,008	5,809	3,407	28,224
Feb	17,862	279	25,576	15,596	1,492	3,652	15,162	8,055	13,754	6,335	5,689	69,735	18,421	5,865	3,385	27,670
Mar	17,996	297	25,285	15,050	1,483	3,738	15,652	8,175	13,958	4,727 (fm)	5,364	68,146 (fm)	19,941	6,017	3,220	29,178
Apr	18,183	304	24,602	14,572	1,472	3,703	15,650	8,257	14,528	4,483	5,516	68,181	18,969	5,985	3,269	28,223
May	18,378	291	22,980	14,689	1,381	4,110	15,425	8,379	14,362	4,864	5,451	68,661	19,055	6,067	3,224	28,346
Jun	18,703	290	23,597	15,635	1,430	4,162	15,599	8,853	14,489	5,192	5,407	70,768	20,268	6,321	3,142	29,731
Jul	18,634	301	24,128	19,123	1,537	3,923	15,838	8,468	15,041	5,110	5,543	74,583	20,051	6,384	2,968	29,404
Aug	18,898	300	24,439	18,993	1,549	3,748	15,913	8,884	14,987	4,990	5,555	74,619	20,494	6,393	2,986	29,874
Sep	18,901	297	25,350	20,118	1,583	3,856	16,139	9,205	15,498	4,925	5,588	76,912	20,864	6,293	2,971	30,128
Oct	19,117	299	25,649	20,987	1,550	3,999	16,204	9,499	15,590	4,847	5,448	78,124	20,961	6,457	2,979	30,397
Nov	19,272	292	25,956	21,971	1,535	3,930	16,675	9,562	15,318	4,909	5,368	79,267	20,890	6,327	3,054	30,270
Dec	19,285	288	26,174	21,735	1,594	3,988	16,349	9,337	15,263	4,991	5,539	78,797	21,230	6,532	2,967	30,730
2015 Jan	19,304	283	27,080	21,588	1,635	3,980	17,082	9,002	15,339	4,935	5,665	79,227	21,333	6,424	3,036	30,793
Feb	19,355	286	26,666	21,272	1,596	4,028	16,253	9,218	15,391	4,795	5,627	78,179	21,656	6,616	2,986	31,258
Mar	19,436	284	27,846	22,795	1,731	4,088	16,741	9,288	15,601	4,926	5,768	80,938	21,587	6,994	3,071	31,652
Apr	23,131 (fk)	289	30,793	23,254	1,750	4,267	16,177	9,221	16,024	4,934	5,700	81,327	21,801	7,091	3,269	32,160

Source: Bank of England

12.4d Industrial analysis of monetary financial institutions' lending to UK residents

£ millions

Amounts outstanding of facilities granted in all currencies

RPM	Development of buildings	Construction					Wholesale and retail trade				Accommodation and food service activities	Transport, storage and communication		
		Construction of commercial buildings	Construction of domestic buildings	Civil Engineering	Other construction activities	Total	Wholesale and retail trade and repair of motor vehicles and motorcycles	Wholesale trade, excluding motor vehicles and motor cycles	Retail trade excluding motor vehicles and motor cycles	Total		Transportation and storage	Information and communication	Total
	B7EH	B3IE	B4PD	B3KK	B5PC	TCAQ	TCAS	TCAT	TCAU	TCAR	TCAV	B3NF	B5PX	TCAW
2013 May	36,076	5,750	7,562	5,019	10,093	64,499	12,737	21,835	29,184	63,756	28,880	26,655	25,967	52,622
Jun	36,102	5,679	7,510	4,971	9,942	64,203	14,012 (fr)	22,446	28,956	65,413 (fr)	28,803	26,054	25,961	52,015
Jul	35,869	5,746	7,281	4,939	9,937	63,771	13,811	22,270	28,809	64,890	28,900	26,322	26,758	53,080
Aug	35,543	5,721	7,350	4,911	9,929	63,453	13,491	22,106	27,599	63,195	28,758	26,117	26,094	52,210
Sep	35,232	5,738	7,457	4,843	9,931	63,201	12,037 (fs)	22,556	28,137	62,730 (fs)	28,611	26,478	25,964	52,442
Oct	35,378	6,044	7,367	5,131	9,503	63,423	11,856	22,280	27,843	61,979	28,297	25,992	26,017	52,009
Nov	42,403 (fm)	7,506 (fp)	7,463	5,204	8,373 (fq)	70,949 (fm)	11,756	22,424	28,388	62,567	29,799 (fx)	25,820	26,096	51,916
Dec	41,079	7,227	7,497	5,050	7,954	68,808	11,726	22,629	28,961	63,316	29,388	26,629	27,227	53,857
2014 Jan	40,844	7,384	7,550	5,163	7,729	68,670	12,187	22,472	29,200	63,860	29,374	25,787	26,566	52,353
Feb	40,151	7,356	7,816	5,179	7,735	68,237	13,732	22,681	29,921	66,333	29,300	25,394	25,356	50,749
Mar	40,083	7,356	7,858	5,834	7,863	68,994	12,314	22,752	29,656	64,722	28,449	25,947	23,815	49,762
Apr	39,379	7,496	7,763	5,681	8,007	68,326	12,786	22,297	29,518	64,601	28,517	25,705	23,924	49,629
May	38,942	7,475	7,827	5,546	7,948	67,738	12,656	22,237	30,172	65,066	28,463	26,337	24,303	50,640
Jun	39,000	7,553	7,862	5,444	7,924	67,784	12,910	23,148	30,424	66,482	28,120	26,700 (fz)	23,946	50,646 (fz)
Jul	38,348	7,473	7,841	5,597	7,897	67,156	13,163	23,337	30,078	66,578	28,279	26,405	28,276	54,681
Aug	38,041	7,387	7,865	5,647	7,983	66,924	13,929	23,520	30,692	68,141 (fw)	28,149	26,614	26,275	52,889
Sep	37,803	7,267	7,887	5,409	8,011	66,378	12,974	24,457	32,689	70,120	28,006	26,703	26,415	53,118
Oct	37,575	7,175	7,825	5,307	7,941	65,824	12,585	24,946	34,209	71,740	27,721	27,386	27,367	54,752
Nov	37,243	7,109	7,609	5,464	7,549	64,974	12,744	25,415	32,907	71,067	27,243	26,258	26,383	52,640
Dec	35,652	6,854	7,631	5,384	7,468	62,989	13,062	24,383	34,258	71,703	27,123	26,280	26,664	52,944
2015 Jan	23,794 (fo)	6,809	7,342	5,345	7,394	50,684 (fo)	13,259	23,543	33,688	70,490	27,062	26,578	26,787	53,365
Feb	23,496	6,783	7,270	5,116	7,357	50,022	14,573	23,344	33,228	71,145	26,838	26,445	26,672	53,118
Mar	23,104	6,718	7,300	5,304	7,286	49,712	13,807	24,308	34,131	72,247	27,135	26,559	28,341	54,901
Apr	23,517	6,816	7,539	5,222	7,823	50,917	14,337	25,791 (ft)	31,956 (fu)(fv)	72,085 (ft)(fu)(fv)	28,941 (fy)	26,430	28,681	55,111

Source: Bank of England

12.4d Industrial analysis of monetary financial institutions' lending to UK residents

£ millions

Amounts outstanding of facilities granted in all currencies

| | Real estate, professional services and support activities | | | | Public administration and defence | Education | Human health and social work | Recreational, personal and community service activities | | | Financial intermediation (excluding insurance and pension funds) | | | | |
| | Buying, selling and renting of real estate | Professional, scientific and technical activities | Administrative and support services | Total | | | | Recreational, cultural and sporting activities | Personal and community service activities | Total | Financial leasing corporations | Non-bank credit grantors excluding credit unions and SPVs | Credit unions | Factoring corporations | Mortgage and housing credit corporations excluding SPVs |
RPM	TCAY	B3QF	B3S3	TCAX	TCBD	TCBE	TCBF	TCBH	TCBG	B3T2	TCBJ	TCBK	TCBL	TCBM	TCBN
2013 May	186,801	25,981	29,136	241,918	11,551	13,891	25,110	9,397	4,824	14,221	31,122	14,086	3	8,374	57,058
Jun	186,296	26,826	29,302	242,425	12,219	13,866	25,081	8,800	4,779	13,578	30,774	14,045	7	9,031	57,233
Jul	184,306	26,089	29,992	240,388	11,864	13,501	24,935	8,860	4,780	13,640	30,266	14,178	3	8,595	57,597
Aug	181,132 (ga)	26,072	29,898	237,102 (ga)	11,274	13,764	24,866	9,103	4,670	13,773	28,953	14,102	3	8,687	57,364
Sep	180,168	26,272	29,696	236,136	12,224	13,489	24,861	8,945	4,691	13,636	28,740	14,215	3	8,373	57,621
Oct	179,057	26,693	29,526	235,276	12,115	13,362	24,643	8,981	4,606	13,587	28,162	14,072	3	8,746	56,639
Nov	167,903 (gb)	24,802 (fq)	33,458 (gj)	226,163 (gj)(gk)	12,484	13,198	24,269	8,679	4,370	13,049	28,315	14,862	3	5,493 (gp)	53,230 (gq)
Dec	167,492	25,818	32,940	226,249	11,530	12,732	23,750	8,701	4,240	12,941	28,066	14,986	3	5,660	51,995 (gr)
2014 Jan	166,192	25,834	32,178	224,204	13,443	12,825	23,731	8,728	4,245	12,973	27,889	14,605	3	4,759	51,981
Feb	165,722	26,196	32,214	224,132	12,360	12,809	23,697	8,736	4,265	13,000	27,844	14,680	3	5,003	51,904
Mar	163,387	26,035	32,817	222,239	12,165	12,870	23,272	8,635	4,248	12,884	28,828	14,857	3	5,060	52,141
Apr	162,055	26,072	32,512	220,639	11,598	13,138	22,897	8,613	4,248	12,860	30,389	14,329	3	5,140	49,877
May	161,345	27,050	33,022	221,417	12,367	13,016	22,717	8,656	4,151	12,807	30,141	14,454	2	5,271	50,427
Jun	160,191	29,088 (gg)	33,416	222,694 (gg)	11,908	13,007	22,836	7,924	4,143	12,067	29,850	14,574	2	5,499	50,620
Jul	159,218	30,411	33,477	223,106	12,036	13,177	22,913	7,901	4,164	12,065	30,049	14,803	2	5,392	51,787
Aug	159,284	30,609	33,682	223,575	12,489	13,193	23,009	8,078	4,168	12,246	30,953	19,316 (gn)	2	5,540	50,733
Sep	156,989	29,335	33,499	219,824	11,649	13,172	22,415	7,783	4,084	11,867	30,529	19,437	3	5,783	50,241
Oct	155,963	29,480	33,468	218,911	13,921	13,117	22,231	7,796	4,121	11,917	30,674	18,255	3	5,527	49,943
Nov	154,405	30,497	33,606	218,508	13,997	13,067	22,167	7,641	4,217	11,858	30,791	18,310	3	5,887	49,528
Dec	152,503 (gc)	30,433	33,018	215,954 (gc)	12,791	13,203	22,162	7,723	4,204	11,928	30,875	17,968	2	5,623	49,476
2015 Jan	163,164 (gd)	31,085	33,176	227,425 (gd)	13,055	12,967	22,267	7,586	4,110	11,695	30,804	17,919	2	5,283	49,759
Feb	162,449	31,238	32,486	226,174	12,493	13,064	22,241	7,565	4,127	11,692	31,094	19,676	2	5,441	49,849
Mar	162,200	31,975	32,139	226,314	14,457	13,245	22,451	8,098	4,149	12,246	30,652	19,368	2	5,247	51,230
Apr	166,822 (ge)(gf)	32,915 (gh)	32,970 (gi)	232,707 (ge)(gf)(gh)(gi)	13,198	13,902	23,590 (gl)	8,289	4,571	12,860	32,466 (gm)	24,263 (go)	2	5,431	51,642

Source: Bank of England

353

12.4d Industrial analysis of monetary financial institutions' lending to UK residents

£ millions

Amounts outstanding of facilities granted in all currencies

RPM	Investment and unit trusts excluding money market mutual funds TCBO	Money market mutual funds TCBP	Financial intermediation (excluding insurance and pension funds)						Insurance companies & pension funds		
			Bank holding companies TCBQ	Securities dealers TCBR	SPVs related to securitisation B7FB	Other financial intermediaries TCBS	of which intragroup activity B7FG	Total TCBI	Insurance companies B7FL	Pension funds B7FQ	Total TCBT
2013 May	21,671	139	31,747	173,583	21,689	276,317	230,997	635,788	20,088	14,736	34,823
Jun	23,876	108	31,642	157,557	21,492	262,839	217,785	608,605	19,507	14,948	34,456
Jul	25,074	135	36,516	154,662	22,532	257,005 (gw)	221,869 (gz)	606,563	18,340	14,134	32,475
Aug	23,235	157	39,329	150,670	22,593	252,345	218,503	597,437	17,105	14,013	31,118
Sep	24,996	145	42,769	134,833	22,765	243,094	210,940	577,553	16,885 (hb)	15,135	32,020 (hb)
Oct	25,297	142	44,742	140,072	22,914	245,022	213,490	585,812	16,937	14,469	31,406
Nov	18,755 (gs)	119	42,246	145,276	23,219	242,759 (gp)	211,288 (gp)	574,277 (gq)(gs)(ha)	17,703	14,397	32,100
Dec	20,468	110	44,400	140,210	22,901	217,053	185,874	545,853 (gr)	20,998	12,996	33,994
2014 Jan	19,808	131	44,512	143,901 (gu)	16,915 (gv)	216,910 (gx)	186,878 (gx)	541,415 (gu)(gv)(gx)	20,809	9,058	29,867
Feb	17,975	144	44,499	146,414	17,069	214,524	184,853	540,059	20,187	9,255	29,442
Mar	14,330	187	44,175	142,988	17,207	165,190	136,048	484,966	19,715	9,150	28,865
Apr	13,229	177	45,470	152,291	17,117	142,766 (gy)	113,545 (gy)	470,788 (gy)	18,105	8,886	26,991
May	13,305	173	44,320	144,437	17,186	135,778	106,713	455,493	18,120	8,328	26,449
Jun	11,784	168	42,869	149,855 (fz)	17,105	120,935	91,596	443,259 (fz)	17,894	9,648	27,542
Jul	11,755	93	41,828	145,665	16,010	121,103	92,766	438,487	18,148	9,314	27,462
Aug	11,715	76	41,937	136,279	17,205	120,580	91,883	434,337 (gn)	20,058	8,956	29,014
Sep	11,792	71	38,403	135,919	19,552	118,468	89,372	430,195	20,966	10,984	31,950
Oct	12,127	21	39,610	134,039	17,779	116,332	86,831	424,309	20,652	11,169	31,821
Nov	12,583	21	28,242	136,295	17,808	116,354	88,078	415,822	21,708	10,182	31,891
Dec	12,767	21	27,230	130,710	20,045	113,402	84,351	408,120	21,567	10,939	32,506
2015 Jan	10,419 (gt)	67	27,349	138,799	18,615	112,220	84,620	411,237 (gt)	24,614	11,532	36,146
Feb	11,028	86	26,730	141,823	17,965	110,858	83,949	414,551	24,030	10,875	34,906
Mar	11,348	106	26,937	144,825	17,543	115,365	88,087	422,623	25,204	12,182	37,386
Apr	12,400	192	31,150	144,653	17,636	113,026	85,899	432,863 (gm)(go)	26,871	11,602	38,473

Source: Bank of England

12.4d Industrial analysis of monetary financial institutions' lending to UK residents

£ millions

Amounts outstanding of facilities granted in all currencies

	Fund management activities	Activities auxiliary to financial intermediation				Total financial and non-financial businesses	Individuals and individual trusts			Total UK residents
		Other			Total		Lending secured on dwellings inc. bridging finance	Other loans and advances	Total	
		Central clearing counterparties	Other auxiliary activities	Total						
RPM	TCBU	B3X7	B3Y5	TCBV	B3ZZ	Z94H	TCBX	TCBY	TCBW	TCAA
2013 May	96,072	155,084	6,824	161,908	257,980	1,584,051	1,085,326	160,936	1,246,261	2,830,312
Jun	87,915	144,755	6,825	151,579	239,495	1,539,303	1,088,203	161,488	1,249,691	2,788,994
Jul	88,021	131,755	6,703	138,458	226,479	1,522,946 (hl)	1,090,237	163,578 (hs)	1,253,815 (hs)	2,776,761
Aug	93,067	141,456	6,879	148,334	241,401	1,519,997	1,091,971	164,140	1,256,111	2,776,108
Sep	93,578	149,667	9,242	158,909	252,487	1,508,895	1,093,595	165,069	1,258,664	2,767,559
Oct	91,583	140,424 (hg)	6,849 (hi)	147,273	238,857	1,502,219	1,097,320	164,663	1,261,983	2,764,202
Nov	94,551 (hc)	145,439	6,241	151,680	246,231 (hc)	1,497,256 (gp)(gq)	1,102,571 (hn)(ho)	165,048	1,267,619 (hn)(ho)	2,764,876 (gp)(gq)(ho)
Dec	98,863	128,727	6,611	135,338	234,201	1,457,287 (gr)	1,103,258	164,441	1,267,700	2,724,987 (gr)
2014 Jan	97,620	151,490 (hh)(hi)	6,318	157,808 (hh)(hi)	255,428 (hh)(hi)	1,469,198 (gu)(gv)(gx)(hh)(hi)	1,103,571	165,171	1,268,742	2,737,940 (gu)(gv)(gx)(hh)(hi)
Feb	100,563	143,557	6,440	149,996	250,559	1,461,800	1,104,828	166,273	1,271,101	2,732,901
Mar	101,497	135,300	6,272	141,572	243,069	1,393,158 (fm)	1,108,646	165,837	1,274,484	2,667,642 (fm)
Apr	105,310	142,148	11,268 (hk)	153,416 (hk)	258,727 (hk)	1,388,203	1,111,319	166,850	1,278,169	2,666,372
May	110,475	145,703	11,295	156,998	267,473	1,382,302	1,113,334	167,335	1,280,669	2,662,971
Jun	112,174	137,885	11,548	149,433	261,607	1,371,038 (gg)(hm)	1,115,846	168,293	1,284,138	2,655,176 (gg)(hm)
Jul	110,348	137,139	12,352	149,491	259,839	1,372,831	1,120,933	168,493	1,289,426	2,662,257
Aug	115,239	134,280	12,561	146,841	262,080	1,374,175 (fw)(gn)	1,122,193	168,704	1,290,898	2,665,073 (fw)(gn)
Sep	113,728 (hd)	139,131	12,932	152,064	265,792 (hd)	1,376,075 (hd)	1,122,802	171,538 (ht)	1,294,340 (ht)	2,670,415 (hd)(ht)
Oct	104,994	140,635	13,157	153,792	258,786	1,368,638	1,126,495	182,553 (hu)	1,308,048 (hu)	2,676,686 (hu)
Nov	113,550	141,302	14,033	155,336	268,886	1,367,175	1,126,946	183,724	1,310,669	2,677,844
Dec	112,857	118,491	14,204	132,695	245,553	1,332,249 (gc)	1,127,095	184,615	1,311,710	2,643,959 (gc)
2015 Jan	118,490 (he)	126,501	14,516	141,016	259,507 (he)	1,352,587	1,124,178 (hp)	184,303	1,308,481 (hp)	2,661,068 (hp)
Feb	116,050	127,173	14,185	141,358	257,407	1,349,395	1,125,302 (hq)	183,245 (hv)	1,308,547	2,657,943
Mar	128,021 (hf)	120,155	14,309	134,464	262,485 (hf)	1,375,356 (hf)	1,128,296	184,659	1,312,955	2,688,311 (hf)
Apr	127,761	123,599	14,218	137,817	265,578	1,407,925 (fk)(ft)(fu)(ge)(gm)(go)	1,127,409 (hr)	192,295 (hw)	1,319,704 (hr)(hw)	2,727,629 (fk)(ft)(fu)(ge)(go)(hr)(hw)

Source: Bank of England

Notes to table

Movements in amounts outstanding can reflect breaks in data series as well as underlying flows. For changes data, users are recommended to refer directly to the appropriate series or data tables.

Further explanation can be found at: www.bankofengland.co.uk/statistics/Pages/iadb/notesiadb/Changes_flows_growth_rates.aspx.

12.4d Industrial analysis of monetary financial institutions' lending to UK residents

(fk) Due to improvements in reporting at one institution, the amounts outstanding increased by £3bn. This effect has been adjusted out of the flows for April 2015.

(fl) Due to improvements in reporting at one institution, the amounts outstanding decreased by £1bn. This effect has been adjusted out of the flows for June 2013.

(fm) Due to a change in accounting treatment at one reporting institution, the amounts outstanding decreased by £1bn. This effect has been adjusted out of the flows for March 2014.

(fn) Due to improvements in reporting at one institution, the amounts outstanding increased by £6bn. This effect has been adjusted out of the flows for November 2013.

(fo) Due to improvements in reporting at one institution, the amounts outstanding decreased by £11bn. This effect has been adjusted out of the flows for January 2015.

(fp) Due to improvements in reporting at one institution, the amounts outstanding increased by £1bn. This effect has been adjusted out of the flows for November 2013.

(fq) Due to improvements in reporting at one institution, the amounts outstanding decreased by £1bn. This effect has been adjusted out of the flows for November 2013.

(fr) Due to improvements in reporting at one institution, the amounts outstanding increased by £0.7bn. This effect has been adjusted out of the flows for June 2013.

(fs) Due to a reclassification by one reporting institution, the amounts outstanding decreased by £1bn. This effect has been adjusted out of the flows for September 2013.

(ft) Due to improvements in reporting at one institution, the amounts outstanding increased by £2bn. This effect has been adjusted out of the flows for April 2015.

(fu) Due to a change in treatment at one institution, the amounts outstanding decreased by £4bn. This effect has been adjusted out of the flows for April 2015.

(fv) Due to improvements in reporting at one institution, the amounts outstanding increased by £1bn. This effect has been adjusted out of the flows for April 2015.

(fw) Due to a change in treatment at one institution, the amounts outstanding increased by £1bn. This effect has been adjusted out of the flows for August 2014.

(fx) Due to improvements in reporting at one institution, the amounts outstanding increased by £2bn. This effect has been adjusted out of the flows for November 2013.

(fy) Due to improvements in reporting at one institution, the amounts outstanding increased by £1bn. This effect has been adjusted out of the flows for April 2015.

(fz) Due to improvements in reporting at one institution, the amounts outstanding increased by £1bn. This effect has been adjusted out of the flows for June 2014.

(ga) Due to loan transfers out of the UK MFI population, the amounts outstanding decreased by £2bn. This effect has been adjusted out of the flows for August 2013.

(gb) Due to improvements in reporting at one institution, the amounts outstanding decreased by £7bn. This effect has been adjusted out of the flows for November 2013.

(gc) Due to a loan transfer by one reporting institution, the amounts outstanding decreased by £1bn. This effect has been adjusted out of the flows for December 2014.

(gd) Due to improvements in reporting at one institution the amounts outstanding increased by £11bn. This effect has been adjusted out of the flows for January 2015.

(ge) Due to improvements in reporting at one institution, the amounts outstanding increased by £3bn. This effect has been adjusted out of the flows for April 2015.

(gf) Due to a change in the reporting population, the amounts outstanding increased by £1bn. This effect has been adjusted out of the flows for April 2015.

(gg) Due to a change in accounting treatment at one reporting institution, the amounts outstanding increased by £2bn. This effect has been adjusted out of the flows for June 2014.

(gh) Due to improvements in reporting at one institution, the amounts outstanding increased by £1bn. This effect has been adjusted out of the flows for April 2015.

(gi) Due to a restructuring at one reporting institution, the amounts outstanding increased by £3bn. This effect has been adjusted out of the flows for November 2013.

(gj) Due to improvements in reporting at one institution, the amounts outstanding increased by £1bn. This effect has been adjusted out of the flows for April 2015.

(gk) Due to improvements in reporting at one institution, the amounts outstanding decreased by £8bn. This effect has been adjusted out of the flows for November 2013.

(gl) Due to improvements in reporting at one institution, the amounts outstanding increased by £1bn. This effect has been adjusted out of the flows for April 2015.

(gm) Due to improvements in reporting at one institution, the amounts outstanding increased by £2bn. This effect has been adjusted out of the flows for April 2015.

(gn) Due to improvements in reporting at one institution, the amounts outstanding increased by £4bn. This effect has been adjusted out of the flows for August 2014.

(go) Due to improvements in reporting at one institution, the amounts outstanding increased by £5bn. This effect has been adjusted out of the flows for April 2015.

(gp) Due to a restructuring at one reporting institution, the amounts outstanding decreased by £3bn. This effect has been adjusted out of the flows for November 2013.

(gq) Due to improvements in reporting at one institution, the amounts outstanding decreased by £1bn. This effect has been adjusted out of the flows for November 2013.

(gr) Due to improvements in reporting at one institution, the amounts outstanding decreased by £2bn. This effect has been adjusted out of the flows for December 2013.

(gs) Due to improvements in reporting at one institution, the amounts outstanding decreased by £4bn. This effect has been adjusted out of the flows for November 2013.

(gt) Due to improvements in reporting at one reporting institution, the amounts outstanding decreased by £2bn. This effect has been adjusted out of the flows for January 2015.

(gu) Due to a restructuring at one reporting institution, the amounts outstanding decreased by £3bn. This effect has been adjusted out of the flows for January 2014.

(gv) Due to improvements in reporting at one institution, the amounts outstanding increased by £4bn. This effect has been adjusted out of the flows for January 2014.

(gw) Due to improvements in reporting at one institution, the amounts outstanding decreased by £7bn. This effect has been adjusted out of the flows for July 2013.

(gx) Due to improvements in reporting at one institution, the amounts outstanding increased by £2bn. This effect has been adjusted out of the flows for January 2014.

(gy) Due to improvements in reporting at one institution, the amounts outstanding decreased by £4bn. This effect has been adjusted out of the flows for April 2014.

(gz) Due to improvements in reporting at one institution, the amounts outstanding increased by £2bn. This effect has been adjusted out of the flows for July 2013.

(ha) Due to a restructuring at one reporting institution, the amounts outstanding decreased by £6bn. This effect has been adjusted out of the flows for November 2013.

(hb) Due to a reclassification by one reporting institution, the amounts outstanding increased by £1bn. This effect has been adjusted out of the flows for September 2013.

(hc) Due to improvements in reporting at one institution, the amounts outstanding increased by £4bn. This effect has been adjusted out of the flows for November 2013.

(hd) Due to improvements in reporting at one institution, the amounts outstanding increased by £1bn. This effect has been adjusted out of the flows for September 2014.

(he) Due to improvements in reporting at one reporting institution, the amounts outstanding increased by £2bn. This effect has been adjusted out of the flows for January 2015.

(hf) Due to improvements in reporting at one institution, the amounts outstanding increased by £2bn. This effect has been adjusted out of the flows for March 2015.

(hg) Due to improvements in reporting at one institution, the amounts outstanding increased by £2bn. This effect has been adjusted out of the flows for October 2013.

(hh) Due to a change in treatment at one institution, the amounts outstanding increased by £17bn. This effect has been adjusted out of the flows for January 2014.

(hi) Due to improvements in reporting at one institution, the amounts outstanding increased by £2bn. This effect has been adjusted out of the flows for January 2014.

(hj) Due to improvements in reporting at one institution, the amounts outstanding decreased by £2bn. This effect has been adjusted out of the flows for October 2013.

(hk) Due to improvements in reporting at one institution, the amounts outstanding increased by £4bn. This effect has been adjusted out of the flows for April 2014.

(hl) Due to improvements in reporting at one institution, the amounts outstanding decreased by £4bn. This effect has been adjusted out of the flows for July 2013.

(hm) Due to improvements in reporting at one institution, the amounts outstanding increased by £2bn. This effect has been adjusted out of the flows for June 2014.

(hn) Due to improvements in reporting at one institution, the amounts outstanding increased by £1bn. This effect has been adjusted out of the flows for November 2013.

(ho) Following a purchase of loans by one reporting institution, the amounts outstanding increased by £2bn. This effect has been adjusted out of the flows for October 2013.

(hp) Due to a loan transfer by one reporting institution, the amounts outstanding decreased by £2bn. This effect has been adjusted out of the flows for January 2015.

(hq) Due to improvements in reporting at one institution, the amounts outstanding decreased by £1bn. This effect has been adjusted out of the flows for February 2015.

(hr) Due to improvements in reporting at one institution, the amounts outstanding decreased by £4bn. This effect has been adjusted out of the flows for April 2015.

(hs) Following a purchase of loans by one reporting institution, the amounts outstanding increased by £2bn. This effect has been adjusted out of the flows for July 2013.

(ht) Due to a change in the reporting population, the amounts outstanding increased by £2bn. This effect has been adjusted out of the flows for September 2014.

(hu) Due to a loan transfer by one reporting institution, the amounts outstanding increased by £10bn. This effect has been adjusted out of the flows for October 2014.

(hv) Due to improvements in reporting at one institution, the amounts outstanding decreased by £1bn. This effect has been adjusted out of the flows for February 2015.

(hw) Due to improvements in reporting at one institution, the amounts outstanding increased by £7bn. This effect has been adjusted out of the flows for April 2015.

12.5a Industrial analysis of monetary financial institutions' deposits from UK residents

£ millions   Not seasonally adjusted

Amounts outstanding of deposit liabilities (including under repo) in sterling

	Agriculture, hunting and forestry	Fishing	Mining and quarrying	Manufacturing: Food, beverages and tobacco	Manufacturing: Textiles, wearing apparel and leather	Manufacturing: Pulp, paper, and printing	Manufacturing: Chemicals, pharmaceuticals, rubber and plastics	Manufacturing: Non-metallic mineral products and metals	Manufacturing: Machinery, equipment and transport equipment	Manufacturing: Electrical, medical and optical equipment	Manufacturing: Other manufacturing	Manufacturing: Total	Electricity, gas and water supply: Electricity, gas steam and air conditioning	Electricity, gas and water supply: Water collection and sewerage	Electricity, gas and water supply: Waste management related services and remediation activities	Total
RPM	TDCB	TDCC	TDCD	TDCF	TDCG	TDCH	TDCI	TDCJ	TDCK	TDCL	TDCM	TDCE	TDCN	TDCO	BE2M	B3FI
2013 May	5,523	243	5,414	3,220	916	1,527	4,163	4,538	7,236	4,496	3,270	29,367	4,517	2,913	1,153	8,583
Jun	5,446	205	5,691	3,290	898	1,462	3,732	4,530	7,629	4,159	3,248	28,949	4,166	2,873	1,187	8,226
Jul	5,411	195	5,007	2,758	907	1,439	3,626	4,527	7,993	4,173	3,432	28,854	3,762	2,845	1,292	7,900
Aug	5,348	186	4,306	2,943	920	1,373	4,213	4,500	7,900	4,056	3,570	29,477	3,975	2,554	1,289	7,817
Sep	5,393	192	4,601	3,179	906	1,366	4,313	4,703	7,552	4,176	3,625	29,820	4,224	2,473	1,249	7,946
Oct	5,248	202	4,529	2,874	924	1,367	4,649	4,821	7,587	4,000	3,648	29,870	4,347	2,365	1,246	7,958
Nov	5,271	239	4,812	3,047	975	1,403	4,509	4,852	7,472	4,063	3,668	29,990	4,649	2,402	1,259	8,311
Dec	6,250	220	4,455	3,545	1,005	1,415	6,076	4,878	8,613	4,139	3,561	33,232	4,270	2,433	1,336	8,039
2014 Jan	6,015	221	4,207	3,061	944	1,478	4,612	4,762	8,449		3,445	30,703	3,875	2,329	1,319	7,523
Feb	5,894	261	4,967	3,140	943	1,288	4,538	4,521	7,802	3,951	3,381	29,578	4,005	2,577	1,341	7,923
Mar	5,875	280	5,131	3,502	953	1,326	4,565	4,766	8,872	4,003 (a)	3,577	31,563 (a)	4,147	2,465	1,363	7,975
Apr	5,777	251	4,789	3,040	954	1,341	4,248	4,974	8,673	4,249	3,537	31,016	4,171	2,416	1,341	7,928
May	5,683	291	4,816	3,383	957	1,338	4,376	4,878	8,176	4,193	3,812	31,114	4,308	2,551	1,331	8,191
Jun	5,673	289	5,222	3,277	951	1,321	4,473	5,002	7,819	4,300	3,582	30,725	4,020	2,629	1,361	8,010
Jul	5,542	259	4,500	3,361	955	1,272	4,478	5,032	8,152	3,995	3,721	30,965	3,942	2,661	1,305	7,908
Aug	5,518	227	4,914	3,309	967	1,249	4,562	5,007	7,433	4,115	3,693	30,335	4,270	2,608	1,360	8,238
Sep	5,552	229	4,674	3,317	988	1,247	5,011	5,316	7,962	4,140	4,097	31,592	3,968	2,801	1,398	8,167
Oct	5,585	232	4,607	3,456	1,019	1,257	4,542	5,431	7,942	4,136	4,211	31,873	3,993	2,876	1,331	8,200
Nov	5,589	269	5,468		1,064	1,363	4,414	5,472		4,219	4,365	32,294	4,056	2,859	1,404	8,318
Dec	6,485	258	5,803	3,739	1,067	1,405	4,852	5,377	8,735	4,285	4,164	33,626	4,768	2,853	1,416	9,036
2015 Jan	6,266	252	4,832	3,295	1,042	1,368	4,215	5,215	8,322	4,244	4,084	31,785	4,308	2,809	1,405	8,523
Feb	6,183	260	5,025	2,945	988	1,318	4,691	5,172	8,345	4,293	3,834	31,587	4,767	2,432	1,363	8,563
Mar	6,070	258	5,820	3,095	1,088	1,425	4,645	5,369	8,326	4,437	4,008	32,393	5,603	2,546	1,426	9,575
Apr	5,930	240	5,789	2,907	1,083	1,418	4,647	5,325	8,728	4,357	4,220	32,685	5,487	2,281	1,430	9,198

Source: Bank of England

12.5a Industrial analysis of monetary financial institutions' deposits from UK residents

£ millions

Amounts outstanding of deposit liabilities (including under repo) in sterling

		Construction					Wholesale and retail trade				Accommodation and food service activities	Transport, storage and communication		
	Development of buildings	Construction of commercial buildings	Construction of domestic buildings	Civil Engineering	Other construction activities	Total	Wholesale and retail trade and repair of motor vehicles and motorcycles	Wholesale trade, excluding motor vehicles and motor cycles	Retail trade excluding motor vehicles and motor cycles	Total		Transportation and storage	Information and communication	Total
RPM	B3FW	B7EK	B3LS	B3JO	B4PS	TDCP	TDCR	TDCS	TDCT	TDCQ	TDCU	B5PF	B3NI	TDCV
2013 May	6,416	2,440	2,022	4,124	8,674	23,676	4,133	12,087	12,936	29,156	5,951	11,700	21,520	33,219
Jun	6,762	2,525	2,370	4,134	8,898	24,690	4,035	12,103	12,231	28,369	5,912	11,626	21,481	33,107
Jul	6,719	2,465	2,124	4,113	8,987	24,407	4,259	12,334	13,590	30,182	6,556	11,150	22,336	33,486
Aug	6,620	2,575	2,254	4,334	9,044	24,825	4,473	12,379	13,215	30,067	6,630	11,027	21,179	32,206
Sep	6,687	2,639	2,230	4,190	9,274	25,020	4,269	12,219	12,861	29,349	6,640	11,405	21,196	32,602
Oct	6,294	3,466 (b)	2,267	4,453	8,563 (c)	25,044	4,220	12,572	12,567	29,360	6,696	11,944	20,210	32,154
Nov	6,599	3,427	2,349	4,625	8,775	25,775	4,194	12,642	13,467	30,302	6,613	11,507	20,303	31,810
Dec	6,763	3,536	2,761	5,113	8,893	27,066	4,133	12,938	16,518	33,590	6,673	11,025	20,481	31,506
2014 Jan	6,615	3,252	2,338	4,535	8,578	25,318	4,083	12,464	13,728	30,276	6,310	10,888	20,141	31,029
Feb	6,653	3,289	2,487	4,506	8,504	25,440	4,430	12,467	14,032	30,929	6,272	12,548	23,747	36,295
Mar	7,011	3,381	2,746	4,589	8,702	26,428	4,519	12,732	14,368	31,618	6,771	11,018	21,264	32,282
Apr	6,392	3,567	2,930	4,360	8,888	26,137	4,564	12,726	13,771	31,062	7,284	11,516	20,310	31,826
May	6,491	3,528	3,060	4,359	8,945	26,383	4,560	12,759	14,317	31,635	7,355	12,287	21,036	33,322
Jun	7,517	3,711	3,648	4,660	9,034	28,570	4,896	13,035	14,164	32,095	7,612	12,058	20,415 (f)	32,472 (f)
Jul	6,951	3,719	3,155	4,352	9,295	27,471	4,876	12,935	14,138	31,949	8,408	13,222	20,385	33,607
Aug	6,788	3,664	3,225	4,489	9,374	27,540	5,064	13,020	15,496 (d)	33,580 (d)	8,145	12,864	19,294	32,159
Sep	7,081	3,813	2,821	4,391	9,574	27,680	5,053	13,115	15,180	33,348	8,338	12,360	20,901	33,261
Oct	7,054	3,634	3,223	4,434	9,874	28,220	5,123	13,798	15,212	34,133	7,534	12,933	21,011	33,944
Nov	6,891	3,678	3,345	4,599	10,120	28,632	5,268	13,842	16,051	35,161	7,380	13,521	20,288	33,810
Dec	6,885	3,895	3,783	5,132	10,390	30,086	4,769	14,647	20,978	40,393	7,443	13,983	21,192	35,175
2015 Jan	6,882	3,692	3,195	4,675	9,947	28,392	4,582	14,209	19,423	38,213	7,066	12,643	23,036	35,679
Feb	6,970	3,708	3,222	4,722	9,865	28,486	4,872	13,841	18,649	37,363	6,877	12,588	22,671	35,259
Mar	7,221	3,862	3,342	5,353	10,208	29,985	5,089	14,326	18,990	38,404	7,013	13,193	22,649	35,842
Apr	7,186	3,815	3,343	4,871	10,218	29,433	5,174	13,942	14,740 (e)	33,856 (e)	7,511	13,314	23,223	36,537

Source: Bank of England

12.5a Industrial analysis of monetary financial institutions' deposits from UK residents

£ millions

Amounts outstanding of deposit liabilities (including under repo) in sterling

	Real estate, professional services and support activities				Public administration and defence	Education	Human health and social work	Recreational, personal and community service activities			Financial intermediation (excluding insurance and pension funds)						
	Buying, selling and renting of real estate	Professional, scientific and technical activities	Administrative and support services	Total				Recreational, cultural and sporting activities	Personal and community service activities	Total	Financial leasing corporations	Non-bank credit grantors excluding credit unions and SPVs	Credit unions	Factoring corporations	Mortgage and housing credit corporations excluding SPVs	Investment and unit trusts excluding money market mutual funds	Money market mutual funds
RPM	TDCX	B3ON	B6PK	TDCW	TDDB	TDDC	TDDD	TDDF	TDDE	B3S6	TDDH	TDDI	TDDJ	TDDK	TDDL	TDDM	TDDN
2013 May	29,861	55,079	21,096	106,036	34,923	18,766	16,185	10,941	16,600	27,541	4,358	2,627	838	990	14,087	23,784	284
Jun	32,250	56,783	21,354	110,387	34,995	18,359	16,327	10,826	16,550	27,376	4,227	2,352	828	1,184	14,143	25,050	295
Jul	30,801	56,097	21,608	108,506	41,078	17,401	16,108	10,851	16,837	27,688	4,204	2,431	848	1,163	14,690	24,373	336
Aug	30,637	55,827	21,350	107,814	36,431	17,507	16,115	11,252	16,625	27,878	4,059	2,461	859	1,082	14,617	31,538	338
Sep	33,601	56,273	21,556	111,430	32,736	18,934	15,688	10,854	16,792	27,646	4,399	2,442	882	1,050	14,527	30,406	307
Oct	31,707	62,364 (g)	18,164 (i)	112,235	36,276	19,409	16,048	10,950	17,062	28,012	4,073	2,315	909	893	14,575	30,985	300
Nov	32,323	62,309 (h)	18,834 (j)	113,466	34,408	18,317	16,165	10,964	17,084	28,048	4,759	2,500	874	950	14,238	30,885	298
Dec	34,900	59,147	19,359	113,406	30,449	17,290	15,907	10,953	17,089	28,042	4,585	2,381	884	1,004	14,523	24,019	317
2014 Jan	33,628	60,620	19,035	113,284	41,454	18,470	15,847	11,647	17,130	28,778	4,044	2,280	894	863	14,552	24,789	296
Feb	33,001	60,915	19,108	113,024	40,872	18,242	15,918	11,555	17,102	28,657	4,209	2,208	926	836	14,309	25,231	626
Mar	35,570	63,620	19,636	118,826	34,521	17,444	16,174	11,347	17,548	28,895	7,889	2,563	948	940	14,421	22,889	631
Apr	34,052	64,189	19,740	117,981	33,108	18,348	16,324	11,676	17,444	29,121	9,901	2,189	952	905	14,541	22,654	506
May	34,017	64,824	19,853	118,694	31,796	19,645	16,537	11,740	17,279	29,020	9,916	2,314	994	909	14,314	23,931	625
Jun	36,277	67,319	20,505	124,101	31,450	19,062	16,845	10,220 (l)	17,318	27,537 (l)	9,778	2,374	985	958	14,401	22,983	386
Jul	34,659	68,719	21,635	125,013	34,991	18,048	16,920	10,325	17,213	27,538	9,744	2,362	954	945	14,646	20,876	787
Aug	34,403	66,758	20,854	122,014	37,323	17,742	17,480	10,658	17,136	27,793	9,695	2,451	944	1,080	14,210	20,888	1,285
Sep	37,325	66,608	20,841	124,774	29,811	18,812	18,074	10,412	17,608	28,020	9,655	2,537	974	998	14,483	19,953	746
Oct	36,374	66,458	20,926	123,758	33,767	19,161	18,590	10,248	17,655	27,903	9,589	2,874	969	992	13,799	18,815	840
Nov	36,100	67,925	20,949	124,974	33,571	18,457	18,611	10,080	17,576	27,657	10,766 (m)	2,836	962	922	13,161	19,646	933
Dec	38,515	63,723	20,878	123,116	28,673	17,851	18,666	10,037	17,504	27,541	11,263	2,429	949	848	13,219	18,722	1,007
2015 Jan	36,697	65,127	20,483	122,307	31,007	18,731	18,579	10,244	17,735	27,979	11,725	2,619	975	950	13,145	18,220	924
Feb	36,538	64,655	22,056	123,250	30,979	18,843	18,456	10,290	17,601	27,891	11,709	2,690	967	889	11,135 (n)	18,334	734
Mar	39,299	68,816	23,477 (k)	131,592 (k)	29,261	17,925	18,693	10,532	17,637	28,169	11,236	2,799	981	913	10,500	18,212	772
Apr	38,258	68,027	22,376	128,660	34,858	18,833	18,695	10,541	17,702	28,243	10,875	2,720	989	929	10,499	18,603	754

Source: Bank of England

12.5a Industrial analysis of monetary financial institutions' deposits from UK residents

£ millions

Amounts outstanding of deposit liabilities (including under repo) in sterling

RPM	Bank holding companies	Securities dealers	SPVs related to securitisation	Other financial intermediaries	of which intragroup activity	Total	Insurance companies	Pension funds	Total	Fund management activities	Central clearing counterparties	Other auxiliary activities	Total	Total	Total financial and non-financial businesses	Individuals and individual trusts	Total UK residents
	TDDO	TDDP	B3T5	TDDQ	B3U3	TDDG	B7FI	B3VH	TDDR	TDDS	B7FT	B7FY	TDDT	B3Y8	Z945	TDDU	TDCA
2013 May	11,530	37,502	188,769	128,804	103,171	413,575	26,437	26,176	52,612	62,100	80,120	13,687	93,806	155,906	966,678	1,050,490	2,017,167
Jun	9,288	35,240	187,968	135,602	108,730	416,178	27,152	26,633	53,785	61,003	73,262	13,689	86,950	147,953	965,956	1,052,750	2,018,706
Jul	16,274 (o)	35,552	186,818	136,531 (t)	110,867 (t)	423,219 (y)	25,158	25,974	51,133	60,754	81,128	13,936	95,064	155,818	982,948 (y)	1,051,967	2,034,914 (y)
Aug	16,768	35,292	185,352	140,889	114,922	433,256	24,923	25,995	50,918	62,727	86,905	13,627	100,532	163,259	994,040	1,058,745 (ad)	2,052,785
Sep	17,972	33,759	185,593	139,973	114,107	431,308	25,575	26,833	52,408	66,164	89,653	14,558	104,211	170,375	1,002,086	1,059,803	2,061,889
Oct	22,004	37,565	179,792	132,313	108,144	425,724	22,844	26,985	49,829	67,239	92,852	13,393	106,245	173,484	1,002,076	1,062,212	2,064,288
Nov	21,131	38,445	182,204	127,889 (u)	101,423 (u)	424,173 (u)	23,510	26,360	49,870	70,185	89,466	12,246	101,713	171,898	999,468 (u)	1,069,457	2,068,925 (u)
Dec	21,178	32,561	177,692 (q)	123,566 (v)	96,146 (v)	402,710	24,870	25,999	50,869	65,205	65,691	12,648	78,339	143,544	953,250	1,068,270	2,021,520
2014 Jan	23,338	38,794	168,049	121,492	95,406	399,389	24,081	25,982	50,064	64,681	97,105 (ac)	12,481	109,585 (ac)	174,267 (ac)	983,153 (ac)	1,066,224	2,049,377 (ac)
Feb	22,871	41,682	165,537	122,216	96,189	400,652	24,913	25,386	50,298	65,790	103,719	12,675	116,394	182,184	997,405	1,073,436	2,070,841
Mar	24,016	38,701	161,129	104,060	77,354	378,187	27,086	26,498	53,584	69,301	75,846	13,246	89,092	158,393	953,948 (a)	1,078,122	2,032,070 (a)
Apr	25,287	36,887	157,530	85,842	58,628	357,194	26,243	26,983	53,226	67,987	86,134	12,976	99,110	167,097	938,468	1,082,528	2,020,996
May	23,151	35,812	159,562	78,450	51,289	349,976	25,129	25,417	50,546	67,768	86,634	13,294	99,928	167,696	932,700	1,087,593	2,020,293
Jun	22,661	40,473	161,946	76,451	49,033	353,395	24,087	26,224	50,311	69,396	81,451	13,860	95,311	164,707	938,077	1,087,856	2,025,932
Jul	22,573	39,975	159,566 (r)	75,663 (r)	48,660	348,090 (r)	23,177	25,289	48,466	66,793	88,068	13,722	101,791	168,584	938,261 (r)	1,087,435	2,025,696 (r)
Aug	22,123	39,890	160,646	71,228 (w)	47,488	344,440 (w)	23,404	25,430	48,834	71,645 (z)	92,719	14,449	107,168	178,813 (z)	945,094 (d)	1,094,664	2,039,757 (d)
Sep	25,035	35,718 (p)	161,388	71,472	45,860	342,958 (p)	24,369	27,164	51,532	74,244 (aa)(ab)	67,418	14,649	82,067	156,311 (aa)(ab)	923,134 (aa)	1,096,138	2,019,272 (aa)
Oct	24,013	32,746	146,377	69,775	46,156	320,791	22,538	25,837	48,374	72,995	83,649	14,032	97,681	170,675	917,346	1,103,466	2,020,812
Nov	15,785	34,240	147,288	70,096 (x)	44,778 (x)	316,636	22,750	26,164	48,914	68,523	88,015	14,476	102,491	171,014	916,755	1,108,105	2,024,860
Dec	11,507	32,184	152,567	72,975	46,331	317,670	23,455	25,171	48,626	67,071	71,857	14,019	85,876	152,947	903,396	1,111,740	2,015,136
2015 Jan	11,878	32,500	130,267	70,950	44,333	294,153	29,112	24,690	53,802	71,770	77,358	13,778	91,137	162,907	890,471	1,104,397	1,994,868
Feb	11,945	31,359	125,635 (s)	69,289	43,582	284,686	26,593	25,184	51,777	75,218	77,902	13,723	91,625	166,843	882,326	1,108,418	1,990,744
Mar	17,842	31,445	124,204	72,274	45,450	291,177	28,741	25,726	54,467	73,305	71,136	14,942	86,078	159,383	896,029 (k)	1,110,461	2,006,490 (k)
Apr	18,247	32,224	119,488	69,847	43,724	285,174	29,168	25,960	55,128	73,660	74,225	15,410	89,635	163,295	894,066 (e)	1,117,221 (ae)	2,011,287 (e)

Financial intermediation (excluding insurance and pension funds) comprises: Bank holding companies, Securities dealers, SPVs related to securitisation, Other financial intermediaries (of which intragroup activity), Total.
Insurance companies & pension funds comprises: Insurance companies, Pension funds, Total.
Activities auxiliary to financial intermediation comprises: Fund management activities, Central clearing counterparties, Other auxiliary activities, Total.

Source: Bank of England

Notes to table

Movements in amounts outstanding can reflect breaks in data series as well as underlying flows. For changes data, users are recommended to refer directly to the appropriate series or data tables.
www.bankofengland.co.uk/statistics/Pages/iadb/notesiadb/Changes_flows_growth_rates.aspx.

12.5a Industrial analysis of monetary financial institutions' deposits from UK residents

(a) Due to a change in accounting treatment at one reporting institution, the amounts outstanding decreased by £1bn. This effect has been adjusted out of the flows for March 2014.

(b) Due to improvements in reporting at one institution, the amounts outstanding increased by £1bn. This effect has been adjusted out of the flows for October 2013.

(c) Due to improvements in reporting at one institution, the amounts outstanding decreased by £1bn. This effect has been adjusted out of the flows for October 2013.

(d) Due to a change in treatment at one institution, the amounts outstanding increased by £1bn. This effect has been adjusted out of the flows for August 2014.

(e) Due to a change in treatment at one institution, the amounts outstanding decreased by £4bn. This effect has been adjusted out of the flows for April 2015.

(f) Due to improvements in reporting at one institution, the amounts outstanding increased by £1bn. This effect has been adjusted out of the flows for June 2014.

(g) Due to improvements in reporting at one institution, the amounts outstanding increased by £4bn. This effect has been adjusted out of the flows for October 2013.

(h) Due to improvements in reporting at one institution, the amounts outstanding decreased by £1bn. This effect has been adjusted out of the flows for November 2013.

(i) Due to improvements in reporting at one institution, the amounts outstanding decreased by £4bn. This effect has been adjusted out of the flows for October 2013.

(j) Due to improvements in reporting at one institution, the amounts outstanding increased by £1bn. This effect has been adjusted out of the flows for November 2013.

(k) Due to improvements in reporting at one institution, the amounts outstanding increased by £1bn. This effect has been adjusted out of the flows for March 2015.

(l) Due to improvements in reporting at one institution, the amounts outstanding decreased by £1bn. This effect has been adjusted out of the flows for June 2014.

(m) Due to improvements in reporting at one institution, the amounts outstanding increased by £1bn. This effect has been adjusted out of the flows for November 2014.

(n) Due to improvements in reporting at one institution, the amounts outstanding decreased by £1bn. This effect has been adjusted out of the flows for February 2015.

(o) Due to improvements in reporting at one institution, the amounts outstanding increased by £7bn. This effect has been adjusted out of the flows for July 2013.

(p) Due to improvements in reporting at one institution, the amounts outstanding decreased by £1bn. This effect has been adjusted out of the flows for September 2014.

(q) Due to improvements in reporting at one institution, the amounts outstanding decreased by £1bn. This effect has been adjusted out of the flows for December 2013.

(r) Due to improvements in reporting at one institution, the amounts outstanding increased by £2bn. This effect has been adjusted out of the flows for July 2014.

(s) Due to improvements in reporting at one institution, the amounts outstanding increased by £1bn. This effect has been adjusted out of the flows for February 2015.

(t) Due to improvements in reporting at one institution, the amounts outstanding increased by £2bn. This effect has been adjusted out of the flows for July 2013.

(u) Due to improvements in reporting at one institution, the amounts outstanding decreased by £3bn. This effect has been adjusted out of the flows for November 2013.

(v) Due to improvements in reporting at one institution, the amounts outstanding increased by £1bn. This effect has been adjusted out of the flows for December 2013.

(w) Due to improvements in reporting at one institution, the amounts outstanding decreased by £1bn. This effect has been adjusted out of the flows for August 2014.

(x) Due to improvements in reporting at one institution, the amounts outstanding decreased by £1bn. This effect has been adjusted out of the flows for November 2014.

(y) Due to improvements in reporting at one institution, the amounts outstanding increased by £9bn. This effect has been adjusted out of the flows for July 2013.

(z) Due to improvements in reporting at one institution, the amounts outstanding increased by £1bn. This effect has been adjusted out of the flows for August 2014.

(aa) Due to improvements in reporting at one institution, the amounts outstanding increased by £1bn. This effect has been adjusted out of the flows for September 2014.

(ab) Due to improvements in reporting at one institution, the amounts outstanding increased by £1bn. This effect has been adjusted out of the flows for September 2014.

(ac) Due to a change in treatment at one institution, the amounts outstanding increased by £17bn. This effect has been adjusted out of the flows for January 2014.

(ad) Due to improvements in reporting at one institution, the amounts outstanding increased by £1bn. This effect has been adjusted out of the flows for August 2013.

(ae) Due to a change in the reporting population, the amounts outstanding increased by the amounts outstanding increased by £1bn. This effect has been adjusted out off the flows for April 2015.

12.5b Industrial analysis of monetary financial institutions' deposits from UK residents

£ millions   Not seasonally adjusted

Amounts outstanding of deposit liabilities (including under repo) in all currencies

| | Agriculture, hunting and forestry | Fishing | Mining and quarrying | Manufacturing | | | | | | | | | Electricity, gas and water supply | | | Total |
				Food, beverages and tobacco	Textiles, wearing apparel and leather	Pulp, paper, and printing	Chemicals, pharmaceuticals, rubber and plastics	Non-metallic mineral products and metals	Machinery, equipment and transport equipment	Electrical, medical and optical equipment	Other manufacturing	Total	Electricity, gas steam and air conditioning	Water collection and sewerage	Waste management related services and remediation activities	
RPM	TDAB	TDAC	TDAD	TDAF	TDAG	TDAH	TDAI	TDAJ	TDAK	TDAL	TDAM	TDAE	TDAN	TDAO	BE2N	B3FJ
2013 May	5,654	250	17,948	4,812	1,259	1,960	6,735	5,592	9,902	8,412	4,443	43,115	5,447	2,927	1,231	9,606
Jun	5,586	213	16,161	4,859	1,218	2,002	7,044	5,501	10,954	8,187	4,033	43,799	4,953	2,894	1,318	9,165
Jul	5,543	203	16,893	4,485	1,128	1,930	6,866	5,585	10,640	7,920	4,400	42,954	4,690	2,872	1,489	9,051
Aug	5,495	192	17,822	4,236	1,155	1,902	7,216	5,580	10,168	7,986	4,364	42,607	4,602	2,586	1,417	8,605
Sep	5,518	201	17,682	5,125	1,158	1,796	7,640	5,781	9,620	8,544	4,443	44,107	4,814	2,501	1,391	8,706
Oct	5,378	210	18,039	4,037	1,203	1,803	8,406	6,033	9,976	7,486	4,300	43,244	5,015	2,385	1,382	8,782
Nov	5,431	251	20,707	4,143	1,235	1,933	7,190	5,836	9,824	8,037	4,424	42,622	5,473	2,427	1,436	9,336
Dec	6,474	232	14,996	4,790	1,275	1,995	8,478	5,961	11,867	7,459	4,281	46,106	5,394	2,453	1,506	9,353
2014 Jan	6,189	234	13,624	4,214	1,267	1,981	7,170	5,799	10,794	7,696	4,023	42,944	4,643	2,348	1,481	8,473
Feb	6,055	278	14,338	5,574	1,328	1,799	7,078	5,586	10,178	7,579	4,220	43,342	4,774	2,597	1,502	8,873
Mar	6,014	294	14,704	4,583	1,337	1,767	7,688	5,949	11,978	6,333 (ak)	4,268	43,903 (ak)	4,948	2,491	1,533	8,973
Apr	5,919	269	15,160	3,958	1,348	1,869	7,333	6,126	11,265	6,464	4,329	42,691	5,041	2,443	1,536	9,019
May	5,838	304	15,542	4,480	1,344	1,881	7,313	6,326	10,731	6,308	4,595	42,976	5,105	2,584	1,478	9,167
Jun	5,829	304	15,864	4,333	1,280	2,042	7,534	6,233	11,301	6,596	4,301	43,620	4,809	2,666	1,501	8,975
Jul	5,710	272	14,909	5,312	1,267	1,954	7,848	6,284	11,031	6,011	4,401	44,107	4,971	2,696	1,452	9,119
Aug	5,666	240	15,739	4,984	1,326	1,953	7,954	6,322	10,427	6,230	4,444	43,641	5,028	2,637	1,487	9,152
Sep	5,815	238	15,672	5,352	1,349	1,840	8,762	6,449	10,159	6,376	4,801	45,090	4,842	2,831	1,530	9,203
Oct	5,756	241	13,555	4,531	1,338	1,840	8,298	6,461	10,980	6,239	4,883	44,571	4,846	2,911	1,466	9,223
Nov	5,721	292	19,023	4,534	1,394	2,005	8,879	6,565	10,540	6,331	5,013	45,261	4,888	2,887	1,522	9,296
Dec	6,674	284	16,533	4,810	1,416	2,248	9,493	6,826	12,189	6,555	5,035	48,571	5,765	2,881	1,577	10,222
2015 Jan	6,431	274	17,353	4,045	1,384	2,151	8,571	6,791	11,009	6,397	4,826	45,173	5,432	2,836	1,577	9,845
Feb	6,325	288	18,510	3,715	1,317	2,052	9,037	6,803	10,895	6,324	4,654	44,797	5,698	2,459	1,536	9,693
Mar	6,205	287	16,210	4,176	1,456	2,002	10,108	6,719	10,919	7,208	4,743	47,331	6,588	2,581	1,650	10,819
Apr	6,073	265	16,203	3,746	1,450	2,009	9,183	6,409	11,212	6,996	4,898	45,903	6,434	2,305	1,619	10,357

Source: Bank of England

12.5b Industrial analysis of monetary financial institutions' deposits from UK residents

£ millions

Amounts outstanding of deposit liabilities (including under repo) in all currencies

RPM	Development of buildings	Construction					Wholesale and retail trade				Accommodation and food service activities	Transport, storage and communication		
		Construction of commercial buildings	Construction of domestic buildings	Civil Engineering	Other construction activities	Total	Wholesale and retail trade and repair of motor vehicles and motorcycles	Wholesale trade, excluding motor vehicles and motor cycles	Retail trade excluding motor vehicles and motor cycles	Total		Transportation and storage	Information and communication	Total
	B3FX	B7EL	B3LT	B4PG	B4PT	TDAP	TDAR	TDAS	TDAT	TDAQ	TDAU	B5PG	B3NJ	TDAV
2013 May	6,443	2,557	2,029	4,283	8,838	24,151	4,406	16,669	14,078	35,153	6,340	16,539	25,783	42,322
Jun	6,790	2,663	2,378	4,258	9,059	25,147	4,351	16,630	13,617	34,598	6,265	15,075	26,152	41,227
Jul	6,744	2,599	2,132	4,290	9,207	24,971	4,497	17,119	14,944	36,559	6,903	14,414	27,930	42,345
Aug	6,655	2,694	2,261	4,503	9,203	25,316	4,728	17,173	14,409	36,310	6,982	14,427	26,466	40,894
Sep	6,724	2,755	2,238	4,347	9,431	25,495	4,541	17,069	14,141	35,751	7,005	14,625	26,108	40,734
Oct	6,336	3,580 (al)	2,277	4,624	8,716 (am)	25,533	4,580	17,465	13,924	35,969	7,022	15,030	24,999	40,029
Nov	6,640	3,501	2,357	4,797	8,933	26,228	4,472	17,913	14,782	37,167	7,148	14,406	25,281	39,687
Dec	6,799	3,613	2,768	5,281	9,048	27,509	4,445	17,902	17,750	40,097	7,246	15,272	24,931	40,202
2014 Jan	6,651	3,330	2,345	4,731	8,723	25,780	4,318	17,469	15,147	36,935	6,824	13,739	24,425	38,164
Feb	6,676	3,362	2,495	4,697	8,662	25,892	4,706	17,455	15,668	37,829	6,838	15,386	38,300	53,686
Mar	7,033	3,463	2,754	4,795	8,869	26,913	4,837	17,389	15,788	38,015	7,497	14,075	26,151	40,226
Apr	6,415	3,659	2,938	4,559	9,048	26,619	4,860	17,578	15,206	37,644	8,006	14,604	24,286	38,890
May	6,511	3,631	3,068	4,527	9,117	26,854	4,868	17,648	15,778	38,293	8,129	15,473	25,124	40,597
Jun	7,536	3,795	3,656	4,883	9,201	29,070	5,227	17,645	15,837	38,708	8,326	15,028	25,021 (ap)	40,049 (ap)
Jul	6,973	3,796	3,165	4,587	9,447	27,967	5,178	18,128	15,373	38,679	9,060	16,208	24,489	40,698
Aug	6,812	3,733	3,236	4,703	9,566	28,050	5,338	17,663	16,645 (an)	39,646 (an)	8,730	15,752	23,323	39,075
Sep	7,106	3,874	2,832	4,617	9,777	28,207	5,395	17,824	16,551	39,769	8,943	15,449	25,346	40,795
Oct	7,079	3,722	3,234	4,628	10,062	28,726	5,426	18,956	16,659	41,041	8,088	16,064	25,480	41,544
Nov	6,914	3,737	3,355	4,923	10,329	29,258	5,613	18,295	17,632	41,540	7,963	16,799	24,175	40,974
Dec	6,911	3,918	3,794	5,529	10,529	30,680	5,078	19,600	22,456	47,135	8,026	17,728	25,407	43,135
2015 Jan	6,909	3,710	3,207	5,045	10,098	28,969	4,906	19,013	20,892	44,811	7,579	15,580	27,579	43,159
Feb	6,997	3,737	3,231	5,071	10,012	29,048	5,168	18,567	20,122	43,857	7,561	15,317	27,426	42,742
Mar	7,246	3,901	3,352	5,709	10,343	30,553	5,431	18,970	20,414	44,814	7,769	16,208	27,698	43,907
Apr	7,211	3,847	3,354	5,229	10,362	30,003	5,695	18,970	16,190 (ao)	40,855 (ao)	8,166	16,116	28,074	44,190

Source: Bank of England

12.5b Industrial analysis of monetary financial institutions' deposits from UK residents

£ millions

Amounts outstanding of deposit liabilities (including under repo) in all currencies

RPM	Buying, selling and renting of real estate	Real estate, professional services and support activities — Professional, scientific and technical activities	Administrative and support services	Total	Public administration and defence	Education	Human health and social work	Recreational, cultural and sporting activities	Personal and community service activities	Total	Financial leasing corporations	Non-bank credit grantors excluding credit unions and SPVs	Credit unions	Factoring corporations	Mortgage and housing credit corporations excluding SPVs	Investment and unit trusts excluding money market mutual funds	Money market mutual funds	Bank holding companies
	TDAX	B3TK	B6PL	TDAW	TDBB	TDBC	TDBD	TDBF	TDBE	B3S7	TDBH	TDBI	TDBJ	TDBK	TDBL	TDBM	TDBN	TDBO
2013 May	30,503	62,826	32,215	125,544	37,942	19,521	16,789	12,377	17,296	29,673	5,016	3,191	838	1,084	15,726	42,370	454	27,690
Jun	32,855	67,817	32,995	133,667	37,657	19,068	16,960	12,330	17,228	29,557	4,922	2,960	828	1,244	15,655	45,882	406	25,336
Jul	31,505	65,652	33,257	130,413	43,587	18,122	16,758	12,256	17,586	29,841	4,943	2,920	848	1,212	16,255	45,638	503	36,245 (az)
Aug	31,327	65,187	32,779	129,292	38,684	18,235	16,806	12,536	17,313	29,849	4,655	2,967	859	1,148	15,976	54,794	639	37,363
Sep	34,286	63,381	26,311	123,978	34,676	19,670	16,340	12,110	17,474	29,584	5,012	2,894	882	1,093	15,721	48,447	388	40,099
Oct	32,412	69,521 (aq)	22,619 (as)	124,552	39,101	20,149	16,682	12,265	17,757	30,022	4,679	2,798	909	935	15,631	47,839	487	44,450
Nov	33,066	69,697 (ar)	22,796 (at)	125,559	37,649	19,083	16,939	12,321	17,802	30,123	5,333	3,025	874	991	15,398	45,221 (ay)	440	42,369
Dec	35,586	67,187	23,097	125,871	33,967	18,093	16,720	12,306	17,788	30,094	5,207	2,837	884	1,064	15,463	37,279	544	41,590
2014 Jan	34,275	68,968	22,746	125,990	44,885	19,240	16,634	12,834	17,815	30,649	4,668	2,674	894	924	15,690	37,499	492	44,621
Feb	33,702	68,600	22,626	124,927	45,031	19,017	16,701	12,716	17,945	30,661	4,846	2,593	926	866	15,181	37,624	729	44,035
Mar	36,349	70,807	23,334	130,490	39,418	18,198	16,958	12,509	18,356	30,865	8,554	3,002	948	982	15,330	31,491	745	46,153
Apr	34,780	71,236	23,149	129,165	36,429	19,091	17,083	12,876	18,220	31,097	10,584	2,684	952	960	15,405	30,277	741	45,368
May	34,649	72,220	23,641	130,511	35,024	20,399	17,305	13,047	18,069	31,116	10,368	2,856	994	961	15,177	31,710	804	45,423
Jun	36,950	74,391	24,486	135,827	34,355	19,790	17,596	11,488 (av)	18,164	29,652 (av)	10,186	2,784	986	1,016	15,244	29,242	603	44,391
Jul	35,378	75,494	25,948	136,820	37,733	18,749	17,683	11,637	18,043	29,680	10,160	2,827	954	1,022	15,301	27,387	887	43,222
Aug	35,184	73,726	24,833	133,744	40,515	18,411	18,267	11,867	17,965	29,832	10,182	2,925	945	1,128	14,901	26,900	1,536	44,282
Sep	38,074	72,888	24,837	135,799	33,495	19,554	18,872	11,576	18,560	30,136	10,137	2,994	974	1,065	15,188	26,071	982	46,514
Oct	37,214	72,814	24,502	134,530	39,361	19,865	19,405	11,365	18,431	29,795	10,082	3,298	976	1,073	13,953	25,320	926	47,015
Nov	36,961	74,234	24,674	135,869	37,965	19,179	19,441	11,195	18,367	29,562	11,209 (aw)	3,329	965	1,019	13,287	26,391	1,123	43,997
Dec	39,318	70,117	24,603	134,038	32,075	18,626	19,580	11,152	18,455	29,607	11,740	2,868	950	936	13,338	25,316	1,155	36,947
2015 Jan	37,495	71,519	24,535	133,549	34,212	19,501	19,500	11,341	18,578	29,919	12,223	3,048	976	1,011	13,244	24,051	1,003	36,628
Feb	37,343	71,132	25,969	134,445	33,780	19,603	19,362	11,392	18,489	29,881	12,242	3,107	968	975	11,221 (ax)	24,129	853	35,921
Mar	40,191	75,806	27,468 (au)	143,465 (au)	33,362	18,629	19,642	11,683	18,636	30,319	11,708	3,290	982	1,012	10,600	24,105	962	43,452
Apr	38,998	74,604	26,277	139,878	37,236	19,548	19,634	11,609	18,675	30,284	11,304	3,230	990	1,063	10,597	25,219	898	45,112

Source: Bank of England

12.5b Industrial analysis of monetary financial institutions' deposits from UK residents

£ millions

Amounts outstanding of deposit liabilities (including under repo) in all currencies

RPM	Securities dealers	SPVs related to securitisation	Other financial intermediaries	of which intragroup activity	Total	Insurance companies	Pension funds	Total	Fund management activities	Central clearing counterparties	Other auxiliary activities	Total	Total	Total financial and non-financial businesses	Individuals and individual trusts	Total UK residents
	TDBP	B3T6	TDBQ	B3U4	TDBG	B3V2	B7FO	TDBR	TDBS	B7FU	B7FZ	TDBT	B5H5	Z82X	TDBU	TDAA
2013 May	128,686	190,268	201,868	164,993	617,193	33,728	28,968	62,695	126,704	160,326	19,829	180,154	306,858	1,400,755	1,055,682	2,456,437
Jun	126,732	189,285	202,088	164,127	615,316	35,459	29,666	65,125	124,203	152,028	19,821	171,849	296,052	1,395,567	1,058,054	2,453,621
Jul	125,808	188,082	200,727 (be)	164,176 (be)	623,182 (bj)	33,718	29,059	62,777	128,264	152,601	20,173	172,774	301,038	1,411,142 (bj)	1,057,268	2,468,410 (bj)
Aug	121,064	186,693	205,291	167,341	631,451	32,923	28,514	61,436	133,624	149,073	19,470	168,543	302,167	1,412,145	1,063,555 (br)	2,475,700
Sep	96,416	187,391	201,308	164,492	599,651	33,276	29,328	62,604	131,932	158,406	20,168	178,574	310,507	1,382,207	1,064,676	2,446,884
Oct	101,984	181,642	193,699	156,869	595,053	31,209	29,334	60,543	129,731	160,498	19,024	179,521	309,252	1,379,560	1,067,179	2,446,739
Nov	106,210	183,855	187,304 (bf)	151,049 (bf)	591,021 (ay)(bf)	31,524	28,938	60,461	132,677 (bk)	163,741	17,893	181,633	314,310 (bk)	1,383,723 (bf)	1,074,465	2,458,188 (bf)
Dec	102,277	179,407 (bb)	182,251 (bg)	144,440 (bg)	568,803	31,719	28,423	60,142	128,734	131,231	18,049	149,280	278,014	1,323,920	1,073,229	2,397,149
2014 Jan	113,903	169,607	178,386	142,714	569,358	30,997	28,397	59,394	133,354	165,282 (bo)(bp)	17,535	182,817 (bo)(bp)	316,170 (bo)(bp)	1,361,487 (bo)(bp)	1,071,344	2,432,830 (bo)(bp)
Feb	117,715	167,063	173,218	139,182	564,796	32,469	29,205	61,674	133,067	173,988	17,718	191,706	324,773	1,384,710	1,078,645	2,463,356
Mar	118,087	162,344	153,487	118,224	541,122	34,149	29,420	63,569	139,703	138,043	18,549	156,591	296,294	1,323,454 (ak)	1,083,381	2,406,835 (ak)
Apr	117,761	158,779	131,232	94,712	514,742	34,026	30,913	64,939	140,765	150,975	18,656	169,631	310,397	1,307,160	1,087,885	2,395,045
May	117,741	160,958	123,157	86,373	510,148	33,344	29,120	62,464	139,066	150,750	18,777	169,527	308,594	1,303,260	1,092,840	2,396,100
Jun	114,540	162,955	110,473	74,060	492,422	31,548	29,790	61,338	140,326	145,581 (bq)	19,263	164,844 (bq)	305,170 (bq)	1,286,898 (bq)	1,093,063	2,379,961 (bq)
Jul	110,575	160,246 (bc)	109,951	73,963	482,531 (bc)	30,062	28,876	58,938	140,071	146,139	19,757	165,896	305,967	1,278,624 (bc)	1,092,663	2,371,287 (bc)
Aug	100,667	161,320	106,066 (bh)	73,682	470,852 (bh)	30,186	29,219	59,405	152,776 (bl)	157,085	21,636	178,721	331,497 (bl)	1,292,463 (an)	1,099,715	2,392,178 (an)
Sep	99,340 (ba)	162,024	106,746	72,156	472,033 (ba)	31,114	31,113	62,227	153,489 (bm)(bn)	129,916	21,281	151,197	304,685 (bm)(bn)	1,270,533 (bm)(bn)	1,101,154	2,371,687 (bm)
Oct	90,671	147,074	104,956	72,920	445,346	30,037	29,370	59,407	150,518	146,295	20,708	167,002	317,521	1,257,976	1,108,417	2,366,392
Nov	93,653	147,918	106,854 (bi)	72,804 (bi)	449,746	29,908	30,309	60,217	147,811	153,498	20,940	174,438	322,249	1,273,556	1,112,655	2,386,211
Dec	94,607	153,201	107,892	73,203	448,950	30,461	28,809	59,271	134,620	132,940	21,081	154,020	288,641	1,242,048	1,116,438	2,358,486
2015 Jan	98,505	130,848	107,008	72,244	428,544	36,849	28,708	65,557	144,357	138,046	21,146	159,192	303,550	1,237,927	1,109,124	2,347,051
Feb	97,206	126,089 (bd)	106,834	73,094	419,544	34,109	29,280	63,390	147,006	140,707	20,703	161,411	308,416	1,231,244	1,113,217	2,344,460
Mar	99,253	124,753	107,702	73,563	427,818	35,935	29,372	65,307	147,860	133,649	22,035	155,684	303,543	1,249,980 (au)	1,115,952	2,365,932 (au)
Apr	96,111	120,021	105,550	71,560	420,094	35,614	30,074	65,688	145,072	138,625	22,967	161,592	306,665	1,241,041 (ao)	1,122,883 (bs)	2,363,924 (ao)

Source: Bank of England

Notes to table

Movements in amounts outstanding can reflect breaks in data series as well as underlying flows.   For changes data, users are recommended to refer directly to the appropriate series or data tables.
www.bankofengland.co.uk/statistics/Pages/iadb/notesiadb/Changes_flows_growth_rates.aspx.

12.5b Industrial analysis of monetary financial institutions' deposits from UK residents

Notes to table

(ak) Due to a change in accounting treatment at one reporting institution, the amounts outstanding decreased by £1bn. This effect has been adjusted out of the flows for March 2014.

(al) Due to improvements in reporting at one institution, the amounts outstanding increased by £1bn. This effect has been adjusted out of the flows for October 2013.

(am) Due to improvements in reporting at one institution, the amounts outstanding decreased by £1bn. This effect has been adjusted out of the flows for October 2013.

(an) Due to a change in treatment at one institution, the amounts outstanding increased by £1bn. This effect has been adjusted out of the flows for August 2014.

(ao) Due to a change in treatment at one institution, the amounts outstanding decreased by £4bn. This effect has been adjusted out of the flows for April 2015.

(ap) Due to improvements in reporting at one institution, the amounts outstanding increased by £1bn. This effect has been adjusted out of the flows for June 2014.

(aq) Due to improvements in reporting at one institution, the amounts outstanding increased by £4bn. This effect has been adjusted out of the flows for October 2013.

(ar) Due to improvements in reporting at one institution, the amounts outstanding decreased by £1bn. This effect has been adjusted out of the flows for November 2013.

(as) Due to improvements in reporting at one institution, the amounts outstanding decreased by £4bn. This effect has been adjusted out of the flows for October 2013.

(at) Due to improvements in reporting at one institution, the amounts outstanding increased by £1bn. This effect has been adjusted out of the flows for November 2013.

(au) Due to improvements in reporting at one institution, the amounts outstanding increased by £1bn. This effect has been adjusted out of the flows for March 2015.

(av) Due to improvements in reporting at one institution, the amounts outstanding decreased by £1bn. This effect has been adjusted out of the flows for June 2014.

(aw) Due to improvements in reporting at one institution, the amounts outstanding increased by £1bn. This effect has been adjusted out of the flows for November 2014.

(ax) Due to improvements in reporting at one institution, the amounts outstanding decreased by £1bn. This effect has been adjusted out of the flows for February 2015.

(ay) Due to improvements in reporting at one institution, the amounts outstanding decreased by £2bn. This effect has been adjusted out of the flows for November 2013.

(az) Due to improvements in reporting at one institution, the amounts outstanding increased by £12bn. This effect has been adjusted out of the flows for July 2013.

(ba) Due to improvements in reporting at one institution, the amounts outstanding decreased by £1bn. This effect has been adjusted out of the flows for September 2014.

(bb) Due to improvements in reporting at one institution, the amounts outstanding decreased by £1bn. This effect has been adjusted out of the flows for December 2013.

(bc) Due to improvements in reporting at one institution, the amounts outstanding increased by £2bn. This effect has been adjusted out of the flows for July 2014.

(bd) Due to improvements in reporting at one institution, the amounts outstanding increased by £1bn. This effect has been adjusted out of the flows for February 2015.

(be) Due to improvements in reporting at one institution, the amounts outstanding increased by £2bn. This effect has been adjusted out of the flows for July 2013.

(bf) Due to improvements in reporting at one institution, the amounts outstanding decreased by £3bn. This effect has been adjusted out of the flows for November 2013.

(bg) Due to improvements in reporting at one institution, the amounts outstanding increased by £1bn. This effect has been adjusted out of the flows for December 2013.

(bh) Due to improvements in reporting at one institution, the amounts outstanding decreased by £1bn. This effect has been adjusted out of the flows for August 2014.

(bi) Due to improvements in reporting at one institution, the amounts outstanding decreased by £14bn. This effect has been adjusted out of the flows for November 2013.

(bj) Due to improvements in reporting at one institution, the amounts outstanding increased by £1bn. This effect has been adjusted out of the flows for July 2013.

(bk) Due to improvements in reporting at one institution, the amounts outstanding increased by £2bn. This effect has been adjusted out of the flows for November 2013.

(bl) Due to improvements in reporting at one institution, the amounts outstanding increased by £1bn. This effect has been adjusted out of the flows for August 2014.

(bm) Due to improvements in reporting at one institution, the amounts outstanding increased by £1bn. This effect has been adjusted out of the flows for September 2014.

(bn) Due to improvements in reporting at one institution, the amounts outstanding increased by £1bn. This effect has been adjusted out of the flows for September 2014.

(bo) Due to a change in treatment at one institution, the amounts outstanding increased by £4bn. This effect has been adjusted out of the flows for January 2014.

(bp) Due to a change in treatment at one institution, the amounts outstanding increased by £17bn. This effect has been adjusted out of the flows for January 2014.

(bq) Due to improvements in reporting at one institution, the amounts outstanding decreased by £2bn. This effect has been adjusted out of the flows for June 2014.

(br) Due to improvements in reporting at one institution, the amounts outstanding increased by £1bn. This effect has been adjusted out of the flows for August 2013.

(bs) Due to a change in the reporting population, the amounts outstanding increased by £1bn. This effect has been adjusted out of the flows for April 2015.

12.6a Components of M4

£ millions   Seasonally adjusted

Amounts outstanding

	Retail deposits and cash in M4			Wholesale deposits in M4		M4	M3
	Deposits	Notes and coin	Total	Deposits	of which repos		(estimate of EMU aggregate for the UK)
LPM	**B3SF**	**VQJO**	**VQWK** (a)	**VRGP**	**VZZQ**	**AUYN**	**VWYZ**
2013 May	1,312,269	58,174	**1,370,443**	727,935	115,973	**2,090,211**	**2,385,336**
Jun	1,317,324	58,204	**1,375,528**	724,377	112,990	**2,089,839**	**2,395,563**
Jul	1,323,741	58,783	**1,382,523**	732,192 (f)	116,874	**2,111,695** (f)	**2,407,172**
Aug	1,328,504	58,809	**1,387,312**	740,110	119,781	**2,129,095**	**2,415,101**
Sep	1,332,900	59,424	**1,392,324**	742,595	120,273	**2,141,995**	**2,387,946**
Oct	1,339,362	59,461	**1,398,823**	734,448	117,056	**2,138,721**	**2,393,148**
Nov	1,349,249	59,334	**1,408,583**	726,096 (g)	112,835	**2,143,799** (g)	**2,395,394**
Dec	1,347,527 (b)	59,756	**1,407,283** (b)	693,209 (h)	108,878	**2,107,003**	**2,367,853**
2014 Jan	1,369,614 (c)(d)	59,629	**1,429,243** (c)(d)	699,342 (i)(j)(k)	127,610 (j)	**2,132,848** (j)	**2,401,196**
Feb	1,378,249	59,835	**1,438,084**	714,271	138,678	**2,150,702**	**2,421,524**
Mar	1,378,424	60,066	**1,438,490**	672,178	120,739	**2,103,039**	**2,370,375**
Apr	1,384,497	60,357	**1,444,854**	657,973	126,146	**2,096,901**	**2,369,333**
May	1,393,280	60,524	**1,453,804**	648,949	120,715	**2,094,844**	**2,358,946**
Jun	1,398,901	61,103	**1,460,004**	650,829 (l)	121,087	**2,104,761** (l)	**2,354,911** (l)
Jul	1,404,853	61,574	**1,466,428**	646,369	116,033	**2,110,115**	**2,357,071**
Aug	1,410,667	61,789	**1,472,456**	644,074	123,215	**2,119,509**	**2,373,650**
Sep	1,414,800	62,542	**1,477,342**	624,883	102,070	**2,108,607**	**2,358,795**
Oct	1,422,518	62,469	**1,484,987**	612,380 (m)	108,651	**2,101,697** (m)	**2,351,052**
Nov	1,425,396	62,920	**1,488,316**	607,065	109,997	**2,102,690**	**2,358,345**
Dec	1,432,073	63,093	**1,495,166**	602,036	109,453	**2,103,011**	**2,358,973**
2015 Jan	1,438,772	63,428	**1,502,200**	586,520	100,187	**2,091,510**	**2,349,502**
Feb	1,442,514	63,964	**1,506,478**	584,582	99,488	**2,089,114**	**2,341,367**
Mar	1,447,239	64,837	**1,512,076**	594,279	103,731	**2,098,522**	**2,363,829**
Apr	1,449,398 (e)	65,249	**1,514,647** (e)	595,097	99,094	**2,102,193** (e)	**2,365,131**

Notes to table   Source: Bank of England

Movements in amounts outstanding can reflect breaks in data series as well as underlying flows. For changes and growth rates data, users are recommended to refer directly to the appropriate series or data tables. Further details can be found at
www.bankofengland.co.uk/statistics/Pages/iadb/notesiadb/Changes_flows_growth_rates.aspx

(a) A minor change was made to the definition of Retail M4 in October 2007. From October data onwards, non-interest-bearing bank deposits are only included in Retail M4 when reporters identify them explicitly as being taken from retail sources. There was also a change to the reporting population in October 2007. Together these led to a break in the amount outstanding of Retail M4 in October 2007. The effect of this has been removed from the flows data.

(b) Due to improvements in reporting at one institution, the amounts outstanding decreased by £4bn. This effect has been adjusted out of the flows for December 2013.

(c) Due to a change in treatment at one institution, the amounts outstanding increased by £10bn. The effect has been adjusted out of the flows for January 2014.

(d) Due to improvements in reporting at one institution, the amounts outstanding increased by £5bn. This effect has been adjusted out of the flows for January 2014.

(e) Due to a change in treatment at one institution, the amounts outstanding decreased by £4bn. This effect has been adjusted out of the flows for April 2015.

(f) Due to improvements in reporting at one institution, the amounts outstanding increased by £8bn. This effect has been adjusted out of the flows for July 2013.

(g) Due to a restructuring at one reporting institution, the amounts outstanding decreased by £3bn. This effect has been adjusted out of the flows for November 2013.

(h) Due to improvements in reporting at one institution, the amounts outstanding increased by £4bn. This effect has been adjusted out of the flows for December 2013.

(i) Due to a change in treatment at one institution, the amounts outstanding decreased by £10bn. The effect has been adjusted out of the flows for January 2014.

(j) Due to a change in treatment at one institution, the amounts outstanding increased by £19bn. This effect has been adjusted out of the flows for January 2014.

(k) Due to improvements in reporting at one institution, the amounts outstanding decreased by £5bn. This effect has been adjusted out of the flows for January 2014.

(l) Due to improvements in reporting at one institution, the amounts outstanding increased by £3bn. This effect has been adjusted out of the flows for June 2014.

(m) Due to a classification change, the amounts outstanding decreased by £5bn. This effect has been adjusted out of the flows for October 2014.

12.6b Components of M4

£ millions   Not seasonally adjusted

Changes

LPM	Retail deposits and cash in M4					Wholesale deposits in M4		M4	M3 (estimate of EMU aggregate for the UK)
	Total	Deposits of which:		Notes and coin	Total	Deposits	of which repos		
		Private non-financial corporations	Household sector						
	VRLW	Z599	Z59A	VQLU	VQZA	VRLR	VWDN	AUZI	VWXK
2013 May	9,065			1,315	10,380	-6,270	185	4,110	20,026
Jun	8,840			418	9,259	-6,530	-7,624	2,728	1,033
Jul	-1,266			-439	-1,705	4,546	8,257	2,841	-9,270
Aug	3,883			442	4,325	15,411	8,592	19,736	15,692
Sep	7,283			250	7,533	2,379	-1	9,912	-6,142
Oct	1,660			-174	1,486	-3,169	887	-1,683	-8,851
Nov	11,986			1,265	13,251	-161	-3,640	13,090	25,877
Dec	6,792			351	7,142	-48,673	-24,791	-41,530	-48,553
2014 Jan	-6,447 (ac)	#	#	-1,416	-7,862 (ac)	7,414 (ad)	14,858	-448	3,644
Feb	9,922	637	6,837	312	10,234	10,775	14,248	21,010	33,967
Mar	13,422	8,043	3,655	574	13,996	-48,676	-32,010	-34,680	-45,646
Apr	2,641	-1,951	4,878	-107	2,534	-10,007	8,893	-7,473	1,875
May	8,061	1,831	6,100	1,051	9,112	-9,778	461	-666	6,283
Jun	8,774	7,736	3,625	257	9,031	-3,223	-5,090	5,808	-5,804
Jul	-2,294	-576	-1,663	176	-2,117	-2,567	2,731	-4,685	-11,762
Aug	6,143	-326	6,043	900	7,043	3,450	5,589	10,493	14,241
Sep	7,501	4,426	10,413	-480	7,022	-21,739	-23,782	-14,717	-13,266
Oct	4,649	839	6,422	960	5,608	-6,070	13,138	-462	-10,493
Nov	6,595	2,073	4,687	1,493	8,088	-1,201	-806	6,887	20,312
Dec	11,349	6,301	3,933	-363	10,986	-15,375	-19,628	-4,388	-23,514
2015 Jan	-11,277	-4,901	-6,403	-909	-12,186	-10,209	7,659	-22,395	-12,424
Feb	4,675	-602	4,421	666	5,342	-6,015	2,061	-673	8,039
Mar	19,730	11,239	494	633	20,362	-1,012	-11,130	19,350	14,186
Apr	2,654	-1,937	6,364	596	3,250	3,598	5,305	6,848	8,796

Notes to table

(ac) Due to improvements in reporting at one institution, this series has been revised upwards by £3bn for January 2014.

(ad) Due to improvements in reporting at one institution, this series has been revised downwards by £3bn for January 2014.

Source: Bank of England

Copyright guidance and the related UK Open Government Licence can be viewed here: www.bankofengland.co.uk/Pages/disclaimer.aspx.

12.7 Counterparts to changes in M4: alternative presentation
£ millions Not seasonally adjusted

Changes

LPM	Public sector net cash requirement (PSNCR)	M4 private sector net purchases (-) of Central Government debt						M4 private sector net purchases of other public sector debt			
		Gilts	Sterling treasury bills	Tax instruments	National Savings	Other	Total	Local government debt (-)	Public corporation debt (-)	Other public sector purchases of M4 private sector debt (+)	Total
	ABEN	AVBY	VQLK	VQLG	VQLJ	VQLI	RCMD	VQLL	VQLO	VQLQ	AVBV
2013 May	9,340	-139	2,318	-28	-572	450	2,029	-389	-	-231	-620
Jun	12,767	-13,957	2,481	-21	-669	1,645	-10,521	90	-	-752	-662
Jul	-8,684	-3,558	2,768	10	-527	10,378	9,071	-177	-	-41	-218
Aug	8,822	-3,920	545	-58	-170	-6,751	-10,352	252	-	-900	-648
Sep	15,078	-10,198	-731	-35	-35	3,863	-7,136	-311	-	-684	-995
Oct	-5,133	-5,933	2,469	-21	-251	14,635	10,899	85	-	-24	61
Nov	12,006	6,161	1,645	-14	-118	585	8,259	132	-	-714	-582
Dec	23,240	3,640	-104	-11	-47	-13,990	-10,512	294	-	-297	-3
2014 Jan	-14,026	-15,101	-114	54	-151	18,221	2,908	12	-	355	367
Feb	4,972	-1,999	-322	-19	-244	7,504	4,921	-59	-	-243	-302
Mar	19,683	10,057	-12,260	-49	-104	-26,532	-28,888	134	-	45	179
Apr	-3,374	-14,459	4,221	-36	-394	11,098	429	-1,337	-	2,869	1,532
May	11,922	4,240	1,630	-276	-261	-9,680	-4,348	-177	-	260	83
Jun	19,422	-16,402	-2,068	-4	-1,502	-2,058	-22,033	-283	-	71	-212
Jul	-4,320	-11,055	-395	-40	-742	15,758	3,527	-409	-	32	-377
Aug	4,509	-11,403	1,637	20	-699	5,252	-5,193	-21	-	196	175
Sep	23,070	10,630	-11,292	-77	-711	-29,595	-31,045	-94	-	-481	-575
Oct	-2,844	-3,244	5,871	-30	-683	12,228	14,141	12	-	-245	-233
Nov	8,406	-2,010	-2,820	-5	-543	1,427	-3,951	208	-	-458	-250
Dec	25,876	-4,427	-4,870	-57	-422	-10,457	-20,233	104	-	-378	-274
2015 Jan	-14,794	-1,114	501	-5	-6,856	1,714	-5,759	-176	-	767	591
Feb	1,748	-1,897	1,592	126	-3,256	-184	-3,618	175	-	402	577
Mar	24,882	2,966	-5,639	105	-2,069	-7,743	-12,381	-101	-	-461	-562
Apr	2,719	-2,748	3,184	6	-2,069	6,199	4,573	-963	-	238	-725

£ millions   Not seasonally adjusted

Changes

LPM	Purchases of public sector net debt (-)	External and foreign currency finance of public sector				Public sector contribution	M4 lending			
		Non-residents' purchases of gilts (-)	Non-residents' purchases of £TBs (-)	Other	Total		Loans	of which reverse repos	Investments	Total
	VQLN	VQCZ	VRME	VQOC	VQDC	VWZL (d)	Z5MB	VWDP	VYAP	BF37
2013 May	1,409	-6,871	870	1,522	-4,479	6,269	-1,880	3,270	-3,643	-5,523
Jun	-11,184	2,607	582	-669	2,520	4,104	-6,029	-3,034	11	-6,018
Jul	8,853	-1,252	1,040	1,008	796	965	-2,042	-4,571	1,251	-791
Aug	-11,001	6,057	128	-462	5,723	3,544	14,262	5,009	2,913	17,174
Sep	-8,131	-2,476	338	-683	-2,821	4,125	12,168	8,137	-3,588	8,580
Oct	10,960	-920	204	624	-92	5,735	-5,585	-11,427	-9,761	-15,347
Nov	7,678	-15,926	513	2,203	-13,210	6,473	4,114	2,741	2,517	6,631
Dec	-10,516	-10,193	290	-160	-10,064	2,661	-25,148	-9,859	-6,118	-31,266
2014 Jan	3,275	5,865	-466	-297	5,103	-5,648	-8,781	-4,825	-198	-8,978
Feb	4,619	-7,232	-368	2,134	-5,466	4,125	4,696	-530	-8,733	-4,037
Mar	-28,709	8,458	-1,965	2,211	8,703	-323	-45,276	-4,310	-3,142	-48,418
Apr	1,962	3,157	765	-2,211	1,712	300	-13,685	264	-2,174	-15,859
May	-4,265	-8,800	84	1,093	-7,623	34	930	4,612	5,361	6,290
Jun	-22,245	4,222	-268	90	4,044	1,221	5,274	4,487	-4,264	1,010
Jul	3,150	-3,206	127	159	-2,919	-4,089	2,283	-1,076	5,245	7,528
Aug	-5,018	514	-55	948	1,407	898	1,918	-3,659	-4,676	-2,759
Sep	-31,619	3,675	-1,284	-880	1,511	-7,038	-732	2,894	-3,989	-4,720
Oct	13,908	347	1,279	1,557	3,183	14,247	-4,833	-123	-7,483	-12,317
Nov	-4,201	-16	-615	2,066	1,435	5,640	-4,034	1,473	2,043	-1,991
Dec	-20,506	-6,151	25	-508	-6,635	-1,265	-12,991	-8,578	12,110	-881
2015 Jan	-5,168	6,044	693	4,320	11,056	-8,906	9,369	4,960	-23,026	-13,656
Feb	-3,041	-5,837	825	4,193	-819	-2,112	1,438	-407	-2,082	-643
Mar	-12,942	-14,772	-2,069	4,029	-12,812	-872	13,371	5,135	-3,126	10,246
Apr	3,847	-6,177	-206	-1,531	-7,914	-1,348	97	-951	2,297	2,395

12.7 Counterparts to changes in M4: alternative presentation

£ millions   Not seasonally adjusted

Changes

| LPM | External and foreign currency flows | | | Total external counterparts | Net non-deposit £ liabilities (-) | M4 |
	Net sterling deposits from non-residents (-)	Net foreign currency liabilities (-)	Total			
	B69P	B72P	AVBW	VQLP	VWZV	AUZI
2013 May	-1,998	-3,368	-5,366	-9,846	8,731	4,110
Jun	10,021	-6,270	3,751	6,271	891	2,728
Jul	-4,528	5,184	656	1,452	2,011	2,841
Aug	12,628	-24,821	-12,193	-6,470	11,211	19,736
Sep	-11,502	-21,267	-32,769	-35,591	29,976	9,912
Oct	17,593	2,466	20,059	19,967	-12,131	-1,683
Nov	-1,015	-10,746	-11,761	-24,971	11,747	13,090
Dec	-9,795	6,566	-3,229	-13,293	-9,696	-41,530
2014 Jan	5,030	43,922	48,952	54,055	-34,774	-448
Feb	19,956	19,108	39,064	33,598	-18,142	21,010
Mar	-2,387	19,188	16,801	25,504	-2,740	-34,680
Apr	-3,428	-3,903	-7,331	-5,619	15,418	-7,473
May	1,073	9,392	10,465	2,842	-17,455	-666
Jun	3,821	-14,898	-11,077	-7,033	14,655	5,808
Jul	-11,586	32,996	21,410	18,491	-29,533	-4,685
Aug	27,569	-11,218	16,351	17,758	-3,998	10,493
Sep	-4,719	-14,402	-19,121	-17,611	16,163	-14,717
Oct	4,879	9,838	14,717	17,900	-17,109	-462
Nov	1,722	1,370	3,092	4,526	146	6,887
Dec	-18,462	27,574	9,112	2,478	-11,354	-4,388
2015 Jan	6,001	-3,783	2,218	13,274	-2,050	-22,395
Feb	15,831	-25,424	-9,593	-10,412	11,675	-673
Mar	-16,840	23,604	6,764	-6,049	3,213	19,350
Apr	-526	-16,948	-17,474	-25,388	23,276	6,848

Notes to table   Source: Bank of England

(d) Net sterling lending to the public sector includes holdings of coin. Coin is a liability of Central Government and therefore outside of the MFIs' consolidated balance sheet. Holdings of coin are a component of M4 and are therefore included here in order to reconcile the counterparts.

(e) Please note that the compilation and descriptions of some credit series have changed from publication of April 2015 data, as described in Bankstats, April 2015, 'Changes to the treatment of loan transfers and lending to housing associations', available at www.bankofengland.co.uk/statistics/Documents/ms/articles/art1apr15.pdf.

Copyright guidance and the related UK Open Government License can be viewed here: www.bankofengland.co.uk/Pages/disclaimer.aspx.

12.8 Selected retail banks' base rate

Daily average of 4 UK Banks' base rates

Date of change	New rate	Date of change	New rate	Date of change	New rate
09-Jan-86	12.5	17-Sep-92	10.5	05-Jul-07	5.75
19-Mar-86	11.5	18-Sep-92	10	06-Dec-07	5.5
08-Apr-86	11.13	22-Sep-92	9	07-Feb-08	5.25
09-Apr-86	11	16-Oct-92	8.25	10-Apr-08	5
21-Apr-86	10.5	19-Oct-92	8	08-Oct-08	4.5
23-May-86	10.25	13-Nov-92	7	06-Nov-08	3
27-May-86	10	26-Jan-93	6	04-Dec-08	2
14-Oct-86	10.5	23-Nov-93	5.5	08-Jan-09	1.5
15-Oct-86	11	08-Feb-94	5.25	05-Feb-09	1
10-Mar-87	10.5	12-Sep-94	5.75	05-Mar-09	0.5
18-Mar-87	10.25	07-Dec-94	6.25	04-Jan-10	0.5
19-Mar-87	10	02-Feb-95	6.63	31-Dec-10	0.5
28-Apr-87	9.88	03-Feb-95	6.75	04-Jan-11	0.5
29-Apr-87	9.5	13-Dec-95	6.5	30-Dec-11	0.5
11-May-87	9	18-Jan-96	6.25	03-Jan-12	0.5
06-Aug-87	9.25	08-Mar-96	6	31-Dec-12	0.5
07-Aug-87	10	06-Jun-96	5.75	02-Jan-13	0.5
23-Oct-87	9.88	30-Oct-96	5.94	31-Dec-13	0.5
26-Oct-87	9.5	31-Oct-96	6		
04-Nov-87	9.38	06-May-97	6.25		
05-Nov-87	9	06-Jun-97	6.44		
04-Dec-87	8.5	09-Jun-97	6.5		
02-Feb-88	9	10-Jul-97	6.75		
17-Mar-88	8.63	07-Aug-97	7		
18-Mar-88	8.5	06-Nov-97	7.25		
11-Apr-88	8	04-Jun-98	7.5		
17-May-88	7.88	08-Oct-98	7.25		
18-May-88	7.5	06-Nov-98	6.75		
02-Jun-88	7.75	10-Dec-98	6.25		
03-Jun-88	8	07-Jan-99	6		
06-Jun-88	8.25	04-Feb-99	5.5		
07-Jun-88	8.5	08-Apr-99	5.25		
22-Jun-88	8.88	10-Jun-99	5		
23-Jun-88	9	08-Sep-99	5.19		
28-Jun-88	9.25	10-Sep-99	5.25		
29-Jun-88	9.5	04-Nov-99	5.5		
04-Jul-88	9.88	14-Jan-00	5.75		
05-Jul-88	10	10-Feb-00	6		
18-Jul-88	10.38	08-Feb-01	5.75		
19-Jul-88	10.5	05-Apr-01	5.5		
08-Aug-88	10.88	10-May-01	5.25		
09-Aug-88	11	02-Aug-01	5		
25-Aug-88	11.75	18-Sep-01	4.75		
26-Aug-88	12	04-Oct-01	4.5		
25-Nov-88	13	08-Nov-01	4		
24-May-89	14	07-Feb-03	3.75		
05-Oct-89	15	11-Jul-03	3.5		
08-Oct-90	14	06-Nov-03	3.75		
13-Feb-91	13.5	05-Feb-04	4		
27-Feb-91	13	07-May-04	4.25		
22-Mar-91	12.5	10-Jun-04	4.5		
12-Apr-91	12	05-Aug-04	4.75		
24-May-91	11.5	04-Aug-05	4.5		
12-Jul-91	11	03-Aug-06	4.75		
04-Sep-91	10.5	09-Nov-06	5		
05-May-92	10	11-Jan-07	5.25		
16-Sep-92	12	10-May-07	5.5		

1 Data obtained from Barclays Bank, Lloyds/TSB Bank, HSBC Bank and National Westminster Bank whose rates are used to compile this series.

2 Where all the rates did not change on the same day a spread is shown.

Source: Bank of England: 020 7601 3644

12.9 Average three month sterling money market rates

	Monthly average rate of discount, 3 month Treasury bills, Sterling IUMAAJNB		Monthly average of Eligible bills discount rate, 3 month (a) IUMAAJND		Monthly average Sterling 3 month mean interbank lending rate IUMAAMIJ		Monthly average of Sterling certificates of deposit interest rate, 3 months, mean offer/bid IUMAVCDA
31-Jan-98	6.8426	31-Jan-98	7.28	31-Jan-98	7.4762	31-Jan-98	7.44
28-Feb-98	6.8778	28-Feb-98	7.24	28-Feb-98	7.4595	28-Feb-98	7.42
31-Mar-98	6.9513	31-Mar-98	7.25	31-Mar-98	7.4774	31-Mar-98	7.43
30-Apr-98	7.0027	30-Apr-98	7.24	30-Apr-98	7.437	30-Apr-98	7.4
31-May-98	7.01	31-May-98	7.2	31-May-98	7.4069	31-May-98	7.37
30-Jun-98	7.2916	30-Jun-98	7.42	30-Jun-98	7.6258	30-Jun-98	7.59
31-Jul-98	7.219	31-Jul-98	7.49	31-Jul-98	7.7088	31-Jul-98	7.66
31-Aug-98	7.194	31-Aug-98	7.4	31-Aug-98	7.6558	31-Aug-98	7.61
30-Sep-98	6.9448	30-Sep-98	7.2	30-Sep-98	7.3825	30-Sep-98	7.34
31-Oct-98	6.5383	31-Oct-98	6.91	31-Oct-98	7.1352	31-Oct-98	7.09
30-Nov-98	6.3118	30-Nov-98	6.52	30-Nov-98	6.8881	30-Nov-98	6.82
31-Dec-98	5.7172	31-Dec-98	6.05	31-Dec-98	6.3817	31-Dec-98	6.32
31-Jan-99	5.2781	31-Jan-99	5.63	31-Jan-99	5.7985	31-Jan-99	5.74
28-Feb-99	5.0407	28-Feb-99	5.28	28-Feb-99	5.4328	28-Feb-99	5.38
31-Mar-99	4.9192	31-Mar-99	5.11	31-Mar-99	5.303	31-Mar-99	5.26
30-Apr-99	4.9003	30-Apr-99	5.02	30-Apr-99	5.2313	30-Apr-99	5.19
31-May-99	4.9302	31-May-99	5.08	31-May-99	5.2482	31-May-99	5.22
30-Jun-99	4.7598	30-Jun-99	4.94	30-Jun-99	5.1234	30-Jun-99	5.09
31-Jul-99	4.7596	31-Jul-99	4.89	31-Jul-99	5.0657	31-Jul-99	5.03
31-Aug-99	4.8495	31-Aug-99	4.94	31-Aug-99	5.1795	31-Aug-99	5.14
30-Sep-99	5.1223	30-Sep-99	5.16	30-Sep-99	5.3168	30-Sep-99	5.28
31-Oct-99	5.2315	31-Oct-99	5.42	31-Oct-99	5.9388	31-Oct-99	5.86
30-Nov-99	5.2018	30-Nov-99	5.43	30-Nov-99	5.7824	30-Nov-99	5.72
31-Dec-99	5.4637	31-Dec-99	5.59	31-Dec-99	5.9656	31-Dec-99	5.89
31-Jan-00	5.7218	31-Jan-00	5.9	31-Jan-00	6.0578	31-Jan-00	6.02
29-Feb-00	5.8346	29-Feb-00	6.01	29-Feb-00	6.1492	29-Feb-00	6.1
31-Mar-00	5.8582	31-Mar-00	5.98	31-Mar-00	6.1458	31-Mar-00	6.09
30-Apr-00	5.9178	30-Apr-00	6.05	30-Apr-00	6.2129	30-Apr-00	6.17
31-May-00	5.9501	31-May-00	6.09	31-May-00	6.2289	31-May-00	6.19
30-Jun-00	5.8535	30-Jun-00	6.03	30-Jun-00	6.1423	30-Jun-00	6.1
31-Jul-00	5.8333	31-Jul-00	5.97	31-Jul-00	6.1146	31-Jul-00	6.08
31-Aug-00	5.8103	31-Aug-00	5.97	31-Aug-00	6.1365	31-Aug-00	6.09
30-Sep-00	5.7798	30-Sep-00	5.95	30-Sep-00	6.1191	30-Sep-00	6.08
31-Oct-00	5.7482	31-Oct-00	5.92	31-Oct-00	6.081	31-Oct-00	6.05
30-Nov-00	5.6833	30-Nov-00	5.88	30-Nov-00	6.0007	30-Nov-00	5.98
31-Dec-00	5.6229	31-Dec-00	5.78	31-Dec-00	5.8882	31-Dec-00	5.85
31-Jan-01	5.4852	31-Jan-01	5.64	31-Jan-01	5.7642	31-Jan-01	5.73
28-Feb-01	5.4582	28-Feb-01	5.56	28-Feb-01	5.6854	28-Feb-01	5.66
31-Mar-01	5.2286	31-Mar-01	5.37	31-Mar-01	5.473	31-Mar-01	5.44
30-Apr-01	5.1158	30-Apr-01	5.21	30-Apr-01	5.3323	30-Apr-01	5.3
31-May-01	4.9765	31-May-01	5.06	31-May-01	5.1727	31-May-01	5.15
30-Jun-01	4.991	30-Jun-01	5.08	30-Jun-01	5.189	30-Jun-01	5.16
31-Jul-01	5.0052	31-Jul-01	5.07	31-Jul-01	5.1917	31-Jul-01	5.17
31-Aug-01	4.7198	31-Aug-01	4.82	31-Aug-01	4.9269	31-Aug-01	4.9
30-Sep-01	4.4297	30-Sep-01	4.57	30-Sep-01	4.6485	30-Sep-01	4.62
31-Oct-01	4.1567	31-Oct-01	4.26	31-Oct-01	4.3594	31-Oct-01	4.33
30-Nov-01	3.7799	30-Nov-01	3.85	30-Nov-01	3.9326	30-Nov-01	3.91
31-Dec-01	3.8296	31-Dec-01	3.88	31-Dec-01	3.9852	31-Dec-01	3.96
31-Jan-02	3.8321	31-Jan-02	3.91	31-Jan-02	3.978	31-Jan-02	3.96
28-Feb-02	3.868	28-Feb-02	3.92	28-Feb-02	3.9805	28-Feb-02	3.96
31-Mar-02	3.9672	31-Mar-02	3.99	31-Mar-02	4.0609	31-Mar-02	4.04
30-Apr-02	3.9693	30-Apr-02	4.04	30-Apr-02	4.1086	30-Apr-02	4.08
31-May-02	3.9525	31-May-02	4.01	31-May-02	4.0795	31-May-02	4.06
30-Jun-02	3.9767	30-Jun-02	4.04	30-Jun-02	4.112	30-Jun-02	4.09

12.9 Average three month sterling money market rates

Monthly average rate of discount, 3 month Treasury bills, Sterling IUMAAJNB		Monthly average of Eligible bills discount rate, 3 month (a) IUMAAJND		Monthly average Sterling 3 month mean interbank lending rate IUMAAMIJ		Monthly average of Sterling certificates of deposit interest rate, 3 months, mean offer/bid IUMAVCDA	
31-Jul-02	3.8408	31-Jul-02	3.94	31-Jul-02	3.9925	31-Jul-02	3.97
31-Aug-02	3.7663	31-Aug-02	3.86	31-Aug-02	3.9174	31-Aug-02	3.9
30-Sep-02	3.7861	30-Sep-02	3.86	30-Sep-02	3.9315	30-Sep-02	3.91
31-Oct-02	3.7509	31-Oct-02	3.82	31-Oct-02	3.9015	31-Oct-02	3.88
30-Nov-02	3.8033	30-Nov-02	3.84	30-Nov-02	3.9091	30-Nov-02	3.89
31-Dec-02	3.8418	31-Dec-02	3.71	31-Dec-02	3.9488	31-Dec-02	3.93
31-Jan-03	3.7993	31-Jan-03	3.87	31-Jan-03	3.9132	31-Jan-03	3.9
28-Feb-03	3.4993	28-Feb-03	3.65	28-Feb-03	3.6888	28-Feb-03	3.68
31-Mar-03	3.4721	31-Mar-03	3.54	31-Mar-03	3.5838	31-Mar-03	3.57
30-Apr-03	3.4537	30-Apr-03	3.52	30-Apr-03	3.576	30-Apr-03	3.57
31-May-03	3.4366	31-May-03	3.52	31-May-03	3.5665	31-May-03	3.56
30-Jun-03	3.4724	30-Jun-03	3.45	30-Jun-03	3.5702	30-Jun-03	3.56
31-Jul-03	3.3119	31-Jul-03	3.39	31-Jul-03	3.42	31-Jul-03	3.41
31-Aug-03	3.3998	31-Aug-03	3.42	31-Aug-03	3.4518	31-Aug-03	3.44
30-Sep-03	3.5239	30-Sep-03	3.59	30-Sep-03	3.6311	30-Sep-03	3.62
31-Oct-03	3.6514	31-Oct-03	3.69	31-Oct-03	3.727	31-Oct-03	3.72
30-Nov-03	3.808	30-Nov-03	3.88	30-Nov-03	3.9085	30-Nov-03	3.9
31-Dec-03	3.8298	31-Dec-03	3.9	31-Dec-03	3.949	31-Dec-03	3.94
31-Jan-04	3.8983	31-Jan-04	3.94	31-Jan-04	3.986	31-Jan-04	3.98
29-Feb-04	3.9788	29-Feb-04	4.06	29-Feb-04	4.101	29-Feb-04	4.09
31-Mar-04	4.1025	31-Mar-04	4.19	31-Mar-04	4.2328	31-Mar-04	4.22
30-Apr-04	4.1862	30-Apr-04	4.28	30-Apr-04	4.3288	30-Apr-04	4.32
31-May-04	4.34	31-May-04	4.42	31-May-04	4.4555	31-May-04	4.45
30-Jun-04	4.5793	30-Jun-04	4.68	30-Jun-04	4.7305	30-Jun-04	4.72
31-Jul-04	4.6424	31-Jul-04	4.75	31-Jul-04	4.7859	31-Jul-04	4.79
31-Aug-04	4.7218	31-Aug-04	4.85	31-Aug-04	4.8938	31-Aug-04	4.89
30-Sep-04	4.6937	30-Sep-04	4.83	30-Sep-04	4.8743	30-Sep-04	4.87
31-Oct-04	4.679	31-Oct-04	4.79	31-Oct-04	4.8336	31-Oct-04	4.83
30-Nov-04	4.6578	30-Nov-04	4.78	30-Nov-04	4.8159	30-Nov-04	4.81
31-Dec-04	4.677	31-Dec-04	4.77	31-Dec-04	4.8057	31-Dec-04	4.8
31-Jan-05	4.6568	31-Jan-05	4.75	31-Jan-05	4.8045	31-Jan-05	4.8
28-Feb-05	4.6858	28-Feb-05	4.78	28-Feb-05	4.822	28-Feb-05	4.82
31-Mar-05	4.7691	31-Mar-05	4.88	31-Mar-05	4.9186	31-Mar-05	4.91
30-Apr-05	4.7047	30-Apr-05	4.84	30-Apr-05	4.8756	30-Apr-05	4.86
31-May-05	4.6618	31-May-05	4.8	31-May-05	4.8253	31-May-05	4.82
30-Jun-05	4.6175	30-Jun-05	4.76	30-Jun-05	4.7777	30-Jun-05	4.78
31-Jul-05	4.4609	31-Jul-05	4.57	31-Jul-05	4.5948	31-Jul-05	4.6
31-Aug-05	4.4057	31-Aug-05	4.51	31-Aug-05	4.533	31-Aug-05	4.53
30-Sep-05	4.4037	30-Sep-05	-	30-Sep-05	4.5359	30-Sep-05	4.54
31-Oct-05	4.402	31-Oct-05	-	31-Oct-05	4.525	31-Oct-05	4.52
30-Nov-05	4.4169	30-Nov-05	-	30-Nov-05	4.5614	30-Nov-05	4.56
31-Dec-05	4.4287	31-Dec-05	-	31-Dec-05	4.587	31-Dec-05	4.58
31-Jan-06	4.3906	31-Jan-06	-	31-Jan-06	4.5369	31-Jan-06	4.54
28-Feb-06	4.3839	28-Feb-06	-	28-Feb-06	4.5203	28-Feb-06	4.52
31-Mar-06	4.3956	31-Mar-06	-	31-Mar-06	4.5263	31-Mar-06	4.53
30-Apr-06	4.4196	30-Apr-06	-	30-Apr-06	4.5725	30-Apr-06	4.57
31-May-06	4.5012	31-May-06	-	31-May-06	4.6519	31-May-06	4.65
30-Jun-06	4.5414	30-Jun-06	-	30-Jun-06	4.6927	30-Jun-06	4.69
31-Jul-06	4.534	31-Jul-06	-	31-Jul-06	4.6838	31-Jul-06	4.68
31-Aug-06	4.7544	31-Aug-06	-	31-Aug-06	4.8968	31-Aug-06	4.89
30-Sep-06	4.8359	30-Sep-06	-	30-Sep-06	4.9819	30-Sep-06	4.98
31-Oct-06	4.9357	31-Oct-06	-	31-Oct-06	5.0909	31-Oct-06	5.09
30-Nov-06	5.0095	30-Nov-06	-	30-Nov-06	5.1791	30-Nov-06	5.18
31-Dec-06	5.0759	31-Dec-06	-	31-Dec-06	5.2453	31-Dec-06	5.24

12.9 Average three month sterling money market rates

Monthly average rate of discount, 3 month Treasury bills, Sterling IUMAAJNB		Monthly average of Eligible bills discount rate, 3 month (a) IUMAAJND		Monthly average Sterling 3 month mean interbank lending rate IUMAAMIJ		Monthly average of Sterling certificates of deposit interest rate, 3 months, mean offer/bid IUMAVCDA	
31-Jan-07	5.304	31-Jan-07	-	31-Jan-07	5.4545	31-Jan-07	5.45
28-Feb-07	5.3393	28-Feb-07	-	28-Feb-07	5.5248	28-Feb-07	5.51
31-Mar-07	5.3274	31-Mar-07	-	31-Mar-07	5.5041	31-Mar-07	5.52
30-Apr-07	5.4329	30-Apr-07	-	30-Apr-07	5.6058	30-Apr-07	5.69
31-May-07	5.5516	31-May-07	-	31-May-07	5.7221	31-May-07	5.84
30-Jun-07	5.6702	30-Jun-07	-	30-Jun-07	5.8348	30-Jun-07	5.94
31-Jul-07	5.7742	31-Jul-07	-	31-Jul-07	5.9789	31-Jul-07	6.11
31-Aug-07	5.7943	31-Aug-07	-	31-Aug-07	6.3389	31-Aug-07	6.35
30-Sep-07	5.6896	30-Sep-07	-	30-Sep-07	6.5813	30-Sep-07	6.54
31-Oct-07	5.6058	31-Oct-07	-	31-Oct-07	6.2122	31-Oct-07	6.21
30-Nov-07	5.4986	30-Nov-07	-	30-Nov-07	6.3564	30-Nov-07	6.34
31-Dec-07	5.3034	31-Dec-07	-	31-Dec-07	6.3542	31-Dec-07	6.35
31-Jan-08	5.1215	31-Jan-08	-	31-Jan-08	5.6071	31-Jan-08	5.61
29-Feb-08	5.0178	29-Feb-08	-	29-Feb-08	5.6083	29-Feb-08	5.6
31-Mar-08	4.8835	31-Mar-08	-	31-Mar-08	5.8555	31-Mar-08	5.85
30-Apr-08	4.8258	30-Apr-08	-	30-Apr-08	5.8961	30-Apr-08	5.89
31-May-08	4.9496	31-May-08	-	31-May-08	5.7933	31-May-08	5.79
30-Jun-08	5.1138	30-Jun-08	-	30-Jun-08	5.9002	30-Jun-08	5.89
31-Jul-08	5.0843	31-Jul-08	-	31-Jul-08	5.803	31-Jul-08	5.8
31-Aug-08	4.9539	31-Aug-08	-	31-Aug-08	5.7588	31-Aug-08	5.75
30-Sep-08	4.7425	30-Sep-08	-	30-Sep-08	5.8698	30-Sep-08	5.86
31-Oct-08	3.6788	31-Oct-08	-	31-Oct-08	6.1772	31-Oct-08	6.16
30-Nov-08	1.9948	30-Nov-08	-	30-Nov-08	4.3955	30-Nov-08	4.4
31-Dec-08	1.2875	31-Dec-08	-	31-Dec-08	3.2143	31-Dec-08	3.21
31-Jan-09	0.8945	31-Jan-09	-	31-Jan-09	2.28	31-Jan-09	2.29
28-Feb-09	0.7177	28-Feb-09	-	28-Feb-09	2.0758	28-Feb-09	2.06
31-Mar-09	0.6035	31-Mar-09	-	31-Mar-09	1.8273	31-Mar-09	1.79
30-Apr-09	0.625	30-Apr-09	-	30-Apr-09	1.4838	30-Apr-09	1.43
31-May-09	0.5271	31-May-09	-	31-May-09	1.3026	31-May-09	1.27
30-Jun-09	0.5037	30-Jun-09	-	30-Jun-09	1.2057	30-Jun-09	1.14
31-Jul-09	0.4397	31-Jul-09	-	31-Jul-09	1.0293	31-Jul-09	0.92
31-Aug-09	0.3946	31-Aug-09	-	31-Aug-09	0.7963	31-Aug-09	0.69
30-Sep-09	0.3761	30-Sep-09	-	30-Sep-09	0.617	30-Sep-09	0.51
31-Oct-09	0.4315	31-Oct-09	-	31-Oct-09	0.5636	31-Oct-09	0.5
30-Nov-09	0.4459	30-Nov-09	-	30-Nov-09	0.5976	30-Nov-09	0.58
31-Dec-09	0.3587	31-Dec-09	-	31-Dec-09	0.6071	31-Dec-09	0.58
31-Jan-10	0.4874	31-Jan-10	-	31-Jan-10	0.6013	31-Jan-10	0.58
28-Feb-10	0.4878	28-Feb-10	-	28-Feb-10	0.5995	28-Feb-10	0.58
31-Mar-10	0.5109	31-Mar-10	-	31-Mar-10	0.6002	31-Mar-10	0.6
30-Apr-10	0.5083	30-Apr-10	-	30-Apr-10	0.6	30-Apr-10	0.63
31-May-10	0.4976	31-May-10	-	31-May-10	0.6645	31-May-10	0.68
30-Jun-10	0.4839	30-Jun-10	-	30-Jun-10	0.7045	30-Jun-10	0.77
31-Jul-10	0.498	31-Jul-10	-	31-Jul-10	0.75	31-Jul-10	0.78
31-Aug-10	0.4945	31-Aug-10	-	31-Aug-10	0.75	31-Aug-10	0.7655
30-Sep-10	0.4966	30-Sep-10	-	30-Sep-10	0.7545	30-Sep-10	0.725
31-Oct-10	0.5061	31-Oct-10	-	31-Oct-10	0.75	31-Oct-10	0.725
30-Nov-10	0.4935	30-Nov-10	-	30-Nov-10	0.75	30-Nov-10	0.725
31-Dec-10	0.4913	31-Dec-10	-	31-Dec-10	0.755	31-Dec-10	0.7655
31-Jan-11	0.5055	31-Jan-11	-	31-Jan-11	0.7785	31-Jan-11	0.825
28-Feb-11	0.5363	28-Feb-11	-	28-Feb-11	0.775	28-Feb-11	0.825
31-Mar-11	0.5603	31-Mar-11	-	31-Mar-11	0.7811	31-Mar-11	0.8315
30-Apr-11	0.5676	30-Apr-11	-	30-Apr-11	0.8	30-Apr-11	0.875
31-May-11	0.5265	31-May-11	-	31-May-11	0.8	31-May-11	0.875
30-Jun-11	0.5174	30-Jun-11	-	30-Jun-11	0.8464	30-Jun-11	0.875

12.9 Average three month sterling money market rates

Monthly average rate of discount, 3 month Treasury bills, Sterling IUMAAJNB		Monthly average of Eligible bills discount rate, 3 month (a) IUMAAJND		Monthly average Sterling 3 month mean interbank lending rate IUMAAMIJ		Monthly average of Sterling certificates of deposit interest rate, 3 months, mean offer/bid IUMAVCDA	
31-Jul-11	0.4996	31-Jul-11	-	31-Jul-11	0.86	31-Jul-11	0.875
31-Aug-11	0.4531	31-Aug-11	-	31-Aug-11	0.8873	31-Aug-11	0.9114
30-Sep-11	0.4649	30-Sep-11	-	30-Sep-11	0.9664	30-Sep-11	1.0077
31-Oct-11	0.4608	31-Oct-11	-	31-Oct-11	1.0179	31-Oct-11	1.0593
30-Nov-11	0.4387	30-Nov-11	-	30-Nov-11	1.0511	30-Nov-11	1.0968
31-Dec-11	0.2996	31-Dec-11	-	31-Dec-11	1.0878	31-Dec-11	1.15
31-Jan-12	0.3239	31-Jan-12	-	31-Jan-12	1.1086	31-Jan-12	1.175
29-Feb-12	0.3912	29-Feb-12	-	29-Feb-12	1.0971	29-Feb-12	1.156
31-Mar-12	0.4248	31-Mar-12	-	31-Mar-12	1.0752	31-Mar-12	1.1164
30-Apr-12	0.4236	30-Apr-12	-	30-Apr-12	1.0558	30-Apr-12	1.0992
31-May-12	0.3561	31-May-12	-	31-May-12	1.0143	31-May-12	1.0891
30-Jun-12	0.3422	30-Jun-12	-	30-Jun-12	0.9658	30-Jun-12	1.0376
31-Jul-12	0.2943	31-Jul-12	-	31-Jul-12	0.8627	31-Jul-12	0.8691
31-Aug-12	0.2398	31-Aug-12	-	31-Aug-12	0.7048	31-Aug-12	0.7405
30-Sep-12	0.2478	30-Sep-12	-	30-Sep-12	0.6418	30-Sep-12	0.6825
31-Oct-12	0.2368	31-Oct-12	-	31-Oct-12	0.535	31-Oct-12	0.575
30-Nov-12	0.2243	30-Nov-12	-	30-Nov-12	0.5034	30-Nov-12	0.575
31-Dec-12	0.249	31-Dec-12	-	31-Dec-12	0.5	31-Dec-12	0.575
31-Jan-13	0.2677	31-Jan-13	-	31-Jan-13	0.4927	31-Jan-13	0.575
28-Feb-13	0.3147	28-Feb-13	-	28-Feb-13	0.49	28-Feb-13	0.575
31-Mar-13	0.3391	31-Mar-13	-	31-Mar-13	0.4865	31-Mar-13	0.5655
30-Apr-13	0.3447	30-Apr-13	-	30-Apr-13	0.485	30-Apr-13	0.5731
31-May-13	0.3065	31-May-13	-	31-May-13	0.485	31-May-13	0.5512
30-Jun-13	0.3066	30-Jun-13	-	30-Jun-13	0.485	30-Jun-13	0.525
31-Jul-13	0.3124	31-Jul-13	-	31-Jul-13	0.4839	31-Jul-13	0.525
31-Aug-13	0.2812	31-Aug-13	-	31-Aug-13	0.485	31-Aug-13	0.525
30-Sep-13	0.289	30-Sep-13	-	30-Sep-13	0.4931	30-Sep-13	0.525
31-Oct-13	0.3141	31-Oct-13	-	31-Oct-13	0.495	31-Oct-13	0.525
30-Nov-13	0.2865	30-Nov-13	-	30-Nov-13	0.5017	30-Nov-13	0.5512
31-Dec-13	0.2555	31-Dec-13	-	31-Dec-13	0.5335	31-Dec-13	0.575
31-Jan-14	0.3211	31-Jan-14	-	31-Jan-14	0.5318	31-Jan-14	0.575
28-Feb-14	0.3624	28-Feb-14	-	28-Feb-14	0.5288	28-Feb-14	0.575
31-Mar-14	0.3882	31-Mar-14	-	31-Mar-14	0.53	31-Mar-14	0.575
30-Apr-14	0.3688	30-Apr-14	-	30-Apr-14	0.532	30-Apr-14	0.575
31-May-14	0.284	31-May-14	-	31-May-14	0.55	31-May-14	0.575
30-Jun-14	0.3586	30-Jun-14	-	30-Jun-14	0.55	30-Jun-14	0.575
31-Jul-14	0.4271	31-Jul-14	-	31-Jul-14	0.5487	31-Jul-14	0.575
31-Aug-14	0.3978	31-Aug-14	-	31-Aug-14	0.545	31-Aug-14	0.575
30-Sep-14	0.4351	30-Sep-14	-	30-Sep-14	0.5505	30-Sep-14	0.567
31-Oct-14	0.3964	31-Oct-14	-	31-Oct-14	0.5426	31-Oct-14	0.5511
30-Nov-14	0.4114	30-Nov-14	-	30-Nov-14	0.53	30-Nov-14	0.5538
31-Dec-14	0.4101	31-Dec-14	-	31-Dec-14	0.53	31-Dec-14	0.5524

Source: Bank of England

Notes:
Data provided is for general reference purposes. Every effort is made to ensure that it is up to date and accurate.
The Bank of England does not warrant, or accept responsibility/liability for, the accuracy/completeness of content, or loss/damage, whether direct, indirect or consequential, which may arise from reliance on said data. We reserve the right to change information published, including timing and methods used. We give no assurance that data currently published will be in the future.

(a) This series discontinued at end of August 2005

12.10 Average Foreign Exchange rates

Monthly average Old IMF-based Effective exchange rate index, Sterling (a) (1990 average = 100) XUMAGBG		Monthly average Effective exchange rate index, Sterling (Jan 2005 = 100) XUMABK67		Monthly average Spot exchange rate, US$ into Sterling XUMAUSS		Monthly average Spot exchange rate, Euro into Sterling XUMAERS	
31-Jan-99	99.57	31-Jan-99	96.0331	31-Jan-99	1.6509	31-Jan-99	1.4236
28-Feb-99	100.84	28-Feb-99	96.8577	28-Feb-99	1.6276	28-Feb-99	1.4534
31-Mar-99	102.84	31-Mar-99	98.4962	31-Mar-99	1.622	31-Mar-99	1.4902
30-Apr-99	103.36	30-Apr-99	98.5196	30-Apr-99	1.6105	30-Apr-99	1.5051
31-May-99	104.25	31-May-99	99.3069	31-May-99	1.6154	31-May-99	1.5185
30-Jun-99	104.71	30-Jun-99	99.2794	30-Jun-99	1.595	30-Jun-99	1.5374
31-Jul-99	103.45	31-Jul-99	98.0968	31-Jul-99	1.5747	31-Jul-99	1.5204
31-Aug-99	103.34	31-Aug-99	98.3371	31-Aug-99	1.6073	31-Aug-99	1.5146
30-Sep-99	104.7	30-Sep-99	99.51	30-Sep-99	1.6243	30-Sep-99	1.5458
31-Oct-99	105.37	31-Oct-99	100.3676	31-Oct-99	1.6572	31-Oct-99	1.5491
30-Nov-99	105.74	30-Nov-99	100.2788	30-Nov-99	1.6214	30-Nov-99	1.5706
31-Dec-99	106.68	31-Dec-99	100.8941	31-Dec-99	1.6132	31-Dec-99	1.5953
31-Jan-00	108.55	31-Jan-00	102.4925	31-Jan-00	1.6402	31-Jan-00	1.6201
29-Feb-00	108.44	29-Feb-00	102.1245	29-Feb-00	1.5998	29-Feb-00	1.6266
31-Mar-00	108.41	31-Mar-00	101.922	31-Mar-00	1.5802	31-Mar-00	1.6377
30-Apr-00	110.06	30-Apr-00	103.2754	30-Apr-00	1.5837	30-Apr-00	1.673
31-May-00	108.52	31-May-00	101.3127	31-May-00	1.5075	31-May-00	1.6655
30-Jun-00	104.64	30-Jun-00	98.2843	30-Jun-00	1.5089	30-Jun-00	1.5882
31-Jul-00	105.63	31-Jul-00	99.0526	31-Jul-00	1.5088	31-Jul-00	1.6052
31-Aug-00	107.38	31-Aug-00	100.1634	31-Aug-00	1.491	31-Aug-00	1.6478
30-Sep-00	106.21	30-Sep-00	98.7213	30-Sep-00	1.4355	30-Sep-00	1.6471
31-Oct-00	109.19	31-Oct-00	101.3133	31-Oct-00	1.4511	31-Oct-00	1.6994
30-Nov-00	107.27	30-Nov-00	99.6371	30-Nov-00	1.4256	30-Nov-00	1.6664
31-Dec-00	106.39	31-Dec-00	99.3875	31-Dec-00	1.4625	31-Dec-00	1.6302
31-Jan-01	104.43	31-Jan-01	98.205	31-Jan-01	1.4769	31-Jan-01	1.5753
28-Feb-01	104.14	28-Feb-01	97.6957	28-Feb-01	1.4529	28-Feb-01	1.5786
31-Mar-01	105.02	31-Mar-01	98.4305	31-Mar-01	1.4454	31-Mar-01	1.5901
30-Apr-01	105.85	30-Apr-01	99.0474	30-Apr-01	1.435	30-Apr-01	1.6084
31-May-01	106.56	31-May-01	99.3667	31-May-01	1.4259	31-May-01	1.6304
30-Jun-01	106.77	30-Jun-01	99.1925	30-Jun-01	1.4014	30-Jun-01	1.6434
31-Jul-01	107.18	31-Jul-01	99.7312	31-Jul-01	1.4139	31-Jul-01	1.6433
31-Aug-01	105.09	31-Aug-01	98.406	31-Aug-01	1.4365	31-Aug-01	1.5955
30-Sep-01	106.08	30-Sep-01	99.5721	30-Sep-01	1.4635	30-Sep-01	1.606
31-Oct-01	105.78	31-Oct-01	99.331	31-Oct-01	1.4517	31-Oct-01	1.6024
30-Nov-01	106.14	30-Nov-01	99.4273	30-Nov-01	1.4358	30-Nov-01	1.6166
31-Dec-01	106.49	31-Dec-01	100.067	31-Dec-01	1.4409	31-Dec-01	1.6151
31-Jan-02	106.9	31-Jan-02	100.2373	31-Jan-02	1.4323	31-Jan-02	1.6222
28-Feb-02	107.36	28-Feb-02	100.4604	28-Feb-02	1.4231	28-Feb-02	1.6348
31-Mar-02	106.48	31-Mar-02	99.7702	31-Mar-02	1.4225	31-Mar-02	1.6224
30-Apr-02	107.13	30-Apr-02	100.4992	30-Apr-02	1.4434	30-Apr-02	1.6282
31-May-02	105.32	31-May-02	99.1344	31-May-02	1.4593	31-May-02	1.5914
30-Jun-02	103.58	30-Jun-02	97.9873	30-Jun-02	1.4863	30-Jun-02	1.5515
31-Jul-02	105.29	31-Jul-02	100.1382	31-Jul-02	1.5546	31-Jul-02	1.5665
31-Aug-02	105.38	31-Aug-02	100.072	31-Aug-02	1.5377	31-Aug-02	1.5723
30-Sep-02	106.46	30-Sep-02	101.2143	30-Sep-02	1.5561	30-Sep-02	1.5861
31-Oct-02	106.67	31-Oct-02	101.427	31-Oct-02	1.5574	31-Oct-02	1.5868
30-Nov-02	105.87	30-Nov-02	100.8689	30-Nov-02	1.5723	30-Nov-02	1.5694
31-Dec-02	105.48	31-Dec-02	100.6495	31-Dec-02	1.5863	31-Dec-02	1.5566
31-Jan-03	104.04	31-Jan-03	99.8874	31-Jan-03	1.6169	31-Jan-03	1.5222
28-Feb-03	102.42	28-Feb-03	98.4617	28-Feb-03	1.6085	28-Feb-03	1.4924
31-Mar-03	100.6	31-Mar-03	96.7912	31-Mar-03	1.5836	31-Mar-03	1.4649
30-Apr-03	99.8	30-Apr-03	95.9455	30-Apr-03	1.5747	30-Apr-03	1.4505
31-May-03	97.9	31-May-03	94.8808	31-May-03	1.623	31-May-03	1.403
30-Jun-03	99.64	30-Jun-03	96.6091	30-Jun-03	1.6606	30-Jun-03	1.4234
31-Jul-03	99.4	31-Jul-03	95.9091	31-Jul-03	1.6242	31-Jul-03	1.4277

12.10 Average Foreign Exchange rates

Monthly average Old IMF-based Effective exchange rate index, Sterling (a) (1990 average = 100) XUMAGBG		Monthly average Effective exchange rate index, Sterling (Jan 2005 = 100) XUMABK67		Monthly average Spot exchange rate, US$ into Sterling XUMAUSS		Monthly average Spot exchange rate, Euro into Sterling XUMAERS	
31-Aug-03	99.01	31-Aug-03	95.2381	31-Aug-03	1.595	31-Aug-03	1.4286
30-Sep-03	99.24	30-Sep-03	95.5568	30-Sep-03	1.6131	30-Sep-03	1.4338
31-Oct-03	99.82	31-Oct-03	96.7126	31-Oct-03	1.6787	31-Oct-03	1.4334
30-Nov-03	100.42	30-Nov-03	97.3113	30-Nov-03	1.6901	30-Nov-03	1.4426
31-Dec-03	100.29	31-Dec-03	97.8575	31-Dec-03	1.7507	31-Dec-03	1.4246
31-Jan-04	102.38	31-Jan-04	100.1746	31-Jan-04	1.8234	31-Jan-04	1.4447
29-Feb-04	104.84	29-Feb-04	102.5018	29-Feb-04	1.8673	29-Feb-04	1.4774
31-Mar-04	104.99	31-Mar-04	102.1856	31-Mar-04	1.8267	31-Mar-04	1.489
30-Apr-04	105.18	30-Apr-04	102.1172	30-Apr-04	1.8005	30-Apr-04	1.5022
31-May-04	104.63	31-May-04	101.7607	31-May-04	1.7876	31-May-04	1.4894
30-Jun-04	105.8	30-Jun-04	103.0553	30-Jun-04	1.8275	30-Jun-04	1.505
31-Jul-04	105.89	31-Jul-04	103.1633	31-Jul-04	1.8429	31-Jul-04	1.5023
31-Aug-04	105.16	31-Aug-04	102.4258	31-Aug-04	1.8216	31-Aug-04	1.4933
30-Sep-04	103.32	30-Sep-04	100.7125	30-Sep-04	1.7922	30-Sep-04	1.4676
31-Oct-04	102.17	31-Oct-04	99.8285	31-Oct-04	1.8065	31-Oct-04	1.4455
30-Nov-04	101.73	30-Nov-04	99.7587	30-Nov-04	1.8603	30-Nov-04	1.4311
31-Dec-04	103.15	31-Dec-04	101.2992	31-Dec-04	1.9275	31-Dec-04	1.4401
31-Jan-05	102.1	31-Jan-05	100	31-Jan-05	1.8764	31-Jan-05	1.4331
28-Feb-05	103.29	28-Feb-05	100.9789	28-Feb-05	1.8871	28-Feb-05	1.4499
31-Mar-05	103.21	31-Mar-05	101.0641	31-Mar-05	1.9078	31-Mar-05	1.444
30-Apr-05	104.38	30-Apr-05	102.0105	30-Apr-05	1.896	30-Apr-05	1.4652
31-May-05	103.55	31-May-05	100.9877	31-May-05	1.8538	31-May-05	1.4611
30-Jun-05	104.92	30-Jun-05	101.7468	30-Jun-05	1.8179	30-Jun-05	1.4952
31-Jul-05	102.14	31-Jul-05	98.8121	31-Jul-05	1.7509	31-Jul-05	1.4547
31-Aug-05	102.85	31-Aug-05	99.6972	31-Aug-05	1.7943	31-Aug-05	1.4592
30-Sep-05	103.91	30-Sep-05	100.6415	30-Sep-05	1.8081	30-Sep-05	1.4761
31-Oct-05	103.09	31-Oct-05	99.6438	31-Oct-05	1.764	31-Oct-05	1.4674
30-Nov-05	103.16	30-Nov-05	99.4137	30-Nov-05	1.7341	30-Nov-05	1.4719
31-Dec-05	103.32	31-Dec-05	99.5015	31-Dec-05	1.7462	31-Dec-05	1.4725
31-Jan-06	102.67	31-Jan-06	99.0536	31-Jan-06	1.7678	31-Jan-06	1.4582
28-Feb-06	102.83	28-Feb-06	98.9111	28-Feb-06	1.747	28-Feb-06	1.4637
31-Mar-06	102.09	31-Mar-06	98.3531	31-Mar-06	1.7435	31-Mar-06	1.45
30-Apr-06	101.87	30-Apr-06	98.3726	30-Apr-06	1.7685	30-Apr-06	1.4402
31-May-06	104.14	31-May-06	101.264	31-May-06	1.8702	31-May-06	1.4637
30-Jun-06	-	30-Jun-06	100.9553	30-Jun-06	1.8428	30-Jun-06	1.456
31-Jul-06	-	31-Jul-06	100.9416	31-Jul-06	1.8447	31-Jul-06	1.454
31-Aug-06	-	31-Aug-06	102.9584	31-Aug-06	1.8944	31-Aug-06	1.4785
30-Sep-06	-	30-Sep-06	103.0138	30-Sep-06	1.8847	30-Sep-06	1.4811
31-Oct-06	-	31-Oct-06	103.1444	31-Oct-06	1.8755	31-Oct-06	1.4869
30-Nov-06	-	30-Nov-06	103.4689	30-Nov-06	1.9119	30-Nov-06	1.4834
31-Dec-06	-	31-Dec-06	104.5367	31-Dec-06	1.9633	31-Dec-06	1.486
31-Jan-07	-	31-Jan-07	105.5736	31-Jan-07	1.9587	31-Jan-07	1.5079
28-Feb-07	-	28-Feb-07	105.032	28-Feb-07	1.9581	28-Feb-07	1.4969
31-Mar-07	-	31-Mar-07	103.5698	31-Mar-07	1.9471	31-Mar-07	1.4703
30-Apr-07	-	30-Apr-07	104.2823	30-Apr-07	1.9909	30-Apr-07	1.4713
31-May-07	-	31-May-07	103.9179	31-May-07	1.9836	31-May-07	1.4677
30-Jun-07	-	30-Jun-07	104.5112	30-Jun-07	1.9864	30-Jun-07	1.4805
31-Jul-07	-	31-Jul-07	105.2441	31-Jul-07	2.0338	31-Jul-07	1.4821
31-Aug-07	-	31-Aug-07	104.542	31-Aug-07	2.0111	31-Aug-07	1.4762
30-Sep-07	-	30-Sep-07	103.3134	30-Sep-07	2.0185	30-Sep-07	1.4515
31-Oct-07	-	31-Oct-07	102.824	31-Oct-07	2.0446	31-Oct-07	1.437
30-Nov-07	-	30-Nov-07	101.9153	30-Nov-07	2.0701	30-Nov-07	1.4106
31-Dec-07	-	31-Dec-07	99.9594	31-Dec-07	2.0185	31-Dec-07	1.3863
31-Jan-08	-	31-Jan-08	96.6679	31-Jan-08	1.9698	31-Jan-08	1.3383
29-Feb-08	-	29-Feb-08	96.1857	29-Feb-08	1.9638	29-Feb-08	1.3316

12.10 Average Foreign Exchange rates

Monthly average Old IMF-based Effective exchange rate index, Sterling (a) (1990 average = 100) XUMAGBG		Monthly average Effective exchange rate index, Sterling (Jan 2005 = 100) XUMABK67		Monthly average Spot exchange rate, US$ into Sterling XUMAUSS		Monthly average Spot exchange rate, Euro into Sterling XUMAERS	
31-Mar-08	-	31-Mar-08	94.8109	31-Mar-08	2.0032	31-Mar-08	1.2897
30-Apr-08	-	30-Apr-08	93.0279	30-Apr-08	1.9817	30-Apr-08	1.258
31-May-08	-	31-May-08	93.0283	31-May-08	1.9641	31-May-08	1.2633
30-Jun-08	-	30-Jun-08	93.1476	30-Jun-08	1.9658	30-Jun-08	1.2636
31-Jul-08	-	31-Jul-08	93.27	31-Jul-08	1.988	31-Jul-08	1.2615
31-Aug-08	-	31-Aug-08	91.6902	31-Aug-08	1.8889	31-Aug-08	1.2614
30-Sep-08	-	30-Sep-08	90.039	30-Sep-08	1.7986	30-Sep-08	1.2531
31-Oct-08	-	31-Oct-08	89.638	31-Oct-08	1.69	31-Oct-08	1.2718
30-Nov-08	-	30-Nov-08	83.8187	30-Nov-08	1.5338	30-Nov-08	1.2041
31-Dec-08	-	31-Dec-08	78.4623	31-Dec-08	1.4859	31-Dec-08	1.1043
31-Jan-09	-	31-Jan-09	77.2888	31-Jan-09	1.4452	31-Jan-09	1.0919
28-Feb-09	-	28-Feb-09	79.1651	28-Feb-09	1.4411	28-Feb-09	1.1264
31-Mar-09	-	31-Mar-09	77.2444	31-Mar-09	1.4174	31-Mar-09	1.0867
30-Apr-09	-	30-Apr-09	79.1244	30-Apr-09	1.4715	30-Apr-09	1.1157
31-May-09	-	31-May-09	80.6572	31-May-09	1.5429	31-May-09	1.1295
30-Jun-09	-	30-Jun-09	84.2033	30-Jun-09	1.6366	30-Jun-09	1.1682
31-Jul-09	-	31-Jul-09	83.787	31-Jul-09	1.6366	31-Jul-09	1.1622
31-Aug-09	-	31-Aug-09	83.6709	31-Aug-09	1.6539	31-Aug-09	1.1597
30-Sep-09	-	30-Sep-09	81.3539	30-Sep-09	1.6328	30-Sep-09	1.1212
31-Oct-09	-	31-Oct-09	79.5725	31-Oct-09	1.6199	31-Oct-09	1.0928
30-Nov-09	-	30-Nov-09	81.134	30-Nov-09	1.6597	30-Nov-09	1.1126
31-Dec-09	-	31-Dec-09	80.4943	31-Dec-09	1.6239	31-Dec-09	1.1127
31-Jan-10	-	31-Jan-10	81.0348	31-Jan-10	1.6162	31-Jan-10	1.1327
28-Feb-10	-	28-Feb-10	80.3095	28-Feb-10	1.5615	28-Feb-10	1.1415
31-Mar-10	-	31-Mar-10	77.5293	31-Mar-10	1.5053	31-Mar-10	1.1092
30-Apr-10	-	30-Apr-10	79.4011	30-Apr-10	1.534	30-Apr-10	1.1436
31-May-10	-	31-May-10	79.251	31-May-10	1.4627	31-May-10	1.1685
30-Jun-10	-	30-Jun-10	81.031	30-Jun-10	1.4761	30-Jun-10	1.2082
31-Jul-10	-	31-Jul-10	81.4246	31-Jul-10	1.5299	31-Jul-10	1.1959
31-Aug-10	-	31-Aug-10	82.64	31-Aug-10	1.566	31-Aug-10	1.2132
30-Sep-10	-	30-Sep-10	81.2171	30-Sep-10	1.5578	30-Sep-10	1.1901
31-Oct-10	-	31-Oct-10	79.5137	31-Oct-10	1.5862	31-Oct-10	1.1412
30-Nov-10	-	30-Nov-10	80.9647	30-Nov-10	1.5961	30-Nov-10	1.1701
31-Dec-10	-	31-Dec-10	80.4131	31-Dec-10	1.5603	31-Dec-10	1.1802
31-Jan-11	-	31-Jan-11	80.7145	31-Jan-11	1.5795	31-Jan-11	1.1817
28-Feb-11	-	28-Feb-11	81.4956	28-Feb-11	1.613	28-Feb-11	1.1815
31-Mar-11	-	31-Mar-11	80.2603	31-Mar-11	1.6159	31-Mar-11	1.1527
30-Apr-11	-	30-Apr-11	79.6844	30-Apr-11	1.6345	30-Apr-11	1.1331
31-May-11	-	31-May-11	79.7862	31-May-11	1.6312	31-May-11	1.1403
30-Jun-11	-	30-Jun-11	78.8891	30-Jun-11	1.6214	30-Jun-11	1.1261
31-Jul-11	-	31-Jul-11	78.7691	31-Jul-11	1.6145	31-Jul-11	1.1308
31-Aug-11	-	31-Aug-11	79.6435	31-Aug-11	1.6348	31-Aug-11	1.1422
30-Sep-11	-	30-Sep-11	79.2594	30-Sep-11	1.5783	30-Sep-11	1.147
31-Oct-11	-	31-Oct-11	79.5312	31-Oct-11	1.576	31-Oct-11	1.1487
30-Nov-11	-	30-Nov-11	80.4688	30-Nov-11	1.5804	30-Nov-11	1.1659
31-Dec-11	-	31-Dec-11	80.8934	31-Dec-11	1.5585	31-Dec-11	1.1843
31-Jan-12	-	31-Jan-12	81.0921	31-Jan-12	1.551	31-Jan-12	1.2034
29-Feb-12	-	29-Feb-12	80.9819	29-Feb-12	1.5802	29-Feb-12	1.1941
31-Mar-12	-	31-Mar-12	81.4057	31-Mar-12	1.5823	31-Mar-12	1.1981
30-Apr-12	-	30-Apr-12	82.5547	30-Apr-12	1.6014	30-Apr-12	1.2161
31-May-12	-	31-May-12	83.7813	31-May-12	1.5905	31-May-12	1.244
30-Jun-12	-	30-Jun-12	83.0566	30-Jun-12	1.5571	30-Jun-12	1.2416
31-Jul-12	-	31-Jul-12	83.9569	31-Jul-12	1.5589	31-Jul-12	1.2688
31-Aug-12	-	31-Aug-12	83.9745	31-Aug-12	1.5719	31-Aug-12	1.2676
30-Sep-12	-	30-Sep-12	84.2006	30-Sep-12	1.6116	30-Sep-12	1.2524

12.10 Average Foreign Exchange rates

Monthly average Old IMF-based Effective exchange rate index, Sterling (a) (1990 average = 100) XUMAGBG		Monthly average Effective exchange rate index, Sterling (Jan 2005 = 100) XUMABK67		Monthly average Spot exchange rate, US$ into Sterling XUMAUSS		Monthly average Spot exchange rate, Euro into Sterling XUMAERS	
31-Oct-12	-	31-Oct-12	83.5987	31-Oct-12	1.6079	31-Oct-12	1.2393
30-Nov-12	-	30-Nov-12	83.6537	30-Nov-12	1.5961	30-Nov-12	1.244
31-Dec-12	-	31-Dec-12	83.5631	31-Dec-12	1.6144	31-Dec-12	1.231
31-Jan-13	-	31-Jan-13	82.1587	31-Jan-13	1.5957	31-Jan-13	1.2
28-Feb-13	-	28-Feb-13	79.6909	28-Feb-13	1.5478	28-Feb-13	1.1594
31-Mar-13	-	31-Mar-13	79.077	31-Mar-13	1.5076	31-Mar-13	1.1634
30-Apr-13	-	30-Apr-13	80.1132	30-Apr-13	1.5316	30-Apr-13	1.175
31-May-13	-	31-May-13	80.4097	31-May-13	1.5285	31-May-13	1.1777
30-Jun-13	-	30-Jun-13	80.9833	30-Jun-13	1.5478	30-Jun-13	1.174
31-Jul-13	-	31-Jul-13	79.9551	31-Jul-13	1.5172	31-Jul-13	1.16
31-Aug-13	-	31-Aug-13	80.9795	31-Aug-13	1.5507	31-Aug-13	1.1649
30-Sep-13	-	30-Sep-13	82.7298	30-Sep-13	1.5865	30-Sep-13	1.1883
31-Oct-13	-	31-Oct-13	82.6643	31-Oct-13	1.6094	31-Oct-13	1.1797
30-Nov-13	-	30-Nov-13	83.5562	30-Nov-13	1.6104	30-Nov-13	1.1938
31-Dec-13	-	31-Dec-13	84.4227	31-Dec-13	1.6375	31-Dec-13	1.1947
31-Jan-14	-	31-Jan-14	85.4224	31-Jan-14	1.647	31-Jan-14	1.2097
28-Feb-14	-	28-Feb-14	85.7435	28-Feb-14	1.6567	28-Feb-14	1.2122
31-Mar-14	-	31-Mar-14	85.539	31-Mar-14	1.6622	31-Mar-14	1.2021
30-Apr-14	-	30-Apr-14	86.186	30-Apr-14	1.6743	30-Apr-14	1.2125
31-May-14	-	31-May-14	86.8526	31-May-14	1.6844	31-May-14	1.2267
30-Jun-14	-	30-Jun-14	87.6924	30-Jun-14	1.6906	30-Jun-14	1.2436
31-Jul-14	-	31-Jul-14	88.7514	31-Jul-14	1.7069	31-Jul-14	1.2611
31-Aug-14	-	31-Aug-14	87.7763	31-Aug-14	1.6709	31-Aug-14	1.2542
30-Sep-14	-	30-Sep-14	87.5131	30-Sep-14	1.6305	30-Sep-14	1.2639
31-Oct-14	-	31-Oct-14	87.3609	31-Oct-14	1.6068	31-Oct-14	1.2678
30-Nov-14	-	30-Nov-14	86.9886	30-Nov-14	1.578	30-Nov-14	1.2646
31-Dec-14	-	31-Dec-14	87.5234	31-Dec-14	1.564	31-Dec-14	1.2686

(a) This series was discontinued in May 2006

Source: Bank of England

12.11 Average zero coupon yields

End month level of yield from British Government Securities, 5 year Nominal Zero Coupon IUMSNZC [a] [b]		End month level of yield from British Government Securities, 10 year Nominal Zero Coupon IUMMNZC [a] [b]		End month level of yield from British Government Securities, 20 year Nominal Zero Coupon IUMLNZC [a] [b]		Monthly average yield from British Government Securities, 10 year Real Zero Coupon IUMAMRZC [a] [b]		Monthly average yield from British Government Securities, 20 year Real Zero Coupon IUMALRZC [a] [b]	
31-Jan-99	4.198	31-Jan-99	4.1264	31-Jan-99	4.2935	31-Jan-99	2.0044	31-Jan-99	2.0654
28-Feb-99	4.6468	28-Feb-99	4.5624	28-Feb-99	4.5413	28-Feb-99	1.8996	28-Feb-99	1.9769
31-Mar-99	4.5823	31-Mar-99	4.5323	31-Mar-99	4.5472	31-Mar-99	1.8371	31-Mar-99	1.9171
30-Apr-99	4.8102	30-Apr-99	4.6291	30-Apr-99	4.5427	30-Apr-99	1.6793	30-Apr-99	1.8048
31-May-99	5.0702	31-May-99	4.9183	31-May-99	4.7684	31-May-99	1.9009	31-May-99	1.9803
30-Jun-99	5.4032	30-Jun-99	5.1012	30-Jun-99	4.58	30-Jun-99	1.8806	30-Jun-99	1.9628
31-Jul-99	5.7292	31-Jul-99	5.3649	31-Jul-99	4.6066	31-Jul-99	1.8961	31-Jul-99	2.0007
31-Aug-99	5.7076	31-Aug-99	5.168	31-Aug-99	4.4194	31-Aug-99	2.2085	31-Aug-99	2.1526
30-Sep-99	6.1497	30-Sep-99	5.6269	30-Sep-99	4.6545	30-Sep-99	2.3324	30-Sep-99	2.273
31-Oct-99	6.0228	31-Oct-99	5.379	31-Oct-99	4.2998	31-Oct-99	2.2768	31-Oct-99	2.2287
30-Nov-99	5.9641	30-Nov-99	5.1532	30-Nov-99	4.107	30-Nov-99	2.0636	30-Nov-99	1.9276
31-Dec-99	6.0376	31-Dec-99	5.3756	31-Dec-99	4.3647	31-Dec-99	1.9953	31-Dec-99	1.8803
31-Jan-00	6.2861	31-Jan-00	5.6139	31-Jan-00	4.479	31-Jan-00	2.1092	31-Jan-00	2.0073
29-Feb-00	6.0103	29-Feb-00	5.335	29-Feb-00	4.3632	29-Feb-00	2.1685	29-Feb-00	1.9533
31-Mar-00	5.8575	31-Mar-00	5.1478	31-Mar-00	4.3495	31-Mar-00	2.0489	31-Mar-00	1.7809
30-Apr-00	5.7047	30-Apr-00	5.0977	30-Apr-00	4.2623	30-Apr-00	2.0737	30-Apr-00	1.8364
31-May-00	5.6958	31-May-00	5.0513	31-May-00	4.3045	31-May-00	2.1386	31-May-00	1.9033
30-Jun-00	5.595	30-Jun-00	5.0731	30-Jun-00	4.3797	30-Jun-00	2.1202	30-Jun-00	1.8707
31-Jul-00	5.6384	31-Jul-00	5.1357	31-Jul-00	4.4363	31-Jul-00	2.1409	31-Jul-00	1.8992
31-Aug-00	5.6807	31-Aug-00	5.2491	31-Aug-00	4.5683	31-Aug-00	2.2278	31-Aug-00	1.9479
30-Sep-00	5.5287	30-Sep-00	5.1367	30-Sep-00	4.6199	30-Sep-00	2.2736	30-Sep-00	1.9532
31-Oct-00	5.4743	31-Oct-00	5.0874	31-Oct-00	4.5168	31-Oct-00	2.3268	31-Oct-00	1.9916
30-Nov-00	5.1547	30-Nov-00	4.7891	30-Nov-00	4.2618	30-Nov-00	2.3179	30-Nov-00	1.9296
31-Dec-00	5.083	31-Dec-00	4.7809	31-Dec-00	4.291	31-Dec-00	2.2104	31-Dec-00	1.8589
31-Jan-01	4.978	31-Jan-01	4.6718	31-Jan-01	4.3694	31-Jan-01	2.2154	31-Jan-01	1.8684
28-Feb-01	4.9824	28-Feb-01	4.7079	28-Feb-01	4.378	28-Feb-01	2.2144	28-Feb-01	1.8523
31-Mar-01	4.8425	31-Mar-01	4.7218	31-Mar-01	4.5984	31-Mar-01	2.2702	31-Mar-01	1.9601
30-Apr-01	5.126	30-Apr-01	5.065	30-Apr-01	4.8872	30-Apr-01	2.5368	30-Apr-01	2.2434
31-May-01	5.2777	31-May-01	5.1627	31-May-01	5.0197	31-May-01	2.5735	31-May-01	2.3112
30-Jun-01	5.4376	30-Jun-01	5.2329	30-Jun-01	5.0078	30-Jun-01	2.5725	30-Jun-01	2.2817
31-Jul-01	5.1702	31-Jul-01	5.0002	31-Jul-01	4.7653	31-Jul-01	2.5826	31-Jul-01	2.2629
31-Aug-01	4.9746	31-Aug-01	4.8652	31-Aug-01	4.682	31-Aug-01	2.3919	31-Aug-01	2.1494
30-Sep-01	4.8735	30-Sep-01	4.9172	30-Sep-01	4.8559	30-Sep-01	2.4992	30-Sep-01	2.3047
31-Oct-01	4.5126	31-Oct-01	4.5368	31-Oct-01	4.4576	31-Oct-01	2.5713	31-Oct-01	2.3376
30-Nov-01	4.6523	30-Nov-01	4.6479	30-Nov-01	4.5089	30-Nov-01	2.3844	30-Nov-01	2.1178
31-Dec-01	5.0788	31-Dec-01	5.0326	31-Dec-01	4.782	31-Dec-01	2.5171	31-Dec-01	2.2145
31-Jan-02	4.9044	31-Jan-02	4.8138	31-Jan-02	4.6689	31-Jan-02	2.4923	31-Jan-02	2.2395
28-Feb-02	4.9428	28-Feb-02	4.923	28-Feb-02	4.7928	28-Feb-02	2.4722	28-Feb-02	2.2767
31-Mar-02	5.3046	31-Mar-02	5.2456	31-Mar-02	5.0823	31-Mar-02	2.5074	31-Mar-02	2.3014
30-Apr-02	5.1522	30-Apr-02	5.1553	30-Apr-02	5.0257	30-Apr-02	2.4157	30-Apr-02	2.2401
31-May-02	5.2156	31-May-02	5.2282	31-May-02	5.1364	31-May-02	2.4142	31-May-02	2.2421
30-Jun-02	5.0148	30-Jun-02	4.9715	30-Jun-02	4.8164	30-Jun-02	2.3162	30-Jun-02	2.1556
31-Jul-02	4.7231	31-Jul-02	4.9201	31-Jul-02	4.8015	31-Jul-02	2.409	31-Jul-02	2.2475
31-Aug-02	4.4976	31-Aug-02	4.6394	31-Aug-02	4.4857	31-Aug-02	2.3109	31-Aug-02	2.1482
30-Sep-02	4.1825	30-Sep-02	4.412	30-Sep-02	4.3797	30-Sep-02	2.1834	30-Sep-02	2.0609
31-Oct-02	4.3315	31-Oct-02	4.5992	31-Oct-02	4.5466	31-Oct-02	2.3919	31-Oct-02	2.236
30-Nov-02	4.5062	30-Nov-02	4.6898	30-Nov-02	4.6549	30-Nov-02	2.3853	30-Nov-02	2.2838
31-Dec-02	4.1583	31-Dec-02	4.3967	31-Dec-02	4.4607	31-Dec-02	2.3083	31-Dec-02	2.2482
31-Jan-03	4.0136	31-Jan-03	4.2807	31-Jan-03	4.374	31-Jan-03	2.0797	31-Jan-03	2.0936
28-Feb-03	3.7987	28-Feb-03	4.227	28-Feb-03	4.4687	28-Feb-03	1.787	28-Feb-03	1.979
31-Mar-03	3.9584	31-Mar-03	4.3549	31-Mar-03	4.5931	31-Mar-03	1.8418	31-Mar-03	2.0679
30-Apr-03	4.0086	30-Apr-03	4.4202	30-Apr-03	4.6491	30-Apr-03	1.9411	30-Apr-03	2.1236
31-May-03	3.7737	31-May-03	4.1579	31-May-03	4.4323	31-May-03	1.7954	31-May-03	2.0315
30-Jun-03	3.8401	30-Jun-03	4.2698	30-Jun-03	4.6015	30-Jun-03	1.6503	30-Jun-03	1.9703
31-Jul-03	4.2291	31-Jul-03	4.6075	31-Jul-03	4.8344	31-Jul-03	1.8311	31-Jul-03	2.1601
31-Aug-03	4.4574	31-Aug-03	4.6562	31-Aug-03	4.6988	31-Aug-03	1.9459	31-Aug-03	2.141
30-Sep-03	4.3404	30-Sep-03	4.5844	30-Sep-03	4.6736	30-Sep-03	2.0465	30-Sep-03	2.1819
31-Oct-03	4.9274	31-Oct-03	5.0093	31-Oct-03	4.859	31-Oct-03	2.1484	31-Oct-03	2.2234
30-Nov-03	4.911	30-Nov-03	5.0473	30-Nov-03	4.8909	30-Nov-03	2.2143	30-Nov-03	2.2058
31-Dec-03	4.612	31-Dec-03	4.7733	31-Dec-03	4.7034	31-Dec-03	2.034	31-Dec-03	2.0784
31-Jan-04	4.7324	31-Jan-04	4.8572	31-Jan-04	4.7485	31-Jan-04	1.9359	31-Jan-04	1.9606
29-Feb-04	4.5996	29-Feb-04	4.735	29-Feb-04	4.7232	29-Feb-04	1.959	29-Feb-04	1.901
31-Mar-04	4.6154	31-Mar-04	4.7184	31-Mar-04	4.6453	31-Mar-04	1.8077	31-Mar-04	1.7684
30-Apr-04	4.8491	30-Apr-04	4.9564	30-Apr-04	4.839	30-Apr-04	1.9295	30-Apr-04	1.848
31-May-04	5.1163	31-May-04	5.1062	31-May-04	4.8917	31-May-04	2.0517	31-May-04	1.8784

12.11 Average zero coupon yields

End month level of yield from British Government Securities, 5 year Nominal Zero Coupon IUMSNZC [a] [b]		End month level of yield from British Government Securities, 10 year Nominal Zero Coupon IUMMNZC [a] [b]		End month level of yield from British Government Securities, 20 year Nominal Zero Coupon IUMLNZC [a] [b]		Monthly average yield from British Government Securities, 10 year Real Zero Coupon IUMAMRZC [a] [b]		Monthly average yield from British Government Securities, 20 year Real Zero Coupon IUMALRZC [a] [b]	
30-Jun-04	5.039	30-Jun-04	5.0587	30-Jun-04	4.84	30-Jun-04	2.1008	30-Jun-04	1.8799
31-Jul-04	5.0958	31-Jul-04	5.0518	31-Jul-04	4.7933	31-Jul-04	2.0733	31-Jul-04	1.8713
31-Aug-04	4.8585	31-Aug-04	4.881	31-Aug-04	4.6547	31-Aug-04	2.0347	31-Aug-04	1.8228
30-Sep-04	4.7433	30-Sep-04	4.7878	30-Sep-04	4.6312	30-Sep-04	1.9736	30-Sep-04	1.798
31-Oct-04	4.6267	31-Oct-04	4.7002	31-Oct-04	4.5693	31-Oct-04	1.8877	31-Oct-04	1.7646
30-Nov-04	4.473	30-Nov-04	4.5606	30-Nov-04	4.4453	30-Nov-04	1.8755	30-Nov-04	1.7059
31-Dec-04	4.4287	31-Dec-04	4.4872	31-Dec-04	4.4097	31-Dec-04	1.7552	31-Dec-04	1.5992
31-Jan-05	4.4769	31-Jan-05	4.5419	31-Jan-05	4.4811	31-Jan-05	1.7474	31-Jan-05	1.5862
28-Feb-05	4.6761	28-Feb-05	4.6514	28-Feb-05	4.5249	28-Feb-05	1.77	28-Feb-05	1.5918
31-Mar-05	4.6106	31-Mar-05	4.6357	31-Mar-05	4.5618	31-Mar-05	1.874	31-Mar-05	1.7246
30-Apr-05	4.444	30-Apr-05	4.4735	30-Apr-05	4.4264	30-Apr-05	1.7638	30-Apr-05	1.6408
31-May-05	4.2051	31-May-05	4.2823	31-May-05	4.3326	31-May-05	1.6959	31-May-05	1.5704
30-Jun-05	4.0387	30-Jun-05	4.1519	30-Jun-05	4.2073	30-Jun-05	1.6498	30-Jun-05	1.5324
31-Jul-05	4.2154	31-Jul-05	4.2892	31-Jul-05	4.3179	31-Jul-05	1.6469	31-Jul-05	1.5442
31-Aug-05	4.0641	31-Aug-05	4.1248	31-Aug-05	4.1705	31-Aug-05	1.6095	31-Aug-05	1.4945
30-Sep-05	4.1884	30-Sep-05	4.2489	30-Sep-05	4.2336	30-Sep-05	1.5097	30-Sep-05	1.4043
31-Oct-05	4.2874	31-Oct-05	4.2833	31-Oct-05	4.238	31-Oct-05	1.5665	31-Oct-05	1.3974
30-Nov-05	4.2061	30-Nov-05	4.1685	30-Nov-05	4.0854	30-Nov-05	1.541	30-Nov-05	1.2925
31-Dec-05	4.1019	31-Dec-05	4.0505	31-Dec-05	3.9626	31-Dec-05	1.4668	31-Dec-05	1.2015
31-Jan-06	4.172	31-Jan-06	4.0817	31-Jan-06	3.8631	31-Jan-06	1.2921	31-Jan-06	0.9687
28-Feb-06	4.2134	28-Feb-06	4.1211	28-Feb-06	3.9088	28-Feb-06	1.3237	28-Feb-06	0.9897
31-Mar-06	4.3946	31-Mar-06	4.3444	31-Mar-06	4.1388	31-Mar-06	1.4135	31-Mar-06	1.1011
30-Apr-06	4.6102	30-Apr-06	4.5855	30-Apr-06	4.3286	30-Apr-06	1.542	30-Apr-06	1.2818
31-May-06	4.6302	31-May-06	4.5395	31-May-06	4.2978	31-May-06	1.6291	31-May-06	1.3321
30-Jun-06	4.7356	30-Jun-06	4.6536	30-Jun-06	4.4151	30-Jun-06	1.6832	30-Jun-06	1.3862
31-Jul-06	4.6631	31-Jul-06	4.5482	31-Jul-06	4.2984	31-Jul-06	1.6457	31-Jul-06	1.3078
31-Aug-06	4.6343	31-Aug-06	4.4391	31-Aug-06	4.163	31-Aug-06	1.5515	31-Aug-06	1.2077
30-Sep-06	4.6412	30-Sep-06	4.4471	30-Sep-06	4.1548	30-Sep-06	1.4912	30-Sep-06	1.1173
31-Oct-06	4.6979	31-Oct-06	4.4201	31-Oct-06	4.0629	31-Oct-06	1.5738	31-Oct-06	1.1275
30-Nov-06	4.6926	30-Nov-06	4.4113	30-Nov-06	4.0858	30-Nov-06	1.4736	30-Nov-06	1.0294
31-Dec-06	4.9131	31-Dec-06	4.6318	31-Dec-06	4.2526	31-Dec-06	1.5561	31-Dec-06	1.1073
31-Jan-07	5.1482	31-Jan-07	4.855	31-Jan-07	4.4219	31-Jan-07	1.7849	31-Jan-07	1.2302
28-Feb-07	4.9735	28-Feb-07	4.6791	28-Feb-07	4.3078	28-Feb-07	1.7983	28-Feb-07	1.2474
31-Mar-07	5.1338	31-Mar-07	4.8548	31-Mar-07	4.4697	31-Mar-07	1.7002	31-Mar-07	1.1947
30-Apr-07	5.194	30-Apr-07	4.9284	30-Apr-07	4.5536	30-Apr-07	1.9068	30-Apr-07	1.3595
31-May-07	5.448	31-May-07	5.1283	31-May-07	4.6951	31-May-07	2.0466	31-May-07	1.4583
30-Jun-07	5.6348	30-Jun-07	5.3604	30-Jun-07	4.8891	30-Jun-07	2.2101	30-Jun-07	1.5415
31-Jul-07	5.3529	31-Jul-07	5.1173	31-Jul-07	4.6572	31-Jul-07	2.1934	31-Jul-07	1.5156
31-Aug-07	5.1209	31-Aug-07	4.9347	31-Aug-07	4.5484	31-Aug-07	1.9666	31-Aug-07	1.3126
30-Sep-07	4.9798	30-Sep-07	4.9495	30-Sep-07	4.6447	30-Sep-07	1.7894	30-Sep-07	1.2421
31-Oct-07	4.9395	31-Oct-07	4.8667	31-Oct-07	4.5916	31-Oct-07	1.7455	31-Oct-07	1.2495
30-Nov-07	4.5718	30-Nov-07	4.6361	30-Nov-07	4.5157	30-Nov-07	1.4823	30-Nov-07	1.095
31-Dec-07	4.4137	31-Dec-07	4.5151	31-Dec-07	4.3859	31-Dec-07	1.4983	31-Dec-07	1.0845
31-Jan-08	4.2964	31-Jan-08	4.4877	31-Jan-08	4.4193	31-Jan-08	1.3032	31-Jan-08	0.9192
29-Feb-08	4.1991	29-Feb-08	4.5274	29-Feb-08	4.503	29-Feb-08	1.3276	29-Feb-08	1.0259
31-Mar-08	3.9541	31-Mar-08	4.424	31-Mar-08	4.6048	31-Mar-08	1.0236	31-Mar-08	0.8844
30-Apr-08	4.4429	30-Apr-08	4.733	30-Apr-08	4.7139	30-Apr-08	1.2032	30-Apr-08	1.0184
31-May-08	4.94	31-May-08	4.9984	31-May-08	4.8293	31-May-08	1.3612	31-May-08	0.9959
30-Jun-08	5.1659	30-Jun-08	5.1663	30-Jun-08	4.8995	30-Jun-08	1.3581	30-Jun-08	0.8405
31-Jul-08	4.7675	31-Jul-08	4.8448	31-Jul-08	4.7434	31-Jul-08	1.2887	31-Jul-08	0.8261
31-Aug-08	4.4108	31-Aug-08	4.5222	31-Aug-08	4.5953	31-Aug-08	1.1652	31-Aug-08	0.6719
30-Sep-08	4.208	30-Sep-08	4.5137	30-Sep-08	4.6924	30-Sep-08	1.2511	30-Sep-08	0.7995
31-Oct-08	3.9697	31-Oct-08	4.713	31-Oct-08	4.9258	31-Oct-08	2.0565	31-Oct-08	1.3285
30-Nov-08	3.3664	30-Nov-08	4.0317	30-Nov-08	4.5731	30-Nov-08	2.58	30-Nov-08	1.3657
31-Dec-08	2.708	31-Dec-08	3.4126	31-Dec-08	4.066	31-Dec-08	2.1901	31-Dec-08	1.2361
31-Jan-09	2.8834	31-Jan-09	4.0861	31-Jan-09	4.7012	31-Jan-09	1.5257	31-Jan-09	1.052
28-Feb-09	2.6227	28-Feb-09	3.8159	28-Feb-09	4.7151	28-Feb-09	1.2501	28-Feb-09	1.1934
31-Mar-09	2.4459	31-Mar-09	3.311	31-Mar-09	4.2558	31-Mar-09	1.1902	31-Mar-09	1.1852
30-Apr-09	2.594	30-Apr-09	3.6361	30-Apr-09	4.5822	30-Apr-09	1.0832	30-Apr-09	1.1448
31-May-09	2.7154	31-May-09	3.8141	31-May-09	4.7127	31-May-09	1.0904	31-May-09	1.0545
30-Jun-09	2.9717	30-Jun-09	3.703	30-Jun-09	4.5708	30-Jun-09	1.0821	30-Jun-09	1.0074
31-Jul-09	3.083	31-Jul-09	3.9125	31-Jul-09	4.7431	31-Jul-09	1.2285	31-Jul-09	0.9964
31-Aug-09	2.6877	31-Aug-09	3.6313	31-Aug-09	4.1118	31-Aug-09	1.1562	31-Aug-09	0.8698
30-Sep-09	2.6807	30-Sep-09	3.7123	30-Sep-09	4.1499	30-Sep-09	1.0559	30-Sep-09	0.8862
31-Oct-09	2.7662	31-Oct-09	3.7684	31-Oct-09	4.2789	31-Oct-09	0.703	31-Oct-09	0.7436

12.11 Average zero coupon yields

End month level of yield from British Government Securities, 5 year Nominal Zero Coupon IUMSNZC [a] [b]		End month level of yield from British Government Securities, 10 year Nominal Zero Coupon IUMMNZC [a] [b]		End month level of yield from British Government Securities, 20 year Nominal Zero Coupon IUMLNZC [a] [b]		Monthly average yield from British Government Securities, 10 year Real Zero Coupon IUMAMRZC [a] [b]		Monthly average yield from British Government Securities, 20 year Real Zero Coupon IUMALRZC [a] [b]	
30-Nov-09	2.6607	30-Nov-09	3.6987	30-Nov-09	4.2359	30-Nov-09	0.774	30-Nov-09	0.7106
31-Dec-09	2.9821	31-Dec-09	4.203	31-Dec-09	4.5939	31-Dec-09	0.8046	31-Dec-09	0.7645
31-Jan-10	2.9411	31-Jan-10	4.1135	31-Jan-10	4.5279	31-Jan-10	0.8237	31-Jan-10	0.8421
28-Feb-10	2.7834	28-Feb-10	4.2373	28-Feb-10	4.7692	28-Feb-10	0.9608	28-Feb-10	1.0657
31-Mar-10	2.7852	31-Mar-10	4.1764	31-Mar-10	4.6577	31-Mar-10	0.8276	31-Mar-10	0.9801
30-Apr-10	2.7534	30-Apr-10	4.1034	30-Apr-10	4.6279	30-Apr-10	0.7118	30-Apr-10	0.9024
31-May-10	2.4101	31-May-10	3.7919	31-May-10	4.4818	31-May-10	0.7264	31-May-10	0.9331
30-Jun-10	2.2133	30-Jun-10	3.5853	30-Jun-10	4.3767	30-Jun-10	0.7631	30-Jun-10	0.9715
31-Jul-10	2.2281	31-Jul-10	3.5691	31-Jul-10	4.4956	31-Jul-10	0.8433	31-Jul-10	1.0381
31-Aug-10	1.7575	31-Aug-10	3.0217	31-Aug-10	3.9415	31-Aug-10	0.6535	31-Aug-10	0.9004
30-Sep-10	1.813	30-Sep-10	3.1512	30-Sep-10	4.0071	30-Sep-10	0.4628	30-Sep-10	0.7343
31-Oct-10	1.878	31-Oct-10	3.3042	31-Oct-10	4.3031	31-Oct-10	0.3775	31-Oct-10	0.7099
30-Nov-10	2.0313	30-Nov-10	3.4591	30-Nov-10	4.4002	30-Nov-10	0.4815	30-Nov-10	0.8143
31-Dec-10	2.314	31-Dec-10	3.6174	31-Dec-10	4.3314	31-Dec-10	0.6754	31-Dec-10	0.8243
31-Jan-11	2.5858	31-Jan-11	3.8827	31-Jan-11	4.5822	31-Jan-11	0.6353	31-Jan-11	0.8637
28-Feb-11	2.6508	28-Feb-11	3.8872	28-Feb-11	4.5184	28-Feb-11	0.7203	28-Feb-11	0.8809
31-Mar-11	2.6575	31-Mar-11	3.8974	31-Mar-11	4.5078	31-Mar-11	0.5424	31-Mar-11	0.8003
30-Apr-11	2.4534	30-Apr-11	3.7116	30-Apr-11	4.3435	30-Apr-11	0.5699	30-Apr-11	0.8156
31-May-11	2.2507	31-May-11	3.5655	31-May-11	4.3125	31-May-11	0.4104	31-May-11	0.793
30-Jun-11	2.2036	30-Jun-11	3.6665	30-Jun-11	4.4964	30-Jun-11	0.2576	30-Jun-11	0.6595
31-Jul-11	1.7512	31-Jul-11	3.1755	31-Jul-11	4.2227	31-Jul-11	0.1927	31-Jul-11	0.5845
31-Aug-11	1.6065	31-Aug-11	2.9038	31-Aug-11	4.0173	31-Aug-11	-0.1442	31-Aug-11	0.4083
30-Sep-11	1.4048	30-Sep-11	2.5096	30-Sep-11	3.5397	30-Sep-11	-0.2071	30-Sep-11	0.3008
31-Oct-11	1.3719	31-Oct-11	2.5642	31-Oct-11	3.4276	31-Oct-11	-0.1245	31-Oct-11	0.337
30-Nov-11	1.2752	30-Nov-11	2.4275	30-Nov-11	3.1294	30-Nov-11	-0.3177	30-Nov-11	0.1173
31-Dec-11	1.001	31-Dec-11	2.105	31-Dec-11	3.0454	31-Dec-11	-0.475	31-Dec-11	-0.0286
31-Jan-12	0.9544	31-Jan-12	2.0983	31-Jan-12	3.0189	31-Jan-12	-0.5915	31-Jan-12	-0.1548
29-Feb-12	1.001	29-Feb-12	2.2582	29-Feb-12	3.2967	29-Feb-12	-0.5785	29-Feb-12	-0.0236
31-Mar-12	1.0698	31-Mar-12	2.3289	31-Mar-12	3.447	31-Mar-12	-0.5281	31-Mar-12	0.0341
30-Apr-12	1.1164	30-Apr-12	2.2516	30-Apr-12	3.3938	30-Apr-12	-0.5759	30-Apr-12	-0.0135
31-May-12	0.6748	31-May-12	1.673	31-May-12	2.8994	31-May-12	-0.6844	31-May-12	-0.0644
30-Jun-12	0.8284	30-Jun-12	1.8661	30-Jun-12	2.9815	30-Jun-12	-0.5935	30-Jun-12	-0.0546
31-Jul-12	0.566	31-Jul-12	1.6099	31-Jul-12	2.7932	31-Jul-12	-0.6427	31-Jul-12	-0.0304
31-Aug-12	0.5849	31-Aug-12	1.6346	31-Aug-12	2.8217	31-Aug-12	-0.6944	31-Aug-12	-0.023
30-Sep-12	0.6798	30-Sep-12	1.6958	30-Sep-12	2.9454	30-Sep-12	-0.6639	30-Sep-12	0.0775
31-Oct-12	0.8255	31-Oct-12	1.879	31-Oct-12	3.0256	31-Oct-12	-0.5872	31-Oct-12	0.1513
30-Nov-12	0.8264	30-Nov-12	1.794	30-Nov-12	2.9544	30-Nov-12	-0.6283	30-Nov-12	0.0967
31-Dec-12	0.8853	31-Dec-12	1.8782	31-Dec-12	3.023	31-Dec-12	-0.7274	31-Dec-12	-0.011
31-Jan-13	1.098	31-Jan-13	2.2055	31-Jan-13	3.3222	31-Jan-13	-0.825	31-Jan-13	-0.0952
28-Feb-13	0.9145	28-Feb-13	2.1054	28-Feb-13	3.2498	28-Feb-13	-1.01	28-Feb-13	-0.1883
31-Mar-13	0.7439	31-Mar-13	1.8933	31-Mar-13	3.0961	31-Mar-13	-1.2531	31-Mar-13	-0.3
30-Apr-13	0.73	30-Apr-13	1.7929	30-Apr-13	2.9541	30-Apr-13	-1.3223	30-Apr-13	-0.4891
31-May-13	1.02	31-May-13	2.1641	31-May-13	3.2631	31-May-13	-1.0738	31-May-13	-0.3514
30-Jun-13	1.3933	30-Jun-13	2.618	30-Jun-13	3.5337	30-Jun-13	-0.6377	30-Jun-13	-0.1279
31-Jul-13	1.2511	31-Jul-13	2.5513	31-Jul-13	3.5392	31-Jul-13	-0.5794	31-Jul-13	-0.0071
31-Aug-13	1.5644	31-Aug-13	2.8265	31-Aug-13	3.6373	31-Aug-13	-0.3798	31-Aug-13	0.0923
30-Sep-13	1.5498	30-Sep-13	2.7601	30-Sep-13	3.5437	30-Sep-13	-0.2206	30-Sep-13	0.1506
31-Oct-13	1.5122	31-Oct-13	2.7053	31-Oct-13	3.4942	31-Oct-13	-0.3819	31-Oct-13	0.0185
30-Nov-13	1.6323	30-Nov-13	2.8783	30-Nov-13	3.6515	30-Nov-13	-0.2983	30-Nov-13	0.0607
31-Dec-13	1.9931	31-Dec-13	3.1577	31-Dec-13	3.7316	31-Dec-13	-0.1979	31-Dec-13	0.1006
31-Jan-14	1.7819	31-Jan-14	2.8386	31-Jan-14	3.5521	31-Jan-14	-0.1654	31-Jan-14	0.127
28-Feb-14	1.798	28-Feb-14	2.8582	28-Feb-14	3.5484	28-Feb-14	-0.1897	28-Feb-14	0.1043
31-Mar-14	1.8714	31-Mar-14	2.8707	31-Mar-14	3.5515	31-Mar-14	-0.3044	31-Mar-14	0.0121
30-Apr-14	1.857	30-Apr-14	2.8105	30-Apr-14	3.4992	30-Apr-14	-0.353	30-Apr-14	-0.0318
31-May-14	1.7997	31-May-14	2.7043	31-May-14	3.412	31-May-14	-0.389	31-May-14	-0.0859
30-Jun-14	1.9945	30-Jun-14	2.8146	30-Jun-14	3.4523	30-Jun-14	-0.296	30-Jun-14	-0.0483
31-Jul-14	1.9847	31-Jul-14	2.7619	31-Jul-14	3.3233	31-Jul-14	-0.3139	31-Jul-14	-0.0823
31-Aug-14	1.6987	31-Aug-14	2.3948	31-Aug-14	2.9663	31-Aug-14	-0.4716	31-Aug-14	-0.2406
30-Sep-14	1.781	30-Sep-14	2.4682	30-Sep-14	3.0612	30-Sep-14	-0.5363	30-Sep-14	-0.2837
31-Oct-14	1.5647	31-Oct-14	2.3054	31-Oct-14	2.9766	31-Oct-14	-0.6198	31-Oct-14	-0.4459
30-Nov-14	1.3003	30-Nov-14	1.9853	30-Nov-14	2.6605	30-Nov-14	-0.7384	30-Nov-14	-0.5418
31-Dec-14	1.1987	31-Dec-14	1.8196	31-Dec-14	2.4808	31-Dec-14	-0.9321	31-Dec-14	-0.7607

Source: Bank of England

Notes:

[a] Calculated by the Bank of England using the Variable Roughness Penalty (VRP) model

[b] There have been small revisions to the UK government VRP curves (nominal, real and inflation) going back to the beginning of November 1998. (30 Nov 1998)

12.12 Consumer credit excluding student loans

£ millions　　　Not seasonally adjusted

Net lending - monthly changes

	Monthly changes of					
	MFIs sterling net unsecured lending for individuals	of which: mutuals	Other consumer credit lenders (excluding Student Loans Company) sterling net unsecured lending for individuals	Total (excluding Student Loans Company) sterling net unsecured lending for individuals	of which: credit card lending to individuals	other consumer credit lending to individuals
	LPMVVXP	LPMB3VC	LPMB4TH	LPMB3PT	LPMVZQS	LPMB4TV
	[a]	[a] [b]	[a]			
31-Jan-11	-961	46	-576	-1537	-896	-641
28-Feb-11	-419	11	-375	-794	-201	-593
31-Mar-11	-230	43	187	-43	-326	283
30-Apr-11	317	33	-26	291	773	-481
31-May-11	21	51	-236	-215	55	-270
30-Jun-11	328	46	-7	321	246	75
31-Jul-11	-208	89	-115	-322	141	-463
31-Aug-11	488	89	-191	298	262	36
30-Sep-11	-193	11	432	239	236	3
31-Oct-11	-125	27	-25	-150	-154	4
30-Nov-11	225	34	167	392	376	17
31-Dec-11	-326	40	231	-94	718	-812
31-Jan-12	-881	10	-203	-1084	-969	-116
29-Feb-12	-973	5	-245	-1219	-518	-701
31-Mar-12	-192	23	755	563	-22	585
30-Apr-12	-19	55	41	22	192	-169
31-May-12	-178	48	180	2	-19	21
30-Jun-12	193	10	407	600	568	33
31-Jul-12	-25	74	70	45	-218	263
31-Aug-12	-337	46	-66	-404	227	-630
30-Sep-12	635	27	830	1465	424	1040
31-Oct-12	-442	24	136	-306	-354	48
30-Nov-12	-1	27	352	352	680	-328
31-Dec-12	1688	61	432	2121	1158	963
31-Jan-13	-534	-6	-277	-811	-1052	241
28-Feb-13	244	75	-447	-202	-22	-180
31-Mar-13	-46	38	901	855	-40	895
30-Apr-13	729	45	93	822	374	448
31-May-13	250	7	171	421	268	153
30-Jun-13	314	13	289	603	522	81
31-Jul-13	718	14	123	841	-43	884
31-Aug-13	584	-1	53	637	544	93
30-Sep-13	941	-9	961	1902	276	1627
31-Oct-13	-327	-27	316	-11	-151	140
30-Nov-13	269	-35	511	780	999	-219
31-Dec-13	1259	-	582	1840	917	924

Notes:　　　　　　　　　　　　　　　　　　　　　　　　　　Source: Bank of England

[a] These series may be affected by securitisations and loan transfers up to December 2009.

[b] This series will be discontinued with effect from December 2013 data. Further information can be found in Bankstats, December 2013, `Changes to publication of data for mutually owned monetary financial institutions', available at www.bankofengland.co.uk/statistics/Documents/ms/articles/art1dec13.pdf.

MFIs - Monetary Financial Institutions

12.13a INVESTMENT TRUSTS' ASSETS AND LIABILITIES AT MARKET VALUES

£ million at end of year

		2002	2003	2004	2005	2006	2007	2008	2009	2010	2011	2012
ASSETS												
British government securities denominated in sterling	RLLT	470	302	466	768	533	715	628	585	466	681	857
Index-linked	AFIS	0	0	0	0	0	0	0	0	8	95	..
Other[1]	K5HJ	470	302	466	768	533	715	628	585	458	586	..
British government securities denominated in foreign currency	CBPP	0	0	0	0	0	0	0	0	0	0	0
UK local authority investments[2]	AHBR	0	0	0	0	0	0	0	0	0	0	0
Other UK public sector investments[3]	AHBS	5	5	0	0	0	0	0	0	0	0	0
UK ordinary shares												
Quoted[4]	AHBM	18,509	22,403	22,598	24,021	21,843	21,848	13,428	16,297	17,547	17,329	18,655
Unquoted	AHBQ	966	889	1,343	1,016	1,027	1,186	938	1,349	1,336	1,437	1,363
Overseas ordinary shares	AHCC	14,453	20,294	18,967	23,065	21,659	25,795	18,385	23,865	29,341	29,083	30,758
Other corporate securities[5]												
UK	CBGZ	946	1,079	1,270	673	1,071	1,259	813	665	560	529	470
Overseas	CBHA	458	603	682	937	741	1,038	623	939	1,304	1,344	1,129
UK authorised unit trust units	AHBT	47	79	149	140	24	0	28	33	42	76	53
Overseas government, provincial and municipal securities	AHBY	137	122	33	168	4	151	410	256	410	254	251
UK existing buildings, property, land and new construction work	CBHB	532	498	39	117	252	154	142	141	197	1,522	1,538
Other longer-term assets not elsewhere classified[6]	AMSE	1,224	1,760	1,665	2,359	2,898	3,462	3,684	3,824	4,618	5,439	5,744
LONGER-TERM ASSETS	**AHBD**	**37,747**	**48,034**	**47,212**	**53,264**	**50,052**	**55,608**	**39,079**	**47,954**	**55,821**	**57,694**	**60,818**
Short-term assets	CBGX	2,626	2,535	3,100	3,032	2,138	3,303	3,397	2,522	2,174	2,893	3,015
TOTAL ASSETS	**CBGW**	**40,373**	**50,569**	**50,312**	**56,296**	**52,190**	**58,911**	**42,476**	**50,476**	**57,995**	**60,587**	**63,833**
LIABILITIES												
Borrowing from UK and overseas banks[7]	CBHD	3,376	3,207	2,797	2,771	2,900	2,708	2,553	2,216	2,359	2,897	2,845
Other UK borrowing[8]	CBHG	1,326	1,189	843	670	952	988	1,012	1,062	1,123	914	865
Other overseas borrowing[9]	CBHI	19	0	0	0	2	0	225	185	186	126	117
Issued share and loan capital[10]	CBHK	8,711	9,873	8,210	7,155	5,492	5,659	3,834	3,627	3,361	4,395	4,345
TOTAL LIABILITIES	**CBHO**	**13,432**	**14,269**	**11,850**	**10,596**	**9,346**	**9,355**	**7,624**	**7,090**	**7,029**	**8,332**	**8,172**
NET ASSETS	**CBHM**	**26,941**	**36,300**	**38,462**	**45,700**	**42,844**	**49,556**	**34,852**	**43,386**	**50,966**	**52,255**	**55,661**

Source: Office for National Statistics

† Data has been revised since previous edition; the period marked is the earliest point of revised data in the table.
1 Includes securities of: 0 up to 15 years maturity; over 15 years maturity and undated maturity. Excludes treasury bills and index-linked securities.
2 Includes local authority securities; negotiable bonds; loans and mortgages.
3 Includes public corporation loans and mortgages and other public sector investments not elsewhere classified.
4 Includes investment trust securities.
5 Includes corporate bonds and preference shares.
6 Includes UK unauthorised unit trust units; UK open-ended investment companies; overseas mutual fund investments; other UK fixed assets; overseas fixed assets; overseas direct investment and other UK and overseas assets not elsewhere classified.
7 Sterling and foreign currency. Includes foreign currency liabilities on back-to-back loans and overdrafts.
8 Includes sterling and foreign currency borrowing from building societies; issue of securities (other than ordinary shares); issue of sterling commercial paper and other borrowing not elsewhere classified (such as borrowing from parent, subsidiary and associate companies and other related concerns).
9 Includes borrowing from banks: related companies and other borrowing not elsewhere classified.
10 Quoted and unquoted. Includes ordinary shares; preference shares; deferred stocks; bonds; debentures and loan stocks.

12.13b UNIT TRUSTS AND PROPERTY UNIT TRUSTS' BALANCE SHEET ASSETS AND LIABILITIES AT MARKET VALUES

£ million at end of year d of year

		2002	2003	2004	2005	2006	2007	2008	2009	2010	2011	2012
ASSETS												
British government securities denominated in sterling[1]	CBHT	7,077	9,125	9,768	25,181	31,603	32,120	33,466	29,331	33,306	37,116	36,033
Ordinary shares[2]												
UK	RLIB	82,851	116,407	130,230	157,149	185,637	195,009	143,550	167,401	204,616	179,940	201,822
Overseas	RLIC	63,152	75,074	81,034	105,443	127,409	142,211	113,667	150,863	200,028	187,714	215,705
Other corporate securities[3]												
UK	CBHU	21,152	23,972	22,467	29,293	29,876	30,626	30,174	36,646	52,786	52,735	63,546
Overseas	CBHV	5,916	9,840	13,142	16,057	25,617	30,029	30,442	43,301	49,098	48,388	62,870
Overseas government, provincial and municipal securities	CBHW	3,278	2,267	2,347	3,412	3,532	3,880	5,754	5,810	9,251	14,797	19,604
UK existing buildings, property, land and new construction work	RLIE	4,026	5,125	5,909	9,623	12,781	12,480	8,518	7,248	9,484	13,220	13,498
Other longer-term assets not elsewhere classified[4]	CBHX	10,151	10,940	14,261	22,327	29,765	38,707	42,670	49,417	60,029	66,640	81,849
Short-term assets	CBHS	8,928	12,090	11,497	16,417	20,653	27,969	35,224	37,263	48,382	45,001	53,734
of which: Derivative contracts with UK and overseas counterparties which have a positive (asset) value[5]	KUU5	719	4,028	2,099	4,745	4,552	7,271	13,151	17,132	25,944	18,168	25,644
TOTAL ASSETS	**CBHR**	**206,531**	**264,840**	**290,655**	**384,902**	**466,873**	**513,031**	**443,465**	**527,280**	**666,980**	**645,551**	**748,661**
LIABILITIES												
Borrowing from UK and overseas banks[6]	RLLF	314	425	413	1,456	2,544	2,603	3,486	1,541	991	1,992	3,430
Other UK borrowing[7]	RLLH	35	85	27	130	16	36	80	26	74	350	83
Other overseas borrowing[8]	RLLI	29	26	1	1	0	0	0	54	0	0	0
Derivative contracts with UK and overseas counterparties which have a negative (liability) value[5]	KUU6	270	2,169	1,611	2,814	3,701	6,382	11,890	15,294	23,676	17,464	22,832
Other creditors, provisions and liabilities not elsewhere classified	KUU7	1,337	1,289	1,835	2,425	3,370	2,562	3,442	5,524	7,228	14,087	5,460
Liability attributable to unit and share holders	RLLG	204,546	260,846	286,768	378,076	457,242	501,448	424,567	504,841	635,011	611,658	716,856
TOTAL LIABILITIES	**RLLE**	**206,531**	**264,840**	**290,655**	**384,902**	**466,873**	**513,031**	**443,465**	**527,280**	**666,980**	**645,551**	**748,661**

Source: Office for National Statistics

1 Includes securities of: 0 up to 15 years maturity; over 15 years maturity; undated maturity and index-linked.
2 UK and overseas. Quoted and unquoted. Includes investment trust securities.
3 Includes corporate bonds and preference shares.
4 UK and overseas. Includes British government securities denominated in foreign currency; local authority and public corporation securities; mutual fund investments; other UK fixed assets; overseas fixed assets; direct investment and other assets not elsewhere classified.
5 Includes credit default products; employee stock options; other options; other swaps; futures; forwards and other derivative contracts not elsewhere classified.
6 Sterling and foreign currency. Includes foreign currency liabilities on back-to-back loans and overdrafts.
7 Includes sterling and foreign currency borrowing from building societies; issue of securities (other than ordinary shares); issue of sterling commercial paper and other borrowing not elsewhere classified (such as borrowing from parent, subsidiary and associate companies and other related concerns).
8 Includes borrowing from banks; related companies and other borrowing not elsewhere classified.

12.14 SELF-ADMINISTERED PENSION FUNDS[1] BALANCE SHEET - ASSETS AND LIABILITIES AT MARKET VALUES

£ million at end of year

		2002	2003	2004	2005	2006	2007	2008	2009	2010	2011	2012
ASSETS												
British government securities denominated in sterling	AHVK	84,461	88,803	87,579	94,325	104,910	113,617	98,577	108,871	122,007	167,372	199,400
Index-linked	AHWC	47,173	52,041	46,333	48,821	53,858	64,797	58,564	70,317	83,016	110,808	142,565
Other[2]	J8Y5	37,288	36,762	41,246	45,504	51,052	48,820	40,013	38,554	38,991	56,564	56,835
British government securities denominated in foreign currency	RYEX	37	0	44	45	27	42	4	126	89	1,287	5,695
UK local authority investments[3]	AHVO	42	8	4	4	2	5	0	2	274	113	263
Other UK public sector investments[4]	JE5J	731	639	656	846	1,118	1,351	1,259	2,347	2,911	1,703	1,611
UK PUBLIC SECTOR SECURITIES	**RYHC**	**85,271**	**89,450**	**88,283**	**95,220**	**106,057**	**115,015**	**99,840**	**111,346**	**125,281**	**170,475**	**206,969**
UK corporate bonds[5]	JX62	30,351	36,918	42,871	47,912	54,626	57,306	55,741	64,351	59,469	61,586	64,508
Sterling	GQFT	29,984	36,415	42,151	47,061	53,190	55,550	53,765	62,073	57,086	59,322	61,896
Foreign currency	GQFU	367	503	720	851	1,436	1,756	1,976	2,278	2,383	2,264	2,612
UK ordinary shares[6]	AHVP	186,437	186,426	180,561	199,199	208,473	152,048	110,571	116,710	121,882	108,631	111,913
UK preference shares[6]	J8YF	99	164	156	153	276	235	775	833	16	11	29
Overseas corporate securities	JRS8	115,778	138,215	156,278	203,562	224,514	215,068	175,747	214,230	222,751	211,562	226,274
Bonds	RLPF	11,119	12,301	15,794	19,891	30,867	44,387	47,612	57,920	60,826	61,129	60,424
Ordinary shares	AHVR	104,392	125,740	140,282	183,060	192,978	169,598	127,525	155,577	161,043	149,638	165,141
Preference shares	RLPC	267	174	202	611	669	1,083	610	733	882	795	709
Mutual fund investments	JRS9	77,372	117,834	144,265	192,033	215,218	254,936	211,724	286,493	369,955	385,337	448,583
UK	J8Y7	60,288	97,218	115,622	150,316	168,635	194,833	148,798	203,523	266,058	264,652	293,071
Unit trust units[7]	JX63	47,083	77,468	86,005	105,429	115,872	147,536	110,558	148,642	178,027	172,120	208,155
Other[8]	JX64	13,205	19,750	29,617	44,887	52,763	47,297	38,240	54,881	88,031	92,532	84,916
Overseas	JE4P	17,084	20,616	28,643	41,717	46,583	60,103	62,926	82,970	103,897	120,685	155,512
CORPORATE SECURITIES	**RYHN**	**410,037**	**479,557**	**524,131**	**642,859**	**703,107**	**679,593**	**554,558**	**682,617**	**774,073**	**767,127**	**851,307**
Overseas government, provincial and municipal securities	AHVT	16,031	16,340	15,075	19,037	21,776	22,434	21,527	16,900	17,335	21,424	23,768
Loans	JRT4	144	35	44	9	42	417	518	1,768	2,343	1,656	1,313
UK[9]	JE5E	0	35	44	6	6	12	0	116	81	77	170
Overseas[10]	AHVZ	144	0	0	3	36	405	518	1,652	2,262	1,579	1,143
Fixed assets[11]	JRT5	31,825	30,775	30,676	31,742	34,608	30,466	22,892	24,957	30,159	32,991	30,705
UK	JE5F	31,662	30,621	30,554	31,616	34,435	30,306	22,818	24,718	28,991	32,178	30,372
Overseas	GOLB	163	154	122	126	173	160	74	239	1,168	813	333
Investment in insurance managed funds, insurance policies and annuities	RYHS	40,593	43,063	67,936	86,336	92,387	103,610	86,541	70,318	80,613	93,823	99,896
Other longer-term assets not elsewhere classified[12]	J8YA	5,845	14,327	17,071	21,423	31,234	41,455	45,301	51,100	69,419	81,562	90,893
OTHER LONGER-TERM ASSETS	**RYHW**	**94,438**	**104,540**	**130,802**	**158,547**	**180,047**	**198,382**	**176,779**	**165,043**	**199,869**	**231,456**	**246,575**
LONGER-TERM ASSETS	**RYHX**	**589,746**	**673,547**	**743,216**	**896,626**	**989,211**	**992,990**	**831,177**	**959,006**	**1,099,223**	**1,169,058**	**1,304,851**

Source: Office for National Statistics

† Data has been revised since previous edition; the period marked is the earliest point of revised data in the table.

1 Combined public and private sector. Data from the pension funds surveys are of lower quality than equivalent data from other institutional groups because of the difficulties in constructing a suitable sampling frame of pension funds.

2 Includes securities of: 0 up to 15 years maturity; over 15 years maturity and undated

3 Includes local authority securities; negotiable

4 Includes public corporation loans and mortgages and other public sector investments

5 Issued by: banks; building societies and other

6 Quoted and unquoted.

7 Authorised and unauthorised.

8 Includes property unit trusts; investment trust securities; open-ended investment companies; hedge funds and other mutual fund investments not elsewhere

9 Includes sterling asset backed loans; loans to individuals secured on dwellings; other loans to individuals (including policy loans); loans to businesses and other loans not elsewhere classified. Excludes loans to UK associate companies; bank term deposits and building society investments.

10 Includes loans to parent companies; subsidiaries; associates and other loans not elsewhere classified. Excludes loans categorised as direct investment; loans covered by Export Credit Guarantee Department (ECGD), specific bank guarantees or ECGD buyer credit guarantees.

11 UK and overseas. Includes existing buildings; property; land; new construction work; vehicles; machinery and equipment; valuables and intangibles. Includes the capital value of assets bought on hire purchase or acquired (as lessee) under a finance leasing arrangement and assets acquired for hiring, renting and operating leasing purposes. Excludes the capital value of assets acquired but leased out to others under finance leasing arrangements.

12 UK and overseas. Includes certificates of tax deposit; insurance policies; annuities and loans covered by Export Credit Guarantee Department (ECGD), specific bank guarantees or ECGD buyer credit guarantees. Excludes pre-payments and debtors.

12.14 SELF-ADMINISTERED PENSION FUNDS[1] BALANCE SHEET
ASSETS AND LIABILITIES AT MARKET VALUES

continued

£ million at end of year

		2002	2003	2004	2005	2006	2007	2008	2009	2010	2011	2012
ASSETS												
Cash	GNOR	0	0	0	0	0	0	0	0	0	0	0
Balances with banks and building societies in the UK	JX5Q	15,079	16,103	16,216	17,789	22,823	25,974	20,133	23,054	23,736	23,854	22,929
Sterling	JX5S	14,094	14,349	14,064	15,510	20,211	22,615	16,802	19,099	20,043	20,159	18,901
Foreign currency	JX5U	985	1,754	2,152	2,279	2,612	3,359	3,331	3,955	3,693	3,695	4,028
Balances with overseas banks	GNOW	226	249	287	361	525	807	351	134	197	72	157
Other liquid deposits[13]	GNOX	992	1,883	1,782	3,010	3,891	5,392	4,300	12,431	9,631	11,956	15,265
Certificates of deposit issued by banks and building societies in the UK[14]	IX8H	1,109	2,063	1,678	2,649	4,932	8,156	6,480	2,269	2,472	6,498	2,069
Money market instruments issued by HM Treasury[15]	IX9J	771	206	69	89	22	304	548	1,709	1,109	1,734	4,116
UK local authority debt	AHVF	365	276	337	270	221	205	323	210	116	157	232
Commercial paper issued by UK companies[16]	GQFR	322	197	175	476	401	857	367	664	1,135	993	1,254
Other UK money market instruments[17]	GOZR	275	497	1,428	883	1,174	1,893	1,959	2,822	3,416	3,936	2,716
Money market instruments issued by non-resident businesses	GOZS	735	441	413	384	449	1,279	911	963	2,067	3,709	2,752
Other short-term assets not elsewhere classified[18]	JX5W	760	721	1,365	1,854	1,898	1,304	3,474	3,113	3,644	2,311	1,904
Balances outstanding from stockbrokers and securities dealers[19]	RYIL	4,584	5,383	8,939	18,879	24,812	28,297	30,536	11,281	7,145	8,241	6,213
Income accrued on investments and rents	RYIM	1,792	2,256	1,921	1,970	2,303	2,744	2,576	2,714	2,761	2,930	2,872
Amounts outstanding from HM Revenue and Customs[19]	RYIN	30	22	28	29	16	15	23	32	37	53	67
Other debtors and assets not elsewhere classified	RYIO	3,660	15,794	22,838	25,006	35,224	22,454	24,565	21,464	13,159	8,902	11,387
Derivative contracts with UK counterparties which have a positive (asset) value[20]	JRO3	1,775	3,089	10,235	22,157	24,357	29,789	35,194	61,862	99,420	170,170	186,184
Derivative contracts with overseas counterparties which have a positive (asset) value[20]	GOJU	696	561	2,962	2,668	5,995	8,652	5,835	20,534	19,803	29,445	38,324
TOTAL ASSETS	**RYIR**	**622,917**	**723,288**	**813,889**	**995,100**	**1,118,254**	**1,131,112**	**968,752**	**1,124,262**	**1,289,071**	**1,444,019**	**1,603,292**
LIABILITIES												
Borrowing[21]	GQED	2,380	5,216	8,133	11,678	14,661	16,180	4,461	3,859	2,830	3,361	10,603
Balances owed to stockbrokers and securities dealers[19]	RYIS	4,424	5,472	9,248	18,722	25,954	33,965	37,912	13,707	7,312	9,688	7,816
Pensions due but not paid[22]	RYIT	173	248	138	86	285	220	167	280	271	300	5,152
Derivative contracts with UK counterparties which have a negative (liability) value[20]	JRP9	1,282	1,817	7,873	16,818	17,231	26,187	27,533	37,689	78,322	147,217	149,493
Derivative contracts with overseas counterparties which have a negative (liability) value[20]	GKGR	392	437	3,082	2,785	7,036	11,275	6,335	41,110	37,345	42,712	60,725
Other creditors, provisions and liabilities not elsewhere classified	RYIU	3,028	16,008	22,107	24,834	36,208	18,327	20,577	21,603	18,889	9,905	9,011
Market value of pension funds[23]	AHVA	611,238	694,090	763,308	920,177	1,016,879	1,024,958	871,767	1,006,014	1,144,102	1,230,836	1,360,492
TOTAL LIABILITIES	**RYIR**	**622,917**	**723,288**	**813,889**	**995,100**	**1,118,254**	**1,131,112**	**968,752**	**1,124,262**	**1,289,071**	**1,444,019**	**1,603,292**

† Data has been revised since previous edition; the period marked is the earliest point of revised data in the table.

Source: Office for National Statistics

1 Combined public and private sector. Data from the pension funds surveys are of lower quality than equivalent data from other institutional groups because of the difficulties in constructing a suitable sampling frame of pension funds.
13 Includes money market funds; liquidity funds and cash liquidity funds.
14 Sterling and foreign currency.
15 Includes treasury bills. Excludes British government securities.
16 Sterling and foreign currency commercial paper issued by: banks; building societies; other financial institutions and other issuing companies.
17 Includes floating rate notes maturing within one year of issue.
18 UK and overseas. Excludes derivative contracts.
19 Gross value.
20 Includes credit default products; employee stock options; other options; other swaps; futures; forwards and other derivative contracts not elsewhere classified.
21 UK and overseas. Includes from a UK perspective: sterling and foreign currency borrowing from UK banks and building societies; borrowing arising from the issue of floating rate notes and preference shares; foreign currency liabilities on back-to-back loans; overdrafts and other borrowing not elsewhere classified. Includes from an overseas perspective: borrowing from banks and other borrowing not elsewhere classified.
22 Excludes any estimated future liabilities.
23 Net value as found in statement of net assets.

12.15a INSURANCE COMPANIES' BALANCE SHEET: LONG-TERM BUSINESS ASSETS AND LIABILITIES AT MARKET VALUES

£ million at end of year

		2002	2003	2004	2005	2006	2007	2008	2009	2010	2011	2012
ASSETS												
British government securities denominated in sterling	AHNJ	131,305	142,920	157,019	161,906	161,641	158,694	166,879	167,247	182,506	205,223	187,145
Index-linked	AHQI	22,359	23,186	28,673	33,722	41,104	45,902	54,387	57,157	66,115	78,354	72,499
Other[1]	J5HZ	108,946	119,734	128,346	128,184	120,537	112,792	112,492	110,090	116,391	126,869	114,646
British government securities denominated in foreign currency	RGBV	36	56	0	206	12	0	0	0	0	0	0
UK local authority investments[2]	AHNN	1,427	1,547	2,044	1,840	1,614	998	776	655	768	813	770
Other UK public sector investments[3]	RGCS	308	613	254	801	651	634	872	1,461	2,189	2,207	2,197
UK PUBLIC SECTOR SECURITIES	RYEK	133,076	145,136	159,317	164,753	163,918	160,326	168,527	169,363	185,463	208,243	190,112
UK corporate bonds[4]	IFLF	146,190	151,703	150,884	165,918	159,073	159,273	159,789	160,532	158,987	163,348	178,627
Sterling	IFLG	142,019	146,410	144,280	158,995	150,907	153,694	154,525	155,184	156,477	160,842	174,682
Foreign currency	IFLH	4,171	5,293	6,604	6,923	8,166	5,579	5,264	5,348	2,510	2,506	3,945
UK ordinary shares[5]	IFLI	228,497	235,601	237,610	273,679	299,717	293,655	188,430	209,992	207,971	177,480	162,949
UK preference shares[5]	RLOL	1,306	1,126	1,198	1,228	1,231	983	724	624	648	536	375
Overseas corporate securities	IFLJ	110,738	110,193	130,098	165,452	194,997	234,388	219,957	266,280	278,930	262,823	303,565
Bonds	RLOP	30,242	32,507	40,281	45,970	57,774	69,696	85,077	111,866	112,338	115,744	127,629
Ordinary shares	AHNQ	80,213	77,501	89,654	119,207	136,652	163,249	134,211	153,500	165,216	145,932	173,982
Preference shares	RLOM	283	185	163	275	571	1,443	669	914	1,376	1,147	1,954
Mutual fund investments[6]	IFLK	73,685	89,523	108,019	168,896	192,516	222,081	186,950	230,247	259,457	265,750	328,657
CORPORATE SECURITIES	RYEO	560,416	588,146	627,809	775,173	847,534	910,380	755,850	867,675	905,993	869,937	974,173
Overseas government, provincial and municipal securities	AHNS	19,762	20,561	20,161	16,065	21,078	25,787	29,053	24,601	25,363	23,727	26,928
Other longer-term assets not elsewhere classified[7]	JX8D	66,835	77,739	89,063	83,665	92,326	99,316	76,139	67,531	74,900	81,916	81,039
OTHER LONGER-TERM ASSETS	RYER	86,597	98,300	109,224	99,730	113,404	125,103	105,192	92,132	100,263	105,643	107,967
LONGER-TERM ASSETS	RYES	780,089	831,582	896,350	1,039,656	1,124,856	1,195,809	1,029,569	1,129,170	1,191,719	1,183,823	1,272,252

Source: Office for National Statistics

1 Includes securities of: 0 up to 15 years maturity; over 15 years maturity and undated maturity. Excludes treasury bills and index-linked securities.
2 Includes local authority securities; negotiable bonds; loans and mortgages.
3 Includes public corporation loans and mortgages and other public sector investments not elsewhere classified.
4 Issued by: banks; building societies and other corporates.
5 Quoted and unquoted.
6 UK and overseas. Includes authorised and unauthorised unit trust units; investment trust securities; open-ended investment companies; hedge funds and other mutual fund investments not elsewhere classified.
7 UK and overseas. Includes loans; fixed assets and other longer-term assets not elsewhere classified.

12.15a INSURANCE COMPANIES' BALANCE SHEET: LONG-TERM BUSINESS ASSETS AND LIABILITIES AT MARKET VALUES

continued

£ million at end of year

		2002	2003	2004	2005	2006	2007	2008	2009	2010	2011	2012
ASSETS												
Cash	HLGW	0	29	15	29	0	0	0	0	0	0	0
Balances with banks and building societies in the UK	JX2C	29,750	26,527	28,018	31,606	34,454	48,619	51,139	44,483	34,026	34,998	35,424
Sterling	JX3R	28,505	24,928	26,116	30,221	32,653	45,948	47,456	42,097	32,387	32,698	33,805
Foreign currency	JX3T	1,245	1,599	1,902	1,385	1,801	2,671	3,683	2,386	1,639	2,300	1,619
Balances with overseas banks	HLHB	1,266	1,067	1,086	1,454	1,022	1,484	2,816	3,758	2,766	1,726	1,381
Other liquid deposits[8]	HLHC	3,170	787	1,522	1,215	333	678	1,638	12,385	14,076	15,891	17,257
Certificates of deposit issued by banks and building societies in the UK[9]	AHND	15,910	19,344	18,733	14,200	17,256	15,177	11,401	8,177	8,622	6,158	5,769
Money market instruments issued by HM Treasury[10]	RGBM	10	334	534	537	685	785	179	1,344	509	1,392	1,081
UK local authority debt	AHNF	0	0	0	0	0	0	0	0	0	0	0
Commercial paper issued by UK companies[11]	JF77	3,555	3,512	2,884	5,130	2,714	2,723	2,268	1,806	646	891	496
Other UK money market instruments[12]	HLHL	984	1,562	1,997	2,670	3,538	3,071	3,159	2,959	3,208	5,501	3,540
Money market instruments issued by non-resident businesses	HLHM	218	1,990	952	1,681	405	859	689	1,755	2,956	1,530	2,068
Other short-term assets not elsewhere classified[13]	JX2E	1,855	1,525	2,615	10,432	10,749	20,965	19,555	10,076	5,232	6,159	6,008
Balances due from stockbrokers and securities dealers[14]	RGBU	577	176	-228	-1,052	-345	140	-399	-1,159	-834	-1,245	-1,145
SHORT-TERM ASSETS (excluding derivatives)	**RYEW**	**57,295**	**56,853**	**58,128**	**67,902**	**70,811**	**94,501**	**92,445**	**85,584**	**71,207**	**73,001**	**71,879**
Derivative contracts with UK and overseas counterparties which have a positive (asset) value[15]	IFKX	5,795	4,545	3,743	5,739	5,937	5,205	17,892	10,317	12,399	24,060	20,805
Agents' balances and outstanding premiums in respect of direct insurance and facultative reinsurance contracts[16]												
UK	RYPA	1,883	635	269	500	669	738	535	467	515	554	620
Overseas	RYPB	49	73	106	-103	-136	-177	0	1	3	3	0
Reinsurance, coinsurance and treaty balances[17]												
UK	RYPC	3,683	3,187	2,965	2,607	3,462	-413	-1,000	3,817	-838	-1,147	-1,778
Overseas	RYPD	758	825	415	929	1,105	836	-7,355	-8,232	-6,020	-6,035	-6,425
Outstanding interest, dividends and rents[18]	RYPH	6,244	6,866	7,476	7,897	7,330	8,690	9,256	9,158	8,591	8,511	8,716
Other debtors and assets not elsewhere classified[19]	RYPF	28,147	28,548	23,028	19,694	44,923	51,373	37,342	33,162	30,366	28,806	27,717
Direct investment for non-insurance subsidiary and associate companies in the UK[20]	RYET	4,577	4,191	3,971	8,390	13,016	9,186	11,484	10,129	5,097	7,249	8,880
Direct investment for UK insurance subsidiary, associate and holding companies[20]	RYEU	4,569	5,054	3,473	2,528	6,114	7,578	7,890	7,234	6,720	7,152	4,275
Direct investment for overseas subsidiaries, associates, branches and agencies[20]	RYEV	5,463	6,330	2,181	4,455	3,341	3,832	5,011	4,141	4,131	3,340	3,470
TOTAL ASSETS	**RKBI**	**898,552**	**948,689**	**1,002,105**	**1,160,194**	**1,281,428**	**1,377,158**	**1,203,069**	**1,284,948**	**1,323,890**	**1,329,317**	**1,410,411**

8 Includes money market funds; liquidity funds and cash liquidity funds.
9 Sterling and foreign currency.
10 Includes treasury bills. Excludes British government securities.
11 Sterling and foreign currency commercial paper issued by: banks; building societies; other financial institutions and other issuing companies.
12 Includes floating rate notes maturing within one year of issue.
13 UK and overseas. Excludes derivative contracts.
14 Net of balances owed. Includes amounts due on securities bought and sold for future settlement.
15 Includes credit default products; employee stock options; other options; other swaps; futures; forwards and other derivative contracts not elsewhere classified.
16 Net of insurance liabilities.
17 Net of reinsurance bought and sold.
18 Net value.
19 Includes deferred acquisition costs.
20 Net asset value of attributable companies.
21 Includes issue of securities (other than ordinary shares); issue of sterling commercial paper and other borrowing not elsewhere classified.
22 Includes borrowing from banks; related companies and other borrowing not elsewhere classified.
23 Net of reinsurers share.
24 UK and overseas. Includes deferred tax net of amounts receivable.
25 UK and overseas. Includes derivative contracts which have a negative (liability) value.
26 Includes unallocated divisible surplus and the 'net worth' of UK branches of overseas companies, including profit and loss account balances.

12.15a INSURANCE COMPANIES' BALANCE SHEET: LONG-TERM BUSINESS ASSETS AND LIABILITIES AT MARKET VALUES

continued

£ million at end of year

		2002	2003	2004	2005	2006	2007	2008	2009	2010	2011	2012
LIABILITIES												
Borrowing	AHNI	13,164	15,617	14,536	15,224	14,369	12,426	12,467	10,866	12,542	12,084	10,660
Banks and building societies in the UK[9]	JX2G	5,390	4,164	5,362	5,043	2,867	3,801	5,089	3,305	2,099	1,980	961
Other UK[21]	ICXU	6,974	10,923	8,381	9,030	9,537	6,699	4,832	5,460	8,112	8,730	9,075
Overseas[22]	RGDD	800	530	793	1,151	1,965	1,926	2,546	2,101	2,331	1,374	624
Long-term business insurance and investment contract liabilities[23]	RKDC	794,177	824,766	873,071	1,037,658	1,125,221	1,205,183	1,069,993	1,153,944	1,178,823	1,171,844	1,241,671
Claims admitted but not paid[23]	RKBM	3,234	3,699	3,579	3,481	3,513	3,848	3,426	4,637	2,946	3,072	3,387
Provisions for taxation and dividends payable[24]	KVE9	2,815	4,084	4,961	8,245	8,120	7,489	60	1,781	2,973	1,993	2,400
Other creditors, provisions and liabilities not elsewhere classified[25]	RYPL	23,261	15,870	16,738	16,907	33,192	39,527	52,849	47,803	53,826	66,466	69,971
Excess of total assets over liabilities in respect of long-term business, minority interests in UK subsidiary companies, shareholders' capital and reserves and any other reserves[26]	A4YP	61,901	84,653	89,220	78,679	97,013	108,685	64,274	65,917	72,780	73,858	82,322
TOTAL LIABILITIES	**RKBI**	**898,552**	**948,689**	**1,002,105**	**1,160,194**	**1,281,428**	**1,377,158**	**1,203,069**	**1,284,948**	**1,323,890**	**1,329,317**	**1,410,411**

Source: Office for National Statistics

8 Includes money market funds; liquidity funds and cash liquidity funds.
9 Sterling and foreign currency.
10 Includes treasury bills. Excludes British government securities.
11 Sterling and foreign currency commercial paper issued by: banks; building societies; other financial institutions and other issuing companies.
12 Includes floating rate notes maturing within one year of issue.
13 UK and overseas. Excludes derivative contracts.
14 Net of balances owed. Includes amounts due on securities bought and sold for future settlement.
15 Includes credit default products; employee stock options; other options; other swaps; futures; forwards and other derivative contracts not elsewhere classified.
16 Net of insurance liabilities.
17 Net of reinsurance bought and sold.
18 Net value.
19 Includes deferred acquisition costs.
20 Net asset value of attributable companies.
21 Includes issue of securities (other than ordinary shares); issue of sterling commercial paper and other borrowing not elsewhere classified.
22 Includes borrowing from banks; related companies and other borrowing not elsewhere classified.
23 Net of reinsurers share.
24 UK and overseas. Includes deferred tax net of amounts receivable.
25 UK and overseas. Includes derivative contracts which have a negative (liability) value.
26 Includes unallocated divisible surplus and the 'net worth' of UK branches of overseas companies, including profit and loss account balances.

12.15b INSURANCE COMPANIES' BALANCE SHEET: GENERAL BUSINESS ASSETS AND LIABILITIES AT MARKET VALUES

£ million at end of year

		2002	2003	2004	2005	2006	2007	2008	2009	2010	2011	2012
ASSETS												
British government securities denominated in sterling	AHMJ	18,390	19,645	19,662	19,818	19,296	16,026	18,441	16,969	13,631	13,384	11,774
Index-linked	AHMZ	733	453	345	538	603	297	1,622	1,991	1,731	1,724	2,150
Other[1]	J8EX	17,657	19,192	19,317	19,280	18,693	15,729	16,819	14,978	11,900	11,660	9,624
British government securities denominated in foreign currency	RYMQ	0	0	35	12	72	69	3	0	0	..	13
UK local authority investments[2]	AHMN	10	10	49	44	0	3	0	0	0	..	0
Other UK public sector investments[3]	RYMU	6	3	54	6	0	10	0	65	249	..	252
UK PUBLIC SECTOR SECURITIES	**RYMV**	**18,406**	**19,658**	**19,800**	**19,880**	**19,368**	**16,108**	**18,444**	**17,034**	**13,880**	**13,907**	**12,039**
UK corporate bonds[4]	IFVV	6,699	7,233	9,826	10,815	11,797	13,397	12,060	13,550	10,487	10,817	12,127
Sterling	IFVW	6,687	7,067	9,637	9,932	11,057	12,647	11,009	12,288	9,544	10,217	11,264
Foreign currency	IFVX	12	166	189	883	740	750	1,051	1,262	943	600	863
UK ordinary shares[5]	IFVY	6,755	6,548	8,724	9,864	10,138	9,006	10,501	9,963	9,525	8,435	8,732
UK preference shares[5]	RLOT	192	143	54	40	9	44	29	26	26	25	21
Overseas corporate securities	IFVZ	7,394	7,124	11,520	12,645	18,636	14,773	20,258	23,002	17,594	18,636	24,380
Bonds	RLOX	5,436	5,473	9,762	10,866	16,128	12,872	18,081	21,017	15,847	16,939	21,872
Ordinary shares	AHMQ	1,924	1,638	1,758	1,779	2,507	1,901	2,175	1,976	1,741	1,692	2,501
Preference shares	RLOU	34	13	0	0	1	0	2	9	6	5	7
Mutual fund investments[6]	IFWA	2,901	1,563	2,470	1,270	1,256	1,780	1,911	3,498	4,878	5,802	4,236
CORPORATE SECURITIES	**RYNF**	**23,941**	**22,611**	**32,594**	**34,634**	**41,836**	**39,000**	**44,759**	**50,039**	**42,510**	**43,715**	**49,496**
Overseas government, provincial and municipal securities	AHMS	7,156	5,720	6,662	7,341	8,035	4,869	8,505	7,204	5,126	5,524	9,355
Other longer-term assets not elsewhere classified[7]	JX8E	2,859	3,335	4,451	6,362	6,746	7,059	8,269	7,338	9,158	9,938	10,148
OTHER LONGER-TERM ASSETS	**RYNO**	**10,015**	**9,055**	**11,113**	**13,703**	**14,781**	**11,928**	**16,774**	**14,542**	**14,284**	**15,462**	**19,503**
LONGER-TERM ASSETS	**RYNP**	**52,362**	**51,324**	**63,507**	**68,217**	**75,985**	**67,036**	**79,977**	**81,615**	**70,674**	**73,084**	**81,038**

Source: Office for National Statistics

.. Suppressed to avoid the disclosure of confidential data.
1 Includes securities of: 0 up to 15 years maturity; over 15 years maturity and undated maturity. Excludes treasury bills and index-linked securities.
2 Includes local authority securities; negotiable bonds; loans and mortgages.
3 Includes public corporation loans and mortgages and other public sector investments not elsewhere classified.
4 Issued by: banks; building societies and other corporates.
5 Quoted and unquoted.
6 UK and overseas. Includes authorised and unauthorised unit trust units; investment trust securities; open-ended investment companies; hedge funds and other mutual fund investments not elsewhere classified.
7 UK and overseas. Includes loans; fixed assets and other longer-term assets not elsewhere classified.

12.15b INSURANCE COMPANIES' BALANCE SHEET: GENERAL BUSINESS ASSETS AND LIABILITIES AT MARKET VALUES

continued   £ million at end of year

		2002	2003	2004	2005	2006	2007	2008	2009	2010	2011	2012
ASSETS												
Cash	HLMN	0	12	23	63	0	0	0	0	0	0	0
Balances with banks and building societies in the UK	JX3H	10,309	12,683	18,051	9,116	9,327	8,949	9,871	10,227	7,961	7,619	7,032
Sterling	JX43	9,280	11,257	16,485	7,952	6,501	6,907	8,170	8,763	6,730	6,532	5,988
Foreign currency	JX45	1,029	1,426	1,566	1,164	2,826	2,042	1,701	1,464	1,231	1,087	1,044
Balances with overseas banks	HLMS	370	700	1,523	1,116	1,031	1,015	1,250	1,138	981	1,150	1,841
Other liquid deposits[8]	HLMT	93	103	204	70	396	375	869	2,476	3,326	2,916	3,753
Certificates of deposit issued by banks and building societies in the UK[9]	IX8K	4,800	3,486	6,808	8,402	7,708	8,264	7,775	2,002	558	843	1,223
Money market instruments issued by HM Treasury[10]	ICWI	172	20	444	1,670	379	342	708	979	327	237	1,675
UK local authority debt	AHMF	0	3	0	0	0	0	0	0	0	0	0
Commercial paper issued by UK companies[11]	JF75	399	607	441	610	732	2,682	1,640	1,630	275	281	509
Other UK money market instruments[12]	HLNC	500	1,209	160	139	68	90	278	346	359	360	253
Money market instruments issued by non-resident businesses	HLND	957	1,239	1,619	2,429	3,516	3,261	2,277	2,321	545	745	449
Other short-term assets not elsewhere classified[13]	JX2I	229	171	138	2,992	1,733	612	1,576	718	725	933	1,064
Balances due from stockbrokers and securities dealers[14]	RYMA	-105	-160	-61	3	-66	25	891	52	90	26	-1
SHORT-TERM ASSETS (excluding derivatives)	**RYME**	17,724	20,073	29,350	26,610	24,824	25,615	27,135	21,889	15,147	15,110	17,798
Derivative contracts with UK and overseas counterparties which have a positive (asset) value[15]	IFVJ	487	104	122	44	45	208	685	455	906	629	3,032
Agents' balances and outstanding premiums in respect of direct insurance and facultative reinsurance contracts[16]												
UK	RYMF	8,081	8,390	8,450	7,991	9,060	8,216	9,022	8,171	8,470	8,222	9,584
Overseas	RYMG	342	816	1,385	572	480	575	55	73	-15	-200	711
Reinsurance, coinsurance and treaty balances[17]												
UK	RYMH	1,182	698	942	934	1,290	1,164	1,092	1,730	-165	-258	-182
Overseas	RYMI	-113	-14	-919	-1,501	-48	-23	537	491	375	921	-4
Outstanding interest, dividends and rents[18]	RYPN	856	982	1,156	905	1,067	1,255	1,108	958	765	726	724
Other debtors and assets not elsewhere classified[19]	RKAC	13,581	12,273	11,462	12,405	15,814	19,096	17,189	10,785	11,064	10,683	14,281
Direct investment for non-insurance subsidiary and associate companies in the UK[20]	RYNR	11,706	13,408	19,028	20,530	20,111	21,954	21,259	21,181	18,206	18,627	19,876
Direct investment for UK insurance subsidiary, associate and holding companies[20]	RYNS	7,190	2,918	2,280	6,071	4,745	6,936	7,669	7,159	6,252	6,795	6,365
Direct investment for overseas subsidiaries, associates, branches and agencies[20]	RYNT	9,014	5,718	5,507	6,446	9,657	9,445	10,815	12,124	9,868	9,073	8,004
TOTAL ASSETS	**RKBY**	122,412	116,690	142,270	149,224	163,030	161,477	176,543	166,631	141,547	143,412	161,227

12.15b INSURANCE COMPANIES' BALANCE SHEET: GENERAL BUSINESS ASSETS AND LIABILITIES AT MARKET VALUES

continued

£ million at end of year

		2002	2003	2004	2005	2006	2007	2008	2009	2010	2011	2012
LIABILITIES												
Borrowing	AHMI	14,772	14,306	17,256	14,790	19,052	18,597	20,214	15,602	14,431	14,281	12,460
Banks and building societies in the UK[9]	JX3J	1,384	2,046	4,519	893	3,148	675	343	744	621	606	819
Other UK[21]	IFHX	10,472	9,342	10,261	11,080	10,445	10,885	13,179	9,965	9,835	8,991	8,401
Overseas[22]	RYMD	2,916	2,918	2,476	2,817	5,459	7,037	6,692	4,893	3,975	4,684	3,240
General business technical reserves[23]	RKCT	62,776	63,463	67,241	71,710	77,221	71,146	76,980	70,947	58,484	57,539	61,771
Provisions for taxation and dividends payable[24]	KVF2	1,904	2,000	2,429	1,806	2,656	2,486	858	345	40	7	240
Other creditors, provisions and liabilities not elsewhere classified[25]	RYPR	8,025	9,567	10,817	10,718	16,226	22,069	21,149	19,976	18,367	19,362	25,757
Excess of total assets over liabilities in respect of minority interests in UK subsidiary companies, shareholders' capital and reserves and any other reserves[26]	A8SI	34,935	27,354	44,527	50,200	47,875	47,179	57,342	59,761	50,225	52,223	60,999
TOTAL LIABILITIES	RKBY	**122,412**	**116,690**	**142,270**	**149,224**	**163,030**	**161,477**	**176,543**	**166,631**	**141,547**	**143,412**	**161,227**

Source: Office for National Statistics

8 Includes money market funds; liquidity funds and cash liquidity funds.
9 Sterling and foreign currency.
10 Includes treasury bills. Excludes British government securities.
11 Sterling and foreign currency commercial paper issued by: banks; building societies; other financial institutions and other issuing companies.
12 Includes floating rate notes maturing within one year of issue.
13 UK and overseas. Excludes derivative contracts.
14 Net of balances owed. Includes amounts due on securities bought and sold for future settlement.
15 Includes credit default products; employee stock options; other options; other swaps; futures; forwards and other derivative contracts not elsewhere classified.
16 Net of insurance liabilities.
17 Net of reinsurance bought and sold.
18 Net value.
19 Includes deferred acquisition costs.
20 Net asset value of attributable companies.
21 Includes issue of securities (other than ordinary shares); issue of sterling commercial paper and other borrowing not elsewhere classified.
22 Includes borrowing from banks; related companies and other borrowing not elsewhere classified.
23 Net of reinsurers share.
24 UK and overseas. Includes deferred tax net of amounts receivable.
25 UK and overseas. Includes derivative contracts which have a negative (liability) value.
26 Includes the 'net worth' of UK branches of overseas companies, including profit and loss account balances.

12.16a Individual insolvencies

England & Wales

Year	Not Seasonally Adjusted			
	Total	Bankruptcy Orders[1]	Debt Relief Orders[2,4]	Individual Voluntary Arrangements[3]
2004	46,652	35,898	:	10,753
2005	67,584	47,291	:	20,293
2006	107,288	62,956	:	44,332
2007	106,645	64,480	:	42,165
2008	106,544	67,428	:	39,116
2009	134,142	74,670	11,831	47,641
2010	135,045	59,173	25,179	50,693
2011	119,943	41,876	29,009	49,058
2012	109,640	31,787	31,179	46,674
2013	100,998	24,571	27,546	48,881

Source: The Insolvency Service

[1] Figures from 2011 Q2 onwards based on the date the bankruptcy order was granted by the court.

[2] Debt Relief Orders (DROs) came into effect on 6 April 2009 as an alternative route into individual insolvency. In April 2011 a change was introduced to the legislation to allow those who have built up value in a pension scheme to apply for debt relief under these provisions.

[3] Includes Deeds of Arrangement.

[4] The data for debt relief orders do not demonstrate a seasonal pattern. The seasonally adjusted data is therefore identical to the unadjusted data.

12.16b Insolvencies

Scotland

Year	not seasonally adjusted		
	Individuals		
	Total	Sequestrations (of which LILA[1])	Protected Trust Deeds
2004	9,321	3,297	6,024
2005	11,897	5,033	6,864
2006	13,789	5,566	8,223
2007	13,924	6,331	7,593
2008	19,991	12,449 (7,133)	7,542
2009	23,541	14,415 (8,774)	9,126
2010	20,344	11,906 (6,801)	8,438
2011	19,650	11,128 (4,812)	8,522
2012	18,402	9,620 (3,886)	8,772
2013	14,250	7,189 (2,728)	7,061

Source: Accountant in Backruptcy

[1] On 1 April 2008, Part 1 of the Bankruptcy and Diligence etc. (Scotland) Act 2007 came into force making significant changes to some aspects of sequestration (bankruptcy), debt relief and debt enforcement in Scotland. This included the introduction of the new route into bankruptcy for people with low income and low assets (LILA). Of the number or sequestrations, individuals who meet LILA criteria are shown in brackets.

12.16c Insolvencies

Northern Ireland

not seasonally adjusted

Year	Total	Individuals		
		Bankruptcy Orders	Debt Relief Orders[1]	Individual Voluntary Arrangements
2004	1,115	666	:	449
2005	1,454	821	:	633
2006	1,809	1,035	:	774
2007	1,338	898	:	440
2008	1,638	1,079	:	559
2009	1,958	1,236	:	722
2010	2,323	1,321	:	1,002
2011	2,839	1,615	112	1,112
2012	3,189	1,452	506	1,231
2013	3,373	1,347	593	1,433

Source: Department for Enterprise, Trade and Investment, Northern Ireland.

[1] Debt relief orders came into effect on 30 June 2011.

12.17a Company insolvencies[1]

England and Wales, not seasonally adjusted

	Total new company insolvencies[2]	Compulsory liquidations[3]	New creditors' voluntary liquidations[2]	Administrations[4]	Company voluntary arrangements	Receivership appointments[5]
2005	16,348	5,233	7,660	2,261	604	590
2006	17,819	5,418	7,719	3,560	534	588
2007	15,774	5,165	7,342	2,512	418	337
2008	21,811	5,494	10,041	4,822	587	867
2009	25,432	5,643	13,434	4,161	726	1,468
2010	20,954	4,792	11,253	2,835	765	1,309
2011	21,858	5,003	11,883	2,808	767	1,397
2012	20,749	4,261	11,895	2,532	839	1,222
2013	18,849	3,632	11,358	2,365	577	917

Sources: Insolvency Service (compulsory liquidations only); Companies House (all other insolvency types).

[1] Includes partnerships.

[2] Excludes creditors' voluntary liquidations following administration

[3] Figures from 2011 Q2 onwards based on the date the winding-up order was granted by the court

[4] Releases prior to 2012 Q4 showed administrations separately as "Administrator Appointments" and "In Administration - Enterprise Act"

[5] Includes Law of Property Act and fixed charge receiverships, which are not insolvencies but which cannot be identified separately to insolvent receiverships. Receivership figures between Q1 2007 and Q1 2008 were previously revised to remove duplication, and are not consistent with those for the earlier period.

12.17b Company insolvencies[1]

Scotland, not seasonally adjusted

	Total company insolvencies[2]	Compulsory liquidations	Creditors' voluntary liquidations[2]	Administrations	Company voluntary arrangements	Receivership appointments
2005	688	420	149	55	8	56
2006	674	416	133	86	5	34
2007	657	439	100	37	6	75
2008	772	437	87	123	4	121
2009	764	432	152	134	6	40
2010	1,340	735	306	243	7	49
2011	1,530	918	319	236	14	43
2012	1,448	926	273	193	25	31
2013	922	450	282	151	16	23

Source: Companies House.

[1] Includes partnerships.

[2] Includes creditors' voluntary liquidations following administration. This is not consistent with the statistics for England and Wales but prior to 2010 it is not possible to separate these CVLs out.

12.17c Company liquidations[1]

Northern Ireland, not seasonally adjusted

	Total company liquidations	Compulsory liquidations[2]	Creditors' voluntary liquidations[3,4]
2005	138	85	53
2006	128	78	50
2007	164	122	42
2008	209	158	51
2009	247	164	83
2010	382	250	132
2011	344	208	136
2012	410	252	158
2013	299	178	121

Sources: Department for Enterprise, Trade and Investment; Companies House

[1] Includes partnerships.

[2] Source: Department for Enterprise, Trade and Investment, Northern Ireland.

[3] Source: Companies House.

[4] Includes creditors' voluntary liquidations following administration. This is not consistent with the statistics for England and Wales but prior to 2011 it is not possible to separate these CVLs out.

12.18a Monetary financial institutions' consolidated balance sheet

£ millions

Not seasonally adjusted

Amounts outstanding of liabilities

LPM	Currency, deposits and money market instruments						Financial derivatives (net)		Other securities issued		Other liabilities		Total liabilities/ assets
	Private sector		Public sector		Non-residents								
	Sterling	Foreign currency	Sterling	Foreign currency	Sterling	Foreign currency	Sterling	Foreign currency	Sterling	Foreign currency	Sterling	Foreign currency	
	VYAX	VYAY	VYAZ	VYBA	VYBB	VYBC	VWKM	VWKN	VWKO	VWKP	VWKQ	VWKR	VYBF
2013 Feb	2,091,791 (aj)	465,991	49,442	5,040	494,660	2,938,407	65,294	-24,995	46,391	235,393	454,767 (aq)	258,655 (ay)	7,080,836
Mar	2,089,138	481,855	36,839	2,690	479,271	2,870,138	44,019	-9,147	45,888	233,296	470,633	262,531	7,007,152
Apr	2,086,636	488,543	43,328	3,445	482,788	2,870,681	43,579	723 (an)	46,096	226,812	467,358 (ar)	234,825 (az)(ba)	6,994,814
May	2,090,823	508,458	43,223	3,564	486,785	2,867,285	34,197	-5,911	44,373	226,022	454,868	237,081	6,990,768
Jun	2,092,997	501,050	45,688	3,185	476,520 (am)	2,798,456 (am)	33,144	-35,673 (ao)	45,110	220,056	438,876	243,678	6,863,086
Jul	2,104,293 (ak)	500,898	50,443	3,079	473,862	2,732,950	33,073	-32,615	44,995	224,621	436,242	248,472	6,820,312
Aug	2,125,268	487,997	46,816	2,973	456,441	2,641,639	6,000	-16,008	44,469	216,531	440,220	234,982	6,687,329
Sep	2,135,808	448,407	44,413	2,394	462,839	2,548,481	-8,715	-941	44,704	212,795	415,178 (as)	247,038 (bb)	6,552,402
Oct	2,134,389	445,933	46,893	3,227	448,102	2,579,764	3,641	-18,222	44,552	213,039	419,465	240,392	6,561,174
Nov	2,144,546	450,727	45,464	3,715	453,865	2,516,546	-9,000	-8,459	44,468	214,099	414,210	259,309	6,529,490
Dec	2,101,999	437,242	42,118	4,107	466,534	2,469,275	-12,032	-9,771	43,042	206,575	412,463	258,154	6,419,706
2014 Jan	2,117,667 (al)	439,870	52,564	4,029	470,946	2,495,753	-11,404	-6,333 (ap)	43,428	200,902	458,797 (at)(au)	228,179 (bc)	6,494,399 (al)(ap)(at)(au)(bc)
Feb	2,138,610	452,053	52,197	4,732	459,100	2,454,141	-14,317	763	42,818	202,494	480,682	192,771	6,466,044
Mar	2,103,891	432,359	46,524	5,395	456,981	2,446,069	-8,795	-11,589	42,794	200,085	469,611	201,766	6,385,091
Apr	2,097,400	433,986	45,842	3,822	445,539	2,441,786	-25,206	-3,256	42,475	203,787	474,046	199,670	6,359,891
May	2,095,978	435,826	44,819	3,795	459,423	2,472,659	-13,119	3,614	42,091	207,292	483,706	186,244	6,422,330
Jun	2,105,099	412,058	43,649	3,365	453,125	2,406,656	-21,592	3,877	41,585	205,036	471,795	199,789	6,324,439
Jul	2,102,819	402,030	48,675	3,300	453,432	2,445,462	-20,437	5,077	42,705	204,005	449,121 (av)(aw)	176,847 (bd)	6,313,035 (av)(aw)(bd)
Aug	2,115,274	412,129	50,544	3,772	443,456	2,481,763	4,302	-4,382	41,626	206,418	453,506 (ax)	166,168	6,374,577 (ax)
Sep	2,102,268	410,435	43,305	4,098	444,223	2,472,728	-2,215	-1,604	41,203	206,296	435,114	196,696	6,352,547
Oct	2,097,658	401,668	49,660	5,797	437,582	2,471,144	472	1,955	41,674	207,615	458,177	167,464	6,340,868
Nov	2,103,021	418,378	50,115	4,932	431,981	2,564,249	22,255	-11,655	39,942	214,203	457,619	175,702	6,470,742
Dec	2,098,499	401,426	46,771	4,655	453,465	2,476,869	23,940	-3,019	39,128	209,595	464,297	165,746	6,381,374
2015 Jan	2,075,141	410,798	47,882	3,509	448,958	2,575,945	41,073	29	39,932	210,609	482,461	154,258	6,490,596

Source: Bank of England

Notes to table

Movements in amounts outstanding can reflect breaks in data series as well as underlying flows. For changes data, users are recommended to refer directly to the appropriate series or data tables. Further explanation can be found at: www.bankofengland.co.uk/statistics/Pages/iadb/notesiadb/Changes_flows_growth_rates.aspx.

(aj) Due to improvements in reporting at one institution, the amounts outstanding increased by £6bn. This effect has been adjusted out of the flows for February 2013.

(ak) Due to improvements in reporting at one institution, the amounts outstanding increased by £8bn. This effect has been adjusted out of the flows for July 2013.

(al) Due to a change in treatment at one institution, the amounts outstanding increased by £19bn. This effect has been adjusted out of the flows for January 2014.

(am) Due to a change in treatment at one reporting institution, the amounts outstanding increased by £11bn. The effect has been adjusted out of the flows for June 2013.

(an) Due to improvements in reporting at one institution, the amounts outstanding decreased by £12bn. The effect has been adjusted out of the flows for April 2013.

(ao) Due to a change in treatment at one reporting institution, the amounts outstanding decreased by £11bn. The effect has been adjusted out of the flows for June 2013.

(ap) Due to a restructuring at one reporting institution, the amounts outstanding decreased by £13bn. The effect has been adjusted out of the flows for January 2014.

(aq) Due to improvements in reporting at one institution, the amounts outstanding increased by £50bn. This effect has been adjusted out of the flows for February 2013.

(ar) Due to improvements in reporting at one institution, the amounts outstanding decreased by £6bn. The effect has been adjusted out of the flows for April 2013.

(as) Due to improvements in reporting at one institution, the amounts outstanding decreased by £8bn. The effect has been adjusted out of the flows for September 2013.

(at) Due to improvements in reporting at one institution, the amounts outstanding increased by £18bn. The effect has been adjusted out of the flows for January 2014.

(au) Due to improvements in reporting at one institution, the amounts outstanding decreased by £18bn. This effect has been adjusted out of the flows for January 2014.

(av) Due to improvements in reporting at one institution, the amounts outstanding decreased by £36bn. The effect has been adjusted out of the flows for July 2014.

(aw) Due to improvements in reporting at one institution, the amounts outstanding decreased by £16bn. The effect has been adjusted out of the flows for July 2014.

(ax) Due to improvements in reporting at one institution, the amounts outstanding increased by £9bn. This effect has been adjusted out of the flows for August 2014.

(ay) Due to improvements in reporting at one institution, the amounts outstanding decreased by £8bn. The effect has been adjusted out of the flows for February 2013.

(az) Due to improvements in reporting at one institution, the amounts outstanding increased by £11bn. The effect has been adjusted out of the flows for April 2013.

(ba) Due to improvements in reporting at one institution, the amounts outstanding decreased by £8bn. The effect has been adjusted out of the flows for April 2013.

(bb) Due to improvements in reporting at one institution, the amounts outstanding increased by £8bn. The effect has been adjusted out of the flows for September 2013.

(bc) Due to a restructuring at one reporting institution, the amounts outstanding increased by £13bn. The effect has been adjusted out of the flows for January 2014.

(bd) Due to improvements in reporting at one institution, the amounts outstanding decreased by £11bn. This effect has been adjusted out of the flows for July 2014.

12.18b Monetary financial institutions' consolidated balances

£ millions   Not seasonally adjusted

Amounts outstanding of assets

	Loans						Securities (other than financial derivatives)						Other assets	
	Private sector		Public sector		Non-residents		Private sector		Public sector		Non-residents			
	Sterling	Foreign currency	Sterling	Foreign currency	Sterling	Foreign currency	Sterling	Foreign currency	Sterling	Foreign currency	Sterling	Foreign currency	Sterling	Foreign currency
LPM	VYBG	VYBH	VYBI	VYBJ	VYBK	VYBL	VYBM	VYBN	VYBO	VYBP	VYBQ	VYBR	VYBS	VYBT
2013 Feb	2,026,750	442,983	16,928	890	246,488	2,748,334	267,718 (bi)(bi)	49,985	494,357	53	46,811	561,548	120,713	57,277 (bq)
Mar	2,016,645	448,213	17,135	952	228,816	2,713,118	264,642	50,123	501,632	122	46,267	540,513	120,215	58,756
Apr	2,003,806	454,057	15,589	1,373	228,736	2,710,246	261,967	50,227	505,596	29	52,522	539,807	119,581	51,278 (br)
May	2,000,758	475,471	17,306	1,483	232,227	2,686,375	258,092	53,119	496,913	7	50,865	545,226	119,494	53,432
Jun	1,994,394	438,196	17,435	1,623	237,729	2,637,951	255,543	52,967	488,631	17	44,022	520,102	122,236	52,241
Jul	1,997,505	420,039	16,001	1,786	230,858	2,598,733	258,168	53,753	498,639	15	43,858	527,678	120,615	52,666
Aug	2,008,057	411,218	14,907	1,591	230,639	2,489,672	259,900	54,854	492,817	2	41,289	509,267	119,159	53,956
Sep	2,019,430	392,819	16,685	1,359	224,858	2,393,271	257,299	53,713	492,922	1	40,694	488,830	119,336	51,185
Oct	2,012,761	395,492	15,966	1,370	226,730	2,373,396	249,717	53,639	505,032	63	42,732	514,771	118,635	50,871
Nov	2,012,915	393,482	14,767	1,428	229,335	2,332,948	252,170	52,409	505,807	83	43,097	521,360	120,737	48,951
Dec	1,984,026	381,250	13,351	2,214	230,884	2,301,474	245,988	52,551	497,773	61	41,140	498,881	119,673	50,439
2014 Jan	1,992,716 (be)(bf)(bg)	391,669	15,406	3,515	238,866	2,348,559	246,572 (bf)(bk)	46,103 (bl)	509,658	74	48,246	486,000	116,826	50,190
Feb	1,995,932	381,393	16,836	2,953	248,046	2,330,718	238,326	45,461	511,401	76	47,536	477,833	118,937	50,596
Mar	1,948,978	362,527	17,596	2,381	243,815	2,341,463	234,654	46,220	500,619	87	47,418	472,507	116,680	50,143
Apr	1,934,268	376,982	16,587	2,136	233,751	2,325,774	232,686	45,246	504,639	91	44,889	476,270	116,015	50,557
May	1,934,236	373,558	15,193	3,161	245,815	2,347,045	238,537	45,683	509,136	70	46,519	496,519	118,871	47,987
Jun	1,940,974 (bh)	349,241	13,431	2,480	243,867	2,282,857	233,839	44,811	505,652	38	46,286	492,948	119,915	48,100
Jul	1,942,994	347,104	12,049	2,472	231,777	2,332,008	238,782	41,071	511,671	91	46,937	479,295 (bm)	70,428 (bn)(bo)	56,356
Aug	1,946,690	344,722	15,790	2,005	250,786	2,351,854	236,781	41,128	525,572	66	45,825	485,931	78,200 (bp)	49,227
Sep	1,946,448	351,903	13,853	2,160	245,441	2,350,666	231,766	41,373	508,206	53	47,814	489,867	75,712	47,284
Oct	1,942,335	343,125	15,767	4,044	243,101	2,323,793	224,241	40,647	529,575	196	48,819	502,371	76,892	45,961
Nov	1,937,096	354,425	17,381	3,600	242,657	2,390,074	227,568	41,665	549,076	247	47,258	534,803	78,602	46,290
Dec	1,920,959	334,404	15,870	2,565	241,383	2,355,947	239,634	28,978	552,494	248	50,371	518,324	78,389	41,809
2015 Jan	1,926,859	349,005	15,027	2,599	244,802	2,422,505	218,896	28,229	569,058	224	50,773	541,298	79,896	41,425

Source: Bank of England

Notes to table

Movements in amounts outstanding can reflect breaks in data series as well as underlying flows. For changes data, users are recommended to refer directly to the appropriate series or data tables. Further explanation can be found at: www.bankofengland.co.uk/statistics/Pages/iadb/notesiadb/Changes_flows_growth_rates.aspx.

(be) Due to a change in treatment at one institution, the amounts outstanding increased by £19bn. This effect has been adjusted out of the flows for January 2014.
(bf) Due to improvements in reporting at one institution, the amounts outstanding decreased by £4bn. This effect has been adjusted out of the flows for January 2014.
(bg) Due to improvements in reporting at one institution, the amounts outstanding increased by £2bn. This effect has been adjusted out of the flows for January 2014.
(bh) Due to a change in accounting treatment at one reporting institution, the amounts outstanding increased by £2bn. This effect has been adjusted out of the flows for June 2014.
(bi) Due to improvements in reporting at one institution, the amounts outstanding increased by £6bn. This effect has been adjusted out of the flows for February 2013.
(bj) Due to improvements in reporting at one institution, the amounts outstanding increased by £5bn. This effect has been adjusted out of the flows for February 2013.
(bk) Due to improvements in reporting at one institution, the amounts outstanding increased by £4bn. This effect has been adjusted out of the flows for January 2014.
(bl) Due to improvements in reporting at one institution, the amounts outstanding decreased by £3bn. This effect has been adjusted out of the flows for January 2014.
(bm) Due to improvements in reporting at one institution, the amounts outstanding decreased by £11bn. This effect has been adjusted out of the flows for July 2014.
(bn) Due to improvements in reporting at one institution, the amounts outstanding decreased by £36bn. This effect has been adjusted out of the flows for July 2014.
(bo) Due to improvements in reporting at one institution, the amounts outstanding decreased by £13bn. This effect has been adjusted out of the flows for July 2014.
(bp) Due to improvements in reporting at one institution, the amounts outstanding increased by £9bn. This effect has been adjusted out of the flows for August 2014.
(bq) Due to improvements in reporting at one institution, the amounts outstanding decreased by £8bn. The effect has been adjusted out of the flows for February 2013
(br) Due to improvements in reporting at one institution, the amounts outstanding decreased by £6bn. The effect has been adjusted out of the flows for April 2013.

12.18c Monetary financial institutions' consolidated balance sheet

£ millions   Not seasonally adjusted

Changes in liabilities

	Currency, deposits and money market instruments						Financial derivatives (net)		Other securities issued		Other liabilities		Total liabilities/ assets
	Private sector		Public sector		Non-residents								
	Sterling	Foreign currency	Sterling	Foreign currency	Sterling	Foreign currency	Sterling	Foreign currency	Sterling	Foreign currency	Sterling	Foreign currency	
LPM	VYAA	VYAB	VYAC	VYAD	VYAE	VYAF	VWKG	VWKH	VWKI	VWKJ	VWKK	VWKL	VYAI
2013 Feb	-1,264	-892	2,216	1,912	-234	-5,447	30,417	-30,214	1,002	439	-19,911	3,182	-18,793
Mar	-3,050	19,686	-12,603	-2,321	-15,336	-43,089	-21,276	15,911	-502	1,990	11,053	4,768	-44,769
Apr	-1,299	7,060	6,489	794	6,310	37,834	-4,183	19,568	207	-4,398	-3,127	-24,251	41,005
May	4,108	12,028	-105	76	4,186	-47,569	-9,439	-6,206	-1,723	-3,299	2,123	6,244	-39,577
Jun	2,724	-7,180	2,466	-387	-10,097	-90,122	-1,053	-12,933	737	-6,121	2,466	15,689	-103,811
Jul	2,833	-10,300	4,754	-142	-2,639	-90,680	357	3,997	-114	1,419	-2,403	12,299	-80,619
Aug	19,712	-1,891	-3,627	-38	-12,572	-33,524	-27,073	14,795	-526	-2,396	15,718	-3,002	-34,424
Sep	9,907	-25,895	-2,403	-499	6,884	-6,410	-14,715	13,023	235	1,690	-15,329	5,694	-27,820
Oct	-1,286	-6,315	2,480	812	-14,922	9,177	-12,356	-16,467	-152	-1,893	-800	-13,043	-30,053
Nov	12,637	14,151	-1,780	556	5,895	-20,812	-12,541	8,849	-52	3,059	4,617	25,981	40,560
Dec	-41,606	-11,624	-3,446	408	11,120	-35,836	-3,282	-1,250	-1,426	-7,015	13,231	-2,511	-83,238
2014 Jan	-453	694	10,446	-61	4,497	36,906	-980	8,984	386	-5,072	36,123	-44,770	46,700
Feb	21,013	17,561	-343	720	-11,201	-21,043	-2,913	6,691	-610	2,314	23,793	-37,832	-1,850
Mar	-34,680	-19,647	-5,673	655	-2,167	-16,329	5,523	-12,164	-24	-3,041	-5,192	9,681	-83,059
Apr	-6,895	5,219	-682	-1,542	-11,295	14,719	-16,411	8,005	-320	5,324	781	-2,672	-5,771
May	-907	2,283	-964	-18	13,898	35,809	12,087	6,431	-384	4,317	6,322	-18,535	60,340
Jun	5,441	-15,968	-1,140	-374	-4,625	-31,184	-8,344	3,147	-603	1,656	-4,691	15,958	-40,726
Jul	-4,711	-11,020	5,089	-63	-311	30,862	1,155	766	1,120	-384	27,463	-22,028	27,937
Aug	10,459	6,950	1,869	448	-10,502	15,786	24,740	-9,431	-1,080	1,283	-21,284	-12,179	7,059
Sep	-14,747	-2,444	-7,285	342	2,245	-16,232	-6,518	2,833	-422	1,075	-11,280	32,542	-19,891
Oct	-110	-11,195	1,681	933	-6,700	-21,602	2,688	3,383	471	27	14,066	-31,383	-47,742
Nov	6,623	12,492	507	-914	-5,347	53,188	21,783	-13,737	-1,732	3,660	-18,439	1,113	59,197
Dec	-4,632	-14,304	-3,344	-236	21,423	-70,965	1,714	8,892	-814	-2,017	4,208	-9,823	-69,896
2015 Jan	-22,522	4,257	1,110	-1,188	-3,826	75,490	17,133	4,846	804	1,863	-10,627	-35,203	32,138

Source: Bank of England

12.18d Monetary financial institutions' consolidated balance sheet

£ millions   Not seasonally adjusted

Changes in assets

	Loans						Securities (other than financial derivatives)						Other assets	
	Private sector		Public sector		Non-residents		Private sector		Public sector		Non-residents			
	Sterling	Foreign currency	Sterling	Foreign currency	Sterling	Foreign currency	Sterling	Foreign currency	Sterling	Foreign currency	Sterling	Foreign currency	Sterling	Foreign currency
	VYAJ	VYAK	VYAL	VYAM	VYAN	VYAO	VYAP	VYAQ	VYAR	VYAS	VYAT	VYAU	VYAV	VYAW
LPM														
2013 Feb	-4,929	6,833	485	323	-1,927	3,939	-3,014	-2,533	-1,114	-98	-3,900	-10,960	-230	-1,667
Mar	-8,732	9,169	146	78	-18,128	-8,244	-4,151	444	1,858	69	-491	-18,363	-234	1,811
Apr	-6,777	12,871	-1,546	421	183	33,140	-3,421	818	-1,573	-91	6,614	457	-235	144
May	-2,014	13,663	1,716	100	3,841	-62,871	-3,643	2,001	4,445	-23	-1,653	3,635	-167	1,392
Jun	-5,837	-37,801	129	135	5,590	-53,749	11	-209	6,436	10	-5,665	-14,461	2,858	-1,259
Jul	-1,745	-13,203	-1,434	129	-6,801	-62,934	1,251	-165	7,146	-2	-366	591	-440	-2,645
Aug	14,348	458	-1,094	-149	1,562	-52,985	2,913	2,156	987	-13	-1,507	-2,540	-756	2,196
Sep	12,151	-4,932	1,777	-203	-5,434	-15,099	-3,588	620	-60	-1	816	-12,897	165	-1,134
Oct	-5,948	-1,071	-669	-5	1,874	-40,375	-9,761	-517	8,879	62	1,603	16,609	-758	25
Nov	6,115	4,952	-1,308	82	2,589	-581	2,517	-300	5,950	22	1,487	17,879	2,175	-1,018
Dec	-25,188	-10,173	-1,481	786	2,607	-19,702	-6,118	428	621	-22	-1,282	-24,383	-1,136	1,805
2014 Jan	-8,513	8,972	2,054	1,337	7,899	38,793	-198	-3,092	2,739	12	1,629	-2,755	484	-2,663
Feb	4,653	-5,952	1,432	-574	9,136	2,209	-8,665	-121	2,353	4	-381	-8,970	2,130	896
Mar	-45,150	-19,781	685	-585	-4,289	4,336	-3,541	597	-6,681	11	-265	-5,638	-2,156	-601
Apr	-14,172	17,459	-1,009	-228	-11,158	3,012	-2,110	-553	615	5	-2,389	4,613	-697	841
May	1,134	-3,113	-1,395	1,038	12,589	26,254	5,218	380	453	-21	1,924	15,524	736	-382
Jun	5,611	-18,316	-1,762	-634	-1,968	-25,969	-4,393	-151	1,835	-31	446	2,613	1,190	804
Jul	2,320	-3,355	-1,351	5	-12,479	41,109	5,302	-250	2,327	52	579	-6,091	138	-370
Aug	1,897	-5,241	3,741	-477	19,539	-970	-4,937	-344	-1,004	-26	-2,476	-3,549	-1,351	2,257
Sep	-126	6,998	-1,937	160	-4,353	-9,183	-4,157	-66	-12,413	-14	1,875	8,011	-2,476	-2,209
Oct	-4,757	-10,276	1,260	593	-2,233	-45,338	-7,976	-977	14,600	34	202	6,798	1,167	-839
Nov	-3,660	6,301	1,614	-506	-309	31,329	1,713	385	4,479	47	-2,868	19,191	1,678	-197
Dec	-12,534	-17,027	-1,511	-985	525	-18,555	11,913	-12,504	-3,131	5	1,580	-13,241	-143	-4,290
2015 Jan	7,336	12,174	-843	93	3,465	32,706	-23,678	-985	-6,910	-22	-2,004	10,301	1,565	-1,060

Source: Bank of England

12.19 Selected interest rates, exchange rates and security prices

Monthly average of 4 UK Banks' base rates IUMAAMIH [a]		Monthly average rate of discount, 3 month Treasury bills, Sterling IUMAAJNB		Monthly average yield from British Government Securities, 20 year Nominal Par Yield IUMALNPY [b] [c]		Monthly average Spot exchange rate, US$ into Sterling XUMAUSS	
31-Jan-06	4.5	31-Jan-06	4.3906	31-Jan-06	3.9287	31-Jan-06	1.7678
28-Feb-06	4.5	28-Feb-06	4.3839	28-Feb-06	3.9954	28-Feb-06	1.747
31-Mar-06	4.5	31-Mar-06	4.3956	31-Mar-06	4.151	31-Mar-06	1.7435
30-Apr-06	4.5	30-Apr-06	4.4196	30-Apr-06	4.3575	30-Apr-06	1.7685
31-May-06	4.5	31-May-06	4.5012	31-May-06	4.4361	31-May-06	1.8702
30-Jun-06	4.5	30-Jun-06	4.5414	30-Jun-06	4.4775	30-Jun-06	1.8428
31-Jul-06	4.5	31-Jul-06	4.534	31-Jul-06	4.4631	31-Jul-06	1.8447
31-Aug-06	4.73	31-Aug-06	4.7544	31-Aug-06	4.4259	31-Aug-06	1.8944
30-Sep-06	4.75	30-Sep-06	4.8359	30-Sep-06	4.3032	30-Sep-06	1.8847
31-Oct-06	4.75	31-Oct-06	4.9357	31-Oct-06	4.3287	31-Oct-06	1.8755
30-Nov-06	4.93	30-Nov-06	5.0095	30-Nov-06	4.2572	30-Nov-06	1.9119
31-Dec-06	5	31-Dec-06	5.0759	31-Dec-06	4.3351	31-Dec-06	1.9633
31-Jan-07	5.17	31-Jan-07	5.304	31-Jan-07	4.5131	31-Jan-07	1.9587
28-Feb-07	5.25	28-Feb-07	5.3393	28-Feb-07	4.5597	28-Feb-07	1.9581
31-Mar-07	5.25	31-Mar-07	5.3274	31-Mar-07	4.5195	31-Mar-07	1.9471
30-Apr-07	5.25	30-Apr-07	5.4329	30-Apr-07	4.735	30-Apr-07	1.9909
31-May-07	5.43	31-May-07	5.5516	31-May-07	4.8163	31-May-07	1.9836
30-Jun-07	5.5	30-Jun-07	5.6702	30-Jun-07	5.0696	30-Jun-07	1.9864
31-Jul-07	5.72	31-Jul-07	5.7742	31-Jul-07	5.026	31-Jul-07	2.0338
31-Aug-07	5.75	31-Aug-07	5.7943	31-Aug-07	4.8049	31-Aug-07	2.0111
30-Sep-07	5.75	30-Sep-07	5.6896	30-Sep-07	4.7407	30-Sep-07	2.0185
31-Oct-07	5.75	31-Oct-07	5.6058	31-Oct-07	4.7394	31-Oct-07	2.0446
30-Nov-07	5.75	30-Nov-07	5.4986	30-Nov-07	4.5924	30-Nov-07	2.0701
31-Dec-07	5.54	31-Dec-07	5.3034	31-Dec-07	4.5916	31-Dec-07	2.0185
31-Jan-08	5.5	31-Jan-08	5.1215	31-Jan-08	4.4578	31-Jan-08	1.9698
29-Feb-08	5.3	29-Feb-08	5.0178	29-Feb-08	4.6173	29-Feb-08	1.9638
31-Mar-08	5.25	31-Mar-08	4.8835	31-Mar-08	4.5401	31-Mar-08	2.0032
30-Apr-08	5.08	30-Apr-08	4.8258	30-Apr-08	4.7315	30-Apr-08	1.9817
31-May-08	5	31-May-08	4.9496	31-May-08	4.8539	31-May-08	1.9641
30-Jun-08	5	30-Jun-08	5.1138	30-Jun-08	5.0261	30-Jun-08	1.9658
31-Jul-08	5	31-Jul-08	5.0843	31-Jul-08	4.9391	31-Jul-08	1.988
31-Aug-08	5	31-Aug-08	4.9539	31-Aug-08	4.7438	31-Aug-08	1.8889
30-Sep-08	5	30-Sep-08	4.7425	30-Sep-08	4.6619	30-Sep-08	1.7986
31-Oct-08	4.61	31-Oct-08	3.6788	31-Oct-08	4.7579	31-Oct-08	1.69
30-Nov-08	3.23	30-Nov-08	1.9948	30-Nov-08	4.6898	30-Nov-08	1.5338
31-Dec-08	2.14	31-Dec-08	1.2875	31-Dec-08	4.1461	31-Dec-08	1.4859
31-Jan-09	1.6	31-Jan-09	0.8945	31-Jan-09	4.2758	31-Jan-09	1.4452
28-Feb-09	1.08	28-Feb-09	0.7177	28-Feb-09	4.3394	28-Feb-09	1.4411
31-Mar-09	0.57	31-Mar-09	0.6035	31-Mar-09	4.007	31-Mar-09	1.4174
30-Apr-09	0.5	30-Apr-09	0.625	30-Apr-09	4.2419	30-Apr-09	1.4715
31-May-09	0.5	31-May-09	0.5271	31-May-09	4.3752	31-May-09	1.5429
30-Jun-09	0.5	30-Jun-09	0.5037	30-Jun-09	4.471	30-Jun-09	1.6366
31-Jul-09	0.5	31-Jul-09	0.4397	31-Jul-09	4.4588	31-Jul-09	1.6366
31-Aug-09	0.5	31-Aug-09	0.3946	31-Aug-09	4.2164	31-Aug-09	1.6539
30-Sep-09	0.5	30-Sep-09	0.3761	30-Sep-09	4.0688	30-Sep-09	1.6328
31-Oct-09	0.5	31-Oct-09	0.4315	31-Oct-09	4.05	31-Oct-09	1.6199
30-Nov-09	0.5	30-Nov-09	0.4459	30-Nov-09	4.2177	30-Nov-09	1.6597
31-Dec-09	0.5	31-Dec-09	0.3587	31-Dec-09	4.3306	31-Dec-09	1.6239
31-Jan-10	0.5	31-Jan-10	0.4874	31-Jan-10	4.4161	31-Jan-10	1.6162
28-Feb-10	0.5	28-Feb-10	0.4878	28-Feb-10	4.5158	28-Feb-10	1.5615
31-Mar-10	0.5	31-Mar-10	0.5109	31-Mar-10	4.5698	31-Mar-10	1.5053
30-Apr-10	0.5	30-Apr-10	0.5083	30-Apr-10	4.558	30-Apr-10	1.534

12.19 Selected interest rates, exchange rates and security prices

Monthly average of 4 UK Banks' base rates IUMAAMIH [a]		Monthly average rate of discount, 3 month Treasury bills, Sterling IUMAAJNB		Monthly average yield from British Government Securities, 20 year Nominal Par Yield IUMALNPY [b] [c]		Monthly average Spot exchange rate, US$ into Sterling XUMAUSS	
31-May-10	0.5	31-May-10	0.4976	31-May-10	4.3143	31-May-10	1.4627
30-Jun-10	0.5	30-Jun-10	0.4839	30-Jun-10	4.2079	30-Jun-10	1.4761
31-Jul-10	0.5	31-Jul-10	0.498	31-Jul-10	4.1754	31-Jul-10	1.5299
31-Aug-10	0.5	31-Aug-10	0.4945	31-Aug-10	3.9824	31-Aug-10	1.566
30-Sep-10	0.5	30-Sep-10	0.4966	30-Sep-10	3.8954	30-Sep-10	1.5578
31-Oct-10	0.5	31-Oct-10	0.5061	31-Oct-10	3.8876	31-Oct-10	1.5862
30-Nov-10	0.5	30-Nov-10	0.4935	30-Nov-10	4.1149	30-Nov-10	1.5961
31-Dec-10	0.5	31-Dec-10	0.4913	31-Dec-10	4.2568	31-Dec-10	1.5603
31-Jan-11	0.5	31-Jan-11	0.5055	31-Jan-11	4.3204	31-Jan-11	1.5795
28-Feb-11	0.5	28-Feb-11	0.5363	28-Feb-11	4.405	28-Feb-11	1.613
31-Mar-11	0.5	31-Mar-11	0.5603	31-Mar-11	4.298	31-Mar-11	1.6159
30-Apr-11	0.5	30-Apr-11	0.5676	30-Apr-11	4.2933	30-Apr-11	1.6345
31-May-11	0.5	31-May-11	0.5265	31-May-11	4.1371	31-May-11	1.6312
30-Jun-11	0.5	30-Jun-11	0.5174	30-Jun-11	4.1277	30-Jun-11	1.6214
31-Jul-11	0.5	31-Jul-11	0.4996	31-Jul-11	4.0974	31-Jul-11	1.6145
31-Aug-11	0.5	31-Aug-11	0.4531	31-Aug-11	3.7132	31-Aug-11	1.6348
30-Sep-11	0.5	30-Sep-11	0.4649	30-Sep-11	3.4205	30-Sep-11	1.5783
31-Oct-11	0.5	31-Oct-11	0.4608	31-Oct-11	3.2581	31-Oct-11	1.576
30-Nov-11	0.5	30-Nov-11	0.4387	30-Nov-11	3.0313	30-Nov-11	1.5804
31-Dec-11	0.5	31-Dec-11	0.2996	31-Dec-11	2.9803	31-Dec-11	1.5585
31-Jan-12	0.5	31-Jan-12	0.3239	31-Jan-12	2.906	31-Jan-12	1.551
29-Feb-12	0.5	29-Feb-12	0.3912	29-Feb-12	3.089	29-Feb-12	1.5802
31-Mar-12	0.5	31-Mar-12	0.4248	31-Mar-12	3.1744	31-Mar-12	1.5823
30-Apr-12	0.5	30-Apr-12	0.4236	30-Apr-12	3.1259	30-Apr-12	1.6014
31-May-12	0.5	31-May-12	0.3561	31-May-12	2.9073	31-May-12	1.5905
30-Jun-12	0.5	30-Jun-12	0.3422	30-Jun-12	2.725	30-Jun-12	1.5571
31-Jul-12	0.5	31-Jul-12	0.2943	31-Jul-12	2.6453	31-Jul-12	1.5589
31-Aug-12	0.5	31-Aug-12	0.2398	31-Aug-12	2.65	31-Aug-12	1.5719
30-Sep-12	0.5	30-Sep-12	0.2478	30-Sep-12	2.7497	30-Sep-12	1.6116
31-Oct-12	0.5	31-Oct-12	0.2368	31-Oct-12	2.7969	31-Oct-12	1.6079
30-Nov-12	0.5	30-Nov-12	0.2243	30-Nov-12	2.7846	30-Nov-12	1.5961
31-Dec-12	0.5	31-Dec-12	0.249	31-Dec-12	2.8391	31-Dec-12	1.6144
31-Jan-13	0.5	31-Jan-13	0.2677	31-Jan-13	3.0069	31-Jan-13	1.5957
28-Feb-13	0.5	28-Feb-13	0.3147	28-Feb-13	3.1035	28-Feb-13	1.5478
31-Mar-13	0.5	31-Mar-13	0.3391	31-Mar-13	2.9654	31-Mar-13	1.5076
30-Apr-13	0.5	30-Apr-13	0.3447	30-Apr-13	2.776	30-Apr-13	1.5316
31-May-13	0.5	31-May-13	0.3065	31-May-13	2.9096	31-May-13	1.5285
30-Jun-13	0.5	30-Jun-13	0.3066	30-Jun-13	3.1584	30-Jun-13	1.5478
31-Jul-13	0.5	31-Jul-13	0.3124	31-Jul-13	3.2719	31-Jul-13	1.5172
31-Aug-13	0.5	31-Aug-13	0.2812	31-Aug-13	3.4083	31-Aug-13	1.5507
30-Sep-13	0.5	30-Sep-13	0.289	30-Sep-13	3.4662	30-Sep-13	1.5865
31-Oct-13	0.5	31-Oct-13	0.3141	31-Oct-13	3.3198	31-Oct-13	1.6094
30-Nov-13	0.5	30-Nov-13	0.2865	30-Nov-13	3.3978	30-Nov-13	1.6104
31-Dec-13	0.5	31-Dec-13	0.2555	31-Dec-13	3.497	31-Dec-13	1.6375

Source: Bank of England

Notes:

[a] Data obtained from Barclays Bank, Lloyds Bank, HSBC, and National Westminster Bank whose rates are used to compile this series. Where all the rates did not change on the same day a spread is shown.

[b] Calculated using the Variable Roughness Penalty (VRP) model.

[c] The monthly average figure is calculated using the available daily observations within each month.

12.20 Mergers and Acquisitions in the UK by other UK Companies: Category of Expenditure

£ million

		Expenditure				Percentage of Expenditure		
		Cash						
	Total	Independent Companies	Subsidiaries	Issues of Ordinary Shares[2]	Issues of Fixed Interest Securities[2]	Cash	Issues of Ordinary Shares	Issues of Fixed Interest Securities
	DUCM	DWVW	DWVX	AIHD	AIHE	DWVY	DWVZ	DWWA
Annual								
2003	18,679	8,956	7,183	1,667	873	86	9	5
2004	31,408	12,080	7,822	10,338	1,168	63	33	4
2005	25,134	13,425	8,510	2,768	431	87	11	2
2006	28,511	..	8,131	..	335	..	..	2
2007	26,778	13,671	6,507	4,909	1,691	76	18	6
2008	36,469	31,333	2,851	1,910	375	94	5	1
2009	12,195	2,937	709	8,435	114	30	69	1
2010[1]	12,605	6,175	4,520	1,560	350	85	12	3
2011	8,089	4,432	2,667	719	271	87	10	4
2012	3,413	1,937	789	419	268	82	10	8
2013	7,665 †	3,690 †	3,475	353	147	92	6	2
Quarterly								
2009 Q2	729	130	150	437	12	38	60	2
2009 Q3	1,886	1,409	214	254	9	87	13	–
2009 Q4	1,374	1,066	217	45	46	94	3	3
2010 Q1[1]	1,361	765	525	58	13	95	4	1
2010 Q2	2,032	986	714	275	57	83	14	3
2010 Q3	2,949	1,165	814	839	131	68	28	4
2010 Q4	6,263	3,259	2,467	388	149	92	6	2
2011 Q1	1,500	552	651	240	57	80	16	4
2011 Q2	3,346	2,355	704	204	83	92	6	2
2011 Q3	1,452	828	462	75	87	89	5	6
2011 Q4	1,791	697	850	200	44	87	11	2
2012 Q1	1,070	518	199	323	30	67	30	3
2012 Q2	1,041	575	269	54	143	81	5	14
2012 Q3	610	409	100	8	93	84	1	15
2012 Q4	692	435	221	34	2	95	5	–
2013 Q1	2,825	567	2,216	26	16	98	1	1
2013 Q2	2,438	1,992	316	80	50	95	3	2
2013 Q3	1,166 †	587 †	332	230	17	79	20	1
2013 Q4	1,236	544	611	17	64	94	1	5
2014 Q1	697	582	95	19	–	97	3	–

† indicates earliest revision, if any
– indicates data is zero or less than £0.5m
Disclosive data indicated by ..

1 The deal identification threshold has been increased from Q1 2010 from £0.1m to £1.0m and as a consequence there may be a discontinuity in the number and value of transactions reported.
2 Issued to the vendor company as payment.

Source: Mergers and Acquisitions Surveys, Office for National Statistics

this page is intentionally blank

Service industry

Chapter 13

Service industry

Annual Business Inquiry (Tables 13.1, 13.3 and 13.4)

The Annual Business Inquiry (ABI) estimates cover all UK businesses registered for Value Added Tax (VAT) and/or Pay As You Earn (PAYE). The businesses are classified to the 2007 Standard Industrial Classification (SIC(2007)) headings listed in the tables. The ABI obtains details on these businesses from the Office for National Statistics (ONS) Inter-Departmental Business Register (IDBR).

As with all its statistical inquiries, ONS is concerned to minimise the form-filling burden of individual contributors and as such the ABI is a sample inquiry. The sample was designed as a stratified random sample of about 66,600 businesses; the inquiry population is stratified by SIC(2007) and employment using the information from the register.

The inquiry results are grossed up to the total population so that they relate to all active UK businesses on the IDBR for the sectors covered.

The results meet a wide range of needs for government, economic analysts and the business community at large. In official statistics the inquiry is an important source for the national accounts and input-output tables, and also provides weights for the indices of production and producer prices. Additionally, inquiry results enable the UK to meet statistical requirements of the European Union.

Data from 1995 and 1996 were calculated on a different basis from those for 1997 and later years. In order to provide a link between the two data series, the 1995 and 1996 data were subsequently reworked to provide estimates on a consistent basis.

Revised ABI results down to SIC(2007) 4 digit class level for 1995–2007, giving both analysis and tabular detail, are available from the ONS website at: www.statistics.gov.uk, with further extracts and bespoke analyses available on request. This service replaces existing publications.

Retail trade: index numbers of value and volume (Table 13.2)

The main purpose of the Retail Sales Inquiry (RSI) is to provide up-to-date information on short period movements in the level of retail sales. In principle, the RSI covers the retail activity of every business classified in the retail sector (Division 52 of the 2007 Standard Industrial Classification (SIC(2007)) in Great Britain. A business will be classified to the retail sector if its main activity is one of the individual 4 digit SIC categories within Division 52. The retail activity of a business is then defined by its retail turnover, that is the sale of all retail goods (note that petrol, for example, is not a retail good).

The RSI is compiled from the information returned to the statutory inquiries into the distribution and services sector. The inquiry is addressed to a stratified sample of 5,000 businesses classified to the retail sector, the stratification being by 'type of store' (the individual 4 digit SIC categories within Division 52) and by size. The sample structure is designed to ensure that the inquiry estimates are as accurate as possible. In terms of the selection, this means that:

• each of the individual 4 digit SIC categories are represented – their coverage depending upon the relative size of the category and the variability of the data

• within each 4 digit SIC category the larger retailers tend to be fully enumerated with decreasing proportions of medium and smaller retailers

The structure of the inquiry is updated periodically by reference to the more comprehensive results of the Annual Business Inquiry (ABI). The monthly inquiry also incorporates a rotation element for the smallest retailers. This helps to spread the burden more fairly, as well as improving the representativeness between successive benchmarks.

13.1a Retail Trade, except of motor vehicles and motorcycles

Standard Industrial Classification (Revised 2007)Division Group Class	Description	Year	Number of enterprises	Total turnover	Approximate gross value added at basic prices (aGVA)	Total purchases of goods materials and services	Total employment - point in time [1]	Total employment - average during the year [1]
			Number	£ million	£ million	£ million	Thousand	Thousand
47	Retail trade, except of motor vehicles and motorcycles	2008	194,677	311,745	65,123	246,237	3,054	3,106
		2009	187,890	319,318	69,924	249,058	3,073	3,139
		2010	187,230	332,131	71,500	261,676	3,016	3,040
		2011	189,119	342,147	70,871	271,203	3,032	3,060
		2012	187,606	348,556	73,187	274,981	3,029	3,062

Standard Industrial Classification (Revised 2007) Division Group Class	Description	Year	Total employment costs	Total net capital expenditure	Total capital expenditure- acquisitions	Total capital expenditure - disposals	Total stocks and work in progress - value at end of year	Total stocks and work in progress - value at beginning of year	Total stocks and work in progress - increase during year
			£ million	£ million	£ million	£ million	£ million	£ million	£ million
47	Retail trade, except of motor vehicles and motorcycles	2008	38,466	9,069	10,495	1,426	26,110	25,519	591
		2009	38,914	7,784	9,113	1,330	26,539	25,759	781
		2010	39,816	6,149	9,258	3,108	28,743	26,425	2,317
		2011	41,592	9,051	10,879	1,828	30,356	28,964	1,392
		2012	42,010	9,443	10,782	1,338	30,563	29,384	1,178

Source: Annual Business Survey (ABS)

The sum of constituent items in tables may not always agree exactly with the totals shown due to rounding.

1. Total employment - point in time and Total employment - average during the year are from the Business Register and Employment Survey (BRES). Caution should be taken when combining financial data from the ABS with employment data from BRES due to differences in methodology. http://www.ons.gov.uk/ons/guide-method/method-quality/specific/business-and-energy/annual-business-survey/quality-and-methods/abs-technical-report.pdf

13.1b Retail trade, except of motor vehicles and motor-cycles

£ million (Inclusive of VAT)

	2008	2009	2010	2011	2012
TOTAL TURNOVER	**346,002**	**350,269**	**367,446**	**385,692**	**393,423**
RETAIL TURNOVER	**325,847**	**331,256**	**347,144**	**363,280**	**368,176**
Fruit (including fresh, chilled, dried, frozen, canned and processed)	5,949	6,469	6,821	7,662	6,846
Vegetables (including fresh, chilled, dried, frozen canned and processed)	10,070	9,949	10,533	10,677	12,380
Meat (including fresh, chilled, smoked, frozen, canned and processed)	17,243	17,855	17,909	19,541	20,254
Fish, crustaceans and molluscs (including fresh, chilled, smoked, frozen, canned and processed)	2,936	2,989	2,978	3,295	3,453
Bakery products and cereals (including rice and pasta products)	15,816	16,719	17,875	18,818	20,078
Sugar, jam, honey, chocolate and confectionery (including ice-cream)	8,192	8,618	8,844	8,688	9,162
Alcoholic drink	14,965	15,609	16,618	17,445	18,184
Non-alcoholic beverages (including tea, coffee, fruit drinks and vegetable drinks)	7,793	7,756	8,018	9,176	9,161
Tobacco (excluding smokers requisites e.g. pipes, lighters etc)	10,343	11,411	11,369	11,838	11,885
Milk, cheese and eggs (including yoghurts and cream)	10,813	11,562	10,918	11,219	11,441
Oils and fats (including butter and margarine)	1,488	1,440	1,444	1,613	1,611
Food products not elsewhere classified (including sauces, herbs spices, soups)	4,969	5,149	4,427	4,528	3,890
Pharmaceutical products	3,519	3,636	3,946	4,390	4,725
National Health Receipts	11,479	11,792	12,067	11,405	11,680
Other medical products and therapeutic appliances and equipment	3,822	3,213	4,210	3,638	4,067
Other appliances, articles and products for personal care	12,596	13,148	14,109	15,107	15,702
Other articles of clothing, accessories for making clothing	3,011	2,505	3,395	3,781	4,051
Garments	34,121	35,556	36,706	37,976	38,730
Footwear (excluding sports shoes)	6,858	7,685	7,458	7,720	8,720
Travel goods and other personal effects not elsewhere classified	1,512	1,722	2,352	2,518	2,506
Household textiles (including furnishing fabrics, curtains etc)	4,368	4,535	4,862	4,188	4,158
Household and personal appliances whether electric or not	6,362	6,736	6,917	7,278	7,367
Glassware, tableware and household utensils (including non-electric)	2,768	2,824	2,754	3,369	3,668
Furniture and furnishings	13,839	13,226	12,313	13,475	12,395
Audio and visual equipment (including radios, televisions and video recorders)	6,215	6,016	6,245	5,353	5,821
Recording material for pictures and sound (including audio and video tapes, blank and pre recorded records etc)	3,622	3,052	2,787	2,547	2,668
Information processing equipment (including printers, software, calculators and typewriters)	4,423	4,384	4,530	5,425	4,862
Decorating and DIY supplies	6,176	6,820	7,319	7,528	5,580
Tools and equipment for house and garden	3,131	2,964	3,088	3,566	3,887
Books	2,497	2,623	2,648	2,579	3,084
Newspapers and periodicals	3,971	3,405	3,947	3,675	3,410
Stationery and drawing materials and miscellaneous printed matter	4,446	4,423	4,025	4,432	4,397
Carpets and other floor coverings (excluding bathroom mats, rush and door mats)	3,493	2,840	2,824	3,159	3,144
Photographic and cinematographic equipment and optical instruments	2,274	1,854	1,625	1,643	1,298
Telephone and telefax equipment (including mobile phones)	3,264	3,249	3,143	3,665	4,437
Jewellery, silverware and plate; watches and clocks	5,091	5,693	6,045	6,235	6,626
Works of art and antiques (including furniture, floor coverings and jewellery)	1,391	1,347	1,756	1,493	1,254
Equipment and accessories for sport, camping, recreation and musical instruments	4,019	4,416	4,864	5,118	4,944
Spare parts and accessories for all types of vehicle and sales of bicycles	1,159	924	1,148	983	950
Games, toys, hobbies (including video game software, video game computers that plug into the tv, video-games cassettes and CD-ROM'S)	7,961	7,484	7,514	7,492	7,154
Other goods not elsewhere classified (including sale of new postage stamps and sales of liquid and solid fuels)	4,307	5,007	5,896	5,929	5,788
Non-durable household goods (including household cleaning, maintenance products) & paper products and other non-durable household goods	4,942	5,280	4,727	4,923	4,936
Natural or artificial plants and flowers	4,192	2,973	3,609	4,023	3,501
Pets and related products (including pet food)	3,601	3,884	3,896	4,166	4,154
Petrol, diesel, lubricating oil and other petroleum products	30,840	30,515	36,664	40,001	40,171

The following symbols and abbreviations are used throughout the ABS releases;

Source: Annual Business Survey (ABS)

*   Information suppressed to avoid disclosure

..   not available

-    nil or less than half the level of rounding

The sum of constituent items in tables may not always agree exactly with the totals shown due to rounding.

13.2 Retail trade: index numbers of value and volume of sales[1]

Great Britain

Non-seasonally adjusted

		Sales in 2013 £ thousand	2003	2004	2005	2006	2007	2008	2009	2010	Weekly average (2011=100)		
											2011	2012	2013
Value													
All retailing	J5AH	359,983,667	77.3	81	82	85.1	88.5	91.8	92.6	95.1	100	102.3	104.9
Large	J5AI	285,712,301	72.4	76.1	77.6	81.2	85.1	89.2	90.7	95	100	102.7	105.7
Small	J5AJ	74,271,354	95.8	99.1	98.6	99.8	101.1	101.8	99.5	95.4	100	100.8	102.2
All retailing excluding automotive fuel	J43S	320,865,851	79.9	83.5	84.5	86.5	89.6	92.4	94.2	96.6	100	102.6	106
Predominantly food stores	EAFS	149,946,364	73	75.9	78.3	81.2	84.6	89.4	94.3	95.8	100	102.8	105.9
Predominantly non-food stores	EAFT	147,560,754	89.3	93.5	93	94.4	97.2	97.7	96.1	98.5	100	101.6	103.4
Non specialised predominantly non-food stores	EAGE	29,551,187	83.5	85.3	85	87.5	90.8	88.3	89.9	96.2	100	106.1	110.8
Textile, clothing, footwear and leather	EAFU	43,770,025	79.6	83.6	84.3	88.2	90.6	90.4	91.5	96.4	100	101.6	104
Household goods stores	EAFV	29,097,122	109.8	113.8	110	110.8	114.6	112.1	106.5	102.3	100	99.1	96
Other specialised non-food stores	EAFW	45,142,420	88.1	94	94.4	93.3	95.5	100.3	97.1	99.3	100	100.5	103.3
Non-store retailing	J596	23,358,733	59	65.2	65	66.4	69.2	73.9	78.7	87.1	100	109.6	128.1
Automotive fuel	J43H	39,117,816	58.4	61.6	63.8	74.6	79.9	87.7	80.2	83.9	100	99.8	96.7
Volume													
All retailing	J5DD	359,983,667	88.1	92.6	93.8	96.8	99.5	99.8	100.2	99.5	100	100.7	102.1
All retailing excluding automotive fuel	J448	320,865,851	86.8	91.7	93.4	95.6	98.2	99	99.6	100	100	101.1	103
Predominantly food stores	EAGW	149,946,364	94.9	98.3	100.4	101.7	102.5	101.8	102.7	101	100	99.7	99.5
Predominantly non-food stores	EAGX	147,560,754	84	89.7	91.2	94.1	97.9	99.5	99.2	100.5	100	101.3	103.2
Non specialised predominantly non-food stores	EAHI	29,551,187	80.9	84.2	85.3	88.8	92.4	90.7	92.1	97.5	100	106.5	112
Textile, clothing, footwear and leather	EAGY	43,770,025	67.2	72.9	75.9	81.3	85.2	88.2	94.1	99.1	100	100.4	101.5
Household goods stores	EAGZ	29,097,122	102.6	109.1	108.4	112.2	117.5	116.5	109.9	103.8	100	98.6	96.3
Other specialised non-food stores	EAHA	45,142,420	90.3	97.1	98.6	97.6	100.4	104.4	100.9	101.2	100	100.7	104.2
Non-store retailing	J5CL	23,358,733	56.4	63.2	64.1	66.4	69.7	74.9	80.7	88.3	100	109.7	128.5
Automotive fuel	J43V	39,117,816	101.8	101.9	97.4	108	112.1	107.8	105.8	95.7	100	97.7	95.2

1 See chapter text.

Please note that the indices have been re-referenced so the value of 100 is in 2011

Source: Office for National Statistics

13.3 Wholesale and retail trade and repair of motor vehicles and motorcycles

Standard Industrial Classification (Revised 2007) Division Group Class	Description	Year	Number of enterprises	Total turnover	Approximate gross value added at basic prices (aGVA)	Total purchases of goods, materials and services	Total employment - point in time [1]	Total employment - average during the year [1]	Total employment costs
			Number	£ million	£ million	£ million	Thousand	Thousand	£ million
45	Wholesale and retail trade and repair of motor vehicles and motorcycles	2008	67,683	135,669	20,957	115,372	532	535	10,925
		2009	66,372	125,764	18,348	105,457	500	539	10,445
		2010	66,239	132,077	22,150	111,243	511	510	10,439
		2011	67,298	137,364	23,419	115,292	523	535	10,658
		2012	67,274	142,461	22,347	120,649	510	522	10,615

Standard Industrial Classification (Revised 2007) Division Group Class	Description	Year	Total net capital expenditure	Total capital expenditure- acquisitions	Total capital expenditure - disposals	Total stocks and work in progress - value at end of year	Total stocks and work in progress - value at beginning of year	Total stocks and work in progress - increase during year
			£ million	£ million	£ million	£ million	£ million	£ million
45	Wholesale and retail trade and repair of motor vehicles and motorcycles	2008	1,044	2,110	1,066	16,136	15,402	735
		2009	885	1,669	784	13,624	15,545	-1,921
		2010	1,035	1,747	711	15,008	13,640	1,368
		2011	1,292	2,067	775	16,451	15,107	1,344
		2012	1,174	1,927	753	17,067	16,490	577

Source: Annual Business Survey (ABS)

The following symbols and abbreviations are used throughout the ABS releases;
* Information suppressed to avoid disclosure
.. not available
- nil or less than half the level of rounding

The sum of constituent items in tables may not always agree exactly with the totals shown due to rounding.

Notes: Total employment - point in time and Total employment - average during the year are from the Business Register and Employment Survey (BRES).
1. Caution should be taken when combining financial data from the ABS with employment data from BRES due to differences in methodology. More information can be found in the ABS Technical Report.

13.4 Accommodation and food service activities

Standard Industrial Classification (Revised 2007) Section Division Group Class	Description	Year	Number of enterprises	Total turnover	Approximate gross value added at basic prices (aGVA)	Total purchases of goods, materials and services	Total employment - point in time [1]	Total employment - average during the year [1]	Total employment costs
			Number	£ million	£ million	£ million	Thousand	Thousand	£ million
I	Accommodation and food service activities	2008	136,504	67,674	31,620	36,047	1,971	1,967	18,737
		2009	129,112	66,195	29,375	36,745	1,919	1,812	19,012
		2010	127,844	68,346	31,435	36,883	1,869	1,855	19,074
		2011	130,336	72,322	34,826	37,563	1,937	1,869	19,987
		2012	128,831	74,355	37,764	37,272	1,970	1,910	21,132
55	Accommodation	2008	15,725	17,532	9,573	7,962	392	389	4,806
		2009	15,157	17,235	9,231	7,973	393	360	4,724
		2010	15,075	17,650	9,087	8,603	388	377	5,075
		2011	15,159	18,566	9,838	8,775	429	407	5,331
		2012	15,205	19,822	11,149	8,677	426	409	5,752
55.1	Hotels and similar accommodation	2008	10,178	13,596	7,732	5,872	328	328	4,011
		2009	9,687	13,624	7,439	6,171	325	297	3,942
		2010	9,559	13,493	7,102	6,399	321	316	4,173
		2011	9,575	14,150	7,619	6,532	358	342	4,424
		2012	9,449	15,186	8,572	6,609	351	339	4,823
55.2	Holiday and other short stay accommodation	2008	2,973	1,313	633	683	27	26	307
		2009	3,351	1,219	661	554	30	29	289
		2010	3,318	1,603	846	776	29	26	339
		2011	3,296	1,476	726	774	33	30	351
		2012	3,247	1,497	913	590	33	31	344
55.3	Camping grounds, recreational vehicle parks and trailer parks	2008	1,728	2,441	1,113	1,321	33	31	433
		2009	1,711	2,230	1,033	1,184	34	31	448
		2010	1,735	2,325	1,031	1,307	*	*	495
		2011	1,775	2,739	1,385	1,378	34	31	507
		2012	1,796	2,771	1,415	1,360	37	34	516
55.9	Other accommodation	2008	846	182	95	86	4	4	55
		2009	408	162	98	64	3	3	46
		2010	463	229	108	121	*	*	69
		2011	513	200	108	92	4	4	49
		2012	713	368	250	118	5	4	70
56	Food and beverage service activities	2008	120,779	50,141	22,047	28,085	1,578	1,578	13,930
		2009	113,955	48,960	20,144	28,772	1,526	1,452	14,288
		2010	112,769	50,696	22,348	28,281	1,481	1,478	13,998
		2011	115,177	53,756	24,988	28,787	1,507	1,462	14,656
		2012	113,626	54,533	26,615	28,594	1,544	1,501	15,380
56.1	Restaurants and mobile food service activities	2008	63,368	22,452	10,018	12,436	753	753	6,255
		2009	61,192	22,658	9,910	12,765	737	644	6,460
		2010	61,387	23,017	10,407	12,623	705	684	6,306
		2011	63,712	25,690	12,301	13,447	767	765	6,886
		2012	64,460	25,934	13,367	13,332	782	783	7,187
56.2	Event catering and other food service activities	2008	7,536	7,539	3,824	3,717	263	260	2,950
		2009	7,049	6,811	2,786	4,029	210	235	2,952
		2010	7,031	7,971	4,003	3,970	227	253	3,149
		2011	7,967	8,553	4,418	4,138	231	212	3,204
		2012	7,651	8,925	4,430	4,521	262	249	3,688
56.21	Event catering activities	2008	6,649	7,000	3,553	3,450	250	247	2,788
		2009	6,070	6,139	2,505	3,636	197	222	2,782
		2010	5,767	7,289	3,710	3,581	211	236	2,957
		2011	6,267	7,837	4,119	3,715	213	196	2,993
		2012	5,514	7,844	3,879	3,968	241	228	3,411
56.29	Other food service activities	2008	887	539	271	268	13	13	162
		2009	979	672	281	393	12	12	170
		2010	1,264	682	293	389	16	17	192
		2011	1,700	716	299	422	18	17	211
		2012	2,137	1,081	551	552	21	20	278
56.3	Beverage serving activities	2008	49,875	20,150	8,204	11,931	562	567	4,726
		2009	45,714	19,491	7,448	11,979	579	574	4,876
		2010	44,351	19,709	7,938	11,688	549	540	4,543
		2011	43,498	19,513	8,269	11,203	509	484	4,566
		2012	41,515	19,675	8,817	10,742	501	469	4,504

13.4 Accommodation and food service

Standard Industrial Classification (Revised 2007) Section Division Group Class	Description	Year	Total net capital expenditure	Total capital expenditure- acquisitions	Total capital expenditure - disposals	Total stocks and work in progress - value at end of year	Total stocks and work in progress - value at beginning of year	Total stocks and work in progress - increase during year
			£ million	£ million	£ million	£ million	£ million	£ million
I	Accommodation and food service activities	2008	4,132	4,634	502	1,393	1,355	37
		2009	3,443	3,803	360	1,318	1,303	15
		2010	2,807	3,804	997	1,481	1,403	79
		2011	3,311	4,339	1,028	1,484	1,368	117
		2012	3,930	4,704	774	1,716	1,713	3
55	Accommodation	2008	2,155	2,289	134	378	379	-1
		2009	1,628	1,728	100	359	391	-32
		2010	1,301	1,489	188	488	445	43
		2011	1,416	1,641	225	506	443	63
		2012	1,898	2,050	152	469	452	17
55.1	Hotels and similar accommodation	2008	1,774	1,848	74	193	187	6
		2009	1,390	1,433	43	181	197	-15
		2010	936	1,072	136	250	231	20
		2011	946	1,137	191	201	176	25
		2012	1,282	1,397	115	185	172	13
55.2	Holiday and other short stay accommodation	2008	111	129	17	50	48	2
		2009	50	67	17	24	29	-5
		2010	186	214	28	75	66	9
		2011	169	184	15	59	45	15
		2012	254	269	16	64	58	6
55.3	Camping grounds, recreational vehicle parks and trailer parks	2008	*	277	*	133	142	-9
		2009	138	*	*	153	164	-11
		2010	160	181	21	159	145	14
		2011	238	257	18	245	222	23
		2012	258	279	21	217	219	-3
55.9	Other accommodation	2008	*	35	*	2	2	-
		2009	50	*	*	1	1	-
		2010	19	22	4	3	3	-
		2011	62	63	1	1	1	-
		2012	104	105	1	3	3	-
56	Food and beverage service activities	2008	1,978	2,346	368	1,015	976	39
		2009	1,815	2,075	260	959	912	47
		2010	1,507	2,316	809	993	958	35
		2011	1,895	2,698	803	978	925	54
		2012	2,032	2,654	622	1,247	1,261	-13
56.1	Restaurants and mobile food service activities	2008	1,021	1,124	103	453	433	20
		2009	1,104	1,250	146	437	408	29
		2010	998	1,185	187	429	402	27
		2011	1,203	1,327	123	412	379	33
		2012	1,380	1,512	132	562	532	30
56.2	Event catering and other food service activities	2008	88	99	10	145	145	1
		2009	44	49	5	103	98	5
		2010	135	176	41	126	122	4
		2011	175	188	14	145	140	5
		2012	127	135	8	158	154	4
56.21	Event catering activities	2008	83	93	10	139	139	1
		2009	33	37	4	87	84	3
		2010	117	155	38	111	107	4
		2011	116	129	13	123	124	-1
		2012	113	120	7	133	131	2
56.29	Other food service activities	2008	5	6	-	6	6	-
		2009	11	12	1	16	14	2
		2010	18	21	2	15	15	-
		2011	59	60	1	22	16	6
		2012	14	15	1	24	23	1
56.3	Beverage serving activities	2008	868	1,123	255	416	398	18
		2009	667	776	109	419	406	13
		2010	374	955	581	438	434	5
		2011	517	1,183	666	421	405	16
		2012	524	1,007	483	527	575	-47

Source: Annual Business Survey (ABS)

The following symbols and abbreviations are used throughout the ABS releases;
* Information suppressed to oid disclosure
.. not available   - nil or less than half the level of rounding
The sum of constituent items in tables may not always agree exactly with the totals shown due to rounding.

1. Total employment - point in time and Total employment - average during the year are from the Business Register and Employment Survey (BRES). Caution should be taken when combining financial data from the ABS with employment data from BRES due to differences in methodology. More information can be found in the ABS Technical Report.

Defence

Chapter 14

Defence

This section includes figures on Defence expenditure, on the size and role of the Armed Forces and on related support activities. Much of the material used in this section can be found in UK Defence Statistics 2012

Table 14.1 United Kingdom Defence Expenditure by Commodity Block

From 2011/12 the MOD reports expenditure against Commodity Blocks and these headings, although similar in some instances, are not directly comparable to the previously used Resource DEL and Capital DEL categories. This table shows a breakdown of Resource and Capital DEL, and AME by Commodity Block. Under Clear Line of Sight (CLoS), the main MOD expenditure categories are now presented as Commodity Blocks. This provides a more meaningful description of the Department's planned and actual spend, which enables a clearer understanding of the MOD's plans and expenditure over the Spending Review period.

Please refer to the Resource Accounting & Budgeting section of UKDS 2012 to view important information relating to the introduction of the International Financial Reporting Standard (IFRS), the implementation of the Clear Line of Sight (CLoS) Alignment project and recent accounting changes for 2011/12, which have led to presentational changes to the reporting of MOD accounts.

Prior to 2011/12, when Commodity Block reporting was first introduced, information contained in this table was reported in Table 1.3a of UK Defence Statistics 2012.

The data are derived directly from the MOD Departmental Resource Accounts .

Table 14.2 Intake to UK Regular Forces by Service and sex
Women accounted for 8.7 per cent of the intake to UK Regular Forces in 2011/12, which represents a gradual decline since 2006/07. This decrease is not uniform across the Officers and Other Ranks with all Services having an increase in the percentage of Officer intake from 15.8 per cent in 2010/11 to 16.8 per cent in 2011/12, notably in the RAF where 36.3 per cent of the 2011/12 intake were female.

The percentage of female intake in the Other Ranks has increased slightly from 7.9 per cent in 2010/11 to 8.1 per cent in 2011/12. When compared to 2010/11, the Naval Service and Army has seen an increase whereas the RAF have decreased.

Table 14.3 provides information on the formation of the United Kingdom's Armed Forces

Table 14.3a shows the number of submarines and ships in the Royal Navy and Royal Fleet Auxiliary, Royal Marine Commando units, squadrons of helicopters and fixed-wing aircraft in the Fleet Air Arm, and Reserve Units at 1 April 2012. The figures show overall unit numbers only; they do not reflect the level of readiness at which the unit is held which changes throughout the year.

Table 14.3b shows the numbers of Regiments and Infantry battalions in the Regular and Territorial Army; and Corps, Divisional and Brigade headquarters. Key points - The number of combat arms regiments in the Army was unchanged between April 2010 and April 2012, when there were 46 Regular Army and 18 Territorial Army combat arms regiments. The number of combat support regiments has increased slightly with an increase in the number of Regular Army Engineers regiments offsetting a fall in the number of Regular Army Signals Regiments. At 1 April 2012 there were 39 Regular Army and 17 Territorial combat support regiments.

Table 14.3c shows the number of squadrons in the Royal Air Force (RAF) and the Royal Auxiliary Air Force (RAuxAF), and units in the RAF Regiment. Key point - here has been a slight fall in the number of RAF squadrons.

Table 14.3d shows the number of regiments and squadrons in the Special Forces, Joint Helicopter Command and Joint Force Harrier. Key points - The number of Joint Forces Squadrons reduced by two between April 2010 and April 2012 due to the disbanding of the Joint Harrier Force Squadrons.

Table 14.4 Outflow from UK Regular Forces by Service and sex
Females as a percentage of total outflow decreased to 8.3 per cent during 2011/12 from 8.8 per cent in 2010/11 and has fallen from 9.7 per cent in 2000/01. Total outflow of females has been fairly stable since 2006/07 in both the Officers and Other Ranks. Females as a proportion of outflow has increased during 2011/12 in the Naval Service and decreased in the Army and the RAF. Naval Service female outflow rose by 0.2 percentage points to 10.1 per cent; Army fell by 0.6 percentage points to 6.3 per cent and RAF fell by 1.4 percentage points to 13.1 per cent.

Table 14.5 United Kingdom Armed Forces Full-time trained strength and requirement, at 1 April each year
The full-time trained strength of the UK Armed Forces was 170,010 at 1 April 2012, down 6,840 (3.9 per cent) since 1 April 2011 and down 20,260 (10.6 per cent) since 1 April 2000.

The requirement for the UK's full-time trained Armed Forces decreased from 198,160 in 2000 to 185,920 in 2006 and 174,840 in 2012. The rate of decrease has been greatest in the RAF, followed by the Naval Service and least in the Army. Contrasting with the other Services, and the Army other ranks, the requirement for Army officers increased between 2011 and 2012, and at 13,480 was higher than it was in 2000.

The deficit between strength and requirement of full-time trained Armed Forces has decreased from 7,880 at 1 April 2000 to 4,830 at 1 April 2012. The deficit at 1 April 2012 is mainly due to a deficit of 4,720 Other Ranks. Officers were also in deficit in 2012, having reduced in strength by 1,150 since 1 April 2011 against a slightly increased requirement. This is the first time that Officers have been in overall deficit since 2005. The largest deficit as a percentage of requirement is in the Naval Service, where the strength has fallen faster than the requirement in the last year.

Table 14.6a Civilian personnel, at 1 April each year
The full-time trained strength of the UK Armed Forces was 170,010 at 1 April 2012, down 6,840 (3.9 per cent) since 1 April 2011 and down 20,260 (10.6 per cent) since 1 April 2000.

The requirement for the UK's full-time trained Armed Forces decreased from 198,160 in 2000 to 185,920 in 2006 and 174,840 in 2012. The rate of decrease has been greatest in the RAF, followed by the Naval Service and least in the Army. Contrasting with the other Services, and the Army other ranks, the requirement for Army officers increased between 2011 and 2012, and at 13,480 was higher than it was in 2000.

The deficit between strength and requirement of full-time trained Armed Forces has decreased from 7,880 at 1 April 2000 to 4,830 at 1 April 2012. The deficit at 1 April 2012 is mainly due to a deficit of 4,720 Other Ranks. Officers were also in deficit in 2012, having reduced in strength by 1,150 since 1 April 2011 against a slightly increased requirement. This is the first time that Officers have been in overall deficit since 2005. The largest deficit as a percentage of requirement is in the Naval Service, where the strength has fallen faster than the requirement in the last year.

Table 14.6b Civilian personnel by budgetary area and grade equivalent, at 1 April each year
A budgetary area is defined as higher level groupings of the Top Level Budgetary areas combined together to allow consistent presentation of data across multiple time periods. Although constituent TLBs in areas such as centralised support and logistic support services have changed in structure across the period, the budgetary area groupings remain the same across the period. The budgetary areas for Navy Command, Land Forces and Air Command each represent individual Service areas. While Defence Equipment & Support covers the departments logistic support systems, with remaining TLB areas falling to Centre covering centralised support services.

As directed by policy deriving from the Strategic Defence and Security Review (SDSR), personnel reductions under the SDSR are set to continue until 2020 from the baseline start point of April 2010. Between 2010 (the start of the current SDSR rundown exercise) and 2012, the total FTE strength of MOD civilian personnel fell by 17.3 per cent. Decreases have been seen within each individual Service Command over this period, with the largest proportionate decrease of 24.5 per cent seen in Air Command and the smallest proportionate decrease of 12.8 per cent in Defence Equipment & Support.

Between 2000 and the start of the current SDSR rundown exercise in 2010, the total FTE strength of MOD civilian personnel fell by 29.2 per cent and between 2000 and 2012 the total FTE strength of MOD civilian personnel fell by 41.5 per cent. Decreases have been seen within each individual Service Command between 2000 and 2012, with the largest proportionate decrease of 43.5 per cent seen in Air Command, while Navy Command and Land Forces showed decreases of similar proportions, by 40.4 per cent and 38.0 per cent respectively. Defence Equipment & Support, decreased significantly by 60.0 per cent across the whole period.

Table 14.7a Land holdings by country and whether owned, leased or with legal rights, at 1 April each year
Table 14.7a shows the area of MOD holdings by country. These holdings include land declared as surplus to defence requirements. A thousand hectares is 3.86 square miles.

Table 14.7b Service Family Accommodation in the United Kingdom, at 31 March each year
The Defence Infrastructure Organisation's Directorate of Operations Accommodation is responsible for Service Family Accommodation (SFA) in the UK, having assumed responsibility for Northern Ireland from 1 April 2008. At 31st March 2012 it managed some 49,000 properties. The planned reduction in UK Permanent Holdings has seen around 300 properties disposed of in the last year which has been partially offset by the procurement of 200 additional properties.

Vacant Properties
There are about 6,500 vacant properties in the UK. A number of these are awaiting incoming deployments particularly from units relocating from Germany, modernisation or disposal, whilst the remainder are available to let or are already under offer to Service families.

The apparent increase in the percentage of properties which are vacant between 2011 and 2012 is explained by uncertainty over the Future Footprint Strategy which has resulted in SFA, previously earmarked for disposal, being retained in certain areas including Scotland and Northern Ireland.

Number of Occupants
DIO Ops Accommodation provides SFA for entitled Service personnel in accordance with Tri-Service Accommodation Regulations, as well as for other entitled/eligible personnel, and for core welfare purposes. SFA can also be utilised for other defence purposes such as Single Living Accommodation.

DIO Ops Accommodation also reports on the number of Substitute Service Family Accommodation (SSFA) properties occupied by entitled Service personnel, i.e. those who would otherwise occupy SFA were it available when and where required. SSFA is private property, is not part of DIO Ops Housing stock, and is provided under contract.

At 1 April 2012 there were around 42,600 entitled and eligible occupants in England, Wales and Scotland in SFA, to which must be added 1,780 in SSFA.

Table 14.8a Location of Service and civilian personnel in the United Kingdom, at 1 April each year
The strength of UK-based civilian personnel has reduced from 67,610 in 2011 to 57,220 in 2012, a decrease of 15.4 per cent. The total strength of MOD service personnel based in Northern Ireland has continued to reduce, falling by 6.8 per cent since last year. Since 2000, the number of Service personnel stationed in Northern Ireland has been reduced by 55.4 per cent, from 8,390 to 3,740, whilst the civilian strength has fallen by 50.6 per cent during the same period from 3,250 to 1,610. The South East Region has the largest population of UK Service personnel, with 43,330, although the South West has the largest population of civilians, with 21,690.

Table 14.8b Global locations of Service and civilian personnel, at 1 April each year
At 1 April 2012, 87.3 per cent of UK Service and 80.6 per cent of MOD civilian personnel were stationed in the UK. The number of UK military personnel stationed overseas has decreased from 37,200 in 2000 to 22,440 in 2012, a decrease of 39.7 per cent. At the same time the number of UK civilian personnel stationed overseas has decreased from 16,800 in 2000 to 11,270 in 2012, a decrease of 32.9 per cent. The percentage of UK military personnel stationed overseas has fallen from 17.4 per cent in 2000 to 12.5 per cent in 2012. Over the same period, the percentage of UK civilian personnel stationed overseas has risen from 13.9 per cent in 2000 to 15.9 per cent in 2012.

Despite the numbers stationed there falling for at least the sixth year in succession, the Germany/Belgium/Netherlands region has the second largest population of MOD personnel after the UK, with 17,480 Service and 5,950 civilians. This amounts to 77.9 per cent of UK military personnel stationed overseas and 52.8 per cent of UK civilian personnel stationed overseas.

Table 14.9a UK regular Armed Forces deaths by Service, Year of occurrence 2004-2012, numbers, age and gender standardised rates
In 2012, there were 129 deaths in the regular Armed Forces. Of these, 19 deaths were in the Naval Service, 95 in the Army and 15 in the RAF. In 2012 the mortality rate for the UK Armed Forces was 71 per 100,000. This was an increase on the 10 year low rate of seen in 2011.

Table 14.10a UK & Overseas Callouts, Incidents and Persons Moved, 2004 to 2012
Table 14.10a shows the number of incidents, callouts and persons moved each year between 2004 and 2013. Between 2004 and 2009 the number of callouts increased year-on-year. Callout numbers peaked in 2009, and since then the number of callouts fell year-on-year.

14.10b Search and Rescue Helicopters - UK & Overseas Callouts and Persons Moved by Unit
This data focuses on SAR helicopter callouts, excluding Mountain Rescue Teams.
Table 14.10b presents the number of callouts by unit and number of Persons moved by Unit between 2004 and 2012. The unit with the highest number of callouts during 2012 was RAF Valley, with 300, closely followed by HMS Gannet with 298. This is the second year in a row that RAF Valley has had the highest number of callouts in a year, although it has been among the top three units with the highest number of callouts for the past five years. HMS Gannet moved the highest number of persons during 2012 with 285, followed by RAF Valley with 284. For the past four years HMS Gannet and RAF Valley have been the two units with the highest number of persons moved.
RAF Wattisham moved the lowest number of persons of the UK units during 2012, with 80.

14.10c Search and Rescue Helicopters: UK & Overseas Callouts by Assistance Type, 2004 to 2012
14.10c presents callout numbers by assistance type between 2004 and 2012. The assistance type with the largest number of callouts during 2012 was Medrescue, representing 45% of all helicopter callouts. Most of the other callout types have very low numbers. The second half of the table shows the number of persons moved by assistance type between 2004 and 2012. In 2012, 56% of persons moved were for Medrescue, a similar proportion to recent years.

14.10d Strength of United Kingdom Medical Staff
The figures shown in 14.10d are for regular personnel only and therefore do not represent the strength of either Reserve or veterinarian personnel.

14.11 Number of vessels boarded by the Royal Navy Fishery Protection Squadron within British fishing limits and convictions arising from these boardings each financial year

This table shows the activities of the Royal Navy Fishery Protection Squadron operating within British fishery limits under contract to the Marine Maritime Organisation (MMO). Boardings carried out by vessels of the Scottish Executive Environment Directorate and the Department of Agriculture and Rural Development for Northern Ireland are not included. The data in this Table are outside the scope of National Statistics since they have not been put forward for assessment by the UK Statistics Authority.

Convictions arising from Royal Navy boardings are convictions of infringements detected by the Royal Navy Fishery Protection vessels in that year operating under contract to DEFRA. Figures may change retrospectively as some cases may not be heard in court until a year or more after the initial Royal Navy boarding.

in financial year 08/09, the Marine and Fisheries Agency introduced the Fisheries Administration Penalty (FAP). This has streamlined the penalty process, and has removed the necessity for most of the crews of vessels that would previously have been sent to Court from actually having to attend Court, where they would probably have been convicted. Convictions from 2008/09 onwards are based on the number of offences addressed by the Courts that resulted in a Court conviction, not the number of fishing vessel crews that attended Court. That is, the same fishing vessel crew could be required to attend Court for one or more offences to be heard and each offence would count separately.

In 2011/12 1,408 vessels were boarded by the Royal Navy Fisheries Protection Squadron, the highest figure in the last six years. This had resulted in 17 court convictions by the time the information was available.

14.1 Defence Expenditure by Commodity Block

This table is an Official Statistic.

	Inclusive of non-recoverable VAT at Current Prices (£ million)	
	Outturn 2011/12	Outturn 2012/13
Defence Spending	**37 169**	**34 260**
Departmental Expenditure Limits (DEL)	**46 994**	**43 718**
Cash Resource DEL	**37 980**	**35 874**
Of which:		
Personnel Costs	12 846	11 921
Of which: Service Personnel Costs[1]	10 101	9 598
Civilian Personnel Costs[2]	2 745	2 323
Infrastructure Costs[3]	4 580	4 594
Inventory Consumption[4]	2 535	2 312
Equipment Support Costs[5]	6 256	5 588
Other Costs & Services[6]	1 850	1 923
Receipts & Other Income[7]	-1 327	-1 277
Depreciation & Impairment[8]	9 825	9 458
Cash Release of Provisions[9]	348	239
Research & Development Costs[10]	833	944
Conflict Pool	46	44
Arm's Length Bodies[11]	187	127
Capital DEL[12]	**9 014**	**7 843**
Of which:		
Single Use Military Equipment[13]	5 284	4 768
Other (Fiscal)[14]	3 883	3 141
Asset/Estate Disposal Costs	- 150	- 64
New Loans and Loan Repayments	- 5	- 6
Arm's Length Bodies	2	3
Annually Managed Expenditure (AME)[15]	**967** r	**1 867**
Of which:		
Depreciation & Impairment	510	1 062
Provisions	- 460	318
Cash Release of Provisions	- 345	- 239
Movement on Fair Value of Financial Instruments	347	- 183
War Pensions Benefits	916	908

Source: Defence Economics (Defence Expenditure Analysis) and Defence Resources

See footnotes over the page:

1. Military and other ranks pay and other allowances; SCAPE; Employer's National Insurance Contributions (ERNIC).
2. Civilian pay and other allowances; pension contributions; Employer's National Insurance Contributions (ERNIC).
3. Property management; service charges; IT & communications costs; utilities costs.
4. Munitions; stores; fuel (marine & aviation); clothing; other materials consumed e.g. stationary, sundries, general stores, etc.
5. Equipment support costs, including leases & hire charges for plant, machinery and transport.
6. Travel & subsistence; professional services & fees; training.
7. Receipts from various sources; costs recoveries; dividends; interest.
8. Depreciation & impairments on Non-Current Assets (Property, SUME, dual purpose).
9. Nuclear and non nuclear provisions e.g. staff redundancies, legal costs, environmental, etc.
10. Research and Development expenditure is incurred mainly for the future benefit of the Department. Such expenditure is primarily incurred on the development of new Single Use Military Equipment (SUME), and on the improvement of the effectiveness and capability of existing SUME.
11. Army Benevolent Fund; Council of Reserve Forces and Cadet Associations; Royal Hospital Chelsea; National Army Museum; RAF Museum; National Museum of the Royal Navy; Commonwealth War Graves Commission.
12. Expenditure on the acquisition of Non-Current Assets.
13. Single Use Military Equipment (SUME) are assets which only have a military use, such as tanks and fighter aircraft. Dual use items (those that also have a civilian use) are recorded under the Other category.
14. Expenditure on Property, Plant and dual use military equipment that could be used by civilian organisations for the production of goods and services
15. The 2011/12 AME figures have been revised following the removal from the total of Capital AME, which is a balance sheet movement which is not voted or included in the outturn.

14.2 Intake[1] to UK Regular Forces by Service and sex

	2000/01	2007/08	2008/09	2009/10	2010/11	2011/12	2012/13
All Services	**23 020**	**21 350**	**23 190**	**21 500**	**12 730**	**14 800**	**14 370**
Percentage female	*11.3%*	*9.9%*	*9.2%*	*8.9%*	*8.8%*	*8.7%*	*8.4%*
Officers	**1 760**	**1 720**	**1 690**	**1 580**	**1 360**	**1 070**	**1 060**
of which female	350	300	300	250	210	180	170
Percentage female	*19.9%*	*17.4%*	*18.0%*	*15.8%*	*15.8%*	*16.8%*	*16.4%*
Other Ranks	**21 260**	**19 630**	**21 500**	**19 920**	**11 370**	**13 730**	**13 310**
of which female	2 260	1 820	1 830	1 660	900	1 110	1 030
Percentage female	*10.6%*	*9.3%*	*8.5%*	*8.4%*	*7.9%*	*8.1%*	*7.7%*
Naval Service	**4 620**	**4 040**	**4 240**	**4 130**	**2 550**	**2 220**	**2 770**
Percentage female	*13.7%*	*12.1%*	*10.5%*	*9.4%*	*6.7%*	*8.3%*	*7.3%*
Officers	**450**	**380**	**310**	**390**	**300**	**280**	**280**
of which female	80	60	50	50	30	40	40
Porcentage female	*18.5%*	*16.0%*	*16.9%*	*13.0%*	*9.4%*	*13.5%*	*12.5%*
Other Ranks	**4 180**	**3 660**	**3 930**	**3 740**	**2 250**	**1 940**	**2 490**
of which female	550	430	390	340	140	150	170
Percentage female	*13.2%*	*11.7%*	*9.9%*	*9.0%*	*6.3%*	*7.5%*	*6.7%*
Army [2]	**14 770**	**14 290**	**14 660**	**13 910**	**8 760**	**11 190**	**10 300**
Percentage female	*9.0%*	*7.8%*	*6.9%*	*6.8%*	*8.1%*	*8.3%*	*8.1%*
Officers	**870**	**940**	**840**	**790**	**780**	**710**	**640**
of which female	170	150	130	120	120	110	100
Percentage female	*19.2%*	*15.8%*	*15.3%*	*15.0%*	*14.8%*	*16.0%*	*15.3%*
Other Ranks	**13 900**	**13 350**	**13 820**	**13 120**	**7 980**	**10 480**	**9 660**
of which female	1 160	960	890	830	590	810	740
Percentage female	*8.3%*	*7.2%*	*6.4%*	*6.3%*	*7.4%*	*7.7%*	*7.6%*
Royal Air Force	**3 630**	**3 020**	**4 300**	**3 460**	**1 410**	**1 390**	**1 310**
Percentage female	*18.0%*	*17.1%*	*15.8%*	*16.7%*	*16.7%*	*13.1%*	*12.9%*
Officers	**440**	**410**	**540**	**400**	**280**	**80**	**140**
of which female	100	90	120	80	70	30	40
Percentage female	*22.8%*	*22.4%*	*22.9%*	*20.3%*	*25.3%*	*36.3%*	*29.7%*
Other Ranks	**3 190**	**2 620**	**3 760**	**3 070**	**1 140**	**1 310**	**1 170**
of which female	560	430	560	500	170	150	130
Percentage female	*17.4%*	*16.3%*	*14.8%*	*16.3%*	*14.6%*	*11.7%*	*10.9%*

Source: Defence Statistics (Tri-Service)

1. Figures show intake to UK Regular Forces which comprises new entrants, re-entrants, direct trained entrants (including professionally qualified officers) and intake from the reserves. They exclude all movements within the Regular Forces; including flows from untrained to trained strength, transfers between Services and flows from ranks to officer due to promotion.

2. From 2009/10 Army intake figures include transfers from the Gurkhas to the UK Regular Forces.

This table is a National Statistic.

14.3a Number of vessels in the Royal Navy and Royal Fleet Auxiliary, and squadrons in the Fleet Air Arm, at 1 April each year

These figures show overall unit numbers only; they do not reflect the level of readiness at which each unit is held, which changes throughout the year. Readiness refers to the length of time it would take for a vessel to be ready for deployment.

This table is a National Statistic.

		2000	2008	2009	2010	2011	2012	2013
Royal Navy submarines	Total	16	13	12	11	11	11	11
Of which:								
Trident / Polaris	Vessels	4	4	4	4	4	4	4
Fleet	Vessels	12	9	8 [2]	7 [3]	7	7	7 [4,5]
Royal Navy ships	Total	89	74	73	71	67	65	66
Of which:								
Aircraft Carriers	Vessels	3	2	2	2	- [6,7]	-	-
Landing Platform Docks / Helicopter	Vessels	3	3	3	3	4 [7]	4	4
Destroyers	Vessels	11	8	7 [8]	6 [9]	6 [10]	5 [11]	6
Frigates	Vessels	21	17	17	17	15 [12]	13 [13]	13
Mine countermeasures vessels	Vessels	21	16	16	16	15 [14]	15	15
Patrol ships and craft	Vessels	23	22 [15]	22	22	22	22	22
Survey ships	Vessels	6	5	5	4 [16]	4	4	4
Ice patrol ships	Vessels	1	1	1	1 [17]	1 [17]	2 [18]	2 [18]
Royal Fleet Auxiliary Service	Total	22	18	16	16	14	13	13
Of which:								
Tankers	Vessels	9 [r]	6 [r,19]	6	6	6 [r,22]	5	5
Fleet Replenishment Ships	Vessels	- [r]	2	2 [r,20]	2 [r,21]	1 [r]	1 [r]	1 [r]
Solid Support Ships	Vessels	4	4	2 [20]	2	2	2	2
Primary Casualty Receiving Ship[23]	Vessels	1	1	1	1	1	1	1
Landing Ships	Vessels	5	4 [24,25]	4	4	3 [26]	3	3
Forward Repair Ships	Vessels	1	1	1	1	1	1	1
Roll-on Roll-off vessels[27]	Vessels	2	- [r]	- [r]	- [r]	- [r]	- [r]	- [r]
Royal Marines								
RM Commando	Commandos	3	3	3	3	3	3	3
Command Support Group	Commandos	1	1	1	1	1	1	1
Infantry Battalion	Battalion	-	1 [28]	1	1	1	1	1
Logistic unit	Regiments	1	1	1	1	1	1	1
Artillery unit	Regiments	1	1	1	1	1	1	1
Engineer unit	Squadrons	1	1	1	1	1	1	1
Nuclear Guarding and Fleet Security	Squadrons	1	3	3	4 [29]	4	4	4
Assault (landing craft)	Squadrons	3	4	4	4	4	4	3 [30]
Naval Aircraft								
Fixed Wing Aircraft[32]	Squadrons	1	- [r]	- [r]	- [r]	-	-	-
Helicopters[33, 34]	Squadrons	10 [r]	8 [r]	8 [r]	8 [r]	8 [r]	8 [r]	8 [r]
Reserve Units								
Royal Navy Reserve Units	Units	..	14	14	14	14	14	14
Royal Marine Reserve Units	Units	..	5	5	5	5	5	5

Source: MOD Finance & Military Capability

Footnotes located on the next page.

14.3a Number of vessels in the Royal Navy and Royal Fleet Auxiliary, and squadrons in the Fleet Air Arm, at 1 April each year

1. HMS Sovereign was withdrawn from service during the year.
2. HMS Superb was withdrawn from service during the year.
3. HMS Trafalgar and HMS Sceptre were withdrawn from service during the year. HMS Astute undergoing sea trials.
4. HMS Turbulent was withdrawn from service in July 2012.
5. HMS Ambush undergoing sea trials.
6. HMS Ark Royal withdrawn from service.
7. HMS Illustrious converted into a Helicopter Landing Platform.
8. HMS Southampton was withdrawn from service during the year.
9. HMS Exeter and HMS Nottingham were withdrawn from service during the year. HMS Daring entered full service during 2010.
10. HMS Dauntless entered service and HMS Manchester was withdrawn from service during the year.
11. HMS Diamond entered service, HMS Gloucester and HMS Liverpool were decommissioned.
12. HMS Chatham and HMS Campbeltown were withdrawn from service during the year.
13. HMS Cumberland and HMS Cornwall were decommissioned in year.
14. HMS Walney was withdrawn from service during the year.
15. HMS Clyde entered service during the year. HMS Dumbarton Castle was withdrawn from service.
16. HMS Roebuck was withdrawn from service during the year.
17. HMS Endurance non-operational while options for her repair or replacement were considered.
18. HMS Endurance non-operational while options for her repair or replacement were considered. Replaced on an operational basis by HMS Protector.
19. RFA Brambleleaf, RFA Oakleaf and RFA Grey Rover were withdrawn from service during this period.
20. Two vessels re-categorised as Fleet Replenishment ships to reflect their primary role.
21. RFA Fort George was withdrawn from service during the year.
22. RFA Bayleaf was withdrawn from service during the year.
23. Secondary role of Aviation Training Ship.
24. RFA Lyme Bay, Cardigan Bay and Mounts Bay entered service 2005/06. RFA Largs Bay entered service 2006/07.
25. The following were withdrawn from service: RFA Sir Geraint 2002, Sir Percivale 2005, Sir Tristram & Sir Galahad 2006, Sir Bedivere 2007.
26. RFA Largs Bay was sold to Australia in January 2011 as a result of SDSR10.
27. This role ceased for the RFA in 2004 and transferred to Chartered Shipping administered by Defence Supply Chain Operational Movements (DSCOM).
28. 1 Rifles became part of 3 Commando Brigade on 1 April 2008.
29. Fleet Protection Group Royal Marines expanded by one squadron (P Sqn) during Mar-Sep 2010.
30. A Landing Craft Assault Squadron has been disestablished as a result of SDSR10.
31. HMS ENDURANCE now withdrawn from service.
32. Excludes Joint Force Harrier squadrons from 1 April 2000.
33. Excludes Joint Helicopter Command squadrons from 1 October 1999.
34. Excludes all Operational Conversion Units (OCU) / Operational Evaluation Units (OEU) from 1 April 2004. Other Training squadrons have also been excluded.

r Some of the figures in this table have been corrected following a review by the MOD Finance and Military Capability branches, due to concerns raised about previously publishe figures. (1) Historic figures of tankers and fleet replenishment ships have been corrected due to the addition of solid support ships. This provides a clearer picture of vessels in the RFA, as each of these types of vessel has a distinct role. (2) Previous editions of this table incorrectly stated the MOD had a number of roll-on roll-off vessels in the Fleet Air Arm. However, the ownership of these vessels transferred from the RFA in 2004 as discussed in footnote 27. (3) Corrections have been made to the number of Naval aircraft squadrons following clarification of the squadrons excluded from these historic figures (see footnotes 32-34).

14.3b Number of Regiments, Infantry Battalions and Major Headquarters in the Regular Army and Army Reserves[1], at 1 April each year

This table is a National Statistic.

		2000	2008	2009	2010	2011	2012	2013
Combat arms								
Armour								
Regular Army	Regiments	10	10	10	10	10	10	10
Army Reserves	Regiments	4	4	4	4	4	4	4
Infantry								
Regular Army[2]	Battalions	40	36	36	36	36	36	36
Army Reserves	Battalions	15	14	14	14	14	14	14
Home Service Forces	Battalions	7	-	-	-	-	-	-
Combat support								
Artillery								
Regular Army[4]	Regiments	15	14	14	14	14	14	13
Army Reserves[5]	Regiments	7	7	7	7	7	7	7
Engineers								
Regular Army	Regiments	11	11	11	12 [6]	12	14	13 [7]
Army Reserves	Regiments	6	6	6	5	5	5	5
Signals								
Regular Army	Regiments	11	12	12	12	12	11	11
Army Reserves	Regiments	11	11	5 [8]	5	5	5	5
Combat service support								
Equipment support								
Regular Army	Battalions	7	7	7	7	7	7	6 [9]
Army Reserves	Battalions	4	2 [10]	2	2	2	2	2
Logistics								
Regular Army	Regiments	22	17	17	17	17	17	16 [11]
Army Reserves	Regiments	17	17	17	17	17	17	17
Medical Regiments / Field Hospitals								
Regular Army	Number	8	8	8	9	9	9	9
Army Reserves	Number	15	15	15	15	15	15	15
Corps, Division & Brigade HQ								
NATO Corps HQ		1	1	1	1	1	1	1
Division / District HQ								
Deployable		2	2	2	2	2	2	2
Non-deployable		4	5	5	5	5	5	4 [14]
Brigade HQ[15]								
Deployable		7	7	7	7	7	7	6 [16]
Non-deployable		15	9	9	10	10	10	10

Source: Army HQ Plans Directorate

1. Previously known as the Territorial Army.
2. Excludes Special Forces Support Group.
3. 1 R WELSH and 2 R WELSH merged Mar 14; 2 YORKS and 3 YORKS merged 2013; 5 SCOTS regiment reduced to a Public Duties Independent Company Mar 14.
4. Excludes 14th Regiment Royal Artillery. Also excludes 40th Regiment Royal Artillery which was disbanded due to Planning Round 2011.
5. Includes the Honourable Artillery Company.
6. 101 Engr Regt (EOD) was 'regularised' under Op ENTIRETY, in order to support ongoing operations in Afghanistan.
7. 38 Engineer Regiment were disbanded in Planning Round 2011.
8. Restructuring of Royal Electrical and Mechanical Engineers was announced in 2008.
9. 19 Combat Service Support Batallion REME disbanded in January 2013 in Planning Round 2011. 01 Bn & 104 Bn REME form a single Regular Force Support Battalion.
10. As a result of Planning Round 2009, six R Signals Regiments (V) were removed from the force structure.
11. 8 Regiment Royal Logistics Corps disbanded in Planning Round 2011.
12. 24 Regiment and 12 Logistic Support Regiment removed from ORBAT as at Mar 14.
13. 168 Pioneer Regiment Royal Logistics Corp disbanded Feb 2014, with effect post 1 Apr 2014.
14. HQ 2 DIV, HQ 4 DIV and HQ 5 DIV all disbanded in 12/13; HQ Sp Comd was established in 12/13.
15. Brigade HQ figures do not include Logistics or Specialist Brigades.
16. HQ 19 Lt Brigade were disbanded in Planning Round 2011.

14.3c Number of Squadrons in the Royal Air Force and the Royal Auxiliary Air Force, at 1 April each year

This table excludes Operational Conversion Units, which train qualified aircrew for different aircraft types.
This table is a National Statistic.

		2000	2008	2009	2010	2011	2012	2013
Regular Air Force								
Multi-roled Fast Jet Squadrons [1,2]	Squadrons	17	11	11	10 [3]	10 [4]	8 [5]	9 [6]
Maritime patrol	Squadrons	3	2	2	2	2	- [7]	-
ISTAR (inc Airborne Early Warning)	Squadrons	2	4	4	4	4	5 [8]	6 [9]
Air transport / Air Refuelling	Squadrons	8	8	8	8	7 [10]	7	7
Search and Rescue	Squadrons	2	2	2	2	2	2	2
RAF FP Wg	HQs	..	7	7	8	8	8	8
RAF Ground based air defence[11]	Squadrons	*	-	-	-	-	-	-
RAF Regiment Field[11]	Squadrons	*	7	7	8	8	8	8
RAF Regt (Jt CBRN)[12]	Squadrons	-	1	1	1	1	-	-
Defence CBRN Wing[12,25]	HQs	-	-	-	-	-	1	1
	Squadrons	-	-	-	-	-	2	2
RAF Police Force[13]	HQs	*	*	*	*	*	* ‖[13]	3
	Squadrons	*	*	*	*	*	* ‖	9
Tactical Provost Wg	HQs	-	1	1	1	1	1 ‖	*
	Squadrons	-	1	1	1	1	1 ‖	*
Specialist Policing Wg	HQs	-	1	1	1	1	1 ‖	*
	Squadrons	-	3	3	3	3	3 ‖	*
General Policing Wg	HQs	-	1	1	1	1	1 ‖	*
	Squadrons	-	4	4	4	4	4 ‖	*
Tactical Communications Wg[14]	Squadrons	*	4	4	4	4	4	4
Auxiliary Air Force[22]								
Air Movements	Squadrons	1	1	1	1	1	1	1
Aeromedical	Squadrons	2	2	2	2	2	2	2
Flight Operations	Squadrons	-	-	-	-	-	1	1
General Support	Squadrons	-	-	-	-	-	-	2 [15]
HQ Augmentation	Squadrons	1	1	1	1	1	1	1 [r]
Intelligence	Squadrons	2	2	2	2	2	2	2
Photographic Interpretation	Squadrons	1	1	1	1	1	1	1
Public Relations	Squadrons	1	1	1	1	1	1	1
RAuxAF Regt Field	Squadrons	4	3	3	3	3	3	4 [16]
FP Operations Support	Squadrons	4	4	4	4	4	4	1 [17]
RAF Police	Squadrons	-	1	1	1	1	1	2 [18]
RAuxAF Regt CBRN[21]	Squadrons	-	1	1	1	1	1	1
A4 - Logs	Squadrons	-	-	-	-	-	-	2 [19]
Reserve Aircrew - Air Mobility	Squadrons	-	-	- -	-	-	-	1
RAF Reserve - Sponsored Reserves								
Meteorological[20]	Units	1	1	1	1	1	1	1

Source: MOD Finance & Military Capability

1. Excludes Joint Force Harrier squadrons.

2. From 2006, four Air Defence squadrons amalgamated with Strike/Attack, Offensive support and Reconnaissance squadrons to form multi-roled fast jet squadrons. One Reconnaissance squadron was re-roled ISTAR. One squadron was disbanded.

3. 43 Sqn was stood down on 1 July 2009.

4. 6 Sqn (Typhoon) stood up 6 Sep 2010. 111 Sqn (Tornado F3) stood down 22 Mar 2011.

5. 13 Sqn and 14 Sqn (both Tornado GR4) were disbanded on 1 Jun 2011. (See further footnote below on 14 Sqn)

6. 1 Sqn (Typhoon) reformed 15 Sep 2012.

7. 201 Sqn and 120 Sqn were disbanded on 26 May 2011.

8. 14 Sqn was subsequently stood up on 14 October 2011. This unit replaced the flight within 5 Sqn operating the R1 Shadow aircraft.

9. 13 Sqn (MQ9) reformed 26 Oct 2012.

10. 70 Sqn disbanded 10 Sep 2010.

11. Delivery of Ground based air defence has been vested with the Army since 2008. The remaining 2 squadrons were combined on 1 Apr 2008 to provide a 7th Field Sqn (15 Sqn RAF Regt).

12. Defence CBRN Wing was established on 14 Dec 2011 on the disbandment of the Joint CBRN Regiment.

13. RAF Police re-brigaded on 1 Apr 2012 following a Planning Round 2011 option that directed a 15% reduction in manning numbers. The previous definitions of Tactical Provost, Specialist and General Wings are no longer appropriate.

14. TCW has existed as a formed unit since 1969 and is currently subordinate to 90 Signals Unit at RAF Leeming. 90 Signals Unit comprises one HQ and 8 Sqns; 4 x TCW and 4 x Force Generation Wg (FGW); it has existed since 2006. All but 2 Sqns have some form of deployable function.

15. 611 Sqn stood up Oct 2012, 502 Sqn stood up Jan 2013

16. 501 Sqn RAuxAF Ops Spt - Regt staff regenerated into newly created 2624 RAuxAF Regt Sqn at BZN.

17. 501 and 504 RAuxAF Ops Spt Sqns transfer to A4. 603 RAuxAF Sqn transfered to RAFP.

18. Reflects the transfer of 603 Sqn to RAF Police.

19. 501 and 504 RAuxAF Logs Sqns.

20. Previously reported as an Royal Auxillary Air Force squadron.

21. CBRN is also known as: Chemical, Biological, Radiological and Nuclear.

22. Note that this is not a comprehensive list of Auxiliary Air Force squadrons, as for example some units that form part of the Air Combat Service Support Units are not included.

r The 2013 edition of UK Defence Statistics incorrectly stated that there were three HQ Augmentation Squadrons in 2013. The reason for this error is that 2 General Support Squadrons were incorrectly declared as HQ Aumentation Squadrons.

14.3d Number of Regiments and Squadrons in selected Joint Units, at 1 April each year

This table excludes Operational Conversion Units, which train qualified aircrew for different aircraft types.
This table is a National Statistic.

		2008	2009	2010	2011	2012	2013
Joint Units							
Joint Nuclear Biological Chemical	Regiments	1	1	1	1	- [3]	-
Special Forces							
Special Air Service	Regiments	1	1	1	1	1	1
Special Air Service - Army Reserves	Regiments	2	2	2	2	2	2
Special Boat Service	Units[1]	1	1	1	1	1	1
Special Forces Support Group Battalion[2]	Battalions	1	1	1	1	1	1
Joint Helicopter Command							
Royal Navy Helicopter	Squadrons[4]	4	4	4	4	4	4
Army Aviation[5]	Regiments	5	5	5	5	5	5
Army Aviation - Army Reserves	Regiments	2	1 [7]	1	1	1	1
Royal Air Force Helicopter	Squadrons[4]	6 [8]	6	6	6	6	6 [r]
Royal Auxiliary Air Force[9]	Squadrons[4]	1	1	1	1	1	1
Joint Special Forces Air Wing	Units	1	1	1	1	1	1
Joint Force Harrier							
Royal Navy	Squadrons[4]	2	2	1 [10]	- [11]	-	-
Royal Air Force	Squadrons[4]	2	2	1 [12]	- [13]	-	-

Source: MOD Finance & Military Capability

1. The units for the Special Boat Service have been changed from Squadrons to Units so that the same level of formation is given for all Special Forces.
2. The Special Forces Support Group was formed as a result of the Ministerial Announcement on 16 Dec 2004 as part of The Future Army Structure. It is a Tri-Service Unit based on 1 PARA, to provide specialist support to Special Forces.
3. The JNBC regiment disbanded on the formation of the Defence CBRN Wing on 14 December 2011.
4. The term "squadron" has different meanings among the three Services: see the Glossary for details.
5. These figures exclude the School of Army Aviation, 667 (D&T) Sqn and 657 Sqn and three independent Army Air Corps flights (7, 25 and 29 Flts).
6. 6 Regt AAC(V) formed on 1 April 2007.
7. 7 Regt AAC(V) was disbanded 31 March 2009.
8. Reflects the standing up of 78 Sqn RAF to accommodate the endorsed increase in Merlin Mk3 crews and aircraft.
9. No 606 (Chiltern) Squadron provides a pool of trained personnel to provide combat service support to the Support Helicopter Force in training and on operations in times of crisis and war.
10. On the reduction in the Joint Force Harrier force from 1 April 2010, the Fleet Air Arm Strike Wing was counted as 1 Sqn.
11. 800 RNAS was disbanded on 28 January 2011.
12. 20 Sqn was disbanded 31 March 2010.
13. 1 Sqn was disbanded on 28 January 2011.

r The 2013 edition of this publication incorrectly stated that there were 7 RAF Helicopter squadrons in 2013.

14.4 Outflow[1] from UK Regular Forces by Service and sex

This table is a National Statistic.

	2000/01	2008/09	2009/10	2010/11	2011/12	2012/13
All Services [2]	**24 950**	**21 650**	**18 270**	**18 140**	**21 370**	**23 520**
of which female	2 430	1 900	1 440	1 590	1 770	1 970
percentage female	*9.7*	*8.8*	*7.9*	*8.8*	*8.3*	*8.4*
Officers: total	**2 290**	**2 380**	**1 880**	**1 930**	**2 560**	**3 040**
of which female	260	300	220	240	290	350
percentage female	*11.1*	*12.7*	*11.5*	*12.2*	*11.5*	*11.5*
Other ranks: total	**22 650**	**19 270**	**16 390**	**16 200**	**18 810**	**20 480**
of which female	2 180	1 600	1 220	1 350	1 480	1 620
percentage female	*9.6*	*8.3*	*7.5*	*8.3*	*7.9*	*7.9*
RN/RM	**5 040**	**4 440**	**3 720**	**3 630**	**4 320**	**4 350**
of which female	550	460	340	360	440	400
percentage female	*11.0*	*10.3*	*9.1*	*9.9*	*10.1*	*9.2*
Officers: total	**480**	**520**	**440**	**460**	**570**	**590**
of which female	40	50	50	50	60	60
percentage female	*9.1*	*9.6*	*11.2*	*10.1*	*11.1*	*9.5*
Other ranks: total	**4 550**	**3 920**	**3 280**	**3 170**	**3 750**	**3 760**
of which female	510	410	290	310	380	340
percentage female	*11.2*	*10.4*	*8.8*	*9.9*	*10.0*	*9.2*
Army [2]	**15 230**	**13 080**	**11 560**	**11 500**	**13 200**	**14 890**
of which female	1 330	920	690	790	830	1 010
percentage female	*8.8*	*7.1*	*6.0*	*6.9*	*6.3*	*6.8*
Officers: total	**1 150**	**1 210**	**980**	**990**	**1 240**	**1 460**
of which female	160	160	100	120	120	150
percentage female	*13.4*	*13.1*	*9.9*	*12.3*	*9.6*	*10.3*
Other ranks: total	**14 080**	**11 870**	**10 580**	**10 510**	**11 960**	**13 430**
of which female	1 180	760	600	670	710	860
percentage female	*8.4*	*6.4*	*5.6*	*6.4*	*5.9*	*6.4*
RAF	**4 680**	**4 120**	**2 990**	**3 010**	**3 850**	**4 280**
of which female	540	520	410	440	510	560
percentage female	*11.6*	*12.5*	*13.6*	*14.5*	*13.1*	*13.0*
Officers: total	**660**	**650**	**460**	**490**	**740**	**990**
of which female	60	90	70	70	110	140
percentage female	*8.5*	*14.3*	*15.3*	*13.9*	*15.1*	*14.4*
Other ranks: total	**4 020**	**3 470**	**2 530**	**2 520**	**3 110**	**3 300**
of which female	490	420	340	370	390	420
percentage female	*12.1*	*12.2*	*13.3*	*14.6*	*12.7*	*12.6*

Source: Defence Statistics (Tri-Service)

1. Figures show outflow from UK Regular Forces, both trained and untrained, including personnel leaving the Services, deaths, recalled reservists on release and outflow to the Home Service battalions of the Royal Irish Regiment (which disbanded on 31 March 2008). They do not include promotion from ranks to officers or flows between Services and are not comparable with gains to trained strength figures in Table 2.19 which include promotion from ranks to officers.

2. Outflow figures up to and including 2006/07 include the net flow of between 100 and 200 personnel from the Regular Army to Long Term Absentee (LTA). Outflow figures from 2007/08 do not include this net flow to LTA. See glossary for more details.

14.5 Full-time trained strength[1] and requirement , at 1 April each year

	2000	2008	2009	2010	2011	2012	2013
All Services							
Requirement	198 160	179 270	178 860	178 750	179 250	174 840	162 940
Strength[2]	190 270	173 530	174 170	177 890	176 860	170 010	160 710
Surplus/Deficit	-7 880	-5 740	-4 690	- 860	-2 390	-4 830	-2 230
Surplus/Deficit as % of requirement	*-4.0*	*-3.2*	*-2.6*	*-0.5*	*-1.3*	*-2.8*	*-1.4*
RN/RM							
Requirement	39 860	36 260	35 760	35 790	35 700	34 800	30 530
Strength[2]	38 880	35 050	35 020	35 500	35 420	33 290	31 420
Surplus/Deficit	- 990	-1 210	- 740	- 290	- 280	-1 510	890
Surplus/Deficit as % of requirement	*-2.5*	*-3.3*	*-2.1*	*-0.8*	*-0.8*	*-4.3*	*2.9*
Army							
Requirement	106 400	101 800	101 790	102 160	102 210	101 210	96 790
Strength[2]	100 190	98 070	99 510	102 260	101 340	98 600	93 940
Surplus/Deficit	-6 210	-3 730	-2 280	100	- 870	-2 610	-2 850
Surplus/Deficit as % of requirement	*-5.8*	*-3.7*	*-2.2*	*0.1*	*-0.8*	*-2.6*	*-2.9*
Royal Air Force							
Requirement	51 900	41 210	41 310	40 800	41 340	38 830	35 620
Strength[2]	51 210	40 400	39 640	40 130	40 090	38 120	35 350
Surplus/Deficit	- 690	- 800	-1 670	- 670	-1 250	- 700	- 270
Surplus/Deficit as % of requirement	*-1.3*	*-1.9*	*-4.1*	*-1.7*	*-3.0*	*-1.8*	*-0.8*

Source: Defence Statistics (Tri-Service)

1. The Full-Time Trained Strength of the UK Armed Forces is defined as comprising of trained UK Regular Forces, trained Gurkhas and elements of the FTRS (Full Time Reserve Service) personnel. It does not include mobilised reservists.

2. From 1 April 2010 some elements of the FTRS are excluded. For a full description of FTRS please refer to the Glossary of Terms and Abbreviations at the end of this publication.

14.6a Civilian Personnel[1], at 1 April each year

This table is a National Statistic.

FTE

	2009	2010	2011	2012	2013	2014
Civilian Level 0[2]	**86 620**	**85 850**	**83 060** e	**71 010** e	**65 400**	**62 500**
Civilian Level 1[3]	**66 440**	**65 920**	**63 130**	**54 510**	**49 980**	**48 400**
Civilian Level 1 - Permanent	63 640	63 270	60 660	52 480	47 950	46 470
Non-industrial	52 680	52 350	50 150	43 890	40 300	38 940
Industrial	10 960	10 930	10 510	8 590	7 650	7 530
Civilian Level 1 - Casual[4]	500	320	120	30	120	120
Non-industrial	360	230	50	20	110	100
Industrial	140	90	70	10	10	10
Civilian Level 1 - RFA[5]	2 300	2 330	2 360	2 000	1 900	1 820
Trading Funds[6]	**9 630**	**9 730**	**9 350**	**7 110**	**7170**	**7110**
Permanent	9 510	9 620	9 290	7 000	7 050	7 000
Casual	110	110	60	110	120	110
Locally engaged civilians	**10 550**	**10 200**	**10 580** e	**9 390** e	**8 250**	**6 990**

Source: Defence Statistics (Civilian)

1. Civilian Level 0 and 1 are defined in footnotes 2 and 3 respectively.
2. **Civilian Level 0** This contains all those at Level 1 plus Trading Funds and Locally Engaged Civilians. This is used for external reporting, including the Quarterly Civilian Personnel Report, Defence Statistics Bulletins and Parliamentary Business.
3. **Civilian Level 1** Permanent and casual civilian personnel and Royal Fleet Auxiliaries, but excludes Trading Funds and Locally Engaged Civilians. This is generally used for MOD internal reporting and planning.
4. Casual staff are usually engaged for less than 12 months.
5. RFA personnel are assumed to be permanent.
6. At 1 October 2011 the Meterological Office transferred to the Department for Business Innovation and Skills (1,800).

14.6b Civilian personnel[1] by Top Level Budget and grade equivalent[2], at 1 April each year

This table is a National Statistic. These statistics have previously been published in the Quarterly Civilian Personnel Report (QCPR). This is a quarterly publication and the latest figures can be found in Quarterly Civilian Personnel Report - July 2014

						FTE
Grade	2009	2010	2011	2012	2013	2014
Civilian Personnel[1]	73 770	73 320	70 130	59 630	55 240	53 690
Non Industrial	53 040	52 570	50 200	43 910	40 410	39 040
of which						
Navy Command	**1 790**	**1 860**	**1 800**	**1 530**	**1 590**	**2 010**
Pay Band C and above	510	540	530	500	540	760
Pay Band D and below	1 280	1 320	1 250	1 020	1 030	1 230
Other non-industrial[3]	-	10	10	10	10	20
Land Command	**11 860**	**11 860**	**10 690**	**9 440**	**7 960**	**7 510**
Pay Band C and above	3 420	3 450	3 170	2 950	2 590	2 350
Pay Band D and below	8 370	8 270	7 530	6 490	5 360	5 150
Other non-industrial[3]	80	150	-	-	10	10
Air Command	**5 720**	**5 810**	**5 670**	**4 770**	**4 050**	**3 830**
Pay Band C and above	1 120	1 150	1 180	1 060	890	850
Pay Band D and below	4 600	4 660	4 480	3 710	3 160	2 980
Other non-industrial[3]	10	-	-	-	-	-
Centre TLB	**16 020**	**16 110**	**15 360**	*	*	*
Pay Band C and above	4 150	4 120	4 180	*	*	*
Pay Band D and below	11 850	11 890	11 180	*	*	*
Other non-industrial[3]	10	100	-	*	*	*
Head Office & Corporate Services	*	*	*	**10 970**	**7 230**	**7 230**
Pay Band C and above	*	*	*	2 680	2 510	2 700
Pay Band D and below	*	*	*	8 300	4 720	4 530
Other non-industrial[3]	*	*	*	-	-	-
Chief of Joint Operations	**290**	**290**	**260**	*	*	*
Pay Band C and above	170	160	150	*	*	*
Pay Band D and below	110	120	110	*	*	*
Other non-industrial[3]	-	-	-	*	*	*
Joint Forces Command	*	*	*	**2 680**	**3 570**	**5 210**
Pay Band C and above	*	*	*	1 210	1 660	2 860
Pay Band D and below	*	*	*	1 450	1 890	2 340
Other non-industrial[3]	*	*	*	20	10	10
Defence Equipment & Support	**14 330**	**13 840**	**13 570**	**12 170**	**11 000**	**8 940**
Pay Band C and above	8 520	8 410	8 610	7 860	7 430	6 110
Pay Band D and below	5 800	5 410	4 950	4 300	3 570	2 800
Other non-industrial[3]	10	20	-	10	-	20
Defence Infrastructure Organisation	**2 550**	**2 700**	**2 850**	**2 350**	**5 010**	**4 240**
Pay Band C and above	1 460	1 500	1 560	1 360	1 380	1 470
Pay Band D and below	1 100	1 200	1 290	990	3 630	2 770
Other non-industrial[3]	-	-	-	-	-	-
Science Innovation & Technology	**350**	*	*	*	*	*
Pay Band C and above	120	*	*	*	*	*
Pay Band D and below	230	*	*	*	*	*
Other non-industrial[3]	-	*	*	*	*	*
Unknown[4]	**120**	**100**	**10**	**10**	**20**	**60**
Pay Band C and above	80	60	-	-	10	40
Pay Band D and below	40	30	10	10	10	20
Other non-industrial[3]	10	10	-	-	-	-

14.6b Civilian personnel[1] by Top Level Budget and grade equivalent[2], at 1 April each year

						FTE
Grade	2009	2010	2011	2012	2013	2014
Industrial	**11 100**	**11 020**	**10 580**	**8 600**	**7 660**	**7 540**
Navy Command	550	570	540	470	440	480
Land Command	4 630	4 620	4 230	3 720	3 460	3 440
Air Command	2 830	2 850	2 760	1 770	1 500	1 410
Centre TLB	550	540	510	*	*	*
Head Office & Corporate Services	*	*	*	80	70	70
Chief of Joint Operations	-	-	-	*	*	*
Joint Forces Command	*	*	*	380	350	360
Defence Equipment & Support	2 400	2 310	2 190	1 920	1 550	1 510
Defence Infrastructure Organisation	120	130	340	260	280	280
Science Innovation & Technology	-	*	*	*	*	*
Unknown	10	-	-	-	-	-
Trading Funds	**9 630**	**9 730**	**9 350**	**7 110**	**7 170**	**7 110**
Defence Science & Technology Laboratory	3 470	3 700	3 640	3 640	3 720	3 690
Defence Support Group	3 350	3 230	2 960	2 490	2 420	2 400
Hydrographic Office	960	970	960	980	1 030	1 020
Met Office[5]	1 850	1 840	1 800	*	*	*

Source: Defence Ststistics (Civilian)

1. Civilian personnel is defined as personnel employed in MOD Main Core TLBs and Trading Funds. Royal Fleet Auxiliary and Locally engaged civilians are excluded from all data in this table.

2. Grade equivalent is shown in terms of the broader banding structure and is based on paid grade.

3. Includes industrial personnel on temporary promotion to non-industrial grades and personnel for whom no grade information is available.

4. Personnel for whom no Top Level Budget (TLB) information is available are included in this section of the table.

5. In October 2011 responsibility for management of the Meteorological Office personnel (1,800) transferred to Department for Business, Innovation and Skills (BIS).

* denotes data not applicable.

14.7a Land holdings by country and whether owned, leased or with legal rights, at 1 April each year

These holdings include land declared as surplus to defence requirements.
A thousand hectares is 3.86 square miles.
This table is a National Statistic.

Thousand hectares

	2000	2008	2009 [1]	2010 [1]	2011 [2]	2012	2013
Total land & foreshore holdings and Rights held[4]	**363.3**	**373.4**	**372.0**	**371.0** ‖	**435.3**	**434.1**	**432.9**
Land and foreshore holdings	238.5	240.3	239.0	238.0 ‖	230.4	229.1	228.0
Freehold	219.9	220.0	219.0	218.0 ‖	209.8	208.8	207.7
Leasehold	18.6	20.3	20.0	20.0 ‖	20.6	20.3	20.3
Rights held[4]	124.8	133.1	133.0	133.0 ‖	204.9	204.9	204.9

Of which:

	2000	2008	2009 [1]	2010 [1]	2011 [2]	2012	2013
England	**226.3**	**223.9**	**223.0**	**221.0** ‖	**263.3**	**262.4**	**261.5**
Land and foreshore holdings	191.8	189.5	188.0	187.0 ‖	179.1	178.2	177.5
Freehold	176.2	172.2	171.0	170.0 ‖	164.5	163.8	163.1
Leasehold	15.6	17.3	17.0	17.0 ‖	14.6	14.4	14.4
Rights held[4]	34.5	34.4	34.0	34.0 ‖	84.1	84.1	84.1
Wales	**23.0**	**22.9**	**23.0**	**23.0** ‖	**23.4**	**23.4**	**23.4**
Land and foreshore holdings	20.8	20.7	21.0	21.0 ‖	20.1	20.1	20.1
Freehold	20.6	20.5	21.0	21.0 ‖	19.8	19.8	19.8
Leasehold	0.2	0.2	-	- ‖	0.3	0.3	0.3
Rights held[4]	2.2	2.2	2.0	2.0 ‖	3.3	3.3	3.3
Scotland	**110.7**	**123.5**	**124.0**	**124.0** ‖	**146.4**	**146.4**	**146.1**
Land and foreshore holdings	22.7	27.2	28.0	28.0 ‖	28.9	28.9	28.6
Freehold	20.2	24.6	25.0	25.0 ‖	23.5	23.5	23.1
Leasehold	2.5	2.6	3.0	3.0 ‖	5.4	5.4	5.5
Rights held[4]	88.0	96.3	96.0	96.0 ‖	117.4	117.5	117.5
Northern Ireland	**3.3**	**3.2**	**3.0**	**3.0** ‖	**2.2**	**1.9**	**1.9**
Land and foreshore holdings	3.2	3.1	3.0	3.0 ‖	2.2	1.8	1.8
Freehold	2.9	2.8	3.0	3.0 ‖	2.0	1.7	1.7
Leasehold	0.3	0.3	-	- ‖	0.2	0.1	0.1
Rights held[4]	0.1	0.1	-	- ‖	-	-	-

	2000	2008	2009	2010	2011	2012	2013
Land and foreshore holdings	**238.5**	**240.3**	**239.0**	**238.0** ‖	**230.4** [5]	**229.1**	**228.0**
Land	**219.9**	**221.7**	**221.0**	**220.0** ‖	..	..	..
England	176.6	174.2	173.0	172.0 ‖	..	..	..
Wales	19.7	19.7	20.0	20.0 ‖	..	..	..
Scotland	20.6	24.9	25.0	25.0 ‖	..	..	..
Northern Ireland	3.0	2.9	3.0	3.0 ‖	..	..	..
Foreshore	**18.6**	**18.6**	**18.0**	**18.0** ‖	..	..	..
England	15.3	15.3	15.0	15.0 ‖	..	..	..
Wales	1.0	1.0	1.0	1.0 ‖	..	..	..
Scotland	2.1	2.1	2.0	2.0 ‖	..	..	..
Northern Ireland	0.2	0.2	-	- ‖	..	..	..

Source: MOD Defence Infrastructure Organisation (DIO)

1. The figures presented for years 2009 and 2010 were rounded to the nearest thousand hectares.
2. Data from 2011 has been compiled using a new spatial dataset which allows for greater accuracy in the measurement of the estate. Because of this new dataset, comparable figures for earlier years are not available. Figures have been rounded to the nearest hundred hectares.
3. Part of the Kinlochleven Training Area in Scotland, over which MOD holds rights, is now included, having been omitted from figures previously reported. It was highlighted by data quality improvement work as a result of the introduction of the DIO's Infrastructure Management System.
4. Rights held are Land and foreshore that are not owned by, or leased to MOD, but over which the Department has limited rights under grants and rights.
5. Separate figures for land and foreshore are no longer recorded.

Defence

14.7b Service Family Accommodation in the United Kingdom at 31 March each year

This table is a National Statistic.

Thousands of dwellings

	2000	2008	2009	2010	2011	2012	2013
Permanent holdings	**64.8**	**51.2**	**49.9**	**49.1**	**49.1**	**49.0**	**49.4**
By country:							
England & Wales	55.9	45.2	44.9	44.1	44.2	44.0	44.5
Scotland	5.7	3.6	3.2	3.2	3.2	3.3	3.3
Northern Ireland	3.2	2.4	1.8	1.8	1.7	1.7	1.6
Vacant properties	**14.7**	**10.5**	**8.4**	**7.3**	**6.0**	**6.5**	**7.7**
By country:							
England & Wales	12.6	8.1	7.3	6.1	5.0	5.0	6.1
Scotland	1.7	0.9	0.6	0.6	0.5	0.7	0.7
Northern Ireland	0.4	1.5	0.5	0.6	0.5	0.8	0.9
Vacant properties as a percentage of all dwellings	*23*	*21*	*17*	*15*	*12*	*13*	*16*
By country:							
England & Wales	*23*	*18*	*16*	*14*	*11*	*11*	*14*
Scotland	*30*	*25*	*19*	*18*	*16*	*24*	*21*
Northern Ireland	*13*	*63*	*28*	*34*	*29*	*40*	*56*

Source: MOD Defence Infrastructure Organisation

430

14.8a Location of Service and civilian personnel[1,2] in the United Kingdom, at 1 April each year

This table is a National Statistic.

FTE

	2000 [3]	2007	2008	2009	2010	2011	2012	2013
United Kingdom	**267 700**	**239 460**	**231 350**	**233 290**	**236 710**	**229 400**	**214 190**	**203 360**
Service	170 300	161 360	158 450	162 670	166 100	161 790	156 970	150 310
Civilian	97 410	78 110	72 900	70 620	70 610	67 610	57 220	53 050
England	**222 560**	**207 550**	**202 710**	**204 400**	**207 890**	**201 320**	**188 810**	**180 080**
Service	143 040	141 360	140 120	143 540	146 950	142 860	139 260	133 810
Civilian	79 520	66 200	62 590	60 860	60 940	58 450	49 560	46 270
Wales	**8 260**	**5 010**	**4 800**	**4 730**	**4 900**	**4 580**	**4 150**	**3 910**
Service	3 220	2 590	2 630	2 720	2 930	2 820	2 780	2 650
Civilian	5 040	2 420	2 170	2 010	1 970	1 760	1 370	1 260
Scotland	**24 680**	**19 190**	**17 960**	**17 880**	**17 840**	**17 630**	**15 880**	**15 340**
Service	15 080	12 640	11 960	12 020	12 080	12 090	11 190	11 310
Civilian	9 600	6 550	5 990	5 860	5 760	5 540	4 690	4 020
Northern Ireland	**11 640**	**7 700**	**5 880**	**6 280**	**6 000**	**5 870**	**5 350**	**4 030**
Service	8 390	4 770	3 730	4 390	4 140	4 010	3 740	2 530
Civilian	3 250	2 940	2 150	1 890	1 930	1 850	1 610	1 500

Source: Defence Statistics (Tri-Service)

Service and Civilian personnel[1,2] by Region

FTE

	Service			Civilian		
	2012	2013	% change	2012	2013	% change
United Kingdom	**156 970**	**150 310**	**-4.2**	**57 220**	**53 050**	**-7.3**
England	**139 260**	**133 810**	**-3.9**	**49 560**	**46 270**	**-6.6**
East of England	17 350	15 210	-12.3	4 600	4 110	-10.6
East Midlands	8 420	8 610	2.3	1 900	1 700	-10.8
London	5 400	5 070	-6.1	3 960	3 690	-6.7
North East	1 400	1 390	-1.1	330	320	-5.3
North West	2 160	2 110	-2.3	1 900	1 810	-4.6
South East	43 330	42 330	-2.3	11 550	11 050	-4.4
South West	39 040	37 230	-4.6	18 100	16 950	-6.4
West Midlands	6 570	6 280	-4.4	3 970	3 690	-7.3
Yorkshire and The Humber	15 600	15 590	0.0	3 230	2 950	-8.7
Wales	**2 780**	**2 650**	**-4.5**	**1 370**	**1 260**	**-7.9**
Scotland	**11 190**	**11 310**	**1.1**	**4 690**	**4 020**	**-14.3**
Northern Ireland	**3 740**	**2 530**	**-32.4**	**1 610**	**1 500**	**-6.5**

Source: Defence Statistics (Tri-Service)

1. Service personnel figures are for UK Regular Forces based in the UK. They include all trained and untrained Personnel and exclude Gurkhas, Full Time Reserve Service personnel and mobilised reservists.

2. Civilian personnel includes Trading Fund staff and exclude RFAs and LECs.

3. 2000 figures are as at 1 July.

14.8b Global locations of Service[1] and civilian personnel[2,3], at 1 April each year

Number: FTE

		2000 [4]	2008	2009	2010	2011	2012	2013
Global Total		**333 960**	**276 410**	**275 220**	**277 560**	**269 420**	**250 810**	**236 110**
	Service	213 220	186 910	188 600	191 710	186 360	179 800	170 710
	Civilian Level 0	120 740	89 500	86 620	85 850	83 060	71 010	65 400
United Kingdom Total		**267 700**	**231 350**	**233 290**	**236 710**	**229 390**	**214 190**	**203 360**
	Service	170 300	158 450	162 670	166 100	161 790	156 970	150 310
	Civilian	97 410	72 900	70 620	70 610	67 610	57 220	53 050
Overseas Total		**54 000**	**41 270**	**38 240**	**37 650**	**36 910**	**33 710**	**30 050**
	Service	37 200	27 590	25 350	25 260	24 230	22 440	20 060
	Civilian	16 800	13 680	12 890	12 400	12 680	11 270	10 000
EUROPE (exc. UK) of which:		..	**36 800**	**33 670**	**33 000**	**31 300**	**29 050**	**25 610**
Germany	Service	..	21 650	19 100	19 100	18 240	16 990	14 840
	Civilian	..	7 820	7 420	7 020	6 470	5 800	5 300
Cyprus	Service	3 510	2 780	2 910	2 880	2 830	2 590	2 400
	Civilian	..	1 850	1 640	1 610	1 570	1 670	1 380
Belgium	Service	..	390	410	410	340	330	330
	Civilian	..	..	..	140	100	100	40
Gibraltar	Service	550	280	260	270	260	230	200
	Civilian	..	750	730	730	750	650	530
Italy	Service	..	250	260	250	210	170	140
	Civilian	..	..	..	60	50	50	20
ASIA (EXC. MIDDLE EAST)		..	**1 430**	**1 600**	**1 920**	**2 080**	**2 110**	**2 020**
	Service	970	260	260	260	280	260	260
	Civilian	..	1 170	1 340	1 660	1 800	1 860	1 760
NORTH AFRICA / MIDDLE EAST		..	**960**	**730**	**460**	**500**	**430**	**420**
	Service	1 300	360	370	380	420	340	330
	Civilian	..	600	360	80	80	90	90
SUB SAHARAN AFRICA of which:		..	**650**	**680**	**690**	**1 540**	**890**	**730**
Kenya[6]	Service	-	30	80	90	140	180	180
	Civilian	..	230	320	360	1 190	640	480
Sierra Leone	Service	-	80	60	30	30	20	20
	Civilian	..	220	150	150	130	-	-

Continued on the next page

14.8b Global locations of Service[1] and civilian personnel[2,3,] at 1 April each year

		2000 [4]	2008	2009	2010	2011	2012	2013
NORTH AMERICA		..	**880**	**920**	**990**	**980**	**990**	**1 000**
of which:								
United States	Service	910	420	470	520	550	560	560
	Civilian	..	180	160	160	150	150	150
Canada	Service	1 610	270	270	270	270	270	280
	Civilian	..	10	10	50	10	10	10
CENTRAL AMERICA / CARIBBEAN		..	**260**	**250**	**240**	**240**	**70**	**70**
	Service	-	80	70	70	70	10	10
	Civilian	..	180	180	170	160	60	60
SOUTH AMERICA		..	**20**	**20**	**20**	**20**	**20**	**20**
	Service	-	10	10	10	10	10	10
	Civilian	..	10	10	10	10	10	10
SOUTH ATLANTIC		..	**190**	**310**	**270**	**180**	**80**	**110**
of which:								
Falkland Islands	Service	780	130	250	220	120	50	70
	Civilian	..	50	50	40	40	30	30
OCEANIA		..	**80**	**60**	**60**	**70**	**70**	**70**
	Service	20	60	50	50	50	60	60
	Civilian	..	20	20	10	20	10	10
Unallocated		-	**1 520**	**1 390**	**860**	**760**	**910**	**800**
	Service	5 720	880	580	350	340	390	350
	Civilian	4 080	650	800	520	420	520	450
Royal Fleet Auxiliaries	Civilian	2 450	2 270	2 300	2 330	2 360	2 000	1 900

Source: Defence Statistics (Tri-Service)

1. Service personnel figures are for UK Regular Forces. They include all trained and untrained Personnel and exclude Gurkhas, Full Time Reserve Service personnel and mobilised reservists.
2. Civilian Level 0 and Level 1 are defined in the Glossary.
3. UK civilian totals include Trading Fund personnel but exclude RFA and LEC personnel and those with an unknown location. Overseas civilian includes LEC personnel.
4. Detailed break down of LEC data for 2000 are not available. The "Overseas Total" for year 2000 subsumes the total LEC figure. 2000 figures as at 1 July.
5. The increase in civilian numbers in 2011 reflects the additional requirements for locally engaged civilian to support military exercises.

14.9a UK regular Armed Forces deaths by Service, Year of occurrence 2005-2013, numbers, age and gender standardised rates.

Year	All		Naval Service		Army		RAF	
	Number	Rate	Number	Rate	Number	Rate	Number	Rate
2005	160	82	27	70	93	91	40	72
2006	191	99	33	85	111	95	47	92
2007	204	106	27	74	145	128	32	74
2008	137	74	40	110	79	74	18	37
2009	205	107	23	58	158	133	24	55
2010	187	97	30	77	136	116	21	50
2011	132	69	19	52	98	88	15	33
2012	130	72	20	59	95	89	15	42
2013	86	50	13	42	63	65	10	23

Source: Defence Statistics (Health)

Rates have been age and gender standardised to the 2014 Armed Forces population, expressed per 100,000 strength.

14.9b UK Regular Armed Forces deaths by Service, 2005-2013, numbers, Standardised Mortality Ratios (SMR) (95% confidence intervals (CI)).

Year	All			Naval Service			Army			RAF		
	Number	SMR	(95% CI)	Number	SMR	(95% CI)	Number	SMR	(95% CI)	Number	SMR	(95% CI)
2005	160	75	(64-88)	27	62	(41-91)	93	87.61154	(71-107)	40	62.48911	(46-85)
2006	191	87	(76-101)	33	73	(52-103)	111	99.70681	(83-120)	47	75.41417	(57-100)
2007	204	96	(84-110)	27	61	(40-89)	145	132.0441	(112-155)	32	55.0789	(39-78)
2008	137	65	(55-76)	40	89		79	71.88922	(58-90)	18	31.54793	(19-50)
2009	205	99	(86-113)	23	53	(33-79)	158	145.5607	(125-170)	24	43.24544	(28-64)
2010	187	94	(81-108)	30	71	(50-102)	136	130.9682	(111-155)	21	39.37523	(24-60)
2011	132	71	(60-84)	19	48	(29-76)	98	100.292	(82-122)	15	30.44807	(17-50)
2012	130	76	(64-90)	20	56	(34-86)	95	104.7419	(86-128)	15	33.68819	(19-56)
2013	86	52	(42-65)	13	37	(20-63)	63	72.59111	(57-93)	10	23.72698	(11-44)

Source: Defence Statistics (Health)

Change in how UK deaths collated, prior to 2006 includes deaths occurred in year, post 2006 includes deaths registered in year.
Standardised mortality ratios have been age and gender standardised.

14.10a Military Search and Rescue - UK & Overseas Callouts, Incidents and Persons Moved, 2005 to 2013

	Incidents			Callouts			Persons Moved		
	All	UK	Overseas	All	UK	Overseas	All	UK	Overseas
2005	1,641	1,584	57	1,766	1,702	64	1,431	1,384	47
2006	1,767	1,703	64	1,948	1,875	73	1,538	1,463	75
2007	1,877	1,803	74	2,065	1,973	92	1,817	1,767	50
2008	2,025	1,941	84	2,179	2,083	96	1,763	1,607	156
2009	2,262	2,191	71	2,418	2,337	81	1,873	1,810	63
2010	1,960	1,901	59	2,050	1,983	67	1,647	1,605	42
2011	1,864	1,801	63	1,921	1,856	65	1,560	1,501	59
2012	1,774	1,733	41	1,879	1,837	42	1,550	1,522	28
2013	1,817	1,777	40	1,918	1,874	44	1,696	1,660	36

Source: UK Defence Statistics, Ministry of Defence

14.10b UK & Overseas Callouts and Persons Moved by Unit, 2005-2013

UK & Overseas Callouts by Unit, 2005 to 2013

	RAF Boulmer	RAF Lossiemouth	RAF Leconfield	RAF Valley	RAF Chivenor	RAF Wattisham	RAF UK Total	RNAS Culdrose	HMS Gannet	RN Total	UK Other	UK Total	Cyprus	Falklands	Overseas Total
2005	144	200	135	218	281	131	1,109	211	267	478	5	**1,592**	39	24	**63**
2006	206	217	147	225	293	163	1,251	228	269	497	8	**1,756**	35	38	**73**
2007	170	188	222	234	256	183	1,253	231	359	590	7	**1,850**	53	39	**92**
2008	211	275	232	222	262	174	1,376	204	382	586	1	**1,963**	30	66	**96**
2009	214	236	204	322	340	162	1,478	311	447	758	1	**2,237**	36	45	**81**
2010	193	175	174	268	339	133	1,282	260	379	639	0	**1,921**	29	38	**67**
2011	181	207	168	276	267	157	1,256	244	298	542	1	**1,799**	24	41	**65**
2012	141	216	129	300	266	160	1,212	251	298	549	0	**1,761**	20	22	**42**
2013	157	231	134	335	238	121	1,216	257	329	586	0	**1,802**	12	32	**44**

UK & Overseas Persons Moved by Unit, 2005 to 2013

	RAF Boulmer	RAF Lossiemouth	RAF Leconfield	RAF Valley	RAF Chivenor	RAF Wattisham	RAF UK Total	RNAS Culdrose	HMS Gannet	RN Total	UK Other	UK Total	Cyprus	Falklands	Overseas Total
2005	136	181	94	195	216	83	905	154	226	380	2	**1,287**	17	30	**47**
2006	132	180	125	202	213	110	962	176	303	479	6	**1,447**	5	70	**75**
2007	136	160	315	236	224	122	1,193	220	286	506	27	**1,726**	11	39	**50**
2008	185	199	163	217	211	87	1,062	169	347	516	0	**1,578**	5	151	**156**
2009	149	171	132	296	304	82	1,134	278	378	656	1	**1,791**	9	54	**63**
2010	169	156	120	263	256	83	1,047	215	324	539	0	**1,586**	5	37	**42**
2011	121	239	125	246	203	96	1,030	219	240	459	0	**1,489**	15	44	**59**
2012	129	205	97	284	187	80	982	235	285	520	0	**1,502**	3	25	**28**
2013	145	219	94	352	191	83	1,084	212	327	539	0	**1,623**	2	34	**36**

Source: UK Defence Statistics; ARCC Database

14.10c Search and Rescue Helicopters: UK & Overseas callouts and Persons Moved by Assistance Type, 2005 to 2013

UK & Overseas Callouts by Assistance Type, 2005 to 2013

	2005	2006	2007	2008	2009	2010	2011	2012	2013
Rescue	115	100	106	99	97	105	87	81	77
Search-Rescue[5]	0	0	30	33	75	40	30	39	56
Medrescue	675	751	703	744	914	839	843	808	873
Search-Medrescue[5]	0	0	38	55	59	61	53	46	54
Medtransfer	157	191	209	229	224	210	182	169	201
Recovery	30	33	15	29	19	13	14	21	13
Search-Recovery[5]	0	0	2	8	16	7	7	8	15
Transfer	28	24	18	16	15	12	10	9	11
Civil Aid	22	23	41	26	17	20	10	5	2
Search	246	289	284	291	297	189	202	178	137
Top Cover	38	28	35	15	28	22	24	19	19
Assist	29	33	25	27	34	31	20	35	21
Search-Assist[5]	0	0	37	53	49	19	27	36	28
Recalled	183	222	212	277	280	243	224	221	209
Not Required	98	83	113	80	104	88	94	97	85
False Alarm	10	9	25	31	36	29	10	9	12
Hoax	6	10	12	14 r	11	15	7	3	5
Precaution	4	8	5	1	2	9	6	5	2
Aborted	14	25	27	23	34	33	9	9	22
Search-Aborted[5]	0	0	5	8	7	3	5	5	4
Total Callouts	**1,655**	**1,829**	**1,942**	**2,059** r	**2,318**	**1,988**	**1,864**	**1,803**	**1,846**

UK & Overseas Persons Moved by Assistance Type, 2005 to 2013

	2005	2006	2007	2008	2009	2010	2011	2012	2013
Rescue	322	407	575	383	289	290	301	287	238
Search-Rescue	0	0	56	70	155	82	55	100	112
Medrescue	791	852	839	821	1,026	917	910	860	949
Search-Medrescue	0	0	56	65	70	68	59	48	62
Medtransfer	159	192	212	243	238	227	190	185	220
Recovery	30	39	16	28	22	15	14	27	24
Search-Recovery	0	0	2	9	20	8	7	10	16
Transfer	32	32	20	115	34	21	12	13	38
Total Persons Moved	**1,334**	**1,522**	**1,776**	**1,734**	**1,854**	**1,628**	**1,548**	**1,530**	**1,659**

5. Here was a change in callout classification in 2007. Prior to 2007, 'Search-Rescue' was included in 'Rescue', 'Search-Medrescue' was included in 'Medrescue', 'Search-Recovery' was included in 'Recovery', 'Search-Assist' was included in 'Assist' and 'Search-Aborted' was included in 'Aborted'.

Source: UK Defence Statistics; ARCC Database

Other Search and Rescue

In addition to the RAF and Royal Navy, a number of non-military organisations provide SAR coverage throughout the UK. The activities of most of these non-military organisations are outside the scope of this report; however background information on some of the organisations involved is provided below.

Maritime and Coastguard Agency

In addition to the eight military aeronautical SAR units, additional aeronautical SAR coverage is provided by four Maritime and Coastguard Agency (MCA) helicopter units. Although these are not part of the military SAR service, the MCA helicopters are coordinated by the ARCC at Kinloss Barracks, to provide integrated coverage across the UK. A summary of callouts for this quarter is provided in this report.

In addition to its aeronautical coverage, the MCA provides maritime SAR coverage throughout the UK. Details of maritime SAR callouts are not included in this report. Further information is available at:

http://www.dft.gov.uk/mca/mcga07-home/emergencyresponse/mcga-searchandrescue.htm

RNLI

The RNLI is a charitable organisation providing 24 hour lifeboat SAR coverage around the coast of the UK and Republic of Ireland, along with a seasonal lifeguard service.

http://www.rnli.org.uk/

Mountain Rescue Teams

A number of voluntary Mountain Rescue services operate throughout the UK. These often work in conjunction with the military SAR service. Details of non-military Mountain Rescue callouts are not included in this report. Further information can be found at:

http://www.mountain.rescue.org.uk/
http://www.mrcofs.org/

Air Ambulance

Air Ambulance services operate throughout the UK, providing emergency medical assistance. Further information is available at:

http://www.associationofairambulances.co.uk/

14.10d Strength of Uniformed United Kingdom Medical Staff, 2011 - 2013

	2011	2012	2013
Qualified Doctors	588	575	578
Qualified Dentists	245	244	226
Nursing Services	1,329	1,461	1,286
Support Staff	4,038	4,000	4,127
Total	**6,200**	**6,280**	**6,217**

Source: Headquarters of the Surgeon General

14.11 Number of vessels boarded by the Royal Navy Fishery Protection Squadron within British fishing limits, each financial year

The data in this Table are outside the scope of National Statistics since they have not been put forward to the UK Statistics Authority for assessment.

Number of Vessels

	2000/01	2006/07	2007/08	2008/09	2009/10	2010/11	2011/12	2012/13
Vessels boarded	**1 603**	**1 335**	**1 309**	**1 102**	**1 201**	**1 399**	**1 408**	**898**
by sea areas[1]:								
North Sea	627	343	367	306	338	411	417	169
Bristol Channel, Celtic Sea, English Channel, Irish Sea and Western Approaches	976	992	942	796	863	988	991	729

Source: Marine Management Organisation

1. The Faroes, Rockall and West of Scotland are not covered by the Royal Navy Fishery Protection Squadron.

Convictions arising from the boarding of vessels by the Royal Navy Fishery Protection Squadron within British fishing limits, each financial year

The data in this Table are outside the scope of National Statistics since they have not been put forward to the UK Statistics Authority for assessment.

Number of Convictions

	2000/01	2006/07	2007/08	2008/09 [1]	2009/10	2010/11	2011/12	2012/13
Convictions arising from boardings	**48**	**53**	**57**	**30**	**10**	**29**	**17**	**10**
by nationality:								
Belgium	4	10	19	5	3	1	2	2
Denmark	3	-	-	-	-	-	-	-
Eire	4	10	6	-	1	3	3	1
Faeroes	3	-	-	-	-	-	-	-
France	8	14	16	12	1	14	6	6
Germany	-	-	-	-	-	2	-	-
Netherlands	6	4	-	2	-	3	2	1
Spain	-	-	-	3	1	1	2	-
United Kingdom	20	15	16	8	4	5	2	-

Source: Marine Management Organisation

1. From 2008/09, these figures include Fisheries Administration Penalties.

Population and vital statistics

Chapter 15

Population and Vital Statistics

This section begins with a summary of population figures for the United Kingdom and constituent countries for 1851 to 2031 and for Great Britain from 1801 (Table 15.1). Table 15.2 analyses the components of population change. Table 15.3 gives details of the national sex and age structures for years up to the present date, with projected figures up to the year 2026. Legal marital condition of the population is shown in Table 15.4. The distribution of population at regional and local levels is summarised in Table 15.5.

In the main, historical series relate to census information, while mid-year estimates, which make allowance for under-enumeration in the census, are given for the recent past and the present (from 1961 onwards).

Population
(Tables 15.1 - 15.3)

Figures shown in these tables relate to the population enumerated at successive censuses, (up to 1951), mid-year estimates (from 1961 to 2008) and population projections (up to 2036). Further information can be found on the National Statistics website www.ons.gov.uk.

Population projections are 2012-based and were published by the Office for National Statistics on 21st October 2009. The 2014-based Projections are not due to be published until Oct/Nov 2015. Further information can be found at www.ons.gov.uk

Definition of resident population

The estimated resident population of an area includes all people who usually live there, whatever their nationality. Members of HM and US Armed Forces in England and Wales are included on a residential basis wherever possible. HM Forces stationed outside England and Wales are not included. Students are taken to be resident at their term time address.

The projections of the resident population of the United Kingdom and constituent countries were prepared by the National Statistics Centre for Demography within ONS, in consultation with the Registrars General, as a common framework for use in national planning in a number of different fields. New projections are made every second year on assumptions regarding future fertility, mortality and migration which seem most appropriate on the basis of the statistical evidence available at the time. The population projections in Tables 15.1 -15.3 are based on the estimates of the population of the United Kingdom at mid-2012 made by the Registrars General.

Marital condition (de jure): estimated population
(Table 15.4)

This table shows population estimates by marital status

**Geographical distribution of the population
(Table 15.5)**

The population enumerated in the censuses for 1911-1951, and the mid-year population estimates for later years, are provided for standard regions of the United Kingdom, for metropolitan areas, for broad groupings of local authority districts by type within England and Wales, and for some of the larger cities. Projections of future sub-national population levels are prepared from time to time by the Registrar General, but are not shown in this publication.

**Migration into and out of the United Kingdom
(Tables 15.7 - 15.8)**

A long-term international migrant is defined as a person who changes his or her country of usual residence for a period of at least a year,so that the country of destination effectively becomes the country of usual residence.

The main source of long-term international migration data is the International Passenger Survey (IPS). This is a continuous voluntary sample survey that provides information on passengers entering and leaving the UK by the principal air, sea and tunnel routes. Being a sample survey, the IPS is subject to some uncertainty; therefore it should be noted that long-term international migration estimates, in particular the difference between inflow and outflow, may be subject to large sampling errors. The IPS excludes routes between the Channel Islands and Isle of Man and the rest of the world.

The IPS data are supplemented with four types of additional information in order to provide a full picture of total long-term international migration, known as Long-Term International Migration or LTIM:

1. The IPS is based on intentions to migrate and intentions are liable to change. Adjustments are made for visitor switchers (those who intend to stay in the UK or abroad for less than one year but subsequently stay for longer and become migrants) and for migrant switchers (those who intend to stay in the UK or abroad for one year or more but then return earlier so are no longer migrants). These adjustments are primarily based on IPS data but for years prior to 2001, Home Office data on short-term visitors who were subsequently granted an extension of stay for a year or longer for other reasons have been incorporated.

2. Home Office data on applications for asylum and dependants of asylum seekers entering the UK are used to estimate inflows of asylum seekers and dependants not already captured by the I PS. In addition, Home Office data on removals and refusals are used to estimate outflows of failed asylum seekers not identified by the IPS.

3. Migration flows between the UK and the Irish Republic were added to the data to 2007 as the IPS did not cover this route until recently. These flows were obtained mainly from the Quarterly National Household Survey and were agreed between the Irish Central Statistics Office and ONS. From 2008 onwards, estimates of migration between the UK and Irish Republic come from the IPS.

4. Migration flows to and from Northern Ireland are added to the IPS data for Great Britain from 2008 onwards. These flows are obtained from the Irish Quarterly National Household Survey (from CSO Ireland) and health card registration data (from Northern Ireland Statistics Research Agency (NISRA)). These data are now deemed a better source for Northern Irish flows than IPS data. Prior to 2008, estimates of migration to and from Northern Ireland came from the IPS.

Grants for settlement in the United Kingdom
(Table 15.9)

This table presents in geographic regions, the statistics of individual countries of nationality, arranged alphabetically within each region. The figures are on a different basis from those derived from IPS (Tables 15.9 and 15.10) and relate only to people subject to immigration control. Persons granted settlement are allowed to stay indefinitely in the United Kingdom. They exclude temporary migrants such as students and generally relate only to non-EEA nationals. Settlement can occur several years after entry to the country.

Applications received for asylum in the United Kingdom, excluding dependants
(Table 15.10)

This table shows statistics of applications for asylum in the United Kingdom. Figures are shown for the main applicant nationalities by geographic region. The basis of assessing asylum applications, and hence of deciding whether to grant asylum in the United Kingdom, is the 1951 United Nations Convention on Refugees.

Marriages
(Table 15.11)
The figures in this table relate to marriages solemnised in England and Wales. They take no account of the growing trend towards marrying abroad.

Births
(Tables 15.14 –15.16)

For Scotland and Northern Ireland the number of births relate to those registered during the year. For England and Wales the figures up to and including 1930-32 are for those registered, while later figures relate to births occurring in each year.

All data for England and Wales and for Scotland include births occurring in those countries to mothers not usually resident in them. Data for Northern Ireland, and hence UK, prior to 1981 include births occurring in Northern Ireland to non-resident mothers; from 1981, such births are excluded.

Deaths
(Tables 15.17 - 15.18)

The figures relate to the number of deaths registered during each calendar year.

Infant and maternal mortality
(Table 15.18)

On 1 October 1992 the legal definition of a stillbirth was altered from a baby born dead after 28 completed weeks gestation or more, to one born after 24 completed weeks of gestation or more. The 258 stillbirths of 24 to 27 weeks gestation that which occurred between 1 October and 31 December 1992 are excluded from this table.

Life tables
(Table 15.19)

The current set of interim life tables are constructed from the estimated populations in 2010-2012 and corresponding data on births, infant deaths and deaths by individual age registered in those years.

Adoptions
(Table 15.20)

The figures shown within these tables relate to the date the adoption was entered in the Adopted Children Register. Figures based on the date of court order are available for England and Wales in the volumes Adoptions in England and Wales, Marriages in England and Wales and Divorces in England and Wales available on the National Statistics website www.statistics.gov.uk.

15.1 Population summary: by country and sex

Thousands

	United Kingdom			England and Wales			Wales	Scotland			Northern Ireland		
	Persons	Males	Females	Persons	Males	Females	Persons	Persons	Males	Females	Persons	Males	Females
Enumerated population: census figures													
1801	..	..	..	8,893	4,255	4,638	587	1,608	739	869	..	..	..
1851	22,259	10,855	11,404	17,928	8,781	9,146	1,163	2,889	1,376	1,513	1,442	698	745
1901	38,237	18,492	19,745	32,528	15,729	16,799	2,013	4,472	2,174	2,298	1,237	590	647
1911	42,082	20,357	21,725	36,070	17,446	18,625	2,421	4,761	2,309	2,452	1,251	603	648
1921 [1]	44,027	21,033	22,994	37,887	18,075	19,811	2,656	4,882	2,348	2,535	1,258	610	648
1931 [1]	46,038	22,060	23,978	39,952	19,133	20,819	2,593	4,843	2,326	2,517	1,243	601	642
1951	50,225	24,118	26,107	43,758	21,016	22,742	2,599	5,096	2,434	2,662	1,371	668	703
1961	52,709	25,481	27,228	46,105	22,304	23,801	2,644	5,179	2,483	2,697	1,425	694	731
Resident population: mid-year estimates													
	DYAY	BBAB	BBAC	BBAD	BBAE	BBAF	KGJM	BBAG	BBAH	BBAI	BBAJ	BBAK	BBAL
1973	56,223	27,332	28,891	49,459	24,061	25,399	2,773	5,234	2,515	2,719	1,530	756	774
1974	56,236	27,349	28,887	49,468	24,075	25,393	2,785	5,241	2,519	2,722	1,527	755	772
1975	56,226	27,361	28,865	49,470	24,091	25,378	2,795	5,232	2,516	2,716	1,524	753	770
1976	56,216	27,360	28,856	49,459	24,089	25,370	2,799	5,233	2,517	2,716	1,524	754	769
1977	56,190	27,345	28,845	49,440	24,076	25,364	2,801	5,226	2,515	2,711	1,523	754	769
1978	56,178	27,330	28,848	49,443	24,067	25,375	2,804	5,212	2,509	2,704	1,523	754	770
1979	56,240	27,373	28,867	49,508	24,113	25,395	2,810	5,204	2,505	2,699	1,528	755	773
1980	56,330	27,411	28,919	49,603	24,156	25,448	2,816	5,194	2,501	2,693	1,533	755	778
1981	56,357	27,412	28,946	49,634	24,160	25,474	2,813	5,180	2,495	2,685	1,543	757	786
1982	56,291	27,364	28,927	49,582	24,119	25,462	2,804	5,165	2,487	2,677	1,545	757	788
1983	56,316	27,371	28,944	49,617	24,133	25,484	2,803	5,148	2,479	2,669	1,551	759	792
1984	56,409	27,421	28,989	49,713	24,185	25,528	2,801	5,139	2,475	2,664	1,557	761	796
1985	56,554	27,489	29,065	49,861	24,254	25,606	2,803	5,128	2,470	2,658	1,565	765	800
1986	56,684	27,542	29,142	49,999	24,311	25,687	2,811	5,112	2,462	2,649	1,574	768	805
1987	56,804	27,599	29,205	50,123	24,371	25,752	2,823	5,099	2,455	2,644	1,582	773	809
1988	56,916	27,652	29,265	50,254	24,434	25,820	2,841	5,077	2,444	2,633	1,585	774	812
1989	57,076	27,729	29,348	50,408	24,510	25,898	2,855	5,078	2,443	2,635	1,590	776	814
1990	57,237	27,819	29,419	50,561	24,597	25,964	2,862	5,081	2,444	2,637	1,596	778	818
1991	57,439	27,909	29,530	50,748	24,681	26,067	2,873	5,083	2,445	2,639	1,607	783	824
1992	57,585	27,977	29,608	50,876	24,739	26,136	2,878	5,086	2,445	2,640	1,623	792	831
1993	57,714	28,039	29,675	50,986	24,793	26,193	2,884	5,092	2,448	2,644	1,636	798	837
1994	57,862	28,108	29,754	51,116	24,853	26,263	2,887	5,102	2,453	2,649	1,644	802	842
1995	58,025	28,204	29,821	51,272	24,946	26,326	2,889	5,104	2,453	2,650	1,649	804	845
1996	58,164	28,287	29,877	51,410	25,030	26,381	2,891	5,092	2,447	2,645	1,662	810	851
1997	58,314	28,371	29,943	51,560	25,113	26,446	2,895	5,083	2,442	2,641	1,671	816	856
1998	58,475	28,458	30,017	51,720	25,201	26,519	2,900	5,077	2,439	2,638	1,678	819	859
1999	58,684	28,578	30,106	51,933	25,323	26,610	2,901	5,072	2,437	2,635	1,679	818	861
2000	58,886	28,690	30,196	52,140	25,438	26,702	2,907	5,063	2,432	2,631	1,683	820	862
2001	59,113	28,832	30,281	52,360	25,574	26,786	2,910	5,064	2,434	2,630	1,689	824	865
2002	59,366	28,973	30,393	52,602	25,708	26,894	2,923	5,066	2,436	2,630	1,697	829	868
2003	59,637	29,125	30,511	52,863	25,854	27,009	2,938	5,069	2,438	2,630	1,705	833	872
2004	59,950	29,297	30,653	53,152	26,012	27,140	2,957	5,084	2,447	2,638	1,714	838	876
2005	60,413	29,541	30,872	53,575	26,234	27,341	2,969	5,110	2,461	2,649	1,728	845	882
2006	60,827	29,762	31,065	53,951	26,433	27,518	2,986	5,133	2,475	2,658	1,743	853	890
2007	61,319	30,028	31,291	54,387	26,669	27,718	3,006	5,170	2,497	2,673	1,762	862	899
2009	62,260	30,532	31,728	55,235	27,122	28,114	3,039	5,232	2,532	2,700	1,793	879	915
2010	62,759	30,805	31,954	55,692	27,373	28,320	3,050	5,262	2,548	2,714	1,805	885	920
2011	63,285	31,097	32,188	56,171	27,638	28,533	3,064	5,300	2,570	2,730	1,814	889	925
2012	63,705	31,315	32,390	56,568	27,843	28,724	3,074	5,314	2,577	2,736	1,824	895	929
2013	64,106	31,533	32,571	56,948	28,049	28,899	3,082	5,328	2,587	2,741	1,830	897	933
Resident population: projections (mid-year) [2]													
	C59J	C59K	C59L	C59M	C59N	C59O	C59P	C59Q	C59R	C59S	C59T	C59U	C59V
2016	65,386	32,244	33,143	58,139	28,710	29,430	3,119	5,386	2,619	2,767	1,861	915	946
2021	67,550	33,414	34,136	60,143	29,793	30,351	3,181	5,497	2,680	2,817	1,910	942	968
2026	69,575	34,497	35,078	62,019	30,795	31,224	3,238	5,606	2,739	2,867	1,950	963	987
2031	71,380	35,457	35,922	63,702	31,689	32,013	3,283	5,698	2,789	2,909	1,980	979	1,001
2036	72,971	36,308	36,663	65,202	32,489	32,713	3,316	5,768	2,829	2,940	2,001	990	1,011

1 Figures for Northern Ireland are estimated. The population at the Census of 1926 was 1,257 thousand (608 thousand males and 648 thousand females).

2 These projections are 2012-based.

Sources: Office for National Statistics: 01329 444661;
National Records of Scotland
Northern Ireland Statistics and Research Agency;

15.2a Population projections by the Office for National Statistics

United Kingdom
PERSONS, thousands

Components of change (mid-year to mid-year), total fertility rate and expectation of life at birth based on the mortality rates for the year

2012-based Principal projection

	2012 -2013	2013 -2014	2014 -2015	2015 -2016	2016 -2017	2017 -2018	2018 -2019	2019 -2020	2020 -2021	2021 -2022	2022 -2023	2023 -2024	2024 -2025	2025 -2026	2026 -2027	2027 -2028
Population at start	63,705	64,087	64,511	64,938	65,386	65,825	66,266	66,697	67,126	67,550	67,969	68,382	68,788	69,186	69,575	69,955
Births	799	807	810	813	815	817	817	816	815	813	812	809	807	805	803	801
Deaths	582	549	548	548	548	549	551	553	556	559	564	569	574	581	588	595
Natural change	218	258	262	265	267	268	266	263	259	254	248	241	233	224	215	206
Net migration	165	166	165	184	171	174	165	165	165	165	165	165	165	165	165	165
Total change	382	424	427	449	438	442	431	428	424	419	413	406	398	389	380	371
Population at end	64,087	64,511	64,938	65,386	65,825	66,266	66,697	67,126	67,550	67,969	68,382	68,788	69,186	69,575	69,955	70,325
Annual growth rate	0.60%	0.66%	0.66%	0.69%	0.67%	0.67%	0.65%	0.64%	0.63%	0.62%	0.61%	0.59%	0.58%	0.56%	0.55%	0.53%
Total fertility rate (TFR)	1.88	1.89	1.89	1.89	1.89	1.89	1.89	1.89	1.89	1.89	1.89	1.89	1.89	1.89	1.89	1.89
EOLB Males	78.7	79.4	79.7	80.0	80.3	80.5	80.8	81.0	81.3	81.5	81.7	81.9	82.1	82.3	82.5	82.7
Females	82.4	83.2	83.5	83.7	83.9	84.1	84.4	84.6	84.8	85.0	85.2	85.3	85.5	85.7	85.9	86.0

Components of change (mid-year to mid-year), total fertility rate and expectation of life at birth based on the mortality rates for the year

2012-based Principal projection — Annual averages for longer-term projections

	2028 -2029	2029 -2030	2030 -2031	2031 -2032	2032 -2033	2033 -2034	2034 -2035	2035 -2036	2036 -2037	2037 -2041	2041 -2046	2046 -2051	2051 -2056	2056 -2061	2061 -2062
Population at start	70,325	70,686	71,037	71,380	71,713	72,037	72,355	72,666	72,971	73,272	74,450	75,879	77,234	78,489	79,671
Births	799	798	797	797	798	799	802	806	811	825	848	859	860	859	860
Deaths	603	611	620	629	638	647	656	666	675	696	727	753	774	788	792
Natural change	196	186	177	168	160	152	146	140	136	129	121	106	86	71	69
Net migration	165	165	165	165	165	165	165	165	165	165	165	165	165	165	165
Total change	361	351	342	333	325	317	311	305	301	294	286	271	251	236	234
Population at end	70,686	71,037	71,380	71,713	72,037	72,355	72,666	72,971	73,272	74,450	75,879	77,234	78,489	79,671	79,904
Annual growth rate	0.51%	0.50%	0.48%	0.47%	0.45%	0.44%	0.43%	0.42%	0.41%	0.40%	0.38%	0.35%	0.32%	0.30%	0.29%
Total fertility rate (TFR)	1.89	1.89	1.89	1.89	1.89	1.89	1.89	1.89	1.89	1.89	1.89	1.89	1.89	1.89	1.89
EOLB Males	82.9	83.0	83.2	83.3	83.5	83.6	83.8	83.9	84.0	84.4	84.9	85.6	86.2	86.8	87.2
Females	86.2	86.3	86.5	86.6	86.8	86.9	87.0	87.2	87.3	87.6	88.1	88.7	89.3	89.9	90.3

15.2a Population projections by the Office for National Statistics

United Kingdom
PERSONS, thousands

	Annual averages for longer-term projections								
	2062 -2066	2066 -2071	2071 -2076	2076 -2081	2081 -2086	2086 -2087	2087 -2092	2092 -2102	2102 -2112
Population at start	79,904	80,855	82,114	83,455	84,831	86,193	86,463	87,808	90,554
Births	864	876	891	903	908	910	913	923	944
Deaths	792	789	788	793	801	806	809	814	831
Natural change	73	87	103	110	107	105	104	110	113
Net migration	165	165	165	165	165	165	165	165	165
Total change	238	252	268	275	272	270	269	275	278
Population at end	80,855	82,114	83,455	84,831	86,193	86,463	87,808	90,554	93,332
Annual growth rate	0.30%	0.31%	0.32%	0.33%	0.32%	0.31%	0.31%	0.31%	0.30%
Total fertility rate (TFR)	1.89	1.89	1.89	1.89	1.89	1.89	1.89	1.89	1.89
EOLB Males	87.5	88.1	88.7	89.4	90.0	90.4	90.7	91.7	92.9
Females	90.5	91.1	91.7	92.2	92.8	93.2	93.5	94.4	95.6

Source: Office for National Statistics

Note: Figures may not add exactly due to rounding.
* Children under 16. Working age and pensionable age populations based on state pension age (SPA) for given year.
Between 2012 and 2018, SPA will change from 65 years for men and 61 years for women, to 65 years for both sexes.
Then between 2019 and 2020, SPA will change from 65 years to 66 years for both men and women. Between 2034 and 2046,
SPA will increase in two stages from 66 years to 68 years for both sexes. This is based on SPA under the 2011 Pensions Act.
** This is consistent with the age-group definitions used in ONS Labour Market Statistics.

National Population Projections are currently produced every two years. The 2014-based Projections are not due to be published until Oct/Nov 2015. Therefore, this table series will be updated in the next edition.

15.2b Population projections by the Office for National Statistics

England & Wales
PERSONS, thousands

2012-based
Principal projection

Components of change (mid-year to mid-year), total fertility rate
and expectation of life at birth based on the mortality rates for the year

	2012 -2013	2013 -2014	2014 -2015	2015 -2016	2016 -2017	2017 -2018	2018 -2019	2019 -2020	2020 -2021	2021 -2022	2022 -2023	2023 -2024	2024 -2025	2025 -2026	2026 -2027	2027 -2028
Population at start	56,568	56,927	57,323	57,721	58,139	58,546	58,956	59,355	59,751	60,143	60,531	60,913	61,289	61,658	62,019	62,372
Births	718	725	727	730	732	732	733	732	731	729	727	726	724	722	720	718
Deaths	511	482	481	481	481	482	483	485	488	491	495	499	504	510	516	523
Natural change	207	244	247	249	251	251	249	247	243	238	233	226	219	212	204	195
Net migration	152	153	151	170	157	159	150	150	150	150	150	150	150	150	150	150
Total change	359	396	398	419	407	410	399	396	392	388	382	376	369	361	353	345
Population at end	56,927	57,323	57,721	58,139	58,546	58,956	59,355	59,751	60,143	60,531	60,913	61,289	61,658	62,019	62,372	62,717
Annual growth rate	0.63%	0.70%	0.69%	0.73%	0.70%	0.70%	0.68%	0.67%	0.66%	0.64%	0.63%	0.62%	0.60%	0.59%	0.57%	0.55%
Total fertility rate (TFR)	1.90	1.91	1.91	1.91	1.91	1.91	1.90	1.90	1.90	1.90	1.90	1.90	1.90	1.90	1.90	1.90
EOLB Males	78.9	79.7	80.0	80.3	80.5	80.8	81.1	81.3	81.5	81.8	82.0	82.2	82.4	82.6	82.8	82.9
Females	82.6	83.4	83.7	83.9	84.1	84.4	84.6	84.8	85.0	85.2	85.4	85.6	85.7	85.9	86.1	86.2

2012-based
Principal projection

Annual averages for longer-term projections

Components of change (mid-year to mid-year), total fertility rate
and expectation of life at birth based on the mortality rates for the year

	2028 -2029	2029 -2030	2030 -2031	2031 -2032	2032 -2033	2033 -2034	2034 -2035	2035 -2036	2036 -2037	2037 -2041	2041 -2046	2046 -2051	2051 -2056	2056 -2061	2061 -2062
Population at start	62,717	63,053	63,382	63,702	64,015	64,320	64,619	64,913	65,202	65,487	66,606	67,971	69,270	70,477	71,616
Births	717	716	716	716	717	719	722	726	731	744	765	776	777	777	779
Deaths	530	537	545	553	561	570	578	586	595	613	642	666	685	698	703
Natural change	187	179	171	163	156	150	144	140	136	130	123	110	92	78	76
Net migration	150	150	150	150	150	150	150	150	150	150	150	150	150	150	150
Total change	337	328	320	313	305	299	294	289	285	280	273	260	241	228	225
Population at end	63,053	63,382	63,702	64,015	64,320	64,619	64,913	65,202	65,487	66,606	67,971	69,270	70,477	71,616	71,842
Annual growth rate	0.54%	0.52%	0.51%	0.49%	0.48%	0.47%	0.45%	0.45%	0.44%	0.42%	0.41%	0.38%	0.35%	0.32%	0.31%
Total fertility rate (TFR)	1.90	1.90	1.90	1.90	1.90	1.90	1.90	1.90	1.90	1.90	1.90	1.90	1.90	1.90	1.90
EOLB Males	83.1	83.3	83.4	83.6	83.7	83.9	84.0	84.1	84.3	84.6	85.1	85.8	86.4	87.0	87.4
Females	86.4	86.6	86.7	86.8	87.0	87.1	87.2	87.4	87.5	87.8	88.3	88.9	89.5	90.1	90.4

15.2b Population projections by the Office for National Statistics

England & Wales
PERSONS, thousands

	2062 -2066	2066 -2071	2071 -2076	2076 -2081	2081 -2086	2086 -2087	2087 -2092	2092 -2102	2102 -2112
				Annual averages for longer-term projections					
Population at start	71,842	72,757	73,965	75,247	76,560	77,860	78,118	79,402	82,019
Births	783	794	809	820	825	828	830	841	861
Deaths	703	702	702	707	715	720	723	729	746
Natural change	79	92	107	113	111	108	107	112	115
Net migration	150	150	150	150	150	150	150	150	150
Total change	229	242	256	263	260	257	257	262	264
Population at end	72,757	73,965	75,247	76,560	77,860	78,118	79,402	82,019	84,659
Annual growth rate	0.32%	0.33%	0.34%	0.35%	0.34%	0.33%	0.33%	0.32%	0.32%
Total fertility rate (TFR)	1.90	1.90	1.90	1.90	1.90	1.90	1.90	1.90	1.90
EOLB Males	87.7	88.3	88.9	89.5	90.1	90.5	90.9	91.8	93.1
Females	90.7	91.2	91.8	92.4	93.0	93.3	93.7	94.6	95.7

Source: Office for National Statistics

Note: Figures may not add exactly due to rounding.

* Children under 16. Working age and pensionable age populations based on state pension age (SPA) for given year.
Between 2012 and 2018, SPA will change from 65 years for men and 61 years for women, to 65 years for both sexes.
Then between 2019 and 2020, SPA will change from 65 years to 66 years for both men and women. Between 2034 and 2046,
SPA will increase in two stages from 66 years to 68 years for both sexes. This is based on SPA under the 2011 Pensions Act.
** This is consistent with the age-group definitions used in ONS Labour Market Statistics.

National Population Projections are currently produced every two years. The 2014-based Projections are not due to be published until Oct/Nov 2015. Therefore, this table series will be updated in the next edition.

15.2c Population projections by the Office for National Statistics

Scotland
PERSONS, thousands

Components of change (mid-year to mid-year), total fertility rate and expectation of life at birth based on the mortality rates for the year

**2012-based
Principal projection**

	2012-2013	2013-2014	2014-2015	2015-2016	2016-2017	2017-2018	2018-2019	2019-2020	2020-2021	2021-2022	2022-2023	2023-2024	2024-2025	2025-2026	2026-2027	2027-2028
Population at start	5,314	5,328	5,346	5,365	5,386	5,407	5,429	5,452	5,474	5,497	5,520	5,542	5,564	5,585	5,606	5,626
Births	57	57	58	59	59	60	60	60	60	61	61	61	60	60	60	60
Deaths	56	53	53	53	53	53	53	53	53	54	54	54	55	55	56	56
Natural change	1	5	5	6	6	7	7	7	7	7	7	6	6	5	5	4
Net migration	13	14	14	14	15	15	16	16	16	16	16	16	16	16	16	16
Total change	14	18	19	20	21	22	23	23	23	23	22	22	21	21	20	19
Population at end	5,328	5,346	5,365	5,386	5,407	5,429	5,452	5,474	5,497	5,520	5,542	5,564	5,585	5,606	5,626	5,645
Annual growth rate	0.27%	0.34%	0.36%	0.38%	0.40%	0.41%	0.42%	0.42%	0.41%	0.41%	0.40%	0.39%	0.38%	0.37%	0.36%	0.34%
Total fertility rate (TFR)	1.64	1.64	1.65	1.67	1.68	1.68	1.69	1.69	1.70	1.70	1.71	1.71	1.72	1.73	1.73	1.74
EOLB Males	76.5	77.2	77.5	77.7	78.0	78.3	78.5	78.8	79.0	79.3	79.5	79.7	79.9	80.1	80.3	80.5
Females	80.4	81.4	81.6	81.8	82.1	82.3	82.5	82.7	82.9	83.1	83.3	83.5	83.6	83.8	84.0	84.1

Components of change (mid-year to mid-year), total fertility rate and expectation of life at birth based on the mortality rates for the year

2012-based Principal projection — **Annual averages for longer-term projections**

	2028-2029	2029-2030	2030-2031	2031-2032	2032-2033	2033-2034	2034-2035	2035-2036	2036-2037	2037-2041	2041-2046	2046-2051	2051-2056	2056-2061	2061-2062
Population at start	5,645	5,664	5,681	5,698	5,714	5,728	5,742	5,756	5,768	5,780	5,826	5,877	5,925	5,972	6,019
Births	60	59	59	59	58	58	58	58	58	59	60	61	61	61	61
Deaths	57	57	58	58	59	60	60	61	62	63	65	67	67	67	67
Natural change	3	2	1	0	-1	-2	-2	-3	-3	-4	-5	-6	-6	-6	-6
Net migration	16	16	16	16	16	16	16	16	16	16	16	16	16	16	16
Total change	18	18	17	16	15	14	13	13	12	11	10	10	9	9	10
Population at end	5,664	5,681	5,698	5,714	5,728	5,742	5,756	5,768	5,780	5,826	5,877	5,925	5,972	6,019	6,029
Annual growth rate	0.33%	0.31%	0.29%	0.28%	0.26%	0.24%	0.23%	0.22%	0.21%	0.19%	0.18%	0.16%	0.16%	0.16%	0.16%
Total fertility rate (TFR)	1.74	1.75	1.75	1.75	1.75	1.75	1.75	1.75	1.75	1.75	1.75	1.75	1.75	1.75	1.75
EOLB Males	80.7	80.8	81.0	81.2	81.3	81.5	81.6	81.8	81.9	82.2	82.9	83.6	84.2	84.9	85.3
Females	84.3	84.5	84.6	84.8	84.9	85.0	85.2	85.3	85.4	85.8	86.3	86.9	87.6	88.2	88.6

15.2c Population projections by the Office for National Statistics

Scotland
PERSONS, thousands

	Annual averages for longer-term projections								
	2062 -2066	2066 -2071	2071 -2076	2076 -2081	2081 -2086	2086 -2087	2087 -2092	2092 -2102	2102 -2112
Population at start	6,029	6,069	6,126	6,188	6,254	6,319	6,332	6,396	6,532
Births	61	61	61	62	62	62	62	62	63
Deaths	66	65	64	64	65	65	65	64	64
Natural change	-5	-4	-3	-2	-2	-3	-3	-2	-1
Net migration	16	16	16	16	16	16	16	16	16
Total change	10	11	13	13	13	13	13	14	14
Population at end	6,069	6,126	6,188	6,254	6,319	6,332	6,396	6,532	6,674
Annual growth rate	0.17%	0.19%	0.20%	0.21%	0.21%	0.20%	0.20%	0.21%	0.22%
Total fertility rate (TFR)	1.75	1.75	1.75	1.75	1.75	1.75	1.75	1.75	1.75
EOLB Males	85.7	86.3	86.9	87.6	88.3	88.7	89.1	90.1	91.4
Females	88.9	89.4	90.0	90.7	91.3	91.7	92.0	93.0	94.2

Source: Office for National Statistics

Note: Figures may not add exactly due to rounding.
* Children under 16. Working age and pensionable age populations based on state pension age (SPA) for given year
Between 2012 and 2018, SPA will change from 65 years for men and 61 years for women, to 65 years for both sexes.
Then between 2019 and 2020, SPA will change from 65 years to 66 years for both men and women. Between 2034 and 2046,
SPA will increase in two stages from 66 years to 68 years for both sexes. This is based on SPA under the 2011 Pensions Act.
** This is consistent with the age-group definitions used in ONS Labour Market Statistics.

National Population Projections are currently produced every two years. The 2014-based Projections are not due to be published until Oct/Nov 2015. Therefore, this table series will be updated in the next edition.

15.2d Population projections by the Office for National Statistics

Northern Ireland
PERSONS, thousands

Components of change (mid-year to mid-year), total fertility rate and expectation of life at birth based on the mortality rates for the year

2012-based
Principal projection

	2012 -2013	2013 -2014	2014 -2015	2015 -2016	2016 -2017	2017 -2018	2018 -2019	2019 -2020	2020 -2021	2021 -2022	2022 -2023	2023 -2024	2024 -2025	2025 -2026	2026 -2027	2027 -2028
Population at start	1,824	1,832	1,842	1,852	1,861	1,871	1,881	1,891	1,900	1,910	1,918	1,927	1,935	1,943	1,950	1,957
Births	25	25	25	25	25	24	24	24	24	24	24	23	23	23	23	22
Deaths	15	14	14	14	14	14	15	15	15	15	15	15	15	16	16	16
Natural change	10	10	10	10	10	10	10	10	9	9	8	8	8	7	7	6
Net migration	-1	-1	-1	-0	-0	-0	0	0	0	0	0	0	0	0	0	0
Total change	9	10	10	10	10	10	10	10	9	9	8	8	8	7	7	6
Population at end	1,832	1,842	1,852	1,861	1,871	1,881	1,891	1,900	1,910	1,918	1,927	1,935	1,943	1,950	1,957	1,963
Annual growth rate	0.48%	0.52%	0.52%	0.53%	0.53%	0.53%	0.52%	0.50%	0.49%	0.46%	0.44%	0.42%	0.40%	0.37%	0.35%	0.33%
Total fertility rate (TFR)	1.98	1.98	1.99	1.99	2.00	2.00	2.00	2.00	2.00	2.00	2.00	2.00	2.00	2.00	2.00	2.00
EOLB Males	77.9	78.5	78.8	79.1	79.4	79.7	79.9	80.2	80.4	80.7	80.9	81.1	81.3	81.5	81.7	81.9
Females	81.9	82.7	82.9	83.2	83.4	83.6	83.8	84.0	84.2	84.4	84.6	84.8	85.0	85.2	85.4	85.5

Components of change (mid-year to mid-year), total fertility rate and expectation of life at birth based on the mortality rates for the year

2012-based
Principal projection

Annual averages for longer-term projections

	2028 -2029	2029 -2030	2030 -2031	2031 -2032	2032 -2033	2033 -2034	2034 -2035	2035 -2036	2036 -2037	2037 -2041	2041 -2046	2046 -2051	2051 -2056	2056 -2061	2061 -2062
Population at start	1,963	1,969	1,975	1,980	1,985	1,989	1,993	1,997	2,001	2,005	2,018	2,032	2,039	2,040	2,035
Births	22	22	22	22	22	22	22	22	22	22	23	23	22	21	21
Deaths	16	17	17	17	17	18	18	18	18	19	20	21	22	22	23
Natural change	6	6	5	5	4	4	4	4	4	3	3	2	0	-1	-1
Net migration	0	0	0	0	0	0	0	0	0	0	0	0	0	0	0
Total change	6	6	5	5	4	4	4	4	4	3	3	2	0	-1	-1
Population at end	1,969	1,975	1,980	1,985	1,989	1,993	1,997	2,001	2,005	2,018	2,032	2,039	2,040	2,035	2,034
Annual growth rate	0.30%	0.28%	0.26%	0.24%	0.23%	0.21%	0.20%	0.19%	0.18%	0.17%	0.14%	0.08%	0.01%	-0.05%	-0.07%
Total fertility rate (TFR)	2.00	2.00	2.00	2.00	2.00	2.00	2.00	2.00	2.00	2.00	2.00	2.00	2.00	2.00	2.00
EOLB Males	82.1	82.2	82.4	82.6	82.7	82.9	83.0	83.1	83.3	83.6	84.2	84.8	85.5	86.1	86.5
Females	85.7	85.8	86.0	86.1	86.3	86.4	86.5	86.7	86.8	87.1	87.6	88.2	88.8	89.4	89.8

15.2d Population projections by the Office for National Statistics

Northern Ireland
PERSONS, thousands

	2062 -2066	2066 -2071	2071 -2076	2076 -2081	2081 -2086	2086 -2087	2087 -2092	2092 -2102	2102 -2112
Population at start	2,034	2,028	2,023	2,020	2,017	2,014	2,014	2,010	2,004
Births	21	21	21	21	21	21	20	20	20
Deaths	22	22	22	22	22	21	21	21	21
Natural change	-1	-1	-1	-0	-1	-1	-1	-1	-1
Net migration	0	0	0	0	0	0	0	0	0
Total change	-1	-1	-1	-0	-1	-1	-1	-1	-1
Population at end	2,028	2,023	2,020	2,017	2,014	2,014	2,010	2,004	1,998
Annual growth rate	-0.07%	-0.05%	-0.03%	-0.02%	-0.03%	-0.04%	-0.04%	-0.03%	-0.03%
Total fertility rate (TFR)	2.00	2.00	2.00	2.00	2.00	2.00	2.00	2.00	2.00
EOLB Males	86.9	87.4	88.1	88.7	89.4	89.8	90.2	91.1	92.4
Females	90.1	90.6	91.2	91.8	92.4	92.7	93.1	94.0	95.1

Source: Office for National Statistics

Note: Figures may not add exactly due to rounding.
* Children under 16. Working age and pensionable age populations based on state pension age (SPA) for given year.
Between 2012 and 2018, SPA will change from 65 years for men and 61 years for women, to 65 years for both sexes.
Then between 2019 and 2020, SPA will change from 65 years to 66 years for both men and women. Between 2034 and 2046,
SPA will increase in two stages from 66 years to 68 years for both sexes. This is based on SPA under the 2011 Pensions Act.
** This is consistent with the age-group definitions used in ONS Labour Market Statistics.

National Population Projections are currently produced every two years. The 2014-based Projections are not due to be published until Oct/Nov 2015. Therefore, this table series will be updated in the next edition.

15.3a Mid-2013 Population Estimates:United Kingdom by sex and single year of age

Ages	Persons	Males	Females	Ages	Persons	Males	Females
All Ages	64,105,654	31,532,873	32,572,781	45	925,320	455,940	469,380
0	792,616	406,642	385,974	46	938,442	464,356	474,086
1	821,578	420,940	400,638	47	938,419	462,099	476,320
2	811,850	415,780	396,070	48	946,556	466,244	480,312
3	797,416	407,819	389,597	49	937,913	462,083	475,830
4	790,401	404,312	386,089	50	919,385	453,913	465,472
5	797,550	408,325	389,225	51	899,847	445,467	454,380
6	770,950	395,097	375,853	52	870,220	430,835	439,385
7	755,033	386,186	368,847	53	836,048	413,932	422,116
8	725,405	371,258	354,147	54	818,743	405,162	413,581
9	712,418	364,761	347,657	55	800,649	396,149	404,500
10	691,840	354,516	337,324	56	772,132	381,665	390,467
11	681,004	348,747	332,257	57	745,333	368,602	376,731
12	699,616	357,259	342,357	58	718,242	354,204	364,038
13	718,222	368,251	349,971	59	720,291	354,257	366,034
14	741,448	379,837	361,611	60	711,437	350,155	361,282
15	751,342	385,011	366,331	61	691,443	339,041	352,402
16	772,514	395,941	376,573	62	697,056	341,369	355,687
17	772,868	398,800	374,068	63	711,354	347,337	364,017
18	777,189	398,570	378,619	64	729,523	356,697	372,826
19	811,390	415,742	395,648	65	768,333	374,770	393,563
20	823,211	419,043	404,168	66	831,774	406,035	425,739
21	857,679	432,908	424,771	67	643,818	313,068	330,750
22	885,632	450,770	434,862	68	624,435	302,312	322,123
23	876,441	446,135	430,306	69	623,087	301,599	321,488
24	869,898	437,953	431,945	70	581,589	278,976	302,613
25	880,638	440,649	439,989	71	521,183	247,897	273,286
26	862,835	428,009	434,826	72	470,131	221,549	248,582
27	872,277	437,032	435,245	73	485,565	228,350	257,215
28	876,318	438,519	437,799	74	480,687	224,850	255,837
29	857,902	427,186	430,716	75	466,283	217,277	249,006
30	866,670	430,050	436,620	76	441,824	203,506	238,318
31	867,766	429,631	438,135	77	419,580	191,087	228,493
32	875,516	434,683	440,833	78	397,411	179,306	218,105
33	876,213	435,292	440,921	79	367,027	163,171	203,856
34	840,702	419,247	421,455	80	347,425	151,831	195,594
35	784,349	391,267	393,082	81	335,545	144,170	191,375
36	772,833	386,344	386,489	82	315,710	132,432	183,278
37	787,837	391,909	395,928	83	290,844	118,504	172,340
38	803,691	399,581	404,110	84	260,378	103,934	156,444
39	818,169	406,009	412,160	85 / 85+	231,430	89,883	141,547
40	855,361	424,782	430,579	86	209,463	79,743	129,720
41	892,511	442,629	449,882	87	187,047	68,706	118,341
42	922,411	454,179	468,232	88	162,812	57,358	105,454
43	901,442	444,455	456,987	89	141,185	47,473	93,712
44	924,544	455,386	469,158	90	527,239	148,137	379,102

Source: Office for National Statistics

Note: It is ONS policy to publish estimates to the nearest hundred persons. Rounded (and particularly unit) estimates cannot be precisely accurate.

: Data not available

15.3b Population projections by the Office for National Statistics

United Kingdom
PERSONS, thousands

2012-based
Principal projection

Projected populations at mid-years by age last birthday

Ages	2012	2013	2014	2015	2016	2017	2018	2019	2020	2021	2022	2023	2024	2025	2026	2027	2028	2029	2030	2031	2032
Thousands																					
0-14	11,214	11,278	11,360	11,466	11,599	11,748	11,887	12,002	12,103	12,172	12,223	12,244	12,270	12,285	12,283	12,268	12,270	12,262	12,250	12,234	12,217
15-29	12,577	12,588	12,596	12,558	12,510	12,442	12,360	12,293	12,223	12,160	12,129	12,147	12,159	12,203	12,261	12,325	12,391	12,473	12,581	12,709	12,857
30-44	12,844	12,778	12,711	12,693	12,663	12,658	12,719	12,819	12,951	13,122	13,295	13,433	13,516	13,538	13,562	13,596	13,609	13,618	13,581	13,526	13,457
45-59	12,606	12,775	12,940	13,087	13,231	13,321	13,347	13,322	13,267	13,166	13,023	12,876	12,768	12,691	12,624	12,551	12,495	12,437	12,426	12,397	12,396
60-74	9,445	9,562	9,688	9,813	9,985	10,140	10,271	10,388	10,524	10,680	10,705	10,810	10,971	11,159	11,354	11,556	11,730	11,897	12,045	12,190	12,284
75 & over	5,020	5,106	5,216	5,319	5,399	5,517	5,682	5,874	6,058	6,249	6,595	6,872	7,104	7,309	7,491	7,657	7,830	7,999	8,155	8,324	8,503
All ages	63,705	64,087	64,511	64,938	65,386	65,825	66,266	66,697	67,126	67,550	67,969	68,382	68,788	69,186	69,575	69,955	70,325	70,686	71,037	71,380	71,713
Percentages																					
0-14	17.6	17.6	17.6	17.7	17.7	17.8	17.9	18.0	18.0	18.0	18.0	17.9	17.8	17.8	17.7	17.5	17.4	17.3	17.2	17.1	17.0
15-29	19.7	19.6	19.5	19.3	19.1	18.9	18.7	18.4	18.2	18.0	17.8	17.8	17.7	17.6	17.6	17.6	17.6	17.6	17.7	17.8	17.9
30-44	20.2	19.9	19.7	19.5	19.4	19.2	19.2	19.2	19.3	19.4	19.6	19.6	19.6	19.6	19.5	19.4	19.4	19.3	19.1	18.9	18.8
45-59	19.8	19.9	20.1	20.2	20.2	20.2	20.1	20.0	19.8	19.5	19.2	18.8	18.6	18.3	18.1	17.9	17.8	17.6	17.5	17.4	17.3
60-74	14.8	14.9	15.0	15.1	15.3	15.4	15.5	15.6	15.7	15.8	15.7	15.8	15.9	16.1	16.3	16.5	16.7	16.8	17.0	17.1	17.1
75 & over	7.9	8.0	8.1	8.2	8.3	8.4	8.6	8.8	9.0	9.3	9.7	10.0	10.3	10.6	10.8	10.9	11.1	11.3	11.5	11.7	11.9
All ages	100.0	100.0	100.0	100.0	100.0	100.0	100.0	100.0	100.0	100.0	100.0	100.0	100.0	100.0	100.0	100.0	100.0	100.0	100.0	100.0	100.0
Mean age	40.1	40.2	40.3	40.4	40.5	40.7	40.8	41.0	41.1	41.2	41.4	41.5	41.7	41.8	42.0	42.1	42.3	42.4	42.6	42.7	42.8
Median age	39.7	39.9	40.0	40.0	40.1	40.1	40.1	40.2	40.4	40.5	40.6	40.8	40.9	41.0	41.2	41.3	41.5	41.6	41.8	41.9	42.1

15.3b Population projections by the Office for National Statistics

United Kingdom
PERSONS, thousands

	Projected populations at mid-years by age last birthday					Annual averages for longer-term projections														
Ages	2033	2034	2035	2036	2037	2041	2046	2051	2056	2061	2062	2066	2071	2076	2081	2086	2087	2092	2102	2112
Thousands																				
0-14	12,198	12,182	12,169	12,161	12,159	12,228	12,472	12,768	12,960	13,018	13,021	13,040	13,120	13,282	13,479	13,644	13,669	13,765	13,934	14,216
15-29	12,993	13,109	13,210	13,279	13,330	13,392	13,345	13,272	13,341	13,586	13,647	13,883	14,075	14,134	14,158	14,239	14,265	14,440	14,790	14,959
30-44	13,373	13,309	13,240	13,180	13,151	13,288	13,740	14,311	14,427	14,384	14,368	14,317	14,384	14,638	14,937	15,132	15,153	15,198	15,332	15,707
45-59	12,458	12,560	12,693	12,863	13,035	13,308	13,285	12,960	13,084	13,544	13,691	14,116	14,243	14,212	14,157	14,240	14,279	14,559	15,026	15,120
60-74	12,318	12,303	12,260	12,175	12,052	11,737	11,600	12,093	12,545	12,555	12,497	12,285	12,458	12,939	13,514	13,667	13,664	13,663	13,808	14,420
75 & over	8,695	8,892	9,093	9,312	9,546	10,497	11,438	11,830	12,132	12,584	12,680	13,213	13,828	14,250	14,587	15,272	15,432	16,183	17,665	18,909
All ages	72,037	72,355	72,666	72,971	73,272	74,450	75,879	77,234	78,489	79,671	79,904	80,855	82,114	83,455	84,831	86,193	86,463	87,808	90,554	93,332
Percentages																				
0-14	16.9	16.8	16.7	16.7	16.6	16.4	16.4	16.5	16.5	16.3	16.3	16.1	16.0	15.9	15.9	15.8	15.8	15.7	15.4	15.2
15-29	18.0	18.1	18.2	18.2	18.2	18.0	17.6	17.2	17.0	17.1	17.1	17.2	17.1	16.9	16.7	16.5	16.5	16.4	16.3	16.0
30-44	18.6	18.4	18.2	18.1	17.9	17.8	18.1	18.5	18.4	18.1	18.0	17.7	17.5	17.5	17.6	17.6	17.5	17.3	16.9	16.8
45-59	17.3	17.4	17.5	17.6	17.8	17.9	17.5	16.8	16.7	17.0	17.1	17.5	17.3	17.0	16.7	16.5	16.5	16.6	16.6	16.2
60-74	17.1	17.0	16.9	16.7	16.4	15.8	15.3	15.7	16.0	15.8	15.6	15.2	15.2	15.5	15.9	15.9	15.8	15.6	15.2	15.5
75 & over	12.1	12.3	12.5	12.8	13.0	14.1	15.1	15.3	15.5	15.8	15.9	16.3	16.8	17.1	17.2	17.7	17.8	18.4	19.5	20.3
All ages	100.0	100.0	100.0	100.0	100.0	100.0	100.0	100.0	100.0	100.0	100.0	100.0	100.0	100.0	100.0	100.0	100.0	100.0	100.0	100.0
Mean age	43.0	43.1	43.2	43.3	43.4	43.8	44.1	44.4	44.6	44.9	44.9	45.1	45.4	45.6	45.9	46.2	46.2	46.5	47.1	47.7
Median age	42.3	42.4	42.6	42.7	42.8	43.1	43.0	43.1	43.4	43.8	43.9	44.2	44.4	44.7	44.8	45.1	45.1	45.5	46.2	46.7

Source: Office for National Statistics

Note: Figures may not add exactly due to rounding.
* Children under 16. Working age and pensionable age populations based on state pension age (SPA) for given year.
Between 2012 and 2018, SPA will change from 65 years for men and 61 years for women, to 65 years for both sexes.
Then between 2019 and 2020, SPA will change from 65 years to 66 years for both men and women. Between 2034 and 2046,
SPA will increase in two stages from 66 years to 68 years for both sexes. This is based on SPA under the 2011 Pensions Act.
** This is consistent with the age-group definitions used in ONS Labour Market Statistics.

National Population Projections are currently produced every two years. The 2014-based Projections are not due to be published until Oct/Nov 2015. Therefore, this table series will be updated in the next edition.

15.3b Population projections by the Office for National Statistics

United Kingdom
MALES, thousands

2012-based
Principal projection

Projected populations at mid-years by age last birthday

Ages	2012	2013	2014	2015	2016	2017	2018	2019	2020	2021	2022	2023	2024	2025	2026	2027	2028	2029	2030	2031	2032
Thousands																					
0-14	5,741	5,774	5,816	5,871	5,940	6,016	6,087	6,147	6,199	6,235	6,261	6,272	6,286	6,295	6,294	6,286	6,287	6,283	6,277	6,269	6,260
15-29	6,357	6,380	6,399	6,393	6,380	6,360	6,330	6,302	6,267	6,236	6,227	6,238	6,244	6,266	6,293	6,327	6,361	6,403	6,458	6,525	6,601
30-44	6,371	6,340	6,310	6,307	6,302	6,302	6,340	6,401	6,483	6,585	6,680	6,763	6,820	6,850	6,882	6,918	6,943	6,962	6,957	6,939	6,919
45-59	6,231	6,309	6,386	6,453	6,518	6,559	6,570	6,555	6,526	6,475	6,405	6,333	6,283	6,246	6,214	6,175	6,149	6,124	6,125	6,121	6,123
60-74	4,572	4,630	4,692	4,754	4,840	4,916	4,980	5,036	5,103	5,178	5,191	5,242	5,319	5,410	5,504	5,602	5,685	5,763	5,832	5,899	5,944
75 &over	2,043	2,099	2,161	2,219	2,265	2,329	2,415	2,514	2,608	2,705	2,875	3,011	3,124	3,223	3,310	3,390	3,472	3,552	3,625	3,704	3,788
All ages	31,315	31,532	31,764	31,998	32,244	32,482	32,722	32,955	33,186	33,414	33,639	33,860	34,077	34,289	34,497	34,699	34,896	35,088	35,275	35,457	35,635
Percentages																					
0-14	18.3	18.3	18.3	18.3	18.4	18.5	18.6	18.7	18.7	18.7	18.6	18.5	18.4	18.4	18.2	18.1	18.0	17.9	17.8	17.7	17.6
15-29	20.3	20.2	20.1	20.0	19.8	19.6	19.3	19.1	18.9	18.7	18.5	18.4	18.3	18.3	18.2	18.2	18.2	18.2	18.3	18.4	18.5
30-44	20.3	20.1	19.9	19.7	19.5	19.4	19.4	19.4	19.5	19.7	19.9	20.0	20.0	20.0	19.9	19.9	19.9	19.8	19.7	19.6	19.4
45-59	19.9	20.0	20.1	20.2	20.2	20.2	20.1	19.9	19.7	19.4	19.0	18.7	18.4	18.2	18.0	17.8	17.6	17.5	17.4	17.3	17.2
60-74	14.6	14.7	14.8	14.9	15.0	15.1	15.2	15.3	15.4	15.5	15.4	15.5	15.6	15.8	16.0	16.1	16.3	16.4	16.5	16.6	16.7
75 &over	6.5	6.7	6.8	6.9	7.0	7.2	7.4	7.6	7.9	8.1	8.5	8.9	9.2	9.4	9.6	9.8	10.0	10.1	10.3	10.4	10.6
All ages	100.0	100.0	100.0	100.0	100.0	100.0	100.0	100.0	100.0	100.0	100.0	100.0	100.0	100.0	100.0	100.0	100.0	100.0	100.0	100.0	100.0
Mean age	39.0	39.1	39.3	39.4	39.5	39.7	39.8	40.0	40.1	40.3	40.4	40.5	40.7	40.8	41.0	41.1	41.3	41.4	41.6	41.7	41.8
Median age	38.7	38.7	38.8	38.8	38.8	38.9	38.9	39.1	39.2	39.3	39.4	39.5	39.6	39.8	39.9	40.0	40.2	40.3	40.5	40.7	40.8

15.3b Population projections by the Office for National Statistics

United Kingdom
MALES, thousands

Ages	Projected populations at mid-years by age last birthday					Annual averages for longer-term projections														
	2033	2034	2035	2036	2037	2041	2046	2051	2056	2061	2062	2066	2071	2076	2081	2086	2087	2092	2102	2112
Thousands																				
0-14	6,251	6,242	6,235	6,231	6,230	6,266	6,391	6,543	6,641	6,671	6,673	6,682	6,724	6,806	6,907	6,992	7,005	7,054	7,141	7,285
15-29	6,671	6,730	6,783	6,819	6,845	6,879	6,855	6,818	6,853	6,979	7,011	7,132	7,230	7,261	7,273	7,315	7,328	7,418	7,597	7,685
30-44	6,887	6,861	6,827	6,798	6,789	6,860	7,094	7,388	7,451	7,430	7,421	7,396	7,434	7,562	7,716	7,816	7,827	7,851	7,920	8,113
45-59	6,162	6,224	6,306	6,407	6,502	6,706	6,769	6,640	6,711	6,951	7,026	7,246	7,315	7,301	7,275	7,319	7,340	7,485	7,726	7,778
60-74	5,960	5,951	5,930	5,888	5,830	5,687	5,645	5,944	6,243	6,321	6,306	6,222	6,321	6,573	6,869	6,954	6,953	6,958	7,041	7,360
75 &over	3,878	3,970	4,063	4,165	4,274	4,711	5,139	5,314	5,457	5,686	5,736	6,043	6,414	6,681	6,895	7,272	7,359	7,760	8,528	9,163
All ages	35,808	35,977	36,144	36,308	36,470	37,108	37,893	38,647	39,357	40,037	40,172	40,721	41,437	42,185	42,936	43,668	43,812	44,525	45,954	47,384
Percentages																				
0-14	17.5	17.4	17.3	17.2	17.1	16.9	16.9	16.9	16.9	16.7	16.6	16.4	16.2	16.1	16.1	16.0	16.0	15.8	15.5	15.4
15-29	18.6	18.7	18.8	18.8	18.8	18.5	18.1	17.6	17.4	17.4	17.5	17.5	17.4	17.2	16.9	16.8	16.7	16.7	16.5	16.2
30-44	19.2	19.1	18.9	18.7	18.6	18.5	18.7	19.1	18.9	18.6	18.5	18.2	17.9	17.9	18.0	17.9	17.9	17.6	17.2	17.1
45-59	17.2	17.3	17.4	17.6	17.8	18.1	17.9	17.2	17.1	17.4	17.5	17.8	17.7	17.3	16.9	16.8	16.8	16.8	16.8	16.4
60-74	16.6	16.5	16.4	16.2	16.0	15.3	14.9	15.4	15.9	15.8	15.7	15.3	15.3	15.6	16.0	15.9	15.9	15.6	15.3	15.5
75 &over	10.8	11.0	11.2	11.5	11.7	12.7	13.6	13.8	13.9	14.2	14.3	14.8	15.5	15.8	16.1	16.7	16.8	17.4	18.6	19.3
All ages	100.0	100.0	100.0	100.0	100.0	100.0	100.0	100.0	100.0	100.0	100.0	100.0	100.0	100.0	100.0	100.0	100.0	100.0	100.0	100.0
Mean age	41.9	42.1	42.2	42.3	42.4	42.8	43.1	43.4	43.7	43.9	44.0	44.2	44.6	44.9	45.2	45.5	45.6	45.9	46.6	47.2
Median age	41.0	41.1	41.3	41.4	41.5	41.8	41.7	42.0	42.4	42.9	42.9	43.3	43.6	43.9	44.1	44.4	44.5	44.9	45.6	46.2

Source: Office for National Statistics

Note: Figures may not add exactly due to rounding.
* Children under 16. Working age and pensionable age populations based on state pension age (SPA) for given year.
Between 2012 and 2018, SPA will change from 65 years for men and 61 years for women, to 65 years for both sexes.
Then between 2019 and 2020, SPA will change from 65 years to 66 years for both men and women. Between 2034 and 2046, SPA will increase in two stages from 66 years to 68 years for both sexes. This is based on SPA under the 2011 Pensions Act.
** This is consistent with the age-group definitions used in ONS Labour Market Statistics.

National Population Projections are currently produced every two years. The 2014-based Projections are not due to be published until Oct/Nov 2015. Therefore, this table series will be updated in the next edition.

457

15.3b Population projections by the Office for National Statistics

United Kingdom

FEMALES, thousands

2012-based

Principal projection

Projected populations at mid-years by age last birthday

Ages	2012	2013	2014	2015	2016	2017	2018	2019	2020	2021	2022	2023	2024	2025	2026	2027	2028	2029	2030	2031	2032
Thousands																					
0-14	5,473	5,504	5,543	5,595	5,659	5,731	5,799	5,855	5,904	5,937	5,962	5,972	5,984	5,990	5,989	5,982	5,983	5,979	5,973	5,965	5,957
15-29	6,220	6,208	6,197	6,166	6,130	6,082	6,030	5,991	5,955	5,924	5,902	5,909	5,915	5,938	5,968	5,999	6,030	6,070	6,122	6,184	6,256
30-44	6,472	6,439	6,402	6,386	6,361	6,356	6,379	6,417	6,468	6,537	6,614	6,670	6,695	6,688	6,680	6,677	6,666	6,655	6,624	6,587	6,538
45-59	6,375	6,466	6,554	6,634	6,713	6,761	6,777	6,767	6,741	6,691	6,618	6,542	6,486	6,445	6,410	6,376	6,346	6,313	6,300	6,277	6,273
60-74	4,873	4,932	4,995	5,059	5,145	5,224	5,291	5,351	5,421	5,502	5,513	5,567	5,651	5,749	5,851	5,954	6,046	6,134	6,212	6,291	6,340
75 &over	2,977	3,007	3,055	3,100	3,134	3,188	3,267	3,360	3,450	3,544	3,720	3,862	3,980	4,086	4,180	4,268	4,358	4,447	4,530	4,619	4,715
All ages	32,390	32,556	32,747	32,940	33,143	33,342	33,544	33,742	33,940	34,136	34,330	34,522	34,711	34,896	35,078	35,256	35,429	35,598	35,762	35,922	36,078
Percentages																					
0-14	16.9	16.9	16.9	17.0	17.1	17.2	17.3	17.4	17.4	17.4	17.4	17.3	17.2	17.2	17.1	17.0	16.9	16.8	16.7	16.6	16.5
15-29	19.2	19.1	18.9	18.7	18.5	18.2	18.0	17.8	17.5	17.4	17.2	17.1	17.0	17.0	17.0	17.0	17.0	17.1	17.1	17.2	17.3
30-44	20.0	19.8	19.5	19.4	19.2	19.1	19.0	19.0	19.1	19.2	19.3	19.3	19.3	19.2	19.0	18.9	18.8	18.7	18.5	18.3	18.1
45-59	19.7	19.9	20.0	20.1	20.3	20.3	20.2	20.1	19.9	19.6	19.3	19.0	18.7	18.5	18.3	18.1	17.9	17.7	17.6	17.5	17.4
60-74	15.0	15.1	15.3	15.4	15.5	15.7	15.8	15.9	16.0	16.1	16.1	16.1	16.3	16.5	16.7	16.9	17.1	17.2	17.4	17.5	17.6
75 &over	9.2	9.2	9.3	9.4	9.5	9.6	9.7	10.0	10.2	10.4	10.8	11.2	11.5	11.7	11.9	12.1	12.3	12.5	12.7	12.9	13.1
All ages	100.0	100.0	100.0	100.0	100.0	100.0	100.0	100.0	100.0	100.0	100.0	100.0	100.0	100.0	100.0	100.0	100.0	100.0	100.0	100.0	100.0
Mean age	41.0	41.1	41.3	41.4	41.5	41.7	41.8	41.9	42.1	42.2	42.4	42.5	42.7	42.8	43.0	43.1	43.3	43.4	43.6	43.7	43.8
Median age	40.8	40.9	41.1	41.2	41.3	41.4	41.4	41.5	41.6	41.7	41.9	42.0	42.2	42.3	42.5	42.6	42.8	42.9	43.1	43.3	43.4

15.3b Population projections by the Office for National Statistics

United Kingdom
FEMALES, thousands

Annual averages for longer-term projections

Ages	Projected populations at mid-years by age last birthday					Annual averages for longer-term projections														
	2033	2034	2035	2036	2037	2041	2046	2051	2056	2061	2062	2066	2071	2076	2081	2086	2087	2092	2102	2112
Thousands																				
0-14	5,948	5,940	5,933	5,929	5,928	5,962	6,081	6,226	6,319	6,347	6,349	6,358	6,397	6,476	6,572	6,652	6,664	6,711	6,793	6,931
15-29	6,322	6,379	6,427	6,460	6,485	6,513	6,490	6,454	6,487	6,607	6,636	6,752	6,845	6,874	6,885	6,924	6,937	7,022	7,192	7,275
30-44	6,486	6,448	6,413	6,382	6,361	6,429	6,646	6,923	6,976	6,955	6,947	6,921	6,955	7,076	7,222	7,316	7,326	7,348	7,411	7,593
45-59	6,297	6,336	6,387	6,457	6,534	6,602	6,516	6,320	6,373	6,593	6,665	6,870	6,928	6,911	6,882	6,920	6,939	7,074	7,300	7,342
60-74	6,359	6,352	6,331	6,287	6,222	6,050	5,955	6,149	6,302	6,234	6,192	6,064	6,137	6,366	6,644	6,713	6,711	6,706	6,767	7,060
75 &over	4,817	4,923	5,030	5,147	5,272	5,786	6,299	6,516	6,675	6,898	6,944	7,170	7,414	7,568	7,691	7,999	8,073	8,423	9,137	9,746
All ages	36,229	36,377	36,522	36,663	36,802	37,341	37,987	38,588	39,132	39,634	39,732	40,134	40,676	41,271	41,896	42,525	42,651	43,283	44,600	45,948
Percentages																				
0-14	16.4	16.3	16.2	16.2	16.1	16.0	16.0	16.1	16.1	16.0	16.0	15.8	15.7	15.7	15.7	15.6	15.6	15.5	15.2	15.1
15-29	17.5	17.5	17.6	17.6	17.6	17.4	17.1	16.7	16.6	16.7	16.7	16.8	16.8	16.7	16.4	16.3	16.3	16.2	16.1	15.8
30-44	17.9	17.7	17.6	17.4	17.3	17.2	17.5	17.9	17.8	17.5	17.5	17.2	17.1	17.1	17.2	17.2	17.2	17.0	16.6	16.5
45-59	17.4	17.4	17.5	17.6	17.8	17.7	17.2	16.4	16.3	16.6	16.8	17.1	17.0	16.7	16.4	16.3	16.3	16.3	16.4	16.0
60-74	17.6	17.5	17.3	17.1	16.9	16.2	15.7	15.9	16.1	15.7	15.6	15.1	15.1	15.4	15.9	15.8	15.7	15.5	15.2	15.4
75 &over	13.3	13.5	13.8	14.0	14.3	15.5	16.6	16.9	17.1	17.4	17.5	17.9	18.2	18.3	18.4	18.8	18.9	19.5	20.5	21.2
All ages	100.0	100.0	100.0	100.0	100.0	100.0	100.0	100.0	100.0	100.0	100.0	100.0	100.0	100.0	100.0	100.0	100.0	100.0	100.0	100.0
Mean age	44.0	44.1	44.2	44.4	44.5	44.8	45.2	45.4	45.6	45.8	45.8	46.0	46.2	46.4	46.6	46.8	46.9	47.1	47.7	48.3
Median age	43.6	43.7	43.9	44.0	44.2	44.5	44.4	44.3	44.5	44.8	44.9	45.1	45.3	45.5	45.6	45.8	45.8	46.1	46.8	47.4

Source: Office for National Statistics

Note: Figures may not add exactly due to rounding.

* Children under 16. Working age and pensionable age populations based on state pension age (SPA) for given year.
Between 2012 and 2018, SPA will change from 65 years for men and 61 years for women, to 65 years for both sexes.
Then between 2019 and 2020, SPA will change from 65 years to 66 years for both men and women. Between 2034 and 2046,
SPA will increase in two stages from 66 years to 68 years for both sexes. This is based on SPA under the 2011 Pensions Act.

** This is consistent with the age-group definitions used in ONS Labour Market Statistics.

National Population Projections are currently produced every two years. The 2014-based Projections are not due to be published until Oct/Nov 2015. Therefore, this table series will be updated in the next edition.

15.3c Mid-2013 Population Estimates: England and Wales by sex and single year of age

Ages	Persons	Males	Females	Ages	Persons	Males	Females
All Ages	56,948,229	28,049,196	28,899,033	45	818,385	404,101	414,284
0	710,927	364,958	345,969	46	830,858	411,749	419,109
1	737,107	377,591	359,516	47	831,304	409,890	421,414
2	725,543	371,703	353,840	48	836,022	412,294	423,728
3	714,192	365,425	348,767	49	828,845	409,131	419,714
4	705,138	360,834	344,304	50	811,201	400,964	410,237
5	712,492	364,949	347,543	51	794,153	393,563	400,590
6	689,504	353,388	336,116	52	766,757	380,153	386,604
7	675,792	345,749	330,043	53	736,210	364,894	371,316
8	647,196	331,031	316,165	54	720,085	356,922	363,163
9	635,523	325,128	310,395	55	704,366	349,091	355,275
10	617,115	316,394	300,721	56	678,567	335,740	342,827
11	606,324	310,660	295,664	57	654,877	324,098	330,779
12	622,567	318,034	304,533	58	631,657	311,644	320,013
13	638,885	327,294	311,591	59	634,904	312,148	322,756
14	658,882	337,499	321,383	60	627,662	309,038	318,624
15	667,216	341,911	325,305	61	610,669	299,450	311,219
16	685,855	351,534	334,321	62	615,531	301,456	314,075
17	686,404	354,191	332,213	63	629,638	307,226	322,412
18	688,070	353,039	335,031	64	646,342	316,060	330,282
19	719,148	368,805	350,343	65	683,241	333,363	349,878
20	729,445	371,910	357,535	66	741,248	362,289	378,959
21	757,441	382,934	374,507	67	572,211	278,365	293,846
22	783,838	399,816	384,022	68	556,110	269,719	286,391
23	778,060	396,916	381,144	69	553,986	268,449	285,537
24	772,934	389,408	383,526	70	515,171	247,788	267,383
25	782,869	391,983	390,886	71	460,702	219,739	240,963
26	767,157	380,756	386,401	72	414,587	196,033	218,554
27	776,985	389,805	387,180	73	429,799	202,883	226,916
28	781,376	391,796	389,580	74	426,011	199,948	226,063
29	765,764	382,003	383,761	75	413,690	193,453	220,237
30	773,620	384,615	389,005	76	391,907	181,474	210,433
31	773,688	383,889	389,799	77	372,021	170,323	201,698
32	781,383	388,526	392,857	78	352,595	159,936	192,659
33	783,401	389,872	393,529	79	325,663	145,477	180,186
34	751,450	375,438	376,012	80	308,811	135,686	173,125
35	700,411	350,384	350,027	81	298,392	129,033	169,359
36	690,208	345,608	344,600	82	281,546	118,670	162,876
37	701,401	349,479	351,922	83	260,165	106,712	153,453
38	716,127	356,870	359,257	84	232,788	93,454	139,334
39	728,796	362,122	366,674	85 / 85+	207,513	81,130	126,383
40	761,192	378,605	382,587	86	187,809	72,014	115,795
41	793,520	394,475	399,045	87	167,975	62,142	105,833
42	819,929	404,688	415,241	88	146,582	51,868	94,714
43	799,780	395,228	404,552	89	127,069	42,983	84,086
44	819,732	404,613	415,119	90	478,217	134,797	343,420

Source: Office for National Statistics

Note: It is ONS policy to publish estimates to the nearest hundred persons. Rounded (and particularly unit) estimates cannot be precisely accurate.

: Data not available

15.3d Population projections by the Office for National Statistics

England
PERSONS, thousands

2012-based
Principal projection

Projected populations at mid-years by age last birthday

Ages	2012	2013	2014	2015	2016	2017	2018	2019	2020	2021	2022	2023	2024	2025	2026	2027	2028	2029	2030	2031	2032
Thousands																					
0-14	9,485	9,550	9,630	9,730	9,851	9,985	10,108	10,210	10,299	10,360	10,405	10,426	10,451	10,465	10,466	10,453	10,453	10,445	10,435	10,422	10,409
15-29	10,567	10,577	10,584	10,554	10,516	10,463	10,401	10,351	10,299	10,258	10,243	10,269	10,287	10,334	10,389	10,455	10,521	10,601	10,702	10,818	10,950
30-44	10,873	10,829	10,783	10,775	10,756	10,756	10,811	10,895	11,006	11,147	11,288	11,400	11,466	11,482	11,503	11,530	11,540	11,546	11,516	11,471	11,417
45-59	10,499	10,647	10,793	10,926	11,057	11,144	11,178	11,169	11,135	11,062	10,954	10,842	10,764	10,711	10,663	10,611	10,573	10,533	10,531	10,512	10,515
60-74	7,857	7,955	8,060	8,165	8,311	8,441	8,550	8,645	8,756	8,885	8,903	8,990	9,127	9,288	9,458	9,632	9,784	9,930	10,062	10,193	10,282
75 & over	4,212	4,285	4,377	4,464	4,528	4,626	4,765	4,929	5,086	5,250	5,546	5,781	5,977	6,150	6,303	6,444	6,589	6,730	6,861	7,001	7,151
All ages	53,494	53,844	54,228	54,613	55,020	55,414	55,812	56,198	56,582	56,962	57,338	57,708	58,073	58,430	58,781	59,124	59,459	59,787	60,107	60,419	60,724
Percentages																					
0-14	17.7	17.7	17.8	17.8	17.9	18.0	18.1	18.2	18.2	18.2	18.1	18.1	18.0	17.9	17.8	17.7	17.6	17.5	17.4	17.2	17.1
15-29	19.8	19.6	19.5	19.3	19.1	18.9	18.6	18.4	18.2	18.0	17.9	17.8	17.7	17.7	17.7	17.7	17.7	17.7	17.8	17.9	18.0
30-44	20.3	20.1	19.9	19.7	19.6	19.4	19.4	19.4	19.5	19.6	19.7	19.8	19.7	19.7	19.6	19.5	19.4	19.3	19.2	19.0	18.8
45-59	19.6	19.8	19.9	20.0	20.1	20.1	20.0	19.9	19.7	19.4	19.1	18.8	18.5	18.3	18.1	17.9	17.8	17.6	17.5	17.4	17.3
60-74	14.7	14.8	14.9	15.0	15.1	15.2	15.3	15.4	15.5	15.6	15.5	15.6	15.7	15.9	16.1	16.3	16.5	16.6	16.7	16.9	16.9
75 & over	7.9	8.0	8.1	8.2	8.2	8.3	8.5	8.8	9.0	9.2	9.7	10.0	10.3	10.5	10.7	10.9	11.1	11.3	11.4	11.6	11.8
All ages	100.0	100.0	100.0	100.0	100.0	100.0	100.0	100.0	100.0	100.0	100.0	100.0	100.0	100.0	100.0	100.0	100.0	100.0	100.0	100.0	100.0
Mean age	39.9	40.0	40.2	40.3	40.4	40.5	40.7	40.8	41.0	41.1	41.2	41.4	41.5	41.7	41.8	42.0	42.1	42.3	42.4	42.6	42.7
Median age	39.5	39.6	39.7	39.8	39.8	39.8	39.9	40.0	40.2	40.3	40.4	40.6	40.7	40.8	41.0	41.1	41.3	41.4	41.6	41.7	41.9

15.3d Population projections by the Office for National Statistics

England
PERSONS, thousands

Annual averages for longer-term projections

Projected populations at mid-years by age last birthday

Ages	2033	2034	2035	2036	2037	2041	2046	2051	2056	2061	2062	2066	2071	2076	2081	2086	2087	2092	2102	2112
Thousands																				
0-14	10,396	10,385	10,378	10,376	10,380	10,461	10,699	10,974	11,151	11,212	11,218	11,246	11,335	11,495	11,682	11,839	11,864	11,960	12,138	12,414
15-29	11,071	11,173	11,263	11,324	11,369	11,431	11,388	11,344	11,430	11,668	11,725	11,943	12,121	12,183	12,218	12,307	12,334	12,505	12,838	13,013
30-44	11,351	11,304	11,253	11,214	11,201	11,350	11,782	12,287	12,398	12,359	12,347	12,318	12,407	12,648	12,925	13,105	13,125	13,175	13,325	13,686
45-59	10,570	10,655	10,767	10,908	11,048	11,268	11,247	11,006	11,155	11,592	11,724	12,099	12,217	12,188	12,157	12,255	12,294	12,560	12,990	13,097
60-74	10,322	10,320	10,295	10,234	10,140	9,914	9,834	10,251	10,618	10,625	10,580	10,428	10,614	11,068	11,574	11,714	11,710	11,710	11,877	12,444
75 & over	7,312	7,477	7,646	7,831	8,029	8,840	9,655	10,022	10,318	10,733	10,817	11,274	11,796	12,162	12,471	13,079	13,224	13,901	15,209	16,311
All ages	61,022	61,315	61,603	61,886	62,166	63,265	64,606	65,883	67,070	68,189	68,411	69,308	70,490	71,744	73,027	74,299	74,552	75,811	78,377	80,965
Percentages																				
0-14	17.0	16.9	16.8	16.8	16.7	16.5	16.6	16.7	16.6	16.4	16.4	16.2	16.1	16.0	16.0	15.9	15.9	15.8	15.5	15.3
15-29	18.1	18.2	18.3	18.3	18.3	18.1	17.6	17.2	17.0	17.1	17.1	17.2	17.2	17.0	16.7	16.6	16.5	16.5	16.4	16.1
30-44	18.6	18.4	18.3	18.1	18.0	17.9	18.2	18.7	18.5	18.1	18.0	17.8	17.6	17.6	17.7	17.6	17.6	17.4	17.0	16.9
45-59	17.3	17.4	17.5	17.6	17.8	17.8	17.4	16.7	16.6	17.0	17.1	17.5	17.3	17.0	16.6	16.5	16.5	16.6	16.6	16.2
60-74	16.9	16.8	16.7	16.5	16.3	15.7	15.2	15.6	15.8	15.6	15.5	15.0	15.1	15.4	15.8	15.8	15.7	15.4	15.2	15.4
75 & over	12.0	12.2	12.4	12.7	12.9	14.0	14.9	15.2	15.4	15.7	15.8	16.3	16.7	17.0	17.1	17.6	17.7	18.3	19.4	20.1
All ages	100.0	100.0	100.0	100.0	100.0	100.0	100.0	100.0	100.0	100.0	100.0	100.0	100.0	100.0	100.0	100.0	100.0	100.0	100.0	100.0
Mean age	42.8	43.0	43.1	43.2	43.3	43.7	44.0	44.3	44.5	44.7	44.8	45.0	45.2	45.5	45.8	46.0	46.1	46.4	47.0	47.6
Median age	42.1	42.2	42.4	42.5	42.6	42.9	42.8	42.9	43.2	43.6	43.7	44.0	44.2	44.4	44.6	44.9	44.9	45.3	46.0	46.5

Source: Office for National Statistics

Note: Figures may not add exactly due to rounding.

* Children under 16. Working age and pensionable age populations based on state pension age (SPA) for given year.

Between 2012 and 2018, SPA will change from 65 years for men and 61 years for women, to 65 years for both sexes.
Then between 2019 and 2020, SPA will change from 65 years to 66 years for both men and women. Between 2034 and 2046,
SPA will increase in two stages from 66 years to 68 years for both sexes. This is based on SPA under the 2011 Pensions Act.

** This is consistent with the age-group definitions used in ONS Labour Market Statistics.

National Population Projections are currently produced every two years. The 2014-based Projections are not due to be published until Oct/Nov 2015. Therefore, this table series will be updated in the next edition.

15.3d Population projections by the Office for National Statistics

England
MALES, thousands

2012-based
Principal projection

Projected populations at mid-years by age last birthday

Ages	2012	2013	2014	2015	2016	2017	2018	2019	2020	2021	2022	2023	2024	2025	2026	2027	2028	2029	2030	2031	2032
Thousands																					
0-14	4,855	4,889	4,931	4,982	5,045	5,114	5,177	5,229	5,276	5,308	5,331	5,342	5,355	5,363	5,364	5,357	5,357	5,353	5,347	5,341	5,334
15-29	5,345	5,363	5,379	5,373	5,363	5,349	5,327	5,307	5,280	5,260	5,257	5,272	5,280	5,304	5,330	5,365	5,399	5,441	5,493	5,554	5,621
30-44	5,407	5,384	5,364	5,365	5,363	5,364	5,397	5,448	5,516	5,600	5,678	5,744	5,790	5,813	5,839	5,868	5,887	5,903	5,897	5,883	5,867
45-59	5,198	5,268	5,337	5,399	5,460	5,501	5,516	5,509	5,491	5,454	5,401	5,347	5,311	5,285	5,262	5,234	5,216	5,199	5,203	5,201	5,204
60-74	3,807	3,856	3,907	3,959	4,031	4,095	4,149	4,195	4,250	4,313	4,323	4,366	4,432	4,511	4,593	4,679	4,752	4,822	4,885	4,946	4,989
75 &over	1,722	1,769	1,821	1,871	1,908	1,961	2,034	2,119	2,199	2,282	2,427	2,542	2,638	2,721	2,794	2,861	2,931	2,997	3,059	3,125	3,195
All ages	26,333	26,530	26,739	26,949	27,170	27,384	27,599	27,807	28,012	28,216	28,416	28,613	28,807	28,997	29,183	29,364	29,541	29,715	29,884	30,049	30,210
Percentages																					
0-14	18.4	18.4	18.4	18.5	18.6	18.7	18.8	18.8	18.8	18.8	18.8	18.7	18.6	18.5	18.4	18.2	18.1	18.0	17.9	17.8	17.7
15-29	20.3	20.2	20.1	19.9	19.7	19.5	19.3	19.1	18.8	18.6	18.5	18.4	18.3	18.3	18.3	18.3	18.3	18.3	18.4	18.5	18.6
30-44	20.5	20.3	20.1	19.9	19.7	19.6	19.6	19.6	19.7	19.8	20.0	20.1	20.1	20.0	20.0	20.0	19.9	19.9	19.7	19.6	19.4
45-59	19.7	19.9	20.0	20.0	20.1	20.1	20.0	19.8	19.6	19.3	19.0	18.7	18.4	18.2	18.0	17.8	17.7	17.5	17.4	17.3	17.2
60-74	14.5	14.5	14.6	14.7	14.8	15.0	15.0	15.1	15.2	15.3	15.2	15.3	15.4	15.6	15.7	15.9	16.1	16.2	16.3	16.5	16.5
75 &over	6.5	6.7	6.8	6.9	7.0	7.2	7.4	7.6	7.9	8.1	8.5	8.9	9.2	9.4	9.6	9.7	9.9	10.1	10.2	10.4	10.6
All ages	100.0	100.0	100.0	100.0	100.0	100.0	100.0	100.0	100.0	100.0	100.0	100.0	100.0	100.0	100.0	100.0	100.0	100.0	100.0	100.0	100.0
Mean age	38.9	39.0	39.2	39.3	39.4	39.6	39.7	39.9	40.0	40.1	40.3	40.4	40.6	40.7	40.9	41.0	41.2	41.3	41.4	41.6	41.7
Median age	38.5	38.5	38.6	38.6	38.6	38.7	38.8	38.9	39.0	39.1	39.2	39.4	39.5	39.6	39.7	39.9	40.0	40.2	40.3	40.5	40.7

15.3d Population projections by the Office for National Statistics

England
MALES, thousands

| | Projected populations at mid-years by age last birthday | | | | | | | | | | Annual averages for longer-term projections | | | | | | | | | |
Ages	2033	2034	2035	2036	2037	2041	2046	2051	2056	2061	2062	2066	2071	2076	2081	2086	2087	2092	2102	2112
Thousands																				
0-14	5,328	5,322	5,319	5,318	5,319	5,361	5,483	5,624	5,715	5,746	5,749	5,764	5,809	5,891	5,987	6,068	6,080	6,130	6,221	6,363
15-29	5,683	5,736	5,783	5,814	5,837	5,871	5,849	5,827	5,871	5,993	6,023	6,134	6,226	6,257	6,275	6,321	6,335	6,423	6,594	6,684
30-44	5,843	5,824	5,798	5,779	5,777	5,853	6,078	6,339	6,398	6,378	6,372	6,358	6,404	6,528	6,670	6,763	6,773	6,800	6,877	7,063
45-59	5,236	5,288	5,357	5,440	5,517	5,681	5,730	5,636	5,717	5,946	6,013	6,207	6,271	6,258	6,244	6,295	6,316	6,453	6,675	6,732
60-74	5,007	5,005	4,993	4,963	4,919	4,817	4,796	5,046	5,289	5,349	5,338	5,279	5,383	5,620	5,882	5,958	5,957	5,961	6,054	6,348
75 &over	3,270	3,348	3,426	3,513	3,605	3,980	4,354	4,520	4,660	4,868	4,911	5,171	5,483	5,710	5,901	6,233	6,310	6,670	7,345	7,906
All ages	30,368	30,523	30,676	30,826	30,976	31,565	32,291	32,991	33,650	34,281	34,406	34,914	35,576	36,265	36,959	37,638	37,772	38,435	39,766	41,095
Percentages																				
0-14	17.5	17.4	17.3	17.3	17.2	17.0	17.0	17.0	17.0	16.8	16.7	16.5	16.3	16.2	16.2	16.1	16.1	15.9	15.6	15.5
15-29	18.7	18.8	18.9	18.9	18.8	18.6	18.1	17.7	17.4	17.5	17.5	17.6	17.5	17.3	17.0	16.8	16.8	16.7	16.6	16.3
30-44	19.2	19.1	18.9	18.7	18.7	18.5	18.8	19.2	19.0	18.6	18.5	18.2	18.0	18.0	18.0	18.0	17.9	17.7	17.3	17.2
45-59	17.2	17.3	17.5	17.6	17.8	18.0	17.7	17.1	17.0	17.3	17.5	17.8	17.6	17.3	16.9	16.7	16.7	16.8	16.8	16.4
60-74	16.5	16.4	16.3	16.1	15.9	15.3	14.9	15.3	15.7	15.6	15.5	15.1	15.1	15.5	15.9	15.8	15.8	15.5	15.2	15.4
75 &over	10.8	11.0	11.2	11.4	11.6	12.6	13.5	13.7	13.8	14.2	14.3	14.8	15.4	15.7	16.0	16.6	16.7	17.4	18.5	19.2
All ages	100.0	100.0	100.0	100.0	100.0	100.0	100.0	100.0	100.0	100.0	100.0	100.0	100.0	100.0	100.0	100.0	100.0	100.0	100.0	100.0
Mean age	41.8	42.0	42.1	42.2	42.3	42.7	43.0	43.3	43.6	43.8	43.9	44.1	44.5	44.8	45.1	45.4	45.5	45.8	46.5	47.1
Median age	40.8	41.0	41.1	41.2	41.3	41.6	41.5	41.8	42.3	42.7	42.8	43.1	43.4	43.7	43.9	44.2	44.3	44.7	45.4	46.0

Source: Office for National Statistics

Note: Figures may not add exactly due to rounding.
* Children under 16. Working age and pensionable age populations based on state pension age (SPA) for given year.
Between 2012 and 2018, SPA will change from 65 years for men and 61 years for women, to 65 years for both sexes.
Then between 2019 and 2020, SPA will change from 65 years to 66 years for both men and women. Between 2034 and 2046, SPA will increase in two stages from 66 years to 68 years for both sexes. This is based on SPA under the 2011 Pensions Act.

** This is consistent with the age-group definitions used in ONS Labour Market Statistics.

National Population Projections are currently produced every two years. The 2014-based Projections are not due to be published until Oct/Nov 2015. Therefore, this table series will be updated in the next edition.

15.3d Population projections by the Office for National Statistics

England
FEMALES, thousands

2012-based
Principal projection

Projected populations at mid-years by age last birthday

Ages	2012	2013	2014	2015	2016	2017	2018	2019	2020	2021	2022	2023	2024	2025	2026	2027	2028	2029	2030	2031	2032
Thousands																					
0-14	4,630	4,661	4,700	4,748	4,806	4,871	4,931	4,980	5,024	5,052	5,074	5,084	5,096	5,102	5,103	5,096	5,096	5,092	5,087	5,081	5,075
15-29	5,223	5,214	5,205	5,181	5,153	5,114	5,074	5,045	5,019	4,998	4,987	4,998	5,007	5,030	5,058	5,090	5,121	5,160	5,209	5,265	5,329
30-44	5,467	5,445	5,419	5,410	5,394	5,392	5,414	5,447	5,489	5,547	5,610	5,656	5,676	5,670	5,663	5,662	5,652	5,644	5,619	5,589	5,550
45-59	5,301	5,379	5,456	5,527	5,597	5,643	5,662	5,660	5,644	5,608	5,553	5,494	5,453	5,426	5,401	5,377	5,357	5,334	5,328	5,311	5,311
60-74	4,050	4,100	4,153	4,206	4,280	4,346	4,401	4,449	4,506	4,572	4,580	4,624	4,695	4,777	4,865	4,953	5,032	5,109	5,178	5,248	5,294
75 &over	2,490	2,516	2,556	2,594	2,620	2,665	2,731	2,810	2,887	2,968	3,118	3,239	3,339	3,429	3,509	3,582	3,658	3,733	3,803	3,877	3,957
All ages	27,160	27,314	27,489	27,665	27,849	28,030	28,213	28,392	28,570	28,747	28,922	29,095	29,266	29,434	29,598	29,760	29,918	30,072	30,223	30,370	30,514
Percentages																					
0-14	17.0	17.1	17.1	17.2	17.3	17.4	17.5	17.5	17.6	17.6	17.5	17.5	17.4	17.3	17.2	17.1	17.0	16.9	16.8	16.7	16.6
15-29	19.2	19.1	18.9	18.7	18.5	18.2	18.0	17.8	17.6	17.4	17.2	17.2	17.1	17.1	17.1	17.1	17.1	17.2	17.2	17.3	17.5
30-44	20.1	19.9	19.7	19.6	19.4	19.2	19.2	19.2	19.2	19.3	19.4	19.4	19.4	19.3	19.1	19.0	18.9	18.8	18.6	18.4	18.2
45-59	19.5	19.7	19.8	20.0	20.1	20.1	20.1	19.9	19.8	19.5	19.2	18.9	18.6	18.4	18.2	18.1	17.9	17.7	17.6	17.5	17.4
60-74	14.9	15.0	15.1	15.2	15.4	15.5	15.6	15.7	15.8	15.9	15.8	15.9	16.0	16.2	16.4	16.6	16.8	17.0	17.1	17.3	17.3
75 &over	9.2	9.2	9.3	9.4	9.4	9.5	9.7	9.9	10.1	10.3	10.8	11.1	11.4	11.7	11.9	12.0	12.2	12.4	12.6	12.8	13.0
All ages	100.0	100.0	100.0	100.0	100.0	100.0	100.0	100.0	100.0	100.0	100.0	100.0	100.0	100.0	100.0	100.0	100.0	100.0	100.0	100.0	100.0
Mean age	40.9	41.0	41.1	41.3	41.4	41.5	41.6	41.8	41.9	42.0	42.2	42.3	42.5	42.6	42.8	42.9	43.1	43.2	43.4	43.5	43.7
Median age	40.5	40.7	40.8	40.9	41.0	41.1	41.1	41.2	41.3	41.4	41.6	41.8	41.9	42.1	42.2	42.4	42.5	42.7	42.9	43.0	43.2

15.3d Population projections by the Office for National Statistics

England
FEMALES, thousands

	Projected populations at mid-years by age last birthday											Annual averages for longer-term projections								
Ages	2033	2034	2035	2036	2037	2041	2046	2051	2056	2061	2062	2066	2071	2076	2081	2086	2087	2092	2102	2112
Thousands																				
0-14	5,068	5,063	5,060	5,059	5,060	5,100	5,216	5,350	5,436	5,466	5,469	5,482	5,526	5,604	5,695	5,772	5,784	5,830	5,917	6,052
15-29	5,388	5,437	5,481	5,509	5,531	5,560	5,539	5,517	5,559	5,675	5,703	5,809	5,896	5,926	5,942	5,986	5,999	6,082	6,244	6,330
30-44	5,509	5,480	5,455	5,435	5,423	5,497	5,704	5,948	6,000	5,981	5,975	5,960	6,003	6,120	6,254	6,342	6,352	6,376	6,448	6,623
45-59	5,333	5,367	5,410	5,468	5,531	5,587	5,517	5,370	5,437	5,647	5,711	5,891	5,946	5,931	5,914	5,960	5,979	6,107	6,315	6,365
60-74	5,315	5,315	5,302	5,271	5,221	5,097	5,038	5,205	5,330	5,276	5,242	5,149	5,231	5,447	5,693	5,756	5,754	5,749	5,823	6,095
75 &over	4,042	4,130	4,220	4,318	4,424	4,860	5,301	5,502	5,658	5,865	5,906	6,103	6,313	6,452	6,570	6,846	6,913	7,231	7,864	8,405
All ages	30,654	30,792	30,927	31,060	31,190	31,700	32,314	32,892	33,420	33,909	34,005	34,395	34,915	35,479	36,068	36,662	36,780	37,376	38,612	39,870
Percentages																				
0-14	16.5	16.4	16.4	16.3	16.2	16.1	16.1	16.3	16.3	16.1	16.1	15.9	15.8	15.8	15.8	15.7	15.7	15.6	15.3	15.2
15-29	17.6	17.7	17.7	17.7	17.7	17.5	17.1	16.8	16.6	16.7	16.8	16.9	16.9	16.7	16.5	16.3	16.3	16.3	16.2	15.9
30-44	18.0	17.8	17.6	17.5	17.4	17.3	17.7	18.1	18.0	17.6	17.6	17.3	17.2	17.2	17.3	17.3	17.3	17.1	16.7	16.6
45-59	17.4	17.4	17.5	17.6	17.7	17.6	17.1	16.3	16.3	16.7	16.8	17.1	17.0	16.7	16.4	16.3	16.3	16.3	16.4	16.0
60-74	17.3	17.3	17.1	17.0	16.7	16.1	15.6	15.8	15.9	15.6	15.4	15.0	15.0	15.4	15.8	15.7	15.6	15.4	15.1	15.3
75 &over	13.2	13.4	13.6	13.9	14.2	15.3	16.4	16.7	16.9	17.3	17.4	17.7	18.1	18.2	18.2	18.7	18.8	19.3	20.4	21.1
All ages	100.0	100.0	100.0	100.0	100.0	100.0	100.0	100.0	100.0	100.0	100.0	100.0	100.0	100.0	100.0	100.0	100.0	100.0	100.0	100.0
Mean age	43.8	43.9	44.1	44.2	44.3	44.7	45.0	45.3	45.5	45.7	45.7	45.8	46.0	46.2	46.4	46.7	46.7	47.0	47.6	48.2
Median age	43.3	43.5	43.6	43.8	43.9	44.2	44.1	44.0	44.3	44.6	44.6	44.9	45.1	45.2	45.4	45.6	45.6	45.9	46.6	47.2

Source: Office for National Statistics

Note: Figures may not add exactly due to rounding.

* Children under 16. Working age and pensionable age populations based on state pension age (SPA) for given year.
Between 2012 and 2018, SPA will change from 65 years for men and 61 years for women, to 65 years for both sexes.
Then between 2019 and 2020, SPA will change from 65 years to 66 years for both men and women. Between 2034 and 2046,
SPA will increase in two stages from 66 years to 68 years for both sexes. This is based on SPA under the 2011 Pensions Act.
** This is consistent with the age-group definitions used in ONS Labour Market Statistics.

National Population Projections are currently produced every two years. The 2014-based Projections are not due to be published until Oct/Nov 2015. Therefore, this table series will be updated in the next edition.

15.3d Population projections by the Office for National Statistics

Wales
PERSONS, thousands

2012-based
Principal projection

Projected populations at mid-years by age last birthday

Ages	2012	2013	2014	2015	2016	2017	2018	2019	2020	2021	2022	2023	2024	2025	2026	2027	2028	2029	2030	2031	2032
Thousands																					
0-14	519	518	519	521	524	529	534	538	542	544	545	545	546	546	545	544	544	544	544	543	541
15-29	599	602	605	605	605	603	599	595	590	584	580	576	574	574	574	573	572	573	575	578	583
30-44	559	553	546	542	537	534	536	540	548	558	569	579	585	588	591	596	599	602	602	601	599
45-59	616	620	624	628	632	632	630	624	617	608	597	586	576	569	562	555	549	542	538	533	531
60-74	514	519	525	529	535	540	544	547	551	556	554	555	559	564	570	576	580	585	588	593	594
75 & over	268	271	276	282	287	293	302	312	322	331	349	364	376	387	396	405	413	421	428	435	442
All ages	3,074	3,083	3,095	3,107	3,119	3,132	3,144	3,157	3,169	3,181	3,193	3,205	3,216	3,227	3,238	3,248	3,258	3,267	3,275	3,283	3,291
Percentages																					
0-14	16.9	16.8	16.8	16.8	16.8	16.9	17.0	17.1	17.1	17.1	17.1	17.0	17.0	16.9	16.8	16.8	16.7	16.7	16.6	16.5	16.4
15-29	19.5	19.5	19.6	19.5	19.4	19.2	19.1	18.8	18.6	18.4	18.2	18.0	17.8	17.8	17.7	17.6	17.6	17.5	17.6	17.6	17.7
30-44	18.2	17.9	17.6	17.4	17.2	17.1	17.0	17.1	17.3	17.5	17.8	18.1	18.2	18.2	18.3	18.4	18.4	18.4	18.4	18.3	18.2
45-59	20.0	20.1	20.2	20.2	20.2	20.2	20.0	19.8	19.5	19.1	18.7	18.3	17.9	17.6	17.4	17.1	16.8	16.6	16.4	16.2	16.1
60-74	16.7	16.8	17.0	17.0	17.1	17.2	17.3	17.3	17.4	17.5	17.4	17.3	17.4	17.5	17.6	17.7	17.8	17.9	18.0	18.1	18.1
75 & over	8.7	8.8	8.9	9.1	9.2	9.4	9.6	9.9	10.2	10.4	10.9	11.4	11.7	12.0	12.2	12.5	12.7	12.9	13.1	13.2	13.4
All ages	100.0	100.0	100.0	100.0	100.0	100.0	100.0	100.0	100.0	100.0	100.0	100.0	100.0	100.0	100.0	100.0	100.0	100.0	100.0	100.0	100.0
Mean age	41.3	41.4	41.5	41.7	41.8	41.9	42.1	42.2	42.3	42.5	42.6	42.7	42.9	43.0	43.1	43.3	43.4	43.5	43.7	43.8	43.9
Median age	41.7	41.9	42.0	42.1	42.2	42.2	42.2	42.1	42.1	42.1	42.2	42.3	42.4	42.4	42.5	42.5	42.6	42.7	42.8	42.9	43.0

15.3d Population projections by the Office for National Statistics

Wales
PERSONS, thousands

| | Projected populations at mid-years by age last birthday | | | | | | | | | | | Annual averages for longer-term projections | | | | | | | | |
Ages	2033	2034	2035	2036	2037	2041	2046	2051	2056	2061	2062	2066	2071	2076	2081	2086	2087	2092	2102	2112
Thousands																				
0-14	540	538	536	535	533	530	532	537	540	539	538	536	533	534	537	538	538	538	536	538
15-29	588	592	596	598	599	599	597	589	584	586	587	592	595	593	590	588	588	589	593	591
30-44	595	591	586	581	576	571	576	595	596	594	593	587	582	584	590	594	594	592	587	591
45-59	532	537	545	555	565	588	598	579	570	575	580	595	597	596	589	584	584	588	597	593
60-74	592	587	581	573	563	534	511	534	567	578	576	560	555	562	582	585	585	585	578	590
75 & over	450	458	466	475	484	520	552	553	549	555	557	579	612	634	646	671	676	699	750	792
All ages	3,298	3,304	3,310	3,316	3,321	3,342	3,365	3,387	3,407	3,427	3,431	3,449	3,475	3,504	3,533	3,561	3,566	3,591	3,641	3,694
Percentages																				
0-14	16.4	16.3	16.2	16.1	16.1	15.9	15.8	15.9	15.9	15.7	15.7	15.5	15.4	15.2	15.2	15.1	15.1	15.0	14.7	14.6
15-29	17.8	17.9	18.0	18.0	18.0	17.9	17.7	17.4	17.1	17.1	17.1	17.2	17.1	16.9	16.7	16.5	16.5	16.4	16.3	16.0
30-44	18.0	17.9	17.7	17.5	17.3	17.1	17.1	17.6	17.5	17.3	17.3	17.0	16.8	16.7	16.7	16.7	16.6	16.5	16.1	16.0
45-59	16.1	16.3	16.5	16.7	17.0	17.6	17.8	17.1	16.7	16.8	16.9	17.3	17.2	17.0	16.5	16.4	16.4	16.4	16.4	16.0
60-74	18.0	17.8	17.6	17.3	17.0	16.0	15.2	15.8	16.6	16.9	16.8	16.3	16.0	16.0	16.5	16.4	16.4	16.3	15.9	16.0
75 & over	13.7	13.9	14.1	14.3	14.6	15.6	16.4	16.3	16.1	16.2	16.2	16.8	17.6	18.1	18.3	18.8	19.0	19.5	20.6	21.4
All ages	100.0	100.0	100.0	100.0	100.0	100.0	100.0	100.0	100.0	100.0	100.0	100.0	100.0	100.0	100.0	100.0	100.0	100.0	100.0	100.0
Mean age	44.0	44.1	44.2	44.3	44.4	44.7	45.0	45.2	45.4	45.6	45.6	45.8	46.1	46.5	46.8	47.1	47.2	47.5	48.1	48.7
Median age	43.2	43.4	43.5	43.7	43.9	44.3	44.4	44.3	44.6	44.9	44.9	45.3	45.7	46.0	46.3	46.5	46.6	46.9	47.6	48.2

Source: Office for National Statistics

Note: Figures may not add exactly due to rounding.
* Children under 16. Working age and pensionable age populations based on state pension age (SPA) for given year.
Between 2012 and 2018, SPA will change from 65 years for men and 61 years for women, to 65 years for both sexes.
Then between 2019 and 2020, SPA will change from 65 years to 66 years for both men and women. Between 2034 and 2046,
SPA will increase in two stages from 66 years to 68 years for both sexes. This is based on SPA under the 2011 Pensions Act.
** This is consistent with the age-group definitions used in ONS Labour Market Statistics.

National Population Projections are currently produced every two years. The 2014-based Projections are not due to be published until Oct/Nov 2015. Therefore, this table series will be updated in the next edition.

15.3d Population projections by the Office for National Statistics

Wales
MALES, thousands

2012-based
Principal projection

Projected populations at mid-years by age last birthday

Ages	2012	2013	2014	2015	2016	2017	2018	2019	2020	2021	2022	2023	2024	2025	2026	2027	2028	2029	2030	2031	2032
Thousands																					
0-14	266	266	266	268	269	272	274	276	278	279	280	280	280	280	280	280	280	280	279	279	278
15-29	306	309	312	313	314	314	313	311	308	306	304	302	301	301	301	301	300	301	302	304	306
30-44	276	273	270	269	267	266	268	272	277	283	289	296	301	304	307	311	314	316	318	318	318
45-59	302	304	305	307	309	309	307	305	301	297	291	286	281	278	275	271	268	265	264	263	262
60-74	250	253	255	257	260	262	263	264	266	268	267	267	269	271	274	276	278	280	282	284	285
75 &over	109	112	115	118	121	125	129	134	139	144	153	160	166	171	175	179	183	187	190	192	196
All ages	1,510	1,516	1,524	1,532	1,539	1,547	1,555	1,562	1,570	1,577	1,585	1,592	1,599	1,605	1,612	1,618	1,624	1,630	1,635	1,640	1,645
Percentages																					
0-14	17.6	17.5	17.5	17.5	17.5	17.6	17.6	17.7	17.7	17.7	17.7	17.6	17.5	17.5	17.4	17.3	17.2	17.2	17.1	17.0	16.9
15-29	20.2	20.4	20.4	20.4	20.4	20.3	20.1	19.9	19.7	19.4	19.2	19.0	18.9	18.8	18.7	18.6	18.5	18.5	18.5	18.5	18.6
30-44	18.3	18.0	17.7	17.6	17.4	17.2	17.2	17.4	17.6	18.0	18.3	18.6	18.8	18.9	19.0	19.2	19.3	19.4	19.4	19.4	19.4
45-59	20.0	20.0	20.0	20.0	20.0	20.0	19.8	19.5	19.2	18.8	18.4	18.0	17.6	17.3	17.1	16.8	16.5	16.3	16.2	16.0	15.9
60-74	16.6	16.7	16.8	16.8	16.9	16.9	16.9	16.9	16.9	17.0	16.9	16.8	16.8	16.9	17.0	17.1	17.1	17.2	17.3	17.3	17.3
75 &over	7.2	7.4	7.5	7.7	7.9	8.1	8.3	8.6	8.9	9.1	9.6	10.0	10.4	10.7	10.9	11.1	11.3	11.5	11.6	11.7	11.9
All ages	100.0	100.0	100.0	100.0	100.0	100.0	100.0	100.0	100.0	100.0	100.0	100.0	100.0	100.0	100.0	100.0	100.0	100.0	100.0	100.0	100.0
Mean age	40.2	40.3	40.4	40.5	40.7	40.8	40.9	41.0	41.2	41.3	41.4	41.6	41.7	41.8	41.9	42.0	42.2	42.3	42.4	42.5	42.6
Median age	40.5	40.5	40.6	40.5	40.5	40.4	40.3	40.3	40.3	40.4	40.4	40.4	40.4	40.4	40.5	40.5	40.6	40.7	40.9	41.0	41.2

15.3d Population projections by the Office for National Statistics

Wales
MALES, thousands

| | Projected populations at mid-years by age last birthday | | | | | | | | | | | Annual averages for longer-term projections | | | | | | | | |
Ages	2033	2034	2035	2036	2037	2041	2046	2051	2056	2061	2062	2066	2071	2076	2081	2086	2087	2092	2102	2112
Thousands																				
0-14	277	277	276	275	274	272	273	276	278	277	277	275	274	275	276	277	277	277	276	276
15-29	309	311	313	314	315	314	313	309	307	308	309	311	313	312	310	309	309	310	312	311
30-44	317	316	313	310	309	306	309	319	320	319	319	315	313	314	317	319	319	318	316	318
45-59	264	267	272	279	285	302	314	307	303	306	309	317	318	317	314	312	312	314	319	317
60-74	284	281	279	275	270	257	248	265	287	299	299	293	291	295	306	308	308	308	305	312
75 &over	199	203	206	210	214	230	243	243	242	247	248	264	286	302	312	328	330	344	372	395
All ages	1,650	1,654	1,658	1,663	1,667	1,682	1,701	1,720	1,738	1,756	1,760	1,775	1,795	1,815	1,835	1,852	1,855	1,870	1,899	1,928
Percentages																				
0-14	16.8	16.7	16.6	16.5	16.4	16.2	16.1	16.1	16.0	15.8	15.7	15.5	15.3	15.1	15.0	14.9	14.9	14.8	14.5	14.3
15-29	18.7	18.8	18.8	18.9	18.9	18.7	18.4	18.0	17.7	17.5	17.5	17.5	17.4	17.2	16.9	16.7	16.7	16.6	16.4	16.1
30-44	19.2	19.1	18.9	18.7	18.5	18.2	18.2	18.6	18.4	18.2	18.1	17.8	17.4	17.3	17.3	17.2	17.2	17.0	16.6	16.5
45-59	16.0	16.2	16.4	16.8	17.1	18.0	18.5	17.8	17.4	17.4	17.5	17.8	17.7	17.5	17.1	16.8	16.8	16.8	16.8	16.4
60-74	17.2	17.0	16.8	16.5	16.2	15.3	14.6	15.4	16.5	17.0	17.0	16.5	16.2	16.3	16.7	16.6	16.6	16.5	16.1	16.2
75 &over	12.1	12.2	12.4	12.6	12.8	13.7	14.3	14.2	14.0	14.0	14.1	14.9	15.9	16.6	17.0	17.7	17.8	18.4	19.6	20.5
All ages	100.0	100.0	100.0	100.0	100.0	100.0	100.0	100.0	100.0	100.0	100.0	100.0	100.0	100.0	100.0	100.0	100.0	100.0	100.0	100.0
Mean age	42.7	42.8	42.9	43.0	43.1	43.4	43.7	43.9	44.2	44.5	44.6	44.9	45.3	45.8	46.2	46.6	46.7	47.0	47.6	48.3
Median age	41.4	41.6	41.8	41.9	42.1	42.5	42.6	42.8	43.3	43.8	43.9	44.3	44.9	45.3	45.7	46.0	46.1	46.4	47.2	47.8

Source: Office for National Statistics

Note: Figures may not add exactly due to rounding.

* Children under 16. Working age and pensionable age populations based on state pension age (SPA) for given year. Between 2012 and 2018, SPA will change from 65 years for men and 61 years for women, to 65 years for both sexes. Then between 2019 and 2020, SPA will change from 65 years to 66 years for both men and women. Between 2034 and 2046, SPA will increase in two stages from 66 years to 68 years for both sexes. This is based on SPA under the 2011 Pensions Act.

** This is consistent with the age-group definitions used in ONS Labour Market Statistics.

National Population Projections are currently produced every two years. The 2014-based Projections are not due to be published until Oct/Nov 2015. Therefore, this table series will be updated in the next edition.

15.3d Population projections by the Office for National Statistics

Wales
FEMALES, thousands

2012-based
Principal projection

Projected populations at mid-years by age last birthday

Ages	2012	2013	2014	2015	2016	2017	2018	2019	2020	2021	2022	2023	2024	2025	2026	2027	2028	2029	2030	2031	2032
Thousands																					
0-14	253	252	253	254	255	258	260	262	263	264	265	265	265	265	265	264	265	264	264	264	263
15-29	293	293	294	293	291	289	286	284	281	278	276	274	273	272	273	272	272	272	273	275	277
30-44	283	280	276	273	270	268	268	269	271	275	279	283	285	285	284	285	285	285	284	283	281
45-59	314	316	318	321	323	323	322	320	316	311	305	300	295	291	287	283	280	276	274	271	269
60-74	263	266	270	272	275	278	280	282	285	288	287	287	290	293	296	299	301	304	306	309	309
75 &over	158	159	161	163	166	169	173	178	183	187	196	204	210	216	221	225	230	235	238	242	247
All ages	1,564	1,567	1,571	1,576	1,580	1,585	1,590	1,594	1,599	1,604	1,609	1,613	1,618	1,622	1,626	1,630	1,634	1,637	1,640	1,643	1,645
Percentages																					
0-14	16.2	16.1	16.1	16.1	16.2	16.3	16.4	16.4	16.5	16.5	16.5	16.4	16.4	16.4	16.3	16.2	16.2	16.2	16.1	16.0	16.0
15-29	18.7	18.7	18.7	18.6	18.4	18.2	18.0	17.8	17.6	17.4	17.1	17.0	16.9	16.8	16.8	16.7	16.6	16.6	16.6	16.7	16.8
30-44	18.1	17.8	17.5	17.3	17.1	16.9	16.8	16.9	17.0	17.1	17.4	17.5	17.6	17.5	17.5	17.5	17.5	17.4	17.3	17.2	17.0
45-59	20.1	20.2	20.3	20.4	20.4	20.4	20.3	20.0	19.8	19.4	19.0	18.6	18.2	18.1	17.7	17.4	17.1	16.9	16.7	16.5	16.3
60-74	16.8	17.0	17.2	17.3	17.4	17.5	17.6	17.7	17.8	17.9	17.8	17.8	17.9	18.1	18.2	18.3	18.5	18.6	18.7	18.8	18.8
75 &over	10.1	10.2	10.3	10.4	10.5	10.7	10.9	11.2	11.4	11.7	12.2	12.7	13.0	13.3	13.6	13.8	14.1	14.3	14.5	14.8	15.0
All ages	100.0	100.0	100.0	100.0	100.0	100.0	100.0	100.0	100.0	100.0	100.0	100.0	100.0	100.0	100.0	100.0	100.0	100.0	100.0	100.0	100.0
Mean age	42.4	42.5	42.6	42.8	42.9	43.0	43.2	43.3	43.5	43.6	43.8	43.9	44.1	44.2	44.4	44.5	44.6	44.8	44.9	45.1	45.2
Median age	42.9	43.0	43.3	43.5	43.7	43.8	43.9	44.0	44.0	44.0	44.1	44.1	44.3	44.4	44.5	44.6	44.7	44.8	44.9	45.0	45.1

15.3d Population projections by the Office for National Statistics

Wales
FEMALES, thousands

Projected populations at mid-years by age last birthday | Annual averages for longer-term projections

Ages	2033	2034	2035	2036	2037	2041	2046	2051	2056	2061	2062	2066	2071	2076	2081	2086	2087	2092	2102	2112
Thousands																				
0-14	262	261	261	260	259	257	258	261	263	262	262	260	259	260	261	261	262	261	260	261
15-29	280	281	283	284	285	284	283	279	277	278	278	281	282	282	280	279	279	279	281	280
30-44	278	275	273	270	267	265	267	276	276	275	275	271	269	270	273	275	275	274	271	273
45-59	269	270	272	276	280	286	284	272	267	269	272	278	279	278	275	273	273	274	278	276
60-74	308	306	303	298	293	277	263	270	280	279	277	268	264	267	276	278	278	277	273	279
75 &over	251	256	260	265	270	290	308	309	307	308	309	315	326	332	334	344	346	355	378	397
All ages	1,648	1,650	1,652	1,653	1,655	1,660	1,664	1,667	1,669	1,671	1,671	1,674	1,680	1,688	1,699	1,709	1,711	1,721	1,742	1,766
Percentages																				
0-14	15.9	15.8	15.8	15.7	15.7	15.5	15.5	15.7	15.7	15.7	15.6	15.5	15.4	15.4	15.3	15.3	15.3	15.2	14.9	14.8
15-29	17.0	17.1	17.1	17.2	17.2	17.1	17.0	16.8	16.6	16.6	16.7	16.8	16.8	16.7	16.5	16.3	16.3	16.2	16.1	15.9
30-44	16.9	16.7	16.5	16.3	16.2	15.9	16.0	16.5	16.5	16.5	16.4	16.2	16.0	16.0	16.1	16.1	16.1	15.9	15.6	15.5
45-59	16.3	16.4	16.5	16.7	16.9	17.2	17.1	16.3	16.0	16.1	16.2	16.6	16.6	16.5	16.3	16.2	16.2	16.1	16.0	15.6
60-74	18.7	18.6	18.3	18.1	17.7	16.7	15.8	16.2	16.7	16.7	16.6	16.0	15.7	15.8	16.3	16.2	16.2	16.1	15.7	15.8
75 &over	15.2	15.5	15.8	16.0	16.3	17.5	18.5	18.6	18.4	18.4	18.5	18.8	19.4	19.7	19.7	20.1	20.2	20.6	21.7	22.5
All ages	100.0	100.0	100.0	100.0	100.0	100.0	100.0	100.0	100.0	100.0	100.0	100.0	100.0	100.0	100.0	100.0	100.0	100.0	100.0	100.0
Mean age	45.3	45.4	45.6	45.7	45.8	46.1	46.3	46.5	46.6	46.7	46.7	46.8	47.0	47.2	47.4	47.7	47.7	48.0	48.5	49.1
Median age	45.2	45.4	45.5	45.6	45.8	46.3	46.4	46.0	46.0	46.1	46.1	46.3	46.6	46.8	47.0	47.2	47.2	47.5	48.2	48.8

Source: Office for National Statistics

Note: Figures may not add exactly due to rounding.
* Children under 16. Working age and pensionable age populations based on state pension age (SPA) for given year. Between 2012 and 2018, SPA will change from 65 years for men and 61 years for women, to 65 years for both sexes. Then between 2019 and 2020, SPA will change from 65 years to 66 years for both men and women. Between 2034 and 2046, SPA will increase in two stages from 66 years to 68 years for both sexes. This is based on SPA under the 2011 Pensions Act.
** This is consistent with the age-group definitions used in ONS Labour Market Statistics.

National Population Projections are currently produced every two years. The 2014-based Projections are not due to be published until Oct/Nov 2015. Therefore, this table series will be updated in the next edition.

15.3e Mid-2013 Population Estimates for Scotland by sex and single year of age

Ages	Persons	Males	Females	Ages	Persons	Males	Females
All Ages	5,327,700	2,586,532	2,741,168	45	80,364	38,799	41,565
0	57,058	29,161	27,897	46	81,019	39,615	41,404
1	58,898	30,258	28,640	47	80,517	39,098	41,419
2	60,762	31,069	29,693	48	83,462	40,686	42,776
3	57,980	29,529	28,451	49	82,452	39,817	42,635
4	59,583	30,266	29,317	50	82,215	39,965	42,250
5	59,457	30,279	29,178	51	80,383	39,491	40,892
6	57,086	29,180	27,906	52	78,537	38,375	40,162
7	56,002	28,523	27,479	53	75,921	37,303	38,618
8	55,553	28,546	27,007	54	75,395	36,727	38,668
9	54,506	28,086	26,420	55	73,359	35,712	37,647
10	52,884	26,967	25,917	56	71,568	35,062	36,506
11	52,706	26,849	25,857	57	69,359	33,986	35,373
12	54,857	27,859	26,998	58	66,474	32,440	34,034
13	56,241	28,969	27,272	59	65,614	32,124	33,490
14	58,432	29,984	28,448	60	64,453	31,498	32,955
15	59,674	30,566	29,108	61	62,186	30,357	31,829
16	61,823	31,755	30,068	62	62,924	30,662	32,262
17	61,892	31,976	29,916	63	63,031	30,919	32,112
18	64,275	32,758	31,517	64	64,733	31,583	33,150
19	67,930	34,380	33,550	65	66,695	32,490	34,205
20	70,057	34,934	35,123	66	72,142	34,941	37,201
21	75,757	37,522	38,235	67	54,591	26,499	28,092
22	77,128	38,479	38,649	68	51,504	24,526	26,978
23	73,666	36,793	36,873	69	52,404	25,114	27,290
24	72,339	36,210	36,129	70	50,408	23,556	26,852
25	72,969	36,357	36,612	71	46,195	21,392	24,803
26	70,669	34,839	35,830	72	42,711	19,508	23,203
27	70,317	34,949	35,368	73	43,358	19,731	23,627
28	69,911	34,385	35,526	74	42,228	19,191	23,037
29	67,468	33,124	34,344	75	40,874	18,456	22,418
30	68,639	33,515	35,124	76	38,583	16,897	21,686
31	69,592	33,819	35,773	77	36,997	16,120	20,877
32	69,168	33,969	35,199	78	34,899	15,035	19,864
33	67,777	33,240	34,537	79	32,220	13,727	18,493
34	65,398	32,395	33,003	80	29,817	12,496	17,321
35	61,018	29,765	31,253	81	28,971	11,798	17,173
36	59,974	29,709	30,265	82	26,479	10,673	15,806
37	63,634	31,333	32,301	83	23,759	9,156	14,603
38	64,228	31,280	32,948	84	21,300	8,131	13,169
39	65,325	32,177	33,148	85 / 85+	18,377	6,754	11,623
40	69,295	33,998	35,297	86	16,625	5,940	10,685
41	73,738	35,714	38,024	87	14,788	5,108	9,680
42	76,636	36,907	39,729	88	12,480	4,231	8,249
43	75,877	36,663	39,214	89	10,772	3,448	7,324
44	78,693	38,049	40,644	90	37,685	10,310	27,375

Source: Office for National Statistics

Note: It is ONS policy to publish estimates to the nearest hundred persons. Rounded (and particularly unit) estimates cannot be precisely accurate.

: Data not available

15.3f Population projections by the Office for National Statistics

Scotland
PERSONS, thousands

2012-based
Principal projection

Projected populations at mid-years by age last birthday

Ages	2012	2013	2014	2015	2016	2017	2018	2019	2020	2021	2022	2023	2024	2025	2026	2027	2028	2029	2030	2031	2032
Thousands																					
0-14	853	851	851	854	859	866	874	881	887	893	897	899	901	904	904	906	909	911	913	913	913
15-29	1,037	1,038	1,039	1,035	1,029	1,020	1,010	1,001	991	979	968	963	959	956	957	955	954	954	957	962	970
30-44	1,040	1,028	1,017	1,012	1,007	1,005	1,011	1,020	1,033	1,049	1,069	1,084	1,094	1,099	1,102	1,104	1,106	1,108	1,105	1,100	1,092
45-59	1,134	1,146	1,155	1,161	1,165	1,164	1,158	1,146	1,133	1,117	1,097	1,075	1,059	1,044	1,033	1,022	1,012	1,002	998	993	992
60-74	830	839	850	861	877	891	905	919	935	951	955	965	978	994	1,007	1,022	1,034	1,044	1,051	1,056	1,057
75 & over	418	426	434	443	450	460	472	484	495	508	535	555	573	589	603	616	630	644	658	674	690
All ages	5,314	5,328	5,346	5,365	5,386	5,407	5,429	5,452	5,474	5,497	5,520	5,542	5,564	5,585	5,606	5,626	5,645	5,664	5,681	5,698	5,714
Percentages																					
0-14	16.1	16.0	15.9	15.9	15.9	16.0	16.1	16.2	16.2	16.2	16.3	16.2	16.2	16.2	16.1	16.1	16.1	16.1	16.1	16.0	16.0
15-29	19.5	19.5	19.4	19.3	19.1	18.9	18.6	18.4	18.1	17.8	17.5	17.4	17.2	17.1	17.1	17.0	16.9	16.8	16.8	16.9	17.0
30-44	19.6	19.3	19.0	18.9	18.7	18.6	18.6	18.7	18.9	19.1	19.4	19.6	19.7	19.7	19.7	19.6	19.6	19.6	19.4	19.3	19.1
45-59	21.3	21.5	21.6	21.6	21.6	21.5	21.3	21.0	20.7	20.3	19.9	19.4	19.0	18.7	18.4	18.2	17.9	17.7	17.6	17.4	17.4
60-74	15.6	15.7	15.9	16.0	16.3	16.5	16.7	16.9	17.1	17.3	17.3	17.4	17.6	17.8	18.0	18.2	18.3	18.4	18.5	18.5	18.5
75 & over	7.9	8.0	8.1	8.3	8.4	8.5	8.7	8.9	9.0	9.2	9.7	10.0	10.3	10.5	10.8	11.0	11.2	11.4	11.6	11.8	12.1
All ages	100.0	100.0	100.0	100.0	100.0	100.0	100.0	100.0	100.0	100.0	100.0	100.0	100.0	100.0	100.0	100.0	100.0	100.0	100.0	100.0	100.0
Mean age	41.0	41.2	41.3	41.5	41.7	41.8	42.0	42.1	42.2	42.4	42.5	42.7	42.8	42.9	43.1	43.2	43.3	43.4	43.6	43.7	43.8
Median age	41.5	41.7	41.9	42.0	42.1	42.2	42.2	42.2	42.2	42.2	42.3	42.4	42.5	42.6	42.7	42.8	42.9	43.0	43.1	43.3	43.4

15.3f Population projections by the Office for National Statistics

Scotland
PERSONS, thousands

Ages	Projected populations at mid-years by age last birthday					Annual averages for longer-term projections														
	2033	2034	2035	2036	2037	2041	2046	2051	2056	2061	2062	2066	2071	2076	2081	2086	2087	2092	2102	2112
Thousands																				
0-14	911	910	908	905	903	896	898	910	922	928	928	927	926	927	933	940	941	946	949	955
15-29	978	985	991	996	1,001	1,008	1,017	1,009	1,000	1,002	1,004	1,014	1,027	1,032	1,032	1,030	1,030	1,033	1,046	1,053
30-44	1,082	1,073	1,064	1,052	1,041	1,031	1,037	1,071	1,083	1,093	1,093	1,086	1,078	1,080	1,092	1,105	1,107	1,111	1,110	1,120
45-59	998	1,008	1,021	1,037	1,057	1,089	1,089	1,044	1,025	1,033	1,041	1,068	1,081	1,091	1,086	1,079	1,078	1,084	1,110	1,116
60-74	1,052	1,043	1,032	1,018	1,000	948	920	967	1,018	1,020	1,014	981	970	981	1,017	1,033	1,035	1,046	1,040	1,064
75 & over	707	724	741	760	779	853	916	925	923	943	950	993	1,045	1,077	1,094	1,132	1,140	1,176	1,277	1,366
All ages	5,728	5,742	5,756	5,768	5,780	5,826	5,877	5,925	5,972	6,019	6,029	6,069	6,126	6,188	6,254	6,319	6,332	6,396	6,532	6,674
Percentages																				
0-14	15.9	15.8	15.8	15.7	15.6	15.4	15.3	15.4	15.4	15.4	15.4	15.3	15.1	15.0	14.9	14.9	14.9	14.8	14.5	14.3
15-29	17.1	17.1	17.2	17.3	17.3	17.3	17.3	17.0	16.8	16.6	16.7	16.7	16.8	16.7	16.5	16.3	16.3	16.1	16.0	15.8
30-44	18.9	18.7	18.5	18.2	18.0	17.7	17.6	18.1	18.1	18.2	18.1	17.9	17.6	17.5	17.5	17.5	17.5	17.4	17.0	16.8
45-59	17.4	17.6	17.7	18.0	18.3	18.7	18.5	17.6	17.2	17.2	17.3	17.6	17.6	17.6	17.4	17.1	17.0	16.9	17.0	16.7
60-74	18.4	18.2	17.9	17.7	17.3	16.3	15.7	16.3	17.1	17.0	16.8	16.2	15.8	15.9	16.3	16.3	16.4	16.4	15.9	15.9
75 & over	12.3	12.6	12.9	13.2	13.5	14.6	15.6	15.6	15.4	15.7	15.8	16.4	17.1	17.4	17.5	17.9	18.0	18.4	19.5	20.5
All ages	100.0	100.0	100.0	100.0	100.0	100.0	100.0	100.0	100.0	100.0	100.0	100.0	100.0	100.0	100.0	100.0	100.0	100.0	100.0	100.0
Mean age	43.9	44.1	44.2	44.3	44.4	44.7	45.0	45.2	45.4	45.5	45.6	45.7	46.0	46.3	46.5	46.8	46.8	47.1	47.7	48.3
Median age	43.6	43.8	43.9	44.1	44.3	44.7	44.8	44.6	44.7	44.8	44.9	45.1	45.4	45.8	46.0	46.2	46.2	46.5	47.2	47.8

Source: Office for National Statistics

Note: Figures may not add exactly due to rounding.

* Children under 16. Working age and pensionable age populations based on state pension age (SPA) for given year.
Between 2012 and 2018, SPA will change from 65 years for men and 61 years for women, to 65 years for both sexes.
Then between 2019 and 2020, SPA will change from 65 years to 66 years for both men and women. Between 2034 and 2046, SPA will increase in two stages from 66 years to 68 years for both sexes. This is based on SPA under the 2011 Pensions Act.
** This is consistent with the age-group definitions used in ONS Labour Market Statistics.

National Population Projections are currently produced every two years. The 2014-based Projections are not due to be published until Oct/Nov 2015. Therefore, this table series will be updated in the next edition.

15.3f Population projections by the Office for National Statistics

Scotland
MALES, thousands

2012-based
Principal projection

Projected populations at mid-years by age last birthday

Ages	2012	2013	2014	2015	2016	2017	2018	2019	2020	2021	2022	2023	2024	2025	2026	2027	2028	2029	2030	2031	2032
Thousands																					
0-14	436	435	435	436	439	443	447	450	453	456	458	459	460	462	462	463	465	466	467	467	467
15-29	519	520	522	521	519	516	511	507	503	497	492	490	488	486	486	485	484	484	486	488	492
30-44	508	502	497	496	494	494	498	504	511	520	530	539	545	549	552	555	557	560	559	558	555
45-59	554	558	562	563	564	563	560	554	547	539	529	519	511	504	499	494	490	485	484	483	484
60-74	397	402	407	413	421	428	435	441	449	456	458	462	468	475	481	487	493	497	499	501	501
75 &over	164	168	173	178	181	186	192	199	205	211	224	235	244	252	259	265	272	278	285	292	300
All ages	2,577	2,586	2,596	2,607	2,619	2,630	2,643	2,655	2,667	2,680	2,692	2,704	2,716	2,728	2,739	2,750	2,760	2,770	2,780	2,789	2,798
Percentages																					
0-14	16.9	16.8	16.8	16.7	16.8	16.8	16.9	17.0	17.0	17.0	17.0	17.0	17.0	16.9	16.9	16.8	16.8	16.8	16.8	16.7	16.7
15-29	20.1	20.1	20.1	20.0	19.8	19.6	19.3	19.1	18.9	18.5	18.3	18.1	18.0	17.8	17.7	17.6	17.6	17.5	17.5	17.5	17.6
30-44	19.7	19.4	19.2	19.0	18.9	18.8	18.8	19.0	19.2	19.4	19.7	19.9	20.0	20.1	20.1	20.2	20.2	20.2	20.1	20.0	19.8
45-59	21.5	21.6	21.6	21.6	21.6	21.4	21.2	20.9	20.5	20.1	19.7	19.2	18.8	18.5	18.2	18.0	17.7	17.5	17.4	17.3	17.3
60-74	15.4	15.5	15.7	15.8	16.1	16.3	16.5	16.6	16.8	17.0	17.0	17.1	17.2	17.4	17.6	17.7	17.8	17.9	18.0	18.0	17.9
75 &over	6.4	6.5	6.7	6.8	6.9	7.1	7.3	7.5	7.7	7.9	8.3	8.7	9.0	9.2	9.4	9.6	9.8	10.1	10.2	10.5	10.7
All ages	100.0	100.0	100.0	100.0	100.0	100.0	100.0	100.0	100.0	100.0	100.0	100.0	100.0	100.0	100.0	100.0	100.0	100.0	100.0	100.0	100.0
Mean age	39.9	40.1	40.2	40.4	40.5	40.7	40.8	41.0	41.1	41.3	41.4	41.5	41.6	41.8	41.9	42.0	42.2	42.3	42.4	42.5	42.6
Median age	40.3	40.5	40.6	40.6	40.7	40.7	40.6	40.6	40.7	40.8	40.9	40.9	41.0	41.1	41.2	41.3	41.4	41.5	41.6	41.8	42.0

15.3f Population projections by the Office for National Statistics

Scotland
MALES, thousands

Ages	Projected populations at mid-years by age last birthday																Annual averages for longer-term projections			
	2033	2034	2035	2036	2037	2041	2046	2051	2056	2061	2062	2066	2071	2076	2081	2086	2087	2092	2102	2112
Thousands																				
0-14	466	465	464	463	462	458	459	465	471	474	474	474	473	474	477	481	481	484	485	488
15-29	497	500	503	506	508	512	517	513	508	509	510	516	522	525	525	524	524	525	532	535
30-44	550	546	543	537	532	527	530	547	554	559	559	555	551	552	559	565	566	569	568	573
45-59	488	493	501	510	520	541	548	529	520	524	528	542	549	555	552	549	549	552	566	569
60-74	499	494	488	482	473	450	440	468	499	506	504	490	485	491	510	519	520	526	524	537
75 &over	307	315	323	332	341	373	400	402	402	414	418	443	474	494	506	527	532	552	604	650
All ages	2,806	2,814	2,821	2,829	2,835	2,862	2,893	2,924	2,955	2,986	2,993	3,019	3,055	3,091	3,129	3,165	3,172	3,207	3,279	3,353
Percentages																				
0-14	16.6	16.5	16.4	16.4	16.3	16.0	15.9	15.9	16.0	15.9	15.9	15.7	15.5	15.3	15.2	15.2	15.2	15.1	14.8	14.6
15-29	17.7	17.8	17.8	17.9	17.9	17.9	17.9	17.5	17.2	17.1	17.0	17.1	17.1	17.0	16.8	16.6	16.5	16.4	16.2	16.0
30-44	19.6	19.4	19.2	19.0	18.8	18.4	18.3	18.7	18.7	18.7	18.7	18.4	18.0	17.9	17.9	17.9	17.9	17.7	17.3	17.1
45-59	17.4	17.5	17.7	18.0	18.3	18.9	18.9	18.1	17.6	17.5	17.6	17.9	18.0	17.9	17.6	17.3	17.3	17.2	17.2	17.0
60-74	17.8	17.6	17.3	17.0	16.7	15.7	15.2	16.0	16.9	16.9	16.8	16.2	15.9	15.9	16.3	16.4	16.4	16.4	16.0	16.0
75 &over	11.0	11.2	11.5	11.7	12.0	13.0	13.8	13.8	13.6	13.9	14.0	14.7	15.5	16.0	16.2	16.7	16.8	17.2	18.4	19.4
All ages	100.0	100.0	100.0	100.0	100.0	100.0	100.0	100.0	100.0	100.0	100.0	100.0	100.0	100.0	100.0	100.0	100.0	100.0	100.0	100.0
Mean age	42.8	42.9	43.0	43.1	43.2	43.5	43.8	44.0	44.2	44.4	44.5	44.7	45.1	45.4	45.7	46.0	46.1	46.4	47.0	47.7
Median age	42.2	42.3	42.5	42.7	42.8	43.2	43.2	43.2	43.4	43.7	43.7	44.1	44.5	44.8	45.1	45.3	45.4	45.7	46.4	47.1

Source: Office for National Statistics

Note: Figures may not add exactly due to rounding.

* Children under 16. Working age and pensionable age populations based on state pension age (SPA) for given year.
Between 2012 and 2018, SPA will change from 65 years for men and 61 years for women, to 65 years for both sexes.
Then between 2019 and 2020, SPA will change from 65 years to 66 years for both men and women. Between 2034 and 2046,
SPA will increase in two stages from 66 years to 68 years for both sexes. This is based on SPA under the 2011 Pensions Act.
** This is consistent with the age-group definitions used in ONS Labour Market Statistics.
SPA will increase in two stages from 66 years to 68 years for both sexes. This is based on SPA under the 2011 Pensions Act

National Population Projections are currently produced every two years. The 2014-based Projections are not due to be published until Oct/Nov 2015. Therefore, this table series will be updated in the next edition.

Population and vital statistics

15.3f Population projections by the Office for National Statistics

Scotland
FEMALES, thousands

2012-based
Principal projection

Projected populations at mid-years by age last birthday

Ages	2012	2013	2014	2015	2016	2017	2018	2019	2020	2021	2022	2023	2024	2025	2026	2027	2028	2029	2030	2031	2032
Thousands																					
0-14	417	416	416	418	420	424	428	431	434	437	439	440	440	442	442	443	444	445	446	446	446
15-29	519	518	517	513	510	505	499	494	488	482	476	473	471	470	471	470	469	470	471	474	477
30-44	533	526	520	516	512	511	513	517	522	529	539	545	549	550	550	549	549	548	545	542	537
45-59	580	587	593	597	600	601	598	592	586	578	567	557	547	539	533	528	522	517	513	510	509
60-74	433	437	443	448	456	463	470	478	486	495	497	503	510	519	526	534	541	547	552	555	556
75 &over	254	257	261	265	269	273	279	285	291	297	310	321	330	337	345	351	359	366	373	381	390
All ages	2,736	2,742	2,750	2,758	2,767	2,777	2,787	2,797	2,807	2,817	2,828	2,838	2,848	2,857	2,867	2,876	2,885	2,893	2,901	2,909	2,916
Percentages																					
0-14	15.2	15.2	15.1	15.1	15.2	15.3	15.3	15.4	15.5	15.5	15.5	15.5	15.5	15.5	15.4	15.4	15.4	15.4	15.4	15.3	15.3
15-29	19.0	18.9	18.8	18.6	18.4	18.2	17.9	17.7	17.4	17.1	16.8	16.7	16.5	16.5	16.4	16.3	16.3	16.2	16.2	16.3	16.4
30-44	19.5	19.2	18.9	18.7	18.5	18.4	18.4	18.5	18.6	18.8	19.1	19.2	19.3	19.2	19.2	19.1	19.0	19.0	18.8	18.6	18.4
45-59	21.2	21.4	21.6	21.6	21.7	21.6	21.5	21.2	20.9	20.5	20.1	19.6	19.2	18.9	18.6	18.4	18.1	17.9	17.7	17.5	17.4
60-74	15.8	16.0	16.1	16.2	16.5	16.7	16.9	17.1	17.3	17.6	17.6	17.7	17.9	18.2	18.4	18.6	18.8	18.9	19.0	19.1	19.1
75 &over	9.3	9.4	9.5	9.6	9.7	9.8	10.0	10.2	10.4	10.5	11.0	11.3	11.6	11.8	12.0	12.2	12.4	12.7	12.9	13.1	13.4
All ages	100.0	100.0	100.0	100.0	100.0	100.0	100.0	100.0	100.0	100.0	100.0	100.0	100.0	100.0	100.0	100.0	100.0	100.0	100.0	100.0	100.0
Mean age	42.1	42.2	42.4	42.6	42.7	42.9	43.0	43.2	43.3	43.5	43.6	43.7	43.9	44.0	44.2	44.3	44.4	44.6	44.7	44.8	45.0
Median age	42.5	42.8	43.0	43.2	43.4	43.5	43.6	43.7	43.7	43.7	43.8	43.8	43.9	44.1	44.2	44.3	44.4	44.5	44.7	44.8	44.9

15.3f Population projections by the Office for National Statistics

Scotland
FEMALES, thousands

	Projected populations at mid-years by age last birthday					Annual averages for longer-term projections														
Ages	2033	2034	2035	2036	2037	2041	2046	2051	2056	2061	2062	2066	2071	2076	2081	2086	2087	2092	2102	2112
Thousands																				
0-14	445	445	444	442	441	438	439	445	451	453	453	453	452	453	456	459	460	462	464	467
15-29	481	485	488	490	493	496	500	496	492	493	494	499	505	507	507	506	506	508	514	517
30-44	532	527	521	515	509	504	507	524	530	534	534	531	527	527	534	540	540	543	542	546
45-59	511	515	520	528	537	548	541	515	505	509	513	526	532	537	534	530	530	532	545	547
60-74	554	549	543	536	527	498	480	499	520	514	510	491	484	490	507	514	515	520	516	527
75 &over	399	409	418	428	438	480	517	522	520	529	532	550	572	583	588	604	608	624	672	716
All ages	2,922	2,928	2,934	2,940	2,945	2,964	2,984	3,002	3,017	3,033	3,036	3,050	3,071	3,097	3,125	3,154	3,160	3,189	3,253	3,321
Percentages																				
0-14	15.2	15.2	15.1	15.0	15.0	14.8	14.7	14.8	14.9	14.9	14.9	14.9	14.7	14.6	14.6	14.6	14.6	14.5	14.3	14.1
15-29	16.5	16.6	16.6	16.7	16.7	16.7	16.8	16.5	16.3	16.3	16.3	16.4	16.4	16.4	16.2	16.1	16.0	15.9	15.8	15.6
30-44	18.2	18.0	17.8	17.5	17.3	17.0	17.0	17.5	17.5	17.6	17.6	17.4	17.1	17.0	17.1	17.1	17.1	17.0	16.7	16.4
45-59	17.5	17.6	17.7	17.9	18.2	18.5	18.1	17.2	16.7	16.8	16.9	17.2	17.3	17.3	17.1	16.8	16.8	16.7	16.8	16.5
60-74	19.0	18.7	18.5	18.2	17.9	16.8	16.1	16.6	17.2	17.0	16.8	16.1	15.8	15.8	16.2	16.3	16.3	16.3	15.9	15.9
75 &over	13.7	14.0	14.2	14.6	14.9	16.2	17.3	17.4	17.2	17.4	17.5	18.0	18.6	18.8	18.8	19.2	19.2	19.6	20.7	21.6
All ages	100.0	100.0	100.0	100.0	100.0	100.0	100.0	100.0	100.0	100.0	100.0	100.0	100.0	100.0	100.0	100.0	100.0	100.0	100.0	100.0
Mean age	45.1	45.2	45.3	45.4	45.5	45.9	46.2	46.4	46.5	46.6	46.6	46.7	46.9	47.1	47.3	47.6	47.6	47.8	48.4	49.0
Median age	45.1	45.2	45.4	45.6	45.7	46.2	46.4	46.1	46.0	46.0	46.0	46.2	46.4	46.7	46.9	47.0	47.1	47.3	47.9	48.6

Source: Office for National Statistics

Note: Figures may not add exactly due to rounding.
* Children under 16. Working age and pensionable age populations based on state pension age (SPA) for given year.
Between 2012 and 2018, SPA will change from 65 years for men and 61 years for women, to 65 years for both sexes.
Then between 2019 and 2020, SPA will change from 65 years to 66 years for both men and women. Between 2034 and 2046, SPA will increase in two stages from 66 years to 68 years for both sexes. This is based on SPA under the 2011 Pensions Act.
** This is consistent with the age-group definitions used in ONS Labour Market Statistics.

National Population Projections are currently produced every two years. The 2014-based Projections are not due to be published until Oct/Nov 2015. Therefore, this table series will be updated in the next edition.

15.3g Mid-2013 Population estimates for Northern Ireland by sex and single year of age

Ages	Persons	Males	Females	Ages	Persons	Males	Females
All Ages	1,829,725	897,145	932,580	45	26,571	13,040	13,531
0	24,631	12,523	12,108	46	26,565	12,992	13,573
1	25,573	13,091	12,482	47	26,598	13,111	13,487
2	25,545	13,008	12,537	48	27,072	13,264	13,808
3	25,244	12,865	12,379	49	26,616	13,135	13,481
4	25,680	13,212	12,468	50	25,969	12,984	12,985
5	25,601	13,097	12,504	51	25,311	12,413	12,898
6	24,360	12,529	11,831	52	24,926	12,307	12,619
7	23,239	11,914	11,325	53	23,917	11,735	12,182
8	22,656	11,681	10,975	54	23,263	11,513	11,750
9	22,389	11,547	10,842	55	22,924	11,346	11,578
10	21,841	11,155	10,686	56	21,997	10,863	11,134
11	21,974	11,238	10,736	57	21,097	10,518	10,579
12	22,192	11,366	10,826	58	20,111	10,120	9,991
13	23,096	11,988	11,108	59	19,773	9,985	9,788
14	24,134	12,354	11,780	60	19,322	9,619	9,703
15	24,452	12,534	11,918	61	18,588	9,234	9,354
16	24,836	12,652	12,184	62	18,601	9,251	9,350
17	24,572	12,633	11,939	63	18,685	9,192	9,493
18	24,844	12,773	12,071	64	18,448	9,054	9,394
19	24,312	12,557	11,755	65	18,397	8,917	9,480
20	23,709	12,199	11,510	66	18,384	8,805	9,579
21	24,481	12,452	12,029	67	17,016	8,204	8,812
22	24,666	12,475	12,191	68	16,821	8,067	8,754
23	24,715	12,426	12,289	69	16,697	8,036	8,661
24	24,625	12,335	12,290	70	16,010	7,632	8,378
25	24,800	12,309	12,491	71	14,286	6,766	7,520
26	25,009	12,414	12,595	72	12,833	6,008	6,825
27	24,975	12,278	12,697	73	12,408	5,736	6,672
28	25,031	12,338	12,693	74	12,448	5,711	6,737
29	24,670	12,059	12,611	75	11,719	5,368	6,351
30	24,411	11,920	12,491	76	11,334	5,135	6,199
31	24,486	11,923	12,563	77	10,562	4,644	5,918
32	24,965	12,188	12,777	78	9,917	4,335	5,582
33	25,035	12,180	12,855	79	9,144	3,967	5,177
34	23,854	11,414	12,440	80	8,797	3,649	5,148
35	22,920	11,118	11,802	81	8,182	3,339	4,843
36	22,651	11,027	11,624	82	7,685	3,089	4,596
37	22,802	11,097	11,705	83	6,920	2,636	4,284
38	23,336	11,431	11,905	84	6,290	2,349	3,941
39	24,048	11,710	12,338	85 / 85+	5,540	1,999	3,541
40	24,874	12,179	12,695	86	5,029	1,789	3,240
41	25,253	12,440	12,813	87	4,284	1,456	2,828
42	25,846	12,584	13,262	88	3,750	1,259	2,491
43	25,785	12,564	13,221	89	3,344	1,042	2,302
44	26,119	12,724	13,395	90	11,337	3,030	8,307

Source: Office for National Statistics

Note: It is ONS policy to publish estimates to the nearest hundred persons. Rounded (and particularly unit) estimates cannot be precisely accurate.

: Data not available

15.3h Population projections by the Office for National Statistics

Northern Ireland
PERSONS, thousands

2012-based
Principal projection

Projected populations at mid-years by age last birthday

Ages	2012	2013	2014	2015	2016	2017	2018	2019	2020	2021	2022	2023	2024	2025	2026	2027	2028	2029	2030	2031	2032
Thousands																					
0-14	357	358	359	361	364	367	370	373	375	376	376	374	372	371	368	366	364	361	359	356	354
15-29	373	371	369	365	360	356	351	347	343	340	338	338	339	340	341	343	344	345	347	350	353
30-44	370	368	366	364	363	363	363	364	365	367	369	370	371	369	366	365	364	362	358	354	350
45-59	357	363	368	373	377	380	382	382	381	379	376	373	370	368	366	364	362	360	359	358	358
60-74	245	249	253	257	263	268	273	277	282	288	293	299	306	313	320	327	333	338	343	347	350
75 & over	122	124	128	130	134	138	143	149	154	159	166	172	177	183	188	193	198	203	208	214	220
All ages	1,824	1,832	1,842	1,852	1,861	1,871	1,881	1,891	1,900	1,910	1,918	1,927	1,935	1,943	1,950	1,957	1,963	1,969	1,975	1,980	1,985
Percentages																					
0-14	19.6	19.5	19.5	19.5	19.6	19.6	19.7	19.7	19.7	19.7	19.6	19.4	19.2	19.1	18.9	18.7	18.5	18.4	18.2	18.0	17.8
15-29	20.5	20.3	20.0	19.7	19.4	19.0	18.6	18.3	18.0	17.8	17.6	17.6	17.5	17.5	17.5	17.5	17.5	17.5	17.6	17.7	17.8
30-44	20.3	20.1	19.9	19.7	19.5	19.4	19.3	19.2	19.2	19.2	19.2	19.2	19.1	19.0	18.8	18.7	18.5	18.4	18.1	17.9	17.6
45-59	19.6	19.8	20.0	20.2	20.3	20.3	20.3	20.2	20.1	19.8	19.6	19.4	19.1	18.9	18.8	18.6	18.4	18.3	18.2	18.1	18.0
60-74	13.4	13.6	13.7	13.9	14.1	14.3	14.5	14.6	14.8	15.1	15.3	15.5	15.8	16.1	16.4	16.7	17.0	17.2	17.4	17.6	17.7
75 & over	6.7	6.8	6.9	7.0	7.2	7.4	7.6	7.9	8.1	8.4	8.6	8.9	9.2	9.4	9.6	9.8	10.1	10.3	10.5	10.8	11.1
All ages	100.0	100.0	100.0	100.0	100.0	100.0	100.0	100.0	100.0	100.0	100.0	100.0	100.0	100.0	100.0	100.0	100.0	100.0	100.0	100.0	100.0
Mean age	38.3	38.5	38.7	38.9	39.1	39.3	39.5	39.7	39.9	40.1	40.3	40.5	40.8	41.0	41.2	41.4	41.6	41.9	42.1	42.3	42.5
Median age	37.6	37.8	38.0	38.2	38.4	38.6	38.8	39.1	39.4	39.6	39.8	40.1	40.3	40.6	40.9	41.1	41.4	41.6	41.9	42.2	42.4

481

15.3h Population projections by the Office for National Statistics

Northern Ireland
PERSONS, thousands

	Projected populations at mid-years by age last birthday											Annual averages for longer-term projections								
Ages	2033	2034	2035	2036	2037	2041	2046	2051	2056	2061	2062	2066	2071	2076	2081	2086	2087	2092	2102	2112
Thousands																				
0-14	351	349	347	345	343	340	343	348	346	339	337	331	327	326	327	326	326	321	312	309
15-29	356	359	361	362	362	354	343	331	326	330	331	334	333	326	318	313	313	313	312	302
30-44	345	341	337	334	333	336	345	357	349	338	335	326	322	326	330	329	328	320	309	310
45-59	358	359	361	363	365	362	351	332	334	343	346	355	348	337	326	322	322	327	328	314
60-74	352	353	352	350	348	341	335	341	342	332	328	315	319	329	341	335	333	323	313	322
75 & over	226	233	240	247	254	284	315	331	342	354	356	367	374	377	376	390	393	406	430	440
All ages	1,989	1,993	1,997	2,001	2,005	2,018	2,032	2,039	2,040	2,035	2,034	2,028	2,023	2,020	2,017	2,014	2,014	2,010	2,004	1,998
Percentages																				
0-14	17.7	17.5	17.4	17.2	17.1	16.9	16.9	17.0	17.0	16.7	16.6	16.3	16.1	16.1	16.2	16.2	16.2	16.0	15.6	15.5
15-29	17.9	18.0	18.1	18.1	18.1	17.6	16.9	16.2	16.0	16.2	16.3	16.5	16.4	16.1	15.7	15.5	15.5	15.6	15.6	15.1
30-44	17.4	17.1	16.9	16.7	16.6	16.7	17.0	17.5	17.1	16.6	16.5	16.1	15.9	16.1	16.4	16.3	16.3	15.9	15.4	15.5
45-59	18.0	18.0	18.1	18.1	18.2	17.9	17.3	16.3	16.4	16.9	17.0	17.5	17.2	16.7	16.2	16.0	16.0	16.3	16.4	15.7
60-74	17.7	17.7	17.6	17.5	17.4	16.9	16.5	16.7	16.7	16.3	16.1	15.5	15.8	16.3	16.9	16.6	16.5	16.1	15.6	16.1
75 & over	11.4	11.7	12.0	12.3	12.7	14.1	15.5	16.2	16.8	17.4	17.5	18.1	18.5	18.7	18.6	19.3	19.5	20.2	21.4	22.0
All ages	100.0	100.0	100.0	100.0	100.0	100.0	100.0	100.0	100.0	100.0	100.0	100.0	100.0	100.0	100.0	100.0	100.0	100.0	100.0	100.0
Mean age	42.7	42.9	43.1	43.3	43.4	44.0	44.6	45.0	45.4	45.8	45.9	46.1	46.4	46.7	46.9	47.2	47.2	47.6	48.3	48.9
Median age	42.7	42.9	43.1	43.3	43.5	44.0	44.3	44.3	44.9	45.5	45.6	46.0	46.4	46.5	46.6	46.8	46.9	47.3	48.2	48.8

Source: Office for National Statistics

Note: Figures may not add exactly due to rounding.
* Children under 16. Working age and pensionable age populations based on state pension age (SPA) for given year.
Between 2012 and 2018, SPA will change from 65 years for men and 61 years for women, to 65 years for both sexes.
Then between 2019 and 2020, SPA will change from 65 years to 66 years for both men and women. Between 2034 and 2046,
SPA will increase in two stages from 66 years to 68 years for both sexes. This is based on SPA under the 2011 Pensions Act.
** This is consistent with the age-group definitions used in ONS Labour Market Statistics.

National Population Projections are currently produced every two years. The 2014-based Projections are not due to be published until Oct/Nov 2015. Therefore, this table series will be updated in the next edition.

5.3h Population projections by the Office for National Statistics

Northern Ireland
MALES, thousands

2012-based
Principal projection

Projected populations at mid-years by age last birthday

Ages	2012	2013	2014	2015	2016	2017	2018	2019	2020	2021	2022	2023	2024	2025	2026	2027	2028	2029	2030	2031	2032
Thousands																					
0-14	183	184	184	185	186	188	190	191	192	192	192	191	190	189	188	187	186	185	183	182	181
15-29	188	188	187	186	184	182	180	178	176	174	174	174	174	175	175	176	177	177	178	180	181
30-44	181	179	178	178	177	177	178	179	180	181	183	184	185	185	184	184	184	183	182	181	179
45-59	177	179	182	184	185	187	187	187	186	185	183	181	180	178	177	176	175	174	174	173	173
60-74	118	120	123	125	128	131	133	135	138	141	143	147	150	153	156	159	162	164	166	168	170
75 &over	48	49	51	53	54	57	59	62	65	68	71	74	77	79	82	84	87	90	92	95	98
All ages	895	900	905	910	915	921	926	931	937	942	946	951	955	959	963	967	970	973	976	979	982
Percentages																					
0-14	20.5	20.4	20.4	20.3	20.4	20.4	20.5	20.5	20.5	20.4	20.3	20.1	19.9	19.7	19.5	19.3	19.1	19.0	18.8	18.6	18.4
15-29	21.0	20.9	20.7	20.4	20.1	19.7	19.4	19.1	18.8	18.5	18.4	18.3	18.2	18.2	18.2	18.2	18.2	18.2	18.2	18.3	18.4
30-44	20.2	20.0	19.7	19.6	19.4	19.3	19.2	19.2	19.2	19.3	19.3	19.4	19.4	19.2	19.1	19.0	19.0	18.8	18.7	18.5	18.2
45-59	19.7	19.9	20.1	20.2	20.2	20.3	20.2	20.1	19.9	19.7	19.4	19.1	18.8	18.6	18.4	18.2	18.0	17.9	17.8	17.7	17.7
60-74	13.2	13.4	13.5	13.8	14.0	14.2	14.4	14.5	14.7	15.0	15.2	15.4	15.7	16.0	16.2	16.5	16.7	16.9	17.0	17.2	17.3
75 &over	5.3	5.5	5.6	5.8	5.9	6.1	6.4	6.7	6.9	7.2	7.5	7.7	8.0	8.3	8.5	8.7	9.0	9.2	9.5	9.7	10.0
All ages	100.0	100.0	100.0	100.0	100.0	100.0	100.0	100.0	100.0	100.0	100.0	100.0	100.0	100.0	100.0	100.0	100.0	100.0	100.0	100.0	100.0
Mean age	37.3	37.5	37.7	37.9	38.1	38.3	38.5	38.7	38.9	39.1	39.4	39.6	39.8	40.0	40.2	40.5	40.7	40.9	41.1	41.3	41.5
Median age	36.5	36.7	36.8	37.0	37.2	37.4	37.7	37.9	38.1	38.3	38.5	38.8	39.0	39.2	39.5	39.7	40.0	40.3	40.5	40.8	41.0

5.3h Population projections by the Office for National Statistics

Northern Ireland
MALES, thousands

Projected populations at mid-years by age last birthday / Annual averages for longer-term projections

Ages	2033	2034	2035	2036	2037	2041	2046	2051	2056	2061	2062	2066	2071	2076	2081	2086	2087	2092	2102	2112
Thousands																				
0-14	179	178	177	176	175	174	175	178	177	173	172	169	167	167	167	167	166	164	159	158
15-29	183	184	185	185	185	181	175	169	167	169	169	171	170	167	162	160	160	160	160	155
30-44	177	175	173	172	171	173	177	183	179	173	172	167	165	167	169	169	168	164	159	159
45-59	174	175	176	178	179	181	178	169	171	175	177	181	177	172	166	164	164	166	167	160
60-74	170	170	170	169	168	163	161	166	169	166	165	159	162	166	172	169	168	163	159	164
75 &over	101	104	107	111	114	128	142	148	152	158	159	166	171	175	176	185	186	194	206	212
All ages	984	986	988	990	992	1,000	1,007	1,013	1,014	1,014	1,014	1,013	1,012	1,013	1,014	1,013	1,013	1,012	1,010	1,008
Percentages																				
0-14	18.2	18.1	17.9	17.8	17.6	17.4	17.4	17.5	17.4	17.1	17.0	16.7	16.5	16.4	16.5	16.4	16.4	16.2	15.8	15.7
15-29	18.6	18.6	18.7	18.7	18.7	18.1	17.4	16.7	16.5	16.6	16.7	16.9	16.8	16.4	16.0	15.8	15.8	15.8	15.8	15.4
30-44	18.0	17.7	17.5	17.3	17.3	17.3	17.6	18.1	17.7	17.1	17.0	16.5	16.3	16.5	16.7	16.6	16.6	16.2	15.7	15.8
45-59	17.7	17.7	17.8	17.9	18.1	18.1	17.6	16.7	16.8	17.3	17.4	17.9	17.5	16.9	16.4	16.2	16.2	16.4	16.6	15.9
60-74	17.3	17.3	17.2	17.0	16.9	16.3	15.9	16.3	16.6	16.4	16.3	15.7	16.0	16.4	17.0	16.7	16.6	16.1	15.7	16.2
75 &over	10.3	10.6	10.9	11.2	11.5	12.8	14.1	14.6	15.0	15.5	15.7	16.3	16.9	17.3	17.4	18.2	18.4	19.2	20.4	21.0
All ages	100.0	100.0	100.0	100.0	100.0	100.0	100.0	100.0	100.0	100.0	100.0	100.0	100.0	100.0	100.0	100.0	100.0	100.0	100.0	100.0
Mean age	41.7	41.9	42.1	42.3	42.4	43.0	43.5	44.0	44.4	44.7	44.8	45.1	45.5	45.8	46.1	46.5	46.5	46.9	47.6	48.3
Median age	41.3	41.5	41.7	41.9	42.1	42.6	42.7	43.1	43.7	44.3	44.5	44.9	45.4	45.6	45.7	46.0	46.1	46.6	47.5	48.0

Source: Office for National Statistics

Note: Figures may not add exactly due to rounding.
* Children under 16. Working age and pensionable age populations based on state pension age (SPA) for given year.
Between 2012 and 2018, SPA will change from 65 years for men and 61 years for women, to 65 years for both sexes.
Then between 2019 and 2020, SPA will change from 65 years to 66 years for both men and women. Between 2034 and 2046,
SPA will increase in two stages from 66 years to 68 years for both sexes. This is based on SPA under the 2011 Pensions Act.
** This is consistent with the age-group definitions used in ONS Labour Market Statistics.

National Population Projections are currently produced every two years. The 2014-based Projections are not due to be published until Oct/Nov 2015. Therefore, this table series will be updated in the next edition.

15.3h Population projections by the Office for National Statistics

Northern Ireland
FEMALES, thousands

2012-based
Principal projection

Projected populations at mid-years by age last birthday

Ages	2012	2013	2014	2015	2016	2017	2018	2019	2020	2021	2022	2023	2024	2025	2026	2027	2028	2029	2030	2031	2032
Thousands																					
0-14	174	174	175	176	178	179	181	182	183	184	184	183	182	181	180	179	178	177	176	174	173
15-29	185	183	182	179	176	174	171	169	167	165	165	164	164	165	166	167	167	168	169	171	172
30-44	189	188	187	186	186	185	185	185	185	186	186	186	186	184	182	181	180	178	176	173	171
45-59	180	183	187	190	192	194	195	195	195	194	193	192	190	190	189	188	187	186	185	185	184
60-74	127	128	130	132	135	137	140	142	144	147	150	153	156	160	164	167	171	174	177	179	181
75 &over	74	75	76	78	79	81	84	86	89	92	95	98	101	103	106	108	111	113	116	118	122
All ages	929	933	937	942	946	950	955	959	964	968	972	976	980	983	987	990	993	996	998	1,001	1,003
Percentages																					
0-14	18.7	18.7	18.7	18.7	18.8	18.9	18.9	19.0	19.0	19.0	18.9	18.8	18.6	18.4	18.3	18.1	17.9	17.8	17.6	17.4	17.3
15-29	19.9	19.7	19.4	19.0	18.7	18.3	17.9	17.6	17.3	17.1	16.9	16.8	16.8	16.8	16.8	16.8	16.8	16.8	16.9	17.0	17.2
30-44	20.4	20.2	20.0	19.8	19.6	19.5	19.4	19.3	19.2	19.2	19.1	19.1	19.0	18.7	18.5	18.3	18.1	17.9	17.6	17.3	17.0
45-59	19.4	19.7	19.9	20.1	20.3	20.4	20.4	20.3	20.2	20.0	19.8	19.6	19.4	19.3	19.1	19.0	18.8	18.7	18.6	18.4	18.4
60-74	13.6	13.8	13.9	14.0	14.2	14.4	14.6	14.8	15.0	15.2	15.4	15.7	15.9	16.3	16.6	16.9	17.2	17.5	17.7	17.9	18.0
75 &over	8.0	8.0	8.2	8.3	8.4	8.5	8.8	9.0	9.2	9.5	9.8	10.0	10.3	10.5	10.7	10.9	11.2	11.4	11.6	11.8	12.1
All ages	100.0	100.0	100.0	100.0	100.0	100.0	100.0	100.0	100.0	100.0	100.0	100.0	100.0	100.0	100.0	100.0	100.0	100.0	100.0	100.0	100.0
Mean age	39.3	39.5	39.7	39.9	40.1	40.3	40.5	40.7	40.9	41.1	41.3	41.5	41.7	41.9	42.2	42.4	42.6	42.8	43.0	43.3	43.5
Median age	38.6	38.9	39.1	39.3	39.5	39.8	40.0	40.2	40.5	40.8	41.1	41.4	41.6	41.9	42.2	42.5	42.7	43.0	43.3	43.6	43.8

15.3h Population projections by the Office for National Statistics

Northern Ireland
FEMALES, thousands

Ages	Projected populations at mid-years by age last birthday											Annual averages for longer-term projections								
	2033	2034	2035	2036	2037	2041	2046	2051	2056	2061	2062	2066	2071	2076	2081	2086	2087	2092	2102	2112
Thousands																				
0-14	172	171	170	169	168	166	168	170	169	166	165	162	160	160	160	160	159	157	153	151
15-29	174	175	176	177	177	173	167	162	159	161	162	163	163	159	155	153	153	153	152	147
30-44	168	166	164	162	162	163	168	174	170	165	163	159	157	159	161	160	160	156	150	151
45-59	184	184	185	185	185	182	173	163	164	168	170	174	171	165	160	158	158	160	161	154
60-74	182	183	182	182	181	178	175	176	173	165	163	156	157	162	168	165	164	159	154	159
75 &over	125	128	132	136	140	156	173	183	190	196	197	201	203	202	199	205	206	212	223	228
All ages	1,005	1,007	1,009	1,011	1,012	1,018	1,024	1,027	1,026	1,021	1,020	1,016	1,010	1,007	1,004	1,001	1,000	998	994	990
Percentages																				
0-14	17.1	17.0	16.8	16.7	16.6	16.4	16.4	16.6	16.5	16.2	16.2	16.0	15.8	15.9	16.0	15.9	15.9	15.7	15.3	15.3
15-29	17.3	17.4	17.5	17.5	17.5	17.0	16.3	15.7	15.5	15.8	15.8	16.1	16.1	15.8	15.5	15.3	15.3	15.3	15.3	14.9
30-44	16.7	16.5	16.3	16.1	16.0	16.0	16.4	16.9	16.6	16.1	16.0	15.7	15.5	15.8	16.0	16.0	16.0	15.6	15.1	15.2
45-59	18.3	18.3	18.3	18.3	18.3	17.8	16.9	15.8	15.9	16.5	16.6	17.2	16.9	16.4	15.9	15.8	15.8	16.1	16.2	15.5
60-74	18.1	18.1	18.1	18.0	17.8	17.4	17.0	17.1	16.8	16.2	16.0	15.3	15.6	16.1	16.8	16.5	16.4	16.0	15.5	16.0
75 &over	12.4	12.8	13.1	13.5	13.8	15.3	16.9	17.8	18.5	19.2	19.3	19.8	20.1	20.1	19.9	20.5	20.6	21.3	22.5	23.1
All ages	100.0	100.0	100.0	100.0	100.0	100.0	100.0	100.0	100.0	100.0	100.0	100.0	100.0	100.0	100.0	100.0	100.0	100.0	100.0	100.0
Mean age	43.7	43.9	44.1	44.3	44.4	45.1	45.6	46.1	46.5	46.8	46.9	47.1	47.3	47.5	47.7	47.9	47.9	48.2	48.9	49.5
Median age	44.1	44.3	44.6	44.8	45.0	45.6	45.9	45.7	46.1	46.6	46.7	47.1	47.4	47.5	47.5	47.6	47.7	48.0	49.0	49.5

Source: Office for National Statistics

Note: Figures may not add exactly due to rounding.
* Children under 16. Working age and pensionable age populations based on state pension age (SPA) for given year.
Between 2012 and 2018, SPA will change from 65 years for men and 61 years for women, to 65 years for both sexes.
Then between 2019 and 2020, SPA will change from 65 years to 66 years for both men and women. Between 2034 and 2046,
SPA will increase in two stages from 66 years to 68 years for both sexes. This is based on SPA under the 2011 Pensions Act.
** This is consistent with the age-group definitions used in ONS Labour Market Statistics.

National Population Projections are currently produced every two years. The 2014-based Projections are not due to be published until Oct/Nov 2015. Therefore, this table series will be updated in the next edition.

15.4 Families by family type and presence of children
United Kingdom, 1997-2013

thousands

Number of families	1997 Estimate	1997 CI+/-	1998 Estimate	1998 CI+/-	1999 Estimate	1999 CI+/-	2000 Estimate	2000 CI+/-	2001 Estimate	2001 CI+/-	2002 Estimate	2002 CI+/-	2003 Estimate	2003 CI+/-	2004 Estimate	2004 CI+/-	2005 Estimate	2005 CI+/-	2006 Estimate	2006 CI+/-	2007 Estimate	2007 CI+/-	2008 Estimate	2008 CI+/-	2009 Estimate	2009 CI+/-	2010 Estimate	2010 CI+/-	2011 Estimate	2011 CI+/-	2012 Estimate	2012 CI+/-	2013 Estimate	2013 CI+/-
Married couple family	12,582	66	12,497	70	12,417	69	12,443	69	12,280	71	12,252	72	12,219	74	12,210	77	12,278	78	12,237	80	12,246	82	12,216	83	12,267	85	12,287	88	12,208	102	12,303	102	12,376	106
No children	5,840	64	5,871	65	5,880	65	5,977	66	5,892	67	5,958	67	5,976	69	5,922	71	6,006	71	6,046	72	5,997	74	6,042	75	5,961	76	6,039	79	5,983	92	5,987	91	5,942	95
Dependent children	5,126	51	5,013	52	4,936	52	4,918	53	4,833	54	4,777	54	4,746	56	4,689	57	4,732	58	4,682	59	4,689	60	4,642	61	4,709	63	4,701	65	4,641	67	4,697	67	4,748	69
Non-dependent children only	1,616	42	1,612	45	1,601	46	1,548	43	1,555	44	1,517	44	1,497	45	1,599	47	1,539	47	1,509	47	1,560	48	1,532	49	1,597	50	1,548	51	1,584	52	1,619	53	1,686	55
Civil partner couple family	N/A	N/A	N/A	N/A	N/A	N/A	N/A	N/A	N/A	N/A	N/A	N/A	N/A	N/A	N/A	N/A	N/A	N/A	13	5	33	9	40	9	41	9	45	10	60	12	67	12	64	13
No children or non-dependent children only	N/A	N/A	N/A	N/A	N/A	N/A	N/A	N/A	N/A	N/A	N/A	N/A	N/A	N/A	N/A	N/A	N/A	N/A	13	5	29	8	37	9	37	8	43	10	54	12	61	12	55	13
Dependent children	N/A	N/A	N/A	N/A	N/A	N/A	N/A	N/A	N/A	N/A	N/A	N/A	N/A	N/A	N/A	N/A	N/A	N/A			4	3	3	2	4	3	2	2	5	3	6	3	9	4
Opposite sex cohabiting couple family	1,674	47	1,728	52	1,855	53	1,984	52	2,129	55	2,156	55	2,242	58	2,298	60	2,392	62	2,457	63	2,549	65	2,653	67	2,689	69	2,749	71	2,863	76	2,880	75	2,826	78
No children	1,035	37	1,036	41	1,083	41	1,184	42	1,260	44	1,267	44	1,354	47	1,331	48	1,409	49	1,419	50	1,480	52	1,522	53	1,564	55	1,556	56	1,632	60	1,619	60	1,524	60
Dependent children	592	28	638	30	718	32	739	32	808	34	809	34	819	36	885	38	899	38	954	40	974	40	1,040	42	1,025	43	1,077	45	1,107	47	1,130	47	1,170	49
Non-dependent children only	46	8	54	9	54	9	61	10	61	10	79	12	68	11	81	12	85	13	85	13	96	14	92	14	101	15	116	16	123	17	130	18	133	18
Same sex cohabiting couple family	28	7	30	7	31	7	38	8	45	9	46	9	53	10	61	11	57	11	68	12	52	11	61	11	54	11	51	11	63	13	70	13	89	16
No children or non-dependent children only	27	7	29	7	30	7	37	8	44	9	45	9	52	10	60	11	54	11	65	12	48	10	58	11	51	11	48	11	61	13	64	13	84	16
Dependent children					1	1											3	3	3	2	4	4	3	2	3	3	3	2	2	2	6	3	5	3
Lone parent family	2,372	53	2,474	55	2,490	55	2,428	55	2,512	58	2,548	57	2,597	60	2,685	62	2,697	63	2,695	63	2,692	64	2,759	66	2,889	68	2,943	70	2,909	71	3,043	74	3,004	77
Dependent children	1,613	41	1,719	43	1,742	43	1,698	44	1,745	45	1,809	45	1,804	47	1,869	49	1,883	49	1,870	50	1,880	50	1,905	52	1,989	54	2,002	54	1,991	56	2,056	57	1,974	58
Non-dependent children only	759	33	755	34	748	34	731	34	767	35	740	35	793	37	817	38	814	39	825	39	812	39	854	41	901	43	942	44	918	45	986	47	1,030	50
Lone mother family	2,055	48	2,163	50	2,162	50	2,108	50	2,159	51	2,207	51	2,250	53	2,320	55	2,352	56	2,347	57	2,339	57	2,414	59	2,512	61	2,562	63	2,565	65	2,637	66	2,597	69
Dependent children	1,463	38	1,558	40	1,579	40	1,550	41	1,575	42	1,636	42	1,626	43	1,686	45	1,708	46	1,701	46	1,713	47	1,736	48	1,803	50	1,813	51	1,826	53	1,878	54	1,806	55
Non-dependent children only	592	29	605	30	583	29	558	29	584	30	571	30	625	32	634	33	644	34	646	34	627	33	678	35	709	37	749	39	739	39	759	40	791	43
Lone father family	317	21	311	21	328	22	320	22	353	24	342	24	347	24	366	26	345	25	347	26	353	26	345	26	377	28	381	28	344	28	405	30	408	31
Dependent children	150	15	161	15	163	16	147	15	170	16	172	17	178	17	183	19	175	18	169	18	167	18	169	18	185	19	188	20	165	19	178	20	168	20
Non-dependent children only	167	16	150	15	165	16	173	17	184	18	169	17	168	17	183	19	170	18	178	18	186	20	176	20	192	20	193	21	179	20	227	24	240	25
All families	16,655	58	16,729	73	16,793	71	16,893	59	16,966	61	17,002	62	17,110	65	17,254	67	17,424	67	17,470	69	17,571	71	17,729	72	17,940	73	18,075	75	18,102	90	18,362	89	18,359	94
No children	6,902	70	6,936	73	6,993	73	7,198	73	7,196	75	7,270	75	7,383	78	7,314	80	7,469	81	7,542	82	7,553	84	7,657	85	7,612	87	7,686	90	7,730	103	7,727	101	7,602	106
Dependent children	7,332	42	7,371	43	7,398	44	7,355	44	7,386	44	7,396	45	7,370	46	7,444	47	7,517	48	7,509	48	7,550	50	7,592	50	7,729	52	7,784	53	7,747	55	7,896	55	7,905	57
Non-dependent children only	2,421	50	2,421	55	2,403	56	2,339	52	2,383	53	2,336	53	2,358	54	2,497	57	2,438	57	2,420	58	2,469	59	2,480	60	2,599	62	2,605	64	2,625	65	2,739	66	2,851	69

1. Totals may not sum due to rounding

2. In the table .. indicates that the data are not sufficiently reliable to be published

3. The robustness of an estimate is presented in two ways.

The coefficient of variation (CV) indicates the robustness of each estimate.

standard error / estimate x 100

Estimates are considered precise
Estimates are reasonably precise
Estimates are considered acceptable
Estimates are not considered reliable for practical purposes

Confidence intervals are also presented. CI+/- is the upper(+) and lower(-) 95% confidence interval. It is defined as **1.96 x standard error**. The confidence interval provides an estimated range of values in which an actual data value is likely to fall around 95 per cent of the time.

For example, there were 12,280,000 married couple families in 2001. This estimate has a confidence interval of 71,000, meaning that there is 95 per cent confidence that the true value is 12,280,000 ± 71,000 or between 12,209,000 and 12,351,000.

where standard error is an estimate of the margin of error associated with a sample survey. The coloured shading on the table indicates the precision of each estimate as follows:

4. Civil partnerships were introduced in the UK in December 2005.

5. Marriages of same sex couples were introduced in England and Wales in March 2014. No married same sex couples were selected in the interview sample in the April to June 2014 quarter of the Labour Force Survey (LFS). Therefore statistics on same sex married couples, their families and their households will not be reported in these 2014 tables.

6. Families with no children and non-dependent children only have been added together for civil partner couple families and same sex cohabiting couple families to improve the robustness of the estimates

7. A **family** is a married, civil partnered or cohabiting couple with or without children, or a lone parent with at least one child. Children may be dependent or non-dependent.

8. **Dependent children** are those living with their parent(s) and either (a) aged under 16, or (b) aged 16 to 18 in full-time education, excluding children aged 16 to 18 who have a spouse, partner or child living in the household

9. **Non-dependent children** are those living with their parent(s) and either (a) aged 19 or over, or (b) aged 16 to 18 who are not in full-time education or who have a spouse, partner or child living in the household. Non-dependent children are sometimes called adult children.

10. Families with **no children** are families where there are no children currently living in the household. This does not necessarily indicate that the adult(s) in the household have never had children.

Source: Labour Force Survey (LFS), Office for National Statistics
Produced by Demographic Analysis Unit, Office for National Statistics
families@ons.gsi.gov.uk

15.5 Geographical distribution of the population
All Persons

Name	Code	Mid-year population estimate [1]	
		2,012	2,013
UNITED KINGDOM	**K02000001**	**63,705,030**	**64,105,654**
GREAT BRITAIN	**K03000001**	**61,881,396**	**62,275,929**
ENGLAND AND WALES	K04000001	56,567,796	56,948,229
ENGLAND	E92000001	53,493,729	53,865,817
WALES	W92000004	3,074,067	3,082,412
SCOTLAND	S92000003	5,313,600	5,327,700
NORTHERN IRELAND	N92000002	1,823,634	1,829,725
NORTH EAST	**E12000001**	**2,602,310**	**2,610,481**
County Durham	E06000047	514,348	515,957
Darlington	E06000005	105,248	105,396
Hartlepool	E06000001	92,238	92,665
Middlesbrough	E06000002	138,744	138,939
Northumberland	E06000057	316,116	315,806
Redcar and Cleveland	E06000003	134,998	134,945
Stockton-on-Tees	E06000004	192,406	193,196
Tyne and Wear (Met County)	E11000007	1,108,212	1,113,577
Gateshead	E08000037	200,153	199,998
Newcastle upon Tyne	E08000021	282,442	286,821
North Tyneside	E08000022	201,446	202,152
South Tyneside	E08000023	148,428	148,526
Sunderland	E08000024	275,743	276,080
NORTH WEST	**E12000002**	**7,084,337**	**7,103,260**
Blackburn with Darwen	E06000008	147,713	147,369
Blackpool	E06000009	141,976	141,400
Cheshire East	E06000049	372,146	372,707
Cheshire West and Chester	E06000050	330,200	331,026
Halton	E06000006	125,692	125,970
Warrington	E06000007	203,652	205,109
Cumbria	E10000006	499,104	498,070
Allerdale	E07000026	96,268	96,208
Barrow-in-Furness	E07000027	68,446	67,831
Carlisle	E07000028	107,952	107,949
Copeland	E07000029	70,329	70,019
Eden	E07000030	52,656	52,607
South Lakeland	E07000031	103,453	103,456
Greater Manchester (Met County)	E11000001	2,702,209	2,714,944
Bolton	E08000001	278,984	280,057
Bury	E08000002	186,199	186,527
Manchester	E08000003	510,772	514,417
Oldham	E08000004	225,875	227,312
Rochdale	E08000005	212,020	212,120
Salford	E08000006	237,085	239,013
Stockport	E08000007	283,897	285,032
Tameside	E08000008	220,241	220,597
Trafford	E08000009	228,466	230,179
Wigan	E08000010	318,670	319,690
Lancashire	E10000017	1,175,979	1,180,076
Burnley	E07000117	87,127	86,894
Chorley	E07000118	109,077	110,505
Fylde	E07000119	76,020	76,442
Hyndburn	E07000120	80,190	80,046
Lancaster	E07000121	139,665	140,575
Pendle	E07000122	89,613	90,131
Preston	E07000123	140,540	140,418
Ribble Valley	E07000124	57,596	57,858
Rossendale	E07000125	68,366	68,744
South Ribble	E07000126	108,971	108,913
West Lancashire	E07000127	110,925	111,314
Wyre	E07000128	107,889	108,236

15.5 Geographical distribution of the population
All Persons

Name	Code	Mid-year population estimate [1]	
		2,012	2,013
Merseyside (Met County)	E11000002	1,385,666	1,386,589
Knowsley	E08000011	145,936	146,086
Liverpool	E08000012	469,690	470,780
Sefton	E08000014	273,697	273,207
St. Helens	E08000013	176,114	176,221
Wirral	E08000015	320,229	320,295
YORKSHIRE AND THE HUMBER	**E12000003**	**5,316,691**	**5,337,710**
East Riding of Yorkshire	E06000011	335,887	336,007
Kingston upon Hull, City of	E06000010	257,204	257,589
North East Lincolnshire	E06000012	159,727	159,827
North Lincolnshire	E06000013	168,372	168,760
York	E06000014	200,018	202,433
North Yorkshire	E10000023	602,628	602,749
Craven	E07000163	55,457	55,540
Hambleton	E07000164	89,748	89,913
Harrogate	E07000165	158,610	158,249
Richmondshire	E07000166	53,935	53,884
Ryedale	E07000167	52,102	52,212
Scarborough	E07000168	108,632	108,223
Selby	E07000169	84,144	84,728
South Yorkshire (Met County)	E11000003	1,352,144	1,358,153
Barnsley	E08000016	233,671	235,757
Doncaster	E08000017	302,739	303,622
Rotherham	E08000018	258,352	258,689
Sheffield	E08000019	557,382	560,085
West Yorkshire (Met County)	E11000006	2,240,711	2,252,192
Bradford	E08000032	524,619	526,369
Calderdale	E08000033	205,293	206,355
Kirklees	E08000034	425,517	428,279
Leeds	E08000035	757,655	761,481
Wakefield	E08000036	327,627	329,708
EAST MIDLANDS	**E12000004**	**4,567,731**	**4,598,729**
Derby	E06000015	250,568	251,423
Leicester	E06000016	331,606	333,812
Nottingham	E06000018	308,735	310,837
Rutland	E06000017	37,015	37,606
Derbyshire	E10000007	773,522	776,160
Amber Valley	E07000032	122,746	123,498
Bolsover	E07000033	76,447	76,729
Chesterfield	E07000034	103,782	104,030
Derbyshire Dales	E07000035	71,336	71,266
Erewash	E07000036	112,809	113,170
High Peak	E07000037	91,118	91,111
North East Derbyshire	E07000038	99,325	99,281
South Derbyshire	E07000039	95,959	97,075
Leicestershire	E10000018	656,698	661,575
Blaby	E07000129	94,593	95,092
Charnwood	E07000130	168,779	170,645
Harborough	E07000131	86,389	87,450
Hinckley and Bosworth	E07000132	106,046	106,613
Melton	E07000133	50,770	50,836
North West Leicestershire	E07000134	94,018	94,814
Oadby and Wigston	E07000135	56,103	56,125
Lincolnshire	E10000019	718,838	724,453
Boston	E07000136	64,793	65,870
East Lindsey	E07000137	136,596	136,711
Lincoln	E07000138	94,588	95,623
North Kesteven	E07000139	109,263	109,906
South Holland	E07000140	88,518	89,243
South Kesteven	E07000141	135,033	136,385

15.5 Geographical distribution of the population
All Persons

Name	Code	Mid-year population estimate [1]	
		2,012	**2,013**
West Lindsey	E07000142	90,047	90,715
Northamptonshire	E10000021	700,576	706,647
Corby	E07000150	63,073	64,212
Daventry	E07000151	78,281	78,556
East Northamptonshire	E07000152	87,365	87,969
Kettering	E07000153	94,841	95,748
Northampton	E07000154	214,566	216,739
South Northamptonshire	E07000155	86,350	87,465
Wellingborough	E07000156	76,100	75,958
Nottinghamshire	E10000024	790,173	796,216
Ashfield	E07000170	120,131	121,553
Bassetlaw	E07000171	113,178	113,654
Broxtowe	E07000172	110,716	111,243
Gedling	E07000173	114,052	114,818
Mansfield	E07000174	104,737	105,296
Newark and Sherwood	E07000175	115,761	116,817
Rushcliffe	E07000176	111,598	112,835
WEST MIDLANDS	**E12000005**	**5,642,569**	**5,674,712**
Herefordshire, County of	E06000019	184,932	186,087
Shropshire	E06000051	308,207	308,567
Stoke-on-Trent	E06000021	249,903	250,227
Telford and Wrekin	E06000020	167,682	168,452
Staffordshire	E10000028	852,123	857,007
Cannock Chase	E07000192	97,940	98,119
East Staffordshire	E07000193	114,388	114,922
Lichfield	E07000194	101,186	101,768
Newcastle-under-Lyme	E07000195	124,183	125,239
South Staffordshire	E07000196	108,441	110,295
Stafford	E07000197	131,630	132,092
Staffordshire Moorlands	E07000198	97,237	97,415
Tamworth	E07000199	77,118	77,157
Warwickshire	E10000031	547,974	548,729
North Warwickshire	E07000218	62,200	62,124
Nuneaton and Bedworth	E07000219	125,805	126,003
Rugby	E07000220	100,751	101,373
Stratford-on-Avon	E07000221	120,578	120,767
Warwick	E07000222	138,640	138,462
West Midlands (Met County)	E11000005	2,762,716	2,783,475
Birmingham	E08000025	1,085,417	1,092,330
Coventry	E08000026	323,132	329,810
Dudley	E08000027	313,589	314,427
Sandwell	E08000028	311,304	314,329
Solihull	E08000029	207,380	208,861
Walsall	E08000030	270,924	272,161
Wolverhampton	E08000031	250,970	251,557
Worcestershire	E10000034	569,032	572,168
Bromsgrove	E07000234	94,285	94,744
Malvern Hills	E07000235	74,980	75,339
Redditch	E07000236	84,419	84,521
Worcester	E07000237	99,604	100,405
Wychavon	E07000238	117,670	118,738
Wyre Forest	E07000239	98,074	98,421
EAST	**E12000006**	**5,907,348**	**5,954,169**
Bedford	E06000055	159,207	161,382
Central Bedfordshire	E06000056	259,969	264,528
Luton	E06000032	205,843	207,989
Peterborough	E06000031	186,372	188,373
Southend-on-Sea	E06000033	174,838	175,798
Thurrock	E06000034	159,533	160,849
Cambridgeshire	E10000003	628,339	632,095

15.5 Geographical distribution of the population
All Persons

Name	Code	Mid-year population estimate [1]	
		2,012	**2,013**
Cambridge	E07000008	125,155	126,480
East Cambridgeshire	E07000009	85,097	85,398
Fenland	E07000010	95,996	96,729
Huntingdonshire	E07000011	171,023	172,056
South Cambridgeshire	E07000012	151,068	151,432
Essex	E10000012	1,406,517	1,416,405
Basildon	E07000066	176,474	178,362
Braintree	E07000067	148,384	149,108
Brentwood	E07000068	74,020	74,460
Castle Point	E07000069	88,218	88,570
Chelmsford	E07000070	169,335	170,256
Colchester	E07000071	176,008	177,626
Epping Forest	E07000072	126,080	127,170
Harlow	E07000073	82,676	83,372
Maldon	E07000074	61,918	62,166
Rochford	E07000075	83,869	83,911
Tendring	E07000076	138,285	138,721
Uttlesford	E07000077	81,250	82,683
Hertfordshire	E10000015	1,129,096	1,140,706
Broxbourne	E07000095	94,497	94,985
Dacorum	E07000096	146,727	148,196
East Hertfordshire	E07000242	139,458	141,076
Hertsmere	E07000098	100,710	101,271
North Hertfordshire	E07000099	128,428	129,318
St Albans	E07000240	141,899	143,094
Stevenage	E07000243	84,798	85,474
Three Rivers	E07000102	88,801	89,495
Watford	E07000103	91,732	93,736
Welwyn Hatfield	E07000241	112,046	114,061
Norfolk	E10000020	865,302	870,146
Breckland	E07000143	131,857	132,587
Broadland	E07000144	125,215	125,499
Great Yarmouth	E07000145	97,570	97,796
King's Lynn and West Norfolk	E07000146	148,628	148,758
North Norfolk	E07000147	101,790	102,043
Norwich	E07000148	134,264	135,893
South Norfolk	E07000149	125,978	127,570
Suffolk	E10000029	732,332	735,898
Babergh	E07000200	87,917	88,289
Forest Heath [1]	E07000201	60,735	63,264
Ipswich	E07000202	134,466	134,693
Mid Suffolk	E07000203	97,611	97,973
St Edmundsbury	E07000204	111,610	111,312
Suffolk Coastal	E07000205	124,323	124,405
Waveney	E07000206	115,670	115,962
LONDON	**E12000007**	**8,308,369**	**8,416,535**
Camden	E09000007	224,962	229,719
City of London	E09000001	7,604	7,648
Hackney	E09000012	252,119	257,379
Hammersmith and Fulham	E09000013	179,850	178,685
Haringey	E09000014	258,912	263,386
Islington	E09000019	211,047	215,667
Kensington and Chelsea	E09000020	155,930	155,594
Lambeth	E09000022	310,200	314,242
Lewisham	E09000023	281,556	286,180
Newham	E09000025	314,084	318,227
Southwark	E09000028	293,530	298,464
Tower Hamlets	E09000030	263,003	272,890
Wandsworth	E09000032	308,312	310,516
Westminster	E09000033	223,858	226,841

15.5 Geographical distribution of the population

All Persons

Name	Code	Mid-year population estimate [1]	
		2,012	**2,013**
Barking and Dagenham	E09000002	190,560	194,352
Barnet	E09000003	363,956	369,088
Bexley	E09000004	234,271	236,687
Brent	E09000005	314,660	317,264
Bromley	E09000006	314,036	317,899
Croydon	E09000008	368,886	372,752
Ealing	E09000009	340,671	342,494
Enfield	E09000010	317,287	320,524
Greenwich	E09000011	260,068	264,008
Harrow	E09000015	242,377	243,372
Havering	E09000016	239,733	242,080
Hillingdon	E09000017	281,756	286,806
Hounslow	E09000018	259,052	262,407
Kingston upon Thames	E09000021	163,906	166,793
Merton	E09000024	202,225	203,223
Redbridge	E09000026	284,617	288,272
Richmond upon Thames	E09000027	189,145	191,365
Sutton	E09000029	193,630	195,914
Waltham Forest	E09000031	262,566	265,797
SOUTH EAST	**E12000008**	**8,724,737**	**8,792,626**
Bracknell Forest	E06000036	115,058	116,567
Brighton and Hove	E06000043	275,762	278,112
Isle of Wight	E06000046	138,748	138,393
Medway	E06000035	268,218	271,105
Milton Keynes	E06000042	252,358	255,692
Portsmouth	E06000044	206,836	207,460
Reading	E06000038	157,112	159,247
Slough	E06000039	141,838	143,024
Southampton	E06000045	239,428	242,141
West Berkshire	E06000037	154,486	155,392
Windsor and Maidenhead	E06000040	145,822	146,335
Wokingham	E06000041	156,663	157,866
Buckinghamshire	E10000002	511,488	516,096
Aylesbury Vale	E07000004	177,793	181,071
Chiltern	E07000005	92,954	93,250
South Bucks	E07000006	67,435	67,941
Wycombe	E07000007	173,306	173,834
East Sussex	E10000011	531,201	534,402
Eastbourne	E07000061	100,049	100,537
Hastings	E07000062	90,345	90,754
Lewes	E07000063	98,690	99,479
Rother	E07000064	91,088	91,054
Wealden	E07000065	151,029	152,578
Hampshire	E10000014	1,330,153	1,337,730
Basingstoke and Deane	E07000084	170,492	171,852
East Hampshire	E07000085	116,400	117,088
Eastleigh	E07000086	126,764	127,722
Fareham	E07000087	112,802	113,614
Gosport	E07000088	83,276	83,503
Hart	E07000089	92,162	92,720
Havant	E07000090	121,271	121,562
New Forest	E07000091	177,382	178,062
Rushmoor	E07000092	94,870	94,971
Test Valley	E07000093	117,032	118,372
Winchester	E07000094	117,702	118,264
Kent	E10000016	1,480,166	1,493,512
Ashford	E07000105	120,116	121,723
Canterbury	E07000106	153,399	155,307
Dartford	E07000107	98,940	100,569
Dover	E07000108	111,765	112,338

15.5 Geographical distribution of the population

All Persons

Name	Code	Mid-year population estimate [1]	
		2,012	2,013
Gravesham	E07000109	102,764	103,752
Maidstone	E07000110	157,297	159,325
Sevenoaks	E07000111	116,400	117,035
Shepway	E07000112	108,700	108,832
Swale	E07000113	137,670	139,171
Thanet	E07000114	135,661	136,766
Tonbridge and Malling	E07000115	121,912	123,001
Tunbridge Wells	E07000116	115,542	115,693
Oxfordshire	E10000025	660,772	666,082
Cherwell	E07000177	142,822	143,659
Oxford	E07000178	152,527	154,773
South Oxfordshire	E07000179	135,541	136,015
Vale of White Horse	E07000180	122,764	123,646
West Oxfordshire	E07000181	107,118	107,989
Surrey	E10000030	1,143,509	1,152,114
Elmbridge	E07000207	131,512	132,179
Epsom and Ewell	E07000208	76,052	77,131
Guildford	E07000209	139,710	141,009
Mole Valley	E07000210	85,846	86,309
Reigate and Banstead	E07000211	139,888	141,073
Runnymede	E07000212	82,189	83,448
Spelthorne	E07000213	96,744	97,456
Surrey Heath	E07000214	86,614	86,904
Tandridge	E07000215	83,693	84,612
Waverley	E07000216	121,884	122,426
Woking	E07000217	99,377	99,567
West Sussex	E10000032	815,119	821,356
Adur	E07000223	61,929	62,505
Arun	E07000224	151,384	152,818
Chichester	E07000225	114,521	115,301
Crawley	E07000226	108,302	108,971
Horsham	E07000227	132,160	132,878
Mid Sussex	E07000228	141,162	142,766
Worthing	E07000229	105,661	106,117
SOUTH WEST	**E12000009**	**5,339,637**	**5,377,595**
Bath and North East Somerset	E06000022	177,643	180,097
Bournemouth	E06000028	186,744	188,733
Bristol, City of	E06000023	432,451	437,492
Cornwall	E06000052	537,914	541,319
Isles of Scilly	E06000053	2,264	2,251
North Somerset	E06000024	204,385	206,135
Plymouth	E06000026	258,026	259,175
Poole	E06000029	148,615	149,009
South Gloucestershire	E06000025	266,147	269,107
Swindon	E06000030	211,934	214,037
Torbay	E06000027	131,492	132,075
Wiltshire	E06000054	476,816	479,634
Devon	E10000008	753,157	758,052
East Devon	E07000040	134,359	134,898
Exeter	E07000041	119,397	121,800
Mid Devon	E07000042	78,335	78,670
North Devon	E07000043	93,847	93,825
South Hams	E07000044	83,597	83,850
Teignbridge	E07000045	125,020	126,001
Torridge	E07000046	64,743	65,089
West Devon	E07000047	53,859	53,919
Dorset	E10000009	414,940	416,721
Christchurch	E07000048	47,987	48,368
East Dorset	E07000049	87,755	87,899
North Dorset	E07000050	69,348	69,883

15.5 Geographical distribution of the population
All Persons

| Name | Code | Mid-year population estimate [1] | |
		2,012	2,013
Purbeck	E07000051	45,289	45,411
West Dorset	E07000052	99,532	100,026
Weymouth and Portland	E07000053	65,029	65,134
Gloucestershire	E10000013	602,159	605,654
Cheltenham	E07000078	116,080	115,900
Cotswold	E07000079	83,562	84,079
Forest of Dean	E07000080	82,731	82,937
Gloucester	E07000081	123,439	124,562
Stroud	E07000082	113,363	113,920
Tewkesbury	E07000083	82,984	84,256
Somerset	E10000027	534,950	538,104
Mendip	E07000187	109,938	110,181
Sedgemoor	E07000188	116,071	117,544
South Somerset	E07000189	163,012	163,943
Taunton Deane	E07000190	111,370	112,116
West Somerset	E07000191	34,559	34,320
WALES	**W92000004**	**3,074,067**	**3,082,412**
Isle of Anglesey	W06000001	70,049	70,091
Gwynedd	W06000002	122,142	121,911
Conwy	W06000003	115,515	115,835
Denbighshire	W06000004	94,066	94,510
Flintshire	W06000005	152,743	153,240
Wrexham	W06000006	135,919	136,399
Powys	W06000023	132,952	132,705
Ceredigion	W06000008	76,046	75,964
Pembrokeshire	W06000009	123,035	123,261
Carmarthenshire	W06000010	184,317	184,681
Swansea	W06000011	239,633	240,332
Neath Port Talbot	W06000012	140,108	139,898
Bridgend	W06000013	139,740	140,480
The Vale of Glamorgan	W06000014	126,831	127,159
Cardiff	W06000015	348,493	351,710
Rhondda Cynon Taf	W06000016	235,599	236,114
Merthyr Tydfil	W06000024	58,898	59,021
Caerphilly	W06000018	179,022	179,247
Blaenau Gwent	W06000019	69,822	69,789
Torfaen	W06000020	91,372	91,407
Monmouthshire	W06000021	91,659	92,100
Newport	W06000022	146,106	146,558
SCOTLAND	**S92000003**	**5,313,600**	**5,327,700**
Aberdeen City	S12000033	224,970	227,130
Aberdeenshire	S12000034	255,540	257,740
Angus	S12000041	116,210	116,240
Argyll and Bute	S12000035	86,900	88,050
Clackmannanshire	S12000005	51,280	51,280
Dumfries and Galloway	S12000006	150,830	150,270
Dundee City	S12000042	147,800	148,170
East Ayrshire	S12000008	122,720	122,440
East Dunbartonshire	S12000045	105,880	105,860
East Lothian	S12000010	100,850	101,360
East Renfrewshire	S12000011	91,030	91,500
City of Edinburgh	S12000036	482,640	487,500
Eilean Siar	S12000013	27,560	27,400
Falkirk	S12000014	156,800	157,140
Fife	S12000015	366,220	366,910
Glasgow City	S12000046	595,080	596,550
Highland	S12000017	232,910	232,950
Inverclyde	S12000018	80,680	80,310

15.5 Geographical distribution of the population
All Persons

Name	Code	Mid-year population estimate [1]	
		2,012	2,013
Midlothian	S12000019	84,240	84,700
Moray	S12000020	92,910	94,350
North Ayrshire	S12000021	137,560	136,920
North Lanarkshire	S12000044	337,870	337,730
Orkney Islands	S12000023	21,530	21,570
Perth and Kinross	S12000024	147,740	147,750
Renfrewshire	S12000038	174,310	173,900
Scottish Borders	S12000026	113,710	113,870
Shetland Islands	S12000027	23,210	23,200
South Ayrshire	S12000028	112,910	112,850
South Lanarkshire	S12000029	314,360	314,850
Stirling	S12000030	91,020	91,260
West Dunbartonshire	S12000039	90,340	89,810
West Lothian	S12000040	175,990	176,140
NORTHERN IRELAND	**N92000002**	**1,823,634**	**1,829,725**
Antrim	95T	53,835	53,978
Ards	95X	78,550	78,549
Armagh	95O	60,147	60,423
Ballymena	95G	64,551	64,762
Ballymoney	95D	31,551	31,659
Banbridge	95Q	48,730	48,905
Belfast	95Z	280,537	281,735
Carrickfergus	95V	39,096	39,015
Castlereagh	95Y	67,716	67,883
Coleraine	95C	58,993	59,043
Cookstown	95I	37,411	37,552
Craigavon	95N	94,597	95,474
Derry	95A	108,586	108,610
Down	95R	70,440	70,825
Dungannon	95M	58,813	59,298
Fermanagh	95L	62,400	62,527
Larne	95F	32,191	32,220
Limavady	95B	33,761	33,886
Lisburn	95S	121,687	121,990
Magherafelt	95H	45,450	45,826
Moyle	95E	17,129	17,111
Newry and Mourne	95P	100,858	101,612
Newtownabbey	95U	85,322	85,558
North Down	95W	79,420	79,424
Omagh	95K	51,830	51,838
Strabane	95J	40,033	40,022

Source: Office for National Statistics

1. The distribution of the foreign armed forces (FAF) special population presented in this release has been incorrectly calculated for certain local authorities in England. This error has a significant impact on the estimate for Forest Heath, where the published population estimate is 3.3% higher than the correct value. The impact in other affected local authorities is much smaller. The error is also reflected in the population estimates of the associated county and region totals which are derived by aggregating the affected local authority figures. Similarly the 'other' category of components of change reflects this difference. Further detail on the error, together with a list of affected local authorities and the size of the error in each area, is available in the Quality and Methodology document.

15.6 UK and non-UK born population by ethnicity in England and Wales, 2011

Ethnic Group	UK born		Non-UK born	
			Number (thousand) and percentage	
White	**44,774**	**92.2**	**3,435**	**45.8**
British	44,186	91.0	949	12.6
Irish	178	0.4	354	4.7
Gypsy or Irish Traveller	51	0.1	7	0.1
Other White	360	0.7	2,126	28.3
Mixed/Multiple ethnic group	**985**	**2.0**	**239**	**3.2**
White and Black Caribbean	401	0.8	26	0.3
White and Black African	113	0.2	53	0.7
White and Asian	271	0.6	71	0.9
Other Mixed	200	0.4	90	1.2
Asian/Asian British	**1,770**	**3.6**	**2,443**	**32.6**
Indian	606	1.2	807	10.7
Pakistani	631	1.3	493	6.6
Bangladeshi	232	0.5	215	2.9
Chinese	93	0.2	300	4.0
Other Asian	207	0.4	628	8.4
Black/African/Caribbean/Black British	**873**	**1.8**	**992**	**13.2**
African	323	0.7	666	8.9
Caribbean	358	0.7	237	3.2
Other Black	192	0.4	89	1.2
Other ethnic group	**168**	**0.3**	**395**	**5.3**
Arab	64	0.1	167	2.2
Any other ethnic group	105	0.2	228	3.0
		100		100
All	**48,571**	**86.6**	**7,505**	**13.4**

Source 2011 Census

15.7 Long-Term International Migration, 1991 to 2013
United Kingdom, England and Wales
Citizenship

thousands

Mid year to mid year	All citizenships 2011 Census Revisions[1] Estimate	+/-CI	British Estimate	+/-CI	Non-British Estimate	+/-CI	European Union[2] Estimate	+/-CI	European Union EU15 Estimate	+/-CI	European Union EU8 Estimate	+/-CI	Non-European Union[3] All Estimate	+/-CI	Commonwealth[4] All[4] Estimate	+/-CI	Old Estimate	+/-CI	New[4] Estimate	+/-CI	Other Foreign[5] Estimate	+/-CI	All citizenships Original Estimates[1] Estimate	+/-CI
United Kingdom																							
Inflow																							
1991	329	23	110	17	219	16	53	11	53	11	z	z	167	12	85	9	26	7	59	5	82	9		
1992	268	20	93	16	175	13	44	9	44	9	z	z	131	9	65	6	18	4	46	5	67	7		
1993	266	19	86	13	179	13	44	7	44	7	z	z	135	11	70	8	23	6	47	4	65	8		
1994	315	23	109	17	206	15	50	9	50	9	z	z	156	12	80	7	21	4	59	5	76	10		
1995	312	22	84	14	228	17	61	11	61	11	z	z	167	13	85	8	27	6	58	5	82	10		
1996	318	25	94	17	224	18	72	13	72	13	z	z	152	12	78	9	29	7	49	5	74	9		
1997	327	27	90	15	237	23	71	18	71	18	z	z	166	13	90	11	31	6	59	9	76	8		
1998	391	27	104	16	287	22	82	15	82	15	z	z	206	16	105	13	54	8	51	10	101	8		
1999	454	31	115	18	338	25	66	16	66	16	z	z	272	19	123	14	55	9	68	11	150	13		
2000	479	31	99	17	379	26	63	14	63	14	z	z	316	22	147	18	56	15	91	9	169	13		
2001	481	30	110	18	370	25	58	16	58	16	z	z	313	19	149	14	65	10	84	10	164	12		
2002	516	32	98	19	418	26	61	16	61	16	z	z	357	20	155	13	63	8	92	10	201	16		
2003	511	33	100	18	411	27	66	18	66	18	z	z	344	20	167	14	62	8	105	11	177	15		
2004	589	40	89	14	500	38	130	22	77	15	53	16	370	30	215	20	73	12	141	16	155	23		
2005	567	37	98	18	469	33	152	23	73	14	76	18	317	24	180	16	62	10	117	13	137	17		
2006	596	39	83	17	513	35	170	26	74	13	92	22	343	24	201	19	62	10	139	16	143	16		
2007	574	40	74	14	500	37	195	29	77	17	112	24	305	23	174	17	45	7	129	15	131	16		
2008	590	39	85	16	505	36	198	28	90	19	89	19	307	22	165	16	44	9	121	13	142	15		
2009	567	30	96	14	471	26	167	19	82	13	68	13	303	18	171	13	30	6	141	12	132	12		
2010	591	31	93	15	498	27	176	21	76	13	86	16	322	17	187	12	31	6	156	11	135	12		
2011	566	28	78	12	488	25	174	18	83	12	77	12	314	18	179	13	29	6	151	12	135	12		
2012	498	27	80	12	418	25	158	18	85	12	60	13	260	17	129	12	31	7	98	10	131	12		
2013	526	29	76	12	450	27	201	20	104	13	70	12	248	18	101	10	23	5	78	8	147	15		
Outflow																							
1991	285	23	154	18	130	15	53	10	53	10	z	z	77	10	35	6	18	4	17	5	43	8		
1992	281	21	155	17	126	13	38	5	38	5	z	z	88	12	31	5	18	4	13	3	57	11		
1993	266	20	149	16	118	11	40	7	40	7	z	z	77	9	34	6	17	4	17	4	43	7		
1994	238	20	125	15	113	13	42	8	42	8	z	z	71	10	31	6	14	4	17	4	40	9		
1995	236	19	135	15	101	11	38	7	38	7	z	z	63	9	29	6	18	5	12	3	34	6		
1996	264	28	156	25	108	11	44	7	44	7	z	z	64	9	32	6	17	4	14	4	32	7		
1997	279	24	149	19	131	15	53	10	53	10	z	z	77	10	40	7	20	6	20	4	37	7		
1998	251	22	126	18	126	12	49	8	49	8	z	z	77	9	33	6	20	4	13	4	44	8		
1999	291	24	139	16	152	18	59	13	59	13	z	z	93	13	41	8	29	7	12	4	52	10		
2000	321	27	161	19	160	19	57	13	57	13	z	z	103	14	47	8	32	6	15	4	55	12		
2001	309	25	159	19	150	17	51	12	51	12	z	z	99	12	51	8	32	6	19	5	49	9		
2002	363	29	186	23	177	19	54	13	54	13	z	z	122	14	58	9	42	8	16	4	64	11		
2003	363	32	191	23	172	22	51	17	51	17	z	z	121	15	59	9	42	8	17	4	62	11		
2004	344	28	196	23	148	16	43	10	39	9	3	3	104	13	53	8	33	6	19	5	52	10		
2005	361	31	186	22	175	21	56	13	40	11	15	8	119	17	60	9	37	7	23	6	59	14		
2006	398	34	207	26	192	22	66	16	44	11	22	11	126	15	66	11	42	8	24	6	60	11		
2007	341	27	171	20	169	18	69	15	41	11	25	10	101	10	58	7	31	4	26	6	43	7		
2008	427	41	173	22	255	34	134	32	54	15	69	21	120	12	66	9	35	6	31	7	55	8		
2009	368	22	140	11	228	18	109	16	53	11	52	12	119	9	66	6	32	5	34	4	53	6		
2010	339	20	136	11	203	16	99	14	58	12	37	8	104	8	52	5	22	4	30	4	52	6		
2011	351	22	149	13	202	17	92	14	49	10	37	9	110	10	60	8	21	4	39	5	50	8		
2012	321	20	143	14	179	14	75	11	41	8	30	8	103	8	53	6	17	3	36	5	51	6		
2013	317	19	134	12	183	15	78	12	47	10	26	7	105	9	53	5	18	3	36	4	52	7		
Balance																							
1991	+ 44	33	- 44	24	+ 89	22	- 1	15	- 1	15	z	z	+ 89	16	+ 50	11	+ 8	8	+ 42	7	+ 39	12		
1992	- 13	29	- 62	23	+ 49	18	+ 5	10	+ 5	10	z	z	+ 44	15	+ 34	8	0~	5	+ 33	6	+ 10	13		
1993	- 1	27	- 62	21	+ 62	17	+ 4	10	+ 4	10	z	z	+ 58	14	+ 36	10	+ 6	8	+ 30	6	+ 22	11		
1994	+ 77	30	- 16	23	+ 94	20	+ 9	12	+ 9	12	z	z	+ 85	16	+ 49	9	+ 7	6	+ 42	7	+ 36	14		
1995	+ 76	29	- 51	21	+ 127	20	+ 23	13	+ 23	13	z	z	+ 104	16	+ 56	10	+ 9	8	+ 46	6	+ 48	12		
1996	+ 55	37	- 62	30	+ 116	21	+ 28	15	+ 28	15	z	z	+ 88	15	+ 47	10	+ 12	8	+ 35	7	+ 41	11		
1997	+ 48	36	- 59	24	+ 107	27	+ 18	21	+ 18	21	z	z	+ 88	17	+ 50	13	+ 11	9	+ 39	10	+ 38	11		
1998	+ 140	35	- 22	24	+ 162	25	+ 33	17	+ 33	17	z	z	+ 129	18	+ 72	14	+ 34	9	+ 38	11	+ 57	11		
1999	+ 163	39	- 24	24	+ 187	31	+ 8	20	+ 8	20	z	z	+ 179	23	+ 82	16	+ 26	11	+ 56	12	+ 98	17		
2000	+ 158	41	- 62	25	+ 220	32	+ 6	19	+ 6	19	z	z	+ 214	26	+ 100	19	+ 24	16	+ 76	10	+ 114	18		
2001	+ 179	:	- 48	26	+ 220	30	+ 7	20	+ 7	20	z	z	+ 213	22	+ 98	16	+ 33	12	+ 65	11	+ 115	15	+ 171	40
2002	+ 172	:	- 88	29	+ 241	32	+ 7	21	+ 7	21	z	z	+ 234	24	+ 97	15	+ 21	11	+ 77	10	+ 137	19	+ 153	43
2003	+ 185	:	- 91	29	+ 239	35	+ 15	25	+ 15	25	z	z	+ 224	25	+ 109	17	+ 20	12	+ 88	12	+ 115	19	+ 148	46
2004	+ 268	:	- 107	27	+ 352	41	+ 87	24	+ 38	18	+ 49	17	+ 266	33	+ 162	22	+ 40	14	+ 122	17	+ 104	25	+ 245	49
2005	+ 267	:	- 88	29	+ 294	39	+ 96	27	+ 33	17	+ 61	20	+ 198	29	+ 120	19	+ 25	12	+ 94	14	+ 78	22	+ 206	49

15.7 Long-Term International Migration, 1991 to 2013
United Kingdom, England and Wales
Citizenship

thousands

United Kingdom

Mid year to mid year	All citizenships 2011 Census Revisions[1]		British		Non-British		European Union[2]		European Union EU15		European Union EU8		Non-European Union[3] All		Commonwealth[4] All[4]		Old		New[4]		Other Foreign[5]		All citizenships Original Estimates[1]	
	Estimate	+/-CI	Estimate	+/-CI	Estimate	+/-CI	Estimate	+/-CI	Estimate	+/-CI	Estimate	+/-CI	Estimate	+/-CI	Estimate	+/-CI	Estimate	+/-CI	Estimate	+/-CI	Estimate	+/-CI	Estimate	+/-CI
2006	+ 265	:	- 124	31	+ 322	41	+ 104	30	+ 30	17	+ 71	24	+ 218	29	+ 135	21	+ 20	13	+ 115	17	+ 83	19	+ 198	52
2007	+ 273	:	- 97	24	+ 330	41	+ 127	33	+ 36	20	+ 87	26	+ 204	25	+ 116	18	+ 13	8	+ 103	16	+ 88	17	+ 233	48
2008	+ 229	:	- 87	28	+ 251	50	+ 63	43	+ 37	24	+ 20	28	+ 187	25	+ 100	18	+ 9	10	+ 91	15	+ 87	17	+ 163	57
2009	+ 229	:	- 44	18	+ 242	32	+ 58	25	+ 29	17	+ 16	18	+ 184	20	+ 105	15	- 2	8	+ 107	12	+ 79	13	+ 198	37
2010	+ 256	:	- 43	18	+ 294	32	+ 77	25	+ 18	17	+ 49	18	+ 217	19	+ 135	13	+ 9	7	+ 126	12	+ 83	13	+ 252	37
2011	+ 205	:	- 70	18	+ 286	31	+ 74	23	+ 34	16	+ 40	15	+ 204	20	+ 119	15	+ 8	7	+ 111	13	+ 85	14	+ 215	35
2012	+ 177	34	- 63	19	+ 239	28	+ 82	21	+ 44	14	+ 30	15	+ 157	19	+ 76	13	+ 15	7	+ 61	11	+ 81	14		
2013	+ 209	35	- 57	16	+ 267	31	+ 123	24	+ 58	16	+ 44	14	+ 143	19	+ 48	11	+ 6	6	+ 42	9	+ 95	16		

England and Wales

Inflow

Year	All cit Est	+/-CI	British Est	+/-CI	Non-British Est	+/-CI	EU[2] Est	+/-CI	EU15 Est	+/-CI	EU8 Est	+/-CI	Non-EU[3] All Est	+/-CI	Comm[4] All Est	+/-CI	Old Est	+/-CI	New[4] Est	+/-CI	Other Foreign[5] Est	+/-CI
1991	304	22	98	15	207	16	50	11	50	11	z	z	157	12	81	9	25	7	57	5	76	8
1992	251	20	87	16	164	12	42	9	42	9	z	z	123	8	60	6	18	4	42	4	63	6
1993	249	18	80	12	170	13	40	6	40	6	z	z	130	11	67	7	22	6	45	4	62	8
1994	292	21	94	15	199	15	47	9	47	9	z	z	151	12	78	6	21	4	58	5	73	10
1995	299	22	79	14	220	17	59	11	59	11	z	z	162	13	83	8	25	6	58	5	79	10
1996	300	23	86	15	214	17	67	13	67	13	z	z	147	12	77	9	29	7	48	5	70	8
1997	310	26	85	15	226	22	69	18	69	18	z	z	157	12	86	10	29	5	57	8	71	7
1998	370	26	96	15	274	21	76	15	76	15	z	z	198	15	101	13	53	8	48	10	97	8
1999	424	29	101	16	323	24	63	16	63	16	z	z	260	18	117	13	51	8	65	11	143	13
2000	446	28	95	16	351	23	53	12	53	12	z	z	298	20	140	17	51	14	89	9	158	11
2001	449	29	99	17	350	24	56	16	56	16	z	z	295	18	139	13	59	9	79	10	156	12
2002	485	31	92	18	394	25	57	16	57	16	z	z	337	19	149	12	61	8	89	9	188	14
2003	480	31	93	17	387	26	61	18	61	18	z	z	326	19	159	13	58	8	101	11	167	14
2004	549	38	82	13	467	36	122	21	72	14	50	16	345	29	199	19	70	12	129	15	146	22
2005	523	36	87	17	436	32	143	22	66	13	74	18	293	22	167	15	56	9	111	13	126	16
2006	549	36	78	16	471	33	149	23	67	12	78	19	322	23	186	18	55	9	131	15	136	15
2007	524	38	65	13	460	35	175	28	68	16	101	23	285	21	163	15	43	7	120	14	122	15
2008	528	36	67	13	461	34	178	27	75	17	84	19	283	21	157	15	40	8	117	13	126	15
2009	507	28	83	13	424	25	142	18	69	12	58	13	282	17	160	12	25	5	135	11	122	11
2010	532	29	80	14	451	26	151	20	68	12	72	15	300	16	175	12	28	5	147	11	124	11
2011	515	26	71	12	445	24	153	17	74	12	67	12	291	17	169	12	27	5	142	11	122	12
2012	451	26	72	11	380	23	138	16	74	11	52	11	241	16	121	11	30	7	92	9	120	12
2013	484	28	70	11	413	26	183	19	94	12	63	12	230	17	95	9	22	5	72	8	135	14

Outflow

Year	All cit Est	+/-CI	British Est	+/-CI	Non-British Est	+/-CI	EU[2] Est	+/-CI	EU15 Est	+/-CI	EU8 Est	+/-CI	Non-EU[3] All Est	+/-CI	Comm[4] All Est	+/-CI	Old Est	+/-CI	New[4] Est	+/-CI	Other Foreign[5] Est	+/-CI
1991	253	21	138	17	115	13	45	9	45	9	z	z	71	9	32	6	17	4	14	4	39	7
1992	248	19	135	15	113	12	34	5	34	5	z	z	79	11	29	5	17	4	12	3	49	9
1993	244	19	137	16	107	11	37	7	37	7	z	z	70	8	31	5	15	4	16	4	39	6
1994	216	19	113	15	103	12	36	7	36	7	z	z	67	10	29	6	13	4	16	4	38	8
1995	216	18	124	15	92	11	33	7	33	7	z	z	59	8	28	6	17	5	11	3	31	6
1996	238	27	141	24	97	11	39	6	39	6	z	z	58	8	28	5	16	4	12	3	30	7
1997	244	21	125	16	120	14	48	10	48	10	z	z	72	10	37	7	19	6	18	4	35	7
1998	223	20	107	16	116	12	44	8	44	8	z	z	72	9	31	5	19	4	12	3	41	7
1999	273	24	129	16	144	18	56	12	56	12	z	z	88	14	39	8	28	7	11	4	49	10
2000	291	26	141	18	151	19	55	13	55	13	z	z	96	14	44	7	30	6	14	4	52	12
2001	282	24	143	18	138	16	46	12	46	12	z	z	93	11	48	8	30	6	18	5	44	8
2002	328	28	168	21	159	18	47	12	47	12	z	z	112	13	52	8	38	7	14	4	60	10
2003	333	31	174	22	159	22	47	16	47	16	z	z	112	14	54	9	38	8	16	4	59	11
2004	311	27	175	22	135	15	41	10	37	9	3	3	94	12	48	7	31	6	17	4	46	9
2005	328	29	171	22	157	19	50	13	35	10	15	8	106	15	55	9	34	7	21	6	51	12
2006	369	33	192	25	177	21	60	15	38	10	22	11	117	15	62	10	39	8	22	6	55	10
2007	307	25	152	19	155	17	60	14	38	11	20	9	94	9	53	6	29	4	23	5	42	7
2008	393	40	157	21	235	34	126	32	49	15	65	20	110	11	59	8	32	5	27	6	50	8
2009	328	20	123	10	205	18	98	16	49	11	46	11	107	8	61	6	31	5	31	4	46	5
2010	308	19	123	10	184	16	89	14	54	11	32	8	95	7	48	5	21	4	27	4	47	5
2011	312	20	134	12	178	16	78	13	42	9	31	9	100	9	55	6	18	3	37	5	45	7
2012	286	19	126	13	160	14	66	11	38	8	24	7	94	8	49	6	16	3	34	5	45	6
2013	280	18	118	11	163	14	68	12	42	9	22	7	95	8	48	5	16	3	32	4	46	6

Balance

Year	All cit Est	+/-CI	British Est	+/-CI	Non-British Est	+/-CI	EU[2] Est	+/-CI	EU15 Est	+/-CI	EU8 Est	+/-CI	Non-EU[3] All Est	+/-CI	Comm[4] All Est	+/-CI	Old Est	+/-CI	New[4] Est	+/-CI	Other Foreign[5] Est	+/-CI
1991	+ 51	31	- 40	23	+ 91	20	+ 5	14	+ 5	14	z	z	+ 86	15	+ 50	10	+ 7	8	+ 42	7	+ 37	10
1992	+ 4	27	- 48	21	+ 51	17	+ 7	10	+ 7	10	z	z	+ 44	14	+ 30	7	+ 1	5	+ 29	5	+ 14	11
1993	+ 5	26	- 57	20	+ 62	16	+ 3	9	+ 3	9	z	z	+ 59	14	+ 36	9	+ 7	7	+ 30	6	+ 23	10
1994	+ 77	28	- 19	20	+ 96	19	+ 12	11	+ 12	11	z	z	+ 84	16	+ 49	9	+ 8	6	+ 42	7	+ 35	13
1995	+ 83	28	- 45	20	+ 129	20	+ 25	13	+ 25	13	z	z	+ 103	15	+ 55	10	+ 8	8	+ 47	6	+ 48	11
1996	+ 62	35	- 55	29	+ 117	20	+ 27	14	+ 27	14	z	z	+ 90	15	+ 49	10	+ 12	8	+ 37	6	+ 41	11
1997	+ 66	34	- 40	22	+ 106	26	+ 21	21	+ 21	21	z	z	+ 85	15	+ 49	12	+ 10	8	+ 39	9	+ 36	10
1998	+ 147	33	- 10	22	+ 157	24	+ 31	17	+ 31	17	z	z	+ 126	18	+ 70	14	+ 34	9	+ 36	10	+ 56	11
1999	+ 151	38	- 28	23	+ 179	30	+ 7	20	+ 7	20	z	z	+ 171	22	+ 77	15	+ 23	10	+ 54	11	+ 94	16
2000	+ 154	38	- 46	24	+ 200	30	- 2	17	- 2	17	z	z	+ 202	24	+ 96	18	+ 22	15	+ 74	10	+ 105	16

15.7 Long-Term International Migration, 1991 to 2013
United Kingdom, England and Wales
Citizenship

thousands

Mid year to mid year	All citizenships 2011 Census Revisions¹ Estimate	+/-CI	British Estimate	+/-CI	Non-British Estimate	+/-CI	European Union² Estimate	+/-CI	European Union EU15 Estimate	+/-CI	European Union EU8 Estimate	+/-CI	Non-European Union³ All Estimate	+/-CI	Commonwealth⁴ All⁴ Estimate	+/-CI	Old Estimate	+/-CI	New⁴ Estimate	+/-CI	Other Foreign⁵ Estimate	+/-CI	All citizenships Original Estimates¹ Estimate	+/-CI
2001	+ 167	38	- 45	24	+ 212	29	+ 10	20	+ 10	20	z	z	+ 202	21	+ 90	16	+ 29	11	+ 61	11	+ 112	14		
2002	+ 158	41	- 77	28	+ 234	30	+ 9	20	+ 9	20	z	z	+ 225	23	+ 97	15	+ 22	11	+ 75	10	+ 128	18		
2003	+ 147	44	- 81	28	+ 228	34	+ 14	24	+ 14	24	z	z	+ 214	24	+ 105	16	+ 21	11	+ 84	12	+ 108	18		
2004	+ 238	47	- 94	26	+ 332	39	+ 81	23	+ 35	17	+ 46	16	+ 251	31	+ 151	20	+ 38	13	+ 112	15	+ 100	24		
2005	+ 195	46	- 84	27	+ 279	37	+ 92	26	+ 31	16	+ 59	20	+ 186	27	+ 112	18	+ 22	11	+ 90	14	+ 75	20		
2006	+ 180	49	- 114	30	+ 294	39	+ 89	27	+ 29	16	+ 56	22	+ 205	28	+ 124	20	+ 16	12	+ 109	16	+ 81	19		
2007	+ 217	45	- 88	23	+ 305	39	+ 115	32	+ 30	19	+ 81	25	+ 190	23	+ 110	17	+ 14	8	+ 97	15	+ 80	16		
2008	+ 135	54	- 90	25	+ 225	48	+ 52	42	+ 26	22	+ 19	28	+ 173	24	+ 97	17	+ 8	10	+ 89	14	+ 76	16		
2009	+ 179	35	- 40	17	+ 219	30	+ 44	24	+ 20	16	+ 12	17	+ 174	18	+ 99	14	- 5	7	+ 104	12	+ 76	12		
2010	+ 224	35	- 43	17	+ 267	30	+ 62	24	+ 14	17	+ 39	17	+ 205	18	+ 127	13	+ 7	6	+ 120	11	+ 78	12		
2011	+ 203	33	- 64	17	+ 267	29	+ 75	21	+ 32	15	+ 37	15	+ 192	19	+ 114	13	+ 8	6	+ 106	12	+ 77	14		
2012	+ 165	32	- 54	18	+ 219	27	+ 73	19	+ 37	13	+ 28	13	+ 147	18	+ 72	13	+ 14	7	+ 58	10	+ 75	13		
2013	+ 203	33	- 47	15	+ 250	29	+ 115	23	+ 52	15	+ 40	13	+ 136	19	+ 47	10	+ 7	6	+ 40	9	+ 89	16		

Source: Office for National Statistics (ONS), Home Office, Central Statistics Office (CSO) Ireland, Northern Ireland Statistics and Research Agency (NISRA).

Totals may not sum due to rounding.

"z" - Not applicable, ":" - Not available, "0~" - Rounds to zero. Please see the Notes worksheet for more information.

1   Net migration ("Balance") figures for the United Kingdom for 2001 to 2011 have been revised in light of the results of the 2011 Census. The original published estimates are shown to the right of the table. The revisions are not reflected in the remainder of the table. The sums of the disaggregated estimates will not therefore match the revised balances. Users should continue to use the estimates in the table to analyse detailed breakdowns of inflows and outflows of long-term international migrants but, in doing so, should bear in mind that the headline net migration estimates have been revised.

2   European Union estimates are for the EU15 (Austria, Belgium, Denmark, Finland, France, Germany, Greece, Republic of Ireland, Italy, Luxembourg, Netherlands, Portugal, Spain and Sweden) up to 2003, the EU25 (the EU15 and the EU8 groupings plus Malta and Cyprus) from 2004 - 2006, the EU27 (the EU25 plus Bulgaria and Romania) from 2007 and the EU28 (the EU27 plus Croatia) from July 2013. Estimates are also shown separately for the EU15, the EU8 (Czech Republic, Estonia, Hungary, Latvia, Lithuania, Poland, Slovakia and Slovenia) and the EU2 (Bulgaria and Romania). British citizens are excluded from all citizenship groupings and are shown separately.

3   Excludes British and other European Union citizens

4   From 2004 onwards, All and New Commonwealth exclude Malta and Cyprus.

5   From 2004 onwards, Other Foreign excludes the eight central and eastern European member states that joined the EU in May 2004 (the EU8). From 2007 onwards, Other Foreign excludes Bulgaria and Romania which joined the EU in January 2007. From July 2013 onwards, Other Foreign excludes Croatia which joined the EU in July 2013.

Statistically Significant Increase   Statistically Significant Decrease

The latest estimates (2013) have been compared with the corresponding estimates for the period one year earlier (2012). Where changes have been found to be statistically significant, the relevant pair of estimates have been highlighted by setting their background colour

Net migration figures for the United Kingdom for 2001 to 2011 have been revised in light of the results of the 2011 Census. These revisions are shown in the body of the table. The original net migration estimates are shown to the right of the table.

15.8 Long-Term International Migration, 1991 to 2013
United Kingdom, England and Wales
Country of Last or Next Residence

United Kingdom

Inflow

Year	All countries 2011 Census Revisions[1] Estimate	+/-CI	European Union[2] Estimate	+/-CI	European Union EU15 Estimate	+/-CI	European Union EU8 Estimate	+/-CI	Non-European Union[3] All Estimate	+/-CI	Commonwealth[4] All[4] Estimate	+/-CI	Old Commonwealth All Estimate	+/-CI	Australia Estimate	+/-CI	Canada Estimate	+/-CI	New Zealand Estimate	+/-CI	South Africa Estimate	+/-CI
1991	329	23	95	17	95	17	z	z	234	16	130	12	51	9	28	6	6	2	10	4	7	4
1992	268	20	89	17	89	17	z	z	179	12	96	8	38	6	20	4	4	2	8	3	6	3
1993	266	19	75	13	75	13	z	z	191	14	103	10	42	8	22	6	5	2	6	2	9	3
1994	315	23	95	17	95	17	z	z	220	16	112	9	42	6	19	4	6	2	8	3	9	3
1995	312	22	89	15	89	15	z	z	223	16	111	10	41	7	19	4	8	4	9	4	5	2
1996	318	25	98	18	98	18	z	z	220	17	112	11	48	8	22	5	7	3	9	4	11	4
1997	327	27	100	22	100	22	z	z	226	16	121	12	53	8	22	5	9	4	10	3	13	4
1998	391	27	109	18	109	18	z	z	282	20	148	16	84	11	38	7	9	5	16	4	20	6
1999	454	31	96	20	96	20	z	z	358	23	174	17	92	12	40	7	6	3	16	5	29	7
2000	479	31	89	19	89	19	z	z	389	25	189	20	85	17	35	7	10	5	18	6	22	13
2001	481	30	84	19	84	19	z	z	397	23	199	17	99	13	52	10	7	3	17	7	23	5
2002	516	32	90	22	90	22	z	z	426	24	188	14	86	10	38	6	8	3	13	4	28	6
2003	511	33	101	23	101	23	z	z	410	23	204	16	92	11	40	7	12	4	12	4	28	6
2004	589	40	153	24	98	18	54	16	436	32	249	21	96	12	39	7	7	4	13	4	37	9
2005	567	37	186	27	107	19	76	18	381	26	219	19	90	12	39	7	7	3	15	6	29	7
2006	596	39	210	30	110	20	93	22	386	25	219	19	80	11	40	8	7	2	12	4	21	6
2007	574	40	220	31	100	19	113	24	354	25	200	18	65	9	31	6	6	3	10	3	17	5
2008	590	39	224	30	114	22	89	19	366	25	196	18	68	11	29	7	10	6	9	2	20	7
2009	567	30	198	21	114	15	67	13	368	21	204	15	56	9	29	6	8	4	8	3	11	4
2010	591	31	208	24	110	17	81	15	383	19	219	14	57	8	30	5	9	3	11	5	7	3
2011	566	28	203	20	107	15	77	12	363	19	204	14	51	8	26	5	9	5	8	3	8	3
2012	498	27	182	20	112	14	57	13	316	19	153	13	51	8	28	6	9	3	9	3	5	3
2013	526	29	220	22	125	17	70	12	306	19	133	11	46	7	29	6	7	3	5	2	5	2

Outflow

Year	All countries Estimate	+/-CI	European Union Estimate	+/-CI	European Union EU15 Estimate	+/-CI	European Union EU8 Estimate	+/-CI	Non-European Union All Estimate	+/-CI	Commonwealth All Estimate	+/-CI	Old Commonwealth All Estimate	+/-CI	Australia Estimate	+/-CI	Canada Estimate	+/-CI	New Zealand Estimate	+/-CI	South Africa Estimate	+/-CI
1991	285	23	95	16	95	16	z	z	189	16	101	12	68	9	38	6	15	5	9	3	7	3
1992	281	21	86	13	86	13	z	z	195	16	87	8	57	7	35	5	7	2	10	3	5	3
1993	266	20	88	14	88	14	z	z	178	14	92	10	61	8	38	6	9	4	10	3	4	2
1994	238	20	76	14	76	14	z	z	162	15	81	10	51	8	28	5	7	3	12	5	4	2
1995	236	19	76	13	76	13	z	z	161	13	81	9	58	7	33	5	7	3	12	3	6	3
1996	264	28	94	23	94	23	z	z	170	15	94	11	63	8	36	5	9	4	13	3	5	2
1997	279	24	92	18	92	18	z	z	187	17	100	11	65	9	35	6	9	4	13	4	8	4
1998	251	22	85	17	85	17	z	z	167	14	83	10	59	8	36	6	7	4	11	3	6	2
1999	291	24	103	17	103	17	z	z	188	17	101	11	80	10	53	8	8	3	12	3	7	3
2000	321	27	103	17	103	17	z	z	217	20	111	12	86	11	54	9	8	3	17	4	7	3
2001	309	25	95	19	95	19	z	z	214	17	114	12	88	11	54	7	10	5	16	4	8	3
2002	363	29	128	23	128	23	z	z	234	19	123	12	94	11	53	7	13	5	18	4	10	4
2003	363	32	123	24	123	24	z	z	240	21	131	14	104	12	62	10	7	4	21	5	14	5
2004	344	28	125	21	111	19	6	4	219	19	125	14	95	12	54	9	12	5	20	5	9	4
2005	361	31	138	23	118	21	17	9	223	21	128	14	99	12	51	8	12	5	22	5	13	4
2006	398	34	145	26	118	23	24	11	253	21	148	16	114	14	68	11	11	5	21	5	14	5
2007	341	27	131	22	98	19	25	10	210	15	127	11	94	9	58	7	8	3	17	4	11	3
2008	427	41	202	38	123	26	66	20	225	15	119	10	86	8	55	6	11	4	13	2	7	3
2009	368	22	144	18	88	14	50	11	224	12	127	9	88	7	57	6	11	3	14	3	6	2
2010	339	20	136	16	92	14	38	8	204	11	102	7	64	6	40	4	9	2	9	2	7	2
2011	351	22	124	16	80	13	36	9	226	15	124	10	74	8	48	5	8	2	14	5	3	1
2012	321	20	114	16	79	13	26	6	207	12	114	8	69	6	48	5	9	3	8	2	4	2
2013	317	19	114	15	79	13	26	7	203	12	109	8	68	7	44	6	11	3	10	3	3	1

Balance

Year	All countries Estimate	+/-CI	European Union Estimate	+/-CI	European Union EU15 Estimate	+/-CI	European Union EU8 Estimate	+/-CI	Non-European Union All Estimate	+/-CI	Commonwealth All Estimate	+/-CI	Old Commonwealth All Estimate	+/-CI	Australia Estimate	+/-CI	Canada Estimate	+/-CI	New Zealand Estimate	+/-CI	South Africa Estimate	+/-CI
1991	+ 44	33	0~	24	0~	24	z	z	+ 44	23	+ 29	16	- 17	12	- 10	8	- 10	6	+ 2	5	+ 1	6
1992	- 13	29	+ 3	21	+ 3	21	z	z	- 16	20	+ 9	12	- 19	9	- 15	6	- 3	3	- 2	4	+ 1	4
1993	- 1	27	- 14	19	- 14	19	z	z	+ 13	19	+ 10	14	- 18	11	- 15	9	- 5	4	- 3	4	+ 5	4
1994	+ 77	30	+ 19	22	+ 19	22	z	z	+ 58	21	+ 31	13	- 9	10	- 9	6	- 2	4	- 4	6	+ 5	4
1995	+ 76	29	+ 13	20	+ 13	20	z	z	+ 63	21	+ 30	13	- 17	10	- 13	6	0~	5	- 3	5	- 1	3
1996	+ 55	37	+ 5	30	+ 5	30	z	z	+ 50	22	+ 17	16	- 15	12	- 14	8	- 2	6	- 4	5	+ 5	5
1997	+ 48	36	+ 9	28	+ 9	28	z	z	+ 39	23	+ 21	16	- 12	12	- 13	8	0~	6	- 4	4	+ 5	6
1998	+ 140	35	+ 24	25	+ 24	25	z	z	+ 116	24	+ 65	19	+ 25	14	+ 3	9	+ 2	6	+ 5	6	+ 15	6
1999	+ 163	39	- 7	27	- 7	27	z	z	+ 170	29	+ 73	20	+ 12	15	- 13	11	- 2	5	+ 5	6	+ 22	8
2000	+ 158	41	- 14	25	- 14	25	z	z	+ 172	32	+ 78	23	- 1	20	- 18	12	+ 2	6	+ 1	7	+ 15	13
2001	+ 179	:	- 11	27	- 11	27	z	z	+ 183	29	+ 85	21	+ 11	17	- 1	12	- 3	6	+ 1	8	+ 14	6
2002	+ 172	:	- 38	31	- 38	31	z	z	+ 191	30	+ 65	19	- 8	14	- 15	10	- 5	6	- 6	6	+ 17	7
2003	+ 185	:	- 23	34	- 23	34	z	z	+ 170	31	+ 74	21	- 12	17	- 23	12	+ 5	6	- 8	6	+ 14	8
2004	+ 268	:	+ 28	32	- 14	26	+ 47	17	+ 217	37	+ 123	26	+ 2	17	- 16	11	- 4	6	- 7	7	+ 28	9
2005	+ 267	:	+ 48	35	- 11	29	+ 59	20	+ 158	34	+ 91	24	- 9	16	- 12	11	- 5	6	- 8	8	+ 15	8
2006	+ 265	:	+ 65	40	- 8	31	+ 69	25	+ 133	33	+ 72	25	- 34	18	- 28	13	- 4	5	- 9	7	+ 7	8
2007	+ 273	:	+ 88	38	+ 2	27	+ 88	26	+ 145	29	+ 73	21	- 29	13	- 27	10	- 2	4	- 7	5	+ 6	6
2008	+ 229	:	+ 21	49	- 9	34	+ 23	28	+ 142	29	+ 76	20	- 18	14	- 26	9	- 1	7	- 4	3	+ 14	7
2009	+ 229	:	+ 54	28	+ 26	21	+ 18	17	+ 144	24	+ 77	17	- 32	12	- 27	9	- 3	4	- 6	4	+ 4	5
2010	+ 256	:	+ 73	29	+ 18	22	+ 43	17	+ 179	23	+ 117	16	- 7	10	- 10	7	0~	4	+ 2	5	+ 1	4
2011	+ 205	:	+ 79	26	+ 27	19	+ 41	15	+ 137	24	+ 80	17	- 23	12	- 22	8	+ 1	6	- 6	6	+ 5	3
2012	+ 177	34	+ 67	26	+ 33	19	+ 31	14	+ 109	22	+ 39	15	- 19	10	- 20	8	+ 1	4	+ 1	4	+ 1	3
2013	+ 209	35	+ 106	26	+ 46	21	+ 44	14	+ 104	23	+ 24	14	- 21	10	- 15	8	- 3	5	- 5	3	+ 2	3

15.8 Long-Term International Migration, 1991 to 2013
United Kingdom, England and Wales
Country of Last or Next Residence

Year	All countries 2011 Census Revisions[1] Estimate	+/-CI	European Union[2] Estimate	+/-CI	European Union EU15 Estimate	+/-CI	European Union EU8 Estimate	+/-CI	Non-European Union[3] All Estimate	+/-CI	Commonwealth[4] All[4] Estimate	+/-CI	Old Commonwealth All Estimate	+/-CI	Australia Estimate	+/-CI	Canada Estimate	+/-CI	New Zealand Estimate	+/-CI	South Africa Estimate	+/-CI
England and Wales																						
Inflow																						
1991	304	22	89	17	89	17	z	z	215	14	120	11	44	8	25	5	5	2	10	4	4	2
1992	251	20	85	17	85	17	z	z	166	11	87	8	35	5	19	4	4	2	7	3	5	2
1993	249	18	67	11	67	11	z	z	183	14	98	10	40	8	22	6	5	2	6	2	8	3
1994	292	21	86	15	86	15	z	z	207	15	108	9	40	6	18	4	6	2	8	3	8	3
1995	299	22	85	15	85	15	z	z	214	15	107	9	37	7	18	4	6	2	9	4	4	2
1996	300	23	89	17	89	17	z	z	210	16	108	11	45	8	21	5	6	3	9	4	9	3
1997	310	26	99	22	99	22	z	z	212	15	116	11	50	7	21	5	7	3	9	2	13	4
1998	370	26	101	18	101	18	z	z	269	19	139	15	79	11	36	7	8	4	16	4	20	6
1999	424	29	92	20	92	20	z	z	332	21	162	16	83	10	37	7	6	3	13	3	27	6
2000	446	28	77	16	77	16	z	z	369	23	182	19	80	16	33	7	6	3	18	6	22	13
2001	449	29	80	19	80	19	z	z	369	22	183	16	89	12	45	8	5	2	17	7	22	4
2002	485	31	84	21	84	21	z	z	401	22	179	14	82	9	36	6	7	2	12	4	27	6
2003	480	31	93	22	93	22	z	z	387	22	192	15	83	10	37	7	9	3	11	3	27	6
2004	549	38	144	24	92	17	51	16	404	30	231	20	91	12	37	7	7	4	12	4	35	8
2005	523	36	175	26	98	19	74	18	348	24	202	18	80	10	35	6	6	2	12	4	28	7
2006	549	36	190	28	104	19	79	19	359	24	203	18	71	10	34	6	7	2	11	4	19	6
2007	524	38	195	30	86	18	102	23	330	23	187	17	60	9	29	6	6	3	10	3	15	5
2008	528	36	199	28	95	19	84	19	329	23	183	16	61	10	27	6	6	3	8	2	19	7
2009	507	28	168	20	95	14	58	13	339	20	188	14	46	7	25	5	7	3	6	2	7	3
2010	532	29	178	23	94	16	69	15	353	18	205	14	53	8	28	5	7	3	10	5	7	3
2011	515	26	179	19	95	14	68	12	336	18	191	13	46	7	24	5	8	3	7	2	7	3
2012	451	26	160	18	98	13	50	11	291	18	142	12	46	8	25	6	9	3	8	3	5	3
2013	484	28	199	21	112	16	63	12	285	19	126	11	44	7	28	6	7	3	5	2	5	2
Outflow																						
1991	253	21	87	16	87	16	z	z	166	14	89	10	58	7	34	5	11	4	8	3	5	2
1992	248	19	78	13	78	13	z	z	170	14	79	8	53	6	32	5	7	2	9	3	4	2
1993	244	19	82	14	82	14	z	z	162	13	85	9	56	7	36	6	8	3	9	3	3	2
1994	216	19	67	13	67	13	z	z	149	14	72	9	44	7	24	4	7	3	9	3	4	2
1995	216	18	69	13	69	13	z	z	147	12	74	8	54	7	30	5	7	3	11	3	6	3
1996	238	27	85	23	85	23	z	z	152	14	83	10	55	7	31	5	6	3	13	3	5	2
1997	244	21	78	15	78	15	z	z	166	15	90	10	58	8	32	5	6	2	12	3	8	4
1998	223	20	74	16	74	16	z	z	148	13	70	8	49	7	30	5	4	2	9	3	6	2
1999	273	24	96	17	96	17	z	z	177	16	95	11	75	10	49	8	7	3	11	3	7	3
2000	291	26	95	17	95	17	z	z	196	19	102	12	78	10	49	9	7	3	15	4	7	3
2001	282	24	89	18	89	18	z	z	193	16	104	11	79	10	48	7	8	4	15	4	8	3
2002	328	28	113	21	113	21	z	z	214	18	110	11	85	10	49	7	11	5	16	4	10	3
2003	333	31	115	24	115	24	z	z	218	20	117	13	92	12	56	9	5	2	18	5	13	5
2004	311	27	116	20	104	19	6	4	195	18	113	13	86	11	49	8	10	5	18	5	13	4
2005	328	29	126	22	106	20	17	9	202	19	116	13	90	11	47	8	10	4	20	5	13	4
2006	369	33	137	26	111	23	24	11	232	20	137	15	105	13	62	10	10	5	19	5	14	5
2007	307	25	119	21	90	19	20	9	188	14	112	10	83	8	50	6	7	3	15	3	11	3
2008	393	40	186	37	111	25	62	20	207	14	111	9	80	7	53	6	9	3	13	2	6	2
2009	328	20	128	17	78	13	43	11	201	11	115	8	79	7	50	6	10	3	13	3	6	2
2010	308	19	122	16	84	13	33	8	186	10	94	7	59	5	36	4	8	2	9	2	6	2
2011	312	20	108	15	71	12	30	8	204	14	112	9	66	8	43	5	8	2	13	5	3	1
2012	286	19	101	16	71	12	20	5	186	11	104	8	63	6	43	5	8	2	7	2	4	2
2013	280	18	101	14	72	12	22	6	180	11	94	8	57	6	37	5	9	3	8	2	3	1
Balance																						
1991	+ 51	31	+ 2	23	+ 2	23	z	z	+ 49	20	+ 32	15	- 14	11	- 9	8	- 6	4	+ 2	5	- 1	3
1992	+ 4	27	+ 8	21	+ 8	21	z	z	- 4	18	+ 8	11	- 18	8	- 13	6	- 3	3	- 2	4	+ 1	3
1993	+ 5	26	- 16	18	- 16	18	z	z	+ 21	18	+ 14	13	- 15	11	- 14	9	- 3	4	- 3	3	+ 5	4
1994	+ 77	28	+ 18	20	+ 18	20	z	z	+ 58	20	+ 36	12	- 4	9	- 6	6	- 1	4	- 2	5	+ 5	4
1995	+ 83	28	+ 16	20	+ 16	20	z	z	+ 67	20	+ 33	12	- 17	9	- 11	6	- 1	4	- 2	5	- 2	3
1996	+ 62	35	+ 4	29	+ 4	29	z	z	+ 58	21	+ 26	15	- 10	10	- 10	7	0~	4	- 4	5	+ 4	4
1997	+ 66	34	+ 21	26	+ 21	26	z	z	+ 45	21	+ 26	15	- 8	11	- 10	7	+ 1	4	- 3	4	+ 5	6
1998	+ 147	33	+ 26	24	+ 26	24	z	z	+ 120	23	+ 69	17	+ 30	13	+ 5	9	+ 3	5	+ 7	5	+ 14	6
1999	+ 151	38	- 4	26	- 4	26	z	z	+ 155	27	+ 68	19	+ 8	14	- 12	10	- 1	5	+ 2	5	+ 20	7
2000	+ 154	38	- 18	24	- 18	24	z	z	+ 172	30	+ 80	23	+ 2	19	- 16	11	0~	4	+ 3	7	+ 15	13
2001	+ 167	38	- 9	27	- 9	27	z	z	+ 176	27	+ 79	19	+ 10	15	- 3	11	- 3	5	+ 1	8	+ 14	5
2002	+ 158	41	- 29	30	- 29	30	z	z	+ 187	29	+ 69	18	- 4	14	- 13	9	- 4	5	- 4	5	+ 18	7
2003	+ 147	44	- 23	33	- 23	33	z	z	+ 169	29	+ 75	20	- 9	15	- 19	11	+ 4	4	- 8	5	+ 13	8
2004	+ 238	47	+ 28	31	- 12	26	+ 45	16	+ 210	35	+ 118	24	+ 5	16	- 12	11	- 3	6	- 6	6	+ 26	9
2005	+ 195	46	+ 49	34	- 8	27	+ 57	20	+ 146	31	+ 85	22	- 10	15	- 12	10	- 4	5	- 8	7	+ 15	8
2006	+ 180	49	+ 52	38	- 7	30	+ 55	22	+ 127	31	+ 66	24	- 34	17	- 28	12	- 4	5	- 8	6	+ 6	8
2007	+ 217	45	+ 76	37	- 4	26	+ 82	25	+ 141	27	+ 75	19	- 23	12	- 21	8	- 1	4	- 5	5	+ 5	5
2008	+ 135	54	+ 12	47	- 16	31	+ 22	27	+ 123	27	+ 71	19	- 20	12	- 25	8	- 3	4	- 4	3	+ 13	7
2009	+ 179	35	+ 41	26	+ 17	19	+ 14	17	+ 138	22	+ 73	16	- 34	10	- 25	8	- 3	4	- 7	3	+ 1	3
2010	+ 224	35	+ 57	27	+ 10	21	+ 36	17	+ 167	21	+ 111	15	- 6	10	- 8	7	- 1	3	+ 2	5	+ 1	4
2011	+ 203	33	+ 71	24	+ 24	18	+ 38	15	+ 132	23	+ 79	16	- 20	11	- 18	7	0~	4	- 6	6	+ 5	3
2012	+ 165	32	+ 59	24	+ 27	18	+ 30	12	+ 106	21	+ 38	15	- 17	10	- 18	8	0~	4	+ 1	3	0~	3
2013	+ 203	33	+ 98	25	+ 41	20	+ 41	13	+ 105	22	+ 31	13	- 13	9	- 9	7	- 3	4	- 3	3	+ 2	3

Source: Office for National Statistics (ONS), Home Office, Central Statistics Office (CSO) Ireland, Northern Ireland Statistics and Research Agency (NISRA).

15.8 Long-Term International Migration, 1991 to 2013
United Kingdom, England and Wales
Country of Last or Next Residence

thousands

Year	Non-European Union[3] Commonwealth[4] New Commonwealth[4] All[4] Est.	+/-CI	Other African Est.	+/-CI	Indian Subcontinent Est.	+/-CI	Other[4] Est.	+/-CI	Other Foreign[5] All[5] Est.	+/-CI	Remainder of Europe[5] Est.	+/-CI	United States of America Est.	+/-CI	Rest of America Est.	+/-CI	Middle East Est.	+/-CI	Other Est.	+/-CI	All countries Original Estimates[1] Est.	+/-CI
United Kingdom																						
Inflow																						
1991	79	8	27	5	33	4	19	4	104	10	23	5	24	5	4	1	11	2	42	7		
1992	57	6	17	2	23	3	17	4	84	8	21	5	18	4	5	1	8	2	32	5		
1993	60	6	18	2	27	5	15	3	88	10	23	7	23	5	4	1	10	2	29	4		
1994	71	6	23	3	27	3	20	4	108	13	26	8	29	7	5	2	12	4	36	6		
1995	71	7	23	2	28	4	21	5	112	12	23	6	27	6	4	1	13	4	45	8		
1996	64	7	19	4	27	4	18	4	109	12	20	5	32	8	4	1	14	4	39	7		
1997	67	9	13	4	31	6	23	5	106	11	23	5	23	6	5	2	15	4	39	6		
1998	64	11	20	9	27	4	17	4	134	12	32	4	37	8	4	2	13	4	48	6		
1999	83	12	24	8	40	7	19	5	183	16	57	11	31	7	7	3	15	3	74	9		
2000	104	11	30	7	50	6	24	5	200	14	50	7	24	5	12	5	30	5	85	9		
2001	101	12	30	7	51	8	19	5	197	15	37	6	25	5	6	2	31	8	99	10		
2002	102	10	41	7	46	6	15	4	237	19	47	9	29	9	7	2	33	4	122	12		
2003	113	12	40	8	58	8	15	4	206	16	35	9	30	6	8	3	26	5	107	11		
2004	152	17	45	9	90	14	17	5	187	24	18	6	27	8	9	5	29	11	104	18		
2005	130	15	32	7	86	13	11	4	162	18	20	7	25	6	7	2	19	5	90	14		
2006	139	16	23	5	102	14	14	5	167	16	21	7	23	5	8	4	21	5	93	12		
2007	135	15	24	5	95	13	16	6	154	17	17	8	23	5	10	4	23	5	82	12		
2008	128	14	31	8	80	10	17	6	171	18	14	5	28	7	12	6	30	9	87	11		
2009	148	12	31	6	101	10	16	4	164	15	13	7	31	8	9	3	26	5	84	9		
2010	162	11	23	4	121	9	19	5	163	13	14	4	22	5	10	4	24	5	94	10		
2011	153	12	19	4	122	10	12	4	159	13	12	4	23	5	6	2	26	5	91	10		
2012	102	10	19	4	69	8	14	4	163	14	16	5	27	6	7	3	24	5	89	10		
2013	87	9	17	3	55	7	15	5	173	16	18	5	21	4	8	3	25	4	102	13		
Outflow																						
1991	33	7	9	5	10	3	14	5	88	12	12	5	35	8	5	2	14	4	23	5		
1992	29	5	8	3	8	2	14	4	108	14	20	8	40	8	5	3	15	4	28	6		
1993	31	5	8	3	9	3	14	4	86	10	12	4	36	7	5	3	11	3	22	4		
1994	30	6	7	3	7	2	16	4	81	11	18	7	27	5	6	3	13	4	18	3		
1995	23	5	5	2	6	2	12	4	80	10	12	4	30	6	3	2	10	3	25	5		
1996	31	8	9	5	6	3	15	5	76	10	16	7	26	5	3	1	8	3	23	5		
1997	35	6	7	3	9	3	18	4	88	13	21	9	28	7	2	1	13	3	22	5		
1998	24	5	5	3	7	2	11	3	84	11	17	6	27	5	4	2	9	3	27	5		
1999	21	5	3	2	5	2	14	5	87	13	16	7	33	8	4	2	10	4	24	6		
2000	26	6	7	4	8	2	10	4	106	16	22	11	33	8	6	3	15	5	30	7		
2001	26	5	5	2	11	3	10	3	100	13	24	7	28	6	4	2	9	3	34	8		
2002	29	6	5	2	11	3	13	5	112	14	28	8	37	8	3	2	12	4	31	7		
2003	27	6	6	3	11	4	10	4	109	15	35	10	27	7	6	3	7	4	34	8		
2004	31	8	6	3	9	4	15	6	93	13	13	5	25	7	7	4	11	4	37	8		
2005	29	7	6	3	16	5	7	4	95	16	17	6	24	9	8	5	11	3	34	10		
2006	33	8	7	3	17	5	10	5	106	15	17	7	29	7	6	3	16	6	38	8		
2007	33	6	5	1	18	5	9	3	83	10	15	6	18	4	7	3	11	2	31	6		
2008	34	6	8	4	17	4	9	3	105	11	15	6	23	5	10	3	21	5	36	5		
2009	39	4	8	2	23	3	8	2	97	8	11	3	27	5	5	2	15	3	39	5		
2010	38	4	8	2	21	3	8	2	102	9	15	4	25	4	5	2	15	3	43	5		
2011	50	6	7	3	29	4	13	3	103	11	17	8	24	4	4	2	17	3	41	5		
2012	45	5	8	3	26	4	10	3	93	8	9	3	20	3	5	2	14	3	45	6		
2013	41	5	7	2	24	3	11	3	94	8	12	4	24	5	4	1	14	3	41	5		
Balance																						
1991	+ 46	11	+ 18	7	+ 23	5	+ 5	7	+ 16	16	+ 11	7	- 10	9	- 1	2	- 3	4	+ 19	9		
1992	+ 28	8	+ 9	4	+ 15	4	+ 3	6	- 25	16	0~	10	- 22	9	0~	3	- 7	4	+ 4	8		
1993	+ 29	8	+ 10	4	+ 19	5	+ 1	5	+ 3	14	+ 12	8	- 13	8	- 1	3	- 1	4	+ 7	6		
1994	+ 41	8	+ 16	4	+ 20	4	+ 4	6	+ 27	17	+ 9	11	+ 2	9	- 1	3	- 1	6	+ 18	7		
1995	+ 47	8	+ 17	3	+ 22	4	+ 8	6	+ 32	16	+ 12	7	- 3	9	+ 1	2	+ 3	5	+ 20	9		
1996	+ 33	11	+ 10	6	+ 20	5	+ 2	7	+ 33	16	+ 4	8	+ 7	9	+ 1	2	+ 5	5	+ 16	9		
1997	+ 32	11	+ 6	5	+ 22	7	+ 5	7	+ 18	17	+ 2	10	- 5	9	+ 3	2	+ 2	5	+ 16	8		
1998	+ 40	12	+ 14	10	+ 20	5	+ 6	6	+ 50	16	+ 15	7	+ 10	10	0~	3	+ 4	5	+ 21	8		
1999	+ 62	13	+ 22	8	+ 35	8	+ 5	7	+ 97	21	+ 41	13	- 2	11	+ 3	4	+ 5	5	+ 50	10		
2000	+ 79	12	+ 23	8	+ 42	7	+ 14	7	+ 94	22	+ 28	13	- 10	9	+ 6	6	+ 15	7	+ 55	12		
2001	+ 74	13	+ 25	7	+ 40	8	+ 10	6	+ 98	20	+ 13	10	- 3	8	+ 2	3	+ 21	8	+ 65	13	+ 171	40
2002	+ 73	12	+ 36	7	+ 36	7	+ 2	6	+ 126	24	+ 19	12	- 9	12	+ 4	3	+ 21	6	+ 91	14	+ 153	43
2003	+ 86	14	+ 34	8	+ 47	9	+ 5	6	+ 97	22	0~	13	+ 3	9	+ 2	4	+ 19	6	+ 73	14	+ 148	46
2004	+ 122	19	+ 39	10	+ 81	14	+ 2	8	+ 94	27	+ 5	8	+ 2	10	+ 2	6	+ 18	12	+ 68	20	+ 245	49
2005	+ 101	17	+ 26	8	+ 70	14	+ 4	6	+ 67	24	+ 3	9	+ 1	11	- 1	5	+ 8	6	+ 56	17	+ 206	49
2006	+ 106	17	+ 16	6	+ 85	15	+ 4	7	+ 61	22	+ 4	10	- 6	9	+ 3	5	+ 6	8	+ 55	14	+ 198	52
2007	+ 103	17	+ 19	6	+ 77	14	+ 7	7	+ 72	20	+ 2	10	+ 4	7	+ 2	5	+ 12	6	+ 51	13	+ 233	48
2008	+ 94	15	+ 23	8	+ 63	11	+ 8	6	+ 65	21	- 2	8	+ 5	8	+ 2	7	+ 9	11	+ 51	13	+ 163	57
2009	+ 109	13	+ 23	6	+ 78	10	+ 8	5	+ 67	17	+ 2	7	+ 4	9	+ 4	4	+ 11	6	+ 46	10	+ 198	37
2010	+ 124	12	+ 15	5	+ 99	10	+ 11	6	+ 62	16	- 1	6	- 3	6	+ 5	4	+ 10	6	+ 52	12	+ 252	37
2011	+ 103	13	+ 12	5	+ 93	11	- 1	5	+ 56	17	- 5	8	- 1	6	+ 2	3	+ 9	6	+ 50	11	+ 215	35
2012	+ 58	11	+ 10	5	+ 43	9	+ 4	5	+ 70	16	+ 7	5	+ 7	7	+ 2	3	+ 10	6	+ 44	12		
2013	+ 46	10	+ 10	4	+ 31	7	+ 4	5	+ 79	18	+ 6	6	- 3	6	+ 4	3	+ 11	5	+ 61	14		

15.8 Long-Term International Migration, 1991 to 2013
United Kingdom, England and Wales
Country of Last or Next Residence

thousands

England and Wales

Year	New Commonwealth All Est.	+/-CI	Other African Est.	+/-CI	Indian Subcontinent Est.	+/-CI	Other[4] Est.	+/-CI	Other Foreign All[5] Est.	+/-CI	Remainder of Europe[5] Est.	+/-CI	United States of America Est.	+/-CI	Rest of America Est.	+/-CI	Middle East Est.	+/-CI	Other Est.	+/-CI
Inflow																				
1991	76	8	26	5	32	4	18	4	95	9	20	4	21	4	4	1	10	2	39	6
1992	52	5	17	2	22	3	13	3	79	8	20	5	17	4	4	1	8	2	30	4
1993	58	6	17	2	27	4	14	3	84	10	22	7	21	4	3	1	10	2	28	4
1994	68	6	23	3	27	3	18	4	99	12	25	8	22	5	5	2	11	4	35	6
1995	70	7	22	2	27	4	20	5	107	12	23	6	23	6	4	1	13	4	44	8
1996	63	7	19	4	26	4	18	4	102	11	18	4	29	7	4	1	12	4	38	7
1997	66	9	13	4	30	6	23	5	96	9	22	5	20	5	5	2	14	3	35	5
1998	60	10	17	8	27	4	16	4	129	11	31	4	35	8	4	2	12	4	47	6
1999	79	12	23	8	38	7	18	5	170	14	56	10	25	5	7	3	14	3	68	7
2000	102	11	30	7	49	6	24	5	187	13	49	7	22	4	9	4	29	5	78	8
2001	94	11	28	7	48	7	17	4	187	15	35	6	22	4	6	2	29	8	95	10
2002	98	10	39	7	45	6	14	4	222	17	45	9	26	8	7	2	30	4	114	11
2003	108	12	39	8	55	7	15	4	196	16	32	8	29	6	7	3	25	5	102	11
2004	139	16	40	8	85	13	15	4	174	23	17	5	25	7	8	4	27	11	96	17
2005	121	15	30	6	81	12	10	4	147	17	18	7	21	5	7	2	17	5	83	14
2006	132	15	22	5	96	13	14	5	157	15	20	7	22	5	7	3	20	5	88	12
2007	126	14	23	5	88	12	16	6	143	16	15	8	21	5	9	4	21	5	77	11
2008	122	13	29	7	78	10	16	6	147	15	12	5	24	7	10	5	23	5	78	11
2009	143	12	30	6	97	9	16	4	150	14	12	7	26	7	9	3	24	5	79	9
2010	152	11	21	4	114	9	17	5	148	12	12	4	19	4	9	3	22	4	87	10
2011	145	11	18	4	116	10	11	3	145	13	12	4	20	4	6	2	24	5	84	10
2012	96	9	17	4	67	8	12	4	149	14	14	4	25	6	6	3	22	5	82	10
2013	82	8	16	3	51	6	14	4	159	15	15	5	19	4	7	3	23	4	96	13
Outflow																				
1991	30	7	8	5	9	3	13	5	78	10	10	5	29	6	5	2	13	4	21	5
1992	27	5	7	2	7	2	12	3	91	12	17	8	31	6	5	3	13	3	25	5
1993	29	5	7	3	8	3	13	4	77	9	10	4	31	5	5	3	10	3	21	4
1994	28	5	7	3	6	2	15	4	77	10	16	7	26	5	6	3	12	4	17	3
1995	20	4	5	2	5	2	11	3	73	9	11	4	28	6	3	2	9	3	22	4
1996	27	7	8	5	5	2	14	5	70	10	14	6	25	5	3	1	7	3	21	4
1997	32	6	7	3	9	3	16	4	76	12	20	9	23	5	2	1	11	3	19	4
1998	21	5	4	3	7	2	10	3	78	10	14	5	25	5	4	2	8	3	27	5
1999	20	5	3	2	5	2	12	4	82	12	16	7	31	7	4	2	10	4	22	5
2000	24	6	6	4	8	2	10	4	95	15	21	11	29	7	5	3	12	4	28	7
2001	25	5	5	2	11	3	9	3	89	11	23	7	26	6	4	2	9	3	27	5
2002	24	6	5	2	10	3	10	4	104	14	27	8	34	7	3	1	11	4	30	7
2003	24	6	5	3	10	3	9	4	101	15	33	9	25	6	5	2	5	3	33	8
2004	27	7	6	3	9	4	12	5	82	12	12	5	22	6	7	4	8	3	33	8
2005	26	7	6	3	14	5	7	4	86	14	16	6	19	6	6	3	10	3	33	10
2006	32	8	6	3	16	5	10	5	95	14	16	7	25	7	5	3	15	6	33	8
2007	29	5	5	1	16	4	8	2	77	10	15	6	16	4	7	3	10	2	28	5
2008	31	6	8	4	15	4	8	3	95	11	15	6	20	4	9	3	19	5	31	5
2009	36	4	7	2	22	3	7	2	86	7	11	3	22	4	5	2	14	3	34	4
2010	35	4	8	2	20	3	8	2	92	8	14	4	23	4	5	2	13	3	38	4
2011	46	5	7	3	27	4	12	3	92	10	15	7	22	4	4	2	15	3	36	4
2012	41	5	8	3	24	4	9	2	82	8	8	3	18	3	5	2	11	3	39	5
2013	38	5	6	2	21	3	10	3	85	8	11	4	20	3	3	1	13	3	38	5
Balance																				
1991	+ 45	11	+ 18	7	+ 23	5	+ 5	7	+ 17	13	+ 11	6	- 7	7	- 1	2	- 2	4	+ 17	8
1992	+ 25	7	+ 9	3	+ 15	4	+ 1	5	- 12	14	+ 3	9	- 14	7	- 1	3	- 5	4	+ 5	7
1993	+ 29	8	+ 10	4	+ 18	5	+ 1	5	+ 7	13	+ 12	8	- 10	7	- 1	3	0~	4	+ 7	6
1994	+ 40	8	+ 17	4	+ 20	4	+ 3	6	+ 22	16	+ 9	10	- 3	7	- 1	3	- 1	5	+ 18	6
1995	+ 49	8	+ 18	3	+ 22	4	+ 9	6	+ 34	15	+ 13	7	- 6	8	+ 1	2	+ 3	5	+ 23	9
1996	+ 36	10	+ 11	6	+ 21	4	+ 3	7	+ 32	15	+ 4	8	+ 4	8	+ 1	2	+ 5	4	+ 18	9
1997	+ 34	10	+ 6	5	+ 21	6	+ 7	6	+ 20	15	+ 2	10	- 3	7	+ 2	2	+ 3	5	+ 16	6
1998	+ 39	12	+ 13	9	+ 20	5	+ 7	5	+ 51	15	+ 17	6	+ 10	9	0~	3	+ 4	5	+ 20	8
1999	+ 59	13	+ 21	8	+ 33	7	+ 6	7	+ 88	19	+ 40	13	- 7	9	+ 3	4	+ 4	5	+ 47	9
2000	+ 79	12	+ 24	8	+ 41	7	+ 14	7	+ 92	20	+ 28	13	- 7	8	+ 4	5	+ 17	6	+ 50	11
2001	+ 69	12	+ 23	7	+ 38	8	+ 8	5	+ 98	19	+ 12	10	- 4	7	+ 2	3	+ 20	8	+ 68	11
2002	+ 73	12	+ 34	7	+ 35	7	+ 4	6	+ 118	22	+ 19	12	- 8	11	+ 4	3	+ 19	6	+ 84	13
2003	+ 84	13	+ 34	8	+ 44	8	+ 6	6	+ 94	22	- 1	13	+ 4	9	+ 3	4	+ 19	6	+ 70	13
2004	+ 112	17	+ 34	8	+ 76	13	+ 3	7	+ 92	26	+ 5	7	+ 3	9	+ 1	6	+ 19	12	+ 64	19
2005	+ 95	16	+ 24	7	+ 67	13	+ 3	6	+ 61	22	+ 1	9	+ 2	8	+ 1	4	+ 7	6	+ 50	17
2006	+ 100	17	+ 16	6	+ 80	14	+ 5	7	+ 62	21	+ 4	10	- 3	8	+ 1	4	+ 4	7	+ 55	14

Column group headings: Non-European Union[3] / Commonwealth[4] / New Commonwealth[4] / All[4]. Other Foreign[5] / All[5]. All countries — Original Estimates[1] (Estimate, +/-CI).

15.8 Long-Term International Migration, 1991 to 2013
United Kingdom, England and Wales
Country of Last or Next Residence

thousands

Year	Non-European Union[3] Commonwealth[4] New Commonwealth[4]								Other Foreign[5]												All countries	
	All[4]		Other African		Indian Subcontinent		Other[4]		All[5]		Remainder of Europe[5]		United States of America		Rest of America		Middle East		Other		Original Estimates[1]	
	Estimate	+/-CI	Estimate	+/-CI	Estimate	+/-CI	Estimate	+/-CI	Estimate	+/-CI	Estimate	+/-CI	Estimate	+/-CI	Estimate	+/-CI	Estimate	+/-CI	Estimate	+/-CI	Estimate	+/-CI
2007	+ 97	15	+ 18	5	+ 72	13	+ 8	7	+ 66	19	0~	10	+ 5	6	+ 2	5	+ 11	5	+ 49	12		
2008	+ 91	14	+ 21	8	+ 62	10	+ 8	6	+ 52	19	- 3	8	+ 3	8	0~	6	+ 4	8	+ 47	12		
2009	+ 107	13	+ 22	6	+ 76	10	+ 9	5	+ 65	16	+ 2	7	+ 4	8	+ 4	4	+ 10	5	+ 45	10		
2010	+ 117	12	+ 14	5	+ 94	9	+ 9	5	+ 56	15	- 3	6	- 4	6	+ 4	4	+ 9	5	+ 49	10		
2011	+ 99	12	+ 11	5	+ 89	11	- 1	4	+ 53	16	- 3	8	- 2	6	+ 2	3	+ 9	6	+ 47	11		
2012	+ 55	11	+ 9	5	+ 42	8	+ 3	4	+ 68	15	+ 6	5	+ 7	7	+ 2	3	+ 10	6	+ 43	11		
2013	+ 44	9	+ 10	4	+ 30	7	+ 4	5	+ 74	17	+ 4	6	- 1	5	+ 4	3	+ 10	5	+ 58	14		

Source: Office for National Statistics (ONS), Home Office, Central Statistics Office (CSO) Ireland, Northern Ireland Statistics and Research Agency (NISRA).

Totals may not sum due to rounding.

"z" - Not applicable, ":" - Not available, "0~" - Rounds to zero.

1 Net migration ("Balance") figures for the United Kingdom for 2001 to 2011 have been revised in light of the results of the 2011 Census. The original published estimates are shown to the right of the table. The revisions are not reflected in the remainder of the table. The sums of the disaggregated estimates will not therefore match the revised balances. Users should continue to use the estimates in the table to analyse detailed breakdowns of inflows and outflows of long-term international migrants but, in doing so, should bear in mind that the headline net migration estimates have been revised.

2 European Union estimates are for the EU15 (Austria, Belgium, Denmark, Finland, France, Germany, Greece, Republic of Ireland, Italy, Luxembourg, Netherlands, Portugal, Spain and Sweden) up to 2003, the EU25 (the EU15 and the EU8 groupings plus Malta and Cyprus) from 2004 - 2006, the EU27 (the EU25 plus Bulgaria and Romania) from 2007 and the EU28 (the EU27 plus Croatia) from July 2013. Estimates are also shown separately for the EU15 and the EU8 (Czech Republic, Estonia, Hungary, Latvia, Lithuania, Poland, Slovakia and Slovenia).

3 Excludes migrants to and from European Union countries

4 From 2004 onwards, All, New and Other Commonwealth exclude Malta and Cyprus.

5 From 2004 onwards, Other Foreign and Remainder of Europe excludes the eight central and eastern European member states that joined the EU in May 2004 (the EU8). From 2007 onwards, Other Foreign and Remainder of Europe excludes Bulgaria and Romania which joined the EU in January 2007. From July 2013 onwards, Other Foreign and Remainder of Europe excludes Croatia which joined the EU in July 2013.

Statistically Significant Changes

The latest estimates (2013) have been compared with the corresponding estimates for the period one year earlier (2012). Where changes have been found to be statistically significant, the relevant pair of estimates have been highlighted by setting their background colour.

15.9 Grants of settlement by country of nationality and category and in-country refusals of settlement

Year	Geographical region	Country of nationality	Total grants of settlement
2013	*Total	*Total	154,689
2013	Africa North	*Total Africa North	3,431
2013	Africa Sub-Saharan	*Total Africa Sub-Saharan	36,565
2013	America North	*Total America North	7,169
2013	America Central and South	*Total America Central and South	6,066
2013	Asia Central	*Total Asia Central	3,920
2013	Asia East	*Total Asia East	10,242
2013	Asia South	*Total Asia South	56,323
2013	Asia South East	*Total Asia South East	9,669
2013	EU 14	*Total EU 14	:
2013	EU 2	*Total EU 2	:
2013	EU 8	*Total EU 8	:
2013	EU Other	*Total EU Other	72
2013	Europe Other	*Total Europe Other	8,377
2013	Middle East	*Total Middle East	6,491
2013	Oceania	*Total Oceania	6,032
2013	Other	*Total Other	332
2013	Asia Central	Afghanistan	3,417
2013	Europe Other	Albania	629
2013	Africa North	Algeria	720
2013	Oceania	American Samoa	0
2013	Europe Other	Andorra	0
2013	Africa Sub-Saharan	Angola	162
2013	Other	Anguilla (British)	0
2013	America Central and South	Antigua and Barbuda	16
2013	America Central and South	Argentina	121
2013	Europe Other	Armenia	45
2013	America Central and South	Aruba	0
2013	Oceania	Australia	3,752
2013	EU 14	Austria	:
2013	Europe Other	Azerbaijan	193
2013	America Central and South	Bahamas, The	11
2013	Middle East	Bahrain	23
2013	Asia South	Bangladesh	4,986
2013	America Central and South	Barbados	77
2013	Europe Other	Belarus	256
2013	EU 14	Belgium	:
2013	America Central and South	Belize	28
2013	Africa Sub-Saharan	Benin	5
2013	Other	Bermuda (British)	0
2013	Asia South	Bhutan	208
2013	America Central and South	Bolivia	110
2013	America Central and South	Bonaire, Sint Eustatius and Saba	0
2013	Europe Other	Bosnia and Herzegovina	74
2013	Africa Sub-Saharan	Botswana	96
2013	America Central and South	Brazil	1,059
2013	Other	British overseas citizens	16
2013	Asia South East	Brunei	13
2013	EU 2	Bulgaria	:
2013	Africa Sub-Saharan	Burkina	7
2013	Asia South East	Burma	572
2013	Africa Sub-Saharan	Burundi	77
2013	Asia South East	Cambodia	22
2013	Africa Sub-Saharan	Cameroon	566
2013	America North	Canada	1,749
2013	Africa Sub-Saharan	Cape Verde	2
2013	Other	Cayman Islands (British)	0
2013	Africa Sub-Saharan	Central African Republic	0
2013	Africa Sub-Saharan	Chad	14
2013	America Central and South	Chile	87
2013	Asia East	China	7,244
2013	Oceania	Christmas Island	0
2013	Oceania	Cocos (Keeling) Islands	0
2013	America Central and South	Colombia	614
2013	Africa Sub-Saharan	Comoros	1
2013	Africa Sub-Saharan	Congo	123
2013	Africa Sub-Saharan	Congo (Democratic Republic)	1,059
2013	Oceania	Cook Islands	0

15.9 Grants of settlement by country of nationality and category and in-country refusals of settlement

Year	Geographical region	Country of nationality	Total grants of settlement
2013	America Central and South	Costa Rica	23
2013	EU Other	Croatia	72
2013	America Central and South	Cuba	92
2013	America Central and South	Curacao	0
2013	EU Other	Cyprus	:
2013	Europe Other	Cyprus (Northern part of)	13
2013	EU 8	Czech Republic	:
2013	EU 14	Denmark	:
2013	Africa Sub-Saharan	Djibouti	16
2013	America Central and South	Dominica	40
2013	America Central and South	Dominican Republic	51
2013	Asia South East	East Timor	1
2013	America Central and South	Ecuador	115
2013	Africa North	Egypt	778
2013	America Central and South	El Salvador	10
2013	Africa Sub-Saharan	Equatorial Guinea	3
2013	Africa Sub-Saharan	Eritrea	3,475
2013	EU 8	Estonia	:
2013	Africa Sub-Saharan	Ethiopia	411
2013	Other	Falkland Islands (British)	0
2013	Europe Other	Faroe Islands	0
2013	Oceania	Fiji	328
2013	EU 14	Finland	:
2013	Europe Other	Former Yugoslavia	12
2013	EU 14	France	:
2013	America Central and South	French Guiana	0
2013	Oceania	French Polynesia	0
2013	Africa Sub-Saharan	Gabon	1
2013	Africa Sub-Saharan	Gambia, The	618
2013	Europe Other	Georgia	139
2013	EU 14	Germany	:
2013	Africa Sub-Saharan	Ghana	2,527
2013	Other	Gibraltar (British)	0
2013	EU 14	Greece	:
2013	Europe Other	Greenland	0
2013	America Central and South	Grenada	82
2013	America Central and South	Guadeloupe	0
2013	Oceania	Guam	0
2013	America Central and South	Guatemala	27
2013	Africa Sub-Saharan	Guinea	148
2013	Africa Sub-Saharan	Guinea-Bissau	8
2013	America Central and South	Guyana	123
2013	America Central and South	Haiti	4
2013	Oceania	Heard Island and McDonald Islands	0
2013	America Central and South	Honduras	17
2013	Asia East	Hong Kong	357
2013	EU 8	Hungary	:
2013	Europe Other	Iceland	:
2013	Asia South	India	26,198
2013	Asia South East	Indonesia	298
2013	Middle East	Iran	2,475
2013	Middle East	Iraq	1,996
2013	EU 14	Ireland	:
2013	Middle East	Israel	386
2013	EU 14	Italy	:
2013	Africa Sub-Saharan	Ivory Coast	211
2013	America Central and South	Jamaica	2,066
2013	Asia East	Japan	1,159
2013	Middle East	Jordan	241
2013	Asia Central	Kazakhstan	186
2013	Africa Sub-Saharan	Kenya	1,096
2013	Oceania	Kiribati	1
2013	Asia East	Korea (North)	341
2013	Asia East	Korea (South)	781
2013	Europe Other	Kosovo	312
2013	Middle East	Kuwait	156
2013	Asia Central	Kyrgyzstan	64
2013	Asia South East	Laos	19

15.9 Grants of settlement by country of nationality and category and in-country refusals of settlement

Year	Geographical region	Country of nationality	Total grants of settlement
2013	EU 8	Latvia	:
2013	Middle East	Lebanon	251
2013	Africa Sub-Saharan	Lesotho	12
2013	Africa Sub-Saharan	Liberia	48
2013	Africa North	Libya	208
2013	Europe Other	Liechtenstein	:
2013	EU 8	Lithuania	:
2013	EU 14	Luxembourg	:
2013	Asia East	Macau	4
2013	Europe Other	Macedonia	59
2013	Africa Sub-Saharan	Madagascar	9
2013	Africa Sub-Saharan	Malawi	252
2013	Asia South East	Malaysia	1,481
2013	Asia South	Maldives	6
2013	Africa Sub-Saharan	Mali	13
2013	EU Other	Malta	:
2013	Oceania	Marshall Islands	0
2013	America Central and South	Martinique	0
2013	Africa North	Mauritania	1
2013	Africa Sub-Saharan	Mauritius	1,031
2013	Africa Sub-Saharan	Mayotte	0
2013	America Central and South	Mexico	333
2013	Oceania	Micronesia	0
2013	Europe Other	Moldova	65
2013	Europe Other	Monaco	0
2013	Asia East	Mongolia	88
2013	Europe Other	Montenegro	13
2013	Other	Montserrat (British)	0
2013	Africa North	Morocco	528
2013	Africa Sub-Saharan	Mozambique	18
2013	Africa Sub-Saharan	Namibia	54
2013	Oceania	Nauru	1
2013	Asia South	Nepal	2,941
2013	EU 14	Netherlands	:
2013	America Central and South	Netherlands Antilles	:
2013	Oceania	New Caledonia	0
2013	Oceania	New Zealand	1,929
2013	America Central and South	Nicaragua	8
2013	Africa Sub-Saharan	Niger	10
2013	Africa Sub-Saharan	Nigeria	7,699
2013	Oceania	Niue	0
2013	Oceania	Norfolk Island	0
2013	Oceania	Northern Mariana Islands	0
2013	Europe Other	Norway	:
2013	Middle East	Occupied Palestinian Territories	198
2013	Middle East	Oman	5
2013	Other	Other and unknown	30
2013	Asia South	Pakistan	18,095
2013	Oceania	Palau	0
2013	America Central and South	Panama	10
2013	Oceania	Papua New Guinea	7
2013	America Central and South	Paraguay	9
2013	America Central and South	Peru	141
2013	Asia South East	Philippines	4,137
2013	Other	Pitcairn Islands (British)	0
2013	EU 8	Poland	:
2013	EU 14	Portugal	:
2013	America North	Puerto Rico	0
2013	Middle East	Qatar	1
2013	Other	Refugee	215
2013	Africa Sub-Saharan	Reunion	0
2013	EU 2	Romania	:
2013	Europe Other	Russia	1,934
2013	Africa Sub-Saharan	Rwanda	65
2013	Oceania	Samoa	2
2013	Europe Other	San Marino	0
2013	Africa Sub-Saharan	Sao Tome and Principe	0
2013	Middle East	Saudi Arabia	66

15.9 Grants of settlement by country of nationality and category and in-country refusals of settlement

Year	Geographical region	Country of nationality	Total grants of settlement
2013	Africa Sub-Saharan	Senegal	57
2013	Europe Other	Serbia	215
2013	Europe Other	Serbia and Montenegro	:
2013	Africa Sub-Saharan	Seychelles	34
2013	Africa Sub-Saharan	Sierra Leone	406
2013	Asia South East	Singapore	286
2013	EU 8	Slovakia	:
2013	EU 8	Slovenia	:
2013	Oceania	Solomon Islands	1
2013	Africa Sub-Saharan	Somalia	4,341
2013	Africa Sub-Saharan	South Africa	5,778
2013	Other	South Georgia and South Sandwich Islands	0
2013	EU 14	Spain	:
2013	Asia South	Sri Lanka	3,889
2013	Other	St. Helena (British)	0
2013	America Central and South	St. Kitts and Nevis	14
2013	America Central and South	St. Lucia	121
2013	America Central and South	St. Maarten (Dutch Part)	0
2013	America Central and South	St. Martin (French Part)	0
2013	America Central and South	St. Pierre and Miquelon	0
2013	America Central and South	St. Vincent and the Grenadines	100
2013	Other	Stateless	71
2013	Africa North	Sudan	936
2013	Africa Sub-Saharan	Sudan (South)	0
2013	America Central and South	Surinam	0
2013	Europe Other	Svalbard and Jan Mayen	0
2013	Africa Sub-Saharan	Swaziland	18
2013	EU 14	Sweden	:
2013	Europe Other	Switzerland	:
2013	Middle East	Syria	384
2013	Asia East	Taiwan	268
2013	Asia Central	Tajikistan	26
2013	Africa Sub-Saharan	Tanzania	340
2013	Asia South East	Thailand	2,336
2013	Africa Sub-Saharan	Togo	36
2013	Oceania	Tokelau	0
2013	Oceania	Tonga	10
2013	America Central and South	Trinidad and Tobago	349
2013	Africa North	Tunisia	260
2013	Europe Other	Turkey	3,518
2013	Asia Central	Turkmenistan	46
2013	Other	Turks and Caicos Islands (British)	0
2013	Oceania	Tuvalu	1
2013	Africa Sub-Saharan	Uganda	653
2013	Europe Other	Ukraine	900
2013	Middle East	United Arab Emirates	3
2013	America North	United States	5,420
2013	America Central and South	Uruguay	18
2013	Asia Central	Uzbekistan	181
2013	Oceania	Vanuatu	0
2013	Europe Other	Vatican City	0
2013	America Central and South	Venezuela	190
2013	Asia South East	Vietnam	504
2013	Other	Virgin Islands (British)	0
2013	America North	Virgin Islands (US)	0
2013	Oceania	Wallis and Futuna	0
2013	Africa North	Western Sahara	0
2013	Middle East	Yemen	306
2013	Africa Sub-Saharan	Zambia	389
2013	Africa Sub-Saharan	Zimbabwe	4,676

Source: Home Office: Immigration Statistics

: = Not applicable.
.. = Not available.

15.10 Asylum applications and initial decisions for main applicants, by country of nationality

Year	Geographical region	Country of nationality	Total applications
2013	*Total	*Total	23,584
2013	Africa North	*Total Africa North	1,499
2013	Africa Sub-Saharan	*Total Africa Sub-Saharan	4,997
2013	America North	*Total America North	31
2013	America Central and South	*Total America Central and South	248
2013	Asia Central	*Total Asia Central	1,075
2013	Asia East	*Total Asia East	813
2013	Asia South	*Total Asia South	7,325
2013	Asia South East	*Total Asia South East	604
2013	EU 14	*Total EU 14	12
2013	EU 2	*Total EU 2	19
2013	EU 8	*Total EU 8	187
2013	EU Other	*Total EU Other	0
2013	Europe Other	*Total Europe Other	1,794
2013	Middle East	*Total Middle East	4,688
2013	Oceania	*Total Oceania	6
2013	Other	*Total Other	286
2013	Asia Central	Afghanistan	1,038
2013	Europe Other	Albania	1,325
2013	Africa North	Algeria	168
2013	Oceania	American Samoa	0
2013	Europe Other	Andorra	0
2013	Africa Sub-Saharan	Angola	47
2013	Other	Anguilla (British)	0
2013	America Central and South	Antigua and Barbuda	2
2013	America Central and South	Argentina	0
2013	Europe Other	Armenia	11
2013	America Central and South	Aruba	0
2013	Oceania	Australia	4
2013	EU 14	Austria	0
2013	Europe Other	Azerbaijan	15
2013	America Central and South	Bahamas, The	1
2013	Middle East	Bahrain	11
2013	Asia South	Bangladesh	1,123
2013	America Central and South	Barbados	4
2013	Europe Other	Belarus	12
2013	EU 14	Belgium	0
2013	America Central and South	Belize	0
2013	Africa Sub-Saharan	Benin	2
2013	Other	Bermuda (British)	0
2013	Asia South	Bhutan	3
2013	America Central and South	Bolivia	6
2013	America Central and South	Bonaire, Sint Eustatius and Saba	0
2013	Europe Other	Bosnia and Herzegovina	4
2013	Africa Sub-Saharan	Botswana	8
2013	America Central and South	Brazil	19
2013	Other	British overseas citizens	0
2013	Asia South East	Brunei	0
2013	EU 2	Bulgaria	1
2013	Africa Sub-Saharan	Burkina	2
2013	Asia South East	Burma	70
2013	Africa Sub-Saharan	Burundi	4
2013	Asia South East	Cambodia	0
2013	Africa Sub-Saharan	Cameroon	118
2013	America North	Canada	6
2013	Africa Sub-Saharan	Cape Verde	0
2013	Other	Cayman Islands (British)	0
2013	Africa Sub-Saharan	Central African Republic	4
2013	Africa Sub-Saharan	Chad	21
2013	America Central and South	Chile	1
2013	Asia East	China	739
2013	Oceania	Christmas Island	0
2013	Oceania	Cocos (Keeling) Islands	0
2013	America Central and South	Colombia	8
2013	Africa Sub-Saharan	Comoros	0
2013	Africa Sub-Saharan	Congo	30
2013	Africa Sub-Saharan	Congo (Democratic Republic)	206
2013	Oceania	Cook Islands	0
2013	America Central and South	Costa Rica	0
2013	EU Other	Croatia	0

509

15.10 Asylum applications and initial decisions for main applicants, by country of nationality

Year	Geographical region	Country of nationality	Total applications
2013	America Central and South	Cuba	3
2013	America Central and South	Curacao	0
2013	EU Other	Cyprus	0
2013	Europe Other	Cyprus (Northern part of)	1
2013	EU 8	Czech Republic	6
2013	EU 14	Denmark	0
2013	Africa Sub-Saharan	Djibouti	0
2013	America Central and South	Dominica	3
2013	America Central and South	Dominican Republic	0
2013	Asia South East	East Timor	0
2013	America Central and South	Ecuador	7
2013	Africa North	Egypt	229
2013	America Central and South	El Salvador	9
2013	Africa Sub-Saharan	Equatorial Guinea	0
2013	Africa Sub-Saharan	Eritrea	1,387
2013	EU 8	Estonia	1
2013	Africa Sub-Saharan	Ethiopia	161
2013	Other	Falkland Islands (British)	0
2013	Europe Other	Faroe Islands	0
2013	Oceania	Fiji	2
2013	EU 14	Finland	0
2013	Europe Other	Former Yugoslavia	2
2013	EU 14	France	3
2013	America Central and South	French Guiana	0
2013	Oceania	French Polynesia	0
2013	Africa Sub-Saharan	Gabon	1
2013	Africa Sub-Saharan	Gambia, The	251
2013	Europe Other	Georgia	33
2013	EU 14	Germany	2
2013	Africa Sub-Saharan	Ghana	172
2013	Other	Gibraltar (British)	0
2013	EU 14	Greece	1
2013	Europe Other	Greenland	0
2013	America Central and South	Grenada	3
2013	America Central and South	Guadeloupe	0
2013	Oceania	Guam	0
2013	America Central and South	Guatemala	0
2013	Africa Sub-Saharan	Guinea	67
2013	Africa Sub-Saharan	Guinea-Bissau	0
2013	America Central and South	Guyana	6
2013	America Central and South	Haiti	0
2013	Oceania	Heard Island and McDonald Islands	0
2013	America Central and South	Honduras	5
2013	Asia East	Hong Kong	3
2013	EU 8	Hungary	2
2013	Europe Other	Iceland	0
2013	Asia South	India	974
2013	Asia South East	Indonesia	4
2013	Middle East	Iran	2,410
2013	Middle East	Iraq	310
2013	EU 14	Ireland	0
2013	Middle East	Israel	8
2013	EU 14	Italy	2
2013	Africa Sub-Saharan	Ivory Coast	74
2013	America Central and South	Jamaica	120
2013	Asia East	Japan	2
2013	Middle East	Jordan	26
2013	Asia Central	Kazakhstan	9
2013	Africa Sub-Saharan	Kenya	67
2013	Oceania	Kiribati	0
2013	Asia East	Korea (North)	33
2013	Asia East	Korea (South)	8
2013	Europe Other	Kosovo	23
2013	Middle East	Kuwait	67
2013	Asia Central	Kyrgyzstan	7
2013	Asia South East	Laos	1
2013	EU 8	Latvia	13
2013	Middle East	Lebanon	44
2013	Africa Sub-Saharan	Lesotho	0
2013	Africa Sub-Saharan	Liberia	5

15.10 Asylum applications and initial decisions for main applicants, by country of nationality

Year	Geographical region	Country of nationality	Total applications
2013	Africa North	Libya	243
2013	Europe Other	Liechtenstein	0
2013	EU 8	Lithuania	25
2013	EU 14	Luxembourg	0
2013	Asia East	Macau	0
2013	Europe Other	Macedonia	0
2013	Africa Sub-Saharan	Madagascar	0
2013	Africa Sub-Saharan	Malawi	109
2013	Asia South East	Malaysia	49
2013	Asia South	Maldives	1
2013	Africa Sub-Saharan	Mali	21
2013	EU Other	Malta	0
2013	Oceania	Marshall Islands	0
2013	America Central and South	Martinique	0
2013	Africa North	Mauritania	5
2013	Africa Sub-Saharan	Mauritius	39
2013	Africa Sub-Saharan	Mayotte	0
2013	America Central and South	Mexico	9
2013	Oceania	Micronesia	0
2013	Europe Other	Moldova	3
2013	Europe Other	Monaco	0
2013	Asia East	Mongolia	25
2013	Europe Other	Montenegro	0
2013	Other	Montserrat (British)	0
2013	Africa North	Morocco	66
2013	Africa Sub-Saharan	Mozambique	1
2013	Africa Sub-Saharan	Namibia	13
2013	Oceania	Nauru	0
2013	Asia South	Nepal	54
2013	EU 14	Netherlands	2
2013	America Central and South	Netherlands Antilles	:
2013	Oceania	New Caledonia	0
2013	Oceania	New Zealand	0
2013	America Central and South	Nicaragua	0
2013	Africa Sub-Saharan	Niger	5
2013	Africa Sub-Saharan	Nigeria	931
2013	Oceania	Niue	0
2013	Oceania	Norfolk Island	0
2013	Oceania	Northern Mariana Islands	0
2013	Europe Other	Norway	0
2013	Middle East	Occupied Palestinian Territories	102
2013	Middle East	Oman	0
2013	Other	Other and unknown	11
2013	Asia South	Pakistan	3,359
2013	Oceania	Palau	0
2013	America Central and South	Panama	0
2013	Oceania	Papua New Guinea	0
2013	America Central and South	Paraguay	0
2013	America Central and South	Peru	3
2013	Asia South East	Philippines	31
2013	Other	Pitcairn Islands (British)	0
2013	EU 8	Poland	138
2013	EU 14	Portugal	2
2013	America North	Puerto Rico	0
2013	Middle East	Qatar	2
2013	Other	Refugee	139
2013	Africa Sub-Saharan	Reunion	0
2013	EU 2	Romania	18
2013	Europe Other	Russia	66
2013	Africa Sub-Saharan	Rwanda	20
2013	Oceania	Samoa	0
2013	Europe Other	San Marino	0
2013	Africa Sub-Saharan	Sao Tome and Principe	0
2013	Middle East	Saudi Arabia	18
2013	Africa Sub-Saharan	Senegal	33
2013	Europe Other	Serbia	3
2013	Europe Other	Serbia and Montenegro	:
2013	Africa Sub-Saharan	Seychelles	1
2013	Africa Sub-Saharan	Sierra Leone	72
2013	Asia South East	Singapore	1

15.10 Asylum applications and initial decisions for main applicants, by country of nationality

Year	Geographical region	Country of nationality	Total applications
2013	EU 8	Slovakia	2
2013	EU 8	Slovenia	0
2013	Oceania	Solomon Islands	0
2013	Africa Sub-Saharan	Somalia	448
2013	Africa Sub-Saharan	South Africa	47
2013	Other	South Georgia and South Sandwich Islands	0
2013	EU 14	Spain	0
2013	Asia South	Sri Lanka	1,811
2013	Other	St. Helena (British)	0
2013	America Central and South	St. Kitts and Nevis	2
2013	America Central and South	St. Lucia	6
2013	America Central and South	St. Maarten (Dutch Part)	0
2013	America Central and South	St. Martin (French Part)	0
2013	America Central and South	St. Pierre and Miquelon	0
2013	America Central and South	St. Vincent and the Grenadines	5
2013	Other	Stateless	136
2013	Africa North	Sudan	743
2013	Africa Sub-Saharan	Sudan (South)	1
2013	America Central and South	Surinam	0
2013	Europe Other	Svalbard and Jan Mayen	0
2013	Africa Sub-Saharan	Swaziland	7
2013	EU 14	Sweden	0
2013	Europe Other	Switzerland	0
2013	Middle East	Syria	1,648
2013	Asia East	Taiwan	3
2013	Asia Central	Tajikistan	1
2013	Africa Sub-Saharan	Tanzania	36
2013	Asia South East	Thailand	11
2013	Africa Sub-Saharan	Togo	8
2013	Oceania	Tokelau	0
2013	Oceania	Tonga	0
2013	America Central and South	Trinidad and Tobago	21
2013	Africa North	Tunisia	39
2013	Europe Other	Turkey	250
2013	Asia Central	Turkmenistan	3
2013	Other	Turks and Caicos Islands (British)	0
2013	Oceania	Tuvalu	0
2013	Africa Sub-Saharan	Uganda	214
2013	Europe Other	Ukraine	46
2013	Middle East	United Arab Emirates	3
2013	America North	United States	25
2013	America Central and South	Uruguay	0
2013	Asia Central	Uzbekistan	17
2013	Oceania	Vanuatu	0
2013	Europe Other	Vatican City	0
2013	America Central and South	Venezuela	5
2013	Asia South East	Vietnam	437
2013	Other	Virgin Islands (British)	0
2013	America North	Virgin Islands (US)	0
2013	Oceania	Wallis and Futuna	0
2013	Africa North	Western Sahara	6
2013	Middle East	Yemen	39
2013	Africa Sub-Saharan	Zambia	24
2013	Africa Sub-Saharan	Zimbabwe	340

: = Not applicable.

.. = Not available.

Source: Home Office: Immigration Statistics

Data, after April 2000 for asylum applications have been taken from the Asylum Case Information Database. Prior to this date manual counts were taken.

The tables do not include grants of asylum or ELR (exceptional leave to remain) or refusals on non-compliance grounds under the backlog criteria in 1999 and 2000 which aimed to reduce the pre-1996 asylum application backlog.

'Fresh claims' are when a human rights or asylum claim has been refused, withdrawn or treated as withdrawn under paragraph 333C of Immigration Rule 353 and any appeal relating to that claim is no longer pending, the decision maker will consider any further submissions and, if rejected, will then determine whether they amount to a fresh claim. The submissions will amount to a fresh claim if they are significantly different from the material that has previously been considered. The submissions will only be significantly different if the content: had not already been considered; and taken together with the previously considered material, created a realistic prospect of success, not withstanding its rejection.

'Pending' cases are those asylum applications, including fresh claims, lodged since 1 April 2006 which are still under consideration at the end of the reference period.

15.11 Previous marital status and manner of solemnisation (numbers and percentages), 1981, 1991, 2001, 2002, 2007–2012

England and Wales

Year of marriage		Total marriages		Civil marriages		Religious marriages	
		Number	Percentage	Number	Percentage	Number	Percentage
2012ᴾ	**Total marriages**	**262,240**	**100.0**	**184,320**	**70.3**	**77,910**	**29.7**
	First marriage for both	175,040	66.7	111,130	42.4	63,910	24.4
	First marriage for one	48,880	18.6	39,750	15.2	9,130	3.5
	Remarriage for both	38,320	14.6	33,450	12.8	4,870	1.9
2011	**Total marriages**	**249,133**	**100.0**	**174,681**	**70.1**	**74,452**	**29.9**
	First marriage for both	165,467	66.4	104,609	42.0	60,858	24.4
	First marriage for one	47,425	19.0	38,557	15.5	8,868	3.6
	Remarriage for both	36,241	14.5	31,515	12.6	4,726	1.9
2010	**Total marriages**	**243,808**	**100.0**	**165,680**	**68.0**	**78,128**	**32.0**
	First marriage for both	161,028	66.0	96,903	39.7	64,125	26.3
	First marriage for one	46,190	18.9	37,069	15.2	9,121	3.7
	Remarriage for both	36,590	15.0	31,708	13.0	4,882	2.0
2009	**Total marriages**	**232,443**	**100.0**	**155,950**	**67.1**	**76,493**	**32.9**
	First marriage for both	151,392	65.1	88,741	38.2	62,651	27.0
	First marriage for one	44,323	19.1	35,469	15.3	8,854	3.8
	Remarriage for both	36,728	15.8	31,740	13.7	4,988	2.1
2008	**Total marriages**	**235,794**	**100.0**	**157,296**	**66.7**	**78,498**	**33.3**
	First marriage for both	149,204	63.3	85,323	36.2	63,881	27.1
	First marriage for one	46,712	19.8	37,238	15.8	9,474	4.0
	Remarriage for both	39,878	16.9	34,735	14.7	5,143	2.2
2007	**Total marriages**	**235,367**	**100.0**	**156,198**	**66.4**	**79,169**	**33.6**
	First marriage for both	146,216	62.1	82,351	35.0	63,865	27.1
	First marriage for one	47,669	20.3	37,941	16.1	9,728	4.1
	Remarriage for both	41,482	17.6	35,906	15.3	5,576	2.4
2002	**Total marriages**	**255,596**	**100.0**	**169,210**	**66.2**	**86,386**	**33.8**
	First marriage for both	151,014	59.1	82,564	32.3	68,450	26.8
	First marriage for one	57,768	22.6	46,207	18.1	11,561	4.5
	Remarriage for both	46,814	18.3	40,439	15.8	6,375	2.5
2001	**Total marriages**	**249,227**	**100.0**	**160,238**	**64.3**	**88,989**	**35.7**
	First marriage for both	148,642	59.6	77,048	30.9	71,594	28.7
	First marriage for one	55,943	22.4	44,601	17.9	11,342	4.6
	Remarriage for both	44,642	17.9	38,589	15.5	6,053	2.4
1991	**Total marriages**	**306,756**	**100.0**	**151,333**	**49.3**	**155,423**	**50.7**
	First marriage for both	192,238	62.7	64,614	21.1	127,624	41.6
	First marriage for one	63,159	20.6	44,643	14.6	18,516	6.0
	Remarriage for both	51,359	16.7	42,076	13.7	9,283	3.0
1981	**Total marriages**	**351,973**	**100.0**	**172,514**	**49.0**	**179,459**	**51.0**
	First marriage for both	227,713	64.7	71,530	20.3	156,183	44.4
	First marriage for one	67,048	19.0	51,628	14.7	15,420	4.4
	Remarriage for both	57,212	16.3	49,356	14.0	7,856	2.2

Figures and percentages may not sum due to rounding.
p Figures for 2012 are provisional.

Source: Office for National Statistics

15.12 Duration of marriage at divorce by age of wife at marriage, 1982-2012

England and Wales **Numbers**

Year of divorce	Age of wife at marriage	All durations	Duration of marriage (completed years)								
			0-2 years	0 years	1 year	2 years	3 years	4 years	5-9 years	5 years	6 years
2012	All ages	118,140	6,268	49	2,033	4,186	5,710	6,550	33,027	6,748	6,542
	Under 20	9,195	193	3	47	143	248	326	1,790	349	316
	20-24	37,445	1,513	7	485	1,021	1,454	1,674	8,183	1,695	1,613
	25-29	34,055	1,937	19	632	1,286	1,738	1,958	9,374	2,038	1,895
	30-44	33,018	2,120	13	689	1,418	1,908	2,160	11,925	2,247	2,349
	45 and over	4,427	505	7	180	318	362	432	1,755	419	369
2011	All ages	117,558	5,803	30	1,748	4,025	5,890	6,654	32,989	6,727	7,111
	Under 20	9,727	238	1	59	178	309	329	1,915	344	400
	20-24	38,327	1,392	10	416	966	1,535	1,681	8,320	1,745	1,751
	25-29	33,379	1,783	11	544	1,228	1,734	1,986	9,406	1,949	2,001
	30-44	31,999	1,924	4	576	1,344	1,931	2,246	11,736	2,332	2,604
	45 and over	4,126	466	4	153	309	381	412	1,612	357	355
2010	All ages	119,589	6,278	17	1,897	4,364	6,109	6,936	33,700	7,418	7,652
	Under 20	10,619	255	-	85	170	332	351	2,085	450	489
	20-24	39,963	1,528	4	429	1,095	1,551	1,849	8,624	1,895	2,072
	25-29	33,309	1,874	3	583	1,288	1,795	1,947	9,609	2,072	2,123
	30-44	31,660	2,134	8	624	1,502	2,009	2,404	11,834	2,597	2,607
	45 and over	4,038	487	2	176	309	422	385	1,548	404	361
2009	All ages	113,949	6,270	21	1,951	4,298	5,884	6,947	31,290	7,561	6,864
	Under 20	10,529	267	1	60	206	293	371	1,943	478	439
	20-24	39,231	1,540	1	472	1,067	1,516	1,813	8,350	2,065	1,889
	25-29	31,400	1,808	8	572	1,228	1,715	1,986	8,994	2,106	1,898
	30-44	29,021	2,184	7	683	1,494	1,981	2,389	10,610	2,554	2,307
	45 and over	3,768	471	4	164	303	379	388	1,393	358	331
2008	All ages	121,708	6,937	27	2,103	4,807	6,776	7,929	31,803	7,369	6,714
	Under 20	11,657	319	1	78	240	365	500	1,948	478	407
	20-24	42,578	1,685	10	463	1,212	1,798	2,103	8,401	2,043	1,879
	25-29	33,050	2,044	7	621	1,416	1,875	2,148	9,287	1,985	1,863
	30-44	30,642	2,379	7	741	1,631	2,349	2,751	10,819	2,512	2,304
	45 and over	3,781	510	2	200	308	389	427	1,348	351	261
2007	All ages	128,131	8,195	38	2,558	5,599	7,206	7,574	32,419	7,164	7,046
	Under 20	13,224	411	1	120	290	417	487	2,053	430	470
	20-24	45,806	2,039	7	623	1,409	1,905	1,977	8,481	1,928	1,814
	25-29	34,564	2,234	13	668	1,553	1,990	2,115	9,987	2,099	2,106
	30-44	30,808	2,942	11	929	2,002	2,521	2,591	10,617	2,403	2,366
	45 and over	3,729	569	6	218	345	373	404	1,281	304	290
2006	All ages	132,140	8,763	37	2,793	5,933	7,226	7,376	33,736	7,398	7,310
	Under 20	14,441	503	2	157	344	376	447	2,232	474	506
	20-24	48,396	2,240	9	668	1,563	1,975	1,997	8,954	1,967	1,901
	25-29	35,054	2,381	13	796	1,572	2,052	2,172	10,416	2,182	2,181
	30-44	30,613	3,087	6	966	2,115	2,441	2,424	10,858	2,473	2,437
	45 and over	3,636	552	7	206	339	382	336	1,276	302	285
2005	All ages	141,322	9,573	49	3,181	6,343	7,520	8,175	36,064	7,920	7,697
	Under 20	16,473	537	2	148	387	515	579	2,389	576	544
	20-24	52,884	2,469	15	783	1,671	2,025	2,203	9,961	2,083	2,016
	25-29	36,992	2,545	9	845	1,691	2,081	2,507	11,296	2,367	2,431
	30-44	31,213	3,413	17	1,171	2,225	2,540	2,554	11,025	2,545	2,406
	45 and over	3,760	609	6	234	369	359	332	1,393	349	300
2004	All ages	152,923	10,101	42	3,345	6,714	8,319	8,894	39,681	8,840	8,375
	Under 20	18,655	626	3	201	422	557	662	2,626	667	581
	20-24	59,356	2,662	7	854	1,801	2,361	2,494	11,818	2,477	2,359
	25-29	39,459	2,871	8	947	1,916	2,480	2,642	12,426	2,674	2,593
	30-44	31,631	3,353	15	1,122	2,216	2,542	2,724	11,356	2,679	2,515
	45 and over	3,822	589	9	221	359	379	372	1,455	343	327
2003	All ages	153,065	10,286	42	3,283	6,961	8,276	8,882	40,497	8,968	8,639
	Under 20	20,008	694	-	198	496	591	662	2,644	614	562
	20-24	60,883	2,735	11	825	1,899	2,352	2,587	12,944	2,636	2,564
	25-29	38,628	2,954	9	903	2,042	2,554	2,715	12,663	2,778	2,716
	30-44	29,873	3,304	10	1,131	2,163	2,444	2,554	10,865	2,600	2,468
	45 and over	3,673	599	12	226	361	335	364	1,381	340	329

15.12 Duration of marriage at divorce by age of wife at marriage, 1982-2012

England and Wales   Numbers

Year of divorce	Age of wife at marriage	7 years	8 years	9 years	10-14 years	15-19 years	20-24 years	25-29 years	30 years and over	Not stated	Median duration
2012	All ages	6,919	6,961	5,857	22,356	15,733	12,215	7,649	8,632	-	11.5
	Under 20	361	406	358	1,259	795	1,056	1,088	2,440	-	..
	20-24	1,700	1,746	1,429	5,523	5,142	5,498	4,024	4,434	-	..
	25-29	1,910	1,843	1,688	7,188	5,426	3,541	1,669	1,224	-	..
	30-44	2,576	2,634	2,119	7,551	4,048	1,984	816	506	-	..
	45 and over	372	332	263	835	322	136	52	28	-	..
2011	All ages	7,263	6,389	5,499	22,126	15,547	12,228	7,712	8,609	-	11.5
	Under 20	487	384	300	1,276	901	1,111	1,130	2,518	-	..
	20-24	1,902	1,619	1,303	5,749	5,361	5,834	4,052	4,403	-	..
	25-29	2,042	1,756	1,658	7,097	5,198	3,370	1,644	1,161	-	..
	30-44	2,488	2,323	1,989	7,267	3,754	1,804	831	506	-	..
	45 and over	344	307	249	737	333	109	55	21	-	..
2010	All ages	7,101	5,995	5,534	22,105	15,772	12,412	7,639	8,638	-	11.4
	Under 20	432	381	333	1,280	1,012	1,305	1,366	2,633	-	..
	20-24	1,825	1,481	1,351	5,967	5,920	5,929	4,117	4,478	-	..
	25-29	2,018	1,690	1,706	7,163	5,134	3,369	1,351	1,067	-	..
	30-44	2,527	2,189	1,914	6,961	3,419	1,693	770	436	-	..
	45 and over	299	254	230	734	287	116	35	24	-	..
2009	All ages	5,968	5,634	5,263	20,591	15,390	11,855	7,490	8,225	7	11.4
	Under 20	355	357	314	1,177	1,092	1,337	1,484	2,565	-	..
	20-24	1,629	1,466	1,301	5,909	5,944	5,964	3,956	4,235	4	..
	25-29	1,679	1,648	1,663	6,704	4,926	2,983	1,299	985	-	..
	30-44	2,068	1,919	1,762	6,090	3,128	1,494	713	429	3	..
	45 and over	237	244	223	711	300	77	38	11	-	..
2008	All ages	6,365	6,034	5,321	21,561	16,945	12,706	8,136	8,907	8	11.5
	Under 20	358	363	342	1,174	1,274	1,526	1,749	2,800	2	..
	20-24	1,619	1,528	1,332	6,315	6,881	6,511	4,247	4,632	5	..
	25-29	1,880	1,862	1,697	7,075	5,204	2,945	1,389	1,082	1	..
	30-44	2,228	2,032	1,743	6,324	3,295	1,620	722	383	-	..
	45 and over	280	249	207	673	291	104	29	10	-	..
2007	All ages	6,560	6,072	5,577	23,427	18,203	13,117	8,701	9,282	7	11.7
	Under 20	423	395	335	1,240	1,542	1,929	2,099	3,045	1	..
	20-24	1,650	1,607	1,482	7,397	7,930	6,757	4,498	4,820	2	..
	25-29	2,021	1,953	1,808	7,777	5,240	2,802	1,377	1,039	3	..
	30-44	2,203	1,890	1,755	6,343	3,219	1,526	686	362	1	..
	45 and over	263	227	197	670	272	103	41	16	-	..
2006	All ages	6,769	6,249	6,010	24,606	18,735	13,472	8,764	9,449	13	11.6
	Under 20	490	397	365	1,491	1,831	2,191	2,241	3,128	1	..
	20-24	1,751	1,681	1,654	8,443	8,470	6,949	4,415	4,947	6	..
	25-29	2,159	2,004	1,890	7,708	5,157	2,745	1,365	1,053	5	..
	30-44	2,107	1,939	1,902	6,263	3,034	1,483	717	305	1	..
	45 and over	262	228	199	701	243	104	26	16	-	..
2005	All ages	7,343	6,801	6,303	26,310	20,310	14,268	9,241	9,852	9	11.6
	Under 20	478	429	362	1,722	2,299	2,605	2,571	3,255	1	..
	20-24	2,007	1,920	1,935	9,570	9,450	7,368	4,636	5,200	2	..
	25-29	2,291	2,173	2,034	8,364	5,146	2,683	1,310	1,058	2	..
	30-44	2,266	2,040	1,768	5,965	3,161	1,526	699	326	4	..
	45 and over	301	239	204	689	254	86	25	13	-	..
2004	All ages	7,900	7,683	6,883	28,984	21,515	15,431	9,705	10,293	-	11.5
	Under 20	498	485	395	2,133	2,737	3,103	2,804	3,407	-	..
	20-24	2,324	2,389	2,269	11,471	10,355	7,893	4,792	5,510	-	..
	25-29	2,517	2,436	2,206	8,671	5,082	2,823	1,427	1,037	-	..
	30-44	2,274	2,111	1,777	6,064	3,093	1,539	639	321	-	..
	45 and over	287	262	236	645	248	73	43	18	-	..
2003	All ages	8,228	7,686	6,976	29,751	20,863	14,974	9,627	9,907	2	11.3
	Under 20	551	495	422	2,613	2,911	3,559	2,985	3,349	-	..
	20-24	2,569	2,622	2,553	12,281	10,413	7,534	4,708	5,327	2	..
	25-29	2,594	2,361	2,214	8,537	4,508	2,409	1,333	955	-	..
	30-44	2,232	1,965	1,600	5,679	2,811	1,391	564	261	-	..
	45 and over	282	243	187	641	220	81	37	15	-	..

15.12 Duration of marriage at divorce by age of wife at marriage, 1982-2012

England and Wales — Numbers

Year of divorce	Age of wife at marriage	All durations	0-2 years	0 years	1 year	2 years	3 years	4 years	5-9 years	5 years	6 years
2002	All ages	147,735	10,239	31	3,326	6,882	8,325	8,780	39,730	8,823	8,370
	Under 20	19,828	684	3	184	497	623	597	2,589	591	541
	20-24	60,353	2,833	6	878	1,949	2,411	2,696	13,727	2,739	2,754
	25-29	36,387	2,903	8	906	1,989	2,581	2,778	12,269	2,795	2,602
	30-44	27,803	3,250	7	1,132	2,111	2,366	2,387	9,865	2,374	2,171
	45 and over	3,364	569	7	226	336	344	322	1,280	324	302
2001	All ages	143,818	10,190	36	3,413	6,741	8,206	8,591	39,079	8,632	8,329
	Under 20	20,218	738	3	225	510	634	560	2,676	574	498
	20-24	60,211	2,809	12	870	1,927	2,472	2,711	14,418	2,900	2,938
	25-29	34,759	3,041	10	973	2,058	2,571	2,737	11,728	2,648	2,600
	30-44	25,405	3,054	6	1,116	1,932	2,177	2,246	9,059	2,202	2,028
	45 and over	3,225	548	5	229	314	352	337	1,198	308	265
2000	All ages	141,135	10,438	52	3,494	6,892	8,296	8,740	38,206	8,506	8,148
	Under 20	20,930	846	2	284	560	598	575	2,937	571	594
	20-24	59,874	2,954	8	925	2,021	2,631	2,978	14,663	3,014	3,021
	25-29	33,282	3,095	17	1,038	2,040	2,567	2,675	11,443	2,625	2,510
	30-44	23,912	2,971	14	1,012	1,945	2,159	2,179	8,082	2,032	1,779
	45 and over	3,137	572	11	235	326	341	333	1,081	264	244
1999	All ages	144,556	11,350	49	3,813	7,488	8,833	9,124	39,676	8,958	8,521
	Under 20	22,486	868	5	268	595	658	625	3,367	604	691
	20-24	62,853	3,445	15	1,125	2,305	2,965	3,366	16,221	3,440	3,404
	25-29	32,867	3,182	6	1,074	2,102	2,710	2,745	11,170	2,670	2,432
	30-44	23,270	3,197	14	1,082	2,101	2,147	2,076	7,898	1,982	1,735
	45 and over	3,080	658	9	264	385	353	312	1,020	262	259
1998	All ages	145,214	12,247	68	4,191	7,988	9,270	9,619	40,239	9,180	8,497
	Under 20	24,276	976	7	327	642	704	785	3,858	753	762
	20-24	64,453	4,000	16	1,303	2,681	3,475	3,737	17,413	3,800	3,586
	25-29	31,533	3,510	21	1,144	2,345	2,697	2,787	10,518	2,569	2,289
	30-44	22,076	3,162	18	1,140	2,004	2,062	2,027	7,478	1,801	1,631
	45 and over	2,876	599	6	277	316	332	283	972	257	229
1997	All ages	146,689	12,596	61	4,369	8,166	9,410	9,761	41,260	9,326	8,580
	Under 20	25,579	1,024	7	359	658	757	809	4,424	857	851
	20-24	66,167	4,412	10	1,449	2,953	3,773	4,114	18,226	3,917	3,736
	25-29	31,022	3,576	13	1,213	2,350	2,706	2,712	10,417	2,591	2,263
	30-44	21,017	2,958	20	1,073	1,865	1,879	1,818	7,241	1,719	1,513
	45 and over	2,904	626	11	275	340	295	308	952	242	217
1996	All ages	157,107	14,021	76	5,010	8,935	10,467	10,436	44,609	10,042	9,850
	Under 20	29,927	1,178	4	383	791	970	1,022	5,543	1,128	1,165
	20-24	71,123	5,289	20	1,744	3,525	4,236	4,392	20,221	4,408	4,417
	25-29	31,396	3,872	23	1,384	2,465	2,901	2,778	10,373	2,557	2,359
	30-44	21,640	3,018	15	1,197	1,806	2,008	1,919	7,480	1,702	1,691
	45 and over	3,021	664	14	302	348	352	325	992	247	218
1995	All ages	155,499	14,015	95	4,944	8,976	10,209	10,283	44,304	10,447	9,812
	Under 20	31,322	1,374	8	418	948	1,090	1,158	5,894	1,224	1,180
	20-24	71,360	5,634	28	1,948	3,658	4,375	4,477	20,360	4,748	4,457
	25-29	29,441	3,568	17	1,257	2,294	2,591	2,576	9,892	2,523	2,255
	30-44	20,506	2,817	26	1,034	1,757	1,842	1,792	7,208	1,684	1,707
	45 and over	2,870	622	16	287	319	311	280	950	268	213
1994	All ages	158,175	13,841	81	4,895	8,865	10,400	11,454	44,769	10,836	9,896
	Under 20	34,069	1,582	6	518	1,058	1,297	1,468	6,805	1,404	1,418
	20-24	73,291	5,689	19	1,956	3,714	4,518	5,106	21,102	4,975	4,681
	25-29	28,360	3,408	24	1,208	2,176	2,520	2,698	9,187	2,414	2,077
	30-44	19,686	2,574	17	959	1,598	1,749	1,838	6,807	1,806	1,523
	45 and over	2,769	588	15	254	319	316	344	868	237	197
1993	All ages	165,018	14,096	74	4,708	9,314	11,357	11,799	46,536	11,137	10,352
	Under 20	38,811	1,867	9	583	1,275	1,668	1,653	8,196	1,713	1,685
	20-24	76,853	6,163	12	2,045	4,106	5,066	5,470	21,731	5,194	4,901
	25-29	27,178	3,051	27	953	2,071	2,439	2,506	8,777	2,282	1,970
	30-44	19,357	2,419	18	878	1,523	1,832	1,827	6,920	1,722	1,562
	45 and over	2,819	596	8	249	339	352	343	912	226	234
1992	All ages	160,385	14,247	62	4,630	9,555	11,299	11,352	43,745	10,417	9,459
	Under 20	39,734	1,990	3	590	1,397	1,736	1,739	8,544	1,798	1,697
	20-24	74,701	6,208	19	1,949	4,240	5,159	5,510	20,464	4,952	4,469
	25-29	25,173	2,992	11	1,010	1,971	2,241	2,213	7,759	1,952	1,796
	30-44	18,011	2,430	16	832	1,582	1,822	1,631	6,054	1,476	1,275
	45 and over	2,766	627	13	249	365	341	259	924	239	222

15.12 Duration of marriage at divorce by age of wife at marriage, 1982-2012

England and Wales
Numbers

Year of divorce	Age of wife at marriage	7 years	8 years	9 years	Duration of marriage (completed years)						Median duration
					10-14 years	15-19 years	20-24 years	25-29 years	30 years and over	Not stated	
2002	All ages	8,020	7,564	6,953	28,592	19,784	13,989	9,106	9,190	-	11.1
	Under 20	481	517	459	2,774	3,160	3,439	2,891	3,071	-	..
	20-24	2,795	2,770	2,669	12,516	9,810	6,845	4,480	5,035	-	..
	25-29	2,514	2,265	2,093	7,524	4,032	2,279	1,175	846	-	..
	30-44	1,985	1,796	1,539	5,249	2,577	1,355	523	231	-	..
	45 and over	245	216	193	529	205	71	37	7	-	..
2001	All ages	7,909	7,463	6,746	28,176	18,603	13,318	8,986	8,667	2	10.9
	Under 20	524	513	567	2,999	3,309	3,607	2,830	2,865	-	..
	20-24	2,925	2,943	2,712	12,875	9,251	6,432	4,505	4,736	2	..
	25-29	2,398	2,183	1,899	7,075	3,587	2,052	1,158	810	-	..
	30-44	1,810	1,612	1,407	4,721	2,270	1,157	475	246	-	..
	45 and over	252	212	161	506	186	70	18	10	-	..
2000	All ages	7,778	7,183	6,591	27,459	17,870	12,907	9,017	8,196	6	10.7
	Under 20	566	604	602	3,230	3,413	3,556	3,003	2,770	2	..
	20-24	2,959	2,909	2,760	12,720	8,839	6,142	4,479	4,465	3	..
	25-29	2,356	2,046	1,906	6,521	3,192	1,995	1,078	715	1	..
	30-44	1,665	1,429	1,177	4,461	2,250	1,145	433	232	-	..
	45 and over	232	195	146	527	176	69	24	14	-	..
1999	All ages	7,861	7,338	6,998	27,384	18,072	12,888	9,349	7,871	9	10.5
	Under 20	620	722	730	3,532	3,886	3,874	3,040	2,633	3	..
	20-24	3,217	3,111	3,049	12,984	8,729	5,960	4,871	4,308	4	..
	25-29	2,205	2,044	1,819	6,209	3,127	1,950	1,053	720	1	..
	30-44	1,622	1,312	1,247	4,191	2,156	1,037	362	205	1	..
	45 and over	197	149	153	468	174	67	23	5	-	..
1998	All ages	7,785	7,757	7,020	26,698	17,934	12,675	9,056	7,468	8	10.2
	Under 20	740	823	780	3,986	4,364	4,020	3,075	2,508	-	..
	20-24	3,435	3,413	3,179	12,757	8,469	5,833	4,738	4,028	3	..
	25-29	2,026	1,955	1,679	5,599	2,955	1,851	896	716	4	..
	30-44	1,398	1,419	1,229	3,907	1,993	911	325	210	1	..
	45 and over	186	147	153	449	153	60	22	6	-	..
1997	All ages	8,324	7,935	7,095	26,215	18,027	13,148	9,058	7,202	12	10.0
	Under 20	923	894	899	4,197	4,648	4,284	2,957	2,476	3	..
	20-24	3,750	3,540	3,283	12,447	8,298	6,082	4,971	3,837	7	..
	25-29	2,065	1,918	1,580	5,353	2,881	1,860	834	681	2	..
	30-44	1,409	1,400	1,200	3,776	2,006	869	274	196	-	..
	45 and over	177	183	133	442	194	53	22	12	-	..
1996	All ages	9,092	8,171	7,454	27,332	19,321	14,236	9,511	7,165	9	9.9
	Under 20	1,120	1,116	1,014	5,084	5,507	4,867	3,294	2,461	1	..
	20-24	4,029	3,776	3,591	12,921	8,558	6,549	5,112	3,841	4	..
	25-29	2,168	1,734	1,555	5,119	2,998	1,882	805	665	3	..
	30-44	1,549	1,375	1,163	3,765	2,087	887	285	190	1	..
	45 and over	226	170	131	443	171	51	15	8	-	..
1995	All ages	8,822	7,965	7,258	27,365	18,943	14,483	8,925	6,962	10	9.6
	Under 20	1,161	1,176	1,153	5,768	5,604	5,009	3,072	2,350	3	..
	20-24	4,051	3,668	3,436	12,640	8,476	6,815	4,860	3,718	5	..
	25-29	2,023	1,664	1,427	4,781	2,832	1,796	711	692	2	..
	30-44	1,426	1,275	1,116	3,727	1,868	795	268	189	-	..
	45 and over	161	182	126	449	163	68	14	13	-	..
1994	All ages	8,881	7,900	7,256	28,073	19,200	14,891	8,801	6,739	7	9.8
	Under 20	1,403	1,327	1,253	6,458	6,077	5,101	3,050	2,230	1	14.6
	20-24	4,222	3,727	3497	12,808	8,351	7,303	4,777	3,633	4	10.1
	25-29	1,774	1,559	1,363	4,733	2,804	1,663	675	670	2	7.6
	30-44	1,315	1,144	1,019	3,693	1,785	761	278	201	-	7.1
	45 and over	167	143	124	381	183	63	21	5	-	5.5
1993	All ages	9,029	8,475	7,543	30,156	20,233	15,503	8,426	6,907	5	9.8
	Under 20	1,593	1,621	1,584	7,812	6,830	5,452	3,065	2,267	1	13.9
	20-24	4,311	3,892	3,433	13,538	8,796	7,909	4,434	3,743	3	10.0
	25-29	1,624	1,627	1,274	4,753	2,808	1,497	671	675	1	7.8
	30-44	1,328	1,177	1,131	3,667	1,648	588	242	214	-	7.0
	45 and over	173	158	121	386	151	57	14	8	-	5.4
1992	All ages	8,708	7,914	7,247	29,285	20,160	15,488	8,098	6,704	7	9.9
	Under 20	1,708	1,670	1,671	8,192	6,920	5,395	3,090	2,125	3	13.5
	20-24	4,090	3,694	3,259	12,837	8,721	8,038	4,067	3,694	3	10.0
	25-29	1,513	1,340	1,158	4,401	2,791	1,448	633	694	1	7.9
	30-44	1,219	1,059	1,025	3,477	1,552	570	289	186	-	6.9
	45 and over	178	151	134	378	176	37	19	5	-	5.6

15.12 Duration of marriage at divorce by age of wife at marriage, 1982-2012

England and Wales   **Numbers**

Year of divorce	Age of wife at marriage	All durations	Duration of marriage (completed years)								
			0-2 years	0 years	1 year	2 years	3 years	4 years	5-9 years	5 years	6 years
1991	All ages	158,745	15,332	62	5,239	10,031	11,321	11,126	42,735	10,049	9,345
	Under 20	40,594	2,387	1	780	1,606	1,894	2,014	9,143	1,857	1,805
	20-24	74,050	6,863	17	2,271	4,575	5,308	5,292	19,926	4,808	4,493
	25-29	24,025	2,942	12	1,003	1,927	2,162	2,014	7,048	1,776	1,571
	30-44	17,359	2,486	16	892	1,578	1,640	1,556	5,765	1,390	1,269
	45 and over	2,717	654	16	293	345	317	250	853	218	207
1990	All ages	153,386	15,122	64	5,142	9,916	10,863	10,314	42,061	9,883	9,025
	Under 20	41,116	2,558	6	788	1,764	1,993	1,961	9,790	2,030	1,917
	20-24	71,489	6,919	20	2,312	4,587	5,115	4,981	19,248	4,702	4,265
	25-29	21,701	2,637	11	906	1,720	1,898	1,721	6,567	1,627	1,462
	30-44	16,387	2,378	16	866	1,496	1,533	1,386	5,608	1,297	1,214
	45 and over	2,693	630	11	270	349	324	265	848	227	167
1989	All ages	150,872	15,231	56	5,420	9,755	10,372	10,116	42,108	9,569	8,928
	Under 20	42,612	2,915	11	980	1,924	2,059	2,144	10,798	2,209	2,199
	20-24	69,424	6,956	18	2,424	4,514	4,886	4,783	18,725	4,377	4,042
	25-29	20,369	2,468	8	887	1,573	1,651	1,580	6,189	1,476	1,360
	30-44	15,774	2,272	12	853	1,407	1,487	1,338	5,535	1,286	1,118
	45 and over	2,693	620	7	276	337	289	271	861	221	209
1988	All ages	152,633	15,003	88	5,403	9,512	10,213	10,376	42,617	9,730	9,080
	Under 20	44,693	3,151	7	1,055	2,089	2,296	2,472	11,676	2,374	2,424
	20-24	69,489	6,676	31	2,339	4,306	4,751	4,777	18,310	4,378	3,936
	25-29	20,267	2,298	16	854	1,428	1,525	1,543	6,167	1,464	1,331
	30-44	15,472	2,207	17	852	1,338	1,328	1,368	5,584	1,302	1,182
	45 and over	2,712	671	17	303	351	313	216	880	212	207
1987	All ages	151,007	14,549	..	..	..	10,248	10,626	43,150	10,262	9,626
	Under 20	46,097	3,387	..	..	..	2,554	2,755	12,428	2,823	2,628
	20-24	68,345	6,393	..	..	..	4,643	4,751	18,180	4,461	4,190
	25-29	19,049	2,045	..	..	..	1,449	1,449	6,088	1,420	1,353
	30-44	14,802	2,085	..	..	..	1,293	1,405	5,549	1,327	1,242
	45 and over	2,714	639	..	..	..	309	266	905	231	213
1986	All ages	153,903	14,596	..	..	..	11,683	12,358	42,187	10,656	9,329
	Under 20	48,621	3,735	..	..	..	3,239	3,618	12,978	3,204	2,863
	20-24	68,387	6,216	..	..	..	5,020	5,257	17,059	4,446	3,713
	25-29	18,990	1,955	..	..	..	1,504	1,561	5,845	1,369	1,296
	30-44	15,064	2,068	..	..	..	1,553	1,583	5,369	1,387	1,248
	45 and over	2,841	622	..	..	..	367	339	936	250	209
1985	All ages	160,300	14,662	..	..	..	16,929	14,185	41,537	10,942	9,352
	Under 20	52,858	4,034	..	..	..	5,320	4,481	13,455	3,471	3,008
	20-24	69,663	5,927	..	..	..	6,983	5,735	16,294	4,374	3,607
	25-29	18,689	1,748	..	..	..	1,894	1,720	5,620	1,408	1,269
	30-44	15,765	2,160	..	..	..	2,187	1,827	5,181	1,403	1,249
	45 and over	3,325	793	..	..	..	545	422	987	286	219
1984	All ages	144,501	1,336	..	..	..	15,296	13,868	40,866	10,434	8,830
	Under 20	49,610	304	..	..	..	5,084	4,577	13,821	3,452	2,994
	20-24	62,642	427	..	..	..	6,107	5,443	15,716	4,020	3,371
	25-29	16,811	183	..	..	..	1,707	1,737	5,477	1,329	1,118
	30-44	12,944	289	..	..	..	1,921	1,739	4,895	1,362	1,126
	45 and over	2,494	133	..	..	..	477	372	957	271	221
1983	All ages	147,479	1,528	..	..	..	15,706	13,863	42,041	10,413	8,785
	Under 20	52,547	389	..	..	..	5,529	4,866	15,084	3,693	3,129
	20-24	63,382	477	..	..	..	6,054	5,228	15,887	3,942	3,294
	25-29	16,351	196	..	..	..	1,723	1,654	5,362	1,270	1,130
	30-44	12,675	326	..	..	..	1,904	1,725	4,726	1,253	1,027
	45 and over	2,524	140	..	..	..	496	390	982	255	205
1982	All ages	146,698	1,712	..	..	..	15,190	13,360	42,499	10,126	8,984
	Under 20	54,067	484	..	..	..	5,580	5,003	15,957	3,720	3,283
	20-24	62,955	491	..	..	..	5,746	4,874	16,225	3,862	3,444
	25-29	15,714	247	..	..	..	1,671	1,581	5,188	1,235	1,116
	30-44	11,604	325	..	..	..	1,707	1,556	4,248	1,076	933
	45 and over	2,358	165	..	..	..	486	346	881	233	208

Source: Office for National Statistics

15.12 Duration of marriage at divorce by age of wife at marriage, 1982-2012

England and Wales — Numbers

| Year of divorce | Age of wife at marriage | Duration of marriage (completed years) | | | | | | | | | Median duration |
		7 years	8 years	9 years	10-14 years	15-19 years	20-24 years	25-29 years	30 years and over	Not stated	
1991	All ages	8,423	7,797	7,121	28,791	20,127	14,957	7,845	6,492	19	9.8
	Under 20	1,808	1,883	1,790	8,295	6,988	5,112	2,825	1,930	6	12.7
	20-24	3,902	3,506	3,217	12,304	8,775	7,924	4,066	3,581	11	9.9
	25-29	1,438	1,228	1,035	4,417	2,686	1,318	685	751	2	8.1
	30-44	1,118	1,033	955	3,355	1,521	553	261	222	-	7.0
	45 and over	157	147	124	420	157	50	8	8	-	5.7
1990	All ages	8,289	7,634	7,230	27,310	19,819	14,186	7,479	6,216	16	9.8
	Under 20	1,950	1,933	1,960	8,313	7,122	4,974	2,648	1,755	2	12.4
	20-24	3,767	3,380	3,134	11,542	8,786	7,500	3,897	3,490	11	9.8
	25-29	1,316	1,144	1,018	3,893	2,416	1,156	639	772	2	8.2
	30-44	1,101	1,016	980	3,163	1,330	514	283	191	1	7.0
	45 and over	155	161	138	399	165	42	12	8	-	6.0
1989	All ages	8,392	7,887	7,332	26,281	19,418	13,575	7,333	6,419	19	9.7
	Under 20	2,233	2,037	2,120	8,289	6,951	4,963	2,632	1,854	7	11.9
	20-24	3,698	3,538	3,070	10,775	8,890	7,051	3,758	3,590	10	9.8
	25-29	1,210	1,113	1,030	3,900	2,201	1,026	640	713	1	8.4
	30-44	1,094	1,054	983	2,885	1,226	491	286	253	1	7.0
	45 and over	157	145	129	432	150	44	17	9	-	5.8
1988	All ages	8,784	7,906	7,117	26,545	20,132	13,723	7,476	6,548	-	9.7
	Under 20	2,410	2,352	2,116	8,648	7,126	4,896	2,571	1,857	-	11.5
	20-24	3,813	3,247	2,936	10,753	9,646	7,074	3,915	3,587	-	10.1
	25-29	1,256	1,083	1,033	3,962	2,046	1,180	698	848	-	8.7
	30-44	1,137	1,069	894	2,787	1,149	527	274	248	-	7.0
	45 and over	168	155	138	395	165	46	18	8	-	5.7
1987	All ages	8,781	7,827	6,654	26,194	19,576	12,970	7,314	6,380	-	9.5
	Under 20	2,592	2,324	2,061	8,925	7,019	4,820	2,472	1,737	-	11.0
	20-24	3,652	3,212	2,665	10,656	9,671	6,602	3,861	3,588	-	10.1
	25-29	1,196	1,127	992	3,723	1,791	1,021	694	789	-	8.5
	30-44	1,163	993	824	2,475	975	488	276	256	-	6.8
	45 and over	178	171	112	415	120	39	11	10	-	5.1
1986	All ages	8,457	7,465	6,280	26,718	19,547	12,909	7,357	6,539	9	9.4
	Under 20	2,616	2,313	1,982	9,208	6,946	4,810	2,317	1,766	4	10.4
	20-24	3,410	2,981	2,509	10,953	9,857	6,376	3,986	3,661	2	10.3
	25-29	1,205	1,044	931	3,679	1,688	1,145	736	874	3	8.6
	30-44	1,034	969	731	2,477	940	541	301	232	-	6.4
	45 and over	192	158	127	401	116	37	17	6	-	5.4
1985	All ages	7,932	6,884	6,427	27,087	19,460	12,463	7,388	6,576	13	8.9
	Under 20	2,553	2,262	2,161	9,658	7,125	4,645	2,347	1,789	4	9.6
	20-24	3,114	2,705	2,494	11,276	9,665	6,122	4,016	3,638	7	10.0
	25-29	1,054	981	908	3,388	1,630	1,122	700	865	2	8.3
	30-44	1,015	781	733	2,348	935	538	315	274	-	6.0
	45 and over	196	155	131	417	105	36	10	10	-	4.8
1984	All ages	7,854	7,105	6,643	27,336	19,108	12,516	7,528	6,637	10	10.1
	Under 20	2,640	2,450	2,285	9,933	7,127	4,614	2,410	1,737	3	10.4
	20-24	3,060	2,687	2,578	11,723	9,412	6,154	3,942	3,711	7	11.5
	25-29	1,048	1,034	948	3,209	1,578	1,159	827	934	-	9.3
	30-44	911	793	703	2,093	884	545	328	250	-	6.8
	45 and over	195	141	129	378	107	44	21	5	-	6.0
1983	All ages	8,072	7,662	7,109	28,432	19,103	12,579	7,529	6,661	37	10.1
	Under 20	2,867	2,752	2,643	10,412	7,596	4,599	2,331	1,728	13	10.2
	20-24	3,111	2,916	2,624	12,764	8,987	6,227	4,045	3,699	14	11.6
	25-29	1,042	997	923	2,999	1,551	1,129	786	943	8	9.2
	30-44	846	825	775	1,899	865	587	355	286	2	7.1
	45 and over	206	172	144	358	104	37	12	5	-	5.9
1982	All ages	8,444	7,747	7,198	28,737	18,855	12,585	7,199	6,517	44	10.1
	Under 20	3,236	2,940	2,778	10,879	7,699	4,512	2,224	1,713	16	10.0
	20-24	3,188	2,936	2,795	13,312	8,606	6,298	3,821	3,559	23	11.5
	25-29	1,034	930	873	2,654	1,498	1,186	761	924	4	9.0
	30-44	817	803	619	1,586	940	552	375	314	1	7.3
	45 and over	169	138	133	306	112	37	18	7	-	5.8

Source: Office for National Statistics

15.13 Duration of marriage at divorce by age of husband at marriage, 2002-2012

England and Wales

Year of divorce	Age of husband at marriage	All durations	Duration of marriage (completed years)								
			0-2 years	0 years	1 year	2 years	3 years	4 years	5-9 years	5 years	6 years
2012	All ages	118,140	6,268	49	2,033	4,186	5,710	6,550	33,027	6,748	6,542
	Under 20	2,710	61	1	19	41	74	96	468	86	92
	20-24	26,783	907	4	257	646	857	1,032	5,132	1,050	985
	25-29	36,697	1,814	21	596	1,197	1,699	1,921	9,215	2,005	1,801
	30-44	44,375	2,706	16	884	1,806	2,483	2,824	15,263	2,949	3,070
	45 and over	7,575	780	7	277	496	597	677	2,949	658	594
2011	All ages	117,558	5,803	30	1,748	4,025	5,890	6,654	32,989	6,727	7,111
	Under 20	2,871	75	-	19	56	87	101	536	108	124
	20-24	27,934	813	4	213	596	910	1,034	5,343	1,092	1,135
	25-29	36,299	1,679	13	489	1,177	1,780	1,890	9,183	1,919	1,883
	30-44	43,304	2,547	6	793	1,748	2,493	2,965	15,209	3,022	3,345
	45 and over	7,150	689	7	234	448	620	664	2,718	586	624
2010	All ages	119,589	6,278	17	1,897	4,364	6,109	6,936	33,700	7,418	7,652
	Under 20	2,958	74	-	20	54	86	97	542	115	120
	20-24	29,661	909	2	251	656	951	1,145	5,437	1,240	1,247
	25-29	36,920	1,740	5	522	1,213	1,723	1,969	9,584	1,998	2,185
	30-44	43,027	2,763	8	829	1,926	2,697	3,070	15,439	3,380	3,468
	45 and over	7,023	792	2	275	515	652	655	2,698	685	632
2009	All ages	113,949	6,270	21	1,951	4,298	5,884	6,947	31,290	7,561	6,864
	Under 20	3,066	74	-	24	50	75	114	543	129	98
	20-24	29,150	883	1	246	636	894	1,193	5,281	1,305	1,221
	25-29	35,305	1,746	4	553	1,189	1,702	1,991	9,186	2,188	1,912
	30-44	39,984	2,810	9	856	1,945	2,623	3,032	13,948	3,370	3,104
	45 and over	6,444	757	7	272	478	590	617	2,332	569	529
2008	All ages	121,708	6,937	27	2,103	4,807	6,776	7,929	31,803	7,369	6,714
	Under 20	3,364	91	-	29	62	98	130	564	125	125
	20-24	32,151	1,006	4	236	766	1,090	1,319	5,161	1,281	1,132
	25-29	37,895	1,978	9	604	1,365	1,889	2,278	9,594	2,013	1,972
	30-44	41,529	3,051	9	941	2,101	3,040	3,544	14,089	3,345	2,979
	45 and over	6,769	811	5	293	513	659	658	2,395	605	506
2007	All ages	128,131	8,195	38	2,558	5,599	7,206	7,574	32,419	7,164	7,046
	Under 20	4,036	132	-	36	96	122	146	611	131	151
	20-24	35,408	1,238	4	364	870	1,214	1,275	5,430	1,198	1,153
	25-29	39,546	2,202	13	659	1,530	1,986	2,109	10,074	2,129	2,133
	30-44	42,408	3,736	12	1,171	2,553	3,279	3,351	13,960	3,163	3,085
	45 and over	6,733	887	9	328	550	605	693	2,344	543	524
2006	All ages	132,140	8,763	37	2,793	5,933	7,226	7,376	33,736	7,398	7,310
	Under 20	4,115	140	-	49	91	119	132	630	142	143
	20-24	38,096	1,400	4	411	985	1,192	1,239	5,727	1,211	1,204
	25-29	40,683	2,304	10	724	1,570	2,054	2,176	10,907	2,285	2,295
	30-44	42,417	4,002	14	1,287	2,701	3,234	3,238	14,093	3,209	3,146
	45 and over	6,829	917	9	322	586	627	591	2,379	551	522
2005	All ages	141,322	9,573	49	3,181	6,343	7,520	8,175	36,064	7,920	7,697
	Under 20	4,685	175	-	53	122	159	139	634	166	134
	20-24	42,354	1,516	5	497	1,014	1,308	1,415	6,526	1,328	1,309
	25-29	43,807	2,625	18	836	1,771	2,175	2,529	11,853	2,547	2,481
	30-44	43,631	4,287	13	1,472	2,802	3,250	3,466	14,547	3,270	3,219
	45 and over	6,845	970	13	323	634	628	626	2,504	609	554
2004	All ages	152,923	10,101	42	3,345	6,714	8,319	8,894	39,681	8,840	8,375
	Under 20	5,392	178	-	52	126	146	187	680	186	136
	20-24	47,794	1,680	7	552	1,121	1,475	1,538	7,762	1,572	1,540
	25-29	48,067	2,863	7	881	1,975	2,568	2,974	13,672	2,982	2,812
	30-44	44,701	4,428	19	1,507	2,902	3,468	3,531	15,035	3,505	3,299
	45 and over	6,969	952	9	353	590	662	664	2,532	595	588
2003	All ages	153,065	10,286	42	3,283	6,961	8,276	8,882	40,497	8,968	8,639
	Under 20	5,764	191	-	58	133	157	169	690	176	148
	20-24	50,015	1,720	4	483	1,233	1,484	1,658	8,685	1,675	1,718
	25-29	47,353	3,021	5	927	2,089	2,702	2,960	13,881	3,000	2,901
	30-44	43,173	4,386	17	1,456	2,913	3,362	3,459	14,702	3,519	3,328
	45 and over	6,760	968	16	359	593	571	636	2,539	598	544
2002	All ages	147,735	10,239	31	3,326	6,882	8,325	8,780	39,730	8,823	8,370
	Under 20	5,572	184	-	54	130	169	146	600	123	109
	20-24	50,028	1,739	5	481	1,253	1,529	1,717	9,494	1,814	1,928
	25-29	45,913	3,173	8	985	2,180	2,886	3,009	13,756	3,089	2,897
	30-44	39,977	4,218	9	1,460	2,749	3,125	3,349	13,589	3,216	2,930
	45 and over	6,245	925	9	346	570	616	559	2,291	581	506

Source: Office for National Statistics

15.13 Duration of marriage at divorce by age of husband at marriage, 2002-2012

England and Wales — Numbers

Year of divorce	Age of husband at marriage	Duration of marriage (completed years) 7 years	8 years	9 years	10-14 years	15-19 years	20-24 years	25-29 years	30 years and over	Not stated	Median duration
2012	All ages	6,919	6,961	5,857	22,356	15,733	12,215	7,649	8,632	-	11.5
	Under 20	99	99	92	359	243	285	296	828	-	..
	20-24	1,095	1,056	946	3,388	3,318	4,039	3,334	4,776	-	..
	25-29	1,810	1,953	1,646	7,133	5,902	4,518	2,447	2,048	-	..
	30-44	3,241	3,277	2,726	10,022	5,629	3,056	1,461	931	-	..
	45 and over	674	576	447	1,454	641	317	111	49	-	..
2011	All ages	7,263	6,389	5,499	22,126	15,547	12,228	7,712	8,609	-	11.5
	Under 20	116	115	73	365	226	309	358	814	-	..
	20-24	1,228	1,024	864	3,599	3,622	4,365	3,444	4,804	-	..
	25-29	2,062	1,766	1,553	7,217	5,803	4,318	2,380	2,049	-	..
	30-44	3,264	2,997	2,581	9,549	5,252	2,962	1,434	893	-	..
	45 and over	593	487	428	1,396	644	274	96	49	-	..
2010	All ages	7,101	5,995	5,534	22,105	15,772	12,412	7,639	8,638	-	11.4
	Under 20	98	123	86	345	277	323	371	843	-	..
	20-24	1,167	904	879	3,769	4,147	4,715	3,596	4,992	-	..
	25-29	2,022	1,726	1,653	7,523	5,757	4,398	2,234	1,992	-	..
	30-44	3,269	2,801	2,521	9,150	5,021	2,738	1,373	776	-	..
	45 and over	545	441	395	1,318	570	238	65	35	-	..
2009	All ages	5,968	5,634	5,263	20,591	15,390	11,855	7,490	8,225	7	11.4
	Under 20	106	108	102	316	296	343	429	876	-	..
	20-24	1,004	912	839	3,716	4,298	4,673	3,545	4,665	2	..
	25-29	1,732	1,719	1,635	7,059	5,566	4,022	2,124	1,907	2	..
	30-44	2,690	2,458	2,326	8,270	4,620	2,617	1,306	755	3	..
	45 and over	436	437	361	1,230	610	200	86	22	-	..
2008	All ages	6,365	6,034	5,321	21,561	16,945	12,706	8,136	8,907	8	11.5
	Under 20	113	90	111	321	342	407	501	909	1	..
	20-24	987	922	839	4,134	4,924	5,257	3,993	5,265	2	..
	25-29	1,910	1,908	1,791	7,677	6,168	4,089	2,233	1,984	5	..
	30-44	2,860	2,697	2,208	8,147	4,911	2,701	1,317	729	-	..
	45 and over	495	417	372	1,282	600	252	92	20	-	..
2007	All ages	6,560	6,072	5,577	23,427	18,203	13,117	8,701	9,282	7	11.7
	Under 20	139	108	82	353	425	516	661	1,070	-	..
	20-24	1,045	1,077	957	4,993	5,878	5,654	4,230	5,494	2	..
	25-29	2,003	1,961	1,848	8,330	6,392	4,045	2,396	2,009	3	..
	30-44	2,892	2,522	2,298	8,441	4,939	2,695	1,332	673	2	..
	45 and over	481	404	392	1,310	569	207	82	36	-	..
2006	All ages	6,769	6,249	6,010	24,606	18,735	13,472	8,764	9,449	13	11.6
	Under 20	145	106	94	370	463	569	666	1,025	1	..
	20-24	1,130	1,099	1,083	5,866	6,495	5,991	4,431	5,752	3	..
	25-29	2,199	2,085	2,043	8,483	6,388	4,053	2,268	2,044	6	..
	30-44	2,783	2,571	2,384	8,503	4,814	2,615	1,317	598	3	..
	45 and over	512	388	406	1,384	575	244	82	30	-	..
2005	All ages	7,343	6,801	6,303	26,310	20,310	14,268	9,241	9,852	9	11.6
	Under 20	116	125	93	445	575	734	761	1,062	1	..
	20-24	1,303	1,317	1,269	6,815	7,425	6,596	4,831	5,921	1	..
	25-29	2,437	2,267	2,121	9,377	6,742	4,049	2,313	2,142	2	..
	30-44	2,951	2,651	2,456	8,448	4,979	2,672	1,274	703	5	..
	45 and over	536	441	364	1,225	589	217	62	24	-	..
2004	All ages	7,900	7,683	6,883	28,984	21,515	15,431	9,705	10,293	-	11.5
	Under 20	127	120	111	596	710	894	849	1,152	-	..
	20-24	1,543	1,585	1,522	8,361	8,403	7,232	5,081	6,262	-	..
	25-29	2,699	2,699	2,480	10,158	6,893	4,251	2,510	2,178	-	..
	30-44	3,016	2,851	2,364	8,605	4,924	2,838	1,200	672	-	..
	45 and over	515	428	406	1,264	585	216	65	29	-	..
2003	All ages	8,228	7,686	6,976	29,751	20,863	14,974	9,627	9,907	2	11.3
	Under 20	127	122	117	705	798	1,064	902	1,087	1	..
	20-24	1,751	1,760	1,781	9,169	8,627	7,216	5,204	6,251	1	..
	25-29	2,781	2,745	2,454	10,243	6,314	3,938	2,330	1,964	-	..
	30-44	3,015	2,616	2,224	8,378	4,617	2,573	1,119	577	-	..
	45 and over	554	443	400	1,256	507	183	72	28	-	..
2002	All ages	8,020	7,564	6,953	28,592	19,784	13,989	9,106	9,190	-	11.1
	Under 20	130	115	123	741	875	1,005	899	953	-	..
	20-24	1,927	1,896	1,929	9,648	8,300	6,801	4,968	5,832	-	..
	25-29	2,760	2,645	2,365	9,594	5,843	3,593	2,193	1,866	-	..
	30-44	2,741	2,509	2,193	7,511	4,281	2,395	983	526	-	..
	45 and over	462	399	343	1,098	485	195	63	13	-	..

Source: Office for National Statistics

15.14 Live births by local authority of usual residence of mother, numbers, sex, General Fertility Rates and Total Fertility Rates, 2013

England and Wales: regions (within England), unitary authorities, counties, districts, London Boroughs, local health boards (within Wales)

	Total Live Births	Male	Female	General Fertility Rate (GFR)[2]	Total Fertility Rate (TFR)[3]
UNITED KINGDOM[P]	778,805	399,600	379,205	61.6	1.83
ENGLAND, WALES AND ELSEWHERE	698,512	358,383	340,129	62.2	1.85
ENGLAND	664,517	340,856	323,661	62.4	1.85
NORTH EAST	28,961	14,970	13,991	58.2	1.75
County Durham UA	5,388	2,814	2,574	56.3	1.72
Darlington UA	1,227	655	572	62.2	1.90
Hartlepool UA	1,021	516	505	58.9	1.76
Middlesbrough UA	1,951	1,021	930	69.8	2.03
Northumberland UA	2,796	1,434	1,362	54.0	1.70
Redcar and Cleveland UA	1,555	780	775	64.9	1.98
Stockton-on-Tees UA	2,414	1,290	1,124	64.9	1.94
Tyne and Wear (Met County)	12,609	6,460	6,149	56.4	1.67
Gateshead	2,297	1,178	1,119	59.6	1.76
Newcastle upon Tyne	3,406	1,743	1,663	51.5	1.60
North Tyneside	2,268	1,164	1,104	59.3	1.77
South Tyneside	1,629	826	803	59.3	1.78
Sunderland	3,009	1,549	1,460	56.5	1.70
NORTH WEST	86,372	44,147	42,225	62.6	1.88
Blackburn with Darwen UA	2,254	1,172	1,082	75.6	2.25
Blackpool UA	1,717	864	853	66.9	2.03
Cheshire East UA	3,770	2,006	1,764	58.9	1.88
Cheshire West and Chester UA	3,577	1,841	1,736	58.9	1.83
Halton UA	1,597	790	807	65.8	1.99
Warrington UA	2,366	1,195	1,171	61.1	1.87
Cumbria	4,814	2,445	2,369	58.0	1.84
Allerdale	879	421	458	56.0	1.82
Barrow-in-Furness	759	396	363	63.3	1.99
Carlisle	1,180	584	596	58.8	1.79
Copeland	752	385	367	63.7	1.97
Eden	447	244	203	55.6	1.86
South Lakeland	797	415	382	51.8	1.70
Greater Manchester (Met County)	37,045	18,882	18,163	65.9	1.92
Bolton	3,812	1,991	1,821	69.8	2.10
Bury	2,453	1,224	1,229	68.8	2.08
Manchester	8,002	4,051	3,951	60.0	1.71
Oldham	3,274	1,672	1,602	73.7	2.20
Rochdale	3,044	1,566	1,478	72.1	2.16
Salford	3,544	1,786	1,758	68.5	1.92
Stockport	3,437	1,770	1,667	66.0	2.01
Tameside	2,918	1,492	1,426	68.0	2.04
Trafford	2,817	1,441	1,376	64.0	1.92
Wigan	3,744	1,889	1,855	61.4	1.87
Lancashire	13,317	6,754	6,563	60.7	1.87
Burnley	1,210	619	591	72.7	2.14
Chorley	1,182	603	579	58.8	1.83
Fylde	645	315	330	56.3	1.78
Hyndburn	1,135	580	555	74.0	2.24
Lancaster	1,482	781	701	51.7	1.68
Pendle	1,278	629	649	74.5	2.18
Preston	1,918	953	965	63.2	1.87
Ribble Valley	427	209	218	45.8	1.56
Rossendale	818	405	413	62.9	1.97
South Ribble	1,138	594	544	57.3	1.78
West Lancashire	1,142	565	577	56.0	1.90
Wyre	942	501	441	55.5	1.79
Merseyside (Met County)	15,915	8,198	7,717	58.4	1.74
Knowsley	1,816	926	890	62.4	1.86
Liverpool	5,646	2,890	2,756	52.8	1.55
Sefton	2,844	1,464	1,380	61.0	1.90
St. Helens	2,049	1,063	986	62.7	1.93
Wirral	3,560	1,855	1,705	62.3	1.92
YORKSHIRE AND THE HUMBER	64,560	33,068	31,492	61.9	1.86
East Riding of Yorkshire UA	2,978	1,565	1,413	55.2	1.83
Kingston upon Hull, City of UA	3,697	1,912	1,785	67.5	1.90
North East Lincolnshire UA	1,941	973	968	65.6	1.96
North Lincolnshire UA	1,840	934	906	61.3	1.87
York UA	2,045	1,052	993	46.3	1.47
North Yorkshire	5,521	2,865	2,656	57.1	1.84

15.14 Live births by local authority of usual residence of mother, numbers, sex, General Fertility Rates and Total Fertility Rates, 2013

England and Wales: regions (within England), unitary authorities, counties, districts, London Boroughs, local health boards (within Wales)

	Total Live Births	Male	Female	General Fertility Rate (GFR)[2]	Total Fertility Rate (TFR)[3]
Craven	463	225	238	54.8	1.84
Hambleton	802	430	372	58.7	1.93
Harrogate	1,453	726	727	55.7	1.79
Richmondshire	511	265	246	61.0	1.89
Ryedale	398	212	186	51.2	1.73
Scarborough	991	519	472	57.5	1.78
Selby	903	488	415	59.6	1.90
South Yorkshire (Met County)	**16,154**	**8,258**	**7,896**	**59.6**	**1.78**
Barnsley	2,807	1,458	1,349	63.6	1.94
Doncaster	3,673	1,916	1,757	65.2	1.95
Rotherham	3,120	1,521	1,599	65.3	1.99
Sheffield	6,554	3,363	3,191	53.5	1.64
West Yorkshire (Met County)	**30,384**	**15,509**	**14,875**	**65.7**	**1.94**
Bradford	8,039	4,025	4,014	75.1	2.21
Calderdale	2,502	1,297	1,205	64.8	2.00
Kirklees	5,658	2,926	2,732	67.1	2.03
Leeds	10,152	5,226	4,926	59.6	1.77
Wakefield	4,033	2,035	1,998	64.5	1.95
EAST MIDLANDS	**52,895**	**26,984**	**25,911**	**60.3**	**1.84**
Derby UA	**3,359**	**1,648**	**1,711**	**64.6**	**1.89**
Leicester UA	**5,096**	**2,550**	**2,546**	**64.9**	**1.87**
Nottingham UA	**4,298**	**2,236**	**2,062**	**55.8**	**1.71**
Rutland UA	**339**	**182**	**157**	**58.6**	**2.04**
Derbyshire	**7,839**	**3,979**	**3,860**	**56.9**	**1.80**
Amber Valley	1,275	675	600	58.0	1.84
Bolsover	887	434	453	62.7	1.96
Chesterfield	1,113	563	550	58.2	1.81
Derbyshire Dales	490	242	248	47.4	1.62
Erewash	1,263	675	588	59.2	1.82
High Peak	866	429	437	54.3	1.74
North East Derbyshire	834	410	424	51.0	1.65
South Derbyshire	1,111	551	560	60.5	1.89
Leicestershire	**6,601**	**3,415**	**3,186**	**54.6**	**1.72**
Blaby	1,000	524	476	58.2	1.80
Charnwood	1,719	908	811	50.2	1.58
Harborough	775	395	380	53.3	1.78
Hinckley and Bosworth	1,092	585	507	57.8	1.79
Melton	497	259	238	57.2	1.86
North West Leicestershire	952	480	472	56.0	1.78
Oadby and Wigston	566	264	302	54.2	1.76
Lincolnshire	**7,550**	**3,847**	**3,703**	**59.5**	**1.85**
Boston	851	425	426	71.2	2.10
East Lindsey	1,259	648	611	62.9	2.03
Lincoln	1,241	622	619	54.6	1.59
North Kesteven	1,064	543	521	57.7	1.88
South Holland	917	451	466	61.0	1.91
South Kesteven	1,371	726	645	57.6	1.86
West Lindsey	847	432	415	57.0	1.90
Northamptonshire	**8,995**	**4,605**	**4,390**	**66.7**	**2.03**
Corby	931	490	441	71.3	2.06
Daventry	815	420	395	62.6	2.10
East Northamptonshire	1,012	511	501	64.9	2.12
Kettering	1,179	593	586	65.0	2.01
Northampton	3,232	1,654	1,578	70.2	2.01
South Northamptonshire	832	419	413	55.8	1.83
Wellingborough	994	518	476	70.3	2.18
Nottinghamshire	**8,818**	**4,522**	**4,296**	**61.3**	**1.90**
Ashfield	1,530	788	742	66.4	2.04
Bassetlaw	1,207	629	578	61.7	1.99
Broxtowe	1,220	621	599	59.6	1.80
Gedling	1,274	635	639	60.9	1.89
Mansfield	1,309	678	631	65.8	1.96
Newark and Sherwood	1,191	601	590	59.2	1.90
Rushcliffe	1,087	570	517	54.6	1.72
WEST MIDLANDS	**71,188**	**36,622**	**34,566**	**64.9**	**1.96**
Herefordshire, County of UA	**1,833**	**963**	**870**	**60.3**	**1.89**
Shropshire UA	**2,843**	**1,485**	**1,358**	**56.7**	**1.82**
Stoke-on-Trent UA	**3,555**	**1,825**	**1,730**	**70.9**	**2.05**
Telford and Wrekin UA	**2,191**	**1,149**	**1,042**	**67.3**	**2.06**
Staffordshire	**8,580**	**4,390**	**4,190**	**56.5**	**1.77**
Cannock Chase	1,172	608	564	62.2	1.91

15.14 Live births by local authority of usual residence of mother, numbers, sex, General Fertility Rates and Total Fertility Rates, 2013

England and Wales: regions (within England), unitary authorities, counties, districts, London Boroughs, local health boards (within Wales)

	Total Live Births	Male	Female	General Fertility Rate (GFR)[2]	Total Fertility Rate (TFR)[3]
East Staffordshire	1,379	708	671	65.8	2.02
Lichfield	936	494	442	55.3	1.78
Newcastle-under-Lyme	1,175	592	583	49.3	1.54
South Staffordshire	942	457	485	53.1	1.74
Stafford	1,229	638	591	54.7	1.71
Staffordshire Moorlands	810	408	402	51.4	1.70
Tamworth	937	485	452	61.2	1.86
Warwickshire	**6,090**	**3,038**	**3,052**	**60.8**	**1.87**
North Warwickshire	676	335	341	62.7	2.01
Nuneaton and Bedworth	1,582	775	807	66.1	2.00
Rugby	1,243	614	629	65.9	2.02
Stratford-on-Avon	1,068	525	543	56.2	1.84
Warwick	1,521	789	732	55.3	1.70
West Midlands (Met County)	**40,026**	**20,615**	**19,411**	**68.9**	**2.03**
Birmingham	17,421	8,881	8,540	71.2	2.08
Coventry	4,495	2,328	2,167	61.8	1.81
Dudley	3,853	1,945	1,908	66.2	2.02
Sandwell	4,844	2,520	2,324	74.8	2.18
Solihull	2,238	1,161	1,077	60.1	1.91
Walsall	3,715	1,953	1,762	70.7	2.11
Wolverhampton	3,460	1,827	1,633	68.2	2.01
Worcestershire	**6,070**	**3,157**	**2,913**	**60.2**	**1.88**
Bromsgrove	871	461	410	55.3	1.81
Malvern Hills	598	312	286	53.2	1.78
Redditch	1,068	554	514	64.0	1.91
Worcester	1,349	703	646	62.6	1.86
Wychavon	1,092	560	532	57.4	1.88
Wyre Forest	1,092	567	525	65.8	2.08
EAST	**71,309**	**36,552**	**34,757**	**63.7**	**1.92**
Bedford UA	**2,074**	**1,018**	**1,056**	**65.7**	**1.97**
Central Bedfordshire UA	**3,214**	**1,629**	**1,585**	**64.5**	**1.95**
Luton UA	**3,481**	**1,896**	**1,585**	**76.5**	**2.14**
Peterborough UA	**3,185**	**1,640**	**1,545**	**81.5**	**2.37**
Southend-on-Sea UA	**2,233**	**1,153**	**1,080**	**66.3**	**2.01**
Thurrock UA	**2,326**	**1,188**	**1,138**	**68.7**	**2.04**
Cambridgeshire	**7,365**	**3,779**	**3,586**	**59.4**	**1.78**
Cambridge	1,380	719	661	42.8	1.34
East Cambridgeshire	1,026	511	515	64.9	1.94
Fenland	1,170	602	568	69.5	2.14
Huntingdonshire	1,985	1,048	937	62.8	1.93
South Cambridgeshire	1,804	899	905	65.4	1.99
Essex	**15,949**	**8,171**	**7,778**	**61.7**	**1.90**
Basildon	2,417	1,219	1,198	69.0	2.07
Braintree	1,659	869	790	60.5	1.88
Brentwood	823	406	417	61.8	1.90
Castle Point	801	430	371	54.9	1.78
Chelmsford	1,857	969	888	57.4	1.71
Colchester	2,210	1,109	1,101	61.0	1.83
Epping Forest	1,553	789	764	65.7	1.98
Harlow	1,219	577	642	72.0	2.10
Maldon	547	291	256	55.9	1.88
Rochford	707	369	338	49.5	1.64
Tendring	1,341	701	640	65.4	2.11
Uttlesford	815	442	373	56.9	1.85
Hertfordshire	**14,503**	**7,439**	**7,064**	**64.4**	**1.90**
Broxbourne	1,258	627	631	67.4	2.02
Dacorum	1,828	943	885	64.1	1.90
East Hertfordshire	1,581	828	753	59.3	1.81
Hertsmere	1,291	646	645	65.4	1.94
North Hertfordshire	1,597	837	760	65.9	1.97
St Albans	1,916	988	928	70.1	1.98
Stevenage	1,149	581	568	65.7	1.93
Three Rivers	1,027	525	502	61.1	1.83
Watford	1,512	752	760	71.3	1.95
Welwyn Hatfield	1,344	712	632	54.5	1.68
Norfolk	**9,187**	**4,709**	**4,478**	**60.7**	**1.86**
Breckland	1,467	747	720	66.5	2.08
Broadland	1,068	565	503	52.8	1.74
Great Yarmouth	1,094	562	532	65.4	2.02
King's Lynn and West Norfolk	1,636	828	808	67.1	2.10
North Norfolk	835	423	412	60.2	1.95
Norwich	1,840	962	878	55.7	1.60
South Norfolk	1,247	622	625	59.3	1.91

15.14 Live births by local authority of usual residence of mother, numbers, sex, General Fertility Rates and Total Fertility Rates, 2013

England and Wales: regions (within England), unitary authorities, counties, districts, London Boroughs, local health boards (within Wales)

	Total Live Births	Male	Female	General Fertility Rate (GFR)[2]	Total Fertility Rate (TFR)[3]
Suffolk	**7,792**	**3,930**	**3,862**	**61.7**	**1.91**
Babergh	740	366	374	53.5	1.81
Forest Heath	953	473	480	76.1	2.08
Ipswich	1,887	958	929	67.5	1.93
Mid Suffolk	876	449	427	56.0	1.84
St Edmundsbury	1,171	586	585	61.0	1.89
Suffolk Coastal	954	472	482	51.6	1.77
Waveney	1,211	626	585	65.2	2.03
LONDON	**128,332**	**65,669**	**62,663**	**64.0**	**1.74**
Inner London	**51,407**	**26,237**	**25,170**	**57.9**	**1.56**
Camden	2,766	1,417	1,349	45.5	1.26
Hackney and City of London [5]	4,500	2,318	2,182	61.5	1.69
Hammersmith and Fulham	2,552	1,299	1,253	52.4	1.41
Haringey	4,141	2,151	1,990	63.3	1.74
Islington	2,819	1,411	1,408	46.0	1.29
Kensington and Chelsea	1,803	937	866	49.5	1.27
Lambeth	4,589	2,370	2,219	53.0	1.46
Lewisham	4,827	2,504	2,323	68.1	1.87
Newham	6,267	3,196	3,071	80.1	2.14
Southwark	4,706	2,393	2,313	57.9	1.58
Tower Hamlets	4,608	2,293	2,315	58.2	1.50
Wandsworth	5,152	2,567	2,585	56.6	1.50
Westminster	2,677	1,381	1,296	48.3	1.25
Outer London	**76,925**	**39,432**	**37,493**	**68.8**	**1.93**
Barking and Dagenham	3,796	1,992	1,804	85.5	2.45
Barnet	5,187	2,699	2,488	63.4	1.74
Bexley	2,959	1,501	1,458	62.1	1.88
Brent	5,170	2,635	2,535	70.6	1.92
Bromley	3,899	2,033	1,866	62.2	1.82
Croydon	5,605	2,871	2,734	69.5	2.00
Ealing	5,395	2,800	2,595	68.8	1.88
Enfield	4,908	2,572	2,336	69.5	1.99
Greenwich	4,442	2,297	2,145	71.1	1.97
Harrow	3,559	1,831	1,728	70.0	1.95
Havering	3,004	1,475	1,529	63.8	1.90
Hillingdon	4,330	2,170	2,160	68.8	1.95
Hounslow	4,443	2,304	2,139	73.3	1.98
Kingston upon Thames	2,112	1,066	1,046	54.4	1.55
Merton	3,370	1,692	1,678	70.9	1.87
Redbridge	4,591	2,357	2,234	71.4	1.97
Richmond upon Thames	2,805	1,381	1,424	69.5	1.80
Sutton	2,629	1,372	1,257	64.0	1.85
Waltham Forest	4,721	2,384	2,337	75.4	2.08
SOUTH EAST	**102,190**	**52,745**	**49,445**	**61.3**	**1.86**
Bracknell Forest UA	**1,468**	**781**	**687**	**61.3**	**1.81**
Brighton and Hove UA	**2,967**	**1,497**	**1,470**	**44.7**	**1.37**
Isle of Wight UA	**1,287**	**655**	**632**	**60.0**	**1.94**
Medway UA	**3,503**	**1,830**	**1,673**	**63.5**	**1.89**
Milton Keynes UA	**3,901**	**1,993**	**1,908**	**72.7**	**2.12**
Portsmouth UA	**2,748**	**1,459**	**1,289**	**59.6**	**1.76**
Reading UA	**2,617**	**1,357**	**1,260**	**68.6**	**1.89**
Slough UA	**2,601**	**1,332**	**1,269**	**78.7**	**2.16**
Southampton UA	**3,272**	**1,716**	**1,556**	**57.5**	**1.66**
West Berkshire UA	**1,744**	**919**	**825**	**61.4**	**1.94**
Windsor and Maidenhead UA	**1,696**	**865**	**831**	**61.7**	**1.83**
Wokingham UA	**1,795**	**909**	**886**	**61.3**	**1.87**
Buckinghamshire	**5,822**	**3,002**	**2,820**	**61.6**	**1.91**
Aylesbury Vale	2,096	1,084	1,012	61.8	1.90
Chiltern	836	437	399	56.0	1.85
South Bucks	724	372	352	62.1	1.92
Wycombe	2,166	1,109	1,057	63.8	1.95
East Sussex	**5,268**	**2,730**	**2,538**	**60.8**	**1.95**
Eastbourne	1,125	560	565	62.7	1.91
Hastings	1,208	614	594	71.1	2.16
Lewes	917	489	428	58.1	1.87
Rother	714	385	329	57.8	1.94
Wealden	1,304	682	622	55.4	1.86
Hampshire	**14,275**	**7,266**	**7,009**	**59.8**	**1.87**
Basingstoke and Deane	2,166	1,081	1,085	64.5	1.93
East Hampshire	1,075	551	524	55.5	1.86
Eastleigh	1,519	802	717	62.7	1.88
Fareham	1,047	538	509	54.7	1.76
Gosport	937	443	494	60.7	1.85
Hart	943	468	475	57.9	1.82
Havant	1,256	650	606	60.7	1.92

15.14 Live births by local authority of usual residence of mother, numbers, sex, General Fertility Rates and Total Fertility Rates, 2013

England and Wales: regions (within England), unitary authorities, counties, districts, London Boroughs, local health boards (within Wales)

	Total Live Births	Male	Female	General Fertility Rate (GFR)[2]	Total Fertility Rate (TFR)[3]
New Forest	1,485	728	757	54.7	1.78
Rushmoor	1,347	704	643	65.7	1.91
Test Valley	1,240	642	598	60.8	1.97
Winchester	1,260	659	601	57.6	1.88
Kent	**16,955**	**8,747**	**8,208**	**61.3**	**1.91**
Ashford	1,452	745	707	64.0	2.02
Canterbury	1,413	767	646	43.2	1.55
Dartford	1,442	736	706	68.7	1.98
Dover	1,150	620	530	61.6	1.95
Gravesham	1,389	681	708	67.8	2.05
Maidstone	1,875	992	883	63.0	1.91
Sevenoaks	1,212	607	605	60.1	1.92
Shepway	1,067	520	547	58.9	1.85
Swale	1,683	871	812	66.0	2.04
Thanet	1,615	835	780	67.7	2.08
Tonbridge and Malling	1,403	722	681	62.2	2.03
Tunbridge Wells	1,254	651	603	59.6	1.89
Oxfordshire	**7,867**	**4,114**	**3,753**	**59.3**	**1.77**
Cherwell	1,777	941	836	64.5	1.94
Oxford	1,919	1,002	917	47.0	1.48
South Oxfordshire	1,548	802	746	66.1	2.07
Vale of White Horse	1,380	722	658	63.4	1.93
West Oxfordshire	1,243	647	596	65.6	2.02
Surrey	**13,569**	**6,958**	**6,611**	**62.9**	**1.90**
Elmbridge	1,848	955	893	77.6	2.27
Epsom and Ewell	909	457	452	61.1	1.85
Guildford	1,535	783	752	52.7	1.63
Mole Valley	826	427	399	58.7	1.88
Reigate and Banstead	1,805	926	879	67.6	1.97
Runnymede	931	464	467	51.9	1.71
Spelthorne	1,327	685	642	71.0	2.09
Surrey Heath	945	514	431	61.3	1.92
Tandridge	892	453	439	59.9	1.88
Waverley	1,240	614	626	60.5	1.92
Woking	1,311	680	631	67.2	1.92
West Sussex	**8,835**	**4,615**	**4,220**	**61.7**	**1.90**
Adur	758	405	353	70.0	2.18
Arun	1,493	747	746	61.9	1.94
Chichester	1,046	539	507	57.6	1.86
Crawley	1,646	876	770	69.6	1.98
Horsham	1,261	676	585	57.6	1.88
Mid Sussex	1,512	788	724	59.5	1.84
Worthing	1,119	584	535	58.3	1.77
SOUTH WEST	**58,710**	**30,099**	**28,611**	**60.7**	**1.87**
Bath and North East Somerset UA	**1,854**	**977**	**877**	**51.0**	**1.74**
Bournemouth UA	**2,366**	**1,260**	**1,106**	**58.7**	**1.69**
Bristol, City of UA	**6,515**	**3,268**	**3,247**	**63.1**	**1.81**
Cornwall UA and Isles of Scilly UA [5]	**5,605**	**2,832**	**2,773**	**61.8**	**1.97**
North Somerset UA	**2,214**	**1,138**	**1,076**	**64.0**	**2.01**
Plymouth UA	**3,163**	**1,649**	**1,514**	**59.2**	**1.76**
Poole UA	**1,622**	**841**	**781**	**61.7**	**1.88**
South Gloucestershire UA	**3,029**	**1,587**	**1,442**	**59.5**	**1.84**
Swindon UA	**2,911**	**1,466**	**1,445**	**67.3**	**1.99**
Torbay UA	**1,474**	**728**	**746**	**69.3**	**2.16**
Wiltshire UA	**5,133**	**2,568**	**2,565**	**61.7**	**1.99**
Devon	**7,185**	**3,792**	**3,393**	**57.7**	**1.83**
East Devon	1,107	584	523	58.1	1.95
Exeter	1,384	741	643	48.6	1.51
Mid Devon	783	418	365	60.7	1.97
North Devon	954	511	443	63.7	2.03
South Hams	648	348	300	54.6	1.80
Teignbridge	1,206	597	609	62.1	2.02
Torridge	630	338	292	63.6	2.06
West Devon	473	255	218	59.6	1.94
Dorset	**3,547**	**1,827**	**1,720**	**58.2**	**1.92**
Christchurch	417	220	197	60.3	1.97
East Dorset	625	317	308	52.0	1.79
North Dorset	664	336	328	60.7	1.99
Purbeck	396	187	209	59.6	1.93
West Dorset	781	421	360	55.6	1.89
Weymouth and Portland	664	346	318	64.0	2.01
Gloucestershire	**6,554**	**3,372**	**3,182**	**60.6**	**1.88**
Cheltenham	1,351	693	658	56.5	1.66
Cotswold	712	350	362	54.2	1.81

15.14 Live births by local authority of usual residence of mother, numbers, sex, General Fertility Rates and Total Fertility Rates, 2013

England and Wales: regions (within England), unitary authorities, counties, districts, London Boroughs, local health boards (within Wales)

	Total Live Births	Male	Female	General Fertility Rate (GFR)[2]	Total Fertility Rate (TFR)[3]
Forest of Dean	734	381	353	55.1	1.87
Gloucester	1,760	920	840	70.1	2.05
Stroud	1,080	560	520	58.6	1.93
Tewkesbury	917	468	449	64.2	1.99
Somerset	**5,538**	**2,794**	**2,744**	**62.0**	**1.98**
Mendip	1,048	535	513	56.6	1.88
Sedgemoor	1,264	641	623	64.3	2.05
South Somerset	1,779	878	901	66.6	2.11
Taunton Deane	1,164	585	579	59.0	1.83
West Somerset	283	155	128	60.7	1.88
WALES	**33,747**	**17,387**	**16,360**	**58.9**	**1.80**
Isle of Anglesey	763	360	403	67.6	2.09
Gwynedd	1,229	659	570	56.3	1.83
Conwy	1,070	534	536	59.6	1.89
Denbighshire	1,017	544	473	64.6	2.05
Flintshire	1,657	836	821	60.1	1.89
Wrexham	1,615	811	804	64.2	1.93
Powys	1,230	643	587	61.5	2.02
Ceredigion	638	341	297	45.6	1.71
Pembrokeshire	1,136	596	540	57.2	1.81
Carmarthenshire	1,815	901	914	57.9	1.79
Swansea	2,488	1,333	1,155	53.6	1.62
Neath Port Talbot	1,495	742	753	59.2	1.80
Bridgend	1,540	807	733	60.2	1.86
The Vale of Glamorgan	1,368	733	635	60.8	1.94
Cardiff	4,624	2,408	2,216	56.0	1.68
Rhondda, Cynon, Taff	2,808	1,423	1,385	61.4	1.83
Merthyr Tydfil	673	343	330	58.6	1.70
Caerphilly	1,990	990	1,000	57.7	1.76
Blaenau Gwent	807	425	382	60.4	1.81
Torfaen	1,039	536	503	60.8	1.85
Monmouthshire	792	417	375	55.2	1.87
Newport	1,953	1,005	948	67.6	2.01
Betsi Cadwaladr University	7,351	3,744	3,607	61.5	1.91
Powys Teaching	1,230	643	587	61.5	2.02
Hywel Dda	3,589	1,838	1,751	55.1	1.73
Abertawe Bro Morgannwg University	5,523	2,882	2,641	56.8	1.72
Cwm Taf	3,481	1,766	1,715	60.8	1.80
Aneurin Bevan	6,581	3,373	3,208	60.8	1.86
Cardiff and Vale University	5,992	3,141	2,851	57.0	1.71
Usual residence outside England and Wales where birth occurred in England and Wales	**248**	**140**	**108**	**0**	**0**

Source: Office for National Statistics (ONS)

Notes:
p United Kingdom are provisional. Figures for England, Wales are final.

A birth to a mother whose usual residence is outside England and Wales is assigned to the country of residence. These births are included in total figures for "England, Wales and elsewhere" but are excluded from any sub-divisions of England and Wales.
The England and Wales and elsewhere figures correspond to figures published at the national level for England and Wales not based on area of usual residence.

The Human Fertilisation and Embryology Act (HFEA) 2008 contained provisions enabling two females in a same-sex couple to register a birth from 1 September 2009 onwards. Due to the small numbers, births registered to a same-sex couple in a civil partnership (655 in 2013) are included with marital births while births registered to a same-sex couple outside a civil partnership (259 in 2013) are included with births outside marriage.

Births registered under HFEA are reported only for England and Wales and no sub division thereof.

1 Live births per 1,000 population (all persons and all ages). This has been calculated using the mid-2013 population estimates.
2 The General Fertility Rate (GFR) is the number of live births per 1,000 women aged 15-44. The GFRs have been calculated using the mid-2013 population estimates.
3 The Total Fertility Rate (TFR) is the average number of live children that a group of women would bear if they experienced the age-specific fertility rates of the calendar year in question throughout their childbearing lifespan.
  The national TFRs have been calculated using the number of live births by single year of age and the mid-2013 population estimates.
  The sub-national TFRs have been calculated using the number of live births by five year age groups and the mid-2013 population estimates.
4 Maternities per 1,000 women aged 15-44. A maternity is a pregnancy resulting in the birth of one or more children, including stillbirths.
5 To preserve confidentiality, counts for City of London and Isles of Scilly have been combined with those for Hackney LB and Cornwall UA respectively
: denotes not available

15.15 Live births by age of mother and registration type[1], 1981-2012

England and Wales

Year	Type of Registration	All ages	Under 20	20-24	25-29	30-34	35-39	40-44	45 and over
					Age of mother at birth				
		Numbers of births							
2012	All	729,674	33,815	132,456	202,370	216,242	114,797	28,019	1,975
	Within Marriage/Civil Partnership[1]	383,189	1,295	29,627	106,555	148,403	78,689	17,380	1,240
	Outside Marriage/Civil Partnership[1]	346,485	32,520	102,829	95,815	67,839	36,108	10,639	735
	Joint Registrations same address	227,337	13,326	62,151	67,031	50,094	26,731	7,528	476
	Joint Registrations different address	77,269	12,327	27,867	18,759	10,872	5,529	1,809	106
	Sole Registrations	41,879	6,867	12,811	10,025	6,873	3,848	1,302	153
2011	All	723,913	36,435	134,946	200,587	207,151	115,444	27,518	1,832
	Within Marriage/Civil Partnership[1]	382,574	1,410	31,785	107,383	143,519	79,951	17,388	1,138
	Outside Marriage/Civil Partnership[1]	341,339	35,025	103,161	93,204	63,632	35,493	10,130	694
	Joint Registrations same address	226,057	14,600	63,287	66,102	47,706	26,688	7,213	461
	Joint Registrations different address	73,464	12,960	26,826	17,379	9,489	5,093	1,603	114
	Sole Registrations	41,818	7,465	13,048	9,723	6,437	3,712	1,314	119
2010	All	723,165	40,591	137,312	199,233	202,457	115,841	25,973	1,758
	Within Marriage/Civil Partnership[1]	384,375	1,684	33,955	108,465	141,873	80,846	16,404	1,148
	Outside Marriage/Civil Partnership[1]	338,790	38,907	103,357	90,768	60,584	34,995	9,569	610
	Joint Registrations same address	224,001	16,401	63,816	64,656	45,498	26,453	6,769	408
	Joint Registrations different address	72,297	14,352	26,184	16,393	8,838	4,903	1,525	102
	Sole Registrations	42,492	8,154	13,357	9,719	6,248	3,639	1,275	100
2009	All	706,248	43,243	136,012	194,129	191,600	114,288	25,357	1,619
	Within Marriage/Civil Partnership[1]	380,069	2,334	35,920	108,499	135,802	80,156	16,318	1,040
	Outside Marriage/Civil Partnership[1]	326,179	40,909	100,092	85,630	55,798	34,132	9,039	579
	Joint Registrations same address	214,189	17,200	61,813	60,876	41,831	25,637	6,444	388
	Joint Registrations different address	68,251	14,778	24,376	14,811	7,991	4,790	1,420	85
	Sole Registrations	43,739	8,931	13,903	9,943	5,976	3,705	1,175	106
2008	All	708,711	44,691	135,971	192,960	192,450	116,220	24,991	1,428
	Within Marriage	387,930	2,739	38,239	110,353	138,066	81,602	15,991	940
	Outside Marriage	320,781	41,952	97,732	82,607	54,384	34,618	9,000	488
	Joint Registrations same address	210,076	17,231	59,913	59,104	41,178	26,036	6,289	325
	Joint Registrations different address	65,241	15,161	23,102	13,543	7,257	4,662	1,441	75
	Sole Registrations	45,464	9,560	14,717	9,960	5,949	3,920	1,270	88
2007	All	690,013	44,805	130,784	182,570	191,124	115,380	24,041	1,309
	Within Marriage	384,463	3,087	38,859	106,603	138,157	81,399	15,484	874
	Outside Marriage	305,550	41,718	91,925	75,967	52,967	33,981	8,557	435
	Joint Registrations same address	198,470	17,036	55,904	54,040	39,783	25,383	6,050	274
	Joint Registrations different address	61,379	14,714	21,415	12,204	7,024	4,587	1,359	76
	Sole Registrations	45,701	9,968	14,606	9,723	6,160	4,011	1,148	85
2006	All	669,601	45,509	127,828	172,642	189,407	110,509	22,512	1,194
	Within Marriage	378,225	3,199	40,126	103,348	137,996	78,269	14,511	776
	Outside Marriage	291,376	42,310	87,702	69,294	51,411	32,240	8,001	418
	Joint Registrations same address	185,461	17,061	52,162	48,474	38,133	23,897	5,469	265
	Joint Registrations different address	60,460	14,870	20,755	11,651	7,159	4,578	1,375	72
	Sole Registrations	45,455	10,379	14,785	9,169	6,119	3,765	1,157	81
2005	All	645,835	44,830	122,145	164,348	188,153	104,113	21,155	1,091
	Within Marriage	369,330	3,654	40,010	99,957	137,401	73,810	13,760	738
	Outside Marriage	276,505	41,176	82,135	64,391	50,752	30,303	7,395	353
	Joint Registrations same address	175,555	16,316	48,755	45,165	37,764	22,265	5,057	233
	Joint Registrations different address	55,780	14,108	18,909	10,320	6,801	4,289	1,287	66
	Sole Registrations	45,170	10,752	14,471	8,906	6,187	3,749	1,051	54
2004	All	639,721	45,094	121,072	159,984	190,550	102,228	19,884	909
	Within Marriage	369,997	4,063	41,285	98,539	139,838	72,555	13,098	619
	Outside Marriage	269,724	41,031	79,787	61,445	50,712	29,673	6,786	290
	Joint Registrations same address	171,498	16,262	47,793	43,038	37,820	21,758	4,648	179
	Joint Registrations different address	52,854	13,608	17,628	9,620	6,713	4,133	1,096	56
	Sole Registrations	45,372	11,161	14,366	8,787	6,179	3,782	1,042	55

15.15 Live births by age of mother and registration type[1], 1981-2012

England and Wales

Year	Type of Registration	All ages	Under 20	20-24	25-29	30-34	35-39	40-44	45 and over
2003	All	621,469	44,236	116,622	156,931	187,214	97,386	18,205	875
	Within Marriage	364,244	4,338	40,887	98,694	138,002	69,595	12,113	615
	Outside Marriage	257,225	39,898	75,735	58,237	49,212	27,791	6,092	260
	Joint Registrations same address	163,374	16,000	45,225	40,867	36,630	20,335	4,151	166
	Joint Registrations different address	48,976	12,706	16,076	8,815	6,488	3,831	1,014	46
	Sole Registrations	44,875	11,192	14,434	8,555	6,094	3,625	927	48
2002	All	596,122	43,467	110,959	153,379	180,532	90,449	16,441	895
	Within Marriage	354,090	4,582	40,712	97,583	134,093	65,369	11,110	641
	Outside Marriage	242,032	38,885	70,247	55,796	46,439	25,080	5,331	254
	Joint Registrations same address	154,086	15,824	42,315	39,554	34,326	18,236	3,656	175
	Joint Registrations different address	44,817	11,832	14,333	8,109	6,164	3,471	866	42
	Sole Registrations	43,129	11,229	13,599	8,133	5,949	3,373	809	37
2001	All	594,634	44,189	108,844	159,926	178,920	86,495	15,499	761
	Within Marriage	356,548	4,640	40,736	103,131	133,710	63,202	10,582	547
	Outside Marriage	238,086	39,549	68,108	56,795	45,210	23,293	4,917	214
	Joint Registrations same address	150,421	16,215	40,843	39,797	33,306	16,790	3,341	129
	Joint Registrations different address	43,921	11,665	13,682	8,416	6,029	3,290	800	39
	Sole Registrations	43,744	11,669	13,583	8,582	5,875	3,213	776	46
2000	All	604,441	45,846	107,741	170,701	180,113	84,974	14,403	663
	Within Marriage	365,836	4,742	40,262	111,606	136,165	62,671	9,910	480
	Outside Marriage	238,605	41,104	67,479	59,095	43,948	22,303	4,493	183
	Joint Registrations same address	149,510	17,011	40,450	41,236	31,795	15,836	3,055	127
	Joint Registrations different address	43,322	11,634	13,110	8,646	6,037	3,158	706	31
	Sole Registrations	45,773	12,459	13,919	9,213	6,116	3,309	732	25
1999	All	621,872	48,375	110,722	181,931	185,311	81,281	13,617	635
	Within Marriage	379,983	5,333	43,190	120,716	140,330	60,470	9,466	478
	Outside Marriage	241,889	43,042	67,532	61,215	44,981	20,811	4,151	157
	Joint Registrations same address	149,584	17,833	40,190	42,126	32,152	14,455	2,725	103
	Joint Registrations different address	44,102	12,015	12,865	9,153	6,214	3,135	695	25
	Sole Registrations	48,203	13,194	14,477	9,936	6,615	3,221	731	29
1998	All	635,901	48,285	113,537	193,144	188,499	78,881	12,980	575
	Within Marriage	395,290	5,278	45,724	130,747	144,599	59,320	9,189	433
	Outside Marriage	240,611	43,007	67,813	62,397	43,900	19,561	3,791	142
	Joint Registrations same address	146,521	17,589	39,818	42,212	30,938	16,410	3,118	114
	Joint Registrations different address	44,130	11,588	13,157	9,513	6,194			
	Sole Registrations	49,960	13,830	14,838	10,672	6,768	3,151	673	28
1997	All	643,095	46,372	118,589	202,792	187,528	74,900	12,332	582
	Within Marriage	404,873	5,233	49,068	139,383	145,293	56,671	8,797	428
	Outside Marriage	238,222	41,139	69,521	63,409	42,235	18,229	3,535	154
	Joint Registrations same address	141,740	16,551	39,784	42,020	28,715	15,179	2,860	122
	Joint Registrations different address	45,900	11,365	14,147	10,374	6,523			
	Sole Registrations	50,582	13,223	15,590	11,015	6,997	3,050	675	32
1996	All	649,485	44,667	125,732	211,103	186,377	69,503	11,516	587
	Within Marriage	416,822	5,365	54,651	148,770	145,898	53,265	8,421	452
	Outside Marriage	232,663	39,302	71,081	62,333	40,479	16,238	3,095	135
	Joint Registrations same address	135,282	15,410	39,978	40,384	26,875	13,347	2,517	107
	Joint Registrations different address	46,365	10,946	14,858	10,599	6,626			
	Sole Registrations	51,016	12,946	16,245	11,350	6,978	2,891	578	28
1995	All	648,138	41,938	130,744	217,418	181,202	65,517	10,779	540
	Within Marriage	428,189	5,623	61,029	157,855	144,200	51,129	7,944	409
	Outside Marriage	219,949	36,315	69,715	59,563	37,002	14,388	2,835	131
	Joint Registrations same address	127,789	14,424	39,274	38,376	24,376	11,859	2,335	99
	Joint Registrations different address	44,244	10,011	14,815	10,323	6,141			
	Sole Registrations	47,916	11,880	15,626	10,864	6,485	2,529	500	32

15.15 Live births by age of mother and registration type[1], 1981-2012

England and Wales

Year	Type of Registration	All ages	Under 20	20-24	25-29	30-34	35-39	40-44	45 and over
1994	All	664,726	42,026	140,240	229,102	179,568	63,061	10,241	488
	Within Marriage	449,190	6,099	69,227	170,605	145,563	49,668	7,662	366
	Outside Marriage	215,536	35,927	71,013	58,497	34,005	13,393	2,579	122
	Joint Registrations same address	123,874	14,168	39,827	37,168	22,288	10,892	2,084	97
	Joint Registrations different address	42,632	9,752	14,778	9,939	5,513			
	Sole Registrations	49,030	12,007	16,408	11,390	6,204	2,501	495	25
1993	All	673,467	45,121	151,975	235,961	171,061	58,824	9,986	539
	Within Marriage	456,919	6,875	76,950	178,456	139,671	46,919	7,621	427
	Outside Marriage	216,548	38,246	75,025	57,505	31,390	11,905	2,365	112
	Joint Registrations same address	118,758	14,134	40,168	35,307	20,084	9,569	1,882	85
	Joint Registrations different address	47,548	11,577	17,381	10,780	5,339			
	Sole Registrations	50,242	12,535	17,476	11,418	5,967	2,336	483	27
1992	All	689,656	47,861	163,311	244,798	166,839	56,650	9,696	501
	Within Marriage	474,431	7,787	86,220	188,928	137,904	45,733	7,456	403
	Outside Marriage	215,225	40,074	77,091	55,870	28,935	10,917	2,240	98
	Joint Registrations same address	119,239	15,236	42,063	34,756	18,673	8,784	1,811	78
	Joint Registrations different address	44,514	11,381	16,658	9,693	4,620			
	Sole Registrations	51,472	13,457	18,370	11,421	5,642	2,133	429	20
1991	All	699,217	52,396	173,356	248,727	161,259	53,644	9,316	519
	Within Marriage	487,923	8,948	95,605	196,281	135,542	43,810	7,294	443
	Outside Marriage	211,294	43,448	77,751	52,446	25,717	9,834	2,022	76
	Joint Registrations same address	115,298	16,351	42,245	32,532	16,468	7,861	1,594	60
	Joint Registrations different address	41,865	11,848	15,835	8,518	3,851			
	Sole Registrations	54,131	15,249	19,671	11,396	5,398	1,973	428	16
1990	All	706,140	55,541	180,136	252,577	156,264	51,905	9,220	497
	Within Marriage	506,141	10,958	106,188	204,701	133,384	43,179	7,302	429
	Outside Marriage	199,999	44,583	73,948	47,876	22,880	8,726	1,918	68
	Joint Registrations same address	106,001	16,311	39,062	29,181	14,585	6,793	1,505	55
	Joint Registrations different address	39,167	12,081	14,751	7,555	3,289			
	Sole Registrations	54,831	16,191	20,135	11,140	5,006	1,933	413	13
1989	All	687,725	55,543	185,239	242,822	145,320	49,465	8,845	491
	Within Marriage	501,921	12,027	114,456	200,961	125,439	41,528	7,079	431
	Outside Marriage	185,804	43,516	70,783	41,861	19,881	7,937	1,766	60
	Joint Registrations same address	95,858	15,686	36,582	24,859	12,543	6,156	1,341	49
	Joint Registrations different address	36,409	11,688	14,022	6,603	2,738			
	Sole Registrations	53,537	16,142	20,179	10,399	4,600	1,781	425	11
1988	All	693,577	58,741	193,726	243,460	140,974	47,649	8,520	507
	Within Marriage	516,225	14,099	125,575	205,292	123,384	40,400	7,025	450
	Outside Marriage	177,352	44,642	68,151	38,168	17,590	7,249	1,495	57
	Joint Registrations same address	87,601	15,304	33,994	22,070	10,765	5,607	1,159	44
	Joint Registrations different address	35,807	12,240	13,807	5,913	2,505			
	Sole Registrations	53,944	17,098	20,350	10,185	4,320	1,642	336	13
1981[2]	All	634,492	56,570	194,500	215,760	126,590	34,210	6,170	690
	Within Marriage	553,509	30,140	165,690	201,460	118,720	31,480	5,340	680
	Outside Marriage	80,983	26,430	28,810	14,300	7,870	2,730	840	20
	Joint Registrations	47,140	12,750	16,820	9,520	5,530	1,940	550	20
	Sole Registrations	33,850	13,670	12,000	4,770	2,340	780	290	-

1. The Human Fertilisation and Embryology Act 2008 contained provisions enabling two females in a same-sex couple to register a birth from 1 September 2009 onwards. Due to the small numbers, births registered to a same-sex couple in a civil partnership (556 in 2012) are included with marital births while births registered to a same-sex couple outside a civil partnership (252 in 2012) are included with births outside marriage.
2. 1981 births for age-groups are based on a 10 per cent sample.

Source: Office for National Statistics

15.16 Legal abortions: by country of procedure (i) age, (ii) gestation weeks, (iii) procedure, (iv) parity, (v) previous abortions, (vi) grounds and (vii) principal medical condition for abortions performed under ground E, 2013

Country of abortion					numbers and percentages	
	England & Wales		Scotland p		Great Britain p	
All legal abortions	**190,800**	*100%*	**11,777**	*100%*	**202,577**	*100%*
(i) Age						
Under 16	2,576	*1*	225	*2*	2,801	*1*
16-17	9,319	*5*	761	*6*	10,080	*5*
18-19	17,664	*9*	1,294	*11*	18,958	*9*
20-24	55,356	*29*	3,556	*30*	58,912	*29*
25-29	44,887	*24*	2,609	*22*	47,496	*23*
30-34	32,470	*17*	1,772	*15*	34,242	*17*
35+	28,528	*15*	1,560	*13*	30,088	*15*
(ii) Gestation weeks						
3 - 9	150,216	*79*	9,281	*79*	159,497	*79*
10 - 12	23,730	*12*	1,588	*13*	25,318	*12*
13 - 19	13,724	*7*	853	*7*	14,577	*7*
20 and over	3,130	*2*	55	*0*	3,185	*2*
(iii) Procedure						
Surgical	99,154	*52*	2,522	*21*	101,676	*50*
Medical	91,646	*48*	9,255	*79*	100,901	*50*
(iv) Parity (number of previous pregnancies resulting in live or stillbirth)						
0	89,916	*47*	5,749	*49*	95,665	*47*
1+	100,884	*53*	6,028	*51*	106,912	*53*
(v) Number of previous pregnancies resulting in abortion under the Act						
0	121,267	*64*	8,159	*69*	129,426	*64*
1+	69,533	*36*	3,618	*31*	73,151	*36*
(vi) Grounds						
A (alone or with B, C or D) or F or G	57	*0*	*	.	*	.
B (alone or with C or D)	136	*0*	*	.	*	.
C (alone)	185,950	*97*	11,610	*99*	197,560	*98*
D (alone or with C)	1,736	*1*	18	*0*	1,754	*1*
E (alone one with A, B, C or D)	2,921	*2*	142	*1*	3,063	*2*
(vii) Principal medical condition for abortions performed under ground E						
Total Ground E	**2,921**	*100%*	**142** [1]	*100%*	**3,063**	*100%*
The nervous system (Q00 - Q07)	720	*25*	37	*26*	757	*25*
Other congenital malformations (Q10-Q89)	664	*23*	28	*20*	692	*23*
Chromosomal abnormalities (Q90 - Q99)	1,087	*37*	47	*33*	1,134	*37*
Other	450	*15*	30	*21*	480	*16*

p Provisional data
Source: ISD Scotland, Department of Health
* Adhering to ISD Statistical Disclosure Control Protocol. See annex B
. Not available
[1] Some notifications record more than one Statutory Ground, therefore totals may not match with the numbers released by ISD Scotland.

Note: percentages are rounded and may not add up to 100

15.17 Death[1] rates per 1,000 population: by age and sex, 2013

England and Wales

Age	Males	Females	Age	Males	Females	Age	Males	Females
All ages	8.76	9.04						
0–4	1.01	0.81	35–39	1.19	0.66	70–74	24.48	16.05
0	4.41	3.49	35	0.95	0.57	70	19.61	12.64
1	0.33	0.30	36	1.03	0.61	71	21.39	13.96
2	0.18	0.14	37	1.21	0.59	72	25.55	16.14
3	0.11	0.12	38	1.30	0.67	73	27.21	18.17
4	0.10	0.09	39	1.42	0.86	74	30.07	20.09
5–9	0.09	0.07	40–44	1.72	1.03	75–79	40.74	28.09
5	0.10	0.09	40	1.43	0.79	75	33.27	22.24
6	0.07	0.08	41	1.61	0.96	76	37.14	25.04
7	0.12	0.06	42	1.76	0.97	77	40.25	27.96
8	0.08	0.08	43	1.81	1.11	78	45.89	31.13
9	0.07	0.06	44	1.95	1.32	79	50.05	35.68
10–14	0.10	0.09	45–49	2.48	1.56	80–84	73.18	53.26
10	0.09	0.10	45	2.26	1.26	80	57.98	41.39
11	0.06 u	0.08	46	2.26	1.34	81	65.12	45.96
12	0.11	0.06 u	47	2.41	1.63	82	75.01	53.11
13	0.12	0.08	48	2.59	1.62	83	83.11	59.52
14	0.13	0.12	49	2.87	1.94	84	92.73	70.15
15–19	0.30	0.14	50–54	3.68	2.48	85–89	129.38	100.41
15	0.15	0.11	50	3.00	2.06	85	106.10	80.25
16	0.21	0.13	51	3.39	2.22	86	118.23	88.54
17	0.28	0.12	52	3.61	2.49	87	130.33	101.77
18	0.39	0.18	53	4.04	2.76	88	148.57	113.18
19	0.46	0.17	54	4.44	2.93	89	167.51	130.97
20–24	0.46	0.21	55–59	5.92	3.96	90 and over	238.28	210.12
20	0.43	0.19	55	4.60	3.36			
21	0.44	0.20	56	5.23	3.60			
22	0.41	0.21	57	6.03	4.04			
23	0.51	0.21	58	6.49	4.38			
24	0.52	0.21	59	7.46	4.50			
25–29	0.60	0.29	60–64	9.61	6.14			
25	0.58	0.24	60	8.09	4.99			
26	0.59	0.26	61	8.69	5.71			
27	0.62	0.29	62	9.71	6.15			
28	0.55	0.33	63	10.28	6.77			
29	0.66	0.30	64	11.23	7.03			
30–34	0.79	0.43	65–69	14.34	9.44			
30	0.66	0.38	65	12.14	7.91			
31	0.78	0.40	66	12.72	8.09			
32	0.81	0.43	67	14.46	9.92			
33	0.81	0.44	68	15.99	10.60			
34	0.89	0.52	69	17.47	11.45			

Notes

Although the male death rate tracks above that of the females at each age group, the overall female death rate is higher than the male rate as there are greater number of female deaths in the population compared to males.

1 Death figures are based on deaths registered rather than deaths occurring in a calendar year. More information on registration delays is available on the ONS website.
u Denotes low reliability

Source: Office for National Statistics

15.18 Stillbirth[1,2] and infant death[3] rates: age at death, 1921-2013

England and Wales

Period	Infant mortality per 1,000 live births[3] at various ages										Stillbirths[2] and infant deaths per 1,000 total births			
	Under 1 year	Neonatal mortality					Postneonatal mortality				Stillbirths	Stillbirths plus deaths under 1 week	Stillbirths plus deaths under 4 weeks	Stillbirths plus deaths under 1 year
		Under 4 weeks	Early neonatal			Late neo-natal	4 weeks and under 1 year	4 weeks and under 3 months	3 months and under 6 months	6 months and under 1 year				
			Under 1 week	Under 1 day	1 day and under 1 week	1 week and under 4 weeks								
1921	82.8	35.3	22.4	10.8	11.6	12.9	47.5	14.8	14.0	18.6	:	:	:	:
1922	77.1	34.1	22.0	10.4	11.6	12.1	43.0	12.7	11.0	19.3	:	:	:	:
1923	69.4	31.9	21.1	10.2	10.9	10.8	37.5	11.3	10.0	16.1	:	:	:	:
1924	75.1	33.1	21.8	10.6	11.2	11.3	42.0	12.5	10.9	18.6	:	:	:	:
1925	75.0	32.3	21.2	10.1	11.1	11.1	42.7	12.6	11.3	18.8	:	:	:	:
1926	70.2	31.9	21.3	10.0	11.3	10.6	38.3	11.6	10.4	16.3	:	:	:	:
1927	69.7	32.3	22.2	10.6	11.6	10.1	37.4	10.7	9.7	16.9	38.8	59.6	69.3	105.3
1928	65.1	31.1	21.6	10.4	11.2	9.5	34.0	10.7	9.2	14.1	40.1	60.8	69.9	102.6
1929	74.4	32.8	22.3	10.4	11.9	10.6	41.5	11.6	10.7	19.3	40.0	61.4	71.6	111.4
1930	60.0	30.9	22.0	10.4	11.6	8.9	29.1	9.6	7.8	11.6	40.8	61.9	70.4	98.3
1931	65.7	31.5	22.1	10.4	11.7	9.5	34.2	10.8	9.2	14.2	40.9	62.1	71.2	104.5
1932	64.5	31.5	22.4	10.6	11.8	9.2	33.0	10.8	9.0	13.2	41.3	62.8	71.6	103.7
1933	62.7	32.1	22.9	11.0	11.8	9.3	30.6	9.8	8.6	12.2	41.4	63.4	72.3	102.5
1934	59.3	31.4	22.7	10.9	11.8	8.7	27.9	8.9	7.7	11.3	40.5	62.2	70.5	96.7
1935	57.0	30.4	22.0	10.7	11.3	8.4	26.6	9.1	7.7	9.8	40.7	61.9	69.9	95.4
1936	58.7	30.2	21.9	10.7	11.3	8.2	28.5	9.3	8.3	10.9	39.7	60.8	68.7	95.9
1937	57.7	29.7	22.0	10.8	11.2	7.8	28.0	9.4	8.3	10.3	39.0	60.2	67.6	94.4
1938	52.8	28.3	21.1	10.3	10.8	7.1	24.5	8.2	7.3	9.0	38.3	58.6	65.5	88.9
1939	50.6	28.3	21.2	10.3	10.9	7.1	22.2	7.9	7.0	7.3	38.1	58.5	65.3	86.9
1940	56.8	29.6	21.3	9.8	11.5	8.3	27.2	9.3	8.2	9.7	37.2	57.7	65.7	92.5
1941	60.0	29.0	20.7	10.1	10.6	8.3	31.1	11.3	9.7	10.1	34.8	54.7	62.7	92.4
1942	50.6	27.2	19.6	9.6	10.0	7.7	23.4	8.7	7.5	7.2	33.2	52.1	59.4	81.1
1943	49.1	25.2	18.3	9.1	9.2	6.9	23.9	8.8	7.8	7.3	30.1	47.9	54.6	77.5
1944	45.4	24.4	17.5	8.8	8.8	6.9	21.1	8.0	7.0	6.1	27.6	44.5	51.1	70.9
1945	46.0	24.8	18.0	9.0	9.0	6.8	21.3	8.2	7.0	6.1	27.6	45.2	51.8	73.4
1946	42.9	24.5	17.8	8.7	9.1	6.7	18.4	7.1	6.1	5.2	27.2	44.3	50.7	66.9
1947	41.4	22.7	16.5	7.8	8.7	6.2	18.6	6.9	6.0	5.7	24.1	40.3	46.4	65.0
1948	33.9	19.7	15.6	7.8	7.9	4.1	14.2	5.5	4.8	3.9	23.2	38.5	42.5	56.8
1949	32.4	19.3	15.6	7.6	8.0	3.7	13.0	4.8	4.4	3.8	22.7	38.0	41.5	54.6
1950	29.6	18.5	15.2	7.2	8.0	3.3	11.1	4.3	3.7	3.1	22.6	37.4	40.7	51.7
1951	29.7	18.8	15.5	7.5	8.0	3.3	10.9	4.1	3.6	3.2	23.0	38.2	41.5	52.2
1952	27.6	18.3	15.2	7.6	7.6	3.2	9.3	3.7	3.0	2.6	22.7	37.5	40.6	49.6
1953	26.8	17.7	14.8	7.4	7.4	2.9	9.1	3.4	3.0	2.7	22.4	36.9	39.7	48.6
1954	25.4	17.7	14.9	7.6	7.4	2.8	7.7	3.0	2.6	2.1	23.5	38.1	40.8	48.4
1955	24.9	17.3	14.6	7.6	7.0	2.6	7.6	2.9	2.6	2.1	23.2	37.4	40.0	47.5
1956	23.7	16.8	14.2	7.4	6.8	2.6	6.9	2.7	2.3	1.8	22.9	36.7	39.3	46.0
1957	23.1	16.5	14.1	7.6	6.5	2.4	6.7	2.6	2.1	1.9	22.5	36.2	38.5	45.1
1958	22.5	16.2	13.8	7.5	6.3	2.4	6.4	2.6	2.1	1.7	21.5	35.0	37.3	43.6
1959	22.2	15.9	13.6	7.6	6.0	2.3	6.3	2.4	2.1	1.8	20.8	34.1	36.3	42.6
1960	21.8	15.5	13.3	7.5	5.8	2.2	6.3	2.5	2.1	1.6	19.8	32.8	35.0	41.1
1961	21.4	15.3	13.3	7.6	5.7	2.1	6.1	2.4	2.0	1.7	19.0	32.0	34.1	40.0
1962	21.7	15.1	13.0	7.4	5.6	2.1	6.6	2.5	2.3	1.8	18.1	30.8	32.9	39.4
1963	21.1	14.3	12.3	7.2	5.1	2.0	6.9	2.7	2.4	1.8	17.2	29.3	31.3	38.0
1964	19.9	13.8	12.0	7.1	4.9	1.8	6.1	2.4	2.1	1.6	16.3	28.2	29.9	35.9
1965	19.0	13.0	11.3	6.6	4.7	1.7	6.0	2.4	2.1	1.6	15.8	26.9	28.6	34.5
1966	19.0	12.9	11.1	6.5	4.6	1.7	6.1	2.5	2.0	1.6	15.3	26.3	28.0	34.1
1967	18.3	12.5	10.7	6.3	4.4	1.8	5.8	2.4	2.0	1.4	14.8	25.4	27.2	32.9
1968	18.3	12.4	10.6	6.3	4.3	1.8	5.9	2.4	2.1	1.5	14.3	24.7	26.4	32.3
1969	18.0	12.0	10.3	6.0	4.3	1.7	6.0	2.5	2.1	1.5	13.2	23.4	25.1	31.0
1970	18.2	12.3	10.6	6.3	4.3	1.7	5.9	2.6	2.0	1.3	13.0	23.5	25.2	31.0
1971	17.5	11.6	9.9	6.0	3.9	1.7	5.9	2.6	2.0	1.3	12.5	22.3	24.0	29.8
1972	17.2	11.5	9.8	5.8	4.1	1.7	5.7	2.4	2.0	1.4	12.0	21.7	23.4	29.0
1973	16.9	11.1	9.5	5.5	4.0	1.6	5.7	2.5	1.9	1.3	11.6	21.0	22.6	28.3
1974	16.3	11.0	9.4	5.2	4.2	1.7	5.3	2.3	1.9	1.1	11.1	20.4	22.0	27.3
1975	15.7	10.7	9.1	5.0	4.1	1.7	5.0	2.2	1.7	1.1	10.3	19.3	20.9	25.9
1976	14.3	9.7	8.2	4.7	3.5	1.5	4.6	1.9	1.6	1.1	9.7	17.7	19.3	23.8
1977	13.8	9.3	7.6	4.2	3.5	1.6	4.5	1.9	1.6	1.1	9.4	17.0	18.6	23.0

15.18 Stillbirth[1,2] and infant death[3] rates: age at death, 1921-2013

England and Wales

Period	Infant mortality per 1,000 live births[3] at various ages										Stillbirths[2] and infant deaths per 1,000 total births			
	Under 1 year	Neonatal mortality					Postneonatal mortality				**Stillbirths**	Stillbirths plus deaths under 1 week	Stillbirths plus deaths under 4 weeks	Stillbirths plus deaths under 1 year
		Under 4 weeks	Early neonatal			Late neo-natal	**4 weeks and under 1 year**	4 weeks and under 3 months	3 months and under 6 months	6 months and under 1 year				
			Under 1 week	Under 1 day	1 day and under 1 week	1 week and under 4 weeks								
1978	**13.2**	**8.7**	**7.1**	3.7	3.4	1.6	**4.5**	1.9	1.6	1.0	**8.5**	15.5	17.1	21.6
1979	**12.8**	**8.2**	**6.8**	3.7	3.0	1.5	**4.6**	1.9	1.7	1.0	**8.0**	14.7	16.1	20.7
1980	**12.0**	**7.7**	**6.2**	3.4	2.8	1.5	**4.4**	1.8	1.5	1.1	**7.2**	13.3	14.8	19.2
1981	**11.1**	**6.7**	**5.3**	2.9	2.3	1.4	**4.4**	1.8	1.6	1.0	**6.6**	11.8	13.2	17.6
1982	**10.8**	**6.3**	**5.0**	2.8	2.2	1.2	**4.6**	1.9	1.6	1.1	**6.3**	11.3	12.5	17.0
1983	**10.1**	**5.9**	**4.7**	2.6	2.1	1.2	**4.3**	1.9	1.5	0.9	**5.7**	10.4	11.6	15.8
1984	**9.5**	**5.6**	**4.4**	2.6	1.9	1.1	**3.9**	1.6	1.3	0.9	**5.7**	10.1	11.2	15.1
1985	**9.4**	**5.4**	**4.3**	2.5	1.9	1.0	**4.0**	1.7	1.4	0.9	**5.5**	9.8	10.9	14.8
1986	**9.6**	**5.3**	**4.3**	2.4	1.8	1.0	**4.3**	1.8	1.5	1.0	**5.3**	9.6	10.6	14.8
1987	**9.2**	**5.1**	**3.9**	2.3	1.6	1.1	**4.1**	1.8	1.5	0.9	**5.0**	8.9	10.0	14.2
1988	**9.0**	**4.9**	**3.9**	2.2	1.7	1.0	**4.1**	1.7	1.5	0.9	**4.9**	8.7	9.8	13.8
1989	**8.4**	**4.8**	**3.7**	2.1	1.6	1.1	**3.7**	1.6	1.3	0.8	**4.7**	8.3	9.4	13.1
1990	**7.9**	**4.6**	**3.5**	2.0	1.5	1.0	**3.3**	1.3	1.2	0.7	**4.6**	8.1	9.1	12.4
1991	**7.4**	**4.4**	**3.4**	2.0	1.4	0.9	**3.0**	1.2	1.0	0.7	**4.6**	8.0	9.0	12.0
1992	**6.6**	**4.3**	**3.3**	2.0	1.4	1.0	**2.3**	1.0	0.8	0.6	**4.3**	7.6	8.5	10.8
1993	**6.3**	**4.2**	**3.2**	1.9	1.3	0.9	**2.1**	0.9	0.7	0.6	**5.7**	8.9	9.8	12.0
1994	**6.2**	**4.1**	**3.2**	1.9	1.4	0.9	**2.1**	0.8	0.7	0.6	**5.7**	8.9	9.8	11.9
1995	**6.1**	**4.2**	**3.2**	1.8	1.5	0.9	**2.0**	0.9	0.6	0.5	**5.5**	8.7	9.7	11.6
1996	**6.1**	**4.1**	**3.2**	1.9	1.3	0.9	**2.0**	0.9	0.6	0.5	**5.4**	8.6	9.5	11.5
1997	**5.9**	**3.9**	**3.0**	1.8	1.2	0.9	**2.0**	0.9	0.6	0.5	**5.3**	8.3	9.2	11.2
1998	**5.7**	**3.8**	**2.9**	1.7	1.2	0.9	**1.9**	0.9	0.6	0.4	**5.3**	8.2	9.1	11.0
1999	**5.8**	**3.9**	**2.9**	1.7	1.2	1.0	**1.9**	0.9	0.6	0.5	**5.3**	8.2	9.2	11.1
2000	**5.6**	**3.9**	**2.9**	1.7	1.2	1.0	**1.7**	0.8	0.5	0.4	**5.3**	8.2	9.1	10.8
2001	**5.4**	**3.6**	**2.7**	1.7	1.0	0.9	**1.9**	0.8	0.5	0.5	**5.3**	8.0	8.9	10.7
2002	**5.2**	**3.6**	**2.7**	1.7	1.0	1.0	**1.7**	0.8	0.0	0.0	**5.6**	8.0	9.0	11.0
2003	**5.3**	**3.6**	**2.8**	1.8	1.0	0.8	**1.7**	0.8	0.4	0.4	**5.8**	8.6	9.4	11.1
2004	**5.0**	**3.5**	**2.7**	1.7	1.0	0.8	**1.6**	0.8	0.4	0.4	**5.7**	8.4	9.2	10.7
2005	**5.0**	**3.4**	**2.6**	1.7	1.0	0.8	**1.6**	0.8	0.5	0.4	**5.4**	8.0	8.8	10.4
2006	**5.0**	**3.5**	**2.6**	1.7	0.9	0.9	**1.5**	0.7	0.4	0.3	**5.4**	8.0	8.8	10.3
2007	**4.7**	**3.3**	**2.5**	1.6	0.9	0.7	**1.5**	0.7	0.4	0.4	**5.2**	7.7	8.4	9.9
2008	**4.6**	**3.2**	**2.4**	1.6	0.8	0.7	**1.4**	0.7	0.4	0.3	**5.1**	7.5	8.3	9.7
2009	**4.5**	**3.1**	**2.4**	1.5	0.9	0.7	**1.4**	0.7	0.4	0.3	**5.2**	7.6	8.3	9.7
2010	**4.3**	**2.9**	**2.3**	1.5	0.8	0.6	**1.3**	0.7	0.3	0.3	**5.1**	7.4	8.0	9.3
2011	**4.2**	**3.0**	**2.3**	1.5	0.7	0.7	**1.2**	0.6	0.3	0.3	**5.2**	7.5	8.2	9.4
2012	**4.0**	**2.8**	**2.2**	1.5	0.6	0.6	**1.2**	0.6	0.3	0.3	**4.9**	7.0	7.6	8.8
2013	**3.8**	**2.7**	**2.0**	1.4	0.6	0.6	**1.2**	0.6	0.3	0.3	**4.7**	6.7	7.3	8.5

1 Registration of stillbirths commenced on 1 July 1927. Annual figures for 1927 are estimated.

2 From 1927 to 30 September 1992 stillbirths relate to fetal deaths at or over 28 weeks gestation, and from 1 October 1992 at or over 24 weeks gestation.

3 Infant deaths are based on the live births occurring in the year, except in the years 1931-56 when they were based on related live births - that is, the combined live births of the associated and preceding years to which they relate.

: denotes not available

Source: Office for National Statistics

15.19 Interim Life Tables
Period expectation of life based on data for the years 2011-2013

United Kingdom

Age x	Males l_x	Males e_x	Females l_x	Females e_x
0	100000.0	78.91	100000.0	82.71
5	99464.3	74.33	99577.4	78.06
10	99418.1	69.37	99541.2	73.09
15	99366.4	64.40	99501.0	68.12
20	99204.5	59.50	99423.3	63.17
25	98954.1	54.65	99315.3	58.23
30	98637.3	49.81	99167.8	53.32
35	98222.0	45.01	98946.5	48.43
40	97624.5	40.27	98614.3	43.58
45	96757.4	35.61	98092.5	38.80
50	95540.5	31.03	97290.8	34.10
55	93727.7	26.58	96021.7	29.52
60	90874.0	22.33	94061.8	25.07
65	86566.3	18.31	91126.2	20.80
70	80239.9	14.54	86692.6	16.72
75	70549.0	11.17	79694.0	12.96
80	57035.1	8.20	68798.7	9.59
85	38998.7	5.80	52237.8	6.78
90	19847.6	4.02	31210.3	4.64
95	6382.7	2.78	12347.9	3.17
100	1024.1	2.01	2594.0	2.27

England & Wales

Age x	Males l_x	Males e_x	Females l_x	Females e_x
0	100000.0	79.15	100000.0	82.92
5	99459.8	74.58	99574.2	78.27
10	99414.0	69.61	99537.9	73.30
15	99363.8	64.65	99496.9	68.33
20	99211.8	59.74	99423.9	63.38
25	98974.1	54.88	99318.7	58.44
30	98681.2	50.03	99178.4	53.52
35	98298.1	45.22	98964.2	48.63
40	97733.0	40.47	98643.7	43.78
45	96902.4	35.79	98137.0	38.99
50	95720.1	31.20	97356.7	34.28
55	93952.6	26.74	96129.6	29.68
60	91170.9	22.47	94217.0	25.23
65	86942.8	18.43	91346.5	20.94
70	80736.3	14.65	87015.9	16.85
75	71201.8	11.25	80184.6	13.06
80	57808.6	8.25	69495.6	9.66
85	39732.3	5.83	53030.6	6.83
90	20356.7	4.03	31882.9	4.67
95	6589.3	2.79	12718.9	3.19
100	1059.9	2.01	2708.9	2.29

Scotland

Age x	Males l_x	Males e_x	Females l_x	Females e_x
0	100000.0	76.77	100000.0	80.89
5	99517.7	72.14	99616.4	76.20
10	99464.9	67.18	99582.0	71.22
15	99409.0	62.21	99545.7	66.25
20	99201.4	57.34	99424.1	61.33
25	98867.0	52.52	99294.0	56.40
30	98351.8	47.78	99072.9	51.52
35	97614.4	43.13	98762.8	46.68
40	96671.6	38.52	98288.9	41.89
45	95434.8	33.99	97626.6	37.16
50	93886.7	29.50	96618.1	32.52
55	91685.1	25.15	94981.4	28.03
60	88219.5	21.03	92629.4	23.68
65	83205.4	17.14	89090.9	19.51
70	75711.6	13.58	83662.5	15.61
75	64623.1	10.46	75159.1	12.07
80	50252.8	7.70	62661.5	8.94
85	32580.4	5.50	45403.1	6.35
90	15499.5	3.92	25490.8	4.37
95	4623.7	2.71	9206.5	2.97
100	722.6	2.04	1701.0	2.11

Northern Ireland

Age x	Males l_x	Males e_x	Females l_x	Females e_x
0	100000.0	78.00	100000.0	82.29
5	99471.3	73.41	99580.9	77.63
10	99426.0	68.44	99539.6	72.66
15	99343.0	63.50	99513.6	67.68
20	99022.5	58.69	99420.9	62.74
25	98628.6	53.92	99293.3	57.82
30	98119.3	49.19	99128.8	52.91
35	97570.0	44.45	98933.0	48.01
40	96918.5	39.73	98640.5	43.14
45	95997.0	35.08	98073.8	38.38
50	94733.4	30.51	97257.5	33.68
55	92784.9	26.10	95891.9	29.12
60	89744.8	21.89	93770.8	24.72
65	85246.6	17.90	90727.8	20.46
70	78818.5	14.15	86189.8	16.39
75	68934.7	10.79	79169.1	12.61
80	54566.9	7.94	67554.6	9.31
85	36638.3	5.56	50492.1	6.57
90	17769.4	3.92	29382.6	4.47
95			11172.8	2.93
100			1923.1	2.06

Data published to age 95 due to very low numbers of deaths and population.

Source: Office for National Statistics

lx is the number of survivors to exact age x of 100,000 live births of the same sex who are assumed to be subject throughout their lives to the mortality rates experienced in the three year period to which the National Life Table relates.

e_x is the average period expectation of life at exact age x, that is the average number of years that those aged x exact will live thereafter based on the mortality rates experienced in the three year period to which the National Life Table relates.

15.20a Adoption Orders[1] granted by sex and age band, 2011-2013

England & Wales

Year	Total adoption orders: All Ages	< 1 year	1-4 yrs	5-9 yrs	10-14 yrs	15-17 yrs	Other[2]
Total							
2011	**4,709**	90	2,924	1,075	457	133	30
2012	**5,260**	121	3,286	1,238	439	158	18
2013	**6,078**	169	4,037	1,338	368	141	25
Males							
2011	2,330	53	530	1465	216	61	5
2012	2,648	58	621	1683	205	70	11
2013	2,985	80	679	1996	173	51	6
Females							
2011	2,365	37	545	1459	241	72	11
2012	2,611	63	617	1603	234	88	6
2013	3,090	89	659	2041	195	90	16
Gender Unknown							
2011	14	0	0	0	0	0	14
2012	1	0	0	0	0	0	1
2013	3	0	0	0	0	0	3

Source: Office for National Statistics

Notes:

1) Figures are for adoption orders only. Figures for orders issued for related non-adoption orders are not included in this summary

2) 'Other' includes those who were aged 18 by the time the order was made, or where the age was not correctly recorded.

Note:

Prior to 2011, National Statistics on Adoptions in england and Wales were published by ONS: http://www.ons.gov.uk/ons/taxonomy/index.html?nscl=AdoptionsData in ONS publications are based on adoption data provided by the General Register Office, which maintains the Adopted Child Register using copies of adoption orders issued by courts. There are small differences between the number of adoptions as recorded by the two sets of statistics.

During the transition period over 2009/2010 when courts were starting to implement the new administrative data systems not all adoption orders made were recorded on the system, resulting in MoJ figures held for adoptions being around 15 per cent lower than those published by ONS. Since 2011 all courts dealing with family matters in England and Wales have been using the Familyman administrative system and hand-written notifications of adoptions to GRO have been phased out. This has resulted in figures for the ONS and MoJ being much closer.

Please see the joint statement produced by MoJ, ONS and GRO on the differences in these adoption statistics attached to the 2012 Q4 edition of Court Statistics Quarterly for further details.

Adoption data is now reported in the Ministry of Justice Family Court Statistics Quarterly.

15.20b Adoptions by age of child and relationship of the adopter(s), 2013

Scotland

Age and sex of child		Total	Relationship of adopter(s)				
			Both parents	Step-parent	Grandparent(s)	Other relation(s)	No relation
All ages	P	489	-	97	4	15	373
	M	258	-	52	-	7	199
	F	231	-	45	4	8	174
Months							
less than 6	M	-	-	-	-	-	-
	F	1	-	1	-	-	-
6-8	M	3	-	1	-	-	2
	F	2	-	1	-	-	1
9-11	M	3	-	-	-	-	3
	F	4	-	-	-	-	4
12-17	M	8	-	-	-	-	8
	F	10	-	-	-	-	10
18-23	M	26	-	1	-	-	25
	F	22	-	-	2	1	19
Years							
2	M	48	-	1	-	3	44
	F	25	-	-	1	1	23
3-4	M	70	-	5	-	1	64
	F	56	-	2	1	3	50
5-9	M	63	-	14	-	2	47
	F	85	-	20	-	3	62
10-14	M	30	-	25	-	-	5
	F	18	-	13	-	-	5
15 and over	M	7	-	5	-	1	1
	F	8	-	8	-	-	-

Source: GRO-Scotland

15.20c Adoptions - Northern Ireland, 2009-2012

Persons	All ages		Under 1		1-4		5-9		10-14		15-17	
Year	Numbers	Percentage	Numbers	Percentage	Numbers	Percentage	Numbers	Percentage	Numbers	Percentage	Numbers	Percentage
2009	116	100%	1	1%	43	37%	46	40%	20	17%	6	5%
2010	116	100%	3	3%	46	40%	46	40%	17	15%	4	3%
2011	104	100%	3	3%	40	38%	40	38%	13	13%	8	8%
2012	127	100%	1	1%	66	52%	39	31%	13	10%	8	6%

Males	All ages		Under 1		1-4		5-9		10-14		15-17	
Year	Numbers	Percentage	Numbers	Percentage	Numbers	Percentage	Numbers	Percentage	Numbers	Percentage	Numbers	Percentage
2009	55	100%	0	0%	24	44%	20	36%	10	18%	1	2%
2010	56	100%	2	4%	26	46%	21	38%	6	11%	1	2%
2011	47	100%	0	0%	19	40%	18	38%	6	13%	4	9%
2012	68	100%	0	0%	33	49%	21	31%	10	15%	4	6%

Females	All ages		Under 1		1-4		5-9		10-14		15-17	
Year	Numbers	Percentage	Numbers	Percentage	Numbers	Percentage	Numbers	Percentage	Numbers	Percentage	Numbers	Percentage
2009	61	100%	1	2%	19	31%	26	43%	10	16%	5	8%
2010	60	100%	1	2%	20	33%	25	42%	11	18%	3	5%
2011	57	100%	3	5%	21	37%	22	39%	7	12%	4	7%
2012	59	100%	1	2%	33	56%	18	31%	3	5%	4	7%

Source: Northern Ireland Statistics and Research Agency (NISRA)

this page is intentionally blank

Health

Health

Deaths: analysed by cause (Table 16.6)
All figures in this table for England and Wales represent the number of deaths occurring in each calendar year. All data for Scotland and Northern Ireland relate to the number of deaths registered during each calendar year. From 2001, all three constituent countries of the UK are coding their causes of death using the latest, tenth, revision of the International Statistical Classification of Diseases and Related Health Problems (ICD-10). All cause of death information from 2001 (also for 2000 for Scotland) presented in this table is based on the revised classification.

To assist users in assessing any discontinuities arising from the introduction of the revised classification, bridge-coding exercises were carried out on all deaths registered in 1999 in England and Wales and also in Scotland. For further information about ICD-10 and the bridge-coding carried out by The Office for National Statistics (ONS), see the ONS Report: Results of the ICD-10 bridge-coding study, England and Wales, Statistics Quarterly 14 (2002), pages 75–83 or log on to the Office for National Statistics (ONS) website at: www.ons.gov.uk. For information on the Scottish bridge-coding exercise, consult the Annual Report of the General Register Office for Scotland or log on to their website at: www.gro-scotland.gov.uk. No bridge-coding exercise was conducted for Northern Ireland.

Neonatal deaths and homicide and assault
For England and Wales, neonatal deaths (those at age under 28 days) are included in the number of total deaths but excluded from the cause figures. This has particular impact on the totals shown for the chapters covered by the ranges P and Q, 'Conditions originating in the perinatal period' and 'Congenital malformations, deformations and chromosomal abnormalities'. These are considerably lower than the actual number of deaths because it is not possible to assign an underlying cause of death from the neonatal death certificate used in England and Wales.
Also, for England and Wales only, the total number shown for Homicide and assault, X85–Y09, will not be a true representation because the registration of these deaths is often delayed by adjourned inquests.

Occupational ill health (Tables 16.8 and 16.9)

There are a number of sources of data on the extent of occupational or work-related ill health in Great Britain. For some potentially severe lung diseases caused by exposures which are highly unlikely to be found in a non-occupational setting, it is useful to count the number of death certificates issued each year. This is also true for mesothelioma, a cancer affecting the lining of the lungs and stomach, for which the number of cases with non-occupational causes is likely to be larger (although still a minority). Table 16.9 shows the number of deaths for mesothelioma and asbestosis (linked to exposure to asbestos), pneumoconiosis (linked to coal dust or silica), byssinosis (linked to cotton dust) and some forms of allergic alveolitis (including farmer's lung). For asbestos-related diseases the figures are derived from a special register maintained by HSE.

Most conditions which can be caused or made worse by work can also arise from other factors. The remaining sources of data on work-related ill health rely on attribution of individual cases of illness to work causes. In The Health and Occupation Reporting Network (THOR), this is done by specialist doctors – either occupational physicians or those working in particular disease specialisms (covering musculoskeletal, psychological, respiratory, skin, audio logical and infectious disease). Table 16.8 presents data from THOR for the last three years. It should be noted that not all cases of occupational disease will be seen by participating specialists; for example, the number of deaths due to mesothelioma (shown in Table 16.9) is known to be greater than the number of cases reported to THOR.

Injuries at work (Table 16.10)

The Reporting of Injuries, Diseases and Dangerous Occurrences Regulations 1995 (RIDDOR) places a legal duty on employers to report injuries arising from work activity to the relevant enforcing authority, namely HSE, local authorities and the Office of Rail Regulation (ORR). These include injuries to employees, self-employed people and members of the public. From 12 September 2011 the reporting of all RIDDOR incidents will move to a predominantly online system.

While the enforcing authorities are informed about almost all relevant fatal workplace injuries, it is known that non-fatal injuries are substantially under-reported. Currently, it is estimated that just over half of all such injuries to employees are actually reported, with the self-employed reporting a much smaller proportion. These results are achieved by comparing reported non-fatal injuries (major as well as over-3-day), with results from the Labour Force Survey (LFS).

16.1a. NHS Hospital and Community Health Services (HCHS): Ambulance staff by type 2004-2014

England as at 30 September each year   Headcount

	2004	2005	2006	2007	2008	2009	2010	2011	2012	2013
Total ambulance staff	26,902	28,180	28,648	28,471	30,518	32,284	33,163	32,902	32,076	32,817
Qualified ambulance staff	17,272	18,117	16,176	17,028	17,451	17,922	18,450	18,687	18,645	18,734
Manager	789	773	614	598	685	692	696	700	657	603
Emergency care practitioner	..	..	438	646	705	750	780	770	742	722
Paramedic	7,536	8,311	8,222	8,241	9,203	10,089	10,678	11,368	11,954	12,556
Ambulance technician	..	..	6,902	7,543	6,858	6,391	6,300	5,853	5,295	4,861
Ambulance personnel (old definition)	8,947	9,033	..	..	..	..	..	..	..	..
Support to ambulance staff	9,630	10,063	12,472	11,443	13,067	14,362	14,738	14,238	13,451	14,112
Ambulance personnel (new definition)	..	..	4,630	4,537	5,438	6,347	6,444	6,398	6,290	6,673
Trainee ambulance technician	..	..	1,829	1,147	1,258	1,415	1,481	1,193	875	666
Trainee ambulance personnel	2,047	2,201	..	..	..	..	..	..	..	..
Clerical & administrative	3,240	3,286	3,247	3,340	3,882	4,161	4,384	4,303	4,382	4,948
Estates (maintenance & works)	265	268	205	166	220	189	226	232	237	226
Healthcare assistant	2,761	2,794	834	992	845	936	960	958	980	919
Support worker	1,317	1,514	1,727	1,261	1,424	1,314	1,254	1,162	695	692

Source: Health and Social Care Information Centre

Notes:
'..' denotes not applicable

These statistics relate to the contracted positions within English NHS organisations and may include those where the person assigned to the position is temporarily absent, for example on maternity leave.

The new headcount methodology is not fully comparable with data for years prior to 2010, due to improvements that make it a more stringent count of absolute staff numbers.

Headcount totals are unlikely to equal the sum of components. Further information on the headcount methodology is available in the Census publication.

In 2006 ambulance staff were collected under new, more detailed, occupation codes. As a result, qualified totals and support to ambulance staff totals are not directly comparable with previous years.

16.1b NHS Labour Turnover and Stability Analysis
Welsh Ambulance Trust

		Headcount
As of 31 Dec 2013	**Occupation Code**	
020 Welsh Ambulance Trust	**Ambulance Officer**	73
	Urgent Care Assistant	125
	Paramedic Practitioner	31
	Paramedic	950
	Ambulance Technician	417
	Staff Group Summary Total	**1596**

Source: Welsh Ambulance Service NHS Trust

16.1c Ambulance Services Staff by Type: Scotland

As of December 2013

Whole time equivalent (WTE)

	Total	Under 20	20 - 24	25 - 29	30 - 34	35 - 39	40 - 44	45 - 49	50 - 54	55 - 59	60 - 64	65 +
Ambulance services	**2,341.5**	**3.0**	**79.2**	**160.4**	**165.9**	**301.6**	**365.8**	**379.1**	**379.3**	**293.4**	**175.8**	**38.0**
Ambulance care assistant	795.2	-	3.0	6.7	11.5	70.8	129.3	130.8	170.3	133.5	107.2	32.1
Auxiliary	-	-	-	-	-	-	-	-	-	-	-	-
Driver	62.3	-	-	1.0	2.3	3.3	4.5	7.4	10.2	13.6	16.1	3.9
EMDC / control	315.4	3.0	22.2	46.7	57.3	48.4	39.6	38.8	28.2	21.7	9.6	-
Paramedic[4]	-	-	-	-	-	-	-	-	-	-	-	-
Technician	1,074.1	-	54.0	106.0	92.8	163.7	179.4	193.1	144.1	99.0	39.9	2.0
Other	94.5	-	-	-	2.0	15.4	13.0	9.0	26.5	25.6	3.0	-
Not assimilated / not known	-	-	-	-	-	-	-	-	-	-	-	-

Source: Scottish Workforce Information Standard System (SWISS)

1. There is a coding issue for management grades (non AfC) for NHS 24 for the three quarters of December 2013 to June 2014. This has been resolved for September 2014 data.

2. Management grade figures include non executive board members.

3. NHS Greater Glasgow & Clyde identified an error in the recording of some portering services staff, these have been corrected and from December 2014 are recorded in general services, previously they were recorded in hotel services.

4. From 1st April 2013 paramedics have been reclassified from ambulance services staff to allied health professions.

Whole time equivalent (WTE) adjusts headcount staff figures to take account of part time staff.

Ambulance services

These figures apply to those staff assimilated to the Agenda for Change (AfC) ambulance services job family and those staff not yet assimilated but where an ambulance services staff group has been identified from their existing payscale.

The ambulance services job family was renamed in 2011, previously it was known as emergency services.

16.1d Ambulance Staff by Type: Northern Ireland

Headcount

		2004	2005	2006	2007	2008	2009	2010	2011	2012	2013
Northern Ireland											
Total Ambulance staff	JHQ9	867	911	989	1,007	1,025	1,036	1026	1045	1052	1086
Emergency Medical Technicians and Paramedics	JHR2	567	576	637	659	625	629	598	610	618	620
Other/Patient care services	JHR3	176	211	220	219	231	227	244	240	231	263
Control Assistants	JHR4	59	61	63	67	94	108	106	102	107	108
Ambulance Officers	JHR5	65	63	69	62	75	72	78	93	96	95

Department of Health, Social Services and Public Safety Northern Ireland

16.2 Hospital and primary care services Scotland

			1999 /00	2000 /01	2001 /02	2002 /03	2003 /04	2004 /05	2005 /06
Hospital and community services In-patients:[1,2]									
Average available staffed beds	KDEA	Thousands	33.5	32.1	30.9	29.8	28.9	28.1	27.4
Average occupied beds:									
All departments	KDEB	"	26.9	25.8	25.1	24.2	23.2	22.5	22.1
Psychiatric and learning disability	KDEC	"	8.3	7.6	7.0	6.4	5.9	5.5	5.2
Discharges or deaths[3]	KDED	"	980	972	969	959	989	1,003	1,015
Outpatients:[2,4]									
New cases	KDEE	"	2,766	2,749	2,728	2,731	2,750	2,718	2,762
Total attendances	KDEF	"	6,451	6,382	6,254	6,193	6,147	5,981	6,060
Medical and dental staff:[5,6,22]	JYXO	Headcount	9,273	9,325	9,644	10,256	10,407	10,658	10,871
Whole-time	KDEG	"	7,185	7,216	7,530	8,115	8,349	8,612	8,796
Part-time	KDEH	"	1,632	1,648	1,681	1,697	1,636	1,630	1,670
Honorary	JYXN	"	495	495	468	468	437	431	418
Professional and technical staff:[6,7,22]									
Whole-time	KDEI	"	11,261	11,261	11,705	12,265	12,942	13,258	13,750
Part-time	KDEJ	"	5,218	5,483	5,852	6,273	6,708	6,968	7,440
Nursing and midwifery staff:[6,8,22]									
Whole-time	KDEK	"	32,356	32,401	33,334	34,294	34,939	35,338	36,093
Part-time	KDEL	"	29,242	29,131	29,004	29,015	29,354	29,484	29,688
Administrative and clerical staff:[6,9,22]									
Whole-time	KDEM	"	14,541	14,710	15,361	16,200	17,260	17,806	18,434
Part-time	KDEN	"	7,456	7,677	8,075	8,630	9,307	9,943	10,707
Domestic, transport, etc, staff:[6,10,22]									
Whole-time	KDEO		7,972	7,848	7,625	7,768	8,234	8,305	8,516
Part-time	KDEP		12 424	12 272	11 522	11 915	12 588	12 324	12 545
Primary care services									
Primary Medical services									
General medical practitioners (GPs):[11,23]	JX4B	Headcount	4,072	4,253	4,346	4,361	4,447	4,456	4,521
Performer[12,23]	KDET	"	3,702	3,710	3,761	3,770	3,805	3,782	3,763
Performer salaried[13,23]	KDEU	"	88	99	108	114	155	188	288
Performer registrar	JX4C	"	283	261	283	284	281	282	300
Performer retainee[14,23]	JX4D	"	-	184	196	194	209	208	176
Expenditure on Primary Medical Services[15,23]	KDEW	£million	378	405	430	468	519	628	701
Pharmaceutical services[16]									
Prescriptions dispensed	KDEX	Millions		63	66	70	72	75	77
Payments to pharmacists (gross)	KDEY	£million		..	..	887	963	984	1016
Average gross cost per prescription	KDEZ	£		11.7	12.2	12.8	13.3	12.6	12.5
Dental services									
Dentists on list[17]	KDFA	Headcount	1,808	1,808	1,844	1,869	1,882	1,900	1,936
Number of courses of treatment completed	KDFB	Thousands	3,338	3,389	3,359	3,420	3,359	3,375	3,348
Payments to dentists (gross)	KDFC	£million	161	163	165	172	170	174	179
Payments bypatients	KDFD	"	49	51	52	55	53	54	54
Payments out of public funds	KDFE	"	112	112	113	118	117	120	125
Average gross cost per course	KDFF	£	38	38	38	40	40	40	41
General ophthalmic services Number of Eye Exams given[18,19]	KDFG	Thousands	850	861	877	907	920	935	960
Number of pairs of glasses supplied[20]	KDFH	"	494	439	463	458	450	457	457
Payments out of public funds forsight testing and dispensing[21]	KDFK	£ million	..	..	..	35	36	38	39

Sources: ISD Scotland, NHS National Services Scotland; 0131 275 7777

16.2   Hospital and primary care services Scotland

			2006 /07	2007 /08	2008 /09	2009 /10	2010 /11	2011 /12	2012 /13
Hospital and community services In-patients:[1,2]									
Average available staffed beds	KDEA	Thousands	26.9	26.3	25.8	24.9	23.9	23.3	22.9
Average occupied beds:					-				
All departments	KDEB	"	21.7	21.0	20.6	19.9	19.2	18.8	18.7
Psychiatric and learning disability	KDEC	"	4.9	4.6	4.3	4.1	3.8	3.6	3.6
Discharges or deaths[3]	KDED	"	1,037	1,066	1,091	1,090	1,096	1,114	1,141
Outpatients:[2,4]									
New cases	KDEE	"	2,827	2,894	3,003	3,026	3,044	3,021	3,028
Total attendances	KDEF	"	6,048	6,093	6,271	6,208	6,206	6,235	6,219
Medical and dental staff:[5,6,22]	JYXO	Headcount	11,201	11,822	12,534	12,619	12,757	13,336	13,317
Whole-time	KDEG	"	9,201	9,828	9,971	9,975	9,973	10,360	10,296
Part-time	KDEH	"	1,607	2,028	2,252	2,444	2,563	2,797	2,849
Honorary	JYXN	"	411	418	377	247	263	252	243
Professional and technical staff:[6,7,22]									
Whole-time	KDEI	"	14,323	13,642	14,567	15,403	15,590	15,021	14,866
Part-time	KDEJ	"	7,990	7,953	8,375	9,036	9,504	9,689	9,924
Nursing and midwifery staff:[6,8,22]									
Whole-time	KDEK	"	37,104	37,071	37,654	37,995	37,165	35,547	35,015
Part-time	KDEL	"	29,995	29,544	29,555	29,949	30,261	30,065	30,518
Administrative and clerical staff:[6,9,22]									
Whole-time	KDEM	"	18,907	18,181	18,158	19,007	18,686	17,639	17,147
Part-time	KDEN	"	11,375	10,836	11,231	11,679	11,703	11,345	11,140
Domestic, transport, etc, staff:[6,10,22]									
Whole-time	KDEO		8,697	10,205	10,623	11,037	10,927	10,522	10,469
Part-time	KDEP		12 675	12,819	12,874	13,138	12,576	12,042	12,051
Primary care services									
Primary Medical services									
General medical practitioners (GPs):[11,23]	JX4B	Headcount	4,597	4,686	4,890	4,907	4,905	4,888	4,856
Performer[12,23]	KDET	"	3,770	3,785	3,783	3,805	3,777	3,748	3,742
Performer salaried[13,23]	KDEU	"	354	418	460	487	482	523	530
Performer registrar	JX4C	"	308	325	490	465	497	478	455
Performer retainee[14,23]	JX4D	"	169	164	164	159	156	145	138
Expenditure on Primary Medical Services[15,23]	KDEW	£million	700	705	701	729	741	747	756
Pharmaceutical services[16]									
Prescriptions dispensed	KDEX	Millions	80	82	86	89	91	95	97
Payments to pharmacists (gross)	KDEY	£million	1045	1067	1107	1139	1160	1177	1118
Average gross cost per prescription	KDEZ	£	12.1	11.7	11.4	11.1	11.0	10.7	9.9
Dental services									
Dentists on list[17]	KDFA	Headcount	2,009	2,099	2,204	2,313	2,354	2,486	2,520
Number of courses of treatment completed	KDFB	Thousands	3,387	3,401	3,548	3,686	3,830	4,100	4,289
Payments to dentists (gross)	KDFC	£million	188	199	220	231	243	255	***
Payments bypatients	KDFD	"	46	47	50	52	55	59	***
Payments out of public funds	KDFE	"	143	152	170	180	188	196	***
Average gross cost per course	KDFF	£	42	43	45				
General ophthalmic services Number of Eye Exams given[18,19]	KDFG	Thousands	1,573	1,626	1,728	1,775	1,805	1,914	1,927
Number of pairs of glasses supplied[20]	KDFH	"	443	451	468	474	466	489	469
Payments out of public funds forsight testing and dispensing[21]	KDFK	£ million	66	79	86	91	90	95	95

Sources: ISD Scotland, NHS National Services Scotland; 0131 275 7777

16.2 Hospital and primary care services Scotland

1 Excludes joint user and contractual hospitals.

2 In year to 31 March.

3 Includes transfers out and emergency inpatients treated in day bed units.

4 Including attendances at accident and emergency consultant clinics.

5 As at 30 September. Figures exclude officers holding honorary locum appointments. Part-time includes maximum part-time appointments. There is an element of double counting of "heads" in this table as doctors can hold more than one contract. For example, they may hold contracts of different type, eg part time and honorary. Doctors holding two or more contracts of the same type, eg part time, are not double counted. Doctors, whose sum of contracts amounts to whole time, are classed as such. Figures have been revised due to coding changes.

6 The change in both collection and presentation of workforce data due to changes to staff groupings under Agenda for Change has inevitably meant that the amount of historical trend analysis of data is limited, though still available for some high level groupings.

7 As at 30 September. Comprises Therapeutic, Healthcare science, Technical and Pharmacy staff.

8 As at 30 September. Includes Health Care Assistants. Figures post 2003 have been amended due to a coding error resulting in some staff previously in this group being moved to the admin and clerical group.

9 As at 30 September. Comprises Senior Management and Administrative and Clerical staff. Figures for 2003 onwards have been amended due to the inclusion of some staff previously in the nursing and midwifery staff group

10 As at 30 September.Comprises Ambulance, Works, Ancillary and Trades.

11 Contracted GP's in post in Scottish general practices, at 1 October up to 2003/04 and 30 Sept for 2004/05 onwards. Excludes GP locums and GPs working only in Out of Hours services. The total may not equal the sum of the figures for individual GP designations as some GPs hold more than one contract. Source: www.isdscotland.org/workforce

12 For 2004/05 onwards this group comprised mainly of Provider (partner) GPs. Known prior to 2004/05 as Principal GPs.

13 Up to 2003/04 this group comprises salaried GPs plus associates, assistants and 'other' GPs. Terminology changed with the introduction of the new GMS contract in April 2004.

14 Data on the number of GP retainees not available prior to 2000.

15 Total expenditure on General Medical Services/Primary Medical Services Source: NHS Scotland Costs Book "R390" tables, www.isdscotland.org/costs Note, the contractual arrangements for payments to many general practices changed with the introduction of the new GMS contract in April 2004.

16 For prescriptions dispensed in financial year by all community pharmacists (including stock orders), dispensing doctors and appliance suppliers. Gross total excludes patient charges.

17 Comprises of non-salaried GDS principal dentists only as at 31 March.

18 Figures represent sight tests paid for by health boards, hospital eye service referrals and GOD(s) ST (v) claimants.

19 Free NHS eye examinations were extended to all on 1st April 2006.

20 Does not include hospital eye service.

21 OPTIX, the electronic system for recording ophtalmic payment information, was introduced in 2002. Information for previous years is now not centrally available from ISD

22 In order to provide additional and more accurate information, ISD revised methodologies. These changes include the revision to the headcount measure. Headcount refers to the actual number of individuals (employees) working within the NHSS. This eliminates any double counting that may exist as a result of an employee holding more than one post. Please note due to revisions in the headcount measure, it is not possible to compare data prior to 2007.

23 Figures have been revised and differ from those previously published due to improvements in source data quality.

*** Figures not yet published.

16.3 Hospital and general health services
Northern Ireland

			2002	2003	2004	2005	2006
Hospital services[1]							
In-patients:							
Beds available[2]	KDGA	Numbers	8,301	8,347	8,323	8,238	7,976
Average daily occupation of beds	KDGB	Percentages	84	84	84	84	83
Discharges or deaths[3]	KDGC	Thousands	327	332	337	296	295
Out-patients:[4]							
New cases	KDGD	"	992	1,014	1,027	1,040	1,081
Total attendances	KDGE	"	2,122	2,161	2,175	2,219	2,233
General health services							
Medical services[1]							
Doctors (principals) on the list[5,6]	KDGF	Numbers	1,076	1,076	1,078	1,084	1,100
Number of patients per doctor	KDGG	"	1,652	1,658	1,663	1,655	1,631
Gross Payments to doctors[7]	KDGH	£ thousand	88,194	96,894	..	..	..
Pharmaceutical services [1]							
Prescription forms dispensed	KDGI	Thousands	14,622	15,158	15,283	15,860	16,393
Number of prescription items	KDGJ	"	25,501	26,656	27,401	28,417	29,599
Gross Cost[9]	KDGK	£ thousand	327,045	362,401	382,789	390,763	408,771
Charges[10]	KDGL	"	9,597	9,798	10,262	10,676	11,298
Net Cost[9]	KDGM	"	317,448	352,602	372,527	380,087	397,473
Average gross cost per prescription item[9]	KDGN	£	13	14	14	14	14
Dental services[1,11]							
Dentists on the list[5]	KDGO	Numbers	689	696	720	722	751
Number of courses of paid treatment	KDGP	Thousands	1,123	1,107	1,086	1,084	1,064
Gross cost	KDGQ	£ thousand	66,201	66,910	67,294	69,480	65,172
Patients	KDGR	Thousands	930	919	907	910	900
Contributions (Net cost)	KDGS	£ thousand	49,376	50,282	50,498	52,308	50,068
Average gross cost per paid treatment	KDGT	£	59	60	62	64	61
Ophthalmic services [1]							
Number of sight tests given[12]	KDGU	Thousands	334	346	347	360	368
Number of optical appliances supplied[13]	KDGV	"	190	192	189	194	196
Cost of service (gross)[14]	KDGW	£ thousand	13,473	13,981	14,395	15,868	16,280
Health and social services[15]							
Medical and dental staff:							
Whole-time	KDGZ	Numbers	2,409	2,606	2,749	2,947	3,152
Part-time	KDHA	"	624	619	626	561	554
Nursing and midwifery staff:							
Whole-time	KDHB	"	10,221	10,709	11,116	11,395	11,454
Part-time	KDHC	"	8,354	8,665	8,850	9,015	9,072
Administrative and clerical staff:							
Whole-time	KDHD	"	7,820	8,188	8,676	8,878	8,938
Part-time	KDHE	"	3,349	3,579	3,828	4,160	4,221
Professional and technical staff:							
Whole-time	KDHF	"	3,968	4,155	4,518	4,685	4,758
Part-time	KDHG	"	1,491	1,605	1,724	1,822	2,021
Social services staff(excluding casual home helps):							
Whole-time	KDHH	"	3,280	3,454	3,709	3,773	3,889
Part-time	KDHI	"	978	1,093	1,197	1,289	1,417
Ancillary and other staff:							
Whole-time	KDHJ	"	3,421	3,413	3,469	3,722	3,833
Part-time	KDHK	"	5,118	5,410	5,580	5,486	5,892
Cost of services (gross)[14]	KDHL	£ thousand	1,868,538	2,113,453	..	..	..
Payments by recipients	KDHM	Thousands	88,860	87,999	..	..	..
Payments out of public funds	KDHN	£ thousand	1,779,678	2,025,454	..	..	..

16.3 Hospital and general health services
Northern Ireland

			2007	2008	2009	2010	2011	2012	2013
Hospital services[1]									
In-patients:									
Beds available[2]	KDGA	Numbers	7,827	7,636	7,274	6,732	6,439	6,288	6,172
Average daily occupation of beds	KDGB	Percentages	83	82	82	83	84	84	83
Discharges or deaths[3]	KDGC	Thousands	306	311	300	295	295	301	304
Out-patients:[4]									
New cases	KDGD	"	1,115	1,149	1,150	1,148	1,123	1,124	1,144
Total attendances	KDGE	"	2,282	2,256	2,231	2,234	2,239	2,247	2,288
General health services									
Medical services[1]									
Doctors (principals) on the list[5,6]	KDGF	Numbers	1,127	1,148	1,156	1,160	1,163	1,170	1,171
Number of patients per doctor	KDGG	"	1,626	1,618	1,615	1,623	1,631	1,631	1,639
Gross Payments to doctors[7]	KDGH	£ thousand	..	..					
Pharmaceutical services[1]									
Prescription forms dispensed	KDGI	Thousands	17,280	17,910	19,241	20,411	20,860	21,416	21,723
Number of prescriptions	KDGJ	"	30,864	32,107	34,263	36,298	36,916	38,614	40,019
Gross Cost[9]	KDGK	£ thousand	425,440	445,184	470,049	490,670	462,947	457,492	463,206
Charges[10]	KDGL	"	11,943	10,243	4,447	0	0	0	0
Net Cost[9]	KDGM	"	413,497	434,940	465,603	490,670	462,947	457,492	463,206
Average gross cost per prescription item[9]	KDGN	£	14	14	14	14	13	12	12
Dental services[1,11]									
Dentists on the list[5]	KDGO	Numbers	763	795	816	889	1,010	1,044	1,049
Number of courses of paid treatment	KDGP	Thousands	1,002	1,034	1,051	1,172	1,231	1,283	1,335
Gross cost	KDGQ	£ thousand	68,775	71,401	73,741	81,621	84,659	90,759	92,984
Patients	KDGR	Thousands	859	868	885	1,001	1,119	1,147	1,166
Contributions (Net cost)	KDGS	£ thousand	53,301	55,801	57,897	64,280	66,533	69,960	73,520
Average gross cost per paid treatment	KDGT	£	69	69	70	70	69	71	70
Ophthalmic services[1]									
Number of sight tests given[12]	KDGU	Thousands	385	404	413	425	435	438	446
Number of optical appliances supplied[13]	KDGV	"	200	210	212	219	226	233	235
Cost of service (gross)[14]	KDGW	£ thousand	16,970	18,468	19,638	19,823	20,220	20,836	21,346
Health and social services[15]									
Medical and dental staff:									
Whole-time	KDGZ	Numbers	3,250	3,278	3,301	3,294	3347	3415	3358
Part-time	KDHA	"	587	603	599	618	649	677	697
Nursing and midwifery staff:									
Whole-time	KDHB	"	11,623	11,512	11,716	11,292	11171	11426	11722
Part-time	KDHC	"	9,310	9,251	9,277	9,470	9356	9422	9453
Administrative and clerical staff:									
Whole-time	KDHD	"	8,683	8,255	8,197	7,880	7795	8106	8201
Part-time	KDHE	"	4,226	4,196	4,286	4,280	4304	4447	4498
Professional and technical staff:									
Whole-time	KDHF	"	4,936	4,619	4,704	4,748	4807	5069	5233
Part-time	KDHG	"	2,076	2,347	2,423	2,533	2639	2725	2859
Social services staff(excluding casual home helps):									
Whole-time	KDHH	"	4,014	4,441	4,619	4,632	4581	4622	4689
Part-time	KDHI	"	2,041	2,808	2,863	2,877	2896	2919	2930
Ancillary and other staff:									
Whole-time	KDHJ	"	3,857	3,831	3,816	3,855	3814	3740	3726
Part-time	KDHK	"	5,667	4,794	4,904	4,805	4582	4598	4636
Cost of services (gross)[14]	KDHL	£ thousand	..	..	..	..	..	..	..
Payments by recipients	KDHM	Thousands	..	..	..	..	..	..	..
Payments out of public funds	KDHN	£ thousand	..	..	..	..	..	..	..

Sources: Business Services Organisation (BSO) Northern Ireland: 028 9053 2975;
Dept of Health, Social Services & Public Safety Northern Ireland: 028 9052 2509;
(Figures on Hospital Services: 028 9052 2800)

16.3 Hospital and general health services
Northern Ireland

1 Financial Year.

2 Average available beds in wards open overnight during the year.

3 Includes transfers to other hospitals. This figure also excludes day case admissions.

4 Includes consultant outpatient clinics and Accident and Emergency departments.

5 At beginning of period for Dentists. Doctors numbers at 2002 (Oct), 2003 (Nov), 2004, 2005 & 2006 (Oct).

6 From 2003 onwards (UPE's).

7 These costs refer to the majority of non-cash limited services: further expenditure under GMS is allocated through HSS Boards on a cash limited basis. Change between 2002 and 2003 is due to advance payments being made in relation to the new GMS contract introduced in April 2004.

9 Gross cost is defined as net ingredient costs plus on-cost, fees and other payments.

10 Excludes amount paid by patients for pre-payment certificates.

11 Due to changes in the Dental Contract which came into force in October 1990 dentists are paid under a combination of headings relating to Capitation and Continuing Care patients. Prior to this, payment was simply on an item of service basis.

12 Excluding sight tests given in hospitals and under the school health service and in the home.

13 Relates to the number of vouchers supplied and excludes repair/replace spectacles.

14 Figures relate to the costs of the hospital, community health and personal social services,and have been estimated from financial year data.

15 Workforce figures are headcounts at 30th September and are taken from the Human Resources Management System. All workforce figures have been revised and now exclude Home Helps, Bank staff, staff on career breaks, Chairperson / Members of Boards and staff with a whole-time equivalent equal to or less than 0.03. The Ancillary and Other staff category includes Ancillary & General staff, Works & Maintenance staff and Ambulance staff for all years, and from 2008 also includes Generic staff who are multidisciplinary staff. Due to Agenda for Change, new grade codes were introduced (from 2007 onwards) which resulted in some staff moving between categories. Backward comparison of the workforce is therefore not advised due to variations in definitions.

16.4 NHS Hospital & Community Health Service (HCHS) and General Practice workforce as at 30 September each specified year

England

headcount & percentages

	2003	2004	2005	2006	2007	2008	2009	2010 [1]	2011	2012	2013	Change 2012-2013	% change 2012-2013	Change 2003-2013	Average Annual % change 2003-2013
Total	1,212,585	1,260,860	1,298,202	1,284,261	1,272,884	1,308,774	1,365,303	1,387,191	1,361,533	1,358,295	1,364,165	5,870	0.4%	151,580	1.2%
Total HCHS medical and dental staff (incl HPCAs)	80,851	86,996	90,630	93,320	94,638	98,703	102,961	103,912	105,711	107,242	108,732	1,490	1.4%	27,881	3.0%
Total HCHS non-medical staff	992,530	1,030,800	1,063,121	1,038,368	1,027,299	1,060,629	1,110,138	1,109,195	1,083,637	1,075,035	1,078,425	3,390	0.3%	85,895	0.8%
Total GPs	33,564	34,855	35,944	36,008	36,420	37,720	40,269	39,409	39,780	40,265	40,236	-29	-0.1%	6,672	1.8%
Total GP Practice staff [6]	110,091	112,254	112,094	119,642	117,375	114,483	114,268	136,831	134,177	137,290	138,056	766	0.6%	27,965	2.3%
Professionally qualified clinical staff	596,233	622,720	643,219	643,906	645,933	661,993	683,703	687,009	686,747	687,810	692,157	4,347	0.6%	95,924	1.5%
All doctors [2]	109,964	117,806	122,987	126,251	128,210	133,662	140,897	141,326	143,836	146,075	147,807	1,732	1.2%	37,843	3.0%
Consultants (including Directors of public health)	28,750	30,650	31,993	32,874	33,674	34,910	36,950	37,752	39,088	40,394	41,220	826	2.0%	12,470	3.7%
Registrars	14,619	16,823	18,006	18,808	30,759	35,042	37,108	38,158	38,891	39,404	40,492	1,088	2.8%	25,873	10.7%
Other doctors in training and equivalents	22,701	24,874	26,305	27,461	16,024	14,136	14,394	14,034	14,018	13,952	14,118	166	1.2%	-8,583	-4.6%
Hospital practitioners and clinical assistants (non-dental specialties) [2]	4,451	4,045	3,587	3,077	2,848	2,761	2,333	2,148	1,782	1,547	1,254	-293	-18.9%	-3,197	-11.9%
Other medical and dental staff	10,330	10,604	10,739	11,100	11,333	11,854	12,176	12,223	12,292	12,302	11,983	-319	-2.6%	1,653	1.5%
GPs total	33,564	34,855	35,944	36,008	36,420	37,720	40,269	39,409	39,780	40,265	40,236	-29	-0.1%	6,672	1.8%
GPs (excluding retainers and registrars)	30,358	31,523	32,738	33,091	33,364	34,010	35,917	35,120	35,415	35,527	35,561	34	0.1%	5,203	1.6%
GP Providers	28,646	28,781	29,340	27,691	27,342	27,347	27,613	27,036	27,218	26,886	26,635	-251	-0.9%	-2,011	-0.7%
Other GPs	1,712	2,742	3,398	5,400	6,022	6,663	8,304	8,319	8,585	8,898	9,153	255	2.9%	7,441	18.3%
GP registrars [5,7]	2,235	2,562	2,564	2,278	2,491	3,203	3,881	3,880	4,013	4,426	4,404	-22	-0.5%	2,169	7.0%
GP retainers	971	770	642	639	565	507	471	419	365	321	284	-37	-11.5%	-687	-11.6%
Total qualified nursing staff [3]	348,246	358,759	367,581	366,981	363,719	368,425	375,505	375,950	372,277	369,868	371,777	1,909	0.5%	23,531	0.7%
Qualified nursing, midwifery & health visiting staff	326,579	336,615	344,677	343,184	340,859	346,377	353,570	352,104	348,693	346,410	347,944	1,534	0.4%	21,365	0.6%
GP practice nurses [6]	21,667	22,144	22,904	23,797	22,860	22,048	21,935	23,846	23,584	23,458	23,833	375	1.6%	2,166	1.0%
Total qualified scientific, therapeutic & technical staff	122,066	128,883	134,534	134,498	136,976	142,455	149,379	151,607	152,216	153,472	154,109	637	0.4%	32,043	2.4%
Qualified Allied Health Professions	62,189	65,515	67,841	67,483	68,687	71,301	73,953	74,374	74,647	74,902	76,163	1,261	1.7%	13,974	2.0%
Qualified Healthcare Scientists	25,649	28,242	30,046	30,453	30,158	30,925	32,161	31,972	31,481	31,173	29,617	-1,556	-5.0%	3,968	1.4%
Other qualified scientific, therapeutic & technical staff	34,228	35,126	36,647	36,562	38,131	40,229	43,265	45,337	46,167	47,490	48,429	939	2.0%	14,201	3.5%
Qualified ambulance staff [4]	15,957	17,272	18,117	16,176	17,028	17,451	17,922	18,450	18,687	18,645	18,734	89	0.5%	2,777	1.6%
Support to clinical staff	327,463	336,044	344,971	334,713	324,249	334,929	352,800	356,410	347,064	343,927	348,999	5,072	1.5%	21,536	0.6%
Support to doctors & nursing staff	265,549	271,389	279,193	267,934	259,547	266,070	278,390	279,522	271,384	269,714	274,144	4,430	1.6%	8,595	0.3%
Support to scientific, therapeutic & technical staff	52,230	55,025	55,715	54,307	53,259	55,792	60,048	62,726	62,057	61,345	61,312	-33	-0.1%	9,082	1.6%
Support to ambulance staff	9,684	9,630	10,063	12,472	11,443	13,067	14,362	14,738	14,238	13,451	14,112	661	4.9%	4,428	3.8%
NHS infrastructure support	199,808	211,489	220,387	209,387	207,778	219,064	236,103	233,342	219,624	215,071	211,185	-3,886	-1.8%	11,377	0.6%
Central functions	92,257	99,831	105,565	101,860	100,177	105,354	115,818	116,846	109,315	106,696	104,130	-2,566	-2.4%	11,873	1.2%
Hotel, property & estates	72,230	73,932	75,431	70,776	71,102	73,797	75,624	74,712	72,283	71,242	70,892	-350	-0.5%	-1,338	-0.2%
Manager & senior manager	35,321	37,726	39,391	36,751	36,499	39,913	44,661	41,962	38,214	37,314	36,360	-954	-2.6%	1,039	0.3%

16.4 NHS Hospital & Community Health Service (HCHS) and General Practice workforce as at 30 September each specified year

England

headcount & percentages

	2003	2004	2005	2006	2007	2008	2009	2010[1]	2011	2012	2013	Change 2012-2013	% change 2012-2013	Change 2003-2013	Average Annual % change 2003-2013
Other non-medical staff or those with unknown classification	657	497	435	410	409	353	364	356	266	237	220	-17	-7.2%	-437	-10.4%
Other GP practice staff [6]	88,424	90,110	89,190	95,845	94,515	92,436	92,333	112,985	110,593	113,832	114,223	391	0.3%	25,799	2.6%

Source: Health and Social Care Information Centre

Notes:

1 The new headcount methodology is not fully comparable with data for years prior to 2010, due to improvements that make it a more stringent count of absolute staff numbers Headcount totals are unlikely to equal the sum of components. Further information on the headcount methodology is available in the Census publication.

2 In order to avoid double counting Hosptial Practitioners & Clinical Assistants (HPCAs) are excluded from the all doctors totals, as they are predominantly GPs that work part time in hospitals (applies to headcount data only).

3 Nursing and midwifery figures exclude students on training courses leading to a first qualification as a nurse or midwife.

4 In 2006 ambulance staff were collected under new, more detailed, occupation codes. As a result, qualified totals and support to ambulance staff totals are not directly comparable with previous years.

5 GP Registrar count from 2008 onwards represents an improvement in data collection processes and comparisons with previous years should be treated with caution

6 Practice staff figures for 2010 & 2011 were revised in 2012. Further details can be found in the data quality statement/methodology. This will affect any related totals and comparisons with years prior to 2010.

7 From 2012 GP Registrars have been removed from the GP Workforce collection where a duplicate record already exists on the Electronic Staff Record. Due to a change in coding practices in some regions GP Registrars are increasingly recorded on the ESR system rather than the GP Exeter Payment System. All these staff are not shown in the GP Registrar totals but are included in the HCHS Medical and Dental Registrars total

These statistics relate to the contracted positions within English NHS organisations and may include those where the person assigned to the position is temporarily absent, for example on maternity leave.

From 2011 the bank staff return was suspended (and formally ceased in 2013). All data (for all years) in these tables excludes bank staff

From April 2013 Public Health England was excluded from workforce publications.

16.5 Staffing summary

Wales

	Unit (a)	2009 (r)	2010 (r)	2011 (r)	2012 (r)	2013
Directly employed NHS staff:						
Medical and dental staff (b):						
Hospital medical staff	Fte	5,291	5,370	5,490	5,544	5,713
Of which consultants	Fte	1,952	2,045	2,128	2,180	2,230
Community/Public health medical staff	Fte	80	84	84	88	79
Hospital dental staff	Fte	163	168	161	161	168
Of which consultants	Fte	40	45	44	44	46
Community/Public health dental staff	Fte	104	104	109	115	114
Total	**Fte**	**5,637**	**5,725**	**5,844**	**5,909**	**6,073**
Nursing, midwifery and health visiting staff	Fte	28,185	28,157	27,980	28,068	28,254
of which qualified	Fte	21,746	21,831	21,748	21,823	22,005
Scientific, therapeutic and technical staff	Fte	11,265	11,507	11,472	11,549	11,616
Health care assistants and other support staff	Fte	9,927	10,033	9,718	9,793	9,699
Administration and estates staff	Fte	16,068	15,472	15,192	15,039	15,120
Ambulance staff	Fte	1,403	1,427	1,457	1,511	1,499
Other (c)	Fte	294	166	173	133	131
Total	**Fte**	**72,778**	**72,487**	**71,836**	**72,002**	**72,393**
Family Practitioners:						
General medical practitioners (d)	Number	1,940	1,991	2,007 (r)	1,996 (r)	2,026
General dental practitioners (e)	Number	1,293	1,310	1,349	1,360	1,392
Ophthalmic medical practitioners (f)	Number	21	16	12	14	8
Ophthalmic opticians (f)	Number	690	740	756	795	773

Source: Health Statistics and Analysis Unit, Welsh Government

(a)   Fte = whole-time equivalent.

(b)   Excludes locum staff.

(c)   Professional advisors and staff on general payments, eg Macmillan and Marie Curie nurses.

(d)   At 30 September,except for 2009 which was counted at 1st October. All practitioners excluding GP registrars, GP Retainers and locums

(e)   Number of dental performers who have any NHS activity recorded against them via FP17 claim forms at any time in the year ending 31 March.

(f)   At 31 December.

(r)   Revised

16.6 Deaths[1]: underlying cause, sex and age-group, Summary

ICD-10 code	England and Wales		2012		2013
	Underlying cause (excludes deaths under 28 days for individual causes)		Age-group		Age-group
			All ages		All ages
A00-R99, U509, V01-Y89	All causes, all ages	M F	240,238 259,093	M F	245,585 261,205
	All causes, ages under 28 days	M F	1,196 904	M F	1,084 813
A00-R99, U509, V01-Y89	All causes, ages 28 days and over	M F	239,042 258,189	M F	244,501 260,392
A00-B99	I Certain infectious and parasitic diseases	M F	2,271 2,838	M F	2,403 2,902
C00-D48	II Neoplasms	M F	76,695 68,700	M F	76,962 68,382
D50-D89	III Diseases of the blood and blood-forming organs and certain disorders involving the immune mechanism	M F	422 521	M F	440 516
E00-E90	IV Endocrine, nutritional and metabolic diseases	M F	3,132 3,578	M F	3,184 3,594
F00-F99	V Mental and behavioural disorders	M F	11,710 24,155	M F	12,655 25,578
G00-G99	VI Diseases of the nervous system	M F	9,499 11,674	M F	10,173 12,331
H00-H59	VII Diseases of the eye and adnexa	M F	11 9	M F	2 10
H60-H95	VIII Diseases of the ear and mastoid process	M F	14 7	M F	12 10
I00-I99	IX Diseases of the circulatory system	M F	69,516 71,846	M F	70,336 69,965
J00-J99	X Diseases of the respiratory system	M F	33,463 37,245	M F	35,115 39,114
K00-K93	XI Diseases of the digestive system	M F	11,766 12,807	M F	11,712 12,646
L00-L99	XII Diseases of the skin and subcutaneous tissue	M F	564 1,111	M F	605 1,115
M00-M99	XIII Diseases of the musculoskeletal system and connective tissue	M F	1,397 2,933	M F	1,368 2,853
N00-N99	XIV Diseases of the genitourinary system	M F	4,080 5,682	M F	4,073 5,558
O00-O99	XV Pregnancy, childbirth and the puerperium	F	46	F	47
P00-P96	XVI Certain conditions originating in the perinatal period	M F	114 91	M F	111 56
Q00-Q99	XVII Congenital malformations, deformations and chromosomal abnormalities	M F	595 554	M F	576 550
R00-R99	XVIII Symptoms, signs and abnormal clinical and laboratory findings, not elsewhere classified	M F	2,800 7,923	M F	2,851 8,167
U509, V01-Y89	XX External causes of morbidity and mortality	M F	10,993 6,469	M F	11,923 6,998

Source: Office for National Statistics

1 Death figures are based on deaths registered rather than deaths occurring in a calendar year. More infomation on registration delays is available on the ONS website.

16.7a Notifications of infectious diseases, 2004-2013

England and Wales

Disease	2004	2005	2006	2007	2008	2009	2010	2011	2012	2013
Acute Meningitis	1267	1381	1494	1251	1181	1219	922	538	522	545
Dysentery	1203	1237	1122	1217	1166	1218	267	.	.	.
Enteric fever (typhoid or paratyphoid fever)	.	.	.	.	.	.	272	224	137	127
Food poisoning	70311	70407	70603	72382	68962	74974	57041	24384	20680	15350
Malaria	609	679	613	426	386	381	327	296	267	226
Measles	2356	2089	3705	3670	5088	5191	2235	2355	4211	6193
Meningococcal septicaemia	691	721	657	673	528	495	367	261	301	300
Mumps	16367	56256	12841	7196	7827	18629	10402	6888	7530	10095
Ophthalmia neonatorum	85	87	100	83	77	90	18	.	.	.
Other	.	.	.	.	.	.	1974	2780	4751	5017
Paratyphoid fever	134	119	185	126	170	130	33	.	.	.
Rubella	1287	1155	1221	1082	1096	1130	631	476	756	553
Scarlet fever	2201	1678	2166	1948	2920	4176	2969	2719	4254	4643
Tuberculosis	6723	7628	7621	6989	7319	7241	8333	9227	9101	8137
Typhoid fever	146	179	201	208	240	210	68	.	.	.
Viral hepatitis	3932	4109	4007	3857	4756	4979	1043	.	.	.
Whooping cough	504	594	550	1089	1512	1155	405	911	6557	3273

Source: Public Health England

1. As from 6th April 2010 the following diseases are no longer notifiable but may still be reported under the Other disease category:

Dysentery, Leptospirosis, Ophthalmia neonatorum, Viral hepatitis

2. As from 6th April 2010 the following diseases became notifiable:

Botulism, Brucellosis, Haemolytic Uraemic Syndrome (HUS), Infectious bloody diarrhoea, Legionnaire's disease,

3. As from 6th April 2010 Typhoid and Paratyphoid fever have been grouped under Enteric fever.

4. As from week 35 of 2010 Food poisoning 'otherwise ascertained' cases are no longer collected.

5. As from 6th April 2010 the Other disease category may be used to notify any cases that may present a significant risk to human health.

6. A proportion of notified cases are shown subsequently not to be the implicated infection.

16.7b Notifications of infectious diseases, 2001-2012

Scotland

Notifiable Disease [1,2,3]	Confirmed notifications											
	2001	2002	2003	2004	2005	2006	2007	2008	2009	2010	2011	2012
Botulism	..	..	..	..	..	..	..	..	..	0	3	0
Anthrax	0	0	0	0	0	1	0	0	4	39	0	4
Brucellosis	..	..	..	..	..	..	..	..	..	1	1	0
Cholera	3	2	1	1	6	3	8	3	5	3	3	1
Clinical Syndrome E.coli O 157 infection	..	..	..	..	..	..	..	..	..	33	4	17
Diphtheria	0	0	0	0	0	0	1	0	0	0	0	0
Haemolytic Uraemic Syndrome (HUS)	..	..	..	..	..	..	..	..	..	5	3	1
Haemophilus influenzae type b (Hib)	..	..	..	..	..	..	..	..	..	3	6	0
Measles	315	399	181	257	186	259	168	219	172	93	82	99
Meningococcal disease	256	175	117	147	139	140	150	120	122	93	103	89
Mumps	155	259	181	3 595	5 698	2 917	2 741	720	1129	727	607	920
Necrotizing fasciitis	..	..	..	..	..	..	..	..	..	2	12	4
Paratyphoid	0	0	0	0	0	0	1	4	2	2	1	0
Pertussis (Whooping cough)	106	99	60	87	51	67	98	134	104	45	85	2068
Poliomyelitis	0	0	0	0	0	0	0	0	0	0	0	0
Rabies	0	1	0	0	0	0	0	0	0	0	0	0
Rubella	234	292	130	222	141	153	146	106	93	39	21	43
Tetanus	0	1	1	1	1	0	0	0	0	0	0	0
Typhoid	3	4	2	2	1	3	3	3	1	6	3	2
Viral haemorrhagic fevers	0	0	0	0	0	0	0	0	0	0	0	1

.. Not available

Source: Health Protection Scotland

Queries to: patriciacassels@nhs.net (tel 0141 300 1148)

1 Figures for all years are confirmed notifications

2 The following diseases were also notifiable but there were no cases in 2012: Plague, Severe Acute Respiratory Syndrome (SARS), Smallpox, Tularemia, West Nile fever, Yellow fever

3 From 2010 the following diseases are no longer notifiable - Bacillary dysentery, Chickenpox, Erysipelas, Food poisoning, Legionellosis, Leptospirosis, Lyme disease, Malaria, Puerperal fever, Scarlet fever, Toxoplasmosis, Typhus fever and Viral hepatitis

16.7c Notifications of Infectious diseases
Northern Ireland

Description	2010	2011	2012	2013
Acute Encephalitis/Meningitis Bacterial	49	28	37	30
Acute Encephalitis/Meningitis Viral	11	13	10	4
Anthrax	0	0	0	2
Chickenpox	2111	1566	2126	1087
Cholera	0	0	0	0
Diphtheria	0	0	0	0
Dysentery	6	7	11	3
Food Poisoning	1550	1575	1777	911
Gastroenteritis (< 2years)	18089	661	799	422
Hepatitis A	4	0	4	2
Hepatitis B	90	129	130	45
Hepatitis Unspecified	0	0	0	0
Legionnaires' Disease	4	4	6	4
Leptospirosis	0	3	3	0
Malaria	6	1	5	3
Measles	72	27	43	49
Meningococcal Septicaemia	38	45	33	18
Mumps	212	123	298	606
Paratyphoid Fever	0	0	0	0
Plague	0	0	0	0
Poliomyelitis (Acute)	0	0	0	0
Poliomyelitis (Paralytic)	0	0	0	0
Rabies	0	0	0	0
Relapsing Fever	0	0	0	0
Rubella	18	18	13	8
Scarlet Fever	154	130	196	139
Smallpox	0	0	0	0
Tetanus	0	1	1	0
Tuberculosis (Non Pulmonary)	32	14	45	22
Tuberculosis (Pulmonary)	34	44	51	19
Typhoid	1	1	1	0
Typhus	0	0	0	0
Viral Haemorraghic Fever	0	0	2	0
Whooping Cough	18	18	394	65
Yellow Fever	0	0	0	0

Public Health Agency, Northern Ireland

16.8a Work-related and occupational respiratory disease: estimated number of cases reported by chest physicians to SWORD 2006-2012 and by occupational physicians to OPRA 2006-2010 by sex and diagnostic category

Sex	Diagnostic category	Chest physicians (SWORD) (d)							Occupational Physicians (OPRA) (c)				
		2006	2007	2008	2009	2010	2011	2012(r)	2006	2007	2008	2009	2010
All cases (b)	Allergic alveolitis	47	19	87	39	29	25	56	-	-	-	13	-
	Asthma	451	251	307	181	205	159	189	145	104	55	47	65
	Bronchitis/emphysema	65	15	18	69	18	52	19	-	2	12	-	-
	Infectious diseases	49	28	24	25	2	60	25	2	36	-	24	12
	Inhalation accidents	16	5	38	50	3	14	3	4	16	1	-	50
	Lung cancer	82	104	91	86	71	133	16	2	-	-	-	-
	Malignant mesothelioma	637	884	611	559	522	472	577	16	1	14	-	-
	Benign pleural disease	1281	1008	1114	893	790	831	711	12	-	-	12	1
	Pneumoconiosis	194	167	145	208	110	224	159	3	5	-	-	-
	Other	53	81	56	100	61	105	61	47	114	80	77	30
	Total diagnoses	**2875**	**2562**	**2491**	**2210**	**1811**	**2075**	**1816**	**231**	**278**	**162**	**173**	**158**
	Total cases (a)	**2829**	**2534**	**2442**	**2135**	**1760**	**2009**	**1750**	**230**	**278**	**161**	**172**	**157**

Source: Health and Safety Executive (HSE)

Notes:

(a) Individuals may have more than one diagnosis.

(b) May not equal males plus females because sex is not recorded for some cases.

(c) The OPRA scheme is no longer running, therefore the latest figures shown are for 2010.

(d) Some physicians report on a sample basis, for one month in each year. Estimated totals for these are calculated by multiplying the actual number of cases reported by 12.

"-" means zero.

(p) Provisional data.

16.8b Work-related Mental ill-health cases reported to THOR-GP by diagnosis 2011-2013

Mental ill-health diagnoses	*Number of cases reported to THOR-GP aggregate total 2011 to 2013	% of all diagnoses
Anxiety/depression	1140	38
Post-traumatic stress disorder (PTSD)	36	1
Other stress	1656	55
Alcohol & drug abuse	60	2
Other diagnoses	84	3
Other stress symptoms	60	2
Total diagnoses	3036	100
Total cases	2940	

Source: Health and Safety Executive (HSE)

* This estimate has an adjustment applied for sample reporting, but not an adjustment for the response rate. This is because there is no evidence indicating that non-responding GPs would report, on average, the same number of cases as those who responded.

THOR-GP is a surveillance scheme in which general practitioners (GPs) are asked to report new cases of work-related ill health

16.8c Work-related skin disease: estimated number of cases reported by dermatologists to EPIDERM 2006 - 2012 and by occupational physicians to OPRA 2006 - 2010, by sex and diagnostic category

Sex	Diagnostic category	Dermatologists (EPIDERM) (d)							Occupational physicians (OPRA) (c)				
		2006	2007	2008	2009	2010	2011	2012 (r)	2006	2007	2008	2009	2010
All cases(b)	Contact dermatitis	1788	1386	1325	1423	1281	1208	1151	596	488	322	373	342
	Contact urticaria	120	73	43	44	55	38	31	26	15	13	14	13
	Folliculitis /acne	16	11	17	3	-	1	-	-	-	1	-	-
	Infective skin disease	16	3	2	13	14	1	-	-	14	36	2	12
	Mechanical skin disease	82	8	9	18	18	14	6	1	-	1	12	-
	Nail conditions	3	25	13	13	1	-	1	-	-	-	-	-
	Skin neoplasia	759	622	418	492	390	231	314	-	-	-	-	-
	Other dermatoses	58	35	30	72	30	72	3	68	40	36	40	37
	Total number of diagnoses	**2842**	**2163**	**1857**	**2078**	**1789**	**1565**	**1506**	**691**	**557**	**409**	**441**	**404**
	Total number of individuals(a)	**2805**	**2137**	**1839**	**2015**	**1745**	**1550**	**1480**	**679**	**556**	**409**	**440**	**392**

Source: Health and Safety Executive (HSE)

Notes:

(a) Individuals may have more than one diagnosis.

(b) May not equal males plus females because sex is not recorded for some cases.

(c) No OPRA data are available for the annual statistics after 2010.

(d) Some physicians report on a sample basis, for one month in each year. Estimated totals for these are calculated by multiplying the actual number of cases reported by 12.

"-" means zero.

r Revised

16.8d Work-related musculoskeletal cases reported to THOR-GP by anatomical site 2010 to 2013

Anatomical site	*Number of cases reported to THOR-GP aggregate total 2011 to 2013	% of all diagnoses
Hand/wrist/arm	768	19
Elbow	468	12
Shoulder	396	10
Neck/thoracic spine	372	9
Lumbar spine/trunk	1260	32
Hip/knee	408	10
Ankle/foot	168	4
Other	144	4
Total diagnoses	3984	100
Total cases	3780	

Source: Health and Safety Executive (HSE)

* This estimate has an adjustment applied for sample reporting, but not an adjustment for the response rate. This is because there is no evidence indicating that non-responding GPs would report, on average, the same number of cases as those who responded.

THOR GP is a surveillance scheme in which general practitioners (GPs) are asked to report new cases of work-related ill health

16.9 Deaths due to occupationally related lung disease Great Britain

Numbers Numbers

		1999	2000	2001	2002	2003	2004	2005	2006	2007	2008	2009	2010	2011(r)	2012(p)
Asbestosis (without mesothelioma)[1,3]	KADY	171	186	233	234	236	268	303	327	320	367	412	414	429	464
Mesothelioma[2,4]	KADZ	1,615	1,633	1,860	1,867	1,887	1,978	2,049	2,060	2,176	2,265	2336	2360	**2311**	**2535**
Pneumoconiosis (other than asbestosis)	KAEA	321	279	240	271	231	214	194	167	149	139	149	134	152	151
Byssinosis	KAEB	6	4	2	-	3	4	3	5	2	1	2	2	1	1
Farmer's lung and other occupational allergic alveolitis	KAEC	9	7	7	6	7	5	13	10	5	7	7	8	9	10
Total	KAED	2,122	2,109	2,342	2,378	2,364	2,469	2,562	2,569	2,652	2,779	2,906	2,918	2902	3161

Sources: Office for National Statistics; Health and Safety Executive

1 Some death certificates mention asbestosis with lung cancer and/or mesothelioma. In some cases - particularly where mesothelioma is mentioned - the word "asbestosis" may have been used incorrectly to indicate the role of asbestos in causing mesothelioma and/or lung cancer.

2 The Office for National Statistics (ONS) discontinued medical enquiries in 1993. Therefore, for deaths registered from 1993 onwards, there is often less information available to accurately code the specific site of the mesothelioma.

3 For inclusion into the Asbestosis register the cause of death on the death certificate must mention the word Asbestosis.

4 Total for Great Britain may include a small number of persons with overseas addresses

16.10 Reported injuries to employees and the self-employed in Great Britain, detailed industry and severity of injury, 2012/13r

Detailed industry classification +	Section	Division	Employees								Self-employed			
			Severity of injury - count				Severity of injury - rate per 100 000				Severity of injury - count			
			Fatal injuries	Non-fatal major injuries	Over-7-day injuries	Total injuries	Fatal injuries	Non-fatal major injuries	Over-7-day injuries	Total injuries	Fatal injuries	Non-fatal major injuries	Over-7-day injuries	Total injuries
Agriculture, Forestry and Fishing (a)	A	01-03	10	361	500	871	6.4	230.4	319.2	556.0	21	65	20	106
Crop and animal production, hunting and related service activities	A	01	9	288	393	690	6.4	205.9	281.0	493.4	20	47	12	79
Forestry and logging	A	02	1	53	71	125	9.4	496.0	664.5	1 169.9	1	17	8	26
Fishing and aquaculture (a)	A	03	-	20	36	56	-	325.9	586.7	912.6	-	1	-	1
Mining and Quarrying	B	05-09	2	160	273	435	2.0	159.1	271.5	432.7	-	1	2	3
Mining of coal and lignite	B	05	-	45	116	161	#	#	#	#	-	-	-	-
Extraction of crude petroleum and natural gas	B	06	-	52	85	137	-	303.4	495.9	799.3	-	-	1	1
Mining of metal ores	B	07	-	-	2	2	#	#	#	#	-	-	-	-
Other mining and quarrying	B	08	2	53	64	119	9.6	254.0	306.7	570.2	-	1	-	1
Mining support service activities	B	09	-	10	6	16	-	18.4	11.0	29.4	-	-	1	1
Manufacturing	C	10-33	20	3 253	10 607	13 880	0.77	124.5	405.9	531.1	1	63	60	124
Manufacture of food products	C	10	-	633	3 011	3 644	-	211.1	1 004.3	1 215.4	1	7	6	14
Manufacture of beverages	C	11	1	53	196	250	1.8	96.1	355.5	453.4	-	1	1	2
Manufacture of tobacco products	C	12	-	1	4	5	#	#	#	#	-	-	-	-
Manufacture of textiles	C	13	-	62	177	239	-	120.8	345.0	465.8	-	1	-	1
Manufacture of wearing apparel	C	14	-	7	11	18	-	24.0	37.7	61.8	-	-	-	-
Manufacture of leather and related products	C	15	-	2	12	14	-	23.7	142.0	165.6	-	-	-	-
Manufacture of wood and of products of wood and cork, except furniture; manufacture of articles of straw and plaiting materials	C	16	2	139	350	491	3.6	252.7	636.3	892.7	-	7	9	16
Manufacture of paper and paper products	C	17	-	76	247	323	-	140.4	456.4	596.8	-	-	2	2
Printing and reproduction of recorded media	C	18	-	94	304	398	-	74.5	240.9	315.4	-	1	2	3
Manufacture of coke and refined petroleum products	C	19	-	17	20	37	-	71.9	84.6	156.6	-	-	-	-
Manufacture of chemicals and chemical products	C	20	1	82	197	280	0.98	80.7	193.9	275.6	-	1	1	2
Manufacture of basic pharmaceutical products and pharmaceutical preparations	C	21	-	32	131	163	-	33.0	135.1	168.1	-	-	-	-
Manufacture of rubber and plastic products	C	22	2	165	598	765	1.3	110.2	399.4	511.0	-	-	2	2
Manufacture of non-metallic mineral products	C	23	1	123	320	444	1.2	146.5	381.2	528.9	-	7	4	11
Manufacture of basic metals	C	24	-	235	583	818	-	251.6	624.3	875.9	-	3	7	10
Manufacture of fabricated metal products, except machinery and equipment	C	25	7	302	916	1 225	3.4	147.6	447.7	598.7	-	6	5	11
Manufacture of computer, electronic and optical products	C	26	-	15	67	82	-	8.1	36.2	44.3	-	1	-	1
Manufacture of electrical equipment	C	27	-	37	141	178	-	49.8	189.8	239.6	-	4	1	5
Manufacture of machinery and equipment not elsewhere classified	C	28	1	185	431	617	0.43	79.0	184.0	263.4	-	4	1	5
Manufacture of motor vehicles, trailers and semi-trailers	C	29	2	173	476	651	1.1	99.2	273.0	373.4	-	3	2	5
Manufacture of other transport equipment	C	30	1	99	300	400	0.55	54.4	164.9	219.9	-	-	2	2
Manufacture of furniture	C	31	-	63	235	298	-	91.0	339.6	430.6	-	1	1	2
Other manufacturing	C	32	1	491	1 450	1 942	1.2	579.5	1 711.4	2 292.1	-	7	9	16
Repair and installation of machinery and equipment	C	33	1	167	430	598	0.58	96.5	248.5	345.6	-	9	5	14
Electricity, Gas, Steam and Air Conditioning Supply	D	35	2	152	188	342	1.2	90.8	112.3	204.4	-	5	4	9
Water Supply; Sewerage; Waste Management and Remediation Activities	E	36-39	9	617	1 968	2 594	4.4	298.7	952.7	1 255.7	1	16	9	26
Water collection, treatment and supply	E	36	-	57	126	183	-	94.5	209.0	303.5	-	4	3	7
Sewerage	E	37	-	36	128	164	-	335.4	1 192.7	1 528.1	-	3	-	3
Waste collection, treatment and disposal activities; materials recovery	E	38	9	507	1 673	2 189	7.8	441.8	1 457.8	1 907.4	1	8	6	15
Remediation activities and other waste management services	E	39	-	17	41	58	-	81.8	197.2	278.9	-	1	-	1
Construction	F	41-43	26	1 937	3 213	5 176	2.1	157.9	262.0	422.0	14	592	481	1 087
Construction of buildings	F	41	15	887	1 247	2 149	3.3	192.6	270.8	466.7	6	383	335	724
Civil engineering	F	42	2	246	453	701	0.81	99.6	183.4	283.9	-	46	36	82
Specialised construction activities	F	43	9	804	1 513	2 326	1.7	154.9	291.5	448.1	8	163	110	281
Service industries	G-U	45-99	30	13 734	43 405	57 169	0.15	67.3	212.7	280.1	14	261	152	427
Wholesale and retail trade and repair of motor vehicles and motorcycles	G	45	4	283	605	892	1.1	80.1	171.2	252.5	4	6	8	18
Wholesale trade, except of motor vehicles and motorcycles	G	46	2	321	854	1 177	0.32	51.1	136.0	187.5	1	4	1	6
Retail trade, except of motor vehicles and motor-cycles	G	47	-	1 730	5 696	7 426	-	67.3	221.7	289.0	1	10	8	19
Land transport and transport via pipelines	H	49	6	581	1 886	2 473	1.2	115.7	375.5	492.4	-	5	3	8
Water transport (b)	H	50	-	39	142	181	-	93.0	338.4	431.4	-	1	1	2
Air transport	H	51	-	105	858	963	-	166.1	1 357.4	1 523.5	-	2	-	2
Warehousing and support activities for transportation	H	52	1	1 154	4 713	5 868	0.33	382.8	1 563.3	1 946.4	-	32	33	65
Postal and courier activities	H	53	1	463	1 628	2 092	0.37	169.5	595.9	765.7	-	4	2	6
Accommodation	I	55	1	383	1 098	1 482	0.33	125.5	359.8	485.7	-	8	4	12
Food and beverage service activities	I	56	-	799	2 811	3 610	-	75.1	264.1	339.2	1	20	9	30
Publishing activities	J	58	-	14	11	25	-	8.1	6.3	14.4	-	1	-	1
Motion picture, video and television programme production, sound recording and music publishing activities	J	59	-	13	25	38	-	18.6	35.8	54.4	-	8	-	8
Programming and broadcasting activities	J	60	-	17	9	26	-	26.8	14.2	41.0	-	3	-	3
Telecommunications	J	61	-	90	286	376	-	58.5	186.0	244.5	-	4	4	8
Computer programming, consultancy and related activities	J	62	-	11	31	42	-	2.4	6.7	9.1	-	1	-	1
Information service activities	J	63	-	33	41	74	-	132.0	164.1	296.1	-	-	-	-
Financial service activities, except insurance and pension funding	K	64	-	138	312	450	-	25.5	57.7	83.2	-	6	3	9
Insurance, reinsurance and pension funding, except compulsory social security	K	65	-	24	60	84	-	10.5	26.2	36.7	-	-	-	-
Activities auxiliary to financial services and insurance activities	K	66	-	4	11	15	-	1.2	3.3	4.5	-	-	-	-
Real estate activities	L	68	-	69	181	250	-	26.7	70.2	96.9	-	3	2	5
Legal and accounting activities	M	69	-	34	63	97	-	9.3	17.2	26.5	-	1	-	1
Activities of head offices; management consultancy activities	M	70	-	33	35	68	-	11.9	12.7	24.6	-	-	-	-
Architectural and engineering activities; technical testing and analysis	M	71	1	11	19	31	0.26	2.8	4.9	8.0	-	1	-	1
Scientific research and development	M	72	-	24	32	56	-	25.9	34.6	60.5	-	-	-	-
Advertising and market research	M	73	-	7	25	32	-	5.4	19.2	24.6	-	2	-	2
Other professional, scientific and technical activities	M	74	-	30	62	92	-	24.8	51.2	75.9	-	3	1	4
Veterinary activities	M	75	-	44	75	119	-	93.3	159.0	252.3	-	3	-	3
Rental and leasing activities	N	77	4	71	239	314	4.2	74.6	251.1	329.9	-	6	-	6
Employment activities	N	78	1	15	16	32	0.57	8.6	9.2	18.3	-	1	-	1
Travel agency, tour operator and other reservation service and related activities	N	79	-	3	7	10	-	3.5	8.1	11.6	-	-	-	-
Security and investigation activities	N	80	-	180	473	653	-	107.7	283.1	390.8	-	7	2	9
Services to buildings and landscape activities	N	81	1	395	1 308	1 704	0.28	109.1	361.2	470.6	2	24	15	41
Office administrative, office support and other business support activities	N	82	-	153	286	439	-	92.7	173.3	266.0	-	4	3	7

16.10 Reported injuries to employees and the self-employed in Great Britain, detailed industry and severity of injury, 2012/13r

Detailed industry classification +	Section	Division	Employees								Self-employed			
			Severity of injury - count				Severity of injury - rate per 100 000				Severity of injury - count			
			Fatal injuries	Non-fatal major injuries	Over-7-day injuries	Total injuries	Fatal injuries	Non-fatal major injuries	Over-7-day injuries	Total injuries	Fatal injuries	Non-fatal major injuries	Over-7-day injuries	Total injuries
Public administration and defence; compulsory social security	O	84	4	1 417	3 822	5 243	0.22	79.4	214.1	293.7	-	7	-	7
Education	P	85	-	1 824	3 177	5 001	-	62.3	108.4	170.7	1	22	11	34
Human health activities	Q	86	-	1 327	7 076	8 403	-	68.6	365.8	434.4	-	9	5	14
Residential care activities	Q	87	-	734	2 718	3 452	-	90.7	335.7	426.4	-	4	5	9
Social work activities without accommodation	Q	88	-	399	1 386	1 785	-	45.6	158.5	204.1	-	2	1	3
Creative, arts and entertainment activities	R	90	-	79	131	210	-	177.2	293.9	471.2	2	15	9	26
Libraries, archives, museums and other cultural activities	R	91	1	47	80	128	1.1	50.6	86.1	137.8	-	1	-	1
Gambling and betting activities	R	92	-	34	84	118	-	44.5	109.9	154.3	-	-	-	-
Sports activities and amusement and recreation activities	R	93	1	398	560	959	0.27	106.1	149.4	255.8	2	16	10	28
Activities of membership organisations	S	94	1	65	110	176	0.42	27.2	46.0	73.5	-	1	3	4
Repair of computers and personal and household goods	S	95	-	14	53	67	-	26.5	100.2	126.7	-	-	-	-
Other personal service activities	S	96	1	125	310	436	0.43	53.6	133.0	187.0	-	14	9	23
Activities of households as employers of domestic personnel	T	97	-	-	-	-	-	-	-	-	-	-	-	-
Undifferentiated goods- and services-producing activities of private households for own use	T	98	-	-	-	-	-	-	-	-	-	-	-	-
Activities of extraterritorial organisations and bodies	U	99	-	-	-	-	-	-	-	-	-	-	-	-
All industries	A-U	01-99	99	20 214	60 154	80 467	0.39	80.5	239.6	320.5	51	1 003	728	1 782

Source: RIDDOR - Reporting of Injuries, Diseases and Dangerous Occurrences Regulations (as amended)

r=revised

Key changes to the reporting system and the legal requirements have occurred in recent years. From September 2011 the RIDDOR notification system used by employers changed, with reporting now being predominantly online, using newly designed forms and online guidance. In April 2012 there was a legislative change to RIDDOR, namely those injuries to workers which result in the person being incapacitated for more than three days, where the reporting threshold changed to over-7-days. The requirement remains for duty-holders to record over-3-day injuries, but not to report them. Further, RIDDOR has recently undergone a more extensive legislative change, which took effect from 1 October 2013. A key change was the introduction of the 'specified injury' category to replace the 'major injury' category. More information on data changes affecting RIDDOR statistics is available at: www.hse.gov.uk/statistics/riddor-notification.htm

+ HSE is now recording and publishing data in Standard Industrial Classification (SIC) 2007 format. Data from previous years which was collected in the SIC1992/2003 formats has been computer recoded to the SIC2007 coding to allow comparisons over time. However, there may be errors as a result of this recoding and care should be taken when interpreting trends over time. Inconsistencies are most likely to be visible in data between 2008/09 and 2009/10. For more information see: www.hse.gov.uk/statistics/industry/sic2007.htm

a) Excludes sea fishing.
b) Injuries arising from shore-based services only. Excludes incidents reported under merchant shipping legislation.

Rates of injury
The Annual Population Survey (APS) is the source of employment data used as the denominator for rates of injury in this document, For more information please go to:
www.hse.gov.uk/statistics/sources.htm#employment

Rates of fatal injury below 1.0 are expressed to two decimal places.
Employment numbers are too small to provide reliable rate estimates.
.. The rate of injury is below 0.1.

this page is intentionally blank

Prices

Chapter 17

Prices

Producer price index numbers
(Tables 17.1 and 17.2)

The producer price indices (PPIs) were published for the first time in August 1983, replacing the former wholesale price indices. Full details of the differences between the two indices were given in an article published in British Business, 15 April 1983. The producer price indices are calculated using the same general methodology as that used by the wholesale price indices.

The high level index numbers in Tables 17.1 and 17.2 are constructed on a net sector basis. That is to say, they are intended to measure only transactions between the sector concerned and other sectors. Within-sector transactions are excluded. Index numbers for the whole of manufacturing are thus not weighted averages of sector index numbers.

The index numbers for selected industries in Tables 17.1 and 17.2 are constructed on a gross sector basis, that is, all transactions are included in deriving the weighting patterns, including sales within the same industry.

Producer Prices has implemented the change to the Standard Industrial Classification 2007 (SIC 2007). The most significant change to PPI output prices involves the reclassification of 'recovered secondary raw materials' and 'publishing'. These are no longer classified in the manufacturing sector, but are classified under services. In addition to this, a new SIC division, 'repair, installation and maintenance of machinery and equipment' has been created. Under SIC 2003 these activities were classified within the output of manufacturing, but as part of the specific industries where this activity took place.

Fundamental changes have been made to the classification of the PPI Trade surveys, Import Price indices (IPI) and Export Price Indices (EPI). As part of the reclassification project the classification of these trade surveys have become compliant with Eurostat's Short Term Statistics Regulation. The collection of IPI and EPI will now be on an SIC basis, a switch from the Standard International Trade Classification (SITC) and Combined Nomenclature (CN) previously used. PPI input prices are heavily dependant on IPI.

Further details are available from the Office for National Statistics website: www.ons.gov.uk.

Purchasing power of the pound
(Table 17.3)

Changes in the internal purchasing power of a currency may be defined as the 'inverse' of changes in the levels of prices; when prices go up, the amount which can be purchased with a given sum of money goes down. Movements in the internal purchasing power of the pound are based on the consumers' expenditure deflator (CED) prior to 1962 and on the general index of retail prices (RPI) from January 1962 onwards. The CED shows the movement in prices implied by the national accounts estimates of consumers' expenditure valued at current and at constant prices, while the RPI is constructed directly by weighting together monthly movements in prices according to a given pattern of household expenditure derived from the Expenditure and Food Survey. If the purchasing power of the pound is taken to be 100p in a particular month (quarter, year), the comparable purchasing power in a subsequent month (quarter, year) is:

$$100 \times \frac{\text{earlier period price index}}{\text{later period price index}}$$

where the price index used is the CED for years 1946–1961

Consumer prices index
(Table 17.4)

The CPI is the main UK domestic measure of consumer price inflation for macroeconomic purposes. It forms the basis for the Government's target for inflation that the Bank of England's Monetary Policy Committee (MPC) is required to achieve. From April 2011 the CPI is also being used for the indexation of benefits, tax credits and public service pensions. The uprating is based on the 12-month change in the September CPI.

Internationally, the CPI is known as the Harmonised Index of Consumer Prices (HICP). HICPs are calculated in each Member State of the European Union, according to rules specified in a series of European regulations developed by Eurostat in conjunction with the EU Member States. HICPs are used to compare inflation rates across the European Union. Since January 1999, the HICP has also been used by the European Central Bank (ECB) as the measure of price stability across the euro area.

The official CPI series starts in 1996 but estimates for earlier periods are available back to 1988. These estimates are broadly consistent with data from 1996 but should be treated with some caution.

A full description of how the CPI is compiled is given in the Consumer Price Indices Technical Manual at: www.ons.gov.uk/ons/guide-method/user-guidance/prices/cpi-and-rpi/index.html

Retail prices index
(Table 17.5)

The all items retail prices index (RPI) is the most long-standing general purpose measure of inflation in the UK. Historically the uses of the RPI include the indexation of various prices and incomes and the uprating of pensions, state benefits and index-linked gilts, as well as the revalorisation of excise duties. Please note, though, that from April 2011 the CPI is being used to uprate benefits, tax credits and public service pensions. RPI data are available back to 1947 but have been re-referenced on several occasions since then, generally accompanied by changes to the coverage and/or structure of the detailed sub-components.

A full description of how the RPI is compiled is given in the Consumer Price Indices Technical Manual at: www.ons.gov.uk/ons/guide-method/user-guidance/prices/cpi-and-rpi/index.html

Further details are available from the Office for National Statistics website: www.ons.gov.uk/ons/taxonomy/index.html?nscl=Price+Indices+and+Inflation

Tax and price index (TPI)
(Table 17.6)

The purpose and methodology of the TPI were described in an article in the August 1979 issue (No. 310) of Economic Trends. The TPI measures the change in gross taxable income needed for taxpayers to maintain their purchasing power, allowing for changes in retail prices. The TPI thus takes account of the changes to direct taxes (and employees' National Insurance (NI) contributions) faced by a representative cross-section of taxpayers as well as changes in the retail prices index (RPI).
When direct taxation or employees' NI contributions change, the TPI will rise by less than or more than the RPI according to the type of changes made. Between Budgets, the monthly increase in the TPI is normally slightly larger than that in the RPI, since all the extra income needed to offset any rise in retail prices is fully taxed.

Index numbers of agricultural prices
(Tables 17.7 and 17.8)

The indices of producer prices of agricultural products are currently based on the calendar year 2005. They are designed to provide short-term and medium-term indications of movements in these prices. All annual series are baseweighted Laspeyres type, using value weights derived from the Economic Accounts for Agriculture prepared for the Statistical Office of the European Union. Prices are measured exclusive of VAT. For Table 17.7, it has generally been necessary to measure the prices of materials (inputs) ex-supplier. For Table 17.8, it has generally been necessary to measure the prices received by producers (outputs) at the first marketing stage. The construction of the indices enables them to be combined with similar indices for other member countries of the EU to provide an overall indication of trends within the Union which appears in the Union's Eurostat series of publications.

Index numbers at a more detailed level and for earlier based series are available from the Department for Environment, Food and Rural Affairs, Room 309, Foss House, Kingspool 1–2 Peasholme Green, York, YO1 7PX, tel 01904 456561

17.1 Producer Price Index (2010=100, SIC2007)

Net Sector Input Price Indices of Materials & Fuel purchased

	6207000050: NSI - All Manufacturing including CCL	6207000010: NSI - All Manufacturing, materials only	6207000060: NSI - Fuel Purchased by Manufacturing Industry including CCL	6207990050: NSI - Materials & Fuels Purchased other than FBTP Industries, NSA	6207998950: NSI - All Manufacturing excl FBTP (incl CCL) - SA	6207990010: NSI - Materials Purchased other than FBTP Industries, NSA
	K646	K644	K647	K655	K658	K653
	NSA	NSA	NSA	NSA	SA	NSA
2009	92.6	90.9	107.4	95.5	95.6	93.6
2010	100.0	100.0	100.0	100.0	100.0	100.0
2011	114.5	115.1	109.7	109.1	109.1	109.1
2012	116.0	115.9	117.6	108.9	108.9	107.5
2013	117.4	116.6	125.0	109.3	109.3	106.8
2011 JAN	108.8	109.0	107.6	106.0	105.4	105.8
FEB	110.0	110.5	106.5	106.3	105.5	106.4
MAR	113.3	113.9	109.1	107.5	106.1	107.4
APR	116.5	117.5	107.9	108.9	108.3	109.2
MAY	115.2	116.1	108.1	109.4	109.0	109.7
JUN	115.4	116.5	107.3	109.5	109.9	110.0
JUL	116.0	117.1	107.8	110.0	110.7	110.5
AUG	114.3	115.2	107.3	110.0	111.0	110.5
SEP	116.4	117.7	106.2	110.6	111.6	111.4
OCT	115.8	116.2	112.9	110.3	110.9	110.0
NOV	116.2	116.3	116.7	110.4	110.8	109.5
DEC	115.8	115.6	118.8	110.0	110.0	108.7
2012 JAN	115.8	115.7	117.7	110.1	109.6	109.0
FEB	118.3	118.1	121.1	111.0	110.0	109.5
MAR	119.8	120.2	117.4	110.9	109.4	110.1
APR	118.3	118.5	117.4	110.1	109.3	109.0
MAY	115.5	115.6	115.3	108.9	108.6	107.9
JUN	113.4	113.3	114.4	108.4	108.8	107.5
JUL	113.1	113.1	113.3	107.3	108.0	106.4
AUG	115.1	115.5	112.3	107.1	108.0	106.3
SEP	115.0	115.0	116.1	107.2	108.2	105.8
OCT	115.6	115.3	119.5	108.0	108.6	106.2
NOV	116.0	115.3	122.8	108.6	108.9	106.3
DEC	116.3	115.4	124.5	108.7	108.9	106.2
2013 JAN	117.7	117.1	123.8	109.9	109.6	107.7
FEB	120.7	120.4	124.0	112.1	111.2	110.1
MAR	120.9	120.0	129.9	112.7	111.3	110.0
APR	118.6	117.6	127.3	111.1	110.4	108.6
MAY	117.1	116.6	121.9	109.3	109.2	107.2
JUN	116.8	116.4	120.4	108.4	108.9	106.4
JUL	118.4	117.9	123.5	109.5	110.1	107.2
AUG	117.2	116.6	122.7	108.6	109.5	106.4
SEP	116.1	115.5	121.5	107.6	108.5	105.3
OCT	115.6	114.4	126.5	107.8	108.2	104.8
NOV	114.9	113.5	127.9	107.5	107.7	104.2
DEC	115.3	113.5	130.8	107.2	107.2	103.4
2014 JAN	114.3	112.6	130.4	106.8	106.5	103.1
FEB	113.7	112.1	127.9	106.4	105.8	102.9
MAR	113.3	111.7	127.5	106.6	105.4	103.2
APR	112.3	111.1	122.4	105.5	105.1	102.6
MAY	112.5	111.6	120.3	105.0	105.1	102.4
JUN	111.4	110.7	117.2	104.6	104.9	102.4

17.1 Producer Price Index (2010=100, SIC2007)

Gross Sector Price Indices of Materials & Fuel purchased

	6107113140: GSI Sub-section - Inputs for Manuf of Textiles & Textile products	6107215000: GSI (excl. CCL) - Inputs for Manuf of Leather & Related products	6107216000: GSI (excl. CCL) - Inputs for Manuf of Wood & products of Wood/Cork	6107117180: GSI Sub-section - Inputs for Manuf of Pulp, Paper & Paper products	6107219000: GSI (excl. CCL) - Inputs for Manuf of Coke & Refined Petroleum products	6107120000: GSI Sub-section - Inputs for Manuf of Chemicals, Chemical products	6107222000: GSI (excl. CCL) - Inputs for Manufacture of Rubber/Plastic products
	MC36 NSA	MC3O NSA	MC3P NSA	MC39 NSA	MC3R NSA	MC3B NSA	MB4R NSA
2009	97.4	97.5	94.9	98.3	78.1	95.8	95.2
2010	100.0	100.0	100.0	100.0	100.0	100.0	100.0
2011	108.2	108.8	106.3	106.9	133.4	111.5	108.7
2012	110.4	110.7	108.5	107.4	136.9	111.8	108.9
2013	111.2	114.0	109.9	108.2	135.5	110.3	108.7
2011 JAN	104.7	104.1	103.6	104.0	118.2	107.6	105.6
FEB	104.7	104.9	104.0	104.1	122.2	107.4	105.5
MAR	106.1	106.9	104.8	105.3	133.2	109.1	106.8
APR	107.5	109.4	105.7	106.2	142.3	111.2	108.6
MAY	108.1	109.8	106.4	106.6	133.9	112.0	109.7
JUN	108.9	110.2	106.8	107.4	134.7	112.6	110.2
JUL	109.1	110.5	107.2	108.1	137.8	113.0	110.5
AUG	108.9	110.0	107.1	108.1	131.2	113.9	110.5
SEP	109.9	110.4	107.4	108.1	138.3	114.1	110.6
OCT	110.2	110.1	107.4	108.4	136.5	112.8	109.4
NOV	110.1	109.8	107.6	108.5	137.6	112.5	109.0
DEC	109.8	109.8	107.5	108.4	135.4	111.3	108.3
2012 JAN	110.2	109.6	107.7	108.6	136.2	111.1	107.9
FEB	110.4	109.7	108.1	108.1	144.1	112.1	109.1
MAR	110.7	109.9	108.5	107.8	151.8	113.4	110.0
APR	109.9	111.1	108.9	107.9	146.1	113.9	110.4
MAY	109.9	111.2	108.6	107.5	136.6	113.3	110.2
JUN	109.5	110.7	108.4	107.4	123.3	111.4	108.9
JUL	110.0	110.3	108.4	107.0	127.3	109.5	107.1
AUG	110.3	110.2	108.6	106.6	137.7	110.7	108.0
SEP	110.7	110.8	108.8	106.6	137.1	111.3	108.5
OCT	111.2	111.4	108.7	106.9	136.4	111.6	108.9
NOV	111.3	111.5	108.6	107.1	134.2	111.6	109.0
DEC	110.4	111.5	108.5	107.2	132.5	111.5	109.1
2013 JAN	110.7	112.0	108.8	107.5	136.5	111.5	109.3
FEB	111.3	112.5	109.4	108.0	144.1	112.1	109.7
MAR	111.9	113.5	109.9	108.8	141.2	113.0	110.6
APR	111.4	114.1	110.0	108.4	132.9	111.6	109.6
MAY	111.3	114.1	109.4	107.9	131.7	110.2	108.5
JUN	111.1	114.3	109.4	107.8	130.0	109.7	108.3
JUL	111.5	114.9	109.8	108.2	137.8	110.0	108.2
AUG	111.3	114.8	109.9	108.1	139.0	110.2	108.5
SEP	111.0	115.0	109.8	108.0	138.0	109.8	108.1
OCT	110.7	114.8	110.6	108.4	133.0	108.9	108.0
NOV	110.7	114.4	110.6	108.5	130.1	108.0	107.5
DEC	110.9	114.1	110.8	108.5	132.1	108.0	107.5
2014 JAN	111.0	114.3	111.0	108.7	129.2	107.8	107.3
FEB	110.9	113.9	111.2	108.6	128.7	108.0	107.3
MAR	111.0	114.0	111.3	108.7	126.6	108.1	107.3
APR	110.8	114.5	112.0	108.1	125.6	107.6	106.7
MAY	110.7	114.2	112.0	107.7	126.5	107.1	106.4
JUN	110.4	113.7	112.0	107.2	127.6	106.4	105.9

17.1 Producer Price Index (2010=100, SIC2007)

Gross Sector Price Indices of Materials & Fuel purchased

	6107123000: GSI - Purchases of materials and fuels for Manufacture of Other Non-Metallic Mineral Products	6107124250: GSI Sub-section - Inputs of Manuf of Basic Metals & Fabricated products	6107126270: GSI Sub-section - Inputs for Manuf of Computer, Elect & Opt products	6107228000: GSI (excl. CCL) - Inputs for Manufacture of Machinery & Equipment	6107129300: GSI Sub-section - Inputs for Manufacture of Motor Vechicles	6107131330: GSI Sub-section - Inputs for Manuf of Other Manufactured Goods n.e.c
	MC3E	MC3F NSA	MC3G NSA	MB4U NSA	MC3I NSA	MC3J NSA
2009	98.0	92.5	97.0	96.8	97.4	96.4
2010	100.0	100.0	100.0	100.0	100.0	100.0
2011	109.1	110.1	103.3	105.3	104.1	104.5
2012	111.7	108.4	103.1	105.3	104.0	105.4
2013	111.9	107.0	103.1	105.6	104.3	106.3
2011 JAN	105.0	106.4	102.1	103.0	102.5	102.9
FEB	104.4	107.7	102.2	103.5	102.7	103.1
MAR	106.4	109.8	102.7	104.3	103.2	103.4
APR	107.0	111.8	103.4	105.6	104.1	104.2
MAY	108.7	111.5	103.5	105.8	104.3	104.6
JUN	108.8	111.1	103.6	105.8	104.5	104.8
JUL	109.2	111.2	103.8	106.0	104.7	105.0
AUG	111.9	110.7	103.8	105.9	104.7	105.3
SEP	111.8	111.6	104.1	106.3	105.1	105.6
OCT	112.2	110.1	103.7	105.7	104.6	105.3
NOV	112.4	110.1	103.6	105.7	104.4	105.2
DEC	111.5	109.5	103.5	105.6	104.2	105.1
2012 JAN	111.9	109.4	103.3	105.6	104.2	105.3
FEB	112.7	111.2	103.7	106.2	104.8	105.8
MAR	113.1	111.6	103.9	106.3	104.9	106.0
APR	113.1	110.5	103.5	106.0	104.3	105.9
MAY	112.1	108.8	103.3	105.5	103.9	105.6
JUN	111.1	107.1	103.0	105.2	104.1	105.5
JUL	110.1	106.6	102.8	104.9	103.6	105.2
AUG	109.6	106.5	102.7	104.5	103.4	105.0
SEP	110.6	107.4	102.6	104.8	103.4	105.0
OCT	111.5	107.5	102.8	104.9	103.7	105.2
NOV	111.9	106.9	102.7	104.7	103.8	105.1
DEC	112.1	107.1	102.3	104.8	103.8	105.0
2013 JAN	112.3	108.0	102.7	105.5	104.6	105.8
FEB	113.1	109.9	103.6	106.7	105.4	106.8
MAR	114.1	110.2	104.2	107.0	105.3	107.2
APR	112.8	108.2	103.8	106.4	104.8	106.8
MAY	111.3	106.9	103.4	105.6	104.4	106.5
JUN	110.7	106.0	103.1	105.3	104.1	106.2
JUL	111.9	106.5	103.3	105.6	104.5	106.6
AUG	111.4	106.8	103.2	105.5	104.3	106.3
SEP	111.2	16.0	102.9	105.0	103.7	105.9
OCT	111.3	105.5	102.7	104.9	103.8	105.8
NOV	111.5	105.2	102.5	104.7	103.6	105.7
DEC	111.5	105.0	102.3	104.5	103.4	105.5
2014 JAN	112.1	104.8	102.8	104.6	103.3	106.3
FEB	111.9	104.6	102.7	104.4	103.3	106.4
MAR	111.9	104.7	102.8	104.7	103.5	106.5
APR	110.3	103.8	102.5	104.2	103.1	106.1
MAY	110.1	103.9	102.4	104.3	103.1	106.1
JUN	109.8	103.9	103.0	104.2	102.9	106.3

Source: Office for National Statistics

Climate change Levy was introduced in April 2001

Rebasing the Producer Price Index, including trade prices (PPI) and the Services Producer Price Index (SPPI) onto 2010=100 occurred at the end of 2013.
Further information can be found at: http://www.ons.gov.uk/ons/rel/ppi2/producer-price-index/ppi-rebasing-2010---100/index.html

Accuracy
Figures for the latest two months are provisional and the latest five months are subject to revisions in light of (a) late and revised respondent data and
(b), for the seasonally adjusted series; revisions to seasonal adjustment factors are re-estimated every month. A routine seasonal adjustment review is normally
conducted in the autumn each year.

Abreviations
NSI - Net Sector Input
FBTP - Food, Beverages and Tobacco Products
NSA - Not Seasonally Adjusted
SA - Seasonally Adjusted
GSI - Gross Sector Input
CCL - Climate Change Levy

17.2 Producer Price Index of Output (2010=100, SIC2007)

	Net Sector Output Price Indices of Materials & Fuel purchased		Gross Sector Output Price Indices of Materials & Fuel purchased (All Manufacturing & Selected Industries)				
	7200700000: Net Sector Output - Output of Manufactured products	7200799000: Net Sector Output - All Manufacturing excl Food, Beverages Tobacco	7111101280: Gross Sector Output - Food Products, Beverages & Tobacco incl duty	7112130000: Textiles	7112140000: Wearing Apparel	7112150000: Leather & related products	7112160000: Wood, Products of Wood & Cork, except Furniture; Articles of Straw
	JVZ7 NSA	K3BI NSA	K65A NSA	K37R NSA	K37S NSA	K37T NSA	K37U NSA
2008	96.9	97.1	95.7	95.6	99.6	98.7	94.8
2009	97.4	98.5	98.9	98.2	99.7	93.7	96.2
2010	100.0	100.0	100.0	100.0	100.0	100.0	100.0
2011	104.8	102.8	106.6	107.0	102.8	116.5	105.2
2012	107.0	103.9	110.9	110.6	106.1	119.0	109.0
2013	108.4	104.8	114.8	111.4	106.9	123.9	110.4
2011 JAN	102.3	101.2	103.5	103.8	100.5	106.0	102.6
FEB	102.8	101.4	104.4	103.9	100.6	109.2	103.2
MAR	103.8	101.8	105.1	104.7	100.6	115.2	103.6
APR	104.8	102.6	105.9	106.1	102.8	120.8	103.9
MAY	104.9	102.7	106.5	106.3	103.3	119.9	105.1
JUN	105.1	102.9	107.0	107.3	103.1	120.6	105.5
JUL	105.4	103.2	107.4	107.4	103.8	120.6	105.9
AUG	105.4	103.5	107.3	107.3	103.8	117.7	106.1
SEP	105.6	103.6	107.7	108.9	103.8	117.8	106.2
OCT	105.6	103.5	108.0	109.7	103.9	117.2	106.8
NOV	105.8	103.4	108.2	109.6	104.0	116.0	106.8
DEC	105.7	103.5	108.3	109.6	104.0	116.4	107.0
2012 JAN	105.9	103.4	108.8	110.6	104.7	114.8	107.6
FEB	106.3	103.7	109.0	110.2	105.1	114.8	107.9
MAR	106.8	103.8	109.8	110.4	105.4	115.6	108.3
APR	107.2	104.0	110.4	108.8	105.7	119.4	108.9
MAY	107.0	104.0	110.8	109.1	106.5	119.6	108.9
JUN	106.6	103.9	110.9	109.2	105.9	120.1	109.1
JUL	106.8	104.0	111.0	111.2	106.7	119.6	109.4
AUG	107.2	104.0	111.3	111.4	106.6	118.9	109.4
SEP	107.5	104.1	111.7	111.9	106.7	119.7	109.6
OCT	107.6	104.1	111.8	112.1	106.7	121.2	109.5
NOV	107.4	104.1	112.5	112.3	106.4	122.2	109.4
DEC	107.2	103.9	112.7	110.5	106.5	122.3	109.6
2013 JAN	107.6	104.2	113.2	110.8	106.6	122.3	109.7
FEB	108.1	104.4	113.4	111.2	106.6	122.4	109.7
MAR	108.4	104.7	114.0	111.2	106.6	122.5	109.9
APR	108.3	104.8	114.7	111.1	106.6	123.6	110.1
MAY	108.3	104.8	115.0	111.8	107.3	124.4	109.7
JUN	108.4	104.8	115.3	111.8	107.3	124.5	109.9
JUL	108.7	104.9	115.5	111.8	107.3	124.3	110.1
AUG	108.8	104.9	115.4	111.7	106.7	124.4	110.5
SEP	108.8	104.9	115.5	111.7	106.7	124.7	110.7
OCT	108.5	104.9	115.2	111.0	106.7	124.7	111.1
NOV	108.3	104.8	115.3	111.3	107.0	124.7	111.4
DEC	108.3	104.9	114.9	111.6	107.0	124.7	111.5
2014 JAN	108.6	105.4	114.9	112.0	109.5	124.5	112.0
FEB	108.7	105.6	114.9	112.1	109.6	124.6	112.9
MAR	108.8	105.8	115.1	112.2	110.0	125.0	113.0
APR	108.9	105.8	115.2	112.6	110.2	125.8	113.2
MAY	108.8	105.8	114.7	112.7	110.2	124.7	113.6
JUN	108.7	105.8	114.0	112.7	111.3	124.3	114.0

17.2 Producer Price Index of Output (2010=100, SIC2007)

Gross Sector Output Price Indices of Materials & Fuel purchased (All Manufacturing & Selected Industries)

	7112170000: Paper & Paper products	7112180000: Printing & Recording Services	7112200000: Chemicals & Chemical products	7112220000: Rubber & Plastics products	7112230000: Other Non-Metallic Mineral products	7112240000: Basic Metals	7112260000: Computer, Electronic & Optical products
	K37V NSA	K37W NSA	K37Z NSA	K383 NSA	K384 NSA	K385 NSA	K387 NSA
2008	97.1	99.6	96.4	96.5	97.2	99.7	97.5
2009	97.4	100.6	98.8	97.8	99.5	90.8	98.3
2010	100.0	100.0	100.0	100.0	100.0	100.0	100.0
2011	107.7	100.4	107.8	105.4	102.7	108.8	98.2
2012	106.9	99.9	108.4	107.0	106.4	104.7	96.5
2013	106.6	99.3	106.5	108.5	107.7	102.0	96.9
2011 JAN	104.0	100.4	105.5	102.2	101.0	105.5	98.2
FEB	104.4	99.9	105.3	103.1	101.5	107.2	98.2
MAR	105.6	100.1	106.1	103.9	101.8	109.1	98.1
APR	106.9	100.1	107.3	104.7	102.4	111.3	98.2
MAY	107.2	100.3	107.7	105.5	102.9	111.6	98.0
JUN	108.5	100.7	108.5	106.1	102.9	110.2	98.0
JUL	109.5	101.0	109.0	106.6	103.1	109.0	98.0
AUG	109.7	100.7	109.7	106.7	103.2	109.3	98.4
SEP	109.6	100.9	109.8	106.7	103.3	110.3	98.5
OCT	109.5	100.0	108.6	106.6	103.5	107.8	98.4
NOV	109.0	100.0	108.5	106.4	103.4	107.3	98.3
DEC	108.9	100.3	107.7	106.3	103.5	106.5	98.3
2012 JAN	109.3	100.4	107.7	106.2	105.0	106.1	97.2
FEB	107.6	100.4	108.6	106.1	105.9	107.6	97.2
MAR	107.5	100.1	109.6	106.5	106.3	107.5	97.2
APR	107.6	100.2	109.9	106.8	106.6	106.8	96.6
MAY	107.4	100.4	109.7	107.0	106.4	105.8	96.5
JUN	107.5	100.2	108.3	106.9	106.3	104.8	96.3
JUL	107.3	100.2	106.9	106.9	106.3	103.9	96.8
AUG	106.4	99.4	107.7	107.1	106.5	102.3	96.6
SEP	105.7	99.5	108.1	107.4	106.6	103.4	96.5
OCT	105.7	99.4	108.0	107.5	106.9	103.2	96.3
NOV	105.6	99.3	107.9	107.3	106.8	102.4	95.9
DEC	105.5	99.3	108.1	107.7	106.7	102.6	94.7
2013 JAN	105.7	99.5	108.0	108.4	107.5	103.3	94.9
FEB	105.6	99.3	107.9	108.3	107.7	104.3	95.1
MAR	106.2	99.2	108.4	108.3	107.7	104.3	95.9
APR	106.3	99.1	107.7	108.4	107.7	102.9	96.9
MAY	106.4	99.0	106.8	108.5	107.2	102.3	97.2
JUN	106.4	99.1	106.2	108.7	107.3	101.3	97.1
JUL	106.4	99.1	105.9	108.4	107.5	100.9	97.2
AUG	106.7	99.0	106.2	108.7	107.6	101.5	97.3
SEP	107.0	99.4	106.0	108.6	107.8	101.1	97.8
OCT	107.2	99.6	105.3	108.7	107.9	100.8	97.8
NOV	107.6	99.4	104.6	108.6	108.2	100.8	97.6
DEC	107.2	99.6	104.6	108.5	108.1	100.4	97.5
2014 JAN	107.4	99.7	105.1	108.6	108.8	100.5	97.4
FEB	107.6	100.5	105.6	109.1	109.5	100.3	97.3
MAR	107.7	100.1	105.7	109.2	109.8	100.6	97.4
APR	107.6	100.0	105.7	108.7	109.9	99.1	97.4
MAY	107.2	100.4	105.6	108.6	109.5	99.4	97.4
JUN	107.0	100.3	105.1	108.6	109.7	100.1	97.2

17.2 Producer Price Index of Output (2010=100, SIC2007)

Gross Sector Output Price Indices of Materials & Fuel purchased (All Manufacturing & Selected Industries)

	7112270000: Electrical Equipment	7112280000: Machinery & Equipment n.e.c.	7112290000: Motor Vehicles, Trailers & Semi-trailers	7112300000: Other Transport Equipment	7112310000: Furniture	7112320000: Other Manufactured Goods	Output in the Construction Industry All New Work *	Monthly index of average price of new dwellings - at mortgage completion stage
	K388 NSA	K389 NSA	K38A NSA	K38B NSA	K38C NSA	K38D NSA		
2008	94.3	97.5	96.2	97.1	96.7	97.2	105.6	164.4
2009	96.9	98.8	99.4	99.1	98.3	98.9	103.2	150.5
2010	100.0	100.0	100.0	100.0	100.0	100.0	98.9	158.1
2011	102.9	103.3	100.9	101.3	102.7	102.0	100.0	170.5
2012	102.8	105.5	101.5	102.9	105.1	104.0	103.3	177.2
2013	103.0	108.2	102.5	105.1	105.8	105.3	106.9	180.3
2011 JAN	102.8	101.0	100.1	100.5	101.2	101.3	98.7	168.1
FEB	103.1	100.9	100.1	100.4	101.4	101.4	98.9	168.0
MAR	103.4	101.6	100.4	100.5	101.8	101.5	99.1	167.5
APR	103.2	103.2	100.7	101.2	102.0	101.3	99.4	168.5
MAY	103.0	103.4	100.8	101.4	102.0	101.8	99.7	167.2
JUN	102.9	103.6	101.1	101.4	102.2	101.9	99.9	167.9
JUL	102.8	104.1	101.2	101.6	103.2	102.0	100.0	172.5
AUG	103.0	104.3	101.5	101.6	103.4	102.1	100.2	170.7
SEP	102.6	104.4	101.6	101.6	103.4	102.3	100.5	172.8
OCT	102.6	104.2	101.5	101.6	103.5	102.3	100.8	172.4
NOV	102.6	104.7	101.1	101.7	103.8	102.5	101.2	172.0
DEC	102.7	104.7	101.0	101.8	103.9	103.5	101.7	178.6
2012 JAN	102.1	104.4	100.9	102.0	104.2	103.5	102.0	183.1
FEB	102.5	104.4	101.2	102.0	104.4	105.3	102.4	181.4
MAR	103.0	105.1	101.2	102.1	104.3	104.1	102.6	179.0
APR	102.9	105.4	101.6	102.0	105.0	104.1	102.7	176.9
MAY	102.8	105.5	101.4	102.5	105.3	104.1	103.0	177.5
JUN	102.6	105.7	101.5	102.9	105.3	104.1	103.2	177.4
JUL	102.8	105.5	101.3	103.9	105.4	104.0	103.5	174.1
AUG	102.9	105.4	101.3	103.8	105.4	103.8	103.9	175.9
SEP	102.8	105.8	101.8	102.9	105.6	103.6	103.9	169.3
OCT	103.0	105.9	101.9	103.5	105.6	103.6	104.0	171.4
NOV	103.0	106.1	101.7	103.7	105.5	103.8	104.2	174.8
DEC	103.0	106.2	101.9	103.7	105.4	104.0	104.4	185.7
2013 JAN	103.3	106.4	102.4	103.8	105.6	104.4	104.8	183.3
FEB	103.3	107.5	102.6	104.5	105.6	104.6	105.2	180.9
MAR	103.4	107.8	102.5	104.9	105.5	104.8	105.6	180.8
APR	103.4	108.2	102.2	105.1	105.6	104.9	105.9	184.8
MAY	103.3	108.2	102.2	105.2	105.7	104.9	106.2	180.1
JUN	103.3	108.3	102.3	105.0	105.6	105.5	106.4	183.3
JUL	103.1	108.8	102.8	105.2	105.8	105.5	106.9	174.6
AUG	102.6	108.6	102.7	105.6	105.8	105.7	107.3	175.8
SEP	102.6	108.4	102.5	105.5	106.0	105.8	107.6	178.1
OCT	102.6	108.6	102.6	105.5	106.0	105.8	108.3	176.9
NOV	102.8	108.7	102.3	105.5	106.0	105.6	108.9	179.1
DEC	102.7	108.5	102.3	105.4	106.2	105.5	109.5	185.7
2014 JAN	103.1	109.1	102.4	106.3	106.8	105.9	108.7	188.0
FEB	103.3	109.3	102.5	106.4	106.8	105.9	109.3	192.1
MAR	103.3	109.5	102.6	106.7	106.9	107.1	109.9	184.7
APR	103.2	109.6	102.2	107.0	107.0	107.1	110.4	189.4
MAY	103.5	109.6	102.3	107.4	107.3	107.2	110.8	192.6
JUN	103.7	109.5	102.0	107.5	107.3	107.2	111.1	190.4

Climate change Levy was introduced in April 2001

Rebasing the Producer Price Index, including trade prices (PPI) and the Services Producer Price Index (SPPI) onto 2010=100 occurred at the end of 2013. Further information can be found at:
http://www.ons.gov.uk/ons/rel/ppi2/producer-price-index/ppi-rebasing-2010---100/index.html

Source: Office for National Statistics
Department for Communities and Local Government

* All New Work uses the base of 2011=100

Accuracy
Figures for the latest two months are provisional and the latest five months are subject to revisions in light of (a) late and revised respondent data and
(b), for the seasonally adjusted series; revisions to seasonal adjustment factors are re-estimated every month. A routine seasonal adjustment review is normally conducted in the autumn each year.

Abreviations
NSI - Net Sector Input
FBTP - Food, Beverages and Tobacco Products
NSA - Not Seasonally Adjusted
SA - Seasonally Adjusted
GSI - Gross Sector Input
CCL - Climate Change Levy
* JYYC 'Quarterly construction output price index' was previously published in Annual Abstract of Statistics has now been replaced by Table 9a, section 'All New Work' from Output in the Construction Industry

17.3 Internal purchasing power of the pound (based on RPI) [1,2,3,4]: 1990 to 2013

pence	1990	1991	1992	1993	1994	1995	1996	1997	1998	1999	2000	2001	2002	2003	2004	2005	2006	2007	2008	2009	2010	2011	2012	2013
1990	100	106	110	112	114	118	121	125	129	131	135	137	140	144	148	152	157	164	170	169	177	186	192	198
1991	94	100	104	105	108	112	114	118	122	124	128	130	132	136	140	144	148	155	161	160	167	176	182	187
1992	91	96	100	102	104	108	110	114	118	119	123	125	127	131	135	139	143	149	155	154	161	170	175	181
1993	90	95	98	100	102	106	109	112	116	118	121	123	125	129	133	136	141	147	153	152	159	167	173	178
1994	88	93	96	98	100	103	106	109	113	115	118	120	122	126	130	133	137	143	149	148	155	163	168	174
1995	85	90	93	94	97	100	102	106	109	111	114	116	118	122	125	129	133	139	144	143	150	158	163	168
1996	83	87	91	92	94	98	100	103	107	108	112	113	115	119	122	126	130	135	141	140	146	154	159	164
1997	80	85	88	89	92	95	97	100	103	105	108	110	112	115	119	122	126	131	136	136	142	149	154	159
1998	77	82	85	86	88	92	94	97	100	102	105	106	108	111	115	118	122	127	132	131	137	144	149	154
1999	76	81	84	85	87	90	92	95	98	100	103	105	107	110	113	116	120	125	130	129	135	142	147	151
2000	74	78	81	83	85	88	90	92	96	97	100	102	103	106	110	113	116	121	126	125	131	138	143	147
2001	73	77	80	81	83	86	88	91	94	95	98	100	102	105	108	111	114	119	124	123	129	136	140	144
2002	72	76	79	80	82	85	87	89	92	94	97	98	100	103	106	109	112	117	122	121	127	133	138	142
2003	70	74	76	78	79	82	84	87	90	91	94	96	97	100	103	106	109	114	118	118	123	130	134	138
2004	68	72	74	75	77	80	82	84	87	89	91	93	94	97	100	103	106	111	115	114	120	126	130	134
2005	66	70	72	73	75	78	80	82	85	86	89	90	92	94	97	100	103	108	112	111	116	123	126	130
2006	64	67	70	71	73	75	77	80	82	83	86	87	89	92	94	97	100	104	108	108	113	119	123	126
2007	61	65	67	68	70	72	74	76	79	80	82	84	85	88	90	93	96	100	104	103	108	114	117	121
2008	59	62	64	65	67	69	71	73	76	77	79	81	82	84	87	89	92	96	100	99	104	109	113	116
2009	59	62	65	66	67	70	71	74	76	77	80	81	82	85	87	90	93	97	101	100	105	110	114	117
2010	56	60	62	63	64	67	68	70	73	74	76	78	79	81	84	86	89	92	96	96	100	105	109	112
2011	54	57	59	60	61	63	65	67	69	70	72	74	75	77	79	82	84	88	91	91	95	100	103	106
2012	52	55	57	58	59	61	63	65	67	68	70	71	73	75	77	79	82	85	89	88	92	97	100	103
2013	50	53	55	56	58	60	61	63	65	66	68	69	70	72	75	77	79	83	86	85	89	94	97	100

1 To find the purchasing power of the pound in 2001, given that it was 100 pence in 1990, select the column headed 1990 and look at the 2001 row. The result is 73 pence.

2 Changes in the internal purchasing power of a currency may be defined as the 'inverse' of changes in the levels of prices; when prices go up, the amount which can be purchased with a given sum of money goes down. The monthly figures of the all items RPI can be used to obtain estimates of the changes in prices or in purchasing power between any 2 months. To find the purchasing power of the pound in one month, given that it was 100p in a previous month the calculation is: 100p multiplied by the earlier month RPI then divided by the later month RPI

3 Comparisons between any 2 years may be made in the same way using the annual averages of the RPI found in table 5.3. These figure are reproduced in the above table.

4 In accordance with the Statistics and Registration Service Act 2007, the Retail Prices Index and its derivatives have been assessed against the Code of Practice for Official Statistics and found not to meet the required standards for designation as National Statistics. A full report can be found at: http://www.statisticsauthority.gov.uk/

Source:
Office for National Statistics
Prices Division
2.001 Cardiff Road
Newport
South Wales
NP10 8XG
Tel: +44 (0) 1633 456900

http://www.ons.gov.uk

17.4 CPI: Detailed figures by division [1,3]

	Food and non-alcoholic beverages	Alcoholic beverages and tobacco	Clothing and footwear	Housing, water, electricity, gas & other fuels	Furniture, household equipment & routine maintenance	Health [2]	Transport	Communic-ation	Recreation and culture	Education [2]	Restaurants and hotels	Miscell-aneous goods and services [2]	CPI (overall index)
COICOP Division	1	2	3	4	5	6	7	8	9	10	11	12	
	CHZR	CHZS	CHZT	CHZU	CHZV	CHZW	CHZX	CHZY	CHZZ	CJUU	CJUV	CJUW	CHZQ
Weights 2014	112	45	72	129	60	24	152	32	144	22	120	88	1000
Monthly indices (2005=100)	D7BU	D7BV	D7BW	D7BX	D7BY	D7BZ	D7C2	D7C3	D7C4	D7C5	D7C6	D7C7	D7BT
Jul 2012	138.2	141.1	76.9	144.2	117.7	123.5	135.5	108.8	100.4	168.3	126.3	118.7	122.5
Aug	138.5	141.4	79.1	144.4	118.6	123.6	137.2	108.8	100.2	168.3	126.5	119.0	123.1
Sep	138.5	142.9	82.8	144.6	119.2	123.8	135.4	108.8	100.8	169.1	126.8	119.9	123.5
Oct	139.1	143.4	83.8	144.8	118.5	124.0	135.3	109.0	101.2	201.5	126.8	119.9	124.2
Nov	140.7	142.7	84.3	145.7	118.4	124.0	133.9	108.8	101.2	201.5	127.5	120.3	124.4
Dec	142.4	141.1	83.1	148.6	119.9	124.2	134.9	108.7	101.1	201.5	127.5	120.4	125.0
Jan 2013	142.6	147.1	78.6	148.4	117.2	124.4	134.0	109.7	101.0	201.5	127.5	119.6	124.4
Feb	143.5	146.3	80.2	149.1	118.9	124.4	135.7	110.8	101.5	201.5	127.8	119.7	125.2
Mar	142.9	145.6	82.1	149.1	119.8	124.7	136.5	110.8	102.0	201.5	128.1	120.0	125.6
Apr	143.9	148.9	82.0	150.1	118.3	126.1	135.6	111.0	102.0	201.5	128.7	120.2	125.9
May	143.9	149.6	83.0	149.8	119.6	126.1	136.2	111.4	101.7	201.5	129.1	120.1	126.1
Jun	143.2	149.1	81.4	149.9	119.0	126.0	136.3	111.5	101.6	201.5	129.3	120.3	125.9
Jul	143.5	150.1	78.8	150.5	117.8	126.9	137.5	111.8	101.1	201.5	129.5	120.4	125.8
Aug	144.2	150.0	80.4	150.5	119.9	127.1	138.9	111.6	101.1	201.5	129.5	120.5	126.4
Sep	144.4	150.7	83.7	150.7	120.1	127.4	137.0	111.7	101.7	205.4	130.1	120.9	126.8
Oct	144.6	151.1	84.6	150.6	119.7	127.2	134.9	112.0	101.9	222.2	130.3	120.7	126.9
Nov	144.6	151.0	85.2	150.6	119.6	127.1	134.2	111.8	102.3	222.2	130.5	121.0	127.0
Dec	145.1	149.2	84.4	154.0	121.6	127.2	135.6	112.2	101.9	222.2	130.5	120.7	127.5
Jan	145.4	153.8	79.9	153.8	117.9	128.0	134.7	112.8	101.4	222.2	130.3	120.4	126.7
Feb	146.1	152.4	80.8	153.9	120.8	128.6	135.1	113.0	102.2	222.2	130.8	120.7	127.4
Mar	145.4	152.8	82.2	153.7	121.1	128.8	135.1	113.3	102.6	222.2	131.4	121.1	127.7
Apr	144.7	154.1	83.0	154.6	120.1	129.8	137.7	113.2	102.5	222.2	131.6	120.6	128.1
May	143.0	156.4	83.0	154.7	120.7	129.9	136.8	112.6	102.9	222.2	132.1	120.4	128.0
Jun	143.2	156.5	83.4	154.7	120.9	130.0	137.6	112.5	102.9	222.2	132.6	120.3	128.3
Jul 2014	143.0	155.4	78.7	155.2	119.2	130.2	139.3	112.6	102.7	222.2	133.1	119.8	127.8
Percentage change on a year earlier	D7G8	D7G9	D7GA	D7GB	D7GC	D7GD	D7GE	D7GF	D7GG	D7GH	D7GI	D7GJ	D7G7
Jul 2012	2.1	5.0	0.1	6.1	3.5	3.0	1.3	4.4	0.4	5.1	3.2	1.7	2.6
Aug	2.2	5.8	-0.7	5.6	2.3	2.6	1.7	4.3	0.6	5.1	3.1	1.6	2.5
Sep	2.0	6.1	-0.5	2.2	1.7	2.4	2.5	3.4	1.2	3.2	3.0	2.3	2.2
Oct	3.4	6.5	-0.1	1.7	1.7	2.5	3.1	3.7	0.8	19.7	2.9	1.9	2.7
Nov	3.9	5.7	-0.6	2.0	0.6	2.5	2.6	3.7	1.0	19.7	3.3	2.3	2.7
Dec	3.8	6.0	0.8	3.9	0.9	2.8	1.1	2.2	0.7	19.7	3.2	2.0	2.7
Jan 2013	4.2	8.5	0.2	3.5	0.8	2.2	1.3	3.5	0.5	19.7	3.2	1.4	2.7
Feb	3.7	7.1	-0.6	4.4	0.7	2.1	1.9	4.0	1.2	19.7	3.1	0.9	2.8
Mar	3.7	6.3	-0.4	4.5	0.2	2.3	1.7	3.3	1.8	19.7	3.1	1.1	2.8
Apr	4.6	5.7	-0.6	4.2	0.1	2.5	-0.1	3.2	1.4	19.7	2.5	1.1	2.4
May	4.3	6.2	0.7	4.2	0.6	2.4	1.1	2.7	1.6	19.7	2.5	1.0	2.7
Jun	3.8	6.4	3.1	4.4	-	2.0	1.7	2.9	1.3	19.7	2.5	1.5	2.9
Jul	3.9	6.3	2.5	4.3	0.1	2.7	1.5	2.8	0.7	19.7	2.5	1.5	2.8
Aug	4.1	6.0	1.6	4.2	1.1	2.9	1.2	2.5	0.9	19.7	2.4	1.2	2.7
Sep	4.3	5.4	1.1	4.2	0.7	2.9	1.1	2.6	0.9	21.4	2.6	0.9	2.7
Oct	3.9	5.4	1.0	4.1	1.0	2.6	-0.3	2.7	0.7	10.3	2.8	0.7	2.2
Nov	2.8	5.8	1.1	3.4	1.0	2.5	0.2	2.8	1.1	10.3	2.3	0.5	2.1
Dec	1.9	5.8	1.6	3.7	1.4	2.5	0.5	3.3	0.8	10.3	2.3	0.3	2.0
Jan	2.0	4.5	1.7	3.6	0.6	2.9	0.5	2.8	0.4	10.3	2.2	0.7	1.9
Feb	1.8	4.1	0.8	3.2	1.6	3.4	-0.4	2.0	0.7	10.3	2.3	0.8	1.7
Mar	1.7	5.0	0.2	3.1	1.1	3.4	-1.0	2.3	0.6	10.3	2.6	0.9	1.6
Apr	0.5	3.5	1.2	3.0	1.5	2.9	1.6	1.9	0.5	10.3	2.3	0.3	1.8
May	-0.6	4.6	-0.1	3.2	0.9	3.1	0.4	1.0	1.1	10.3	2.3	0.3	1.5
Jun	-	5.0	2.4	3.2	1.6	3.1	0.9	0.9	1.3	10.3	2.6	-	1.9
Jul 2014	-0.4	3.6	-0.2	3.2	1.1	2.6	1.3	0.7	1.5	10.3	2.8	-0.6	1.6

Source: Office for National Statistics

Key: - zero or negligible

1. Inflation rates prior to 1997 and index levels prior to 1996 are estimated. (Details are given in Economic Trends No. 541 December 1998 available on the Office for National Statistics website)

2. The coverage of these categories was extended in January 2000; further extensions to coverage came into effect in January 2001 for health and miscellaneous goods and services; the coverage of miscellaneous goods and services was further extended with effect from January 2002. (Details are given in a series of Economic Trends articles available on the National Statistics website)

3. More detailed CPI data are available at: http://www.ons.gov.uk

17.5 Retail Prices Index[1] United Kingdom

Indices (13 January 1987=100)

	All items (RPI)	All items excluding		Housing	All items excluding Food	All items excluding Seasonal food[2]	Food and catering	Alcohol and tobacco	Housing and household expenditure	Pesonal expend-iture	Travel and leisure	Consumer durables[4]	All items excluding mortgage interest payments and indirect taxes (RPIY)[3]
		mortgage interest payments (RPIX)	mortgage interest payments and depreci-ation										
Weights													
	CZGU	CZGY	DOGZ	CZGX	CZGV	CZGW	CBVV	CBVW	CBVX	CBVY	CBVZ	CBWA	
2001	1000	954	914	795	884	982	169	97	362	96	276	125	
2002	1000	964	924	801	886	980	166	99	363	94	278	126	
2003	1000	961	919	797	891	983	160	98	365	92	285	126	
2004	1000	961	914	791	889	981	160	97	367	93	283	121	
2005	1000	950	901	776	890	981	159	96	387	89	269	122	
2006	1000	950	906	778	895	983	155	96	392	90	267	117	
2007	1000	945	895	762	895	981	152	95	408	83	262	109	
2008	1000	940	885	746	889	980	158	86	417	83	256	104	
2009	1000	959	909	764	882	979	168	90	416	80	246	106	
2010	1000	966	911	763	888	981	159	91	403	81	266	105	
2011	1000	968	914	762	882	980	165	88	408	82	257	106	
2012	1000	971	915	763	886	981	161	85	412	84	258	100	
2013	1000	971	913	746	884	980	163	91	419	83	244	96	
2014	1000	970	912	747	886	981	161	87	424	85	243	98	
Annual averages													
	CHAW	CHMK	CHON	CHAZ	CHAY	CHAX	CHBS	CHBT	CHBU	CHBV	CHBW	CHBY	CBZW
2001	173.3	171.3	169.5	163.7	178.0	174.3	162.2	216.9	180.0	135.7	172.0	105.0	163.7
2002	176.2	175.1	172.5	166.0	181.1	177.2	164.8	222.3	184.6	133.2	174.2	101.9	167.5
2003	181.3	180.0	176.2	168.9	186.7	182.4	167.9	228.0	194.3	133.2	177.0	99.8	172.0
2004	186.7	184.0	179.1	170.9	192.8	187.9	170.0	233.6	207.4	131.5	178.1	97.7	175.5
2005	192.0	188.2	182.6	173.7	198.7	193.3	172.9	239.8	219.4	131.0	179.2	95.3	179.4
2006	198.1	193.7	187.8	178.3	205.2	199.5	176.9	247.1	231.8	131.7	181.1	94.0	184.8
2007	206.6	199.9	193.3	183.2	213.9	207.9	184.3	256.2	248.1	132.9	183.8	93.3	190.8
2008	214.8	208.5	201.9	191.3	221.2	216.0	198.5	266.7	258.6	132.4	189.0	91.6	199.2
2009	213.7	212.6	207.2	196.3	218.3	214.6	207.6	276.7	247.4	131.4	191.2	90.7	204.8
2010	223.6	222.7	217	206.5	228.8	224.5	214.1	289.9	253.8	138.2	207.6	94.4	211.9
2011	235.2	234.5	229.3	219.6	240.5	236.3	225.6	311.3	262.5	149.8	220.1	99.7	220.4
2012	242.7	242.0	237.0	227.4	248.2	243.9	232.9	327.1	270.9	158.2	224.1	104.1	227.7
2013	250.1	249.4	244.4	235.1	255.5	251.2	240.8	341.9	279.7	166.8	226.8	108.8	235.0
Monthly figures													
2013 July	249.7	249.0	244.0	234.4	255.2	250.8	240.6	343.4	279.4	163.7	227.0	106.2	234.5
Aug	251.0	250.3	245.2	235.8	256.5	252.1	241.5	343.5	280.6	166.0	228.4	108.5	235.8
Sep	251.9	251.2	246.0	236.8	257.5	253.0	241.6	345.0	281.3	170.5	228.2	111.2	236.8
Oct	251.9	251.2	246.0	236.7	257.4	252.9	242.1	346.0	281.6	171.5	226.6	111.2	236.7
Nov	252.1	251.5	246.2	236.9	257.7	253.2	242.2	346.6	281.9	172.6	226.3	111.7	237.0
Dec	253.4	252.8	247.5	238.4	259.1	254.5	242.8	344.7	284.9	171.8	227.5	112.4	238.5
2014 Jan	252.6	251.9	246.5	237.2	258.0	253.6	243.6	349.9	283.7	166.9	226.6	107.4	237.6
Feb	254.2	253.6	248.2	239.2	259.8	255.3	244.6	348.7	285.6	171.2	227.7	112.3	239.4
Mar	254.8	254.3	248.7	239.9	260.5	255.9	244.3	349.9	285.8	174.3	228.0	114.0	240.0
Apr	255.7	255.2	249.6	240.4	261.7	257.0	243.5	352.1	286.4	175.8	229.6	113.7	240.6
May	255.9	255.4	249.6	240.4	262.2	257.2	242.0	355.4	287.1	175.8	229.4	114.4	240.8
June	256.3	255.8	250.0	240.7	262.7	257.7	242.5	355.7	288.0	176.3	229.4	115.0	241.3
July	256.0	255.5	249.4	239.9	262.5	257.4	242.1	354.7	288.2	171.2	230.9	110.8	241.1

1 See chapter text.

2 Seasonal food is defined as items of food the prices of which show significant seasonal variations. These are fresh fruit and vegetables, fresh fish, eggs and home-killed lamb.

3 There are no weights available for RPIY. The taxes excluded are council tax, VAT, duties, car purchase tax and vehicle excise duty, insurance premium tax and airport tax.

4 Consumer durables: Furniture, furnishings, electrical appliances and other household equipment, men's, women's and children's outerwear, footwear, audio-visual equipment, CDs and tapes, toys, photographic and sports goods.

Source: Office for National Statistics: 020 7533 5874

In accordance with the *Statistics and Registration Service Act 2007*, the Retail Prices Index and its derivatives have been assessed against the Code of Practice for Official Statistics and found not to meet the required standards for designation as National Statistics. A full report can be found at:
http://www.statisticsauthority.gov.uk/

17.6 Tax and Price Index[1] United Kingdom

Indices and percentages

Tax and Price Index: (January 1987=100)
DQAB

	1999	2000	2001	2002	2003	2004	2005	2006	2007	2008	2009	2010	2011	2012	2013	2014
January	150.5	152.7	156.7	156.5	161.4	166.9	172.1	175.9	183.3	190.7	188.6	194.7	205.5	212.8	218.8	222.7
February	150.8	153.7	157.6	157.0	162.3	167.6	172.8	176.7	184.8	192.3	189.8	196.0	207.7	214.6	220.5	224.2
March	151.2	154.6	157.8	157.7	163.0	168.4	173.7	177.4	186.1	192.9	189.7	197.4	208.8	215.6	221.6	224.8
April	151.2	155.7	156.3	158.6	164.9	168.9	174.1	178.3	186.3	192.2	188.5	199.5	209.2	215.6	219.7	224.2
May	151.7	156.3	157.4	159.1	165.2	169.7	174.5	179.5	187.1	193.4	189.7	200.3	210.0	215.5	220.2	224.4
June	151.7	156.7	157.6	159.1	165.0	170.0	174.7	180.3	188.2	195.1	190.2	200.8	210.0	214.9	219.9	224.8
July	151.1	156.1	156.5	158.8	165.0	170.0	174.7	180.3	187.0	194.8	190.2	200.3	209.5	215.2	219.9	224.5
August	151.5	156.1	157.2	159.3	165.4	170.6	175.1	181.0	188.2	195.5	191.3	201.2	210.9	216.1	221.1	225.5
September	152.3	157.3	157.8	160.6	166.3	171.3	175.6	181.9	188.9	196.7	192.2	201.9	212.7	217.2	222.0	226.1
October	152.6	157.2	157.5	160.9	166.4	171.8	175.8	182.2	189.8	196.0	192.9	202.4	212.8	218.6	222.0	226.1
November	152.8	157.7	156.8	161.2	166.5	172.2	176.1	182.8	190.6	194.3	193.4	203.4	213.2	218.6	222.2	225.6
December	153.4	157.8	156.6	161.5	167.3	173.1	176.6	184.4	191.8	191.2	194.8	204.9	214.1	219.8	223.5	226.0

Retail Prices Index: (January 1987=100)
CHAW

	1999	2000	2001	2002	2003	2004	2005	2006	2007	2008	2009	2010	2011	2012	2013	2014
January	163.4	166.6	171.1	173.3	178.4	183.1	188.9	193.4	201.6	209.8	210.1	217.9	229.0	238.0	245.8	252.6
February	163.7	167.5	172.0	173.8	179.3	183.8	189.6	194.2	203.1	211.4	211.4	219.2	231.3	239.9	247.6	254.2
March	164.1	168.4	172.2	174.5	179.9	184.6	190.5	195.0	204.4	212.1	211.3	220.7	232.5	240.8	248.7	254.8
April	165.2	170.1	173.1	175.7	181.2	185.7	191.6	196.5	205.4	214.0	211.5	222.8	234.4	242.5	249.5	255.7
May	165.6	170.7	174.2	176.2	181.5	186.5	192.0	197.7	206.2	215.1	212.8	223.6	235.2	242.4	250.0	255.9
June	165.6	171.1	174.4	176.2	181.3	186.8	192.2	198.5	207.3	216.8	213.4	224.1	235.2	241.8	249.7	256.3
July	165.1	170.5	173.3	175.9	181.3	186.8	192.2	198.5	206.1	216.5	213.4	223.6	234.7	242.1	249.7	256.0
August	165.5	170.5	174.0	176.4	181.6	187.4	192.6	199.2	207.3	217.2	214.4	224.5	236.1	243.0	251.0	257.0
September	166.2	171.7	174.6	177.6	182.5	188.1	193.1	200.1	208.0	218.4	215.3	225.3	237.9	244.2	251.9	257.6
October	166.5	171.6	174.3	177.9	182.6	188.6	193.3	200.4	208.9	217.7	216.0	225.8	238.0	245.6	251.9	257.7
November	166.7	172.1	173.6	178.2	182.7	189.0	193.6	201.1	209.7	216.0	216.6	226.8	238.5	245.6	252.1	257.1
December	167.3	172.2	173.4	178.5	183.5	189.9	194.1	202.7	210.9	212.9	218.0	228.4	239.4	246.8	253.4	257.5

Percentage changes on one year earlier[1] CZVL

Tax and Price Index[1]

	1999	2000	2001	2002	2003	2004	2005	2006	2007	2008	2009	2010	2011	2012	2013	2014
January	2.3	1.5	2.6	-0.1	3.1	3.4	3.1	2.2	4.2	4.0	-1.1	3.2	5.5	3.6	2.8	1.8
February	2.0	1.9	2.5	-0.4	3.4	3.3	3.1	2.3	4.6	4.1	-1.3	3.3	6.0	3.3	2.7	1.7
March	1.9	2.2	2.1	-0.1	3.4	3.3	3.1	2.1	4.9	3.7	-1.7	4.1	5.8	3.3	2.8	1.4
April	1.0	3.0	0.4	1.5	4.0	2.4	3.1	2.4	4.5	3.2	-1.9	5.8	4.9	3.1	1.9	2.0
May	0.7	3.0	0.7	1.1	3.8	2.7	2.8	2.9	4.2	3.4	-1.9	5.6	4.8	2.6	2.2	1.9
June	0.8	3.3	0.6	1.0	3.7	3.0	2.8	3.2	4.4	3.7	-2.5	5.6	4.6	2.3	2.3	2.2
July	0.7	3.3	0.3	1.5	3.9	3.0	2.8	3.2	3.7	4.2	-2.4	5.3	4.6	2.7	2.2	2.1
August	0.5	3.0	0.7	1.3	3.8	3.1	2.6	3.4	4.0	3.9	-2.1	5.2	4.8	2.5	2.3	2.0
September	0.5	3.3	0.3	1.8	3.5	3.0	2.5	3.6	3.8	4.1	-2.3	5.0	5.3	2.1	2.2	1.8
October	0.7	3.0	0.2	2.2	3.4	3.2	2.3	3.6	4.2	3.3	-1.6	4.9	5.1	2.7	1.6	1.8
November	0.9	3.2	-0.6	2.8	3.3	3.4	2.3	3.8	4.3	1.9	-0.5	5.2	4.8	2.5	1.6	1.5
December	1.3	2.9	-0.8	3.1	3.6	3.5	2.0	4.4	4.0	-0.3	1.9	5.2	4.5	2.7	1.7	1.1

Retail Prices Index - CZBH

	1999	2000	2001	2002	2003	2004	2005	2006	2007	2008	2009	2010	2011	2012	2013	2014
January	2.4	2.0	2.7	1.3	2.9	2.6	3.2	2.4	4.2	4.1	0.1	3.7	5.1	3.9	3.3	2.8
February	2.1	2.3	2.7	1.0	3.2	2.5	3.2	2.4	4.6	4.1	-	3.7	5.5	3.7	3.2	2.7
March	2.1	2.6	2.3	1.3	3.1	2.6	3.2	2.4	4.8	3.8	-0.4	4.4	5.3	3.6	3.3	2.5
April	1.6	3.0	1.8	1.5	3.1	2.5	3.2	2.6	4.5	4.2	-1.2	5.3	5.2	3.5	2.9	2.5
May	1.3	3.1	2.1	1.1	3.0	2.8	2.9	3.0	4.3	4.3	-1.1	5.1	5.2	3.1	3.1	2.4
June	1.3	3.3	1.9	1.0	2.9	3.0	2.9	3.3	4.4	4.6	-1.6	5.0	5.0	2.8	3.3	2.6
July	1.3	3.3	1.6	1.5	3.1	3.0	2.9	3.3	3.8	5.0	-1.4	4.8	5.0	3.2	3.1	2.5
August	1.1	3.0	2.1	1.4	2.9	3.2	2.8	3.4	4.1	4.8	-1.3	4.7	5.2	2.9	3.3	2.4
September	1.1	3.3	1.7	1.7	2.8	3.1	2.7	3.6	3.9	5.0	-1.4	4.6	5.6	2.6	3.2	2.3
October	1.2	3.1	1.6	2.1	2.6	3.3	2.5	3.7	4.2	4.2	-0.8	4.5	5.4	3.2	2.6	2.3
November	1.4	3.2	0.9	2.6	2.5	3.4	2.4	3.9	4.3	3.0	0.3	4.7	5.2	3.0	2.6	2.0
December	1.8	2.9	0.7	2.9	2.8	3.5	2.2	4.4	4.0	0.9	2.4	4.8	4.8	3.1	2.7	1.6

Source: Office for National Statistics: 020 7533 5874 [7]533 5874

Key: - zero or negligible   .. not available

1. In accordance with the *Statistics and Registration Service Act 2007*, the Retail Prices Index and its derivatives have been assessed against the Code of Practice for Official Statistics and found not to meet the required standards for designation as National Statistics. A full report can be found at: http://www.statisticsauthority.gov.uk/

17.7 Index of Producer Prices of Agricultural Products, UK (2010=100)

		2004	2005	2006	2007	2008	2009	2010	2011	2012	2013
Total Inputs	a	72.9	75.3	78.1	84.8	103.2	95.9	100.0	112.2	114.0	116.9
All goods and services currently consumed in agriculture	a	70.8	73.2	76.2	83.6	105.0	95.7	100.0	113.9	116.4	119.7
Seeds	a	82.5	93.5	86.3	97.2	111.2	105.0	100.0	105.8	98.5	110.2
Energy and lubricants		54.3	67.3	75.8	78.2	107.0	88.3	100.0	118.2	122.4	123.4
Electricity		58.6	64.9	79.7	84.4	100.5	102.2	100.0	108.8	113.4	121.9
Fuels for heating		43.6	58.6	68.2	75.0	101.4	81.4	100.0	110.7	120.0	128.1
Motor fuels		54.3	69.2	75.5	76.7	109.6	85.0	100.0	122.0	125.4	123.3
Fertilisers and soil improvers		53.8	58.9	62.6	67.8	148.5	102.3	100.0	130.4	125.2	113.1
Straight fertilisers		54.4	61.3	66.0	69.8	152.9	93.7	100.0	140.7	128.2	115.2
Straight fertilisers - nitrogenous		56.2	63.7	68.8	71.6	151.8	89.1	100.0	144.5	130.7	118.0
Straight fertilisers - phosphatic		45.0	48.0	48.0	69.0	184.3	111.3	100.0	131.0	120.2	97.5
Straight fertilisers - potassic		38.9	42.1	44.8	51.3	148.2	134.6	100.0	105.2	105.5	94.7
Compound fertilisers		49.5	52.9	55.4	62.4	147.1	112.6	100.0	120.5	123.6	111.3
Other fertilisers and soil improvers		92.8	93.0	96.2	100.8	105.6	105.8	100.0	100.0	102.4	105.5
Plant protection products	a	92.1	94.9	97.3	98.8	100.9	102.8	100.0	100.7	102.0	97.7
Fungicides		95.7	96.8	98.3	99.6	101.9	103.5	100.0	110.6	109.3	99.9
Insecticides		71.1	80.6	85.7	89.6	91.4	102.2	100.0	89.5	67.3	61.0
Herbicides	a	91.3	95.2	98.4	99.8	101.9	102.3	100.0	95.1	89.1	91.6
Other plant protection products		96.3	96.4	96.5	97.8	99.5	102.7	100.0	98.6	151.3	137.3
Veterinary services	a	84.5	83.9	89.8	91.2	87.6	88.0	100.0	102.0	103.5	106.1
Animal feedingstuffs	q	68.9	63.7	66.0	80.1	103.7	95.4	100.0	120.7	128.5	139.4
Straight feedingstuffs		66.9	60.0	62.6	81.7	106.1	90.1	100.0	122.9	135.7	147.6
Cereal and milling by products		73.2	61.3	69.0	96.7	127.2	90.5	100.0	151.6	153.8	161.4
Feed wheat		70.2	57.2	65.5	91.2	123.8	91.3	100.0	143.8	144.6	157.0
Feed barley		77.7	66.5	73.5	105.1	132.5	90.0	100.0	159.9	163.7	165.8
Feed oats		67.7	68.8	74.3	90.8	111.7	80.3	100.0	184.8	198.4	180.7
Oilcakes		57.4	51.9	51.2	64.7	93.8	90.5	100.0	96.6	124.2	138.7
Soya bean meal		49.5	44.0	49.8	66.2	108.6	93.4	100.0	117.3	134.4	137.3
Sunflower seed meal		58.4	52.0	49.8	60.6	90.9	97.1	100.0	97.8	126.0	141.3
Rape seed meal		54.4	54.8	53.9	72.9	99.1	77.6	100.0	91.6	113.4	131.2
Products of animal origin (incl. white fish meal)		40.2	42.3	61.0	58.0	58.6	67.2	100.0	101.9	103.5	108.8
Other straights		71.5	68.9	68.8	84.9	96.6	90.0	100.0	120.8	128.4	142.8
Field peas		66.8	58.5	55.6	99.3	119.9	93.2	100.0	126.4	140.4	171.1
Field beans		65.7	56.4	54.8	97.7	114.9	88.8	100.0	125.3	141.1	177.4
Soya beans		51.6	56.8	60.1	59.3	67.8	81.1	100.0	103.9	110.6	122.0
Compound feedingstuffs	q	70.3	66.2	68.2	79.1	102.2	98.9	100.0	119.2	123.7	134.0
Compound feedingstuffs for cattle and calves	q	72.0	68.9	69.8	80.1	103.8	101.0	100.0	117.8	125.6	135.6
Compound feedingstuffs for pigs	q	69.5	64.6	68.1	79.3	98.6	95.3	100.0	118.7	123.5	128.6
Compound feedingstuffs for poultry	q	67.6	62.7	65.8	77.4	101.5	97.3	100.0	120.8	121.2	132.9
Compound feedingstuffs for sheep	q	76.4	72.9	72.7	81.9	103.8	103.3	100.0	119.8	127.3	142.2
Maintenance of Materials		74.2	79.0	83.5	86.6	91.6	95.8	100.0	104.9	106.5	108.3
Maintenance of Buildings		73.7	76.8	81.6	87.7	94.0	93.8	100.0	107.4	109.8	110.1
Other goods and services	a	76.8	81.1	83.6	88.3	93.0	93.3	100.0	106.0	107.2	109.6
Goods and services contributing to investment	a	83.6	86.2	87.9	90.9	94.3	96.9	100.0	103.6	101.7	102.9
Materials	a	87.2	89.4	90.0	91.8	94.3	97.3	100.0	103.0	99.1	100.4
Machinery and other equipment	a	83.0	87.5	88.5	92.1	97.4	99.7	100.0	103.8	94.3	96.8
Plant and machinery for cultivation		80.6	85.0	86.2	90.4	96.6	99.5	100.0	104.7	93.4	95.9
Farm machinery and installations	a	92.0	96.7	96.8	98.2	100.3	100.1	100.0	100.6	97.4	100.4
Transport Equipment		90.3	90.8	91.1	91.6	92.0	95.6	100.0	102.4	102.8	103.0
Tractors		84.5	86.6	87.8	89.1	91.4	95.9	100.0	103.7	104.6	105.3
Other vehicles		113.7	107.7	104.8	102.1	95.1	94.4	100.0	98.2	96.3	95.0
Buildings		75.5	79.0	83.7	89.3	95.0	95.2	100.0	105.8	107.4	107.7
Other (Engineering and soil improvement operations)		80.0	83.4	84.9	89.0	93.1	97.9	100.0	102.5	104.5	107.2

Source: Department for Environment, Food and Rural Affairs
Enquiries Defra prices team. Tel: ++44(0)1904 455331

a:- Part or all of the series is made up of annual data
q:- Part or all of the series is made up of quarterly data

17.8 Index of Producer Prices of Agricultural Products, UK (2010=100)

Outputs annual series		2004	2005	2006	2007	2008	2009	2010	2011	2012	2013
Total Outputs	a	71.6	69.6	72.3	82.2	98.9	95.0	100.0	113.0	118.6	125.4
Crop products	a	71.9	67.4	73.2	88.0	103.6	89.1	100.0	117.8	124.1	128.6
Cereals	a	69.4	59.5	66.2	96.8	124.0	89.6	100.0	144.8	149.7	153.1
Wheat	a	68.5	57.0	64.2	93.2	121.5	90.5	100.0	141.7	144.3	151.9
Wheat - Feeding	a	67.9	56.6	65.1	92.1	120.0	89.5	100.0	141.0	143.7	152.8
Wheat - Breadmaking		68.1	58.3	60.2	95.5	124.0	95.7	100.0	138.3	141.7	141.9
Wheat - Other Milling		73.6	58.2	63.4	98.6	129.1	90.0	100.0	152.2	152.7	158.4
Barley	a	72.5	66.1	71.5	107.9	132.6	88.0	100.0	150.3	160.9	154.4
Barley - Feeding	a	73.8	65.2	71.4	103.8	126.0	86.3	100.0	155.5	159.9	158.6
Barley - Malting		69.4	67.9	71.6	117.1	147.1	91.7	100.0	138.9	163.2	145.2
Oats	a	64.0	67.6	73.6	91.9	113.1	82.7	100.0	177.8	190.1	173.7
Oats - Milling		60.3	65.6	71.6	91.1	110.0	82.6	100.0	170.4	183.2	155.8
Oats - Feeding	a	69.9	70.8	76.6	93.1	118.0	82.7	100.0	189.7	201.0	202.0
Potatoes		90.2	70.3	92.1	104.4	108.7	86.6	100.0	107.1	121.9	156.1
Potatoes - Earlies		71.8	55.5	79.3	61.7	89.4	61.4	100.0	65.9	125.2	122.6
Potatoes - Main Crop		92.4	71.6	93.6	108.6	110.9	88.5	100.0	111.1	122.2	160.7
Industrial Crops	a	69.9	62.4	64.7	73.6	112.4	93.5	100.0	132.0	130.0	121.5
Oilseed Rape (non set aside)		58.8	49.3	58.9	69.7	118.7	91.5	100.0	143.3	139.1	127.0
Sugar Beet	a	104.9	101.5	81.2	83.7	93.6	99.0	100.0	99.9	104.3	105.7
Forage plants		57.6	62.6	62.8	73.7	80.5	84.1	100.0	112.6	106.2	114.8
Hay and dried grass		53.3	53.7	54.8	69.0	65.0	69.5	100.0	136.9	100.4	86.3
Straw		43.1	54.8	51.4	63.1	70.9	80.1	100.0	113.5	100.6	104.3
Other forage plants		65.3	56.3	54.9	94.3	111.1	87.6	100.0	127.5	136.9	168.3
Fresh Vegetables		76.1	79.3	85.3	93.3	91.9	87.8	100.0	92.7	108.6	110.2
Cauliflowers		66.5	78.5	77.9	91.5	93.4	89.4	100.0	96.3	118.4	102.0
Tomatoes		65.6	73.3	80.8	82.3	87.1	75.9	100.0	78.9	90.7	88.3
Cabbages		69.4	77.2	83.1	102.5	99.2	92.0	100.0	108.4	120.3	113.4
Lettuce		70.2	74.5	82.8	78.7	91.4	79.4	100.0	85.5	110.1	104.9
Carrots		71.0	85.7	91.9	106.4	110.7	114.7	100.0	108.0	124.2	124.4
Onions		52.9	41.6	56.1	77.1	56.1	57.1	100.0	94.1	68.3	96.9
Beans (Green)		79.1	69.0	87.9	106.2	94.8	84.4	100.0	89.8	132.6	124.1
Mushrooms		114.4	109.2	100.9	95.0	79.6	86.0	100.0	87.4	104.4	117.7
Fresh Fruit		77.3	73.9	77.3	84.0	96.6	95.6	100.0	98.7	103.7	104.8
Dessert Apples		73.8	68.3	76.1	86.7	92.1	96.6	100.0	107.0	118.0	117.1
Cooking Apples		97.4	78.2	87.0	97.5	122.5	99.6	100.0	104.0	132.0	158.1
Dessert Pears		77.2	76.2	82.2	80.3	106.2	113.3	100.0	101.2	116.9	129.4
Strawberries		68.5	73.8	70.5	73.1	83.8	90.9	100.0	91.8	87.4	84.0
Raspberries		83.3	76.7	83.9	96.6	97.7	99.0	100.0	102.2	96.5	96.2
Flowers and plants	a	70.9	71.5	73.6	77.5	83.6	86.6	100.0	99.1	109.3	110.9
Other crop products	a	45.5	89.3	93.1	83.7	79.1	103.7	100.0	93.3	98.7	98.7
Seeds	a	45.5	89.3	93.1	83.7	79.1	103.7	100.0	93.3	98.7	98.7
Animals and animal products	a	71.4	71.1	71.7	78.0	95.6	99.3	100.0	109.5	114.7	123.2
Animals (for slaughter & export)		68.8	69.0	71.0	73.9	90.2	100.8	100.0	109.6	114.6	120.0
Cattle and calves		66.7	67.3	73.8	75.0	98.4	104.9	100.0	116.4	129.3	137.7
Cattle (clean)		68.8	69.5	75.2	76.3	98.4	105.0	100.0	115.1	129.0	139.0
Cows and Bulls		54.5	55.2	65.7	67.5	92.3	103.9	100.0	123.8	131.2	131.1
Calves		86.5	63.4	80.1	84.7	102.5	128.6	100.0	112.7	126.7	118.4
Pigs		73.2	73.5	74.2	76.0	89.5	103.1	100.0	102.1	106.3	116.7
Pigs (clean)		73.0	73.3	74.0	76.3	89.2	102.9	100.0	102.2	106.2	116.9
Sows and Boars		75.7	75.5	76.5	60.8	97.3	114.1	100.0	96.1	114.1	107.2
Sheep and lambs		67.0	61.8	63.4	56.7	72.1	91.1	100.0	112.3	105.1	102.0
Sheep and lambs (clean)		68.5	64.1	65.4	58.0	74.5	92.0	100.0	111.7	104.7	104.2
Ewes and Rams		55.9	45.5	48.3	47.2	54.7	84.0	100.0	116.2	108.6	85.8
All Poultry	a	71.0	73.4	70.1	81.0	89.5	99.5	100.0	102.9	105.0	109.3
Chickens	a	72.0	74.6	70.5	82.1	87.4	99.3	100.0	102.1	103.7	107.5
Turkeys		64.8	64.3	63.7	74.2	101.4	101.6	100.0	106.8	112.4	118.5
Animal products	a	75.5	74.5	72.7	84.3	104.1	96.9	100.0	109.4	114.8	128.1
Milk		74.9	74.9	72.8	84.3	105.2	96.1	100.0	111.0	113.8	128.2
Eggs	q	81.0	74.7	76.9	87.8	103.2	105.7	100.0	99.9	124.0	130.8
Intensive eggs	q	76.0	66.1	71.4	80.6	98.1	103.5	100.0	101.6	135.7	139.6
Free range eggs	q	84.3	80.5	80.7	92.6	106.6	107.2	100.0	98.7	116.2	124.9
Wool clip	a	53.0	45.6	16.6	35.4	32.4	47.1	100.0	121.6	75.5	101.0

a:- Part or all of the series is made up of annual data
q:- Part or all of the series is made up of quarterly data

Source: Department for Environment, Food and Rutal Affairs
Enquiries Defra prices team. Tel: ++44(0)1904 455331
or email: prices@defra.gsi.gov.uk

17.9 Harmonised Indices of Consumer Prices (HICPs) - International Comparisons: EU Countries: 2009 to 2014 Percentage change over 12 months

per cent

	Austria	Belgium	Bulgaria	Cyprus	Czech Republic	Denmark	Estonia	Finland	France	Germany	Greece	Hungary	Ireland	Italy	Latvia
Annual average															
	D7SK	D7SL	GHY8	D7RO	D7RP	D7SM	D7RQ	D7SN	D7SO	D7SP	D7SQ	D7RR	D7SS	D7ST	D7RS
2009	0.4	-	2.5	0.2	0.6	1.1	0.2	1.6	0.1	0.2	1.3	4.0	-1.7	0.8	3.3
2010	1.7	2.3	3.0	2.6	1.2	2.2	2.7	1.7	1.7	1.2	4.7	4.7	-1.6	1.6	-1.2
2011	3.6	3.4	3.4	3.5	2.1	2.7	5.1	3.3	2.3	2.5	3.1	3.9	1.2	2.9	4.2
2012	2.6	2.6	2.4	3.1	3.5	2.4	4.2	3.2	2.2	2.1	1.0	5.7	1.9	3.3	2.3
2013	2.1	1.2	0.4	0.4	1.4	0.5	3.2	2.2	1.0	1.6	-0.9	1.7	0.5	1.3	-
Monthly															
Jul 2013	2.1	1.6	0.0	0.7	1.4	0.4	3.9	2.5	1.2	1.9	-0.5	1.7	0.7	1.2	0.5
Aug	2.0	1.1	-0.7	0.1	1.2	0.1	3.6	2.0	1.0	1.6	-1.0	1.6	0.0	1.2	-0.1
Sep	1.8	1.0	-1.3	0.3	1.0	0.2	2.6	1.8	1.0	1.6	-1.0	1.6	0.0	0.9	-0.4
Oct	1.5	0.7	-1.1	-0.5	0.8	0.3	2.2	1.7	0.7	1.2	-1.9	1.1	-0.1	0.8	0.0
Nov	1.5	0.9	-1.0	-0.8	1.0	0.3	2.1	1.8	0.8	1.6	-2.9	0.4	0.3	0.7	-0.3
Dec	2.0	1.2	-0.9	-1.3	1.5	0.4	2.0	1.9	0.8	1.2	-1.8	0.6	0.4	0.7	-0.4
Jan	1.5	1.1	-1.4	-1.6	0.3	0.8	1.6	1.9	0.8	1.2	-1.4	0.8	0.3	0.6	0.5
Feb	1.5	1.0	-2.1	-1.3	0.3	0.3	1.1	1.6	1.1	1.0	-0.9	0.3	0.1	0.4	0.5
Mar	1.4	0.9	-2.0	-0.9	0.3	0.2	0.7	1.3	0.7	0.9	-1.5	0.2	0.3	0.3	0.3
Apr	1.6	0.9	-1.3	-0.4	0.2	0.5	0.8	1.3	0.8	1.1	-1.6	-0.2	0.4	0.5	0.8
May	1.5	0.8	-1.8	-0.1	0.5	0.3	0.6	1.0	0.8	0.6	-2.1	0.0	0.4	0.4	0.8
Jun	1.7*	0.7	-1.8	0.0	0.0	0.4	0.4	1.1	0.6	1.0	-1.5	-0.1	0.5	0.2	0.8
Jul 2014	..	..	..	..	..	..	..	..	..	..	..	..	..	..	..

per cent

	Lithuania	Luxem-bourg	Malta	Nether-lands	Poland	Portugal	Romania	Slovakia	Slovenia	Spain	Sweden	United Kingdom[1]	EICP[2] EU 25 average[3]	EICP[2] EU 27 average[3]	MUICP average[4]
Annual average															
	D7RT	D7SU	D7RU	D7SV	D7RV	D7SX	GHY7	D7RW	D7RX	D7SY	D7SZ	D7G7	D7RY	GJ2E	D7SR
2009	4.2	-	1.8	1.0	4.0	-0.9	5.6	0.9	0.9	-0.2	1.9	2.2	..	1.0	0.3
2010	1.2	2.8	2.0	0.9	2.7	1.4	6.1	0.7	2.1	2.0	1.9	3.3	..	2.1	1.6
2011	4.1	3.7	2.5	2.5	3.9	3.6	5.8	4.1	2.1	3.1	1.4	4.5	..	3.1	2.7
2012	3.2	2.9	3.2	2.8	3.7	2.8	3.4	3.7	2.8	2.4	0.9	2.8	..	2.6	2.5
2013	1.2	1.7	1.0	2.6	0.8	0.4	3.2	1.5	1.9	1.5	0.4	2.6	..	1.5	1.3
Monthly															
Jul 2013	0.6	1.8	0.9	3.1	0.9	0.8	3.4	1.6	2.8	1.9	0.8	2.8	..	1.7	1.6
Aug	0.5	1.7	0.7	2.8	0.9	0.2	2.6	1.4	2.2	1.6	0.8	2.7	..	1.5	1.3
Sep	0.5	1.5	0.6	2.4	0.9	0.3	1.1	1.1	1.5	0.5	0.5	2.7	..	1.3	1.1
Oct	0.5	1.0	0.5	1.3	0.7	0.0	1.2	0.7	1.1	0.0	0.2	2.2	..	0.9	0.7
Nov	0.5	1.1	0.3	1.2	0.5	0.1	1.3	0.5	1.2	0.3	0.3	2.1	..	1.0	0.9
Dec	0.4	1.5	1.0	1.4	0.6	0.2	1.3	0.4	0.9	0.3	0.4	2.0	..	1.0	0.8
Jan	0.2	1.5	0.9	0.8	0.6	0.1	1.2	-	0.9	0.3	0.2	1.9	..	0.9	0.8
Feb	0.3	0.8	1.6	0.4	0.7	-0.1	1.3	-0.1	0.2	0.1	0.1	1.7	..	0.8	0.7
Mar	0.4	0.8	1.4	0.1	0.6	-0.4	1.3	-0.2	0.6	-0.2	-0.4	1.6	..	0.6	0.5
Apr	0.3	0.9	0.5	0.6	0.3	-0.1	1.6	-0.2	0.5	0.3	0.3	1.8	..	0.8	0.7
May	0.1	1.4	0.4	0.1	0.3	-0.3	1.3	0.0	1.0	0.2	0.1	1.5	..	0.6	0.5
Jun	0.3	1.2	0.7	0.3	0.3	-0.2	0.9	-0.1	1.0	0.0	0.5	1.9	..	0.7*	0.5*
Jul 2014	..	..	..	..	..	..	..	..	..	..	..	1.6	..	..	0.4

Key: - zero or negligible .. Not available * Provisional
† Date of earliest revision ᵠ Estimated

1. Published as the CPI in the UK.

2. The EICP (European Index of Consumer Prices) is the official EU aggregate. It covers 15 member states until April 2004, 25 member states from May 2004 to Dec 2006, and 27 member states from Jan 2007. The EU 25 annual average for 2004 is calculated from the EU 15 average from January to Apri and the EU 25 average from May to December.

3. The coverage of the European Union was extended to include Cyprus, Czech Republic, Estonia, Hungary, Latvia, Lithuania, Malta, Poland, Slovakia and Slovenia with effect from 1 May 2004, and Bulgaria and Romania from 1 Jan 2007. Data for the EU 25 average is available from May 2004 and for the EU 27 average from Jan 2007.

4. The coverage of the Monetary Union Indices of Consumer Prices (MUICP) was extended to include Greece with effect from Jan 2001 and Slovakia from Jan 2009.

Source:
Office for National Statistics
Prices Division
2.001 Cardiff Road
Newport
South Wales
NP10 8XG

http://www.ons.gov.uk

Eurostat
www.ec.europa.eu/eurostat

this page is intentionally blank

Production

Chapter 18

Production

Annual Business Survey
(Table 18.1)

The Annual Business Survey (ABS) estimates cover all UK businesses registered for Value Added Tax (VAT) and/or Pay As You Earn (PAYE) classified to the 2007 Standard Industrial Classification (SIC (2007)) headings listed in the tables. The ABS obtains details on these businesses from the Office for National Statistics (ONS) Inter-Departmental Business Register (IDBR).

As with all its statistical inquiries, ONS is concerned to minimise the form-filling burden of individual contributors and as such the ABS is a sample inquiry. The sample was designed as a stratified random sample of about 66,300 businesses; the inquiry population is stratified by SIC (2007) and employment using the information from the register.

The inquiry results are grossed up to the total population so that they relate to all active UK businesses on the IDBR for the sectors covered.

The results meet a wide range of needs for government, economic analysts and the business community at large. In official statistics the inquiry is an important source for the national accounts and input-output tables, and also provides weights for the indices of production and producer prices. Inquiry results also enable the UK to meet statistical requirements of the European Union.

Revised ABS results down to SIC (2007) 4 digit class level for 2008-2009, giving both analysis and tabular detail, are available from the ONS website at: www.ons.gov.uk with further extracts and bespoke analyses available on request.

UK Manufacturer's Sales by Industry
(Table 18.2)

Table 18.2 lists total UK manufacturers' sales by industry.

Number of local units in manufacturing industries
(Table 18.3)

The table shows the number of local units (sites) in manufacturing by employment size band. The classification breakdown is at division level (two digit) as classified to SIC(2003) held on the Inter-Departmental Business Register (IDBR). This register became fully operational in 1995 and combines information on VAT traders and PAYE employers in a statistical register comprising 2.1 million enterprises (businesses) representing nearly 99 per cent of economic activity.
UK Business: Activity, Size and Location provides further details and contains detailed information regarding enterprises in the UK including size, classification, and local units in the UK including size, classification and location.

For further information on the IDBR see the ONS website at: www.ons.gov.uk/idbr

Production of primary fuels
(Table 18.4)

This table shows indigenous production of primary fuels. It includes the extraction or capture of primary commodities and the generation or manufacture of secondary commodities. Production is always gross; that is, it includes the quantities used during the extraction or manufacturing process. Primary fuels are coal, natural gas (including colliery methane), oil, primary electricity (that is, electricity generated by hydro, nuclear wind and tide stations and also electricity imported from France through the interconnector) and renewables (includes solid renewables such as wood, straw and waste and gaseous renewables such as landfill gas and sewage gas). The figures are presented on a common basis expressed in million tonnes of oil equivalent. Estimates of the gross calorific values used for converting the statistics for the various fuels to these are given in the Digest of UK Energy Statistics available at:
www.decc.gov.uk/en/content/cms/statistics/publications/dukes/dukes.aspx

Total inland energy consumption
(Table 18.5)

This table shows energy consumption by fuel and final energy consumption by fuel and class of consumer. Primary energy consumption covers consumption of all primary fuels (defined above) for energy purposes. This measure of energy consumption includes energy that is lost by converting primary fuels into secondary fuels (the energy lost burning coal to generate electricity or the energy used by refineries to separate crude oil into fractions) in addition to losses in distribution. The other common way of measuring energy consumption is to measure the energy content of the fuels supplied to consumers. This is called final energyconsumption. It is net of fuel used by the energy industries, conversion, transmission and distribution losses. The figures are presented on a common basis, measured as energy supplied and expressed in million tonnes of oil equivalent. Estimates of the gross calorific values used for converting the statistics for the various fuels to these are given in the Digest of UK Energy Statistics available at:
www.decc.gov.uk/ en/content/cms/statistics/publications/dukes/dukes.aspx

So far as practicable the user categories have been grouped on the basis of the SIC(2007) although the methods used by each of the supply industries to identify end users are slightly different. Chapter 1 of the Digest of UK Energy Statistics gives more information on these figures.

Coal
(Table 18.6)

Since 1995, aggregate data on coal production have been obtained from the Coal Authority. In addition, main coal producers provide data in response to an annual Department of Energy and Climate Change (DECC) inquiry which covers production (deepmined and opencast), trade, stocks and disposals. HM Revenue & Customs (HMRC) also provides trade data for solid fuels. DECC collects information on the use of coal from the UK Iron and Steel Statistics Bureau and consumption of coal for electricity generation is covered by data provided by the electricity generators.

Gas
(Table 18.7)

Production figures, covering the production of gas from the UK Continental Shelf offshore and onshore gas fields and gas obtained during the production of oil, are obtained from returns made under the DECC's Petroleum Production Reporting System. Additional information is used on imports and exports of gas and details from the operators of gas terminals in the UK to complete the picture.

It is no longer possible to present information on fuels input into the gas industry and gas output and sales in the same format as in previous editions of this table. As such, users are directed to Chapter 4 of the 2002 edition of the Digest of UK Energy Statistics, where more detailed information on gas production and consumption in the UK is available.

DECC carry out an annual survey of gas suppliers to obtain details of gas sales to the various categories of consumer. Estimates are included for the suppliers with the smallest market share, since the DECC inquiry covers only the largest suppliers (that is, those known to supply more than 1,750 GWh per year).

Electricity
(Tables 18.8–18.10)

Tables 18.8 to 18.10 cover all generators and suppliers of electricity in the UK. The relationship between generation, supply, availability and consumption is as follows:

Electricity generated

less electricity used on works

equals electricity supplied (gross)

less electricity used in pumping at pumped storage stations.

equals electricity supplied (net)

plus imports (net of exports) of electricity

equals electricity available

less losses and statistical differences

equals electricity consumed

In Table 18.8 'major power producers' are those generating companies corresponding to the old
public sector supply system:
- AES Electric Ltd.
- Baglan Generation Ltd.
- Barking Power Ltd.
- British Energy plc
- Centrica Energy
- Coolkeeragh ESB Ltd.
- Corby Power Ltd.
- Coryton Energy Company Ltd.
- Derwent Cogeneration Ltd.
- Drax Power Ltd.
- EDF Energy plc
- E.ON UK plc
- Energy Power Resources Ltd.
- Gaz De France
- GDF Suez Teesside Power Ltd
- Immingham CHP
- International Power plc
- Magnox Electric Ltd.
- Premier Power Ltd.
- RGS Energy Ltd.
- Rocksavage Power Company Ltd.
- RWE Npower plc
- Scottish Power plc
- Scottish and Southern Energy plc
- Seabank Power Ltd.
- SELCHP Ltd.
- Spalding Energy Company Ltd.
- Uskmouth Power Company Ltd.
- Western Power Generation Ltd.

Additionally, from 2007, the following major wind farm companies are included as 'major power
producers':

- Airtricity
- Cumbria Wind Farms
- Fred Olsen
- H G Capital
- Renewable Energy Systems
- Vattenfall Wind

In Table 18.10 all fuels are converted to the common unit of million tonnes of oil equivalent, that is,
the amounts of oil which would be needed to produce the output of electricity generated from those fuels.

More detailed statistics on energy are given in the Digest of United Kingdom Energy Statistics. Readers may wish to note that the production and consumption of fuels are presented using commodity balances. A commodity balance shows the flows of an individual fuel through from production to final consumption, showing its use in transformation and energy industry own use.

**Oil and oil products
(Tables 18.11–18.13)**

Data on the production of crude oil, condensates and natural gases given in Table 19.11 are collected by DECC direct from the operators of production facilities and terminals situated on UK territory, either onshore or offshore, that is, on the UK Continental Shelf. Data are also collected from the companies on their trade in oil and oil products. These data are used in preference to the foreign trade as recorded by HMRC in Overseas Trade Statistics.

Data on the internal UK oil industry (that is, on the supply, refining and distribution of oil and oil products in the UK) are collected by the UK Petroleum Industry Association. These data, reported by individual refining companies and wholesalers and supplemented where necessary by data from other sources, provide the contents of Tables 19.12 and 19.13. The data are presented in terms of deliveries to the inland UK market. This is regarded as an acceptable proxy for actual consumption of products. The main shortcoming is that, while changes in stocks held by companies in central storage areas are taken into account, changes in the levels of stocks further down the retail ladder (such as stocks held on petrol station forecourts) are not. This is not thought to result in a significant degree of difference in the data.

**Iron and steel
(Tables 18.14–18.16)**
Iron and steel industry
The general definition of the UK iron and steel industry is based on groups 271 'ECSC iron and steel', 272 'Tubes', and 273 'Primary Transformation' of the UK SIC(92), except those parts of groups 272 and 273 which cover cast iron pipes, drawn wire, cold formed sections and Ferro alloys.

The definition excludes certain products which may be made by works within the industry, such as refined iron, finished steel castings, steel tyres, wheels, axles and rolled rings, open and closed die forgings, colliery arches and springs. Iron foundries and steel stockholders are also considered to be outside of the industry.

Statistics

The statistics for the UK iron and steel industry are compiled by the Iron and Steel Statistics Bureau (ISSB) Ltd from data collected from UK steel producing companies, with the exception of trade data which is based on HMRC data.

'Crude steel' is the total of usable ingots, usable continuously cast semi-finished products and liquid steel for castings.

'Production of finished products' is the total production at the mill of that product after deduction of any material which is immediately scrapped

'Deliveries' are based on invoiced tonnages and will include deliveries made to steel stockholders and service centres by the UK steel industry.

For more detailed information on definitions etc please contact ISSB Ltd. on 020 7343 3900.

Fertilisers
(Table 18.17)

Table 18.17 gives the quantity of the fertiliser nutrients nitrogen (N), phosphate (P2O5) and potash (K2O) used by UK farmers during the growing season, or fertiliser year, which is taken as the year ending in June.

Minerals
(Table 18.18)

Table 18.18 gives, separately for Great Britain and Northern Ireland, the production of minerals extracted from the ground. The figures for chemicals and metals are estimated from the quality of the ore which is extracted. The data come from an annual census of the quarrying industry, which, for Great Britain, is conducted by ONS for Communities and Local Government and Business, Innovation and Skills (BIS) –formally known as Business, Enterprise and Regulatory Reform (BERR)

Building materials
(Table 18.19)

Table 18.19 gives the production and deliveries of a number of building materials, including bricks, concrete blocks, sand and gravel, slate, cement, concrete roofing tiles and ready mixed cement. This data comes from the Monthly Bulletin of Building Materials and Components.

Construction
(Tables 18.20–18.21)

Figures for the construction industry are based on SIC(2003).

The value of output represents the value of construction work done during the quarter in Great Britain and is derived from returns made by private contractors and public authorities with their own direct labour forces. The series (and the accompanying index of the volume of output) include estimates of the output of small firms and self-employed workers not recorded in the regular quarterly output inquiry.

The new orders statistics are collected from private contractors and analysed by the principal types of construction work involved. The series includes speculative work for eventual sale or lease undertaken on the initiative of the respondent where no formal contract or order is involved.

Engineering turnover and orders
(Tables 18.22–18.23)

The figures represent the output of UK-based manufacturers classified to Subsections DK and DL of the SIC(2007). They are derived from the monthly production inquiry (MPI) and include estimates for non-responders and for establishments which are not sampled.

Drink and tobacco
(Tables 18.24–18.25)

Data for these tables are derived by HMRC from the systems for collecting excise duties.
Alcoholic drinks and tobacco products become liable for duty when released for consumption in the
UK. Figures for releases include both home-produced products and commercial imports. Production
figures are also available for potable spirits distilled and beer brewed in the UK.

Alcoholic drink
(Table 18.24)

The figures for imported ad other spirits released for home consumption include gin and other
UK produced spirits for which a breakdown is not available.

Since June 1993 beer duty has been charged when the beer leaves the brewery or other registered
premises. Previously duty was chargeable at an earlier stage (the worts stage) in the brewing process
and an allowance was made for wastage. Figures for years prior to 1994 include adjustments to bring
them into line with current data. The change in June 1993 also led to the availability of data on the
strength; a series in hectolitres of pure alcohol is shown from 1994.

Made wine with alcoholic strength from 1.2 per cent to 5.5 per cent is termed 'coolers'. Included in
'coolers' are alcoholic lemonade and similar products of appropriate strength. From 28 April 2002
duty on spirit-based 'coolers' (ready to drink products) is charged at the same rate as spirits per litre
of alcohol. Made wine coolers include only wine based 'coolers' from this period.

Tobacco products
(Table 18.25)

Releases of cigarettes and other tobacco products tend to be higher in the period before a Budget.
Products may then be stocked, duty paid, before being sold.

The industries are now grouped according to the 2007 Standard Industrial Classification at 2-digit level.

18.1 Production and Construction Industries

	Description	Year	Number of enterprises	Total turnover	Approximate gross value added at basic prices (aGVA)	Total purchases of goods, materials and services	Total employment point in time[1]	Total employment average during the year[1]
Standard Industrial Classification (Revised 2007)			Number	£ million	£ million	£ million	Thousand	Thousand
B-F	Production and Construction	2010	397,056	835,034	276,229	537,030	4,168	4,222
		2011	396,645	892,106	285,411	591,093	4,203	4,244
		2012	391,516	893,690	288,925	587,760	4,156	4,161
B-E	Production industries	2010	131,774	652,941	208,870	425,519	2,821	2,864
		2011	131,430	702,639	215,261	471,926	2,851	2,854
		2012	134,410	703,277	215,117	470,931	2,855	2,865
B	Mining and quarrying	2010	1,152	47,785	26,488	21,882	60	61
		2011	1,206	53,951	28,597	26,469	65	63
		2012	1,263	51,173	24,581	27,945	76	75
05	Mining of coal and lignite	2010	23	917	350	552	6	6
		2011	21	*	*	744	6	7
		2012	*	*	*	*	7	8
06	Extraction of crude petroleum and natural gas	2010	99	36,950	22,198	15,402	12	15
		2011	124	42,317	24,589	18,928	13	13
		2012	151	37,430	19,720	19,167	16	15
07	Mining of metal ores	2010	-	-	-	-	-	-
		2011	4	*	*	4	-	-
		2012	*	*	*	*	*	*
08	Other mining and quarrying	2010	708	3,394	927	2,327	17	17
		2011	718	4,097	1,205	2,793	*	*
		2012	703	5,359	1,501	3,726	27	27
09	Mining support service activities	2010	322	6,524	3,013	3,601	25	23
		2011	339	6,358	2,367	4,001	*	*
		2012	378	7,083	2,961	4,189	*	*
C	Manufacturing	2010	123,979	482,086	145,997	317,333	2,479	2,523
		2011	122,591	516,408	149,313	349,623	2,495	2,510
		2012	124,514	513,437	149,498	344,634	2,482	2,500
10	Manufacture of food products	2010	6,377	70,560	18,979	51,622	377	380
		2011	6,444	73,175	19,271	54,355	377	376
		2012	6,642	76,445	18,664	57,977	363	359
11	Manufacture of beverages	2010	975	17,795	5,627	8,952	*	*
		2011	1,034	17,635	*	*	*	*
		2012	1,127	18,396	*	*	43	43
12	Manufacture of tobacco products	2010	10	10,248	1,647	832	*	*
		2011	10	10,418	*	*	*	*
		2012	11	10,990	*	*	*	*
13	Manufacture of textiles	2010	3,935	5,304	1,934	3,463	*	*
		2011	3,871	5,473	1,847	3,668	54	54
		2012	3,778	5,313	2,262	3,053	55	54
14	Manufacture of wearing apparel	2010	3,389	2,816	885	1,928	38	40
		2011	3,378	2,834	831	2,009	29	30
		2012	3,384	2,653	744	1,895	29	29
15	Manufacture of leather and related products	2010	525	893	325	593	*	*
		2011	540	976	365	642	*	*
		2012	559	970	313	647	*	*

587

18.1 Production and Construction Industries

Description Standard Industrial Classification (Revised 2007)	Year	Number of enterprises	Total turnover	Approximate gross value added at basic prices (aGVA)	Total purchases of goods, materials and services	Total employment point in time[1]	Total employment average during the year[1]
16 Manufacture of wood and of produc of wood and cork, except furniture; manufacture of articles of straw and plaiting materials	2010	7,583	6,693	2,372	4,385	74	76
	2011	7,321	6,806	2,454	4,363	61	58
	2012	7,105	6,752	2,673	4,136	68	66
17 Manufacture of paper and paper products	2010	1,770	10,796	3,541	7,298	54	54
	2011	1,679	11,507	4,049	7,561	56	58
	2012	1,576	10,827	3,859	6,910	56	58
18 Printing and reproduction of recorded media	2010	14,465	11,388	5,087	6,300	134	139
	2011	13,923	11,411	5,337	6,113	121	127
	2012	13,259	10,943	4,966	5,955	115	120
19 Manufacture of coke and refined petroleum products	2010	174	39,300	2,248	26,597	*	*
	2011	164	49,895	2,232	38,281	10	9
	2012	149	53,725	2,226	42,590	11	10
20 Manufacture of chemicals and chemical products	2010	2,565	37,764	10,326	28,061	106	110
	2011	2,464	38,874	8,910	30,330	114	117
	2012	2,468	31,201	8,500	22,758	109	111
21 Manufacture of basic pharmaceutical products and pharmaceutical preparations	2010	444	18,716	9,629	9,163	44	48
	2011	448	17,248	7,417	9,863	44	45
	2012	510	16,027	6,736	9,402	50	50
22 Manufacture of rubber and plastic products	2010	5,994	19,789	7,118	12,824	153	148
	2011	5,809	22,182	7,881	14,478	156	154
	2012	5,696	21,925	8,048	13,969	155	154
23 Manufacture of other non-metallic mineral products	2010	3,958	14,164	4,502	9,568	93	90
	2011	3,799	14,248	3,987	10,187	96	96
	2012	3,625	12,462	3,735	8,680	86	87
24 Manufacture basic metals	2010	1,452	17,964	4,370	14,078	72	76
	2011	1,403	19,661	4,600	15,320	75	76
	2012	1,400	17,548	3,628	13,653	71	71
25 Manufacture of fabricated metal products, except machinery and equipment	2010	25,592	30,335	12,042	18,554	281	290
	2011	24,801	31,745	13,170	18,866	305	302
	2012	24,050	33,093	14,483	18,711	292	296
26 Manufacture of computer, electronic and optical products	2010	6,384	20,033	8,314	11,781	128	133
	2011	6,117	19,592	8,560	11,289	122	128
	2012	5,874	18,358	8,025	10,403	123	128
27 Manufacture of electrical equipment	2010	2,928	12,824	4,503	8,580	92	93
	2011	2,951	14,016	4,450	9,561	97	95
	2012	2,971	14,446	4,869	9,567	87	86
28 Manufacture of machinery and equipment n.e.c	2010	8,644	33,389	12,249	21,386	184	190
	2011	8,251	37,833	13,423	24,879	201	199
	2012	7,948	37,173	14,455	22,696	208	205
29 Manufacture of motor vehicles, and semi-trailers	2010	2,794	46,500	10,045	36,799	134	135
	2011	2,703	54,375	11,253	43,546	131	129
	2012	2,614	55,353	10,856	44,758	137	135
30 Manufacture of other transport equipment	2010	1,856	26,819	8,081	18,631	137	141
	2011	1,817	28,208	9,605	18,436	139	134
	2012	1,876	29,197	9,680	19,839	134	131
31 Manufacture of furniture	2010	6,207	7,091	2,873	4,239	70	67
	2011	6,129	6,460	2,599	3,913	75	81
	2012	6,131	6,589	2,585	4,026	79	86

18.1 Production and Construction Industries

Description	Year	Number of enterprises	Total turnover	Approximate gross value added at basic prices (aGVA)	Total purchases of goods, materials and services	Total employment point in time[1]	Total employment average during the year[1]
Standard Industrial Classification (Revised 2007)							
32 Other manufacturing	2010	9,732	8,712	3,938	4,760	89	88
	2011	9,838	9,502	3,987	5,615	88	95
	2012	9,988	8,949	3,812	5,194	91	100
33 Repair and installation of machinery and equipment	2010	6,226	12,191	5,364	6,938	99	102
	2011	7,697	12,336	5,634	6,651	86	89
	2012	11,773	14,104	6,564	7,686	107	109
D Electricity, gas, steam and air conditioning supply	2010	647	94,424	21,561	72,362	130	125
	2011	1,219	100,735	21,206	80,139	131	123
	2012	1,825	106,916	24,151	82,879	136	129
E Water supply, sewerage, waste management, and remediation activities	2010	5,996	28,646	14,824	13,942	152	156
	2011	6,414	31,544	16,145	15,695	159	158
	2012	6,808	31,751	16,887	15,473	162	161
36 Water collection, treatment and	2010	118	10,138	7,623	2,754	*	*
	2011	119	10,246	8,024	2,485	*	*
	2012	120	11,049	9,033	2,681	*	*
37 Sewerage	2010	935	2,424	1,859	724	12	12
	2011	896	2,361	1,927	608	11	11
	2012	899	2,586	1,921	818	15	15
38 Waste collection, treatment and disposal activities; materials recovery	2010	4,596	15,895	5,245	10,373	102	104
	2011	4,940	18,789	6,098	12,546	111	110
	2012	5,186	17,804	5,734	11,851	105	104
39 Remediation activities and other waste management services	2010	347	189	97	90	*	*
	2011	459	148	96	55	*	*
	2012	603	311	199	123	*	*
F Construction	2010	265,282	182,093	67,359	111,511	1,347	1,358
	2011	265,215	189,467	70,150	119,168	1,352	1,391
	2012	257,106	190,413	73,807	116,829	1,300	1,296
41 Construction of buildings	2010	76,980	71,933	22,624	46,489	385	384
	2011	73,696	71,561	23,440	47,483	393	403
	2012	67,554	75,292	27,312	47,548	369	376
42 Civil engineering	2010	21,430	36,935	12,033	24,691	208	214
	2011	20,093	39,332	12,446	27,322	200	202
	2012	19,682	37,025	12,485	24,794	207	205
43 Specialised construction activities	2010	166,872	73,225	32,702	40,331	755	760
	2011	171,426	78,575	34,264	44,362	759	786
	2012	169,870	78,095	34,010	44,487	725	715

18.1 Production and Construction Industries

	Description	Year	Total employment costs	Total net capital expenditure	Total capital expenditure acquisitions	Total capital expenditure disposals	Total stocks and work in progress - value at end of year	Total stocks and work in progress - value at beginning of year	Total stocks and work in progress - increase during year
Standard Industrial Classification (Revised 2007)			£ million	£ million	£ million	£ million	£ million	£ million	£ million
B-F	Production and Construction	2010	123,557	32,410	38,564	6,154	94,199	93,994	205
		2011	125,296	43,208	50,673	7,465	93,752	88,680	5,072
		2012	127,164	42,749	54,088	11,339	95,112	93,980	1,131
B-E	Production industries	2010	87,944	28,443	31,571	3,127	55,498	52,372	3,126
		2011	89,836	36,431	39,446	3,015	59,943	54,897	5,047
		2012	92,982	40,694	44,742	4,048	59,641	58,850	791
B	Mining and quarrying	2010	4,275	5,988	6,311	323	1,570	1,467	103
		2011	4,681	8,910	9,184	274	1,970	1,774	195
		2012	5,263	9,402	10,887	1,484	2,019	1,906	113
05	Mining of coal and lignite	2010	313	107	*	*	103	118	-15
		2011	303	*	126	*	110	107	3
		2012	*	*	*	*	*	*	*
06	Extraction of crude petroleum and natural gas	2010	1,921	5,493	*	*	853	832	21
		2011	2,120	*	8,445	*	1,137	953	184
		2012	2,388	8,927	10,201	1,274	1,055	979	76
07	Mining of metal ores	2010	-	-	-	-	-	-	-
		2011	2	3	3	-	-	-	-
		2012	*	*	*	*	*	*	*
08	Other mining and quarrying	2010	591	155	191	36	274	276	-2
		2011	705	202	256	54	321	328	-7
		2012	854	160	238	78	417	418	-1
09	Mining support service activities	2010	1,450	234	340	107	341	241	100
		2011	1,552	331	355	24	401	387	15
		2012	1,665	360	398	38	476	402	74
C	Manufacturing	2010	74,231	9,707	11,885	2,178	50,095	46,562	3,533
		2011	74,964	11,573	13,707	2,133	53,680	49,401	4,278
		2012	76,955	12,589	14,614	2,026	53,081	52,507	575
10	Manufacture of food products	2010	9,429	1,946	2,205	259	4,661	4,391	270
		2011	9,433	1,739	1,958	219	4,725	4,219	507
		2012	9,609	1,822	1,989	167	5,013	4,801	212
11	Manufacture of beverages	2010	1,719	533	664	131	5,092	4,890	203
		2011	1,820	659	*	*	5,406	5,047	359
		2012	1,780	714	*	*	5,729	5,392	337
12	Manufacture of tobacco products	2010	145	94	96	2	220	224	-4
		2011	132	50	*	*	175	222	-48
		2012	135	84	*	*	177	173	4
13	Manufacture of textiles	2010	1,113	87	131	44	754	650	104
		2011	1,144	137	153	16	745	696	48
		2012	1,086	131	143	12	710	703	7
14	Manufacture of wearing apparel	2010	450	24	28	4	482	476	6
		2011	479	49	52	3	369	352	18
		2012	444	13	29	16	336	348	-13
15	Manufacture of leather and related products	2010	156	26	28	1	133	105	28
		2011	186	25	25	1	179	146	34
		2012	199	29	31	2	160	166	-6

18.1 Production and Construction Industries

Description	Year	Total employment costs	Total net capital expenditure	Total capital expenditure acquisitions	Total capital expenditure disposals	Total stocks and work in progress - value at end of year	Total stocks and work in progress - value at beginning of year	Total stocks and work in progress - increase during year
Standard Industrial Classification (Revised 2007)								
16 Manufacture of wood and of products of wood and cork, except furniture; manufacture of articles of straw and plaiting materials	2010	1,343	89	159	70	602	542	60
	2011	1,398	128	192	64	608	623	-15
	2012	1,403	122	171	49	659	621	38
17 Manufacture of paper and paper products	2010	1,851	166	233	67	904	857	47
	2011	1,889	310	354	43	920	828	91
	2012	1,794	340	379	39	831	897	-66
18 Printing and reproduction of recorded media	2010	3,034	248	361	113	503	501	2
	2011	2,842	280	420	140	498	485	13
	2012	2,811	288	458	170	428	437	-10
19 Manufacture of coke and refined petroleum products	2010	810	206	382	176	2,332	1,881	451
	2011	969	535	560	25	3,854	2,842	1,012
	2012	1,111	509	531	22	2,841	3,759	-919
20 Manufacture of chemicals and chemical products	2010	4,273	917	1,004	87	3,660	3,225	435
	2011	4,381	953	1,101	148	4,005	3,665	340
	2012	4,293	1,174	1,266	92	3,473	3,426	46
21 Manufacture of basic pharmaceutical products and pharmaceutical preparations	2010	2,191	505	553	48	1,937	1,876	61
	2011	1,847	438	465	27	1,893	1,878	14
	2012	2,478	428	453	24	2,075	1,984	90
22 Manufacture of rubber and plastic products	2010	4,046	458	518	61	1,797	1,665	132
	2011	4,143	508	609	100	2,004	1,835	170
	2012	4,222	610	725	115	1,986	1,900	85
23 Manufacture of other non-metallic mineral products	2010	2,789	292	392	100	1,661	1,615	46
	2011	2,732	347	423	76	1,504	1,431	73
	2012	2,527	353	522	168	1,380	1,339	41
24 Manufacture basic metals	2010	2,811	258	287	29	2,649	2,166	483
	2011	2,863	431	489	58	2,728	2,460	268
	2012	2,766	454	495	42	2,474	2,746	-272
25 Manufacture of fabricated metal products, except machinery and equipment	2010	7,629	608	743	134	3,322	3,094	228
	2011	7,809	908	1,051	143	3,511	3,235	276
	2012	8,287	896	1,068	172	3,596	3,513	83
26 Manufacture of computer, electronic and optical products	2010	4,037	416	492	75	2,441	2,356	85
	2011	4,168	480	553	73	2,601	2,338	263
	2012	4,138	542	610	68	2,623	2,563	60
27 Manufacture of electrical equipment	2010	2,568	224	299	75	1,619	1,356	263
	2011	2,545	158	236	78	1,743	1,730	13
	2012	2,727	190	297	107	1,729	1,722	7
28 Manufacture of machinery and equipment n.e.c	2010	6,870	537	752	215	3,875	3,620	255
	2011	7,016	471	847	376	4,409	3,927	482
	2012	6,674	853	962	109	4,054	4,082	-28
29 Manufacture of motor vehicles, and semi-trailers	2010	4,922	1,001	1,128	127	3,196	2,771	425
	2011	5,077	1,662	1,715	53	3,770	3,277	492
	2012	5,889	1,650	1,945	295	4,092	3,755	337
30 Manufacture of other transport equipment	2010	5,572	672	794	122	5,193	5,363	-170
	2011	5,322	709	858	149	5,109	5,305	-196
	2012	5,544	802	920	118	5,463	5,149	314
31 Manufacture of furniture	2010	1,634	116	140	25	608	587	21
	2011	1,663	124	168	44	587	533	54
	2012	1,613	124	137	13	680	656	24

18.1 Production and Construction Industries

	Description	Year	Total employment costs	Total net capital expenditure	Total capital expenditure acquisitions	Total capital expenditure disposals	Total stocks and work in progress - value at end of year	Total stocks and work in progress - value at beginning year	Total stocks and work in progress - increase during year
Standard Industrial Classification (Revised 2007)									
32	Other manufacturing	2010	1,986	196	276	79	1,163	1,175	-12
		2011	2,139	275	319	45	1,202	1,140	62
		2012	2,069	266	308	42	1,125	1,069	57
33	Repair and installation of machinery and equipment	2010	2,854	87	221	134	1,290	1,176	114
		2011	2,969	198	260	62	1,138	1,187	-50
		2012	3,356	193	298	105	1,448	1,304	144
D	Electricity, gas, steam and air conditioning supply	2010	5,286	7,434	7,811	378	2,889	3,574	-685
		2011	5,765	9,801	10,256	455	3,381	2,935	446
		2012	6,028	11,961	12,357	396	3,557	3,446	111
E	Water supply, sewerage, waste management, and remediation activities	2010	4,152	5,315	5,563	248	944	769	174
		2011	4,426	6,147	6,299	152	913	786	127
		2012	4,736	6,742	6,884	142	983	991	-8
36	Water collection, treatment and	2010	1,363	3,305	3,345	41	145	137	8
		2011	1,391	4,000	4,028	27	175	193	-17
		2012	1,534	4,330	4,356	26	180	175	5
37	Sewerage	2010	423	*	*	39	21	20	1
		2011	355	*	*	27	18	13	5
		2012	395	*	*	24	18	18	-
38	Waste collection, treatment and disposal activities; materials recovery	2010	2,331	*	*	167	774	607	167
		2011	2,611	*	*	98	715	579	137
		2012	2,740	*	*	91	766	791	-24
39	Remediation activities and other waste management services	2010	34	10	12	1	3	5	-2
		2011	68	30	30	-	4	1	3
		2012	67	11	13	2	18	7	11
F	Construction	2010	35,612	3,966	6,993	3,027	38,701	41,622	-2,921
		2011	35,460	6,777	11,227	4,451	33,809	33,784	25
		2012	34,182	2,055	9,346	7,291	35,471	35,130	341
41	Construction of buildings	2010	10,123	2,701	4,943	2,242	32,305	35,040	-2,734
		2011	10,463	4,902	8,474	3,572	27,601	28,156	-554
		2012	9,636	165	6,675	6,510	28,637	29,005	-368
42	Civil engineering	2010	7,836	352	658	307	3,028	3,193	-165
		2011	7,673	598	867	268	2,721	2,362	359
		2012	7,576	597	848	251	2,829	2,604	226
43	Specialised construction activities	2010	17,653	914	1,392	478	3,368	3,389	-21
		2011	17,324	1,276	1,887	610	3,486	3,266	220
		2012	16,970	1,293	1,823	530	4,004	3,522	483

* Information suppressed to avoid disclosure

.. not available

- nil or less than half the level of rounding

Source: Annual Business Survey (ABS)

The sum of constituent items in tables may not always agree exactly with the totals shown due to rounding.

1.Total employment - point in time and Total employment - average during the year are from the Business Register and Employment Survey (BRES). Caution should be taken when combining financial data from the ABS with employment data from BRES due to differences in methodology. More information can be found in the ABS Technical Report.

18.2 UK Manufacturer's Sales by Industry

Industry	SIC(07)	2008	2009	2010	2011	2012	£ million 2013
Other mining and quarrying							
Quarrying of ornamental and building stone, limestone, gypsum, chalk and slate	08110	12	9	S	12	383	S
Operation of gravel and sand pits; mining of clays and kaolin	08120	95	68	74	54	1,330	S
Mining of chemical and fertiliser minerals	08910	S	S	S	S	S	S
Extraction of salt	08930	S	S	S	S	331	S
Other mining and quarrying n.e.c.	08990	S	S	S	S	33	36
Manufacture of food products							
Processing and preserving of meat	10110	4,489	4,473	4,637	5,035	5,835	6,192
Processing and preserving of poultry meat	10120	2,618	2,682	2,732	2,894	2,947	3,369
Production of meat and poultry meat products	10130	5,084	5,222	5,383	5,318	5,593	5,281
Processing and preserving of fish, crustaceans and molluscs	10200	1,700	1,620	1,887	2,106	2,220	2,095
Processing and preserving of potatoes	10310	S	S	S	S	S	1,117
Manufacture of fruit and vegetable juice	10320	592	491	495	549	574	613
Other processing and preserving of fruit and vegetables	10390	2,580	2,720	2,841	2,910	2,900	3,049
Manufacture of oils and fats	10410	2,256	981	930	1,198	1,150	1,119
Manufacture of margarine and similar edible fats	10420	S	S	S	S	484	466
Operation of dairies and cheese making	10510	6,637	6,445	6,829	7,075	6,792	7,094
Manufacture of ice cream	10520	593	562	600	566	591	635
Manufacture of grain mill products	10610	3,583	3,506	3,410	3,770	3,736	S
Manufacture of starches and starch products	10620	437	374	304	S	319	395
Manufacture of bread; manufacture of fresh pastry goods and cakes	10710	5,581	5,282	S	S	5,752	6,062
Manufacture of rusks and biscuits; manufacture of preserved pastry goods and cakes	10720	3,229	S	3,695	S	3,958	4,131
Manufacture of macaroni, noodles, couscous and similar farinaceous products	10730	30	S	35	S	S	S
Manufacture of sugar	10810	1,108	1,128	1,076	S	1,183	1,210
Manufacture of cocoa, chocolate and sugar confectionery	10820	3,704	3,528	3,781	2,707	2,613	2,611
Processing of tea and coffee	10830	1,618	S	S	S	S	S
Manufacture of condiments and seasonings	10840	1,453	1,416	1,482	1,636	1,812	1,901
Manufacture of prepared meals and dishes	10850	1,781	2,302	2,477	2,546	S	S
Manufacture of homogenised food preparations and dietetic food	10860	S	30	29	33	30	29
Manufacture of other food products n.e.c.	10890	2,773	2,991	3,019	3,295	3,588	3,805
Manufacture of prepared feeds for farm animals	10910	3,173	3,002	3,278	3,811	3,787	4,274
Manufacture of prepared pet foods	10920	1,385	1,508	1,536	1,541	1,537	1,698
Manufacture of beverages							
Distilling, rectifying and blending of spirits	11010	2,662	2,502	S	S	3,723	S
Manufacture of wine from grape	11020	S	S	S	S	S	S
Manufacture of cider and other fruit wines	11030	547	641	574	760	771	813
Manufacture of other non-distilled fermented beverages	11040	0	0	0	0	0	S
Manufacture of beer	11050	3,757	4,766	3,914	4,081	3,269	3,300
Manufacture of malt	11060	S	418	S	377	S	S
Manufacture of soft drinks; production of mineral waters and other bottled waters	11070	S	3,538	3,963	S	S	S
Manufacture of tobacco products							
Manufacture of tobacco products	12000	1,735	1,912	1,626	1,673	1,793	1,723
Manufacture of textiles							
Preparation and spinning of textile fibres	13100	591	315	367	384	385	401
Weaving of textiles	13200	548	469	542	591	608	616
Finishing of textiles	13300	538	414	490	517	492	499
Manufacture of knitted and crocheted fabrics	13910	155	134	S	S	S	S
Manufacture of made-up textile articles, except apparel	13920	1,340	1,042	1,094	1,064	1,169	1,095
Manufacture of carpets and rugs	13930	735	691	675	S	700	738
Manufacture of cordage, rope, twine and netting	13940	88	64	46	52	56	50
Manufacture of non-wovens and articles made from non-wovens, except apparel	13950	S	S	S	172	S	185
Manufacture of other technical and industrial textiles	13960	S	S	279	309	293	285
Manufacture of other textiles n.e.c.	13990	129	102	108	108	106	112
Manufacture of wearing apparel							
Manufacture of leather clothes	14110	4	6	S	S	4	4

18.2 UK Manufacturer's Sales by Industry

Industry	SIC(07)	£ million					
		2008	2009	2010	2011	2012	2013
Manufacture of workwear	14120	255	214	191	171	147	118
Manufacture of other outerwear	14130	667	551	538	474	595	614
Manufacture of underwear	14140	448	397	S	388	415	465
Manufacture of other wearing apparel and accessories	14190	250	242	215	198	223	254
Manufacture of articles of fur	14200	S	0	S	S	1	S
Manufacture of knitted and crocheted hosiery	14310	110	S	108	95	86	81
Manufacture of other knitted and crocheted apparel	14390	138	113	124	159	162	179

Manufacture of leather and related products

Industry	SIC(07)						
Tanning and dressing of leather; dressing and dyeing of fur	15110	183	150	228	263	248	296
Manufacture of luggage, handbags and the like, saddlery and harness	15120	130	111	134	119	147	S
Manufacture of footwear	15200	S	S	S	236	252	284

Manufacture of wood and of products of wood and cork; except furniture; manufacture of articles of straw and plaiting materials

Industry	SIC(07)						
Sawmilling and planing of wood	16100	891	797	897	968	985	1,056
Manufacture of veneer sheets and wood-based panels	16210	959	801	836	856	928	910
Manufacture of assembled parquet floors	16220	2	S	S	2	3	5
Manufacture of other builders' carpentry and joinery	16230	3,588	2,803	3,212	3,014	2,983	3,370
Manufacture of wooden containers	16240	463	388	434	401	513	535
Manufacture of other products of wood; manufacture of articles of cork, straw and plaiting materials	16290	441	334	332	336	328	337

Manufacture of paper and paper products

Industry	SIC(07)						
Manufacture of pulp	17110	S	S	S	S	S	S
Manufacture of paper and paperboard	17120	2,664	2,309	2,437	2,507	2,481	2,423
Manufacture of corrugated paper and paperboard and of containers of paper and paperboard	17210	3,551	3,097	3,399	3,815	3,921	3,952
Manufacture of household and sanitary goods and of toilet requisites	17220	1,985	2,201	S	2,302	S	2,012
Manufacture of paper stationery	17230	756	641	548	548	531	474
Manufacture of wallpaper	17240	S	113	136	132	134	141
Manufacture of other articles of paper and paperboard	17290	1,296	970	962	989	945	1,000

Printing and reproduction of recorded media

Industry	SIC(07)						
Printing of newspapers	18110	304	217	218	219	S	159
Other printing	18120	7,726	7,478	7,659	7,965	7,722	6,993
Pre-press and pre-media services	18130	837	470	455	404	387	388
Binding and related services	18140	320	275	271	232	238	243
Reproduction of recorded media	18200	214	167	111	S	S	112

Manufacture of coke and refined petroleum products

Industry	SIC(07)						
Manufacture of coke oven products	19100	S	S	S	S	S	S

Manufacture of chemicals and chemical products

Industry	SIC(07)						
Manufacture of industrial gases	20110	581	528	594	623	631	649
Manufacture of dyes and pigments	20120	1,124	930	1,001	1,066	914	933
Manufacture of other inorganic basic chemicals	20130	1,235	1,100	1,187	1,209	949	973
Manufacture of other organic basic chemicals	20140	4,529	3,111	3,579	3,597	2,940	2,869
Manufacture of fertilisers and nitrogen compounds	20150	1,362	1,118	1,294	1,550	1,603	1,645
Manufacture of plastics in primary forms	20160	3,564	3,038	3,518	3,930	3,524	3,510
Manufacture of synthetic rubber in primary forms	20170	503	298	392	S	S	302
Manufacture of pesticides and other agrochemical products	20200	520	624	577	582	605	623
Manufacture of paints, varnishes and similar coatings, printing ink and mastics	20300	2,977	2,761	2,847	3,086	2,950	3,022
Manufacture of soap and detergents, cleaning and polishing preparations	20410	1,550	1,662	1,755	1,752	1,784	1,748
Manufacture of perfumes and toilet preparations	20420	2,267	2,243	2,380	2,356	2,392	2,536
Manufacture of explosives	20510	163	186	171	159	154	S
Manufacture of glues	20520	340	340	342	357	382	388
Manufacture of essential oils	20530	S	642	690	878	860	683
Manufacture of other chemical products n.e.c.	20590	2,681	2,645	2,612	2,606	2,456	2,632
Manufacture of man-made fibres	20600	287	211	208	256	300	201

18.2 UK Manufacturer's Sales by Industry

							£ million
Industry	SIC(07)	2008	2009	2010	2011	2012	2013
Manufacture of basic pharmaceutical products and pharmaceutical preparations							
Manufacture of basic pharmaceutical products	21100	797	495	559	936	794	797
Manufacture of pharmaceutical preparations	21200	9,396	12,702	14,159	12,965	11,495	11,274
Manufacture of rubber and plastic products							
Manufacture of rubber tyres and tubes; retreading and rebuilding of rubber tyres	22110	S	S	S	S	S	S
Manufacture of other rubber products	22190	1,542	1,276	1,399	1,607	1,602	1,590
Manufacture of plastic plates, sheets, tubes and profiles	22210	4,613	4,065	4,471	4,574	4,707	4,744
Manufacture of plastic packing goods	22220	2,878	2,651	2,852	3,295	3,441	3,268
Manufacture of builders' ware of plastic	22230	4,104	3,634	3,795	3,478	3,368	3,960
Manufacture of other plastic products	22290	3,129	2,762	3,011	3,424	3,537	4,218
Manufacture of other non-metallic mineral products							
Manufacture of flat glass	23110	S	S	S	S	S	177
Shaping and processing of flat glass	23120	1,347	1,143	1,237	1,115	1,123	1,098
Manufacture of hollow glass	23130	585	635	654	694	724	726
Manufacture of glass fibres	23140	405	374	424	432	423	401
Manufacture and processing of other glass, including technical glassware	23190	153	119	125	172	174	170
Manufacture of refractory products	23200	247	237	234	276	259	245
Manufacture of ceramic tiles and flags	23310	91	88	76	74	78	87
Manufacture of bricks, tiles and construction products, in baked clay	23320	532	S	S	478	465	526
Manufacture of ceramic household and ornamental articles	23410	248	205	236	S	S	S
Manufacture of ceramic sanitary fixtures	23420	S	S	S	110	S	S
Manufacture of ceramic insulators and insulating fittings	23430	36	34	35	31	S	S
Manufacture of other technical ceramic products	23440	S	S	26	28	S	S
Manufacture of other ceramic products	23490	S	18	19	27	28	22
Manufacture of cement	23510	1,046	814	S	714	702	673
Manufacture of lime and plaster	23520	235	S	184	S	208	S
Manufacture of concrete products for construction purposes	23610	S	S	S	1,474	S	S
Manufacture of plaster products for construction purposes	23620	S	S	S	S	S	S
Manufacture of ready-mixed concrete	23630	1,384	1,208	1,095	1,127	1,088	1,172
Manufacture of mortars	23640	S	104	118	S	S	S
Manufacture of fibre cement	23650	89	S	S	S	76	70
Manufacture of other articles of concrete, plaster and cement	23690	163	134	S	146	167	S
Cutting, shaping and finishing of stone	23700	445	463	402	420	414	404
Production of abrasive products	23910	S	109	90	100	S	143
Manufacture of other non-metallic mineral products n.e.c.	23990	1,063	1,280	1,320	1,484	1,517	1,479
Manufacture of basic metals							
Manufacture of tubes, pipes, hollow profiles and related fittings, of steel	24200	1,603	S	1,266	1,544	1,557	1,322
Cold drawing of bars	24310	153	76	128	190	168	149
Cold rolling of narrow strip	24320	98	31	S	S	S	S
Cold forming or folding	24330	S	S	S	S	S	S
Cold drawing of wire	24340	S	S	S	S	157	146
Precious metals production	24410	504	443	643	875	481	371
Aluminium production	24420	2,061	1,211	1,478	1,646	1,259	1,097
Lead, zinc and tin production	24430	461	S	541	529	507	532
Copper production	24440	735	454	637	727	615	575
Other non-ferrous metal production	24450	1,317	923	1,046	1,011	1,017	960
Casting of iron	24510	427	256	316	421	415	418
Casting of steel	24520	332	299	287	388	333	343
Casting of light metals	24530	421	294	362	388	359	407
Casting of other non-ferrous metals	24540	206	157	184	224	224	191
Manufacture of fabricated metal products; except machinery and equipment							
Manufacture of metal structures and parts of structures	25110	6,944	5,801	5,418	5,682	5,463	5,408
Manufacture of doors and windows of metal	25120	1,597	1,278	1,235	1,217	1,286	1,354
Manufacture of central heating radiators and boilers	25210	832	S	787	798	803	923
Manufacture of other tanks, reservoirs and containers of metal	25290	455	379	324	395	430	420
Manufacture of steam generators, except central heating hot water boilers	25300	578	S	S	S	S	S
Manufacture of weapons and ammunition	25400	2,709	2,912	2,032	1,941	1,881	1,903

18.2 UK Manufacturer's Sales by Industry

Industry	SIC(07)	2008	2009	2010	2011	2012	£ million 2013
Forging, pressing, stamping and roll-forming of metal; powder metallurgy	25500	1,958	1,319	1,608	1,839	1,968	1,928
Treatment and coating of metals	25610	1,223	1,054	1,045	1,187	1,263	1,291
Machining	25620	4,098	3,383	3,629	4,243	4,559	4,675
Manufacture of cutlery	25710	S	21	20	23	25	22
Manufacture of locks and hinges	25720	573	491	537	561	514	515
Manufacture of tools	25730	857	730	796	799	825	860
Manufacture of steel drums and similar containers	25910	113	96	107	112	106	S
Manufacture of light metal packaging	25920	1,357	S	1,533	1,499	1,395	S
Manufacture of wire products, chain and springs	25930	937	768	857	904	782	784
Manufacture of fasteners and screw machine products	25940	412	340	364	454	469	460
Manufacture of other fabricated metal products n.e.c.	25990	1,836	1,386	1,595	1,747	1,810	1,909
Manufacture of computer; electronic and optical products							
Manufacture of electronic components	26110	1,378	1,048	1,296	1,301	897	1,031
Manufacture of loaded electronic boards	26120	576	937	1,044	1,256	1,167	1,042
Manufacture of computers and peripheral equipment	26200	1,373	1,359	1,182	1,270	1,182	1,212
Manufacture of communication equipment	26300	2,085	1,754	1,736	1,691	1,460	1,344
Manufacture of consumer electronics	26400	1,382	S	S	404	383	354
Manufacture of instruments and appliances for measuring, testing and navigation	26510	4,838	4,817	5,112	5,544	5,658	5,626
Manufacture of watches and clocks	26520	31	S	34	30	31	30
Manufacture of irradiation, electromedical and electrotherapeutic equipment	26600	837	787	S	S	S	S
Manufacture of optical instruments and photographic equipment	26700	357	304	332	394	374	349
Manufacture of magnetic and optical media	26800	11	12	9	S	13	S
Manufacture of electrical equipment							
Manufacture of electric motors, generators and transformers	27110	2,749	2,187	2,602	3,153	3,060	2,689
Manufacture of electricity distribution and control apparatus	27120	1,664	1,465	1,891	2,086	2,173	2,392
Manufacture of batteries and accumulators	27200	S	224	247	S	259	S
Manufacture of fibre optic cables	27310	110	92	124	S	114	93
Manufacture of other electronic and electric wires and cables	27320	1,240	952	1,263	1,399	1,311	1,214
Manufacture of wiring devices	27330	656	423	576	601	S	564
Manufacture of electric lighting equipment	27400	1,324	1,020	1,142	1,293	1,334	1,310
Manufacture of electric domestic appliances	27510	1,424	1,272	1,277	1,268	1,156	1,194
Manufacture of non-electric domestic appliances	27520	S	406	427	463	346	360
Manufacture of other electrical equipment	27900	1,436	1,101	1,356	1,211	1,231	1,209
Manufacture of machinery and equipment n.e.c.							
Manufacture of engines and turbines, except aircraft, vehicle and cycle engines	28110	4,364	3,263	3,662	4,303	4,232	4,158
Manufacture of fluid power equipment	28120	887	606	791	977	1,037	962
Manufacture of other pumps and compressors	28130	2,282	1,984	2,175	2,447	2,215	2,159
Manufacture of other taps and valves	28140	1,141	1,063	1,103	1,303	1,400	1,445
Manufacture of bearings, gears, gearing and driving elements	28150	1,105	812	903	1,027	1,004	986
Manufacture of ovens, furnaces and furnace burners	28210	289	239	222	271	295	S
Manufacture of lifting and handling equipment	28220	2,684	1,965	1,842	2,132	2,326	2,373
Manufacture of office machinery and equipment (except computers and peripheral equipment)	28230	419	410	524	548	607	S
Manufacture of power-driven hand tools	28240	S	70	100	S	151	159
Manufacture of non-domestic cooling and ventilation equipment	28250	2,717	S	2,502	2,371	2,260	2,393
Manufacture of other general-purpose machinery n.e.c.	28290	2,246	1,969	1,990	2,090	2,125	2,161
Manufacture of agricultural and forestry machinery	28300	1,378	1,177	1,275	1,483	1,767	1,610
Manufacture of metal forming machinery	28410	488	334	389	554	679	689
Manufacture of other machine tools	28490	300	247	280	329	351	312
Manufacture of machinery for metallurgy	28910	S	60	76	97	82	70
Manufacture of machinery for mining, quarrying and construction	28920	4,108	2,171	2,894	4,087	4,471	4,297
Manufacture of machinery for food, beverage and tobacco processing	28930	481	424	467	461	428	479
Manufacture of machinery for textile, apparel and leather production	28940	91	77	67	82	59	58
Manufacture of machinery for paper and paperboard production	28950	126	109	134	135	126	127
Manufacture of plastics and rubber machinery	28960	107	51	68	86	78	74
Manufacture of other special-purpose machinery n.e.c.	28990	1,415	972	1,181	1,252	1,227	1,042
Manufacture of motor vehicles; trailers and semi-trailers							
Manufacture of motor vehicles	29100	24,382	18,506	25,590	27,516	28,004	33,860
trailers and semi-trailers	29200	2,634	1,890	2,097	2,165	2,153	2,127

18.2 UK Manufacturer's Sales by Industry

Industry	SIC(07)	2008	2009	2010	2011	2012	£ million 2013
Manufacture of electrical and electronic equipment for motor vehicles	29310	666	515	S	544	346	313
Manufacture of other parts and accessories for motor vehicles	29320	8,970	6,345	8,301	8,222	8,794	8,650
Manufacture of other transport equipment							
Building of ships and floating structures	30110	2,171	2,456	2,756	2,903	S	3,787
Building of pleasure and sporting boats	30120	945	842	850	792	824	744
Manufacture of railway locomotives and rolling stock	30200	S	S	S	1,366	S	1,657
Manufacture of air and spacecraft and related machinery	30300	14,283	15,815	15,378	15,853	17,265	20,274
Manufacturer of military fighting vehicles	30400	412	430	513	S	S	S
Manufacture of motorcycles	30910	S	S	S	S	S	S
Manufacture of bicycles and invalid carriages	30920	101	115	115	113	129	136
Manufacture of other transport equipment n.e.c.	30990	72	51	41	S	S	46
Manufacture of furniture							
Manufacture of office and shop furniture	31010	1,452	1,032	1,011	1,100	1,217	1,095
Manufacture of kitchen furniture	31020	1,098	1,016	1,036	1,055	1,094	1,301
Manufacture of mattresses	31030	536	544	587	S	579	610
Manufacture of other furniture	31090	3,170	2,783	2,988	3,084	3,208	3,268
Other manufacturing							
Striking of coins	32110	S	184	206	S	S	S
Manufacture of jewellery and related articles	32120	370	S	411	437	420	390
Manufacture of imitation jewellery and related articles	32130	S	44	48	45	37	37
Manufacture of musical instruments	32200	27	24	16	18	20	22
Manufacture of sports goods	32300	293	S	324	369	344	345
Manufacture of games and toys	32400	205	210	171	162	155	273
Manufacture of medical and dental instruments and supplies	32500	2,753	2,783	2,667	2,541	2,629	2,571
Manufacture of brooms and brushes	32910	112	105	105	91	85	79
Other manufacturing n.e.c.	32990	606	589	531	572	662	685
Repair and installation of machinery and equipment							
Repair of fabricated metal products	33110	666	455	800	977	1,017	S
Repair of machinery	33120	3,251	3,130	2,759	2,983	3,034	3,195
Repair of electronic and optical equipment	33130	S	654	618	631	598	635
Repair of electrical equipment	33140	619	522	439	476	528	478
Repair and maintenance of ships and boats	33150	378	327	338	331	404	420
Repair and maintenance of aircraft and spacecraft	33160	2,767	2,904	2,557	S	3,333	3,527
Repair and maintenance of other transport equipment	33170	747	S	S	S	855	942
Repair of other equipment	33190	3	S	S	S	S	S
Installation of industrial machinery and equipment	33200	3,307	2,914	S	3,379	3,273	3,326
Total		331,894	299,845	324,799	341,031	341,985	354,521

Source: Office for National Statistics

Information in this table relate to products corresponding to an industry irrespective of which SIC the business making the product is classified.

S - A volume or unit value suppressed as disclosive

Suppression of data

Statistical disclosure control methodology is applied to PRODCOM data. This ensures that information attributable to an individual or individual organisation is not identifiable in any published outputs. The Code of Practice for Official Statistics, and specifically the Principle on Confidentiality (P.C) set out practices for how ONS protects data from being disclosed. The P.C includes the statement that ONS outputs should "ensure that official statistics do not reveal the identity of an individual or organisation, or any private information relating to them, taking into account other relevant sources of information". More information can be found in National Statistician's Guidance: Confidentiality of Official Statistics, on the statistical disclosure control methodology page of the ONS website.

Previous PRODCOM codes and the incorporation of additional back data

Following user feedback for a longer time series to aid statistical analysis of trends, 2008 and 2009 back data have been included to these reference tables, in addition to the 2010 to 2013 data. However, caution should be exercised when comparing certain values, due to the continuously evolving nature of the PRODCOM question list which is set by Eurostat, the European Union's Statistical Authority, in the face of new or changing products and industries. The changes can make backwards comparability difficult, as some codes may appear or disappear in future publications. In this publication, only products included in the most recent PRODCOM list have been included. This leads to difficulties with some aggregate figures in previous years, where the parts do not sum to the whole; this is caused by some of those parts being now-defunct product codes that are not included here, so the sum of the actual values in the table may not equal the aggregate total.

This sheet contains 2013 Intermediate estimates, and 2008 to 2012 Final estimates.

18.3 United Kingdom - Number of local units in VAT and/or PAYE based entreprises in 2013

STANDARD INDUSTRIAL CLASSIFICATION (UK SIC 2007) DIVISION by EMPLOYMENT SIZE BAND

Division	Employment size									TOTAL
	0 - 4	5 - 9	10 - 19	20 - 49	50 - 99	100 - 249	250 - 499	500 - 999	1,000 +	
01 Crop and animal production, hunting and related service activities Enterprises	122,980	12,015	3,040	955	230	110	40	5	0	139,375
02 Forestry and logging Enterprises	3,125	365	145	65	20	0	0	0	0	3,720
03 Fishing and aquaculture Enterprises	3,540	310	105	20	0	0	0	0	0	3,975
05 Mining of coal and lignite Enterprises	5	10	10	10	10	10	0	5	0	60
06 Extraction of crude petroleum and natural gas Enterprises	70	25	15	20	10	10	10	5	0	165
07 Mining of metal ores Enterprises	5	0	0	0	0	0	0	0	0	5
08 Other mining and quarrying Enterprises	780	315	240	160	35	15	0	0	0	1,545
09 Mining support service activities Enterprises	360	35	30	30	30	20	5	5	5	520
10 Manufacture of food products Enterprises	3,335	1,550	1,145	925	470	415	225	115	25	8,205
11 Manufacture of beverages Enterprises	825	200	155	105	55	45	25	10	0	1,420
12 Manufacture of tobacco products Enterprises	0	5	0	0	0	0	0	5	0	10
13 Manufacture of textiles Enterprises	2,300	730	460	330	110	85	10	0	0	4,025
14 Manufacture of wearing apparel Enterprises	2,225	680	360	200	60	20	5	0	0	3,550
15 Manufacture of leather and related products Enterprises	365	95	55	55	20	5	5	0	0	600
16 Manufacture of wood and of products of wood and cork, except furniture; manufacture of articles of straw and plaiting materials Enterprises	4,830	1,290	810	465	145	50	5	5	0	7,600
17 Manufacture of paper and paper products Enterprises	715	235	245	245	145	130	30	0	0	1,745
18 Printing and reproduction of recorded media Enterprises	9,185	2,180	1,205	725	235	115	30	5	0	13,680
19 Manufacture of coke and refined petroleum products Enterprises	75	20	20	20	15	10	0	5	0	165
20 Manufacture of chemicals and chemical products Enterprises	1,235	435	370	430	225	160	50	20	0	2,925
21 Manufacture of basic pharmaceutical products and pharmaceutical preparations Enterprises	330	45	40	35	40	35	30	15	5	575
22 Manufacture of rubber and plastic products Enterprises	2,480	1,180	1,025	850	415	260	55	10	0	6,275
23 Manufacture of other non-metallic mineral products Enterprises	2,775	840	645	440	205	105	35	5	0	5,050
24 Manufacture of basic metals Enterprises	670	225	210	260	115	85	20	10	5	1,600
25 Manufacture of fabricated metal products, except machinery and equipment Enterprises	14,705	4,485	3,300	2,275	720	295	35	15	5	25,835
26 Manufacture of computer, electronic and optical products Enterprises	3,600	915	660	615	285	165	50	15	5	6,310

18.3 United Kingdom - Number of local units in VAT and/or PAYE based entreprises in 2013

STANDARD INDUSTRIAL CLASSIFICATION (UK SIC 2007) DIVISION by EMPLOYMENT SIZE BAND

Division		Employment size									
		0 - 4	5 - 9	10 - 19	20 - 49	50 - 99	100 - 249	250 - 499	500 - 999	1,000 +	TOTAL
27	Manufacture of electrical equipment Enterprises	1,460	450	460	455	210	140	30	10	5	3,220
28	Manufacture of machinery and equipment n.e.c. Enterprises	4,285	1,470	1,105	970	425	260	75	25	5	8,620
29	Manufacture of motor vehicles, trailers and semi-trailers Enterprises	1,445	430	310	275	165	120	60	20	15	2,840
30	Manufacture of other transport equipment Enterprises	1,355	245	135	140	100	90	50	25	20	2,160
31	Manufacture of furniture Enterprises	3,795	1,070	680	465	175	95	25	5	0	6,310
32	Other manufacturing Enterprises	7,040	1,710	795	410	135	90	25	5	0	10,210
33	Repair and installation of machinery and equipment Enterprises	11,195	1,310	800	480	165	95	35	15	5	14,100
35	Electricity, gas, steam and air conditioning supply Enterprises	1,915	295	235	200	125	130	50	30	20	3,000
36	Water collection, treatment and supply Enterprises	435	180	145	120	55	35	10	10	0	990
37	Sewerage Enterprises	760	230	180	160	45	25	0	0	0	1,400
38	Waste collection, treatment and disposal activities; materials recovery Enterprises	4,035	1,340	965	880	355	170	25	10	0	7,780
39	Remediation activities and other waste management services Enterprises	480	110	55	30	0	5	0	0	0	680
41	Construction of buildings Enterprises	60,815	6,905	2,960	1,480	585	340	70	15	5	73,175
42	Civil engineering Enterprises	15,220	2,730	1,435	1,005	425	240	65	20	10	21,150
43	Specialised construction activities Enterprises	142,090	17,565	7,875	3,610	950	350	65	20	5	172,530
45	Wholesale and retail trade and repair of motor vehicles and motorcycles Enterprises	52,025	14,290	5,985	4,190	1,025	225	25	10	0	77,775
46	Wholesale trade, except of motor vehicles and motorcycles Enterprises	77,390	21,990	13,605	7,535	2,135	940	235	65	20	123,915
47	Retail trade, except of motor vehicles and motorcycles Enterprises	164,305	64,815	32,850	15,395	3,775	2,265	1,195	260	25	284,885
49	Land transport and transport via pipelines Enterprises	33,155	5,640	3,695	2,440	925	595	230	60	5	46,745
50	Water transport Enterprises	1,155	210	140	85	20	25	5	0	0	1,640
51	Air transport Enterprises	775	125	110	65	50	60	25	15	10	1,235
52	Warehousing and support activities for transportation Enterprises	9,115	3,025	2,160	1,840	790	505	155	75	25	17,690
53	Postal and courier activities Enterprises	12,450	1,645	985	1,110	750	350	80	30	15	17,415
55	Accommodation Enterprises	7,900	3,480	3,215	3,080	1,205	665	95	15	5	19,660

18.3 United Kingdom - Number of local units in VAT and/or PAYE based entreprises in 2013

STANDARD INDUSTRIAL CLASSIFICATION (UK SIC 2007) DIVISION by EMPLOYMENT SIZE BAND

Division		Employment size									
		0 - 4	5 - 9	10 - 19	20 - 49	50 - 99	100 - 249	250 - 499	500 - 999	1,000 +	TOTAL
56	Food and beverage service activities										
	Enterprises	66,315	39,440	24,365	14,285	2,180	560	75	30	10	147,260
58	Publishing activities										
	Enterprises	7,840	1,235	795	520	195	115	45	30	15	10,790
59	Motion picture, video and television programme production, sound recording and music publishing activities										
	Enterprises	17,380	940	605	495	215	70	15	10	5	19,735
60	Programming and broadcasting activities										
	Enterprises	1,630	160	120	75	50	25	5	10	5	2,080
61	Telecommunications										
	Enterprises	7,855	1,185	750	625	260	200	95	45	20	11,035
62	Computer programming, consultancy and related activities										
	Enterprises	108,855	5,995	3,665	2,310	755	390	120	40	20	122,150
63	Information service activities										
	Enterprises	6,365	690	380	210	80	55	25	10	5	7,820
64	Financial service activities, except insurance and pension funding										
	Enterprises	15,545	6,505	4,180	2,050	375	255	140	105	80	29,235
65	Insurance, reinsurance and pension funding, except compulsory social security										
	Enterprises	5,660	315	205	155	90	95	65	35	15	6,635
66	Activities auxiliary to financial services and insurance activities										
	Enterprises	20,725	4,095	2,185	1,400	585	385	150	80	30	29,635
68	Real estate activities										
	Enterprises	72,375	12,955	5,245	1,730	545	365	75	20	5	93,315
69	Legal and accounting activities										
	Enterprises	52,010	9,985	5,870	2,970	865	415	140	65	30	72,350
70	Activities of head offices; management consultancy activities										
	Enterprises	123,420	6,660	3,445	2,030	720	450	140	55	30	136,950
71	Architectural and engineering activities; technical testing and analysis										
	Enterprises	68,040	6,455	3,805	2,100	675	315	85	35	10	81,520
72	Scientific research and development										
	Enterprises	2,990	495	375	315	175	125	60	30	10	4,575
73	Advertising and market research										
	Enterprises	17,665	1,975	1,075	655	220	155	50	25	10	21,830
74	Other professional, scientific and technical activities										
	Enterprises	56,765	3,725	1,515	585	140	50	10	5	0	62,795
75	Veterinary activities										
	Enterprises	2,205	1,345	1,090	510	60	10	0	0	0	5,220
77	Rental and leasing activities										
	Enterprises	13,280	3,720	1,970	980	235	125	15	5	0	20,330
78	Employment activities										
	Enterprises	13,925	2,935	2,240	2,390	1,690	1,280	375	130	60	25,025
79	Travel agency, tour operator and other reservation service and related activities										
	Enterprises	5,800	3,030	1,055	445	180	90	30	5	0	10,635
80	Security and investigation activities										
	Enterprises	5,780	1,080	720	525	270	215	85	40	20	8,735
81	Services to buildings and landscape activities										
	Enterprises	35,490	7,375	3,910	2,115	775	490	195	80	80	50,510
82	Office administrative, office support and other business support activities										
	Enterprises	51,710	5,905	3,040	1,390	495	340	115	55	15	63,065
84	Public administration and defence; compulsory social security										
	Enterprises	9,670	3,600	3,755	3,935	2,105	1,660	795	345	145	26,010

18.3 United Kingdom - Number of local units in VAT and/or PAYE based entreprises in 2013

STANDARD INDUSTRIAL CLASSIFICATION (UK SIC 2007) DIVISION by EMPLOYMENT SIZE BAND

Division		Employment size									
		0 - 4	5 - 9	10 - 19	20 - 49	50 - 99	100 - 249	250 - 499	500 - 999	1,000 +	TOTAL
85	Education Enterprises	22,550	8,450	8,395	15,015	8,255	4,445	640	200	120	68,070
86	Human health activities Enterprises	28,800	12,045	10,365	7,440	2,025	1,230	365	150	325	62,745
87	Residential care activities Enterprises	7,920	4,405	5,915	7,845	3,240	710	55	15	5	30,110
88	Social work activities without accommodation Enterprises	22,300	13,370	11,675	7,850	2,240	940	160	35	10	58,580
90	Creative, arts and entertainment activities Enterprises	26,165	1,425	630	340	180	75	10	5	0	28,830
91	Libraries, archives, museums and other cultural activities Enterprises	2,845	1,425	900	680	220	95	30	15	0	6,210
92	Gambling and betting activities Enterprises	4,000	6,525	450	430	120	95	5	5	0	11,630
93	Sports activities and amusement and recreation activities Enterprises	17,975	4,915	3,845	2,885	1,045	455	75	30	10	31,235
94	Activities of membership organisations Enterprises	15,990	4,510	2,425	1,270	370	210	45	15	5	24,840
95	Repair of computers and personal and household goods Enterprises	6,610	770	365	195	65	35	15	0	5	8,060
96	Other personal service activities Enterprises	47,310	14,115	4,865	1,290	185	80	15	5	0	67,865
97	Activities of households as employers of domestic personnel Enterprises	0	0	0	0	0	0	0	0	0	0
98	Undifferentiated goods- and services-producing activities of private households for own use Enterprises	0	0	0	0	0	0	0	0	0	0
99	Activities of extraterritorial organisations and bodies Enterprises	5	0	0	0	0	5	0	0	0	10
	TOTAL ALL INDUSTRIES **Enterprises**	**1,786,875**	**383,200**	**221,360**	**145,695**	**50,065**	**26,570**	**7,615**	**2,760**	**1,345**	**2,625,485**

Source: Office for National Statistics

18.4 Production of primary fuels

United Kingdom   **Million tonnes of oil equivalent**

	1998	1999	2000	2001	2002	2003	2004	2005	2006	2007	2008	2009	2010	2011	2012	2013
Coal	25.8	23.2	19.6	20.0	18.8	17.6	15.6	12.7	11.4	10.7	11.3	11.0	11.4r	11.5r	10.6r	8.0r
Petroleum [1]	145.3	150.2	138.3	127.8	127.0	116.2	104.5	92.9	84.0	83.9	78.7r	74.7	69.0	56.9	48.8	44.5
Natural Gas [2]	90.2	99.1	108.4	105.9	103.6	103.0	96.4	88.2	80.0	72.1	69.7	59.7	57.2	45.3	38.9	36.5
Primary electricity [3]	24.0	22.9	20.2	21.2	20.6	20.4	18.7	19.0	17.9	14.9	13.0r	16.5r	15.1r	17.5r	17.5r	18.5r
Renewable energy [4]	2.1	2.2	2.3	2.5	2.8	3.0	3.1	3.7	4.0	4.3	5.0r	5.4r	5.9r	6.1r	6.8r	7.5r
Total Production	287.2	297.7	288.7	277.4	272.9	260.3	238.4	216.5	197.2	186.0	177.7r	167.4r	158.6r	137.3r	122.6r	114.9r

r - revised data

Source: Department of Energy and Climate Change

(1) Crude oil plus all condensates and petroleum gases extracted at gas separation plants.

(2) Includes colliery methane.

(3) Nuclear and natural flow hydro electricty excluding generation of pumped storage stations. Includes generation at wind stations

(4) Includes solar and geothermal heat, solid renewable sources (wood, waste, etc), and gaseous renewable sources (landfill gas, sewage gas)

Datasource	Location
DUKES 1.1.2	https://www.gov.uk/government/statistics/energy-chapter-1-digest-of-united-kingdom-energy-statistics-dukes

18.5 Total inland energy consumption
United Kingdom

Million tonnes of oil equivalent

	1998	1999	2000	2001	2002	2003	2004	2005	2006	2007	2008	2009	2010	2011	2012	2013
Inland energy consumption of primary fuels and equivalents	230.7	231.3	234.8	236.9	229.6	231.9	233.6	236.3	233.1	227.5	224.7	211.5	219.2	202.9	206.9	205.7
Coal	41.0	36.0	38.5	40.8	37.7	40.5	39.1	39.9	43.4	41.0	38.2	31.2	32.6	32.2	40.9	39.1
Petroleum	75.4	76.4	76.7	75.9	73.5	73.0	75.1	78.2	77.4	76.3	74.4	70.9	70.2	67.8	67.0	66.1
Primary electricity	25.0	24.2	21.4	22.1	21.3	20.6	19.4	19.8	18.5	15.4	13.0	16.5	15.1	17.5	17.5	18.5
Natural gas	87.3	92.5	95.9	95.6	94.3	94.6	96.6	94.3	89.4	90.2	93.2	86.3	93.6	77.6	73.3	72.7
Renewables and waste	2.1	2.2	2.3	2.5	2.8	3.1	3.5	4.2	4.4	4.7	6.0	6.7	7.6	7.7	8.3	9.4
less Energy used by fuel producers and losses in conversion and distribution	74.7	74.1	74.5	75.4	73.2	73.8	73.6	74.4	74.2	73.4	70.8	67.9	68.1	65.4	65.7	63.9
Total consumption by final users	155.9	156.5	159.4	160.9	156.5	158.1	159.9	159.7	157.0	154.3	154.5	144.0	150.6	138.4	142.4	143.3
Final energy consumption by type of fuel																
Coal (direct use)	3.7	3.5	2.7	2.7	2.2	2.1	2.0	1.7	1.6	1.8	1.8	1.7	1.9	1.8	1.7	1.9
Coke and breeze	0.9	0.9	0.8	0.8	0.7	0.7	0.6	0.6	0.5	0.5	0.5	0.4	0.3	0.3	0.4	0.5
Other solid fuel	0.7	0.6	0.6	0.5	0.5	0.4	0.4	0.4	0.4	0.4	0.4	0.2	0.2	0.2	0.2	0.2
Coke oven gas	0.4	0.2	0.2	0.2	0.1	0.1	0.1	0.1	0.1	0.1	0.1	0.0	0.1	0.1	0.0	0.1
Natural gas (direct use)	55.9	55.1	57.1	57.8	55.2	56.7	57.1	55.4	52.6	50.0	51.8	46.6	51.9	42.8	47.1	47.4
Electricity	27.1	27.8	28.3	28.6	28.7	28.9	29.1	30.0	29.7	29.4	29.4	27.7	28.3	27.3	27.3	27.3
Petroleum (direct use)	66.1	65.1	66.3	67.1	66.1	66.8	68.6	69.5	69.8	69.5	66.5	63.4	63.2	61.5	61.1	60.8
Renewables[6]	0.9	0.7	0.7	0.7	0.7	0.7	0.7	0.8	1.0	1.2	2.4	2.7	3.3	3.1	3.2	3.8
Heat	..	2.5	2.5	2.3	2.1	1.8	1.3	1.3	1.2	1.3	1.5	1.2	1.3	1.2	1.2	1.4
Final energy consumption by class of consumer																
Agriculture	1.4	1.3	1.2	1.3	1.2	0.9	0.9	1.0	0.9	0.9	0.9	0.9	1.0	0.9	1.0	1.0
Iron and steel industry	4.0	3.8	2.2	2.3	2.0	1.9	1.9	1.8	1.9	1.8	1.6	1.2	1.4	1.3	1.2	1.3
Other industries	30.5	30.5	33.3	33.2	31.8	32.1	31.0	30.5	29.6	28.8	27.5	23.2	24.7	23.1	22.7	22.9
Railways	0.6	1.4	1.4	1.4	1.4	1.4	1.0	1.0	1.0	1.0	1.0	1.0	1.0	1.0	1.0	1.0
Road transport	41.0	41.4	41.1	41.1	41.9	41.8	42.2	42.6	42.7	43.2	41.9	40.7	40.4	39.8	39.5	39.3
Water transport	1.2	1.1	1.0	0.8	0.7	1.2	1.2	1.4	1.8	1.6	1.0	1.0	0.9	0.9	0.8	0.8
Air transport	53.8	11.0	12.0	11.8	11.7	11.9	12.9	13.9	14.0	13.9	13.4	12.8	12.3	12.8	12.4	12.4
Domestic	46.1	46.1	46.9	48.2	47.5	48.3	49.3	47.8	46.6	44.9	46.0	44.6	49.3	39.5	44.5	44.6
Public administration	8.1	8.2	8.1	8.0	7.0	6.7	7.2	7.1	6.6	6.3	7.0	6.2	6.4	6.1	6.2	6.3
Commercial and other services	13.4	11.8	12.2	12.8	11.3	11.8	12.2	12.7	12.0	11.8	14.1	12.6	13.2	13.0	13.2	13.6

Source: Department of Energy and Climate Change

Datasource	Location
DUKES 1.1.2	https://www.gov.uk/government/publications/energy-chapter-1-digest-of-united-kingdom-energy-statistics-dukes
DUKES 1.1.5	https://www.gov.uk/government/publications/energy-chapter-1-digest-of-united-kingdom-energy-statistics-dukes
DUKES 1.1-1.3	https://www.gov.uk/government/publications/energy-chapter-1-digest-of-united-kingdom-energy-statistics-dukes

((-Transformation in total column) + industry use + losses) in DUKES 1.1-1.3

18.6 Coal: supply and demand

United Kingdom   **Million tonnes**

	1998	1999	2000	2001	2002	2003	2004	2005	2006	2007	2008	2009	2010	2011	2012	2013
Supply																
Production of deep-mined coal	25.7	20.9	17.2	17.3	16.4	15.6	12.5	9.6	9.4	7.7	8.1	7.5	7.4	7.3	6.2	4.1
Production of opencast coal	14.3	15.3	13.4	14.2	13.1	12.1	12.0	10.4	8.6	8.9	9.5	9.9	10.4	10.6	10.1	8.6
Total	40.0	36.2	30.6	31.5	29.5	27.8	24.5	20.0	18.1	16.5	17.6	17.4	17.8	17.9	16.3	12.7
Recovered slurry, fines, etc	1.1	0.9	0.6	0.4	0.4	0.5	0.6	0.5	0.4	0.5	0.4	0.5	0.5	0.7	0.7	0.1
Imports	21.2	20.3	23.4	35.5	28.7	31.9	36.2	44.0	50.5	43.4	43.9	38.2	26.5	32.5	44.8	49.4
Total	62.4	57.4	54.6	67.5	58.7	60.2	61.2	64.5	69.0	60.4	61.9	56.0	44.9	51.1	61.8	62.2
Change in stocks at collieries and opencast sites	0.2	-0.6	3.5	0.1	-0.9	0.9	0.4	0.1	0.3	0.0	-0.1	-0.6	-0.1	0.6	-0.2	0.4
Total supply	62.7	56.8	58.2	67.5	57.8	61.0	61.7	64.6	69.4	60.4	61.8	55.4	44.8	51.7	61.6	62.6
Home consumption																
Total home consumption	62.9	55.4	59.8	63.5	58.6	62.9	60.6	61.8	67.3	62.9	58.2	48.8	51.4	51.4	64.3	60.2
Overseas shipments and bunkers	1.0	0.8	0.7	0.5	0.5	0.5	0.6	0.5	0.4	0.5	0.6	0.6	0.7	0.5	0.5	0.6
Total consumption and shipments	63.8	56.2	60.5	64.1	59.2	63.4	61.2	62.3	67.8	63.4	58.8	49.4	52.1	51.9	64.7	60.8
Change in distributed stocks	1.2	-0.6	2.3	-3.5	1.4	2.4	-0.5	-1.9	-1.9	3.0	-3.0	-6.2	7.3	0.3	3.2	-1.7
Balance	0.0	0.0	0.0	0.0	0.0	0.0	0.0	0.3	-0.3	0.0	0.0	-0.2	0.0	0.0	0.1	0.0
Stocks at end of year																
Distributed	14.2	14.8	12.4	15.9	14.5	12.1	12.6	14.5	16.4	13.4	16.4	22.6	15.4	15.1	11.9	13.6
At collieries and opencast sites	4.6	5.2	1.6	1.6	2.5	1.6	1.2	1.1	0.8	0.7	0.9	1.4	1.5	0.9	1.1	0.7
Total stocks	18.8	19.9	14.1	17.5	17.0	13.7	13.8	15.6	17.2	14.2	17.2	24.1	16.9	16.0	13.0	14.3

Source: Department of Energy and Climate Change

Datasource
DUKES 2.4
location
https://www.gov.uk/government/publications/solid-fuels-and-derived-gases-chapter-2-digest-of-united-kingdom-energy-statistics-dukes

18.7 Fuel input and gas output: gas consumption

United Kingdom   **Giga-watt hours**

	2000	2001	2002	2003	2004	2005	2006	2007	2008	2009	2010	2011	2012	2013
Analysis of gas consumption														
Transformation sector	349,454	336,525	351,856	344,410	362,668	354,146	333,431	379,518	402,236	382,061r	397,293	330,076	239,729r	225,483
Electricity generation	324,563	312,939	329,847	324,580	340,824	331,658	311,408	355,878	376,810	359,303r	373,586	307,140	214,638r	202,325
Heat generation	24,891	23,586	22,009	19,830	21,844	22,488	22,023	23,640	25,426	22,758	23,707	22,936	25,091r	23,158
Energy industry use total	77,941	91,451	91,260	88,907	88,468	87,161	81,859	76,025	72,280	70,597r	73,219r	64,605r	57,333r	54,873r
Oil and gas extraction	65,555	78,457	79,364	76,837	77,753	73,372	69,252	64,230	61,292	61,110r	61,124r	53,163r	48,461r	46,556
Petroleum refineries	3,641	4,189	3,350	2,773	3,076	5,163	5,161	5,206	4,971	1,601r	1,785r	1,757r	1,619r	1,151
Coal extraction and coke manufacture	241	220	196	188	150	114	112	91	95	217r	260r	223r	194r	158
Blast furnaces	712	375	222	539	728	941	611	719	718	450	641	453	266	363
Other	7,792	8,210	8,128	8,570	6,761	7,572	6,723	5,779	5,204	7,218r	9,409r	9,009r	6,793r	6,645
Final consumption total	678,142	683,753	653,151	669,457	673,860	652,024	620,035	591,274	599,018	550,142r	612,526r	505,062r	555,268r	563,154
Iron and steel industry	8,953	8,502	8,791	10,327	9,715	8,453	8,391	7,323	6,920	5,346r	6,124r	5,829r	5,091r	5,338
Other industries	174,488	171,341	156,375	155,890	144,238	142,988	136,150	126,028	127,013	4,900r	5,373r	5,155r	5,069r	5,220
Domestic	369,909	379,426	376,372	386,486	396,411	381,879	366,928	352,868	359,554	344,499r	389,595	293,400	345,080r	344,501
Public administration	44,552	46,232	42,998	44,362	51,934	50,319	45,803	42,444	45,665	42,372r	45,473r	42,960r	43,243r	44,495
Commercial	36,216	37,098	36,224	39,537	37,595	38,197	34,273	33,098	38,448	53,025r	57,320r	55,757r	57,377r	60,286
Agriculture	1,522	2,329	2,346	2,324	2,355	2,261	2,013	1,998	2,161	1,468r	1,619r	1,351r	1,162r	1,097
Miscellaneous	28,166	27,452	19,265	20,510	21,591	20,014	18,564	17,286	11,052	10,627r	11,501r	11,130r	11,111r	13,871
Non energy use	14,336	11,373	10,780	10,021	10,021	7,913	7,913	10,228	8,206	6,887	8,089	5,949	5,771r	5,598
Total gas consumption	1,105,537	1,111,729	1,096,267	1,102,774	1,124,996	1,093,331	1,035,325	1,046,817	1,073,535	1,013,943r	1,095,833r	909,669r	860,222r	850,984

Source: Department of Energy and Climate Change

Data source   Location
DUKES 4.2 - Supply and consumption of natural gas and colliery methane   https://www.gov.uk/government/publications/natural-gas-chapter-4-digest-of-united-kingdom-energy-statistics-dukes

18.8 Electricity: generation, supply and consumption

United Kingdom

Gigawatt-hours

	2001	2002	2003	2004	2005	2006	2007	2008	2009	2010	2011	2012	2013
Electricity generated													
Major power producers: total	353,066	353,994	362,600	358,313	362,212	361,232	361,317	355,209	342,374	347,846	332,312	328,270	324,725
Conventional thermal and other	132,744	135,579	147,536	140,576	143,091	160,566	146,706	128,944	106,939	111,127	111,255	147,946	141,114
Combined cycle gas turbine stations	123,846	123,987	121,076	131,182	130,748	117,669	140,011	160,109	151,454	160,518	131,886	85,647	82,533
Nuclear stations	90,093	87,848	88,686	79,999	81,618	75,451	63,028	52,486	69,098	62,140	68,980	70,405	70,607
Hydro-electric stations:													
Natural flow	3,215	3,927	2,568	3,908	3,826	3,693	4,144	4,224	4,294	2,703	4,594	4,169	3,609
Pumped storage	2,422	2,652	2,734	2,649	2,930	3,853	3,859	4,089	3,685	3,150	2,906	2,966	2,904
Renewables other than hydro	738	856	1,154	1,471	2,744	2,928	5,910	7,966	9,574	11,893	17,358	23,204	33,243
Other generators: total	31,721	33,252	35,609	35,616	36,148	36,050	35,513	33,663	34,378	33,926	34,960	35,309	34,443
Conventional thermal and other	16,621	15,788	17,244	14,419	13,407	12,354	13,865	19,457	20,218	18,862	20,258	20,065	17,813
Combined cycle gas turbine stations	8,979	10,577	10,879	11,852	11,792	11,561	11,516	11,522	10,790	12,113	10,560	10,074	9,078
Hydro-electric stations (natural flow)	840	860	660	936	1,096	900	933	931	947	862	1,086	1,116	1,093
Renewables other than hydro	5,283	6,028	6,825	8,408	9,853	11,235	8,702	8,680	10,428	10,325	11,491	12,635	15,332
All generating companies: total	384,787	387,246	398,209	393,929	398,360	397,282	396,830	388,872	376,753	381,772	367,272	363,579	359,168
Conventional thermal and other	149,365	151,367	164,780	154,995	156,498	172,920	160,571	148,401	127,157	129,989	131,513	168,011	158,927
Combined cycle gas turbine stations	132,825	134,564	131,955	143,034	142,540	129,230	151,527	171,631	162,244	172,631	142,447	95,721	91,611
Nuclear stations	90,093	87,848	88,686	79,999	81,618	75,451	63,028	52,486	69,098	62,140	68,980	70,405	70,607
Hydro-electric stations:													
Natural flow	4,055	4,787	3,228	4,844	4,922	4,593	5,077	5,155	5,241	3,565	5,680	5,285	4,702
Pumped storage	2,422	2,652	2,734	2,649	2,930	3,853	3,859	4,089	3,685	3,150	2,906	2,966	2,904
Renewables other than hydro	6,021	6,884	7,979	9,879	12,597	14,164	14,612	16,645	20,002	22,218	28,849	35,839	48,575
Electricity used on works: Total	17,394	17,126	18,136	17,032	17,873	18,503	17,694	16,340	16,571	16,112	16,430	17,967	17,891
Major generating companies	16,066	15,746	16,747	15,582	16,265	17,031	16,090	14,662	14,750	14,403	14,479	15,859	15,669
Other generators	1,328	1,380	1,389	1,451	1,608	1,472	1,605	1,678	1,821	1,710	1,951	2,108	2,222
Electricity supplied (gross)													
Major power producers: total	336,999	338,248	345,854	342,732	345,947	344,201	345,227	340,547	327,624	333,443	317,983	312,411	309,056
Conventional thermal and other	127,119	128,795	140,196	133,607	135,999	151,866	138,793	121,816	101,100	105,142	105,345	139,994	133,330
Combined cycle gas turbine stations	121,344	121,886	118,546	128,983	128,179	115,695	137,657	157,417	148,907	157,818	129,669	84,207	81,145
Nuclear stations	82,985	81,090	81,911	73,682	75,173	69,237	57,249	47,673	62,762	56,442	62,655	63,949	64,133
Hydro-electric stations:													
Natural flow	3,203	3,914	2,559	3,901	3,821	3,680	4,114	4,209	4,279	2,694	4,578	4,168	3,596
Pumped storage	2,340	2,562	2,641	2,559	2,776	3,722	3,846	4,075	3,672	3,139	2,895	2,956	2,894
Renewables other than hydro	692	802	1,059	1,367	2,486	2,643	5,675	7,704	9,306	11,523	16,904	22,595	32,311
Other generators: total	30,393	31,873	34,220	34,165	34,539	34,578	33,908	31,985	32,558	32,216	33,009	33,200	32,221
Conventional thermal and other	20,066	19,716	21,942	20,046	19,494	18,598	19,801	18,371	18,952	17,771	18,854	18,480	16,066
Combined cycle gas turbine stations	8,531	10,049	10,336	11,260	11,204	10,859	11,471	10,947	10,251	11,509	10,033	9,571	8,625
Hydro-electric stations (natural flow)	829	849	653	919	930	885	918	915	930	847	1,066	1,095	1,071
Renewables other than hydro	5,037	5,764	6,519	8,000	9,380	10,702	8,147	8,000	9,584	9,584	10,502	11,452	13,836
All generating companies: total	367,392	370,121	380,074	376,896	380,486	378,779	379,136	372,532	360,182	365,660	350,992	345,611	341,277
Conventional thermal and other	147,185	148,511	162,138	153,653	155,493	170,464	158,594	140,186	120,052	122,913	124,199	158,474	149,396
Combined cycle gas turbine stations	129,875	131,935	128,882	140,243	139,382	126,554	149,127	168,364	159,159	169,327	139,702	93,778	89,770
Nuclear stations	82,985	81,090	81,911	73,682	75,173	69,237	57,249	47,673	62,762	56,442	62,655	63,949	64,133
Hydro-electric stations:													
Natural flow	4,032	4,763	3,212	4,821	4,750	4,566	5,032	5,124	5,209	3,541	5,643	5,263	4,667
Pumped storage	2,340	2,562	2,641	2,559	2,776	3,722	3,846	4,075	3,672	3,139	2,895	2,956	2,894
Renewables other than hydro	5,729	6,566	7,578	9,367	11,867	13,345	13,822	15,704	18,889	21,107	27,406	34,047	46,147
Electricity used in pumping													
Major power producers	3,210	3,463	3,546	3,497	3,707	4,918	5,071	5,371	4,843	4,212	3,843	3,978	3,930
Electricity supplied (net): Total	364,182	366,657	376,528	373,399	376,780	373,861	374,064	367,161	355,339	361,448	347,149	341,633	337,348
Major power producers	333,789	334,785	342,308	339,235	342,240	339,283	340,156	335,175	322,781	329,231	314,140	308,433	305,127
Other generators	30,393	31,873	34,220	34,165	34,539	34,578	33,908	31,985	32,558	32,216	33,009	33,200	32,221
Net imports	10,399	8,415	2,160	7,490	8,321	7,517	5,215	11,022	2,861	2,663	6,222	11,871	14,430
Electricity available	374,581	375,072	378,687	380,889	385,101	381,378	379,279	378,183	358,200	364,111	353,371	353,504	351,777
Losses in transmission etc	30,902	29,980	29,862	30,728	27,674	27,410	28,223	27,849	28,043	27,032	28,128	28,905	27,725
Electricity consumption: Total	341,619	343,608	346,126	347,246	356,685	353,367	350,970	349,648	329,555	337,203	325,620	324,801	324,651
Fuel industries	8,898	10,206	9,908	8,299	8,010	8,137	9,313	7,825	7,807	8,377	7,793	6,841	7,673
Final users: total	332,721	333,401	336,218	338,948	348,675	345,229	341,656	341,822	321,748	328,825	317,827	317,959	316,978
Industrial sector	111,337	110,168	109,278	111,467	116,024	114,896	112,799	114,151	99,738	104,523	102,361	98,175	97,669
Domestic sector	115,337	120,014	123,001	124,200	125,711	124,704	123,076	119,800	118,541	118,833	111,591	114,667	113,445
Other sectors	106,047	103,219	103,939	103,280	106,939	105,629	105,781	107,871	103,469	105,470	103,875	105,117	105,863

Source: Department of Energy and Climate Change

Datasource
Electricity fuel use, generation and supply (DUKES 5.5)
https://www.gov.uk/government/publications/electricity-chapter-5-digest-of-united-kingdom-energy-statistics-dukes
Electricity commodity balances : (DUKES 5.1)
https://www.gov.uk/government/publications/electricity-chapter-5-digest-of-united-kingdom-energy-statistics-dukes
Electricity supply, electricity supplied (net), electricity available, electricity consumption and electricity sales (DUKES 5.4)
https://www.gov.uk/government/publications/electricity-chapter-5-digest-of-united-kingdom-energy-statistics-dukes
DUKES 5.5 and DUKES 5.1.3
https://www.gov.uk/government/publications/electricity-chapter-5-digest-of-united-kingdom-energy-statistics-dukes

18.9 Electricity: plant capacity and demand

United Kingdom
At end of December

Megawatts

	2000	2001	2002	2003	2004	2005	2006	2007	2008	2009	2010	2011	2012	2013
Major power producers														
Total declared net capability	72,193	73,382	70,369	71,471	73,293	73,941	74,996	75,979	76,993	77,881	83,438	81,789	81,879	78,508
Conventional steam stations	34,835	34,835	32,227	31,867	31,982	32,292	33,608	34,134	32,823	32,831	32,839	31,763	28,523	24,337
Combined cycle gas turbine stations	19,349	20,517	20,260	21,452	23,178	23,678	24,274	24,269	26,203	26,785	31,724	30,183	33,113	32,967
Nuclear stations	12,486	12,486	12,240	11,852	11,852	11,852	10,969	10,979	10,979	10,858	10,865	10,663	9,946	9,906
Gas turbines and oil engines	1,291	1,291	1,432	1,582	1,540	1,541	1,629	1,630	1,641	1,779	1,779	1,706	1,651	1,783
Hydro-electric stations:														
Natural flow	1,327	1,348	1,304	1,273	1,276	1,273	1,294	1,293	1,392	1,395	1,397	1,397	1,398	1,399
Pumped storage	2,788	2,788	2,788	2,788	2,788	2,788	2,726	2,744	2,744	2,744	2,744	2,744	2,744	2,744
Renewables other than hydro	117	117	117	117	117	117	96	929	1,210	1,488	2,090	3,333	4,504	5,373
Other generators:														
Total capacity of own generating plant	6,258	6,296	6,336	6,793	6,829	7,422	7,407	6,763	6,700	6,945	7,035	7,241	7,420	7,692
Conventional steam stations	3,544	3,464	3,325	3,480	3,275	3,269	3,059	2,924	2,749	2,408	2,475	2,401	2,464	2,095
Combined cycle gas turbine stations	1,709	1,777	1,854	1,927	1,968	2,182	2,106	2,076	1,988	2,267	2,302	2,212	2,244	2,162
Hydro-electric stations (natural flow)	158	160	162	129	132	127	123	126	125	127	129	153	158	162
Renewables other than hydro	847	895	995	1,257	1,454	1,852	2,118	1,637	1,837	2,144	2,129	2,475	2,553	3,273
All generating companies: Total capacity	78,451	79,678	76,705	78,264	80,122	81,363	82,403	82,742	83,693	84,826	90,473	89,031	89,299	86,200
Conventional steam stations	38,379	38,299	35,552	35,347	35,257	35,561	36,667	37,058	35,572	35,239	35,315	34,164	30,988	26,432
Combined cycle gas turbine stations	21,058	22,294	22,114	23,379	25,146	25,860	26,380	26,345	28,191	29,051	34,026	32,395	35,357	35,129
Nuclear stations	12,486	12,486	12,240	11,852	11,852	11,852	10,969	10,979	10,979	10,858	10,865	10,663	9,946	9,906
Gas turbines and oil engines	1,291	1,291	1,432	1,582	1,540	1,541	1,629	1,630	1,641	1,779	1,779	1,706	1,651	1,783
Hydro-electric stations:														
Natural flow	1,485	1,508	1,466	1,402	1,408	1,400	1,417	1,419	1,517	1,523	1,526	1,550	1,556	1,561
Pumped storage	2,788	2,788	2,788	2,788	2,788	2,788	2,726	2,744	2,744	2,744	2,744	2,744	2,744	2,744
Renewables other than hydro	964	1,012	1,112	1,374	1,571	1,969	2,214	2,566	3,048	3,632	4,218	5,808	7,057	8,645
Major power producers:														
Simultaneous maximum load met	58,452	58,589	61,717	60,501	61,013	61,697	59,071	61,527	60,289	60,231	60,893	57,086	57,490	53,420
System load factor (percentages)	67	69	65	67	67	66	69	66	68	64	65	67	66	71

Source: Department of Energy and Climate Change

Data source
DUKES Table 5.6 - Plant capacity
DUKES Table 5.9 - Plant loads, demand
and efficiency

Location
https://www.gov.uk/government/publications/electricity-chapter-5-digest-of-united-kingdom-energy-statistics-dukes

https://www.gov.uk/government/publications/electricity-chapter-5-digest-of-united-kingdom-energy-statistics-dukes

18.10 Electricity: fuel used in generation

United Kingdom
At end of December

Million tonnes of oil equivalent

	1998	1999	2000	2001	2002	2003	2004	2005	2006	2007	2008	2009	2010	2011	2012	2013
Major power producers: total all fuels	74.9	73.6	74.4	77.4	75.8	77.5	76.8	78.2	78.7	76.0	74.2	70.2	70.9	68.2	69.6	67.8
Coal	28.7	24.5	27.8	30.6	28.6	31.6	30.4	31.7	35.0	32.0	29.0	23.8	24.8	25.2	33.7	31.3
Oil	0.8	0.8	0.8	0.8	0.7	0.7	0.6	0.9	1.0	0.7	1.1	1.0	0.6	0.3	0.4	0.2
Gas	20.3	24.2	24.4	23.8	25.0	24.5	26.2	25.4	23.9	27.5	29.6	28.2	29.4	23.7	15.7	14.8
Nuclear	23.4	22.2	19.6	20.8	20.1	20.0	18.2	18.4	17.1	14.0	11.9	15.2	13.9	15.6	15.2	15.4
Hydro (natural flow)	0.4	0.4	0.4	0.3	0.3	0.2	0.3	0.3	0.3	0.4	0.4	0.4	0.2	0.4	0.4	0.3
Wind							-	-	-	0.3	0.5	0.6	0.7	1.1	1.5	2.0
Other renewables	0.2	0.2	0.2	0.3	0.3	0.4	0.5	0.8	0.7	0.6	0.8	0.7	1.0	1.3	1.8	2.4
Net imports	1.1	1.2	1.2	0.9	0.7	0.2	0.6	0.7	0.6	0.4	0.9	0.2	0.2	0.5	1.0	1.2
Other generators: total all fuels	7.1	7.3	8.0	7.6	8.0	8.7	8.4	9.2	9.0	8.8	8.3	8.5	8.4	8.7	8.6	8.5
Transport under takings																
Gas	0.220	0.215	0.189	0.192	0.154	0.008	0.002	0.003	0.002	0.002	0.002	0.001	0.002	0.001	0.001	0.001
Under takings in industrial sector																
Coal	1.2	1.0	0.9	1.0	1.0	1.0	0.9	0.9	0.9	0.9	1.0	0.9	0.8	0.8	0.7	0.1
Oil	0.7	0.7	0.8	0.6	0.6	0.5	0.5	0.4	0.5	0.5	0.5	0.5	0.5	0.4	0.3	0.3
Gas	2.5	2.7	3.3	2.9	3.2	3.4	3.1	3.1	2.9	3.1	2.8	2.7	2.7	2.7	2.8	2.6
Hydro (natural flow)	0.1	0.1	0.1	0.1	0.1	0.1	0.1	0.1	0.1	0.1	0.1	0.1	0.1	0.1	0.1	0.1
Wind, wave and solar photovoltaics	0.1	0.1	0.1	0.1	0.1	0.1	0.2	0.3	0.4	0.1	0.2	0.2	0.2	0.3	0.3	0.6
Other renewables	1.0	1.2	1.3	1.6	1.8	2.0	2.2	2.5	2.7	2.8	2.7	3.1	3.3	3.4	3.3	3.4
Other fuels	1.4	1.4	1.4	1.0	1.1	1.5	1.4	1.9	1.6	1.3	1.1	1.0	0.8	1.0	1.1	1.3
All generating companies: total fuels	82.0	80.9	82.4	84.9	83.8	86.2	85.2	87.4	87.7	84.7	82.5	78.7	79.3	76.9	78.2	76.3
Coal	29.9	25.5	28.7	31.6	29.6	32.5	31.3	32.6	35.9	32.9	30.0	24.7	25.6	26.0	34.3	31.4
Oil	1.5	1.5	1.5	1.4	1.3	1.2	1.1	1.3	1.4	1.2	1.6	1.5	1.2	0.8	0.7	0.6
Gas	23.0	27.1	27.9	26.9	28.4	27.9	29.3	28.5	26.8	30.6	32.4	30.9	32.1	26.4	18.5	17.4
Nuclear	23.4	22.2	19.6	20.8	20.1	20.0	18.2	18.4	17.1	14.0	11.9	15.2	13.9	15.6	15.2	15.4
Hydro (natural flow)	0.4	0.5	0.4	0.3	0.4	0.3	0.4	0.4	0.4	0.4	0.4	0.4	0.3	0.5	0.5	0.4
Wind, wave and solar photovoltaics	0.1	0.1	0.1	0.1	0.1	0.1	0.2	0.3	0.4	0.5	0.6	0.8	0.9	1.4	1.8	2.6
Other renewables	1.1	1.4	1.6	1.9	2.1	2.4	2.8	3.4	3.5	3.4	3.5	3.9	4.3	4.6	5.1	5.8
Other fuels	1.4	1.4	1.4	1.0	1.1	1.5	1.4	1.9	1.6	1.3	1.1	1.0	0.8	1.0	1.1	1.3
Net imports	1.1	1.2	1.2	0.9	0.7	0.2	0.6	0.7	0.6	0.4	0.9	0.2	0.2	0.5	1.0	1.2

Source: Department of Energy and Climate Change

Data source   Location
DUKES 5.3 - Fuel used in generation   https://www.gov.uk/government/publications/electricity-chapter-5-digest-of-united-kingdom-energy-statistics-dukes

18.11 Indigenous petroleum production, refinery receipts, imports and exports of oil

Thousand tonnes

	1999	2000	2001	2002	2003	2004	2005	2006	2007	2008	2009	2010	2011	2012	2013
Total indigenous petroleum production	137099	126245	116678	115944	106073	95374	84721	76578	76575	71665	68199	62962	51972	44561	40646
Crude petroleum:															
Refinery receipts total	88286	88013	83343	84784	84585	89821	86134	83213	81477	81034	75604	73543	75080	68862	65034
Foreign trade															
Imports	44869	54386	53551	56968	54177	62517	58885	59443	57357	60335	55056	55064	58092	60559	59137
Exports	91797	92917	86930	87144	74898	64504	54099	50195	50999	48401	45444	42196	33745	33961	33844
Net imports	-46928	-38531	-33378	-30176	-20720	-1987	4786	9249	6357	11934	9612	12868	24348	26598	25293
Petroleum products															
Foreign trade															
Imports	13896	14212	17234	14900	16472	18545	22481	26836	25110	23741	22172	23665	22656	26028	28245
Exports	21730	20677	19088	23444	23323	30495	29722	28945	29983	28803	25491	26065	27800	27083	26223
Net imports	-7834	-6464	-1854	-8544	-6851	-11950	-7241	-2109	-4874	-5062	-3319	-2400	-5145	-1055	2022
International marine bunkers	2329	2079	2274	1913	1764	2085	2055	2348	2371	3472	3306	2807	3130	2663	2540

Source: Department of Energy and Climate Change

Data source
DUKES 3.1 - Primary oil commodity balances
https://www.gov.uk/government/publications/petroleum-chapter-3-digest-of-united-kingdom-energy-statistics-dukes

DUKES 3.2-3.4 - Petroleum products commodity balances
https://www.gov.uk/government/publications/petroleum-chapter-3-digest-of-united-kingdom-energy-statistics-dukes

18.12 Throughput of crude and process oils and output of refined products from refineries

United Kingdom   Thousand tonnes

	1999	2000	2001	2002	2003	2004	2005	2006	2007	2008	2009	2010	2011	2012	2013
Throughput of crude and process oils	88432	88627	83438	84356	84814	89710	86069	83130	81509	81241	75754	73555	74809	68738	64990
less: Refinery fuel:	5538	5252	5059	5677	5456	5417	5601	4879	4676	4706	4304	4378	4585	4299	3768
Losses	1553	1633	1233	788	56	-7	371	374	293	470	777	566	373	222	305
Total output of refined products	81341	81743	77146	77891	79302	84301	80097	77877	76541	76065	70674	68612	69851	64217	60917
Gases:															
Butane and propane	1976	1919	1770	2149	2300	2170	2222	2142	2298	2250	2113	2247	2598	2512	2326
Other petroleum	361	289	272	537	715	520	427	661	517	369	449	518	434	285	320
Naphtha and other feedstock	2430	3082	3428	3153	3503	3168	3019	2734	2561	1863	1287	1596	1493	1488	1587
Aviation spirit	16	30	101	28	26	31	32	25	0	0	0	0	0	0	0
Motor spirit	25230	23445	21455	22944	22627	24589	22604	21443	21313	20319	20404	19918	19856	17013	17572
Industrial and white spirit	129	122	121	121	104	100	136	107	70	55	61	66	65	72	106
Kerosene:															
Aviation turbine fuel	7249	6484	5910	5365	5277	5615	5167	6261	6176	6549	6022	5781	6411	5775	4527
Burning oil	3553	3078	3088	3506	3521	3613	3325	3374	2968	3092	2830	2570	2377	2268	2705
DERV							19056	15821	16138	16350	15908	15332	16801	15772	14831
Gas/diesel oil	25755	28229	26748	28343	27380	28646	9430	10215	10165	10566	9487	9505	8683	8941	8193
Fuel oil	10446	10296	10179	8507	9495	11308	10155	11280	10433	10483	8043	7004	7432	6818	6151
Lubr icating oil	907	702	656	509	576	1136	936	617	547	514	530	412	430	457	377
Bitumen	1644	1438	1707	1918	1925	2196	1912	1749	1628	1485	1338	1276	1476	1222	777
Petroleum coke	648	657	513	441	612	633	660	606	676	781	847	817	654	467	528
Other products	854	1379	1140	818	1030	702	1103	964	1058	1182	1204	1557	1412	1252	1017

Source: Department of Energy and Climate Change

Data source
DUKES 3.5 - Supply and disposal of petroleum
https://www.gov.uk/government/publications/petroleum-chapter-3-digest-of-united-kingdom-energy-statistics-dukes

DUKES 3.2-3.4 - Petroleum product
https://www.gov.uk/government/publications/petroleum-chapter-3-digest-of-united-kingdom-energy-statistics-dukes

18.13 Deliveries of petroleum products for inland consumption
United Kingdom

	2001	2002	2003	2004	2005	2006	2007	2008	2009	2010	2011	2012	2013
Total (including refinery fuel)	76413	76233	77154	79066	80736	79812	77424	75160	71252	70582	68763	67070	66114
Total (excluding refinery fuel)	71354	70557	71697	73649	75135	74933	72748	70455	66948	66204	64178	62771	62346
Butane and propane	2061	2553	3017	3115	3310	3123	2823	3390	3112	2935	2976	2388	2538
Other Petroleum Gases (includes Ethane)	1898	1953	1885	1737	1838	1714	1563	1459	1344	1199	1003	899	986
Naphtha	1592	1592	2332	2029	1916	2278	1608	856	988	1037	1046	1060	1140
Aviation spirit	59	50	46	49	52	46	33	30	22	21	21	17	16
Motor spirit													
Retail deliveries													
Lead Replacement Petrol/Super premium unleaded	1258	1107	1044	884	851	737	787	757	745	647	560	446	-
Premium unleaded	19100	19167	18291	17795	17221	16615	16322	15250	14300	13435	12870	12357	-
Total retail deliveries	20358	20274	19335	18679	18071	17351	17109	16007	15045	14082	13430	12803	-
Commercial consumers													
Lead Replacement Petrol/Super premium unleaded (6)	44	36	41	40	22	21	16	12	12	11	11	2	-
Premium unleaded	538	499	542	765	759	719	624	523	555	509	454	426	-
Total commercial consumers	581	535	583	805	781	739	641	535	567	520	465	428	-
Total motor spirit	20940	20808	19918	19484	18852	18091	17615	16542	15613	14602	13895	13231	12574
Industrial and white spirits	151	157	147	281	284	156	167	145	174	224	143	219	279
Kerosene													
Aviation turbine fuel	10614	10519	10765	11637	12497	12641	12574	12142	11533	11116	11574	11221	11083
Burning oil	4236	3578	3569	3950	3870	4017	3629	3681	3732	4012	3288	3329	3460
Gas/diesel oil													
DERV fuel													
Retail deliveries	7846	8153	9057	9517	10532	11501	12685	12777	12669	13157	13549	13965	-
Commercial consumers	8213	8774	8655	8997	8845	8660	8730	7724	7443	7583	7442	7573	-
Total DERV fuel	16059	16926	17712	18514	19377	20161	21038	20501	20112	20740	20991	21538	21926
Other gas/diesel oil (includes MDF)	6959	6099	6326	6023	6719	6525	6116	5632	5034	5059	4759	4990	4631
Fuel oil	4262	3767	3562	3743	3780	3248	3228	2660	2113	1892	1415	1052	913
Lubricating oils	846	829	868	914	750	713	672	510	510	580	491	412	418
Bitumen	1935	2002	1959	1991	1906	1610	1563	1741	1381	1370	1621	1355	1358
Petroleum coke	702	893	880	1145	1042	925	366	281	207	301	262	154	127
Miscellaneous products	508	647	506	526	556	437	338	590	573	671	592	541	361

Source: Department for Energy and Climate Change

- Data no longer available

Datasource

Supply and demand of petroleum (DUKES Table 3.5)

https://www.gov.uk/government/publications/petroleum-chapter-3-digest-of-united-kingdom-energy-statistics-dukes

Additional information on inland deliveries of selected products (DUKES 3.6)

https://www.gov.uk/government/publications/petroleum-chapter-3-digest-of-united-kingdom-energy-statistics-dukes

Additional information on inland deliveries for non-energy uses (DUKES 3.8)

https://www.gov.uk/government/publications/petroleum-chapter-3-digest-of-united-kingdom-energy-statistics-dukes

Inland deliveries of petroleum (DUKES 3.1.2)

https://www.gov.uk/government/publications/petroleum-chapter-3-digest-of-united-kingdom-energy-statistics-dukes

Commodity (DUKES 3.2-3.4)

https://www.gov.uk/government/publications/petroleum-chapter-3-digest-of-united-kingdom-energy-statistics-dukes

18.14 Iron and steel:[1] summary of steel supplies, deliveries and stocks
United Kingdom

		2010	2011	2012	2013
Supply, disposal and consumption -(Finished product weight -Thousand tonnes)					
UK producers' home deliveries	**KLTA**	4685	4604	4256	4166
Imports excluding steelworks receipts	**KLTB**	5168	5613	5554	5420
Total deliveries to home market (a)	**KLTC**	9853	10217	9810	9586
Total exports (producers, consumers, merchants)	**KLTD**	5830	5779	6185	8162
Exports by UK producers	**KLTE**	4767	4614	4950	7041
Derived consumers' and merchants' exports (b)	**KLTF**	1063	1165	1235	1121
Net home disposals (a)-(b)	**KLTG**	8790	9052	8575	8465
Estimated home consumption	**KLTI**	8790	9052	8575	8465
Stocks -(Finished product weight - Thousand tonnes)					
Producers					
-ingots & semis	**KLTJ**	552	470	564	507
-finished steel	**KLTK**	704	632	632	705
Estimated home consumption -(Crude steel equivalent -Million tonnes)					
Crude steel production[2]	**KLTN**	9.71	9.48	9.58	11.86
Producers' stock change	**KLTO**	-0.18	-0.20	0.14	0.01
Re-usable material	**KLTP**	0.00	0.00	0.00	0.00
Total supply from home sources	**KLTQ**	9.89	9.68	9.44	11.85
Total imports	**KLTR**	6.86	8.03	7.83	6.95
Total exports	**KLTS**	6.67	6.66	7.02	9.11
Net home disposals	**KLTT**	10.08	11.05	10.25	9.69
Estimated home consumption	**KLTV**	10.08	11.05	10.25	9.69

Source: International Steel Statistics Bureau (ISSB)

1 The figures relate to periods of 52 weeks.
2 Includes liquid steel for castings only up to 2003.

18.15 Iron and steel:[1] iron ore, manganese ore, pig iron and iron and steel scrap

United Kingdom				Thousand tonnes	
		2010	2011	2012	2013
Iron ore consumption	**KLOF**	10572	9735	10511	14034
Manganese ore consumption	**KLOG**	0	0	0	3
Pig iron (and blast furnace ferro-alloys)					
Average number of furnaces in blast during period	**KLOH**	5	5	5	4
Production					
Steelmaking iron	**KLOI**	7233	6625	7183	9471
In blast furnaces: total	**KLOL**	7233	6625	7183	9471
In steel works	**KLOM**	7233	6625	7183	9471
Consumption of pig iron: total	**KLOO**	7233	6625	7183	9471
Iron and steel scrap					
Steelworks and steel foundries					
Circulating scrap	**KLOQ**	1256	1317	1413	1689
Purchased receipts	**KLOR**	2507	2517	2384	2456
Consumption	**KLOS**	3713	3890	3675	4085
Stocks (end of period)	**KLOT**	179	123	245	306

Source: International Steel Statistics Bureau (ISSB)

1 The figures relate to periods of 52 weeks.

18.16 Iron and steel:[1] furnaces and production of steel

United Kingdom   Number and thousand tonnes

		2010	2011	2012	2013
Steel furnaces (numbers[2])	**KLPA**				
Oxygen converters	**KLPC**				
Electric	**KLPD**				
Production of crude steel	**KLPF**	9708	9478	9579	11858
by process					
Oxygen converters	**KLPH**	7323	6946	7525	9915
Electric	**KLPI**	2385	2532	2054	1943
by cast method					
Cast to ingot	**KLPK**	153	205	189	146
Continuously cast	**KLPL**	9555	9273	9390	11699
Steel for castings	**KLPM**				
by quality					
Non alloy steel	**KLPN**	9201	8835	8992	11303
Stainless and other alloy steel	**KLPO**	508	643	587	555
Production of finished steel products (All quantities)					
Rods and bars for reinforcement (in coil and lengths)	**KLPP**	792	637	606	578
Wire rods and other rods and bars in coil	**KLPQ**	874	787	728	738
Hot rolled bars in lengths	**KLPR**	887	1002	849	809
Bright steel bars	**KLPS**	154	187	168	163
Light sections other than rails	**KLPT**	129	117	112	125
Heavy sections	**KGQZ**	1069	978	883	927
Hot rolled plates, sheets and strip in coil and lengths	**KLPW**	4733	4575	3962	4944
Cold rolled plates and sheets in coil and lengths	**KLPX**	2200	2215	1939	2848
Cold rolled strip	**KLPZ**	45	42	38	38
Tinplate	**KLQW**	468	411	411	401
Other coated sheet	**KLQX**	1278	1262	1161	1373
Tubes and pipes	**KLQY**	702	803	832	619
Forged bars	**KLQZ**				

1 The figures relate to periods of 52 weeks.

2 Includes steel furnaces at steel foundries, only up to 2003.

Source: International Steel Statistics Bureau (ISSB)

18.17 Fertilisers - UK consumption

Years ending 30 June   Thousand tonnes

Nutrient Content		2000	2001	2002	2003	2004	2005	2006	2007	2008	2009	2010	2011	2012	2013[e]
Nitrogen (N):	**XXXX**	1268	1162	1197	1131	1125	1061	1003	1008	1001	948	1016	1022	1000	995
Straight	**KGRM**	819	714	751	664	662	691	631	656	744	733	771			
Compounds	**KGRN**	449	448	446	467	463	370	372	352	292	180	245			
Phosphate (P2O5)	**KGRO**	317	279	283	282	278	259	235	224	215	129	184	192	188	194
Potash (K2O)	**KGRP**	409	369	391	375	375	352	325	317	325	208	251	283	259	267
Compounds - total product	**KGRQ**	2,851	2,471	2,511	2,558	2,550	2,221	2,134	2,039	1,827	1,116	1,529			

Source: British Survey of Fertiliser Practice (Defra)

e - data for 2013 are estimates

Table 18.17 gives the quantity of the fertiliser nutrients nitrogen (N), phosphate (P2O5) and potash (K2O) used by UK farmers during the fertiliser year, which runs from 1st July to 30th June. The year shown in the table is the year in which the harvest takes place, at the end of each fertiliser year.

18.18a United Kingdom production of minerals 2006–2012

Thousand tonnes

Mineral	2006	2007	2008	2009	2010	2011	2012
Coal:							
Deep-mined	9,444	7,674	8,096	7,520	7,390	7,312	6,153
Opencast	8,635	8,866	9,509	9,854	10,426	10,580	10,134
Other (a)	438	467	449	500	600	735	760
Natural gas and oil:							
Methane (oil equivalent)							
Colliery	65	62	63	67	63	58	61
Onshore	91	105	92	89	88	27	15
Offshore	79,856	71,957	69,525	59,581	57,036	45,204	38,858
Crude oil							
Onshore	1,379	1,271	1,248	1,181	941	678	870
Offshore	68,287	69,086	64,249	61,639	57,106	47,893	41,182
Condensates and other (c)							
Onshore	41	38	33	32	17	0	13
Offshore	6,872	6,180	6,135	5,346	4,898	3,401	2,495
Iron ore	0.4	0.3	0.1	—	—	—	—
Non-ferrous ores (metal content):							
Tin	—	—	—	—	—	—	—
Lead (h)	0.4	0.3	0.3	0.2	0.3	0.3	0.1
Gold (kg)	...	88	163	187	177	202	102
Silver (kg)	—	212	398	514	506	531	230
Chalk (e)	7,376	7,566	5,874	4,047	3,626	3,996	3,473
Clay and shale (e)	10,432	10,104	8,459	5,310	5,934	6,154	5,497
Igneous rock (j) (k)	53,954	58,909	53,490	44,618	44,876	(l) 44 400	(l) 40 200
Limestone (excluding dolomite)	80,228	83,491	74,145	60,111	56,985	(l) 58 100	(l) 54 800
Dolomite (excluding limestone)	12,101	7,622	5,509	3,164	4,540	4,490	4,896
Sand and gravel:							
Land	71,418	72,810	66,640	50,973	47,167	(l) 45 800	(l) 41 800
Marine (i)	20,689	20,426	18,833	15,253	14,533	17,287	14,840
Sandstone	18,038	16,806	12,255	12,335	11,556	(l) 12 300	(l) 11 500
Slate (g)	865	1,428	1,058	683	695	763	701
Ball clay (sales)	1,015	1,022	1,020	727	(h) 900	(h) 930	(h) 748
Barytes	48	53	43	36	34	31	30
Chert and flint	2	1	1	1	...	...	...
China clay (sales) (d)	1,762	1,671	1,355	1,060	(h) 1 140	(h) 1 290	(h) 1 150
China stone	1	1	0.5	0.0	0.0	0.0	0.0
Fireclay (e)	228	338	180	129	110	162	96
Fluorspar (h)	50	45	37	19	26	—	—
Gypsum (natural) (h)	1,700	1,700	1,200	1,200	1,200	1,200	1,200
Lignite	...	...	...	...	...	...	...
Peat (000 m^3)	1,593	885	760	887	1,004	825	568
Potash (b)	716	712	673	(h) 700	(h) 700	(h) 770	(h) 900
Salt	5,499	5,600	5,565	6,166	6,666	6,060	6,152
Silica sand	5,174	4,909	4,777	3,755	4,070	3,969	3,888
Talc	4	3	2	3	3	4	4

(a) Slurry etc. recovered from dumps, ponds, rivers etc.

(b) Marketable product (KCl).

(c) Including ethane, propane and butane, in addition to condensates.

(d) Dry weight.

(e) Excluding a small production in Northern Ireland.

(f) BGS estimates based on data from producing companies.

(g) Slate figures include waste used for constructional fill and powder and granules used in industry.

(h) BGS estimate.

(i) Including marine-dredged landings at foreign ports (exports).

(j) Excluding a small production of granite in Northern Ireland.

(k) In addition, the following amounts of igneous rock were produced in Guernsey (thousand tonnes): 2006: 136; 2007: 160; 2008: 139; 2009: 120; 2010: 116; 2011: 156; 2012: 169 and Jersey: 2007: 295; 2008: 325; 2009: 249; 2010: 238; 2011: 220; 2012: 239

(l) Contains estimate related to Northern Ireland production

Sources: Office for National Statistics, Department of Business, Innovation and Skills, Dept. of Enterprise, Trade & Investment (Northern Ireland), Crown Estate Commissioners (marine sand and gravel produced for export), and company data.

18.18b Minerals produced in Northern Ireland, the Isle of Man, Guernsey and Jersey 2008-2012

Thousand tonnes

	2008	2009	2010	2011	2012
Northern Ireland					
Gold (kg)	163	187	177	202	102
Silver (kg)	398	514	506	531	230
Lead	(c) 200	243	251	280	60
Limestone	3,739	3,972	3,689	...	...
Sand and gravel	7,134	4,856	2,178	...	...
Basalt and igneous rock (a)	6,481	5,758	5,438	...	...
Sandstone	2,697	3,793	2,768	...	...
Granite	...	...	...	...	...
Clay and shale	...	...	...	...	...
Others (b)	2,931	1,998	2,087	...	...
Total	**22,982**	**20,377**	**16,160**	...	...
Isle of Man					
Limestone	113	352	71	82	72
Sand and gravel	197	171	145	141	101
Igneous rock	158	132	109	96	94
Slate	64	45	28	29	23
Total	**532**	**701**	**353**	**347**	**290**
Guernsey					
Igneous rock	139	120	116	156	169
Jersey					
Igneous rock (c)	325	249	238	220	239
Sand and gravel	67	67	57	74	46

(a) Excluding granite.
(b) Including rock salt, chalk, dolomite, fireclay and granite
(c) BGS estimates.

Sources: Department of Enterprise, Trade & Investment (Northern Ireland), Department of Economic Development (Isle of Man), Company data (Guernsey and Jersey).

18.19a: Building materials and components

Bricks - Production, Deliveries and Stocks

Great Britain | Millions

(a) Brick Type

	Production	Deliveries (from)	Stocks*	Production	Deliveries (from)	Stocks*	Production	Deliveries (from)	Stocks*	Production	Deliveries (from)	Stocks*
	All Types			Commons			Facings			Engineerings		
2009	1,257	1,469	887	185	224	108	973	1,135	732	99	109	48
2010	1,430	1,606	702	182	194	94	1,124	1,280	570	124	132	39
2011	1,554	1,646	610	172	185	82	1,230	1,304	494	152	157	34
2012	1,459	1,551	515	137	166	52	1,172	1,239	425	150	146	38
2013	1,555	1,736	339	151	169	35	1,244	1,384	288	160	183	16
2013 Q3	416	498	362	44	47	38	332	397	304	41	53	20
Q4	408	434	339	39	41	35	327	347	288	41	46	16
2014 Q1	442	437	343	43	41	38	360	358	290	39	39	15
Q2	466	476	336	43	48	32	380	384	289	43	45	15
Q3	475	479	330	43	47	26	386	386	289	46	46	15
2013 November	149	152	336	13	14	35	120	121	283	16	17	19
December	107	108	339	11	10	35	89	88	288	7	10	16
2014 January	133	138	334	14	13	35	107	112	283	13	13	15
February	144	137	341	14	12	37	119	114	289	11	12	15
March	165	162	343	16	15	38	134	132	290	15	14	15
April	151	156	341	14	16	36	124	125	291	13	15	14
May	160	158	342	14	15	35	130	129	293	16	15	15
June	156	162	336	16	18	32	126	130	289	14	15	15
July	160	169	325	15	17	28	130	137	282	15	15	15
August	151	145	331	13	14	27	123	117	288	16	14	16
September	163	164	330	15	16	26	133	132	289	15	17	15
October	161	168	323	15	16	25	132	137	285	14	16	13
November p	161	138	343	15	12	28	132	113	301	13	13	14

(b) Material Type

	Production	Deliveries (from)	Stocks*	Production	Deliveries (from)	Stocks*	Production	Deliveries (from)	Stocks*	Production	Deliveries (from)	Stocks*
	All Materials			Clay#			Sand-Lime#			Concrete		
2009	1,257	1,469	887	c	c	c	c	c	c	c	c	c
2010	1,430	1,606	702	c	c	c	c	c	c	c	c	c
2011	1,554	1,646	610	c	c	c	c	c	c	c	c	c
2012	1,459	1,551	515	c	c	c	c	c	c	c	c	c
2013	1,555	1,736	339	c	c	c	c	c	c	c	c	c
												c
2013 Q3	416	498	362	c	c	c	c	c	c	c	c	c
Q4	408	434	339	c	c	c	c	c	c	c	c	c
2014 Q1	442	437	343	c	c	c	c	c	c	c	c	c
Q2	466	476	336	c	c	c	c	c	c	c	c	c
Q3	475	479	330	c	c	c	c	c	c	c	c	c
												c
2013 November	149	152	336	c	c	c	c	c	c	c	c	c
December	107	108	339	c	c	c	c	c	c	c	c	c
2014 January	133	138	334	c	c	c	c	c	c	c	c	c
February	144	137	341	c	c	c	c	c	c	c	c	c
March	165	162	343	c	c	c	c	c	c	c	c	c
April	151	156	341	c	c	c	c	c	c	c	c	c
May	160	158	342	c	c	c	c	c	c	c	c	c
June	156	162	336	c	c	c	c	c	c	c	c	c
July	160	169	325	c	c	c	c	c	c	c	c	c
August	151	145	331	c	c	c	c	c	c	c	c	c
September	163	164	330	c	c	c	c	c	c	c	c	c
October	161	168	323	c	c	c	c	c	c	c	c	c
November p	161	138	343	c	c	c	c	c	c	c	c	c

* Refers to stocks at end of period

Sand-lime bricks are included with clay bricks

p Provisional

r Revised

c Confidential

Source: Department for Business, Innovation and Skills (BIS)

Note: Data covering January 2009 to February 2011 were revised in the December 2011 edition of this bulletin. These data are included in this table. Additionally, data covering January 2013 to November 2013 were revised for the February 2014 edition of this bulletin. These revisions were due to the receipt of more accurate data from sites already sampled. For more information on revisions, see the 'Pre-announcements and Summary of Revisions to Monthly Statistics of Building Materials and Components Publication' document on our website.

18.19b Building and components

Concrete Blocks - Production, Deliveries and Stocks

Great Britain

Thousand square metres

	All Types			Dense			Lightweight			Aerated		
	Production	Deliveries (from)	Stocks*	Production	Deliveries (from)	Stocks*	Production	Deliveries (from)	Stocks*	Production	Deliveries (from)	Stocks*
2003	95,675	96,383	8,513	36,775	37,175	3,684	24,991	25,161	2,107	33,909	34,047	2,721
2004	96,256	94,854	10,088	37,677	37,444	3,690	25,462	25,736	2,271	33,117	31,674	4,127
2005	89,997	89,551	9,680	36,188	36,473	3,465	25,561	25,673	2,173	28,248	27,405	4,042
2006	87,510	87,015	:	34,956	34,741	:	25,345	25,222	:	27,209	27,051	:
2007	89,951	88,746	:	36,686	35,396	:	25,965	25,667	:	27,300	27,682	:
2008	67,743	67,136	8,920	29,675	29,889	3,498	18,168	18,363	2,149	19,900	18,884	3,273
2009	50,394	50,639	8,320	22,607	22,748	3,291	13,421	13,989	1,522	14,367	13,903	3,507
2010	53,629	51,758	10,152	22,393	21,731	3,833	14,415	13,923	2,044	16,822	16,104	4,276
2011	54,583	52,901	10,810	22,940	22,101	4,486	15,153	14,821	1,728	16,490	15,978	4,596
2012	51,693	52,021	10,700	21,551	22,323	3,808	14,383	14,103	2,024	15,759	15,595	4,868
2013	56,031	57,995	4,171	23,599	24,340	1,894	17,055	17,508	1,208	15,377	16,147	1,069
2009 Q3	12,771	13,924	8,203	5,811	6,255	3,390	3,293	3,765	1,544	3,667	3,903	3,269
Q4	12,066	11,874	8,320	4,969	5,023	3,291	3,416	3,412	1,522	3,681	3,439	3,507
2010 Q1	12,614	12,072	8,740	5,033	4,896	3,333	3,344	3,252	1,601	4,238	3,924	3,806
Q2	14,956	14,753	8,990	6,343	6,176	3,513	4,031	3,950	1,692	4,582	4,627	3,785
Q3	15,172	14,343	9,832	6,477	6,125	3,837	4,208	3,899	2,023	4,487	4,319	3,971
Q4	10,887	10,590	10,152	4,541	4,534	3,833	2,832	2,822	2,044	3,515	3,234	4,276
2011 Q1	13,982	12,795	11,516	5,642	5,278	4,197	3,916	3,665	2,301	4,423	3,852	5,017
Q2	14,761	13,911	12,510	6,217	5,871	4,647	4,008	3,827	2,507	4,537	4,212	5,357
Q3	14,208	14,076	12,352	6,217	5,931	4,862	3,908	3,970	2,218	4,083	4,175	5,272
Q4	11,632	12,120	10,810	4,864	5,021	4,486	3,321	3,359	1,728	3,447	3,739	4,596
2012 Q1	13,323	12,642	11,493	5,374	5,426	4,456	3,559	3,314	1,964	4,389	3,903	5,074
Q2	13,268	13,235	11,595	5,535	5,824	4,209	3,487	3,437	2,006	4,245	3,973	5,380
Q3	12,584	13,795	10,471	5,360	5,773	3,773	3,756	3,887	1,904	3,467	4,135	4,794
Q4	12,519	12,349	10,700	5,281	5,300	3,808	3,580	3,465	2,024	3,658	3,584	4,868
2013 Q1	12,125	12,713	10,165	5,212	5,430	3,643	3,094	3,389	1,730	3,818	3,893	4,793
Q2	14,960	16,188	4,401	6,351	6,655	2,190	4,691	4,809	1,303	3,918	4,723	908
Q3	15,333	16,042	3,683	6,345	6,609	1,875	5,079	5,162	1,210	3,909	4,271	597
Q4	13,614	13,052	4,171	5,691	5,646	1,894	4,191	4,147	1,208	3,732	3,259	1,069
2014 Q1	14,021	12,907	5,311	5,918	5,595	2,236	4,164	4,058	1,320	3,939	3,254	1,755
Q2	14,867	15,095	5,228	6,257	6,627	1,867	4,503	4,710	1,256	4,107	3,758	2,104
Q3	15,399	16,038	4,610	7,012	7,112	1,784	4,854	4,794	1,322	3,533	4,133	1,504
2012 November	4,726	4,582	:	2,022	1,943	:	1,333	1,308	:	1,371	1,330	:
December	3,151	2,900	10,700	1,314	1,283	3,808	854	704	2,024	983	914	4,868
2013 January	3,751	3,432	:	1,696	1,500	:	930	927	:	1,125	1,006	:
February	3,793	4,431	:	1,506	1,885	:	1,048	1,211	:	1,239	1,334	:
March	4,580	4,850	10,165	2,010	2,045	3,643	1,116	1,252	1,730	1,454	1,553	4,793
April	4,966	5,451	:	2,250	2,375	:	1,436	1,518	:	1,280	1,558	:
May	5,303	5,695	:	2,305	2,329	:	1,805	1,771	:	1,192	1,594	:
June	4,691	5,042	4,401	1,796	1,952	2,190	1,449	1,520	1,303	1,446	1,571	908
July	5,458	5,935	:	2,265	2,422	:	1,853	1,947	:	1,340	1,566	:
August	4,561	4,904	:	1,869	2,076	:	1,597	1,577	:	1,095	1,251	:
September	5,314	5,203	3,683	2,211	2,111	1,875	1,629	1,638	1,210	1,474	1,454	597
October	5,207	5,211	:	2,198	2,243	:	1,686	1,634	:	1,323	1,335	:
November	4,989	4,545	:	2,031	1,986	:	1,604	1,481	:	1,354	1,078	:
December	3,418	3,296	4,171	1,462	1,418	1,894	901	1,032	1,208	1,055	847	1,069
2014 January	4,376	3,749	:	1,984	1,738	:	1,324	1,104	:	1,068	908	:
February	4,596	4,093	:	1,856	1,679	:	1,383	1,379	:	1,357	1,036	:
March	5,049	5,064	5,311	2,078	2,178	2,236	1,457	1,575	1,320	1,514	1,311	1,755
April	4,960	4,825	:	2,011	2,132	:	1,602	1,625	:	1,346	1,068	:
May	4,773	5,009	:	2,080	2,258	:	1,396	1,529	:	1,298	1,223	:
June	5,134	5,261	5,228	2,165	2,237	1,867	1,505	1,556	1,256	1,463	1,467	2,104
July	5,288	5,692	:	2,444	2,585	:	1,770	1,712	:	1,074	1,395	:
August	4,728	4,905	:	2,211	2,172	:	1,480	1,478	:	1,036	1,256	:
September	5,384	5,441	4,610	2,357	2,355	1,784	1,605	1,604	1,322	1,422	1,481	1,504
October p	5,214	5,042	:	2,272	2,246	:	1,620	1,605	:	1,323	1,191	:
November p	4,904	4,352	:	2,086	1,893	:	1,464	1,358	:	1,354	1,101	:

* Refers to stocks at end of period

: Not available

p Provisional

r Revised

c Confidential

Source: Department for Business, Innovation and Skills (BIS)

Data from December 2011 to June 2012 has been revised following receipt of corrected data. The period August 2007 to November 2011 may also be affected, but non-availability of a back-series of corrected data means that this period cannot be revised, and should be treated with caution. Full details are available in the 'Summary of revision to monthly statistics of building materials and components publication' document on the BIS website.

18.19c Building materials and components

Other building materials

		Great Britain			United Kingdom
		Concrete Roofing Tiles (Th.sq.m. of roof area covered)			Ready-Mixed Concrete # (Th.cu.m.)
	Production	Deliveries	Stocks *		Deliveries
2003	21,437	21,401	2,982		22,289
2004	20,739	19,403	2,850		22,856
2005	25,719	24,489	4,902		22,432
2006	23,730	24,118	4,426		23,029
2007	23,551	23,812	3,646		23,548
2008	20,084	19,926	3,899		20,051
2009	14,079	15,612	2,344		14,069
2010	17,817	17,146	3,023		14,038
2011	17,712	17,684	3,126		15,121
2012	17,476	17,578	3,061		13,758
2013	18,745	19,580	2,214		15,089
2005 Q3	6,135	7,103	4,850		5,920
Q4	6,295	6,200	4,902		5,381
2006 Q1	6,792	6,252	5,418		5,445
Q2	6,002	5,709	5,708		5,995
Q3	5,448	6,371	4,688		6,047
Q4	5,489	5,787	4,426		5,542
2007 Q1	6,618	5,629	5,368		5,554
Q2	5,775	5,728	5,360		6,103
Q3	5,129	6,541	3,929		6,205
Q4	6,028	5,914	3,646		5,686
2008 Q1	5,708	5,421	3,922		5,193
Q2	5,815	5,679	4,488		5,773
Q3	4,657	4,977	3,840		4,902
Q4	3,903	3,849	3,899		4,183
2009 Q1	3,664	3,281	4,273		3,583
Q2	3,055	3,936	3,391		3,637
Q3	3,580	4,447	2,522		3,628
Q4	3,779	3,949	2,344		3,221
2010 Q1	4,129	3,505	2,967		3,328
Q2	4,961	4,922	3,008		3,819
Q3	4,783	4,824	2,967		3,831
Q4	3,945	3,894	3,023		3,060
2011 Q1	4,820	4,079	3,858		3,827
Q2	4,565	4,398	4,022		3,907
Q3	4,210	4,901	3,316		3,908
Q4	4,116	4,306	3,126		3,479
2012 Q1	4,673	3,928	3,872		3,463
Q2	4,236	4,100	4,008		3,399
Q3	4,095	5,004	3,136		3,556
Q4	4,471	4,547	3,061		3,340
2013 Q1	4,514	4,055	3,520		3,325
Q2	4,209	4,598	3,131		4,108
Q3	4,550	5,468	2,214		3,972
Q4	5,471	5,459	2,214		3,684
2014 Q1	6,151	5,414	2,932		3,475

Source: Department for Business, Innovation and Skills (BIS)

* Refers to stocks at the end of the period.

In April 2012, the Mineral Products Association (who provide these figures), estimated that data understates UK deliveries by around 20-25%. Previously, they had estimated that figures understate UK deliveries by 14-18%.

Concrete roofing tiles data have included imputation for non-responders in each quarter since 2012Q1.

18.19d Building materials and components

Slate - Production, Deliveries and Stocks

Great Britain   Tonnes

| | Production | | | Deliveries | | | Stocks [1] | | | Deliveries |
	Roofing [2]	Other [3]	Powder & Granules	Roofing [2]	Other [3]	Powder & Granules	Roofing [2]	Other [3]	Powder & Granules	Fill & Other Uses
2002	32,182	18,348	44,424	32,653	19,069	43,947	2,674	7,850	3,275	498,212
2003	34,471	15,623	29,003	34,700	14,576	29,240	2,477	8,849	3,416	669,818
2004	c	c	c	c	c	c	c	c	c	c
2005	c	c	c	c	c	c	2,824	10,281	5,347	c
2006	c	61,612	22,967	c	64,037	22,719	c	6,454	4,274	860,395
2007	c	65,260	19,141	c	62,646	19,431	2,563	2,521	3,746	c
2008	c	59,644	16,915	c	58,129	18,402	c	2,749	2,253	c
2009	c	33,759	9,150	22,555	34,322	10,637	2,420	2,186	766	615,346
2010	c	28,001	c	c	27,355	c	c	3,063	c	582,111
2011	c	30,665	c	c	30,437	c	c	3,245	c	662,003
2012	c	29,634	c	c	28,083	c	c	1,351	c	607,127
2013	c	32,419	c	c	31,375	c	c	c	665	692,319
2006 Q3	c	16,170	5,194	c	16,803	5,094	c	6,792	4,090	251,314
Q4	c	19,044	6,147	c	19,372	5,962	c	6,454	4,274	189,623
2007 Q1	c	17,787	5,571	c	16,829	5,036	6,984	4,996	4,571	376,876
Q2	c	16,577	4,315	c	14,765	4,875	3,066	5,850	4,011	346,426
Q3	c	16,017	4,672	c	15,475	4,929	2,977	6,391	3,754	c
Q4	c	14,879	4,583	c	15,577	4,591	2,563	2,521	3,746	255,249
2008 Q1	c	18,608	4,282	c	18,071	4,414	c	3,059	3,594	246,495
Q2	c	15,465	4,738	c	14,457	4,862	c	3,801	3,484	c
Q3	c	13,811	3,843	c	13,841	5,511	3,851	2,749	1,816	c
Q4	c	11,760	4,052	c	11,760	3,615	c	2,749	2,253	c
2009 Q1	c	7,370	2,128	5,315	7,688	2,724	c	2,431	1,658	148,722
Q2	5,084	9,124	2,046	5,328	9,319	3,385	4,142	2,236	318	169,661
Q3	5,503	8,263	2,046	6,534	8,267	2,163	3,111	2,232	201	154,862
Q4	4,687	9,002	2,930	5,378	9,048	2,365	2,420	2,186	766	142,101
2010 Q1	c	6,772	c	c	6,662	c	c	2,296	c	88,805
Q2	c	7,517	c	c	7,388	c	2,049	3,284	683	175,098
Q3	c	7,335	c	c	7,184	c	1,326	3,332	281	159,574
Q4	4,907	6,377	c	4,909	6,121	c	c	3,063	c	158,634
2011 Q1	4,736	6,516	3,314	4,449	6,504	3,399	c	3,029	c	198,547
Q2	4,677	8,167	3,370	4,630	8,187	3,094	2,012	3,009	472	216,524
Q3	c	9,851	c	c	9,732	c	c	3,128	c	139,359
Q4	c	6,131	c	c	6,014	c	c	3,245	c	107,573
2012 Q1	c	9,247	c	c	8,829	c	c	2,646	c	131,311
Q2	c	8,216	c	c	9,677	c	c	1,154	c	177,748
Q3	c	6,219	c	c	6,167	c	c	1,206	c	146,152
Q4	c	5,952	c	c	3,410	c	c	1,351	c	151,916
2013 Q1	c	6,052	c	c	9,220	c	c	c	802	157,215
Q2	c	9,638	c	c	9,440	c	c	c	736	216,035
Q3	c	10,429	c	c	6,843	c	c	c	537	169,995
Q4	c	6,300	c	c	5,872	c	c	c	665	149,074
2014 Q1	4,670	5,639	4,036	4,337	5,637	4,209	2,721	1,134	492	159,818

Source: Department for Business, Innovation and Skills (BIS)

Note : 1) We have improved our sampling panel to include some new sites and have removed some non-pure slate sites. In line with the Code of Practice we have revised the data for Q2, Q3 and Q4 2010.

2) From Q1 1995, the coverage of 'powder & granules' has been extended to include non-quarry manufacture; and 'crude blocks' are included in 'other' maufacture slate.

[1]   Refers to stocks at the end of the period.

[2]   Consists of all slate tiles which could be used as roofing tiles.

[3]   Consists of all slate products for cladding and decorative uses

: Not available

p Provisional

r Revised

c Confidential

18.19e Building materials and components

Cement & Clinker - Production and Deliveries

Great Britain   Thousand tonnes

		Cement								Clinker
		Production		Deliveries	Imports *(into GB)*		Cementitious Material			Production
		of which :	**Exports**	*(into GB from*	by	by				
			(from GB)	*GB production)*	*'Manuf.*	*Others**	other	total		
2007		11,887	74	11,638	255	1,121	2,769	15,783		10,227
2008		10,071	61	9,937	283	1,084	2,432	13,660		8,700
2009		7,623	21	7,474	99	1,085	1,680	10,338		6,421
2010		7,883	0	7,767	61	1,153	1,535	10,515		6,598
2011		8,529	0	8,318	86	1,173	1,736	11,312		7,096
2012		7,952	0	7,728	61	1,122	1,605	10,515		6,555
2013		8,203	0	8,204	117	1,322	1,892	11,535		6,712
2007	Q4	2,891	16	2,787	69	259	681	3,796		2,643
2008	Q1	2,609	18	2,551	88	268	598	3,505		2,267
	Q2	2,803	18	2,816	94	327	682	3,917		2,366
	Q3	2,520	13	2,496	72	263	648	3,445		2,202
	Q4	2,139	12	2,074	29	226	505	2,793		1,865
2009	Q1	1,762	14	1,782	37	256	410	2,485		1,378
	Q2	2,004	1	1,970	21	279	451	2,721		1,587
	Q3	1,998	5	1,999	25	283	453	2,760		1,831
	Q4	1,859	1	1,723	17	268	366	2,373		1,624
2010	Q1	1,726	0	1,744	24	246	336	2,350		1,261
	Q2	2,157	0	2,154	8	345	416	2,923		1,745
	Q3	2,203	0	2,195	17	310	450	2,971		1,880
	Q4	1,796	0	1,674	12	252	332	2,270		1,713
2011	Q1	1,979	0	2,043	12	281	402	2,738		1,427
	Q2	2,245	0	2,165	25	319	448	2,956		1,791
	Q3	2,246	0	2,200	25	303	494	3,022		2,015
	Q4	2,059	0	1,909	24	270	392	2,595		1,863
2012	Q1	1,880	0	1,928	16	285	370	2,599		1,366
	Q2	2,073	0	1,974	13	277	389	2,653		1,736
	Q3	2,120	0	2,021	13	302	444	2,780		1,722
	Q4	1,879	0	1,805	20	257	400	2,483		1,731
2013	Q1	1,425	0	1,724	16	259	393	2,393		1,198
	Q2	2,212	0	2,171	17	310	518	3,016		1,821
	Q3	2,324	0	2,251	38	..	..	..		1,884
2012	Sep	701	0	642	4	..	..	..		545
	Oct	692	0	733	4	..	..	..		566
	Nov	674	0	668	8	..	..	..		536
	Dec	513	0	404	8	..	..	..		629
2013	Jan	423	0	467	4	..	..	..		290
	Feb	617	0	620	8	..	..	..		427
	Mar	676	0	622	4	..	..	..		479
	Apr	693	0	714	4	..	..	..		622
	May	759	0	735	9	..	..	..		631
	Jun	760	0	723	4	..	..	..		568
	Jul	795	0	800	10	..	..	..		598
	Aug	779	0	714	17	..	..	..		672
	Sep	749	0	738	11	..	..	..		613

Monthly data no longer available1

Source: Department of Business, Innovation and Skills (BIS)

1. Arrangements for publication of the cementitious data have been revised following discussion and agreement by the Mineral

Products Association (MPA) Cement members. Data are now provided on an annual basis.

Monthly data ceased publication in the December 2013

2. Where the coverage is for Great Britain, the figures for imports & exports are defined accordingly and have been estimated.

Cementitious material covers cement itself, fly ash to EN 450 Part 1 where used as part of the cement in concrete

(previously known as pulverised fuel ash (pfa) to BS 3892 Part 1) and ground granulated blast furnace slag (ggbs) to

EN 15167 Part 1 (previously BS 6699)

18.19f Building materials and components

Sales of Sand and Gravel in Great Britain

Great Britain   Thousand tonnes

	Sand		Gravel	Sand & Gravel	Sand, Gravel & Hoggin	Sand & Gravel	of which
	for Building	for Concreting	for Concreting & other uses	for Coating	for Fill	Total	Marine-Dredged
2003	11,474	31,349	31,725	1,493	6,498	82,539	12,249
2004	11,017	32,366	30,184	1,380	6,399	81,346	12,996
2005	12,419	30,704	30,648	1,569	5,173	80,513	13,025
2006	9,499	29,893	31,963	2,346	4,195	77,896	13,974
2007	8,649	29,803	31,114	1,695	4,254	75,515	13,777
2008	8,864	28,922	28,297	c	c	74,651	12,582
2009	7,270	21,582	c	c	c	58,482	9,589
2010	6,074	19,887	c	c	c	54,530	9,341
2011	6,041	23,489	c	c	c	57,062	11,169
2012	6,499	21,994	23,077	c	c	57,972	10,320
2013	5,722	19,036	18,890	c	c	52,591	10,489
2008 Q3	2,279	7,644	7,091	c	c	19,341	3,337
Q4	2,049	6,398	6,252	490	1,695	16,884	2,669
2009 Q1	1,727	5,313	5,330	695	1,566	14,631	2,389
Q2	1,916	5,637	5,756	c	c	15,359	2,637
Q3	1,992	5,598	c	c	c	14,878	2,457
Q4	1,635	5,034	c	c	1,432	13,614	2,106
2010 Q1	1,539	4,952	c	c	c	13,711	2,131
Q2	1,585	4,983	c	c	c	13,940	2,444
Q3	1,584	5,268	c	c	c	14,112	2,592
Q4	1,366	4,684	c	c	c	12,767	2,174
2011 Q1	1,572	5,665	c	c	c	14,150	2,746
Q2	1,579	6,127	5,291	c	c	14,831	2,923
Q3	1,533	6,085	5,160	c	c	14,684	2,937
Q4	1,357	5,612	4,719	c	c	13,397	2,563
2012 Q1	1,481	5,635	5,039	c	c	13,894	2,675
Q2	1,712	5,608	5,633	c	c	14,474	2,609
Q3	1,778	5,612	6,259	c	c	15,192	2,749
Q4	1,528	5,139	6,146	c	c	14,412	2,287
2013 Q1	1,380	4,854	5,107	c	c	12,957	2,260
Q2	1,570	4,665	4,908	c	c	13,662	2,681
Q3	1,545	5,007	4,760	322	2,264	13,898	2,914
Q4	1,227	4,510	4,115	c	c	12,074	2,634
2014 Q1	1,379 r	4,221 r	4,393 r	394 r	1,533 r	11,919 r	2,447
Q2	1,472 r	4,744 r	5,627 r	302 r	1,379 r	13,524 r	3,296 r
Q3	1,593	5,456	5,511	387	1,388	14,334	3,138

The figures above are from a quarterly sample inquiry whereas those below are from the Annual Minerals Raised Inquiry, a census. The two inquiries differ because some respondents are only able to provide estimated information for the quarterly inquiry.

From May 2014, values for each quarter will no longer be adjusted to ensure that rounded values sum to the total value. Thus, in any given quarter, the sum of all sub-categories of sand and gravel may not exactly match that shown in the total column. Please see the 'Pre-announcements and Summary of Revisions to Monthly Statistics of Building Materials and Components Publication' document on the BIS website for further details.

1999	11,356	31,730	31,614	2,585	10,924	88,209	13,424
2000	11,758	31,167	31,797	2,461	12,051	89,234	14,356
2001	11,515	31,656	35,135	2,257	7,647	88,210	13,611
2002	11,190	31,224	32,434	2,031	5,842	82,721	12,832
2003	11,851	31,411	30,236	1,766	4,957	80,221	12,131
2004	10,688	32,529	32,346	2,437	8,058	86,057	12,996
2005	11,558	29,848	32,163	2,172	6,651	82,392	13,024
2006	9,907	29,815	31,002	2,648	6,869	80,242	13,974

18.19f Building materials and components

Sales of Sand and Gravel in Great Britain

Great Britain — Thousand tonnes

	Sand		Gravel	Sand & Gravel	Sand, Gravel & Hoggin	Sand & Gravel	of which
	for Building	for Concreting	for Concreting & other uses	for Coating	for Fill	Total	Marine-Dredged
2007	9,877	30,202	29,350	2,636	6,436	78,501	13,777
2008	8,527	26,885	23,388	2,222	11,106	72,127	12,621
2009	6,296	21,570	19,553	2,270	6,021	55,709	9,592
2010	6,110	20,947	18,540	2,112	6,621	54,330	9,341
2011	6,140	22,591	18,712	1,913	5,659	55,015	11,189
2012	5,474	19,697	18,072	1,817	4,985	50,044	10,291

: Not available

p Provisional

r Revised

c Confidential

Source: Department for Business, Innovation and Skills (BIS)

18.20 Volume of construction output in Great Britain. Constant (2010) prices, seasonally adjusted index numbers by sector

£million

PERIOD	New Housing			Infras-tructure	Other New Work			All New Work	Repair and Maintenance			Non Housing R&M	All Repair and Maintenance	All Work
	Public	Private	Total Housing		Excluding Infrastructure				Housing					
					Public	Private Industrial	Private Commercial		Public	Private	Total			
2009 Q1	53.8	81.4	75.0	63.0	70.9	103.7	111.7	84.9	96.2	95.2	95.5	106.3	100.9	90.5
Q2	56.3	78.2	73.2	68.6	77.1	96.6	104.9	84.1	100.3	91.6	94.5	103.7	99.1	89.4
Q3	66.2	74.3	72.4	73.4	86.1	95.3	93.9	82.8	107.5	97.8	101.0	111.5	106.3	91.0
Q4	77.1	77.9	77.7	86.7	94.5	101.9	85.9	85.9	103.0	86.4	92.0	102.0	97.0	89.8
2010 Q1	88.9	83.4	84.6	94.8	103.9	106.5	94.7	94.0	109.9	91.6	97.7	88.7	93.2	93.8
Q2	96.9	89.4	91.1	97.4	109.7	110.0	96.7	98.1	111.5	97.7	102.3	95.4	98.9	98.4
Q3	102.6	96.6	98.0	93.0	107.8	123.7	101.0	100.8	107.5	104.6	105.5	97.5	101.5	101.0
Q4	103.0	97.4	98.7	83.8	111.3	101.4	98.0	98.0	106.3	102.8	103.9	93.1	98.5	98.2
2011 Q1	106.9	98.5	100.4	96.6	111.0	102.5	96.8	100.5	103.7	100.7	101.6	98.2	99.9	100.3
Q2	103.8	100.2	101.0	104.3	102.4	103.3	99.6	101.5	101.5	98.7	99.6	98.2	98.9	100.6
Q3	95.9	102.1	100.7	100.0	96.3	95.1	100.9	99.6	97.2	98.4	98.0	105.1	101.5	100.3
Q4	93.3	99.3	97.9	99.2	90.3	99.3	102.7	98.4	97.7	102.3	100.8	98.6	99.7	98.9
2012 Q1	88.2	101.0	98.1	87.3	85.1	102.2	94.1	92.7	99.3	100.8	100.4	100.2	100.3	95.4
Q2	81.1	95.0	91.8	81.4	79.2	104.2	93.3	88.6	100.6	94.0	96.1	100.7	98.4	92.1
Q3	82.0	93.6	90.9	89.6	76.0	106.0	83.9	86.6	104.2	92.9	96.6	101.6	99.1	91.1
Q4	81.9	97.2	93.7	91.3	73.4	115.4	87.0	88.6	102.8	91.1	94.9	97.0	96.0	91.2
2013 Q1	80.5	95.8	92.2	86.5	69.7	100.8	89.6	86.8	100.5	88.4	92.3	97.8	95.0	89.7
Q2	87.6	103.4	99.8	86.7	71.4	91.2	89.0	88.6	97.8	93.2	94.7	101.0	97.8	91.9
Q3	90.8	107.5	103.7	86.3	72.5	89.2	93.6	91.1	95.4	94.9	95.0	107.0	100.9	94.7
Q4	101.9	112.3	109.9	88.9	68.7	89.4	92.3	92.3	97.2	96.1	96.4	103.0	99.7	95.0
2014 Q1	109.7	121.4	118.7	85.6	68.5	103.8	93.8	95.1	98.9	107.1	104.5	106.4	105.4	98.9

Source: Office for National Statistics

18.21 Value of orders for new construction obtained by main contractors in Great Britain: current prices by sector

£ Million		New Housing			Other New Work					All New Work	Period on period growths	Period on same period one year ago growths
		Public	Private	All New Housing	Infra-structure	Excluding Infrastructure			All Other Work			
						Public	Private Industrial	Private Commercial				
2008		3,082	9,201	12,283	7,897	14,671	4,346	23,353	50,267	62,550	-17.8%	
2009		3,107	6,393	9,500	11,032	14,709	2,653	12,886	41,280	50,780	-18.8%	
2010		3,482	9,953	13,435	9,774	13,430	2,131	13,580	38,915	52,350	3.1%	
2011		2,690	10,507	13,197	8,499	9,064	2,146	13,005	32,714	45,911	-12.3%	
2012		2,450	10,805	13,255	12,510	8,028	2,659	11,973	35,169	48,423	5.5%	
2013		3,989	14,576	18,566	10,818	9,045	3,605	13,539	37,006	55,571	14.8%	
2008	Q1	992	3,217	4,210	2,220	3,588	1,267	7,066	14,141	18,351	6.3%	-5.5%
	Q2	829	2,732	3,562	2,379	3,498	942	6,268	13,087	16,648	-9.3%	-20.5%
	Q3	709	1,778	2,487	1,695	4,123	1,166	5,832	12,816	15,303	-8.1%	-17.1%
	Q4	551	1,473	2,024	1,603	3,463	971	4,187	10,223	12,248	-20.0%	-29.1%
2009	Q1	765	1,422	2,186	2,474	2,793	554	3,297	9,117	11,303	-7.7%	-38.4%
	Q2	638	1,668	2,306	3,265	4,091	738	3,433	11,527	13,833	22.4%	-16.9%
	Q3	907	1,456	2,363	3,089	4,405	630	2,926	11,050	13,413	-3.0%	-12.4%
	Q4	797	1,847	2,645	2,204	3,420	732	3,230	9,586	12,231	-8.8%	-0.1%
2010	Q1	1,333	2,294	3,627	3,350	3,712	492	3,348	10,902	14,529	18.8%	28.5%
	Q2	738	2,182	2,920	2,533	3,465	603	3,586	10,187	13,106	-9.8%	-5.3%
	Q3	544	2,913	3,457	1,501	2,882	526	3,650	8,559	12,016	-8.3%	-10.4%
	Q4	867	2,564	3,431	2,390	3,371	510	2,997	9,267	12,698	5.7%	3.8%
2011	Q1	1,203	2,798	4,001	2,110	2,927	530	3,279	8,846	12,847	1.2%	-11.6%
	Q2	535	2,594	3,129	1,461	2,141	551	3,225	7,379	10,508	-18.2%	-19.8%
	Q3	533	2,573	3,105	1,726	2,355	537	3,928	8,546	11,652	10.9%	-3.0%
	Q4	420	2,541	2,961	3,202	1,642	527	2,573	7,943	10,904	-6.4%	-14.1%
2012	Q1	736	2,524	3,260	3,347	1,709	778	3,550	9,383	12,643	15.9%	-1.6%
	Q2	490	2,631	3,121	1,941	2,103	578	2,833	7,456	10,577	-16.3%	0.7%
	Q3	592	2,644	3,236	2,681	2,128	734	2,716	8,259	11,494	8.7%	-1.4%
	Q4	632	3,006	3,638	4,541	2,088	569	2,874	10,071	13,709	19.3%	25.7%
2013	Q1	1,032	3,240	4,272	2,022	2,572	627	3,277	8,497	12,769	-6.9%	1.0%
	Q2	892	3,811	4,704	2,958	2,210	750	3,476	9,393	14,097	10.4%	33.3%
	Q3	1,058	3,605	4,663	2,974	2,032	992	3,363	9,362	14,024	-0.5%	22.0%
	Q4	1,007	3,920	4,927	2,864	2,231	1,236	3,423	9,754	14,681	4.7%	7.1%
2014	Q1	766	4,264	5,030	1,893	2,531	1,060	3,608	9,092	14,123	-3.8%	10.6%

Office for National Statistics

18.22 Total engineering[1]

Values at current prices

£ million

	Turnover			New Orders		
	Export	Home	Total	Export	Home	Total
	JWO5	JWO6	JWO7	JWO8	JWO9	JWP2
2007	33,202.3	67,167.5	100,370.1	32,938.0	52,618.8	85,556.6
2008	33,929.2	68,053.8	101,983.0	30,512.2	54,571.6	85,084.4
2009	29,994.1	56,556.9	86,550.6	26,189.2	44,661.1	70,850.7
2010	37,532.0	61,679.2	99,211.2	35,537.8	54,997.3	90,535.1
2011	40,021.3	63,718.0	103,739.3	38,364.0	53,445.6	91,809.6
2012	40,458.8	66,938.9	107,397.7	38,569.9	52,650.2	91,220.1
2013	41,248.8	61,547.6	102,796.4	-	-	-
2008 Q1	8,142.2	17,060.6	25,203.3	7,687.2	14,276.8	21,964.2
Q2	8,770.8	17,362.6	26,133.1	8,176.6	13,830.9	22,007.5
Q3	8,394.8	17,295.0	25,689.6	7,371.0	14,296.0	21,667.3
Q4	8,621.4	16,335.6	24,957.0	7,277.4	12,167.9	19,445.4
2009 Q1	7,396.6	14,414.2	21,810.7	6,415.1	10,982.5	17,398.1
Q2	7,065.8	13,824.1	20,889.9	6,452.2	10,589.0	17,041.3
Q3	7,094.7	14,005.9	21,100.4	6,328.2	11,271.4	17,599.5
Q4	8,437.0	14,312.7	22,749.6	6,993.7	11,818.2	18,811.8
2010 Q1	8,405.6	14,561.7	22,967.3	8,184.8	13,131.0	21,315.8
Q2	9,268.8	15,326.0	24,594.8	9,293.0	14,418.4	23,711.4
Q3	9,498.2	16,005.1	25,503.3	8,595.8	13,589.2	22,185.0
Q4	10,359.4	15,786.4	26,145.8	9,464.2	13,858.7	23,322.9
2011 Q1	10,003.1	15,286.3	25,289.4	10,198.5	12,874.7	23,073.2
Q2	10,216.5	15,953.7	26,170.2	10,357.6	13,311.0	23,668.6
Q3	9,737.5	16,471.0	26,208.5	8,777.4	13,159.5	21,936.9
Q4	10,064.2	16,007.0	26,071.2	9,030.5	14,100.4	23,130.9
2012 Q1	9784.2	16,486.3	26,270.5	10,167.2	13,636.5	23,803.7
Q2	10224.1	17,159.1	27,383.2	9,528.5	13,034.2	22,562.7
Q3	9862.7	16,861.3	26,724.0	8,794.5	12,945.7	21,740.2
Q4	10587.8	16,432.2	27,020.0	10,079.7	13,033.8	23,113.5
2013 Q1	10,034.20	14,750.6	24,784.8	-	-	-
Q2	10,682.30	15,189.0	25,871.3	-	-	-
Q3	10,154.90	15,767.1	25,922.0	-	-	-
Q4	10,377.40	15,840.9	26,218.3	-	-	-
2012 Jan	2,897.7	5,056.4	7,954.1	3,460.1	4,114.6	7,574.7
Feb	3,152.0	5,229.0	8,381.0	3,283.4	4,555.9	7,839.3
Mar	3,734.5	6,200.9	9,935.4	3,423.7	4,966.0	8,389.7
Apr	3,262.3	5,165.3	8,427.6	3,110.9	4,509.0	7,619.9
May	3,490.6	5,819.0	9,309.6	3,203.9	4,294.2	7,498.1
June	3,471.2	6,174.8	9,646.0	3,213.7	4,231.0	7,444.7
July	3,275.6	5,913.4	9,189.0	2,986.2	4,677.5	7,663.7
August	3,101.7	5,514.2	8,615.9	2,733.5	4,078.9	6,812.4
September	3,485.4	5,433.7	8,919.1	3,074.8	4,189.3	7,264.1
October	3,567.0	5,847.2	9,414.2	3,176.5	4,528.9	7,705.4
November	3,591.7	5,835.4	9,427.1	3,404.6	4,414.0	7,818.6
December	3,429.1	4,749.6	8,178.7	3,498.6	4,090.9	7,589.5
2013 Jan	2,907.2	5,056.4	7,963.6	-	-	-
Feb	3,066.0	5,229.0	8,295.0	-	-	-
Mar	4,061.0	6,200.9	10,261.9	-	-	-
Apr	3,604.2	5,165.3	8,769.5	-	-	-
May	3,391.1	5,819.0	9,210.1	-	-	-
June	3,687.0	6,174.8	9,861.8	-	-	-
July	3,539.3	5,913.4	9,452.7	-	-	-
August	3,008.5	5,514.2	8,522.7	-	-	-
September	3,607.1	5,433.7	9,040.8	-	-	-
October	3,428.0	5,847.2	9,275.2	-	-	-
November	3,395.9	5,835.4	9,231.3	-	-	-
December	3,553.5	4,749.6	8,303.1	-	-	-

Source: Office for National Statistics : 01633 646659

- As of January 2013, New Orders data is no longer being collected
1 The data for this table is based on SIC 2007 (the Industrial Classification for 2007). The change is a result of the SIC 2003 based MPI survey (which provided figures up to the April edition of the Monthly Digest) becoming part of the SIC 2007 based Monthly Business Survey (MBS). This is part of an ONS wide project to convert all data series to the latest SIC. This means that this table is now Total engineering (SIC 07 25-28) Please note this new table does not include Orders on Hand.

18.23 Manufacture of fabricated metal products and machinery and equipment n.e.c.[1]

Values at current prices

£ million

	Turnover			New Orders		
	Export	Home	Total	Export	Home	Total
	JWM9	JWN2	JWN3	JWN4	JWN5	JWN6
2007	18,628.0	45,697.2	64,325.5	17,322.7	32,001.5	49,324.0
2008	20,022.2	46,615.9	66,638.5	16,445.4	36,125.6	52,571.6
2009	16,407.4	37,694.8	54,102.1	14,092.0	26,752.2	40,844.4
2010	22,257.5	42,731.1	64,988.6	21,727.5	34,866.8	56,594.3
2011	24,209.6	46,149.6	70,359.2	24,884.9	35,766.8	60,651.7
2012	24,794.0	47,704.2	72,498.2	24,489.3	34,234.2	58,723.5
2013	23,644.6	43,936.4	67,581.0	-	-	-
2008 Q1	4,920.2	11,586.7	16,507.3	4,337.7	9,049.0	13,386.9
Q2	5,340.0	11,958.4	17,298.4	4,470.1	9,120.8	13,591.0
Q3	4,968.4	12,009.0	16,977.3	4,004.0	10,027.5	14,031.7
Q4	4,793.6	11,061.8	15,855.5	3,633.6	7,928.3	11,562.0
2009 Q1	3,975.4	9,812.2	13,787.6	3,238.9	6,990.6	10,229.9
Q2	3,776.4	9,349.0	13,125.4	3,620.6	6,259.2	9,879.8
Q3	3,866.1	9,359.6	13,225.5	3,398.0	6,789.5	10,187.4
Q4	4,789.5	9,174.0	13,963.6	3,834.5	6,712.9	10,547.3
2010 Q1	4,838.8	9,902.9	14,741.7	4,810.6	8,203.9	13,014.5
Q2	5,567.2	10,577.9	16,145.1	5,852.1	9,155.6	15,007.7
Q3	5,622.2	11,313.3	16,935.5	5,113.6	8,520.7	13,634.3
Q4	6,229.3	10,937.0	17,166.3	5,951.2	8,986.6	14,937.8
2011 Q1	6,033.3	10,736.0	16,769.3	6,554.6	8,407.0	14,961.6
Q2	6,110.9	11,745.8	17,856.7	6,830.3	9,006.5	15,836.8
Q3	5,978.8	12,137.6	18,116.4	5,756.8	8,804.5	14,561.3
Q4	6,086.6	11,530.2	17,616.8	5,743.2	9,548.8	15,292.0
2012 Q1	5,995.6	11,728.6	17,724.2	6,493.8	8,721.4	15,215.2
Q2	6,327.4	12,382.9	18,710.3	6,089.3	8,674.9	14,764.2
Q3	6,095.4	12,006.9	18,102.3	5,459.0	8,355.3	13,814.3
Q4	6,375.6	11,585.8	17,961.4	6,447.2	8,482.6	14,929.8
2013 Q1	10,034.2	14,750.6	24,784.8	-	-	-
Q2	10,682.3	15,189.0	25,871.3	-	-	-
Q3	10,154.9	15,767.1	25,922.0	-	-	-
Q4	10,377.4	15,840.9	26,218.3	-	-	-
2012 Jan	1,752.4	3,643.4	5,395.8	2,278.6	2,645.7	4,924.3
Feb	1,942.9	3,701.6	5,644.5	2,036.8	2,968.6	5,005.4
Mar	2,300.3	4,383.6	6,683.9	2,178.4	3,107.1	5,285.5
Apr	2,011.2	3,659.0	5,670.2	1,953.1	3,175.2	5,128.3
May	2,204.1	4,150.0	6,354.1	2,142.6	2,826.0	4,968.6
June	2,112.1	4,573.9	6,686.0	1,993.6	2,673.7	4,667.3
July	2,080.5	4,274.4	6,354.9	1,821.7	3,096.4	4,918.1
August	1,869.3	3,909.3	5,778.6	1,746.4	2,605.7	4,352.1
September	2,145.6	3,823.2	5,968.8	1,890.9	2,653.2	4,544.1
October	2,122.9	4,126.2	6,249.1	2,101.6	2,871.7	4,973.3
November	2,211.1	4,162.6	6,373.7	2,092.9	2,851.4	4,944.3
December	2,041.6	3,297.0	5,338.6	2,252.7	2,759.5	5,012.2
2013 Jan	2,907.2	4,635.9	7,543.1	-	-	-
Feb	3,066.0	4,667.6	7,733.6	-	-	-
Mar	4,061.0	5,447.1	9,508.1	-	-	-
Apr	3,604.2	4,954.2	8,558.4	-	-	-
May	3,391.1	5,006.6	8,397.7	-	-	-
June	3,687.0	5,228.2	8,915.2	-	-	-
July	3,539.3	5,401.1	8,940.4	-	-	-
August	3,008.5	4,975.0	7,983.5	-	-	-
September	3,607.1	5,391.0	8,998.1	-	-	-
October	3,428.0	5,814.0	9,242.0	-	-	-
November	3,395.9	5,313.3	8,709.2	-	-	-
December	3,553.5	4,713.6	8,267.1	-	-	-

Source: Office for National Statistics : 01633 646659

- As of Jan 2013, new orders data is no longer collected

1 The data for this table is based on SIC 2007 (the Industrial Classification for 2007). The change is a result of the SIC 2003 based MPI survey (which provided figures up to the April edition of the Monthly Digest) becoming part of the SIC 2007 based Monthly Business Survey (MBS). This is part of an ONS wide project to convert all data series to the latest SIC. Manufacture of fabricated metal products and machinery and equipment n.e.c. (SIC 07 25, 28). Please note this new table does not include Orders on Hand.

623

18.24 Alcoholic drink

Calendar Year	Spirits					Beer			
	Production (hl of pure alcohol)	Whisky (hl of pure alcohol)	RTD (hl of pure alcohol)	Imported and other (hl of pure alcohol)	Total (hl of pure alcohol)	Production (thousand hl)	Released for home consumption (thousand hl)	Production (thousand hl of pure alcohol)	Clearances (thousand hl of pure alcohol)
2002	4508	321	105	689	1115	56672	59384	2352	2473
2003	4553	318	124	744	1187	58014	60301	2414	2515
2004	4081	319	114	792	1226	57461	59194	2433	2499
2005	4365	301	84	822	1206	56255	57572	2338	2398
2006	4485	283	65	767	1114	53768	55751	2250	2335
2007	5498	286	52	832	1170	51341	53465	2160	2247
2008	6072	289	42	817	1148	49611	51498	2062	2145
2009	5757	258	32	802	1091	45141	46817	1891	1957
2010	5074	267	35	842	1144	44997	45872	1905	1932
2011	5697	252	30	828	1111	45694	44844	1934	1888
2012	6185	252	24	836	1112	42049	43187	1752	1794

Calendar Year	Wine of Fresh Grapes				Made Wine				Cider and Perry
	Fortified (hl)	Still table (hl)	Sparkling (hl)	Total (hl)	Still (hl)	Sparkling (hl)	Coolers (hl)	Total (hl)	Released for home consumption (thousand hl)
2002	325	10319	578	11222	366	2	1606	1974	5939
2003	296	10647	640	11584	338	1	423	762	5876
2004	298	11768	676	12742	351	1	508	859	6139
2005	306	12117	721	13143	334	0	597	931	6377
2006	302	11655	715	12672	316	1	528	844	7523
2007	305	12559	838	13702	343	5	720	1068	8046
2008	324	12402	757	13483	374	7	611	993	8412
2009	219	11729	731	12680	390	2	597	989	9404
2010	220	11870	810	12900	400	5	758	1162	9399
2011	220	11827	812	12860	440	7	828	1275	9280
2012	226	11692	882	12801	424	3	1000	1427	8735

HL = Hectolitres

Source: Her Majesty's Revenue and Customs
Published in the HMRC Alcohol Bulletin

18.25 Tobacco products: released for home consumption

Calendar Year	Cigarettes			Other			Overall Total (thousand kg)
	Home Produced (million sticks)	Imported (million sticks)	Total (million sticks)	Cigars (thousand kg)	HRT (thousand kg)	Other (thousand kg)	
2008	7005	579	7585	86	473	27	8171
2009	7473	578	8051	92	607	29	8779
2010	7590	662	8252	86	683	29	9051
2011	7899	657	8556	87	845	28	9517
2012	7954	637	8591	88	991	29	9699

Source: Her Majesty's Revenue and Customs
Published in the HMRC Tobacco Bulletin

National accounts

Chapter 19

National accounts

The tables are based on those in The Blue Book 2014 Edition. The Blue Book presents the full set of economic accounts for the United Kingdom. The accounts are based on the European System of Accounts 1995 (ESA 95), a system of national accounts that all European Union members have agreed to use. ESA 95 is fully compliant with the System of National Accounts 1993 (SNA93), which was unanimously approved by the Statistical Commission of the United Nations, and is used by statistical offices throughout the world.

The Blue Book contains an introduction which provides an overview of the accounts and an explanation of the underlying framework. A detailed description of the structure of the accounts and the methods used to derive the figures is provided in a separate Office for National Statistics (ONS) publication United Kingdom National Accounts: Concepts, Sources and Methods (TSO 1998). Further information on the financial accounts is given in the Financial Statistics Explanatory Handbook.

Brief definitions of some national accounting terms used in this chapter are included here. Current prices (or, more precisely, current price estimates) describe values during the period of the observation. Hence, in a time series, they will describe changes to price and to volume. Chain volume measures exclude the effects of price change. Basic prices do not include taxes and subsidies on products, whereas these are included in market prices.

**Gross Domestic Product and Gross National Income
(Tables 19.1, 19.2, 19.3)**

Table 19.1 shows three of the most important economic aggregates: Gross Domestic Product (GDP), Gross National Income (GNI) and Gross National Disposable Income (GNDI). In all three cases 'gross' denotes that depreciation (or consumption) of fixed capital is ignored. GDP is the total value of the UK's output. GNI is GDP plus primary incomes received from the rest of the world minus primary incomes paid to the rest of the world. Primary income comprises taxes on production and imports, property income and compensation of employees. These measures are given as current price estimates and chained volume measures. GNDI equals GNI plus net current transfers to the rest of the world. Transfers are unrequited payments such as taxes, social benefits and remittances.

There are three different approaches to measuring GDP: output, income and expenditure. Table 19.2 shows the various money flows which are used in these different approaches, and those that are used to measure GNI at current prices. The output approach to measuring GDP takes the gross value added for the entire economy (that is, the value of the UK's output minus the goods and services consumed in the productive process) to give gross value added at basic prices. This figure is then adjusted to include taxes and exclude subsidies on products. This gives gross value added at market prices for the UK, which is equivalent to GDP.

The expenditure approach to GDP shows consumption expenditure by households and government, gross capital formation and expenditure on UK exports. The sum of these items overstates the amount of income generated in the UK by the value of imported goods and services. This item is therefore subtracted to produce GDP at market prices.

The income approach to GDP shows gross operating surplus, mixed income and compensation of employees (previously known as income from employment). Production taxes less subsidies are added to produce the total of the income-based components at market prices.

Table 19.2 also shows the primary incomes received from the rest of the world, which are added to GDP, and primary incomes payable to non-resident units, which are deducted from GDP, to arrive at GNI. Primary income comprises compensation of employees, taxes less subsidies on production, and property and entrepreneurial income. The data in Table 19.2 are in current prices. This means that changes between years will be driven by a combination of price effects and changes in the volume of production. The second of these components is often referred to as 'real growth'.

Table 19.3 shows the expenditure approach to the chained volume measure of GDP, that is to say the effects of price change have been removed. In chained volume series, volume measures for each year are produced in prices of the previous year. These volume measures are then 'chain-linked' together to produce a continuous time series.

Industrial analysis
(Tables 19.4, 19.5)

The analysis of gross value added by industry at current prices shown in Table 19.4 reflects the estimates based on the 2007 Standard Industrial Classification (SIC2007). The table is based on current price data reconciled through the input–output process for 2005 to 2012.

Table 19.5 shows chained volume measures of gross value added by industry. These indices are based on basic price measures. Chained volume measures of gross value added provides a lead economic indicator. The analysis of gross value added is estimated in terms of change and expressed in index number form.

Sector analysis – Distribution of income accounts and capital account
(Tables 19.6 to 19.13)

The National Accounts accounting framework includes the sector accounts which provide, by institutional sector, a description of the different stages of the economic process, from the income generated by production and its distribution and re-distribution to different economic units, and finally, capital accumulation and financing. Tables 19.6 to 19.12 show the 'allocation of primary income account' and the 'secondary distribution of income account' for the non-financial corporations, financial corporations, government and households sectors. Additionally, Table 19.12 shows the 'use of income account' for the households sector and Table 19.13 provides a summary of the capital account. The full sequence of accounts is shown in The Blue Book.

The allocation of primary income account shows the resident units and institutional sectors as recipients rather than producers of primary income. The balancing item of this account is the gross balance of primary income (B.5g) for each sector and, if the gross balance is aggregated across all sectors of the economy, the result is Gross National Income.

The secondary distribution of income account describes how the balance of income for each sector is allocated by redistribution; through transfers such as taxes on income, social contributions and benefits, and other current transfers. The balancing item of this account is Gross Disposable Income (GDI). For the households sector, the chained volume measure of GDI is shown as real household disposable income.

Table 19.12 shows, for the household sector, the use of disposable income where the balancing item is saving (B.8g). For the non-financial corporations sector the balancing item of the secondary distribution of income account, gross disposable income (B.6g), is equal to saving (B.8g).

The summary capital account (Table 19.13) brings together the saving and investment of the sectors of the economy. It shows saving, capital transfers, gross capital formation and net acquisition of non-financial assets for each of these.

Households' and non-profit institutions serving households' consumption expenditure at current market prices and chained volume measures (Tables 19.14 to 19.17)

Households' and non-profit institutions serving households' (NPISH) final consumption expenditure is a major component of the expenditure measure of GDP. In Table 19.2 this expenditure is given at current market prices, broken down by the type of good or service purchased. Table 19.3 supplies the same breakdown in chain volume measures. Household final consumption expenditure includes the value of income-in-kind and imputed rent of owner-occupied dwellings. It includes expenditure on durable goods (for instance motor cars) which, from the point of view of the individual might more appropriately be treated as capital expenditure. The purchase of land and dwellings (including costs incurred in connection with the transfer of their ownership) and expenditure on major improvements by occupiers are treated as personal capital expenditure. Other goods and services purchased by the household sector (with the exception of goods and services that are to be used in self-employment) are treated as final consumption expenditure. The most detailed figures are published quarterly in Consumer Trends

Change in inventories (previously known as value of physical increase in stocks and work in progress)(Table 19.18)

This table gives a broad analysis by industry of the value of entries less withdrawals and losses of inventories (stocks), and analysis by asset for manufacturing industry.

Gross fixed capital formation (Table 19.19 to 19.22)

Gross fixed capital formation is the total value of the acquisition less disposal of fixed assets, and improvements to land.

19.1 UK national and domestic product
Main aggregates: index numbers and values
Current prices and chained volume measures (reference year 2011)

		2000	2001	2002	2003	2004	2005	2006
INDICES (2011=100)								
VALUES AT CURRENT PRICES								
B.1*g Gross domestic product at current market prices ("money GDP")	YBEU	63.3	65.7	69.1	73.6	77.6	82.0	86.8
B.1g Gross value added at current basic prices	YBEX	63.2	65.8	69.3	74.0	77.9	82.5	87.3
CHAINED VOLUME MEASURES								
B.1*g Gross domestic product at market prices	YBEZ	82.9	85.1	87.2	90.9	93.2	95.8	98.7
B.6*g Gross national disposable income at market prices	YBFP	82.7	85.8	88.5	92.6	95.1	98.1	99.7
B.1g Gross value added at basic prices	CGCE	83.0	85.0	86.8	90.7	92.7	95.5	98.4
PRICES								
Implied deflator of GDP at market prices	YBGB	76.3	77.2	79.2	80.9	83.3	85.6	87.9

VALUES AT CURRENT PRICES (£ million)

Gross measures (before deduction of Consumption of fixed capital) at current market prices

		2000	2001	2002	2003	2004	2005	2006
B.1*g **Gross domestic product ("money GDP")**	YBHA	1 023 512	1 062 262	1 117 171	1 190 525	1 255 191	1 326 660	1 403 726
D.1+D.4 Employment, property and entrepreneurial income from the rest of the world (receipts *less* payments)	YBGG	5 431	9 117	16 277	17 607	20 416	29 541	13 610
-D.21+D.31 Subsidies (receipts) *less* taxes (payments) on products from/to the rest of the world	QZOZ	−106	3	−449	−680	−687	2 261	2 329
+D.29-D.39 Other subsidies on production from/to the rest of the world	IBJL	−335	−582	−519	−592	−592	−3 408	−3 221
B.5*g **Gross balance of primary incomes/Gross national income (GNI)**	ABMX	1 029 380	1 071 959	1 134 416	1 209 404	1 276 887	1 357 351	1 418 225
D.5,6,7 Current transfers from the rest of the world (receipts *less* payments)	YBGF	10 216	6 971	9 427	10 841	11 096	12 893	12 680
B.6*g **Gross national disposable income**	NQCO	1 019 164	1 064 988	1 124 989	1 198 563	1 265 791	1 344 458	1 405 545

Adjustment to current basic prices

		2000	2001	2002	2003	2004	2005	2006
B.1*g **Gross domestic product (at current market prices)**	YBHA	1 023 512	1 062 262	1 117 171	1 190 525	1 255 191	1 326 660	1 403 726
D.21 D.31 Adjustment to current basic prices (*less* taxes *plus* subsidies on products)	NQBU	112 399	114 069	118 158	124 251	131 954	137 488	144 642
B.1g **Gross value added (at current basic prices)**	ABML	911 113	948 193	999 013	1 066 274	1 123 237	1 189 172	1 259 084

Net measures (after deduction of Consumption of fixed capital) at market prices

		2000	2001	2002	2003	2004	2005	2006
P.51c	NQAE	135 374	144 703	154 579	160 954	171 150	179 144	193 231
B.1*n Net domestic product	NHRK	888 138	917 559	962 592	1 029 571	1 084 041	1 147 516	1 210 495
B.5*n Net national income	NSRX	894 010	927 255	979 837	1 048 450	1 105 736	1 178 204	1 224 997
B.6*n Net national disposable income	NQCP	883 794	920 284	970 410	1 037 609	1 094 640	1 165 311	1 212 317

CHAINED VOLUME MEASURES (reference year 2011, £ million)

Gross measures (before deduction of Consumption of fixed capital) at market prices

		2000	2001	2002	2003	2004	2005	2006
B.1*g **Gross domestic product**	ABMI	1 340 947	1 376 677	1 410 437	1 471 091	1 507 191	1 549 491	1 596 628
TGL Terms of trade effect ("Trading gain or loss")	YBGJ	−154	4 480	8 203	13 853	14 753	13 424	10 612
GDI Real gross domestic income	YBGL	1 340 793	1 381 157	1 418 640	1 484 944	1 521 944	1 562 915	1 607 240
D.1+D.4 Real employment, property and entrepreneurial income from the rest of the world (receipts *less* payments)	YBGI	7 106	11 852	20 675	21 975	24 799	34 865	15 621
-D.21+D.31 Subsidies (receipts) *less* taxes (payments) on products from/to the rest of the world	QZPB	−125	4	−572	−850	−835	2 669	2 674
+D.29-D.39 Other subsidies on production from/to the rest of the world	IBJN	−438	−757	−659	−739	−719	−4 024	−3 698
B.5*g **Gross balance of primary incomes/Gross national income (GNI)**	YBGM	1 348 430	1 393 719	1 440 502	1 508 461	1 548 248	1 599 071	1 623 856
D.5,6,7 Real current transfers from the rest of the world (receipts *less* payments)	YBGP	13 371	9 063	11 978	13 534	13 480	15 220	14 557
B.6*g **Gross national disposable income**	YBGO	1 335 047	1 384 648	1 428 516	1 494 920	1 534 759	1 583 845	1 609 291

Adjustment to basic prices

		2000	2001	2002	2003	2004	2005	2006
B.1*g **Gross domestic product (at market prices)**	ABMI	1 340 947	1 376 677	1 410 437	1 471 091	1 507 191	1 549 491	1 596 628
D.21 D.31 Adjustment to basic prices (*less* taxes *plus* subsidies on products)	NTAQ	144 934	152 191	159 670	164 413	171 640	172 658	177 997
B.1g **Gross value added (at basic prices)**	ABMM	1 196 650	1 225 077	1 251 491	1 307 278	1 336 401	1 377 383	1 419 204

Net measures (after deduction of Consumption of fixed capital) at market prices

		2000	2001	2002	2003	2004	2005	2006
P.51c	CIHA	169 677	177 058	186 429	194 296	204 499	209 180	219 992
B.5*n Net national income at market prices	YBET	1 179 862	1 217 720	1 254 910	1 315 098	1 343 861	1 389 956	1 403 761
B.6*n Net national disposable income at market prices	YBEY	1 166 492	1 208 698	1 242 947	1 301 572	1 330 390	1 374 746	1 389 212

19.1
continued

UK national and domestic product
Main aggregates: index numbers and values
Current prices and chained volume measures (reference year 2011)

			2007	2008	2009	2010	2011	2012	2013
INDICES (2011=100)									
VALUES AT CURRENT PRICES									
B.1*g Gross domestic product at current market prices									
("money GDP")		YBEU	91.5	93.9	91.6	96.3	100.0	102.3	105.9
B.1g Gross value added at current basic prices		YBEX	92.1	94.9	93.3	97.2	100.0	102.4	105.8
CHAINED VOLUME MEASURES									
B.1*g Gross domestic product at market prices		YBEZ	101.2	100.9	96.5	98.4	100.0	100.7	102.4
B.6*g Gross national disposable income at market prices		YBFP	101.9	99.9	95.9	98.7	100.0	99.3	100.5
B.1g Gross value added at basic prices		CGCE	100.9	100.8	96.3	98.3	100.0	100.7	102.3
PRICES									
Implied deflator of GDP at market prices		YBGB	90.4	93.1	94.9	97.9	100.0	101.7	103.4

VALUES AT CURRENT PRICES (£ million)

Gross measures (before deduction of Consumption of fixed capital) at current market prices

			2007	2008	2009	2010	2011	2012	2013
B.1*g	Gross domestic product ("money GDP")	YBHA	1 480 956	1 518 675	1 482 144	1 558 365	1 617 677	1 655 384	1 713 302
D.1+D.4	Employment, property and entrepreneurial income from the rest of the world (receipts *less* payments)	YBGG	13 525	2 161	1 772	17 056	18 500	−4 988	−12 662
-D.21+D.31	Subsidies (receipts) *less* taxes (payments) on products from/to the rest of the world	QZOZ	2 412	2 636	2 645	2 945	2 937	2 898	2 926
+D.29-D.39	Other subsidies on production from/to the rest of the world	IBJL	−2 952	−3 051	−3 411	−3 059	−3 166	−2 625	−2 455
B.5*g	Gross balance of primary incomes/Gross national income (GNI)	ABMX	1 495 025	1 521 251	1 484 682	1 575 535	1 636 409	1 650 124	1 700 170
D.5,6,7	Current transfers from the rest of the world (receipts *less* payments)	YBGF	13 996	14 112	15 826	20 696	21 937	22 195	27 162
B.6*g	**Gross national disposable income**	NQCO	1 481 029	1 507 139	1 468 856	1 554 839	1 614 472	1 627 929	1 673 008

Adjustment to current basic prices

			2007	2008	2009	2010	2011	2012	2013
B.1*g	**Gross domestic product (at current market prices)**	YBHA	1 480 956	1 518 675	1 482 144	1 558 365	1 617 677	1 655 384	1 713 302
D.21 D.31	Adjustment to current basic prices (*less* taxes *plus* subsidies on products)	NQBU	153 012	149 958	137 098	157 681	176 079	179 436	187 998
B.1g	**Gross value added (at current basic prices)**	ABML	1 327 944	1 368 717	1 345 046	1 400 684	1 441 598	1 475 948	1 525 304

Net measures (after deduction of Consumption of fixed capital) at current market prices

			2007	2008	2009	2010	2011	2012	2013
P.51c		NQAE	202 582	199 645	203 460	207 522	212 991	218 749	227 981
B.1*n	Net domestic product	NHRK	1 278 374	1 319 030	1 278 684	1 350 843	1 404 686	1 436 635	1 485 321
B.5*n	Net national income	NSRX	1 292 439	1 321 606	1 281 222	1 368 013	1 423 415	1 431 374	1 472 189
B.6*n	Net national disposable income	NQCP	1 278 443	1 307 494	1 265 396	1 347 317	1 401 478	1 409 179	1 445 027

CHAINED VOLUME MEASURES
(reference year 2011, £ million)

Gross measures (before deduction of Consumption of fixed capital) at market prices

			2007	2008	2009	2010	2011	2012	2013
B.1*g	**Gross domestic product**	ABMI	1 637 432	1 631 995	1 561 646	1 591 494	1 617 677	1 628 338	1 656 498
TGL	Terms of trade effect ("Trading gain or loss")	YBGJ	7 945	−6 545	506	5 653	−	2 045	4 970
GDI	Real gross domestic income	YBGL	1 645 377	1 625 450	1 562 152	1 597 147	1 617 677	1 630 383	1 661 468
D.1+D.4	Real employment, property and entrepreneurial income from the rest of the world (receipts *less* payments)	YBGI	15 072	2 315	1 869	17 493	18 500	−4 914	−12 281
-D.21+D.31	Subsidies (receipts) *less* taxes (payments) on products from/to the rest of the world	QZPB	2 689	2 825	2 790	3 021	2 937	2 855	2 838
+D.29-D.39	Other subsidies on production from/to the rest of the world	IBJN	−3 291	−3 270	−3 598	−3 137	−3 166	−2 586	−2 381
B.5*g	**Gross balance of primary incomes/Gross national income (GNI)**	YBGM	1 661 025	1 628 223	1 564 842	1 614 757	1 636 406	1 625 200	1 648 730
D.5,6,7	Real current transfers from the rest of the world (receipts *less* payments)	YBGP	15 601	15 126	16 695	21 226	21 937	21 866	26 347
B.6*g	**Gross national disposable income**	YBGO	1 645 418	1 613 091	1 548 143	1 593 530	1 614 469	1 603 334	1 622 383

Adjustment to basic prices

			2007	2008	2009	2010	2011	2012	2013
B.1*g	**Gross domestic product (at market prices)**	ABMI	1 637 432	1 631 995	1 561 646	1 591 494	1 617 677	1 628 338	1 656 498
D.21 D.31	Adjustment to basic prices (*less* taxes *plus* subsidies on products)	NTAQ	183 142	178 658	173 691	174 195	176 079	176 643	181 529
B.1g	**Gross value added (at basic prices)**	ABMM	1 454 928	1 453 645	1 388 546	1 417 380	1 441 598	1 451 695	1 474 969

Net measures (after deduction of Consumption of fixed capital) at market prices

			2007	2008	2009	2010	2011	2012	2013
P.51c		CIHA	227 263	213 629	208 822	212 191	212 991	215 746	219 258
B.5*n	Net national income at market prices	YBET	1 433 588	1 414 324	1 355 754	1 402 284	1 423 415	1 409 454	1 429 472
B.6*n	Net national disposable income at market prices	YBEY	1 417 997	1 399 207	1 339 072	1 381 057	1 401 478	1 387 588	1 403 125

Source: Office for National Statistics, Blue Book 2014

19.2 UK gross domestic product and national income
Current prices

£ million

		Code	2000	2001	2002	2003	2004	2005	2006
	GROSS DOMESTIC PRODUCT								
	Gross domestic product: production								
B.1g	Gross value added, at basic prices								
P.1	Output of goods and services	KN26	1 818 752	1 900 124	1 990 060	2 090 923	2 205 505	2 302 784	2 494 245
P.2	*less* intermediate consumption	KN25	907 639	951 931	991 047	1 024 649	1 082 268	1 113 612	1 235 161
B.1g	**Total gross value added**	ABML	911 113	948 193	999 013	1 066 274	1 123 237	1 189 172	1 259 084
D.211	Value added taxes (VAT) on products	QYRC	64 202	67 100	71 066	77 343	81 544	83 425	87 758
D.212,4	Other taxes on products	NSUI	54 127	52 940	54 271	54 977	58 446	59 376	63 102
D.31	*less* subsidies on products	NZHC	5 930	5 971	7 179	8 069	8 036	5 313	6 218
B.1*g	**Gross domestic product at market prices**	YBHA	1 023 512	1 062 262	1 117 171	1 190 525	1 255 191	1 326 660	1 403 726
	Gross domestic product: expenditure								
P.3	Final consumption expenditure								
P.41	Actual individual consumption								
P.3	Household final consumption expenditure	ABPB	636 745	662 037	693 295	730 090	771 312	812 501	850 835
P.3	Final consumption expenditure of NPISH[1]	ABNV	24 694	27 502	30 528	32 985	36 307	39 095	41 259
P.31	Individual govt. final consumption expenditure	NNAQ	103 088	111 183	123 461	136 319	148 425	159 891	172 495
P.41	Total actual individual consumption	NQEO	764 527	800 722	847 284	899 394	956 044	1 011 487	1 064 589
P.32	Collective govt. final consumption expenditure	NQEP	75 909	81 608	88 174	97 009	102 321	107 863	112 663
P.3	Total final consumption expenditure	ABKW	840 436	882 330	935 458	996 403	1 058 365	1 119 350	1 177 252
P.3	Households and NPISH	NSSG	661 439	689 539	723 823	763 075	807 619	851 596	892 094
P.3	Central government	NMBJ	107 688	115 862	127 673	140 115	149 639	158 790	170 538
P.3	Local government	NMMT	71 309	76 929	83 961	93 213	101 107	108 964	114 620
P.5	Gross capital formation								
P.51g	Gross fixed capital formation	NPQX	195 830	198 438	208 470	216 587	227 247	238 837	254 926
P.52	Changes in inventories	ABMP	7 074	6 298	4 017	5 634	4 299	3 547	5 311
P.53	Acquisitions *less* disposals of valuables	NPJO	310	94	−735	−865	666	−431	−544
P.5	Total gross capital formation	NQFM	203 214	204 830	211 752	221 356	232 212	241 953	259 693
P.6	Exports of goods and services	KTMW	269 290	277 813	280 684	293 760	305 768	341 690	390 394
P.7	*less* imports of goods and services	KTMX	289 428	302 711	310 723	320 994	341 154	376 333	423 613
B.11	External balance of goods and services	KTMY	−20 138	−24 898	−30 039	−27 234	−35 386	−34 643	−33 219
de	Statistical discrepancy between expenditure components and GDP	RVFD	–	–	–	–	–	–	–
B.1*g	**Gross domestic product at market prices**	YBHA	1 023 512	1 062 262	1 117 171	1 190 525	1 255 191	1 326 660	1 403 726
	Gross domestic product: income								
B.2g	Operating surplus, gross								
	Non-financial corporations								
	Public non-financial corporations	NRJT	8 039	8 209	7 746	8 587	7 925	9 722	10 698
	Private non-financial corporations	NRJK	200 412	194 023	209 336	224 574	234 797	245 920	259 257
	Financial corporations	NQNV	12 541	13 450	18 362	26 599	32 447	44 348	42 092
	General government	NMXV	13 249	13 728	14 487	15 810	16 260	17 222	18 251
	Households and NPISH	QWLS	60 683	63 950	67 360	71 869	78 065	82 325	87 628
B.2g	Total operating surplus, gross	ABNF	294 924	293 359	317 291	347 439	369 494	399 537	417 927
B.3	Mixed income	QWLT	64 573	68 779	74 286	81 289	81 674	88 116	93 645
D.1	Compensation of employees	HAEA	535 352	569 907	590 527	620 975	655 379	687 776	733 152
D.2	Taxes on production and imports	NZGX	135 503	137 443	143 666	150 754	158 749	162 401	171 534
D.3	*less* subsidies	AAXJ	6 840	7 226	8 599	9 932	10 105	11 170	12 532
di	Statistical discrepancy between income components and GDP	RVFC	–	–	–	–	–	–	–
B.1*g	**Gross domestic product at market prices**	YBHA	1 023 512	1 062 262	1 117 171	1 190 525	1 255 191	1 326 660	1 403 726
	GROSS NATIONAL INCOME at market prices								
B.1*g	**Gross domestic product at market prices**	YBHA	1 023 512	1 062 262	1 117 171	1 190 525	1 255 191	1 326 660	1 403 726
D.1	Compensation of employees								
	receipts from the rest of the world	KTMN	1 034	1 089	1 123	1 118	934	977	942
	less payments to the rest of the world	KTMO	884	1 023	1 056	1 059	1 427	1 586	1 898
D.1	Total	KTMP	150	66	67	59	−493	−609	−956
	Subsidies (receipts) *less* taxes (payments) on								
-D.21+D.31	products from/to the rest of the world	QZOZ	−106	3	−449	−680	−687	2 261	2 329
+D.29-D.39	Other subsidies on production from/to the rest of the world	IBJL	−335	−582	−519	−592	−592	−3 408	−3 221
D.4	Property and entrepreneurial income								
	from the rest of the world	HMBN	134 317	139 686	124 002	124 710	140 745	192 849	249 122
	(receipts *less* payments)	HMBO	129 036	130 635	107 792	107 162	119 836	162 699	234 556
D.4	Total	HMBM	5 281	9 051	16 210	17 548	20 909	30 150	14 566
B.5*g	**Gross balance of primary incomes/Gross national income (GNI)**	ABMX	1 029 380	1 071 959	1 134 416	1 209 404	1 276 887	1 357 351	1 418 225

1 Non-profit institutions serving households

19.2 UK gross domestic product and national income
Current prices
continued

£ million

			2007	2008	2009	2010	2011	2012	2013
	GROSS DOMESTIC PRODUCT								
	Gross domestic product: production								
B.1g	Gross value added, at basic prices								
P.1	Output of goods and services[2]	KN26	2 654 898	2 727 947	2 685 754	2 777 408	2 865 888	2 928 137	..
P.2	*less* intermediate consumption[2]	KN25	1 326 954	1 359 230	1 340 708	1 376 724	1 424 290	1 452 189	..
B.1g	**Total gross value added**	ABML	1 327 944	1 368 717	1 345 046	1 400 684	1 441 598	1 475 948	1 525 304
D.211	Value added taxes (VAT) on products	QYRC	92 025	92 002	79 900	95 865	111 437	113 892	118 296
D.212,4	Other taxes on products	NSUI	66 911	63 638	63 683	68 753	70 937	72 746	76 439
D.31	*less* subsidies on products	NZHC	5 924	5 682	6 485	6 937	6 295	7 202	6 737
B.1*g	**Gross domestic product at market prices**	YBHA	1 480 956	1 518 675	1 482 144	1 558 365	1 617 677	1 655 384	1 713 302
	Gross domestic product: expenditure								
P.3	Final consumption expenditure								
P.41	Actual individual consumption								
P.3	Household final consumption expenditure	ABPB	897 836	926 562	908 137	953 264	985 843	1 022 159	1 059 073
P.3	Final consumption expenditure of NPISH[1]	ABNV	43 718	46 893	50 205	50 885	53 259	50 386	51 734
P.31	Individual govt. final consumption expenditure	NNAQ	181 190	193 838	206 294	211 682	213 300	216 111	216 828
P.41	Total actual individual consumption	NQEO	1 122 744	1 167 293	1 164 636	1 215 831	1 252 402	1 288 656	1 327 635
P.32	Collective govt. final consumption expenditure	NQEP	115 456	122 087	123 772	124 899	123 994	127 767	129 946
P.3	Total final consumption expenditure	ABKW	1 238 200	1 289 380	1 288 408	1 340 731	1 376 396	1 416 423	1 457 581
P.3	Households and NPISH	NSSG	941 554	973 455	958 342	1 004 149	1 039 102	1 072 545	1 110 807
P.3	Central government	NMBJ	176 412	189 253	198 084	202 681	207 912	218 216	221 013
P.3	Local government	NMMT	120 233	126 672	131 982	133 901	129 382	125 662	125 761
P.5	Gross capital formation								
P.51g	Gross fixed capital formation	NPQX	273 750	272 516	239 078	250 198	260 779	268 823	281 519
P.52	Changes in inventories	ABMP	7 538	535	−16 039	4 285	2 751	1 767	8 826
P.53	Acquisitions *less* disposals of valuables	NPJO	2 162	1 145	−1 188	209	1 576	2 840	1 372
P.5	Total gross capital formation	NQFM	283 450	274 196	221 851	254 692	265 106	273 430	291 717
P.6	Exports of goods and services	KTMW	379 768	420 900	400 260	447 057	499 452	500 735	511 275
P.7	*less* imports of goods and services	KTMX	420 462	465 801	428 375	484 115	523 277	535 204	543 375
B.11	External balance of goods and services	KTMY	−40 694	−44 901	−28 115	−37 058	−23 825	−34 469	−32 100
de	Statistical discrepancy between expenditure components and GDP	RVFD	–	–	–	–	–	–	−3 896
B.1*g	**Gross domestic product at market prices**	YBHA	1 480 956	1 518 675	1 482 144	1 558 365	1 617 677	1 655 384	1 713 302
	Gross domestic product: income								
B.2g	Operating surplus, gross								
	Non-financial corporations								
	Public non-financial corporations	NRJT	11 317	10 742	9 682	9 589	9 309	10 061	10 471
	Private non-financial corporations	NRJK	265 598	280 887	256 407	273 005	292 086	291 378	302 742
	Financial corporations	NQNV	51 078	46 155	61 356	49 389	54 256	56 150	58 811
	General government	NMXV	18 911	20 152	21 081	22 208	23 525	24 630	25 872
	Households and NPISH	QWLS	96 155	107 667	93 875	110 945	118 022	125 773	125 455
B.2g	Total operating surplus, gross	ABNF	443 059	465 603	442 401	465 137	497 198	507 992	523 351
B.3	Mixed income	QWLT	92 417	94 690	93 620	96 603	96 574	96 644	98 848
D.1	Compensation of employees	HAEA	777 590	792 428	791 986	816 958	827 828	849 423	877 883
D.2	Taxes on production and imports	NZGX	180 399	178 622	167 751	192 552	207 846	213 877	222 991
D.3	*less* subsidies	AAXJ	12 509	12 668	13 614	12 885	11 769	12 552	12 275
di	Statistical discrepancy between income components and GDP	RVFC	–	–	–	–	–	–	2 504
B.1*g	**Gross domestic product at market prices**	YBHA	1 480 956	1 518 675	1 482 144	1 558 365	1 617 677	1 655 384	1 713 302
	GROSS NATIONAL INCOME at market prices								
B.1*g	**Gross domestic product at market prices**	YBHA	1 480 956	1 518 675	1 482 144	1 558 365	1 617 677	1 655 384	1 713 302
D.1	Compensation of employees								
	receipts from the rest of the world	KTMN	987	1 050	1 179	1 100	1 124	1 127	1 097
	less payments to the rest of the world	KTMO	1 720	1 763	1 437	1 488	1 295	1 274	1 422
D.1	Total	KTMP	−733	−713	−258	−388	−171	−147	−325
	Subsidies (receipts) *less* taxes (payments) on								
-D.21+D.31	products from/to the rest of the world	QZOZ	2 412	2 636	2 645	2 945	2 937	2 898	2 926
+D.29-D.39	Other subsidies on production from/to the rest of the world	IBJL	−2 952	−3 051	−3 411	−3 059	−3 166	−2 625	−2 455
D.4	Property and entrepreneurial income								
	from the rest of the world	HMBN	307 686	287 572	174 559	173 484	199 905	168 708	158 204
	(receipts *less* payments)	HMBO	293 428	284 698	172 529	156 040	181 234	173 549	170 541
D.4	Total	HMBM	14 258	2 874	2 030	17 444	18 671	−4 841	−12 337
B.5*g	**Gross balance of primary incomes/Gross national income (GNI)**	ABMX	1 495 025	1 521 251	1 484 682	1 575 535	1 636 409	1 650 124	1 700 170

1 Non-profit institutions serving households
2 These series are not available for the latest year

Source: Office for National Statistics, Blue Book 2014

19.3 UK gross domestic product
Chained volume measures (reference year 2011)

£ million

			2000	2001	2002	2003	2004	2005	2006
	GROSS DOMESTIC PRODUCT								
	Gross domestic product: expenditure approach								
P.3	Final consumption expenditure								
P.41	Actual individual consumption								
P.3	Household final consumption expenditure	ABPF	812 921	842 907	876 541	911 950	944 478	973 087	994 192
P.3	Final consumption expenditure of non-profit institutions serving households	ABNU	42 567	44 984	46 869	47 726	49 811	50 656	50 769
P.31	Individual government final consumption expenditure	NSZK	163 857	170 156	175 652	181 784	187 154	192 165	196 111
P.41	Total actual individual consumption	YBIO	1 018 408	1 056 841	1 097 969	1 140 572	1 180 533	1 215 053	1 240 273
P.32	Collective government final consumption expenditure	NSZL	101 815	106 023	111 994	118 785	121 790	123 931	126 947
P.3	Total final consumption expenditure	ABKX	1 120 281	1 162 921	1 210 051	1 259 493	1 302 425	1 339 042	1 367 298
P.5	Gross capital formation								
P.51g	Gross fixed capital formation	NPQR	248 115	244 769	250 837	258 536	266 891	271 284	280 162
P.52	Changes in inventories	ABMQ	1 243	9 684	2 749	4 094	−44	−2 760	1 793
P.53	Acquisitions *less* disposals of valuables	NPJP	−158	55	−187	920	698	1 482	764
P.5	Total gross capital formation	NPQU	243 215	247 555	246 357	259 259	264 097	266 505	279 498
	Gross domestic final expenditure	YBIK	1 366 636	1 413 273	1 458 469	1 521 162	1 568 747	1 607 490	1 649 311
P.6	Exports of goods and services	KTMZ	354 691	361 882	371 707	382 108	400 284	434 031	487 663
	Gross final expenditure	ABME	1 724 403	1 778 350	1 833 473	1 906 877	1 972 564	2 043 802	2 136 977
P.7	*less* imports of goods and services	KTNB	380 660	398 814	420 235	432 574	463 372	493 829	542 748
de	Statistical discrepancy between expenditure components and GDP	GIXS	–	–	–	–	–	–	–
B.1*g	**Gross domestic product at market prices**	ABMI	**1 340 947**	**1 376 677**	**1 410 437**	**1 471 091**	**1 507 191**	**1 549 491**	**1 596 628**
B.11	*of which* External balance of goods and services	KTNC	−25 969	−36 932	−48 528	−50 466	−63 088	−59 798	−55 085

Source: Office for National Statistics, Blue Book 2014

continued

£ million

			2007	2008	2009	2010	2011	2012	2013
	GROSS DOMESTIC PRODUCT								
	Gross domestic product: expenditure approach								
P.3	Final consumption expenditure								
P.41	Actual individual consumption								
P.3	Household final consumption expenditure	ABPF	1 021 686	1 016 524	982 490	986 956	985 843	1 000 859	1 017 251
P.3	Final consumption expenditure of non-profit institutions serving households	ABNU	50 739	50 869	52 081	51 337	53 259	49 936	50 651
P.31	Individual government final consumption expenditure	NSZK	198 818	203 338	208 170	210 422	213 300	217 941	219 972
P.41	Total actual individual consumption	YBIO	1 270 427	1 270 082	1 242 557	1 248 578	1 252 402	1 268 736	1 287 874
P.32	Collective government final consumption expenditure	NSZL	128 055	130 073	129 105	126 877	123 994	127 219	127 736
P.3	Total final consumption expenditure	ABKX	1 398 501	1 400 211	1 371 752	1 375 487	1 376 396	1 395 955	1 415 610
P.5	Gross capital formation								
P.51g	Gross fixed capital formation	NPQR	294 888	281 041	240 605	254 861	260 779	262 697	271 018
P.52	Changes in inventories	ABMQ	49	−8 616	−17 629	5 482	2 751	3 597	9 020
P.53	Acquisitions *less* disposals of valuables	NPJP	−1 818	−2 379	1 664	236	1 576	2 885	1 632
P.5	Total gross capital formation	NPQU	294 441	273 296	223 206	260 658	265 106	269 179	281 670
	Gross domestic final expenditure	YBIK	1 696 083	1 675 081	1 593 167	1 636 136	1 641 502	1 665 134	1 697 280
P.6	Exports of goods and services	KTMZ	477 211	484 990	445 090	472 829	499 452	502 793	505 498
	Gross final expenditure	ABME	2 174 848	2 160 376	2 039 442	2 109 552	2 140 954	2 167 927	2 202 778
P.7	*less* imports of goods and services	KTNB	538 275	528 370	476 614	518 175	523 277	539 589	542 516
de	Statistical discrepancy between expenditure components and GDP	GIXS	–	–	–	–	–	–	−3 763
B.1*g	**Gross domestic product at market prices**	ABMI	**1 637 432**	**1 631 995**	**1 561 646**	**1 591 494**	**1 617 677**	**1 628 338**	**1 656 498**
B.11	*of which* External balance of goods and services	KTNC	−61 064	−43 380	−31 524	−45 346	−23 825	−36 796	−37 018

Source: Office for National Statistics, Blue Book 2014

19.4 Output and capital formation: by industry[1,2]
Gross value added at current basic prices

£ million

			2005	2006	2007	2008	2009	2010	2011	2012
	Agriculture									
	Output									
D.1	Compensation of employees	KLR2	3 339	3 432	3 962	3 994	4 146	4 248	4 744	4 690
D.29-D.39	Taxes *less* subsidies on production other than those on products	KLR3	−3 219	−3 049	−2 845	−2 675	−3 512	−2 606	−2 552	−2 173
B.2g+B.3g	Operating surplus and mixed income, gross	KLR4	7 282	7 157	7 117	7 764	6 871	7 840	7 032	7 480
B.1g	Gross value added at basic prices	KLR5	7 402	7 540	8 234	9 083	7 505	9 482	9 224	9 997
P.2	Intermediate consumption at purchasers' prices	KLR6	10 987	11 470	13 194	13 723	15 550	14 861	16 115	15 813
P.1	Total output at basic prices	KLR7	18 389	19 010	21 428	22 806	23 055	24 343	25 339	25 810
P.5	Gross capital formation	KLR8	4 294	4 359	5 714	5 901	6 164	5 755	5 904	6 926
	Production									
	Output									
D.1	Compensation of employees	KLR9	110 385	116 696	118 735	119 577	115 376	118 671	121 723	126 438
D.29-D.39	Taxes *less* subsidies on production other than those on products	KLS4	3 758	3 971	3 850	4 190	4 238	4 204	4 254	4 375
B.2g+B.3g	Operating surplus and mixed income, gross	KLS3	79 322	83 082	82 273	88 937	81 243	82 704	84 876	82 393
B.1g	Gross value added at basic prices	KLS5	193 465	203 749	204 858	212 704	200 857	205 579	210 853	213 206
P.2	Intermediate consumption at purchasers' prices	KLS6	321 573	349 198	363 878	379 629	358 960	388 219	423 844	433 468
P.1	Total output at basic prices	KLS7	515 038	552 947	568 736	592 333	559 817	593 798	634 697	646 674
P.5	Gross capital formation	KLS8	48 899	37 540	40 289	42 394	33 335	36 748	47 539	54 690
	Construction									
	Output									
D.1	Compensation of employees	KLS9	37 212	40 993	46 678	45 824	44 292	44 922	45 543	46 871
D.29-D.39	Taxes *less* subsidies on production other than those on products	KLT3	672	750	819	924	968	1 015	926	1 137
B.2g+B.g	Operating surplus and mixed income, gross	KLT2	42 670	44 294	43 571	43 217	35 560	37 671	45 048	40 708
B.1g	Gross value added at basic prices	KLT4	80 554	86 037	91 068	89 965	80 820	83 608	91 517	88 716
P.2	Intermediate consumption at purchasers' prices	KLT5	111 243	119 415	134 456	135 736	116 656	117 775	119 182	119 411
P.1	Total output at basic prices	KLT6	191 797	205 452	225 524	225 701	197 476	201 383	210 699	208 127
P.5	Gross capital formation	KLT7	5 962	5 628	7 795	4 235	−4 478	1 592	3 089	3 280

1 The contribution of each industry to the gross domestic product before providing for consumption of fixed capital. The industrial composition in this table is consistent with the Supply-Use Tables in Table 2.1, which show data from 2009-2012.
2 Components may not sum to totals due to rounding.

Source: Office for National Statistics, Blue Book 2014

19.4

Output and capital formation: by industry[1,2]
Gross value added at current basic prices

continued

£ million

			2005	2006	2007	2008	2009	2010	2011	2012
	Distribution, transport, hotels & restaurants									
	Output									
D.1	Compensation of employees	KLT8	144 451	152 022	160 627	167 070	164 146	167 529	169 422	176 072
D.29-D.39	Taxes *less* subsidies on production other than those on products	KLU2	8 848	8 881	8 806	9 810	10 907	11 001	11 781	12 027
B.2g+B.3g	Operating surplus and mixed income, gross	KLT9	76 159	76 426	80 012	76 322	72 242	79 115	80 300	79 363
B.1g	Gross value added at basic prices	KLU3	229 458	237 329	249 445	253 202	247 295	257 645	261 503	267 462
P.2	Intermediate consumption at purchasers' prices	KLU4	214 519	229 095	241 684	248 813	243 112	245 967	250 631	262 742
P.1	Total output at basic prices	KLU5	443 977	466 424	491 129	502 015	490 407	503 612	512 134	530 204
P.5	Gross capital formation	KLU6	32 342	35 556	38 494	40 424	31 829	44 216	38 394	36 580
	Information and communication									
	Output									
D.1	Compensation of employees	KLU7	47 709	47 768	51 408	52 915	50 000	51 345	54 170	57 040
D.29-D.39	Taxes *less* subsidies on production other than those on products	KLU9	1 118	1 204	1 264	1 195	1 129	1 177	1 189	1 112
B.2g+B.3g	Operating surplus and mixed income, gross	KLU8	29 945	31 918	32 344	34 113	32 307	33 913	33 999	34 062
B.1g	Gross value added at basic prices	KLV2	78 772	80 890	85 016	88 223	83 436	86 435	89 358	92 214
P.2	Intermediate consumption at purchasers' prices	KLV3	57 188	61 663	64 060	64 368	63 973	68 763	69 718	68 418
P.1	Total output at basic prices	KLV4	135 960	142 553	149 076	152 591	147 409	155 198	159 076	160 632
P.5	Gross capital formation	KLV5	18 622	20 069	19 344	19 884	18 043	17 319	17 607	16 826
	Financial and insurance									
	Output									
D.1	Compensation of employees	KLV6	48 281	59 115	65 679	58 944	61 197	63 941	61 445	59 698
D.29-D.39	Taxes *less* subsidies on production other than those on products	KLV8	1 471	1 566	1 667	1 803	1 790	5 475	1 870	2 701
B.2g+B.3g	Operating surplus and mixed income, gross	KLV7	45 704	43 536	52 394	47 658	62 708	50 615	55 425	57 362
B.1g	Gross value added at basic prices	KLV9	95 456	104 217	119 740	108 405	125 695	120 031	118 740	119 761
P.2	Intermediate consumption at purchasers' prices	KLW2	84 258	118 704	141 458	133 792	122 284	117 085	119 635	124 265
P.1	Total output at basic prices	KLW3	179 714	222 921	261 198	242 197	247 979	237 116	238 375	244 026
P.5	Gross capital formation	KLW4	7 628	6 629	7 499	8 202	6 451	8 313	8 024	9 627

1 The contribution of each industry to the gross domestic product before providing for consumption of fixed capital. The industrial composition in this table is consistent with the Supply-Use Tables in Table 2.1, which show data from 2009-2012.

2 Components may not sum to totals due to rounding.

Source: Office for National Statistics, Blue Book 2014

19.4

Output and capital formation: by industry[1,2]
Gross value added at current basic prices

continued

£ million

			2005	2006	2007	2008	2009	2010	2011	2012
	Real estate									
	Output									
D.1	Compensation of employees	KLW5	7 807	8 574	9 334	9 955	9 025	9 547	9 677	11 082
D.29-D.39	Taxes *less* subsidies on production other than those on products	KLW7	−799	−1 250	−1 052	−1 752	−1 088	−861	−386	−401
B.2g+B.3g	Operating surplus and mixed income, gross	KLW6	96 720	103 384	111 556	128 223	115 694	137 446	146 122	156 604
B.1g	Gross value added at basic prices	KLW8	103 728	110 708	119 838	136 426	123 631	146 132	155 413	167 285
P.2	Intermediate consumption at purchasers' prices	KLW9	35 960	39 673	42 513	34 485	61 547	65 504	62 176	60 116
P.1	Total output at basic prices	KLX2	139 688	150 381	162 351	170 911	185 178	211 636	217 589	227 401
P.5	Gross capital formation	KLX3	4 176	4 154	5 383	5 939	4 047	2 831	2 518	2 546
	Professional and support									
	Output									
D.1	Compensation of employees	KLX4	81 597	86 383	93 610	96 426	95 713	96 212	97 748	102 858
D.29-D.39	Taxes *less* subsidies on production other than those on products	KLX6	923	1 181	1 325	1 325	1 225	1 250	1 617	1 578
B.2g+B.3g	Operating surplus and mixed income, gross	KLX5	50 200	58 814	60 271	63 937	59 680	63 141	68 928	71 341
B.1g	Gross value added at basic prices	KLX7	132 720	146 378	155 206	161 688	156 618	160 603	168 293	175 777
P.2	Intermediate consumption at purchasers' prices	KLX8	94 247	104 187	113 661	122 092	117 131	119 445	124 381	127 455
P.1	Total output at basic prices	KLX9	226 967	250 565	268 867	283 780	273 749	280 048	292 674	303 232
P.5	Gross capital formation	KLY2	15 901	16 958	19 137	16 575	13 886	16 451	20 186	20 109
	Government, health and education									
	Output									
D.1	Compensation of employees	KLY3	183 644	193 671	201 505	210 507	220 430	228 223	230 701	231 416
D.29-D.39	Taxes *less* subsidies on production other than those on products	KLY5	298	344	340	408	375	456	436	509
B.2g+B.3g	Operating surplus and mixed income, gross	KLY4	37 617	40 667	43 138	45 830	46 606	46 146	48 069	49 952
B.1g	Gross value added at basic prices	KLY6	221 559	234 682	244 983	256 745	267 411	274 825	279 206	281 877
P.2	Intermediate consumption at purchasers' prices	KLY7	154 399	169 415	178 920	190 622	206 309	206 477	205 551	208 117
P.1	Total output at basic prices	KLY8	375 958	404 097	423 903	447 367	473 720	481 302	484 757	489 994
P.5	Gross capital formation	KLY9	18 668	36 909	39 197	47 424	48 806	48 549	45 527	45 125

1 The contribution of each industry to the gross domestic product before providing for consumption of fixed capital. The industrial composition in this table is consistent with the Supply-Use Tables in Table 2.1, which show data from 2009-2012.
2 Components may not sum to totals due to rounding.

Source: Office for National Statistics, Blue Book 2014

19.4 Output and capital formation: by industry[1,2]
Gross value added at current basic prices

continued

£ million

			2005	2006	2007	2008	2009	2010	2011	2012
	Other services									
	Output									
D.1	Compensation of employees	KLZ2	23 351	24 498	26 052	27 216	27 661	32 320	32 655	33 258
D.29-D.39	Taxes *less* subsidies on production other than those on products	KLZ4	673	762	704	768	1 007	875	863	1 024
B.2g+B.3g	Operating surplus and mixed income, gross	KLZ3	22 034	22 294	22 800	24 292	23 110	23 149	23 973	25 371
B.1g	Gross value added at basic prices	KLZ5	46 058	47 554	49 556	52 276	51 778	56 344	57 491	59 653
P.2	Intermediate consumption at purchasers' prices	KLZ6	29 238	32 341	33 130	35 970	35 186	32 628	33 057	32 384
P.1	Total output at basic prices	KLZ7	75 296	79 895	82 686	88 246	86 964	88 972	90 548	92 037
P.5	Gross capital formation	KLZ8	5 549	5 609	6 094	6 354	6 303	5 532	5 515	5 388
	Not allocated to industries									
P.5	Gross capital formation[3]	KN28	79 912	86 282	94 504	76 864	57 465	67 386	70 803	72 333
	All industries									
	Output									
D.1	Compensation of employees	HAEA	687 776	733 152	777 590	792 428	791 986	816 958	827 828	849 423
D.29-D.39	Taxes *less* subsidies on production other than those on products	KN22	13 743	14 360	14 878	15 996	17 039	21 986	19 998	21 889
B.2g	Operating surplus, gross	ABNF	399 537	417 927	443 059	465 603	442 401	465 137	497 198	507 992
B.3g	Mixed income, gross	QWLT	88 116	93 645	92 417	94 690	93 620	96 603	96 574	96 644
di	Statistical discrepancy between income and GDP	RVFC	–	–	–	–	–	–	–	–
B.1g	Gross value added at basic prices	ABML	1 189 172	1 259 084	1 327 944	1 368 717	1 345 046	1 400 684	1 441 598	1 475 948
P.2	Intermediate consumption at purchasers' prices	KN25	1 113 612	1 235 161	1 326 954	1 359 230	1 340 708	1 376 724	1 424 290	1 452 189
P.1	Total output at basic prices	KN26	2 302 784	2 494 245	2 654 898	2 727 947	2 685 754	2 777 408	2 865 888	2 928 137
	Gross capital formation									
P.51g	Gross fixed capital formation	NPQX	238 837	254 926	273 750	272 516	239 078	250 198	260 779	268 823
P.52	Changes in inventories	ABMP	3 547	5 311	7 538	535	–16 039	4 285	2 751	1 767
P.53	Acquisitions less disposals of valuables	NPJO	–431	–544	2 162	1 145	–1 188	209	1 576	2 840
P.5	Total gross capital formation	NQFM	241 953	259 693	283 450	274 196	221 851	254 692	265 106	273 430

1 The contribution of each industry to the gross domestic product before providing for consumption of fixed capital. The industrial composition in this table is consistent with the Supply-Use Tables in Table 2.1, which show data from 2009-2012.
2 Components may not sum to totals due to rounding.
3 GFCF of dwellings and costs associated with the transfer of non-produced as and acquisitions less disposals of valuables.

Source: Office for National Statistics, Blue Book 2014

19.5 Gross value added at basic prices: by industry[1,2,3]
Chained volume indices

Indices 2011=100

		Weight per 1000[1]		2005	2006	2007	2008	2009	2010	2011	2012	2013
		2011										
A	**Agriculture**	6.4	L2KL	95.7	92.8	89.5	98.9	92.3	92.2	100.0	95.4	91.5
B-F	**Production and Construction**											
B-E	Production											
B	Mining and quarrying	22.9	L2KR	154.6	145.7	141.2	133.2	121.1	116.5	100.0	89.2	87.0
C	Manufacturing											
CA	Food products, beverages and tobacco	14.8	KN3D	96.1	95.2	95.0	92.1	90.8	94.5	100.0	98.1	96.1
CB	Textiles, wearing apparel and leather products	3.3	KN3E	106.6	106.9	105.1	105.4	95.9	98.9	100.0	96.6	92.1
CC	Wood, paper products and printing	7.2	KN3F	119.8	118.3	117.8	113.2	105.1	105.9	100.0	94.8	96.9
CD	Coke and refined petroleum products	2.0	KN3G	117.0	110.9	110.0	106.3	100.2	98.7	100.0	89.9	88.2
CE	Chemicals and chemical products	5.8	KN3H	105.6	107.3	109.1	108.6	94.6	93.5	100.0	96.8	96.5
CF	Basic pharmaceutical products and preparations	8.7	KN3I	113.1	119.8	114.8	117.0	124.3	115.7	100.0	94.1	92.3
CG	Rubber, plastic and other non-metallic mineral products	7.7	KN3J	117.9	122.7	121.9	116.0	100.1	100.2	100.0	95.8	93.0
CH	Basic metals and metal products	10.8	KN3K	113.9	116.7	119.1	113.9	91.9	97.6	100.0	101.8	102.0
CI	Computer, electronic and optical products	6.5	KN3L	117.3	118.0	117.9	110.4	105.8	101.2	100.0	100.6	100.2
CJ	Electrical equipment	2.9	KN3M	115.1	120.4	122.8	120.1	93.3	104.0	100.0	110.9	105.9
CK	Machinery and equipment n. e. c.	7.9	KN3N	90.0	94.8	97.4	96.8	77.0	92.1	100.0	101.1	89.4
CL	Transport equipment	15.0	KN3O	81.0	85.4	87.9	85.1	74.2	90.7	100.0	104.0	112.7
CM	Other manufacturing and repair	8.9	KN3P	94.6	97.1	99.2	95.8	91.2	95.0	100.0	93.7	98.1
C	Total manufacturing	101.4	L2KX	103.5	105.8	106.6	103.5	93.8	98.2	100.0	98.7	98.6
D	Electricity, gas, steam and air conditioning supply	10.4	L2MW	102.8	102.2	103.1	105.0	102.5	106.6	100.0	99.2	99.4
E	Water supply, sewerage, waste mgmt and remediation	11.5	L2N2	101.7	100.0	103.5	103.5	95.2	95.0	100.0	99.1	102.4
B - E	Total production	146.3	L2KQ	109.1	109.8	110.2	107.2	97.8	100.8	100.0	97.3	97.2
F	Construction	63.5	L2N8	103.6	104.4	106.7	103.9	90.2	97.9	100.0	92.5	93.9
B - F	Total production and construction	209.7	L2KP	107.4	108.2	109.1	106.2	95.5	100.0	100.0	95.8	96.2

1 The weights shown are in proportion to total gross value added (GVA) in 2011 and are used to combine the industry output indices to calculate the totals. For 2010 and earlier, totals are calculated using the equivalent weights for the previous year (e.g. totals for 2009 use 2008 weights). Weights may not sum to totals due to rounding.

2 As GVA is expressed in index number form, it is inappropriate to show as a statistical adjustment any divergence from the other measures of GDP. Such an adjustment does, however, exist implicitly.

3 Because of differences in the annual and monthly production inquiries, estimates of current price output and gross value added by industry derived from the current price Input-Output Supply and Use Tables are not consistent with the equivalent measures of chained volume measures growth given in 19.5. These differences do not affect GDP totals.

Source: Office for National Statistics, Blue Book 2014

19.5 Gross value added at basic prices: by industry[1,2,3]
Chained volume indices

continued

Indices 2011=100

		Weight per 1000[1]										
		2011		2005	2006	2007	2008	2009	2010	2011	2012	2013
G-T	**Services**											
G-I	Distribution, transport, hotels and restaurants											
G	Wholesale, retail, repair of motor vehicles and m/cycles	110.8	L2NE	97.9	101.4	105.6	102.7	97.0	98.3	100.0	100.9	106.2
H	Transportation and storage	42.0	L2NI	112.2	112.9	113.8	111.6	100.4	99.2	100.0	99.4	100.3
I	Accommodation and food service activities	28.5	L2NQ	94.3	99.0	101.4	99.8	94.6	97.2	100.0	104.0	101.2
G - I	Total distribution, transport, hotels and restaurants	181.4	L2ND	100.5	103.6	106.8	104.3	97.4	98.3	100.0	101.0	104.0
J	Information and communication											
JA	Publishing, audiovisual and broadcasting activities	16.4	L2NU	97.7	99.7	103.3	101.8	94.4	96.8	100.0	103.4	107.7
JB	Telecommunications	17.5	L2NZ	76.1	78.0	84.1	87.9	90.5	95.7	100.0	100.4	97.4
JC	IT and other information service activities	28.0	L2O3	83.9	87.7	94.3	96.3	90.0	99.2	100.0	103.9	107.2
J	Total information and communication	62.0	L2NT	84.8	87.5	93.2	95.0	91.3	97.6	100.0	102.8	104.5
K	Financial and insurance	82.4	L2O6	92.5	100.7	104.9	107.7	107.3	100.4	100.0	99.7	97.1
L	Real estate	107.7	L2OC	87.1	89.7	91.1	92.6	95.4	97.5	100.0	103.1	104.9
M-N	Professional and support											
M	Professional, scientific and technical activities											
MA	Legal, accounting, mgmt, architect, engineering etc	52.7	L2OJ	81.0	89.5	101.0	103.0	95.0	95.5	100.0	103.1	111.1
MB	Scientific research and development	6.8	L2OQ	91.1	98.3	101.0	99.3	94.8	106.2	100.0	102.4	108.8
MC	Other professional, scientific and technical activities	13.0	L2OS	91.8	90.2	91.5	89.9	80.0	85.8	100.0	106.2	107.1
M	Total professional, scientific and technical activities	72.5	L2OI	83.5	90.2	99.0	99.9	91.9	94.4	100.0	103.6	110.2
N	Administrative and support service activities	44.3	L2OX	82.6	87.3	95.3	95.5	83.3	93.4	100.0	108.1	114.2
M - N	Total professional and support	116.7	L2OH	83.0	88.9	97.3	98.0	88.3	94.0	100.0	105.3	111.7
O-Q	Government, health and education											
O	Public admin, defence, compulsory social security	54.7	L2P8	103.9	103.9	102.4	103.9	105.1	104.2	100.0	98.4	96.5
P	Education	68.0	L2PA	104.1	103.0	100.8	100.4	100.0	99.2	100.0	102.9	103.4
Q	Human health and social work activities											
QA	Human health activities	53.5	L2PD	81.6	84.5	86.4	89.7	94.3	96.9	100.0	103.6	105.7
QB	Residential care and social work activities	17.5	L2PF	94.2	96.2	96.1	92.6	91.7	97.8	100.0	101.3	102.8
Q	Total human health and social work activities	70.9	L2PC	84.6	87.4	88.7	90.4	93.6	97.2	100.0	103.0	104.9
O - Q	Total government, health and education	193.7	L2P7	96.3	97.1	96.5	97.5	98.9	99.8	100.0	101.7	102.0
R-T	Other services											
R	Arts, entertainment and recreation	14.6	L2PJ	104.3	105.5	105.5	108.1	98.8	96.7	100.0	104.5	107.5
S	Other service activities	21.2	L2PP	89.3	96.8	90.5	93.5	96.1	93.4	100.0	95.9	94.3
T	Activities of households as employers, undiff. goods	4.1	L2PT	105.7	103.3	99.8	103.9	94.4	105.6	100.0	105.0	107.9
R - T	Total other services	39.9	L2PI	96.2	100.4	96.7	99.7	96.7	95.7	100.0	99.9	100.5
G - T	Total service industries	783.9	L2NC	92.4	95.9	98.9	99.4	96.6	98.0	100.0	102.0	103.9
B.1g	**All industries**	1 000.0	CGCE	95.5	98.4	100.9	100.8	96.3	98.3	100.0	100.7	102.3

1 The weights shown are in proportion to total gross value added (GVA) in 2011 and are used to combine the industry output indices to calculate the totals. For 2010 and earlier, totals are calculated using the equivalent weights for the previous year (e.g. totals for 2009 use 2008 weights). Weights may not sum to totals due to rounding.

2 As GVA is expressed in index number form, it is inappropriate to show as a statistical adjustment any divergence from the other measures of GDP. Such an adjustment does, however, exist implicitly.

3 Because of differences in the annual and monthly production inquiries, estimates of current price output and gross value added by industry derived from the current price Input-Output Supply and Use Tables are not consistent with the equivalent measures of chained volume measures growth given in 19.5. These differences do not affect GDP totals.

Source: Office for National Statistics, Blue Book 2014

19.6 Non-financial corporations
ESA 2010 sector S.11

£ million

			2005	2006	2007	2008	2009	2010	2011	2012	2013
II.1.2	**ALLOCATION OF PRIMARY INCOME ACCOUNT**										
	Resources										
B.2g	Operating surplus, gross	NQBE	255 642	269 955	276 915	291 629	266 089	282 594	301 395	301 439	313 213
D.4	Property income, received										
D.41g	Interest before FISIM allocation	J4WQ	17 217	23 639	26 480	26 005	9 111	8 989	9 143	8 633	11 097
P.119	*plus* FISIM	IV89	3 212	4 131	3 728	5 769	3 305	2 664	3 749	3 584	3 108
D.41	Interest	EABC	20 429	27 770	30 208	31 774	12 416	11 653	12 892	12 217	14 205
D.42	Distributed income of corporations	EABD	46 724	43 927	38 964	47 124	62 614	57 887	68 097	65 267	64 153
D.43	Reinvested earnings on direct foreign investment	WEYD	33 354	36 725	50 749	37 714	12 455	26 240	27 262	11 726	6 440
D.44	Other investment income										
D.441	Attributable to insurance policy holders	L8GM	1 363	943	715	972	975	430	297	218	197
D.443	Attributable to collective investment fund shareholders										
D.4431	Dividends	L8H9	6	8	8	6	2	5	4	–	2
D.4432	Retained earnings	L8HG	8	12	16	8	4	8	4	4	4
D.443	Total	L8H2	14	20	24	14	6	13	8	4	6
D.44	Total other investment income	FAOF	1 377	963	739	986	981	443	305	222	203
D.45	Rent	FAOG	122	124	123	126	132	130	132	132	132
D.4	Total	FAKY	102 006	109 509	120 783	117 724	88 598	96 353	108 688	89 564	85 133
Total	Total resources	FBXJ	357 648	379 464	397 698	409 353	354 687	378 947	410 083	391 003	398 346
	Uses										
D.4	Property income, paid										
D.41g	Interest before FISIM allocation	J4WS	49 758	58 001	69 689	75 847	51 712	40 298	38 266	37 700	39 738
P.119	*less* FISIM	IV88	4 899	5 917	7 672	5 588	9 081	9 521	8 466	7 967	7 989
D.41	Interest	EABG	44 859	52 084	62 017	70 259	42 631	30 777	29 800	29 733	31 749
D.42	Distributed income of corporations	NVCS	104 164	108 003	108 076	113 715	119 722	122 352	141 152	141 824	151 305
D.43	Reinvested earnings on direct foreign investment	HDVB	4 983	15 452	15 049	3 656	−4 539	156	−5 971	702	1 482
D.45	Rent	FBXO	224	220	229	215	240	236	244	258	267
D.4	Total	FBXK	154 230	175 759	185 371	187 845	158 054	153 521	165 225	172 517	184 803
B.5g	**Balance of primary incomes, gross**	NQBG	**203 418**	**203 705**	**212 327**	**221 508**	**196 633**	**225 426**	**244 858**	**218 486**	**213 543**
Total	Total uses	FBXJ	357 648	379 464	397 698	409 353	354 687	378 947	410 083	391 003	398 346
P.51c	*less* Consumption of fixed capital	DBGF	96 833	101 785	104 350	108 317	112 113	112 700	115 782	117 922	121 187
B.5n	Balance of primary incomes, net	FBXQ	106 585	101 920	107 977	113 191	84 520	112 726	129 076	100 564	92 356

Source: Office for National Statistics, Blue Book 2014

19.7 Non-financial corporations
ESA 2010 sector S.11

£ million

			2005	2006	2007	2008	2009	2010	2011	2012	2013
II.2	**SECONDARY DISTRIBUTION OF INCOME ACCOUNT**										
	Resources										
B.5g	**Balance of primary incomes, gross**	NQBG	**203 418**	**203 705**	**212 327**	**221 508**	**196 633**	**225 426**	**244 858**	**218 486**	**213 543**
D.61	Net social contributions										
D.612	Employers' imputed social contributions	L8RD	3 423	3 348	3 479	3 864	4 339	3 483	3 247	3 163	3 251
D61	Total net social contributions	L8TP	3 423	3 348	3 479	3 864	4 339	3 483	3 247	3 163	3 251
D.7	Current transfers other than taxes, social contributions and benefits										
D.72	Non-life insurance claims	FCBP	6 631	5 361	5 595	5 230	4 030	5 267	3 386	3 331	4 935
D.75	Miscellaneous current transfers	CY8C	–	–	–	–	–	–	–	724	136
D.7	Total	NRJB	6 631	5 361	5 595	5 230	4 030	5 267	3 386	4 055	5 071
Total	Total resources	FCBR	213 472	212 414	221 401	230 602	205 002	234 176	251 491	225 704	221 865
	Uses										
D.5	Current taxes on income, wealth etc.										
D.51	Taxes on income	FCBS	33 594	37 204	38 309	40 826	33 925	35 685	38 573	35 089	33 565
D.62	Social benefits other than social transfers in kind										
D.622	Other social insurance benefits	L8S3	3 423	3 348	3 479	3 864	4 339	3 483	3 247	3 163	3 251
D.62	Total	L8TD	3 423	3 348	3 479	3 864	4 339	3 483	3 247	3 163	3 251
D.7	Current transfers other than taxes, social contributions and benefits										
D.71	Net non-life insurance premiums	FCBY	6 631	5 361	5 595	5 230	4 030	5 267	3 386	3 331	4 935
D.75	Miscellaneous current transfers	CY8B	488	477	488	488	488	488	488	488	488
D.7	Total, other current transfers	FCBX	7 119	5 838	6 083	5 718	4 518	5 755	3 874	3 819	5 423
B.6g	**Gross Disposable Income**	NRJD	**169 336**	**166 024**	**173 530**	**180 194**	**162 220**	**189 253**	**205 797**	**183 633**	**179 626**
Total	Total uses	FCBR	213 472	212 414	221 401	230 602	205 002	234 176	251 491	225 704	221 865
P.51c	*less* Consumption of fixed capital	DBGF	96 833	101 785	104 350	108 317	112 113	112 700	115 782	117 922	121 187
B.6n	Disposable income, net	FCCF	72 503	64 239	69 180	71 877	50 107	76 553	90 015	65 711	58 439

Source: Office for National Statistics, Blue Book 2014

19.8 Private non-financial corporations
ESA 2010 sectors S.11002 National controlled and S.11003 Foreign controlled

£ million

			2005	2006	2007	2008	2009	2010	2011	2012	2013
II.1.2	**ALLOCATION OF PRIMARY INCOME ACCOUNT** before deduction of fixed capital consumption										
	Resources										
B.2g	Operating surplus, gross[1]	NRJK	245 920	259 257	265 598	280 887	256 407	273 005	292 086	291 378	302 742
D.4	Property income, received										
D.41g	Interest before FISIM allocation	I69R	15 463	22 776	25 741	25 171	8 834	8 693	8 906	8 413	10 920
P.119	*plus* FISIM	IV87	3 201	4 105	3 727	5 765	3 313	2 662	3 745	3 573	3 095
D.41	Interest	DSZR	18 664	26 881	29 468	30 936	12 147	11 355	12 651	11 986	14 015
D.42	Distributed income of corporations	DSZS	46 683	43 889	38 473	46 389	62 589	57 803	68 011	65 182	64 074
D.43	Reinvested earnings on direct foreign investment	HDVR	33 199	36 511	50 598	37 890	12 337	26 179	27 201	11 665	6 379
D.44	Other investment income										
D.441	Attributable to insurance policy holders	KZI4	1 363	943	715	972	975	430	297	218	197
D.443	Attributable to collective investment fund shares										
D.4431	Dividends	KZI6	6	8	8	6	2	5	4	–	2
D.4432	Retained earnings	KZI7	8	12	16	8	4	8	4	4	4
D.443	Total	L5U6	14	20	24	14	6	13	8	4	6
D.44	Total other investment income	FCFP	1 377	963	739	986	981	443	305	222	203
D.45	Rent	FAOL	122	124	123	126	132	130	132	132	132
D.4	Total	FACV	100 045	108 368	119 401	116 327	88 186	95 910	108 300	89 187	84 803
Total	Total resources	FCFQ	345 965	367 625	384 999	397 214	344 593	368 915	400 386	380 565	387 545
	Uses										
D.4	Property income, paid										
D.41g	Interest before FISIM allocation	I6A2	48 492	56 569	67 975	73 642	49 975	39 198	37 482	37 098	38 888
P.119	*less* FISIM	IV86	4 879	5 877	7 600	5 518	9 023	9 483	8 424	7 943	7 976
D.41	Interest	DSZV	43 613	50 692	60 375	68 124	40 952	29 715	29 058	29 155	30 912
D.42	Distributed income of corporations	NVDC	103 369	107 325	107 450	113 218	119 045	121 764	140 232	140 539	149 880
D.421	*Of which:* Dividend payments	NETZ	82 891	83 684	83 911	88 150	84 631	82 601	103 901	102 007	107 579
D.43	Reinvested earnings on direct foreign investment	HDVB	4 983	15 452	15 049	3 656	–4 539	156	–5 971	702	1 482
D.45	Rent	FCFU	224	220	229	215	240	236	244	258	267
D.4	Total	FCFR	152 189	173 689	183 103	185 213	155 698	151 871	163 563	170 654	182 541
B.5g	**Balance of primary incomes, gross**	NRJM	**193 776**	**193 936**	**201 896**	**212 001**	**188 895**	**217 044**	**236 823**	**209 911**	**205 004**
Total	Total uses	FCFQ	345 965	367 625	384 999	397 214	344 593	368 915	400 386	380 565	387 545
P.51c	*less* Consumption of fixed capital	NSRK	89 557	94 220	96 679	100 365	103 966	104 701	107 734	109 881	112 834
B.5n	Balance of primary incomes, net	FCFW	104 219	99 716	105 217	111 636	84 929	112 343	129 089	100 030	92 170

1 Companies gross trading profits and rental of buildings less holding gains of inventories, details of which are shown at Table C: The Sector Accounts Key Economic Indicators.

Source: Office for National Statistics, Blue Book 2014

19.9 Private non-financial corporations
ESA 2010 sectors S.11002 National controlled and S.11003 Foreign controlled

£ million

			2005	2006	2007	2008	2009	2010	2011	2012	2013
II.2	**SECONDARY DISTRIBUTION OF INCOME ACCOUNT**										
	Resources											
B.5g	**Balance of primary incomes, gross**	NRJM	**193 776**	**193 936**	**201 896**	**212 001**	**188 895**	**217 044**	**236 823**	**209 911**	**205 004**
D.61	Net social contributions										
D.612	Employers' imputed social contributions	L8RJ	3 294	3 227	3 363	3 718	4 182	3 364	3 138	3 049	3 146
D.61	Total net social contributions	L8TV	3 294	3 227	3 363	3 718	4 182	3 364	3 138	3 049	3 146
D.7	Other current transfers										
D.72	Net non-life insurance claims	FDBA	6 631	5 361	5 595	5 230	4 030	5 267	3 386	3 331	4 935
Total	Total resources	FDBC	203 701	202 524	210 854	220 949	197 107	225 675	243 347	216 291	213 085
	Uses										
D.5	Current taxes on income, wealth etc.										
D.51	Taxes on income	FCCP	33 453	36 832	38 084	40 572	33 674	35 536	38 464	34 983	33 492
D.62	Social security benefits other than social transfers in kind										
D.622	Other social insurance benefits	L8S9	3 294	3 227	3 363	3 718	4 182	3 364	3 138	3 049	3 146
D.62	Total	L8TH	3 294	3 227	3 363	3 718	4 182	3 364	3 138	3 049	3 146
D.7	Current transfers other than taxes, social contributions and benefits										
D.71	Net non-life insurance premiums	FDBH	6 631	5 361	5 595	5 230	4 030	5 267	3 386	3 331	4 935
D.75	Miscellaneous current transfers	CY88	488	477	488	488	488	488	488	488	488
D.7	Total	FCCN	7 119	5 838	6 083	5 718	4 518	5 755	3 874	3 819	5 423
B.6g	**Gross Disposable Income**	NRJQ	**159 835**	**156 627**	**163 324**	**170 941**	**154 733**	**181 020**	**197 871**	**174 440**	**171 024**
Total	Total uses	FDBC	203 701	202 524	210 854	220 949	197 107	225 675	243 347	216 291	213 085
P.51c	*less* Consumption of fixed capital	NSRK	89 557	94 220	96 679	100 365	103 966	104 701	107 734	109 881	112 834
B.6n	Disposable income, net	FDBK	70 278	62 407	66 645	70 576	50 767	76 319	90 137	64 559	58 190

Source: Office for National Statistics, Blue Book 2014

19.10 Households and non-profit institutions serving households
ESA 2010 sectors S.14 and S.15

£ million

			2006	2007	2008	2009	2010	2011	2012	2013
II.1.2	**ALLOCATION OF PRIMARY INCOME ACCOUNT** before deduction of fixed capital consumption									
	Resources									
B.2g	Operating surplus, gross	QWLS	87 628	96 155	107 667	93 875	110 945	118 022	125 773	125 455
B.3g	Mixed income, gross	QWLT	93 645	92 417	94 690	93 620	96 603	96 574	96 644	98 848
D.1	Compensation of employees									
D.11	Wages and salaries	QWLW	608 399	644 194	661 747	659 209	668 790	678 088	693 953	714 805
D.12	Employers' social contributions	QWLX	123 795	132 662	129 966	132 518	147 779	149 568	155 322	162 753
D.1	Total	QWLY	732 194	776 856	791 713	791 727	816 569	827 656	849 275	877 558
D.4	Property income, received									
D.41g	Interest before FISIM allocation	J4WY	34 403	43 018	42 320	19 950	19 340	21 149	22 233	20 125
P.119	*plus* FISIM	IV8W	13 527	14 734	23 517	3 015	−695	548	216	−629
D.41	Interest	QWLZ	47 930	57 752	65 837	22 965	18 645	21 697	22 449	19 496
D.42	Distributed income of corporations	QWMA	47 022	47 826	43 248	51 010	54 660	54 873	52 168	54 957
D.44	Other investment income									
D.441	Attributable to insurance policy holders	L8GL	20 852	28 802	28 990	24 219	24 936	24 505	22 195	21 796
D.442	Payable on pension entitlements	L8GS	69 956	80 172	79 922	69 283	80 106	77 775	70 167	68 192
D.443	Attributable to collective investment fund shareholders									
D.4431	Dividends	L8H8	2 740	3 250	1 656	773	1 660	1 044	675	677
D.4432	Retained earnings	L8HF	4 285	5 083	2 588	1 206	2 596	1 633	1 059	1 062
D.443	Total	L8GZ	7 025	8 333	4 244	1 979	4 256	2 677	1 734	1 739
D.44	Total other investment income	QWMC	97 833	117 307	113 156	95 481	109 298	104 957	94 096	91 727
D.45	Rent	QWMD	110	110	115	115	118	123	127	128
D.4	Total	QWME	192 895	222 995	222 356	169 571	182 721	181 650	168 840	166 308
Total	Total resources	QWMF	1 106 362	1 188 423	1 216 426	1 148 793	1 206 838	1 223 902	1 240 532	1 268 169
	Uses									
D.4	Property income, paid									
D.41g	Interest before FISIM allocation	J4WZ	80 307	94 682	98 724	72 196	64 957	62 132	61 750	61 600
P.119	*less* FISIM	IV8X	18 387	16 959	9 958	44 708	44 908	38 619	36 341	39 798
D.41	Interest	QWMG	61 920	77 723	88 766	27 488	20 049	23 513	25 409	21 802
D.45	Rent	QWMH	226	225	233	239	239	243	247	248
D.4	Total	QWMI	62 146	77 948	88 999	27 727	20 288	23 756	25 656	22 050
B.5g	**Balance of primary incomes, gross**	QWMJ	**1 044 216**	**1 110 475**	**1 127 427**	**1 121 066**	**1 186 550**	**1 200 146**	**1 214 876**	**1 246 119**
Total	Total uses	QWMF	1 106 362	1 188 423	1 216 426	1 148 793	1 206 838	1 223 902	1 240 532	1 268 169
P.51c	*less* Consumption of fixed capital	QWLL	67 503	73 493	64 820	63 322	65 502	66 260	68 581	73 257
B.5n	Balance of primary incomes, net	QWMK	976 713	1 036 982	1 062 607	1 057 744	1 121 048	1 133 886	1 146 295	1 172 862

Source: Office for National Statistics, Blue Book 2014

19.11 Households and non-profit institutions serving households
ESA 2010 sectors S.14 and S.15

£ million

			2006	2007	2008	2009	2010	2011	2012	2013
II.2	**SECONDARY DISTRIBUTION OF INCOME ACCOUNT**									
	Resources									
B.5g	**Balance of primary incomes, gross**	QWMJ	**1 044 216**	**1 110 475**	**1 127 427**	**1 121 066**	**1 186 550**	**1 200 146**	**1 214 876**	**1 246 119**
D.612	Employers' imputed social contributions	L8RF	525	520	689	754	652	608	635	827
D.62	Social benefits other than social transfers in kind									
D.621	Social security benefits in cash	L8QF	65 054	69 037	73 871	80 826	82 117	83 826	88 939	91 151
D.622	Other social insurance benefits	L8QT	84 351	88 727	93 492	100 176	105 974	108 280	116 941	120 118
D.623R	Social assistance benefits in cash	MT3B	78 800	83 033	88 889	99 920	107 461	111 240	116 066	117 088
D.62	Total	QWML	228 205	240 797	256 252	280 922	295 552	303 346	321 946	328 357
D.7	Other current transfers									
D.72	Non-life insurance claims	QWMM	18 840	24 141	21 674	20 062	27 927	28 853	28 040	28 045
D.75	Miscellaneous current transfers	QWMN	37 346	38 650	37 899	39 502	40 728	39 451	43 741	39 373
D.7	Total	QWMO	56 186	62 791	59 573	59 564	68 655	68 304	71 781	67 418
	Total resources	QWMP	1 329 132	1 414 583	1 443 941	1 462 306	1 551 409	1 572 404	1 609 238	1 642 721
	Uses									
D.5	Current taxes on income, wealth, etc									
D.51	Taxes on income	QWMQ	139 215	150 948	154 602	145 672	146 847	152 627	150 395	156 188
D.59	Other current taxes	NVCO	29 831	31 586	32 931	33 776	34 588	34 924	35 315	36 468
D.5	Total	QWMS	169 046	182 534	187 533	179 448	181 435	187 551	185 710	192 656
D.61	Net social contributions									
D.611	Employers' actual social contributions	L8NJ	102 172	109 483	106 047	106 770	121 198	123 512	128 823	136 765
D.612	Employers' imputed social contributions	M9X2	21 619	23 180	23 918	25 746	26 581	26 056	26 499	25 988
D.613	Households' actual social contributions	L8PR	59 525	59 794	60 186	57 155	58 668	59 983	63 496	65 841
D.614	Households' social contribution supplements	L8Q7	69 956	80 172	79 922	69 283	80 106	77 775	70 167	68 192
D.61SC	Social insurance scheme service charge	L8LT	−11 872	−12 686	−12 777	−11 101	−12 568	−14 740	−17 046	−17 651
D.61	Total	QWMY	241 400	259 943	257 296	247 853	273 985	272 586	271 939	279 135
D.62	Social benefits other than social transfers in kind									
D.622	Other social insurance benefits	L8S5	525	520	689	754	652	608	635	827
D.623U	Social assistance benefits in cash	MT3D	496	496	496	494	486	496	496	496
D.62	Total	QWMZ	1 021	1 016	1 185	1 248	1 138	1 104	1 131	1 323
D.7	Other current transfers									
D.71	Net non-life insurance premiums	QWNA	18 840	24 141	21 674	20 062	27 926	28 853	28 040	28 045
D.75	Miscellaneous current transfers	QWNB	13 121	14 247	13 616	13 939	14 113	14 387	15 378	15 936
D.7	Total	QWNC	31 961	38 388	35 290	34 001	42 039	43 240	43 418	43 981
B.6g	**Gross Disposable Income**[1]	QWND	**885 704**	**932 702**	**962 637**	**999 756**	**1 052 812**	**1 067 923**	**1 107 040**	**1 125 626**
	Total uses	QWMP	1 329 132	1 414 583	1 443 941	1 462 306	1 551 409	1 572 404	1 609 238	1 642 721
P.51c	*less* Consumption of fixed capital	QWLL	67 503	73 493	64 820	63 322	65 502	66 260	68 581	73 257
B.6n	Disposable income, net	QWNE	818 201	859 209	897 817	936 434	987 310	1 001 663	1 038 459	1 052 369

1 Gross household disposable income revalued by the implied household and
NPISH final consumption expenditure deflator is as follows:

			2006	2007	2008	2009	2010	2011	2012	2013
Real household disposable income: (Chained volume measures)										
£ million (reference year 2011)		RVGK	1 037 377	1 062 306	1 055 488	1 079 270	1 088 559	1 067 923	1 084 591	1 082 149
Index (2011 = 100)		OSXR	97.1	99.5	98.8	101.1	101.9	100.0	101.6	101.3

Source: Office for National Statistics, Blue Book 2014

19.12 Households and non-profit institutions serving households
ESA 2010 sectors S.14 and S.15

£ million

			2006	2007	2008	2009	2010	2011	2012	2013
II.3	**REDISTRIBUTION OF INCOME IN KIND ACCOUNT**									
	Resources									
B.6g	**Gross Disposable Income**	QWND	**885 704**	**932 702**	**962 637**	**999 756**	**1 052 812**	**1 067 923**	**1 107 040**	**1 125 626**
D.63	Social transfers in kind	NSSB	213 754	224 908	240 731	256 499	262 567	266 559	266 497	268 562
Total	Total resources	NSSC	1 099 458	1 157 610	1 203 368	1 256 255	1 315 379	1 334 482	1 373 537	1 394 188
	Uses									
D.63	Social transfers in kind	HAEK	41 259	43 718	46 893	50 205	50 885	53 259	50 386	51 734
B.7g	Adjusted disposable income, gross	NSSD	1 058 199	1 113 892	1 156 475	1 206 050	1 264 494	1 281 223	1 323 151	1 342 454
Total	Total uses	NSSC	1 099 458	1 157 610	1 203 368	1 256 255	1 315 379	1 334 482	1 373 537	1 394 188

£ million

			2006	2007	2008	2009	2010	2011	2012	2013
II.4	**USE OF INCOME ACCOUNT**									
II.4.1	**USE OF DISPOSABLE INCOME ACCOUNT**									
	Resources									
B.6g	**Gross Disposable Income**	QWND	**885 704**	**932 702**	**962 637**	**999 756**	**1 052 812**	**1 067 923**	**1 107 040**	**1 125 626**
D.8	Adjustment for the change in pension entitlements	NSSE	68 394	80 669	68 265	56 907	75 076	68 913	58 912	61 647
Total	Total resources	NSSF	954 098	1 013 371	1 030 902	1 056 663	1 127 888	1 136 836	1 165 952	1 187 273
	Uses									
P.3	Final consumption expenditure									
P.31	Individual consumption expenditure	NSSG	892 094	941 554	973 455	958 342	1 004 149	1 039 102	1 072 545	1 110 807
B.8g	**Gross Saving**	NSSH	**62 004**	**71 817**	**57 447**	**98 321**	**123 739**	**97 734**	**93 407**	**76 466**
Total	Total uses	NSSF	954 098	1 013 371	1 030 902	1 056 663	1 127 888	1 136 836	1 165 952	1 187 273
P.51c	*less* Consumption of fixed capital	QWLL	67 503	73 493	64 820	63 322	65 502	66 260	68 581	73 257
B.8n	Saving, net	NSSI	−5 499	−1 676	−7 373	34 999	58 237	31 474	24 826	3 209
II.4.2	**USE OF ADJUSTED DISPOSABLE INCOME ACCOUNT**									
	Resources									
B.7g	Adjusted disposable income, gross	NSSD	1 058 199	1 113 892	1 156 475	1 206 050	1 264 494	1 281 223	1 323 151	1 342 454
D.8	Adjustment for the change in pension entitlements	NSSE	68 394	80 669	68 265	56 907	75 076	68 913	58 912	61 647
Total	Total resources	NSSJ	1 126 593	1 194 561	1 224 740	1 262 957	1 339 570	1 350 136	1 382 063	1 404 101
	Uses									
P.4	Actual final consumption									
P.41	Actual individual consumption	ABRE	1 064 589	1 122 744	1 167 293	1 164 636	1 215 831	1 252 402	1 288 656	1 327 635
B.8g	**Gross Saving**[1]	NSSH	**62 004**	**71 817**	**57 447**	**98 321**	**123 739**	**97 734**	**93 407**	**76 466**
Total	Total uses	NSSJ	1 126 593	1 194 561	1 224 740	1 262 957	1 339 570	1 350 136	1 382 063	1 404 101

1 Household saving as a percentage of total available household resources is as follows:

		2006	2007	2008	2009	2010	2011	2012	2013
Household saving ratio (per cent)	RVGL	6.5	7.1	5.6	9.3	11.0	8.6	8.0	6.4

Source: Office for National Statistics, Blue Book 2014

19.13 The sector accounts: Key economic indicators

£ million

			2005	2006	2007	2008	2009	2010	2011	2012	2013
Net lending(+)/borrowing(-) by:											
B.9	Non-financial corporations	EABO	45 107	36 002	28 462	40 152	64 941	63 631	71 204	41 700	18 284
B.9	Financial corporations	NHCQ	−5 975	−9 140	−8 333	−5 183	8 515	−17 784	−5 647	9 225	−1 705
B.9	General government	NNBK	−46 134	−41 258	−44 677	−76 198	−162 295	−150 084	−122 979	−137 010	−94 751
B.9	Households and NPISH[1]	NSSZ	−10 280	−18 085	−15 763	−14 423	48 351	64 564	31 229	24 996	−92
B.9	Rest of the world	NHRB	17 285	32 478	40 315	55 652	40 488	39 674	26 196	61 090	71 864
	Private non-financial corporations											
	Gross trading profits											
	Continental shelf profits	CAGD	24 918	27 611	25 896	30 317	23 055	26 988	30 198	25 409	23 132
	Others	CAED	204 384	214 883	221 738	228 483	212 632	223 519	239 327	247 477	259 918
	Rental of buildings	DTWR	16 910	17 345	18 910	22 406	21 626	22 814	22 510	20 496	20 404
	less Holding gains of inventories	DLRA	292	581	946	319	907	316	−51	2 004	712
B.2g	Gross operating surplus	CAER	245 920	259 258	265 598	280 887	256 406	273 005	292 086	291 378	302 742
	Households and NPISH											
B.6g	Disposable income, gross	QWND	847 486	885 704	932 702	962 637	999 756	1 052 812	1 067 923	1 107 040	1 125 626
	Implied deflator of household and NPISH individual consumption expenditure index (2011=100)[2]	YBFS	83.2	85.4	87.8	91.2	92.6	96.7	100.0	102.1	104.0
	Real household disposable income:											
	Chained volume measures (reference year 2011)	RVGK	1 018 634	1 037 377	1 062 306	1 055 488	1 079 270	1 088 559	1 067 923	1 084 591	1 082 149
	Index (2011=100)[2]	OSXR	95.4	97.1	99.5	98.8	101.1	101.9	100.0	101.6	101.3
B.8g	Gross saving	NSSH	64 478	62 004	71 817	57 447	98 321	123 739	97 734	93 407	76 466
	Households total resources	NSSJ	1 075 965	1 126 593	1 194 561	1 224 740	1 262 957	1 339 570	1 350 136	1 382 063	1 404 101
	Saving ratio, per cent	RVGL	7.0	6.5	7.1	5.6	9.3	11.0	8.6	8.0	6.4

1 Non-profit institutions serving households
2 Rounded to one decimal place

Source: Office for National Statistics, Blue Book 2014

647

19.14 Household final consumption expenditure: classified by purpose at current market prices

£ million

			2006	2007	2008	2009	2010	2011	2012	2013
P.31	**FINAL CONSUMPTION EXPENDITURE OF HOUSEHOLDS**									
	Durable goods									
05.	Furnishings, household equipment and routine maintenance of the house	LLIJ	22 414	23 217	23 017	20 420	20 677	21 788	22 316	23 133
06.	Health	LLIK	2 834	2 952	3 070	3 170	2 979	3 042	3 168	3 278
07.	Transport	LLIL	36 989	39 154	35 377	35 017	35 366	35 420	39 016	42 107
08.	Communication	LLIM	792	717	803	872	761	780	738	762
09.	Recreation and culture	LLIN	22 608	22 647	24 247	23 139	23 608	22 877	23 764	24 325
12.	Miscellaneous goods and services	LLIO	5 555	5 376	5 530	5 324	5 688	6 540	7 522	8 212
D	Total durable goods	UTIA	91 192	94 063	92 044	87 942	89 079	90 447	96 524	101 817
	Semi-durable goods									
03.	Clothing and footwear	LLJL	45 129	46 635	48 357	48 124	50 044	53 768	55 194	58 836
05.	Furnishings, household equipment and routine maintenance of the house	LLJM	14 088	14 545	13 781	13 923	14 427	14 373	14 927	15 262
07.	Transport	LLJN	3 716	3 700	4 084	4 114	3 928	3 802	4 295	4 794
09.	Recreation and culture	LLJO	27 434	29 638	30 117	27 790	27 815	26 335	26 694	28 710
12.	Miscellaneous goods and services	LLJP	3 585	3 463	3 256	3 550	5 508	5 676	5 441	5 691
SD	Total semi-durable goods	UTIQ	93 952	97 981	99 595	97 501	101 722	103 954	106 551	113 293
	Non-durable goods									
01.	Food & drink	ABZV	70 281	73 284	78 107	79 802	82 805	86 436	90 931	95 146
02.	Alcoholic beverages, tobacco & narcotics	ADFL	37 072	37 844	37 145	37 296	37 671	40 719	41 956	42 133
04.	Housing, water, electricity, gas and other fuels	LLIX	26 828	28 493	33 583	34 086	35 498	34 225	37 445	39 611
05.	Furnishings, household equipment and routine maintenance of the house	LLIY	3 871	3 880	3 886	4 278	4 303	4 221	4 076	4 152
06.	Health	LLIZ	4 435	4 621	4 647	4 765	5 896	5 334	5 951	6 315
07.	Transport	LLJA	24 855	26 625	29 709	26 575	30 737	35 341	35 748	33 411
09.	Recreation and culture	LLJB	15 463	15 657	15 899	15 150	15 108	15 094	15 052	14 859
12.	Miscellaneous goods and services	LLJC	15 367	16 079	15 871	16 025	16 154	16 999	17 756	19 209
ND	Total non-durable goods	UTII	198 172	206 483	218 847	217 977	228 172	238 369	248 915	254 836
	Total goods	UTIE	383 316	398 527	410 486	403 420	418 973	432 770	451 990	469 946
	Services									
03.	Clothing and footwear	LLJD	841	905	1 032	1 090	989	858	865	855
04.	Housing, water, electricity, gas and other fuels	LLJE	141 292	152 756	160 887	174 612	200 188	206 685	212 850	219 294
05.	Furnishings, household equipment and routine maintenance of the house	LLJF	5 951	6 041	6 459	5 959	6 760	6 588	6 737	7 156
06.	Health	LLJG	6 228	6 960	6 554	7 056	7 426	7 702	7 530	7 356
07.	Transport	LLJH	52 931	56 852	57 432	56 030	58 429	61 657	64 294	67 263
08.	Communication	LLJI	17 420	18 163	18 084	17 634	18 737	19 332	19 690	20 807
09.	Recreation and culture	LLJJ	32 593	34 744	36 188	35 216	35 621	38 085	39 581	39 759
10.	Education	ADIE	10 667	12 380	13 665	14 893	15 252	15 826	16 749	19 212
11.	Restaurants and hotels	ADIF	83 242	86 945	87 952	82 708	87 276	93 572	97 362	101 523
12.	Miscellaneous goods and services	LLJK	104 374	110 646	113 474	98 864	94 106	94 739	97 063	100 287
S	Total services	UTIM	455 539	486 392	501 727	494 062	524 784	545 044	562 721	583 503
0.	Final consumption expenditure in the UK by resident and non-resident households (domestic concept)	ABQI	838 855	884 919	912 213	897 482	943 757	977 814	1 014 711	1 053 449
P.33	Final consumption expenditure outside the UK by UK resident households	ABTA	30 979	32 406	34 146	30 207	30 676	30 118	30 829	31 704
P.34	Final consumption expenditure in the UK by households resident in the rest of the world	CDFD	–18 999	–19 489	–19 797	–19 552	–21 169	–22 089	–23 381	–26 080
P.31	Final consumption expenditure by UK resident households in the UK and abroad (national concept)	ABPB	850 835	897 836	926 562	908 137	953 264	985 843	1 022 159	1 059 073

Source: Office for National Statistics, Blue Book 2014

19.15 Household final consumption expenditure: classified by purpose
Chained volume measures (reference year 2011)

£ million

			2006	2007	2008	2009	2010	2011	2012	2013
P.31	**FINAL CONSUMPTION EXPENDITURE OF HOUSEHOLDS**									
	Durable goods									
	Furnishings, household equipment and									
05.	routine maintenance of the house	LLME	25 690	26 195	25 357	21 744	21 340	21 788	21 769	22 412
06.	Health	LLMF	2 956	3 043	3 131	3 219	2 995	3 042	3 152	3 287
07.	Transport	LLMG	40 051	42 312	39 380	39 854	36 802	35 420	38 424	42 100
08.	Communication	LLMH	807	761	879	949	791	780	714	717
09.	Recreation and culture	LLMI	13 210	15 302	19 318	20 063	21 403	22 877	25 838	27 921
12.	Miscellaneous goods and services	LLMJ	7 341	6 863	6 686	6 115	6 118	6 540	7 018	7 501
D	Total durable goods	UTIC	85 615	91 046	93 510	91 234	89 284	90 447	96 915	103 938
	Semi-durable goods									
03.	Clothing and footwear	LLNG	37 818	40 625	45 172	48 725	51 144	53 768	54 799	57 922
	Furnishings, household equipment and									
05.	routine maintenance of the house	LLNH	15 571	16 114	15 319	15 210	15 354	14 373	14 501	14 784
07.	Transport	LLNI	4 263	4 228	4 566	4 454	4 082	3 802	4 253	4 706
09.	Recreation and culture	LLNJ	25 206	27 582	28 745	26 927	27 045	26 335	26 806	28 612
12.	Miscellaneous goods and services	LLNK	3 736	3 543	3 290	3 543	5 536	5 676	5 364	5 509
SD	Total semi-durable goods	UTIS	85 817	91 489	96 905	98 803	103 157	103 954	105 723	111 533
	Non-durable goods									
01.	Food & drink	ADIP	92 047	91 818	89 742	86 975	87 439	86 436	88 185	88 901
02.	Alcoholic beverages, tobacco & narcotics	ADIS	44 402	41 954	42 950	41 883	40 801	40 719	39 679	38 262
	Housing, water, electricity, gas and									
04.	other fuels	LLMS	38 284	37 584	37 988	36 118	38 571	34 225	34 824	34 759
	Furnishings, household equipment and									
05.	routine maintenance of the house	LLMT	4 815	4 726	4 577	4 696	4 579	4 221	3 964	3 987
06.	Health	LLMU	4 734	4 871	4 856	4 901	5 969	5 334	5 854	6 153
07.	Transport	LLMV	36 679	38 181	36 858	35 740	34 431	35 341	35 436	33 449
09.	Recreation and culture	LLMW	18 304	18 288	17 946	16 452	15 721	15 094	14 716	14 185
12.	Miscellaneous goods and services	LLMX	17 231	17 656	17 145	16 857	16 581	16 999	17 606	19 078
ND	Total non-durable goods	UTIK	256 112	254 471	251 674	243 244	244 120	238 369	240 264	238 774
	Total goods	UTIG	422 644	434 469	441 094	432 904	436 341	432 770	442 902	454 245
	Services									
03.	Clothing and footwear	LLMY	967	1 008	1 115	1 152	1 027	858	850	823
	Housing, water, electricity, gas and									
04.	other fuels	LLMZ	193 136	196 217	198 981	201 753	203 693	206 685	209 330	212 729
	Furnishings, household equipment and									
05.	routine maintenance of the house	LLNA	6 902	6 682	6 835	6 188	6 879	6 588	6 640	6 938
06.	Health	LLNB	7 402	7 965	7 308	7 547	7 655	7 702	7 363	6 955
07.	Transport	LLNC	64 087	66 176	64 164	60 744	61 651	61 657	62 214	61 851
08.	Communication	LLND	18 105	19 511	19 921	19 223	19 475	19 332	18 872	19 350
09.	Recreation and culture	LLNE	39 476	40 502	40 974	38 369	37 366	38 085	38 454	37 312
10.	Education	ADMJ	16 169	16 491	16 303	16 492	16 037	15 826	15 427	15 072
11.	Restaurants and hotels	ADMK	98 253	98 979	96 329	88 427	91 280	93 572	92 960	94 342
12.	Miscellaneous goods and services	LLNF	104 110	108 124	102 496	97 570	95 545	94 739	96 858	99 642
S	Total services	UTIO	550 954	564 682	556 140	537 710	540 628	545 044	548 968	555 014
	Final consumption expenditure in the UK by resident and non-resident households									
0.	(domestic concept)	ABQJ	972 909	998 513	997 067	970 563	976 926	977 814	991 870	1 009 259
P.33	Final consumption expenditure outside the UK by UK resident households	ABTC	44 043	46 026	41 277	32 640	32 009	30 118	31 598	32 592
P.34	Final consumption expenditure in the UK by households resident in the rest of the world	CCHX	–21 280	–21 215	–21 118	–20 721	–21 963	–22 089	–22 609	–24 600
P.3	**Final consumption expenditure by UK resident households in the UK and abroad** (national concept)	ABPF	994 192	1 021 686	1 016 524	982 490	986 956	985 843	1 000 859	1 017 251

Source: Office for National Statistics, Blue Book 2014

649

19.16 Individual consumption expenditure at current market prices by households, non-profit institutions serving households and general government

Classified by function (COICOP/COPNI/COFOG) [1]

£ million

			2006	2007	2008	2009	2010	2011	2012	2013
P.31	**FINAL CONSUMPTION EXPENDITURE OF HOUSEHOLDS**									
01.	**Food and non-alcoholic beverages**	ABZV	70 281	73 284	78 107	79 802	82 805	86 436	90 931	95 146
01.1	Food	ABZW	61 540	64 335	69 046	70 478	73 121	75 897	80 052	84 173
01.2	Non-alcoholic beverages	ADFK	8 741	8 949	9 061	9 324	9 684	10 539	10 879	10 973
02.	**Alcoholic beverages, tobacco and narcotics**	ADFL	37 072	37 844	37 145	37 296	37 671	40 719	41 956	42 133
02.1	Alcoholic beverages	ADFM	13 844	14 068	14 004	14 160	14 389	15 530	16 447	16 780
02.2	Tobacco	ADFN	15 556	15 781	15 902	15 869	17 182	18 286	18 724	18 679
02.3	Narcotics	MNC2	7 672	7 995	7 239	7 267	6 100	6 903	6 785	6 674
03.	**Clothing and footwear**	ADFP	45 970	47 540	49 389	49 214	51 033	54 626	56 059	59 691
03.1	Clothing	ADFQ	39 340	40 634	42 170	41 697	43 376	46 716	47 745	50 882
03.2	Footwear	ADFR	6 630	6 906	7 219	7 517	7 657	7 910	8 314	8 809
04.	**Housing, water, electricity, gas and other fuels**	ADFS	168 120	181 249	194 470	208 698	235 686	240 910	250 295	258 905
04.1	Actual rentals for housing	ADFT	34 902	38 494	40 908	43 466	48 503	51 526	55 031	57 464
04.2	Imputed rentals for housing	ADFU	101 400	108 949	114 720	125 805	146 097	149 390	152 004	155 621
04.3	Maintenance and repair of the dwelling	ADFV	2 413	2 361	2 032	1 931	2 047	2 149	2 088	2 405
04.4	Water supply and miscellaneous dwelling services	ADFW	6 929	7 619	8 040	8 231	8 600	8 943	9 210	9 484
04.5	Electricity, gas and other fuels	ADFX	22 476	23 826	28 770	29 265	30 439	28 902	31 962	33 931
05.	**Furnishings, household equipment and routine maintenance of the house**	ADFY	46 324	47 683	47 143	44 580	46 167	46 970	48 056	49 703
05.1	Furniture, furnishings, carpets and other floor coverings	ADFZ	17 414	18 186	17 540	15 693	15 616	16 637	16 619	17 692
05.2	Household textiles	ADGG	5 013	5 443	5 500	5 714	6 305	5 193	5 258	5 505
05.3	Household appliances	ADGL	6 111	5 960	6 076	5 697	6 066	6 465	6 845	6 559
05.4	Glassware, tableware and household utensils	ADGM	4 751	4 509	4 342	4 267	4 177	4 906	5 069	5 248
05.5	Tools and equipment for house and garden	ADGN	3 810	4 226	3 809	3 434	3 450	3 590	4 042	3 946
05.6	Goods and services for routine household maintenance	ADGO	9 225	9 359	9 876	9 775	10 553	10 179	10 223	10 753
06.	**Health**	ADGP	13 497	14 533	14 271	14 991	16 301	16 078	16 649	16 949
06.1	Medical products, appliances and equipment	ADGQ	7 269	7 573	7 717	7 935	8 875	8 376	9 119	9 593
06.2	Out-patient services	ADGR	3 603	4 247	3 756	3 940	4 291	4 680	4 467	4 306
06.3	Hospital services	ADGS	2 625	2 713	2 798	3 116	3 135	3 022	3 063	3 050
07.	**Transport**	ADGT	118 491	126 331	126 602	121 736	128 460	136 220	143 353	147 575
07.1	Purchase of vehicles	ADGU	36 989	39 154	35 377	35 017	35 366	35 420	39 016	42 107
07.2	Operation of personal transport equipment	ADGV	50 300	52 928	57 139	54 066	59 473	64 267	65 547	63 513
07.3	Transport services	ADGW	31 202	34 249	34 086	32 653	33 621	36 533	38 790	41 955
08.	**Communication**	ADGX	18 212	18 880	18 887	18 506	19 498	20 112	20 428	21 569
08.1	Postal services	CDEF	1 041	1 076	1 013	1 051	961	1 062	1 245	1 317
08.2	Telephone & telefax equipment	ADWO	792	717	803	872	761	780	738	762
08.3	Telephone & telefax services	ADWP	16 379	17 087	17 071	16 583	17 776	18 270	18 445	19 490
09.	**Recreation and culture**	ADGY	98 098	102 686	106 451	101 295	102 152	102 391	105 091	107 644
09.1	Audio-visual, photographic and information processing equipment	ADGZ	22 604	21 660	22 891	20 747	20 520	19 838	20 660	20 322
09.2	Other major durables for recreation and culture	ADHL	6 497	6 765	7 146	7 371	7 713	7 243	7 684	8 656
09.3	Other recreational items and equipment; flowers, garden and pets	ADHZ	26 018	29 427	30 454	29 157	30 087	28 624	28 887	30 624
09.4	Recreational and cultural services	ADIA	30 138	31 926	33 464	32 316	32 382	35 077	36 370	36 832
09.5	Newspapers, books and stationery	ADIC	12 841	12 908	12 496	11 704	11 450	11 609	11 490	11 210
09.6	Package holidays [2]	ADID	–	–	–	–	–	–	–	–
10.	**Education**									
10.	Education services	ADIE	10 667	12 380	13 665	14 893	15 252	15 826	16 749	19 212
11.	**Restaurants and hotels**	ADIF	83 242	86 945	87 952	82 708	87 276	93 572	97 362	101 523
11.1	Catering services	ADIG	71 573	73 667	74 360	70 871	74 087	78 430	80 977	83 682
11.2	Accommodation services	ADIH	11 669	13 278	13 592	11 837	13 189	15 142	16 385	17 841
12.	**Miscellaneous goods and services**	ADII	128 881	135 564	138 131	123 763	121 456	123 954	127 782	133 399
12.1	Personal care	ADIJ	21 788	22 509	22 264	22 700	23 494	24 206	24 989	26 726
12.2	Prostitution	MNC8	4 628	4 914	5 178	5 305	5 453	5 612	5 741	5 838
12.3	Personal effects n.e.c.	ADIK	7 998	7 700	7 815	7 707	9 832	10 804	11 582	12 366
12.4	Social protection	ADIL	12 107	12 676	13 419	13 044	13 164	13 043	13 417	14 000
12.5	Insurance	ADIM	21 128	23 858	19 235	21 460	20 319	20 521	23 781	27 000
12.6	Financial services n.e.c.	ADIN	52 463	54 635	61 031	45 083	41 440	41 515	39 461	38 474
12.7	Other services n.e.c.	ADIO	8 769	9 272	9 189	8 464	7 754	8 253	8 811	8 995
0.	**Final consumption expenditure in the UK by resident and non-resident households (domestic concept)**	ABQI	838 855	884 919	912 213	897 482	943 757	977 814	1 014 711	1 053 449
P.33	Final consumption expenditure outside the UK by UK resident households	ABTA	30 979	32 406	34 146	30 207	30 676	30 118	30 829	31 704
P.34	Final consumption expenditure in the UK by households resident in the rest of the world	CDFD	−18 999	−19 489	−19 797	−19 552	−21 169	−22 089	−23 381	−26 080
P.31	**Final consumption expenditure by UK resident households in the UK and abroad (national concept)**	ABPB	850 835	897 836	926 562	908 137	953 264	985 843	1 022 159	1 059 073

19.16

Individual consumption expenditure at current market prices by households, non-profit institutions serving households and general government
Classified by function (COICOP/COPNI/COFOG) [1]

continued

£ million

			2006	2007	2008	2009	2010	2011	2012	2013
P.31	**CONSUMPTION EXPENDITURE OF UK RESIDENT HOUSEHOLDS**									
P.31	Final consumption expenditure of UK resident households in the UK and abroad	ABPB	850 835	897 836	926 562	908 137	953 264	985 843	1 022 159	1 059 073
13.	**FINAL INDIVIDUAL CONSUMPTION EXPENDITURE OF NPISH**									
P.31	Final individual consumption expenditure of NPISH	ABNV	41 259	43 718	46 893	50 205	50 885	53 259	50 386	51 734
14.	**FINAL INDIVIDUAL CONSUMPTION EXPENDITURE OF GENERAL GOVERNMENT**									
14.1	Health	IWX5	88 895	93 652	100 875	109 076	112 387	115 316	117 162	120 257
14.2	Recreation and culture	IWX6	5 813	6 186	6 122	6 225	6 100	6 151	6 279	5 563
14.3	Education	IWX7	49 070	51 648	55 327	58 483	60 294	59 458	60 094	60 215
14.4	Social protection	IWX8	28 717	29 704	31 514	32 510	32 901	32 375	32 576	30 793
P.31	Final individual consumption expenditure of general government	NNAQ	172 495	181 190	193 838	206 294	211 682	213 300	216 111	216 828
P.31 P.41	Total, individual consumption expenditure/ actual individual consumption	ABRE	1 064 589	1 122 744	1 167 293	1 164 636	1 215 831	1 252 402	1 288 656	1 327 635

1 "Purpose" or "function" classifications are designed to indicate the "socio-economic objectives" that institutional units aim to achieve through various kinds of outlays. COICOP is the Classification of Individual Consumption by Purpose and applies to households. COPNI is the Classification of the Purposes of Non-profit Institutions Serving Households and COFOG the Classification of the Functions of Government.
2 Package holidays data are dispersed between components (transport etc).

Source: Office for National Statistics, Blue Book 2014

19.17

Individual consumption expenditure by households, NPISH and general government
Chained volume measures (reference year 2011)

Classified by function (COICOP/COPNI/COFOG)

£ million

		2006	2007	2008	2009	2010	2011	2012	2013
P.31 FINAL CONSUMPTION EXPENDITURE OF HOUSEHOLDS									
01. **Food and non-alcoholic beverages**	ADIP	92 047	91 818	89 742	86 975	87 439	86 436	88 185	88 901
01.1 Food	ADIQ	80 810	80 760	78 824	76 229	76 900	75 897	77 728	78 535
01.2 Non-alcoholic beverages	ADIR	11 240	11 063	10 922	10 760	10 535	10 539	10 457	10 366
02. **Alcoholic beverages, tobacco and narcotics**	ADIS	44 402	41 954	42 950	41 883	40 801	40 719	39 679	38 262
02.1 Alcoholic beverages	ADIT	16 741	16 990	16 505	15 823	15 781	15 530	15 465	15 284
02.2 Tobacco	ADIU	21 407	20 541	19 663	18 823	19 002	18 286	17 428	16 306
02.3 Narcotics	MNC4	7 008	5 527	6 893	7 212	6 102	6 903	6 786	6 672
03. **Clothing and footwear**	ADIW	38 763	41 618	46 272	49 866	52 168	54 626	55 649	58 745
03.1 Clothing	ADIX	32 922	35 437	39 564	42 640	44 758	46 716	47 320	49 835
03.2 Footwear	ADIY	5 850	6 185	6 707	7 227	7 419	7 910	8 329	8 910
04. **Housing, water, electricity, gas and other fuels**	ADIZ	231 144	233 570	236 737	237 453	241 997	240 910	244 154	247 488
04.1 Actual rentals for housing	ADJA	45 297	47 019	48 933	49 759	49 796	51 526	53 244	54 260
04.2 Imputed rentals for housing	ADJB	141 862	143 118	144 386	146 520	148 152	149 390	150 531	152 781
04.3 Maintenance and repair of the dwelling	ADJC	2 958	2 781	2 276	2 091	2 139	2 149	2 051	2 382
04.4 Water supply and miscellaneous dwelling services	ADJD	8 620	8 919	8 843	8 611	8 893	8 943	8 729	8 573
04.5 Electricity, gas and other fuels	ADJE	32 787	31 975	32 538	30 929	33 304	28 902	29 599	29 492
05. **Furnishings, household equipment and routine maintenance of the house**	ADJF	52 949	53 718	52 090	47 794	48 127	46 970	46 874	48 121
05.1 Furniture, furnishings, carpets and other floor coverings	ADJG	19 993	20 511	19 150	16 673	16 132	16 637	16 122	17 053
05.2 Household textiles	ADJH	5 114	5 704	5 889	6 102	6 649	5 193	5 164	5 383
05.3 Household appliances	ADJI	6 940	6 710	6 847	6 068	6 203	6 465	6 817	6 499
05.4 Glassware, tableware and household utensils	ADJJ	5 452	5 100	4 854	4 651	4 379	4 906	4 991	5 124
05.5 Tools and equipment for house and garden	ADJK	4 605	5 051	4 511	3 979	3 869	3 590	3 766	3 709
05.6 Goods and services for routine household maintenance	ADJL	11 030	10 770	10 924	10 375	10 933	10 179	10 014	10 353
06. **Health**	ADJM	15 085	15 851	15 303	15 671	16 616	16 078	16 369	16 395
06.1 Medical products, appliances and equipment	ADJN	7 691	7 914	7 989	8 123	8 961	8 376	9 006	9 440
06.2 Out-patient services	ADJO	3 972	4 551	3 988	4 076	4 358	4 680	4 446	4 182
06.3 Hospital services	ADJP	3 471	3 404	3 344	3 501	3 308	3 022	2 917	2 773
07. **Transport**	ADJQ	145 046	150 922	144 868	140 707	137 051	136 220	140 327	142 106
07.1 Purchase of vehicles	ADJR	40 051	42 312	39 380	39 854	36 802	35 420	38 424	42 100
07.2 Operation of personal transport equipment	ADJS	67 447	68 521	67 337	65 435	64 482	64 267	64 838	62 690
07.3 Transport services	ADJT	37 523	39 821	38 146	35 406	35 739	36 533	37 065	37 316
08. **Communication**	ADJU	18 913	20 270	20 800	20 172	20 267	20 112	19 586	20 067
08.1 Postal services	CCGZ	1 542	1 448	1 279	1 219	1 050	1 062	1 050	994
08.2 Telephone & telefax equipment	ADQF	807	761	879	949	791	780	714	717
08.3 Telephone & telefax services	ADQG	16 674	18 114	18 653	18 013	18 424	18 270	17 822	18 356
09. **Recreation and culture**	ADJV	92 297	98 883	105 917	101 346	101 420	102 391	105 814	108 030
09.1 Audio-visual, photographic and information processing equipment	ADJW	11 507	12 873	16 497	17 034	18 059	19 838	22 791	23 989
09.2 Other major durables for recreation and culture	ADJX	7 516	7 771	8 049	8 027	8 021	7 243	7 437	8 282
09.3 Other recreational items and equipment; flowers, gardens and pets	ADJY	26 066	29 733	30 968	29 125	29 780	28 624	28 936	30 610
09.4 Recreational and cultural services	ADJZ	36 438	37 117	37 851	35 199	33 962	35 077	35 306	34 515
09.5 Newspapers, books and stationery	ADKM	15 000	14 853	13 830	12 543	11 805	11 609	11 344	10 634
09.6 Package holidays[2]	ADMI	–	–	–	–	–	–	–	–
10. **Education**									
10. Education services	ADMJ	16 169	16 491	16 303	16 492	16 037	15 826	15 427	15 072
11. **Restaurants and Hotels**	ADMK	98 253	98 979	96 329	88 427	91 280	93 572	92 960	94 342
11.1 Catering services	ADML	85 545	84 867	82 129	76 041	77 706	78 430	77 006	77 304
11.2 Accommodation services	ADMM	12 849	14 150	14 202	12 423	13 595	15 142	15 954	17 038
12. **Miscellaneous goods and services**	ADMN	132 389	136 350	129 700	124 121	123 807	123 954	126 846	131 730
12.1 Personal care	ADMO	24 633	24 827	24 042	23 937	24 161	24 206	24 741	26 415
12.2 Prostitution	MND2	5 372	5 430	5 483	5 503	5 548	5 612	5 652	5 651
12.3 Personal effects n.e.c.	ADMP	9 580	8 957	8 722	8 287	10 263	10 804	11 014	11 487
12.4 Social protection	ADMQ	14 829	14 730	14 915	13 855	13 554	13 043	13 082	13 392
12.5 Insurance	ADMR	26 841	29 017	22 575	24 052	21 451	20 521	23 587	26 316
12.6 Financial services n.e.c.	ADMS	41 258	43 250	43 302	39 846	40 839	41 515	40 214	40 029
12.7 Other services n.e.c.	ADMT	10 807	10 794	10 010	9 021	8 035	8 253	8 556	8 440
0. Final consumption expenditure in the UK by resident and non-resident households (domestic concept)	ABQJ	972 909	998 513	997 067	970 563	976 926	977 814	991 870	1 009 259
P.33 Final consumption expenditure outside the UK by UK resident households	ABTC	44 043	46 026	41 277	32 640	32 009	30 118	31 598	32 592
P.34 Final consumption expenditure in the UK by households resident in the rest of the world	CCHX	−21 280	−21 215	−21 118	−20 721	−21 963	−22 089	−22 609	−24 600
P.31 Final consumption expenditure by UK resident households in the UK and abroad (national concept)	ABPF	994 192	1 021 686	1 016 524	982 490	986 956	985 843	1 000 859	1 017 251

19.17

Individual consumption expenditure by households, NPISH and general government
Chained volume measures (reference year 2011)

continued   Classified by function (COICOP/COPNI/COFOG)   £ million

			2006	2007	2008	2009	2010	2011	2012	2013
P.31	**CONSUMPTION EXPENDITURE OF UK RESIDENT HOUSEHOLDS**									
P.31	Final consumption expenditure of UK resident households in the UK and abroad	ABPF	994 192	1 021 686	1 016 524	982 490	986 956	985 843	1 000 859	1 017 251
13.	**FINAL INDIVIDUAL CONSUMPTION EXPENDITURE OF NPISH**									
P.31	Final individual consumption expenditure of NPISH	ABNU	50 769	50 739	50 869	52 081	51 337	53 259	49 936	50 651
14.	**FINAL INDIVIDUAL CONSUMPTION EXPENDITURE OF GENERAL GOVERNMENT**									
14.1	Health	K4CP	97 280	100 493	105 819	110 357	112 723	115 316	118 923	121 206
14.2	Recreation and culture	K4CQ	6 468	6 596	6 345	6 374	6 150	6 151	6 224	5 486
14.3	Education	K4CR	58 404	58 216	57 881	58 027	58 336	59 458	60 841	61 802
14.4	Social protection	K4CS	34 283	33 673	33 322	33 441	33 235	32 375	31 953	31 479
P.31	Final individual consumption expenditure of general government	NSZK	196 111	198 818	203 338	208 170	210 422	213 300	217 941	219 972
P.31 P.41	Total, individual consumption expenditure/ actual individual consumption	YBIO	1 240 273	1 270 427	1 270 082	1 242 557	1 248 578	1 252 402	1 268 736	1 287 874

1 "Purpose" or "function" classifications are designed to indicate the "socio-economic objectives" that institutional units aim to achieve through various kinds of outlays. COICOP is the Classification of Individual Consumption by Purpose and applies to households. COPNI is the Classification of the Purposes of Non-profit Institutions Serving Households and COFOG the Classification of the Functions of Government.

2 Package holidays data are dispersed between components (transport etc)

Source: Office for National Statistics, Blue Book 2014

19.18 Change in inventories at chained volume measures [1]

Reference year 2011, £ million

	Mining and quarrying	Manufacturing industries				Electricity, gas and water supply	Distributive trades		Other industries	Changes in inventories [3]
		Materials and fuel	Work in progress	Finished goods	Total		Wholesale [2]	Retail [2]		
Level of inventories held at end-December 2012 [4]	1 326	20 094	17 344	19 742	57 193	5 508	36 974	36 039	74 439	212 531
	FAEA	FBNF	FBNG	FBNH	DHBM	FAEB	FAJX	FBYN	DLWX	CAFU
Seasonally adjusted										
1997	1 251	200	- 1 427	- 104	- 1 331	- 501	2 631	368	745	2 685
1998	5 876	833	- 323	2 016	2 526	37	6 373	580	- 6 469	4 874
1999	- 7 600	794	- 325	- 1 614	- 1 145	- 112	- 5 411	1 174	15 552	7 847
2000	- 1 076	2 105	1 288	206	3 599	1 016	- 1 034	464	- 1 610	1 243
2001	2 184	- 3 559	1 214	2 585	241	- 407	4 316	1 976	2 152	9 684
2002	- 1 580	- 511	- 719	- 866	- 2 097	188	- 208	1 970	3 699	2 749
2003	56	- 304	- 1 010	- 497	- 1 810	- 183	205	972	4 517	4 093
2004	- 1 101	- 488	- 731	- 1 101	- 2 321	- 824	- 73	1 361	1 731	- 44
2005	- 1 788	127	- 287	- 997	- 1 158	- 1 584	- 1 237	675	899	- 2 760
2006	276	- 86	629	205	749	- 46	2 272	242	- 1 042	1 793
2007	- 999	- 312	- 1 403	- 675	- 2 389	168	115	877	1 627	49
2008	1 426	- 1 641	- 1 091	- 1 653	- 4 387	- 343	- 6 358	309	511	- 8 616
2009	- 1 450	- 3 292	- 949	- 4 296	- 8 536	5 796	- 3 624	118	- 10 955	- 17 629
2010	- 507	1 046	- 1 050	- 744	- 749	- 918	- 55	287	7 420	5 481
2011	262	1 294	- 423	141	1 012	- 75	1 546	351	- 345	2 751
2012	179	- 1 174	743	738	307	- 238	1 586	235	1 528	3 597
2013	- 197	736	773	- 162	1 347	434	5 342	- 973	2 812	8 765

1. Estimates are given to the nearest £ million but cannot be regarded as accurate to this degree.

2. Wholesaling and retailing estimates exclude the motor trades.

3. Quarterly alignment adjustment included in this series.

4. Estimates of level based on previously available data.

Source: Office for National Statistics

19.19
Gross fixed capital formation at current purchasers' prices[1]
Analysis by broad sector and type of asset
Total economy

£ million

			2005	2006	2007	2008	2009	2010	2011	2012	2013
	Private sector										
	New dwellings, excluding land	L5ZQ	48 268	48 572	51 112	50 998	42 338	46 510	50 658	50 199	54 127
	Other buildings and structures	EQBU	28 039	31 795	37 984	45 428	40 213	37 314	43 572	48 152	50 094
	Transport equipment	EQBV	9 692	11 836	10 508	10 855	9 344	13 050	8 261	9 692	10 341
	ICT equipment and other machinery and equipment										
	and cultivated biological resources	EQBW	39 525	40 733	45 014	44 752	36 381	37 234	43 835	46 379	48 227
	Intellectual property products	EQBX	42 082	43 852	46 928	49 728	46 368	48 209	51 909	53 260	57 554
	Costs associated with the transfer of										
	ownership of non-produced assets	L5ZR	33 217	38 850	40 866	20 289	8 439	12 657	11 520	12 138	13 774
P.51g	Total	EQBZ	200 823	215 638	232 412	222 050	183 083	194 974	209 755	219 820	234 117
S.11001	**Public non-financial corporations**										
	New dwellings, excluding land	L5YQ	3 574	4 048	3 897	4 033	4 184	3 992	3 366	3 135	3 297
	Other buildings and structures	DEES	2 617	2 432	2 228	1 446	1 571	1 157	977	650	1 402
	Transport equipment	DEEP	327	173	145	368	301	472	465	343	149
	ICT equipment and other machinery and equipment										
	and cultivated biological resources	DEEQ	16 454	966	1 246	1 997	1 516	1 412	1 295	1 019	913
	Intellectual property products	DLXJ	2 044	2 028	2 067	2 081	2 055	2 055	2 024	2 022	2 013
	Costs associated with the transfer of										
	ownership of non-produced assets	L5ZL	−4 226	−3 589	−3 062	−1 654	−370	−406	−363	−387	−418
P.51g	Total	FCCJ	20 790	6 058	6 521	8 271	9 257	8 682	7 764	6 782	7 356
S.13	**General government**										
	New dwellings, excluding land	L5ZU	46	9	3	15	1	−5	−8	115	98
	Other buildings and structures	EQCH	20 787	22 006	23 912	26 901	28 061	24 948	22 530	22 408	20 025
	Transport equipment	EQCI	726	519	500	515	611	702	534	509	484
	ICT equipment, other machinery and equipment,										
	cultivated biological resources, weapons	EQCJ	−6 676	8 551	7 555	9 035	10 130	11 309	11 248	10 017	9 997
	Intellectual property products	EQCK	2 877	3 209	3 321	3 691	3 874	5 159	4 902	4 879	4 805
	Costs associated with the transfer of										
	ownership of non-produced assets	L5ZV	−536	−1 064	−474	2 038	4 061	4 429	4 054	4 293	4 637
P.51g	Total	NNBF	17 224	33 230	34 817	42 195	46 738	46 542	43 260	42 221	40 046
P.51g	Total gross fixed capital formation	NPQX	238 837	254 926	273 750	272 516	239 078	250 198	260 779	268 823	281 519

1 Components may not sum to totals due to rounding.

Source: Office for National Statistics, Blue Book 2014

19.20
Gross fixed capital formation at current purchasers' prices[1]
Analysis by type of asset
Total economy

£ million

		2005	2006	2007	2008	2009	2010	2011	2012	2013
Tangible fixed assets										
New dwellings, excluding land	DFDK	51 888	52 629	55 012	55 046	46 523	50 497	54 016	53 449	57 522
Other buildings and structures	DLWS	51 443	56 233	64 124	73 775	69 845	63 419	67 079	71 210	71 521
Transport equipment	DLWZ	10 745	12 528	11 153	11 738	10 256	14 224	9 260	10 544	10 974
ICT equipment, other machinery and equipment,										
cultivated biological resources, weapons	DLXI	49 303	50 250	53 815	55 784	48 027	49 955	56 378	57 415	59 137
Total	EQCQ	163 379	171 640	184 104	196 343	174 651	178 095	186 733	192 618	199 154
Intellectual property products	DLXP	47 003	49 089	52 316	55 500	52 297	55 423	58 835	60 161	64 372
Costs associated with the transfer of										
ownership of non-produced assets	DFBH	28 455	34 197	37 330	20 673	12 130	16 680	15 211	16 044	17 993
P.51g Total gross fixed capital formation	NPQX	238 837	254 926	273 750	272 516	239 078	250 198	260 779	268 823	281 519

1 Components may not sum to totals due to rounding.

Source: Office for National Statistics, Blue Book 2014

19.21 Gross fixed capital formation[1,2]
Chained volume measures (reference year 2011)
Total economy: Analysis by broad sector and type of asset

£ million

			2005	2006	2007	2008	2009	2010	2011	2012	2013
	Private sector										
	New dwellings, excluding land	L62K	61 326	57 669	57 690	54 030	43 469	47 482	50 658	48 349	50 541
	Other buildings and structures	EQCU	29 796	31 651	36 356	41 953	37 866	37 220	43 572	46 426	46 585
	Transport equipment	EQCV	10 485	12 928	11 432	11 339	9 641	13 494	8 261	9 773	10 477
	ICT equipment and other machinery and equipment and cultivated biological resources	EQCW	48 169	49 938	55 959	53 207	38 988	40 440	43 835	45 883	48 442
	Intellectual property products	EQCX	47 105	48 052	50 420	51 978	48 320	49 387	51 909	52 716	56 640
	Costs associated with the transfer of ownership of non-produced assets	L62L	39 078	45 328	46 864	22 477	8 834	13 013	11 520	11 872	13 332
P.51g	Total	EQCZ	235 421	245 860	261 271	230 868	181 005	192 772	209 755	215 019	226 017
S.11001	**Public non-financial corporations**										
	New dwellings, excluding land	L62M	4 535	4 807	4 399	4 270	4 288	4 068	3 366	3 015	3 074
	Other buildings and structures	DEEX	2 836	2 420	2 180	1 374	1 511	1 153	977	643	1 324
	Transport equipment	DEEU	353	189	158	383	310	489	465	345	150
	ICT equipment and other machinery and equipment and cultivated biological resources	DEEV	20 030	1 160	1 505	2 250	1 536	1 458	1 295	1 007	903
	Intellectual property products	EQDE	2 424	2 416	2 393	2 309	2 189	2 124	2 024	1 945	1 847
	Costs associated with the transfer of ownership of non-produced assets	L62N	−4 971	−4 187	−3 511	−1 832	−388	−418	−363	−378	−406
P.51g	Total	EQDG	25 303	7 140	7 376	8 765	9 467	8 876	7 764	6 577	6 892
S.13	**General government**										
	New dwellings, excluding landcosts	L62O	60	11	3	16	–	−5	−8	111	92
	Other buildings and structures	EQDI	22 303	21 997	23 373	24 664	26 217	24 728	22 530	21 558	18 445
	Transport equipment	EQDJ	774	563	539	535	622	725	534	510	487
	ICT equipment,other machinery and equipment, cultivated biological resources, weapons	EQDK	−8 508	9 956	8 817	9 924	10 249	11 625	11 248	9 884	9 827
	Intellectual property services	EQDL	3 336	3 612	3 647	3 853	4 032	5 314	4 902	4 839	4 760
	Costs associated with the transfer of ownership of non-produced assets	L62P	−631	−1 242	−544	2 258	4 252	4 554	4 054	4 199	4 498
P.51g	Total	EQDN	18 537	35 009	36 036	41 500	45 553	46 935	43 260	41 101	38 109
P.51g	Total gross fixed capital formation	NPQR	271 284	280 162	294 888	281 041	240 605	254 861	260 779	262 697	271 018

1 For the years before 2011, totals differ from the sum of their components.
2 Components may not sum to totals due to rounding.

Source: Office for National Statistics, Blue Book 2014

19.22 Gross fixed capital formation[1,2]
Chained volume measures (reference year 2011)
Total economy: Analysis by type of asset

£ million

		2005	2006	2007	2008	2009	2010	2011	2012	2013
Tangible fixed assets										
New dwellings, excluding land	DFDV	65 922	62 490	62 095	58 320	47 758	51 548	54 016	51 475	53 707
Other buildings and structures	EQDP	54 666	55 978	61 375	68 132	65 768	63 260	67 079	68 627	66 354
Transport equipment	DLWJ	11 617	13 681	12 132	12 258	10 575	14 708	9 260	10 628	11 114
ICT equipment, other machinery and equipment, cultivated biological resources, weapons	DLWM	57 009	58 273	64 018	63 007	48 797	51 513	56 378	56 774	59 172
Total	EQDS	186 598	187 866	197 481	200 550	173 279	180 930	186 733	187 504	190 347
Intellectual property products	EQDT	52 839	54 047	56 437	58 115	54 511	56 808	58 835	59 500	63 247
Costs associated with the transfer of ownership of non-produced assets	DFDW	33 477	39 901	42 809	22 903	12 698	17 148	15 211	15 693	17 424
P.51g Total gross fixed capital formation	NPQR	271 284	280 162	294 888	281 041	240 605	254 861	260 779	262 697	271 018

1 For the years before 2011, totals differ from the sum of their components.
2 Components may not sum to totals due to rounding.

Source: Office for National Statistics, Blue Book 2014

Education

Chapter 20

Education

Educational establishments in the UK are administered and financed in several ways. Most schools are controlled by local authorities, which are part of the structure of local government, but some are 'assisted', receiving grants direct from central government sources and being controlled by governing bodies who have a substantial degree of autonomy. Completely outside the public sector are non.maintained schools run by individuals, companies or charitable institutions.

For the purposes of UK education statistics, schools fall under the following broad categories:

Mainstream state schools
(In Northern Ireland, grant-aided mainstream schools)

These schools work in partnership with other schools and local authorities and they receive funding from local authorities. Since 1 September 1999, the categories (typically in England) are:

Community – schools formerly known as 'county' plus some former grant-maintained (GM) schools

Foundation – most former GM schools

Voluntary Aided – schools formerly known as 'aided' and some former GM schools

Voluntary Controlled – schools formerly known as 'controlled'

Non-maintained mainstream schools

These consist of:

(a) Independent schools

Schools which charge fees and may also be financed by individuals, companies or charitable institutions. These include Direct Grant schools, where the governing bodies are assisted by departmental grants and a proportion of the pupils attending them do so free or under an arrangement by which local authorities meet tuition fees. City Technology Colleges (CTCs) and Academies (applicable in England only) are also included as independent schools.

(b) Non-maintained schools
Run by voluntary bodies who may receive some grant from central government for capital work and for equipment, but their current expenditure is met primarily from the fees charged to local authorities for pupils placed in schools.

Special schools

Special schools provide education for children with Special Educational Needs (SEN) (in Scotland, Record of Needs or a Coordinated Support Plan), who cannot be educated satisfactorily in an ordinary school. Maintained special schools are run by local authorities, while non-maintained special schools are financed as described at (b) above.

Pupil Referral Units

Pupil Referral Units (PRUs) operate in England and Wales and provide education outside of a mainstream or special school setting, to meet the needs of difficult or disruptive children.

Schools in Scotland are categorised as Education Authority, Grant-aided, Opted-out/Self-governing (these three being grouped together as 'Publicly funded' schools), Independent schools and Partnership schools.

The home government departments dealing with education statistics are:

Department for Education (DfE)
Department for Business, Innovation and Skills (BIS)
Welsh Government (WG)
Scottish Government (SG)
Northern Ireland Department of Education (DENI)
Northern Ireland Department for Employment and Learning (DELNI)

Each of the home education departments in Great Britain, along with the Northern Ireland Department of Education, have overall responsibility for funding the schools sectors in their own country.

Up to March 2001, further education (FE) courses in FE sector colleges in England and in Wales were largely funded through grants from the respective FE funding councils. In April 2001, however, the Learning and Skills Council (LSC) took over the responsibility for funding the FE sector in England, and the National Council for Education and Training for Wales (part of Education and Learning Wales – ELWa) did so for Wales. The Apprenticeships, Skills, Children and Learning Act 2009 received Royal Assent on 12 November 2009 for the dissolution of the Learning and Skills Council by 2010 and the transfer of its functions on 1 April 2010 to local authorities and two new agencies: the Young People's Learning Agency (YPLA) and the Skills Funding Agency. The YPLA champions young people's learning by providing financial support to young learners; by funding academies, general FE and sixth form colleges and other 16 to 19 providers; and supporting local authorities to secure sufficient education and training places for all 16 to 19 year olds in England. The Skills Funding Agency funds further education colleges and training providers in England to deliver adult skills and apprenticeships. In Wales, the National Council – ELWa, funds FE provision made by FE institutions via a third party or sponsored arrangements. The Scottish Further Education Funding Council (SFEFC) funds FE colleges in Scotland, while the Department for Employment and Learning funds FE colleges in Northern Ireland.

From 1 April 2012, funding for the education and training of 3 to 19 year olds in England will become the responsibility of the Education Funding Agency (EFA), which will be a new executive agency of the Department for Education. The EFA will directly fund academies, free schools, university technology colleges, studio schools and 16 to 19 providers. It will distribute funding to local authorities for them to pass on to their maintained schools and it will also be responsible for the distribution of capital funding.

Higher education (HE) courses in higher education establishments are largely publicly funded through block grants from the HE funding councils in England and Scotland, the Higher Education Council – ELWa in Wales, and the Department for Employment and Learning in Northern Ireland. In addition, some designated HE (mainly HND/HNC Diplomas and Certificates of HE) is also funded by these sources. The FE sources mentioned above fund the remainder.

Statistics for the separate systems obtained in England, Wales, Scotland and Northern Ireland are collected and processed separately in accordance with the particular needs of the responsible departments. Since 1994/95 the Higher Education Statistics Agency (HESA) has undertaken the data collection for all higher education institutions (HEIs) in the UK. This includes the former Universities Funding Council (UFC) funded UK universities previously collected by the Universities Statistical Record. There are some structural differences in the information collected for schools, FE and HE in each of the four home countries and in some tables the GB/UK data presented are amalgamations from sources that are not entirely comparable.

Stages of education

There are five stages of education: early years, primary, secondary, FE and HE, and education is compulsory for all children between the ages of 5 (4 in Northern Ireland) and 16. The non-compulsory fourth stage, FE, covers non-advanced education, which can be taken at further (including tertiary) education colleges, HE institutions (HEIs) and increasingly in secondary schools. The fifth stage, HE, is study beyond GCE A levels and their equivalent which, for most full-time students, takes place in universities and other HEIs.

Early years education

Children under 5 attend a variety of settings including state nursery schools, nursery classes within primary schools and, in England and Wales, reception classes within primary schools, as well as s ettings outside the state sector such as voluntary pre-schools or privately run nurseries. In recent years there has been a major expansion of early years education, and the Education Act 2002 extended the National Curriculum for England to include the foundation stage. The foundation stage was introduced in September 2000, and covered children's education from the age of 3 to the end of the reception year, when most are just 5 and some almost 6 years old. The Early Years Foundation Stage (EYFS), came into force in September 2008, and is a single regulatory and quality framework for the provision of learning, development and care for children in all registered early years settings between birth and the academic year in which they turn 5.

Children born in Scotland between March and December are eligible for early years education at the time the Pre-School Education and Day Care Census is carried out. In Scotland, early years education is called ante-pre-school education for those aged 3 to 4 years old, and pre-school education for those aged 4.

Primary education

The primary stage covers three age ranges: nursery (under 5), infant (5 to 7 or 8) and junior (up to 11 or 12) but in Scotland and Northern Ireland there is generally no distinction between infant and junior schools. Most public sector primary schools take both boys and girls in mixed classes. It is usual to transfer straight to secondary school at age 11 (in England, Wales and Northern Ireland) or 12 (in Scotland), but in England some children make the transition via middle schools catering for various age ranges between 8 and 14. Depending on their individual age ranges middle schools are classified as either primary or secondary.

Secondary education

Public provision of secondary education in an area may consist of a combination of different types of school, the pattern reflecting historical circumstance and the policy adopted by the local authority. Comprehensive schools largely admit pupils without reference to ability or aptitude and cater for all the children in a neighbourhood, but in some areas they co.exist with grammar, secondary modern or technical schools. In 2005/06, 88 per cent of secondary pupils in England attended comprehensive schools while all secondary schools in Wales are comprehensive schools.

The majority of education authority secondary schools in Scotland are comprehensive in character and offer six years of secondary education; however, in remote areas there are several two-year and four-year secondary schools.

In Northern Ireland, post-primary education is provided by grammar schools and non-selective secondary schools.

In England, the Specialist Schools Programme helps schools, in partnership with private sector sponsors and supported by additional government funding, to establish distinctive identities through their chosen specialisms and achieve their targets to raise standards. Specialist schools have a special focus on their chosen subject area but must meet the National Curriculum requirements and deliver a broad and balanced education to all pupils. Any maintained secondary school in England can apply to be designated as a specialist school in one of ten specialist areas: arts, business & enterprise, engineering, humanities, languages, mathematics & computing, music, science, sports and technology. Schools can also combine any two specialisms.

Academies, operating in England, are publicly funded independent local schools that provide free education. They are all-ability schools established by sponsors from business, faith or voluntary groups working with partners from the local community.

Academies benefit from greater freedoms to help innovate and raise standards. These include freedom from local authority control, ability to set pay and conditions for staff, freedom from following the National Curriculum and the ability to change the lengths of terms and school days.

The Academies Programme was first introduced in March 2000 with the objective of replacing poorly performing schools. Academies were established and driven by external sponsors, to achieve a transformation in education performance.

The Academies Programme was expanded through legislation in the Academies Act 2010. This enables all maintained primary, secondary and special schools to apply to become an Academy. The early focus is on schools rated outstanding by Ofsted and the first of these new academies opened in September 2010. These schools do not have a sponsor but instead are expected to work with underperforming schools to help raise standards.

Special schools

Special schools (day or boarding) provide education for children who require specialist support to complete their education, for example because they have physical or other difficulties. Many pupils with special educational needs are educated in mainstream schools. All children attending special schools are offered a curriculum designed to overcome their learning difficulties and to enable them to become self-reliant. Since December 2005, special schools have also been able to apply for the Special Educational Needs (SEN) specialism, under the Specialist Schools Programme. They can apply for a curriculum specialism, but not for both the SEN and a curriculum specialism.

Further education

The term further education may be used in a general sense to cover all non.advanced courses taken after the period of compulsory education, but more commonly it excludes those staying on at secondary school and those in higher education, that is, courses in universities and colleges leading to qualifications above GCE A Level, Scottish Certificate of Education (SCE) Higher Grade, GNVQ/NVQ level 3, and their equivalents. Since 1 April 1993, sixth form colleges in England and Wales have been included in the further education sector.

Higher education

Higher education is defined as courses that are of a standard that is higher than GCE A level, the Higher Grade of the SCE/National Qualification, GNVQ/NVQ level 3 or the Edexcel (formerly BTEC) or SQA National Certificate/Diploma. There are three main levels of HE course:

(i) Postgraduate courses leading to higher degrees, diplomas and certificates (including postgraduate certificates of education (PGCE) and professional qualifications) which usually require a first degree as entry qualification.

(ii) Undergraduate courses which include first degrees, first degrees with qualified teacher status, enhanced first degrees, first degrees obtained concurrently with a diploma, and intercalated first degrees (where first degree students, usually in medicine, dentistry or veterinary medicine, interrupt their studies to complete a one-year course of advanced studies in a related topic).

(iii) Other undergraduate courses which include all other higher education courses, for example HNDs and Diplomas in HE.

As a result of the Further and Higher Education Act 1992, former polytechnics and some other HEIs were designated as universities in 1992/93. Students normally attend HE courses at HEIs, but some attend at FE colleges. Some also attend institutions which do not receive public grant (such as the University of Buckingham) and these numbers are excluded from the tables. However, the University of Buckingham is included in Tables 20.6 and 20.7.

20.1: Number of schools, by type of school - time series

United Kingdom

Numbers

	Academic years			
	2000/01	2010/11[14]	2011/12[14]	2012/13[14]
UNITED KINGDOM				
Public sector mainstream				
Nursery[1]	3,228	3,130	3,095	3,085
Primary	22,902	21,281	21,165	21,069
Middle [2]	.	.	.	4
Secondary[3,4,5]	4,352	4,121	4,072	4,077
of which Middle deemed secondary	316	225	196	189
Non-maintained mainstream	2,397	2,498	2,502	2,497
Special schools	1,498	1,293	1,281	1,269
of which state-funded	1,401	1,218	1,209	1,198
of which non-maintained	97	75	72	71
Pupil referral units	338	427	403	400
ALL SCHOOLS	34,715	32,750	32,518	32,401
ENGLAND				
Public sector mainstream				
Maintained nursery	506	423	423	417
State-funded primary[6]	18,069	16,884	16,818	16,784
State-funded secondary[3,4,5]	3,496	3,310	3,268	3,281
of which Middle deemed secondary	316	225	196	189
Non-maintained mainstream[7]	2,190	2,417	2,421	2,414
Special schools	1,175	1,046	1,039	1,032
of which state-funded[8]	1,113	971	967	961
of which non-maintained	62	75	72	71
Pupil referral units	308	427	403	400
ALL SCHOOLS	25,744	24,507	24,372	24,328
WALES				
Public sector mainstream				
Nursery	41	23	22	20
Primary	1,631	1,435	1,412	1,374
Middle[2]	.	.	.	4
Secondary[3,9]	229	222	221	216
Non-maintained mainstream	54	66	66	68
Special (maintained)	45	43	43	42
Pupil referral units	30	..	..	..
ALL SCHOOLS	2,030	1,789	1,764	1,724
SCOTLAND				
Public sector mainstream				
Nursery[1,10]	2,586	2,586	2,553	2,551
Primary	2,278	2,099	2,081	2,064
Secondary[9]	389	372	367	365
Non-maintained mainstream[11]	127	..	..	..
Special schools	230	163	158	155
of which maintained	195	163	158	155
of which non-maintained[11]	35	..	..	..
ALL SCHOOLS	5,610	5,220	5,159	5,135
NORTHERN IRELAND				
Grant aided mainstream				
Nursery[12]	95	98	97	97
Primary[13]	924	863	854	847
Secondary	238	217	216	215
Non-maintained mainstream	26	15	15	15
Special (maintained)	48	41	41	40
ALL SCHOOLS	1,331	1,234	1,223	1,214

Sources: Department for Education; Welsh Government; Scottish Government; Northern Ireland Department of Education

1 Nursery schools figures for Scotland prior to 1998/99 only include data for Local Authority pre-schools. Data thereafter include partnership pre-schools.
  From 2005/06, figures exclude pre-school education centres not in partnership with the local authority.
2 In Wales, the Middle School for pupils of both primary and secondary school age was introduced in 2012/13.
3 Time series revised to show State-funded secondary schools (i.e. including CTCs and Academies, previously included in the 'Non-maintained mainstream' category).
4 From 1993/94, excludes sixth form colleges in England and Wales which were reclassified as further education colleges on 1 April 1993.
  In 1990/91, there were 114 sixth form colleges in England and 2 in Wales.
5 In England includes secondary sponsor-led academies, secondary converter academies and secondary free schools.
6 In England includes middle deemed primary schools as well as primary sponsor-led academies, primary convertor academies and primary free schools
7 In England includes direct grant nurseries.
8 In England includes special converter academies. Excludes general hospital schools.
9 All secondary schools are classed as Comprehensive.
10 In Scotland, there was a change in the timing of the Pre-School Education Census in 2010 from January to September. Please note that due to changes in timing, figures for
   September 2010 (provided for 2010/11) may not be directly comparable with previously published January figures.   For 2010/11, September 2010 census figure provided.
   For 2011/12, September 2011 census figure provided. For 2012/13, September 2012 census figure provided.
11 Figures for non-maintained schools are not available as the relevant publication was discontinued in 2010.
12 Excludes voluntary and private pre-school education centres.
13 From 1995/96, includes Preparatory Departments in Grammar Schools.
14 For Scotland data 2010, 2011 and 2012 primary and pre-school teacher figures and 2012 pre-school centre figures have been revised.

20.2 Full-time and part-time pupils by age, gender[1,2] and school type, 2013/14

Thousands

United Kingdom

| | Maintained schools[3] | | | | | | | | | Non-maintained[4] | | | |
| | Nursery Schools[8,9] | Primary Schools[5,6,7] | | | Middle Schools[11] | Secondary Schools[5,12] | Special schools[13] | Pupil Referral Units[14] | All maintained schools | Special schools | Other Schools[15] | All non-maintained schools | All schools[19] |
		Nursery Classes	Other Classes[10]	Total[6]									
Age at 31 August 2013[16]													
All													
2-4[17]	150.0	272.3	574.7	1,031.0	0.3	7.4	6.6	-	1,195.3	0.1	64.4	64.5	1,259.8
5[18]	-	-	634.5	746.2	0.1	4.5	5.0	0.1	755.8	0.1	29.2	29.3	785.1
6	-	0.0	618.0	724.7	0.1	3.7	5.2	0.1	733.8	0.1	30.5	30.5	764.3
7	0.0	0.0	593.0	699.2	0.1	3.5	5.8	0.1	708.8	0.1	32.4	32.5	741.3
8	0.0	0.0	580.0	684.4	0.1	3.1	6.3	0.2	694.0	0.1	33.5	33.6	727.6
9	0.0	0.0	555.7	656.1	0.1	17.2	6.7	0.2	680.3	0.1	36.0	36.1	716.5
10	0.0	0.0	538.0	635.1	0.1	19.6	7.1	0.3	662.1	0.2	36.9	37.1	699.2
11	0.0	0.0	52.3	52.7	0.4	571.9	9.8	0.2	635.0	0.3	41.9	42.2	677.1
12	0.0	0.0	4.9	5.2	0.4	624.7	10.4	0.7	641.5	0.3	43.4	43.7	685.3
13	0.0	0.0	0.3	0.3	0.5	641.9	11.2	1.5	655.4	0.4	45.7	46.0	701.4
14	0.0	0.0	0.1	0.1	0.5	658.2	11.8	2.8	673.5	0.5	49.2	49.7	723.1
15	0.0	0.0	0.2	0.2	0.5	659.9	12.1	6.4	679.0	0.5	51.3	51.8	730.9
16	0.0	0.0	0.0	0.0	0.2	311.4	6.7	0.2	318.5	0.5	42.9	43.3	361.8
17	0.0	0.0	-	-	0.2	245.1	5.2	0.1	250.6	0.4	40.1	40.5	291.1
18	0.0	0.0	0.0	0.0	-	27.5	3.6	-	31.2	0.3	7.9	8.2	39.4
19 and over	0.0	0.0	-	-	-	1.2	0.1	-	1.2	0.2	3.0	3.2	4.4
Total[19]	150.0	272.3	4,151.7	5,235.1	3.5	3,800.9	113.5	12.9	9,316.0	4.1	588.3	592.3	9,908.4
of which													
England	40.0	263.3	3,611.7	4,416.7	.	3,181.4	97.4	12.9	7,748.3	4.1	579.0	583.1	8,331.4
Wales	1.4	..	..	269.4	3.5	186.4	4.3	..	465.1	0.0	8.6	8.6	473.7
Scotland	102.9		377.4	377.4	.	289.2	7.0	.	776.4	..	..	..	776.4
Northern Ireland	5.9	9.0	162.6	171.5	.	144.0	4.8	.	326.2	.	0.7	0.7	326.9
	0.0	0.0	0.0	0.0	0.0	0.0	0.0	0.0	0.0	0.0	0.0	0.0	0.0
Males[1]													
2-4[17]	24.4	138.2	293.5	525.7	0.1	3.7	4.6	-	558.6	0.1	32.3	32.3	590.9
5[18]	-	-	323.5	380.7	0.1	2.2	3.6	-	386.6	-	14.7	14.7	401.3
6	-	0.0	315.7	370.1	-	1.9	3.8	0.1	375.9	-	15.5	15.5	391.4
7	0.0	0.0	302.5	356.8	-	1.8	4.2	0.1	362.9	0.1	16.4	16.5	379.4
8	0.0	0.0	295.6	348.9	0.1	1.6	4.5	0.1	355.3	0.1	17.2	17.3	372.6
9	0.0	0.0	283.4	334.8	-	8.7	4.8	0.2	348.6	0.1	18.4	18.5	367.1
10	0.0	0.0	274.2	323.7	0.1	10.0	5.2	0.3	339.2	0.2	19.3	19.4	358.7
11	0.0	0.0	26.6	26.9	0.2	290.9	7.1	0.2	325.2	0.2	21.5	21.7	346.9
12	0.0	0.0	3.1	3.2	0.2	316.5	7.5	0.6	328.0	0.2	22.3	22.5	350.6
13	0.0	0.0	0.1	0.1	0.2	326.0	8.2	1.1	335.6	0.3	23.4	23.7	359.3
14	0.0	0.0	0.1	0.1	0.2	334.2	8.5	2.0	345.0	0.3	25.3	25.6	370.6
15	0.0	0.0	0.1	0.1	0.2	334.2	8.6	4.2	347.3	0.4	26.3	26.7	374.1
16	0.0	0.0	0.0	0.0	0.1	149.8	4.5	0.1	154.5	0.3	21.9	22.3	176.7
17	0.0	0.0	-	-	0.1	115.7	3.3	-	119.1	0.3	20.7	21.0	140.0
18	0.0	0.0	0.0	0.0	-	14.7	2.3	-	17.0	0.2	4.3	4.5	21.5
19 and over	0.0	0.0	0.0	0.0	0.0	0.5	-	-	0.5	0.1	1.8	1.9	2.4
Total[19]	24.4	138.2	2,118.4	2,671.2	1.6	1,912.4	80.6	9.0	4,699.3	2.9	301.3	304.2	5,003.5
of which													
England	20.8	133.6	1,842.6	2,252.9	.	1,601.2	69.4	9.0	3,953.2	2.9	296.4	299.3	4,252.5
Wales	0.7	..	..	137.9	1.6	94.2	3.1	..	237.5	0.0	4.5	4.5	242.0
Scotland	..		192.8	192.8	.	145.5	4.9	.	343.2	..	..	..	343.2
Northern Ireland	2.9	4.6	83.0	87.6	.	71.5	3.3	.	165.4	.	0.3	0.3	165.8
	0.0	0.0	0.0	0.0	0.0	0.0	0.0	0.0	0.0	0.0	0.0	0.0	0.0
Females[1]													
2-4[17]	22.7	134.1	281.2	505.3	0.1	3.7	2.1	-	533.9	-	32.2	32.2	566.1
5[18]	-	-	311.0	365.5	0.1	2.2	1.4	-	369.2	-	14.5	14.5	383.7
6	-	0.0	302.3	354.5	0.1	1.8	1.4	-	357.8	-	15.0	15.0	372.9
7	0.0	0.0	290.5	342.4	0.1	1.8	1.6	-	345.9	-	16.0	16.0	361.8
8	0.0	0.0	284.4	335.4	-	1.5	1.7	-	338.7	-	16.2	16.3	355.0
9	0.0	0.0	272.3	321.3	0.1	8.5	1.8	-	331.7	-	17.6	17.6	349.4
10	0.0	0.0	263.8	311.3	-	9.6	1.9	-	322.9	-	17.6	17.6	340.5
11	0.0	0.0	25.6	25.8	0.2	281.1	2.7	-	309.8	0.1	20.4	20.5	330.3
12	0.0	0.0	1.9	2.0	0.2	308.3	2.9	0.1	313.5	0.1	21.1	21.2	334.7
13	0.0	0.0	0.2	0.2	0.2	316.0	3.1	0.4	319.8	0.1	22.3	22.4	342.2
14	0.0	0.0	0.1	0.1	0.3	324.0	3.3	0.9	328.5	0.1	24.0	24.1	352.5
15	0.0	0.0	0.1	0.1	0.3	325.7	3.5	2.2	331.7	0.1	25.0	25.1	356.8
16	0.0	0.0	0.0	0.0	0.1	161.6	2.2	0.1	164.0	0.1	21.0	21.1	185.1
17	0.0	0.0	-	-	0.1	129.4	1.9	0.1	131.5	0.1	19.4	19.6	151.1
18	0.0	0.0	0.0	0.0	-	12.8	1.4	-	14.2	0.1	3.6	3.7	17.9
19 and over	0.0	0.0	-	-	-	0.6	-	-	0.7	0.1	1.2	1.3	2.0
Total[19]	22.7	134.1	2,033.3	2,563.9	1.9	1,888.5	32.9	3.9	4,513.8	1.2	287.0	288.2	4,802.0
of which													
England	19.2	129.7	1,769.1	2,163.8	.	1,580.2	28.0	3.9	3,795.1	1.2	282.6	283.8	4,078.9
Wales	0.6	..	..	131.5	1.9	92.3	1.3	..	227.6	0.0	4.1	4.1	231.7
Scotland	..		184.6	184.6	.	143.6	2.1	.	330.4	..	..	..	330.4
Northern Ireland	2.9	4.3	79.6	83.9	.	72.4	1.5	.	160.8	.	0.3	0.3	161.1

Sources: Department for Education; Welsh Government; Scottish Government; Northern Ireland Department of Education

1 In Scotland gender split is not collected by age but has been calculated according to figures collected in September each year. There are a small number of pupils for whom it has not been possible to assign an age; these pupils are included in the Scotland total but excluded from the age breakdowns.
2 In Northern Ireland a gender split is not available by age but is available by year group and so this is used as a proxy. For example pupils in Year 1 are counted as age 4, pupils in Year 2 are counted as age 5 etc.
3 Maintained school figures includes all state-funded schools (Grant-aided schools in Northern Ireland)
4 In Scotland figures for the Non-maintained sector have not been provided, the collection was discontinued in 2010.
5 In England includes middle schools as deemed.
6 In England includes primary converter academies, primary sponsor led academies and primary free schools.
7 A Primary school breakdown by class type is not available in Wales.
8 Excludes 8,410 children in total at voluntary and private pre-school centres in Northern Ireland in places funded under the Pre-School Expansion Programme which began in 1998/99.
9 For centres providing early learning and childcare in Scotland (this includes nursery classes within schools); children are counted once for each centre they are registered with. Only the 'All' figures are provided for early learning and childcare registrations in Scotland, as these cannot be split by gender.
10 Includes reception pupils in primary classes and, in Northern Ireland, pupils in preparatory departments of grammar schools.
11 In Wales, the Middle School for pupils of both primary and secondary school age was introduced in 2012/13.
12 Includes City Technology Colleges (CTCs) and Academies in England. Also includes secondary free schools, university technical colleges and studio schools.
13 Includes general hospital schools. Also includes special converter academies, special sponsored academies and special free schools. Hospital schools not included in Northern Ireland figures.
14 England and Wales only. Figures exclude dually registered pupils. In PRUs also includes pupils registered with other providers and further education colleges. Includes alternative provision academies and alternative provision free schools.
15 Includes pupils less than 2 years of age in England.
16 1 July for Northern Ireland, 28 February for maintained primary and secondary school pupils in Scotland and age at census date in September for pupils in early learning and childcare provision in Scotland.
17 Includes the so-called rising five's (i.e. those pupils who became 5 during the autumn term).
18 In Scotland, includes some 4-year-olds.
19 Some figures do not equal the sum of the component parts due to rounding

20.3 Pupil: teacher ratios (PTRs) and pupil: adult ratios (PARs) within schools, by type of school - time series

United Kingdom   Numbers

	Pupil: teacher ratio within schools[1]					Pupil: adult ratio within schools[2]			
	1995/96 [3]	2000/01	2010/11	2011/12	2012/13	2000/01	2010/11	2011/12	2012/13
United Kingdom									
Public sector mainstream									
Nursery schools[10]	21.3	23.1	17.2	17.7	17.5	..	..	..	..
Primary schools[5,12]	22.7	22.3	20.4	20.5	20.5	..	..	..	..
Middle[16]	.	.	.	.	16.2	.	.	.	.
Secondary schools[6,7]	16.1	16.5	15.3	15.3	15.2	..	..	..	..
Pupil Referral Units (PRUs)	..	..	3.5	3.1	3.4	.	.	.	.
Non-maintained mainstream schools	10.3	9.7	10.6	8.0	8.0	.	.	.	.
Special schools									
Maintained[15]	6.3	6.4	6.1	6.0	5.9	.	.	.	.
Non-maintained	.	.	..	..	..	.	.	.	.
All schools[8]	18.0	17.9	16.3	16.2	16.2	.	.	.	.
England[9,14]									
Public sector mainstream									
Nursery schools	19.2	17.7	16.1	16.7	16.5	6.8	..	4.9	4.9
State-funded primary schools[12]	23.2	22.9	20.9	21.0	20.9	15.7	..	11.9	11.5
State-funded secondary schools[6,7]	16.6	17.1	15.6	15.6	15.5	14.0	..	10.6	10.5
Pupil Referral Units (PRUs)	4.3	4.4	3.5	3.1	3.4	.	.	.	.
Non-maintained mainstream schools	10.2	9.7	10.6	8.0	8.0	.	.	.	.
Special schools									
State-funded[14]	6.7	6.7	6.4	6.3	6.2	.	.	.	.
Non-maintained	4.6	4.8	..	..	..	.	.	.	.
All schools	18.2	18.1	16.4	16.3	16.2	.	.	.	.
Wales									
Public sector mainstream									
Nursery schools	19.5	17.3	15.7	15.2	15.1	..	5.6	5.6	5.4
Primary schools	22.5	21.5	20.5	20.7	20.7	..	10.5	10.2	9.9
Middle[15]	.	.	.	.	16.2	.	.	.	10.6
Secondary schools[6]	16.0	16.6	16.6	16.7	16.3	..	12.0	11.9	11.5
Pupil Referral Units (PRUs)	..	..	..	..	..	.	.	.	.
Non-maintained mainstream schools	10.1	9.6	8.0	8.1	7.9	.	.	.	.
Special schools (maintained)	6.7	6.8	6.4	6.6	6.7	.	.	.	.
All schools[8]	18.7	18.4	17.8	17.9	17.8	.	.	.	.
Scotland									
Public sector mainstream									
Nursery schools[10]	24.3	28.5	..	..	..	..	..	..	..
Primary schools	19.5	19.0	15.8	16.0	16.3	..	11.4	11.7	11.8
Secondary schools	12.9	13.0	12.1	12.3	12.2	..	10.2	9.9	10.3
Non-maintained mainstream schools	11.0	10.1	..	..	..	..	..	..	..
Special schools									
Maintained	4.8	4.2	3.6	3.5	3.4	.	.	.	.
Non-maintained[13]	3.7	3.3	..	..	..	..	..	..	..
All schools	15.5	15.4	13.3	13.7	13.8	.	.	.	.
Northern Ireland[4]									
Grant-aided sector mainstream									
Nursery schools	24.1	24.4	25.9	26.1	25.6	..	..	..	..
Primary schools[5]	20.7	20.1	21.1	21.4	21.1	..	..	..	..
Secondary schools	14.8	14.5	15.0	15.2	15.3	..	..	..	..
Non-maintained mainstream schools	10.9	9.3	6.6	6.7	6.8	.	.	.	.
Special schools (maintained)	6.7	5.9	6.3	6.3	6.0	.	.	.	.
All schools	17.2	16.6	17.3	17.5	17.5	.	.	.	.

Sources: Department for Education; Welsh Government; Scottish Government; Northern Ireland Department of Education

1 The within-schools PTR is calculated by dividing the total full-time equivalent (FTE) number of pupils on roll in schools by the total FTE number of **qualified teachers** regularly employed in schools. The UK PTR excludes Pupil Referral Units and non-maintained special schools.

2 The within-schools PAR is calculated by dividing the total FTE number of pupils on roll in schools by the total FTE number of **all teachers** and support staff employed in schools, excluding administrative and clerical staff.

3 Nursery schools figures for Scotland exclude pre-school education centres and are not therefore directly comparable with figures from 1999/00.

4 Since 2003/04, data on teacher numbers in Northern Ireland have been compiled on a new, improved basis. Pupil/teacher ratios in Northern Ireland from 2003/04 onwards are not comparable with previous years.

5 Includes preparatory departments attached to grammar schools in Northern Ireland.

6 Excludes sixth form colleges in England and Wales which were reclassified as further education colleges from 1 April 1993.

7 From 2011/12, State-funded secondary schools (i.e. including City Technology Colleges (CTCs), secondary converter academies, secondary sponsor-led academies and secondary free schools in England, which were previously included under 'Non-maintained'). All through academies are included with secondary academies. Pupil adult ratio figure amended for 2011/12.

8 Excludes Pupil Referral Units as information on teachers is not collected for Wales.

9 Teacher numbers up to and including 2009 are sourced from 'Form 618g' in January of each year. From 2010 onwards figures are derived from the 'School Workforce Census in November of each year and are not directly comparable with earlier data

10   Excluding pre-school education figures for Scotland as FTE pupil numbers are not available.

11 The figures for Northern Ireland exclude temporary teachers i.e. teachers filling vacant posts, secondments or career breaks

12 Since 2011/12, includes primary converter academies, primary sponsor-led academies and primary free schools in England, previously included under 'Non-maintained

13 Figures on Non-maintained schools are not included, the collection was discontinued in 2010

14 Since 2011/12, includes special academies in England.

15 In Wales, the Middle School for pupils of both primary and secondary school age was introduced in 2012/13

20.4 Pupils with statements of Special Educational Needs (SEN) (1)
As at January each year: 2008-2013
England

	2008	2009	2010	2011	2012	2013
ALL SCHOOLS						
Pupils with statements	227,315	225,400	223,945	224,210	226,125	229,390
Pupils on roll	8,121,955	8,092,280	8,098,360	8,123,865	8,178,200	8,249,810
Incidence (%) (2)	2.8	2.8	2.8	2.8	2.8	2.8
STATE-FUNDED SCHOOLS						
Maintained nursery						
Pupils with statements	265	285	265	250	305	245
Pupils on roll	37,440	37,285	37,575	38,830	39,395	38,820
Incidence (%) (2)	0.7	0.8	0.7	0.6	0.8	0.6
Placement (%) (3)	0	0	0.1	0.1	0.1	0.1
State-funded primary (4)(5)						
Pupils with statements	59,695	58,505	57,850	57,855	58,535	59,710
Pupils on roll	4,090,400	4,077,350	4,096,580	4,137,755	4,217,000	4,309,580
Incidence (%) (2)	1.5	1.4	1.4	1.4	1.4	1.4
Placement (%) (3)	26.3	26.0	25.8	25.8	25.9	26.0
State-funded secondary (4)(6)						
Pupils with statements	67,875	65,890	64,605	63,720	62,630	61,615
Pupils on roll	3,294,575	3,278,130	3,278,485	3,262,635	3,234,875	3,210,120
Incidence (%) (2)	2.1	2.0	2.0	2.0	1.9	1.9
Placement (%) (3)	29.9	29.2	28.8	28.4	27.7	26.9
Maintained special (7)						
Pupils with statements	83,600	84,295	85,445	86,660	88,230	90,845
Pupils on roll	87,135	87,615	88,690	89,860	91,590	94,350
Incidence (%) (2)	95.9	96.2	96.3	96.4	96.3	96.3
Placement (%) (3)	36.8	37.4	38.2	38.7	39.0	39.6
Pupil Referral Units (8)						
Pupils with statements	3,260	3,230	1,910	1,695	1,610	1,630
Pupils on roll	25,290	24,760	15,550	14,050	13,495	12,950
Incidence (%) (2)	12.9	13.0	12.3	12.1	11.9	12.6
Placement (%) (3)	1.4	1.4	0.9	0.8	0.7	0.7
OTHER SCHOOLS						
Independent (9)						
Pupils with statements	8,055	8,690	9,470	9,750	10,630	11,265
Pupils on roll	582,425	582,490	576,940	576,325	577,515	579,740
Incidence (%) (2)	1.4	1.5	1.6	1.7	1.8	1.9
Placement (%) (3)	3.5	3.9	4.2	4.3	4.7	4.9
Non-maintained special						
Pupils with statements	4,565	4,500	4,400	4,280	4,185	4,085
Pupils on roll	4,695	4,655	4,540	4,415	4,325	4,245
Incidence (%) (2)	97.3	96.7	97.0	97.0	96.7	96.1
Placement (%) (3)	2.0	2.0	2.0	1.9	1.9	1.8

Source: School Census

(1) Includes pupils who are sole or dual main registrations.
(2) Incidence of pupils - the number of pupils with statements expressed as a proportion of the number of pupils on roll.
(3) Placement of pupils - the number of pupils with statements expressed as a proportion of the number of pupils with statements in all schools.
(4) Includes middle schools as deemed.
(5) Includes all primary academies, including free schools.
(6) Includes city technology colleges, university technology colleges, studio schools and all secondary academies, including free schools. Includes all-through schools.
(7) Includes general hospital schools and special academies, including free schools.
(8) Includes pupils registered with other providers, in alternative provision academies, including free schools and in further education colleges. Prior to 2010 includes dual subsidiary registered pupils.
(9) Includes direct grant nursery schools.

Totals may not appear to equal the sum of the component parts because numbers have been rounded to the nearest 5.

20.5 GCE, GCSE, SCE/NQ[1] and vocational qualifications obtained by pupils and students - time series

United Kingdom   **Percentages and thousands**

	1995/96	2000/01	2009/10	2010/11	2011/12
All					
Pupils in their last year of compulsory education[2]					
England, Wales and Northern Ireland[8]					
Percentage achieving GCSE or equivalent					
5 or more grades A*-C[3]	45.5	51.0	73.6	78.7	81.2
5 or more grades A*-C incl English and Maths	..	..	52.9	58.5	59.0
Any Passes	..	..	98.9	99.1	99.4
Scotland[9]					
Percentage of pupils in S4, last year of compulsory education achieving					
5 or more qualifications at SCQF level 3 or better	..	90.7	92.4	92.7	93.9
5 or more qualifications at SCQF level 4 or better	..	76.8	78.3	78.8	80.2
5 or more qualifications at SCQF level 5 or better	..	33.8	36.1	36.4	37.4
Pupils/students in education[4,5]					
England, Wales and Northern Ireland[8]					
Percentage achieving GCE A Levels and equivalent[6,7]					
2 or more passes[9]	29.6	37.4	52.7	52.8	54.7
Population aged 17 (thousands)[11]	672.1	717.9	800.0	707.4	700.4
Scotland[10]					
Percentage of pupils from relevant S4 roll achieving					
3 or more qualifications at SCQF level 6 or better by end of S5	..	..	25	26.3	27.2
1 or more qualifications at SCQF level 7 or better by end of S6	..	..	14.6	15.8	16.4
Males					
Pupils in their last year of compulsory education[2]					
England, Wales and Northern Ireland[8]					
Percentage achieving GCSE or equivalent					
5 or more grades A*-C[3]	40.6	45.7	69.5	75	77.6
5 or more grades A*-C incl English and Maths	..	..	48.9	54.8	54.3
Any Passes	..	..	98.4	98.9	99.1
Scotland[9]					
Percentage of pupils in S4, last year of compulsory education achieving					
5 or more qualifications at SCQF level 3 or better	..	89.7	91.8	92.3	93.4
5 or more qualifications at SCQF level 4 or better	..	73.8	75.6	76.6	77.6
5 or more qualifications at SCQF level 5 or better	..	28.7	31.8	32.4	32.8
Pupils/students in education[4,5]					
England, Wales and Northern Ireland[8]					
Percentage achieving GCE A Levels and equivalent[6,7]					
2 or more passes[9]	26.7	33.4	47.3	48.0	49.7
Population aged 17 (thousands)[11]	345.8	366.6	411.0	364.0	359.9
Scotland[10]					
Percentage of pupils from relevant S4 roll achieving					
3 or more qualifications at SCQF level 6 or better by end of S5	..	..	21.6	22.6	23.6
1 or more qualifications at SCQF level 7 or better by end of S6	..	..	13.0	13.9	14.6
Females					
Pupils in their last year of compulsory education[2]					
England, Wales and Northern Ireland[8]					
Percentage achieving GCSE or equivalent					
5 or more grades A*-C[3]	50.5	56.5	77.9	82.6	85.0
5 or more grades A*-C incl English and Maths	..	..	57.1	62.4	63.9
Any Passes	..	..	99.4	99.4	99.8
Scotland[9]					
Percentage of pupils in S4, last year of compulsory education achieving					
5 or more qualifications at SCQF level 3 or better	..	91.7	92.9	93.1	94.5
5 or more qualifications at SCQF level 4 or better	..	79.9	81.1	81.1	82.9
5 or more qualifications at SCQF level 5 or better	..	39.1	40.5	40.6	42.2
Pupils/students in education[4,5]					
England, Wales and Northern Ireland[8]					
Percentage achieving GCE A Levels and equivalent[6,7]					
2 or more passes[9]	32.7	41.6	58.5	57.9	60.1
Population aged 17 (thousands)[11]	326.3	351.3	389.0	343.4	340.4
Scotland[10]					
Percentage of pupils from relevant S4 roll achieving					
3 or more qualifications at SCQF level 6 or better by end of S5	..	..	28.4	30	30.9
1 or more qualifications at SCQF level 7 or better by end of S6	..	..	16.3	17.7	18.3

20.5 GCE, GCSE, SCE/NQ[1] and vocational qualifications obtained by pupils and students - time series

Source: Department for Education; Welsh Government; Scottish Government; Northern Ireland Department of Education

1 National Qualifications (NQ) include Standard Grades, Intermediate 1 & 2 and Higher Grades. The figures for Higher Grades combine the new NQ Higher and the old SCE Higher and include Advanced Highers.
2 Pupils aged 15 at the start of the academic year; pupils in Year S4 in Scotland; Year 12 Pupils in Northern Ireland. From 2004/05, pupils at the end of Key Stage 4 in England.
3 Standard Grades 1-3/Intermediate 2 A-C/Intermediate 1 A in Scotland for 2009/10 and earlier.
4 Pupils in schools and students in further education institutions generally aged 16-18 at the start of the academic year in England, Wales and Northern Ireland as a percentage of the 17-year-old population. Data from 2002/03 for Wales and Northern Ireland, however, relate to schools only. Pupils in Scotland generally sit Highers one year earlier than those sitting A levels in the rest of the UK, and the figures relate to the results of pupils in Year S5/S6.
5 Figures, other than for Scotland, include Vocational Certificates of Education (VCE) and, previously, Advanced level GNVQ, which is equivalent to 2 GCE A levels or AS equivalents. From 2005/06, figures included for England cover achievements in all Level 3 qualifications approved under Section 96 of the Learning and Skills Act (2000), therefore UK aggregates are not comparable with previous years.
6 2 AS levels or 2 Highers/1 Advanced Higher or 1 each in Scotland, count as 1 A level pass for 2009/10 and earlier.
7 3 or more SCE/NQ Higher Grades/2 or more Advanced Highers/1 Advanced Higher with 2 or more Higher Passes in Scotland for 2009/10 and earlier.
8 Also includes Scotland for 2009/10 and earlier.
9 In Scotland a number of qualifications cover the Scottish Credit and Qualifications Framework (SCQF) levels 3-5. Standard Grades span SCQF levels 3-5 depending on the results, whereas Intermediate 1 is at SCQF level 4 and Intermediate 2 is at SCQF level 5
10 In Scotland, pupils stay on into S5 and S6 to take additional qualifications or qualifications at a higher level. Most pupils will take Highers, SCQF level 5 qualifications in S5. If pupils stay on into S6 they may take more highers and/or Advanced Higher qualifications (SCQF level 7). Not all schools offer advanced highers and pupils can enter university with Highers
11 For 2011/12, based on mid-2010 based population projections. These do not take into account the 2011 UK Census. Census-based estimates following the publication of mid-2012 will not be available until after the UK volume is published.

Notes on population data
1 National population estimates and projections are the responsibility of the Office for National Statistics.
2 It is ONS policy to publish population estimates rounded to at least the nearest hundred persons. Estimates are sometimes provided in units to facilitate further calculations. They cannot be guaranteed to be as exact as the level of detail implied by unit figures and should be re-rounded prior to further presentation or publication.
3 The data are Crown copyright. They may be reproduced freely within your organisation. They must not be used for sale or advertising purposes.
   Source: ONS mid-2010 based population projections adjusted within DfE to academic age at January. These will be superseded by ONS mid-2012 based population projections in November 2013.
   Method: The age and count adjustment takes account of the actual distribution of births across the year, using monthly birth data for each nation.
      The figures for UK are derived by summation of England, Wales, Northern Ireland and Scotland.
      The figures for UK excluding Scotland are derived by summation of England, Wales and Northern Ireland.
      This is an improvement to the method used in 2012, which only considered the distribution of births at a UK level.
      Differences from the previous method are small - less than 10 persons at the UK level.

20.6 HE qualifications obtained by sex, subject area**, level of qualification obtained and class of first degree 2009/10 to 2012/13

	2009/10 All levels	2010/11 All levels	2011/12 All levels	2012/13							All levels
				Postgraduate			Undergraduate				
				Postgraduate research	Postgraduate taught	Total postgraduate	First degree	Foundation degree	Other undergraduate	Total undergraduate	
Female											
Medicine & dentistry	9705	10145	10650	1330	3435	4765	5755	0	235	5990	10755
Subjects allied to medicine	65535	66695	68470	1075	12435	13510	31690	2080	23155	56930	70440
Biological sciences	31155	33210	34450	2165	7675	9840	23425	785	2640	26845	36685
Veterinary science	740	820	875	45	80	125	660	0	15	675	800
Agriculture & related subjects	3215	3860	3635	120	740	860	1840	830	390	3060	3920
Physical sciences	10030	10840	11110	1245	2325	3570	6790	255	785	7825	11395
Mathematical sciences	3970	4445	4720	205	910	1115	3490	0	405	3895	5015
Computer science	5445	5860	5750	255	1790	2045	2675	180	555	3410	5455
Engineering & technology	7545	8315	8595	735	3580	4315	3830	190	420	4440	8755
Architecture, building & planning	7315	7270	7340	140	3165	3305	3140	130	555	3820	7125
Total - Science subject areas	144660	151465	155590	7320	36130	43455	83290	4445	29150	116885	160340
Percentage - Science subject areas	36%	35%	35%	61%	27%	29%	37%	30%	49%	39%	36%
Social studies	42770	44920	46255	1095	13360	14455	24490	1870	5905	32265	46720
Law	18470	19080	19585	220	6790	7015	10995	55	1530	12580	19590
Business & administrative studies	58355	64445	69655	470	30450	30920	30700	1825	6390	38915	69835
Mass communications & documentation	9590	11125	11815	105	4385	4490	6455	200	500	7160	11645
Languages	22750	25035	25345	910	4845	5755	16980	10	2810	19800	25555
Historical & philosophical studies	13185	14110	15000	750	3150	3900	9490	200	1190	10880	14780
Creative arts & design	33150	35905	37755	365	7135	7500	26080	2185	2400	30665	38165
Education	58760	60335	61430	800	29685	30485	15840	4230	8265	28335	58815
Combined	4180	3870	4100	0	55	55	2815	10	1145	3970	4025
Total - All subject areas	405865	430295	446520	12035	135990	148025	227130	15030	59285	301450	449470
Male											
Medicine & dentistry	6760	7190	7555	1055	2080	3135	4425	0	105	4530	7670
Subjects allied to medicine	15480	16495	17280	760	4005	4765	7790	860	4230	12875	17640
Biological sciences	18215	19795	20970	1345	3455	4795	15515	1040	2105	18660	23460
Veterinary science	205	250	255	30	45	70	190	0	0	190	260
Agriculture & related subjects	2135	2370	2255	110	520	630	935	540	275	1750	2380
Physical sciences	13565	15055	15100	2000	2715	4715	9610	240	1205	11055	15770
Mathematical sciences	6005	6415	6765	495	1305	1795	4940	0	695	5635	7430
Computer science	23675	25265	24765	785	5575	6360	12890	875	2755	16520	22880
Engineering & technology	38855	41230	42085	2495	11790	14285	20920	1685	4695	27300	41585
Architecture, building & planning	15385	15190	14405	215	4375	4590	6900	445	1665	9010	13600
Total - Science subject areas	140285	149260	151440	9285	35865	45150	84115	5680	17730	107520	152675
Percentage - Science subject areas	45%	45%	44%	67%	36%	40%	48%	56%	47%	48%	45%
Social studies	24440	26305	27485	1125	8500	9620	15615	530	2085	18230	27850
Law	12865	13295	13480	250	5200	5450	6500	40	1110	7650	13100
Business & administrative studies	61220	66825	70370	665	28890	29555	30190	1815	7090	39095	68650
Mass communications & documentation	7030	7855	8090	110	1810	1915	5155	280	515	5950	7870
Languages	10305	11390	11495	650	1980	2630	6790	5	1975	8770	11400
Historical & philosophical studies	11840	12720	13170	980	2750	3730	8655	160	895	9705	13440
Creative arts & design	20965	22300	23535	400	4045	4440	15410	1345	1805	18560	23000
Education	19515	19725	18915	400	11055	11455	2430	345	3730	6510	17965
Combined	2610	2565	2705	0	20	20	1740	5	645	2390	2410
Total - All subject areas	311070	332245	340685	13865	100110	113975	176595	10205	37580	224380	338355
All sexes											
Medicine & dentistry	16470	17335	18200	2385	5520	7900	10180	0	340	10520	18425
Subjects allied to medicine	81015	83190	85750	1840	16440	18275	39480	2940	27385	69805	88085
Biological sciences	49370	53000	55420	3510	11130	14635	38945	1825	4745	45515	60150
Veterinary science	945	1075	1135	75	120	195	845	0	15	865	1060
Agriculture & related subjects	5350	6235	5885	230	1260	1490	2775	1370	665	4810	6300
Physical sciences	23595	25895	26210	3250	5040	8285	16400	495	1990	18885	27170
Mathematical sciences	9975	10860	11485	700	2215	2915	8430	0	1095	9530	12445
Computer science	29120	31125	30520	1040	7370	8410	15565	1055	3310	19930	28340
Engineering & technology	46405	49550	50680	3230	15370	18600	24755	1875	5115	31740	50345
Architecture, building & planning	22700	22460	21745	355	7545	7900	10040	575	2215	12830	20730
Total - Science subject areas	284940	300725	307025	16610	72000	88610	167420	10130	46885	224435	313045
Percentage - Science subject areas	40%	39%	39%	64%	30%	34%	41%	40%	48%	43%	40%
Social studies	67210	71225	73740	2220	21865	24080	40115	2400	7990	50505	74585
Law	31335	32380	33065	470	11990	12465	17495	95	2645	20230	32695
Business & administrative studies	119575	131270	140020	1135	59345	60475	60890	3640	13480	78015	138490
Mass communications & documentation	16620	18980	19905	210	6195	6405	11615	480	1015	13110	19515
Languages	33050	36430	36845	1560	6825	8385	23770	15	4785	28570	36955
Historical & philosophical studies	25025	26830	28170	1730	5900	7635	18145	360	2085	20590	28220
Creative arts & design	54115	58205	61285	760	11180	11940	41495	3535	4210	49235	61175
Education	78280	80060	80340	1205	40740	41940	18270	4580	11995	34845	76785
Combined	6785	6435	6810	0	75	75	4555	15	1790	6355	6435
Total - All subject areas*	716940	762540	787205	25900	236115	262015	403770	25240	96875	525885	787900

Higher Education Statistics Agency Limited

In this table 0,1, 2 are rounded to 0. All other numbers are rounded up or down to the nearest multiple of 5.

Percentages are calculated on un-rounded data. Percentages are rounded to the nearest whole number. Percentages calculated on populations which contain fewer than 22.5 individuals are suppressed and

* Students with a sex of 'other' are included in total figures but not in separate breakdowns.

** Analyses of subject information show Full-person equivalent (FPE). These are derived by splitting student instances between the different subjects that make up their course aim.

20.7 Qualifications obtained by students on HE courses at HEIs in the UK by sex, level of qualification obtained, mode of study and domicile 2008/09 to 2012/13

	2008/09 All modes	2009/10 All modes	2010/11 All modes	2011/12		
				Full-time	Part-time	All modes
All UK HEIs						
Female						
Postgraduate research	9270	9820	10440	8930	2255	11190
Postgraduate taught	101580	110510	122880	87100	44915	132015
..of which Postgraduate Certificate in Education	14925	15690	14895	13545	945	14490
First degree	188925	198530	208890	197570	24315	221885
Foundation degree	11590	15015	16370	9435	6955	16390
Other undergraduate	75335	71990	71715	27875	37170	65045
..of which Professional Graduate Certificate in Education	4540	4970	4470	2515	1410	3925
Total female	**386700**	**405865**	430295	**330915**	**115610**	**446520**
Male						
Postgraduate research	11300	11860	12615	10710	2220	12925
Postgraduate taught	82410	94140	106220	77080	30880	107960
..of which Postgraduate Certificate in Education	5780	6340	6320	5430	355	5785
First degree	144795	152325	160125	153235	15870	169105
Foundation degree	7260	9850	10935	7065	3690	10755
Other undergraduate	41950	42895	42350	19550	20385	39940
..of which Professional Graduate Certificate in Education	1975	2465	2185	1120	720	1840
Total male	**287710**	**311070**	332245	**267635**	**73045**	**340685**
All sexes						
Postgraduate research	20570	21680	23055	19640	4475	24115
Postgraduate taught	183990	204650	229100	164180	75795	239975
..of which Postgraduate Certificate in Education	20705	22030	21215	18980	1300	20275
First degree	333720	350860	369010	350805	40185	390990
Foundation degree	18850	24865	27305	16500	10645	27145
Other undergraduate	117280	114885	114070	47430	57555	104985
..of which Professional Graduate Certificate in Education	6515	7435	6655	3630	2130	5760
Total all sexes(#2)	**674415**	**716940**	762540	**598550**	**188655**	**787205**

In this table 0,1, 2 are rounded to 0. All other numbers are rounded up or down to the nearest multiple of 5.
Percentages are not subject to rounding. ".." represents a percentage calculated on a population of between 0 and 52 inclusive.

© Higher Education Statistics Agency Limited

20.8 Students[1] in further[2] and higher[3] education - time series

United Kingdom

Thousands

Further education	2008/09	2009/10	2010/11	2011/12	2012/13
All					
United Kingdom					
England - participation[4]	4,837.1	4,635.5	4264.9	4216.6	4320.3
Wales[5]	218.1	187.3	212.7	211.3	197.5
Scotland	381.0	353.2	311	256.5	235.8
Northern Ireland	132.2	151.9	144.4	141.7	145.4
Males					
United Kingdom					
England - participation[4]	2,141.9	2,089.3	1941.2	1940.9	1985.9
Wales[5]	83.2	79.6	94	92.1	86.5
Scotland	172.0	160.6	144.8	121.0	113.1
Northern Ireland	64.7	75.0	72.2	71.1	73.9
Females					
United Kingdom					
England - participation[4]	2,695.2	2,546.2	2323.7	2275.7	2334.4
Wales[5]	117.8	107.7	118.7	119.3	111.1
Scotland	209.0	192.6	166.2	135.5	122.7
Northern Ireland	67.6	76.9	72.3	70.8	71.5

Higher education	2008/09		2009/10		2010/11		2011/12		2012/13	
	Full-time	Part-time	Full-time	Part-time	Full-time	Part-time	Full-time	Part-time	Full-time	Part-time
All										
Postgraduate	268.7	273.8	298.9	284.6	310.5	282.5	309.7	261.8	297.0	242.7
of which										
PhD & equivalent	58.6	23.1	61.4	23.9	65.5	24.5	69.5	25.5	71.3	25.3
Masters and Others	210.1	250.7	237.5	260.8	245	257.9	240.2	236.3	225.6	217.3
First Degree	1,154.0	214.6	1,215.9	222.7	1,258.0	224.7	1,319.8	241.3	1319.6	229.8
Other Undergraduate	174.1	471.3	177.9	458.2	170.5	413.1	151.1	378.5	123.6	301.4
Total	**1,596.9**	**959.7**	**1,692.7**	**965.5**	**1,739.0**	**920.3**	**1,780.6**	**881.6**	**1,740.1**	**773.8**
Males										
Postgraduate	136.5	113.8	151.5	118.5	155.5	115.9	148.8	108.2	139.3	100.0
of which										
PhD & equivalent	32.1	11.6	33.4	11.7	35.7	12.0	38.0	12.4	39.0	12.2
Masters and Others	104.4	102.2	118.1	106.8	119.8	103.9	110.8	95.8	100.3	87.8
First Degree	524.7	86.5	553.3	91.2	573.9	92.9	601.9	100.0	599.8	95.5
Other Undergraduate	68.7	175.3	73.3	168.2	70.7	154	63.8	142.3	54.4	114.5
Total	**729.9**	**375.5**	**778.1**	**378.0**	**800.1**	**362.8**	**814.5**	**350.5**	**793.5**	**310.1**
Females										
Postgraduate	132.2	160.0	147.3	166.1	155	166.5	160.9	153.6	157.6	142.7
of which										
PhD & equivalent	26.5	11.5	27.9	12.2	29.8	12.6	31.5	13.1	32.3	13.1
Masters and Others	105.7	148.5	119.4	153.9	125.2	154	129.4	140.5	125.3	129.6
First Degree	629.3	128.1	662.6	131.4	684	131.8	717.9	141.3	719.8	134.3
Other Undergraduate	105.5	296.1	104.6	289.9	99.8	259.2	87.3	236.2	69.2	186.9
Total	**867.0**	**584.2**	**914.5**	**587.5**	**938.9**	**557.5**	**966.1**	**531.1**	**946.6**	**463.8**

Sources: Department for Business, Innovation and Skills; Welsh Government; Scottish Funding Council; Northern Ireland Department for Employment and Learning

1 Home and overseas students.
2 Further education (FE) institution figures are based on whole year enrolments (excluding England which are based on headcounts).
3 Higher education (HE) figures include Open University students. Part-time figures include dormant modes (up to 2003/04), those writing up at home and on sabbaticals. Full-time includes sandwich. Part-time comprises both day and evening, including block release and open/distance learning. In Scotland, full-time at HE level covers programmes of at least 480 hours of planned notional hours. Part-time includes short full-time, block/day release, evenings/weekends assessment of work based learning, distance/locally based learning, college based private study, other open learning and flexible learning. In Wales, full-time learners are those with at least 450 guided contact hours in the academic year.
4 Learner Participation rate. Information on full-time and part-time learners in England is not available across all of the funding streams covered under Further Education.
5 From 2010/11, includes students in Wales FE colleges undertaking work based learning (WBL).

20.9 Students in higher[1] education by level, mode of study,[2] gender and subject group, 2012/13[3,4,5,6]

United Kingdom — Home and Overseas Students — Thousands

	PhD & equivalent[7]		Masters and Others[8]		Total Postgraduate		First degree[9]		Other Undergraduate[10]		Total higher education students	
	Full-time	Part-time	Full-time	Part-time	Full-time	Part-time	Full-time	Part-time	Full-time	Part-time	Full-time	Part-time
All												
Medicine & Dentistry	5.3	2.4	3.8	8.6	9.1	11.0	45.9	0.2	0.5	0.4	55.4	11.6
Subjects Allied to Medicine	3.7	2.4	11.9	40.3	15.6	42.6	125.9	22.6	22.9	52.0	164.3	117.2
Biological Sciences	10.6	2.2	10.1	9.7	20.6	11.9	135.3	22.9	4.5	7.0	160.4	41.8
Vet. Science, Agriculture & related	0.9	0.1	1.4	1.6	2.3	1.7	13.5	0.6	3.6	3.8	19.4	6.1
Physical Sciences	10.1	0.7	5.8	2.6	15.8	3.4	62.8	7.2	1.3	2.8	79.9	13.3
Mathematical and Computing Sciences	5.6	0.8	10.7	5.1	16.3	6.0	86.2	16.3	6.5	4.5	109.0	26.8
	0.0	0.0	0.0	0.0	0.0	0.0	0.0	0.0	0.0	0.0	0.0	0.0
Engineering & Technology	11.1	1.4	16.5	9.8	27.7	11.2	91.5	12.6	8.3	13.9	127.4	37.7
Architecture, Building & Planning	1.3	0.5	7.2	5.5	8.5	6.0	27.6	6.0	2.7	3.6	38.7	15.6
Social Sciences (inc Law)	7.6	2.8	35.2	22.8	42.8	25.6	183.9	30.4	10.3	17.4	237.0	73.4
Business & Administrative Studies	3.6	2.4	61.7	38.2	65.3	40.6	180.3	23.0	17.0	24.0	262.6	87.6
Mass Communications & Documentation	0.6	0.3	6.2	2.8	6.8	3.1	37.5	1.4	2.1	0.6	46.4	5.1
Languages	3.7	1.3	7.2	3.6	10.9	4.9	79.3	12.1	2.6	14.5	92.8	31.5
	0.0	0.0	0.0	0.0	0.0	0.0	0.0	0.0	0.0	0.0	0.0	0.0
Historical and Philosophical Studies	3.9	2.0	5.6	5.5	9.5	7.5	54.2	14.7	0.5	6.2	64.3	28.4
Creative Arts & Design	1.8	1.2	13.0	6.0	14.8	7.2	135.9	5.3	15.7	3.4	166.3	15.9
Education[11]	1.6	4.7	28.8	51.3	30.3	56.0	49.8	11.8	6.6	27.3	86.7	95.1
Other subjects[12]	-	-	-	1.6	-	1.6	3.8	31.0	2.8	34.9	6.6	67.5
Unknown[13]	-	-	0.5	2.3	0.5	2.3	6.3	12.1	15.9	85.0	22.7	99.4
All subjects	71.3	25.3	225.6	217.3	297.0	242.7	1,319.6	229.8	123.6	301.4	1,740.1	773.8
	0.0	0.0	0.0	0.0	0.0	0.0	0.0	0.0	0.0	0.0	0.0	0.0
of which overseas students	34.3	5.6	135.2	23.9	169.5	29.5	196.1	8.8	10.9	15.8	376.5	54.0
	0.0	0.0	0.0	0.0	0.0	0.0	0.0	0.0	0.0	0.0	0.0	0.0
Males												
Medicine & Dentistry	2.1	1.2	1.4	3.9	3.5	5.2	20.5	-	0.1	0.2	24.0	5.4
Subjects Allied to Medicine	1.6	0.8	2.9	10.2	4.5	11.0	26.0	4.6	3.7	7.9	34.3	23.5
Biological Sciences	3.9	0.8	3.5	3.1	7.4	3.8	55.4	6.9	2.7	2.2	65.6	13.0
Vet. Science, Agriculture & related	0.4	0.1	0.6	0.6	1.0	0.7	4.0	0.2	1.4	2.0	6.4	2.9
Physical Sciences	6.5	0.4	3.2	1.5	9.6	1.9	38.1	4.1	0.7	1.6	48.4	7.6
Mathematical and Computing Sciences	4.1	0.6	7.7	4.0	11.9	4.6	65.6	12.4	5.5	3.3	82.9	20.3
	0.0	0.0	0.0	0.0	0.0	0.0	0.0	0.0	0.0	0.0	0.0	0.0
Engineering & Technology	8.5	1.1	12.6	8.0	21.1	9.0	77.7	11.4	7.4	12.8	106.2	33.3
Architecture, Building & Planning	0.7	0.3	4.1	3.5	4.9	3.8	18.1	4.7	2.0	2.8	25.0	11.3
Social Sciences (inc Law)	3.8	1.3	14.4	8.2	18.2	9.5	73.2	9.8	2.6	4.1	94.1	23.4
Business & Administrative Studies	2.1	1.5	30.0	20.7	32.1	22.2	92.8	11.2	7.8	11.2	132.6	44.6
Mass Communications & Documentation	0.3	0.2	1.8	0.9	2.1	1.1	16.3	0.6	1.3	0.3	19.6	2.0
Languages	1.5	0.5	2.2	1.1	3.7	1.6	23.2	3.3	1.3	5.9	28.2	10.8
	0.0	0.0	0.0	0.0	0.0	0.0	0.0	0.0	0.0	0.0	0.0	0.0
Historical and Philosophical Studies	2.2	1.1	2.7	2.7	4.9	3.8	26.1	6.1	0.3	2.3	31.2	12.2
Creative Arts & Design	0.9	0.6	4.7	2.2	5.6	2.9	50.9	2.0	6.1	1.0	62.6	5.9
Education[11]	0.5	1.7	8.3	15.7	8.8	17.4	8.0	1.2	1.5	7.0	18.3	25.6
Other subjects[12]	-	-	-	0.7	-	0.7	1.5	12.3	1.8	12.9	3.3	25.9
Unknown[13]	-	-	0.2	0.8	0.2	0.8	2.3	4.4	8.2	37.1	10.8	42.3
All subjects	39.0	12.2	100.3	87.8	139.3	100.0	599.8	95.5	54.4	114.5	793.5	310.1
	0.0	0.0	0.0	0.0	0.0	0.0	0.0	0.0	0.0	0.0	0.0	0.0
of which overseas students	19.6	3.0	63.5	13.0	83.1	16.0	97.3	4.7	5.6	6.9	186.0	27.7
	0.0	0.0	0.0	0.0	0.0	0.0	0.0	0.0	0.0	0.0	0.0	0.0
Females												
Medicine & Dentistry	3.2	1.2	2.4	4.7	5.6	5.9	25.4	0.1	0.4	0.2	31.4	6.2
Subjects Allied to Medicine	2.2	1.5	8.9	30.1	11.1	31.6	99.8	17.9	19.1	44.1	130.0	93.7
Biological Sciences	6.6	1.4	6.6	6.6	13.2	8.0	79.8	16.0	1.7	4.8	94.8	28.8
Vet. Science, Agriculture & related	0.5	0.1	0.8	1.0	1.4	1.0	9.5	0.3	2.2	1.8	13.0	3.2
Physical Sciences	3.6	0.3	2.6	1.2	6.2	1.5	24.7	3.1	0.6	1.1	31.5	5.7
Mathematical and Computing Sciences	1.5	0.2	3.0	1.1	4.5	1.4	20.6	3.9	1.0	1.2	26.1	6.4
	0.0	0.0	0.0	0.0	0.0	0.0	0.0	0.0	0.0	0.0	0.0	0.0
Engineering & Technology	2.6	0.3	3.9	1.9	6.6	2.2	13.7	1.1	0.9	1.1	21.2	4.4
Architecture, Building & Planning	0.5	0.2	3.0	2.0	3.6	2.1	9.5	1.3	0.6	0.9	13.7	4.3
Social Sciences (inc Law)	3.8	1.5	20.8	14.6	24.6	16.1	110.6	20.5	7.7	13.3	142.9	49.9
Business & Administrative Studies	1.5	0.9	31.7	17.5	33.2	18.4	87.5	11.8	9.2	12.8	130.0	43.0
Mass Communications & Documentation	0.3	0.1	4.4	1.9	4.8	2.0	21.2	0.8	0.9	0.3	26.8	3.1
Languages	2.2	0.8	5.0	2.5	7.2	3.3	56.1	8.8	1.3	8.6	64.6	20.7
	0.0	0.0	0.0	0.0	0.0	0.0	0.0	0.0	0.0	0.0	0.0	0.0
Historical and Philosophical Studies	1.7	0.9	2.9	2.8	4.7	3.7	28.2	8.5	0.3	3.9	33.1	16.1
Creative Arts & Design	0.9	0.6	8.2	3.8	9.2	4.4	85.0	3.2	9.6	2.3	103.7	10.0
Education[11]	1.1	3.0	20.4	35.6	21.5	38.6	41.8	10.6	5.1	20.3	68.5	69.4
Other subjects[12]	-	-	-	0.9	-	0.9	2.3	18.7	1.0	22.1	3.3	41.6
Unknown[13]	-	-	0.3	1.6	0.3	1.6	4.0	7.6	7.6	48.0	11.9	57.1
All subjects	32.3	13.1	125.3	129.6	157.6	142.7	719.8	134.3	69.2	186.9	946.6	463.8
	0.0	0.0	0.0	0.0	0.0	0.0	0.0	0.0	0.0	0.0	0.0	0.0
of which overseas students	14.8	2.5	71.7	10.9	86.4	13.4	98.8	4.0	5.3	8.8	190.5	26.3

Sources: Department for Business, Innovation and Skills; Welsh Government; Scottish Funding Council; Northern Ireland Department for Employment and Learning

1 Higher Education Statistics Agency (HESA) higher education institutions include Open University students.
The field "gender" has changed to be consistent with the MIAP (Managing Information Across Partners) common data definitions coding frame. Students of "indeterminate gender" are now included in total figures but not in separate breakdowns. "Indeterminate" means unable to be classified as either male or female and is not related in any way to trans-gender

20.9 Students in higher[1] education by level, mode of study,[2] gender and subject group, 2012/13[3,4,5,6]

2 Full-time includes sandwich. Part-time comprises both day and evening, including block release and open/distance learning. In Scotland, full-time at HE level covers programmes of

   at least 480 hours of planned notional hours. Part-time includes short full-time, block/day release, evenings/weekends, assessment of work based learning,distance/locally based learning, college based private study,other open learning and flexible learning. In Wales, full-time learners are those with at least 450 guided contact hours in the academic year

3 Figures for higher education (HE) institutions are based on the HESA 'standard registration' count. Figures for FE institutions and colleges are whole year enrolments

4 Further education (FE) institution figures for England include Learning and Skills Council (LSC) funded students only

5 FE insititution figures for Wales are counts of unique learners. As a learner may pursue more than one course, only one subject per learner has been selected (based on the most recently started course of the learner where applicable). Students have been assigned a level on the basis of learning programme type. For the purpose of this table, HE learners are those pursuing a (non-WBL) overarching HElearning programme. (It excludes learners pursuing HE level activities within an FE or WBL programme.)

6 Figures for Northern Ireland further education colleges are professional and technical course enrolments rather than headcounts. Figures for Scotland do not include students with under 25% attendance rate.

7 Defined as 'Doctorate' in Scotland.

8 For Scotland includes masters (research/taught) and postgraduate diploma/certificate.

9 For Scotland includes first degree honours/ordinary

10 For Scotland includes 'SVQ or NVQ: Level 4 and Level 5,' 'Diploma (HNC/D level for diploma and degree holders),' and 'HND/C or equivalent.

11 Including Initial Teacher Training (ITT) and In-Service Education and Training (INSET).

12 Includes Combined and general programmes and programmes not otherwise classified

13 Includes data for higher education students in further education institutions in England and Wales, which cannot be split by subject group.

20.10 Qualified teachers by type of school and gender - time series

United Kingdom			(i) Full-time teachers					Thousands
	2000/01[3,4]	2011/12	2012/13	2013/14				
				Total	of which			
					England[1]	Wales	Scotland[10,14]	Northern Ireland[11]
All								
Public sector mainstream								
Nursery[5,6] and Primary[15]	211.2	198.6	205.2	209.6	171.2	10.9	20.6	7.0
Middle[17]	..	..	0.2	0.2	.	0.2	.	.
Secondary[7,12]	225.7	218.8	222.9	220.2	180.1	10.5	21.3	8.4
Non-maintained mainstream[13]	52.3	55.5	56.9	57.3	56.4	0.9	..	0.1
All Special[16]	16.5	14.8	15.4	18.8	15.8	0.6	1.7	0.7
All schools[9]	**505.7**	**487.7**	**500.6**	**506.1**	**423.4**	**23.0**	**43.6**	**16.1**
Males								
Public sector mainstream								
Nursery[5,6] and Primary[15]	32.1	30.2	31.9	33.2	28.1	2.0	1.9	1.2
Middle[17]	..	..	0.1	0.1	.	0.1	.	.
Secondary[7,12]	102.9	89.8	90.8	89.3	73.8	4.1	8.4	3.0
Non-maintained mainstream[13]	21.3	22.3	22.8	23.0	22.6	0.3	..	0.0
All Special[16]	5.0	4.1	4.2	5.4	4.7	0.2	0.4	0.1
All schools[9]	**161.3**	**146.4**	**149.8**	**151.0**	**129.3**	**6.7**	**10.6**	**4.3**
Females								
Public sector mainstream								
Nursery[5,6] and Primary[15]	179.1	166.8	171.7	175.1	143.0	8.9	17.5	5.7
Middle[17]	..	..	0.1	0.1	.	0.1	.	.
Secondary[7,12]	122.8	128.8	131.8	130.7	106.1	6.4	12.9	5.4
Non-maintained mainstream[13]	30.9	33.2	34.1	34.4	33.8	0.5	..	0.1
All Special[16]	11.6	10.7	11.2	13.4	11.1	0.4	1.3	0.5
All schools[9]	**344.4**	**339.5**	**349.0**	**353.7**	**294.0**	**16.3**	**31.7**	**11.7**

			(ii) Full-time equivalent (FTE) of part-time teachers					Thousands
	2000/01[3,4]	2011/12	2012/13	2013/14				
				Total	of which			
					England[1]	Wales	Scotland	Northern Ireland[11]
All								
Public sector mainstream								
Nursery[5,6] and Primary[15]	21.9	39.5	39.7	41.4	34.2	2.9	3.6	0.8
Middle[17]	..	..	0.0	0.0	.	0.0	.	.
Secondary[7,12]	16.7	27.3	27.4	28.5	23.5	1.9	2.4	0.7
Non-maintained mainstream[13, 8]	10.2	13.0	12.7	12.4	12.0	0.4	..	0.0
All Special[16]	1.6	2.6	2.5	3.3	2.8	0.1	0.3	0.1
All schools[9]	**50.4**	**82.3**	**82.4**	**85.7**	**72.5**	**5.3**	**6.3**	**1.6**

Sources: Department for Education; Welsh Government; Scottish Government; Northern Ireland Department of Education

1 Pre 2009/10 teacher numbers in England were derived from the 618g survey and the Database of Teacher Records. From 2009/10 figures are derived from the School Workforce survey and are not directly comparable with earlier data. Totals include gender unspecified or not known, therefore totals may not equal the sum of component parts.

2 Includes 1994/95 data for Northern Ireland.

3 Includes 1999/00 pre-school data for Scotland.

4 Includes 2001/02 data for Northern Ireland.

5 From 2005/06, data for Scotland include only centres providing pre-school education as a local authority centre or in partnership with the local authority. Figures are not therefore directly comparable with previous years.

6 From 2005/06, for Scotland pre-school education centres, the total full-time equivalent (FTE) of General Teaching Council of Scotland (GTC) registered staff has been provided within the 'full-time' section only because information on full-time/part-time split is not available. Teachers are counted once for each centre they work for, so the number of teachers contains some double counting. However, as each centre calculates the teacher's FTE as the time they spend working in that centre, the FTE should not be double-counted. Full-time/part-time figures for 2004/05 are estimates based on the headcount of all GTC registered staff.

7 From 1993/94 excludes sixth form colleges in England and Wales which were reclassified as further education colleges on 1 April 1993.

8 Figures refer to Great Britain.

9 Excludes Pupil Referral Units (PRUs).

10 For Scotland pre-school education centres FTE staff, a gender split is not available. Gender figures for 2004/05 are estimates based on the headcount of all GTC registered staff.

11 The figures for Northern Ireland exclude temporary teachers i.e. teachers filling vacant posts, secondments or career breaks.

12 From 2010/11, State-funded secondary schools (i.e. including City Technology Colleges (CTCs), secondary converter academies, secondary sponsor-led academies and secondary free schools in England, which were previously included under 'Non-maintained'). All through academies are included with secondary academies.

13 For Scotland, figures on non-maintained schools are not included, the collection was discontinued in 2010.

14 For Scotland, due to the change in the timing of the Pre-school Education Census from January to September, nursery figures for September 2010 (provided for 2010/11) are not directly comparable with previously published January figures. This is because some centres may take on additional teachers, or teachers may have their hours increased, once new children become eligible and start receiving pre-school education from the start of the January term.

15 Since 2010/11, includes primary converter academies, primary sponsor-led academies and primary free schools in England, previously included under 'Non-maintained'.

16 Includes PRU figures for England

Crime and Justice

Chapter 21

Crime and Justice

There are differences in the legal and judicial systems of England and Wales, Scotland and Northern Ireland which make it impossible to provide tables covering the UK as a whole in this section. These differences concern the classification of offences, the meaning of certain terms used in the statistics, the effects of the several Criminal Justice Acts and recording practices.

Recorded crime statistics
(Table 21.3)

Crimes recorded by the police provide a measure of the amount of crime committed. For a variety of reasons, many offences are either not reported to the police or not recorded by them. The changes in the number of offences recorded do not necessarily provide an accurate reflection of changes in the amount of crime committed.

The recorded crime statistics include all indictable and triable-either-way offences together with a few summary offences which are closely linked to these offences. The revised rules changed the emphasis of measurement more towards one crime per victim, and also increased the coverage of offences.

In order to further improve the consistency of recorded crime statistics and to take a more victim-oriented approach to crime recording, the National Crime Recording Standard (NCRS) was introduced across all forces in England, Wales and Northern Ireland from 1 April 2002. Some police forces implemented the principles of NCRS in advance of its introduction across all forces. The NCRS had the effect of increasing the number of offences recorded by the police and data before and after 2002/03 are not directly comparable.

For a variety of reasons many offences are either not reported to the police or not recorded by them. The changes in the number of offences recorded do not necessarily provide an accurate reflection of changes in the amount of crime committed.

Similarly, the Scottish Crime Recording Standard (SCRS) was introduced by the eight Scottish police forces with effect from 1 April 2004. This means that no corroborative evidence is required initially to record a crime-related incident as a crime if the victim perceived it as a crime. Again, the introduction of this new recording standard was expected to increase the numbers of minor crimes recorded by the police, such as minor crimes of vandalism and minor thefts and offences of petty assault and breach of the peace. However, it was expected that the SCRS would not have much impact on the figures for the more serious crimes such as serious assault, sexual assault, robbery or housebreaking.

The Sexual Offences Act 2003 introduced in May 2004 altered the definition and coverage of sexual offences. In particular, it redefined indecent exposure as a sexual offence, which is likely to account for much of the increase in sexual offences.

The Sexual Offences (Scotland) Act 2009 introduced in 1 December 2010 repealed a number of common law crimes including rape, clandestine injury to women and sodomy and replaced them with new statutory sexual offences. The Act created a number of new "protective" offences, which criminalise sexual activity with children and mentally disordered persons. Protective offences are placed into categories concerning young children (under 13) and older (13-15 years). The new legislation may result in some increases in Group 2 crimes. For example, the offences of voyeurism or indecent communication towards an adult would previously have been classified as breach of the peace. It is likely that the effect will be to change the distribution of these crimes among the sub classifications. For example, some crimes previously categorised as lewd and libidinous practices will now be classified as sexual assault. The standard breakdown provided in response to information requests on sexual offences has had to be revised to accommodate these changes. Details of changes are provided below.

Offences committed before 1 December 2010:

Rape & attempted rape includes:

- Rape
- Assault with intent to rape

Indecent assault includes:

- Indecent assault

Lewd and indecent behaviour includes:

- Public indecency

'Other' includes:

- Incest
- Unnatural crimes
- Prostitution
- Procuration and other sexual offences

Offences committed on or after 1 December 2010:

Rape & attempted rape includes:

- Rape
- Attempted rape

Sexual assault includes:

- Contact sexual assault (13-15 years old or adult 16+)
- other sexually coercive conduction (adult 16+)
- Sexual offences against children under 13
- Sexual activity with children aged 13-15
- Other sexual offences involving children aged 13-15
- Lewd and libidinous practices

Prostitution

- Offences relating to prostitution

'Other' includes:

- Incest
- Unnatural crimes
- Public indecency
- Sexual exposure
- Procuration and other sexual offences

Further information is available from Crime in England and Wales.

Court proceedings and police cautions
(Tables 21.4 to 21.8, 21.12 to 21.16, 21.19 to 21.20

The statistical basis of the tables of court proceedings is broadly similar in England and Wales, Scotland and Northern Ireland; the tables show the number of persons found guilty, recording a person under the heading of the principal offence of which they were found guilty, excluding additional findings of guilt at the same proceedings. A person found guilty at a number of separate court proceedings is included more than once.

The statistics on offenders cautioned in England and Wales cover only those who, on admission of guilt, were given a formal caution by, or on the instructions of, a senior police officer as an alternative to prosecution. Written warnings by the police for motor offences and persons paying fixed penalties for certain motoring offences are excluded. Formal cautions are not issued in Scotland. There are no statistics on cautioning available for Northern Ireland.

The Crime and Disorder Act 1998 created provisions in relation to reprimands and final warnings, new offences and orders which have been implemented nationally since 1 June 2000. They replace the system of cautioning for offenders aged under 18. Reprimands can be given to first-time offenders for minor offences. Any further offending results in either a final warning or a charge.

For persons proceeded against in Scotland, the statistics relate to the High Court of Justiciary, the sheriff courts and the district courts. The High Court deals with serious solemn (that is, jury) cases and has unlimited sentencing power. Sheriff courts are limited to imprisonment of 3 years for solemn cases, or 3 months (6 months when specified in legislation for second or subsequent offences and 12 months for certain statutory offences) for summary (that is, non-jury) cases. District courts deal only with summary cases and are limited to 60 days imprisonment and level 4 fines. Stipendiary magistrates sit in Glasgow District Court and have the summary sentencing powers of a sheriff.

In England and Wales, indictable offences are offences which are:

• triable only on indictment. These offences are the most serious breaches of the criminal law and must be tried at the Crown Court. 'Indictable-only' offences include murder, manslaughter, rape and robbery
• triable either way. These offences may be tried at the Crown Court or a magistrates' court

The Criminal Justice Act 1991 led to the following main changes in the sentences available to the courts in England and Wales:

• introduction of combination orders
• introduction of the 'unit fine scheme' at magistrates' courts
• abolishing the sentence of detention in a young offender institution for 14-year-old boys and changing the minimum and maximum sentence lengths for 15 to 17-year-olds to 10 and 12 months respectively, and
• abolishing partly suspended sentences of imprisonment and restricting the use of a fully suspended sentence

(The Criminal Justice Act 1993 abolished the 'unit fine scheme' in magistrates' courts, which had been introduced under the Criminal Justice Act 1991.

A charging standard for assault was introduced in England and Wales on 31 August 1994 with the aim of promoting consistency between the police and prosecution on the appropriate level of charge to be brought.

The Criminal Justice and Public Order Act 1994 created several new offences in England and Wales, mainly in the area of public order, but also including male rape (there is no statutory offence of male rape in Scotland, although such a crime may be charged as serious assault). The Act also:

• extended the provisions of section 53 of the Children and Young Persons Act 1993 for 10 to 13-year-olds
• increased the maximum sentence length for 15 to 17-year-olds to 2 years
• increased the upper limit from £2,000 to £5,000 for offences of criminal damage proceeded against as if triable only summarily
• introduced provisions for the reduction of sentences for early guilty pleas, and
• increased the maximum sentence length for certain firearm offences

Provisions within the Crime (Sentences) Act 1997 (as amended by the Powers of Criminal Courts Sentencing Act 2000) in England and Wales, and the Crime and Punishment (Scotland) Act 1997 in Scotland, included:

• an automatic life sentence for a second serious violent or sexual offence unless there are exceptional circumstances (this provision has not been enacted in Scotland)
• a minimum sentence of 7 years for an offender convicted for a third time of a class A drug trafficking offence unless the court considers this to be unjust in all the circumstances, and
• in England and Wales, the new section 38A of the Magistrates' Courts' Act 1980 extending the circumstances in which a magistrates' court may commit a person convicted of an offence triable-either-way to the Crown Court for sentence – it was implemented in conjunction with section 49 of the Criminal Procedure and Investigations Act 1996, which involves the magistrates' courts in asking defendants to indicate a plea before the mode of trial decision is taken and compels the court to sentence, or commit for sentence, any defendant who indicates a guilty plea.

Under the Criminal Justice and Court Service Act 2000 new terms were introduced for certain orders. Community rehabilitation order is the new name for a probation order. A community service order is now known as a community punishment order. Finally, the new term for a combination order is community punishment and rehabilitation order. In April 2000 the secure training order was replaced by the detention and training order. Section 53 of the Children and Young Persons Act 1993 was repealed on 25 August 2000 and its provisions were transferred to sections 90 to 92 of the Powers of Criminal Courts (Sentencing) Act 2000. Reparation and action plan orders were implemented nationally from 1 June 2000. The drug treatment and testing order was introduced in England, Scotland and Wales from October 2000. The referral order was introduced in England, Scotland and Wales from April 2000. Youth rehabilitation orders came into effect in November 2009 as part of the Criminal Justice and Immigration Act 2008. These changes are now reflected in Table 21.8.

Following the introduction of the Libra case management system during 2008, offenders at magistrates' courts can now be recorded as sex 'Not Stated'. In 2008 one per cent of offenders sentenced were recorded as sex 'Not Stated' as well as 'Male', 'Female', or 'Other'. Amendments to the data tables have been made to accommodate this new category.

The system of magistrates' courts and Crown courts in Northern Ireland operates in a similar way to that in England and Wales. A particularly significant statutory development, however, has been the Criminal Justice (NI) Order 1996 which introduced a new sentencing regime into Northern Ireland, largely replicating that which was introduced into England and Wales by the Criminal Justice Acts of 1991 and 1993. The order makes many changes to both community and custodial sentences, while introducing new orders such as the combination order, the custody probation order, and orders for release on licence of sexual offenders.

Abbreviations
(Tables 21.4a, 21.6a-c, 21.6d-f)

Every effort is made to ensure that the figures presented are accurate and complete. However, it is important to note that these data have been extracted from large administrative data systems generated by the police forces and courts.

As a consequence, care should be taken to ensure data collection processes and their inevitable limitations are taken into account when those data are used.

Abbreviation	Description
Total Proc Against	Total Proceeded Against
Proc Disc	Proceedings Discontinued
Proc Disc	Discharge Section 6 Magistrates' Courts Act 1980
Charge Wdrn	Charge Withdrawn
Charge Dism	Charge Dismissed
Comm For Trial	Committed for Trial
Comm For Sent	Committed for Sentence
Total For Sent	Total for Sentence
Abslt Disch	Absolute Discharge
Condl Disch	Conditional Discharge
CRO	Community Rehabilitation Order
YRO	Youth Rehabilitation Order
SO	Supervision Order
CPO	Community Punishment Order
ACO	Attendance Centre Order
CP & RO	Community Punishment Order and Rehabilitation Order
Curf Order	Curfew Order
Rep Order	Reparation Order
APO	Action Plan Order
DTTO	Drug Treatment and Test Order
Ref Order	Referral Order
Comm Order	Community Order
YRO	Youth Rehabilitation Order
SS	Suspended Sentence
DTO	Detention and Training Order
YOI	Young Offender Institution
Unsus Sent Impri	Unsuspended sentence of imprisonment
Imm Cust	Immediate Custody
ODW	Otherwise dealt with

21.1a Police officers in england and Wales, by police force area, as at 31 March 2014

Police force	All officers (full-time equivalent)[1]			Officers available for duty[2] (headcount)		
	Male	Female	Total	Male	Female	Total
Avon and Somerset	2,048	752	2,800	2,022	781	2,803
Bedfordshire	704	314	1,019	689	292	981
Cambridgeshire	985	386	1,370	967	382	1,349
Cheshire	1,383	542	1,925	1,357	519	1,876
Cleveland	1,059	322	1,382	976	276	1,252
Cumbria	748	402	1,150	741	407	1,148
Derbyshire	1,280	508	1,788	1,259	495	1,754
Devon and Cornwall	2,237	860	3,096	2,214	901	3,115
Dorset	909	308	1,217	889	315	1,204
Durham	918	370	1,288	901	366	1,267
Essex	2,263	933	3,196	2,228	924	3,152
Gloucestershire	833	355	1,188	825	361	1,186
Greater Manchester	5,046	1,951	6,997	4,952	1,854	6,806
Hampshire	2,265	982	3,247	2,222	979	3,201
Hertfordshire	1,319	608	1,927	1,290	582	1,872
Humberside	1,209	492	1,701	1,184	505	1,689
Kent	2,351	918	3,268	2,317	917	3,234
Lancashire	2,184	891	3,074	2,123	861	2,984
Leicestershire	1,508	535	2,043	1,491	529	2,020
Lincolnshire	796	295	1,091	776	272	1,048
London, City of	582	164	746	573	159	732
Merseyside	2,904	1,050	3,954	2,844	1,025	3,869
Metropolitan Police	23,063	7,868	30,932	22,617	7,649	30,266
Norfolk	1,163	419	1,582	1,147	429	1,576
Northamptonshire	867	372	1,239	867	375	1,242
Northumbria	2,629	1,017	3,646	2,581	986	3,567
North Yorkshire	1,002	406	1,408	987	400	1,387
Nottinghamshire	1,565	593	2,158	1,537	588	2,125
South Yorkshire	1,932	791	2,722	1,890	787	2,677
Staffordshire	1,267	462	1,729	1,253	462	1,715
Suffolk	895	330	1,226	889	339	1,228
Surrey	1,303	635	1,938	1,297	614	1,911
Sussex	1,958	847	2,805	1,933	850	2,783
Thames Valley	3,041	1,305	4,346	3,003	1,286	4,289
Warwickshire	580	221	802	564	216	780
West Mercia	1,390	576	1,966	1,384	570	1,954
West Midlands	5,116	2,172	7,288	5,018	2,144	7,162
West Yorkshire	3,388	1,469	4,857	3,327	1,441	4,768
Wiltshire	696	325	1,020	683	318	1,001
Dyfed-Powys	813	310	1,123	802	309	1,111
Gwent	941	389	1,330	917	388	1,305
North Wales	1,035	430	1,464	1,030	422	1,452
South Wales	2,083	778	2,861	2,040	764	2,804
Total 43 forces	**92,256**	**35,653**	**127,909**	**90,606**	**35,039**	**125,645**
Central service secondments	354	83	437	359	86	445
British Transport Police (BTP)	2,431	480	2,912	2,391	482	2,873
Total	95,042	36,216	131,258	93,356	35,607	128,963

Source: Home Office

1. Full-time equivalent figures. There may appear to be small discrepancies between the totals and the sums of the constituent items as the figures are presented to the nearest whole number but are actually provided unrounded.
2. Officers available for duty is the number of officers in post excluding long-term absentees.

21.1b Special constables, by police force area and gender, as at 31 March 2014

England and Wales
Headcount[1]

	Total			Minority Ethnic			Joiners			Leavers		
	Male	Female	Total	Male	Female	Total	Male	Female	Total	Male	Female	Total
Avon and Somerset	358	171	529	5	1	6	50	31	81	55	39	94
Bedfordshire	131	65	196	5	3	8	23	16	39	27	11	38
Cambridgeshire	198	86	284	4	2	6	67	36	103	36	16	52
Cheshire	245	118	363	6	2	8	76	31	107	63	28	91
Cleveland	56	26	82	1	0	1	0	1	1	10	7	17
Cumbria	83	43	126	2	1	3	22	16	38	26	21	47
Derbyshire	190	81	271	9	2	11	36	25	61	47	19	66
Devon and Cornwall	404	223	627	2	2	4	129	57	186	66	41	107
Dorset	148	63	211	1	1	2	50	28	78	47	23	70
Durham	61	24	85	2	0	2	21	11	32	15	8	23
Essex	312	114	426	11	4	15	30	15	45	75	39	114
Gloucestershire	87	35	122	3	0	3	5	3	8	33	20	53
Greater Manchester	530	200	730	56	10	66	153	76	229	141	60	201
Hampshire	429	147	576	7	5	12	90	36	126	80	45	125
Hertfordshire	315	98	413	25	5	30	104	46	150	99	46	145
Humberside	237	164	401	3	3	6	58	59	117	30	29	59
Kent	241	48	289	9	1	10	70	20	90	106	50	156
Lancashire	340	150	490	24	4	28	135	78	213	75	43	118
Leicestershire	220	87	307	30	6	36	88	34	122	65	39	104
Lincolnshire	160	90	250	0	1	1	55	26	81	35	18	53
London, City of	58	24	82	0	0	0	8	3	11	6	5	11
Merseyside	275	145	420	9	4	13	103	51	154	190	110	300
Metropolitan Police	3,110	1,477	4,587	978	372	1,350	815	441	1,256	1,214	589	1,803
Norfolk	181	59	240	3	0	3	35	18	53	67	37	104
Northamptonshire	231	80	311	6	4	10	73	41	114	9	10	19
Northumbria	226	82	308	2	1	3	64	28	92	73	33	106
North Yorkshire	101	54	155	3	0	3	30	17	47	30	18	48
Nottinghamshire	217	102	319	10	3	13	41	29	70	75	54	129
South Yorkshire	245	165	410	11	8	19	104	88	192	55	50	105
Staffordshire	270	132	402	12	2	14	57	36	93	95	52	147
Suffolk	165	68	233	5	0	5	39	17	56	48	24	72
Surrey	141	41	182	5	2	7	10	5	15	62	35	97
Sussex	248	118	366	5	3	8	77	49	126	66	40	106
Thames Valley	482	185	667	28	6	34	120	60	180	168	86	254
Warwickshire	193	87	280	13	6	19	22	12	34	31	12	43
West Mercia	211	102	313	4	3	7	49	26	75	40	28	68
West Midlands	318	104	422	67	21	88	30	10	40	73	31	104
West Yorkshire	321	131	452	39	17	56	75	59	134	113	56	169
Wiltshire	203	115	318	6	2	8	31	17	48	10	7	17
Dyfed-Powys	131	65	196	1	0	1	17	9	26	18	4	22
Gwent	102	41	143	2	1	3	22	12	34	13	13	26
North Wales	70	56	126	0	0	0	23	24	47	22	10	32
South Wales	66	13	79	2	1	3	0	0	0	0	0	0
Total all 43 forces	**12,310**	**5,479**	**17,789**	**1,416**	**509**	**1,925**	**3,107**	**1,697**	**4,804**	**3,609**	**1,906**	**5,515**
British Transport Police (BTP)	236	44	280	25	0	25	71	22	93	40	8	48
Total	12,546	5,523	18,069	1,441	509	1,950	3,178	1,719	4,897	3,649	1,914	5,563

Source: Home Office

1. Special constable figures are provided on a headcount basis.

21.1c Police forces strength:[1] by country and sex

As at 31 March

Numbers

		2001	2002	2003	2004	2005	2006	2007	2008	2009	2010	2011	2012	2013	2014
Northern Ireland															
Regular police[2,3]															
Strength:															
Men	KERU	6,227	6,057	6,171	6,108	6,016	5,992	5,949	5,761	5,669	5,548	5,371	5238	5085	4988
Women	KERV	1,009	1,080	1,266	1,418	1,547	1,534	1,600	1,653	1,735	1,837	1,922	1907	1877	1882
Reserve[4]															
Strength:															
Men	KERW	2,629	2,223	1,983	1,824	1,431	1,424	1,212	1,119	930	774	597	333	313	278
Women	KERX	556	510	453	485	410	402	400	382	345	311	283	247	222	184

1. All figures are full-time equivalent strength figures that have been rounded to the nearest whole

2 Does not include officers on secondment.

3 Also includes student officers.

4 As at 31/03/12 No longer any FTR in PSNI, As at 31/03/12 Reserve figures only include Con PT (Formerly known as PTR)

Source: Police Service of Northern Ireland

21.1d Number of Police Officers (Full-time Equivalent) in Scotland[1,2], and by Local Policing Divisions, as at 31 March 2014

as at 31 March	Scotland
2014	17,244

Police Officer Distribution

The chart below outlines the distribution of officers across each of the 14 local policing divisions together with the available regional and national resources.

POLICE OFFICER DISTRIBUTION (FTE)

1. All figures are expressed in terms of full-time equivalent (FTE) police officers, rounded to the nearest whole number.

2. Police Officers in Scotland - includes all officers deployed with the 14 local policing divisions, specialist and operational support, central functions, officers undertaking Scottish Police College training, long-term sick leave and maternity/adoption leave, officers at ports and airports paid either wholly or partially by the port/airport authority, and additional officers either wholly or partially funded by the local authority or an external body, and all officers otherwise seconded to Scottish Government, Her Majesty's Inspectorate of Constabulary for Scotland (HMICS), Scottish Police Authority and elsewhere.

Sources: Scottish Government Justice Analytical Services;
Police Scotland

21.2 Prison Population International Comparisons with other EU Countries

	Prison population total (no in penal institutions incl. Pre-trial detainees/remand prisoners)	Date	Estimated national population	Prison population rate (per 100,000 of national population)	Source of Prison Population Total
Northern Europe					
Denmark	3,481	at 1.5.2015	5.66M	62	NPA
Estonia	2,862	at 27.7.2015	1.31M	218	NPA
Finland	3,105	at 16.5.2015	5.47M	57	NPA
Iceland	147	at 1.1.2014	325,700	45	NPA
Ireland	3,770	at 25.6.2015	4.62M	82	NPA
Latvia	5,280	at April 2014	2.0M	264	NPA
Lithuania	9,261	at 1.1.2014	2.94M	315	C of E
Norway	3,710	at 13.5.2015	5.19M	71	NPA
Sweden	5,779	at 1.10.2014	9.71M	60	NPA
United Kingdom					
- England & Wales	85,743	at 19.6.2015	57.85M	148	Ministry of Justice
- Northern Ireland	1,715	at 29.5.2015	1.84M	93	NPA
- Scotland	7,732	at 19.6.2015	5.37M	144	NPA
Faeroe Islands (Denmark)	9	average for 2013	48,120	19	Danish NPA
Guernsey (UK)	96	at 24.10.2014	64,800	148	Guernsey Prison Administration
Isle of Man (UK)	86	at 11.3.2015	86,700	99	Home Affairs Minister
Jersey (UK)	133	at 17.11.2014	100,700	132	Jersey Prison Administration
Southern Europe					
Albania	5,734	at December 2014	2.89M	198	NPA
Andorra	45	at 1.1.2014	76,250	59	C of E
Bosnia & Hertzegovina					
- Federation	1,883	at 1.1.2013	2.35M	80	C of E
- Republika Srpska	940	at 31.12.2014	1.32M	71	Rep.Srpska Prison Administration
Croatia	3,853	at 25.11.2014	4.24M	91	NPA
Cyprus	811	at 1.9.2013	860,600	94	C of E Annual Penal Statistics
Greece	13,147	at November 2013	11M	120	NPA
Italy	53,283	at 31.5.2015	62.34M	85	Ministry of Justice
Kosovo/Kosova	1,695	at 15.11.2013	1.83M	93	U.S. State Dept. human rights report
Macedonia (FYR)	2,880	at 31.12.2013	2.06M	140	NPA
Malta	582	at 31.1.2015	429,740	135	Home Affairs Minister
Montenegro	1,064	at 31.12.2013	624,300	170	United Nations Survey
Portugal	14,214	at 30.4.2015	10.35M	137	NPA
San Marino	2 *	01.09.2013	33,700	6	C of E Annual Penal Statistics
	* most prisoners serve their sentences in Italian prisons and are not included in prison population for San Marino				
Serbia	10,034	at 31.12.2013	7.15M	140	NPA
Slovenia	1,511	at 25.5.2015	2.06M	73	NPA
Spain	65,581	at 29.5.2015	46.38M	141	NPA
Gibraltar (UK)	48	at 31.12.2013	32,800	146	Government of Gibraltar
Western Europe					
Austria	8,241	at 1.11.2014	8.55M	96	NPA
Belgium	11,769	1.3.2014	11.24M	105	Service Public Federal
France	66,761*	at 1.4.2015	67M	100	NPA
	* including French overseas departments and territories; excluding 11,695 persons not detained in penal institutions (écrouées non détenues)				
Germany	61,872	at 30.11.2014	81.0M	76	German Federal Statistical Office
Liechtenstein	7*	at 1.1.2014	37,130	19	C of E
	* additional prisoners, serving more than two years (11 at November 2013), are held in Austrian & Swiss prisons in accordance with treaty agreements				
Luxembourg	631	at 1.1.2015	562,400	112	NPA
Monaco	23	at 1.1.2014	36,950	62	C of E
Netherlands	12,638	at 30.9.2013	16.82M	75	NPA
Switzerland	6,923	at 3.9.2014	8.2M	84	Swiss Federal Statistical Office
Europe/Asia					
Armenia	3,923	1.1.2014	2.98M	132	C of E
Azerbaijan	20,669	at 31.12.2013	9.48M	218	United Nations survey
Georgia	10,493	at 30.4.2015	3.73M	281	National Statistical Office
Russian Federation	656,618	at 01.07.2015	144.3M	455	NPA
Turkey	165,033	at 2.3.2015	77.88M	212	NPA
Central and Eastern Europe					
Belarus	31,700	at 1.10.2012	9.45M	335	NPA
Bulgaria	10,006	at October 2013	7.25M	138	U.S. State Dept. Human Rights Report
Czech Republic	20,071	at 19.6.2015	10.51M	191	NPA
Hungary	17,716	at 1.7.2015	9.83M	180	NPA
Moldova	7,548	at 1.4.2015	3.56M	212	NPA
Poland	76,145	at 31.5.2015	38.44M	198	NPA
Romania	29,291	at 23.6.2015	19.83M	148	NPA
Slovakia	10,146	at 1.6.2015	5.42M	187	NPA
Ukraine	71,327*	at 1.7.2015	36.5M	c. 195	NPA
	* not including prisoners in Crimea, Sebastopol and those Donetsk & Luhansk areas that are not under the control of the Ukrainian authorities				

Source: International Centre for Prison Studies

C of E - Council of Europe
NPA - National Prison Administration

21.3 Police recorded crime by offence, 2003/04 to year ending December 2013 and year to December 2014 and percentage change between year to December 2013 and year to December 2014

England and Wales

Offence		2003/04	2004/05	2005/06	2006/07	2007/08	2008/09	2009/10	2010/11	2011/12	2012/13	2013/14	12 months to Dec 2013	12 months to Dec 2014	% change between years [1]
	VICTIM BASED CRIME	5,422,954	5,022,946	4,910,238	4,788,218	4,338,484	4,091,230	3,760,387	3,598,145	3,454,955	3,150,551	3,107,541	3,107,941	3,142,935	1
1	Murder														
4.1	Manslaughter														
4.10	Corporate manslaughter	904	868	764	758	775	664	620	639	553	558	534	552	515	-7
4.2	Infanticide														
	Homicide [3,4]	904	868	764	758	775	664	620	639	553	558	534	552	515	-7
2	Attempted murder [4]	888	740	920	633	621	574	591	523	483	412	500	488	523	7
	Intentional destruction of viable unborn child	8	4	5	5	4	2	3	3	3	1	4	1	7	-
4.3	Causing death by dangerous driving	:	:	:	:	:	373	296	213	200	174	284	275	347	26
4.4	Causing death by careless driving when under the influence of drink or drugs	:	:	:	:	:	29	36	25	24	14	23	25	12	-
4.6	Causing death by careless or inconsiderate driving	:	:	:	:	:	35	188	172	179	139	136	142	151	6
4.8	Causing death by dangerous or careless driving	445	441	432	459	422	:	:	:	:	:	:	:	:	:
4.4/6/8	More serious wounding or other act endangering life [5]	19,528	19,612	18,825	17,276	15,118	:	:	:	:	:	:	:	:	:
5	Inflicting grievous bodily harm (GBH) with intent [5,6]	:	:	:	:	:	22,663	22,795	19,489	17,777	:	:	:	:	:
5A	Use of substance or object to endanger life [5,6]	:	:	:	:	:	462	416	371	315	:	:	:	:	:
5B	Possession of items to endanger life [5,6]	:	:	:	:	:	266	331	329	298	:	:	:	:	:
5C	Assault with intent to cause serious harm [6]	:	:	:	:	:	:	:	:	:	17,006	17,924	17,514	20,010	14
5D	Endangering life [6]	:	:	:	:	:	:	:	:	:	778	800	791	958	21
5E	Endangering railway passengers [6]	811	718	646	484	402	320	231	257	214	:	:	:	:	:
6	Endangering life at sea [6]	2	3	13	5	10	8	6	4	6	:	:	:	:	:
7	Inflicting grievous bodily harm (GBH) without intent [7,8]	:	:	:	:	:	17,159	16,482	15,112	14,409	:	:	:	:	:
8F	Racially or religiously aggravated inflicting GBH without intent [7,8]	:	:	:	:	:	384	224	188	169	:	:	:	:	:
8H	Causing death by aggravated vehicle taking	63	40	24	18	18	14	5	14	7	8	4	8	3	-
37.1	Causing or allowing death of child or vulnerable person	:	:	:	3	3	7	3	5	6	8	22	18	14	-
4.7	Causing death by driving: unlicensed or disqualified or uninsured drivers	:	:	:	:	1	8	16	6	6	10	5	5	1	-
4.9	Less serious wounding [7]	431,056	488,135	516,523	481,822	430,818	:	:	:	:	:	:	:	:	:
8A	Actual bodily harm (ABH) and other injury [7,8]	:	:	:	:	:	374,255	355,962	328,463	301,223	:	:	:	:	:
8G	Racially or religiously aggravated less serious wounding [7]	4,930	5,426	6,107	5,620	4,830	:	:	:	:	:	:	:	:	:
8D	Racially or religiously aggravated ABH or other injury [7,8]	:	:	:	:	:	3,921	3,521	2,985	2,688	:	:	:	:	:
8J	Poisoning or female genital mutilation [7,8]	:	:	:	:	:	163	138	118	118	:	:	:	:	:
8K	Assault with injury [8]	:	:	:	:	:	:	:	:	:	290,956	300,584	293,653	338,224	15
8N	Racially or religiously aggravated assault with injury [8]	:	:	:	:	:	:	:	:	:	2,579	2,451	2,476	2,602	5
	Violence with injury	457,731	515,119	543,500	506,325	452,247	420,643	401,244	368,277	338,125	312,085	322,737	315,396	362,852	15
3	Threat or conspiracy to murder [9]	22,299	23,758	18,683	12,822	9,966	:	:	:	:	:	:	:	:	:
3A	Conspiracy to murder [9]	:	:	:	:	:	56	45	36	36	28	30	20	42	-
3B	Threats to kill [9]	:	:	:	:	:	9,448	9,523	9,480	7,643	7,347	8,477	7,906	11,712	48
8L	Harassment [10,11]	38,434	49,815	54,644	55,493	52,107	48,363	52,959	51,173	48,141	54,532	61,175	58,467	74,999	28
8M	Racially or religiously aggravated harassment [10,11]	2,088	2,302	2,548	2,657	2,424	2,395	2,370	1,971	1,625	1,500	1,446	1,384	1,743	26
8Q	Stalking [10]	:	:	:	:	:	:	:	:	:	:	:	:	2,187	-
11	Cruelty to and neglect of children [12]	6,083	5,724	5,045	4,917	5,287	6,204	6,611	6,087	6,081	6,370	7,998	7,781	8,449	9
11A	Cruelty to children/young persons [12]	:	:	:	:	:	:	:	:	12	:	:	:	:	:
12	Abandoning a child under the age of two years [12]	49	49	49	23	19	23	9	6	6	5	6	6	4	-
13	Child abduction	930	1,035	919	696	595	567	560	548	532	513	568	560	756	35
14	Procuring illegal abortion	9	7	6	6	6	3	3	5	3	5	6	6	4	-
36	Kidnapping	3,141	2,814	2,799	2,367	1,991	2,035	1,860	1,717	1,516	1,388	1,728	1,669	2,071	24
104	Assault without injury on a constable	22,189	23,604	22,217	21,749	20,384	17,384	15,781	15,510	15,873	14,527	14,452	14,578	14,399	-1
105A	Assault without injury	241,229	216,712	183,555	202,701	198,653	197,035	203,098	205,975	202,509	198,390	211,208	202,103	256,436	27
105B	Racially or religiously aggravated assault without injury	4,161	3,866	3,945	4,351	4,325	4,186	4,328	4,062	4,071	3,898	4,102	3,988	4,637	16
	Violence without injury	340,612	329,686	294,410	307,782	295,757	287,701	297,147	296,570	288,042	288,498	311,190	298,462	377,435	26
	TOTAL VIOLENCE AGAINST THE PERSON	799,247	845,673	838,674	814,865	748,779	709,008	699,011	665,486	626,720	601,141	634,461	614,410	740,802	21

21.3 Police recorded crime by offence, 2003/04 to year ending December 2014 and percentage change between year to December 2013 and year to December 2014

England and Wales

Offence		2003/04	2004/05	2005/06	2006/07	2007/08	2008/09	2009/10	2010/11	2011/12	2012/13	2013/14	12 months to Dec 2013	12 months to Dec 2014	% change between years
19A	Rape of a female [13,14]	12,378	693	61	25	145	170	9,027	9,469	9,773	9,646	12,306	11,150	16,628	49
19C	Rape of a female aged 16 or over [13]	:	8,192	8,725	8,222	7,610	7,768	2,908	2,877	2,777	2,803	3,401	3,189	3,988	25
19D	Rape of a female child under 16 [13]	:	3,014	3,153	2,853	2,422	2,537	1,967	2,243	2,212	2,372	2,836	2,736	3,262	19
19E	Rape of a female child under 13 [13]	:	970	1,388	1,524	1,487	1,658	:	:	:	:	:	:	:	:
19B	Rape of a male [13,14]	894	81	22	18	10	22	368	387	387	413	661	544	956	76
19F	Rape of a male aged 16 or over [13]	:	444	438	413	332	317	241	246	288	352	416	413	582	41
19G	Rape of a male child under 16 [13]	:	322	292	261	237	216	563	670	601	788	1,125	1,067	1,287	21
19H	Rape of a male child under 13 [13]	:	297	364	458	430	408	:	:	:	:	:	:	:	:
	Rape	**13,272**	**14,013**	**14,443**	**13,774**	**12,673**	**13,096**	**15,074**	**15,892**	**16,038**	**16,374**	**20,745**	**19,099**	**26,703**	**40**
16	Buggery [13,14]	247	73	39	35	49	36	:	:	:	:	:	:	:	:
17	Indecent assault on a male [13,14]	4,110	1,003	347	76	209	158	:	:	:	:	:	:	:	:
17A	Sexual assault on a male aged 13 and over [13]	:	1,316	1,428	1,450	1,323	1,161	1,208	1,285	1,261	1,400	1,962	1,794	2,624	46
17B	Sexual assault on a male child under 13 [13]	:	1,227	1,394	1,237	1,121	1,004	1,054	1,126	1,011	1,270	1,648	1,656	2,093	26
18	Gross indecency between males [13]	260	49	20	12	17	14	:	:	:	:	:	:	:	:
20	Indecent assault on a female [13,14]	27,240	5,152	1,215	267	768	575	:	:	:	:	:	:	:	:
20A	Sexual assault on a female aged 13 and over [13]	:	15,087	17,158	16,883	15,793	15,500	15,693	16,346	15,794	15,518	17,373	16,672	21,506	29
20B	Sexual assault on a female child under 13 [13]	:	4,391	4,647	4,245	3,984	3,665	4,148	4,298	3,991	4,177	5,124	4,880	5,799	19
21	Unlawful sexual intercourse with a girl under 13 [13]	212	436	138	67	33	51	:	:	:	:	:	:	:	:
21	Sexual activity involving a child under 13 [13]	:	1,510	1,950	1,936	1,836	1,650	1,817	1,769	1,808	2,173	2,881	2,746	3,845	40
22	Unlawful sexual intercourse with a girl under 16 [13,14]	1,911	713	595	:	:	:	:	:	:	:	:	:	:	:
22B	Sexual activity involving a child under 16 [13]	:	2,546	3,208	3,208	3,123	3,318	3,992	4,039	3,971	4,468	5,879	5,520	7,394	34
22A	Causing sexual activity without consent [13,15]	:	239	224	224	217	151	130	167	203	191	275	257	429	67
23	Incest or familial sexual offences [13]	105	86	966	1,344	1,125	1,041	1,111	803	637	509	491	492	571	16
25	Abduction of female [13,14]	403	104	36	21	4	4	:	:	:	:	:	:	:	:
70	Sexual activity with a person with a mental disorder [13]	:	99	139	163	127	131	124	130	101	115	134	134	187	40
71	Abuse of children through prostitution and pornography [13]	:	21	124	101	108	116	134	153	159	176	290	263	320	22
72	Trafficking for sexual exploitation [13]	:	:	33	43	57	52	58	66	59	70	124	117	133	14
73	Abuse of position of trust of a sexual nature [13]	792	682	463	361	328	195	185	146	176	192	194	201	217	8
74	Gross indecency with a child [13,14]	1,987	398	120	64	149	121	:	:	:	:	:	:	:	:
88A	Sexual grooming [13]	:	186	237	322	274	313	393	309	371	370	462	446	607	36
88B	Other miscellaneous sexual offences [13,16,17]	9,873	11,593	11,363	10,209	8,848	:	:	:	:	:	:	:	:	:
88C	Other miscellaneous sexual offences [13,17]	:	:	:	:	:	298	354	198	163	160	199	172	211	23
88D	Unnatural sexual offences [13,17]	:	:	:	:	:	5	15	12	11	16	17	16	16	-
88E	Exposure and voyeurism [13,17]	:	:	:	:	:	7,530	7,516	7,201	7,006	6,420	6,407	6,372	7,607	19
	Other sexual offences [13]	**47,140**	**46,911**	**45,844**	**42,268**	**39,493**	**37,089**	**37,932**	**38,048**	**36,722**	**37,225**	**43,460**	**41,738**	**53,559**	**28**
	TOTAL SEXUAL OFFENCES [13]	**60,412**	**60,924**	**60,287**	**56,042**	**52,166**	**50,185**	**53,006**	**53,940**	**52,760**	**53,599**	**64,205**	**60,837**	**80,262**	**32**
34A	Robbery of business property	10,110	7,934	8,760	9,454	9,173	9,350	8,182	7,729	6,770	6,120	5,786	5,783	5,778	0
34B	Robbery of personal property	93,626	83,076	89,438	91,922	75,600	70,780	66,923	68,460	67,918	59,035	52,028	53,643	45,807	-15
	TOTAL ROBBERY	**103,736**	**91,010**	**98,198**	**101,376**	**84,773**	**80,130**	**75,105**	**76,189**	**74,688**	**65,155**	**57,814**	**59,426**	**51,585**	**-13**
28	Burglary in a dwelling	398,945	318,969	298,355	290,454	279,125	282,977	:	:	:	:	:	:	:	:
28A	Burglary in a dwelling	:	:	:	:	:	:	214,889	208,484	198,853	185,147	171,415	176,277	160,895	-9
28B	Attempted burglary in a dwelling	:	:	:	:	:	:	44,706	42,298	40,287	37,386	36,359	36,969	35,348	-4
28C	Distraction burglary in a dwelling	:	:	:	:	:	:	6,936	5,480	4,467	3,305	2,847	2,825	3,067	9
28D	Attempted distraction burglary in a dwelling	:	:	:	:	:	:	722	543	368	257	189	207	212	2
29	Aggravated burglary in a dwelling	3,400	2,538	2,162	1,806	1,571	1,454	1,353	1,360	1,337	1,181	1,175	1,208	1,263	5
	Domestic burglary	402,345	321,507	300,517	292,260	280,696	284,431	268,606	258,165	245,312	227,276	211,985	217,486	200,785	-8
	of which: distraction burglary	15,716	13,258	11,552	12,750	10,058	9,092	7,658	6,023	4,835	3,562	3,036	3,032	3,279	8

21.3 Police recorded crime by offence, 2003/04 to year ending December 2014 and percentage change between year to December 2013 and year to December 2014

England and Wales

Offence		2003/04	2004/05	2005/06	2006/07	2007/08	2008/09	2009/10	2010/11	2011/12	2012/13	2013/14	12 months to Dec 2013	12 months to Dec 2014	% change between years
30	Burglary in a building other than a dwelling	417,133	358,398	344,195	329,473	302,799	296,970	236,019	230,868	223,153	202,440	200,552	199,504	189,311	-5
30A	Burglary in a building other than a dwelling	..	..	..	..	..	..	35,868	33,515	32,473	29,959	30,545	30,128	29,097	-3
30B	Attempted burglary in a building other than a dwelling	535	453	356	279	215	183	152	135	110	120	105	117	157	34
31	Aggravated burglary in a building other than a dwelling														
	Non-domestic burglary	417,668	358,851	344,551	329,752	303,014	297,153	272,039	264,518	255,736	232,519	231,202	229,749	218,565	-5
	Burglary	**820,013**	**680,358**	**645,068**	**622,012**	**583,710**	**581,584**	**540,645**	**522,683**	**501,048**	**459,795**	**443,187**	**447,235**	**419,350**	**-6**
37.2	Aggravated vehicle taking	11,570	11,409	10,943	10,920	10,334	9,730	8,000	6,954	6,253	5,652	5,252	5,269	5,438	3
45	Theft from a vehicle	603,256	500,360	507,239	502,651	432,412	396,976	339,170	313,467	300,377	285,047	276,352	281,600	245,851	-13
48	Theft or unauthorised taking of a motor vehicle	280,288	231,323	203,239	182,464	159,704	137,508	109,684	99,208	85,803	74,168	70,056	70,389	69,547	-1
126	Vehicle interference [18]	89,892	77,004	71,400	68,980	54,003	47,639	38,019	29,987	25,009	22,492	20,367	20,872	32,472	56
	Vehicle offences	**985,006**	**820,096**	**792,821**	**765,015**	**656,453**	**591,853**	**494,873**	**449,616**	**417,442**	**387,359**	**372,027**	**378,130**	**353,308**	**-7**
39	Theft from the person	137,154	122,081	123,867	114,852	101,660	89,652	92,247	92,902	100,588	109,757	98,272	104,725	80,728	-23
	Theft from the person	**137,154**	**122,081**	**123,867**	**114,852**	**101,660**	**89,652**	**92,247**	**92,902**	**100,588**	**109,757**	**98,272**	**104,725**	**80,728**	**-23**
44	Theft or unauthorised taking of a pedal cycle	105,467	105,953	113,192	110,526	104,000	104,169	109,847	108,962	115,902	97,286	97,679	96,662	94,251	-2
	Bicycle theft	**105,467**	**105,953**	**113,192**	**110,526**	**104,000**	**104,169**	**109,847**	**108,962**	**115,902**	**97,286**	**97,679**	**96,662**	**94,251**	**-2**
46	Shoplifting	303,235	281,127	295,999	294,282	290,653	320,739	307,823	305,896	308,326	300,623	321,023	317,047	325,504	3
	Shoplifting	**303,235**	**281,127**	**295,999**	**294,282**	**290,653**	**320,739**	**307,823**	**305,896**	**308,326**	**300,623**	**321,023**	**317,047**	**325,504**	**3**
35	Blackmail [20]	1,497	1,465	1,645	2,481	1,201	1,363	1,450	1,491	1,369	1,497	2,134	1,846	3,164	71
40	Theft in a dwelling other than from an automatic machine or meter	61,099	57,713	54,757	54,471	51,336	51,220	53,338	54,798	54,518	52,384	50,510	50,420	51,241	2
41	Theft by an employee	17,700	17,251	17,048	16,323	15,864	15,467	13,169	12,141	11,589	10,446	10,315	10,348	10,666	3
42	Theft of mail	20,537	22,509	9,351	4,740	3,051	3,724	3,098	2,792	2,447	2,878	2,162	2,153	2,038	-5
43	Dishonest use of electricity	1,309	1,296	1,299	1,497	2,024	1,785	1,736	1,860	1,948	2,007	2,228	2,150	2,357	10
47	Theft from automatic machine or meter [19]	29,515	35,918	42,049	33,721	11,932	7,651	7,753	6,215	6,692	6,394	4,951	5,185	4,212	-19
49	Other theft	634,491	589,189	554,368	536,603	526,949	472,325	436,244	481,585	491,559	419,685	389,027	396,018	364,749	-8
49A	Making off without payment [35]	132,624	102,906	87,767	82,261	73,895	80,048	70,397	66,505	61,351	50,833	51,560	50,641	58,833	16
	All other theft offences	**898,772**	**828,247**	**768,284**	**732,097**	**686,252**	**633,583**	**587,185**	**627,387**	**631,473**	**546,124**	**512,887**	**518,761**	**497,260**	**-4**
	TOTAL THEFT OFFENCES	**3,249,647**	**2,837,862**	**2,739,231**	**2,638,784**	**2,422,728**	**2,321,580**	**2,132,620**	**2,107,446**	**2,074,779**	**1,900,944**	**1,845,075**	**1,862,560**	**1,770,401**	**-5**
56	Arson [21]	57,546	48,368	45,731	43,100	39,327									
56A	Arson endangering life [21]	..	..	..	..	..	3,629	3,623	3,325	3,100	2,588	2,571	2,570	2,656	3
56B	Arson not endangering life [21]	..	..	..	..	..	31,198	28,957	25,791	24,119	16,717	16,003	16,133	16,278	1
	Arson	**57,546**	**48,368**	**45,731**	**43,100**	**39,327**	**34,827**	**32,580**	**29,116**	**27,219**	**19,305**	**18,574**	**18,703**	**18,934**	**1**
58A	Criminal damage to a dwelling	321,613	308,973	297,579	288,285	256,804	235,424	198,623	172,916	155,982	131,157	121,519	124,849	116,712	-7
58B	Criminal damage to a building other than a dwelling	186,784	174,489	161,436	160,207	131,146	109,440	88,687	75,677	67,329	57,631	52,596	53,829	50,533	-6
58C	Criminal damage to a vehicle	457,950	461,346	468,143	483,237	425,632	389,719	336,927	289,045	259,871	222,770	217,989	217,159	215,827	-1
58D	Other criminal damage	180,411	188,842	195,069	197,036	173,127	157,109	140,575	125,751	113,478	97,008	93,436	94,312	96,095	2
58E	Racially or religiously aggravated criminal damage to a dwelling [22]	1,982	1,845	1,742	1,543	1,150	999	849	639	499					..
58F	Racially or religiously aggravated criminal damage to a building other than a dwelling [22]	1,185	1,137	1,274	1,079	833	778	663	534	431					..
58G	Racially or religiously aggravated criminal damage to a vehicle [22]	1,603	1,640	1,899	1,711	1,338	1,304	1,135	869	788					..
58H	Racially or religiously aggravated other criminal damage [22]	838	837	975	953	681	727	606	537	411					..
58J	Racially or religiously aggravated other criminal damage [22]	..	..	..	..	..	..	..	..	..	1,841	1,872	1,856	1,784	-4
	Criminal damage	**1,152,366**	**1,139,109**	**1,128,117**	**1,134,051**	**990,711**	**895,500**	**768,065**	**665,968**	**598,789**	**510,407**	**487,412**	**492,005**	**480,951**	**-2**
	TOTAL CRIMINAL DAMAGE AND ARSON	**1,209,912**	**1,187,477**	**1,173,848**	**1,177,151**	**1,030,038**	**930,327**	**800,645**	**695,084**	**626,008**	**529,712**	**505,986**	**510,708**	**499,885**	**-2**

21.3 Police recorded crime by offence, 2003/04 to year ending December 2013 and year to December 201 and percentage change between year to December 2013 and year to December 201

England and Wales

Offence	2003/04	2004/05	2005/06	2006/07	2007/08	2008/09	2009/10	2010/11	2011/12	2012/13	2013/14	12 months to Dec 2013	12 months to Dec 2014	% change between years
OTHER CRIMES AGAINST SOCIETY	420,595	453,825	515,453	534,159	542,656	539,153	504,649	480,330	448,626	402,617	398,436	397,662	401,293	1
92A Trafficking in controlled drugs	24,628	24,190	25,276	26,550	28,323	29,885	33,223	32,336	31,316	29,746	29,351	29,592	28,021	-5
Trafficking of drugs	24,628	24,190	25,276	26,550	28,323	29,885	33,223	32,336	31,316	29,746	29,351	29,592	28,021	-5
92B Possession of controlled drugs [23]	118,006													
92C Other drug offences	877	781	601	680	817	1,123	1,122	1,142	1,127	1,034	1,197	1,203	869	-28
92D Possession of controlled drugs (excluding cannabis) [23]		32,603	32,685	36,608	42,519	44,578	38,439	38,711	36,453	34,596	34,044	33,961	32,492	-4
92E Possession of cannabis [23]		88,263	119,917	130,395	158,254	167,950	162,800	160,733	160,203	142,627	133,552	136,416	117,337	-14
Possession of drugs	118,883	121,647	153,203	167,683	201,590	213,651	202,361	200,586	197,783	178,257	168,793	171,580	150,698	-12
TOTAL DRUG OFFENCES	143,511	145,837	178,479	194,233	229,913	243,536	235,584	232,922	229,099	208,003	198,144	201,172	178,719	-11
8B Possession of weapons [24]	35,669	36,374	35,590	34,689	32,513									
10A Possession of firearms with intent [24]						1,973	1,587	1,385	1,151	998	1,076	1,118	1,152	3
10B Possession of firearms offences [26]						4,460	4,070	3,650	3,402	3,052	2,924	2,958	3,048	3
10C Possession of other weapons [24]						14,944	11,950	10,564	9,138	7,274	7,328	7,419	7,341	-1
10D Possession of article with blade or point [24]	3,322	4,210	4,106	4,239	4,560	13,985	10,885	10,474	9,762	8,425	9,047	8,825	9,635	9
81 Other firearms offences [25]	30	21	15	9	6	293	253	254	229	160	237	196	194	-1
90 Other knives offences						7	13	0	6	1	2	1	1	-
TOTAL POSSESSION OF WEAPONS OFFENCES	39,021	40,605	39,711	38,937	37,079	35,662	28,758	26,327	23,688	19,910	20,614	20,517	21,371	4
9A Public fear, alarm or distress [10, 11]	116,566	147,801	164,061	173,152	158,045	142,246	126,597	114,781	97,085	81,139	79,561	78,778	89,838	14
9B Racially or religiously aggravated public fear, alarm or distress [10, 11]	18,887	21,061	24,057	25,828	24,086	23,355	23,226	20,967	20,188	20,420	21,676	21,094	24,966	18
62 Treason [27]	1	0	0	0	0	0	0	0	0					
62A Violent disorder [27]									0	656	638	590	752	27
63 Treason felony [27]	0	0	0	0	0	0	0	0	0					
64 Riot [27]	8	4	7	4	2	3	0	2	3					
65 Violent disorder [27]	2,790	2,636	2,457	1,742	1,180	1,022	859	751	696					
66 Other offences against the State or public order	19,926	20,370	31,999	35,935	35,067	37,663	37,572	36,580	32,886	29,990	32,467	31,509	35,527	13
TOTAL PUBLIC ORDER OFFENCES	158,178	191,872	222,581	236,661	218,380	204,289	188,254	173,081	150,858	132,205	134,342	131,971	151,083	14
15 Concealing an infant death close to birth	6	6	8	4	8	8	6	9	5	2	2	2	4	-
24 Exploitation of prostitution [13]	186	117	153	190	184	173	148	153	110	120	124	124	130	5
26 Bigamy	71	104	101	61	74	64	60	44	31	39	40	38	50	
27 Soliciting for prostitution [13]	1,944	1,821	1,640	1,290	1,216	1,071	1,190	826	797	883	750	876	785	-10
33 Going equipped for stealing, etc.	5,706	4,567	4,382	4,253	3,781	3,791	3,647	4,129	3,765	3,473	3,472	3,452	3,178	-8
33A Making, supplying or possessing articles for use in fraud [28]	69	438	1,548	1,961	2,382	2,505	2,609	2,344	1,779	1,427	2,928	2,129	2,622	11
38 Profiting from or concealing proceeds of crime [28]					183	611	862	975	1,301	1,384	1,485	1,347	1,492	11
53H Making or supplying articles for use in fraud [29]														
53J Possession of articles for use in fraud [29]					1,108	1,466	1,564	1,559	1,366	1,287		341	328	-
54 Handling stolen goods	17,308	14,157	12,714	11,826	11,335	10,766	9,448	9,184	9,769	8,134	8,529	8,445	7,082	-16
59 Threat etc. to commit criminal damage	8,612	10,066	10,501	7,889	6,318	6,034	5,996	5,916	5,214	4,950	5,788	5,397	7,997	48
60 Forgery or use of drug prescription	805	747	693	593	440	446	343	298	361	379	413	459	428	-7
61 Other forgery	7,992	10,249	10,627	8,479	4,211	4,241	2,526	1,632	2,124	2,984	2,864	3,105	2,310	-26
61A Possession of false documents					2,301	2,646	2,263	1,770	1,378	962	935	762	1,095	44
67 Perjury	206	265	245	197	193	177	184	339	151	134	96	117	91	-22
68 Libel [30]	0	0	1	1	0	1	0	4						
69 Offender Management Act offences [30]							533	518	583	1,024	1,111	1,049	1,417	35
75 Betting, gaming and lotteries [30]	1	12	6	13	11	22	21	14	12	11	12	13	19	-
76 Aiding suicide [30]	11	6	11	13	9	7	17	7	10	11	12	13	19	-
78 Immigration offences [30]	451	550	935	792	661	573	411	445	344					
79 Perverting the course of justice	11,894	11,567	12,712	11,114	9,131	8,396	7,997	6,890	5,698	4,947	5,366	5,180	6,097	18
80 Absconding from lawful custody	1,721	1,362	1,272	979	828	651	557	499	414	482	370	400	459	15

21.3 Police recorded crime by offence, 2003/04 to year ending December 2014 and percentage change between year to December 2013 and year to December 2014

England and Wales

Offence		2003/04	2004/05	2005/06	2006/07	2007/08	2008/09	2009/10	2010/11	2011/12	2012/13	2013/14	12 months to Dec 2013	12 months to Dec 2014	% change between years
82	Customs and Revenue offences [30]	49	30	49	27	10	13	10	3	5	..	..	..	..	..
83	Bail offences	212	202	177	83	25	3	4	6	3	2	3	4	5	-
84	Trade descriptions, etc [30]	513	1,344	1,360	1,353	1,321	1,143	809	486	263	..	..	..	..	..
85	Health and Safety offences [30]	4	15	8	9	8	15	6	2	8	..	..	..	..	..
86	Obscene publications, etc and protected sexual material [30]	2,881	2,861	2,592	2,378	2,672	2,775	3,215	3,342	3,335	3,506	4,581	4,261	6,383	50
87	Protection from eviction [30]	75	70	75	69	81	71	81	73	68	..	..	..	..	..
89	Adulteration of food [30]	34	29	45	32	44	13	4	9	0	..	..	..	..	..
91	Public health offences [30, 31]	86	112	128	50	44	115	488	398	289	..	..	..	..	..
94	Planning laws [30]	3	4	5	0	0	1	0	1	1	..	..	..	..	..
95	Disclosure, obstruction, false or misleading statements etc	22	144	368	266	425	506	426	348	363	294	357	341	343	1
96	Wildlife crime [36]	..	..	..	..	..	..	..	..	..	..	..	..	26	..
99	Other indictable or triable-either-way offences [30, 37]	3,440	2,577	2,197	1,915	1,391	1,735	1,629	1,569	1,589	2,510	2,514	2,269	4,508	99
802	Dangerous driving	7,567	6,669	5,923	5,353	4,725	4,240	3,941	3,475	3,239	3,092	3,152	3,085	3,209	4
814	Fraud, forgery associated with vehicle driver records	8,016	5,420	4,206	3,138	2,164	1,387	1,058	733	606	473	444	478	390	-18
	TOTAL MISCELLANEOUS CRIMES AGAINST SOCIETY	79,885	75,511	74,682	64,328	57,284	55,666	52,053	48,000	44,981	42,499	45,336	44,002	50,120	14
	TOTAL RECORDED CRIME – ALL OFFENCES EXCLUDING FRAUD [32]	5,843,549	5,476,771	5,425,691	5,322,377	4,881,140	4,630,383	4,265,036	4,078,475	3,903,581	3,553,168	3,505,977	3,505,603	3,544,228	1
FRAUD OFFENCES [33]															
51	Fraud by company director [34]	80	51	626	101	162	815	85	207	45	103	0	1	..	..
52	False accounting	721	541	487	462	251	146	155	108	75	59	1	9	1	-
53A	Cheque and credit card fraud (pre Fraud Act 2006) [29]	131,022	121,376	87,860	59,011	..	..	..	..	..	..	..	..	..	..
53B	Preserved other fraud and repealed fraud offences (pre-Fraud Act 2006) [29 35]	38,378	38,761	40,415	45,593	1,880	1,152	1,042	..	..	..	..	..	..	..
53C	Fraud by false representation: cheque, plastic card and online bank accounts [19, 29]	..	..	..	..	9,984	3,494	3,666	3,342	3,799	3,027	..	400	..	..
53D	Fraud by false representation: other frauds [29]	..	..	..	..	23,345	26,578	27,148	24,942	22,703	17,873	3	1,410	..	..
53E	Fraud by failing to disclose information [29]	..	..	..	..	34,544	38,884	39,626	42,460	44,719	40,325	8	3,027	1	..
53F	Fraud by abuse of position [29]	..	..	..	..	265	304	364	339	246	163	1	15	..	..
53G	Obtaining services dishonestly [29]	..	..	..	..	675	926	1,160	1,033	1,170	927	1	80	1	..
55	Bankruptcy and insolvency offences	9	11	93	14	31	15	13	10	11	12	0	5	..	..
	TOTAL FRAUD OFFENCES RECORDED BY THE POLICE [29,33]	170,210	160,740	129,481	105,181	71,137	72,314	73,259	72,441	72,768	62,489	14	4,947	3	..
	FRAUD OFFENCES RECORDED BY ACTION FRAUD [33]	..	..	..	..	..	..	..	..	46,658	117,402	211,221	202,216	224,944	11
	TOTAL FRAUD OFFENCES	170,210	160,740	129,481	105,181	71,137	72,314	73,259	72,441	119,426	179,891	211,235	207,163	224,947	9
	TOTAL RECORDED CRIME – ALL OFFENCES INCLUDING FRAUD [32]	6,013,759	5,637,511	5,555,172	5,427,558	4,952,277	4,702,697	4,338,295	4,150,916	4,023,007	3,733,059	3,717,212	3,712,766	3,769,175	2

Source: Police recorded crime, Home Office

Police recorded crime data are not designated as National Statistics.

NOTES TO ACCOMPANY TABLE 21.3

1   The National Crime Recording Standard (NCRS) was introduced in April 2002, although some forces adopted NCRS practices before the standard was formally introduced. Figures before and after that date are not directly comparable. The introduction of NCRS led to a rise in recording in 2002/03 and, particularly for violent crime, in the following years as forces continued to improve compliance with the new standard.

2   Includes the British Transport Police from 2002/03 onward

3   The homicide figure for 2002/03 includes 172 homicides attributed to Harold Shipman in previous years but coming to light in the official inquiry in 2002.

4   The homicide figure in 2005/06 of 764 includes 52 homicide victims of the 7 July London bombings, which also accounted for approximately one-quarter of the total of 920 attempted murders.

5   Offence classifications 5A, 5B and 5C were introduced from 1 April 2008 and replaced classification 5. Classification 5A was influenced by a clarification in recording rules that had the effect of significantly increasing levels of recording in some forces. Classification 5A also includes some other offences of endangering life as well as GBH with intent, though GBH with intent is the major part of this category

6   Offence classification 5D was introduced from 1 April 2012 and replaced classification 5A offences. Offence classification 5E was also introduced and replaced the remaining classification 5A offences, 5B, 5C, 6 and 7.

7   Offence classifications 8F, 8G, 8H, 8J and 8K were introduced from 1 April 2008 and had previously been recorded as part of classifications 8A or 8D.

8   Offence classification 8N was introduced from 1 April 2012 and replaced classifications 8F, 8G and 8K. Offence classification 8P was also introduced and replaced classifications 8H and 8J.

9   Offence classifications 3A and 3B were introduced from 1 April 2008 and had previously been recorded as classification 3.

10   Prior to 2008/09, the police sent combined figures for harassment (8L, 8M) and public fear, alarm and distress (9A, 9B) offences. For the years 2002/03 to 2007/08, figures for these offence groups are estimated based upon the proportionate split between the offences in 2008/09. Stalking (8Q) was introduced as a separate crime classification in April 2014, following the introduction of the Protection of Freedoms Act 2012 section 111. Before this, stalking offences were included within harassment offences (8L).

11   Prior to 2008/09, the police sent combined figures for harassment (8L, 8M) and public fear, alarm and distress (9A, 9B) offences. For the years 2002/03 to 2007/08, figures for these offence groups are estimated based upon the proportionate split between the offences in 2008/09.

12   Offence classification 11A was introduced from 1 April 2012 and replaced classifications 11 and 12.

13   The Sexual Offences Act 2003, introduced in May 2004, altered the definition and coverage of sexual offences.

14   Prior to 2009/10, a small number of offences continued to be recorded relating to offences repealed by the Sexual Offences Act 2003. While these may have been legitimately recorded for offences committed prior to May 2004 it is also possible that some may have been recorded in these old categories in error, so any changes based on small numbers should be interpreted with caution.

15   The increase in 2005/06 was accounted for by a large number of offences that were dealt with by the Norfolk Constabulary.

16   This offence consists solely of the former offence of 'Indecent Exposure' for years prior to 2004/05. This became the offence of 'Exposure' and was included within 'Other miscellaneous sexual offences' from May 2004.

17   Offence classification 88B was split into 88C–E with effect from 2008/09. Since that time offences of exposure have been recorded as classification 88E.

18   Includes tampering with a motor vehicle

19   Following a change in the implementation of the Fraud Act 2006, offences involving theft from an automatic machine using a plastic card are now regarded as false representation and recorded under classification 53C.

20   The large increase in 2006/07 was due to the recording of threats made against shareholders of GlaxoSmithKline by animal rights activists.

21   Offence classifications 56A and 56B were introduced from 1 April 2008 and had previously been recorded as classification 56.

22   Offence classifications 58E-58H were amalgamated on 1 April 2012 to form classification 58J.

23   Possession of controlled drugs offences were split with effect from April 2004 into possession of cannabis and possession of drugs other than cannabis.

24   Offence classifications 10A, 10C and 10D were introduced from 1 April 2008 and had previously been recorded as classification 8B.

25   These are offences under the Firearms Act 1968 and other Firearms Acts connected with licensing and certification of firearms. Such offences are not included in the firearms offences statistics.

26   Offence classification 10B was introduced from 1 April 2008. Possession of firearms offences are those offences where the weapon has not been used during the commission of another offence.

27   Offence classifications 62-65 were amalgamated on 1 April 2012 to form classification 62A.

28   These offences were added to the series from 1 April 2003.

29   New offences were introduced under the Fraud Act 2006, which came into force on 15 January 2007.

30   Offence classifications 68, 75, 78, 82, 84, 85, 87, 89, 91 and 94 were included with classification 99 with effect from 1 April 2012.

31   The large increase in this offence from 2008/09 is mainly due to the recording of fly-tipping by some forces following advice that this offence is notifiable.

32   Some forces have revised their data and totals may therefore not agree with those previously published.

33   Action Fraud have taken over the recording of fraud offences on behalf of individual police forces. This process began in April 2011 and was rolled out to all police forces by March 2013. Due to this change caution should be applied when comparing data over this transitional period and with earlier years. There were 14 cases in 2013/14 where police forces recorded a fraud offence after the transfer of responsibility to Action Fraud. These cases are likely to be revised in future quarters. See the User Guide for more details including information on transfer date to Action Fraud for each force

34   The large increase in this offence in 2005/06 was due to one large-scale fraud recorded by the Cambridgeshire Constabulary. The increase in 2007/08 was due to a fraud recorded by North Yorkshire Police. The large increase in 2008/09 was due to large-scale frauds recorded by Gwent Police, Leicestershire Constabulary and the Metropolitan Police. The increase in 2010/11 was due to a large-scale fraud recorded by North Yorkshire Police.

35   Offence classification 49A was introduced as a separate theft classification in 2013/14. Before this, it was recorded under the fraud offence classification 53B. Data for 49A are provided for all years following a special request to forces. In some cases, these have been estimated where forces were unable to provide data.

36   Wildlife crime (96) was introduced as a separate crime classification in April 2014. This saw a number of offences that were previously recorded under "Other notifiable offences" (99) brought together.

37   Due to the introduction of fly-tipping as an offence under "Other notifiable offences" (99) in April 2014, percentage changes may appear high in certain publications.

-       Indicates that data are not reported because the base number of offences is less than 50.

21.4 Persons sentenced at all courts by type of sentence and offence group, 2004 to 2013

England and Wales

Persons Sentenced

Year ending and type of sentence	Violence against the person	Sexual offences	Robbery	Theft Offences	Criminal damage and arson	Drug offences	Possession of weapons	Public order offences	Miscellaneous crimes against society	Fraud offences	All Indictable Offences	Summary Motoring	Summary Non-Motoring	All Summary Offences	All offences
2004 All Sentenced	**27,363**	**4,794**	**7,513**	**125,302**	**10,907**	**39,146**	**13,944**	**9,128**	**64,470**	**13,239**	**315,806**	**520,623**	**700,397**	**1,221,020**	**1,536,826**
Immediate custody	10,585	2,829	5,063	31,445	1,140	7,981	2,455	2,850	12,926	2,664	79,938	11,215	15,169	26,384	106,322
Suspended sentence	443	62	33	378	48	254	106	111	386	322	2,143	320	392	712	2,855
Community sentence	12,378	1,395	2,292	48,514	5,251	8,983	6,122	4,762	15,208	6,108	111,013	50,859	39,631	90,490	201,503
Fine	1,295	191	7	18,493	1,524	14,019	2,502	679	23,646	1,643	63,999	393,171	615,332	1,008,503	1,072,502
Absolute discharge	77	16	3	683	69	448	106	26	1,130	31	2,589	4,146	8,049	12,195	14,784
Conditional discharge	1,525	227	39	22,345	2,117	6,687	2,434	537	4,993	2,285	43,189	45,604	9,442	55,046	98,235
Compensation	360	3	14	1,003	454	-	1	46	66	101	2,048	4,694	3,519	8,213	10,261
Otherwise dealt with	700	71	62	2,441	304	774	218	117	6,115	85	10,887	10,614	8,863	19,477	30,364
Average custodial sentence[1]	21.5	40.0	38.4	8.7	17.0	37.3	11.6	10.0	6.4	10.7	16.1	2.8	3.5	3.2	12.9
2005 All Sentenced	**28,873**	**4,719**	**7,139**	**118,059**	**10,777**	**38,898**	**14,028**	**8,775**	**61,217**	**13,019**	**305,504**	**507,149**	**660,622**	**1,167,771**	**1,473,275**
Immediate custody	10,996	2,689	4,407	28,167	1,155	7,783	2,601	2,697	13,153	2,643	76,291	12,075	12,870	24,945	101,236
Suspended sentence	1,078	115	60	1,746	107	516	344	270	876	499	5,611	1,515	2,540	4,055	9,666
Community sentence	13,057	1,438	2,539	47,500	5,360	9,693	6,644	4,552	14,961	5,980	111,724	58,029	34,494	92,523	204,247
Fine	1,114	178	21	16,087	1,347	13,539	2,032	599	20,999	1,466	57,382	374,417	584,409	958,826	1,016,208
Absolute discharge	79	11	7	675	82	370	100	34	909	31	2,298	3,919	6,779	10,698	12,996
Conditional discharge	1,330	196	17	20,870	2,121	6,400	2,108	475	4,657	2,212	40,386	43,853	8,431	52,284	92,670
Compensation	488	10	12	1,110	371	7	4	35	73	103	2,213	4,720	3,477	8,197	10,410
Otherwise dealt with	731	82	76	1,904	234	590	195	113	5,589	85	9,599	8,621	7,622	16,243	25,842
Average custodial sentence[1]	20.8	41.6	35.0	8.6	16.1	35.8	11.8	10.6	6.9	11.2	15.8	2.8	3.4	3.1	12.6
2006 All Sentenced	**29,798**	**4,880**	**8,169**	**114,200**	**11,864**	**39,478**	**14,123**	**8,735**	**57,131**	**13,016**	**301,394**	**493,888**	**617,564**	**1,111,452**	**1,412,846**
Immediate custody	10,479	2,787	4,802	27,147	1,238	7,532	2,616	2,322	12,345	2,260	73,528	12,571	9,914	22,485	96,013
Suspended sentence	4,449	290	264	6,622	398	1,848	1,303	1,205	3,043	1,376	20,798	6,041	6,669	12,710	33,508
Community sentence	11,198	1,332	2,957	43,310	5,794	9,127	6,625	4,176	13,101	5,332	102,952	59,585	28,281	87,866	190,818
Fine	999	164	13	13,465	1,306	13,271	1,505	475	17,994	1,411	50,603	354,941	548,556	903,497	954,100
Absolute discharge	53	17	7	729	88	334	81	20	838	32	2,199	3,692	5,858	9,550	11,749
Conditional discharge	1,229	139	26	19,013	2,302	6,532	1,757	371	4,297	2,349	38,015	41,996	7,340	49,336	87,351
Compensation	593	14	23	1,305	479	4	4	59	68	122	2,671	5,030	3,922	8,952	11,623
Otherwise dealt with	798	137	77	2,609	259	830	232	107	5,445	134	10,628	10,032	7,024	17,056	27,684
Average custodial sentence[1]	19.5	41.1	32.3	8.4	13.2	33.8	11.3	10.3	7.2	11.9	15.3	2.8	3.4	3.0	12.4
2007 All Sentenced	**30,161**	**4,986**	**8,862**	**121,965**	**11,700**	**44,500**	**14,090**	**9,041**	**52,066**	**13,820**	**311,191**	**489,882**	**605,715**	**1,095,597**	**1,406,788**
Immediate custody	10,615	2,777	4,772	27,284	1,225	8,186	2,709	2,356	12,115	1,998	74,037	13,277	7,892	21,169	95,206
Suspended sentence	5,928	423	452	8,346	490	2,678	1,466	1,816	3,662	1,993	27,254	7,266	6,168	13,434	40,688
Community sentence	10,127	1,359	3,470	46,697	5,308	10,296	6,619	3,837	12,045	5,384	105,142	65,188	26,094	91,282	196,424
Fine	1,004	130	33	14,036	1,135	14,190	1,243	414	14,782	1,485	48,452	342,011	543,354	885,365	933,817
Absolute discharge	58	11	4	815	89	379	70	24	738	28	2,216	3,609	5,161	8,770	10,986
Conditional discharge	1,145	157	30	20,980	2,424	7,825	1,721	372	4,627	2,625	41,906	45,934	6,171	52,105	94,011
Compensation	480	20	26	1,465	691	6	6	54	94	119	2,962	5,161	3,965	9,126	12,088
Otherwise dealt with	804	109	75	2,342	338	939	256	168	4,003	188	9,222	7,436	6,910	14,346	23,568
Average custodial sentence[1]	19.7	43.2	31.3	8.1	13.0	31.9	12.1	10.6	7.4	11.4	15.2	2.7	3.3	3.0	12.4
2008[2] All Sentenced	**29,147**	**5,049**	**8,495**	**127,484**	**9,006**	**52,909**	**14,576**	**8,559**	**46,300**	**13,416**	**314,941**	**492,451**	**546,545**	**1,038,996**	**1,353,937**
Immediate custody	10,897	2,952	5,095	29,324	1,062	9,488	3,374	2,382	12,306	2,178	79,058	14,089	6,378	20,467	99,525
Suspended sentence	5,943	406	444	8,376	407	2,958	1,813	1,908	3,951	2,249	28,455	7,696	5,000	12,696	41,151
Community sentence	9,553	1,360	2,832	47,146	3,982	12,273	6,661	3,450	10,725	4,801	102,783	65,687	21,702	87,389	190,172
Fine	832	89	6	14,174	980	17,674	1,082	386	11,942	1,571	48,736	342,845	490,923	833,768	882,504
Absolute discharge	54	7	2	721	90	382	67	19	538	20	1,900	3,274	4,505	7,779	9,679
Conditional discharge	881	125	23	21,405	1,741	8,099	1,253	271	3,872	2,242	39,912	43,183	4,553	47,736	87,648
Compensation	337	7	13	1,204	492	2	1	19	81	109	2,265	4,402	3,232	7,634	9,899
Otherwise dealt with	650	103	80	5,134	252	2,033	325	124	2,885	246	11,832	11,275	10,252	21,527	33,359
Average custodial sentence[1]	20.6	44.5	32.5	8.3	15.4	32.7	13.4	11.2	7.8	13.2	16.0	2.7	3.2	2.8	13.3
2009 All Sentenced	**30,493**	**5,028**	**8,664**	**128,137**	**7,274**	**56,656**	**15,054**	**16,852**	**43,749**	**14,685**	**326,592**	**513,321**	**558,365**	**1,071,686**	**1,398,278**
Immediate custody	11,530	2,940	5,155	28,424	944	9,426	3,462	5,147	10,583	2,654	80,265	14,698	5,268	19,966	100,231

21.4 Persons sentenced at all courts by type of sentence and offence group, 2004 to 2013

England and Wales

Persons Sentenced

Year ending and type of sentence	Violence against the person	Sexual offences	Robbery	Theft Offences	Criminal damage and arson	Drug offences	Possession of weapons	Public order offences	Miscellaneous crimes against society	Fraud offences	All Indictable Offences	Summary Motoring	Summary Non-Motoring	All Summary Offences	All offences
Suspended sentence	6,385	402	476	8,676	368	3,119	2,449	2,586	4,084	2,586	31,131	8,970	5,056	14,026	45,157
Community sentence	9,937	1,388	2,915	48,290	3,317	13,657	6,785	5,938	10,246	5,522	107,995	67,820	20,162	87,982	195,977
Fine	909	84	8	15,684	873	20,993	1,035	1,707	12,396	1,662	55,351	368,443	513,963	882,406	937,757
Absolute discharge	39	8	5	549	55	353	51	134	421	31	1,646	2,961	4,292	7,253	8,899
Conditional discharge	839	86	15	22,574	1,350	7,207	912	796	3,169	2,053	39,001	41,253	3,630	44,883	83,884
Compensation	280	6	9	1,071	201	-	360	18	50	97	1,732	3,543	2,313	5,856	7,588
Otherwise dealt with	574	114	81	2,869	166	1,901	360	526	2,800	80	9,471	5,633	3,681	9,314	18,785
Average custodial sentence[1]	21.0	49.3	33.6	9.0	19.9	32.1	12.7	7.2	8.2	12.2	16.5	2.6	3.1	2.8	13.7
2010 All Sentenced	**32,438**	**5,720**	**8,514**	**138,065**	**7,127**	**61,435**	**12,990**	**19,338**	**46,314**	**15,481**	**347,422**	**492,345**	**517,833**	**1,010,178**	**1,357,600**
Immediate custody	11,730	3,259	4,946	30,993	1,000	9,693	2,953	5,483	10,225	2,657	82,939	14,634	3,940	18,574	101,513
Suspended sentence	7,069	450	505	9,757	382	3,820	2,061	3,016	4,302	2,814	34,176	9,560	4,382	13,942	48,118
Community sentence	10,411	1,641	2,768	48,645	2,981	13,418	5,779	6,537	10,296	6,031	108,507	64,723	16,103	80,826	189,333
Fine	945	106	4	16,848	772	23,354	999	2,168	12,434	1,807	59,437	343,650	483,234	826,884	886,321
Absolute discharge	41	7	4	588	56	425	49	179	465	21	1,835	2,909	4,068	6,977	8,812
Conditional discharge	1,016	127	13	24,585	1,410	8,526	864	945	3,400	1,917	42,803	44,597	3,033	47,630	90,433
Compensation	562	8	196	1,769	293	3	2	58	69	100	3,060	4,703	192	4,895	7,955
Otherwise dealt with	664	122	78	4,880	233	2,196	283	952	5,123	134	14,665	7,569	2,881	10,450	25,115
Average custodial sentence[1]	20.9	49.0	34.5	8.7	18.5	30.7	13.2	7.1	8.2	13.4	16.2	2.6	3.1	2.7	13.7
2011 All Sentenced	**30,452**	**5,928**	**9,333**	**139,548**	**6,430**	**61,094**	**12,439**	**17,970**	**43,780**	**14,884**	**341,858**	**493,115**	**470,697**	**963,812**	**1,305,670**
Immediate custody	12,120	3,413	5,584	33,817	1,067	9,788	3,196	5,513	10,113	2,947	87,558	15,161	3,451	18,612	106,170
Suspended sentence	6,405	503	541	10,325	396	4,205	2,083	2,644	4,321	2,999	34,422	9,510	4,221	13,731	48,153
Community sentence	8,761	1,646	2,937	47,539	2,595	12,724	5,170	5,639	9,732	5,445	102,188	60,846	14,569	75,415	177,603
Fine	1,124	120	1	16,995	715	23,317	920	2,165	11,351	1,580	58,288	351,819	439,729	791,548	849,836
Absolute discharge	42	8	1	572	48	428	46	157	486	17	1,805	2,721	3,626	6,347	8,152
Conditional discharge	978	89	12	24,139	1,161	8,345	755	889	3,161	1,683	41,212	42,356	2,731	45,087	86,299
Compensation	414	10	173	1,662	225	1	4	55	72	91	2,707	3,918	155	4,073	6,780
Otherwise dealt with	608	139	84	4,499	223	2,286	265	908	4,544	122	13,678	6,784	2,215	8,999	22,677
Average custodial sentence[1]	21.8	53.5	35.4	9.1	19.8	30.7	13.1	7.3	8.8	14.9	16.8	2.5	3.1	2.6	14.3
2012 All Sentenced	**26,189**	**5,715**	**8,342**	**126,366**	**5,374**	**57,601**	**10,164**	**16,313**	**37,828**	**12,218**	**306,110**	**469,284**	**447,838**	**917,122**	**1,223,232**
Immediate custody	11,322	3,397	5,002	32,507	899	9,011	2,651	5,021	8,638	2,631	81,079	13,953	3,012	16,965	98,044
Suspended sentence	5,561	477	555	9,709	300	4,215	1,793	2,320	4,111	2,843	31,884	9,007	3,752	12,759	44,643
Community sentence	6,366	1,512	2,583	39,402	2,018	11,513	4,075	4,828	8,132	4,122	84,551	53,799	12,833	66,632	151,183
Fine	1,296	101	1	15,911	674	21,344	783	2,252	10,134	1,171	53,667	342,435	420,724	763,159	816,826
Absolute discharge	59	8	2	530	47	407	33	157	337	23	1,603	2,592	3,301	5,893	7,496
Conditional discharge	915	92	17	22,263	998	8,816	576	852	2,797	1,210	38,536	38,979	2,350	41,329	79,865
Compensation	202	18	74	2,466	250	3	3	43	65	122	3,247	3,721	173	3,894	7,141
Otherwise dealt with	468	110	108	3,578	188	2,291	250	840	3,614	96	11,543	4,798	1,693	6,491	18,034
Average custodial sentence[1]	23.2	54.5	35.8	9.2	23.6	28.7	13.0	7.4	9.1	14.6	17.0	2.6	3.1	2.7	14.5
2013 All Sentenced	**24,149**	**5,634**	**6,767**	**121,637**	**4,054**	**56,323**	**9,932**	**16,343**	**34,364**	**12,099**	**291,302**	**435,500**	**443,883**	**879,383**	**1,170,685**
Immediate custody	10,357	3,360	4,298	31,718	722	9,024	2,621	4,799	8,525	2,535	77,959	12,318	2,689	15,007	92,966
Suspended sentence	5,561	581	499	11,140	296	5,173	2,108	2,558	4,522	3,097	35,535	9,551	3,679	13,230	48,765
Community sentence	5,262	1,354	1,838	31,978	1,412	9,388	3,557	4,342	6,680	3,963	69,774	46,080	10,681	56,761	126,535
Fine	1,366	125	28	16,500	503	20,712	823	2,838	9,124	1,166	53,185	320,479	419,737	740,216	793,401
Absolute discharge	59	5	1	580	19	346	33	116	352	13	1,525	2,368	3,107	5,475	7,000
Conditional discharge	866	91	19	21,629	783	9,396	488	971	2,377	1,089	37,709	36,191	1,943	38,134	75,843
Compensation	187	19	8	3,958	181	4	2	102	73	141	4,675	4,520	127	4,647	9,322
Otherwise dealt with	490	99	76	4,134	138	2,280	300	617	2,711	95	10,940	3,993	1,920	5,913	16,853
Average custodial sentence[1]	24.7	59.1	39.6	9.2	26.7	31.2	13.3	7.5	9.6	14.9	18.0	2.6	3.1	2.7	15.5

(1) Excludes life and indeterminate sentences.
(2) Excludes data for Cardiff magistrates' court for April, July and August 2008.

Source: Ministry of Justice

21.5 Persons cautioned for summary offences (excluding motoring) by offence, sex and age, 2013

Offence	Ages					Total
	10-11	12-14	15-17	18-20	21+	
104 Assaulting, resisting or obstructing a constable or designated officer in execution of duty	**4**	**69**	**333**	**672**	**2159**	**3237**
Female	1	36	144	232	873	1286
Male	3	32	186	437	1283	1941
Unstated	0	1	3	3	3	10
105 Common assault and battery	**116**	**1495**	**2631**	**4920**	**33417**	**42579**
Female	18	546	933	1386	8114	10997
Male	97	942	1672	3516	25230	31457
Unstated	1	7	26	18	73	125
106 Betting or Gaming Offence	**0**	**0**	**0**	**2**	**29**	**31**
Female	0	0	0	0	0	0
Male	0	0	0	2	29	31
Other	0	0	0	0	0	0
Unstated	0	0	0	0	0	0
107 Brothel Keeping	**0**	**0**	**0**	**0**	**12**	**12**
Female	0	0	0	0	9	9
Male	0	0	0	0	3	3
108 Cruelty to Animal	**0**	**3**	**2**	**2**	**18**	**25**
Female	0	0	0	0	4	4
Male	0	3	2	2	14	21
Other	0	0	0	0	0	0
Unstated	0	0	0	0	0	0
111A Offences under Dangerous Dogs Acts - summary	**0**	**0**	**1**	**4**	**72**	**77**
Female	0	0	1	3	39	43
Male	0	0	0	1	32	33
Unstated	0	0	0	0	1	1
111B Other offences relating to dogs	**0**	**0**	**0**	**0**	**2**	**2**
Female	0	0	0	0	2	2
Male	0	0	0	0	0	0
Unstated	0	0	0	0	0	0
112A Education Acts - Truancy	**0**	**0**	**0**	**0**	**0**	**0**
Female	0	0	0	0	0	0
Male	0	0	0	0	0	0
Unstated	0	0	0	0	0	0
112B Education Acts - Other	**0**	**3**	**2**	**4**	**2**	**11**
Female	0	2	0	0	0	2
Male	0	1	2	4	2	9
Unstated	0	0	0	0	0	0
115 Firearms Acts - summary offences	**1**	**5**	**31**	**47**	**162**	**246**
Female	0	0	1	0	4	5
Male	1	5	30	46	158	240
Unstated	0	0	0	1	0	1
118 Night Poaching	**0**	**0**	**0**	**2**	**6**	**8**
Female	0	0	0	0	0	0
Male	0	0	0	2	6	8
119 Day Poaching	**0**	**0**	**1**	**4**	**9**	**14**
Female	0	0	0	0	0	0
Male	0	0	1	4	9	14
121B Other offences related to Game Law	**0**	**0**	**0**	**0**	**2**	**2**
Male	0	0	0	0	2	2
122 Obstruction (of highways, etc, other than by vehicle	**0**	**0**	**1**	**0**	**1**	**2**
Female	0	0	0	0	0	0
Male	0	0	1	0	1	2
Other	0	0	0	0	0	0
Unstated	0	0	0	0	0	0
123 Nuisance (other than by vehicle)	**2**	**4**	**5**	**1**	**2**	**14**
Female	0	1	0	0	0	1
Male	2	3	5	1	2	13
Other	0	0	0	0	0	0
Unstated	0	0	0	0	0	0

21.5 Persons cautioned for summary offences (excluding motoring) by offence, sex and age, 2013

Offence	10-11	12-14	15-17	18-20	21+	Total
			Ages			
125A Causing intentional harassment, alarm or distress - summary	**6**	**40**	**121**	**134**	**777**	**1078**
Female	0	9	30	25	159	223
Male	6	30	88	109	615	848
Unstated		1	3	0	3	7
125B Causing fear or provocation of violence - summary	**3**	**58**	**277**	**897**	**2860**	**4095**
Female	1	14	43	101	392	551
Male	2	44	234	792	2457	3529
Unstated	0	0	0	4	11	15
125C Causing harassment, alarm or distress - summary	**10**	**189**	**719**	**650**	**2568**	**4136**
Female	0	65	187	109	586	947
Male	10	123	524	537	1977	3171
Unstated	0	1	8	4	5	18
125D Racially or religiously aggravated harassment, alarm or distress - summary	**0**	**10**	**17**	**33**	**97**	**157**
Female	0	2	3	10	34	49
Male	0	8	14	23	63	108
Unstated	0	0	0	0	0	0
125E Public Order Act 1986 - other offences	**0**	**2**	**31**	**40**	**132**	**205**
Female	0	0	2	3	17	22
Male	0	2	29	37	115	183
Other	0	0	0	0	0	0
Unstated	0	0	0	0	0	0
126 Interference with Motor Vehicles	**0**	**6**	**30**	**28**	**51**	**115**
Female	0	0	2	0	4	6
Male	0	6	28	28	47	109
Unstated	0	0	0	0	0	0
130 Theft of a motor vehicle (excl. aggravated vehicle taking) - summary (MOT)	**1**	**73**	**299**	**265**	**352**	**990**
Female	0	5	38	27	49	119
Male	1	65	259	237	303	865
Unstated	0	3	2	1	0	6
137 Pedal cycle - Careless driving	**0**	**0**	**0**	**0**	**0**	**0**
Female	0	0	0	0	0	0
Male	0	0	0	0	0	0
137 Pedal cycle - Neglect of traffic directions	**0**	**0**	**0**	**0**	**0**	**0**
Female	0	0	0	0	0	0
Male	0	0	0	0	0	0
Unstated	0	0	0	0	0	0
137 Pedal cycle - Other offences	**0**	**7**	**17**	**21**	**28**	**73**
Female	0	0	1	2	3	6
Male	0	7	16	19	25	67
Unstated	0	0	0	0	0	0
137 Pedal cycle - Reckless and dangerous driving	**0**	**0**	**0**	**0**	**0**	**0**
Male	0	0	0	0	0	0
Unstated	0	0	0	0	0	0
137 Pedal cycle - Riding on footpath	**0**	**0**	**0**	**0**	**0**	**0**
Female	0	0	0	0	0	0
Male	0	0	0	0	0	0
Unstated	0	0	0	0	0	0
138 Offences involving impersonation, giving false or misleading information, failing to supply information, etc	**0**	**1**	**2**	**0**	**6**	**9**
Female	0	1		0	1	2
Male	0	0	2	0	5	7
Other	0	0	0	0	0	0
Unstated	0	0	0	0	0	0
140 Drunkenness, simple	**0**	**1**	**12**	**15**	**227**	**255**
Female	0	0	1	1	23	25
Male	0	1	11	14	204	230
Unstated	0	0	0	0	0	0

21.5 Persons cautioned for summary offences (excluding motoring) by offence, sex and age, 2013

Offence	10-11	12-14	15-17	18-20	21+	Total
141 Drunkenness, with aggravation - disorderly in a public place	**0**	**38**	**543**	**754**	**3072**	**4407**
Female	0	20	171	144	653	988
Male	0	18	371	610	2413	3412
Unstated	0	0	1	0	6	7
141 Drunkenness, with aggravation - other	**0**	**0**	**1**	**6**	**258**	**265**
Female	0	0	0	5	186	191
Male	0	0	1	1	70	72
Unstated	0	0	0	0	2	2
142 Other offences by licenced persons	**0**	**0**	**0**	**0**	**0**	**0**
Female	0	0	0	0	0	0
Male	0	0	0	0	0	0
Other	0	0	0	0	0	0
Unstated	0	0	0	0	0	0
142A Responsible person allowing individual aged under 18 to sell or supply alcohol	**0**	**0**	**0**	**0**	**0**	**0**
Male	0	0	0	0	0	0
143A Sale of alcohol to a person aged under 18	**0**	**0**	**0**	**0**	**11**	**11**
Female	0	0	0	0	2	2
Male	0	0	0	0	9	9
Other	0	0	0	0	0	0
Unstated	0	0	0	0	0	0
143B Buying, attempting to buy or delivering alcohol to persons aged under 18	**0**	**0**	**0**	**1**	**1**	**2**
Female	0	0	0	0	0	0
Male	0	0	0	1	1	2
143C Purchase of alcohol by a person aged under 18	**0**	**0**	**1**	**0**	**0**	**1**
Male	0	0	1	0	0	1
143D Sale of alcohol to, or obtaining alcohol for a person who is drunk	**0**	**0**	**0**	**0**	**2**	**2**
Female	0	0	0	0	1	1
Male	0	0	0	0	1	1
143E Other offences related to the sale of alcohol and licensed premises	**0**	**0**	**5**	**39**	**161**	**205**
Female	0	0	0	3	11	14
Male	0	0	5	36	147	188
Other	0	0	0	0	0	0
Unstated	0	0	0	0	3	3
149 Summary Criminal or Malicious Damage Offence	**110**	**939**	**1785**	**2506**	**10162**	**15502**
Female	6	189	327	360	1759	2641
Male	102	735	1445	2138	8383	12803
Unstated	2	15	13	8	20	58
151 Benefit fraud offences - summary	**0**	**0**	**0**	**2**	**14**	**16**
Female	0	0	0	0	3	3
Male	0	0	0	2	11	13
Unstated	0	0	0	0	0	0
153-155 Offences against Military Law - Army, Navy and Air Force	**0**	**0**	**1**	**2**	**1**	**4**
Female	0	0	0	0	0	0
Male	0	0	1	2	1	4
Other	0	0	0	0	0	0
Unstated	0	0	0	0	0	0
160 Pedlars Act - Acting without certificate, refusal to produce certificate, etc	**0**	**0**	**0**	**1**	**1**	**2**
Female	0	0	0	0	0	0
Male	0	0	0	1	1	2
162 Disorderly Behaviour	**0**	**0**	**4**	**4**	**16**	**24**
Female	0	0	3	0	3	6
Male	0	0	1	4	13	18
Other	0	0	0	0	0	0
Unstated	0	0	0	0	0	0

21.5 Persons cautioned for summary offences (excluding motoring) by offence, sex and age, 2013

Offence	Ages					
	10-11	12-14	15-17	18-20	21+	Total
166 Offence by Prostitute	**0**	**0**	**0**	**15**	**100**	**115**
Female	0	0	0	14	86	100
Male	0	0	0	1	14	15
Unstated	0	0	0	0	0	0
167 Aiding, etc. Offence by Prostitute	**0**	**0**	**5**	**32**	**666**	**703**
Female	0	0	0	0	3	3
Male	0	0	5	32	658	695
Unstated	0	0	0	0	5	5
168 Public Health Offence	**0**	**0**	**0**	**0**	**1**	**1**
Female	0	0	0	0	0	0
Male	0	0	0	0	1	1
Other	0	0	0	0	0	0
Unstated	0	0	0	0	0	0
169A Travelling by railway without paying correct fare, failing to show ticket, failing to give name and address, etc	**0**	**15**	**170**	**471**	**987**	**1643**
Female	0	4	28	61	104	197
Male	0	10	141	405	874	1430
Unstated	0	1	1	5	9	16
169B Other railway offences	**0**	**7**	**13**	**16**	**107**	**143**
Female	0	1	3	4	18	26
Male	0	6	9	12	87	114
Other	0	0	0	0	0	0
Unstated	0	0	1	0	2	3
173 Stage Carriage or Public Service Vehicle Offence	**0**	**2**	**2**	**3**	**299**	**306**
Female	0	0	0	0	5	5
Male	0	2	2	3	294	301
Other	0	0	0	0	0	0
Unstated	0	0	0	0	0	0
175 Sexual Offences- Miscellaneous	**0**	**0**	**0**	**2**	**37**	**39**
Female	0	0	0	0	1	1
Male	0	0	0	2	36	38
182 Begging	**0**	**4**	**7**	**12**	**354**	**377**
Female	0	4	4	7	101	116
Male	0	0	3	5	253	261
Unstated	0	0	0	0	0	0
183 Sleeping Out	**0**	**0**	**0**	**0**	**1**	**1**
Female	0	0	0	0	1	1
Male	0	0	0	0	0	0
185 Being on enclosed premises for an unlawful purpose	**0**	**5**	**25**	**28**	**60**	**118**
Female	0	0	1	3	2	6
Male	0	5	24	25	58	112
Unstated	0	0	0	0	0	0
193 Drug offences - summary	**0**	**0**	**0**	**3**	**34**	**37**
Female	0	0	0	2	6	8
Male	0	0	0	0	28	28
Unstated	0	0	0	1	0	1
194 Immigration Offence	**0**	**0**	**0**	**0**	**5**	**5**
Female	0	0	0	0	1	1
Male	0	0	0	0	4	4
Unstated	0	0	0	0	0	0
Other summary non-motoring offences	**2**	**10**	**28**	**22**	**214**	**276**
Female	0	1	3	3	31	38
Male	2	9	24	18	182	235
Other	0	0	0	0	0	0
Unstated	0	0	1	1	1	3

Source: Ministry of Justice
CJS Outcomes by Offence 2004 to 2014: Pivot Table Analytical Tool for England and Wales

21.6a Offenders found guilty at all courts by offence group, sex and age group, 2013

England and Wales   Number of offenders (thousands)

Offence group	All offenders[1]	Males			Females			Other offenders[2]
		All ages	Aged 10-17	Aged 18 & over	All ages	Aged 10-17	Aged 18 & over	
Indictable offences								
Violence against the person	24.3	21.6	1.2	20.4	2.6	0.2	2.4	0.1
Sexual offences	5.7	5.6	0.4	5.2	0.0	0.0	0.0	0.0
Robbery	6.8	6.2	2.1	4.1	0.5	0.2	0.3	0.0
Theft Offences	122.4	98.4	7.1	91.3	23.3	1.2	22.0	0.8
Criminal damage and arson	4.1	3.6	0.6	3.0	0.5	0.1	0.4	0.0
Drug offences	57.0	52.7	3.4	49.4	4.0	0.1	3.8	0.3
Possession of weapons	10.0	9.2	1.2	8.1	0.7	0.1	0.6	0.0
Public order offences	16.4	14.9	0.9	14.0	1.4	0.1	1.3	0.1
Miscellaneous crimes against society	35.2	29.3	1.5	27.9	4.2	0.2	4.1	1.6
Fraud Offences	12.3	7.8	0.1	7.7	3.7	0.1	3.7	0.7
Total indictable	294.1	249.5	18.5	231.0	41.0	2.4	38.7	3.6
Summary offences								
Offences (excluding motoring offences)	429.4	245.7	10.1	235.6	158.8	2.6	156.2	24.8
Motoring offences	448.5	333.7	2.1	331.6	83.4	0.2	83.2	31.4
Total summary	877.8	579.4	12.1	567.3	242.2	2.8	239.5	56.2
All offences	**1,172.0**	**828.9**	**30.6**	**798.3**	**283.3**	**5.1**	**278.1**	**59.8**

Source: Ministry of Justice

(1) Includes males, females, persons where sex "Not Stated" and other offenders, ie companies, public bodies, etc.

(2) Includes sex 'not stated' and other offenders, i.e. companies, public bodies, etc.

Note:

May not sum due to rounding.

For the first time, annual data are presented using offence groups defined by the Office for National Statistics (ONS). Previously published versions of this table used Ministry of Justice offence groups. The Office for National Statistics (ONS) re-designed the classifications used to present police recorded crime statistics to provide a more coherent and consistent set of offence categories and a clearer picture for users. This follows the National Statistician's review of Crime Statistics in England and Wales in June 2011 which included recommendations for improving the presentation of crime statistics to give users and the public a clearer understanding of the overall picture of crime.

21.6b Persons found guilty at all courts or cautioned [1] for indictable offences and number per 100,000 population in the age group by sex and age, 2003 - 2013

England and Wales   Number of persons

Year	All persons [2]	Males						Females					
		All ages	Aged 10-11	Aged 12-14	Aged 15-17	Aged 18-20	Aged 21 & over	All ages	Aged 10-11	Aged 12-14	Aged 15-17	Aged 18-20	Aged 21 & over
					Number of persons cautioned (thousands)								
2003	150.7	109.8	2.5	14.3	24.1	19.4	49.4	41.0	0.7	7.9	9.1	4.9	18.4
2004	156.3	110.0	2.6	16.1	25.9	16.7	48.7	46.3	0.8	9.8	10.6	5.2	19.9
2005	182.9	129.9	3.0	18.1	28.0	19.8	61.1	53.0	0.9	11.3	12.2	5.8	22.8
2006	203.8	147.6	2.9	18.7	30.2	22.9	72.8	56.2	0.9	11.6	12.7	6.2	24.7
2007	205.1	148.5	2.7	17.0	30.0	23.7	75.1	56.6	0.9	11.7	13.0	6.3	24.8
2008[3]	181.2	133.4	2.1	12.5	24.5	21.7	72.5	47.8	0.6	8.4	10.2	5.6	23.1
2009	159.5	114.9	1.4	9.5	20.2	19.2	64.6	44.7	0.5	7.6	9.3	5.3	22.0
2010	133.5	98.6	0.8	6.2	15.5	16.9	59.2	35.0	0.2	4.0	5.8	4.5	20.6
2011	123.9	94.4	0.5	5.3	13.8	15.9	58.9	29.5	0.1	2.2	4.0	3.8	19.3
2012	105.6	81.2	0.4	3.8	10.6	13.0	53.3	24.5	0.1	1.4	2.8	3.0	17.1
2013	94.1	71.7	0.3	3.1	9.3	11.1	48.1	21.9	0.1	1.0	2.2	2.5	16.0
					Number of persons found guilty (thousands)								
2003	333.7	283.4	0.5	7.6	31.4	43.8	200.2	50.2	0.1	1.6	4.9	6.2	37.5
2004	316.7	268.4	0.4	8.0	31.8	39.9	188.2	48.4	0.1	1.6	5.0	5.7	35.9
2005	307.4	261.3	0.4	8.1	32.0	38.5	182.2	46.1	0.0	1.7	5.5	5.3	33.6
2006	302.2	258.4	0.4	7.9	32.5	39.0	178.7	43.7	0.0	1.6	5.1	4.8	32.1
2007	312.3	266.9	0.4	8.1	35.0	40.6	182.9	45.3	0.0	1.7	5.5	4.6	33.4
2008[3]	316.0	267.7	0.3	7.3	31.9	38.3	189.8	46.4	0.0	1.6	4.9	4.7	35.3
2009	328.4	277.6	0.2	6.3	30.8	39.8	200.4	49.0	0.0	1.4	5.0	5.0	37.6
2010	349.8	296.8	0.1	5.4	30.3	41.5	219.5	51.1	0.0	1.1	4.4	5.1	40.5
2011	343.7	295.1	0.1	4.8	27.3	38.5	224.4	48.5	0.0	0.8	3.6	4.4	39.8
2012	308.1	265.4	0.1	3.7	20.8	31.4	209.5	42.7	0.0	0.6	2.7	3.5	35.9
2013	293.4	249.5	0.0	2.5	15.9	26.3	204.8	41.0	0.0	0.4	2.0	2.8	35.9
					Number of persons found guilty or cautioned (thousands)								
2003	484.4	393.2	3.0	21.9	55.5	63.3	249.6	91.2	0.8	9.5	14.0	11.0	55.9
2004	473.0	378.4	3.0	24.2	57.8	56.5	236.9	94.6	0.8	11.4	15.7	10.9	55.8
2005	490.3	391.2	3.4	26.2	60.1	58.3	243.3	99.1	0.9	13.0	17.7	11.1	56.4
2006	506.0	406.1	3.3	26.7	62.7	61.9	251.5	99.9	1.0	13.2	17.8	11.0	56.8
2007	517.4	415.4	3.1	25.1	65.0	64.3	257.9	101.9	0.9	13.4	18.5	10.9	58.2
2008[3]	497.1	401.1	2.4	19.8	56.4	60.1	262.3	94.2	0.6	9.9	15.0	10.3	58.4
2009	488.0	392.5	1.6	15.7	51.1	59.0	265.0	93.7	0.5	9.0	14.3	10.3	59.6
2010	483.4	395.3	0.9	11.6	45.8	58.4	278.6	86.1	0.2	5.0	10.2	9.5	61.1
2011	467.6	389.6	0.7	10.1	41.1	54.4	283.2	78.0	0.1	3.0	7.6	8.2	59.0
2012	413.8	346.6	0.5	7.5	31.4	44.4	262.8	67.1	0.1	2.0	5.5	6.5	53.0
2013	387.4	321.2	0.3	5.6	25.2	37.3	252.8	62.9	0.1	1.4	4.2	5.3	51.9
					Number of persons found guilty or cautioned per 100,000 population								
2003	1,041	1,737	427	2,047	5,256	6,137	1,329	381	122	935	1,403	1,142	276
2004	1,010	1,659	445	2,253	5,408	5,301	1,252	394	127	1,128	1,549	1,094	274
2005	1,039	1,700	505	2,463	5,574	5,378	1,272	410	149	1,292	1,730	1,081	275
2006	1,065	1,751	494	2,563	5,767	5,622	1,303	411	155	1,343	1,746	1,060	275
2007	1,081	1,777	468	2,467	5,961	5,749	1,323	417	142	1,391	1,810	1,039	280
2008[3]	1,033	1,703	372	1,979	5,235	5,365	1,331	383	100	1,043	1,479	966	279
2009	1,008	1,655	253	1,581	4,842	5,256	1,332	379	83	949	1,428	968	283
2010	998	1,667	140	1,166	4,337	5,205	1,400	348	38	532	1,017	893	290
2011	944	1,608	106	990	3,869	4,816	1,390	309	20	312	758	752	273
2012	832	1,423	82	751	2,978	3,992	1,278	264	14	212	552	608	244
2013	779	1,319	49	557	2,390	3,357	1,230	248	10	151	419	498	238

(1) Motoring offences may attract written warnings, which are excluded from this table.

(2) Includes sex 'not stated'.

(3) Excludes convictions data for Cardiff Magistrates' court for April, July and August 2008.

Source: Ministry of Justice

May not sum due to rounding.

For the first time, annual data are presented using offence groups defined by the Office for National Statistics (ONS). Previously published versions of this table used Ministry of Justice offence groups. The Office for National Statistics (ONS) re-designed the classifications used to present police recorded crime statistics to provide a more coherent and consistent set of offence categories and a clearer picture for users. This follows the National Statistician's review of Crime Statistics in England and Wales in June 2011 which included recommendations for improving the presentation of crime statistics to give users and the public a clearer understanding of the overall picture of crime.

England and Wales

Persons

21.7 Persons found guilty at all courts or cautioned for indictable offences(1) and number per 100,000 population(2) in age group, by sex and age, 2009 - 2013

Sex and age	Number per 100,000 population(2) found guilty or cautioned					Number of persons (thousands)														
						Found guilty or cautioned					Found guilty					Cautioned				
	2009	2010	2011	2012(3)	2013(3)	2009	2010	2011	2012	2013	2009	2010	2011	2012	2013	2009	2010	2011	2012	2013
Males																				
10	144	78	50	44	17	0.5	0.2	0.2	0.1	0.1	0.0	0.0	0.0	0.0	0.0	0.4	0.2	0.1	0.1	0.0
11	360	201	161	118	80	1.2	0.6	0.5	0.4	0.3	0.2	0.1	0.1	0.1	0.0	1.0	0.5	0.4	0.3	0.2
12	739	469	407	311	207	2.5	1.6	1.4	1.0	0.7	0.7	0.5	0.4	0.3	0.2	1.8	1.1	0.9	0.7	0.5
13	1,410	1,066	856	658	467	4.7	3.5	2.9	2.2	1.6	1.7	1.5	1.2	1.0	0.7	2.9	2.0	1.7	1.2	0.9
14	2,590	1,962	1,678	1,264	980	8.6	6.5	5.8	4.3	3.3	3.9	3.4	3.1	2.4	1.6	4.7	3.2	2.8	2.0	1.7
15	3,940	3,293	2,661	2,129	1,653	13.5	11.3	9.3	7.5	5.8	7.2	6.8	5.6	4.5	3.3	6.3	4.5	3.7	2.9	2.5
16	4,896	4,410	3,927	2,884	2,387	17.1	15.4	13.7	10.2	8.4	10.2	10.2	9.0	6.7	5.3	6.9	5.2	4.7	3.5	3.1
17	5,640	5,251	4,979	3,919	3,127	20.5	19.1	18.1	13.8	11.0	13.4	13.3	12.7	9.6	7.3	7.1	5.8	5.4	4.2	3.7
18	5,368	5,167	4,783	3,895	3,183	20.1	19.4	17.4	14.2	11.6	12.8	13.2	11.8	9.6	7.8	7.3	6.1	5.5	4.6	3.9
19	5,359	5,387	4,988	4,073	3,467	20.1	20.2	18.7	15.0	12.8	13.8	14.6	13.4	10.7	9.1	6.3	5.6	5.3	4.3	3.7
20	5,040	5,061	4,681	4,005	3,419	18.8	18.9	18.3	15.2	13.0	13.2	13.7	13.3	11.0	9.4	5.6	5.2	5.1	4.2	3.5
21 and under 25	4,064	4,167	4,392	3,872	3,352	63.0	64.7	67.3	60.6	52.5	45.4	48.7	51.1	46.2	40.3	17.7	15.9	16.2	14.4	12.2
25 and under 30	3,249	3,364	3,280	2,994	2,885	61.0	63.2	63.0	57.5	55.4	46.6	49.9	49.8	45.7	44.7	14.5	13.3	13.2	11.8	10.7
30 and under 40	2,164	2,297	2,266	2,126	2,125	78.6	83.4	83.8	78.2	78.2	61.7	68.0	68.5	64.4	65.3	17.0	15.5	15.3	13.9	12.8
40 and under 50	1,081	1,153	1,175	1,107	1,101	43.4	46.3	47.7	44.9	44.6	33.3	37.1	38.6	36.5	37.0	10.1	9.2	9.2	8.3	7.6
50 and under 60	418	472	465	463	477	13.6	15.4	15.7	16.0	16.5	10.0	11.8	12.3	12.5	13.1	3.6	3.6	3.4	3.5	3.3
60 and over	95	101	99	96	98	5.3	5.6	5.7	5.7	5.8	3.5	4.0	4.2	4.2	4.3	1.7	1.6	1.5	1.5	1.5
All males	1,655	1,667	1,608	1,423	1,319	392.5	395.3	389.6	346.6	321.2	277.6	296.8	295.1	265.4	249.5	114.9	98.6	94.4	81.2	71.7
Females																				
10	33	17	8	7	3	0.1	0.1	0.0	0.0	-	0.0	0.0	0.0	0.0	-	0.1	0.0	0.0	0.0	0.0
11	132	59	32	20	17	0.4	0.2	0.1	0.1	0.1	0.0	0.0	0.0	0.0	0.0	0.4	0.2	0.1	0.1	0.0
12	394	212	110	70	55	1.2	0.7	0.4	0.2	0.2	0.1	0.1	0.0	0.0	0.0	1.2	0.6	0.3	0.2	0.2
13	918	489	282	193	135	2.9	1.5	0.9	0.6	0.4	0.4	0.3	0.2	0.2	0.1	2.5	1.3	0.7	0.5	0.3
14	1,535	897	535	366	258	4.8	2.8	1.8	1.2	0.8	1.0	0.7	0.6	0.4	0.2	3.9	2.1	1.2	0.8	0.6
15	1,668	1,084	709	511	359	5.4	3.5	2.3	1.7	1.2	1.5	1.3	1.0	0.7	0.5	3.9	2.2	1.4	1.0	0.7
16	1,419	1,017	780	555	407	4.7	3.4	2.6	1.8	1.3	1.7	1.4	1.2	0.9	0.6	3.0	1.9	1.4	1.0	0.7
17	1,210	954	783	590	490	4.2	3.3	2.7	2.0	1.6	1.8	1.7	1.4	1.1	0.9	2.4	1.6	1.3	0.9	0.8
18	1,006	904	736	579	470	3.6	3.2	2.6	2.0	1.6	1.5	1.5	1.3	1.0	0.8	2.0	1.6	1.3	1.0	0.9
19	958	897	768	624	512	3.4	3.2	2.8	2.2	1.8	1.7	1.8	1.5	1.2	1.0	1.7	1.4	1.3	1.0	0.8
20	941	880	750	620	510	3.4	3.1	2.8	2.3	1.9	1.8	1.8	1.6	1.3	1.1	1.6	1.4	1.2	1.0	0.8
21 and under 25	784	794	727	615	547	11.6	11.8	11.0	9.4	8.3	6.7	7.2	6.7	5.7	5.1	4.9	4.6	4.3	3.7	3.2
25 and under 30	723	724	639	565	563	13.1	13.1	12.3	10.9	10.8	8.5	9.0	8.4	7.4	7.6	4.6	4.2	3.9	3.5	3.3
30 and under 40	523	530	510	461	464	19.0	19.2	18.9	17.1	17.2	12.7	13.5	13.6	12.5	12.6	6.2	5.7	5.3	4.6	4.5
40 and under 50	272	289	280	253	251	11.1	11.8	11.6	10.5	10.4	7.0	7.9	7.9	7.2	7.3	4.1	3.9	3.7	3.3	3.1
50 and under 60	107	117	117	112	111	3.6	3.9	4.0	3.9	3.9	2.0	2.3	2.5	2.5	2.5	1.6	1.6	1.5	1.5	1.4
60 and over	17	19	18	18	18	1.2	1.3	1.3	1.3	1.2	0.5	0.7	0.7	0.7	0.7	0.6	0.6	0.6	0.6	0.5
All females	379	348	309	264	248	93.7	86.1	78.0	67.1	62.9	49.0	51.1	48.5	42.7	41.0	44.7	35.0	29.5	24.5	21.9

' = Nil

(1) Motoring offences may attract written warnings, which are excluded from this table.

(2) Population estimates were taken from the Office for National Statistics (ONS).

(3) ONS 2012 population estimates were used to calculate the number of persons found guilty or cautions per 100,000 population for 2013 and 2012.

Source: Ministry of Justice

For the first time, annual data are presented using offence groups defined by the Office for National Statistics (ONS). Previously published versions of this table used Ministry of Justice offence groups. The Office for National Statistics (ONS) re-designed the classifications used to present crime statistics to provide a more coherent and consistent set of offence categories and a clearer picture for users. This follows the National Statistician's review of Crime Statistics in England and Wales in June 2011 which included recommendations for improving the presentation of crime statistics to give users and the public a clearer understanding of the overall picture of crime.

21.8 Persons sentenced to immediate custody at all courts by length of sentence and average custodial sentence length, 2004 to 2013

England and Wales | | | | | | | | | | Number of persons

All Offences	2004	2005	2006	2007	2008[1]	2009	2010	2011	2012	2013
Up to and including 3 months	39,688	37,100	34,711	34,427	35,738	36,071	38,316	39,419	36,442	34,821
Over 3 months and up to and including 6 months	28,491	26,756	24,421	23,109	22,338	21,321	20,181	20,269	19,332	18,236
Over 6 months and less than 12 months	5,678	5,851	5,728	6,154	6,920	7,177	7,052	7,891	6,787	6,431
12 months	5,244	5,414	5,245	5,479	5,652	5,837	5,618	5,947	4,788	4,380
Over 12 months and up to and including 18 months	6,366	6,258	6,232	6,271	6,751	7,289	7,343	8,022	7,343	6,375
Over 18 months and up to and including 3 years	10,695	10,385	10,372	10,470	11,516	12,077	12,358	13,138	12,621	12,225
Over 3 years and less than 4 years	2,082	1,745	1,533	1,458	1,629	1,811	1,937	1,990	1,973	2,092
4 years	2,146	1,745	1,607	1,603	1,903	1,977	1,934	2,094	1,787	1,704
Over 4 years and up to and including 5 years	2,161	1,920	1,670	1,611	1,998	1,980	2,061	2,208	1,913	1,945
Over 5 years and up to and including 10 years	2,772	2,658	2,190	2,109	2,614	2,784	2,796	3,307	3,238	3,417
Over 10 years and less than life	409	353	309	316	405	485	514	671	661	936
Indeterminate sentence[2]	-	426	1,445	1,707	1,538	1,001	1,019	819	747	9
Life	590	625	550	492	523	421	384	395	412	395
Number given immediate custody	**106,322**	**101,236**	**96,013**	**95,206**	**99,525**	**100,231**	**101,513**	**106,170**	**98,044**	**92,966**
Average custodial sentence length (months)[3]	12.9	12.6	12.4	12.4	13.3	13.7	13.7	14.3	14.5	15.5

Indictable Offences	2004	2005	2006	2007	2008[1]	2009	2010	2011	2012	2013
Up to and including 3 months	25,417	23,808	22,378	22,421	23,533	23,692	26,290	27,245	25,676	25,437
Over 3 months and up to and including 6 months	16,380	15,109	14,284	13,952	14,083	13,768	13,684	13,900	13,146	12,619
Over 6 months and less than 12 months	5,677	5,848	5,725	6,150	6,916	7,158	7,023	7,824	6,778	6,427
12 months	5,243	5,412	5,241	5,477	5,650	5,828	5,607	5,947	4,786	4,378
Over 12 months and up to and including 18 months	6,366	6,257	6,230	6,271	6,750	7,284	7,337	8,020	7,341	6,375
Over 18 months and up to and including 3 years	10,695	10,385	10,369	10,470	11,516	12,076	12,353	13,138	12,621	12,225
Over 3 years and less than 4 years	2,082	1,745	1,532	1,458	1,629	1,811	1,937	1,990	1,973	2,092
4 years	2,146	1,745	1,607	1,603	1,903	1,977	1,934	2,094	1,787	1,704
Over 4 years and up to and including 5 years	2,161	1,920	1,670	1,611	1,998	1,980	2,061	2,208	1,913	1,945
Over 5 years and up to and including 10 years	2,772	2,658	2,189	2,109	2,614	2,784	2,796	3,307	3,238	3,417
Over 10 years and less than life	409	353	309	316	405	485	514	671	661	936
Indeterminate sentence[2]	-	426	1,444	1,707	1,538	1,001	1,019	819	747	9
Life	590	625	550	492	523	421	384	395	412	395
Number given immediate custody	**79,938**	**76,291**	**73,528**	**74,037**	**79,058**	**80,265**	**82,939**	**87,558**	**81,079**	**77,959**
Average custodial sentence length (months)[3]	16.1	15.8	15.3	15.2	16.0	16.5	16.2	16.8	17.0	18.0

Source: Ministry of Justice

(1) Excludes data for Cardiff magistrates' court for April, July and August 2008.
(2) Sentences of imprisonment for public protection introduced by the Criminal Justice Act 2003 on 4 April 2005.
(3) Excludes life and indeterminate sentences.

21.9a Persons sentenced to life imprisonment[1] by sex and age, 2002 to 2013

England and Wales												Number of persons
Sex and age	2002	2003	2004	2005	2006	2007	2008	2009	2010	2011	2012	2013
Males												
Aged 10-17	21	11	15	27	16	23	24	22	17	13	13	13
Aged 18-20	21	47	24	50	46	70	54	57	39	30	47	33
Aged 21 and over	494	431	509	517	469	378	417	322	308	328	316	320
All ages	536	489	548	594	531	471	495	401	364	371	376	366
Females												
Aged 10-17	1	-	1	1	-	3	1	1	2	2	1	0
Aged 18-20	2	4	2	4	2	3	2	1	2	5	1	0
Aged 21 and over	16	20	19	26	14	15	25	18	16	17	30	29
All ages	19	24	22	31	16	21	28	20	20	24	32	29
All persons												
Aged 10-17	22	11	16	28	16	26	25	23	19	15	14	13
Aged 18-20	23	51	26	54	48	73	56	58	41	35	48	33
Aged 21 and over	510	451	528	543	483	393	442	340	324	345	346	349
All ages	555	513	570	625	547	492	523	421	384	395	408	395

(1) Includes detention under the Powers of Criminal Courts (Sentencing) Act 2000, Secs 90-92 (Children and Young Persons Act 1933, Secs 53(1) and (2) prior to August 2000) (persons aged 10-17), custody for life under the Powers of Criminal Courts (Sentencing) Act 2000, Secs 93 and 94(1) (persons aged 18-20), mandatory life sentences under the Powers of Criminal Courts (Sentencing) Act 2000, Sec 109 (persons aged 18 and over) and immediate imprisonment (persons aged 21 and over). Indeterminate sentences for public protection under the Criminal Justice Act 2003 are excluded.

Note: Excludes data for Cardiff magistrates' court for April, July and August 2008.

Source: Ministry of Justice

21.9b persons sentenced to determinate an indeterminate custodial sentences by age group, sex and type of sentence, 2009 to 2013

Sex and age	Year	Determinate Sentence	Extended sentence of imprisonment - EPP	Imprisonment for public protection - IPP	Life sentence	Total Immediate Custody
Male						
Aged Under 18	2009	4,485	17	25	22	4,549
	2010	3,877	10	41	17	3,945
	2011	3,864	26	28	13	3,931
	2012	2,819	6	30	13	2,868
	2013	2,196	0	0	13	2,209
Aged 18-20	2009	12,978	59	120	57	13,214
	2010	12,296	58	107	39	12,500
	2011	11,555	94	70	30	11,749
	2012	9,262	34	76	47	9,419
	2013	7,591	6	0	33	7,630
Aged 21 and over	2009	72,957	346	835	322	74,460
	2010	75,491	370	845	308	77,014
	2011	80,817	502	703	328	82,350
	2012	76,628	280	620	320	77,848
	2013	75,159	24	9	320	75,512
Female						
Aged Under 18	2009	378	0	2	1	381
	2010	256	0	0	2	258
	2011	266	1	1	2	270
	2012	181	0	0	1	182
	2013	117	0	0	0	117
Aged 18 - 20	2009	803	2	2	1	808
	2010	734	0	3	2	739
	2011	582	3	0	5	590
	2012	509	0	2	1	512
	2013	329	0	0	0	329
Aged 21 and over	2009	6,878	10	17	18	6,923
	2010	7,160	15	23	16	7,214
	2011	7,528	22	17	17	7,584
	2012	6,966	12	19	30	7,027
	2013	6,663	1	0	29	6,693
Sex not Stated						
Aged under 18	2009	27	0	0	0	27
	2010	26	0	0	0	26
	2011	31	0	0	0	31
	2012	41	0	0	0	41
	2013	27	0	0	0	27
Aged 18-20	2009	56	0	0	0	56
	2010	43	0	0	0	43
	2011	38	0	0	0	38
	2012	62	0	0	0	62
	2013	45	0	0	0	45
Aged 21 and over	2009	247	0	0	0	247
	2010	227	0	0	0	227
	2011	275	0	0	0	275
	2012	417	0	0	0	417
	2013	435	0	0	0	435

21.9b persons sentenced to determinate an indeterminate custodial sentences by age group, sex and type of sentence, 2009 to 2013

Sex and age	Year	Determinate Sentence	Extended sentence of imprisonment - EPP	Imprisonment for public protection - IPP	Life sentence	Total Immediate Custody
All Persons						
Aged Under 18	2009	4,890	17	27	23	4,957
	2010	4,159	10	41	19	4,229
	2011	4,161	27	29	15	4,232
	2012	3,041	6	30	14	3,091
	2013	2,340	0	0	13	2,353
Aged 18 - 20	2009	13,837	61	122	58	14,078
	2010	13,073	58	110	41	13,282
	2011	12,175	97	70	35	12,377
	2012	9,833	34	78	48	9,993
	2013	7,965	6	0	33	8,004
Aged 21 and over	2009	80,082	356	852	340	81,630
	2010	82,878	385	868	324	84,455
	2011	88,620	524	720	345	90,209
	2012	84,011	292	639	350	85,292
	2013	82,257	25	9	349	82,640
All Ages	2009	98,809	434	1,001	421	100,665
	2010	100,110	453	1,019	384	101,966
	2011	104,956	648	819	395	106,818
	2012	96,885	332	747	412	98,376
	2013	92,562	31	9	395	92,997

Source: Ministry of Justice

Criminal Justice System Statistics publication: Sentencing: Pivot Table Analytical Tool for England and Wales

a) The figures given relate to persons for whom these offences were the principal offences for which they were dealt with. When a defendant has been found guilty of two or more offences it is the offence for which the heaviest penalty is imposed. Where the same disposal is imposed for two or more offences, the offence selected is the offence for which the statutory maximum penalty is the most severe.

b) Every effort is made to ensure that the figures presented are accurate and complete. However, it is important to note that these data have been extracted from large administrative data systems generated by the courts. As a consequence, care should be taken to ensure data collection processes and their inevitable limitations are taken into account when those data are used.

21.10 Prison receptions and population in custody

England and Wales

Numbers[1]

		2003	2004	2005	2006	2007	2008	2009	2010*	2011	2012	2013
Receptions												
Type of inmate:												
Untried	**KEDA**	58,696	54,556	55,455	55,809	55,305	57,417	55,207	-	54,837	**50,227**	**48,875**
Convicted, unsentenced	**KEDB**	53,246	50,115	49,104	47,995	43,566	44,773	37,003	-	39,391	**36,646**	**33,692**
Sentenced	**KEDE**	93,495	95,161	92,452	90,038	91,736	100,348	94,964	-	90,955	**86,479**	**82,305**
Immediate custodial sentence	**KEDF**	92,245	93,326	90,414	88,134	90,261	98,820	93,621	-	89,822	**85,364**	**81,442**
ADULTS												
Remand - untried		**45,400**	**41,684**	**42,692**	**42,772**	**42,546**	**44,953**	**43,505**	..	**44,681**	**41,955**	**42,203**
Remand - convicted unsentenced		**42,592**	**40,088**	**39,333**	**38,312**	**34,656**	**35,832**	**30,012**	..	**32,213**	**30,771**	**29,039**
Prisoners under sentence		**75,200**	**76,742**	**74,471**	**71,935**	**72,622**	**80,758**	**77,146**	..	**75,170**	**73,243**	**71,798**
Fine defaulter		1,134	1,680	1,876	1,786	1,383	1,427	1,270	..	1,079	1,070	827
Less than or equal to 6 months		43,046	43,927	42,288	39,474	39,949	44,954	41,345	..	37,048	34,811	33,208
Greater than 6 months to less than 12 months		5,916	5,887	5,902	6,294	6,757	7,377	7,195	..	7,224	7,452	7,531
12 months to less than 4 years		17,968	17,988	17,397	16,970	17,233	19,061	19,804	..	21,855	21,692	21,603
4 years or more (excluding Indeterminate)		6,694	6,754	6,130	5,613	5,472	6,394	6,426	..	7,252	7,589	8,308
Indeterminate sentences		442	506	878	1,798	1,828	1,545	1,107	..	712	629	321
18-20 YEAR OLDS												
Remand - untried		**9,013**	**8,517**	**8,405**	**8,499**	**8,299**	**8,413**	**8,205**	..	**7,255**	**6,269**	**5,610**
Remand - convicted unsentenced		**8,359**	**7,598**	**7,391**	**7,239**	**6,706**	**6,782**	**5,566**	..	**5,794**	**4,917**	**4,117**
Prisoners under sentence		**13,377**	**13,247**	**12,806**	**12,812**	**13,758**	**14,300**	**13,804**	..	**12,788**	**10,941**	**8,879**
Fine defaulter		116	155	162	118	92	101	73	..	54	45	35
Less than or equal to 6 months		7,491	7,275	6,892	6,857	7,442	7,816	7,202	..	6,092	4,859	3,720
Greater than 6 months to less than 12 months		1,162	1,239	1,227	1,212	1,295	1,381	1,323	..	1,273	1,137	884
12 months to less than 4 years		3,825	3,764	3,726	3,691	3,939	3,988	4,226	..	4,406	3,965	3,433
4 years or more (excluding Indeterminate)		728	756	671	639	629	778	818	..	890	866	780
Indeterminate sentences		55	58	128	295	361	236	162	..	73	69	27
15-17 YEAR OLDS												
Remand - untried		**4,283**	**4,355**	**4,358**	**4,538**	**4,460**	**4,051**	**3,497**	..	**2,901**	**2,003**	**1,062**
Remand - convicted unsentenced		**2,295**	**2,429**	**2,380**	**2,444**	**2,204**	**2,159**	**1,425**	..	**1,384**	**958**	**536**
Prisoners under sentence		**4,918**	**5,172**	**5,175**	**5,291**	**5,356**	**5,290**	**4,014**	..	**2,997**	**2,295**	**1,628**
Fine defaulter		0	0	0	0	0	0	0	..	0	0	1
Less than or equal to 6 months		2,321	2,474	2,637	2,593	2,669	2,563	1,895	..	1,242	913	599
Greater than 6 months to less than 12 months		876	867	854	864	889	894	677	..	538	409	266
12 months to less than 4 years		1,587	1,662	1,517	1,626	1,591	1,585	1,249	..	1,056	851	650
4 years or more (excluding Indeterminate)		122	151	126	143	117	177	147	..	134	102	102
Indeterminate sentences		12	18	41	65	90	71	46	..	27	20	10
Non-criminal prisoners	**KEDM**	3,142	3,669	3,668	4,734	3,888	3,836	4,282	-	2,565	2,495	2,766
Immigration Act 1971	**KEDN**	2,457	3,041	3,093	4,073	3,347	3,466	-	-	2,304	2,238	2,521
Others	**KEDO**	685	628	575	661	541	370	-	-	261	257	245

21.10 Prison receptions and population in custody
England and Wales

Numbers[1]

		2003	2004	2005	2006	2007	2008	2009	2010*	2011	2012	2013
Population (30 June)												
Total in prison service establishments	**KFBQ**	73,657	74,488	76,190	77,982	79,734	83,193	83,454	85,002	85,374	86,048	83,842
Untried	**KEDQ**	7,896	7,716	8,084	8,064	8,387	8,750	8,933	8,487	8,299	7,671	7,743
Convicted, unsentenced	**KEDR**	5,177	4,779	4,780	5,003	4,457	4,690	4,523	4,517	4,165	3,653	3,228
Total sentenced	**KEDU**	59,439	60,976	62,257	63,493	65,601	68,233	68,488	71,000	71,964	73,562	70,913
Total Immediate custodial sentence	**KFBR**	59,393	60,924	62,179	63,404	65,533	68,123	68,375	70,871	71,835	73,435	70,781
Young offenders	**KFBS**	7,823	7,644	7,700	7,852	8,518	8,689	8,405	7,808	7,305	6,846	5,557
Determinate sentence	**I7IJ**	7,679	7,498	7,541	7,533	7,936	7,984	7,781	6,877	6,442	6,125	5,022
Indeterminate sentence	**I7IL**	144	146	159	319	582	705	624	454	358	300	226
Recalls		0	0	0	0	0	0	0	477	505	421	309
Adults	**KFCO**	51,570	53,280	54,479	55,552	57,015	59,434	59,970	63,063	64,530	66,589	65,224
Determinate sentence	**I7IK**	46,293	47,832	48,756	48,596	48,116	48,757	48,073	45,510	46,103	48,139	47,469
Indeterminate sentence	**I7IM**	5,277	5,448	5,723	6,956	8,899	10,677	11,897	12,680	13,286	13,454	12,956
Recalls		0	0	0	0	0	0	0	4,873	5,141	4,996	4,799
Committed in default of payment of a fine	**KFCS**	46	52	78	89	68	110	113	129	129	127	132
Young offenders	**KFEW**	3	5	3	5	4	6	5	5	6	4	3
Adults	**KFEX**	43	47	75	84	64	104	108	124	123	123	129
Non-criminal prisoners	**KEEB**	1,145	1,017	1,069	1,422	1,289	1,520	1,510	998	946	1,162	1,958
Immigration Act 1971	**KEEC**	1,079	957	996	1,366	1,218	1,473	1,465	963	918	1,140	1,928
Others	**KEED**	66	60	73	56	71	47	45	35	28	22	30

Source: Ministry of Justice

1 Due to the introduction of a new prison IT system the 2010 prison population data is now taken from a different source and recalls are shown separately (they were previously included in the relevant sentence length band). See OMCS 2010 for more details.

* Data for 2010 is unavailable due to problems in the supply of data for statistical purposes

21.11 Prison population under an immediate custodial sentence by offence group, age group and sex, 2002 to 2013, England and Wales

	30-Jun-05	30-Jun-06	30-Jun-07	30-Jun-08	30-Jun-09	30-Jun-09[1]	30-Jun-10	30-Jun-11	30-Jun-12	30-Jun-13
Males and females	**62,179**	**63,404**	**65,533**	**68,124**	**68,375**	**68,461**	**70,871**	**71,835**	**73,435**	**70,781**
Violence against the person	15,178	16,215	17,616	18,930	19,946	19,762	20,247	20,431	20,437	19,473
Sexual offences	6,185	6,598	7,336	7,616	7,972	8,176	9,304	9,850	10,473	10,540
Robbery	8,378	8,415	8,747	8,733	9,049	8,738	8,834	9,141	9,279	8,873
Burglary	8,082	7,791	7,920	7,935	7,884	7,403	6,857	7,102	7,345	7,073
Theft and handling	4,126	4,125	3,706	3,836	3,382	3,134	3,850	4,198	4,646	4,500
Fraud and forgery	1,454	1,692	1,738	2,020	1,875	1,923	1,544	1,376	1,454	1,320
Drug offences	10,661	10,647	10,613	10,982	10,696	10,420	11,064	10,621	10,682	10,175
Motoring offences	2,163	1,920	1,484	1,377	1,149	1,050	931	841	798	723
Other offences	5,289	5,594	5,991	6,439	6,117	6,186	7,353	7,755	7,826	7,625
Offence not recorded	664	408	383	256	304	1,669	887	520	495	479
Adults	**54,479**	**55,552**	**57,015**	**59,435**	**59,970**	**60,186**	**63,063**	**64,530**	**66,589**	**65,224**
Violence against the person	13,229	14,187	15,323	16,483	17,515	17,433	17,997	18,496	18,686	18,010
Sexual offences	5,933	6,314	6,986	7,242	7,597	7,822	8,841	9,396	10,044	10,187
Robbery	6,573	6,450	6,627	6,688	6,942	6,780	7,055	7,398	7,545	7,460
Burglary	7,056	6,790	6,808	6,770	6,711	6,329	5,808	6,052	6,379	6,316
Theft and handling	3,479	3,500	3,100	3,308	2,949	2,738	3,454	3,797	4,216	4,168
Fraud and forgery	1,388	1,634	1,688	1,973	1,828	1,881	1,513	1,352	1,425	1,298
Drug offences	10,038	10,021	9,951	10,144	9,926	9,695	10,382	10,002	10,124	9,670
Motoring offences	1,826	1,633	1,288	1,210	1,029	943	842	766	743	672
Other offences	4,411	4,676	4,931	5,404	5,215	5,221	6,403	6,813	6,984	7,011
Offence not recorded	547	347	313	212	258	1,344	768	458	443	432
18-20 year olds	**5,865**	**5,987**	**6,634**	**6,757**	**6,846**	**6,669**	**6,623**	**6,155**	**5,851**	**4,876**
Violence against the person	1,561	1,638	1,871	1,942	2,050	1,947	1,934	1,696	1,526	1,298
Sexual offences	187	216	277	300	298	281	406	406	382	326
Robbery	1,367	1,461	1,611	1,561	1,656	1,521	1,491	1,450	1,431	1,190
Burglary	737	719	828	846	922	816	848	846	815	676
Theft and handling	413	434	415	375	306	268	318	315	358	288
Fraud and forgery	55	47	40	43	46	41	28	22	29	21
Drug offences	545	554	588	727	685	641	618	560	524	471
Motoring offences	279	218	152	141	107	93	84	67	53	50
Other offences	621	652	800	788	734	760	784	745	690	518
Offence not recorded	99	48	51	35	42	301	112	48	43	38
15-17 year olds	**1,835**	**1,865**	**1,883**	**1,932**	**1,559**	**1,606**	**1,185**	**1,150**	**995**	**681**
Violence against the person	389	391	422	505	381	382	316	239	225	165
Sexual offences	65	68	73	74	77	73	57	48	47	27
Robbery	438	503	509	485	451	437	288	293	303	223
Burglary	289	282	283	319	251	258	201	204	151	81
Theft and handling	233	192	191	153	127	128	78	86	72	44
Fraud and forgery	11	11	10	4	1	1	3	2	0	1
Drug offences	79	71	74	111	86	84	64	59	34	34
Motoring offences	58	69	44	26	13	14	5	8	2	1
Other offences	257	265	259	247	168	205	166	197	152	96
Offence not recorded	18	13	19	9	4	24	7	14	9	9

1) Due to the introduction of a new prison IT system the 2010 prison population data is now taken from a different source. The 2009 figures from both the old and new systems have been presented to aid comparison.

	30-Jun-05	30-Jun-06	30-Jun-07	30-Jun-08	30-Jun-09	30-Jun-09[1]	30-Jun-10	30-Jun-11	30-Jun-12	30-Jun-13
Males	**58,703**	**59,898**	**62,188**	**64,600**	**64,993**	**65,047**	**67,450**	**68,424**	**69,976**	**67,587**
Violence against the person	14,541	15,537	16,929	18,159	19,108	18,913	19,349	19,520	19,488	18,568
Sexual offences	6,146	6,561	7,287	7,569	7,918	8,116	9,221	9,767	10,390	10,463
Robbery	8,035	8,100	8,437	8,437	8,715	8,406	8,562	8,840	8,951	8,551
Burglary	7,844	7,563	7,723	7,733	7,678	7,202	6,706	6,931	7,137	6,874
Theft and handling	3,716	3,691	3,332	3,373	2,963	2,741	3,412	3,747	4,141	4,034
Fraud and forgery	1,281	1,456	1,512	1,725	1,628	1,669	1,359	1,202	1,249	1,166
Drug offences	9,427	9,484	9,569	9,992	9,803	9,561	10,235	9,899	10,108	9,704
Motoring offences	2,124	1,887	1,453	1,356	1,130	1,034	910	824	778	701
Other offences	4,954	5,242	5,598	6,024	5,758	5,797	6,895	7,219	7,284	7,090
Offence not recorded	636	378	348	232	291	1,608	801	475	450	436
Adults	**51,327**	**52,368**	**54,007**	**56,270**	**56,882**	**57,088**	**59,951**	**61,394**	**63,374**	**62,181**
Violence against the person	12,682	13,594	14,755	15,830	16,792	16,707	17,223	17,673	17,832	17,162
Sexual offences	5,896	6,281	6,939	7,195	7,546	7,765	8,765	9,321	9,967	10,112
Robbery	6,306	6,200	6,383	6,448	6,663	6,507	6,828	7,143	7,254	7,165
Burglary	6,839	6,581	6,625	6,587	6,520	6,144	5,667	5,887	6,187	6,125
Theft and handling	3,100	3,090	2,754	2,880	2,559	2,371	3,039	3,365	3,734	3,719
Fraud and forgery	1,224	1,406	1,469	1,688	1,583	1,628	1,329	1,180	1,222	1,146
Drug offences	8,861	8,925	8,951	9,214	9,078	8,882	9,593	9,315	9,570	9,209
Motoring offences	1,788	1,602	1,259	1,191	1,010	927	822	749	723	651
Other offences	4,110	4,366	4,590	5,047	4,886	4,871	5,987	6,341	6,482	6,500
Offence not recorded	522	323	280	190	245	1,286	698	420	403	392
18-20 year olds	**5,596**	**5,716**	**6,354**	**6,454**	**6,593**	**6,398**	**6,337**	**5,896**	**5,623**	**4,733**
Violence against the person	1,493	1,563	1,772	1,843	1,949	1,840	1,820	1,615	1,439	1,244
Sexual offences	186	213	276	300	295	279	399	399	376	324

21.11 Prison population under an immediate custodial sentence by offence group, age group and sex, 2002 to 2013, England and Wales

	30-Jun-05	30-Jun-06	30-Jun-07	30-Jun-08	30-Jun-09	30-Jun-09[1]	30-Jun-10	30-Jun-11	30-Jun-12	30-Jun-13
Robbery	1,307	1,413	1,558	1,517	1,611	1,473	1,451	1,408	1,396	1,165
Burglary	719	707	817	831	909	803	838	840	800	669
Theft and handling	385	412	392	346	281	245	296	296	335	271
Fraud and forgery	48	39	34	33	45	40	27	21	27	19
Drug offences	491	491	546	672	643	598	579	525	506	461
Motoring offences	278	216	150	139	107	93	83	67	53	49
Other offences	592	619	758	739	711	729	746	684	652	495
Offence not recorded	96	43	51	34	42	298	98	41	39	36
15-17 year olds	**1,780**	**1,814**	**1,827**	**1,876**	**1,517**	**1,561**	**1,162**	**1,134**	**979**	**673**
Violence against the person	366	381	402	486	366	366	306	232	217	162
Sexual offences	65	67	73	74	77	72	57	47	47	27
Robbery	422	486	495	472	440	426	283	289	301	221
Burglary	285	275	281	315	248	255	201	204	150	80
Theft and handling	230	189	185	147	124	125	77	86	72	44
Fraud and forgery	10	11	9	4	1	1	3	1	0	1
Drug offences	76	68	71	106	82	81	63	59	32	34
Motoring offences	58	69	44	26	13	14	5	8	2	1
Other offences	252	258	250	238	161	197	162	194	150	95
Offence not recorded	18	12	17	8	4	24	5	14	8	8

1) Due to the introduction of a new prison IT system the 2010 prison population data is now taken from a different source. The 2009 figures from both the old and new systems have been presented to aid comparison.

	30-Jun-05	30-Jun-06	30-Jun-07	30-Jun-08	30-Jun-09	30-Jun-09[1]	30-Jun-10	30-Jun-11	30-Jun-12	30-Jun-13
Females	**3,476**	**3,506**	**3,345**	**3,524**	**3,382**	**3,414**	**3,421**	**3,411**	**3,459**	**3,194**
Violence against the person	637	678	687	771	839	849	898	911	949	905
Sexual offences	38	37	48	47	54	60	83	83	83	77
Robbery	343	315	310	295	334	332	272	301	328	322
Burglary	238	228	197	203	207	201	151	171	208	199
Theft and handling	410	435	374	462	418	393	438	451	505	466
Fraud and forgery	173	236	227	295	246	254	185	174	205	154
Drug offences	1,234	1,163	1,044	990	893	859	829	722	574	471
Motoring offences	39	33	31	22	19	16	21	17	20	22
Other offences	335	352	392	416	359	389	458	536	542	535
Offence not recorded	29	30	35	24	13	61	86	45	45	43
Adults	**3,153**	**3,185**	**3,009**	**3,164**	**3,088**	**3,098**	**3,112**	**3,136**	**3,215**	**3,043**
Violence against the person	547	593	568	653	723	726	774	823	854	848
Sexual offences	37	33	47	47	51	57	76	75	77	75
Robbery	267	250	244	239	279	273	227	255	291	295
Burglary	216	209	183	183	191	185	141	165	192	191
Theft and handling	379	410	346	428	391	367	415	432	482	449
Fraud and forgery	165	227	219	285	245	253	184	172	203	152
Drug offences	1,177	1,097	999	930	847	813	789	687	554	461
Motoring offences	38	31	29	20	19	16	20	17	20	21
Other offences	301	310	341	358	329	350	416	472	502	511
Offence not recorded	26	24	33	22	13	58	70	38	40	40
18-20 year olds	**269**	**271**	**280**	**303**	**253**	**271**	**286**	**259**	**228**	**143**
Violence against the person	68	75	99	99	101	107	114	81	87	54
Sexual offences	2	3	1	0	3	2	7	7	6	2
Robbery	59	48	54	43	45	48	40	42	35	25
Burglary	18	13	11	15	13	13	10	6	15	7
Theft and handling	28	22	23	29	25	23	22	19	23	17
Fraud and forgery	7	8	6	9	1	1	1	1	2	2
Drug offences	54	62	42	56	42	43	39	35	18	10
Motoring offences	1	2	2	2	0	0	1	0	0	1
Other offences	29	34	43	49	23	31	38	61	38	23
Offence not recorded	3	5	0	1	0	3	14	7	4	2
15-17 year olds	**55**	**50**	**56**	**57**	**42**	**45**	**23**	**16**	**16**	**8**
Violence against the person	23	11	20	19	15	16	10	7	8	3
Sexual offences	0	1	0	0	0	1	0	1	0	0
Robbery	16	17	13	13	10	11	5	4	2	2
Burglary	4	7	2	5	3	3	0	0	1	1
Theft and handling	3	3	6	6	3	3	1	0	0	0
Fraud and forgery	1	0	1	0	0	0	0	1	0	0
Drug offences	3	4	3	5	4	3	1	0	2	0
Motoring offences	0	0	0	0	0	0	0	0	0	0
Other offences	5	7	9	9	7	8	4	3	2	1
Offence not recorded	0	1	2	1	0	0	2	0	1	1

Source: Ministry of Justice

1) Due to the introduction of a new prison IT system the 2010 prison population data is now taken from a different source. The 2009 figures from both the old and new systems have been presented to aid comparison.

21.12 Crimes recorded by the police, Scotland, 2004-05 to 2013-14

Number & Percentage

Crime group	2004-05	2005-06	2006-07	2007-08	2008-09	2009-10	2010-11	2011-12	2012-13	2013-14	% change 12-13 to 13-
Total Crimes	438,123	417,785	419,257	385,509	377,433	338,124	323,247	314,188	273,053	270,397	-1
Non-sexual crimes of violence	14,728	13,726	14,099	12,874	12,612	11,228	11,438	9,533	7,530	6,785	-10
Homicide etc.[1] (incl. causing death by driving)	165	121	159	142	134	106	122	121	91	106	16
Attempted murder & serious assault[2]	7,603	7,030	7,345	6,711	6,472	5,621	5,493	4,693	3,643	3,268	-10
Robbery	3,736	3,553	3,578	3,064	2,963	2,496	2,557	2,244	1,832	1,499	-18
Other violence	3,224	3,022	3,017	2,957	3,043	3,005	3,266	2,475	1,964	1,912	-3
Sexual crimes[3]	7,325	6,558	6,726	6,552	6,331	6,527	6,696	7,361	7,693	8,604	12
Rape & attempted rape	1,109	1,161	1,123	1,053	963	996	1,131	1,274	1,462	1,808	24
Sexual assault	3,470	3,392	3,452	3,502	3,297	3,412	3,220	2,908	3,008	3,405	13
Crimes associated with prostitution	1,458	730	779	682	765	661	576	567	534	490	-8
Other sexual crimes	1,288	1,275	1,372	1,315	1,306	1,458	1,769	2,612	2,689	2,901	8
Crimes of dishonesty	210,365	187,798	183,760	166,718	167,812	153,256	155,870	154,337	135,899	137,324	1
Housebreaking[4]	34,959	31,319	30,580	25,443	25,496	23,774	25,017	24,222	21,515	22,272	4
Theft by opening a lockfast place (OLP)	7,849	8,263	7,422	6,378	6,952	5,074	4,059	3,529	3,239	3,218	-1
Theft from a motor vehicle by OLP	20,403	16,453	16,060	15,217	13,649	10,173	9,495	8,988	6,159	6,189	0
Theft of a motor vehicle	15,633	14,041	15,000	12,105	11,551	9,304	8,716	7,060	5,731	5,976	4
Shoplifting	28,534	28,247	28,750	29,186	32,048	30,332	29,660	29,758	26,449	27,693	5
Other theft	77,586	72,128	70,241	64,645	64,384	61,008	64,680	66,681	58,704	58,794	0
Fraud	18,307	11,074	9,332	8,409	8,316	8,283	8,983	8,892	8,898	8,088	-9
Other dishonesty	7,094	6,273	6,375	5,335	5,416	5,308	5,260	5,207	5,204	5,094	-2
Fire-raising, vandalism etc.	128,566	127,889	129,734	118,025	109,430	93,443	82,020	75,201	59,479	54,418	-9
Fire-raising	4,698	4,856	4,976	4,635	4,651	4,244	3,966	3,755	3,066	2,549	-17
Vandalism etc.	123,868	123,033	124,758	113,390	104,779	89,199	78,054	71,446	56,413	51,869	-8
Other crimes	77,139	81,814	84,938	81,340	81,248	73,670	67,223	67,756	62,452	63,266	1
Crimes against public justice	25,616	27,668	32,052	31,353	29,493	26,885	26,294	26,635	23,401	23,610	1
Handling an offensive weapon	9,545	9,628	10,110	8,989	8,980	7,042	6,283	5,631	4,015	3,795	-5
Drugs	41,823	44,247	42,422	40,746	42,509	39,408	34,347	35,157	34,688	35,616	3
Other	155	271	354	252	266	335	299	333	348	245	-30

Source: Scottish Government

Notes:

1. Includes Murder, and Culpable homicide, which includes Culpable homicide (common law), Causing death by dangerous driving, Causing death by careless driving while under the influence of drink or drugs, Causing death by careless driving, Illegal driver involved in fatal accident and Corporate homicide.

2. For the definition of Serious assault please see Annex 1 of recorded crime in Scotland

3. Implementation of Sexual Offences (Scotland) Act will have an effect on comparability of breakdown of Sexual offences over time.

4. Includes dwellings, non-dwellings and other premises.

21.13 People with a charge proved by main crime/offence, 2004-05 to 2013-14, Scotland

Main crime or offence	2004-05	2005-06	2006-07	2007-08	2008-09	2009-10	2010-11	2011-12	2012-13	2013-14 [1]	% change 2012-13 to 2013-14	All offences proved, 2013-14 [2]
All crimes and offences	129,733	128,204	134,413	133,608	125,895	121,042	115,576	108,388	101,013	105,549	4	138,722
All crimes	46,219	44,882	48,798	48,640	46,805	43,570	42,301	40,651	36,996	36,158	-2	47,764
Non-sexual crimes of violence	2,429	2,459	2,461	2,749	2,658	2,462	2,539	2,438	2,136	1,782	-17	1,961
Homicide etc	143	111	121	136	116	118	117	111	113	90	-20	92
Attempted murder and serious assault	1,376	1,561	1,496	1,731	1,709	1,511	1,418	1,352	1,283	1,029	-20	1,087
Robbery	610	512	529	548	562	532	526	596	517	441	-15	526
Other non-sexual crimes of violence	300	275	315	334	271	301	478	379	223	222	0	256
Sexual crimes	839	864	855	727	915	831	756	784	864	1,053	22	1,769
Rape and attempted rape	70	61	60	49	42	57	36	49	77	87	13	148
Sexual assault	197	185	184	145	182	158	160	151	204	235	15	528
Crimes associated with prostitution	229	292	306	254	335	250	245	200	142	169	19	176
Other sexual crimes	343	326	305	279	356	366	315	384	441	562	27	917
Crimes of dishonesty	19,610	17,997	18,381	17,728	17,429	15,951	15,614	14,772	13,250	12,546	-5	16,436
Housebreaking	2,372	2,074	2,025	1,867	1,860	1,604	1,540	1,498	1,365	1,034	-24	1,303
Theft by opening lockfast places	458	366	398	389	349	312	284	291	247	216	-13	306
Theft from a motor vehicle	649	489	408	447	387	297	270	250	200	142	-29	229
Theft of a motor vehicle	942	847	851	776	733	572	484	450	373	269	-28	583
Shoplifting	8,427	8,162	8,548	8,457	8,287	8,098	7,853	7,267	6,500	6,517	0	8,071
Other theft	3,668	3,289	3,430	3,260	3,113	2,768	2,871	2,961	2,720	2,572	-5	3,248
Fraud	1,537	1,457	1,355	1,337	1,438	1,142	1,065	811	624	681	9	1,252
Other dishonesty	1,557	1,313	1,366	1,195	1,262	1,158	1,247	1,244	1,221	1,115	-9	1,444
Fire-raising, vandalism, etc.	5,028	5,000	5,438	5,392	4,375	3,836	3,362	3,016	2,584	2,500	-3	3,145
Fire-raising	192	192	251	224	244	190	159	146	134	128	-4	160
Vandalism etc.	4,836	4,808	5,187	5,168	4,131	3,646	3,203	2,870	2,450	2,372	-3	2,985
Other crimes	18,313	18,562	21,663	22,044	21,428	20,490	20,030	19,641	18,162	18,277	1	24,453
Crimes against public justice	7,280	7,347	9,018	9,825	10,349	9,744	9,821	10,169	9,767	9,691	-1	13,465
Handling offensive weapons	3,447	3,500	3,550	3,422	3,539	2,863	2,465	2,278	1,734	1,697	-2	2,027
Drugs	7,555	7,606	8,892	8,529	7,302	7,694	7,525	6,981	6,449	6,713	4	8,753
Other crime	31	109	203	268	238	189	219	213	212	176	-17	208
All offences	83,514	83,322	85,615	84,968	79,090	77,472	73,275	67,737	64,017	69,391	8	90,958
Miscellaneous offences	35,957	38,083	40,501	39,612	34,159	31,491	29,168	29,453	28,564	29,133	2	40,695
Common assault	12,138	12,919	13,717	13,834	13,647	12,968	12,600	12,757	11,649	11,203	-4	14,999
Breach of the peace etc.	16,172	16,894	18,104	17,494	16,004	14,077	12,113	12,544	12,961	13,723	6	19,747
Drunkenness and other disorderly conduct	311	293	261	235	129	146	160	124	102	85	-17	186
Urinating etc.	257	345	473	514	81	47	43	20	32	41	28	92
Other miscellaneous	7,079	7,632	7,946	7,535	4,298	4,253	4,252	4,008	3,820	4,081	7	5,671
Motor vehicle offences	47,557	45,239	45,114	45,356	44,931	45,981	44,107	38,284	35,453	40,258	14	50,263
Dangerous and careless driving	3,774	3,620	3,774	3,967	3,696	3,405	3,167	2,858	2,811	3,574	27	3,956
Driving under the influence	7,997	7,970	8,066	7,820	7,222	6,232	5,351	5,287	4,735	4,087	-14	4,537
Speeding	13,512	12,252	13,395	14,156	13,589	14,357	12,955	12,381	12,034	14,117	17	14,422
Unlawful use of motor vehicle	16,592	14,703	13,450	13,609	12,741	12,175	11,053	9,002	7,855	8,507	8	14,068
Vehicle defect offences	1,786	1,652	1,707	1,414	1,483	1,662	1,723	1,504	1,243	1,610	30	2,781
Seat belt offences	978	1,234	1,211	1,010	1,257	2,199	2,673	1,982	2,052	2,537	24	2,744
Mobile phone offences	251	631	814	1,197	2,266	2,856	3,603	2,641	2,663	3,094	16	3,314
Other motor vehicle offences	2,667	3,177	2,697	2,183	2,677	3,095	3,582	2,629	2,060	2,732	33	4,441

Source: Scottish Government

1. Figures for some categories dealt with by the High Court - including homicide, rape and major drug cases - may be underestimated due to late recording of disposals

2. Number of individual offences relating to people with a charge proved, whether or not the main crime/offence involved. Breaches of social work orders are not counted as individual offences.

21.14 People with a charge proved by type of court, 2004-05 to 2013-14

Number

Type of court	2004-05	2005-06	2006-07	2007-08	2008-09	2009-10	2010-11	2011-12	2012-13	2013-14
All court types[1]	129,733	128,204	134,413	133,608	125,895	121,042	115,576	108,388	101,013	105,549
High court [2,3]	974	885	908	861	810	771	702	732	703	661
Sheriff solemn	3,670	3,967	4,682	5,195	4,532	4,222	4,020	4,138	4,303	4,228
Sheriff summary	77,196	75,989	80,503	79,981	73,898	65,585	61,573	60,677	56,239	55,347
Justice of the Peace court [4,5]	47,891	47,358	48,319	47,569	46,632	50,448	49,281	42,841	39,768	45,313

Per cent

Type of court	2004-05	2005-06	2006-07	2007-08	2008-09	2009-10	2010-11	2011-12	2012-13	2013-14
All court types[1]	100	100	100	100	100	100	100	100	100	100
High court [2,3]	1	1	1	1	1	1	1	1	1	1
Sheriff solemn	3	3	3	4	4	3	3	4	4	4
Sheriff summary	60	59	60	60	59	54	53	56	56	52
Justice of the Peace court [4,5]	37	37	36	36	37	42	43	40	39	43

Index: 2004-05=100

Type of court	2004-05	2005-06	2006-07	2007-08	2008-09	2009-10	2010-11	2011-12	2012-13	2013-14
All court types[1]	100	99	104	103	97	93	89	84	78	81
High court [2,3]	100	91	93	88	83	79	72	75	72	68
Sheriff solemn	100	108	128	142	123	115	110	113	117	115
Sheriff summary	100	98	104	104	96	85	80	79	73	72
Justice of the Peace court [4,5]	100	99	101	99	97	105	103	89	83	95

Source: Scottish Government

1. Includes court type unknown.
2. Includes cases remitted to the High court from the Sheriff court.
3. The figures for 2013-14, and to an extent earlier years, may be underestimates due to late recording of high court disposals
4. Includes the stipendiary magistrates court in Glasgow.
5. Includes District courts up to 2009-10

21.15 People with a charge proved by main penalty, 2004-05 to 2013-14

Number

Main penalty	2004-05	2005-06	2006-07	2007-08	2008-09	2009-10	2010-11	2011-12	2012-13	2013-14	% change 2012-13 to 2013-14
Total[1]	129,733	128,204	134,413	133,608	125,895	121,042	115,576	108,388	101,013	105,549	4
Custody	15,011	15,082	16,758	16,761	16,944	15,801	15,314	15,921	14,783	14,101	-5
Prison	12,306	12,155	13,489	13,593	13,905	13,017	13,121	13,703	13,066	12,768	-2
Young offenders institution	2,685	2,903	3,245	3,142	3,017	2,753	2,168	2,202	1,690	1,311	-22
Other custody	20	24	24	26	21	22	12	6	10	5	-50
Order for life-long restriction	-	-	-	-	1	9	13	10	17	17	-
Community sentence	15,316	15,973	16,077	16,709	17,922	16,350	15,617	16,934	17,264	18,231	6
Community payback order	-	-	-	-	-	-	461	10,380	14,940	16,317	9
Community service order	4,850	5,183	5,286	5,601	5,784	5,471	5,308	2,642	479	141	-71
Probation	8,623	8,785	8,614	9,002	9,912	8,893	7,935	2,305	293	82	-72
Restriction of liberty order	1,097	1,136	1,179	1,155	1,143	931	831	845	919	1,074	17
Drug treatment & testing order	713	758	865	822	885	808	806	642	608	610	0
Supervised attendance order [2]	33	99	112	129	198	247	276	120	25	7	-72
Community reparation order	-	11	15	-	-	-	-	-	-	-	-
Anti-social behaviour order	-	1	6	-	-	-	-	-	-	-	-
Financial penalty	84,932	82,194	84,820	83,345	73,993	72,491	67,575	59,320	53,429	57,812	8
Fine	83,237	80,723	83,445	82,020	72,840	71,452	66,491	58,395	52,661	56,938	8
Compensation order	1,695	1,471	1,375	1,325	1,153	1,039	1,084	925	768	874	14
Other sentence[1]	14,474	14,955	16,758	16,793	17,036	16,400	17,070	16,213	15,537	15,405	-1
Insanity, hospital, guardianship order	95	115	65	20	16	15	19	24	32	19	-41
Admonition[3]	13,744	14,175	15,967	16,084	16,399	15,687	16,421	15,577	15,011	14,834	-1
Absolute discharge, no order made	403	401	413	430	412	523	460	472	361	458	27
Remit to children's hearing	221	260	313	259	209	175	170	140	133	94	-29
Average amount of penalty[4]											
Custody (days)[5]	238	229	232	248	263	284	278	287	284	292	
Fine[6,7] (£)	217	211	213	219	229	217	215	241	245	224	
Compensation order [7,8](£)	247	282	335	322	378	394	391	426	439	442	

1. Includes a small number of sentences unknown for the years 2004-05 and 2005-06.
2. Of first instance.
3. Includes a small number of court cautions and dog-related disposals.
4. Excludes indeterminate/not known sentences.
5. Figures for 2013-14 may be underestimates due to delayed reporting.
6. Excludes company fines.
7. Excludes a small number of large fines.
8. As main or secondary penalty.

Percentage

Main penalty	2004-05	2005-06	2006-07	2007-08	2008-09	2009-10	2010-11	2011-12	2012-13	2013-14
Total										
Custody	12	12	12	13	13	13	13	15	15	13
Prison	9	9	10	10	11	11	11	13	13	12
Young offenders institution	2	2	2	2	2	2	2	2	2	1
Other custody	*	*	*	*	*	*	*	*	*	*
Order for life-long restriction	-	-	-	-	*	*	*	*	*	*
Community sentence	12	12	12	13	14	14	14	16	17	17
Community payback order	-	-	-	-	-	-	*	10	15	15
Community service order	4	4	4	4	5	5	5	2	*	*
Probation	7	7	6	7	8	7	7	2	*	*
Restriction of liberty order	1	1	1	1	1	1	1	1	1	1
Drug treatment & testing order	1	1	1	1	1	1	1	1	1	1
Supervised attendance order	*	*	*	*	*	*	*	*	*	*
Financial penalty	65	64	63	62	59	60	58	55	53	55
Fine	64	63	62	61	58	59	58	54	52	54
Compensation order	1	1	1	1	1	1	1	1	1	1
Other sentence	11	12	12	13	14	14	15	15	15	15
Insanity, hospital, guardianship order	*	*	*	*	*	*	*	*	*	*
Admonition	11	11	12	12	13	13	14	14	15	14
Absolute discharge, no order made	*	*	*	*	*	*	*	*	*	*
Remit to children's hearing	*	*	*	*	*	*	*	*	*	*

Source: Scottish Government

711

21.16 People with a charge proved by main penalty, sex and age, 2004-05 to 2013-14, Scotland

		2004-05	2005-06	2006-07	2007-08	2008-09	2009-10	2010-11	2011-12	2012-13	2013-14	% change 12-13 to 13-14
Total[1]		129,235	127,843	134,113	133,353	125,881	121,038	115,556	108,303	100,897	105,464	5
Males[4]	Total	108,460	107,804	113,511	112,788	106,301	101,614	97,027	90,866	84,342	87,896	4
	Under 21	23,205	24,185	25,639	24,525	20,535	17,328	15,144	13,130	10,358	9,182	-11
	21-30	39,337	38,079	40,404	41,222	38,899	37,315	35,174	32,742	30,336	30,679	1
	Over 30	45,912	45,537	47,466	47,041	46,867	46,971	46,708	44,994	43,646	48,035	10
Females[4]	Total	20,775	20,039	20,602	20,565	19,580	19,424	18,529	17,437	16,555	17,568	6
	Under 21	2,909	2,937	3,264	3,306	2,830	2,511	2,228	1,952	1,616	1,431	-11
	21-30	7,652	7,387	7,401	7,387	7,313	7,010	6,572	5,989	5,872	5,647	-4
	Over 30	10,214	9,715	9,935	9,872	9,437	9,903	9,727	9,496	9,067	10,490	16
Custody[2,3]		15,010	15,082	16,758	16,761	16,944	15,801	15,313	15,921	14,783	14,101	-5
Males[4]	Total	13,809	13,939	15,583	15,486	15,591	14,521	14,011	14,553	13,495	12,895	-4
	Under 21	2,521	2,803	3,070	2,986	2,856	2,601	2,014	2,049	1,588	1,234	-22
	21-30	6,478	6,030	6,684	6,864	6,718	6,154	6,074	6,043	5,487	4,995	-9
	Over 30	4,809	5,106	5,829	5,636	6,017	5,766	5,923	6,461	6,420	6,666	4
Females	Total	1,201	1,143	1,175	1,275	1,353	1,280	1,302	1,368	1,288	1,206	-6
	Under 21	191	125	200	182	182	175	168	160	116	83	-28
	21-30	611	563	592	615	682	581	588	620	598	488	-18
	Over 30	399	455	383	478	489	524	546	588	574	635	11
Community sentence[2,3]		15,316	15,973	16,077	16,709	17,921	16,350	15,617	16,934	17,264	18,231	6
Males[4]	Total	12,821	13,355	13,566	13,886	14,955	13,484	12,979	14,087	14,396	15,218	6
	Under 21	3,914	4,158	4,486	4,471	4,608	3,640	3,446	3,292	2,743	2,632	-4
	21-30	4,832	4,920	4,878	4,935	5,303	5,037	4,697	5,246	5,590	5,662	1
	Over 30	4,075	4,277	4,202	4,480	5,044	4,807	4,836	5,549	6,063	6,924	14
Females[4]	Total	2,495	2,618	2,511	2,823	2,966	2,866	2,638	2,847	2,868	3,013	5
	Under 21	529	532	633	667	593	559	453	433	428	340	-21
	21-30	1,042	1,126	926	1,092	1,176	1,013	1,020	1,014	1,063	1,024	-4
	Over 30	924	960	952	1,064	1,197	1,294	1,165	1,400	1,377	1,649	20
Monetary[2,3]		84,468	81,862	84,541	83,105	73,980	72,487	67,558	59,243	53,317	57,734	8
Males[4]	Total	71,134	69,505	72,051	71,058	63,241	61,480	57,350	50,260	45,143	48,452	7
	Under 21	13,765	14,029	14,646	13,597	9,886	8,462	7,070	5,365	4,061	3,699	-9
	21-30	24,840	23,884	25,214	25,791	23,102	22,258	20,357	17,798	15,810	16,489	4
	Over 30	32,524	31,589	32,189	31,670	30,253	30,760	29,922	27,097	25,270	28,264	12
Females[4]	Total	13,334	12,357	12,490	12,047	10,739	11,007	10,208	8,983	8,174	9,282	14
	Under 21	1,494	1,507	1,572	1,569	1,206	1,061	909	746	530	521	-2
	21-30	4,611	4,254	4,253	4,140	3,754	3,818	3,381	2,907	2,705	2,774	3
	Over 30	7,229	6,596	6,663	6,338	5,779	6,128	5,916	5,330	4,939	5,987	21
Other sentence[2,3]		14,441	14,926	16,737	16,778	17,036	16,400	17,068	16,205	15,533	15,398	-1
Males[4]	Total	10,696	11,005	12,311	12,358	12,514	12,129	12,687	11,966	11,308	11,331	*
	Under 21	3,005	3,195	3,437	3,471	3,185	2,625	2,614	2,424	1,966	1,617	-18
	21-30	3,187	3,245	3,628	3,632	3,776	3,866	4,046	3,655	3,449	3,533	2
	Over 30	4,504	4,565	5,246	5,255	5,553	5,638	6,027	5,887	5,893	6,181	5
	Total	3,745	3,921	4,426	4,420	4,522	4,271	4,381	4,239	4,225	4,067	-4
	Under 21	695	773	859	888	849	716	698	613	542	487	-10
	21-30	1,388	1,444	1,630	1,540	1,701	1,598	1,583	1,448	1,506	1,361	-10
	Over 30	1,662	1,704	1,937	1,992	1,972	1,957	2,100	2,178	2,177	2,219	2

1. Includes people with sentence unknown.
2. Sentence type breakdowns exclude people with gender unknown.
3. Sentence type breakdowns exclude companies.
4. Gender totals include people with age unknown

Source: Scottish Government

21.17a Average daily population in penal establishments by type of custody: 2002-03 to 2011-12

	2002-03	2003-04	2004-05	2005-06	2006-07	2007-08	2008-09	2009-10	2010-11	2011-12	% change over past year
Total	**6,453**	**6,606**	**6,776**	**6,856**	**7,187**	**7,376**	**7,826**	**7,963**	**7,853**	**8,178**	*4*
Remand	1,207	1,237	1,223	1,250	1,572	1,561	1,679	1,522	1,474	1,600	*9*
Untried	1,055	1,075	1,036	1,032	1,329	1,306	1,415	1,170	1,112	1,237	*11*
Convicted awaiting sentence	152	163	188	218	243	255	264	352	362	363	*
Young offenders	273	256	261	285	361	355	334	305	262	258	*-1*
Adults	933	981	962	965	1,211	1,206	1,344	1,217	1,212	1,342	*11*
Sentenced	5,246	5,369	5,553	5,605	5,615	5,815	6,147	6,441	6,379	6,578	*3*
Young offenders (direct sentence)	569	539	544	607	621	658	657	690	576	534	*-7*
Adults (direct sentence)	4,379	4,474	4,599	4,553	4,433	4,518	4,879	5,120	5,111	5,332	*4*
Fine defaulters	56	55	51	47	46	28	11	9	9	9	*-4*
Recalls from supervision/licence	235	293	351	397	514	610	599	621	681	701	*3*
Others	6	7	5	1	*	*	-	-	-	*	-
Sentenced by court martial	*	*	1	-	-	*	1	-	1	1	-
Civil prisoners	1	1	1	1	1	1	*	1	*	1	-
Men	**6,171**	**6,293**	**6,444**	**6,521**	**6,833**	**7,005**	**7,414**	**7,539**	**7,419**	**7,710**	*4*
Remand	1,125	1,150	1,138	1,166	1,471	1,444	1,545	1,417	1,369	1,492	*9*
Untried	1,000	1,016	980	976	1,257	1,232	1,330	1,107	1,044	1,170	*12*
Convicted awaiting sentence	126	134	159	191	213	213	215	311	325	322	*-1*
Sentenced	5,046	5,143	5,306	5,355	5,363	5,561	5,869	6,122	6,050	6,218	*3*
Young offenders (direct sentence)	548	515	515	583	591	634	633	662	545	506	*-7*
Adults (direct sentence)	4,206	4,279	4,387	4,333	4,219	4,296	4,633	4,836	4,827	5,013	*4*
Fine defaulters	51	50	47	43	43	26	10	8	9	8	*-5*
Recalls from supervision/licence	235	291	350	395	510	603	592	614	669	689	*3*
Others	5	7	5	1	*	*	-	-	-	*	-
Sentenced by court martial	*	*	1	-	-	*	1	-	1	1	-
Civil prisoners	1	1	1	*	*	1	*	1	*	*	-
Women	**282**	**314**	**332**	**334**	**353**	**371**	**412**	**424**	**434**	**468**	*8*
Remand	81	88	85	84	101	117	133	105	105	108	*2*
Untried	55	59	56	57	72	74	85	63	68	67	*-1*
Convicted awaiting sentence	26	29	29	27	29	42	49	41	38	41	*8*
Sentenced	200	226	247	250	252	255	278	319	329	360	*9*
Young offenders (direct sentence)	20	24	30	24	30	24	25	28	32	28	*-12*
Adults (direct sentence)	173	196	212	221	215	222	246	284	284	319	*12*
Fine defaulters	5	4	4	4	3	2	1	1	*	*	-
Recalls from supervision/licence	1	2	1	2	4	7	7	6	13	13	-
Others	1	*	*	*	-	-	-	-	-	-	-
Sentenced by court martial	-	-	-	-	-	-	-	-	-	-	-
Civil prisoners	*	*	*	*	*	*	*	*	*	*	-

Source: Prison Statistics and Population Projections Scotland: 2011-12

Data for 2012-2013 not yet published expected October 2015

21.17b Average daily population of sentenced offenders by sentence length: 2002-03 to 2011-12

	2002-03	2003-04	2004-05	2005-06	2006-07	2007-08	2008-09	2009-10	2010-11	2011-12	% change over past year
Total	**5,245**	**5,367**	**5,551**	**5,605**	**5,614**	**5,814**	**6,146**	**6,440**	**6,377**	**6,576**	*3*
Fine default	56	55	51	47	46	28	11	9	9	9	*-4*
Less than 3 months	88	68	81	101	124	116	98	89	78	50	*-36*
3 months - less than 6 months	433	403	450	442	444	426	402	350	347	383	*10*
6 months - less than 2 years	1,176	1,163	1,161	1,214	1,159	1,226	1,567	1,767	1,682	1,822	*8*
2 years - less than 4 years	814	857	884	913	959	1,058	1,099	1,211	1,183	1,172	*-1*
4 years or over (excluding life)	1,839	1,932	1,957	1,841	1,702	1,654	1,643	1,631	1,597	1,600	*
Life/Section 205/206 sentences	599	590	612	650	666	696	726	763	800	838	*5*
Persons recalled from supervision/licence	235	293	351	397	514	610	599	621	681	701	*3*
Others	6	7	5	1	*	*	-	-	-	-	-
Young offenders	**579**	**552**	**558**	**624**	**644**	**684**	**686**	**719**	**604**	**556**	*-8*
Fine default	7	6	5	5	5	2	1	1	1	1	-
Less than 3 months	13	9	9	14	13	13	11	8	6	3	*-56*
3 months - less than 6 months	63	51	55	57	58	59	50	45	37	34	*-8*
6 months - less than 2 years	231	216	212	241	241	243	267	307	242	246	*2*
2 years - less than 4 years	112	111	118	142	136	175	165	182	164	137	*-16*
4 years or over (excluding life)	131	132	130	127	143	136	134	126	103	94	*-9*
Life/Section 205/206 sentences	19	19	19	26	30	31	30	22	23	19	*-18*
Persons recalled from supervision/licence	3	7	8	11	19	25	28	28	26	22	*-19*
Others	*	1	1	*	-	-	-	-	-	-	-
Adults	**4,666**	**4,816**	**4,993**	**4,981**	**4,970**	**5,130**	**5,460**	**5,722**	**5,774**	**6,020**	*4*
Fine default	49	49	46	43	41	26	10	8	8	8	*-1*
Less than 3 months	76	59	71	87	111	102	88	81	72	47	*-35*
3 months - less than 6 months	370	353	395	386	386	367	352	305	310	349	*13*
6 months - less than 2 years	945	947	949	972	918	983	1,300	1,460	1,440	1,576	*9*
2 years - less than 4 years	702	746	766	771	823	883	935	1,029	1,019	1,035	*2*
4 years or over (excluding life)	1,708	1,799	1,827	1,713	1,559	1,518	1,510	1,505	1,493	1,507	*1*
Life/Section 205/206 sentences	579	571	592	623	637	664	696	741	776	819	*6*
Persons recalled from supervision/licence	233	286	343	385	495	585	571	593	655	680	*4*
Others	5	6	4	1	*	*	-	-	-	-	-
Men	**5,045**	**5,142**	**5,304**	**5,355**	**5,362**	**5,560**	**5,868**	**6,121**	**6,049**	**6,216**	*3*
Fine default	51	50	47	43	43	26	10	8	9	8	*-5*
Less than 3 months	83	62	75	94	116	108	91	83	73	45	*-38*
3 months - less than 6 months	407	378	421	415	419	402	375	324	319	352	*10*
6 months - less than 2 years	1,119	1,084	1,075	1,120	1,070	1,133	1,464	1,644	1,554	1,689	*9*
2 years - less than 4 years	766	817	831	862	904	1,002	1,035	1,128	1,114	1,096	*-2*
4 years or over (excluding life)	1,793	1,878	1,905	1,792	1,652	1,607	1,595	1,582	1,539	1,529	*-1*
Life/Section 205/206 sentences	586	573	595	633	649	678	707	739	773	807	*4*
Persons recalled from supervision/licence	235	291	350	395	510	603	592	614	669	689	*3*
Others	5	7	5	1	*	*	-	-	-	-	-
Women	**200**	**226**	**247**	**250**	**252**	**254**	**278**	**319**	**329**	**360**	*9*
Fine default	5	4	4	4	3	2	1	1	*	*	-
Less than 3 months	5	5	6	7	8	8	7	7	5	5	*-9*
3 months - less than 6 months	26	25	30	27	25	24	28	26	28	31	*10*
6 months - less than 2 years	57	79	86	94	90	92	103	123	129	133	*3*
2 years - less than 4 years	48	41	52	51	55	56	64	83	70	76	*9*
4 years or over (excluding life)	46	54	52	49	49	47	48	49	58	71	*23*
Life/Section 205/206 sentences	13	17	16	17	18	18	19	24	26	31	*18*
Persons recalled from supervision/licence	1	2	1	2	4	7	7	6	13	13	*1*
Others	1	*	*	*	-	-	-	-	-	-	-

Source: Prison Statistics and Population Projections Scotland: 2011-12

Civil and court martial prisoners are excluded from this table.

Data for 2012-2013 not yet published expected October 2015

21.17c Receptions to penal establishments by type of custody: 2002-03 to 2011-12

	2002-03	2003-04	2004-05	2005-06	2006-07	2007-08	2008-09	2009-10	2010-11	2011-12	% change over past year
Total	**39,783**	**39,076**	**38,347**	**38,746**	**43,506**	**40,450**	**38,986**	**36,521**	**36,012**	**37,002**	3
Remand	18,595	18,385	18,539	19,105	22,812	22,136	22,303	20,637	21,023	21,659	3
Unruly certificate [1]	26	22	20	24	29	15	10	5	-	-	-
Sentenced	20,957	20,437	19,652	19,488	20,430	18,229	16,566	15,824	14,943	15,331	3
Young offenders	3,299	2,880	2,674	2,933	2,985	2,760	2,449	2,324	1,862	1,805	-3
Direct sentenced	2,225	2,004	1,948	2,162	2,287	2,357	2,264	2,144	1,709	1,688	-1
Fine defaulters	1,074	876	726	771	698	403	185	180	153	117	-24
Adults	17,438	17,293	16,708	16,209	16,977	15,057	13,696	13,060	12,560	13,035	4
Direct sentenced	10,604	10,517	10,627	10,759	11,705	11,846	12,374	11,907	11,461	11,989	5
Fine defaulters	6,834	6,776	6,081	5,450	5,272	3,211	1,322	1,153	1,099	1,046	-5
Recalls from supervision/licence	220	264	270	346	468	412	421	440	521	491	-6
Sentenced by court martial	3	1	6	-	-	2	1	-	2	-	n/a
Civil prisoners	11	12	6	4	4	11	4	12	22	12	-45
Legalised police cells [2]	191	219	124	125	231	57	102	43	n/a	n/a	n/a
Men	**36,674**	**35,856**	**35,201**	**35,692**	**40,089**	**37,059**	**35,603**	**33,545**	**32,980**	**33,902**	3
Remand	16,881	16,601	16,787	17,374	20,810	19,966	20,057	18,792	19,130	19,680	3
Unruly certificate [1]	24	21	19	24	26	14	10	5	-	-	-
Sentenced	19,569	19,020	18,265	18,171	19,042	17,013	15,433	14,699	13,828	14,210	3
Young offenders	3,126	2,707	2,520	2,818	2,811	2,629	2,321	2,193	1,725	1,697	-2
Direct sentenced	2,102	1,885	1,827	2,074	2,157	2,244	2,145	2,019	1,576	1,588	1
Fine defaulters	1,024	822	693	744	654	385	176	174	149	109	-27
Adults	16,224	16,053	15,479	15,012	15,775	13,982	12,701	12,079	11,592	12,032	4
Direct sentenced	10,014	9,858	9,897	10,015	10,902	11,017	11,468	11,010	10,568	11,045	5
Fine defaulters	6,210	6,195	5,582	4,997	4,873	2,965	1,233	1,069	1,024	987	-4
Recalls from supervision/licence	219	260	266	341	456	402	411	427	511	481	-6
Sentenced by court martial	3	1	6	-	-	2	1	-	2	-	n/a
Civil prisoners	11	12	6	4	3	10	3	11	20	12	-40
Legalised police cells [2]	186	201	118	119	208	54	99	38	n/a	n/a	n/a
Women	**3,109**	**3,220**	**3,146**	**3,054**	**3,417**	**3,391**	**3,383**	**2,976**	**3,010**	**3,100**	3
Remand	1,714	1,784	1,752	1,731	2,002	2,170	2,246	1,845	1,893	1,979	5
Unruly certificate [1]	2	1	1	-	3	1	-	-	-	-	-
Sentenced	1,388	1,417	1,387	1,317	1,388	1,216	1,133	1,125	1,115	1,121	1
Young offenders	173	173	154	115	174	131	128	131	137	108	-21
Direct sentenced	123	119	121	88	130	113	119	125	133	100	-25
Fine defaulters	50	54	33	27	44	18	9	6	4	8	100
Adults	1,214	1,240	1,229	1,197	1,202	1,075	995	981	968	1,003	4
Direct sentenced	590	659	730	744	803	829	906	897	893	944	6
Fine defaulters	624	581	499	453	399	246	89	84	75	59	-21
Recalls from supervision/licence	1	4	4	5	12	10	10	13	10	10	-
Sentenced by court martial	-	-	-	-	-	-	-	-	-	-	-
Civil prisoners	-	-	-	-	1	1	1	1	2	-	n/a
Legalised police cells [2]	5	18	6	6	23	3	3	5	n/a	n/a	n/a

Source: Prison Statistics and Population Projections Scotland: 2011-12

Notes: Receptions do not equate to persons received since someone receiving a custodial sentence after a period on remand, or several custodial sentences at different times or from different courts, will be counted more than once.
1. The legislation under which children may be remanded in custody on an unruly certificate was repealed in 2010.
2. Figures from 2010-11 onward are not available due to technical difficulties.

Data for 2012-2013 not yet published expected October 2015

21.18 Scottish Prison Service Statement of Comprehensive Net Expenditure for the year ended 31 March 2013

	2012-13 £000	Restated 2011-12 £000
Income		
Income from all sources	-7,493	-6,630
Expenditure		
Staff costs	144,421	136,813
Running costs	176,593	128,442
Other current expenditure	28,280	25,779
Total Expenditure	349,094	291,034
Operating cost	341,601	284,404
Interest payable and similar charges	11,455	10,952
Net operating cost	353,056	295,356
Other comprehensive Expenditure		
Net (surplus)/loss on revaluation of property, plant and equipment	7,715	-48,802
Total comprenensive expenditure for the year ending 31 March 2013	360,771	246,554

Source: Scottish Prison Service Annual Report & Accounts 2012-13

21.19 Number of recorded crimes 2013/14 and 2014/15 - Northern Ireland

Offence group	Recorded crime		Number and percentage changes	
	2013/14	2014/15	change between years	% change between years[1]
VICTIM-BASED CRIME				
VIOLENCE AGAINST THE PERSON	32,403	34,253	1,850	5.7
Homicide	21	24	3	-
Violence with injury	14,136	14,455	319	2.3
Violence without injury	18,246	19,774	1,528	8.4
SEXUAL OFFENCES	2,234	2,734	500	22.4
Rape	550	737	187	34.0
Other sexual offences	1,684	1,997	313	18.6
ROBBERY	958	880	-78	-8.1
Robbery of personal property	715	632	-83	-11.6
Robbery of business property	243	248	5	2.1
THEFT OFFENCES	36,023	35,444	-579	-1.6
Burglary	9,067	8,937	-130	-1.4
Domestic burglary	5,753	5,873	120	2.1
Non-domestic burglary	3,314	3,064	-250	-7.5
Theft from the person	576	514	-62	-10.8
Vehicle offences	5,609	5,089	-520	-9.3
Bicycle theft	1,097	966	-131	-11.9
Shoplifting	6,372	6,495	123	1.9
All other theft offences	13,302	13,443	141	1.1
CRIMINAL DAMAGE	19,889	19,830	-59	-0.3
OTHER CRIMES AGAINST SOCIETY				
DRUG OFFENCES	4,732	5,048	316	6.7
Trafficking of drugs	968	871	-97	-10.0
Possession of drugs	3,764	4,177	413	11.0
POSSESSION OF WEAPONS OFFENCES	727	772	45	6.2
PUBLIC ORDER OFFENCES	1,536	1,447	-89	-5.8
MISCELLANEOUS CRIMES AGAINST SOCIETY	2,415	2,768	353	14.6
OTHER FRAUD[2]	1,829	1,896	67	3.7
TOTAL RECORDED CRIME – ALL OFFENCES	**102,746**	**105,072**	**2,326**	**2.3**

Source: Police Service Northern Ireland

[1] '-' indicates that for offences recorded a percentage change is not reported because the base number of offences is less than 50.
[2] In England & Wales offences such as fraud by false representation (deception) are reported to Action Fraud and from April 2013 these figures are no longer included in police recorded crime statistics. However in Northern Ireland these offences are still reported to the police and so continue to be included in the PSNI recorded crime statistics.

21.20 Northern Ireland Prison Receptions by Prisoner Type, Gender and Establishment

		2009	2010	2011	2012	2013
Remand	Maghaberry	2,104	2,347	2,600	2,688	2,236
	Hydebank Wood YOC Males	633	784	730	544	420
	Hydebank Wood Females	143	169	222	208	209
	Total	2,880	3,300	3,552	3,440	2,865
Immediate Custody	Maghaberry	1,241	1,197	1,457	1,689	1,783
	Hydebank Wood YOC Males	270	286	328	276	258
	Hydebank Wood Females	59	64	70	107	132
	Total	1,570	1,547	1,855	2,072	2,173
Fine Defaulter	Maghaberry	1,168	1,615	1,832	1,936	244
	Hydebank Wood YOC Males	268	332	343	276	33
	Hydebank Wood Females	118	188	209	261	27
	Total	1,554	2,135	2,384	2,473	304
Non Criminal	Maghaberry	67	27	22	17	17
	Hydebank Wood YOC Males	4	3	2	0	1
	Hydebank Wood Females	12	4	1	2	1
	Total	83	34	25	19	19
Males[1]		5,755	6,591	7,313	7,426	4,992
Females[2]		332	425	503	578	369
Establishment	Maghaberry	4,580	5,186	5,911	6,330	4,280
	Hydebank Wood YOC Males	1,175	1,405	1,403	1,096	712
	Hydebank Wood Females	332	425	502	578	369
	Total	6,087	7,016	7,816	8,004	5,361

Northern Ireland Prison Population 2013

Notes: (1) A small number of transgender persons may be included in the male category.
(2) One female was received into Maghaberry during 2011.

Transport and communications

Chapter 22

Transport and communication

Road data (Tables 22.4 & 22.5)

The Department for Transport has undertaken significant development work over the last few years to improve its traffic estimates and measurement of traffic flow on particular stretches of the road network. This work has previously been outlined in a number of publications (Road Traffic Statistics: 2001 SB(02)23, Traffic in Great Britain Q4 2002 Data SB(03)5 and Traffic in Great Britain Q1 2003 SB(03)6).

The main point to note is that figures for 1993 to 2004 have been calculated on a different basis from years prior to 1993. Therefore, figures prior to 1993 are not directly comparable with estimates for later years. Estimates on the new basis for 1993 and subsequent years were first published by the Department on 8 May 2003 in Traffic in Great Britain Q1 2003 SB(03)6. A summary of the main methodological changes to take place over the last couple of years appears below.

Traffic estimates are now disaggregated for roads in urban and rural areas rather than between built-up and non built-up roads. Built-up roads were defined as those with a speed limit of 40 mph or lower. This created difficulties in producing meaningful disaggregated traffic estimates because an increasing number of clearly rural roads were subject to a 40 mph speed limit for safety reasons. The urban/rural split of roads is largely determined by whether roads lie within the boundaries of urban areas with a population of 10,000 or more with adjustments in some cases for major roads at the boundary.

Traffic estimates are based on the results of many 12-hour manual counts in every year, which are grossed up to estimates of annual average daily flows using expansion factors based on data from automatic traffic counters on similar roads. These averages are needed so that traffic in off-peak times, at weekends and in the summer and winter months (when only special counts are undertaken) can be taken into account when assessing the traffic at each site. For this purpose roads are now sorted into 22 groupings (previously there were only seven) and this allows a better match of manual count sites with our automatic count sites. These groupings are based on a detailed analysis of the results from all the individual automatic count sites and take into account regional groupings, road category (that is, both the urban/rural classification of the road and the road class) and traffic flow levels. The groupings range from lightly trafficked, rural minor roads in holiday areas such as Cornwall and Devon, to major roads in central London.

With the increasing interest in sub-regional statistics, we have undertaken a detailed study of traffic counts on minor roads carried out in the last ten years. This has been done in conjunction with a Geographic Information System to enable us to establish general patterns of minor road traffic in each local authority. As a result of this, we have been able to produce more reliable estimate of traffic levels in each authority in our base year of 1999. This in turn has enabled us to produce better estimates of traffic levels back to 1993, as well as more reliable estimates for 1999 onwards.

The Department created a database for major roads based on a Geographic Information System and Ordnance Survey data. This was checked by local authorities and discussed with government regional offices and the Highways Agency to ensure that good local knowledge supplemented the available technical data.

Urban major and minor roads, from 1993 onwards, are defined as being within an urban area with a population of more than 10,000 people, based on the 2001 urban settlements. The definition for urban settlement can be found on the CLG web site at:
www.communities.gov.uk/planningandbuilding/planningbuilding/planningstatistics/urbanrural.

Rural major and minor roads, from 1993 onwards, are defined as being outside an urban settlement.

New vehicle registrations (Table 22.8)

Special concession group
Various revisions to the vehicle taxation system were introduced on 1 July 1995 and on 29 November 1995. Separate taxation classes for farmers' goods vehicles were abolished on 1 July 1995; after this date new vehicles of this type were registered as Heavy Goods Vehicles (HGVs). The total includes 5,900 vehicles registered between 1 January and 30 June in the (now abolished) agricultural and special machines group in classes which were not eligible to register in the special concession group. The old agricultural and special machines taxation group was abolished at end June 1995. The group includes agricultural and mowing machines, snow ploughs and gritting vehicles. Electric vehicles are also included in this group and are no longer exempt from Vehicle Excise Duty (VED). Steam propelled vehicles were added to this group from November 1995.

Other licensed vehicles
Includes three wheelers, pedestrian controlled vehicles, general haulage and showmen's tractors and recovery vehicles. Recovery vehicle tax class introduced January 1988.

Special vehicles group
The special vehicles group was created on 1 July 1995 and consists of various vehicle types over 3.5 tonnes gross weight but not required to pay VED as heavy goods vehicles. The group includes mobile cranes, work trucks, digging machines, road rollers and vehicles previously taxed as showman's goods and haulage. The figure shown for 1995 covers the period from 1 July to 31 December only.

National Travel Survey data (Tables 22.1 & 22.11)
The National Travel Survey (NTS) is designed to provide a databank of personal travel information for Great Britain. It has been conducted as a continuous survey since July 1988, following ad hoc surveys since the mid-1960s. The survey is designed to identify long-term trends and is not suitable for monitoring short-term trends.

In 2006, a weighting strategy was introduced to the NTS and applied retrospectively to data back to 1995. The weighting methodology adjusts for non-response bias and also adjusts for the drop-off in the number of trips recorded by respondents during the course of the travel week. All results now published for 1995 onwards are based on weighted data, and direct comparisons cannot be made to earlier years or previous publications.

During 2008, over 8,000 households provided details of their personal travel by filling in travel diaries over the course of a week. The drawn sample size from 2002 was nearly trebled compared with previous years following recommendations in a National Statistics Review of the NTS. This enables most results to be presented on a single year basis from 2002.

Travel included in the NTS covers all trips by British residents within Great Britain for personal reasons, including travel in the course of work.

A trip is defined as a one-way course of travel having a single main purpose. It is the basic unit of personal travel defined in the survey.

A round trip is split into two trips, with the first ending at a convenient point about half-way round as a notional stopping point for the outward destination and return origin.

A stage is that portion of a trip defined by the use of a specific method of transport or of a specific ticket (a new stage being defined if either the mode or ticket changes). The main mode of a trip is that used for the longest stage of the trip. With stages of equal length, the mode of the latest stage is used. Walks of less than 50 yards are excluded.

Travel details provided by respondents include trip purpose, method of travel, time of day and trip length. The households also provided personal information, such as their age, sex, working status, driving licence holding, and details of the cars available for their use.

Because estimates made from a sample survey depend on the particular sample chosen, they generally differ from the true values of the population. This is not usually a problem when considering large samples (such as all car trips in Great Britain), but it may give misleading information when considering data from small samples even after weighting.

The most recent editions of all NTS publications are available on the DfT website at: www.dft.gov.uk/transtat/personaltravel. Bulletins of key results are published annually. The most recent bulletin is National Travel Survey: 2013.

Households with regular use of cars (Table 22.11)

The mid-year estimates of the percentage of households with regular use of a car or van are based on combined data from the NTS, the Expenditure and Food Survey (previously the Family Expenditure Survey) and the General Household Survey. The method for calculating these figures was changed slightly in 2006, to incorporate weighted data from the NTS and the GHS. Figures since have also been revised to incorporate weighted data. Results by area type are based on weighted data from the NTS only.

Continuing Survey of Road Goods Transport (Tables 22.2, 22.17 & 22.18)

The estimates are derived from the Continuing Survey of Road Goods Transport (CSRGT) which in 2005 was based on an average weekly returned sample of some 330 HGVs. The samples are drawn from the computerised vehicle licence records held by the Driver and Vehicle Licensing Agency. Questionnaires are sent to the registered keepers of the sampled vehicles asking for a description of the vehicle and its activity during the survey week. The estimates are grossed to the vehicle population,, and at the overall national level have a 2 per cent margin of error (at 95 per cent confidence level). Further details and results are published in Road Freight Statistics, and previously in Transport of Goods by Road in Great Britain.

Methodological changes

A key component of National Statistics outputs is a programme of quality reviews carried out at least every five years to ensure that such statistics are fit for purpose and that their quality and value continue to improve. A quality review of the Department for Transport's road freight surveys, including the CSRGT, was carried out in 2003. A copy of the report can be accessed at: www.statistics.gov.uk/nsbase/methods_quality/quality_review/downloads/NSQR30FinalReport.doc

The quality review made a number of recommendations about the CSRGT. The main methodological recommendation was that, to improve the accuracy of survey estimates, the sample strata should be amended to reflect current trends in vehicle type, weight and legislative groups. These new strata are described more fully in Appendix C of the survey report. For practical and administrative reasons, changes were also made to the sample selection methodology (see Appendix B of the report). These changes have resulted in figures from 2004 not being fully comparable with those for 2003 and earlier years. Detailed comparisons should therefore be made with caution.

Railways: permanent way and rolling stock (Table 22.21)

1) Locomotives - locos owned by Northern Ireland Railways (NIR), does not include those from the Republic of Ireland Railway System.

2) Diesel electric etc rail motor vehicles - powered passenger carrying vehicles, includes diesel electric (DE) power cars and all Construcciones y Auxiliar de Ferocarriles (CAF) vehicles. (Note: only 16 of the CAF sets were delivered to NIR at the time.)

3) Loco hauled coaches - NIR owned De Dietrich plus Gatwick but not including gen van.

4) Rail car trailers - 80 class and 450 class trailers. Not CAF, they are all powered.

5) Rolling stock for maintenance and repair - a 'standalone' figure - may or may not be included in the above totals. Anything listed as 'repair' or 'workshop' in the motive power sheets is included. Also, those CAF vehicles not yet delivered at the time.

6) The information is a 'snapshot' taken from the motive power sheets at end of March, together with any other known information.

22.23 - 22.26

All data from Airline Statistics, Civil Aviation Authority

22.1 Average number of trips (trip rates) by purpose and main mode: England, 2013

Purpose	Walk	Bicycle	Car / van driver	Car / van passenger	Motorcycle	Other private transport[1]	Local bus	Rail[2]	Other public transport[3]	All modes
Commuting	14	5	83	15	1	-	11	13	2	145
Business	2	-	21	2	-	-	1	3	-	30
Education / escort education	45	1	23	25	-	3	13	2	1	112
Shopping	38	1	81	39	-	1	16	2	2	180
Other escort	10	-	48	25	-	-	2	-	1	86
Personal business	18	1	38	22	-	1	7	1	1	89
Leisure[4]	36	5	88	82	1	2	13	8	6	240
Other including just walk	40	0	-	-	-	0	0	0	0	40
All purposes	203	14	380	210	3	7	63	30	13	923
Unweighted sample size: trips ('000s)	62	4	113	63	1	2	18	8	4	274

Source: National Travel Survey

1 Mostly private hire bus (including school buses).
2 Surface rail and London Underground.
3 Non-local bus, taxi / minicab and other public transport (air, ferries, light rail).
4 Visit friends at home and elsewhere, entertainment, sport, holiday and day trip.

Telephone: 020 7944 3097
Email: national.travelsurvey@dft.gsi.gov.uk

The figures in this table are National Statistics

Note:
The results presented in this table are weighted. The base (unweighted sample size) is shown in the table for information.
Weights are applied to adjust for non-response to ensure the characteristics of the achieved sample match the population of Great Britain (1995-2012) or England (2013 onwards) and for the drop off in trip recording in diary data.
The survey results are subject to sampling error.

22.2 Domestic freight transport[1]: by mode: 2000-2012

	2000	2001	2002	2003	2004	2005	2006	2007	2008	2009	2010	2011[2]	2012[2]
(a) Goods moved											Billion tonne kilometres/percentage		
Petroleum products													
Road [3]	6.4	5.8	5.2	5.5|	5.7	5.5	5.5	5.0	6.2	4.5	6.0	..	..
Rail [4]	1.4	1.2	1.2	1.2	1.2	1.2	1.5	1.6	1.5	1.4	1.3	1.2	1.2
Water	52.7	43.5	51.7	46.9	46.9	47.2	37.8	36.4	36.4	36.4	28.3	29.6	22.1
ow: coastwise	26.0	23.1	24.2	23.3	26.6	30.3	22.8	25.1	26.5	27.1	20.6	22.6	15.6
Pipeline	11.4	11.5	10.9	10.5	10.7	10.8	10.4	10.2	10.2	10.2	10.3	10.1	..
All modes	**71.9**	**62.0**	**69.0**	**64.1|**	**64.5**	**64.7**	**55.2**	**53.2**	**54.3**	**52.5**	**45.9**	**..**	**..**
Coal and coke													
Road [3]	1.5	2.1	1.5	1.5|	1.2	1.5	1.3	1.5	1.0	0.9	1.4	..	..
Rail [4]	4.8	6.2	5.7	5.8	6.7	8.3	8.6	7.7	7.9	6.2	5.5	6.4	7.5
Water	0.2	0.5	0.3	0.5	0.3	0.4	0.5	0.5	0.5	0.3	1.0	0.4	0.3
All modes	**6.5**	**8.8**	**7.5**	**7.9|**	**8.2**	**10.2**	**10.4**	**9.7**	**9.4**	**7.5**	**7.9**	**..**	**..**
Other freight													
Road [3]	151.5	150.6	152.7	154.7|	155.6	156.4	156.6	162.3	150.2	131.3	143.1	..	..
Rail [4]	11.9	12.0	11.7	11.9	12.5	12.2	11.8	11.9	11.2	11.4	12.5	13.4	14.0
Water	14.6	14.8	15.2	13.5	12.2	13.3	13.5	13.9	12.7	11.9	12.6	13.1	12.6
All modes	**178.1**	**177.4**	**179.6**	**180.0|**	**180.3**	**181.9**	**182.0**	**188.1**	**174.1**	**154.6**	**168.2**	**..**	**..**
All traffic													
Road [3]	159.4	158.5	159.4	161.7|	162.5	163.4	163.4	168.8	157.4	136.8	150.5	..	..
Rail [4]	18.1	19.4	18.5	18.9	20.3	21.7	21.9	21.2	20.6	19.1	19.2	21.1	21.5
Water	67.4	58.8	67.2	60.9	59.4	60.9	51.8	50.8	49.7	48.6	41.9	43.0	35.0
Pipeline	11.4	11.5	10.9	10.5	10.7	10.8	10.4	10.2	10.2	10.2	10.3	10.1	..
All modes	**256.3**	**248.2**	**256.0**	**252.0|**	**253.0**	**256.8**	**247.6**	**251.0**	**237.8**	**214.6**	**221.9**	**..**	**..**
Percentage of all traffic													
Road [3]	62	64	62	64	64	64	66	67	66	64	68	..	..
Rail [4]	7	8	7	7	8	8	9	8	9	9	9	..	..
Water	26	24	26	24	24	24	21	20	21	23	19	..	..
Pipeline	4	5	4	4	4	4	4	4	4	5	5	..	..
All modes	**100**	**100**	**100**	**100**	**100**	**100**	**100**	**100**	**100**	**100**	**100**	**..**	**..**
(b) Goods lifted											Million tonnes/percentage		
Petroleum products													
Road [3]	75	74	59	64|	67	70	66	69	76	57	67	..	..
Rail [4]	..	..	..	..|	..|	..	..|	..	..	..	..	..	..
Water	72	60	67	64	63	66	57	56	58	55	46	46	41
ow: coastwise	40	34	36	35	38	42	34	35	36	35	28	28	23
Pipeline	151	151	146	141	158	168	159	146	147	148	149	151	..
All modes	**298**	**285**	**272**	**269|**	**288|**	**304**	**282|**	**272**	**281**	**259**	**263**	**..**	**..**
Coal and coke													
Road [3]	22	21	17	22|	14	21	16	23	14	10	11	..	..
Rail [4]	35	39	34	35|	44|	48	49|	43	47	38	39	44	52
Water	3	3	2	2	1	2	2	2	2	1	2	1	1
All modes	**60**	**63**	**53**	**59|**	**59|**	**71**	**68|**	**68**	**63**	**49**	**52**	**..**	**..**
Other freight													
Road [3]	1,596	1,587	1,658	1,667|	1,782	1,777	1,819	1,861	1,709	1,422	1,543	..	..
Rail [4]	60	54	53	54|	57|	58	59|	59	56	49	51	57	61
Water [3]	62	68	70	67	63	65	66	68	63	54	57	57	54
All modes	**1,718**	**1,709**	**1,781**	**1,788|**	**1,902**	**1,900**	**1,945|**	**1,988**	**1,828**	**1,525**	**1,651**	**..**	**..**
All traffic													
Road [3]	1,693	1,682	1,734	1,753|	1,863	1,868	1,901	1,953	1,800	1,488	1,621	..	..
Rail [4]	96	94	87	89|	101|	105	108|	102	103	87	90	102	113
Water	137	131	139	133	127	133	126	126	123	110	106	104	96
Pipeline	151	151	146	141	158	168	159	146	147	148	149	151	..
All modes	**2,077**	**2,058**	**2,106**	**2,116|**	**2,249|**	**2,275**	**2,294|**	**2,328**	**2,173**	**1,833**	**1,966**	**..**	**..**
Percentage of all traffic													
Road [3]	82	82	82	83	83	82	83	84	83	81	82	..	..
Rail [4]	5	5	4	4	4	5	5	4	5	5	5	..	..
Water	7	6	7	6	6	6	6	5	6	6	5	..	..
Pipeline	7	7	7	7	7	7	7	6	7	8	8	..	..
All modes	**100**	**100**	**100**	**100**	**100**	**100**	**100**	**100**	**100**	**100**	**100**	**..**	**..**

Sources: Road and water - DfT; Rail - ORR; Pipeline - DECC

1. Discontinuities in the series (denoted by lines) are described in detail in the Notes and Definitions.
2. Road freight data are not currently available.
3. Statistics for all goods vehicles, including those 3.5 tonnes gross vehicle weight or less.
4. Figures for rail are for financial years (e.g. 2012 will be 2012/13).
See Notes and Definitions at: https://www.gov.uk/government/statistical-data-sets/tsgb04-freight

Telephone:
Rail: 020 7944 2419
Road: 020 7944 3180
Pipeline: 020 7215 2718

22.3 Passenger transport: by mode, annual from 2000

Billion passenger kilometres/*percentage*

Year	Buses & coaches	%	Cars, vans & taxis	%	Motor cycles	%	Pedal cycles	%	All Road	%	Rail[1]	%	Air (UK)[2]	%	All modes [3]	%
2000	47	6	639	85	5	1	4	1	694	93	47	6	8	1.0	749	100
2001	47	6	651	85	5	1	4	1	707	93	48	6	8	1.0	763	100
2002 R	41	5	673	86	5	1	4	1	723	93	48	6	8	1.1	780	100
2003 R	45	6	669	86	5	1	4	1	723	92	50	6	9	1.2	782	100
2004 R	41	5	673	86	6	1	4	1	724	92	50	6	10	1.2	784	100
2005 R	43	5	667	85	5	1	4	1	719	92	52	7	10	1.3	781	100
2006 R	41	5	672	85	6	1	5	1	723	92	55	7	10	1.3	788	100
2007 R	41	5	674	85	5	1	4	1	724	91	59	7	10	1.2	792	100
2008 R	43	5	666	84	6	1	5	1	720	91	61	8	9	1.1	789	100
2009 R	44	6	661	84	5	1	5	1	716	91	61	8	8	1.1	785	100
2010 R	45	6	644	83	5	1	5	1	699	91	65	8	8	1.0	771	100
2011 R	43	6	642	83	5	1	5	1	694	90	68	9	8	1.1	770	100
2012 R	42	5	642	83	5	1	5	1	694	90	70	9	8	1.1	772	100
2013 P	40	5	638	83	5	1	5	1	688	90	72	9	8	1.1	768	100

Sources: Road - DfT Traffic Estimates, National Travel Survey; Rail - ORR; Air - CAA
Email: publicationgeneral.enq@dft.gsi.gov.uk

1. Financial years. National Rail (franchised operators only to 2008, franchised and non-franchised operators from 2009), urban metros and modern trams.
2. UK airlines, domestic passengers uplifted on scheduled and non-scheduled flights.
3. Excluding travel by water.

R Road figures have been revised from 2002 due to the revision of population estimates.

See Notes and Definitions for details of discontinuity in road passengers figures from 1993 and 1996 onwards.
https://www.gov.uk/government/publications/transport-statistics-great-britain-guidance

Telephone:
Road: 020 7944 3097
Rail: 020 7944 2419
Air: 020 7944 3088

The Rail and Air figures in this table are outside the scope of National Statistics

22.4 Motor vehicle traffic (vehicle kilometres) by road class in Great Britain, annual from 2000

Billion vehicle kilometres

	Major roads					Minor roads			
		'A' roads							
	Motorway [1]	Rural	Urban [2]	All 'A' roads	All major roads	Rural	Urban [2]	All minor roads	All roads
2000	88.3	130.0	81.7	211.7	300.0	61.3	104.8	166.1	**466.2**
2001	90.8	133.3	81.8	215.1	305.9	61.2	105.5	166.7	**472.6**
2002	92.6	136.4	82.2	218.6	311.2	63.9	108.6	172.5	**483.7**
2003	93.0	139.3	81.8	221.0	314.0	63.6	109.0	172.6	**486.7**
2004	96.6	141.3	82.8	224.1	320.7	64.9	108.3	173.3	**493.9**
2005	97.0	141.4	81.8	223.1	320.2	65.6	108.1	173.7	**493.9**
2006	99.5	143.6	82.5	226.1	325.5	67.9	107.6	175.5	**501.1**
2007	100.6	143.5	81.3	224.9	325.4	70.3	109.7	180.0	**505.4**
2008	100.1	142.8	80.1	222.8	323.0	70.3	107.3	177.6	**500.6**
2009	99.5	142.0	80.4	222.4	321.9	68.3	105.7	174.0	**495.8**
2010	98.2	139.8	79.7	219.5	317.7	68.1	102.1	170.2	**487.9**
2011	99.5	141.2	79.3	220.4	319.9	66.3	102.7	169.0	**488.9**
2012	100.4	140.4	78.1	218.5	319.0	64.6	103.5	168.1	**487.1**
2013	101.9	140.5	78.1	218.6	320.5	66.4	101.9	168.3	**488.8**

1 Includes trunk motorways and principal motorways
2 Urban roads: Major and minor roads within an urban area with a population of 10,000 or more. These are based on the 2001 urban settlements. The definition for 'urban settlement' is in 'Urban and rural area definitions: a user guide' which can be found on the Notes & definitions (www.gov.uk/transport-statistics-notes-and-guidance-road-traffic)

Source: DfT National Road Traffic Survey
Telephone: 020 7944 3095
Email: roadtraff.stats@dft.gsi.gov.uk

The figures in this table are National Statistics.

22.5 Road lengths (kilometres) by road type in Great Britain, 2000-2013

Kilometres

Year	Motorways			'A' roads			All major roads	Minor roads				All minor roads	All roads
	Trunk	Principal	Total	Trunk	Principal	Total		'B' road	C' road	U' road	'C' and 'U' roads		
2000	3,422	45	3,467	11,701	34,906	46,607	**50,074**	30,200	84,624	225,339	309,963	**340,163**	**390,237**
2001[1]	3,431	45	3,476	11,369	35,285	46,654	**50,130**	30,196	84,742	225,901	310,643	**340,839**	**390,969**
2002	3,433	45	3,478	10,679	35,995	46,674	**50,152**	30,192	84,858	226,462	311,320	**341,512**	**391,663**
2003	3,432	46	3,478	9,615	37,037	46,652	**50,130**	30,188	84,976	227,048	312,024	**342,212**	**392,342**
2004[2]	3,478	46	3,523	9,147	37,521	46,668	**50,192**	30,178	84,223	223,082	307,305	**337,483**	**387,674**
2005	3,471	48	3,518	8,708	38,019	46,727	**50,246**	30,189	84,459	223,183	307,642	**337,830**	**388,076**
2006[2]	3,508	48	3,555	8,706	38,030	46,735	**50,291**	30,018	84,469	229,605	314,074	**344,092**	**394,383**
2007	3,518	41	3,559	8,670	38,073	46,743	**50,302**	30,265	84,423	229,889	314,312	**344,577**	**394,879**
2008	3,518	41	3,559	8,634	38,057	46,691	**50,249**	30,161	84,574	229,482	314,056	**344,217**	**394,467**
2009	3,519	41	3,560	8,596	38,173	46,770	**50,329**	30,141	84,813	229,145	313,958	**344,099**	**394,428**
2010	3,517	41	3,558	8,489	38,218	46,707	**50,265**	30,192	84,827	228,970	313,797	**343,989**	**394,253**
2011	3,529	41	3,570	8,508	38,225	46,734	**50,304**	30,208	84,831	228,953	313,784	**343,992**	**394,296**
2012	3,576	41	3,617	8,507	38,235	46,742	**50,359**	30,214	84,903	229,414	314,317	**344,531**	**394,890**
2013[3]	3,600	41	3,641	8,505	38,245	46,749	**50,391**	30,217	..	..	314,853	**345,070**	**395,461**

1. Figures for trunk and principal 'A' roads in England, from 2001 onwards, are affected by the detrunking programme.
2. New information from 2004 and from 2006 enabled better estimates of road lengths to be made - see Notes and definitions.
3. Minor roads figures in 2013 have been derived differently, with 'C' and 'U' roads combined, as no R199b road length consultation took place.
.. Sufficient data unavailable.

Source: Department for Transport
Telephone: 020 7944 5032
Email: road.length@dft.gsi.gov.uk

Notes and definitions
https://www.gov.uk/government/uploads/system/uploads/attachment_data/file/230605/road-length-notes-definitions.pdf

Methodology note
https://www.gov.uk/government/uploads/system/uploads/attachment_data/file/230607/road-length-statistics-methodology.pdf

The figures in this table are National Statistics

22.6 Road traffic (vehicle kilometres) by vehicle type in Great Britain, annual from 2000

Billion vehicle kilometres

	Cars and taxis	Light vans [1]	Goods vehicles [2]	Other Vehicles			All motor vehicles
				Motorcycles	Buses & Coaches	Total [3]	
2000	376.0	52.2	28.2	4.6	5.1	9.7	**466.2**
2001	381.2	53.4	28.0	4.8	5.1	9.9	**472.6**
2002	390.6	54.7	28.3	5.0	5.2	10.2	**483.7**
2003	390.0	57.4	28.4	5.6	5.3	10.9	**486.7**
2004	394.2	60.2	29.3	5.1	5.1	10.2	**493.9**
2005	392.7	61.8	28.9	5.3	5.1	10.4	**493.9**
2006	397.4	64.3	29.0	5.1	5.3	10.4	**501.1**
2007	397.9	67.4	29.3	5.5	5.4	10.9	**505.4**
2008	395.0	66.9	28.6	5.0	5.0	10.1	**500.6**
2009	394.0	65.5	26.2	5.1	5.0	10.1	**495.8**
2010	385.9	66.1	26.3	4.6	5.0	9.6	**487.9**
2011	387.4	66.6	25.6	4.6	4.7	9.3	**488.9**
2012	386.7	66.4	25.0	4.6	4.4	8.9	**487.1**
2013	386.2	68.5	25.2	4.3	4.5	8.8	**488.8**

1 Not exceeding 3,500 kgs gross vehicle weight, post 1982
2 Over 3,500 kgs gross vehicle weight, post 1982
3 Total of all other vehicles (i.e. motorcycles, buses, and coaches)

Source: DfT National Road Traffic Survey
Telephone: 020 7944 3095
Email: roadtraff.stats@dft.gsi.gov.uk

Notes & definitions (www.gov.uk/transport-statistics-notes-and-guidance-road-traffic)

The figures in this table are National Statistics.

22.7 Cars licensed by propulsion / fuel type, Great Britain, annually: 1994 to 2012

Thousands/*Percentages*

Year	Petrol	Diesel	Hybrid Electric	Gas[1]	Electric	Other[2]	Total
Total number of cars							
1994	19,620.9	1,576.2	0.0	1.8	0.1	0.2	21,199.2
1995	19,499.8	1,891.3	0.0	2.9	0.1	0.1	21,394.1
1996	20,051.6	2,181.6	0.0	4.1	0.1	0.1	22,237.5
1997	20,384.7	2,440.5	0.0	6.2	0.1	0.1	22,831.7
1998	20,590.5	2,692.9	0.0	9.6	0.2	0.1	23,293.3
1999	21,031.0	2,929.9	0.0	13.8	0.2	0.1	23,974.9
2000	21,232.6	3,152.7	-	20.0	0.2	-	24,405.5
2001	21,641.1	3,459.5	0.6	24.4	0.3	0.1	25,125.9
2002	21,839.5	3,912.4	0.9	28.8	0.3	0.1	25,781.9
2003	21,805.5	4,399.6	1.2	33.7	0.3	0.1	26,240.4
2004	21,976.6	5,010.6	2.8	37.6	0.4	0.1	27,028.1
2005	21,876.0	5,596.1	8.1	39.5	0.6	0.1	27,520.4
2006	21,465.8	6,083.3	16.6	42.4	0.8	0.2	27,609.2
2007	21,264.4	6,657.4	31.8	45.1	1.2	0.3	28,000.3
2008	20,899.1	7,163.5	46.7	49.6	1.3	0.4	28,160.7
2009	20,491.2	7,641.4	61.1	50.9	1.5	0.4	28,246.5
2010	20,083.1	8,202.7	82.1	51.0	1.5	0.5	28,420.9
2011	19,548.5	8,763.5	102.3	50.0	2.6	0.4	28,467.3
2012	19,158.8	9,385.1	125.3	48.7	4.1	0.4	28,722.5
Percentage of cars							
1994	92.6	7.4	0.0	-	-	-	100.0
1995	91.1	8.8	0.0	-	-	-	100.0
1996	90.2	9.8	0.0	-	-	-	100.0
1997	89.3	10.7	0.0	-	-	-	100.0
1998	88.4	11.6	0.0	-	-	-	100.0
1999	87.7	12.2	0.0	0.1	-	-	100.0
2000	87.0	12.9	-	0.1	-	-	100.0
2001	86.1	13.8	-	0.1	-	-	100.0
2002	84.7	15.2	-	0.1	-	-	100.0
2003	83.1	16.8	-	0.1	-	-	100.0
2004	81.3	18.5	-	0.1	-	-	100.0
2005	79.5	20.3	-	0.1	-	-	100.0
2006	77.7	22.0	0.1	0.2	-	-	100.0
2007	75.9	23.8	0.1	0.2	-	-	100.0
2008	74.2	25.4	0.2	0.2	-	-	100.0
2009	72.5	27.1	0.2	0.2	-	-	100.0
2010	70.7	28.9	0.3	0.2	-	-	100.0
2011	68.7	30.8	0.4	0.2	-	-	100.0
2012	66.7	32.7	0.4	0.2	-	-	100.0

1. Includes gas, gas bi-fuel, petrol/gas and gas-diesel
2. Includes vehicles propelled by steam

Source: DVLA/DfT
Telephone: 020 7944 3077
Email : vehicles.stats@dft.gsi.gov.uk

Notes & definitions (https://www.gov.uk/government/publications/vehicles-statistics-guidance)

22.8 Motor vehicles registered for the first time by tax class: Great Britain, annually: 2000 to 2012

Thousands

| Year | Private and light goods[1] | | Goods vehicles | Motor cycles, scooters and mopeds | Buses[2] | Special machines etc[5] | Other vehicles[3,4,5] | Total |
	Private cars[1]	Other vehicles[1]						
2000	2,430.0		50.0	183.0	8.0	24.0	176.0	2,871.0
2001	2,431.8	277.9	48.6	177.1	6.8	26.8	168.8	3,137.7
2002	2,528.8	286.8	44.9	162.2	7.8	:	199.0	3,229.0
2003	2,497.1	323.5	48.4	157.3	8.4	:	197.1	3,231.9
2004	2,437.4	347.3	48.0	133.7	8.3	:	210.7	3,185.4
2005	2,266.3	337.2	51.2	132.3	8.9	:	225.5	3,021.4
2006	2,160.7	338.4	47.9	131.9	7.6	:	227.1	2,913.6
2007	2,191.5	347.8	41.1	143.0	9.0	:	264.6	2,996.9
2008	1,891.9	296.4	47.0	138.4	8.3	:	290.2	2,672.2
2009	1,765.5	193.5	27.0	111.5	7.2	:	266.3	2,371.2
2010	1,765.3	229.3	27.0	97.1	6.4	:	292.7	2,417.8
2011	1,663.8	264.8	36.9	96.2	5.8	:	314.0	2,381.5
2012	1,784.1	244.4	38.0	96.6	7.8	:	299.0	2,469.8

Source: DVLA/DfT

1. From 1980 onwards figures refer to the October 1990 taxation classes.
2. Prior to 1995 this tax class was called 'Public Transport' and taxis and Hackney Carriages were included. Prior to 1969, tram cars were also included.
3. Includes crown and exempt vehicles, three wheelers, pedestrian controlled vehicles and showmen's goods vehicles.
4. Excludes vehicles officially registered by the armed forces.
5. Special Machines became part of the 'Crown and Exempt' taxation class with effect from January 2002.

Telephone: 020 7944 3077
Email : vehicles.stats@dft.gsi.gov.uk
Notes & definitions (https://www.gov.uk/government/publications/vehicles-statistics-guidance)

22.9a Practical car pass rates by gender Great Britain, 2007/08 to 2013/14

| | Male tests | | | Female tests | | | Total tests | | |
	Conducted	Passes	Pass rate (%)	Conducted	Passes	Pass rate (%)	Conducted	Passes	Pass rate (%)
2007/08	865,614	409,329	47.3	896,341	369,798	41.3	1,762,363	779,317	44.2
2008/09	849,997	413,160	48.6	888,942	374,462	42.1	1,739,257	787,760	45.3
2009/10	753,838	370,148	49.1	780,087	333,805	42.8	1,534,039	703,994	45.9
2010/11	772,537	383,405	49.6	833,035	360,637	43.3	1,605,599	744,044	46.3
2011/12	744,487	374,472	50.3	824,572	361,685	43.9	1,569,069	736,158	46.9
2012/13	682,699	345,599	50.6	753,774	331,653	44.0	1,436,481	677,255	47.1
2013/14	706,757	358,143	50.7	770,823	337,436	43.8	1,477,585	695,580	47.1

Source: Driver & Vehicle Standards Agency DVSA; Department for Transport

These statistics includes test categories B and B1

Gender statistics - Any gender based statistics are based on recorded information. In the case of GB licence holders, details of gender are reliant upon the correct information being held on the DVLA database as this is our source.

Gender details about licence holders from other countries (such as Northern Ireland) are reliant upon information being captured accurately at the time of booking a test. In some cases, gender will not have been captured. Where a gender has not been captured these candidates will be recorded in total tests conducted there will therefore be small anomalies where the totals of gender do not match overall totals.

22.9b Practical motorcycle test[1] (Module 1) pass rates by gender, Great Britain: 2009/10 to 2013/14

Numbers / *Per cent*

	Male tests			Female tests			Total tests		
	Conducted	Passes	Pass rate (%)	Conducted	Passes	Pass rate (%)	Conducted	Passes	Pass rate (%)
Annually (financial years)									
2009/10[1]	44,165	28,123	63.7	6,655	2,765	41.5	50,823	30,891	60.8
2010/11	50,046	33,735	67.4	7,665	3,498	45.6	57,711	37,233	64.5
2011/12	52,726	38,325	72.7	6,868	3,706	54.0	59,594	42,031	70.5
2012/13	58,280	42,490	72.9	7,770	4,092	52.7	66,050	46,582	70.5
2013/14	41,299	29,366	71.1	4,964	2,458	49.5	46,263	31,824	68.8

Source: DVSA/DfT

1 All test data excludes mopeds.

2 The two-part modular motorcycle test was introduced on 27 April 2009. The figures for April 2009 only includes tests conducted between 27 and 30 April 2009.

Please note that all statistics are provisional until information for the whole financial year is published. Until that point, data for months / quarters from within the current financial year can be revised.

Telephone: 020 7944 3077

Email : vehicles.stats@dft.gsi.gov.uk

Notes & definitions (https://www.gov.uk/government/organisations/department-for-transport/series/driving-tests-and-instructors-statistics)

22.9c Practical motorcycle test[1] (Module 2) pass rates by gender, Great Britain: 2009/10 to 2013/14

Numbers / *Per cent*

	Male tests			Female tests			Total tests		
	Conducted	Passes	Pass rate (%)	Conducted	Passes	Pass rate (%)	Conducted	Passes	Pass rate (%)
Annually (financial years)									
2009/10[1]	34,550	24,122	69.8	3,363	2,352	69.9	37,914	26,474	69.8
2010/11	44,991	31,236	69.4	4,654	3,249	69.8	49,645	34,485	69.5
2011/12	52,619	36,367	69.1	5,292	3,559	67.3	57,911	39,926	68.9
2012/13	59,237	40,871	69.0	5,891	4,018	68.2	65,128	44,889	68.9
2013/14	40,052	28,110	70.2	3,423	2,343	68.4	43,475	30,453	70.0

Source: DVSA/DfT

1 All test data excludes mopeds.

2 The two-part modular motorcycle test was introduced on 27 April 2009. The figures for April 2009 only includes tests conducted between 27 and 30 April 2009.

Please note that all statistics are provisional until information for the whole financial year is published. Until that point, data for months / quarters from within thecurrent financial year can be revised.

Telephone: 020 7944 3077

Email : vehicles.stats@dft.gsi.gov.uk

Notes & definitions (https://www.gov.uk/government/organisations/department-for-transport/series/driving-tests-and-instructors-statistics)

22.9d Practical large goods vehicle (LGV) CPC test[1] rates by gender, Great Britain: 2009/10 to 2013/14

Numbers / *Per cent*

	Male tests			Female tests			Total tests		
	Conducted	Passes	Pass rate (%)	Conducted	Passes	Pass rate (%)	Conducted	Passes	Pass rate (%)
Annually (financial years)									
2009/10	1,778	1,322	74.4	45	37	82.2	1,823	1,359	74.5
2010/11	6,361	5,070	79.7	194	162	83.5	6,556	5,233	79.8
2011/12	7,724	6,410	83.0	244	202	82.8	7,970	6,614	83.0
2012/13	9,336	8,015	85.9	305	267	87.5	9,641	8,282	85.9
2013/14	11,388	9,957	87.4	395	342	86.6	11,784	10,300	87.4

1. Includes all LGV CPC mod 4 tests   Source: DVSA/DfT

Please note that all statistics are provisional until information for the whole financial year is published. Until that point, data for months / quarters from within the current financial year can be revised.

Telephone: 020 7944 3077

Email : vehicles.stats@dft.gsi.gov.uk

Notes & definitions (https://www.gov.uk/government/organisations/department-for-transport/series/driving-tests-and-instructors-statistics)

22.9e Practical passenger carrying vehicle (PCV) CPC test[1] rates by gender, Great Britain: 2008/09 to 2013/14

Numbers / *Per cent*

	Male tests			Female tests			Total tests		
	Conducted	Passes	Pass rate (%)	Conducted	Passes	Pass rate (%)	Conducted	Passes	Pass rate (%)
Annually (financial years)									
2008/09	1,089	763	70.1	123	92	74.8	1,212	855	70.5
2009/10	2,436	1,881	77.2	273	225	82.4	2,709	2,106	77.7
2010/11	2,280	1,892	83.0	265	230	86.8	2,545	2,122	83.4
2011/12	2,177	1,852	85.1	296	263	88.9	2,474	2,116	85.5
2012/13	2,626	2,254	85.8	309	259	83.8	2,935	2,513	85.6
2013/14	3,179	2,760	86.8	372	330	88.7	3,551	3,090	87.0

1. Includes all PCV CPC mod 4 tests   Source: DVSA/DfT

Please note that all statistics are provisional until information for the whole financial year is published. Until that point, data for months / quarters from within the current financial year can be revised.

Telephone: 020 7944 3077

Email : vehicles.stats@dft.gsi.gov.uk

Notes & definitions (https://www.gov.uk/government/organisations/department-for-transport/series/driving-tests-and-instructors-statistics)

22.10 Full car driving licence holders by age and gender: England, 1975/76 to 2013

	All aged 17+	17-20	21-29	30-39	40-49	50-59	60-69	70+	Estimated licence holders (millions)	Unweighted sample size (individuals aged 17+)
All adults:										
1975/76	48	28	59	67	60	50	35	15	19.4	17,064
1985/86	57	33	63	74	71	60	47	27	24.3	19,835
1989/91[1]	64	44	74	78	79	68	55	32	24.1	17,466
1992/94	67	48	75	82	80	74	59	33	25.4	16,401
1995/97[2]	69	44	74	82	82	76	64	39	26.3	16,716
1998/00	71	41	75	85	83	78	68	40	27.3	17,156
2002	71	32	67	83	83	81	70	45	27.6	13,836
2003	71	29	67	82	84	81	72	44	27.8	14,556
2004	70	27	65	82	83	81	73	46	27.8	14,228
2005	72	31	65	82	84	83	75	52	28.8	15,063
2006	72	35	67	82	84	82	76	51	29.3	14,815
2007	72	38	66	81	84	82	76	53	29.5	14,693
2008	73	36	64	83	84	83	78	53	30.0	14,290
2009	73	36	64	80	84	83	80	55	30.2	14,791
2010	73	33	63	81	85	83	80	57	30.6	14,118
2011	72	31	64	78	84	83	80	59	30.7	13,723
2012	73	36	64	78	85	82	80	59	31.1	14,578
2013	74	31	66	80	85	84	82	62	31.9	14,694
Males:										
1975/76	69	36	78	85	83	75	58	32	13.4	8,113
1985/86	74	37	73	86	87	81	72	51	15.1	9,367
1989/91[1]	80	54	83	88	90	86	79	58	14.5	8,306
1992/94	82	55	83	90	89	88	82	59	14.8	7,652
1995/97[2]	82	51	81	90	89	89	83	65	14.9	7,934
1998/00	82	44	81	90	91	89	83	66	15.2	8,117
2002	80	34	72	89	89	89	85	68	15.2	6,586
2003	81	34	72	87	91	91	88	69	15.4	6,950
2004	80	29	69	87	89	90	87	72	15.3	6,723
2005	81	36	68	86	90	91	88	74	15.7	7,159
2006	81	37	71	87	88	90	90	77	15.9	7,078
2007	81	41	69	86	90	90	88	77	16.0	6,978
2008	81	36	67	88	90	91	90	75	16.2	6,818
2009	80	38	67	85	89	91	91	77	16.3	7,021
2010	80	34	66	86	90	89	90	78	16.4	6,769
2011	80	31	68	81	89	90	90	79	16.4	6,521
2012	80	40	67	81	88	89	90	80	16.6	6,981
2013	81	30	67	83	90	90	91	82	16.9	7,048
Females:										
1975/76	29	20	43	48	37	24	15	4	6.0	8,951
1985/86	41	29	54	62	56	41	24	11	9.2	10,468
1989/91[1]	50	35	65	68	67	50	33	15	9.7	9,160
1992/94	55	42	69	74	71	59	38	16	10.8	8,749
1995/97[2]	58	36	68	74	74	63	46	22	11.4	8,781
1998/00	61	38	70	79	75	67	54	22	12.1	9,039
2002	61	30	62	77	77	74	55	28	12.5	7,250
2003	61	24	62	77	77	71	58	26	12.4	7,606
2004	61	24	61	77	77	71	60	28	12.5	7,505
2005	64	26	61	77	79	75	62	36	13.2	7,904
2006	64	32	62	78	80	74	64	32	13.4	7,737
2007	64	35	63	76	78	74	64	36	13.4	7,715
2008	65	35	61	78	80	76	67	37	13.8	7,472
2009	65	33	62	76	79	75	69	38	13.9	7,770
2010	66	32	60	77	80	77	70	41	14.2	7,349
2011	66	30	59	74	79	76	71	44	14.3	7,202
2012	66	31	62	75	81	75	71	43	14.5	7,597
2013	68	31	64	77	80	77	73	47	14.9	7,646

1 Figures prior to 1989 for Great Britain, rather than England only.
2 Figures prior to 1995 are based on unweighted data.

Source: National Travel Survey
Telephone: 020 7944 3097
Email: national.travelsurvey@dft.gsi.gov.uk

Notes and definitions: https://www.gov.uk/government/publications/national-travel-survey-2013
The figures in this table are National Statistics

The results presented in this table are weighted. The base (unweighted sample size) is shown in the table for information.
Weights are applied to adjust for non-response to ensure the characteristics of the achieved sample match the population of Great Britain (1995-2012) or England (2013 onwards) and for the drop off in trip recording in diary data.
The survey results are subject to sampling error.

22.11a Household car availability: Great Britain 2002 to 2013 and England 2013

Percentage/number

Year	No car / van	One car / van	Two or more cars / vans	All households	Cars / vans per household	Cars / vans per adult (17+)	Unweighted sample size (households
			Percentage				
2002	26	44	30	100	1.09	0.59	7,535
2003	26	42	31	100	1.11	0.60	7,853
2004	25	44	30	100	1.11	0.59	7,692
2005	25	43	33	100	1.16	0.61	8,065
2006	24	44	32	100	1.16	0.61	7,884
2007	25	43	33	100	1.16	0.61	7,879
2008	25	43	33	100	1.15	0.61	7,665
2009	25	43	32	100	1.15	0.60	7,858
2010	25	42	33	100	1.17	0.61	7,534
2011	25	43	32	100	1.15	0.60	7,289
2012	25	44	31	100	1.14	0.60	7,724
2013	25	43	32	100	1.15	0.60	7,820

Source: National Travel Survey
Telephone: 020 7944 3097
Email: national.travelsurvey@dft.gsi.gov.uk

The results presented in this table are weighted. The base (unweighted sample size) is shown in the table for information. Weights are applied to adjust for non-response to ensure the characteristics of the achieved sample match the population of Great Britain (1995-2012) or England (2013 onwards) and for the drop off in trip recording in diary data.
The survey results are subject to sampling error.

The figures in this table are National Statistics
Note and definitions: https://www.gov.uk/government/publications/national-travel-survey-2013

22.11b Household car ownership by region and area type: Great Britain, 1995/97[1] and 2011/12[2]

Percentage /number

	No car / van		One car / van		Two or more cars / vans		Cars / vans per household		Unweighted sample size (households)	
	1995/97	2011/12	1995/97	2011/12	1995/97	2011/12	1995/97	2011/12	1995/97	2011/12
Region of residence:										
North East	45	29	41	41	14	30	0.70	1.08	490	816
North West	31	28	44	43	25	29	0.99	1.07	1,292	2,114
Yorkshire and The Humber	34	25	45	44	21	31	0.90	1.12	886	1,440
East Midlands	28	20	40	45	31	34	1.09	1.21	770	1,298
West Midlands	29	21	42	43	28	35	1.05	1.22	975	1,562
East of England	22	18	47	44	31	37	1.17	1.30	740	1,714
London	39	45	43	40	17	16	0.81	0.75	1,387	2,155
South East	21	16	45	45	34	40	1.20	1.32	1,544	2,367
South West	22	17	48	48	30	36	1.16	1.28	898	1,547
England	30	25	44	44	26	32	1.02	1.14	8,982	15,013
Wales	32	24	44	40	24	36	0.97	1.22	534	860
Scotland	38	29	45	43	17	27	0.81	1.06	945	1,558
Great Britain excluding London	29	22	44	44	27	34	1.03	1.20	9,074	15,276
Great Britain	30	25	44	43	25	31	1.00	1.14	10,461	17,431
Area type of residence:										
London Boroughs	39	45	43	40	17	16	0.81	0.75	1,387	2,155
Metropolitan built-up areas	40	33	40	42	20	25	0.83	0.97	1,635	2,736
Large urban (over 250k population)	35	27	44	43	22	30	0.92	1.09	1,494	2,441
Medium urban (25k to 250k population)	29	23	46	47	24	30	1.00	1.14	2,834	4,419
Small / medium urban (10k to 25k population)[3]	25	19	47	47	28	34	1.07	1.23	947	1,631
Small urban (3k to 10k population)[3]	20	16	45	46	35	38	1.22	1.30	1,023	1,223
Rural areas	15	9	45	40	40	52	1.36	1.58	1,141	2,826
All areas	30	25	44	43	25	31	1.00	1.14	10,461	17,431

Source: National Travel Survey
Telephone: 020 7944 3097
Email: national.travelsurvey@dft.gsi.gov.uk

1 Three calendar years combined, e.g. 1995, 1996 and 1997.
2 Two survey years combined, e.g. 2011 and 2012. A survey year runs from mid-January to mid-January.
3 Due to a change in the definition of small urban areas used in data collection after 1995, some additional assumptions have been used to provide these estimates for comparison.

Notes & definitions (including information about revisions) https://www.gov.uk/government/publications/national-travel-survey-2012
The figures in this table are National Statistics

Note: The results presented in this table are weighted. The base (unweighted sample size) is shown in the table for information. Weights are applied to adjust for non-response to ensure the characteristics of the achieved sample match the population of Great Britain and for the drop off in trip recording. The survey results are subject to sampling error.

22.12 Vehicles currently licensed by taxation group: 2009-2013 Northern Ireland

Number at 31 December

Taxation Group (Taxation Classes)	2009		2010		2011		2012[r]		2013	
	Number	%	Number	%	Number	%	Number	%	Number	%
Private Light Goods (11, 36, 39, 48, 49, 59, 91, 92)	873,562	83.7	877,034	83.5	879,787	83.5	885,976	83.6	901,357	84.5
Motorcycles, Scooters & Mopeds (17, 18, 93)	28,080	2.7	26,771	2.5	25,196	2.4	23,560	2.2	22,745	2.1
General (HGV) Goods (1, 2, 10, 23, 45, 46, 53)	24,534	2.4	23,863	2.3	23,084	2.2	22,114	2.1	22,052	2.1
Bus (34, 38)	2,987	0.3	3,035	0.3	3,015	0.3	3,094	0.3	3,315	0.3
Agricultural/Tractors (40 & 44)	15,526	1.5	17,059	1.6	18,555	1.8	19,775	1.9	20,784	1.9
Other (14-16, 19, 37, 47, 50, 55-58, 79, 81, 82)	2,244	0.2	2,180	0.2	2,159	0.2	2,154	0.2	2,200	0.2
Crown (60)	7,215	0.7	7,488	0.7	7,646	0.7	7,862	0.7	1,936	0.2
Exempt (>60 except 79, 81, 82, 91, 92, 93)	89,757	8.6	93,051	8.9	93,896	8.9	95,793	9.0	92,115	8.6
All Vehicles	**1,043,905**	**100.0**	**1,050,481**	**100.0**	**1,053,338**	**100.0**	**1,060,328**	**100.0**	**1,066,504**	**100.0**

Source: Driver and Vehicle Agency (DVA);
N.I Transport Statistics

22.13   Motor vehicles registered for the first time in NI by vehicle type: 2009-2013

Number at 31 December

Vehicle type	2009	2010	2011	2012	2013
Private cars					
New cars	42,693	42,416	35,330	36,365	40,353
New cars exempt - Govt owned	12	8	29	3	22
New cars exempt - Non Govt owned	10,154	12,019	12,407	11,622	12,576
Used cars	32,901	29,422	29,070	30,625	33,955
Used cars exempt - Govt owned	1	1	0	1	0
Used cars exempt - Non Govt owned	1,182	1,027	1,059	975	859
All private cars	**86,943**	**84,893**	**77,895**	**79,591**	**87,765**
Buses	**477**	**486**	**319**	**411**	**584**
Light goods					
Light goods	9,139	7,807	8,645	8,179	9,175
Light goods exempt - Govt owned	34	38	24	74	27
Light goods exempt - Non Govt owned	208	213	315	356	371
All light goods	**9,381**	**8,058**	**8,984**	**8,609**	**9,573**
Heavy goods					
Heavy goods	2,797	2,546	2,462	2,453	2,878
Heavy goods exempt - Govt owned	46	17	5	24	29
Heavy goods exempt - Non Govt owned	77	43	42	54	66
All heavy goods	**2,920**	**2,606**	**2,509**	**2,531**	**2,973**
Tractors					
Tractors	3	0	2	1	5
Tractors exempt - Govt Owned	0	10	2	6	2
Tractors exempt - Non Govt owned	1,811	1,953	1,981	2,092	2,015
All tractors	**1,814**	**1,963**	**1,985**	**2,099**	**2,022**
Motorcycles					
Motorcycles	3,403	2,528	2,009	1,874	1,908
Motorcycles exempt - Govt owned	29	22	19	0	1
Motorcycles exempt - Non Govt owned	129	98	170	137	139
All motorcycles	**3,561**	**2,648**	**2,198**	**2,011**	**2,048**
Other exempt	**0**	**0**	**0**	**0**	**0**
Other non exempt	**0**	**0**	**0**	**0**	**0**
General Haulage and Special Types	**26**	**25**	**23**	**15**	**21**
All vehicles	**105,122**	**100,679**	**93,913**	**95,267**	**104,986**

Source: DVA;
N.I Transport Statistics

22.14 Vehicle kilometres on local bus services by metropolitan area status and country: Great Britain, 2000/01 to 2013/14

Millions

Year	Estimation method[1]	London	English metropolitan areas	English non-metropolitan areas	England	Scotland	Wales	Great Britain	England outside London
2000/01		371	654	1,134	2,158	369	126	2,653	1,788
2001/02		381	646	1,102	2,129	368	126	2,622	1,748
2002/03		404	630	1,088	2,122	374	123	2,619	1,718
2003/04		444	596	1,069	2,109	369	113	2,590	1,665
2004/05	Old	..	575	1,077	2,122	357	116	2,594	1,652
2004/05 R	New	470	592	1,061	2,122	359	130	2,611	1,653
2005/06 R		461	589	1,071	2,121	374	128	2,623	1,660
2006/07 R		465	591	1,066	2,122	384	124	2,630	1,657
2007/08 R		465	597	1,068	2,129	397	124	2,650	1,665
2008/09 R		474	589	1,077	2,139	386	126	2,651	1,666
2009/10 R		479	569	1,071	2,119	377	125	2,620	1,640
2010/11 R		481	567	1,073	2,121	346	125	2,592	1,640
2011/12 R		485	563	1,055	2,103	338	117	2,559	1,618
2012/13 R		486	554	1,052	2,092	327	117	2,535	1,606
2013/14		486	547	1,052	2,085	330	114	2,529	1,599

Source: DfT Public Service Vehicle Survey, Transport for London
Telephone: 020 7944 3094
Email: bus.statistics@dft.gsi.gov.uk

1 Break in the local bus series (outside London) due to changes in the estimation methodology from 2004/05

2 Deregulation of the bus market took place in October 1986. For more information see the technical information

R Previously published figures have been revised. For details of the revisions (which include planned updates) please see the technical information

Notes and definitions http://www.dft.gov.uk/statistics/series/buses/
The figures in this table are National Statistics

22.15 Local bus fares index (at current prices[2]) by metropolitan area status and country: Great Britain, annual from 2000

March 2005=100

Year[1]	All items Retail Prices Index[3]	Local bus fares index							England outside London
		London	English metropolitan areas	English non-metropolitan areas	England	Scotland	Wales	Great Britain	
2000	88.4	83.2	79.1	78.4	79.6	89.6	80.3	80.9	78.7
2001	90.4	83.9	83.3	82.7	82.9	92.2	84.7	84.1	82.9
2002	91.6	81.5	87.3	86.6	85.3	93.5	88.6	86.4	86.9
2003	94.4	81.8	90.3	90.8	88.0	96.1	91.6	89.2	90.6
2004	96.9	86.9	94.7	95.3	92.7	97.1	95.8	93.4	95.1
2005	100.0	100.0	100.0	100.0	100.0	100.0	100.0	100.0	100.0
2006	102.4	105.7	111.9	107.8	108.3	105.1	105.0	107.9	109.6
2007	107.3	116.6	113.6	102.0	110.2	111.4	111.5	110.4	106.9
2008	111.3	111.2	121.6	106.7	112.8	116.7	117.5	113.4	113.0
2009	110.9	120.0	136.5	113.9	122.5	126.5	125.3	123.1	123.2
2010	115.9	135.2	137.6	115.6	128.8	129.5	128.7	129.0	124.7
2011	122.0	144.5	146.4	119.4	135.7	132.2	130.1	135.2	130.3
2012	126.4	152.3	156.2	127.0	144.0	139.1	137.8	143.4	138.9
2013	130.6	159.4	161.3	134.3	150.8	145.1	147.2	150.1	145.4
2014	133.8	164.3	165.3	138.9	155.5	149.8	149.5	154.7	149.8

1 Index as at March.
2 Not adjusted for inflation.
3 These figures are not National Statistics

Source: DfT Fares Survey, Office for National Statistics
Telephone: 020 7944 3094
Email: bus.statistics@dft.gsi.gov.uk

Bus Statistics - Notes & Definitions (https://www.gov.uk/government/publications/buses-statistics-guidance)
The figures in this table are National Statistics except where indicated

22.16 Reported road accident casualties by road user type and severity, Great Britain, 2003-2013

Number of casualties

	2003	2004	2005	2006	2007	2008	2009	2010	2011	2012	2013
Pedestrians											
Killed	774	671	671	675	646	572	500	405	453	420	398
KSI[1]	7,933	7,478	7,129	7,051	6,924	6,642	6,045	5,605	5,907	5,979	5,396
All severities	36,405	34,881	33,281	30,982	30,191	28,482	26,887	25,845	26,198	25,218	24,033
of which, children [2]											
Killed	74	77	63	71	57	57	37	26	33	20	26
KSI	2,381	2,339	2,134	2,025	1,899	1,784	1,660	1,646	1,602	1,545	1,358
All severities	12,544	12,234	11,250	10,131	9,527	8,648	7,983	7,929	7,807	6,999	6,396
Pedal cyclists											
Killed	114	134	148	146	136	115	104	111	107	118	109
KSI	2,411	2,308	2,360	2,442	2,564	2,565	2,710	2,771	3,192	3,340	3,252
All severities	17,033	16,648	16,561	16,196	16,195	16,297	17,064	17,185	19,215	19,091	19,438
of which, children											
Killed	18	25	20	31	13	12	14	7	6	13	6
KSI	595	577	527	503	522	417	458	398	398	324	282
All severities	4,769	4,682	4,286	3,765	3,633	3,306	3,204	2,828	2,881	2,198	1,958
Motorcyclists users [3]											
Killed	105	83	569	599	588	493	472	403	362	328	331
KSI	2,474	2,301	6,508	6,484	6,737	6,049	5,822	5,183	5,609	5,328	5,197
All severities	12,459	11,885	24,824	23,326	23,459	21,550	20,703	18,686	20,150	19,310	18,752
Car occupants											
Killed	16	8	1,675	1,612	1,432	1,257	1,059	835	883	801	785
KSI	100	99	14,617	14,254	12,967	11,968	11,112	9,749	9,225	9,033	8,426
All severities	1,100	1,001	178,302	171,000	161,433	149,188	143,412	133,205	124,924	119,708	109,787
Bus and coach occupants											
Killed	11	20	9	19	12	6	14	9	7	11	10
KSI	500	488	363	426	455	432	370	401	332	323	342
All severities	9,068	8,820	7,920	7,253	7,079	6,929	6,317	6,268	6,177	5,234	4,873
Van occupants											
Killed	72	62	54	52	58	43	36	34	34	33	37
KSI	765	631	587	564	494	445	417	359	340	363	371
All severities	6,897	6,166	6,048	5,914	5,340	4,913	4,743	4,494	4,499	4,533	4,426
HGV occupants											
Killed	44	47	55	39	52	23	14	28	28	29	21
KSI	429	406	395	383	363	240	189	212	195	198	168
All severities	3,061	2,883	2,843	2,530	2,476	1,930	1,519	1,578	1,415	1,339	1,296
All road users [4]											
Killed	3,508	3,221	3,201	3,172	2,946	2,538	2,222	1,850	1,901	1,754	1,713
KSI	37,215	34,351	32,155	31,845	30,720	28,572	26,912	24,510	25,023	24,793	23,370
All severities	290,607	280,840	271,017	258,404	247,780	230,905	222,146	208,648	203,950	195,723	183,670

1. Killed and seriously injured.
2. Casualties aged 0 -15.
3. Includes mopeds and scooters.
4. Includes other motor or non-motor vehicle users, and unknown road user type and casualty age

Source: DfT STATS19
Telephone: 020 7944 6595
Email: roadacc.stats@dft.gsi.gov.uk

The figures in this table are National Statistics

note and definitions
https://www.gov.uk/government/uploads/system/uploads/attachment_data/file/48822/reported-road-casualties-gb-notes-definitions.pd

22.17a Goods lifted and goods moved by mode of working: by GB HGVs in the UK
UK activity of GB registered heavy goods vehicles

	Tonnes lifted (millions)					Tonne kilometres (billions)				
Year	Mainly public haulage	% of total	Mainly own account	% of total	All modes	Mainly public haulage	% of total	Mainly own account	% of total	All modes
1999	991	64	576	36	1,567	111	75	38	25	149
2000	1,038	65	556	35	1,593	113	75	37	25	150
2001	1,052	67	529	33	1,581	115	77	35	23	149
2002	1,019	63	608	37	1,627	111	74	39	26	150
2003	1,053	64	590	36	1,643	114	75	37	25	152
2004	1,101	63	643	37	1,744	111	73	41	27	152
2005	1,079	62	667	38	1,746	110	72	43	28	153
2006	1,104	62	671	38	1,776	110	72	43	28	152
2007	1,116	61	706	39	1,822	113	72	45	28	157
2008	948	57	720	43	1,668	99	68	47	32	146
2009	690	51	666	49	1,356	77	62	48	38	125
2010	800	54	689	46	1,489	89	64	50	36	139
2011	789	51	770	49	1,559	86	60	59	40	145
2012	858	54	729	46	1,587	97	65	53	35	150

Source: Continuing Survey of Road Goods Transport (Great Britain)
Telephone: 020 7944 3903
Email: roadfreight.stats@dft.gsi.gov.uk

Note: discontinuities in the series (denoted by lines) are described in detail within the methodology note; comparisons across years where methodological changes have occurred should be treated with caution.
Methodology note: https://www.gov.uk/government/collections/road-freight-domestic-and-international-statistics

Notes & definitions
https://www.gov.uk/government/collections/road-freight-domestic-and-international-statistics

22.17b Goods moved by type and weight of vehicle: by GB HGVs in the UK
UK activity of GB registered heavy goods vehicles

Billion tonne kilometres

	Rigids					Articulated vehicles			
Year	Over 3.5t to 7.5t	Over 7.5t to 17t	Over 17t to 25t	Over 25t	All Rigids	Over 3.5t to 33t	Over 33t	All artics	All vehicles
1999	5	13	4	15	37	14	98	112	149
2000	5	11	5	15	36	14	100	114	150
2001	5	9	6	16	34	13	102	115	149
2002	5	7	6	17	36	10	104	114	150
2003	4	6	7	18	35	9	108	116	152
2004	4	5	7	19	36	7	109	116	152
2005	4	4	8	21	37	6	110	116	153
2006	4	3	8	20	36	6	111	117	152
2007	3	3	9	22	37	6	115	120	157
2008	3	2	8	20	33	5	108	113	146
2009	3	2	7	17	30	5	91	96	125
2010	3	2	7	18	31	4	104	108	139
2011	3	2	8	23	36	5	105	109	145
2012	3	2	8	22	35	4	111	115	150

Source: Continuing Survey of Road Goods Transport (Great Britain)
Telephone: 020 7944 3903
Email: roadfreight.stats@dft.gsi.gov.uk

Note: discontinuities in the series (denoted by lines) are described in detail within the methodology note; comparisons across years where methodological changes have occurred should be treated with caution.
Methodology note: https://www.gov.uk/government/collections/road-freight-domestic-and-international-statistics

Notes & definitions
https://www.gov.uk/government/collections/road-freight-domestic-and-international-statistics

22.17c Goods moved by commodity[1]
UK activity of GB registered heavy goods vehicles

Billion tonne kilometres

Commodity	2004	2005	2006	2007	2008	2009	2010	2011	2012
Products of agriculture, forestry, raw materials									
Agricultural products	12.8	11.9	11.5	12.3	11.7	10.1	10.7	11.8	13.1
Coal and lignite	1.2	1.5	1.4	1.5	1.7	1.2	1.5	0.7	1.0
Metal ore and other mining and quarrying	15.1	16.3	16.3	16.8	14.4	11.5	13.6	10.9	12.5
Subtotal	**29.1**	**29.6**	**29.2**	**30.6**	**27.9**	**22.8**	**25.8**	**23.5**	**26.5**
Food products, includ. beverages and tobacco									
Food products	30.3	29.9	30.7	32.8	31.2	32.2	34.3	33.7	38.2
Textile, leather and wood products									
Textiles and textile products; leather and leather products	2.0	1.9	2.2	2.2	1.6	2.0	2.0	1.5	1.4
Wood products	13.4	12.6	12.8	11.8	10.6	9.0	10.3	9.3	7.9
Subtotal	**15.4**	**14.5**	**15.0**	**14.0**	**12.3**	**11.0**	**12.3**	**10.8**	**9.3**
Metal, mineral and chemical products									
Coke and refined petroleum products	5.7	5.5	5.4	5.0	5.5	4.3	5.9	5.8	7.1
Chemical products	7.0	8.8	7.1	7.7	6.9	6.1	5.9	7.8	7.7
Glass, cement and other non-metallic mineral products	12.2	11.0	11.5	11.5	10.8	8.2	9.1	9.8	8.1
Metal products	7.3	7.3	6.7	8.2	5.7	4.9	5.0	5.1	7.2
Subtotal	**32.2**	**32.5**	**30.7**	**32.4**	**28.9**	**23.6**	**25.9**	**28.4**	**30.0**
Machinery and equipment, consumer durables									
Machinery and equipment	4.2	4.5	4.5	4.8	4.1	3.6	3.7	4.1	3.4
Transport equipment	4.7	4.7	4.7	4.5	4.4	3.3	3.8	3.7	4.3
Furniture	6.5	5.9	5.8	5.8	4.3	3.4	2.9	2.5	2.4
Subtotal	**15.4**	**15.2**	**15.1**	**15.1**	**12.8**	**10.3**	**10.4**	**10.2**	**10.2**
Other products									
Waste related products	5.5	6.4	6.4	7.4	6.3	4.6	5.6	9.3	9.0
Mail, parcels	4.3	4.1	4.2	3.6	3.8	3.0	3.9	5.8	4.3
Empty containers, pallets and other packaging	3.6	3.4	3.4	3.5	3.7	3.7	3.9	3.9	4.4
Household and office removals	0.1	0.2	0.2	0.1	0.1	~	0.1	1.0	1.6
Grouped goods	16.1	16.7	17.6	17.8	18.9	13.9	16.7	16.8	15.5
Unidentifiable goods	0.1	0.1	:	:	:	:	:	1.8	1.2
Other goods	:	:	:	:	:	:	:	:	~
Subtotal	**29.7**	**30.9**	**31.8**	**32.4**	**32.8**	**25.3**	**30.2**	**38.6**	**36.0**
All commodities	**152.1**	**152.6**	**152.4**	**157.3**	**145.8**	**125.2**	**138.9**	**145.2**	**150.1**

Source: Continuing Survey of Road Goods Transport (Great Britain)
Telephone: 020 7944 3903
Email: roadfreight.stats@dft.gsi.gov.uk

1. The commodity groups have been revised since the last publication
':' = none recorded in the sample or not available due to small sample size
'~' = rounds to zero but different from a real zero

Note: discontinuities in the series (denoted by lines) are described in detail within the methodology note; comparisons across years where methodological changes have occurred should be treated with caution.

Methodology note https://www.gov.uk/government/collections/road-freight-domestic-and-international-statistics

Notes & definitions
https://www.gov.uk/government/collections/road-freight-domestic-and-international-statistics

22.18a Goods lifted by type and weight of vehicle: by GB HGVs in the UK
UK activity of GB registered heavy goods vehicles

Million tonnes

Year	Rigids					Articulated vehicles			
	Over 3.5t to 7.5t	Over 7.5t to 17t	Over 17t to 25t	Over 25t	All Rigids	Over 3.5t to 33t	Over 33t	All artics	All vehicles
2000	77	152	87	424	741	107	746	852	1,593
2001	80	123	86	443	733	97	751	848	1,581
2002	77	111	90	491	768	81	778	859	1,627
2003	70	89	100	506	765	69	809	878	1,643
2004	77	87	108	540	812	59	873	932	1,744
2005	70	70	110	562	812	51	883	934	1,746
2006	64	64	118	585	831	49	896	945	1,776
2007	54	52	127	614	848	49	926	975	1,822
2008	56	44	118	513	731	44	892	937	1,668
2009	56	37	102	377	572	38	746	785	1,356
2010	54	37	103	414	607	33	848	881	1,489
2011	55	36	108	479	677	39	844	883	1,559
2012	50	29	112	454	645	37	905	942	1,587

Source: Continuing Survey of Road Goods Transport (Great Britain)
Telephone: 020 7944 3903
Email: roadfreight.stats@dft.gsi.gov.uk

Note: discontinuities in the series (denoted by lines) are described in detail within the methodology note; comparisons across years where methodological changes have occurred should be treated with caution.

Methodology note: https://www.gov.uk/government/collections/road-freight-domestic-and-international-statistics

Notes & definitions
https://www.gov.uk/government/collections/road-freight-domestic-and-international-statistics

22.18b Goods lifted by commodity[1]
UK activity of GB registered heavy goods vehicles

Million tonnes

Commodity	2004	2005	2006	2007	2008	2009	2010	2011	2012
Products of agriculture, forestry, raw materials									
Agricultural products	117	112	103	107	102	100	106	111	119
Coal and lignite	12	20	17	23	21	13	12	9	10
Metal ore and other mining and quarrying	381	394	390	398	335	234	270	232	236
Subtotal	**510**	**526**	**510**	**529**	**458**	**347**	**389**	**352**	**365**
Food products, includ. beverages and tobacco									
Food products	245	236	257	266	261	259	285	295	311
Textile, leather and wood products									
Textiles and textile products; leather and leather products	15	14	15	13	11	15	15	12	11
Wood products	103	95	89	92	89	71	74	67	59
Subtotal	**118**	**109**	**104**	**104**	**100**	**85**	**89**	**78**	**70**
Metal, mineral and chemical products									
Coke and refined petroleum products	68	69	66	69	69	53	67	66	82
Chemical products	53	64	55	56	53	46	44	63	57
Glass, cement and other non-metallic mineral products	187	170	177	173	173	121	140	136	121
Metal products	62	61	61	65	51	44	46	41	58
Subtotal	**369**	**364**	**360**	**363**	**346**	**264**	**296**	**306**	**318**
Machinery and equipment, consumer durables									
Machinery and equipment	38	44	46	48	40	39	39	40	32
Transport equipment	31	32	32	34	33	26	29	30	33
Furniture	43	40	41	40	29	26	22	16	16
Subtotal	**112**	**116**	**119**	**122**	**101**	**90**	**90**	**86**	**82**
Other products									
Waste related products	169	195	220	239	178	131	140	196	194
Mail, parcels	36	32	31	29	29	22	33	38	34
Empty containers, pallets and other packaging	41	39	37	41	40	36	37	40	39
Household and office removals	2	2	1	1	1	1	1	14	21
Grouped goods	140	128	135	129	152	121	128	143	145
Unidentifiable goods	2	1	:	:	:	:	:	12	8
Other goods	:	:	:	:	:	:	:	:	~
Subtotal	**389**	**396**	**426**	**439**	**401**	**310**	**340**	**442**	**441**
All commodities	**1,744**	**1,746**	**1,776**	**1,822**	**1,668**	**1,356**	**1,489**	**1,559**	**1,587**

Source: Continuing Survey of Road Goods Transport (Great Britain)
Telephone: 020 7944 3903
Email: roadfreight.stats@dft.gsi.gov.uk

1. The commodity groups have been revised since the last publication
':' = none recorded in the sample or not available due to small sample size
'~' = rounds to zero but different from a real zero

Note: discontinuities in the series (denoted by lines) are described in detail within the methodology note; comparisons across years where methodological changes have occurred should be treated with caution.

Methodology note: https://www.gov.uk/government/collections/road-freight-domestic-and-international-statistics

Notes & definitions
https://www.gov.uk/government/collections/road-freight-domestic-and-international-statistics

22.19a Passenger journeys by sector - Great Britain

Great Britain annual data from 2002-03- number of passenger journeys made (millions)

Financial year	Franchised long distance operators	Franchised London and South East operators	Franchised regional operators	Total franchised passenger journeys	Non franchised
2002-03	77.2	679.1	219.2	975.5	-
2003-04	81.5	690.0	240.2	1011.7	-
2004-05	83.7	704.5	251.3	1039.5	-
2005-06	89.5	719.7	267.3	1076.5	-
2006-07	99.0	769.5	276.5	1145.0	-
2007-08	103.9	828.4	285.8	1218.1	-
2008-09	109.4	854.3	302.8	1266.5	-
2009-10	111.6	842.2	304.0	1257.9	1.4
2010-11	117.9	917.6	318.2	1353.8	1.8
2011-12	125.3	993.8	340.9	1460.0	1.5
2012-13	127.7	1,032.4	340.9	1500.9	1.7

Source: Office of Rail and Road; LENNON Database and train operating companies

Data can be subject to revisions indicated by (R). For the latest information on data revisions, please see the revisions log: http://www.rail-reg.gov.uk/upload/xls/stats-revisions-log.xls

This dataset is used in the passenger rail usage statistical release. To view or download the statistical release: http://www.rail-reg.gov.uk/server/show/nav.3016

The quality report relating to this dataset can be found at http://www.rail-reg.gov.uk/server/show/nav.3016.

The quality report pulls together the key qualitative information on relevance, accuracy and reliability, timeliness and punctuality, accessibility and clarity and coherence and comparability. It also includes information on some additional quality principles on user needs and perceptions, confidentiality, transparency and security of data.

Passenger journeys on light rail and trams by system[1]: England

Millions

Financial year	Docklands Light Railway	Croydon Tramlink	Nottingham Express Transit	Midland Metro	Sheffield Supertram	Tyne and Wear Metro	Manchester Metrolink[2]	Blackpool Tramway	England
1998/99	27.6	.	.	.	10.4	33.8	13.2	4.4	89.3
1999/00	31.3	.	.	4.8	10.9	32.7	14.2	4.3	98.2
2000/01	38.4	15.0	.	5.4	11.1	32.5	17.2	4.1	123.6
2001/02	41.3	18.2	.	4.8	11.4	33.4	18.2	4.9	132.2
2002/03	45.7	18.7	.	4.9	11.5	36.6	18.8	4.5	140.7
2003/04	48.5	19.8	0.4	5.1	12.3	37.9	18.9	3.7	146.5
2004/05	50.1	22.0	8.5	5.0	12.8	36.8	19.7	3.9	158.7
2005/06	53.5	22.5	9.8	5.1	13.1	35.8	19.9	3.6	163.4
2006/07	63.9	24.6	10.1	4.9	14.0	37.9	19.8	3.4	178.6
2007/08	66.6	27.2	10.2	4.8	14.8	39.8	20.0	2.9	186.2
2008/09	67.8	27.2	9.8	4.7	15.0	40.6	21.1	2.3	188.6
2009/10	69.4	25.8	9.0	4.7	14.7	40.8	19.6	2.2	186.2
2010/11	78.3	27.9	9.7	4.8	15.0	39.9	19.2	1.6	196.5
2011/12	86.1	28.6	9.0	4.9	15.0	37.9	22.3	1.1	204.8
2012/13	100.0	30.1	7.4	4.8	14.4	37.0	25.0	3.7	222.5
2013/14	101.6	31.2	7.9	4.7	12.6	35.7	29.2	4.3	227.1

Source: DfT Light Rail and Tram Survey
Telephone: 020 7944 3094
Email: bus.statistics@dft.gsi.gov.uk

1 For further information on these systems including network and infrastructure changes that may affect the figures, please refer to the technical information.

2 Manchester Metrolink have revised their method for calculation of passenger boardings so the figures from 2010/11 are not directly comparable with previous years.

Notes and Definitions (www.gov.uk/transport-statistics-notes-and-guidance-light-rail-and-tram-statistics)

The figures in this table are National Statistics

22.19b Passenger revenue by sector

Great Britain annual from 2002-03 - passenger revenue by sector (£ millions)

Financial year	Franchised long distance operators	Franchised London andSouth East operators	Franchised regional operators	Total franchised passenger revenue	Non franchised
2002-03	1,279	1,848	535	3,663	-
2003-04	1,384	1,932	585	3,901	-
2004-05	1,465	2,059	634	4,158	-
2005-06	1,609	2,197	687	4,493	-
2006-07	1,842	2,437	733	5,012	-
2007-08	2,036	2,717	801	5,555	-
2008-09	2,168	2,963	872	6,004	-
2009-10	2,216	3,046	916	6,179	36.7
2010-11	2,366	3,264	990	6,620	45.5
2011-12	2,533	3,602	1,094	7,229	43.9
2012-13	2,652	3,888	1,167	7,707	49.9

Source: Office for Rail and Road; LENNON database and train operating companies

Data can be subject to revisions indicated by (R). For the latest information on data revisions, please see the revisions log: http://www.rail-reg.gov.uk/upload/xls/stats-revisions-log.xls

This dataset is used in the passenger rail usage statistical release. To view or download the statistical release: http://www.rail-reg.gov.uk/server/show/nav.3016

The quality report relating to this dataset can be found at http://www.rail-reg.gov.uk/server/show/nav.3016.

The quality report pulls together the key qualitative information on relevance, accuracy and reliability, timeliness and punctuality, accessibility and clarity and coherence and comparability. It also includes information on some additional quality principles on user needs and perceptions, confidentiality, transparency and security of data.

Passenger revenue at 2014/15 prices[1] on light rail and trams by system[2]: England

£ Millions

Financial year	Docklands Light Railway	London Tramlink	Nottingham Express Transit	Midland Metro	Sheffield Supertram	Tyne and Wear Metro	Manchester Metrolink	Blackpool Tramway	England
1998/99	28.6	:	:	:	8.7	32.3	22.1	6.0	97.7
1999/00	29.7	:	:	3.5	9.6	32.9	24.0	6.0	105.7
2000/01	39.8	16.8	:	4.3	9.8	33.4	25.1	5.9	135.0
2001/02	43.9	17.6	:	5.3	10.3	34.1	27.4	6.4	145.0
2002/03	47.3	19.9	:	6.6	13.5	38.1	27.8	6.1	159.2
2003/04	48.4	21.0	:	6.7	12.0	40.9	27.2	5.1	161.3
2004/05	50.9	22.7	7.4	6.9	13.9	41.0	27.9	5.4	176.2
2005/06	56.5	23.1	9.0	7.3	12.8	42.2	27.8	5.3	183.9
2006/07	64.3	22.6	9.0	7.5	14.8	42.0	28.2	5.4	193.8
2007/08	73.2	24.2	9.2	7.3	15.9	43.3	26.0	4.6	203.6
2008/09	72.4	20.5	9.7	7.5	17.2	46.7	25.4	3.9	203.3
2009/10	82.6	17.9	8.7	7.2	16.6	45.0	25.9	3.3	207.1
2010/11	95.3	20.5	9.7	7.5	16.4	44.6	29.4	2.6	226.1
2011/12	111.1	22.4	8.9	7.8	16.2	44.5	35.5	1.8	248.2
2012/13	129.6	23.4	8.8	8.1	15.0	45.3	43.5	5.2	278.8

Source: DfT Light Rail and Tram Survey
Telephone: 020 7944 3094
Email: bus.statistics@dft.gsi.gov.uk

[1] Adjusted for inflation using the GDP market price deflator (as at 31 March 2015).

[2] For further information on these systems including infrastructure changes that may affect the figures, please refer to the technical information.

Notes and Definitions
https://www.gov.uk/government/publications/light-rail-and-tram-statistics-guidance
The figures in this table are National Statistics

22.19c Passenger kilometres by sector

Great Britain annual from 2002-03- number of passenger kilometres travelled (billions)

Financial year	Franchised long distance operators	Franchised London and South East operators	Franchised regional operators	Total franchised passenger kilometres	Non franchised
2002-03	12.9	19.8	6.9	39.7	-
2003-04	13.3	20.1	7.5	40.9	-
2004-05	13.4	20.5	7.8	41.7	-
2005-06	14.2	20.7	8.2	43.1	-
2006-07	15.6	22.2	8.4	46.2	-
2007-08	16.5	23.5	8.9	48.9	-
2008-09	17.0	24.2	9.4	50.6	-
2009-10	17.6	23.8	9.7	51.1	0.3
2010-11	18.6	25.0	10.4	54.1	0.4
2011-12	19.2	26.4	11.1	56.7	0.4
2012-13	19.5	27.3	11.0	57.8	0.4

Source: Office for Road and Rail; LENNON database and train operating companies

Data can be subject to revisions indicated by (R). For the latest information on data revisions, please see the revisions log: http://www.rail-reg.gov.uk/upload/xls/stats-revisions-log.xls

Data are provisional (P) as train operating companies can revise their data.

This dataset is used in the passenger rail usage statistical release. To view or download the statistical release: http://www.rail-reg.gov.uk/server/show/nav.3016

The quality report relating to this dataset can be found at http://www.rail-reg.gov.uk/server/show/nav.3016.

The quality report pulls together the key qualitative information on relevance, accuracy and reliability, timeliness and punctuality, accessibility and clarity and coherence and comparability. It also includes information on some additional quality principles on user needs and perceptions, confidentiality, transparency and security of data.

Passenger miles on light rail and trams by system[1]: England

Millions

Financial year	Docklands Light Railway	London Tramlink	Nottingham Express Transit	Midland Metro	Sheffield Supertram	Tyne and Wear Metro	Manchester Metrolink[2]	Blackpool Tramway[3]	England
1998/99	89.7	:	:	:	45.0	147.8	72.7	8.3	363.4
1999/00	106.9	:	:	31.0	47.3	142.9	78.3	8.1	414.6
2000/01	124.3	59.7	:	34.7	48.1	142.4	94.6	7.8	511.6
2001/02	128.5	61.5	:	31.1	49.7	148.1	100.2	9.3	528.5
2002/03	144.2	62.1	:	31.1	50.0	170.8	103.5	8.5	570.3
2003/04	146.3	65.2	1.2	33.3	53.5	176.4	105.0	7.0	588.0
2004/05	152.5	69.7	23.0	32.5	55.7	176.0	126.8	7.4	643.7
2005/06	160.0	72.7	25.9	33.5	57.0	173.4	128.0	6.9	657.4
2006/07	186.8	79.5	26.9	31.9	60.9	183.2	129.0	6.5	704.7
2007/08	202.8	87.9	27.3	31.4	64.4	194.4	130.5	5.4	744.1
2008/09	197.5	89.2	26.1	31.0	65.2	198.5	137.1	4.4	749.0
2009/10	226.5	83.5	23.6	30.8	64.0	203.2	128.1	4.1	763.8
2010/11	257.2	90.0	25.7	31.3	60.5	195.8	124.8	3.1	788.4
2011/12	283.0	92.2	24.9	31.7	60.3	188.8	141.9	2.1	824.9
2012/13	316.8	97.2	20.5	31.3	58.0	186.0	162.6	9.9	882.2

Source: DfT Light Rail and Tram Survey;
Telephone: 020 7944 3094; Email: bus.statistics@dft.gsi.gov.uk

[1] For further information on these systems including infrastructure changes that may affect the figures, please refer to the technical information.

[2] Manchester Metrolink have revised their approach calculation of passenger boardings so the figure for 2010/11 is not directly comparable with previous years.

[3] 1983/84 to 1998/99 Blackpool Tramway data are imputed. The figures use passenger journeys data and an assumed average distance.

Notes and Definitions:
https://www.gov.uk/government/publications/light-rail-and-tram-statistics-guidance

22.19d Infrastructure on the railways

Great Britain

Year	Route open for traffic (km)	Of which electrified (km)	Route Open for Passenger & Freight Traffic	Route Open for Freight Traffic Only (km)	Passenger Stations
1986-87	16,670	4,156	14,304	2,366	2,405
1987-88	16,633	4,207	14,302	2,331	2,426
1988-89	16,599	4,376	14,309	2,290	2,470
1989-90	16,587	4,546	14,318	2,269	2,471
1990-91	16,584	4,912	14,317	2,267	2,488
1991-92	16,588	4,886	14,291	2,267	2,468
1992-93	16,528	4,910	14,317	2,211	2,468
1993-94	16,536	4,968	14,357	2,179	2,493
1994-95	16,542	4,970	14,359	2,183	2,489
1995-96	16,666	5,163	15,002	1,664	2,497
1996-97	16,666	5,176	15,034	1,632	2,498
1997-98	16,656	5,166	15,024	1,632	2,495
1998-99	16,659	5,166	15,038	1,621	2,499
1999-00	16,649	5,167	15,038	1,610	2,503
2000-01	16,652	5,167	15,042	1,610	2,508
2001-02	16,652	5,167	15,042	1,610	2,508
2002-03	16,670	5,167	15,042	1,610	2,508
2003-04	16,493	5,200	14,883	1,610	2,507
2004-05	16,116	5,200	14,328	1,788	2,508
2005-06	15,810	5,205	14,356	1,454	2,510
2006-07	15,795	5,250	14,353	1,442	2,520
2007-08	15,814	5,250	14,484	1,330	2,516
2008-09	15,814	5,250	14,494	1,320	2,516
2009-10	15,753	5,239	14,482	1,271	2,516
2010-11	15,777	5,262	14,506	1,271	2,532
2011-12	15,742	5,261	14,506	1,236	2,535
2012-13	15,753	5,265	14,504	1,249	2,532

Source: Network Rail

Data can be subject to revisions indicated by (R). For the latest information on data revisions, please see the revisions log: http://www.rail-reg.gov.uk/upload/xls/stats-revisions-log.xls

This dataset is used in the rail infrastructure, assets, and environment statistical release. To view or download the statistical release: http://www.rail-reg.gov.uk/server/show/nav.3016

The quality report relating to this dataset can be found at http://www.rail-reg.gov.uk/server/show/nav.3016.

The quality report pulls together the key qualitative information on relevance, accuracy and reliability, timeliness and punctuality, accessibility and clarity and coherence and comparability. It also includes information on some additional quality principles on user needs and perceptions, confidentiality, transparency and security of data.

22.19d Vehicle miles on light rail and trams by system[1]: England

Millions

Financial year	Docklands Light Railway	London Tramlink	Nottingham Express Transit	Midland Metro	Sheffield Supertram	Tyne and Wear Metro	Manchester Metrolink[2]	Blackpool Tramway	England
1999/00	1.8	:	:	1.1	1.5	3.0	2.3	0.7	10.3
2000/01	1.8	1.3	:	1.2	1.5	2.9	2.7	0.8	12.2
2001/02	1.8	1.5	:	1.0	1.5	2.9	2.8	0.8	12.4
2002/03	2.0	1.5	:	1.1	1.6	3.9	2.9	0.7	13.7
2003/04	2.1	1.6	0.0	1.0	1.5	3.6	2.8	0.6	13.2
2004/05	2.0	1.5	0.6	1.0	1.5	3.5	2.8	0.5	13.5
2005/06	2.1	1.5	0.7	1.0	1.5	3.4	2.8	0.5	13.5
2006/07	2.7	1.6	0.7	1.0	1.5	3.6	2.3	0.6	14.1
2007/08	2.8	1.4	0.7	1.0	1.5	3.8	2.5	0.5	14.1
2008/09	2.5	1.4	0.7	1.0	1.5	3.5	2.4	0.5	13.5
2009/10	2.8	1.6	0.7	1.0	1.5	3.5	2.1	0.4	13.6
2010/11	2.9	1.6	0.7	1.0	1.5	3.5	2.3	0.3	13.9
2011/12	3.1	1.7	0.7	1.0	1.5	3.5	2.9	0.1	14.5
2012/13	3.6	1.8	0.7	1.0	1.5	3.4	3.6	0.5	16.1

Source: DfT Light Rail and Tram Survey

Telephone: 020 7944 3094

Email: bus.statistics@dft.gsi.gov.uk

[1] For further information on these systems including infrastructure changes that may affect the figures, please refer to the technical information.

[2] Figures for Manchester Metrolink represent total mileage of each tram 'set'. Where two sets are joined to form one train, the vehicle miles run will therefore be counted twice. Based on information supplied by the operator, this affects approximately 7% of services to 2012 and around 12% in 12/1, meaning that figures for later years are not directly comparable with earlier ones (or with other systems). We estimate that the increasing use of double sets to form trains contributes around a third of the overall increase in vehicle mileage shown for this system since 2011/12.

Notes & Definitions

https://www.gov.uk/government/publications/light-rail-and-tram-statistics-guidance

The figures in this table are National Statistics

22.19e Number of stations or stops on light rail and trams by system[1]: England

Financial year	Docklands Light Railway	London Tramlink	Nottingham Express Transit	Midland Metro	Sheffield Supertram	Tyne and Wear Metro	Manchester Metrolink	Blackpool Tramway[2,3]	England
1995/96	28	:	:	:	45	46	26	62	207
1996/97	28	:	:	:	45	46	26	62	207
1997/98	29	:	:	:	46	46	26	62	209
1998/99	29	:	:	:	47	46	26	62	210
1999/00	34	:	:	23	47	46	36	62	248
2000/01	34	38	:	23	47	46	36	62	286
2001/02	34	38	:	23	48	58	36	62	299
2002/03	34	38	:	23	48	58	37	62	300
2003/04	34	38	23	23	48	58	37	62	323
2004/05	34	38	23	23	48	58	37	62	323
2005/06	38	39	23	23	48	59	37	62	329
2006/07	34	39	23	23	48	59	37	61	324
2007/08	39	38	23	23	48	60	37	61	329
2008/09	40	39	23	23	48	60	37	61	331
2009/10	40	39	23	23	48	60	37	59	329
2010/11	40	39	23	23	48	60	38	59	330
2011/12	45	39	23	23	48	60	42	31	311
2012/13	45	39	23	23	48	60	65	37	340

Source: DfT Light Rail and Tram Survey
Telephone: 020 7944 3094
Email: bus.statistics@dft.gsi.gov.uk

[1] For further information on these systems including infrastructure changes that may affect the figures, please refer to the technical information.

[2] The number of stops has been shown for one direction of the route (as is the case with the other systems). In publications prior to 2011/12 the figures shown covered both directions.

[3] In 2012/13 Blackpool Tramway had 37 stops on the outward journey and 36 stops on the inward journey, as Fleetwood Ferry only had one platform.

Notes and Definitions: https://www.gov.uk/government/publications/light-rail-and-tram-statistics-guidance
The figures in this table are National Statistics

22.19f London Underground statistics, annual

	Passenger Journeys (millions)								Receipts (£ million)					
	Ordinary[1]	Season ticket	All journeys	Passenger miles (millions)	Loaded train miles (millions)	Stations	Rail carriages	Route miles	Ordinary[1]	Season ticket	Traffic receipts	Traffic receipts at 2014/15 prices[2]	Receipts per journey (£)	Receipts per jny at 2014/15 prices[2]
2000/01	486	484	970	4,642	40	274	3,954	254	610	519	1,129	1,561	1.16	1.61
2001/02	491	462	953	4,630	40	274	3,954	254	636	515	1,151	1,567	1.21	1.64
2002/03	495	446	942	4,578	41	274	3,954	254	628	510	1,138	1,510	1.21	1.60
2003/04	491	457	948	4,561	43	274	3,959	254	625	536	1,161	1,510	1.22	1.59
2004/05	486	490	976	4,726	43	274	3,959	254	663	578	1,241	1,564	1.27	1.60
2005/06	460	510	970	4,714	43	274	4,070	254	678	630	1,308	1,604	1.35	1.65
2006/07	519	521	1,040	4,938	43	273	4,070	254	782	635	1,417	1,692	1.36	1.63
2007/08	581	515	1,096	5,190	43	268	4,070	254	880	645	1,525	1,769	1.39	1.61
2008/09	616	473	1,089	5,372	44	270	4,070	254	962	654	1,615	1,828	1.48	1.68
2009/10	634	425	1,059	5,255	43	270	4,078	249	840	612	1,635	1,804	1.54	1.70
2010/11	660	447	1,107	5,515	43	270	4,134	249	1,087	672	1,759	1,888	1.59	1.71
2011/12	685	486	1,171	5,915	45	270	4,127	249	1,208	774	1,982	2,090	1.69	1.78
2012/13	723	506	1,229	6,275	47	270	4,180	249	1,293	833	2,125	2,206	1.73	1.79

Source: Transport for London
Telephone: 020 7944 3094
Email: bus.statistics@dft.gsi.gov.uk

1. Ordinary journeys include daily travelcards and those where concessionary fares apply.
2. Adjustment to values using the HM Treasury GDP Deflator (as at 31 March 2015). 'Other' income no longer available on the same basis as previously published.

The figures in this table are outside the scope of National Statistics

22.19g Glasgow Underground statistics, annual

	Passenger journeys (millions)	Passenger miles (millions)	Loaded train or tram miles [also referred to as vehicle miles] (millions) [1]	Stations or stops served	Passenger carriages or tramcars	Route miles open for passenger traffic	Passenger revenue at 2014/15 prices (£ millions)
1998/99	14.6	29.0	0.7	15	41	6.8	13.3
1999/00	14.7	29.2	0.7	15	41	6.8	14.1
2000/01	14.4	28.6	0.7	15	41	6.8	13.8
2001/02	13.8	27.4	0.7	15	41	6.8	13.7
2002/03	13.4	26.6	0.7	15	41	6.8	13.5
2003/04	13.3	26.5	0.6	15	41	6.8	13.4
2004/05	13.3	26.5	0.6	15	41	6.8	13.8
2005/06	13.2	26.2	0.6	15	41	6.5	13.7
2006/07	13.5	26.8	0.6	15	41	6.5	14.8
2007/08	14.5	28.8	0.6	15	41	6.5	15.0
2008/09	14.1	28.1	0.7	15	41	6.5	16.6
2009/10	13.1	26.0	0.6	15	41	6.5	15.5
2010/11	13.0	25.9	0.6	15	41	6.5	15.2
2011/12	12.9	25.6	0.7	15	41	6.5	15.1
2012/13	12.6	25.0	0.7	15	41	6.5	15.1

Source: DfT Light Rail and Tram Survey
Telephone: 020 7944 3094
Email: bus.statistics@dft.gsi.gov.uk

[1] Loaded tram kilometers are only available as rolling stock totals, to calculate vehicle kilometres the figure provided by Glasgow is divided by 3, as all trams run with three carriages.

Notes and Definitions: https://www.gov.uk/government/publications/light-rail-and-tram-statistics-guidance

The figures in this table are outside the scope of National Statistics

22.20a Freight moved
Great Britain annual data from 2002-03 - amount of freight moved on the rail network (billion net tonne kilometres)

Financial year	Coal	Metals	Construction	Oil and petroleum	International	Domestic intermodal	Other	Total (1)	Infrastructure (2)
2002-03	5.66	2.64	2.51	1.15	0.46	3.38	2.72	18.52	1.18
2003-04	5.82	2.41	2.68	1.19	0.48	3.53	2.77	18.87	1.23
2004-05	6.66	2.59	2.86	1.22	0.54	3.96	2.53	20.35	1.29
2005-06	8.26	2.22	2.91	1.22	0.46	4.33	2.29	21.70	1.38
2006-07	8.56	2.04	2.70	1.53	0.44	4.72	1.89	21.88	1.36
2007-08	7.73	1.83	2.79	1.58	0.37	5.15	1.73	21.18	1.70
2008-09	7.91	1.53	2.70	1.52	0.42	5.17	1.38	20.63	1.55
2009-10	6.23	1.64	2.78	1.45	0.44	5.51	1.01	19.06	1.43
2010-11	5.46	2.23	3.19	1.32	0.42	5.68	0.94	19.23	1.54
2011-12	6.41	2.24	3.45	1.20	0.45	6.31	0.99	21.06	1.86

Source: Network Rail

(1) Infrastructure data are not included in the total.
(2) This series excludes some possession trains used during engineering works.

Data can be subject to revisions indicated by (R). For the latest information on data revisions, please see the revisions log: http://www.rail-reg.gov.uk/upload/xls/stats-revisions-log.xls

This dataset is used in the freight rail usage statistical release. To view or download the statistical release please see: http://www.rail-reg.gov.uk/server/show/nav.3016

The quality report relating to this dataset can be found at http://www.rail-reg.gov.uk/server/show/nav.3016

The quality report pulls together the key qualitative information on relevance, accuracy and reliability, timeliness and punctuality, accessibility and clarity and coherence and comparability. It also includes information on some additional quality principles on user needs and perceptions, confidentiality, transparency and security of data.

22.20b Freight lifted

Great Britain annual data from 1999-00 - mass of freight goods carried on the rail network (million tonnes)

Financial year	Coal	Other	Total
1999-00	35.9	60.6	96.5
2000-01	35.3	60.3	95.6
2001-02	39.5	54.5	93.9
2002-03	34.0	53.0	87.0
2003-04	35.2	53.7	88.9
2004-05	44.1	56.8	100.9
2005-06	47.6	57.7	105.3
2006-07	48.7	59.5	108.2
2007-08	43.3	59.1	102.4
2008-09	46.6	56.1	102.7
2009-10	37.9	49.3	87.2
2010-11	38.8	51.1	89.9
2011-12	44.4	57.3	101.7

Source: Freight Operating Companies

Data can be subject to revisions indicated by (R). For the latest information on data revisions, please see the revisions log:
http://www.rail-reg.gov.uk/upload/xls/stats-revisions-log.xls

This dataset is used in the freight rail usage statistical release. To view or download the statistical release please see:
http://www.rail-reg.gov.uk/server/show/nav.3016

The quality report relating to this dataset can be found at http://www.rail-reg.gov.uk/server/show/nav.3016

The quality report pulls together the key qualitative information on relevance, accuracy and reliability, timeliness and punctuality, accessibility and clarity and coherence and comparability. It also includes information on some additional quality principles on user needs and perceptions, confidentiality, transparency and security of data.

22.21 Railways: permanent way and rolling stock
Northern Ireland
At end of year

Numbers

		1999	2000	2001	2002	2003	2004	2005	2006	2007	2008	2009/10	2010/11	2011/12	2012/13
Length of road open for traffic[1] (Km)	KNRA	335	356	334	334	334	299	299	299	299	299	299	299	299	299
Length of track open for traffic (Km)															
Total	KNRB	526	547	480	480	480	445	445	445	445	445	445	445	445	445
Running lines	KNRC	484	505	464	464	464	427	427	427	427	427	427	427	427	427
Sidings (as single track)	KNRD	42	42	16	16	16	18	18	18	18	18	18	18	18	18
Locomotives															
Diesel-electrics	KNRE	6	6	6	6	5	6	5	5	5	5	5	5	5	5
Passenger carrying vehicles															
Total	KNRF	105	105	106	100	100	102	124	125	128	130	130	130	130	156
Rail motor vehicles:															
Diesel-electric,etc	KNRG	30	30	29	28	28	28	70	85	84	84	84	84	84	110
Trailer carriages:															
Total locomotive hauled	KNRH	21	21	25	22	22	22	22	22	22	22	22	22	22	22
Ordinary coaches	KNRI	19	19	23	20	20	20	20	20	20	20	20	20	20	20
Restaurant cars	KNRJ	2	2	2	2	2	2	2	2	2	2	2	2	2	2
Rail car trailers	KNRK	54	54	52	50	50	52	32	18	22	24	24	24	24	10
Rolling stock for maintenance and repair	KNRT	18	18	18	18	39	46	48	48	48	48	48	48	48	50

Sources: Department for Regional Development;
Northern Ireland: 02890 540981

1 The total length of railroad open for traffic irrespective of the number of tracks comprising the road.

22.22 Operating statistics of railways
Northern Ireland

		Unit	2001	2002	2003	2004	2005 /06	2006 /07	2007 /08	2008 /09	2009 /10	2010 /11	2011 /12	2012 /13	2013 /14
Maintenance of way and works															
Material used:															
Ballast	KNSA	Thousand m^2	80.0	40.0	130.0	70.0	90.0	30.0	15.0	10.0	35.0	10.0	16.2	46.2	10.0
Rails	KNSB	Thousand tonnes	2.5	1.0	4.5	1.0	3.2	1.0	1.0	0.1	1.4	1.2	3.4	0.2	0.1
Sleepers	KNSC	Thousands	50.0	5.0	40.0	28.0	45.0	2.0	5.0	2.0	2.0	2.0	27.7	2.7	0.3
Track renewed	KNSD	Km	15.0	5.0	25.8	2.0	29.0	1.0	-	..	6.0	1.0	0.5	21.6	0.0
New Track laid	KPGD	Km	-	-	-	-	-	-	-	..	–	0.0	-	-	-
Engine kilometres															
Total[1]	KNSE	Thousand Km	4,056	4,056	4,170	4,110	4,618	4,677	5,108	5,047	4,899	5,088	5,082	5,258	5,760
Train kilometres:															
Total	KNSF	"	3,626	3,626	3,704	4,110	4,618	4,677	5,108	5,047	4,899	5,088	5,082	5,258	5,760
Coaching	KNSG	"	3,622	3,622	3,700	4,110	4,618	4,677	5,108	5,047	4,899	5,088	5,082	5,258	5,760
Freight	KNSH	"	4	4	4	-	-	-	-	-	-	-	-	-	-

1 Including shunting, assisting, light, departmental, maintenance and repair.

Sources: Department for Regional Development;
Northern Ireland: 02890 540981

22.23 Main Outputs of UK Airlines (1994 - 2013) in Tonne-kilometres Available and Used (a)

Year	Available Tonne-Kilometres						Tonne-Kilometres Used					
	Total (000 000)	Percentage growth on previous year	Scheduled services (000 000)	Percentage growth on previous year	Non-scheduled services (000 000)	Percentage growth on previous year	Total (000 000)	Percentage growth on previous year	Scheduled services (000 000)	Percentage growth on previous year	Non-scheduled services (000 000)	Percentage growth on previous year
1994	27 713	10.5	20 359	9.5	7 354	13.2	19 350	11.4	13 314	11.3	6 035	11.6
1995	29 901	7.9	22 016	8.1	7 885	7.2	21 306	10.1	14 890	11.8	6 416	6.3
1996	32 214	7.7	23 795	8.1	8 419	6.8	23 001	8.0	16 198	8.8	6 803	6.0
1997	35 571	10.4	26 507	11.4	9 064	7.7	25 091	9.1	17 914	10.6	7 176	5.5
1998	40 022	12.5	29 762	12.3	10 261	13.2	27 552	9.8	19 598	9.4	7 954	10.8
1999	41 911	4.7	31 856	7.0	10 055	-2.0	28 530	3.5	20 596	5.1	7 934	-0.3
2000	43 393	3.5	32 950	3.4	10 443	3.9	29 989	5.1	21 846	6.1	8 143	2.6
2001	42 374	-2.3	31 864	-3.3	10 510	0.6	28 118	-6.2	19 907	-8.9	8 211	0.8
2002	40 550	-4.3	30 433	-4.5	10 117	-3.7	27 913	-0.7	20 032	0.6	7 881	-4.0
2003	42 784	5.5	31 513	3.6	11 271	11.4	29 325	5.1	20 671	3.2	8 654	9.8
2004	43 904	2.6	32 442	2.9	11 462	1.7	29 923	2.0	20 963	1.4	8 960	3.5
2005	48 294	10.0	36 937	13.9	11 357	-0.9	29 494	-1.4	21 133	0.8	8 362	-6.7
2006	50 396	4.4	38 590	4.5	11 806	4.0	30 932	4.9	22 404	6.0	8 528	2.0
2007	54 190	7.5	40 979	6.2	13 211	11.9	32 863	6.2	23 557	5.1	9 306	9.1
2008	53 392	-1.5	41 316	0.8	12 076	-8.6	32 509	-1.1	24 107	2.3	8 402	-9.7
2009	49 150	-7.9	39 207	-5.1	9 944	-17.7	30 411	-6.5	23 427	-2.8	6 984	-16.9
2010	47 168	-4.0	38 059	-2.9	9 109	-8.4	29 915	-1.6	23 263	-0.7	6 651	-4.8
2011	50 120	6.3	41 043	7.8	9 078	-0.3	31 405	5.0	24 796	6.6	6 609	-0.6
2012	50 348	0.5	41 694	1.6	8 653	-4.7	31 621	0.7	25 251	1.8	6 370	-3.6
2013	50 111	-0.5	42 098	1.0	8 014	-7.4	31 704	0.3	25 684	1.7	6 019	-5.5

(a) Excludes Small Airlines Public Transport Operations
(b) Excludes Air Europe Operations

Source: Civil Aviation Authority

22.24a Air Transport Movements(a) by Type and Nationality of Operator 2013

	Total	<----- Scheduled Services ----->			<-------- Charter Flights -------->		
		UK Operators	Other EU Operators	Other Overseas Operators	UK Operators	Other EU Operators	Other Overseas Operators
London Area Airports							
GATWICK	244 301	172 029	21 627	27 326	20 894	1 941	484
HEATHROW	469 565	260 160	100 099	107 118	604	1 543	41
LONDON CITY	68 118	25 059	34 181	8 868	-	1	9
LUTON	70 889	36 560	27 534	908	3 824	1 892	171
SOUTHEND	9 475	7 477	1 949	-	1	46	2
STANSTED	131 925	23 608	93 555	2 647	6 848	661	4 606
Total London Area Airports	994 273	524 893	278 945	146 867	32 171	6 084	5 313
Other UK Airports							
ABERDEEN	99 893	39 721	10 547	3 057	46 057	408	103
BARRA	880	880	-	-	-	-	-
BELFAST CITY (GEORGE BEST)	36 866	29 507	7 226	-	131	2	-
BELFAST INTERNATIONAL	36 596	29 942	17	558	3 824	2 163	92
BENBECULA	1 887	1 887	-	-	-	-	-
BIGGIN HILL	8	-	-	-	6	2	-
BIRMINGHAM	84 851	37 786	31 838	5 637	8 077	765	748
BLACKPOOL	10 282	1 642	2 246	-	6 388	6	-
BOURNEMOUTH	6 824	272	3 431	-	3 080	41	-
BRISTOL	53 966	30 435	17 082	328	5 814	305	2
CAMBRIDGE	763	1	-	714	43	5	-
CAMPBELTOWN	1 022	1 018	-	-	-	4	-
CARDIFF WALES	14 024	6 480	4 167	-	3 076	265	36
CITY OF DERRY (EGLINTON)	3 011	4	2 930	-	77	-	-
COVENTRY	604	-	-	-	604	-	-
DONCASTER SHEFFIELD	4 291	64	1 790	1	2 281	81	74
DUNDEE	1 357	14	1 296	-	41	5	1
DURHAM TEES VALLEY	4 327	2 069	2 002	-	242	13	1
EAST MIDLANDS INTERNATIONAL	57 043	17 494	13 498	2	13 218	10 858	1 973
EDINBURGH	103 828	68 192	25 978	3 092	4 642	1 827	97
EXETER	12 511	10 083	2	-	2 156	195	75
GLASGOW	72 506	55 269	7 432	3 188	5 561	444	612
GLOUCESTERSHIRE	1 256	-	1 256	-	-	-	-
HUMBERSIDE	11 672	2 051	2 116	-	7 276	163	66
INVERNESS	10 011	9 891	-	26	67	19	8
ISLAY	1 558	1 558	-	-	-	-	-
ISLES OF SCILLY (ST.MARYS)	10 816	10 816	-	-	-	-	-
KIRKWALL	10 786	10 639	-	-	144	1	2
LANDS END (ST JUST)	6 985	6 985	-	-	-	-	-
LEEDS BRADFORD	30 393	20 320	9 020	199	743	103	8
LERWICK (TINGWALL)	1 329	1 329	-	-	-	-	-
LIVERPOOL (JOHN LENNON)	32 947	18 591	14 033	197	91	28	7
LYDD	127	120	-	-	6	1	-
MANCHESTER	161 050	77 431	45 119	16 723	19 194	1 580	1 003
MANSTON (KENT INT)	1 640	8	1 078	-	15	254	285
NEWCASTLE	42 974	26 230	8 419	1 166	6 386	309	464
NEWQUAY	4 966	4 929	32	-	-	5	-
NORWICH	22 056	5 040	2 426	-	7 308	988	6 294
OXFORD (KIDLINGTON)	579	31	3	510	24	9	2
PRESTWICK	8 606	4	8 518	2	2	25	55
SCATSTA	13 174	-	-	-	13 174	-	-
SHOREHAM	664	-	-	-	664	-	-
SOUTHAMPTON	36 056	35 828	-	-	204	24	-
STORNOWAY	6 340	6 316	-	-	22	2	-
SUMBURGH	9 197	6 604	-	-	2 508	85	-
TIREE	985	985	-	-	-	-	-
WICK JOHN O GROATS	3 337	1 930	-	-	184	1 221	2
Total Other UK Airports	1 036 844	580 396	223 502	35 400	163 330	22 206	12 010
Total All Reporting UK Airports	2 031 117	1 105 289	502 447	182 267	195 501	28 290	17 323
Non UK Reporting Airports							
ALDERNEY	6 379	6 379	-	-	-	-	-
GUERNSEY	32 982	30 660	156	-	2 144	14	8
ISLE OF MAN	20 372	13 489	6 274	-	582	27	-
JERSEY	34 299	31 772	482	-	1 873	163	9
Total Non UK Reporting Airports	94 032	82 300	6 912	-	4 599	204	17

Note
(a) Excludes Air Taxi operations

Source: Civil Aviation Authority

22.24b Air Passengers by Type and Nationality of Operator 2013

	Total Terminal and Transit Passengers	Scheduled Services — UK Operators Terminal	UK Operators Transit	Other EU Operators Terminal	Other EU Operators Transit	Other Overseas Operators Terminal	Other Overseas Operators Transit	Charter Flights — UK Operators Terminal	UK Operators Transit	Other EU Operators Terminal	Other EU Operators Transit	Other Overseas Operators Terminal	Other Overseas Operators Transit
London Area Airports													
GATWICK	35 444 206	23 756 271	5 049	2 597 895	1 355	4 338 381	2 008	4 375 398	6 860	279 600	386	81 003	-
HEATHROW	72 367 054	38 146 123	548	11 948 920	319	22 141 871	34 497	88 609	-	4 142	-	2 025	-
LONDON CITY	3 379 753	1 357 994	-	1 458 657	-	562 631	-	-	-	59	-	412	-
LUTON	9 697 944	5 019 884	3 171	4 116 458	351	100 100	-	439 154	864	14 715	52	3 176	19
SOUTHEND	969 912	902 469	-	62 175	-	-	-	75	-	5 005	-	188	-
STANSTED	17 852 393	3 008 762	2 325	13 907 355	369	348 972	-	518 300	805	44 615	-	20 867	23
Total London Area Airports	139 711 262	72 191 503	11 093	34 091 460	2 394	27 491 955	36 505	5 421 536	8 529	348 136	438	107 671	42
Other UK Airports													
ABERDEEN	3 440 765	1 792 528	25	713 114	-	117 569	-	766 623	368	36 965	31	13 526	16
BARRA	9 410	9 410	-	-	-	-	-	-	-	-	-	-	-
BELFAST CITY (GEORGE BEST)	2 541 759	2 004 038	37	524 199	-	-	-	13 432	-	53	-	-	-
BELFAST INTERNATIONAL	4 023 336	3 591 857	2	2 012	-	85 146	-	302 010	584	33 673	199	7 771	82
BENBECULA	30 738	30 612	126	-	-	-	-	-	-	-	-	-	-
BIGGIN HILL	326	-	-	-	-	-	-	226	-	100	-	-	-
BIRMINGHAM	9 120 201	3 218 478	1 324	3 177 041	606	1 017 997	890	1 593 691	2 507	94 366	628	12 653	20
BLACKPOOL	262 630	201 028	-	35 473	-	-	-	25 758	-	371	-	-	-
BOURNEMOUTH	660 272	27 074	899	455 124	167	-	-	171 706	185	5 117	-	-	-
BRISTOL	6 131 896	3 486 601	387	1 806 596	137	13 443	-	775 603	5 618	42 796	605	110	-
CAMBRIDGE	9 307	23	-	-	-	7 517	-	1 244	58	465	-	-	-
CAMPBELTOWN	9 550	9 303	123	-	-	-	-	-	-	124	-	-	-
CARDIFF WALES	1 072 062	231 201	14 129	260 880	-	-	-	528 333	453	29 173	407	7 486	-
CITY OF DERRY (EGLINTON)	384 973	317	-	371 315	-	-	-	13 341	-	-	-	-	-
DONCASTER SHEFFIELD	690 351	3 922	124	265 296	-	-	-	398 235	31	11 043	269	11 265	166
DUNDEE	27 595	165	24	25 637	11	-	-	1 714	-	41	3	-	-
DURHAM TEES VALLEY	161 092	36 359	1 111	97 798	23	-	-	23 317	647	1 791	-	46	-
EAST MIDLANDS INTERNATIONAL	4 334 117	1 390 422	1 913	1 983 143	291	-	251	918 163	1 920	23 149	2 186	12 679	-
EDINBURGH	9 775 443	6 328 717	398	2 805 632	19	385 093	-	201 481	-	41 860	-	12 243	-
EXETER	741 465	505 335	3 399	136	-	-	-	200 447	147	18 749	-	13 252	-
GLASGOW	7 363 764	4 892 270	1 366	551 757	839	684 380	1 990	1 141 357	181	56 033	280	32 302	1 009
GLOUCESTERSHIRE	14 168	-	-	14 129	39	-	-	-	-	-	-	-	-
HUMBERSIDE	236 083	38 814	888	114 876	-	-	-	51 626	159	19 046	395	10 279	-
INVERNESS	608 184	599 711	1 457	-	-	2 164	-	2 117	5	2 274	-	456	-
ISLAY	26 085	25 721	364	-	-	-	-	-	-	-	-	-	-
ISLES OF SCILLY (ST.MARYS)	89 170	89 170	-	-	-	-	-	-	-	-	-	-	-
KIRKWALL	159 325	149 148	9 273	-	-	-	-	320	478	10	-	96	-
LANDS END (ST JUST)	46 626	46 299	327	-	-	-	-	-	-	-	-	-	-
LEEDS BRADFORD	3 318 358	2 035 226	3 754	1 115 399	3	31 021	-	121 231	1	10 495	205	1 023	-
LERWICK (TINGWALL)	3 784	3 784	-	-	-	-	-	-	-	-	-	-	-
LIVERPOOL (JOHN LENNON)	4 187 493	2 209 553	504	1 953 551	427	16 158	-	3 695	805	2 534	-	266	-
LYDD	670	627	-	-	-	-	-	30	-	13	-	-	-
MANCHESTER	20 751 581	8 402 515	3 414	4 844 883	3 068	3 090 976	41 513	4 116 411	19 959	172 195	1 696	53 487	1 464
MANSTON (KENT INT)	40 391	479	248	35 995	-	-	-	1 255	-	2 414	-	-	-
NEWCASTLE	4 420 839	2 474 752	3 243	673 898	4	217 538	-	999 904	6	37 143	2 324	12 027	-
NEWQUAY	174 891	171 514	259	2 407	-	-	-	-	-	711	-	-	-
NORWICH	463 401	123 809	16	131 901	-	-	-	91 866	120	43 040	52	72 413	184

22.24b Air Passengers by Type and Nationality of Operator 2013

	Total Terminal and Transit Passengers	Scheduled Services UK Operators Terminal	Scheduled Services UK Operators Transit	Scheduled Services Other EU Operators Terminal	Scheduled Services Other EU Operators Transit	Scheduled Services Other Overseas Operators Terminal	Scheduled Services Other Overseas Operators Transit	Charter Flights UK Operators Terminal	Charter Flights UK Operators Transit	Charter Flights Other EU Operators Terminal	Charter Flights Other EU Operators Transit	Charter Flights Other Overseas Operators Terminal	Charter Flights Other Overseas Operators Transit
Other UK Airports (Continued)													
OXFORD (KIDLINGTON)	6 847	235	7	-	-	6 304	-	71	-	138	-	92	-
PRESTWICK	1 145 836	120	-	1 143 212	645	5	302	143	-	1 088	321	-	-
SCATSTA	298 308	-	-	-	-	-	-	298 308	-	-	-	-	-
SHOREHAM	732	-	-	-	-	-	-	732	-	-	-	-	-
SOUTHAMPTON	1 722 758	1 702 986	171	-	-	-	-	18 834	116	651	-	-	-
STORNOWAY	122 410	119 088	2 506	-	-	-	-	802	-	14	-	-	-
SUMBURGH	212 233	153 104	390	-	-	-	-	53 896	2 096	2 747	-	-	-
TIREE	8 560	8 270	290	-	-	-	-	-	-	-	-	-	-
WICK JOHN O GROATS	33 639	23 275	5	-	-	-	-	1 107	543	8 558	-	151	-
Total Other UK Airports	88 883 424	46 137 860	52 503	23 105 404	6 279	5 675 311	44 946	12 839 029	36 987	698 940	9 598	273 626	2 941
Total All Reporting UK Airports	228 594 686	118 329 363	63 596	57 196 864	8 673	33 167 266	81 451	18 260 565	45 516	1 047 076	10 036	381 297	2 983
Non UK Reporting Airports													
ALDERNEY	62 855	62 855	28 429	-	-	-	-	-	66	-	-	-	-
GUERNSEY	886 396	849 156	51	4 793	1 170	-	-	2 688	-	39	-	55	-
ISLE OF MAN	739 683	641 851	22 710	90 192	1 110	-	-	2 892	854	3 587	-	-	-
JERSEY	1 453 863	1 375 836	-	30 469	826	-	-	6 300	-	16 749	95	24	-
Total Non UK Reporting Airports	3 142 797	2 929 698	51 190	125 454	3 106	-	-	11 880	920	20 375	95	79	-

Source: Civil Aviation Authority

22.25 Scheduled and Non-Scheduled Services All Services 2013 (a)

	Aircraft-Km (000)	Stage Flights	A/C Hours	(b) Number of Passengers Uplifted	Seat-Km Available (000)	Seat-Km Used (000)	As % of Avail	(b) Cargo Uplifted Tonnes	Tonne-Km Available (000)	Tonne-Kilometres Used Total (000)	Mail (000)	Freight (000)	Passenger (000)	As % of Avail
Passenger Services														
ACROPOLIS AVIATION LTD	387	125	550	1 124	7 340	3 810	51.9	-	4 635	331	-	-	331	7.1
AIRTANKER SERVICES LTD	1 434	329	1 940	45 557	417 108	195 157	46.8	2 494	58 484	30 310	-	11 798	18 512	51.8
ARAVCO LTD	96	35	129	247	1 466	574	39.2	285	165	47	-	-	47	28.5
AURIGNY AIR SERVICES	3 022	20 488	13 938	487 525	166 200	114 802	69.1	1	16 901	8 589	12	20	8 557	50.8
BA CITYFLYER LTD	18 546	23 893	36 916	1 371 993	1 639 121	1 135 679	69.3	25	164 397	94 944	-	-	94 944	57.8
BLUE ISLANDS LIMITED	2 498	11 414	8 517	219 518	93 232	51 274	55.0	45	8 323	4 579	-	11	4 568	55.0
BMI REGIONAL	14 230	20 543	29 333	447 975	660 290	323 963	49.1	-	75 178	27 579	-	39	27 540	36.7
BRITISH AIRWAYS (BA) LTD	5 379	1 445	7 631	21 816	172 378	121 952	70.7	-	17 334	6 087	-	-	6 087	35.1
BRITISH AIRWAYS PLC	675 058	283 832	1 002 894	38 412 127	158 549 539	129 247 922	81.5	553 494	22 927 597	12 991 631	126 756	3 631 415	9 233 460	56.7
CELLO AVIATION LTD	346	380	696	10 182	21 369	15 213	71.2	-	2 684	1 520	-	-	1 520	56.6
EASTERN AIRWAYS	10 879	27 801	29 516	508 387	423 113	220 119	52.0	-	43 815	16 323	-	-	16 323	37.3
EASYJET AIRLINE COMPANY LTD	407 190	367 517	710 953	50 963 923	66 497 193	58 468 902	87.9	-	5 652 261	4 630 179	-	-	4 630 179	81.9
EXECUTIVE JET CHARTER LTD	102	59	136	201	1 302	298	22.9	-	102	24	-	-	24	23.5
FLYBE LTD	63 103	139 256	161 497	7 369 336	5 641 623	3 745 240	66.4	925	616 920	318 359	-	249	318 110	51.6
GAMA AVIATION	291	206	418	669	3 594	1 298	36.1	1	324	121	-	-	121	37.3
ISLES OF SCILLY SKYBUS	885	10 035	4 013	89 479	14 149	8 810	62.3	-	1 117	645	-	-	645	57.7
JET2.COM LTD	66 275	36 064	105 720	5 515 021	12 029 764	10 807 283	89.8	-	1 189 871	918 641	-	-	918 641	77.2
LOGANAIR	7 534	34 675	27 965	574 322	236 987	154 697	65.3	774	21 190	13 298	14	157	13 127	62.8
MONARCH AIRLINES	81 414	38 421	121 628	6 821 668	17 953 083	15 281 207	85.1	2 014	1 812 391	1 207 038	-	5 611	1 201 427	66.6
ORYX JET LTD	292	118	356	301	2 988	621	20.8	-	466	60	-	-	60	12.9
TAG AVIATION (UK) LTD	3 335	2 355	4 290	9 725	39 466	13 901	35.2	-	10 422	1 199	-	-	1 199	11.5
THOMAS COOK AIRLINES LTD	85 635	28 438	122 124	6 084 315	21 285 491	19 808 698	93.1	3 354	2 293 141	1 704 848	-	20 805	1 684 043	74.3
THOMSON AIRWAYS LTD	156 906	54 926	224 579	10 548 952	34 162 680	31 574 748	92.4	6 903	2 858 552	2 410 129	-	45 433	2 364 696	84.3
TITAN AIRWAYS LTD	5 952	3 155	7 611	105 933	1 183 981	875 001	73.9	-	123 962	61 160	-	-	61 160	49.3
TRIAIR (BERMUDA) LTD	310	82	407	275	3 727	1 488	39.9	-	684	148	-	-	148	21.6
TWINJET AIRCRAFT	274	112	441	2 063	9 130	4 940	54.1	-	4 497	368	-	-	368	8.2
VIRGIN ATLANTIC AIRWAYS LTD	154 483	28 373	202 237	5 888 045	50 330 854	39 538 277	78.6	209 235	8 398 122	4 581 502	-	1 516 159	3 065 343	54.6
Total Passenger Services	1 765 856	1 134 077	2 826 432	135 500 679	371 547 168	311 715 874	83.9	779 550	46 303 535	29 029 659	126 782	5 231 697	23 671 180	62.7
Cargo Services														
AIRTANKER SERVICES LTD	87	32	128	-	-	-	:	126	3 552	452	-	452	-	12.7
ATLANTIC AIRLINES LTD	3 455	8 982	11 009	-	-	-	:	33 128	32 507	14 881	4 159	10 722	-	45.8
BRITISH AIRWAYS PLC	12 805	4 702	19 159	-	-	-	:	140 759	1 260 267	872 642	-	872 642	-	69.2
DHL AIR LTD	26 529	18 141	42 636	-	-	-	:	119 108	1 079 447	744 695	-	744 695	-	69.0
GLOBAL SUPPLY SYSTEMS LTD	10 615	2 363	13 598	-	-	-	:	-	1 384 637	1 023 940	-	1 023 940	-	74.0
JET2.COM LTD	1 728	4 554	4 557	-	-	-	:	29 107	27 658	10 043	10 043	-	-	36.3
TITAN AIRWAYS LTD	1 522	2 748	2 078	-	-	-	:	12 389	19 804	7 220	7 220	-	-	36.5
Total Cargo Services	56 741	41 522	93 165	-	-	-	:	334 616	3 807 872	2 673 873	21 422	2 652 451	-	70.2
Grand Total	1 822 597	1 175 599	2 919 597	135 500 679	371 547 168	311 715 874	83.9	1 114 167	50 111 407	31 703 532	148 204	7 884 148	23 671 180	63.3

Source: Civil Aviation Authority

(a) Excludes small airlines' public transport operations (see table 1.13)
(b) Excludes passengers and cargo uplifted on sub-charter operations
(c) Excludes some charter operations performed by aircraft below 15 MTOM

22.26a Aircraft Movements 2013

	Total	Commercial Movements				Non-Commercial Movements						
		Air Transport	Of Which Air Taxi	Positioning Flights	Local Movements	Other Flights by Air Transport Operators	Test and Training	Aero Club	Private	Official	Military	Business Aviation
London Area Airports												
GATWICK	250 520	244 354	53	4 002	8	174	75	-	75	24	9	1 799
HEATHROW	471 936	469 736	171	1 167	8	107	46	-	5	281	42	544
LONDON CITY	74 006	73 122	5 004	462	-	7	144	-	-	-	-	271
LUTON	95 763	74 795	3 906	5 155	2	458	252	-	74	76	44	14 951
SOUTHEND	29 443	10 703	1 228	792	362	334	1 166	10 490	4 276	374	36	902
STANSTED	146 324	135 159	3 234	4 612	1	44	109	-	48	144	-	6 171
Total London Area Airports	1 067 992	1 007 869	13 596	16 190	381	1 124	1 792	10 490	4 478	899	131	24 638
METRO LONDON HELIPORT	7 650	1 895	1 895	1 832	422	823	-	-	2 253	12	124	289
Other UK Airports												
ABERDEEN	118 219	106 755	6 862	4 314	2	89	4 293	2 346	82	2	73	263
BARRA	966	881	1	2	-	1	-	-	78	-	4	-
BELFAST CITY (GEORGE BEST)	38 051	37 621	755	170	18	15	18	-	150	29	22	8
BELFAST INTERNATIONAL	54 003	38 044	1 448	1 283	4 506	1	48	1 140	1 635	16	6 494	837
BENBECULA	3 708	3 286	1 399	280	4	1	6	-	101	-	28	2
BIGGIN HILL	41 493	6 404	6 396	152	3 386	-	12	22 430	7 414	-	130	4 951
BIRMINGHAM	95 713	86 632	1 781	1 967	49	54	89	-	914	3	168	2 503
BLACKPOOL	41 406	12 045	1 763	730	10	8	2 508	19 172	5 281	-	457	1 153
BOURNEMOUTH	47 174	7 229	405	968	-	8 107	21 224	1 219	4 568	-	561	3 288
BRISTOL	65 299	55 640	1 674	802	1 852	14	-	2 848	5 769	6	219	7
CAMBRIDGE	19 785	778	15	18	1	-	351	10 992	2 722	-	424	2 642
CAMPBELTOWN	1 596	1 123	101	96	-	-	6	-	197	-	173	-
CARDIFF WALES	24 879	14 070	46	790	-	-	110	4 766	5 035	4	108	399
CARLISLE	17 280	558	558	120	172	-	80	11 206	3 360	4	1 381	-
CITY OF DERRY (EGLINTON)	7 103	3 156	145	45	97	6	907	1 366	1 399	-	17	106
COVENTRY	41 629	1 596	992	758	-	6	29 581	2 227	7 457	3	4	-
DONCASTER SHEFFIELD	11 197	4 634	343	219	227	2	2 006	2 395	917	5	879	142
DUNDEE	40 427	1 543	186	250	868	110	540	36 597	719	565	31	405
DURHAM TEES VALLEY	18 298	5 156	829	61	6	23	133	5 113	5 849	5	530	4 637
EAST MIDLANDS INTERNATIONAL	76 563	61 141	4 098	3 003	4	5 902	793	1	966	10	114	2 386
EDINBURGH	111 736	106 748	2 920	1 610	339	29	58	447	287	10	162	1 668
EXETER	31 458	13 200	689	597	6	493	1 184	8 750	4 803	3	414	421
GLASGOW	79 520	75 585	3 079	1 757	751	54	146	1 224	118	59	199	1 388
GLOUCESTERSHIRE	73 857	1 440	184	329	2 050	461	10 278	44 606	14 400	8	201	2 348
HAWARDEN	15 662	-	-	21	-	2 086	544	5 338	2 644	-	572	488
HUMBERSIDE	27 178	12 231	559	3 669	20	1 396	3 503	-	5 799	11	83	767
INVERNESS	28 947	14 425	4 414	1 396	-	158	1 925	8 530	1 664	6	62	5
ISLAY	2 637	1 739	181	150	-	-	2	-	583	-	158	-
ISLES OF SCILLY (ST.MARYS)	12 238	10 953	137	54	-	2	101	-	975	-	144	10
KIRKWALL	14 403	12 951	2 165	726	14	27	292	63	312	16	8	-
LANDS END (ST JUST)	8 586	7 251	266	87	56	12	515	-	647	-	12	-
LEEDS BRADFORD	45 627	31 057	664	1 440	856	21	3 692	5 510	2 889	-	73	73
LERWICK (TINGWALL)	2 084	1 748	419	288	1	9	8	4	17	-	9	9
LIVERPOOL (JOHN LENNON)	55 839	33 611	664	326	-	8	46	16 761	3 290	10	378	1 409
LYDD	16 347	649	522	171	361	-	1 006	4 018	9 932	25	107	78
MANCHESTER	169 497	161 306	256	3 977	23	102	21	-	495	-	50	3 523

22.26a Aircraft Movements 2013

	Total	Air Transport	Of Which Air Taxi	Positioning Flights	Local Movements	Test and Training	Other Flights by Air Transport Operators	Aero Club	Private	Official	Military	Business Aviation
		← Commercial Movements →						← Non-Commercial Movements →				
Other UK Airports(Continued)												
MANSTON (KENT INT)	17 504	2 073	433	1 068	34	2 028	4	5 571	6 190	2	478	56
NEWCASTLE	59 962	43 150	176	1 323	1 024	698	29	-	11 040	2 225	346	127
NEWQUAY	5 118	4 973	7	110	-	32	1	-	2	-	-	-
NORWICH	40 702	24 338	2 282	5 477	644	5 185	258	3 411	1 268	1	113	7
OXFORD (KIDLINGTON)	37 553	1 120	541	4 919	144	22 795	383	271	5 978	-	18	1 925
PRESTWICK	24 305	8 623	17	302	-	2 610	1	6 886	2 045	-	3 838	-
SCATSTA	14 668	13 338	164	1 007	-	310	13	-	-	-	-	-
SHOREHAM	55 500	664	-	129	1 322	202	37	40 942	12 151	-	53	-
SOUTHAMPTON	40 501	36 626	570	1 149	3	79	73	-	448	1	99	2 023
STORNOWAY	11 049	8 644	2 304	357	294	883	1	-	454	-	412	4
SUMBURGH	16 771	13 606	4 409	1 073	328	1 683	4	-	49	-	28	-
SWANSEA	20 731	870	870	72	63	16	-	12 624	4 327	-	2 665	94
TIREE	1 247	1 111	126	12	-	-	-	1	121	-	2	-
WICK JOHN O GROATS	7 787	4 276	939	1 227	5	1 126	1	-	1 111	-	36	5
Total Other UK Airports	1 813 803	1 096 598	59 754	50 851	19 541	123 673	19 999	288 775	148 652	3 029	22 528	40 157
Total All Reporting UK Airports	2 889 445	2 106 362	75 245	68 873	20 344	125 465	21 946	299 265	155 383	3 940	22 783	65 084
Non UK Reporting Airports												
ALDERNEY	10 460	6 816	437	165	839	66	14	693	1 861	4	2	-
GUERNSEY	49 403	34 540	1 558	1 642	4 284	254	309	5 344	2 839	70	102	19
ISLE OF MAN	29 857	22 231	1 859	842	-	130	25	2 366	2 866	10	105	1 282
JERSEY	54 878	35 903	1 604	1 220	-	262	708	5 226	11 249	-	264	46
Total Non UK Reporting Airports	144 598	99 490	5 458	3 869	5 123	712	1 056	13 629	18 815	84	473	1 347

Source: Civil Aviation Authority

Note
Business Aviation was collected under a category in its own right with effect from June 2001 data. However, currently it is not possible for all airports to report using this category

22.26b Terminal and Transit Passengers 2013 Comparison with the Previous Year

	Terminal and Transit Passengers			Terminal Passengers			Transit Passengers		
	2013	2012	Percentage Change	2013	2012	Percentage Change	2013	2012	Percentage Change
London Area Airports									
GATWICK	35 444 206	34 235 982	4	35 428 548	34 218 668	4	15 658	17 314	-10
HEATHROW	72 367 054	70 037 417	3	72 331 690	69 983 139	3	35 364	54 278	-35
LONDON CITY	3 379 753	3 016 664	12	3 379 753	3 016 664	12	-	-	-
LUTON	9 697 944	9 617 027	1	9 693 487	9 614 175	1	4 457	3 522	27
SOUTHEND	969 912	617 027	57	969 912	616 974	57	-	53	..
STANSTED	17 852 393	17 472 699	2	17 848 871	17 464 792	2	3 522	7 907	-55
Total London Area Airports	139 711 262	134 997 486	3	139 652 261	134 914 412	4	59 001	83 074	-29
Other UK Airports									
ABERDEEN	3 440 765	3 330 126	3	3 440 325	3 328 533	3	440	1 593	-72
BARRA	9 410	11 415	-18	9 410	11 414	-18	-	1	..
BELFAST CITY (GEORGE BEST)	2 541 759	2 246 202	13	2 541 722	2 246 202	13	37	-	..
BELFAST INTERNATIONAL	4 023 336	4 313 685	-7	4 022 469	4 312 441	-7	867	1 244	-30
BENBECULA	30 738	31 364	-2	30 612	30 849	-1	126	515	-76
BIGGIN HILL	326	-	..	326	-	..	-	-	-
BIRMINGHAM	9 120 201	8 922 539	2	9 114 226	8 916 209	2	5 975	6 330	-6
BLACKPOOL	262 630	235 238	12	262 630	235 191	12	-	47	..
BOURNEMOUTH	660 272	692 545	-5	659 021	689 755	-4	1 251	2 790	-55
BRISTOL	6 131 896	5 921 530	4	6 125 149	5 916 258	4	6 747	5 272	28
CAMBRIDGE	9 307	2 130	337	9 249	2 130	334	58	-	..
CAMPBELTOWN	9 550	9 144	4	9 427	8 689	8	123	455	-73
CARDIFF WALES	1 072 062	1 028 123	4	1 057 073	1 013 386	4	14 989	14 737	2
CITY OF DERRY (EGLINTON)	384 973	398 209	-3	384 973	398 209	-3	-	-	-
DONCASTER SHEFFIELD	690 351	693 661	0	689 761	693 129	0	590	532	11
DUNDEE	27 595	54 655	-50	27 560	54 642	-50	35	13	169
DURHAM TEES VALLEY	161 092	166 251	-3	159 311	164 826	-3	1 781	1 425	25
EAST MIDLANDS INTERNATIONAL	4 334 117	4 076 178	6	4 327 556	4 067 915	6	6 561	8 263	-21
EDINBURGH	9 775 443	9 195 061	6	9 775 026	9 194 334	6	417	727	-43
EXETER	741 465	701 743	6	737 919	694 963	6	3 546	6 780	-48
GLASGOW	7 363 764	7 157 859	3	7 358 099	7 150 095	3	5 665	7 764	-27
GLOUCESTERSHIRE	14 168	15 292	-7	14 129	15 245	-7	39	47	-17
HUMBERSIDE	236 083	234 142	1	234 641	233 589	0	1 442	553	161
INVERNESS	608 184	604 098	1	606 722	601 550	1	1 462	2 548	-43
ISLAY	26 085	21 609	21	25 721	21 230	21	364	379	-4
ISLES OF SCILLY (ST.MARYS)	89 170	97 012	-8	89 170	97 012	-8	-	-	-
ISLES OF SCILLY (TRESCO)	-	25 563	..	-	24 175	..	-	1 388	..
KIRKWALL	159 325	140 683	13	149 574	132 235	13	9 751	8 448	15
LANDS END (ST JUST)	46 626	33 108	41	46 299	31 964	45	327	1 144	-71
LEEDS BRADFORD	3 318 358	2 990 517	11	3 314 395	2 968 700	12	3 963	21 817	-82
LERWICK (TINGWALL)	3 784	5 041	-25	3 784	5 041	-25	-	-	-
LIVERPOOL (JOHN LENNON)	4 187 493	4 463 257	-6	4 185 757	4 458 500	-6	1 736	4 757	-64
LYDD	670	445	51	670	445	51	-	-	-
MANCHESTER	20 751 581	19 736 502	5	20 680 467	19 654 100	5	71 114	82 402	-14
MANSTON (KENT INT)	40 391	8 595	370	40 143	8 262	386	248	333	-26
NEWCASTLE	4 420 839	4 366 196	1	4 415 262	4 354 648	1	5 577	11 548	-52
NEWQUAY	174 891	166 609	5	174 632	166 272	5	259	337	-23

22.26b Terminal and Transit Passengers 2013 Comparison with the Previous Year

	Terminal and Transit Passengers			Terminal Passengers			Transit Passengers		
	2013	2012	Percentage Change	2013	2012	Percentage Change	2013	2012	Percentage Change
Other UK Airports(Continued)									
NORWICH	463 401	396 676	17	463 029	396 646	17	372	30	1140
OXFORD (KIDLINGTON)	6 847	7 223	-5	6 840	6 577	4	7	646	-99
PENZANCE HELIPORT	-	61 747	::	-	61 747	::	-	-	::
PRESTWICK	1 145 836	1 067 933	7	1 144 568	1 066 917	7	1 268	1 016	25
SCATSTA	298 308	304 480	-2	298 308	304 426	-2	-	54	::
SHOREHAM	732	480	53	732	480	53	-	-	::
SOUTHAMPTON	1 722 758	1 694 120	2	1 722 471	1 693 350	2	287	770	-63
STORNOWAY	122 410	119 411	3	119 904	115 860	3	2 506	3 551	-29
SUMBURGH	212 233	150 567	41	209 747	148 861	41	2 486	1 706	46
TIREE	8 560	7 545	13	8 270	7 317	13	290	228	27
WICK JOHN O GROATS	33 639	24 976	35	33 091	24 920	33	548	56	879
Total Other UK Airports	88 883 424	85 931 485	3	88 730 170	85 729 239	4	153 254	202 246	-24
Total All Reporting UK Airports	228 594 686	220 928 971	3	228 382 431	220 643 651	4	212 255	285 320	-26
Non UK Reporting Airports									
ALDERNEY	62 855	64 165	-2	62 855	64 165	-2	-	-	::
GUERNSEY	886 396	890 746	0	856 731	862 330	-1	29 665	28 416	4
ISLE OF MAN	739 883	697 123	6	738 522	695 610	6	1 161	1 513	-23
JERSEY	1 453 863	1 468 333	-1	1 429 378	1 441 671	-1	24 485	26 662	-8
Total Non UK Reporting Airports	3 142 797	3 120 367	1	3 087 486	3 063 776	1	55 311	56 591	-2

Notes

Please note that figures may change overtime as each new version is produced. Information relating to an airport that has ceased to handle regular traffic/closed will be excluded from this table completely. For data concerning historical years it is recommended that you use earlier produced versions of this table.

Source: Civil Aviation Authority

759

22.26c Freight by Type and Nationality of Operator 2013 Tonnes

		Scheduled Services						Charter Flights					
		UK Operators		Other EU Operators		Other Overseas Operators		UK Operators		Other EU Operators		Other Overseas Operators	
	Total	Set Down	Picked Up	Set Down	Picked Up	Set Down	Picked Up	Set Down	Picked Up	Set Down	Picked Up	Set Down	Picked Up
London Area Airports													
GATWICK	96 724	20 773	25 636	1 121	575	24 209	17 721	3 758	2 863	26	42	-	-
HEATHROW	1 422 939	313 839	322 207	10 763	9 271	373 627	356 910	48	22	19 096	17 037	29	89
LUTON	29 074	89	117	7	16	2 886	1 637	900	1 170	15 137	7 058	10	47
SOUTHEND	1	-	-	-	-	-	-	-	-	1	-	-	-
STANSTED	211 952	44 799	12 593	5 015	1 995	3 308	3 610	306	198	2 798	1 708	73 029	62 594
Total London Area Airports	1 760 690	379 500	360 554	16 907	11 857	404 028	379 879	5 011	4 252	37 059	25 844	73 068	62 731
Other UK Airports													
ABERDEEN	7 102	32	498	323	323	109	113	2 851	2 838	4	2	9	1
BARRA	22	22	-	-	-	-	-	-	-	-	-	-	-
BELFAST CITY (GEORGE BEST)	527	131	272	67	57	-	-	-	-	-	-	-	-
BELFAST INTERNATIONAL	29 288	1	-	-	-	76	2	116	19	17 912	10 360	374	428
BENBECULA	42	37	5	-	-	-	-	-	-	-	-	-	-
BIRMINGHAM	21 067	108	265	229	163	7 940	6 460	75	90	37	10	2 875	2 816
BOURNEMOUTH	1 818	-	-	-	-	-	-	5	1 792	21	-	-	-
CARDIFF WALES	48	-	-	-	-	-	-	44	1	3	-	-	-
COVENTRY	2 355	-	-	-	-	-	-	1 151	1 204	-	-	-	-
DONCASTER SHEFFIELD	354	-	-	-	-	65	1	4	1	6	6	46	226
EAST MIDLANDS INTERNATIONAL	266 968	2	13	-	-	16	25	22 405	22 536	87 684	86 513	26 624	21 191
EDINBURGH	18 624	142	49	35	82	-	-	234	203	9 353	8 486	-	-
EXETER	1	1	-	-	-	-	-	-	-	-	-	-	-
GLASGOW	11 837	414	424	45	50	2 549	7 534	42	95	-	-	364	319
HUMBERSIDE	153	-	24	-	-	-	-	40	89	-	-	-	-
ISLAY	207	102	105	-	-	-	-	-	-	-	-	-	-
ISLES OF SCILLY (ST.MARYS)	69	59	10	-	-	-	-	-	-	-	-	-	-
KIRKWALL	38	9	29	-	-	-	-	-	-	-	-	-	-
LANDS END (ST JUST)	61	8	53	-	-	-	-	-	-	-	-	-	-
LEEDS BRADFORD	324	5	18	2	1	270	28	-	-	-	-	-	-
LIVERPOOL (JOHN LENNON)	278	26	57	2	187	-	-	-	-	-	-	-	-
MANCHESTER	96 373	3 261	3 785	1 022	716	41 674	31 975	2 192	1 730	2 617	3 451	1 307	2 643
MANSTON (KENT INT)	29 306	-	-	-	-	-	-	4	2	13 156	96	13 973	2 076
NEWCASTLE	3 701	1	2	9	4	998	2 265	-	3	-	-	202	217
NORWICH	160	-	-	-	-	-	-	48	112	-	-	-	-
PRESTWICK	9 526	-	-	4 825	3 460	-	-	-	-	19	21	105	1 096
SCATSTA	849	-	-	-	-	-	-	396	453	-	1	-	-
SOUTHAMPTON	133	17	114	-	-	-	-	-	-	1	1	-	-
STORNOWAY	114	82	32	-	-	-	-	-	-	-	-	-	-
SUMBURGH	329	297	17	-	-	-	-	8	6	-	-	-	-
TIREE	21	21	1	-	-	-	-	-	-	-	-	-	-
Total Other UK Airports	501 696	4 778	5 770	6 559	5 043	53 696	48 402	29 618	31 174	130 812	108 946	45 884	31 014
Total All Reporting UK Airports	2 262 386	384 279	366 324	23 466	16 900	457 724	428 280	34 629	35 426	167 871	134 790	118 952	93 744

22.26c Freight by Type and Nationality of Operator 2013 Tonnes

	Total	Scheduled Services						Charter Flights					
		UK Operators		Other EU Operators		Other Overseas Operators		UK Operators		Other EU Operators		Other Overseas Operators	
		Set Down	Picked Up	Set Down	Picked Up	Set Down	Picked Up	Set Down	Picked Up	Set Down	Picked Up	Set Down	Picked Up
Non UK Reporting Airports (Continued)													
Non UK Reporting Airports													
ALDERNEY	128	87	41	-	-	-	-	-	-	-	-	-	-
GUERNSEY	2 026	233	134	-	-	-	-	1 476	184	-	-	-	-
ISLE OF MAN	447	173	57	3	-	-	-	210	5	-	-	-	-
JERSEY	2 823	236	115	-	-	-	-	2 116	357	-	-	-	-
Total Non UK Reporting Airports	5 425	730	346	3	-	-	-	3 801	545	-	-	-	-

Source: Civil Aviation Authority

22.26d Mail by Type and Nationality of Operator 2013 Tonnes

	Total	Scheduled Services						Charter Flights					
		UK Operators		Other EU Operators		Other Overseas Operators		UK Operators		Other EU Operators		Other Overseas Operators	
		Set Down	Picked Up	Set Down	Picked Up	Set Down	Picked Up	Set Down	Picked Up	Set Down	Picked Up	Set Down	Picked Up
London Area Airports													
GATWICK	4 314	305	1 106	601	1 537	171	586	2	5	-	-	-	-
HEATHROW	92 037	9 049	15 328	5 699	6 323	21 050	34 550	3	-	-	1	5	27
STANSTED	24 707	-	10	32	1	9	3	9 785	14 687	-	56	115	9
Total London Area Airports	121 057	9 354	16 443	6 332	7 861	21 231	35 139	9 790	14 693	-	58	120	36
Other UK Airports													
ABERDEEN	362	1	22	-	-	-	-	213	124	2	-	-	-
BELFAST INTERNATIONAL	14 776	1	-	-	-	-	-	8 570	6 160	18	-	-	28
BENBECULA	1	-	-	-	-	-	-	-	-	-	-	-	-
BIRMINGHAM	15	1	-	-	1	-	12	-	-	-	-	-	-
BOURNEMOUTH	7 608	1	-	-	-	-	-	3 470	4 131	6	-	-	-
CARDIFF WALES	986	-	-	-	-	-	-	986	-	-	-	-	-
EAST MIDLANDS INTERNATIONAL	30 131	3	483	3	-	-	-	12 981	16 663	-	-	-	-
EDINBURGH	19 458	120	60	-	16	20	16	10 876	8 296	25	16	5	5
EXETER	5 237	-	-	-	-	-	-	3 016	2 221	-	-	-	-
GLASGOW	155	22	73	-	-	-	-	31	29	-	-	-	-
INVERNESS	8	-	-	-	-	-	-	8	-	-	-	-	-
ISLAY	67	40	28	-	-	-	-	-	-	-	-	-	-
ISLES OF SCILLY (ST.MARYS)	170	111	58	-	-	-	-	-	-	-	-	-	-
KIRKWALL	27	8	19	-	-	-	-	-	-	-	-	-	-
LANDS END (ST JUST)	138	43	95	-	-	-	-	-	-	-	-	-	-
MANCHESTER	726	2	1	4	10	47	660	1	-	-	-	-	-
NEWCASTLE	6 512	-	-	-	-	-	-	3 624	2 888	-	-	-	-
TIREE	32	27	5	-	-	-	-	-	-	-	-	-	-
Total Other UK Airports	86 411	379	844	9	27	67	689	43 776	40 514	51	16	5	33
Total All Reporting UK Airports	207 468	9 734	17 287	6 341	7 888	21 298	35 828	53 566	55 206	51	74	125	69
Non UK Reporting Airports													
ALDERNEY	89	57	32	-	-	-	-	-	-	-	-	-	-
GUERNSEY	2 646	33	56	-	-	-	-	1 371	1 187	-	-	-	-
ISLE OF MAN	2 511	-	-	-	-	-	-	1 465	1 046	-	-	-	-
JERSEY	1 565	-	-	-	-	-	-	1 116	449	-	-	-	-
Total Non UK Reporting Airports	6 811	90	89	-	-	-	-	3 952	2 681	-	-	-	-

Source: Civil Aviation Authority

Government finance

Chapter 23

Government Finance

Public sector (Tables 23.1 to 23.3 and 23.6)

In Table 23.1 the term public sector describes the consolidation of central government, local government and public corporations. General government is the consolidated total of central government and local government. The table shows details of the key public sector finances' indicators, consistent with the European System of Accounts 1995 (ESA95), by sub-sector.

The concepts in Table 23.1 are consistent with the format for public finances in the Economic and Fiscal Strategy Report (EFSR), published by HM Treasury on 11 June 1998, and the Budget. The public sector current budget is equivalent to net saving in national accounts plus capital tax receipts. Net investment is gross capital formation, plus payments less receipts of investment grants, less depreciation. Net borrowing is net investment less current budget. Net borrowing differs from the net cash requirement (see below) in that it is measured on an accruals basis whereas the net cash requirement is mainly a cash measure which includes some financial transactions.

Table 23.2 shows the public sector key fiscal balances. The table shows the component detail of the public sector key fiscal balance by economic category. The tables are consistent with the Budget.

Table 23.3 shows public sector net debt. Public sector net debt consists of the public sector's financial liabilities at face value, minus its liquid assets – mainly foreign currency exchange reserves and bank deposits. General government gross debt (consolidated) in Table 23.3 is consistent with the definition of general government gross debt reported to the European Commission under the requirements of the Maastricht Treaty.

More information on the concepts in Table 23.1, 23.2 and 23.3 can be found in a guide to monthly public sector finance statistics, GSS Methodology Series No 12, the ONS First Releases Public Sector Finances and Financial Statistics Explanatory Handbook.

Table 23.6 shows the taxes and National Insurance contributions paid to central government, local government, and to the institutions of the European Union. The table is the same as Table 11.1 of the National Accounts Blue Book. More information on the data and concepts in the table can be found in Chapter 11 of the Blue Book.

Consolidated Fund and National Loans Fund (Tables 23.4, 23.5 and 23.7)

The central government embraces all bodies for whose activities a Minister of the Crown, or other responsible person, is accountable to Parliament. It includes, in addition to the ordinary government departments, a number of bodies administering public policy, but without the substantial degree of financial independence which characterises the public corporations. It also includes certain extra-budgetary funds and accounts controlled by departments.

The government's financial transactions are handled through a number of statutory funds or accounts. The most important of these is the Consolidated Fund, which is the government's main account with the Bank of England. Up to 31 March 1968 the Consolidated Fund was virtually synonymous with the term 'Exchequer', which was then the government's central cash account. From 1 April 1968 the National Loans Fund, with a separate account at the Bank of England, was set up by the National Loans Act 1968. The general effect of this Act was to remove from the Consolidated Fund most of the government's domestic lending and the whole of the government's borrowing transactions, and to provide for them to be brought to account in the National Loans Fund.

Revenue from taxation and miscellaneous receipts, including interest and dividends on loans made from votes, continue to be paid into the Consolidated Fund.

After meeting the ordinary expenditure on Supply Services and the Consolidated Fund Standing Services, the surplus or deficit of the Consolidated Fund (Table 23.4), is payable into or met by the National Loans Fund. Table 23.4 also provides a summary of the transactions of the National Loans Fund. The service of the National Debt, previously borne by the Consolidated Fund, is now met from the National Loans Fund which receives:

• interest payable on loans to the nationalised industries, local authorities and other bodies, whether the loans were made before or after 1 April 1968 and

• the profits of the Issue Department of the Bank of England, mainly derived from interest on government securities, which were formerly paid into the Exchange Equalisation Account.

The net cost of servicing the National Debt after applying these interest receipts and similar items is a charge on the Consolidated Fund as part of the standing services. Details of National Loans Fund loans outstanding are shown in Table 23.5. Details of borrowing and repayments of debt, other than loans from the National Loans Fund, are shown in Table 23.7.

Income tax (Table 23.10, 23.11)

Following the introduction of Independent Taxation from 1990/91, the Married Couple's Allowance was introduced. It is payable in addition to the Personal Allowance and between 1990/91 and 1992/93 went to the husband unless the transfer condition was met. The condition was that the husband was unable to make full use of the allowance himself and, in that case, he could transfer only part or all of the Married Couple's Allowance to his wife. In 1993/94 all or half of the allowance could be transferred to the wife if the couple had agreed beforehand. The wife has the right to claim half the allowance. The Married Couple's Allowance, and allowances linked to it, were restricted to 20 per cent in 1994/95 and to 15 per cent from 1995/96. From 2000/01 only people born before 6 April 1935 are entitled to Married Couple's Allowance.

The age allowance replaces the single allowance, provided the taxpayer's income is below the limits shown in the table. From 1989/90, for incomes in excess of the limits, the allowance is reduced by £1 for each additional £2 of income until the ordinary limit is reached (before it was £2 for each £3 of additional income). The relief is due where the taxpayer is aged 65 or over in the year of assessment.

The additional Personal Allowance could be claimed by a single parent (or by a married man if his wife was totally incapacitated) who maintained a resident child at his or her own expense. Widow's Bereavement Allowance was due to a widow in the year of her husband's death and in the following year provided the widow had not remarried before the beginning of that year. Both the additional Personal Allowance and the Widow's Bereavement Allowance were abolished from April 2000.

The Blind Person's Allowance may be claimed by blind persons (in England and Wales, registered as blind by a local authority) and surplus Blind Person's Allowance may be transferred to a husband or wife. Relief on life assurance premiums is given by deduction from the premium payable. From 1984/85, it is confined to policies made before 14 March 1984.

From 1993/94 until 1998/99 a number of taxpayers with taxable income in excess of the lower rate limit only paid tax at the lower rate. This was because it was only their dividend income and (from 1996/97) their savings income which took their taxable income above the lower rate limit but below the basic rate limit, and such income was chargeable to tax at the lower rate and not the basic rate.

In 1999/2000 the 10 per cent starting rate replaced the lower rate and taxpayers with savings or dividend income at the basic rate of tax are taxed at 20 per cent and 10 per cent respectively. Before 1999/2000 these people would have been classified as lower rate taxpayers.

Rateable values (Table 23.12)

Major changes to local government finance in England and Wales took effect from 1 April 1990. These included the abolition of domestic rating (replaced by the Community Charge, then replaced in 1993 by the Council Tax), the revaluation of all non-domestic properties, and the introduction of the Uniform Business Rate. Also in 1990, a new classification scheme was introduced which has resulted in differences in coverage. Further differences are caused by legislative changes which have changed the treatment of certain types of property. There was little change in the total rateable value of non-domestic properties when all these properties were re-valued in April 1995. Rateable values for offices fell and there was a rise for all other property types shown in the table.

With effect from 1 April 2000, all non-domestic properties were re-valued. Overall there was an increase in rateable values of over 25 per cent compared with the last year of the 1995 list. The largest proportionate increase was for offices and cinemas, with all property types given in the table showing rises.

The latest revaluation affecting all non-domestic properties took effect from 1 April 2010. In this revaluation the overall increase in rateable values between 1 April of the first year of the new list and the same day on the last year of the 2005 list was 21 per cent. The largest proportionate increase was for offices and educational properties, with all property types in the table showing rises.

Local authority capital expenditure and receipts (Table 23.16)

Authorities finance capital spending in a number of ways, including use of their own revenue funds, borrowing or grants and contributions from elsewhere. Until 31 March 2004, the capital finance system laid down in Part 4 of the Local Government and Housing Act 1989 (the '1989 Act') provided the framework within which authorities were permitted to finance capital spending from sources other than revenue - that is by the use of borrowing, long-term credit or capital receipts.

Until 31 March 2004, capital spending could be financed by:

• revenue resources – either the General Fund Revenue Account, the Housing Revenue Account (HRA) or the Major Repairs Reserve – but an authority could not charge council tenants for spending on general services, or spending on council houses to local taxpayers

• borrowing or long-term credit as authorised by the credit approvals issued by central government. Credit approvals were normally accompanied by an element of Revenue Support Grant (RSG) covering most of the costs of borrowing

• grants received from central government

• contributions or grants from elsewhere – including the National Lottery and non-departmental public bodies (NDPBs) such as Sport England, English Heritage and Natural England, as well as private sector partners, capital receipts (that is, proceeds from the sale of land, buildings or other fixed assets) and sums set aside as Provision for Credit Liabilities (PCL). This required the use of a credit approval, unless the authority was debt-free

From 1 April 2004, capital spending can be financed in the same ways, except that central government no longer issues credit approvals to allow authorities to finance capital spending by borrowing. However, it continues to provide financial support in the usual way, via RSG or HRA subsidy, towards some capital spending financed by borrowing that is Supported Capital Expenditure (Revenue). Authorities are now free to finance capital spending by self-financed borrowing within limits of affordability set, having regard to the 2003 Act and the CIPFA Prudential Code. The concept of PCL has not been carried forward into the new system, although authorities that were debt-free and had a negative credit ceiling at the end of the old system could still spend amounts of PCL built up under the old rules.

Local authority financing for capital expenditure (Table 23.16, 23.17)

Capital spending by local authorities is mainly for buying, constructing or improving physical assets such as:
• buildings – schools, houses, libraries and museums, police and fire stations
• land – for development, roads, playing fields
• vehicles, plant and machinery – including street lighting and road signs

It also includes grants and advances made to the private sector or the rest of the public sector for capital purposes, such as advances to Registered Social Landlords Local authority capital expenditure more than doubled between 2001/02 and 2007/08.

The underlying trend in capital expenditure shows an increase of 8 per cent from 2008/09 to 2009/10. The exceptional event was the payment by the Greater London Authority (Transport for London) of £1.7 billion to Metronet in 2007/08.

New construction, conversion and renovation forms the major part of capital spending. The largest increases in capital expenditure in 2008/09 were in police (44 per cent), and education (22 per cent). Capital expenditure on transport increased by 14 per cent, allowing for the Greater London Authority's grant payment via TfL in respect of Metronet in 2007/08. Between 2004/05 and 2008/09 capital expenditure on transport had risen from 20 per cent to 24 per cent of the total, while capital expenditure on housing has fallen from 28 per cent to 25 per cent of the total.

The largest percentage increase in capital expenditure in 2009/10 was in transport (24 per cent). Capital expenditure on housing and police fell by 8 per cent and 11 per cent respectively. Between 2005/06 and 2009/10 capital expenditure on transport has risen from 21 per cent to 28 per cent of the total, while capital expenditure on housing has fallen from 27 per cent to 21 per cent of the total.

23.1

Sector analysis of key fiscal balances[1]
United Kingdom

Not seasonally adjusted

£ million[2]

		2008 /09	2009 /10	2010 /11	2011 /12	2012 /13	2013 /14
Surplus on current budget[3]							
Central Government	ANLV	−46 497	−100 936	−96 334	−86 250	−85 613	−69 159
Local government	NMMX	−7 536	−8 167	−6 298	−5 296	−3 096	−1 683
General Government	ANLW	−54 325	−109 237	−102 380	−91 211	−87 803	−70 179
Public corporations	IL6M	15 103	16 335	18 902	18 982	13 023	8 484
Public sector	ANMU	−37 875	−86 149	−74 938	−62 325	−71 288	−62 227
Net investment[4]							
Central government	-ANNS	48 705	55 970	43 391	27 857	40 270	33 969
Local government	-ANNT	590	−1 666	−1 172	6 525	−1 961	−2 867
General Government	-ANNV	48 962	54 045	41 092	33 300	34 855	27 144
Public corporations	-JSH6	−8 773	−9 027	−986	−1 915	−1 911	−3 021
Public sector	-ANNW	40 191	45 045	40 106	31 410	32 891	24 173
Net borrowing[5]							
Central government	-NMFJ	95 161	156 781	138 346	112 690	121 523	98 507
Local government	-NMOE	8 126	6 501	5 126	11 821	1 135	−1 184
General Government	-NNBK	103 287	163 282	143 472	124 511	122 658	97 323
Public corporations	-IL6E	−23 876	−25 361	−19 888	−20 897	−14 934	−11 505
Public sector	-ANNX	78 399	131 424	116 176	94 801	107 710	89 649
Net cash requirement							
Central government[6]	RUUX	163 909	197 488	132 069	108 644	94 596	79 832
Local government	ABEG	4 401	4 958	773	8 816	1 647	−3 114
General Government	RUUS	166 914	202 673	138 454	126 325	..	..
Public corporations	IL6F	14 178	−105 774	−120 697	−164 127	−105 402	−66 659
Public sector	RURQ	181 599	92 387	4 765	−57 919	−21 738	−2 628
Public sector debt							
Public sector net debt	BKQK	2 132 221	2 245 262	2 261 767	2 185 009	2 211 873	1 975 216
Public sector net debt (£ billion)	RUTN	2 132.2	2 245.3	2 261.8	2 185.0	2 211.9	1 975.2
Public sector net debt as a percentage of GDP	RUTO	144.1	145.6	141.2	132.6	130.6	111.4
Excluding financial interventions							
Net debt	HF6W	724.4	956.4	1 101.1	1 191.0	1 299.1	1 402.1
Net debt as a % GDP	HF6X	49.0	62.0	68.7	72.3	76.7	79.1

1 Consistent with the latest Public Sector Finances data, compliant with the European System of Accounts 2010 (ESA10)
2 Unless otherwise stated.
3 Net saving *plus* capital taxes.
4 Gross capital formation *plus* payments *less* receipts of investment grants *less* depreciation.

5 Net investment *less* surplus on current budget. A version of General government net borrowing is reported to the European Commision under the requirements of the Maastricht Treaty.
6 Central government net cash requirement (own account).

Source: Office for National Statistics: 020 7014 2124

23.2 Public sector transactions and fiscal balances[1]
United Kingdom

£ million

		2008 /09	2009 /10	2010 /11	2011 /12	2012 /13	2013 /14
Current receipts							
Taxes on income and wealth	ANSO	205 546	183 282	196 409	197 534	195 592	199 793
Taxes on production	NMYE	170 151	172 284	194 006	206 927	211 910	223 584
Other current taxes[2]	MJBC	33 281	33 968	34 618	36 936	37 107	39 170
Taxes on capital	NMGI	26 552	2 431	2 722	2 955	3 150	4 413
Social contributions	ANBO	96 613	96 638	97 747	101 597	104 483	107 306
Gross operating surplus	ANBP	44 427	44 756	50 305	50 181	48 467	49 236
Interest and dividends from private sector and Rest of World	ANBQ	49 284	54 120	45 786	49 720	45 054	34 693
Rent and other current transfers[3]	ANBS	−94	766	−1 180	−1 993	109	−708
Total current receipts	ANBT	602 140	588 247	620 413	643 857	645 872	657 487
Current expenditure							
Current expenditure on goods and services[4]	GZSN	320 038	332 693	339 475	339 739	341 254	347 208
Subsidies	NMRL	9 044	10 735	9 179	8 496	9 927	9 957
Social benefits	ANLY	172 206	188 693	196 850	205 872	217 206	220 127
Net current grants abroad[5]	GZSI	−1 347	976	3 244	2 862	3 027	3 788
Other current grants	NNAI	25 548	28 711	27 345	25 981	23 921	22 041
Interest and dividends paid to private sector and Rest of World	ANLO	74 917	70 037	73 828	76 747	72 341	63 851
Total current expenditure	ANLT	611 421	643 550	663 224	673 090	682 415	683 014
Saving, gross plus capital taxes	ANSP	−9 282	−55 303	−42 810	−29 233	−36 543	−25 527
Depreciation	-ANNZ	−29 517	−31 285	−32 700	−33 986	−34 851	−35 728
Surplus on current budget	ANMU	−37 875	−86 149	−74 938	−62 325	−71 288	−62 227
Net investment							
Gross fixed capital formation[6]	ANSQ	51 986	57 026	56 147	50 681	45 556	47 265
Less depreciation	-ANNZ	−29 517	−31 285	−32 700	−33 986	−34 851	−35 728
Increase in inventories and valuables	ANSR	325	−30	101	−	−100	118
Capital grants to private sector and Rest of World	ANSS	44 410	20 540	17 504	15 523	23 604	14 527
Capital grants from private sector and Rest of World	-ANST	−27 013	−1 206	−946	−808	−1 318	−2 009
Total net investment	-ANNW	40 191	45 045	40 106	31 410	32 891	24 173
Net borrowing[7]	-ANNX	78 399	131 424	116 176	94 801	107 710	89 649
Financial transactions determining net cash requirement							
Net lending to private sector and Rest of World	ANSU	−9 975	−34 383	−56 915	−29 980	−48 955	−8 671
Net acquisition of UK company securities	ANSV	54 029	53 275	−28 571	−67 232	−56 262	−76 027
Accounts receivable/payable	ANSW	5 443	23 360	−1 477	−3 646	642	−92
Adjustment for interest on gilts	ANSX	−4 885	1 817	−7 819	−2 291	−5 126	1 761
Other financial transcations[8]	ANSY	58 588	−83 106	−16 629	−49 571	−19 748	−9 251
Public sector net cash requirement	RURQ	181 599	92 387	4 765	−57 919	−21 738	−2 628

1 See chapter text.
2 Includes domestic rates, council tax, community charge, motor vehicle duty paid by household and some licence fees.
3 ESA10 transactions D44, D45, D74, D75 and D72-D71: includes rent of land, oil royalties, other property income and fines.
4 Includes non-trading capital consumption.

5 Net of current grants received from abroad.
6 Including net acquisition of land.
7 Net investment *less* surplus on current budget.
8 Includes statistical discrepancy, finance leasing and similar borrowing, insurance technical reserves and some other minor adjustments.

Source: Office for National Statistics: 020 7014 2124

23.3 Public sector net debt[1]
United Kingdom

£ million

		2008 /09	2009 /10	2010 /11	2011 /12	2012 /13	2013 /14
Central government sterling gross debt:							
British government stock							
Conventional gilts	BKPK	426 107	608 511	697 968	788 568	..	..
Index linked gilts	BKPL	154 038	178 170	220 631	253 779	..	..
Total	BKPM	580 145	786 681	918 599	1 042 347	1 142 442	1 244 355
Sterling Treasury bills	BKPJ	43 748	62 866	63 174	69 933	56 370	56 453
National savings	ACUA	97 231	98 804	98 886	102 903	102 238	105 663
Tax instruments	ACRV	1 121	819	679	638	633	880
Other sterling debt[2]	BKSK	64 612	39 934	34 068	42 506	34 260	35 257
Central government sterling gross debt total	BKSL	786 857	989 104	1 115 406	1 258 327	1 335 943	1 442 608
Central government foreign currency gross debt:							
US$ bonds	BKPG	–	–	–	–	–	–
ECU bonds	EYSJ	–	–	–	–	..	..
ECU/Euro Treasury notes	EYSV	–	–	–	–	..	..
Other foreign currency debt	BKPH	–	–	–	–	–	–
Central government foreign currency gross debt total	BKPI	–	–	–	–	–	–
Central government gross debt total	BKPW	809 649	1 059 345	1 196 643	1 329 736	1 403 501	1 504 820
Local government gross debt total	EYKP	67 353	68 589	70 977	81 604	84 705	85 458
less							
Central government holdings of local government debt	-EYKZ	–50 508	–50 889	–52 848	–61 641	..	..
Local government holdings of central government debt	-EYLA	–2 960	–2 689	–2 076	–3 415	..	..
General government gross debt (consolidated)	BKPX	823 314	1 073 796	1 212 111	1 345 202	1 420 611	1 521 156
Public corporations gross debt	EYYD	13 669	10 518	10 405	10 820	10 127	7 743
less:							
Central government holdings of public corporations debt	-EYXY	–4 879	–5 617	–5 604	–5 839	..	..
Local government holdings of public corporations debt	-EYXZ	–107	–153	–155	–152	..	..
Public corporations holdings of central government debt	-BKPZ	–3 947	–3 352	–3 301	–4 383	..	..
Public corporations holdings of local government debt	-EYXV	–33	–63	–150	–110	..	..
Public sector gross debt (consolidated)	BKQA	2 806 708	2 870 234	2 889 398	2 872 251	2 802 165	2 449 407
Public sector liquid assets:							
Official reserves	AIPD	31 527	44 652	52 969	..	..	..
Central government deposits[3]	BKSM	5 242	4 351	5 783	6 672	6 034	8 280
Other central government	BKSN	39 075	48 143	21 204	45 634	31 813	45 572
Local government deposits[3]	BKSO	21 781	18 177	19 145	18 123	21 109	23 169
Other local government short term assets	BKQG	2 072	1 780	3 227	4 733	4 119	4 722
Public corporations deposits[3]	BKSP	1 781	2 203	1 923	2 910	2 701	2 214
Other public corporations short term assets	BKSQ	2 166	2 284	2 170	2 296	2 280	2 169
Public sector liquid assets total	BKQJ	673 963	637 424	632 261	681 778	612 635	515 713
Public sector net debt	BKQK	2 132 221	2 245 262	2 261 767	2 185 009	2 211 873	1 975 216
as percentage of GDP[4]	RUTO	*144.1*	*145.6*	*141.2*	*132.6*	*130.6*	*111.4*

1 See chapter text.
2 Including overdraft with Bank of England.
3 Bank and building society deposits.
4 Gross domestic product at market prices from 12 months centred on the end
of the month.

Source: Office for National Statistics: 020 7014 2124

23.4a Central government surplus on current budget and net borrowing

£ million

| | Taxes on production | of which | Taxes on income and wealth | | | | | | Asset | | |
| | | | Income and capital gains | | | | | Interest and | Purchase | Other | |
	Total	VAT	Total	tax[1]	Other[2]	Other taxes	NICs[3]	dividends	Facility	receipts[4]	Total
	NMBY	NZGF	NMCU	LIBR	LIBP	LIQR	AIIH	LIQP	L6BD	LIQQ	ANBV
2002	141,549	71,066	142,814	112,440	30,374	9,569	63,410	7,154	0	11,930	376,426
2003	148,641	77,343	147,034	116,509	30,525	10,118	71,540	7,697	0	12,713	397,743
2004	156,416	81,544	158,434	125,032	33,402	10,862	79,224	7,426	0	13,246	425,608
2005	159,958	83,425	176,676	135,867	40,809	11,481	84,459	7,125	0	14,013	453,712
2006	169,003	87,758	196,494	145,608	50,886	12,262	89,550	6,747	0	14,516	488,572
2007	177,720	92,025	203,646	157,084	46,562	13,213	93,210	7,970	0	14,927	510,686
2008	175,685	92,002	212,166	161,624	50,542	12,939	98,319	9,746	0	15,863	524,718
2009	164,831	79,900	190,476	152,553	37,923	12,295	94,445	9,085	0	16,476	487,608
2010	189,232	95,865	197,699	153,507	44,192	12,881	97,346	7,920	0	17,057	522,135
2011	204,550	111,437	204,710	159,070	45,640	14,798	101,441	8,078	0	17,918	551,495
2012	210,414	113,892	198,590	155,278	43,312	15,248	104,319	11,885	0	19,556	560,012
2013	219,626	118,296	203,004	160,695	42,309	17,115	106,085	26,673	18,609	20,563	593,066
2002/03	142,550	71,604	143,256	112,373	30,883	9,588	63,529	7,735	0	12,503	379,161
2003/04	151,777	79,207	149,400	119,146	30,254	10,309	75,148	7,660	0	12,244	406,538
2004/05	156,816	81,864	164,727	128,714	36,013	10,950	80,923	7,054	0	13,615	434,085
2005/06	161,866	83,507	184,158	139,116	45,042	11,760	85,559	7,048	0	14,123	464,514
2006/07	171,793	90,008	198,045	150,325	47,720	12,520	90,916	6,779	0	14,601	494,654
2007/08	178,630	92,469	211,697	162,356	49,341	13,264	95,437	8,683	0	15,100	522,811
2008/09	169,840	87,805	205,759	158,685	47,074	12,717	96,613	9,681	0	16,109	510,719
2009/10	171,965	84,825	187,833	149,640	38,193	12,389	96,638	8,580	0	16,560	493,965
2010/11	193,649	99,523	202,063	156,851	45,212	12,882	97,747	8,011	0	17,319	531,671
2011/12	206,464	112,067	202,767	157,043	45,724	15,355	101,597	9,612	0	18,134	553,929
2012/13	211,447	114,465	198,967	156,222	42,745	15,361	104,483	16,668	6,428	19,932	566,858
2013/14	223,244	120,226	203,566	161,528	42,038	17,444	107,306	20,295	12,181	20,759	592,614
2007 Q1	42,871	22,568	63,943	52,924	11,019	3,260	24,995	1,940	0	3,705	140,714
2007 Q2	43,996	22,676	40,152	31,564	8,588	3,311	22,354	1,767	0	3,734	115,314
2007 Q3	45,363	23,368	52,067	38,859	13,208	3,438	22,560	1,789	0	3,712	128,929
2007 Q4	45,490	23,413	47,484	33,737	13,747	3,204	23,301	2,474	0	3,776	125,729
2008 Q1	43,781	23,012	71,994	58,196	13,798	3,311	27,222	2,653	0	3,878	152,839
2008 Q2	45,596	24,683	40,634	31,513	9,121	3,315	23,784	2,113	0	3,918	119,360
2008 Q3	43,837	22,938	54,410	40,019	14,391	3,293	23,597	2,427	0	4,039	131,603
2008 Q4	42,471	21,369	45,128	31,896	13,232	3,020	23,716	2,553	0	4,028	120,916
2009 Q1	37,936	18,815	65,587	55,257	10,330	3,089	25,516	2,588	0	4,124	138,840
2009 Q2	40,363	19,079	37,265	30,160	7,105	3,040	22,990	2,659	0	4,048	110,365
2009 Q3	42,555	20,658	45,250	36,786	8,464	3,243	22,535	1,779	0	4,124	119,486
2009 Q4	43,977	21,348	42,374	30,350	12,024	2,923	23,404	2,059	0	4,180	118,917
2010 Q1	45,070	23,740	62,944	52,344	10,600	3,183	27,709	2,083	0	4,208	145,197
2010 Q2	49,602	23,810	38,677	30,987	7,690	3,202	23,115	1,591	0	4,216	120,403
2010 Q3	46,910	24,090	50,785	38,451	12,334	3,391	22,983	2,256	0	4,284	130,609
2010 Q4	47,650	24,225	45,293	31,725	13,568	3,105	23,539	1,990	0	4,349	125,926
2011 Q1	49,487	27,398	67,308	55,688	11,620	3,184	28,110	2,174	0	4,470	154,733
2011 Q2	49,997	27,363	40,091	32,055	8,036	3,394	24,484	1,874	0	4,444	124,284
2011 Q3	52,652	28,427	51,360	38,637	12,723	4,494	24,326	2,129	0	4,485	139,446
2011 Q4	52,414	28,249	45,951	32,690	13,261	3,726	24,521	1,901	0	4,519	133,032
2012 Q1	51,401	28,028	65,365	53,661	11,704	3,741	28,266	3,708	0	4,686	157,167
2012 Q2	51,084	28,143	39,465	31,481	7,984	3,684	25,631	4,244	0	4,886	128,994
2012 Q3	53,042	28,038	49,272	38,314	10,958	4,046	25,201	1,981	0	4,956	138,498
2012 Q4	54,887	29,683	44,488	31,822	12,666	3,777	25,221	1,952	0	5,028	135,353
2013 Q1	52,434	28,601	65,742	54,605	11,137	3,854	28,430	8,491	6,428	5,062	164,013
2013 Q2	53,416	29,109	41,876	34,026	7,850	4,946	26,556	13,679	11,655	5,054	145,527
2013 Q3	56,448	30,079	49,916	38,764	11,152	4,252	25,239	2,732	526	5,088	143,675
2013 Q4	57,328	30,507	45,470	33,300	12,170	4,063	25,860	1,771	0	5,359	139,851
2014 Q1	56,052	30,531	66,304	55,438	10,866	4,183	29,651	2,113	0	5,258	163,561

Source: Office for National Statistics; HM Treasury

1. Includes capital gains tax paid by households. Includes income tax and capital gains tax paid by corporations.
2. Mainly comprises corporation tax and petroleum revenue tax.
3. Formerly titled compulsory social contributions.
Consists 4. largely of gross operating surplus, equates to depreciation for government. Also includes rent receipts.

23.4a Central government surplus on current budget and net borrowing

£ million

	Current expenditure				Saving, gross plus capital taxes	Depreciation	Current budget deficit	Net investment	Net borrowing
	Interest	Net Social Benefits	Other	Total					
	NMFX	GZSJ	LIQS	ANLP	ANPM	NSRN	-ANLV	-ANNS	-NMFJ
2002	20,912	107,799	238,563	367,274	9,152	9,834	682	19,539	20,221
2003	21,837	117,683	262,624	402,144	-4,401	10,905	15,306	24,214	39,520
2004	23,420	126,449	280,690	430,559	-4,951	11,494	16,445	23,615	40,060
2005	26,259	130,527	300,192	456,978	-3,266	12,207	15,473	25,113	40,586
2006	27,413	134,482	322,240	484,135	4,437	12,849	8,412	29,857	38,269
2007	31,520	143,582	332,047	507,149	3,537	13,296	9,759	30,811	40,570
2008	32,831	154,145	349,518	536,494	-11,776	14,289	26,065	44,652	70,717
2009	27,698	170,873	368,980	567,551	-79,943	14,836	94,779	57,075	151,854
2010	44,756	178,158	386,909	609,823	-87,688	15,488	103,176	44,160	147,336
2011	51,160	183,643	383,012	617,815	-66,320	16,390	82,710	36,435	119,145
2012	47,828	193,223	396,707	637,758	-77,746	17,123	94,869	35,151	130,020
2013	49,071	195,678	394,455	639,204	-46,138	17,363	63,501	31,045	94,546
2002/03	20,726	109,144	243,711	373,581	5,580	10,465	4,885	22,052	26,937
2003/04	22,025	120,876	266,638	409,539	-3,001	10,592	13,593	23,209	36,802
2004/05	24,570	126,997	287,475	439,042	-4,957	11,826	16,783	25,454	42,237
2005/06	26,293	131,741	305,298	463,332	1,182	12,328	11,146	24,881	36,027
2006/07	28,579	135,745	322,470	486,794	7,860	12,939	5,079	31,094	36,173
2007/08	31,220	145,283	339,263	515,766	7,045	13,499	6,454	36,113	42,567
2008/09	31,520	159,241	352,467	543,228	-32,509	14,541	47,050	47,708	94,758
2009/10	31,566	172,792	376,129	580,487	-86,522	14,895	101,417	55,000	156,417
2010/11	46,609	178,825	387,246	612,680	-81,009	15,790	96,799	42,078	138,877
2011/12	49,704	186,180	388,172	624,056	-70,127	16,607	86,734	26,708	113,442
2012/13	48,856	194,768	391,748	635,372	-68,514	17,126	85,640	39,445	125,085
2013/14	48,669	196,343	399,829	644,841	-52,227	17,440	69,667	32,300	101,967
2007 Q1	7,400	33,150	80,445	120,995	19,719	3,273	-16,446	10,889	-5,557
2007 Q2	7,912	35,360	84,632	127,904	-12,590	3,300	15,890	4,929	20,819
2007 Q3	7,164	36,403	83,586	127,153	1,776	3,328	1,552	6,944	8,496
2007 Q4	9,044	38,669	83,384	131,097	-5,368	3,395	8,763	8,049	16,812
2008 Q1	7,100	34,851	87,661	129,612	23,227	3,476	-19,751	16,191	-3,560
2008 Q2	8,869	38,220	89,218	136,307	-16,947	3,551	20,498	7,396	27,894
2008 Q3	7,716	39,340	85,651	132,707	-1,104	3,613	4,717	9,957	14,674
2008 Q4	9,146	41,734	86,988	137,868	-16,952	3,649	20,601	11,108	31,709
2009 Q1	5,789	39,947	90,610	136,346	2,494	3,728	1,234	19,247	20,481
2009 Q2	7,886	42,077	95,369	145,332	-34,967	3,661	38,628	12,336	50,964
2009 Q3	4,348	43,141	91,298	138,787	-19,301	3,701	23,002	10,282	33,284
2009 Q4	9,675	45,708	91,703	147,086	-28,169	3,746	31,915	15,210	47,125
2010 Q1	9,657	41,866	97,759	149,282	-4,085	3,787	7,872	17,172	25,044
2010 Q2	12,259	43,631	98,107	153,997	-33,594	3,837	37,431	7,822	45,253
2010 Q3	10,092	44,979	94,518	149,589	-18,980	3,901	22,881	9,390	32,271
2010 Q4	12,748	47,682	96,525	156,955	-31,029	3,963	34,992	9,776	44,768
2011 Q1	11,510	42,533	98,096	152,139	2,594	4,089	1,495	15,090	16,585
2011 Q2	14,081	45,523	99,487	159,091	-34,807	4,064	38,871	6,108	44,979
2011 Q3	11,147	47,206	92,863	151,216	-11,770	4,103	15,873	7,366	23,239
2011 Q4	14,422	48,381	92,566	155,369	-22,337	4,134	26,471	7,871	34,342
2012 Q1	10,054	45,070	103,256	158,380	-1,213	4,306	5,519	5,363	10,882
2012 Q2	14,219	48,459	98,232	160,910	-31,916	4,209	36,125	16,249	52,374
2012 Q3	9,600	49,047	96,303	154,950	-16,452	4,270	20,722	6,552	27,274
2012 Q4	13,955	50,647	98,916	163,518	-28,165	4,338	32,503	6,987	39,490
2013 Q1	11,082	46,615	98,297	155,994	8,019	4,309	-3,710	9,657	5,947
2013 Q2	14,427	48,596	105,307	168,330	-22,803	4,336	27,139	5,833	32,972
2013 Q3	10,229	49,611	93,882	153,722	-10,047	4,359	14,406	7,532	21,938
2013 Q4	13,333	50,856	96,969	161,158	-21,307	4,359	25,666	8,023	33,689
2014 Q1	10,680	47,280	103,671	161,631	1,930	4,386	2,456	10,912	13,368

Source: Office for National Statistics; HM Treasury

1. Includes capital gains tax paid by households. Includes income tax and capital gains tax paid by corporations.
2. Mainly comprises corporation tax and petroleum revenue tax.
3. Formerly titled compulsory social contributions.
4. Consists largely of gross operating surplus, equates to depreciation for government. Also includes rent receipts.

23.4b Central government surplus on current budget and net borrowing

£ million

Current receipts

| | Taxes on production | of which | Taxes on income and wealth | | | | | | Asset | | |
	Total	VAT	Total	Income and capital gains tax[1]	Other[2]	Other taxes	NICs[3]	Interest and dividends	Purchase Facility	Other receipts[4]	Total
	NMBY	NZGF	NMCU	LIBR	LIBP	LIQR	AIIH	LIQP	L6BD	LIQQ	ANBV
2012 Jan	16,335	9,253	34,521	25,300	9,221	1,186	8,710	562	0	1,562	62,876
2012 Feb	16,685	9,109	16,040	14,795	1,245	1,457	9,077	493	0	1,563	45,315
2012 Mar	18,381	9,666	14,804	13,566	1,238	1,098	10,479	2,653	0	1,561	48,976
2012 Apr	16,549	9,304	15,854	10,682	5,172	1,157	8,670	3,116	0	1,652	46,998
2012 May	16,943	9,304	11,271	9,778	1,493	1,279	8,150	644	0	1,606	39,893
2012 Jun	17,592	9,535	12,340	11,021	1,319	1,248	8,811	484	0	1,628	42,103
2012 Jul	17,894	9,379	23,650	16,563	7,087	1,431	8,486	614	0	1,660	53,735
2012 Aug	17,399	9,145	12,841	11,398	1,443	1,418	8,214	553	0	1,655	42,080
2012 Sep	17,749	9,514	12,781	10,353	2,428	1,197	8,501	814	0	1,641	42,683
2012 Oct	18,166	9,775	18,426	10,368	8,058	1,427	8,157	799	0	1,677	48,652
2012 Nov	18,072	9,758	11,089	9,510	1,579	1,187	8,136	578	0	1,675	40,737
2012 Dec	18,649	10,150	14,973	11,944	3,029	1,163	8,928	575	0	1,676	45,964
2013 Jan	16,984	9,621	34,484	26,458	8,026	1,209	8,716	4,271	3,757	1,702	67,366
2013 Feb	16,872	9,287	16,371	14,781	1,590	1,228	8,995	3,118	2,671	1,716	48,300
2013 Mar	18,578	9,693	14,887	13,366	1,521	1,417	10,719	1,102	0	1,644	48,347
2013 Apr	17,274	9,613	17,038	12,123	4,915	1,281	9,175	4,653	3,885	1,707	51,128
2013 May	17,880	9,639	12,089	10,626	1,463	2,304	8,503	4,524	3,885	1,662	46,962
2013 Jun	18,262	9,857	12,749	11,277	1,472	1,361	8,878	4,502	3,885	1,685	47,437
2013 Jul	19,069	10,117	23,844	16,820	7,024	1,450	8,332	1,151	526	1,695	55,541
2013 Aug	18,576	9,887	12,742	11,229	1,513	1,452	8,350	561	0	1,695	43,376
2013 Sep	18,803	10,075	13,330	10,715	2,615	1,350	8,557	1,020	0	1,698	44,758
2013 Oct	18,892	9,788	18,030	10,623	7,407	1,482	8,231	513	0	1,866	49,014
2013 Nov	18,809	10,138	11,958	10,495	1,463	1,271	8,400	671	0	1,799	42,908
2013 Dec	19,627	10,581	15,482	12,182	3,300	1,310	9,229	587	0	1,694	47,929
2014 Jan	18,454	10,359	32,687	25,163	7,524	1,369	8,969	537	0	1,782	63,798
2014 Feb	18,140	9,922	17,119	15,462	1,657	1,379	9,490	488	0	1,740	48,356
2014 Mar	19,458	10,250	16,498	14,813	1,685	1,435	11,192	1,088	0	1,736	51,407
2014 Apr	18,516	10,230	16,520	11,199	5,321	1,336	8,762	4,691	4,107	1,746	51,571
2014 May	18,903	10,138	11,942	10,224	1,718	1,527	8,503	618	0	1,747	43,240
2014 Jun	19,062	10,211	13,110	11,377	1,733	1,425	9,094	647	0	1,749	45,087

| | Current expenditure | | | | Saving, gross plus capital taxes | Depreciation | Current budget deficit | Net investment | Net borrowing |
	Interest	Net Social Benefits	Other	Total					
	NMFX	GZSJ	LIQS	ANLP	ANPM	NSRN	-ANLV	-ANNS	-NMFJ
2012 Jan	4,075	15,084	31,374	50,533	12,343	1,434	-10,909	2,862	-8,047
2012 Feb	4,001	14,711	33,006	51,718	-6,403	1,434	7,837	3,083	10,920
2012 Mar	1,978	15,275	38,876	56,129	-7,153	1,438	8,591	-582	8,009
2012 Apr	5,363	16,106	32,393	53,862	-6,864	1,427	8,291	3,348	11,639
2012 May	4,752	16,700	33,151	54,603	-14,710	1,381	16,091	2,036	18,127
2012 Jun	4,104	15,653	32,688	52,445	-10,342	1,401	11,743	10,865	22,608
2012 Jul	3,665	16,400	29,793	49,858	3,877	1,431	-2,446	2,523	77
2012 Aug	2,908	16,478	33,407	52,793	-10,713	1,427	12,140	1,695	13,835
2012 Sep	3,027	16,169	33,103	52,299	-9,616	1,412	11,028	2,334	13,362
2012 Oct	4,487	16,351	31,860	52,698	-4,046	1,447	5,493	2,388	7,881
2012 Nov	4,455	17,970	31,767	54,192	-13,455	1,445	14,900	1,767	16,667
2012 Dec	5,013	16,326	35,289	56,628	-10,664	1,446	12,110	2,832	14,942
2013 Jan	3,816	16,161	32,445	52,422	14,944	1,460	-13,484	3,788	-9,696
2013 Feb	4,669	14,490	31,195	50,354	-2,054	1,459	3,513	909	4,422
2013 Mar	2,597	15,964	34,657	53,218	-4,871	1,390	6,261	4,960	11,221
2013 Apr	5,211	16,145	42,673	64,029	-12,901	1,469	14,370	2,442	16,812
2013 May	4,691	16,680	30,678	52,049	-5,087	1,423	6,510	1,546	8,056
2013 Jun	4,525	15,771	31,956	52,252	-4,815	1,444	6,259	1,845	8,104
2013 Jul	3,707	16,902	31,380	51,989	3,552	1,453	-2,099	3,167	1,068
2013 Aug	3,454	16,371	30,681	50,506	-7,130	1,453	8,583	1,940	10,523
2013 Sep	3,068	16,338	31,821	51,227	-6,469	1,453	7,922	2,425	10,347
2013 Oct	5,131	16,484	31,357	52,972	-3,958	1,454	5,412	2,912	8,324
2013 Nov	4,630	17,565	31,320	53,515	-10,607	1,452	12,059	2,359	14,418
2013 Dec	3,572	16,807	34,292	54,671	-6,742	1,453	8,195	2,752	10,947
2014 Jan	3,691	16,404	32,426	52,521	11,277	1,485	-9,792	2,872	-6,920
2014 Feb	4,388	14,831	35,959	55,178	-6,822	1,485	8,307	3,157	11,464
2014 Mar	2,601	16,045	35,286	53,932	-2,525	1,416	3,941	4,883	8,824
2014 Apr	5,421	16,875	40,972	63,268	-11,697	1,488	13,185	2,483	15,668
2014 May	4,280	16,777	31,343	52,400	-9,160	1,488	10,648	1,767	12,415
2014 Jun	4,370	16,132	33,530	54,032	-8,945	1,488	10,433	2,315	12,748

1. Includes capital gains tax paid by households. Includes income tax and capital gains tax paid by corporations. Source: Office for National Statistics; HM Treasury
2. Mainly comprises corporation tax and petroleum revenue tax.
3. Formerly titled compulsory social contributions.
4. Consists largely of gross operating surplus, equates to depreciation for government. Also includes rent receipts.

23.5 National Loans Fund: assets and liabilities
United Kingdom as at 31 March 2014

	At 31 March 2014 £m	At 31 March 2013 £m
Assets		
Advances	**217,820**	171,596
Loans	**2,542**	2,997
Other assets	**67,412**	76,429
IMF Quota Subscription & Lending	**12,186**	12,958
Total assets	**299,960**	263,980
Liabilities		
Gilt-edged stock	**1,408,776**	1,315,472
National Savings and Investments	**105,663**	102,238
products Liabilities to the IMF	**7,554**	7,244
Other debt payable in sterling:		
FLS Treasury Bills	**61,707**	35,259
Other	**44,496**	46,485
Total liabilities	**1,628,196**	1,506,698
Net liabilities	**1,328,236**	1,242,718
Liability of the Consolidated Fund to the National Loans Fund	**1,328,236**	1,242,718

Nick Macpherson
Accounting Officer
HM Treasury

7 July 2014

Source: HM Treasury

23.6a Taxes paid by UK residents to general government and the European Union

Total economy sector S.1

£ million

			2005	2006	2007	2008	2009	2010	2011	2012	2013
Part	**GENERATION OF INCOME**										
	Uses										
D.2	Taxes on production and imports										
D.21	Taxes on products and imports										
D.211	Value added tax (VAT)										
	Paid to central government	NZGF	83 425	87 758	92 025	92 002	79 900	95 865	111 437	113 892	118 296
D.211	Total	QYRC	83 425	87 758	92 025	92 002	79 900	95 865	111 437	113 892	118 296
D.212	Taxes and duties on imports excluding VAT										
D.2121	Paid to CG: import duties[1]	NMXZ	–	–	–	–	–	–	–	–	–
D.2121	Paid to EU: import duties	FJWE	2 237	2 329	2 412	2 636	2 645	2 933	2 925	2 885	2 914
D.212	Total	QYRB	2 237	2 329	2 412	2 636	2 645	2 933	2 925	2 885	2 914
D.214	Taxes on products excluding VAT and import duties										
	Paid to central government										
	Customs & excise revenue										
	Beer	GTAM	3 072	3 065	3 042	3 140	3 189	3 278	3 429	3 425	3 337
	Wines, cider, perry & spirits	GTAN	4 802	4 779	5 008	5 533	5 728	6 075	6 439	6 775	7 063
	Tobacco	GTAO	8 036	8 072	7 862	8 203	9 056	9 076	9 361	9 897	9 479
	Hydrocarbon oils	GTAP	23 346	23 448	24 512	24 790	25 894	27 013	26 923	26 703	26 698
	Car tax	GTAT	–	–	–	–	–	–	–	–	–
	Betting, gaming & lottery	CJQY	864	958	959	989	1 013	1 092	1 206	1 207	1 538
	Air passenger duty	CWAA	896	961	1 883	1 876	1 800	2 094	2 605	2 766	2 960
	Insurance premium tax	CWAD	2 343	2 314	2 306	2 281	2 259	2 401	2 942	3 022	3 018
	Landfill tax	BKOF	733	804	877	954	842	1 065	1 090	1 094	1 191
	Other	ACDN	–	–	–	–	–	–	–	–	–
	Fossil fuel levy	CIQY	–	–	–	–	–	–	–	–	–
	Gas levy	GTAZ	–	–	–	–	–	–	–	–	–
	Stamp duties	GTBC	9 910	13 074	14 634	9 499	7 141	9 098	8 831	8 918	11 542
	Levies on exports (third country trade)	CUDF	–	–	–	–	–	–	–	–	–
	Camelot payments to national lottery distribution fund	LIYH	1 349	1 440	1 310	1 405	1 553	1 625	1 793	1 832	1 644
	Purchase tax	EBDB	–	–	–	–	–	–	–	–	–
	Hydro-benefit	LITN	10	–	–	–	–	–	–	–	–
	Aggregates levy	MDUQ	327	321	339	334	275	290	290	264	282
	Milk super levy	DFT3	19	1	–	–	–	–	–	–	–
	Climate change levy	LSNT	747	711	690	717	693	666	675	624	1 098
	Channel 4 funding formula	EG9G	–	–	–	–	–	–	–	–	–
	Renewable energy obligations	EP89	563	700	833	996	1 099	1 243	1 423	2 046	2 388
	Rail franchise premia	LITT	98	125	244	285	496	792	993	1 275	1 275
	Other taxes and levies	GCSP	–	–	–	–	–	–	–	–	–
	Total paid to central government	NMYB	57 115	60 773	64 499	61 002	61 038	65 808	68 000	69 848	73 513
	Paid to the European Union										
	Sugar levy	GTBA	24	–	–	–	–	12	12	13	12
	European Coal & Steel Community levy	GTBB	–	–	–	–	–	–	–	–	–
	Total paid to the European Union	FJWG	24	–	–	–	–	12	12	13	12
D.214	Total taxes on products excluding VAT & import duties	QYRA	57 139	60 773	64 499	61 002	61 038	65 820	68 012	69 861	73 525
D.21	Total taxes on products and imports	NZGW	142 801	150 860	158 936	155 640	143 583	164 618	182 374	186 638	194 735
D.29	Production taxes other than on products										
	Paid to central government										
	Consumer credit act fees	CUDB	197	223	281	328	435	480	480	480	480
	National non-domestic rates	CUKY	17 813	18 762	19 344	20 607	21 361	21 507	22 426	23 581	24 445
	Northern Ireland non-domestic rates	NSEZ	286	318	353	328	325	361	368	366	373
	Levies paid to cg levy-funded bodies	LITK	235	232	261	459	746	569	508	600	585
	London regional transport levy	GTBE	–	–	–	–	–	–	–	–	–
	IBA levy	GTAL	–	–	–	–	–	–	–	–	–
	Motor vehicle duties paid by businesses	EKED	809	865	878	885	908	937	931	940	977
	Regulator fees	GCSQ	78	72	76	70	72	90	78	81	84
	Northern Ireland driver vehicle agency	IY9N	–	–	3	4	4	4	4	4	4
	Bank payroll tax: accrued receipts	JT2Q	–	–	–	–	–	3 413	–	–	–
	Emissions trading scheme	M98G	–	–	–	–	–	244	341	257	356
	Carbon reduction commitment	L8UA	–	–	–	–	–	–	–	586	602
	Total	NMBX	19 418	20 472	21 196	22 681	23 851	27 605	25 136	26 895	27 906
	Paid to local government										
	Non-domestic rates[2]	NMYH	182	202	267	301	317	329	336	344	350
D.29	Total production taxes other than on products	NMYD	19 600	20 674	21 463	22 982	24 168	27 934	25 472	27 239	28 256
D.2	Total taxes on production and imports, paid										
	Paid to central government	NMBY	159 958	169 003	177 720	175 685	164 789	189 278	204 573	210 635	219 715
	Paid to local government	NMYH	182	202	267	301	317	329	336	344	350
	Paid to the European Union	FJWB	2 261	2 329	2 412	2 636	2 645	2 945	2 937	2 898	2 926
D.2	Total	NZGX	162 401	171 534	180 399	178 622	167 751	192 552	207 846	213 877	222 991

1 These taxes existed before the UK's entry into the EEC in 1973.
2 From 1990/1991 onwards these series only contain rates paid in Northern Ireland.

Source: Office for National Statistics, The Blue Book 2014

23.6b Taxes paid by UK residents to general government and the European Union

Total economy sector S.1

£ million

			2005	2006	2007	2008	2009	2010	2011	2012	2013
Part	**SECONDARY DISTRIBUTION OF INCOME**										
	Uses										
D.5	Current taxes on income, wealth etc										
D.51	Taxes on income										
	Paid to central government										
	Household income taxes	DRWH	127 884	136 686	147 371	149 575	137 964	144 478	149 104	146 127	152 409
	Corporation tax	ACCD	37 820	47 108	43 912	46 487	35 402	41 253	42 267	39 710	39 367
	Petroleum revenue tax	DBHA	1 799	2 546	1 387	2 663	1 047	1 349	1 775	2 106	1 296
	Windfall tax	EYNK	–	–	–	–	–	–	–	–	–
	Other taxes on income	BMNX	4 778	5 787	6 601	8 190	10 387	5 041	6 593	7 308	7 144
D.51	Total	NMCU	172 281	192 127	199 271	206 915	184 800	192 121	199 739	195 251	200 216
D.59	Other current taxes										
	Paid to central government										
	Motor vehicle duty paid by households	CDDZ	3 953	4 145	4 506	4 639	4 722	4 903	4 889	4 933	5 124
	Northern Ireland domestic rates	NSFA	233	244	265	329	355	335	391	416	409
	Boat licences	NSNP	–	–	–	–	–	–	–	–	–
	Fishing licences	NRQB	20	20	20	20	20	20	23	21	21
	National non-domestic rates paid by non-market sectors[1]	BMNY	1 191	1 260	1 304	1 354	1 423	1 481	1 637	1 649	1 639
	Passport fees	E8A6	279	322	377	376	351	400	368	362	343
	Television licence fee	DH7A	2 655	2 696	2 862	2 949	3 009	3 088	3 088	3 117	3 082
	Northern Ireland Driver Vehicle Agency	IY9O	–	–	12	15	14	12	12	12	12
	Bank levy	KIH3	–	–	–	–	–	–	1 454	1 609	2 171
	Total	NMCV	8 331	8 687	9 346	9 682	9 894	10 239	11 862	12 119	12 801
	Paid to local government										
	Domestic rates[2]	NMHK	147	155	127	122	131	146	157	164	170
	Community charge	NMHL	–	–	–	–	–	–	–	–	–
	Council tax	NMHM	20 931	22 064	23 224	24 274	24 940	25 439	25 715	26 030	27 057
	Total	NMIS	21 078	22 219	23 351	24 396	25 071	25 585	25 872	26 194	27 227
D.59	Total	NVCM	29 409	30 906	32 697	34 078	34 965	35 824	37 734	38 313	40 028
D.5	Total current taxes on income, wealth etc										
	Paid to central government	NMCP	180 612	200 814	208 617	216 597	194 694	202 360	211 601	207 370	213 017
	Paid to local government	NMIS	21 078	22 219	23 351	24 396	25 071	25 585	25 872	26 194	27 227
D.5	Total	NMZL	201 690	223 033	231 968	240 993	219 765	227 945	237 473	233 564	240 244
D.61	Social contributions										
	Actual social contributions										
	Paid to central government										
	(National Insurance Contributions)										
	Employers' compulsory contributions	CEAN	46 475	49 568	53 765	57 080	54 411	55 887	58 604	60 689	62 013
	Employees' compulsory contributions	GCSE	35 159	37 052	36 585	38 186	37 184	38 703	40 196	41 037	41 492
	Self- and non-employed persons' compulsory contributions	NMDE	2 825	2 930	2 860	3 053	2 850	2 756	2 641	2 593	2 580
	Total	AIIH	84 459	89 550	93 210	98 319	94 445	97 346	101 441	104 319	106 085
Part	**CAPITAL ACCOUNT**										
	Changes in liabilities and net worth										
D.91	Other capital taxes										
	Paid to central government										
	Inheritance tax	GILF	3 100	3 471	3 764	3 130	2 305	2 592	2 856	3 041	3 293
	Tax on other capital transfers	GILG	50	50	50	50	50	50	50	50	50
	Tax on Swiss bank accounts[3]	KW69	–	–	–	–	–	–	–	–	870
	Development land tax and other	GCSV	–	–	–	–	–	–	–	–	–
	Tax paid on LG equal pay settlements	C625	–	54	53	77	46	–	30	38	36
	Fscs levies on private sector[4]	HZQ4	–	–	–	21 816	1 805	–	–	–	–
D.91	Total	NMGI	3 150	3 575	3 867	25 073	4 206	2 642	2 936	3 129	4 249
	TOTAL TAXES AND COMPULSORY SOCIAL CONTRIBUTIONS										
	Paid to central government	GCSS	428 179	462 942	483 414	515 674	458 134	491 626	520 551	525 453	543 066
	Paid to local government	GCST	21 260	22 421	23 618	24 697	25 388	25 914	26 208	26 538	27 577
	Paid to the European Union	FJWB	2 261	2 329	2 412	2 636	2 645	2 945	2 937	2 898	2 926
	Total	GCSU	451 700	487 692	509 444	543 007	486 167	520 485	549 696	554 889	573 569

1 Up until 1995/96 these payments are included in national non-domestic rates under production taxes other than on products.
2 From 1990/1991 onwards these series only contain rates paid in Northern Ireland.
3 Tax liable from banking deposits of UK residents held in Swiss banks.
4 Financial Services Compensation Scheme.

Source: Office for National Statistics, The Blue Book 2014

23.7 Central government
ESA 2010 sector S.1311 Unconsolidated

£ million

			2005	2006	2007	2008	2009	2010	2011	2012	2013
III.2	**FINANCIAL ACCOUNT**										
F.A	**Net acquisition of financial assets**										
F.1	Monetary gold and special drawing rights										
F.11	Monetary gold	NARO	–	–4	–	–	–	–	–	–	–
F.12	Special drawing rights	NARP	–8	51	–50	–24	8 522	18	333	111	43
F.1	Total	NWXM	–8	47	–50	–24	8 522	18	333	111	43
F.2	Currency and deposits										
F.22	Transferable deposits										
F.22N1	with UK monetary financial institutions	NART	493	1 993	2 183	17 018	6 809	–4 302	4 347	3 729	–1 902
F.22N12	*of which*: foreign currency deposits with UK MFIs[1]	NARV	–92	289	456	–1 208	–782	28	1 737	–271	901
F.22N9	with rest of the world monetary financial institutions	NARX	–1 516	–671	–579	2 913	540	423	140	935	142
F.29	Other deposits	RYWO	–	161	3 761	11 021	7 075	–9 754	7 583	–898	9 863
F.2	Total	NARQ	–1 023	1 483	5 365	30 952	14 424	–13 633	12 070	3 766	8 103
F.3	Debt securities										
F.31	Short-term										
F.31N5	Issued by UK monetary financial institutions	NSUN	213	1 768	–2 038	1 974	–2 144	–400	–	–	–
	Money market instruments										
F.31N6	Issued by other UK residents	NSRI	–	1 192	–1 142	–	882	1 349	3 336	–3 404	1 459
F.31N9	Issued by the rest of the world	NASM	1 465	1 363	2 125	–1 029	471	466	315	–967	–2 314
F.32	Long-term										
	Issued by UK monetary financial institutions										
F.32N5-6	and other UK residents	NASV	856	–601	–21	4 978	–5 236	–	–	1 152	–327
F.32N9	Issued by the rest of the world	NASW	370	–854	2 155	–1 085	–820	5 439	4 099	5 182	–2 864
F.3	Total	NARZ	2 904	2 868	1 079	4 838	–6 847	6 854	7 750	1 963	–4 046
F.4	Loans										
F.42	Long-term										
F.422	Secured on dwellings	NATM	–	–	–	–	–	–6 616	–9 162	–6 649	–6 500
F.424N1	Other loans by UK residents	NATR	4 678	3 448	5 530	6 449	3 753	8 710	5 513	16 890	6 547
F.424N9	Other loans by the rest of the world	NATS	–	–	–	–	–	–	–	–	–
F.4	Total	NATB	4 678	3 448	5 530	6 449	3 753	2 094	–3 649	10 241	47
F.5	Equity and investment fund shares/units										
F.51	Equity										
F.511N1	Listed UK shares	NATY	–177	–755	–727	11 323	45 164	–1 257	–1 508	–1 170	–5 622
F.512N1	Unlisted UK shares	NATZ	–550	–	–2 102	–1 548	–279	–	–	–	–21 969
F.519	Other equity										
F.519N6	Other UK equity	NAUA	–1 249	–1 356	–2 416	–	–4 421	–	–	–	–10
F.519N7	UK shares and bonds issued by other UK residents	NSOX	–	–	–	–	–	–	–	–	–
F.519N9	Shares and other equity issued by rest of the world	NAUD	656	792	693	949	1 107	1 305	1 556	1 218	147
F.5	Total[2]	NATT	–1 320	–1 319	–4 552	10 724	41 571	48	48	2 750	–28 816
F.7	Financial derivatives and employee stock options	MN5T	137	–419	–284	538	936	254	213	–18	–
F.71	*of which:* financial derivatives	CFZG	137	–419	–284	538	936	254	213	–18	–
F.8	Other accounts receivable	NAUN	5 288	2 205	–2 035	18 788	144	3 326	431	2 100	5 018
F.A	**Total net acquisition of financial assets**	NARM	10 656	8 313	5 053	72 265	62 503	–1 039	17 196	20 913	–19 651

1 Monetary financial institutions
2 Total F.5 does not always equal the sum of the components
listed as some equity components are omitted from this table

Source: Office for National Statistics, The Blue Book 2014

23.7
continued

Central government
ESA 2010 sector S.1311 Unconsolidated

£ million

			2005	2006	2007	2008	2009	2010	2011	2012	2013
III.2	**FINANCIAL ACCOUNT** continued										
F.L	**Net acquisition of financial liabilities**										
F.12	Special drawing rights	M98C	–	–	–	–	8 654	–	–	–	–
F.2	Currency and deposits										
F.21	Currency	NAUV	121	129	57	95	48	82	30	158	197
F.29	Other deposits	NAVC	5 604	5 219	7 971	21 013	8 236	–7 118	9 209	–2 348	–7 972
F.2	Total	NAUU	5 725	5 348	8 028	21 108	8 284	–7 036	9 239	–2 190	–7 775
F.3	Debt securities										
F.31	Short-term										
F.31N1	Issued by UK central government	NAVF	–3 902	–1 752	–1 367	13 494	25 975	–2 077	14 454	–18 729	–14 491
F.32	Long-term										
F.32N11	UK central government securities	NAVT	39 716	40 970	39 095	97 323	195 725	170 951	121 587	129 373	103 137
F.32N12	Other UK central government bonds	NAVU	17	13	25	–1 490	–7	27	30	29	25
F.32N5-6	Bonds issued by UK MFIs[1] and other UK residents	MNR7	–	–	–	–	–	–5 416	–10 967	–5 296	–11 682
F.3	Total	NAVD	35 831	39 231	37 753	109 327	221 693	163 485	125 104	105 377	76 989
F.4	Loans										
F.41	Short-term										
F.41N1	by UK monetary financial institutions	NAWH	2 567	–3 277	–568	7 605	–19 414	–1 794	238	–601	846
F.41N9	by rest of the world	NAWL	777	451	–217	504	–1 731	–44	–208	911	–825
F.42	Long-term										
F.423	Finance leasing	NAWU	502	299	410	86	50	145	–	–	–
F.424N1	Other loans by UK residents	NAWV	–12	–7	–6	–7	–18	–9	–9	–5	–12
F.424N9	Other loans by the rest of the world	NAWW	–65	7	–3	32	5	–495	–1 834	36	479
F.4	Total	NAWF	3 769	–2 527	–384	8 220	–21 108	–2 197	–1 813	341	488
F.8	Other accounts payable	NAXR	4 750	5 944	1 206	2 343	–609	–8 592	4 211	46 535	1 178
F.L	**Total net acquisition of financial liabilities**	NAUQ	50 075	47 996	46 603	140 998	216 914	145 660	136 741	150 063	70 880
B.9	**Net lending(+) / net borrowing(-)**										
F.A	Total net acquisition of financial assets	NARM	10 656	8 313	5 053	72 265	62 503	–1 039	17 196	20 913	–19 651
F.L	less Total net acquisition of financial liabilities	NAUQ	50 075	47 996	46 603	140 998	216 914	145 660	136 741	150 063	70 880
B.9f	Net lending(+) / borrowing(-) from the financial account	NZDX	–39 419	–39 683	–41 550	–68 733	–154 411	–146 699	–119 545	–129 150	–90 531
dB.9	Statistical discrepancy between the financial and non-financial accounts	NZDW	–372	962	607	–947	720	62	663	218	925
B.9n	**Net lending (+) / borrowing (-) from non-financial accounts**	NMFJ	–39 791	–38 721	–40 943	–69 680	–153 691	–146 637	–118 882	–128 932	–89 606

1 Monetary financial institutions

Source: Office for National Statistics, The Blue Book 2014

23.8 Central government net cash requirement on own account (receipts and outlays on a cash basis)

£ million

	Cash receipts								Cash outlays				
	HM Revenue and Customs												
	Total paid over[1]	Income tax[2]	Corpora-tion tax[2]	NICs[3]	V.A.T.[4]	Interest and dividends	Other receipts[5]	Total	Interest payments	Net acquisition of company securities[6]	Net departmental outlays[7]	Total	Own account net cash requirement
	1	2	3	4	5	6	7	8	9	10	11	12	13
	MIZX	RURC	ACCD	ABLP	EYOO	RUUL	RUUM	RUUN	RUUO	ABIF	RUUP	RUUQ	RUUX
2002	315987	111559	28866	63992	63000	6954	25310	348251	19343	0	347612	366955	-2485
2003	325138	113712	28489	69360	67525	7335	25329	357802	20348	-39	379418	399727	-39062
2004	347514	121493	31160	77026	71907	6855	25137	379506	21027	0	400631	421658	-2667
2005	372567	130818	37820	83612	73012	6549	26341	405457	22434	0	421021	443455	18704
2006	401362	140616	47108	87156	76103	6640	28115	436117	25834	-347	448131	473618	41925
2007	422465	149968	43912	96656	80301	8251	30083	460799	25537	-2340	470169	493366	42152
2008	428380	157500	46487	98504	80709	9354	30556	468290	26033	19714	544720	590467	37998
2009	384875	147425	35402	95053	68637	6666	31282	422823	29304	41809	548810	619923	37501
2010	411846	147659	41253	95860	80865	5274	34063	451183	34008	0	569599	603607	32567
2011	434438	152095	42267	101033	95208	5757	42235	482430	43923	0	557494	601417	122177
2012	436196	151091	39710	102232	98619	9806	38399	484401	39016	-14287	565882	590611	197100
2013	451668	156928	39367	106702	103726	46577	36469	534714	47108	-5212	577535	619431	146437
2002 Q1	87576	36973	6795	17037	15329	1853	5579	95008	3457	0	85219	88676	-2016
2002 Q2	74585	24145	5793	16649	15779	1688	5472	81745	6254	0	84027	90281	-5307
2002 Q3	78319	27737	7138	15720	15171	1797	7516	87632	3682	0	85156	88838	6123
2002 Q4	75507	22704	9140	14586	16721	1616	6743	83866	5950	0	93210	99160	-1940
2003 Q1	88763	36516	7197	17598	15780	2324	4994	96081	3801	-39	91497	95259	-4530
2003 Q2	76531	25184	5869	17760	16529	1547	6240	84318	7053	0	95376	102429	-5997
2003 Q3	81637	28919	7262	17404	17047	1728	6901	90266	4167	0	93496	97663	4791
2003 Q4	78207	23093	8161	16598	18169	1736	7194	87137	5327	0	99049	104376	-2801
2004 Q1	94758	38998	6785	20695	17330	2161	5013	101932	4704	0	97198	101902	1522
2004 Q2	82029	25114	7110	20601	18039	1546	5791	89366	5140	0	98121	103261	-14176
2004 Q3	87673	31464	8045	18585	17707	1549	7474	96696	5192	0	98424	103616	-12488
2004 Q4	83054	25917	9220	17145	18831	1599	6859	91512	5991	0	106888	112879	-15909
2005 Q1	103161	42707	9266	21767	18449	1939	4950	110050	5487	0	99835	105322	3511
2005 Q2	86274	28884	7766	20941	17342	1469	6592	94335	5568	0	105729	111297	-12365
2005 Q3	94524	32042	9765	22007	18188	1611	7430	103565	5836	0	105215	111051	6567
2005 Q4	88608	27185	11023	18897	19033	1530	7369	97507	5543	0	110242	115785	-5625
2006 Q1	112661	45408	13275	23677	18293	1783	5631	120075	6174	-347	107430	113257	8756
2006 Q2	91224	30604	7882	22211	18021	1497	6459	99180	5298	0	117434	122732	-6332
2006 Q3	100664	35891	12958	20798	18731	1428	8403	110495	8628	0	108129	116757	8536
2006 Q4	96813	28713	12993	20470	21058	1932	7622	106367	5734	0	115138	120872	1206
2007 Q1	117636	51926	10475	23795	19550	1897	4875	124408	6619	0	110361	116980	15294
2007 Q2	96004	29417	8015	25932	20123	1864	8204	106072	5959	-2340	121026	124645	-822
2007 Q3	107134	37488	12465	24165	19301	1986	9934	119054	6486	0	114418	120904	18111
2007 Q4	101691	31137	12957	22764	21327	2504	7070	111265	6473	0	124364	130837	7397
2008 Q1	126971	54549	12946	27550	19850	2646	5997	135614	6472	0	118768	125240	17239
2008 Q2	97153	34333	8509	23517	20087	2252	8154	107559	6449	0	131441	137890	-30
2008 Q3	108990	39286	12742	24801	21235	2266	9143	120399	6566	-255	150477	156788	13895
2008 Q4	95266	29332	12290	22636	19537	2190	7262	104718	6546	19969	144034	170549	6920
2009 Q1	115103	52753	9536	25930	17580	2016	3449	120568	6386	12536	131608	150530	21367
2009 Q2	85699	31277	6362	22727	16102	1892	9626	97217	8534	-2021	145058	151571	-4728
2009 Q3	93410	35562	8049	23574	16847	1357	9721	104488	7577	0	133158	140735	16962
2009 Q4	90663	27833	11455	22822	18108	1401	8486	100550	6807	31294	138986	177087	7486
2010 Q1	112559	47102	9939	26393	19103	1551	4493	118603	9271	0	139909	149180	18278
2010 Q2	94699	34366	7173	22870	19886	1049	8868	104616	6956	0	147380	154336	-6818
2010 Q3	107569	37334	11294	23950	20564	1370	11557	120496	10782	0	136851	147633	23552
2010 Q4	97019	28857	12847	22647	21312	1304	9145	107468	6999	0	145459	152458	6262
2011 Q1	120293	50993	10807	27081	21737	1836	9019	131148	11840	0	135142	146982	14505
2011 Q2	99487	33246	7345	24283	24084	1229	10614	111330	7392	0	145667	153059	-7428
2011 Q3	110502	37608	11600	25861	23984	1506	13346	125354	17071	0	137097	154168	18573
2011 Q4	104156	30248	12515	23808	25403	1186	9256	114598	7620	0	139588	147208	1850
2012 Q1	123458	49463	10691	27665	24821	3331	6142	132931	12421	-747	135613	147287	19572
2012 Q2	100129	33526	7271	24669	24469	3547	11978	115654	7542	-11109	147450	143883	-10374
2012 Q3	109251	37934	9843	25873	24524	1462	10843	121556	12622	-1174	136553	148001	30331
2012 Q4	103358	30168	11905	24025	24805	1466	9436	114260	6431	-1257	146266	151440	36389
2013 Q1	124619	51345	10435	27470	26772	13219	12683	150521	12701	639	153613	166953	65831
2013 Q2	105685	36268	7221	27227	24915	13088	8780	127553	7110	-382	148767	155495	29962
2013 Q3	114459	38409	10266	26916	25681	14898	8414	137771	20372	-3355	135380	152397	54354
2013 Q4	106905	30906	11445	25089	26358	5372	6592	118869	6925	-2114	139775	144586	36247
2014 Q1	129449	52479	10339	28459	27486	4136	48400	181985	13707	-4217	186206	195696	76537

Relationships between columns 1+6+7=8; 9+10+11=12; 12-8=13

Sources: HM Revenue & Customs; Office for National Statistics

1 Comprises payments into the Consolidated Fund and all payovers of NICS excluding those for Northern Ireland.

2 Income tax includes capital gains tax and is net of any tax credits treated by HM Revenue and Customs as tax deductions.

3 UK receipts net of personal pension rebates; gross of Statutory Maternity Pay and Statutory Sick Pay.

4 Payments into Consolidated Fund.

5 Including some elements of expenditure not separately identified.

6 Mainly comprises privatisation proceeds.

7 Net of certain receipts, and excluding on-lending to local authorities and public corporations.

23.9 HM Revenue and Customs receipts (Revised 1st July)

Amounts: £ million

Year	Total Paid Over 1 receipts 2,3,9	Total HMRC receipts 2,3,9	Total Income Tax 4	Of which: PAYE Income Tax**	Of which: SA Income Tax**	Capital Gains Tax	NICs	VAT	Total Corporation Tax 5	Of which offshore** 6	Bank Levy	Bank payroll tax	Petroleum Revenue Tax	Fuel duties	IHT 7	Shares	Stamp Duty Land Tax	Annual Tax on Enveloped Dwellings	Tobacco duties
		MIZX		BKMR	LISB	BKLO	ABLP	EYOO	ACCD			JT2R	ACCJ	ACDD	ACCH	BKST	BKSU		ACDE
2002-03	317,174	324,505	109,506	94,243	16,059	1,596	64,553	63,451	29,268	3,662			958	22,147	2,354	2,538	5,011		8,054
2003-04	331,133	347,563	117,917	101,389	15,772	2,225	72,457	69,075	28,077	3,057			1,179	22,786	2,504	2,559	4,986		8,091
2004-05	355,917	375,411	127,294	108,699	17,141	2,282	78,098	73,026	33,641	3,831			1,284	23,313	2,922	2,715	6,251		8,100
2005-06	382,067	402,347	134,916	113,894	18,077	3,042	85,522	72,856	41,829	7,307			2,016	23,438	3,259	3,465	7,454		7,959
2006-07	406,337	428,063	147,712	124,799	20,306	3,830	87,274	77,360	44,308	6,709			2,155	23,585	3,545	3,757	9,635		8,149
2007-08	431,800	455,468	151,738	126,760	22,443	5,268	100,410	80,599	46,383	5,728			1,680	24,905	3,824	4,167	9,958		8,094
2008-09	416,512	444,681	153,442	128,470	22,531	7,852	96,882	78,439	43,077	9,826			2,567	24,615	2,839	3,203	4,796		8,219
2009-10	382,331	414,097	144,881	122,584	21,708	2,491	95,517	70,160	35,805	4,998			923	26,197	2,384	3,017	4,886		8,813
2010-11	419,580	452,695	153,491	132,263	22,108	3,601	96,548	83,502	42,121	6,864		3,416	1,458	27,256	2,717	2,971	5,961		9,144
2011-12	437,603	471,336	150,939	132,189	20,334	4,337	101,617	98,292	42,151	8,840	1,612	-2	2,032	26,800	2,903	2,794	6,125		9,551
2012-13	437,357	472,749	152,030	132,433	20,550	3,927	102,037	100,572	39,454	4,393	1,595	0	1,737	26,571	3,105	2,234	6,907		9,681
2013-14	456,498	492,593	156,898	134,686	20,854	3,908	107,690	104,718	39,274	3,556	2,200	0	1,118	26,881	3,402	3,108	9,273	100	9,531
Apr-10	43,631	46,157	15,679	15,578	97	4	9,285	9,465	5,207	-	-	0	-4	2,378	216	265	464		1,331
May-10	26,282	28,692	9,905	10,191	8	3	7,450	5,463	744	-		0	57	2,233	206	282	386		234
Jun-10	24,786	27,772	10,126	10,175	-8	4	6,135	4,957	1,222	-		0	48	2,245	245	251	485		645
Jul-10	45,103	49,020	16,960	10,931	5,898	3	8,499	8,447	8,515	-		0	30	2,304	283	276	647		1,275
Aug-10	35,405	37,084	11,534	10,060	1,503	3	7,897	7,527	1,069	-		3,107	44	2,306	217	294	616		386
Sep-10	27,061	30,282	10,286	10,185	39	5	7,554	4,591	1,710	2,359		295	560	2,307	216	163	525		731
Oct-10	40,076	42,395	10,644	10,158	-25	10	7,542	8,689	9,298	-		0	82	2,367	206	268	527		1,035
Nov-10	29,608	32,132	9,395	10,273	-74	11	7,595	7,623	1,260	-		0	115	2,381	209	256	519		581
Dec-10	27,335	30,656	10,204	10,123	305	4	7,510	5,000	2,289	2,294		-50	123	2,243	233	282	539		677
Jan-11	52,321	56,720	21,996	10,873	10,860	2,696	9,101	8,803	8,270	-		30	86	2,141	196	163	444		1,012
Feb-11	38,809	39,629	14,867	11,499	3,152	786	8,832	8,384	1,141	-		43	64	2,203	230	217	374		797
Mar-11	29,163	32,158	11,894	12,216	352	72	9,148	4,551	1,396	2,211		-9	253	2,148	259	253	435		440
Apr-11	44,593	46,528	13,440	13,709	85	7	9,916	10,608	5,594	-		1	124	2,384	221	267	552		1,492
May-11	29,847	33,035	10,570	10,548	-61	5	7,990	7,999	1,094	-		0	83	2,157	241	244	415		185
Jun-11	25,047	28,186	10,426	10,584	-72	9	6,377	5,474	657	-		0	99	2,269	257	218	377		651
Jul-11	47,037	51,227	17,069	11,238	5,104	6	9,484	9,960	8,561	-	42	0	63	2,254	254	289	573		805
Aug-11	34,904	37,055	12,220	10,803	1,723	6	8,476	8,552	1,278	-		8	70	2,187	277	241	571		808
Sep-11	28,561	31,052	9,545	10,283	86	2	7,901	5,470	1,761	3,272		0	577	2,311	275	252	581		878
Oct-11	42,789	44,859	10,224	10,421	-24	2	8,017	10,560	8,658	-	1,098	-9	114	2,305	234	244	566		935
Nov-11	32,548	36,024	10,671	10,378	-64	6	7,983	9,465	1,071	-		-3	117	2,302	239	201	548		1,037
Dec-11	28,819	32,118	10,540	10,157	441	4	7,808	5,381	2,786	2,787		0	125	2,262	215	233	572		478
Jan-12	56,559	60,524	21,929	11,112	10,184	3,324	9,693	10,343	9,039	-	472	0	67	2,100	222	140	461		855
Feb-12	37,279	38,549	13,112	11,291	2,650	868	9,000	8,796	1,060	-		0	72	2,197	252	208	431		668
Mar-12	29,620	32,179	11,192	11,666	281	97	8,972	5,684	592	2,781		0	521	2,070	218	257	478		760
Apr-12	44,065	46,781	14,148	14,179	19	11	9,798	10,232	4,890	-	287	0	150	2,386	236	204	479		1,818
May-12	30,304	33,324	10,166	10,912	-103	4	8,335	8,363	1,244	-		0	127	2,119	261	75	534		136

23.9 HM Revenue and Customs receipts (Revised 1st July)

Amounts: £ million

Year	Total Paid Over 1 receipts	Total HMRC receipts 2,3,9	Total Income Tax 4	Of which: PAYE Income Tax**	Of which: SA Income Tax**	Capital Gains Tax	NICs	VAT	Total Corporation Tax 5	Of which offshore** 6	Bank Levy	Bank payroll tax	Petroleum Revenue Tax	Fuel duties	IHT 7	Shares	Stamp Duty Land Tax	Annual Tax on Enveloped Dwellings	Tobacco duties
	MIZX			BKMR	LISB	BKLO	ABLP	EYOO	ACCD			JT2R	ACCJ	ACDD	ACCH	BKST	BKSU		ACDE
Jun-12	25,760	28,841	9,956	10,264	-67	3	6,536	5,873	1,137	-	-	0	53	2,247	255	213	509		600
Jul-12	46,840	50,713	17,464	11,290	6,146	4	9,699	10,058	6,861	-	526	0	101	2,212	288	189	666		759
Aug-12	33,976	36,968	11,443	10,648	977	4	8,287	9,047	1,208	-	-	0	108	2,237	335	218	683		1,054
Sep-12	28,435	30,903	9,794	10,318	28	2	7,887	5,420	1,774	1,573	-	0	533	2,260	235	166	588		680
Oct-12	41,068	43,956	11,030	10,772	-12	9	8,259	10,248	7,806	-	366	0	126	2,220	282	174	624		979
Nov-12	31,877	34,009	9,265	10,301	-67	4	7,890	8,756	1,304	-	-	0	141	2,324	256	231	611		769
Dec-12	30,413	33,002	10,596	10,204	409	4	7,876	5,803	2,795	1,493	-	0	107	2,331	237	188	591		622
Jan-13	57,228	62,216	23,578	11,103	10,685	2,971	9,926	11,210	7,818	-	416	0	75	2,008	221	159	623		1,052
Feb-13	36,473	39,141	13,588	11,018	2,347	820	8,751	9,129	1,352	-	-	0	115	2,155	163	145	502		566
Mar-13	30,918	32,896	11,002	11,426	189	90	8,793	6,434	1,265	1,327	334	0	101	2,072	337	271	496	-	648
Apr-13	44,225	47,305	14,785	14,051	52	2	9,916	10,177	4,689	-	-	0	77	2,258	309	222	660	-	1,725
May-13	32,327	35,726	11,858	12,048	-132	3	8,528	8,263	1,234	-	-	0	91	2,267	293	323	646	-	201
Jun-13	29,133	32,334	10,309	10,405	-79	3	8,783	6,505	1,298	-	-	0	45	2,319	304	225	560	-	560
Jul-13	49,068	53,026	17,840	11,267	6,548	3	10,543	10,230	6,902	-	658	0	-1	2,187	339	304	886	-	724
Aug-13	35,214	36,882	10,947	10,338	862	2	8,254	9,192	1,297	-	-	0	80	2,317	266	207	803	-	880
Sep-13	30,177	33,162	10,329	10,371	12	3	8,119	6,259	2,067	1,306	-	0	410	2,260	251	191	817	2	822
Oct-13	42,906	45,724	10,931	10,537	-77	3	8,495	11,546	7,173	-	624	0	98	2,226	312	312	852	76	964
Nov-13	32,907	35,721	9,982	10,136	-81	2	8,219	9,056	1,236	-	-	0	84	2,347	270	249	781	6	858
Dec-13	31,092	34,155	10,679	10,366	414	2	8,375	5,756	3,036	1,229	-	0	121	2,282	259	256	960	8	530
Jan-14	58,102	61,425	22,539	11,488	10,673	3,006	10,246	11,139	7,390	-	584	0	-1	2,070	263	244	843	1	1,001
Feb-14	39,569	42,091	14,048	11,285	2,427	732	9,157	10,432	1,450	-	-	0	69	2,215	271	276	721	2	625
Mar-14	31,778	35,042	12,650	12,395	235	149	9,056	6,162	1,499	1,021	-	0	45	2,134	264	299	743	5	640
Apr-14*	46,696	49,925	15,344	14,822	103	2	10,001	11,192	5,105	-	485	0	83	2,303	362	233	872	40	1,751

23.9 HM Revenue and Customs receipts (Revised 1st July)

Amounts: £ million

Year	Spirits duties	Beer duties	Wines duties	Cider duties	Betting & Gaming	Air Passenger Duty	Insurance Premium Tax	Landfill Tax	Climate Change Levy	Aggregates Levy	Swiss Capital Tax	Misc	Customs Duties	Child and Working Tax Credits (Expenditure)	Child Benefit Payments 8
	ACDF	ACDG	ACDH	ACDI	ACDJ	ACDP	ACDO	DOLC	LSNS	MDUP			ADET		
2002-03	2,273	2,935	1,936	153	1,292	816	2,138	541	829	247		2	1,907	13,361	9,425
2003-04	2,362	3,044	2,006	153	1,347	791	2,294	607	832	339		-8	1,941	15,896	9,593
2004-05	2,385	3,101	2,233	157	1,421	864	2,359	672	764	334		0	2,195	17,332	9,770
2005-06	2,309	3,076	2,308	168	1,421	905	2,343	733	744	326		1	2,258	18,684	10,156
2006-07	2,256	3,072	2,385	200	1,391	971	2,314	804	712	321		1	2,325	20,030	10,603
2007-08	2,374	3,067	2,641	220	1,481	1,994	2,306	877	688	339		0	2,456	24,099	11,262
2008-09	2,358	3,127	2,741	244	1,474	1,862	2,281	954	716	334		0	2,659	27,601	11,824
2009-10	2,570	3,182	2,949	311	1,439	1,856	2,259	842	695	275		0	2,646	28,879	12,160
2010-11	2,675	3,296	3,101	324	1,533	2,155	2,400	1,065	674	288		0	2,998	29,830	12,177
2011-12	2,889	3,463	3,356	329	1,633	2,607	2,941	1,090	676	290	0	0	2,912	29,888	12,160
2012-13	2,931	3,426	3,537	326	1,680	2,791	3,021	1,092	635	265	342	0	2,854	29,710	12,167
2013-14	3,056	3,346	3,713	340	2,098	3,013	3,014	1,189	1,068	285	466	0	2,901		11,438
Apr-10	330	300	311	36	120	156	108	181	61	31		0	232	2,178	932
May-10	116	285	212	21	139	106	436	44	141	20		0	212	2,265	1,012
Jun-10	170	380	255	42	124	190	2	3	1	15		0	226	2,591	1,014
Jul-10	217	273	274	38	142	180	121	185	53	42		0	256	2,711	1,052
Aug-10	170	250	259	28	159	214	500	105	115	24		0	258	2,400	1,093
Sep-10	196	288	237	27	99	201	2	9	1	14		0	265	2,398	1,024
Oct-10	219	254	261	23	129	183	120	182	40	41		0	274	2,297	993
Nov-10	306	267	291	24	155	185	485	87	93	23		0	274	2,423	960
Dec-10	363	295	343	22	106	188	0	0	3	14		0	267	2,689	1,061
Jan-11	238	306	255	28	132	196	114	202	41	36		0	235	2,149	955
Feb-11	137	182	203	16	123	91	510	30	120	17		0	262	2,259	981
Mar-11	213	217	203	20	106	267	4	37	5	12		0	236	2,521	1,082
Apr-11	322	345	314	32	118	182	123	192	26	32		0	236	2,403	1,075
May-11	128	287	230	28	174	216	531	58	161	22		0	216	2,439	1,037
Jun-11	180	302	271	31	104	227	7	7	4	15		0	231	2,660	938
Jul-11	228	293	270	31	156	226	150	188	45	41		0	239	2,667	1,040
Aug-11	194	290	268	29	186	274	621	102	120	23		0	254	2,599	1,038
Sep-11	225	317	291	30	109	255	12	12	3	14		0	230	2,390	991
Oct-11	235	278	278	27	134	233	157	215	40	42		0	272	2,417	932
Nov-11	310	285	321	28	154	234	605	52	103	21		0	274	2,453	1,058
Dec-11	402	320	404	29	106	177	3	19	2	13		0	240	2,657	1,155
Jan-12	231	313	259	23	167	223	149	194	46	39		0	235	2,258	900
Feb-12	154	193	215	18	122	179	576	34	122	17		0	255	2,409	973
Mar-12	281	240	236	23	105	180	14	17	3	11		0	230	2,478	1,040
Apr-12	352	386	381	36	147	213	133	186	54	33	0	0	220	2,378	943
May-12	115	238	217	22	154	223	574	45	139	18	0	0	216	2,881	1,180

23.9 HM Revenue and Customs receipts (Revised 1st July)

Amounts: £ million

Year	Spirits duties	Beer duties	Wines duties	Cider duties	Betting & Gaming	Air Passenger Duty	Insurance Premium Tax	Landfill Tax	Climate Change Levy	Aggregates Levy	Swiss Capital Tax	Misc	Customs Duties	Child and Working Tax Credits (Expenditure)	Child Benefit Payments 8
	ACDF	ACDG	ACDH	ACDI	ACDJ	ACDP	ACDO	DOLC	LSNS	MDUP			ADET		
Jun-12	202	336	284	35	105	231	8	11	2	12	0	0	231	2,401	949
Jul-12	202	286	259	28	163	246	157	219	55	39	0	0	231	2,766	1,042
Aug-12	184	287	291	31	188	284	627	57	108	19	0	0	268	2,666	1,059
Sep-12	228	308	282	31	118	272	16	38	2	12	0	0	261	2,220	987
Oct-12	222	251	261	23	127	246	189	184	44	37	0	0	252	2,527	1,009
Nov-12	365	289	355	27	164	260	561	60	82	19	0	0	278	2,418	996
Dec-12	430	318	427	29	124	195	12	68	2	14	0	0	234	2,532	1,027
Jan-13	217	293	291	24	147	237	163	153	48	36	342	0	209	2,351	1,016
Feb-13	151	205	236	20	150	119	562	66	97	16	0	0	232	2,302	895
Mar-13	263	230	252	21	95	263	20	6	3	11	0	0	225	2,446	1,064
Apr-13	387	283	370	33	161	242	171	198	57	30	0	0	217	2,394	886
May-13	125	267	229	24	212	217	544	53	117	18	0	0	213	2,655	1,003
Jun-13	192	310	287	33	112	227	11	13	2	12	0	0	224	2,450	968
Jul-13	206	271	276	30	226	289	212	183	185	36	258	0	238	2,932	989
Aug-13	211	319	323	40	206	302	568	98	135	26	147	0	263	2,412	1,010
Sep-13	228	285	310	34	125	308	8	43	4	14	0	0	274	2,348	861
Oct-13	237	255	287	22	198	273	216	168	102	40	35	0	279	2,539	1,034
Nov-13	391	286	378	28	191	265	532	89	162	21	10	0	278	2,275	943
Dec-13	419	298	455	30	137	216	21	39	10	14	8	0	246	2,729	965
Jan-14	224	328	291	23	222	239	158	242	107	40	0	0	225	2,373	986
Feb-14	161	208	236	22	188	222	545	53	183	20	5	0	251	2,286	883
Mar-14	276	235	272	22	121	213	28	12	6	13	4	0	194	2,317	911
Apr-14*	271	257	371	28	191	232	184	184	115	35	58	0	228	2,654	1,023

Source: HM Revenue & Customs

1 Comprises of payments into the Consolidated Fund and all payovers of NICs excluding those of Northern Ireland.

2 Total HMRC Receipts includes payments into the Consolidated Fund and all payovers of NICs including those of Northern Ireland. As of January 2015, total now gross of all Child & Working Tax Credits (Expenditure): this follows the changes generated by revisions to the European System of Accounts (ESA2010) and the Public Sector Finances Review.

3 Consistent with the OBR definition published in the supplementary fiscal table 2.8 i.e. on a cash basis.

4 Gross of tax credits and includes other smaller elements of income tax.

5 Gross of tax credits classed as expenditure (payable) and net of tax credits treated as negative (offset against tax liabilities). As from November 2014 Bank Levy receipts are shown seperately and no longer included within the CT total.

6 The majority of UK Oil & Gas companies payments are due in three instalments, (Jul, Oct and Jan): receipts are reported in a similar pattern following each instalment.

7 Excludes non cash elements which are shown in the table Inheritance Tax: Analysis of Receipts

8 From April 2011, the Child Benefit series has been revised to ensure consistency with HMRC Resource Accounts.

9 Total of columns D, G to J, and L to AG

* Provisional

** Figures in italic are included with the relevant total for either income tax or corporation tax

Archived tables can be found here: https://www.gov.uk/government/collections/hm-revenue-customs-receipts

For any queries regarding this table, please email Karen Mason
Room 2/62, 100 Parliament Street, London, WC1A 2BQ

23.10 INCOME TAX PERSONAL ALLOWANCES AND RELIEFS, 1990-91 TO 2014-15

Financial years	Non-aged allowances			Aged allowances				
				Personal		Married couple's		
	Personal	Married couple's (1)	Blind person's (2)	65-74	75+	65-74	75+	Income limit (3)
1990-91	3,005	1,720	1,080	3,670	3,820	2,145	2,185	12,300
1991-92	3,295	1,720	1,080	4,020	4,180	2,355	2,395	13,500
1992-93	3,445	1,720	1,080	4,200	4,370	2,465	2,505	14,200
1993-94	3,445	1,720	1,080	4,200	4,370	2,465	2,505	14,200
1994-95	3,445	1,720 (4)	1,200	4,200	4,370	2,665 (4)	2,705 (4)	14,200
1995-96	3,525	1,720 (5)	1,200	4,630	4,800	2,995 (5)	3,035 (5)	14,600
1996-97	3,765	1,790 (5)	1,250	4,910	5,090	3,115 (5)	3,155 (5)	15,200
1997-98	4,045	1,830 (5)	1,280	5,220	5,400	3,185 (5)	3,225 (5)	15,600
1998-99	4,195	1,900 (5)	1,330	5,410	5,600	3,305 (5)	3,345 (5)	16,200
1999-00	4,335	1,970 (6)	1,380	5,720	5,980	5,125 (6)	5,195 (6)	16,800
2000-01	4,385	-	1,400	5,790	6,050	5,185 (6,7)	5,255 (6,7)	17,000
2001-02	4,535	-	1,450	5,990	6,260	5,365 (6,7)	5,435 (6,7)	17,600
2002-03	4,615	-	1,480	6,100	6,370	5,465 (6,7)	5,535 (6,7)	17,900
2003-04	4,615	-	1,510	6,610	6,720	5,565 (6,7)	5,635 (6,7)	18,300
2004-05	4,745	-	1,560	6,830	6,950	5,725 (6,7)	5,795 (6,7)	18,900
2005-06	4,895	-	1,610	7,090	7,220	5,905 (6,7)	5,975 (6,7)	19,500
2006-07	5,035	-	1,660	7,280	7,420	6,065 (6,7)	6,135 (6,7)	20,100
2007-08	5,225	-	1,730	7,550	7,690	6,285 (6,7)	6,365 (6,7)	20,900
2008-09	6,035	-	1,800	9,030	9,180	6,535 (6,7)	6,625 (6,7)	21,800
2009-10	6,475	-	1,890	9,490	9,640	-	6,965 (6,7)	22,900
2010-11	6,475 (8)	-	1,890	9,490	9,640	-	6,965 (6,7)	22,900
2011-12	7,475 (8)	-	1,980	9,940	10,090	-	7,295 (6,7)	24,000
2012-13	8,105 (8)	-	2,100	10,500	10,660	-	7,705 (6,7)	25,400
2013-14	9,440 (8)	-	2,160	10,500 (9)	10,660 (10)	-	7,915 (6,7)	26,100
2014-15	10,000 (8)	-	2,230	10,500 (9)	10,660 (10)	-	8,165 (6,7)	27,000

Source: HM Revenue & Customs

Table updated March 2015

(1) Given in addition to the personal allowance to married couples. The additional personal allowance and the widow's bereavement allowance have the same value as the married couple's allowance.

(2) Married couples where both spouses are blind get double the single amount.

(3) Where an individual's income exceeds the income limit, their aged personal allowance is reduced by £1 for every £2 above the income limit, potentially down to the non aged allowance level.

(4) Allowance available at a flat rate of 20%.

(5) Allowance available at a flat rate of 15%.

(6) Allowance available at a flat rate of 10%.

(7) At least one of the partners must have been born before 6 April 1935.

(8) The Personal Allowance reduces where an individuals income is above £100,000 - by £1 for every £2 of income above the £100,000 limit. This reduction applies irrespective of age or date of birth.

(9) Available to people born in the period 6 April 1938 to 5 April 1948.

(10) Available to people born on or before 5 April 1938.

23.11 RATES OF INCOME TAX: 2000-01 TO 2014-15

	2000-01 Bands of taxable income(1) £	Rate of tax %		2001-02 Bands of taxable income(1) £	Rate of tax %		2002-03 Bands of taxable income(1) £	Rate of tax %	
Starting rate	1-1,520	10		1-1,880	10		1-1,920	10	
Basic rate	1,521-28,400	22	(5)	1,881-29,400	22	(5)	1,921-29,900	22	(5)
Higher rate	Over 28,400	40	(6)	Over 29,400	40	(6)	Over 29,900	40	(6)

	2003-04 Bands of taxable income(1) £	Rate of tax %		2004-05 Bands of taxable income(1) £	Rate of tax %		2005-06 Bands of taxable income(1) £	Rate of tax %	
Starting rate	1-1,960	10		1-2,020.	10		1-2.090	10	
Basic rate	1,961-30,500	22	(5)	2,021-31,400	22	(5)	2,091-32,400	22	(5)
Higher rate	Over 30,500	40	(6)	Over 31,400	40	(6)	Over 32,400	40	(6)

	2006-07 Bands of taxable income(1) £	Rate of tax %		2007-08 Bands of taxable income(1) £	Rate of tax %		2008-09 Bands of taxable income(1) £	Rate of tax %	
Starting rate	1-2,150	10		1-2,230	10		1-34,800	20	(8)
Basic rate	2,151-33,300	22	(5)	2,231-34,600	22	(5)	Over 34,800	40	(6)
Higher rate	Over 33,300	40	(6)	Over 34,600	40	(6)	Not Applicable		

	2009-10 Bands of taxable income(1) £	Rate of tax %		2010-11 Bands of taxable income(1) £	Rate of tax %		2011-12 Bands of taxable income(1) £	Rate of tax %	
Basic rate (7)	1-37,400	20	(8)	1-37,400	20	(8)	1-35,000	20	(8)
Higher rate	Over 37,400	40	(6)	Over 37,400	40	(6)	Over 35,000	40	(6)
Additional Rate	Not Applicable			Over 150,000	50	(9)	Over 150,000	50	(9)

	2012-13 Bands of taxable income(1) £	Rate of tax %		2013-14 Bands of taxable income(1) £	Rate of tax %		2014-15 Bands of taxable income(1) £	Rate of tax %	
Basic rate (7)	1-34,370	20	(8)	1-32,010	20	(8)	1-31,865	20	(8)
Higher rate	Over 34,370	40	(6)	Over 32,010	40	(6)	Over 31,865	40	(6)
Additional Rate	Over 150,000	50	(9)	Over 150,000	45	(10)	Over 150,000	45	(10)

Source: HM Revenue & Customs
Table updated March 2015

(1) Taxable income is defined as gross income for income tax purposes less any allowances and reliefs available at the taxpayer's marginal rate.

(2) Applies to the income of discretionary and accumulation trusts. Prior to 1993-94 trusts paid tax at the basic rate, with an additional rate of 10%.

(3) The basic rate of tax on dividend income is 20%.

(4) The basic rate of tax on dividends and savings income is 20%.

(5) The basic rate of tax on dividends is 10% and savings income is 20%.

(6) The higher rate of tax on dividends is 32.5%.

(7) From 2008-09 the starting rate is abolished for all non-savings income (e.g. employment, self-employed trading profits, pensions and property income), which is the first slice of income to be charged to income tax. The starting rate and the starting rate limit for savings is shown in the table below. Where taxable non-savings income does not fully occupy the starting rate limit the remainder of the starting rate limit is available for savings income.

(8) The basic rate of tax on dividends is 10%.

(9) The additional rate of tax on dividends is 42.5%.

(10) The additional rate of tax on dividends is 37.5%.

23.12 Non-domestic rating in England & Wales
Analysis of 2010 rating lists. Number of rateable properties, total rateable values by detailed property type by country as at 31 March 2014

Property Type[1]	England Rateable property[2] Count (thousands)	England Rateable value Total (£millions)	Wales Rateable property[2] Count (thousands)	Wales Rateable value Total (£millions)	England & Wales Rateable property[2] Count (thousands)	England & Wales Rateable value Total (£millions)
Commercial						
Advertising rights	37	68	1	1	38	69
Holiday sites	6	190	1	27	7	217
Garages & petrol stations	38	1,087	3	52	41	1,139
Hotels etc.	51	1,494	5	56	56	1,550
Pubs & wine bars	55	1,605	5	87	59	1,692
Markets	2	38	-	2	2	40
Offices	349	13,532	16	276	365	13,808
Car parks	58	534	2	19	59	552
Restaurants & cafes	38	1,135	2	44	40	1,179
Showroom and premises	8	213	-	7	8	220
Hypermarket and premises	-	94	-	5	-	99
Superstore and premises	2	2,700	-	169	2	2,869
Other Shops	462	10,095	28	413	489	10,509
Shops[3]	471	13,103	28	595	500	13,698
Warehouses & stores[4]	211	8,036	12	353	223	8,389
Other commercial	37	817	3	25	40	843
All commercial	*1,353*	*41,639*	*78*	*1,535*	*1,431*	*43,174*
Educational, training & cultural						
Local authority schools & colleges	22	1,789	2	96	24	1,885
Libraries and museums	4	259	-	10	5	269
Private schools & colleges	3	404	-	4	4	408
Universities	1	442	-	25	1	467
Other educational, training and cultural	12	278	1	8	13	286
All educational, training & cultural	*43*	*3,172*	*3*	*143*	*47*	*3,315*
Utilities						
Docks	-	76	-	6	-	81
Electricity companies	1	1,295	-	154	1	1,449
British Gas - Transco[5]	0	89	0	5	0	94
Railways[5]	0	347	0	14	0	360
Telecommunications[5]	0	197	0	8	0	205
Water companies[5]	0	736	0	45	0	781
Bus stations, moorings etc.	2	52	-	1	2	53
Other utilities[5]	7	1,047	1	54	7	1,100
All utilities[6]	*9*	*3,838*	*1*	*285*	*10*	*4,123*
Industrial						
Factories, mills & workshops[7]	226	5,188	15	338	241	5,525
Quarries, mines etc.	5	450	-	23	6	473
Other industrial	3	478	-	35	4	513
All industrial	*234*	*6,115*	*15*	*395*	*250*	*6,511*
Leisure						
Community centres & halls	32	597	3	29	35	626
Sports centres & stadia	1	181	-	12	1	193
Sports grounds, golf courses etc	10	247	1	13	11	260
Cinemas, theatres etc.	2	214	-	12	3	226
Other leisure	37	387	1	15	38	402
All leisure	*83*	*1,626*	*5*	*81*	*88*	*1,707*
Miscellaneous						
Cemeteries and crematoria	2	32	-	1	3	33
Medical facilities	26	1,303	2	68	28	1,371
Local government offices[8]	2	194	-	17	2	210
Police stations & courts	2	396	-	19	3	415
Hostels & homes	1	23	-	2	2	25
Other properties	50	1,654	3	58	54	1,712
All miscellaneous	*84*	*3,602*	*6*	*165*	*90*	*3,766*
All properties	1,806	59,992	109	2,605	1,915	62,596

Source: Valuation Office Agency

Table notes

Counts are rounded to the nearest thousand with counts fewer than 500 but greater than 0 reported as negligible and denoted by '-'.
Total rateable values are rounded to the nearest £1million with amounts smaller than £0.5million but larger than £0 reported as negligible and denoted by '-'.
Totals may not sum due to rounding.
Figures include rateable properties in the local rating list only, except where stated, (see footnote 3 and 4).

Footnotes

[1] The property type groupings has been derived from the property codes used for the rating lists. The individual codes are grouped into broad classes, which have been used to provide six broad groupings. Within each grouping various categories are identified, with the remaining properties assigned to an 'miscellaneous' category.

[2] In other publications "rateable property" was referred to as "hereditament"
[3] This is the total of showrooms, hypermarket, superstore and premises including "other shops".
[4] In tables 2, 3 and 4 warehouses and stores are labelled as warehouses.
[5] Includes rateable properties from the central rating list. Further details are provided in the accompanying Release Notes.
[6] Includes rateable properties from both the central and local Rating Lists. Further details are provided in the accompanying Release Notes.
[7] In tables 2, 3 and 4 factories, mills and workshops are labelled as factories.
[8]Local government offices are shown in the table under the 'Miscellaneous' category but are included in the figures for property type 'Offices' in all other tables.

23.13 Revenue expenditure of local authorities

£ million

	2008-09 [1] outturn	2009-10 [2] outturn	2010-11 [3] outturn	2011-12 [3] outturn	2012-13 [3] outturn	2013/14 [3] outturn	2014/15 budget	2015/16 budget
England								
Education [4,5]	42,148	44,471	45,283	40,219	37,109	35,881	35,835	34,976
Highways and Transport	5,679	6,541	5,669	5,380	4,868	4,795	4,814	4,922
Social care [6,7]	19,604	20,963	21,062	21,160	21,127	21,480	22,090	21,779
Public Health [8]						2,508	2,849	3,321
Housing (excluding HRA) [9]	16,964	20,022	21,032	21,868	22,730	23,006	22,946	22,836
Cultural, environmental and planning	10,474	11,083	10,676	9,741	9,444	9,176	9,029	8,695
of which:								
Cultural	3,297	3,465	3,278	3,021	2,945	2,831	2,614	2,496
Environmental	5,087	5,308	5,201	5,068	5,065	4,992	5,139	5,048
Planning and development	2,091	2,310	2,197	1,652	1,434	1,353	1,276	1,151
Police	11,555	12,022	11,948	11,650	11,335	10,920	11,121	10,951
Fire	2,104	2,177	2,165	2,118	2,120	2,089	2,123	2,080
Central services [10]	3,846	3,771	3,608	3,344	3,420	3,238	3,686	3,112
Other	643	9	-267	-267	-202	-247	224	281
Appropriations to (+) / from (-) accumulated absences account			64	6	21	39	-4	-6
Reversal of revenue expenditure funded from capital under statue (RECS) [11]		-1,883						
Net current expenditure	**113,018**	**119,176**	**121,240**	**115,220**	**111,972**	**112,885**	**114,711**	**113,089**
Capital financing	2,974	3,710	4,135	4,639	4,343	4,468	4,482	4,463
Capital Expenditure charged to Revenue Account	1,706	1,964	2,598	2,915	1,288	2,778	3,120	1,320
Interest receipts	-1,926	-780	-663	-860	-821	-839	-744	-793
Pension Interest Costs and expected return on Pension assets	7,042							
Appropriation to/from Pension Reserves	-6,395							
Other non-current expenditure [12,13]	3,459	4,163	4,136	3,905	4,218	-68	199	215
Specific grants outside Aggregate External Finance (AEF)	-21,772	-24,958	-27,191	-26,541	-26,651	-22,805	-22,617	-22,427
Revenue expenditure	**98,107**	**103,276**	**104,256**	**99,278**	**94,350**	**96,419**	**98,753**	**95,437**
Specific and special grants inside AEF	-42,920	-45,639	-45,750	-45,502	-41,982	-41,760	-40,763	-39,653
Area Based Grant (ABG)	-3,050	-3,314	-4,363					
Local Services Support Grant (LSSG)				-253	-221	-77	33	28
Net revenue expenditure	**52,137**	**54,323**	**54,143**	**53,523**	**52,147**	**54,582**	**57,957**	**55,756**
Appropriation to/from reserves (excluding pension reserves)	248	-308	1,261	2,553	2,551	2,379	2,107	1,834
Other adjustments	2	1	-23	0	0	1	0	0
Formula Grant [13,14]	-27,495	-28,269	-29,012	-29,436	-27,802	-33,459	31,603	28,798
of which:								
Police grant	-4,136	-4,253	-4,374	-4,546	-4,224	-7,565	-7,784	-7,421
Revenue support grant	-2,854	-4,501	-3,122	-5,873	-448	-15,175	-12,675	-9,509
Redistributed non-domestic rates	-20,506	-19,515	-21,517	-19,017	-23,129			
Retained income from Rate Retention Scheme						-10,719	-11,144	-11,867
General Greater London Authority Grant	-48	-48	-48	-63	-50			
Other items	-85	-65	-65	-126	-131	-130	-281	-392
Council tax requirement	**24,759**	**25,633**	**26,254**	**26,451**	**26,715**	**23,371**	**23,965**	**24,734**

1 Produced on a Financial Reporting Standard 17 (FRS17) basis

2 Produced on a non-FRS17 and PFI off balance sheet basis.

3 Produced on a non-International Accounting Standard 19 (IAS19) and PFI off balance sheet basis.

4 Education expenditure for 2011-12 and 2012-13 are not comparable to previous years due to a number of schools changing their status to become academies, which are centrally funded rather than funded by local authorities.

5 Includes mandatory student awards and inter-authority education recoupment.

6 Social Care expenditure for 2011-12 is not comparable to previous years due to a change in responsibility between NHS and local government for adults with learning disabilities, where from 1st April 2011 the transfer of funding was made directly from Department of Health to LAs, where they now receive a new non-ring fenced grant which amounts to £1.2 billion in 2011-12.

7 Includes supported employment.

8 There was a transfer of Public Health duties to local authorities in 2013-14, following the Health and Social Care Act 2012

9 Includes mandatory rent allowances and rent rebates.

10 Includes court services.

11 Net current expenditure estimates for 2009-10 are not fully comparable to 2010-11 figures owing to revenue expenditure funded from capital by statute (RECS) distributed across all services. Furthermore 2010-11 net current expenditure figures include liabilities for short term accumulated compensated absences (e.g. untaken annual leave entitlement), distributed across all the services, which makes comparisons against previous years not fully comparable. However total net current expenditure has been adjusted for both 2009-10 and 2010-11 so that they can be compared.

12 Includes:

(i) Gross expenditure on council tax benefit.

(ii) Expenditure on council tax reduction scheme.

(iii) Discretionary (non-domestic) rate relief.

(iv) Flood defence payments to the Environment Agency.

(v) Bad debt provision.

(vi) Appropriations to(+)/ from(-) financial instruments adjustment account

(vii) Appropriations to(+)/ from(-) unequal pay back pay account

(viii) Private Finance Initiative (PFI) schemes - difference from service charge

(ix) Business Rates Supplement

(x) Community Infrastructure Levy

(xi) Carbon Reduction Commitment

13 Localisation of council tax support; prior to 2013-14, local authorities were given a grant outside AEF by the Department for Work and Pensions (DWP) to cover the cost of council tax benefit in their area. In 2013-14, local authorities and local policing bodies in England will receive £3.7 billion towards the cost of local council tax support schemes. The funding is now provided as part of the revenue support grant system and reduces the council tax requirement to local authorities.

14 Business Rates; from April 2013 local authorities, except police authorities, now retain a share of business rates and keep the growth on that share, thereby giving them a significant financial incentive to help deliver growth locally. This will have a significant effect on the amount of Revenue Support Grant each authority receives in 2013-14.

In addition, police authorities, which are not part of the rates retention scheme, will receive all of their funding through Police Grant from 2013-14 onwards.

23.13 Revenue expenditure of local authorities

	2009/10 outturn	2010/11 outturn	2011/12 outturn	2012/13 outturn	2013/14 outturn	2014/15 budget	2015/16 budget
Scotland [21, 22]							
Net revenue expenditure on general fund	13,135,364	13,004,704	12,696,622	12,799,446	11,674,901	11,898,827	11,877,050
Wales [15]							
Education	2,550.4	2,584.3	2,590.5	2,630	2,641 (r)	2,630	2,555
Personal social services	1,418.0	1,461.1	1,486.5	1,536	1,565	1,599	1,639
Housing [16]	985.3	999.5	1,058.6	1,110	1,098	1,140	1,141
Local environmental services [17]	419.6	423.9	419.4	432	420	413	378
Roads and transport	325.3	330.7	317.9	315	307	302	287
Libraries, culture, heritage, sport and recreation	296.0	288.2	284.2	283	263	243	219
Planning, economic development and community development	152.4	159.0	147.9	132	125	110	81
Council tax benefit and administration [18]	32.4	31.3	28.9	30	34	40	36
Debt financing costs: counties	316.4	321.3	314.1	321	334	337	338
Central administrative and other revenue expenditure: counties [19]	190.1	205.9	275.0	310	307	295	313
Total county and county borough council expenditure	6,685.8	6,805.3	6,923.2	7,099	7,093 (r)	7,109	6,987
Total police expenditure	670.9	666.6	655.9	656	698	668	667
Total fire expenditure	150.1	148.0	145.6	146	149	148	145
Total national park expenditure	16.1	16.0	16.0	18	17	15	15
Gross revenue expenditure	7,522.9	7,636.0	7,740.6	7,919	7,958 (r)	7,940	7,813
less specific and special government grants (except council tax benefit grant)	1,987.2	2,019.6	2,013.8	2,112	1,933 (r)	1,981	1,935
Net revenue expenditure	5,535.7	5,616.4	5,726.8	5,806	6,025	5,959	5,878
Putting to (+)/drawing from (-) reserves	23.9	135.8	28.3	-32	-66	-72	-85
Council tax reduction scheme [20]	.	.	.	.	244	247	256
Budget requirement	5,559.6	5,752.2	5,755.1	5,774	6,203	6,134	6,049
Plus discretionary non-domestic rate relief	2.6	2.8	3.1	3	3	4	4
less revenue support grant	3,191.7	3,282.4	3,382.1	3,257	3,489	3,364	3,304
council tax reduction scheme grant	.	.	.	.	22	.	.
less police grant	236.3	242.2	245.7	228	240	236	222
less re-distributed non-domestic rates income	894.0	935.0	787.0	911	1,032	1,041	956
Council tax requirement	1,240.2	1,295.4	1,343.3	1,381	1,423	1,497	1,571
of which:							
Paid by council tax reduction scheme grant. [20]	218.6	230.9	242.2	247	244	247	256
Paid directly by council tax payers	1,021.6	1,064.5	1,101.2	1,134	1,179	1,250	1,315

Sources: Communities and Local Government: 0303 444 1333
Scottish Government, Statistical Support for Local Government: 0131 245 7034
Welsh Government: 02920 825355

15 Service expenditure is shown excluding that financed by sales, fees and charges, but including that financed by specific and special government grants.

16 Includes housing benefit and private sector costs such as provision for the homeless. Includes rent rebates granted to HRA tenants which is 100% grant funded. Excludes council owned housing.

17 Includes cemeteries and crematoria, community safety, environmental health, consumer protection, waste collection/disposal and central services to the public such as birth registration and elections.

18 Excludes council tax benefit expenditure funded by the specific grant from the Department for Work and Pensions.

19 Includes agricultural services, coastal and flood defence and community councils.Also includes central administrative costs of corporate management,democratic representation and certain costs, such as those relating to back year or additional pension contributions which should not be allocated to individual services, capital expenditure charged to the revenue account and is net of any interest expected to accrue on balances.

20 In 2013-14 council tax reduction scheme, funded by the Welsh Government, replaced council tax benefit grant funded from the Department for Work & Pensions.

22 Following the Police and Fire Reform (Scotland) Act 2012 figures from 2013-14 are not to be compared to previous years

(r) revised

Service expenditure for 2009-10 are not fully comparable to later years due to revenue expenditure funded from capital by statute (RECS) distributed across all services. 2008-09 years and earlier include FRS17 pension costs.

. Data not applicable

23.14 Financing of revenue expenditure England and Wales

England and Wales
Years ending 31 March

£ million

		2003 /04	2004 /05	2005 /06	2006 /07	2007 /08	2008 /09	2009 /10	2010 /11[a]	2011 /12[a]	2012 /13[a]	2013 /14 [1,a]	2014 /15 [1,a]
England[2]													
Revenue expenditure[3]													
Cash £m	**KRTN**	75,244	79,303	84,422	88,172	92,384	98,107	103,276	104,256	99,278	94,350	102,165	98,753
Government grants													
Cash £m	**KRTO**	41,777	45,258	45,838	49,093	51,657	53,007	57,755	57,657	56,237	46,926	66,724	61,255
Percentage of revenue expenditure	**KRTP**	56	57	54	56	56	54	56	55	57	50	65	62
Redistributed business rates[4]													
Cash £m	**KRTQ**	15,611	15,004	18,004	17,506	18,506	20,506	19,515	21,517	19,017	23,129	N/A	N/A
Percentage of revenue expenditure	**KRTR**	21	19	21	20	20	21	19	21	19	25	N/A	N/A
Retained income from rate retention													
Cash £m		N/A	N/A	N/A	N/A	N/A	N/A	N/A	N/A	N/A	N/A	10,763	11,144
Percentage of revenue expenditure		N/A	N/A	N/A	N/A	N/A	N/A	N/A	N/A	N/A	N/A	11	11
Council tax													
Cash £m	**KRTS**	18,946	20,299	21,315	22,453	23,608	24,759	25,633	26,254	26,451	26,715	23,371	23,965
Percentage of revenue expenditure	**KRTT**	25	26	25	25	26	25	25	25	27	28	23	24
Wales													
Gross revenue expenditure[5]	**ZBXH**	5,243	5,786	6,128	6,472	6,739	7,184	7,523	7,636	7,741	7,919	7,958 (r)	7,940
General government grants[6]	**ZBXI**	2,743	2,817	2,987	3,169	3,287	3,335	3,428	3,525	3,628	3,485	3,507	3,352.3
Specific government grants[7]	**ZBXG**	1,005	1,381	1,473	1,530	1,630	1,809	1,987	2,020	2,014	2,112	1,933 (r)	1,981.1
Share of redistributed business rates	**ZBXJ**	660	672	672	730	791	868	894	935	787	911	1,032	1,041.0
Council tax income[8]	**ZBXK**	861	924	1,012	1,071	1,131	1,188	1,240	1,295	1,343	1,381	1,423	1,497.0
Other[9]	**ZBXL**	-25	-8	-16	-27	-99	-16	-26	-139	-31	29	63	69

Sources: Communities and Local Government: 0303 444 1333;
Welsh Government 02920 825355

1 Budget estimates.
2 Produced on a non-Financial Reporting Standard 17 (FRS17) basis.
3 The sum of government grants, business rates and local taxes does not normally equal revenue expenditure because of the use of reserves.
4 1993-94 to 2003-04 includes City of London Offset.

5 Gross revenue expenditure is total local authority expenditure on services, plus capital charges, but net of any income from sales, fees, and charges and other non-grant sources. It includes expenditure funded by specific grants. The figures have been adjusted to account for FRS17 pension costs.
6 Includes all unhypothecated grants, namely revenue support grant, police grant, council tax reduction scheme grant, transitional grant and the adjustment to reverse the transfer.
7 Comprises specific and supplementary grants,excluding police grant.
8 This includes community council precepts, and income covered by charge/council tax benefit grant, but excludes council tax reduction scheme (2013-14).
9 Includes use of reserves and discretionary non-domestic rate relief

a - produced on a non-international Accounting Standard 19 basis.

23.15 Financing of capital expenditure

£ million

	2009-10	2010-11	2011-12	2012-13	2013-14	2014-15 (F)
Central government grants	7,494	8,063	7,170 [a]	8,481	7,483	8,718
EU structural funds grants	43	38	77	55	57	124
Grants and contributions from private developers and from leaseholders etc	502	634	747	693	750	929
Grants and contributions from NDPBs [b]	602	753	522	442	443	547
National lottery grants	119	104	121	67	49	69
Use of capital receipts	1,603	1,409	1,647	1,294	1,516	2,505
Revenue financing of capital expenditure	3,532	3,984	4,504 [a]	3,167	4,920	6,187
of which:						
Housing Revenue Account (CERA)	*247*	*235*	*324*	*466*	*578*	*1,291*
Major Repairs Reserve	*1,377*	*1,069*	*1,160*	*1,259*	*1,491*	*1,357*
General Fund (CERA)	*1,908*	*2,680*	*3,020*	*1,442*	*2,851*	*3,538*
Capital expenditure financed by borrowing/credit	7,931	8,399	18,819	4,842	4,454	8,025
of which:						
SCE(R) Single Capital Pot [c]	*2,181*	*1,581*	*338*	*88*	*70*	*44*
SCE(R) Separate Programme Element [c]	*748*	*484*	*74*	*30*	*8*	*16*
Other borrowing & credit arrangements not supported by central government [e]	*5,002*	*6,335*	*18,406 [d]*	*4,724*	*4,376*	*7,965*
Total	**21,826**	**23,385**	**33,606 [d]**	**19,042**	**19,671**	**27,103**

Source: Department for Communities and Local Government

(a) There is a discontinuity from 2010-11 owing to a change in the treatment of expenditure by GLA. Previously this was recorded as 'Central government grant' but for 2011-12 it has been recorded as CERA to align with figures received on the Revenue Outturn

(b) Non-Departmental Public Bodies, organisations that are not government departments but which have a role in the processes of national government, such as Sport England, English Heritage and the Natural England.

(c) Supported capital expenditure (SCE) financed by borrowing that is attracting central government support has been discontinued as of March 31 2011. This may have a bearing on the financing of capital expenditure. A residue of schemes in 2011-12 and 2012-13 will continue to be financed in reliance of supported borrowing from earlier years.

(d) It is estimated that approximately £13 billion is associated with the financing of the HRA self-financing determination payment.

(e) The Prudential System, which came into effect on 1 April 2004, allows local authorities to raise finance for capital expenditure - without Government consent - where they can afford to service the debt without extra Government support.

23.16a Capital receipts: all services: England 2012-13: 2nd provisional outturn

£ thousand

	Sales & disposal of tangible fixed assets (10)	Sales of intangible assets (11)	Repayments of grants loans & financial assistance (12)	Total receipts(a) (10+11+12)
Pre-primary & Primary Education	42,656	0	0	42,656
Secondary Education	161,531	0	532	162,063
Special Education	17,518	0	0	17,518
Non-school funding	43,196	0	8,662	51,858
Education	**264,901**	**0**	**9,194**	**274,095**
Roads, Street Lights & Safety	11,191	0	11	11,202
Parking of Vehicles	8,570	0	90	8,660
Public Passenger Transport-Bus	101	0	894	995
Public Passenger Transport-Rail & Other	14,197	2,311	0	16,508
Airports	9	0	822	831
Local Authority Ports and Piers	0	0	2	2
Tolled Road bridges,tunnels,ferries, public transport companies	218	0	1	219
Highways & transport	**34,286**	**2,311**	**1,820**	**38,417**
Social services	**76,075**	**0**	**1,287**	**77,362**
Housing	**729,945**	**3,877**	**27,305**	**761,127**
Culture and heritage	4,424	0	419	4,843
Recreation and sport	28,634	267	1,485	30,386
Open spaces	22,643	0	46	22,689
Tourism	325	0	0	325
Library Services	3,755	0	106	3,861
Total Culture and related services	**59,781**	**267**	**2,056**	**62,104**
Cemeteries, cremation and mortuary	2,024	0	0	2,024
Coast protection	0	0	0	0
Community safety	0	0	0	0
Community safety (CCTV)	0	0	0	0
Flood defence and land drainage	89	0	0	89
Agriculture and fisheries services	35,553	0	0	35,553
Regulatory services (environmental health)	815	0	16	831
Regulatory services (trading standards)	0	0	0	0
Street cleaning not chargeable to highways	5,980	0	0	5,980
Waste collection	2,963	0	370	3,333
Waste disposal	3,465	0	973	4,438
Trade waste	4	0	469	473
Recycling	175	0	0	175
Waste minimisation	249	0	0	249
Climate change costs	0	0	319	319
Total environmental and regulatory services	**51,317**	**0**	**2,147**	**53,464**
Planning and development services	**123,179**	**15**	**11,872**	**135,066**
Police	**116,318**	**0**	**788**	**117,106**
Fire and rescue services	**9,890**	**86**	**0**	**9,976**
Central services	**378,152**	**2,161**	**7,713**	**388,026**
Industrial and commercial trading	181,464	0	93	181,557
Other trading	8,004	0	11,631	19,635
Total Trading	**189,468**	**0**	**11,724**	**201,192**
Total all services	**2,033,312**	**8,717**	**75,906**	**2,117,935**

Source: Department for Communities and Local Government

(a) Figures in this column do not include disposals of share and loan capital

23.16b Capital expenditure: all services: England 2012-13: 2nd provisional outturn

£ thousand

	Total expenditure on fixed & intangible assets (6) (1+2+3+4+5)	Expenditure on grants (7)	Expenditure on loans & other financial assistance (8)	Total Expenditure[a] (9) (6+7+8)
Pre-primary & Primary Education	1,762,955	110,671	399	1,874,025
Secondary Education	1,906,645	293,952	18,628	2,219,225
Special Education	241,362	5,193	0	246,555
Non-school funding	160,615	14,178	5,700	180,493
Education	**4,071,578**	**423,994**	**24,727**	**4,520,299**
Roads, Street Lights & Safety	2,268,801	35,254	830	2,304,885
Parking of Vehicles	62,912	2,901	0	65,813
Public Passenger Transport-Bus	269,350	19,184	0	288,534
Public Passenger Transport-Rail & Other	201,979	1,271,379	648,470	2,121,828
Airports	1,338	0	11,919	13,257
Local Authority Ports and Piers	15,606	0	800	16,406
Tolled Road bridges,tunnels,ferries, public transport companies	24,321	0	0	24,321
Highways & transport	**2,844,307**	**1,328,718**	**662,019**	**4,835,044**
Social services	**177,418**	**29,009**	**218**	**206,645**
Housing	**2,648,917**	**1,036,311**	**45,554**	**3,730,782**
Culture and heritage	181,608	19,687	1,392	202,687
Recreation and sport	358,771	17,393	853	377,017
Open spaces	132,878	5,544	181	138,603
Tourism	7,232	1,390	0	8,622
Library Services	148,627	1,348	0	149,975
Total Culture and related services	**829,116**	**45,362**	**2,426**	**876,904**
Cemeteries, cremation and mortuary	51,252	90	882	52,224
Coast protection	18,892	457	0	19,349
Community safety	4,611	423	0	5,034
Community safety (CCTV)	10,138	215	0	10,353
Flood defence and land drainage	17,141	6,573	1,313	25,027
Agriculture and fisheries	7,325	19	0	7,344
Regulatory services (environmental health)	18,307	617	0	18,924
Regulatory services (trading standards)	281	0	0	281
Street cleaning (not chargeable to highways)	12,246	0	0	12,246
Waste collection	105,949	1,665	0	107,614
Waste disposal	92,437	157	25,000	117,594
Trade waste	1,536	29	0	1,565
Recycling	112,139	2,648	121	114,908
Waste minimisation	1,258	11	0	1,269
Climate change costs	25,370	5,892	835	32,097
Total environmental services	**478,882**	**18,796**	**28,151**	**525,829**
Planning and development services	**646,172**	**212,374**	**16,932**	**875,478**
Police	**499,907**	**21**	**0**	**499,928**
Fire and rescue services	**171,280**	**1,094**	**0**	**172,374**
Central services	**1,159,520**	**32,251**	**70,637**	**1,262,408**
Industrial and commercial trading	136,792	4,198	18,022	159,012
Other trading	40,620	793	10	41,423
Total Trading	**177,412**	**4,991**	**18,032**	**200,435**
Total all services	**13,704,509**	**3,132,921**	**868,696**	**17,706,126**

Source: Department for Communities and Local Government

(a) Figures in this column do not include acquisitions of share and loan capital

23.17 Capital outturn expenditure, by service (£ thousand)
Wales

	2001 -02	2002 -03	2003 -04 (4)	2004 -05	2005 -06	2006 -07	2007 -08	2008 -09	2009 -10	2010 -11	2011 -12	2012 -13
Total capital expenditure/receipts	595,279	638,698	741,073	860,323	982,266	1,076,976	1,145,861	1,128,396	934,125	997,663	1,036,261	1,088,056
Total all services	597,381	637,848	739,864	859,323	980,845	1,061,728	1,128,516	1,123,578	932,217	993,058	1,027,215	1,085,049
Total education	96,077	96,933	115,863	143,757	161,085	185,828	189,771	203,552	215,542	233,275	260,584	267,384
Personal social services (1)	9,841	10,800	13,953	16,830	20,459	18,731	18,520	22,119	21,897	22,325	18,777	22,948
Total transport	111,216	109,893	127,389	141,188	203,417	213,950	237,630	231,376	203,962	210,947	206,929	231,510
Total housing	201,724	219,282	220,918	242,328	257,461	267,013	247,097	238,170	217,445	210,084	230,148	216,368
General administration (2)	23,173	36,369	49,084	51,931	56,311	74,540	66,956	61,668	47,411	50,618	42,579	63,374
Planning and development (3)	45,645	34,608	48,793	71,610	77,999	79,607	111,584	95,584	56,520	73,902	94,657	109,165
Total other local services	84,072	102,226	124,651	148,257	162,568	185,515	213,851	209,473	124,853	138,742	135,677	140,425
Total law, order and protective services	25,633	27,737	39,209	43,418	41,542	36,543	43,104	61,632	44,585	53,161	37,861	33,872
Other transactions	-2,103	849	1,209	1,000	1,421	15,248	17,345	4,818	1,908	4,605	9,046	3,007

Source: Capital outturn (COR) data collection, Welsh Government

Email: stats.finance@wales.gsi.gov.uk

1. Expenditure and receipts on sheltered employment and workshops. Excludes port health. Where premises are provided for both educational and personal social services for children under five, only the expenditure/receipts attributable to personal social services are included.

2. Expenditure on an authority's own properties, transportation, equipment and material generally, which can not properly be set against some other specific service.

3. Expenditure on planning departments' payments on development control, building regulations and planning implementation; direct expenditure on conservation, environmental improvements, conversion and commercial development; gypsy sites; advances and grants for industrial and commercial enterprises and industrial development; and tourism. Excludes expenditure in respect of industrial trading estates.

4. From 2003-04 onwards data was also collected from National park authorities.

23.18 Service Analysis of General Fund Revenue Expenditure and Income, 2012-13

£ thousands

Scotland	Revenue Contributions to Capital	Support Service Costs	All other Expenditure	Adjustment for Inter Account and Inter Authority Transfers	Total Expenditure	Total Income	Net Revenue Expenditure
Education	**14,798**	**184,132**	**4,601,660**	**-26,136**	**4,774,454**	**188,205**	**4,586,249**
Pre-primary education	761	11,015	303,603	-999	314,380	13,388	300,992
Primary education	8,056	69,989	1,751,069	-7,511	1,821,603	61,534	1,760,069
Secondary education	4,313	72,105	1,878,586	-8,716	1,946,288	74,566	1,871,722
Special education	1,549	16,923	498,627	-6,591	510,508	13,643	496,865
Community Learning	68	7,798	134,451	-1,244	141,073	18,783	122,290
Other non-school funding	51	6,302	35,324	-1,075	40,602	6,291	34,311
Cultural and related services	**4,321**	**42,135**	**698,459**	**-41,808**	**703,107**	**89,432**	**613,675**
Museums and galleries	33	2,520	43,671	-66	46,158	3,671	42,487
Other cultural and heritage services	418	4,418	59,024	-828	63,032	15,634	47,398
Library service	351	8,511	108,937	-491	117,308	4,640	112,668
Tourism	9	692	29,496	-270	29,927	4,748	25,179
Countryside recreation and management	576	1,821	24,657	-502	26,552	2,756	23,796
Sport facilities	611	7,779	196,376	-1,943	202,823	33,036	169,787
Community parks and open spaces	1,746	11,924	174,712	-36,251	152,131	13,856	138,275
Other recreation and sport	577	4,470	61,586	-1,457	65,176	11,091	54,085
Social work	**2,414**	**198,150**	**3,619,993**	**-35,081**	**3,785,476**	**823,859**	**2,961,617**
Service Strategy	465	2,794	25,652	-3,318	25,593	3,063	22,530
Children's Panel	0	448	2,068	-20	2,496	260	2,236
Children and families	207	43,532	801,216	-7,849	837,106	20,723	816,383
Older persons	1,093	83,705	1,606,741	-9,895	1,681,644	388,352	1,293,292
Adults with physical or sensory disabilities	359	12,023	201,691	-2,289	211,784	28,179	183,605
Adults with learning disabilities	207	36,130	666,636	-6,474	696,499	193,470	503,029
Adults with mental health needs	33	8,209	149,011	-762	156,491	62,705	93,786
Adults with other needs	8	3,141	62,376	-2,409	63,116	22,342	40,774
Criminal justice social work services	42	8,168	104,602	-2,065	110,747	104,765	5,982
Police[1]	**7,027**	**56,114**	**1,184,101**	**-6,493**	**1,240,749**	**726,933**	**513,816**
Local Policing	3,260	33,849	697,633	-5,353	729,389	414,004	315,385
Dealing with the Public	337	3,729	83,566	-77	87,555	42,844	44,711
Criminal Justice Arrangements	380	3,818	79,375	-89	83,484	43,670	39,814
Road Policing	1,476	2,882	56,330	-634	60,054	35,792	24,262
Specialist Operations	217	1,982	50,128	-42	52,285	36,321	15,964
Intelligence	204	2,415	51,750	-35	54,334	29,734	24,600
Specialist Investigations	400	4,624	91,984	-106	96,902	54,964	41,938
Investigative Support	18	260	4,387	-9	4,656	2,624	2,032
National Policing	735	2,555	68,948	-148	72,090	66,980	5,110
Fire[1]	**4,422**	**9,193**	**337,877**	**-4,817**	**346,675**	**50,011**	**296,664**
Fire fighting and rescue	4,185	6,577	247,627	-503	257,886	10,047	247,839
Community fire safety	237	2,554	20,362	-52	23,101	1,848	21,253
Fire fighters' pensions	0	0	68,554	-4,262	64,292	38,115	26,177
Fire service emergency planning	0	62	1,334	0	1,396	1	1,395
Roads and transport[2]	**18,800**	**41,047**	**768,774**	**-132,777**	**695,844**	**208,566**	**487,278**
Road construction	1,728	291	11,150	-1,323	11,846	5,375	6,471
Winter maintenance	62	2,683	88,910	-88	91,567	2,982	88,585
Maintenance & repairs	2,591	17,133	256,787	-54,422	222,089	40,018	182,071
Road lighting	576	3,484	79,932	-3,706	80,286	7,463	72,823
School crossing patrols	0	559	13,273	-113	13,719	48	13,671
Other network and traffic management	345	9,242	62,709	-12,645	59,651	15,416	44,235
Parking	596	2,364	30,353	-723	32,590	61,622	-29,032
Non-LA PT: Concessionary fares	0	286	7,804	-13	8,077	1,071	7,006
Non-LA PT: Support to operators	0	1,874	96,001	-9,756	88,119	7,593	80,526
Non-LA PT: Co-ordination	12,902	2,856	93,539	-47,969	61,328	60,035	1,293
Local authority Transport	0	275	28,316	-2,019	26,572	6,943	19,629

23.18 Service Analysis of General Fund Revenue Expenditure and Income, 2012-13

£ thousands

Scotland	Revenue Contributions to Capital	Support Service Costs	All other Expenditure	Adjustment for Inter Account and Inter Authority Transfers	Total Expenditure	Total Income	Net Revenue Expenditure
Environmental services	**11,147**	**59,827**	**741,663**	**-28,306**	**784,331**	**128,769**	**655,562**
Cemetery, cremation and mortuary services	200	4,001	34,751	-815	38,137	29,593	8,544
Coast protection	2	226	2,266	-3	2,491	652	1,839
Flood defence and land drainage	366	828	8,451	-386	9,259	833	8,426
Environmental Health	235	14,127	90,790	-4,742	100,410	15,831	84,579
Trading Standards	17	4,304	28,198	-1,011	31,508	1,934	29,574
Waste Collection	2,445	15,064	197,793	-6,060	209,242	41,976	167,266
Waste Disposal	7,576	10,902	272,135	-7,270	283,343	34,871	248,472
Other waste management	306	10,375	107,279	-8,019	109,941	3,079	106,862
Planning and economic development	**4,011**	**49,979**	**452,037**	**-22,389**	**483,638**	**201,088**	**282,550**
Planning: Building control	3	6,579	35,014	-664	40,932	25,180	15,752
Planning: Development control	205	8,661	41,831	-318	50,379	24,785	25,594
Planning: Policy	156	5,381	71,407	-3,272	73,672	36,478	37,194
Planning: Environmental initiatives	147	2,619	24,789	-2,145	25,410	10,193	15,217
Economic development	3,500	26,739	278,996	-15,990	293,245	104,452	188,793
Non-HRA Housing	**530**	**30,672**	**2,320,242**	**-24,625**	**2,326,819**	**2,020,080**	**306,739**
Private sector housing renewal	178	2,958	69,734	-1,452	71,418	42,732	28,686
Housing benefits: Rent allowances	0	0	1,108,430	0	1,108,430	1,073,853	34,577
Housing benefits: Rent rebate	0	0	611,977	0	611,977	638,290	-26,313
Homelessness	7	8,163	181,235	-3,933	185,472	114,385	71,087
Welfare Services	0	40	5,841	-242	5,639	681	4,958
Administration of housing advances	0	90	71	-82	79	361	-282
Housing Support Services	0	4,755	158,050	-1,022	161,783	8,026	153,757
Other non-HRA housing (excl admin of Housing Benefits)	345	14,666	184,904	-17,894	182,021	141,752	40,269
Central Services[3]	**26,259**	**133,693**	**648,892**	**-235,773**	**573,071**	**210,842**	**362,229**
Council tax collection	49	25,032	61,349	-1,808	84,622	52,090	32,532
Council tax benefit administration	25	10,722	25,490	-2,432	33,805	19,405	14,400
Non-domestic rates collection	2	4,084	5,832	-125	9,793	1,577	8,216
Housing benefit administration	111	13,248	26,516	-2,149	37,726	22,407	15,319
Registration of births, deaths and marriages	2	5,117	10,168	-147	15,140	9,662	5,478
Emergency Planning (non Police or Fire)	0	608	4,109	-316	4,401	426	3,975
Licensing	1	5,826	14,767	-218	20,376	20,205	171
Conducting Elections	0	1,318	10,135	-592	10,861	1,861	9,000
Registration of electors	39	795	9,121	-505	9,450	160	9,290
Council tax valuation	57	519	9,743	-27	10,292	61	10,231
Non-domestic lands valuation	63	1,139	16,125	-60	17,267	276	16,991
Local Land Charges	0	1	55	0	56	25	31
Non-road lighting	0	374	11,718	-10	12,082	3,490	8,592
General grants, bequests and donations	10	535	8,131	0	8,676	35	8,641
Corporate and democratic core costs	270	105,788	67,235	-4,588	168,705	1,816	166,889
Non-distributed costs	1,173	-52,242	127,482	-12,129	64,284	2,728	61,556
Other	24,457	10,829	240,916	-210,667	65,535	74,618	-9,083
Trading Services	**422**	**1,564**	**62,664**	**-10,093**	**54,557**	**58,115**	**-3,558**
Add Ring Fenced Grants Back In	.	.	.	.	**0**	**-524,957**	**524,957**
Interest and investment income	.	.	.	.	**683,665**	**64,529**	**619,136**
Surplus/deficit from Significant Trading Operations	.	.	.	.	**-2,811**	**0**	**-2,811**
Statutory repayment of debt	.	.	.	.	**595,343**		**595,343**
All services	**94,151**	**806,506**	**15,436,362**	**-568,298**	**17,044,918**	**4,245,472**	**12,799,446**

1. Police and fire expenditure is apportioned to councils using the amount that the Joint Boards requisition from them
2. Regional Transport Partnerships expenditure is apportioned to councils by population (NRS 2012 mid-year population estimates)
3. Expenditure on council tax and non-domestic valuation and registration of electors is apportioned to councils using the amount that the Valuation Joint Boards requisition from them

Source: Scottish Local Government Finance Statistics

23.19a Local Government Revenue Income by Source, 2008-09 to 2012-13, Scotland

£ millions

	2008-09	2009-10	2010-11	2011-12	2012-13
General Revenue Funding[1]	7,426	7,757	8,149	7,790	7,782
Council Tax	1,909	1,910	1,923	1,926	1,947
Council Tax Benefit Subsidy	351	368	375	376	371
Non Domestic Rates	1,963	2,165	2,068	2,182	2,263
Sales, Rents, Fees & Charges	2,262	2,287	2,179	2,298	2,342
Other Income	3,363	3,390	3,348	3,300	3,244
Total revenue income	**17,274**	**17,877**	**18,043**	**17,872**	**17,949**

1. Prior to 2008-09 this was Revenue Support Grant

Sources: General Revenue Funding (Up to 2010-11) – Finance Circulars; Non-Domestic Rates – Non Domestic Rates Returns (NDRI); All Other Data – Local Financial Returns (LFRs)

Source: Scottish Local Government Financial Statistics

23.19b Total Capital Expenditure and Financing, 2008-09 to 2012-13

£ thousands

	2008-09	2009-10	2010-11	2011-12	2012-13
Scottish Government General Capital Grant	364,039	462,640	352,652	565,541	450,088
Scottish Government Specific Capital Grants	262,093	268,370	228,865	234,365	217,281
Grants from Scottish Government Agencies and NDPBs	141,590	160,281	115,726	82,764	141,311
Other Grants and Contributions	115,871	104,575	94,486	85,714	124,311
Borrowing from Loans fund	1,206,318	1,091,548	1,113,929	1,261,468	1,165,387
Capital receipts used from asset sales/disposals	204,048	164,746	114,722	94,020	105,937
Capital Fund applied	40,609	28,616	14,916	21,653	36,867
Capital funded from current revenue	196,836	166,141	208,894	209,122	294,087
Assets acquired under credit arrangements (e.g. finance leases, PPP/PFI)	737	824,442	103,972	106,888	14,055
Total Financing	**2,532,141**	**3,271,359**	**2,348,162**	**2,661,534**	**2,549,324**

1. From 2009-10 onwards assets acquired through PPP/PFI are included. In addition, figures for 2009-10 include assets acquired through PPP/PFI for past years. (more information on the changes can be found here - http://www.scotland.gov.uk/Topics/Government/local-government/17999/LACapital/CapExReport200910)

Source: Capital Returns (CR Final)

Source: Scottish Local Government Financial Statistics

23.20 Subjective Analysis of General Fund Revenue Expenditure and Income, 2012-13

£thousands

	Education Services	Culture and Related Services	Social Work Services	Police Service	Fire Service	Roads and Transport	Environmental Services	Planning and Development Services	Central Services	Housing Services (Non-HRA)	Trading with the Public	Total General Fund Services	HRA Housing Services	Total General Fund Services (inc HRA)
INCOME														
Government Grants														
Ring-fenced Revenue Grants	8,361	0		507,631	0	0	0	0	0	8,965	0	524,957	2,840	527,797
General Capital Grant used to fund grants to third parties	0	1,965	2	3,663	0	16,390	0	3,385	0	105,954	0	131,359	0	131,359
Other Central Government Grants (excl GRG)	31,358	2,977	94,493	100,020	21,003	24,071	5,895	24,378	67,734	1,591,239	0	1,963,168	6,690	1,969,858
Total Government Grants	**39,719**	**4,942**	**94,495**	**611,314**	**21,003**	**40,461**	**5,895**	**27,763**	**67,734**	**1,706,158**	**0**	**2,619,484**	**9,530**	**2,629,014**
Other Grants reimbursements and Contributions														
Contributions from Health Authorities			398,370									398,370		398,370
All other grants, reimbursements and contributions	35,131	13,130	54,539	6,569	26,066	13,988	4,905	56,576	32,219	148,510	70	391,703	10,567	402,270
Total Other Grants reimbursements and Contributions	**35,131**	**13,130**	**452,909**	**6,569**	**26,066**	**13,988**	**4,905**	**56,576**	**32,219**	**148,510**	**70**	**790,073**	**10,567**	**800,640**
Customer and Client Receipts														
Income from charges to service users	46,625	35,158	247,614	22,473	99	79,886	45,458	20,709	20,700	24,254	19,447	562,423	65,937	628,360
Rent Income	1,370	5,809	7,100	4,160	138	11,958	1,035	47,707	10,280	93,026	1,094	183,677	947,540	1,131,217
Other Sales, Fees and Charges	65,360	30,390	21,736	82,417	2,705	62,273	71,476	48,125	79,909	48,132	37,504	550,027	20,829	570,856
Total Customer and Client Receipts	**113,355**	**71,357**	**276,450**	**109,050**	**2,942**	**154,117**	**117,969**	**116,541**	**110,889**	**165,412**	**58,045**	**1,296,127**	**1,034,306**	**2,330,433**
Credits resulting from soft loans	0	3	5	0	0	0	0	208	0	0	0	216	0	216
Total Income	**188,205**	**89,432**	**823,859**	**726,933**	**50,011**	**208,566**	**128,769**	**201,088**	**210,842**	**2,020,080**	**58,115**	**4,705,900**	**1,054,403**	**5,760,303**

Source: Scottish Local Government Financial Statistics

23.21 Expenditure of local authorities

Northern Ireland
Years ending 31 March

£ thousand

	1998 /99	1999 /00	2000 /01	2001 /02	2002 /03	2003 /04	2004 /05	2005 /06	2006 /07	2007 /08	2008 /09[1]	2009 /10	2010 /11	2011 /12	2012 /13
Libraries,museums and art galleries	14,571	19,900	23,097	24,181	32,728	30,062	30,481	33,516	28,655	31,557	36,527	35,549	37,163	40,321	48,852
Environmental health services:															
Refuse collection and disposal	56,360	62,226	65,289	73,336	90,148	94,715	102,633	113,768	121,879	136,181	142,071	151,332	155,540	159,518	159,753
Public baths	2,634	1,750	1,724	1,423	..	..	..	..	..	..	..	..	..	..	..
Parks, recreation grounds,etc	118,396	158,304	170,999	184,406	194,224	193,617	205,734	221,298	198,314	213,780	265,720	257,522	278,716	263,211	278,729
Other sanitary services	42,923	44,214	45,552	48,784	52,075	55,349	59,906	66,294	68,641	74,624	86,428	87,000	90,966	91,358	88,817
Housing (grants and small dwellings acquisition)	358	37	28	27	12	21	18	10	15	17	8	15	79	13,474	0
Trading services:															
Cemeteries	5,887	5,973	6,151	6,538	7,208	7,980	8,455	8,520	7,752	8,726	9,125	9,353	10,994	10,274	10,350
Other trading services (including markets, fairs and harbours)	10,779	9,366	7,209	7,769	18,281	17,489	18,776	19,596	15,240	17,498	27,711	21,115	15,610	13,222	14,667
Miscellaneous	161,790	86,649	89,881	98,244	79,645	114,971	105,031	128,304	141,717	160,606	263,230	183,563	107,841	129,889	130,318
Total expenditure	413,698	388,419	409,930	444,708	474,321	490,619	531,034	591,306	582,213	642,991	830,820	745,450	696,909	707,809	731,490
Total loan charges	26,413	..	..	..	..	..	..	..	..	..	..	..	..	..	..

Source: Department of the Environment for Northern Ireland: 028 9025 6086

1. The overall expenditure figure for 2008/2009 is much higher than 2009/2010 substantially due to the Capital Finance Reserve of one particular council.

Agriculture

Chapter 24

Agriculture

Input and Output (Tables 24.1 and 24.2)

For both tables, output is net of VAT collected on the sale of non-edible products. Figures for total output include subsidies on products, that is, payments that have the purpose of influencing production, their prices or remuneration of the factors of production. Unspecified crops include turf, other minor crops and arable area payments for fodder maize. Eggs include the value of duck eggs and exports of eggs for hatching. Landlords' expenses are included within farm maintenance, miscellaneous expenditure and depreciation of buildings and works. Also included within 'Other farming costs' are livestock and crop costs, water costs, insurance premia, bank charges, professional fees, rates, and other farming costs.

Non-subsidy payments

Payments other than subsidies on products from which farmers can benefit as a consequence of engaging in agriculture. This includes:
• environment and countryside management schemes
• organic farming schemes
• support schemes for less favoured areas
• Single Payment Scheme
• animal disease compensation attributable to income
• other payments

Compensation of employees and interest charges

Total compensation of employees excludes the value of work done by farm labour on own account capital formation in buildings and work. 'Interest' relates to interest charges on loans for current farming purposes and buildings, less interest on money held on short-term deposit.

Rent

Rent paid (after deductions) is the rent paid on all tenanted land including 'conacre' land in Northern Ireland, less landlords' expenses and the benefit value of dwellings on that land. Rent received (after deductions) is the rent received by farming landowners from renting of land to other farmers, less landlords' expenses and the benefit value of dwellings on that land. Total net rent is the net rent flowing out of the agricultural sector paid to non-farming landowners, including that part of tenanted land in Northern Ireland.

Agricultural censuses and surveys (Tables 24.3 and 24.5 and 24.12)

Data in thse tables are sourced primarily from the June Surveys of Agriculture carried out in the four UK countries each year. The exceptions to this are the holder age data (sourced from the EU Farm Structure Survey) and land use data in Scotland (sourced from Single Application Form (SAF) subsidy data). Also, cattle data are sourced from the Cattle Tracing System (CTS) in England, Wales and Scotland (from 2013) and from the equivalent Animal and Public Health Administration (APHIS) system in Northern Ireland. Prior to 2013 Scottish cattle data was sourced from agricultural surveys.

From 2009 onwards, England data relate to "commercial" holdings only. The term "commercial" covers all English holdings which have more than 5 hectares of agricultural land, 1 hectare of orchards, 0.5 hectares of vegetables or 0.1 hectares of protected crops, or more than 10 cattle, 50 pigs, 20 sheep, 20 goats, or 1,000 poultry. These thresholds are specified in the EU Farm Structure Survey Regulation EC 1166/2008.

Estimated quantity of crops and grass harvested
(Table 24.4)

The estimated yield of sugar beet is obtained from production figures supplied by British Sugar plc in England and Wales. In Great Britain, potato yields are estimated in consultation with the Potato Council Limited.

Forestry
(Table 24.6)

Statistics for state forestry are from Forestry Commission and Forest Service management information systems. For private forestry in Great Britain, statistics on new planting and restocking are based on records of grant aid and estimates of planting undertaken without grant aid, and softwood production is estimated from a survey of the largest timber harvesting companies. Hardwood production is estimated from deliveries of roundwood to primary wood processors and others, based on surveys of the UK timber industry, data provided by trade associations and estimates provided by the Expert Group on Timber and Trade Statistics.

Fisheries
(Table 24.14)
Figures show the number of registered and licensed fishing vessels based on information provided by the Marine Management Organisation.

Estimated average household food consumption – 'Family Food' Expenditure and Food Survey
(Table 24.15)
In 2008 the Expenditure and Food Survey (EFS) was renamed as the Living Costs and Food Survey (LCFS) when it became part of the Integrated Household Survey (IHS). The Expenditure and Food Survey started in April 2001, having been preceded by the National Food Survey (NFS) and the Family Expenditure Survey (FES). Both surveys were brought into one to provide value for money without compromising data quality. The EFS was effectively a continuation of the FES extended to record quantities of purchases. This extension is now known as the Family Food Module of the LCFS. Estimates from the NFS prior to 2000 have been adjusted by aligning estimates for the year 2000 with corresponding estimates from the FES. From 2006 the survey moved onto a calendar year basis (from the previous financial year basis) in preparation for its integration to the Integrated Household Survey from January 2008.

The Living Costs and Food Survey is a voluntary sample survey of private households throughout the UK. The basic unit of the survey is the household which is defined as a group of people living at the same address and sharing common catering arrangements. The survey is continuous, interviews being spread evenly over the year to ensure that seasonal effects are covered. Each household member over the age of seven keeps a diary of all their expenditure over a two-week period. A simplified version of the diary is used by those aged between seven and 15. The diaries record expenditure and quantities of purchases of food and drink rather than consumption of food and drink. Items of food and drink are defined as either household or eating out and are recorded in the form the item was purchased not how it was consumed. 'Household' covers all food that is brought into the household. 'Eating out' covers all food that never enters the household, for example restaurant meals, school meals and snacks eaten away from home.

24.1 Production and income account at current prices; United Kingdom

Enquiries: Helen Mason on +44 (0)1904 455096
Email: helen.mason@defra.gsi.gov.uk

£ million

Calendar years

	2002	2003	2004	2005	2006	2007	2008	2009	2010	2011	2012	2013
1 Output of cereals	1 535	1 491	1 707	1 434	1 507	1 949	3 180	2 312	2 267	3 230	3 201	3 391
of which: wheat	1 095	1 001	1 232	1 018	1 066	1 325	2 270	1 562	1 680	2 322	2 162	2 090
barley	392	446	433	380	384	555	817	675	521	809	920	1 135
oats	45	43	40	34	54	65	90	72	63	94	114	160
2 Output of industrial crops	612	719	683	679	597	702	1 010	913	1 051	1 524	1 356	1 183
of which: oilseed rape	220	314	266	278	318	431	641	502	697	1 137	1 002	768
protein crops	80	93	109	94	72	81	131	136	127	103	98	123
sugar beet	285	283	280	278	178	162	208	246	197	251	227	270
3 Output of forage plants	116	141	142	155	167	132	143	190	189	186	146	217
4 Output of vegetables and horticultural products	1 586	1 662	1 613	1 682	1 738	1 822	1 909	1 966	2 263	2 337	2 398	2 530
of which: fresh vegetables	837	898	834	912	1 001	1 054	1 090	1 088	1 266	1 224	1 255	1 340
plants and flowers	748	764	779	770	737	768	819	879	997	1 114	1 142	1 191
5 Output of potatoes (including seeds)	512	562	715	535	650	708	793	681	598	711	659	947
6 Output of fruit	251	310	318	390	377	459	535	570	585	604	573	602
7 Output of other crop products incl. seeds	340	203	238	271	252	189	335	383	439	475	644	581
Total crop output (sum 1-7)	**4 953**	**5 087**	**5 416**	**5 147**	**5 288**	**5 961**	**7 904**	**7 016**	**7 392**	**9 067**	**8 977**	**9 451**
8 Output of livestock	4 573	4 814	4 814	5 093	5 067	5 149	6 374	7 030	7 316	8 169	8 637	9 171
primarily for meat	3 866	4 084	4 157	4 299	4 364	4 432	5 504	5 846	6 108	6 904	7 242	7 765
of which: cattle	1 146	1 227	1 279	1 466	1 561	1 623	2 071	2 131	2 154	2 573	2 792	2 893
pigs	687	671	680	677	685	736	866	968	978	1 070	1 139	1 274
sheep	613	696	726	686	709	641	798	967	979	1 149	1 020	1 045
poultry	1 262	1 328	1 306	1 300	1 233	1 249	1 579	1 590	1 799	1 904	2 075	2 326
gross fixed capital formation	707	730	657	794	703	716	870	1 184	1 208	1 265	1 395	1 406
of which: cattle	392	448	337	545	419	410	577	750	714	631	868	870
pigs	7	7	8	6	8	5	6	8	8	8	8	6
sheep	178	146	176	112	146	153	125	238	295	413	316	334
poultry	129	129	136	131	131	149	162	188	191	213	203	195
9 Output of livestock products	2 834	3 031	3 038	3 009	2 918	3 286	4 019	3 711	3 973	4 387	4 485	5 072
of which: milk	2 466	2 628	2 610	2 592	2 497	2 823	3 447	3 123	3 329	3 738	3 767	4 271
eggs	315	336	378	349	362	410	520	531	561	559	662	718
Total livestock output (8+9)	**7 407**	**7 845**	**7 852**	**8 103**	**7 985**	**8 434**	**10 393**	**10 740**	**11 289**	**12 556**	**13 123**	**14 243**
10 Other agricultural activities	642	632	717	638	622	680	790	868	918	1 026	1 015	1 052
11 Inseparable non-agricultural activities	560	592	637	678	684	763	813	897	936	1 003	1 041	1 176
12 Output (at market prices) (sum 1 to 11) (a)	13 561	14 156	14 621	14 566	14 579	15 838	19 900	19 522	20 535	23 652	24 155	25 922
13 Total subsidies (less taxes) on product (b)	1 944	1 978	2 172	214	87	62	57	38	29	28	20	21
14 Gross output at basic prices (12+13)	**15 506**	**16 134**	**16 794**	**14 780**	**14 666**	**15 900**	**19 957**	**19 559**	**20 563**	**23 679**	**24 176**	**25 942**
Intermediate consumption												
15 Seeds	555	540	692	723	635	683	790	779	737	761	742	867
16 Energy	647	600	669	779	831	897	1 166	1 101	1 216	1 380	1 429	1 450
of which: electricity and fuels for heating	235	204	209	235	258	274	340	344	357	369	386	386
motor and machinery fuels	412	395	460	544	573	623	826	758	859	1 012	1 043	1 065
17 Fertilisers	808	746	734	785	791	792	1 455	1 176	1 339	1 589	1 523	1 511
18 Plant protection products	531	501	576	547	518	571	656	674	711	772	839	856
19 Veterinary expenses	250	253	279	280	284	302	338	364	405	401	420	447
20 Animal feed	2 396	2 547	2 716	2 490	2 595	2 983	3 863	3 694	4 087	4 508	4 891	5 567
of which: compounds	1 377	1 348	1 450	1 318	1 426	1 702	2 186	2 088	2 255	2 622	2 876	3 290
straights	729	849	883	807	785	879	1 197	1 156	1 387	1 374	1 448	1 574
feed produced & used on farm or purchased from other farms	290	350	384	365	384	401	480	450	444	512	566	703
21 Total maintenance	976	991	1 035	1 010	1 029	1 104	1 221	1 297	1 379	1 459	1 455	1 513
of which: materials	629	633	654	644	645	687	734	789	846	900	903	937
buildings	348	358	381	366	384	416	487	507	533	559	552	575
22 Agricultural services	599	592	635	629	621	679	789	868	918	1 025	1 015	1 052
23 FISIM	86	86	90	111	115	122	115	71	86	89	95	88
24 Other goods and services (c)	2 066	2 120	2 361	2 348	2 323	2 387	2 619	2 717	2 807	3 013	3 118	3 140
25 Total intermediate consumption (sum 15 to 24)	**8 914**	**8 976**	**9 787**	**9 703**	**9 741**	**10 521**	**13 013**	**12 741**	**13 684**	**14 999**	**15 528**	**16 491**
26 Gross value added at market prices (12-25)	**4 648**	**5 180**	**4 834**	**4 863**	**4 838**	**5 317**	**6 886**	**6 781**	**6 850**	**8 653**	**8 627**	**9 430**
27 Gross value added at basic prices (14-25)	**6 592**	**7 158**	**7 006**	**5 077**	**4 925**	**5 379**	**6 944**	**6 818**	**6 879**	**8 681**	**8 648**	**9 451**
28 Total consumption of Fixed Capital	2 730	2 813	2 712	2 914	2 962	3 024	3 428	3 522	3 480	3 822	3 956	3 939
of which: equipment	1 318	1 256	1 194	1 207	1 208	1 222	1 280	1 363	1 440	1 535	1 610	1 675
buildings	779	806	852	928	956	993	1 056	983	886	925	949	926
livestock	633	750	667	779	798	809	1 091	1 176	1 154	1 362	1 398	1 338
cattle	353	441	364	490	499	503	743	731	679	791	870	857
pigs	8	8	9	7	7	6	7	8	8	8	8	7
sheep	141	173	167	151	162	157	188	269	291	358	301	268
poultry	130	128	127	132	129	142	153	167	176	205	220	206

24.1 Production and income account at current prices; United Kingdom

Enquiries: Helen Mason on +44 (0)1904 455096
Email: helen.mason@defra.gsi.gov.uk

£ million   Calendar years

	2002	2003	2004	2005	2006	2007	2008	2009	2010	2011	2012	2013
29 Net value added at market prices (26-28)	**1 917**	**2 368**	**2 122**	**1 949**	**1 877**	**2 294**	**3 459**	**3 258**	**3 370**	**4 831**	**4 671**	**5 491**
30 Net value added at basic prices (27-28)	**3 862**	**4 345**	**4 294**	**2 163**	**1 964**	**2 356**	**3 516**	**3 296**	**3 399**	**4 859**	**4 691**	**5 512**
31 Other taxes on production	- 80	- 83	- 95	- 101	- 99	- 101	- 102	- 106	- 112	- 121	- 121	- 118
32 Other subsidies on production (b)	712	781	781	2 852	3 042	2 932	3 237	3 616	3 472	3 482	3 262	3 334
33 Net value added at factor cost (30+31+32)	**4 493**	**5 044**	**4 980**	**4 914**	**4 907**	**5 187**	**6 651**	**6 806**	**6 759**	**8 219**	**7 832**	**8 728**
34 Compensation of employees	1 836	1 827	1 894	1 944	1 973	2 004	2 065	2 165	2 226	2 341	2 353	2 402
35 Rent	378	373	385	366	372	356	383	397	415	453	467	493
36 Interest (d)	367	340	391	403	372	417	349	220	230	253	289	302
37 Total Income from Farming (33-34-35-36)	**1 912**	**2 504**	**2 310**	**2 201**	**2 191**	**2 410**	**3 853**	**4 024**	**3 888**	**5 172**	**4 723**	**5 530**
GDP deflator (a) 2011 = 100	79	81	83	86	88	90	93	95	98	100	102	104
Total Income from Farming in real terms	2 542	3 259	2 921	2 707	2 624	2 808	4 358	4 466	4 182	5 446	4 890	5 626

Source: Defra

- means 'nil' or 'negligible' (less than half the last digit shown).

.. means 'not available' or 'not applicable'.

(a) Output is net of VAT collected on the sale of non-edible products. Figures for output at market prices exclude subsidies on products.

(b) "Subsidies (less taxes) on product": payments linked to the production of agricultural products. "Other subsidies on production": payments not linked to production from which agricultural producers can benefit as a consequence of engaging in agricultural activities e.g. Single Payment Scheme, agri-environment schemes.

(c) Includes livestock and crop costs, water costs, insurance premiums, bank charges, professional fees, rates, and other farming costs.

(d) Interest charges on loans for current farming purposes and buildings and works less interest on money held on short term deposit.

24.2 Total factor productivity volume indices (2010=100)

Enquiries: Nick Olney on +44 (0) 1904 455355
email: nick.olney@defra.gsi.gov.uk

	2002	2003	2004	2005	2006	2007	2008	2009	2010	2011	2012	2013
1 Output of cereals	109.0	100.2	101.8	96.6	96.3	89.2	116.7	102.4	100.0	105.0	92.6	92.9
wheat	109.0	95.1	100.6	96.7	96.4	86.8	113.7	93.6	100.0	104.2	88.2	76.4
rye	90.9	86.4	86.4	86.4	86.4	86.4	86.4	86.4	100.0	100.0	68.2	90.9
barley	113.4	125.2	113.6	103.6	97.9	100.4	132.4	141.2	100.0	110.7	111.3	154.2
oats and summer cereal mixtures	114.6	110.0	84.9	71.1	106.6	103.0	119.5	109.7	100.0	92.1	93.2	150.4
other cereals	84.5	83.0	79.9	80.8	80.8	67.9	77.5	120.2	100.0	99.5	93.3	106.0
2 Output of industrial crops	100.1	107.7	102.8	109.5	99.5	97.7	93.9	99.5	100.0	118.3	104.4	97.3
oil seeds	70.5	87.2	79.6	95.5	92.9	101.7	86.8	87.0	100.0	122.9	112.9	95.2
oilseed rape	72.4	87.5	79.9	94.2	93.8	104.5	88.5	87.5	100.0	123.7	114.6	95.4
other oil seeds	22.6	81.4	73.5	124.3	70.1	27.3	41.2	75.4	100.0	98.9	58.0	86.4
protein crops	114.7	121.6	119.2	125.9	102.5	71.1	93.0	117.2	100.0	76.0	55.5	68.9
sugar beet	146.4	140.5	138.5	133.1	113.4	103.2	117.1	129.6	100.0	130.3	111.7	129.2
other industrial crops	113.2	109.1	107.0	105.1	105.3	101.8	99.7	98.1	100.0	101.1	57.1	57.1
3 Output of forage plants	114.8	112.2	115.2	114.3	112.2	117.8	104.1	105.3	100.0	107.1	109.0	121.3
4 Output of vegetables and horticultural products	108.1	105.2	103.4	103.4	97.7	96.6	98.5	96.4	100.0	97.7	95.0	97.8
fresh vegetables	98.4	98.0	91.9	95.9	94.3	89.9	92.2	96.4	100.0	98.1	93.4	97.9
plants and flowers	121.1	115.0	119.1	113.6	101.9	106.1	107.2	96.4	100.0	97.2	96.7	97.7
5 Output of potatoes	142.1	131.4	137.8	125.6	118.3	114.9	124.1	125.8	100.0	116.4	90.3	111.1
6 Output of fruit	53.9	59.3	70.0	80.0	78.2	92.5	94.8	99.7	100.0	101.3	93.0	100.1
7 Output of other crop products	59.5	58.5	62.8	97.8	97.7	78.8	98.8	103.5	100.0	114.4	126.9	119.1
Total crop output (sum 1 - 7)	**103.6**	**100.8**	**101.8**	**101.5**	**97.0**	**95.1**	**105.8**	**101.7**	**100.0**	**105.5**	**95.4**	**97.7**
8 Output of livestock (meat)	99.2	98.0	98.5	102.5	99.9	100.6	99.6	96.7	100.0	102.8	102.6	103.0
cattle	87.8	90.6	89.4	101.7	97.5	99.8	98.1	95.4	100.0	102.8	101.7	98.0
pigs	107.0	94.7	95.6	95.0	94.8	99.8	98.7	95.3	100.0	106.4	107.8	111.1
sheep	105.5	107.5	114.2	115.9	115.4	114.8	111.7	108.1	100.0	105.9	101.1	104.2
poultry	104.4	103.2	102.3	101.2	98.0	100.1	94.7	95.7	100.0	99.5	102.2	105.2
other animals	100.7	100.1	100.0	100.4	99.9	100.1	99.9	100.0	100.0	100.0	100.0	100.0
9 Output of livestock products	103.0	104.2	101.7	101.9	100.6	98.3	97.0	96.2	100.0	101.3	98.9	100.2
milk	106.6	107.8	104.5	103.8	102.8	100.9	98.6	97.5	100.0	101.5	99.9	100.5
eggs	81.9	80.2	86.7	88.1	85.0	83.0	88.3	89.2	100.0	99.6	96.5	99.5
raw wool	132.2	129.2	131.2	134.7	121.8	112.2	108.2	99.0	100.0	105.2	110.7	97.5
other animal products	108.6	135.3	81.9	135.1	135.2	107.2	87.8	92.9	100.0	98.7	57.5	84.2
Total livestock output (8 + 9)	**100.8**	**100.6**	**99.9**	**102.3**	**100.3**	**99.7**	**98.6**	**96.5**	**100.0**	**102.2**	**101.2**	**101.9**
10 Inseparable non-agricultural activities	82.8	84.6	87.0	88.8	85.5	90.4	91.0	100.5	100.0	101.5	103.1	115.4
11 All outputs	**100.6**	**99.5**	**99.6**	**101.0**	**98.0**	**97.2**	**100.8**	**98.6**	**100.0**	**103.4**	**99.0**	**100.9**
12 Seeds	74.6	73.5	65.7	78.1	84.9	98.4	94.2	92.6	100.0	97.6	101.3	106.4
13 Energy	117.4	99.7	102.0	95.0	90.0	94.0	89.9	102.5	100.0	96.3	96.3	97.0
electricity and fuels for heating	143.7	116.1	109.5	104.2	94.9	94.0	94.0	100.5	100.0	94.5	93.8	87.4
motor and machinery fuels	106.4	92.8	98.8	91.1	87.8	94.0	88.2	103.4	100.0	96.9	97.2	100.9
14 Fertilisers	128.3	126.8	123.2	115.1	108.4	109.7	97.6	88.4	100.0	103.2	97.9	99.2
15 Plant protection products	83.7	79.0	88.3	81.2	74.9	81.3	91.5	92.3	100.0	108.1	117.9	124.9
16 Veterinary expenses	78.2	76.3	81.6	82.5	78.3	81.9	95.5	102.4	100.0	97.2	100.3	104.1
17 Animal feed	88.8	91.5	93.3	91.6	90.9	88.3	92.5	92.6	100.0	93.0	94.7	99.1
compounds	90.8	90.7	91.7	88.4	92.7	95.5	95.5	93.7	100.0	97.7	103.0	109.3
straights	85.5	93.0	96.2	97.3	87.9	76.3	88.2	90.9	100.0	85.3	81.3	82.5
18 Total maintenance	101.5	97.7	97.8	90.7	87.5	90.0	95.0	98.7	100.0	99.8	99.3	100.4
materials	111.9	106.3	104.2	96.3	91.3	93.7	94.7	97.4	100.0	101.4	100.2	102.2
buildings	86.2	85.0	88.3	82.3	81.9	84.4	95.6	100.8	100.0	97.2	97.8	97.6
19 FISIM	100.0	100.0	100.0	100.0	100.0	100.0	100.0	100.0	100.0	100.0	100.0	100.0
20 Other goods and services	96.0	102.9	109.9	105.1	100.7	102.0	100.4	103.7	100.0	103.4	96.0	99.6
21 Intermediate consumption (excl Agricultural services)	**95.4**	**95.4**	**97.5**	**94.8**	**92.3**	**94.2**	**95.0**	**96.4**	**100.0**	**98.6**	**98.0**	**101.3**
22 Consumption fixed capital (excluding livestock)	**101.9**	**100.3**	**99.4**	**98.4**	**97.4**	**97.1**	**97.8**	**98.8**	**100.0**	**102.3**	**104.0**	**106.0**
equipment	99.0	96.9	95.8	94.8	93.5	93.6	95.5	97.7	100.0	104.0	107.2	110.9
buildings	105.6	104.9	104.2	103.5	102.8	102.0	101.1	100.4	100.0	99.6	99.0	98.3
23 All Labour	**110.7**	**107.5**	**105.8**	**104.6**	**103.1**	**102.4**	**101.9**	**100.4**	**100.0**	**101.6**	**101.7**	**100.9**
Compensation of employees	113.9	108.4	106.9	105.3	102.0	101.2	102.0	100.7	100.0	102.3	102.4	101.7
Entrepreneurial workers (farm and specialist contractor)	109.0	107.0	105.2	104.2	103.7	103.0	101.9	100.3	100.0	101.3	101.3	100.5
24 Land	**100.5**	**100.2**	**99.9**	**100.0**	**101.6**	**100.7**	**100.5**	**100.5**	**100.0**	**99.6**	**99.7**	**100.1**
25 All Inputs and Entrepreneurial Labour	**101.0**	**99.8**	**100.3**	**98.4**	**96.7**	**97.3**	**97.7**	**98.1**	**100.0**	**99.9**	**99.8**	**101.6**
Total factor productivity (11 divided by26)	**99.6**	**99.7**	**99.3**	**102.6**	**101.4**	**99.9**	**103.3**	**100.5**	**100.0**	**103.5**	**99.2**	**99.3**
Partial factor productivity indicators												
Productivity by intermediate consumption (11 divided by 21)	105.4	104.3	102.1	106.5	106.2	103.1	106.2	102.4	100.0	104.9	101.1	99.6
Productivity by capital consumption (11 divided by 22)	98.8	99.2	100.3	102.6	100.6	100.1	103.1	99.8	100.0	101.1	95.1	95.1
Productivity by labour (11 divided by 23)	90.9	92.6	94.2	96.5	95.0	94.9	98.9	98.2	100.0	101.8	97.3	100.0
Productivity by land (11 divided by 24)	100.1	99.4	99.7	101.0	96.4	96.5	100.3	98.1	100.0	103.8	99.2	100.7

Source: Department for Environment, Food and Rural Affairs

24.3 Agricultural land use (a)

Enquiries: Joanne Gardiner on +44 (0)1904 455681
email: farming-statistics@defra.gsi.gov.uk

Thousand hectares

At June of each year

	2002	2003	2004	2005	2006	2007	2008	2009	2010	2011	2012	2013
Utilised agricultural area (UAA) (b)	**17 701**	**17 644**	**17 606**	**17 614**	**17 897**	**17 737**	**17 703**	**17 325**	**17 234**	**17 172**	**17 190**	**17 259**
UAA as a proportion of total UK area	72%	72%	72%	72%	73%	73%	73%	71%	71%	70%	70%	71%
Total agricultural area	**18 507**	**18 465**	**18 431**	**18 486**	**18 770**	**18 692**	**18 697**	**18 296**	**18 282**	**18 263**	**18 349**	**18 449**
Common rough grazing	**1 234**	**1 236**	**1 237**	**1 236**	**1 241**	**1 238**	**1 238**	**1 237**	**1 228**	**1 199**	**1 200**	**1 198**
Total area on agricultural holdings	**17 272**	**17 228**	**17 194**	**17 250**	**17 529**	**17 453**	**17 459**	**17 060**	**17 054**	**17 064**	**17 149**	**17 250**
Total croppable area	**6 460**	**6 395**	**6 423**	**6 313**	**6 197**	**6 215**	**6 070**	**6 092**	**6 015**	**6 106**	**6 258**	**6 310**
Total crops	**4 574**	**4 476**	**4 589**	**4 421**	**4 397**	**4 440**	**4 735**	**4 607**	**4 610**	**4 673**	**4 748**	**4 665**
Arable crops (c)	4 398	4 301	4 413	4 251	4 231	4 271	4 565	4 437	4 441	4 497	4 576	4 502
Cereals	3 245	3 057	3 130	2 919	2 864	2 885	3 274	3 076	3 013	3 075	3 142	3 028
Oilseeds (includes linseed and borage)	369	492	528	564	605	687	621	600	686	742	785	752
Potatoes	158	145	148	137	140	140	144	144	138	146	149	139
Other crops	625	607	607	631	623	559	527	616	604	534	500	582
Horticultural crops	176	176	175	170	166	169	170	170	169	175	172	163
Uncropped arable land (d)(e)	**644**	**718**	**589**	**699**	**663**	**599**	**194**	**244**	**174**	**156**	**153**	**255**
Temporary grass under 5 years old	**1 243**	**1 200**	**1 246**	**1 193**	**1 137**	**1 176**	**1 141**	**1 241**	**1 232**	**1 278**	**1 357**	**1 390**
Total permanent grassland	**10 006**	**10 013**	**9 946**	**10 065**	**10 458**	**10 284**	**10 395**	**9 996**	**9 980**	**9 858**	**9 725**	**9 742**
Grass over 5 years old	5 519	5 683	5 620	5 711	5 967	5 965	6 036	5 865	5 925	5 877	5 799	5 802
Sole right rough grazing (f)	4 488	4 329	4 326	4 354	4 491	4 319	4 359	4 131	4 055	3 981	3 926	3 940
Other land on agricultural holdings	**806**	**821**	**825**	**872**	**874**	**954**	**994**	**972**	**1 059**	**1 100**	**1 166**	**1 198**
Woodland	524	544	563	583	606	663	705	726	774	786	827	865
Land used for outdoor pigs	. .	. .	. .	. .	. .	. .	. .	. .	10	9	7	9
All other non-agricultural land	282	276	262	289	268	291	289	246	274	305	332	324

Source: June Surveys/Census of Agriculture/SAF land data Scotland

Please note that totals may not add up to the sum of components due to rounding. Totals may not agree across tables for the same reason.

\#: The 2011 UK totals for other arable crops and glasshouse crops were revised in May 2012 to account for calculation changes in the Scotland and Northern Ireland figures. As a result some subtotals have also been revised.

(a) Figures for England from 2009 onwards relate to commercial holdings only.

(b) UAA includes all arable and horticultural crops, uncropped arable land, common rough grazing, temporary and permanent grassland and land used for outdoor pigs (it excludes woodland and other non-agricultural land).

(c) Includes crops grown on previous set-aside land for England for 2007.

(d) Includes uncropped set-aside land for 2007.

(e) Includes all arable land not in production, including land managed in Good Agricultural and Environmental Condition (GAEC12), wild bird cover and game cover. In the 2009 form guidance notes for England, bird cover and game strips were for the first time explicitly stated as belonging in this category, so the 2009 figure may have captured more of this land than in previous years.

(f) Also includes mountains, hills, heathland or moorland.

- means 'nil' or 'negligible' (less than half the last digit shown).

. . means 'not available' or 'not applicable'.

24.4a Estimated quantity of crops and grass harvested

United Kingdom — Thousand tonnes

		2001	2002	2003	2004	2005	2006	2007	2008	2009	2010	2011	2012	2013
Agricultural crops														
Wheat	BADO	11 580	15 973	14 288	15 473	14 863	14 755	13 221	17 227	14 076	14 878	15 257	13 261	11 921
Barley (Winter and Spring)	BADP	6 660	6 128	6 370	5 816	5 495	5 239	5 079	6 144	6 668	5 252	5 494	5 522	7 092
Oats	BADQ	621	753	749	627	528	728	712	784	744	685	613	627	964
Sugar beet	BADR	8 335	9 557	9 168	9 042	8 687	7 400	6 733	7 641	8 457	6 527	8 504	7 291	8 432
Potatoes	BADS	6 674	6 921	6 058	6 246	5 979	5 727	5 564	6 132	6 396	6 056	6 310	4 658	5 902

Source: Department for Environment, Food and Rural Affairs

24.4b Fruit: Home Production marketed for the calendar year in the UK

(Thousand tonnes)

CALENDAR YEAR	2002	2003	2004	2005	2006	2007	2008	2009	2010	2011	2012	2013 Provisional
ORCHARD FRUIT												
Dessert Apples -												
Cox's Orange Pippin	41.4	34.5	46.6	60.1	64.0	39.2	50.8	46.5	46.4	45.9	32.0	35.1
Worcester Pearmain	2.5	2.0	2.6	2.6	2.3	1.8	1.9	2.3	2.1	1.9	1.6	1.9
Discovery	2.9	2.4	2.2	2.9	3.0	2.9	2.8	2.8	3.0	2.7	2.2	2.7
Early Season	1.0	0.9	1.7	1.9	2.3	2.2	2.0	2.0	2.2	2.0	1.7	2.1
Mid Season Desserts	7.1	6.8	7.3	7.8	7.7	7.4	6.7	7.5	7.2	6.8	5.7	6.8
Late Season Desserts	29.1	22.4	31.7	42.8	50.0	52.7	54.3	60.7	63.9	68.6	73.0	82.3
Total Dessert Apples :	**84.0**	**69.0**	**92.2**	**118.0**	**129.3**	**106.2**	**118.4**	**121.7**	**124.9**	**127.9**	**116.2**	**130.8**
Culinary Apples -												
Bramley's Seedling	94.0	73.3	76.6	98.5	109.9	135.3	123.0	105.9	109.0	110.8	86.4	83.0
Other Culinary (a)	1.3	1.6	1.2	1.2	1.1	1.0	1.1	1.2	1.1	1.0	0.9	1.1
Total Culinary Apples :	**95.3**	**74.9**	**77.8**	**99.7**	**111.0**	**136.3**	**124.1**	**107.1**	**110.1**	**111.8**	**87.2**	**84.0**
Pears -												
Conference	29.6	26.6	20.8	19.6	24.6	17.7	17.2	16.6	27.1	26.9	21.1	18.2
Williams Bon Chretien	0.1	0.1	n/a	n/a	n/a	n/a	n/a	n/a	n/a	n/a	n/a	n/a
Comice	3.8	1.6	n/a	n/a	n/a	n/a	n/a	n/a	n/a	n/a	n/a	n/a
Others (b)	0.7	1.3	1.9	3.8	3.9	2.9	2.5	3.9	4.3	5.3	4.5	3.5
Total Pears :	**34.2**	**29.6**	**22.7**	**23.4**	**28.4**	**20.6**	**19.8**	**20.5**	**31.4**	**32.2**	**25.6**	**21.7**
Plums -												
Victoria	6.0	7.1	8.1	7.3	6.9	6.8	1.1	6.2	6.1	6.0	2.5	5.5
Marjorie's Seedling	1.8	2.2	n/a	n/a	n/a	n/a	n/a	n/a	n/a	n/a	n/a	n/a
Pershore Yellow Egg (c)	n/a	n/a	n/a	n/a	n/a	n/a	n/a	n/a	n/a	n/a	n/a	n/a
Damsons (d)	0.5	0.7	n/a	n/a	n/a	n/a	n/a	n/a	n/a	n/a	n/a	n/a
Other Plums (e)	4.2	5.1	5.5	6.2	6.3	6.2	1.4	6.7	7.1	7.0	3.1	6.9
Total Plums :	**12.6**	**15.1**	**13.6**	**13.5**	**13.2**	**13.0**	**2.5**	**13.0**	**13.2**	**12.9**	**5.6**	**12.4**
Cherries (f):	**1.3**	**1.0**	**1.1**	**1.1**	**1.1**	**1.2**	**n/a**	**n/a**	**n/a**	**n/a**	**n/a**	**n/a**
Others & Mixed :	**2.3**	**1.9**	**2.9**	**3.3**	**3.8**	**4.8**	**6.1**	**6.7**	**6.4**	**6.9**	**5.9**	**7.2**
TOTAL ORCHARD FRUIT :	**229.7**	**191.5**	**210.2**	**259.0**	**286.9**	**282.2**	**270.9**	**268.9**	**286.0**	**291.8**	**240.6**	**256.1**
Soft Fruit												
Strawberries	41.4	47.1	52.5	68.6	67.5	83.1	94.0	98.5	95.7	101.9	94.8	94.4
Raspberries	7.3	8.5	10.0	12.2	12.2	14.8	15.5	15.6	15.9	15.5	15.6	13.8
Blackcurrants	13.0	19.1	18.2	19.7	15.6	12.3	13.7	15.8	17.7	11.7	11.9	16.3
Other Soft Fruit:	5.3	5.2	5.4	5.1	6.0	7.8	7.8	8.9	8.9	7.7	7.5	8.0
TOTAL SOFT FRUIT (g):	**67.1**	**79.9**	**86.0**	**105.5**	**101.3**	**118.1**	**130.9**	**138.9**	**138.3**	**136.8**	**129.9**	**132.5**
TOTAL FRUIT :	**296.7**	**271.3**	**296.2**	**364.4**	**388.2**	**400.3**	**401.9**	**407.8**	**424.3**	**428.6**	**370.4**	**388.6**

Source: Basic Horticultural Statistics, Department for Environment, Food and Rural Affairs

(a) Data for both 'Early' and 'Mid/Late Season Culinary' apples has been combined under 'Total Other Culinary'.
(b) Data for 'other' includes Williams & Comice
(c) Data for 'Pershore Yellow Egg' included in 'Other Plums' from 2000.
(d) Data for 'Damsons' included in Other plums from 2004.
(e) Other plums - Includes other varieties from 2004.
(f) Data for 'Cherries' included in 'Others & Mixed' from 2008
(g) Excludes Glasshouse Fruit.
(h) All Import data for strawberries relates to fresh produce only.
(i) Trade figures, where distinguishable, relate to fresh produce.
(j) Value for 'Cider Apples and Perry Pears' only included in 'total orchard fruit' from 2008.
n/a This crop data is no longer available for the individual category and is now combined with other data.
... Blanks in data indicate that the information is not available.

24.4c Field Vegetables: Home production marketed for the calendar year in the UK

(Thousand Tonnes)

CALENDAR YEAR	2002	2003	2004	2005	2006	2007	2008	2009	2010	2011	2012	2013 Provisional
Roots and Onions												
Beetroot	56	59	53	51	57	57	55	55	57	59	62	69
Carrots	718	602	676	710	712	727	711	695	768	688	664	696
Parsnips	102	92	77	72	84	86	90	86	90	87	83	82
Turnips and Swedes	104	97	97	103	115	101	106	109	113	102	87	101
Onions, Dry Bulb	283	374	341	414	359	304	349	355	364	313	374	354
Onions, Spring	11	16	14	24	24	20	15	14	14	15	14	14
Total :	1,275	1,239	1,259	1,374	1,351	1,294	1,327	1,314	1,408	1,263	1,284	1,316
Brassicas												
Brussels Sprouts	43	56	44	46	50	41	43	44	43	47	44	51
Cabbage, Spring	22	29	34	32	36	35	30	28	24	24	23	24
Cabbage, Summer and Autumn	44	41	44	77	61	56	56	62	61	60	49	57
Cabbage, Winter	178	159	143	157	158	126	149	146	162	151	151	140
Cauliflower	117	126	168	133	124	122	116	108	109	102	90	88
Broccoli	53	62	66	87	72	68	73	78	79	78	67	68
Total :	456	473	500	532	500	448	468	465	479	463	424	428
Legumes												
Beans, Broad (d)	10	12	10	10	10	10	9	12	12	11	11	12
Beans, Runner and Dwarf (a)	19	20	23	21	18	17	16	15	16	15	14	15
Peas, Green for Market	7	6	6	6	6	6	6	6	6	6	6	6
Peas, Green for Processing (b,d)	169	168	131	130	124	98	153	168	156	178	127	153
Peas, Harvested Dry (e)	24	16	30	37	24	33	25	40	49	57	22	44
Total :	230	222	199	204	182	163	209	241	239	268	180	228
Others												
Asparagus	2	2	2	2	3	3	3	4	4	5	5	5
Celery	32	37	41	47	36	47	50	49	51	51	51	51
Leeks	38	36	41	51	47	50	42	37	42	41	37	35
Lettuce	110	126	143	133	126	108	117	128	127	126	116	117
Rhubarb (c)	19	18	21	19	17	16	16	20	21	20	22	24
Watercress	2	2	2	2	2	2	2	2	2	2	2	2
Others (f)	104	104	110	124	116	113	116	144	141	128	118	123
Total :	307	325	360	378	348	339	346	384	388	373	352	358
TOTAL FIELD VEGETABLES :	2,268	2,260	2,318	2,488	2,382	2,244	2,349	2,405	2,513	2,366	2,240	2,330

Source: Basic Horticultural Statistics, Department for Environment, Food and Rural Affairs

(a) Dwarf beans are sometimes called French beans.
(b) Vining peas.
(c) Including forced rhubarb grown in sheds.
(d) Shelled weight.
(e) Dried shelled weight, excluding factory waste; for human consumption only.
(f) Includes all smaller field grown crops.

24.5 Crop areas and livestock numbers (a)

Enquiries: Joanne Gardiner on +44 (0)1904 455681

email: farming-statistics@defra.gsi.gov.uk

At June of each year

	2002	2003	2004	2005	2006	2007	2008	2009	2010	2011	2012	2013
Crop areas (thousand hectares)												
Total area of arable crops (b)	4 398	4 301	4 413	4 251	4 231	4 271	4 565	4 437	4 441	4 497	4 576	4 502
of which: wheat	1 996	1 836	1 990	1 867	1 836	1 830	2 080	1 775	1 939	1 969	1 992	1 615
barley	1 101	1 076	1 007	938	881	898	1 032	1 143	921	970	1 002	1 213
oats	126	121	108	90	121	129	135	129	124	109	122	177
rye, mixed corn and triticale	..	..	..	..	25	27	27	28	29	27	26	24
oilseed rape	357	460	498	519	568	674	598	570	642	705	756	715
linseed	12	32	29	45	36	13	16	28	44	36	29	34
potatoes	158	145	148	137	140	140	144	144	138	146	149	139
sugar beet (not for stockfeeding)	169	162	154	148	130	125	120	114	118	113	120	117
peas for harvesting dry and field beans	249	235	242	239	231	161	148	228	210	155	120	147
maize	121	119	118	131	137	146	153	163	164	164	158	194
Total area of horticultural crops	176	176	175	170	166	169	170	170	169	175	172	163
of which: vegetables grown outdoors	124	125	125	121	119	121	122	125	121	129	123	116
orchard fruit (c)	26	25	24	23	23	23	24	22	24	24	24	23
soft fruit & wine grapes	9	9	9	9	10	10	10	10	10	10	9	10
outdoor plants and flowers	15	14	15	14	12	13	13	11	12	11	12	12
glasshouse crops	2	2	2	2	2	2	2	2	2	2	3	3
Livestock numbers (thousand head)												
Total cattle and calves (d)	10 345	10 508	10 588	10 770	10 644	10 370	10 163	10 082	10 170	9 988	9 952	9 844
of which: cows in the dairy herd (e)	2 227	2 191	2 129	1 998	1 963	1 937	1 892	1 838	1 830	1 796	1 796	1 782
cows in the beef herd (f)	1 657	1 698	1 736	1 751	1 745	1 709	1 678	1 633	1 668	1 687	1 666	1 611
Total sheep and lambs	35 834	35 812	35 817	35 416	34 722	33 946	33 131	31 445	31 084	31 634	32 215	32 856
of which: ewes and shearlings	17 630	17 580	17 630	16 935	16 637	16 064	15 616	14 636	14 740	14 868	15 229	15 561
lambs under one year old	17 310	17 322	17 238	17 488	17 058	16 855	16 574	15 892	15 431	15 990	16 229	16 381
Total pigs	5 588	5 046	5 159	4 862	4 933	4 834	4 714	4 540	4 460	4 441	4 481	4 885
of which: sows in pig and other sows for breeding	483	442	449	403	401	398	365	379	360	362	357	355
gilts in pig	74	73	66	67	67	57	55	48	67	70	66	66
Total poultry	168 996	178 800	181 759	173 909	173 081	167 667	166 200	152 753	163 867	162 551	160 061	162 609
of which: table fowl	105 137	116 738	119 888	111 475	110 672	109 794	109 859	98 754	105 309	102 461	102 558	104 576
laying flock (including pullets)	38 562	37 560	37 811	40 472	38 257	36 257	35 253	33 266	37 497	38 357	36 646	35 841
breeding flock	11 307	10 988	10 125	8 561	9 273	11 461	9 068	9 397	9 610	10 253	9 987	11 184
turkeys, ducks, geese and all other poultry	13 991	13 514	13 935	13 400	14 879	10 154	12 019	11 335	11 451	11 481	10 870	11 008

Source: June Surveys/Census of Agriculture/SAF land data Scotland. Also Cattle Tracing System/APHIS (for cattle data).
Department for Environment, Food and Rural Afairs

Please note that totals may not add up to the sum of components due to rounding. Totals may not agree across tables for the same reason.

#: The 2011 UK totals for other arable crops and glasshouse crops were revised in May 2012 to account for calculation changes in the Scotland and Northern Ireland figures. As a result some subtotals have also been revised.
(a) Figures for England from 2009 onwards relate to commercial holdings only.
(b) Includes arable crops grown on set-aside land in 2007 for England only.
(c) Includes non-commercial orchards.
(d) Cattle figures in this table are based on all agricultural holdings.
(e) Dairy cows are defined as female dairy cows over 2 years old with offspring.
(f) Beef cows are defined as female beef cows over 2 years old with offspring.

- means 'nil' or 'negligible' (less than half the last digit shown).
.. means 'not available' or 'not applicable'.

24.6 Forestry

United Kingdom

Woodland area[1] - (Thousand hectares)

		2000	2004	2005	2006	2007	2008	2009	2010	2011	2012	2013	2014
United Kingdom	C5OF	2793	2816	2825	2829	2837	2841	2841	3059	3067	3110	3125	3138
England	C5OG	1103	1114	1119	1121	1124	1127	1128	1290	1292	1298	1298	1302
Wales	C5OI	289	286	286	285	285	285	284	303	304	305	305	306
Scotland	C5OH	1318	1330	1334	1337	1341	1342	1341	1378	1383	1403	1411	1419
Northern Ireland[2]	C5OJ	83	86	85	86	87	87	88	88	88	105	111	111
Forestry Commission/Forest Service	C5OK	886	842	838	832	827	821	814	868	869	874	874	870
Private Sector Woodland [3]	C5OL	1907	1974	1987	1997	2010	2020	2027	2191	2199	2236	2252	2268
Conifer	C5OM	1663	1651	1647	1642	1640	1635	1628	1603	1604	1617	1619	1608
Broadleaved[4]	C5ON	1131	1165	1178	1187	1197	1207	1213	1457	1463	1493	1508	1531

		2000 /01	2001 /02	2002 /03	2003 /04	2004 /05	2005 /06	2006 /07	2007 /08	2008 /09	2009 /10	2010 /11	2011 /12	2012 /13	2013 /14
New Planting[5,6] - (Thousand hectares)															
United Kingdom	C5OO	18.7	14.4	13.7	12.4	12.0	8.8	10.8	7.5	6.4	5.4	8.2	12.7	10.8	12.9
England	C5OP	5.9	5.4	5.9	4.6	5.3	3.7	3.2	2.6	2.5	2.3	2.5	2.6	2.6	3.3
Wales	C5OR	0.5	0.3	0.5	0.4	0.6	0.5	0.6	0.2	0.2	0.2	0.3	0.8	0.9	0.9
Scotland	C5OQ	11.7	8.0	6.7	6.8	5.7	4.0	6.6	4.2	3.4	2.7	5.1	9.0	7.0	8.3
Northern Ireland	C5OS	0.7	0.7	0.6	0.5	0.4	0.6	0.5	0.6	0.3	0.2	0.3	0.3	0.3	0.3
Forestry Commission/Forest Service/Natural Resources Wales[8]	C5OT	0.3	0.8	0.9	0.2	0.1	0.3	0.2	0.2	0.9	0.7	0.8	1.3	0.9	0.6
Private Sector Woodland [3]	C5OU	18.4	13.6	12.8	12.1	11.9	8.5	10.6	7.4	5.5	4.7	7.3	11.4	9.9	12.3
Conifer	C5OV	4.9	3.9	3.8	2.9	2.1	1.1	2.1	0.9	1.2	0.5	1.5	3.5	1.9	2.2
Broadleaved[4]	C5OW	13.8	10.5	9.9	9.4	9.9	7.7	8.7	6.7	5.2	4.9	6.6	9.2	8.9	10.7
Restocking[5,7] - (Thousand hectares)															
United Kingdom	C5OX	15.3	13.9	14.5	14.9	16.1	15.9	19.0	18.9	16.1	15.1	14.0	12.3	13.1	15.8
England	C5OY	4.0	3.4	3.4	3.2	2.8	3.2	2.8	3.5	3.5	2.8	4.0	3.6	4.0	4.5
Wales	C5P2	2.2	1.9	1.9	1.8	1.8	2.8	3.0	2.3	2.2	2.1	2.1	2.0	2.0	2.3
Scotland	C5OZ	8.0	7.8	8.5	8.9	10.4	9.0	12.4	12.6	9.6	9.5	6.9	5.7	6.0	7.9
Northern Ireland	C5P3	1.1	0.9	0.7	1.1	1.0	0.9	0.8	0.5	0.8	0.7	1.0	1.0	1.2	1.2
Forestry Commission/Forest Service/Natural Resources Wales[8]	C5P4	8.9	9.2	9.1	9.9	10.6	10.4	11.0	10.4	9.2	7.1	10.0	8.9	9.3	10.9
Private Sector Woodland [3]	C5P5	6.4	4.7	5.3	5.0	5.5	5.5	8.0	8.5	6.9	8.0	4.1	3.3	3.8	4.9
Conifer	C5P6	12.3	11.5	12.0	12.1	13.0	12.5	15.3	14.8	12.1	11.5	10.3	9.0	9.7	11.6
Broadleaved [4]	C5P7	3.0	2.4	2.4	2.8	3.0	3.4	3.6	4.1	4.0	3.6	3.8	3.3	3.4	4.2

		2002	2003	2004	2005	2006	2007	2008	2009	2010	2011	2012	2013
Wood Production (volume - Thousand green tonnes)													
United Kingdom	C5P8	8060	8470	8650	8670	8680	9180	8670	8930	9760	10540	10627	11469
Softwood total	C5PA	7440	7910	8140	8080	8240	8740	8240	8390	9220	10000	10095	10940
Forestry Commission/Forest Service/Natural Resources Wales[8]	C5PB	4770	4940	5000	4680	4630	4690	4460	5220	4700	4950	4891	5163
Private Sector[9]	C5PC	3290	3540	3650	3990	4050	4480	4210	3720	5070	5600	5737	6307
Hardwood[10]	C5PD	620	560	510	590	440	440	430	540	540	540	532	529

Source: Forestry Commission, Natural Resources Wales, Forest Service, National Forest Inventory.

1. Figures for England, Wales and Scotland are based on data obtained from the National Forest Inventory (NFI) and adjusted
   for new planting, but at present no adjustment is made for woodland recently converted to another land use.
2. Figures for Northern Ireland are obtained from the Northern Ireland Woodland Register.
3. Used to be called "other"
4. Broadleaves include coppice and coppice with standards.
5. Private sector figures are based on areas for which grants were paid during the year. Estimate of areas planted without grant aid are also
   included (where possible), although private sector non grant-aided planting may be under-represented in the figures. Figures for grant-aided
   planting under Rural Development Contracts in Scotland relate to calendar years.
6. The planting season lies both sides of 31 March, and the weather can cause planting to be advanced or delayed.
7. Includes natural colonisation and natural regeneration.
8. Forestry Commission (England, Scotland, and until March 2013, Wales), Natural Resources Wales (from April 2013), Forest Service (Northern Ireland).
9. Private sector: removals from all other woodland (including some publicly owned woodland).
10. Most hardwood production in the UK comes from private sector woodland; the figures are estimates based on reported deliveries to wood processing industries and others.

24.7 Sales for food of agricultural produce and livestock

			2001	2002	2003	2004 (e)	2005	2006	2007	2008	2009	2010 (e)	2011	2012	2013
Milk:															
Utilised for liquid consumption	KCQO	Million litres	6 748	6 825	6 753	6 693	6 652	6 734	6 724	6 678	6 626	6 836	6 892	6 816	6 861
Utilised for manufacture	KCQP	"	6 752	6 883	7 140	6 724	6 490	6 266	6 085	5 840	5 699	6 112	6 260	6 089	6 220
Total available for domestic use [a]	KCQQ	"	13 940	14 100	14 290	13 765	13 478	13 325	13 146	12 816	12 777	13 131	13 292	13 113	13 200
Hen eggs in shell	KCQR	Million dozens	753	747	730	773	772	742	720	754	751	826	821	797	829
Cattle and calves:															
Cattle	KCQS	Thousands	2 072	2 184	2 188	2 290	2 302	2 593	2 616	2 588	2 470	2 698	2 757	2 607	2 534
Calves	KCQT	"	92	98	87	103	111	51	46	44	43	62	81	74	91
Total	KCQU	"	2 164	2 282	2 275	2 393	2 413	2 644	2 661	2 632	2 513	2 760	2 838	2 681	2 625
Sheep and lambs	KCQV	"	12 964	14 993	15 095	15 492	16 284	16 414	15 804	16 697	15 600	14 289	14 477	13 746	14 517
Pigs:															
Clean pigs	MBGD	"	10 446	10 260	9 133	9 150	8 971	8 900	9 274	9 192	8 824	9 411	9 813	10 035	10 050
Sows and boars [d]	KCQZ	"	180	314	241	240	202	196	210	235	207	c	c	265	252
Total [d]	KCRA	"	10 626	10 575	9 374	9 390	9 173	9 097	9 484	9 427	9 031	c	c	10 300	10 302
Poultry [b]	KCRB	Millions	867	862	882	881	903	886	874	862	868	933	931	952	976

Source: Defra statistics, Agriculture in the UK and slaugher statistics: 01904 455096

(a) The totals of liquid consumption and milk used for manufacture may not add up to total available for domestic use because of adjustments for dairy wastage, stock changes and other uses such as famhouse consumption, milk fed to stock and on farm waste.

(b) fowls, turkeys, ducks and geese

(c) provisional data

(d) data marked as "C" are confidential

(e) denotes a 53 week year for slaughter of livestock

Totals of categories may not agree due to rounding

(p) Provisional data

24.8 Organic and In Conversion Livestock Numbers in the UK

										Thousand Heads
	2004	2005	2006	2007	2008	2009	2010	2011	2012	2013
Cattle	174 751	214 276	244 752	250 376	319 587	331 156	350 183	334 759	290 212	283 336
Sheep [a]	n/a	n/a	n/a	n/a	n/a	884 810	981 223	1 161 717	1 152 097	999 200
Pigs	43 733	29 995	32 926	50 435	71 229	49 398	47 387	52 640	34 648	30 165
Poultry	2 431 555	3 439 548	4 421 326	4 440 698	4 362 939	3 958 669	3 870 891	2 838 150	2 457 656	2 487 640
Other livestock [b]	1 696	2 030	4 903	3 954	4 781	3 404	4 509	4 983	4 150	4 133

(a) We are unable to provide full historical data for sheep as there are some inconsistencies in the historical data

(b) "Other Livestock" includes goats, farmed deer, horses, camelids and any livestock not recorded elsewhere.

Source: Department for Environment, Food and Rural Affairs

Keith Seabridge, E-mail organic-stats@defra.gsi.gov.uk
Department for Environment, Food and Rural Affairs

24.9 Number of organic producers and processors

Number

	2005	2006	2007	2008	2009	2010	2011	2012	2013
United Kingdom	**6 413**	**7 043**	**7 631**	**7 896**	**7 567**	**7 287**	**6 929**	**6 487**	**6072**
England	4 554	5 005	5 516	5 474	5 278	5 131	4 897	4 592	4419
Wales	800	835	953	1 230	1 176	1 166	1 119	1 080	913
Scotland	792	911	860	889	820	737	679	611	551
Northern Ireland	267	292	302	303	293	253	234	204	189
North East	129	161	173	179	167	160	152	137	127
North West	311	332	367	367	333	315	301	273	253
Yorkshire & Humberside	279	319	356	330	308	302	278	262	240
East Midlands	416	446	487	449	422	408	383	366	351
West Midlands	478	520	556	555	507	494	476	442	426
Eastern	508	556	574	551	529	515	481	456	449
South East (Inc London)	901	939	1 042	1 041	1 024	984	975	950	957
South West	1 532	1 732	1 961	2 002	1 988	1 953	1 851	1 706	1616

Source: Department for Environment, Food and Rural Affairs
Enquiries : Keith Seabridge
organic-stats@defra.gsi.gov.uk

24.10a Organic and In-Conversion Land

Thousand hectares

	2004	2005	2006	2007	2008	2009	2010	2011	2012	2013
In conversion land area										
North East	4.6	6.6	6.9	4.8	9.8	6.5	4.0	2.9	2.7	1.0
North West	2.5	3.2	1.8	3.3	3.8	3.4	2.4	1.4	1.1	0.9
Yorkshire & Humberside	1.3	2.3	3.4	4.1	3.8	2.7	0.9	0.7	0.6	0.5
East Midlands	1.2	2.4	2.1	3.1	3.7	3.1	1.0	0.5	0.6	0.7
West Midlands	2.4	3.2	4.0	5.7	8.2	5.7	2.1	1.8	1.4	0.8
Eastern	2.4	2.6	3.6	5.3	4.8	4.1	1.4	1.0	0.7	0.7
South East (inc. London)	5.4	10.7	13.2	14.6	10.4	7.3	4.3	3.7	3.1	3.0
South West	9.1	22.0	31.6	48.2	46.5	34.7	13.6	13.5	8.9	6.3
England	**28.8**	**53.2**	**66.5**	**89.0**	**91.1**	**67.6**	**29.8**	**25.4**	**19.2**	**14.0**
Wales	8.6	12.8	15.4	30.9	49.5	36.8	4.0	2.4	1.5	1.9
Scotland	13.7	16.7	35.2	34.8	6.2	12.0	12.6	5.1	8.0	8.4
Northern Ireland	1.6	3.2	4.0	3.2	2.3	3.0	4.4	4.0	3.6	0.1
United Kingdom	**52.7**	**86.0**	**121.1**	**157.9**	**149.1**	**119.4**	**50.8**	**36.9**	**32.2**	**24.4**
Fully organic land area										
North East	25.3	29.3	22.6	25.8	25.6	26.8	30.6	28.1	27.3	26.9
North West	19.8	18.9	19.4	20.4	21.2	19.8	20.0	16.4	15.5	14.0
Yorkshire & Humberside	8.6	9.0	9.0	9.6	10.9	11.9	13.8	12.5	9.9	10.2
East Midlands	13.4	13.2	12.5	13.2	12.2	14.4	16.3	15.2	15.5	14.1
West Midlands	26.8	27.0	26.3	28.2	29.7	32.0	35.4	28.9	30.6	30.8
Eastern	10.3	11.8	10.8	12.7	13.2	14.2	17.3	15.8	14.1	14.1
South East (inc. London)	34.9	35.2	35.8	42.5	47.2	51.6	54.1	51.4	46.5	48.1
South West	90.5	94.0	93.4	106.3	123.9	140.4	174.6	157.2	145.5	144.2
England	**229.6**	**238.4**	**229.9**	**258.7**	**284.0**	**311.2**	**362.0**	**325.6**	**304.8**	**302.4**
Wales	55.6	58.0	63.5	65.1	75.1	88.6	118.8	120.4	118.4	100.0
Scotland	331.6	231.2	200.1	193.1	225.1	209.3	176.3	164.8	143.7	140.0
Northern Ireland	5.0	6.3	5.1	7.3	10.1	10.3	10.4	8.3	6.6	9.3
United Kingdom	**621.8**	**533.9**	**498.6**	**524.3**	**594.4**	**619.3**	**667.6**	**619.1**	**573.4**	**551.7**
Total fully organic and in conversion land area										
North East	29.9	35.9	29.5	30.6	35.4	33.3	34.6	31.1	30.0	27.9
North West	22.3	22.1	21.2	23.7	25.0	23.2	22.4	17.8	16.6	14.9
Yorkshire & Humberside	9.8	11.3	12.4	13.7	14.7	14.6	14.6	13.2	10.5	10.7
East Midlands	14.6	15.6	14.5	16.3	16.0	17.6	17.3	15.7	16.1	14.8
West Midlands	29.1	30.2	30.3	33.9	37.9	37.7	37.5	30.7	31.9	31.6
Eastern	12.7	14.4	14.4	18.0	18.0	18.4	18.7	16.7	14.8	14.9
South East (inc. London)	40.3	46.0	49.0	57.1	57.6	58.9	58.4	55.1	49.6	51.1
South West	99.6	116.0	125.0	154.5	170.5	175.1	188.2	170.7	154.4	150.4
England	**258.5**	**291.6**	**296.4**	**347.8**	**375.1**	**378.8**	**391.8**	**351.0**	**323.9**	**316.4**
Wales	64.2	70.8	79.0	96.0	124.6	125.4	122.9	122.7	119.9	101.9
Scotland	345.3	247.9	235.3	227.9	231.3	221.3	188.9	169.9	151.7	148.4
Northern Ireland	6.6	9.5	9.1	10.5	12.5	13.3	14.8	12.3	10.1	9.4
United Kingdom	**674.5**	**619.9**	**619.8**	**682.2**	**743.5**	**738.7**	**718.3**	**656.0**	**605.7**	**576.0**

Source: Department for Environment, Food and Rural Affairs

Enquiries : Keith Seabridge

organic-stats@defra.gsi.gov.uk

24.10b Fully organic and in conversion land use in England

Hectares

	2004	2005	2006	2007	2008	2009	2010	2011	2012	2013
England										
In-conversion area										
Cereals	3,290	8,580	8,412	8,983	8,420	5,295	1,646	971	1,060	1,128
Other crops	2,480	3,166	2,915	2,880	1,969	1,490	540	387	221	152
Fruit & nuts	164	146	192	376	367	307	220	169	103	89
Vegetables [a]	1,190	1,043	1,636	2,042	1,739	1,224	431	239	208	142
Herbaceous & ornamentals	11	174	77	124	475	524	900	436	252	493
Temporary pasture	7,874	12,902	19,095	28,553	27,751	16,026	6,410	5,248	4,994	3,389
Permanent pasture [b]	10,634	21,337	27,948	37,929	45,951	38,615	16,828	14,117	10,203	7,379
Woodland	423	3,263	3,513	4,802	2,196	1,658	1,597	1,578	844	551
Unutilised land	2,766	2,613	2,738	3,349	2,208	2,450	1,198	2,274	1,296	630
Total	**28,832**	**53,223**	**66,525**	**89,037**	**91,074**	**67,588**	**29,769**	**25,418**	**19,181**	**13,952**
Fully organic area										
Cereals	27,241	30,769	28,702	31,101	35,534	41,092	43,636	40,418	36,806	34,101
Other crops	8,778	6,043	5,285	6,004	5,659	6,412	7,244	6,569	5,741	5,428
Fruit & nuts	1,415	1,447	1,490	1,489	1,477	1,843	1,988	1,925	1,973	1,920
Vegetables [a]	9,879	10,254	10,775	11,438	13,447	13,228	13,230	11,932	9,504	9,027
Herbaceous & ornamentals	219	607	606	421	3,710	3,812	3,877	4,557	4,838	5,318
Temporary pasture	63,142	64,711	62,868	72,914	78,549	87,096	96,678	90,856	82,129	77,856
Permanent pasture [b]	112,156	118,833	114,184	126,955	138,952	148,158	182,561	159,047	152,870	155,851
Woodland	1,900	1,800	2,293	4,281	2,115	3,270	4,503	4,623	4,564	4,816
Unutilised land	4,896	3,892	3,658	4,140	4,550	6,263	8,276	5,639	6,334	7,342
Total	**229,626**	**238,355**	**229,861**	**258,744**	**283,993**	**311,176**	**361,992**	**325,566**	**304,758**	**301,658**
Total fully organic and in conversion land use										
Cereals	30,531	39,349	37,114	40,084	43,954	46,387	45,282	41,389	37,866	35,228
Other crops	11,258	9,208	8,200	8,884	7,628	7,902	7,784	6,956	5,962	5,579
Fruit & nuts	1,580	1,593	1,683	1,865	1,844	2,150	2,207	2,094	2,077	2,009
Vegetables [a]	11,070	11,297	12,410	13,481	15,185	14,452	13,661	12,171	9,712	9,169
Herbaceous & ornamentals	230	780	682	545	4,185	4,336	4,777	4,993	5,090	5,811
Temporary pasture	71,016	77,613	81,963	101,467	106,300	103,122	103,088	96,105	87,123	81,245
Permanent pasture [b]	122,790	140,170	142,133	164,884	184,903	186,773	199,389	173,164	163,073	163,230
Woodland	2,323	5,063	5,805	9,082	4,310	4,928	6,100	6,200	5,407	5,366
Unutilised land	7,662	6,505	6,395	7,489	6,758	8,713	9,474	7,913	7,630	7,972
Total	**258,458**	**291,578**	**296,386**	**347,781**	**375,067**	**378,764**	**391,761**	**350,984**	**323,939**	**315,610**

Source: Department for Environment, Food and Rural Affairs

(a) including potatoes

(b) Including rough grazing

Enquiries : Keith Seabridge

organic-stats@defra.gsi.gov.uk

24.11 Wages in Agriculture: Minimum weekly rates of pay

Minimum weekly rates of pay in force in 2013 for workers working standard weekly hours

1 January to 30 September 2013					
Grade 6	**Grade 5**	**Grade 4**	**Grade 3**	**Grade 2**	**Grade 1**
£	**£**	**£**	**£**	**£**	**£**
366.60	339.30	320.19	298.74	271.44	242.19

Grade 1 - Initial Grade
Grade 2 - Standard Grade
Grade 3 - Lead Worker
Grade 4 - Craft Grade
Grade 5 - Supervisory Grade
Grade 6 - Farm Management Grade

Higher rates apply to Full Time and Part Time Flexible Workers.

Source: Department for Environment, Food and Rural Affairs

24.12 Agricultural labour force on commercial holdings (a)

Thousands

										At June of each year		
	2002	2003	2004	2005	2006	2007	2008	2009	2010	2011	2012	2013
Total labour force on commercial holdings (incl. farmers and spouses) (a)	507	491	501	494	491	481	483	464	466	476	481	464
Farmers, business partners, directors and spouses	319	313	315	311	313	305	302	289	295	299	298	290
Full time	160	155	151	149	146	141	140	137	134	140	141	138
Part time (b)	160	158	164	162	167	165	161	152	161	159	158	152
Salaried managers	12	11	14	15	14	15	14	11	11	11	11	11
Other workers	175	166	171	169	164	161	167	164	160	166	172	162
Full time	76	69	66	66	63	61	64	63	64	64	65	63
Male	64	60	57	56	53	51	54	52	..	..	..	-
Female	11	10	9	10	10	10	11	11	..	..	..	-
Part time (b)	38	36	38	39	39	43	43	42	39	39	41	39
Male	21	20	22	23	23	27	27	27	..	..	..	-
Female	17	16	16	16	16	16	16	16	..	..	..	-
Seasonal, casual or gang labour	62	61	66	64	62	57	60	59	56	62	67	61
Male	45	44	48	45	43	40	42	42	40	44	48	40
Female	17	17	18	18	19	17	18	17	17	18	19	21

Source: June Surveys/Census of Agriculture.
Enquiries: Lisa Richardson on +44 (0)1904 455075
email: farming-statistics@defra.gsi.gov.uk

Please note that totals may not add up to the sum of components due to rounding.

(a) Figures for England relate to commercial holdings only. More information on commercial holdings can be found in the introduction
(b) Part time is defined as less than 39 hours per week in England and Wales, less than 38 hours per week in Scotland and less than 30 hours per week in Northern Ireland.

- means 'nil' or 'negligible' (less than half the last digit shown).
. . means 'not available' or 'not applicable'.

24.13 Summary of UK fishing industry: 2003 to 2013

£ million (unless otherwise specified)

	2003	2004	2005	2006	2007	2008	2009	2010	2011	2012	2013
Fleet size at end of year [a]											
(no. of vessels)	7,096	7,022	6,716	6,752	6,763	6,573	6,500	6,477	6,444	6,406	6,399
Employment											
(no. of fishermen)	13,122	13,453	12,831	12,934	12,871	12,614	12,212	12,703	12,405	12,445	12,152
Total landings by UK vessels [b]											
Quantity ('000 tonnes)	639.7	653.7	715.7	619.6	613.9	587.2	582.9	605.3 R	595.9 R	627.8 R	623.7
Value (£ million)	528.3	513.0	574.6	614.3	646.3	634.5	679.6	720.3 R	832.0 R	771.8 R	717.6
Imports											
Quantity ('000 tonnes)	631.5	671.3	720.4	753.3	747.9	781.7	720.6	703.8	720.2	754.5 R	738.9
Value (£ million) [c]	1,439.0	1,474.0	1,696.0	1,920.6	1,993.9	2,210.1	2,177.2	2,254.7	2,558.6	2,570.0 R	2,754.8
Exports											
Quantity ('000 tonnes)	479.5	477.8	461.4	415.6	466.9	415.8	479.7	516.7	436.1	465.9 R	452.8
Value (£ million) [c]	891.0	886.0	939.0	942.2	982.0	1009.4	1,166.1	1,345.7	1,463.9	1,343.9 R	1,462.7
Total household consumption											
of fish ('000 tonnes) [d]	473	480	509	519	515	510	501	483	472	467 R	nd
Population ('000 persons) [j]	58,142	58,313	58,473	58,603	59,737	60,816	60,907	61,464	61,528	61,946 R	nd
Total consumer expenditure											
on fish (£ million)	2,848	3,011	3,179	3,410	3,599	3,650	3,711	3,742	3,866	3,998 R	nd
on food (£ million) [e]	68,728	70,085	71,833	74,193	77,716	67,635	70,143	72,587	73,744	77,523 R	nd
Fish as a % of food [e]	4.1%	4.3%	4.4%	4.6%	4.6%	5.4%	5.3%	5.2%	5.2%	5.2% R	nd
Landed Price Index [f]	105.7	109.3	123.8	134.4	136.2	141.1	141.7	152.2	163.7	153.9	146.9
Retail Price Index [g]	103.5	101.7	102.3	108.5	115.7	123.9	130.3	138.2	151.0	157.4	163.4
Consumer Price Index [h]	103.3	101.6	103.2	111.4	120.7	126.7	131.5	140.1	153.0	158.4	163.6
GDP for Fishing [i]											
Current price gross value added at basic prices (KK37)	368	377	407	435	491	506	493	523	404	479	476
Output index (chain volume measures) (L2KO) (2009=100)	108.7	100.9	100.5	92.7	99.4	94.6	96.8	100.0	100.5	100.4	100.4
GDP for Agriculture, Forestry and Fishing											
Current price gross value added at basic prices (KKD5)	8,841	9,588	7,174	7,156	8,005	9,093	7,392	9,054	9,438	9,040	9,106
Output index (chain volume measures) (L2KL) (2010=100)	101.0	100.1	106.0	102.5	98.6	108.2	100.7	100.0	110.6	106.9	102.4
GDP at Market Prices											
Current price GDP at market prices (KKP5) (£ billion)	1,024	1,081	1,139	1,205	1,275	1,312	1,280	1,328	1,361	1,381	1,377
Chain volume measures index (YBEZ) (2010=100)	92.3	95.3	98.4	101.1	104.5	103.7	98.4	100.0	101.1	101.3	103.2
Percentage contribution of GVA from fishing to GVA for agriculture, hunting, forestry and fishing											
Current prices (%)	4.2%	3.9%	5.7%	6.1%	6.1%	5.6%	6.7%	5.8%	4.3%	5.3%	5.2%

Source: Fisheries Administrations in the UK, H.M. Customs and Excise, Expenditure and Food Survey, Office for National Statistics

(a) The number of vessels includes those registered in the Channel Islands and Isle of Man.

(b) The quantity of landed fish is expressed in terms of liveweight. The figures relate to landings both into the UK and abroad.

(c) Imports are valued at cost, including insurance and freight terms whereas exports are valued at free on board terms.

(d) Figures for 2001 to 2005 are based on financial year data.

(e) Including non-alcoholic beverages.

(f) The landed price index has been calculated on an annual basis with 2000 = 100.

(g) The fish component of the RPI which includes canned and processed fish. The index has been re-based such that 2000 = 100.

(h) The fish component of the CPI which includes canned and processed fish. The index has been re-based such that 2000 = 100.

(i) GDP for fishing includes landings abroad, according to the KK37 index.

(j) The population estimate has been updated to be consistent with the Living Costs and Food Survey figures, which provide the basis for the household consumption and consumers expenditure figures given in this table

24.14 UK Fishing Fleet[1]

AT 1st January each year

	2003	2004	2005	2006[2]	2007	2008	2009	2010	2011	2012	2013
By Size											
10m and under	5661	5498	5445	5210	5238	5280	5137	5078	5042	5038	5034
10.01 - 11.99m	494	466	446	433	425	424	410	405	396	399	406
12.00 - 14.99m	284	295	304	303	306	310	312	307	304	299	291
15.00 - 17.99m	288	263	239	224	220	217	211	208	201	193	191
18.00 - 23.99m	371	315	300	296	284	283	287	286	274	252	245
24.00 - 39.99m	323	280	267	253	246	228	218	210	200	190	187
40m and over	69	74	70	69	62	62	57	57	57	57	58
By Segment (based on activity in previous year)											
Drift and/or fixed netters	178	177	229	214	468	618	678	665	676	719	704
Dredgers	176	181	169	243	244	219	235	246	245	274	260
Demersal trawlers and/or demersal seiners	1135	1052	1037	985	1047	1076	1057	1005	926	886	878
Vessels using pots and/or traps	1084	1100	1061	1073	2208	2186	2186	2031	2067	2083	2023
Vessels using hooks	238	147	266	270	224	382	387	488	524	508	548
Vessels using polyvalent active gears only	13	11	20	14	11	16	14	14	19	37	37
Vessels using polyvalent passive gears only	18	18	23	20	68	71	83	85	65	82	76
Vessels using active and passive gears	6	3	5	7	12	9	6	5	14	7	8
Purse seiners	44	45	41	50	34	31	34	40	44	39	41
Beam trawlers	171	175	155	131	126	135	136	124	117	81	95
Pelagic trawlers	1	1	1	1	1	1	1		1		
Inactive during previous year	4426	4281	4064	3780	2338	2060	1815	1848	1776	1712	1742
Total UK Fleet	7490	7191	7071	6788	6781	6804	6632	6551	6474	6428	6412

Source: Marine Management Organisation

1 Includes Channel Islands and Isle of Man

2 Pre 2006 data on activity by under 10m vessels was collected as grouped landings - as such for a significant number of vessels did not have activity listed against them. From September 2005 sales notes were required for sales by individual vessels leading to a reduction in the number of vessels regarded as inactive each year from 2006 onwards.

24.15 Estimated household food consumption[1]

Grammes per person per week

		Great Britain				United Kingdom				
		1998	1999	2000		2001 /02	2002 /03	2003 /04	2004 /05	2005 /06
Liquid wholemilk[2] (ml)	KPQM	693	634	664	VQEW	599	555	585	484	460
Fully skimmed (ml)	KZBH	164	167	164	VQEX	160	166	154	158	159
Semi skimmed (ml)	KZBI	945	958	975	VQEZ	931	919	926	975	1008
Other milk and cream (ml)	KZBJ	243	248	278	VQFA	333	350	358	366	385
Cheese	KPQO	104	104	110	VQFB	112	112	113	110	116
Butter	KPQP	39	37	39	VQFC	41	37	35	35	38
Margarine	KPQQ	26	20	21	VQFD	13	13	12	11	20
Low and reduced fat spreads	KZBK	69	71	68	VQFE	72	70	71	68	55
All other oils and fats (ml for oils)	KPQR	62	58	58	VQFF	70	70	68	68	70
Eggs (number)	KPQS	2	2	2	VQFG	2	2	2	2	2
Preserves and honey	KPQT	38	33	33	VQFH	35	35	33	34	35
Sugar	KPQU	119	107	105	VQFI	112	111	102	99	94
Beef and veal	KPQV	109	110	124	VQFJ	118	118	119	123	120
Mutton and lamb	KPQW	59	57	55	VQFK	51	51	49	50	53
Pork	KPQX	76	69	68	VQFL	61	61	56	56	52
Bacon and ham, uncooked	KPQY	76	68	71	VQFM	68	69	70	70	68
Bacon and ham, cooked (including canned)	KPQZ	40	39	41	VQFN	45	45	47	43	44
Poultry uncooked	JZCH	218	201	214	VQFO	206	199	200	197	212
Cooked poultry (not purchased in cans)	KYBP	33	35	39	VQFQ	44	45	48	49	48
Other cooked and canned meats	KPRB	49	48	51	VQFR	54	58	60	58	56
Offals	KPRC	5	5	5	VQFS	6	6	7	5	5
Sausages, uncooked	KPRD	60	58	60	VQFT	66	66	70	67	64
Other meat products	KPRE	216	221	239	VQFU	313	319	335	330	323
Fish, fresh and processed (including shellfish)	KPRF	70	70	67						
Canned fish	KPRG	29	31	32						
Fish and fish products, frozen	KPRH	46	42	44						
Fish, fresh chilled or frozen					VQAI	51	48	45	42	45
Other fish and fish products					VQAJ	105	107	111	115	122
Potatoes (excluding processed)	KPRI	715	673	707	VQFY	647	617	600	570	587
Fresh green vegetables	KPRJ	246	245	240	VQAK	229	231	228	225	235
Other fresh vegetables	KPRK	486	500	492	VQAL	502	505	505	536	567
Frozen potato products	KYBQ	111	113	120						
Other frozen vegetables	KPRL	88	87	80						
Potato products not frozen	JZCF	89	86	82						
Canned beans	KPRM	118	112	114						
Other canned vegetables (excl. potatoes)	KPRN	99	92	97						
Other processed vegetables (excl. potatoes)	LQZH	54	59	54						
All processed vegetables					VQAM	628	621	611	597	608
Apples	KPRO	181	169	180	VQGN	175	172	171	173	179
Bananas	KPRP	198	202	206	VQGO	203	208	211	217	225
Oranges	KPRQ	63	50	54	VQGP	55	62	64	57	59
All other fresh fruit	KPRR	274	290	304	VQGS	318	351	343	358	392
Canned fruit	KPRS	37	38	38	VQGT	40	39	40	38	36
Dried fruit, nuts and fruit and nut products	KPRT	34	30	35	VQGU	39	41	40	46	51
Fruit juices (ml)	KPRU	304	284	303	VQGX	327	333	322	280	350
Flour	KPRV	55	56	67	VQGY	55	61	52	55	60
Bread	KPRW	742	717	720	VQGZ	770	757	728	695	701
Buns, scones and teacakes	KPRX	41	40	43	VQHA	37	41	44	47	46
Cakes and pastries	KPRY	88	87	89	VQHB	126	122	120	117	122
Biscuits	KPRZ	137	132	141	VQHC	166	174	163	165	165
Breakfast cereals	KPSA	136	134	143	VQHE	133	132	134	131	135
Oatmeal and oat products	KPSB	11	13	15	VQHF	12	13	12	14	19
Other cereals and cereal products	JZCG	270	284	291	VQHG	365	370	360	354	378
Tea	KPSC	35	32	34	VQHK	34	34	31	31	33
Instant coffee	KPSD	12	11	11	VQHL	13	12	13	13	13
Canned soups	KPSE	71	67	71	VQHM	79	80	77	76	82
Pickles and sauces	KPSF	96	91	107	VQHN	121	123	121	120	125

1 See chapter text.

2 Including also school and welfare milk (pre-2001-02)

24.15 Estimated household food consumption[15]

Grammes per person per week
United Kingdom

		2006	2007	2008	2009	2010	2011	2012	2013
Liquid wholemilk[2] (ml)	VQEW	477	420	410	412	352	355	297	285
Fully skimmed (ml)	VQEX	163	173	158	165	172	167	158	155
Semi skimmed (ml)	VQEZ	974	982	987	991	985	984	1051	996
Other milk and cream (ml)	VQFA	395	397	392	427	389	398	394	410
Cheese	VQFB	116	119	111	116	118	118	114	118
Butter	VQFC	40	41	40	39	40	40	41	42
Margarine	VQFD	18	19	22	24	23	20	24	23
Low and reduced fat spreads	VQFE	57	53	51	48	49	46	43	38
All other oils and fats (ml for oils)	VQFF	69	68	72	71	71	63	71	67
Eggs (number)	VQFG	2	2	2	2	2	2	2	2
Preserves and honey	VQFH	34	33	34	35	36	33	32	31
Sugar	VQFI	92	92	93	90	90	93	91	91
Beef and veal	VQFJ	128	126	111	112	114	112	104	97
Mutton and lamb	VQFK	54	55	45	46	44	37	36	35
Pork	VQFL	55	54	55	54	53	56	55	51
Bacon and ham, uncooked	VQFM	66	64	63	68	70	69	68	64
Bacon and ham, cooked (including canned)	VQFN	45	45	45	43	43	43	40	39
Poultry uncooked	VQFO	207	208	207	205	201	206	214	203
Cooked poultry (not purchased in cans)	VQFQ	48	43	44	41	41	41	37	38
Other cooked and canned meats	VQFR	53	50	51	51	48	46	44	43
Offals	VQFS	5	5	5	6	5	7	6	5
Sausages, uncooked	VQFT	65	65	62	65	66	64	67	61
Other meat products	VQFU	315	316	311	309	331	318	317	313
Fish, fresh and processed (including shellfish)									
Canned fish									
Fish and fish products, frozen									
Fish, fresh chilled or frozen	VQAI	47	43	43	41	38	34	37	36
Other fish and fish products	VQAJ	123	122	118	117	113	113	108	110
Potatoes (excluding processed)	VQFY	565	537	535	514	501	496	478	439
Fresh green vegetables	VQAK	221	224	203	201	192	189	183	179
Other fresh vegetables	VQAL	566	566	557	552	565	550	551	569
Frozen potato products									
Other frozen vegetables									
Potato products not frozen									
Canned beans									
Other canned vegetables (excl. potatoes)									
Other processed vegetables (excl. potatoes)									
All processed vegetables	VQAM	601	594	599	597	592	601	597	597
Apples	VQGN	180	178	162	163	156	149	135	137
Bananas	VQGO	226	230	219	205	204	220	214	219
Oranges	VQGP	55	59	49	45	47	48	50	47
All other fresh fruit	VQGS	394	389	360	348	348	347	346	340
Canned fruit	VQGT	39	35	32	29	30	30	29	26
Dried fruit, nuts and fruit and nut products	VQGU	53	51	52	51	52	49	51	56
Fruit juices (ml)	VQGX	366	340	325	302	296	307	282	288
Flour	VQGY	54	54	63	58	58	71	73	57
Bread	VQGZ	692	677	659	656	634	621	615	607
Buns, scones and teacakes	VQHA	45	44	43	47	45	46	45	47
Cakes and pastries	VQHB	120	115	111	111	108	105	105	103
Biscuits	VQHC	165	163	170	169	162	164	160	165
Breakfast cereals	VQHE	135	130	130	133	133	132	128	127
Oatmeal and oat products	VQHF	17	19	20	21	21	20	22	24
Other cereals and cereal products	VQHG	378	387	386	393	402	395	392	398
Tea	VQHK	30	30	30	29	28	27	26	25
Instant coffee	VQHL	14	13	14	15	15	14	13	14
Canned soups	VQHM	79	79	76	78	76	75	85	79
Pickles and sauces	VQHN	128	129	130	132	131	131	129	130

1 See chapter text.
2 Including also school and welfare milk (pre-2001-02)

Sources: Living Costs and Food Survey;
Department for Environment Food and Rural Affairs;
Office for National Statistics.
Contact: 01904 455303
familyfood@defra.gsi.gov.uk

Sources:

This index of sources gives the titles of official publications or other sources containing statistics allied to those in the tables of this Annual Abstract. These publications provide more detailed analyses than are shown in the Annual Abstract. This index includes publications to which reference should be made for short–term (monthly or quarterly) series.

Table number	Government department or other organisation

Chapter 1: Area

1.1	ONS Geography Codes; Office for National Statistics - Standard Area Measurement for UK Local Authority Districts (SAM 2013)

Chapter 2: Parliamentary elections

2.1	British Electoral Facts 1832-2012; Plymouth University for the Electoral Commission
2.2	Plymouth University for the Electoral Commission
2.3	British Electoral Facts 1832-2012; Plymouth University for the Electoral Commission
2.4	Electoral Facts 1832-2012; Plymouth University for the Electoral Commission

Chapter 3 International Development

3.1a	Department for International Development
3.1b	Department for International Development
3.2a	Department for International Development
3.2b	Department for International Development
3.2c	Department for International Development
3.2d	Department for International Development
3.2e	Department for International Development
3.3	Department for International Development

Chapter 4 Labour Market

4.1	Labour Force Survey, Office for National Statistics
4.2	Labour Force Survey, Office for National Statistics
4.3	Labour Force Survey, Office for National Statistics
4.4	Labour Force Survey, Office for National Statistics
4.5a	Labour market statistics, Office for National Statistics; Eurostat
4.5b	Labour Disputes Inquiry, Office for National Statistics
4.6	Annual Civil Service Employment Survey, Office for National Statistics
4.7	Labour Force Survey, Office for National Statistics
4.8	Labour Force Survey, Office for National Statistics
4.9	Office for National Statistics
4.10	Jobcentre Plus administrative system; Labour Market Statistics,Office for National Statistics
4.11a	Annual Survey of Hours and Earnings, Office for National Statistics
4.11b	Annual Survey of Hours and Earnings, Office for National Statistics
4.12a	Annual Survey of Hours and Earnings, Office for National Statistics
4.12b	Annual Survey of Hours and Earnings, Office for National Statistics
4.13	Office for National Statistics
4.14a	Monthly Wages & Salaries Survey, Office for National Statistics
4.14b	Monthly Wages & Salaries Survey, Office for National Statistics
4.14c	Monthly Wages & Salaries Survey, Office for National Statistics
4.14d	Monthly Wages & Salaries Survey, Office for National Statistics
4.15a	Annual Survey of Hours and Earnings, Office for National Statistics
4.15b	Annual Survey of Hours and Earnings, Office for National Statistics
4.16	Annual Survey of Hours and Earnings, Office for National Statistics
4.17	Certification Office

Chapter 5 Social Protection

5.1	HM Revenue and Customs; Department for Work and Pensions
5.2	HM Revenue and Customs; Department for Work and Pensions (Information Governance and Security Directorate)
5.3	HM Revenue and Customs
5.4	Department for Work and Pensions
5.5	Department for Work and Pensions
5.6	Department for Work and Pensions
5.7	Department for Work and Pensions Work and Pensions Longitudinal Study 100% data
5.8	DWP Information, Governance and Security, Work and Pensions Longitudinal Study
5.9a	HM Revenue and Customs

Table number	Government department or other organisation
5.9b	HM Revenue and Customs
5.10	HM Revenue and Customs
5.11	HM Revenue and Customs
5.12	DWP Information, Governance and Security, Work and Pensions Longitudinal Study.
5.13	DWP Information, Governance and Security, Work and Pensions Longitudinal Study.
5.14	DWP Information, Governance and Security, Work and Pensions Longitudinal Study.
5.15a	Ministry of Defence/DASA
5.15b	Ministry of Defence/DASA
5.16	DWP Information, Governance and Security, Work and Pensions Longitudinal Study
5.17	DWP Information, Governance and Security, Work and Pensions Longitudinal Study
5.18	DWP Information, Governance and Security, Work and Pensions Longitudinal Study
5.19	DWP Information, Governance and Security, Work and Pensions Longitudinal Study

Chapter 6 External Trade

6.1	Office for National Statistics
6.2a	Office for National Statistics
6.3	Office for National Statistics
6.4	Office for National Statistics
6.5	Office for National Statistics
6.6	Office for National Statistics
6.7	Office for National Statistics
6.8	Office for National Statistics
6.9	Pink Book 2013, Office for National Statistics
6.10	Pink Book 2013, Office for National Statistics
6.11	Pink Book 2013, Office for National Statistics
6.12	Pink Book 2013, Office for National Statistics
6.13	Office for National Statistics
6.14	Office for National Statistics
6.15	Office for National Statistics
6.16	Office for National Statistics
6.17	Office for National Statistics
6.18	Office for National Statistics

Chapter 7 Research and development

7.1a	Office for National Statistics
7.1b	Office for National Statistics
7.2	Office for National Statistics
7.3	Office for National Statistics
7.4	Office for National Statistics
7.5a	Office for National Statistics
7.5b	Office for National Statistics

Chapter 8 Personal income, expendiure & wealth

8.1	Survey of Personal Incomes, HM Revenue and Customs
8.2	Office for National Statistics
8.3	Family Spending 2013, Office for National Statistics
8.4	Family Spending 2013, Office for National Statistics
8.5	Family Spending 2013, Office for National Statistics

Chapter 9 Lifestyles

9.1	Department for Culture, Media and Sport
9.2	National Readership Surveys Ltd.
9.3	Annual Population Survey 2012, Office for National Statistics
9.4	Taking Part Survey, Department for Culture, Media and Sport
9.5	BFI RSU Analysis; BVA; Official Charts Company; Attentional, IHS
9.6	Rentrak, BFI RSU analysis.
9.7	International Passenger Survey, Office for National Statistics
9.8	International Passenger Survey, Office for National Statistics
9.9	International Passenger Survey, Office for National Statistics
9.10	Visit England
9.11	The GB Tourist 2013, Visit England
9.12	National Lottery Commission; Gambling Commission; Department for Culture, Media and Sport
9.13	Office for National Statistics
9.14a	Taking Part Survey, Department for Culture, Media and Sport
9.14b	Taking Part Survey, Department for Culture, Media and Sport
9.14c	Taking Part Survey, Department for Culture, Media and Sport
9.15	Taking Part Survey, Department for Culture, Media and Sport

Table number	Government department or other organisation
9.16	Community Life Survey, Cabinet Office
9.17	International Passenger Survey, Office for National Statistics
9.18	Office for National Statistics
9.19	RAJAR

Chapter 10 Environment

10.1	AEA Energy & Environment, Office for National Statistics
10.2	Ricardo-AEA, Office for National Statistics
10.3	Department for Energy and Climate Change
10.4	Ricardo-AEA, Department of Energy & Climate Change, Office for National Statistics
10.5	Department for Energy and Climate Change
10.6	Department for Energy and Climate Change
10.7	Department for Energy and Climate Change
10.8	Office for National Statistics; Department for Environment, Food and Rural Affairs
10.9	Met Office; National Hydrological Monitoring Programme, Centre for Ecology and Hydrology
10.10	Met Office
10.11	Environment Agency
10.12	Scottish Environment Protection Agency
10.13	Water PLCs; Environment Agency; National Hydrological Monitoring Programme, Centre for Ecology and Hydrology
10.14a	Office of Water Services (OFWAT)
10.14b	Office of Water Services (OFWAT)
10.15	Environment Agency
10.16a	Department for Environment, Food and Rural Affairs
10.16b	Department for Environment, Food and Rural Affairs
10.17	Environment Agency
10.18	Office for National Statistics; Department of Energy and Climate Change
10.19a	Department for Environment, Food and Rural Affairs
10.19b	WasteDataFlow, Natural Resources Wales
10.19c	Scottish Environment Protection Agency
10.19d	Northern Ireland Environment Agency, NISRA, DSD
10.20a	WasteDataFlow, Department for Environment Food and Rural affairs
10.20b	WasteDataFlow, Natural Resources Wales
10.20c	WasteDataFlow, Scottish Environment Protection Agency
10.20d	Northern Ireland Environment Agency
10.21	The Chartered Institute of Environmental Health
10.22	Office for National Statistics; Department for Energy and Climate Change

Chapter 11 Housing

11.1a	Department for Communities and Local Government
11.1b	Welsh Assembly Government
11.1c	Scottish Government
11.1d	Department for Social Development (NI)
11.2	Department or Communities and Local Government; Welsh Assembly Government; Scottish Government; Department for Social Development (NI)
11.3	National House Building Council (NHBC);Welsh Assembly Government; Scottish Government; Department for Social Development (NI); Northern Ireland Housing Executive; Local Authority Building Control (NI)
11.4a	Department for Communities and Local Government
11.4b	Welsh Government
11.5	HM Courts and Tribunals Service CaseMan; Possession Claim OnLine (PCOL); Council of Mortgage Lenders (CML)
11.6	Compendium of Housing Finance Statistics & Housing Finance, Council of Mortgage Lenders; Janet Ford, Roof
11.7	Department for Communities and Local Government
11.8	Statutory Homelessness data collection from local authorities, Welsh Government
11.9	Scottish Government

Chapter 12 Banking and Finance

12.1a	Bank of England
12.1b	Bank of England
12.1c	Bank of England
12.1d	Bank of England
12.1e	Bank of England
12.1f	Bank of England
12.2a	UK Payments Administration Ltd
12.2b	UK Payments Administration Ltd
12.2c	UK Payments Administration Ltd
12.2d	UK Payments Administration Ltd
12.2e	UK Payments Administration Ltd
12.2f	UK Payments Administration Ltd
12.2g	UK Payments Administration Ltd

Table number	Government department or other organisation
12.2h	UK Payments Administration Ltd
12.2i	UK Payments Administration Ltd
12.2j	UK Payments Administration Ltd
12.3a	Bank of England
12.3b	Bank of England
12.3c	Bank of England
12.3d	Bank of England
12.3e	Bank of England
12.3f	Bank of England
12.3g	Bank of England
12.3h	Bank of England
12.4a	Bank of England
12.4b	Bank of England
12.4c	Bank of England
12.4d	Bank of England
12.5a	Bank of England
12.5b	Bank of England
12.6a	Bank of England
12.6b	Bank of England
12.7	Bank of England
12.8	Bank of England
12.9	Bank of England
12.10	Bank of England
12.11	Bank of England
12.12	Bank of England
12.13a	Office for National Statistics
12.13b	Office for National Statistics
12.14	Office for National Statistics
12.15a	Office for National Statistics
12.15b	Office for National Statistics
12.16a	Insolvency Service
12.16b	Accountant in Bankruptcy (AiB), Companies House
12.16c	Department for Enterprise, Trade and Investment, Northern Ireland (DETINI)
12.17a	Insolvency Service; Companies House
12.17b	Companies House
12.17c	Department for Enterprise, Trade and Investment Northern Ireland (DETINI); Companies House
12.18a	Bank of England
12.18b	Bank of England
12.18c	Bank of England
12.18d	Bank of England
12.19	Bank of England
12.20	Mergers and Acquisitions Surveys, Office for National Statistics

Chapter 13 Services

13.1a	Annual Business Survey (ABS), Office for National Statistics
13.1b	Annual Business Survey (ABS), Office for National Statistics
13.2	Office for National Statistics
13.3	Annual Business Survey (ABS), Office for National Statistics
13.4	Annual Business Survey (ABS), Office for National Statistics

Chapter 14 Defence

14.1	Defence Economics (Defence Expenditure Analysis) and Defence Resources, Ministry of Defence
14.2	Defence Statistics (Tri-Service), Ministry of Defence
14.3a	Finance & Military Capability, Ministry of Defence
14.3b	Army HQ Plans Directorate, Ministry of Defence
14.3c	Finance & Military Capability, Ministry of Defence
14.3d	Finance & Military Capability, Ministry of Defence
14.4	Defence Statistics (Tri-Service), Ministry of Defence
14.5	Defence Statistics (Tri-Service), Ministry of Defence
14.6a	Defence Statistics (Civilian), Ministry of Defence
14.6b	Defence Statistics (Civilian), Ministry of Defence
14.7a	MOD Defence Infrastructure Organisation, Ministry of Defence
14.7b	MOD Defence Infrastructure Organisation, Ministry of Defence
14.8a	Defence Statistics (Tri-Service), Ministry of Defence
14.8b	Defence Statistics (Tri-Service), Ministry of Defence
14.9a	Defence Statistics (Health), Ministry of Defence
14.9b	Defence Statistics (Health), Ministry of Defence
14.10a	UK Defence Statistics, Ministry of Defence
14.10b	UK Defence Statistics, ARCC Database, Ministry of Defence
14.10c	UK Defence Statistics, ARCC Database, Ministry of Defence
14.10d	HQ Surgeon General

Table number	Government department or other organisation
14.11	Marine Management Organisation

Chapter 15 Population

15.1	Office for National Statistics; National Records of Scotland; Northern Ireland Statistics and Research Agency
15.2a	National Population Projections, Office for National Statistics
15.2b	National Population Projections, Office for National Statistics
15.2c	National Population Projections, Office for National Statistics
15.2d	National Population Projections, Office for National Statistics
15.3a	Office for National Statistics
15.3b	National Population Projections, Office for National Statistics
15.3c	Office for National Statistics
15.3d	National Population Projections, Office for National Statistics
15.3e	Office for National Statistics
15.3f	National Population Projections, Office for National Statistics
15.3g	Office for National Statistics
15.3h	National Population Projections, Office for National Statistics
15.4	Labour Force Survey, Office for National Statistics
15.5	Office for National Statistics
15.6	2011 Census
15.7	ONS; Home Office; Central Statistics Office (CSO) Ireland; Northern Ireland Statistics and Research Agency (NISRA)
15.8	ONS; Home Office; Central Statistics Office (CSO) Ireland; Northern Ireland Statistics and Research Agency (NISRA)
15.9	Immigration Statistics, Home Office
15.10	Immigration Statistics, Home Office
15.11	Office for National Statistics
15.12	Office for National Statistics
15.13	Office for National Statistics
15.14	Office for National Statistics
15.15	Office for National Statistics
15.16	ISD Scotland; Department of Health
15.17	Office for National Statistics
15.18	Office for National Statistics
15.19	Office for National Statistics
15.20a	Office for National Statistics
15.20b	GRO-Scotland
15.20c	Northern Ireland Statistics and Research Agency (NISRA)

Chapter 16 Health

16.1a	Health and Social Care Information Centre
16.1b	Welsh Ambulance Service NHS Trust
16.1c	Scottish Workforce Information Standard System (SWISS)
16.1d	Department of Health, Social Services and Public Safety Northern Ireland
16.2	ISD Scotland, NHS National Services Scotland
16.3	Business Services Organisation (BSO) Northern Ireland; Dept of Health, Social Services & Public Safety Northern Ireland
16.4	Health and Social Care Information Centre
16.5	Health Statistics and Analysis Unit, Welsh Government
16.6	Office for National Statistics
16.7a	Public Health England
16.7b	Health Protection Scotland
16.7c	Public Health Agency, Northern Ireland
16.8a	Health and Safety Executive (HSE)
16.8b	Health and Safety Executive (HSE)
16.8c	Health and Safety Executive (HSE)
16.8d	Health and Safety Executive (HSE)
16.9	Office for National Statistics; Health and Safety Executive
16.10	RIDDOR - Reporting of Injuries, Diseases and Dangerous Occurrences Regulations 1995, Health and Safety Executive (HSE)

Chapter 17 Prices

17.1	Office for National Statistics
17.2	Office for National Statistics; Department for Communities and Local Government
17.3	Office for National Statistics
17.4	Office for National Statistics
17.5	Office for National Statistics
17.6	Office for National Statistics
17.7	Department for Environment, Food and Rural Affairs
17.8	Department for Environment, Food and Rural Affairs
17.9	Eurostat; Office for National Statistics

Chapter 18 Production

Table number	Government department or other organisation
18.1	Annual Business Survey (ABS), Office for National Statistics
18.2	PRODCOM , Office for National Statistics
18.3	Office for National Statistics
18.4	Department of Energy and Climate Change
18.5	Department of Energy and Climate Change
18.6	Department of Energy and Climate Change
18.7	Department of Energy and Climate Change
18.8	Department of Energy and Climate Change
18.9	Department of Energy and Climate Change
18.10	Department of Energy and Climate Change
18.11	Department of Energy and Climate Change
18.12	Department of Energy and Climate Change
18.13	Department of Energy and Climate Change
18.14	International Steel Statistics Bureau
18.15	International Steel Statistics Bureau
18.16	International Steel Statistics Bureau
18.17	British Survey of Fertiliser Practice (Defra)
18.18a	Office for National Statistics, Department of Business, Innovation and Skills;
	Dept. of Enterprise, Trade & Investment (Northern Ireland)
18.18b	Department of Enterprise, Trade & Investment (Northern Ireland);
	Department of Economic Development (Isle of Man), Company data (Guernsey and Jersey)
18.19a	Department for Business,Innovation and Skills (BIS)
18.19b	Department for Business,Innovation and Skills (BIS)
18.19c	Department for Business,Innovation and Skills (BIS)
18.19d	Department for Business,Innovation and Skills (BIS)
18.19e	Department for Business,Innovation and Skills (BIS)
18.19f	Department for Business,Innovation and Skills (BIS)
18.20	Output in the Construction Industry, Office for National Statistics
18.21	Orders for New Construction, Office for National Statistics
18.22	Office for National Statistics
18.23	Office for National Statistics
18.24	Her Majesty's Revenue and Customs
18.25	Her Majesty's Revenue and Customs

Chapter 19 National Accounts

19.1	Blue Book 2014, Office for National Statistics
19.2	Blue Book 2014, Office for National Statistics
19.3	Blue Book 2014, Office for National Statistics
19.4	Blue Book 2014, Office for National Statistics
19.5	Blue Book 2014, Office for National Statistics
19.6	Blue Book 2014, Office for National Statistics
19.7	Blue Book 2014, Office for National Statistics
19.8	Blue Book 2014, Office for National Statistics
19.9	Blue Book 2014, Office for National Statistics
19.10	Blue Book 2014, Office for National Statistics
19.11	Blue Book 2014, Office for National Statistics
19.12	Blue Book 2014, Office for National Statistics
19.13	Blue Book 2014, Office for National Statistics
19.14	Blue Book 2014, Office for National Statistics
19.15	Blue Book 2014, Office for National Statistics
19.16	Blue Book 2014, Office for National Statistics
19.17	Blue Book 2014, Office for National Statistics
19.18	Office for National Statistics
19.19	Blue Book 2014, Office for National Statistics
19.20	Blue Book 2014, Office for National Statistics
19.21	Blue Book 2014, Office for National Statistics
19.22	Blue Book 2014, Office for National Statistics

Chapter 20 Education

20.1	Department for Education; Welsh Government; Scottish Government; Northern Ireland Department of Education
20.2	Department for Education; Welsh Government; Scottish Government; Northern Ireland Department of Education
20.3	Department for Education; Welsh Government; Scottish Government; Northern Ireland Department of Education
20.4	School Census, Department for Education
20.5	Department for Education; Welsh Government; Scottish Government; Northern Ireland Department of Education
20.6	Higher Education Statistics Agency Limited
20.7	Higher Education Statistics Agency Limited
20.8	Department for Business, Innovation and Skills; Welsh Government;
	Scottish Funding Council; Northern Ireland Department for Employment and Learning

Table number	Government department or other organisation
20.9	Department for Business, Innovation and Skills; Welsh Government;
	Scottish Funding Council; Northern Ireland Department for Employment and Learning
20.10	Department for Education; Welsh Government; Scottish Government; Northern Ireland Department of Education

Chapter 21 Crime and Justice

21.1a	Home Office
21.1b	Home Office
21.1c	The Police Service of Northern Ireland
21.1d	Scottish Government Justice Analytical Services; Police Scotland
21.2	International Centre for Prison Studies
21.3	Police Recorded Crime, Home Office
21.4	Ministry of Justice
21.5	Ministry of Justice
21.6a	Ministry of Justice
21.6b	Ministry of Justice
21.6c	Ministry of Justice
21.6d	Ministry of Justice
21.6e	Ministry of Justice
21.7	Ministry of Justice
21.8	Ministry of Justice
21.9a	Ministry of Justice
21.9b	Ministry of Justice
21.10	Ministry of Justice
21.11	Ministry of Justice
21.12	Scottish Government
21.13	Scottish Government
21.14	Scottish Government
21.15	Scottish Government
21.16	Scottish Government
21.17a	Prison Statistics and Population Projections, Scottish Government
21.17b	Prison Statistics and Population Projections, Scottish Government
21.17c	Prison Statistics and Population Projections, Scottish Government
21.18	Scottish Prison Service
21.19	Police Service Northern Ireland
21.20	Northern Ireland Prison Population, Department of Justice Northern Ireland

Chapter 22 Transport

22.1	National Travel Survey, Department for Transport
22.2	Department for Transport; Office of Rail Regulation; Department of Energy and Climate Change
22.3	Department for Transport; Office of Rail Regulation; Civil Aviation Authority
22.4	National Road Traffic Survey, Department for Transport
22.5	Department for Transport
22.6	National Road Traffic Survey, Department for Transport
22.7	Department for Transport; Driver and Vehicle Licensing Agency
22.8	Department for Transport; Driver and Vehicle Licensing Agency
22.9a	Driver & Vehicle Standards Agency DVSA; Department for Transport
22.9b	Driver & Vehicle Standards Agency DVSA; Department for Transport
22.9c	Driver & Vehicle Standards Agency DVSA; Department for Transport
22.9d	Driver & Vehicle Standards Agency DVSA; Department for Transport
22.9e	Driver & Vehicle Standards Agency DVSA; Department for Transport
22.10	National Travel Survey, Department for Transport
22.11a	National Travel Survey, Department for Transport
22.11b	National Travel Survey, Department for Transport
22.12	Driver and Vehicle Agency; Northern Ireland Transport Statistics
22.13	Driver and Vehicle Agency; Northern Ireland Transport Statistics
22.14	DfT Public Service Vehicle Survey, Transport for London
22.15	Dft Fares survey; Office for National Statistics
22.16	Department for Transport
22.17a	Continuing Survey of Road Goods Transport, Department for Transport
22.17b	Continuing Survey of Road Goods Transport, Department for Transport
22.17c	Continuing Survey of Road Goods Transport, Department for Transport
22.18a	Continuing Survey of Road Goods Transport, Department for Transport
22.18b	Continuing Survey of Road Goods Transport, Department for Transport
22.19a	Office of Rail and Road; LENNON Database and train operating companies; DfT Light Rail and Tram Survey
22.19b	Office of Rail and Road; LENNON Database and train operating companies; DfT Light Rail and Tram Survey
22.19c	Office of Rail and Road; LENNON Database and train operating companies; DfT Light Rail and Tram Survey
22.19d	Network Rail; DfT Light Rail and Tram Survey
22.19e	DfT Light Rail and Tram Survey
22.19f	Transport for London
22.19g	Light Rail and Tram Survey, Department for Transport
22.20a	Network Rail
22.20b	Freight operating companies